SO-AGV-259

# Baseball america

## 1994 ALMANAC

A Comprehensive Review
Of the 1993 Season,
Featuring Statistics
And Commentary

Copyright by Baseball America, Inc.
Distributed by Simon & Schuster

No portion of this book may be reprinted or reproduced without the written consent of the publisher.
For additional copies, send $12.95 to Baseball America, P.O. Box 2089, Durham, N.C 27702

# BaseBall america's
# 1994
# ALMANAC

**PUBLISHED BY**
Baseball America, Inc.

**EDITOR**
Allan Simpson

**ASSISTANT EDITOR**
David Hardee

**ASSOCIATE EDITORS**
Mike Berardino
Jim Callis
John Royster
Alan Schwarz

**CONTRIBUTING WRITERS**
Maureen Delany, Jeff Garretson, Wayne Graczyk, Rubin Grant, Sean Kernan, Mike Klis, Chris Krug, Bill Palmer, Tim Pearrell, Curt Rallo, Tracy Ringolsby, George Rorrer, Gene Sapakoff

**STATISTICAL PRODUCTION CONSULTANT**
Howe Sportsdata International,
Boston, Mass.

## BaseBall america

| **EDITOR** | **PUBLISHER** | **PRODUCTION MANAGER** |
|---|---|---|
| Allan Simpson | Dave Chase | Joy C. Tempkins |
| **MANAGING EDITOR** | **ADVERTISING DIRECTOR** | **PRODUCTION ASSISTANT** |
| Jim Callis | Kris Grubbs | Susan Merrell |

**EDITOR'S NOTE**
   Major league statistics are based on final, unofficial 1993 averages. Minor league statistics are official.
   The organization statistics, which begin on page 48, include all players who participated in at least one game during the 1993 season. Pitchers' batting statistics are not included, nor are the pitching statistics of field players who pitched on rare occasions. For players who played with more than one team in the same league, the player's cumulative statistics appear on the line immediately after the player's second-team statistics.
   Innings have been rounded off to the nearest full inning.

*lefthanded batter, pitcher   #switch hitter

# CONTENTS

## MAJOR LEAGUES

## ORGANIZATIONS

## MINOR LEAGUES

## FOREIGN/INDEPENDENT LEAGUES

## COLLEGE BASEBALL

## AMATEUR BASEBALL

## AMATEUR DRAFT

**Cover Photograph:** John Olerud by Michael Ponzini

# MAJOR LEAGUES

# Record-Breaking Year Marred By Tragedy

**By JOHN ROYSTER**

Off the field, 1993 was a landmark year in baseball. But the beauty of the game is that what happened on the field is what will be remembered.

The year gave us quite an offensive show, a sizzling pennant race in the National League West and the first games of two expansion teams, the Colorado Rockies and Florida Marlins.

The most significant story of the year, realignment of the major leagues into six divisions instead of four, and the accompanying new playoff system, will be thought of as a 1994 event. Because that is the first year it'll be manifest on the field.

But in 1993, it had all the suspense and intrigue of a prize-winning novel. When the year opened, realignment was just one of several hot-button issues, sharing billing with revenue sharing, a salary cap, television, the lack of a commissioner. Congress was looking into repealing baseball's antitrust exemption.

Realignment, it turned out, was the only one of those issues that would be truly resolved in 1993. And even that may not be true: As the season ended, there was talk of another round of expansion in the not-too-distant future. The owners may have to figure out who plays where again.

"We're not going to solve the situation until we have more expansion," Rockies owner Jerry McMorris said. "We need to have another team in each league, which would give us three five-team divisions, and then expand to eight divisions with four teams in each. It's inevitable, and so is interleague play. What we are doing now are just steps along the way."

## Tragedy In Florida

All the action in the boardrooms and on the playing fields paled to insignificance March 22, when Cleveland Indians pitchers Tim Crews and Steve Olin were killed in a boating accident.

Crews' boat, with Crews driving, hit a dock just after dark on Little Lake Nellie, outside Orlando. A third pitcher, Bob Ojeda, was seriously injured. The players were on a fishing outing on the Indians' only off day of spring training.

**Bob Ojeda**

Crews and Olin were the first active major leaguers killed in an accident since New York Yankees catcher Thurman Munson died in an airplane crash Aug. 2, 1979.

Ojeda recovered to make an emotional season debut Aug. 7 in Baltimore. He pitched two innings in middle relief against the Orioles, and went 2-1 with a 4.40 ERA over the season's last two months.

The accident was another blow for an Indians fran-

**Tragedy Rocks Indians.** Cleveland pitchers Steve Olin, left, and Tim Crews were killed in a spring training boating accident.

chise plagued by tragedy and losses seemingly forever. The Indians are the only major league team to have a player killed during a game: Ray Chapman, who was killed by a pitched ball in 1920. In 1957, promising pitcher Herb Score was hit in the eye by a line drive. Walter Bond, who was supposed to be the next Rocky Colavito, died of leukemia in 1967. Tony Horton hit 27 home runs at age 24 for the 1969 Indians. One year and one nervous breakdown later, he was out of baseball.

The loss of Olin still had a definite effect on the field. The Indians were in the midst of assembling a good team of position players, but their weakness is pitching. Olin, 27, had 29 saves and eight wins in 1992. He was a young pitcher to build around.

■ Another young team suffered a tragedy before it even played a game. Marlins president Carl Barger, 62, collapsed and died Dec. 9, 1992, at the Winter Meetings in Louisville.

It was Barger who convinced Marlins owner Wayne Huizenga to seek the expansion franchise in the first place. Once it was awarded, Barger had much to do with its design until his death.

Before that, Barger was president of the Pittsburgh Pirates when that franchise rose from perennial doormat to three straight NL East championships.

■ Baseball lost one of its best when Royals owner Ewing Kauffman, 76, died Aug. 1.

Kauffman, who owned at least half the team from its inception in 1969 until his death, didn't buy the team with borrowed money, wasn't motivated by ego and ran it in an effective, understated way.

"Ewing Kauffman was the prototype of what an owner should be," said Brewers owner Bud Selig, the de facto commissioner. "He was completely unselfish, devoted to his city and devoted to the game of baseball."

He also was one of the richest people in America, having made his fortune in pharmaceuticals. He founded Marion Laboratories in 1950.

## A New Day

The owners made baseball history Sept. 8-9 in Boston, when they created the new alignment and an extra tier of playoffs. The old two-division format lasted exactly 25 seasons.

Under the new setup, each division winner, plus a wild-card, second-place finisher from each league, will make the playoffs. The new divisions:

**American League East:** Baltimore, Boston, Detroit, New York, Toronto.

**AL Central:** Chicago, Cleveland, Kansas City, Milwaukee, Minnesota.

**AL West:** California, Oakland, Seattle, Texas.

**National League East:** Atlanta, Florida, Montreal, New York, Philadelphia.

**NL Central:** Chicago, Cincinnati, Houston, Pittsburgh, St. Louis.

**NL West:** Colorado, Los Angeles, San Diego, San Francisco.

It previously was unimaginable that the 28 owners could agree on a change so radical, let alone get approval for it from the Major League Players Association. Suffice it to say that everyone in baseball gets more efficient when they see a chance for TV money.

The realignment was as much a creation of the networks and the players' union as it was the owners. The television executives wanted the extra tier of playoffs, and the union wanted to see it achieved through three divisions in each league, rather than two larger ones.

Otherwise, the television package agreed to with NBC and ABC in May is significantly different from past contracts, to wit:

■ Baseball gets no up-front money in the form of rights fees. Instead, it enters into a partnership with NBC and ABC, billed as The Baseball Network, to produce the games and sell the commercial time. How much each makes depends on how much they get for all those Bud Light and Weed Eater commercials.

■ The extra tier of playoff games won't all be telecast nationally. They'll be regionalized, a first for baseball.

■ The Game of the Week is back, sort of. That, too, will be regionalized, much like National Football League broadcasts. And it'll be on a weeknight, and only after the all-star break.

■ Afternoon baseball on the networks is history. Regular season, playoffs, anytime, anywhere.

Baseball also re-upped with ESPN, which will show fewer games than it did under its first contract. ESPN's Sunday night games will continue, with the addition of a season opener on the day before the traditional Opening Day. But the Tuesday games and Friday doubleheaders will be dropped in favor of Wednesday doubleheaders.

Still unresolved is the question of pay-per-view television—whether the public, literally, will buy it.

Revenue-sharing and salary-cap

**Remember When?** Baseball had a commissioner until the owners ousted Fay Vincent, left, on Labor Day weekend in 1992. Brewers owner Bud Selig has served as de facto commissioner.

issues also remained unresolved, and that required an even bigger miracle than realignment or the television contract. Large-market and small-market owners will have to agree, to say nothing of convincing the players to approve.

When the owners met to discuss revenue sharing in August in Kohler, Wis., they quite literally split into two camps. The large-market people met in one place, the small-market people in another. Needless to say, they didn't come up with a revenue-sharing plan.

Still, after the meeting one owner sounded a note of optimism: "I really believe that when we meet in Boston (in September), we will finally have this done and can move forward."

Nope. Didn't happen. But more meetings were scheduled before the end of the year.

By the way, remember when baseball had something called a commissioner? It hasn't since Fay Vincent was ousted by the owners on Labor Day weekend in 1992. Since then, the assistant commissioner and both major league presidents have resigned, though the latter two, the AL's Bobby Brown and the NL's Bill White, are staying on until their successors are named.

The owners don't expect to fill any of the positions until after they resolve the revenue-sharing and salary-cap issues.

Both Steve Greenberg, the assistant commissioner, and White took some loud parting shots when they resigned over the winter.

"The game is permeated by selfish, greedy interests," Greenberg said, "as opposed to focusing on the history and beauty of the game and trying to draw the next generation to the game."

"It's a mess and it's going to get worse," White said. "You can't make an impact, so you get out. I haven't made an impact. I don't think anybody can today because of the division of ownership. So I'm going to get on with my life.

"We plead poverty and go out and spend millions. The players don't believe disaster is happening. There's

| CAREER STRIKEOUTS | |
| :--- | ---: |

Baseball's career strikeout leader Nolan Ryan wound up a distinguished career in 1993. The game's career leaders:

| Player | Strikeouts |
| :--- | ---: |
| 1. Nolan Ryan | 5,714 |
| 2. Steve Carlton | 4,136 |
| 3. Bert Blyleven | 3,701 |
| 4. Tom Seaver | 3,640 |
| 5. Don Sutton | 3,574 |
| 6. Gaylord Perry | 3,524 |
| 7. Walter Johnson | 3,509 |
| 8. Phil Niekro | 3,342 |
| 9. Ferguson Jenkins | 3,117 |
| 10. Bob Gibson | 3,117 |
| 11. Jim Bunning | 2,855 |
| 12. Mickey Lolich | 2,832 |
| 13. Cy Young | 2,803 |
| 14. Frank Tanana | 2,773 |
| 15. Warren Spahn | 2,583 |
| 16. Bob Feller | 2,581 |
| 17. Jerry Koosman | 2,556 |
| 18. Tim Keefe | 2,521 |
| 19. Christy Mathewson | 2,502 |
| 20. Don Drysdale | 2,486 |

no cooperation between players and ownership. Everybody wants to get his little piece of the pie and worry about the game later. That's owners, players, umpires, administrators. It's sad."

There is one group in the United States which moves more slowly than baseball's owners: the U.S. Congress. And it is interested in baseball.

Sen. Howard Metzenbaum, D-Ohio, early in the year introduced a bill to kill baseball's antitrust exemption. It followed a round of hearings late in 1992. Metzenbaum's bill finally was killed in committee Sept. 30. The Senate Judiciary Committee opted instead for, you guessed it, more hearings.

## Grand Old Men

On the field, the game continued to thrive in 1992, timeless as ever. Four likely Hall of Famers said goodbye, and another of the all-time greats reached 3,000 hits.

Nolan Ryan's farewell tour made a lot of detours, but that shouldn't diminish the man's accomplishments. A maddening series of injuries limited Ryan to 13 starts in his 27th and final season, and his last pitch tore the ulnar-collateral ligament in his elbow.

It's a mark of his greatness that his exit seemed dignified anyway. Everyone knows Ryan's career strikeout record (5,714) probably never will be broken. But some more arcane statistics compiled by Baseball America columnist Jayson Stark express things even better:

■ The player who made the last out of Ryan's seventh and final no-hitter (Roberto Alomar) was the son of the man who made the first out in his first no-hitter (Sandy Alomar Sr.).

■ He won games in 12 ballparks that weren't built yet when he threw his first major league pitch.

■ Of the 19 players in history who have gotten 3,000 hits, Ryan struck out more than half of them (10).

■ He struck out 47 MVPs, 21 Hall of Famers, 10

LINDA KAYE

**Greats Go Out Together.** The retirements of George Brett, left, and Nolan Ryan marked the end of an era.

members of the 1964 Phillies and nine members of the 1993 Phillies.

■ His abrupt departure on Sept. 22 in Seattle, with a 3-1 count on the Mariners' Dave Magadan, gave rookie Steve Dreyer the bizarre distinction of throwing the last pitch of Ryan's final walk. Dreyer wasn't yet alive for Ryan's first 131 walks.

The Royals' George Brett, who reached 3,000 hits in 1992, called it quits after the 1993 season. It's a mark of *his* greatness that he lamented his .270 average when he made his retirement announcement. Of course, he went out the next night and hit two home runs, including a game-winner in the 10th inning.

For the record, Brett's last at-bat was a two-hop single up the middle.

The Twins' Dave Winfield, 41, has no plans to retire, preferring instead to keep banging out hits. No. 3,000 came Sept. 16, off Dennis Eckersley, no less.

Two other greats left the game earlier in the season, though, sadly, not on their own terms.

Dale Murphy retired May 27, rather than suffer the indignity of a release by the Rockies. He was ineffective in limited 1993 action, and finished his career two home runs short of 400.

Carlton Fisk had feuded with White Sox owner Jerry

### 3,000-HIT CLUB

Minnesota's Dave Winfield joined an exclusive club when he drilled a single Sept. 16, 1993 for career hit No. 3,000. The list:

| Player | Hits | At-Bats | Avg. |
|---|---|---|---|
| 1. Pete Rose | 4,256 | 14,053 | .303 |
| 2. Ty Cobb | 4,191 | 11,429 | .367 |
| 3. Hank Aaron | 3,771 | 12,364 | .305 |
| 4. Stan Musial | 3,630 | 10,972 | .331 |
| 5. Tris Speaker | 3,615 | 10,208 | .344 |
| 6. Honus Wagner | 3,430 | 10,427 | .329 |
| 7. Carl Yastrzemski | 3,419 | 11,988 | .285 |
| 8. Eddie Collins | 3,309 | 9,946 | .333 |
| 9. Willie Mays | 3,283 | 10,881 | .302 |
| 10. Nap Lajoie | 3,252 | 9,589 | .339 |
| 11. George Brett | 3,154 | 10,349 | .305 |
| 12. Paul Waner | 3,152 | 9,459 | .333 |
| 13. Robin Yount | 3,142 | 11,008 | .285 |
| 14. Cap Anson | 3,081 | 9,084 | .339 |
| 15. Rod Carew | 3,053 | 9,315 | .328 |
| 16. Lou Brock | 3,023 | 10,332 | .293 |
| 17. Dave Winfield | 3,014 | 10,594 | .285 |
| 18. Al Kaline | 3,007 | 10,116 | .297 |
| 19. Roberto Clemente | 3,000 | 9,454 | .317 |

TOM DiPACE

**Dave Winfield**

# 1993 MAJOR LEAGUE ALL-STAR GAME

## American League Scores Sixth Consecutive Victory

After more than 25 years of All-Star Game domination by the National League, the pendulum has clearly swung in the junior circuit's favor. The 64th contest, played at Baltimore's majestic Oriole Park at Camden Yards, did nothing to slow the American League's momentum as it registered its second straight blowout victory, and sixth straight over the National League, 9-3.

The game may be best remembered for its bizarre conclusion. With the game well in hand, Toronto manager Cito Gaston, who skippered the AL, had Blue Jays closer Duane Ward

**Kirby Puckett**

finish the game, while hometown favorite Mike Mussina, one of only two Baltimore players selected, warmed in the bullpen. Baltimore fans boisterously booed Gaston for not bringing Mussina in the game, barely pausing to cheer when the six-run victory was clinched.

Minnesota outfielder Kirby Puckett earned game MVP honors by collecting a double, home run and two RBIs. Chicago White Sox righthander Jack McDowell worked a scoreless fifth inning to earn the victory. Gary Sheffield homered in the first inning in the first-ever All-Star Game at-bat by a Florida Marlin.

### TOP VOTE GETTERS
#### AMERICAN LEAGUE

**CATCHER:** 1. Ivan Rodriguez, Rangers (1,380,005); 2. Sandy Alomar, Indians (969,583); 3. Pat Borders, Blue Jays (902,570).

**FIRST BASE:** 1. John Olerud, Blue Jays (1,285,334); 2. Cecil Fielder, Tigers (946,792); 3. Mark McGwire, Athletics (853,409).

**SECOND BASE:** 1. Roberto Alomar, Blue Jays (1,852,280); 2. Carlos Baerga, Indians (858,381); 3. Chuck Knoblauch, Twins (729,687).

**THIRD BASE:** 1. Wade Boggs, Yankees (1,523,805); 2. Robin Ventura, White Sox (920,007); 3. Dean Palmer, Rangers (870,293).

**SHORTSTOP:** 1. Cal Ripken, Orioles (2,077,482); 2. Travis Fryman, Tigers (848,610); 3. Ozzie Guillen, White Sox (499,590).

**OUTFIELD:** 1. Ken Griffey, Mariners (2,696,918); 2. Kirby Puckett, Twins (2,362,551); 3. Joe Carter, Blue Jays (1,407,179); 4. Albert Belle, Indians (999,730); 5. Dave Winfield, Twins (973,495); 6. Jose Canseco, Rangers (922,919); 7. Juan Gonzalez, Rangers (899,539); 9. Devon White, Blue Jays (847,993); 9. Rickey Henderson, Athletics (602,429).

#### NATIONAL LEAGUE

**CATCHER:** 1. Darren Daulton, Phillies (2,061,255); 2. Benito Santiago, Marlins (1,227,232); 3. Mike Piazza, Dodgers (644,823).

**FIRST BASE:** 1. John Kruk, Phillies (1,200,219); 2. Fred McGriff, Padres (1,080,347); 3. Will Clark, Giants (992,420).

**SECOND BASE:** 1. Ryne Sandberg, Cubs (1,770,559); 2. Delino DeShields, Expos (1,259,713); 3. Craig Biggio, Astros (744,885).

**THIRD BASE:** 1. Gary Sheffield, Marlins (1,512,548); 2. Matt Williams, Giants (1,063,392); 3. Terry Pendleton, Braves (910,977).

**SHORTSTOP:** 1. Barry Larkin, Reds (1,259,939); 2. Ozzie Smith, Cardinals (1,147,552); 3. Jeff Blauser, Braves (796,981).

**OUTFIELD:** 1. Barry Bonds, Giants (3,074,603); 2. Andy Van Slyke, Pirates (1,125,615); 3. David Justice, Braves (1,056,324); 4. Lenny Dykstra, Phillies (838,406); 5.Darryl Strawberry,

Dodgers (816,148); 6. Derek Bell, Padres (806,954); 7. Tony Gwynn, Padres (757,154); 8. Ron Gant, Braves (694,542); 9. Larry Walker, Expos (654,789).

### ROSTERS

#### AMERICAN LEAGUE

**MANAGER:** Cito Gaston, Blue Jays.

**PITCHERS:** Rick Aguilera, Twins; Pat Hentgen, Blue Jays; Randy Johnson, Mariners; **Mark Langston, Angels;** Jack McDowell, White Sox; Jeff Montgomery, Royals; Mike Mussina, Orioles; Duane Ward, Blue Jays; Jimmy Key, Yankees.

**CATCHERS: Ivan Rodriguez, Rangers;** Terry Steinbach, Athletics.

**INFIELDERS: Roberto Alomar (2b), Blue Jays;** Carlos Baerga, Indians; **Wade Boggs (3b), Yankees;** Scott Cooper, Red Sox; Cecil Fielder, Tigers; Travis Fryman, Tigers; **Paul Molitor (dh), Blue Jays; John Olerud (1b), Blue Jays; Cal Ripken (ss), Orioles;** Frank Thomas, White Sox.

**OUIFIELDERS:** Albert Belle, Indians; **Joe Carter (rf), Blue Jays;** Juan Gonzalez, Rangers; **Ken Griffey (cf), Mariners; Kirby Puckett (lf), Twins;** Greg Vaughn, Brewers; Devon White, Blue Jays.

#### NATIONAL LEAGUE

**MANAGER:** Bobby Cox, Braves.

**PITCHERS:** Steve Avery, Braves; Rod Beck, Giants; Andy Benes, Padres; John Burkett, Giants; Tom Glavine, Braves; Bryan Harvey, Marlins; Darryl Kile, Astros; **Terry Mulholland, Phillies;** Lee Smith, Cardinals; John Smoltz, Braves.

**CATCHERS: Darren Daulton, Phillies;** Mike Piazza, Dodgers.

**INFIELDERS:** Jay Bell, Pirates; Jeff Blauser, Braves; Andres Galarraga, Rockies; **Mark Grace, Cubs;** Gregg Jefferies, Cardinals; **John Kruk (1b), Phillies; Barry Larkin (ss), Reds; Ryne Sandberg (2b), Cubs; Gary Sheffield (3b), Marlins;** Robby Thompson, Giants.

**OUTFIELDERS: Barry Bonds (lf), Giants;** Bobby Bonilla, Mets; **Marquis Grissom (cf), Expos;** Tony Gwynn, Padres; **David Justice (rf), Braves;** Bobby Kelly, Reds.

Starters in **boldface** type

### BOX SCORE
#### July 13 in Baltimore
#### American League 9, National League 3

| NATIONAL | ab | r | h | bi | bb | so | AMERICAN | ab | r | h | bi | bb | so |
|---|---|---|---|---|---|---|---|---|---|---|---|---|---|
| Grissom cf | 3 | 0 | 0 | 0 | 0 | 1 | Alomar 2b | 3 | 1 | 1 | 1 | 0 | 0 |
| Kelly cf | 1 | 0 | 0 | 0 | 0 | 1 | Baerga 2b | 2 | 1 | 0 | 0 | 0 | 1 |
| Bonds lf | 3 | 2 | 2 | 0 | 0 | 0 | Molitor dh | 1 | 0 | 0 | 0 | 1 | 0 |
| Bonilla lf | 1 | 0 | 1 | 0 | 0 | 0 | Belle dh | 1 | 2 | 1 | 1 | 1 | 0 |
| Sheffield 3b | 3 | 1 | 2 | 2 | 0 | 0 | Thomas dh | 1 | 0 | 1 | 0 | 0 | 0 |
| Hollins 3b | 1 | 0 | 1 | 0 | 0 | 0 | Griffey cf | 3 | 1 | 1 | 1 | 0 | 1 |
| Kruk 1b | 3 | 0 | 0 | 0 | 0 | 2 | White cf | 2 | 1 | 1 | 0 | 0 | 0 |
| Galarraga 1b | 1 | 0 | 0 | 0 | 0 | 0 | Carter rf | 3 | 0 | 1 | 0 | 0 | 1 |
| Larkin ss | 2 | 0 | 0 | 1 | 0 | 1 | Gonzalez rf | 1 | 0 | 0 | 0 | 1 | 1 |
| Blauser ss | 1 | 0 | 0 | 0 | 0 | 0 | Olerud 1b | 2 | 0 | 0 | 0 | 0 | 0 |
| Grace dh | 3 | 0 | 0 | 0 | 0 | 1 | Fielder 1b | 1 | 0 | 0 | 0 | 0 | 0 |
| Jefferies dh | 1 | 0 | 0 | 0 | 0 | 1 | Puckett lf | 3 | 1 | 2 | 2 | 0 | 0 |
| Justice rf | 3 | 0 | 1 | 0 | 0 | 0 | Vaughn lf | 1 | 1 | 1 | 0 | 0 | 0 |
| Gwynn rf | 1 | 0 | 0 | 0 | 0 | 0 | Ripken ss | 3 | 0 | 0 | 0 | 0 | 1 |
| Daulton c | 3 | 0 | 0 | 0 | 0 | 1 | Fryman ss | 1 | 0 | 0 | 0 | 0 | 0 |
| Piazza c | 1 | 0 | 0 | 0 | 0 | 0 | Boggs 3b | 1 | 0 | 0 | 0 | 1 | 0 |
| Sandberg 2b | 1 | 0 | 0 | 0 | 1 | 0 | Cooper 3b | 2 | 0 | 0 | 0 | 0 | 1 |
| Bell 2b | 1 | 0 | 0 | 0 | 0 | 0 | Rodriguez c | 2 | 1 | 1 | 0 | 0 | 0 |
| | | | | | | | Steinbach c | 2 | 0 | 1 | 0 | 1 | 0 |
| **Totals** | **33** | **3** | **7** | **3** | **1** | **9** | **Totals** | **35** | **9** | **11** | **7** | **4** | **7** |

| | | | |
|---|---|---|---|
| National | 200 | 001 | 000—3 |
| American | 011 | 033 | 10x—9 |

E—Justice, Blauser. LOB—National 5, American 7. 2B—Bonds 2, Rodriguez, Puckett, White, Steinbach, Hollins. HR—Sheffield, Alomar, Puckett. SB—White. SF—Larkin.

| National | ip | h | r | er | bb | so | American | ip | h | r | er | bb | so |
|---|---|---|---|---|---|---|---|---|---|---|---|---|---|
| Mulholland | 2 | 1 | 1 | 1 | 2 | 0 | Langston | 2 | 3 | 2 | 2 | 1 | 2 |
| Benes | 2 | 1 | 0 | 0 | 0 | 2 | Johnson | 2 | 0 | 0 | 0 | 0 | 1 |
| Burkett L | ⅔ | 4 | 3 | 3 | 0 | 1 | McDowell W | 1 | 0 | 0 | 0 | 0 | 0 |
| Avery | 1 | 1 | 3 | 0 | 1 | 1 | Key | 1 | 2 | 1 | 1 | 0 | 1 |
| Smoltz | ⅓ | 0 | 0 | 0 | 1 | 0 | Montgomery | 1 | 0 | 0 | 0 | 0 | 1 |
| Beck | 1 | 2 | 1 | 1 | 0 | 1 | Aguilera | 1 | 2 | 0 | 0 | 0 | 2 |
| Harvey | 1 | 1 | 0 | 0 | 0 | 2 | Ward | 1 | 0 | 0 | 0 | 0 | 2 |

WP—Smoltz 2. HBP—Fielder (by Burkett).

T—2:49. A—48,147. Umpires: HP—McKean; 1B—Davidson; 2B—Reilly; 3B—Darling.

Reinsdorf for a few years. Reinsdorf got the last word by releasing Fisk six days after he broke Bob Boone's major league record of 2,225 games caught.

It had been a while since baseball had a player flirt with a season batting average of .400. In 1993 it had two, one in each league.

Andres Galarraga of the Rockies and John Olerud of the Toronto Blue Jays stayed within striking distance of .400 for the season's first half.

Neither had enough speed to really stand a chance, but it was fun for a while and both players won batting titles. Galarraga finished at .370, Olerud at .363.

## A Year For High Numbers

The Galarraga-Olerud story was part of a definite surge in offense.

**End Of The Line.** The 1993 season marked the end for two of baseball's most distinguished veterans: catcher Carlton Fisk, left, and outfielder Dale Murphy.

Home runs increased 16.8 percent in the AL, and an eye-popping 55 percent in the NL, aided by the two expansion teams and the fact that one of them was located in the mile-high air of Colorado. But even if you factor out the 236 homers hit by the Marlins and Rockies, the NL increase still would have been 36.3 percent over 1992.

Indeed, the impact of expansion wasn't as great as might have been expected. The total of 4,030 homers in both leagues represented a 32.7-percent increase over 1992. But in 1977, the last time the majors expanded, home runs increased 63 percent.

The National League ERA rose from 3.50 in 1992 to 4.04, the highest since a 4.08 figure in offense-crazy 1977. In the American League, the ERA went from 3.94 to 4.32, the highest since a 4.46 mark in 1987.

All that scoring put a big dent in Major League

Baseball's plan to shorten games. The average game time dipped by just one minute in each league, from 2:53 to 2:52 in the American and 2:45 to 2:44 in the National. Better luck next year.

## Last Days For Two Parks

Two major league ballparks saw their last games in 1993, but in neither case did a lot of people get misty-eyed.

Cleveland Stadium and Arlington Stadium weren't classic baseball parks, and each will be remembered as the home of mostly lousy teams.

Even the Indians were slow to warm up to Cleveland Stadium. They moved in for the 1933 season, but after that moved out again and played mostly at League Park until 1947.

They will move to the new Indians Ballpark at Gateway in 1994. The Stadium, as the old place is known locally, will remain the home of the National Football League's Cleveland Browns.

Arlington Stadium was built as a minor league park in the mid-1960s, and expanded when the Rangers came to town in 1972. Only 20,105 showed up for the opener, and the first capacity crowd was more than a year later, for the debut of pitching phenom David Clyde.

The Rangers' new home, located adjacent to the old one, wil be called The Ballpark. Arlington Stadium was being torn down to make room for parking.

## Turnstiles Spin

For all the talk about its prob-

**Flirting With .400.** Toronto's John Olerud and Colorado's Andres Galarraga hit better than .400 much of the 1993 season. Both won their respective league's batting title.

# 1993 MAJOR LEAGUE FREE AGENTS

Ninety-seven players with six or more seasons of major league service filed for free agency following the 1993 season, per baseball's Basic Agreement. Players whose signing by another club requires draft-pick compensation—provided the player's former club offers salary arbitration—are indicated by Types A, B or C:

### ATLANTA (3)
| Player, Pos. | 1993 Salary |
| --- | --- |
| Sid Bream (C), 1b | $1,600,000 |
| +Jay Howell, rhp | $1,000,000 |
| Otis Nixon (B), of | $2,815,000 |

### BALTIMORE (6)
| Player, Pos. | 1993 Salary |
| --- | --- |
| Harold Baines (A), of | $1,100,000 |
| +Mike Pagliarulo, 3b | $400,000 |
| +Harold Reynolds, 2b | $1,650,000 |
| +Lonnie Smith, of | $1,000,000 |
| +Rick Sutcliffe, rhp | $2,000,000 |
| Fernando Valenzuela, lhp | $250,000 |

### BOSTON (6)
| Player, Pos. | 1993 Salary |
| --- | --- |
| +Rob Deer, of | $2,066,667 |
| John Dopson, rhp | $750,000 |
| Steve Lyons, inf | $109,000 |
| +Tony Pena, c | $2,200,000 |
| Ernest Riles, 3b | $400,000 |
| Luis Rivera, ss | $1,075,000 |

### CALIFORNIA (3)
| Player, Pos. | 1993 Salary |
| --- | --- |
| Rene Gonzales (B), 3b | $600,000 |
| Stan Javier, of | $600,000 |
| Luis Polonia (C), of | $2,475,000 |

### CHICAGO—AL (6)
| Player, Pos. | 1993 Salary |
| --- | --- |
| Tim Belcher (A), rhp | $3,750,000 |
| Ellis Burks (A), of | $500,000 |
| Ivan Calderon, of | $3,000,000 |
| Jose DeLeon, rhp | $275,000 |
| Bo Jackson, of | $910,000 |
| Tim Raines (A), of | $3,500,000 |

### CINCINNATI (4)
| Player, Pos. | 1993 Salary |
| --- | --- |
| +Jeff Reardon, rhp | $500,000 |
| Bip Roberts (A), 2b | $3,900,000 |
| Chris Sabo (B), 3b | $3,100,000 |
| Juan Samuel, 2b | $700,000 |

### CLEVELAND (3)
| Player, Pos. | 1993 Salary |
| --- | --- |
| Bob Ojeda, lhp | $1,700,000 |
| +Junior Ortiz, c | $335,000 |
| Jeff Treadway, 2b | $300,000 |

### COLORADO (3)
| Player, Pos. | 1993 Salary |
| --- | --- |
| +Daryl Boston, of | $550,000 |
| Andres Galarraga (A), 1b | $600,000 |
| Bruce Hurst (C), lhp | $3,000,000 |

### DETROIT (4)
| Player, Pos. | 1993 Salary |
| --- | --- |
| +Storm Davis, rhp | $900,000 |
| +Kirk Gibson, of | $500,000 |
| Dan Gladden (B), of | $1,150,000 |
| David Wells (C), lhp | $900,000 |

### FLORIDA (3)
| Player, Pos. | 1993 Salary |
| --- | --- |
| Henry Cotto, of | $900,000 |
| +Charlie Hough, rhp | $800,000 |
| Walt Weiss (B), ss | $825,000 |

**Will Clark,** San Francisco

### HOUSTON (3)
| Player, Pos. | 1993 Salary |
| --- | --- |
| +Kevin Bass, of | $500,000 |
| Mark Portugal (A), rhp | $1,875,000 |
| +Jose Uribe, ss | $400,000 |

### KANSAS CITY (5)
| Player, Pos. | 1993 Salary |
| --- | --- |
| +Hubie Brooks, of | $250,000 |
| Greg Cadaret, lhp | $1,190,000 |
| Gary Gaetti (C), 3b | $3,000,000 |
| Mark Gubicza (B), rhp | $1,250,000 |
| +Dennis Rasmussen, lhp | $325,000 |

### LOS ANGELES (1)
| Player, Pos. | 1993 Salary |
| --- | --- |
| Jody Reed (A), 2b | $2,500,000 |

### MILWAUKEE (3)
| Player, Pos. | 1993 Salary |
| --- | --- |
| +Kevin Seitzer, 3b | $109,000 |
| Dickie Thon (C), ss | $250,000 |
| +Robin Yount, of | $2,700,000 |

### MINNESOTA (1)
| Player, Pos. | 1993 Salary |
| --- | --- |
| Brian Harper (A), c | $2,400,000 |

### MONTREAL (2)
| Player, Pos. | 1993 Salary |
| --- | --- |
| Dennis Martinez (A), rhp | $2,833,334 |
| Randy Ready, 2b | $109,000 |

### NEW YORK—AL (5)
| Player, Pos. | 1993 Salary |
| --- | --- |
| +Steve Farr, rhp | $1,500,000 |
| Dion James (B), of | $350,000 |
| Lee Smith (A), rhp | $2,666,667 |
| +Frank Tanana, lhp | $1,500,000 |
| Mike Witt, rhp | $2,166,667 |

### NEW YORK—NL (4)
| Player, Pos. | 1993 Salary |
| --- | --- |
| Sid Fernandez (A), lhp | $2,100,000 |
| Howard Johnson (B), 3b | $2,100,000 |
| +Eddie Murray, 1b | $3,375,000 |
| Charlie O'Brien (C), c | $500,000 |

### OAKLAND (6)
| Player, Pos. | 1993 Salary |
| --- | --- |
| Mike Aldrete, of | $125,000 |
| Jerry Browne (B), 2b | $625,000 |
| +Rich Gossage, rhp | $325,000 |
| Dave Henderson, of | $2,250,000 |
| +Rick Honeycutt, lhp | $725,000 |
| +Edwin Nunez, rhp | $200,000 |

### PHILADELPHIA (3)
| Player, Pos. | 1993 Salary |
| --- | --- |
| +Larry Andersen, rhp | $700,000 |
| +Jim Eisenreich, of | $600,000 |

Bobby Thigpen, rhp ............ $3,416,667

### PITTSBURGH (1)
| Player, Pos. | 1993 Salary |
| --- | --- |
| Bob Walk (B), rhp | $2,175,000 |

### ST. LOUIS (3)
| Player, Pos. | 1993 Salary |
| --- | --- |
| Lee Guetterman, lhp | $200,000 |
| Les Lancaster, rhp | $350,000 |
| Gerald Perry, 1b | $966,667 |

### SAN DIEGO (1)
| Player, Pos. | 1993 Salary |
| --- | --- |
| Tim Teufel (C), 2b | $762,500 |

### SAN FRANCISCO (4)
| Player, Pos. | 1993 Salary |
| --- | --- |
| Will Clark (A), 1b | $4,750,000 |
| Jim Deshaies, lhp | $700,000 |
| +Scott Sanderson, rhp | $500,000 |
| Robby Thompson (A), 2b | $1,900,000 |

### SEATTLE (3)
| Player, Pos. | 1993 Salary |
| --- | --- |
| +Tim Leary, rhp | $1,800,000 |
| +Ted Power, rhp | $450,000 |
| Dave Valle (A), c | $1,866,667 |

### TEXAS (5)
| Player, Pos. | 1993 Salary |
| --- | --- |
| Julio Franco (B), 2b | $3,000,000 |
| +Craig Lefferts, lhp | $1,080,000 |
| Charlie Leibrandt, lhp | $2,833,334 |
| Rafael Palmeiro (A), 1b | $4,550,000 |
| +Geno Petralli, c | $650,000 |

### TORONTO (6)
| Player, Pos. | 1993 Salary |
| --- | --- |
| Danny Cox (B), rhp | $625,000 |
| +Mark Eichhorn, rhp | $700,000 |
| Tony Fernandez (A), ss | $2,300,000 |
| Alfredo Griffin, ss | $500,000 |
| +Rickey Henderson, of | $3,250,000 |
| Jack Morris (B), rhp | $5,425,000 |

**COMPENSATION: Type A**—Teams signing a Type A free agent must compensate his former team with a 1994 first-round pick (or a second-round pick if the signing team selects in the first half of the rotation). The player's former team also receives a supplemental pick at the end of the first round. **Type B**—The player's former team receives the same compensation it would for a Type A free agent, except it does not get the supplemental pick. **Type C**—The player's former team receives a supplemental pick at the end of the second round.

+Repeater rights free agent.

**Rafael Palmeiro,** Texas

**Out With The Old . . .** and in with new stadiums in Cleveland and Texas. At left, construction on Cleveland's new Indians Ballpark at Gateway, scheduled to open in 1994. Texas' Arlington Stadium saw its final game in 1993.

lems, baseball enjoyed a record year in attendance. The total was 70,257,938, a 26.5-percent increase over 1992, leading opponents of the realignment to shout, "If it ain't broke, don't fix it."

However, there were some unusual circumstances. First and foremost was the addition of the Marlins and Rockies, both of whom drew extremely well. The Rockies broke the record for one team, drawing 4,483,350 to 76,000-seat Mile High Stadium.

Also, the NL changed its method of counting. It formerly used its actual turnstile count, but switched in 1993 to tickets sold, the method used by the AL for years.

If you factor out the Rockies and Marlins (3,064,847), and figure the counting change meant a 10 percent increase, attendance would be about 59.8 million. That makes the increase just 7 percent over 1992, but still 5.2 percent more than the previous record attendance of 56,813,760 in 1991.

## Jackson Enters Hall

Reggie Jackson never was one to share the spotlight during his 21-year playing career, so it was fitting that he was the year's only Hall of Fame inductee.

Jackson was remembered as the consummate clutch performer, especially in the 1977 World Series, in which he homered on his last four swings as his Yankees finished off the Dodgers.

Mr. October hit 563 regular season home runs, and 10 more in five World Series. Almost lost to history is the fact that an injured Jackson didn't play the first time one of his teams reached the World Series. The 1972 Athletics beat the Reds in seven games without him.

**Reggie Jackson**

## Step Right Up, Buy A Team

Baltimore Orioles owner Eli Jacobs found a new way to sell a major league team. Jacobs went bankrupt, and the team went under the auctioneer's gavel.

The winning bid was $173 million, from a group led by Baltimore lawyer Peter Angelos and Cincinnati businessman William DeWitt. The group also included some interesting minority partners: movie director Barry Levinson, author Tom Clancy, sports broadcaster Jim McKay and tennis pro Pam Shriver.

Their bid destroyed the previous record price for a major league team, the $106 million paid by the Nintendo group for the Seattle Mariners just a year

| ATTENDANCE INCREASE | | | |
| --- | --- | --- | --- |

Major League Baseball shattered its all-time single-season attendance record in 1993, drawing more than 70 million. Here's how '93 attendance compared to 1992, a 26.5 percent increase:

| Club | '93 Attend. | '92 Attend. | +/- |
| --- | --- | --- | --- |
| Colorado* | 4,483,270 | — | +4,483,270 |
| Toronto | 4,057,947 | 4,028,318 | +29,629 |
| Atlanta | 3,884,720 | 3,077,400 | +807,320 |
| Baltimore | 3,644,965 | 3,567,819 | +77,146 |
| Los Angeles | 3,162,506 | 2,473,266 | +689,310 |
| Philadelphia | 3,137,539 | 1,927,448 | +1,210,091 |
| Florida* | 3,064,847 | — | +3,064,847 |
| St. Louis | 2,841,028 | 2,418,483 | +422,545 |
| Chicago (NL) | 2,653,763 | 2,126,720 | +527,043 |
| San Francisco | 2,606,354 | 1,560,998 | +1,045,356 |
| Chicago (AL) | 2,581,091 | 2,681,156 | -100,065 |
| Cincinnati | 2,453,232 | 2,315,946 | +137,286 |
| Boston | 2,422,021 | 2,468,574 | -46,553 |
| New York (AL) | 2,416,942 | 1,748,737 | +668,205 |
| Texas | 2,244,616 | 2,198,231 | +46,385 |
| Cleveland | 2,177,908 | 1,224,094 | +953,814 |
| Houston | 2,084,528 | 1,211,412 | +873,116 |
| California | 2,057,460 | 2,065,444 | -7,984 |
| Seattle | 2,052,638 | 1,651,367 | +401,271 |
| Minnesota | 2,048,673 | 2,482,428 | -433,755 |
| Oakland | 2,035,025 | 2,494,160 | -459,135 |
| Detroit | 1,970,791 | 1,423,963 | +546,828 |
| Kansas City | 1,934,578 | 1,867,689 | +66,889 |
| New York (NL) | 1,873,183 | 1,779,534 | +93,649 |
| Milwaukee | 1,688,080 | 1,857,351 | -169,271 |
| Pittsburgh | 1,650,593 | 1,829,395 | -178,802 |
| Montreal | 1,641,437 | 1,669,127 | -27,690 |
| San Diego | 1,375,432 | 1,721,406 | -345,974 |
| **Totals** | **70,245,237** | **55,870,466** | **+14,374,771** |

*Expansion franchise

# MAJOR LEAGUE DEBUTS, 1993

MEL BAILEY

**Brian Anderson.** First 1993 draftee to reach majors.

| Player, Pos. | Club | Debut |
| --- | --- | --- |
| Abbott, Kurt, inf | Athletics | Aug. 8 |
| Anderson, Brian, lhp | Angels | Sept. 10 |
| Anderson, Mike, rhp | Reds | Sept. 7 |
| Armas, Marcos, of | Athletics | May 25 |
| Arocha, Rene, rhp | Cardinals | April 9 |
| Aude, Rich, 1b | Pirates | Sept. 9 |
| Ausmus, Brad, c | Padres | July 28 |
| Bailey, Cory, rhp | Red Sox | Sept. 1 |
| Batchelor, Rich, rhp | Cardinals | Sept. 3 |
| Bautista, Danny, of | Tigers | Sept. 15 |
| Becker, Rich, of | Twins | Sept. 10 |
| Bergman, Sean, rhp | Tigers | July 7 |
| Bere, Jason, rhp | White Sox | May 27 |
| Blosser, Greg, of | Red Sox | Sept. 5 |
| Bogar, Tim, ss | Mets | April 21 |
| Bolick, Frank, 3b | Expos | April 5 |
| Bolton, Rod, rhp | White Sox | April 10 |
| Brewer, Billy, lhp | Royals | April 8 |
| Bronkey, Jeff, rhp | Rangers | May 2 |
| Brooks, Jerry, of | Dodgers | Sept. 6 |
| Brow, Scott, rhp | Blue Jays | April 28 |
| Brummett, Greg, rhp | Giants | May 29 |
| Buford, Damon, of | Orioles | May 4 |
| Burgos, Enrique, lhp | Royals | July 15 |
| Burnitz, Jeromy, of | Mets | June 21 |
| Bushing, Chris, rhp | Reds | Sept. 3 |
| Butler, Rob, of | Blue Jays | June 12 |
| Byrd, Jim, ss | Red Sox | May 31 |
| Canate, Willie, of | Blue Jays | April 16 |
| Caraballo, Ramon, 2b | Braves | Sept. 9 |
| Carey, Paul, 1b | Orioles | May 25 |
| Castellano, Pedro, 3b | Rockies | May 30 |
| Cedeno, Domingo, ss | Blue Jays | May 19 |
| Converse, Jim, rhp | Mariners | May 22 |
| Cook, Andy, rhp | Yankees | May 9 |
| Correia, Rod, ss | Angels | June 20 |
| Cromer, Tripp, ss | Cardinals | Sept. 7 |
| Cummings, John, lhp | Mariners | April 10 |
| Cummings, Midre, of | Pirates | Sept. 10 |
| Daal, Omar, lhp | Dodgers | April 24 |
| Delgado, Carlos, c | Blue Jays | Oct. 1 |
| DeSilva, John, rhp | Tigers | Aug. 15 |
| DiPoto, Jerry, rhp | Indians | May 11 |
| Dixon, Steve, lhp | Cardinals | Sept. 7 |
| Draper, Mike, rhp | Mets | April 10 |
| Dreyer, Steve, rhp | Rangers | Aug. 8 |
| Edmonds, Jim, of | Angels | Sept. 9 |
| Everett, Carl, of | Marlins | July 1 |
| Ettles, Mark, rhp | Padres | June 5 |
| Faneyte, Rikkert, of | Giants | Aug. 29 |
| Flener, Huck, lhp | Blue Jays | Sept. 14 |
| Fletcher, Paul, rhp | Phillies | July 11 |
| Floyd, Cliff, 1b | Expos | Sept. 18 |
| Foster, Kevin, rhp | Phillies | Sept. 12 |
| Frazier, Lou, of | Expos | April 8 |
| Fredrickson, Scott, rhp | Rockies | April 30 |
| Gainer, Jay, 1b | Rockies | May 14 |
| Gates, Brent, 2b | Athletics | May 5 |
| Gil, Benji, ss | Rangers | April 5 |
| Gohr, Greg, rhp | Tigers | April 7 |
| Gomez, Chris, ss | Tigers | July 19 |
| Gomez, Pat, lhp | Padres | April 6 |
| Gonzales, Larry, c | Angels | June 13 |
| Gordon, Keith, of | Reds | July 8 |
| Granger, Jeff, lhp | Royals | Sept. 16 |
| Green, Shawn, of | Blue Jays | Sept. 28 |
| Green, Tyler, rhp | Phillies | April 9 |
| Greer, Kenny, rhp | Mets | Sept. 29 |
| Guardado, Eddie, lhp | Twins | June 13 |
| Gutierrez, Ricky, ss | Padres | April 13 |
| Hamelin, Bob, 1b | Royals | Sept. 12 |
| Hammonds, Jeffrey, of | Orioles | June 25 |
| Hampton, Mike, lhp | Mariners | April 17 |
| Helfand, Eric, c | Athletics | Sept. 4 |
| Hiatt, Phil, 3b | Royals | April 7 |
| Higgins, Kevin, c | Padres | May 29 |
| Hocking, Denny, ss | Twins | Sept. 10 |
| Hoffman, Trevor, rhp | Marlins | April 6 |
| Holman, Brad, rhp | Mariners | July 4 |
| Holzemer, Mark, rhp | Angels | Aug. 21 |
| Hope, John, rhp | Pirates | Aug. 29 |
| Howard, Chris, rhp | White Sox | Sept. 21 |
| Huskey, Butch, 3b | Mets | Sept. 8 |
| Hutton, Mark, rhp | Yankees | July 23 |
| Jean, Domingo, rhp | Yankees | Aug. 8 |
| Jimenez, Miguel, rhp | Athletics | Sept. 12 |
| Johnson, Erik, ss | Giants | July 8 |
| Johnstone, John, rhp | Marlins | Sept. 3 |
| Jones, Bobby, rhp | Mets | Aug. 14 |
| Jones, Chipper, ss | Braves | Sept. 11 |
| Jones, Todd, rhp | Astros | July 7 |
| Karsay, Steve, rhp | Athletics | Aug. 17 |
| Kessinger, Keith, ss | Reds | Sept. 15 |
| Kiefer, Mark, rhp | Brewers | Sept. 20 |
| King, Kevin, lhp | Mariners | Sept. 2 |
| Kmak, Joe, c | Brewers | April 6 |
| Koelling, Brian, 2b | Reds | Aug. 21 |
| Lansing, Mike, 2b | Expos | April 7 |
| Lee, Derek, of | Twins | June 27 |
| Leftwich, Phil, rhp | Angels | July 29 |
| Leskanic, Curtis, rhp | Rockies | June 27 |
| Lloyd, Graeme, lhp | Brewers | April 11 |
| Longmire, Tony, of | Phillies | Sept. 3 |
| Looney, Brian, lhp | Expos | Sept. 26 |
| Lopez, Albie, rhp | Indians | July 6 |
| Lopez, Luis, 2b | Padres | Sept. 7 |
| Luebbers, Larry, rhp | Reds | July 3 |
| Lyden, Mitch, c | Marlins | June 16 |
| Lydy, Scott, of | Athletics | May 18 |
| Maclin, Lonnie, of | Cardinals | Sept. 5 |
| Marrero, Oreste, 1b | Expos | Aug. 12 |
| Martin, Norberto, 2b | White Sox | Sept. 20 |
| Martinez, Pedro, ss | Padres | June 29 |
| McCarty, David, of | Twins | May 17 |
| McGehee, Kevin, rhp | Orioles | Aug. 23 |
| McMichael, Greg, rhp | Braves | April 12 |
| McNeely, Jeff, of | Red Sox | Sept. 5 |
| Meares, Pat, ss | Twins | May 5 |
| Mejia, Roberto, 2b | Rockies | July 15 |
| Merriman, Brett, rhp | Twins | April 8 |
| Miceli, Dan, rhp | Pirates | Sept. 3 |
| Mieske, Matt, of | Brewers | May 3 |
| Minchey, Nate, rhp | Red Sox | Sept. 12 |
| Miranda, Angel, lhp | Brewers | June 5 |
| Mohler, Mike, lhp | Athletics | April 7 |
| Mondesi, Raul, of | Dodgers | July 19 |
| Montoyo, Charlie, inf | Expos | Sept. 7 |
| Moore, Marcus, rhp | Rockies | July 9 |
| Munoz, Bobby, rhp | Yankees | May 29 |
| Navarro, Tito, ss | Mets | Sept. 6 |
| Nen, Robb, rhp | Rangers | April 10 |
| Newfield, Marc, 1b | Mariners | July 6 |
| Obando, Sherman, of | Orioles | April 10 |
| O'Donoghue, John, lhp | Orioles | June 27 |
| O'Leary, Troy, of | Brewers | May 9 |
| Oliver, Darren, lhp | Rangers | Sept. 1 |
| Oquist, Mike, rhp | Orioles | Aug. 14 |
| Ortiz, Luis, 3b | Red Sox | Aug. 31 |
| Owens, J., c | Rockies | June 6 |
| Painter, Lance, lhp | Rockies | May 19 |
| Paquette, Craig, 3b | Athletics | June 1 |
| Pennington, Brad, lhp | Orioles | April 14 |
| Perez, Eduardo, 3b | Angels | July 27 |
| Phillips, J.R., 1b | Giants | Sept. 3 |
| Pirkl, Greg, 1b | Mariners | Aug. 13 |
| Plantenberg, Erik, lhp | Mariners | July 31 |
| Pose, Scott, of | Marlins | April 5 |
| Powell, Ross, lhp | Reds | Sept. 5 |
| Pride, Curtis, of | Expos | Sept. 14 |
| Ramirez, Manny, of | Indians | Sept. 2 |
| Roberson, Kevin, of | Cubs | July 15 |
| Robertson, Rich, lhp | Pirates | April 30 |
| Ronan, Marc, c | Cardinals | Sept. 21 |
| Roper, John, rhp | Reds | May 16 |
| Rueter, Kirk, lhp | Expos | July 7 |
| Ruffcorn, Scott, rhp | White Sox | June 19 |
| Ruffin, Johnny, rhp | Reds | Aug. 8 |
| Salkeld, Roger, rhp | Mariners | Sept. 8 |
| Sanders, Scott, rhp | Padres | Aug. 6 |
| Saunders, Doug, 2b | Mets | June 13 |
| Schwarz, Jeff, rhp | White Sox | April 24 |
| Scott, Darryl, rhp | Angels | May 31 |
| Sele, Aaron, rhp | Red Sox | June 23 |
| Shave, Jon, 2b | Rangers | May 15 |
| Shelton, Ben, 1b | Pirates | June 16 |
| Sherman, Darrell, of | Padres | April 8 |
| Shinall, Zak, rhp | Mariners | May 12 |
| Shouse, Brian, lhp | Pirates | July 31 |
| Siddall, Joe, c | Expos | July 28 |
| Smithberg, Roger, rhp | Athletics | Sept. 1 |
| Spradlin, Jerry, rhp | Reds | July 2 |
| Stahoviak, Scott, 3b | Twins | Sept. 10 |
| Staton, Dave, 1b | Padres | Sept. 8 |
| Stocker, Kevin, ss | Phillies | July 7 |
| Swingle, Paul, rhp | Angels | Sept. 7 |
| Tarasco, Tony, of | Braves | April 30 |
| Tavarez, Julian, rhp | Indians | Aug. 7 |
| Taylor, Kerry, rhp | Padres | April 13 |
| Telgheder, David, rhp | Mets | June 12 |
| Tinsley, Lee, of | Mariners | April 6 |
| Tomberlin, Andy, of | Pirates | Aug. 12 |
| Torres, Salomon, rhp | Giants | Aug. 29 |
| Trachsel, Steve, rhp | Cubs | Sept. 19 |
| Tsamis, George, lhp | Twins | April 26 |
| Tubbs, Greg, of | Reds | Aug. 1 |
| Turang, Brian, of | Mariners | Aug. 13 |
| Turner, Chris, c | Angels | Aug. 27 |
| Turner, Matt, rhp | Marlins | April 23 |
| Urbani, Tom, lhp | Cardinals | April 21 |
| Van Burkleo, Ty, 1b | Angels | July 28 |
| Vina, Fernando, 2b | Mariners | April 10 |
| Walbeck, Matt, c | Cubs | April 7 |
| Watson, Allen, lhp | Cardinals | July 8 |
| Wendell, Turk, rhp | Cubs | June 17 |
| Wertz, Bill, rhp | Indians | May 22 |
| White, Derrick, 1b | Expos | July 22 |
| White, Rondell, of | Expos | Sept. 1 |
| Whitmore, Darrell, of | Marlins | June 25 |
| Williams, Woody, rhp | Blue Jays | May 14 |
| Wilson, Nigel, of | Marlins | Sept. 8 |
| Womack, Tony, ss | Pirates | Sept. 10 |
| Worrell, Tim, rhp | Padres | June 25 |
| Zambrano, Eddie, of | Cubs | Sept. 19 |

**Mark Hutton.** First Australian pitcher to start a big league game.

before. The Orioles were the only major league team sold in 1993.

## Salaries Stabilize, Sort Of

Major league salaries stayed high in 1993, but the owners began showing some signs of restraint.

The average salary was $1.07 million in 1993, down slightly from $1.08 million the year before. The number of players making $1 million or more also fell a bit, from 268 to 262. And the owners were changing the way they parceled the money out, giving more to a few big stars and less to most players.

The new salary champion was Barry Bonds, who signed with the San Francisco Giants in December 1992 for six years and $43.75 million. If it's possible to be worth that much money, Bonds was. He batted .336, hit 46 home runs and in the first year of the contract actually made less than teammate Will Clark, the 1993-94 offseason's marquee free agent. With Bonds producing an MVP season, the Giants won 103 games just a year after they appeared headed out of town.

And of course, cutting salaries doesn't necessarily make an owner popular. The Padres' Tom Werner certainly proved that.

Werner rid himself of Benito Santiago, Tony

### TOP-PAID PLAYERS

Barry Bonds signed baseball's richest-ever contract—a multiyear $43.75 million deal—with the San Francisco Giants, but his 1993 salary of $4,219,175 didn't even rank him among baseball's best-paid players in 1993. Here's how the 20 ranked in 1993:

| Rank, Club | '93 Contract |
|---|---|
| 1. Bobby Bonilla, of, Mets | $6,450,000 |
| 2. Ryne Sandberg, 2b, Cubs | 6,025,000 |
| 3. Dwight Gooden, rhp, Mets | 5,916,667 |
| 4. Barry Larkin, ss, Reds | 5,750,000 |
| 5. Joe Carter, of, Blue Jays | 5,550,000 |
| Greg Maddux, rhp, Braves | 5,550,000 |
| 7. Jack Morris, rhp, Blue Jays | 5,425,000 |
| 8. Chuck Finley, lhp, Angels | 5,375,000 |
| 9. Kirby Puckett, of, Twins | 5,300,000 |
| 10. Cal Ripken, ss, Orioles | 5,150,000 |
| 11. Danny Tartabull, of, Yankees | 5,050,000 |
| 12. David Cone, rhp, Royals | 5,000,000 |
| 13. Jimmy Key, lhp, Yankees | 4,900,000 |
| Andy Van Slyke, of, Pirates | 4,900,000 |
| 15. Roberto Alomar, 2b, Blue Jays | 4,883,333 |
| 16. Andre Dawson, of, Red Sox | 4,875,000 |
| 17. Tom Glavine, lhp, Braves | 4,850,000 |
| 18. Frank Viola, lhp, Red Sox | 4,833,333 |
| 19. Jose Canseco, of, Rangers | 4,800,000 |
| 20. Will Clark, 1b, Giants | 4,750,000 |

**Bobby Bonilla**

Fernandez, Darrin Jackson and Randy Myers before the season started, either through trade or free agency. After the 1993 season began, Werner unloaded Fred McGriff, Gary Sheffield, Bruce Hurst, Greg Harris and Kurt Stillwell, the latter of whom certainly wasn't a star but made $1.75 million.

The Padres finished last in the NL West, behind even the expansion Rockies, and San Diego fans were outraged. When the season closed, Tony Gwynn and Andy Benes were the team's only seven-figure players, and Benes figured to be the next to go.

## Schott Goes, Returns

Another owner making negative headlines was the Reds' Marge Schott, who was suspended for the season for making racially insensitive remarks, some of them about her own players.

General manager Jim Bowden ran the team in Schott's absence, and had a tumultuous year. Bowden fired popular manager Tony Perez just 44 games into the season, and replaced him with Davey Johnson.

Schott's suspension ended in the fall, and more fireworks were expected after that. She and Johnson reportedly don't get along.

**Marge Schott**

## Bye-Bye Bureau

Cost-conscious owners began dismantling the Major League Scouting Bureau, a 1970s creation designed to supplement the work of organizations' own scouts.

Contracts weren't renewed for all 21 part-time scouts and most of the full-timers. Cross-checkers, regional supervisors and professional scouting were eliminated entirely. The only scouts remaining were ones whose contracts had another year left.

Also eliminated was the bureau's scouting school, which brought many young scouts into the business over the years.

### TEAM SALARIES

The World Series champion Toronto Blue Jays had baseball's highest payroll in 1993. Here's how the teams ranked, factoring in prorated shares of signing bonuses and earned performance bonuses, but not award bonuses. Termination pay for players who were traded, plus any cash payments to club receiving a traded players, is indicated:

| Rank, Club | Active | Term. Pay | '93 Payroll |
|---|---|---|---|
| 1. Toronto | $48,018,166 | $3,556,868 | $51,575,034 |
| 2. New York (AL) | 46,736,000 | (-172,209) | 46,563,791 |
| 3. Boston | 38,978,250 | 7,186,538 | 46,164,788 |
| 4. Atlanta | 43,856,416 | 1,000,000 | 44,856,416 |
| 5. Chicago (AL) | 39,368,498 | 2,582,225 | 41,950,723 |
| 6. Cincinnati | 39,803,167 | 1,828,220 | 41,631,387 |
| 7. New York (NL) | 40,622,667 | 200,000 | 40,822,667 |
| 8. Kansas City | 38,081,499 | 1,983,379 | 40,064,878 |
| 9. Detroit | 37,929,498 | 109,000 | 38,038,498 |
| 10. San Francisco | 36,155,509 | 61,813 | 36,217,322 |
| 11. Texas | 35,656,739 | 255,951 | 35,912,690 |
| 12. Chicago (NL) | 35,211,333 | 544,643 | 35,755,976 |
| 13. Oakland | 32,751,334 | 2,600,000 | 35,351,334 |
| 14. Los Angeles | 36,079,000 | (-2,550,000) | 33,529,000 |
| 15. Seattle | 30,533,333 | 2,677,709 | 33,211,042 |
| 16. Houston | 30,075,000 | 5,233 | 30,080,233 |
| 17. Baltimore | 29,164,000 | 39,066 | 29,203,066 |
| 18. Philadelphia | 31,203,001 | (-2,707,143) | 28,495,858 |
| 19. California | 24,675,834 | 2,809,065 | 27,444,899 |
| 20. Minnesota | 26,802,933 | 264,835 | 27,067,768 |
| 21. Milwaukee | 23,467,123 | 2,168,264 | 25,635,387 |
| 22. St. Louis | 21,626,667 | 2,298,000 | 24,190,667 |
| 23. Pittsburgh | 20,474,667 | 3,694,000 | 24,168,667 |
| 24. Florida | 20,972,545 | 200,000 | 21,172,545 |
| 25. Montreal | 14,616,334 | 3,005,706 | 17,622,040 |
| 26. Cleveland | 15,783,167 | 757,830 | 16,540,997 |
| 27. Colorado | 14,275,500 | 597,088 | 14,872,588 |
| 28. San Diego | 10,592,333 | 2,250,000 | 12,842,333 |
| **TOTALS** | **863,106,513** | **37,876,081** | **900,982,594** |

# OBITUARIES

## November 1993-October 1992

**Ethan Allen**, 89, who hit .300 in 13 major league seasons and had a storied career after his playing days ended, died Sept. 15 in Brookings, Ore. Allen, an outfielder, batted .300 in 1,281 games with the Reds, New York Giants, Cardinals, Phillies, Cubs and St. Louis Browns. He became head baseball coach at Yale in 1946, and his 1947 and 1948 teams played in the first NCAA championships, losing to Southern California and California in the finals. Former President George Bush was the captain and first baseman on the 1948 team.

**Carl Barger**, 62, Florida Marlins president virtually since the club's inception, died Dec. 9, 1992, of a ruptured aorta while attending the Winter Meetings in Louisville. Barger didn't join baseball until the mid-1980s, when he was involved in the sale of the Pirates to Doug Danforth. He became president of the Pirates Oct. 2, 1987. Barger helped convince Blockbuster Video mogul Wayne Huizenga to pursue one of the National League's expansion franchises and then lobbied on Huizenga's behalf. On July 8, 1991, three days after the Marlins were approved as an expansion team, Barger was named club president.

**Roy Campanella**, 71, a three-time Most Valuable Player as a catcher with the Dodgers in the 1950s, died June 26 in Woodland Hills, Calif., of a heart attack. He was just the fourth black player in major league history when he joined the Dodgers in 1948, following nine seasons in the Negro Leagues. In 1961, he followed teammate Jackie Robinson as the second black inducted into the Hall of Fame. Campanella set single-season major league records for catchers with 41 home runs and 142 RBIs in 1953. He was the starting backstop for five National League champions and the Dodgers' first World Series winning team in 1955. He hit 242 home runs and drove in 856 runs in his brief career that was cut short first by baseball's color barrier and then by a crippling accident. Campenella was paralyzed from the chest down on Jan. 28, 1958, when the rental car he was driving skidded on a rain-slicked road, hit a telephone pole and turned over, pinning Campanella underneath.

**Ben Chapman**, 84, who played next to Babe Ruth during the Babe's final five seasons with the Yankees, died July 7 in Hoover, Ala., of an apparent heart attack. Chapman posted a career average of .302 and stole 287 bases in his 15-year major league career. Four times Chapman led the American League in stolen bases. Chapman also was the first-ever batter in baseball's All-Star game, batting leadoff for the AL in 1933.

**Tim Crews**, 31, and **Steve Olin**, 27, pitchers for the Cleveland Indians, died following a March 22 accident in which the 18-foot fishing boat Crews was piloting struck a pier on Little Lake Nellie, about 25 miles west of Orlando.

**Don Drysdale**, 56, half of one of the greatest pitching duos in baseball history with the Los Angeles Dodgers, died July 3 in Montreal of a heart attack. Along with Sandy Koufax, Drysdale formed a 1-2 punch that led the Dodgers to World Series titles in 1959, 1963 and 1965. Drysdale went 209-166 in 14 seasons, starting with the Brooklyn Dodgers in 1956. He led the National League in strikeouts three times, posted a lifetime ERA of 2.95 and recorded 58⅔ straight scoreless innings in 1968. Drysdale was inducted into the Hall of Fame in 1984.

**Don Drysdale**

**Charlie Gehringer**, 89, considered one of the greatest second basemen in baseball history, died Jan. 23 in Bloomfield Hills, Mich. He had suffered a stroke Dec. 23, 1992.

Gehringer spent all 19 of his major league seasons with Detroit from 1924-42, appearing in three World Series, including 1935, when the Tigers won their last championship prior to 1968. Gehringer was the starting second baseman for the American League in the first six All-Star games, hit .300 or better 13 times, was the AL's MVP in 1937 and collected 2,839 hits in his career.

**Granny Hamner**, 66, the shortstop on the Philadelphia Phillies' Whiz Kids team of 1950, died of an apparent heart attack Sept. 12 in Philadelphia. Hamner batted .262 in 17 big league seasons and was a three-time all-star.

**Tex Hughson**, 77, a two-time 20-game winner with the Red Sox, died Aug. 6 of kidney failure in Austin. Hughson pitched in eight major league seasons, all with Boston. He had his best years during World War II, including 1942, when he led the American League in wins (22), complete games (22), innings (281) and strikeouts (113).

**Ewing Kauffman**, 76, owner of the Kansas City Royals since the team's inception in 1969, died of bone cancer in Kansas City Aug. 1. Kauffman made his fortune in the pharmaceutical business. After serving as the sole owner of the Royals for 14 years, he sold 49 percent of the club to Avron Fogelman in 1983 and an additional one percent to Fogelman in 1988. In 1991, however, Kauffman bought back the shares to again become sole owner when Fogelman ran into financial trouble. The Royals changed the name of their home park from Royals Stadium to Kauffman Stadium.

**Ewing Kauffman**

**Mark Koenig**, 88, the last survivor from what is considered the greatest baseball team in history, the 1927 New York Yankees, died April 22 in Willows, Calif., of cancer.

**Bob Miller**, 54, the Giants' advance scout and a former major league pitcher for 17 seasons, died Aug. 6 in a car crash near San Diego. Miller and his mother were in a car that collided with another in the San Diego suburb of Rancho Bernardo. Miller was killed instantly, and his mother, Norma Jean Miller, was injured. Miller was on the first Mets team in 1962, and tied the National League record for losses at the start of a season, 12. The record was broken in 1993 by another Met, Anthony Young.

**Johnny Mize**, 80, who hit 359 home runs in a 15-year career for the St. Louis Cardinals, New York Giants and New York Yankees, died June 2 in Demorest, Ga., of cardiac arrest. Mize, inducted into the Hall of Fame, hit three home runs in a game a major league record six times (tied with Joe Carter). "The Big Cat" led the National League in home runs four times, including 1948, when he hit a career-best 51. Mize also won the 1939 NL batting title, hitting .349. He retired with a career batting average of .312 and a career slugging percentage of .562, the eighth-best in major league history.

**Diego Ruiz**, 22, a Springfield Cardinals reliever, died in a May 22 auto accident in Springfield. Cardinals catcher Eddie Williams was driving the car when it hit a steel pole, went airborne and crashed into a liquor store. Police said alcohol was involved in the accident, but did not press charges.

**Hal Schumacher**, 82, who pitched for the New York Giants for 13 seasons in the 1930s and '40s, died April 21 in Cooperstown, N.Y. Schumacher posted a 158-120 career mark, pitched in two All-Star Games and appeared in three World Series.

**Bob Wright**, 101, the second-oldest former major league player, died of pneumonia July 30 in Carmichael, Calif. Wright made two relief appearances for the 1915 Cubs.

# Carter's Heroics Lift Jays To Second Title

**By TRACY RINGOLSBY**

On the day they were honored in Toronto as 1992 World Series champions, the Blue Jays began rebuilding in hopes of repeating. And it wasn't just a cosmetic change or two that general manager Pat Gillick had in mind.

By the time the Blue Jays opened the 1993 regular season, the team had been redesigned. Twelve members from the previous year were gone. By season's end, however, the Blue Jays had a familiar look— the look of a World Series winner.

With the constant attention of Gillick, the steady hand of manager Cito Gaston and a positive impact from the new faces that were added to the roster, the Blue Jays beat the Philadelphia Phillies in six games, becoming the first team to win consecutive championships since the 1977-78 New York Yankees.

In the end it was Paul Molitor, the veteran free agent signed when Dave Winfield went home to Minnesota, who was honored as the World Series MVP. He hit .500 with two home runs and eight RBIs in the series, while scoring 10 runs, including the run that clinched the title.

Molitor was on first base—Rickey Henderson on third—when Joe Carter delivered a dramatic game-winning three-run home run in the bottom of the ninth inning of the Jays 8-6 victory in Game Six. The homer was just the second to end a World Series and the first since Bill Mazeroski of Pittsburgh took Ralph Terry of the Yankees deep in the bottom of the ninth of Game Seven in 1960.

"You saw me jumping up and down last year at first base," said Carter, who took the throw from pitcher Mike Timlin to record the final out in the Game Six clincher at Atlanta the previous October. "And you saw me jump up and down again this year, only this time it was all around the bases."

## Phillies Fight To The End

It was only fitting that a big hit would provide an end to this offensive roller-coaster of a World Series. The two teams combined to score 81 runs—one short of the all-time record set by the Pirates and Yankees, who played a seventh game back in 1960.

And it featured the highest-scoring and the longest game in Series history when the Blue Jays rode a six-run, eighth inning to a 15-14 victory at Philadelphia in Game Four. The game lasted four hours and 14 minutes.

Phillies center fielder Lenny Dykstra did everything he could to produce the first World Series winner from the National League East since the 1986 New York Mets. As a leadoff hitter, he had a .348 average, and

**Jays Win! Jays Win!** Toronto's Joe Carter launched one of the most dramatic home runs in World Series history, winning the '93 Series for the Blue Jays.

produced only the fourth four-home run effort in Series history.

Even in the final game, it was Dykstra's three-run homer that helped the Phillies become the first team since 1925 to rally from a four-run deficit. Philadelphia trailed 5-1 when it scored five times in the seventh to go ahead 6-5. The Jays, however, had one final rally within them.

"We don't quit until they tell us it is time to quit," Phillies first baseman John Kruk said. "Like when we were in a bar until 2 a.m. They tell us to get up and go home and we do. Joe Carter told us it was time to go home."

That message was delivered to Mitch Williams, the erratic and emotional Philadelphia closer, who went from a cult hero to a scapegoat for the city's disappointment. It was Williams who let a 6-5 lead disappear in the ninth inning of Game Six, and it was also "Wild Thing" who was on the mound as the Jays scored the final five runs in that six-run eighth inning in Game Four.

Williams, in fact, converted only three of seven save

# WORLD SERIES
## YEAR-BY-YEAR

| Year | Winner | Manager | Loser | Manager | Result | MVP |
|---|---|---|---|---|---|---|
| 1903 | Boston (AL) | Jimmy Collins | Pittsburgh (NL) | Fred Clarke | 5-3 | None Selected |
| 1904 | NO SERIES | | | | | |
| 1905 | New York (NL) | John McGraw | Philadelphia (AL) | Connie Mack | 4-1 | None Selected |
| 1906 | Chicago (AL) | Fielder Jones | Chicago (NL) | Frank Chance | 4-2 | None Selected |
| 1907 | Chicago (NL) | Frank Chance | Detroit (AL) | Hugh Jennings | 4-0 | None Selected |
| 1908 | Chicago (NL) | Frank Chance | Detroit (AL) | Hugh Jennings | 4-1 | None Selected |
| 1909 | Pittsburgh (NL) | Fred Clarke | Detroit (AL) | Hugh Jennings | 4-3 | None Selected |
| 1910 | Philadelphia (AL) | Connie Mack | Chicago (NL) | Frank Chance | 4-1 | None Selected |
| 1911 | Philadelphia (AL) | Connie Mack | New York (NL) | John McGraw | 4-2 | None Selected |
| 1912 | Boston (AL) | Jake Stahl | New York (NL) | John McGraw | 4-3-1 | None Selected |
| 1913 | Philadelphia (AL) | Connie Mack | New York (NL) | John McGraw | 4-1 | None Selected |
| 1914 | Boston (NL) | George Stallings | Philadelphia (AL) | Connie Mack | 4-0 | None Selected |
| 1915 | Boston (AL) | Bill Carrigan | Philadelphia (NL) | Pat Moran | 4-1 | None Selected |
| 1916 | Boston (AL) | Bill Carrigan | Brooklyn (NL) | Wilbert Robinson | 4-1 | None Selected |
| 1917 | Chicago (AL) | Pants Rowland | New York (NL) | John McGraw | 4-2 | None Selected |
| 1918 | Boston (AL) | Ed Barrow | Chicago (NL) | Fred Mitchell | 4-2 | None Selected |
| 1919 | Cincinnati (NL) | Pat Moran | Chicago (AL) | Kid Gleason | 5-3 | None Selected |
| 1920 | Cleveland (AL) | Tris Speaker | Brooklyn (NL) | Wilbert Robinson | 5-2 | None Selected |
| 1921 | New York (NL) | John McGraw | New York (AL) | Miller Huggins | 5-3 | None Selected |
| 1922 | New York (NL) | John McGraw | New York (AL) | Miller Huggins | 4-0 | None Selected |
| 1923 | New York (AL) | Miller Huggins | New York (NL) | John McGraw | 4-2 | None Selected |
| 1924 | Washington (AL) | Bucky Harris | New York (NL) | John McGraw | 4-3 | None Selected |
| 1925 | Pittsburgh (NL) | Bill McKechnie | Washington (AL) | Bucky Harris | 4-3 | None Selected |
| 1926 | St. Louis (NL) | Rogers Hornsby | New York (AL) | Miller Huggins | 4-3 | None Selected |
| 1927 | New York (AL) | Miller Huggins | Pittsburgh (NL) | Donie Bush | 4-0 | None Selected |
| 1928 | New York (AL) | Miller Huggins | St. Louis (NL) | Bill McKechnie | 4-0 | None Selected |
| 1929 | Philadelphia (AL) | Connie Mack | Chicago (NL) | Joe McCarthy | 4-1 | None Selected |
| 1930 | Philadelphia (AL) | Connie Mack | St. Louis (NL) | Gabby Street | 4-2 | None Selected |
| 1931 | St. Louis (NL) | Gabby Street | Philadelphia (AL) | Connie Mack | 4-3 | None Selected |
| 1932 | New York (AL) | Joe McCarthy | Chicago (NL) | Charlie Grimm | 4-0 | None Selected |
| 1933 | New York (NL) | Bill Terry | Washington (AL) | Joe Cronin | 4-1 | None Selected |
| 1934 | St. Louis (NL) | Frankie Frisch | Detroit (AL) | Mickey Cochrane | 4-3 | None Selected |
| 1935 | Detroit (AL) | Mickey Cochrane | Chicago (NL) | Charlie Grimm | 4-2 | None Selected |
| 1936 | New York (AL) | Joe McCarthy | New York (NL) | Bill Terry | 4-2 | None Selected |
| 1937 | New York (AL) | Joe McCarthy | New York (NL) | Bill Terry | 4-1 | None Selected |
| 1938 | New York (AL) | Joe McCarthy | Chicago (NL) | Gabby Hartnett | 4-0 | None Selected |
| 1939 | New York (AL) | Joe McCarthy | Cincinnati (NL) | Bill McKechnie | 4-0 | None Selected |
| 1940 | Cincinnati (NL) | Bill McKechnie | Detroit (AL) | Del Baker | 4-3 | None Selected |
| 1941 | New York (AL) | Joe McCarthy | Brooklyn (NL) | Leo Durocher | 4-1 | None Selected |
| 1942 | St. Louis (NL) | Billy Southworth | New York (AL) | Joe McCarthy | 4-1 | None Selected |
| 1943 | New York (AL) | Joe McCarthy | St. Louis (NL) | Billy Southworth | 4-1 | None Selected |
| 1944 | St. Louis (NL) | Billy Southworth | St. Louis (AL) | Luke Sewell | 4-2 | None Selected |
| 1945 | Detroit (AL) | Steve O'Neill | Chicago (NL) | Charlie Grimm | 4-3 | None Selected |
| 1946 | St. Louis (NL) | Eddie Dyer | Boston (AL) | Joe Cronin | 4-3 | None Selected |
| 1947 | New York (AL) | Bucky Harris | Brooklyn (NL) | Burt Shotton | 4-3 | None Selected |
| 1948 | Cleveland (AL) | Lou Boudreau | Boston (NL) | Billy Southworth | 4-2 | None Selected |
| 1949 | New York (AL) | Casey Stengel | Brooklyn (NL) | Burt Shotton | 4-1 | None Selected |
| 1950 | New York (AL) | Casey Stengel | Philadelphia (NL) | Eddie Sawyer | 4-0 | None Selected |
| 1951 | New York (AL) | Casey Stengel | New York (NL) | Leo Durocher | 4-2 | None Selected |
| 1952 | New York (AL) | Casey Stengel | Brooklyn (NL) | Chuck Dressen | 4-3 | None Selected |
| 1953 | New York (AL) | Casey Stengel | Brooklyn (NL) | Chuck Dressen | 4-2 | None Selected |
| 1954 | New York (NL) | Leo Durocher | Cleveland (AL) | Al Lopez | 4-0 | None Selected |
| 1955 | Brooklyn (NL) | Walter Alston | New York (AL) | Casey Stengel | 4-3 | Johnny Podres, p, Brooklyn |
| 1956 | New York (AL) | Casey Stengel | Brooklyn (NL) | Walter Alston | 4-3 | Don Larsen, p, New York |
| 1957 | Milwaukee (NL) | Fred Haney | New York (AL) | Casey Stengel | 4-3 | Lew Burdette, p, Milwaukee |
| 1958 | New York (AL) | Casey Stengel | Milwaukee (NL) | Fred Haney | 4-3 | Bob Turley, p, New York |
| 1959 | Los Angeles (NL) | Walter Alston | Chicago (AL) | Al Lopez | 4-2 | Larry Sherry, p, Los Angeles |
| 1960 | Pittsburgh (NL) | Danny Murtaugh | New York (AL) | Casey Stengel | 4-3 | Bobby Richardson, 2b, New York |
| 1961 | New York (AL) | Ralph Houk | Cincinnati (NL) | Fred Hutchinson | 4-1 | Whitey Ford, p, New York |
| 1962 | New York (AL) | Ralph Houk | San Francisco (NL) | Alvin Dark | 4-3 | Ralph Terry, p, New York |
| 1963 | Los Angeles (NL) | Walter Alston | New York (AL) | Ralph Houk | 4-0 | Sandy Koufax, p, Los Angeles |
| 1964 | St. Louis (NL) | Johnny Keene | New York (AL) | Yogi Berra | 4-3 | Bob Gibson, p, St. Louis |
| 1965 | Los Angeles (NL) | Walter Alston | Minnesota (AL) | Sam Mele | 4-3 | Sandy Koufax, p, Los Angeles |
| 1966 | Baltimore (AL) | Hank Bauer | Los Angeles (NL) | Walter Alston | 4-0 | Frank Robinson, of, Baltimore |
| 1967 | St. Louis (NL) | Red Schoendienst | Boston (AL) | Dick Williams | 4-3 | Bob Gibson, p, St. Louis |
| 1968 | Detroit (AL) | Mayo Smith | St. Louis (NL) | Red Schoendienst | 4-3 | Mickey Lolich, p, Detroit |
| 1969 | New York (NL) | Gil Hodges | Baltimore (AL) | Earl Weaver | 4-1 | Donn Clendenon, 1b, New York |
| 1970 | Baltimore (AL) | Earl Weaver | Cincinnati (NL) | Sparky Anderson | 4-1 | Brooks Robinson, 3b, Baltimore |
| 1971 | Pittsburgh (NL) | Danny Murtaugh | Baltimore (AL) | Earl Weaver | 4-3 | Roberto Clemente, of, Pittsburgh |
| 1972 | Oakland (AL) | Dick Williams | Cincinnati (NL) | Sparky Anderson | 4-3 | Gene Tenace, c, Oakland |
| 1973 | Oakland (AL) | Dick Williams | New York (NL) | Yogi Berra | 4-3 | Reggie Jackson, of, Oakland |
| 1974 | Oakland (AL) | Alvin Dark | Los Angeles (NL) | Walter Alston | 4-1 | Rollie Fingers, p, Oakland |
| 1975 | Cincinnati (NL) | Sparky Anderson | Boston (AL) | Darrell Johnson | 4-3 | Pete Rose, 3b, Cincinnati |
| 1976 | Cincinnati (NL) | Sparky Anderson | New York (AL) | Billy Martin | 4-0 | Johnny Bench, c, Cincinnati |
| 1977 | New York (AL) | Billy Martin | Los Angeles (NL) | Tom Lasorda | 4-2 | Reggie Jackson, of, New York |
| 1978 | New York (AL) | Bob Lemon | Los Angeles (NL) | Tom Lasorda | 4-2 | Bucky Dent, ss, New York |
| 1979 | Pittsburgh (NL) | Chuck Tanner | Baltimore (AL) | Earl Weaver | 4-3 | Willie Stargell, 1b, Pittsburgh |
| 1980 | Philadelphia (NL) | Dallas Green | Kansas City (AL) | Jim Frey | 4-2 | Mike Schmidt, 3b, Philadelphia |
| 1981 | Los Angeles (NL) | Tom Lasorda | New York (AL) | Bob Lemon | 4-2 | Cey/Guerrero/Yeager, Los Angeles |
| 1982 | St. Louis (NL) | Whitey Herzog | Milwaukee (AL) | Harvey Kuenn | 4-3 | Darrell Porter, c, St. Louis |
| 1983 | Baltimore (AL) | Joe Altobelli | Philadelphia (NL) | Paul Owens | 4-1 | Rick Dempsey, c, Baltimore |
| 1984 | Detroit (AL) | Sparky Anderson | San Diego (NL) | Dick Williams | 4-1 | Alan Trammell, ss, Detroit |
| 1985 | Kansas City (AL) | Dick Howser | St. Louis (NL) | Whitey Herzog | 4-3 | Bret Saberhagen, p, Kansas City |
| 1986 | New York (NL) | Dave Johnson | Boston (AL) | John McNamara | 4-3 | Ray Knight, 3b, New York |
| 1987 | Minnesota (AL) | Tom Kelly | St. Louis (NL) | Whitey Herzog | 4-3 | Frank Viola, p, Minnesota |
| 1988 | Los Angeles (NL) | Tom Lasorda | Oakland (AL) | Tony La Russa | 4-1 | Orel Hershiser, p, Los Angeles |
| 1989 | Oakland (AL) | Tony La Russa | San Francisco (NL) | Roger Craig | 4-0 | Dave Stewart, p, Oakland |
| 1990 | Cincinnati (NL) | Lou Piniella | Oakland (AL) | Tony La Russa | 4-0 | Jose Rijo, p, Cincinnati |
| 1991 | Minnesota (AL) | Tom Kelly | Atlanta (NL) | Bobby Cox | 4-3 | Jack Morris, p, Minnesota |
| 1992 | Toronto (AL) | Cito Gaston | Atlanta (NL) | Bobby Cox | 4-2 | Pat Borders, c, Toronto |
| 1993 | Toronto (AL) | Cito Gaston | Philadelphia (NL) | Jim Fregosi | 4-2 | Paul Molitor, dh, Toronto |

opportunities during postseason play. Manager Jim Fregosi, however, never wavered in his belief in Williams. Not even in Game Six after Dykstra's home run gave the Phillies a 6-5 lead and hope of forcing a seventh game did Fregosi lose faith in the man who converted all but four of his 47 regular season save opportunities.

"Mitch has been our closer all year and I wasn't going to change things at the end," Fregosi said.

Williams' fastball was so tempered that Carter thought he had hit a slider for the game-winning homer.

The decisive ninth began with a walk to Henderson. After Devon White flied out, Molitor, whose fifth-inning home run had given Toronto a 5-1 lead, singled to center. Up stepped Carter. Five pitches later, Carter drove a 2-2 pitch from Williams over the fence down the left field line and the celebration began.

"That's something you dream about," Carter said. "Bottom of the ninth, two strikes, you hit a home run to win the World Series."

## Leiter Quiets Phillies' Bats

The tone for the Series was set in Game One. Al Leiter, a middle reliever, was the pitching star in the Blue Jays' 8-5 victory. Leiter, a lefthander, shut down a Philadelphia lineup loaded with lefthanded bats and deflated the Phillies with a two-out, bases-loaded strikeout of Kruk in the sixth. The Blue Jays offense came to life after that. John Olerud tied the score with a home run in the sixth, and the Jays put the game away with three more runs in the seventh.

Just as it looked like Toronto might breeze to another title, the Phillies stunned American League Championship Series MVP Dave Stewart with a 6-4 victory in Game 2. Stewart was blitzed by a five-run fifth capped off by Jim Eisenreich's three-run home run—more runs in an inning than Stewart had allowed in 19 other postseason games, 17 of which were starts.

The Phillies got out of a potentially damaging jam in the eighth, thanks to the work of advance scouts Jimmy Stewart and Ray Shore. After Roberto Alomar stole second base, he was ready to try for third on the next pitch—a Blue Jays play the scouts had warned the Phillies about—and Williams was able to wheel and

**Series MVP.** Veteran Paul Molitor did it all for the Blue Jays—in the field and at the plate (.500, six extra-base hits).

throw out Alomar before he could slide into third. It ended Alomar's postseason-record stolen base streak at 16. It would be Williams' last converted save opportunity of the Series.

The postseason—and basically his entire stay in Toronto—was a bust for Henderson, picked up in an August trade. But there was one night of redemption, in Game Three of the World Series.

Henderson was the igniter and first baseman-for-a-game Molitor the detonator in Toronto's 10-3 rain-delayed explosion against Philadelphia, the series' only blowout.

"It looks to me like Cito made the right choice," Fregosi said of Gaston's decision to put Molitor at first in place of Olerud, the AL batting champ, against lefthander Danny Jackson. Molitor would move to third base in place of Ed Sprague in games Four and Five at Philadelphia, where the designated hitter was not allowed.

In Game Three, Molitor was 3-for-4 with a walk, triple and home run, driving in three runs and scoring three, numbers that supported Gaston's decision.

## Pitchers' Nightmare

The clock at Veterans Stadium was about to strike midnight, and the Blue Jays were in a bind in Game Four.

"I'm figuring we'll come back and get them tomorrow," White thought with his team five runs down heading to the eighth.

MEL BAILEY

**Goat Horns.** Phillies lefthander Mitch Williams was victimized by Toronto comebacks in Games Four and Six.

The Blue Jays, however, didn't have to wait that long for their third victory. Night ran into early morning and Toronto pulled out a midst-shrouded 15-14 victory. A six-run eighth inning that White capped off with a two-run triple as the scoreboard clock flashed midnight was the difference in the highest scoring and longest game in World Series history.

"This will go down in the annals as one of the all-time World Series games," said Fregosi. "It was unbelievable."

It was dreamlike for the two offenses, particularly Blue Jays shortstop Tony Fernandez and Phillies left fielder Milt Thompson, who drove in five runs apiece, one short of a Series record. Dykstra tied a Series record by scoring four runs. He also drove in four runs, hit two home runs and drew a leadoff walk in what became a four-run Phillies first that wiped out a 3-0 Toronto lead.

Neither starting pitcher survived the third inning.

Toronto's Todd Stottlemyre walked four batters, three in a row in the first, and departed after giving up six runs in just two innings.

Philadelphia's Tommy Greene was knocked out with one out in the third, having given up seven runs.

"Like Nightmare on Elm Street," said Jays closer Duane Ward, who provided the final successful act in this rendition to earn the save. "Everyone who came out kept giving up runs until Timlin came in."

Even the bullpen phone from the Blue Jays' dugout

**Rises To Occasion.** One of baseball's best money players, Blue Jays second baseman Roberto Alomar hit .480 in the 1993 Series.

MICHAEL PONZINI

went on the blink. When Gaston went out in the sixth to bring in Tony Castillo, it was Mark Eichhorn who came trotting in. After a talk with the umpires, Eichhorn returned to the bullpen, and Castillo was allowed to take as long as he wanted on the mound. Castillo was the winning pitcher, despite walking three and giving up three hits in 2⅓ innings.

## Series Returns To SkyDome

Philadelphia righthander Curt Schilling personally forced the Blue Jays back to Toronto's SkyDome for Game Six. With the Phillies bullpen worn thin in the first four games, Schilling turned in a 148-pitch, five-hitter in a 2-0 victory against the Blue Jays in Game Five.

It was only the second time the Blue Jays were shut out in 1993, the first time by a righthander.

"We're 10 games into a postseason we're not supposed to be in," Schilling said of the Phillies, who finished last in the NL East in 1992. "There's no pressure on us. This is the World Series. This is fun."

Fun? Knowing that the Phillies' season rested on his right arm?

"After the seventh, (pitching coach) Johnny Podres told me how many pitches he had thrown," Fregosi said, "and I told him, 'Let me know when he gets to 150 or 160.'"

Schilling didn't allow a Blue Jay into scoring position until the sixth, when he walked Henderson and White but got Alomar to ground into a double play. The big test came in the eighth. Singles by Pat Borders and pinch-hitter Rob Butler put Jays on first and third with no outs.

"I glanced at the bullpen to see who was warming up and nobody was up," Schilling said. "That got me pumped up. I knew it was up to me whether we were going to Toronto or going home."

MORRIS FOSTOFF

**Not His Fault.** Even though his team lost, Phillies center fielder Lenny Dykstra had an exemplary Series: .348 with four homers.

# WORLD SERIES
## BOX SCORES

BOB ROSATO

**Steady.** Blue Jays center fielder Devon White enjoyed a solid World Series, hitting .292 with six extra-base hits.

### Game One: October 16
### Blue Jays 8, Phillies 5

| PHIL. | ab | r | h | bi | bb | so | TORONTO | ab | r | h | bi | bb | so |
|---|---|---|---|---|---|---|---|---|---|---|---|---|---|
| Dykstra cf | 4 | 1 | 1 | 0 | 1 | 0 | Henderson lf | 3 | 1 | 1 | 0 | 1 | 0 |
| Duncan 2b | 5 | 2 | 3 | 0 | 0 | 2 | White cf | 4 | 3 | 2 | 2 | 0 | 0 |
| Kruk 1b | 4 | 2 | 3 | 2 | 1 | 1 | Alomar 2b | 4 | 0 | 1 | 2 | 0 | 1 |
| Hollins 3b | 4 | 0 | 0 | 0 | 1 | 0 | Carter rf | 3 | 1 | 1 | 1 | 1 | 0 |
| Daulton c | 4 | 0 | 1 | 1 | 1 | 2 | Olerud 1b | 3 | 2 | 2 | 1 | 1 | 0 |
| Eisenreich rf | 5 | 0 | 1 | 1 | 0 | 2 | Molitor dh | 4 | 0 | 1 | 1 | 0 | 0 |
| Jordan dh | 5 | 0 | 1 | 0 | 0 | 2 | Fernandez ss | 3 | 0 | 0 | 1 | 1 | 0 |
| Thompson lf | 3 | 0 | 0 | 0 | 0 | 1 | Sprague 3b | 4 | 0 | 1 | 0 | 0 | 2 |
| Incaviglia ph-lf | 1 | 0 | 0 | 0 | 0 | 0 | Borders c | 4 | 1 | 1 | 0 | 0 | 1 |
| Stocker ss | 3 | 0 | 1 | 0 | 1 | 0 | | | | | | | |
| Totals | 38 | 5 | 11 | 4 | 5 | 11 | Totals | 32 | 8 | 10 | 8 | 3 | 5 |

| | | |
|---|---|---|
| Philadelphia | | 201 010 001—5 |
| Toronto | | 021 011 30x—8 |

E—Thompson (1), Alomar (1), Carter (1), Sprague (1). DP—Philadelphia 1, Toronto 1. LOB—Philadelphia 11, Toronto 4. 2B—White (1), Alomar (1). 3B—Duncan (1). HR—White (1), Olerud (1). SB—Dykstra (1), Duncan (1), Alomar (1). CS—Fernandez (1). SF—Carter.

| Phil. | ip | h | r | er | bb | so | Toronto | ip | h | r | er | bb | so |
|---|---|---|---|---|---|---|---|---|---|---|---|---|---|
| Schilling L | 6⅓ | 8 | 7 | 6 | 2 | 3 | Guzman | 5 | 5 | 4 | 4 | 4 | 6 |
| West | 0 | 2 | 1 | 1 | 0 | 0 | Leiter W | 2⅔ | 4 | 0 | 0 | 1 | 2 |
| Andersen | ⅔ | 0 | 0 | 1 | 1 | 0 | Ward S | 1⅓ | 2 | 1 | 0 | 0 | 3 |
| Mason | 1 | 0 | 0 | 0 | 0 | 1 | | | | | | | |

West pitched to two batters in 7th.
WP—Guzman PB—Daulton.
Umpires: HP—Phillips; 1B—Runge; 2B—Johnson; 3B—Williams; LF—McClelland; RP—DeMuth.
T—3:27. A—52,011.

### Game Two: October 17
### Phillies 6, Blue Jays 4

| PHIL. | ab | r | h | bi | bb | so | TORONTO | ab | r | h | bi | bb | so |
|---|---|---|---|---|---|---|---|---|---|---|---|---|---|
| Dykstra cf | 4 | 2 | 2 | 1 | 1 | 0 | Henderson lf | 3 | 0 | 0 | 0 | 1 | 1 |
| Duncan 2b | 4 | 1 | 1 | 0 | 1 | 2 | White cf | 4 | 0 | 1 | 0 | 0 | 2 |
| Kruk 1b | 5 | 1 | 2 | 1 | 0 | 1 | Molitor dh | 3 | 2 | 2 | 0 | 1 | 0 |
| Hollins 3b | 4 | 1 | 2 | 1 | 1 | 2 | Carter rf | 4 | 1 | 1 | 2 | 0 | 1 |
| Batiste 3b | 0 | 0 | 0 | 0 | 0 | 0 | Olerud 1b | 3 | 0 | 0 | 1 | 0 | 0 |
| Daulton c | 5 | 0 | 1 | 0 | 1 | 0 | Alomar 2b | 3 | 1 | 1 | 0 | 1 | 1 |
| Eisenreich rf | 4 | 1 | 1 | 3 | 1 | 1 | Fernandez ss | 3 | 0 | 2 | 1 | 1 | 0 |
| Incaviglia lf | 4 | 0 | 1 | 0 | 0 | 2 | Sprague 3b | 4 | 0 | 0 | 0 | 0 | 1 |
| Thompson pr-lf | 0 | 0 | 0 | 0 | 0 | 0 | Griffin pr | 0 | 0 | 0 | 0 | 0 | 0 |
| Jordan dh | 4 | 0 | 1 | 0 | 0 | 0 | Borders c | 4 | 0 | 1 | 0 | 0 | 0 |
| Stocker ss | 3 | 0 | 1 | 0 | 1 | 0 | | | | | | | |
| Totals | 37 | 6 | 12 | 6 | 5 | 8 | Totals | 31 | 4 | 8 | 4 | 4 | 6 |

| | | |
|---|---|---|
| Philadelphia | | 005 000 100—6 |
| Toronto | | 000 201 010—4 |

DP—Philadelphia 1, Toronto 1. LOB—Philadelphia 9, Toronto 5. 2B—White (2), Molitor (1), Fernandez (1). HR—Carter (1), Dykstra (1), Eisenreich (1). SB—Molitor (1), Alomar (2). CS—Stocker (1), Henderson (1), Alomar (1). SF—Olerud.

| Phil. | ip | h | r | er | bb | so | Toronto | ip | h | r | er | bb | so |
|---|---|---|---|---|---|---|---|---|---|---|---|---|---|
| Mulholland W | 5⅔ | 7 | 3 | 3 | 2 | 4 | Stewart L | 6 | 6 | 5 | 5 | 4 | 6 |
| Mason | 1⅓ | 1 | 1 | 1 | 0 | 2 | Castillo | 1 | 3 | 1 | 1 | 0 | 0 |
| Williams S | 1⅓ | 0 | 0 | 0 | 2 | 0 | Eichhorn | ⅓ | 1 | 0 | 0 | 1 | 0 |
| | | | | | | | Timlin | 1⅔ | 2 | 0 | 0 | 0 | 2 |

WP—Stewart. Balk—Stewart.
Umpires: HP—Runge; 1B—Johnson; 2B—Williams; 3B—McClelland; LF—DeMuth; RF—Phillips.
T—3:35. A—52,062.

### Game Three: October 19
### Blue Jays 10, Phillies 3

| TORONTO | ab | r | h | bi | bb | so | PHIL. | ab | r | h | bi | bb | so |
|---|---|---|---|---|---|---|---|---|---|---|---|---|---|
| Henderson lf | 4 | 2 | 2 | 0 | 0 | 0 | Dykstra cf | 5 | 0 | 1 | 0 | 0 | 1 |
| White cf | 4 | 2 | 1 | 1 | 1 | 0 | Duncan 2b | 5 | 0 | 2 | 1 | 0 | 1 |
| Molitor 1b | 4 | 3 | 3 | 3 | 1 | 0 | Kruk 1b | 3 | 1 | 2 | 0 | 2 | 1 |
| Carter rf | 4 | 1 | 1 | 1 | 0 | 1 | Hollins 3b | 3 | 0 | 0 | 0 | 1 | 1 |
| Alomar 2b | 5 | 2 | 4 | 2 | 0 | 0 | Daulton c | 3 | 0 | 0 | 0 | 1 | 1 |
| Fernandez ss | 3 | 0 | 2 | 2 | 1 | 0 | Eisenreich rf | 4 | 0 | 1 | 1 | 0 | 0 |
| Sprague 3b | 4 | 0 | 0 | 1 | 0 | 2 | Incaviglia lf | 3 | 0 | 0 | 0 | 0 | 2 |
| Borders c | 4 | 0 | 0 | 0 | 1 | 0 | Thigpen p | 0 | 0 | 0 | 0 | 0 | 1 |
| Hentgen p | 3 | 0 | 0 | 0 | 0 | 1 | Morandini ph | 0 | 0 | 0 | 0 | 1 | 0 |
| Cox p | 1 | 0 | 0 | 0 | 0 | 0 | Andersen p | 0 | 0 | 0 | 0 | 0 | 0 |
| Ward p | 0 | 0 | 0 | 0 | 0 | 0 | Stocker ss | 4 | 0 | 1 | 0 | 0 | 2 |
| | | | | | | | Jackson p | 1 | 0 | 0 | 0 | 0 | 1 |
| | | | | | | | Cham'lain ph | 1 | 0 | 0 | 0 | 0 | 0 |
| | | | | | | | Rivera p | 0 | 0 | 0 | 0 | 0 | 0 |
| | | | | | | | Thompson lf | 2 | 2 | 2 | 1 | 0 | 0 |
| Totals | 36 | 10 | 13 | 10 | 4 | 4 | Totals | 34 | 3 | 9 | 3 | 5 | 10 |

| | | |
|---|---|---|
| Toronto | | 301 001 302—10 |
| Philadelphia | | 000 001 101— 3 |

E—Carter (2). DP—Toronto 2. LOB—Toronto 7, Philadelphia 9. 2B—Henderson (1), Kruk (1). 3B—White (1), Molitor (1), Alomar (1). HR—Molitor (1), Thompson (1). SB—Alomar 2 (4). SF—Sprague, Fernandez, Carter.

| Toronto | ip | h | r | er | bb | so | Phil. | ip | h | r | er | bb | so |
|---|---|---|---|---|---|---|---|---|---|---|---|---|---|
| Hentgen W | 6 | 5 | 1 | 1 | 3 | 6 | Jackson L | 5 | 6 | 4 | 4 | 1 | 1 |
| Cox | 2 | 3 | 1 | 1 | 2 | 2 | Rivera | 1⅓ | 4 | 4 | 4 | 2 | 3 |
| Ward | 1 | 1 | 1 | 0 | 2 | 2 | Thigpen | 1⅔ | 0 | 0 | 0 | 1 | 0 |
| | | | | | | | Andersen | 1 | 3 | 2 | 2 | 0 | 0 |

HBP—Henderson (by Thigpen).
Umpires: HP—Johnson; 1B—Williams; 2B—McClelland; 3B—DeMuth; LF—Phillips; RF—Runge.
T—3:16. A—62,689.

### Game Four: October 20
### Blue Jays 15, Phillies 14

| TORONTO | ab | r | h | bi | bb | so | PHIL. | ab | r | h | bi | bb | so |
|---|---|---|---|---|---|---|---|---|---|---|---|---|---|
| Henderson lf | 5 | 2 | 2 | 2 | 1 | 1 | Dykstra cf | 5 | 4 | 3 | 4 | 1 | 1 |
| White cf | 5 | 2 | 3 | 4 | 1 | 1 | Duncan 2b | 6 | 1 | 3 | 1 | 0 | 0 |
| Alomar 2b | 6 | 1 | 2 | 1 | 0 | 1 | Kruk 1b | 5 | 0 | 0 | 0 | 1 | 2 |
| Carter rf | 6 | 2 | 3 | 0 | 0 | 0 | Hollins 3b | 4 | 3 | 2 | 0 | 2 | 0 |
| Olerud 1b | 4 | 2 | 1 | 0 | 2 | 0 | Daulton c | 3 | 2 | 1 | 3 | 1 | 1 |
| Molitor 3b | 4 | 2 | 1 | 1 | 1 | 0 | Eisenreich rf | 4 | 2 | 1 | 1 | 1 | 0 |
| Griffin 3b | 0 | 0 | 0 | 0 | 0 | 0 | Thompson lf | 5 | 1 | 3 | 5 | 0 | 0 |
| Fernandez ss | 6 | 2 | 3 | 5 | 0 | 1 | Stocker ss | 4 | 0 | 0 | 0 | 1 | 1 |
| Borders c | 4 | 1 | 1 | 1 | 1 | 0 | Greene p | 1 | 1 | 1 | 0 | 0 | 0 |
| Stottlemyre p | 0 | 0 | 0 | 0 | 1 | 0 | Mason p | 1 | 0 | 0 | 0 | 0 | 0 |
| Butler ph | 1 | 1 | 0 | 0 | 0 | 0 | Jordan ph | 1 | 0 | 0 | 0 | 0 | 0 |
| Leiter p | 1 | 0 | 1 | 0 | 0 | 0 | West p | 0 | 0 | 0 | 0 | 0 | 0 |
| Castillo p | 1 | 0 | 0 | 0 | 0 | 1 | Chamberlain ph | 1 | 0 | 0 | 0 | 0 | 1 |
| Sprague ph | 1 | 0 | 0 | 0 | 0 | 1 | Andersen p | 0 | 0 | 0 | 0 | 0 | 0 |
| Timlin p | 0 | 0 | 0 | 0 | 0 | 0 | Williams p | 0 | 0 | 0 | 0 | 0 | 0 |
| Ward p | 0 | 0 | 0 | 0 | 0 | 0 | Morandini ph | 1 | 0 | 0 | 0 | 0 | 1 |
| | | | | | | | Thigpen p | 0 | 0 | 0 | 0 | 0 | 0 |
| Totals | 44 | 15 | 17 | 14 | 7 | 6 | Totals | 41 | 14 | 14 | 14 | 7 | 7 |

| | | |
|---|---|---|
| Toronto | | 304 002 060—15 |
| Philadelphia | | 420 151 100—14 |

E—Hollins (1). LOB—Toronto 10, Philadelphia 8. 2B—Henderson (2), White (3), Carter (1), Leiter (1), Dykstra (1), Hollins (1), Thompson (1). 3B—White (2), Thompson (1). HR—Dykstra 2 (3), Daulton (1). SB—Henderson (1), White (1), Dykstra (2), Duncan (2).

| Toronto | ip | h | r | er | bb | so | Phil. | ip | h | r | er | bb | so |
|---|---|---|---|---|---|---|---|---|---|---|---|---|---|
| Stottlemyre | 2 | 3 | 6 | 6 | 4 | 1 | Greene | 2⅓ | 7 | 7 | 7 | 4 | 1 |
| Leiter | 2⅔ | 8 | 6 | 6 | 0 | 1 | Mason | 2⅔ | 2 | 0 | 0 | 1 | 2 |
| Castillo W | 2⅓ | 3 | 2 | 2 | 3 | 1 | West | 1 | 3 | 2 | 2 | 0 | 0 |
| Timlin | ⅔ | 0 | 0 | 0 | 0 | 2 | Andersen | 1⅓ | 1 | 3 | 1 | 1 | 2 |
| Ward S | 1⅓ | 0 | 0 | 0 | 0 | 2 | Williams L | ⅔ | 3 | 3 | 3 | 1 | 1 |
|  |  |  |  |  |  |  | Thigpen | 1 | 1 | 0 | 0 | 0 | 0 |

HBP—Daulton (by Castillo), Molitor (by West).

Umpires: HP—Williams; 1B—McClelland; 2B—DeMuth; 3B—Phillips; LF—Runge; RF—Johnson.

T—4:14. A—62,731.

## Game Five: October 21
### Phillies 2, Blue Jays 0

| TORONTO | ab | r | h | bi | bb | so | PHIL. | ab | r | h | bi | bb | so |
|---|---|---|---|---|---|---|---|---|---|---|---|---|---|
| Henderson lf | 3 | 0 | 0 | 0 | 1 | 0 | Dykstra cf | 2 | 1 | 0 | 0 | 2 | 1 |
| White cf | 3 | 0 | 0 | 0 | 1 | 2 | Duncan 2b | 4 | 0 | 0 | 0 | 0 | 1 |
| Alomar 2b | 3 | 0 | 1 | 0 | 1 | 0 | Kruk 1b | 3 | 0 | 1 | 1 | 1 | 1 |
| Carter rf | 4 | 0 | 0 | 0 | 0 | 1 | Hollins 3b | 3 | 0 | 1 | 0 | 1 | 1 |
| Olerud 1b | 4 | 0 | 0 | 0 | 0 | 1 | Batiste 3b | 0 | 0 | 0 | 0 | 0 | 0 |
| Molitor 3b | 4 | 0 | 1 | 0 | 0 | 0 | Daulton c | 4 | 1 | 1 | 0 | 0 | 1 |
| Fernandez ss | 3 | 0 | 0 | 0 | 0 | 1 | Eisenreich rf | 4 | 0 | 0 | 0 | 0 | 1 |
| Borders c | 3 | 0 | 2 | 0 | 0 | 0 | Thompson lf | 3 | 0 | 0 | 0 | 1 | 1 |
| Canate pr | 0 | 0 | 0 | 0 | 0 | 0 | Stocker ss | 2 | 0 | 1 | 1 | 1 | 1 |
| Knorr c | 0 | 0 | 0 | 0 | 0 | 0 | Schilling p | 2 | 0 | 1 | 0 | 0 | 1 |
| Guzman p | 2 | 0 | 0 | 0 | 0 | 1 |  |  |  |  |  |  |  |
| Butler ph | 1 | 0 | 1 | 0 | 0 | 0 |  |  |  |  |  |  |  |
| Cox p | 0 | 0 | 0 | 0 | 0 | 0 |  |  |  |  |  |  |  |
| Totals | 30 | 0 | 5 | 0 | 3 | 6 | Totals | 27 | 2 | 5 | 2 | 6 | 9 |

| Toronto | | | | | | | | 000 | 000 | 000—0 |
|---|---|---|---|---|---|---|---|---|---|---|
| Philadelphia | | | | | | | | 110 | 000 | 00x—2 |

E—Borders (1), Duncan (1). DP—Toronto 1, Philadelphia 3. LOB—Toronto 6, Philadelphia 8. 2B—Daulton (1), Stocker (1). SB—Dykstra (3). CS—Alomar (2). S—Schilling.

| Toronto | ip | h | r | er | bb | so | Phil. | ip | h | r | er | bb | so |
|---|---|---|---|---|---|---|---|---|---|---|---|---|---|
| Guzman L | 7 | 5 | 2 | 1 | 4 | 6 | Schilling W | 9 | 5 | 0 | 0 | 3 | 6 |
| Cox | 1 | 0 | 0 | 0 | 2 | 3 |  |  |  |  |  |  |  |

Umpires: HP—McClelland; 1B—DeMuth; 2B—Phillips; 3B—Runge; LF—Johnson; RF—Williams.

T—2:53. A—62,706.

## Game Six: October 23
### Blue Jays 8, Phillies 6

| PHIL. | ab | r | h | bi | bb | so | TORONTO | ab | r | h | bi | bb | so |
|---|---|---|---|---|---|---|---|---|---|---|---|---|---|
| Dykstra cf | 3 | 1 | 1 | 3 | 2 | 1 | Henderson lf | 4 | 1 | 0 | 0 | 1 | 0 |
| Duncan dh | 5 | 1 | 1 | 0 | 0 | 1 | White cf | 4 | 1 | 0 | 1 | 1 | 2 |
| Kruk 1b | 3 | 0 | 0 | 0 | 2 | 1 | Molitor dh | 5 | 3 | 3 | 2 | 0 | 0 |
| Hollins 3b | 5 | 1 | 1 | 1 | 0 | 0 | Carter rf | 4 | 1 | 1 | 4 | 0 | 0 |
| Batiste 3b | 0 | 0 | 0 | 0 | 0 | 0 | Olerud 1b | 3 | 1 | 1 | 0 | 1 | 0 |
| Daulton c | 4 | 1 | 1 | 0 | 0 | 0 | Griffin pr-3b | 0 | 0 | 0 | 0 | 0 | 0 |
| Eisenreich rf | 5 | 0 | 2 | 1 | 0 | 0 | Alomar 2b | 4 | 1 | 3 | 1 | 0 | 0 |
| Thompson lf | 3 | 0 | 0 | 0 | 0 | 0 | Fernandez ss | 3 | 0 | 0 | 0 | 0 | 1 |
| Incaviglia ph-lf | 0 | 0 | 0 | 1 | 0 | 0 | Sprague 3b-1b | 2 | 0 | 0 | 1 | 1 | 0 |
| Stocker ss | 3 | 1 | 0 | 0 | 1 | 1 | Borders c | 4 | 0 | 2 | 0 | 0 | 0 |
| Morandini 2b | 4 | 1 | 1 | 0 | 0 | 1 |  |  |  |  |  |  |  |
| Totals | 35 | 6 | 7 | 6 | 5 | 5 | Totals | 33 | 8 | 10 | 8 | 4 | 3 |

| Philadelphia | | | | | | | | 000 | 100 | 500—6 |
|---|---|---|---|---|---|---|---|---|---|---|
| Toronto | | | | | | | | 300 | 110 | 003—8 |

E—Alomar (2), Sprague (2). LOB—Philadelphia 9, Toronto 7. 2B—Daulton (2), Olerud (1), Alomar (2). 3B—Molitor (2). HR—Molitor (2), Carter (2), Dykstra (4). SB—Dykstra (4), Duncan (3). SF—Incaviglia, Carter, Sprague.

| Phil. | ip | h | r | er | bb | so | Toronto | ip | h | r | er | bb | so |
|---|---|---|---|---|---|---|---|---|---|---|---|---|---|
| Mulholland | 5 | 7 | 5 | 5 | 1 | 1 | Stewart | 6 | 4 | 4 | 4 | 4 | 2 |
| Mason | 2⅓ | 1 | 0 | 0 | 2 | 0 | Cox | ⅓ | 3 | 2 | 2 | 1 | 0 |
| West | 0 | 0 | 0 | 0 | 1 | 0 | Leiter | 1⅔ | 0 | 0 | 0 | 1 | 2 |
| Andersen | ⅔ | 0 | 0 | 0 | 1 | 0 | Ward W | 1 | 0 | 0 | 0 | 0 | 0 |
| Williams L | ⅓ | 2 | 3 | 3 | 1 | 0 |  |  |  |  |  |  |  |

Stewart pitched to three batters in 7th. West pitched to one batter in 8th.

HBP—Fernandez (by Andersen).

Umpires: HP—DeMuth; 1B—Phillips; 2B—Runge; 3B—Johnson; LF—Williams; RF—McClelland.

T—3:26. A—52,195.

# COMPOSITE BOX
## PHILADELPHIA

| Player, Pos. | AVG. | G | AB | R | H | 2B | 3B | HR | RBI | BB | SO | SB |
|---|---|---|---|---|---|---|---|---|---|---|---|---|
| Tommy Greene, p.... | 1.000 | 1 | 1 | 1 | 1 | 0 | 0 | 0 | 0 | 0 | 0 | 0 |
| Curt Schilling, p......... | .500 | 2 | 2 | 0 | 1 | 0 | 0 | 0 | 0 | 0 | 1 | 0 |
| Len Dykstra, cf ......... | .348 | 6 | 23 | 9 | 8 | 1 | 0 | 4 | 8 | 7 | 4 | 4 |
| John Kruk, 1b............ | .348 | 6 | 23 | 4 | 8 | 1 | 0 | 0 | 4 | 7 | 7 | 0 |
| M. Duncan, 2b-dh ..... | .345 | 6 | 29 | 5 | 10 | 0 | 1 | 0 | 2 | 1 | 7 | 3 |
| Milt Thompson, lf-pr .. | .313 | 5 | 16 | 3 | 5 | 1 | 1 | 1 | 6 | 1 | 2 | 0 |
| Dave Hollins, 3b........ | .261 | 6 | 23 | 5 | 6 | 1 | 0 | 0 | 2 | 6 | 5 | 0 |
| Jim Eisenreich, rf ...... | .231 | 6 | 26 | 3 | 6 | 0 | 0 | 1 | 7 | 2 | 4 | 0 |
| Darren Daulton, c ...... | .217 | 6 | 23 | 4 | 5 | 2 | 0 | 1 | 4 | 4 | 5 | 0 |
| Kevin Stocker, ss ...... | .211 | 6 | 19 | 1 | 4 | 0 | 0 | 0 | 1 | 5 | 5 | 0 |
| Ricky Jordan, dh-ph ... | .200 | 3 | 10 | 0 | 2 | 0 | 0 | 0 | 0 | 0 | 2 | 0 |
| M. Morandini, ph-2b... | .200 | 3 | 5 | 1 | 1 | 0 | 0 | 0 | 0 | 1 | 2 | 0 |
| Pete Incaviglia, ph-lf... | .125 | 4 | 8 | 0 | 1 | 0 | 0 | 0 | 1 | 0 | 4 | 0 |
| Wes Chamberlain, ph | .000 | 2 | 2 | 0 | 0 | 0 | 0 | 0 | 0 | 0 | 1 | 0 |
| Danny Jackson, p ...... | .000 | 1 | 1 | 0 | 0 | 0 | 0 | 0 | 0 | 0 | 1 | 0 |
| Roger Mason, p ........ | .000 | 4 | 1 | 0 | 0 | 0 | 0 | 0 | 0 | 0 | 1 | 0 |
| Kim Batiste, 3b.......... | .000 | 5 | 5 | 0 | 0 | 0 | 0 | 0 | 0 | 0 | 0 | 0 |
| TOTALS.................... | .274 | 6 | 212 | 36 | 58 | 7 | 2 | 7 | 35 | 34 | 50 | 7 |

| Pitcher | W | L | ERA | G | GS | CG | SV | IP | H | R | ER | BB | SO |
|---|---|---|---|---|---|---|---|---|---|---|---|---|---|
| Bobby Thigpen... | 0 | 0 | 0.00 | 2 | 0 | 0 | 0 | 2⅔ | 1 | 0 | 0 | 0 | 1 |
| Roger Mason...... | 0 | 0 | 1.17 | 4 | 0 | 0 | 0 | 7⅔ | 4 | 1 | 1 | 7 | 7 |
| Curt Schilling..... | 1 | 1 | 3.52 | 2 | 2 | 1 | 0 | 15⅓ | 13 | 7 | 6 | 5 | 9 |
| Terry Mulholland.. | 1 | 0 | 6.75 | 2 | 2 | 0 | 0 | 10⅔ | 14 | 8 | 8 | 3 | 5 |
| Danny Jackson.... | 0 | 1 | 7.20 | 1 | 1 | 0 | 0 | 5 | 6 | 4 | 4 | 1 | 1 |
| Larry Andersen.... | 0 | 0 | 12.27 | 4 | 0 | 0 | 0 | 3⅔ | 5 | 5 | 5 | 3 | 3 |
| Mitch Williams.... | 0 | 2 | 20.25 | 3 | 0 | 0 | 1 | 2⅔ | 5 | 6 | 6 | 4 | 1 |
| Tommy Greene.... | 0 | 0 | 27.00 | 1 | 0 | 0 | 0 | 2⅓ | 7 | 7 | 7 | 4 | 1 |
| Ben Rivera.......... | 0 | 0 | 27.00 | 1 | 0 | 0 | 0 | 1⅓ | 4 | 4 | 4 | 2 | 3 |
| David West.......... | 0 | 0 | 27.00 | 3 | 0 | 0 | 1 | 5 | 3 | 3 | 1 | 0 |
| TOTALS............ | 2 | 4 | 7.57 | 6 | 6 | 1 | 1 | 52⅓ | 64 | 45 | 44 | 25 | 30 |

## TORONTO

| Player, Pos. | AVG. | G | AB | R | H | 2B | 3B | HR | RBI | BB | SO | SB |
|---|---|---|---|---|---|---|---|---|---|---|---|---|
| Al Leiter, p ................ | 1.000 | 3 | 1 | 0 | 1 | 1 | 0 | 0 | 0 | 0 | 0 | 0 |
| Paul Molitor, dh-1b-3b | .500 | 6 | 24 | 10 | 12 | 2 | 2 | 2 | 8 | 3 | 0 | 1 |
| Rob Butler, ph ......... | .500 | 2 | 2 | 1 | 1 | 0 | 0 | 0 | 0 | 0 | 0 | 0 |
| Roberto Alomar, 2b... | .480 | 6 | 25 | 5 | 12 | 1 | 0 | 1 | 6 | 2 | 3 | 4 |
| Tony Fernandez, ss ... | .333 | 6 | 21 | 2 | 7 | 1 | 0 | 0 | 9 | 3 | 3 | 0 |
| Pat Borders, c .......... | .304 | 6 | 23 | 2 | 7 | 0 | 0 | 0 | 1 | 2 | 1 | 0 |
| Devon White, cf ........ | .292 | 6 | 25 | 8 | 7 | 3 | 2 | 1 | 7 | 4 | 7 | 1 |
| Joe Carter, rf ........... | .280 | 6 | 25 | 6 | 7 | 1 | 0 | 2 | 8 | 0 | 4 | 0 |
| John Olerud, 1b ........ | .235 | 5 | 17 | 5 | 4 | 1 | 0 | 1 | 2 | 4 | 1 | 0 |
| Rickey Henderson, lf.. | .227 | 6 | 22 | 6 | 5 | 2 | 0 | 0 | 2 | 5 | 2 | 1 |
| Ed Sprague, 3b-ph-1b | .067 | 5 | 15 | 0 | 1 | 0 | 0 | 0 | 2 | 1 | 6 | 0 |
| Pat Hentgen, p .......... | .000 | 1 | 3 | 0 | 0 | 0 | 0 | 0 | 0 | 0 | 0 | 0 |
| Juan Guzman, p ........ | .000 | 2 | 2 | 0 | 0 | 0 | 0 | 0 | 0 | 0 | 1 | 0 |
| Tony Castillo, p ......... | .000 | 2 | 1 | 0 | 0 | 0 | 0 | 0 | 0 | 0 | 0 | 0 |
| Danny Cox, p ............ | .000 | 3 | 1 | 0 | 0 | 0 | 0 | 0 | 0 | 0 | 0 | 0 |
| Alfredo Griffin, pr-3b.. | .000 | 1 | 0 | 0 | 0 | 0 | 0 | 0 | 0 | 0 | 0 | 0 |
| William Canate, pr...... | .000 | 1 | 0 | 1 | 0 | 0 | 0 | 0 | 0 | 0 | 0 | 0 |
| Todd Stottlemyre, p.... | .000 | 1 | 0 | 0 | 0 | 0 | 0 | 0 | 0 | 0 | 0 | 0 |
| TOTALS.................... | .311 | 6 | 206 | 45 | 64 | 13 | 5 | 6 | 45 | 25 | 30 | 7 |

| Pitcher | W | L | ERA | G | GS | CG | SV | IP | H | R | ER | BB | SO |
|---|---|---|---|---|---|---|---|---|---|---|---|---|---|
| Mike Timlin............ | 0 | 0 | 0.00 | 2 | 0 | 0 | 0 | 2⅓ | 2 | 0 | 0 | 0 | 4 |
| Mark Eichhorn........ | 0 | 0 | 0.00 | 1 | 0 | 0 | 0 | ⅓ | 1 | 0 | 0 | 1 | 0 |
| Pat Hentgen........... | 0 | 1 | 1.50 | 1 | 1 | 0 | 0 | 6 | 5 | 1 | 1 | 3 | 6 |
| Duane Ward............ | 1 | 0 | 1.93 | 4 | 0 | 0 | 2 | 4⅔ | 3 | 2 | 1 | 0 | 7 |
| Juan Guzman.......... | 0 | 1 | 3.75 | 2 | 2 | 0 | 0 | 12 | 10 | 6 | 5 | 8 | 12 |
| Dave Stewart.......... | 1 | 0 | 6.75 | 2 | 2 | 0 | 0 | 12 | 10 | 9 | 9 | 8 | 8 |
| Al Leiter................. | 1 | 0 | 7.71 | 3 | 0 | 0 | 0 | 7 | 12 | 6 | 6 | 2 | 5 |
| Tony Castillo.......... | 1 | 0 | 8.10 | 2 | 0 | 0 | 0 | 3⅓ | 6 | 3 | 3 | 3 | 1 |
| Danny Cox.............. | 0 | 0 | 8.10 | 3 | 0 | 0 | 0 | 3⅓ | 6 | 3 | 3 | 5 | 6 |
| Todd Stottlemyre..... | 0 | 0 | 27.00 | 1 | 1 | 0 | 0 | 2 | 3 | 6 | 6 | 4 | 1 |
| TOTALS................ | 4 | 2 | 5.77 | 6 | 6 | 0 | 2 | 53 | 58 | 36 | 34 | 34 | 50 |

| Philadelphia | | | | | | | | | 7 | 3 | 6 | 2 | 6 | 2 | 8 | 0 | 2—6 |
|---|---|---|---|---|---|---|---|---|---|---|---|---|---|---|---|---|---|
| Toronto | | | | | | | | | 9 | 2 | 6 | 3 | 2 | 5 | 6 | 7 | 5—45 |

E—Duncan, Thompson, Alomar 2, Borders, Carter 2, Sprague 2. DP—Philadelphia 5, Toronto 5. LOB—Philadelphia 54, Toronto 39. CS—Fernandez, Henderson, Stocker, Alomar 2. S—Schilling. SF—Carter 3, Olerud, Fernandez, Sprague 2, Incaviglia. HBP—Henderson (by Thigpen); Molitor (by West); Daulton (by Castillo); Fernandez (by Andersen). Balk—Stewart. PB—Daulton. Umpires—Dave Phillips (AL), Paul Runge (NL), Mark Johnson (AL), Charlie Williams (NL), Tim McClelland (AL), Dana DeMuth (NL). Official Scorers—Neil Hohlfeld (Houston Chronicle), Dave Nightingale, Joe Sawchuk (Toronto Blue Jays), Bob Kenney (Camden Courier-Post).

**Young Talent Abounds.** In 1993, the American League showcased some of its best young talent in years. From left, 40-home-run sluggers Juan Gonzalez (Rangers), Fronk Thomas (White Sox) and Ken Griffey (Mariners).

# Trio of Sluggers Steal The Headlines

**By MIKE BERARDINO**

American League fans were treated to an incredible offensive display in 1993.

From the Detroit Tigers' early onslaught that kept them close to first place for much of the first half to the Toronto Blue Jays' late push that offset pitching problems and brought them their second straight AL pennant, it was wall-to-wall scoring in the junior circuit.

Three players in particular, all age 25 or younger, staged a memorable season-long war for offensive supremacy. Chicago White Sox first baseman Frank Thomas ended up with slightly superior overall numbers, and his team won its first division title in 10 years.

But Seattle Mariners center fielder Ken Griffey Jr. and Texas Rangers left fielder Juan Gonzalez chased The Big Hurt and the White Sox right down to wire. For the first time since the expansion season of 1969, the AL had three players hit 40 or more home runs in the same year. An AL trio nearly reached the 45-homer plateau for the first time since 1961, the year of Maris, Mantle and Colavito.

Thomas batted .317 with 41 home runs and 128 RBIs to finish sixth in average, third in home runs and second in RBIs. He also hit 36 doubles and scored 106 runs, but perhaps the most amazing statistic from Thomas was his walks-to-strikeouts ratio: 112-to-54.

For his efforts, Thomas was named Baseball America's American League Player of the Year. He was probably more excited, though, about the four-year, $28 million contract extension the White Sox gave him in late October.

"He's a big man with a small man's hitting philosophy," White Sox hitting coach Walt Hriniak said of Thomas. "His approach to each at-bat is no different than Joey Cora."

In most other years, either Griffey or Gonzalez would have been good enough to win. Griffey, blessed with remarkable natural talent and enviable bloodlines, finally began to reach his potential in 1993. Griffey batted .309 with 45 home runs and 109 RBIs with 38 doubles and 113 runs scored.

Most remarkable, though, was Griffey's string of home runs in eight straight games. Griffey capped the surge July 28, tying Don Mattingly (1987) and Dale Long (1956) for most consecutive games with a home run.

"Junior" battled Thomas and eventual winner Gonzalez for the league home run championship all year, despite what he termed a derrière disadvantage.

"I'm the little guy in the group," Griffey said. "I can hit them, but I've got to get my whole little body behind it. They just get their big butts and big legs and big bats going. Juan and Frank hit fly balls that go out because they're so strong."

Gonzalez, he of the geri curls and the huge forearms, ended up winning his second straight home run title. He batted .310 with 46 homers and 118 RBIs for the Rangers, who, like the Mariners, fared surprisingly well in the AL West race.

Beloved in his native Puerto Rico, Gonzalez seemed destined to succeed where his countryman and former Rangers teammate Ruben Sierra failed. Unlike Sierra, Gonzalez seemed a good bet to sustain the greatness of his early seasons.

Already Gonzalez—nicknamed Igor, after Igor the Magnificent, his favorite wrestler as a youth—had made strides in maturity.

"He's not a laid-back type guy. He's high-strung,"

| Page | EAST | W | L | PCT | GB | Manager | General Manager | Attendance/Dates | Last Pennant |
|---|---|---|---|---|---|---|---|---|---|
| 210 | Toronto Blue Jays | 95 | 67 | .586 | — | Cito Gaston | Pat Gillick | 4,057,947 (81) | 1993 |
| 149 | New York Yankees | 88 | 74 | .543 | 7 | Buck Showalter | Gene Michael | 2,416,942 (80) | 1981 |
| 54 | Baltimore Orioles | 85 | 77 | .525 | 10 | John Oates | Roland Hemond | 3,644,965 (80) | 1983 |
| 102 | Detroit Tigers | 85 | 77 | .525 | 10 | Sparky Anderson | Jerry Walker | 1,970,791 (81) | 1984 |
| 60 | Boston Red Sox | 80 | 82 | .494 | 15 | Butch Hobson | Lou Gorman | 2,422,021 (80) | 1986 |
| 91 | Cleveland Indians | 76 | 86 | .469 | 19 | Mike Hargrove | John Hart | 2,177,908 (80) | 1954 |
| 131 | Milwaukee Brewers | 69 | 93 | .426 | 26 | Phil Garner | Sal Bando | 1,688,080 (78) | 1982 |

| Page | WEST | W | L | PCT | GB | Manager | General Manager | Attendance/Dates | Last Pennant |
|---|---|---|---|---|---|---|---|---|---|
| 72 | Chicago White Sox | 94 | 68 | .580 | — | Gene Lamont | Ron Schueler | 2,581,091 (79) | 1959 |
| 204 | Texas Rangers | 86 | 76 | .531 | 8 | Kevin Kennedy | Tom Grieve | 2,244,616 (79) | None |
| 119 | Kansas City Royals | 84 | 78 | .519 | 10 | Hal McRae | Herk Robinson | 1,934,578 (80) | 1985 |
| 198 | Seattle Mariners | 82 | 80 | .506 | 12 | Lou Piniella | Woody Woodward | 2,052,638 (81) | None |
| 66 | California Angels | 71 | 91 | .438 | 23 | Buck Rodgers | Whitey Herzog | 2,057,460 (81) | None |
| 137 | Minnesota Twins | 71 | 91 | .438 | 23 | Tom Kelly | Andy MacPhail | 2,048,673 (81) | 1991 |
| 161 | Oakland Athletics | 68 | 94 | .420 | 26 | Tony LaRussa | Sandy Alderson | 2,035,025 (79) | 1990 |

**LEAGUE CHAMPIONSHIP SERIES:** Toronto defeated Chicago, 4-2, in best-of-7 final.
**NOTE:** Team's individual batting, pitching and fielding statistics can be found on page indicated in lefthand column.

Rangers general manager Tom Grieve said. "He's a thoroughbred. He's learning to harness his emotions."

As for his talent, it's already been harnessed. Of course, the same is true of Griffey and Thomas. Together, these three sluggers may wage offensive shootouts through the remainder of the 1990s. If so, fans may look back at 1993 as the year the rivalry first blossomed.

"I read the stat sheets," Thomas said. "I see what the other guys (Griffey and Gonzalez) are doing. I think we all respect each other. I think we feed off each other."

**Dave Stewart**

## Deja Stew

If these were the playoffs, and they were, then it must have been Dave Stewart time.

The 36-year-old righthander delivered exactly what the Blue Jays desired when they signed him as a free agent over the winter of 1992-93: rock-solid pitching with the AL pennant on the line. Stewart won Games Two and Six to turn back the bickering White Sox, four games to two, in the American League Championship Series.

Stewart allowed only three earned runs in 13⅓ innings to run his career ALCS record to 8-0, 2.03. Four times, including three times for the Oakland Athletics, Stewart has pitched the game that put his team into the World Series.

"There's not a nerve in his body," Blue Jays third baseman Ed Sprague said. "He sure knows how to focus for the big game."

Knowledge and experience, combined with a still-nasty split-finger fastball, give Stewart a great advantage against hitters facing the most important at-bats of their careers.

"I'm older and there's less velocity, no doubt about it," Stewart said. "I used to throw the ball between 94 and 95 mph. Now I'm about average, 87, maxing out at 90.

"But I'm smarter now. That doesn't show in the statistics. I have a better idea of setting up the hitters and getting them out with my second and third pitches. I can trick hitters now. I can make adjustments to what I think they're adjusting to."

Stewart beat the White Sox 3-1 in Game Two, wriggling out of a bases-loaded, no-outs jam in the sixth inning to give the Jays a 2-0 lead in games. Then, with the White Sox in position to win the last two games at home and steal a berth in the World Series, Stewart slammed the door shut with 7⅓ innings of four-hit ball to win 6-3.

While the veteran Stewart shined, 22-game winner Jack McDowell laid an egg in his first postseason opportunity for the White Sox. The goateed righthander, who had been so strong during the season, was shelled for seven earned runs in 6⅔ innings in the series opener, a 7-3 Jays win at Comiskey Park.

Fortunately for McDowell, Chicagoans were too busy lamenting the retirement of basketball superstar Michael Jordan to focus on their stopper's failure. Rumors of Jordan's impending retirement hit the airwaves in the middle of Game One, and those in

**Jack McDowell.** White Sox righthander had a Cy Young-type regular season but bombed in postseason play.

R&R SPORTS GROUP

Comiskey Park spent the rest of the game buzzing about the news.

Jordan had thrown out the first pitch before the opener, but left his luxury-suite perch in the seventh inning with the Sox far behind.

McDowell had a chance at redemption in Game Five in Toronto. The White Sox had rallied to knot the series at 2-2 with back-to-back road wins in Games Three and Four, but once again, Black Jack fell on his face.

Toronto scratched out a run in each of the first four innings and held on for a 5-3 win behind righthander Juan Guzman, who allowed just three hits and one earned run in seven innings.

The series also featured the much-anticipated post-season baseball debut of Bo Jackson, who came back from hip replacement surgery after being sidelined for two full seasons. Would Bo, who batted .232 with 16 home runs during the regular season as the White Sox' DH and sometimes outfielder, again display his flair for the dramatic?

Nope. With Dan Pasqua playing first base and Frank Thomas (bruised left forearm) forced to DH in Games One and Two, Jackson sat on the White Sox' bench next to another part-time DH, George Bell. Jackson publicly criticized manager Gene Lamont's decision not to play him, then went 0-for-10 with six strikeouts once he got into the lineup.

## Pair O' No-Nos

More than four months separated the American League's two no-hitters. Mariners righthander Chris Bosio got the first one April 22 against the Red Sox. Bosio walked the first two batters, then retired the final 27.

In his next outing, Bosio tripped covering first base and broke his collarbone, missing more than a month before reinjuring himself in a June 6 Mariners-Orioles brawl. That mishap capped a strange period which began in spring training, when Bosio learned someone had broken into his California home and was living there.

Then there was Jim Abbott's emotional gem on Sept. 4 in New York. The Yankees lefthander struggled all season, but on that Saturday afternoon against the Indians, he was in complete control.

"I never expected to throw one," Abbott said. "I'm just thrilled to death. I didn't know how to react out there, whether to be extremely confident or extremely thankful. I guess I was a little bit of both."

That Abbott has just one hand made his feat all the more amazing. It was the first Yankees no-hitter since Dave Righetti's Fourth of July gem against the Red Sox in 1983, and only the second since Don Larsen's perfect game in the 1956 World Series.

## The Pain Lingers

As he walked out to the mound for the bottom of the fourth inning, a low buzz began to spread through the stands at Camden Yards. After a warmup pitch or two, the capacity crowd began to stand and applaud this opposing pitcher, the one wearing the Cleveland Indians uniform.

Bob Ojeda was back.

The standing ovation lasted for close to a minute, growing louder and more impassioned by the second.

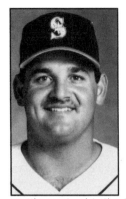 

**No-Hitters.** Seattle's Chris Bosio, left, and New York's Jim Abbott spun the American League's two no-hitters in 1993.

Ojeda, overcome by emotion, had to step off the mound in the middle of his warmup tosses. He doffed his cap in appreciation of the gesture.

Ojeda, 35, was the lone survivor of the spring training boating accident that killed Indians relievers Tim Crews and Steve Olin. After the tragedy, Laurie Crews and Patti Olin made Ojeda promise to pitch again. His scalp severely torn, his body wracked by survivor's guilt, he said he would try.

It took Ojeda until Aug. 7, a Saturday night in Baltimore, to make good on that promise. Activated earlier in the day from the 60-day disabled list, the veteran lefthander allowed two runs on four hits in two innings.

"The fact that two people are gone is there and always will be," Ojeda said in a pregame statement. "I don't know how much that will affect me when I go out there. I have to do this for me and for my friends who aren't here to do it for themselves.

"The void that was left with the accident won't be filled if I throw one more game, 100 more games or 1,000 more games."

Ojeda went on to make eight more appearances in the season's final two months, including seven starts. He went 2-1 with a 4.40 ERA in 43 innings of work. The numbers, though, weren't important. What was important was that he returned.

## Tragedy Averted

Baseball got another scare on July 11, when Blue Jays third-base coach Rich Hacker suffered a head injury and a fractured right ankle in a car collision.

Hacker, 45, was driving alone in a borrowed van from the St. Louis airport to his home in nearby Belleville, Ill., when struck by a vehicle that police believe was racing another vehicle. Hacker was going home for the three-day all-star break.

Hacker was in serious but stable condition for several days in the intensive-care unit at St. Louis University Hospital before his condition was upgraded to fair. After several months of recovery, Hacker was able to rejoin the Jays for the playoffs and World Series.

## Jose, Will You Please?

For someone who batted just .255 with 10 home runs in 1993, Jose Canseco got quite a bit of ink.

# AMERICAN LEAGUE
## CHAMPIONS, 1901-93

| Year | Pennant | Pct. | GA |
|---|---|---|---|
| 1901 | Chicago | .610 | 4 |
| 1902 | Philadelphia | .610 | 5 |
| 1903 | Boston | .659 | 14½ |
| 1904 | Boston | .617 | 1½ |
| 1905 | Philadelphia | .622 | 2 |
| 1906 | Chicago | .616 | 3 |
| 1907 | Detroit | .613 | 1½ |
| 1908 | Detroit | .588 | ½ |
| 1909 | Detroit | .645 | 3½ |
| 1910 | Philadelphia | .680 | 14½ |
| 1911 | Philadelphia | .669 | 13½ |
| 1912 | Boston | .691 | 14 |
| 1913 | Philadelphia | .627 | 6½ |
| 1914 | Philadelphia | .651 | 8½ |
| 1915 | Boston | .669 | 2½ |
| 1916 | Boston | .591 | 2 |
| 1917 | Chicago | .649 | 9 |
| 1918 | Boston | .595 | 2½ |
| 1919 | Chicago | .629 | 3½ |
| 1920 | Cleveland | .636 | 2 |
| 1921 | New York | .641 | 4½ |
| 1922 | New York | .610 | 1 |
| 1923 | New York | .645 | 16 |
| 1924 | Washington | .597 | 2 |
| 1925 | Washington | .636 | 8½ |
| 1926 | New York | .591 | 3 |
| 1927 | New York | .714 | 19 |
| 1928 | New York | .656 | 2½ |
| 1929 | Philadelphia | .693 | 18 |
| 1930 | Philadelphia | .662 | 8 |

| Year | Pennant | Pct. | GA | MVP |
|---|---|---|---|---|
| 1931 | Philadelphia | .704 | 13½ | Lefty Grove, lhp, Philadelphia |
| 1932 | New York | .695 | 13 | Jimmie Foxx, 1b, Philadelphia |
| 1933 | Washington | .651 | 7 | Jimmie Foxx, 1b, Philadelphia |
| 1934 | Detroit | .656 | 7 | Mickey Cochrane, c, Detroit |
| 1935 | Detroit | .616 | 3 | Hank Greenberg, 1b, Detroit |
| 1936 | New York | .667 | 19½ | Lou Gehrig, 1b, New York |
| 1937 | New York | .662 | 13 | Charlie Gehringer, 2b, Detroit |
| 1938 | New York | .651 | 9½ | Jimmie Foxx, 1b, Boston |
| 1939 | New York | .702 | 17 | Joe DiMaggio, of, New York |
| 1940 | Detroit | .584 | 1 | Hank Greenberg, 1b, Detroit |
| 1941 | New York | .656 | 17 | Joe DiMaggio, of, New York |
| 1942 | New York | .669 | 9 | Joe Gordon, 2b, New York |
| 1943 | New York | .636 | 13½ | Spud Chandler, rhp, New York |
| 1944 | St. Louis | .578 | 1 | Hal Newhouser, lhp, Detroit |
| 1945 | Detroit | .575 | 1½ | Hal Newhouser, lhp, Detroit |
| 1946 | Boston | .675 | 12 | Ted Williams, of, Boston |
| 1947 | New York | .630 | 12 | Joe DiMaggio, of, New York |
| 1948 | Cleveland | .626 | 1 | Lou Boudreau, ss, Cleveland |
| 1949 | New York | .630 | 1 | Ted Williams, of, Boston |
| 1950 | New York | .636 | 3 | Phil Rizzuto, ss, New York |
| 1951 | New York | .636 | 5 | Yogi Berra, c, New York |
| 1952 | New York | .617 | 2 | Bobby Shantz, lhp, Philadelphia |
| 1953 | New York | .656 | 8½ | Al Rosen, 3b, Cleveland |
| 1954 | Cleveland | .721 | 8 | Yogi Berra, c, New York |
| 1955 | New York | .623 | 3 | Yogi Berra, c, New York |
| 1956 | New York | .630 | 9 | Mickey Mantle, of, New York |
| 1957 | New York | .636 | 8 | Mickey Mantle, of, New York |
| 1958 | New York | .597 | 10 | Jackie Jensen, of, Boston |
| 1959 | Chicago | .610 | 5 | Nellie Fox, 2b, Chicago |
| 1960 | New York | .630 | 8 | Roger Maris, of, New York |
| 1961 | New York | .673 | 8 | Roger Maris, of, New York |
| 1962 | New York | .593 | 5 | Mickey Mantle, of, New York |
| 1963 | New York | .646 | 10½ | Elston Howard, c, New York |
| 1964 | New York | .611 | 1 | Brooks Robinson, 3b, Baltimore |
| 1965 | Minnesota | .630 | 7 | Zoilo Versalles, ss, Minnesota |
| 1966 | Baltimore | .606 | 9 | Frank Robinson, of, Baltimore |
| 1967 | Boston | .568 | 1 | Carl Yastrzemski, of, Boston |
| 1968 | Detroit | .636 | 12 | Denny McLain, rhp, Detroit |

| Year | East. Div. | PCT | GA | West. Div. | PCT | GA | Pennant | | MVP |
|---|---|---|---|---|---|---|---|---|---|
| 1969 | Baltimore | .673 | 19 | Minnesota | .599 | 9 | Baltimore | 3-0 | Harmon Killebrew, 1b-3b, Minnesota |
| 1970 | Baltimore | .667 | 15 | Minnesota | .605 | 9 | Baltimore | 3-0 | Boog Powell, 1b, Baltimore |
| 1971 | Baltimore | .639 | 12 | Oakland | .627 | 16 | Baltimore | 3-0 | Vida Blue, lhp, Oakland |
| 1972 | Detroit | .551 | ½ | Oakland | .600 | 5½ | Oakland | 3-2 | Dick Allen, 1b, Chicago |
| 1973 | Baltimore | .599 | 8 | Oakland | .580 | 6 | Oakland | 3-2 | Reggie Jackson, of, Oakland |
| 1974 | Baltimore | .562 | 2 | Oakland | .556 | 5 | Oakland | 3-1 | Jeff Burroughs, of, Texas |
| 1975 | Boston | .594 | 4½ | Oakland | .605 | 7 | Boston | 3-0 | Fred Lynn, of, Boston |
| 1976 | New York | .610 | 10½ | Kansas City | .556 | 2½ | New York | 3-2 | Thurman Munson, c, New York |
| 1977 | New York | .617 | 2½ | Kansas City | .630 | 8 | New York | 3-2 | Rod Carew, 1b, Minnesota |
| 1978 | New York | .613 | 1 | Kansas City | .568 | 5 | New York | 3-1 | Jim Rice, of, Boston |
| 1979 | Baltimore | .642 | 8 | California | .543 | 3 | Baltimore | 3-1 | Don Baylor, dh, California |
| 1980 | New York | .636 | 3 | Kansas City | .599 | 14 | Kansas City | 3-0 | George Brett, 3b, Kansas City |
| 1981 | New York* | .607 | 2 | Oakland** | .587 | — | New York | 3-0 | Rollie Fingers, rhp, Milwaukee |
| | Milwaukee | .585 | 1½ | Kansas City | .566 | 1 | | | |
| 1982 | Milwaukee | .586 | 1 | California | .574 | 3 | Milwaukee | 3-2 | Robin Yount, ss, Milwaukee |
| 1983 | Baltimore | .605 | 6 | Chicago | .611 | 20 | Baltimore | 3-1 | Cal Ripken Jr., ss, Baltimore |
| 1984 | Detroit | .642 | 15 | Kansas City | .519 | 3 | Detroit | 3-0 | Willie Hernandez, lhp, Detroit |
| 1985 | Toronto | .615 | 2 | Kansas City | .562 | 1 | Kansas City | 4-3 | Don Mattingly, 1b, New York |
| 1986 | Boston | .590 | 5½ | California | .568 | 5 | Boston | 4-3 | Roger Clemens, rhp, Boston |
| 1987 | Detroit | .605 | 2 | Minnesota | .525 | 2 | Minnesota | 4-1 | George Bell, of, Toronto |
| 1988 | Boston | .549 | 1 | Oakland | .642 | 13 | Oakland | 4-0 | Jose Canseco, of, Oakland |
| 1989 | Toronto | .549 | 2 | Oakland | .611 | 7 | Oakland | 4-1 | Robin Yount, of, Milwaukee |
| 1990 | Boston | .543 | 2 | Oakland | .636 | 9 | Oakland | 4-0 | Rickey Henderson, of, Oakland |
| 1991 | Toronto | .562 | 7 | Minnesota | .586 | 8 | Minnesota | 4-1 | Cal Ripken Jr., ss, Baltimore |
| 1992 | Toronto | .593 | 4 | Oakland | .593 | 6 | Toronto | 4-2 | Dennis Eckersley, rhp, Oakland |
| 1993 | Toronto | .586 | 7 | Chicago | .580 | 8 | Toronto | 4-2 | Frank Thomas, 1b, Chicago |

NOTE: Most Valuable Player award formally recognized in 1931.
GA—Games ahead of second-place team

*Won first half; defeated Milwaukee 3-2 in best-of-5 playoff.
**Won first half, defeated Kansas City 3-0 in best-of-5 playoff.

It started May 29 in Fenway Park. It was a Saturday afternoon, and Canseco's Texas Rangers were in the midst of a 15-1 loss to the Red Sox. That's when first-year Rangers manager Kevin Kennedy made a decision he'd regret the rest of the season, letting Canseco pitch the eighth inning.

**Jose Canseco**

Actually, Canseco had pitched once before in 1993, April 15 in an exhibition game at Oklahoma City. But this time was different. For one thing, he threw about 50 warmup pitches in the bullpen.

Zany Jose threw 33 more pitches in the game, using almost as many different deliveries, and allowed two hits, three walks and two runs. Everyone was still laughing when, several days later, Canseco headed a fly ball over the right-field fence for an Indians home run.

Soon thereafter came the news that Canseco would need elbow surgery and would be out for the year. So much for the Humor Jose campaign.

"There was a lot more goodwill involved than the average fan realizes," Kennedy said. "This wasn't a decision that was made without a lot of thought. Nobody's happy it happened, but it's done with. Life goes on."

## . . . Ready To Rumble!

Nolan Ryan's final season was forgettable in every way but one: his Aug. 6 brawl with a mound-charging Robin Ventura.

Ryan, making one of just 13 starts in his injury-plagued swan song, hit the White Sox third baseman on the forearm. Ventura threw the bat down and charged a waiting Ryan. The 46-year-old legend put Ventura in a head lock and peppered him with six uppercuts, most of which landed harmlessly atop Ventura's helmetless scalp.

"When someone comes out to the mound, they are

R&R SPORTS GROUP

**Streak Intact.** Baltimore shortstop Cal Ripken continued his iron-man role in 1993, playing in his 1,897th consecutive game.

coming out there with the intent to hurt you," Ryan said. "I'm not going to be passive about it. I learned that against Dave Winfield. I decided I was going to be the aggressor."

Winfield charged Ryan after a 1981 plunking and connected with a haymaker on a retreating Ryan's face. Ryan-Ventura went differently, to say the least, though the White Sox had plenty of fighting words afterward.

"The whole world stops when that guy pitches," Jack McDowell said of Ryan. "He pulls that stuff off wherever he goes and people are gutless to do anything about it. I was glad Robin went out. Someone had to do it."

Ventura received a three-game suspension while Ryan went scot-free. That only caused the controversy

# AMERICAN LEAGUE ALL-STARS

Selected by Baseball America

| Pos. | Player, Team | B-T | Ht. | Wt. | Age | '93 Salary | AVG | AB | R | H | 2B | 3B | HR | RBI | SB |
|------|--------------|-----|-----|-----|-----|------------|-----|-----|-----|-----|-----|-----|-----|-----|-----|
| C | Chris Hoiles, Baltimore | R-R | 6-0 | 213 | 28 | $350,000 | .310 | 419 | 80 | 130 | 28 | 0 | 29 | 82 | 1 |
| 1B | John Olerud, Toronto | L-L | 6-5 | 218 | 25 | 1,487,500 | .363 | 551 | 109 | 200 | 54 | 2 | 24 | 107 | 0 |
| 2B | Roberto Alomar, Toronto | B-R | 6-0 | 175 | 25 | 4,833,333 | .326 | 589 | 109 | 192 | 35 | 6 | 17 | 93 | 55 |
| 3B | Travis Fryman, Detroit | R-R | 6-1 | 194 | 24 | 650,000 | .300 | 607 | 98 | 182 | 37 | 5 | 22 | 97 | 9 |
| SS | Cal Ripken, Baltimore | R-R | 6-4 | 225 | 33 | 5,100,000 | .257 | 641 | 87 | 165 | 26 | 3 | 24 | 90 | 1 |
| OF | Albert Belle, Cleveland | R-R | 6-2 | 200 | 27 | 1,600,000 | .290 | 594 | 93 | 172 | 36 | 3 | 38 | 129 | 23 |
| | Juan Gonzalez, Texas | R-R | 6-3 | 210 | 23 | 525,000 | .310 | 536 | 105 | 166 | 33 | 1 | 46 | 118 | 4 |
| | Ken Griffey, Seattle | L-L | 6-3 | 220 | 23 | 4,000,000 | .309 | 582 | 113 | 180 | 38 | 3 | 45 | 109 | 17 |
| DH | Frank Thomas, Chicago | R-R | 6-5 | 240 | 25 | 900,000 | .317 | 549 | 106 | 174 | 36 | 0 | 41 | 128 | 4 |

| | | | | | | | W | L | ERA | G | SV | IP | H | BB | SO |
|---|---|---|---|---|---|---|---|---|---|---|---|---|---|---|---|
| P | Kevin Appier, Kansas City | R-R | 6-2 | 200 | 25 | 2,000,000 | 18 | 8 | 2.56 | 34 | 0 | 239 | 183 | 81 | 186 |
| | Randy Johnson, Seattle | R-L | 6-10 | 225 | 29 | 2,625,000 | 19 | 8 | 3.24 | 35 | 1 | 255 | 185 | 99 | 308 |
| | Jimmy Key, New York | R-L | 6-1 | 190 | 32 | 4,750,000 | 18 | 6 | 3.00 | 34 | 0 | 237 | 219 | 43 | 173 |
| | Jack McDowell, Chicago | R-R | 6-5 | 185 | 27 | 4,000,000 | 22 | 10 | 3.37 | 34 | 0 | 257 | 261 | 69 | 158 |
| | Duane Ward, Toronto | R-R | 6-4 | 215 | 29 | 3,250,000 | 2 | 3 | 2.13 | 71 | 45 | 72 | 49 | 25 | 97 |

**Player of Year:** Frank Thomas, 1b, Chicago.    **Pitcher of Year:** Randy Johnson, lhp, Seattle.    **Rookie of Year:** Tim Salmon, California.
**Manager of Year:** Buck Showalter, New York.    **Executive of Year:** Pat Gillick, Toronto.

**Tim Salmon.** AL's top rookie hit 31 homers.

R&R SPORTS GROUP

# AL: BEST TOOLS

A Baseball America survey of American League managers, conducted at midseason 1993, ranked AL players with the best tools:

**BEST HITTER**
1. John Olerud, Blue Jays
2. Paul Molitor, Blue Jays
3. Ken Griffey Jr., Mariners

**BEST POWER HITTER**
1. Cecil Fielder, Tigers
2. Juan Gonzalez, Rangers
3. Albert Belle, Indians

**BEST BUNTER**
1. Kenny Lofton, Indians
2. Roberto Alomar, Blue Jays
3. Luis Polonia, Angels

**BEST HIT-AND-RUN ARTIST**
1. Chuck Knoblauch, Twins
2. Scott Fletcher, Red Sox
3. Roberto Alomar, Blue Jays

**BEST BASERUNNER**
1. Roberto Alomar, Blue Jays
2. Paul Molitor, Blue Jays
3. Kenny Lofton, Indians

**FASTEST BASERUNNER**
1. Kenny Lofton, Indians
2. Devon White, Blue Jays
3. Rickey Henderson, Athletics

**BEST PITCHER**
1. Mike Mussina, Orioles
2. Jack McDowell, White Sox
3. Roger Clemens, Red Sox

**BEST FASTBALL**
1. Randy Johnson, Mariners
2. Roger Clemens, Red Sox
3. Juan Guzman, Blue Jays

**BEST CURVEBALL**
1. Gregg Olson, Orioles
2. Erik Hanson, Mariners
3. Mark Langston, Angels

**BEST SLIDER**
1. Duane Ward, Blue Jays
2. Kevin Brown, Rangers
3. Juan Guzman, Blue Jays

**BEST CHANGEUP**
1. Jimmy Key, Yankees
2. Frank Viola, Red Sox
3. Mike Mussina, Orioles

**BEST CONTROL**
1. Jimmy Key, Yankees
2. Dennis Eckersley, Athletics
3. Mike Mussina, Orioles

**BEST PICKOFF MOVE**
1. Jimmy Key, Yankees
2. Mark Langston, Angels
3. Jack McDowell, White Sox

**BEST RELIEVER**
1. Duane Ward, Blue Jays
2. Jeff Montgomery, Royals
3. Rick Aguilera, Twins

**BEST DEFENSIVE C**
1. Ivan Rodriguez, Rangers
2. Ron Karkovice, White Sox
3. Terry Steinbach, Athletics

**BEST DEFENSIVE 1B**
1. Don Mattingly, Yankees
2. Mark McGuire, Athletics
3. J.T. Snow, Angels

**BEST DEFENSIVE 2B**
1. Roberto Alomar, Blue Jays
2. Jose Lind, Royals
3. Carlos Baerga, Indians

**BEST DEFENSIVE 3B**
1. Robin Ventura, White Sox
2. Dean Palmer, Rangers
3. Wade Boggs, Yankees

**BEST DEFENSIVE SS**
1. Omar Vizquel, Mariners
2. Greg Gagne, Royals
3. Cal Ripken, Orioles

**BEST INFIELD ARM**
1. Scott Cooper, Red Sox
2. Travis Fryman, Tigers
3. Dean Palmer, Rangers

**BEST DEFENSIVE OF**
1. Devon White, Blue Jays
2. Ken Griffey Jr., Mariners
3. Kenny Lofton, Indians

**BEST OUTFIELD ARM**
1. Jay Buhner, Mariners
2. Ken Griffey Jr., Mariners
3. Tim Salmon, Angels

**MOST EXCITING PLAYER**
1. Kenny Lofton, Indians
2. Ken Griffey Jr., Mariners
3. Kirby Puckett, Twins

**BEST MANAGER**
1. Tony La Russa, Athletics
2. Sparky Anderson, Tigers
3. Johnny Oates, Orioles

to drag on for the rest of August and almost to the last pitch of Ryan's career, Sept. 22 in Seattle.

The Rangers-White Sox brawl was just one of several ugly on-field incidents in 1993. On June 6 the Mariners and Orioles fought at Camden Yards after Mike Mussina plunked Bill Haselman. Seven players were ejected following a 20-minute scuffle that featured actual punching, as opposed to baseball's usual square-dance approach to fighting.

## Achievements, Etc.

Angels right fielder Tim Salmon lived up to expectations, batting .283 with 31 homers and 95 RBIs to win AL rookie-of-the-year honors. Salmon's numbers would have been even more impressive had his season not ended Sept. 15, when he fractured a finger in a game against the Mariners.

Tigers manager Sparky Anderson picked up the 2,000th win of his managerial career April 15 in a 3-2 win over the Athletics. Anderson finished the year with 2,081 wins, fifth on the all-time list. In winning 85 games and finishing tied for third in the AL East, Anderson's Tigers scored 899 runs. No big league team has scored 900 since the 1953 Brooklyn Dodgers.

Blue Jays hitters finished 1-2-3 in the AL batting race, marking the first time that's happened in either league in exactly 100 years. John Olerud (.363), Paul Molitor (.332) and Roberto Alomar (.326) did the honors for Toronto as the Blue Jays joined the 1893 Phillies.

Blue Jays second baseman Alomar reached 1,000 hits at age 25, prompting talk of his one day reaching 3,000 hits. Only two second basemen, Eddie Collins and Nap Lajoie, have had 3,000 hits.

Indians second baseman Carlos Baerga became the only player in big league history to homer from both sides of the plate in the same inning. Baerga's April 8 blasts came off Yankees relievers Steve Howe and Steve Farr.

Blue Jays outfielder Joe Carter hit three home runs against his former team, the Indians, on Aug. 23. It was the fifth three-homer game of his career, setting a new AL record.

Twins righthander Scott Erickson went 8-19 and narrowly avoided becoming the first major leaguer since Oakland's Brian Kingman in 1980 to lose 20 games. Erickson had no-decisions in his last two starts.

# AMERICAN LEAGUE
## 1993 BATTING, PITCHING STATISTICS

### CLUB BATTING

| | AVG | G | AB | R | H | 2B | 3B | HR | BB | SO | SB |
|---|---|---|---|---|---|---|---|---|---|---|---|
| New York | .279 | 162 | 5615 | 821 | 1568 | 294 | 24 | 178 | 629 | 910 | 39 |
| Toronto | .279 | 162 | 5579 | 847 | 1556 | 317 | 42 | 159 | 588 | 861 | 170 |
| Cleveland | .275 | 162 | 5619 | 790 | 1547 | 264 | 31 | 141 | 488 | 843 | 159 |
| Detroit | .275 | 162 | 5620 | 899 | 1546 | 282 | 38 | 178 | 765 | 1122 | 104 |
| Texas | .267 | 162 | 5510 | 835 | 1472 | 284 | 39 | 181 | 483 | 984 | 113 |
| Baltimore | .267 | 162 | 5508 | 786 | 1470 | 287 | 24 | 157 | 655 | 930 | 73 |
| Chicago | .265 | 162 | 5483 | 776 | 1454 | 228 | 44 | 162 | 604 | 834 | 106 |
| Minnesota | .264 | 162 | 5601 | 693 | 1480 | 261 | 27 | 121 | 493 | 850 | 83 |
| Boston | .264 | 162 | 5496 | 686 | 1451 | 219 | 29 | 114 | 508 | 871 | 73 |
| Kansas City | .263 | 162 | 5522 | 675 | 1455 | 294 | 35 | 125 | 428 | 936 | 100 |
| Seattle | .260 | 162 | 5494 | 734 | 1429 | 272 | 24 | 161 | 624 | 901 | 91 |
| California | .260 | 162 | 5391 | 684 | 1399 | 259 | 24 | 114 | 564 | 930 | 169 |
| Milwaukee | .258 | 162 | 5525 | 733 | 1426 | 240 | 25 | 125 | 555 | 932 | 138 |
| Oakland | .254 | 162 | 5543 | 715 | 1408 | 260 | 21 | 158 | 622 | 1048 | 131 |

### CLUB PITCHING

| | ERA | G | CG | SHO | SV | IP | H | R | ER | BB | SO |
|---|---|---|---|---|---|---|---|---|---|---|---|
| Chicago | 3.72 | 162 | 16 | 11 | 48 | 1454 | 1398 | 664 | 601 | 566 | 974 |
| Boston | 3.77 | 162 | 9 | 11 | 44 | 1452 | 1379 | 698 | 609 | 552 | 997 |
| Kansas City | 4.04 | 162 | 16 | 6 | 48 | 1445 | 1379 | 694 | 649 | 571 | 985 |
| Seattle | 4.20 | 162 | 22 | 10 | 41 | 1454 | 1421 | 731 | 678 | 605 | 1083 |
| Toronto | 4.21 | 162 | 11 | 11 | 50 | 1441 | 1441 | 742 | 674 | 620 | 1023 |
| Texas | 4.28 | 162 | 20 | 6 | 45 | 1438 | 1476 | 751 | 684 | 562 | 957 |
| Baltimore | 4.31 | 162 | 21 | 10 | 42 | 1443 | 1427 | 745 | 691 | 579 | 900 |
| California | 4.34 | 162 | 26 | 6 | 41 | 1430 | 1482 | 770 | 690 | 550 | 843 |
| New York | 4.35 | 162 | 11 | 13 | 38 | 1438 | 1467 | 761 | 695 | 552 | 899 |
| Milwaukee | 4.45 | 162 | 26 | 6 | 29 | 1447 | 1511 | 792 | 716 | 522 | 810 |
| Cleveland | 4.58 | 162 | 7 | 8 | 45 | 1446 | 1591 | 813 | 735 | 591 | 888 |
| Detroit | 4.65 | 162 | 11 | 7 | 36 | 1437 | 1547 | 837 | 742 | 542 | 828 |
| Minnesota | 4.71 | 162 | 5 | 3 | 44 | 1444 | 1591 | 830 | 756 | 514 | 901 |
| Oakland | 4.90 | 162 | 8 | 2 | 42 | 1452 | 1551 | 846 | 791 | 680 | 864 |

### CLUB FIELDING

| | PCT | PO | A | E | DP | | PCT | PO | A | E | DP |
|---|---|---|---|---|---|---|---|---|---|---|---|
| Seattle | .985 | 4361 | 1726 | 90 | 173 | Chicago | .982 | 4362 | 1665 | 112 | 153 |
| Kansas City | .984 | 4336 | 1709 | 97 | 150 | California | .980 | 4291 | 1694 | 120 | 161 |
| Baltimore | .984 | 4328 | 1789 | 100 | 169 | Boston | .980 | 4357 | 1692 | 122 | 155 |
| Minnesota | .984 | 4333 | 1755 | 100 | 167 | Texas | .979 | 4315 | 1779 | 132 | 145 |
| New York | .983 | 4315 | 1889 | 105 | 166 | Detroit | .979 | 4310 | 1777 | 132 | 148 |
| Toronto | .982 | 4324 | 1582 | 107 | 144 | Milwaukee | .979 | 4341 | 1632 | 131 | 148 |
| Oakland | .982 | 4357 | 1626 | 111 | 161 | Cleveland | .976 | 4337 | 1661 | 148 | 174 |

### INDIVIDUAL BATTING LEADERS
(Minimum 502 Plate Appearances)

| | AVG | G | AB | R | H | 2B | 3B | HR | RBI | BB | SO | SB | CS |
|---|---|---|---|---|---|---|---|---|---|---|---|---|---|
| *Olerud, John, Toronto | .363 | 158 | 551 | 109 | 200 | 54 | 2 | 24 | 107 | 114 | 65 | 0 | 2 |
| Molitor, Paul, Toronto | .332 | 160 | 636 | 121 | 211 | 37 | 5 | 22 | 111 | 77 | 71 | 22 | 4 |
| #Alomar, Roberto, Toronto | .326 | 153 | 589 | 109 | 192 | 35 | 6 | 17 | 93 | 80 | 67 | 55 | 15 |
| *Lofton, Kenny, Cleveland | .325 | 148 | 569 | 116 | 185 | 28 | 8 | 1 | 42 | 81 | 83 | 70 | 14 |
| #Baerga, Carlos, Cleveland | .321 | 154 | 624 | 105 | 200 | 28 | 6 | 21 | 114 | 34 | 68 | 15 | 4 |
| Thomas, Frank, Chicago | .317 | 153 | 549 | 106 | 174 | 36 | 0 | 41 | 128 | 112 | 54 | 4 | 2 |
| *Greenwell, Mike, Boston | .315 | 146 | 540 | 77 | 170 | 38 | 6 | 13 | 72 | 54 | 46 | 5 | 4 |
| #Phillips, Tony, Detroit | .313 | 151 | 566 | 113 | 177 | 27 | 0 | 7 | 57 | 132 | 102 | 16 | 11 |
| *O'Neill, Paul, New York | .311 | 141 | 498 | 71 | 155 | 34 | 1 | 20 | 75 | 44 | 69 | 2 | 4 |
| *Johnson, Lance, Chicago | .311 | 147 | 540 | 75 | 168 | 18 | 14 | 0 | 47 | 36 | 33 | 35 | 7 |

### INDIVIDUAL PITCHING LEADERS
(Minimum 162 Innings)

| | W | L | ERA | G | GS | CG | SV | IP | H | R | ER | BB | SO |
|---|---|---|---|---|---|---|---|---|---|---|---|---|---|
| Appier, Kevin, Kansas City | 18 | 8 | 2.56 | 34 | 34 | 5 | 0 | 239 | 183 | 74 | 68 | 81 | 186 |
| *Alvarez, Wilson, Chicago | 15 | 8 | 2.95 | 31 | 31 | 1 | 0 | 208 | 168 | 78 | 68 | 122 | 155 |
| *Key, Jimmy, New York | 18 | 6 | 3.00 | 34 | 34 | 4 | 0 | 237 | 219 | 84 | 79 | 43 | 173 |
| Fernandez, Alex, Chicago | 18 | 9 | 3.13 | 34 | 34 | 3 | 0 | 247 | 221 | 95 | 86 | 67 | 169 |
| *Viola, Frank, Boston | 11 | 8 | 3.14 | 29 | 29 | 2 | 0 | 184 | 180 | 76 | 64 | 72 | 91 |
| *Finley, Chuck, California | 16 | 14 | 3.15 | 35 | 35 | 13 | 0 | 251 | 243 | 108 | 88 | 82 | 187 |
| *Langston, Mark, California | 16 | 11 | 3.20 | 35 | 35 | 7 | 0 | 256 | 220 | 100 | 91 | 85 | 196 |
| *Johnson, Randy, Seattle | 19 | 8 | 3.24 | 35 | 34 | 10 | 1 | 255 | 185 | 97 | 92 | 99 | 308 |
| Darwin, Danny, Boston | 15 | 11 | 3.26 | 34 | 34 | 2 | 0 | 229 | 196 | 93 | 83 | 49 | 130 |
| Cone, David, Kansas City | 11 | 14 | 3.33 | 34 | 34 | 6 | 0 | 254 | 205 | 102 | 94 | 114 | 191 |

---

# AWARD WINNERS
Selected by Baseball Writers Association of America

## MVP

| Player, Team | 1st | 2nd | 3rd | Total |
|---|---|---|---|---|
| Frank Thomas, Chi. | 28 | 0 | 0 | 392 |
| Paul Molitor, Toronto | 0 | 13 | 5 | 209 |
| John Olerud, Toronto | 0 | 4 | 11 | 198 |
| Juan Gonzalez, Texas | 0 | 4 | 4 | 185 |
| Ken Griffey, Seattle | 0 | 4 | 5 | 182 |
| Roberto Alomar, Tor. | 0 | 3 | 2 | 102 |
| Albert Belle, Cleve. | 0 | 0 | 0 | 81 |
| Rafael Palmeiro, Texas | 0 | 0 | 0 | 52 |
| Jack McDowell, Chi. | 0 | 0 | 0 | 51 |
| Carlos Baerga, Cleve. | 0 | 0 | 1 | 50 |
| Jimmy Key, New York | 0 | 0 | 0 | 29 |
| Joe Carter, Toronto | 0 | 0 | 0 | 25 |
| Mike Stanley, N.Y. | 0 | 0 | 0 | 15 |
| Jeff Montgomery, K.C. | 0 | 0 | 0 | 15 |
| Kenny Lofton, Cleve. | 0 | 0 | 0 | 11 |
| Tony Phillips, Detroit | 0 | 0 | 0 | 10 |
| Chris Hoiles, Balt. | 0 | 0 | 0 | 10 |
| Mo Vaughn, Boston | 0 | 0 | 0 | 8 |
| Don Mattingly, N.Y. | 0 | 0 | 0 | 7 |
| Cal Ripken, Balt. | 0 | 0 | 0 | 7 |
| Alex Fernandez, Chi. | 0 | 0 | 0 | 4 |
| Duane Ward, Toronto | 0 | 0 | 0 | 3 |
| Greg Gagne, K.C. | 0 | 0 | 0 | 3 |
| Kevin Appier, K.C. | 0 | 0 | 0 | 1 |
| Cecil Fielder, Detroit | 0 | 0 | 0 | 1 |
| Randy Johnson, Sea. | 0 | 0 | 0 | 1 |

## Cy Young Award

| Pitcher, Team | 1st | 2nd | 3rd | Total |
|---|---|---|---|---|
| Jack McDowell, Chi. | 21 | 6 | 1 | 124 |
| Randy Johnson, Sea. | 6 | 14 | 3 | 75 |
| Kevin Appier, K.C. | 1 | 4 | 13 | 30 |
| Jimmy Key, N.Y. | 0 | 2 | 8 | 14 |
| Duane Ward, Toronto | 0 | 1 | 2 | 5 |
| Pat Hentgen, Toronto | 0 | 1 | 0 | 3 |
| Juan Guzman, Toronto | 0 | 0 | 1 | 1 |

## Rookie of the Year

| Player, Team | 1st | 2nd | 3rd | Total |
|---|---|---|---|---|
| Tim Salmon, Calif. | 28 | 0 | 0 | 140 |
| Jason Bere, Chicago | 0 | 18 | 5 | 59 |
| Aaron Sele, Boston | 0 | 3 | 10 | 19 |
| Wayne Kirby, Cleve. | 0 | 3 | 3 | 12 |
| Rich Amaral, Seattle | 0 | 2 | 2 | 8 |
| Brent Gates, Oakland | 0 | 1 | 4 | 7 |
| Troy Neel, Oakland | 0 | 1 | 2 | 5 |
| Jerry DiPoto, Cleve. | 0 | 0 | 1 | 1 |
| David Hulse, Texas | 0 | 0 | 1 | 1 |

## Manager of the Year

| Manager, Team | 1st | 2nd | 3rd | Total |
|---|---|---|---|---|
| Gene Lamont, Chi. | 8 | 9 | 5 | 72 |
| Buck Showalter, N.Y. | 7 | 8 | 4 | 63 |
| Cito Gaston, Toronto | 6 | 5 | 4 | 49 |
| Kevin Kennedy, Texas | 3 | 3 | 4 | 28 |
| Lou Piniella, Seattle | 3 | 2 | 3 | 24 |
| Mike Hargrove, Cleve. | 1 | 0 | 5 | 10 |
| Johnny Oates, Balt. | 0 | 1 | 2 | 5 |
| Butch Hobson, Boston | 0 | 0 | 1 | 1 |

**NOTE:** MVP balloting based on 14 points for first-place vote, nine for second, eight for third, etc.; Cy Young Award, Rookie of the Year and Manager of the Year balloting based on five points for first-place vote, three for second and one for third.

# DEPARTMENT LEADERS
## AMERICAN LEAGUE

### BATTING

#### RUNS
Rafael Palmeiro, Texas ...................... 124
Paul Molitor, Toronto ........................ 121
Kenny Lofton, Cleveland .................. 116
Devon White, Toronto ...................... 116
Rickey Henderson, Oakland-Toronto . 114

#### HITS
Paul Molitor, Toronto .......................... 211
Carlos Baerga, Cleveland ................ 200
John Olerud, Toronto ........................ 200
Roberto Alomar, Toronto.................. 192
Kenny Lofton, Cleveland .................. 185

#### TOTAL BASES
Ken Griffey, Seattle ........................... 359
Juan Gonzalez, Texas ...................... 339
Frank Thomas, Chicago .................... 333
Rafael Palmeiro, Texas ..................... 331
John Olerud, Toronto ........................ 330

#### DOUBLES
John Olerud, Toronto ...................... 54
Devon White, Toronto ......................... 42
Rafael Palmeiro, Texas ...................... 40
John Valentin, Boston ......................... 40
Kirby Puckett, Minnesota ................... 39

#### TRIPLES
Lance Johnson, Chicago..................... 14
Joey Cora, Chicago ............................. 13
David Hulse, Texas .............................. 10
Tony Fernandez, Toronto...................... 9
Brian McRae, Kansas City ................... 9

#### HOME RUNS
Juan Gonzalez, Texas ......................... 46
Ken Griffey, Seattle ............................ 45
Frank Thomas, Chicago....................... 41
Albert Belle, Cleveland ....................... 38
Rafael Palmeiro, Texas........................ 37

#### RUNS BATTED IN
Albert Belle, Cleveland ...................... 129
Frank Thomas, Chicago ..................... 128
Joe Carter, Toronto ........................... 121
Juan Gonzalez, Texas ....................... 118
Cecil Fielder, Detroit.......................... 117

#### SACRIFICE BUNTS
Joey Cora, Chicago ............................ 19
John Valentin, Boston........................... 16
Brian McRae, Kansas City .................. 14
Ozzie Guillen, Chicago........................ 13
Jose Lind, Kansas City ........................ 13
Tony Pena, Boston ............................... 13
Omar Vizquel, Seattle.......................... 13

#### SACRIFICE FLIES
Albert Belle, Cleveland ....................... 14
Carlos Baerga, Cleveland ................... 13
Frank Thomas, Chicago ...................... 13
George Brett, Kansas City................... 10
Joe Carter, Toronto ............................. 10
Ruben Sierra, Oakland........................ 10

#### HIT BY PITCH
Dave Valle, Seattle .............................. 17
Mike Macfarlane, Kansas City............. 16
Andre Dawson, Boston........................ 13
Juan Gonzalez, Texas.......................... 13
Mike Bordick, Oakland......................... 11
Billy Hatcher, Boston ........................... 11

#### WALKS
Tony Phillips, Detroit........................... 132
Rickey Henderson, Oakland-Toronto.. 120
John Olerud, Toronto........................... 114
Frank Thomas, Chicago ..................... 112
Mickey Tettleton, Detroit..................... 109

**John Olerud.** Toronto first baseman flirted with .400 much of 1993 before finally settling at .363.

BOB ROSATO

#### INTENTIONAL WALKS
John Olerud, Toronto............................ 33
Ken Griffey, Seattle .............................. 25
Frank Thomas, Chicago ...................... 23
Mo Vaughn, Boston .............................. 23
Rafael Palmeiro, Texas ........................ 22

#### STRIKEOUTS
Rob Deer, Detroit-Boston .................. 169
Danny Tartabull, New York ................ 156
Dean Palmer, Texas........................... 154
Jay Buhner, Seattle ............................ 144
Mickey Tettleton, Detroit..................... 139

#### STOLEN BASES
Kenny Lofton, Cleveland ...................... 70
Roberto Alomar, Toronto...................... 55
Luis Polonia, California ........................ 55
Rickey Henderson, Oakland-Toronto.... 53
Chad Curtis, California ......................... 48

#### CAUGHT STEALING
Chad Curtis, California ......................... 24
Luis Polonia, California ........................ 24
Roberto Alomar, Toronto...................... 15
Mark McLemore, Baltimore ................. 15
Kenny Lofton, Cleveland ...................... 14
Brian McRae, Kansas City ................... 14
Omar Vizquel, Seattle........................... 14

#### GIDP
Ed Sprague, Toronto ............................ 23

Cecil Fielder, Detroit .............................. 22
Mark McLemore, Baltimore ................. 21
George Brett, Kansas City.................... 20
Don Mattingly, New York...................... 20

#### HITTING STREAKS
John Olerud, Toronto............................ 26
Bernie Williams, New York ................... 21
Brian Harper, Minnesota....................... 19
Three tied at................................. 18

#### MULTI-HIT GAMES
Carlos Baerga, Cleveland .................... 64
Paul Molitor, Toronto ........................... 63
Kenny Lofton, Cleveland ...................... 59
Roberto Alomar, Toronto...................... 57
Kirby Puckett, Minnesota...................... 56

#### SLUGGING PERCENTAGE
Juan Gonzalez, Texas.........................632
Ken Griffey, Seattle ............................617
Frank Thomas, Chicago .....................607
John Olerud, Toronto...........................599
Chris Hoiles, Baltimore .......................585

#### ON-BASE PERCENTAGE
John Olerud, Toronto............................473
Tony Phillips, Detroit............................443
Rickey Henderson, Oakland-Toronto. .432
Frank Thomas, Chicago ......................426
Chris Hoiles, Baltimore .......................416

## PITCHING

### WINS
Jack McDowell, Chicago ...................... 22
Randy Johnson, Seattle ....................... 19
Pat Hentgen, Toronto .......................... 19
Jimmy Key, New York .......................... 18
Kevin Appier, Kansas City ................... 18
Alex Fernandez, Chicago ..................... 18

### LOSSES
Scott Erickson, Minnesota ................... 19
Cal Eldred, Milwaukee ......................... 16
Kevin Tapani, Minnesota ...................... 15
Jim Abbott, New York ........................... 14
Roger Clemens, Boston ....................... 14
David Cone, Kansas City ..................... 14
Chuck Finley, California ....................... 14
Ben McDonald, Baltimore .................... 14
Melido Perez, New York ....................... 14
Bill Wegman, Milwaukee ...................... 14

### WINNING PERCENTAGE
Juan Guzman, Toronto ...................... .824
Bob Wickman, New York .................. .778
Jimmy Key, New York ....................... .750
Jason Bere, Chicago ........................ .706
Dave Fleming, Seattle ...................... .706

### GAMES
Greg Harris, Boston ............................. 80
Scott Radinsky, Chicago ...................... 73
Tony Fossas, Boston ........................... 71
Jeff Nelson, Seattle ............................. 71
Duane Ward, Toronto ........................... 71

### GAMES STARTED
Cal Eldred, Milwaukee .......................... 36
Mike Moore, Detroit .............................. 36
Chuck Finley, California ....................... 35
Mark Langston, California .................... 35
Kevin Tapani, Minnesota ...................... 35

### COMPLETE GAMES
Chuck Finley, California ....................... 13
Kevin Brown, Texas .............................. 12
Randy Johnson, Seattle ....................... 10
Jack McDowell, Chicago ...................... 10
Cal Eldred, Milwaukee ........................... 8

### SHUTOUTS
Jack McDowell, Chicago ........................ 4
Kevin Brown, Texas ................................ 3
Randy Johnson, Seattle ......................... 3
Mike Moore, Detroit ............................... 3
Five tied at ............................................ 2

### GAMES FINISHED
Duane Ward, Toronto ............................ 70
Roberto Hernandez, Chicago ............... 67
Jeff Montgomery, Kansas City .............. 63
Rick Aguilera, Minnesota ..................... 61

**Albert Belle.** Cleveland slugger led AL in RBIs with 129.

**Randy Johnson.** Mariners lefty led AL with 308 strikeouts.

Tom Henke, Texas ................................ 60

### SAVES
Jeff Montgomery, Kansas City .............. 45
Duane Ward, Toronto ........................... 45
Tom Henke, Texas ................................ 40
Roberto Hernandez, Chicago ............... 38
Dennis Eckersley, Oakland .................. 36

### INNINGS PITCHED
Cal Eldred, Milwaukee ........................ 258
Jack McDowell, Chicago ..................... 257
Mark Langston, California ................... 256
Randy Johnson, Seattle ...................... 255
David Cone, Kansas City .................... 254

### HITS ALLOWED
Scott Erickson, Minnesota ................. 266
Jack McDowell, Chicago ..................... 261
Jaime Navarro, Milwaukee .................. 254
Chuck Finley, California ...................... 243
Kevin Tapani, Minnesota ..................... 243

### RUNS ALLOWED
Scott Erickson, Minnesota ................. 138
Mike Moore, Detroit ............................ 135
Jaime Navarro, Milwaukee .................. 135
Kevin Tapani, Minnesota ..................... 123
Ricky Bones, Milwaukee ..................... 122
Jose Mesa, Cleveland ........................ 122

### HOME RUNS ALLOWED
Mike Moore, Detroit .............................. 35
Cal Eldred, Milwaukee .......................... 32
Danny Darwin, Boston ......................... 31
Ricky Bones, Milwaukee ...................... 28
Bill Gullickson, Detroit ......................... 28

### WALKS
Wilson Alvarez, Chicago ..................... 122
David Cone, Kansas City .................... 114
Juan Guzman, Toronto ........................ 110
Randy Johnson, Seattle ....................... 99
Cal Eldred, Milwaukee .......................... 91
Bobby Witt, Oakland ............................. 91

### HIT BATSMEN
Randy Johnson, Seattle ....................... 16
Kevin Brown, Texas .............................. 15
Roger Clemens, Boston ....................... 11
Jaime Navarro, Milwaukee ................... 11
David Cone, Kansas City ..................... 10
Cal Eldred, Milwaukee .......................... 10
Scott Erickson, Minnesota ................... 10
Greg Harris, Boston ............................. 10

### STRIKEOUTS
Randy Johnson, Seattle ..................... 308
Mark Langston, California ................... 196
Juan Guzman, Toronto ........................ 194
David Cone, Kansas City .................... 191

Chuck Finley, California ...................... 187

### WILD PITCHES
Juan Guzman, Toronto ........................ 26
Tom Gordon, Kansas City .................... 17
David Cone, Kansas City ..................... 14
Jack Morris, Toronto ............................ 14
David Wells, Detroit ............................. 13

### BALKS
Willie Banks, Minnesota ........................ 5
Kenny Rogers, Texas ............................. 5
Jim Deshaies, Minnesota ...................... 4
Scott Radinsky, Chicago ....................... 4
John Dopson, Boston ............................ 3
Mark Guthrie, Minnesota ...................... 3
Ted Higuera, Milwaukee ....................... 3
Hipolito Pichardo, Kansas City ............. 3

### OPPONENTS BATTING AVERAGE
Randy Johnson, Seattle ..................... .203
Kevin Appier, Kansas City .................. .212
David Cone, Kansas City .................... .223
Ben McDonald, Baltimore ................... .228
Chris Bosio, Seattle ........................... .229

## FIELDING

### PITCHER
PCT Alex Fernandez, Chicago ....... 1.000
PO Kevin Brown, Texas.................... 29
A Mark Langston, California .............. 47
E Willie Banks, Minnesota ............... 6
TC Kevin Brown, Texas..................... 74
DP Charlie Leibrandt, Texas .............. 5
    Bobby Witt, Oakland ..................... 5

### CATCHER
PCT Mike Stanley, New York ........... .996
PO Dave Valle, Seattle .................. 881
A Pat Borders, Toronto .............. 80
E Pat Borders, Toronto .............. 13
TC Pat Borders, Toronto ............ 962
DP Junior Ortiz, Cleveland ............. 13
    Dave Valle, Seattle ............... 13
PB Brian Harper, Minnesota............. 18

### FIRST BASE
PCT Don Mattingly, New York .......... .998
PO Rafael Palmeiro, Texas ......... 1,389
A Rafael Palmeiro, Texas ............. 146
E Mo Vaughn, Boston ..................... 16
TC Rafael Palmeiro, Texas ......... 1,540
DP Rafael Palmeiro, Texas ........... 133

### SECOND BASE
PCT Jose Lind, Kansas City ............ .994
PO Carlos Baerga, Cleveland ........ 347
A Carlos Baerga, Cleveland ....... 445
E Joey Cora, Chicago .................. 19
TC Carlos Baerga, Cleveland ....... 809
DP Harold Reynolds, Baltimore....... 110

### THIRD BASE
PCT Wade Boggs, New York ........... .970
PO Ed Sprague, Toronto .............. 127
A Wade Boggs, New York .......... 311
E Dean Palmer, Texas.................. 29
TC Robin Ventura, Chicago .......... 404
DP Wade Boggs, New York ........... 29

### SHORTSTOP
PCT Greg Gagne, Kansas City ........ .986
PO Mike Bordick, Oakland.............. 280
A Cal Ripken, Baltimore .............. 495
E Felix Fermin, Cleveland ............. 23
TC Cal Ripken, Baltimore .............. 738
DP Mike Bordick, Oakland.............. 108
    Omar Vizquel, Seattle............... 108

### OUTFIELD
PCT Tim Raines, Chicago ............. 1.000
PO Lance Johnson, Chicago.......... 427
A Wayne Kirby, Cleveland ........... 19
E Chad Curtis, California ............. 9
    Lance Johnson, Chicago........... 9
    Kenny Lofton, Cleveland ........... 9
TC Chad Curtis, California ............ 448
DP Albert Belle, Cleveland ............ 7

# AMERICAN LEAGUE
## YEAR-BY-YEAR LEADERS: BATTING

| Year | Batting Average | | Home Runs | | RBIs | |
|---|---|---|---|---|---|---|
| 1901 | Nap Lajoie, Phil. | .422 | Nap Lajoie, Phil. | 14 | Nap Lajoie, Phil. | 125 |
| 1902 | Ed Delahanty, Wash. | .376 | Socks Seybold, Phil. | 16 | Buck Freeman, Boston. | 121 |
| 1903 | Nap Lajoie, Cleveland. | .355 | Buck Freeman, Boston. | 13 | Buck Freeman, Boston. | 104 |
| 1904 | Nap Lajoie, Cleveland. | .381 | Harry Davis, Phil. | 10 | Nap Lajoie, Cleveland. | 102 |
| 1905 | Elmer Flick, Cleveland. | .306 | Harry Davis, Phil. | 8 | Harry Davis, Phil. | 83 |
| 1906 | George Stone, St. Louis. | .358 | Harry Davis, Phil. | 12 | Harry Davis, Phil. | 96 |
| 1907 | Ty Cobb, Detroit. | .350 | Harry Davis, Phil. | 8 | Ty Cobb, Detroit. | 116 |
| 1908 | Ty Cobb, Detroit. | .324 | Sam Crawford, Detroit | 7 | Ty Cobb, Detroit. | 101 |
| 1909 | Ty Cobb, Detroit. | .377 | Ty Cobb, Detroit. | 9 | Ty Cobb, Detroit. | 115 |
| 1910 | Ty Cobb, Detroit. | .385 | Jake Stahl, Boston | 10 | Sam Crawford, Detroit. | 115 |
| 1911 | Ty Cobb, Detroit. | .420 | Frank Baker, Phil. | 11 | Ty Cobb, Detroit. | 144 |
| 1912 | Ty Cobb, Detroit. | .410 | 2 tied at. | 10 | Frank Baker, Phil. | 133 |
| 1913 | Ty Cobb, Detroit. | .390 | Frank Baker, Phil. | 12 | Frank Baker, Phil. | 126 |
| 1914 | Ty Cobb, Detroit. | .368 | Frank Baker, Phil. | 9 | Sam Crawford, Detroit. | 112 |
| 1915 | Ty Cobb, Detroit. | .370 | Braggo Roth, Cleveland | 7 | Sam Crawford, Detroit. | 116 |
| 1916 | Tris Speaker, Cleveland. | .386 | Wally Pipp, New York. | 12 | Wally Pipp, New York. | 99 |
| 1917 | Ty Cobb, Detroit. | .383 | Wally Pipp, New York. | 9 | Bob Veach, Detroit. | 115 |
| 1918 | Ty Cobb, Detroit. | .382 | 2 tied at. | 11 | 2 tied at. | 74 |
| 1919 | Ty Cobb, Detroit. | .384 | Babe Ruth, Boston. | 29 | Babe Ruth, Boston. | 112 |
| 1920 | George Sisler, St. Louis | .407 | Babe Ruth, New York. | 54 | Babe Ruth, New York. | 137 |
| 1921 | Harry Heilmann, Detroit | .394 | Babe Ruth, New York. | 59 | Babe Ruth, New York. | 171 |
| 1922 | George Sisler, St. Louis. | .420 | Ken Williams, St. Louis. | 39 | Kenny Williams, St. Louis. | 155 |
| 1923 | Harry Heilmann, Detroit | .403 | Babe Ruth, New York. | 41 | Babe Ruth, New York. | 131 |
| 1924 | Babe Ruth, New York. | .378 | Babe Ruth, New York. | 46 | Goose Goslin, Wash. | 129 |
| 1925 | Harry Heilmann, Detroit | .393 | Bob Meusel, New York | 33 | Bob Meusel, New York | 138 |
| 1926 | Heinie Manush, Detroit | .377 | Babe Ruth, New York. | 47 | Babe Ruth, New York. | 145 |
| 1927 | Harry Heilmann, Detroit | .398 | Babe Ruth, New York. | 60 | Lou Gehrig, New York. | 175 |
| 1928 | Goose Goslin, Wash. | .379 | Babe Ruth, New York. | 54 | Babe Ruth, New York. | 142 |
| 1929 | Lew Fonseca, Cleveland | .369 | Babe Ruth, New York. | 46 | Al Simmons, Phil. | 157 |
| 1930 | Al Simmons, Phil | .381 | Babe Ruth, New York. | 49 | Lou Gehrig, New York. | 174 |
| 1931 | Al Simmons, Phil. | .390 | 2 tied at. | 46 | Lou Gehrig, New York. | 184 |
| 1932 | Dale Alexander, Det.-Bos. | .367 | Jimmie Foxx, Phil. | 58 | Jimmie Foxx, Phil. | 169 |
| 1933 | Jimmie Foxx, Phil. | .356 | Jimmie Foxx, Phil. | 48 | Jimmie Foxx, Phil. | 163 |
| 1934 | Lou Gehrig, New York. | .363 | Lou Gehrig, New York. | 49 | Lou Gehrig, New York. | 165 |
| 1935 | Buddy Myer, Wash. | .349 | 2 tied at. | 36 | Hank Greenberg, Detroit. | 170 |
| 1936 | Luke Appling, Chicago. | .388 | Lou Gehrig, New York. | 49 | Hal Trosky, Cleveland. | 162 |
| 1937 | Charlie Gehringer, Det. | .371 | Joe DiMaggio, N.Y. | 46 | Hank Greenberg, Detroit. | 183 |
| 1938 | Jimmie Foxx, Boston. | .349 | Hank Greenberg, Det. | 58 | Jimmie Foxx, Boston. | 175 |
| 1939 | Joe DiMaggio, New York. | .381 | Jimmie Foxx, Boston. | 35 | Ted Williams, Boston. | 145 |
| 1940 | Joe DiMaggio, N.Y. | .352 | Hank Greenberg, Detroit. | 41 | Hank Greenberg, Detroit. | 150 |
| 1941 | Ted Williams, Boston. | .406 | Ted Williams, Boston. | 37 | Joe DiMaggio, N.Y. | 125 |
| 1942 | Ted Williams, Boston. | .356 | Ted Williams, Boston. | 36 | Ted Williams, Boston. | 137 |
| 1943 | Luke Appling, Chicago. | .328 | Rudy York, Detroit. | 34 | Rudy York, Detroit. | 118 |
| 1944 | Lou Boudreau, Cleve. | .327 | Nick Etten, New York. | 22 | Vern Stephens, St. Louis | 109 |
| 1945 | Snuffy Stirnweiss, N.Y. | .309 | Vern Stephens, St. Louis | 24 | Nick Etten, N.Y. | 111 |
| 1946 | Mickey Vernon, Wash. | .352 | Hank Greenberg, Detroit. | 44 | Hank Greenberg, Detroit | 127 |
| 1947 | Ted Williams, Boston. | .343 | Ted Williams, Boston. | 32 | Ted Williams, Boston. | 114 |
| 1948 | Ted Williams, Boston. | .369 | Joe DiMaggio, N.Y. | 39 | Joe DiMaggio, New York. | 155 |
| 1949 | George Kell, Detroit. | .343 | Ted Williams, Boston. | 43 | 2 tied at. | 159 |
| 1950 | Billy Goodman, Boston. | .354 | Al Rosen, Cleveland. | 37 | 2 tied at. | 144 |
| 1951 | Ferris Fain, Phil. | .344 | Gus Zernial, Chi.-Phil. | 33 | Gus Zernial, Chi.-Phil. | 129 |
| 1952 | Ferris Fain, Phil. | .327 | Larry Doby, Cleveland. | 32 | Al Rosen, Cleveland. | 105 |
| 1953 | Mickey Vernon, Wash. | .337 | Al Rosen, Cleveland. | 43 | Al Rosen, Cleveland. | 145 |
| 1954 | Bobby Avila, Cleveland. | .341 | Larry Doby, Cleveland. | 32 | Larry Doby, Cleveland. | 126 |
| 1955 | Al Kaline, Detroit. | .340 | Mickey Mantle, N.Y. | 37 | 2 tied at. | 116 |
| 1956 | Mickey Mantle, N.Y. | .353 | Mickey Mantle, N.Y. | 52 | Mickey Mantle, N.Y. | 130 |
| 1957 | Ted Williams, Boston. | .388 | Roy Sievers, Wash. | 42 | Roy Sievers, Wash. | 114 |
| 1958 | Ted Williams, Boston. | .328 | Mickey Mantle, N.Y. | 42 | Jackie Jensen, Boston. | 122 |
| 1959 | Harvey Kuenn, Detroit | .353 | 2 tied at. | 42 | Jackie Jensen, Boston. | 112 |
| 1960 | Pete Runnels, Boston. | .320 | Mickey Mantle, N.Y. | 40 | Roger Maris, New York | 112 |
| 1961 | Norm Cash, Detroit. | .361 | Roger Maris, New York. | 61 | Roger Maris, New York | 142 |
| 1962 | Pete Runnels, Boston. | .326 | Harmon Killebrew, Minn. | 48 | Harmon Killebrew, Minn. | 126 |
| 1963 | Carl Yastrzemski, Bos. | .321 | Harmon Killebrew, Minn. | 45 | Dick Stuart, Boston. | 118 |
| 1964 | Tony Oliva, Minnesota | .323 | Harmon Killebrew, Minn. | 49 | Brooks Robinson, Balt. | 118 |
| 1965 | Tony Oliva, Minnesota | .321 | Tony Conigliaro, Bos. | 32 | Rocky Colavito, Cleve. | 108 |
| 1966 | Frank Robinson, Balt. | .316 | Frank Robinson, Balt. | 49 | Frank Robinson, Balt. | 122 |
| 1967 | Carl Yastrzemski, Bos. | .326 | 2 tied at. | 44 | Carl Yastrzemski, Boston. | 121 |
| 1968 | Carl Yastrzemski, Boston | .301 | Frank Howard, Wash. | 44 | Ken Harrelson, Boston. | 109 |
| 1969 | Rod Carew, Minnesota | .332 | Harmon Killebrew, Minn. | 49 | Harmon Killebrew, Minn. | 140 |
| 1970 | Alex Johnson, Cal. | .329 | Frank Howard, Wash. | 44 | Frank Howard, Wash. | 126 |
| 1971 | Tony Oliva, Minnesota | .337 | Bill Melton, Chicago. | 33 | Harmon Killebrew, Minn. | 119 |
| 1972 | Rod Carew, Minnesota | .318 | Dick Allen, Chicago | 37 | Dick Allen, Chicago | 113 |
| 1973 | Rod Carew, Minnesota | .350 | Reggie Jackson, Oakland | 32 | Reggie Jackson, Oakland | 117 |
| 1974 | Rod Carew, Minnesota | .364 | Dick Allen, Chicago | 32 | Jeff Burroughs, Texas | 118 |
| 1975 | Rod Carew, Minnesota | .359 | 2 tied at. | 36 | George Scott, Mil. | 109 |
| 1976 | George Brett, K.C. | .333 | Graig Nettles, New York. | 32 | Lee May, Baltimore | 109 |
| 1977 | Rod Carew, Minnesota | .388 | Jim Rice, Boston. | 39 | Larry Hisle, Minnesota | 119 |
| 1978 | Rod Carew, Minnesota | .333 | Jim Rice, Boston. | 46 | Jim Rice, Boston. | 139 |
| 1979 | Fred Lynn, Boston | .333 | Gorman Thomas, Mil. | 45 | Don Baylor, California | 139 |
| 1980 | George Brett, K.C. | .390 | 2 tied at. | 41 | Cecil Cooper, Milwaukee | 122 |
| 1981 | Carney Lansford, Boston. | .336 | 4 tied at. | 22 | Eddie Murray, Balt. | 78 |
| 1982 | Willie Wilson, K.C. | .332 | 2 tied at. | 39 | Hal McRae, K.C. | 133 |
| 1983 | Wade Boggs, Boston. | .361 | Jim Rice, Boston. | 39 | 2 tied at. | 126 |
| 1984 | Don Mattingly, N.Y. | .343 | Tony Armas, Boston. | 43 | Tony Armas, Boston. | 123 |
| 1985 | Wade Boggs, Boston. | .368 | Darrell Evans, Detroit. | 40 | Don Mattingly, N.Y. | 145 |
| 1986 | Wade Boggs, Boston. | .357 | Jesse Barfield, Toronto. | 40 | Joe Carter, Cleveland. | 121 |
| 1987 | Wade Boggs, Boston. | .363 | Mark McGwire, Oakland. | 49 | George Bell, Toronto. | 134 |
| 1988 | Wade Boggs, Boston. | .366 | Jose Canseco, Oakland | 42 | Jose Canseco, Oakland | 124 |
| 1989 | Kirby Puckett, Minn. | .339 | Fred McGriff, Toronto. | 36 | Ruben Sierra, Texas | 119 |
| 1990 | George Brett, K.C. | .329 | Cecil Fielder, Detroit. | 51 | Cecil Fielder, Detroit. | 132 |
| 1991 | Julio Franco, Texas | .341 | 2 tied at. | 44 | Cecil Fielder, Detroit. | 133 |
| 1992 | Edgar Martinez, Seattle | .343 | Juan Gonzalez, Texas | 43 | Cecil Fielder, Detroit. | 124 |
| 1993 | John Olerud, Toronto | .363 | Juan Gonzalez, Texas | 46 | Albert Belle, Cleveland. | 129 |

# AMERICAN LEAGUE
## YEAR-BY-YEAR LEADERS: PITCHING

| Year | Wins | | ERA | | Strikeouts | |
|---|---|---|---|---|---|---|
| 1901 | Cy Young, Boston | 33 | Cy Young, Boston | 1.63 | Cy Young, Boston | 158 |
| 1902 | Cy Young, Boston | 32 | Ed Siever, Detroit | 1.91 | Rube Waddell, Phil. | 210 |
| 1903 | Cy Young, Boston | 28 | Earl Moore, Cleveland | 1.77 | Rube Waddell, Phil. | 302 |
| 1904 | Jack Chesbro, N.Y. | 41 | Addie Joss, Cleveland | 1.59 | Rube Waddell, Phil. | 349 |
| 1905 | Rube Waddell, Phil. | 26 | Rube Waddell, Phil. | 1.48 | Rube Waddell, Phil. | 287 |
| 1906 | Al Orth, New York | 27 | Doc White, Chicago | 1.52 | Rube Waddell, Phil. | 196 |
| 1907 | 2 tied at... | 27 | Ed Walsh, Chicago | 1.60 | Rube Waddell, Phil. | 232 |
| 1908 | Ed Walsh, Chicago | 40 | Addie Joss, Cleveland | 1.16 | Ed Walsh, Chicago | 269 |
| 1909 | George Mullin, Detroit | 29 | Harry Krause, Phil. | 1.39 | Frank Smith, Chicago | 177 |
| 1910 | Jack Coombs, Phil. | 31 | Ed Walsh, Chicago | 1.27 | Walter Johnson, Wash. | 313 |
| 1911 | Jack Coombs, Phil. | 28 | Vean Gregg, Cleveland | 1.81 | Ed Walsh, Chicago | 255 |
| 1912 | Joe Wood, Boston | 34 | Walter Johnson, Wash. | 1.39 | Walter Johnson, Wash. | 303 |
| 1913 | Walter Johnson, Wash. | 36 | Walter Johnson, Wash. | 1.14 | Walter Johnson, Wash. | 243 |
| 1914 | Walter Johnson, Wash. | 28 | Dutch Leonard, Bos. | 1.00 | Walter Johnson, Wash. | 225 |
| 1915 | Walter Johnson, Wash. | 27 | Joe Wood, Boston | 1.49 | Walter Johnson, Wash. | 203 |
| 1916 | Walter Johnson, Wash. | 25 | Babe Ruth, Boston. | 1.75 | Walter Johnson, Wash. | 228 |
| 1917 | Ed Cicotte, Chicago | 28 | Ed Cicotte, Chicago | 1.53 | Walter Johnson, Wash. | 188 |
| 1918 | Walter Johnson, Wash. | 23 | Walter Johnson, Wash. | 1.27 | Walter Johnson, Wash. | 162 |
| 1919 | Ed Cicotte, Chicago | 29 | Walter Johnson, Wash. | 1.49 | Walter Johnson, Wash. | 147 |
| 1920 | Jim Bagby, Cleveland | 31 | Bob Shawkey, N.Y. | 2.45 | Stan Coveleski, Cleve. | 133 |
| 1921 | 2 tied at... | 27 | Red Faber, Chicago | 2.48 | Walter Johnson, Wash. | 143 |
| 1922 | Eddie Rommel, Phil. | 27 | Red Faber, Chicago | 2.80 | Urban Shocker, St. Louis | 149 |
| 1923 | George Uhle, Cleveland. | 26 | Stan Coveleski, Cleve. | 2.76 | Walter Johnson, Wash. | 130 |
| 1924 | Walter Johnson, Wash. | 23 | Walter Johnson, Wash. | 2.72 | Walter Johnson, Wash. | 158 |
| 1925 | 2 tied at... | 21 | Stan Coveleski, Wash. | 2.84 | Lefty Grove, Phil. | 116 |
| 1926 | George Uhle, Cleve. | 27 | Lefty Grove, Phil. | 2.51 | Lefty Grove, Phil. | 194 |
| 1927 | 2 tied at... | 22 | Wilcy Moore, N.Y. | 2.28 | Lefty Grove, Phil. | 174 |
| 1928 | 2 tied at... | 24 | Garland Braxton, Wash. | 2.52 | Lefty Grove, Phil. | 183 |
| 1929 | George Earnshaw, Phil. | 24 | Lefty Grove, Phil. | 2.82 | Lefty Grove, Phil. | 170 |
| 1930 | Lefty Grove, Phil. | 28 | Lefty Grove, Phil. | 2.54 | Lefty Grove, Phil. | 209 |
| 1931 | Lefty Grove, Phil. | 31 | Lefty Grove, Phil. | 2.05 | Lefty Grove, Phil. | 175 |
| 1932 | General Crowder, Wash. | 26 | Lefty Grove, Phil. | 2.84 | Red Ruffing, New York. | 190 |
| 1933 | 2 tied at... | 24 | Monte Pearson, Cleve. | 2.33 | Lefty Gomez, New York | 163 |
| 1934 | Lefty Gomez, New York | 26 | Lefty Gomez, New York | 2.33 | Lefty Gomez, New York | 158 |
| 1935 | Wes Ferrell, Boston. | 25 | Lefty Grove, Boston. | 2.70 | Tommy Bridges, Detroit | 163 |
| 1936 | Tommy Bridges, Detroit | 23 | Lefty Grove, Boston. | 2.81 | Tommy Bridges, Detroit | 175 |
| 1937 | Lefty Gomez, New York | 21 | Lefty Gomez, New York | 2.33 | Lefty Gomez, New York | 194 |
| 1938 | Red Ruffing, N.Y. | 21 | Lefty Grove, Phil. | 3.07 | Bob Feller, Cleveland | 240 |
| 1939 | Bob Feller, Cleveland. | 24 | Lefty Grove, Phil. | 2.54 | Bob Feller, Cleveland | 246 |
| 1940 | Bob Feller, Cleveland. | 27 | Bob Feller, Cleveland. | 2.62 | Bob Feller, Cleveland | 261 |
| 1941 | Bob Feller, Cleveland | 25 | Thornton Lee, Chicago. | 2.37 | Bob Feller, Cleveland | 260 |
| 1942 | Tex Hughson, Boston. | 22 | Ted Lyons, Chicago | 2.10 | Bob Feller, Cleveland | 113 |
| 1943 | 2 tied at... | 20 | Spud Chandler, N.Y. | 1.64 | Allie Reynolds, Cleve. | 151 |
| 1944 | Hal Newhouser, Detroit | 29 | Dizzy Trout, Detroit. | 2.12 | Hal Newhouser, Detroit | 187 |
| 1945 | Hal Newhouser, Detroit | 25 | Hal Newhouser, Detroit. | 1.81 | Hal Newhouser, Detroit | 212 |
| 1946 | 2 tied at... | 26 | Hal Newhouser, Detroit | 1.94 | Bob Feller, Cleveland | 348 |
| 1947 | Bob Feller, Cleveland. | 20 | Spud Chandler, N.Y. | 2.46 | Bob Feller, Cleveland | 196 |

| Year | Wins | | ERA | | Strikeouts | |
|---|---|---|---|---|---|---|
| 1948 | Hal Newhouser, Detroit. | 21 | Gene Bearden, Cleveland | 2.43 | Bob Feller, Cleveland. | 164 |
| 1949 | Mel Parnell, Boston. | 25 | Mel Parnell, Boston. | 2.78 | Virgil Trucks, Detroit | 153 |
| 1950 | Bob Lemon, Cleveland. | 23 | Early Wynn, Cleveland. | 3.20 | Bob Lemon, Cleveland. | 170 |
| 1951 | Bob Feller, Cleveland. | 22 | Saul Rogovin, Det.-Chi. | 2.78 | Vic Raschi, New York. | 164 |
| 1952 | Bobby Shantz, Phil. | 24 | Allie Reynolds, N.Y. | 2.07 | Allie Reynolds, New York. | 160 |
| 1953 | Bob Porterfield, Wash. | 22 | Eddie Lopat, N.Y. | 2.43 | Billy Pierce, Chicago | 186 |
| 1954 | 2 tied at... | 23 | Mike Garcia, Cleveland | 2.64 | Bob Turley, Baltimore. | 185 |
| 1955 | 3 tied at... | 18 | Billy Pierce, Chicago | 1.97 | Herb Score, Cleveland | 245 |
| 1956 | Frank Lary, Detroit. | 21 | Whitey Ford, New York | 2.47 | Herb Score, Cleveland | 263 |
| 1957 | 2 tied at... | 20 | Bobby Shantz, N.Y. | 2.45 | Early Wynn, Chicago | 184 |
| 1958 | Bob Turley, New York | 21 | Whitey Ford, New York | 2.01 | Early Wynn, Chicago. | 179 |
| 1959 | Early Wynn, Chicago. | 22 | Hoyt Wilhelm, Balt. | 2.19 | Jim Bunning, Detroit | 201 |
| 1960 | 2 tied at... | 18 | Frank Baumann, Chicago | 2.68 | Jim Bunning, Detroit | 201 |
| 1961 | Whitey Ford, New York. | 25 | Dick Donovan, Wash. | 2.40 | Camilo Pascual, Minn. | 221 |
| 1962 | Ralph Terry, New York. | 23 | Hank Aguirre, Detroit. | 2.21 | Camilo Pascual, Minn. | 206 |
| 1963 | Whitey Ford, New York. | 24 | Gary Peters, Chicago | 2.33 | Camilo Pascual, Minn. | 202 |
| 1964 | 2 tied at... | 20 | Dean Chance, L.A. | 1.65 | Al Downing, New York | 217 |
| 1965 | Mudcat Grant, Minnesota. | 21 | Sam McDowell, Cleve. | 2.18 | Sam McDowell, Cleve. | 325 |
| 1966 | Jim Kaat, Minnesota | 25 | Gary Peters, Chicago | 1.98 | Sam McDowell, Cleve. | 225 |
| 1967 | 2 tied at... | 22 | Joel Horlen, Chicago | 2.06 | Jim Lonborg, Boston. | 246 |
| 1968 | Denny McLain, Detroit | 31 | Luis Tiant, Cleveland. | 1.60 | Sam McDowell, Cleve. | 283 |
| 1969 | Denny McLain, Detroit | 24 | Dick Bosman, Wash. | 2.19 | Sam McDowell, Cleve. | 279 |
| 1970 | 3 tied at... | 24 | Diego Segui, Oakland | 2.56 | Sam McDowell, Cleve. | 304 |
| 1971 | Mickey Lolich, Detroit. | 25 | Vida Blue, Oakland | 1.82 | Mickey Lolich, Detroit. | 308 |
| 1972 | 2 tied at... | 24 | Luis Tiant, Boston. | 1.91 | Nolan Ryan, California | 329 |
| 1973 | Wilbur Wood, Chicago | 24 | Jim Palmer, Baltimore. | 2.40 | Nolan Ryan, California | 383 |
| 1974 | 2 tied at... | 25 | Catfish Hunter, Oakland. | 2.49 | Nolan Ryan, California | 367 |
| 1975 | 2 tied at... | 25 | Jim Palmer, Baltimore. | 2.09 | Frank Tanana, California | 269 |
| 1976 | Jim Palmer, Baltimore | 22 | Mark Fidrych, Detroit | 2.34 | Nolan Ryan, California | 327 |
| 1977 | 3 tied at... | 20 | Frank Tanana, Calif. | 2.54 | Nolan Ryan, California | 341 |
| 1978 | Ron Guidry, New York | 25 | Ron Guidry, New York | 1.74 | Nolan Ryan, California | 260 |
| 1979 | Mike Flanagan, Baltimore | 23 | Ron Guidry, New York | 2.78 | Nolan Ryan, California | 223 |
| 1980 | Steve Stone, Baltimore | 25 | Rudy May, New York | 2.47 | Len Barker, Cleveland | 187 |
| 1981 | Steve McCatty, Oak. | 14 | Steve McCatty, Oak. | 2.32 | Len Barker, Cleveland | 127 |
| 1982 | LaMarr Hoyt, Chicago | 19 | Rick Sutcliffe, Cleve. | 2.96 | Floyd Bannister, Seattle | 209 |
| 1983 | LaMarr Hoyt, Chicago | 24 | Rick Honeycutt, Texas | 2.42 | Jack Morris, Detroit. | 232 |
| 1984 | Mike Boddicker, Balt. | 20 | Mike Boddicker, Balt. | 2.79 | Mark Langston, Seattle. | 204 |
| 1985 | Ron Guidry, New York | 22 | Dave Stieb, Toronto. | 2.48 | Bert Blyleven, Cleve.-Minn. | 206 |
| 1986 | Roger Clemens, Boston | 24 | Roger Clemens, Boston | 2.48 | Mark Langston, Seattle | 245 |
| 1987 | 2 tied at... | 20 | Jimmy Key, Toronto. | 2.76 | Mark Langston, Seattle | 262 |
| 1988 | Frank Viola, Minn. | 24 | Allan Anderson, Minn. | 2.45 | Roger Clemens, Boston | 291 |
| 1989 | Bret Saberhagen, K.C. | 23 | Bret Saberhagen, K.C. | 2.16 | Nolan Ryan, Texas. | 301 |
| 1990 | Bob Welch, Oakland | 27 | Roger Clemens, Boston. | 1.93 | Nolan Ryan, Texas | 232 |
| 1991 | 2 tied at... | 20 | Roger Clemens, Boston | 2.62 | Roger Clemens, Boston | 241 |
| 1992 | 2 tied at... | 21 | Roger Clemens, Boston. | 2.41 | Randy Johnson, Seattle | 241 |
| 1993 | Jack McDowell, Chicago | 22 | Kevin Appier, K.C. | 2.56 | Randy Johnson, Seattle | 308 |

# AMERICAN LEAGUE CHAMPIONSHIP SERIES
## BOX SCORES

TOM DiPACE

**Juan Guzman.** Blue Jays righthander was one of two Toronto pitchers to win two games in the ALCS.

| TORONTO | ip | h | r | er | bb | so | CHICAGO | ip | h | r | er | bb | so |
|---|---|---|---|---|---|---|---|---|---|---|---|---|---|
| Guzman W | 6 | 5 | 3 | 2 | 8 | 3 | McDowell L | 6⅔ | 13 | 7 | 7 | 2 | 4 |
| Cox | 2 | 1 | 0 | 0 | 0 | 2 | DeLeon | 1 | 2 | 0 | 0 | 0 | 1 |
| Ward | 1 | 0 | 0 | 0 | 2 | 2 | Radinsky | ½ | 0 | 0 | 0 | 0 | 1 |
| | | | | | | | McCaskill | 1 | 2 | 0 | 0 | 0 | 2 |

HBP—Pasqua (by Guzman). WP—Guzman 3.
Umpires: HP—Evans; 1B—Kosc; 2B—Shulock; 3B—Hendry; LF—Tschida; RF—Kaiser.
T—3:38. A—46,246.

### Game Two: October 6
### Blue Jays 3, White Sox 1

| TORONTO | ab | r | h | bi | bb | so | CHICAGO | ab | r | h | bi | bb | so |
|---|---|---|---|---|---|---|---|---|---|---|---|---|---|
| Henderson lf | 3 | 1 | 0 | 0 | 1 | 1 | Raines lf | 4 | 1 | 1 | 0 | 1 | 1 |
| White cf | 4 | 0 | 2 | 0 | 0 | 1 | Cora 2b | 5 | 0 | 0 | 0 | 0 | 2 |
| Alomar 2b | 4 | 0 | 0 | 1 | 0 | 1 | Thomas dh | 3 | 0 | 2 | 0 | 1 | 0 |
| Carter rf | 4 | 0 | 1 | 0 | 0 | 1 | Ventura 3b-1b | 3 | 0 | 1 | 0 | 1 | 2 |
| Olerud 1b | 4 | 0 | 1 | 0 | 0 | 0 | Burks rf | 2 | 0 | 0 | 0 | 2 | 0 |
| Molitor dh | 4 | 1 | 2 | 0 | 0 | 1 | Pasqua 1b | 3 | 0 | 0 | 0 | 0 | 1 |
| Fernandez ss | 3 | 1 | 1 | 1 | 0 | 0 | Grebeck ph-3b | 1 | 0 | 1 | 0 | 0 | 0 |
| Sprague 3b | 3 | 0 | 0 | 1 | 0 | 0 | Johnson cf | 4 | 0 | 1 | 0 | 0 | 0 |
| Borders c | 4 | 0 | 1 | 0 | 0 | 0 | Karkovice c | 1 | 0 | 0 | 0 | 0 | 1 |
| | | | | | | | Newson ph | 1 | 0 | 0 | 0 | 0 | 0 |
| | | | | | | | LaValliere c | 1 | 0 | 1 | 0 | 0 | 0 |
| | | | | | | | Guillen ss | 4 | 0 | 0 | 0 | 0 | 0 |
| **Totals** | **33** | **3** | **8** | **2** | **3** | **5** | **Totals** | **32** | **1** | **7** | **0** | **5** | **7** |

Toronto 100 200 000—3
Chicago 100 000 000—1

E—Cora (2), Pasqua (1). DP—Toronto 1, Chicago 2. LOB—Toronto 6, Chicago 10. 2B—Molitor (1), Johnson (1). S—Karkovice.

| TORONTO | ip | h | r | er | bb | so | CHICAGO | ip | h | r | er | bb | so |
|---|---|---|---|---|---|---|---|---|---|---|---|---|---|
| Stewart W | 6 | 4 | 1 | 1 | 4 | 5 | Fernandez L | 8 | 8 | 3 | 1 | 3 | 5 |
| Leiter | 2 | 2 | 0 | 0 | 1 | 2 | Hernandez | 1 | 0 | 0 | 0 | 0 | 0 |
| Ward S | 1 | 1 | 0 | 0 | 0 | 0 | | | | | | | |

WP—Stewart.
Umpires: HP—Kosc; 1B—Shulock; 2B—Hendry; 3B—Tschida; LF—Kaiser; RF—Evans.
T—3:00. A—46,101.

### Game Three: October 8
### White Sox 6, Blue Jays 1

| CHICAGO | ab | r | h | bi | bb | so | TORONTO | ab | r | h | bi | bb | so |
|---|---|---|---|---|---|---|---|---|---|---|---|---|---|
| Raines lf | 5 | 1 | 4 | 0 | 0 | 0 | Henderson lf | 3 | 1 | 1 | 0 | 1 | 1 |
| Cora 2b | 3 | 1 | 2 | 0 | 0 | 0 | White cf | 4 | 0 | 1 | 1 | 0 | 0 |
| Thomas 1b | 3 | 1 | 1 | 1 | 2 | 0 | Molitor dh | 4 | 0 | 1 | 0 | 0 | 1 |
| Ventura 3b | 2 | 1 | 0 | 1 | 2 | 1 | Carter rf | 4 | 0 | 0 | 0 | 0 | 1 |
| Burks rf | 5 | 1 | 2 | 2 | 0 | 1 | Olerud 1b | 4 | 0 | 2 | 0 | 0 | 0 |
| Jackson dh | 4 | 0 | 0 | 0 | 1 | 3 | Alomar 2b | 3 | 0 | 1 | 0 | 1 | 0 |
| Johnson cf | 5 | 0 | 2 | 2 | 0 | 0 | Fernandez ss | 3 | 0 | 1 | 0 | 0 | 1 |
| Karkovice c | 4 | 0 | 0 | 0 | 0 | 3 | Sprague 3b | 3 | 0 | 0 | 0 | 0 | 0 |
| Guillen ss | 4 | 1 | 1 | 0 | 0 | 0 | Borders c | 3 | 0 | 0 | 0 | 0 | 2 |
| **Totals** | **35** | **6** | **12** | **6** | **5** | **8** | **Totals** | **31** | **1** | **7** | **1** | **2** | **6** |

Chicago 005 100 000—6
Toronto 001 000 000—1

E—Henderson (1). DP—Chicago 2, Toronto 1. LOB—Chicago 10, Toronto 5. 2B—Raines 2 (2), Henderson (1). SB—Johnson (1), Henderson (1). CS—Burks (1), White (1). S—Cora 2. SF—Ventura.

| CHICAGO | ip | h | r | er | bb | so | TORONTO | ip | h | r | er | bb | so |
|---|---|---|---|---|---|---|---|---|---|---|---|---|---|
| Alvarez W | 9 | 7 | 1 | 1 | 2 | 6 | Hentgen L | 3 | 9 | 6 | 6 | 2 | 3 |
| | | | | | | | Cox | 3 | 2 | 0 | 0 | 2 | 3 |
| | | | | | | | Eichhorn | 2 | 1 | 0 | 0 | 1 | 1 |
| | | | | | | | Castillo | 1 | 0 | 0 | 0 | 0 | 1 |

Hentgen pitched to 2 batters in the 4th.
Umpires: HP—Shulock; 1B—Hendry; 2B—Tschida; 3B—Kaiser; LF—Evans; RF—Kosc.
T—2:56. A—51,783.

### Game Four: October 9
### White Sox 7, Blue Jays 4

| CHICAGO | ab | r | h | bi | bb | so | TORONTO | ab | r | h | bi | bb | so |
|---|---|---|---|---|---|---|---|---|---|---|---|---|---|
| Raines lf | 5 | 1 | 3 | 0 | 0 | 0 | Henderson lf | 3 | 1 | 0 | 0 | 2 | 1 |
| Cora 2b | 5 | 0 | 1 | 1 | 0 | 1 | White cf | 4 | 1 | 2 | 0 | 1 | 0 |
| Thomas 1b | 3 | 1 | 1 | 1 | 2 | 1 | Alomar 2b | 5 | 1 | 2 | 2 | 0 | 1 |
| Ventura 3b | 5 | 0 | 2 | 1 | 0 | 0 | Carter rf | 4 | 0 | 2 | 1 | 0 | 0 |
| Burks rf | 4 | 2 | 1 | 0 | 1 | 1 | Olerud 1b | 4 | 0 | 0 | 0 | 0 | 0 |
| Jackson dh | 2 | 1 | 0 | 0 | 2 | 1 | Molitor dh | 4 | 0 | 0 | 0 | 1 | 0 |
| Johnson cf | 4 | 1 | 2 | 4 | 0 | 0 | Fernandez ss | 3 | 0 | 2 | 0 | 1 | 1 |
| Karkovice c | 4 | 0 | 0 | 0 | 0 | 0 | Sprague 3b | 4 | 0 | 0 | 0 | 0 | 1 |
| Guillen ss | 4 | 1 | 1 | 0 | 0 | 2 | Borders c | 4 | 1 | 1 | 0 | 0 | 1 |
| **Totals** | **36** | **7** | **11** | **7** | **5** | **6** | **Totals** | **35** | **4** | **9** | **4** | **6** | **5** |

Chicago 020 003 101—7
Toronto 003 001 000—4

DP—Toronto 1. LOB—Chicago 7, Toronto 11. 2B—Alomar (1). 3B—Johnson (1), White (1). HR—Thomas (1), Johnson (1).

### Game One: October 5
### Blue Jays 7, White Sox 3

| TORONTO | ab | r | h | bi | bb | so | CHICAGO | ab | r | h | bi | bb | so |
|---|---|---|---|---|---|---|---|---|---|---|---|---|---|
| Henderson lf | 6 | 0 | 0 | 0 | 0 | 0 | Raines lf | 5 | 0 | 2 | 1 | 0 | 0 |
| White cf | 5 | 0 | 2 | 0 | 0 | 2 | Cora 2b | 3 | 0 | 0 | 0 | 2 | 1 |
| Alomar 2b | 4 | 1 | 0 | 0 | 1 | 1 | Thomas dh | 1 | 0 | 1 | 0 | 4 | 0 |
| Carter rf | 5 | 1 | 2 | 0 | 0 | 0 | Ventura 3b | 3 | 0 | 0 | 2 | 2 | 2 |
| Olerud 1b | 4 | 3 | 3 | 2 | 1 | 1 | Burks rf | 5 | 0 | 1 | 0 | 0 | 1 |
| Molitor dh | 5 | 2 | 4 | 3 | 0 | 0 | Pasqua 1b | 3 | 1 | 0 | 0 | 1 | 1 |
| Fernandez ss | 5 | 0 | 1 | 0 | 0 | 2 | Johnson cf | 4 | 1 | 0 | 0 | 1 | 1 |
| Sprague 3b | 5 | 0 | 4 | 2 | 0 | 1 | Karkovice c | 3 | 0 | 0 | 0 | 0 | 1 |
| Borders c | 5 | 0 | 1 | 0 | 0 | 1 | Guillen ss | 4 | 1 | 2 | 2 | 0 | 0 |
| **Totals** | **44** | **7** | **17** | **7** | **2** | **8** | **Totals** | **31** | **3** | **6** | **3** | **10** | **7** |

Toronto 000 230 200—7
Chicago 000 300 000—3

E—Olerud (1), Cora (1). DP—Toronto 1. LOB—Toronto 12, Chicago 13. 2B—Olerud (1), Burks (1). 3B—Sprague (1). HR—Molitor (1). SB—Raines (1), Guillen (1). CS—Raines (1). S—Karkovice.

| CHICAGO | ip | h | er | bb | so |  | TORONTO | ip | h | r | er | bb | so |
|---|---|---|---|---|---|---|---|---|---|---|---|---|---|
| Bere | 2⅓ | 5 | 3 | 3 | 2 | 3 | Stottlemyre L | 6 | 6 | 5 | 5 | 4 | 4 |
| Belcher W | 3⅔ | 3 | 1 | 1 | 3 | 1 | Leiter | ⅔ | 2 | 1 | 1 | 1 | 0 |
| McCaskill | 1⅓ | 1 | 0 | 0 | 1 | 1 | Timlin | 2⅓ | 3 | 1 | 1 | 0 | 2 |
| Radinsky | ⅔ | 0 | 0 | 0 | 0 | 0 |  |  |  |  |  |  |  |
| Hernandez S | 1 | 0 | 0 | 0 | 0 | 0 |  |  |  |  |  |  |  |

HBP—Olerud (by Bere). WP—Belcher. Balk—Stottlemyre.
Umpires: HP—Hendry; 1B—Tschida; 2B—Kaiser; 3B—Evans; LF—Kosc; RF—Shulock.
T—3:30. A—51,889.

## Game Five: October 10
### Blue Jays 5, White Sox 3

| CHICAGO | ab | r | h | bi | bb | so |  | TORONTO | ab | r | h | bi | bb | so |
|---|---|---|---|---|---|---|---|---|---|---|---|---|---|---|
| Raines lf | 4 | 1 | 1 | 0 | 0 | 1 | Henderson lf | 5 | 1 | 2 | 0 | 0 | 1 |
| Cora 2b | 3 | 0 | 0 | 1 | 1 | 1 | White cf | 5 | 1 | 2 | 0 | 0 | 1 |
| Thomas 1b | 4 | 0 | 0 | 0 | 0 | 3 | Alomar 2b | 3 | 1 | 3 | 1 | 2 | 0 |
| Ventura 3b | 4 | 1 | 1 | 2 | 0 | 0 | Carter rf | 5 | 0 | 1 | 0 | 0 | 2 |
| Burks rf | 3 | 1 | 2 | 1 | 0 | 1 | Olerud 1b | 3 | 0 | 1 | 1 | 2 | 0 |
| Jackson dh | 4 | 0 | 0 | 0 | 0 | 2 | Molitor dh | 3 | 2 | 1 | 0 | 1 | 0 |
| Johnson cf | 3 | 0 | 0 | 0 | 0 | 0 | Fernandez ss | 4 | 0 | 2 | 0 | 0 | 0 |
| Karkovice c | 2 | 0 | 0 | 1 | 1 | 1 | Sprague 3b | 3 | 0 | 1 | 2 | 0 | 1 |
| Guillen ss | 3 | 0 | 1 | 0 | 0 | 0 | Borders c | 4 | 0 | 1 | 0 | 0 | 2 |
| **Totals** | **30** | **3** | **5** | **3** | **2** | **9** | **Totals** | **35** | **5** | **14** | **4** | **5** | **7** |

| Chicago | 000 | 000 | 000—3 |
|---|---|---|---|
| Toronto | 111 | 100 | 10x—5 |

E—McDowell (1). DP—Chicago 1, Toronto 2. LOB—Chicago 3, Toronto 12. 2B—Henderson (2), White (1), Molitor (2). HR—Ventura (1), Burks (1). SB—Henderson (2), Alomar 3 (3), Borders (1). CS—Henderson (1). SF—Sprague.

| CHICAGO | ip | h | r | er | bb | so |  | TORONTO | ip | h | r | er | bb | so |
|---|---|---|---|---|---|---|---|---|---|---|---|---|---|---|
| McDowell L | 2⅓ | 5 | 3 | 3 | 3 | 1 | Guzman W | 7 | 3 | 1 | 1 | 1 | 6 |
| DeLone | 3⅔ | 5 | 1 | 1 | 1 | 5 | Castillo | 1 | 0 | 0 | 0 | 1 | 0 |
| Radinsky | ⅓ | 1 | 1 | 1 | 1 | 0 | Ward | 1 | 2 | 2 | 2 | 0 | 3 |
| Hernandez | 1⅔ | 3 | 0 | 0 | 0 | 1 |  |  |  |  |  |  |  |

HBP—Burks (by Ward). WP—McDowell.
Umpires: HP—Tschida; 1B—Kaiser; 2B—Evans; 3B—Kosc; LF—Shulock; RF—Hendry.
T—3:09. A—51,375.

## Game Six: October 12
### Blue Jays 6, White Sox 3

| TORONTO | ab | r | h | bi | bb | so |  | CHICAGO | ab | r | h | bi | bb | so |
|---|---|---|---|---|---|---|---|---|---|---|---|---|---|---|
| Henderson lf | 5 | 0 | 0 | 0 | 0 | 1 | Raines lf | 4 | 1 | 1 | 0 | 1 | 0 |
| White cf | 5 | 1 | 3 | 1 | 0 | 1 | Cora 2b | 3 | 0 | 0 | 0 | 0 | 1 |
| Alomar 2b | 5 | 0 | 1 | 0 | 0 | 0 | Thomas 1b | 3 | 0 | 1 | 1 | 1 | 1 |
| Carter rf | 5 | 1 | 1 | 0 | 0 | 1 | Ventura 3b | 3 | 0 | 0 | 1 | 1 | 1 |
| Olerud 1b | 4 | 2 | 1 | 0 | 0 | 2 | Burks rf | 4 | 0 | 1 | 0 | 0 | 0 |
| Molitor dh | 3 | 2 | 1 | 2 | 1 | 1 | Newson dh | 4 | 1 | 1 | 1 | 0 | 4 |
| Fernandez ss | 4 | 0 | 0 | 0 | 0 | 0 | Johnson cf | 3 | 0 | 0 | 0 | 1 | 0 |
| Sprague 3b | 3 | 0 | 1 | 0 | 1 | 1 | LaValliere c | 2 | 0 | 0 | 0 | 0 | 1 |
| Borders c | 4 | 0 | 2 | 3 | 0 | 0 | Karkovice pr-c | 1 | 0 | 0 | 0 | 0 | 1 |
|  |  |  |  |  |  |  | Guillen ss | 3 | 1 | 1 | 0 | 0 | 0 |
| **Totals** | **38** | **6** | **10** | **6** | **3** | **5** | **Totals** | **30** | **3** | **5** | **3** | **5** | **6** |

| Toronto | 020 | 100 | 003—6 |
|---|---|---|---|
| Chicago | 002 | 000 | 001—3 |

E—Cora (3), Ventura (1), Radinsky (1). DP—Toronto 1. LOB—Toronto 10, Chicago 7. 2B—Borders (1), Guillen (1). 3B—Molitor (1). HR—Newson (1), White (1). SB—Alomar (4). S—Fernandez, Guillen.

| TORONTO | ip | h | r | er | bb | so |  | CHICAGO | ip | h | r | er | bb | so |
|---|---|---|---|---|---|---|---|---|---|---|---|---|---|---|
| Stewart W | 7⅓ | 4 | 2 | 2 | 4 | 3 | Fernandez L | 7 | 7 | 3 | 2 | 3 | 5 |
| Ward S | 1⅔ | 1 | 1 | 1 | 1 | 3 | McCaskill | 1⅓ | 0 | 0 | 0 | 0 | 0 |
|  |  |  |  |  |  |  | Radinsky | ⅓ | 2 | 3 | 1 | 0 | 0 |
|  |  |  |  |  |  |  | Hernandez | ⅓ | 1 | 0 | 0 | 0 | 1 |

HBP—Cora (by Stewart), Molitor (by Fernandez). WP—Stewart.
Umpires: HP—Kaiser; 1B—Evans; 2B—Kosc; 3B—Shulock; LF—Hendry; RF—Tschida.
T—3:31. A—45,527.

# COMPOSITE BOX

## TORONTO

| Player, Pos. | AVG. | G | AB | R | H | 2B | 3B | HR | RBI | BB | SO | SB |
|---|---|---|---|---|---|---|---|---|---|---|---|---|
| Devon White, cf | .444 | 6 | 27 | 3 | 12 | 1 | 1 | 1 | 2 | 1 | 5 | 0 |
| Paul Molitor, dh | .391 | 6 | 23 | 7 | 9 | 2 | 1 | 1 | 5 | 3 | 3 | 0 |
| John Olerud, 1b | .348 | 6 | 23 | 5 | 8 | 1 | 0 | 0 | 3 | 4 | 1 | 0 |
| Tony Fernandes, ss | .318 | 6 | 22 | 1 | 7 | 0 | 0 | 0 | 1 | 2 | 4 | 0 |
| Roberto Alomar, 2b | .292 | 6 | 24 | 3 | 7 | 1 | 0 | 0 | 4 | 4 | 3 | 4 |
| Ed Sprague, 3b | .286 | 6 | 21 | 0 | 6 | 0 | 1 | 0 | 4 | 2 | 4 | 0 |
| Joe Carter, rf | .259 | 6 | 27 | 2 | 7 | 0 | 0 | 0 | 2 | 1 | 5 | 0 |
| Pat Borders, c | .250 | 6 | 24 | 1 | 6 | 1 | 0 | 0 | 3 | 0 | 6 | 1 |
| Rickey Henderson, lf | .120 | 6 | 25 | 4 | 3 | 2 | 0 | 0 | 0 | 4 | 5 | 2 |
| **TOTALS** | **.301** | **6** | **216** | **26** | **65** | **8** | **3** | **2** | **24** | **21** | **36** | **7** |

| Pitcher | W | L | ERA | G | GS | SV | IP | H | R | ER | BB | SO |
|---|---|---|---|---|---|---|---|---|---|---|---|---|
| Danny Cox | 0 | 0 | 0.00 | 2 | 0 | 0 | 5 | 3 | 0 | 0 | 2 | 5 |
| Tony Castillo | 0 | 0 | 0.00 | 2 | 0 | 0 | 2 | 0 | 0 | 0 | 1 | 1 |
| Mark Eichhorn | 0 | 0 | 0.00 | 1 | 0 | 0 | 2 | 1 | 0 | 0 | 1 | 1 |
| Dave Stewart | 2 | 0 | 2.03 | 2 | 2 | 0 | 13⅓ | 8 | 3 | 3 | 8 | 8 |
| Juan Guzman | 2 | 0 | 2.08 | 2 | 2 | 0 | 13 | 8 | 4 | 3 | 9 | 9 |
| Al Leiter | 0 | 0 | 3.38 | 2 | 0 | 0 | 2⅔ | 4 | 1 | 1 | 2 | 0 |
| Mike Timlin | 0 | 0 | 3.86 | 1 | 0 | 0 | 2⅓ | 3 | 1 | 1 | 0 | 2 |
| Duane Ward | 0 | 0 | 5.79 | 4 | 0 | 2 | 4⅔ | 4 | 3 | 3 | 3 | 8 |
| Todd Stottlemyre | 0 | 1 | 7.50 | 1 | 1 | 0 | 6 | 6 | 5 | 5 | 4 | 4 |
| Pat Hentgen | 0 | 1 | 18.00 | 1 | 1 | 0 | 3 | 9 | 6 | 6 | 2 | 3 |
| **TOTALS** | **4** | **2** | **3.67** | **6** | **6** | **2** | **54** | **46** | **23** | **22** | **32** | **43** |

## CHICAGO

| Player, Pos. | AVG. | G | AB | R | H | 2B | 3B | HR | RBI | BB | SO | SB |
|---|---|---|---|---|---|---|---|---|---|---|---|---|
| Craig Grebeck, ph-3b | 1.000 | 1 | 1 | 0 | 1 | 0 | 0 | 0 | 0 | 0 | 0 | 0 |
| Tim Raines, lf | .444 | 6 | 27 | 5 | 12 | 3 | 0 | 0 | 1 | 2 | 2 | 1 |
| Frank Thomas, dh-1b | .353 | 6 | 17 | 2 | 6 | 0 | 0 | 1 | 3 | 10 | 5 | 0 |
| Mike LaValliere, c | .333 | 2 | 3 | 0 | 1 | 0 | 0 | 0 | 0 | 0 | 1 | 0 |
| Ellis Burks, rf | .304 | 6 | 23 | 4 | 7 | 1 | 0 | 1 | 3 | 3 | 5 | 0 |
| Ozzie Guillen, ss | .273 | 6 | 22 | 4 | 6 | 1 | 0 | 0 | 2 | 0 | 2 | 1 |
| Lance Johnson, cf | .217 | 6 | 23 | 2 | 5 | 1 | 1 | 0 | 1 | 6 | 2 | 1 |
| Robin Ventura, 3b-1b | .200 | 6 | 20 | 2 | 4 | 0 | 0 | 1 | 5 | 6 | 6 | 0 |
| Warren Newson, ph-dh | .200 | 2 | 5 | 1 | 1 | 0 | 0 | 1 | 1 | 0 | 1 | 0 |
| Joey Cora, 2b | .136 | 6 | 22 | 1 | 3 | 0 | 0 | 0 | 1 | 3 | 6 | 0 |
| Ron Karkovice, c-pr | .000 | 6 | 15 | 0 | 0 | 0 | 0 | 0 | 0 | 1 | 7 | 0 |
| Bo Jackson, dh | .000 | 3 | 10 | 1 | 0 | 0 | 0 | 0 | 0 | 3 | 6 | 0 |
| Dan Pasqua, 1b | .000 | 2 | 6 | 1 | 0 | 0 | 0 | 0 | 0 | 1 | 2 | 0 |
| **TOTALS** | **.237** | **6** | **194** | **23** | **46** | **6** | **1** | **5** | **22** | **32** | **43** | **3** |

| Pitcher | W | L | ERA | G | GS | SV | IP | H | R | ER | BB | SO |
|---|---|---|---|---|---|---|---|---|---|---|---|---|
| Roberto Hernandez | 0 | 0 | 0.00 | 4 | 0 | 1 | 4 | 4 | 0 | 0 | 0 | 1 |
| Kirk McCaskill | 0 | 0 | 0.00 | 2 | 0 | 0 | 3⅔ | 3 | 0 | 0 | 1 | 3 |
| Wilson Alvarez | 1 | 0 | 1.00 | 1 | 1 | 0 | 9 | 7 | 1 | 1 | 2 | 6 |
| Alex Fernandez | 0 | 2 | 1.80 | 2 | 2 | 0 | 15 | 15 | 3 | 3 | 6 | 10 |
| Jose DeLeon | 0 | 0 | 1.93 | 2 | 0 | 0 | 4⅔ | 7 | 1 | 1 | 1 | 6 |
| Tim Belcher | 1 | 0 | 2.45 | 1 | 0 | 0 | 3⅔ | 3 | 1 | 1 | 3 | 1 |
| Jack McDowell | 0 | 2 | 10.00 | 2 | 2 | 0 | 9 | 18 | 10 | 10 | 5 | 5 |
| Scott Radinsky | 0 | 0 | 10.80 | 4 | 0 | 0 | 1⅔ | 4 | 2 | 1 | 1 | 0 |
| Jason Bere | 0 | 0 | 11.57 | 1 | 1 | 0 | 2⅓ | 5 | 3 | 3 | 2 | 3 |
| **TOTALS** | **2** | **4** | **3.57** | **6** | | | **53** | **65** | **26** | **21** | **21** | **36** |

| Toronto | | | | | | 2 | 3 | 5 | | 6 | 3 | 1 | 3 | 0 | 3—26 |
|---|---|---|---|---|---|---|---|---|---|---|---|---|---|---|---|---|
| Chicago | | | | | | 1 | 2 | 7 | | 4 | 1 | 3 | 1 | 0 | 4—23 |

E—Olerud, Henderson, Ventura, Cora 3, Pasqua, McDowell, Radinsky. DP—Toronto 7, Chicago 5. LOB—Toronto 56, Chicago 50. S—Karkovice 2, Cora 2, Guillen, T. Fernandez. SF—Ventura, Sprague. HBP—Pasqua (by Guzman), Olerud (by Bere), Burks (by Ward), Molitor (by A. Fernandez), Cora (by Stewart). WP—Stewart 2, Guzman 3, Belcher, McDowell. Balk—Stottlemyre. Umpires—Jim Evans, Greg Kosc, John Shulock, Ted Hendry, Tim Tschida, Ken Kaiser.

# Upstart Phillies Pull Rank On Braves

**By ALAN SCHWARZ**

First, it appeared obvious. The Atlanta Braves were the easy preseason choice to win the National League West.

Then it looked impossible. Slowed by a sluggish offense, the Braves spent most of the first half of the 1993 season hovering six or seven games behind the surprising San Francisco Giants. They fell to 10 behind July 22.

But the July 20 trade for slugger Fred McGriff, coupled with the Braves' outstanding pitching staff, helped the Braves go on a furious dog-day run to catch San Francisco and lead by four games Sept. 17. The Giants came back, though, and the two teams went into the last day of the season tied. When Atlanta beat the Rockies 5-3 and the Giants lost to Los Angeles 12-1, the Braves emerged with their third straight division title.

It was one of the best pennant races baseball had seen in years.

**Big Boppers.** Ex-San Diego first baseman Fred McGriff, left, joined Dave Justice to give Atlanta a dynamic 1-2 left-side home run punch.

"It's definitely gratifying to do it the way we did it," first baseman Sid Bream said, "chasing them all year, catching them and then finishing it on the last day."

The Braves gave up three prospects to San Diego to get McGriff—righthander Donnie Elliott and outfielders Melvin Nieves and Vince Moore—and found out quickly he would add heat to the club. The day he arrived in Atlanta, July 21, a fire raged through a section of Atlanta-Fulton County Stadium 90 minutes before a game against the Cardinals, sending fans and players scurrying for safety as black smoke poured out of the press box.

McGriff hit seven home runs in his first 10 games for the Braves, and his heroics helped jump-start the Atlanta offense. Right fielder Dave Justice hit .300 after McGriff's arrival, finishing with .270-40-120 numbers, and left fielder Ron Gant went on a ferocious tear Sept. 12-15 by driving in 15 runs in four games. Justice ultimately placed second in the NL RBI race, Gant third with 117.

The Braves' front four pitchers, Tom Glavine (22-6, 3.20), Greg Maddux (20-10, 2.36), Steve Avery (18-6, 2.94) and John Smoltz (15-11, 3.62) remained dominating throughout the season.

Helped by winning five of six games against the Giants in a showdown Aug. 23-Sept. 2, the Braves mounted their four-game lead with two weeks left. But the Giants won 14 of 16 games down the stretch to pull even with one game each left to play.

The Braves express kept on rolling over the Padres, and the Giants finally ran out of steam, losing to rival Los Angeles and the two-homer heroics of Dodgers rookie Mike Piazza. San Francisco's amazing season had come to a crushing end.

"It just kind of snowballed," Giants second baseman

Robby Thompson said. "Standing out there, you feel it's slowly slipping away."

The Braves' comeback couldn't detract from San Francisco's amazing resurgence as a franchise. In fact, because of the new expanded playoff format, the Giants probably became the last excellent team to miss out on the postseason.

One year earlier, they were ready to move to Tampa-St. Petersburg. But under the leadership of new owner Peter Magowan, San Francisco rejuvenated itself with a cleaned-up Candlestick Park and the daily heroics of the best player in baseball, Barry Bonds.

Signed as a free agent the previous December, Bonds hit .336 and led the NL in home runs (46), RBIs (123), slugging (.677) and on-base percentage (.458).

While Bonds was the flashy hero, Thompson stepped forward, hit .312 and finally made the all-star team (he didn't play because of injury). Third baseman Matt Williams hit .294 with 38 homers and 110 RBIs, and center fielder Darren Lewis played 136 games without an error to key a splendid all-around defense.

The Giants also saw two righthanders emerge as top-flight starters: Bill Swift (21-8, 2.82) and John Burkett (22-7, 3.65). Rod Beck played the closer role to perfection with his menacing facial hair and 48 saves.

But it all seemingly went for naught when the Braves began celebrating.

"Everybody was running on empty already," said rookie manager Dusty Baker, later named NL manager of the year. "And it showed."

## Phils Upstage Braves in NLCS

Atlanta's celebration didn't last long. The upstart Phillies, in a series as rich and full as their beards and

| Page | EAST | W | L | PCT | GB | Manager(s) | General Manager | Attendance/Dates | Last Pennant |
|---|---|---|---|---|---|---|---|---|---|
| 167 | Philadelphia Phillies | 97 | 65 | .599 | — | Jim Fregosi | Lee Thomas | 3,137,539 (80) | 1993 |
| 143 | Montreal Expos | 94 | 68 | .580 | 3 | Felipe Alou | Dan Duquette | 1,641,437 (81) | None |
| 179 | St. Louis Cardinals | 87 | 75 | .537 | 10 | Joe Torre | Dal Maxvill | 2,841,028 (81) | 1987 |
| 78 | Chicago Cubs | 84 | 78 | .519 | 13 | Jim Lefebvre | Larry Himes | 2,653,763 (80) | 1945 |
| 173 | Pittsburgh Pirates | 75 | 87 | .463 | 22 | Jim Leyland | T. Simmons, C. Bonifay | 1,650,593 (79) | 1979 |
| 108 | Florida Marlins | 64 | 98 | .395 | 33 | Rene Lachemann | Dave Dombrowski | 3,064,847 (80) | None |
| 155 | New York Mets | 59 | 103 | .364 | 38 | J. Torborg, D. Green | A.Harazin, J.McIlvaine | 1,873,183 (79) | 1986 |

| Page | WEST | W | L | PCT | GB | Manager(s) | General Manager | Attendance/Dates | Last Pennant |
|---|---|---|---|---|---|---|---|---|---|
| 48 | Atlanta Braves | 104 | 58 | .642 | — | Bobby Cox | John Schuerholz | 3,884,720 (81) | 1992 |
| 192 | San Francisco Giants | 103 | 59 | .636 | 1 | Dusty Baker | Bob Quinn | 2,606,354 (81) | 1989 |
| 113 | Houston Astros | 85 | 77 | .525 | 19 | Art Howe | Bill Wood | 2,084,528 (81) | None |
| 125 | Los Angeles Dodgers | 81 | 81 | .500 | 23 | Tommy Lasorda | Fred Claire | 3,162,576 (81) | 1988 |
| 85 | Cincinnati Reds | 73 | 89 | .451 | 31 | T.Perez, D.Johnson | Jim Bowden | 2,453,232 (79) | 1990 |
| 97 | Colorado Rockies | 67 | 95 | .414 | 37 | Don Baylor | Bob Gebhard | 4,483,270 (79) | None |
| 186 | San Diego Padres | 61 | 101 | .377 | 43 | Jim Riggleman | J.McIlvaine, R.Smith | 1,375,432 (80) | 1984 |

**LEAGUE CHAMPIONSHIP SERIES:** Philadelphia defeated Atlanta 4-2, in best-of-7 final.
**NOTE:** Team's individual batting, pitching and fielding statistics can be found on page indicated in lefthand column.

bellies, stood undaunted against the clear favorite and snatched away a trip to the World Series with a 4-games-to-2 win in the NL playoffs.

The Phillies became the third team to go from last place one season to first place the next. In the process, a clubhouse full of characters, foremost among them jiggling first baseman John Kruk, sparkplug Len Dykstra and closer Mitch Williams, showed it could have fun and win at the same time.

And finally, at the Braves' expense. Two outstanding starts by righthander Curt Schilling—a 1.69 ERA  in Games One and Five, earning him series MVP honors despite not getting a win—helped stymie Atlanta's offense and let the Phillies win in 10 innings both times. Philadelphia was led offensively by Dykstra, who hit .280 in the series with eight RBIs and two home runs. The second home run won Game Five in the 10th, 4-3, and began pounding the Nails in Atlanta's

**Lee Thomas**

coffin. The Braves lost Game Six 6-3 and were left scratching their heads after a dizzying season.

"You can't say this is a team that choked when we put on a barrage in the second half to even get here," Justice said. "That was the playoffs right there. This team just didn't play its best for six games."

"I still think we're the better team," Maddux said, "but they beat us."

## Promise Fulfilled

The Phillies' roster essentially was the same as in 1992, with only platoon additions and the midseason promotion of rookie Kevin Stocker, who solidified the shortstop position and hit a surprising .324-2-31. Overall, Philadelphia's talent finally stayed healthy and played together for most of the season. It was the Phillies' first division title since 1983.

The key player was Dykstra. The Phillies already had recognized his importance, as they had gone 76-71 in games with him and 72-105 without him the past two years. Dykstra played all but one game in 1993, and was the perfect table-setter. He scored a phenome-

**MVP Credentials.** In his first season as a San Francisco Giant, Barry Bonds put up MVP numbers: .336-46-123.

nal 143 runs, the most in the NL since fellow Phillie Chuck Klein's 152 in 1932, and hit .305 with 19 homers and 37 stolen bases to emerge as an MVP candidate during Bonds' September slide.

Catcher Darren Daulton proved that his excellent 1992 season was no fluke. He hit 24 homers and drove in 105 and again was an iron man behind the plate, playing 147 games.

The Phillies also enjoyed excellent starting pitching. General manager Lee Thomas, who arrived at Veterans Stadium in 1988, put together his front five entirely through trades. Tommy Greene (16-4, 3.42), Terry Mulholland (12-9, 3.25), Schilling (16-7, 4.02), Danny Jackson (12-11, 3.77) and Ben Rivera (13-9, 5.02) stayed healthy enough to win the division by three games over the Expos.

LES BALDWIN

# NATIONAL LEAGUE
## CHAMPIONS, 1901-93

| | Pennant | Pct. | GA |
|---|---|---|---|
| 1901 | Pittsburgh | .647 | 1½ |
| 1902 | Pittsburgh | .741 | 27½ |
| 1903 | Pittsburgh | .650 | 6½ |
| 1904 | New York | .693 | 13 |
| 1905 | New York | .686 | 9 |
| 1906 | Chicago | .763 | 20 |
| 1907 | Chicago | .704 | 17 |
| 1908 | Chicago | .643 | 1 |
| 1909 | Pittsburgh | .724 | 6½ |
| 1910 | Chicago | .675 | 13 |
| 1911 | New York | .647 | 7½ |
| 1912 | New York | .682 | 10 |
| 1913 | New York | .664 | 12½ |
| 1914 | Boston | .614 | 10½ |
| 1915 | Philadelphia | .592 | 7 |
| 1916 | Brooklyn | .610 | 2½ |
| 1917 | New York | .636 | 10 |
| 1918 | Chicago | .651 | 10½ |
| 1919 | Cincinnati | .686 | 9 |
| 1920 | Brooklyn | .604 | 7 |
| 1921 | New York | .614 | 4 |
| 1922 | New York | .604 | 7 |
| 1923 | New York | .621 | 4½ |
| 1924 | New York | .608 | 1½ |
| 1925 | Pittsburgh | .621 | 8½ |
| 1926 | St. Louis | .578 | 2 |
| 1927 | Pittsburgh | .610 | 1½ |
| 1928 | St. Louis | .617 | 2 |
| 1929 | Chicago | .645 | 10½ |
| 1930 | St. Louis | .597 | 2 |

| | Pennant | Pct. | GA | MVP |
|---|---|---|---|---|
| 1931 | St. Louis | .656 | 13 | Frankie Frisch, 2b, St.Louis |
| 1932 | Chicago | .584 | 4 | Chuck Klein, of, Philadelphia |
| 1933 | New York | .599 | 5 | Carl Hubbell, lhp, New York |
| 1934 | St. Louis | .621 | 2 | Dizzy Dean, rhp, St.Louis |
| 1935 | Chicago | .649 | 4 | Gabby Hartnett, c, Chicago |
| 1936 | New York | .597 | 5 | Carl Hubbell, lhp, New York |
| 1937 | New York | .625 | 3 | Joe Medwick, of, St. Louis |
| 1938 | Chicago | .586 | 2 | Ernie Lombardi, c, Cincinnati |
| 1939 | Cincinnati | .630 | 4½ | Bucky Walters, rhp, Cincinnati |
| 1940 | Cincinnati | .654 | 12 | Frank McCormick, 1b, Cincinnati |
| 1941 | Brooklyn | .649 | 2½ | Dolf Camilli, 1b, Brooklyn |
| 1942 | St. Louis | .688 | 2 | Mort Cooper, rhp, St. Louis |
| 1943 | St. Louis | .682 | 18 | Stan Musial, of, St. Louis |
| 1944 | St. Louis | .682 | 14½ | Marty Marion, ss, St. Louis |
| 1945 | Chicago | .636 | 3 | Phil Cavarretta, 1b, Chicago |
| 1946 | St. Louis | .628 | 2 | Stan Musial, 1b, St. Louis |
| 1947 | Brooklyn | .610 | 5 | Bob Elliott, 3b, Boston |
| 1948 | Boston | .595 | 6½ | Stan Musial, of, St. Louis |
| 1949 | Brooklyn | .630 | 1 | Jackie Robinson, 2b, Brooklyn |
| 1950 | Philadelphia | .591 | 2 | Jim Konstanty, rhp, Philadelphia |
| 1951 | New York | .624 | 1 | Roy Campanella, c, Brooklyn |
| 1952 | Brooklyn | .627 | 4½ | Hank Sauer, of, Chicago |
| 1953 | Brooklyn | .682 | 13 | Roy Campanella, c, Brooklyn |
| 1954 | New York | .630 | 5 | Willie Mays, of, New York |
| 1955 | Brooklyn | .641 | 13½ | Roy Campanella, c, Brooklyn |
| 1956 | Brooklyn | .604 | 1 | Don Newcombe, rhp, Brooklyn |
| 1957 | Milwaukee | .617 | 8 | Hank Aaron, of, Milwaukee |
| 1958 | Milwaukee | .597 | 8 | Ernie Banks, ss, Chicago |
| 1959 | Los Angeles | .564 | 2 | Ernie Banks, ss, Chicago |
| 1960 | Pittsburgh | .617 | 7 | Dick Groat, ss, Pittsburgh |
| 1961 | Cincinnati | .604 | 4 | Frank Robinson, of, Cincinnati |
| 1962 | San Francisco | .624 | 1 | Maury Wills, ss, Los Angeles |
| 1963 | Los Angeles | .611 | 6 | Sandy Koufax, lhp, Los Angeles |
| 1964 | St. Louis | .574 | 1 | Ken Boyer, 3b, St. Louis |
| 1965 | Los Angeles | .599 | 2 | Willie Mays, of, San Francisco |
| 1966 | Los Angeles | .586 | 1½ | Roberto Clemente, of, Pittsburgh |
| 1967 | St. Louis | .627 | 10½ | Orlando Cepeda, 1b, St. Louis |
| 1968 | St. Louis | .599 | 9 | Bob Gibson, rhp, St. Louis |

| | East. Div. | PCT | GA | West. Div. | PCT | GA | Pennant | | MVP |
|---|---|---|---|---|---|---|---|---|---|
| 1969 | New York | .617 | 8 | Atlanta | .574 | 3 | New York | 3-0 | Willie McCovey, 1b, San Francisco |
| 1970 | Pittsburgh | .549 | 5 | Cincinnati | .630 | 14½ | Cincinnati | 3-0 | Johnny Bench, c, Cincinnati |
| 1971 | Pittsburgh | .599 | 7 | San Francisco | .556 | 1 | Pittsburgh | 3-1 | Joe Torre, 3b, St. Louis |
| 1972 | Pittsburgh | .619 | 11 | Cincinnati | .617 | 10½ | Cincinnati | 3-2 | Johnny Bench, c, Cincinnati |
| 1973 | New York | .509 | 1½ | Cincinnati | .611 | 3½ | New York | 3-2 | Pete Rose, of, Cincinnati |
| 1974 | Pittsburgh | .543 | 1½ | Los Angeles | .630 | 4 | Los Angeles | 3-1 | Steve Garvey, 1b, Los Angeles |
| 1975 | Pittsburgh | .571 | 6½ | Cincinnati | .667 | 20 | Cincinnati | 3-0 | Joe Morgan, 2b, Cincinnati |
| 1976 | Philadelphia | .623 | 9 | Cincinnati | .630 | 10 | Cincinnati | 3-0 | Joe Morgan, 2b, Cincinnati |
| 1977 | Philadelphia | .623 | 5 | Los Angeles | .605 | 10 | Los Angeles | 3-1 | George Foster, of, Cincinnati |
| 1978 | Philadelphia | .556 | 1½ | Los Angeles | .586 | 2½ | Los Angeles | 3-1 | Dave Parker, of, Pittsburgh |
| 1979 | Pittsburgh | .605 | 2 | Cincinnati | .559 | 1½ | Pittsburgh | 3-0 | Hernandez, St. Louis; Stargell, Pittsburgh |
| 1980 | Philadelphia | .562 | 1 | Houston | .571 | 1 | Philadelphia | 3-2 | Mike Schmidt, 3b, Philadelphia |
| 1981 | Montreal* | .566 | ½ | Los Angeles** | .632 | ½ | Los Angeles | 3-2 | Mike Schmidt, 3b, Philadelphia |
| | Philadelphia | .618 | 1½ | Houston | .623 | 1 | | | |
| 1982 | St. Louis | .568 | 3 | Atlanta | .549 | 1 | St. Louis | 3-0 | Dale Murphy, of, Atlanta |
| 1983 | Philadelphia | .556 | 6 | Los Angeles | .562 | 3 | Philadelphia | 3-1 | Dale Murphy, of, Atlanta |
| 1984 | Chicago | .596 | 6½ | San Diego | .568 | 12 | San Diego | 3-2 | Ryne Sandberg, 2b, Chicago |
| 1985 | St. Louis | .623 | 3 | Los Angeles | .586 | 5½ | St. Louis | 4-2 | Willie McGee, of, St. Louis |
| 1986 | New York | .667 | 21½ | Houston | .593 | 10 | New York | 4-2 | Mike Schmidt, 3b, Philadelphia |
| 1987 | St. Louis | .586 | 3 | San Francisco | .556 | 6 | St. Louis | 4-3 | Andre Dawson, of, Chicago |
| 1988 | New York | .625 | 15 | Los Angeles | .584 | 7 | Los Angeles | 4-3 | Kirk Gibson, of, Los Angeles |
| 1989 | Chicago | .571 | 6 | San Francisco | .568 | 3 | San Francisco | 4-1 | Kevin Mitchell, of, San Francisco |
| 1990 | Pittsburgh | .586 | 4 | Cincinnati | .562 | 5 | Cincinnati | 4-2 | Barry Bonds, of, Pittsburgh |
| 1991 | Pittsburgh | .605 | 14 | Atlanta | .580 | 1 | Atlanta | 4-3 | Terry Pendleton, 3b, Atlanta |
| 1992 | Pittsburgh | .593 | 9 | Atlanta | .605 | 8 | Atlanta | 4-3 | Barry Bonds, of, Pittsburgh |
| 1993 | Philadelphia | .599 | 3 | Atlanta | .642 | 1 | Philadelphia | 4-2 | Barry Bonds, of, San Francisco |

NOTE: Most Valuable Player award formally recognized in 1931
GA—Games ahead of second-place team

*Won second half; defeated Philadelphia 3-2 in best-of-5 playoff.
**Won first half; defeated Houston 3-2 in best-of-5 playoff.

"A certain attitude has evolved over four or five years on this team," Mulholland said. "Lee Thomas has brought survivors in here. It's gone beyond having a chip on your shoulder against your former team. It's more like a chip on your shoulder against the rest of the league.

"We've been in the basement long enough to realize nobody out there really respected us at all. If a guy here comes from another team and has something against that team, we all feel that way.

"We take the attitude, 'The Mets didn't want Lenny Dykstra, so screw the Mets.' Or, 'The Braves were dumb enough to let Ben Rivera and Tommy Greene go, so the heck with them.' What it comes down to is we don't like the rest of the league."

## First-Year Fun

The rest of the National League found out it didn't like the expansion Marlins and Rockies as much as they had expected to.

Each club enjoyed success in its inaugural season. The Marlins, who generally were regarded as having made the best personnel moves, finished ahead of the dismal Mets with a 64-98 record. The Rockies rebounded from a poor first half, especially on the mound, and finished with a strong run to clip the Marlins at 67-95 and finish ahead of the Padres in the West.

The year began with some sadness for the Marlins, whose president, Carl Barger, collapsed and died during the previous December's Winter Meetings. But the excitement of a budding franchise soon reasserted itself. And how exciting it was.

The Marlins began the season 34-42 behind rejuvenated closer Bryan Harvey (45 saves by year's end), and obtained all-star third baseman Gary Sheffield from the Padres in June. Center fielder Chuck Carr, with 58 stolen bases, became the first member of an expansion team to lead his league in any offensive category.

Meanwhile, the Rockies looked exactly like an expansion team early on. The thin air at Mile High Stadium hurt a thin pitching staff, and double-digit scores became commonplace. Colorado usually found itself on the wrong end of those ugly games.

Patience won out, though, as the Rockies went 31-21 behind manager Don Baylor after Aug. 8 to become respectable again. (That record was the NL's third-best during that period behind Atlanta's 39-11 and Montreal's 34-17.) Three Rockies hitters enjoyed fine years in the climate's friendly confines.

First baseman Andres Galarraga, picked up from the Cardinals scrap heap over the winter, underwent some swing tinkering from Baylor and made a run at .400 before settling in at .370. Outfielder Dante Bichette batted .310. Third baseman Charlie Hayes hit .305 and led the NL with 45 doubles.

## A Piazza With Everything

The league's best rookie story, and one of its finest overall, was the enormous success Los Angeles catcher Mike Piazza enjoyed in his first full major league season.

Quick-wristed but slow afoot, Piazza was selected by Los Angeles in the 62nd round of the 1988 draft solely as a favor to a good friend of his father, Dodgers

**Mike Piazza.** Dodgers catcher hit .318 with 35 homers and 112 RBIs to cop NL rookie of the year honors.

manager Tom Lasorda. But he worked his way up the minor league ladder and was named 1993 Baseball America and National League Rookie of the Year.

Piazza's 35 home runs set a Los Angeles Dodgers record—with no consideration for position or being a rookie. He added a .318 average (seventh in the NL) and 112 RBIs (fourth) while catching 141 games.

Piazza became just the sixth player in the storied, 103-year history of the Dodgers to post a .300-30-100 season, joining Roy Campanella, Pedro Guerrero, Babe Herman, Gil Hodges and Duke Snider.

"It's just a dream season," Piazza said after crushing the Giants' division-title hopes on the season's last day. "I'm just as happy, if not more so, with the way I caught. There were always questions: Can he catch? Can he handle the pitching staff? For me, that'll probably get overlooked. For me, that was no less important."

## Hard-Hittin' Whiten

Cardinals outfielder Mark Whiten misplayed a line drive in the first game of a Sept. 7 doubleheader at Cincinnati and probably cost St. Louis a win. Then he made up for the mistake.

Whiten broke out for the finest one-game offensive show in major league history. He hit four titanic home runs in the Cardinals' 15-2 victory.

"Every time I hit it, I was like, amazed," Whiten said.

"You don't see too many guys get curtain calls on the road at midnight," Cardinals catcher Tom Pagnozzi said. "But he earned it."

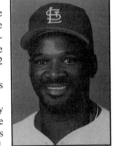

**Mark Whiten**

Whiten became the first player to hit four home runs in a game since Atlanta's Bob Horner in 1986. No one had driven in 12 runs in one game since the Cardinals' Jim Bottomley in 1924.

## Stupid Met Tricks

The year 1993 also will be remembered as when the Mets became an embarrassment to baseball on and off the field.

It began with some hope. Ace Dwight Gooden wore his old No. 64 in spring training to somewhat recapture his glory days of youth a decade before. Little did he know, though, that New York would win fewer than 64 *games*. They fininshed 59-103, the worst record in the majors, behind bad hitting, bad pitching and bad defense. Replacing manager Jeff Torborg with fiery Dallas Green during the season didn't help.

The bigger stories came off the field. Bobby Bonilla threateningly told New York Daily News columnist Bob Klapisch he would "show him the Bronx" after Klapisch's co-authored, unflattering book "The Worst Team Money Could Buy" detailed the Mets' equally bad 1992 season.

On July 7, pitcher Bret Saberhagen threw a firecracker near a group of reporters. No one was injured.

On July 24, in an incident outside the players' parking lot at Dodger Stadium, a two-year-old girl allegedly suffered facial injuries when an explosive device identified as an M-100 by the Los Angeles Fire Department detonated. Mets outfielder Vince Coleman was charged with possession of an explosive, and later apologized for whatever injuries might have resulted from the incident, saying, "I personally in the last few days have been portrayed as an insensitive, non-caring athlete. Nothing could be further from the truth." Coleman played only sparingly after the incident and was placed on administrative leave with six weeks remaining in the season. The Mets said he never will play for them again.

On July 27, a Met squirted a reporter with bleach from a water gun. Saberhagen first denied responsibility but later admitted it.

## Pride Of The Expos

With the Expos breathing down the Phillies' necks in September, Montreal rookie outfielder Curtis Pride provided one of the season's most emotional moments.

Pride was born 95 percent deaf. He fought his way to the major leagues by hitting hitting .324 with 21

**Disaster.** Mets pitcher Anthony Young, left, lost a record 27 games in a row; Vince Coleman was suspended.

homers and 50 stolen bases at Double-A Harrisburg and Triple-A Ottawa in 1993. He previously had spent seven nondescript years in the Mets chain and was signed by the Expos as a six-year free agent.

On Sept. 17, Pride delivered a clutch pinch-double to help Montreal beat Philadelphia 8-7. A monstrous standing ovation cascaded from the stands while Pride stood at second unaware.

As the Phillies prepared for a pitching change, Pride looked at third-base coach Jerry Manuel and asked if he had the green light to steal.

"Tip your cap," Manuel said.

"What?"

"They're cheering for you. Tip your cap."

## Unsatisfied Astros Clean House

Houston began the 1993 season with plenty of hope. The club had been sold from thrifty John McMullen to the more ambitious Drayton McLane, and free-agent pitchers Doug Drabek and Greg Swindell had been brought back to their home state after spending time in Pittsburgh and Cincinnati, respectively.

But the Astros finished 85-77, 19 games behind the Braves, and McLane decided that wasn't enough. He fired general manager Bill Wood and manager Art Howe two days after the season.

Assistant GM Bob Watson was moved up to GM, becoming just the second black man to serve in that

# NATIONAL LEAGUE ALL-STARS

Selected by Baseball America

| Pos. | Player, Team | B-T | Ht. | Wt. | Age | '93 Salary | AVG | AB | R | H | 2B | 3B | HR | RBI | SB |
|---|---|---|---|---|---|---|---|---|---|---|---|---|---|---|---|
| C | Mike Piazza, Los Angeles | R-R | 6-3 | 220 | 24 | $126,000 | .318 | 547 | 81 | 174 | 24 | 2 | 35 | 112 | 3 |
| 1B | Andres Galarraga, Colorado | R-R | 6-3 | 225 | 32 | 600,000 | .370 | 470 | 71 | 174 | 35 | 4 | 22 | 98 | 2 |
| 2B | Robby Thompson, S.F. | R-R | 5-11 | 170 | 31 | 1,900,000 | .312 | 494 | 85 | 154 | 30 | 2 | 19 | 65 | 4 |
| 3B | Matt Williams, San Francisco | R-R | 6-2 | 205 | 27 | 2,250,000 | .294 | 579 | 105 | 170 | 33 | 4 | 38 | 110 | 1 |
| SS | Jeff Blauser, Atlanta | R-R | 6-0 | 170 | 27 | 2,000,000 | .305 | 597 | 110 | 182 | 29 | 2 | 15 | 73 | 16 |
| OF | Barry Bonds, San Francisco | L-L | 6-1 | 185 | 29 | 4,416,666 | .336 | 539 | 129 | 181 | 38 | 4 | 46 | 123 | 29 |
| | Lenny Dykstra, Philadelphia | L-L | 5-10 | 160 | 30 | 2,466,667 | .305 | 637 | 143 | 194 | 44 | 6 | 19 | 66 | 37 |
| | Ron Gant, Atlanta | R-R | 6-0 | 172 | 28 | 3,700,000 | .274 | 606 | 113 | 166 | 27 | 4 | 36 | 117 | 26 |

| | | | | | | | W | L | ERA | G | SV | IP | H | BB | SO |
|---|---|---|---|---|---|---|---|---|---|---|---|---|---|---|---|
| P | Rod Beck, San Francisco | R-R | 6-1 | 215 | 25 | 250,000 | 3 | 1 | 2.16 | 76 | 48 | 79 | 57 | 13 | 86 |
| | Tom Glavine, Atlanta | L-L | 6-0 | 175 | 27 | 4,750,000 | 22 | 6 | 3.20 | 36 | 0 | 239 | 236 | 90 | 120 |
| | Greg Maddux, Atlanta | R-R | 6-0 | 150 | 27 | 5,500,000 | 20 | 10 | 2.36 | 36 | 0 | 267 | 228 | 52 | 197 |
| | Billy Swift, San Francisco | R-R | 6-0 | 180 | 31 | 3,316,667 | 21 | 8 | 2.82 | 34 | 0 | 233 | 195 | 55 | 157 |
| | John Wetteland, Montreal | R-R | 6-2 | 195 | 27 | 315,000 | 9 | 3 | 1.37 | 70 | 43 | 85 | 58 | 28 | 113 |

**Player of Year:** Barry Bonds, of, San Francisco. **Pitcher of Year:** Greg Maddux, rhp, Atlanta. **Rookie of Year:** Mike Piazza, c, Los Angeles. **Manager of Year:** Dusty Baker, San Francisco. **Executive of Year:** Lee Thomas, Philadelphia.

**Bryan Harvey.** Relief ace had 45 saves for expansion Florida Marlins.

capacity.

Wood had rebuilt a team that was purged of its veterans two years before to slash its payroll, and could be a contender in the NL Central in 1994. Ironically, the players McLane bought to put Houston over the top, Drabek and Swindell, went 21-31 combined.

## Miscellaneous

■ The fire sale in San Diego to trim its payroll continued, as management traded Sheffield to Florida in midseason for prospects Trevor Hoffman, Andres Berumen and Jose Martinez. GM Joe McIlvaine was fired, later to join the Mets.

Finally, McGriff was jettisoned to the Braves. That capped a series of moves that lopped $13 million off the Padres' payroll since Opening Day 1992. It also left right fielder Tony Gwynn and righthander Andy Benes as the core of a last-place team.

"We've probably set some sort of world record for going from a contender to an expansion club in one winter," one Padres official said. "Everyone's frustrated with what's going on around here."

■ The Mets' dismal season was personified by righthander Anthony Young, who lost a major league-record 27 games before finally getting the win in New York's 5-4 win over Florida July 28.

"That wasn't even a big monkey off my back," said Young, mobbed by his teammates after the game. "It was a zoo."

The old record of 23 had belonged to the Boston Braves' Clifton Curtis since 1911.

After loss No. 23, Young asked the media: "You saw me. Am I *that* bad?"

■ Not long after free agency cost the Pirates three

MORRIS FOSTOFF

# NL: BEST TOOLS

A Baseball America survey of National League managers, conducted at midseason 1993, ranked NL players with the best tools:

**BEST HITTER**
1. Barry Bonds, Giants
2. Tony Gwynn, Padres
3. John Kruk, Phillies

**BEST POWER HITTER**
1. Barry Bonds, Giants
2. Fred McGriff, Padres
3. Matt Williams, Giants

**BEST BUNTER**
1. Brett Butler, Dodgers
2. Jay Bell, Pirates
3. Otis Nixon, Braves

**BEST HIT-AND-RUN ARTIST**
1. Barry Larkin, Reds
2. Jody Reed, Dodgers
3. Tony Gwynn, Padres

**BEST BASERUNNER**
1. Barry Bonds, Giants
2. Marquis Grissom, Expos
3. Ryne Sandberg, Cubs

**FASTEST BASERUNNER**
1. Marquis Grissom, Expos
2. Deion Sanders, Braves
3. Vince Coleman, Mets

**BEST PITCHER**
1. John Burkett, Giants
2. Tom Glavine, Braves
3. Greg Maddux, Braves

**BEST FASTBALL**
1. Rob Dibble, Reds
2. Bret Saberhagen, Mets
3. John Wetteland, Expos

**BEST CURVEBALL**
1. Dwight Gooden, Mets
2. Dennis Martinez, Expos
3. John Smoltz, Braves

**BEST SLIDER**
1. Jose Rijo, Reds
2. John Smoltz, Braves
3. Andy Benes, Padres

**BEST CHANGEUP**
1. Tom Glavine, Braves
2. Greg Maddux, Braves
3. Mark Portugal, Astros

**BEST CONTROL**
1. Bob Tewksbury, Cardinals
2. Greg Maddux, Braves
3. Tom Glavine, Braves

**BEST PICKOFF MOVE**
1. Terry Mulholland, Phillies
2. Armando Reynoso, Rockies
3. Tom Glavine, Braves

**BEST RELIEVER**
1. Bryan Harvey, Marlins
2. Lee Smith, Cardinals
3. Randy Myers, Cubs

**BEST DEFENSIVE C**
1. Tom Pagnozzi, Cardinals
2. Kirt Manwaring, Giants
3. Darren Daulton, Phillies

**BEST DEFENSIVE 1B**
1. Will Clark, Giants
2. Mark Grace, Cubs
3. Andres Galarraga, Rockies

**BEST DEFENSIVE 2B**
1. Ryne Sandberg, Cubs
2. Robby Thompson, Giants
3. Mark Lemke, Braves

**BEST DEFENSIVE 3B**
1. Matt Williams, Giants
2. Ken Caminiti, Astros
3. Terry Pendleton, Braves

**BEST DEFENSIVE SS**
1. Barry Larkin, Reds
2. Ozzie Smith, Cardinals
3. Jay Bell, Pirates

**BEST INFIELD ARM**
1. Ken Caminiti, Astros
2. Jay Bell, Pirates
3. Gary Sheffield, Marlins

**BEST DEFENSIVE OF**
1. Barry Bonds, Giants
2. Andy Van Slyke, Pirates
3. Marquis Grissom, Expos

**BEST OUTFIELD ARM**
1. Mark Whiten, Cardinals
2. Larry Walker, Expos
3. Andy Van Slyke, Pirates

**MOST EXCITING PLAYER**
1. Barry Bonds, Giants
2. Gary Sheffield, Marlins
3. Marquis Grissom, Expos

**BEST MANAGER**
1. Jim Leyland, Pirates
2. Dusty Baker, Giants
3. Joe Torre, Cardinals

stars in Bonilla, Bonds and Drabek and left them in little position to defend their three straight NL East titles, Pittsburgh went through more upheaval, this time in the front office.

General manager Ted Simmons resigned for health reasons June 19, 11 days after undergoing emergency heart surgery. Assistant GM Cam Bonifay replaced him, and Simmons later hooked on with Cleveland as a scout.

■ The Cardinals' Lee Smith broke the major league saves record with his 358th, on April 13 against the Dodgers. The next night, he broke the National League record with No. 301.

# NATIONAL LEAGUE
## 1993 BATTING, PITCHING STATISTICS

### CLUB BATTING

| | AVG | G | AB | R | H | 2B | 3B | HR | BB | SO | SB |
|---|---|---|---|---|---|---|---|---|---|---|---|
| San Francisco | .276 | 162 | 5557 | 808 | 1534 | 269 | 33 | 168 | 516 | 930 | 120 |
| Philadelphia | .274 | 162 | 5685 | 877 | 1555 | 297 | 51 | 156 | 665 | 1049 | 91 |
| Colorado | .273 | 162 | 5517 | 758 | 1507 | 278 | 59 | 142 | 388 | 944 | 146 |
| St. Louis | .272 | 162 | 5551 | 758 | 1508 | 262 | 34 | 118 | 588 | 882 | 153 |
| Chicago | .270 | 163 | 5627 | 738 | 1521 | 259 | 32 | 161 | 446 | 923 | 100 |
| Pittsburgh | .267 | 162 | 5549 | 707 | 1482 | 267 | 50 | 110 | 536 | 972 | 92 |
| Houston | .267 | 162 | 5464 | 716 | 1459 | 288 | 37 | 138 | 497 | 911 | 103 |
| Cincinnati | .264 | 162 | 5517 | 722 | 1457 | 261 | 28 | 137 | 485 | 1025 | 142 |
| Atlanta | .262 | 162 | 5515 | 767 | 1444 | 239 | 29 | 169 | 560 | 946 | 125 |
| Los Angeles | .261 | 162 | 5588 | 675 | 1458 | 234 | 28 | 130 | 492 | 937 | 126 |
| Montreal | .257 | 163 | 5493 | 732 | 1410 | 270 | 36 | 122 | 542 | 860 | 228 |
| San Diego | .252 | 162 | 5503 | 679 | 1386 | 239 | 28 | 153 | 443 | 1046 | 92 |
| New York | .248 | 162 | 5448 | 672 | 1350 | 228 | 37 | 158 | 448 | 879 | 79 |
| Florida | .248 | 162 | 5475 | 581 | 1356 | 197 | 61 | 94 | 498 | 1054 | 117 |

### CLUB PITCHING

| | ERA | G | CG | SHO | SV | IP | H | R | ER | BB | SO |
|---|---|---|---|---|---|---|---|---|---|---|---|
| Atlanta | 3.14 | 162 | 18 | 16 | 46 | 1455 | 1297 | 559 | 507 | 480 | 1036 |
| Houston | 3.49 | 162 | 18 | 14 | 42 | 1441 | 1363 | 630 | 559 | 476 | 1056 |
| Los Angeles | 3.50 | 162 | 17 | 9 | 36 | 1473 | 1406 | 662 | 573 | 567 | 1043 |
| Montreal | 3.55 | 163 | 8 | 7 | 61 | 1457 | 1369 | 682 | 574 | 521 | 934 |
| San Francisco | 3.61 | 162 | 4 | 9 | 50 | 1457 | 1385 | 636 | 585 | 442 | 982 |
| Philadelphia | 3.95 | 162 | 24 | 11 | 46 | 1473 | 1419 | 740 | 647 | 573 | 1117 |
| New York | 4.05 | 162 | 16 | 8 | 22 | 1438 | 1483 | 744 | 647 | 434 | 867 |
| St. Louis | 4.09 | 162 | 5 | 7 | 54 | 1453 | 1553 | 744 | 660 | 383 | 775 |
| Florida | 4.13 | 162 | 4 | 5 | 48 | 1440 | 1437 | 724 | 661 | 598 | 945 |
| San Diego | 4.23 | 162 | 8 | 6 | 32 | 1438 | 1470 | 772 | 675 | 558 | 957 |
| Cincinnati | 4.51 | 162 | 11 | 8 | 37 | 1434 | 1510 | 785 | 718 | 508 | 996 |
| Pittsburgh | 4.77 | 162 | 12 | 5 | 34 | 1446 | 1557 | 806 | 766 | 485 | 832 |
| Chicago | 5.27 | 163 | 8 | 5 | 56 | 1150 | 1514 | 739 | 673 | 470 | 905 |
| Colorado | 5.41 | 162 | 9 | 0 | 35 | 1431 | 1664 | 967 | 860 | 609 | 913 |

### CLUB FIELDING

| | PCT | PO | A | E | DP | | PCT | PO | A | E | DP |
|---|---|---|---|---|---|---|---|---|---|---|---|
| San Francisco | .984 | 4370 | 1733 | 101 | 169 | Los Angeles | .979 | 4418 | 1838 | 133 | 141 |
| Pittsburgh | .983 | 4337 | 1816 | 105 | 161 | Philadelphia | .979 | 4418 | 1536 | 141 | 123 |
| Atlanta | .983 | 4365 | 1769 | 108 | 146 | St. Louis | .975 | 4359 | 1890 | 159 | 117 |
| Chicago | .982 | 4349 | 1889 | 115 | 162 | New York | .975 | 4314 | 1781 | 156 | 143 |
| Cincinnati | .980 | 4302 | 1633 | 121 | 133 | Montreal | .975 | 4370 | 1827 | 159 | 144 |
| Florida | .980 | 4321 | 1703 | 125 | 125 | San Diego | .974 | 4313 | 1616 | 160 | 129 |
| Houston | .979 | 4324 | 1652 | 126 | 141 | Colorado | .973 | 4294 | 1760 | 167 | 149 |

### INDIVIDUAL BATTING LEADERS
#### (Minimum 502 Plate Appearances)

| | AVG | G | AB | R | H | 2B | 3B | HR | RBI | BB | SO | SB | CS |
|---|---|---|---|---|---|---|---|---|---|---|---|---|---|
| Galarraga, Andres, Colorado | .370 | 120 | 470 | 71 | 174 | 35 | 4 | 22 | 98 | 24 | 73 | 2 | 4 |
| *Gywnn, Tony, San Diego | .358 | 122 | 489 | 70 | 175 | 41 | 3 | 7 | 59 | 36 | 19 | 14 | 1 |
| #Jefferies, Gregg, St. Louis | .342 | 142 | 544 | 89 | 186 | 24 | 3 | 16 | 83 | 62 | 32 | 46 | 9 |
| *Bonds, Barry, San Francisco | .336 | 159 | 539 | 129 | 181 | 38 | 4 | 46 | 123 | 126 | 79 | 29 | 12 |
| *Grace, Mark, Chicago | .325 | 155 | 594 | 86 | 193 | 39 | 4 | 14 | 98 | 71 | 32 | 8 | 4 |
| Bagwell, Jeff, Houston | .320 | 142 | 535 | 76 | 171 | 37 | 4 | 20 | 88 | 62 | 73 | 13 | 4 |
| Piazza, Mike, Los Angeles | .318 | 149 | 547 | 81 | 174 | 24 | 2 | 35 | 112 | 46 | 86 | 3 | 4 |
| *Kruk, John, Philadelphia | .316 | 150 | 535 | 100 | 169 | 33 | 5 | 14 | 85 | 111 | 87 | 6 | 2 |
| #Merced, Orlando, Pittsburgh | .313 | 137 | 447 | 68 | 140 | 26 | 4 | 8 | 70 | 77 | 64 | 3 | 3 |
| Thompson, Robby, S.F. | .312 | 128 | 494 | 85 | 154 | 30 | 2 | 19 | 65 | 45 | 97 | 10 | 4 |

### INDIVIDUAL PITCHING LEADERS
#### (Minimum 162 Innings)

| | W | L | ERA | G | GS | CG | SV | IP | H | R | ER | BB | SO |
|---|---|---|---|---|---|---|---|---|---|---|---|---|---|
| Maddux, Greg, Atlanta | 20 | 10 | 2.36 | 36 | 36 | 8 | 0 | 267 | 228 | 85 | 70 | 52 | 197 |
| Rijo, Jose, Cincinnati | 14 | 9 | 2.48 | 36 | 36 | 2 | 0 | 257 | 218 | 76 | 71 | 62 | 227 |
| Portugal, Mark, Houston | 18 | 4 | 2.77 | 33 | 33 | 1 | 0 | 208 | 194 | 75 | 64 | 77 | 131 |
| Swift, Bill, San Francisco | 21 | 8 | 2.82 | 34 | 34 | 1 | 0 | 233 | 195 | 82 | 73 | 55 | 157 |
| *Avery, Steve, Atlanta | 18 | 6 | 2.94 | 35 | 35 | 3 | 0 | 223 | 216 | 81 | 73 | 43 | 125 |
| Harnisch, Pete, Houston | 16 | 9 | 2.98 | 33 | 33 | 5 | 0 | 218 | 171 | 84 | 72 | 79 | 185 |
| Candiotti, Tom, Los Angeles | 8 | 10 | 3.12 | 33 | 32 | 2 | 0 | 214 | 192 | 86 | 74 | 71 | 155 |
| *Glavine, Tom, Atlanta | 22 | 6 | 3.20 | 36 | 36 | 4 | 0 | 240 | 236 | 91 | 85 | 90 | 120 |
| Hill, Ken, Montreal | 9 | 7 | 3.23 | 28 | 28 | 2 | 0 | 184 | 163 | 84 | 66 | 74 | 90 |
| *Mulholland, Terry, Philadelphia | 12 | 9 | 3.25 | 29 | 28 | 7 | 0 | 191 | 177 | 80 | 69 | 40 | 116 |

## AWARD WINNERS

Selected by Baseball Writers Association of America

### MVP

| Player, Team | 1st | 2nd | 3rd | Total |
|---|---|---|---|---|
| Barry Bonds, S.F. | 24 | 4 | 0 | 372 |
| Len Dykstra, Phil. | 4 | 20 | 3 | 267 |
| David Justice, Atlanta | 0 | 3 | 5 | 183 |
| Fred McGriff, Atlanta | 0 | 1 | 12 | 177 |
| Ronnie Gant, Atlanta | 0 | 0 | 8 | 176 |
| Matt Williams, S.F. | 0 | 0 | 0 | 103 |
| Darren Daulton, Phil. | 0 | 0 | 0 | 79 |
| Marquis Grissom, Mtl. | 0 | 0 | 0 | 70 |
| Mike Piazza, L.A. | 0 | 0 | 0 | 49 |
| Andres Galarraga, Col. | 0 | 0 | 0 | 45 |
| Gregg Jefferies, St.L. | 0 | 0 | 0 | 28 |
| Rod Beck, S.F. | 0 | 0 | 0 | 23 |
| Greg Maddux, Atlanta | 0 | 0 | 0 | 17 |
| Bryan Harvey, Fla. | 0 | 0 | 0 | 14 |
| Robby Thompson, S.F. | 0 | 0 | 0 | 11 |
| Jeff Blauser, Atlanta | 0 | 0 | 0 | 9 |
| John Kruk, Phil. | 0 | 0 | 0 | 9 |
| Mark Grace, Chicago | 0 | 0 | 0 | 8 |
| Jay Bell, Pittsburgh | 0 | 0 | 0 | 4 |
| Jeff Bagwell, Hou. | 0 | 0 | 0 | 3 |
| Tony Gwynn, S.D. | 0 | 0 | 0 | 2 |
| Randy Myers, Chicago | 0 | 0 | 0 | 2 |
| Jose Rijo, Cin. | 0 | 0 | 0 | 2 |
| John Burkett, S.F. | 0 | 0 | 0 | 1 |
| Tom Glavine, Atlanta | 0 | 0 | 0 | 1 |
| John Wetteland, Mtl. | 0 | 0 | 0 | 1 |

### Cy Young Award

| Pitcher, Team | 1st | 2nd | 3rd | Total |
|---|---|---|---|---|
| Greg Maddux, Atlanta | 22 | 2 | 3 | 119 |
| Bill Swift, S.F. | 2 | 15 | 6 | 61 |
| Tom Glavine, Atlanta | 4 | 7 | 8 | 49 |
| John Burkett, S.F. | 0 | 3 | 0 | 9 |
| Jose Rijo, Cincinnati | 0 | 1 | 5 | 8 |
| Tommy Greene, Phil. | 0 | 2 | 2 | 2 |
| Mark Portugal, Hou. | 0 | 0 | 2 | 2 |
| Bryan Harvey, Fla. | 0 | 0 | 1 | 1 |
| Randy Myers, Chicago | 0 | 0 | 1 | 1 |

### Rookie of the Year

| Player, Team | 1st | 2nd | 3rd | Total |
|---|---|---|---|---|
| Mike Piazza, L.A. | 28 | 0 | 0 | 140 |
| Greg McMichael, Atl. | 0 | 12 | 4 | 40 |
| Jeff Conine, Florida | 0 | 7 | 10 | 31 |
| Chuck Carr, Florida | 0 | 4 | 6 | 18 |
| Al Martin, Pitt. | 0 | 2 | 0 | 6 |
| Kevin Stocker, Phil. | 0 | 1 | 1 | 4 |
| Will Cordero, Montreal | 0 | 1 | 0 | 3 |
| Kirk Rueter, Montreal | 0 | 1 | 0 | 3 |
| Carlos Garcia, Pitt. | 0 | 0 | 2 | 2 |
| Pedro Martinez, L.A. | 0 | 0 | 2 | 2 |
| Steve Cooke, Pitt. | 0 | 0 | 1 | 1 |
| Ricky Gutierrez, S.D. | 0 | 0 | 1 | 1 |
| Armando Reynoso, Col. | 0 | 0 | 1 | 1 |

### Manager of the Year

| Manager, Team | 1st | 2nd | 3rd | Total |
|---|---|---|---|---|
| Dusty Baker, S.F. | 15 | 9 | 3 | 105 |
| Jim Fregosi, Phil. | 11 | 11 | 4 | 92 |
| Felipe Alou, Montreal | 2 | 2 | 11 | 27 |
| Bobby Cox, Atlanta | 0 | 6 | 9 | 27 |
| Don Baylor, Colorado | 0 | 0 | 1 | 1 |

**NOTE:** MVP balloting based on 14 points for first-place vote, nine for second, eight for third, etc.; Cy Young Award, Rookie of the Year and Manager of the Year balloting based on five points for first-place vote, three for second and one for third.

# NATIONAL LEAGUE
## YEAR-BY-YEAR LEADERS: BATTING

| Year | Batting Average | Home Runs | RBIs |
|---|---|---|---|
| 1901 | Jesse Burkett, St. Louis .382 | Sam Crawford, Cin. 16 | Honus Wagner, Pitt. 126 |
| 1902 | Ginger Beaumont, Pitt. .357 | Tom Leach, Pittsburgh 6 | Honus Wagner, Pitt. 91 |
| 1903 | Honus Wagner, Pitt. .355 | Jim Sheckard, Brooklyn 9 | Sam Mertes, New York 104 |
| 1904 | Honus Wagner, Pitt. .349 | Harry Lumley, Brooklyn 9 | Bill Dahlen, N.Y. 80 |
| 1905 | Cy Seymour, Cin. .377 | Fred Odwell, Cin. 9 | Cy Seymour, Cin. 121 |
| 1906 | Honus Wagner, Pitt. .339 | Tim Jordan, Brooklyn 12 | 2 tied at 83 |
| 1907 | Honus Wagner, Pitt. .350 | Dave Brain, Boston 10 | Sherry Magee, Phil. 85 |
| 1908 | Honus Wagner, Pitt. .354 | Tim Jordan, Brooklyn 12 | Honus Wagner, Pitt. 109 |
| 1909 | Honus Wagner, Pitt. .339 | Red Murray, New York 7 | Honus Wagner, Pitt. 100 |
| 1910 | Sherry Magee, Phil. .331 | 2 tied at 10 | Sherry Magee, Phil. 123 |
| 1911 | Honus Wagner, Pitt. .334 | Wildfire Schulte, Chicago 21 | Wildfire Schulte, Chicago 121 |
| 1912 | Heinie Zimmerman, Chi. .372 | Heinie Zimmerman, Chi. 14 | Heinie Zimmerman, Chi. 103 |
| 1913 | Jake Daubert, Brook. .350 | Gavvy Cravath, Phil. 19 | Gavvy Cravath, Phil. 128 |
| 1914 | Jake Daubert, Brook. .329 | Gavvy Cravath, Phil. 19 | Sherry Magee, Phil. 103 |
| 1915 | Larry Doyle, New York .320 | Gavvy Cravath, Phil. 24 | Gavvy Cravath, Phil. 115 |
| 1916 | Hal Chase, Cincinnati .339 | 2 tied at 12 | Heinie Zimmerman, Chi.-N.Y. 83 |
| 1917 | Edd Roush, Cincinnati .341 | Gavvy Cravath, Phil. 12 | Heinie Zimmerman, N.Y. 102 |
| 1918 | Zack Wheat, Brooklyn .335 | Gavvy Cravath, Phil. 8 | Sherry Magee, Cin. 76 |
| 1919 | Edd Roush, Cincinnati .321 | Gavvy Cravath, Phil. 12 | Hy Myers, Brooklyn 73 |
| 1920 | Rogers Hornsby, St.L. .370 | Cy Williams, Phil. 15 | 2 tied at 94 |
| 1921 | Rogers Hornsby, St.L. .397 | George Kelly, New York 23 | Rogers Hornsby, St. Louis 126 |
| 1922 | Rogers Hornsby, St.L. .401 | Rogers Hornsby, St.L. 42 | Rogers Hornsby, St. Louis 152 |
| 1923 | Rogers Hornsby, St.L. .384 | Cy Williams, Phil. 41 | Emil Meusel, N.Y. 125 |
| 1924 | Rogers Hornsby, St.L. .424 | Jack Fournier, Brook. 27 | George Kelly, New York 136 |
| 1925 | Rogers Hornsby, St.L. .403 | Rogers Hornsby, St.L. 39 | Rogers Hornsby, St. Louis 143 |
| 1926 | Bubbles Hargrave, Cin. .353 | Hack Wilson, Chicago 21 | Jim Bottomley, St. Louis 120 |
| 1927 | Paul Waner, Pittsburgh .380 | 2 tied at 30 | Paul Waner, Pittsburgh 131 |
| 1928 | Rogers Hornsby, St.L. .387 | 2 tied at 31 | Jim Bottomley, St. Louis 136 |
| 1929 | Lefty O'Doul, Phil. .398 | Chuck Klein, Phil. 43 | Hack Wilson, Chicago 159 |
| 1930 | Bill Terry, New York .401 | Hack Wilson, Chicago 56 | Hack Wilson, Chicago 190 |
| 1931 | Chick Hafey, St. Louis .349 | Chuck Klein, Phil. 31 | Chuck Klein, Phil. 121 |
| 1932 | Lefty O'Doul, Phil. .368 | 2 tied at 38 | Frank Hurst, Phil. 143 |
| 1933 | Chuck Klein, Phil. .368 | Chuck Klein, Phil. 28 | Chuck Klein, Phil. 135 |
| 1934 | Paul Waner, Pittsburgh .362 | Mel Ott, New York 35 | Mel Ott, New York 135 |
| 1935 | Arky Vaughan, Pitt. .385 | Wally Berger, Boston 34 | Wally Berger, Boston 130 |
| 1936 | Paul Waner, Pittsburgh .373 | Mel Ott, New York 33 | Joe Medwick, St. Louis 138 |
| 1937 | Joe Medwick, St. Louis .374 | Joe Medwick, St. Louis 31 | Joe Medwick, St. Louis 154 |
| 1938 | Ernie Lombardi, Cin. .342 | Mel Ott, New York 36 | Joe Medwick, St. Louis 122 |
| 1939 | Johnny Mize, St. Louis .349 | Johnny Mize, St. Louis 28 | Frank McCormick, Cin. 128 |
| 1940 | Debs Garms, Pittsburgh .355 | Johnny Mize, St. Louis 43 | Johnny Mize, St. Louis 137 |
| 1941 | Pete Reiser, Brooklyn .343 | Dolf Camilli, Brooklyn 34 | Dolf Camilli, Brooklyn 120 |
| 1942 | Ernie Lombardi, Boston .330 | Mel Ott, New York 30 | Johnny Mize, New York 110 |
| 1943 | Stan Musial, St. Louis .357 | Bill Nicholson, Chicago 29 | Bill Nicholson, Chicago 128 |
| 1944 | Dixie Walker, Brooklyn .357 | Bill Nicholson, Chicago 33 | Bill Nicholson, Chicago 122 |
| 1945 | Phil Cavarretta, Chicago .355 | Tommy Holmes, Boston 28 | Dixie Walker, Brooklyn 124 |
| 1946 | Stan Musial, St. Louis .365 | Ralph Kiner, Pittsburgh 23 | Enos Slaughter, St. Louis 130 |
| 1947 | Harry Walker, St.L.-Phil. .363 | 2 tied at 51 | Johnny Mize, New York 138 |
| 1948 | Stan Musial, St. Louis .376 | 2 tied at 40 | Stan Musial, St. Louis 131 |
| 1949 | Jackie Robinson, Brook. .342 | Ralph Kiner, Pittsburgh 54 | Ralph Kiner, Pittsburgh 127 |
| 1950 | Stan Musial, St. Louis .346 | Ralph Kiner, Pittsburgh 47 | Del Ennis, Phil. 126 |
| 1951 | Stan Musial, St. Louis .355 | Ralph Kiner, Pittsburgh 42 | Monte Irvin, New York 121 |
| 1952 | Stan Musial, St. Louis .336 | 2 tied at 37 | Hank Sauer, Chicago 121 |
| 1953 | Carl Furillo, Brooklyn .344 | Eddie Mathews, Mil. 47 | Roy Campanella, Brook. 142 |
| 1954 | Willie Mays, New York .345 | Ted Kluszewski, Cin. 49 | Ted Kluszewski, Cin. 141 |
| 1955 | Richie Ashburn, Phil. .338 | Willie Mays, New York 51 | Duke Snider, Brooklyn 136 |
| 1956 | Hank Aaron, Milwaukee .328 | Duke Snider, Brooklyn 43 | Stan Musial, St. Louis 109 |
| 1957 | Stan Musial, St. Louis .351 | Hank Aaron, Milwaukee 44 | Hank Aaron, Milwaukee 132 |
| 1958 | Richie Ashburn, Phil. .350 | Ernie Banks, Chicago 47 | Ernie Banks, Chicago 129 |
| 1959 | Hank Aaron, Milwaukee .355 | Eddie Mathews, Mil. 46 | Ernie Banks, Chicago 143 |
| 1960 | Dick Groat, Pittsburgh .325 | Ernie Banks, Chicago 41 | Hank Aaron, Milwaukee 126 |
| 1961 | Roberto Clemente, Pitt. .351 | Orlando Cepeda, S.F. 46 | Orlando Cepeda, S.F. 142 |
| 1962 | Tommy Davis, L.A. .346 | Willie Mays, S.F. 49 | Tommy Davis, Los Angeles 153 |
| 1963 | Tommy Davis, L.A. .326 | Hank Aaron, Milwaukee 44 | 2 tied at 130 |
| 1964 | Roberto Clemente, Pitt. .339 | Willie Mays, S.F. 47 | Ken Boyer, St. Louis 119 |
| 1965 | Roberto Clemente, Pitt. .329 | Willie Mays, S.F. 52 | Deron Johnson, Cin. 130 |
| 1966 | Matty Alou, Pittsburgh .342 | Hank Aaron, Atlanta 44 | Hank Aaron, Atlanta 127 |
| 1967 | Roberto Clemente, Pitt. .357 | Hank Aaron, Atlanta 39 | Orlando Cepeda, S.F. 111 |
| 1968 | Pete Rose, Cincinnati .335 | Willie McCovey, S.F. 36 | Willie McCovey, S.F. 105 |
| 1969 | Pete Rose, Cincinnati .348 | Willie McCovey, S.F. 45 | Willie McCovey, S.F. 126 |
| 1970 | Rico Carty, Atlanta .366 | Johnny Bench, Cincinnati 45 | Johnny Bench, Cincinnati 148 |
| 1971 | Joe Torre, St. Louis .363 | Willie Stargell, Pitt. 48 | Joe Torre, St. Louis 137 |
| 1972 | Billy Williams, Chicago .333 | Johnny Bench, Cincinnati 40 | Johnny Bench, Cincinnati 125 |
| 1973 | Pete Rose, Cincinnati .338 | Willie Stargell, Pitt. 44 | Willie Stargell, Pitt. 119 |
| 1974 | Ralph Garr, Atlanta .353 | Mike Schmidt, Phil. 36 | Johnny Bench, Cincinnati 129 |
| 1975 | Bill Madlock, Chicago .354 | Mike Schmidt, Phil. 38 | Greg Luzinski, Phil. 120 |
| 1976 | Bill Madlock, Chicago .339 | Mike Schmidt, Phil. 38 | George Foster, Cincinnati 121 |
| 1977 | Dave Parker, Pitt. .338 | George Foster, Cincinnati 52 | George Foster, Cincinnati 149 |
| 1978 | Dave Parker, Pitt. .334 | George Foster, Cincinnati 40 | George Foster, Cincinnati 120 |
| 1979 | Keith Hernandez, St.L. .344 | Dave Kingman, Chicago 48 | Dave Winfield, San Diego 118 |
| 1980 | Bill Buckner, Chicago .324 | Mike Schmidt, Phil. 48 | Mike Schmidt, Phil. 121 |
| 1981 | Bill Madlock, Pitt. .341 | Mike Schmidt, Phil. 31 | Mike Schmidt, Phil. 91 |
| 1982 | Al Oliver, Montreal .331 | Dave Kingman, N.Y. 37 | Dale Murphy, Atlanta 109 |
| 1983 | Bill Madlock, Pitt. .323 | Mike Schmidt, Phil. 40 | Dale Murphy, Atlanta 121 |
| 1984 | Tony Gwynn, San Diego .351 | Dale Murphy, Atlanta 36 | 2 tied at 106 |
| 1985 | Willie McGee, St. Louis .353 | Dale Murphy, Atlanta 37 | Dave Parker, Cin. 125 |
| 1986 | Tim Raines, Montreal .334 | Mike Schmidt, Phil. 37 | Mike Schmidt, Phil. 119 |
| 1987 | Tony Gwynn, San Diego .370 | Andre Dawson, Chicago 49 | Andre Dawson, Chicago 137 |
| 1988 | Tony Gwynn, San Diego .313 | Darryl Strawberry, N.Y. 39 | Will Clark, S.F. 109 |
| 1989 | Tony Gwynn, San Diego .336 | Kevin Mitchell, S.F. 47 | Kevin Mitchell, S.F. 125 |
| 1990 | Willie McGee, St. Louis .335 | Ryne Sandberg, Chicago 40 | Matt Williams, S.F. 122 |
| 1991 | Terry Pendleton, Atlanta .319 | Howard Johnson, N.Y. 38 | Howard Johnson, N.Y. 117 |
| 1992 | Gary Sheffield, S.D. .330 | Fred McGriff, S.D. 35 | Darren Daulton, Phil. 109 |
| 1993 | Andres Galarraga, Col. .370 | Barry Bonds, S.F. 46 | Barry Bonds, S.F. 123 |

# DEPARTMENT LEADERS
## NATIONAL LEAGUE

### BATTING

#### RUNS
Lenny Dykstra, Philadelphia .............. 143
Barry Bonds, San Francisco .............. 129
Ron Gant, Atlanta .............................. 113
Fred McGriff, San Diego-Atlanta ........ 111
Jeff Blauser, Atlanta ........................... 110

#### HITS
Lenny Dykstra, Philadelphia .............. 194
Mark Grace, Chicago ......................... 193
Marquis Grissom, Montreal ................ 188
Jay Bell, Pittsburgh ........................... 187
Gregg Jefferies, St. Louis .................. 186

#### TOTAL BASES
Barry Bonds, San Francisco .............. 365
Matt Williams, San Francisco ............ 325
Ron Gant, Atlanta .............................. 309
Lenny Dykstra, Philadelphia .............. 307
Mike Piazza, Los Angeles ................. 307

#### DOUBLES
Charlie Hayes, Colorado ..................... 45
Lenny Dykstra, Philadelphia ................ 44
Dante Bichette, Colorado .................... 43
Craig Biggio, Houston ........................ 41
Tony Gwynn, San Diego ..................... 41

#### TRIPLES
Steve Finley, Houston ......................... 13
Brett Butler, Los Angeles .................... 10
Jay Bell, Pittsburgh .............................. 9
Mickey Morandini, Philadelphia ............. 9
Vince Coleman, New York ..................... 8
Al Martin, Pittsburgh ............................. 8
Eric Young, Colorado ............................ 8

#### HOME RUNS
Barry Bonds, San Francisco ................ 46
Dave Justice, Atlanta ........................... 40
Matt Williams, San Francisco .............. 38
Fred McGriff, San Diego-Atlanta .......... 37
Ron Gant, Atlanta ................................ 36

#### RUNS BATTED IN
Barry Bonds, San Francisco .............. 123
Dave Justice, Atlanta ......................... 120
Ron Gant, Atlanta .............................. 117
Mike Piazza, Los Angeles ................. 112
Matt Williams, San Francisco ............ 110

#### SACRIFICE BUNTS
Jose Offerman, Los Angeles ................ 25
Jody Reed, Los Angeles ...................... 17
Andy Benes, San Diego ....................... 14
Brett Butler, Los Angeles .................... 14
Ken Hill, Montreal ............................... 14

#### SACRIFICE FLIES
Luis Gonzalez, Houston ....................... 10
Jeff Bagwell, Houston ............................ 9
Mark Grace, Chicago ............................ 9
Eddie Murray, New York ......................... 9
Joe Oliver, Cincinnati ............................ 9
Jose Vizcaino, Chicago .......................... 9
Tim Wallach, Los Angeles ...................... 9
Matt Williams, San Francisco ................. 9
Kevin Young, Pittsburgh ........................ 9

#### HIT BY PITCH
Jeff Blauser, Atlanta ............................ 16
Derek Bell, San Diego .......................... 12
Craig Biggio, Houston .......................... 10
Jerald Clark, Colorado ......................... 10
Luis Gonzalez, Houston ....................... 10

#### WALKS
Lenny Dykstra, Philadelphia .............. 129
Barry Bonds, San Francisco .............. 126
Darren Daulton, Philadelphia ............. 117
John Kruk, Philadelphia ...................... 111
Brett Butler, Los Angeles ..................... 86

**Andres Galarraga.** Rockies first baseman had highest average in NL since Stan Musial in 1948.

#### INTENTIONAL WALKS
Barry Bonds, San Francisco ................ 43
Larry Walker, Montreal ........................ 20
Mark Grace, Chicago ........................... 14
Mark Lemke, Atlanta ........................... 13
Kirt Manwaring, San Francisco ............ 13
Walt Weiss, Florida ............................. 13
Rick Wilkins, Chicago .......................... 13

#### STRIKEOUTS
Cory Snyder, Los Angeles .................. 147
Jeff Conine, Florida ............................ 135
Sammy Sosa, Chicago ....................... 135
Orestes Destrade, Florida .................. 130
Phil Plantier, San Diego ..................... 124

#### STOLEN BASES
Chuck Carr, Florida ............................ 58
Marquis Grissom, Montreal ................. 53
Otis Nixon, Atlanta ............................. 47
Gregg Jefferies, St. Louis ................... 46
Darren Lewis, San Francisco .............. 46

#### CAUGHT STEALING
Chuck Carr, Florida ............................ 22
Brett Butler, Los Angeles .................... 19
Eric Young, Colorado .......................... 19
Craig Biggio, Houston ......................... 17
Darren Lewis, San Francisco .............. 15

#### GIDP
Mark Grace, Chicago ........................... 25
Charlie Hayes, Colorado ..................... 25

Eddie Murray, New York ...................... 24
Mark Lemke, Atlanta ........................... 21
Jeff Bagwell, Houston .......................... 20

#### HITTING STREAKS
Delino DeShields, Montreal ................. 21
Robby Thompson, San Francisco ........ 21
Kevin Mitchell, Cincinnati ................... 20
Mariano Duncan, Philadelphia ............. 18
Two tied at .......................................... 17

#### MULTI-HIT GAMES
Andres Galarraga, Colorado ............... 56
Marquis Grissom, Montreal ................. 55
Jay Bell, Pittsburgh ............................ 55
Eddie Murray, New York ...................... 55
Jeff Bagwell, Houston .......................... 54
Jeff Conine, Florida ............................ 54
Lenny Dykstra, Philadelphia ............... 54
Tony Gwynn, San Diego ..................... 54

#### SLUGGING PERCENTAGE
Barry Bonds, San Francisco .............. .677
Andres Galarraga, Colorado .............. .602
Matt Williams, San Francisco ............ .561
Mike Piazza, Los Angeles ................. .561
Fred McGriff, San Diego-Atlanta ........ .549

#### ON-BASE PERCENTAGE
Barry Bonds, San Francisco .............. .458
John Kruk, Philadelphia ..................... .430
Lenny Dykstra, Philadelphia .............. .420
Orlando Merced, Pittsburgh ............... .414
Gregg Jefferies, St. Louis .................. .408

**Billy Swift.** Righthander won 21 games for second-place Giants.

## PITCHING

### WINS

| | |
|---|---|
| Tom Glavine, Atlanta | 22 |
| John Burkett, San Francisco | 22 |
| Billy Swift, San Francisco | 21 |
| Greg Maddux, Atlanta | 20 |
| Steve Avery, Atlanta | 18 |
| Mark Portugal, Houston | 18 |

### LOSSES

| | |
|---|---|
| Doug Drabek, Houston | 18 |
| Jack Armstrong, Florida | 17 |
| Charlie Hough, Florida | 16 |
| Anthony Young, New York | 16 |
| Andy Benes, San Diego | 15 |
| Dwight Gooden, New York | 15 |
| Mike Morgan, Chicago | 15 |
| Tim Pugh, Cincinnati | 15 |
| Frank Tanana, New York | 15 |

### WINNING PERCENTAGE

| | |
|---|---|
| Mark Portugal, Houston | .818 |
| Tommy Greene, Philadelphia | .800 |
| Tom Glavine, Atlanta | .786 |
| John Burkett, San Francisco | .759 |
| Steve Avery, Atlanta | .750 |

### GAMES

| | |
|---|---|
| Mike Jackson, San Francisco | 81 |
| Rod Beck, San Francisco | 76 |
| David West, Philadelphia | 76 |
| Greg McMichael, Atlanta | 74 |
| Rob Murphy, St. Louis | 73 |
| Randy Myers, Chicago | 73 |

### GAMES STARTED

| | |
|---|---|
| Tom Glavine, Atlanta | 36 |
| Greg Maddux, Atlanta | 36 |
| Jose Rijo, Cincinnati | 36 |
| Steve Avery, Atlanta | 35 |
| John Smoltz, Atlanta | 35 |

### COMPLETE GAMES

| | |
|---|---|
| Greg Maddux, Atlanta | 8 |
| Doug Drabek, Houston | 7 |
| Dwight Gooden, New York | 7 |
| Tommy Greene, Philadelphia | 7 |
| Terry Mulholland, Philadelphia | 7 |
| Curt Schilling, Philadelphia | 7 |

### SHUTOUTS

| | |
|---|---|
| Pete Harnisch, Houston | 4 |
| Ramon Martinez, Los Angeles | 3 |
| 11 tied at | 2 |

### GAMES FINISHED

| | |
|---|---|
| Rod Beck, San Francisco | 71 |
| Randy Myers, Chicago | 69 |
| Doug Jones, Houston | 60 |
| John Wetteland, Montreal | 58 |
| Mitch Williams, Philadelphia | 57 |

### SAVES

| | |
|---|---|
| Randy Myers, Chicago | 53 |
| Rod Beck, San Francisco | 48 |
| Bryan Harvey, Florida | 45 |
| Lee Smith, St. Louis | 43 |
| John Wetteland, Montreal | 43 |
| Mitch Williams, Philadelphia | 43 |

### INNINGS PITCHED

| | |
|---|---|
| Greg Maddux, Atlanta | 267 |
| Jose Rijo, Cincinnati | 257 |
| John Smoltz, Atlanta | 244 |
| Tom Glavine, Atlanta | 239 |
| Doug Drabek, Houston | 238 |

### HITS ALLOWED

| | |
|---|---|
| Bob Tewksbury, St. Louis | 258 |
| Doug Drabek, Houston | 242 |
| Tom Glavine, Atlanta | 236 |
| Curt Schilling, Philadelphia | 234 |
| Greg Maddux, Atlanta | 228 |

### RUNS ALLOWED

| | |
|---|---|
| Bob Walk, Pittsburgh | 121 |
| Curt Schilling, Philadelphia | 114 |
| Andy Benes, San Diego | 111 |
| Kevin Gross, Los Angeles | 110 |
| Dennis Martinez, Montreal | 110 |
| Charlie Hough, Florida | 109 |

### HOME RUNS ALLOWED

| | |
|---|---|
| Jack Armstrong, Florida | 29 |
| Dennis Martinez, Montreal | 27 |
| Frank Tanana, New York | 26 |
| Jose Guzman, Chicago | 25 |
| Kent Bottenfield, Montreal-Colorado | 24 |
| Greg Swindell, Houston | 24 |

### WALKS

| | |
|---|---|
| Ramon Martinez, Los Angeles | 104 |
| John Smoltz, Atlanta | 100 |
| Tom Glavine, Atlanta | 90 |
| Ryan Bowen, Florida | 87 |
| Andy Benes, San Diego | 86 |

### HIT BATSMEN

| | |
|---|---|
| Darryl Kile, Houston | 15 |
| John Burkett, San Francisco | 11 |
| Dennis Martinez, Montreal | 11 |
| Six tied at | 9 |

**Randy Myers.** Cubs lefthander set NL record with 53 saves.

### STRIKEOUTS

| | |
|---|---|
| Jose Rijo, Cincinnati | 227 |
| John Smoltz, Atlanta | 208 |
| Greg Maddux, Atlanta | 197 |
| Curt Schilling, Philadelphia | 186 |
| Pete Harnisch, Houston | 185 |

### WILD PITCHES

| | |
|---|---|
| Tommy Greene, Philadelphia | 15 |
| Andy Benes, San Diego | 14 |
| Ben Rivera, Philadelphia | 13 |
| John Smoltz, Atlanta | 13 |
| Doug Drabek, Houston | 12 |
| Paul Wagner, Pittsburgh | 12 |

### BALKS

| | |
|---|---|
| Pedro Astacio, Los Angeles | 9 |
| Armando Reynoso, Colorado | 6 |
| Kevin Gross, Los Angeles | 5 |
| Jose Guzman, Chicago | 5 |
| Chris Hammond, Florida | 5 |

### OPPONENTS BATTING AVERAGE

| | |
|---|---|
| Pete Harnisch, Houston | .214 |
| Billy Swift, San Francisco | .226 |
| Jose Rijo, Cincinnati | .230 |
| John Smoltz, Atlanta | .230 |
| Andy Benes, San Diego | .232 |
| Greg Maddux, Atlanta | .232 |

## FIELDING

### PITCHER

| | | |
|---|---|---|
| PCT | Bob Tewksbury, St. Louis | 1.000 |
| PO | Greg Maddux, Atlanta | 39 |
| A | Greg Maddux, Atlanta | 59 |
| E | Greg Maddux, Atlanta | 7 |
| TC | Greg Maddux, Atlanta | 105 |
| DP | Jose Rijo, Cincinnati | 8 |

### CATCHER

| | | |
|---|---|---|
| PCT | Kirt Manwaring, San Francisco | .998 |
| PO | Darren Daulton, Philadelphia | 981 |
| A | Mike Piazza, Los Angeles | 98 |
| E | Mike Piazza, Los Angeles | 11 |
| | Benito Santiago, Florida | 11 |
| TC | Darren Daulton, Philadelphia | 1,057 |
| DP | Darren Daulton, Philadelphia | 19 |
| PB | Benito Santiago, Florida | 23 |

### FIRST BASE

| | | |
|---|---|---|
| PCT | Kevin Young, Pittsburgh | .998 |
| PO | Mark Grace, Chicago | 1,456 |
| A | Eric Karros, Los Angeles | 147 |
| E | Orestes Destrade, Florida | 19 |
| TC | Mark Grace, Chicago | 1,573 |
| DP | Mark Grace, Chicago | 134 |

### SECOND BASE

| | | |
|---|---|---|
| PCT | Jody Reed, Los Angeles | .993 |
| PO | Mark Lemke, Atlanta | 329 |
| A | Craig Biggio, Houston | 447 |
| E | Jeff Kent, New York | 18 |
| TC | Mark Lemke, Atlanta | 785 |
| DP | Mark Lemke, Atlanta | 100 |

### THIRD BASE

| | | |
|---|---|---|
| PCT | Steve Buechele, Chicago | .975 |
| PO | Terry Pendleton, Atlanta | 128 |
| A | Jeff King, Pittsburgh | 353 |
| E | Gary Sheffield, San Diego-Fla. | 34 |
| TC | Jeff King, Pittsburgh | 475 |
| DP | Matt Williams, San Francisco | 34 |

### SHORTSTOP

| | | |
|---|---|---|
| PCT | Jay Bell, Pittsburgh | .986 |
| PO | Jay Bell, Pittsburgh | 255 |
| A | Jay Bell, Pittsburgh | 527 |
| E | Jose Offerman, Los Angeles | 37 |
| TC | Jay Bell, Pittsburgh | 793 |
| DP | Royce Clayton, San Francisco | 103 |

### OUTFIELD

| | | |
|---|---|---|
| PCT | Brett Butler, Los Angeles | 1.000 |
| PO | Lenny Dykstra, Philadelphia | 469 |
| A | Bernard Gilkey, St. Louis | 19 |
| E | Ron Gant, Atlanta | 11 |
| TC | Lenny Dykstra, Philadelphia | 481 |
| DP | Orlando Merced, Pittsburgh | 5 |

# NATIONAL LEAGUE
## YEAR-BY-YEAR LEADERS: PITCHING

| Year | Wins | ERA | Strikeouts |
|---|---|---|---|
| 1948 | Johnny Sain, Boston...24 | Harry Brecheen, St.L....2.24 | Harry Brecheen, St.L....149 |
| 1949 | Warren Spahn, Boston...21 | Dave Koslo, New York...2.50 | Warren Spahn, Boston...151 |
| 1950 | Warren Spahn, Boston...21 | Jim Hearn, St.L.-N.Y....2.49 | Warren Spahn, Boston...191 |
| 1951 | 2 tied at...23 | Chet Nichols, Boston...2.88 | 2 tied at...164 |
| 1952 | Robin Roberts, Phil....28 | Hoyt Wilhelm, N.Y....2.43 | Warren Spahn, Boston...183 |
| 1953 | Robin Roberts, Phil....23 | Warren Spahn, Mil....2.10 | Robin Roberts, Phil....198 |
| 1954 | Robin Roberts, Phil....23 | John Antonelli, N.Y....2.29 | Robin Roberts, Phil....185 |
| 1955 | Robin Roberts, Phil....23 | Bob Friend, Pitt....2.84 | Sam Jones, Chicago...198 |
| 1956 | Don Newcombe, Brooklyn...27 | Lew Burdette, Mil....2.71 | Sam Jones, Chicago...176 |
| 1957 | Warren Spahn, Mil....21 | Johnny Podres, Brooklyn...2.66 | Jack Sanford, Phil....188 |
| 1958 | 2 tied at...22 | Stu Miller, S.F....2.47 | Sam Jones, St. Louis...225 |
| 1959 | 3 tied at...21 | Sam Jones, S.F....2.82 | Don Drysdale, L.A....242 |
| 1960 | 2 tied at...21 | Mike McCormick, S.F....2.70 | Don Drysdale, L.A....246 |
| 1961 | 2 tied at...21 | Warren Spahn, Mil....3.01 | Sandy Koufax, L.A....269 |
| 1962 | Don Drysdale, L.A....25 | Sandy Koufax, L.A....2.54 | Don Drysdale, L.A....232 |
| 1963 | Sandy Koufax, L.A....25 | Sandy Koufax, L.A....1.88 | Sandy Koufax, L.A....306 |
| 1964 | Larry Jackson, Chicago...24 | Sandy Koufax, L.A....1.74 | Bob Veale, Pittsburgh...250 |
| 1965 | Sandy Koufax, L.A....26 | Sandy Koufax, L.A....2.04 | Sandy Koufax, L.A....382 |
| 1966 | Sandy Koufax, L.A....27 | Sandy Koufax, L.A....1.73 | Jim Bunning, Phil....317 |
| 1967 | Mike McCormick, S.F....22 | Phil Niekro, Atlanta...1.87 | Jim Bunning, Phil....253 |
| 1968 | Juan Marichal, S.F....26 | Bob Gibson, St. Louis...1.12 | Bob Gibson, St. Louis...268 |
| 1969 | Tom Seaver, New York...25 | Juan Marichal, S.F....2.10 | Ferguson Jenkins, Chi....273 |
| 1970 | Bob Gibson, St. Louis...23 | Tom Seaver, New York...2.81 | Tom Seaver, New York...283 |
| 1971 | Ferguson Jenkins, Chi....24 | Tom Seaver, New York...1.76 | Tom Seaver, New York...289 |
| 1972 | Steve Carlton, Phil....27 | Steve Carlton, Phil....1.98 | Steve Carlton, Phil....310 |
| 1973 | Ron Bryant, S.F....24 | Tom Seaver, New York...2.08 | Tom Seaver, New York...251 |
| 1974 | 2 tied at...20 | Buzz Capra, Atlanta...2.28 | Steve Carlton, Phil....240 |
| 1975 | Tom Seaver, New York...22 | Randy Jones, S.D....2.24 | Tom Seaver, New York...243 |
| 1976 | Randy Jones, S.D....22 | John Denny, St. Louis...2.52 | Tom Seaver, New York...235 |
| 1977 | Steve Carlton, Phil....23 | John Candelaria, Pitt....2.34 | Phil Niekro, Atlanta...252 |
| 1978 | Gaylord Perry, S.D....21 | Craig Swan, New York...2.43 | J.R. Richard, Houston...303 |
| 1979 | 2 tied at...21 | J.R. Richard, Houston...2.71 | J.R. Richard, Houston...313 |
| 1980 | Steve Carlton, Phil....24 | Don Sutton, L.A....2.21 | Steve Carlton, Phil....286 |
| 1981 | Tom Seaver, Cincinnati...14 | Nolan Ryan, Houston...1.69 | Fernando Valenzuela, L.A....180 |
| 1982 | Steve Carlton, Phil....23 | Steve Rogers, Montreal...2.40 | Steve Carlton, Phil....286 |
| 1983 | John Denny, Phil....19 | Atlee Hammaker, S.F....2.25 | Steve Carlton, Phil....275 |
| 1984 | Joaquin Andujar, St.L....20 | Alejandro Pena, L.A....2.48 | Dwight Gooden, N.Y....276 |
| 1985 | Dwight Gooden, N.Y....24 | Dwight Gooden, N.Y....1.53 | Dwight Gooden, N.Y....268 |
| 1986 | Fernando Valenzuela, L.A....21 | Mike Scott, Houston...2.22 | Mike Scott, Houston...306 |
| 1987 | Rick Sutcliffe, Chicago...18 | Nolan Ryan, Houston...2.76 | Nolan Ryan, Houston...270 |
| 1988 | 2 tied at...23 | Joe Magrane, St. Louis...2.18 | Nolan Ryan, Houston...228 |
| 1989 | Mike Scott, Houston...20 | Scott Garrelts, S.F....2.28 | Jose DeLeon, St. Louis...201 |
| 1990 | Doug Drabek, Pitt....22 | Danny Darwin, Houston...2.21 | David Cone, New York...233 |
| 1991 | 2 tied at...20 | Dennis Martinez, Mon....2.39 | David Cone, New York...241 |
| 1992 | 2 tied at...20 | Bill Swift, S.F....2.08 | John Smoltz, Atlanta...215 |
| 1993 | 2 tied at...22 | Greg Maddux, Atlanta...2.36 | Jose Rijo, Cincinnati...227 |

| Year | Wins | ERA | Strikeouts |
|---|---|---|---|
| 1901 | Bill Donovan, Bklyn....25 | Jesse Tannehill, Pitt....2.18 | Noodles Hahn, Cin....233 |
| 1902 | Jack Chesbro, Pitt....28 | Jack Taylor, Chicago...1.33 | Vic Willis, Boston...226 |
| 1903 | Joe McGinnity, N.Y....31 | Sam Leever, Pitt....2.06 | Christy Mathewson, N.Y....267 |
| 1904 | Joe McGinnity, N.Y....35 | Joe McGinnity, N.Y....1.61 | Christy Mathewson, N.Y....212 |
| 1905 | Christy Mathewson, N.Y....32 | Christy Mathewson, N.Y....1.27 | Christy Mathewson, N.Y....206 |
| 1906 | Joe McGinnity, N.Y....27 | Mordecai Brown, Chicago...1.04 | Fred Beebe, Chi.-St.L....171 |
| 1907 | Christy Mathewson, N.Y....24 | Jack Pfiester, Chicago...1.15 | Christy Mathewson, N.Y....178 |
| 1908 | Christy Mathewson, N.Y....37 | Christy Mathewson, N.Y....1.43 | Christy Mathewson, N.Y....259 |
| 1909 | Mordecai Brown, Chicago...27 | Christy Mathewson, N.Y....1.14 | Orval Overall, Chicago...205 |
| 1910 | Christy Mathewson, N.Y....27 | George McQuillan, Phil....1.60 | Christy Mathewson, N.Y....190 |
| 1911 | Grover Alexander, Phil....28 | Christy Mathewson, N.Y....1.99 | Rube Marquard, N.Y....237 |
| 1912 | 2 tied at...26 | Jeff Tesreau, N.Y....1.96 | Grover Alexander, Phil....195 |
| 1913 | Tom Seaton, Phil....27 | Christy Mathewson, N.Y....2.06 | Tom Seaton, Phil....168 |
| 1914 | 2 tied at...27 | Bill Doak, St. Louis...1.72 | Grover Alexander, Phil....214 |
| 1915 | Grover Alexander, Phil....31 | Grover Alexander, Phil....1.22 | Grover Alexander, Phil....241 |
| 1916 | Grover Alexander, Phil....33 | Grover Alexander, Phil....1.55 | Grover Alexander, Phil....167 |
| 1917 | Grover Alexander, Phil....30 | Grover Alexander, Phil....1.85 | Grover Alexander, Phil....200 |
| 1918 | Hippo Vaughn, Chicago...22 | Hippo Vaughn, Chicago...1.74 | Hippo Vaughn, Chicago...148 |
| 1919 | Jesse Barnes, N.Y....25 | Grover Alexander, Chi....1.72 | Hippo Vaughn, Chicago...141 |
| 1920 | Grover Alexander, Chi....27 | Grover Alexander, Chi....1.91 | Grover Alexander, Chi....173 |
| 1921 | 2 tied at...22 | Bill Doak, St. Louis...2.58 | Burleigh Grimes, Bklyn....136 |
| 1922 | Eppa Rixey, Cincinnati...25 | Rosy Ryan, N.Y....3.00 | Dazzy Vance, Brooklyn...134 |
| 1923 | Dolf Luque, Cincinnati...27 | Dolf Luque, Cincinnati...1.93 | Dazzy Vance, Brooklyn...197 |
| 1924 | Dazzy Vance, Brooklyn...28 | Dazzy Vance, Brooklyn...2.16 | Dazzy Vance, Brooklyn...262 |
| 1925 | Dazzy Vance, Brooklyn...22 | Dolf Luque, Cincinnati...2.63 | Dazzy Vance, Brooklyn...221 |
| 1926 | 4 tied at...20 | Ray Kremer, Pittsburgh...2.61 | Dazzy Vance, Brooklyn...140 |
| 1927 | Charlie Root, Chicago...26 | Ray Kremer, Pittsburgh...2.47 | Dazzy Vance, Brooklyn...184 |
| 1928 | 2 tied at...25 | Dazzy Vance, Brooklyn...2.09 | Dazzy Vance, Brooklyn...200 |
| 1929 | Pat Malone, Chicago...22 | Bill Walker, New York...3.08 | Pat Malone, Chicago...166 |
| 1930 | 2 tied at...20 | Dazzy Vance, Brooklyn...2.61 | Bill Hallahan, St. Louis...177 |
| 1931 | 3 tied at...19 | Bill Hallahan, St. Louis...2.26 | Bill Hallahan, St. Louis...159 |
| 1932 | Lon Warneke, Chicago...22 | Lon Warneke, Chicago...2.37 | Dizzy Dean, St. Louis...191 |
| 1933 | Carl Hubbell, New York...23 | Carl Hubbell, New York...1.66 | Dizzy Dean, St. Louis...199 |
| 1934 | Dizzy Dean, St. Louis...30 | Carl Hubbell, New York...2.30 | Dizzy Dean, St. Louis...195 |
| 1935 | Dizzy Dean, St. Louis...28 | Cy Blanton, Pitt....2.59 | Dizzy Dean, St. Louis...182 |
| 1936 | Carl Hubbell, New York...26 | Carl Hubbell, New York...2.31 | Van Lingle Mungo, Bklyn....238 |
| 1937 | Carl Hubbell, New York...22 | Jim Turner, Boston...2.38 | Carl Hubbell, New York...159 |
| 1938 | Bill Lee, Chicago...22 | Bill Lee, Chicago...2.66 | Clay Bryant, Chicago...135 |
| 1939 | Bucky Walters, Cin....27 | Bucky Walters, Cin....2.29 | 2 tied at...137 |
| 1940 | Bucky Walters, Cin....22 | Bucky Walters, Cin....2.48 | Kirby Higbe, Phil....137 |
| 1941 | 2 tied at...22 | Elmer Riddle, Cin....2.24 | Johnny Vander Meer, Cin....202 |
| 1942 | Mort Cooper, St. Louis...22 | Mort Cooper, St. Louis...1.77 | Johnny Vander Meer, Cin....186 |
| 1943 | 3 tied at...21 | Howie Pollet, St. Louis...1.75 | Johnny Vander Meer, Cin....174 |
| 1944 | Bucky Walters, Cin....23 | Ed Heusser, Cin....2.38 | Bill Voiselle, N.Y....161 |
| 1945 | Red Barrett, Bos.-St.L....23 | Hank Borowy, Chicago...2.14 | Preacher Roe, Pitt....148 |
| 1946 | Howie Pollet, St. Louis...21 | Howie Pollet, St. Louis...2.10 | John Schmitz, Chicago...135 |
| 1947 | Ewell Blackwell, Cin....22 | Warren Spahn, Boston...2.33 | Ewell Blackwell, Cin....193 |

# NATIONAL LEAGUE CHAMPIONSHIP SERIES
## BOX SCORES

### Game One: October 6
### Phillies 4, Braves 3

| ATLANTA | ab | r | h | bi | bb | so | PHIL. | ab | r | h | bi | bb | so |
|---|---|---|---|---|---|---|---|---|---|---|---|---|---|
| Nixon cf | 4 | 0 | 2 | 2 | 1 | 1 | Dykstra cf | 4 | 1 | 1 | 0 | 1 | 1 |
| Blauser ss | 4 | 0 | 0 | 0 | 1 | 3 | Duncan 2b | 5 | 0 | 1 | 0 | 0 | 2 |
| Gant lf | 4 | 1 | 1 | 0 | 1 | 3 | Kruk 1b | 4 | 2 | 1 | 1 | 1 | 0 |
| McMichael p | 0 | 0 | 0 | 0 | 0 | 0 | Hollins 3b | 4 | 0 | 1 | 0 | 0 | 0 |
| McGriff 1b | 5 | 0 | 1 | 0 | 0 | 2 | Batiste 3b | 1 | 0 | 1 | 1 | 0 | 0 |
| Justice rf | 4 | 0 | 0 | 1 | 0 | 1 | Daulton c | 3 | 0 | 0 | 0 | 1 | 1 |
| Pendleton 3b | 5 | 0 | 1 | 0 | 0 | 0 | Incaviglia lf | 4 | 1 | 2 | 1 | 0 | 1 |
| Berryhill c | 3 | 0 | 0 | 0 | 0 | 1 | Thompson pr-lf | 0 | 0 | 0 | 0 | 0 | 0 |
| Pecota ph | 0 | 1 | 0 | 0 | 1 | 0 | Chamberlain rf | 3 | 0 | 2 | 0 | 1 | 1 |
| Olson c | 1 | 0 | 1 | 0 | 0 | 0 | Williams p | 0 | 0 | 0 | 0 | 0 | 0 |
| Lemke 2b | 4 | 0 | 1 | 0 | 0 | 0 | Stocker ss | 3 | 0 | 0 | 0 | 1 | 0 |
| Tarasco pr-lf | 1 | 0 | 0 | 0 | 0 | 1 | Schilling p | 3 | 0 | 0 | 0 | 0 | 1 |
| Avery p | 2 | 1 | 2 | 0 | 0 | 0 | Eisenreich rf | 1 | 0 | 0 | 0 | 0 | 0 |
| Sanders ph | 1 | 0 | 0 | 0 | 0 | 0 | | | | | | | |
| Mercker p | 0 | 0 | 0 | 0 | 0 | 0 | | | | | | | |
| Belliard ph-2b | 0 | 0 | 0 | 0 | 0 | 0 | | | | | | | |
| **Totals** | 38 | 3 | 9 | 3 | 4 | 12 | **Totals** | 35 | 4 | 9 | 3 | 5 | 7 |

| | | |
|---|---|---|
| Atlanta | 001 100 001 0—3 | |
| Philadelphia | 100 101 000 1—4 | |

E—Batiste (1). DP—Atlanta 1. LOB—Atlanta 11, Philadelphia 8. 2B—Nixon (1), Olson (1), Avery (1), Dykstra (1), Kruk (1), Hollins (1), Chamberlain 2 (2). HR—Incaviglia (1). S—Belliard. SF—Justice.

| ATLANTA | ip | h | r | er | bb | so | PHIL. | ip | h | r | er | bb | so |
|---|---|---|---|---|---|---|---|---|---|---|---|---|---|
| Avery | 6 | 5 | 3 | 3 | 4 | 5 | Schilling | 8 | 7 | 2 | 2 | 2 | 10 |
| Mercker | 2 | 2 | 0 | 0 | 1 | 2 | Williams W | 2 | 2 | 1 | 0 | 2 | 2 |
| McMichael L | 1⅓ | 2 | 1 | 1 | 0 | 0 | | | | | | | |

WP—Avery.
Umpires: HP—Froemming.; 1B—Pulli; 2B—Tata; 3B—Quick; LF—Crawford; RF—West.
T—3:33. A—62,012.

### Game Two: October 7
### Braves 14, Phillies 3

| ATLANTA | ab | r | h | bi | bb | so | PHIL. | ab | r | h | bi | bb | so |
|---|---|---|---|---|---|---|---|---|---|---|---|---|---|
| Nixon cf | 4 | 2 | 3 | 2 | 2 | 0 | Dykstra cf | 4 | 1 | 1 | 1 | 1 | 2 |
| Wohlers p | 0 | 0 | 0 | 0 | 0 | 0 | Morandini 2b | 5 | 0 | 1 | 0 | 0 | 2 |
| Blauser ss | 5 | 1 | 2 | 1 | 0 | 1 | Kruk 1b | 3 | 1 | 2 | 0 | 1 | 0 |
| Belliard pr-ss | 1 | 1 | 0 | 0 | 0 | 1 | Hollins 3b | 3 | 1 | 1 | 2 | 1 | 0 |
| Gant lf | 5 | 1 | 2 | 3 | 0 | 1 | Daulton c | 4 | 0 | 1 | 0 | 0 | 1 |
| McGriff 1b | 5 | 2 | 3 | 2 | 0 | 1 | Andersen p | 0 | 0 | 0 | 0 | 0 | 0 |
| Stanton p | 0 | 0 | 0 | 0 | 0 | 0 | Eisenreich rf | 4 | 0 | 0 | 0 | 0 | 1 |
| Tarasco rf | 0 | 0 | 0 | 0 | 0 | 0 | Thompson lf | 4 | 0 | 0 | 0 | 0 | 0 |
| Justice rf | 3 | 1 | 0 | 0 | 2 | 0 | Stocker ss | 4 | 0 | 1 | 0 | 0 | 1 |
| Sanders cf | 0 | 0 | 0 | 0 | 0 | 0 | Greene p | 0 | 0 | 0 | 0 | 0 | 0 |
| Pendleton 3b | 5 | 2 | 3 | 3 | 0 | 1 | Thigpen p | 0 | 0 | 0 | 0 | 0 | 0 |
| Berryhill c | 5 | 1 | 1 | 3 | 0 | 2 | Longmire ph | 1 | 0 | 0 | 0 | 0 | 1 |
| Lemke 2b | 5 | 0 | 0 | 1 | 0 | 1 | Rivera p | 0 | 0 | 0 | 0 | 0 | 0 |
| Maddux p | 4 | 1 | 1 | 0 | 0 | 1 | Chamberlain ph | 1 | 0 | 0 | 0 | 0 | 1 |
| Bream 1b | 1 | 1 | 1 | 0 | 0 | 0 | Mason p | 0 | 0 | 0 | 0 | 0 | 0 |
| | | | | | | | Jordan ph | 0 | 0 | 0 | 0 | 1 | 0 |
| | | | | | | | West p | 0 | 0 | 0 | 0 | 0 | 0 |
| | | | | | | | Pratt c | 1 | 0 | 0 | 0 | 0 | 0 |
| **Totals** | 43 | 14 | 16 | 14 | 4 | 9 | **Totals** | 34 | 3 | 7 | 3 | 4 | 11 |

| | | |
|---|---|---|
| Atlanta | 206 010 041—14 | |
| Philadelphia | 000 200 001— 3 | |

E—Morandini (1), Stocker (1). LOB—Atlanta 6, Philadelphia 8. 2B—Nixon (2), Gant 2 (2). HR—Dykstra (1), Hollins (1), Blauser (1), McGriff (1), Pendleton (1), Berryhill (1). SB—Morandini (1). CS—Nixon (1).

| ATLANTA | ip | h | r | er | bb | so | PHIL. | ip | h | r | er | bb | so |
|---|---|---|---|---|---|---|---|---|---|---|---|---|---|
| Maddux W | 7 | 5 | 2 | 2 | 3 | 8 | Greene L | 2⅓ | 7 | 7 | 7 | 2 | 2 |
| Stanton | 1 | 1 | 0 | 0 | 1 | 0 | Thigpen | ⅔ | 1 | 1 | 1 | 0 | 1 |
| Wohlers | 1 | 1 | 1 | 1 | 0 | 3 | Rivera | 2 | 1 | 1 | 1 | 2 | 1 |
| | | | | | | | Mason | 2 | 1 | 0 | 0 | 0 | 1 |
| | | | | | | | West | 1 | 4 | 4 | 3 | 1 | 2 |
| | | | | | | | Andersen | 1 | 2 | 1 | 1 | 0 | 1 |

PB—Daulton.
Umpires: HP—Pulli; 1B—Tata; 2B—Quick; 3B—Crawford; LF—West; RF—Froemming.
T—3:14. A—62,436.

**Curt Schilling.** Phillies righthander never won a game in the NLCS, but was selected MVP.

DAN ARNOLD

### Game Three: October 9
### Braves 9, Phillies 4

| PHIL. | ab | r | h | bi | bb | so | ATLANTA | ab | r | h | bi | bb | so |
|---|---|---|---|---|---|---|---|---|---|---|---|---|---|
| Dykstra cf | 5 | 0 | 1 | 0 | 0 | 2 | Nixon cf | 5 | 0 | 1 | 0 | 0 | 2 |
| Duncan 2b | 5 | 2 | 2 | 0 | 0 | 1 | Blauser ss | 4 | 2 | 2 | 0 | 1 | 0 |
| Kruk 1b | 4 | 1 | 2 | 3 | 0 | 0 | Gant lf | 4 | 1 | 1 | 0 | 1 | 0 |
| Hollins 3b | 3 | 0 | 0 | 1 | 0 | 0 | McGriff 1b | 4 | 2 | 2 | 1 | 1 | 1 |
| Daulton c | 4 | 0 | 0 | 0 | 0 | 0 | Pendleton 3b | 4 | 2 | 2 | 0 | 0 | 0 |
| Incaviglia lf | 4 | 0 | 0 | 0 | 0 | 1 | Justice rf | 4 | 1 | 1 | 2 | 0 | 1 |
| Chamberlain rf | 4 | 1 | 1 | 0 | 0 | 0 | Berryhill c | 3 | 1 | 1 | 0 | 1 | 0 |
| Stocker ss | 4 | 0 | 3 | 0 | 0 | 0 | Lemke 2b | 4 | 0 | 2 | 3 | 0 | 1 |
| Mulholland p | 2 | 0 | 0 | 0 | 0 | 1 | Glavine p | 3 | 0 | 0 | 0 | 0 | 0 |
| Mason p | 0 | 0 | 0 | 0 | 0 | 1 | Cabrera ph | 1 | 0 | 0 | 0 | 0 | 1 |
| Thompson ph | 1 | 0 | 0 | 0 | 0 | 1 | Mercker p | 0 | 0 | 0 | 0 | 0 | 0 |
| Andersen p | 0 | 0 | 0 | 0 | 0 | 0 | McMichael p | 0 | 0 | 0 | 0 | 0 | 0 |
| West p | 0 | 0 | 0 | 0 | 0 | 0 | | | | | | | |
| Thigpen p | 0 | 0 | 0 | 0 | 0 | 0 | | | | | | | |
| Eisenreich ph | 1 | 0 | 1 | 1 | 0 | 0 | | | | | | | |
| **Totals** | 37 | 4 | 10 | 4 | 1 | 6 | **Totals** | 36 | 9 | 12 | 8 | 4 | 7 |

| | | |
|---|---|---|
| Philadelphia | 000 101 011—4 | |
| Atlanta | 000 005 40x—9 | |

E—Duncan (1). LOB—Philadelphia 7, Atlanta 7. 2B—Chamberlain (3), Stocker (1), Eisenreich (1), Blauser (1), Gant (3), McGriff (1), Justice (1), Lemke (1). 3B—Duncan 2 (2), Kruk (1). HR—Kruk (1). SB—Hollins (1). CS—Nixon (2).

| PHIL. | ip | h | r | er | bb | so | ATLANTA | ip | h | r | er | bb | so |
|---|---|---|---|---|---|---|---|---|---|---|---|---|---|
| Mulholland L | 5 | 9 | 5 | 4 | 1 | 2 | Glavine W | 7 | 6 | 2 | 2 | 0 | 5 |
| Mason | 1 | 0 | 0 | 0 | 0 | 0 | Mercker | 1 | 1 | 1 | 1 | 1 | 0 |
| Andersen | ⅓ | 2 | 3 | 3 | 1 | 0 | McMichael | 1 | 3 | 1 | 1 | 0 | 1 |
| West | ⅔ | 1 | 1 | 1 | 1 | 2 | | | | | | | |
| Thigpen | 1 | 0 | 0 | 1 | 0 | 2 | | | | | | | |

Mulholland pitched to one batter in 6th
Umpires: HP—Tata; 1B—Quick; 2B—Crawford; 3B—West; LF—Froemming; RF—Pulli.
T—2:44. A—52,032.

### Game Four: October 10
### Phillies 2, Braves 1

| PHIL. | ab | r | h | bi | bb | so | ATLANTA | ab | r | h | bi | bb | so |
|---|---|---|---|---|---|---|---|---|---|---|---|---|---|
| Dykstra cf | 3 | 0 | 2 | 0 | 2 | 1 | Nixon cf | 3 | 0 | 1 | 0 | 0 | 1 |
| Morandini 2b | 5 | 0 | 2 | 0 | 0 | 1 | Blauser ss | 4 | 0 | 0 | 1 | 0 | 1 |
| Kruk 1b | 5 | 0 | 0 | 0 | 0 | 4 | Gant lf | 5 | 0 | 0 | 0 | 0 | 2 |
| Hollins 3b | 4 | 0 | 1 | 0 | 1 | 3 | McGriff 1b | 4 | 1 | 2 | 0 | 0 | 1 |
| Batiste 3b | 0 | 0 | 0 | 0 | 0 | 0 | Pendleton 3b | 4 | 0 | 1 | 0 | 0 | 0 |
| Daulton c | 1 | 1 | 0 | 0 | 4 | 0 | Justice rf | 4 | 0 | 2 | 0 | 0 | 0 |
| Eisenreich rf | 5 | 0 | 1 | 0 | 0 | 1 | Olson c | 2 | 0 | 0 | 0 | 0 | 1 |
| Thompson lf | 4 | 1 | 1 | 1 | 1 | 1 | Berryhill c | 1 | 0 | 1 | 0 | 0 | 0 |
| Stocker ss | 4 | 0 | 0 | 1 | 0 | 1 | Lemke 2b | 4 | 0 | 1 | 0 | 0 | 0 |
| Jackson p | 4 | 0 | 1 | 1 | 0 | 3 | Smoltz p | 1 | 0 | 0 | 0 | 1 | 1 |
| Williams p | 0 | 0 | 0 | 0 | 0 | 0 | Mercker p | 0 | 0 | 0 | 0 | 0 | 0 |
| | | | | | | | Cabrera ph | 1 | 0 | 1 | 0 | 0 | 0 |
| | | | | | | | Sanders pr | 0 | 0 | 0 | 0 | 0 | 0 |
| | | | | | | | Wohlers p | 0 | 0 | 0 | 0 | 0 | 0 |
| | | | | | | | Pecota ph | 1 | 0 | 1 | 0 | 0 | 0 |
| **Totals** | 35 | 2 | 8 | 2 | 8 | 15 | **Totals** | 34 | 1 | 10 | 1 | 2 | 6 |

| | | |
|---|---|---|
| **Philadelphia** | | **000 200 000—2** |
| **Atlanta** | | **010 000 000—1** |

E—Williams (1), Lemke (1). DP—Philadelphia 1. LOB—Philadelphia 15, Atlanta 11. 2B—Thompson (1), McGriff (2), Pendleton (1), Lemke (2). CS—Gant (1). S—Nixon 2. SF—Stocker.

| PHIL. | ip | h | r | er | bb | so | ATLANTA | ip | h | r | er | bb | so |
|---|---|---|---|---|---|---|---|---|---|---|---|---|---|
| Jackson W | 7⅔ | 9 | 1 | 1 | 2 | 6 | Smoltz L | 6⅓ | 8 | 2 | 0 | 5 | 10 |
| Williams S | 1⅓ | 1 | 0 | 0 | 0 | 0 | Mercker | ⅔ | 0 | 0 | 0 | 0 | 0 |
| | | | | | | | Wohlers | 2 | 0 | 0 | 0 | 3 | 5 |

HBP—Olson (by Jackson). WP—Wohlers.

Umpires: HP—Quick; 1B—Crawford; 2B—West; 3B—Froemming; LF—Pulli; RF—Tata.

T—3:33. A—52,032.

### Game Five: October 11
### Phillies 4, Braves 3

| PHIL. | ab | r | h | bi | bb | so | ATLANTA | ab | r | h | bi | bb | so |
|---|---|---|---|---|---|---|---|---|---|---|---|---|---|
| Dykstra cf | 5 | 1 | 1 | 1 | 0 | 0 | Nixon cf | 4 | 0 | 0 | 0 | 1 | 1 |
| Duncan 2b | 5 | 1 | 1 | 0 | 0 | 2 | Blauser ss | 4 | 1 | 1 | 0 | 1 | 2 |
| Andersen p | 0 | 0 | 0 | 0 | 0 | 0 | Gant lf | 5 | 1 | 1 | 0 | 0 | 1 |
| Kruk 1b | 4 | 0 | 1 | 1 | 1 | 1 | McGriff 1b | 4 | 1 | 2 | 1 | 0 | 1 |
| Hollins 3b | 4 | 0 | 0 | 0 | 0 | 1 | Justice rf | 2 | 0 | 0 | 1 | 1 | 1 |
| Batiste 3b | 0 | 0 | 0 | 0 | 0 | 0 | Pendleton 3b | 4 | 0 | 1 | 0 | 0 | 1 |
| Daulton c | 3 | 1 | 2 | 1 | 1 | 1 | Berryhill c | 3 | 0 | 1 | 0 | 0 | 1 |
| Incaviglia lf | 4 | 1 | 0 | 0 | 0 | 1 | Cabrera ph-c | 1 | 0 | 1 | 1 | 0 | 0 |
| Thompson lf | 0 | 0 | 0 | 0 | 0 | 0 | Lemke 2b | 4 | 0 | 0 | 0 | 0 | 3 |
| Chamberlain rf | 3 | 0 | 1 | 1 | 0 | 1 | Avery p | 2 | 0 | 0 | 0 | 0 | 1 |
| Eisenreich rf | 0 | 0 | 0 | 0 | 0 | 0 | Mercker p | 0 | 0 | 0 | 0 | 0 | 0 |
| Stocker ss | 4 | 0 | 0 | 0 | 0 | 0 | Sanders ph | 1 | 0 | 0 | 0 | 0 | 0 |
| Schilling p | 2 | 0 | 0 | 0 | 0 | 1 | McMichael p | 0 | 0 | 0 | 0 | 0 | 0 |
| Williams p | 0 | 0 | 0 | 0 | 0 | 0 | Pecota ph | 1 | 0 | 0 | 0 | 0 | 0 |
| Morandini ph-2b | 1 | 0 | 0 | 0 | 0 | 0 | Wohlers p | 0 | 0 | 0 | 0 | 0 | 0 |
| **Totals** | **35** | **4** | **6** | **4** | **2** | **8** | **Totals** | **35** | **3** | **7** | **3** | **3** | **12** |

| | | |
|---|---|---|
| **Philadelphia** | | **100 100 001 1—4** |
| **Atlanta** | | **000 000 003 0—3** |

E—Batiste (2), Gant (1). LOB—Philadelphia 5, Atlanta 6. 2B—Kruk (2). HR—Dykstra (2). S—Schilling. SF—Chamberlain, Justice.

| PHIL. | ip | h | r | er | bb | so | ATLANTA | ip | h | r | er | bb | so |
|---|---|---|---|---|---|---|---|---|---|---|---|---|---|
| Schilling | 8 | 4 | 2 | 1 | 3 | 9 | Avery | 7 | 4 | 2 | 1 | 2 | 5 |
| Williams W | 1 | 3 | 1 | 1 | 0 | 1 | Mercker | 1 | 0 | 0 | 0 | 0 | 2 |
| Andersen S | 1 | 0 | 0 | 0 | 0 | 2 | McMichael | 1 | 1 | 1 | 1 | 0 | 0 |
| | | | | | | | Wohlers L | 1 | 1 | 1 | 1 | 0 | 1 |

Schilling pitched to two batters in 9th

WP—Avery.

Umpires: HP—Crawford; 1B—West; 2B—Froemming; 3B—Pulli; LF—Tata; RF—Quick.

T—3:21. A—52,032.

### Game Six: October 13
### Phillies 6, Braves 3

| ATLANTA | ab | r | h | bi | bb | so | PHIL. | ab | r | h | bi | bb | so |
|---|---|---|---|---|---|---|---|---|---|---|---|---|---|
| Nixon cf | 3 | 1 | 1 | 0 | 1 | 1 | Dykstra cf | 4 | 2 | 1 | 0 | 1 | 2 |
| Blauser ss | 4 | 1 | 2 | 3 | 0 | 1 | Morandini 2b | 5 | 1 | 1 | 2 | 0 | 0 |
| Gant lf | 4 | 0 | 0 | 0 | 0 | 1 | Kruk 1b | 4 | 0 | 0 | 0 | 1 | 0 |
| McGriff 1b | 1 | 0 | 0 | 0 | 3 | 1 | Hollins 3b | 2 | 1 | 1 | 2 | 2 | 0 |
| Justice rf | 4 | 0 | 0 | 0 | 0 | 0 | Batiste 3b | 0 | 0 | 0 | 0 | 0 | 0 |
| Pendleton 3b | 4 | 0 | 1 | 0 | 0 | 0 | Daulton c | 4 | 0 | 2 | 2 | 0 | 0 |
| Berryhill c | 4 | 0 | 0 | 0 | 0 | 1 | Eisenreich rf | 4 | 0 | 0 | 0 | 0 | 0 |
| Lemke 2b | 3 | 1 | 1 | 0 | 1 | 1 | Thompson lf | 4 | 1 | 2 | 0 | 0 | 0 |
| Maddux p | 0 | 0 | 0 | 0 | 0 | 0 | Stocker ss | 3 | 0 | 0 | 0 | 1 | 2 |
| Mercker p | 0 | 0 | 0 | 0 | 0 | 0 | Greene p | 0 | 1 | 0 | 0 | 1 | 0 |
| Sanders ph | 1 | 0 | 0 | 0 | 0 | 1 | Jordan ph | 1 | 0 | 0 | 0 | 0 | 0 |
| McMichael p | 0 | 0 | 0 | 0 | 0 | 0 | West p | 0 | 0 | 0 | 0 | 0 | 0 |
| Wohlers p | 0 | 0 | 0 | 0 | 0 | 0 | Williams p | 0 | 0 | 0 | 0 | 0 | 0 |
| Pecota ph | 1 | 0 | 0 | 0 | 0 | 1 | | | | | | | |
| **Totals** | **29** | **3** | **5** | **3** | **5** | **8** | **Totals** | **31** | **6** | **7** | **6** | **6** | **4** |

| | | |
|---|---|---|
| **Atlanta** | | **000 010 200—3** |
| **Philadelphia** | | **002 022 00x—6** |

E—Justice (1), Lemke (2), Maddux (1), Thompson (1). DP—Philadelphia 1. LOB—Atlanta 6, Philadelphia 9. 2B—Daulton (1). 3B—Morandini (1). HR—Blauser (2), Hollins (2). S—Maddux 2, Greene 2.

| ATLANTA | ip | h | r | er | bb | so | PHIL. | ip | h | r | er | bb | so |
|---|---|---|---|---|---|---|---|---|---|---|---|---|---|
| Maddux L | 5⅔ | 6 | 6 | 5 | 4 | 3 | Greene W | 7 | 5 | 3 | 3 | 5 | 5 |
| Mercker | ⅓ | 0 | 0 | 0 | 0 | 0 | West | 1 | 0 | 0 | 0 | 0 | 1 |
| McMichael | ⅔ | 1 | 0 | 0 | 2 | 0 | Williams S | 1 | 0 | 0 | 0 | 0 | 2 |
| Wohlers | 1⅓ | 0 | 0 | 0 | 0 | 1 | | | | | | | |

PB—Daulton. Umpires: HP—West; 1B—Froemming; 2B—Pulli; 3B—Tata; LF—Quick; RF—Crawford.

T—3:04. A—62,502.

# COMPOSITE BOX

### ATLANTA

| Player, Pos. | AVG. | G | AB | R | H | 2B | 3B | HR | RBI | BB | SO | SB |
|---|---|---|---|---|---|---|---|---|---|---|---|---|
| Sid Bream, 1b | 1.000 | 1 | 1 | 1 | 1 | 0 | 0 | 0 | 0 | 0 | 0 | 0 |
| F. Cabrera, ph-c | .667 | 3 | 3 | 0 | 2 | 0 | 0 | 0 | 1 | 0 | 1 | 0 |
| Steve Avery, p | .500 | 2 | 4 | 1 | 2 | 1 | 0 | 0 | 0 | 0 | 1 | 0 |
| Fred McGriff, 1b | .435 | 6 | 23 | 6 | 10 | 2 | 0 | 1 | 4 | 4 | 7 | 0 |
| Otis Nixon, cf | .348 | 6 | 23 | 3 | 8 | 2 | 0 | 0 | 4 | 5 | 6 | 0 |
| Terry Pendleton, 3b | .346 | 6 | 26 | 4 | 9 | 1 | 0 | 1 | 5 | 0 | 2 | 0 |
| Greg Olson, c | .333 | 2 | 3 | 0 | 1 | 1 | 0 | 0 | 0 | 0 | 1 | 0 |
| Bill Pecota, ph | .333 | 4 | 3 | 1 | 1 | 0 | 0 | 0 | 0 | 1 | 1 | 0 |
| Jeff Blauser, ss | .280 | 6 | 25 | 5 | 7 | 1 | 0 | 2 | 4 | 4 | 7 | 0 |
| Greg Maddux, p | .250 | 2 | 4 | 1 | 1 | 0 | 0 | 0 | 0 | 0 | 1 | 0 |
| Damon Berryhill, c | .211 | 6 | 19 | 2 | 4 | 0 | 0 | 1 | 3 | 1 | 5 | 0 |
| Mark Lemke, 2b | .208 | 6 | 24 | 2 | 5 | 2 | 0 | 0 | 4 | 1 | 6 | 0 |
| Ron Gant, lf | .185 | 6 | 27 | 4 | 5 | 3 | 0 | 0 | 3 | 2 | 9 | 0 |
| Dave Justice, rf | .143 | 6 | 21 | 2 | 3 | 1 | 0 | 0 | 4 | 3 | 3 | 0 |
| Tom Glavine, p | .000 | 1 | 3 | 0 | 0 | 0 | 0 | 0 | 0 | 0 | 0 | 0 |
| D. Sanders, ph-cf-pr | .000 | 5 | 3 | 0 | 0 | 0 | 0 | 0 | 0 | 0 | 1 | 0 |
| R. Belliard, ph-2b-ss | .000 | 2 | 1 | 1 | 0 | 0 | 0 | 0 | 0 | 0 | 1 | 0 |
| John Smoltz, p | .000 | 1 | 1 | 0 | 0 | 0 | 0 | 0 | 0 | 0 | 1 | 1 |
| Tony Tarasco, pr-lf-rf | .000 | 2 | 1 | 0 | 0 | 0 | 0 | 0 | 0 | 0 | 1 | 0 |
| **TOTALS** | **.274** | **6** | **215** | **33** | **59** | **14** | **0** | **5** | **32** | **22** | **54** | **0** |

| Pitcher | W | L | ERA | G | GS | SV | IP | H | R | ER | BB | SO |
|---|---|---|---|---|---|---|---|---|---|---|---|---|
| John Smoltz | 0 | 1 | 0.00 | 1 | 1 | 0 | 6⅓ | 8 | 2 | 0 | 5 | 10 |
| Mike Stanton | 0 | 0 | 0.00 | 1 | 0 | 0 | 1 | 1 | 0 | 0 | 1 | 0 |
| Kent Mercker | 0 | 0 | 1.80 | 5 | 0 | 0 | 5 | 3 | 1 | 1 | 2 | 4 |
| Tom Glavine | 1 | 0 | 2.57 | 1 | 1 | 0 | 7 | 6 | 2 | 2 | 0 | 5 |
| Steve Avery | 0 | 0 | 2.77 | 2 | 2 | 0 | 13 | 9 | 5 | 4 | 6 | 10 |
| Mark Wohlers | 0 | 1 | 3.38 | 4 | 0 | 0 | 5⅓ | 2 | 2 | 2 | 3 | 10 |
| Greg Maddux | 1 | 1 | 4.97 | 2 | 2 | 0 | 12⅔ | 11 | 8 | 7 | 7 | 11 |
| Greg McMichael | 0 | 1 | 6.75 | 4 | 0 | 0 | 4 | 7 | 3 | 3 | 2 | 1 |
| **TOTALS** | **2** | **4** | **3.15** | **6** | **6** | **0** | **54⅓** | **47** | **23** | **19** | **26** | **51** |

### PHILADELPHIA

| Player, Pos. | AVG. | G | AB | R | H | 2B | 3B | HR | RBI | BB | SO | SB |
|---|---|---|---|---|---|---|---|---|---|---|---|---|
| Kim Batiste, 3b | 1.000 | 4 | 1 | 0 | 1 | 0 | 0 | 0 | 1 | 0 | 0 | 0 |
| W. Chamberlain, rf-ph | .364 | 4 | 11 | 1 | 4 | 3 | 0 | 0 | 1 | 1 | 3 | 0 |
| Len Dykstra, cf | .280 | 6 | 25 | 5 | 7 | 1 | 0 | 2 | 2 | 5 | 8 | 0 |
| Mariano Duncan, 2b | .267 | 3 | 15 | 3 | 4 | 0 | 2 | 0 | 0 | 0 | 5 | 0 |
| Darren Daulton, c | .263 | 6 | 19 | 2 | 5 | 1 | 0 | 1 | 3 | 6 | 3 | 0 |
| Danny Jackson, p | .250 | 1 | 4 | 0 | 1 | 0 | 0 | 0 | 1 | 0 | 3 | 0 |
| John Kruk, 1b | .250 | 6 | 24 | 4 | 6 | 2 | 1 | 1 | 5 | 4 | 5 | 0 |
| M. Morandini, 2b-ph | .250 | 4 | 16 | 1 | 4 | 0 | 1 | 0 | 2 | 0 | 3 | 1 |
| M. Thompson, pr-lf-ph | .231 | 6 | 13 | 2 | 3 | 1 | 0 | 0 | 0 | 1 | 2 | 0 |
| Dave Hollins, 3b | .200 | 6 | 20 | 2 | 4 | 1 | 0 | 2 | 4 | 5 | 4 | 1 |
| Kevin Stocker, ss | .182 | 6 | 22 | 0 | 4 | 1 | 0 | 0 | 1 | 2 | 5 | 0 |
| Pete Incaviglia, lf | .167 | 3 | 12 | 2 | 2 | 0 | 0 | 1 | 1 | 0 | 3 | 0 |
| Jim Eisenreich, rf-ph | .133 | 6 | 15 | 0 | 2 | 1 | 0 | 0 | 1 | 0 | 2 | 0 |
| Curt Schilling, p | .000 | 2 | 5 | 0 | 0 | 0 | 0 | 0 | 0 | 0 | 2 | 0 |
| Terry Mulholland, p | .000 | 1 | 2 | 0 | 0 | 0 | 0 | 0 | 0 | 0 | 1 | 0 |
| Ricky Jordan, ph | .000 | 2 | 1 | 0 | 0 | 0 | 0 | 0 | 0 | 1 | 0 | 0 |
| Tony Longmire, ph | .000 | 1 | 1 | 0 | 0 | 0 | 0 | 0 | 0 | 0 | 1 | 0 |
| Todd Pratt, c | .000 | 1 | 1 | 0 | 0 | 0 | 0 | 0 | 0 | 0 | 1 | 0 |
| Tommy Greene, p | .000 | 2 | 0 | 1 | 0 | 0 | 0 | 0 | 0 | 1 | 0 | 0 |
| **TOTALS** | **.227** | **6** | **207** | **23** | **47** | **11** | **4** | **7** | **22** | **26** | **51** | **2** |

| Pitcher | W | L | ERA | G | GS | SV | IP | H | R | ER | BB | SO |
|---|---|---|---|---|---|---|---|---|---|---|---|---|
| Roger Mason | 0 | 0 | 0.00 | 2 | 0 | 0 | 3 | 1 | 0 | 0 | 0 | 2 |
| Danny Jackson | 1 | 0 | 1.17 | 1 | 1 | 0 | 7⅔ | 9 | 1 | 1 | 2 | 6 |
| Curt Schilling | 0 | 0 | 1.67 | 2 | 2 | 0 | 16 | 11 | 4 | 3 | 5 | 19 |
| Mitch Williams | 2 | 0 | 1.69 | 4 | 0 | 2 | 5⅓ | 6 | 2 | 1 | 2 | 5 |
| Ben Rivera | 0 | 0 | 4.50 | 1 | 0 | 0 | 2 | 1 | 1 | 1 | 1 | 2 |
| Bobby Thigpen | 0 | 0 | 5.40 | 2 | 0 | 0 | 1⅔ | 1 | 1 | 1 | 1 | 3 |
| Terry Mulholland | 0 | 1 | 7.20 | 1 | 1 | 0 | 5 | 9 | 5 | 4 | 1 | 2 |
| Tommy Greene | 1 | 1 | 9.64 | 2 | 2 | 0 | 9⅓ | 12 | 10 | 10 | 7 | 7 |
| David West | 0 | 0 | 13.50 | 3 | 0 | 0 | 2⅔ | 5 | 5 | 4 | 2 | 5 |
| Larry Andersen | 0 | 0 | 15.43 | 3 | 0 | 1 | 2⅓ | 4 | 4 | 4 | 1 | 3 |
| **TOTALS** | **4** | **2** | **4.75** | **6** | **6** | **3** | **55** | **59** | **33** | **29** | **22** | **54** |

| | | | | |
|---|---|---|---|---|
| **Atlanta** | **2 1 7** | **1 2 5** | **6 4 5** | **0—33** |
| **Philadelphia** | **2 0 2** | **7 2 2** | **2 1 3** | **2—23** |

**E**—Maddux, Lemke 2, Gant, Justice, Batiste 2, Duncan, Morandini, Thompson, Stocker, Mit. Williams. **DP**—Atlanta 1, Philadelphia 2. **LOB**—Atlanta 47, Philadelphia 52. **S**—Belliard, Nixon 2, Maddux 2, Schilling, Greene 2. **SF**—Justice 2, Stocker, Chamberlain. **HBP**—Olson (by Jackson). **PB**—Daulton 2. **Umpires**—Bruce Froemming, Frank Pulli, Terry Tata, Jim Quick, Jerry Crawford, Joe West.

# ORGANIZATION STATISTICS

# ATLANTA BRAVES

**Manager:** Bobby Cox.   **1993 Record:** 104-58, .642 (1st, NL West).

| BATTING | AVG | G | AB | R | H | 2B | 3B | HR | RBI | BB | SO | SB | CS | B | T | HT | WT | DOB | 1st Yr | Resides |
|---|---|---|---|---|---|---|---|---|---|---|---|---|---|---|---|---|---|---|---|---|
| Belliard, Rafael........... | .228 | 91 | 79 | 6 | 18 | 5 | 0 | 0 | 6 | 4 | 13 | 0 | 0 | R | R | 5-6 | 160 | 10-24-61 | 1980 | Boca Raton, Fla. |
| Berryhill, Damon ....... | .245 | 115 | 335 | 24 | 82 | 18 | 2 | 8 | 43 | 21 | 64 | 0 | 0 | S | R | 6-0 | 205 | 12-3-63 | 1984 | Luguna Niguel, Calif. |
| Blauser, Jeff ............. | .305 | 161 | 597 | 110 | 182 | 29 | 2 | 15 | 73 | 85 | 109 | 16 | 6 | R | R | 6-0 | 170 | 11-8-65 | 1984 | Alpharetta, Ga. |
| Bream, Sid ................ | .260 | 117 | 277 | 33 | 72 | 14 | 1 | 9 | 35 | 31 | 43 | 4 | 2 | L | L | 6-4 | 220 | 8-3-60 | 1981 | Wexford, Pa. |
| Cabrera, Francisco ..... | .241 | 70 | 83 | 8 | 20 | 3 | 0 | 4 | 11 | 8 | 21 | 0 | 0 | R | R | 6-4 | 195 | 10-10-66 | 1986 | Santo Domingo, D.R. |
| Caraballo, Ramon....... | .000 | 6 | 0 | 0 | 0 | 0 | 0 | 0 | 0 | 0 | 0 | 0 | 0 | S | R | 5-7 | 150 | 5-23-69 | 1989 | Santo Domingo, D.R. |
| Gant, Ron................. | .274 | 157 | 606 | 113 | 166 | 27 | 4 | 36 | 117 | 67 | 117 | 26 | 9 | R | R | 6-0 | 172 | 3-2-65 | 1983 | Smyrna, Ga. |
| Hunter, Brian............. | .138 | 37 | 80 | 4 | 11 | 3 | 1 | 0 | 8 | 2 | 15 | 0 | 0 | R | L | 6-0 | 195 | 3-4-68 | 1987 | Long Beach, Calif. |
| Jones, Chipper........... | .667 | 8 | 3 | 2 | 2 | 1 | 0 | 0 | 0 | 1 | 1 | 0 | 0 | S | R | 6-3 | 185 | 4-24-72 | 1990 | Pierson, Fla. |
| Justice, Dave ............ | .270 | 157 | 585 | 90 | 158 | 15 | 4 | 40 | 120 | 78 | 90 | 3 | 5 | L | L | 6-3 | 195 | 4-14-66 | 1985 | Atlanta, Ga. |
| Klesko, Ryan............. | .353 | 22 | 17 | 3 | 6 | 1 | 0 | 2 | 5 | 3 | 4 | 0 | 0 | L | L | 6-3 | 220 | 6-12-71 | 1989 | Westminster, Calif. |
| Lemke, Mark ............. | .252 | 151 | 493 | 52 | 124 | 19 | 2 | 7 | 49 | 65 | 50 | 1 | 2 | S | R | 5-9 | 167 | 8-13-65 | 1983 | Whitesboro, N.Y. |
| Lopez, Javy............... | .375 | 8 | 16 | 1 | 6 | 1 | 1 | 1 | 2 | 0 | 2 | 0 | 0 | R | R | 6-3 | 185 | 11-5-70 | 1988 | Ponce, P.R. |
| McGriff, Fred ............. | .310 | 68 | 255 | 59 | 79 | 18 | 1 | 19 | 55 | 34 | 51 | 1 | 0 | L | L | 6-3 | 215 | 10-31-63 | 1981 | Tampa, Fla. |
| 2-team (83 S.D.)...... | .291 | 151 | 557 | 111 | 162 | 29 | 2 | 37 | 101 | 76 | 106 | 5 | 3 |  |  |  |  |  |  |  |
| Nixon, Otis............... | .269 | 134 | 461 | 77 | 124 | 12 | 3 | 1 | 24 | 61 | 63 | 47 | 13 | S | R | 6-2 | 180 | 1-9-59 | 1979 | Alpharetta, Ga. |
| Olson, Greg............... | .225 | 83 | 262 | 23 | 59 | 10 | 0 | 4 | 24 | 29 | 27 | 1 | 0 | R | R | 6-0 | 200 | 9-6-60 | 1982 | Edina, Minn. |
| Pecota, Bill .............. | .323 | 72 | 62 | 17 | 20 | 2 | 1 | 0 | 5 | 2 | 5 | 1 | 1 | R | R | 6-2 | 195 | 2-16-60 | 1981 | Overland Park, Kan. |
| Pendleton, Terry ........ | .272 | 161 | 633 | 81 | 172 | 33 | 1 | 17 | 84 | 36 | 97 | 5 | 1 | S | R | 5-9 | 195 | 7-16-60 | 1982 | Duluth, Ga. |
| Sanders, Deion .......... | .276 | 95 | 272 | 42 | 75 | 18 | 6 | 6 | 28 | 16 | 42 | 19 | 7 | L | L | 6-1 | 195 | 8-9-67 | 1988 | Alpharetta, Ga. |
| Tarasco, Tony ........... | .229 | 24 | 35 | 6 | 8 | 2 | 0 | 0 | 2 | 0 | 5 | 0 | 1 | L | R | 6-1 | 205 | 12-9-70 | 1988 | Chino Hills, Calif. |

| PITCHING | W | L | ERA | G | GS | CG | SV | IP | H | R | ER | BB | SO | B | T | HT | WT | DOB | 1st Yr | Resides |
|---|---|---|---|---|---|---|---|---|---|---|---|---|---|---|---|---|---|---|---|---|
| Avery, Steve ............... | 18 | 6 | 2.94 | 35 | 35 | 3 | 0 | 223 | 216 | 81 | 73 | 43 | 125 | L | L | 6-4 | 190 | 4-14-70 | 1988 | Taylor, Mich. |
| Bedrosian, Steve ........ | 5 | 2 | 1.63 | 49 | 0 | 0 | 0 | 50 | 34 | 11 | 9 | 14 | 33 | R | R | 6-3 | 205 | 12-6-57 | 1978 | Duluth, Ga. |
| Borbon, Pedro ............ | 0 | 0 | 21.60 | 3 | 0 | 0 | 0 | 2 | 3 | 4 | 4 | 3 | 2 | L | L | 6-1 | 205 | 11-15-67 | 1988 | Texas City, Texas |
| Freeman, Marvin ......... | 2 | 0 | 6.08 | 21 | 0 | 0 | 0 | 24 | 24 | 16 | 16 | 10 | 25 | R | R | 6-7 | 222 | 4-10-63 | 1984 | Chicago, Ill. |
| Glavine, Tom .............. | 22 | 6 | 3.20 | 36 | 36 | 4 | 0 | 239 | 236 | 91 | 85 | 90 | 120 | L | L | 6-1 | 190 | 3-25-66 | 1984 | Alpharetta, Ga. |
| Howell, Jay ............... | 3 | 3 | 2.31 | 54 | 0 | 0 | 0 | 58 | 48 | 16 | 15 | 16 | 37 | R | R | 6-3 | 215 | 11-26-55 | 1976 | Cumming, Ga. |
| Maddux, Greg............. | 20 | 10 | 2.36 | 36 | 36 | 8 | 0 | 267 | 228 | 85 | 70 | 52 | 197 | R | R | 6-0 | 175 | 4-14-66 | 1984 | Las Vegas, Nev. |
| McMichael, Greg ......... | 2 | 3 | 2.06 | 74 | 0 | 0 | 19 | 92 | 68 | 22 | 21 | 29 | 89 | R | R | 6-3 | 215 | 12-1-66 | 1988 | Knoxville, Tenn. |
| Mercker, Kent ............ | 3 | 1 | 2.86 | 43 | 6 | 0 | 0 | 66 | 52 | 24 | 21 | 36 | 59 | L | L | 6-2 | 195 | 2-1-68 | 1986 | Dublin, Ohio |
| Smith, Pete ............... | 4 | 8 | 4.37 | 20 | 14 | 0 | 0 | 91 | 92 | 45 | 44 | 36 | 53 | R | R | 6-2 | 200 | 2-27-66 | 1984 | Smyrna, Ga. |
| Smoltz, John .............. | 15 | 11 | 3.62 | 35 | 35 | 3 | 0 | 244 | 208 | 104 | 98 | 100 | 208 | R | R | 6-3 | 185 | 5-15-67 | 1986 | Alpharetta, Ga. |
| Stanton, Mike ............ | 4 | 6 | 4.67 | 63 | 0 | 0 | 27 | 52 | 51 | 35 | 27 | 29 | 43 | L | L | 5-10 | 190 | 6-2-67 | 1987 | Houston, Texas |
| Wohlers, Mark ............ | 6 | 2 | 4.50 | 46 | 0 | 0 | 0 | 48 | 37 | 25 | 24 | 22 | 45 | R | R | 6-4 | 207 | 1-23-70 | 1988 | Holyoke, Mass. |

## FIELDING

| Catcher | PCT | G | PO | A | E | DP |
|---|---|---|---|---|---|---|
| Berryhill .......... | .990 | 105 | 570 | 52 | 6 | 2 |
| Cabrera ....... | 1.000 | 2 | 4 | 0 | 0 | 0 |
| Lopez ............. | .975 | 7 | 37 | 2 | 1 | 0 |
| Olson ............. | .988 | 81 | 445 | 35 | 6 | 6 |

| First Base | PCT | G | PO | A | E | DP |
|---|---|---|---|---|---|---|
| Bream............. | .996 | 90 | 627 | 62 | 3 | 62 |
| Cabrera ....... | 1.000 | 12 | 61 | 10 | 0 | 4 |
| Hunter ......... | .994 | 29 | 164 | 13 | 1 | 19 |
| Klesko .......... | 1.000 | 3 | 8 | 0 | 0 | 0 |
| McGriff........... | .992 | 66 | 563 | 45 | 5 | 52 |

| Second Base | PCT | G | PO | A | E | DP |
|---|---|---|---|---|---|---|
| Belliard ....... | .987 | 24 | 26 | 50 | 1 | 7 |
| Caraballo....... | 1.000 | 5 | 4 | 3 | 0 | 0 |
| Lemke ............ | .982 | 150 | 329 | 442 | 14 | 100 |
| Pecota ........ | 1.000 | 4 | 5 | 1 | 0 | 1 |

| Third Base | PCT | G | PO | A | E | DP |
|---|---|---|---|---|---|---|
| Pecota ........... | 1.000 | 23 | 3 | 12 | 0 | 0 |
| Pendleton...... | .959 | 161 | 128 | 319 | 19 | 32 |

| Shortstop | PCT | G | PO | A | E | DP |
|---|---|---|---|---|---|---|
| Belliard ....... | 1.000 | 58 | 27 | 49 | 0 | 11 |
| Blauser.......... | .970 | 161 | 189 | 426 | 19 | 86 |

| | PCT | G | PO | A | E | DP |
|---|---|---|---|---|---|---|
| Jones............. | 1.000 | 3 | 1 | 1 | 0 | 0 |

| Outfield | PCT | G | PO | A | E | DP |
|---|---|---|---|---|---|---|
| Gant ................ | .962 | 155 | 271 | 5 | 11 | 1 |
| Hunter .......... | 1.000 | 2 | 4 | 0 | 0 | 0 |
| Justice ........... | .985 | 157 | 323 | 9 | 5 | 2 |
| Klesko ........... | .000 | 2 | 0 | 0 | 0 | 0 |
| Nixon ............. | .990 | 116 | 308 | 4 | 3 | 1 |
| Pecota ........... | 1.000 | 1 | 1 | 0 | 0 | 0 |
| Sanders.......... | .986 | 60 | 137 | 1 | 2 | 1 |
| Tarasco ......... | 1.000 | 12 | 11 | 0 | 0 | 0 |

# BRAVES FARM SYSTEM

| Class | Club | League | W | L | Pct. | Finish* | Manager | First Year |
|---|---|---|---|---|---|---|---|---|
| AAA | Richmond (Va.) Braves | International | 80 | 62 | .563 | 2nd (10) | Grady Little | 1966 |
| AA | Greenville (S.C.) Braves | Southern | 75 | 67 | .528 | 2nd (10) | Bruce Kimm | 1984 |
| A# | Durham (N.C.) Bulls | Carolina | 69 | 69 | .500 | 5th (8) | Leon Roberts | 1980 |
| A | Macon (Ga.) Braves | South Atlantic | 74 | 67 | .525 | 6th (14) | Randy Ingle | 1991 |
| Rookie# | Danville (Va.) Braves | Appalachian | 38 | 30 | .559 | 3rd (10) | Bruce Benedict | 1993 |
| Rookie# | Idaho Falls (Idaho) Braves | Pioneer | 36 | 40 | .474 | 6th (8) | Paul Runge | 1986 |
| Rookie | West Palm Beach (Fla.) Braves | Gulf Coast | 32 | 26 | .552 | 4th (15) | Jim Saul | 1976 |

*Finish in overall standings (No. of teams in league)   #Advanced level

**Jeff Blauser.** Braves shortstop had an all-star season, hitting .305 and scoring 110 runs.

**Tom Glavine.** Braves lefthander won 22 games, the third year in a row he has reached 20 victories.

# RICHMOND AAA
## INTERNATIONAL LEAGUE

| BATTING | AVG | G | AB | R | H | 2B | 3B | HR | RBI | BB | SO | SB | CS | B | T | HT | WT | DOB | 1st Yr | Resides |
|---|---|---|---|---|---|---|---|---|---|---|---|---|---|---|---|---|---|---|---|---|
| Caraballo, Ramon | .272 | 126 | 470 | 73 | 128 | 25 | 9 | 3 | 41 | 30 | 81 | 20 | 14 | S | R | 5-7 | 150 | 5-23-69 | 1989 | Santo Domingo, D.R. |
| Houston, Tyler | .139 | 13 | 36 | 4 | 5 | 1 | 1 | 1 | 3 | 1 | 8 | 0 | 0 | L | R | 6-2 | 210 | 1-17-71 | 1989 | Las Vegas, Nev. |
| Hunter, Brian | .242 | 30 | 99 | 16 | 24 | 7 | 0 | 6 | 26 | 10 | 21 | 4 | 2 | R | L | 6-0 | 195 | 3-4-68 | 1987 | Long Beach, Calif. |
| Jones, Barry | .167 | 11 | 30 | 1 | 5 | 0 | 0 | 0 | 4 | 2 | 6 | 0 | 0 | L | R | 6-2 | 197 | 2-14-65 | 1984 | Walker Springs, Ala. |
| Jones, Chipper | .325 | 139 | 536 | 97 | 174 | 31 | 12 | 13 | 89 | 57 | 70 | 23 | 8 | S | R | 6-3 | 185 | 4-24-72 | 1990 | Pierson, Fla. |
| Jones, Ron | .291 | 79 | 203 | 25 | 59 | 9 | 0 | 10 | 41 | 25 | 29 | 0 | 1 | L | R | 5-10 | 200 | 6-11-64 | 1985 | Seguin, Texas |
| Kelly, Mike | .243 | 123 | 424 | 63 | 103 | 13 | 1 | 19 | 58 | 36 | 109 | 11 | 7 | R | R | 6-4 | 195 | 6-2-70 | 1991 | Los Alamitos, Calif. |
| Klesko, Ryan | .274 | 98 | 343 | 59 | 94 | 14 | 2 | 22 | 74 | 47 | 69 | 4 | 3 | L | L | 6-3 | 220 | 6-12-71 | 1989 | Westminster, Calif. |
| Kowitz, Brian | .267 | 12 | 45 | 10 | 12 | 1 | 3 | 0 | 8 | 5 | 8 | 1 | 0 | L | L | 5-10 | 175 | 8-17-69 | 1990 | Owings Mills, Md. |
| Lopez, Javy | .305 | 100 | 380 | 56 | 116 | 23 | 2 | 17 | 74 | 12 | 53 | 1 | 6 | R | R | 6-3 | 185 | 11-5-70 | 1988 | Ponce, P.R. |
| Mitchell, Keith | .232 | 110 | 353 | 59 | 82 | 23 | 1 | 4 | 44 | 44 | 48 | 9 | 5 | R | R | 5-10 | 180 | 8-6-69 | 1987 | San Diego, Calif. |
| Moore, Bobby | .667 | 1 | 3 | 2 | 2 | 0 | 0 | 0 | 0 | 1 | 0 | 1 | 0 | R | R | 5-11 | 165 | 10-27-65 | 1987 | Cincinnati, Ohio |
| Mordecai, Mike | .268 | 72 | 205 | 29 | 55 | 8 | 1 | 2 | 14 | 14 | 33 | 10 | 2 | R | R | 5-11 | 175 | 12-13-67 | 1989 | Birmingham, Ala. |
| Nieves, Melvin | .278 | 78 | 273 | 38 | 76 | 10 | 3 | 10 | 36 | 25 | 84 | 4 | 3 | S | R | 6-2 | 186 | 12-28-71 | 1988 | Bayamon, P.R. |
| Oliva, Jose | .235 | 125 | 412 | 63 | 97 | 20 | 6 | 21 | 65 | 35 | 134 | 1 | 5 | R | R | 6-1 | 150 | 3-3-71 | 1988 | San Pedro de Macoris, D.R. |
| Rodriguez, Boi | .267 | 88 | 236 | 34 | 63 | 13 | 1 | 10 | 22 | 26 | 55 | 4 | 1 | L | R | 6-0 | 165 | 4-14-66 | 1987 | Dorado Beach, P.R. |
| Tarasco, Tony | .330 | 93 | 370 | 73 | 122 | 15 | 7 | 15 | 53 | 36 | 54 | 19 | 11 | L | R | 6-1 | 205 | 12-9-70 | 1988 | Chino Hills, Calif. |
| Willard, Jerry | .319 | 107 | 317 | 37 | 101 | 21 | 0 | 8 | 44 | 60 | 63 | 0 | 0 | L | R | 6-2 | 195 | 3-14-60 | 1980 | Port Hueneme, Calif. |

| PITCHING | W | L | ERA | G | GS | CG | SV | IP | H | R | ER | BB | SO | B | T | HT | WT | DOB | 1st Yr | Resides |
|---|---|---|---|---|---|---|---|---|---|---|---|---|---|---|---|---|---|---|---|---|
| Bark, Brian | 12 | 9 | 3.67 | 29 | 28 | 1 | 0 | 162 | 153 | 81 | 66 | 72 | 110 | L | L | 5-9 | 160 | 8-26-68 | 1990 | Randallstown, Md. |
| Birkbeck, Mike | 13 | 8 | 3.11 | 27 | 26 | 1 | 0 | 159 | 143 | 67 | 55 | 41 | 136 | R | R | 6-2 | 190 | 3-10-61 | 1983 | Canton, Ohio |
| Borbon, Pedro | 5 | 5 | 4.23 | 52 | 0 | 0 | 1 | 77 | 71 | 40 | 36 | 42 | 95 | L | L | 6-1 | 205 | 11-15-67 | 1988 | Texas City, Texas |
| Burlingame, Dennis | 2 | 0 | 4.91 | 6 | 1 | 0 | 0 | 15 | 12 | 9 | 8 | 14 | 5 | R | R | 6-4 | 200 | 6-17-69 | 1988 | Mullica Hill, N.J. |
| Elliott, Donnie | 8 | 5 | 4.72 | 18 | 18 | 1 | 0 | 103 | 108 | 65 | 54 | 39 | 99 | R | R | 6-4 | 190 | 9-20-68 | 1988 | Deer Park, Texas |
| Freeman, Marvin | 0 | 0 | 2.25 | 2 | 2 | 0 | 0 | 4 | 4 | 1 | 1 | 1 | 5 | R | R | 6-7 | 222 | 4-10-63 | 1984 | Chicago, Ill. |
| Holman, Shawn | 12 | 7 | 4.18 | 37 | 22 | 0 | 0 | 155 | 174 | 88 | 72 | 46 | 101 | R | R | 6-1 | 200 | 11-10-64 | 1982 | Sewickley, Pa. |
| Hostetler, Mike | 1 | 3 | 5.06 | 9 | 9 | 0 | 0 | 48 | 50 | 29 | 27 | 18 | 36 | R | R | 6-2 | 195 | 6-5-70 | 1991 | Marietta, Ga. |
| Johnson, Judd | 4 | 2 | 2.65 | 49 | 2 | 0 | 0 | 85 | 85 | 28 | 25 | 22 | 55 | R | L | 6-0 | 185 | 5-4-66 | 1988 | Peebles, Ohio |
| Lovelace, Vance | 0 | 0 | 5.00 | 5 | 0 | 0 | 0 | 9 | 10 | 5 | 5 | 6 | 7 | L | L | 6-5 | 235 | 8-9-63 | 1981 | Tampa, Fla. |
| Loynd, Mike | 8 | 5 | 3.85 | 18 | 18 | 1 | 0 | 108 | 98 | 53 | 46 | 34 | 85 | R | R | 6-4 | 210 | 3-26-64 | 1986 | North Palm Beach, Fla. |
| Polley, Dale | 1 | 0 | 3.93 | 10 | 0 | 0 | 0 | 18 | 21 | 9 | 8 | 11 | 14 | R | L | 6-0 | 165 | 8-9-65 | 1987 | Frankfort, Ky. |
| Reyes, Carlos | 1 | 0 | 3.77 | 18 | 1 | 0 | 1 | 29 | 30 | 12 | 12 | 11 | 30 | S | R | 6-1 | 190 | 4-19-69 | 1991 | Macon, Ga. |
| Robinson, Nap | 4 | 6 | 4.88 | 19 | 6 | 0 | 0 | 52 | 55 | 31 | 28 | 25 | 42 | R | R | 6-3 | 195 | 1-26-66 | 1988 | Smyrna, Ga. |
| St.Claire, Randy | 0 | 0 | 2.79 | 8 | 0 | 0 | 0 | 10 | 14 | 6 | 3 | 2 | 3 | R | R | 6-3 | 190 | 8-23-60 | 1979 | Whitehall, N.Y. |
| Strange, Don | 1 | 2 | 3.88 | 34 | 0 | 0 | 1 | 46 | 45 | 24 | 20 | 19 | 34 | R | R | 6-0 | 195 | 5-26-67 | 1989 | Springfield, Mass. |
| Taylor, Billy | 2 | 4 | 1.98 | 59 | 0 | 0 | 26 | 68 | 56 | 19 | 15 | 26 | 81 | R | R | 6-8 | 200 | 10-16-61 | 1980 | Thomasville, Ga. |
| Wohlers, Mark | 1 | 3 | 1.84 | 25 | 0 | 0 | 4 | 29 | 21 | 7 | 6 | 11 | 39 | R | R | 6-4 | 207 | 1-23-70 | 1988 | Holyoke, Mass. |
| Woodall, Brad | 5 | 3 | 4.21 | 10 | 9 | 0 | 0 | 58 | 59 | 32 | 27 | 16 | 45 | S | L | 6-0 | 175 | 6-25-69 | 1991 | Columbia, S.C. |

# BRAVES: ORGANIZATION LEADERS

## MAJOR LEAGUERS

**BATTING**

| | | |
|---|---|---|
| *AVG | Fred McGriff | .310 |
| R | Ron Gant | 113 |
| H | Jeff Blauser | 182 |
| TB | Ron Gant | 309 |
| 2B | Terry Pendleton | 33 |
| 3B | Deion Sanders | 6 |
| HR | Dave Justice | 40 |
| RBI | Dave Justice | 120 |
| BB | Jeff Blauser | 85 |
| SO | Ron Gant | 117 |
| SB | Otis Nixon | 47 |

**PITCHING**

| | | |
|---|---|---|
| W | Tom Glavine | 22 |
| L | John Smoltz | 11 |
| #ERA | Greg Maddux | 2.36 |
| G | Greg McMichael | 74 |
| CG | Greg Maddux | 8 |
| SV | Mike Stanton | 27 |
| IP | Greg Maddux | 267 |
| BB | John Smoltz | 100 |
| SO | John Smoltz | 208 |

MORRIS FOSTOFF

**Greg McMichael**
Rookie appeared in 74 games

## MINOR LEAGUERS

**BATTING**

| | | |
|---|---|---|
| *AVG | Tony Tarasco, Richmond | .330 |
| R | Chipper Jones, Richmond | 97 |
| H | Chipper Jones, Richmond | 174 |
| TB | Chipper Jones, Richmond | 268 |
| 2B | Jose Olmeda, Greenville | 33 |
| 3B | Chipper Jones, Richmond | 12 |
| HR | Ryan Klesko, Richmond | 22 |
| RBI | Chipper Jones, Richmond | 89 |
| BB | Ed Giovanola, Greenville | 84 |
| SO | Jose Oliva, Richmond | 134 |
| SB | Mike Warner, Durham-Greenville | 31 |

**PITCHING**

| | | |
|---|---|---|
| W | Darrell May, Macon-Durham | 15 |
| L | Blase Sparma, Greenville | 12 |
| #ERA | Darrell May, Macon-Durham | 2.19 |
| G | Don Strange, Richmond-Greenville | 61 |
| CG | Matt Murray, Macon | 3 |
| SV | Billy Taylor, Richmond | 26 |
| IP | Mike Hostetler, Greenville-Richmond | 184 |
| BB | Mike Potts, Greenville | 86 |
| SO | Terrell Wade, Macon-Durham-G'ville | 208 |

*Minimum 250 At-Bats  #Minimum 75 Innings

## FIELDING

| Catcher | PCT | G | PO | A | E | DP |
|---|---|---|---|---|---|---|
| Houston | .959 | 12 | 69 | 2 | 3 | 1 |
| Lopez | .987 | 96 | 718 | 70 | 10 | 8 |
| Mordecai | 1.000 | 3 | 2 | 0 | 0 | 0 |
| Willard | .993 | 47 | 254 | 25 | 2 | 3 |

| First Base | PCT | G | PO | A | E | DP |
|---|---|---|---|---|---|---|
| Hunter | 1.000 | 22 | 165 | 15 | 0 | 14 |
| Klesko | .985 | 66 | 569 | 42 | 9 | 60 |
| Mordecai | 1.000 | 1 | 8 | 1 | 0 | 1 |
| Rodriguez | .984 | 35 | 281 | 20 | 5 | 25 |
| Willard | .982 | 34 | 248 | 23 | 5 | 17 |

| Second Base | PCT | G | PO | A | E | DP |
|---|---|---|---|---|---|---|
| Caraballo | .960 | 121 | 211 | 345 | 23 | 64 |

| | PCT | G | PO | A | E | DP |
|---|---|---|---|---|---|---|
| Mordecai | .973 | 27 | 62 | 83 | 4 | 25 |
| **Third Base** | **PCT** | **G** | **PO** | **A** | **E** | **DP** |
| Mordecai | .900 | 15 | 3 | 24 | 3 | 0 |
| Oliva | .929 | 121 | 44 | 205 | 19 | 13 |
| Rodriguez | .881 | 24 | 3 | 34 | 5 | 3 |
| **Shortstop** | **PCT** | **G** | **PO** | **A** | **E** | **DP** |
| C.Jones | .931 | 129 | 195 | 381 | 43 | 74 |
| Mordecai | .966 | 17 | 19 | 37 | 2 | 11 |
| Oliva | 1.000 | 1 | 0 | 1 | 0 | 0 |
| **Outfield** | **PCT** | **G** | **PO** | **A** | **E** | **DP** |
| Caraballo | .000 | 1 | 0 | 0 | 0 | 0 |

| | PCT | G | PO | A | E | DP |
|---|---|---|---|---|---|---|
| Hunter | 1.000 | 5 | 9 | 0 | 0 | 0 |
| B. Jones | .933 | 14 | 0 | 1 | 0 | 0 |
| R. Jones | 1.000 | 23 | 25 | 1 | 0 | 0 |
| Kelly | .993 | 117 | 270 | 6 | 2 | 1 |
| Klesko | .875 | 18 | 18 | 3 | 3 | 0 |
| Kowitz | .955 | 12 | 20 | 1 | 1 | 0 |
| Mitchell | .960 | 102 | 138 | 7 | 6 | 1 |
| Moore | 1.000 | 1 | 1 | 0 | 0 | 0 |
| Mordecai | 1.000 | 7 | 4 | 0 | 0 | 0 |
| Nieves | .949 | 68 | 124 | 5 | 7 | 1 |
| Tarasco | .987 | 92 | 143 | 8 | 2 | 3 |

# GREENVILLE                                                          AA

## SOUTHERN LEAGUE

**BATTING**

| | AVG | G | AB | R | H | 2B | 3B | HR | RBI | BB | SO | SB | CS | B | T | HT | WT | DOB | 1st Yr | Resides |
|---|---|---|---|---|---|---|---|---|---|---|---|---|---|---|---|---|---|---|---|---|
| Alicea, Edwin, 2b-of | .065 | 14 | 31 | 5 | 2 | 0 | 0 | 0 | 2 | 5 | 9 | 1 | 0 | S | R | 5-10 | 175 | 3-9-67 | 1988 | Guaynabo, P.R. |
| Bradley, Scott, c-1b | .333 | 26 | 57 | 6 | 19 | 2 | 0 | 1 | 11 | 5 | 8 | 0 | 0 | L | R | 5-11 | 185 | 3-22-60 | 1981 | Redmond, Wash. |
| Gillis, Tim, 1b-3b | .251 | 135 | 451 | 58 | 113 | 22 | 3 | 14 | 62 | 51 | 103 | 1 | 6 | R | R | 6-2 | 195 | 2-9-68 | 1990 | Crestview, Fla. |
| Giovanola, Ed, 3b-2b | .281 | 120 | 384 | 70 | 108 | 21 | 5 | 5 | 43 | 84 | 49 | 6 | 7 | L | R | 5-10 | 175 | 3-4-69 | 1990 | San Jose, Calif. |
| Heath, Lee, of | .243 | 112 | 432 | 47 | 105 | 15 | 6 | 6 | 36 | 23 | 108 | 16 | 18 | S | R | 5-10 | 170 | 12-26-69 | 1988 | Cincinnati, Ohio |
| Houston, Tyler, c-dh | .279 | 84 | 262 | 27 | 73 | 14 | 1 | 5 | 33 | 13 | 50 | 5 | 3 | L | R | 6-2 | 210 | 1-17-71 | 1989 | Las Vegas, Nev. |
| Hughes, Troy, of | .266 | 109 | 383 | 49 | 102 | 20 | 4 | 14 | 59 | 44 | 67 | 7 | 3 | R | R | 6-4 | 195 | 1-3-71 | 1989 | Mt. Vernon, Ill. |
| Kelly, Pat, inf | .255 | 72 | 212 | 23 | 54 | 10 | 1 | 0 | 17 | 14 | 30 | 2 | 3 | R | R | 5-11 | 175 | 1-22-67 | 1988 | Waukegan, Ill. |
| Kowitz, Brian, of | .278 | 122 | 450 | 63 | 125 | 20 | 5 | 5 | 48 | 60 | 56 | 13 | 10 | L | L | 5-10 | 175 | 8-17-69 | 1990 | Owings Mills, Md. |
| O'Connor, Kevin, of-1b | .189 | 122 | 355 | 63 | 67 | 15 | 2 | 7 | 30 | 62 | 63 | 18 | 10 | L | R | 6-0 | 180 | 6-8-69 | 1990 | Huntington Beach, Calif. |
| Olmeda, Jose, 2b-ss | .279 | 122 | 451 | 61 | 126 | 33 | 2 | 9 | 51 | 29 | 63 | 15 | 7 | S | R | 5-9 | 155 | 6-20-68 | 1989 | San Lorenzo, P.R. |
| Perez, Eddie, 1b-c | .333 | 28 | 84 | 15 | 28 | 6 | 0 | 6 | 17 | 2 | 8 | 1 | 0 | R | R | 6-1 | 210 | 5-4-68 | 1987 | Maracaibo, Venez. |
| Rippelmeyer, Brad, c | .191 | 95 | 277 | 25 | 53 | 14 | 0 | 4 | 27 | 31 | 74 | 0 | 2 | R | R | 6-2 | 190 | 2-6-70 | 1991 | Valmeyer, Ill. |
| Roa, Hector, ss | .246 | 123 | 447 | 50 | 110 | 28 | 4 | 6 | 58 | 24 | 72 | 6 | 7 | R | R | 5-10 | 145 | 6-11-69 | 1988 | Santo Domingo, D.R. |
| Sanchez, Ozzie, of-dh | .220 | 33 | 100 | 8 | 22 | 3 | 0 | 4 | 13 | 12 | 28 | 2 | 0 | L | L | 6-2 | 175 | 12-24-69 | 1987 | Caguas, P.R. |
| Swann, Pedro, of-dh | .306 | 44 | 157 | 19 | 48 | 9 | 2 | 3 | 21 | 9 | 23 | 2 | 2 | L | R | 6-0 | 195 | 10-27-70 | 1991 | Townsend, Del. |
| Warner, Mike, of | .350 | 5 | 20 | 4 | 7 | 0 | 2 | 0 | 3 | 2 | 4 | 2 | 1 | L | L | 5-9 | 170 | 5-9-71 | 1992 | Palm Beach Gardens, Fla. |

**PITCHING**

| | W | L | ERA | G | GS | CG | SV | IP | H | R | ER | BB | SO | B | T | HT | WT | DOB | 1st Yr | Resides |
|---|---|---|---|---|---|---|---|---|---|---|---|---|---|---|---|---|---|---|---|---|
| Boltz, Brian | 1 | 2 | 3.23 | 9 | 8 | 0 | 0 | 39 | 36 | 15 | 14 | 17 | 22 | L | L | 6-2 | 195 | 10-13-68 | 1989 | Salisbury, N.C. |
| Burlingame, Dennis | 4 | 4 | 5.00 | 15 | 12 | 0 | 0 | 67 | 76 | 52 | 37 | 37 | 35 | R | R | 6-4 | 200 | 6-17-69 | 1988 | Mullica Hill, N.J. |
| Hassinger, Brad | 3 | 1 | 1.57 | 12 | 0 | 0 | 0 | 23 | 19 | 4 | 4 | 8 | 11 | R | R | 6-0 | 195 | 11-29-67 | 1990 | Berrysburg, Pa. |
| Hostetler, Mike | 8 | 5 | 2.72 | 19 | 19 | 2 | 0 | 136 | 122 | 48 | 41 | 36 | 105 | R | R | 6-2 | 195 | 6-5-70 | 1991 | Marietta, Ga. |
| Lomon, Kevin | 3 | 4 | 3.86 | 13 | 13 | 1 | 0 | 79 | 76 | 41 | 34 | 31 | 68 | R | R | 6-1 | 195 | 11-20-71 | 1991 | Cameron, Okla. |
| Lovelace, Vance | 2 | 0 | 1.65 | 11 | 0 | 0 | 0 | 16 | 10 | 4 | 3 | 12 | 21 | L | L | 6-5 | 235 | 8-9-63 | 1981 | Tampa, Fla. |
| Polley, Dale | 4 | 4 | 4.12 | 42 | 0 | 0 | 2 | 59 | 44 | 28 | 27 | 21 | 66 | L | L | 6-0 | 165 | 9-9-65 | 1987 | Frankfort, Ky. |
| Potts, Mike | 7 | 6 | 3.88 | 25 | 25 | 1 | 0 | 142 | 131 | 79 | 61 | 86 | 116 | L | L | 5-9 | 165 | 9-5-70 | 1991 | Lithonia, Ga. |
| Reyes, Carlos | 8 | 1 | 2.06 | 33 | 2 | 0 | 2 | 70 | 64 | 22 | 16 | 24 | 57 | S | R | 6-1 | 190 | 4-19-69 | 1991 | Macon, Ga. |
| Ritter, Darren | 4 | 6 | 6.06 | 35 | 3 | 0 | 3 | 65 | 81 | 48 | 44 | 26 | 49 | R | R | 6-5 | 220 | 2-20-68 | 1989 | Baltimore, Md. |
| Schutz, Carl | 2 | 1 | 5.06 | 22 | 0 | 0 | 3 | 21 | 17 | 17 | 12 | 22 | 19 | L | L | 5-11 | 200 | 8-22-71 | 1993 | Paulina, La. |
| Sparma, Blase | 5 | 12 | 4.85 | 28 | 27 | 1 | 0 | 150 | 170 | 95 | 81 | 68 | 97 | R | R | 6-2 | 185 | 7-6-70 | 1991 | Dublin, Ohio |
| Strange, Don | 1 | 1 | 3.65 | 17 | 0 | 0 | 18 | 25 | 27 | 11 | 10 | 9 | 27 | R | R | 6-0 | 195 | 5-26-67 | 1989 | Springfield, Mass. |
| Upshaw, Lee | 9 | 9 | 3.29 | 34 | 14 | 0 | 2 | 120 | 109 | 49 | 44 | 56 | 99 | L | L | 6-5 | 210 | 12-30-66 | 1988 | Lithonia, Ga. |
| Vasquez, Marcos | 4 | 5 | 4.61 | 43 | 4 | 0 | 3 | 82 | 96 | 47 | 42 | 37 | 61 | R | R | 5-10 | 170 | 11-5-68 | 1987 | Rio Piedras, P.R. |
| Wade, Terrell | 2 | 1 | 3.21 | 8 | 8 | 1 | 0 | 42 | 32 | 16 | 15 | 29 | 40 | L | L | 6-3 | 204 | 1-25-73 | 1991 | Rembert, S.C. |
| Williams, Dave | 2 | 4 | 4.15 | 45 | 0 | 0 | 3 | 56 | 51 | 29 | 26 | 27 | 35 | R | R | 6-1 | 210 | 7-12-69 | 1990 | Marked Tree, Ark. |
| Woodall, Brad | 2 | 4 | 3.38 | 8 | 7 | 1 | 0 | 53 | 43 | 24 | 20 | 14 | 38 | S | L | 6-0 | 175 | 6-25-69 | 1991 | Columbia, S.C. |

# DURHAM  A
## CAROLINA LEAGUE

| BATTING | AVG | G | AB | R | H | 2B | 3B | HR | RBI | BB | SO | SB | CS | B | T | HT | WT | DOB | 1st Yr | Resides |
|---|---|---|---|---|---|---|---|---|---|---|---|---|---|---|---|---|---|---|---|---|
| Ayrault, Joe, c | .254 | 119 | 390 | 45 | 99 | 21 | 0 | 6 | 52 | 23 | 103 | 1 | 4 | R | R | 6-3 | 210 | 10-8-71 | 1990 | Sarasota, Fla. |
| Coates, Tom, of | .267 | 93 | 221 | 31 | 59 | 10 | 3 | 7 | 24 | 28 | 63 | 8 | 4 | R | R | 5-10 | 190 | 9-11-68 | 1991 | Lexington, Ky. |
| Graffanino, Tony, 2b | .275 | 123 | 459 | 78 | 126 | 30 | 5 | 15 | 69 | 45 | 78 | 24 | 11 | R | R | 6-1 | 175 | 6-6-72 | 1990 | Clemson, S.C. |
| Jimenez, Manny, ss | .225 | 127 | 427 | 55 | 96 | 16 | 4 | 6 | 29 | 21 | 93 | 7 | 9 | R | R | 5-11 | 175 | 7-4-70 | 1991 | Pueblo Nuevo Mao, D.R. |
| Kelly, Pat, 3b-2b | .281 | 35 | 128 | 27 | 36 | 6 | 0 | 1 | 12 | 13 | 19 | 5 | 4 | R | R | 5-11 | 175 | 1-22-67 | 1989 | Waukegan, Ill. |
| Marks, Lance, 1b | .213 | 113 | 385 | 55 | 82 | 21 | 2 | 10 | 56 | 40 | 111 | 6 | 5 | R | R | 6-1 | 195 | 8-12-71 | 1990 | Laguna Niguel, Calif. |
| Moore, Vince, of | .292 | 87 | 319 | 53 | 93 | 14 | 1 | 14 | 64 | 29 | 93 | 21 | 8 | L | L | 5-11 | 177 | 9-22-71 | 1991 | Houston, Texas |
| Robinson, Don, of | .228 | 117 | 390 | 52 | 89 | 11 | 3 | 10 | 47 | 45 | 112 | 15 | 9 | L | R | 6-0 | 185 | 1-16-72 | 1990 | Haynesville, La. |
| Sanchez, Ozzie, dh-1b | .243 | 14 | 37 | 8 | 9 | 2 | 0 | 2 | 5 | 11 | 8 | 0 | 0 | L | L | 6-2 | 175 | 12-24-69 | 1987 | Caguas, P.R. |
| Swail, Steve, c | .263 | 48 | 133 | 16 | 35 | 6 | 0 | 1 | 12 | 12 | 39 | 1 | 3 | R | R | 6-4 | 215 | 4-28-67 | 1989 | Somerset, Ky. |
| Swann, Pedro, dh-of | .346 | 61 | 182 | 27 | 63 | 8 | 2 | 6 | 27 | 19 | 38 | 6 | 12 | L | R | 6-0 | 195 | 10-27-70 | 1991 | Townsend, Del. |
| Therrien, Dom, 3b | .300 | 117 | 387 | 53 | 116 | 26 | 3 | 6 | 55 | 34 | 49 | 10 | 7 | L | R | 5-9 | 195 | 6-9-72 | 1991 | Cap-de-la-Madeleine, Que. |
| Waldrop, Tom, of | .441 | 11 | 34 | 9 | 15 | 5 | 0 | 1 | 3 | 4 | 8 | 0 | 1 | L | L | 6-3 | 195 | 1-10-70 | 1992 | Decatur, Ill. |
| Warner, Mike, of | .319 | 77 | 263 | 55 | 84 | 18 | 4 | 5 | 32 | 50 | 45 | 29 | 12 | L | L | 5-9 | 170 | 5-9-71 | 1992 | Palm Beach Gardens, Fla. |
| Williams, Juan, of | .231 | 124 | 403 | 49 | 93 | 16 | 2 | 11 | 44 | 36 | 120 | 11 | 12 | L | R | 6-0 | 180 | 10-9-72 | 1990 | Riverside, Calif. |
| Wollenburg, Doug, 1b | .299 | 113 | 361 | 49 | 108 | 21 | 4 | 5 | 42 | 27 | 61 | 6 | 7 | R | R | 6-4 | 205 | 10-11-70 | 1992 | Newark, Ohio |
| Zimmerman, Phil, 3b-ss | .208 | 39 | 72 | 9 | 15 | 3 | 0 | 0 | 1 | 7 | 20 | 1 | 0 | R | R | 6-0 | 170 | 12-30-69 | 1992 | Denver, Colo. |

| PITCHING | W | L | ERA | G | GS | CG | SV | IP | H | R | ER | BB | SO | B | T | HT | WT | DOB | 1st Yr | Resides |
|---|---|---|---|---|---|---|---|---|---|---|---|---|---|---|---|---|---|---|---|---|
| Blair, Dirk | 4 | 5 | 3.21 | 44 | 0 | 0 | 12 | 81 | 78 | 32 | 29 | 17 | 69 | R | R | 6-3 | 215 | 5-19-69 | 1991 | Durant, Okla. |
| Boltz, Brian | 3 | 0 | 3.67 | 15 | 5 | 0 | 1 | 42 | 35 | 21 | 17 | 11 | 27 | L | L | 6-2 | 195 | 10-13-68 | 1989 | Salisbury, N.C. |
| Brock, Chris | 5 | 2 | 2.51 | 12 | 12 | 1 | 0 | 79 | 63 | 28 | 22 | 35 | 67 | R | R | 6-1 | 180 | 2-5-71 | 1992 | Altamonte Springs, Fla. |
| Burgess, Kurt | 6 | 5 | 4.40 | 48 | 0 | 0 | 5 | 76 | 84 | 40 | 37 | 20 | 61 | L | L | 6-0 | 175 | 6-10-69 | 1991 | Tulsa, Okla. |
| Chiles, Barry | 1 | 0 | 5.03 | 14 | 2 | 0 | 0 | 34 | 31 | 21 | 19 | 10 | 10 | R | R | 6-3 | 195 | 1-6-71 | 1989 | Jupiter, Fla. |
| Clontz, Brad | 1 | 7 | 2.75 | 51 | 0 | 0 | 10 | 75 | 69 | 32 | 23 | 26 | 79 | R | R | 6-1 | 180 | 4-25-71 | 1992 | Patrick Spring, Va. |
| Hassinger, Brad | 4 | 1 | 2.08 | 14 | 0 | 0 | 0 | 30 | 20 | 12 | 7 | 4 | 25 | R | R | 6-0 | 195 | 11-29-67 | 1990 | Berrysburg, Pa. |
| Koller, Jerry | 8 | 10 | 4.57 | 27 | 26 | 1 | 0 | 158 | 168 | 91 | 80 | 47 | 102 | R | R | 6-3 | 190 | 6-30-72 | 1990 | Martinsville, Ind. |
| Leahy, Tom | 1 | 7 | 5.28 | 28 | 0 | 0 | 4 | 44 | 40 | 30 | 26 | 24 | 36 | R | R | 6-2 | 190 | 11-2-69 | 1991 | Boulder, Colo. |
| Lomon, Kevin | 4 | 2 | 3.71 | 14 | 14 | 1 | 0 | 85 | 80 | 36 | 35 | 30 | 68 | R | R | 6-1 | 195 | 11-20-71 | 1991 | Cameron, Okla. |
| May, Darrell | 5 | 2 | 2.09 | 9 | 9 | 0 | 0 | 52 | 44 | 18 | 12 | 16 | 47 | L | L | 6-2 | 172 | 6-13-72 | 1992 | Rogue River, Ore. |
| Place, Mike | 1 | 2 | 3.13 | 5 | 5 | 0 | 0 | 32 | 30 | 15 | 11 | 9 | 26 | R | R | 6-4 | 170 | 8-13-70 | 1990 | Seminole, Fla. |
| Ramirez, Leo | 0 | 1 | 6.75 | 8 | 0 | 0 | 0 | 11 | 13 | 10 | 8 | 10 | 10 | R | R | 6-3 | 185 | 9-25-68 | 1993 | Downey, Calif. |
| Ryder, Scott | 0 | 0 | 5.48 | 10 | 0 | 0 | 1 | 23 | 23 | 14 | 14 | 15 | 26 | R | R | 6-2 | 210 | 6-17-69 | 1990 | Clifton, N.J. |
| Schmidt, Jason | 7 | 11 | 4.94 | 22 | 22 | 0 | 0 | 117 | 128 | 69 | 64 | 47 | 110 | R | R | 6-5 | 185 | 1-29-73 | 1991 | Kelso, Wash. |
| Seelbach, Chris | 9 | 9 | 4.93 | 25 | 25 | 0 | 0 | 131 | 133 | 85 | 72 | 74 | 112 | R | R | 6-4 | 180 | 12-18-72 | 1991 | Lufkin, Texas |
| Steinmetz, Earl | 0 | 0 | 12.27 | 6 | 0 | 0 | 0 | 11 | 21 | 15 | 15 | 11 | 10 | R | R | 6-4 | 205 | 5-17-71 | 1989 | San Antonio, Texas |
| Wade, Terrell | 2 | 1 | 3.27 | 5 | 5 | 0 | 0 | 33 | 26 | 13 | 12 | 18 | 47 | L | L | 6-3 | 204 | 1-25-73 | 1991 | Rembert, S.C. |
| Wilder, John | 5 | 3 | 3.86 | 35 | 8 | 0 | 3 | 77 | 75 | 36 | 33 | 36 | 58 | R | R | 6-0 | 180 | 10-17-70 | 1991 | Florence, S.C. |
| Woodall, Brad | 3 | 1 | 3.00 | 6 | 5 | 1 | 0 | 30 | 21 | 10 | 10 | 6 | 27 | S | L | 6-0 | 175 | 6-25-69 | 1991 | Columbia, S.C. |

# MACON  A
## SOUTH ATLANTIC LEAGUE

| BATTING | AVG | G | AB | R | H | 2B | 3B | HR | RBI | BB | SO | SB | CS | B | T | HT | WT | DOB | 1st Yr | Resides |
|---|---|---|---|---|---|---|---|---|---|---|---|---|---|---|---|---|---|---|---|---|
| Buckley, Terrell, of | .196 | 42 | 107 | 10 | 21 | 3 | 1 | 0 | 9 | 14 | 30 | 9 | 6 | R | R | 5-10 | 180 | 6-7-71 | 1993 | Pascagoula, Miss. |
| Chambers, Mark, of | .205 | 15 | 39 | 6 | 8 | 0 | 0 | 0 | 4 | 3 | 11 | 4 | 1 | R | R | 6-1 | 185 | 9-13-69 | 1990 | East St. Louis, Ill. |
| Correa, Miguel, of | .265 | 131 | 495 | 58 | 131 | 26 | 8 | 10 | 61 | 30 | 84 | 18 | 17 | S | R | 6-2 | 170 | 9-10-71 | 1990 | Arroyo, P.R. |
| Garcia, Adrian, c | .267 | 47 | 105 | 13 | 28 | 4 | 2 | 1 | 11 | 6 | 44 | 2 | 3 | R | R | 5-11 | 165 | 9-12-72 | 1990 | Elizabeth, N.J. |
| Garr, Ralph, of | .224 | 57 | 143 | 19 | 32 | 10 | 2 | 1 | 23 | 21 | 54 | 5 | 1 | R | R | 6-0 | 170 | 5-14-72 | 1990 | Missouri City, Texas |
| Grijak, Kevin, 1b | .296 | 120 | 389 | 50 | 115 | 26 | 5 | 7 | 58 | 37 | 37 | 9 | 5 | L | R | 6-2 | 195 | 8-6-70 | 1991 | Sterling Heights, Mich. |
| Keeline, Jason, ss | .215 | 121 | 353 | 35 | 76 | 4 | 0 | 0 | 28 | 35 | 70 | 6 | 5 | R | R | 6-2 | 190 | 4-13-69 | 1991 | Hemet, Calif. |
| Knott, John, 1b-3b | .262 | 113 | 309 | 66 | 81 | 16 | 3 | 14 | 49 | 71 | 96 | 9 | 12 | R | R | 5-11 | 180 | 12-7-70 | 1993 | St. Louis, Mo. |
| Malloy, Marty, 2b | .293 | 109 | 355 | 55 | 110 | 19 | 3 | 2 | 36 | 39 | 70 | 24 | 8 | L | R | 5-10 | 155 | 7-6-72 | 1992 | Trenton, Fla. |
| Noel, Jason, of | .228 | 118 | 373 | 48 | 85 | 15 | 2 | 6 | 44 | 33 | 109 | 23 | 19 | R | R | 6-1 | 180 | 3-4-71 | 1992 | Fort Myers, Fla. |
| Nunez, Ramon, dh-1b | .286 | 115 | 377 | 57 | 108 | 18 | 5 | 7 | 40 | 37 | 73 | 6 | 5 | R | R | 6-0 | 150 | 9-22-72 | 1990 | Manzanillo, D.R. |
| Paulino, Nelson, 2b-ss | .231 | 99 | 325 | 45 | 75 | 10 | 1 | 3 | 24 | 19 | 93 | 24 | 5 | S | R | 5-11 | 155 | 1-28-73 | 1990 | San Pedro de Macoris, D.R. |
| Sly, Kian, of | .179 | 21 | 56 | 2 | 10 | 2 | 0 | 2 | 7 | 4 | 25 | 2 | 1 | L | R | 6-2 | 171 | 1-22-73 | 1990 | San Diego, Calif. |
| Smith, Bobby, 3b | .245 | 108 | 384 | 53 | 94 | 16 | 7 | 4 | 38 | 23 | 81 | 12 | 8 | R | R | 6-3 | 190 | 5-10-74 | 1992 | Oakland, Calif. |
| Soto, Miguel, c | .221 | 40 | 104 | 10 | 23 | 3 | 0 | 1 | 10 | 7 | 18 | 1 | 1 | R | R | 6-3 | 190 | 8-13-72 | 1990 | Maracaibo, Venez. |
| Toth, David, c | .246 | 104 | 353 | 38 | 87 | 22 | 0 | 4 | 40 | 28 | 53 | 6 | 5 | R | R | 6-1 | 195 | 12-8-69 | 1990 | West Keansburg, N.J. |
| Waldrop, Tom, of | .246 | 107 | 342 | 46 | 84 | 16 | 5 | 11 | 52 | 36 | 90 | 7 | 4 | L | L | 6-3 | 195 | 1-10-70 | 1992 | Decatur, Ill. |

# BRAVES: MOST COMMON LINEUPS

| | Atlanta | Richmond | Greenville | Durham | Macon |
|---|---|---|---|---|---|
| | Majors | AAA | AA | A | A |
| C | Damon Berryhill (105) | Javy Lopez (96) | Brad Ripplemeyer (78) | Joe Ayrault (108) | David Toth (101) |
| 1B | Sid Bream (90) | Ryan Klesko (66) | Tim Gillis (108) | Lance Marks (98) | Kevin Grijak (84) |
| 2B | Mark Lemke (150) | Ramon Caraballo (121) | Jose Olmeda (98) | Tony Graffanino (103) | Marty Malloy (99) |
| 3B | Terry Pendleton (161) | Jose Oliva (121) | Ed Giovanola (107) | Dom Therrien (98) | Bobby Smith (92) |
| SS | Jeff Blauser (161) | Chipper Jones (129) | Hector Roa (112) | Manny Jimenez (126) | Jason Keeline (120) |
| OF | Dave Justice (157) | Mike Kelly (117) | Brian Kowitz (117) | Juan Williams (112) | Miguel Correa (128) |
| | Ron Gant (155) | Keith Mitchell (106) | Lee Heath (103) | Don Robinson (105) | Jason Noel (119) |
| | Otis Nixon (116) | Tony Tarasco (92) | Troy Hughes (98) | Vince Moore (86) | Tom Waldrop (95) |
| DH | N/A | Ron Jones (33) | Tyler Houston (17) | Pedro Swann (34) | Ramon Nunez (50) |
| SP | Glavine/Maddux (36) | Brian Bark (28) | Blase Sparma (27) | Jerry Koller (26) | Jamie Arnold (27) |
| RP | Greg McMichael (74) | Billy Taylor (59) | Dave Williams (45) | Brad Clontz (51) | Tom Thobe (43) |
| | Full-season farm clubs only | No. of games at position in parenthesis | | | |

# BRAVES
## TOP 10 PROSPECTS

**Chipper Jones**
.325 at Richmond

How the Braves Top 10 prospects, as judged by Baseball America prior to the 1993 season, fared in 1993:

| Player, Pos. | Club (Class) | AVG | AB | H | HR | RBI | SB |
|---|---|---|---|---|---|---|---|
| 1. Chipper Jones, ss | Richmond (AAA) | .325 | 536 | 174 | 13 | 89 | 23 |
| | Atlanta | .667 | 3 | 2 | 0 | 0 | 0 |
| 2. Javy Lopez, c | Richmond (AAA) | .305 | 380 | 116 | 17 | 74 | 1 |
| | Atlanta | .375 | 16 | 6 | 1 | 2 | 0 |
| 3. Ryan Klesko, 1b-of | Richmond (AAA) | .274 | 343 | 94 | 22 | 74 | 4 |
| | Atlanta | .353 | 17 | 6 | 2 | 5 | 0 |
| 4. Mike Kelly, of | Richmond (AAA) | .243 | 424 | 103 | 19 | 58 | 11 |
| 5. Melvin Nieves, of* | Richmond (AAA) | .278 | 273 | 76 | 10 | 36 | 4 |
| | Las Vegas (AAA) | .308 | 159 | 49 | 7 | 24 | 2 |
| | San Diego | .191 | 47 | 9 | 2 | 3 | 0 |
| 7. Jose Oliva, 3b | Richmond (AAA) | .235 | 412 | 97 | 21 | 65 | 1 |

| Player, Pos. | Club (Class) | W | L | ERA | IP | H | BB | SO |
|---|---|---|---|---|---|---|---|---|
| 6. Jamie Arnold, rhp | Macon (A) | 8 | 9 | 3.12 | 164 | 142 | 56 | 124 |
| 8. Chris Seelbach, rhp | Durham (A) | 9 | 4 | 4.93 | 131 | 133 | 74 | 112 |
| 9. Donnie Elliott, rhp* | Richmond (AAA) | 8 | 5 | 4.72 | 103 | 108 | 39 | 99 |
| | Las Vegas (AAA) | 2 | 5 | 6.37 | 41 | 48 | 24 | 44 |
| 10. Jason Schmidt, rhp | Durham (A) | 7 | 11 | 4.94 | 117 | 128 | 47 | 110 |

*Traded to San Diego Padres

| PITCHING | W | L | ERA | G | GS | CG | SV | IP | H | R | ER | BB | SO | B | T | HT | WT | DOB | 1st Yr | Resides |
|---|---|---|---|---|---|---|---|---|---|---|---|---|---|---|---|---|---|---|---|---|
| Arnold, Jamie | 8 | 9 | 3.12 | 27 | 27 | 1 | 0 | 164 | 142 | 67 | 57 | 56 | 124 | R | R | 6-2 | 188 | 3-24-74 | 1992 | Kissimmee, Fla. |
| Bock, Jeff | 2 | 1 | 2.16 | 3 | 3 | 1 | 0 | 17 | 12 | 9 | 4 | 8 | 11 | R | R | 6-5 | 200 | 4-26-71 | 1993 | Cary, N.C. |
| Brock, Chris | 7 | 5 | 2.70 | 14 | 14 | 1 | 0 | 80 | 61 | 37 | 24 | 33 | 92 | R | R | 6-1 | 180 | 2-5-71 | 1992 | Altamonte Springs, Fla. |
| Burlingame, Dennis | 4 | 1 | 2.03 | 6 | 6 | 1 | 0 | 40 | 34 | 13 | 9 | 19 | 30 | R | R | 6-4 | 200 | 6-17-69 | 1988 | Mullica Hill, N.J. |
| Butler, Jason | 2 | 6 | 4.54 | 31 | 9 | 2 | 1 | 83 | 74 | 54 | 42 | 49 | 61 | L | L | 5-11 | 170 | 4-6-71 | 1991 | Harrisburg, Ill. |
| Cromer, Burke | 0 | 0 | 3.19 | 17 | 0 | 0 | 3 | 31 | 33 | 18 | 11 | 22 | 16 | R | R | 6-1 | 190 | 1-8-70 | 1992 | Lexington, S.C. |
| D'Andrea, Mike | 8 | 7 | 4.03 | 26 | 23 | 0 | 0 | 136 | 129 | 68 | 61 | 55 | 156 | R | R | 5-10 | 195 | 12-23-69 | 1992 | Old Town, Maine |
| Giard, Ken | 1 | 7 | 3.84 | 41 | 1 | 0 | 2 | 68 | 59 | 37 | 29 | 27 | 58 | R | R | 6-3 | 200 | 4-2-73 | 1991 | Warwick, R.I. |
| May, Darrell | 10 | 4 | 2.24 | 17 | 17 | 0 | 0 | 104 | 81 | 29 | 26 | 22 | 111 | L | L | 6-2 | 172 | 6-13-72 | 1992 | Rogue River, Ore. |
| Murray, Matt | 7 | 3 | 1.83 | 15 | 15 | 3 | 0 | 84 | 70 | 24 | 17 | 27 | 77 | L | R | 6-6 | 200 | 9-26-70 | 1988 | Swampscott, Mass. |
| Place, Mike | 6 | 5 | 2.35 | 31 | 9 | 1 | 2 | 100 | 91 | 44 | 26 | 23 | 74 | R | R | 6-4 | 170 | 8-13-70 | 1990 | Seminole, Fla. |
| Ramirez, Leo | 4 | 4 | 3.10 | 36 | 0 | 0 | 17 | 41 | 34 | 18 | 14 | 13 | 43 | R | R | 6-3 | 185 | 9-25-68 | 1993 | Downey, Calif. |
| Rusciano, Chris | 0 | 2 | 5.86 | 19 | 1 | 0 | 1 | 35 | 34 | 26 | 23 | 24 | 33 | R | R | 6-5 | 205 | 12-13-71 | 1992 | Staten Island, N.Y. |
| Simmons, John | 0 | 5 | 2.66 | 35 | 0 | 0 | 3 | 68 | 49 | 25 | 20 | 25 | 59 | L | L | 6-6 | 205 | 10-12-70 | 1992 | Tinley Park, Ill. |
| Thobe, Tom | 7 | 5 | 2.69 | 43 | 0 | 0 | 5 | 70 | 70 | 25 | 21 | 16 | 55 | L | L | 6-5 | 195 | 9-3-69 | 1988 | Huntington Beach, Calif. |
| Turnier, Aaron | 0 | 1 | 4.88 | 12 | 2 | 0 | 1 | 24 | 21 | 18 | 13 | 20 | 14 | L | L | 6-3 | 190 | 9-30-70 | 1992 | Las Vegas, Nev. |
| Wade, Terrell | 8 | 2 | 1.73 | 14 | 14 | 0 | 0 | 83 | 57 | 16 | 16 | 36 | 121 | L | L | 6-3 | 204 | 1-25-73 | 1991 | Rembert, S.C. |

## DANVILLE
### APPALACHIAN LEAGUE
R

| BATTING | AVG | G | AB | R | H | 2B | 3B | HR | RBI | BB | SO | SB | CS | B | T | HT | WT | DOB | 1st Yr | Resides |
|---|---|---|---|---|---|---|---|---|---|---|---|---|---|---|---|---|---|---|---|---|
| Benitez, Fernando, c | .286 | 20 | 49 | 8 | 14 | 3 | 0 | 0 | 2 | 6 | 14 | 1 | 0 | S | R | 6-0 | 178 | 1-20-74 | 1992 | Lindsay, Calif. |
| Brennan, Shawn, of | .107 | 29 | 56 | 6 | 6 | 1 | 0 | 0 | 4 | 4 | 16 | 0 | 0 | R | R | 6-3 | 190 | 9-25-73 | 1992 | Cincinnati, Ohio |
| Columna, Jose, ss-2b | .289 | 43 | 149 | 26 | 43 | 9 | 2 | 2 | 13 | 18 | 36 | 1 | 3 | R | R | 5-11 | 160 | 12-2-74 | 1993 | Santo Domingo, D.R. |
| Cox, Chris, 3b | .242 | 19 | 66 | 12 | 16 | 5 | 0 | 2 | 8 | 8 | 26 | 1 | 0 | R | R | 6-0 | 175 | 9-10-70 | 1993 | Winston-Salem, N.C. |
| Dailey, Jason, dh-of | .185 | 12 | 27 | 3 | 5 | 2 | 0 | 0 | 0 | 0 | 9 | 0 | 0 | R | R | 6-4 | 215 | 9-29-72 | 1993 | Roanoke, Va. |
| Dye, Jermaine, of | .277 | 25 | 94 | 6 | 26 | 6 | 1 | 2 | 18 | 8 | 10 | 4 | 1 | R | R | 6-4 | 195 | 1-28-74 | 1993 | Vacaville, Calif. |
| Garcia, Luis, ss-3b | .240 | 30 | 104 | 14 | 25 | 4 | 0 | 0 | 8 | 6 | 13 | 2 | 0 | R | R | 6-0 | 190 | 6-21-74 | 1992 | Punto Fijo Falcon, Venez. |
| Hollins, Damon, of | .321 | 62 | 240 | 37 | 77 | 15 | 2 | 7 | 51 | 19 | 30 | 10 | 2 | R | L | 5-11 | 187 | 6-12-74 | 1992 | Vallejo, Calif. |
| King, Andre, of | .309 | 60 | 223 | 41 | 69 | 10 | 6 | 0 | 18 | 36 | 40 | 15 | 5 | R | R | 6-1 | 190 | 11-26-73 | 1993 | Fort Lauderdale, Fla. |
| Magee, Danny, ss | .243 | 10 | 37 | 4 | 9 | 1 | 0 | 0 | 1 | 0 | 10 | 3 | 0 | R | R | 6-2 | 175 | 11-25-74 | 1993 | Denham Springs, La. |
| Paragin, Bill, c | .135 | 16 | 37 | 6 | 5 | 2 | 0 | 0 | 0 | 5 | 10 | 0 | 0 | R | R | 6-2 | 215 | 6-22-71 | 1992 | Hamilton, Ohio |
| Reece, John, of-dh | .160 | 29 | 81 | 11 | 13 | 0 | 1 | 0 | 4 | 8 | 25 | 1 | 0 | L | L | 6-1 | 195 | 1-24-71 | 1993 | Houston, Texas |
| Saturnino, Sherton, of | .254 | 45 | 142 | 25 | 36 | 6 | 1 | 2 | 15 | 7 | 39 | 9 | 4 | S | R | 5-9 | 175 | 10-16-71 | 1991 | Curacao, Neth. Antilles |
| Selmo, Feliberto, ss | .236 | 16 | 55 | 5 | 13 | 2 | 0 | 0 | 7 | 7 | 15 | 3 | 2 | R | R | 5-10 | 160 | 10-6-73 | 1991 | Villa Mella, D.R. |
| Shelley, Jason, of | .111 | 14 | 18 | 4 | 2 | 1 | 0 | 0 | 1 | 8 | 9 | 3 | 1 | R | R | 6-2 | 178 | 8-5-74 | 1992 | Vallejo, Calif. |
| Simon, Randall, 1b | .254 | 61 | 232 | 28 | 59 | 17 | 1 | 3 | 31 | 10 | 34 | 1 | 2 | L | L | 6-0 | 198 | 5-26-75 | 1993 | Curacao, Neth. Antilles |
| Smith, Sean, c | .287 | 49 | 157 | 17 | 45 | 5 | 1 | 2 | 23 | 21 | 21 | 1 | 3 | L | R | 5-10 | 185 | 2-15-74 | 1992 | Oconomowoc, Wis. |
| Stutts, Angelo, dh-of | .244 | 29 | 78 | 10 | 19 | 3 | 0 | 0 | 8 | 3 | 21 | 2 | 2 | R | R | 5-11 | 190 | 8-6-73 | 1992 | Hammond, La. |
| Warner, Ken, 2b | .235 | 60 | 221 | 37 | 52 | 5 | 2 | 0 | 35 | 28 | 47 | 16 | 7 | R | R | 5-10 | 175 | 7-1-72 | 1992 | Amite, La. |
| Wieser, Mike, 3b-1b | .243 | 58 | 206 | 27 | 50 | 11 | 8 | 3 | 21 | 23 | 76 | 2 | 4 | R | R | 6-4 | 200 | 3-24-73 | 1991 | Fargo, N.D. |

| PITCHING | W | L | ERA | G | GS | CG | SV | IP | H | R | ER | BB | SO | B | T | HT | WT | DOB | 1st Yr | Resides |
|---|---|---|---|---|---|---|---|---|---|---|---|---|---|---|---|---|---|---|---|---|
| Betti, Rick | 2 | 1 | 2.10 | 11 | 5 | 0 | 0 | 34 | 20 | 13 | 8 | 19 | 28 | R | L | 5-11 | 170 | 9-16-73 | 1993 | Milford, Mass. |
| Bock, Jeff | 0 | 0 | 7.11 | 5 | 0 | 0 | 0 | 6 | 6 | 5 | 5 | 3 | 2 | R | R | 6-5 | 200 | 4-26-71 | 1993 | Cary, N.C. |
| Bradshaw, Craig | 3 | 1 | 2.63 | 22 | 0 | 0 | 1 | 38 | 33 | 15 | 11 | 10 | 33 | R | L | 5-11 | 193 | 8-21-70 | 1993 | Alexandria, La. |
| Brown, Darold | 1 | 0 | 1.42 | 11 | 1 | 0 | 0 | 19 | 12 | 8 | 3 | 19 | 19 | L | L | 6-0 | 175 | 8-16-73 | 1993 | Richmond, Calif. |
| Byrd, Matt | 5 | 2 | 1.96 | 25 | 0 | 0 | 7 | 41 | 23 | 10 | 9 | 17 | 57 | R | R | 6-2 | 200 | 5-17-71 | 1993 | Brighton, Mich. |
| Christmas, Maurice | 7 | 5 | 4.32 | 14 | 14 | 1 | 0 | 81 | 94 | 50 | 39 | 15 | 60 | R | R | 6-4 | 188 | 2-26-74 | 1992 | Winchester, Mass. |
| Cromer, Burke | 0 | 1 | 3.86 | 3 | 0 | 0 | 0 | 2 | 4 | 2 | 1 | 1 | 1 | R | R | 6-1 | 190 | 1-8-70 | 1992 | Lexington, S.C. |
| Danley, Mike | 2 | 1 | 8.69 | 13 | 1 | 0 | 0 | 20 | 21 | 25 | 19 | 25 | 17 | L | L | 6-3 | 215 | 8-8-69 | 1993 | Papillion, Neb. |
| Havens, Will | 1 | 1 | 3.82 | 13 | 2 | 0 | 0 | 35 | 38 | 20 | 15 | 14 | 22 | R | R | 6-2 | 175 | 12-2-72 | 1991 | San Antonio, Texas |
| Hostetler, Marcus | 0 | 1 | 2.05 | 20 | 0 | 0 | 5 | 31 | 18 | 8 | 7 | 5 | 36 | R | R | 6-3 | 215 | 7-4-69 | 1993 | Kalona, Iowa |
| Howard, Jamie | 9 | 8 | 0 | 39 | 31 | 29 | 17 | 26 | 31 | R | R | 6-1 | 200 | 12-7-73 | 1992 | Lafayette, La. |
| Jacobs, Ryan | 4 | 3 | 4.01 | 10 | 10 | 0 | 0 | 43 | 35 | 24 | 19 | 25 | 32 | R | L | 6-2 | 175 | 2-3-74 | 1993 | Winston-Salem, N.C. |
| Paige, Carey | 2 | 4 | 4.21 | 13 | 13 | 0 | 0 | 66 | 59 | 37 | 31 | 32 | 58 | R | R | 6-3 | 175 | 3-2-74 | 1992 | Abilene, Texas |
| Schutz, Carl | 1 | 0 | 0.66 | 12 | 0 | 0 | 4 | 14 | 6 | 1 | 1 | 6 | 25 | L | L | 5-11 | 200 | 8-22-71 | 1993 | Paulina, La. |
| Shafer, Bill | 4 | 1 | 2.32 | 23 | 0 | 0 | 6 | 50 | 38 | 18 | 13 | 11 | 43 | R | R | 6-4 | 215 | 10-6-72 | 1991 | Arlington, Texas |
| Yan, Esteban | 4 | 7 | 3.03 | 14 | 14 | 0 | 0 | 71 | 73 | 46 | 24 | 24 | 50 | R | R | 6-4 | 180 | 6-22-74 | 1991 | La Higuera, D.R. |

## PIONEER LEAGUE

| BATTING | AVG | G | AB | R | H | 2B | 3B | HR | RBI | BB | SO | SB | CS | B | T | HT | WT | DOB | 1st Yr | Resides |
|---|---|---|---|---|---|---|---|---|---|---|---|---|---|---|---|---|---|---|---|---|
| Benitez, Fernando, c | .400 | 3 | 10 | 3 | 4 | 2 | 0 | 0 | 2 | 1 | 2 | 0 | 0 | S | R | 6-0 | 178 | 1-20-74 | 1992 | Lindsay, Calif. |
| Bishop, Stephen, 1b-3b | .382 | 20 | 68 | 13 | 26 | 6 | 0 | 2 | 10 | 9 | 11 | 1 | 2 | R | R | 6-4 | 205 | 9-14-70 | 1993 | Atlanta, Ga. |
| Browder, Cam, 1b | .273 | 54 | 128 | 28 | 35 | 12 | 0 | 4 | 17 | 32 | 23 | 2 | 4 | L | L | 6-3 | 200 | 10-19-70 | 1993 | Kernersville, N.C. |
| Bugg, Jason, 3b-of | .245 | 56 | 200 | 37 | 49 | 17 | 2 | 3 | 29 | 21 | 45 | 8 | 2 | L | R | 5-10 | 180 | 6-12-71 | 1993 | San Jose, Calif. |
| Burrill, Casey, 1b-c | .296 | 44 | 152 | 16 | 45 | 9 | 0 | 5 | 25 | 6 | 12 | 1 | 1 | R | R | 6-3 | 231 | 8-31-70 | 1993 | Saugus, Calif. |
| Burton, Adam, ss-3b | .262 | 64 | 202 | 46 | 53 | 16 | 4 | 9 | 48 | 43 | 75 | 19 | 5 | R | R | 5-9 | 175 | 3-17-72 | 1992 | Melbourne, Australia |
| Denman, Ralph, of-dh | .217 | 37 | 115 | 18 | 25 | 5 | 1 | 1 | 9 | 6 | 22 | 5 | 2 | L | R | 6-2 | 190 | 8-2-72 | 1993 | Crockett, Texas |
| Diieso, Tony, dh-of | .264 | 32 | 72 | 18 | 19 | 5 | 0 | 1 | 8 | 5 | 24 | 2 | 2 | R | R | 5-11 | 190 | 9-28-73 | 1992 | Copiague, N.Y. |
| Eaglin, Michael, 2b | .326 | 66 | 236 | 50 | 77 | 5 | 4 | 2 | 35 | 29 | 48 | 28 | 11 | R | R | 5-10 | 170 | 4-25-73 | 1992 | San Pablo, Calif. |
| Garcia, Luis, ss | .215 | 27 | 107 | 17 | 23 | 4 | 1 | 0 | 13 | 4 | 15 | 3 | 1 | R | R | 6-0 | 190 | 6-21-74 | 1992 | Punto Fijo Falcon, Venez. |
| McBride, Gator, 3b-of | .289 | 49 | 142 | 25 | 41 | 6 | 4 | 2 | 20 | 13 | 27 | 8 | 3 | R | R | 5-10 | 170 | 8-12-73 | 1993 | Hurricane, W.Va. |
| Monds, Wonderful, of | .299 | 60 | 214 | 47 | 64 | 13 | 8 | 4 | 35 | 25 | 43 | 17 | 5 | R | R | 6-2 | 193 | 1-11-73 | 1993 | Fort Pierce, Fla. |
| Moreno, Erik, c | .283 | 49 | 138 | 21 | 39 | 4 | 0 | 3 | 20 | 31 | 24 | 0 | 1 | R | R | 5-11 | 195 | 10-1-69 | 1993 | Tucson, Ariz. |
| Newman, Bruce, of | .295 | 45 | 122 | 17 | 36 | 5 | 1 | 3 | 22 | 12 | 29 | 6 | 4 | L | R | 6-2 | 185 | 5-14-73 | 1993 | Sacramento, Calif. |
| Perez, Eddie, of | .308 | 43 | 117 | 20 | 36 | 4 | 0 | 3 | 10 | 15 | 25 | 6 | 3 | R | R | 6-3 | 175 | 9-14-73 | 1992 | San Juan, D.R. |
| Rodriguez, Jose, c-1b | .272 | 54 | 195 | 30 | 53 | 10 | 1 | 3 | 35 | 20 | 41 | 1 | 2 | R | R | 6-1 | 205 | 3-6-74 | 1991 | Cayey, P.R. |
| Ruff, Tony, of | .295 | 40 | 132 | 21 | 39 | 4 | 1 | 1 | 18 | 7 | 21 | 9 | 7 | R | R | 5-11 | 160 | 12-1-72 | 1993 | Moreno Valley, Calif. |
| Valdez, Miguel, of | .358 | 39 | 134 | 29 | 48 | 5 | 2 | 1 | 28 | 15 | 24 | 7 | 9 | L | L | 5-11 | 175 | 3-18-75 | 1992 | La Romana, D.R. |
| Vazquetelles, D., ss | .253 | 37 | 87 | 16 | 22 | 0 | 1 | 0 | 15 | 14 | 13 | 5 | 2 | R | R | 5-10 | 160 | 10-18-69 | 1992 | Guaynabo, P.R. |

| PITCHING | W | L | ERA | G | GS | CG | SV | IP | H | R | ER | BB | SO | B | T | HT | WT | DOB | 1st Yr | Resides |
|---|---|---|---|---|---|---|---|---|---|---|---|---|---|---|---|---|---|---|---|---|
| Blaine, Jim | 0 | 0 | 7.50 | 14 | 0 | 0 | 1 | 24 | 31 | 27 | 20 | 11 | 19 | R | R | 6-4 | 198 | 5-9-73 | 1992 | Cypress, Texas |
| Bock, Jeff | 3 | 2 | 2.84 | 15 | 1 | 0 | 1 | 32 | 31 | 16 | 10 | 12 | 21 | R | R | 6-5 | 200 | 4-26-71 | 1993 | Cary, N.C. |
| Evangelista, Alberto | 4 | 2 | 6.15 | 15 | 11 | 0 | 0 | 60 | 68 | 46 | 41 | 35 | 41 | S | R | 6-1 | 172 | 6-10-73 | 1993 | Sanchez Ramirez, D.R. |
| Gagnon, Clint | 3 | 3 | 8.10 | 13 | 8 | 0 | 0 | 47 | 69 | 49 | 42 | 21 | 42 | R | R | 6-3 | 220 | 9-12-73 | 1992 | Bourbonnais, Ill. |
| Martineau, Yves | 3 | 8 | 5.01 | 16 | 15 | 1 | 0 | 83 | 91 | 53 | 46 | 29 | 75 | S | R | 6-2 | 168 | 4-13-71 | 1991 | Point-Aux-Tremble, Que. |
| Nelson, Earl | 5 | 7 | 4.38 | 16 | 15 | 2 | 0 | 76 | 82 | 50 | 37 | 48 | 72 | R | L | 6-2 | 210 | 5-12-72 | 1991 | San Antonio, Texas |
| Randall, Jim | 1 | 1 | 5.85 | 13 | 9 | 0 | 0 | 48 | 51 | 34 | 31 | 22 | 36 | L | L | 6-0 | 185 | 8-5-71 | 1993 | Ava, N.Y. |
| Rusciano, Chris | 1 | 0 | 0.00 | 1 | 1 | 0 | 0 | 6 | 4 | 0 | 0 | 1 | 6 | R | R | 6-5 | 205 | 12-13-71 | 1992 | Staten Island, N.Y. |
| Simmons, Jason | 2 | 4 | 3.95 | 21 | 0 | 0 | 2 | 43 | 53 | 28 | 19 | 15 | 21 | R | R | 6-3 | 200 | 12-1-71 | 1993 | Tinley Park, Ill. |
| Stoeckle, Tony | 3 | 2 | 2.42 | 27 | 0 | 0 | 8 | 45 | 36 | 14 | 12 | 14 | 51 | R | L | 6-1 | 178 | 9-10-70 | 1992 | Wood River, Ill. |
| Thomas, Jason | 3 | 1 | 4.19 | 26 | 0 | 0 | 3 | 43 | 48 | 23 | 20 | 17 | 36 | L | L | 6-1 | 195 | 11-29-71 | 1993 | Danville, Ill. |
| Turnier, Aaon | 4 | 0 | 4.50 | 9 | 3 | 0 | 0 | 30 | 27 | 15 | 15 | 9 | 24 | L | R | 6-3 | 190 | 9-30-70 | 1992 | Las Vegas, Nev. |
| Tyner, Mar | 2 | 3 | 6.06 | 21 | 4 | 0 | 1 | 52 | 61 | 43 | 35 | 22 | 64 | R | R | 6-2 | 200 | 4-11-72 | 1993 | Richmond, Calif. |
| Wells, David | 2 | 7 | 5.52 | 18 | 9 | 0 | 0 | 62 | 90 | 51 | 38 | 22 | 44 | R | R | 6-5 | 200 | 6-20-72 | 1993 | Logansport, Ind. |

## GULF COAST LEAGUE

| BATTING | AVG | G | AB | R | H | 2B | 3B | HR | RBI | BB | SO | SB | CS | B | T | HT | WT | DOB | 1st Yr | Resides |
|---|---|---|---|---|---|---|---|---|---|---|---|---|---|---|---|---|---|---|---|---|
| Brewer, Doug, of | .282 | 41 | 142 | 17 | 40 | 4 | 2 | 0 | 16 | 2 | 17 | 5 | 1 | R | R | 6-2 | 185 | 10-16-74 | 1993 | Snowflake, Ariz. |
| Brown, Roosevelt, dh-of | .113 | 26 | 80 | 4 | 9 | 1 | 2 | 0 | 5 | 2 | 9 | 2 | 0 | L | R | 5-11 | 170 | 8-3-75 | 1993 | Vicksburg, Miss. |
| Carter, Rickey, dh-of | .138 | 25 | 87 | 8 | 12 | 1 | 0 | 1 | 9 | 4 | 20 | 2 | 1 | R | R | 6-2 | 210 | 5-26-74 | 1993 | Sparr, Fla. |
| Catlett, David, 1b | .311 | 54 | 193 | 33 | 60 | 11 | 2 | 5 | 33 | 31 | 19 | 11 | 5 | R | R | 6-0 | 215 | 4-6-74 | 1993 | Oakland, Calif. |
| Cruz, Brian, c | .211 | 22 | 57 | 11 | 12 | 5 | 0 | 0 | 5 | 11 | 6 | 0 | 0 | R | R | 5-10 | 190 | 12-10-70 | 1993 | Gas City, Ind. |
| Domingo, Tyrone, ss | .067 | 4 | 15 | 3 | 1 | 0 | 0 | 0 | 0 | 1 | 6 | 1 | 0 | R | R | 5-8 | 169 | 10-22-74 | 1991 | Los Angeles, Calif. |
| Dye, Jermaine, of-3b | .347 | 31 | 124 | 17 | 43 | 14 | 0 | 0 | 27 | 5 | 13 | 5 | 0 | R | R | 6-4 | 195 | 1-28-74 | 1993 | Vacaville, Calif. |
| Franklin, James, of | .236 | 41 | 148 | 18 | 35 | 4 | 1 | 2 | 22 | 15 | 48 | 4 | 1 | R | R | 6-1 | 210 | 9-14-74 | 1993 | Hodgenville, Ky. |
| Hofer, Ray, 3b | .240 | 27 | 96 | 12 | 23 | 1 | 1 | 0 | 8 | 3 | 16 | 1 | 2 | R | R | 6-2 | 205 | 9-29-74 | 1993 | Zaandam, Neth. Antilles |
| Lee, Jason, 2b | .206 | 27 | 97 | 8 | 20 | 1 | 0 | 0 | 6 | 4 | 12 | 1 | 1 | R | R | 5-6 | 160 | 10-24-73 | 1993 | Edmonton, Alberta |
| Magee, Danny, ss | .283 | 16 | 60 | 14 | 17 | 4 | 1 | 1 | 8 | 5 | 12 | 4 | 0 | R | R | 6-2 | 175 | 11-25-74 | 1993 | Denham Springs, La. |
| Mathews, Del, p-1b | .147 | 25 | 34 | 4 | 5 | 0 | 0 | 0 | 2 | 5 | 8 | 0 | 0 | L | L | 6-4 | 195 | 10-31-74 | 1993 | Fernandina Beach, Fla. |
| Matos, Pasqual, c | .227 | 36 | 119 | 12 | 27 | 5 | 1 | 0 | 15 | 3 | 32 | 3 | 1 | R | R | 6-2 | 167 | 12-26-74 | 1992 | Barahona, D.R. |
| Rennspies, Dustin, c | .286 | 15 | 28 | 7 | 8 | 1 | 0 | 0 | 5 | 7 | 3 | 1 | 0 | R | R | 6-1 | 195 | 8-12-73 | 1992 | Pensacola, Fla. |
| Roberson, Gerald, 2b | .281 | 42 | 153 | 34 | 43 | 7 | 3 | 0 | 8 | 21 | 17 | 14 | 3 | R | R | 5-10 | 170 | 8-22-74 | 1993 | Pontotoc, Miss. |
| Sasser, Robert, 3b | .239 | 33 | 113 | 19 | 27 | 4 | 0 | 0 | 7 | 6 | 25 | 2 | 1 | R | R | 6-3 | 190 | 3-6-75 | 1993 | Oakland, Calif. |
| Selmo, Feliberto, ss-2b | .263 | 33 | 118 | 16 | 31 | 5 | 2 | 1 | 12 | 18 | 15 | 1 | 6 | R | R | 5-10 | 160 | 10-6-73 | 1991 | Villa Mella, D.R. |
| Thomas, Rob, of | .500 | 2 | 2 | 0 | 1 | 0 | 0 | 0 | 0 | 0 | 0 | 0 | 0 | R | R | 6-0 | 170 | 11-2-73 | 1993 | Chicopee, Mass. |
| Tillman, Bennie, of | .259 | 33 | 116 | 18 | 30 | 1 | 4 | 2 | 14 | 13 | 31 | 3 | 3 | L | R | 6-3 | 191 | 11-22-72 | 1993 | Bay St. Louis, Miss. |
| Tolbert, Andrew, of | .189 | 29 | 90 | 10 | 17 | 1 | 0 | 0 | 7 | 14 | 17 | 4 | 1 | R | R | 6-2 | 203 | 12-23-75 | 1993 | San Antonio, Texas |
| Vazquez, Jorge, of | .239 | 16 | 46 | 10 | 11 | 4 | 0 | 0 | 4 | 8 | 22 | 2 | 0 | R | R | 6-2 | 195 | 10-17-73 | 1993 | Esperanza, Mexico |
| Williams, Richard, of | .000 | 2 | 3 | 0 | 0 | 0 | 0 | 0 | 0 | 0 | 0 | 0 | 0 | S | R | 6-0 | 175 | 1-8-74 | 1992 | Hesperia, Calif. |

| PITCHING | W | L | ERA | G | GS | CG | SV | IP | H | R | ER | BB | SO | B | T | HT | WT | DOB | 1st Yr | Resides |
|---|---|---|---|---|---|---|---|---|---|---|---|---|---|---|---|---|---|---|---|---|
| Barrera, Davy | 0 | 3 | 2.94 | 12 | 4 | 0 | 0 | 34 | 28 | 20 | 11 | 21 | 22 | R | R | 5-10 | 165 | 12-29-75 | 1993 | Merida, Mexico |
| Betti, Rick | 1 | 0 | 0.89 | 9 | 2 | 0 | 2 | 20 | 10 | 5 | 2 | 8 | 27 | R | L | 5-11 | 170 | 9-16-73 | 1993 | Milford, Mass. |
| Bryant, Shane | 4 | 4 | 2.97 | 14 | 8 | 0 | 3 | 64 | 66 | 30 | 21 | 13 | 40 | R | R | 6-3 | 175 | 6-5-74 | 1992 | Reno, Nev. |
| Cain, Travis | 1 | 2 | 4.50 | 9 | 4 | 0 | 0 | 30 | 24 | 24 | 15 | 20 | 33 | L | R | 6-3 | 190 | 8-10-75 | 1993 | Anderson, S.C. |
| Danley, Mike | 0 | 0 | 7.20 | 3 | 0 | 0 | 0 | 5 | 6 | 6 | 4 | 3 | 4 | L | L | 6-3 | 215 | 8-8-69 | 1993 | Papillion, Neb. |
| Faile, William | 3 | 0 | 1.73 | 11 | 0 | 0 | 2 | 26 | 15 | 9 | 5 | 18 | 9 | R | R | 6-4 | 190 | 6-25-75 | 1993 | Greenwich, N.Y. |
| Gann, Charlie | 1 | 0 | 5.55 | 17 | 0 | 0 | 4 | 24 | 31 | 17 | 15 | 9 | 14 | R | R | 6-0 | 175 | 8-28-75 | 1993 | Mira Loma, Calif. |
| Green, Jason | 3 | 2 | 2.91 | 12 | 10 | 0 | 0 | 43 | 27 | 21 | 14 | 36 | 63 | R | R | 6-3 | 195 | 11-15-73 | 1993 | Hercules, Calif. |
| Hostetler, Marcus | 2 | 0 | 1.00 | 3 | 0 | 0 | 0 | 9 | 2 | 1 | 1 | 2 | 12 | R | R | 6-3 | 215 | 7-4-69 | 1993 | Kalona, Wash. |
| Leroy, John | 2 | 2 | 2.05 | 10 | 2 | 0 | 1 | 26 | 21 | 9 | 6 | 8 | 32 | R | R | 6-3 | 195 | 4-19-75 | 1993 | Bellevue, Wash. |
| Lollie, Adrian | 0 | 0 | 0.00 | 3 | 0 | 0 | 0 | 4 | 2 | 1 | 0 | 3 | 3 | R | R | 6-2 | 173 | 1-1-75 | 1993 | Kirkwood, N.Y. |
| Mathews, Del | 2 | 4 | 4.50 | 14 | 12 | 0 | 0 | 62 | 66 | 42 | 31 | 26 | 59 | L | L | 6-4 | 195 | 10-31-74 | 1993 | Fernandina Beach, Fla. |
| Miller, Jerrod | 5 | 2 | 1.07 | 13 | 7 | 0 | 0 | 51 | 31 | 12 | 6 | 16 | 43 | R | R | 6-3 | 205 | 8-29-75 | 1993 | Spokane, Wash. |
| Millwood, Kevin | 3 | 3 | 3.06 | 12 | 9 | 0 | 0 | 50 | 36 | 27 | 17 | 28 | 49 | R | R | 6-4 | 205 | 12-24-74 | 1993 | Bessemer City, N.C. |
| Olszewski, Eric | 3 | 3 | 5.58 | 13 | 0 | 0 | 0 | 31 | 33 | 25 | 19 | 20 | 26 | L | R | 6-2 | 190 | 11-4-74 | 1993 | Spring, Texas |
| Rigney, Justin | 2 | 1 | 3.47 | 11 | 0 | 0 | 2 | 23 | 22 | 10 | 9 | 14 | 18 | R | L | 6-0 | 210 | 11-8-72 | 1993 | Goochland, Va. |
| Warner, Michael | 0 | 0 | 9.00 | 1 | 0 | 0 | 0 | 1 | 0 | 1 | 1 | 1 | 1 | R | R | 6-3 | 185 | 9-7-74 | 1993 | Bellaire, Texas |

# BALTIMORE ORIOLES

**Manager:** Johnny Oates.  **1993 Record:** 85-77, .525 (T-3rd, AL East).

| BATTING | AVG | G | AB | R | H | 2B | 3B | HR | RBI | BB | SO | SB | CS | B | T | HT | WT | DOB | 1st Yr | Resides |
|---|---|---|---|---|---|---|---|---|---|---|---|---|---|---|---|---|---|---|---|---|
| Alexander, Manny | .000 | 3 | 0 | 1 | 0 | 0 | 0 | 0 | 0 | 0 | 0 | 0 | 0 | R | R | 5-10 | 160 | 3-20-71 | 1988 | San Pedro de Macoris, D.R. |
| Anderson, Brady | .263 | 142 | 560 | 87 | 147 | 36 | 8 | 13 | 66 | 82 | 99 | 24 | 12 | L | L | 6-1 | 195 | 1-18-64 | 1985 | Newport Beach, Calif. |
| Baines, Harold | .313 | 118 | 416 | 64 | 130 | 22 | 0 | 20 | 78 | 57 | 52 | 0 | 0 | L | L | 6-2 | 195 | 3-15-59 | 1977 | St. Michael's, Md. |
| Buford, Damon | .228 | 53 | 79 | 18 | 18 | 5 | 0 | 2 | 9 | 9 | 19 | 2 | 2 | R | R | 5-10 | 170 | 6-12-70 | 1990 | Sherman Oaks, Calif. |
| Carey, Paul | .213 | 18 | 47 | 1 | 10 | 1 | 0 | 0 | 3 | 5 | 14 | 0 | 0 | R | L | 6-4 | 215 | 1-8-68 | 1990 | Weymouth, Mass. |
| Davis, Glenn | .177 | 30 | 113 | 8 | 20 | 3 | 0 | 1 | 9 | 7 | 29 | 0 | 1 | R | R | 6-3 | 212 | 3-28-61 | 1981 | Hunt Valley, Md. |
| Devereaux, Mike | .250 | 131 | 527 | 72 | 132 | 31 | 3 | 14 | 75 | 43 | 99 | 3 | 3 | R | R | 6-0 | 195 | 4-10-63 | 1985 | Scottsdale, Ariz. |
| Gomez, Leo | .197 | 71 | 244 | 30 | 48 | 7 | 0 | 10 | 25 | 32 | 60 | 0 | 1 | R | R | 6-0 | 208 | 3-2-67 | 1986 | Canovanas, P.R. |
| Hammonds, Jeffrey | .305 | 33 | 105 | 10 | 32 | 8 | 0 | 3 | 19 | 2 | 16 | 4 | 0 | R | R | 6-0 | 180 | 3-5-71 | 1992 | Scotch Plains, N.J. |
| Hoiles, Chris | .310 | 126 | 419 | 80 | 130 | 28 | 0 | 29 | 82 | 69 | 94 | 1 | 1 | R | R | 6-0 | 213 | 3-20-65 | 1986 | Cockeysville, Md. |
| Hulett, Tim | .300 | 85 | 260 | 40 | 78 | 15 | 0 | 2 | 23 | 23 | 56 | 1 | 2 | R | R | 6-0 | 199 | 1-12-60 | 1980 | Springfield, Ill. |
| Leonard, Mark | .067 | 10 | 15 | 1 | 1 | 1 | 0 | 0 | 3 | 3 | 7 | 0 | 0 | L | R | 6-0 | 212 | 8-14-64 | 1986 | San Jose, Calif. |
| Martinez, Chito | .000 | 8 | 15 | 0 | 0 | 0 | 0 | 0 | 0 | 4 | 4 | 0 | 0 | L | L | 5-10 | 175 | 12-19-65 | 1984 | Metairie, La. |
| McLemore, Mark | .284 | 148 | 581 | 81 | 165 | 27 | 5 | 4 | 72 | 64 | 92 | 21 | 15 | S | R | 5-11 | 207 | 10-4-64 | 1982 | Gilbert, Ariz. |
| Mercedes, Luis | .292 | 10 | 24 | 1 | 7 | 2 | 0 | 0 | 0 | 5 | 4 | 1 | 1 | R | R | 6-3 | 183 | 2-20-68 | 1987 | San Pedro de Macoris, D.R. |
| Obando, Sherman | .272 | 31 | 92 | 8 | 25 | 2 | 0 | 3 | 15 | 4 | 26 | 0 | 0 | R | R | 6-4 | 215 | 1-23-70 | 1988 | Changuinola, Panama |
| Pagliarulo, Mike | .325 | 33 | 117 | 24 | 38 | 9 | 0 | 6 | 21 | 8 | 15 | 0 | 0 | L | R | 6-2 | 195 | 3-15-60 | 1981 | Melrose, Mass. |
| 2-team (83 Minn.) | .303 | 116 | 370 | 55 | 112 | 25 | 4 | 9 | 44 | 26 | 49 | 6 | 6 | | | | | | | |
| Parent, Mark | .259 | 22 | 54 | 7 | 14 | 2 | 0 | 4 | 12 | 3 | 14 | 0 | 0 | R | R | 6-5 | 225 | 9-16-61 | 1979 | San Diego, Calif. |
| Reynolds, Harold | .252 | 145 | 485 | 64 | 122 | 20 | 4 | 4 | 47 | 66 | 47 | 12 | 11 | S | R | 5-11 | 165 | 11-26-60 | 1981 | Baltimore, Md. |
| Ripken, Cal | .257 | 162 | 641 | 87 | 165 | 26 | 3 | 24 | 90 | 65 | 58 | 1 | 4 | R | R | 6-4 | 220 | 8-24-60 | 1978 | Reisterstown, Md. |
| Segui, David | .273 | 146 | 450 | 54 | 123 | 27 | 0 | 10 | 60 | 58 | 53 | 2 | 1 | S | L | 6-1 | 202 | 7-19-66 | 1988 | Kansas City, Kan. |
| Smith, Lonnie | .208 | 9 | 24 | 8 | 5 | 1 | 0 | 2 | 3 | 8 | 10 | 0 | 0 | R | R | 5-9 | 195 | 12-22-55 | 1974 | Atlanta, Ga. |
| Tackett, Jeff | .172 | 39 | 87 | 8 | 15 | 3 | 0 | 0 | 9 | 13 | 28 | 0 | 1 | R | R | 6-2 | 205 | 12-1-65 | 1984 | Camarillo, Calif. |
| Voigt, Jack | .296 | 64 | 152 | 32 | 45 | 11 | 1 | 6 | 23 | 25 | 33 | 1 | 0 | R | R | 6-1 | 170 | 5-17-66 | 1987 | Venice, Fla. |

| PITCHING | W | L | ERA | G | GS | CG | SV | IP | H | R | ER | BB | SO | B | T | HT | WT | DOB | 1st Yr | Resides |
|---|---|---|---|---|---|---|---|---|---|---|---|---|---|---|---|---|---|---|---|---|
| Cook, Mike | 0 | 0 | 0.00 | 2 | 0 | 0 | 0 | 3 | 1 | 0 | 0 | 2 | 3 | L | R | 6-3 | 225 | 8-14-63 | 1985 | Charleston, S.C. |
| Frohwirth, Todd | 6 | 7 | 3.83 | 70 | 0 | 0 | 3 | 96 | 91 | 47 | 41 | 44 | 50 | R | R | 6-4 | 204 | 9-28-62 | 1984 | Milwaukee, Wis. |
| McDonald, Ben | 13 | 14 | 3.39 | 34 | 34 | 7 | 0 | 220 | 185 | 92 | 83 | 86 | 171 | R | R | 6-7 | 210 | 11-24-67 | 1989 | Denham Springs, La. |
| McGehee, Kevin | 0 | 0 | 5.94 | 5 | 0 | 0 | 0 | 17 | 18 | 11 | 11 | 7 | 7 | R | R | 6-0 | 190 | 1-18-69 | 1990 | Pineville, La. |
| Mills, Alan | 5 | 4 | 3.23 | 45 | 0 | 0 | 4 | 100 | 80 | 39 | 36 | 51 | 68 | S | R | 6-1 | 192 | 10-18-66 | 1986 | Lakeland, Fla. |
| Moyer, Jamie | 12 | 9 | 3.43 | 25 | 25 | 3 | 0 | 152 | 154 | 63 | 58 | 38 | 90 | L | L | 6-0 | 170 | 11-18-62 | 1984 | Granger, Ill. |
| Mussina, Mike | 14 | 6 | 4.46 | 25 | 25 | 3 | 0 | 168 | 163 | 84 | 83 | 44 | 117 | R | R | 6-2 | 185 | 12-8-68 | 1990 | Montoursville, Pa. |
| O'Donoghue, John | 0 | 1 | 4.58 | 11 | 1 | 0 | 0 | 20 | 22 | 12 | 10 | 10 | 16 | L | L | 6-6 | 198 | 5-26-69 | 1990 | Elkton, Md. |
| Olson, Gregg | 0 | 2 | 1.60 | 50 | 0 | 0 | 29 | 45 | 37 | 9 | 8 | 18 | 44 | R | R | 6-4 | 212 | 10-11-66 | 1988 | Omaha, Neb. |
| Oquist, Mike | 0 | 0 | 3.86 | 5 | 0 | 0 | 0 | 12 | 12 | 5 | 5 | 4 | 8 | R | R | 6-2 | 170 | 5-30-68 | 1989 | LaJunta, Colo. |
| Pennington, Brad | 3 | 2 | 6.55 | 34 | 0 | 0 | 4 | 33 | 34 | 25 | 24 | 25 | 39 | L | L | 6-5 | 205 | 4-14-69 | 1989 | Salem, Ind. |
| Poole, Jim | 2 | 1 | 2.15 | 55 | 0 | 0 | 2 | 50 | 50 | 18 | 12 | 21 | 29 | L | L | 6-2 | 203 | 4-28-66 | 1988 | Cockeysville, Md. |
| Rhodes, Arthur | 5 | 6 | 6.51 | 17 | 17 | 0 | 0 | 86 | 91 | 62 | 62 | 49 | 49 | L | L | 6-2 | 204 | 10-24-69 | 1988 | Sarasota, Fla. |
| Sutcliffe, Rick | 10 | 10 | 5.75 | 29 | 28 | 3 | 0 | 166 | 212 | 112 | 106 | 74 | 80 | L | R | 6-7 | 239 | 6-21-56 | 1974 | Lee's Summit, Mo. |
| Telford, Anthony | 0 | 0 | 9.82 | 3 | 0 | 0 | 0 | 7 | 11 | 8 | 8 | 1 | 6 | R | R | 6-0 | 189 | 3-6-66 | 1987 | San Jose, Calif. |
| Valenzuela, Fernando | 8 | 10 | 4.94 | 32 | 31 | 5 | 0 | 179 | 179 | 104 | 98 | 79 | 78 | L | L | 5-11 | 202 | 11-1-60 | 1978 | Los Angeles, Calif. |
| Williamson, Mark | 7 | 5 | 4.91 | 48 | 1 | 0 | 0 | 88 | 106 | 54 | 48 | 25 | 45 | R | R | 6-0 | 177 | 7-21-59 | 1982 | Timonium, Md. |

## FIELDING

| Catcher | PCT | G | PO | A | E | DP |
|---|---|---|---|---|---|---|
| Hoiles | .993 | 124 | 696 | 64 | 5 | 11 |
| Parent | .989 | 21 | 83 | 5 | 1 | 0 |
| Tackett | .989 | 38 | 167 | 16 | 2 | 1 |

| First Base | PCT | G | PO | A | E | DP |
|---|---|---|---|---|---|---|
| Carey | .970 | 9 | 64 | 1 | 2 | 7 |
| Davis | .990 | 22 | 190 | 12 | 2 | 19 |
| Pagliarulo | 1.000 | 4 | 26 | 2 | 0 | 3 |
| Segui | .996 | 144 | 1152 | 98 | 5 | 122 |
| Voigt | 1.000 | 5 | 26 | 2 | 0 | 3 |

| Second Base | PCT | G | PO | A | E | DP |
|---|---|---|---|---|---|---|
| Hulett | 1.000 | 4 | 10 | 8 | 0 | 3 |

| | PCT | G | PO | A | E | DP |
|---|---|---|---|---|---|---|
| McLemore | 1.000 | 25 | 53 | 59 | 0 | 19 |
| Reynolds | .986 | 141 | 306 | 396 | 10 | 110 |

| Third Base | PCT | G | PO | A | E | DP |
|---|---|---|---|---|---|---|
| Gomez | .951 | 70 | 48 | 145 | 10 | 16 |
| Hulett | .963 | 75 | 48 | 161 | 8 | 23 |
| McLemore | .800 | 4 | 0 | 8 | 2 | 0 |
| Pagliarulo | .937 | 28 | 27 | 47 | 5 | 6 |
| Voigt | 1.000 | 3 | 0 | 1 | 0 | 0 |

| Shortstop | PCT | G | PO | A | E | DP |
|---|---|---|---|---|---|---|
| Hulett | 1.000 | 8 | 0 | 7 | 0 | 0 |
| Ripken | .977 | 162 | 226 | 495 | 17 | 101 |

| Outfield | PCT | G | PO | A | E | DP |
|---|---|---|---|---|---|---|
| Anderson | .993 | 140 | 296 | 7 | 2 | 0 |
| Buford | .984 | 30 | 61 | 2 | 1 | 1 |
| Devereaux | .988 | 130 | 311 | 8 | 4 | 3 |
| Hammonds | .961 | 23 | 47 | 2 | 2 | 0 |
| Leonard | .833 | 4 | 5 | 0 | 1 | 0 |
| Martinez | 1.000 | 5 | 2 | 0 | 0 | 0 |
| McLemore | .987 | 124 | 282 | 13 | 4 | 4 |
| Mercedes | 1.000 | 8 | 11 | 1 | 0 | 1 |
| Obando | .929 | 8 | 13 | 0 | 1 | 0 |
| Smith | 1.000 | 4 | 5 | 1 | 0 | 0 |
| Voigt | .987 | 43 | 75 | 3 | 1 | 0 |

# ORIOLES FARM SYSTEM

| Class | Club | League | W | L | Pct. | Finish* | Manager | First Year |
|---|---|---|---|---|---|---|---|---|
| AAA | Rochester (N.Y.) Red Wings | International | 74 | 67 | .525 | 4th (10) | Bob Miscik | 1961 |
| AA | Bowie (Md.) BaySox | Eastern | 72 | 68 | .514 | 3rd (8) | Don Buford | 1993 |
| A# | Frederick (Md.) Keys | Carolina | 78 | 62 | .557 | 1st (8) | Pete Mackanin | 1989 |
| A | Albany (Ga.) Polecats | South Atlantic | 71 | 71 | .500 | 8th (14) | Mike O'Berry | 1993 |
| Rookie# | Bluefield (W.Va.) Orioles | Appalachian | 44 | 24 | .647 | T-1st (10) | Andy Etchebarren | 1958 |
| Rookie | Sarasota (Fla.) Orioles | Gulf Coast | 30 | 28 | .517 | 8th (15) | Oneri Fleita | 1991 |

*Finish in overall standings (No. of teams in league)  #Advanced level

**Powerful Battery.** Righthander Ben McDonald, left, led Baltimore with 171 strikeouts while batterymate Chris Hoiles led Orioles hitters with 29 home runs.

## ROCHESTER                                                        AAA
## INTERNATIONAL LEAGUE

| BATTING | AVG | G | AB | R | H | 2B | 3B | HR | RBI | BB | SO | SB | CS | B | T | HT | WT | DOB | 1st Yr | Resides |
|---|---|---|---|---|---|---|---|---|---|---|---|---|---|---|---|---|---|---|---|---|
| Alexander, Manny | .244 | 120 | 471 | 55 | 115 | 23 | 8 | 6 | 51 | 22 | 60 | 19 | 7 | R | R | 5-10 | 160 | 3-20-71 | 1988 | San Pedro de Macoris, D.R. |
| Alstead, Jason | .178 | 23 | 45 | 8 | 8 | 1 | 0 | 0 | 4 | 5 | 8 | 2 | 1 | L | R | 6-0 | 190 | 8-7-68 | 1990 | Paynesville, Minn. |
| Buford, Damon | .284 | 27 | 116 | 24 | 33 | 6 | 1 | 1 | 4 | 7 | 16 | 10 | 2 | R | R | 5-10 | 170 | 6-12-70 | 1990 | Sherman Oaks, Calif. |
| Campbell, Darrin | .183 | 54 | 115 | 21 | 21 | 9 | 1 | 1 | 11 | 11 | 30 | 0 | 0 | R | R | 5-9 | 180 | 7-1-67 | 1988 | Cleveland, Ohio |
| Carey, Paul | .311 | 96 | 325 | 63 | 101 | 20 | 4 | 12 | 50 | 65 | 92 | 0 | 0 | R | L | 6-4 | 215 | 1-8-68 | 1990 | Weymouth, Mass. |
| Coolbaugh, Scott | .245 | 118 | 421 | 52 | 103 | 26 | 4 | 18 | 67 | 27 | 110 | 0 | 0 | R | R | 5-11 | 195 | 6-13-66 | 1987 | Seguin, Texas |
| Davis, Glenn | .250 | 7 | 24 | 2 | 6 | 1 | 1 | 0 | 3 | 2 | 8 | 0 | 0 | R | R | 6-3 | 212 | 3-28-61 | 1981 | Hunt Valley, Md. |
| Dickerson, Bobby | .250 | 40 | 88 | 12 | 22 | 3 | 1 | 3 | 18 | 4 | 18 | 0 | 1 | R | R | 6-0 | 182 | 9-4-65 | 1987 | La Place, La. |
| Dostal, Bruce | .296 | 88 | 297 | 46 | 88 | 12 | 5 | 3 | 29 | 39 | 73 | 13 | 7 | L | L | 6-0 | 195 | 3-10-65 | 1987 | Towaco, N.J. |
| 2-team (6 Scranton) | .294 | 94 | 310 | 46 | 91 | 12 | 5 | 3 | 30 | 41 | 78 | 14 | 8 | | | | | | | |
| Gomez, Leo | .200 | 4 | 15 | 3 | 3 | 1 | 0 | 0 | 1 | 3 | 4 | 0 | 0 | R | R | 6-0 | 208 | 3-2-67 | 1986 | Canovanas, P.R. |
| Hammonds, Jeffrey | .311 | 36 | 151 | 25 | 47 | 9 | 1 | 5 | 23 | 5 | 27 | 6 | 3 | R | R | 6-0 | 180 | 3-5-71 | 1992 | Scotch Plains, N.J. |
| Hinzo, Tommy | .271 | 136 | 560 | 83 | 152 | 25 | 5 | 6 | 69 | 37 | 78 | 29 | 12 | S | R | 5-11 | 175 | 6-18-64 | 1986 | Chula Vista, Calif. |
| Holland, Tim | .107 | 9 | 28 | 4 | 3 | 2 | 0 | 0 | 1 | 3 | 10 | 0 | 0 | R | R | 6-3 | 180 | 6-15-69 | 1987 | Sacramento, Calif. |
| Leonard, Mark | .276 | 97 | 330 | 57 | 91 | 23 | 1 | 17 | 58 | 60 | 81 | 0 | 1 | L | R | 6-0 | 212 | 8-14-64 | 1986 | San Jose, Calif. |
| Martinez, Chito | .262 | 43 | 145 | 14 | 38 | 11 | 0 | 5 | 23 | 11 | 34 | 0 | 0 | L | L | 5-10 | 185 | 12-19-65 | 1984 | Metairie, La. |
| Palacios, Rey | .000 | 1 | 1 | 0 | 0 | 0 | 0 | 0 | 0 | 0 | 0 | 0 | 0 | R | R | 5-10 | 190 | 11-8-62 | 1983 | Lakeland, Fla. |
| Parent, Mark | .247 | 92 | 332 | 47 | 82 | 15 | 0 | 14 | 56 | 40 | 71 | 0 | 1 | R | R | 6-5 | 225 | 9-16-61 | 1979 | San Diego, Calif. |
| Ready, Randy | .289 | 84 | 305 | 48 | 88 | 17 | 3 | 9 | 46 | 50 | 37 | 4 | 0 | R | R | 5-11 | 180 | 1-8-60 | 1980 | Cardiff, Calif. |
| Smith, Mark | .280 | 129 | 485 | 69 | 136 | 27 | 1 | 12 | 68 | 37 | 90 | 4 | 6 | R | R | 6-3 | 205 | 5-7-70 | 1991 | Arcadia, Calif. |
| Tackett, Jeff | .320 | 8 | 25 | 1 | 8 | 2 | 0 | 0 | 2 | 3 | 8 | 0 | 0 | R | R | 6-2 | 205 | 12-1-65 | 1984 | Camarillo, Calif. |
| Voigt, Jack | .361 | 18 | 61 | 16 | 22 | 6 | 1 | 3 | 11 | 9 | 14 | 0 | 1 | R | R | 6-1 | 170 | 5-17-66 | 1987 | Venice, Fla. |
| Wearing, Mel | .235 | 112 | 379 | 52 | 89 | 14 | 2 | 14 | 61 | 55 | 109 | 5 | 1 | R | R | 6-3 | 230 | 4-19-67 | 1989 | West Haven, Conn. |
| Yacopino, Ed | .149 | 17 | 47 | 6 | 7 | 1 | 0 | 0 | 5 | 1 | 6 | 0 | 0 | S | L | 6-0 | 170 | 9-19-65 | 1987 | Aliquippa, Pa. |
| Zaun, Greg | .256 | 21 | 78 | 10 | 20 | 4 | 2 | 1 | 11 | 6 | 11 | 0 | 0 | S | R | 5-10 | 170 | 4-14-71 | 1989 | Glendale, Calif. |

| PITCHING | W | L | ERA | G | GS | CG | SV | IP | H | R | ER | BB | SO | B | T | HT | WT | DOB | 1st Yr | Resides |
|---|---|---|---|---|---|---|---|---|---|---|---|---|---|---|---|---|---|---|---|---|
| Bielecki, Mike | 5 | 3 | 5.03 | 9 | 9 | 0 | 0 | 48 | 56 | 33 | 27 | 16 | 31 | R | R | 6-3 | 200 | 7-31-59 | 1979 | Crownsville, Md. |
| Clements, Pat | 0 | 0 | 5.91 | 8 | 0 | 0 | 1 | 11 | 14 | 7 | 7 | 8 | 8 | R | L | 6-0 | 180 | 2-2-62 | 1983 | Chico, Calif. |
| Cook, Mike | 6 | 7 | 3.10 | 57 | 0 | 0 | 13 | 81 | 77 | 39 | 28 | 48 | 74 | L | R | 6-3 | 225 | 8-14-63 | 1985 | Charleston, S.C. |
| Dedrick, Jim | 1 | 0 | 2.57 | 1 | 1 | 1 | 0 | 7 | 6 | 2 | 2 | 0 | 3 | S | R | 6-0 | 185 | 4-4-68 | 1990 | Everett, Wash. |
| Dubois, Brian | 0 | 2 | 9.00 | 3 | 3 | 0 | 0 | 13 | 20 | 13 | 13 | 4 | 10 | L | L | 5-8 | 160 | 4-18-67 | 1985 | Sarasota, Fla. |
| Krivda, Rick | 3 | 0 | 1.89 | 5 | 5 | 0 | 0 | 33 | 20 | 7 | 7 | 16 | 23 | R | L | 6-1 | 180 | 1-19-70 | 1991 | McKeesport, Pa. |
| Manuel, Barry | 1 | 1 | 3.66 | 9 | 0 | 0 | 0 | 20 | 14 | 8 | 8 | 7 | 11 | R | R | 5-11 | 185 | 8-12-65 | 1987 | Mamou, La. |
| McGehee, Kevin | 7 | 6 | 2.96 | 20 | 20 | 2 | 0 | 134 | 124 | 53 | 44 | 37 | 92 | R | R | 6-0 | 190 | 1-18-69 | 1990 | Pineville, La. |
| Moyer, Jamie | 6 | 0 | 1.67 | 8 | 8 | 1 | 0 | 54 | 42 | 13 | 10 | 13 | 41 | L | L | 6-0 | 170 | 11-18-62 | 1984 | Granger, Ill. |

# ORIOLES: ORGANIZATION LEADERS

## MAJOR LEAGUERS

### BATTING
| | | |
|---|---|---|
| *AVG | Harold Baines | .313 |
| R | Two tied at | 87 |
| H | Two tied at | 165 |
| TB | Cal Ripken | 269 |
| 2B | Brady Anderson | 36 |
| 3B | Brady Anderson | 8 |
| HR | Chris Hoiles | 29 |
| RBI | Cal Ripken | 90 |
| BB | Brady Anderson | 82 |
| SO | Two tied at | 99 |
| SB | Brady Anderson | 24 |

### PITCHING
| | | |
|---|---|---|
| W | Mike Mussina | 14 |
| L | Ben McDonald | 14 |
| #ERA | Alan Mills | 3.23 |
| G | Todd Frohwirth | 70 |
| CG | Ben McDonald | 7 |
| SV | Gregg Olson | 29 |
| IP | Ben McDonald | 220 |
| BB | Ben McDonald | 86 |
| SO | Ben McDonald | 171 |

**Brady Anderson**
Stole 24 bases

R&R SPORTS GROUP

## MINOR LEAGUERS

### BATTING
| | | |
|---|---|---|
| *AVG | Bryan Link, Bluefield-Frederick | .338 |
| R | Curtis Goodwin, Frederick | 98 |
| H | Billy Owens, Albany-Frederick | 157 |
| TB | Alex Ochoa, Frederick | 225 |
| 2B | Eric Chavez, Albany | 38 |
| 3B | Brad Tyler, Bowie | 17 |
| HR | Stanton Cameron, Bowie | 21 |
| RBI | Alex Ochoa, Frederick | 90 |
| BB | Two tied at | 84 |
| SO | Tim Holland, Bowie-Rochester | 132 |
| SB | Curtis Goodwin, Frederick | 61 |

### PITCHING
| | | |
|---|---|---|
| W | Garrett Stephenson, Albany | 16 |
| L | Two tied at | 13 |
| #ERA | Dave Paveloff, Bowie-Frederick | 1.43 |
| G | Mike Cook, Rochester | 57 |
| CG | Matt Jarvis, Albany | 8 |
| SV | Rafael Chaves, Bowie | 20 |
| IP | Matt Jarvis, Albany | 185 |
| BB | Matt Jarvis, Albany | 82 |
| SO | Rick Forney, Frederick-Bowie | 179 |

*Minimum 250 At-Bats #Minimum 75 Innings

### PITCHING
| | W | L | ERA | G | GS | CG | SV | IP | H | R | ER | BB | SO | B | T | HT | WT | DOB | 1st Yr | Resides |
|---|---|---|---|---|---|---|---|---|---|---|---|---|---|---|---|---|---|---|---|---|
| O'Donoghue, John | 7 | 4 | 3.88 | 22 | 20 | 2 | 0 | 128 | 122 | 60 | 55 | 41 | 111 | L | L | 6-6 | 198 | 5-26-69 | 1990 | Elkton, Md. |
| Oquist, Mike | 9 | 8 | 3.50 | 28 | 21 | 2 | 0 | 149 | 144 | 62 | 58 | 41 | 128 | R | R | 6-2 | 170 | 5-30-68 | 1989 | LaJunta, Colo. |
| Pennington, Brad | 1 | 2 | 3.45 | 17 | 0 | 0 | 8 | 16 | 12 | 11 | 6 | 13 | 19 | L | L | 6-5 | 205 | 4-14-69 | 1989 | Salem, Ind. |
| Rhodes, Arthur | 1 | 1 | 4.05 | 6 | 6 | 0 | 0 | 27 | 26 | 12 | 12 | 15 | 33 | L | L | 6-2 | 204 | 10-24-69 | 1988 | Sarasota, Fla. |
| Ricci, Chuck | 0 | 0 | 5.63 | 4 | 0 | 0 | 0 | 8 | 11 | 5 | 5 | 3 | 6 | R | R | 6-2 | 180 | 11-20-68 | 1987 | Naples, Fla. |
| Satre, Jason | 4 | 5 | 5.85 | 15 | 15 | 0 | 0 | 80 | 87 | 57 | 52 | 45 | 42 | R | R | 6-1 | 180 | 8-24-70 | 1988 | Abilene, Texas |
| Schulze, Don | 8 | 5 | 4.10 | 39 | 9 | 1 | 7 | 97 | 111 | 49 | 44 | 24 | 65 | R | R | 6-3 | 235 | 9-27-62 | 1980 | Dixon, Ill. |
| Searcy, Steve | 2 | 1 | 6.00 | 16 | 0 | 0 | 1 | 15 | 19 | 10 | 10 | 15 | 12 | L | L | 6-1 | 190 | 6-4-64 | 1985 | Knoxville, Tenn. |
| Stephan, Todd | 3 | 7 | 5.10 | 29 | 10 | 0 | 1 | 95 | 98 | 58 | 54 | 35 | 71 | L | R | 6-3 | 195 | 5-28-66 | 1989 | Baltimore, Md. |
| Telford, Anthony | 7 | 7 | 4.27 | 38 | 6 | 0 | 2 | 91 | 98 | 51 | 43 | 33 | 66 | R | R | 6-0 | 189 | 3-6-66 | 1987 | San Jose, Calif. |
| Valenzuela, Fernando | 0 | 1 | 10.80 | 1 | 1 | 0 | 0 | 3 | 6 | 4 | 4 | 3 | 1 | L | L | 5-11 | 202 | 11-1-60 | 1978 | Los Angeles, Calif. |
| Williams, Jeff | 2 | 5 | 5.76 | 33 | 5 | 0 | 1 | 86 | 95 | 59 | 55 | 47 | 59 | R | R | 6-4 | 230 | 4-16-69 | 1990 | Wichita, Kan. |
| Wood, Brian | 1 | 2 | 2.70 | 30 | 0 | 0 | 3 | 53 | 47 | 20 | 16 | 32 | 59 | L | R | 6-2 | 200 | 7-29-65 | 1986 | Shepersdville, Ky. |

### FIELDING

| Catcher | PCT | G | PO | A | E | DP |
|---|---|---|---|---|---|---|
| Campbell | .992 | 51 | 243 | 13 | 2 | 1 |
| Palacios | 1.000 | 1 | 4 | 1 | 0 | 0 |
| Parent | .995 | 86 | 549 | 63 | 3 | 11 |
| Tackett | .967 | 8 | 56 | 3 | 2 | 0 |
| Zaun | .975 | 21 | 141 | 18 | 4 | 4 |

| First Base | PCT | G | PO | A | E | DP |
|---|---|---|---|---|---|---|
| Carey | .993 | 91 | 752 | 53 | 6 | 70 |
| Coolbaugh | 1.000 | 7 | 65 | 3 | 0 | 4 |
| Davis | 1.000 | 5 | 28 | 7 | 0 | 2 |
| Dickerson | .900 | 7 | 6 | 3 | 1 | 1 |
| Ready | 1.000 | 12 | 94 | 9 | 0 | 6 |
| Voigt | 1.000 | 2 | 18 | 1 | 0 | 1 |
| Wearing | .988 | 32 | 240 | 11 | 3 | 17 |

| Second Base | PCT | G | PO | A | E | DP |
|---|---|---|---|---|---|---|
| Dickerson | 1.000 | 2 | 4 | 5 | 0 | 1 |
| Hinzo | .966 | 136 | 267 | 415 | 24 | 75 |
| Ready | 1.000 | 3 | 7 | 11 | 0 | 3 |

| Third Base | PCT | G | PO | A | E | DP |
|---|---|---|---|---|---|---|
| Coolbaugh | .912 | 110 | 82 | 253 | 23 | 18 |
| Dickerson | .909 | 9 | 1 | 9 | 1 | 2 |
| Gomez | 1.000 | 3 | 1 | 5 | 0 | 0 |
| Ready | .930 | 27 | 18 | 48 | 5 | 4 |
| Voigt | 1.000 | 3 | 2 | 3 | 0 | 1 |

| Shortstop | PCT | G | PO | A | E | DP |
|---|---|---|---|---|---|---|
| Alexander | .966 | 119 | 184 | 335 | 18 | 71 |
| Dickerson | .957 | 18 | 19 | 47 | 3 | 10 |

| | PCT | G | PO | A | E | DP |
|---|---|---|---|---|---|---|
| Holland | .939 | 8 | 10 | 21 | 2 | 5 |

| Outfield | PCT | G | PO | A | E | DP |
|---|---|---|---|---|---|---|
| Alstead | 1.000 | 21 | 29 | 2 | 0 | 0 |
| Buford | .962 | 27 | 73 | 3 | 3 | 1 |
| Dostal | .990 | 83 | 185 | 6 | 2 | 1 |
| Hammonds | 1.000 | 30 | 72 | 1 | 0 | 0 |
| Leonard | .985 | 69 | 127 | 2 | 2 | 1 |
| Martinez | .911 | 29 | 36 | 5 | 4 | 2 |
| Ready | .975 | 25 | 37 | 2 | 1 | 0 |
| Smith | .975 | 127 | 261 | 9 | 7 | 1 |
| Voigt | .950 | 14 | 18 | 1 | 1 | 0 |
| Wearing | 1.000 | 16 | 26 | 1 | 0 | 0 |
| Yacopino | 1.000 | 14 | 24 | 1 | 0 | 0 |

# BOWIE                                                                 AA

## EASTERN LEAGUE

### BATTING
| | AVG | G | AB | R | H | 2B | 3B | HR | RBI | BB | SO | SB | CS | B | T | HT | WT | DOB | 1st Yr | Resides |
|---|---|---|---|---|---|---|---|---|---|---|---|---|---|---|---|---|---|---|---|---|
| Alfonzo, Ed, 3b-2b | .264 | 130 | 459 | 45 | 121 | 22 | 3 | 5 | 49 | 37 | 49 | 14 | 4 | R | R | 6-0 | 187 | 6-10-67 | 1985 | Santa Teresa, Venez. |
| Alstead, Jason, of | .298 | 53 | 124 | 25 | 37 | 4 | 3 | 2 | 13 | 11 | 18 | 12 | 5 | L | R | 6-0 | 190 | 8-7-68 | 1990 | Paynesville, Minn. |
| Baines, Harold, dh | .000 | 2 | 6 | 0 | 0 | 0 | 0 | 0 | 0 | 1 | 1 | 0 | 0 | L | L | 6-2 | 195 | 3-15-59 | 1977 | St. Michael's, Md. |
| Cameron, Stanton, of | .276 | 118 | 384 | 65 | 106 | 27 | 1 | 21 | 64 | 84 | 103 | 6 | 7 | R | R | 6-5 | 195 | 7-5-69 | 1987 | Powell, Tenn. |
| Davis, Glenn, 1b | .333 | 2 | 6 | 2 | 2 | 1 | 0 | 1 | 1 | 1 | 0 | 0 | 0 | R | R | 6-3 | 212 | 3-28-61 | 1981 | Hunt Valley, Md. |
| Devaraz, Cesar, c | .224 | 57 | 174 | 14 | 39 | 7 | 1 | 0 | 17 | 5 | 21 | 5 | 1 | R | R | 5-10 | 175 | 9-22-69 | 1988 | San Pedro de Macoris, D.R. |
| Devereaux, Mike, of | .286 | 2 | 7 | 1 | 2 | 1 | 0 | 0 | 2 | 0 | 2 | 0 | 0 | R | R | 6-0 | 195 | 4-10-63 | 1985 | Scottsdale, Ariz. |
| Ferretti, Sam, 3b-ss | .238 | 60 | 164 | 24 | 39 | 6 | 0 | 4 | 18 | 18 | 30 | 2 | 2 | R | R | 5-10 | 175 | 8-25-65 | 1987 | Rutherford, N.J. |
| Hammonds, Jeffrey, of | .283 | 24 | 92 | 13 | 26 | 3 | 0 | 3 | 10 | 9 | 18 | 4 | 3 | R | R | 6-0 | 180 | 3-5-71 | 1992 | Scotch Plains, N.J. |
| Holland, Tim, ss | .249 | 130 | 449 | 49 | 112 | 17 | 5 | 9 | 53 | 25 | 123 | 9 | 8 | R | R | 6-3 | 180 | 6-15-69 | 1987 | Sacramento, Calif. |
| Lewis, T.R., dh-1b | .304 | 127 | 480 | 73 | 146 | 26 | 2 | 5 | 64 | 36 | 80 | 22 | 8 | R | R | 6-0 | 180 | 4-15-71 | 1989 | Jacksonville, Fla. |
| Martinez, Chito, dh-of | .077 | 5 | 13 | 5 | 1 | 0 | 0 | 0 | 0 | 2 | 2 | 0 | 0 | L | L | 5-10 | 185 | 12-19-65 | 1984 | Metairie, La. |
| Millares, Jose, 2b | .280 | 30 | 50 | 6 | 14 | 1 | 2 | 0 | 5 | 1 | 9 | 1 | 1 | R | R | 5-11 | 190 | 3-24-68 | 1990 | Alhambra, Calif. |
| Miller, Brent, 1b | .257 | 113 | 404 | 35 | 104 | 13 | 0 | 11 | 66 | 19 | 41 | 6 | 1 | L | R | 6-0 | 190 | 11-12-70 | 1990 | Columbus, Ga. |
| Obando, Sherman, of | .241 | 19 | 58 | 8 | 14 | 2 | 0 | 3 | 12 | 9 | 11 | 1 | 0 | R | R | 6-4 | 215 | 1-23-70 | 1988 | Changuinola, Panama |
| Ortiz, Basilio, of | .200 | 8 | 30 | 1 | 6 | 0 | 1 | 0 | 3 | 1 | 5 | 0 | 0 | R | R | 5-11 | 170 | 4-4-70 | 1991 | Hartford, Conn. |
| Ramirez, Danny, 2b | .065 | 15 | 31 | 3 | 2 | 0 | 0 | 0 | 1 | 6 | 0 | 0 | 0 | R | R | 5-10 | 165 | 6-30-68 | 1990 | Montebello, Calif. |
| Roso, Jimmy, c | .231 | 52 | 117 | 12 | 27 | 5 | 0 | 0 | 9 | 10 | 35 | 2 | 1 | S | R | 6-2 | 185 | 10-2-69 | 1989 | Portland, Ore. |
| Tyler, Brad, 2b-of | .236 | 139 | 437 | 85 | 103 | 24 | 17 | 10 | 44 | 89 | 124 | 11 | 5 | L | R | 6-2 | 175 | 3-3-69 | 1990 | Aurora, Ind. |
| Washington, Kyle, of | .252 | 120 | 389 | 50 | 98 | 23 | 4 | 7 | 33 | 39 | 96 | 16 | 12 | R | R | 6-2 | 190 | 12-9-69 | 1988 | Claremont, Calif. |
| Wawruck, Jim, of | .297 | 128 | 475 | 59 | 141 | 21 | 5 | 4 | 44 | 43 | 66 | 28 | 12 | L | L | 5-11 | 185 | 4-23-70 | 1991 | Glastonbury, Conn. |

| BATTING | AVG | G | AB | R | H | 2B | 3B | HR | RBI | BB | SO | SB | CS | B | T | HT | WT | DOB | 1st Yr | Resides |
|---|---|---|---|---|---|---|---|---|---|---|---|---|---|---|---|---|---|---|---|---|
| Zaun, Greg, c | .306 | 79 | 258 | 25 | 79 | 10 | 0 | 3 | 38 | 27 | 26 | 4 | 7 | S | R | 5-10 | 170 | 4-14-71 | 1989 | Glendale, Calif. |

| PITCHING | W | L | ERA | G | GS | CG | SV | IP | H | R | ER | BB | SO | B | T | HT | WT | DOB | 1st Yr | Resides |
|---|---|---|---|---|---|---|---|---|---|---|---|---|---|---|---|---|---|---|---|---|
| Borowski, Joe | 3 | 0 | 0.00 | 9 | 0 | 0 | 0 | 18 | 11 | 0 | 0 | 11 | 17 | R | R | 6-2 | 225 | 5-4-71 | 1989 | Bayonne, N.J. |
| Chaves, Rafael | 2 | 5 | 3.94 | 45 | 0 | 0 | 20 | 48 | 56 | 23 | 21 | 16 | 39 | R | R | 6-0 | 195 | 11-1-68 | 1986 | Isabela, P.R. |
| Dedrick, Jim | 8 | 3 | 2.54 | 38 | 6 | 1 | 3 | 106 | 84 | 36 | 30 | 32 | 78 | S | R | 6-0 | 185 | 4-4-68 | 1990 | Everett, Wash. |
| Dubois, Brian | 6 | 1 | 2.52 | 13 | 13 | 0 | 0 | 75 | 71 | 36 | 21 | 29 | 37 | L | L | 5-8 | 160 | 4-18-67 | 1985 | Sarasota, Fla. |
| Farrar, Terry | 7 | 7 | 3.49 | 24 | 21 | 2 | 0 | 116 | 114 | 51 | 45 | 40 | 85 | S | L | 6-1 | 180 | 9-10-69 | 1991 | St. Louis, Mo. |
| Forney, Rick | 0 | 0 | 1.29 | 1 | 1 | 0 | 0 | 7 | 1 | 1 | 1 | 1 | 4 | R | R | 6-4 | 210 | 10-24-71 | 1991 | Arnold, Md. |
| Krivda, Rick | 7 | 5 | 3.08 | 22 | 22 | 0 | 0 | 126 | 114 | 46 | 43 | 50 | 108 | R | L | 6-1 | 180 | 1-19-70 | 1991 | McKeesport, Pa. |
| Mercedes, Jose | 6 | 8 | 4.78 | 26 | 23 | 3 | 0 | 147 | 170 | 86 | 78 | 65 | 75 | R | R | 6-1 | 180 | 3-5-71 | 1990 | Las Palmillas, D.R. |
| Mussina, Mike | 1 | 0 | 2.25 | 2 | 2 | 0 | 0 | 8 | 5 | 2 | 2 | 1 | 10 | R | R | 6-2 | 185 | 12-8-68 | 1990 | Montoursville, Pa. |
| Paveloff, Dave | 5 | 4 | 1.73 | 32 | 0 | 0 | 1 | 57 | 50 | 21 | 11 | 19 | 31 | R | R | 6-2 | 190 | 12-6-67 | 1990 | Palm Desert, Calif. |
| Ricci, Chuck | 7 | 4 | 3.20 | 34 | 1 | 0 | 5 | 82 | 72 | 35 | 29 | 20 | 83 | R | R | 6-2 | 185 | 11-20-68 | 1987 | Naples, Fla. |
| Ryan, Kevin | 3 | 10 | 5.30 | 16 | 15 | 2 | 0 | 88 | 106 | 67 | 52 | 34 | 40 | R | R | 6-1 | 180 | 9-23-70 | 1991 | Oklahoma City, Okla. |
| Satre, Jason | 7 | 3 | 3.11 | 13 | 13 | 2 | 0 | 84 | 68 | 35 | 29 | 20 | 65 | R | R | 6-1 | 180 | 8-24-70 | 1988 | Abilene, Texas |
| Schullstrom, Erik | 5 | 10 | 4.27 | 24 | 14 | 2 | 1 | 110 | 119 | 63 | 52 | 45 | 78 | R | R | 6-5 | 220 | 3-25-69 | 1990 | San Leandro, Calif. |
| Smith, Daryl | 0 | 0 | 2.45 | 3 | 3 | 0 | 0 | 22 | 14 | 7 | 6 | 11 | 23 | R | R | 6-4 | 220 | 7-29-60 | 1980 | Baltimore, Md. |
| Smith, Mark | 0 | 1 | 8.22 | 5 | 1 | 0 | 0 | 8 | 11 | 7 | 7 | 1 | 4 | R | R | 6-4 | 195 | 4-9-68 | 1990 | Houston, Texas |
| Taylor, Tom | 4 | 7 | 5.62 | 40 | 4 | 0 | 4 | 90 | 90 | 65 | 56 | 47 | 69 | R | R | 6-1 | 180 | 7-16-70 | 1989 | Louisa, Va. |
| Valenzuela, Fernando | 0 | 0 | 1.50 | 1 | 1 | 0 | 0 | 6 | 4 | 1 | 1 | 0 | 4 | L | L | 5-11 | 202 | 11-1-60 | 1978 | Los Angeles, Calif. |
| Wood, Brian | 1 | 0 | 3.38 | 8 | 0 | 0 | 1 | 13 | 13 | 6 | 5 | 8 | 15 | L | R | 6-2 | 200 | 7-29-65 | 1986 | Shepardsville, Ky. |

## FREDERICK A
## CAROLINA LEAGUE

| BATTING | AVG | G | AB | R | H | 2B | 3B | HR | RBI | BB | SO | SB | CS | B | T | HT | WT | DOB | 1st Yr | Resides |
|---|---|---|---|---|---|---|---|---|---|---|---|---|---|---|---|---|---|---|---|---|
| Alstead, Jason, of | .228 | 21 | 57 | 6 | 13 | 1 | 0 | 0 | 1 | 12 | 8 | 1 | 2 | L | R | 6-0 | 190 | 8-7-68 | 1990 | Paynesville, Minn. |
| Castaldo, Gregg, 2b-ss | .216 | 75 | 208 | 23 | 45 | 8 | 0 | 0 | 13 | 27 | 61 | 2 | 3 | R | R | 6-0 | 180 | 3-14-71 | 1992 | Creve Coeur, Mo. |
| Davis, Glenn, 1b-dh | .273 | 3 | 11 | 1 | 3 | 1 | 0 | 0 | 2 | 1 | 3 | 0 | 0 | R | R | 6-3 | 212 | 3-28-61 | 1981 | Hunt Valley, Md. |
| Devarez, Cesar, c | .290 | 38 | 124 | 15 | 36 | 8 | 0 | 2 | 16 | 12 | 18 | 1 | 4 | R | R | 5-10 | 175 | 9-22-69 | 1988 | San Pedro de Macoris, D.R. |
| Goodwin, Curtis, of | .281 | 138 | 555 | 98 | 156 | 15 | 10 | 2 | 42 | 52 | 90 | 61 | 15 | L | L | 5-11 | 180 | 9-30-72 | 1991 | San Leandro, Calif. |
| Gresham, Kris, c | .218 | 66 | 188 | 22 | 41 | 13 | 1 | 4 | 17 | 13 | 41 | 1 | 0 | R | R | 6-1 | 193 | 8-30-71 | 1991 | Charlotte, N.C. |
| Hodge, Roy, of | .205 | 67 | 166 | 17 | 34 | 9 | 1 | 0 | 12 | 18 | 29 | 4 | 1 | R | R | 6-2 | 175 | 6-22-71 | 1990 | St. Thomas, V.I. |
| Link, Bryan, of | .333 | 6 | 24 | 3 | 8 | 3 | 0 | 1 | 2 | 3 | 5 | 0 | 0 | L | L | 6-1 | 185 | 1-9-71 | 1993 | Nashville, Tenn. |
| McClain, Scott, 3b | .260 | 133 | 427 | 65 | 111 | 22 | 2 | 9 | 54 | 70 | 88 | 10 | 6 | R | R | 6-3 | 200 | 5-19-72 | 1990 | Atascadero, Calif. |
| McConathy, Doug, dh | .217 | 100 | 322 | 25 | 70 | 13 | 2 | 7 | 41 | 30 | 37 | 1 | 0 | L | R | 6-2 | 185 | 2-18-71 | 1991 | Buena Park, Calif. |
| Mercedes, Feliciano, ss | .228 | 123 | 400 | 45 | 91 | 17 | 6 | 2 | 35 | 44 | 91 | 17 | 7 | S | R | 5-10 | 145 | 7-9-73 | 1990 | Villa Magdalena, D.R. |
| Millares, Jose, 2b | .251 | 85 | 299 | 38 | 75 | 11 | 0 | 9 | 36 | 23 | 44 | 4 | 4 | R | R | 5-11 | 190 | 3-24-68 | 1990 | Alhambra, Calif. |
| Ochoa, Alex, of | .276 | 137 | 532 | 84 | 147 | 29 | 5 | 13 | 90 | 46 | 67 | 34 | 13 | R | R | 6-0 | 173 | 3-29-72 | 1991 | Miami Lakes, Fla. |
| Ortiz, Basilio, of | .282 | 104 | 351 | 72 | 99 | 18 | 7 | 10 | 60 | 44 | 65 | 12 | 11 | R | R | 5-11 | 170 | 4-4-70 | 1991 | Hartford, Conn. |
| Owens, Billy, 1b-dh | .350 | 17 | 60 | 8 | 21 | 4 | 0 | 0 | 8 | 3 | 6 | 0 | 0 | S | R | 6-1 | 210 | 4-12-71 | 1992 | Fresno, Calif. |
| Ramirez, Dan, 2b-ss | .215 | 41 | 130 | 11 | 28 | 4 | 0 | 0 | 9 | 7 | 26 | 3 | 3 | R | R | 5-10 | 165 | 6-30-68 | 1990 | Montebello, Calif. |
| Seitzer, Brad, 1b | .253 | 130 | 439 | 44 | 111 | 24 | 3 | 10 | 68 | 58 | 95 | 3 | 3 | R | R | 6-2 | 195 | 2-2-70 | 1991 | Lincoln, Ill. |
| Tallman, Troy, c | .189 | 55 | 143 | 16 | 27 | 7 | 0 | 3 | 12 | 19 | 48 | 3 | 0 | R | R | 6-0 | 195 | 3-17-70 | 1991 | Napa, Calif. |
| Waszgis, B.J., c | .248 | 31 | 109 | 12 | 27 | 3 | 0 | 3 | 9 | 9 | 21 | 0 | 1 | R | R | 6-2 | 225 | 8-24-70 | 1991 | Omaha, Neb. |

| PITCHING | W | L | ERA | G | GS | CG | SV | IP | H | R | ER | BB | SO | B | T | HT | WT | DOB | 1st Yr | Resides |
|---|---|---|---|---|---|---|---|---|---|---|---|---|---|---|---|---|---|---|---|---|
| Benavides, Al | 1 | 2 | 5.17 | 25 | 0 | 0 | 0 | 38 | 42 | 27 | 22 | 21 | 31 | R | R | 6-1 | 170 | 1-1-68 | 1991 | Corpus Christi, Texas |
| Benitez, Armando | 3 | 0 | 0.66 | 12 | 0 | 0 | 4 | 14 | 7 | 1 | 1 | 4 | 29 | R | R | 6-4 | 180 | 11-3-72 | 1990 | Santo Domingo, D.R. |
| Borowski, Joe | 1 | 1 | 3.61 | 42 | 0 | 0 | 11 | 62 | 61 | 30 | 25 | 37 | 70 | R | R | 6-2 | 225 | 5-4-71 | 1989 | Bayonne, N.J. |
| Cusey, Lee | 1 | 1 | 3.58 | 16 | 1 | 0 | 1 | 28 | 27 | 13 | 11 | 9 | 16 | R | R | 6-0 | 160 | 12-21-70 | 1992 | Santa Fe Springs, Calif. |
| Dubois, Brian | 6 | 2 | 1.55 | 10 | 8 | 1 | 0 | 58 | 50 | 19 | 10 | 13 | 55 | L | L | 5-8 | 160 | 4-18-67 | 1985 | Sarasota, Fla. |
| Eshelman, Vaughn | 7 | 10 | 3.89 | 24 | 24 | 2 | 0 | 143 | 128 | 70 | 62 | 59 | 122 | L | L | 6-3 | 205 | 5-22-69 | 1991 | Houston, Texas |
| Forney, Rick | 14 | 8 | 2.78 | 27 | 27 | 2 | 0 | 165 | 156 | 64 | 51 | 64 | 175 | R | R | 6-4 | 210 | 10-24-71 | 1991 | Arnold, Md. |
| Haynes, Jimmy | 12 | 8 | 3.03 | 27 | 27 | 2 | 0 | 172 | 139 | 73 | 58 | 61 | 174 | R | R | 6-4 | 175 | 9-5-72 | 1991 | LaGrange, Ga. |
| Jones, Stacy | 0 | 2 | 9.95 | 4 | 2 | 0 | 0 | 13 | 24 | 17 | 14 | 1 | 7 | R | R | 6-6 | 225 | 5-26-67 | 1988 | Attalla, Ala. |
| Klingenbeck, Scott | 13 | 4 | 2.98 | 23 | 23 | 0 | 0 | 139 | 151 | 62 | 46 | 35 | 146 | R | R | 6-2 | 200 | 2-3-71 | 1992 | Cincinnati, Ohio |
| Lemp, Chris | 4 | 1 | 3.56 | 52 | 0 | 0 | 8 | 61 | 51 | 32 | 24 | 35 | 51 | R | R | 6-0 | 175 | 7-23-71 | 1991 | Sacramento, Calif. |
| Paveloff, Dave | 2 | 1 | 0.73 | 24 | 0 | 0 | 15 | 25 | 16 | 4 | 2 | 8 | 18 | R | R | 6-2 | 190 | 12-6-67 | 1990 | Palm Desert, Calif. |
| Polasek, John | 3 | 4 | 3.36 | 55 | 0 | 0 | 5 | 59 | 39 | 24 | 22 | 31 | 56 | L | L | 6-2 | 195 | 8-30-68 | 1990 | Anchorage, Alaska |
| Ryan, Kevin | 0 | 3 | 2.43 | 15 | 2 | 0 | 1 | 33 | 28 | 11 | 9 | 9 | 23 | R | R | 6-1 | 180 | 9-23-70 | 1991 | Oklahoma City, Okla. |
| Sackinsky, Brian | 6 | 8 | 3.20 | 18 | 18 | 1 | 0 | 121 | 117 | 55 | 43 | 37 | 112 | R | R | 6-4 | 220 | 6-22-71 | 1992 | Library, Pa. |
| Smith, Mark | 5 | 6 | 3.84 | 31 | 6 | 0 | 0 | 82 | 84 | 35 | 35 | 21 | 64 | R | R | 6-4 | 195 | 4-9-68 | 1990 | Houston, Texas |

# ORIOLES: MOST COMMON LINEUPS

| | Baltimore<br>Majors | Rochester<br>AAA | Bowie<br>AA | Frederick<br>A | Albany<br>A |
|---|---|---|---|---|---|
| C | Chris Hoiles (124) | Mark Parent (86) | Gregg Zaun (61) | Troy Tallman (51) | Marco Manrique (88) |
| 1B | David Segui (144) | Paul Carey (91) | Brent Miller (87) | Brad Seitzer (99) | Billy Owens (113) |
| 2B | Harold Reynolds (141) | Tommy Hinzo (136) | Brad Tyler (112) | Jose Millares (73) | Jose Serra (106) |
| 3B | Tim Hulett (75) | Scott Coolbaugh (110) | Ed Alfonzo (108) | Scott McClain (132) | Eric Chavez (131) |
| SS | Cal Ripken (162) | Manny Alexander (119) | Tim Holland (128) | Feliciano Mercedes (120) | Juan Bautista (133) |
| OF | Brady Anderson (140) | Mark Smith (128) | Jim Wawruck (121) | Curtis Goodwin (136) | Clayton Byrne (122) |
| | Mike Devereaux (130) | Bruce Dostal (80) | Stanton Cameron (115) | Alex Ochoa (133) | Kyle Yeske (104) |
| | Mark McLemore (124) | Mark Leonard (70) | Kyle Washington (106) | Basilio Ortiz (98) | Keith Eaddy (56) |
| DH | Harold Baines (140) | Mel Wearing (54) | T.R. Lewis (73) | Doug McConathy (62) | Scott Metcalf (52) |
| SP | Ben McDonald (34) | Mike Oquist (21) | Jose Mercedes (23) | Forney/Haynes (27) | Matt Jarvis (29) |
| RP | Todd Frohwirth (70) | Mike Cook (57) | Rafael Chaves (45) | John Polasek (55) | Larry Shenk (53) |

Full-season farm clubs only   No. of games at position in parenthesis

## ORIOLES TOP 10 PROSPECTS

How the Orioles Top 10 prospects, as judged by Baseball America prior to the 1993 season, fared in 1993:

| Player, Pos. | Club (Class) | AVG | AB | H | HR | RBI | SB |
|---|---|---|---|---|---|---|---|
| 2. Jeffrey Hammonds, of | Bowie (AA) | .283 | 92 | 26 | 3 | 10 | 4 |
| | Rochester (AAA) | .311 | 151 | 47 | 5 | 23 | 6 |
| | Baltimore | .305 | 105 | 32 | 3 | 19 | 4 |
| 3. Manny Alexander, ss | Rochester (AAA) | .244 | 471 | 115 | 6 | 51 | 19 |
| | Baltimore | .000 | 0 | 0 | 0 | 0 | 0 |
| 4. Alex Ochoa, of | Frederick (A) | .276 | 532 | 147 | 13 | 90 | 34 |
| 7. Mark Smith, of | Rochester (AAA) | .280 | 485 | 136 | 12 | 68 | 4 |
| 9. Luis Mercedes, of* | Phoenix (AAA) | .291 | 244 | 71 | 0 | 15 | 14 |
| | Baltimore | .292 | 24 | 7 | 0 | 0 | 1 |
| | San Francisco | .160 | 25 | 4 | 0 | 3 | 0 |
| 10. T.R. Lewis, 1b | Bowie (AA) | .304 | 480 | 146 | 5 | 64 | 22 |

| | | W | L | ERA | IP | H | BB | SO |
|---|---|---|---|---|---|---|---|---|
| 1. Brad Pennington, lhp | Rochester (AAA) | 1 | 2 | 3.45 | 16 | 12 | 13 | 19 |
| | Baltimore | 3 | 2 | 6.55 | 33 | 34 | 25 | 39 |
| 5. Jimmy Haynes, rhp | Frederick (A) | 12 | 8 | 3.03 | 172 | 139 | 61 | 174 |
| 6. Jose Mercedes, rhp | Bowie (AA) | 6 | 8 | 4.78 | 147 | 170 | 65 | 75 |
| 8. J. O'Donoghue, lhp | Rochester (AAA) | 7 | 4 | 3.88 | 128 | 122 | 41 | 111 |
| | Baltimore | 0 | 1 | 4.58 | 20 | 22 | 10 | 16 |

*Traded to San Francisco Giants

**Brad Pennington**
3-2 at Baltimore

---

## ALBANY — A
### SOUTH ATLANTIC LEAGUE

| BATTING | AVG | G | AB | R | H | 2B | 3B | HR | RBI | BB | SO | SB | CS | B | T | HT | WT | DOB | 1st Yr | Resides |
|---|---|---|---|---|---|---|---|---|---|---|---|---|---|---|---|---|---|---|---|---|
| Barnden, Myles, dh-3b | .362 | 12 | 47 | 6 | 17 | 3 | 0 | 2 | 11 | 6 | 5 | 0 | 1 | L | R | 6-0 | 190 | 6-27-72 | 1992 | Springvale, Australia |
| Bautista, Juan, ss | .237 | 98 | 295 | 24 | 70 | 17 | 2 | 0 | 28 | 14 | 72 | 11 | 3 | R | R | 6-1 | 190 | 6-24-72 | 1992 | San Pedro de Macoris, D.R. |
| Berrios, Harry, of | .207 | 46 | 145 | 16 | 30 | 5 | 1 | 3 | 16 | 18 | 20 | 2 | 0 | R | R | 5-11 | 205 | 12-2-71 | 1993 | Grand Rapids, Mich. |
| Byrne, Clayton, of | .276 | 122 | 457 | 64 | 126 | 26 | 3 | 6 | 55 | 42 | 69 | 23 | 11 | R | R | 6-1 | 180 | 2-12-72 | 1991 | Perth, Australia |
| Chavez, Eric, 3b | .250 | 139 | 476 | 74 | 119 | 38 | 2 | 18 | 74 | 79 | 124 | 3 | 3 | R | R | 5-11 | 212 | 9-7-70 | 1992 | Carlsbad, N.M. |
| Clark, Howie, 2b | .235 | 7 | 17 | 2 | 4 | 0 | 0 | 0 | 1 | 0 | 3 | 1 | 0 | L | R | 5-10 | 171 | 2-13-74 | 1992 | Huntington Beach, Calif. |
| Curtis, Kevin, of | .200 | 59 | 180 | 26 | 36 | 7 | 0 | 7 | 27 | 38 | 36 | 4 | 3 | R | R | 6-2 | 210 | 8-19-75 | 1993 | Upland, Calif. |
| Delgado, Geno, 2b-ss | .209 | 78 | 206 | 33 | 43 | 9 | 3 | 0 | 14 | 28 | 35 | 14 | 5 | R | R | 5-11 | 155 | 12-21-71 | 1992 | Hialeah, Fla. |
| Eaddy, Keith, of | .262 | 86 | 229 | 40 | 60 | 13 | 2 | 3 | 18 | 41 | 69 | 12 | 9 | R | R | 5-10 | 165 | 11-23-70 | 1992 | Newark, N.J. |
| Hodge, Roy, of | .258 | 29 | 97 | 25 | 25 | 3 | 2 | 0 | 11 | 13 | 21 | 1 | 0 | R | R | 6-2 | 175 | 6-22-71 | 1990 | St. Thomas, V.I. |
| Manrique, Marco, c | .216 | 100 | 319 | 26 | 69 | 14 | 0 | 4 | 48 | 20 | 44 | 3 | 2 | R | R | 6-2 | 188 | 2-16-72 | 1991 | Caracas, Venez. |
| Mejia, Miguel, of | .165 | 23 | 79 | 11 | 13 | 0 | 3 | 0 | 2 | 4 | 22 | 7 | 2 | R | R | 6-1 | 155 | 3-25-75 | 1992 | San Pedro de Macoris, D.R. |
| Metcalf, Scott, dh-of | .256 | 115 | 375 | 48 | 96 | 16 | 2 | 4 | 45 | 35 | 69 | 6 | 0 | R | R | 6-4 | 205 | 1-11-72 | 1992 | Willerton, Australia |
| Michael, Jeff, ss-3b | .270 | 49 | 163 | 20 | 44 | 6 | 0 | 0 | 14 | 14 | 21 | 5 | 1 | R | R | 6-0 | 174 | 8-8-71 | 1993 | Hamilton, Ohio |
| Owens, Billy, 1b | .297 | 120 | 458 | 64 | 136 | 23 | 2 | 11 | 66 | 49 | 70 | 3 | 5 | S | R | 6-1 | 210 | 4-12-71 | 1992 | Fresno, Calif. |
| Riemer, Matt, ss-of | .130 | 11 | 23 | 1 | 3 | 0 | 0 | 0 | 2 | 2 | 5 | 1 | 1 | R | R | 6-3 | 180 | 9-1-72 | 1992 | Baltimore, Md. |
| Schmidt, Keith, of | .152 | 18 | 46 | 3 | 7 | 1 | 0 | 0 | 1 | 3 | 14 | 1 | 0 | L | R | 6-2 | 195 | 2-25-71 | 1989 | Burton, Texas |
| Serra, Jose, 2b | .213 | 111 | 390 | 62 | 83 | 15 | 1 | 1 | 23 | 35 | 51 | 26 | 6 | R | R | 5-11 | 160 | 3-28-73 | 1991 | San Pedro de Macoris, D.R. |
| Thomas, Duane, of | .077 | 8 | 13 | 2 | 1 | 0 | 1 | 0 | 0 | 1 | 11 | 0 | 1 | R | R | 6-0 | 190 | 8-8-71 | 1991 | Rocky Mount, N.C. |
| Tobin, Sean, 1b | .229 | 20 | 35 | 3 | 8 | 0 | 0 | 0 | 4 | 3 | 1 | 1 | 0 | R | R | 6-2 | 200 | 8-12-71 | 1993 | Concord, Maine |
| Waszgis, B.J., c-dh | .307 | 86 | 300 | 45 | 92 | 25 | 3 | 8 | 52 | 27 | 55 | 4 | 0 | R | R | 6-2 | 210 | 8-24-70 | 1991 | Omaha, Neb. |
| Yeske, Kyle, of | .224 | 109 | 313 | 36 | 70 | 13 | 2 | 3 | 40 | 35 | 92 | 6 | 6 | R | R | 6-4 | 205 | 2-20-70 | 1992 | Onalaska, Wis. |

| PITCHING | W | L | ERA | G | GS | CG | SV | IP | H | R | ER | BB | SO | B | T | HT | WT | DOB | 1st Yr | Resides |
|---|---|---|---|---|---|---|---|---|---|---|---|---|---|---|---|---|---|---|---|---|
| Benitez, Armando | 5 | 1 | 1.52 | 40 | 0 | 0 | 14 | 53 | 31 | 10 | 9 | 19 | 83 | R | R | 6-4 | 180 | 11-3-72 | 1990 | Santo Domingo, D.R. |
| Brewer, Brian | 0 | 3 | 2.57 | 6 | 3 | 0 | 0 | 21 | 19 | 14 | 6 | 21 | 19 | L | L | 6-0 | 207 | 12-10-71 | 1993 | Fairfield, Calif. |
| Chatterton, Chris | 3 | 2 | 5.00 | 25 | 1 | 0 | 1 | 45 | 53 | 35 | 25 | 24 | 47 | R | R | 6-0 | 165 | 4-23-70 | 1991 | Silver Spring, Md. |
| Chavez, Carlos | 1 | 3 | 5.29 | 20 | 0 | 0 | 3 | 34 | 33 | 20 | 20 | 18 | 28 | R | R | 6-1 | 190 | 8-25-72 | 1992 | El Paso, Texas |
| Conner, Scott | 6 | 6 | 5.14 | 37 | 13 | 0 | 0 | 116 | 133 | 92 | 66 | 71 | 90 | R | R | 6-2 | 182 | 3-22-72 | 1991 | Irvine, Calif. |
| Cusey, Lee | 2 | 0 | 2.22 | 11 | 0 | 0 | 0 | 24 | 23 | 8 | 6 | 5 | 20 | R | R | 6-0 | 160 | 12-21-70 | 1992 | Santa Fe Springs, Calif. |
| Devereux, Charles | 3 | 2 | 4.33 | 27 | 1 | 0 | 1 | 62 | 69 | 38 | 30 | 15 | 48 | R | R | 6-2 | 185 | 7-22-70 | 1992 | Derwood, Md. |
| Emerson, Scott | 10 | 9 | 3.54 | 27 | 27 | 1 | 0 | 147 | 143 | 72 | 58 | 62 | 115 | S | L | 6-5 | 180 | 12-22-71 | 1992 | Phoenix, Ariz. |
| Fregoso, Danny | 3 | 1 | 1.93 | 6 | 6 | 0 | 0 | 28 | 17 | 7 | 6 | 17 | 23 | R | R | 6-0 | 175 | 11-11-73 | 1991 | Tucson, Ariz. |
| Griffin, Ryan | 0 | 0 | 0.00 | 2 | 0 | 0 | 0 | 2 | 1 | 0 | 0 | 0 | 2 | R | R | 6-2 | 195 | 10-15-73 | 1991 | Dunedin, Fla. |
| Jarvis, Matt | 11 | 13 | 3.06 | 29 | 29 | 8 | 0 | 185 | 173 | 82 | 63 | 82 | 118 | R | L | 6-4 | 185 | 2-22-72 | 1991 | Albuquerque, N.M. |
| Lane, Aaron | 2 | 10 | 4.97 | 29 | 11 | 0 | 0 | 76 | 92 | 62 | 42 | 48 | 42 | L | L | 6-1 | 180 | 6-2-71 | 1992 | Taylorville, Ill. |
| Lombardi, John | 0 | 2 | 5.40 | 4 | 4 | 0 | 0 | 20 | 25 | 14 | 12 | 18 | 9 | R | R | 6-3 | 210 | 4-24-73 | 1993 | Warwick, R.I. |
| Porter, Mike | 0 | 0 | 4.80 | 10 | 0 | 0 | 0 | 15 | 14 | 19 | 8 | 25 | 11 | R | R | 6-3 | 210 | 9-21-69 | 1992 | Lawton, Okla. |
| Powell, Jay | 0 | 2 | 4.55 | 6 | 6 | 0 | 0 | 28 | 29 | 19 | 14 | 13 | 29 | R | R | 6-4 | 220 | 1-29-72 | 1993 | Meridian, Miss. |
| Sackinsky, Brian | 3 | 4 | 3.20 | 9 | 8 | 0 | 0 | 51 | 50 | 29 | 18 | 16 | 41 | R | R | 6-4 | 220 | 6-22-71 | 1992 | Library, Pa. |
| Shenk, Larry | 5 | 2 | 2.10 | 53 | 0 | 0 | 9 | 86 | 57 | 25 | 20 | 11 | 101 | R | R | 6-0 | 185 | 6-13-69 | 1992 | Federal Way, Wash. |
| Stephenson, Garrett | 16 | 7 | 2.84 | 30 | 24 | 3 | 1 | 171 | 142 | 65 | 54 | 44 | 147 | R | R | 6-4 | 185 | 1-2-72 | 1992 | Kimberly, Md. |
| Walker, Jim | 1 | 4 | 2.96 | 10 | 9 | 1 | 0 | 49 | 49 | 24 | 16 | 21 | 29 | R | R | 6-0 | 180 | 2-26-71 | 1993 | Nickerson, Kan. |

---

## BLUEFIELD — R
### APPALACHIAN LEAGUE

| BATTING | AVG | G | AB | R | H | 2B | 3B | HR | RBI | BB | SO | SB | CS | B | T | HT | WT | DOB | 1st Yr | Resides |
|---|---|---|---|---|---|---|---|---|---|---|---|---|---|---|---|---|---|---|---|---|
| Asermely, Bill, dh-of | .244 | 30 | 90 | 10 | 22 | 1 | 2 | 1 | 10 | 17 | 26 | 1 | 1 | R | R | 5-10 | 178 | 2-25-71 | 1993 | Pawtucket, R.I. |
| Barnden, Myles, 3b | .288 | 65 | 212 | 52 | 61 | 13 | 2 | 6 | 53 | 58 | 46 | 5 | 5 | L | R | 6-0 | 190 | 6-27-72 | 1992 | Springvale, Australia |
| Bartee, Kimera, of | .246 | 66 | 264 | 59 | 65 | 15 | 2 | 4 | 37 | 44 | 66 | 27 | 6 | R | R | 6-0 | 180 | 7-21-72 | 1993 | Omaha, Neb. |
| Bridgers, Brandon, of | .249 | 63 | 205 | 39 | 51 | 6 | 2 | 0 | 26 | 31 | 36 | 22 | 8 | R | R | 5-11 | 170 | 8-31-72 | 1993 | Fayetteville, N.C. |
| Castaneda, Hector, c | .179 | 22 | 56 | 8 | 10 | 4 | 0 | 0 | 6 | 2 | 19 | 0 | 2 | L | R | 6-2 | 190 | 11-1-71 | 1992 | Mexico City, Mexico |
| Clark, Howie, dh-2b | .294 | 58 | 180 | 29 | 53 | 10 | 1 | 3 | 30 | 26 | 34 | 2 | 2 | L | R | 5-10 | 171 | 2-13-74 | 1992 | Huntington Beach, Calif. |
| Foster, Jim, c | .326 | 61 | 218 | 59 | 71 | 21 | 1 | 10 | 45 | 42 | 34 | 3 | 1 | R | R | 6-4 | 220 | 8-18-71 | 1993 | Warwick, R.I. |

| BATTING | AVG | G | AB | R | H | 2B | 3B | HR | RBI | BB | SO | SB | CS | B | T | HT | WT | DOB | 1st Yr | Resides |
|---|---|---|---|---|---|---|---|---|---|---|---|---|---|---|---|---|---|---|---|---|
| Hawkins, Wes, of | .246 | 49 | 179 | 29 | 44 | 10 | 1 | 2 | 37 | 26 | 39 | 10 | 1 | R | R | 6-0 | 195 | 12-10-71 | 1993 | Mansfield, La. |
| Jones, Paul, 1b | .286 | 9 | 35 | 9 | 10 | 2 | 0 | 3 | 5 | 2 | 8 | 0 | 0 | L | L | 6-4 | 210 | 5-22-70 | 1992 | Russellville, Ky. |
| Link, Bryan, 1b-of | .338 | 68 | 266 | 64 | 90 | 17 | 1 | 14 | 60 | 42 | 38 | 9 | 9 | L | L | 6-1 | 185 | 1-9-71 | 1993 | Nashville, Tenn. |
| Martin, Lincoln, 2b | .273 | 64 | 245 | 50 | 67 | 15 | 0 | 6 | 34 | 44 | 52 | 26 | 7 | S | R | 5-10 | 170 | 10-20-71 | 1993 | Douglasville, Ga. |
| Reed, Ken, 1b-3b | .217 | 21 | 46 | 9 | 10 | 1 | 0 | 3 | 15 | 3 | 20 | 1 | 0 | R | R | 6-1 | 194 | 3-4-72 | 1993 | Hamilton, Ohio |
| Riemer, Matt, ss | .241 | 61 | 224 | 38 | 54 | 6 | 1 | 6 | 35 | 18 | 65 | 8 | 6 | R | R | 6-3 | 180 | 9-1-72 | 1992 | Baltimore, Md. |
| Shankle, Ron, ss-3b | .275 | 29 | 80 | 14 | 22 | 3 | 1 | 1 | 8 | 10 | 25 | 0 | 1 | R | R | 6-1 | 190 | 5-13-74 | 1993 | Frederick, Md. |
| White, Jarvis, of | .222 | 16 | 36 | 6 | 8 | 0 | 0 | 0 | 5 | 10 | 9 | 0 | 0 | R | R | 5-11 | 185 | 11-8-72 | 1993 | Palmetto, Fla. |

| PITCHING | W | L | ERA | G | GS | CG | SV | IP | H | R | ER | BB | SO | B | T | HT | WT | DOB | 1st Yr | Resides |
|---|---|---|---|---|---|---|---|---|---|---|---|---|---|---|---|---|---|---|---|---|
| Barrett, Rick | 0 | 0 | 15.00 | 2 | 0 | 0 | 0 | 3 | 6 | 5 | 5 | 4 | 1 | L | L | 6-3 | 207 | 7-14-71 | 1993 | Milwaukee, Wis. |
| Brewer, Bryan | 3 | 0 | 1.38 | 6 | 3 | 1 | 0 | 26 | 18 | 8 | 4 | 10 | 18 | L | L | 6-0 | 207 | 12-10-71 | 1993 | Fairfield, Calif. |
| Brown, Cory | 2 | 5 | 5.79 | 9 | 9 | 0 | 0 | 47 | 56 | 31 | 30 | 17 | 37 | R | R | 6-3 | 166 | 6-29-73 | 1992 | St. Petersburg, Fla. |
| Chavez, Carlos | 6 | 3 | 3.73 | 14 | 13 | 0 | 0 | 82 | 80 | 43 | 34 | 37 | 71 | R | R | 6-1 | 190 | 8-25-72 | 1992 | El Paso, Texas |
| Dawley, Joe | 3 | 1 | 3.52 | 20 | 0 | 0 | 3 | 31 | 34 | 20 | 12 | 14 | 30 | R | R | 6-4 | 200 | 9-19-71 | 1993 | Moreno Valley, Calif. |
| Fregoso, Danny | 3 | 2 | 4.33 | 6 | 5 | 0 | 0 | 27 | 22 | 15 | 13 | 13 | 22 | R | R | 6-0 | 175 | 11-11-73 | 1991 | Tucson, Ariz. |
| Griffin, Ryan | 3 | 2 | 2.91 | 15 | 4 | 0 | 5 | 46 | 42 | 22 | 15 | 13 | 29 | R | R | 6-2 | 195 | 10-15-73 | 1991 | Dunedin, Fla. |
| Kitchen, Ron | 1 | 2 | 5.18 | 16 | 0 | 0 | 0 | 40 | 49 | 33 | 23 | 7 | 24 | R | R | 6-1 | 218 | 7-4-71 | 1993 | Belleveron, Pa. |
| Knott, Shawn | 1 | 0 | 3.00 | 4 | 0 | 0 | 0 | 6 | 5 | 2 | 2 | 1 | 6 | R | R | 6-1 | 180 | 1-17-70 | 1992 | Hollywood, Md. |
| Maduro, Calvin | 9 | 4 | 3.96 | 14 | 14 | 3 | 0 | 91 | 90 | 46 | 40 | 17 | 83 | R | R | 6-0 | 175 | 9-5-74 | 1992 | Santa Cruz, Aruba |
| Percibal, William | 6 | 0 | 3.81 | 13 | 13 | 2 | 0 | 83 | 71 | 48 | 35 | 33 | 81 | R | R | 6-1 | 160 | 2-2-74 | 1992 | Santo Domingo, D.R. |
| Porter, Mike | 0 | 0 | 5.56 | 9 | 0 | 0 | 3 | 11 | 11 | 7 | 7 | 13 | 12 | R | R | 6-3 | 210 | 9-21-69 | 1992 | Lawton, Okla. |
| Rinderknecht, Robert | 0 | 0 | 5.14 | 11 | 0 | 0 | 0 | 14 | 17 | 9 | 8 | 3 | 11 | L | L | 5-11 | 180 | 1-29-71 | 1993 | Cedar Rapids, Iowa |
| Saneaux, Francisco | 2 | 1 | 3.62 | 6 | 6 | 0 | 0 | 32 | 30 | 14 | 13 | 14 | 28 | R | R | 6-4 | 170 | 2-16-74 | 1991 | El Seibo, D.R. |
| Trimarco, Michael | 3 | 3 | 4.21 | 19 | 0 | 0 | 2 | 36 | 35 | 26 | 17 | 11 | 24 | R | R | 6-0 | 160 | 12-22-71 | 1993 | Aurora, Ill. |
| Ziegler, Shane | 2 | 1 | 4.13 | 14 | 1 | 0 | 2 | 24 | 18 | 12 | 11 | 9 | 30 | R | R | 6-7 | 223 | 3-30-72 | 1993 | Minot, N.D. |

## SARASOTA R

## GULF COAST LEAGUE

| BATTING | AVG | G | AB | R | H | 2B | 3B | HR | RBI | BB | SO | SB | CS | B | T | HT | WT | DOB | 1st Yr | Resides |
|---|---|---|---|---|---|---|---|---|---|---|---|---|---|---|---|---|---|---|---|---|
| Alonso, Marcelino, of | .256 | 36 | 78 | 9 | 20 | 2 | 1 | 0 | 6 | 8 | 15 | 4 | 0 | R | R | 5-11 | 170 | 2-8-74 | 1992 | Chitre Herrera, Panama |
| Baker, Keivi, c | .172 | 29 | 64 | 9 | 11 | 2 | 0 | 0 | 5 | 13 | 16 | 2 | 0 | R | R | 6-1 | 184 | 1-10-74 | 1992 | Gretna, Fla. |
| Bowman, Delshon, of | .127 | 31 | 79 | 8 | 10 | 1 | 0 | 0 | 5 | 11 | 36 | 8 | 4 | R | R | 5-10 | 157 | 12-25-75 | 1993 | Tampa, Fla. |
| Brea, Vincente, c | .324 | 12 | 34 | 5 | 11 | 1 | 0 | 0 | 2 | 4 | 11 | 0 | 0 | R | R | 6-1 | 185 | 6-5-73 | 1991 | Bani, D.R. |
| Chancey, Robert, of | .143 | 29 | 84 | 7 | 12 | 3 | 0 | 0 | 3 | 4 | 39 | 3 | 0 | R | R | 5-11 | 243 | 9-7-72 | 1992 | Millbrook, Ala. |
| Freeberger, George, c | .133 | 26 | 60 | 5 | 8 | 1 | 0 | 0 | 4 | 9 | 30 | 1 | 1 | R | R | 6-3 | 190 | 3-25-74 | 1992 | Baltimore, Md. |
| Gabriel, Denio, 3b | .221 | 44 | 154 | 19 | 34 | 4 | 4 | 2 | 8 | 7 | 40 | 11 | 7 | S | R | 6-0 | 150 | 10-25-75 | 1993 | La Romana, D.R. |
| Garcia, Jesus, 2b-ss | .237 | 48 | 156 | 20 | 37 | 4 | 0 | 0 | 16 | 21 | 32 | 14 | 6 | R | R | 5-9 | 155 | 9-24-73 | 1993 | Robstown, Texas |
| Gargiulo, Mike, dh-c | .162 | 26 | 74 | 8 | 12 | 1 | 0 | 0 | 6 | 8 | 16 | 1 | 3 | L | R | 6-1 | 174 | 1-22-75 | 1993 | Harrisburg, Pa. |
| Hidalgo, Jose, 1b | .205 | 38 | 122 | 12 | 25 | 4 | 2 | 0 | 15 | 9 | 16 | 5 | 2 | R | R | 6-0 | 180 | 7-4-74 | 1993 | Maracaibo, Venez. |
| Lamb, David, ss-3b | .179 | 16 | 56 | 4 | 10 | 1 | 0 | 0 | 6 | 10 | 8 | 2 | 0 | S | R | 6-2 | 165 | 6-6-75 | 1993 | Newbury Park, Calif. |
| Linares, Ruben, 1b | .157 | 24 | 70 | 7 | 20 | 0 | 0 | 0 | 5 | 6 | 29 | 3 | 3 | R | R | 6-0 | 175 | 11-20-74 | 1993 | Panama City, Panama |
| Mejia, Miguel, of | .246 | 35 | 130 | 21 | 32 | 3 | 3 | 0 | 12 | 13 | 23 | 18 | 5 | R | R | 6-1 | 155 | 3-25-75 | 1992 | San Pedro de Macoris, D.R. |
| Melendez, Osmin, 2b | .193 | 48 | 140 | 13 | 27 | 2 | 1 | 0 | 6 | 19 | 18 | 9 | 1 | S | R | 5-10 | 152 | 3-26-75 | 1992 | Barquisimeto, Venez. |
| Pagan, Angel, ss | .278 | 34 | 115 | 12 | 32 | 5 | 3 | 1 | 30 | 17 | 33 | 7 | 1 | S | R | 6-1 | 166 | 4-23-74 | 1992 | Arecibo, P.R. |
| Simmons, Edwon, 3b | .208 | 27 | 77 | 10 | 16 | 1 | 0 | 0 | 5 | 6 | 20 | 2 | 0 | R | R | 6-0 | 210 | 8-15-75 | 1993 | Chicago, Ill. |
| Ulises, Pedro, of | .220 | 40 | 132 | 13 | 29 | 5 | 0 | 0 | 8 | 13 | 38 | 10 | 2 | S | R | 6-0 | 165 | 3-6-75 | 1992 | La Romana, D.R. |
| Valdez, Trovin, of-dh | .212 | 39 | 151 | 16 | 32 | 2 | 2 | 0 | 6 | 9 | 23 | 21 | 5 | S | R | 5-10 | 163 | 11-18-73 | 1993 | New York, N.Y. |
| White, Jarvis, of-dh | .263 | 5 | 19 | 2 | 5 | 0 | 0 | 0 | 0 | 2 | 5 | 1 | 0 | R | R | 5-11 | 185 | 11-8-72 | 1993 | Palmetto, Fla. |

| PITCHING | W | L | ERA | G | GS | CG | SV | IP | H | R | ER | BB | SO | B | T | HT | WT | DOB | 1st Yr | Resides |
|---|---|---|---|---|---|---|---|---|---|---|---|---|---|---|---|---|---|---|---|---|
| Anderson, Matt | 0 | 0 | 0.00 | 3 | 3 | 0 | 0 | 4 | 3 | 0 | 0 | 2 | 5 | L | L | 6-3 | 180 | 6-3-71 | 1989 | Ventura, Calif. |
| Barrett, Ricky | 0 | 1 | 0.98 | 6 | 0 | 0 | 2 | 18 | 13 | 2 | 2 | 3 | 11 | L | L | 6-3 | 207 | 7-14-71 | 1993 | Milwaukee, Wis. |
| Cafaro, Rocco | 2 | 2 | 1.79 | 14 | 8 | 1 | 1 | 81 | 58 | 21 | 16 | 12 | 57 | R | R | 6-0 | 175 | 12-12-72 | 1993 | Brandon, Fla. |
| Dykhoff, Radhomes | 1 | 2 | 3.40 | 14 | 3 | 0 | 1 | 45 | 37 | 22 | 17 | 11 | 29 | L | L | 6-0 | 160 | 9-27-74 | 1993 | Parendera, Aruba |
| Galvez, Rey | 1 | 1 | 6.60 | 15 | 0 | 0 | 1 | 30 | 32 | 28 | 22 | 15 | 13 | R | R | 6-1 | 165 | 9-24-73 | 1991 | La Romana, D.R. |
| Gulledge, Derek | 4 | 1 | 3.62 | 18 | 0 | 0 | 4 | 32 | 41 | 14 | 13 | 5 | 19 | R | R | 6-2 | 195 | 10-17-72 | 1993 | Bartow, Fla. |
| Hale, Shane | 0 | 0 | 0.00 | 3 | 3 | 0 | 0 | 4 | 2 | 0 | 0 | 0 | 2 | R | L | 6-1 | 180 | 12-30-68 | 1990 | Mobile, Ala. |
| Holter, Brian | 1 | 0 | 1.93 | 9 | 0 | 0 | 2 | 14 | 7 | 5 | 3 | 9 | 8 | R | R | 6-4 | 200 | 9-20-72 | 1992 | Benton, Ark. |
| Karns, Tim | 5 | 4 | 4.09 | 11 | 9 | 0 | 0 | 55 | 47 | 32 | 25 | 39 | 28 | R | R | 6-3 | 195 | 5-21-72 | 1993 | Lakewood, Colo. |
| Kitchen, Ron | 0 | 0 | 0.00 | 2 | 0 | 0 | 0 | 2 | 3 | 0 | 0 | 1 | 2 | R | R | 6-1 | 218 | 7-4-71 | 1993 | Belleveron, Pa. |
| Lane, Mike | 3 | 7 | 7.09 | 11 | 10 | 0 | 0 | 47 | 56 | 49 | 37 | 34 | 36 | R | R | 5-11 | 192 | 5-18-71 | 1993 | Franklin, Ky. |
| Lombardi, John | 7 | 1 | 0.92 | 10 | 10 | 0 | 0 | 59 | 32 | 10 | 6 | 27 | 45 | R | R | 6-3 | 185 | 4-24-73 | 1993 | Warwick, R.I. |
| Pena, Alex | 3 | 1 | 2.68 | 19 | 0 | 0 | 1 | 37 | 38 | 18 | 11 | 8 | 28 | R | R | 6-0 | 175 | 9-9-72 | 1993 | El Paso, Texas |
| Price, Tobias | 2 | 5 | 5.54 | 13 | 6 | 1 | 1 | 37 | 36 | 27 | 23 | 43 | 28 | L | L | 6-2 | 225 | 8-11-74 | 1992 | San Diego, Calif. |
| Romano, Manuel | 0 | 2 | 3.55 | 7 | 6 | 0 | 1 | 25 | 22 | 14 | 10 | 12 | 15 | R | R | 6-6 | 170 | 11-6-73 | 1991 | El Seibo, D.R. |
| Singleton, Kendrick | 1 | 1 | 5.19 | 5 | 0 | 0 | 0 | 9 | 10 | 8 | 5 | 5 | 6 | S | R | 6-2 | 185 | 10-10-75 | 1993 | Tampa, Fla. |
| Smith, Hut | 0 | 0 | 0.00 | 3 | 0 | 0 | 1 | 4 | 0 | 0 | 0 | 1 | 5 | R | R | 6-3 | 195 | 6-8-73 | 1992 | Kannapolis, N.C. |
| Trimarco, Michael | 0 | 0 | 9.00 | 1 | 0 | 0 | 0 | 1 | 3 | 1 | 1 | 0 | 0 | R | R | 6-0 | 160 | 12-22-71 | 1993 | Aurora, Ill. |

# BOSTON RED SOX

**Manager:** Butch Hobson.  **1993 Record:** 80-82, .494 (5th, AL East).

| BATTING | AVG | G | AB | R | H | 2B | 3B | HR | RBI | BB | SO | SB | CS | B | T | HT | WT | DOB | 1st Yr | Resides |
|---|---|---|---|---|---|---|---|---|---|---|---|---|---|---|---|---|---|---|---|---|
| Blosser, Greg | .071 | 17 | 28 | 1 | 2 | 1 | 0 | 0 | 1 | 2 | 7 | 1 | 0 | L | L | 6-3 | 200 | 6-26-71 | 1989 | Sarasota, Fla. |
| Byrd, Jim | .000 | 1 | 0 | 0 | 0 | 0 | 0 | 0 | 0 | 0 | 0 | 0 | 0 | R | R | 6-1 | 186 | 10-3-68 | 1988 | Lawton, Okla. |
| Calderon, Ivan | .221 | 73 | 213 | 25 | 47 | 8 | 2 | 1 | 19 | 21 | 28 | 4 | 2 | R | R | 6-1 | 221 | 3-19-62 | 1980 | Loiza, P.R. |
| Cooper, Scott | .279 | 156 | 526 | 67 | 147 | 29 | 3 | 9 | 63 | 58 | 81 | 5 | 2 | L | R | 6-3 | 205 | 10-13-67 | 1986 | St. Charles, Mo. |
| Dawson, Andre | .273 | 121 | 461 | 44 | 126 | 29 | 1 | 13 | 67 | 17 | 49 | 2 | 1 | R | R | 6-3 | 195 | 7-10-54 | 1975 | Miami, Fla. |
| Deer, Rob | .196 | 38 | 143 | 18 | 28 | 6 | 1 | 7 | 16 | 20 | 49 | 2 | 0 | R | R | 6-3 | 225 | 9-29-60 | 1978 | Scottsdale, Ariz. |
| 2-team (90 Detroit) | .210 | 128 | 466 | 66 | 98 | 17 | 1 | 21 | 55 | 58 | 169 | 5 | 2 | | | | | | | |
| Flaherty, John | .120 | 13 | 25 | 3 | 3 | 2 | 0 | 0 | 2 | 2 | 6 | 0 | 0 | R | R | 6-1 | 195 | 10-21-67 | 1988 | West Nyack, N.Y. |
| Fletcher, Scott | .285 | 121 | 480 | 81 | 137 | 31 | 5 | 5 | 45 | 37 | 35 | 16 | 3 | R | R | 5-11 | 173 | 7-30-58 | 1979 | Arlington, Texas |
| Greenwell, Mike | .315 | 146 | 540 | 77 | 170 | 38 | 6 | 13 | 72 | 54 | 46 | 5 | 4 | L | R | 6-0 | 205 | 7-18-63 | 1982 | Cape Coral, Fla. |
| Hatcher, Billy | .287 | 136 | 508 | 71 | 146 | 24 | 3 | 9 | 57 | 28 | 46 | 14 | 7 | R | R | 5-10 | 190 | 10-4-60 | 1981 | Cincinnati, Ohio |
| Lyons, Steve | .130 | 28 | 23 | 4 | 3 | 1 | 0 | 0 | 0 | 2 | 5 | 1 | 2 | L | R | 6-3 | 190 | 6-3-60 | 1981 | Scottsdale, Ariz. |
| McNeely, Jeff | .297 | 21 | 37 | 10 | 11 | 1 | 0 | 0 | 1 | 7 | 9 | 6 | 0 | R | R | 6-2 | 190 | 10-18-69 | 1989 | Monroe, N.C. |
| Melvin, Bob | .222 | 77 | 176 | 13 | 39 | 7 | 0 | 3 | 23 | 7 | 44 | 0 | 0 | R | R | 6-4 | 205 | 10-28-61 | 1981 | Germantown, Tenn. |
| Naehring, Tim | .331 | 39 | 127 | 14 | 42 | 10 | 0 | 1 | 17 | 10 | 26 | 1 | 0 | R | R | 6-2 | 190 | 2-1-67 | 1988 | Cincinnati, Ohio |
| Ortiz, Luis | .250 | 9 | 12 | 0 | 3 | 0 | 0 | 0 | 1 | 0 | 2 | 0 | 0 | R | R | 6-0 | 188 | 5-25-70 | 1991 | Santo Domingo, D.R. |
| Pena, Tony | .181 | 126 | 304 | 20 | 55 | 11 | 0 | 4 | 19 | 25 | 46 | 1 | 3 | R | R | 6-0 | 184 | 6-4-57 | 1976 | Santiago, D.R. |
| Quintana, Carlos | .244 | 101 | 303 | 31 | 74 | 5 | 0 | 1 | 19 | 31 | 52 | 1 | 0 | R | R | 6-2 | 220 | 8-26-65 | 1985 | Miranda, Venez. |
| Richardson, Jeff | .208 | 15 | 24 | 3 | 5 | 2 | 0 | 0 | 2 | 1 | 3 | 0 | 0 | R | R | 6-1 | 172 | 8-26-65 | 1986 | Lincoln, Neb. |
| Riles, Ernest | .189 | 94 | 143 | 15 | 27 | 8 | 0 | 5 | 20 | 20 | 40 | 1 | 3 | L | R | 6-1 | 180 | 10-2-60 | 1981 | Tallahassee, Fla. |
| Rivera, Luis | .208 | 62 | 130 | 13 | 27 | 8 | 1 | 1 | 7 | 11 | 36 | 1 | 2 | R | R | 5-10 | 172 | 1-3-64 | 1982 | Cidra, P.R. |
| Valentin, John | .278 | 144 | 468 | 50 | 130 | 40 | 3 | 11 | 66 | 49 | 77 | 3 | 4 | R | R | 6-0 | 170 | 2-18-67 | 1988 | Jersey City, N.J. |
| Vaughn, Mo. | .297 | 152 | 539 | 86 | 160 | 34 | 1 | 29 | 101 | 79 | 130 | 4 | 3 | L | R | 6-1 | 225 | 12-15-67 | 1989 | Norwalk, Conn. |
| Zupcic, Bob | .241 | 141 | 286 | 40 | 69 | 24 | 2 | 2 | 26 | 27 | 54 | 5 | 2 | R | R | 6-4 | 220 | 8-18-66 | 1987 | Charlotte, N.C. |

| PITCHING | W | L | ERA | G | GS | CG | SV | IP | H | R | ER | BB | SO | B | T | HT | WT | DOB | 1st Yr | Resides |
|---|---|---|---|---|---|---|---|---|---|---|---|---|---|---|---|---|---|---|---|---|
| Bailey, Cory | 0 | 1 | 3.45 | 11 | 0 | 0 | 0 | 16 | 12 | 7 | 6 | 12 | 11 | R | R | 6-1 | 210 | 1-24-71 | 1991 | Marion, Ill. |
| Bankhead, Scott | 2 | 1 | 3.50 | 40 | 0 | 0 | 0 | 64 | 59 | 28 | 25 | 29 | 47 | R | R | 5-10 | 185 | 7-31-63 | 1985 | Asheboro, N.C. |
| Clemens, Roger | 11 | 14 | 4.46 | 29 | 29 | 2 | 0 | 192 | 175 | 99 | 95 | 67 | 160 | R | R | 6-4 | 220 | 8-4-62 | 1983 | Houston, Texas |
| Darwin, Danny | 15 | 11 | 3.26 | 34 | 34 | 2 | 0 | 229 | 196 | 93 | 83 | 49 | 130 | R | R | 6-3 | 190 | 10-25-55 | 1976 | Valley View, Texas |
| Dopson, John | 7 | 11 | 4.97 | 34 | 28 | 1 | 0 | 156 | 170 | 93 | 86 | 59 | 89 | L | R | 6-4 | 225 | 7-14-63 | 1982 | Finksburg, Md. |
| Fossas, Tony | 1 | 1 | 5.18 | 71 | 0 | 0 | 0 | 40 | 38 | 28 | 23 | 15 | 39 | L | L | 6-0 | 187 | 9-23-57 | 1979 | Fort Lauderdale, Fla. |
| Harris, Greg | 6 | 7 | 3.77 | 80 | 0 | 0 | 8 | 112 | 95 | 55 | 47 | 60 | 103 | S | R | 6-0 | 175 | 11-2-55 | 1977 | Las Vegas, Nev. |
| Hesketh, Joe | 3 | 4 | 5.06 | 28 | 5 | 0 | 1 | 53 | 62 | 35 | 30 | 29 | 34 | L | L | 6-2 | 170 | 2-15-59 | 1980 | Palm Harbor, Fla. |
| Melendez, Jose | 2 | 1 | 2.25 | 9 | 0 | 0 | 0 | 16 | 10 | 4 | 4 | 5 | 14 | R | R | 6-2 | 175 | 9-2-65 | 1984 | Naguabo, P.R. |
| Minchey, Nate | 1 | 2 | 3.55 | 5 | 5 | 1 | 0 | 33 | 35 | 16 | 13 | 8 | 18 | R | R | 6-7 | 200 | 8-31-69 | 1987 | Pflugerville, Texas |
| Quantrill, Paul | 6 | 12 | 3.91 | 49 | 14 | 1 | 1 | 138 | 151 | 73 | 60 | 44 | 66 | L | R | 6-1 | 185 | 11-3-68 | 1989 | Mansfield, Mass. |
| Russell, Jeff | 1 | 4 | 2.70 | 51 | 0 | 0 | 33 | 47 | 39 | 16 | 14 | 14 | 45 | R | R | 6-3 | 205 | 9-2-61 | 1980 | Colleyville, Texas |
| Ryan, Ken | 7 | 2 | 3.60 | 47 | 0 | 0 | 1 | 50 | 43 | 23 | 20 | 29 | 49 | R | R | 6-3 | 215 | 10-24-68 | 1986 | Seekonk, Mass. |
| Sele, Aaron | 7 | 2 | 2.74 | 18 | 18 | 0 | 0 | 112 | 100 | 42 | 34 | 48 | 93 | R | R | 6-5 | 205 | 6-25-70 | 1991 | Suquamish, Wash. |
| Taylor, Scott | 0 | 1 | 8.18 | 16 | 0 | 0 | 0 | 11 | 14 | 10 | 10 | 12 | 8 | L | L | 6-1 | 190 | 8-2-67 | 1988 | Defiance, Ohio |
| Viola, Frank | 11 | 8 | 3.14 | 29 | 29 | 2 | 0 | 184 | 180 | 76 | 64 | 72 | 91 | L | L | 6-4 | 209 | 4-19-60 | 1981 | Longwood, Fla. |

## FIELDING

| Catcher | PCT | G | PO | A | E | DP |
|---|---|---|---|---|---|---|
| Flaherty | 1.000 | 13 | 35 | 9 | 0 | 1 |
| Lyons | .000 | 1 | 0 | 0 | 0 | 0 |
| Melvin | .994 | 76 | 304 | 18 | 2 | 4 |
| Pena | .995 | 125 | 698 | 53 | 4 | 8 |

| First Base | PCT | G | PO | A | E | DP |
|---|---|---|---|---|---|---|
| Cooper | 1.000 | 2 | 1 | 0 | 0 | 1 |
| Lyons | .000 | 1 | 0 | 0 | 0 | 0 |
| Melvin | 1.000 | 1 | 5 | 1 | 0 | 1 |
| Quintana | .991 | 53 | 320 | 21 | 3 | 30 |
| Riles | 1.000 | 1 | 1 | 0 | 0 | 0 |
| Vaughn | .987 | 131 | 1110 | 70 | 16 | 104 |

| Second Base | PCT | G | PO | A | E | DP |
|---|---|---|---|---|---|---|
| Fletcher | .982 | 116 | 217 | 371 | 11 | 68 |
| Hatcher | .000 | 2 | 0 | 0 | 0 | 0 |
| Lyons | 1.000 | 9 | 6 | 15 | 0 | 2 |

| | PCT | G | PO | A | E | DP |
|---|---|---|---|---|---|---|
| Naehring | .973 | 15 | 36 | 35 | 2 | 10 |
| Richardson | 1.000 | 8 | 9 | 24 | 0 | 3 |
| Riles | 1.000 | 20 | 22 | 45 | 0 | 8 |
| Rivera | .969 | 27 | 36 | 57 | 3 | 13 |

| Third Base | PCT | G | PO | A | E | DP |
|---|---|---|---|---|---|---|
| Cooper | .937 | 154 | 111 | 244 | 24 | 22 |
| Fletcher | .000 | 1 | 0 | 0 | 0 | 0 |
| Lyons | .000 | 1 | 0 | 0 | 0 | 0 |
| Naehring | 1.000 | 9 | 6 | 6 | 0 | 2 |
| Ortiz | 1.000 | 5 | 2 | 2 | 0 | 1 |
| Richardson | 1.000 | 1 | 1 | 0 | 0 | 0 |
| Riles | 1.000 | 11 | 3 | 8 | 0 | 0 |
| Rivera | 1.000 | 2 | 1 | 3 | 0 | 1 |

| Shortstop | PCT | G | PO | A | E | DP |
|---|---|---|---|---|---|---|
| Cooper | .000 | 1 | 0 | 0 | 0 | 0 |

| | PCT | G | PO | A | E | DP |
|---|---|---|---|---|---|---|
| Fletcher | .000 | 2 | 0 | 0 | 0 | 0 |
| Naehring | 1.000 | 4 | 3 | 3 | 0 | 3 |
| Richardson | 1.000 | 5 | 2 | 6 | 0 | 2 |
| Rivera | .963 | 27 | 28 | 51 | 3 | 14 |
| Valentin | .971 | 144 | 238 | 432 | 20 | 96 |

| Outfield | PCT | G | PO | A | E | DP |
|---|---|---|---|---|---|---|
| Blosser | 1.000 | 9 | 11 | 1 | 0 | 0 |
| Dawson | 1.000 | 20 | 42 | 0 | 0 | 0 |
| Deer | .970 | 36 | 94 | 2 | 3 | 0 |
| Greenwell | .993 | 134 | 261 | 6 | 2 | 1 |
| Hatcher | .993 | 130 | 284 | 6 | 2 | 2 |
| Lyons | 1.000 | 10 | 5 | 0 | 0 | 0 |
| McNeely | .917 | 13 | 22 | 0 | 2 | 0 |
| Quintana | 1.000 | 51 | 92 | 4 | 0 | 1 |
| Zupcic | .979 | 122 | 179 | 7 | 4 | 2 |

# RED SOX FARM SYSTEM

| Class | Club | League | W | L | Pct. | Finish* | Manager | First Year |
|---|---|---|---|---|---|---|---|---|
| AAA | Pawtucket (R.I.) Red Sox | International | 60 | 82 | .423 | 9th (10) | Buddy Bailey | 1973 |
| AA | New Britain (Conn.) Red Sox | Eastern | 52 | 88 | .371 | 8th (8) | Jim Pankovits | 1983 |
| A# | Lynchburg (Va.) Red Sox | Carolina | 65 | 74 | .468 | 7th (8) | Mark Meleski | 1988 |
| A# | Ft. Lauderdale (Fla.) Red Sox | Florida State | 46 | 85 | .351 | 13th (13) | DeMarlo Hale | 1993 |
| A | Utica (N.Y.) Blue Sox | New York-Penn | 38 | 38 | .500 | 6th (14) | Dave Holt | 1993 |
| Rookie | Fort Myers (Fla.) Red Sox | Gulf Coast | 32 | 28 | .533 | T-6th (15) | Felix Maldonado | 1993 |

*Finish in overall standings (No. of teams in league)   #Advanced level

R&R SPORTS GROUP

**Lefthanded Punch.** Mo Vaughn, left, who hit .297 with 29 home runs and 101 RBIs, and Mike Greenwell, a .315 hitter, were Boston's offensive leaders in 1993.

## PAWTUCKET
### INTERNATIONAL LEAGUE

| BATTING | AVG | G | AB | R | H | 2B | 3B | HR | RBI | BB | SO | SB | CS | B | T | HT | WT | DOB | 1st Yr | Resides |
|---|---|---|---|---|---|---|---|---|---|---|---|---|---|---|---|---|---|---|---|---|
| Blosser, Greg | .228 | 130 | 478 | 66 | 109 | 22 | 2 | 23 | 66 | 58 | 139 | 3 | 3 | L | L | 6-3 | 200 | 6-26-71 | 1989 | Sarasota, Fla. |
| Byrd, Jim | .177 | 117 | 378 | 33 | 67 | 12 | 4 | 3 | 26 | 18 | 111 | 10 | 9 | R | R | 6-1 | 186 | 10-3-68 | 1988 | Lawton, Okla. |
| Chick, Bruce | .305 | 29 | 82 | 8 | 25 | 6 | 0 | 2 | 12 | 6 | 24 | 0 | 3 | R | R | 6-4 | 210 | 3-7-69 | 1990 | St. Petersburg, Fla. |
| Crowley, Jim | .171 | 12 | 35 | 2 | 6 | 0 | 0 | 0 | 2 | 2 | 10 | 0 | 0 | R | R | 6-0 | 190 | 10-16-69 | 1991 | Cockeysville, Md. |
| Flaherty, John | .271 | 105 | 365 | 29 | 99 | 22 | 0 | 6 | 35 | 26 | 41 | 0 | 2 | R | R | 6-1 | 195 | 10-21-67 | 1988 | West Nyack, N.Y. |
| Garcia, Cheo | .260 | 96 | 373 | 48 | 97 | 16 | 3 | 4 | 32 | 24 | 45 | 3 | 8 | R | R | 5-11 | 165 | 4-27-68 | 1988 | Maracaibo, Venez. |
| Hatteberg, Scott | .189 | 18 | 53 | 6 | 10 | 0 | 0 | 1 | 2 | 6 | 12 | 0 | 0 | L | R | 6-1 | 185 | 12-14-69 | 1991 | Yakima, Wash. |
| Lyons, Steve | .213 | 67 | 197 | 24 | 42 | 6 | 0 | 4 | 18 | 26 | 50 | 3 | 4 | L | R | 6-3 | 190 | 6-3-60 | 1981 | Scottsdale, Ariz. |
| Malzone, John | .237 | 75 | 207 | 14 | 49 | 7 | 0 | 2 | 15 | 12 | 24 | 2 | 1 | L | R | 5-10 | 170 | 10-29-67 | 1989 | Needham, Mass. |
| Martin, Jeff | .211 | 9 | 19 | 5 | 4 | 1 | 0 | 1 | 2 | 4 | 9 | 1 | 0 | R | R | 6-4 | 220 | 7-14-70 | 1992 | Goodlettsville, Tenn. |
| McNeely, Jeff | .261 | 129 | 498 | 65 | 130 | 14 | 3 | 2 | 35 | 43 | 102 | 40 | 7 | R | R | 6-2 | 190 | 10-18-69 | 1989 | Monroe, N.C. |
| Milstien, Dave | .252 | 88 | 258 | 28 | 65 | 8 | 3 | 1 | 18 | 10 | 31 | 1 | 3 | R | R | 6-0 | 190 | 9-11-68 | 1986 | Simi Valley, Calif. |
| Naehring, Tim | .307 | 55 | 202 | 38 | 62 | 9 | 1 | 7 | 36 | 35 | 27 | 0 | 2 | R | R | 6-0 | 188 | 2-1-67 | 1988 | Cincinnati, Ohio |
| Ortiz, Luis | .294 | 102 | 402 | 45 | 118 | 28 | 1 | 18 | 81 | 13 | 74 | 1 | 1 | R | R | 6-1 | 172 | 8-26-65 | 1986 | Santo Domingo, D.R. |
| Richardson, Jeff | .321 | 9 | 28 | 2 | 9 | 1 | 0 | 0 | 1 | 1 | 6 | 0 | 0 | R | R | 6-1 | 180 | 8-26-65 | 1986 | Lincoln, Neb. |
| Riles, Ernie | .278 | 6 | 18 | 4 | 5 | 0 | 0 | 2 | 6 | 3 | 0 | 0 | 0 | L | R | 6-1 | 180 | 10-2-60 | 1981 | Tallahassee, Fla. |
| Rodriguez, Ruben | .320 | 32 | 97 | 12 | 31 | 5 | 0 | 1 | 10 | 1 | 14 | 1 | 1 | R | R | 6-1 | 180 | 8-4-64 | 1982 | Santo Domingo, D.R. |
| Ross, Sean | .225 | 26 | 80 | 14 | 18 | 2 | 0 | 2 | 5 | 2 | 12 | 4 | 2 | L | L | 6-2 | 185 | 10-21-67 | 1986 | Wilmington, N.C. |
| Sparks, Greg | .172 | 58 | 198 | 7 | 34 | 6 | 0 | 4 | 21 | 14 | 54 | 0 | 3 | L | L | 6-0 | 185 | 3-31-64 | 1984 | Phoenix, Ariz. |
| Stubbs, Franklin | .237 | 94 | 334 | 47 | 79 | 18 | 1 | 15 | 58 | 51 | 82 | 3 | 3 | L | L | 6-2 | 208 | 10-21-60 | 1982 | Chino Hills, Calif. |
| Tatum, Willie | .083 | 7 | 24 | 5 | 2 | 1 | 1 | 0 | 2 | 3 | 4 | 0 | 0 | S | R | 6-7 | 200 | 11-5-66 | 1988 | Sacramento, Calif. |
| Thoutsis, Paul | .319 | 60 | 216 | 30 | 69 | 10 | 1 | 4 | 27 | 24 | 28 | 1 | 1 | L | R | 6-1 | 185 | 10-23-65 | 1983 | Worcester, Mass. |
| Valentin, John | .333 | 2 | 9 | 3 | 3 | 0 | 0 | 1 | 1 | 0 | 1 | 0 | 0 | R | R | 6-0 | 170 | 2-18-67 | 1988 | Jersey City, N.J. |
| Winningham, Herm | .257 | 59 | 214 | 31 | 55 | 6 | 1 | 5 | 24 | 22 | 52 | 8 | 2 | L | R | 5-11 | 190 | 12-1-61 | 1981 | Orangeburg, S.C. |

| PITCHING | W | L | ERA | G | GS | CG | SV | IP | H | R | ER | BB | SO | B | T | HT | WT | DOB | 1st Yr | Resides |
|---|---|---|---|---|---|---|---|---|---|---|---|---|---|---|---|---|---|---|---|---|
| Bailey, Cory | 4 | 5 | 2.88 | 52 | 0 | 0 | 20 | 66 | 48 | 21 | 21 | 31 | 59 | R | R | 6-1 | 210 | 1-24-71 | 1991 | Marion, Ill. |
| Caruso, Joe | 5 | 10 | 5.44 | 36 | 17 | 2 | 0 | 122 | 138 | 82 | 74 | 68 | 65 | R | R | 6-3 | 195 | 9-16-70 | 1991 | Petaluma, Calif. |
| Ciccarella, Joe | 0 | 1 | 5.60 | 12 | 0 | 0 | 0 | 18 | 27 | 13 | 11 | 12 | 8 | L | L | 6-3 | 190 | 12-29-69 | 1991 | Huntington Beach, Calif. |
| Clemens, Roger | 0 | 0 | 0.00 | 1 | 1 | 0 | 0 | 4 | 1 | 0 | 0 | 4 | 8 | R | R | 6-4 | 220 | 8-4-62 | 1983 | Houston, Texas |
| Conroy, Brian | 5 | 7 | 5.86 | 19 | 19 | 0 | 0 | 106 | 126 | 74 | 69 | 40 | 64 | S | R | 6-2 | 180 | 8-29-68 | 1989 | Needham, Mass. |
| Finnvold, Gar | 5 | 9 | 3.77 | 24 | 24 | 0 | 0 | 136 | 128 | 68 | 57 | 51 | 123 | R | R | 6-5 | 195 | 3-11-68 | 1990 | Boca Raton, Fla. |
| Florence, Don | 7 | 8 | 3.36 | 57 | 0 | 0 | 2 | 59 | 56 | 24 | 22 | 18 | 46 | R | L | 6-0 | 195 | 3-16-67 | 1988 | Manchester, N.H. |
| Gakeler, Dan | 0 | 1 | 7.50 | 6 | 0 | 0 | 0 | 12 | 21 | 11 | 10 | 9 | 8 | R | R | 6-6 | 215 | 5-1-64 | 1984 | Greensboro, N.C. |
| Livernois, Derek | 2 | 6 | 5.72 | 27 | 14 | 0 | 0 | 85 | 89 | 55 | 54 | 37 | 69 | L | R | 6-0 | 170 | 4-17-67 | 1985 | Port Casselberry, Fla. |
| Melendez, Jose | 2 | 3 | 5.40 | 19 | 0 | 0 | 2 | 35 | 37 | 24 | 21 | 7 | 31 | R | R | 6-2 | 175 | 9-2-65 | 1984 | Naguabo, P.R. |

| PITCHING | W | L | ERA | G | GS | CG | SV | IP | H | R | ER | BB | SO | B | T | HT | WT | DOB | 1st Yr | Resides |
|---|---|---|---|---|---|---|---|---|---|---|---|---|---|---|---|---|---|---|---|---|
| Minchey, Nate | 7 | 14 | 4.02 | 29 | 29 | 7 | 0 | 195 | 182 | 103 | 87 | 50 | 113 | R | R | 6-7 | 200 | 8-31-69 | 1986 | Pflugerville, Texas |
| Plympton, Jeff | 2 | 1 | 4.44 | 30 | 0 | 0 | 1 | 51 | 54 | 33 | 25 | 15 | 48 | R | R | 6-2 | 205 | 11-24-65 | 1987 | Plainville, Mass. |
| Riley, Ed | 4 | 4 | 5.01 | 14 | 13 | 2 | 0 | 70 | 90 | 45 | 39 | 23 | 44 | L | L | 6-2 | 195 | 2-10-70 | 1988 | Worcester, Mass. |
| Ryan, Ken | 0 | 2 | 2.49 | 18 | 0 | 0 | 8 | 25 | 18 | 9 | 7 | 17 | 22 | R | R | 6-3 | 215 | 10-24-68 | 1986 | Seekonk, Mass. |
| Sele, Aaron | 8 | 2 | 2.19 | 14 | 14 | 2 | 0 | 94 | 74 | 30 | 23 | 23 | 87 | R | R | 6-5 | 205 | 6-25-70 | 1991 | Suquamish, Wash. |
| Shea, John | 2 | 2 | 7.00 | 12 | 3 | 0 | 0 | 36 | 51 | 31 | 28 | 19 | 20 | R | L | 6-6 | 210 | 6-23-66 | 1986 | Dunedin, Fla. |
| Taylor, Scott | 7 | 7 | 4.04 | 47 | 8 | 0 | 1 | 123 | 132 | 61 | 55 | 48 | 88 | L | L | 6-1 | 190 | 8-2-67 | 1988 | Defiance, Ohio |

### FIELDING

| Catcher | PCT | G | PO | A | E | DP |
|---|---|---|---|---|---|---|
| Flaherty | .986 | 101 | 626 | 78 | 10 | 7 |
| Hatteberg | .964 | 18 | 131 | 4 | 5 | 0 |
| Lyons | 1.000 | 1 | 1 | 0 | 0 | 0 |
| Martin | 1.000 | 7 | 31 | 2 | 0 | 0 |
| Rodriguez | .983 | 27 | 157 | 15 | 3 | 1 |

| First Base | PCT | G | PO | A | E | DP |
|---|---|---|---|---|---|---|
| Lyons | .978 | 14 | 129 | 2 | 3 | 14 |
| Milstien | .992 | 36 | 242 | 20 | 2 | 21 |
| Rodriguez | 1.000 | 3 | 7 | 0 | 0 | 0 |
| Sparks | .982 | 46 | 354 | 30 | 7 | 36 |
| Stubbs | .983 | 49 | 389 | 28 | 7 | 52 |
| Tatum | 1.000 | 7 | 60 | 10 | 0 | 10 |
| Thoutsis | 1.000 | 1 | 1 | 0 | 0 | 0 |

| Second Base | PCT | G | PO | A | E | DP |
|---|---|---|---|---|---|---|
| Crowley | .969 | 9 | 13 | 18 | 1 | 1 |
| Garcia | .957 | 90 | 205 | 220 | 19 | 70 |
| Lyons | .929 | 2 | 4 | 9 | 1 | 1 |

|  | PCT | G | PO | A | E | DP |
|---|---|---|---|---|---|---|
| Malzone | .935 | 18 | 21 | 22 | 3 | 4 |
| Milstien | .974 | 22 | 53 | 58 | 3 | 16 |
| Naehring | .988 | 15 | 36 | 48 | 1 | 10 |
| Richardson | .900 | 3 | 3 | 6 | 1 | 3 |
| Riles | 1.000 | 1 | 1 | 2 | 0 | 0 |

| Third Base | PCT | G | PO | A | E | DP |
|---|---|---|---|---|---|---|
| Crowley | .857 | 3 | 1 | 5 | 1 | 0 |
| Lyons | .929 | 6 | 3 | 10 | 1 | 1 |
| Malzone | .876 | 50 | 30 | 69 | 14 | 10 |
| Milstien | .914 | 14 | 7 | 25 | 3 | 3 |
| Naehring | .967 | 20 | 18 | 40 | 2 | 5 |
| Ortiz | .928 | 63 | 41 | 114 | 12 | 11 |
| Richardson | 1.000 | 2 | 1 | 4 | 0 | 0 |
| Riles | 1.000 | 1 | 2 | 4 | 0 | 0 |

| Shortstop | PCT | G | PO | A | E | DP |
|---|---|---|---|---|---|---|
| Byrd | .940 | 116 | 202 | 314 | 33 | 64 |
| Garcia | .000 | 1 | 0 | 0 | 0 | 0 |

|  | PCT | G | PO | A | E | DP |
|---|---|---|---|---|---|---|
| Milstein | .933 | 12 | 21 | 35 | 4 | 7 |
| Naehring | .986 | 16 | 25 | 45 | 1 | 13 |
| Richardson | .889 | 4 | 4 | 12 | 2 | 1 |
| Riles | .900 | 2 | 2 | 7 | 1 | 2 |
| Valentin | 1.000 | 2 | 8 | 9 | 0 | 4 |

| Outfield | PCT | G | PO | A | E | DP |
|---|---|---|---|---|---|---|
| Blosser | .968 | 115 | 199 | 13 | 7 | 1 |
| Chick | .981 | 29 | 51 | 0 | 1 | 0 |
| Garcia | 1.000 | 1 | 1 | 0 | 0 | 0 |
| Lyons | .970 | 42 | 57 | 7 | 2 | 3 |
| McNeely | .963 | 127 | 284 | 6 | 11 | 1 |
| Ortiz | 1.000 | 6 | 4 | 0 | 0 | 0 |
| Ross | 1.000 | 19 | 32 | 0 | 0 | 0 |
| Sparks | 1.000 | 2 | 2 | 1 | 0 | 0 |
| Thoutsis | .968 | 54 | 90 | 0 | 3 | 0 |
| Winningham | .981 | 55 | 102 | 3 | 2 | 1 |

# NEW BRITAIN
## EASTERN LEAGUE

**AA**

| BATTING | AVG | G | AB | R | H | 2B | 3B | HR | RBI | BB | SO | SB | CS | B | T | HT | WT | DOB | 1st Yr | Resides |
|---|---|---|---|---|---|---|---|---|---|---|---|---|---|---|---|---|---|---|---|---|
| Beams, Mike, of | .236 | 84 | 263 | 26 | 62 | 16 | 1 | 5 | 36 | 28 | 74 | 3 | 4 | R | R | 6-0 | 190 | 6-8-67 | 1986 | Altamonte Springs, Fla. |
| Bethea, Scott, ss-2b | .228 | 117 | 395 | 47 | 90 | 13 | 1 | 0 | 30 | 32 | 48 | 3 | 4 | L | R | 5-10 | 165 | 6-17-69 | 1990 | Austin, Texas |
| Brown, Bryan, of | .230 | 34 | 113 | 13 | 26 | 5 | 1 | 3 | 17 | 11 | 20 | 0 | 0 | R | R | 6-2 | 180 | 7-1-70 | 1991 | Metairie, La. |
| Carroll, Kevin, c | .149 | 56 | 168 | 9 | 25 | 6 | 0 | 0 | 6 | 6 | 58 | 1 | 1 | R | R | 5-11 | 200 | 1-25-67 | 1989 | South Lafayette, N.Y. |
| Chick, Bruce, of | .259 | 55 | 193 | 20 | 50 | 8 | 1 | 3 | 14 | 8 | 39 | 2 | 3 | R | R | 6-4 | 210 | 3-7-69 | 1990 | St. Petersburg, Fla. |
| Crowley, Jim, 2b | .241 | 109 | 369 | 49 | 89 | 19 | 1 | 11 | 51 | 59 | 95 | 3 | 7 | R | R | 6-0 | 190 | 10-16-69 | 1991 | Cockeysville, Md. |
| Delgado, Alex, c | .184 | 33 | 87 | 10 | 16 | 2 | 0 | 1 | 9 | 4 | 11 | 2 | 1 | R | R | 6-0 | 160 | 1-11-71 | 1988 | Palmarejo, Venez. |
| Dixon, Colin, 3b-1b | .210 | 66 | 214 | 11 | 45 | 10 | 0 | 3 | 22 | 9 | 47 | 1 | 2 | R | R | 6-5 | 215 | 8-27-68 | 1989 | West Vancouver, B.C. |
| Friedman, Jason, 1b | .248 | 81 | 294 | 22 | 73 | 15 | 1 | 1 | 24 | 20 | 50 | 2 | 0 | L | L | 6-1 | 200 | 8-8-69 | 1989 | Cypress, Calif. |
| Hatteberg, Scott, c | .278 | 68 | 227 | 35 | 63 | 10 | 2 | 7 | 28 | 42 | 38 | 1 | 3 | L | R | 6-1 | 185 | 12-14-69 | 1991 | Yakima, Wash. |
| Mahay, Ron, of | .120 | 8 | 25 | 2 | 3 | 0 | 0 | 1 | 2 | 1 | 6 | 1 | 0 | L | L | 6-2 | 185 | 6-28-71 | 1991 | Crestwood, Ill. |
| Moore, Boo, of-dh | .209 | 96 | 301 | 35 | 63 | 8 | 1 | 11 | 32 | 32 | 102 | 7 | 3 | R | R | 6-4 | 200 | 1-23-70 | 1988 | La Puente, Calif. |
| Morrison, Jim, of | .221 | 77 | 249 | 30 | 55 | 10 | 1 | 4 | 25 | 29 | 81 | 11 | 8 | R | R | 5-11 | 170 | 10-28-67 | 1986 | Anna, Ill. |
| Norris, Bill, 3b | .259 | 119 | 398 | 43 | 103 | 17 | 4 | 3 | 36 | 21 | 69 | 4 | 6 | L | R | 5-10 | 180 | 1-29-69 | 1990 | Clifton Park, N.Y. |
| Rappoli, Paul, of | .213 | 115 | 356 | 49 | 76 | 16 | 5 | 3 | 26 | 64 | 77 | 6 | 9 | L | R | 6-1 | 195 | 10-4-71 | 1990 | Stoughton, Mass. |
| Rodriguez, Tony, ss | .228 | 99 | 355 | 37 | 81 | 16 | 4 | 0 | 31 | 16 | 52 | 8 | 7 | R | R | 5-11 | 165 | 8-15-70 | 1991 | Cidra, P.R. |
| Tatum, Willie, 1b | .276 | 43 | 152 | 25 | 42 | 7 | 0 | 1 | 21 | 20 | 38 | 4 | 5 | S | R | 6-7 | 200 | 11-5-66 | 1988 | Sacramento, Calif. |
| Thoutsis, Paul, of | .291 | 64 | 213 | 17 | 62 | 12 | 2 | 0 | 21 | 27 | 24 | 0 | 2 | L | R | 6-1 | 185 | 10-23-65 | 1983 | Worcester, Mass. |
| Wallin, Les, dh-1b | .231 | 69 | 195 | 22 | 45 | 10 | 0 | 3 | 23 | 26 | 37 | 1 | 3 | L | L | 6-4 | 210 | 6-16-66 | 1988 | Danbury, Conn. |

| PITCHING | W | L | ERA | G | GS | CG | SV | IP | H | R | ER | BB | SO | B | T | HT | WT | DOB | 1st Yr | Resides |
|---|---|---|---|---|---|---|---|---|---|---|---|---|---|---|---|---|---|---|---|---|
| Carter, Glenn | 5 | 4 | 3.14 | 12 | 12 | 2 | 0 | 80 | 67 | 31 | 28 | 35 | 55 | R | R | 6-0 | 175 | 11-29-67 | 1988 | Melrose Park, Ill. |
| Ciccarella, Joe | 0 | 4 | 4.22 | 30 | 0 | 0 | 15 | 32 | 31 | 19 | 15 | 23 | 34 | L | L | 6-3 | 190 | 12-29-69 | 1991 | Huntington Beach, Calif. |

# RED SOX: ORGANIZATION LEADERS

**Roger Clemens**
Struck out 160 despite injuries

MORRIS FOSTOFF

## MAJOR LEAGUERS

**BATTING**
| | | |
|---|---|---|
| *AVG | Mike Greenwell | .315 |
| R | Mo Vaughn | 86 |
| H | Mike Greenwell | 170 |
| TB | Mo Vaughn | 283 |
| 2B | John Valentin | 40 |
| 3B | Mike Greenwell | 6 |
| HR | Mo Vaughn | 29 |
| RBI | Mo Vaughn | 101 |
| BB | Mo Vaughn | 79 |
| SO | Mo Vaughn | 130 |
| SB | Scott Fletcher | 16 |

**PITCHING**
| | | |
|---|---|---|
| W | Danny Darwin | 15 |
| L | Roger Clemens | 14 |
| #ERA | Aaron Sele | 2.74 |
| G | Greg Harris | 80 |
| CG | Three tied at | 2 |
| SV | Jeff Russell | 33 |
| IP | Danny Darwin | 229 |
| BB | Frank Viola | 72 |
| SO | Roger Clemens | 160 |

## MINOR LEAGUERS

**BATTING**
| | | |
|---|---|---|
| *AVG | T.J. O'Donnell, Utica | .329 |
| R | Steve Rodriguez, Lynchburg | 78 |
| H | Steve Rodriguez, Lynchburg | 135 |
| TB | Doug Hecker, Lynchburg | 208 |
| 2B | Luis Ortiz, Pawtucket | 28 |
| 3B | Two tied at | 7 |
| HR | Greg Blosser, Pawtucket | 23 |
| RBI | Luis Ortiz, Pawtucket | 81 |
| BB | Bob Juday, Lynchburg | 83 |
| SO | Doug Hecker, Lynchburg | 149 |
| SB | Jeff McNeely, Pawtucket | 40 |

**PITCHING**
| | | |
|---|---|---|
| W | Scott Bakkum, Lynchburg | 12 |
| L | Brent Hansen, New Britain-Ft. Laud. | 17 |
| #ERA | Aaron Sele, Pawtucket | 2.19 |
| G | John Shea, New Britain | 60 |
| CG | Two tied at | 7 |
| SV | Cory Bailey, Pawtucket | 20 |
| IP | Brent Hansen, New Britain-Ft. Laud. | 196 |
| BB | Frank Rodriguez, New Britain | 78 |
| SO | Joel Bennett, Lynchburg | 221 |

*Minimum 250 At-Bats   #Minimum 75 Innings

# RED SOX: MOST COMMON LINEUPS

| | Boston | Pawtucket | New Britain | Lynchburg | Fort Lauderdale |
|---|---|---|---|---|---|
| | Majors | AAA | AA | A | A |
| C | Tony Pena (125) | John Flaherty (101) | Scott Hatteberg (67) | Walt McKeel (70) | Dana LeVangie (73) |
| 1B | Mo Vaughn (131) | Franklin Stubbs (49) | Jason Friedman (67) | Doug Hecker (110) | Ryan McGuire (56) |
| 2B | Scott Fletcher (116) | Cheo Garcia (90) | Jim Crowley (102) | Steve Rodriguez (119) | Pat Murphy (42) |
| 3B | Scott Cooper (154) | Luis Ortiz (63) | Bill Norris (116) | Bill Selby (73) | Jim Larkin (41) |
| SS | John Valentin (144) | Jim Byrd (116) | Tony Rodriguez (96) | Randy Brown (126) | Todd Carey (107) |
| OF | Mike Greenwell (134) | Jeff McNeely (127) | Paul Rappoli (110) | John Eierman (114) | Derek Vinyard (79) |
| | Billy Hatcher (130) | Greg Blosser (117) | Jim Morrison (74) | Jose Malave (77) | Brian Bright (58) |
| | Bob Zupcic (122) | Herm Winningham (57) | Mike Beams (70) | Ron Mahay (71) | Gino Dimare (50) |
| DH | Andre Dawson (97) | Franklin Stubbs (45) | Les Wallin (38) | Felix Colon (55) | Bryan Brown (32) |
| SP | Danny Darwin (34) | Nate Minchey (29) | Tim Vanegmond (29) | Joel Bennett (29) | Klvac/Nies (19) |
| RP | Greg Harris (80) | Don Florence (57) | Peter Hoy (51) | Joe Hudson (48) | Chad Amos (42) |

Full-season farm clubs only No. of games at position in parenthesis

| PITCHING | W | L | ERA | G | GS | CG | SV | IP | H | R | ER | BB | SO | B | T | HT | WT | DOB | 1st Yr | Resides |
|---|---|---|---|---|---|---|---|---|---|---|---|---|---|---|---|---|---|---|---|---|
| Dzafic, Zack | 2 | 7 | 4.04 | 45 | 0 | 0 | 2 | 65 | 86 | 38 | 29 | 17 | 31 | R | R | 6-3 | 200 | 1-19-68 | 1988 | Carlinville, Ill. |
| Fischer, Tom | 0 | 2 | 12.46 | 16 | 0 | 0 | 0 | 17 | 36 | 25 | 24 | 15 | 12 | L | L | 5-11 | 195 | 3-23-67 | 1988 | Madison, Wis. |
| Hansen, Brent | 2 | 11 | 4.92 | 15 | 15 | 1 | 0 | 93 | 99 | 55 | 51 | 30 | 56 | R | R | 6-2 | 195 | 8-4-70 | 1992 | Carlsbad, Calif. |
| Hoy, Peter | 9 | 4 | 3.84 | 51 | 0 | 0 | 0 | 80 | 86 | 38 | 34 | 41 | 37 | L | R | 6-7 | 220 | 6-29-66 | 1989 | Cardinal, Ontario |
| Mintz, Steve | 2 | 4 | 2.08 | 43 | 1 | 0 | 7 | 69 | 52 | 22 | 16 | 30 | 51 | L | R | 5-11 | 190 | 11-24-68 | 1990 | Leland, N.C. |
| Mitchell, John | 1 | 1 | 1.04 | 8 | 1 | 0 | 1 | 17 | 15 | 2 | 2 | 2 | 8 | R | R | 6-2 | 165 | 8-11-65 | 1983 | Nashville, Tenn. |
| Mosley, Tony | 0 | 0 | 6.17 | 15 | 0 | 0 | 0 | 12 | 12 | 9 | 8 | 9 | 11 | S | L | 6-4 | 175 | 6-2-69 | 1987 | Fort Meade, Fla. |
| Painter, Gary | 3 | 6 | 4.06 | 14 | 14 | 0 | 0 | 78 | 76 | 44 | 35 | 29 | 57 | R | R | 6-2 | 196 | 4-30-68 | 1990 | Bowling Green, Fla. |
| Riley, Ed | 4 | 6 | 3.55 | 14 | 14 | 1 | 0 | 84 | 85 | 39 | 33 | 29 | 50 | L | L | 6-2 | 195 | 2-10-70 | 1988 | Worcester, Mass. |
| Rodriguez, Frank | 7 | 11 | 3.74 | 28 | 26 | 4 | 0 | 171 | 147 | 79 | 71 | 78 | 151 | R | R | 6-0 | 175 | 12-11-72 | 1991 | Oviedo, Fla. |
| Shea, John | 4 | 2 | 3.65 | 48 | 0 | 0 | 1 | 57 | 48 | 27 | 23 | 22 | 62 | R | L | 6-6 | 210 | 6-23-66 | 1986 | Dunedin, Fla. |
| Smith, Tim | 7 | 13 | 3.79 | 28 | 28 | 3 | 0 | 180 | 192 | 91 | 76 | 44 | 81 | R | R | 6-4 | 190 | 8-9-68 | 1990 | Cumberland, R.I. |
| Uhrhan, Kevin | 0 | 1 | 11.57 | 9 | 0 | 0 | 0 | 9 | 14 | 12 | 12 | 6 | 3 | R | R | 6-0 | 175 | 7-19-66 | 1989 | Chaffee, Mo. |
| Vanegmond, Tim | 6 | 12 | 3.97 | 29 | 29 | 1 | 0 | 190 | 182 | 99 | 84 | 44 | 163 | R | R | 6-2 | 175 | 5-31-69 | 1991 | Senoia, Ga. |

# LYNCHBURG                                                                     A
## CAROLINA LEAGUE

| BATTING | AVG | G | AB | R | H | 2B | 3B | HR | RBI | BB | SO | SB | CS | B | T | HT | WT | DOB | 1st Yr | Resides |
|---|---|---|---|---|---|---|---|---|---|---|---|---|---|---|---|---|---|---|---|---|
| Baez, Diogenes, of | .231 | 13 | 26 | 2 | 6 | 1 | 0 | 0 | 1 | 3 | 1 | 1 | 1 | L | R | 6-0 | 185 | 2-28-71 | 1991 | Manhattan, N.Y. |
| Brown, Randy, ss | .236 | 128 | 483 | 57 | 114 | 25 | 7 | 2 | 45 | 25 | 127 | 10 | 8 | R | R | 5-11 | 160 | 5-1-70 | 1989 | Houston, Texas |
| Carey, Tim, c-dh | .220 | 49 | 141 | 9 | 31 | 7 | 0 | 0 | 11 | 17 | 45 | 1 | 0 | L | R | 6-2 | 225 | 4-17-70 | 1992 | Cumberland, R.I. |
| Colon, Felix, dh-1b | .320 | 98 | 319 | 52 | 102 | 22 | 0 | 16 | 58 | 45 | 65 | 0 | 1 | R | R | 6-0 | 176 | 9-15-70 | 1989 | Levittown, P.R. |
| Eierman, John, of | .273 | 119 | 399 | 56 | 109 | 20 | 2 | 15 | 62 | 62 | 97 | 2 | 2 | L | R | 6-1 | 190 | 5-30-70 | 1991 | Chicago, Ill. |
| Graham, Tim, of | .130 | 8 | 23 | 6 | 3 | 1 | 0 | 0 | 3 | 13 | 8 | 0 | 2 | L | R | 6-0 | 170 | 9-4-71 | 1990 | Lancaster, Ohio |
| Hecker, Doug, 1b | .237 | 127 | 490 | 57 | 116 | 23 | 3 | 21 | 73 | 36 | 149 | 0 | 0 | R | R | 6-4 | 210 | 1-21-71 | 1992 | Wantagh, N.Y. |
| Johnson, J.J., of | .255 | 25 | 94 | 10 | 24 | 3 | 0 | 4 | 17 | 7 | 20 | 1 | 2 | R | R | 6-0 | 195 | 8-31-73 | 1991 | Pine Plains, N.Y. |
| Juday, Bob, 3b-ss | .297 | 114 | 354 | 67 | 105 | 15 | 1 | 4 | 32 | 83 | 58 | 5 | 5 | S | R | 6-0 | 180 | 12-29-70 | 1992 | Midland, Mich. |
| Mahay, Ron, of | .213 | 73 | 254 | 28 | 54 | 8 | 1 | 5 | 23 | 11 | 63 | 2 | 2 | L | L | 6-2 | 185 | 6-28-71 | 1991 | Crestwood, Ill. |
| Malave, Jose, of | .301 | 82 | 312 | 42 | 94 | 27 | 1 | 8 | 54 | 36 | 54 | 2 | 3 | R | R | 6-2 | 194 | 5-31-71 | 1990 | Cumana, Venez. |
| Martin, Jeff, c | .182 | 62 | 192 | 25 | 35 | 7 | 2 | 6 | 22 | 23 | 78 | 0 | 0 | R | R | 6-4 | 210 | 7-14-70 | 1992 | Goodlettsville, Tenn. |
| McKeel, Walt, c | .239 | 80 | 247 | 28 | 59 | 17 | 2 | 5 | 32 | 26 | 40 | 0 | 1 | R | R | 6-2 | 200 | 1-17-72 | 1990 | Stantonsburg, N.C. |
| Rodriguez, Steve, 2b | .274 | 120 | 493 | 78 | 135 | 26 | 3 | 3 | 42 | 31 | 69 | 20 | 13 | R | R | 5-9 | 170 | 11-29-70 | 1991 | Las Vegas, Nev. |
| Schmidt, David, 3b-2b | .158 | 6 | 19 | 2 | 3 | 0 | 0 | 2 | 4 | 0 | 7 | 0 | 0 | R | R | 6-1 | 185 | 7-22-70 | 1990 | San Diego, Calif. |
| Scott, George, of | .230 | 80 | 196 | 26 | 45 | 6 | 2 | 1 | 21 | 18 | 32 | 1 | 3 | R | R | 5-8 | 175 | 6-20-69 | 1992 | South Dartmouth, Mass. |
| Selby, Bill, 3b-dh | .251 | 113 | 394 | 57 | 99 | 22 | 1 | 7 | 38 | 24 | 66 | 1 | 2 | L | R | 5-9 | 190 | 6-11-70 | 1992 | Walls, Miss. |
| Smith, Dave, 2b | .308 | 4 | 13 | 1 | 4 | 0 | 1 | 0 | 2 | 0 | 1 | 0 | 0 | R | R | 5-10 | 160 | 2-18-72 | 1993 | Cheektowaga, N.Y. |
| Zambrano, Jose, of | .245 | 72 | 233 | 32 | 57 | 16 | 2 | 9 | 27 | 20 | 70 | 0 | 2 | R | R | 6-0 | 165 | 3-18-71 | 1988 | Maracaibo, Venez. |

| PITCHING | W | L | ERA | G | GS | CG | SV | IP | H | R | ER | BB | SO | B | T | HT | WT | DOB | 1st Yr | Resides |
|---|---|---|---|---|---|---|---|---|---|---|---|---|---|---|---|---|---|---|---|---|
| Bakkum, Scott | 12 | 11 | 3.77 | 26 | 26 | 6 | 0 | 170 | 201 | 87 | 71 | 31 | 98 | R | R | 6-4 | 205 | 11-20-69 | 1991 | LaCrosse, Wis. |
| Bennett, Joel | 7 | 12 | 3.83 | 29 | 29 | 3 | 0 | 181 | 151 | 93 | 77 | 67 | 221 | R | R | 6-1 | 170 | 1-31-70 | 1991 | Kirkwood, N.Y. |
| Donovan, Bret | 3 | 10 | 5.72 | 31 | 16 | 0 | 0 | 107 | 136 | 82 | 68 | 33 | 63 | L | L | 6-5 | 205 | 8-23-69 | 1992 | Atlanta, Ga. |
| Faino, Jeff | 6 | 3 | 3.16 | 40 | 8 | 0 | 1 | 105 | 93 | 45 | 37 | 37 | 79 | R | L | 6-0 | 185 | 11-22-72 | 1992 | Danvers, Mass. |
| Gakeler, Dan | 3 | 3 | 1.49 | 30 | 0 | 0 | 9 | 42 | 31 | 13 | 7 | 11 | 28 | R | R | 6-6 | 215 | 5-1-64 | 1984 | Greensboro, N.C. |
| Glaze, Gettys | 5 | 12 | 3.97 | 27 | 25 | 2 | 1 | 163 | 191 | 90 | 72 | 49 | 137 | R | R | 6-1 | 185 | 9-23-70 | 1992 | Charleston, S.C. |
| Henkel, Rob | 8 | 7 | 4.18 | 18 | 7 | 0 | 0 | 113 | 120 | 60 | 54 | 27 | 96 | R | R | 6-3 | 190 | 11-23-70 | 1991 | Norris, Tenn. |
| Hudson, Joe | 1 | 4 | 4.06 | 49 | 1 | 0 | 6 | 84 | 97 | 49 | 38 | 38 | 62 | R | R | 6-1 | 180 | 9-29-70 | 1992 | Medford, N.J. |
| Johnston, Danny | 0 | 1 | 6.33 | 20 | 0 | 0 | 3 | 27 | 37 | 23 | 19 | 13 | 21 | L | R | 6-0 | 170 | 6-14-68 | 1989 | Indianapolis, Ind. |
| Maloney, Ryan | 0 | 0 | 7.07 | 18 | 0 | 0 | 0 | 28 | 41 | 25 | 22 | 18 | 13 | L | L | 6-3 | 190 | 1-24-72 | 1990 | Lancaster, Ohio |
| Miller, Todd | 4 | 0 | 3.38 | 25 | 0 | 0 | 0 | 51 | 54 | 22 | 19 | 17 | 23 | R | R | 6-3 | 210 | 9-26-69 | 1990 | Coplay, Pa. |
| Niles, Tommy | 7 | 7 | 5.07 | 32 | 15 | 0 | 0 | 108 | 121 | 68 | 61 | 53 | 82 | R | R | 6-1 | 185 | 10-19-68 | 1991 | South China, Maine |
| Painter, Gary | 2 | 2 | 2.15 | 15 | 1 | 0 | 5 | 29 | 24 | 8 | 7 | 8 | 26 | R | R | 6-2 | 196 | 4-30-68 | 1990 | Bowling Green, Fla. |

# FORT LAUDERDALE                                                               A
## FLORIDA STATE LEAGUE

| BATTING | AVG | G | AB | R | H | 2B | 3B | HR | RBI | BB | SO | SB | CS | B | T | HT | WT | DOB | 1st Yr | Resides |
|---|---|---|---|---|---|---|---|---|---|---|---|---|---|---|---|---|---|---|---|---|
| Bright, Brian, of | .301 | 75 | 259 | 25 | 78 | 11 | 0 | 5 | 35 | 10 | 47 | 1 | 2 | R | R | 6-1 | 190 | 1-6-70 | 1991 | Revere, Mass. |
| Brown, Bryan, dh-of | .312 | 55 | 205 | 24 | 64 | 9 | 2 | 5 | 29 | 19 | 37 | 0 | 1 | R | R | 6-2 | 180 | 7-1-70 | 1991 | Metairie, La. |
| Carey, Todd, ss | .245 | 118 | 444 | 41 | 109 | 14 | 5 | 3 | 31 | 24 | 44 | 2 | 6 | L | R | 6-1 | 180 | 8-14-71 | 1992 | Cumberland, R.I. |
| Chick, Bruce, of | .289 | 39 | 159 | 13 | 46 | 9 | 0 | 1 | 14 | 4 | 34 | 1 | 2 | R | R | 6-4 | 210 | 3-7-69 | 1990 | St. Petersburg, Fla. |
| Davis, Tim, 2b | .071 | 4 | 14 | 0 | 1 | 0 | 0 | 0 | 1 | 1 | 2 | 0 | 0 | R | R | 5-9 | 170 | 6-17-68 | 1990 | DuQuoin, Ill. |
| Delgado, Alex, c | .253 | 63 | 225 | 26 | 57 | 9 | 0 | 2 | 25 | 9 | 21 | 2 | 2 | R | R | 6-0 | 160 | 1-11-71 | 1988 | Palmarejo, Venez. |
| DiMare, Gino, of-dh | .230 | 81 | 278 | 36 | 64 | 3 | 0 | 0 | 23 | 41 | 41 | 12 | 8 | L | L | 5-11 | 175 | 7-21-69 | 1992 | Miami, Fla. |
| Dorante, Luis, c | .074 | 14 | 27 | 1 | 2 | 1 | 0 | 0 | 1 | 7 | 8 | 0 | 0 | R | R | 6-0 | 165 | 10-25-68 | 1987 | Coro, Venez. |

# RED SOX TOP 10 PROSPECTS

**How the Red Sox Top 10 prospects, as judged by Baseball America prior to the 1993 season, fared in 1993:**

| Player, Pos. | Club (Class) | AVG | AB | H | HR | RBI | SB |
|---|---|---|---|---|---|---|---|
| 2. Greg Blosser, of | Pawtucket (AAA) | .228 | 478 | 109 | 23 | 66 | 3 |
| | Boston | .071 | 28 | 2 | 0 | 1 | 1 |
| 4. Luis Ortiz, 3b | Pawtucket (AAA) | .294 | 402 | 118 | 18 | 81 | 1 |
| | Boston | .250 | 12 | 3 | 0 | 1 | 0 |
| 6. Jeff McNeely, of | Pawtucket (AAA) | .261 | 498 | 130 | 2 | 35 | 40 |
| | Boston | .297 | 37 | 11 | 0 | 1 | 6 |
| 9. Jose Malave, of | Lynchburg (A) | .301 | 312 | 94 | 8 | 54 | 2 |
| 10. Scott Hatteberg, c | New Britain (AA) | .278 | 227 | 63 | 7 | 28 | 1 |
| | Pawtucket (AAA) | .189 | 53 | 10 | 1 | 2 | 0 |

| Player, Pos. | Club (Class) | W | L | ERA | IP | H | BB | SO |
|---|---|---|---|---|---|---|---|---|
| 1. F. Rodriguez, rhp | New Britain (AA) | 7 | 11 | 3.74 | 171 | 147 | 78 | 151 |
| 3. Aaron Sele, rhp | Pawtucket (AAA) | 8 | 2 | 2.19 | 94 | 74 | 23 | 87 |
| | Boston | 7 | 2 | 2.74 | 112 | 100 | 48 | 93 |
| 5. Joe Caruso, rhp | Pawtucket (AAA) | 5 | 10 | 5.30 | 122 | 138 | 68 | 85 |
| 7. Ken Ryan, rhp | Pawtucket (AAA) | 0 | 2 | 2.49 | 25 | 18 | 17 | 22 |
| | Boston | 7 | 2 | 3.60 | 50 | 43 | 29 | 49 |
| 8. Rob Henkel, rhp | Lynchburg (A) | 8 | 7 | 4.29 | 113 | 120 | 27 | 96 |

**Frank Rodriguez** 7-11 at New Britain

## BATTING

| | AVG | G | AB | R | H | 2B | 3B | HR | RBI | BB | SO | SB | CS | B | T | HT | WT | DOB | 1st Yr | Resides |
|---|---|---|---|---|---|---|---|---|---|---|---|---|---|---|---|---|---|---|---|---|
| Durkin, Marty, of-3b | .259 | 97 | 332 | 43 | 86 | 16 | 3 | 5 | 32 | 21 | 73 | 15 | 5 | S | R | 6-2 | 180 | 11-5-67 | 1989 | Fort Lauderdale, Fla. |
| Ferreira, Tony, 2b | .185 | 42 | 124 | 10 | 23 | 2 | 1 | 0 | 6 | 25 | 30 | 2 | 3 | S | R | 5-10 | 160 | 11-3-69 | 1991 | Sarasota, Fla. |
| Graham, John, of | .237 | 55 | 177 | 23 | 42 | 6 | 3 | 2 | 14 | 18 | 53 | 2 | 2 | L | L | 5-10 | 170 | 5-7-71 | 1993 | North Abington, Mass. |
| Graham, Tim, of | .259 | 53 | 162 | 34 | 42 | 5 | 7 | 0 | 11 | 32 | 31 | 8 | 3 | L | R | 6-0 | 170 | 9-4-71 | 1989 | Lancaster, Ohio |
| Larkin, Jim, 3b | .203 | 47 | 158 | 11 | 32 | 7 | 0 | 0 | 8 | 7 | 34 | 1 | 0 | R | R | 6-1 | 185 | 2-16-71 | 1993 | Mendon, Mass. |
| LeVangie, Dana, c | .188 | 80 | 250 | 17 | 47 | 5 | 0 | 0 | 11 | 26 | 46 | 0 | 2 | R | R | 5-10 | 185 | 8-11-69 | 1991 | Whitman, Mass. |
| McGuire, Ryan, 1b | .324 | 58 | 213 | 23 | 69 | 12 | 2 | 4 | 38 | 27 | 34 | 2 | 4 | L | L | 6-1 | 195 | 11-23-71 | 1993 | Woodland Hills, Calif. |
| Merloni, Lou, 3b-ss | .244 | 44 | 156 | 14 | 38 | 1 | 1 | 2 | 21 | 13 | 26 | 1 | 1 | R | R | 5-9 | 180 | 4-6-71 | 1993 | Framingham, Mass. |
| Murphy, Pat, 2b | .296 | 54 | 186 | 28 | 55 | 4 | 2 | 0 | 21 | 24 | 23 | 9 | 9 | L | R | 5-10 | 160 | 3-24-72 | 1993 | Mobile, Ala. |
| Ortiz, Nick, 3b-ss | .205 | 36 | 112 | 9 | 23 | 9 | 1 | 1 | 14 | 9 | 39 | 2 | 1 | R | R | 6-0 | 165 | 7-9-73 | 1991 | Cidra, P.R. |
| Perozo, Ed, 1b-of | .219 | 49 | 160 | 18 | 35 | 5 | 1 | 3 | 18 | 11 | 35 | 0 | 0 | S | R | 6-4 | 215 | 1-15-70 | 1989 | Maracaibo, Venez. |
| Smith, David, 2b-dh | .225 | 36 | 120 | 22 | 27 | 2 | 1 | 0 | 8 | 17 | 31 | 7 | 1 | R | R | 5-10 | 160 | 2-18-72 | 1993 | Cheektowaga, N.Y. |
| Soto, Emison, 3b-of | .151 | 45 | 139 | 13 | 21 | 5 | 0 | 4 | 12 | 6 | 36 | 1 | 1 | R | R | 6-0 | 175 | 8-3-71 | 1990 | Maracaibo, Venez. |
| Vinyard, Derek, of | .210 | 85 | 281 | 34 | 59 | 3 | 1 | 0 | 19 | 33 | 65 | 26 | 8 | S | R | 6-2 | 185 | 2-9-71 | 1992 | Salem, Ore. |
| Wallin, Les, 1b | .297 | 47 | 155 | 23 | 46 | 16 | 0 | 4 | 25 | 27 | 13 | 0 | 1 | L | L | 6-4 | 210 | 6-16-66 | 1988 | Danbury, Conn. |
| Zambrano, Jose, of | .158 | 23 | 57 | 6 | 9 | 3 | 0 | 1 | 6 | 6 | 24 | 0 | 1 | R | R | 6-0 | 165 | 3-18-71 | 1988 | Maracaibo, Venez. |

## PITCHING

| | W | L | ERA | G | GS | CG | SV | IP | H | R | ER | BB | SO | B | T | HT | WT | DOB | 1st Yr | Resides |
|---|---|---|---|---|---|---|---|---|---|---|---|---|---|---|---|---|---|---|---|---|
| Allen, Ron | 6 | 5 | 5.03 | 26 | 10 | 1 | 0 | 79 | 80 | 48 | 44 | 56 | 45 | L | L | 5-11 | 172 | 11-1-72 | 1991 | Plant City, Fla. |
| Amos, Chad | 3 | 2 | 6.97 | 42 | 0 | 0 | 4 | 50 | 53 | 43 | 39 | 30 | 40 | R | R | 6-6 | 230 | 10-8-71 | 1992 | New Matamoras, Ohio |
| Bennett, Shayne | 1 | 2 | 1.72 | 23 | 0 | 0 | 6 | 31 | 26 | 8 | 6 | 11 | 23 | R | R | 6-5 | 195 | 4-23-72 | 1993 | Downers Grove, Ill. |
| Blais, Mike | 1 | 1 | 1.50 | 3 | 0 | 0 | 0 | 6 | 4 | 1 | 1 | 3 | 7 | R | R | 6-5 | 226 | 10-2-71 | 1993 | East Lyme, Conn. |
| Brooks, Wes | 8 | 5 | 3.89 | 19 | 18 | 4 | 0 | 127 | 124 | 62 | 55 | 42 | 85 | R | R | 6-3 | 200 | 1-11-72 | 1992 | Lebanon, Ill. |
| Davis, Chris | 2 | 6 | 6.96 | 8 | 8 | 0 | 0 | 43 | 69 | 42 | 33 | 8 | 10 | R | R | 6-2 | 190 | 11-7-71 | 1992 | Cordova, Tenn. |
| Gonzalez, Melvin | 0 | 4 | 4.84 | 21 | 2 | 0 | 2 | 48 | 52 | 31 | 26 | 34 | 37 | R | R | 6-2 | 190 | 10-9-70 | 1989 | Arecibo, P.R. |
| Hansen, Brent | 4 | 6 | 2.63 | 14 | 14 | 4 | 0 | 103 | 94 | 37 | 30 | 37 | 59 | R | R | 6-2 | 195 | 8-4-70 | 1992 | Carlsbad, Calif. |
| Hayward, Steve | 1 | 4 | 5.18 | 13 | 5 | 0 | 0 | 40 | 43 | 25 | 23 | 32 | 37 | R | R | 6-2 | 185 | 1-1-71 | 1993 | Washington Township, N.J. |
| Hoy, Peter | 0 | 0 | 0.00 | 4 | 0 | 0 | 1 | 4 | 2 | 0 | 0 | 0 | 4 | L | R | 6-7 | 220 | 6-29-66 | 1989 | Cardinal, Ontario |
| Johnson, Jeff | 0 | 2 | 6.61 | 14 | 0 | 0 | 1 | 16 | 17 | 19 | 12 | 15 | 10 | R | R | 6-2 | 210 | 4-18-71 | 1991 | Clovis, Calif. |
| Kennedy, Greg | 3 | 6 | 3.66 | 12 | 12 | 1 | 0 | 79 | 79 | 41 | 32 | 43 | 44 | L | L | 6-1 | 180 | 1-26-72 | 1993 | Quitman, Miss. |
| Kivac, Dave | 4 | 9 | 4.46 | 21 | 19 | 3 | 0 | 127 | 138 | 76 | 63 | 59 | 72 | R | L | 6-4 | 205 | 4-11-70 | 1991 | Medway, Mass. |
| Lawrence, Randy | 0 | 0 | 22.50 | 5 | 0 | 0 | 0 | 8 | 27 | 22 | 20 | 4 | 5 | R | R | 6-4 | 230 | 3-5-70 | 1992 | Ferrum, Va. |
| Martinez, Cesar | 3 | 11 | 5.47 | 18 | 16 | 2 | 0 | 97 | 124 | 65 | 59 | 44 | 45 | L | L | 6-2 | 175 | 4-29-73 | 1991 | San Diego, Calif. |
| Mosley, Tony | 2 | 1 | 4.78 | 17 | 0 | 0 | 0 | 26 | 36 | 18 | 14 | 10 | 19 | S | L | 6-4 | 175 | 6-2-69 | 1987 | Fort Meade, Fla. |
| Nies, Joel | 5 | 9 | 3.55 | 20 | 19 | 3 | 0 | 127 | 123 | 60 | 50 | 31 | 85 | R | R | 6-2 | 200 | 6-23-70 | 1993 | Wenham, Mass. |
| Osterkamp, Ken | 1 | 1 | 1.81 | 39 | 0 | 0 | 3 | 50 | 51 | 12 | 10 | 20 | 19 | R | L | 6-2 | 195 | 11-14-69 | 1993 | Cincinnati, Ohio |
| Perez, Hilario | 0 | 4 | 7.90 | 6 | 6 | 0 | 0 | 27 | 50 | 29 | 24 | 18 | 12 | R | R | 6-2 | 175 | 10-11-72 | 1991 | Elias Pina, D.R. |
| Santa Maria, Silverio | 2 | 7 | 3.91 | 41 | 2 | 0 | 3 | 71 | 61 | 37 | 31 | 35 | 61 | R | R | 6-3 | 180 | 6-20-70 | 1989 | La Victoria, D.R. |

# UTICA
## NEW YORK-PENN LEAGUE — A

### BATTING

| | AVG | G | AB | R | H | 2B | 3B | HR | RBI | BB | SO | SB | CS | B | T | HT | WT | DOB | 1st Yr | Resides |
|---|---|---|---|---|---|---|---|---|---|---|---|---|---|---|---|---|---|---|---|---|
| Aguado, Victor, ss-2b | .208 | 9 | 24 | 3 | 5 | 2 | 0 | 0 | 1 | 1 | 5 | 0 | 2 | R | R | 5-11 | 145 | 5-6-73 | 1991 | Caracas, Venez. |
| Baez, Diogenes, of | .272 | 50 | 151 | 30 | 41 | 9 | 1 | 2 | 20 | 13 | 20 | 5 | 4 | L | R | 6-0 | 185 | 2-28-71 | 1991 | Manhattan, N.Y. |
| Borrero, Richie, c | .158 | 44 | 120 | 10 | 19 | 2 | 0 | 2 | 14 | 11 | 39 | 3 | 1 | R | R | 6-1 | 195 | 1-5-73 | 1990 | Hormigueros, P.R. |
| Collier, Daniel, of | .217 | 67 | 226 | 39 | 49 | 11 | 1 | 15 | 48 | 29 | 95 | 4 | 0 | R | R | 6-3 | 205 | 8-13-70 | 1991 | Ozark, Ala. |
| Debrand, Juan, ss-2b | .500 | 4 | 2 | 1 | 1 | 0 | 0 | 0 | 1 | 0 | 0 | 0 | 0 | R | R | 5-11 | 160 | 12-4-69 | 1993 | Tuscaloosa, Ala. |
| DePastino, Joey, 3b-1b | .253 | 62 | 221 | 28 | 56 | 9 | 1 | 2 | 32 | 16 | 51 | 3 | 2 | R | R | 6-2 | 210 | 9-4-73 | 1992 | Sarasota, Fla. |
| Ford, Eric, 1b-of | .194 | 33 | 103 | 14 | 20 | 9 | 1 | 1 | 16 | 6 | 28 | 1 | 1 | R | R | 6-2 | 195 | 10-4-71 | 1993 | Brandon, Miss. |
| Fuller, Aaron, of | .250 | 53 | 176 | 31 | 44 | 3 | 0 | 1 | 17 | 20 | 26 | 24 | 4 | S | R | 5-10 | 170 | 9-7-71 | 1993 | Sacramento, Calif. |
| Hayward, Joe, dh | .243 | 36 | 74 | 7 | 18 | 5 | 0 | 0 | 2 | 21 | 18 | 1 | 0 | L | R | 6-1 | 195 | 8-5-70 | 1993 | Osterville, Mass. |
| Johnson, J.J., of | .288 | 43 | 170 | 33 | 49 | 17 | 4 | 2 | 27 | 9 | 34 | 5 | 3 | R | R | 6-0 | 195 | 8-31-73 | 1991 | Pine Plains, N.Y. |
| Jones, Donny, of | .200 | 21 | 65 | 6 | 13 | 2 | 0 | 1 | 4 | 1 | 18 | 0 | 2 | R | R | 6-2 | 190 | 9-14-72 | 1991 | Poway, Calif. |
| Milligan, Ricky, of | .228 | 53 | 123 | 18 | 28 | 7 | 3 | 2 | 12 | 20 | 47 | 4 | 4 | R | R | 6-3 | 210 | 10-25-72 | 1992 | Stockton, Calif. |
| Moore, Andy, 1b | .130 | 7 | 23 | 3 | 3 | 1 | 0 | 2 | 2 | 2 | 10 | 0 | 1 | R | R | 6-3 | 210 | 11-13-70 | 1992 | West Chester, Pa. |
| O'Donnell, T.J., 2b-1b | .329 | 68 | 255 | 47 | 84 | 22 | 1 | 4 | 33 | 18 | 24 | 5 | 5 | R | R | 6-0 | 180 | 10-7-70 | 1992 | Hazlet, N.J. |
| Ortiz, Nick, 3b-ss | .269 | 63 | 197 | 31 | 53 | 14 | 1 | 2 | 26 | 19 | 56 | 4 | 1 | R | R | 6-0 | 165 | 7-9-73 | 1991 | Cidra, P.R. |
| Patton, Greg, ss | .225 | 54 | 169 | 22 | 38 | 8 | 1 | 3 | 24 | 23 | 45 | 0 | 2 | R | R | 6-3 | 195 | 3-8-72 | 1991 | Springfield, Va. |
| Senkowitz, Mark, c-dh | .285 | 42 | 137 | 25 | 39 | 8 | 1 | 2 | 23 | 14 | 28 | 2 | 3 | R | R | 6-0 | 205 | 10-27-70 | 1992 | Warren, Ohio |
| Stratton, John, c-1b | .249 | 53 | 173 | 22 | 43 | 14 | 1 | 2 | 19 | 17 | 44 | 2 | 2 | L | R | 6-1 | 185 | 1-10-71 | 1993 | Stratford, Conn. |

| BATTING | AVG | G | AB | R | H | 2B | 3B | HR | RBI | BB | SO | SB | CS | B | T | HT | WT | DOB | 1st Yr | Resides |
|---|---|---|---|---|---|---|---|---|---|---|---|---|---|---|---|---|---|---|---|---|
| Walker, John, 2b ........... | .298 | 37 | 94 | 14 | 28 | 5 | 1 | 0 | 12 | 15 | 13 | 6 | 4 | L | R | 5-9 | 170 | 11-4-71 | 1993 | Grand Rapids, Mich. |

| PITCHING | W | L | ERA | G | GS | CG | SV | IP | H | R | ER | BB | SO | B | T | HT | WT | DOB | 1st Yr | Resides |
|---|---|---|---|---|---|---|---|---|---|---|---|---|---|---|---|---|---|---|---|---|
| Berryman, Robb ............ | 2 | 3 | 3.65 | 21 | 0 | 0 | 5 | 25 | 23 | 14 | 10 | 15 | 30 | L | R | 6-0 | 210 | 4-19-72 | 1992 | Yorktown, Va. |
| Bogott, Kurt.................... | 1 | 7 | 4.45 | 13 | 10 | 0 | 0 | 57 | 64 | 37 | 28 | 23 | 53 | L | L | 6-4 | 195 | 9-30-72 | 1993 | Sterling, Ill. |
| Bush, Craig ................... | 3 | 3 | 5.35 | 16 | 12 | 0 | 0 | 66 | 67 | 44 | 39 | 28 | 51 | R | R | 6-3 | 195 | 8-13-73 | 1991 | Lancaster, Ohio |
| Cormier, Eric................. | 7 | 5 | 3.10 | 18 | 15 | 1 | 0 | 105 | 95 | 39 | 36 | 39 | 93 | R | R | 6-4 | 218 | 5-26-74 | 1992 | Milford, Mass. |
| Johnson, Jeff ................ | 0 | 2 | 5.40 | 19 | 0 | 0 | 3 | 28 | 20 | 22 | 17 | 19 | 23 | R | R | 6-2 | 210 | 4-18-71 | 1991 | Clovis, Calif. |
| Johnston, Danny............ | 0 | 0 | 2.35 | 4 | 0 | 0 | 2 | 8 | 3 | 2 | 2 | 5 | 10 | L | R | 6-0 | 170 | 6-14-68 | 1989 | Indianapolis, Ind. |
| Lawrence, Randy........... | 1 | 1 | 5.56 | 14 | 0 | 0 | 0 | 23 | 28 | 20 | 14 | 15 | 13 | R | R | 6-4 | 230 | 3-5-70 | 1992 | Ferrum, Va. |
| McKinley, Leif ............... | 2 | 1 | 4.23 | 21 | 3 | 0 | 3 | 45 | 58 | 26 | 21 | 7 | 28 | R | R | 6-5 | 175 | 7-7-71 | 1992 | Willamina, Ore. |
| Orellano, Rafael ............ | 1 | 2 | 5.79 | 11 | 0 | 0 | 2 | 19 | 22 | 15 | 12 | 7 | 13 | L | L | 6-2 | 160 | 4-28-73 | 1993 | Humacao, P.R. |
| Perez, Hilario ............... | 3 | 2 | 3.03 | 16 | 3 | 0 | 0 | 30 | 39 | 20 | 10 | 11 | 15 | R | R | 6-2 | 175 | 10-11-72 | 1991 | Elias Pina, D.R. |
| Peterson, Dean............. | 1 | 4 | 5.36 | 16 | 5 | 0 | 2 | 42 | 45 | 28 | 25 | 7 | 26 | R | R | 6-3 | 200 | 8-3-72 | 1993 | Cortland, Ohio |
| Renfroe, Chad .............. | 7 | 4 | 2.78 | 16 | 15 | 0 | 0 | 91 | 69 | 40 | 28 | 39 | 73 | L | R | 6-2 | 195 | 9-10-73 | 1991 | Pedro, Ohio |
| Senior, Shawn ............... | 7 | 2 | 3.89 | 13 | 13 | 1 | 0 | 76 | 84 | 40 | 33 | 34 | 77 | L | L | 6-1 | 195 | 3-17-72 | 1993 | Cherry Hill, N.J. |
| Telgheder, Jim ............... | 0 | 0 | 0.00 | 2 | 0 | 0 | 0 | 2 | 0 | 1 | 0 | 1 | 0 | R | R | 6-3 | 210 | 3-22-71 | 1993 | Slate Hill, N.Y. |
| Tyrell, Jim ..................... | 3 | 2 | 3.38 | 28 | 0 | 0 | 3 | 35 | 27 | 17 | 13 | 18 | 25 | R | L | 5-11 | 170 | 10-14-72 | 1992 | Poughkeepsie, N.Y. |

## FORT MYERS
## GULF COAST LEAGUE

| BATTING | AVG | G | AB | R | H | 2B | 3B | HR | RBI | BB | SO | SB | CS | B | T | HT | WT | DOB | 1st Yr | Resides |
|---|---|---|---|---|---|---|---|---|---|---|---|---|---|---|---|---|---|---|---|---|
| Abad, Andy, of-1b ........ | .248 | 59 | 230 | 24 | 57 | 9 | 2 | 1 | 28 | 25 | 27 | 2 | 2 | L | L | 6-1 | 185 | 8-25-72 | 1993 | Jupiter, Fla. |
| Arias, Ramon, c............ | .200 | 14 | 20 | 3 | 4 | 1 | 0 | 0 | 2 | 8 | 6 | 0 | 0 | S | R | 5-11 | 170 | 11-18-73 | 1991 | Santo Domingo, D.R. |
| Arrollado, Courtney, ss . | .161 | 17 | 56 | 6 | 9 | 0 | 0 | 0 | 1 | 7 | 16 | 2 | 2 | R | R | 6-1 | 175 | 9-5-74 | 1993 | El Cajon, Calif. |
| Bowles, John, 1b.......... | .191 | 48 | 152 | 14 | 29 | 4 | 0 | 1 | 13 | 18 | 20 | 0 | 1 | L | R | 5-11 | 188 | 9-6-74 | 1992 | Rockville, Md. |
| Clark, Kevin, c.............. | .204 | 40 | 137 | 14 | 28 | 9 | 0 | 1 | 19 | 16 | 24 | 1 | 1 | R | R | 6-1 | 185 | 4-30-73 | 1993 | Henderson, Nev. |
| Faggett, Ethan, of-dh .... | .172 | 23 | 58 | 4 | 10 | 2 | 1 | 0 | 2 | 10 | 15 | 5 | 1 | L | L | 6-0 | 190 | 8-21-74 | 1992 | Burleson, Texas |
| Ford, Eric, 1b-of .......... | .273 | 8 | 33 | 5 | 9 | 1 | 1 | 0 | 3 | 5 | 8 | 0 | 0 | R | R | 6-2 | 185 | 10-4-71 | 1993 | Brandon, Miss. |
| Fuller, Aaron, dh........... | .545 | 6 | 11 | 5 | 6 | 0 | 1 | 0 | 2 | 3 | 0 | 3 | 0 | S | R | 5-10 | 170 | 9-7-71 | 1993 | Sacramento, Calif. |
| Gibralter, David, 3b ...... | .267 | 49 | 180 | 23 | 48 | 14 | 0 | 3 | 27 | 11 | 34 | 1 | 1 | R | R | 6-3 | 215 | 6-19-75 | 1993 | Duncanville, Texas |
| Graham, John, of .......... | .385 | 9 | 39 | 7 | 15 | 4 | 1 | 1 | 6 | 4 | 5 | 3 | 2 | L | L | 5-10 | 170 | 5-7-71 | 1993 | North Abington, Mass. |
| Hamilton, Joe, 3b-dh..... | .170 | 15 | 47 | 3 | 8 | 0 | 0 | 1 | 2 | 8 | 13 | 0 | 0 | L | R | 6-0 | 185 | 7-12-74 | 1992 | Rehoboth, Mass. |
| Hayward, Joe, dh-of...... | .333 | 8 | 24 | 7 | 8 | 1 | 0 | 2 | 6 | 7 | 2 | 0 | 0 | L | R | 6-1 | 195 | 8-5-70 | 1993 | Osterville, Mass. |
| Jackson, Gavin, ss ........ | .318 | 41 | 157 | 29 | 50 | 7 | 2 | 0 | 11 | 14 | 18 | 11 | 5 | R | R | 5-10 | 170 | 7-19-73 | 1993 | Sylvester, Ga. |
| Larkin, Jim, 3b.............. | .276 | 8 | 29 | 6 | 8 | 1 | 0 | 0 | 3 | 2 | 5 | 1 | 1 | R | R | 6-1 | 195 | 2-16-71 | 1993 | Mendon, Mass. |
| Lebron, Ruben, 2b ........ | .294 | 14 | 34 | 4 | 10 | 1 | 0 | 0 | 2 | 0 | 7 | 0 | 1 | S | R | 5-10 | 140 | 8-10-75 | 1992 | San Pedro de Macoris, D.R. |
| Lorenzo, Wilson, c......... | .169 | 24 | 65 | 2 | 11 | 3 | 0 | 0 | 7 | 3 | 12 | 0 | 0 | R | R | 6-2 | 175 | 1-13-72 | 1993 | San Cristobal, D.R. |
| Martinez, Humberto, of . | .197 | 26 | 66 | 7 | 13 | 1 | 1 | 0 | 5 | 9 | 20 | 0 | 0 | R | R | 6-2 | 175 | 12-26-74 | 1993 | San Pedro de Macoris, D.R. |
| Merloni, Lou, ss............ | .357 | 4 | 14 | 4 | 5 | 1 | 0 | 0 | 1 | 1 | 1 | 1 | 1 | R | R | 5-9 | 180 | 4-6-71 | 1993 | Framingham, Mass. |
| Murphy, Pat, 2b............ | .273 | 5 | 22 | 4 | 6 | 0 | 0 | 0 | 1 | 2 | 1 | 1 | 1 | L | R | 5-10 | 160 | 3-24-72 | 1993 | Mobile, Ala. |
| Norman, Tyrone, 2b ....... | .185 | 22 | 65 | 8 | 12 | 2 | 0 | 0 | 2 | 7 | 7 | 5 | 1 | R | R | 5-11 | 165 | 6-29-74 | 1992 | Haddock, Ga. |
| Patton, Greg, ss............ | .563 | 4 | 16 | 6 | 9 | 2 | 0 | 0 | 5 | 2 | 2 | 0 | 2 | R | R | 6-3 | 195 | 3-8-72 | 1993 | Springfield, Va. |
| Rivera, Wilfredo, of........ | .268 | 53 | 183 | 17 | 49 | 15 | 1 | 0 | 21 | 19 | 29 | 2 | 2 | R | R | 6-2 | 200 | 5-12-74 | 1993 | Vega Alta, P.R. |
| Rounsifer, Aaron, 1b ...... | .267 | 23 | 60 | 3 | 16 | 4 | 0 | 0 | 6 | 2 | 17 | 2 | 0 | R | R | 6-2 | 195 | 6-21-74 | 1992 | Cape Coral, Fla. |
| Sheffield, Tony, of......... | .177 | 43 | 130 | 11 | 23 | 3 | 2 | 1 | 17 | 17 | 47 | 6 | 2 | L | L | 6-1 | 175 | 2-17-74 | 1992 | Tullahoma, Tenn. |
| Smith, David, 2b-ss ....... | .300 | 3 | 10 | 3 | 3 | 0 | 0 | 0 | 1 | 2 | 2 | 0 | 0 | R | R | 5-10 | 160 | 2-18-72 | 1993 | Cheektowaga, N.Y. |
| Tebbs, Nathan, of.......... | .260 | 43 | 146 | 21 | 38 | 4 | 1 | 0 | 4 | 15 | 16 | 7 | 1 | S | R | 5-11 | 175 | 12-14-72 | 1993 | Twin Falls, Idaho |
| Walker, John, 2b ........... | .250 | 1 | 4 | 1 | 1 | 0 | 0 | 0 | 1 | 0 | 1 | 0 | 0 | L | R | 5-9 | 170 | 11-4-71 | 1993 | Grand Rapids, Mich. |

| PITCHING | W | L | ERA | G | GS | CG | SV | IP | H | R | ER | BB | SO | B | T | HT | WT | DOB | 1st Yr | Resides |
|---|---|---|---|---|---|---|---|---|---|---|---|---|---|---|---|---|---|---|---|---|
| Amos, Chad................... | 3 | 0 | 1.50 | 11 | 0 | 0 | 2 | 18 | 13 | 3 | 3 | 4 | 21 | R | R | 6-6 | 230 | 10-8-71 | 1992 | New Matamoras, Ohio |
| Asher, Ray .................... | 2 | 1 | 1.60 | 6 | 6 | 1 | 0 | 34 | 21 | 13 | 6 | 14 | 28 | S | R | 6-4 | 175 | 10-2-74 | 1993 | Vallejo, Calif. |
| Becker, Kevin................ | 4 | 3 | 4.75 | 14 | 5 | 0 | 2 | 53 | 58 | 35 | 28 | 28 | 45 | R | R | 6-7 | 180 | 10-18-72 | 1991 | Galloway, Ohio |
| Bennett, Shayne ........... | 0 | 0 | 1.29 | 2 | 1 | 0 | 1 | 7 | 2 | 1 | 1 | 1 | 4 | R | R | 6-5 | 195 | 4-23-72 | 1993 | Downers Grove, Ill. |
| Blais, John ................... | 3 | 1 | 1.38 | 22 | 0 | 0 | 4 | 26 | 15 | 6 | 4 | 8 | 22 | R | R | 6-5 | 226 | 10-2-71 | 1993 | East Lyme, Conn. |
| Bogott, Kurt.................. | 0 | 1 | 1.80 | 3 | 2 | 0 | 0 | 15 | 10 | 3 | 3 | 4 | 20 | L | L | 6-4 | 195 | 9-30-72 | 1993 | Sterling, Ill. |
| Bonilla, Welnis .............. | 0 | 1 | 13.50 | 3 | 0 | 0 | 0 | 5 | 12 | 8 | 8 | 1 | 1 | R | R | 6-3 | 175 | 10-18-75 | 1993 | Mao Valverde, D.R. |
| Cook, Jake ................... | 1 | 1 | 2.03 | 8 | 1 | 0 | 0 | 13 | 8 | 3 | 3 | 13 | 10 | R | R | 6-6 | 205 | 8-31-74 | 1993 | Greenville, Ohio |
| DeWalt, Mark................. | 1 | 1 | 3.54 | 6 | 2 | 0 | 1 | 20 | 16 | 11 | 8 | 6 | 12 | R | R | 6-6 | 215 | 6-16-75 | 1993 | Upper Arlington, Ohio |
| Fernandes, James......... | 2 | 0 | 0.86 | 6 | 2 | 0 | 0 | 21 | 14 | 3 | 2 | 8 | 17 | R | R | 6-5 | 240 | 8-4-71 | 1993 | Waltham, Mass. |
| Hayward, Steve ............ | 1 | 1 | 1.17 | 2 | 0 | 0 | 0 | 8 | 7 | 3 | 1 | 1 | 3 | R | R | 6-2 | 185 | 1-1-71 | 1993 | Washington Township, N.J. |
| Hobson, Dennis ............ | 0 | 0 | 0.00 | 1 | 0 | 0 | 0 | 1 | 1 | 0 | 0 | 0 | 2 | R | R | 6-3 | 205 | 7-12-71 | 1992 | Meridian, Miss. |
| Kennedy, Greg .............. | 0 | 0 | 2.77 | 3 | 2 | 0 | 0 | 13 | 12 | 4 | 4 | 3 | 14 | L | L | 6-1 | 180 | 1-26-72 | 1993 | Quitman, Miss. |
| Kivac, David ................. | 0 | 3 | 2.92 | 7 | 5 | 1 | 0 | 37 | 27 | 15 | 12 | 15 | 26 | R | L | 6-4 | 175 | 4-11-70 | 1991 | Medway, Mass. |
| Martinez, Cesar ............ | 0 | 0 | 0.00 | 1 | 1 | 0 | 0 | 3 | 1 | 0 | 0 | 2 | 3 | L | L | 6-2 | 175 | 4-29-73 | 1993 | San Diego, Calif. |
| Mejia, Carlos ................ | 5 | 4 | 3.20 | 12 | 9 | 0 | 0 | 56 | 43 | 25 | 20 | 31 | 59 | L | L | 6-2 | 170 | 11-14-73 | 1992 | La Vega, D.R. |
| Padilla, Roy.................. | 0 | 1 | 2.35 | 13 | 1 | 0 | 0 | 31 | 25 | 10 | 8 | 17 | 18 | L | L | 6-5 | 185 | 8-4-75 | 1993 | Panama City, Panama |
| Peterson, Dean............. | 1 | 0 | 3.60 | 3 | 2 | 0 | 0 | 15 | 14 | 8 | 6 | 4 | 10 | R | R | 6-3 | 200 | 8-3-72 | 1993 | Cortland, Ohio |
| Phillip, Craig ................. | 1 | 1 | 4.50 | 3 | 2 | 0 | 0 | 8 | 13 | 6 | 4 | 2 | 9 | R | R | 6-3 | 180 | 9-13-72 | 1993 | Aurora, Ill. |
| Pinango, Simon ............. | 0 | 4 | 1.73 | 10 | 7 | 0 | 0 | 52 | 36 | 17 | 10 | 17 | 57 | L | L | 6-1 | 175 | 12-9-73 | 1991 | Sucre, Venez. |
| Senior, Shawn ............... | 3 | 0 | 1.93 | 3 | 2 | 0 | 0 | 14 | 10 | 7 | 3 | 6 | 17 | L | L | 6-1 | 195 | 3-17-72 | 1993 | Cherry Hill, N.J. |
| Suppan, Jeff.................. | 4 | 3 | 2.18 | 10 | 9 | 2 | 0 | 58 | 52 | 20 | 14 | 16 | 64 | R | R | 6-1 | 200 | 1-2-75 | 1993 | West Hills, Calif. |
| Telgheder, Jim ............... | 1 | 2 | 3.38 | 7 | 1 | 0 | 1 | 19 | 16 | 11 | 7 | 2 | 17 | R | R | 6-3 | 210 | 3-22-71 | 1993 | Slate Hill, N.Y. |

# CALIFORNIA ANGELS

**Manager:** Buck Rodgers.  **1993 Record:** 71-91, .438 (T-5th, AL West).

| BATTING | AVG | G | AB | R | H | 2B | 3B | HR | RBI | BB | SO | SB | CS | B | T | HT | WT | DOB | 1st Yr | Resides |
|---|---|---|---|---|---|---|---|---|---|---|---|---|---|---|---|---|---|---|---|---|
| Correia, Ron | .266 | 64 | 128 | 12 | 34 | 5 | 0 | 0 | 9 | 6 | 20 | 2 | 4 | R | R | 5-11 | 180 | 9-13-67 | 1988 | Rehoboth, Mass. |
| Curtis, Chad | .285 | 152 | 583 | 94 | 166 | 25 | 3 | 6 | 59 | 70 | 89 | 48 | 24 | R | R | 5-10 | 175 | 11-6-68 | 1989 | Benson, Ariz. |
| Davis, Chili | .243 | 153 | 573 | 74 | 139 | 32 | 0 | 27 | 112 | 71 | 135 | 4 | 1 | S | R | 6-3 | 217 | 1-17-60 | 1978 | Scottsdale, Ariz. |
| DiSarcina, Gary | .238 | 126 | 416 | 44 | 99 | 20 | 1 | 3 | 45 | 15 | 38 | 5 | 7 | R | R | 6-1 | 178 | 11-19-67 | 1988 | Billerica, Mass. |
| Easley, Damion | .313 | 73 | 230 | 33 | 72 | 13 | 2 | 2 | 22 | 28 | 35 | 6 | 6 | R | R | 5-11 | 155 | 11-11-69 | 1989 | Long Beach, Calif. |
| Edmonds, Jim | .246 | 18 | 61 | 5 | 15 | 4 | 1 | 0 | 4 | 2 | 16 | 0 | 2 | L | L | 6-1 | 190 | 6-27-70 | 1988 | Diamond Bar, Calif. |
| Gaetti, Gary | .180 | 20 | 50 | 3 | 9 | 2 | 0 | 0 | 4 | 5 | 12 | 1 | 0 | R | R | 6-0 | 200 | 8-19-58 | 1979 | Eden Prairie, Minn. |
| Gonzales, Larry | .500 | 2 | 2 | 0 | 1 | 0 | 0 | 0 | 1 | 1 | 0 | 0 | 0 | R | R | 6-3 | 200 | 3-28-67 | 1988 | West Covina, Calif. |
| Gonzales, Rene | .251 | 118 | 335 | 34 | 84 | 17 | 0 | 2 | 31 | 49 | 45 | 5 | 5 | R | R | 6-3 | 215 | 9-3-62 | 1982 | Balboa Island, Calif. |
| Gruber, Kelly | .277 | 18 | 65 | 10 | 18 | 3 | 0 | 3 | 9 | 2 | 11 | 0 | 0 | R | R | 6-0 | 185 | 2-26-62 | 1980 | Austin, Texas |
| Javier, Stan | .291 | 92 | 237 | 33 | 69 | 10 | 4 | 3 | 28 | 27 | 33 | 12 | 2 | S | R | 6-0 | 185 | 1-9-64 | 1981 | Santo Domingo, D.R. |
| Lovullo, Torey | .251 | 116 | 367 | 42 | 92 | 20 | 0 | 6 | 30 | 36 | 49 | 7 | 6 | S | R | 6-0 | 185 | 7-25-65 | 1987 | Northridge, Calif. |
| Myers, Greg | .255 | 108 | 290 | 27 | 74 | 10 | 0 | 7 | 40 | 17 | 47 | 3 | 3 | L | R | 6-2 | 215 | 4-14-66 | 1984 | Riverside, Calif. |
| Orton, John | .189 | 37 | 95 | 5 | 18 | 5 | 0 | 1 | 4 | 7 | 24 | 1 | 2 | R | R | 6-1 | 192 | 12-8-65 | 1987 | Atascadero, Calif. |
| Perez, Eduardo | .250 | 52 | 180 | 16 | 45 | 6 | 2 | 4 | 30 | 9 | 39 | 5 | 4 | R | R | 6-4 | 215 | 9-11-69 | 1991 | Santurce, P.R. |
| Polonia, Luis | .271 | 152 | 576 | 75 | 156 | 17 | 6 | 1 | 32 | 48 | 53 | 55 | 24 | L | L | 5-8 | 150 | 10-12-64 | 1984 | Santiago, D.R. |
| Salmon, Tim | .283 | 142 | 515 | 93 | 146 | 35 | 1 | 31 | 95 | 82 | 135 | 5 | 6 | R | R | 6-3 | 220 | 8-24-68 | 1989 | Phoenix, Ariz. |
| Snow, J.T. | .241 | 129 | 419 | 60 | 101 | 18 | 2 | 16 | 57 | 55 | 88 | 3 | 0 | S | L | 6-2 | 202 | 2-26-68 | 1989 | Seal Beach, Calif. |
| Stillwell, Kurt | .262 | 22 | 61 | 2 | 16 | 2 | 2 | 0 | 3 | 4 | 11 | 2 | 0 | S | R | 5-11 | 185 | 6-4-65 | 1983 | Poway, Calif. |
| Tingley, Ron | .200 | 58 | 90 | 7 | 18 | 7 | 0 | 0 | 12 | 9 | 22 | 1 | 2 | R | R | 6-2 | 194 | 5-27-59 | 1977 | Riverside, Calif. |
| Turner, Chris | .280 | 25 | 75 | 9 | 21 | 5 | 0 | 1 | 13 | 9 | 16 | 1 | 1 | R | R | 6-1 | 190 | 3-23-69 | 1991 | Bowling Green, Ky. |
| Van Burkleo, Ty | .152 | 12 | 33 | 2 | 5 | 3 | 0 | 1 | 1 | 6 | 9 | 1 | 0 | L | L | 6-4 | 210 | 10-7-63 | 1982 | Mesa, Ariz. |
| Walewander, Jim | .125 | 12 | 8 | 2 | 1 | 0 | 0 | 0 | 3 | 5 | 1 | 1 | 1 | S | R | 5-10 | 158 | 5-2-61 | 1983 | Tampa, Fla. |
| Walton, Jerome | .000 | 5 | 2 | 2 | 0 | 0 | 0 | 0 | 0 | 1 | 2 | 1 | 0 | R | R | 6-1 | 175 | 7-8-65 | 1986 | Fairburn, Ga. |

| PITCHING | W | L | ERA | G | GS | CG | SV | IP | H | R | ER | BB | SO | B | T | HT | WT | DOB | 1st Yr | Resides |
|---|---|---|---|---|---|---|---|---|---|---|---|---|---|---|---|---|---|---|---|---|
| Anderson, Brian | 0 | 0 | 3.97 | 4 | 1 | 0 | 0 | 11 | 11 | 5 | 5 | 2 | 4 | S | L | 6-1 | 180 | 4-26-71 | 1993 | Geneva, Ohio |
| Butcher, Mike | 1 | 0 | 2.86 | 23 | 0 | 0 | 8 | 28 | 21 | 12 | 9 | 15 | 24 | R | R | 6-1 | 200 | 5-10-65 | 1986 | East Moline, Ill. |
| Crim, Chuck | 2 | 2 | 5.87 | 11 | 0 | 0 | 0 | 15 | 17 | 11 | 10 | 5 | 10 | R | R | 6-0 | 185 | 7-23-61 | 1982 | Gilbert, Ariz. |
| Farrell, John | 3 | 12 | 7.35 | 21 | 17 | 0 | 0 | 91 | 110 | 74 | 74 | 44 | 45 | R | R | 6-4 | 210 | 8-4-62 | 1984 | Westlake, Ohio |
| Finley, Chuck | 16 | 14 | 3.15 | 35 | 35 | 13 | 0 | 251 | 243 | 108 | 88 | 82 | 187 | L | L | 6-6 | 212 | 11-26-62 | 1985 | Newport Beach, Calif. |
| Frey, Steve | 2 | 3 | 2.98 | 55 | 0 | 0 | 13 | 48 | 41 | 20 | 16 | 26 | 22 | R | L | 5-9 | 170 | 7-29-63 | 1983 | Newtown, Pa. |
| Grahe, Joe | 4 | 1 | 2.86 | 45 | 0 | 0 | 11 | 57 | 54 | 22 | 18 | 25 | 31 | R | R | 6-0 | 200 | 8-14-67 | 1989 | Lake Park, Fla. |
| Hathaway, Hilly | 4 | 3 | 5.02 | 11 | 11 | 0 | 0 | 57 | 71 | 35 | 32 | 26 | 11 | L | L | 6-4 | 195 | 9-12-69 | 1990 | Jacksonville, Fla. |
| Holzemer, Mark | 0 | 3 | 8.87 | 5 | 4 | 0 | 0 | 23 | 34 | 24 | 23 | 13 | 10 | L | L | 6-0 | 165 | 8-20-69 | 1988 | Littleton, Colo. |
| Langston, Mark | 16 | 11 | 3.20 | 35 | 35 | 7 | 0 | 256 | 220 | 100 | 91 | 85 | 196 | R | L | 6-2 | 184 | 8-20-60 | 1981 | Anaheim Hills, Calif. |
| Leftwich, Phil | 4 | 6 | 3.79 | 12 | 12 | 1 | 0 | 81 | 81 | 35 | 34 | 27 | 31 | R | R | 6-5 | 215 | 5-19-69 | 1990 | Lynchburg, Va. |
| Lewis, Scott | 1 | 2 | 4.22 | 15 | 4 | 0 | 0 | 32 | 37 | 16 | 15 | 12 | 10 | R | R | 6-3 | 178 | 12-5-65 | 1988 | Medford, Ore. |
| Linton, Doug | 2 | 0 | 7.71 | 19 | 0 | 0 | 0 | 26 | 35 | 22 | 22 | 14 | 16 | R | R | 6-1 | 190 | 9-2-65 | 1987 | Kingsport, Tenn. |
| 2-team (4 Toronto) | 2 | 1 | 7.36 | 23 | 1 | 0 | 0 | 37 | 46 | 30 | 30 | 23 | 23 | | | | | | | |
| Magrane, Joe | 3 | 2 | 3.94 | 8 | 8 | 0 | 0 | 48 | 48 | 27 | 21 | 21 | 24 | R | L | 6-6 | 225 | 7-2-64 | 1985 | Morehead, Ky. |
| Nelson, Gene | 0 | 5 | 3.08 | 46 | 0 | 0 | 4 | 53 | 50 | 25 | 18 | 23 | 31 | R | R | 6-0 | 174 | 12-3-60 | 1978 | Dade City, Fla. |
| Nielsen, Jerry | 0 | 0 | 8.03 | 10 | 0 | 0 | 0 | 12 | 18 | 13 | 11 | 4 | 8 | L | L | 6-3 | 185 | 8-5-66 | 1988 | Fair Oaks, Calif. |
| Patterson, Ken | 1 | 1 | 4.58 | 46 | 0 | 0 | 1 | 59 | 54 | 30 | 30 | 35 | 36 | L | L | 6-4 | 210 | 7-8-64 | 1985 | McGregor, Texas |
| Sanderson, Scott | 7 | 11 | 4.46 | 21 | 21 | 4 | 0 | 135 | 153 | 77 | 67 | 27 | 66 | R | R | 6-5 | 192 | 7-22-56 | 1977 | Northbrook, Ill. |
| Scott, Darryl | 1 | 2 | 5.85 | 16 | 0 | 0 | 0 | 20 | 19 | 13 | 13 | 11 | 13 | R | R | 6-1 | 185 | 8-6-68 | 1990 | Prior Lake, Minn. |
| Springer, Russ | 1 | 6 | 7.20 | 14 | 9 | 1 | 0 | 60 | 73 | 48 | 48 | 32 | 31 | R | R | 6-4 | 195 | 11-7-68 | 1989 | Pollack, La. |
| Swingle, Paul | 0 | 1 | 8.38 | 9 | 0 | 0 | 0 | 10 | 15 | 9 | 9 | 6 | 6 | R | R | 6-0 | 185 | 12-21-66 | 1989 | Mesa, Ariz. |
| Valera, Julio | 3 | 6 | 6.62 | 19 | 5 | 0 | 4 | 53 | 77 | 44 | 39 | 15 | 28 | R | R | 6-2 | 215 | 10-13-68 | 1986 | San Sebastian, P.R. |

## FIELDING

| Catcher | PCT | G | PO | A | E | DP |
|---|---|---|---|---|---|---|
| L. Gonzales | 1.000 | 2 | 4 | 0 | 0 | 0 |
| Myers | .986 | 97 | 369 | 44 | 6 | 5 |
| Orton | .980 | 35 | 184 | 17 | 4 | 4 |
| Tingley | .995 | 58 | 200 | 20 | 1 | 3 |
| Turner | .992 | 25 | 116 | 14 | 1 | 0 |

| First Base | PCT | G | PO | A | E | DP |
|---|---|---|---|---|---|---|
| Gaetti | 1.000 | 6 | 37 | 2 | 0 | 2 |
| R. Gonzales | .989 | 31 | 163 | 10 | 2 | 24 |
| Javier | .971 | 12 | 64 | 2 | 2 | 2 |
| Lovullo | .000 | 1 | 0 | 0 | 0 | 0 |
| Snow | .995 | 129 | 1010 | 81 | 6 | 103 |
| Van Burkleo | 1.000 | 12 | 99 | 3 | 0 | 8 |

| Second Base | PCT | G | PO | A | E | DP |
|---|---|---|---|---|---|---|
| Correia | 1.000 | 11 | 30 | 19 | 0 | 6 |
| Curtis | 1.000 | 3 | 2 | 1 | 0 | 0 |

| | PCT | G | PO | A | E | DP |
|---|---|---|---|---|---|---|
| Easley | .978 | 54 | 101 | 125 | 5 | 26 |
| R. Gonzales | 1.000 | 4 | 4 | 3 | 0 | 1 |
| Javier | 1.000 | 2 | 2 | 0 | 0 | 0 |
| Lovullo | .981 | 91 | 184 | 220 | 8 | 67 |
| Stillwell | .952 | 39 | 41 | 4 | 6 |  |
| Walewander | 1.000 | 2 | 2 | 3 | 0 | 1 |

| Third Base | PCT | G | PO | A | E | DP |
|---|---|---|---|---|---|---|
| Correia | 1.000 | 3 | 1 | 0 | 0 | 0 |
| Easley | .977 | 14 | 10 | 32 | 1 | 3 |
| Gaetti | .857 | 7 | 1 | 5 | 1 | 1 |
| R. Gonzales | .956 | 79 | 63 | 156 | 10 | 20 |
| Gruber | .938 | 17 | 18 | 42 | 4 | 3 |
| Lovullo | .929 | 14 | 14 | 25 | 3 | 2 |
| Perez | .962 | 45 | 24 | 101 | 5 | 7 |

| Shortstop | PCT | G | PO | A | E | DP |
|---|---|---|---|---|---|---|
| Correia | .981 | 40 | 56 | 102 | 3 | 16 |

| | PCT | G | PO | A | E | DP |
|---|---|---|---|---|---|---|
| DiSarcina | .975 | 126 | 193 | 362 | 14 | 77 |
| R. Gonzales | 1.000 | 5 | 3 | 1 | 0 | 1 |
| Lovullo | 1.000 | 9 | 4 | 4 | 0 | 1 |
| Stillwell | .944 | 7 | 7 | 10 | 1 | 3 |
| Walewander | 1.000 | 6 | 7 | 10 | 0 | 3 |

| Outfield | PCT | G | PO | A | E | DP |
|---|---|---|---|---|---|---|
| Curtis | .980 | 151 | 426 | 13 | 9 | 6 |
| Edmonds | .981 | 17 | 47 | 4 | 1 | 2 |
| Gruber | 1.000 | 1 | 2 | 0 | 0 | 0 |
| Javier | .981 | 64 | 101 | 2 | 2 | 0 |
| Lovullo | 1.000 | 2 | 6 | 0 | 0 | 0 |
| Orton | 1.000 | 1 | 1 | 0 | 0 | 0 |
| Polonia | .983 | 141 | 286 | 12 | 5 | 3 |
| Salmon | .980 | 140 | 335 | 12 | 7 | 2 |
| Walton | 1.000 | 1 | 2 | 0 | 0 | 0 |

**Sixteen-Game Winners.** Lefthanders Mark Langston, left, and Chuck Finley led California pitchers with 16 victories apiece. Langston (16-11, 3.20) also contributed 196 strikeouts, while Finley (16-14, 3.15) was right behind at 187.

# ANGELS FARM SYSTEM

| Class | Club | League | W | L | Pct. | Finish* | Manager | First Year |
|---|---|---|---|---|---|---|---|---|
| AAA | Vancouver (B.C.) Canadians | Pacific Coast | 72 | 68 | .514 | 3rd (10) | Max Oliveras | 1993 |
| AA | Midland (Texas) Angels | Texas | 67 | 67 | .500 | 3rd (8) | Don Long | 1985 |
| A# | Palm Springs (Calif.) Angels | California | 61 | 75 | .449 | T-8th (10) | Mario Mendoza | 1986 |
| A | Cedar Rapids (Iowa) Kernels | Midwest | 54 | 80 | .403 | 14th (14) | Mitch Seoane | 1993 |
| A | Boise (Idaho) Hawks | Northwest | 41 | 35 | .539 | 3rd† (8) | Tom Kotchman | 1990 |
| Rookie | Mesa (Ariz.) Angels | Arizona | 29 | 26 | .527 | 4th (8) | Bill Lachemann | 1989 |

*Finish in overall standings (No. of teams in league)   #Advanced level   †Won league championship

# VANCOUVER                                                                    AAA
## PACIFIC COAST LEAGUE

| BÁTTING | AVG | G | AB | R | H | 2B | 3B | HR | RBI | BB | SO | SB | CS | B | T | HT | WT | DOB | 1st Yr | Resides |
|---|---|---|---|---|---|---|---|---|---|---|---|---|---|---|---|---|---|---|---|---|
| Anderson, Garret | .293 | 124 | 467 | 57 | 137 | 34 | 4 | 4 | 71 | 31 | 95 | 3 | 4 | L | L | 6-3 | 190 | 6-30-72 | 1990 | Newhall, Calif. |
| Correia, Rod | .271 | 60 | 207 | 43 | 56 | 10 | 4 | 4 | 28 | 15 | 25 | 11 | 4 | R | R | 5-11 | 180 | 9-13-67 | 1988 | Rehoboth, Mass. |
| Dalesandro, Mark | .299 | 26 | 107 | 16 | 32 | 8 | 1 | 2 | 15 | 6 | 13 | 1 | 0 | R | R | 6-0 | 185 | 5-14-68 | 1990 | Chicago, Ill. |
| Davis, Kevin | .271 | 62 | 210 | 24 | 57 | 8 | 3 | 2 | 25 | 7 | 41 | 3 | 4 | S | R | 5-9 | 180 | 7-6-64 | 1982 | Charlotte, N.C. |
| Dodge, Tom | .235 | 7 | 17 | 3 | 4 | 1 | 0 | 0 | 4 | 1 | 2 | 3 | 0 | S | R | 6-0 | 195 | 9-19-68 | 1991 | McHenry, Ill. |
| Edmonds, Jim | .315 | 95 | 356 | 59 | 112 | 28 | 4 | 9 | 74 | 41 | 81 | 6 | 8 | L | L | 6-1 | 190 | 6-27-70 | 1988 | Diamond Bar, Calif. |
| Fabregas, Jorge | .231 | 4 | 13 | 1 | 3 | 1 | 0 | 0 | 1 | 1 | 3 | 0 | 0 | L | R | 6-3 | 205 | 3-13-70 | 1991 | Miami, Fla. |
| Flora, Kevin | .330 | 30 | 94 | 17 | 31 | 2 | 0 | 1 | 12 | 10 | 20 | 6 | 2 | R | R | 6-0 | 185 | 6-10-69 | 1987 | Chandler, Ariz. |
| Forbes, P.J. | .250 | 5 | 16 | 1 | 4 | 2 | 0 | 0 | 3 | 0 | 3 | 0 | 0 | R | R | 5-9 | 160 | 9-22-67 | 1990 | Pittsburg, Kan. |
| Gonzales, Larry | .261 | 81 | 264 | 30 | 69 | 9 | 0 | 2 | 27 | 26 | 28 | 5 | 1 | R | R | 6-3 | 200 | 3-28-67 | 1988 | West Covina, Calif. |
| Gruber, Kelly | .458 | 8 | 24 | 4 | 11 | 1 | 0 | 1 | 5 | 1 | 2 | 0 | 0 | R | R | 6-0 | 185 | 2-26-62 | 1980 | Austin, Texas |
| Hill, Orsino | .222 | 9 | 36 | 4 | 8 | 3 | 1 | 1 | 4 | 0 | 11 | 0 | 0 | L | R | 6-4 | 190 | 2-25-62 | 1982 | Altadena, Calif. |
| Jackson, John | .289 | 55 | 201 | 28 | 58 | 9 | 4 | 2 | 20 | 17 | 29 | 12 | 4 | L | L | 6-0 | 185 | 1-2-67 | 1990 | Diamond Bar, Calif. |
| Kipila, Jeff | .313 | 32 | 99 | 18 | 31 | 7 | 0 | 5 | 21 | 15 | 20 | 2 | 1 | R | R | 6-4 | 230 | 9-13-65 | 1988 | Sewaren, N.J. |
| Martinez, Ray | .252 | 114 | 357 | 54 | 90 | 24 | 2 | 3 | 35 | 35 | 64 | 5 | 6 | R | R | 6-0 | 165 | 10-1-68 | 1987 | Los Angeles, Calif. |
| Perez, Eduardo | .306 | 96 | 363 | 66 | 111 | 23 | 6 | 12 | 70 | 28 | 83 | 21 | 7 | R | R | 6-4 | 215 | 9-11-69 | 1991 | Santurce, P.R. |
| Snow, J.T. | .340 | 23 | 94 | 19 | 32 | 9 | 1 | 5 | 24 | 10 | 13 | 0 | 0 | S | L | 6-2 | 202 | 2-26-68 | 1989 | Seal Beach, Calif. |
| Tejero, Fausto | .153 | 20 | 59 | 2 | 9 | 0 | 0 | 0 | 2 | 4 | 12 | 1 | 1 | R | R | 6-2 | 205 | 10-26-68 | 1990 | Hialeah, Fla. |
| Turner, Chris | .276 | 90 | 283 | 50 | 78 | 12 | 1 | 4 | 57 | 49 | 44 | 6 | 1 | R | R | 6-1 | 190 | 3-23-69 | 1991 | Bowling Green, Ky. |
| Van Burkleo, Ty | .274 | 105 | 361 | 47 | 99 | 19 | 2 | 6 | 56 | 51 | 89 | 7 | 3 | L | L | 6-4 | 210 | 10-7-63 | 1982 | Mesa, Ariz. |
| Walewander, Jim | .305 | 102 | 351 | 77 | 107 | 12 | 1 | 1 | 43 | 60 | 57 | 36 | 6 | S | R | 5-10 | 158 | 5-2-61 | 1983 | Tampa, Fla. |

## MAJOR LEAGUERS

**BATTING**

| | | |
|---|---|---|
| *AVG | Chad Curtis | .285 |
| R | Chad Curtis | 94 |
| H | Chad Curtis | 166 |
| TB | Tim Salmon | 276 |
| 2B | Tim Salmon | 35 |
| 3B | Luis Polonia | 6 |
| HR | Tim Salmon | 31 |
| RBI | Chili Davis | 112 |
| BB | Tim Salmon | 82 |
| SO | 2 tied at | 135 |
| SB | Luis Polonia | 55 |

**PITCHING**

| | | |
|---|---|---|
| W | Two tied at | 16 |
| L | Chuck Finley | 14 |
| #ERA | Chuck Finley | 3.15 |
| G | Steve Frey | 55 |
| CG | Chuck Finley | 13 |
| SV | Steve Frey | 13 |
| IP | Mark Langston | 256 |
| BB | Mark Langston | 85 |
| SO | Mark Langston | 196 |

**Chad Curtis**
Scored 94 runs

*RON VESELY*

## MINOR LEAGUERS

**BATTING**

| | | |
|---|---|---|
| *AVG | Mark Sweeney, Palm Springs-Midland | .356 |
| R | Marquis Riley, Palm Springs | 93 |
| H | Two tied at | 163 |
| TB | P.J. Forbes, Midland-Vancouver | 237 |
| 2B | Garret Anderson, Vancouver | 34 |
| 3B | Jay Simpson, Palm Springs | 7 |
| HR | Two tied at | 17 |
| RBI | Luis Raven, Palm Springs-Midland | 82 |
| BB | Marquis Riley, Palm Springs | 90 |
| SO | Luis Raven, Palm Springs-Midland | 129 |
| SB | Marquis Riley, Palm Springs | 69 |

**PITCHING**

| | | |
|---|---|---|
| W | Keith Morrison, Palm Springs | 14 |
| L | Jeff Schmidt, Cedar Rapids | 14 |
| #ERA | Bryan Harris, Boise | 1.89 |
| G | Jose Musset, Midland | 59 |
| CG | Mark Ratekin, Palm Springs-Midland | 8 |
| SV | John Pricher, Palm Springs | 26 |
| IP | Mark Ratekin, Palm Springs-Midland | 188 |
| BB | Two tied at | 70 |
| SO | Kyle Sebach, Cedar Rapids | 138 |

*Minimum 250 At-Bats    #Minimum 75 Innings

| BATTING | AVG | G | AB | R | H | 2B | 3B | HR | RBI | BB | SO | SB | CS | B | T | HT | WT | DOB | 1st Yr | Resides |
|---|---|---|---|---|---|---|---|---|---|---|---|---|---|---|---|---|---|---|---|---|
| Walton, Jerome | .313 | 54 | 176 | 34 | 55 | 11 | 1 | 2 | 20 | 16 | 24 | 5 | 4 | R | R | 6-1 | 175 | 7-8-65 | 1986 | Fairburn, Ga. |
| Williams, Reggie | .274 | 130 | 481 | 92 | 132 | 17 | 6 | 2 | 53 | 88 | 99 | 50 | 17 | S | R | 6-1 | 180 | 5-5-66 | 1988 | Laurens, S.C. |

| PITCHING | W | L | ERA | G | GS | CG | SV | IP | H | R | ER | BB | SO | B | T | HT | WT | DOB | 1st Yr | Resides |
|---|---|---|---|---|---|---|---|---|---|---|---|---|---|---|---|---|---|---|---|---|
| Anderson, Brian | 0 | 1 | 12.38 | 2 | 2 | 0 | 0 | 8 | 13 | 12 | 11 | 6 | 2 | S | L | 6-1 | 180 | 4-26-71 | 1993 | Geneva, Ohio |
| Bennett, Erik | 6 | 6 | 6.05 | 18 | 12 | 0 | 1 | 80 | 101 | 57 | 54 | 21 | 51 | R | R | 6-2 | 205 | 9-13-68 | 1989 | Yreka, Calif. |
| Burcham, Tim | 0 | 2 | 11.30 | 13 | 0 | 0 | 1 | 14 | 29 | 19 | 18 | 8 | 11 | R | R | 6-0 | 175 | 10-7-63 | 1985 | Hampton, Va. |
| Butcher, Mike | 3 | 4 | 4.44 | 14 | 1 | 0 | 3 | 24 | 21 | 16 | 12 | 12 | 12 | R | R | 6-1 | 200 | 5-10-65 | 1986 | East Moline, Ill. |
| Charland, Colin | 3 | 2 | 3.86 | 6 | 6 | 0 | 0 | 33 | 37 | 22 | 14 | 17 | 27 | L | L | 6-3 | 205 | 11-13-65 | 1986 | Duncanville, Texas |
| Edenfield, Ken | 0 | 0 | 0.00 | 2 | 0 | 0 | 0 | 4 | 1 | 0 | 0 | 1 | 5 | R | R | 6-1 | 165 | 3-18-67 | 1990 | Knoxville, Tenn. |
| Egloff, Bruce | 0 | 0 | 3.50 | 12 | 0 | 0 | 0 | 18 | 20 | 10 | 7 | 3 | 9 | R | R | 6-2 | 215 | 4-10-65 | 1986 | Denver, Colo. |
| Farrell, John | 4 | 5 | 3.99 | 12 | 12 | 2 | 0 | 86 | 83 | 44 | 38 | 28 | 71 | R | R | 6-4 | 210 | 8-4-62 | 1984 | Westlake, Ohio |
| Fritz, John | 3 | 1 | 4.07 | 8 | 7 | 0 | 0 | 42 | 52 | 22 | 19 | 18 | 29 | R | R | 6-1 | 170 | 3-6-69 | 1988 | Koppel, Pa. |
| Gamez, Bob | 1 | 0 | 4.73 | 9 | 0 | 0 | 0 | 13 | 11 | 9 | 7 | 9 | 15 | L | L | 6-5 | 190 | 11-18-68 | 1988 | Newark, Calif. |
| Grahe, Joe | 1 | 1 | 4.50 | 4 | 2 | 0 | 0 | 6 | 4 | 3 | 3 | 2 | 5 | R | R | 6-0 | 200 | 8-14-67 | 1989 | Lake Park, Fla. |
| Grant, Mark | 0 | 0 | 0.00 | 1 | 0 | 0 | 0 | 2 | 0 | 0 | 0 | 2 | 1 | R | R | 6-2 | 215 | 10-24-63 | 1981 | Alpine, Calif. |
| 2-team (4 Tucson) | 1 | 0 | 0.87 | 5 | 0 | 0 | 0 | 10 | 5 | 1 | 1 | 6 | 11 | | | | | | | |
| Green, Otis | 2 | 8 | 5.61 | 25 | 18 | 1 | 0 | 109 | 109 | 71 | 68 | 53 | 97 | L | L | 6-2 | 192 | 3-11-64 | 1983 | Miami, Fla. |
| Hathaway, Hilly | 7 | 0 | 4.09 | 12 | 12 | 0 | 0 | 70 | 60 | 38 | 32 | 27 | 44 | L | L | 6-4 | 195 | 9-12-69 | 1990 | Jacksonville, Fla. |
| Holzemer, Mark | 9 | 6 | 4.82 | 24 | 23 | 2 | 0 | 146 | 158 | 94 | 78 | 70 | 80 | L | L | 6-0 | 165 | 8-20-69 | 1988 | Littleton, Colo. |
| Leftwich, Phil | 7 | 7 | 4.64 | 20 | 20 | 3 | 0 | 126 | 138 | 74 | 65 | 45 | 102 | R | R | 6-5 | 205 | 5-19-69 | 1990 | Lynchburg, Va. |
| Lewis, Scott | 3 | 1 | 1.37 | 24 | 0 | 0 | 9 | 39 | 31 | 7 | 6 | 9 | 38 | R | R | 6-3 | 178 | 12-5-65 | 1988 | Medford, Ore. |
| Nielsen, Jerry | 2 | 5 | 4.20 | 33 | 5 | 0 | 0 | 56 | 70 | 32 | 26 | 20 | 45 | L | L | 6-3 | 185 | 4-4-66 | 1988 | Fair Oaks, Calif. |
| Peck, Steve | 5 | 3 | 4.85 | 31 | 7 | 0 | 0 | 72 | 91 | 47 | 39 | 29 | 47 | R | R | 6-3 | 190 | 11-20-67 | 1989 | Mesa, Ariz. |
| Percival, Troy | 0 | 1 | 6.27 | 18 | 0 | 0 | 4 | 19 | 24 | 14 | 13 | 13 | 19 | R | R | 6-3 | 200 | 8-9-69 | 1990 | Moreno Valley, Calif. |
| Pico, Jeff | 3 | 1 | 4.21 | 18 | 0 | 0 | 0 | 26 | 35 | 17 | 12 | 20 | 16 | R | R | 6-2 | 175 | 2-12-66 | 1984 | Antioch, Calif. |
| Scott, Darryl | 7 | 1 | 2.09 | 46 | 0 | 0 | 15 | 52 | 35 | 12 | 12 | 19 | 57 | R | R | 6-1 | 185 | 8-6-68 | 1990 | Prior Lake, Minn. |
| Springer, Russ | 5 | 4 | 4.27 | 11 | 9 | 1 | 0 | 59 | 58 | 37 | 28 | 33 | 40 | R | R | 6-4 | 195 | 11-7-68 | 1989 | Pollack, La. |
| Swingle, Paul | 2 | 9 | 6.92 | 37 | 4 | 0 | 1 | 68 | 85 | 61 | 52 | 32 | 61 | R | R | 6-0 | 185 | 12-21-66 | 1989 | Mesa, Ariz. |
| Zappelli, Mark | 0 | 1 | 3.91 | 17 | 0 | 0 | 1 | 25 | 31 | 12 | 11 | 5 | 13 | R | R | 6-0 | 185 | 7-21-66 | 1989 | Santa Rosa, Calif. |

### FIELDING

| Catcher | PCT | G | PO | A | E | DP |
|---|---|---|---|---|---|---|
| Dodge | 1.000 | 7 | 31 | 3 | 0 | 0 |
| Fabregas | 1.000 | 3 | 30 | 3 | 0 | 0 |
| Gonzales | 1.000 | 52 | 289 | 31 | 0 | 1 |
| Tejero | .991 | 14 | 96 | 13 | 1 | 0 |
| Turner | .990 | 74 | 469 | 52 | 5 | 4 |

| First Base | PCT | G | PO | A | E | DP |
|---|---|---|---|---|---|---|
| Anderson | 1.000 | 5 | 37 | 3 | 0 | 4 |
| Gonzales | 1.000 | 10 | 67 | 7 | 0 | 6 |
| Kipila | 1.000 | 1 | 3 | 1 | 0 | 0 |
| Perez | .972 | 10 | 62 | 8 | 2 | 3 |
| Snow | .991 | 23 | 200 | 13 | 2 | 27 |
| Turner | .983 | 8 | 55 | 4 | 1 | 5 |
| Van Burkleo | .984 | 96 | 765 | 51 | 13 | 68 |

| Second Base | PCT | G | PO | A | E | DP |
|---|---|---|---|---|---|---|
| Correia | .963 | 17 | 38 | 39 | 3 | 8 |
| Davis | .992 | 26 | 58 | 68 | 1 | 23 |

| | PCT | G | PO | A | E | DP |
|---|---|---|---|---|---|---|
| Flora | .950 | 11 | 16 | 22 | 2 | 5 |
| Forbes | 1.000 | 5 | 15 | 13 | 0 | 2 |
| Martinez | .986 | 14 | 40 | 28 | 1 | 9 |
| Walewander | .980 | 73 | 155 | 193 | 7 | 47 |

| Third Base | PCT | G | PO | A | E | DP |
|---|---|---|---|---|---|---|
| Dalesandro | .918 | 26 | 19 | 59 | 7 | 8 |
| Davis | .884 | 14 | 7 | 31 | 5 | 4 |
| Gonzales | .889 | 9 | 3 | 13 | 2 | 0 |
| Gruber | 1.000 | 2 | 0 | 4 | 0 | 0 |
| Martinez | .936 | 14 | 6 | 38 | 3 | 5 |
| Perez | .905 | 77 | 35 | 166 | 21 | 11 |
| Walewander | .941 | 7 | 1 | 15 | 1 | 1 |

| Shortstop | PCT | G | PO | A | E | DP |
|---|---|---|---|---|---|---|
| Correia | .944 | 43 | 67 | 120 | 11 | 20 |
| Davis | .881 | 13 | 12 | 25 | 5 | 7 |

| | PCT | G | PO | A | E | DP |
|---|---|---|---|---|---|---|
| Martinez | .943 | 85 | 120 | 241 | 22 | 40 |
| Walewander | 1.000 | 7 | 8 | 15 | 0 | 4 |

| Outfield | PCT | G | PO | A | E | DP |
|---|---|---|---|---|---|---|
| Anderson | .988 | 106 | 161 | 10 | 2 | 1 |
| Davis | 1.000 | 4 | 2 | 1 | 0 | 0 |
| Edmonds | .983 | 76 | 167 | 4 | 3 | 0 |
| Flora | 1.000 | 2 | 5 | 0 | 0 | 0 |
| Hill | 1.000 | 6 | 5 | 1 | 0 | 0 |
| Jackson | .989 | 46 | 90 | 3 | 1 | 0 |
| Kipila | 1.000 | 6 | 10 | 0 | 0 | 0 |
| Perez | 1.000 | 1 | 1 | 0 | 0 | 0 |
| Van Burkleo | 1.000 | 12 | 16 | 0 | 0 | 0 |
| Walewander | 1.000 | 4 | 1 | 1 | 0 | 0 |
| Walton | 1.000 | 47 | 82 | 3 | 0 | 0 |
| Williams | .987 | 127 | 293 | 6 | 4 | 4 |

## TEXAS LEAGUE

| BATTING | AVG | G | AB | R | H | 2B | 3B | HR | RBI | BB | SO | SB | CS | B | T | HT | WT | DOB | 1st Yr | Resides |
|---|---|---|---|---|---|---|---|---|---|---|---|---|---|---|---|---|---|---|---|---|
| Boykin, Tyrone, of-dh | .280 | 35 | 132 | 29 | 37 | 3 | 3 | 2 | 17 | 17 | 17 | 1 | 0 | R | R | 6-0 | 195 | 4-25-68 | 1991 | Hamden, Conn. |
| Brakebill, Mark, 3b | .230 | 62 | 222 | 21 | 51 | 9 | 1 | 5 | 32 | 4 | 60 | 0 | 6 | R | R | 6-1 | 185 | 8-15-69 | 1989 | Phoenix, Ariz. |

| BATTING | AVG | G | AB | R | H | 2B | 3B | HR | RBI | BB | SO | SB | CS | B | T | HT | WT | DOB | 1st Yr | Resides |
|---|---|---|---|---|---|---|---|---|---|---|---|---|---|---|---|---|---|---|---|---|
| Claus, Todd, 3b | .188 | 18 | 32 | 7 | 6 | 1 | 1 | 0 | 3 | 10 | 10 | 1 | 0 | S | R | 5-10 | 170 | 3-24-69 | 1991 | Oakland Park, Fla. |
| Cohick, Emmitt, of | .270 | 105 | 356 | 59 | 96 | 18 | 5 | 11 | 53 | 35 | 91 | 6 | 2 | L | L | 6-2 | 175 | 8-8-68 | 1991 | Yorba Linda, Calif. |
| Dalesandro, Mark, 3b-c | .294 | 57 | 235 | 33 | 69 | 9 | 0 | 2 | 36 | 8 | 30 | 1 | 1 | R | R | 6-0 | 185 | 5-14-68 | 1990 | Chicago, Ill. |
| Davis, Kevin, ss | .276 | 47 | 156 | 29 | 43 | 5 | 1 | 7 | 28 | 18 | 31 | 6 | 3 | S | R | 5-9 | 180 | 7-6-64 | 1982 | Charlotte, N.C. |
| Fabregas, Jorge, c | .289 | 113 | 409 | 63 | 118 | 26 | 3 | 6 | 56 | 31 | 60 | 1 | 1 | L | R | 6-3 | 205 | 3-13-70 | 1991 | Miami, Fla. |
| Forbes, P.J., 2b | .319 | 126 | 498 | 90 | 159 | 23 | 2 | 15 | 64 | 26 | 50 | 6 | 8 | R | R | 5-9 | 160 | 9-22-67 | 1990 | Pittsburg, Kan. |
| Garrett, Clifton, of | .359 | 11 | 39 | 3 | 14 | 2 | 0 | 0 | 5 | 4 | 4 | 2 | 0 | L | L | 5-11 | 170 | 9-2-70 | 1989 | Chicago, Ill. |
| Grebeck, Brian, ss | .294 | 118 | 405 | 65 | 119 | 20 | 4 | 5 | 54 | 64 | 81 | 6 | 1 | R | R | 5-7 | 160 | 8-31-67 | 1990 | Cerritos, Calif. |
| Jackson, John, of | .325 | 70 | 243 | 43 | 79 | 18 | 2 | 3 | 34 | 40 | 43 | 12 | 8 | L | L | 6-0 | 185 | 1-2-67 | 1990 | Diamond Bar, Calif. |
| Kipila, Jeff, dh-of | .232 | 59 | 203 | 32 | 47 | 7 | 1 | 12 | 47 | 32 | 67 | 0 | 0 | R | R | 6-4 | 230 | 9-13-65 | 1988 | Sewaren, N.J. |
| Munoz, Orlando, 3b-ss | .263 | 36 | 118 | 24 | 31 | 8 | 1 | 0 | 10 | 20 | 23 | 0 | 4 | S | R | 5-11 | 175 | 5-4-71 | 1989 | Guatire, Venez. |
| Palmeiro, Orlando, of | .305 | 131 | 535 | 85 | 163 | 19 | 5 | 0 | 64 | 42 | 35 | 18 | 14 | L | L | 5-11 | 155 | 1-19-69 | 1991 | Miami, Fla. |
| Pritchett, Chris, 1b | .308 | 127 | 464 | 61 | 143 | 30 | 6 | 2 | 66 | 61 | 72 | 3 | 7 | L | R | 6-4 | 185 | 1-31-70 | 1991 | Modesto, Calif. |
| Raven, Luis, of-dh | .257 | 43 | 167 | 21 | 43 | 12 | 1 | 2 | 30 | 5 | 45 | 4 | 2 | R | R | 6-4 | 230 | 11-19-68 | 1989 | La Guaira, Venez. |
| Rumsey, Dan, of | .059 | 19 | 51 | 3 | 3 | 1 | 0 | 0 | 1 | 4 | 15 | 0 | 0 | L | R | 5-10 | 185 | 8-1-67 | 1989 | Mesa, Ariz. |
| Sweeney, Mark, of | .356 | 51 | 188 | 41 | 67 | 13 | 2 | 9 | 32 | 27 | 22 | 1 | 1 | L | L | 6-1 | 195 | 10-26-69 | 1991 | Holliston, Mass. |
| Tejero, Fausto, c | .130 | 26 | 69 | 3 | 9 | 1 | 1 | 1 | 7 | 8 | 17 | 0 | 0 | R | R | 6-2 | 205 | 10-26-68 | 1990 | Hialeah, Fla. |
| Wasinger, Mark, dh-3b | .214 | 39 | 117 | 17 | 25 | 4 | 0 | 2 | 17 | 15 | 26 | 0 | 1 | R | R | 6-0 | 165 | 8-4-61 | 1982 | Duluth, Ga. |

| PITCHING | W | L | ERA | G | GS | CG | SV | IP | H | R | ER | BB | SO | B | T | HT | WT | DOB | 1st Yr | Resides |
|---|---|---|---|---|---|---|---|---|---|---|---|---|---|---|---|---|---|---|---|---|
| Anderson, Brian | 0 | 1 | 3.38 | 2 | 2 | 0 | 0 | 11 | 16 | 5 | 4 | 0 | 9 | S | L | 6-1 | 180 | 4-26-71 | 1993 | Geneva, Ohio |
| Bennett, Erik | 5 | 4 | 6.49 | 11 | 11 | 0 | 0 | 69 | 87 | 57 | 50 | 17 | 33 | R | R | 6-2 | 205 | 9-13-68 | 1989 | Yreka, Calif. |
| Charland, Colin | 6 | 2 | 5.01 | 10 | 10 | 0 | 0 | 59 | 66 | 37 | 33 | 17 | 54 | L | L | 6-3 | 205 | 11-13-65 | 1986 | Duncanville, Texas |
| Chavez, Tony | 0 | 0 | 4.15 | 5 | 0 | 0 | 1 | 9 | 11 | 5 | 4 | 4 | 9 | R | R | 5-10 | 175 | 10-27-70 | 1992 | Merced, Calif. |
| Edenfield, Ken | 5 | 8 | 4.61 | 48 | 3 | 1 | 4 | 94 | 93 | 56 | 48 | 35 | 84 | R | R | 6-1 | 165 | 3-18-67 | 1990 | Knoxville, Tenn. |
| Fritz, John | 9 | 5 | 3.61 | 20 | 20 | 2 | 0 | 130 | 125 | 61 | 52 | 42 | 85 | R | R | 6-1 | 170 | 3-6-69 | 1988 | Koppel, Pa. |
| Gamez, Bob | 5 | 2 | 3.26 | 44 | 0 | 0 | 0 | 61 | 68 | 27 | 22 | 18 | 50 | L | L | 6-5 | 190 | 11-18-68 | 1988 | Newark, Calif. |
| Gledhill, Chance | 6 | 11 | 5.41 | 28 | 23 | 1 | 0 | 141 | 169 | 102 | 85 | 41 | 66 | R | R | 6-3 | 195 | 2-20-69 | 1991 | Monroe, Utah |
| Heredia, Julian | 5 | 3 | 3.12 | 46 | 1 | 0 | 0 | 89 | 77 | 42 | 31 | 19 | 89 | R | R | 6-1 | 160 | 9-22-69 | 1989 | La Romana, D.R. |
| Holdridge, David | 8 | 10 | 6.08 | 27 | 27 | 1 | 0 | 151 | 202 | 117 | 102 | 55 | 123 | R | R | 6-3 | 195 | 2-5-69 | 1988 | Huntington Beach, Calif. |
| Lewis, Scott | 1 | 0 | 1.50 | 1 | 1 | 0 | 0 | 6 | 6 | 1 | 1 | 0 | 2 | R | R | 6-3 | 178 | 12-5-65 | 1988 | Medford, Ore. |
| Musset, Jose | 2 | 6 | 5.49 | 59 | 0 | 0 | 21 | 62 | 59 | 38 | 38 | 32 | 59 | R | R | 6-3 | 186 | 9-18-68 | 1987 | Monte Plata, D.R. |
| Perez, Beban | 0 | 1 | 19.64 | 3 | 0 | 0 | 0 | 4 | 8 | 8 | 8 | 2 | 1 | L | L | 5-10 | 170 | 6-15-67 | 1987 | La Romana, D.R. |
| Purdy, Shawn | 2 | 2 | 5.06 | 5 | 5 | 1 | 0 | 32 | 38 | 19 | 18 | 9 | 18 | R | R | 6-0 | 205 | 7-30-68 | 1991 | St. Cloud, Fla. |
| Ratekin, Mark | 3 | 1 | 4.67 | 7 | 6 | 2 | 0 | 44 | 50 | 25 | 23 | 11 | 24 | R | R | 6-4 | 215 | 11-14-70 | 1991 | Tehachapi, Calif. |
| Stroud, Derek | 1 | 1 | 4.61 | 13 | 0 | 0 | 0 | 14 | 16 | 7 | 7 | 9 | 13 | L | L | 6-0 | 190 | 6-6-66 | 1987 | Paso Robles, Calif. |
| Watson, Ron | 2 | 1 | 3.88 | 36 | 0 | 0 | 3 | 46 | 39 | 22 | 20 | 43 | 41 | L | R | 6-5 | 240 | 9-12-68 | 1990 | Gilford, N.H. |
| Williams, Shad | 7 | 10 | 4.71 | 27 | 27 | 2 | 0 | 176 | 192 | 100 | 92 | 65 | 91 | R | R | 6-0 | 185 | 3-10-71 | 1991 | Fresno, Calif. |

## PALM SPRINGS   A
### CALIFORNIA LEAGUE

| BATTING | AVG | G | AB | R | H | 2B | 3B | HR | RBI | BB | SO | SB | CS | B | T | HT | WT | DOB | 1st Yr | Resides |
|---|---|---|---|---|---|---|---|---|---|---|---|---|---|---|---|---|---|---|---|---|
| Anderson, Chris, 3b-ss | .238 | 103 | 353 | 51 | 84 | 19 | 6 | 2 | 45 | 30 | 50 | 3 | 5 | R | R | 6-0 | 180 | 8-7-69 | 1992 | Coral Gables, Fla. |
| Boykin, Tyrone, of | .325 | 77 | 286 | 48 | 93 | 13 | 1 | 3 | 40 | 51 | 52 | 22 | 8 | R | R | 6-0 | 195 | 4-25-68 | 1991 | Hamden, Conn. |
| Claus, Todd, 3b | .190 | 42 | 105 | 17 | 20 | 4 | 1 | 1 | 8 | 13 | 24 | 1 | 0 | S | R | 5-10 | 170 | 3-24-69 | 1991 | Oakland Park, Fla. |
| Dalesandro, Mark, c-1b | .244 | 46 | 176 | 22 | 43 | 5 | 3 | 1 | 25 | 15 | 20 | 3 | 2 | R | R | 6-0 | 185 | 5-14-68 | 1990 | Chicago, Ill. |
| Dodge, Tom, c-1b | .270 | 97 | 366 | 47 | 99 | 9 | 2 | 1 | 44 | 35 | 38 | 13 | 10 | R | R | 6-0 | 195 | 9-19-68 | 1991 | McHenry Ill. |
| Gruber, Kelly, 3b-dh | .222 | 5 | 9 | 0 | 2 | 0 | 0 | 1 | 1 | 2 | 0 | 0 | R | R | 6-0 | 185 | 2-26-62 | 1980 | Austin, Texas |
| Hagy, Gary, ss | .179 | 104 | 340 | 35 | 61 | 8 | 1 | 0 | 24 | 42 | 61 | 6 | 6 | R | R | 6-3 | 195 | 4-7-69 | 1991 | Ephrata, Wash. |
| Hirsch, Chris, c | .276 | 44 | 145 | 19 | 40 | 10 | 1 | 6 | 22 | 23 | 35 | 1 | 2 | R | R | 6-0 | 195 | 11-12-68 | 1990 | Palm Beach Gardens, Fla. |
| McCaffery, Dennis, of | .251 | 75 | 239 | 25 | 60 | 6 | 2 | 0 | 25 | 26 | 59 | 10 | 6 | R | R | 6-2 | 190 | 5-27-69 | 1991 | Roselle Park, N.J. |
| Munoz, Orlando, 2b-ss | .270 | 64 | 237 | 38 | 64 | 8 | 3 | 0 | 24 | 47 | 25 | 23 | 14 | S | R | 5-11 | 175 | 5-4-71 | 1989 | Guatire, Venez. |
| Orton, John, c | .000 | 2 | 7 | 0 | 0 | 0 | 0 | 0 | 0 | 1 | 1 | 0 | 0 | R | R | 6-1 | 192 | 12-8-65 | 1987 | Atascadero, Calif. |
| Raven, Luis, 1b-of | .277 | 85 | 343 | 38 | 95 | 20 | 2 | 7 | 52 | 22 | 84 | 15 | 11 | R | R | 6-4 | 230 | 11-19-68 | 1989 | La Guaira, Venez. |
| Riley, Marquis, of | .264 | 130 | 508 | 93 | 134 | 10 | 2 | 1 | 42 | 90 | 117 | 69 | 25 | R | R | 5-10 | 170 | 12-27-70 | 1992 | Ashdown, Ark. |
| Simmons, Nelson, 1b | .329 | 20 | 76 | 13 | 25 | 8 | 0 | 5 | 23 | 10 | 7 | 0 | 1 | S | R | 6-1 | 215 | 6-27-63 | 1981 | Spring Valley, Calif. |
| Simpson, Jay, of | .260 | 77 | 246 | 31 | 64 | 12 | 7 | 3 | 29 | 12 | 54 | 14 | 8 | S | R | 5-11 | 190 | 5-29-70 | 1992 | Zachary, La. |
| Smith, Chris, 3b | .279 | 40 | 154 | 27 | 43 | 7 | 2 | 2 | 21 | 16 | 20 | 3 | 4 | R | R | 5-11 | 180 | 1-14-74 | 1992 | Vallejo, Calif. |
| Smith, Joel, dh-1b | .234 | 86 | 295 | 37 | 69 | 16 | 2 | 6 | 47 | 24 | 61 | 2 | 2 | R | R | 5-10 | 185 | 12-12-68 | 1992 | Tallahassee, Fla. |
| Stela, Jose, c | .261 | 10 | 23 | 4 | 6 | 1 | 0 | 0 | 4 | 7 | 4 | 2 | 0 | R | R | 5-11 | 175 | 10-23-69 | 1988 | Maracaibo, Venez. |
| Swanson, John, 1b-of | .293 | 29 | 92 | 17 | 27 | 8 | 1 | 1 | 13 | 19 | 17 | 3 | 1 | L | L | 6-0 | 165 | 7-8-71 | 1993 | Lakewood, Calif. |
| Sweeney, Mark, of | .355 | 66 | 245 | 41 | 87 | 18 | 3 | 3 | 47 | 42 | 29 | 9 | 6 | L | L | 6-1 | 195 | 10-26-69 | 1991 | Holliston, Mass. |
| Tejero, Fausto, c | .300 | 7 | 20 | 2 | 6 | 2 | 0 | 0 | 1 | 2 | 1 | 0 | 1 | R | R | 6-2 | 205 | 10-26-68 | 1990 | Hialeah, Fla. |
| Urso, Joe, 2b | .257 | 96 | 346 | 51 | 89 | 17 | 1 | 2 | 41 | 57 | 53 | 9 | 5 | R | R | 5-7 | 160 | 7-28-70 | 1992 | Tampa, Fla. |

## ANGELS: MOST COMMON LINEUPS

| | California | Vancouver | Midland | Palm Springs | Cedar Rapids |
|---|---|---|---|---|---|
| | Majors | AAA | AA | A | A |
| C | Greg Myers (97) | Chris Turner (74) | Jorge Fabregas (106) | Tom Dodge (49) | Robert Tucker (73) |
| 1B | J.T. Snow (129) | Ty Van Burkleo (96) | Chris Pritchett (126) | Luis Raven (56) | Brandon Markiewicz (86) |
| 2B | Torey Lovullo (91) | Jim Walewander (73) | P.J. Forbes (122) | Joe Urso (84) | Mark Simmons (57) |
| 3B | Rene Gonzales (79) | Eduardo Perez (77) | Mark Brakebill (58) | Chris Anderson (72) | Georgie Arias (72) |
| SS | Gary DiSarcina (126) | Ray Martinez (85) | Brian Grebeck (97) | Gary Hagy (104) | Chris Smith (66) |
| OF | Chad Curtis (151) | Reggie Williams (133) | Orlando Palmeiro (130) | Marquis Riley (129) | Morisse Daniels (106) |
| | Luis Polonia (141) | Garret Anderson (108) | Emmitt Cohick (91) | Tyrone Boykin (76) | Mike Wolff (96) |
| | Tim Salmon (140) | Jim Edmonds (76) | John Jackson (62) | Jay Simpson (64) | Hardwick/Kerns (61) |
| DH | Chili Davis (150) | Jeff Kipila (35) | Jeff Kipila (35) | Joel Smith (57) | Orsino Holl (53) |
| SP | Finley/Langston (35) | Mark Holzemer (23) | Holdridge/Williams (27) | Butler/Morrison (27) | Kyle Sebach (26) |
| RP | Steve Frey (55) | Darryl Scott (46) | Jose Musset (59) | John Pricher (49) | Chavez/White (41) |

Full-season farm clubs only    No. of games at position in parenthesis

| PITCHING | W | L | ERA | G | GS | CG | SV | IP | H | R | ER | BB | SO | B | T | HT | WT | DOB | 1st Yr | Resides |
|---|---|---|---|---|---|---|---|---|---|---|---|---|---|---|---|---|---|---|---|---|
| Burcham, Tim | 6 | 5 | 3.43 | 21 | 12 | 0 | 0 | 94 | 95 | 43 | 36 | 34 | 68 | R | R | 6-0 | 175 | 10-7-63 | 1985 | Hampton, Va. |
| Butler, Mike | 8 | 10 | 4.62 | 27 | 27 | 4 | 0 | 179 | 197 | 112 | 92 | 61 | 123 | L | L | 6-0 | 187 | 12-14-70 | 1991 | Denton, Md. |
| Ferguson, Jim | 0 | 2 | 7.94 | 11 | 1 | 0 | 0 | 11 | 9 | 10 | 10 | 16 | 7 | R | R | 6-6 | 240 | 6-22-69 | 1991 | Anaheim, Calif. |
| Janicki, Pete | 0 | 0 | 10.80 | 1 | 1 | 0 | 0 | 2 | 3 | 2 | 2 | 2 | 2 | R | R | 6-4 | 200 | 1-26-71 | 1992 | Placentia, Calif. |
| Johnson, Dom | 2 | 4 | 5.72 | 45 | 0 | 0 | 0 | 50 | 51 | 34 | 32 | 39 | 47 | R | R | 6-5 | 230 | 8-9-68 | 1987 | Poway, Calif. |
| Keling, Korey | 8 | 8 | 3.29 | 31 | 21 | 2 | 0 | 159 | 152 | 69 | 58 | 62 | 131 | R | R | 6-5 | 210 | 11-24-68 | 1991 | Shawnee, Kan. |
| Marcon, David | 0 | 1 | 5.06 | 8 | 0 | 0 | 0 | 11 | 15 | 7 | 6 | 4 | 6 | L | L | 6-4 | 205 | 9-26-67 | 1990 | Dearborn, Mich. |
| Montoya, Norm | 1 | 3 | 4.81 | 28 | 4 | 0 | 0 | 64 | 83 | 38 | 34 | 21 | 35 | L | L | 6-1 | 190 | 9-24-70 | 1990 | Newark, Calif. |
| Morrison, Keith | 14 | 6 | 4.14 | 27 | 27 | 2 | 0 | 176 | 200 | 108 | 81 | 55 | 107 | R | R | 6-4 | 190 | 11-22-69 | 1990 | Suwanee, Ga. |
| Perez, Beban | 3 | 3 | 5.11 | 33 | 0 | 0 | 0 | 49 | 52 | 36 | 28 | 30 | 27 | L | L | 5-10 | 170 | 6-15-67 | 1987 | La Romana, D.R. |
| Pricher, John | 3 | 5 | 3.17 | 49 | 0 | 0 | 26 | 54 | 41 | 20 | 19 | 25 | 61 | S | R | 5-10 | 200 | 11-13-70 | 1992 | Orlando, Fla. |
| Purdy, Shawn | 1 | 1 | 3.67 | 5 | 3 | 0 | 1 | 27 | 30 | 12 | 11 | 5 | 17 | R | R | 6-0 | 205 | 7-30-68 | 1991 | St. Cloud, Fla. |
| Ratekin, Mark | 7 | 7 | 3.89 | 21 | 21 | 6 | 0 | 143 | 151 | 78 | 62 | 46 | 66 | R | R | 6-4 | 215 | 11-14-70 | 1991 | Tehachapi, Calif. |
| Rinehart, Dallas | 1 | 4 | 11.92 | 7 | 6 | 0 | 0 | 26 | 37 | 34 | 34 | 16 | 14 | R | R | 6-3 | 180 | 10-15-71 | 1992 | Kingsport, Tenn. |
| Silverio, Victor | 1 | 6 | 6.08 | 19 | 12 | 0 | 0 | 67 | 88 | 50 | 45 | 45 | 28 | R | R | 6-4 | 186 | 9-20-68 | 1987 | Santo Domingo, D.R. |
| Szczepanski, Joe | 2 | 3 | 4.86 | 26 | 0 | 0 | 0 | 33 | 48 | 19 | 18 | 14 | 13 | L | L | 6-2 | 220 | 6-18-68 | 1991 | Covina, Calif. |
| Trujillo, Jose | 3 | 6 | 4.72 | 36 | 0 | 0 | 0 | 34 | 32 | 19 | 18 | 13 | 30 | R | R | 5-9 | 175 | 6-9-66 | 1989 | Bayamon, P.R. |
| Wernig, Pat | 1 | 1 | 6.75 | 13 | 1 | 0 | 0 | 21 | 24 | 17 | 16 | 18 | 15 | L | L | 6-1 | 186 | 4-18-65 | 1987 | Vienna, Va. |

## CEDAR RAPIDS    A
### MIDWEST LEAGUE

| BATTING | AVG | G | AB | R | H | 2B | 3B | HR | RBI | BB | SO | SB | CS | B | T | HT | WT | DOB | 1st Yr | Resides |
|---|---|---|---|---|---|---|---|---|---|---|---|---|---|---|---|---|---|---|---|---|
| Arias, Georgie, 3b | .217 | 74 | 253 | 31 | 55 | 13 | 3 | 9 | 41 | 31 | 65 | 6 | 1 | R | R | 6-4 | 200 | 1-1-73 | 1991 | Santiago, D.R. |
| Castro, Antonio, p-3b | .087 | 34 | 46 | 8 | 4 | 2 | 0 | 0 | 3 | 8 | 22 | 2 | 0 | R | R | 6-2 | 175 | 7-9-71 | 1989 | Santo Domingo, D.R. |
| Connell, Lino, 2b-3b | .179 | 75 | 240 | 20 | 43 | 1 | 0 | 0 | 24 | 31 | 70 | 6 | 6 | S | R | 6-2 | 182 | 3-12-72 | 1990 | Maracaibo, Venez. |
| Daniels, Morisse, of | .242 | 110 | 368 | 53 | 89 | 7 | 2 | 7 | 36 | 54 | 113 | 25 | 8 | R | R | 6-2 | 190 | 1-14-71 | 1992 | Tallahassee, Fla. |
| Dunckel, Bill, 1b-of | .125 | 12 | 32 | 2 | 4 | 2 | 0 | 0 | 3 | 4 | 5 | 0 | 0 | R | R | 5-11 | 190 | 9-6-68 | 1991 | Fallbrook, Calif. |
| Garrett, Clifton, of-dh | .323 | 36 | 127 | 26 | 41 | 4 | 2 | 0 | 11 | 30 | 22 | 14 | 6 | L | L | 5-11 | 170 | 9-2-70 | 1989 | Chicago, Ill. |
| Guzik, Brian, 1b | .252 | 36 | 115 | 20 | 29 | 5 | 0 | 3 | 10 | 15 | 29 | 0 | 1 | R | R | 6-4 | 175 | 4-8-72 | 1990 | Latrobe, Pa. |
| Hardwick, Joe, of | .227 | 62 | 194 | 44 | 44 | 5 | 3 | 1 | 14 | 34 | 57 | 22 | 7 | R | R | 5-7 | 145 | 7-19-72 | 1991 | Nashua, N.H. |
| Harkrider, Tim, ss | .253 | 54 | 190 | 29 | 48 | 11 | 0 | 0 | 14 | 22 | 28 | 7 | 4 | S | R | 6-0 | 180 | 9-5-71 | 1993 | Carthage, Texas |
| Hill, Orsino, dh | .271 | 54 | 199 | 36 | 54 | 17 | 0 | 7 | 30 | 19 | 51 | 0 | 0 | L | R | 6-4 | 190 | 2-25-62 | 1982 | Altadena, Calif. |
| Hirsch, Chris, dh-c | .194 | 13 | 36 | 4 | 7 | 1 | 0 | 1 | 6 | 10 | 15 | 0 | 0 | R | R | 6-0 | 195 | 11-12-68 | 1990 | Palm Beach Gardens, Fla. |
| Kerns, Mickey, of | .193 | 91 | 300 | 30 | 58 | 15 | 1 | 9 | 34 | 19 | 85 | 8 | 7 | R | R | 6-1 | 185 | 3-1-70 | 1992 | Hancock, Md. |
| Kessler, David, c-dh | .265 | 13 | 34 | 5 | 9 | 0 | 0 | 0 | 5 | 11 | 9 | 1 | 0 | R | R | 6-4 | 210 | 8-4-69 | 1992 | Rancho Cordova, Calif. |
| Markiewicz, Brandon, 1b | .264 | 120 | 425 | 56 | 112 | 18 | 5 | 9 | 55 | 37 | 68 | 6 | 8 | R | R | 6-3 | 205 | 6-15-72 | 1990 | St. Petersburg, Fla. |
| Martin, Steve, of | .265 | 56 | 181 | 33 | 48 | 7 | 2 | 5 | 15 | 27 | 56 | 11 | 1 | R | R | 6-1 | 190 | 12-20-67 | 1989 | Tucson, Ariz. |
| Martinez, Javier, 2b | .155 | 33 | 97 | 15 | 15 | 3 | 0 | 0 | 7 | 13 | 17 | 1 | 2 | S | R | 5-11 | 170 | 4-24-72 | 1990 | Levittown, P.R. |
| Puchkov, Yevgeny, 2b | .116 | 19 | 43 | 2 | 5 | 0 | 0 | 0 | 1 | 7 | 11 | 0 | 0 | L | R | 6-0 | 172 | 3-3-69 | 1992 | Moscow, Russia |
| Rumsey, Dan, of | .178 | 16 | 45 | 3 | 8 | 2 | 0 | 1 | 5 | 5 | 20 | 1 | 0 | L | R | 5-10 | 185 | 8-1-67 | 1989 | Mesa, Ariz. |
| Simmons, Mark, 2b | .192 | 58 | 203 | 25 | 39 | 6 | 0 | 0 | 23 | 33 | 57 | 8 | 4 | R | R | 6-0 | 180 | 9-23-72 | 1990 | Chicago, Ill. |
| Smith, Chris, ss | .260 | 70 | 246 | 29 | 64 | 11 | 2 | 5 | 39 | 28 | 35 | 1 | 2 | R | R | 5-11 | 180 | 1-14-74 | 1992 | Vallejo, Calif. |
| Stela, Jose, c | .231 | 53 | 173 | 12 | 40 | 9 | 0 | 2 | 15 | 15 | 22 | 3 | 2 | R | R | 5-11 | 175 | 10-23-69 | 1988 | Maracaibo, Venez. |
| Tucker, Robert, c | .226 | 81 | 266 | 34 | 60 | 10 | 1 | 3 | 29 | 38 | 56 | 2 | 2 | R | R | 6-0 | 200 | 6-29-71 | 1991 | Santee, Calif. |
| Wolff, Mike, of-1b | .246 | 120 | 407 | 63 | 100 | 18 | 5 | 17 | 72 | 74 | 104 | 8 | 8 | R | R | 6-1 | 195 | 12-19-70 | 1992 | Wilmington, N.C. |

| PITCHING | W | L | ERA | G | GS | CG | SV | IP | H | R | ER | BB | SO | B | T | HT | WT | DOB | 1st Yr | Resides |
|---|---|---|---|---|---|---|---|---|---|---|---|---|---|---|---|---|---|---|---|---|
| Castro, Antonio | 2 | 1 | 7.27 | 13 | 2 | 0 | 0 | 26 | 25 | 22 | 21 | 23 | 22 | R | R | 6-2 | 175 | 7-9-71 | 1989 | Santo Domingo, D.R. |
| Chavez, Tony | 4 | 5 | 1.52 | 41 | 0 | 0 | 16 | 59 | 44 | 17 | 10 | 24 | 87 | R | R | 5-10 | 175 | 10-27-70 | 1992 | Merced, Calif. |
| Fermin, Miguel | 2 | 1 | 3.33 | 9 | 2 | 0 | 0 | 24 | 23 | 10 | 9 | 4 | 27 | R | R | 6-0 | 152 | 12-26-71 | 1991 | Santiago, D.R. |
| Hingle, Larry | 9 | 13 | 4.91 | 28 | 24 | 1 | 1 | 147 | 146 | 103 | 80 | 64 | 115 | L | L | 6-3 | 200 | 12-12-70 | 1992 | Ormond Beach, Fla. |
| Marcon, Dave | 10 | 5 | 2.96 | 30 | 5 | 1 | 1 | 82 | 87 | 34 | 27 | 17 | 60 | L | L | 6-4 | 205 | 9-26-67 | 1990 | Dearborn, Mich. |
| Mejia, Juan | 0 | 2 | 4.76 | 13 | 1 | 0 | 0 | 28 | 38 | 17 | 15 | 13 | 30 | L | L | 5-8 | 144 | 7-28-71 | 1992 | El Seibo, D.R. |
| Rinehart, Dallas | 1 | 2 | 5.29 | 16 | 4 | 0 | 0 | 48 | 59 | 37 | 28 | 17 | 40 | R | R | 6-3 | 180 | 10-15-71 | 1992 | Kingsport, Tenn. |
| Schmidt, Jeff | 3 | 14 | 4.90 | 26 | 25 | 3 | 0 | 152 | 166 | 105 | 83 | 58 | 107 | R | R | 6-5 | 190 | 2-21-71 | 1992 | LaCrosse, Wis. |
| Sebach, Kyle | 6 | 9 | 3.04 | 26 | 26 | 4 | 0 | 154 | 138 | 73 | 52 | 70 | 138 | R | R | 6-4 | 175 | 9-6-71 | 1991 | Santee, Calif. |
| Simas, Billy | 4 | 8 | 4.95 | 35 | 6 | 0 | 6 | 80 | 93 | 60 | 44 | 36 | 62 | L | R | 6-3 | 200 | 11-28-71 | 1992 | LeMoore, Calif. |
| Snyder, John | 5 | 6 | 5.91 | 21 | 16 | 1 | 0 | 99 | 125 | 88 | 65 | 39 | 79 | R | R | 6-3 | 175 | 8-16-74 | 1992 | Thousand Oaks, Calif. |
| Valencia, Max | 0 | 2 | 5.75 | 14 | 0 | 0 | 0 | 20 | 21 | 17 | 13 | 15 | 14 | R | R | 5-10 | 175 | 6-6-70 | 1991 | San Francisco, Calif. |
| Van Dyke, Rod | 0 | 0 | 10.03 | 7 | 0 | 0 | 0 | 12 | 14 | 18 | 13 | 10 | 14 | S | R | 6-1 | 185 | 2-25-68 | 1991 | Jacksonville, Fla. |
| White, Steve | 2 | 4 | 4.60 | 41 | 0 | 0 | 2 | 76 | 84 | 52 | 39 | 31 | 41 | R | R | 6-2 | 205 | 2-7-70 | 1992 | Brandon, Fla. |
| Williard, Brian | 5 | 8 | 4.76 | 23 | 23 | 1 | 0 | 125 | 130 | 79 | 66 | 57 | 111 | R | R | 6-2 | 200 | 5-1-73 | 1991 | St. Petersburg, Fla. |

## ANGELS TOP 10 PROSPECTS

**How the Angels Top 10 prospects, as judged by Baseball America prior to the 1993 season, fared in 1993:**

| Player, Pos. | Club (Class) | AVG | AB | H | HR | RBI | SB |
|---|---|---|---|---|---|---|---|
| 1. Tim Salmon, of | California | .283 | 515 | 146 | 31 | 95 | 5 |
| 4. Eduardo Perez, 3b | Vancouver (AAA) | .306 | 363 | 111 | 12 | 70 | 21 |
| | California | .250 | 180 | 45 | 4 | 30 | 5 |
| 6. J.T. Snow, 1b | Vancouver (AAA) | .340 | 94 | 32 | 5 | 24 | 0 |
| | California | .241 | 419 | 101 | 18 | 57 | 3 |
| 9. Kevin Flora, 2b | Vancouver (AAA) | .330 | 94 | 31 | 1 | 12 | 6 |

| | | W | L | ERA | IP | H | BB | SO |
|---|---|---|---|---|---|---|---|---|
| 2. Troy Percival, rhp | Vancouver (AAA) | 0 | 1 | 6.27 | 19 | 24 | 13 | 19 |
| 3. Ron Watson, rhp | Midland (AA) | 2 | 1 | 3.88 | 46 | 39 | 43 | 41 |
| 5. Russ Springer, rhp | Vancouver (AAA) | 5 | 4 | 4.27 | 59 | 58 | 33 | 40 |
| | California | 1 | 6 | 7.20 | 60 | 73 | 32 | 31 |
| 7. Hilly Hathaway, lhp | Vancouver (AAA) | 7 | 0 | 4.09 | 70 | 60 | 27 | 44 |
| | California | 4 | 3 | 5.02 | 57 | 71 | 26 | 11 |
| 8. Pete Janicki, rhp | Palm Springs (A) | 0 | 0 | 10.80 | 2 | 3 | 2 | 2 |
| 10. D. Warren, lhp | AZL Angels (R) | 2 | 4 | 4.10 | 42 | 27 | 34 | 63 |

**Tim Salmon**
AL Rookie of Year

DAN ARNOLD

### NORTHWEST LEAGUE

| BATTING | AVG | G | AB | R | H | 2B | 3B | HR | RBI | BB | SO | SB | CS | B | T | HT | WT | DOB | 1st Yr | Resides |
|---|---|---|---|---|---|---|---|---|---|---|---|---|---|---|---|---|---|---|---|---|
| Barwick, Lyall, of | .286 | 59 | 210 | 31 | 60 | 13 | 4 | 2 | 31 | 12 | 27 | 2 | 6 | R | R | 6-0 | 175 | 4-23-71 | 1992 | Willetton, Australia |
| Buckley, Mat, ss | .214 | 19 | 56 | 9 | 12 | 0 | 0 | 0 | 6 | 10 | 7 | 2 | 0 | R | R | 6-2 | 170 | 1-22-73 | 1993 | Lismore Hts., Australia |
| Burke, Jamie, 3b | .301 | 66 | 226 | 32 | 68 | 11 | 1 | 1 | 30 | 39 | 28 | 2 | 3 | R | R | 6-0 | 195 | 9-24-71 | 1993 | Roseburg, Ore. |
| Cavalli, Brian, c | .235 | 14 | 34 | 4 | 8 | 2 | 0 | 1 | 4 | 3 | 12 | 0 | 1 | R | R | 6-2 | 205 | 12-8-70 | 1993 | Alameda, Calif. |
| Diaz, Freddie, ss | .293 | 26 | 75 | 13 | 22 | 4 | 1 | 2 | 14 | 9 | 11 | 1 | 3 | S | R | 5-11 | 165 | 9-10-72 | 1992 | El Monte, Calif. |
| Donati, John, 1b | .193 | 52 | 109 | 15 | 21 | 3 | 0 | 3 | 16 | 19 | 37 | 2 | 4 | R | R | 6-1 | 200 | 5-4-73 | 1991 | Concord, Calif. |
| Doty, Derrin, of | .261 | 64 | 211 | 50 | 55 | 13 | 2 | 3 | 33 | 46 | 45 | 11 | 3 | R | R | 6-2 | 220 | 6-3-70 | 1993 | Oak Harbor, Wash. |
| Greene, Todd, of | .269 | 76 | 305 | 55 | 82 | 15 | 3 | 15 | 71 | 34 | 44 | 4 | 3 | R | R | 5-10 | 195 | 5-8-71 | 1993 | Martinez, Ga. |
| Guiel, Aaron, 2b-of | .298 | 35 | 104 | 24 | 31 | 6 | 4 | 2 | 12 | 26 | 21 | 3 | 0 | L | R | 5-10 | 190 | 10-5-72 | 1993 | Langley, B.C. |
| Harkrider, Tim, ss | .400 | 3 | 10 | 4 | 4 | 2 | 0 | 0 | 1 | 5 | 0 | 0 | 0 | S | R | 6-0 | 180 | 9-5-71 | 1993 | Carthage, Texas |
| Iatarola, Aaron, of | .289 | 57 | 218 | 36 | 63 | 12 | 2 | 7 | 39 | 28 | 46 | 4 | 1 | L | L | 5-11 | 189 | 9-28-71 | 1993 | Longwood, Fla. |
| Kennedy, David, 1b-dh | .238 | 74 | 248 | 53 | 59 | 14 | 2 | 10 | 49 | 65 | 63 | 2 | 0 | R | R | 6-4 | 215 | 9-3-70 | 1992 | Glen Ridge, N.J. |
| Kessler, David, c | .269 | 9 | 26 | 4 | 7 | 0 | 0 | 0 | 4 | 1 | 5 | 0 | 0 | R | R | 6-4 | 210 | 8-4-69 | 1992 | Rancho Cordova, Calif. |
| Kim, Bobby, dh-c | .167 | 8 | 18 | 0 | 3 | 0 | 0 | 0 | 1 | 0 | 6 | 1 | 0 | R | R | 6-1 | 202 | 5-5-72 | 1992 | West Hills, Calif. |
| King, Hank, ss-2b | .165 | 54 | 139 | 14 | 23 | 1 | 1 | 0 | 11 | 22 | 31 | 3 | 4 | R | R | 6-0 | 175 | 2-26-71 | 1993 | Fall City, Wash. |
| Martinez, Javier, 2b | .083 | 7 | 24 | 3 | 2 | 0 | 0 | 0 | 2 | 0 | 5 | 0 | 0 | S | R | 5-11 | 170 | 4-24-72 | 1990 | Levittown, P.R. |
| Simmons, Mark, 2b-3b | .304 | 58 | 230 | 46 | 70 | 9 | 1 | 2 | 24 | 39 | 57 | 18 | 5 | R | R | 6-0 | 180 | 9-23-72 | 1993 | Chicago, Ill. |
| Speakman, Willie, c | .233 | 70 | 227 | 31 | 53 | 7 | 0 | 3 | 28 | 32 | 46 | 2 | 4 | S | R | 6-0 | 180 | 4-12-70 | 1991 | San Clemente, Calif. |
| Vizcaino, Julian, 2b-3b | .140 | 23 | 57 | 8 | 8 | 1 | 0 | 1 | 5 | 16 | 19 | 2 | 1 | R | R | 5-11 | 169 | 5-10-74 | 1992 | San Pedro de Macoris, D.R. |

| PITCHING | W | L | ERA | G | GS | CG | SV | IP | H | R | ER | BB | SO | B | T | HT | WT | DOB | 1st Yr | Resides |
|---|---|---|---|---|---|---|---|---|---|---|---|---|---|---|---|---|---|---|---|---|
| Blanchette, Bill | 2 | 0 | 1.64 | 20 | 0 | 0 | 0 | 22 | 20 | 5 | 4 | 6 | 14 | L | L | 5-10 | 175 | 9-1-70 | 1992 | Honolulu, Hawaii |
| Brown, Willard | 5 | 4 | 3.87 | 15 | 15 | 0 | 0 | 84 | 64 | 41 | 36 | 42 | 68 | R | R | 6-4 | 215 | 4-14-72 | 1993 | Marblehead, Mass. |
| Drysdale, Brooks | 2 | 2 | 2.73 | 18 | 0 | 0 | 11 | 26 | 22 | 8 | 8 | 5 | 32 | R | R | 5-10 | 185 | 6-15-71 | 1993 | Petaluma, Calif. |
| Edsell, Geoff | 4 | 3 | 6.89 | 13 | 13 | 1 | 0 | 64 | 64 | 52 | 49 | 40 | 63 | L | R | 6-2 | 195 | 12-10-72 | 1993 | Montoursville, Pa. |
| Fontes, Brian | 2 | 5 | 6.10 | 14 | 9 | 0 | 0 | 52 | 43 | 45 | 35 | 29 | 41 | S | R | 6-2 | 200 | 11-29-70 | 1993 | Fresno, Calif. |
| Grenert, Geoff | 3 | 4 | 4.30 | 26 | 1 | 0 | 1 | 46 | 51 | 24 | 22 | 20 | 44 | R | R | 6-3 | 181 | 2-18-71 | 1993 | Scottsdale, Ariz. |
| Hancock, Ryan | 1 | 0 | 3.31 | 3 | 3 | 0 | 0 | 16 | 14 | 9 | 6 | 8 | 18 | R | R | 6-2 | 210 | 11-11-71 | 1993 | Cupertino, Calif. |
| Harris, Bryan | 8 | 3 | 1.89 | 16 | 16 | 1 | 0 | 105 | 80 | 29 | 22 | 29 | 96 | L | L | 6-2 | 205 | 9-11-71 | 1993 | Peachtree City, Ga. |
| Kane, Mike | 0 | 1 | 9.95 | 12 | 0 | 0 | 0 | 13 | 11 | 18 | 14 | 18 | 14 | R | R | 6-5 | 215 | 12-5-70 | 1993 | Carmichael, Calif. |
| Knox, Jeff | 0 | 0 | 0.00 | 3 | 0 | 0 | 0 | 2 | 1 | 0 | 0 | 2 | 3 | R | R | 6-2 | 205 | 8-1-72 | 1991 | Deltona, Fla. |
| Lloyd, Johnny | 0 | 3 | 5.09 | 13 | 8 | 0 | 0 | 53 | 60 | 41 | 30 | 27 | 54 | R | R | 6-2 | 190 | 11-30-73 | 1992 | Jacksonville, Fla. |
| Lorraine, Andrew | 4 | 1 | 1.29 | 6 | 6 | 3 | 0 | 42 | 33 | 6 | 6 | 6 | 39 | L | L | 6-3 | 195 | 8-11-72 | 1993 | Valencia, Calif. |
| Mejia, Juan | 1 | 2 | 2.40 | 3 | 3 | 0 | 0 | 15 | 14 | 8 | 4 | 4 | 13 | L | L | 5-8 | 144 | 7-28-71 | 1992 | El Seibo, D.R. |
| Myers, Matt | 0 | 0 | 4.09 | 11 | 0 | 0 | 0 | 11 | 10 | 5 | 5 | 11 | 10 | R | R | 6-0 | 186 | 1-25-73 | 1991 | Chino, Calif. |
| Nedeau, John | 2 | 3 | 3.26 | 24 | 0 | 0 | 0 | 39 | 33 | 15 | 14 | 9 | 26 | R | R | 6-2 | 175 | 2-19-71 | 1993 | Tallahassee, Fla. |
| Puffer, Aaron | 4 | 2 | 5.40 | 19 | 0 | 0 | 1 | 28 | 29 | 21 | 17 | 14 | 28 | R | R | 6-2 | 230 | 12-10-70 | 1993 | Lombard, Ill. |
| Purdy, Shawn | 1 | 0 | 0.00 | 1 | 1 | 0 | 0 | 6 | 2 | 2 | 0 | 5 | 1 | R | R | 6-0 | 205 | 7-30-68 | 1991 | St. Cloud, Fla. |
| Razhigaev, Rudy | 0 | 0 | 6.35 | 9 | 0 | 0 | 0 | 6 | 13 | 4 | 4 | 6 | 3 | R | L | 6-1 | 188 | 7-15-68 | 1992 | Moscow, Russia |
| Runzi, Andrew | 0 | 0 | 9.00 | 5 | 1 | 0 | 0 | 7 | 10 | 7 | 7 | 5 | 10 | R | R | 6-2 | 205 | 2-10-71 | 1993 | Herculaneum, Mo. |
| Slade, Shawn | 2 | 2 | 5.33 | 24 | 0 | 0 | 5 | 27 | 34 | 20 | 16 | 15 | 26 | R | R | 6-2 | 195 | 10-26-70 | 1993 | Seekonk, Mass. |

### ARIZONA LEAGUE

| BATTING | AVG | G | AB | R | H | 2B | 3B | HR | RBI | BB | SO | SB | CS | B | T | HT | WT | DOB | 1st Yr | Resides |
|---|---|---|---|---|---|---|---|---|---|---|---|---|---|---|---|---|---|---|---|---|
| Bogatyrev, Ilya, dh-2b | .274 | 25 | 62 | 12 | 17 | 1 | 0 | 0 | 6 | 11 | 16 | 1 | 2 | R | R | 6-0 | 165 | 3-22-69 | 1992 | Moscow, Russia |
| Cullen, Geoff, dh-c | .118 | 15 | 34 | 2 | 4 | 2 | 0 | 0 | 3 | 4 | 1 | 0 | 0 | L | R | 6-0 | 180 | 5-5-73 | 1993 | Mississauga, Ontario |
| Denny, Shawn, dh-2b | .167 | 2 | 6 | 1 | 1 | 0 | 0 | 0 | 2 | 2 | 1 | 0 | 0 | R | R | 5-9 | 170 | 7-7-73 | 1993 | Lenoir, N.C. |
| Goebel, Matt, dh-c | .273 | 9 | 11 | 1 | 3 | 1 | 0 | 0 | 0 | 0 | 4 | 1 | 0 | R | R | 6-2 | 170 | 4-19-74 | 1992 | Simi Valley, Calif. |
| Ham, Kevin, of | .220 | 49 | 150 | 18 | 33 | 8 | 0 | 2 | 14 | 17 | 36 | 1 | 2 | R | R | 6-1 | 195 | 9-14-74 | 1993 | El Paso, Texas |
| Henderson, Juan, ss | .323 | 54 | 192 | 37 | 62 | 11 | 3 | 1 | 16 | 29 | 29 | 10 | 6 | R | R | 5-10 | 160 | 4-17-74 | 1993 | Santo Domingo, D.R. |
| Herdocia, Harold, 1b | .280 | 52 | 186 | 18 | 52 | 5 | 0 | 2 | 27 | 25 | 38 | 0 | 1 | R | R | 6-3 | 175 | 2-6-71 | 1990 | Diez Bara, Nicaragua |
| Herrick, Jason, c | .301 | 56 | 196 | 34 | 59 | 9 | 4 | 3 | 36 | 41 | 51 | 5 | 4 | L | L | 6-0 | 175 | 7-29-73 | 1991 | Franklin, Wis. |
| Leger, Gus, of | .125 | 14 | 32 | 4 | 4 | 1 | 2 | 0 | 2 | 5 | 12 | 1 | 0 | R | R | 5-11 | 200 | 10-12-74 | 1993 | Auckland, New Zealand |
| Mazara, Hommy, 3b | .217 | 54 | 207 | 29 | 45 | 7 | 5 | 0 | 21 | 18 | 38 | 3 | 5 | R | R | 5-11 | 175 | 8-3-74 | 1992 | San Pedro de Macoris, D.R. |
| Molina, Ben, dh-c | .263 | 27 | 80 | 9 | 21 | 6 | 2 | 0 | 10 | 10 | 4 | 0 | 2 | R | R | 5-11 | 190 | 7-20-74 | 1993 | Vega Alta, P.R. |
| Monday, Mike, c | .175 | 24 | 63 | 13 | 11 | 2 | 0 | 0 | 7 | 10 | 18 | 1 | 1 | R | R | 6-4 | 186 | 9-14-72 | 1992 | Santa Ana, Calif. |
| Perozo, Jose, 2b | .235 | 55 | 221 | 31 | 52 | 6 | 4 | 0 | 14 | 20 | 24 | 5 | 3 | R | R | 5-11 | 150 | 4-14-71 | 1989 | Maracaibo, Venez. |
| Rodriguez, Orlando, c | .202 | 41 | 124 | 18 | 25 | 5 | 2 | 0 | 18 | 22 | 22 | 0 | 0 | L | R | 6-1 | 190 | 11-5-74 | 1993 | Vega Alta, P.R. |
| Taylor, Sam, of | .245 | 52 | 159 | 27 | 39 | 4 | 3 | 1 | 21 | 26 | 29 | 9 | 4 | R | R | 6-0 | 175 | 4-8-72 | 1993 | El Cerrito, Calif. |
| Tiffany, Ted, of-1b | .161 | 24 | 56 | 7 | 9 | 1 | 0 | 0 | 3 | 8 | 11 | 1 | 0 | L | L | 6-2 | 170 | 6-18-74 | 1993 | Glendale, Ariz. |

| PITCHING | W | L | ERA | G | GS | CG | SV | IP | H | R | ER | BB | SO | B | T | HT | WT | DOB | 1st Yr | Resides |
|---|---|---|---|---|---|---|---|---|---|---|---|---|---|---|---|---|---|---|---|---|
| Aguirre, Jose | 5 | 5 | 2.75 | 11 | 11 | 5 | 0 | 72 | 51 | 29 | 22 | 18 | 62 | R | L | 5-11 | 165 | 11-25-73 | 1992 | Anaheim, Calif. |
| Andujar, Guillermo | 0 | 0 | 4.00 | 5 | 0 | 0 | 0 | 9 | 8 | 5 | 4 | 2 | 8 | R | R | 5-11 | 185 | 6-15-73 | 1990 | San Pedro de Macoris, D.R. |
| Bawlson, Jeff | 4 | 2 | 3.51 | 15 | 6 | 2 | 0 | 59 | 55 | 32 | 23 | 21 | 54 | L | L | 6-2 | 170 | 8-24-73 | 1993 | Tampa, Fla. |
| Blyleven, Todd | 4 | 4 | 3.60 | 11 | 11 | 1 | 0 | 70 | 69 | 35 | 28 | 17 | 49 | R | R | 6-5 | 220 | 9-27-72 | 1993 | Villa Park, Calif. |
| Carrasco, Jose | 3 | 3 | 1.54 | 18 | 1 | 0 | 4 | 35 | 28 | 10 | 6 | 14 | 43 | R | R | 6-2 | 160 | 9-9-73 | 1991 | Azua, D.R. |
| Cintron, Jose | 0 | 3 | 2.81 | 12 | 2 | 0 | 0 | 32 | 27 | 14 | 10 | 10 | 17 | L | R | 6-2 | 185 | 9-12-75 | 1993 | Yabucoa, P.R. |
| Egloff, Bruce | 1 | 0 | 0.00 | 4 | 0 | 0 | 0 | 6 | 6 | 0 | 0 | 1 | 6 | R | R | 6-2 | 215 | 4-10-65 | 1986 | Denver, Colo. |
| Knox, Jeff | 2 | 1 | 3.51 | 13 | 3 | 0 | 1 | 33 | 28 | 16 | 13 | 9 | 32 | R | R | 6-2 | 205 | 8-1-72 | 1991 | Deltona, Fla. |
| Mayer, Aaron | 0 | 1 | 4.82 | 17 | 0 | 0 | 3 | 19 | 10 | 11 | 10 | 13 | 14 | R | R | 6-5 | 175 | 8-13-74 | 1993 | San Ramon, Calif. |
| Perisho, Matt | 7 | 3 | 3.66 | 11 | 11 | 1 | 0 | 64 | 58 | 32 | 26 | 23 | 65 | L | L | 6-0 | 175 | 6-8-75 | 1993 | Tempe, Ariz. |
| Purdy, Shawn | 1 | 0 | 2.08 | 2 | 2 | 0 | 0 | 13 | 7 | 3 | 3 | 1 | 11 | R | R | 6-0 | 205 | 7-30-68 | 1991 | St. Cloud, Fla. |
| Thurmond, Travis | 0 | 0 | 4.26 | 12 | 0 | 0 | 0 | 19 | 20 | 14 | 9 | 8 | 18 | R | R | 6-2 | 170 | 12-8-73 | 1992 | Beaverton, Ore. |
| Vega, Orlando | 0 | 0 | 6.97 | 6 | 0 | 0 | 0 | 10 | 11 | 12 | 8 | 13 | 7 | R | R | 6-1 | 190 | 11-4-74 | 1993 | Rio Piedras, P.R. |
| Warren, Deshawn | 2 | 4 | 4.10 | 9 | 9 | 1 | 0 | 42 | 27 | 26 | 19 | 34 | 63 | R | L | 6-0 | 172 | 5-5-74 | 1992 | Butler, Ala. |

# CHICAGO WHITE SOX

**Manager:** Gene Lamont.    **1993 Record:** 94-68, .580 (1st, AL West).

| BATTING | AVG | G | AB | R | H | 2B | 3B | HR | RBI | BB | SO | SB | CS | B | T | HT | WT | DOB | 1st Yr | Resides |
|---|---|---|---|---|---|---|---|---|---|---|---|---|---|---|---|---|---|---|---|---|
| Bell, George | .217 | 102 | 410 | 36 | 89 | 17 | 2 | 13 | 64 | 13 | 49 | 1 | 1 | R | R | 6-1 | 210 | 10-21-59 | 1978 | San Pedro de Macoris, D.R. |
| Burks, Ellis | .275 | 146 | 499 | 75 | 137 | 24 | 4 | 17 | 74 | 60 | 97 | 6 | 9 | R | R | 6-2 | 205 | 9-11-64 | 1983 | Fort Worth, Texas |
| Calderon, Ivan | .115 | 9 | 26 | 1 | 3 | 2 | 0 | 0 | 3 | 0 | 5 | 0 | 0 | R | R | 6-1 | 221 | 3-19-62 | 1980 | Loiza, P.R. |
| 2-team (73 Boston) | .209 | 82 | 239 | 26 | 50 | 10 | 2 | 1 | 22 | 21 | 33 | 4 | 2 | | | | | | | |
| Cora, Joey | .268 | 153 | 579 | 95 | 155 | 15 | 13 | 2 | 51 | 67 | 63 | 20 | 8 | S | R | 5-8 | 155 | 5-14-65 | 1985 | Caguas, P.R. |
| Denson, Drew | .200 | 4 | 5 | 0 | 1 | 0 | 0 | 0 | 0 | 0 | 2 | 0 | 0 | R | R | 6-5 | 220 | 11-16-65 | 1984 | Cincinnati, Ohio |
| Fisk, Carlton | .189 | 25 | 53 | 2 | 10 | 0 | 0 | 1 | 4 | 2 | 11 | 0 | 1 | R | R | 6-2 | 235 | 12-26-47 | 1967 | Lockport, Ill. |
| Grebeck, Craig | .226 | 72 | 190 | 25 | 43 | 5 | 0 | 1 | 12 | 26 | 26 | 1 | 2 | R | R | 5-7 | 148 | 12-29-64 | 1987 | Cerritos, Calif. |
| Guillen, Ozzie | .280 | 134 | 457 | 44 | 128 | 23 | 4 | 4 | 50 | 10 | 41 | 5 | 4 | L | R | 5-11 | 164 | 1-20-64 | 1981 | Guarenas, Venez. |
| Huff, Mike | .182 | 43 | 44 | 4 | 8 | 2 | 0 | 1 | 6 | 9 | 15 | 1 | 0 | R | R | 6-1 | 190 | 8-11-63 | 1985 | Chicago, Ill. |
| Jackson, Bo | .232 | 85 | 284 | 32 | 66 | 9 | 0 | 16 | 45 | 23 | 106 | 0 | 2 | R | R | 6-1 | 228 | 11-30-62 | 1986 | Burr Ridge, Ill. |
| Johnson, Lance | .311 | 147 | 540 | 75 | 168 | 18 | 14 | 0 | 47 | 36 | 33 | 35 | 7 | L | L | 5-11 | 160 | 7-6-63 | 1984 | Mobile, Ala. |
| Karkovice, Ron | .228 | 128 | 403 | 60 | 92 | 17 | 1 | 20 | 54 | 29 | 126 | 2 | 2 | R | R | 6-1 | 215 | 8-8-63 | 1982 | Orlando, Fla. |
| LaValliere, Mike | .258 | 37 | 97 | 6 | 25 | 2 | 0 | 0 | 8 | 4 | 14 | 0 | 1 | L | R | 5-10 | 210 | 8-18-60 | 1981 | Bradenton, Fla. |
| Lindsey, Doug | .000 | 2 | 1 | 0 | 0 | 0 | 0 | 0 | 0 | 0 | 0 | 0 | 0 | R | R | 6-2 | 232 | 9-22-67 | 1987 | Austin, Texas |
| Martin, Norberto | .357 | 8 | 14 | 3 | 5 | 0 | 0 | 0 | 2 | 1 | 1 | 0 | 0 | S | R | 5-10 | 164 | 12-10-66 | 1984 | Hato Rey, P.R. |
| Merullo, Matt | .050 | 8 | 20 | 1 | 1 | 0 | 0 | 0 | 0 | 1 | 0 | 0 | 0 | L | R | 6-2 | 200 | 8-4-65 | 1986 | Ridgefield, Conn. |
| Newson, Warren | .300 | 26 | 40 | 9 | 12 | 0 | 0 | 2 | 6 | 9 | 12 | 0 | 0 | L | L | 5-7 | 202 | 7-3-64 | 1986 | Newnan, Ga. |
| Pasqua, Dan | .205 | 78 | 176 | 22 | 36 | 10 | 1 | 5 | 20 | 26 | 51 | 2 | 2 | L | L | 6-0 | 205 | 10-17-61 | 1982 | Palos Hills, Ill. |
| Raines, Tim | .306 | 115 | 415 | 75 | 127 | 16 | 4 | 16 | 54 | 64 | 35 | 21 | 7 | S | R | 5-8 | 185 | 9-16-59 | 1977 | Heathrow, Fla. |
| Sax, Steve | .235 | 57 | 119 | 20 | 28 | 5 | 0 | 1 | 8 | 8 | 6 | 7 | 3 | R | R | 5-11 | 185 | 1-29-60 | 1978 | Loomis, Calif. |
| Thomas, Frank | .317 | 153 | 549 | 106 | 174 | 36 | 0 | 41 | 128 | 112 | 54 | 4 | 2 | R | R | 6-5 | 257 | 5-27-68 | 1989 | Burr Ridge, Ill. |
| Ventura, Robin | .262 | 157 | 554 | 85 | 145 | 27 | 1 | 22 | 94 | 105 | 82 | 1 | 6 | L | R | 6-1 | 185 | 7-14-67 | 1989 | Santa Maria, Calif. |
| Wrona, Rick | .125 | 4 | 8 | 0 | 1 | 0 | 0 | 0 | 1 | 0 | 4 | 0 | 0 | R | R | 6-0 | 180 | 12-10-63 | 1985 | Tulsa, Okla. |

| PITCHING | W | L | ERA | G | GS | CG | SV | IP | H | R | ER | BB | SO | B | T | HT | WT | DOB | 1st Yr | Resides |
|---|---|---|---|---|---|---|---|---|---|---|---|---|---|---|---|---|---|---|---|---|
| Alvarez, Wilson | 15 | 8 | 2.95 | 31 | 31 | 1 | 0 | 208 | 168 | 78 | 68 | 122 | 155 | L | L | 6-1 | 235 | 3-24-70 | 1987 | Maracaibo, Venez. |
| Belcher, Tim | 3 | 5 | 4.40 | 12 | 11 | 1 | 0 | 72 | 64 | 36 | 35 | 27 | 34 | R | R | 6-3 | 220 | 10-19-61 | 1984 | Mt. Gilead, Ohio |
| Bere, Jason | 12 | 5 | 3.47 | 24 | 24 | 1 | 0 | 143 | 109 | 60 | 55 | 81 | 129 | R | R | 6-3 | 185 | 5-26-71 | 1990 | Wilmington, Mass. |
| Bolton, Rod | 2 | 6 | 7.44 | 9 | 8 | 0 | 0 | 42 | 55 | 40 | 35 | 16 | 17 | R | R | 6-2 | 190 | 9-23-68 | 1990 | Chattanooga, Tenn. |
| Cary, Chuck | 1 | 0 | 5.23 | 16 | 0 | 0 | 0 | 21 | 22 | 12 | 12 | 11 | 10 | L | L | 6-4 | 210 | 3-3-60 | 1981 | Destin, Fla. |
| DeLeon, Jose | 0 | 0 | 1.74 | 11 | 0 | 0 | 0 | 10 | 5 | 2 | 2 | 3 | 6 | R | R | 6-3 | 215 | 12-20-60 | 1979 | Boca Raton, Fla. |
| Drahman, Brian | 0 | 0 | 0.00 | 5 | 0 | 0 | 1 | 5 | 7 | 0 | 0 | 2 | 3 | R | R | 6-3 | 231 | 11-7-66 | 1986 | Fort Lauderdale, Fla. |
| Fernandez, Alex | 18 | 9 | 3.13 | 34 | 34 | 3 | 0 | 247 | 221 | 95 | 86 | 67 | 169 | R | R | 6-0 | 195 | 8-13-69 | 1990 | Hialeah, Fla. |
| Hernandez, Roberto | 3 | 4 | 2.29 | 70 | 0 | 0 | 38 | 79 | 66 | 21 | 20 | 20 | 71 | R | R | 6-4 | 235 | 11-11-64 | 1986 | Cobo Rojo, P.R. |
| Howard, Chris | 1 | 0 | 0.00 | 3 | 0 | 0 | 0 | 2 | 2 | 0 | 0 | 1 | 5 | R | L | 6-0 | 185 | 11-18-65 | 1986 | Nahant, Mass. |
| Jones, Barry | 0 | 1 | 8.59 | 6 | 0 | 0 | 0 | 7 | 14 | 8 | 7 | 3 | 7 | R | R | 6-4 | 225 | 2-15-63 | 1984 | Anna Maria, Fla. |
| Leach, Terry | 0 | 0 | 2.81 | 14 | 0 | 0 | 1 | 16 | 15 | 5 | 5 | 2 | 3 | R | R | 6-0 | 195 | 3-13-54 | 1976 | Seminole, Fla. |
| McCaskill, Kirk | 4 | 8 | 5.23 | 30 | 14 | 0 | 2 | 114 | 144 | 71 | 66 | 36 | 65 | R | R | 6-1 | 205 | 4-9-61 | 1982 | Corona Del Mar, Calif. |
| McDowell, Jack | 22 | 10 | 3.37 | 34 | 34 | 10 | 0 | 257 | 261 | 104 | 96 | 69 | 158 | R | R | 6-5 | 185 | 1-16-66 | 1987 | Chicago, Ill. |
| Pall, Donn | 2 | 3 | 3.22 | 39 | 0 | 0 | 1 | 59 | 62 | 25 | 21 | 11 | 29 | R | R | 6-1 | 180 | 1-11-62 | 1985 | Bloomingdale, Ill. |
| Radinsky, Scott | 8 | 2 | 4.28 | 73 | 0 | 0 | 4 | 55 | 61 | 33 | 26 | 19 | 44 | L | L | 6-3 | 204 | 3-3-68 | 1986 | Simi Valley, Calif. |
| Ruffcorn, Scott | 0 | 2 | 8.10 | 3 | 2 | 0 | 0 | 10 | 9 | 11 | 9 | 10 | 2 | R | R | 6-4 | 215 | 12-29-69 | 1991 | Austin, Texas |
| Schwarz, Jeff | 2 | 2 | 3.71 | 41 | 0 | 0 | 0 | 51 | 35 | 21 | 21 | 38 | 41 | R | R | 6-5 | 190 | 5-20-64 | 1982 | Fort Pierce, Fla. |
| Stieb, Dave | 1 | 3 | 6.04 | 4 | 4 | 0 | 0 | 22 | 27 | 17 | 15 | 14 | 11 | R | R | 6-0 | 195 | 7-22-57 | 1978 | Gilroy, Calif. |
| Thigpen, Bobby | 0 | 0 | 5.71 | 25 | 0 | 0 | 1 | 35 | 51 | 25 | 22 | 12 | 19 | R | R | 6-3 | 195 | 7-17-63 | 1985 | St. Petersburg, Fla. |

## FIELDING

| Catcher | PCT | G | PO | A | E | DP |
|---|---|---|---|---|---|---|
| Fisk | 1.000 | 25 | 75 | 5 | 0 | 0 |
| Karkovice | .994 | 127 | 769 | 63 | 5 | 4 |
| LaValliere | 1.000 | 37 | 164 | 28 | 0 | 2 |
| Lindsey | 1.000 | 2 | 3 | 0 | 0 | 0 |
| Wrona | 1.000 | 4 | 12 | 0 | 0 | 0 |

| First Base | PCT | G | PO | A | E | DP |
|---|---|---|---|---|---|---|
| Denson | .800 | 3 | 4 | 0 | 1 | 0 |
| Pasqua | .987 | 32 | 147 | 9 | 2 | 14 |
| Thomas | .989 | 150 | 1222 | 83 | 15 | 128 |
| Ventura | 1.000 | 4 | 7 | 0 | 0 | 1 |

| Second Base | PCT | G | PO | A | E | DP |
|---|---|---|---|---|---|---|
| Cora | .974 | 151 | 295 | 410 | 19 | 85 |
| Grebeck | 1.000 | 16 | 29 | 53 | 0 | 13 |
| Martin | .957 | 5 | 13 | 9 | 1 | 4 |
| Sax | 1.000 | 1 | 0 | 3 | 0 | 0 |

| Third Base | PCT | G | PO | A | E | DP |
|---|---|---|---|---|---|---|
| Cora | 1.000 | 3 | 1 | 3 | 0 | 0 |
| Grebeck | .923 | 14 | 6 | 18 | 2 | 2 |
| Ventura | .965 | 155 | 112 | 278 | 14 | 26 |

| Shortstop | PCT | G | PO | A | E | DP |
|---|---|---|---|---|---|---|
| Grebeck | .983 | 46 | 56 | 114 | 3 | 25 |

| | PCT | G | PO | A | E | DP |
|---|---|---|---|---|---|---|
| Guillen | .972 | 133 | 189 | 361 | 16 | 82 |

| Outfield | PCT | G | PO | A | E | DP |
|---|---|---|---|---|---|---|
| Burks | .982 | 146 | 313 | 6 | 6 | 1 |
| Calderon | 1.000 | 47 | 94 | 2 | 0 | 0 |
| Huff | 1.000 | 43 | 40 | 0 | 0 | 0 |
| Jackson | .989 | 47 | 89 | 5 | 1 | 2 |
| Johnson | .980 | 146 | 427 | 7 | 9 | 1 |
| Newson | 1.000 | 5 | 5 | 0 | 0 | 0 |
| Pasqua | .984 | 37 | 57 | 3 | 1 | 1 |
| Raines | 1.000 | 112 | 200 | 5 | 0 | 2 |
| Sax | 1.000 | 32 | 39 | 0 | 0 | 0 |

# WHITE SOX FARM SYSTEM

| Class | Club | League | W | L | Pct. | Finish* | Manager | First Year |
|---|---|---|---|---|---|---|---|---|
| AAA | Nashville (Tenn.) Sounds | American Assoc. | 81 | 62 | .566 | 2nd (8) | Rick Renick | 1993 |
| AA | Birmingham (Ala.) Barons | Southern | 78 | 64 | .549 | 1st† (10) | Terry Francona | 1986 |
| A# | Sarasota (Fla.) White Sox | Florida State | 77 | 57 | .575 | 3rd (13) | Dave Huppert | 1989 |
| A | South Bend (Ind.) White Sox | Midwest | 77 | 59 | .566 | 5th† (14) | Tony Franklin | 1988 |
| A | Hickory (N.C.) Crawdads | South Atlantic | 52 | 88 | .371 | 13th (14) | Fred Kendall | 1993 |
| Rookie | Sarasota (Fla.) White Sox | Gulf Coast | 32 | 27 | .542 | 5th (15) | Mike Rojas | 1964 |

*Finish in overall standings (No. of teams in league)    #Advanced level    †Won league championship

# NASHVILLE AAA

## AMERICAN ASSOCIATION

| BATTING | AVG | G | AB | R | H | 2B | 3B | HR | RBI | BB | SO | SB | CS | B | T | HT | WT | DOB | 1st Yr | Resides |
|---|---|---|---|---|---|---|---|---|---|---|---|---|---|---|---|---|---|---|---|---|
| Alvarez, Clemente | .207 | 11 | 29 | 1 | 6 | 0 | 0 | 0 | 2 | 1 | 4 | 0 | 0 | R | R | 5-11 | 180 | 5-18-68 | 1987 | Anzoategui, Venez. |
| Beltre, Esteban | .292 | 134 | 489 | 67 | 143 | 24 | 4 | 8 | 52 | 33 | 102 | 18 | 6 | R | R | 5-10 | 172 | 12-26-67 | 1984 | San Pedro de Macoris, D.R. |
| Brady, Doug | .000 | 2 | 3 | 0 | 0 | 0 | 0 | 0 | 0 | 0 | 0 | 0 | 0 | S | R | 5-11 | 165 | 11-23-69 | 1991 | Las Vegas, Nev. |
| Cepicky, Scott | .212 | 45 | 137 | 22 | 29 | 3 | 1 | 12 | 27 | 19 | 51 | 0 | 1 | L | R | 6-4 | 220 | 7-29-66 | 1989 | St. Louis, Mo. |
| Coomer, Ron | .313 | 59 | 211 | 34 | 66 | 19 | 0 | 13 | 51 | 10 | 29 | 1 | 2 | R | R | 5-11 | 195 | 11-18-66 | 1987 | Crest Hill, Ill. |
| Coughlin, Kevin | .571 | 2 | 7 | 0 | 4 | 1 | 0 | 0 | 3 | 0 | 1 | 0 | 0 | L | L | 6-0 | 175 | 9-7-70 | 1989 | Clarksburg, Md. |
| Cron, Chris | .257 | 126 | 460 | 69 | 118 | 27 | 0 | 22 | 68 | 61 | 114 | 2 | 1 | R | R | 6-2 | 200 | 3-31-64 | 1984 | Placentia, Calif. |
| Denson, Drew | .281 | 136 | 513 | 82 | 144 | 36 | 0 | 24 | 103 | 46 | 98 | 0 | 0 | R | R | 6-5 | 220 | 11-16-65 | 1984 | Cincinnati, Ohio |
| Gilbert, Shawn | .227 | 104 | 278 | 28 | 63 | 17 | 2 | 0 | 17 | 12 | 41 | 6 | 2 | R | R | 5-9 | 170 | 3-12-65 | 1987 | Glendale, Ariz. |
| Hall, Joe | .290 | 116 | 424 | 66 | 123 | 33 | 5 | 10 | 58 | 52 | 56 | 10 | 9 | R | R | 6-0 | 180 | 3-6-66 | 1988 | Paducah, Ky. |
| Huff, Mike | .294 | 92 | 344 | 65 | 101 | 12 | 6 | 8 | 32 | 64 | 43 | 18 | 7 | R | R | 6-1 | 190 | 8-11-63 | 1985 | Chicago, Ill. |
| Jeter, Shawn | .208 | 43 | 149 | 14 | 31 | 2 | 2 | 2 | 22 | 6 | 38 | 6 | 3 | L | R | 6-2 | 185 | 6-28-66 | 1985 | New York, N.Y. |
| Komminsk, Brad | .266 | 118 | 383 | 55 | 102 | 18 | 2 | 11 | 49 | 52 | 92 | 7 | 8 | R | R | 6-2 | 205 | 4-4-61 | 1979 | Lima, Ohio |
| Martin, Norberto | .309 | 137 | 580 | 87 | 179 | 21 | 6 | 9 | 74 | 26 | 59 | 31 | 5 | S | R | 5-10 | 164 | 12-10-66 | 1984 | Hato Rey, P.R. |
| Merullo, Matt | .332 | 103 | 352 | 50 | 117 | 30 | 1 | 12 | 65 | 28 | 47 | 0 | 2 | L | R | 6-2 | 200 | 8-4-65 | 1986 | Ridgefield, Conn. |
| Newson, Warren | .341 | 61 | 176 | 40 | 60 | 8 | 2 | 4 | 21 | 38 | 38 | 5 | 2 | L | L | 5-7 | 202 | 7-3-64 | 1986 | Newnan, Ga. |
| Raines, Tim | .455 | 3 | 11 | 3 | 5 | 1 | 0 | 0 | 2 | 2 | 0 | 2 | 1 | S | R | 5-8 | 185 | 9-16-59 | 1977 | Heathrow, Fla. |
| Tedder, Scott | .288 | 47 | 111 | 24 | 32 | 5 | 0 | 3 | 15 | 14 | 15 | 2 | 2 | L | L | 6-4 | 195 | 6-1-66 | 1988 | Whitehall, Ohio |
| Wrona, Rick | .212 | 73 | 184 | 24 | 39 | 13 | 0 | 3 | 22 | 11 | 35 | 0 | 1 | R | R | 6-0 | 180 | 12-10-63 | 1985 | Tulsa, Okla. |

| PITCHING | W | L | ERA | G | GS | CG | SV | IP | H | R | ER | BB | SO | B | T | HT | WT | DOB | 1st Yr | Resides |
|---|---|---|---|---|---|---|---|---|---|---|---|---|---|---|---|---|---|---|---|---|
| Alvarez, Wilson | 0 | 1 | 2.84 | 1 | 1 | 0 | 0 | 6 | 7 | 7 | 2 | 2 | 8 | L | L | 6-1 | 235 | 3-24-70 | 1987 | Maracaibo, Venez. |
| Baldwin, James | 5 | 4 | 2.61 | 10 | 10 | 1 | 0 | 69 | 43 | 21 | 20 | 36 | 61 | R | R | 6-4 | 210 | 7-15-71 | 1990 | Southern Pines, N.C. |
| Barfield, John | 3 | 1 | 4.11 | 14 | 4 | 0 | 1 | 35 | 36 | 19 | 16 | 11 | 15 | L | L | 6-1 | 195 | 10-15-64 | 1986 | Pine Bluff, Ark. |
| Bere, Jason | 5 | 1 | 2.37 | 8 | 8 | 0 | 0 | 49 | 36 | 19 | 13 | 25 | 52 | R | R | 6-3 | 185 | 5-26-71 | 1990 | Wilmington, Mass. |
| Bolton, Rod | 10 | 1 | 2.88 | 18 | 16 | 1 | 1 | 116 | 108 | 40 | 37 | 37 | 75 | R | R | 6-2 | 190 | 9-23-68 | 1990 | Chattanooga, Tenn. |
| Campos, Frank | 7 | 5 | 3.55 | 19 | 19 | 2 | 0 | 117 | 104 | 60 | 46 | 58 | 86 | R | R | 6-1 | 168 | 5-11-68 | 1987 | Caracas, Venez. |
| Carter, Jeff | 2 | 4 | 6.99 | 11 | 6 | 0 | 0 | 37 | 43 | 30 | 29 | 17 | 21 | R | R | 6-3 | 195 | 12-3-64 | 1987 | Brandon, Fla. |
| Cary, Chuck | 0 | 1 | 9.00 | 1 | 0 | 0 | 0 | 2 | 4 | 2 | 2 | 2 | 1 | L | L | 6-4 | 210 | 3-3-60 | 1981 | Destin, Fla. |
| Dabney, Fred | 2 | 5 | 4.86 | 51 | 0 | 0 | 3 | 63 | 65 | 43 | 34 | 21 | 44 | R | L | 6-3 | 180 | 11-20-67 | 1988 | Lawton, Okla. |
| Drahman, Brian | 9 | 4 | 2.91 | 54 | 0 | 0 | 20 | 56 | 59 | 29 | 18 | 19 | 49 | R | R | 6-3 | 231 | 11-7-66 | 1986 | Fort Lauderdale, Fla. |
| Garcia, Ramon | 4 | 1 | 4.01 | 7 | 7 | 1 | 0 | 43 | 45 | 22 | 19 | 11 | 25 | R | R | 6-2 | 200 | 12-9-69 | 1987 | Guanare, Venez. |
| Howard, Chris | 4 | 3 | 3.38 | 43 | 0 | 0 | 3 | 67 | 55 | 32 | 25 | 16 | 53 | R | L | 6-0 | 185 | 11-18-65 | 1986 | Nahant, Mass. |
| Jones, Barry | 0 | 0 | 2.60 | 7 | 0 | 0 | 2 | 17 | 16 | 5 | 5 | 2 | 19 | R | R | 6-4 | 225 | 2-15-63 | 1984 | Anna Maria, Fla. |
| Keyser, Brian | 9 | 5 | 4.66 | 30 | 18 | 2 | 1 | 122 | 142 | 70 | 63 | 27 | 44 | R | R | 6-1 | 180 | 10-31-66 | 1989 | Walnut Creek, Calif. |
| Leach, Terry | 0 | 0 | 3.18 | 5 | 0 | 0 | 1 | 6 | 4 | 2 | 2 | 0 | 4 | R | R | 6-0 | 195 | 3-13-54 | 1976 | Seminole, Fla. |
| Merigliano, Frank | 0 | 1 | 6.48 | 7 | 0 | 0 | 0 | 8 | 7 | 6 | 6 | 6 | 10 | R | R | 6-2 | 180 | 11-10-66 | 1988 | Pittsburgh, Pa. |
| Mongiello, Mike | 6 | 4 | 4.25 | 39 | 9 | 1 | 7 | 91 | 88 | 44 | 43 | 41 | 73 | R | R | 6-2 | 215 | 1-19-68 | 1989 | Secaucus, N.J. |
| Ruffcorn, Scott | 2 | 2 | 2.80 | 7 | 6 | 1 | 0 | 45 | 30 | 16 | 14 | 8 | 44 | R | R | 6-4 | 215 | 12-29-69 | 1991 | Austin, Texas |
| Ruffin, Johnny | 3 | 4 | 3.30 | 29 | 0 | 0 | 1 | 60 | 48 | 24 | 22 | 16 | 69 | R | R | 6-3 | 174 | 7-29-71 | 1988 | Butler, Ala. |
| Schrenk, Steve | 6 | 8 | 3.90 | 21 | 20 | 0 | 0 | 122 | 117 | 61 | 53 | 47 | 78 | R | R | 6-3 | 185 | 11-20-68 | 1987 | Aurora, Ore. |
| Schwarz, Jeff | 0 | 0 | 2.45 | 7 | 0 | 0 | 0 | 11 | 1 | 3 | 3 | 12 | 8 | R | R | 6-5 | 190 | 5-20-64 | 1982 | Fort Pierce, Fla. |
| Stieb, Dave | 0 | 1 | 3.86 | 1 | 1 | 0 | 0 | 7 | 9 | 3 | 3 | 2 | 3 | R | R | 6-0 | 195 | 7-22-57 | 1978 | Gilroy, Calif. |
| Thomas, Larry | 4 | 6 | 5.99 | 18 | 18 | 1 | 0 | 101 | 114 | 73 | 67 | 32 | 67 | L | L | 6-1 | 190 | 10-25-69 | 1991 | Mobile, Ala. |

### FIELDING

| Catcher | PCT | G | PO | A | E | DP |
|---|---|---|---|---|---|---|
| Alvarez | 1.000 | 11 | 75 | 0 | 0 | 0 |
| Hall | 1.000 | 5 | 15 | 2 | 0 | 0 |
| Merullo | .985 | 83 | 427 | 40 | 7 | 3 |
| Wrona | .989 | 72 | 400 | 52 | 5 | 7 |

| First Base | PCT | G | PO | A | E | DP |
|---|---|---|---|---|---|---|
| Cepicky | .929 | 2 | 13 | 0 | 1 | 2 |
| Cron | .993 | 91 | 766 | 63 | 6 | 67 |
| Denson | .981 | 56 | 534 | 48 | 11 | 38 |
| Merullo | .889 | 1 | 8 | 0 | 1 | 0 |
| Tedder | 1.000 | 1 | 1 | 0 | 0 | 0 |

| Second Base | PCT | G | PO | A | E | DP |
|---|---|---|---|---|---|---|
| Brady | .800 | 2 | 1 | 3 | 1 | 0 |

| | PCT | G | PO | A | E | DP |
|---|---|---|---|---|---|---|
| Gilbert | 1.000 | 7 | 12 | 22 | 0 | 4 |
| Huff | 1.000 | 1 | 1 | 2 | 0 | 0 |
| Martin | .976 | 137 | 291 | 438 | 18 | 86 |

| Third Base | PCT | G | PO | A | E | DP |
|---|---|---|---|---|---|---|
| Coomer | .895 | 58 | 30 | 107 | 16 | 6 |
| Cron | .924 | 32 | 24 | 61 | 7 | 6 |
| Gilbert | .909 | 41 | 12 | 68 | 8 | 7 |
| Hall | .926 | 28 | 7 | 56 | 5 | 4 |

| Shortstop | PCT | G | PO | A | E | DP |
|---|---|---|---|---|---|---|
| Beltre | .952 | 134 | 190 | 404 | 30 | 77 |
| Gilbert | .873 | 13 | 17 | 31 | 7 | 7 |
| Martin | 1.000 | 1 | 1 | 4 | 0 | 0 |

| Outfield | PCT | G | PO | A | E | DP |
|---|---|---|---|---|---|---|
| Cepicky | .960 | 24 | 20 | 4 | 1 | 0 |
| Coughlin | 1.000 | 2 | 3 | 0 | 0 | 0 |
| Gilbert | .955 | 33 | 40 | 2 | 2 | 0 |
| Hall | .989 | 85 | 169 | 7 | 2 | 1 |
| Huff | .986 | 88 | 206 | 9 | 3 | 5 |
| Jeter | .955 | 41 | 80 | 4 | 4 | 1 |
| Komminsk | .983 | 108 | 160 | 9 | 3 | 2 |
| Newson | .968 | 49 | 74 | 7 | 1 | 1 |
| Raines | 1.000 | 2 | 3 | 0 | 0 | 0 |
| Tedder | 1.000 | 41 | 65 | 3 | 0 | 0 |

# BIRMINGHAM AA

## SOUTHERN LEAGUE

| BATTING | AVG | G | AB | R | H | 2B | 3B | HR | RBI | BB | SO | SB | CS | B | T | HT | WT | DOB | 1st Yr | Resides |
|---|---|---|---|---|---|---|---|---|---|---|---|---|---|---|---|---|---|---|---|---|
| Alvarez, Clemente, c | .225 | 35 | 111 | 8 | 25 | 4 | 0 | 1 | 8 | 11 | 28 | 0 | 4 | R | R | 5-11 | 180 | 5-18-68 | 1987 | Anzoategui, Venez. |
| Belcher, Kevin, of | .222 | 111 | 360 | 38 | 80 | 13 | 2 | 13 | 50 | 45 | 81 | 11 | 6 | R | R | 6-0 | 175 | 8-8-67 | 1987 | Waco, Texas |
| Cairo, Sergio, of | .228 | 68 | 189 | 20 | 43 | 2 | 0 | 2 | 13 | 28 | 28 | 6 | 3 | R | R | 6-1 | 165 | 10-22-70 | 1988 | San Pedro de Macoris, D.R. |
| Cepicky, Scott, dh-of | .242 | 66 | 236 | 30 | 57 | 12 | 1 | 7 | 35 | 34 | 67 | 4 | 0 | L | R | 6-4 | 220 | 7-29-66 | 1989 | St. Louis, Mo. |
| Coleman, Ken, 2b-ss | .233 | 50 | 129 | 11 | 30 | 3 | 0 | 0 | 14 | 13 | 25 | 2 | 1 | S | R | 5-10 | 175 | 2-6-67 | 1988 | Jersey City, N.J. |
| Coomer, Ron, 3b | .324 | 69 | 262 | 44 | 85 | 18 | 0 | 13 | 50 | 15 | 43 | 1 | 1 | R | R | 5-11 | 195 | 11-18-66 | 1987 | Crest Hill, Ill. |
| DiSarcina, Glenn, ss | .400 | 3 | 5 | 1 | 2 | 0 | 0 | 0 | 1 | 2 | 1 | 0 | 1 | R | R | 6-1 | 180 | 4-29-70 | 1991 | Billerica, Mass. |
| Durham, Ray, 2b | .271 | 137 | 528 | 83 | 143 | 22 | 10 | 3 | 37 | 42 | 100 | 39 | 25 | S | R | 5-8 | 165 | 11-30-71 | 1990 | Charlotte, N.C. |
| Hood, Randy, of | .250 | 11 | 20 | 6 | 5 | 3 | 1 | 0 | 2 | 3 | 6 | 0 | 0 | R | R | 5-11 | 185 | 8-9-68 | 1990 | Goldsboro, N.C. |
| Manning, Henry, c | .179 | 30 | 106 | 7 | 19 | 3 | 1 | 2 | 9 | 3 | 25 | 0 | 1 | R | R | 5-11 | 185 | 7-3-68 | 1991 | Rutherford, N.J. |
| Miranda, Geovany, 2b-ss | .094 | 12 | 32 | 2 | 3 | 0 | 0 | 0 | 0 | 1 | 6 | 0 | 0 | R | R | 5-11 | 170 | 2-16-70 | 1988 | Chiriqui, Panama |
| Nunez, Rogelio, of | .214 | 83 | 257 | 22 | 55 | 10 | 3 | 0 | 21 | 5 | 82 | 1 | 2 | S | R | 6-0 | 180 | 5-6-70 | 1988 | Santiago, D.R. |
| Pledger, Kinnis, of | .242 | 125 | 393 | 70 | 95 | 16 | 6 | 14 | 56 | 74 | 120 | 19 | 6 | L | R | 6-4 | 215 | 7-17-68 | 1987 | Benton, Ark. |
| Robertson, Mike, 1b | .270 | 138 | 511 | 73 | 138 | 31 | 3 | 11 | 73 | 59 | 97 | 10 | 5 | L | L | 6-0 | 180 | 10-9-70 | 1991 | Placentia, Calif. |
| Saenz, Olmedo, 3b | .347 | 49 | 173 | 30 | 60 | 17 | 2 | 6 | 29 | 20 | 21 | 2 | 1 | R | R | 6-2 | 185 | 10-8-70 | 1990 | Chitre Herrera, Panama |
| Strange, Keith, c | .235 | 6 | 17 | 1 | 4 | 0 | 0 | 0 | 3 | 0 | 5 | 0 | 0 | R | R | 6-1 | 200 | 7-9-69 | 1990 | Eugene, Ore. |

## MAJOR LEAGUERS

**BATTING**

| | | |
|---|---|---|
| *AVG | Frank Thomas | .317 |
| R | Frank Thomas | 106 |
| H | Frank Thomas | 174 |
| TB | Frank Thomas | 333 |
| 2B | Frank Thomas | 36 |
| 3B | Lance Johnson | 14 |
| HR | Frank Thomas | 41 |
| RBI | Frank Thomas | 128 |
| BB | Frank Thomas | 112 |
| SO | Ron Karkovice | 126 |
| SB | Lance Johnson | 35 |

**PITCHING**

| | | |
|---|---|---|
| W | Jack McDowell | 22 |
| L | Jack McDowell | 10 |
| #ERA | Roberto Hernandez | 2.29 |
| G | Scott Radinsky | .73 |
| CG | Jack McDowell | 10 |
| SV | Roberto Hernandez | 38 |
| IP | Jack McDowell | 257 |
| BB | Wilson Alvarez | 122 |
| SO | Alex Fernandez | 169 |

MORRIS FOSTOFF

**Roberto Hernandez**
Saved 38 games

## MINOR LEAGUERS

**BATTING**

| | | |
|---|---|---|
| *AVG | Matt Merullo, Nashville | .332 |
| R | Essex Burton, South Bend | 95 |
| H | Norberto Martin, Nashville | 179 |
| TB | Ron Coomer, Birmingham-Nashville | 266 |
| 2B | Ron Coomer, Birmingham-Nashville | 37 |
| 3B | Ray Durham, Birmingham | 10 |
| HR | Ron Coomer, Birmingham-Nashville | 26 |
| RBI | Drew Denson, Nashville | 103 |
| BB | Chris Mader, Hickory-South Bend | 92 |
| SO | Jimmy Hurst, South Bend | 141 |
| SB | Essex Burton, South Bend | 74 |

**PITCHING**

| | | |
|---|---|---|
| W | Mike Call, South Bend | 15 |
| L | Robert Ellis, Sarasota-Birmingham | 11 |
| #ERA | Barry Johnson, Sarasota-Birmingham | 1.42 |
| G | Brian Drahman, Nashville | 54 |
| CG | Robert Ellis, Sarasota-Birmingham | 10 |
| SV | Brian Drahman, Nashville | 20 |
| IP | James Baldwin, Birmingham-Nashville | 189 |
| BB | Frank Campos, Nashville | 84 |
| SO | Two tied at | 185 |

*Minimum 250 At-Bats    #Minimum 75 Innings

| BATTING | AVG | G | AB | R | H | 2B | 3B | HR | RBI | BB | SO | SB | CS | B | T | HT | WT | DOB | 1st Yr | Resides |
|---|---|---|---|---|---|---|---|---|---|---|---|---|---|---|---|---|---|---|---|---|
| Tedder, Scott, of | .254 | 39 | 118 | 20 | 30 | 5 | 0 | 1 | 12 | 19 | 15 | 1 | 4 | L | L | 6-4 | 195 | 6-1-66 | 1988 | Whitehall, Ohio |
| Walker, Dennis, 3b | .214 | 46 | 126 | 10 | 27 | 4 | 2 | 2 | 16 | 1 | 32 | 2 | 0 | R | R | 6-0 | 210 | 10-31-66 | 1988 | Martindale, Texas |
| Wilson, Brandon, ss | .270 | 137 | 500 | 76 | 135 | 19 | 5 | 2 | 48 | 52 | 77 | 43 | 10 | R | R | 6-1 | 175 | 2-26-69 | 1990 | Owensboro, Ky. |
| Wolak, Jerry, of | .305 | 137 | 525 | 78 | 160 | 35 | 4 | 9 | 64 | 26 | 95 | 16 | 12 | R | R | 5-10 | 170 | 7-27-70 | 1988 | West Covina, Calif. |

| PITCHING | W | L | ERA | G | GS | CG | SV | IP | H | R | ER | BB | SO | B | T | HT | WT | DOB | 1st Yr | Resides |
|---|---|---|---|---|---|---|---|---|---|---|---|---|---|---|---|---|---|---|---|---|
| Adkins, Steve | 1 | 4 | 4.14 | 26 | 3 | 0 | 2 | 50 | 46 | 25 | 23 | 20 | 40 | R | L | 6-6 | 215 | 10-26-64 | 1986 | Devon, Pa. |
| Andujar, Luis | 5 | 0 | 1.82 | 6 | 6 | 0 | 0 | 40 | 31 | 9 | 8 | 18 | 48 | R | R | 6-2 | 175 | 11-22-72 | 1991 | Bani, D.R. |
| Baldwin, James | 8 | 5 | 2.25 | 17 | 17 | 4 | 0 | 120 | 94 | 48 | 30 | 43 | 107 | R | R | 6-4 | 180 | 7-15-71 | 1990 | Southern Pines, N.C. |
| Barfield, John | 5 | 2 | 3.86 | 13 | 5 | 1 | 1 | 42 | 57 | 24 | 18 | 5 | 18 | L | L | 6-1 | 195 | 10-15-64 | 1986 | Pine Bluff, Ark. |
| Boehringer, Brian | 2 | 1 | 3.54 | 7 | 7 | 1 | 0 | 41 | 41 | 20 | 16 | 14 | 29 | S | R | 6-2 | 180 | 1-8-69 | 1991 | Fenton, Mo. |
| Campos, Frank | 2 | 4 | 3.25 | 9 | 9 | 0 | 0 | 55 | 49 | 29 | 20 | 26 | 41 | R | R | 6-1 | 168 | 5-11-68 | 1987 | Caracas, Venez. |
| Carter, Jeff | 2 | 1 | 1.02 | 13 | 0 | 0 | 8 | 18 | 9 | 2 | 2 | 6 | 21 | R | R | 6-3 | 195 | 12-3-64 | 1987 | Brandon, Fla. |
| Ellis, Robert | 6 | 3 | 3.10 | 12 | 12 | 2 | 0 | 81 | 68 | 33 | 28 | 21 | 77 | R | R | 6-5 | 220 | 12-15-70 | 1990 | Baton Rouge, La. |
| Gajkowski, Steve | 0 | 0 | 0.00 | 1 | 0 | 0 | 0 | 2 | 0 | 0 | 0 | 0 | 2 | R | R | 6-2 | 200 | 12-30-69 | 1990 | Bellevue, Wash. |
| Gardner, John | 0 | 4 | 6.21 | 19 | 1 | 0 | 1 | 38 | 36 | 31 | 26 | 20 | 27 | R | R | 6-3 | 210 | 11-23-65 | 1987 | Michigan City, Ind. |
| 2-team (7 Orlando) | 5 | 5 | 5.50 | 26 | 8 | 0 | 1 | 75 | 70 | 52 | 46 | 43 | 46 | | | | | | | |
| Gordon, Anthony | 3 | 2 | 2.58 | 37 | 0 | 0 | 1 | 45 | 32 | 17 | 13 | 35 | 49 | R | L | 6-1 | 185 | 12-8-68 | 1988 | Avon Park, Fla. |
| Johnson, Barry | 2 | 0 | 3.32 | 13 | 1 | 0 | 1 | 22 | 27 | 11 | 8 | 6 | 16 | R | R | 6-4 | 200 | 8-21-69 | 1991 | Joliet, Ill. |
| Keyser, Brian | 0 | 2 | 5.73 | 2 | 2 | 1 | 0 | 11 | 15 | 9 | 7 | 5 | 8 | R | R | 6-1 | 180 | 10-31-66 | 1989 | Walnut Creek, Calif. |
| Leach, Terry | 0 | 0 | 4.15 | 4 | 0 | 0 | 1 | 4 | 4 | 2 | 2 | 2 | 5 | R | R | 6-0 | 195 | 3-13-54 | 1976 | Seminole, Fla. |
| Locklear, Dean | 2 | 0 | 6.14 | 9 | 2 | 0 | 0 | 22 | 29 | 17 | 15 | 11 | 20 | R | L | 6-1 | 190 | 10-12-69 | 1990 | Granite, Okla. |
| Manon, Ramon | 10 | 7 | 3.63 | 25 | 22 | 2 | 0 | 131 | 134 | 63 | 53 | 65 | 88 | R | R | 6-0 | 170 | 1-20-68 | 1986 | Santo Domingo, D.R. |
| Merigliano, Frank | 0 | 1 | 27.00 | 2 | 0 | 0 | 0 | 2 | 4 | 5 | 5 | 2 | 3 | R | R | 6-2 | 180 | 11-10-66 | 1988 | Pittsburgh, Pa. |
| Mongiello, Mike | 0 | 1 | 1.54 | 7 | 1 | 0 | 1 | 12 | 5 | 6 | 2 | 4 | 9 | R | R | 6-2 | 215 | 1-19-68 | 1989 | Secaucus, N.J. |
| Olsen, Steve | 10 | 9 | 4.75 | 25 | 25 | 1 | 0 | 142 | 156 | 87 | 75 | 52 | 92 | R | R | 6-4 | 225 | 11-2-69 | 1991 | LaGrange, Ky. |
| Perigny, Don | 3 | 4 | 4.22 | 48 | 0 | 0 | 3 | 70 | 69 | 38 | 33 | 15 | 57 | R | R | 5-11 | 175 | 1-8-69 | 1990 | Lowell, Mass. |
| Pierce, Jeff | 3 | 4 | 2.59 | 33 | 0 | 0 | 18 | 49 | 34 | 16 | 14 | 7 | 45 | R | R | 6-1 | 195 | 6-7-69 | 1991 | Staatsburg, N.Y. |
| Ruffcorn, Scott | 9 | 4 | 2.73 | 20 | 20 | 3 | 0 | 135 | 108 | 47 | 41 | 52 | 141 | R | R | 6-4 | 215 | 12-29-69 | 1991 | Austin, Texas |
| Ruffin, Johnny | 0 | 4 | 2.82 | 11 | 0 | 0 | 2 | 22 | 16 | 9 | 7 | 9 | 23 | R | R | 6-3 | 174 | 7-29-71 | 1988 | Butler, Ala. |
| Schrenk, Steve | 5 | 1 | 1.17 | 8 | 8 | 2 | 0 | 62 | 31 | 11 | 8 | 7 | 51 | R | R | 6-3 | 185 | 11-20-68 | 1987 | Aurora, Ore. |
| Thomas, Larry | 0 | 1 | 5.14 | 1 | 1 | 0 | 0 | 7 | 9 | 5 | 4 | 1 | 5 | R | L | 6-1 | 190 | 10-25-69 | 1991 | Mobile, Ala. |

## SARASOTA    A

### FLORIDA STATE LEAGUE

| BATTING | AVG | G | AB | R | H | 2B | 3B | HR | RBI | BB | SO | SB | CS | B | T | HT | WT | DOB | 1st Yr | Resides |
|---|---|---|---|---|---|---|---|---|---|---|---|---|---|---|---|---|---|---|---|---|
| Blackburn, Tyres, of | .000 | 1 | 2 | 0 | 0 | 0 | 0 | 0 | 0 | 0 | 0 | 0 | 0 | R | R | 5-11 | 185 | 5-19-71 | 1992 | Dallas, Texas |
| Bradish, Mike, 1b | .226 | 32 | 106 | 6 | 24 | 3 | 0 | 1 | 17 | 15 | 23 | 0 | 0 | R | R | 6-4 | 220 | 4-5-68 | 1990 | Brea, Calif. |
| Brady, Doug, 2b | .252 | 115 | 449 | 75 | 113 | 16 | 6 | 5 | 44 | 55 | 54 | 26 | 9 | S | R | 5-11 | 165 | 11-23-69 | 1991 | Las Vegas, Nev. |
| Buchanan, Shawn, of | .274 | 30 | 106 | 18 | 29 | 5 | 2 | 0 | 11 | 23 | 23 | 1 | 3 | R | R | 6-0 | 190 | 2-1-69 | 1991 | Gary, Ind. |
| Cappuccio, Carmine, of | .189 | 24 | 90 | 9 | 17 | 2 | 2 | 1 | 12 | 4 | 10 | 3 | 0 | L | R | 5-8 | 185 | 2-1-70 | 1992 | Malden, Mass. |
| Coleman, Ken, inf | .188 | 11 | 32 | 4 | 6 | 0 | 0 | 0 | 2 | 6 | 4 | 1 | 1 | S | R | 5-10 | 175 | 2-6-67 | 1988 | Jersey City, N.J. |
| Coughlin, Kevin, of-1b | .308 | 112 | 415 | 53 | 128 | 19 | 2 | 2 | 32 | 42 | 51 | 4 | 4 | L | L | 6-0 | 175 | 9-7-70 | 1989 | Clarksburg, Md. |
| DiSarcina, Glenn, ss | .283 | 120 | 477 | 73 | 135 | 29 | 5 | 4 | 47 | 33 | 77 | 11 | 5 | L | R | 6-1 | 180 | 4-29-70 | 1991 | Billerica, Mass. |
| Faircloth, Wayne, c | .222 | 5 | 9 | 1 | 2 | 1 | 0 | 0 | 1 | 1 | 2 | 1 | 0 | R | R | 6-3 | 185 | 6-3-71 | 1992 | Winston-Salem, N.C. |
| Fryman, Troy, 1b | .239 | 78 | 285 | 42 | 68 | 16 | 3 | 5 | 46 | 31 | 55 | 0 | 0 | L | R | 6-4 | 195 | 10-2-71 | 1991 | Pensacola, Fla. |
| Henry, Harold, of | .203 | 37 | 123 | 16 | 25 | 9 | 0 | 1 | 7 | 12 | 34 | 7 | 5 | R | R | 6-2 | 200 | 8-31-69 | 1991 | Downsville, La. |
| Hood, Randy, of | .182 | 47 | 143 | 14 | 26 | 6 | 1 | 0 | 9 | 12 | 36 | 3 | 2 | R | R | 5-11 | 185 | 8-9-68 | 1990 | Goldsboro, N.C. |
| LaValliere, Mike, c-dh | .306 | 32 | 108 | 6 | 33 | 2 | 0 | 0 | 14 | 19 | 5 | 2 | 0 | L | R | 5-10 | 210 | 8-18-60 | 1981 | Bradenton, Fla. |
| Manning, Ramon, of | .228 | 27 | 79 | 8 | 18 | 3 | 0 | 0 | 4 | 7 | 12 | 0 | 0 | R | R | 5-11 | 185 | 7-3-68 | 1991 | Rutherford, N.J. |
| Miranda, Geovany, 2b-ss | .175 | 19 | 63 | 7 | 11 | 0 | 1 | 0 | 2 | 1 | 8 | 3 | 0 | R | R | 5-11 | 170 | 2-16-70 | 1988 | Chiriqui, Panama |
| Poe, Charles, of | .249 | 95 | 313 | 45 | 78 | 16 | 6 | 11 | 47 | 33 | 91 | 5 | 8 | R | R | 6-0 | 185 | 11-9-71 | 1990 | West Covina, Calif. |
| Reyes, Jimmy, 2b-3b | .256 | 17 | 43 | 2 | 11 | 0 | 1 | 0 | 0 | 6 | 8 | 2 | 0 | S | R | 6-1 | 165 | 5-6-72 | 1991 | New York, N.Y. |
| Robledo, Nilson, c | .259 | 74 | 259 | 35 | 67 | 18 | 1 | 7 | 34 | 13 | 63 | 0 | 1 | R | R | 6-1 | 165 | 11-3-68 | 1989 | Entrega General, Pan. |
| Saenz, Olmedo, 3b | .256 | 33 | 121 | 13 | 31 | 9 | 4 | 0 | 34 | 7 | 9 | 18 | 3 | 1 | R | R | 6-2 | 185 | 10-8-70 | 1990 | Chitre Herrera, Panama |

| BATTING | AVG | G | AB | R | H | 2B | 3B | HR | RBI | BB | SO | SB | CS | B | T | HT | WT | DOB | 1st Yr | Resides |
|---|---|---|---|---|---|---|---|---|---|---|---|---|---|---|---|---|---|---|---|---|
| Snopek, Chris, 3b-ss | .245 | 107 | 371 | 61 | 91 | 21 | 4 | 10 | 50 | 65 | 67 | 3 | 2 | R | R | 6-1 | 185 | 9-20-70 | 1992 | Cynthiana, Ky. |
| Tremie, Chris, c | .162 | 14 | 37 | 2 | 6 | 1 | 0 | 0 | 5 | 2 | 4 | 0 | 0 | R | R | 6-0 | 200 | 10-17-69 | 1992 | Houston, Texas |
| Valrie, Kerry, of | .212 | 115 | 386 | 47 | 82 | 14 | 2 | 12 | 52 | 17 | 81 | 19 | 7 | R | R | 5-10 | 195 | 10-31-68 | 1990 | Loxley, Ala. |
| Vinas, Julio, c | .246 | 18 | 65 | 5 | 16 | 2 | 1 | 1 | 7 | 5 | 13 | 0 | 0 | R | R | 6-0 | 200 | 2-14-73 | 1991 | Hialeah, Fla. |
| Vogel, Mike, dh-1b | .239 | 71 | 247 | 21 | 59 | 7 | 0 | 0 | 21 | 29 | 48 | 2 | 0 | S | R | 6-2 | 190 | 1-15-72 | 1990 | Brooklyn Park, Minn. |
| Walker, Dennis, dh-3b | .355 | 30 | 107 | 16 | 38 | 5 | 1 | 1 | 13 | 7 | 25 | 2 | 2 | R | R | 6-0 | 210 | 10-31-66 | 1988 | Martindale, Texas |

| PITCHING | W | L | ERA | G | GS | CG | SV | IP | H | R | ER | BB | SO | B | T | HT | WT | DOB | 1st Yr | Resides |
|---|---|---|---|---|---|---|---|---|---|---|---|---|---|---|---|---|---|---|---|---|
| Andujar, Luis | 6 | 6 | 1.99 | 18 | 11 | 2 | 1 | 86 | 67 | 26 | 19 | 28 | 76 | R | R | 6-2 | 175 | 11-22-72 | 1991 | Bani, D.R. |
| Boehringer, Brian | 10 | 4 | 2.80 | 18 | 17 | 3 | 0 | 119 | 103 | 47 | 37 | 51 | 92 | S | R | 6-2 | 180 | 1-8-69 | 1991 | Fenton, Mo. |
| Christmann, Scott | 0 | 1 | 0.87 | 2 | 2 | 0 | 0 | 10 | 5 | 4 | 1 | 5 | 6 | L | L | 6-3 | 190 | 12-3-71 | 1993 | Vancouver, Wash. |
| Dunne, Mike | 1 | 1 | 5.47 | 7 | 1 | 0 | 0 | 25 | 30 | 17 | 15 | 8 | 11 | L | R | 6-4 | 212 | 10-27-62 | 1985 | Peoria, Ill. |
| Ellis, Robert | 7 | 8 | 2.51 | 15 | 15 | 8 | 0 | 104 | 81 | 37 | 29 | 31 | 79 | R | R | 6-5 | 220 | 12-15-70 | 1990 | Baton Rouge, La. |
| Fordham, Tom | 0 | 0 | 0.00 | 2 | 0 | 0 | 0 | 5 | 3 | 1 | 0 | 3 | 5 | L | L | 6-2 | 210 | 2-20-74 | 1993 | El Cajon, Calif. |
| Gajkowski, Steve | 3 | 3 | 2.07 | 43 | 0 | 0 | 15 | 70 | 52 | 21 | 16 | 17 | 46 | R | R | 6-2 | 200 | 12-30-69 | 1990 | Bellevue, Wash. |
| Gordon, Anthony | 0 | 0 | 1.50 | 2 | 0 | 0 | 0 | 6 | 4 | 1 | 1 | 4 | 6 | R | L | 6-1 | 185 | 12-8-68 | 1988 | Avon Park, Fla. |
| Heathcott, Mike | 11 | 10 | 3.61 | 26 | 26 | 6 | 0 | 179 | 174 | 90 | 72 | 62 | 83 | R | R | 6-3 | 185 | 5-16-69 | 1991 | Chicago, Ill. |
| Johnson, Barry | 5 | 0 | 0.66 | 18 | 1 | 0 | 1 | 54 | 33 | 5 | 4 | 8 | 35 | R | R | 6-4 | 200 | 8-21-69 | 1991 | Joliet, Ill. |
| Johnston, Sean | 6 | 5 | 4.50 | 12 | 12 | 1 | 0 | 72 | 74 | 43 | 36 | 30 | 29 | L | L | 6-2 | 185 | 12-10-70 | 1992 | Berlin, Conn. |
| Keating, David | 2 | 0 | 3.55 | 22 | 0 | 0 | 3 | 33 | 37 | 16 | 13 | 16 | 28 | R | L | 6-1 | 195 | 11-6-67 | 1989 | Salinas, Calif. |
| Levine, Alan | 11 | 8 | 3.68 | 27 | 26 | 5 | 0 | 161 | 169 | 87 | 66 | 50 | 129 | L | R | 6-3 | 185 | 5-22-68 | 1991 | Hanover Park, Ill. |
| Locklear, Dean | 7 | 0 | 3.69 | 18 | 2 | 1 | 0 | 54 | 55 | 25 | 22 | 16 | 37 | R | L | 6-1 | 190 | 10-12-69 | 1990 | Granite, Okla. |
| Merigliano, Frank | 0 | 1 | 2.10 | 18 | 0 | 0 | 8 | 26 | 12 | 6 | 6 | 12 | 21 | R | R | 6-2 | 180 | 11-10-66 | 1988 | Pittsburgh, Pa. |
| Stieb, Dave | 1 | 1 | 5.84 | 2 | 2 | 0 | 0 | 12 | 18 | 10 | 8 | 2 | 14 | R | R | 6-0 | 195 | 7-22-57 | 1978 | Gilroy, Calif. |
| Tagle, Hank | 1 | 1 | 2.87 | 17 | 0 | 0 | 0 | 16 | 13 | 8 | 5 | 10 | 9 | L | L | 6-0 | 175 | 4-24-68 | 1991 | Sierra Vista, Ariz. |
| Thomas, Larry | 4 | 2 | 2.48 | 8 | 8 | 3 | 0 | 62 | 52 | 19 | 17 | 15 | 27 | R | L | 6-1 | 190 | 10-25-69 | 1991 | Mobile, Ala. |
| Tolar, Kevin | 2 | 6 | 5.35 | 23 | 11 | 0 | 1 | 77 | 75 | 55 | 46 | 51 | 60 | R | L | 6-3 | 225 | 1-28-71 | 1989 | Panama City, Fla. |

# SOUTH BEND  A
## MIDWEST LEAGUE

| BATTING | AVG | G | AB | R | H | 2B | 3B | HR | RBI | BB | SO | SB | CS | B | T | HT | WT | DOB | 1st Yr | Resides |
|---|---|---|---|---|---|---|---|---|---|---|---|---|---|---|---|---|---|---|---|---|
| Bell, George, dh | .125 | 2 | 8 | 1 | 1 | 0 | 0 | 0 | 0 | 1 | 0 | 0 | 0 | R | R | 6-1 | 210 | 10-21-59 | 1978 | San Pedro de Macoris, D.R. |
| Bowrosen, Ricky, 3b | .159 | 32 | 88 | 9 | 14 | 5 | 0 | 2 | 9 | 11 | 37 | 0 | 1 | R | R | 6-1 | 185 | 12-11-70 | 1991 | Port Orange, Fla. |
| Bradish, Mike, 1b-3b | .285 | 47 | 172 | 21 | 49 | 11 | 0 | 3 | 26 | 9 | 46 | 0 | 1 | R | R | 6-4 | 220 | 4-5-68 | 1990 | Brea, Calif. |
| Burton, Essex, 2b | .255 | 134 | 501 | 95 | 128 | 6 | 8 | 1 | 36 | 85 | 94 | 74 | 24 | S | R | 5-9 | 155 | 5-16-69 | 1991 | San Diego, Calif. |
| Cameron, Mike, of | .238 | 122 | 411 | 52 | 98 | 14 | 5 | 0 | 30 | 27 | 101 | 19 | 10 | R | R | 6-1 | 170 | 1-8-73 | 1991 | LaGrange, Ga. |
| Cappuccio, Carmine, of | .305 | 101 | 383 | 59 | 117 | 26 | 5 | 4 | 52 | 42 | 56 | 2 | 6 | L | R | 6-3 | 185 | 2-1-70 | 1992 | Malden, Mass. |
| Devers, Edgar, of | .197 | 33 | 66 | 9 | 13 | 3 | 0 | 0 | 10 | 6 | 21 | 0 | 0 | L | R | 6-0 | 155 | 5-31-72 | 1991 | San Pedro de Macoris, D.R. |
| Faircloth, Wayne, c | .250 | 2 | 4 | 0 | 1 | 0 | 0 | 0 | 0 | 0 | 3 | 0 | 0 | R | R | 6-3 | 185 | 6-3-71 | 1992 | Winston-Salem, N.C. |
| Fraraccio, Dan, 3b | .274 | 49 | 135 | 23 | 37 | 10 | 0 | 0 | 21 | 6 | 29 | 0 | 1 | R | R | 5-11 | 175 | 9-18-70 | 1992 | Bradenton, Fla. |
| Fryman, Troy, 1b | .318 | 51 | 173 | 34 | 55 | 7 | 6 | 7 | 41 | 33 | 45 | 2 | 0 | L | R | 6-4 | 195 | 10-2-71 | 1991 | Pensacola, Fla. |
| Hood, Randy, of | .235 | 6 | 17 | 5 | 4 | 2 | 0 | 0 | 1 | 6 | 3 | 1 | 1 | R | R | 5-11 | 185 | 8-9-68 | 1990 | Goldsboro, N.C. |
| Hurst, Jimmy, of-dh | .244 | 123 | 464 | 79 | 113 | 26 | 4 | 20 | 79 | 37 | 141 | 15 | 2 | R | R | 6-6 | 225 | 3-1-72 | 1991 | Tuscaloosa, Ala. |
| Machado, Robert, c | .306 | 75 | 281 | 34 | 86 | 14 | 3 | 2 | 33 | 19 | 59 | 1 | 2 | R | R | 6-1 | 150 | 6-3-73 | 1991 | Carabobo, Venez. |
| Mader, Chris, 3b | .262 | 18 | 61 | 6 | 16 | 2 | 0 | 1 | 8 | 11 | 8 | 2 | 0 | R | R | 6-0 | 195 | 10-6-70 | 1992 | Tewksbury, Mass. |
| Mathews, Byron, of | .245 | 131 | 518 | 75 | 127 | 10 | 7 | 2 | 58 | 48 | 110 | 30 | 13 | S | R | 6-2 | 175 | 11-30-70 | 1992 | Ballwin, Mo. |
| Mumma, Bob, c | .160 | 9 | 25 | 5 | 4 | 0 | 0 | 0 | 0 | 3 | 9 | 0 | 1 | R | R | 6-2 | 200 | 3-16-71 | 1992 | Rising Sun, Md. |
| Pearson, Gene, c | .326 | 48 | 190 | 23 | 62 | 16 | 0 | 1 | 26 | 13 | 29 | 0 | 1 | S | R | 6-3 | 225 | 1-31-74 | 1992 | Mobile, Ala. |
| Polidor, Wil, 3b-ss | .283 | 42 | 120 | 14 | 34 | 2 | 4 | 0 | 9 | 1 | 15 | 0 | 1 | S | R | 6-1 | 158 | 9-23-73 | 1991 | Caracas, Venez. |
| Rich, Ted, 1b | .228 | 26 | 79 | 5 | 18 | 1 | 1 | 2 | 11 | 6 | 23 | 1 | 1 | R | R | 6-1 | 210 | 8-13-69 | 1992 | Orange Park, Fla. |
| Saenz, Olmedo, 3b | .360 | 13 | 50 | 3 | 18 | 4 | 1 | 0 | 7 | 7 | 7 | 1 | 1 | R | R | 6-0 | 185 | 10-8-70 | 1990 | Chitre Herrera, Panama |
| Snopek, Chris, 3b | .389 | 22 | 72 | 20 | 28 | 8 | 1 | 5 | 18 | 15 | 13 | 1 | 1 | R | R | 6-1 | 185 | 9-20-70 | 1992 | Cynthiana, Ky. |
| Vinas, Julio, c | .319 | 55 | 188 | 24 | 60 | 15 | 1 | 9 | 37 | 12 | 29 | 1 | 1 | R | R | 6-0 | 200 | 2-14-73 | 1991 | Hialeah, Fla. |
| Vogel, Mike, dh-c | .269 | 24 | 78 | 7 | 21 | 7 | 0 | 1 | 8 | 8 | 24 | 1 | 0 | S | R | 6-2 | 190 | 1-15-72 | 1990 | Brooklyn Park, Minn. |
| Wilson, Craig, ss | .259 | 132 | 455 | 56 | 118 | 27 | 2 | 5 | 59 | 49 | 50 | 4 | 4 | R | R | 6-1 | 190 | 9-3-70 | 1992 | Phoenix, Ariz. |

| PITCHING | W | L | ERA | G | GS | CG | SV | IP | H | R | ER | BB | SO | B | T | HT | WT | DOB | 1st Yr | Resides |
|---|---|---|---|---|---|---|---|---|---|---|---|---|---|---|---|---|---|---|---|---|
| Bertotti, Mike | 5 | 7 | 3.49 | 17 | 16 | 2 | 0 | 111 | 93 | 51 | 43 | 44 | 108 | L | L | 6-1 | 185 | 1-18-70 | 1991 | Highland Mills, N.Y. |
| Call, Mike | 15 | 7 | 3.78 | 26 | 26 | 4 | 0 | 176 | 187 | 87 | 74 | 31 | 109 | R | R | 6-0 | 180 | 11-6-68 | 1991 | Seattle, Wash. |
| Cary, Chuck | 1 | 1 | 2.00 | 8 | 3 | 0 | 1 | 18 | 13 | 4 | 4 | 1 | 28 | L | L | 6-4 | 210 | 3-3-60 | 1981 | Destin, Fla. |
| Culberson, Don | 0 | 1 | 9.60 | 9 | 1 | 0 | 1 | 15 | 24 | 18 | 16 | 14 | 7 | R | R | 6-2 | 195 | 12-31-70 | 1990 | Philadelphia, Miss. |
| Dixon, Jim | 0 | 0 | 4.85 | 10 | 0 | 0 | 0 | 13 | 17 | 8 | 7 | 5 | 10 | R | R | 6-2 | 210 | 10-7-72 | 1993 | Raton, N.M. |
| Fritz, Greg | 2 | 7 | 5.18 | 11 | 10 | 3 | 0 | 66 | 88 | 44 | 38 | 35 | 20 | L | L | 6-5 | 190 | 11-22-67 | 1990 | River Vale, N.J. |
| Gay, Chris | 0 | 0 | 5.16 | 12 | 0 | 0 | 1 | 23 | 25 | 16 | 13 | 9 | 14 | S | L | 6-0 | 190 | 12-24-69 | 1992 | Bedford, Texas |
| Jenkins, Jon | 2 | 1 | 1.93 | 16 | 0 | 0 | 1 | 23 | 10 | 9 | 5 | 26 | 31 | R | R | 5-8 | 210 | 6-3-68 | 1990 | Culpeper, Va. |

# WHITE SOX: MOST COMMON LINEUPS

| | Chicago | Nashville | Birmingham | Sarasota | South Bend | Hickory |
|---|---|---|---|---|---|---|
| | Majors | AAA | AA | A | A | A |
| C | Ron Karkovice (128) | Matt Merullo (83) | Rogelio Nunez (80) | Nilson Robledo (59) | Robert Machado (73) | Nerio Rodriguez (72) |
| 1B | Frank Thomas (150) | Chris Cron (91) | Mike Robertson (137) | Troy Fryman (74) | Troy Fryman (51) | Eddie Pearson (64) |
| 2B | Joey Cora (151) | Norberto Martin (137) | Ray Durham (120) | Doug Brady (110) | Essex Burton (132) | Frank Menechino (49) |
| 3B | Robin Ventura (155) | Ron Coomer (58) | Ron Coomer (54) | Chris Snopek (88) | Dan Fraraccio (35) | Chris Mader (71) |
| SS | Ozzie Guillen (133) | Esteban Beltre (134) | Brandon Wilson (133) | Glenn DiSarcina (114) | Craig Wilson (132) | Jimmy Reyes (47) |
| OF | Ellis Burks (146) | Brad Komminsk (100) | Jerry Wolak (136) | Kerry Valrie (114) | Byron Mathews (127) | Eric Richardson (118) |
| | Lance Johnson (146) | Mike Huff (87) | Kinnis Pledger (113) | Charles Poe (90) | Mike Cameron (112) | Marc Harris (75) |
| | Tim Raines (146) | Joe Hall (83) | Kevin Belcher (84) | Kevin Coughlin (89) | Carmine Cappuccio (86) | Maggio Ordonez (72) |
| DH | George Bell (102) | Drew Denson (79) | Scott Cepicky (83) | Mike Vogel (59) | Jimmy Hurst (34) | Juan Thomas (44) |
| SP | Fernandez/McDowell (34) | Steve Schrenk (20) | Steve Olsen (25) | Heathcott/Levine (26) | Call/Moore (26) | David Elsbernd (19) |
| RP | Scott Radinsky (73) | Brian Drahman (54) | Don Perigny (48) | Steve Gajkowski (43) | Jason Watkins (37) | Ricky Bennett (37) |

Full-season farm clubs only    No. of games at position in parenthesis

## WHITE SOX TOP 10 PROSPECTS

**How the White Sox Top 10 prospects, as judged by Baseball America prior to the 1993 season, fared in 1993:**

| Player, Pos. | Club (Class) | AVG | AB | H | HR | RBI | SB |
|---|---|---|---|---|---|---|---|
| 7. Chris Snopek, 3b | South Bend (A) | .389 | 72 | 28 | 5 | 18 | 1 |
| | Sarasota (A) | .245 | 371 | 91 | 10 | 50 | 3 |
| 8. Mike Robertson, 1b | Birmingham (AA) | .270 | 511 | 138 | 11 | 73 | 10 |
| 10 Brandon Wilson, ss | Birmingham (AA) | .270 | 500 | 135 | 2 | 48 | 43 |

| Player, Pos. | Club (Class) | W | L | ERA | IP | H | BB | SO |
|---|---|---|---|---|---|---|---|---|
| 1. Jason Bere, rhp | Nashville (AAA) | 5 | 1 | 2.37 | 49 | 36 | 25 | 52 |
| | Chicago | 12 | 5 | 3.47 | 143 | 109 | 81 | 129 |
| 2. James Baldwin, rhp | Birmingham (AA) | 8 | 5 | 2.25 | 120 | 94 | 43 | 107 |
| | Nashville (AAA) | 5 | 4 | 2.61 | 69 | 43 | 36 | 61 |
| 3. Scott Ruffcorn, rhp | Birmingham (AA) | 9 | 4 | 2.73 | 135 | 108 | 52 | 141 |
| | Nashville (AAA) | 2 | 2 | 2.80 | 45 | 30 | 8 | 44 |
| | Chicago | 0 | 2 | 8.10 | 10 | 9 | 10 | 2 |
| 4. Larry Thomas, lhp | Birmingham (AA) | 0 | 1 | 5.14 | 7 | 9 | 1 | 5 |
| | Nashville (AAA) | 4 | 6 | 5.99 | 101 | 114 | 32 | 67 |
| 5. Steve Olsen, rhp | Birmingham (AA) | 10 | 4 | 4.75 | 142 | 156 | 52 | 92 |
| 6. Johnny Ruffin, rhp* | Birmingham (AA) | 0 | 4 | 2.82 | 22 | 16 | 9 | 23 |
| | Nashville (AAA) | 3 | 4 | 3.30 | 60 | 48 | 16 | 69 |
| | Indy (AAA) | 1 | 1 | 1.35 | 7 | 3 | 2 | 6 |
| | Cincinnati | 2 | 1 | 3.58 | 38 | 36 | 11 | 30 |
| 9. Rod Bolton, rhp | Nashville (AAA) | 10 | 1 | 2.88 | 116 | 108 | 37 | 75 |
| | Chicago | 2 | 6 | 7.44 | 42 | 55 | 16 | 17 |

*Traded to Cincinnati Reds

**Jason Bere**
12-5 at Chicago

### PITCHING

| | W | L | ERA | G | GS | CG | SV | IP | H | R | ER | BB | SO | B | T | HT | WT | DOB | 1st Yr | Resides |
|---|---|---|---|---|---|---|---|---|---|---|---|---|---|---|---|---|---|---|---|---|
| Johnston, Sean | 8 | 3 | 2.20 | 15 | 15 | 2 | 0 | 98 | 83 | 30 | 24 | 28 | 59 | L | L | 6-0 | 185 | 12-10-70 | 1992 | Berlin, Conn. |
| Keating, David | 1 | 0 | 3.12 | 6 | 0 | 0 | 1 | 9 | 6 | 3 | 3 | 2 | 6 | R | L | 6-1 | 195 | 11-6-67 | 1989 | Salinas, Calif. |
| Lindemann, Wayne | 3 | 2 | 4.26 | 12 | 11 | 1 | 0 | 70 | 76 | 37 | 33 | 21 | 48 | L | L | 6-1 | 205 | 12-19-69 | 1992 | Longview, Wash. |
| McCaskill, Kirk | 1 | 0 | 1.50 | 1 | 1 | 0 | 0 | 6 | 3 | 2 | 1 | 3 | 5 | R | R | 6-1 | 205 | 4-9-61 | 1982 | Corona Del Mar, Calif. |
| McDermott, Jim | 1 | 0 | 5.56 | 6 | 0 | 0 | 1 | 11 | 11 | 7 | 7 | 1 | 5 | R | R | 5-11 | 180 | 10-1-70 | 1992 | Plymouth, Pa. |
| Moore, Tim | 11 | 9 | 4.52 | 26 | 26 | 4 | 0 | 165 | 156 | 89 | 83 | 52 | 108 | R | R | 6-4 | 190 | 9-4-70 | 1992 | Irving, Texas |
| Pierson, Jason | 13 | 9 | 4.70 | 26 | 25 | 2 | 0 | 147 | 160 | 92 | 77 | 43 | 107 | R | L | 6-0 | 190 | 1-6-71 | 1992 | Berwyn, Pa. |
| Sirotka, Mike | 0 | 1 | 6.10 | 7 | 1 | 0 | 0 | 10 | 12 | 8 | 7 | 6 | 12 | L | L | 6-1 | 190 | 5-13-71 | 1993 | Houston, Texas |
| Tagle, Hank | 0 | 1 | 2.51 | 11 | 0 | 0 | 1 | 14 | 12 | 7 | 4 | 3 | 10 | L | L | 6-0 | 175 | 4-24-68 | 1991 | Sierra Vista, Ariz. |
| Watkins, Jason | 6 | 3 | 1.57 | 37 | 0 | 0 | 16 | 63 | 37 | 13 | 11 | 24 | 57 | R | R | 6-0 | 185 | 3-26-70 | 1992 | Longview, Texas |
| Winiarski, Chip | 4 | 4 | 4.85 | 34 | 0 | 0 | 3 | 56 | 59 | 38 | 30 | 18 | 31 | R | R | 6-2 | 190 | 7-30-68 | 1990 | South Amherst, Ohio |
| Woodfin, Chris | 0 | 0 | 1.62 | 11 | 0 | 0 | 4 | 17 | 10 | 3 | 3 | 3 | 34 | R | R | 6-1 | 190 | 2-23-68 | 1991 | Statesville, N.C. |
| Woods, Brian | 0 | 1 | 3.86 | 2 | 1 | 0 | 0 | 7 | 7 | 5 | 3 | 3 | 4 | L | R | 6-6 | 212 | 6-7-71 | 1993 | West Caldwell, N.J. |
| Worrell, Steve | 4 | 2 | 1.68 | 36 | 0 | 0 | 10 | 59 | 37 | 12 | 11 | 23 | 57 | L | L | 6-2 | 190 | 11-25-69 | 1992 | Cape May, N.J. |

## HICKORY       A

### SOUTH ATLANTIC LEAGUE

#### BATTING

| | AVG | G | AB | R | H | 2B | 3B | HR | RBI | BB | SO | SB | CS | B | T | HT | WT | DOB | 1st Yr | Resides |
|---|---|---|---|---|---|---|---|---|---|---|---|---|---|---|---|---|---|---|---|---|
| Aquino, Geronimo, of | .000 | 4 | 10 | 0 | 0 | 0 | 0 | 0 | 0 | 0 | 8 | 0 | 0 | R | R | 6-1 | 160 | 7-9-71 | 1990 | San Pedro de Macoris, D.R. |
| Boulware, Ben, 2b | .193 | 18 | 57 | 6 | 11 | 2 | 0 | 0 | 3 | 8 | 10 | 2 | 1 | R | R | 5-11 | 185 | 2-25-72 | 1993 | Los Gatos, Calif. |
| Evans, Jason, of-2b | .212 | 82 | 274 | 26 | 58 | 6 | 1 | 1 | 29 | 31 | 56 | 11 | 4 | S | R | 5-11 | 187 | 2-11-71 | 1992 | Venice, Calif. |
| Faircloth, Wayne, c | .173 | 25 | 81 | 4 | 14 | 2 | 0 | 0 | 4 | 3 | 25 | 0 | 0 | R | R | 6-3 | 185 | 6-3-71 | 1992 | Winston-Salem, N.C. |
| Fraraccio, Dan, ss | .211 | 41 | 147 | 13 | 31 | 9 | 1 | 1 | 15 | 6 | 21 | 2 | 2 | R | R | 5-11 | 175 | 9-18-70 | 1992 | Bradenton, Fla. |
| Harris, Marc, of | .188 | 79 | 250 | 24 | 47 | 10 | 4 | 0 | 14 | 21 | 74 | 15 | 8 | R | R | 6-3 | 185 | 2-19-73 | 1991 | Camden, Del. |
| Hollrah, Scot, 2b-3b | .236 | 59 | 148 | 23 | 35 | 4 | 0 | 0 | 8 | 18 | 34 | 10 | 6 | L | R | 5-10 | 165 | 8-21-70 | 1992 | St. Charles, Mo. |
| Levias, Andres, of | .165 | 25 | 85 | 8 | 14 | 2 | 0 | 1 | 7 | 6 | 17 | 6 | 2 | S | R | 6-1 | 195 | 10-1-73 | 1992 | Hawthorne, Calif. |
| Mader, Chris, 3b-dh | .270 | 120 | 396 | 54 | 107 | 25 | 1 | 7 | 49 | 81 | 90 | 2 | 0 | R | R | 6-0 | 195 | 10-6-70 | 1992 | Tewksbury, Mass. |
| McKinnon, Sandy, of | .251 | 64 | 263 | 29 | 66 | 10 | 3 | 0 | 21 | 21 | 47 | 17 | 12 | R | R | 5-8 | 175 | 9-20-73 | 1993 | Nicholls, Ga. |
| Menechino, Frank, 2b | .281 | 50 | 178 | 35 | 50 | 6 | 3 | 4 | 19 | 33 | 28 | 11 | 2 | R | R | 5-9 | 175 | 1-7-71 | 1993 | Staten Island, N.Y. |
| Miranda, Geovany, ss | .234 | 33 | 107 | 13 | 25 | 3 | 0 | 0 | 6 | 5 | 8 | 4 | 2 | R | R | 5-11 | 170 | 2-16-70 | 1988 | Chiriqui, Panama |
| Mumma, Bob, c-1b | .213 | 23 | 61 | 8 | 13 | 3 | 1 | 1 | 5 | 10 | 16 | 0 | 1 | R | R | 6-2 | 200 | 3-16-71 | 1992 | Rising Sun, Md. |
| Norton, Greg, 3b-ss | .244 | 71 | 254 | 36 | 62 | 12 | 2 | 4 | 36 | 41 | 44 | 0 | 2 | S | R | 6-1 | 182 | 7-6-72 | 1993 | Walnut Creek, Calif. |
| Ordonez, Magglio, of | .216 | 84 | 273 | 32 | 59 | 14 | 4 | 3 | 20 | 26 | 66 | 5 | 5 | R | R | 5-11 | 155 | 1-28-74 | 1991 | Coro Falcon, Venez. |
| Patton, Scott, of | .181 | 38 | 116 | 13 | 21 | 3 | 0 | 0 | 11 | 22 | 50 | 5 | 3 | R | R | 6-0 | 190 | 10-7-73 | 1992 | Mission Viejo, Calif. |
| Pearson, Eddie, 1b | .242 | 87 | 343 | 37 | 83 | 15 | 3 | 4 | 40 | 20 | 59 | 5 | 1 | S | R | 6-3 | 225 | 1-31-74 | 1992 | Mobile, Ala. |
| Polidor, Wil, ss | .233 | 15 | 43 | 4 | 10 | 0 | 0 | 0 | 3 | 2 | 7 | 0 | 1 | S | R | 6-1 | 158 | 9-23-73 | 1991 | Caracas, Venez. |
| Randle, Mike, 2b-3b | .000 | 3 | 6 | 1 | 0 | 0 | 0 | 0 | 0 | 0 | 2 | 0 | 0 | R | R | 5-9 | 170 | 8-4-70 | 1992 | St. Louis, Mo. |
| Reyes, Jimmy, ss-2b | .218 | 77 | 262 | 38 | 57 | 1 | 7 | 0 | 23 | 42 | 64 | 9 | 8 | S | R | 6-1 | 165 | 5-6-72 | 1991 | New York, N.Y. |
| Rich, Ted, 1b | .164 | 16 | 55 | 5 | 9 | 1 | 0 | 2 | 5 | 4 | 21 | 0 | 0 | R | R | 6-1 | 210 | 8-13-69 | 1992 | Orange Park, Fla. |
| Richardson, Eric, of | .231 | 119 | 412 | 40 | 95 | 9 | 1 | 2 | 30 | 19 | 75 | 42 | 15 | R | R | 6-0 | 179 | 9-6-72 | 1991 | Brenham, Texas |
| Rodriguez, Nerio, c | .206 | 82 | 262 | 31 | 54 | 9 | 2 | 4 | 32 | 27 | 70 | 4 | 0 | R | R | 6-0 | 180 | 3-22-73 | 1991 | San Pedro de Macoris, D.R. |
| Starks, Fred, p-dh | .150 | 20 | 20 | 2 | 3 | 0 | 0 | 0 | 0 | 3 | 9 | 0 | 0 | L | R | 6-4 | 205 | 2-18-71 | 1991 | Rockledge, Fla. |
| Thomas, Juan, 1b-dh | .229 | 90 | 328 | 51 | 75 | 14 | 6 | 12 | 46 | 35 | 124 | 2 | 4 | R | R | 6-5 | 240 | 4-17-72 | 1991 | Ashland, Ky. |
| Tremie, Chris, c | .187 | 49 | 155 | 7 | 29 | 6 | 1 | 1 | 17 | 9 | 26 | 0 | 0 | R | R | 6-0 | 200 | 10-17-69 | 1992 | Houston, Texas |

#### PITCHING

| | W | L | ERA | G | GS | CG | SV | IP | H | R | ER | BB | SO | B | T | HT | WT | DOB | 1st Yr | Resides |
|---|---|---|---|---|---|---|---|---|---|---|---|---|---|---|---|---|---|---|---|---|
| Bennett, Ricky | 8 | 7 | 3.29 | 41 | 4 | 0 | 6 | 112 | 112 | 50 | 41 | 23 | 98 | R | R | 6-3 | 195 | 1-23-70 | 1992 | Cincinnati, Ohio |
| Bertotti, Mike | 3 | 3 | 2.11 | 9 | 9 | 2 | 0 | 60 | 42 | 19 | 14 | 29 | 77 | L | L | 6-1 | 185 | 1-18-70 | 1991 | Highland Mills, N.Y. |
| Brincks, Mark | 2 | 4 | 3.84 | 30 | 0 | 0 | 0 | 68 | 64 | 32 | 29 | 26 | 60 | R | R | 5-11 | 190 | 1-8-70 | 1992 | Calamar, Iowa |
| Culberson, Don | 2 | 1 | 4.56 | 29 | 0 | 0 | 5 | 53 | 49 | 33 | 27 | 32 | 43 | R | R | 6-2 | 195 | 12-31-70 | 1990 | Philadelphia, Miss. |
| Elsbernd, David | 2 | 9 | 4.37 | 19 | 19 | 2 | 0 | 105 | 107 | 74 | 51 | 41 | 71 | R | R | 6-4 | 210 | 4-22-71 | 1992 | Arlington, Texas |
| Fitzpatrick, Dave | 0 | 1 | 7.50 | 6 | 0 | 0 | 1 | 12 | 17 | 11 | 10 | 3 | 13 | R | R | 6-2 | 200 | 1-22-73 | 1991 | Kingsport, Tenn. |
| Fordham, Tom | 4 | 3 | 3.88 | 8 | 8 | 1 | 0 | 49 | 36 | 21 | 21 | 21 | 27 | L | L | 6-2 | 210 | 2-20-74 | 1993 | El Cajon, Calif. |
| Gay, Chris | 3 | 2 | 3.06 | 13 | 8 | 2 | 0 | 71 | 67 | 30 | 24 | 19 | 43 | S | L | 6-0 | 190 | 12-24-69 | 1992 | Bedford, Texas |
| Lehman, Toby | 3 | 3 | 3.51 | 39 | 7 | 1 | 7 | 103 | 64 | 40 | 57 | 91 | R | R | 6-0 | 200 | 8-12-71 | 1992 | Vista, Calif. |

| PITCHING | W | L | ERA | G | GS | CG | SV | IP | H | R | ER | BB | SO | B | T | HT | WT | DOB | 1st Yr | Resides |
|---|---|---|---|---|---|---|---|---|---|---|---|---|---|---|---|---|---|---|---|---|
| Lindemann, Wayne ....... | 6 | 8 | 3.62 | 15 | 15 | 2 | 0 | 99 | 95 | 51 | 40 | 32 | 58 | L | L | 6-1 | 205 | 12-19-69 | 1992 | Longview, Wash. |
| Malaver, Johnny ............. | 1 | 1 | 10.38 | 9 | 0 | 0 | 0 | 13 | 20 | 19 | 15 | 14 | 6 | R | R | 6-4 | 170 | 2-11-73 | 1990 | Caracas, Venez. |
| McCormack, Andy ........ | 4 | 7 | 4.64 | 14 | 14 | 1 | 0 | 83 | 89 | 47 | 43 | 26 | 67 | L | L | 6-1 | 205 | 2-4-74 | 1993 | Raynham, Mass. |
| McGraw, Doug................ | 1 | 0 | 1.38 | 5 | 1 | 0 | 0 | 13 | 13 | 4 | 2 | 7 | 14 | R | R | 6-4 | 190 | 4-25-72 | 1990 | Duncanville, Texas |
| McKinion, Mickey ......... | 2 | 8 | 5.04 | 17 | 15 | 0 | 0 | 86 | 83 | 57 | 48 | 48 | 54 | S | R | 6-2 | 180 | 10-14-73 | 1992 | Wilmer, Ala. |
| Ogden, Jason ................ | 0 | 1 | 3.24 | 9 | 0 | 0 | 0 | 17 | 19 | 8 | 6 | 8 | 18 | R | R | 6-1 | 190 | 10-3-69 | 1992 | Houston, Texas |
| Pratt, Rich ...................... | 1 | 4 | 3.68 | 13 | 4 | 0 | 2 | 44 | 36 | 23 | 18 | 24 | 29 | L | L | 6-3 | 201 | 5-7-71 | 1993 | East Hartford, Conn. |
| Proctor, William.............. | 3 | 4 | 6.75 | 21 | 0 | 0 | 1 | 29 | 29 | 23 | 22 | 18 | 19 | R | R | 6-2 | 205 | 12-2-70 | 1993 | Lebanon, Ore. |
| Quirk, John .................... | 3 | 4 | 4.97 | 10 | 10 | 0 | 0 | 51 | 55 | 34 | 28 | 31 | 30 | L | L | 6-4 | 210 | 11-20-70 | 1993 | Bronx, N.Y. |
| Soto, Juan ..................... | 0 | 2 | 3.60 | 3 | 3 | 0 | 0 | 15 | 13 | 7 | 6 | 8 | 9 | R | R | 6-1 | 160 | 7-15-72 | 1988 | Bani, D.R. |
| Starks, Fred ................... | 1 | 7 | 7.43 | 14 | 5 | 0 | 0 | 40 | 44 | 40 | 33 | 47 | 34 | R | R | 6-5 | 240 | 4-17-72 | 1991 | Rockledge, Fla. |
| Theodile, Robert ............ | 0 | 4 | 6.75 | 8 | 8 | 0 | 0 | 45 | 63 | 40 | 34 | 21 | 23 | R | R | 6-3 | 190 | 9-16-72 | 1992 | Jeanerette, La. |
| Woods, Brian ................. | 2 | 5 | 2.51 | 10 | 10 | 0 | 0 | 61 | 49 | 20 | 17 | 31 | 53 | L | R | 6-6 | 212 | 6-7-71 | 1993 | West Caldwell, N.J. |

## SARASOTA   R
### GULF COAST LEAGUE

| BATTING | AVG | G | AB | R | H | 2B | 3B | HR | RBI | BB | SO | SB | CS | B | T | HT | WT | DOB | 1st Yr | Resides |
|---|---|---|---|---|---|---|---|---|---|---|---|---|---|---|---|---|---|---|---|---|
| Alvarez, Clemente, c ..... | .000 | 2 | 5 | 0 | 0 | 0 | 0 | 0 | 0 | 1 | 2 | 0 | 1 | R | R | 5-11 | 180 | 5-18-68 | 1987 | Anzoategui, Venez. |
| Aquino, Geronimo, of .... | .103 | 13 | 29 | 1 | 3 | 1 | 0 | 0 | 2 | 1 | 12 | 0 | 1 | R | R | 6-1 | 160 | 7-9-71 | 1990 | San Pedro de Macoris, D.R. |
| Blackburn, Tyres, of ...... | .256 | 31 | 78 | 9 | 20 | 1 | 1 | 0 | 5 | 6 | 22 | 6 | 1 | R | R | 5-11 | 185 | 5-19-71 | 1992 | Dallas, Texas |
| Boulware, Ben, 2b......... | .208 | 33 | 106 | 19 | 22 | 3 | 0 | 2 | 11 | 20 | 11 | 13 | 1 | R | R | 5-11 | 185 | 2-25-72 | 1993 | Los Gatos, Calif. |
| Carone, Rich, c ............. | .239 | 27 | 88 | 12 | 21 | 4 | 1 | 2 | 14 | 8 | 19 | 2 | 0 | R | R | 6-0 | 195 | 1-17-71 | 1993 | Cary, Ill. |
| Friedrich, Steve, 2b....... | .262 | 28 | 84 | 10 | 22 | 2 | 0 | 0 | 11 | 6 | 12 | 7 | 5 | R | R | 6-0 | 175 | 5-29-73 | 1993 | Yorba Linda, Calif. |
| Goligoski, Jason, ss ...... | .258 | 54 | 163 | 30 | 42 | 12 | 2 | 2 | 27 | 34 | 18 | 16 | 9 | L | R | 6-1 | 180 | 10-2-71 | 1993 | Hamilton, Mont. |
| Hall, Todd, 3b-dh........... | .241 | 34 | 83 | 15 | 20 | 8 | 1 | 0 | 11 | 16 | 7 | 4 | 2 | R | R | 6-0 | 175 | 10-5-71 | 1993 | Placerville, Calif. |
| Hobert, Billy Joe, of ...... | .256 | 15 | 39 | 3 | 10 | 2 | 0 | 0 | 4 | 6 | 5 | 1 | 1 | | | 6-3 | 225 | 1-8-71 | 1993 | Puyallup, Wash. |
| Izquierdo, Nelson, 3b..... | .318 | 11 | 22 | 5 | 7 | 1 | 0 | 0 | 3 | 3 | 2 | 0 | 0 | R | R | 6-1 | 180 | 7-22-70 | 1992 | Hialeah, Fla. |
| Levias, Andres, of ......... | .209 | 39 | 86 | 18 | 18 | 2 | 3 | 0 | 5 | 14 | 15 | 9 | 4 | S | R | 6-1 | 195 | 10-1-73 | 1992 | Hawthorne, Calif. |
| McClure, Craig, of ........ | .245 | 58 | 200 | 36 | 49 | 8 | 3 | 2 | 25 | 40 | 66 | 17 | 8 | R | R | 6-1 | 175 | 8-4-75 | 1993 | Littleton, Colo. |
| McKinnon, Sandy, of ..... | .182 | 6 | 11 | 2 | 2 | 0 | 0 | 0 | 3 | 2 | 4 | 0 | 0 | R | R | 5-8 | 175 | 9-20-73 | 1993 | Nicholls, Ga. |
| Menechino, Frank, 2b ... | .244 | 17 | 45 | 10 | 11 | 4 | 1 | 1 | 9 | 12 | 4 | 3 | 1 | R | R | 5-9 | 175 | 1-7-71 | 1993 | Staten Island, N.Y. |
| Moore, David, 3b........... | .239 | 47 | 134 | 16 | 32 | 3 | 1 | 1 | 16 | 21 | 47 | 4 | 4 | R | R | 6-3 | 185 | 10-9-74 | 1993 | Windemere, Fla. |
| Norton, Greg, 3b .......... | .222 | 3 | 9 | 1 | 2 | 0 | 0 | 0 | 2 | 1 | 1 | 0 | 0 | S | R | 6-1 | 182 | 7-6-72 | 1993 | Walnut Creek, Calif. |
| Patton, Scott, of............ | .189 | 50 | 159 | 19 | 30 | 8 | 2 | 0 | 16 | 31 | 46 | 10 | 7 | R | R | 6-0 | 190 | 10-7-73 | 1992 | Mission Viejo, Calif. |
| Poe, Charles, of-dh ....... | .308 | 3 | 13 | 2 | 4 | 3 | 0 | 1 | 2 | 1 | 3 | 0 | 1 | R | R | 6-0 | 185 | 11-9-71 | 1990 | West Covina, Calif. |
| Ridenour, Jim, c ........... | .308 | 7 | 13 | 3 | 4 | 0 | 0 | 0 | 2 | 2 | 2 | 0 | 0 | R | R | 5-11 | 190 | 11-29-70 | 1993 | Hope Mills, N.C. |
| Sanchez, Dan, ss .......... | .179 | 26 | 28 | 0 | 5 | 1 | 1 | 0 | 7 | 3 | 5 | 1 | 1 | S | R | 6-0 | 165 | 1-8-71 | 1989 | San Pedro de Macoris, D.R. |
| Spry, Shane, 1b-dh ....... | .239 | 43 | 117 | 19 | 28 | 6 | 0 | 0 | 10 | 15 | 24 | 6 | 3 | L | L | 5-11 | 185 | 9-4-75 | 1993 | Spearwood, Australia |
| Starks, Fred, dh-of ....... | .294 | 9 | 17 | 2 | 5 | 0 | 2 | 0 | 6 | 3 | 1 | 0 | 0 | L | R | 6-4 | 205 | 2-18-71 | 1991 | Rockledge, Fla. |
| Thomas, Juan, 1b.......... | .305 | 19 | 59 | 12 | 18 | 3 | 2 | 1 | 9 | 12 | 12 | 5 | 5 | R | R | 6-0 | 240 | 4-17-72 | 1991 | Ashland, Ky. |
| Tremie, Chris, c ............ | .000 | 2 | 4 | 0 | 0 | 0 | 0 | 0 | 0 | 0 | 0 | 0 | 0 | R | R | 6-0 | 200 | 10-17-69 | 1992 | Houston, Texas |
| Vollmer, Scott, c ........... | .273 | 43 | 132 | 19 | 36 | 9 | 0 | 0 | 11 | 17 | 11 | 3 | 4 | R | R | 6-1 | 175 | 2-9-71 | 1993 | Thousand Oaks, Calif. |
| Williams, Harold, 1b-dh . | .280 | 52 | 186 | 18 | 52 | 6 | 4 | 1 | 21 | 17 | 40 | 4 | 5 | L | L | 6-4 | 200 | 2-14-71 | 1993 | Garyville, La. |

| PITCHING | W | L | ERA | G | GS | CG | SV | IP | H | R | ER | BB | SO | B | T | HT | WT | DOB | 1st Yr | Resides |
|---|---|---|---|---|---|---|---|---|---|---|---|---|---|---|---|---|---|---|---|---|
| Baldwin, Will ................. | 0 | 2 | 6.75 | 4 | 0 | 0 | 0 | 13 | 11 | 11 | 10 | 17 | 12 | R | R | 6-4 | 210 | 8-27-70 | 1993 | Chicago, Ill. |
| Bales, Joe ..................... | 0 | 0 | 6.19 | 4 | 4 | 0 | 0 | 16 | 19 | 11 | 11 | 10 | 11 | R | R | 6-5 | 175 | 9-13-74 | 1993 | Reno, Nev. |
| Broome, Curtis .............. | 5 | 3 | 2.57 | 15 | 4 | 1 | 0 | 63 | 56 | 24 | 18 | 25 | 32 | R | R | 6-2 | 195 | 4-30-72 | 1993 | Gary, Ind. |
| Christman, Scott............ | 0 | 0 | 0.00 | 4 | 2 | 0 | 1 | 11 | 3 | 1 | 0 | 4 | 15 | L | L | 6-3 | 190 | 12-3-71 | 1993 | Vancouver, Wash. |
| Dixon, James................. | 0 | 1 | 0.90 | 3 | 0 | 0 | 0 | 10 | 8 | 2 | 1 | 1 | 7 | R | R | 6-2 | 210 | 10-7-72 | 1993 | Raton, N.M. |
| Dunne, Mike.................. | 0 | 0 | 0.00 | 3 | 2 | 0 | 0 | 6 | 3 | 1 | 0 | 1 | 9 | L | R | 6-4 | 212 | 10-27-62 | 1985 | Peoria, Ill. |
| Fitzpatrick, Dave ............ | 1 | 0 | 0.00 | 3 | 0 | 0 | 0 | 6 | 3 | 2 | 0 | 1 | 10 | R | R | 6-2 | 200 | 1-22-73 | 1991 | Kingsport, Tenn. |
| Forbes, Adam ................ | 0 | 1 | 2.31 | 7 | 0 | 0 | 1 | 12 | 4 | 5 | 3 | 4 | 16 | L | L | 6-3 | 175 | 1-27-75 | 1993 | Cambridge, Australia |
| Fordham, Tom ............... | 1 | 1 | 1.80 | 3 | 0 | 0 | 0 | 10 | 9 | 2 | 2 | 3 | 12 | L | L | 6-2 | 210 | 2-20-74 | 1993 | El Cajon, Calif. |
| Garcia, Ariel ................. | 5 | 2 | 3.15 | 12 | 11 | 0 | 0 | 69 | 71 | 34 | 24 | 12 | 36 | R | R | 6-0 | 158 | 10-3-75 | 1993 | Panama City, Panama |
| Gomez, Gus .................. | 1 | 0 | 2.08 | 13 | 0 | 0 | 6 | 17 | 10 | 4 | 4 | 9 | 28 | R | R | 5-10 | 170 | 10-28-73 | 1991 | Caracas, Venez. |
| Hassen, Ted .................. | 3 | 3 | 2.74 | 14 | 0 | 0 | 1 | 23 | 17 | 12 | 7 | 18 | 19 | R | R | 6-0 | 190 | 10-22-70 | 1993 | College Park, Ga. |
| Leiber, Zane ................. | 0 | 2 | 2.66 | 15 | 0 | 0 | 3 | 20 | 12 | 10 | 6 | 21 | 11 | R | R | 6-2 | 190 | 7-15-73 | 1993 | Tucson, Ariz. |
| Lundquist, Dave ............ | 5 | 3 | 3.14 | 11 | 10 | 0 | 0 | 63 | 70 | 26 | 22 | 15 | 40 | R | R | 6-2 | 200 | 6-4-73 | 1993 | Carson City, Nev. |
| Matznick, Dan ............... | 0 | 2 | 2.13 | 9 | 9 | 0 | 0 | 25 | 17 | 11 | 6 | 12 | 35 | R | R | 6-2 | 190 | 7-9-71 | 1989 | Sterling, Ill. |
| McCormack, Andy .......... | 0 | 0 | 0.00 | 1 | 1 | 0 | 0 | 6 | 1 | 0 | 0 | 0 | 7 | L | L | 6-1 | 205 | 2-4-74 | 1993 | Raynham, Mass. |
| McKinion, Mickey............ | 1 | 1 | 3.06 | 6 | 2 | 0 | 2 | 18 | 13 | 6 | 6 | 5 | 10 | S | R | 6-2 | 180 | 10-14-73 | 1992 | Wilmer, Ala. |
| Merigliano, Frank............ | 1 | 1 | 2.25 | 3 | 0 | 0 | 0 | 4 | 2 | 1 | 1 | 1 | 8 | R | R | 6-2 | 180 | 11-10-66 | 1988 | Pittsburgh, Pa. |
| Ogden, Jason ................ | 0 | 0 | 1.50 | 4 | 0 | 0 | 0 | 6 | 4 | 2 | 1 | 1 | 3 | R | R | 6-1 | 190 | 10-3-69 | 1992 | Houston, Texas |
| Pratt, Rich .................... | 0 | 1 | 2.70 | 3 | 0 | 0 | 0 | 10 | 10 | 3 | 3 | 2 | 10 | L | L | 6-3 | 201 | 5-7-71 | 1993 | East Hartford, Conn. |
| Proctor, William.............. | 0 | 0 | 0.00 | 2 | 0 | 0 | 0 | 4 | 4 | 1 | 0 | 2 | 1 | R | R | 6-2 | 205 | 12-2-70 | 1993 | Lebanon, Ore. |
| Quirk, John ................... | 2 | 0 | 0.86 | 4 | 4 | 0 | 0 | 21 | 16 | 2 | 2 | 2 | 10 | L | L | 6-4 | 210 | 11-20-70 | 1993 | Bronx, N.Y. |
| Sirotka, Mike ................. | 0 | 0 | 0.00 | 3 | 0 | 0 | 0 | 5 | 4 | 1 | 0 | 2 | 8 | L | L | 6-1 | 190 | 5-13-71 | 1993 | Houston, Texas |
| Theodile, Robert ............ | 5 | 2 | 2.59 | 10 | 8 | 1 | 1 | 66 | 45 | 24 | 19 | 23 | 42 | R | R | 6-3 | 190 | 9-16-72 | 1992 | Jeanerette, La. |
| Woodfin, Chris ............... | 1 | 0 | 0.00 | 4 | 0 | 0 | 0 | 5 | 1 | 1 | 0 | 0 | 7 | R | R | 6-1 | 190 | 2-23-68 | 1991 | Statesville, N.C. |
| Woods, Brian ................. | 0 | 0 | 2.25 | 2 | 2 | 0 | 0 | 8 | 4 | 3 | 2 | 6 | 6 | L | R | 6-6 | 212 | 6-7-71 | 1993 | West Caldwell, N.J. |

# CHICAGO CUBS

**Manager:** Jim Lefebvre.  **1993 Record:** 84-78, .519 (4th, NL East).

| BATTING | AVG | G | AB | R | H | 2B | 3B | HR | RBI | BB | SO | SB | CS | B | T | HT | WT | DOB | 1st Yr | Resides |
|---|---|---|---|---|---|---|---|---|---|---|---|---|---|---|---|---|---|---|---|---|
| Buechele, Steve | .272 | 133 | 460 | 53 | 125 | 27 | 2 | 15 | 65 | 48 | 87 | 1 | 1 | R | R | 6-2 | 200 | 9-26-61 | 1982 | Arlington, Texas |
| Dunston, Shawon | .400 | 7 | 10 | 3 | 4 | 2 | 0 | 0 | 2 | 0 | 1 | 0 | 0 | R | R | 6-1 | 175 | 3-21-63 | 1982 | Fremont, Calif. |
| Grace, Mark | .325 | 155 | 594 | 86 | 193 | 39 | 4 | 14 | 98 | 71 | 32 | 8 | 4 | L | L | 6-2 | 190 | 6-28-64 | 1986 | Pacific Palisades, Calif. |
| Hill, Glenallen | .345 | 31 | 87 | 14 | 30 | 7 | 0 | 10 | 22 | 6 | 21 | 1 | 0 | R | R | 6-2 | 210 | 3-22-65 | 1983 | Boca Raton, Fla. |
| Jennings, Doug | .250 | 42 | 52 | 8 | 13 | 3 | 1 | 2 | 8 | 3 | 10 | 0 | 0 | L | L | 5-10 | 170 | 9-30-64 | 1984 | Tallahassee, Fla. |
| Lake, Steve | .225 | 44 | 120 | 11 | 27 | 6 | 0 | 5 | 13 | 4 | 19 | 0 | 0 | R | R | 6-1 | 180 | 3-14-57 | 1975 | Glendale, Ariz. |
| Maldonado, Candy | .186 | 70 | 140 | 8 | 26 | 5 | 0 | 3 | 15 | 13 | 40 | 0 | 0 | R | R | 5-11 | 195 | 9-5-60 | 1978 | Arecibo, P.R. |
| May, Derrick | .295 | 128 | 465 | 62 | 137 | 25 | 2 | 10 | 77 | 31 | 41 | 10 | 3 | L | R | 6-4 | 200 | 7-14-68 | 1986 | Newark, Del. |
| Rhodes, Karl | .288 | 15 | 52 | 12 | 15 | 2 | 1 | 3 | 7 | 11 | 9 | 2 | 0 | L | L | 5-11 | 170 | 8-21-68 | 1986 | Cincinnati, Ohio |
| 2-team (5 Houston) | .278 | 20 | 54 | 12 | 15 | 2 | 1 | 3 | 7 | 11 | 9 | 2 | 0 | | | | | | | |
| Roberson, Kevin | .189 | 62 | 180 | 23 | 34 | 4 | 1 | 9 | 27 | 12 | 48 | 0 | 1 | S | R | 6-4 | 210 | 1-29-68 | 1988 | Decatur, Ill. |
| Sanchez, Rey | .282 | 105 | 344 | 35 | 97 | 11 | 2 | 0 | 28 | 15 | 22 | 1 | 1 | R | R | 5-9 | 180 | 10-5-67 | 1986 | Rio Piedras, P.R. |
| Sandberg, Ryne | .309 | 117 | 456 | 67 | 141 | 20 | 6 | 9 | 45 | 37 | 62 | 9 | 2 | R | R | 6-1 | 175 | 9-18-59 | 1978 | Phoenix, Ariz. |
| Shields, Tommy | .176 | 20 | 34 | 4 | 6 | 1 | 0 | 0 | 1 | 2 | 10 | 0 | 0 | R | R | 6-0 | 175 | 8-14-64 | 1986 | Devon, Pa. |
| Smith, Dwight | .300 | 111 | 310 | 51 | 93 | 17 | 5 | 11 | 35 | 25 | 51 | 8 | 6 | L | R | 5-11 | 177 | 11-8-63 | 1984 | Atlanta, Ga. |
| Sosa, Sammy | .261 | 159 | 598 | 92 | 156 | 25 | 5 | 33 | 93 | 38 | 135 | 36 | 11 | R | R | 6-0 | 165 | 11-12-68 | 1986 | San Pedro de Macoris, D.R. |
| Vizcaino, Jose | .287 | 151 | 551 | 74 | 158 | 19 | 4 | 4 | 54 | 46 | 71 | 12 | 9 | S | R | 6-1 | 180 | 3-26-68 | 1987 | El Cajon, Calif. |
| Walbeck, Matt | .200 | 11 | 30 | 2 | 6 | 2 | 0 | 1 | 6 | 1 | 6 | 0 | 0 | S | R | 6-0 | 192 | 10-2-69 | 1987 | Sacramento, Calif. |
| Wilkins, Rick | .303 | 136 | 446 | 78 | 135 | 23 | 1 | 30 | 73 | 50 | 99 | 2 | 1 | L | R | 6-2 | 210 | 6-4-67 | 1987 | Jacksonville, Fla. |
| Wilson, Willie | .258 | 105 | 221 | 29 | 57 | 11 | 3 | 1 | 11 | 11 | 40 | 7 | 2 | S | R | 6-3 | 195 | 7-9-55 | 1974 | Leawood, Kan. |
| Yelding, Eric | .204 | 69 | 108 | 14 | 22 | 5 | 1 | 1 | 10 | 11 | 22 | 3 | 2 | R | R | 5-11 | 165 | 2-22-65 | 1984 | Daphne, Ala. |
| Zambrano, Eddie | .294 | 8 | 17 | 1 | 5 | 0 | 0 | 2 | 1 | 3 | 0 | 0 | 0 | R | R | 6-2 | 175 | 2-1-66 | 1985 | Maracaibo, Venez. |

| PITCHING | W | L | ERA | G | GS | CG | SV | IP | H | R | ER | BB | SO | B | T | HT | WT | DOB | 1st Yr | Resides |
|---|---|---|---|---|---|---|---|---|---|---|---|---|---|---|---|---|---|---|---|---|
| Assenmacher, Paul | 2 | 1 | 3.49 | 46 | 0 | 0 | 0 | 39 | 44 | 15 | 15 | 13 | 34 | L | L | 6-3 | 195 | 12-10-60 | 1983 | Stone Mountain, Ga. |
| Bautista, Jose | 10 | 3 | 2.82 | 58 | 7 | 1 | 2 | 112 | 105 | 38 | 35 | 27 | 63 | R | R | 6-2 | 207 | 7-25-64 | 1981 | Cooper City, Fla. |
| Boskie, Shawn | 5 | 3 | 3.43 | 39 | 2 | 0 | 0 | 66 | 63 | 30 | 25 | 21 | 39 | R | R | 6-3 | 205 | 3-28-67 | 1986 | Reno, Nev. |
| Brennan, Bill | 2 | 1 | 4.20 | 8 | 1 | 0 | 0 | 15 | 16 | 8 | 7 | 8 | 11 | R | R | 6-3 | 185 | 1-15-63 | 1985 | Kenesaw, Ga. |
| Bullinger, Jim | 1 | 0 | 4.32 | 15 | 0 | 0 | 1 | 17 | 18 | 9 | 8 | 9 | 10 | R | R | 6-2 | 180 | 8-21-65 | 1986 | Sarasota, Fla. |
| Castillo, Frank | 5 | 8 | 4.84 | 29 | 25 | 2 | 0 | 141 | 162 | 83 | 76 | 39 | 84 | R | R | 6-1 | 185 | 4-1-69 | 1987 | El Paso, Texas |
| Guzman, Jose | 12 | 10 | 4.34 | 30 | 30 | 2 | 0 | 191 | 188 | 98 | 92 | 74 | 163 | R | R | 6-3 | 195 | 4-9-63 | 1981 | Arlington, Texas |
| Harkey, Mike | 10 | 10 | 5.26 | 28 | 28 | 1 | 0 | 157 | 187 | 100 | 92 | 43 | 67 | R | R | 6-5 | 220 | 10-25-66 | 1987 | Chino Hills, Calif. |
| Hibbard, Greg | 15 | 11 | 3.96 | 31 | 31 | 1 | 0 | 191 | 209 | 96 | 84 | 47 | 82 | L | L | 6-0 | 190 | 9-13-64 | 1986 | Gulfport, Miss. |
| McElroy, Chuck | 2 | 2 | 4.56 | 49 | 0 | 0 | 0 | 47 | 51 | 30 | 24 | 25 | 31 | L | L | 6-0 | 180 | 10-1-67 | 1986 | Beaumont, Texas |
| Morgan, Mike | 10 | 15 | 4.03 | 32 | 32 | 1 | 0 | 208 | 206 | 100 | 93 | 74 | 111 | R | R | 6-2 | 222 | 10-8-59 | 1978 | Ogden, Utah |
| Myers, Randy | 2 | 4 | 3.11 | 73 | 0 | 0 | 53 | 75 | 65 | 26 | 26 | 26 | 86 | L | L | 6-1 | 210 | 9-19-62 | 1982 | Vancouver, Wash. |
| Plesac, Dan | 2 | 1 | 4.74 | 57 | 0 | 0 | 0 | 63 | 74 | 37 | 33 | 21 | 47 | L | L | 6-5 | 215 | 2-4-62 | 1983 | Hales Corners, Wis. |
| Scanlan, Bob | 4 | 5 | 4.54 | 70 | 0 | 0 | 0 | 75 | 79 | 41 | 38 | 28 | 44 | R | R | 6-8 | 215 | 8-9-66 | 1984 | Beverly Hills, Calif. |
| Slocumb, Heath | 1 | 0 | 3.38 | 10 | 0 | 0 | 0 | 11 | 7 | 5 | 4 | 4 | 4 | R | R | 6-3 | 180 | 6-7-66 | 1984 | Jamaica, N.Y. |
| Trachsel, Steve | 0 | 2 | 4.58 | 3 | 3 | 0 | 0 | 20 | 16 | 10 | 10 | 3 | 14 | R | R | 6-3 | 185 | 10-31-70 | 1991 | Yorba Linda, Calif. |
| Wendell, Turk | 1 | 2 | 4.37 | 7 | 4 | 0 | 0 | 23 | 24 | 13 | 11 | 8 | 15 | S | R | 6-2 | 175 | 5-19-67 | 1988 | Dalton, Mass. |

## FIELDING

| Catcher | PCT | G | PO | A | E | DP |
|---|---|---|---|---|---|---|
| Lake | .985 | 41 | 168 | 27 | 3 | 1 |
| Walbeck | 1.000 | 11 | 49 | 2 | 0 | 0 |
| Wilkins | .996 | 133 | 717 | 89 | 3 | 9 |

| First Base | PCT | G | PO | A | E | DP |
|---|---|---|---|---|---|---|
| Buechele | 1.000 | 6 | 18 | 0 | 0 | 3 |
| Grace | .997 | 154 | 1456 | 112 | 5 | 134 |
| Jennings | 1.000 | 10 | 80 | 2 | 0 | 8 |
| Shields | 1.000 | 1 | 0 | 1 | 0 | 0 |
| Zambrano | .929 | 2 | 13 | 0 | 1 | 1 |

| Second Base | PCT | G | PO | A | E | DP |
|---|---|---|---|---|---|---|
| Sandberg | .988 | 115 | 209 | 347 | 7 | 76 |
| Shields | 1.000 | 7 | 6 | 12 | 0 | 3 |

| | PCT | G | PO | A | E | DP |
|---|---|---|---|---|---|---|
| Vizcaino | .986 | 34 | 66 | 76 | 2 | 23 |
| Yelding | .984 | 32 | 48 | 76 | 2 | 14 |

| Third Base | PCT | G | PO | A | E | DP |
|---|---|---|---|---|---|---|
| Buechele | .975 | 129 | 79 | 232 | 8 | 24 |
| Shields | 1.000 | 7 | 2 | 9 | 0 | 1 |
| Vizcaino | .979 | 44 | 25 | 70 | 2 | 6 |
| Yelding | .923 | 7 | 3 | 9 | 1 | 1 |

| Shortstop | PCT | G | PO | A | E | DP |
|---|---|---|---|---|---|---|
| Dunston | 1.000 | 2 | 5 | 0 | 0 | 0 |
| Sanchez | .969 | 98 | 158 | 316 | 15 | 60 |
| Vizcaino | .968 | 81 | 126 | 264 | 13 | 43 |
| Yelding | .500 | 1 | 0 | 1 | 1 | 0 |

| Outfield | PCT | G | PO | A | E | DP |
|---|---|---|---|---|---|---|
| Hill | .957 | 21 | 42 | 2 | 2 | 1 |
| Maldonado | .914 | 41 | 50 | 3 | 5 | 2 |
| May | .970 | 122 | 220 | 8 | 7 | 1 |
| Rhodes | .970 | 14 | 31 | 1 | 1 | 0 |
| Roberson | .963 | 51 | 77 | 2 | 3 | 0 |
| Shields | .000 | 1 | 0 | 0 | 0 | 0 |
| Smith | .955 | 89 | 163 | 5 | 8 | 2 |
| Sosa | .976 | 158 | 344 | 17 | 9 | 4 |
| Wilson | .991 | 82 | 109 | 1 | 1 | 0 |
| Yelding | 1.000 | 1 | 1 | 0 | 0 | 0 |
| Zambrano | 1.000 | 4 | 1 | 0 | 0 | 0 |

# CUBS FARM SYSTEM

| Class | Club | League | W | L | Pct. | Finish* | Manager | First Year |
|---|---|---|---|---|---|---|---|---|
| AAA | Iowa Cubs | American Assoc. | 85 | 59 | .590 | 1st† (8) | Marv Foley | 1981 |
| AA | Orlando (Fla.) Cubs | Southern | 71 | 70 | .504 | T-6th (10) | Tommy Jones | 1993 |
| A# | Daytona (Fla.) Cubs | Florida State | 57 | 76 | .429 | 10th (13) | Bill Hayes | 1993 |
| A | Peoria (Ill.) Chiefs | Midwest | 59 | 79 | .428 | 12th (14) | Steve Roadcap | 1985 |
| A | Geneva (N.Y.) Cubs | New York-Penn | 43 | 34 | .558 | 4th (14) | Jerry Weinstein | 1977 |
| Rookie# | Huntington (W.Va.) Cubs | Appalachian | 33 | 35 | .485 | 6th (10) | Steve Kolinsky | 1990 |
| Rookie | St. Lucie (Fla.) Cubs | Gulf Coast | 19 | 40 | .322 | 15th (15) | Butch Hughes | 1993 |

*Finish in overall standings (No. of teams in league)  #Advanced level  †Won league championship

**Mark Grace.** Cubs first baseman hit .325 and finished second in National League with 193 hits.

**Sammy Sosa.** With 33 homers and 36 stolen bases, Sosa was only 30-30 player in baseball in 1993.

# IOWA       AAA
## AMERICAN ASSOCIATION

| BATTING | AVG | G | AB | R | H | 2B | 3B | HR | RBI | BB | SO | SB | CS | B | T | HT | WT | DOB | 1st Yr | Resides |
|---|---|---|---|---|---|---|---|---|---|---|---|---|---|---|---|---|---|---|---|---|
| Anderson, Kent | .250 | 69 | 212 | 28 | 53 | 11 | 0 | 3 | 18 | 22 | 26 | 2 | 2 | R | R | 6-1 | 180 | 8-12-63 | 1984 | Timmonsville, S.C. |
| Chance, Tony | .282 | 101 | 294 | 50 | 83 | 23 | 1 | 16 | 46 | 38 | 73 | 5 | 5 | R | R | 6-1 | 191 | 10-26-64 | 1983 | Charleston, W.Va. |
| Dauphin, Phil | .222 | 20 | 54 | 5 | 12 | 4 | 1 | 1 | 2 | 10 | 9 | 2 | 0 | L | L | 6-1 | 180 | 5-11-69 | 1990 | Worthington, Ohio |
| Franco, Matt | .291 | 62 | 199 | 24 | 58 | 17 | 4 | 5 | 29 | 16 | 30 | 4 | 1 | L | R | 6-3 | 195 | 8-19-69 | 1987 | Thousand Oaks, Calif. |
| Gomez, Rudy | .150 | 9 | 20 | 0 | 3 | 0 | 0 | 0 | 0 | 1 | 8 | 0 | 0 | R | R | 5-10 | 165 | 6-8-69 | 1991 | Tempe, Ariz. |
| Grayum, Richie | .143 | 4 | 7 | 0 | 1 | 0 | 0 | 0 | 0 | 0 | 2 | 0 | 0 | L | R | 5-10 | 185 | 9-17-68 | 1989 | Green Cove Springs, Fla. |
| Hernandez, Jose | .250 | 6 | 24 | 3 | 6 | 1 | 0 | 0 | 3 | 0 | 2 | 0 | 0 | R | R | 6-0 | 180 | 7-14-69 | 1987 | Vega Alta, P.R. |
| Jennings, Doug | .294 | 65 | 228 | 38 | 67 | 20 | 1 | 7 | 37 | 29 | 64 | 3 | 4 | L | L | 5-10 | 170 | 9-30-64 | 1984 | Tallahassee, Fla. |
| Jensen, John | .177 | 25 | 62 | 5 | 11 | 3 | 0 | 2 | 8 | 7 | 18 | 2 | 1 | L | R | 6-2 | 215 | 11-30-66 | 1988 | Galveston, Texas |
| Lewis, Dan | .197 | 42 | 122 | 10 | 24 | 7 | 0 | 3 | 13 | 7 | 23 | 0 | 0 | L | L | 6-0 | 202 | 12-14-67 | 1986 | Hawthorne, Calif. |
| Lonigro, Greg | .254 | 43 | 114 | 14 | 29 | 5 | 0 | 3 | 10 | 10 | 16 | 2 | 2 | R | R | 6-1 | 180 | 11-20-65 | 1986 | Connellsville, Pa. |
| Mercado, Orlando | .357 | 8 | 28 | 4 | 10 | 2 | 0 | 1 | 5 | 1 | 6 | 0 | 0 | R | R | 6-0 | 195 | 11-7-61 | 1978 | Arecibo, P.R. |
| Pedre, George | .211 | 68 | 232 | 27 | 49 | 12 | 1 | 7 | 21 | 13 | 47 | 2 | 1 | R | R | 5-11 | 210 | 10-12-66 | 1987 | Buena Park, Calif. |
| Ramsey, Fernando | .270 | 134 | 545 | 76 | 147 | 30 | 7 | 5 | 42 | 25 | 72 | 13 | 13 | R | R | 6-2 | 180 | 12-20-65 | 1987 | Ciudad Arcoiris, Panama |
| Rhodes, Karl | .320 | 35 | 125 | 31 | 40 | 12 | 1 | 7 | 25 | 20 | 22 | 6 | 3 | L | L | 5-11 | 170 | 8-21-68 | 1986 | Cincinnati, Ohio |
|   2-team (88 Omaha) | .318 | 123 | 490 | 112 | 156 | 43 | 3 | 30 | 89 | 58 | 82 | 16 | 8 | | | | | | | |
| Roberson, Kevin | .304 | 67 | 263 | 48 | 80 | 20 | 1 | 16 | 50 | 19 | 66 | 3 | 2 | S | R | 6-4 | 210 | 1-29-68 | 1988 | Decatur, Ill. |
| Shields, Tommy | .287 | 84 | 314 | 48 | 90 | 16 | 1 | 9 | 48 | 26 | 46 | 10 | 6 | R | R | 6-0 | 175 | 8-14-64 | 1986 | Devon, Pa. |
| Smith, Greg | .282 | 131 | 500 | 82 | 141 | 27 | 1 | 9 | 54 | 53 | 61 | 25 | 11 | S | R | 5-11 | 170 | 4-5-67 | 1985 | Sykesville, Md. |
| Wade, Scott | .170 | 47 | 147 | 14 | 25 | 8 | 0 | 3 | 15 | 12 | 42 | 9 | 3 | R | R | 6-2 | 200 | 4-26-63 | 1984 | Seabrook, Md. |
| Walbeck, Matt | .281 | 87 | 331 | 31 | 93 | 18 | 2 | 6 | 43 | 18 | 47 | 1 | 2 | S | R | 6-0 | 192 | 10-2-69 | 1987 | Sacramento, Calif. |
| Worthington, Craig | .273 | 132 | 469 | 63 | 128 | 23 | 0 | 13 | 66 | 59 | 91 | 1 | 1 | R | R | 6-0 | 200 | 4-17-65 | 1985 | Anaheim, Calif. |
| Zambrano, Eddie | .303 | 133 | 469 | 95 | 142 | 29 | 2 | 32 | 115 | 54 | 93 | 10 | 7 | R | R | 6-2 | 175 | 2-1-66 | 1985 | Maracaibo, Venez. |

| PITCHING | W | L | ERA | G | GS | CG | SV | IP | H | R | ER | BB | SO | B | T | HT | WT | DOB | 1st Yr | Resides |
|---|---|---|---|---|---|---|---|---|---|---|---|---|---|---|---|---|---|---|---|---|
| Boskie, Shawn | 6 | 1 | 4.27 | 11 | 11 | 1 | 0 | 72 | 70 | 35 | 34 | 21 | 35 | R | R | 6-3 | 205 | 3-28-67 | 1986 | Reno, Nev. |
| Brennan, Bill | 10 | 7 | 4.42 | 28 | 28 | 2 | 0 | 179 | 180 | 96 | 88 | 64 | 143 | R | R | 6-3 | 185 | 1-15-63 | 1985 | Kenesaw, Ga. |
| Bullinger, Jim | 4 | 6 | 3.42 | 49 | 3 | 0 | 20 | 74 | 64 | 29 | 28 | 43 | 74 | R | R | 6-2 | 180 | 8-21-65 | 1986 | Sarasota, Fla. |
| Corbett, Sherm | 0 | 1 | 3.77 | 8 | 0 | 0 | 0 | 14 | 11 | 6 | 6 | 4 | 9 | L | L | 6-4 | 203 | 11-3-62 | 1984 | Converse, Texas |
| Czajkowski, Jim | 7 | 5 | 3.84 | 42 | 0 | 0 | 0 | 70 | 64 | 31 | 30 | 32 | 43 | S | R | 6-4 | 215 | 12-18-63 | 1986 | Cary, N.C. |
| Dickson, Lance | 0 | 1 | 10.38 | 2 | 2 | 0 | 0 | 4 | 6 | 5 | 5 | 1 | 3 | R | L | 6-1 | 185 | 10-19-69 | 1990 | La Mesa, Calif. |
| Dyer, Mike | 1 | 0 | 4.81 | 14 | 0 | 0 | 0 | 24 | 18 | 14 | 13 | 20 | 18 | R | R | 6-3 | 200 | 9-8-66 | 1986 | Covina, Calif. |
| Hartsock, Jeff | 0 | 4 | 6.32 | 9 | 9 | 0 | 0 | 47 | 68 | 35 | 33 | 20 | 17 | R | R | 6-0 | 190 | 11-19-66 | 1988 | Greensboro, N.C. |
| Ilsley, Blaise | 12 | 7 | 3.94 | 48 | 16 | 0 | 4 | 135 | 147 | 61 | 59 | 32 | 78 | L | L | 6-1 | 185 | 4-9-64 | 1985 | Alpena, Mich. |
| Johnson, Earnie | 1 | 1 | 3.21 | 9 | 0 | 0 | 1 | 14 | 12 | 5 | 5 | 4 | 11 | L | L | 6-2 | 190 | 10-18-67 | 1989 | El Dorado Springs, Mo. |
| McElroy, Chuck | 1 | 0 | 4.60 | 9 | 0 | 0 | 2 | 16 | 19 | 10 | 8 | 9 | 13 | L | L | 6-0 | 180 | 10-1-67 | 1986 | Beaumont, Texas |
| Slocumb, Heath | 1 | 0 | 1.50 | 10 | 0 | 0 | 7 | 12 | 7 | 2 | 2 | 8 | 10 | R | R | 6-3 | 180 | 6-7-66 | 1984 | Jamaica, N.Y. |
| Steenstra, Kennie | 1 | 0 | 6.75 | 1 | 1 | 0 | 0 | 7 | 9 | 5 | 5 | 4 | 6 | R | R | 6-5 | 220 | 10-13-70 | 1992 | Lynchburg, Mo. |
| Stevens, Dave | 4 | 0 | 4.19 | 24 | 0 | 0 | 4 | 34 | 24 | 16 | 16 | 14 | 29 | R | R | 6-3 | 200 | 3-4-70 | 1990 | La Habra, Calif. |
| Swartzbaugh, Dave | 4 | 6 | 5.30 | 26 | 9 | 0 | 1 | 87 | 90 | 57 | 51 | 44 | 69 | R | R | 6-2 | 195 | 2-11-68 | 1989 | Middletown, Ohio |
| Trachsel, Steve | 13 | 6 | 3.96 | 27 | 26 | 1 | 0 | 171 | 170 | 78 | 75 | 45 | 135 | R | R | 6-3 | 185 | 10-31-70 | 1991 | Yorba Linda, Calif. |

# CUBS TOP 10 PROSPECTS

How the Cubs Top 10 prospects, as judged by Baseball America prior to the 1993 season, fared in 1993:

| Player, Pos. | Club (Class) | AVG | AB | H | HR | RBI | SB |
|---|---|---|---|---|---|---|---|
| 4. Kevin Roberson, of | Iowa (AAA) | .304 | 263 | 80 | 16 | 50 | 3 |
| | Chicago | .189 | 180 | 34 | 9 | 27 | 0 |
| 6. Doug Glanville, of | Daytona (A) | .293 | 239 | 70 | 2 | 21 | 18 |
| | Orlando (AA) | .264 | 295 | 78 | 9 | 40 | 15 |
| 7. Jose Viera, 3b | Orlando (AA) | .091 | 11 | 1 | 0 | 1 | 0 |
| 8. Matt Walbeck, c | Iowa (AAA) | .281 | 331 | 93 | 6 | 43 | 1 |
| | Chicago | .200 | 30 | 6 | 1 | 6 | 0 |
| 9. Brant Brown, 1b | Daytona (A) | .342 | 266 | 91 | 3 | 33 | 8 |
| | Orlando (AA) | .318 | 110 | 35 | 4 | 23 | 2 |
| 10. Ozzie Timmons, of | Orlando (AA) | .284 | 359 | 102 | 18 | 58 | 5 |

| | | W | L | ERA | IP | H | BB | SO |
|---|---|---|---|---|---|---|---|---|
| 1. Jessie Hollins, rhp | Injured—Did Not Play | | | | | | | |
| 2. Steve Trachsel, rhp | Iowa (AAA) | 13 | 6 | 3.96 | 171 | 170 | 45 | 135 |
| | Chicago | 0 | 2 | 4.58 | 20 | 16 | 3 | 14 |
| 3. Derek Wallace, rhp | Daytona (A) | 5 | 6 | 4.20 | 79 | 85 | 23 | 34 |
| | Orlando (AA) | 5 | 7 | 5.03 | 97 | 105 | 28 | 69 |
| | Iowa (AAA) | 0 | 0 | 11.25 | 4 | 8 | 1 | 2 |
| 5. Dave Stevens, rhp | Orlando (AA) | 6 | 1 | 4.22 | 70 | 69 | 35 | 49 |
| | Iowa (AAA) | 4 | 0 | 4.19 | 34 | 24 | 14 | 29 |

**Jessie Hollins**
Injured

## PITCHING

| | W | L | ERA | G | GS | CG | SV | IP | H | R | ER | BB | SO | B | T | HT | WT | DOB | 1st Yr | Resides |
|---|---|---|---|---|---|---|---|---|---|---|---|---|---|---|---|---|---|---|---|---|
| Vosberg, Ed | 5 | 1 | 3.57 | 52 | 0 | 0 | 3 | 63 | 67 | 32 | 25 | 22 | 64 | L | L | 6-1 | 190 | 9-28-61 | 1983 | Tucson, Ariz. |
| Walker, Mike | 1 | 1 | 2.70 | 12 | 0 | 0 | 0 | 23 | 22 | 8 | 7 | 9 | 11 | R | R | 6-1 | 195 | 10-4-66 | 1986 | Brooksville, Fla. |
| Wallace, Derek | 0 | 0 | 11.25 | 1 | 1 | 0 | 0 | 4 | 8 | 5 | 5 | 1 | 2 | R | R | 6-3 | 200 | 9-1-71 | 1992 | Oxnard, Calif. |
| Wendell, Turk | 10 | 8 | 4.60 | 25 | 25 | 3 | 0 | 149 | 148 | 88 | 76 | 47 | 110 | S | R | 6-2 | 175 | 5-19-67 | 1988 | Dalton, Mass. |
| Williams, Jimmy | 5 | 3 | 3.46 | 17 | 13 | 0 | 0 | 78 | 74 | 32 | 30 | 37 | 49 | L | L | 6-7 | 232 | 5-18-65 | 1984 | Butler, Ala. |

### FIELDING

| Catcher | PCT | G | PO | A | E | DP |
|---|---|---|---|---|---|---|
| Mercado | 1.000 | 8 | 73 | 5 | 0 | 0 |
| Pedre | .998 | 60 | 383 | 40 | 1 | 3 |
| Walbeck | .998 | 79 | 496 | 64 | 1 | 9 |

| First Base | PCT | G | PO | A | E | DP |
|---|---|---|---|---|---|---|
| Chance | .000 | 1 | 0 | 0 | 0 | 0 |
| Franco | .996 | 52 | 445 | 39 | 2 | 47 |
| Jennings | .996 | 48 | 433 | 36 | 2 | 50 |
| Lewis | 1.000 | 8 | 62 | 8 | 0 | 9 |
| Lonigro | 1.000 | 1 | 3 | 0 | 0 | 1 |
| Pedre | .000 | 1 | 0 | 0 | 0 | 0 |
| Worthington | 1.000 | 2 | 6 | 1 | 0 | 0 |
| Zambrano | .988 | 48 | 391 | 32 | 5 | 44 |

| Second Base | PCT | G | PO | A | E | DP |
|---|---|---|---|---|---|---|
| Anderson | .975 | 9 | 13 | 26 | 1 | 5 |

| | PCT | G | PO | A | E | DP |
|---|---|---|---|---|---|---|
| Franco | 1.000 | 1 | 0 | 0 | 0 | 0 |
| Gomez | 1.000 | 1 | 2 | 2 | 0 | 0 |
| Lonigro | .984 | 12 | 27 | 34 | 1 | 10 |
| Smith | .983 | 126 | 241 | 396 | 11 | 98 |

| Third Base | PCT | G | PO | A | E | DP |
|---|---|---|---|---|---|---|
| Gomez | .833 | 3 | 0 | 10 | 2 | 2 |
| Lonigro | 1.000 | 4 | 2 | 8 | 0 | 0 |
| Pedre | 1.000 | 1 | 0 | 1 | 0 | 0 |
| Shields | .980 | 17 | 10 | 40 | 1 | 3 |
| Worthington | .940 | 124 | 71 | 240 | 20 | 22 |

| Shortstop | PCT | G | PO | A | E | DP |
|---|---|---|---|---|---|---|
| Anderson | .966 | 58 | 84 | 145 | 8 | 38 |
| Gomez | 1.000 | 2 | 2 | 8 | 0 | 3 |
| Hernandez | .976 | 6 | 14 | 26 | 1 | 7 |

| | PCT | G | PO | A | E | DP |
|---|---|---|---|---|---|---|
| Lonigro | .957 | 20 | 28 | 60 | 4 | 13 |
| Shields | .950 | 66 | 121 | 186 | 16 | 55 |

| Outfield | PCT | G | PO | A | E | DP |
|---|---|---|---|---|---|---|
| Chance | .985 | 75 | 130 | 5 | 2 | 1 |
| Dauphin | .931 | 16 | 27 | 0 | 2 | 0 |
| Franco | 1.000 | 3 | 5 | 0 | 0 | 0 |
| Grayum | 1.000 | 1 | 2 | 0 | 0 | 0 |
| Jennings | 1.000 | 6 | 9 | 0 | 0 | 0 |
| Jensen | .923 | 20 | 23 | 1 | 2 | 0 |
| Ramsey | .977 | 127 | 292 | 7 | 7 | 5 |
| Rhodes | .968 | 35 | 57 | 4 | 2 | 0 |
| Roberson | .968 | 64 | 110 | 4 | 4 | 0 |
| Wade | 1.000 | 34 | 67 | 3 | 0 | 1 |
| Zambrano | .984 | 70 | 112 | 8 | 2 | 0 |

# ORLANDO
## SOUTHERN LEAGUE
**AA**

### BATTING

| | AVG | G | AB | R | H | 2B | 3B | HR | RBI | BB | SO | SB | CS | B | T | HT | WT | DOB | 1st Yr | Resides |
|---|---|---|---|---|---|---|---|---|---|---|---|---|---|---|---|---|---|---|---|---|
| Brown, Adam, dh-c | .500 | 2 | 6 | 0 | 3 | 1 | 0 | 0 | 1 | 0 | 1 | 0 | 0 | L | R | 6-0 | 203 | 8-10-66 | 1986 | Monroe, Ga. |
| Brown, Brant, 1b | .315 | 28 | 111 | 17 | 35 | 11 | 3 | 4 | 23 | 6 | 19 | 2 | 1 | L | L | 6-3 | 220 | 6-22-71 | 1992 | Porterville, Calif. |
| Busby, Wayne, ss-3b | .203 | 27 | 74 | 8 | 15 | 5 | 0 | 0 | 4 | 10 | 16 | 1 | 1 | R | R | 6-2 | 184 | 11-24-67 | 1988 | Jackson, Miss. |
| Crockett, Russ, 2b-ss | .204 | 33 | 98 | 15 | 20 | 4 | 0 | 0 | 3 | 7 | 14 | 1 | 1 | R | R | 5-8 | 150 | 9-22-66 | 1988 | Crescent, Okla. |
| Dauphin, Phil, of | .264 | 81 | 299 | 53 | 79 | 16 | 2 | 11 | 35 | 30 | 40 | 7 | 10 | L | L | 6-1 | 180 | 5-11-69 | 1990 | Worthington, Ohio |
| Davisson, Sean, 2b | .000 | 2 | 1 | 0 | 0 | 0 | 0 | 0 | 0 | 0 | 0 | 0 | 0 | R | R | 5-9 | 165 | 9-17-71 | 1993 | Sacramento, Calif. |
| Ebright, Chris, 1b | .283 | 113 | 318 | 49 | 90 | 21 | 1 | 10 | 56 | 50 | 61 | 0 | 1 | L | L | 6-1 | 190 | 9-1-67 | 1989 | Tulsa, Okla. |
| Erdman, Brad, c | .181 | 69 | 171 | 12 | 31 | 5 | 0 | 1 | 17 | 18 | 42 | 2 | 2 | R | R | 6-3 | 190 | 2-23-70 | 1989 | Casper, Wyo. |
| Franco, Matt, 1b | .316 | 68 | 237 | 31 | 75 | 20 | 1 | 7 | 37 | 29 | 26 | 2 | 1 | L | R | 6-3 | 195 | 8-19-69 | 1987 | Thousand Oaks, Calif. |
| Glanville, Doug, of | .264 | 73 | 296 | 42 | 78 | 14 | 4 | 9 | 40 | 12 | 41 | 15 | 7 | R | R | 6-2 | 170 | 8-25-70 | 1991 | Teaneck, N.J. |
| Gomez, Pat, 2b-ss | .329 | 56 | 140 | 26 | 46 | 8 | 0 | 1 | 17 | 25 | 31 | 5 | 3 | R | R | 5-10 | 165 | 6-8-69 | 1991 | Tempe, Ariz. |
| Grace, Mike, 3b | .271 | 120 | 425 | 65 | 115 | 29 | 3 | 13 | 76 | 35 | 56 | 2 | 3 | R | R | 6-1 | 180 | 12-9-67 | 1989 | Houston, Texas |
| Grayum, Richie, of | .295 | 92 | 234 | 45 | 69 | 13 | 1 | 10 | 33 | 45 | 66 | 1 | 10 | L | R | 5-10 | 185 | 9-17-68 | 1989 | Green Cove Springs, Fla. |
| Hernandez, Jose, ss | .304 | 71 | 263 | 42 | 80 | 8 | 3 | 8 | 33 | 20 | 60 | 8 | 4 | R | R | 6-0 | 180 | 7-14-69 | 1987 | Vega Alta, P.R. |
| Jensen, John, of | .266 | 62 | 192 | 27 | 51 | 10 | 2 | 6 | 34 | 18 | 45 | 4 | 3 | L | R | 6-2 | 215 | 11-30-66 | 1988 | Galveston, Texas |
| Johnson, Jack, c | .232 | 33 | 82 | 9 | 19 | 6 | 0 | 0 | 5 | 12 | 22 | 0 | 1 | R | R | 6-3 | 205 | 3-24-70 | 1991 | Chicago, Ill. |
| Kapano, Corey, of | .255 | 89 | 263 | 46 | 67 | 12 | 1 | 8 | 35 | 22 | 58 | 17 | 4 | R | R | 6-2 | 200 | 5-28-70 | 1989 | Diamond Bar, Calif. |
| Kieschnick, Brooks, of | .341 | 25 | 91 | 12 | 31 | 8 | 0 | 2 | 10 | 7 | 19 | 1 | 2 | L | R | 6-4 | 217 | 6-6-72 | 1993 | Caldwell, Texas |
| Lewis, Mica, of | .244 | 42 | 86 | 14 | 21 | 3 | 0 | 1 | 10 | 14 | 19 | 3 | 1 | R | R | 5-11 | 170 | 1-12-67 | 1988 | Los Angeles, Calif. |
| Lonigro, Greg, ss-2b | .273 | 62 | 216 | 20 | 59 | 12 | 0 | 4 | 22 | 5 | 33 | 4 | 5 | R | R | 6-1 | 180 | 11-20-65 | 1986 | Connellsville, Pa. |
| Magallanes, Willie, of | .176 | 7 | 17 | 1 | 3 | 0 | 0 | 0 | 0 | 2 | 3 | 1 | 0 | R | R | 6-2 | 200 | 7-10-66 | 1985 | Miranda, Venez. |
| Mann, Kelly, c | .244 | 28 | 82 | 11 | 20 | 3 | 1 | 1 | 7 | 11 | 11 | 0 | 0 | R | R | 6-3 | 215 | 8-17-67 | 1985 | Pacific Palisades, Calif. |
| McDonnell, Shawn, c | .213 | 18 | 47 | 2 | 10 | 2 | 0 | 0 | 8 | 4 | 14 | 0 | 0 | S | R | 6-2 | 205 | 4-4-70 | 1993 | Estell Manor, N.J. |
| Raasch, Glen, c | .214 | 5 | 14 | 0 | 3 | 0 | 0 | 0 | 1 | 0 | 4 | 0 | 0 | R | R | 6-0 | 200 | 11-1-68 | 1989 | Burbank, Calif. |
| Robinson, Jim, c | .231 | 20 | 52 | 3 | 12 | 2 | 0 | 0 | 6 | 1 | 14 | 1 | 0 | R | R | 6-0 | 190 | 8-14-69 | 1990 | Chicago, Ill. |
| Sandberg, Ryne, dh-2b | .222 | 4 | 9 | 0 | 2 | 0 | 0 | 1 | 3 | 1 | 0 | 1 | 0 | R | R | 6-1 | 175 | 9-18-59 | 1978 | Phoenix, Ariz. |
| Timmons, Ozzie, of | .284 | 107 | 359 | 65 | 102 | 22 | 2 | 18 | 58 | 62 | 80 | 5 | 11 | R | R | 6-2 | 205 | 9-18-70 | 1991 | Tampa, Fla. |
| Torres, Paul, of | .255 | 19 | 55 | 10 | 14 | 4 | 0 | 3 | 10 | 7 | 18 | 3 | 0 | R | R | 6-3 | 210 | 10-19-70 | 1989 | San Lorenzo, Calif. |
| Vice, Darryl, 2b-3b | .273 | 62 | 220 | 36 | 60 | 15 | 2 | 3 | 24 | 28 | 31 | 6 | 5 | S | R | 5-11 | 170 | 12-30-66 | 1989 | Santa Rosa, Calif. |
| Viera, Jose, 3b | .091 | 3 | 11 | 1 | 0 | 0 | 0 | 1 | 0 | 0 | 1 | 0 | 0 | R | R | 6-1 | 190 | 2-23-71 | 1990 | Arecibo, P.R. |
| White, Billy, 2b | .242 | 40 | 120 | 14 | 29 | 11 | 1 | 2 | 14 | 15 | 28 | 1 | 2 | R | R | 6-0 | 185 | 7-3-68 | 1989 | Louisville, Ky. |
| Zambrano, Roberto, 3b | .135 | 13 | 37 | 4 | 5 | 1 | 0 | 0 | 1 | 6 | 3 | 0 | 0 | R | R | 6-0 | 175 | 4-23-67 | 1985 | Maracaibo, Venez. |

| PITCHING | W | L | ERA | G | GS | CG | SV | IP | H | R | ER | BB | SO | B | T | HT | WT | DOB | 1st Yr | Resides |
|---|---|---|---|---|---|---|---|---|---|---|---|---|---|---|---|---|---|---|---|---|
| Corbett, Sherm | 2 | 1 | 3.16 | 5 | 4 | 0 | 0 | 26 | 32 | 11 | 9 | 9 | 16 | L | L | 6-4 | 203 | 11-3-62 | 1984 | Converse, Texas |
| Czajkowski, Jim | 1 | 2 | 2.84 | 10 | 0 | 0 | 1 | 19 | 15 | 7 | 6 | 3 | 16 | S | R | 6-4 | 215 | 12-18-63 | 1986 | Cary, N.C. |
| Delgado, Tim | 1 | 3 | 5.90 | 9 | 6 | 0 | 0 | 40 | 53 | 28 | 26 | 9 | 23 | R | R | 6-6 | 230 | 8-6-67 | 1990 | Birmingham, Mich. |
| Dickson, Lance | 2 | 3 | 3.83 | 9 | 9 | 0 | 0 | 49 | 37 | 22 | 21 | 17 | 46 | R | L | 6-1 | 185 | 10-19-69 | 1990 | La Mesa, Calif. |
| Galvez, Balvino | 0 | 1 | 8.44 | 3 | 2 | 0 | 0 | 11 | 16 | 14 | 10 | 3 | 9 | R | R | 6-0 | 170 | 3-31-64 | 1982 | San Pedro de Macoris, D.R. |
| Gardner, John | 2 | 1 | 4.78 | 7 | 7 | 0 | 0 | 38 | 34 | 21 | 20 | 23 | 19 | R | R | 6-3 | 210 | 11-23-65 | 1987 | Michigan City, Ind. |
| Harkey, Mike | 0 | 0 | 1.69 | 1 | 1 | 0 | 0 | 5 | 4 | 1 | 1 | 2 | 5 | R | R | 6-5 | 220 | 10-25-66 | 1987 | Chino Hills, Calif. |
| Hartsock, Jeff | 3 | 4 | 3.47 | 8 | 8 | 1 | 0 | 49 | 43 | 24 | 19 | 17 | 24 | R | R | 6-0 | 190 | 11-19-66 | 1988 | Greensboro, N.C. |
| Johnson, Chris | 0 | 1 | 2.96 | 15 | 1 | 0 | 1 | 27 | 31 | 12 | 9 | 15 | 14 | R | R | 6-3 | 215 | 12-7-68 | 1987 | Hixson, Tenn. |
| Johnson, Earnie | 6 | 5 | 5.94 | 53 | 0 | 0 | 2 | 67 | 84 | 47 | 44 | 31 | 58 | L | L | 6-2 | 190 | 10-18-67 | 1989 | El Dorado Springs, Mo. |
| Melvin, Bill | 0 | 1 | 3.88 | 36 | 1 | 0 | 1 | 65 | 57 | 34 | 28 | 40 | 60 | R | R | 6-3 | 192 | 10-13-66 | 1986 | Raleigh, N.C. |
| Morones, Geno | 2 | 2 | 4.88 | 4 | 4 | 1 | 0 | 24 | 29 | 14 | 13 | 9 | 14 | R | R | 5-11 | 197 | 3-26-71 | 1991 | San Leandro, Calif. |
| Salles, John | 11 | 9 | 4.38 | 33 | 26 | 1 | 1 | 177 | 203 | 103 | 86 | 50 | 115 | R | R | 6-0 | 175 | 8-11-67 | 1988 | Fresno, Calif. |
| Steenstra, Kennie | 8 | 3 | 3.59 | 14 | 14 | 2 | 0 | 100 | 103 | 47 | 40 | 25 | 60 | R | R | 6-5 | 220 | 10-13-70 | 1992 | Lynchburg, Mo. |
| Stevens, Dave | 6 | 1 | 4.22 | 11 | 11 | 1 | 0 | 70 | 69 | 36 | 33 | 19 | 49 | R | R | 6-3 | 220 | 3-4-70 | 1990 | La Habra, Calif. |
| Strauss, Julio | 0 | 2 | 3.54 | 15 | 0 | 0 | 0 | 28 | 22 | 12 | 11 | 15 | 21 | R | R | 6-1 | 185 | 1-31-67 | 1989 | Aragua, Venez. |
| Swartzbaugh, Dave | 1 | 3 | 4.23 | 10 | 9 | 1 | 0 | 66 | 52 | 33 | 31 | 18 | 59 | R | R | 6-2 | 195 | 2-11-68 | 1989 | Middletown, Ohio |
| Taylor, Aaron | 5 | 4 | 4.85 | 28 | 3 | 0 | 0 | 56 | 73 | 37 | 30 | 15 | 37 | R | R | 6-4 | 185 | 2-13-71 | 1989 | Reno, Nev. |
| Trinidad, Hector | 1 | 3 | 6.57 | 4 | 4 | 1 | 0 | 25 | 34 | 19 | 18 | 7 | 13 | R | R | 6-2 | 190 | 9-8-73 | 1991 | Whittier, Calif. |
| Walker, Mike | 2 | 3 | 7.31 | 16 | 2 | 0 | 1 | 28 | 42 | 26 | 23 | 9 | 21 | R | R | 6-1 | 195 | 10-4-66 | 1986 | Brooksville, Fla. |
| Wallace, Derek | 5 | 7 | 5.03 | 15 | 15 | 2 | 0 | 97 | 105 | 59 | 54 | 28 | 69 | R | R | 6-3 | 200 | 9-1-71 | 1992 | Oxnard, Calif. |
| Williams, Jimmy | 5 | 5 | 2.48 | 15 | 14 | 0 | 0 | 91 | 84 | 29 | 25 | 38 | 65 | L | L | 6-7 | 232 | 5-18-65 | 1984 | Butler, Ala. |
| Willis, Travis | 8 | 6 | 2.84 | 61 | 1 | 0 | 24 | 82 | 91 | 37 | 26 | 22 | 56 | R | R | 6-2 | 185 | 11-28-68 | 1989 | Somis, Calif. |

# DAYTONA A

## FLORIDA STATE LEAGUE

| BATTING | AVG | G | AB | R | H | 2B | 3B | HR | RBI | BB | SO | SB | CS | B | T | HT | WT | DOB | 1st Yr | Resides |
|---|---|---|---|---|---|---|---|---|---|---|---|---|---|---|---|---|---|---|---|---|
| Brown, Adam, dh-c | .284 | 36 | 109 | 17 | 31 | 8 | 0 | 4 | 23 | 15 | 21 | 0 | 1 | L | R | 6-0 | 203 | 8-10-66 | 1986 | Monroe, Ga. |
| Brown, Brant, 1b | .342 | 75 | 266 | 26 | 91 | 8 | 7 | 3 | 33 | 11 | 38 | 8 | 7 | L | L | 6-3 | 220 | 6-22-71 | 1992 | Porterville, Calif. |
| Busby, Wayne, 3b-dh | .231 | 9 | 26 | 5 | 6 | 1 | 1 | 0 | 3 | 5 | 9 | 1 | 0 | R | R | 6-2 | 184 | 11-24-67 | 1988 | Jackson, Miss. |
| Davisson, Sean, dh-of | .184 | 33 | 76 | 9 | 14 | 2 | 0 | 0 | 6 | 7 | 21 | 6 | 2 | R | R | 5-9 | 165 | 9-17-71 | 1993 | Sacramento, Calif. |
| Glanville, Doug, of | .293 | 61 | 239 | 47 | 70 | 10 | 1 | 2 | 21 | 28 | 24 | 18 | 15 | R | R | 6-2 | 170 | 8-25-70 | 1991 | Teaneck, N.J. |
| Gomez, Rudy, 2b-3b | .265 | 40 | 147 | 20 | 39 | 4 | 1 | 0 | 12 | 19 | 24 | 3 | 5 | R | R | 5-10 | 165 | 6-8-69 | 1991 | Tempe, Ariz. |
| Hartung, Andy, dh-3b | .295 | 44 | 173 | 24 | 51 | 10 | 1 | 4 | 32 | 23 | 33 | 1 | 1 | R | R | 6-1 | 205 | 2-12-69 | 1990 | Stoneham, Mass. |
| Hubbard, Mike, c | .294 | 68 | 245 | 25 | 72 | 10 | 3 | 1 | 20 | 18 | 41 | 10 | 6 | R | R | 6-1 | 180 | 2-16-71 | 1992 | Madison Heights, Va. |
| Johnson, Jack, c | .111 | 3 | 9 | 0 | 1 | 0 | 0 | 0 | 0 | 0 | 3 | 0 | 0 | R | R | 6-3 | 205 | 3-24-70 | 1991 | Chicago, Ill. |
| Kapano, Corey, 1b-c | .200 | 7 | 25 | 2 | 5 | 1 | 0 | 0 | 3 | 0 | 8 | 3 | 1 | R | R | 6-2 | 200 | 5-28-70 | 1989 | Diamond Bar, Calif. |
| Kieschnick, Brooks, of | .182 | 6 | 22 | 1 | 4 | 2 | 0 | 0 | 2 | 1 | 4 | 0 | 1 | L | R | 6-4 | 217 | 6-6-72 | 1993 | Caldwell, Texas |
| Larregui, Ed, of | .237 | 95 | 329 | 26 | 78 | 10 | 5 | 2 | 34 | 15 | 24 | 1 | 11 | R | R | 6-0 | 185 | 12-1-72 | 1990 | Carolina, P.R. |
| McDonnell, Shawn, c | .277 | 42 | 141 | 18 | 39 | 2 | 0 | 2 | 14 | 20 | 18 | 2 | 2 | S | R | 6-2 | 205 | 4-4-70 | 1993 | Estell Manor, N.J. |
| Molina, Jose, c | .143 | 3 | 7 | 0 | 1 | 0 | 0 | 0 | 1 | 2 | 0 | 0 | 1 | R | R | 6-1 | 180 | 6-3-75 | 1993 | Vega Alta, P.R. |
| Montero, Danny, of | 1.000 | 1 | 1 | 1 | 1 | 0 | 0 | 0 | 0 | 0 | 0 | 0 | 0 | R | R | 5-10 | 170 | 10-9-73 | 1992 | Jobillo, D.R. |
| Nunez, Bernie, of | .231 | 124 | 458 | 51 | 106 | 18 | 2 | 15 | 73 | 37 | 119 | 5 | 3 | R | R | 6-2 | 190 | 8-6-68 | 1987 | Puerto Plata, D.R. |
| Petersen, Chris, ss | .214 | 130 | 473 | 66 | 101 | 10 | 0 | 0 | 28 | 58 | 105 | 19 | 11 | R | R | 5-10 | 160 | 11-6-70 | 1992 | Southington, Conn. |
| Sandberg, Ryne, 2b | .200 | 2 | 5 | 2 | 1 | 0 | 0 | 1 | 2 | 1 | 0 | 0 | 0 | R | R | 6-1 | 175 | 9-18-59 | 1978 | Phoenix, Ariz. |
| Smith, Dan, 3b | .249 | 102 | 334 | 50 | 83 | 11 | 4 | 8 | 36 | 25 | 65 | 15 | 5 | R | R | 6-0 | 165 | 5-25-70 | 1992 | Thousand Oaks, Calif. |
| Smith, Dwight, of-dh | .313 | 5 | 16 | 3 | 5 | 4 | 0 | 0 | 2 | 3 | 4 | 0 | 1 | L | R | 5-11 | 177 | 11-8-63 | 1984 | Atlanta, Ga. |
| Stutheit, Tim, 2b | .167 | 5 | 12 | 1 | 2 | 0 | 0 | 0 | 0 | 5 | 7 | 1 | 0 | R | R | 6-1 | 185 | 7-8-69 | 1992 | Omaha, Neb. |
| Terilli, Joey, of | .213 | 70 | 216 | 29 | 46 | 10 | 3 | 0 | 19 | 40 | 27 | 4 | 2 | L | L | 5-10 | 175 | 3-1-69 | 1991 | Dallas, Texas |
| Torres, Paul, of-1b | .278 | 100 | 353 | 63 | 98 | 17 | 5 | 13 | 43 | 52 | 94 | 5 | 4 | R | R | 6-3 | 210 | 10-19-70 | 1989 | San Lorenzo, Calif. |
| Tredaway, Chad, 2b | .256 | 66 | 242 | 32 | 62 | 12 | 0 | 0 | 21 | 27 | 25 | 4 | 3 | S | R | 6-0 | 180 | 6-18-72 | 1992 | Edinburg, Texas |
| Valdez, Pedro, of-dh | .287 | 60 | 230 | 27 | 66 | 16 | 1 | 8 | 49 | 9 | 30 | 3 | 4 | L | L | 6-1 | 160 | 6-29-73 | 1991 | Loiza, P.R. |
| Ventress, Leroy, dh-of | .183 | 17 | 60 | 8 | 11 | 1 | 0 | 0 | 4 | 10 | 17 | 2 | 1 | S | R | 6-0 | 173 | 8-14-68 | 1986 | Maringouin, La. |
| White, Billy, 2b | .336 | 38 | 125 | 19 | 42 | 9 | 2 | 3 | 22 | 16 | 23 | 2 | 0 | R | R | 6-0 | 185 | 7-3-68 | 1989 | Louisville, Ky. |
| Wolff, Jim, c | .224 | 24 | 67 | 5 | 15 | 5 | 0 | 1 | 8 | 5 | 13 | 1 | 1 | R | R | 6-2 | 210 | 12-22-69 | 1990 | Boca Raton, Fla. |

| PITCHING | W | L | ERA | G | GS | CG | SV | IP | H | R | ER | BB | SO | B | T | HT | WT | DOB | 1st Yr | Resides |
|---|---|---|---|---|---|---|---|---|---|---|---|---|---|---|---|---|---|---|---|---|
| Adams, Terry | 3 | 5 | 4.97 | 13 | 13 | 0 | 0 | 71 | 78 | 47 | 39 | 43 | 35 | R | R | 6-3 | 180 | 3-6-73 | 1991 | Semmes, Ala. |
| Bradford, Troy | 3 | 5 | 5.53 | 11 | 10 | 0 | 0 | 54 | 58 | 35 | 33 | 27 | 39 | R | R | 6-2 | 200 | 2-25-69 | 1990 | St. David, Ariz. |
| Broome, John | 0 | 1 | 4.50 | 1 | 1 | 0 | 0 | 6 | 6 | 3 | 3 | 0 | 1 | R | R | 6-0 | 185 | 6-26-73 | 1993 | Maple Shade, N.J. |
| Burlingame, Ben | 0 | 1 | 7.79 | 8 | 1 | 0 | 0 | 17 | 27 | 16 | 15 | 9 | 10 | R | R | 6-5 | 210 | 1-31-70 | 1991 | Newton, Mass. |
| Corbett, Sherm | 0 | 3 | 3.04 | 5 | 4 | 0 | 0 | 27 | 26 | 15 | 9 | 11 | 20 | L | L | 6-4 | 203 | 11-3-62 | 1984 | Converse, Texas |
| Daniel, Chuck | 2 | 2 | 3.00 | 15 | 0 | 0 | 2 | 24 | 17 | 10 | 8 | 9 | 9 | R | R | 6-1 | 190 | 3-11-69 | 1992 | Metairie, La. |
| Delgado, Tim | 6 | 7 | 1.70 | 17 | 13 | 1 | 0 | 85 | 78 | 31 | 16 | 28 | 44 | R | R | 6-6 | 230 | 8-6-67 | 1990 | Birmingham, Mich. |
| Dickson, Lance | 1 | 2 | 3.18 | 3 | 3 | 0 | 0 | 17 | 17 | 7 | 6 | 3 | 18 | R | L | 6-1 | 185 | 10-19-69 | 1990 | La Mesa, Calif. |

# CUBS: MOST COMMON LINEUPS

| | Chicago Majors | Iowa AAA | Orlando AA | Daytona A | Peoria A |
|---|---|---|---|---|---|
| C | Rick Wilkins (133) | Matt Walbeck (79) | Brad Erdman (66) | Mike Hubbard (67) | Glen Raasch (39) |
| 1B | Mark Grace (154) | Matt Franco (52) | Chris Ebright (72) | Brant Brown (75) | Mark Kingston (62) |
| 2B | Ryne Sandberg (115) | Greg Smith (126) | Darryl Vice (46) | Chad Tredaway (65) | Richard Perez (92) |
| 3B | Steve Buechele (129) | Craig Worthington (124) | Mike Grace (112) | Dan Smith (95) | Byron Bradley (46) |
| SS | Rey Sanchez (98) | Tommy Shields (66) | Jose Hernandez (71) | Chris Peterson (130) | Rafael Soto (80) |
| OF | Sammy Sosa (158) | Fernando Ramsey (127) | Ozzie Timmons (101) | Bernie Nunez (118) | Steve Walker (127) |
| | Derrick May (122) | Tony Chance (73) | Phil Dauphin (77) | Ed Larregui (84) | Robin Jennings (121) |
| | Dwight Smith (89) | Eddie Zambrano (70) | Doug Glanville (70) | Doug Glanville (60) | Dan Madsen (79) |
| DH | N/A | Dan Lewis (23) | Ebright/Kapano (14) | Andy Hartung (26) | Pedro Valdez (38) |
| SP | Mike Morgan (32) | Bill Brennan (28) | John Salles (26) | Jay Franklin (15) | Amaury Telemaco (23) |
| RP | Randy Myers (73) | Ed Vosberg (52) | Travis Willis (60) | Mike Tidwell (39) | Daryle Gavlick (51) |
| | Full-season farm clubs only | No. of games at position in parenthesis | | | |

| PITCHING | W | L | ERA | G | GS | CG | SV | IP | H | R | ER | BB | SO | B | T | HT | WT | DOB | 1st Yr | Resides |
|---|---|---|---|---|---|---|---|---|---|---|---|---|---|---|---|---|---|---|---|---|
| Dreyer, Darren | 2 | 2 | 1.80 | 4 | 4 | 1 | 0 | 30 | 22 | 8 | 6 | 3 | 17 | R | R | 6-0 | 208 | 5-21-71 | 1992 | Taft, Texas |
| Franklin, Jay | 3 | 11 | 4.49 | 39 | 15 | 4 | 3 | 132 | 146 | 80 | 66 | 39 | 64 | R | R | 6-2 | 190 | 8-5-68 | 1989 | Spiro, Okla. |
| Howze, Ben | 2 | 7 | 4.55 | 20 | 13 | 1 | 1 | 85 | 95 | 53 | 43 | 46 | 29 | R | R | 6-4 | 205 | 12-10-69 | 1988 | Pensacola, Fla. |
| James, Todd | 0 | 1 | 8.44 | 5 | 0 | 0 | 0 | 5 | 10 | 6 | 5 | 2 | 1 | L | L | 6-2 | 190 | 5-23-68 | 1989 | Fair Oaks, Calif. |
| Kirk, Chuck | 1 | 2 | 6.08 | 20 | 0 | 0 | 4 | 27 | 38 | 23 | 18 | 6 | 20 | R | R | 6-0 | 195 | 9-26-67 | 1990 | Jacksonville, Fla. |
| Meyer, Jay | 3 | 2 | 3.47 | 33 | 1 | 0 | 2 | 49 | 48 | 23 | 19 | 23 | 29 | L | L | 6-2 | 170 | 6-15-71 | 1991 | Independence, Mo. |
| Morones, Geno | 5 | 1 | 1.76 | 13 | 6 | 1 | 0 | 51 | 44 | 10 | 10 | 16 | 27 | R | R | 5-11 | 197 | 3-26-71 | 1991 | San Leandro, Calif. |
| Ratliff, Jon | 2 | 4 | 3.95 | 8 | 8 | 0 | 0 | 41 | 50 | 29 | 18 | 23 | 15 | R | R | 6-4 | 195 | 12-22-71 | 1993 | Clay, N.Y. |
| Rodriguez, Chris | 1 | 1 | 3.18 | 29 | 0 | 0 | 4 | 40 | 30 | 15 | 14 | 16 | 31 | R | R | 6-1 | 195 | 10-8-71 | 1991 | Caguas, P.R. |
| Schramm, Carl | 8 | 4 | 3.50 | 34 | 13 | 0 | 2 | 121 | 119 | 58 | 47 | 29 | 89 | R | R | 6-4 | 200 | 6-10-70 | 1991 | Crete, Ill. |
| Steenstra, Kennie | 5 | 3 | 2.55 | 13 | 13 | 1 | 0 | 81 | 64 | 26 | 23 | 12 | 57 | R | R | 6-5 | 220 | 10-13-70 | 1992 | Lynchburg, Mo. |
| Strauss, Julio | 0 | 1 | 3.79 | 14 | 0 | 0 | 3 | 19 | 12 | 9 | 8 | 5 | 19 | R | R | 6-1 | 185 | 1-31-67 | 1989 | Aragua, Venez. |
| Taylor, Aaron | 1 | 0 | 4.56 | 15 | 1 | 0 | 2 | 24 | 21 | 13 | 12 | 8 | 17 | R | R | 6-4 | 185 | 2-13-71 | 1989 | Reno, Nev. |
| Tidwell, Mike | 4 | 2 | 3.07 | 39 | 0 | 0 | 2 | 59 | 40 | 25 | 20 | 19 | 41 | L | L | 6-3 | 175 | 7-3-70 | 1991 | Charlotte, N.C. |
| Wallace, Derek | 5 | 6 | 4.20 | 14 | 12 | 0 | 1 | 79 | 85 | 50 | 37 | 23 | 34 | R | R | 6-3 | 200 | 9-1-71 | 1992 | Oxnard, Calif. |
| White, Fred | 0 | 3 | 8.15 | 7 | 2 | 0 | 0 | 18 | 22 | 16 | 16 | 11 | 5 | R | R | 6-2 | 180 | 8-24-68 | 1986 | Compton, Calif. |
| Whitfill, Mike | 0 | 0 | 0.00 | 1 | 0 | 0 | 0 | 5 | 0 | 0 | 0 | 0 | 1 | R | R | 6-3 | 185 | 10-24-74 | 1993 | Bryson, Texas |

# PEORIA  A
## MIDWEST LEAGUE

| BATTING | AVG | G | AB | R | H | 2B | 3B | HR | RBI | BB | SO | SB | CS | B | T | HT | WT | DOB | 1st Yr | Resides |
|---|---|---|---|---|---|---|---|---|---|---|---|---|---|---|---|---|---|---|---|---|
| Bradley, Byron, 3b | .301 | 49 | 176 | 28 | 53 | 13 | 0 | 1 | 22 | 15 | 33 | 4 | 3 | R | R | 6-0 | 190 | 11-15-70 | 1992 | Barrington, Ill. |
| Cunningham, Earl, dh-of | .194 | 43 | 139 | 15 | 27 | 6 | 1 | 5 | 15 | 10 | 38 | 2 | 1 | R | R | 6-2 | 225 | 6-3-70 | 1989 | Lancaster, S.C. |
| Deutsch, John, 1b | .246 | 43 | 130 | 18 | 32 | 10 | 0 | 5 | 13 | 22 | 32 | 0 | 5 | L | L | 6-5 | 235 | 11-11-66 | 1989 | Phillipsburg, N.J. |
| Erdman, Brad, c | .246 | 20 | 57 | 7 | 14 | 1 | 0 | 1 | 10 | 6 | 12 | 2 | 0 | R | R | 6-3 | 190 | 2-23-70 | 1989 | Casper, Wyo. |
| Hightower, Vee, dh-of | .200 | 2 | 10 | 0 | 2 | 0 | 0 | 0 | 0 | 1 | 1 | 0 | 0 | S | R | 6-5 | 205 | 4-26-72 | 1993 | Pittsburgh, Pa. |
| Jennings, Robin, of | .308 | 132 | 474 | 64 | 146 | 29 | 5 | 3 | 65 | 46 | 73 | 11 | 11 | L | L | 6-2 | 190 | 4-11-72 | 1992 | Miami, Fla. |
| Johnson, Jack, c | .188 | 39 | 96 | 10 | 18 | 7 | 0 | 0 | 10 | 23 | 33 | 3 | 0 | R | R | 6-3 | 205 | 3-24-70 | 1991 | Chicago, Ill. |
| Kingston, Mark, 1b | .254 | 64 | 224 | 25 | 57 | 14 | 1 | 4 | 24 | 28 | 44 | 3 | 0 | S | R | 6-4 | 210 | 5-16-70 | 1992 | Midland, Ga. |
| Madsen, Dan, of | .211 | 80 | 265 | 39 | 56 | 16 | 4 | 0 | 32 | 37 | 60 | 9 | 8 | S | L | 6-0 | 185 | 2-10-71 | 1992 | Carson City, Nev. |
| McGinnis, Shane, 3b | .184 | 38 | 103 | 5 | 19 | 2 | 0 | 0 | 11 | 10 | 31 | 2 | 3 | R | R | 6-2 | 200 | 1-21-71 | 1993 | Ocala, Fla. |
| Medina, Ricardo, 3b-1b | .254 | 88 | 283 | 30 | 72 | 14 | 0 | 3 | 29 | 40 | 37 | 0 | 5 | R | R | 6-1 | 205 | 11-4-71 | 1989 | Panama City, Panama |
| Mendez, Emilio, ss | .190 | 14 | 21 | 3 | 4 | 0 | 0 | 0 | 1 | 2 | 8 | 0 | 0 | R | R | 6-0 | 160 | 5-17-73 | 1992 | Miami Beach, Fla. |
| Morales, Francisco, c | .204 | 19 | 49 | 9 | 10 | 1 | 1 | 3 | 11 | 9 | 16 | 0 | 0 | R | R | 6-3 | 180 | 1-31-73 | 1991 | San Pedro de Macoris, D.R. |
| Orie, Kevin, ss | .269 | 65 | 238 | 28 | 64 | 17 | 1 | 7 | 45 | 21 | 51 | 3 | 5 | R | R | 6-4 | 205 | 9-1-72 | 1993 | Pittsburgh, Pa. |
| Perez, Richard, 2b-3b | .243 | 109 | 370 | 60 | 90 | 12 | 1 | 0 | 34 | 31 | 64 | 5 | 8 | R | R | 6-2 | 175 | 1-30-73 | 1991 | Lara, Venez. |
| Pico, Brandon, of | .156 | 8 | 32 | 5 | 5 | 1 | 1 | 0 | 3 | 1 | 6 | 0 | 0 | L | L | 6-1 | 185 | 1-2-74 | 1992 | Newport, R.I. |
| Raasch, Glen, c | .274 | 53 | 197 | 17 | 54 | 13 | 0 | 3 | 18 | 7 | 47 | 1 | 2 | R | R | 6-0 | 200 | 11-1-68 | 1992 | Burbank, Calif. |
| Rodgers, John, c | .220 | 37 | 91 | 16 | 20 | 3 | 0 | 0 | 5 | 25 | 24 | 2 | 1 | R | R | 6-2 | 185 | 12-2-70 | 1993 | Waxahachie, Texas |
| Simmons, Josh, 2b-dh | .290 | 30 | 69 | 20 | 20 | 4 | 1 | 0 | 4 | 29 | 23 | 1 | 2 | S | R | 5-11 | 175 | 10-31-72 | 1992 | San Luis Obispo, Calif. |
| Smith, Coleman, of | .056 | 6 | 18 | 4 | 1 | 0 | 0 | 0 | 1 | 3 | 6 | 0 | 0 | R | R | 6-2 | 180 | 9-30-69 | 1992 | Lithonia, Ga. |
| Smith, Dan, 3b-2b | .276 | 8 | 29 | 2 | 8 | 1 | 0 | 1 | 3 | 1 | 7 | 1 | 0 | R | R | 6-0 | 165 | 5-25-70 | 1992 | Thousand Oaks, Calif. |
| Soto, Rafael, ss-2b | .236 | 114 | 330 | 39 | 78 | 3 | 2 | 0 | 25 | 18 | 43 | 8 | 6 | S | R | 5-9 | 155 | 10-2-72 | 1990 | Gomes, D.R. |
| Stutheit, Tim, dh-2b | .119 | 19 | 42 | 4 | 5 | 2 | 0 | 1 | 4 | 8 | 11 | 1 | 0 | R | R | 6-1 | 185 | 7-8-69 | 1992 | Omaha, Neb. |
| Terilli, Joe, of | .246 | 21 | 65 | 11 | 16 | 3 | 0 | 1 | 10 | 21 | 12 | 2 | 0 | L | L | 5-10 | 175 | 3-1-69 | 1991 | Dallas, Texas |
| Valdez, Pedro, dh-of | .316 | 34 | 234 | 33 | 74 | 11 | 1 | 7 | 36 | 10 | 40 | 2 | 2 | L | L | 6-1 | 160 | 6-29-73 | 1991 | Loiza, P.R. |
| Vaske, Terry, ss-of | .213 | 21 | 47 | 10 | 10 | 4 | 0 | 1 | 7 | 11 | 13 | 0 | 0 | L | R | 6-5 | 185 | 3-1-71 | 1992 | Dyersville, Iowa |
| Walker, Steve, of | .249 | 128 | 466 | 60 | 116 | 27 | 2 | 7 | 58 | 21 | 123 | 15 | 6 | S | R | 6-1 | 180 | 2-11-72 | 1991 | Leesburg, Ga. |
| Zarate, Vince, of | .260 | 61 | 123 | 16 | 32 | 4 | 0 | 0 | 13 | 14 | 25 | 3 | 0 | R | R | 6-0 | 170 | 10-6-71 | 1990 | New York, N.Y. |

| PITCHING | W | L | ERA | G | GS | CG | SV | IP | H | R | ER | BB | SO | B | T | HT | WT | DOB | 1st Yr | Resides |
|---|---|---|---|---|---|---|---|---|---|---|---|---|---|---|---|---|---|---|---|---|
| Bliss, Bill | 3 | 4 | 5.56 | 12 | 12 | 0 | 0 | 66 | 67 | 49 | 41 | 41 | 38 | R | R | 6-6 | 205 | 10-10-69 | 1991 | Stoneboro, Pa. |
| Broome, John | 0 | 1 | 7.88 | 6 | 0 | 0 | 0 | 8 | 12 | 8 | 7 | 4 | 3 | R | R | 6-0 | 185 | 6-26-73 | 1993 | Maple Shade, N.J. |
| Burlingame, Ben | 9 | 7 | 3.56 | 20 | 20 | 4 | 0 | 126 | 122 | 59 | 50 | 32 | 102 | R | R | 6-5 | 210 | 1-31-70 | 1991 | Newton, Mass. |
| Daniel, Chuck | 1 | 1 | 1.86 | 19 | 0 | 0 | 10 | 19 | 14 | 4 | 4 | 5 | 19 | R | R | 6-1 | 190 | 3-11-69 | 1992 | Metairie, La. |
| Gardner, Scott | 5 | 6 | 5.40 | 39 | 9 | 1 | 3 | 88 | 81 | 60 | 53 | 36 | 99 | S | R | 6-5 | 210 | 9-30-71 | 1990 | El Centro, Calif. |
| Gavlick, Daryle | 6 | 7 | 1.30 | 51 | 0 | 0 | 9 | 55 | 43 | 17 | 8 | 18 | 49 | L | L | 6-1 | 185 | 8-28-69 | 1992 | Wormleysburg, Pa. |
| Guerra, Esmili | 1 | 4 | 5.79 | 27 | 0 | 0 | 0 | 37 | 37 | 28 | 24 | 14 | 25 | L | L | 5-11 | 180 | 5-12-72 | 1991 | Anzuategui, Venez. |
| Hassel, Jay | 3 | 5 | 5.82 | 12 | 11 | 0 | 0 | 56 | 75 | 41 | 36 | 20 | 37 | R | R | 6-3 | 215 | 8-10-71 | 1992 | San Diego, Calif. |
| Hutcheson, David | 4 | 3 | 2.33 | 15 | 12 | 1 | 0 | 89 | 71 | 26 | 23 | 29 | 82 | R | R | 6-2 | 185 | 8-29-71 | 1993 | Tampa, Fla. |
| Kenny, Brian | 0 | 0 | 3.68 | 5 | 0 | 0 | 0 | 7 | 8 | 3 | 3 | 1 | 9 | L | R | 6-4 | 195 | 4-8-69 | 1991 | River Vale, N.J. |
| Kerley, Collin | 6 | 9 | 4.41 | 31 | 17 | 1 | 0 | 135 | 148 | 75 | 66 | 44 | 129 | R | R | 6-3 | 200 | 3-26-70 | 1992 | Houston, Texas |
| Lee, Anthony | 1 | 4 | 5.19 | 41 | 3 | 0 | 1 | 76 | 72 | 56 | 44 | 46 | 53 | R | R | 6-4 | 185 | 4-29-71 | 1990 | Las Vegas, Nev. |
| Lopez, Orlando | 1 | 1 | 5.11 | 4 | 4 | 1 | 0 | 25 | 22 | 16 | 14 | 7 | 16 | L | L | 6-0 | 185 | 3-28-73 | 1992 | Isabela, P.R. |
| Morones, Geno | 0 | 2 | 2.45 | 13 | 0 | 0 | 0 | 18 | 12 | 8 | 5 | 7 | 21 | R | R | 5-11 | 197 | 3-26-71 | 1991 | San Leandro, Calif. |
| Rodriguez, Chris | 3 | 2 | 2.67 | 17 | 1 | 0 | 2 | 30 | 26 | 13 | 9 | 14 | 28 | R | R | 6-1 | 195 | 10-8-71 | 1991 | Caguas, P.R. |
| Sanchez, Adrian | 1 | 2 | 12.13 | 16 | 0 | 0 | 0 | 23 | 44 | 35 | 31 | 16 | 12 | R | R | 6-1 | 170 | 1-15-72 | 1990 | Albuquerque, N.M. |
| Schulhofer, Adam | 0 | 4 | 10.34 | 4 | 4 | 0 | 0 | 16 | 19 | 18 | 18 | 12 | 12 | R | R | 6-2 | 185 | 12-22-69 | 1992 | Woodland Hills, Calif. |
| Telemaco, Amaury | 8 | 11 | 3.45 | 23 | 23 | 3 | 0 | 144 | 129 | 69 | 55 | 54 | 133 | R | R | 6-3 | 180 | 1-19-74 | 1991 | La Romana, D.R. |
| Trinidad, Hector | 7 | 6 | 2.47 | 22 | 22 | 4 | 0 | 153 | 142 | 56 | 42 | 29 | 118 | R | R | 6-2 | 190 | 9-8-73 | 1991 | Whittier, Calif. |

# GENEVA  A
## NEW YORK-PENN LEAGUE

| BATTING | AVG | G | AB | R | H | 2B | 3B | HR | RBI | BB | SO | SB | CS | B | T | HT | WT | DOB | 1st Yr | Resides |
|---|---|---|---|---|---|---|---|---|---|---|---|---|---|---|---|---|---|---|---|---|
| Alongi, Doug, of | .275 | 60 | 182 | 29 | 50 | 6 | 2 | 1 | 22 | 33 | 32 | 17 | 9 | L | L | 6-0 | 170 | 11-17-70 | 1993 | Spotswood, N.J. |
| Biernat, Joe, 3b | .287 | 69 | 247 | 44 | 71 | 8 | 2 | 4 | 26 | 28 | 40 | 23 | 15 | L | R | 5-11 | 190 | 12-10-70 | 1993 | New Brighton, Minn. |
| Bonneau, Britt, 2b | .208 | 9 | 24 | 5 | 5 | 2 | 0 | 0 | 5 | 2 | 7 | 2 | 1 | S | R | 5-9 | 160 | 5-11-71 | 1993 | Farmers Branch, Texas |
| Booker, Kevin, of | .255 | 52 | 157 | 28 | 40 | 8 | 1 | 3 | 17 | 10 | 52 | 11 | 4 | R | R | 6-2 | 194 | 8-18-71 | 1992 | Memphis, Tenn. |
| Cabrera, Alex, of-1b | .246 | 53 | 167 | 29 | 41 | 5 | 0 | 5 | 27 | 9 | 49 | 4 | 5 | R | R | 6-2 | 217 | 12-24-71 | 1991 | El Tigre, Venez. |
| Dowler, Demetrius, of | .271 | 75 | 291 | 49 | 79 | 26 | 2 | 6 | 33 | 28 | 54 | 21 | 11 | R | R | 5-9 | 175 | 7-23-71 | 1993 | Indianapolis, Ind. |
| Duross, Gabe, 1b | .276 | 62 | 225 | 35 | 62 | 15 | 2 | 6 | 41 | 6 | 14 | 9 | 5 | L | L | 6-1 | 195 | 4-6-72 | 1992 | Kingston, N.Y. |

| BATTING | AVG | G | AB | R | H | 2B | 3B | HR | RBI | BB | SO | SB | CS | B | T | HT | WT | DOB | 1st Yr | Resides |
|---|---|---|---|---|---|---|---|---|---|---|---|---|---|---|---|---|---|---|---|---|
| Galvez, Ricardo, ph | .333 | 2 | 3 | 1 | 1 | 0 | 0 | 0 | 0 | 0 | 2 | 0 | 0 | R | R | 6-0 | 200 | 3-9-71 | 1993 | Fullerton, Calif. |
| Gibson, Michael, of | .177 | 30 | 62 | 11 | 11 | 1 | 0 | 3 | 14 | 16 | 3 | 2 | | R | R | 5-10 | 175 | 11-1-70 | 1993 | Gaithersburg, Md. |
| Jackson, Kuron, ss-2b | .263 | 50 | 133 | 25 | 35 | 6 | 1 | 3 | 17 | 11 | 22 | 7 | 6 | R | R | 5-9 | 170 | 5-3-71 | 1993 | Fairhope, Ala. |
| Jones, Ken, of | .240 | 13 | 25 | 4 | 6 | 2 | 0 | 0 | 1 | 2 | 11 | 0 | 0 | R | R | 6-3 | 220 | 5-19-72 | 1993 | Pelham, Ga. |
| Kingston, Mark, dh-1b | .222 | 3 | 9 | 0 | 2 | 0 | 0 | 0 | 0 | 0 | 3 | 0 | 0 | S | R | 6-4 | 210 | 5-16-70 | 1992 | Midland, Ga. |
| Kulpa, Steve, 3b | .230 | 56 | 165 | 18 | 38 | 10 | 0 | 1 | 17 | 18 | 45 | 4 | 3 | R | R | 6-4 | 205 | 5-4-71 | 1993 | Wyckoff, N.J. |
| McCabe, Brett, dh-1b | .271 | 38 | 107 | 20 | 29 | 4 | 0 | 1 | 15 | 20 | 25 | 3 | 0 | R | R | 6-2 | 195 | 9-1-71 | 1993 | Sacramento, Calif. |
| McGinnis, Shane, 3b-dh | .318 | 13 | 44 | 9 | 14 | 1 | 0 | 0 | 3 | 7 | 12 | 0 | 1 | R | R | 6-2 | 200 | 1-21-71 | 1993 | Ocala, Fla. |
| Mendez, Emilio, ss | .144 | 51 | 139 | 18 | 20 | 2 | 0 | 0 | 11 | 11 | 46 | 5 | 4 | R | R | 6-0 | 160 | 5-17-73 | 1992 | Miami Beach, Fla. |
| Montero, Danny, c | .063 | 9 | 16 | 1 | 1 | 1 | 0 | 0 | 1 | 2 | 7 | 0 | 1 | R | R | 5-10 | 170 | 10-9-73 | 1992 | Jobillo, D.R. |
| Morales, Francisco, c | .195 | 45 | 123 | 12 | 24 | 4 | 0 | 2 | 20 | 15 | 41 | 1 | 0 | R | R | 6-3 | 180 | 1-31-73 | 1991 | San Pedro de Macoris, D.R. |
| Pico, Brandon, of | .269 | 45 | 167 | 22 | 45 | 7 | 2 | 4 | 24 | 8 | 29 | 7 | 4 | L | L | 6-1 | 185 | 1-2-74 | 1992 | Newport, R.I. |
| Sigler, Brad, 3b | .154 | 6 | 13 | 3 | 2 | 0 | 0 | 0 | 1 | 6 | 5 | 0 | 1 | L | R | 6-0 | 180 | 7-30-71 | 1993 | Mobile, Ala. |
| Snyder, Jared, c | .209 | 51 | 148 | 15 | 31 | 7 | 0 | 2 | 22 | 16 | 29 | 5 | 1 | R | R | 6-2 | 215 | 3-8-70 | 1993 | Saugus, Calif. |
| Young, James, of | .181 | 43 | 72 | 19 | 13 | 1 | 0 | 1 | 9 | 17 | 26 | 8 | 3 | S | R | 5-10 | 185 | 6-6-70 | 1993 | Weaver, Ala. |

| PITCHING | W | L | ERA | G | GS | CG | SV | IP | H | R | ER | BB | SO | B | T | HT | WT | DOB | 1st Yr | Resides |
|---|---|---|---|---|---|---|---|---|---|---|---|---|---|---|---|---|---|---|---|---|
| Ball, Thomas | 5 | 2 | 4.55 | 15 | 11 | 0 | 0 | 61 | 85 | 48 | 31 | 23 | 43 | L | L | 6-2 | 180 | 10-29-71 | 1993 | Sylmar, Calif. |
| Bobbitt, Greg | 2 | 0 | 3.42 | 6 | 4 | 0 | 0 | 24 | 27 | 11 | 9 | 8 | 16 | R | L | 6-3 | 175 | 10-25-70 | 1993 | Rocky Mount, N.C. |
| Donnelly, Brendan | 4 | 0 | 6.28 | 21 | 3 | 0 | 1 | 43 | 39 | 34 | 30 | 29 | 29 | R | R | 6-3 | 200 | 7-4-71 | 1992 | Albuquerque, N.M. |
| Dreyer, Darren | 2 | 1 | 3.66 | 3 | 3 | 0 | 0 | 20 | 22 | 9 | 8 | 4 | 10 | R | R | 6-0 | 208 | 5-21-71 | 1992 | Taft, Texas |
| Farrow, James | 3 | 6 | 4.65 | 15 | 12 | 0 | 1 | 72 | 76 | 48 | 37 | 23 | 52 | R | R | 6-4 | 215 | 8-28-71 | 1993 | Swainsboro, Ga. |
| Hill, Shawn | 5 | 4 | 2.25 | 34 | 0 | 0 | 12 | 40 | 26 | 12 | 10 | 18 | 55 | R | R | 5-11 | 190 | 5-4-70 | 1993 | Nashua, N.H. |
| Hillman, Greg | 3 | 5 | 3.30 | 14 | 14 | 0 | 0 | 76 | 76 | 51 | 28 | 42 | 85 | L | L | 6-2 | 195 | 5-20-70 | 1993 | Austin, Texas |
| Hogan, Sean | 1 | 1 | 7.25 | 17 | 0 | 0 | 0 | 22 | 27 | 25 | 18 | 21 | 23 | L | L | 6-2 | 215 | 9-28-71 | 1993 | Sarasota, Fla. |
| Jenkins, Mike | 3 | 3 | 4.25 | 20 | 0 | 0 | 1 | 36 | 30 | 21 | 17 | 14 | 30 | R | R | 6-2 | 185 | 12-4-70 | 1993 | Simi Valley, Calif. |
| Kendrick, Scott | 0 | 0 | 18.00 | 1 | 0 | 0 | 0 | 1 | 1 | 2 | 2 | 1 | 1 | R | R | 6-3 | 185 | 11-21-75 | 1993 | Monroe, N.Y. |
| Locey, Anthony | 2 | 2 | 3.34 | 29 | 0 | 0 | 4 | 62 | 52 | 29 | 23 | 32 | 61 | R | R | 6-4 | 234 | 4-19-71 | 1993 | Columbus, Ga. |
| Ratliff, Jon | 1 | 1 | 3.21 | 3 | 3 | 0 | 0 | 14 | 12 | 8 | 5 | 8 | 7 | R | R | 6-4 | 195 | 12-22-71 | 1993 | Clay, N.Y. |
| Twiggs, Greg | 5 | 6 | 3.16 | 14 | 14 | 2 | 0 | 80 | 65 | 39 | 28 | 37 | 67 | R | L | 5-10 | 155 | 10-15-71 | 1993 | Winter Springs, Fla. |
| Walker, Wade | 5 | 2 | 3.12 | 13 | 13 | 1 | 0 | 84 | 76 | 38 | 29 | 36 | 47 | R | R | 6-1 | 190 | 9-18-71 | 1993 | Gonzalez, La. |
| Woodall, Brent | 2 | 1 | 1.30 | 23 | 0 | 0 | 1 | 35 | 19 | 6 | 5 | 20 | 44 | R | L | 6-4 | 245 | 7-20-70 | 1993 | La Jolla, Calif. |

# HUNTINGTON R
## APPALACHIAN LEAGUE

| BATTING | AVG | G | AB | R | H | 2B | 3B | HR | RBI | BB | SO | SB | CS | B | T | HT | WT | DOB | 1st Yr | Resides |
|---|---|---|---|---|---|---|---|---|---|---|---|---|---|---|---|---|---|---|---|---|
| Bonneau, Britt, 2b | .255 | 51 | 153 | 25 | 39 | 7 | 2 | 4 | 26 | 22 | 34 | 4 | 4 | S | R | 5-9 | 160 | 5-11-71 | 1993 | Farmers Branch, Texas |
| Chambers, Brad, of-dh | .100 | 3 | 10 | 1 | 1 | 0 | 0 | 0 | 2 | 0 | 1 | 0 | 0 | L | R | 6-2 | 195 | 11-23-73 | 1993 | Midlothian, Va. |
| Cline, Pat, c | .188 | 33 | 96 | 17 | 18 | 6 | 0 | 2 | 13 | 17 | 28 | 0 | 0 | R | R | 6-3 | 220 | 10-9-74 | 1993 | Bradenton, Fla. |
| Ellis, Kevin, 3b | .267 | 59 | 225 | 44 | 60 | 11 | 2 | 13 | 48 | 25 | 43 | 6 | 5 | R | R | 6-0 | 210 | 11-21-71 | 1993 | Waco, Texas |
| Eusebio, Ralph, of | .216 | 47 | 116 | 25 | 25 | 2 | 0 | 2 | 12 | 25 | 25 | 4 | 4 | R | R | 6-0 | 170 | 1-20-73 | 1993 | Hoboken, N.J. |
| Fric, Sean, of | .268 | 63 | 190 | 36 | 51 | 8 | 1 | 8 | 37 | 29 | 41 | 5 | 1 | R | R | 6-1 | 190 | 6-7-73 | 1993 | Port Lavaca, Texas |
| Johnson, Artis, of | .294 | 33 | 102 | 17 | 30 | 6 | 0 | 0 | 10 | 8 | 20 | 2 | 3 | R | R | 6-1 | 180 | 9-12-72 | 1993 | Delray Beach, Fla. |
| Khoury, Tony, c-p | .293 | 30 | 41 | 8 | 12 | 0 | 1 | 1 | 11 | 4 | 8 | 1 | 0 | R | R | 6-1 | 185 | 6-16-71 | 1993 | Toledo, Ohio |
| King, Anthony, of | .189 | 28 | 74 | 8 | 14 | 2 | 0 | 1 | 6 | 8 | 23 | 2 | 2 | L | L | 6-2 | 205 | 6-4-71 | 1993 | Jackson, Miss. |
| King, Thomas, of | .266 | 44 | 124 | 16 | 33 | 6 | 0 | 2 | 21 | 13 | 35 | 7 | 2 | S | R | 6-1 | 212 | 9-6-70 | 1993 | Albany, Ga. |
| Martin, Ariel, 1b-dh | .232 | 45 | 151 | 18 | 35 | 5 | 1 | 1 | 13 | 14 | 35 | 2 | 1 | S | L | 6-5 | 247 | 8-14-71 | 1993 | Los Angeles, Calif. |
| Maxwell, Jason, ss | .291 | 61 | 179 | 50 | 52 | 7 | 2 | 7 | 38 | 35 | 39 | 6 | 4 | R | R | 6-0 | 175 | 3-21-72 | 1993 | Lewisburg, Tenn. |
| Mercedes, Juan, ss | .157 | 39 | 102 | 11 | 16 | 0 | 0 | 0 | 5 | 8 | 24 | 3 | 3 | R | R | 6-3 | 150 | 5-21-74 | 1992 | San Pedro de Macoris, D.R. |
| Montero, Danny, c | .292 | 33 | 89 | 20 | 26 | 3 | 2 | 1 | 9 | 12 | 16 | 4 | 3 | R | R | 5-10 | 170 | 10-9-73 | 1992 | Jobillo, D.R. |
| Morris, Bob, 2b | .288 | 50 | 170 | 29 | 49 | 8 | 3 | 1 | 24 | 24 | 29 | 6 | 8 | L | R | 6-0 | 180 | 11-22-72 | 1993 | Munster, Ind. |
| Serrato, Jacob, c | .071 | 12 | 14 | 0 | 1 | 1 | 0 | 0 | 1 | 1 | 3 | 0 | 0 | R | R | 6-2 | 185 | 5-14-74 | 1993 | Chicago, Ill. |
| Sigler, Brad, dh-3b | .250 | 9 | 20 | 4 | 5 | 1 | 0 | 0 | 2 | 7 | 4 | 1 | 0 | L | R | 6-0 | 180 | 7-30-71 | 1993 | Mobile, Ala. |
| Smith, Ronald, 1b | .205 | 49 | 156 | 22 | 32 | 4 | 0 | 7 | 26 | 19 | 28 | 3 | 0 | L | R | 6-2 | 230 | 8-8-71 | 1993 | Decatur, Ga. |
| Whatley, Gabe, 3b-of | .263 | 51 | 175 | 30 | 46 | 12 | 1 | 5 | 25 | 26 | 32 | 3 | 3 | L | R | 6-0 | 180 | 12-29-71 | 1993 | Stone Mountain, Ga. |

# CUBS: ORGANIZATION LEADERS

## MAJOR LEAGUERS

**BATTING**

| | | |
|---|---|---|
| *AVG | Mark Grace | .325 |
| R | Sammy Sosa | 92 |
| H | Mark Grace | 193 |
| TB | Sammy Sosa | 290 |
| 2B | Mark Grace | 39 |
| 3B | Two tied at | 5 |
| HR | Sammy Sosa | 33 |
| RBI | Mark Grace | 98 |
| BB | Mark Grace | 71 |
| SO | Sammy Sosa | 135 |
| SB | Sammy Sosa | 36 |

**PITCHING**

| | | |
|---|---|---|
| W | Greg Hibbard | 15 |
| L | Mike Morgan | 15 |
| #ERA | Jose Bautista | 2.82 |
| G | Randy Myers | 73 |
| CG | Two tied at | 2 |
| SV | Randy Myers | 53 |
| IP | Mike Morgan | 208 |
| BB | Two tied at | 74 |
| SO | Jose Guzman | 163 |

**Greg Hibbard**
Career-high 15 wins

MEL BAILEY

## MINOR LEAGUERS

**BATTING**

| | | |
|---|---|---|
| *AVG | Brant Brown, Daytona-Orlando | .334 |
| R | Eddie Zambrano, Iowa | 95 |
| H | Doug Glanville, Daytona-Orlando | 148 |
| TB | Eddie Zambrano, Iowa | 271 |
| 2B | Matt Franco, Orlando-Iowa | 37 |
| 3B | Brant Brown, Daytona-Orlando | 10 |
| HR | Eddie Zambrano, Iowa | 32 |
| RBI | Eddie Zambrano, Iowa | 115 |
| BB | Ozzie Timmons, Orlando | 62 |
| SO | Steve Walker, Peoria | 123 |
| SB | Doug Glanville, Daytona-Orlando | 33 |

**PITCHING**

| | | |
|---|---|---|
| W | Kennie Steenstra, Day.-Orlando-Iowa | 14 |
| L | Derek Wallace, Daytona-Orlando-Iowa | 13 |
| #ERA | David Hutcheson, Peoria | 2.33 |
| G | Earnie Johnson, Orlando-Iowa | 62 |
| CG | Hector Trinidad, Peoria-Orlando | 5 |
| SV | Travis Willis, Orlando | 24 |
| IP | Kennie Steenstra, Day.-Orlando-Iowa | 188 |
| BB | Jimmy Williams, Iowa-Orlando | 75 |
| SO | Bill Brennan, Iowa | 143 |

*Minimum 250 At-Bats  #Minimum 75 Innings

| PITCHING | W | L | ERA | G | GS | CG | SV | IP | H | R | ER | BB | SO | B | T | HT | WT | DOB | 1st Yr | Resides |
|---|---|---|---|---|---|---|---|---|---|---|---|---|---|---|---|---|---|---|---|---|
| Bobbitt, Greg | 3 | 2 | 3.56 | 10 | 10 | 0 | 0 | 61 | 54 | 27 | 24 | 9 | 30 | R | L | 6-3 | 175 | 10-25-70 | 1993 | Rocky Mount, N.C. |
| Bryant, Chris | 5 | 4 | 3.18 | 12 | 12 | 0 | 0 | 65 | 57 | 28 | 23 | 37 | 56 | L | L | 6-1 | 180 | 8-13-75 | 1993 | Tampa, Fla. |
| Childress, Billy | 4 | 1 | 2.49 | 16 | 0 | 0 | 6 | 43 | 37 | 19 | 12 | 16 | 57 | R | L | 6-2 | 210 | 10-22-70 | 1992 | Richmond, Va. |
| Garcia, Alfredo | 1 | 2 | 4.95 | 3 | 3 | 0 | 0 | 20 | 23 | 11 | 11 | 1 | 11 | S | R | 6-2 | 175 | 6-11-74 | 1993 | Buena Park, Calif. |
| Gonzalez, Geremis | 3 | 9 | 6.25 | 12 | 12 | 1 | 0 | 68 | 82 | 59 | 47 | 38 | 42 | R | R | 6-1 | 180 | 1-8-75 | 1992 | Maracaibo, Venez. |
| Hennessy, Sean | 0 | 1 | 8.83 | 11 | 0 | 0 | 0 | 17 | 36 | 20 | 17 | 4 | 17 | L | L | 6-2 | 190 | 6-23-71 | 1993 | Pt. Pleasant Beach, N.J. |
| Khoury, Tony | 0 | 1 | 3.63 | 12 | 0 | 0 | 1 | 22 | 17 | 9 | 9 | 12 | 22 | R | R | 6-1 | 185 | 6-16-71 | 1993 | Toledo, Ohio |
| Kurtz, Rodd | 4 | 3 | 4.75 | 11 | 11 | 0 | 0 | 61 | 71 | 42 | 32 | 18 | 42 | L | L | 6-6 | 215 | 7-7-72 | 1993 | San Antonio, Texas |
| Lavenia, Mark | 2 | 3 | 4.24 | 21 | 0 | 0 | 5 | 34 | 27 | 19 | 16 | 14 | 35 | R | L | 6-1 | 175 | 8-30-72 | 1993 | Latham, N.Y. |
| Lopez, Orlando | 7 | 1 | 3.19 | 9 | 8 | 2 | 0 | 54 | 55 | 28 | 19 | 17 | 46 | L | L | 6-0 | 185 | 3-28-73 | 1992 | Isabela, P.R. |
| Lynch, Mike | 2 | 1 | 5.70 | 14 | 3 | 0 | 2 | 36 | 29 | 26 | 23 | 25 | 40 | R | R | 6-4 | 230 | 5-5-72 | 1993 | Chicago, Ill. |
| Ortiz, Dan | 1 | 2 | 4.79 | 17 | 0 | 0 | 1 | 36 | 33 | 25 | 19 | 24 | 42 | L | L | 6-2 | 174 | 5-4-73 | 1992 | Hoboken, N.J. |
| Weber, David | 1 | 5 | 4.66 | 14 | 9 | 0 | 0 | 56 | 73 | 48 | 29 | 18 | 25 | R | R | 5-11 | 175 | 11-19-74 | 1993 | Jersey City, N.J. |

## ST. LUCIE — R

### GULF COAST LEAGUE

| BATTING | AVG | G | AB | R | H | 2B | 3B | HR | RBI | BB | SO | SB | CS | B | T | HT | WT | DOB | 1st Yr | Resides |
|---|---|---|---|---|---|---|---|---|---|---|---|---|---|---|---|---|---|---|---|---|
| Avalos, Gil, ss-2b | .297 | 33 | 111 | 22 | 33 | 6 | 1 | 1 | 8 | 14 | 17 | 14 | 2 | R | R | 5-11 | 175 | 3-26-73 | 1993 | Houston, Texas |
| Castle, Ryan, 2b | .275 | 25 | 80 | 15 | 22 | 3 | 0 | 2 | 10 | 9 | 11 | 6 | 1 | R | R | 5-9 | 175 | 12-7-71 | 1993 | Carmel, N.Y. |
| Chambers, Brad, dh-1b | .297 | 24 | 74 | 9 | 22 | 6 | 0 | 1 | 10 | 9 | 7 | 0 | 2 | L | R | 6-2 | 195 | 11-23-73 | 1993 | Midlothian, Va. |
| Cicero, Frank, c-dh | .241 | 29 | 83 | 13 | 20 | 2 | 1 | 0 | 9 | 7 | 14 | 2 | 1 | R | R | 6-1 | 175 | 11-25-74 | 1993 | La Mirada, Calif. |
| Cunningham, Jamil, 2b | .179 | 40 | 106 | 16 | 19 | 1 | 1 | 1 | 12 | 6 | 25 | 9 | 6 | R | R | 5-10 | 163 | 6-27-72 | 1993 | DeLeon Springs, Fla. |
| DeJesus, Jose, 3b | .150 | 33 | 80 | 13 | 12 | 2 | 0 | 0 | 4 | 10 | 20 | 1 | 0 | R | R | 6-2 | 175 | 10-31-74 | 1993 | Patillas, P.R. |
| Garcia, Eduard, of | .211 | 45 | 133 | 13 | 28 | 4 | 1 | 1 | 13 | 8 | 29 | 2 | 1 | R | R | 6-1 | 175 | 6-13-75 | 1992 | Azua, D.R. |
| Gil, Dan, of | .272 | 48 | 151 | 13 | 41 | 3 | 0 | 0 | 19 | 20 | 25 | 4 | 8 | R | R | 6-3 | 190 | 7-3-74 | 1993 | San Diego, Calif. |
| Hunter, Burt, 2b-3b | .226 | 9 | 31 | 2 | 7 | 1 | 0 | 0 | 2 | 2 | 8 | 2 | 0 | S | R | 5-11 | 168 | 2-13-73 | 1992 | Hopewell, Va. |
| Kieschnick, Brooks, of-dh | .222 | 3 | 9 | 0 | 2 | 1 | 0 | 0 | 0 | 1 | 0 | 0 | 0 | L | R | 6-4 | 217 | 6-6-72 | 1993 | Caldwell, Texas |
| Knighten, Dwon, of | .250 | 34 | 88 | 12 | 22 | 1 | 1 | 0 | 14 | 10 | 14 | 6 | 3 | R | R | 5-10 | 170 | 10-24-73 | 1993 | Cerritos, Calif. |
| Molina, Jose, c | .218 | 33 | 78 | 5 | 17 | 2 | 0 | 0 | 4 | 12 | 12 | 3 | 2 | R | R | 6-1 | 180 | 6-3-75 | 1993 | Vega Alta, P.R. |
| Montilla, Miguel, ss | .216 | 40 | 125 | 15 | 27 | 1 | 1 | 0 | 7 | 23 | 35 | 3 | 4 | R | R | 6-1 | 180 | 12-18-73 | 1993 | North Bergen, N.J. |
| Nelson, Andre, of | .200 | 4 | 15 | 3 | 3 | 0 | 0 | 0 | 0 | 2 | 7 | 2 | 0 | R | R | 6-1 | 218 | 5-7-71 | 1992 | Ridgeway, S.C. |
| Pico, Brandon, of | .385 | 10 | 39 | 3 | 15 | 3 | 1 | 0 | 9 | 2 | 2 | 3 | 3 | L | L | 6-1 | 185 | 1-2-74 | 1992 | Newport, R.I. |
| Reynolds, Paul, 1b-c | .261 | 48 | 142 | 16 | 37 | 8 | 0 | 0 | 13 | 28 | 33 | 4 | 7 | R | R | 6-2 | 195 | 11-17-73 | 1993 | Tarpon Springs, Fla. |
| Salazar, Marlon, 3b | .000 | 2 | 1 | 0 | 0 | 0 | 0 | 0 | 0 | 0 | 0 | 0 | 0 | R | R | 6-2 | 196 | 7-19-74 | 1992 | Barquisimeto, Venez. |
| Sanchez, Juan, of | .232 | 27 | 69 | 9 | 16 | 1 | 0 | 0 | 6 | 9 | 10 | 2 | 2 | R | R | 6-1 | 160 | 6-26-73 | 1991 | San Pedro de Macoris, D.R. |
| Sauer, John, of | .169 | 29 | 65 | 12 | 11 | 1 | 0 | 0 | 1 | 10 | 17 | 5 | 1 | R | R | 6-2 | 210 | 5-14-75 | 1993 | Baltimore, Md. |
| Scopio, Joe, of | .156 | 43 | 90 | 18 | 14 | 1 | 0 | 0 | 2 | 15 | 21 | 14 | 5 | S | R | 6-1 | 170 | 1-7-73 | 1993 | Maple Shade, N.J. |
| Thomas, Nate, p-1b | .200 | 7 | 5 | 0 | 1 | 0 | 0 | 0 | 0 | 1 | 0 | 1 | 0 | L | L | 6-1 | 165 | 1-16-74 | 1993 | Virginia Beach, Va. |
| Vaske, Terry, 1b-p | .261 | 31 | 88 | 16 | 23 | 3 | 2 | 2 | 10 | 12 | 17 | 2 | 5 | L | R | 6-5 | 185 | 3-1-71 | 1992 | Dyersville, Iowa |
| Vielleux, Billy, 3b | .283 | 36 | 99 | 11 | 28 | 2 | 2 | 0 | 10 | 10 | 18 | 6 | 4 | R | R | 6-3 | 180 | 1-25-74 | 1993 | White River Junction, Vt. |
| Wolff, James, c-dh | .212 | 11 | 33 | 4 | 7 | 2 | 2 | 0 | 5 | 1 | 8 | 2 | 0 | R | R | 6-2 | 210 | 12-22-69 | 1990 | Boca Raton, Fla. |
| Zuleta, Julio, dh-c | .245 | 17 | 53 | 3 | 13 | 0 | 1 | 0 | 6 | 3 | 12 | 0 | 0 | R | R | 6-4 | 200 | 3-28-75 | 1993 | Juan Diaz, Panama |

| PITCHING | W | L | ERA | G | GS | CG | SV | IP | H | R | ER | BB | SO | B | T | HT | WT | DOB | 1st Yr | Resides |
|---|---|---|---|---|---|---|---|---|---|---|---|---|---|---|---|---|---|---|---|---|
| Beashore, Gary | 0 | 1 | 6.75 | 3 | 1 | 0 | 1 | 8 | 10 | 7 | 6 | 1 | 6 | R | R | 6-0 | 193 | 6-17-71 | 1993 | Kansas City, Kan. |
| Blanco, Rosmel | 0 | 5 | 11.44 | 6 | 6 | 0 | 0 | 20 | 22 | 33 | 25 | 30 | 5 | R | R | 6-6 | 206 | 11-9-73 | 1991 | La Sabana, Venez. |
| Broome, John | 3 | 6 | 5.66 | 11 | 11 | 0 | 0 | 56 | 79 | 42 | 35 | 16 | 29 | R | R | 6-0 | 185 | 6-26-73 | 1993 | Maple Shade, N.J. |
| Castro, Gabby | 2 | 3 | 2.88 | 13 | 0 | 0 | 1 | 41 | 35 | 21 | 13 | 19 | 31 | S | L | 6-2 | 180 | 8-26-75 | 1993 | Aguadilla, P.R. |
| Garcia, Alfredo | 2 | 6 | 3.40 | 10 | 8 | 0 | 0 | 56 | 54 | 29 | 21 | 7 | 38 | S | R | 6-2 | 175 | 6-11-74 | 1993 | Buena Park, Calif. |
| Kendrick, Scott | 1 | 2 | 7.32 | 9 | 7 | 0 | 0 | 36 | 44 | 37 | 29 | 15 | 17 | L | R | 6-3 | 185 | 11-21-75 | 1993 | Monroe, N.C. |
| Liriano, Orlando | 1 | 1 | 3.89 | 12 | 3 | 0 | 1 | 35 | 40 | 18 | 15 | 10 | 24 | R | R | 6-0 | 195 | 8-8-75 | 1993 | New York, N.Y. |
| Love, Farley | 1 | 0 | 3.00 | 5 | 0 | 0 | 0 | 9 | 12 | 8 | 3 | 6 | 7 | R | R | 6-6 | 200 | 4-21-73 | 1993 | Eight Mile, Ala. |
| Pacheco, Jose | 0 | 0 | 4.50 | 4 | 2 | 0 | 2 | 18 | 18 | 10 | 9 | 3 | 11 | R | R | 6-2 | 190 | 4-14-74 | 1991 | Yuaco, P.R. |
| Pimentel, Robert | 0 | 1 | 2.25 | 4 | 0 | 0 | 0 | 8 | 8 | 7 | 2 | 6 | 9 | R | R | 6-1 | 160 | 5-27-74 | 1991 | Azua, D.R. |
| Porzio, Mike | 1 | 3 | 3.83 | 10 | 8 | 0 | 0 | 42 | 42 | 26 | 18 | 30 | 30 | L | L | 6-3 | 190 | 8-20-72 | 1993 | Norwalk, Conn. |
| Rain, Steve | 1 | 3 | 3.89 | 10 | 6 | 0 | 0 | 37 | 37 | 20 | 16 | 17 | 29 | R | R | 6-6 | 225 | 6-2-75 | 1993 | Walnut, Calif. |
| Rose, Tim | 2 | 2 | 3.04 | 10 | 1 | 0 | 0 | 24 | 25 | 9 | 8 | 6 | 22 | R | R | 6-2 | 185 | 6-9-75 | 1993 | Chesapeake, Va. |
| Ruiz, Jose | 0 | 0 | 1.86 | 4 | 1 | 0 | 1 | 10 | 7 | 2 | 2 | 2 | 6 | L | L | 6-2 | 165 | 2-13-73 | 1992 | Valcon, Venez. |
| Sabino, Miguel | 0 | 0 | 5.59 | 3 | 0 | 0 | 0 | 10 | 13 | 10 | 6 | 4 | 9 | R | R | 6-4 | 188 | 12-27-74 | 1992 | San Pedro de Macoris, D.R. |
| Thomas, Nate | 0 | 0 | 8.31 | 5 | 2 | 0 | 0 | 13 | 15 | 15 | 12 | 14 | 10 | L | L | 6-1 | 165 | 1-16-74 | 1993 | Virginia Beach, Va. |
| Tomberlin, Lance | 2 | 2 | 4.02 | 14 | 2 | 0 | 0 | 47 | 49 | 29 | 21 | 19 | 18 | L | R | 6-1 | 180 | 9-30-73 | 1993 | Ocilla, Ga. |
| Vaske, Terry | 1 | 1 | 1.29 | 4 | 0 | 0 | 0 | 7 | 8 | 1 | 1 | 1 | 4 | L | R | 6-5 | 185 | 3-1-71 | 1992 | Dyersville, Iowa |
| Whitfill, Mike | 2 | 2 | 1.91 | 13 | 1 | 0 | 1 | 33 | 33 | 16 | 7 | 5 | 24 | R | R | 6-3 | 185 | 10-24-74 | 1993 | Bryson, Texas |

# CINCINNATI REDS

**Managers:** Tony Perez, Dave Johnson.    **1993 Record:** 73-89, .451 (5th, NL West).

| BATTING | AVG | G | AB | R | H | 2B | 3B | HR | RBI | BB | SO | SB | CS | B | T | HT | WT | DOB | 1st Yr | Resides |
|---|---|---|---|---|---|---|---|---|---|---|---|---|---|---|---|---|---|---|---|---|
| Branson, Jeff | .241 | 125 | 381 | 40 | 92 | 15 | 1 | 3 | 22 | 19 | 73 | 4 | 1 | L | R | 6-0 | 180 | 1-26-67 | 1989 | Silas, Ala. |
| Brumfield, Jacob | .268 | 103 | 272 | 40 | 73 | 17 | 3 | 6 | 23 | 21 | 47 | 20 | 8 | R | R | 6-0 | 180 | 5-27-65 | 1983 | Atlanta, Ga. |
| Costo, Tim | .224 | 31 | 98 | 13 | 22 | 5 | 0 | 3 | 12 | 4 | 17 | 0 | 0 | R | R | 6-5 | 230 | 2-16-69 | 1990 | Glen Ellyn, Ill. |
| Daugherty, Jack | .220 | 46 | 59 | 7 | 13 | 2 | 0 | 2 | 9 | 11 | 15 | 0 | 0 | S | L | 6-0 | 190 | 7-3-60 | 1983 | San Diego, Calif. |
| 2-team (4 Houston) | .226 | 50 | 62 | 7 | 14 | 2 | 0 | 2 | 9 | 11 | 15 | 0 | 0 | | | | | | | |
| Dorsett, Brian | .254 | 25 | 63 | 7 | 16 | 4 | 0 | 2 | 12 | 3 | 14 | 0 | 0 | R | R | 6-3 | 220 | 4-9-61 | 1983 | Terre Haute, Ind. |
| Espy, Cecil | .233 | 40 | 60 | 6 | 14 | 2 | 0 | 0 | 5 | 14 | 13 | 2 | 2 | S | R | 6-3 | 195 | 1-20-63 | 1980 | Fort Worth, Texas |
| Gordon, Keith | .167 | 3 | 6 | 0 | 1 | 0 | 0 | 0 | 0 | 0 | 2 | 0 | 0 | R | R | 6-1 | 205 | 1-22-69 | 1990 | Olney, Md. |
| Greene, Willie | .160 | 15 | 50 | 7 | 8 | 1 | 1 | 2 | 5 | 2 | 19 | 0 | 0 | L | R | 5-11 | 180 | 9-23-71 | 1989 | Haddock, Ga. |
| Gregg, Tommy | .167 | 10 | 12 | 1 | 2 | 0 | 0 | 0 | 1 | 0 | 0 | 0 | 0 | L | L | 6-1 | 190 | 7-29-63 | 1985 | Smyrna, Ga. |
| Hernandez, Cesar | .083 | 27 | 24 | 3 | 2 | 0 | 0 | 0 | 1 | 1 | 8 | 1 | 2 | R | R | 6-0 | 170 | 9-28-66 | 1985 | Santo Domingo, D.R. |
| Howard, Tom | .277 | 38 | 141 | 22 | 39 | 8 | 3 | 4 | 13 | 12 | 21 | 5 | 6 | S | R | 6-2 | 205 | 12-11-64 | 1986 | Middletown, Ohio |
| Hughes, Keith | .000 | 3 | 4 | 0 | 0 | 0 | 0 | 0 | 0 | 0 | 0 | 0 | 0 | L | L | 6-3 | 210 | 9-12-63 | 1982 | Berwyn, Pa. |
| Kelly, Bobby | .319 | 78 | 320 | 44 | 102 | 17 | 3 | 9 | 35 | 17 | 43 | 21 | 5 | R | R | 6-2 | 192 | 10-1-64 | 1982 | Panama City, Panama |
| Kessinger, Keith | .259 | 11 | 27 | 4 | 7 | 1 | 0 | 1 | 3 | 4 | 4 | 0 | 0 | S | R | 6-2 | 185 | 2-19-67 | 1989 | Oxford, Miss. |
| Koelling, Brian | .067 | 7 | 15 | 2 | 1 | 0 | 0 | 0 | 0 | 0 | 2 | 0 | 0 | R | R | 6-1 | 185 | 6-11-69 | 1991 | Cleves, Ohio |
| Larkin, Barry | .315 | 100 | 384 | 57 | 121 | 20 | 3 | 8 | 51 | 51 | 33 | 14 | 1 | R | R | 6-0 | 190 | 4-28-64 | 1985 | Cincinnati, Ohio |
| Milligan, Randy | .274 | 83 | 234 | 30 | 64 | 11 | 1 | 6 | 29 | 46 | 49 | 0 | 2 | R | R | 6-1 | 225 | 11-27-61 | 1981 | Baltimore, Md. |
| Mitchell, Kevin | .341 | 93 | 323 | 56 | 110 | 21 | 3 | 19 | 64 | 25 | 48 | 1 | 0 | R | R | 5-11 | 210 | 1-13-62 | 1981 | Chula Vista, Calif. |
| Morris, Hal | .317 | 101 | 379 | 48 | 120 | 18 | 0 | 7 | 49 | 34 | 51 | 2 | 2 | L | L | 6-4 | 215 | 4-9-65 | 1986 | Union, Ky. |
| Oliver, Joe | .239 | 139 | 482 | 40 | 115 | 28 | 0 | 14 | 75 | 27 | 91 | 0 | 0 | R | R | 6-3 | 210 | 7-24-65 | 1983 | Orlando, Fla. |
| Roberts, Bip | .240 | 83 | 292 | 46 | 70 | 13 | 0 | 1 | 18 | 38 | 46 | 26 | 6 | S | R | 5-7 | 160 | 10-27-63 | 1982 | San Diego, Calif. |
| Sabo, Chris | .259 | 148 | 552 | 86 | 143 | 33 | 2 | 21 | 82 | 43 | 105 | 6 | 4 | R | R | 6-0 | 185 | 1-19-62 | 1983 | Cincinnati, Ohio |
| Samuel, Juan | .230 | 103 | 261 | 31 | 60 | 10 | 4 | 4 | 26 | 23 | 53 | 9 | 1 | R | R | 5-11 | 180 | 12-9-60 | 1980 | Santo Domingo, D.R. |
| Sanders, Reggie | .274 | 138 | 496 | 90 | 136 | 16 | 4 | 20 | 83 | 51 | 118 | 27 | 10 | R | R | 6-1 | 180 | 12-1-67 | 1985 | Cincinnati, Ohio |
| Tubbs, Greg | .186 | 35 | 59 | 10 | 11 | 0 | 0 | 1 | 2 | 14 | 10 | 3 | 1 | R | R | 5-9 | 185 | 8-31-62 | 1984 | Cookeville, Tenn. |
| Varsho, Gary | .232 | 77 | 95 | 8 | 22 | 6 | 2 | 1 | 11 | 9 | 19 | 1 | 0 | L | R | 5-10 | 180 | 6-20-61 | 1982 | Marshfield, Wis. |
| Wilson, Dan | .224 | 36 | 76 | 6 | 17 | 3 | 0 | 0 | 8 | 9 | 16 | 0 | 0 | R | R | 6-3 | 190 | 3-25-69 | 1990 | St. Louis Park, Ill. |

| PITCHING | W | L | ERA | G | GS | CG | SV | IP | H | R | ER | BB | SO | B | T | HT | WT | DOB | 1st Yr | Resides |
|---|---|---|---|---|---|---|---|---|---|---|---|---|---|---|---|---|---|---|---|---|
| Anderson, Mike | 0 | 0 | 18.56 | 3 | 0 | 0 | 0 | 5 | 12 | 11 | 11 | 3 | 4 | R | R | 6-3 | 205 | 7-30-66 | 1988 | Georgetown, Texas |
| Ayala, Bobby | 7 | 10 | 5.60 | 43 | 9 | 0 | 3 | 98 | 106 | 72 | 61 | 45 | 65 | R | R | 6-3 | 200 | 7-8-69 | 1988 | Oxnard, Calif. |
| Belcher, Tim | 9 | 6 | 4.47 | 22 | 22 | 4 | 0 | 137 | 134 | 72 | 68 | 47 | 101 | R | R | 6-3 | 220 | 10-19-61 | 1984 | Mt. Gilead, Ohio |
| Browning, Tom | 7 | 7 | 4.74 | 21 | 20 | 0 | 0 | 114 | 159 | 61 | 60 | 20 | 53 | L | L | 6-1 | 195 | 4-28-60 | 1982 | Edgewood, Ky. |
| Bushing, Chris | 0 | 0 | 12.46 | 6 | 0 | 0 | 0 | 4 | 9 | 7 | 6 | 4 | 3 | R | R | 6-0 | 190 | 11-4-67 | 1986 | Plantation, Fla. |
| Cadaret, Greg | 2 | 1 | 4.96 | 34 | 0 | 0 | 1 | 33 | 40 | 19 | 18 | 23 | 23 | L | L | 6-3 | 215 | 2-27-62 | 1983 | Mesa, Ariz. |
| Dibble, Rob | 1 | 4 | 6.48 | 45 | 0 | 0 | 19 | 42 | 34 | 33 | 30 | 42 | 49 | L | R | 6-4 | 230 | 1-24-64 | 1983 | Cincinnati, Ohio |
| Foster, Steve | 2 | 2 | 1.75 | 17 | 0 | 0 | 0 | 26 | 23 | 8 | 5 | 5 | 16 | R | R | 6-0 | 180 | 8-16-66 | 1988 | Waxahachie, Texas |
| Henry, Dwayne | 0 | 1 | 3.86 | 3 | 0 | 0 | 0 | 5 | 6 | 8 | 2 | 4 | 2 | R | R | 6-3 | 205 | 2-16-62 | 1980 | Glen Allen, Va. |
| Hill, Milt | 3 | 0 | 5.65 | 19 | 0 | 0 | 0 | 29 | 34 | 18 | 18 | 9 | 23 | R | R | 6-0 | 180 | 8-22-65 | 1987 | Dawsonville, Ga. |
| Kaiser, Jeff | 0 | 0 | 2.70 | 3 | 0 | 0 | 0 | 3 | 4 | 1 | 1 | 2 | 4 | R | L | 6-3 | 205 | 7-24-60 | 1982 | Trenton, Mich. |
| Landrum, Bill | 0 | 2 | 3.74 | 14 | 0 | 0 | 0 | 22 | 18 | 9 | 9 | 6 | 14 | R | R | 6-2 | 200 | 8-17-58 | 1980 | Chapin, S.C. |
| Luebbers, Larry | 2 | 5 | 4.54 | 14 | 14 | 0 | 0 | 77 | 74 | 49 | 39 | 38 | 38 | R | R | 6-6 | 190 | 10-11-69 | 1990 | Florence, Ky. |
| Powell, Ross | 0 | 3 | 4.41 | 9 | 1 | 0 | 0 | 16 | 13 | 8 | 8 | 6 | 17 | L | L | 6-0 | 180 | 1-24-68 | 1989 | Sand Lake, Mich. |
| Pugh, Tim | 10 | 15 | 5.26 | 31 | 27 | 3 | 0 | 164 | 200 | 102 | 96 | 59 | 94 | R | R | 6-5 | 225 | 1-26-67 | 1989 | Bartlesville, Okla. |
| Reardon, Jeff | 4 | 6 | 4.09 | 58 | 0 | 0 | 8 | 62 | 66 | 34 | 28 | 10 | 35 | R | R | 6-0 | 200 | 10-1-55 | 1977 | Palm Beach Gardens, Fla. |
| Rijo, Jose | 14 | 9 | 2.48 | 36 | 36 | 2 | 0 | 257 | 218 | 76 | 71 | 62 | 227 | R | R | 6-2 | 210 | 5-13-65 | 1981 | Boca Raton, Fla. |
| Roper, John | 2 | 5 | 5.63 | 16 | 15 | 0 | 0 | 80 | 92 | 51 | 50 | 36 | 54 | R | R | 6-0 | 175 | 11-21-71 | 1990 | Raeford, N.C. |
| Ruffin, Johnny | 2 | 1 | 3.58 | 21 | 0 | 0 | 2 | 38 | 36 | 16 | 15 | 11 | 30 | R | R | 6-3 | 174 | 7-29-71 | 1988 | Butler, Ala. |
| Ruskin, Scott | 0 | 0 | 18.00 | 4 | 0 | 0 | 0 | 1 | 3 | 2 | 2 | 2 | 0 | R | L | 6-2 | 195 | 6-8-63 | 1986 | Jacksonville, Fla. |
| Service, Scott | 2 | 2 | 3.70 | 26 | 0 | 0 | 2 | 41 | 36 | 19 | 17 | 15 | 40 | R | R | 6-6 | 235 | 2-26-67 | 1986 | Cincinnati, Ohio |
| 2-team (3 Colorado) | 2 | 2 | 4.30 | 29 | 0 | 0 | 2 | 46 | 44 | 24 | 22 | 16 | 43 | | | | | | | |
| Smiley, John | 3 | 9 | 5.62 | 18 | 18 | 2 | 0 | 106 | 117 | 69 | 66 | 31 | 60 | L | L | 6-4 | 215 | 3-17-65 | 1983 | Wexford, Pa. |
| Spradlin, Jerry | 2 | 1 | 3.49 | 37 | 0 | 0 | 2 | 49 | 44 | 20 | 19 | 9 | 24 | S | R | 6-7 | 230 | 6-14-67 | 1988 | Anaheim, Calif. |
| Wickander, Kevin | 1 | 0 | 6.75 | 33 | 0 | 0 | 0 | 25 | 32 | 20 | 19 | 14 | 23 | L | L | 6-3 | 200 | 1-4-65 | 1986 | Glendale, Ariz. |

## FIELDING

| Catcher | PCT | G | PO | A | E | DP |
|---|---|---|---|---|---|---|
| Dorsett | 1.000 | 18 | 111 | 5 | 0 | 0 |
| Oliver | .992 | 133 | 791 | 68 | 7 | 8 |
| Wilson | .994 | 35 | 146 | 9 | 1 | 2 |

| First Base | PCT | G | PO | A | E | DP |
|---|---|---|---|---|---|---|
| Branson | 1.000 | 1 | 10 | 1 | 0 | 0 |
| Costo | 1.000 | 2 | 2 | 1 | 0 | 0 |
| Daugherty | 1.000 | 2 | 20 | 2 | 0 | 1 |
| Dorsett | 1.000 | 3 | 8 | 0 | 0 | 0 |
| Milligan | .994 | 61 | 468 | 56 | 3 | 47 |
| Morris | .994 | 98 | 746 | 75 | 5 | 61 |
| Oliver | 1.000 | 12 | 34 | 2 | 0 | 5 |
| Samuel | 1.000 | 6 | 11 | 3 | 0 | 0 |

| Second Base | PCT | G | PO | A | E | DP |
|---|---|---|---|---|---|---|
| Branson | .974 | 94 | 105 | 5 | 28 | |
| Brumfield | .842 | 4 | 6 | 10 | 3 | 3 |
| Koelling | .941 | 3 | 4 | 12 | 1 | 1 |

| | PCT | G | PO | A | E | DP |
|---|---|---|---|---|---|---|
| Roberts | .984 | 64 | 136 | 172 | 5 | 31 |
| Samuel | .971 | 70 | 135 | 164 | 9 | 33 |

| Third Base | PCT | G | PO | A | E | DP |
|---|---|---|---|---|---|---|
| Branson | .958 | 14 | 7 | 16 | 1 | 0 |
| Costo | 1.000 | 2 | 0 | 1 | 0 | 0 |
| Greene | 1.000 | 5 | 2 | 9 | 0 | 0 |
| Roberts | 1.000 | 3 | 1 | 4 | 0 | 0 |
| Sabo | .967 | 148 | 79 | 242 | 11 | 16 |
| Samuel | 1.000 | 4 | 2 | 4 | 0 | 0 |

| Shortstop | PCT | G | PO | A | E | DP |
|---|---|---|---|---|---|---|
| Branson | .978 | 59 | 88 | 138 | 5 | 28 |
| Greene | .978 | 10 | 17 | 28 | 1 | 8 |
| Kessinger | .935 | 11 | 7 | 22 | 2 | 5 |
| Koelling | 1.000 | 2 | 2 | 0 | 0 | 0 |
| Larkin | .965 | 99 | 159 | 281 | 16 | 56 |
| Roberts | .000 | 1 | 0 | 0 | 0 | 0 |

| Outfield | PCT | G | PO | A | E | DP |
|---|---|---|---|---|---|---|
| Brumfield | .978 | 96 | 172 | 6 | 4 | 1 |
| Costo | .980 | 26 | 49 | 1 | 1 | 0 |
| Daugherty | .917 | 16 | 11 | 0 | 1 | 0 |
| Espy | .931 | 18 | 25 | 2 | 2 | 0 |
| Gordon | 1.000 | 2 | 2 | 0 | 0 | 0 |
| Gregg | 1.000 | 4 | 2 | 0 | 0 | 0 |
| Hernandez | .970 | 23 | 30 | 2 | 1 | 0 |
| Howard | .987 | 37 | 73 | 4 | 1 | 1 |
| Hughes | .000 | 2 | 0 | 0 | 0 | 0 |
| Kelly | .995 | 77 | 198 | 3 | 1 | 1 |
| Milligan | .833 | 9 | 9 | 1 | 2 | 0 |
| Mitchell | .957 | 87 | 149 | 7 | 7 | 2 |
| Oliver | .000 | 1 | 0 | 0 | 0 | 0 |
| Roberts | .938 | 11 | 15 | 0 | 1 | 0 |
| Samuel | .800 | 3 | 3 | 1 | 1 | 0 |
| Sanders | .975 | 137 | 312 | 3 | 8 | 0 |
| Tubbs | .975 | 21 | 38 | 1 | 1 | 0 |
| Varsho | 1.000 | 22 | 27 | 1 | 0 | 1 |

**Tough Season.** Jose Rijo, left, won 14 games and led the National League with 227 strikeouts, but Barry Larkin's season was cut short by injuries which contributed to Cincinnati's 73-win season.

## INDIANAPOLIS AAA
### AMERICAN ASSOCIATION

| BATTING | AVG | G | AB | R | H | 2B | 3B | HR | RBI | BB | SO | SB | CS | B | T | HT | WT | DOB | 1st Yr | Resides |
|---|---|---|---|---|---|---|---|---|---|---|---|---|---|---|---|---|---|---|---|---|
| Afenir, Troy | .240 | 84 | 254 | 29 | 61 | 14 | 2 | 8 | 35 | 11 | 53 | 2 | 1 | R | R | 6-4 | 210 | 9-21-63 | 1983 | San Diego, Calif. |
| Anderson, Kent | .197 | 24 | 61 | 6 | 12 | 2 | 0 | 0 | 4 | 3 | 9 | 1 | 0 | R | R | 6-1 | 180 | 8-12-63 | 1984 | Timmonsville, S.C. |
| 2-team (69 Iowa) | .238 | 93 | 273 | 34 | 65 | 13 | 0 | 3 | 22 | 25 | 35 | 3 | 2 | | | | | | | |
| Brumfield, Jacob | .325 | 33 | 126 | 23 | 41 | 14 | 1 | 4 | 19 | 6 | 14 | 11 | 0 | R | R | 6-0 | 180 | 5-27-65 | 1983 | Atlanta, Ga. |
| Canate, William | .000 | 3 | 5 | 0 | 0 | 0 | 0 | 0 | 0 | 0 | 1 | 0 | 0 | R | R | 6-0 | 170 | 12-11-71 | 1989 | Maracaibo, Venez. |
| Carter, Steve | .269 | 68 | 212 | 21 | 57 | 13 | 0 | 3 | 22 | 10 | 27 | 6 | 0 | L | R | 6-4 | 205 | 12-12-64 | 1987 | Charlottesville, Va. |
| Costo, Tim | .326 | 106 | 362 | 49 | 118 | 30 | 2 | 11 | 57 | 22 | 60 | 3 | 2 | R | R | 6-5 | 230 | 2-16-69 | 1990 | Glen Ellyn, Ill. |
| Dauphin, Phil | .286 | 8 | 21 | 0 | 6 | 0 | 0 | 0 | 2 | 2 | 4 | 0 | 0 | L | L | 6-1 | 180 | 5-11-69 | 1990 | Worthington, Ohio |
| 2-team (20 Iowa) | .240 | 20 | 75 | 5 | 18 | 4 | 1 | 1 | 4 | 12 | 13 | 2 | 0 | | | | | | | |
| Dorsett, Brian | .299 | 77 | 278 | 38 | 83 | 27 | 0 | 18 | 57 | 28 | 53 | 2 | 0 | R | R | 6-3 | 220 | 4-9-61 | 1983 | Terre Haute, Ind. |
| Espy, Cecil | .229 | 25 | 83 | 10 | 19 | 3 | 0 | 0 | 7 | 6 | 16 | 2 | 0 | S | R | 6-3 | 195 | 1-20-63 | 1980 | Fort Worth, Texas |
| Green, Gary | .188 | 72 | 218 | 15 | 41 | 7 | 0 | 2 | 14 | 11 | 30 | 1 | 1 | R | R | 6-3 | 180 | 1-14-62 | 1985 | Arlington, Texas |
| Greene, Willie | .267 | 98 | 341 | 62 | 91 | 19 | 0 | 22 | 58 | 51 | 83 | 2 | 4 | L | R | 5-11 | 180 | 9-23-71 | 1989 | Haddock, Ga. |
| Gregg, Tommy | .318 | 71 | 198 | 34 | 63 | 12 | 5 | 7 | 30 | 26 | 28 | 3 | 5 | L | L | 6-1 | 190 | 7-29-63 | 1985 | Smyrna, Ga. |
| Hernandez, Cesar | .257 | 84 | 272 | 30 | 70 | 12 | 4 | 5 | 22 | 9 | 63 | 5 | 7 | R | R | 6-0 | 170 | 9-28-66 | 1985 | Santo Domingo, D.R. |
| Hughes, Keith | .286 | 82 | 283 | 55 | 81 | 28 | 4 | 13 | 42 | 41 | 61 | 5 | 0 | L | L | 6-3 | 210 | 9-12-63 | 1982 | Berwyn, Pa. |
| Kessinger, Keith | .283 | 35 | 120 | 17 | 34 | 9 | 0 | 2 | 15 | 14 | 14 | 0 | 1 | S | R | 6-2 | 185 | 2-19-67 | 1989 | Oxford, Miss. |
| Koelling, Brian | .222 | 2 | 9 | 1 | 2 | 0 | 0 | 0 | 0 | 0 | 1 | 0 | 1 | R | R | 6-1 | 185 | 6-11-69 | 1991 | Cleves, Ohio |
| Kremblas, Frank | .243 | 108 | 341 | 38 | 83 | 15 | 4 | 8 | 46 | 42 | 78 | 7 | 4 | R | R | 5-11 | 180 | 10-25-66 | 1989 | Carroll, Ohio |
| Lofton, Rod | .667 | 2 | 3 | 0 | 2 | 0 | 0 | 0 | 2 | 0 | 1 | 0 | 0 | R | R | 6-0 | 175 | 10-7-67 | 1988 | East St. Louis, Ill. |
| Merchant, Mark | .167 | 3 | 6 | 2 | 1 | 0 | 0 | 0 | 0 | 2 | 3 | 0 | 0 | S | R | 6-2 | 185 | 1-23-69 | 1987 | Chuluota, Fla. |
| Morris, Hal | .462 | 3 | 13 | 4 | 6 | 0 | 1 | 1 | 5 | 1 | 2 | 0 | 1 | L | L | 6-4 | 215 | 4-9-65 | 1986 | Union, Ky. |
| Noboa, Junior | .283 | 45 | 180 | 27 | 51 | 11 | 1 | 0 | 14 | 14 | 8 | 2 | 0 | R | R | 5-10 | 165 | 11-10-64 | 1981 | Santo Domingo, D.R. |
| Scott, Gary | .211 | 77 | 284 | 39 | 60 | 12 | 1 | 3 | 18 | 21 | 33 | 2 | 1 | R | R | 6-0 | 175 | 8-22-68 | 1989 | Pelham, N.Y. |
| Shines, Razor | .276 | 65 | 192 | 24 | 53 | 13 | 0 | 5 | 35 | 18 | 27 | 1 | 0 | S | R | 6-1 | 210 | 7-18-56 | 1978 | Durham, N.C. |
| Tubbs, Greg | .305 | 97 | 334 | 59 | 102 | 21 | 4 | 10 | 45 | 42 | 65 | 15 | 11 | R | R | 5-9 | 185 | 8-31-62 | 1984 | Cookeville, Tenn. |
| Varsho, Gary | .289 | 32 | 121 | 19 | 35 | 8 | 1 | 3 | 18 | 15 | 13 | 1 | 2 | L | R | 5-10 | 180 | 6-20-61 | 1982 | Marshfield, Wis. |
| Wilson, Dan | .262 | 51 | 191 | 18 | 50 | 11 | 1 | 1 | 17 | 19 | 31 | 1 | 0 | R | R | 6-3 | 190 | 3-25-69 | 1990 | St. Louis Park, Ill. |
| Young, Gerald | .301 | 32 | 103 | 15 | 31 | 10 | 0 | 1 | 6 | 18 | 7 | 7 | 2 | S | R | 6-2 | 185 | 10-22-64 | 1982 | Santa Ana, Calif. |

| PITCHING | W | L | ERA | G | GS | CG | SV | IP | H | R | ER | BB | SO | B | T | HT | WT | DOB | 1st Yr | Resides |
|---|---|---|---|---|---|---|---|---|---|---|---|---|---|---|---|---|---|---|---|---|
| Anderson, Mike | 10 | 6 | 3.75 | 23 | 23 | 2 | 0 | 151 | 150 | 73 | 63 | 56 | 111 | R | R | 6-3 | 205 | 7-30-66 | 1988 | Georgetown, Texas |
| Arnsberg, Brad | 0 | 0 | 9.00 | 6 | 0 | 0 | 0 | 10 | 17 | 10 | 10 | 2 | 2 | R | R | 6-4 | 210 | 8-20-63 | 1984 | Arlington, Texas |
| Ayala, Bobby | 0 | 2 | 5.67 | 5 | 5 | 0 | 0 | 27 | 36 | 19 | 17 | 12 | 19 | R | R | 6-3 | 200 | 7-8-69 | 1988 | Oxnard, Calif. |
| Bennett, Chris | 0 | 0 | 4.85 | 3 | 2 | 0 | 0 | 13 | 21 | 8 | 7 | 1 | 10 | R | R | 6-6 | 205 | 9-8-65 | 1986 | Yreka, Calif. |
| Culberson, Calvain | 1 | 0 | 0.69 | 2 | 2 | 0 | 0 | 13 | 9 | 2 | 1 | 7 | 9 | R | R | 5-10 | 195 | 11-14-66 | 1988 | Rome, Ga. |
| Grott, Matt | 7 | 5 | 3.59 | 33 | 9 | 0 | 1 | 100 | 88 | 45 | 40 | 40 | 73 | L | L | 6-1 | 190 | 12-5-67 | 1988 | Glendale, Ariz. |
| Hill, Milt | 3 | 5 | 4.08 | 20 | 5 | 0 | 2 | 53 | 53 | 27 | 24 | 17 | 45 | R | R | 6-0 | 180 | 8-22-65 | 1987 | Dawsonville, Ga. |
| Kaiser, Jeff | 0 | 0 | 0.00 | 1 | 0 | 0 | 0 | 1 | 0 | 0 | 0 | 2 | 4 | R | L | 6-3 | 205 | 7-24-60 | 1982 | Trenton, Mich. |
| Kennedy, Bo | 3 | 7 | 4.96 | 39 | 14 | 0 | 1 | 118 | 135 | 76 | 65 | 47 | 79 | R | R | 5-11 | 180 | 1-4-68 | 1986 | Elvins, Mo. |
| Luebbers, Larry | 4 | 7 | 4.16 | 15 | 15 | 0 | 0 | 84 | 81 | 45 | 39 | 47 | 51 | R | R | 6-6 | 190 | 10-11-69 | 1990 | Florence, Ky. |
| Lynch, David | 9 | 4 | 3.21 | 59 | 0 | 0 | 1 | 84 | 73 | 41 | 30 | 48 | 76 | R | L | 6-3 | 205 | 10-7-65 | 1987 | Redondo Beach, Calif. |

## PITCHING

| PITCHING | W | L | ERA | G | GS | CG | SV | IP | H | R | ER | BB | SO | B | T | HT | WT | DOB | 1st Yr | Resides |
|---|---|---|---|---|---|---|---|---|---|---|---|---|---|---|---|---|---|---|---|---|
| Moore, Brad | 0 | 1 | 5.86 | 21 | 1 | 0 | 0 | 43 | 46 | 28 | 28 | 22 | 22 | R | R | 6-0 | 185 | 6-20-64 | 1986 | Loveland, Colo. |
| Newman, Alan | 1 | 3 | 8.55 | 8 | 3 | 0 | 0 | 20 | 24 | 23 | 19 | 27 | 15 | L | L | 6-6 | 225 | 10-2-69 | 1988 | La Habra, Calif. |
| Powell, Ross | 10 | 10 | 4.11 | 28 | 27 | 4 | 0 | 180 | 159 | 89 | 82 | 71 | 133 | L | L | 6-0 | 180 | 1-24-68 | 1989 | Sand Lake, Mich. |
| Robinson, Scott | 2 | 5 | 6.42 | 9 | 9 | 0 | 0 | 48 | 55 | 43 | 34 | 24 | 29 | R | R | 6-2 | 200 | 11-15-68 | 1990 | Cordova, Ala. |
| Roper, John | 3 | 5 | 4.45 | 12 | 12 | 0 | 0 | 55 | 56 | 33 | 27 | 30 | 42 | R | R | 6-0 | 175 | 11-21-71 | 1990 | Raeford, N.C. |
| Ruffin, Johnny | 1 | 1 | 1.35 | 3 | 0 | 0 | 1 | 7 | 3 | 1 | 1 | 2 | 6 | R | R | 6-3 | 174 | 7-29-71 | 1988 | Butler, Ala. |
| 2-team (29 Nashville) | 4 | 5 | 3.11 | 32 | 0 | 0 | 2 | 67 | 51 | 25 | 23 | 18 | 75 | | | | | | | |
| Ruskin, Scott | 1 | 5 | 5.14 | 49 | 2 | 0 | 28 | 56 | 60 | 34 | 32 | 22 | 41 | R | L | 6-2 | 195 | 6-8-63 | 1986 | Jacksonville, Fla. |
| Sauveur, Rich | 2 | 0 | 1.82 | 5 | 5 | 0 | 0 | 35 | 41 | 10 | 7 | 7 | 21 | L | L | 6-4 | 170 | 11-23-63 | 1983 | Bradenton, Fla. |
| Service, Scott | 4 | 2 | 4.45 | 21 | 1 | 0 | 2 | 30 | 25 | 16 | 15 | 17 | 28 | R | R | 6-6 | 235 | 2-26-67 | 1988 | Cincinnati, Ohio |
| Spradlin, Jerry | 3 | 2 | 3.49 | 34 | 0 | 0 | 1 | 57 | 58 | 24 | 22 | 12 | 46 | S | R | 6-7 | 230 | 6-14-67 | 1988 | Anaheim, Calif. |
| Tracy, Jim | 2 | 7 | 6.00 | 12 | 7 | 2 | 0 | 42 | 50 | 35 | 28 | 22 | 16 | R | R | 6-3 | 180 | 11-30-65 | 1985 | Lynn, Mass. |
| 2-team (15 Buffalo) | 4 | 9 | 5.24 | 27 | 10 | 2 | 0 | 77 | 85 | 54 | 45 | 32 | 36 | | | | | | | |
| Wickander, Kevin | 0 | 0 | 0.00 | 1 | 1 | 0 | 0 | 3 | 2 | 0 | 0 | 1 | 2 | L | L | 6-3 | 200 | 1-4-65 | 1986 | Glendale, Ariz. |

## FIELDING

| Catcher | PCT | G | PO | A | E | DP |
|---|---|---|---|---|---|---|
| Afenir | .979 | 37 | 219 | 13 | 5 | 0 |
| Dorsett | .993 | 61 | 389 | 45 | 3 | 4 |
| Wilson | .994 | 50 | 314 | 24 | 2 | 2 |

| First Base | PCT | G | PO | A | E | DP |
|---|---|---|---|---|---|---|
| Afenir | .989 | 10 | 86 | 7 | 1 | 8 |
| Costo | .992 | 67 | 468 | 30 | 4 | 41 |
| Dorsett | .932 | 7 | 50 | 5 | 4 | 2 |
| Gregg | .980 | 43 | 312 | 29 | 7 | 32 |
| Hughes | 1.000 | 5 | 24 | 2 | 0 | 1 |
| Morris | 1.000 | 3 | 26 | 3 | 0 | 1 |
| Shines | .967 | 23 | 199 | 9 | 7 | 17 |
| Varsho | 1.000 | 3 | 21 | 0 | 0 | 3 |

| Second Base | PCT | G | PO | A | E | DP |
|---|---|---|---|---|---|---|
| Anderson | 1.000 | 1 | 0 | 1 | 0 | 0 |
| Kessinger | 1.000 | 6 | 9 | 10 | 0 | 0 |
| Kroelling | 1.000 | 2 | 5 | 8 | 0 | 1 |
| Kremblas | .982 | 21 | 47 | 64 | 2 | 13 |
| Noboa | .989 | 42 | 73 | 112 | 2 | 28 |

| | PCT | G | PO | A | E | DP |
|---|---|---|---|---|---|---|
| Scott | .964 | 77 | 161 | 187 | 13 | 40 |

| Third Base | PCT | G | PO | A | E | DP |
|---|---|---|---|---|---|---|
| Anderson | .923 | 9 | 6 | 18 | 2 | 2 |
| Costo | .897 | 13 | 6 | 29 | 4 | 7 |
| Greene | .905 | 92 | 69 | 150 | 23 | 6 |
| Kremblas | .951 | 35 | 29 | 87 | 6 | 9 |
| Lofton | .833 | 2 | 2 | 3 | 1 | 0 |
| Noboa | 1.000 | 1 | 0 | 2 | 0 | 0 |
| Shines | .900 | 5 | 2 | 7 | 1 | 1 |

| Shortstop | PCT | G | PO | A | E | DP |
|---|---|---|---|---|---|---|
| Anderson | .980 | 11 | 22 | 26 | 1 | 6 |
| Carter | .000 | 1 | 0 | 0 | 0 | 0 |
| Costo | .500 | 1 | 0 | 1 | 1 | 0 |
| Green | .951 | 71 | 76 | 176 | 13 | 28 |
| Greene | 1.000 | 6 | 8 | 21 | 0 | 4 |
| Kessinger | .985 | 28 | 41 | 91 | 2 | 22 |
| Kremblas | .916 | 41 | 47 | 84 | 12 | 14 |

| Outfield | PCT | G | PO | A | E | DP |
|---|---|---|---|---|---|---|
| Afenir | .000 | 2 | 0 | 0 | 0 | 0 |
| Brumfield | .951 | 33 | 74 | 4 | 4 | 0 |
| Canate | .000 | 1 | 0 | 0 | 0 | 0 |
| Carter | .971 | 53 | 95 | 4 | 3 | 0 |
| Costo | 1.000 | 29 | 42 | 1 | 0 | 0 |
| Dauphin | 1.000 | 7 | 13 | 1 | 0 | 1 |
| Espy | 1.000 | 19 | 33 | 2 | 0 | 0 |
| Gregg | 1.000 | 12 | 18 | 0 | 0 | 0 |
| Hernandez | .985 | 75 | 183 | 9 | 3 | 1 |
| Hughes | .965 | 72 | 136 | 3 | 5 | 1 |
| Kremblas | .909 | 20 | 29 | 1 | 3 | 0 |
| Merchant | 1.000 | 1 | 1 | 0 | 0 | 0 |
| Moore | .000 | 1 | 0 | 0 | 0 | 0 |
| Noboa | .000 | 1 | 0 | 0 | 0 | 0 |
| Tubbs | .971 | 91 | 195 | 7 | 6 | 2 |
| Varsho | .923 | 26 | 48 | 0 | 4 | 0 |
| Young | 1.000 | 28 | 53 | 0 | 0 | 0 |

# CHATTANOOGA                                                                    AA
## SOUTHERN LEAGUE

| BATTING | AVG | G | AB | R | H | 2B | 3B | HR | RBI | BB | SO | SB | CS | B | T | HT | WT | DOB | 1st Yr | Resides |
|---|---|---|---|---|---|---|---|---|---|---|---|---|---|---|---|---|---|---|---|---|
| Arias, Amador, 2b-ss | .215 | 18 | 65 | 6 | 14 | 1 | 1 | 0 | 2 | 4 | 23 | 1 | 1 | S | R | 5-10 | 160 | 5-28-72 | 1990 | Maracay, Venez. |
| Beauchamp, Kash, of | .400 | 18 | 60 | 16 | 24 | 6 | 1 | 5 | 15 | 10 | 9 | 1 | 1 | R | R | 6-3 | 165 | 1-8-63 | 1982 | Fortston, Ga. |
| Buckley, Troy, c | .256 | 14 | 43 | 4 | 11 | 1 | 0 | 1 | 4 | 1 | 5 | 0 | 0 | R | R | 6-4 | 215 | 3-3-68 | 1990 | Campbell, Calif. |
| Cox, Darron, c | .217 | 89 | 300 | 35 | 65 | 9 | 5 | 3 | 26 | 38 | 63 | 7 | 4 | R | R | 6-1 | 210 | 11-21-67 | 1989 | Norman, Okla. |
| Dismuke, Jamie, 1b | .306 | 136 | 497 | 69 | 152 | 22 | 1 | 20 | 91 | 48 | 60 | 4 | 2 | L | R | 6-1 | 215 | 10-17-69 | 1989 | Syracuse, N.Y. |
| Fuller, Jon, c | .270 | 46 | 148 | 22 | 40 | 8 | 1 | 3 | 17 | 12 | 41 | 3 | 1 | R | R | 6-1 | 210 | 5-7-69 | 1988 | Gig Harbor, Wash. |
| Garner, Kevin, dh | .151 | 19 | 53 | 6 | 8 | 1 | 0 | 2 | 5 | 9 | 26 | 2 | 1 | L | R | 6-2 | 200 | 10-21-65 | 1987 | Austin, Texas |
| Gibralter, Steve, of | .237 | 132 | 477 | 65 | 113 | 25 | 3 | 11 | 47 | 20 | 108 | 7 | 12 | R | R | 6-0 | 170 | 10-9-72 | 1990 | Duncanville, Texas |
| Gill, Chris, ss | .000 | 1 | 2 | 0 | 0 | 0 | 0 | 0 | 0 | 0 | 0 | 0 | 0 | R | R | 5-10 | 180 | 9-26-66 | 1989 | Santa Ana, Calif. |
| Gillum, K.C., of | .245 | 66 | 216 | 31 | 53 | 9 | 1 | 6 | 24 | 19 | 61 | 3 | 6 | L | R | 6-0 | 180 | 5-27-70 | 1990 | Oxford, Ohio |
| Gordon, Keith, of | .291 | 116 | 419 | 69 | 122 | 26 | 3 | 14 | 59 | 19 | 132 | 13 | 18 | R | R | 6-1 | 205 | 1-22-69 | 1990 | Olney, Md. |
| Hammond, Greg, c | .281 | 9 | 32 | 3 | 9 | 3 | 0 | 0 | 5 | 2 | 6 | 0 | 1 | R | R | 6-0 | 205 | 3-25-68 | 1990 | Birmingham, Ala. |
| Houk, Tom, 3b-2b | .245 | 43 | 147 | 19 | 36 | 3 | 3 | 1 | 13 | 22 | 29 | 4 | 4 | R | R | 6-0 | 165 | 6-14-69 | 1989 | Bloomington, Ill. |
| 2-team (48 Nashville) | .237 | 91 | 278 | 36 | 66 | 6 | 4 | 2 | 29 | 48 | 57 | 6 | 6 | | | | | | | |
| Jenkins, Bernie, of | .252 | 102 | 290 | 31 | 73 | 9 | 1 | 3 | 26 | 21 | 71 | 18 | 7 | R | R | 6-4 | 195 | 9-12-67 | 1988 | Brooklyn, N.Y. |
| Jones, Motorboat, of | .225 | 26 | 89 | 10 | 20 | 4 | 0 | 1 | 10 | 9 | 17 | 3 | 2 | R | R | 6-1 | 175 | 3-15-69 | 1987 | Gadsden, Ala. |
| Kessinger, Keith, ss-2b | .311 | 56 | 161 | 24 | 50 | 9 | 0 | 3 | 28 | 24 | 18 | 0 | 3 | S | R | 6-2 | 185 | 2-19-67 | 1989 | Oxford, Miss. |
| Koelling, Brian, 2b | .277 | 110 | 430 | 64 | 119 | 17 | 6 | 4 | 47 | 32 | 105 | 34 | 13 | R | R | 6-1 | 185 | 6-11-69 | 1991 | Cleves, Ohio |
| Lane, Brian, 3b | .264 | 114 | 425 | 60 | 112 | 29 | 4 | 10 | 57 | 41 | 134 | 1 | 1 | R | R | 6-3 | 215 | 6-15-69 | 1987 | Waco, Texas |

MEL BAILEY

**Willie Greene**
.267-22-58 at Indy

## REDS TOP 10 PROSPECTS

### How the Reds Top 10 prospects, as judged by Baseball America prior to the 1993 season, fared in 1993:

| Player, Pos. | Club (Class) | AVG | AB | H | HR | RBI | SB |
|---|---|---|---|---|---|---|---|
| 1. Willie Greene, 3b | Indianapolis (AAA) | .267 | 341 | 91 | 22 | 58 | 2 |
| | Cincinnati | .160 | 50 | 8 | 2 | 5 | 0 |
| 3. Chad Mottola, of | Winston-Salem (A) | .280 | 493 | 138 | 21 | 91 | 13 |
| 4. Calvin Reese, ss | Chattanooga (AA) | .212 | 345 | 73 | 3 | 37 | 8 |
| 5. Dan Wilson, c | Indianapolis (AAA) | .262 | 191 | 50 | 1 | 17 | 1 |
| | Cincinnati | .224 | 76 | 17 | 0 | 8 | 0 |
| 6. Steve Gibralter, of | Chattanooga (AA) | .237 | 477 | 113 | 11 | 47 | 7 |
| 7. Tim Costo, 1b | Indianapolis (AAA) | .326 | 362 | 118 | 11 | 57 | 3 |
| | Cincinnati | .224 | 98 | 22 | 3 | 12 | 0 |
| 10. Brian Koelling, ss | Chattanooga (AA) | .277 | 430 | 119 | 4 | 47 | 34 |
| | Indianapolis (AAA) | .222 | 9 | 2 | 0 | 0 | 0 |
| | Cincinnati | .067 | 15 | 1 | 0 | 0 | 0 |

| | W | L | ERA | IP | H | BB | SO |
|---|---|---|---|---|---|---|---|
| 2. John Roper, rhp | Indianapolis (AAA) | 3 | 5 | 4.45 | 55 | 56 | 30 | 42 |
| | Cincinnati | 2 | 5 | 5.63 | 80 | 92 | 36 | 54 |
| 8. Tim Pugh, rhp | Cincinnati | 10 | 15 | 5.26 | 164 | 200 | 59 | 94 |
| 9. Bobby Ayala, rhp | Indianapolis (AAA) | 0 | 2 | 5.67 | 27 | 36 | 12 | 19 |
| | Cincinnati | 7 | 10 | 5.60 | 98 | 106 | 45 | 65 |

# REDS: MOST COMMON LINEUPS

| | Cincinnati<br>Majors | Indianapolis<br>AAA | Chattanooga<br>AA | Winston-Salem<br>A | Charleston<br>A |
|---|---|---|---|---|---|
| C | Joe Oliver (133) | Brian Dorsett (61) | Darron Cox (88) | Mike Harrison (68) | John Bess (79) |
| 1B | Hal Morris (98) | Tim Costo (67) | Jamie Dismuke (135) | Tim Belk (122) | Dan Frye (71) |
| 2B | Juan Samuel (70) | Gary Scott (77) | Brian Koelling (105) | Mateo Ozuna (81) | Dee Jenkins (129) |
| 3B | Chris Sabo (148) | Willie Greene (92) | Brian Lane (104) | Bobby Perna (134) | Dan Kopriva (77) |
| SS | Barry Larkin (99) | Gary Green (71) | Calvin Reese (102) | Eric Owens (121) | Ricky Magdaleno (131) |
| OF | Reggie Sanders (137) | Greg Tubbs (86) | Steve Gibralter (131) | Chad Mottola (137) | Mike Meggers (111) |
| | Jacob Brumfield (59) | Cesar Hernandez (71) | Keith Gordon (111) | Cleveland Ladell (124) | Wayne Wilkerson (87) |
| | Kevin Mitchell (87) | Keith Hughes (70) | Bernie Jenkins (86) | Motorboat Jones (77) | Micah Franklin (76) |
| DH | N/A | Troy Afenir (24) | Mark Merchant (64) | Bubba Smith (73) | Toby Rumfield (26) |
| SP | Jose Rijo (36) | Ross Powell (27) | Ferry/Hook (28) | Rod Steph (28) | Chad Fox (26) |
| RP | Jeff Reardon (58) | Dave Lynch (59) | Chris Bushing (61) | John Hrusovsky (52) | Louis Maberry (57) |

Full-season farm clubs only   No. of games at position in parenthesis

## BATTING

| | AVG | G | AB | R | H | 2B | 3B | HR | RBI | BB | SO | SB | CS | B | T | HT | WT | DOB | 1st Yr | Resides |
|---|---|---|---|---|---|---|---|---|---|---|---|---|---|---|---|---|---|---|---|---|
| Lofton, Rod, inf | .111 | 10 | 27 | 1 | 3 | 0 | 0 | 0 | 2 | 7 | 11 | 2 | 0 | R | R | 6-0 | 175 | 10-7-67 | 1988 | East St. Louis, Ill. |
| Merchant, Mark, dh-of | .301 | 109 | 336 | 56 | 101 | 16 | 0 | 17 | 61 | 50 | 79 | 3 | 5 | S | R | 6-2 | 185 | 1-23-69 | 1987 | Chuluota, Fla. |
| Reese, Calvin, ss | .212 | 102 | 345 | 35 | 73 | 17 | 4 | 3 | 37 | 23 | 77 | 8 | 5 | R | R | 6-0 | 160 | 6-10-73 | 1991 | Columbia, S.C. |
| Spann, Tookie, of-dh | .071 | 8 | 14 | 0 | 1 | 0 | 0 | 0 | 0 | 0 | 6 | 0 | 0 | R | R | 6-2 | 200 | 2-18-67 | 1988 | New Orleans, La. |

## PITCHING

| | W | L | ERA | G | GS | CG | SV | IP | H | R | ER | BB | SO | B | T | HT | WT | DOB | 1st Yr | Resides |
|---|---|---|---|---|---|---|---|---|---|---|---|---|---|---|---|---|---|---|---|---|
| Anderson, Mike | 1 | 1 | 1.20 | 2 | 2 | 1 | 0 | 15 | 10 | 3 | 2 | 1 | 14 | R | R | 6-3 | 205 | 7-30-66 | 1988 | Georgetown, Texas |
| Buckley, Travis | 0 | 1 | 3.38 | 2 | 2 | 0 | 0 | 8 | 7 | 6 | 3 | 4 | 6 | R | R | 6-4 | 208 | 6-15-70 | 1989 | Overland Park, Kan. |
| Burgos, John | 2 | 2 | 3.56 | 31 | 1 | 0 | 1 | 48 | 33 | 21 | 19 | 14 | 35 | L | L | 5-11 | 170 | 8-2-67 | 1986 | Humacao, P.R. |
| Bushing, Chris | 6 | 1 | 2.31 | 61 | 0 | 0 | 29 | 70 | 50 | 20 | 18 | 23 | 84 | R | R | 6-0 | 190 | 11-4-67 | 1986 | Plantation, Fla. |
| Courtright, John | 5 | 11 | 3.50 | 27 | 27 | 1 | 0 | 175 | 179 | 81 | 68 | 70 | 96 | L | L | 6-2 | 185 | 5-30-70 | 1991 | Columbus, Ohio |
| Culberson, Calvain | 6 | 6 | 2.99 | 37 | 7 | 0 | 1 | 105 | 82 | 38 | 35 | 36 | 86 | R | R | 5-10 | 195 | 11-14-66 | 1988 | Rome, Ga. |
| Ferry, Mike | 13 | 8 | 3.42 | 28 | 28 | 4 | 0 | 187 | 176 | 85 | 71 | 30 | 111 | R | R | 6-3 | 195 | 7-26-69 | 1990 | Tuscaloosa, Ala. |
| Garcia, Victor | 0 | 2 | 5.85 | 15 | 0 | 0 | 0 | 20 | 24 | 15 | 13 | 11 | 14 | R | R | 6-2 | 205 | 9-15-69 | 1988 | Bonao, D.R. |
| Holcomb, Scott | 0 | 2 | 13.50 | 6 | 0 | 0 | 0 | 4 | 5 | 6 | 6 | 5 | 3 | L | L | 6-1 | 170 | 8-23-68 | 1986 | Placentia, Calif. |
| Hook, Chris | 12 | 8 | 3.62 | 28 | 28 | 1 | 0 | 167 | 163 | 85 | 67 | 66 | 122 | S | R | 6-5 | 195 | 8-4-68 | 1989 | Florence, Ky. |
| Jarvis, Kevin | 3 | 1 | 1.69 | 7 | 3 | 2 | 0 | 37 | 26 | 7 | 7 | 11 | 18 | L | R | 6-2 | 190 | 8-1-69 | 1991 | Lexington, Ky. |
| Kennedy, Bo | 1 | 1 | 6.75 | 2 | 2 | 0 | 0 | 9 | 12 | 7 | 7 | 5 | 10 | R | R | 5-11 | 180 | 1-4-68 | 1986 | Elvins, Mo. |
| Kilgo, Rusty | 11 | 7 | 2.80 | 53 | 1 | 0 | 6 | 80 | 92 | 30 | 25 | 31 | 61 | L | L | 6-0 | 175 | 8-9-66 | 1989 | Houston, Texas |
| Lynch, David | 0 | 0 | 0.00 | 3 | 0 | 0 | 1 | 2 | 0 | 0 | 0 | 0 | 3 | R | L | 6-3 | 205 | 10-7-65 | 1987 | Redondo Beach, Calif. |
| Pierce, Jeff | 0 | 0 | 2.61 | 13 | 0 | 0 | 4 | 21 | 17 | 6 | 6 | 9 | 22 | R | R | 6-1 | 195 | 6-7-69 | 1991 | Staatsburg, N.Y. |
| 2-team (33 Birm.) | 3 | 4 | 2.60 | 46 | 0 | 0 | 22 | 69 | 51 | 22 | 20 | 16 | 67 | | | | | | | |
| Ray, Johnny | 3 | 7 | 6.82 | 30 | 8 | 0 | 0 | 62 | 79 | 55 | 47 | 28 | 46 | R | R | 6-3 | 215 | 10-28-67 | 1989 | Holly Springs, Miss. |
| Robinson, Scott | 6 | 5 | 3.54 | 20 | 18 | 0 | 0 | 112 | 114 | 60 | 44 | 40 | 58 | R | R | 6-2 | 200 | 11-15-68 | 1990 | Cordova, Ala. |
| Shaw, Kevin | 0 | 1 | 3.82 | 25 | 0 | 0 | 0 | 38 | 50 | 19 | 16 | 9 | 14 | R | R | 6-4 | 235 | 7-2-69 | 1987 | Yorba Linda, Calif. |
| Stewart, Carl | 3 | 4 | 5.03 | 10 | 10 | 1 | 0 | 54 | 57 | 35 | 30 | 24 | 47 | R | R | 6-3 | 190 | 12-8-70 | 1988 | Plano, Texas |
| Tatar, Kevin | 0 | 1 | 1.93 | 4 | 4 | 0 | 0 | 14 | 9 | 4 | 3 | 5 | 7 | R | R | 6-3 | 190 | 7-3-68 | 1990 | Wheeling, W.Va. |

# WINSTON-SALEM                                                                              A

## CAROLINA LEAGUE

### BATTING

| | AVG | G | AB | R | H | 2B | 3B | HR | RBI | BB | SO | SB | CS | B | T | HT | WT | DOB | 1st Yr | Resides |
|---|---|---|---|---|---|---|---|---|---|---|---|---|---|---|---|---|---|---|---|---|
| Arias, Amador, 2b-ss | .263 | 58 | 179 | 25 | 47 | 3 | 0 | 0 | 12 | 7 | 28 | 5 | 6 | S | R | 5-10 | 160 | 5-28-72 | 1990 | Maracay, Venez. |
| Ashton, Jeff, 2b | .500 | 4 | 2 | 1 | 1 | 0 | 0 | 0 | 0 | 2 | 0 | 0 | 0 | R | R | 5-11 | 175 | 11-20-70 | 1992 | North Royalton, Ohio |
| Belk, Tim, 1b | .306 | 134 | 509 | 89 | 156 | 23 | 3 | 14 | 65 | 48 | 76 | 9 | 7 | R | R | 6-3 | 200 | 4-6-70 | 1992 | Houston, Texas |
| Bess, John, c | .242 | 11 | 33 | 4 | 8 | 0 | 0 | 2 | 7 | 6 | 7 | 2 | 1 | S | R | 6-1 | 190 | 4-6-70 | 1992 | Grand Junction, Colo. |
| Buckley, Troy, c-dh | .265 | 64 | 215 | 19 | 57 | 10 | 1 | 4 | 29 | 15 | 31 | 0 | 3 | R | R | 6-4 | 215 | 3-3-68 | 1990 | Campbell, Calif. |
| Franklin, Micah, of | .232 | 20 | 69 | 10 | 16 | 1 | 1 | 3 | 6 | 10 | 19 | 0 | 1 | S | R | 6-0 | 195 | 4-25-72 | 1990 | San Francisco, Calif. |
| Gill, Chris, 2b-ss | .161 | 49 | 93 | 10 | 15 | 3 | 0 | 1 | 6 | 10 | 21 | 0 | 4 | R | R | 5-10 | 180 | 9-26-66 | 1989 | Santa Ana, Calif. |
| Gonzalez, Ricky, ss-2b | .276 | 10 | 29 | 5 | 8 | 0 | 0 | 0 | 0 | 4 | 7 | 1 | 0 | R | R | 5-10 | 165 | 4-3-70 | 1993 | Maracaibo, Venez. |
| Hammond, Greg, c | .190 | 46 | 137 | 11 | 26 | 5 | 0 | 2 | 11 | 9 | 47 | 1 | 0 | R | R | 6-0 | 205 | 3-25-68 | 1990 | Birmingham, Ala. |
| Harrison, Mike, c | .252 | 72 | 238 | 20 | 60 | 10 | 0 | 4 | 23 | 15 | 46 | 2 | 1 | R | R | 6-2 | 210 | 11-30-69 | 1991 | Moraga, Calif. |
| Jones, Motorboat, of | .300 | 90 | 330 | 58 | 99 | 21 | 4 | 19 | 69 | 30 | 47 | 8 | 4 | R | R | 6-1 | 185 | 3-15-69 | 1987 | Gadsden, Ala. |
| Ladell, Cleveland, of | .284 | 132 | 531 | 90 | 151 | 15 | 7 | 20 | 66 | 16 | 95 | 24 | 7 | R | S | 5-11 | 170 | 9-19-70 | 1992 | Dallas, Texas |
| Mottola, Chad, of | .280 | 137 | 493 | 76 | 138 | 25 | 3 | 21 | 91 | 62 | 109 | 13 | 7 | R | R | 6-3 | 215 | 10-15-71 | 1992 | Pembroke Pines, Fla. |
| Owens, Eric, ss | .271 | 122 | 487 | 74 | 132 | 25 | 4 | 10 | 63 | 53 | 69 | 21 | 12 | R | R | 6-1 | 184 | 2-3-71 | 1992 | Danville, Va. |
| Ozuna, Mateo, 2b | .306 | 93 | 304 | 54 | 93 | 17 | 2 | 4 | 29 | 26 | 36 | 32 | 7 | R | R | 5-11 | 165 | 1-1-71 | 1989 | La Romana, D.R. |
| Perna, Bobby, 3b | .265 | 138 | 525 | 88 | 139 | 27 | 0 | 18 | 70 | 64 | 116 | 6 | 5 | S | R | 6-0 | 195 | 9-17-68 | 1990 | Philadelphia, Pa. |
| Pueschner, Craig, of | .182 | 33 | 99 | 14 | 18 | 0 | 1 | 1 | 6 | 2 | 34 | 5 | 1 | R | R | 6-4 | 180 | 11-20-70 | 1989 | Tucson, Ariz. |
| Ramey, Arthur, of | .071 | 6 | 14 | 0 | 1 | 0 | 0 | 0 | 0 | 0 | 7 | 0 | 1 | R | R | 5-11 | 190 | 3-24-71 | 1992 | Portsmouth, Ohio |
| Smith, Bubba, dh-1b | .301 | 92 | 342 | 55 | 103 | 16 | 0 | 27 | 81 | 35 | 109 | 1 | 0 | R | R | 6-2 | 225 | 12-18-69 | 1991 | Riverside, Calif. |
| Vasquez, Chris, of-dh | .262 | 67 | 233 | 29 | 61 | 10 | 1 | 10 | 31 | 11 | 52 | 1 | 1 | L | R | 5-11 | 170 | 10-23-71 | 1990 | Saugus, Calif. |

### PITCHING

| | W | L | ERA | G | GS | CG | SV | IP | H | R | ER | BB | SO | B | T | HT | WT | DOB | 1st Yr | Resides |
|---|---|---|---|---|---|---|---|---|---|---|---|---|---|---|---|---|---|---|---|---|
| Angel, Jason | 3 | 5 | 6.75 | 10 | 10 | 0 | 0 | 43 | 53 | 37 | 32 | 25 | 14 | R | R | 6-4 | 205 | 9-8-71 | 1992 | Glen Allen, Va. |
| Cullop, Glen | 6 | 0 | 1.52 | 39 | 0 | 0 | 2 | 65 | 37 | 12 | 11 | 21 | 48 | R | R | 6-7 | 180 | 10-4-71 | 1992 | Kingsport, Tenn. |
| Dodd, Scott | 0 | 0 | 18.00 | 1 | 0 | 0 | 0 | 1 | 3 | 2 | 2 | 1 | 1 | L | L | 6-2 | 195 | 8-4-69 | 1991 | Glendale, Ariz. |
| Duff, Scott | 2 | 0 | 10.57 | 7 | 0 | 0 | 0 | 8 | 20 | 13 | 9 | 6 | 10 | S | L | 5-11 | 175 | 6-26-68 | 1990 | Franklin, Tenn. |
| Garcia, Victor | 1 | 0 | 3.53 | 26 | 0 | 0 | 1 | 43 | 33 | 20 | 17 | 10 | 41 | R | R | 6-2 | 205 | 9-15-69 | 1988 | Bonao, D.R. |
| Hrusovsky, John | 2 | 4 | 3.86 | 52 | 0 | 0 | 25 | 58 | 53 | 27 | 25 | 27 | 61 | R | R | 6-1 | 190 | 9-12-70 | 1991 | Vero Beach, Fla. |
| Jarvis, Kevin | 8 | 7 | 3.41 | 21 | 20 | 2 | 0 | 145 | 133 | 68 | 55 | 48 | 101 | L | R | 6-2 | 190 | 8-1-69 | 1991 | Lexington, Ky. |
| Kummerfeldt, Jason | 1 | 1 | 5.32 | 5 | 4 | 0 | 0 | 24 | 31 | 16 | 14 | 9 | 21 | R | R | 6-4 | 220 | 12-17-69 | 1992 | Billings, Mont. |
| Loftin, Bo | 3 | 2 | 3.41 | 24 | 0 | 0 | 3 | 34 | 30 | 17 | 13 | 22 | 23 | R | R | 6-5 | 225 | 2-8-69 | 1991 | Jacksonville, Ala. |
| McCann, Joe | 11 | 8 | 4.67 | 32 | 23 | 0 | 1 | 160 | 185 | 92 | 83 | 47 | 84 | R | R | 6-3 | 205 | 10-16-68 | 1989 | Roswell, Ga. |
| McClain, Charlie | 2 | 6 | 6.38 | 10 | 7 | 0 | 0 | 42 | 46 | 40 | 30 | 31 | 30 | R | R | 6-3 | 205 | 12-2-67 | 1990 | Wynnburg, Tenn. |
| Nix, James | 3 | 3 | 3.57 | 11 | 6 | 0 | 0 | 35 | 37 | 24 | 14 | 15 | 33 | R | R | 5-11 | 175 | 9-6-70 | 1992 | Burton, Texas |
| O'Laughlin, Chad | 0 | 1 | 6.75 | 3 | 1 | 0 | 0 | 9 | 17 | 9 | 7 | 5 | 8 | L | L | 6-5 | 220 | 1-7-72 | 1991 | Lake Havasu, Ariz. |

| PITCHING | W | L | ERA | G | GS | CG | SV | IP | H | R | ER | BB | SO | B | T | HT | WT | DOB | 1st Yr | Resides |
|---|---|---|---|---|---|---|---|---|---|---|---|---|---|---|---|---|---|---|---|---|
| Quinones, Rene | 3 | 1 | 3.95 | 50 | 0 | 0 | 1 | 71 | 76 | 41 | 31 | 21 | 65 | L | L | 6-0 | 185 | 3-13-70 | 1991 | El Paso, Texas |
| Ruyak, Todd | 1 | 0 | 4.32 | 7 | 0 | 0 | 3 | 8 | 9 | 4 | 4 | 1 | 4 | L | L | 6-3 | 215 | 9-18-70 | 1992 | Hamilton Square, N.J. |
| Shaw, Kevin | 2 | 3 | 4.30 | 25 | 0 | 0 | 3 | 46 | 46 | 24 | 22 | 18 | 34 | R | R | 6-4 | 235 | 7-2-69 | 1987 | Yorba Linda, Calif. |
| Steph, Rod | 7 | 11 | 3.92 | 28 | 28 | 4 | 0 | 168 | 166 | 101 | 73 | 57 | 130 | R | R | 5-11 | 185 | 8-27-69 | 1991 | Houston, Texas |
| Stewart, Carl | 5 | 2 | 3.24 | 14 | 14 | 1 | 0 | 81 | 65 | 38 | 29 | 35 | 69 | R | R | 6-3 | 190 | 12-8-70 | 1988 | Plano, Texas |
| Sutko, Glenn | 5 | 7 | 4.30 | 28 | 14 | 2 | 0 | 98 | 112 | 54 | 47 | 33 | 68 | R | R | 6-3 | 225 | 5-9-69 | 1988 | Alpharetta, Ga. |
| Tuttle, Dave | 7 | 7 | 5.53 | 15 | 15 | 2 | 0 | 86 | 98 | 61 | 53 | 39 | 58 | R | R | 6-3 | 190 | 9-29-69 | 1992 | Los Gatos, Calif. |

# CHARLESTON          A
## SOUTH ATLANTIC LEAGUE

| BATTING | AVG | G | AB | R | H | 2B | 3B | HR | RBI | BB | SO | SB | CS | B | T | HT | WT | DOB | 1st Yr | Resides |
|---|---|---|---|---|---|---|---|---|---|---|---|---|---|---|---|---|---|---|---|---|
| Ashton, Jeff, 2b | .167 | 5 | 6 | 1 | 1 | 0 | 0 | 0 | 2 | 3 | 3 | 0 | 0 | R | R | 5-11 | 175 | 11-20-70 | 1992 | North Royalton, Ohio |
| Bess, John, c-1b | .229 | 106 | 358 | 35 | 82 | 16 | 7 | 5 | 67 | 47 | 107 | 10 | 5 | S | R | 6-1 | 190 | 4-6-70 | 1992 | Grand Junction, Colo. |
| Cradle, Cobi, of | .352 | 44 | 159 | 34 | 56 | 9 | 0 | 1 | 12 | 35 | 19 | 16 | 6 | L | L | 5-11 | 165 | 7-7-71 | 1993 | Cerritos, Calif. |
| Franklin, Micah, of | .262 | 102 | 343 | 56 | 90 | 14 | 4 | 17 | 68 | 47 | 109 | 6 | 1 | S | R | 6-0 | 195 | 4-25-72 | 1990 | San Francisco, Calif. |
| Frye, Dan, 1b-3b | .267 | 134 | 472 | 64 | 126 | 35 | 7 | 9 | 70 | 76 | 122 | 13 | 15 | R | R | 6-0 | 180 | 2-22-70 | 1992 | Logansport, Ind. |
| Gill, Chris, 3b | .000 | 1 | 2 | 1 | 0 | 0 | 0 | 0 | 0 | 1 | 0 | 0 | 0 | R | R | 5-10 | 180 | 9-26-66 | 1989 | Santa Ana, Calif. |
| Gonzalez, Ricky, 2b-ss | .115 | 34 | 52 | 6 | 6 | 1 | 0 | 0 | 5 | 9 | 8 | 2 | 1 | R | R | 5-10 | 165 | 4-3-70 | 1993 | Maracaibo, Venez. |
| Jenkins, Dee, 2b | .292 | 133 | 480 | 93 | 140 | 32 | 4 | 8 | 58 | 73 | 104 | 27 | 6 | L | R | 5-9 | 175 | 6-28-73 | 1991 | Columbia, S.C. |
| Jesperson, Bob, p-of | .209 | 53 | 91 | 7 | 19 | 4 | 1 | 1 | 7 | 4 | 30 | 3 | 2 | R | R | 6-1 | 195 | 5-25-69 | 1991 | White Lake, Wis. |
| Keenan, Brad, 1b | .198 | 29 | 96 | 13 | 19 | 5 | 1 | 0 | 6 | 11 | 24 | 0 | 0 | R | R | 6-5 | 215 | 3-29-71 | 1992 | Moorhead, Minn. |
| Kopriva, Dan, 3b-1b | .244 | 121 | 402 | 69 | 98 | 22 | 7 | 3 | 70 | 75 | 57 | 6 | 6 | R | R | 5-11 | 190 | 11-6-69 | 1992 | Traer, Iowa |
| Magdaleno, Ricky, ss | .239 | 131 | 447 | 49 | 107 | 15 | 4 | 3 | 25 | 37 | 103 | 8 | 8 | R | R | 6-1 | 170 | 7-6-74 | 1993 | Baldwin Park, Calif. |
| Manship, Jeff, of | .244 | 84 | 287 | 45 | 70 | 12 | 1 | 7 | 36 | 32 | 80 | 8 | 3 | R | R | 6-2 | 185 | 3-2-70 | 1992 | Fullerton, Calif. |
| Martin, Matt, ss-2b | .223 | 58 | 121 | 19 | 27 | 6 | 0 | 1 | 10 | 18 | 23 | 1 | 2 | S | R | 6-1 | 170 | 7-18-69 | 1991 | Lubbock, Texas |
| Meggers, Mike, of | .206 | 116 | 388 | 43 | 80 | 14 | 2 | 12 | 49 | 33 | 118 | 3 | 5 | R | R | 6-2 | 200 | 7-6-70 | 1992 | Sacramento, Calif. |
| Nagy, Jeff, of | .160 | 29 | 100 | 19 | 16 | 1 | 0 | 1 | 8 | 20 | 31 | 10 | 4 | R | R | 5-11 | 180 | 8-1-70 | 1992 | Toledo, Ohio |
| Pueschner, Craig, of | .182 | 26 | 99 | 24 | 18 | 2 | 1 | 2 | 5 | 12 | 22 | 10 | 6 | R | R | 6-4 | 180 | 11-20-70 | 1989 | Tucson, Ariz. |
| Rumfield, Toby, c-1b | .225 | 97 | 333 | 36 | 75 | 20 | 1 | 5 | 50 | 26 | 74 | 6 | 4 | R | R | 6-3 | 190 | 9-4-72 | 1991 | Belton, Texas |
| Silvia, Brian, c | .264 | 23 | 53 | 7 | 14 | 2 | 1 | 0 | 4 | 4 | 12 | 0 | 0 | R | R | 6-0 | 195 | 9-13-71 | 1992 | Columbia, Miss. |
| Wilkerson, Wayne, of | .216 | 102 | 287 | 39 | 62 | 10 | 1 | 4 | 27 | 30 | 55 | 11 | 3 | L | L | 6-0 | 170 | 10-15-69 | 1991 | Richmond, Va. |

| PITCHING | W | L | ERA | G | GS | CG | SV | IP | H | R | ER | BB | SO | B | T | HT | WT | DOB | 1st Yr | Resides |
|---|---|---|---|---|---|---|---|---|---|---|---|---|---|---|---|---|---|---|---|---|
| Angel, Jason | 3 | 2 | 5.13 | 19 | 7 | 0 | 0 | 60 | 62 | 39 | 34 | 33 | 28 | R | R | 6-4 | 205 | 9-8-71 | 1992 | Glen Allen, Va. |
| Brothers, John | 5 | 3 | 4.43 | 46 | 4 | 0 | 1 | 89 | 94 | 58 | 44 | 40 | 70 | R | R | 6-1 | 180 | 11-12-69 | 1990 | Douglasville, Ga. |
| Brunson, William | 5 | 6 | 3.93 | 37 | 15 | 0 | 0 | 124 | 119 | 68 | 54 | 50 | 103 | L | L | 6-4 | 185 | 3-20-70 | 1992 | DeSoto, Texas |
| Etheridge, Roger | 3 | 3 | 7.21 | 13 | 8 | 0 | 0 | 44 | 43 | 41 | 35 | 35 | 28 | L | L | 6-5 | 215 | 5-31-72 | 1992 | Linden, Ala. |
| Fox, Chad | 9 | 12 | 5.37 | 27 | 26 | 0 | 0 | 136 | 138 | 100 | 81 | 97 | 81 | R | R | 6-2 | 180 | 9-3-70 | 1992 | Houston, Texas |
| Garcia, Fermin | 6 | 7 | 4.33 | 35 | 12 | 0 | 0 | 116 | 127 | 74 | 56 | 51 | 79 | R | R | 6-0 | 170 | 1-6-72 | 1990 | Los Pasos, D.R. |
| Jesperson, Bob | 3 | 1 | 1.37 | 20 | 0 | 0 | 0 | 26 | 13 | 10 | 4 | 15 | 19 | R | R | 6-1 | 195 | 5-25-69 | 1991 | White Lake, Wis. |
| Kummerfeldt, Jason | 5 | 6 | 3.89 | 23 | 13 | 1 | 0 | 83 | 102 | 54 | 36 | 32 | 67 | R | R | 6-4 | 220 | 12-17-69 | 1992 | Billings, Mont. |
| Langford, Rich | 0 | 1 | 1.33 | 4 | 4 | 0 | 0 | 20 | 12 | 5 | 3 | 10 | 34 | R | R | 6-4 | 195 | 9-14-71 | 1990 | Simi Valley, Calif. |
| Lister, Martin | 1 | 2 | 2.08 | 51 | 0 | 0 | 32 | 52 | 38 | 16 | 12 | 31 | 57 | L | L | 6-2 | 210 | 6-12-72 | 1992 | Pensacola, Fla. |
| Loftin, Bo | 4 | 1 | 1.94 | 9 | 9 | 0 | 0 | 51 | 47 | 24 | 11 | 22 | 19 | R | R | 6-5 | 225 | 2-8-69 | 1991 | Jacksonville, Ala. |
| Maberry, Louis | 8 | 4 | 1.62 | 57 | 0 | 0 | 4 | 95 | 55 | 23 | 17 | 28 | 103 | R | R | 5-11 | 180 | 12-6-70 | 1992 | Abilene, Texas |
| Nix, James | 7 | 2 | 2.23 | 26 | 5 | 1 | 5 | 61 | 28 | 19 | 15 | 24 | 75 | R | R | 5-11 | 175 | 9-6-70 | 1992 | Burton, Texas |
| O'Laughlin, Chad | 0 | 0 | 0.00 | 2 | 0 | 0 | 0 | 1 | 2 | 0 | 0 | 0 | 0 | L | L | 6-5 | 220 | 1-7-72 | 1991 | Lake Havasu, Ariz. |
| Pickett, Ricky | 1 | 2 | 6.75 | 44 | 1 | 0 | 0 | 44 | 42 | 40 | 33 | 48 | 65 | L | L | 6-0 | 185 | 1-19-70 | 1992 | Fort Worth, Texas |
| Reed, Chris | 7 | 9 | 4.09 | 21 | 21 | 0 | 0 | 112 | 99 | 63 | 51 | 58 | 84 | R | R | 6-3 | 206 | 8-25-73 | 1991 | Anaheim, Calif. |
| Ruyak, Todd | 1 | 0 | 1.74 | 14 | 0 | 0 | 2 | 21 | 12 | 5 | 4 | 9 | 21 | L | L | 6-3 | 215 | 9-18-70 | 1992 | Hamilton Square, N.J. |
| Stewart, Carl | 0 | 0 | 0.84 | 2 | 2 | 0 | 0 | 11 | 4 | 2 | 1 | 4 | 9 | R | R | 6-3 | 190 | 12-8-70 | 1988 | Plano, Texas |
| Tuttle, Dave | 8 | 3 | 3.54 | 13 | 13 | 0 | 0 | 81 | 66 | 37 | 32 | 36 | 74 | R | R | 6-3 | 190 | 9-29-69 | 1992 | Los Gatos, Calif. |

# REDS: ORGANIZATION LEADERS

**Reggie Sanders**
Scored 90, drove in 83

## MAJOR LEAGUERS

**BATTING**

| | | |
|---|---|---|
| *AVG | Kevin Mitchell | .341 |
| R | Reggie Sanders | 90 |
| H | Chris Sabo | 143 |
| TB | Chris Sabo | 243 |
| 2B | Chris Sabo | 33 |
| 3B | Two tied at | 4 |
| HR | Chris Sabo | 21 |
| RBI | Reggie Sanders | 83 |
| BB | Two tied at | 51 |
| SO | Reggie Sanders | 118 |
| SB | Reggie Sanders | 27 |

**PITCHING**

| | | |
|---|---|---|
| W | Jose Rijo | 14 |
| L | Tim Pugh | 10 |
| #ERA | Jose Rijo | 2.48 |
| G | Jeff Reardon | 58 |
| CG | Tim Belcher | 4 |
| SV | Rob Dibble | 19 |
| IP | Jose Rijo | 257 |
| BB | Jose Rijo | 62 |
| SO | Jose Rijo | 227 |

## MINOR LEAGUERS

**BATTING**

| | | |
|---|---|---|
| *AVG | Chris Sexton, Billings | .333 |
| R | Dee Jenkins, Charleston | 93 |
| H | Tim Belk, Winston-Salem | 156 |
| TB | Cleveland Ladell, Winston-Salem | 240 |
| 2B | Dan Frye, Charleston | 35 |
| 3B | Two tied at | 7 |
| HR | Bubba Smith, Winston-Salem | 27 |
| RBI | Jamie Dismuke, Chattanooga | 91 |
| BB | Dan Frye, Charleston | 76 |
| SO | Brian Lane, Chattanooga | 134 |
| SB | Brian Koelling, Chatt.-Indianapolis | 34 |

**PITCHING**

| | | |
|---|---|---|
| W | Dave Tuttle, Winston-Salem/Charleston | 15 |
| L | Chad Fox, Charleston | 12 |
| #ERA | Louis Maberry, Charleston | 1.61 |
| G | David Lynch, Indianapolis-Chatt. | 62 |
| CG | Two tied at | 4 |
| SV | Martin Lister, Charleston | 32 |
| IP | Mike Ferry, Chattanooga | 187 |
| BB | Chad Fox, Charleston | 97 |
| SO | Ross Powell, Indianapolis | 133 |

*Minimum 250 At-Bats    #Minimum 75 Innings

R&R SPORTS GROUP

## APPALACHIAN LEAGUE

### BATTING

| BATTING | AVG | G | AB | R | H | 2B | 3B | HR | RBI | BB | SO | SB | CS | B | T | HT | WT | DOB | 1st Yr | Resides |
|---|---|---|---|---|---|---|---|---|---|---|---|---|---|---|---|---|---|---|---|---|
| Broach, Donald, of | .232 | 55 | 181 | 29 | 42 | 5 | 1 | 1 | 19 | 15 | 31 | 8 | 3 | R | R | 6-0 | 185 | 7-18-71 | 1993 | Cincinnati, Ohio |
| Carvajal, Jhonny, 2b-ss | .292 | 67 | 253 | 41 | 74 | 10 | 5 | 0 | 16 | 29 | 31 | 7 | 11 | R | R | 5-10 | 165 | 7-24-74 | 1993 | Barcelona, Venez. |
| Concepcion, Yamil, 3b | .153 | 32 | 85 | 6 | 13 | 3 | 0 | 1 | 8 | 2 | 24 | 1 | 2 | R | R | 6-1 | 195 | 1-22-73 | 1991 | Florida, P.R. |
| Cradle, Cobi, of | .238 | 27 | 105 | 21 | 25 | 4 | 4 | 1 | 11 | 14 | 15 | 7 | 2 | L | L | 5-11 | 165 | 7-7-71 | 1993 | Cerritos, Calif. |
| DeBruhl, Randy, c-dh | .272 | 58 | 184 | 37 | 50 | 12 | 2 | 5 | 36 | 32 | 67 | 0 | 3 | R | R | 6-3 | 210 | 6-28-70 | 1993 | Monroe, La. |
| Dold, Jon, of | .244 | 44 | 127 | 12 | 31 | 6 | 1 | 1 | 21 | 13 | 18 | 5 | 1 | R | R | 6-4 | 215 | 7-24-71 | 1993 | Richmond, Minn. |
| Domino, Rob, c | .244 | 34 | 86 | 8 | 21 | 4 | 0 | 2 | 7 | 7 | 14 | 1 | 1 | R | R | 6-2 | 200 | 2-12-71 | 1993 | Bridgeview, Ill. |
| Duke, Mitch, c-dh | .156 | 26 | 64 | 7 | 10 | 2 | 0 | 0 | 3 | 11 | 12 | 0 | 0 | L | R | 5-10 | 190 | 2-20-70 | 1993 | Falkville, Ala. |
| Hall, Darran, of | .197 | 49 | 142 | 17 | 28 | 3 | 0 | 0 | 5 | 14 | 40 | 17 | 3 | S | L | 5-10 | 160 | 9-8-75 | 1993 | San Diego, Calif. |
| LaBarca, Argenis, 3b | .224 | 31 | 98 | 11 | 22 | 5 | 1 | 1 | 13 | 2 | 14 | 0 | 1 | R | R | 5-11 | 165 | 4-23-75 | 1993 | Maracaibo, Venez. |
| Lofton, James, ss | .224 | 50 | 174 | 26 | 39 | 4 | 2 | 1 | 13 | 19 | 41 | 11 | 5 | S | R | 5-9 | 163 | 3-6-74 | 1993 | Los Angeles, Calif. |
| McCroskey, Jackie, of | .253 | 29 | 95 | 21 | 24 | 10 | 1 | 4 | 12 | 15 | 26 | 0 | 3 | L | L | 5-10 | 177 | 8-23-73 | 1993 | Louisville, Ky. |
| Moon, Ray, of | .224 | 26 | 67 | 8 | 15 | 1 | 0 | 1 | 10 | 10 | 9 | 1 | 3 | R | R | 6-2 | 180 | 8-29-72 | 1992 | New Haven, Ind. |
| Ordaz, Luis, 3b-ss | .300 | 57 | 217 | 28 | 65 | 9 | 7 | 2 | 39 | 7 | 32 | 3 | 1 | R | R | 5-11 | 170 | 9-21-75 | 1993 | Maracaibo, Venez. |
| Ramey, Jeff, 1b | .271 | 63 | 240 | 31 | 65 | 10 | 3 | 0 | 43 | 23 | 36 | 17 | 3 | R | R | 5-11 | 190 | 3-24-71 | 1992 | Portsmouth, Ohio |
| Sanders, Rod, of | .183 | 40 | 82 | 8 | 15 | 2 | 0 | 0 | 5 | 5 | 25 | 0 | 1 | R | R | 5-9 | 175 | 9-27-73 | 1992 | Florence, S.C. |
| Silvia, Brian, c-dh | .176 | 5 | 17 | 1 | 3 | 0 | 0 | 0 | 1 | 2 | 1 | 1 | 1 | R | R | 6-0 | 195 | 9-13-71 | 1992 | Columbia, Miss. |
| White, Maximo, inf | .176 | 12 | 17 | 3 | 3 | 0 | 1 | 0 | 1 | 2 | 9 | 1 | 0 | R | R | 5-10 | 160 | 11-13-74 | 1993 | Santo Domingo, D.R. |

### PITCHING

| PITCHING | W | L | ERA | G | GS | CG | SV | IP | H | R | ER | BB | SO | B | T | HT | WT | DOB | 1st Yr | Resides |
|---|---|---|---|---|---|---|---|---|---|---|---|---|---|---|---|---|---|---|---|---|
| Chandler, Jason | 2 | 6 | 4.04 | 14 | 14 | 1 | 0 | 76 | 77 | 47 | 34 | 23 | 53 | R | R | 6-4 | 210 | 6-14-71 | 1993 | Jackson, Ky. |
| Etheridge, Roger | 3 | 2 | 1.49 | 9 | 9 | 1 | 0 | 54 | 40 | 14 | 9 | 28 | 60 | L | L | 6-5 | 215 | 5-31-72 | 1992 | Linden, Ala. |
| Fernandez, Luis | 0 | 1 | 5.74 | 15 | 0 | 0 | 1 | 27 | 28 | 18 | 17 | 20 | 13 | L | L | 6-2 | 185 | 1-25-74 | 1993 | Lamarovilla, Venez. |
| Franklin, Joel | 3 | 1 | 3.42 | 16 | 0 | 0 | 1 | 24 | 20 | 16 | 9 | 13 | 30 | S | R | 6-3 | 200 | 4-18-73 | 1993 | Coronado, Calif. |
| Fuccillo, Joe | 1 | 2 | 9.45 | 13 | 0 | 0 | 1 | 13 | 10 | 22 | 14 | 19 | 14 | L | L | 6-0 | 185 | 8-21-71 | 1993 | Brooklyn, N.Y. |
| Hagan, Danny | 2 | 1 | 3.17 | 17 | 6 | 0 | 1 | 60 | 44 | 23 | 21 | 35 | 63 | R | L | 6-2 | 205 | 6-14-72 | 1993 | Louisville, Ky. |
| Keenan, Brad | 1 | 1 | 6.05 | 14 | 0 | 0 | 2 | 19 | 16 | 16 | 13 | 20 | 21 | R | R | 6-5 | 215 | 3-29-71 | 1992 | Moorhead, Minn. |
| Meier, Pat | 1 | 3 | 8.24 | 14 | 0 | 0 | 0 | 20 | 26 | 20 | 18 | 18 | 18 | R | R | 6-4 | 180 | 11-15-72 | 1993 | Aurora, Colo. |
| Morales, Armando | 0 | 0 | 36.00 | 1 | 0 | 0 | 0 | 1 | 4 | 4 | 4 | 0 | 2 | S | R | 6-2 | 195 | 8-22-70 | 1991 | Levittown, P.R. |
| Mullins, Sam | 3 | 7 | 4.60 | 14 | 14 | 0 | 0 | 74 | 87 | 58 | 38 | 49 | 51 | R | R | 6-2 | 185 | 2-20-73 | 1991 | Chapmanville, W.Va. |
| Murphy, Jeff | 4 | 4 | 3.84 | 16 | 0 | 0 | 0 | 70 | 79 | 36 | 30 | 20 | 52 | R | R | 6-3 | 210 | 8-13-72 | 1991 | Greenville, Texas |
| Robbins, Jason | 1 | 5 | 6.55 | 17 | 5 | 0 | 1 | 44 | 50 | 41 | 32 | 20 | 34 | R | R | 6-3 | 195 | 12-20-72 | 1993 | South Bend, Ind. |
| Rutledge, Murry | 4 | 5 | 3.80 | 12 | 10 | 2 | 0 | 64 | 63 | 43 | 27 | 25 | 42 | R | R | 6-3 | 205 | 3-2-72 | 1993 | Olathe, Kan. |
| Sullivan, Jason | 1 | 4 | 5.30 | 27 | 0 | 0 | 3 | 37 | 38 | 25 | 22 | 28 | 30 | R | R | 6-1 | 185 | 9-21-71 | 1992 | Greenville, Fla. |

## PIONEER LEAGUE

### BATTING

| BATTING | AVG | G | AB | R | H | 2B | 3B | HR | RBI | BB | SO | SB | CS | B | T | HT | WT | DOB | 1st Yr | Resides |
|---|---|---|---|---|---|---|---|---|---|---|---|---|---|---|---|---|---|---|---|---|
| Akers, Chad, dh-2b | .267 | 65 | 247 | 54 | 66 | 14 | 3 | 2 | 35 | 24 | 26 | 14 | 7 | S | R | 5-8 | 160 | 5-30-72 | 1993 | Lake, W.Va. |
| Ashton, Jeff, 2b-3b | .235 | 58 | 183 | 28 | 43 | 10 | 2 | 6 | 29 | 33 | 42 | 13 | 1 | R | R | 5-11 | 175 | 11-20-70 | 1992 | North Royalton, Ohio |
| Baker, Jason, of | .308 | 34 | 91 | 18 | 28 | 3 | 1 | 0 | 9 | 8 | 16 | 1 | 3 | R | R | 6-2 | 175 | 9-22-72 | 1993 | Renfren, Pa. |
| Bako, Paul, c | .314 | 57 | 194 | 34 | 61 | 11 | 0 | 4 | 30 | 22 | 37 | 5 | 1 | L | R | 6-2 | 205 | 6-20-72 | 1993 | Lafayette, La. |
| Durrwachter, Doug, ss | .256 | 18 | 43 | 12 | 11 | 1 | 0 | 1 | 4 | 12 | 6 | 6 | 1 | R | R | 6-0 | 160 | 6-25-72 | 1993 | Duncanville, Texas |
| Eddie, Steve, 1b | .286 | 67 | 231 | 31 | 66 | 8 | 1 | 3 | 38 | 23 | 33 | 5 | 9 | R | R | 6-3 | 185 | 1-6-71 | 1993 | Storm Lake, Iowa |
| Gann, Stephen, 3b | .301 | 71 | 266 | 46 | 80 | 14 | 2 | 5 | 51 | 22 | 33 | 14 | 6 | R | R | 6-1 | 185 | 6-19-70 | 1993 | Houston, Texas |
| Moon, Ray, of | .214 | 16 | 42 | 6 | 9 | 1 | 0 | 0 | 3 | 3 | 5 | 1 | 1 | R | R | 6-2 | 180 | 8-29-72 | 1992 | New Haven, Ind. |
| Oyas, Dan, of | .271 | 68 | 255 | 35 | 69 | 17 | 2 | 6 | 49 | 29 | 44 | 15 | 3 | R | R | 6-0 | 180 | 3-19-73 | 1992 | San Bernardino, Calif. |
| Robinson, Eli, 1b-dh | .128 | 13 | 39 | 7 | 5 | 0 | 0 | 1 | 5 | 4 | 17 | 4 | 0 | R | R | 6-3 | 210 | 12-15-72 | 1991 | Joliet, Ill. |
| Sexton, Chris, ss | .333 | 72 | 273 | 63 | 91 | 14 | 4 | 4 | 46 | 35 | 27 | 13 | 4 | R | R | 5-11 | 180 | 8-3-71 | 1993 | Cincinnati, Ohio |
| Thomas, Rod, of | .257 | 65 | 230 | 38 | 59 | 11 | 2 | 8 | 35 | 23 | 68 | 1 | 6 | R | R | 6-1 | 195 | 8-22-73 | 1993 | Reddick, Fla. |
| Towle, Justin, c | .263 | 47 | 137 | 29 | 36 | 6 | 0 | 7 | 23 | 27 | 37 | 4 | 4 | R | R | 6-3 | 210 | 2-21-74 | 1992 | Seattle, Wash. |
| Watkins, Pat, of | .268 | 66 | 235 | 46 | 63 | 10 | 3 | 6 | 30 | 22 | 44 | 15 | 4 | R | R | 6-2 | 185 | 9-2-72 | 1993 | Garner, N.C. |

### PITCHING

| PITCHING | W | L | ERA | G | GS | CG | SV | IP | H | R | ER | BB | SO | B | T | HT | WT | DOB | 1st Yr | Resides |
|---|---|---|---|---|---|---|---|---|---|---|---|---|---|---|---|---|---|---|---|---|
| Connors, Chad | 2 | 2 | 2.12 | 19 | 0 | 0 | 5 | 30 | 20 | 9 | 7 | 20 | 32 | R | R | 6-0 | 200 | 10-18-71 | 1993 | Dayton, Ohio |
| Etler, Todd | 8 | 1 | 2.71 | 15 | 15 | 1 | 0 | 90 | 75 | 33 | 27 | 30 | 55 | R | R | 6-0 | 205 | 4-18-74 | 1992 | Villa Hills, Ky. |
| Fussell, Denny | 1 | 0 | 8.22 | 18 | 0 | 0 | 1 | 23 | 39 | 22 | 21 | 13 | 15 | L | L | 6-1 | 190 | 5-11-71 | 1992 | San Antonio, Texas |
| Harvell, Pete | 5 | 3 | 4.62 | 19 | 8 | 0 | 1 | 60 | 61 | 45 | 31 | 40 | 45 | L | L | 6-2 | 190 | 10-14-71 | 1993 | San Jose, Calif. |
| Hebel, Jon | 6 | 2 | 3.45 | 12 | 11 | 2 | 0 | 63 | 61 | 32 | 24 | 24 | 65 | R | R | 6-0 | 175 | 9-8-70 | 1993 | Dalton, Ga. |
| Lyons, Curt | 7 | 3 | 3.00 | 15 | 12 | 2 | 0 | 84 | 89 | 35 | 28 | 20 | 64 | R | R | 6-5 | 228 | 10-17-74 | 1992 | Richmond, Ky. |
| Magre, Pete | 2 | 5 | 4.56 | 14 | 8 | 0 | 2 | 49 | 49 | 32 | 25 | 22 | 34 | R | R | 6-1 | 180 | 10-31-70 | 1993 | Cameron, Texas |
| McKenzie, David | 1 | 2 | 3.60 | 14 | 1 | 0 | 0 | 30 | 27 | 16 | 12 | 14 | 37 | R | R | 6-0 | 185 | 9-30-70 | 1993 | Mansfield, Texas |
| Moses, Michael | 3 | 0 | 1.63 | 18 | 1 | 1 | 0 | 39 | 30 | 13 | 7 | 15 | 27 | L | L | 6-0 | 175 | 5-20-71 | 1993 | Glendora, Calif. |
| Sullivan, Scott | 5 | 0 | 1.67 | 18 | 7 | 2 | 3 | 54 | 33 | 13 | 10 | 25 | 79 | R | R | 6-3 | 210 | 3-13-71 | 1993 | Carrollton, Ala. |
| Tweedlie, Brad | 3 | 3 | 4.30 | 11 | 8 | 0 | 1 | 44 | 28 | 22 | 21 | 31 | 31 | R | R | 6-2 | 215 | 12-9-71 | 1993 | Enfield, Conn. |
| Wilkerson, Steve | 2 | 2 | 3.00 | 15 | 3 | 0 | 2 | 30 | 28 | 15 | 10 | 18 | 26 | R | R | 6-2 | 200 | 11-8-72 | 1993 | Farmington, N.M. |
| Witzel, Shane | 4 | 3 | 2.34 | 22 | 0 | 0 | 2 | 42 | 34 | 12 | 11 | 15 | 36 | R | R | 6-0 | 170 | 4-17-70 | 1993 | Woodlawn, Ill. |

# CLEVELAND INDIANS

**Manager:** Mike Hargrove.     **1993 Record:** 76-86, .469 (6th, AL East).

| BATTING | AVG | G | AB | R | H | 2B | 3B | HR | RBI | BB | SO | SB | CS | B | T | HT | WT | DOB | 1st Yr | Resides |
|---|---|---|---|---|---|---|---|---|---|---|---|---|---|---|---|---|---|---|---|---|
| Alomar, Sandy | .270 | 64 | 215 | 24 | 58 | 7 | 1 | 6 | 32 | 11 | 28 | 3 | 1 | R | R | 6-5 | 215 | 6-18-66 | 1984 | Westlake, Ohio |
| Baerga, Carlos | .321 | 154 | 624 | 105 | 200 | 28 | 6 | 21 | 114 | 34 | 68 | 15 | 4 | S | R | 5-11 | 200 | 11-4-68 | 1986 | Westlake, Ohio |
| Belle, Albert | .290 | 159 | 594 | 93 | 172 | 36 | 3 | 38 | 129 | 76 | 96 | 23 | 12 | R | R | 6-2 | 210 | 8-25-66 | 1987 | Euclid, Ohio |
| Espinoza, Alvaro | .278 | 129 | 263 | 34 | 73 | 15 | 0 | 4 | 27 | 8 | 36 | 2 | 2 | R | R | 6-0 | 190 | 2-19-62 | 1979 | Bergenfield, N.J. |
| Fermin, Felix | .263 | 140 | 480 | 48 | 126 | 16 | 2 | 2 | 45 | 24 | 14 | 4 | 5 | R | R | 5-11 | 170 | 10-9-63 | 1983 | Santiago, D.R. |
| Hill, Glenallen | .224 | 66 | 174 | 19 | 39 | 7 | 2 | 5 | 25 | 11 | 50 | 7 | 3 | R | R | 6-2 | 210 | 3-22-65 | 1983 | Boca Raton, Fla. |
| Horn, Sam | .455 | 12 | 33 | 8 | 15 | 1 | 0 | 4 | 8 | 1 | 5 | 0 | 0 | L | L | 6-5 | 250 | 11-2-63 | 1982 | Bessemer, Ala. |
| Howard, Tom | .236 | 74 | 178 | 26 | 42 | 7 | 0 | 3 | 23 | 12 | 42 | 5 | 1 | S | R | 6-2 | 205 | 12-11-64 | 1986 | Middletown, Ohio |
| Jefferson, Reggie | .249 | 113 | 366 | 35 | 91 | 11 | 2 | 10 | 34 | 28 | 78 | 1 | 3 | S | L | 6-4 | 215 | 9-25-68 | 1986 | Tallahassee, Fla. |
| Kirby, Wayne | .269 | 131 | 458 | 71 | 123 | 19 | 5 | 6 | 60 | 37 | 58 | 17 | 5 | L | R | 5-10 | 185 | 1-22-64 | 1983 | Yorktown, Va. |
| Levis, Jesse | .175 | 31 | 63 | 7 | 11 | 2 | 0 | 0 | 4 | 2 | 10 | 0 | 0 | L | R | 5-9 | 180 | 4-14-68 | 1989 | Philadelphia, Pa. |
| Lewis, Mark | .250 | 14 | 52 | 6 | 13 | 2 | 0 | 1 | 5 | 0 | 7 | 3 | 0 | R | R | 6-1 | 190 | 11-30-69 | 1988 | Hamilton, Ohio |
| Lofton, Kenny | .325 | 148 | 569 | 116 | 185 | 28 | 8 | 1 | 42 | 81 | 83 | 70 | 14 | L | L | 6-0 | 180 | 5-31-67 | 1988 | East Chicago, Ind. |
| Maldonado, Candy | .247 | 28 | 81 | 11 | 20 | 2 | 0 | 5 | 20 | 11 | 18 | 0 | 1 | R | R | 5-11 | 195 | 9-5-60 | 1978 | Arecibo, P.R. |
| Martinez, Dave | .244 | 80 | 262 | 26 | 64 | 10 | 0 | 5 | 31 | 20 | 29 | 1 | 1 | R | R | 6-5 | 215 | 8-11-65 | 1984 | La Guaira, Venez. |
| Milligan, Randy | .426 | 19 | 47 | 7 | 20 | 7 | 0 | 0 | 7 | 14 | 4 | 0 | 0 | R | R | 6-1 | 225 | 11-27-61 | 1981 | Baltimore, Md. |
| Ortiz, Junior | .221 | 95 | 249 | 19 | 55 | 13 | 0 | 0 | 20 | 11 | 26 | 1 | 0 | R | R | 5-11 | 185 | 10-24-59 | 1977 | Humacao, P.R. |
| Parrish, Lance | .200 | 10 | 20 | 2 | 4 | 1 | 0 | 1 | 2 | 4 | 5 | 1 | 0 | R | R | 6-3 | 220 | 6-15-56 | 1974 | Yorba Linda, Calif. |
| Ramirez, Manny | .170 | 22 | 53 | 5 | 9 | 1 | 0 | 2 | 5 | 2 | 8 | 0 | 0 | R | R | 6-0 | 190 | 5-30-72 | 1991 | Brooklyn, N.Y. |
| Sorrento, Paul | .257 | 148 | 463 | 75 | 119 | 26 | 1 | 18 | 65 | 58 | 121 | 3 | 1 | L | R | 6-2 | 205 | 11-17-65 | 1986 | Peabody, Mass. |
| Thome, Jim | .266 | 47 | 154 | 28 | 41 | 11 | 0 | 7 | 22 | 29 | 36 | 2 | 1 | L | R | 6-4 | 200 | 8-27-70 | 1989 | Peoria, Ill. |
| Treadway, Jeff | .303 | 97 | 221 | 25 | 67 | 14 | 1 | 2 | 27 | 14 | 21 | 1 | 1 | L | R | 5-11 | 175 | 1-22-63 | 1984 | Griffin, Ga. |

| PITCHING | W | L | ERA | G | GS | CG | SV | IP | H | R | ER | BB | SO | B | T | HT | WT | DOB | 1st Yr | Resides |
|---|---|---|---|---|---|---|---|---|---|---|---|---|---|---|---|---|---|---|---|---|
| Abbott, Paul | 0 | 1 | 6.38 | 5 | 5 | 0 | 0 | 18 | 19 | 15 | 13 | 11 | 7 | R | R | 6-3 | 180 | 9-15-67 | 1985 | Fullerton, Calif. |
| Bielecki, Mike | 4 | 5 | 5.90 | 13 | 13 | 0 | 0 | 69 | 90 | 47 | 45 | 23 | 38 | R | R | 6-3 | 200 | 7-31-59 | 1979 | Crownsville, Md. |
| Christopher, Mike | 0 | 0 | 3.86 | 9 | 0 | 0 | 0 | 12 | 14 | 6 | 5 | 2 | 8 | R | R | 6-5 | 205 | 11-3-63 | 1985 | Church Road, Va. |
| Clark, Mark | 7 | 5 | 4.28 | 26 | 15 | 1 | 0 | 109 | 119 | 55 | 52 | 25 | 57 | R | R | 6-5 | 225 | 5-12-68 | 1988 | Bath, Ill. |
| Cook, Dennis | 5 | 5 | 5.67 | 25 | 6 | 0 | 0 | 54 | 62 | 36 | 34 | 16 | 34 | L | L | 6-3 | 190 | 10-4-62 | 1985 | Austin, Texas |
| DiPoto, Jerry | 4 | 4 | 2.40 | 46 | 0 | 0 | 11 | 56 | 57 | 21 | 15 | 30 | 41 | R | R | 6-2 | 200 | 5-24-68 | 1989 | Leawood, Kan. |
| Grimsley, Jason | 3 | 4 | 5.31 | 10 | 6 | 0 | 0 | 42 | 52 | 26 | 25 | 20 | 27 | R | R | 6-3 | 180 | 8-7-67 | 1985 | Cleveland, Texas |
| Hernandez, Jeremy | 6 | 5 | 3.14 | 49 | 0 | 0 | 8 | 77 | 75 | 33 | 27 | 27 | 44 | R | R | 6-5 | 195 | 7-6-66 | 1987 | Yuma, Ariz. |
| Kramer, Tom | 7 | 3 | 4.02 | 39 | 16 | 1 | 0 | 121 | 126 | 60 | 54 | 59 | 71 | S | R | 6-0 | 205 | 1-9-68 | 1987 | St. Bernard, Ohio |
| Lilliquist, Derek | 4 | 4 | 2.25 | 56 | 2 | 0 | 10 | 64 | 64 | 20 | 16 | 19 | 40 | L | L | 5-10 | 195 | 2-20-66 | 1987 | Vero Beach, Fla. |
| Lopez, Albie | 3 | 1 | 5.98 | 9 | 9 | 0 | 0 | 50 | 49 | 34 | 33 | 32 | 25 | R | R | 6-1 | 205 | 8-18-71 | 1991 | Mesa, Ariz. |
| Mesa, Jose | 10 | 12 | 4.92 | 34 | 33 | 3 | 0 | 209 | 232 | 122 | 114 | 62 | 118 | R | R | 6-3 | 225 | 5-22-66 | 1982 | Westlake, Ohio |
| Milacki, Bob | 1 | 1 | 3.38 | 5 | 2 | 0 | 0 | 16 | 19 | 8 | 6 | 11 | 7 | R | R | 6-4 | 230 | 7-28-64 | 1984 | Lake Havasu, Ariz. |
| Mlicki, Dave | 0 | 0 | 3.38 | 3 | 3 | 0 | 0 | 13 | 11 | 6 | 5 | 6 | 7 | R | R | 6-4 | 190 | 6-8-68 | 1990 | Galloway, Ohio |
| Mutis, Jeff | 3 | 6 | 5.78 | 17 | 13 | 1 | 0 | 81 | 93 | 56 | 52 | 33 | 29 | L | L | 6-2 | 185 | 12-20-66 | 1988 | Allentown, Pa. |
| Nagy, Charles | 2 | 6 | 6.29 | 9 | 9 | 1 | 0 | 49 | 66 | 38 | 34 | 13 | 30 | L | R | 6-3 | 200 | 5-5-67 | 1989 | Westlake, Ohio |
| Ojeda, Bobby | 2 | 1 | 4.40 | 9 | 7 | 0 | 0 | 43 | 48 | 22 | 21 | 21 | 27 | L | L | 6-1 | 195 | 12-17-57 | 1978 | Holmdale, N.J. |
| Plunk, Eric | 4 | 5 | 2.79 | 70 | 0 | 0 | 15 | 71 | 61 | 29 | 22 | 30 | 77 | R | R | 6-6 | 220 | 9-3-63 | 1981 | Riverside, Calif. |
| Power, Ted | 0 | 2 | 7.20 | 20 | 0 | 0 | 0 | 20 | 30 | 17 | 16 | 8 | 11 | R | R | 6-4 | 215 | 1-31-55 | 1976 | Cincinnati, Ohio |
| Scudder, Scott | 0 | 1 | 9.00 | 2 | 1 | 0 | 0 | 4 | 5 | 4 | 4 | 4 | 1 | R | R | 6-2 | 190 | 2-14-68 | 1986 | Austin, Texas |
| Slocumb, Heathcliff | 3 | 1 | 4.28 | 20 | 0 | 0 | 0 | 27 | 28 | 14 | 13 | 16 | 18 | R | R | 6-3 | 180 | 6-7-66 | 1984 | Jamaica, N.Y. |
| Tavarez, Julian | 2 | 2 | 6.57 | 8 | 7 | 0 | 0 | 37 | 53 | 29 | 27 | 13 | 19 | R | R | 6-2 | 165 | 5-22-73 | 1990 | Santiago, D.R. |
| Wertz, Bill | 2 | 3 | 3.62 | 34 | 0 | 0 | 0 | 60 | 54 | 28 | 24 | 32 | 53 | R | R | 6-6 | 220 | 1-15-67 | 1989 | Cleveland, Ohio |
| Wickander, Kevin | 0 | 0 | 4.15 | 11 | 0 | 0 | 0 | 9 | 15 | 7 | 4 | 3 | 3 | L | L | 6-3 | 200 | 1-4-65 | 1986 | Glendale, Ariz. |
| Young, Cliff | 3 | 3 | 4.62 | 21 | 7 | 0 | 1 | 60 | 74 | 35 | 31 | 18 | 31 | L | L | 6-4 | 210 | 8-2-64 | 1983 | Willis, Texas |
| Young, Matt | 1 | 6 | 5.21 | 22 | 8 | 0 | 0 | 74 | 75 | 45 | 43 | 57 | 65 | L | L | 6-3 | 205 | 8-9-58 | 1980 | La Canada, Calif. |

## FIELDING

| Catcher | PCT | G | PO | A | E | DP |
|---|---|---|---|---|---|---|
| Alomar | .984 | 64 | 342 | 25 | 6 | 4 |
| Levis | .991 | 29 | 109 | 7 | 1 | 4 |
| Ortiz | .990 | 95 | 441 | 58 | 5 | 13 |
| Parrish | .950 | 10 | 47 | 10 | 3 | 1 |

| First Base | PCT | G | PO | A | E | DP |
|---|---|---|---|---|---|---|
| Jefferson | .976 | 15 | 112 | 10 | 3 | 10 |
| Martinez | .973 | 22 | 135 | 7 | 4 | 12 |
| Milligan | 1.000 | 18 | 101 | 7 | 0 | 16 |
| Sorrento | .995 | 144 | 1012 | 86 | 6 | 107 |

| Second Base | PCT | G | PO | A | E | DP |
|---|---|---|---|---|---|---|
| Baerga | .979 | 150 | 347 | 445 | 17 | 108 |

| | PCT | G | PO | A | E | DP |
|---|---|---|---|---|---|---|
| Espinoza | .900 | 2 | 6 | 3 | 1 | 2 |
| Treadway | .949 | 19 | 29 | 45 | 4 | 8 |
| **Third Base** | **PCT** | **G** | **PO** | **A** | **E** | **DP** |
| Espinoza | .937 | 99 | 42 | 107 | 10 | 9 |
| Martinez | .934 | 35 | 27 | 44 | 5 | 5 |
| Thome | .950 | 47 | 29 | 86 | 6 | 10 |
| Treadway | .933 | 42 | 17 | 66 | 6 | 5 |
| **Shortstop** | **PCT** | **G** | **PO** | **A** | **E** | **DP** |
| Espinoza | .985 | 35 | 18 | 47 | 1 | 13 |
| Fermin | .960 | 140 | 211 | 346 | 23 | 87 |
| Lewis | .964 | 13 | 22 | 31 | 2 | 10 |

| Outfield | PCT | G | PO | A | E | DP |
|---|---|---|---|---|---|---|
| Belle | .986 | 150 | 338 | 16 | 5 | 7 |
| Hill | .940 | 39 | 62 | 1 | 4 | 0 |
| Howard | .977 | 47 | 81 | 3 | 2 | 1 |
| Kirby | .983 | 123 | 273 | 19 | 5 | 5 |
| Lofton | .979 | 146 | 402 | 11 | 9 | 3 |
| Maldonado | .976 | 26 | 39 | 1 | 1 | 0 |
| Ramirez | 1.000 | 1 | 3 | 0 | 0 | 0 |
| Sorrento | 1.000 | 3 | 3 | 0 | 0 | 0 |

# INDIANS FARM SYSTEM

| Class | Club | League | W | L | Pct. | Finish* | Manager | First Year |
|---|---|---|---|---|---|---|---|---|
| AAA | Charlotte (N.C.) Knights | International | 86 | 55 | .610 | 1st† (10) | Charlie Manuel | 1993 |
| AA | Canton-Akron (Ohio) Indians | Eastern | 75 | 63 | .543 | 2nd (8) | Brian Graham | 1989 |
| A# | Kinston (N.C.) Indians | Carolina | 71 | 67 | .514 | 3rd (8) | Dave Keller | 1987 |

TOM DiPACE

**Kenny Lofton.** Indians speedy center fielder hit .325 and led American League with 70 stolen bases.

R&R SPORTS GROUP

**Carlos Baerga.** Big 1993 season included a .321 average, 200 hits and 114 RBIs.

| Class | Club | League | W | L | Pct. | Finish* | Manager | First Year |
|---|---|---|---|---|---|---|---|---|
| A# | Kinston (N.C.) Indians | Carolina | 71 | 67 | .514 | 3rd (8) | Dave Kelier | 1987 |
| A | Columbus (Ga.) RedStixx | South Atlantic | 86 | 56 | .606 | 2nd (14) | Mike Brown | 1991 |
| A | Watertown (N.Y.) Indians | New York-Penn | 46 | 32 | .590 | 3rd (14) | Mike Young | 1989 |
| Rookie# | Burlington (N.C.) Indians | Appalachian | 44 | 24 | .647 | T-1st† (10) | Jim Gabella | 1986 |

*Finish in overall standings (No. of teams in league) #Advanced level †Won league championship

## CHARLOTTE AAA

### INTERNATIONAL LEAGUE

| BATTING | AVG | G | AB | R | H | 2B | 3B | HR | RBI | BB | SO | SB | CS | B | T | HT | WT | DOB | 1st Yr | Resides |
|---|---|---|---|---|---|---|---|---|---|---|---|---|---|---|---|---|---|---|---|---|
| Allred, Beau | .245 | 120 | 347 | 59 | 85 | 13 | 3 | 20 | 61 | 45 | 57 | 4 | 3 | L | L | 6-0 | 190 | 6-4-65 | 1987 | Safford, Ariz. |
| Alomar, Sandy | .364 | 12 | 44 | 8 | 16 | 5 | 0 | 1 | 8 | 5 | 8 | 0 | 0 | R | R | 6-5 | 215 | 6-18-66 | 1984 | Westlake, Ohio |
| Canale, George | .216 | 73 | 208 | 32 | 45 | 8 | 0 | 6 | 27 | 26 | 47 | 2 | 1 | L | R | 6-1 | 195 | 8-11-65 | 1986 | Roanoke, Va. |
| Cockrell, Alan | .276 | 96 | 275 | 31 | 76 | 12 | 2 | 8 | 39 | 23 | 59 | 0 | 0 | R | R | 6-2 | 210 | 12-5-62 | 1984 | Galena, Kan. |
| Davidson, Mark | .281 | 101 | 263 | 39 | 74 | 12 | 2 | 9 | 36 | 27 | 52 | 1 | 1 | R | R | 6-2 | 190 | 2-15-61 | 1982 | Statesville, N.C. |
| Horn, Sam | .269 | 122 | 402 | 62 | 108 | 17 | 1 | 38 | 96 | 60 | 131 | 1 | 0 | L | L | 6-5 | 250 | 11-2-63 | 1982 | Bessemer, Ala. |
| Kirby, Wayne | .289 | 17 | 76 | 10 | 22 | 6 | 2 | 3 | 7 | 3 | 10 | 4 | 2 | L | R | 5-10 | 185 | 1-22-64 | 1983 | Yorktown, Va. |
| Kunkel, Jeff | .281 | 115 | 430 | 65 | 121 | 34 | 3 | 11 | 46 | 13 | 104 | 12 | 8 | R | R | 6-2 | 180 | 3-25-62 | 1983 | Arlington, Texas |
| Levis, Jesse | .248 | 47 | 129 | 10 | 32 | 6 | 1 | 2 | 20 | 15 | 12 | 0 | 2 | L | R | 5-9 | 180 | 4-14-68 | 1989 | Philadelphia, Pa. |
| Lewis, Mark | .284 | 126 | 507 | 93 | 144 | 30 | 4 | 17 | 67 | 34 | 76 | 9 | 5 | R | R | 6-1 | 190 | 11-30-69 | 1988 | Hamilton, Ohio |
| Lopez, Luis | .314 | 67 | 242 | 36 | 76 | 15 | 0 | 12 | 37 | 6 | 17 | 0 | 0 | R | R | 6-1 | 190 | 9-1-64 | 1983 | Brooklyn, N.Y. |
| Martinez, Carlos | .367 | 20 | 79 | 17 | 29 | 7 | 1 | 3 | 12 | 4 | 15 | 2 | 0 | R | R | 6-5 | 215 | 8-11-65 | 1984 | La Guaira, Venez. |
| Marzano, John | .111 | 3 | 9 | 0 | 1 | 0 | 0 | 0 | 0 | 1 | 1 | 0 | 0 | R | R | 5-11 | 195 | 2-14-63 | 1985 | Philadelphia, Pa. |
| Mercado, Orlando | .143 | 10 | 21 | 0 | 3 | 0 | 0 | 0 | 0 | 2 | 5 | 0 | 0 | R | R | 6-0 | 195 | 11-7-61 | 1978 | Arecibo, P.R. |
| Mota, Carlos | .200 | 14 | 25 | 4 | 5 | 1 | 0 | 0 | 1 | 2 | 6 | 1 | 0 | R | R | 6-0 | 170 | 1-10-68 | 1987 | Haina, D.R. |
| Nixon, Donell | .333 | 20 | 24 | 8 | 8 | 0 | 0 | 0 | 1 | 2 | 3 | 3 | 1 | R | R | 6-1 | 185 | 12-31-61 | 1981 | Evergreen, N.C. |
| Ramirez, Manny | .317 | 40 | 145 | 38 | 46 | 12 | 0 | 14 | 36 | 27 | 35 | 1 | 1 | R | R | 6-0 | 190 | 5-30-72 | 1991 | Brooklyn, N.Y. |
| Ramos, Ken | .292 | 132 | 480 | 77 | 140 | 16 | 11 | 3 | 41 | 47 | 41 | 12 | 8 | L | L | 6-1 | 185 | 6-8-67 | 1989 | Pueblo, Colo. |
| Schaefer, Jeff | .279 | 133 | 448 | 53 | 125 | 20 | 3 | 7 | 43 | 21 | 61 | 5 | 8 | R | R | 5-10 | 170 | 5-31-60 | 1981 | Charlotte, N.C. |
| Stinnett, Kelly | .274 | 98 | 288 | 42 | 79 | 10 | 3 | 6 | 33 | 17 | 52 | 0 | 0 | R | R | 5-11 | 195 | 2-14-70 | 1990 | Lawton, Okla. |
| Thome, Jim | .332 | 115 | 410 | 85 | 136 | 21 | 4 | 25 | 102 | 76 | 94 | 1 | 3 | L | R | 6-4 | 200 | 8-27-70 | 1989 | Peoria, Ill. |

| PITCHING | W | L | ERA | G | GS | CG | SV | IP | H | R | ER | BB | SO | B | T | HT | WT | DOB | 1st Yr | Resides |
|---|---|---|---|---|---|---|---|---|---|---|---|---|---|---|---|---|---|---|---|---|
| Abbott, Paul | 0 | 1 | 6.63 | 4 | 4 | 0 | 0 | 19 | 25 | 16 | 14 | 7 | 12 | R | R | 6-3 | 180 | 9-15-67 | 1985 | Fullerton, Calif. |
| Anderson, Allan | 0 | 0 | 9.64 | 7 | 0 | 0 | 0 | 14 | 30 | 15 | 15 | 4 | 5 | L | L | 6-0 | 180 | 1-7-64 | 1983 | Lancaster, Ohio |
| August, Don | 3 | 1 | 5.48 | 14 | 5 | 0 | 0 | 44 | 57 | 29 | 27 | 10 | 24 | R | R | 6-3 | 190 | 7-3-63 | 1985 | New Berlin, Wis. |
| Byrd, Paul | 7 | 4 | 3.89 | 14 | 14 | 1 | 0 | 81 | 80 | 43 | 35 | 30 | 54 | R | R | 6-1 | 185 | 12-3-70 | 1991 | Louisville, Ky. |
| Charland, Colin | 1 | 0 | 6.75 | 6 | 1 | 0 | 0 | 15 | 20 | 12 | 11 | 5 | 16 | L | L | 6-3 | 205 | 11-13-65 | 1986 | Duncanville, Texas |
| Christopher, Mike | 3 | 6 | 3.22 | 50 | 0 | 0 | 22 | 50 | 51 | 21 | 18 | 6 | 36 | R | R | 6-5 | 205 | 11-3-63 | 1985 | Church Road, Va. |
| Clark, Mark | 1 | 0 | 2.08 | 2 | 2 | 0 | 0 | 13 | 9 | 5 | 3 | 2 | 12 | R | R | 6-5 | 225 | 5-12-68 | 1988 | Bath, Ill. |
| Cook, Dennis | 3 | 2 | 5.06 | 12 | 6 | 0 | 0 | 43 | 46 | 26 | 24 | 6 | 40 | L | L | 6-3 | 190 | 10-4-62 | 1985 | Austin, Texas |
| Curtis, Mike | 2 | 1 | 5.23 | 7 | 0 | 0 | 0 | 10 | 10 | 6 | 6 | 3 | 10 | L | L | 6-3 | 180 | 3-12-65 | 1986 | Mt. Gilead, Ohio |
| DiPoto, Jerry | 6 | 3 | 1.93 | 34 | 0 | 0 | 12 | 47 | 34 | 10 | 10 | 13 | 44 | R | R | 6-2 | 200 | 5-24-68 | 1989 | Leawood, Kan. |
| Eiland, Dave | 1 | 3 | 5.30 | 8 | 8 | 0 | 0 | 36 | 42 | 22 | 21 | 12 | 13 | R | R | 6-3 | 205 | 7-5-66 | 1987 | Dade City, Fla. |
| Grimsley, Jason | 6 | 6 | 3.39 | 28 | 19 | 3 | 0 | 135 | 138 | 64 | 51 | 49 | 102 | R | R | 6-3 | 180 | 8-7-67 | 1985 | Cleveland, Texas |

| PITCHING | W | L | ERA | G | GS | CG | SV | IP | H | R | ER | BB | SO | B | T | HT | WT | DOB | 1st Yr | Resides |
|---|---|---|---|---|---|---|---|---|---|---|---|---|---|---|---|---|---|---|---|---|
| Lopez, Albie .................. | 1 | 0 | 2.25 | 3 | 2 | 0 | 0 | 12 | 8 | 3 | 3 | 2 | 7 | R | R | 6-1 | 205 | 8-18-71 | 1991 | Mesa, Ariz. |
| McCarthy, Tom .............. | 6 | 5 | 4.11 | 45 | 2 | 0 | 2 | 105 | 104 | 55 | 48 | 26 | 61 | R | R | 6-0 | 180 | 6-18-61 | 1979 | Lexington, N.C. |
| Milacki, Bob ................ | 4 | 3 | 3.39 | 21 | 7 | 0 | 4 | 72 | 59 | 31 | 27 | 19 | 46 | R | R | 6-4 | 230 | 7-28-64 | 1984 | Lake Havasu, Ariz. |
| Mutis, Jeff ..................... | 6 | 0 | 2.62 | 12 | 11 | 3 | 0 | 76 | 64 | 27 | 22 | 25 | 59 | L | L | 6-2 | 185 | 12-20-66 | 1988 | Allentown, Pa. |
| Ogea, Chad ................. | 13 | 8 | 3.81 | 29 | 29 | 2 | 0 | 182 | 169 | 91 | 77 | 54 | 135 | R | R | 6-2 | 200 | 11-9-70 | 1991 | Lake Charles, La. |
| Robinson, Nap................ | 0 | 0 | 54.00 | 1 | 0 | 0 | 0 | 1 | 7 | 6 | 6 | 1 | 1 | R | R | 6-3 | 195 | 1-26-66 | 1988 | Smyrna, Ga. |
| 2-team (19 Richmond) | 4 | 6 | 5.81 | 20 | 6 | 0 | 0 | 53 | 62 | 37 | 34 | 26 | 43 | | | | | | | |
| Scudder, Scott ............ | 7 | 7 | 5.03 | 23 | 22 | 2 | 0 | 136 | 148 | 92 | 76 | 52 | 64 | R | R | 6-2 | 190 | 2-14-68 | 1986 | Austin, Texas |
| Shinall, Zak ................... | 0 | 0 | 54.00 | 1 | 0 | 0 | 0 | 1 | 3 | 4 | 4 | 1 | 0 | R | R | 6-3 | 215 | 10-14-68 | 1987 | Vero Beach, Fla. |
| Slocumb, Heath ............ | 3 | 2 | 3.56 | 23 | 0 | 0 | 1 | 30 | 25 | 14 | 12 | 11 | 25 | R | R | 6-3 | 180 | 6-7-66 | 1984 | Jamaica, N.Y. |
| Solano, Julio ................ | 0 | 0 | 7.50 | 3 | 0 | 0 | 0 | 6 | 7 | 5 | 5 | 3 | 5 | R | R | 6-1 | 170 | 1-8-60 | 1980 | La Romana, D.R. |
| Wells, Terry .................. | 0 | 0 | 4.26 | 6 | 0 | 0 | 0 | 6 | 9 | 5 | 3 | 6 | 5 | L | L | 6-5 | 205 | 9-10-63 | 1985 | Chicago, Ill. |
| Wertz, Bill ................... | 7 | 2 | 1.95 | 28 | 1 | 0 | 0 | 51 | 42 | 18 | 11 | 14 | 47 | R | R | 6-6 | 220 | 1-15-67 | 1989 | Cleveland, Ohio |
| Young, Cliff .................. | 3 | 1 | 2.15 | 5 | 5 | 1 | 0 | 38 | 30 | 10 | 9 | 2 | 21 | L | L | 6-4 | 210 | 8-2-64 | 1983 | Willis, Texas |
| Young, Matt .................. | 3 | 0 | 2.55 | 3 | 3 | 1 | 0 | 18 | 11 | 5 | 5 | 5 | 17 | L | L | 6-3 | 205 | 8-9-58 | 1980 | La Canada, Calif. |

### FIELDING

| Catcher | PCT | G | PO | A | E | DP |
|---|---|---|---|---|---|---|
| Alomar.......... | 1.000 | 5 | 20 | 1 | 0 | 0 |
| Levis............... | .986 | 45 | 266 | 22 | 4 | 1 |
| Marzano.......... | .929 | 3 | 12 | 1 | 1 | 0 |
| Mercado.......... | 1.000 | 10 | 51 | 3 | 0 | 0 |
| Mota ............... | .959 | 13 | 44 | 3 | 2 | 0 |
| Stinnett.......... | .985 | 95 | 495 | 48 | 8 | 4 |

| First Base | PCT | G | PO | A | E | DP |
|---|---|---|---|---|---|---|
| Allred........... | 1.000 | 1 | 2 | 0 | 0 | 0 |
| Canale........... | .986 | 63 | 532 | 23 | 8 | 45 |
| Cockrell ........ | 1.000 | 8 | 33 | 4 | 0 | 5 |
| Horn ............. | .983 | 7 | 58 | 0 | 1 | 5 |
| Kunkel ........... | .992 | 39 | 234 | 21 | 2 | 26 |
| Lopez ............. | .990 | 52 | 396 | 20 | 4 | 32 |

| | PCT | G | PO | A | E | DP |
|---|---|---|---|---|---|---|
| Martinez .......... | .988 | 17 | 78 | 6 | 1 | 8 |
| Mercado ........ | 1.000 | 1 | 11 | 0 | 0 | 0 |

| Second Base | PCT | G | PO | A | E | DP |
|---|---|---|---|---|---|---|
| Kunkel ............ | .982 | 31 | 34 | 75 | 2 | 13 |
| Lopez ............. | 1.000 | 3 | 3 | 2 | 0 | 0 |
| Schaefer.......... | .970 | 129 | 250 | 386 | 20 | 91 |

| Third Base | PCT | G | PO | A | E | DP |
|---|---|---|---|---|---|---|
| Kunkel ............ | .943 | 26 | 8 | 25 | 2 | 0 |
| Lopez ............. | .800 | 7 | 4 | 4 | 2 | 0 |
| Martinez .......... | .960 | 12 | 7 | 17 | 1 | 0 |
| Thome ............. | .951 | 114 | 67 | 226 | 15 | 18 |

| Shortstop | PCT | G | PO | A | E | DP |
|---|---|---|---|---|---|---|
| Kunkel ............. | .983 | 14 | 14 | 45 | 1 | 6 |
| Lewis ............... | .961 | 125 | 168 | 403 | 23 | 81 |
| Schaefer........ | 1.000 | 5 | 3 | 7 | 0 | 3 |

| Outfield | PCT | G | PO | A | E | DP |
|---|---|---|---|---|---|---|
| Allred............. | .978 | 115 | 212 | 9 | 5 | 4 |
| Cockrell ........... | .955 | 68 | 100 | 6 | 5 | 0 |
| Davidson ......... | .987 | 88 | 147 | 8 | 2 | 2 |
| Kirby ............... | 1.000 | 17 | 38 | 1 | 0 | 1 |
| Kunkel ............. | .982 | 30 | 54 | 2 | 1 | 0 |
| Lopez ............. | 1.000 | 8 | 17 | 0 | 0 | 0 |
| Ramirez............ | .961 | 39 | 70 | 3 | 3 | 0 |
| Ramos............. | .991 | 124 | 205 | 11 | 2 | 0 |

# CANTON-AKRON                                                    AA
## EASTERN LEAGUE

| BATTING | AVG | G | AB | R | H | 2B | 3B | HR | RBI | BB | SO | SB | CS | B | T | HT | WT | DOB | 1st Yr | Resides |
|---|---|---|---|---|---|---|---|---|---|---|---|---|---|---|---|---|---|---|---|---|
| Bell, David, 3b-2b ....... | .292 | 129 | 483 | 69 | 141 | 20 | 2 | 9 | 60 | 43 | 54 | 3 | 4 | R | R | 5-10 | 170 | 9-14-72 | 1990 | Cincinnati, Ohio |
| Flores, Miguel, 2b....... | .292 | 116 | 435 | 73 | 127 | 20 | 5 | 3 | 54 | 59 | 39 | 36 | 9 | R | R | 5-11 | 185 | 8-16-70 | 1990 | Monterrey, Mexico |
| Giles, Brian, of.............. | .327 | 123 | 425 | 64 | 139 | 17 | 6 | 8 | 64 | 57 | 43 | 18 | 12 | L | L | 5-11 | 195 | 1-20-71 | 1989 | El Cajon, Calif. |
| Harvey, Ray, 1b ........ | .244 | 14 | 41 | 5 | 10 | 1 | 0 | 0 | 4 | 7 | 5 | 0 | 1 | L | L | 6-1 | 185 | 1-1-69 | 1991 | Brentwood, Tenn. |
| Hernandez, Jose, ss ..... | .200 | 45 | 150 | 19 | 30 | 6 | 0 | 2 | 17 | 10 | 39 | 9 | 2 | R | R | 6-0 | 180 | 7-14-69 | 1987 | Vega Alta, P.R. |
| Lennon, Pat, of.............. | .257 | 45 | 152 | 24 | 39 | 7 | 1 | 4 | 23 | 30 | 45 | 4 | 2 | R | R | 6-2 | 200 | 4-27-68 | 1986 | Whiteville, N.C. |
| Lopez, Luis, 1b-dh ...... | .277 | 60 | 231 | 30 | 64 | 16 | 0 | 2 | 41 | 13 | 16 | 0 | 3 | R | R | 6-1 | 190 | 9-1-64 | 1983 | Brooklyn, N.Y. |
| Martindale, Ryan, c ....... | .219 | 105 | 310 | 44 | 68 | 19 | 1 | 10 | 39 | 23 | 71 | 1 | 3 | R | R | 6-3 | 215 | 12-2-68 | 1991 | Omaha, Neb. |
| Mota, Carlos, c ............. | .286 | 35 | 84 | 12 | 24 | 1 | 0 | 0 | 10 | 4 | 12 | 2 | 2 | R | R | 6-0 | 170 | 1-10-68 | 1987 | Haina, D.R. |
| Odor, Rouglas, ss-2b ..... | .209 | 86 | 263 | 39 | 55 | 9 | 2 | 3 | 18 | 22 | 65 | 10 | 3 | R | R | 5-11 | 165 | 1-26-68 | 1988 | New Orleans, La. |
| Peguero, Julio, of........ | .226 | 65 | 177 | 19 | 40 | 6 | 5 | 0 | 14 | 17 | 32 | 5 | 1 | S | R | 5-11 | 160 | 9-7-68 | 1987 | Elbonito, D.R. |
| Perry, Herbert, 1b-3b ..... | .269 | 89 | 327 | 52 | 88 | 21 | 1 | 9 | 55 | 37 | 47 | 7 | 4 | R | R | 6-2 | 210 | 9-15-69 | 1991 | Mayo, Fla. |
| Ramirez, Manny, of..... | .340 | 89 | 344 | 67 | 117 | 32 | 0 | 17 | 79 | 45 | 68 | 2 | 2 | R | R | 6-0 | 190 | 5-30-72 | 1991 | Brooklyn, N.Y. |
| Ramirez, Omar, of........ | .314 | 125 | 516 | 116 | 162 | 24 | 6 | 7 | 53 | 53 | 49 | 24 | 6 | R | R | 5-9 | 170 | 11-2-70 | 1990 | Santiago, D.R. |
| Sanders, Tracy, of......... | .213 | 42 | 136 | 20 | 29 | 6 | 2 | 5 | 20 | 31 | 30 | 4 | 1 | L | R | 6-2 | 200 | 7-26-69 | 1990 | Dallas, N.C. |
| Sarbaugh, Mike, inf-of ... | .249 | 85 | 277 | 29 | 69 | 13 | 5 | 6 | 31 | 20 | 44 | 3 | 3 | R | R | 6-0 | 180 | 4-25-67 | 1989 | Mount Joy, Pa. |
| Skinner, Joel, c-dh ........ | .239 | 15 | 46 | 6 | 11 | 3 | 0 | 2 | 5 | 6 | 16 | 0 | 0 | R | R | 6-4 | 204 | 2-21-61 | 1980 | Bay Village, Ohio |
| Sparks, Greg, 1b ......... | .231 | 35 | 117 | 11 | 27 | 9 | 0 | 4 | 23 | 18 | 33 | 0 | 1 | L | L | 6-0 | 185 | 3-31-64 | 1984 | Phoenix, Ariz. |
| Sued, Nick, c ................. | .254 | 24 | 63 | 5 | 16 | 2 | 0 | 1 | 6 | 4 | 8 | 0 | 0 | R | R | 5-10 | 170 | 6-6-72 | 1990 | Santiago, D.R. |
| Vargas, Hector, ss-2b ... | .222 | 29 | 90 | 9 | 20 | 2 | 0 | 1 | 8 | 12 | 22 | 3 | 0 | R | R | 5-11 | 155 | 6-3-66 | 1986 | Arecibo, P.R. |

| PITCHING | W | L | ERA | G | GS | CG | SV | IP | H | R | ER | BB | SO | B | T | HT | WT | DOB | 1st Yr | Resides |
|---|---|---|---|---|---|---|---|---|---|---|---|---|---|---|---|---|---|---|---|---|
| Abbott, Paul ................... | 4 | 5 | 4.06 | 13 | 12 | 1 | 0 | 75 | 72 | 34 | 34 | 28 | 86 | R | R | 6-3 | 180 | 9-15-67 | 1985 | Fullerton, Calif. |
| Alexander, Gerald......... | 1 | 0 | 6.00 | 6 | 0 | 0 | 1 | 9 | 8 | 7 | 6 | 7 | 6 | R | R | 6-1 | 185 | 3-26-68 | 1989 | Donaldsonville, La. |
| Allen, Chad .................. | 0 | 1 | 5.16 | 18 | 0 | 0 | 1 | 23 | 34 | 20 | 13 | 12 | 10 | S | R | 6-4 | 200 | 8-15-68 | 1989 | Richland, Wash. |
| Bryant, Shawn .............. | 10 | 5 | 3.72 | 27 | 27 | 0 | 0 | 172 | 179 | 80 | 71 | 61 | 111 | R | L | 6-3 | 205 | 6-10-69 | 1990 | Oklahoma City, Okla. |
| Byrd, Paul .................... | 0 | 0 | 3.60 | 2 | 1 | 0 | 0 | 10 | 7 | 4 | 4 | 3 | 8 | R | R | 6-1 | 185 | 12-3-70 | 1991 | Louisville, Ky. |
| Charland, Colin .............. | 2 | 2 | 7.43 | 5 | 5 | 0 | 0 | 23 | 33 | 20 | 19 | 8 | 18 | L | L | 6-3 | 205 | 11-13-65 | 1986 | Duncanville, Texas |
| Dyer, Mike .................. | 7 | 4 | 5.55 | 17 | 17 | 0 | 0 | 94 | 90 | 64 | 58 | 55 | 75 | R | R | 6-3 | 200 | 9-8-66 | 1986 | Covina, Calif. |
| Embree, Alan ................ | 0 | 0 | 3.38 | 1 | 1 | 0 | 0 | 5 | 3 | 2 | 2 | 3 | 4 | L | L | 6-2 | 190 | 1-23-70 | 1990 | Brush Prairie, Wash. |
| Garcia, Apolinar............. | 8 | 4 | 3.89 | 42 | 7 | 0 | 3 | 111 | 103 | 53 | 48 | 37 | 110 | R | R | 5-11 | 165 | 1-30-68 | 1988 | Santo Domingo, D.R. |

# INDIANS: MOST COMMON LINEUPS

| | Cleveland | Charlotte | Canton-Akron | Kinston | Columbus |
|---|---|---|---|---|---|
| | Majors | AAA | AA | A | A |
| C | Junior Ortiz (95) | Kelly Stinnett (95) | Ryan Martindale (101) | Mike Crosby (71) | Mitch Meluskey (99) |
| 1B | Paul Sorrento (144) | George Canale (63) | Herbert Perry (46) | Chop Pough (72) | Chad Townsend (101) |
| 2B | Carlos Baerga (150) | Jeff Schaefer (129) | Miguel Flores (109) | Pat Maxwell (102) | Jonathon Nunnally (75) |
| 3B | Alvaro Espinoza (99) | Jim Thome (114) | David Bell (103) | Pete Rose (74) | Jamie Taylor (102) |
| SS | Felix Fermin (140) | Mark Lewis (125) | Rouglas Odor (73) | Juan Andujar (111) | Damian Jackson (106) |
| OF | Albert Belle (125) | Ken Ramos (125) | Omar Ramirez (120) | John Cotton (125) | Pat Bryant (113) |
| | Kenny Lofton (146) | Beau Allred (124) | Brian Giles (100) | Marc Marini (117) | Andre White (108) |
| | Wayne Kirby (123) | Mark Davidson (89) | Manny Ramirez (84) | Tony Mitchell (85) | Patricio Claudio (88) |
| DH | Reggie Jefferson (88) | Sam Horn (107) | Luis Lopez (23) | Ray Harvey (45) | Derek Hacopian (88) |
| SP | Jose Mesa (33) | Chad Ogea (29) | Shawn Bryant (27) | Carlos Crawford (28) | John Carter (29) |
| RP | Eric Plunk (70) | Mike Christopher (50) | Calvin Jones (43) | Ian Doyle (47) | Rod Koller (47) |
| | Full-season farm clubs only | No. of games at position in parenthesis | | | |

# INDIANS: ORGANIZATION LEADERS

## MAJOR LEAGUERS

**BATTING**

| | | |
|---|---|---|
| *AVG | Kenny Lofton | .325 |
| R | Kenny Lofton | 116 |
| H | Carlos Baerga | 200 |
| TB | Albert Belle | 328 |
| 2B | Albert Belle | 36 |
| 3B | Kenny Lofton | 8 |
| HR | Albert Belle | 38 |
| RBI | Albert Belle | 129 |
| BB | Kenny Lofton | 81 |
| SO | Paul Sorrento | 121 |
| SB | Kenny Lofton | 70 |

**PITCHING**

| | | |
|---|---|---|
| W | Jose Mesa | 10 |
| L | Jose Mesa | 12 |
| #ERA | Jeremy Hernandez | 3.14 |
| G | Eric Plunk | 70 |
| CG | Jose Mesa | 3 |
| SV | Eric Plunk | 15 |
| IP | Jose Mesa | 209 |
| BB | Jose Mesa | 62 |
| SO | Jose Mesa | 118 |

**Jose Mesa**
Led Tribe with 10 wins, 12 losses

DAN ARNOLD

## MINOR LEAGUERS

**BATTING**

| | | |
|---|---|---|
| *AVG | Manny Ramirez, Canton-Akron/Char. | .333 |
| R | Omar Ramirez, Canton-Akron | 116 |
| H | Manny Ramirez, Canton-Akron/Char. | 163 |
| TB | Manny Ramirez, Canton-Akron/Char. | 300 |
| 2B | Manny Ramirez, Canton-Akron/Char. | 44 |
| 3B | Ken Ramos, Charlotte | 11 |
| HR | Sam Horn, Charlotte | 38 |
| RBI | Manny Ramirez, Canton-Akron/Char. | 115 |
| BB | Jim Thome, Charlotte | 76 |
| SO | Sam Horn, Charlotte | 131 |
| SB | Pat Bryant, Columbus | 43 |

**PITCHING**

| | | |
|---|---|---|
| W | John Carter, Columbus | 17 |
| L | Matt Williams, Kinston | 12 |
| #ERA | J.J. Thobe, Columbus-Kinston | 2.09 |
| G | Cesar Perez, Columbus-Kinston | 55 |
| CG | Carlos Crawford, Kinston | 4 |
| SV | Cesar Perez, Columbus-Kinston | 35 |
| IP | Chad Ogea, Charlotte | 182 |
| BB | Matt Williams, Kinston | 100 |
| SO | Charles York, Columbus | 182 |

*Minimum 250 At-Bats   #Minimum 75 Innings

| PITCHING | W | L | ERA | G | GS | CG | SV | IP | H | R | ER | BB | SO | B | T | HT | WT | DOB | 1st Yr | Resides |
|---|---|---|---|---|---|---|---|---|---|---|---|---|---|---|---|---|---|---|---|---|
| Gardella, Mike | 2 | 1 | 4.37 | 21 | 0 | 0 | 4 | 23 | 26 | 14 | 11 | 22 | 14 | L | L | 5-10 | 195 | 1-18-67 | 1989 | Sapulpa, Okla. |
| Hernandez, Fernando | 0 | 1 | 11.74 | 2 | 2 | 0 | 0 | 8 | 14 | 11 | 10 | 5 | 8 | R | R | 6-2 | 185 | 6-16-71 | 1990 | Santiago, D.R. |
| Jones, Calvin | 5 | 5 | 3.30 | 43 | 0 | 0 | 22 | 63 | 40 | 25 | 23 | 26 | 73 | R | R | 6-3 | 185 | 9-26-63 | 1984 | Perris, Calif. |
| Lopez, Albie | 9 | 4 | 3.11 | 16 | 16 | 2 | 0 | 110 | 79 | 44 | 38 | 47 | 80 | R | R | 6-1 | 205 | 8-18-71 | 1991 | Mesa, Ariz. |
| McCarthy, Greg | 2 | 3 | 4.72 | 33 | 0 | 0 | 6 | 34 | 28 | 18 | 18 | 37 | 39 | L | L | 6-2 | 193 | 10-30-68 | 1987 | Shelton, Conn. |
| Mlicki, Dave | 2 | 1 | 0.39 | 6 | 6 | 0 | 0 | 23 | 15 | 2 | 1 | 8 | 21 | R | R | 6-4 | 190 | 6-8-68 | 1990 | Galloway, Ohio |
| Nagy, Charles | 0 | 0 | 1.13 | 2 | 2 | 0 | 0 | 8 | 8 | 1 | 1 | 2 | 4 | L | R | 6-3 | 200 | 5-5-67 | 1989 | Westlake, Ohio |
| Power, Ted | 0 | 0 | 4.67 | 7 | 3 | 0 | 0 | 17 | 22 | 10 | 9 | 8 | 16 | R | R | 6-4 | 215 | 1-31-55 | 1976 | Cincinnati, Ohio |
| Rivera, Roberto | 0 | 1 | 5.02 | 8 | 0 | 0 | 0 | 14 | 22 | 8 | 8 | 3 | 6 | L | L | 6-0 | 175 | 1-1-69 | 1988 | Bayamon, P.R. |
| Robinson, Nap | 3 | 2 | 4.56 | 9 | 7 | 0 | 0 | 47 | 49 | 28 | 24 | 18 | 26 | R | R | 6-3 | 195 | 1-26-66 | 1988 | Smyrna, Ga. |
| Romanoli, Paul | 1 | 2 | 4.54 | 30 | 0 | 0 | 0 | 40 | 37 | 22 | 20 | 21 | 38 | L | L | 6-2 | 182 | 9-22-69 | 1991 | Germantown, Tenn. |
| Shuey, Paul | 4 | 8 | 7.30 | 27 | 7 | 0 | 0 | 62 | 76 | 50 | 50 | 36 | 61 | R | R | 6-3 | 215 | 9-16-70 | 1992 | Raleigh, N.C. |
| Soper, Mike | 1 | 3 | 5.63 | 8 | 0 | 0 | 4 | 8 | 8 | 5 | 5 | 4 | 11 | R | R | 5-11 | 180 | 10-13-66 | 1989 | Saugus, Mass. |
| Stone, Eric | 3 | 0 | 3.05 | 14 | 0 | 0 | 0 | 21 | 17 | 8 | 7 | 17 | 15 | R | R | 6-2 | 195 | 7-29-67 | 1988 | Dallas, Texas |
| Tavarez, Julian | 2 | 1 | 0.95 | 3 | 2 | 1 | 0 | 19 | 14 | 2 | 2 | 1 | 11 | R | R | 6-2 | 165 | 5-22-73 | 1990 | Santiago, D.R. |
| Trice, Wally | 3 | 2 | 5.61 | 19 | 3 | 0 | 1 | 51 | 65 | 36 | 32 | 24 | 30 | L | L | 6-4 | 175 | 7-28-66 | 1988 | El Cajon, Calif. |
| Turek, Joe | 1 | 0 | 2.25 | 3 | 3 | 0 | 0 | 16 | 11 | 4 | 4 | 7 | 7 | R | R | 6-1 | 175 | 11-1-66 | 1987 | West Chester, Pa. |
| Valdez, Rafael | 1 | 0 | 0.00 | 5 | 0 | 0 | 1 | 11 | 7 | 1 | 0 | 2 | 12 | R | R | 5-11 | 185 | 12-17-68 | 1985 | Bani, D.R. |
| Veres, Randy | 1 | 5 | 4.89 | 13 | 12 | 0 | 0 | 57 | 59 | 33 | 31 | 19 | 49 | R | R | 6-3 | 187 | 11-25-65 | 1985 | Rancho Cordova, Calif. |
| Wilkins, Mike | 3 | 3 | 3.89 | 11 | 5 | 0 | 0 | 44 | 44 | 30 | 19 | 13 | 37 | R | R | 6-3 | 175 | 8-30-66 | 1987 | Livonia, Mich. |

# KINSTON

A

## CAROLINA LEAGUE

| BATTING | AVG | G | AB | R | H | 2B | 3B | HR | RBI | BB | SO | SB | CS | B | T | HT | WT | DOB | 1st Yr | Resides |
|---|---|---|---|---|---|---|---|---|---|---|---|---|---|---|---|---|---|---|---|---|
| Andujar, Juan, ss | .253 | 111 | 407 | 42 | 103 | 12 | 5 | 3 | 31 | 17 | 92 | 15 | 9 | R | R | 6-0 | 150 | 8-14-71 | 1989 | Bani, D.R. |
| Arntzen, Brian, c | .220 | 20 | 50 | 1 | 11 | 2 | 0 | 1 | 6 | 4 | 17 | 3 | 1 | R | R | 6-3 | 205 | 1-8-70 | 1992 | Redding, Calif. |
| Azuaje, Jesus, 2b | .455 | 3 | 11 | 1 | 5 | 2 | 0 | 0 | 2 | 1 | 2 | 0 | 0 | R | R | 5-10 | 170 | 1-16-73 | 1992 | Bolivar, Venez. |
| Charbonnet, Mark, of | .245 | 96 | 319 | 35 | 78 | 13 | 5 | 7 | 34 | 11 | 89 | 8 | 8 | L | L | 6-1 | 185 | 4-5-71 | 1989 | Norwalk, Calif. |
| Cotton, John, of | .264 | 127 | 454 | 81 | 120 | 16 | 3 | 13 | 51 | 59 | 130 | 28 | 24 | L | R | 5-11 | 170 | 10-30-70 | 1989 | Huntsville, Texas |
| Crosby, Mark, c | .217 | 72 | 203 | 20 | 44 | 9 | 0 | 3 | 17 | 7 | 45 | 1 | 2 | L | R | 6-1 | 200 | 2-24-69 | 1992 | Warwick, R.I. |
| George, Curtis, 3b-ss | .214 | 31 | 70 | 11 | 15 | 5 | 0 | 0 | 2 | 6 | 17 | 1 | 1 | R | R | 6-3 | 185 | 11-12-71 | 1992 | Stone Mountain, Ga. |
| Harvey, Bill, dh-of | .284 | 88 | 335 | 36 | 95 | 19 | 2 | 3 | 39 | 28 | 43 | 3 | 6 | L | L | 6-1 | 185 | 1-1-69 | 1991 | Brentwood, Tenn. |
| Marini, Marc, of | .300 | 124 | 466 | 77 | 140 | 34 | 4 | 5 | 53 | 63 | 70 | 7 | 6 | L | L | 6-1 | 185 | 3-17-70 | 1991 | Tunkhannock, Pa. |
| Maxwell, Pat, 2b | .293 | 103 | 400 | 46 | 117 | 17 | 3 | 4 | 35 | 22 | 32 | 6 | 4 | L | R | 6-0 | 170 | 3-28-70 | 1991 | Wichita Falls, Texas |
| McCall, Rod, 1b | .208 | 71 | 245 | 32 | 51 | 13 | 0 | 9 | 33 | 32 | 85 | 3 | 1 | L | L | 6-7 | 220 | 11-4-71 | 1990 | Stanton, Calif. |
| Meade, Paul, 3b-2b | .240 | 117 | 404 | 47 | 97 | 17 | 1 | 9 | 45 | 23 | 80 | 5 | 5 | S | R | 6-0 | 175 | 2-14-69 | 1991 | Urbandale, Iowa |
| Mitchell, Tony, of | .245 | 96 | 318 | 43 | 78 | 16 | 2 | 8 | 44 | 33 | 88 | 5 | 4 | S | R | 6-4 | 225 | 10-14-70 | 1989 | Detroit, Mich. |
| Patrizi, Mike, c | .133 | 7 | 15 | 1 | 2 | 1 | 0 | 0 | 0 | 2 | 4 | 0 | 1 | R | R | 6-1 | 190 | 11-1-71 | 1990 | Pennsauken, N.J. |
| Pough, Chop, 3b-dh | .270 | 120 | 418 | 66 | 113 | 18 | 1 | 13 | 57 | 59 | 95 | 8 | 3 | R | R | 6-0 | 173 | 12-25-69 | 1988 | Avon Park, Fla. |
| Ramirez, Alex, of | .167 | 3 | 12 | 0 | 2 | 0 | 0 | 0 | 1 | 0 | 5 | 0 | 1 | R | R | 5-11 | 176 | 10-3-74 | 1991 | Miranda, Venez. |
| Rose, Pete, 3b | .218 | 74 | 284 | 33 | 62 | 10 | 1 | 7 | 30 | 25 | 34 | 1 | 3 | L | R | 6-1 | 180 | 11-16-69 | 1989 | Cincinnati, Ohio |
| Sued, Nick, c | .249 | 62 | 189 | 24 | 47 | 5 | 1 | 2 | 25 | 26 | 22 | 2 | 3 | R | R | 5-10 | 170 | 6-6-72 | 1990 | Santiago, D.R. |

| PITCHING | W | L | ERA | G | GS | CG | SV | IP | H | R | ER | BB | SO | B | T | HT | WT | DOB | 1st Yr | Resides |
|---|---|---|---|---|---|---|---|---|---|---|---|---|---|---|---|---|---|---|---|---|
| Brown, Dickie | 4 | 3 | 3.29 | 31 | 8 | 0 | 2 | 82 | 77 | 40 | 30 | 42 | 62 | R | R | 6-0 | 160 | 8-13-70 | 1990 | Little Rock, Ark. |
| Crawford, Carlos | 7 | 9 | 3.65 | 28 | 28 | 4 | 0 | 165 | 158 | 87 | 67 | 46 | 124 | R | R | 6-1 | 185 | 10-4-71 | 1990 | Charlotte, N.C. |
| Doyle, Ian | 5 | 1 | 3.08 | 47 | 0 | 0 | 23 | 53 | 44 | 20 | 18 | 29 | 51 | R | R | 6-2 | 200 | 9-11-71 | 1991 | Brecksville, Ohio |
| Fleet, Joe | 2 | 2 | 4.34 | 40 | 1 | 0 | 0 | 66 | 61 | 37 | 32 | 36 | 54 | R | R | 6-1 | 185 | 10-17-69 | 1990 | Hammond, La. |
| Fronio, Jason | 7 | 9 | 2.41 | 32 | 20 | 2 | 0 | 138 | 95 | 46 | 37 | 66 | 147 | R | R | 6-2 | 205 | 12-26-69 | 1991 | Riverside, Conn. |
| Hernandez, Fernando | 2 | 3 | 1.76 | 8 | 8 | 0 | 0 | 51 | 34 | 15 | 10 | 18 | 53 | R | R | 6-2 | 185 | 6-16-71 | 1990 | Santiago, D.R. |
| Logsdon, Kevin | 6 | 7 | 6.14 | 31 | 20 | 1 | 3 | 125 | 146 | 94 | 85 | 57 | 105 | S | L | 6-0 | 200 | 12-23-70 | 1991 | Baker, Ore. |
| McCarthy, Greg | 0 | 0 | 1.69 | 9 | 0 | 0 | 2 | 11 | 8 | 4 | 2 | 13 | 14 | L | L | 6-2 | 193 | 10-30-68 | 1987 | Shelton, Conn. |
| Morgan, Scott | 2 | 3 | 4.10 | 28 | 0 | 0 | 3 | 42 | 28 | 19 | 19 | 15 | 54 | R | R | 6-2 | 190 | 6-20-68 | 1990 | Carrboro, N.C. |
| Perez, Cesar | 0 | 0 | 2.70 | 10 | 0 | 0 | 0 | 13 | 7 | 4 | 4 | 7 | 20 | R | R | 5-11 | 175 | 8-13-70 | 1988 | Greensboro, N.C. |
| Ramos, Cesar | 0 | 0 | 27.00 | 2 | 0 | 0 | 0 | 2 | 6 | 7 | 6 | 2 | 1 | R | R | 6-0 | 160 | 12-2-73 | 1992 | Monte Cristi, D.R. |

| PITCHING | W | L | ERA | G | GS | CG | SV | IP | H | R | ER | BB | SO | B | T | HT | WT | DOB | 1st Yr | Resides |
|---|---|---|---|---|---|---|---|---|---|---|---|---|---|---|---|---|---|---|---|---|
| Rivera, Roberto ............. | 2 | 3 | 6.17 | 19 | 1 | 0 | 0 | 35 | 44 | 26 | 24 | 4 | 32 | L | L | 6-0 | 175 | 1-1-69 | 1988 | Bayamon, P.R. |
| Ruyak, Todd ................. | 0 | 1 | 4.76 | 18 | 0 | 0 | 2 | 23 | 21 | 13 | 12 | 10 | 16 | L | L | 6-3 | 215 | 9-18-70 | 1992 | Hamilton Square, N.J. |
| 2-team (7 Win.-Salem) | 1 | 1 | 4.65 | 25 | 0 | 0 | 5 | 31 | 30 | 17 | 16 | 11 | 20 | | | | | | | |
| Shuey, Paul ................... | 1 | 0 | 4.84 | 15 | 0 | 0 | 0 | 22 | 29 | 12 | 12 | 8 | 27 | R | R | 6-3 | 215 | 9-16-70 | 1992 | Raleigh, N.C. |
| Tavarez, Julian ........... | 11 | 5 | 2.42 | 18 | 18 | 2 | 0 | 119 | 102 | 48 | 32 | 28 | 107 | R | R | 6-2 | 165 | 5-22-73 | 1990 | Santiago, D.R. |
| Thobe, J.J ...................... | 1 | 2 | 3.13 | 4 | 4 | 0 | 0 | 23 | 26 | 11 | 8 | 9 | 11 | R | R | 6-6 | 200 | 11-19-70 | 1992 | Huntington Beach, Calif. |
| Welch, David................. | 9 | 6 | 3.47 | 46 | 2 | 0 | 0 | 83 | 62 | 38 | 32 | 34 | 83 | L | L | 6-3 | 210 | 4-30-70 | 1992 | Violet, La. |
| Williams, Greg .............. | 0 | 1 | 9.00 | 2 | 1 | 0 | 0 | 3 | 6 | 3 | 3 | 1 | 2 | L | L | 6-1 | 195 | 4-30-72 | 1993 | Portland, Ore. |
| Williams, Matt .............. | 12 | 12 | 3.17 | 27 | 27 | 2 | 0 | 153 | 125 | 65 | 54 | 100 | 134 | S | L | 6-0 | 175 | 4-12-71 | 1992 | Virginia Beach, Va. |

## COLUMBUS      A
## SOUTH ATLANTIC LEAGUE

| BATTING | AVG | G | AB | R | H | 2B | 3B | HR | RBI | BB | SO | SB | CS | B | T | HT | WT | DOB | 1st Yr | Resides |
|---|---|---|---|---|---|---|---|---|---|---|---|---|---|---|---|---|---|---|---|---|
| Arntzen, Brian, c............ | .188 | 35 | 112 | 10 | 21 | 5 | 0 | 1 | 10 | 11 | 24 | 0 | 1 | R | R | 6-3 | 205 | 1-8-70 | 1992 | Redding, Calif. |
| Bryant, Pat, of............... | .263 | 121 | 483 | 82 | 127 | 26 | 2 | 16 | 61 | 43 | 117 | 43 | 11 | R | R | 5-11 | 182 | 10-27-72 | 1990 | Sherman Oaks, Calif. |
| Cardenas, Epi, 2b-3b .... | .242 | 119 | 472 | 53 | 114 | 25 | 5 | 4 | 68 | 26 | 72 | 1 | 3 | R | R | 5-10 | 160 | 1-28-72 | 1992 | Pandera, Texas |
| Claudio, Patricio, of ....... | .256 | 98 | 312 | 48 | 80 | 8 | 6 | 0 | 26 | 23 | 67 | 40 | 12 | R | R | 6-0 | 160 | 4-12-72 | 1991 | Santiago, D.R. |
| Diaz, Einar, c ................. | .000 | 1 | 5 | 0 | 0 | 0 | 0 | 0 | 0 | 0 | 1 | 0 | 0 | R | R | 5-10 | 165 | 12-28-72 | 1991 | Chiriqui, Panama |
| Duplessis, Dave, 1b-dh . | .289 | 52 | 187 | 26 | 54 | 7 | 2 | 8 | 32 | 12 | 60 | 0 | 1 | L | L | 6-6 | 225 | 2-8-70 | 1991 | Pittsburg, Calif. |
| Duran, Felipe, ss .......... | .185 | 48 | 119 | 15 | 22 | 2 | 0 | 3 | 15 | 6 | 22 | 4 | 2 | R | R | 6-2 | 175 | 8-10-71 | 1991 | Tijuana, Mexico |
| Hacopian, Derek, dh-of . | .315 | 131 | 454 | 81 | 143 | 29 | 0 | 24 | 82 | 60 | 69 | 4 | 2 | R | R | 6-0 | 200 | 1-1-70 | 1992 | Potomac, Md. |
| Hence, Sam, of .............. | .299 | 88 | 268 | 36 | 80 | 16 | 2 | 6 | 33 | 10 | 57 | 5 | 7 | R | R | 6-0 | 185 | 1-3-71 | 1990 | Wiggins, Miss. |
| Jackson, Damian, ss...... | .269 | 108 | 350 | 70 | 94 | 19 | 3 | 6 | 45 | 41 | 61 | 26 | 7 | R | R | 5-10 | 160 | 8-16-73 | 1992 | Concord, Calif. |
| Marshall, Jason, c ......... | .130 | 15 | 46 | 3 | 6 | 1 | 0 | 1 | 5 | 1 | 13 | 1 | 0 | R | R | 5-11 | 195 | 8-28-70 | 1993 | Leonard, Texas |
| Meluskey, Mitch, c......... | .246 | 101 | 342 | 36 | 84 | 18 | 3 | 3 | 47 | 35 | 69 | 1 | 1 | S | R | 6-0 | 185 | 9-18-73 | 1992 | Yakima, Wash. |
| Mercado, Rafael, 1b....... | .152 | 36 | 99 | 14 | 15 | 2 | 0 | 3 | 13 | 5 | 27 | 0 | 1 | R | R | 6-3 | 170 | 3-12-70 | 1990 | Santiago, D.R. |
| Nunnally, Jon, 2b-of ...... | .251 | 125 | 438 | 81 | 110 | 15 | 2 | 15 | 56 | 63 | 108 | 17 | 11 | L | R | 5-10 | 185 | 11-9-71 | 1992 | Pelham, N.C. |
| Taylor, Jamie, 3b........... | .226 | 111 | 402 | 46 | 91 | 21 | 0 | 8 | 46 | 36 | 115 | 4 | 2 | L | R | 6-2 | 220 | 10-10-70 | 1992 | Bloomingdale, Ohio |
| Townsend, Chad, 1b....... | .236 | 104 | 314 | 43 | 74 | 15 | 3 | 10 | 40 | 23 | 84 | 1 | 0 | L | L | 6-5 | 222 | 7-7-71 | 1992 | Palm Desert, Calif. |
| White, Andre, of ............ | .278 | 115 | 367 | 55 | 102 | 15 | 2 | 3 | 35 | 19 | 48 | 29 | 12 | L | L | 6-2 | 185 | 10-25-70 | 1991 | Oakland, Calif. |
| White, Eric, 3b.............. | .143 | 2 | 7 | 1 | 1 | 0 | 0 | 0 | 0 | 0 | 1 | 0 | 0 | R | R | 6-1 | 180 | 10-13-72 | 1992 | Diamond Bar, Calif. |

| PITCHING | W | L | ERA | G | GS | CG | SV | IP | H | R | ER | BB | SO | B | T | HT | WT | DOB | 1st Yr | Resides |
|---|---|---|---|---|---|---|---|---|---|---|---|---|---|---|---|---|---|---|---|---|
| Beauchamp, Jim........... | 5 | 6 | 4.43 | 27 | 22 | 0 | 0 | 130 | 148 | 85 | 64 | 76 | 78 | R | R | 6-4 | 200 | 5-5-70 | 1993 | Arnold, Calif. |
| Cabrera, Jose ............... | 11 | 6 | 2.67 | 26 | 26 | 1 | 0 | 155 | 122 | 54 | 46 | 53 | 105 | R | R | 6-0 | 160 | 3-24-72 | 1991 | Santiago, D.R. |
| Campbell, Camp............ | 0 | 0 | 27.00 | 1 | 0 | 0 | 0 | 2 | 4 | 5 | 5 | 1 | 1 | R | R | 6-3 | 195 | 12-24-70 | 1993 | Ocala, Fla. |
| Carter, John ................. | 17 | 7 | 2.79 | 29 | 29 | 1 | 0 | 180 | 147 | 72 | 56 | 48 | 134 | R | R | 6-1 | 195 | 2-16-72 | 1991 | Chicago, Ill. |
| Diaz, German ................ | 0 | 2 | 5.91 | 5 | 0 | 0 | 0 | 11 | 10 | 9 | 7 | 12 | 11 | L | R | 6-4 | 177 | 12-2-70 | 1989 | San Sebastian, P.R. |
| Gibbs, Paul ................... | 1 | 1 | 1.63 | 23 | 0 | 0 | 3 | 55 | 32 | 15 | 10 | 27 | 68 | R | R | 6-4 | 210 | 2-18-70 | 1991 | Hillsborough, N.C. |
| Harris, Pep .................... | 7 | 8 | 4.24 | 26 | 17 | 0 | 0 | 119 | 113 | 67 | 56 | 44 | 82 | R | R | 6-2 | 185 | 9-23-72 | 1991 | Lancaster, S.C. |
| Koller, Rod.................... | 9 | 5 | 2.24 | 47 | 0 | 0 | 9 | 68 | 51 | 21 | 17 | 19 | 37 | R | R | 6-4 | 195 | 7-13-70 | 1991 | Texarkana, Texas |
| Neilson, Mike ............... | 0 | 0 | 6.00 | 5 | 0 | 0 | 0 | 9 | 6 | 6 | 6 | 6 | 2 | R | L | 6-1 | 210 | 1-7-71 | 1992 | Burnaby, B.C. |
| Perez, Cesar ................. | 0 | 0 | 0.59 | 45 | 0 | 0 | 35 | 46 | 21 | 4 | 3 | 19 | 50 | R | R | 5-11 | 175 | 8-13-70 | 1988 | Greensboro, N.C. |
| Resendez, Oscar........... | 7 | 3 | 4.75 | 32 | 2 | 1 | 2 | 66 | 61 | 43 | 35 | 45 | 49 | R | R | 6-1 | 175 | 9-1-71 | 1991 | Alice, Texas |
| Ruyak, Todd .................. | 3 | 0 | 3.13 | 9 | 1 | 0 | 0 | 23 | 19 | 8 | 8 | 5 | 20 | L | L | 6-3 | 215 | 9-18-70 | 1992 | Hamilton Square, N.J. |
| 2-team (14 Char, WV). | 4 | 0 | 2.47 | 23 | 1 | 0 | 2 | 44 | 31 | 13 | 12 | 14 | 41 | | | | | | | |
| Sharts, Scott ................. | 3 | 3 | 3.99 | 43 | 0 | 0 | 6 | 65 | 66 | 39 | 29 | 39 | 45 | R | R | 6-6 | 220 | 12-12-69 | 1991 | Simi Valley, Calif. |
| Smith, Fred ................... | 1 | 6 | 7.17 | 18 | 0 | 0 | 1 | 21 | 24 | 21 | 17 | 18 | 20 | R | R | 5-10 | 200 | 11-16-71 | 1992 | Brooklyn, N.Y. |
| Thobe, J.J. ................... | 11 | 2 | 1.91 | 19 | 19 | 2 | 0 | 132 | 105 | 36 | 28 | 25 | 106 | R | R | 6-6 | 200 | 11-19-70 | 1992 | Huntington Beach, Calif. |
| Williams, Jeff................. | 1 | 0 | 15.43 | 6 | 0 | 0 | 0 | 5 | 11 | 8 | 8 | 2 | 4 | L | L | 6-1 | 188 | 9-14-69 | 1993 | Fort Worth, Texas |
| York, Charles ................ | 10 | 7 | 2.79 | 26 | 26 | 1 | 0 | 158 | 127 | 59 | 49 | 78 | 182 | L | L | 6-4 | 240 | 12-5-70 | 1992 | Orange Park, Fla. |

## WATERTOWN      A
## NEW YORK-PENN LEAGUE

| BATTING | AVG | G | AB | R | H | 2B | 3B | HR | RBI | BB | SO | SB | CS | B | T | HT | WT | DOB | 1st Yr | Resides |
|---|---|---|---|---|---|---|---|---|---|---|---|---|---|---|---|---|---|---|---|---|
| Cawhorn, Gerad, 3b-1b | .254 | 66 | 232 | 28 | 59 | 9 | 2 | 1 | 29 | 26 | 51 | 3 | 4 | R | R | 6-1 | 185 | 8-27-71 | 1993 | Brea, Calif. |

INDIANS TOP 10 PROSPECTS

How the Indians Top 10 prospects, as judged by Baseball America prior to the 1993 season, fared in 1993:

| Player, Pos. | Club (Class) | AVG | AB | H | HR | RBI | SB |
|---|---|---|---|---|---|---|---|
| 1. Manny Ramirez, of | Can.-Akron (AA) | .340 | 344 | 117 | 17 | 79 | 2 |
| | Charlotte (AAA) | .317 | 145 | 46 | 14 | 36 | 1 |
| | Cleveland | .170 | 53 | 9 | 2 | 5 | 0 |
| 9. Tracy Sanders, of* | Can.-Akron (AA) | .213 | 136 | 29 | 5 | 20 | 4 |
| | Wichita (AA) | .323 | 266 | 86 | 13 | 47 | 6 |
| 10. Tony Mitchell, of | Kinston (A) | .245 | 318 | 78 | 8 | 44 | 5 |

| | W | L | ERA | IP | H | BB | SO |
|---|---|---|---|---|---|---|---|
| 2. Alan Embree, lhp | Can.-Akron (AA) | 0 | 0 | 3.38 | 5 | 3 | 3 | 4 |
| 3. Paul Shuey, rhp | Can.-Akron (AA) | 4 | 8 | 7.30 | 62 | 76 | 36 | 41 |
| | Kinston (A) | 1 | 0 | 4.84 | 22 | 29 | 8 | 27 |
| 4. Chad Ogea, rhp | Charlotte (AAA) | 13 | 8 | 3.81 | 182 | 169 | 54 | 135 |
| 5. Paul Byrd, rhp | Can.-Akron (AA) | 0 | 0 | 3.60 | 10 | 7 | 3 | 8 |
| | Charlotte (AAA) | 7 | 4 | 3.89 | 81 | 80 | 30 | 54 |
| 6. Dave Mlicki, rhp | Can.-Akron (AA) | 2 | 1 | 0.39 | 23 | 15 | 8 | 21 |
| | Cleveland | 1 | 1 | 3.38 | 16 | 19 | 11 | 7 |
| 7. Albie Lopez, rhp | Charlotte (AAA) | 1 | 0 | 2.25 | 12 | 8 | 2 | 7 |
| | Can.-Akron (AA) | 9 | 4 | 3.11 | 110 | 79 | 47 | 80 |
| | Cleveland | 3 | 1 | 5.98 | 50 | 49 | 32 | 25 |

8. Mike Matthews, lhp     Injured—Did Not Play

*Traded to San Diego Padres

DAN ARNOLD

**Manny Ramirez**
33 homers, 120 RBIs

| BATTING | AVG | G | AB | R | H | 2B | 3B | HR | RBI | BB | SO | SB | CS | B | T | HT | WT | DOB | 1st Yr | Resides |
|---|---|---|---|---|---|---|---|---|---|---|---|---|---|---|---|---|---|---|---|---|
| Chapman, Eric, of | .233 | 64 | 215 | 28 | 50 | 4 | 3 | 4 | 24 | 21 | 62 | 14 | 4 | R | R | 6-1 | 178 | 9-9-71 | 1993 | Charlottesville, Va. |
| Garrett, Bryan, of | .221 | 69 | 217 | 40 | 48 | 4 | 3 | 0 | 24 | 24 | 62 | 17 | 4 | S | R | 6-0 | 180 | 10-28-71 | 1993 | Mascoufall, Ill. |
| George, Curtis, ss | .200 | 2 | 5 | 1 | 1 | 0 | 0 | 0 | 0 | 0 | 2 | 1 | 0 | R | R | 6-3 | 185 | 11-12-71 | 1992 | Stone Mountain, Ga. |
| Haag, Jeff, dh-c | .200 | 5 | 10 | 1 | 2 | 0 | 0 | 0 | 1 | 2 | 1 | 0 | 0 | L | R | 6-2 | 190 | 2-26-71 | 1993 | Shoemakersville, Pa. |
| Hodson, Blair, dh-1b | .288 | 60 | 191 | 34 | 55 | 13 | 0 | 2 | 27 | 19 | 33 | 4 | 1 | L | R | 6-2 | 200 | 1-13-72 | 1993 | Logan, Utah |
| Holland, Rod, of | .051 | 13 | 39 | 3 | 2 | 0 | 0 | 0 | 1 | 1 | 12 | 0 | 0 | L | R | 5-10 | 165 | 5-1-71 | 1993 | New Braunfels, Texas |
| Kulle, Robert, of | .211 | 45 | 128 | 18 | 27 | 6 | 1 | 4 | 19 | 12 | 48 | 2 | 1 | R | R | 6-3 | 200 | 9-21-71 | 1993 | Endicott, N.Y. |
| Lefebvre, Ryan, of | .150 | 6 | 20 | 1 | 3 | 0 | 0 | 0 | 2 | 5 | 2 | 0 | 1 | L | L | 5-10 | 170 | 2-12-71 | 1993 | Los Angeles, Calif. |
| Lewis, Robert, c-3b | .268 | 59 | 198 | 30 | 53 | 10 | 0 | 2 | 29 | 30 | 38 | 4 | 1 | R | R | 5-11 | 190 | 12-15-70 | 1993 | El Segundo, Calif. |
| Lyman, Jason, ss-2b | .213 | 31 | 80 | 14 | 17 | 3 | 2 | 0 | 7 | 14 | 25 | 2 | 1 | R | R | 6-0 | 185 | 8-2-69 | 1993 | Riverside, Calif. |
| Marte, Pedro, of | .263 | 43 | 133 | 41 | 35 | 1 | 0 | 0 | 11 | 34 | 38 | 23 | 5 | S | R | 5-7 | 145 | 10-16-71 | 1993 | Los Amina, D.R. |
| Neal, Mike, ss | .291 | 67 | 234 | 47 | 68 | 15 | 3 | 4 | 43 | 55 | 45 | 7 | 1 | R | R | 6-1 | 180 | 11-5-71 | 1993 | Hammond, La. |
| Oram, Jon, 2b-3b | .189 | 29 | 74 | 11 | 14 | 2 | 0 | 1 | 5 | 5 | 21 | 0 | 1 | R | R | 6-1 | 180 | 10-29-73 | 1993 | Olympia, Wash. |
| Prieto, Richard, 2b | .292 | 68 | 219 | 53 | 64 | 15 | 4 | 4 | 40 | 39 | 61 | 11 | 1 | S | R | 5-10 | 175 | 8-24-72 | 1993 | Carmel, Calif. |
| Schulz, Pat, of | .198 | 24 | 86 | 14 | 17 | 6 | 0 | 0 | 9 | 13 | 16 | 4 | 2 | R | R | 6-1 | 180 | 11-30-70 | 1993 | Evansville, Ind. |
| Soliz, Steve, c | .297 | 56 | 209 | 30 | 62 | 12 | 0 | 3 | 35 | 15 | 41 | 2 | 0 | R | R | 5-10 | 180 | 1-27-71 | 1993 | Oxnard, Calif. |
| Thomas, Greg, 1b | .307 | 73 | 277 | 48 | 85 | 20 | 5 | 9 | 63 | 27 | 47 | 3 | 4 | L | L | 6-3 | 200 | 7-19-72 | 1993 | Orlando, Fla. |

| PITCHING | W | L | ERA | G | GS | CG | SV | IP | H | R | ER | BB | SO | B | T | HT | WT | DOB | 1st Yr | Resides |
|---|---|---|---|---|---|---|---|---|---|---|---|---|---|---|---|---|---|---|---|---|
| Augustine, Rob | 0 | 1 | 6.43 | 19 | 0 | 0 | 1 | 28 | 26 | 25 | 20 | 29 | 29 | R | R | 6-4 | 200 | 8-19-70 | 1992 | Franklin, La. |
| Dempsey, Dalton | 2 | 4 | 4.50 | 20 | 0 | 0 | 2 | 24 | 26 | 16 | 12 | 14 | 27 | L | L | 6-3 | 203 | 8-4-71 | 1993 | Pasadena, Texas |
| De la Maza, Roland | 10 | 3 | 2.52 | 15 | 15 | 1 | 0 | 100 | 90 | 39 | 28 | 14 | 81 | R | R | 6-2 | 195 | 11-11-71 | 1993 | Arleta, Calif. |
| Diaz, German | 0 | 0 | 2.91 | 11 | 0 | 0 | 1 | 22 | 22 | 10 | 7 | 12 | 20 | L | R | 6-4 | 177 | 12-2-70 | 1989 | San Sebastian, P.R. |
| Driskill, Travis | 5 | 4 | 4.14 | 21 | 8 | 0 | 3 | 63 | 62 | 38 | 29 | 21 | 53 | R | R | 6-0 | 195 | 8-1-71 | 1993 | Austin, Texas |
| Garza, Roberto | 1 | 2 | 6.05 | 11 | 0 | 0 | 0 | 19 | 29 | 22 | 13 | 5 | 12 | R | R | 6-4 | 210 | 6-20-72 | 1992 | Monterrey, Mexico |
| Hanson, Kris | 4 | 2 | 3.43 | 9 | 9 | 0 | 0 | 45 | 44 | 23 | 17 | 13 | 31 | R | R | 6-5 | 240 | 1-5-71 | 1993 | Stevens Point, Wis. |
| Key, Denny | 2 | 1 | 6.14 | 3 | 2 | 0 | 0 | 15 | 18 | 11 | 10 | 4 | 5 | R | R | 6-5 | 215 | 9-21-70 | 1991 | Winston-Salem, N.C. |
| Kirkreit, Daron | 4 | 1 | 2.23 | 7 | 7 | 1 | 0 | 36 | 33 | 14 | 9 | 11 | 44 | R | R | 6-6 | 225 | 8-7-72 | 1993 | Norco, Calif. |
| Kline, Steve | 5 | 4 | 3.19 | 13 | 13 | 2 | 0 | 79 | 77 | 36 | 28 | 12 | 45 | S | L | 6-2 | 195 | 8-22-72 | 1993 | Winfield, Pa. |
| Neilson, Mike | 0 | 0 | 4.61 | 10 | 0 | 0 | 1 | 14 | 10 | 13 | 7 | 14 | 15 | R | L | 6-1 | 210 | 1-7-71 | 1992 | Burnaby, B.C. |
| Plumlee, Chris | 1 | 2 | 5.21 | 23 | 0 | 0 | 15 | 19 | 13 | 11 | 16 | 15 | 16 | R | R | 6-0 | 200 | 4-4-72 | 1993 | Olive Beach, Miss. |
| Runion, Tony | 0 | 1 | 6.75 | 4 | 1 | 0 | 0 | 8 | 7 | 9 | 6 | 9 | 8 | R | R | 6-3 | 220 | 12-6-71 | 1993 | Florence, Ky. |
| Sexton, Jeff | 1 | 1 | 2.67 | 17 | 1 | 1 | 2 | 34 | 35 | 15 | 10 | 10 | 30 | R | R | 6-2 | 190 | 10-4-71 | 1993 | Indianola, Okla. |
| Sides, Craig | 0 | 0 | 8.74 | 3 | 3 | 0 | 0 | 11 | 16 | 15 | 11 | 7 | 8 | R | R | 6-1 | 175 | 9-15-72 | 1990 | Montgomery, Ala. |
| Sinner, Greg | 0 | 0 | 9.00 | 1 | 0 | 0 | 0 | 1 | 2 | 2 | 1 | 1 | 1 | R | R | 6-4 | 200 | 12-11-70 | 1992 | Carmel, Ind. |
| Smith, Fred | 0 | 0 | 6.75 | 1 | 0 | 0 | 0 | 3 | 1 | 2 | 2 | 6 | 1 | R | R | 5-10 | 200 | 11-16-71 | 1992 | Brooklyn, N.Y. |
| Whitten, Casey | 6 | 3 | 2.42 | 14 | 14 | 0 | 0 | 82 | 75 | 28 | 22 | 18 | 81 | L | L | 6-0 | 175 | 5-23-72 | 1993 | Haubstadt, Ind. |
| Williams, Greg | 0 | 1 | 0.00 | 1 | 0 | 0 | 0 | 0 | 1 | 1 | 0 | 2 | 0 | L | L | 6-1 | 195 | 4-30-72 | 1993 | Portland, Ore. |
| Williams, Jeff | 5 | 2 | 3.77 | 19 | 5 | 1 | 1 | 62 | 63 | 34 | 26 | 11 | 52 | L | L | 6-1 | 188 | 9-14-69 | 1993 | Fort Worth, Texas |

## BURLINGTON     R

## APPALACHIAN LEAGUE

| BATTING | AVG | G | AB | R | H | 2B | 3B | HR | RBI | BB | SO | SB | CS | B | T | HT | WT | DOB | 1st Yr | Resides |
|---|---|---|---|---|---|---|---|---|---|---|---|---|---|---|---|---|---|---|---|---|
| Azuaje, Jesus, 2b-ss | .280 | 62 | 254 | 46 | 71 | 10 | 1 | 7 | 41 | 22 | 53 | 19 | 2 | R | R | 5-10 | 170 | 1-16-73 | 1992 | Bolivar, Venez. |
| Batiste, Darnell, 1b | .286 | 13 | 14 | 4 | 4 | 0 | 0 | 0 | 6 | 7 | 4 | 0 | 0 | L | R | 6-1 | 195 | 10-6-75 | 1993 | Arlington, Texas |
| Betts, Todd, 3b | .232 | 56 | 168 | 40 | 39 | 9 | 0 | 7 | 27 | 32 | 26 | 6 | 1 | L | R | 6-0 | 185 | 4-3-74 | 1993 | Scarborough, Ontario |
| Chambers, Mack, 2b | .132 | 28 | 53 | 9 | 7 | 0 | 0 | 0 | 3 | 7 | 18 | 2 | 0 | R | R | 5-10 | 155 | 2-8-73 | 1993 | Spiro, Okla. |
| Coleman, Ronnie, of | .189 | 42 | 74 | 25 | 14 | 2 | 1 | 1 | 3 | 37 | 30 | 12 | 8 | S | R | 5-11 | 170 | 4-11-72 | 1991 | Chicago, Ill. |
| Diaz, Einar, c | .299 | 60 | 231 | 40 | 69 | 15 | 3 | 5 | 33 | 8 | 7 | 7 | 3 | R | R | 5-10 | 165 | 12-28-72 | 1991 | Chiriqui, Panama |
| Hobbie, Matt, of | .282 | 25 | 85 | 15 | 24 | 1 | 0 | 2 | 14 | 15 | 16 | 6 | 4 | L | L | 5-10 | 180 | 12-12-74 | 1993 | Sarasota, Fla. |
| Johnson, Todd, c-dh | .299 | 52 | 184 | 33 | 55 | 11 | 0 | 2 | 27 | 20 | 27 | 7 | 2 | R | R | 5-11 | 195 | 12-18-70 | 1993 | Fresno, Calif. |
| Lemons, Rich, of | .329 | 51 | 155 | 31 | 51 | 9 | 1 | 4 | 24 | 21 | 41 | 8 | 5 | L | R | 6-4 | 215 | 9-9-71 | 1993 | Tucson, Ariz. |
| Lewandowski, John, 1b | .000 | 1 | 2 | 0 | 0 | 0 | 0 | 0 | 0 | 0 | 0 | 0 | 0 | R | R | 6-3 | 185 | 12-3-71 | 1992 | Lansing, Ill. |
| Moyle, Mike, dh-c | .250 | 4 | 8 | 1 | 2 | 0 | 0 | 0 | 0 | 1 | 1 | 0 | 0 | R | R | 6-2 | 200 | 9-8-71 | 1992 | Dionelia, Australia |
| Ramirez, Alex, of | .270 | 64 | 252 | 44 | 68 | 14 | 4 | 13 | 58 | 13 | 52 | 12 | 9 | R | R | 5-11 | 176 | 10-3-74 | 1991 | Miranda, Venez. |
| Ramirez, Richard, ss | .227 | 64 | 203 | 30 | 46 | 9 | 1 | 2 | 23 | 21 | 35 | 3 | 5 | R | R | 5-11 | 160 | 11-19-75 | 1993 | Santiago, D.R. |
| Sexson, Richie, 1b | .186 | 40 | 97 | 11 | 18 | 3 | 0 | 1 | 5 | 18 | 21 | 1 | 1 | R | R | 6-6 | 200 | 12-29-74 | 1993 | Brush Prairie, Wash. |
| Thompson, Leroy, of-dh | .243 | 54 | 169 | 23 | 41 | 9 | 3 | 4 | 32 | 17 | 54 | 3 | 3 | L | L | 6-0 | 180 | 10-25-74 | 1992 | Fernandina Beach, Fla. |
| White, Eric, 1b-3b | .321 | 68 | 249 | 41 | 80 | 19 | 1 | 1 | 45 | 27 | 37 | 14 | 9 | R | R | 6-1 | 180 | 10-13-72 | 1992 | Diamond Bar, Calif. |
| Williams, Norman, of | .209 | 37 | 91 | 9 | 19 | 2 | 0 | 0 | 7 | 4 | 22 | 6 | 2 | R | R | 5-11 | 175 | 11-17-73 | 1993 | Adel, Ga. |

| PITCHING | W | L | ERA | G | GS | CG | SV | IP | H | R | ER | BB | SO | B | T | HT | WT | DOB | 1st Yr | Resides |
|---|---|---|---|---|---|---|---|---|---|---|---|---|---|---|---|---|---|---|---|---|
| Brabant, Daniel | 5 | 3 | 4.82 | 12 | 12 | 1 | 0 | 65 | 64 | 38 | 35 | 34 | 48 | R | R | 6-1 | 211 | 4-16-73 | 1993 | Longueuil, Quebec |
| Campbell, Camp | 4 | 5 | 3.57 | 23 | 6 | 0 | 0 | 63 | 60 | 33 | 25 | 29 | 50 | R | R | 6-3 | 195 | 12-24-70 | 1993 | Ocala, Fla. |
| De la Rosa, Maximo | 7 | 2 | 3.77 | 14 | 14 | 2 | 0 | 76 | 53 | 38 | 32 | 37 | 69 | R | R | 5-11 | 170 | 7-12-71 | 1990 | Villa Mella, D.R. |
| Dinnen, Kevin | 3 | 2 | 3.00 | 30 | 0 | 0 | 1 | 45 | 45 | 19 | 15 | 20 | 38 | R | R | 6-1 | 175 | 12-1-72 | 1993 | Pembroke Pines, Fla. |
| Done, J.J. | 0 | 0 | 6.00 | 1 | 1 | 0 | 0 | 3 | 2 | 2 | 2 | 3 | 1 | R | R | 6-1 | 160 | 10-23-75 | 1993 | Miami, Fla. |
| Hritz, Derrick | 2 | 2 | 4.50 | 9 | 8 | 0 | 0 | 44 | 44 | 25 | 22 | 30 | 39 | L | L | 6-0 | 195 | 9-21-72 | 1993 | Gahanna, Ohio |
| Kline, Steve | 1 | 1 | 4.91 | 2 | 1 | 0 | 0 | 7 | 11 | 4 | 4 | 2 | 4 | S | L | 6-2 | 195 | 8-22-72 | 1993 | Winfield, Pa. |
| Leyva, Damian | 0 | 1 | 4.91 | 17 | 0 | 0 | 1 | 26 | 32 | 18 | 14 | 17 | 22 | L | L | 5-11 | 200 | 8-26-70 | 1992 | Miami, Fla. |
| Mackey, Jason | 6 | 0 | 2.15 | 22 | 5 | 0 | 1 | 54 | 28 | 14 | 13 | 36 | 53 | R | L | 6-2 | 185 | 4-8-74 | 1993 | Kelso, Wash. |
| Martinez, Johnny | 6 | 1 | 2.22 | 11 | 10 | 1 | 0 | 73 | 63 | 21 | 18 | 25 | 54 | R | R | 6-3 | 168 | 11-25-72 | 1993 | Guayabin, D.R. |
| Palmer, Brett | 0 | 1 | 7.04 | 10 | 0 | 0 | 0 | 15 | 18 | 17 | 12 | 13 | 13 | L | L | 6-3 | 180 | 3-8-73 | 1993 | Idaho Falls, Idaho |
| Ramos, Cesar | 3 | 3 | 1.88 | 29 | 0 | 0 | 14 | 38 | 32 | 8 | 8 | 10 | 38 | R | R | 6-0 | 160 | 12-2-73 | 1992 | Monte Cristi, D.R. |
| Runion, Tony | 0 | 0 | 3.00 | 3 | 2 | 0 | 0 | 12 | 10 | 4 | 4 | 6 | 6 | R | R | 6-3 | 220 | 12-6-71 | 1993 | Florence, Ky. |
| Williams, Greg | 3 | 1 | 4.39 | 11 | 4 | 0 | 0 | 2 | 41 | 31 | 30 | 20 | 48 | L | L | 6-1 | 195 | 4-30-72 | 1993 | Portland, Ore. |
| Wisler, Brian | 1 | 1 | 3.60 | 4 | 0 | 0 | 0 | 5 | 7 | 4 | 2 | 2 | 10 | L | R | 6-1 | 180 | 1-3-73 | 1993 | Alderwood Manor, Wash. |
| Zubiri, Jon | 3 | 1 | 3.81 | 5 | 5 | 0 | 0 | 26 | 23 | 12 | 11 | 8 | 15 | R | R | 6-2 | 170 | 11-15-74 | 1992 | Hanford, Calif. |

# COLORADO ROCKIES

**Manager:** Don Baylor.   **1993 Record:** 67-95, .414 (6th, NL West).

| BATTING | AVG | G | AB | R | H | 2B | 3B | HR | RBI | BB | SO | SB | CS | B | T | HT | WT | DOB | 1st Yr | Resides |
|---|---|---|---|---|---|---|---|---|---|---|---|---|---|---|---|---|---|---|---|---|
| Benavides, Freddie | .286 | 74 | 213 | 20 | 61 | 10 | 3 | 3 | 26 | 6 | 27 | 3 | 2 | R | R | 6-2 | 180 | 4-7-66 | 1987 | Laredo, Texas |
| Bichette, Dante | .310 | 141 | 538 | 93 | 167 | 43 | 5 | 21 | 89 | 28 | 99 | 14 | 8 | R | R | 6-3 | 212 | 11-18-63 | 1984 | Lake Park, Fla. |
| Boston, Daryl | .261 | 124 | 291 | 46 | 76 | 15 | 1 | 14 | 40 | 26 | 57 | 1 | 6 | L | L | 6-3 | 210 | 1-4-63 | 1981 | Cincinnati, Ohio |
| Castellano, Pete | .183 | 34 | 71 | 12 | 13 | 2 | 0 | 3 | 7 | 8 | 16 | 1 | 1 | R | R | 6-1 | 175 | 3-11-70 | 1988 | Lara, Venez. |
| Castilla, Vinny | .255 | 105 | 337 | 36 | 86 | 9 | 7 | 9 | 30 | 13 | 45 | 2 | 5 | R | R | 6-1 | 175 | 7-4-67 | 1990 | Oaxaca, Mexico |
| Clark, Jerald | .282 | 140 | 478 | 65 | 135 | 26 | 6 | 13 | 67 | 20 | 60 | 9 | 6 | R | R | 6-4 | 202 | 8-10-63 | 1985 | Crockett, Texas |
| Cole, Alex | .256 | 126 | 348 | 50 | 89 | 9 | 4 | 0 | 24 | 43 | 58 | 30 | 13 | L | L | 6-2 | 183 | 8-17-65 | 1985 | St. Petersburg, Fla. |
| Gainer, Jay | .171 | 23 | 41 | 4 | 7 | 0 | 0 | 3 | 6 | 4 | 12 | 1 | 1 | L | L | 6-0 | 188 | 10-8-66 | 1990 | Panama City, Fla. |
| Galarraga, Andres | .370 | 120 | 470 | 71 | 174 | 35 | 4 | 22 | 98 | 24 | 73 | 2 | 4 | R | R | 6-3 | 235 | 6-18-61 | 1979 | Caracas, Venez. |
| Girardi, Joe | .290 | 86 | 310 | 35 | 90 | 14 | 5 | 3 | 31 | 24 | 41 | 6 | 6 | R | R | 5-11 | 195 | 10-14-64 | 1986 | Lake Forest, Ill. |
| Hayes, Charlie | .305 | 157 | 573 | 89 | 175 | 45 | 2 | 25 | 98 | 43 | 82 | 11 | 6 | R | R | 6-0 | 207 | 5-29-65 | 1983 | Hattiesburg, Miss. |
| Jones, Chris | .273 | 86 | 209 | 29 | 57 | 11 | 4 | 6 | 31 | 10 | 48 | 9 | 4 | R | R | 6-2 | 205 | 12-16-65 | 1984 | Liverpool, N.Y. |
| Liriano, Nelson | .305 | 48 | 151 | 28 | 46 | 6 | 3 | 2 | 15 | 18 | 22 | 6 | 4 | S | R | 5-10 | 165 | 6-3-64 | 1983 | Santo Domingo, D.R. |
| Mejia, Roberto | .231 | 65 | 229 | 31 | 53 | 14 | 5 | 5 | 20 | 13 | 63 | 4 | 1 | R | R | 5-11 | 160 | 4-14-72 | 1989 | Hato Mayor, D.R. |
| Murphy, Dale | .143 | 26 | 42 | 1 | 6 | 1 | 0 | 0 | 7 | 5 | 15 | 0 | 0 | R | R | 6-5 | 210 | 3-12-56 | 1974 | Portland, Ore. |
| Owens, J. | .209 | 33 | 86 | 12 | 18 | 5 | 0 | 3 | 6 | 6 | 30 | 1 | 0 | R | R | 6-0 | 200 | 2-10-69 | 1990 | Sardinia, Ohio |
| Sheaffer, Danny | .278 | 82 | 216 | 26 | 60 | 9 | 1 | 4 | 32 | 8 | 15 | 2 | 3 | R | R | 6-2 | 190 | 8-21-61 | 1981 | Winston-Salem, N.C. |
| Tatum, Jim | .204 | 92 | 98 | 7 | 20 | 5 | 0 | 1 | 12 | 5 | 27 | 0 | 0 | R | R | 6-2 | 200 | 10-9-67 | 1985 | Lakeside, Calif. |
| Wedge, Eric | .182 | 9 | 11 | 2 | 2 | 0 | 0 | 0 | 1 | 0 | 4 | 0 | 0 | R | R | 6-3 | 215 | 1-27-68 | 1989 | Malden, Mass. |
| Young, Eric | .269 | 144 | 490 | 82 | 132 | 16 | 8 | 3 | 42 | 63 | 41 | 42 | 19 | R | R | 5-9 | 180 | 5-18-67 | 1989 | New Brunswick, N.J. |
| Young, Gerald | .053 | 19 | 19 | 5 | 1 | 0 | 0 | 0 | 1 | 4 | 1 | 0 | 1 | S | R | 6-2 | 185 | 10-22-64 | 1982 | Santa Ana, Calif. |

| PITCHING | W | L | ERA | G | GS | CG | SV | IP | H | R | ER | BB | SO | B | T | HT | WT | DOB | 1st Yr | Resides |
|---|---|---|---|---|---|---|---|---|---|---|---|---|---|---|---|---|---|---|---|---|
| Aldred, Scott | 0 | 0 | 10.80 | 5 | 0 | 0 | 0 | 7 | 10 | 10 | 8 | 9 | 5 | L | L | 6-4 | 195 | 6-12-68 | 1987 | Lakeland, Fla. |
| Ashby, Andy | 0 | 4 | 8.50 | 20 | 9 | 0 | 1 | 54 | 89 | 54 | 51 | 32 | 33 | R | R | 6-5 | 180 | 7-11-67 | 1986 | Kansas City, Mo. |
| Blair, Willie | 6 | 10 | 4.75 | 46 | 18 | 1 | 0 | 146 | 184 | 90 | 77 | 42 | 84 | R | R | 6-1 | 185 | 12-18-65 | 1986 | Lexington, Ky. |
| Bottenfield, Kent | 3 | 5 | 6.10 | 14 | 14 | 1 | 0 | 77 | 86 | 53 | 52 | 38 | 30 | S | R | 6-3 | 215 | 11-14-68 | 1986 | Portland, Ore. |
| 2-team (23 Mtl.) | 5 | 10 | 5.07 | 37 | 25 | 1 | 0 | 160 | 179 | 102 | 90 | 71 | 63 |  |  |  |  |  |  |  |
| Fredrickson, Scott | 0 | 1 | 6.21 | 25 | 0 | 0 | 0 | 29 | 33 | 25 | 20 | 17 | 20 | R | R | 6-3 | 215 | 8-19-67 | 1990 | San Antonio, Texas |
| Grant, Mark | 0 | 1 | 12.56 | 14 | 0 | 0 | 1 | 14 | 23 | 20 | 20 | 6 | 8 | R | R | 6-2 | 215 | 10-24-63 | 1981 | Alpine, Calif. |
| Harris, Greg W. | 1 | 8 | 6.50 | 13 | 13 | 0 | 0 | 73 | 88 | 62 | 53 | 30 | 40 | R | R | 6-2 | 195 | 12-1-63 | 1985 | Cary, N.C. |
| 2-team (22 S.D.) | 11 | 17 | 4.59 | 35 | 35 | 4 | 0 | 225 | 239 | 127 | 115 | 69 | 123 |  |  |  |  |  |  |  |
| Henry, Butch | 2 | 8 | 6.59 | 20 | 15 | 1 | 0 | 85 | 117 | 66 | 62 | 24 | 39 | L | L | 6-1 | 195 | 10-7-68 | 1987 | El Paso, Texas |
| Holmes, Darren | 3 | 3 | 4.05 | 62 | 0 | 0 | 25 | 67 | 56 | 31 | 30 | 20 | 60 | R | R | 6-0 | 199 | 4-25-66 | 1984 | Fletcher, N.C. |
| Hurst, Bruce | 0 | 1 | 5.19 | 3 | 3 | 0 | 0 | 9 | 6 | 5 | 5 | 3 | 6 | L | L | 6-3 | 219 | 3-24-58 | 1976 | Rancho Sante Fe, Calif. |
| 2-team (2 S.D.) | 0 | 2 | 7.62 | 5 | 5 | 0 | 0 | 13 | 15 | 12 | 11 | 6 | 9 |  |  |  |  |  |  |  |
| Knudson, Mark | 0 | 0 | 22.24 | 4 | 0 | 0 | 0 | 6 | 16 | 14 | 14 | 5 | 3 | R | R | 6-5 | 200 | 10-28-60 | 1982 | Westminster, Colo. |
| Leskanic, Curt | 1 | 5 | 5.37 | 18 | 8 | 0 | 0 | 57 | 59 | 40 | 34 | 27 | 30 | R | R | 6-0 | 180 | 4-2-68 | 1990 | Pineville, La. |
| Moore, Marcus | 3 | 1 | 6.84 | 27 | 0 | 0 | 0 | 26 | 30 | 25 | 20 | 20 | 13 | S | R | 6-5 | 195 | 11-2-70 | 1989 | Oakland, Calif. |
| Munoz, Mike | 2 | 1 | 4.50 | 21 | 0 | 0 | 0 | 18 | 21 | 12 | 9 | 9 | 16 | L | L | 6-2 | 190 | 7-12-65 | 1986 | West Covina, Calif. |
| Nied, David | 5 | 9 | 5.17 | 16 | 16 | 1 | 0 | 87 | 99 | 53 | 50 | 42 | 46 | R | R | 6-2 | 185 | 12-22-68 | 1988 | Duncanville, Texas |
| Painter, Lance | 2 | 2 | 6.00 | 10 | 6 | 1 | 0 | 39 | 52 | 26 | 26 | 9 | 16 | L | L | 6-1 | 195 | 7-21-67 | 1990 | Milwaukee, Wis. |
| Parrett, Jeff | 3 | 3 | 5.38 | 40 | 6 | 0 | 1 | 74 | 78 | 47 | 44 | 45 | 66 | R | R | 6-3 | 185 | 8-26-61 | 1983 | Lexington, Ky. |
| Reed, Steve | 9 | 5 | 4.48 | 64 | 0 | 0 | 3 | 84 | 80 | 47 | 42 | 30 | 51 | R | R | 6-2 | 195 | 3-11-66 | 1988 | Lewiston, Idaho |
| Reynoso, Armando | 12 | 11 | 4.00 | 30 | 30 | 4 | 0 | 189 | 206 | 101 | 84 | 63 | 117 | R | R | 6-0 | 185 | 5-1-66 | 1989 | Jalisco, Mexico |
| Ruffin, Bruce | 6 | 5 | 3.87 | 59 | 12 | 0 | 2 | 140 | 145 | 71 | 60 | 69 | 126 | S | L | 6-2 | 213 | 10-4-63 | 1985 | Austin, Texas |
| Sanford, Mo | 1 | 2 | 5.30 | 11 | 6 | 0 | 0 | 36 | 37 | 25 | 21 | 27 | 36 | R | R | 6-5 | 225 | 12-24-66 | 1988 | Cincinnati, Ohio |
| Service, Scott | 0 | 0 | 9.64 | 3 | 0 | 0 | 0 | 5 | 8 | 5 | 5 | 1 | 3 | R | R | 6-6 | 235 | 2-26-67 | 1986 | Cincinnati, Ohio |
| Shepherd, Keith | 1 | 1 | 6.98 | 14 | 1 | 0 | 1 | 19 | 26 | 16 | 15 | 4 | 7 | R | R | 6-2 | 197 | 1-21-68 | 1986 | Wabash, Ind. |
| Smith, Bryn | 2 | 4 | 8.49 | 11 | 5 | 0 | 0 | 30 | 47 | 29 | 28 | 11 | 9 | R | R | 6-2 | 205 | 8-11-55 | 1975 | Santa Maria, Calif. |
| Wayne, Gary | 5 | 3 | 5.05 | 65 | 0 | 0 | 1 | 62 | 68 | 40 | 35 | 26 | 49 | L | L | 6-3 | 185 | 11-30-62 | 1984 | Dearborn Heights, Mich. |

## FIELDING

| Catcher | PCT | G | PO | A | E | DP |
|---|---|---|---|---|---|---|
| Girardi | .989 | 84 | 478 | 46 | 6 | 7 |
| Owens | .957 | 32 | 138 | 19 | 7 | 3 |
| Sheaffer | .994 | 65 | 331 | 28 | 2 | 5 |
| Wedge | 1.000 | 1 | 6 | 1 | 0 | 0 |

| First Base | PCT | G | PO | A | E | DP |
|---|---|---|---|---|---|---|
| Benavides | 1.000 | 1 | 2 | 0 | 0 | 1 |
| Castellano | .955 | 10 | 37 | 5 | 2 | 6 |
| Clark | .984 | 37 | 284 | 16 | 5 | 29 |
| Gainer | .982 | 7 | 52 | 2 | 1 | 3 |
| Galarraga | .990 | 119 | 1018 | 103 | 11 | 88 |
| Sheaffer | 1.000 | 7 | 6 | 4 | 0 | 1 |
| Tatum | .978 | 12 | 41 | 4 | 1 | 6 |

| Second Base | PCT | G | PO | A | E | DP |
|---|---|---|---|---|---|---|
| Benavides | .986 | 19 | 30 | 39 | 1 | 7 |

| | PCT | G | PO | A | E | DP |
|---|---|---|---|---|---|---|
| Castellano | 1.000 | 4 | 10 | 7 | 0 | 2 |
| Liriano | .944 | 16 | 19 | 32 | 3 | 7 |
| Mejia | .963 | 65 | 126 | 184 | 12 | 38 |
| E. Young | .962 | 79 | 153 | 228 | 15 | 43 |

| Third Base | PCT | G | PO | A | E | DP |
|---|---|---|---|---|---|---|
| Benavides | 1.000 | 5 | 0 | 6 | 0 | 0 |
| Castellano | .909 | 13 | 4 | 16 | 2 | 1 |
| Hayes | .954 | 154 | 123 | 292 | 20 | 22 |
| Liriano | 1.000 | 1 | 1 | 0 | 0 | 0 |
| Sheaffer | .000 | 1 | 0 | 0 | 0 | 0 |
| Tatum | .800 | 6 | 3 | 1 | 1 | 1 |

| Shortstop | PCT | G | PO | A | E | DP |
|---|---|---|---|---|---|---|
| Benavides | .937 | 48 | 66 | 113 | 12 | 19 |
| Castellano | 1.000 | 5 | 4 | 5 | 0 | 1 |

| | PCT | G | PO | A | E | DP |
|---|---|---|---|---|---|---|
| Castilla | .975 | 104 | 141 | 282 | 11 | 67 |
| Hayes | .000 | 1 | 0 | 0 | 0 | 0 |
| Liriano | .975 | 35 | 45 | 71 | 3 | 13 |

| Outfield | PCT | G | PO | A | E | DP |
|---|---|---|---|---|---|---|
| Bichette | .973 | 137 | 308 | 14 | 9 | 3 |
| Boston | .985 | 79 | 124 | 5 | 2 | 1 |
| Clark | .966 | 96 | 192 | 7 | 7 | 1 |
| Cole | .982 | 93 | 219 | 5 | 4 | 1 |
| Jones | .983 | 70 | 114 | 2 | 2 | 0 |
| Murphy | 1.000 | 13 | 16 | 1 | 0 | 0 |
| Sheaffer | 1.000 | 2 | 0 | 0 | 0 | 0 |
| Tatum | 1.000 | 3 | 1 | 0 | 0 | 0 |
| E. Young | .972 | 52 | 101 | 2 | 3 | 1 |
| G. Young | .882 | 11 | 15 | 0 | 2 | 0 |

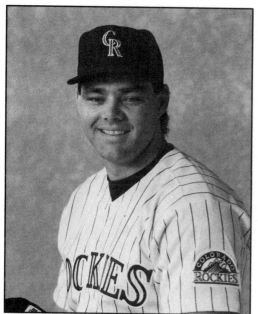

ALLEN KEE

**Offensive Stalwarts.** The Rockies set a record for wins by a National League expansion team, thanks largely to outfielder Dante Bichette (.310-21-89, 43 doubles), left, and third baseman Charlie Hayes (.305-25-98, 45 doubles).

# ROCKIES FARM SYSTEM

| Class | Club | League | W | L | Pct. | Finish* | Manager | First Year |
|---|---|---|---|---|---|---|---|---|
| AAA | Colo. Springs (Colo.) Sky Sox | Pacific Coast | 66 | 75 | .468 | 8th (10) | Brad Mills | 1993 |
| A# | Central Valley (Calif.) Rockies | California | 61 | 75 | .449 | T-8th (10) | Paul Zuvella | 1993 |
| A | Bend (Ore.) Rockies | Northwest | 35 | 41 | .461 | T-6th (8) | Howie Bedell | 1992 |
| Rookie | Chandler (Ariz.) Rockies | Arizona | 21 | 32 | .396 | 7th (8) | P.J. Carey | 1992 |

*Finish in overall standings (No. of teams in league)    #Advanced level

## COLORADO SPRINGS                                    AAA
### PACIFIC COAST LEAGUE

| BATTING | AVG | G | AB | R | H | 2B | 3B | HR | RBI | BB | SO | SB | CS | B | T | HT | WT | DOB | 1st Yr | Resides |
|---|---|---|---|---|---|---|---|---|---|---|---|---|---|---|---|---|---|---|---|---|
| Alicea, Edwin | .337 | 67 | 205 | 44 | 69 | 8 | 4 | 1 | 23 | 20 | 30 | 3 | 5 | S | R | 5-10 | 175 | 3-9-67 | 1988 | Guaynabo, P.R. |
| Ausmus, Brad | .270 | 76 | 241 | 31 | 65 | 10 | 4 | 2 | 33 | 27 | 41 | 10 | 6 | R | R | 5-11 | 185 | 4-14-69 | 1988 | Cheshire, Conn. |
| Bates, Jason | .267 | 122 | 449 | 76 | 120 | 21 | 2 | 13 | 62 | 45 | 99 | 9 | 8 | S | R | 5-11 | 170 | 1-15-71 | 1992 | Norwalk, Calif. |
| Benavides, Fred | .438 | 5 | 16 | 3 | 7 | 1 | 0 | 0 | 2 | 1 | 0 | 0 | 0 | R | R | 6-2 | 180 | 4-7-66 | 1987 | Laredo, Texas |
| Canale, George | .287 | 39 | 115 | 15 | 33 | 9 | 1 | 5 | 15 | 10 | 20 | 2 | 1 | L | R | 6-1 | 195 | 8-11-65 | 1986 | Roanoke, Va. |
| Case, Mike | .333 | 3 | 3 | 0 | 1 | 0 | 0 | 0 | 0 | 0 | 0 | 0 | 0 | R | R | 6-2 | 185 | 12-26-68 | 1992 | Yorba Linda, Calif. |
| Castellano, Pedro | .313 | 90 | 304 | 61 | 95 | 21 | 2 | 12 | 60 | 36 | 63 | 3 | 5 | R | R | 6-1 | 175 | 3-11-70 | 1988 | Lara, Venez. |
| Castillo, Braulio | .359 | 39 | 156 | 34 | 56 | 16 | 3 | 2 | 22 | 17 | 40 | 8 | 3 | R | R | 6-0 | 160 | 5-13-68 | 1986 | Elias Pina, D.R. |
| Cole, Stu | .281 | 104 | 324 | 54 | 91 | 22 | 3 | 5 | 35 | 36 | 36 | 10 | 6 | R | R | 6-2 | 190 | 2-7-66 | 1987 | Charlotte, N.C. |
| Gainer, Jay | .294 | 86 | 293 | 51 | 86 | 11 | 3 | 10 | 74 | 22 | 70 | 4 | 2 | L | L | 6-0 | 188 | 10-8-66 | 1990 | Panama City, Fla. |
| Girardi, Joe | .484 | 8 | 31 | 6 | 15 | 1 | 1 | 1 | 6 | 0 | 3 | 1 | 0 | R | R | 5-11 | 195 | 10-14-64 | 1986 | Lake Forest, Ill. |
| Hubbard, Trent | .314 | 117 | 439 | 83 | 138 | 24 | 8 | 7 | 56 | 47 | 57 | 33 | 18 | R | R | 5-8 | 180 | 5-11-66 | 1986 | Chicago, Ill. |
| Jones, Chris | .280 | 46 | 168 | 41 | 47 | 5 | 5 | 12 | 40 | 19 | 47 | 8 | 2 | R | R | 6-2 | 205 | 12-16-65 | 1984 | Liverpool, N.Y. |
| Liriano, Nelson | .358 | 79 | 293 | 48 | 105 | 23 | 6 | 6 | 46 | 32 | 34 | 9 | 13 | S | R | 5-10 | 165 | 6-3-64 | 1983 | Santo Domingo, D.R. |
| List, Paul | .300 | 18 | 50 | 9 | 15 | 7 | 1 | 0 | 5 | 3 | 8 | 0 | 0 | R | R | 6-3 | 200 | 11-17-65 | 1987 | North Hollywood, Calif. |
| Mejia, Roberto | .299 | 77 | 291 | 51 | 87 | 15 | 2 | 14 | 48 | 18 | 56 | 12 | 5 | R | R | 5-11 | 160 | 4-14-72 | 1989 | Hato Mayor, D.R. |
| Mota, Andy | .344 | 70 | 262 | 36 | 90 | 23 | 4 | 7 | 50 | 13 | 38 | 6 | 3 | R | R | 5-10 | 180 | 3-4-66 | 1987 | Glendale, Calif. |
| 3-team (3 Tuc; 29 Phx) | .301 | 102 | 345 | 46 | 104 | 29 | 4 | 7 | 61 | 21 | 57 | 8 | 5 | | | | | | | |
| Olander, Jim | .300 | 57 | 200 | 43 | 60 | 16 | 3 | 6 | 25 | 31 | 40 | 4 | 1 | R | R | 6-2 | 175 | 2-21-63 | 1981 | Tucson, Ariz. |
| Owens, J. | .310 | 55 | 174 | 24 | 54 | 11 | 3 | 6 | 43 | 21 | 56 | 5 | 3 | R | R | 6-0 | 200 | 2-10-69 | 1990 | Sardinia, Ohio |
| Reyes, Gilberto | .236 | 73 | 174 | 22 | 41 | 6 | 2 | 9 | 29 | 22 | 36 | 1 | 1 | R | R | 6-2 | 200 | 12-10-63 | 1980 | Santo Domingo, D.R. |
| Ricker, Troy | .045 | 9 | 22 | 0 | 1 | 0 | 0 | 0 | 1 | 2 | 5 | 2 | 0 | R | R | 6-4 | 245 | 8-23-66 | 1985 | Colton, Calif. |
| Ross, Sean | .303 | 34 | 119 | 15 | 36 | 13 | 3 | 1 | 14 | 5 | 20 | 3 | 3 | L | L | 6-2 | 185 | 10-21-67 | 1986 | Wilmington, N.C. |
| Strittmatter, Mark | .200 | 5 | 10 | 1 | 2 | 1 | 0 | 0 | 2 | 0 | 2 | 0 | 0 | R | R | 6-1 | 200 | 4-4-69 | 1992 | Ridgewood, N.J. |
| Tatum, Jim | .222 | 13 | 45 | 5 | 10 | 2 | 0 | 2 | 7 | 2 | 9 | 0 | 1 | R | R | 6-2 | 200 | 10-9-67 | 1985 | Lakeside, Calif. |
| Ward, Kevin | .233 | 23 | 73 | 12 | 17 | 2 | 2 | 3 | 13 | 9 | 16 | 1 | 1 | R | R | 6-1 | 195 | 9-28-61 | 1983 | Chalfont, Pa. |
| Wedge, Eric | .267 | 38 | 90 | 17 | 24 | 6 | 0 | 3 | 13 | 16 | 22 | 0 | 0 | R | R | 6-3 | 215 | 1-27-68 | 1989 | Malden, Mass. |

| PITCHING | W | L | ERA | G | GS | CG | SV | IP | H | R | ER | BB | SO | B | T | HT | WT | DOB | 1st Yr | Resides |
|---|---|---|---|---|---|---|---|---|---|---|---|---|---|---|---|---|---|---|---|---|
| Allen, Steve | 5 | 4 | 3.92 | 35 | 0 | 0 | 2 | 62 | 70 | 32 | 27 | 26 | 31 | R | R | 6-3 | 210 | 7-27-66 | 1988 | Nashua, N.H. |
| 2-team (2 Albu.) | 6 | 4 | 4.10 | 37 | 0 | 0 | 2 | 64 | 73 | 34 | 29 | 28 | 32 | | | | | | | |
| Ashby, Andy | 4 | 2 | 4.10 | 7 | 6 | 1 | 0 | 42 | 45 | 25 | 19 | 12 | 35 | R | R | 6-5 | 180 | 7-11-67 | 1986 | Kansas City, Mo. |
| Bochtler, Doug | 1 | 4 | 6.93 | 12 | 11 | 0 | 0 | 51 | 71 | 41 | 39 | 26 | 38 | R | R | 6-3 | 200 | 7-5-70 | 1989 | West Palm Beach, Fla. |

| PITCHING | W | L | ERA | G | GS | CG | SV | IP | H | R | ER | BB | SO | B | T | HT | WT | DOB | 1st Yr | Resides |
|---|---|---|---|---|---|---|---|---|---|---|---|---|---|---|---|---|---|---|---|---|
| Buckley, Travis .............. | 1 | 2 | 6.00 | 6 | 1 | 0 | 0 | 9 | 12 | 13 | 6 | 7 | 5 | R | R | 6-4 | 208 | 6-15-70 | 1989 | Overland Park, Kan. |
| Burke, John.................... | 3 | 2 | 3.14 | 8 | 8 | 0 | 0 | 49 | 44 | 22 | 17 | 23 | 38 | S | R | 6-4 | 220 | 2-9-70 | 1992 | Englewood, Colo. |
| Fredrickson, Scott.......... | 1 | 3 | 5.47 | 23 | 0 | 0 | 7 | 26 | 25 | 16 | 16 | 19 | 20 | R | R | 6-3 | 215 | 8-19-67 | 1990 | San Antonio, Texas |
| Hawblitzel, Ryan ............. | 8 | 13 | 6.15 | 29 | 28 | 2 | 0 | 165 | 221 | 129 | 113 | 49 | 90 | R | R | 6-2 | 170 | 4-30-71 | 1990 | Lake Worth, Fla. |
| Holmes, Darren ............. | 1 | 0 | 0.00 | 3 | 2 | 0 | 0 | 9 | 1 | 1 | 0 | 1 | 9 | R | R | 6-0 | 199 | 4-25-66 | 1984 | Fletcher, N.C. |
| Hurst, Bruce................... | 1 | 1 | 7.36 | 3 | 3 | 0 | 0 | 15 | 22 | 13 | 12 | 4 | 8 | L | L | 6-3 | 219 | 3-24-58 | 1976 | Rancho Sante Fe, Calif. |
| 2-team (1 Las Vegas) . | 1 | 2 | 7.78 | 4 | 4 | 0 | 0 | 20 | 30 | 19 | 17 | 4 | 15 | | | | | | | |
| Knudson, Mark .............. | 3 | 1 | 2.25 | 5 | 5 | 1 | 0 | 28 | 30 | 12 | 7 | 8 | 15 | R | R | 6-5 | 200 | 10-28-60 | 1982 | Westminster, Colo. |
| Leskanic, Curt............... | 4 | 3 | 4.47 | 9 | 7 | 1 | 0 | 44 | 39 | 24 | 22 | 26 | 38 | R | R | 6-0 | 180 | 4-2-68 | 1990 | Pineville, La. |
| Marshall, Randy.............. | 1 | 0 | 3.86 | 11 | 1 | 0 | 1 | 21 | 35 | 20 | 9 | 6 | 12 | L | L | 6-3 | 170 | 10-12-66 | 1989 | Ypsilanti, Mich. |
| Metzinger, Bill ................ | 1 | 0 | 10.07 | 12 | 0 | 0 | 0 | 20 | 25 | 24 | 22 | 19 | 21 | R | R | 6-4 | 215 | 11-30-69 | 1992 | Youngstown, Ohio |
| Moore, Marcus.............. | 1 | 5 | 4.47 | 30 | 0 | 0 | 4 | 44 | 54 | 26 | 22 | 29 | 38 | S | R | 6-5 | 195 | 11-2-70 | 1989 | Oakland, Calif. |
| Munoz, Mike .................. | 1 | 2 | 1.67 | 40 | 0 | 0 | 3 | 38 | 46 | 10 | 7 | 9 | 30 | L | L | 6-2 | 190 | 7-12-65 | 1986 | West Covina, Calif. |
| Nied, David ................... | 0 | 2 | 9.00 | 3 | 3 | 0 | 0 | 15 | 24 | 17 | 15 | 6 | 11 | R | R | 6-2 | 185 | 12-22-68 | 1988 | Duncanville, Texas |
| Painter, Lance .............. | 9 | 7 | 4.30 | 23 | 22 | 4 | 0 | 138 | 165 | 90 | 66 | 44 | 91 | L | L | 6-1 | 195 | 7-21-67 | 1990 | Milwaukee, Wis. |
| Reed, Steve .................. | 0 | 0 | 0.00 | 11 | 0 | 0 | 7 | 12 | 8 | 1 | 0 | 3 | 10 | R | R | 6-2 | 195 | 3-11-66 | 1988 | Lewiston, Idaho |
| Reynoso, Armando........ | 2 | 1 | 3.22 | 4 | 4 | 0 | 0 | 22 | 19 | 10 | 8 | 8 | 22 | R | R | 6-0 | 185 | 5-1-66 | 1989 | Jalisco, Mexico |
| Ridenour, Dana ............. | 8 | 8 | 5.21 | 39 | 16 | 1 | 0 | 121 | 156 | 83 | 70 | 58 | 105 | R | R | 6-2 | 205 | 11-15-65 | 1986 | Sylmar, Calif. |
| Sanford, Mo .................. | 3 | 6 | 5.23 | 20 | 17 | 0 | 0 | 105 | 103 | 64 | 61 | 57 | 104 | R | R | 6-6 | 225 | 12-24-66 | 1988 | Cincinnati, Ohio |
| Seanez, Rudy ................ | 0 | 0 | 9.00 | 3 | 0 | 0 | 0 | 3 | 3 | 3 | 3 | 1 | 5 | R | R | 5-10 | 185 | 10-20-68 | 1986 | El Centro, Calif. |
| Shepherd, Keith ............ | 3 | 6 | 6.78 | 37 | 1 | 0 | 8 | 68 | 90 | 61 | 51 | 44 | 57 | R | R | 6-2 | 197 | 1-21-68 | 1986 | Wabash, Ind. |
| Thompson, Mark............ | 3 | 0 | 2.70 | 4 | 4 | 2 | 0 | 33 | 31 | 13 | 10 | 11 | 22 | R | R | 6-2 | 205 | 4-7-71 | 1992 | Russellville, Ky. |
| Wassenaar, Rob............ | 0 | 0 | 11.74 | 13 | 0 | 0 | 1 | 15 | 32 | 21 | 20 | 10 | 9 | R | R | 6-2 | 200 | 4-28-65 | 1987 | Orinda, Calif. |
| Wells, Terry................... | 2 | 3 | 6.67 | 16 | 2 | 0 | 1 | 27 | 33 | 23 | 20 | 25 | 22 | L | L | 6-3 | 205 | 9-10-63 | 1985 | Chicago, Ill. |
| Zavaras, Clint................ | 0 | 0 | 2.25 | 6 | 0 | 0 | 0 | 8 | 5 | 3 | 2 | 11 | 9 | R | R | 6-1 | 175 | 1-4-67 | 1985 | Federal Way, Wash. |

### FIELDING

| Catcher | PCT | G | PO | A | E | DP |
|---|---|---|---|---|---|---|
| Ausmus ........... | .987 | 63 | 391 | 57 | 6 | 4 |
| Girardi ............. | .977 | 8 | 40 | 3 | 1 | 0 |
| Owens ............. | .959 | 35 | 191 | 17 | 9 | 2 |
| Reyes .............. | .972 | 46 | 217 | 27 | 7 | 2 |
| Strittmatter .... | 1.000 | 4 | 15 | 1 | 0 | 0 |
| Wedge............. | .986 | 12 | 60 | 12 | 1 | 0 |

| First Base | PCT | G | PO | A | E | DP |
|---|---|---|---|---|---|---|
| Canale............. | .995 | 29 | 203 | 15 | 1 | 15 |
| Castellano ....... | .981 | 35 | 281 | 30 | 6 | 29 |
| Cole................. | 1.000 | 1 | 4 | 0 | 0 | 0 |
| Gainer............. | .989 | 65 | 504 | 49 | 6 | 54 |
| Mota ............... | .900 | 3 | 9 | 0 | 1 | 0 |
| Owens ............. | 1.000 | 1 | 6 | 0 | 0 | 1 |
| Reyes.............. | .971 | 12 | 94 | 6 | 3 | 14 |
| Tatum.............. | 1.000 | 1 | 0 | 0 | 0 | 0 |
| Ward............... | 1.000 | 1 | 12 | 0 | 0 | 0 |
| Wedge............. | .977 | 12 | 74 | 10 | 2 | 8 |

| Second Base | PCT | G | PO | A | E | DP |
|---|---|---|---|---|---|---|
| Bates ............. | 1.000 | 7 | 13 | 26 | 0 | 8 |

| | PCT | G | PO | A | E | DP |
|---|---|---|---|---|---|---|
| Cole................ | 1.000 | 11 | 22 | 23 | 0 | 5 |
| Hubbard .......... | .909 | 8 | 12 | 8 | 2 | 3 |
| Liriano ............ | .975 | 50 | 103 | 173 | 7 | 38 |
| Mejia............... | .979 | 72 | 166 | 204 | 8 | 49 |
| Mota ............... | 1.000 | 2 | 2 | 4 | 0 | 1 |

| Third Base | PCT | G | PO | A | E | DP |
|---|---|---|---|---|---|---|
| Alicea ............. | 1.000 | 6 | 0 | 4 | 0 | 0 |
| Castellano ....... | .954 | 52 | 31 | 115 | 7 | 10 |
| Cole................. | .892 | 66 | 38 | 111 | 18 | 11 |
| Hubbard .......... | 1.000 | 5 | 2 | 10 | 0 | 1 |
| Liriano ............ | .913 | 13 | 7 | 14 | 2 | 1 |
| Mota ............... | 1.000 | 1 | 0 | 1 | 0 | 0 |
| Tatum.............. | .903 | 11 | 7 | 21 | 3 | 3 |

| Shortstop | PCT | G | PO | A | E | DP |
|---|---|---|---|---|---|---|
| Alicea ............. | .946 | 8 | 8 | 27 | 2 | 7 |
| Bates .............. | .940 | 112 | 161 | 293 | 29 | 66 |
| Benavides ..... | 1.000 | 5 | 4 | 12 | 0 | 1 |
| Cole................. | .880 | 7 | 9 | 13 | 3 | 3 |
| Hubbard .......... | 1.000 | 1 | 1 | 2 | 0 | 1 |

| | PCT | G | PO | A | E | DP |
|---|---|---|---|---|---|---|
| Liriano ............ | .929 | 17 | 33 | 45 | 6 | 14 |

| Outfield | PCT | G | PO | A | E | DP |
|---|---|---|---|---|---|---|
| Alicea .............. | .891 | 47 | 51 | 6 | 7 | 1 |
| Ausmus ........... | 1.000 | 3 | 2 | 0 | 0 | 0 |
| Canale............. | 1.000 | 9 | 17 | 2 | 0 | 1 |
| Castillo ............ | .952 | 38 | 57 | 2 | 3 | 0 |
| Cole................. | .800 | 6 | 4 | 0 | 1 | 0 |
| Hubbard .......... | .981 | 95 | 193 | 9 | 4 | 1 |
| Jones............... | .974 | 46 | 107 | 5 | 3 | 0 |
| List.................. | .944 | 16 | 16 | 1 | 1 | 0 |
| Moore .............. | .000 | 1 | 0 | 0 | 0 | 0 |
| Mota ............... | .969 | 68 | 120 | 6 | 4 | 1 |
| Olander ........... | .988 | 47 | 81 | 1 | 1 | 0 |
| Owens ............. | .917 | 10 | 10 | 1 | 1 | 0 |
| Ricker.............. | .500 | 8 | 3 | 0 | 3 | 0 |
| Ross................ | .942 | 31 | 64 | 1 | 4 | 0 |
| Ward............... | 1.000 | 20 | 32 | 2 | 0 | 0 |

## CENTRAL VALLEY       A
### CALIFORNIA LEAGUE

| BATTING | AVG | G | AB | R | H | 2B | 3B | HR | RBI | BB | SO | SB | CS | B | T | HT | WT | DOB | 1st Yr | Resides |
|---|---|---|---|---|---|---|---|---|---|---|---|---|---|---|---|---|---|---|---|---|
| Alicea, Edwin, of-3b .......... | .306 | 12 | 49 | 5 | 15 | 2 | 0 | 1 | 5 | 2 | 5 | 0 | 2 | S | R | 5-10 | 175 | 3-9-67 | 1988 | Guaynabo, P.R. |
| Case, Mike, 1b-of ........ | .276 | 124 | 449 | 54 | 124 | 20 | 2 | 11 | 80 | 53 | 120 | 21 | 6 | R | R | 6-2 | 185 | 12-26-68 | 1992 | Yorba Linda, Calif. |
| Counsell, Craig, ss ........ | .280 | 131 | 471 | 79 | 132 | 26 | 3 | 5 | 59 | 95 | 68 | 14 | 8 | L | R | 6-0 | 177 | 8-21-70 | 1992 | Whitefish Bay, Wis. |
| De la Cruz, Marcelino, dh | .176 | 11 | 34 | 6 | 6 | 2 | 0 | 0 | 2 | 6 | 6 | 0 | 0 | R | R | 5-11 | 165 | 1-16-73 | 1990 | Gilbert, Ariz. |
| Echevarria, Angel, of.......... | .271 | 104 | 358 | 45 | 97 | 16 | 2 | 6 | 52 | 44 | 74 | 6 | 5 | R | R | 6-4 | 215 | 5-25-71 | 1992 | Bridgeport, Conn. |
| Gonzalez, Mauricio, dh .. | .281 | 83 | 263 | 30 | 74 | 8 | 2 | 3 | 27 | 19 | 37 | 1 | 5 | L | R | 5-11 | 160 | 2-13-72 | 1990 | Santo Domingo, D.R. |
| Jones, Terry, of ............. | .288 | 21 | 73 | 16 | 21 | 1 | 0 | 0 | 7 | 10 | 15 | 5 | 0 | R | R | 5-10 | 160 | 2-15-71 | 1993 | Pinson, Ala. |
| Krenke, Keith, of-dh .. | .125 | 15 | 40 | 3 | 5 | 2 | 0 | 0 | 4 | 4 | 9 | 0 | 0 | R | R | 5-11 | 195 | 12-28-68 | 1992 | Owatonna, Minn. |

## ROCKIES TOP 10 PROSPECTS

How the Rockies Top 10 prospects, as judged by Baseball America prior to the 1993 season, fared in 1993:

| Player, Pos. | Club (Class) | AVG | AB | H | HR | RBI | SB |
|---|---|---|---|---|---|---|---|
| 3. Roberto Mejia, 2b | Colo. Spr. (AAA) | .299 | 291 | 87 | 14 | 48 | 12 |
| | Colorado | .231 | 229 | 53 | 5 | 20 | 12 |
| 9. Jason Bates, ss | Colo. Spr. (AAA) | .267 | 449 | 120 | 13 | 62 | 9 |
| 10. Pedro Castellano, 3b | Colo. Spr. (AAA) | .313 | 304 | 95 | 12 | 60 | 3 |
| | Colorado | .183 | 71 | 13 | 3 | 7 | 1 |

| Player, Pos. | Club (Class) | W | L | ERA | IP | H | BB | SO |
|---|---|---|---|---|---|---|---|---|
| 1. David Nied, rhp | Cent. Valley (A) | 0 | 1 | 3.00 | 3 | 3 | 3 | 3 |
| | Colo. Spr. (AAA) | 0 | 2 | 9.00 | 15 | 24 | 6 | 11 |
| | Colorado | 5 | 9 | 5.17 | 87 | 99 | 42 | 46 |
| 2. Mark Thompson, rhp | Cent. Valley (A) | 3 | 2 | 2.20 | 70 | 46 | 18 | 72 |
| | Colo. Spr. (AAA) | 3 | 0 | 2.70 | 33 | 31 | 11 | 22 |
| 4. Jason Hutchins, rhp | Cent. Valley (A) | 1 | 3 | 9.15 | 21 | 14 | 37 | 27 |
| 5. John Burke, rhp | Cent. Valley (A) | 7 | 8 | 3.18 | 119 | 104 | 64 | 114 |
| | Colo. Spr. (AAA) | 3 | 2 | 3.14 | 49 | 44 | 23 | 38 |
| 6. Roger Bailey, rhp | Cent. Valley (A) | 4 | 7 | 4.84 | 112 | 139 | 56 | 84 |
| 7. Ryan Hawblitzel, rhp | Colo. Spr. (AAA) | 8 | 13 | 6.15 | 165 | 221 | 49 | 90 |
| 8. Garvin Alston, rhp | Cent. Valley (A) | 5 | 9 | 5.46 | 117 | 124 | 70 | 90 |

**David Nied**
5-9 at Colorado

## BATTING

| | AVG | G | AB | R | H | 2B | 3B | HR | RBI | BB | SO | SB | CS | B | T | HT | WT | DOB | 1st Yr | Resides |
|---|---|---|---|---|---|---|---|---|---|---|---|---|---|---|---|---|---|---|---|---|
| Liriano, Nelson, ss-3b | .364 | 6 | 22 | 3 | 8 | 0 | 2 | 0 | 4 | 6 | 0 | 0 | 2 | S | R | 5-10 | 165 | 6-3-64 | 1983 | Santo Domingo, D.R. |
| List, Paul, of | .292 | 33 | 120 | 21 | 35 | 6 | 2 | 8 | 27 | 17 | 19 | 0 | 3 | R | R | 6-3 | 200 | 11-17-65 | 1987 | North Hollywood, Calif. |
| Martin, Darryl, of | .212 | 10 | 33 | 6 | 7 | 2 | 0 | 0 | 1 | 1 | 5 | 1 | 1 | R | R | 6-2 | 205 | 10-26-67 | 1986 | Lombard, Ill. |
| McCracken, Quinton, of | .292 | 127 | 483 | 94 | 141 | 17 | 7 | 2 | 58 | 78 | 90 | 60 | 19 | S | R | 5-8 | 170 | 3-16-70 | 1992 | Southport, N.C. |
| Oakland, Mike, 1b | .235 | 62 | 221 | 20 | 52 | 10 | 0 | 2 | 27 | 22 | 35 | 0 | 3 | R | R | 6-4 | 215 | 7-18-70 | 1992 | San Leandro, Calif. |
| Ortman, Ben, of | .130 | 7 | 23 | 3 | 3 | 0 | 0 | 0 | 0 | 3 | 7 | 1 | 0 | R | R | 5-10 | 175 | 2-13-71 | 1993 | Corvallis, Ore. |
| Pineiro, Mike, c-dh | .308 | 34 | 117 | 19 | 36 | 3 | 0 | 3 | 14 | 17 | 22 | 0 | 0 | R | R | 6-0 | 200 | 2-25-72 | 1990 | West Covina, Calif. |
| Pozo, Yohel, c | .333 | 1 | 3 | 1 | 1 | 0 | 0 | 0 | 0 | 0 | 1 | 0 | 0 | R | R | 6-1 | 187 | 10-17-73 | 1992 | Maracaibo, Venez. |
| Ricker, Troy, of | .222 | 27 | 90 | 11 | 20 | 2 | 0 | 1 | 9 | 11 | 31 | 2 | 2 | R | R | 6-4 | 245 | 8-23-66 | 1985 | Colton, Calif. |
| Rogers, Lamarr, 2b | .264 | 112 | 406 | 68 | 107 | 14 | 2 | 2 | 33 | 68 | 54 | 29 | 15 | R | R | 5-8 | 165 | 6-24-71 | 1992 | Plano, Texas |
| Ross, Sean, of | .314 | 9 | 35 | 5 | 11 | 0 | 1 | 2 | 11 | 5 | 5 | 2 | 0 | L | L | 6-2 | 185 | 10-21-67 | 1986 | Wilmington, N.C. |
| Scalzitti, Will, c | .242 | 75 | 248 | 25 | 60 | 10 | 0 | 2 | 17 | 17 | 40 | 0 | 1 | R | R | 6-0 | 190 | 8-29-72 | 1992 | Hollywood, Fla. |
| Schmidt, Tom, 3b | .245 | 126 | 478 | 61 | 117 | 15 | 1 | 19 | 62 | 40 | 107 | 5 | 3 | R | R | 6-3 | 200 | 2-12-73 | 1992 | Perry Hall, Md. |
| Strittmatter, Mark, c | .263 | 59 | 179 | 21 | 47 | 8 | 0 | 2 | 15 | 31 | 29 | 3 | 0 | R | R | 6-1 | 200 | 4-4-69 | 1992 | Ridgewood, N.J. |
| Turner, Ryan, of | .294 | 112 | 422 | 64 | 124 | 23 | 1 | 13 | 67 | 62 | 88 | 11 | 5 | R | R | 6-4 | 200 | 4-24-69 | 1991 | San Jose, Calif. |
| Wedge, Eric, c-dh | .304 | 6 | 23 | 6 | 7 | 0 | 0 | 3 | 11 | 2 | 6 | 0 | 0 | R | R | 6-3 | 215 | 1-27-68 | 1989 | Malden, Mass. |

## PITCHING

| | W | L | ERA | G | GS | CG | SV | IP | H | R | ER | BB | SO | B | T | HT | WT | DOB | 1st Yr | Resides |
|---|---|---|---|---|---|---|---|---|---|---|---|---|---|---|---|---|---|---|---|---|
| Acevedo, Juan | 9 | 8 | 4.40 | 27 | 20 | 1 | 0 | 119 | 119 | 68 | 58 | 58 | 107 | R | R | 6-2 | 195 | 5-5-70 | 1992 | Carpentersville, Ill. |
| Alston, Garvin | 5 | 9 | 5.46 | 25 | 24 | 1 | 0 | 117 | 124 | 81 | 71 | 70 | 90 | R | R | 6-2 | 185 | 12-8-71 | 1992 | Mt. Vernon, N.Y. |
| Bailey, Roger | 4 | 7 | 4.84 | 22 | 22 | 1 | 0 | 112 | 139 | 78 | 60 | 56 | 84 | R | R | 6-1 | 180 | 10-3-70 | 1992 | Chattahoochee, Fla. |
| Bochtler, Doug | 3 | 1 | 3.40 | 8 | 8 | 0 | 0 | 48 | 40 | 23 | 18 | 28 | 43 | R | R | 6-3 | 200 | 7-5-70 | 1989 | West Palm Beach, Fla. |
| Burke, John | 7 | 8 | 3.18 | 20 | 20 | 2 | 0 | 119 | 104 | 62 | 42 | 64 | 114 | S | R | 6-4 | 220 | 2-9-70 | 1992 | Englewood, Colo. |
| Duke, Kyle | 3 | 3 | 3.07 | 28 | 0 | 0 | 0 | 41 | 42 | 14 | 14 | 12 | 40 | S | L | 6-2 | 197 | 9-26-70 | 1990 | Carrollton, Texas |
| Eiffert, Mike | 1 | 4 | 7.65 | 13 | 1 | 0 | 0 | 20 | 19 | 20 | 17 | 28 | 12 | L | L | 6-4 | 215 | 10-13-69 | 1992 | Mission, Texas |
| Ericson, Mike | 0 | 5 | 5.78 | 38 | 1 | 0 | 0 | 67 | 90 | 46 | 43 | 27 | 51 | L | R | 6-2 | 200 | 1-15-68 | 1990 | Sterling Heights, Mich. |
| Grimes, Mike | 1 | 3 | 4.92 | 26 | 0 | 0 | 1 | 53 | 52 | 33 | 29 | 22 | 52 | R | R | 6-2 | 195 | 6-29-68 | 1989 | Dallas, Texas |
| Hovey, James | 1 | 4 | 8.10 | 23 | 0 | 0 | 0 | 40 | 62 | 45 | 36 | 27 | 23 | S | L | 6-1 | 210 | 4-18-71 | 1992 | Eau Claire, Wis. |
| Hutchins, Jason | 1 | 3 | 9.15 | 20 | 0 | 0 | 1 | 21 | 14 | 21 | 21 | 37 | 27 | R | R | 6-1 | 185 | 3-20-70 | 1992 | Irvine, Calif. |
| Johnson, Jason | 3 | 1 | 2.45 | 7 | 6 | 0 | 0 | 40 | 31 | 12 | 11 | 13 | 33 | R | R | 6-6 | 225 | 1-7-71 | 1993 | Williamsport, Pa. |
| Kotarski, Mike | 6 | 2 | 3.87 | 52 | 0 | 0 | 11 | 88 | 87 | 44 | 38 | 37 | 81 | L | L | 6-1 | 195 | 9-18-70 | 1992 | Peabody, Mass. |
| Metzinger, Bill | 0 | 1 | 7.24 | 14 | 0 | 0 | 0 | 27 | 31 | 25 | 22 | 25 | 28 | R | R | 6-2 | 215 | 11-30-69 | 1992 | Youngstown, Ohio |
| Mineer, David | 0 | 0 | 6.97 | 8 | 0 | 0 | 0 | 10 | 12 | 8 | 8 | 13 | 8 | R | R | 6-6 | 205 | 3-10-71 | 1993 | Murray, Utah |
| Moore, Marcus | 1 | 0 | 0.75 | 8 | 0 | 0 | 2 | 12 | 7 | 3 | 1 | 9 | 15 | S | R | 6-5 | 195 | 11-2-70 | 1989 | Oakland, Calif. |
| Nied, David | 0 | 1 | 3.00 | 1 | 1 | 0 | 0 | 3 | 3 | 2 | 1 | 3 | 5 | R | R | 6-2 | 185 | 12-22-68 | 1988 | Duncanville, Texas |
| Peever, Lloyd | 2 | 4 | 4.19 | 16 | 7 | 1 | 4 | 67 | 65 | 31 | 31 | 17 | 69 | R | R | 5-11 | 185 | 9-15-71 | 1992 | Stonewall, Okla. |
| Schneider, Phil | 8 | 1 | 3.11 | 19 | 0 | 0 | 0 | 38 | 30 | 16 | 13 | 25 | 42 | L | L | 6-1 | 215 | 4-26-71 | 1993 | Westbury, N.Y. |
| Seanez, Rudy | 0 | 2 | 9.72 | 5 | 1 | 0 | 0 | 8 | 9 | 9 | 9 | 11 | 7 | R | R | 5-10 | 205 | 10-20-68 | 1988 | El Centro, Calif. |
| Thompson, Mark | 3 | 2 | 2.20 | 11 | 11 | 0 | 0 | 70 | 46 | 19 | 17 | 18 | 72 | R | R | 6-2 | 205 | 4-7-71 | 1992 | Russellville, Ky. |
| Voisard, Mark | 3 | 6 | 6.12 | 21 | 14 | 0 | 0 | 82 | 72 | 58 | 56 | 53 | 61 | R | R | 6-5 | 210 | 11-4-69 | 1992 | Sidney, Ohio |

# BEND   A

## NORTHWEST LEAGUE

| | AVG | G | AB | R | H | 2B | 3B | HR | RBI | BB | SO | SB | CS | B | T | HT | WT | DOB | 1st Yr | Resides |
|---|---|---|---|---|---|---|---|---|---|---|---|---|---|---|---|---|---|---|---|---|
| Anderson, Jamie, 2b-ss | .063 | 7 | 16 | 1 | 1 | 0 | 0 | 0 | 2 | 2 | 2 | 0 | 1 | R | R | 5-11 | 155 | 9-5-71 | 1993 | Lexington, Ky. |
| Bernhardt, Steven, 3b | .191 | 54 | 162 | 16 | 31 | 7 | 0 | 1 | 9 | 19 | 24 | 5 | 3 | R | R | 6-0 | 180 | 10-9-70 | 1993 | Timonium, Md. |
| Boyd, Greg, 1b-dh | .223 | 70 | 224 | 39 | 50 | 6 | 1 | 10 | 33 | 40 | 61 | 3 | 2 | L | R | 6-2 | 250 | 6-28-71 | 1992 | Scottsburg, Va. |
| Cristopher, Carlos, 2b | .293 | 22 | 41 | 13 | 12 | 1 | 1 | 1 | 5 | 7 | 8 | 5 | 2 | L | R | 5-10 | 160 | 9-17-74 | 1993 | Mao Esperanza, D.R. |
| Dermendziev, Tony, of | .217 | 19 | 60 | 8 | 13 | 0 | 0 | 0 | 5 | 6 | 19 | 8 | 1 | L | R | 6-0 | 185 | 2-3-73 | 1993 | San Jose, Calif. |
| Giudice, John, of | .234 | 57 | 184 | 28 | 43 | 8 | 0 | 5 | 17 | 36 | 57 | 5 | 2 | R | R | 6-1 | 205 | 6-19-71 | 1993 | New Britain, Conn. |
| Grunewald, Keith, 2b-ss | .275 | 56 | 182 | 29 | 50 | 4 | 2 | 3 | 22 | 30 | 43 | 7 | 2 | S | R | 6-1 | 185 | 10-15-71 | 1993 | Marietta, Ga. |
| Higgins, Mike, c | .269 | 51 | 167 | 23 | 45 | 10 | 1 | 7 | 19 | 20 | 47 | 3 | 4 | R | R | 6-0 | 210 | 6-3-71 | 1993 | Nutley, N.J. |
| Holdren, Nate, 1b-dh | .227 | 62 | 203 | 30 | 46 | 10 | 2 | 12 | 43 | 24 | 78 | 8 | 0 | R | R | 6-5 | 245 | 12-8-71 | 1993 | Richland, Wash. |
| Jones, Terry, of | .290 | 33 | 138 | 21 | 40 | 5 | 4 | 0 | 18 | 12 | 19 | 16 | 6 | R | R | 5-10 | 160 | 2-15-71 | 1993 | Pinson, Ala. |
| Munoz, Mario, 3b | .235 | 58 | 187 | 28 | 44 | 10 | 1 | 3 | 11 | 17 | 49 | 5 | 2 | R | R | 5-11 | 180 | 4-27-71 | 1993 | Phoenix, Ariz. |

# ROCKIES: ORGANIZATION LEADERS

## MAJOR LEAGUERS

**BATTING**

| *AVG | Andres Galarraga | .370 |
|---|---|---|
| R | Dante Bichette | 93 |
| H | Charlie Hayes | 175 |
| TB | Charlie Hayes | 299 |
| 2B | Charlie Hayes | 45 |
| 3B | Eric Young | 8 |
| HR | Charlie Hayes | 25 |
| RBI | Two tied at | 98 |
| BB | Eric Young | 63 |
| SO | Dante Bichette | 99 |
| SB | Eric Young | 42 |

**PITCHING**

| W | Armando Reynoso | 12 |
|---|---|---|
| L | Armando Reynoso | 11 |
| #ERA | Bruce Ruffin | 3.87 |
| G | Gary Wayne | 65 |
| CG | Armando Reynoso | 4 |
| SV | Darren Holmes | 25 |
| IP | Armando Reynoso | 189 |
| BB | Two tied at | 69 |
| SO | Bruce Ruffin | 126 |

**Armando Reynoso**
One win shy of expansion record

FRANK RAGSDALE

## MINOR LEAGUERS

**BATTING**

| *AVG | Nelson Liriano, Colo. Spr.-Cent. Valley | .359 |
|---|---|---|
| R | Quinton McCracken, Central Valley | 94 |
| H | Quinton McCracken, Central Valley | 141 |
| TB | Trent Hubbard, Colorado Springs | 199 |
| 2B | Trent Hubbard, Colorado Springs | 24 |
| 3B | Two tied at | 8 |
| HR | Tom Schmidt, Central Valley | 19 |
| RBI | Mike Case, Cent. Valley-Colo. Springs | 80 |
| BB | Craig Counsell, Central Valley | 95 |
| SO | Mike Case, Central Valley | 120 |
| SB | Quinton McCracken, Central Valley | 60 |

**PITCHING**

| W | John Burke, Cent. Valley-Colo. Springs | 10 |
|---|---|---|
| L | Ryan Hawblitzel, Colorado Springs | 13 |
| #ERA | Mark Thompson, Cent. Valley-Colo. Spr. | 2.36 |
| G | Mike Kotarski, Central Valley | 52 |
| CG | Lance Painter, Colorado Springs | 4 |
| SV | Mike Kotarski, Central Valley | 11 |
| IP | John Burke, Cent. Valley-Colo. Springs | 168 |
| BB | John Burke, Cent. Valley-Colo. Springs | 87 |
| SO | John Burke, Cent. Valley-Colo. Springs | 152 |

*Minimum 250 At-Bats   #Minimum 75 Innings

# ROCKIES: MOST COMMON LINEUPS

| | Colorado<br>Majors | Colorado Springs<br>AAA | Central Valley<br>A |
|---|---|---|---|
| C | Joe Girardi (84) | Brad Ausmus (63) | Will Scalzitti (66) |
| 1B | Andres Galarraga (119) | Jay Gainer (65) | Mike Case (86) |
| 2B | Eric Young (79) | Roberto Mejia (72) | Lamarr Rogers (97) |
| 3B | Charlie Hayes (154) | Stu Cole (66) | Tom Schmidt (122) |
| SS | Vinny Castilla (104) | Jason Bates (112) | Craig Counsell (124) |
| OF | Dante Bichette (137) | Trent Hubbard (95) | Ryan Turner (98) |
| | Jerald Clark (96) | Andy Mota (68) | Angel Echevarria (92) |
| | Alex Cole (93) | Edwin Alicea (50) | Quinton McCracken (82) |
| DH | N/A | Jay Gainer (10) | Mauricio Gonzalez (34) |
| SP | Armando Reynoso (30) | Ryan Hawblitzel (28) | Garvin Alston (24) |
| RP | Gary Wayne (65) | Mike Munoz (40) | Mike Kotarski (52) |
| | Full-season farm clubs only | No. of games at position in parenthesis | |

| BATTING | AVG | G | AB | R | H | 2B | 3B | HR | RBI | BB | SO | SB | CS | B | T | HT | WT | DOB | 1st Yr | Resides |
|---|---|---|---|---|---|---|---|---|---|---|---|---|---|---|---|---|---|---|---|---|
| Myrow, John, of............ | .200 | 70 | 260 | 27 | 52 | 12 | 0 | 4 | 24 | 16 | 62 | 12 | 5 | R | R | 6-0 | 180 | 2-11-72 | 1993 | Pacific Palisades, Calif. |
| Ortman, Ben, of............ | .288 | 63 | 226 | 38 | 65 | 5 | 5 | 4 | 27 | 34 | 44 | 18 | 12 | R | R | 5-10 | 175 | 2-13-71 | 1993 | Corvallis, Ore. |
| Perez, Neifi, ss-2b........ | .260 | 75 | 296 | 35 | 77 | 11 | 4 | 3 | 32 | 19 | 43 | 19 | 14 | S | R | 6-0 | 164 | 6-2-75 | 1993 | Santo Domingo, D.R. |
| Pineiro, Mike, c............ | .077 | 5 | 13 | 1 | 1 | 0 | 0 | 0 | 1 | 1 | 0 | 1 | 0 | R | R | 6-0 | 200 | 2-25-72 | 1990 | West Covina, Calif. |
| Porter, Jason, c............ | .000 | 6 | 8 | 1 | 0 | 0 | 0 | 0 | 1 | 1 | 0 | 0 | 0 | R | R | 5-11 | 195 | 8-19-70 | 1993 | Portland, Ore. |
| Smith, Jason, c-dh........ | .211 | 46 | 152 | 22 | 32 | 5 | 0 | 9 | 36 | 24 | 59 | 1 | 2 | R | R | 6-4 | 225 | 9-12-70 | 1993 | Beaumont, Texas |

| PITCHING | W | L | ERA | G | GS | CG | SV | IP | H | R | ER | BB | SO | B | T | HT | WT | DOB | 1st Yr | Resides |
|---|---|---|---|---|---|---|---|---|---|---|---|---|---|---|---|---|---|---|---|---|
| Calvin, Derrick ............. | 0 | 2 | 3.91 | 13 | 0 | 0 | 0 | 23 | 22 | 10 | 10 | 12 | 11 | R | R | 6-2 | 190 | 6-17-72 | 1993 | New Orleans, La. |
| Conley, Curt................. | 2 | 1 | 3.57 | 20 | 0 | 0 | 2 | 35 | 30 | 18 | 14 | 16 | 27 | L | L | 6-2 | 210 | 2-19-71 | 1993 | Clayton, Ohio |
| Dewett, Martin.............. | 1 | 2 | 2.92 | 14 | 0 | 0 | 0 | 37 | 30 | 14 | 12 | 30 | 36 | L | L | 5-10 | 185 | 1-29-73 | 1993 | Aurora, Colo. |
| Eiffert, Mike ................ | 0 | 1 | 10.80 | 7 | 3 | 0 | 0 | 8 | 15 | 21 | 10 | 17 | 4 | L | L | 6-4 | 215 | 10-13-69 | 1992 | Mission, Texas |
| Goodrich, Jon ............... | 1 | 2 | 4.91 | 17 | 0 | 0 | 0 | 22 | 30 | 18 | 12 | 9 | 13 | R | R | 6-3 | 195 | 12-6-72 | 1992 | Sonoma, Calif. |
| Henderson, Chris........... | 4 | 3 | 2.36 | 27 | 0 | 0 | 8 | 42 | 34 | 14 | 11 | 16 | 38 | R | R | 6-2 | 205 | 12-15-71 | 1992 | Boca Raton, Fla. |
| Holland, Jay ................ | 0 | 0 | 10.80 | 2 | 0 | 0 | 0 | 2 | 1 | 3 | 2 | 4 | 1 | R | R | 6-1 | 185 | 1-26-70 | 1992 | Everett, Wash. |
| Johnson, Jason ............. | 4 | 1 | 0.79 | 8 | 4 | 0 | 3 | 34 | 30 | 10 | 3 | 10 | 27 | R | R | 6-6 | 225 | 1-7-71 | 1993 | Williamsport, Pa. |
| Lasbury, Bob................ | 0 | 1 | 6.29 | 13 | 1 | 0 | 1 | 24 | 31 | 22 | 17 | 19 | 16 | R | R | 6-2 | 185 | 8-5-72 | 1993 | Waterbury, Conn. |
| McClinton, Pat .............. | 3 | 2 | 4.98 | 18 | 1 | 0 | 0 | 34 | 34 | 23 | 19 | 22 | 30 | L | L | 6-5 | 210 | 8-9-71 | 1993 | Louisville, Ky. |
| Moore, Joel ................. | 4 | 7 | 3.21 | 15 | 15 | 0 | 0 | 90 | 75 | 35 | 32 | 31 | 79 | L | R | 6-3 | 200 | 8-13-72 | 1993 | Elgin, Ill. |
| Neier, Chris................. | 3 | 5 | 4.79 | 15 | 15 | 0 | 0 | 77 | 90 | 55 | 41 | 32 | 58 | R | R | 6-3 | 205 | 11-19-71 | 1992 | Palo Alto, Calif. |
| Rekar, Bryan ............... | 3 | 5 | 4.08 | 13 | 13 | 1 | 0 | 75 | 81 | 36 | 34 | 18 | 59 | S | R | 6-3 | 200 | 6-3-72 | 1993 | Mokena, Ill. |
| Schneider, Phil.............. | 1 | 0 | 0.00 | 4 | 0 | 0 | 0 | 7 | 1 | 1 | 0 | 0 | 9 | L | L | 6-1 | 215 | 4-26-71 | 1993 | Westbury, N.Y. |
| Sobkoviak, Jeff ............. | 4 | 6 | 4.44 | 15 | 15 | 1 | 0 | 77 | 90 | 50 | 38 | 38 | 34 | R | R | 6-7 | 220 | 8-22-71 | 1992 | Iroquois, Ill. |
| Wehn, Kevin ................. | 1 | 0 | 7.03 | 13 | 1 | 0 | 0 | 24 | 30 | 20 | 19 | 15 | 14 | R | R | 6-2 | 205 | 8-23-72 | 1993 | Cooper City, Fla. |
| Zolecki, Mike ............... | 4 | 3 | 4.42 | 14 | 8 | 1 | 1 | 55 | 47 | 35 | 27 | 30 | 78 | R | R | 6-2 | 185 | 12-6-71 | 1993 | South Milwaukee, Wis. |

# CHANDLER      R
## ARIZONA LEAGUE

| BATTING | AVG | G | AB | R | H | 2B | 3B | HR | RBI | BB | SO | SB | CS | B | T | HT | WT | DOB | 1st Yr | Resides |
|---|---|---|---|---|---|---|---|---|---|---|---|---|---|---|---|---|---|---|---|---|
| Cedeno, Jose, 1b.......... | .205 | 46 | 156 | 21 | 32 | 7 | 2 | 3 | 14 | 17 | 49 | 8 | 3 | R | R | 6-0 | 150 | 6-29-75 | 1993 | Santo Domingo, D.R. |
| De la Cruz, Marcelino, 3b | .203 | 23 | 74 | 10 | 15 | 4 | 0 | 0 | 5 | 10 | 16 | 6 | 3 | R | R | 5-11 | 165 | 1-16-73 | 1990 | Gilbert, Ariz. |
| Dermendziev, Tony, of.. | .318 | 30 | 110 | 24 | 35 | 2 | 3 | 1 | 18 | 14 | 23 | 17 | 0 | L | R | 6-0 | 185 | 2-3-73 | 1993 | San Jose, Calif. |
| Diaz, Javier, 3b............ | .215 | 39 | 135 | 17 | 29 | 8 | 2 | 2 | 16 | 16 | 29 | 6 | 1 | R | R | 6-2 | 163 | 6-27-75 | 1992 | Santo Domingo, D.R. |
| Edwards, Randy, of......... | .132 | 24 | 68 | 10 | 9 | 2 | 2 | 0 | 8 | 11 | 22 | 7 | 0 | R | R | 6-1 | 193 | 9-18-73 | 1992 | West Covina, Calif. |
| Figueroa, Danny, ss-2b.. | .273 | 28 | 88 | 22 | 24 | 4 | 1 | 0 | 6 | 11 | 19 | 8 | 1 | R | R | 5-11 | 160 | 3-6-74 | 1992 | Rio Piedras, P.R. |
| Gambill, Chad, of .......... | .214 | 46 | 159 | 23 | 34 | 8 | 0 | 4 | 24 | 21 | 39 | 1 | 2 | R | R | 6-2 | 190 | 11-27-74 | 1993 | Clearwater, Fla. |
| Garcia, Vincente, 2b....... | .299 | 38 | 137 | 13 | 41 | 10 | 0 | 0 | 13 | 18 | 27 | 12 | 2 | R | R | 6-0 | 170 | 2-14-75 | 1993 | Maracaibo, Venez. |
| Gibson, Derrick, of-dh .... | .151 | 34 | 119 | 13 | 18 | 2 | 2 | 0 | 10 | 5 | 55 | 3 | 0 | R | R | 6-2 | 227 | 2-5-75 | 1993 | Winter Haven, Fla. |
| Hatfield, Rick, c-1b ........ | .167 | 36 | 108 | 9 | 18 | 6 | 0 | 0 | 12 | 5 | 12 | 1 | 1 | L | R | 6-0 | 185 | 10-13-74 | 1992 | Marianna, W.Va. |
| Hoover, Will, c .............. | .100 | 18 | 40 | 6 | 4 | 1 | 0 | 0 | 3 | 9 | 23 | 1 | 0 | R | R | 6-2 | 190 | 12-10-74 | 1993 | Camp Hill, Pa. |
| Houser, Kyle, ss ........... | .176 | 37 | 119 | 14 | 21 | 2 | 0 | 0 | 11 | 14 | 16 | 1 | 1 | R | R | 6-0 | 160 | 1-21-75 | 1993 | Dallas, Texas |
| Machado, Mike, dh-of .... | .130 | 13 | 46 | 4 | 6 | 1 | 0 | 0 | 1 | 4 | 15 | 3 | 2 | R | R | 6-2 | 205 | 9-11-73 | 1992 | Antioch, Calif. |
| Medina, Alger, of-dh....... | .291 | 29 | 79 | 19 | 23 | 3 | 3 | 0 | 5 | 26 | 21 | 26 | 6 | R | R | 6-0 | 178 | 6-30-74 | 1993 | Santo Domingo, D.R. |
| Melendez, Enrique, 2b.... | .188 | 15 | 32 | 3 | 6 | 1 | 0 | 0 | 3 | 7 | 14 | 1 | 2 | S | R | 6-1 | 175 | 8-21-75 | 1993 | Ensenada, P.R. |
| Pozo, Yohel, c.............. | .284 | 21 | 74 | 5 | 21 | 4 | 0 | 1 | 17 | 4 | 13 | 1 | 1 | R | R | 6-1 | 187 | 10-17-73 | 1992 | Maracaibo, Venez. |
| Pridgen, Matt, of ........... | .263 | 19 | 38 | 8 | 10 | 1 | 1 | 0 | 1 | 4 | 15 | 2 | 1 | S | R | 5-11 | 175 | 9-13-74 | 1993 | Phoenix, Ariz. |
| Velazquez, Edgard, of..... | .245 | 39 | 147 | 20 | 36 | 4 | 2 | 2 | 20 | 16 | 35 | 7 | 5 | R | R | 6-0 | 170 | 12-15-75 | 1993 | Guaynabo, P.R. |

| PITCHING | W | L | ERA | G | GS | CG | SV | IP | H | R | ER | BB | SO | B | T | HT | WT | DOB | 1st Yr | Resides |
|---|---|---|---|---|---|---|---|---|---|---|---|---|---|---|---|---|---|---|---|---|
| Barnes, Keith ................ | 5 | 4 | 2.67 | 11 | 11 | 1 | 0 | 61 | 60 | 30 | 18 | 14 | 38 | L | L | 6-3 | 189 | 8-9-74 | 1992 | Hixson, Tenn. |
| Barry, Dan .................... | 1 | 1 | 3.66 | 12 | 0 | 0 | 0 | 20 | 26 | 15 | 8 | 6 | 15 | L | L | 6-2 | 190 | 5-14-71 | 1993 | Manalapan, N.J. |
| Burdick, Morgan ............ | 1 | 0 | 4.94 | 16 | 2 | 0 | 0 | 27 | 39 | 19 | 15 | 12 | 14 | R | R | 6-2 | 175 | 5-15-75 | 1993 | Clovis, Calif. |
| Dewett, Martin ............... | 0 | 0 | 0.00 | 3 | 0 | 0 | 1 | 4 | 3 | 0 | 0 | 2 | 9 | L | L | 5-10 | 185 | 1-29-73 | 1993 | Aurora, Colo. |
| Fernandez, Fernando .... | 1 | 4 | 1.00 | 16 | 0 | 0 | 1 | 27 | 19 | 14 | 3 | 9 | 14 | R | R | 6-3 | 188 | 5-16-75 | 1993 | San Cristobal, D.R. |
| Garrett, Neil ................. | 1 | 1 | 2.91 | 11 | 10 | 1 | 0 | 56 | 50 | 27 | 18 | 10 | 42 | R | R | 6-1 | 172 | 7-4-74 | 1992 | Joliet, Ill. |
| Hutchins, Jason ............ | 0 | 1 | 0.00 | 1 | 0 | 0 | 0 | 0 | 6 | 6 | 4 | 4 | 0 | R | R | 6-1 | 185 | 3-20-70 | 1992 | Irvine, Calif. |
| Matos, Jose ................. | 0 | 2 | 4.97 | 18 | 1 | 0 | 0 | 25 | 32 | 19 | 14 | 12 | 15 | R | R | 6-3 | 168 | 7-9-74 | 1993 | Baranona, D.R. |
| McAdams, Denny .......... | 3 | 1 | 4.08 | 22 | 0 | 0 | 5 | 29 | 34 | 14 | 13 | 10 | 35 | R | R | 5-10 | 171 | 11-20-73 | 1993 | San Marcos, Calif. |
| Mineer, Dave ................ | 2 | 1 | 2.19 | 10 | 0 | 0 | 0 | 12 | 11 | 6 | 3 | 5 | 6 | R | R | 6-5 | 205 | 3-10-71 | 1993 | Murray, Utah |
| Mora, Jaihe .................. | 0 | 1 | 11.05 | 14 | 0 | 0 | 0 | 15 | 21 | 22 | 18 | 16 | 6 | R | R | 6-4 | 190 | 6-23-74 | 1993 | Maracaibo, Venez. |
| Tafoya, Greg................. | 0 | 0 | 3.07 | 9 | 0 | 0 | 0 | 15 | 20 | 5 | 5 | 4 | 14 | R | L | 6-2 | 208 | 7-15-73 | 1992 | Holbrook, Ariz. |
| Thomson, John ............. | 3 | 5 | 4.62 | 11 | 11 | 0 | 0 | 51 | 43 | 40 | 26 | 31 | 36 | R | R | 6-3 | 185 | 10-1-73 | 1993 | Sulphur, La. |
| Viano, Jacob ................ | 2 | 2 | 3.27 | 22 | 1 | 0 | 1 | 33 | 24 | 15 | 12 | 6 | 32 | R | R | 5-10 | 170 | 9-4-73 | 1993 | Long Beach, Calif. |
| Walls, Doug .................. | 2 | 7 | 4.56 | 10 | 10 | 0 | 0 | 47 | 51 | 40 | 24 | 26 | 50 | L | R | 6-2 | 200 | 3-21-74 | 1993 | Union, Ohio |
| Wright, Jamey................ | 1 | 3 | 4.00 | 8 | 8 | 0 | 0 | 36 | 35 | 19 | 16 | 9 | 26 | R | R | 6-5 | 202 | 12-24-74 | 1993 | Oklahoma City, Okla. |

# DETROIT TIGERS

**Manager:** Sparky Anderson.     **1993 Record:** 85-77, .525 (T-3rd, AL East).

| BATTING | AVG | G | AB | R | H | 2B | 3B | HR | RBI | BB | SO | SB | CS | B | T | HT | WT | DOB | 1st Yr | Resides |
|---|---|---|---|---|---|---|---|---|---|---|---|---|---|---|---|---|---|---|---|---|
| Barnes, Skeeter | .281 | 84 | 160 | 24 | 45 | 8 | 1 | 2 | 27 | 11 | 19 | 5 | 5 | R | R | 5-10 | 180 | 3-7-57 | 1978 | Indianapolis, Ind. |
| Bautista, Danny | .311 | 17 | 61 | 6 | 19 | 3 | 0 | 1 | 9 | 1 | 10 | 3 | 1 | R | R | 5-11 | 170 | 5-24-72 | 1989 | Santo Domingo, D.R. |
| Cuyler, Milt | .213 | 82 | 249 | 46 | 53 | 11 | 7 | 0 | 19 | 19 | 53 | 13 | 2 | S | R | 5-10 | 185 | 10-7-68 | 1986 | Farmington Hills, Mich. |
| Davis, Eric | .253 | 23 | 75 | 14 | 19 | 1 | 1 | 6 | 15 | 14 | 18 | 2 | 2 | R | R | 6-3 | 185 | 5-29-62 | 1980 | Cincinnati, Ohio |
| Deer, Rob | .217 | 90 | 323 | 48 | 70 | 11 | 0 | 14 | 39 | 38 | 120 | 3 | 2 | R | R | 6-3 | 225 | 9-29-60 | 1978 | Scottsdale, Ariz. |
| Fielder, Cecil | .267 | 154 | 573 | 80 | 153 | 23 | 0 | 30 | 117 | 90 | 125 | 0 | 1 | R | R | 6-3 | 250 | 9-21-63 | 1982 | Irving, Texas |
| Fryman, Travis | .300 | 151 | 607 | 98 | 182 | 37 | 5 | 22 | 97 | 77 | 128 | 9 | 4 | R | R | 6-1 | 194 | 3-25-69 | 1987 | Pensacola, Fla. |
| Gibson, Kirk | .261 | 116 | 403 | 62 | 105 | 18 | 6 | 13 | 62 | 44 | 87 | 15 | 6 | L | L | 6-3 | 225 | 5-28-57 | 1978 | Grosse Pointe, Mich. |
| Gladden, Dan | .267 | 91 | 356 | 52 | 95 | 16 | 2 | 13 | 56 | 21 | 50 | 8 | 5 | R | R | 5-11 | 180 | 7-7-57 | 1979 | Eden Prairie, Minn. |
| Gomez, Chris | .250 | 46 | 128 | 11 | 32 | 7 | 1 | 0 | 11 | 9 | 17 | 2 | 2 | R | R | 6-1 | 183 | 6-16-71 | 1992 | Lakewood, Calif. |
| Kreuter, Chad | .286 | 119 | 374 | 59 | 107 | 23 | 3 | 15 | 51 | 49 | 92 | 2 | 1 | R | R | 6-2 | 190 | 8-26-64 | 1985 | Arlington, Texas |
| Livingstone, Scott | .293 | 98 | 304 | 39 | 89 | 10 | 2 | 2 | 39 | 19 | 32 | 1 | 3 | L | R | 6-0 | 184 | 7-15-65 | 1988 | Dallas, Texas |
| Phillips, Tony | .313 | 151 | 566 | 113 | 177 | 27 | 0 | 7 | 57 | 132 | 102 | 16 | 11 | S | R | 5-10 | 175 | 4-25-59 | 1978 | Scottsdale, Ariz. |
| Rowland, Rich | .217 | 21 | 46 | 2 | 10 | 3 | 0 | 0 | 4 | 5 | 16 | 0 | 0 | R | R | 6-1 | 210 | 2-25-67 | 1988 | Cloverdale, Calif. |
| Tettleton, Mickey | .245 | 152 | 522 | 79 | 128 | 25 | 4 | 32 | 110 | 109 | 139 | 3 | 7 | S | R | 6-2 | 195 | 9-16-60 | 1981 | Pauls Valley, Okla. |
| Thurman, Gary | .213 | 75 | 89 | 22 | 19 | 2 | 2 | 0 | 13 | 11 | 30 | 7 | 0 | R | R | 5-10 | 175 | 11-12-64 | 1983 | Indianapolis, Ind. |
| Trammell, Alan | .329 | 112 | 401 | 72 | 132 | 25 | 3 | 12 | 60 | 38 | 38 | 12 | 8 | R | R | 6-0 | 185 | 2-21-58 | 1976 | Birmingham, Ala. |
| Whitaker, Lou | .290 | 119 | 383 | 72 | 111 | 32 | 1 | 9 | 67 | 78 | 46 | 3 | 3 | L | R | 5-11 | 180 | 5-12-57 | 1975 | Lakeland, Fla. |

| PITCHING | W | L | ERA | G | GS | CG | SV | IP | H | R | ER | BB | SO | B | T | HT | WT | DOB | 1st Yr | Resides |
|---|---|---|---|---|---|---|---|---|---|---|---|---|---|---|---|---|---|---|---|---|
| Bergman, Sean | 1 | 4 | 5.67 | 9 | 6 | 1 | 0 | 40 | 47 | 29 | 25 | 23 | 19 | R | R | 6-4 | 205 | 4-11-70 | 1991 | Joliet, Ill. |
| Boever, Joe | 2 | 1 | 2.74 | 19 | 0 | 0 | 3 | 23 | 14 | 10 | 7 | 11 | 14 | R | R | 6-1 | 200 | 10-4-60 | 1982 | Palm Harbor, Fla. |
| 2-team (42 Oak.) | 3 | 3 | 3.61 | 61 | 0 | 0 | 3 | 102 | 101 | 50 | 41 | 44 | 63 | | | | | | | |
| Bolton, Tom | 6 | 6 | 4.47 | 43 | 8 | 0 | 0 | 103 | 113 | 57 | 51 | 45 | 66 | L | L | 6-3 | 185 | 5-6-62 | 1980 | Smyrna, Tenn. |
| Davis, Storm | 0 | 2 | 3.06 | 24 | 0 | 0 | 4 | 35 | 25 | 12 | 12 | 15 | 36 | R | R | 6-4 | 225 | 12-26-61 | 1979 | Atlantic Beach, Fla. |
| 2-team (19 Oak.) | 2 | 8 | 5.05 | 43 | 8 | 0 | 4 | 98 | 93 | 57 | 55 | 48 | 73 | | | | | | | |
| DeSilva, John | 0 | 0 | 9.00 | 1 | 0 | 0 | 0 | 1 | 2 | 1 | 1 | 0 | 0 | R | R | 6-0 | 193 | 9-30-67 | 1989 | Fort Bragg, Calif. |
| Doherty, John | 14 | 11 | 4.44 | 32 | 31 | 3 | 0 | 185 | 205 | 104 | 91 | 48 | 63 | R | R | 6-4 | 200 | 6-11-67 | 1989 | Tuckahoe, N.Y. |
| Gardiner, Mike | 0 | 0 | 3.97 | 10 | 0 | 0 | 0 | 11 | 12 | 5 | 5 | 7 | 4 | R | R | 6-0 | 185 | 10-19-65 | 1987 | Sarnia, Ontario |
| Gohr, Greg | 0 | 0 | 5.96 | 16 | 0 | 0 | 0 | 23 | 26 | 15 | 15 | 14 | 23 | R | R | 6-3 | 205 | 10-29-67 | 1989 | Campbell, Calif. |
| Grater, Mark | 0 | 0 | 5.40 | 4 | 0 | 0 | 0 | 5 | 6 | 3 | 3 | 4 | 4 | R | R | 5-10 | 205 | 1-19-64 | 1986 | Monaca, Pa. |
| Groom, Buddy | 0 | 2 | 6.14 | 19 | 3 | 0 | 0 | 37 | 48 | 25 | 25 | 13 | 15 | L | L | 6-2 | 200 | 7-10-65 | 1987 | Red Oak, Texas |
| Gullickson, Bill | 13 | 9 | 5.37 | 28 | 28 | 2 | 0 | 159 | 186 | 106 | 95 | 44 | 70 | R | R | 6-3 | 225 | 2-20-59 | 1977 | Brentwood, Tenn. |
| Haas, Dave | 1 | 2 | 6.11 | 20 | 0 | 0 | 0 | 28 | 45 | 20 | 19 | 8 | 17 | R | R | 6-1 | 200 | 10-19-65 | 1988 | Wichita, Kan. |
| Henneman, Mike | 5 | 3 | 2.64 | 63 | 0 | 0 | 24 | 72 | 69 | 28 | 21 | 32 | 58 | R | R | 6-4 | 205 | 12-11-61 | 1984 | Colleyville, Texas |
| Johnson, Dave | 1 | 1 | 12.96 | 6 | 0 | 0 | 0 | 8 | 13 | 13 | 12 | 5 | 7 | R | R | 5-11 | 180 | 10-24-59 | 1982 | Middle River, Md. |
| Kiely, John | 0 | 2 | 7.71 | 8 | 0 | 0 | 0 | 12 | 13 | 11 | 10 | 13 | 5 | R | R | 6-3 | 210 | 10-4-64 | 1988 | Brockton, Mass. |
| Knudsen, Kurt | 3 | 2 | 4.78 | 30 | 0 | 0 | 2 | 38 | 41 | 22 | 20 | 24 | 31 | R | R | 6-2 | 184 | 2-20-67 | 1988 | Carmichael, Calif. |
| Krueger, Bill | 6 | 4 | 3.40 | 32 | 7 | 0 | 0 | 82 | 90 | 43 | 31 | 30 | 60 | L | L | 6-5 | 205 | 4-24-58 | 1980 | Seattle, Wash. |
| Leiter, Mark | 6 | 6 | 4.73 | 27 | 13 | 1 | 0 | 107 | 111 | 61 | 56 | 44 | 70 | R | R | 6-3 | 210 | 4-13-63 | 1983 | West Caldwell, N.J. |
| MacDonald, Bob | 3 | 3 | 5.35 | 68 | 0 | 0 | 3 | 66 | 67 | 42 | 39 | 33 | 39 | L | L | 6-2 | 208 | 4-27-65 | 1987 | Toms River, N.J. |
| Moore, Mike | 13 | 9 | 5.22 | 36 | 36 | 4 | 0 | 214 | 227 | 135 | 124 | 89 | 89 | R | R | 6-4 | 205 | 11-26-59 | 1981 | Costa Mesa, Calif. |
| Munoz, Mike | 0 | 1 | 6.00 | 8 | 0 | 0 | 0 | 3 | 4 | 2 | 2 | 6 | 1 | L | L | 6-2 | 190 | 7-12-65 | 1986 | West Covina, Calif. |
| Wells, David | 11 | 9 | 4.19 | 32 | 30 | 0 | 0 | 187 | 183 | 93 | 87 | 42 | 139 | L | L | 6-4 | 225 | 5-20-63 | 1982 | San Diego, Calif. |

## FIELDING

| Catcher | PCT | G | PO | A | E | DP |
|---|---|---|---|---|---|---|
| Kreuter | .988 | 112 | 517 | 69 | 7 | 10 |
| Rowland | .988 | 17 | 75 | 7 | 1 | 1 |
| Tettleton | .997 | 56 | 268 | 19 | 1 | 1 |

| First Base | PCT | G | PO | A | E | DP |
|---|---|---|---|---|---|---|
| Barnes | .984 | 27 | 113 | 9 | 2 | 6 |
| Fielder | .991 | 119 | 971 | 78 | 10 | 84 |
| Kreuter | 1.000 | 1 | 5 | 1 | 0 | 0 |
| Tettleton | .992 | 59 | 364 | 24 | 3 | 41 |

| Second Base | PCT | G | PO | A | E | DP |
|---|---|---|---|---|---|---|
| Barnes | 1.000 | 10 | 7 | 10 | 0 | 1 |
| Gomez | .988 | 17 | 37 | 45 | 1 | 7 |
| Phillips | .985 | 51 | 106 | 159 | 4 | 33 |

| | PCT | G | PO | A | E | DP |
|---|---|---|---|---|---|---|
| Whitaker | .981 | 110 | 236 | 322 | 11 | 75 |

| Third Base | PCT | G | PO | A | E | DP |
|---|---|---|---|---|---|---|
| Barnes | .963 | 13 | 9 | 17 | 1 | 0 |
| Fryman | .976 | 69 | 44 | 120 | 4 | 10 |
| Livingstone | .955 | 62 | 33 | 94 | 6 | 6 |
| Phillips | .333 | 1 | 0 | 1 | 2 | 0 |
| Trammell | .938 | 35 | 19 | 56 | 5 | 7 |

| Shortstop | PCT | G | PO | A | E | DP |
|---|---|---|---|---|---|---|
| Barnes | .500 | 2 | 0 | 1 | 1 | 0 |
| Fryman | .953 | 81 | 125 | 262 | 19 | 60 |
| Gomez | .963 | 29 | 32 | 73 | 4 | 16 |
| Trammell | .989 | 63 | 79 | 181 | 3 | 24 |

| Outfield | PCT | G | PO | A | E | DP |
|---|---|---|---|---|---|---|
| Barnes | 1.000 | 18 | 29 | 0 | 0 | 0 |
| Bautista | 1.000 | 16 | 38 | 2 | 0 | 0 |
| Cuyler | .968 | 80 | 211 | 2 | 7 | 1 |
| E. Davis | .981 | 18 | 52 | 0 | 1 | 0 |
| Deer | .975 | 86 | 192 | 5 | 5 | 3 |
| Gibson | .987 | 32 | 76 | 0 | 1 | 0 |
| Gladden | .986 | 86 | 196 | 9 | 3 | 1 |
| Phillips | .969 | 108 | 215 | 5 | 7 | 1 |
| Tettleton | .980 | 55 | 92 | 4 | 2 | 1 |
| Thurman | .950 | 53 | 54 | 3 | 3 | 1 |
| Trammell | .941 | 8 | 15 | 1 | 1 | 0 |

# TIGERS FARM SYSTEM

| Class | Club | League | W | L | Pct. | Finish* | Manager | First Year |
|---|---|---|---|---|---|---|---|---|
| AAA | Toledo (Ohio) Mud Hens | International | 65 | 77 | .458 | 7th (10) | Joe Sparks | 1987 |
| AA | London (Ont.) Tigers | Eastern | 63 | 75 | .457 | 6th (8) | Tom Runnels | 1989 |
| A# | Lakeland (Fla.) Tigers | Florida State | 65 | 63 | .508 | 7th (13) | Gerry Groninger | 1960 |
| A | Fayetteville (N.C.) Generals | South Atlantic | 75 | 66 | .532 | 5th (14) | Mark Wagner | 1987 |
| A | Niagara Falls (N.Y.) Rapids | New York-Penn | 47 | 31 | .603 | 2nd† (14) | Larry Parrish | 1989 |
| Rookie# | Bristol (Va.) Tigers | Appalachian | 28 | 39 | .418 | 8th (10) | Ruben Amaro | 1969 |

*Finish in overall standings (No. of teams in league)   #Advanced level   †Won league championship

**Cecil Fielder.** He didn't lead the American League in RBIs for the first time in four years, but his 117 led the Tigers.

MICHAEL YELMAN

**Travis Fryman.** Splitting the 1993 season between shortstop and third base, Fryman hit .300 with 22 home runs and 97 RBIs.

MORRIS FOSTOFF

# TOLEDO                                                                    AAA
## INTERNATIONAL LEAGUE

| BATTING | AVG | G | AB | R | H | 2B | 3B | HR | RBI | BB | SO | SB | CS | B | T | HT | WT | DOB | 1st Yr | Resides |
|---|---|---|---|---|---|---|---|---|---|---|---|---|---|---|---|---|---|---|---|---|
| Brogna, Rico | .273 | 129 | 483 | 55 | 132 | 30 | 3 | 11 | 59 | 31 | 94 | 7 | 5 | L | L | 6-2 | 202 | 4-18-70 | 1988 | Watertown, Conn. |
| Cangelosi, John | .292 | 113 | 439 | 73 | 128 | 23 | 4 | 6 | 42 | 56 | 59 | 39 | 18 | S | L | 5-8 | 150 | 3-10-63 | 1982 | Chicago, Ill. |
| Cruz, Ivan | .226 | 115 | 402 | 44 | 91 | 18 | 4 | 13 | 50 | 30 | 85 | 1 | 1 | L | L | 6-3 | 210 | 5-3-68 | 1989 | Fajardo, P.R. |
| Givens, Jim | .257 | 44 | 148 | 18 | 38 | 4 | 2 | 0 | 13 | 10 | 19 | 6 | 3 | S | R | 6-1 | 177 | 11-11-67 | 1991 | Findlay, Ohio |
| Gladden, Dan | .393 | 7 | 28 | 6 | 11 | 1 | 0 | 1 | 7 | 0 | 6 | 1 | 0 | R | R | 5-11 | 180 | 7-7-57 | 1979 | Eden Prairie, Minn. |
| Gomez, Chris | .245 | 87 | 277 | 29 | 68 | 12 | 2 | 0 | 20 | 23 | 37 | 6 | 2 | R | R | 6-1 | 183 | 6-16-71 | 1992 | Lakewood, Calif. |
| Hare, Shawn | .264 | 130 | 470 | 81 | 124 | 29 | 3 | 20 | 76 | 34 | 90 | 8 | 4 | L | L | 6-2 | 190 | 3-26-67 | 1989 | Rochester Hills, Mich. |
| Hurst, Jody | .250 | 61 | 200 | 26 | 50 | 6 | 2 | 6 | 27 | 17 | 35 | 15 | 1 | R | L | 6-4 | 185 | 3-11-67 | 1989 | Meridian, Miss. |
| Ingram, Riccardo | .270 | 123 | 415 | 41 | 112 | 20 | 4 | 13 | 62 | 32 | 66 | 9 | 7 | R | R | 6-0 | 198 | 9-10-66 | 1988 | Douglas, Ga. |
| Paredes, Johnny | .257 | 133 | 471 | 70 | 121 | 19 | 4 | 2 | 41 | 47 | 45 | 21 | 13 | R | R | 5-11 | 175 | 9-2-62 | 1982 | Maracaibo, Venez. |
| Pevey, Marty | .274 | 62 | 175 | 11 | 48 | 8 | 1 | 2 | 18 | 16 | 36 | 3 | 3 | L | R | 6-1 | 190 | 9-18-61 | 1982 | Savannah, Ga. |
| Reimink, Bob | .197 | 66 | 193 | 18 | 38 | 7 | 0 | 1 | 10 | 23 | 41 | 4 | 0 | S | R | 6-0 | 180 | 6-28-67 | 1989 | Hamilton, Mich. |
| Robertson, Rod | .235 | 121 | 409 | 54 | 96 | 13 | 2 | 12 | 48 | 27 | 76 | 15 | 7 | S | R | 5-9 | 175 | 1-16-68 | 1986 | Orange, Texas |
| Rowland, Rich | .268 | 96 | 325 | 58 | 87 | 24 | 2 | 21 | 59 | 51 | 72 | 1 | 6 | R | R | 6-1 | 210 | 2-25-67 | 1988 | Cloverdale, Calif. |
| Sellers, Rick | .283 | 18 | 46 | 6 | 13 | 4 | 1 | 2 | 7 | 3 | 8 | 0 | 1 | R | R | 6-0 | 215 | 2-22-67 | 1989 | Remus, Mich. |
| Williams, Ted | .247 | 68 | 194 | 21 | 48 | 7 | 3 | 1 | 16 | 10 | 45 | 22 | 5 | S | R | 6-1 | 160 | 2-23-65 | 1986 | Columbus, Miss. |

| PITCHING | W | L | ERA | G | GS | CG | SV | IP | H | R | ER | BB | SO | B | T | HT | WT | DOB | 1st Yr | Resides |
|---|---|---|---|---|---|---|---|---|---|---|---|---|---|---|---|---|---|---|---|---|
| Bergman, Sean | 8 | 9 | 4.38 | 19 | 19 | 3 | 0 | 117 | 124 | 62 | 57 | 53 | 91 | R | R | 6-4 | 205 | 4-11-70 | 1991 | Joliet, Ill. |
| Blomdahl, Ben | 3 | 4 | 4.88 | 11 | 10 | 0 | 0 | 63 | 67 | 34 | 34 | 19 | 27 | R | R | 6-2 | 185 | 12-30-70 | 1991 | Riverside, Calif. |
| Carlyle, Kenny | 2 | 10 | 6.42 | 15 | 14 | 1 | 0 | 76 | 88 | 59 | 54 | 36 | 43 | R | R | 6-1 | 185 | 4-16-69 | 1992 | Cordova, Tenn. |
| Corbett, Sherm | 0 | 0 | 4.76 | 5 | 0 | 0 | 0 | 6 | 6 | 3 | 3 | 2 | 6 | L | L | 6-4 | 203 | 11-3-62 | 1984 | Converse, Texas |
| DeSilva, John | 7 | 10 | 3.69 | 25 | 24 | 1 | 0 | 161 | 145 | 73 | 66 | 60 | 136 | R | R | 6-0 | 193 | 9-30-67 | 1989 | Fort Bragg, Calif. |
| Fraser, Willie | 10 | 7 | 4.69 | 53 | 1 | 0 | 8 | 71 | 79 | 44 | 37 | 24 | 63 | R | R | 6-1 | 206 | 5-26-64 | 1985 | Newburgh, N.Y. |
| Gardiner, Mike | 0 | 1 | 5.40 | 4 | 0 | 0 | 1 | 5 | 6 | 3 | 3 | 2 | 10 | R | R | 6-0 | 185 | 10-19-65 | 1987 | Sarnia, Ontario |
| 2-team (5 Ottawa) | 1 | 2 | 2.70 | 9 | 3 | 0 | 1 | 30 | 23 | 11 | 9 | 11 | 35 | | | | | | | |
| Gohr, Greg | 3 | 10 | 5.80 | 18 | 17 | 2 | 0 | 107 | 127 | 74 | 69 | 38 | 77 | R | R | 6-3 | 205 | 10-29-67 | 1989 | Campbell, Calif. |
| Gomez, Henrique | 1 | 1 | 6.61 | 6 | 2 | 1 | 0 | 16 | 21 | 12 | 12 | 4 | 15 | R | R | 6-3 | 170 | 4-14-68 | 1986 | Maracay, Venez. |
| Gonzales, Frank | 6 | 3 | 3.95 | 29 | 15 | 2 | 0 | 109 | 116 | 56 | 48 | 37 | 71 | R | L | 6-0 | 185 | 3-12-68 | 1989 | La Junta, Colo. |
| Grater, Mark | 1 | 2 | 8.13 | 28 | 0 | 0 | 4 | 31 | 42 | 31 | 28 | 12 | 31 | R | R | 5-10 | 205 | 1-19-64 | 1986 | Monaca, Pa. |
| Groom, Buddy | 9 | 3 | 2.74 | 16 | 15 | 0 | 0 | 102 | 98 | 34 | 31 | 30 | 78 | L | L | 6-2 | 200 | 7-10-65 | 1987 | Red Oak, Texas |
| Gullickson, Bill | 1 | 0 | 9.00 | 1 | 1 | 0 | 0 | 6 | 8 | 6 | 6 | 0 | 4 | R | R | 6-3 | 225 | 2-20-59 | 1977 | Brentwood, Conn. |
| Haas, David | 0 | 0 | 18.69 | 2 | 2 | 0 | 0 | 4 | 8 | 9 | 9 | 6 | 2 | R | R | 6-1 | 200 | 10-19-65 | 1988 | Wichita, Kan. |
| Hudek, John | 1 | 3 | 5.82 | 16 | 5 | 0 | 0 | 39 | 44 | 26 | 25 | 22 | 32 | S | R | 6-1 | 200 | 8-8-66 | 1988 | Orlando, Fla. |
| Johnson, Dave | 1 | 0 | 0.00 | 9 | 0 | 0 | 0 | 17 | 6 | 0 | 0 | 5 | 8 | R | R | 5-11 | 180 | 10-24-59 | 1982 | Middle River, Md. |
| Kiely, John | 3 | 4 | 3.88 | 37 | 0 | 0 | 4 | 58 | 65 | 34 | 25 | 25 | 48 | R | R | 6-3 | 210 | 10-4-64 | 1988 | Brockton, Mass. |
| Knudsen, Kurt | 2 | 2 | 3.78 | 23 | 0 | 0 | 6 | 33 | 24 | 15 | 14 | 11 | 39 | R | R | 6-2 | 184 | 2-20-67 | 1988 | Carmichael, Calif. |
| Krueger, Bill | 1 | 0 | 1.59 | 3 | 3 | 0 | 0 | 11 | 11 | 2 | 2 | 3 | 8 | L | L | 6-5 | 205 | 4-24-58 | 1980 | Seattle, Wash. |
| Lira, Felipe | 1 | 2 | 4.60 | 5 | 5 | 0 | 0 | 31 | 32 | 18 | 16 | 11 | 23 | R | R | 6-0 | 170 | 4-26-72 | 1990 | Miranda, Venez. |
| Lumley, Mike | 0 | 2 | 6.57 | 6 | 2 | 0 | 0 | 12 | 13 | 10 | 9 | 8 | 7 | R | R | 6-1 | 185 | 1-29-67 | 1988 | Lucan, Ontario |
| Rightnowar, Ron | 2 | 2 | 3.55 | 22 | 6 | 0 | 1 | 58 | 57 | 32 | 23 | 19 | 32 | R | R | 6-0 | 190 | 9-5-64 | 1987 | Toledo, Ohio |
| Ritchie, Wally | 1 | 0 | 4.76 | 62 | 0 | 0 | 4 | 45 | 44 | 26 | 24 | 15 | 29 | L | L | 6-2 | 180 | 7-12-65 | 1985 | Glendale, Calif. |
| Warren, Brian | 2 | 2 | 3.44 | 24 | 1 | 0 | 0 | 37 | 40 | 17 | 14 | 11 | 26 | R | R | 6-0 | 170 | 4-26-67 | 1990 | Bridgewater, Mass. |

### FIELDING

| Catcher | PCT | G | PO | A | E | DP |
|---|---|---|---|---|---|---|
| Pevey | .985 | 53 | 298 | 25 | 5 | 4 |
| Rowland | .988 | 88 | 569 | 64 | 8 | 6 |
| Sellers | 1.000 | 14 | 74 | 7 | 0 | 2 |

| First Base | PCT | G | PO | A | E | DP |
|---|---|---|---|---|---|---|
| Brogna | .992 | 116 | 937 | 97 | 8 | 102 |
| Cruz | .993 | 28 | 268 | 27 | 2 | 23 |
| Hare | 1.000 | 2 | 1 | 0 | 0 | 0 |

| Second Base | PCT | G | PO | A | E | DP |
|---|---|---|---|---|---|---|
| Paredes | .980 | 132 | 270 | 369 | 13 | 91 |

| | PCT | G | PO | A | E | DP |
|---|---|---|---|---|---|---|
| Robertson | .886 | 14 | 21 | 41 | 8 | 11 |

| Third Base | PCT | G | PO | A | E | DP |
|---|---|---|---|---|---|---|
| Ingram | .000 | 1 | 0 | 0 | 0 | 0 |
| Pevey | 1.000 | 1 | 1 | 0 | 0 | 0 |
| Reimink | .924 | 58 | 30 | 92 | 10 | 6 |
| Robertson | .930 | 90 | 59 | 154 | 16 | 21 |

| Shortstop | PCT | G | PO | A | E | DP |
|---|---|---|---|---|---|---|
| Givens | .957 | 43 | 57 | 119 | 8 | 23 |
| Gomez | .961 | 87 | 133 | 261 | 16 | 57 |

| | PCT | G | PO | A | E | DP |
|---|---|---|---|---|---|---|
| Robertson | .984 | 15 | 18 | 42 | 1 | 7 |

| Outfield | PCT | G | PO | A | E | DP |
|---|---|---|---|---|---|---|
| Cangelosi | .973 | 112 | 251 | 5 | 7 | 0 |
| Gladden | .846 | 7 | 11 | 0 | 2 | 0 |
| Hare | .975 | 106 | 189 | 5 | 5 | 1 |
| Hurst | .933 | 55 | 93 | 5 | 7 | 1 |
| Ingram | .988 | 104 | 167 | 2 | 2 | 0 |
| Pevey | .714 | 4 | 5 | 0 | 2 | 0 |
| Robertson | .875 | 5 | 7 | 0 | 1 | 0 |
| Williams | .941 | 60 | 94 | 2 | 6 | 0 |

# LONDON
## EASTERN LEAGUE

**AA**

| BATTING | AVG | G | AB | R | H | 2B | 3B | HR | RBI | BB | SO | SB | CS | B | T | HT | WT | DOB | 1st Yr | Resides |
|---|---|---|---|---|---|---|---|---|---|---|---|---|---|---|---|---|---|---|---|---|
| Alder, Jimmy, 3b-of | .193 | 42 | 119 | 8 | 23 | 7 | 1 | 0 | 7 | 11 | 42 | 2 | 1 | R | R | 6-4 | 205 | 5-11-72 | 1990 | Kingsport, Tenn. |
| Bautista, Danny, of | .285 | 117 | 424 | 55 | 121 | 21 | 1 | 6 | 48 | 32 | 69 | 28 | 12 | R | R | 5-11 | 170 | 5-24-72 | 1989 | Santo Domingo, D.R. |
| Cornelius, Brian, of | .262 | 64 | 229 | 21 | 60 | 11 | 0 | 4 | 24 | 23 | 36 | 1 | 4 | L | R | 6-0 | 170 | 2-16-67 | 1989 | Homestead, Fla. |
| Decillis, Dean, dh-3b | .293 | 54 | 208 | 28 | 61 | 13 | 0 | 5 | 26 | 25 | 22 | 1 | 0 | R | R | 5-11 | 180 | 7-9-67 | 1987 | Pembroke Pines, Fla. |
| Givens, Jim, ss | .263 | 82 | 262 | 24 | 69 | 8 | 3 | 3 | 28 | 16 | 45 | 17 | 8 | S | R | 6-1 | 177 | 11-11-67 | 1991 | Findlay, Ohio |
| Gonzalez, Pete, c | .156 | 25 | 64 | 5 | 10 | 3 | 0 | 0 | 6 | 14 | 12 | 0 | 0 | R | R | 6-0 | 185 | 11-24-69 | 1989 | Hialeah, Fla. |
| Higginson, Bob, of | .308 | 63 | 224 | 25 | 69 | 15 | 4 | 4 | 35 | 19 | 37 | 3 | 4 | L | R | 5-11 | 180 | 8-18-70 | 1992 | Philadelphia, Pa. |
| Mendenhall, Kirk, ss-3b | .204 | 97 | 275 | 41 | 56 | 5 | 1 | 1 | 18 | 30 | 45 | 21 | 4 | R | R | 5-9 | 160 | 9-17-67 | 1990 | Rochester, Ill. |
| Milne, Darren, dh | .050 | 5 | 20 | 2 | 1 | 0 | 0 | 0 | 1 | 2 | 7 | 0 | 0 | R | R | 6-1 | 195 | 3-24-71 | 1992 | Sandy, Utah |
| Pemberton, Rudy, of | .276 | 124 | 471 | 70 | 130 | 22 | 4 | 15 | 67 | 24 | 80 | 14 | 12 | R | R | 6-1 | 185 | 12-17-69 | 1987 | San Pedro de Macoris, D.R. |
| Penn, Shannon, 2b | .260 | 128 | 493 | 78 | 128 | 13 | 6 | 0 | 36 | 54 | 95 | 53 | 17 | S | R | 5-10 | 155 | 9-11-69 | 1989 | Cincinnati, Ohio |
| Perona, Joe, c-1b | .269 | 102 | 349 | 34 | 94 | 17 | 2 | 5 | 29 | 28 | 56 | 2 | 5 | R | R | 6-0 | 190 | 2-8-70 | 1991 | Spring Valley, Ill. |
| Pratte, Evan, 3b-2b | .238 | 121 | 408 | 44 | 97 | 24 | 2 | 3 | 46 | 45 | 77 | 5 | 2 | S | R | 5-10 | 175 | 12-18-68 | 1991 | Ballwin, Mo. |
| Rendina, Mike, 1b | .282 | 135 | 475 | 59 | 134 | 30 | 1 | 10 | 77 | 55 | 96 | 8 | 4 | L | L | 6-4 | 200 | 9-28-70 | 1988 | El Cajon, Calif. |
| Saltzgaber, Brian, of | .212 | 87 | 241 | 28 | 51 | 9 | 1 | 2 | 17 | 41 | 59 | 13 | 3 | R | R | 5-11 | 175 | 3-31-68 | 1990 | Tekonsha, Mich. |
| Sellers, Rick, c-dh | .264 | 72 | 239 | 31 | 63 | 11 | 0 | 6 | 31 | 45 | 55 | 5 | 3 | R | R | 6-0 | 215 | 2-22-67 | 1989 | Remus, Mich. |
| Williams, Ted, of-dh | .240 | 32 | 125 | 17 | 30 | 8 | 0 | 0 | 9 | 9 | 21 | 10 | 5 | S | R | 6-1 | 160 | 2-23-65 | 1986 | Columbus, Miss. |

| PITCHING | W | L | ERA | G | GS | CG | SV | IP | H | R | ER | BB | SO | B | T | HT | WT | DOB | 1st Yr | Resides |
|---|---|---|---|---|---|---|---|---|---|---|---|---|---|---|---|---|---|---|---|---|
| Blomdahl, Ben | 6 | 6 | 3.71 | 17 | 17 | 3 | 0 | 119 | 108 | 58 | 49 | 42 | 72 | R | R | 6-2 | 185 | 12-30-70 | 1991 | Riverside, Calif. |
| Braley, Jeff | 1 | 2 | 4.73 | 9 | 0 | 0 | 2 | 13 | 19 | 10 | 7 | 6 | 6 | R | R | 6-2 | 200 | 8-1-67 | 1989 | Bay City, Mich. |
| Carlyle, Kenny | 4 | 6 | 3.69 | 12 | 12 | 1 | 0 | 78 | 72 | 40 | 32 | 35 | 50 | R | R | 6-1 | 185 | 4-16-69 | 1992 | Cordova, Tenn. |
| Edmondson, Brian | 0 | 4 | 6.26 | 5 | 5 | 1 | 0 | 23 | 30 | 23 | 16 | 13 | 17 | R | R | 6-2 | 165 | 1-29-73 | 1991 | Riverside, Calif. |
| Garcia, Mike | 1 | 0 | 5.56 | 6 | 0 | 0 | 0 | 11 | 12 | 8 | 7 | 6 | 12 | R | R | 6-2 | 195 | 5-11-68 | 1989 | Moreno Valley, Calif. |
| Gomez, Henrique | 4 | 3 | 3.53 | 29 | 6 | 0 | 1 | 71 | 56 | 30 | 28 | 27 | 67 | R | R | 6-3 | 170 | 4-14-68 | 1986 | Maracay, Venez. |
| Greene, Rick | 2 | 2 | 6.52 | 23 | 0 | 0 | 0 | 29 | 31 | 22 | 21 | 20 | 19 | R | R | 6-5 | 200 | 1-2-71 | 1992 | Miami, Fla. |
| Guilfoyle, Mike | 1 | 2 | 3.73 | 49 | 0 | 0 | 3 | 41 | 43 | 19 | 17 | 16 | 35 | L | L | 5-11 | 187 | 4-29-68 | 1990 | Bayonne, N.J. |
| Henry, Jim | 1 | 3 | 5.28 | 33 | 0 | 0 | 0 | 31 | 33 | 20 | 18 | 28 | 25 | L | L | 6-3 | 195 | 10-25-70 | 1990 | Forest Hill, Calif. |
| Kelley, Rich | 0 | 0 | 9.00 | 7 | 0 | 0 | 0 | 5 | 7 | 5 | 5 | 5 | 3 | L | L | 6-3 | 200 | 5-27-70 | 1991 | Scituate, Mass. |
| Lima, Jose | 8 | 13 | 4.07 | 27 | 27 | 2 | 0 | 177 | 160 | 96 | 80 | 59 | 138 | R | R | 6-2 | 170 | 9-30-72 | 1993 | Santiago, D.R. |
| Lira, Felipe | 10 | 4 | 3.38 | 22 | 22 | 2 | 0 | 152 | 157 | 63 | 57 | 39 | 122 | R | R | 6-0 | 170 | 4-26-72 | 1990 | Miranda, Venez. |
| Lumley, Mike | 4 | 2 | 4.57 | 26 | 1 | 0 | 0 | 41 | 32 | 22 | 21 | 20 | 26 | R | R | 6-1 | 185 | 1-29-67 | 1988 | Lucan, Ontario |
| Pfaff, Jason | 6 | 9 | 5.73 | 23 | 23 | 1 | 0 | 132 | 176 | 90 | 84 | 45 | 62 | R | R | 6-2 | 205 | 10-19-69 | 1991 | Cincinnati, Ohio |
| Schwarber, Tom | 5 | 2 | 5.03 | 48 | 0 | 0 | 16 | 54 | 54 | 34 | 30 | 28 | 58 | R | R | 6-4 | 205 | 12-19-67 | 1991 | Cincinnati, Ohio |
| Stidham, Phil | 2 | 2 | 2.38 | 33 | 0 | 0 | 2 | 34 | 40 | 18 | 9 | 19 | 39 | R | R | 6-0 | 170 | 11-13-68 | 1991 | Tulsa, Okla. |
| Thompson, Justin | 3 | 6 | 4.09 | 14 | 14 | 1 | 0 | 84 | 96 | 51 | 38 | 37 | 72 | L | L | 6-3 | 175 | 3-8-73 | 1991 | Spring, Texas |
| Undorf, Bob | 0 | 1 | 3.58 | 19 | 0 | 0 | 1 | 33 | 37 | 17 | 13 | 6 | 15 | R | R | 6-2 | 220 | 9-21-67 | 1990 | Tampa, Fla. |
| Warren, Brian | 3 | 3 | 5.83 | 22 | 1 | 0 | 5 | 29 | 36 | 19 | 19 | 9 | 21 | R | R | 6-0 | 170 | 4-26-67 | 1990 | Bridgewater, Mass. |
| Wolf, Steve | 2 | 5 | 4.99 | 14 | 10 | 1 | 0 | 61 | 56 | 39 | 34 | 45 | 55 | R | R | 6-2 | 200 | 12-16-68 | 1990 | Lodi, Calif. |

# TIGERS: ORGANIZATION LEADERS

## MAJOR LEAGUERS

**BATTING**
| *AVG | Alan Trammell | .329 |
|---|---|---|
| R | Tony Phillips | 113 |
| H | Travis Fryman | 182 |
| TB | Travis Fryman | 295 |
| 2B | Travis Fryman | 37 |
| 3B | Kirk Gibson | 6 |
| HR | Mickey Tettleton | 32 |
| RBI | Cecil Fielder | 117 |
| BB | Tony Phillips | 132 |
| SO | Mickey Tettleton | 139 |
| SB | Tony Phillips | 16 |

**PITCHING**
| W | John Doherty | 14 |
|---|---|---|
| L | John Doherty | 11 |
| #ERA | Bill Krueger | 3.40 |
| G | Bob MacDonald | 68 |
| CG | Mike Moore | 4 |
| SV | Mike Henneman | 24 |
| IP | Mike Moore | 214 |
| BB | Mike Moore | 89 |
| SO | David Wells | 139 |

**Mickey Tettleton**
Third straight 30-homer season

R&R SPORTS GROUP

## MINOR LEAGUERS

**BATTING**
| *AVG | Mike Wiseley, Niagara Falls | .321 |
|---|---|---|
| R | Tim Thomas, Fayetteville-Lakeland | 85 |
| H | Brian Dubose, Lakeland | 140 |
| TB | Shawn Hare, Toledo | 219 |
| 2B | Tim Thomas, Fayetteville-Lakeland | 32 |
| 3B | Two tied at | 11 |
| HR | Rich Rowland, Toledo | 21 |
| RBI | Matt Evans, Fayetteville | 94 |
| BB | Tim Thomas, Fayetteville-Lakeland | 90 |
| SO | Keith Kimsey, Fayetteville | 168 |
| SB | Shannon Penn, London | 53 |

**PITCHING**
| W | Clint Sodowsky, Fayetteville | 14 |
|---|---|---|
| L | Kenny Carlyle, Toledo-London | 16 |
| #ERA | John Rosengren, Niagara Falls | 2.41 |
| G | Wally Ritchie, Toledo | 62 |
| CG | Two tied at | 3 |
| SV | Tom Schwarber, London | 16 |
| IP | Felipe Lira, London-Toledo | 183 |
| BB | Kenny Carlyle, Toledo-London | 71 |
| SO | Felipe Lira, London-Toledo | 145 |

*Minimum 250 At-Bats   #Minimum 75 Innings

# FLORIDA STATE LEAGUE

| BATTING | AVG | G | AB | R | H | 2B | 3B | HR | RBI | BB | SO | SB | CS | B | T | HT | WT | DOB | 1st Yr | Resides |
|---|---|---|---|---|---|---|---|---|---|---|---|---|---|---|---|---|---|---|---|---|
| Alder, Jimmy, 3b .......... | .200 | 41 | 135 | 13 | 27 | 6 | 1 | 4 | 16 | 14 | 39 | 2 | 2 | R | R | 6-4 | 205 | 5-11-72 | 1990 | Kingsport, Tenn. |
| Ayala, Moises, c .......... | .500 | 3 | 2 | 1 | 1 | 0 | 0 | 1 | 4 | 1 | 0 | 0 | 0 | R | R | 6-2 | 195 | 12-28-73 | 1992 | Sabana Grande, P.R. |
| Burguillos, Carlos, of ..... | .286 | 15 | 28 | 6 | 8 | 1 | 0 | 0 | 5 | 7 | 2 | 1 | 1 | R | R | 6-0 | 180 | 10-23-71 | 1991 | Caracas, Venez. |
| Clark, Tony, of-dh ......... | .265 | 36 | 117 | 14 | 31 | 4 | 1 | 1 | 22 | 18 | 32 | 0 | 1 | S | R | 6-8 | 205 | 6-15-72 | 1990 | El Cajon, Calif. |
| DuBose, Brian, 1b ......... | .313 | 122 | 448 | 74 | 140 | 27 | 11 | 8 | 68 | 49 | 97 | 18 | 18 | L | R | 6-3 | 210 | 5-17-71 | 1990 | Detroit, Mich. |
| Facione, Chris, of ......... | .333 | 3 | 6 | 1 | 2 | 0 | 1 | 0 | 1 | 0 | 2 | 0 | 0 | R | R | 6-3 | 190 | 9-21-70 | 1993 | Millbrae, Calif. |
| Fermin, Carlos, 3b-ss ..... | .252 | 86 | 278 | 25 | 70 | 11 | 1 | 0 | 19 | 25 | 38 | 3 | 2 | R | R | 5-9 | 140 | 7-12-73 | 1990 | Mao Valverde, D.R. |
| Gonzalez, Pedro, c......... | .250 | 63 | 200 | 20 | 50 | 4 | 1 | 2 | 25 | 31 | 28 | 7 | 2 | R | R | 6-0 | 185 | 11-24-69 | 1989 | Hialeah, Fla. |
| Higginson, Bob, of ........ | .300 | 61 | 223 | 42 | 67 | 11 | 7 | 3 | 25 | 40 | 31 | 8 | 3 | L | R | 5-11 | 180 | 8-18-70 | 1992 | Philadelphia, Pa. |
| Killen, Brent, 3b .......... | .243 | 45 | 136 | 17 | 33 | 10 | 0 | 1 | 18 | 36 | 22 | 2 | 3 | L | R | 6-1 | 225 | 5-25-70 | 1992 | St. Paul, Minn. |
| Lamar, Johnny, of ........ | .269 | 102 | 346 | 43 | 93 | 16 | 6 | 4 | 37 | 35 | 67 | 10 | 2 | L | R | 6-3 | 204 | 5-29-70 | 1992 | Indianapolis, Ind. |
| Landry, Lonny, dh-of ...... | .500 | 2 | 4 | 0 | 2 | 2 | 0 | 0 | 1 | 0 | 1 | 0 | 0 | R | R | 5-11 | 185 | 11-2-72 | 1993 | Broussard, La. |
| Marrero, Kenny, c.......... | .250 | 9 | 8 | 0 | 2 | 0 | 0 | 0 | 2 | 2 | 0 | 0 | 0 | R | R | 6-3 | 205 | 5-13-70 | 1991 | Dorado, P.R. |
| Mashore, Justin, of ....... | .256 | 118 | 442 | 64 | 113 | 11 | 4 | 3 | 30 | 37 | 92 | 26 | 13 | R | R | 5-9 | 190 | 2-14-72 | 1991 | Concord, Calif. |
| McConnell, Tim, c-dh ..... | .273 | 81 | 253 | 34 | 69 | 16 | 3 | 3 | 43 | 41 | 48 | 9 | 3 | R | R | 5-11 | 195 | 10-3-68 | 1992 | Marine City, Mich. |
| Milne, Darren, of.......... | .196 | 71 | 204 | 19 | 40 | 6 | 1 | 5 | 18 | 23 | 33 | 6 | 5 | R | R | 6-1 | 195 | 3-24-71 | 1992 | Sandy, Utah |
| Moreno, Jorge, dh......... | .000 | 2 | 1 | 0 | 0 | 0 | 0 | 0 | 0 | 0 | 1 | 0 | 0 | S | R | 6-2 | 150 | 8-19-72 | 1989 | Santo Domingo, D.R. |
| Morgan, Kevin, ss ........ | .237 | 112 | 417 | 45 | 99 | 12 | 2 | 2 | 34 | 32 | 84 | 9 | 7 | R | R | 6-1 | 170 | 12-3-70 | 1991 | Duson, La. |
| O'Neal, Kelley, 2b ........ | .275 | 117 | 436 | 66 | 120 | 14 | 3 | 3 | 36 | 48 | 73 | 28 | 10 | L | R | 5-10 | 160 | 12-19-70 | 1989 | Belleville, Mich. |
| Rea, Clarke, c-dh ......... | .141 | 24 | 71 | 4 | 10 | 2 | 0 | 0 | 8 | 10 | 21 | 1 | 0 | L | R | 6-2 | 190 | 1-9-70 | 1991 | Scottsdale, Ariz. |
| Rodriguez, Adam, c ....... | .167 | 3 | 6 | 4 | 1 | 0 | 0 | 1 | 2 | 3 | 2 | 3 | 0 | R | R | 5-10 | 190 | 3-16-71 | 1993 | Tucson, Ariz. |
| Ruff, Dan, of ............. | .284 | 101 | 349 | 47 | 99 | 17 | 6 | 9 | 65 | 36 | 65 | 1 | 5 | L | R | 6-1 | 195 | 1-2-69 | 1991 | Bremen, Ohio |
| Thomas, Tim, 3b-2b ....... | .167 | 15 | 48 | 5 | 8 | 1 | 1 | 0 | 2 | 8 | 13 | 1 | 1 | R | R | 6-2 | 185 | 7-21-69 | 1992 | St. Paul, Minn. |
| Yelton, Rob, of............ | .300 | 24 | 90 | 14 | 27 | 4 | 0 | 0 | 13 | 8 | 9 | 0 | 2 | R | R | 5-11 | 180 | 11-14-69 | 1991 | Elsmere, Ky. |

| PITCHING | W | L | ERA | G | GS | CG | SV | IP | H | R | ER | BB | SO | B | T | HT | WT | DOB | 1st Yr | Resides |
|---|---|---|---|---|---|---|---|---|---|---|---|---|---|---|---|---|---|---|---|---|
| Ahearne, Pat................ | 6 | 15 | 4.46 | 25 | 24 | 2 | 0 | 147 | 160 | 87 | 73 | 48 | 51 | R | R | 6-3 | 195 | 12-10-69 | 1992 | Atascadero, Calif. |
| Berlin, Mike ................ | 1 | 5 | 9.69 | 9 | 8 | 1 | 0 | 39 | 62 | 45 | 42 | 23 | 18 | R | R | 6-1 | 185 | 2-14-71 | 1992 | Moundsville, W.Va. |
| Coppeta, Greg ............. | 3 | 4 | 2.41 | 36 | 3 | 0 | 1 | 67 | 63 | 20 | 18 | 21 | 37 | L | L | 6-2 | 205 | 8-27-69 | 1990 | Methuen, Mass. |
| Edmondson, Brian ......... | 8 | 5 | 2.99 | 19 | 19 | 1 | 0 | 114 | 115 | 44 | 38 | 43 | 64 | R | R | 6-5 | 200 | 1-2-71 | 1992 | Miami, Fla. |
| Greene, Rick............... | 2 | 3 | 6.20 | 26 | 0 | 0 | 2 | 41 | 57 | 28 | 28 | 16 | 32 | R | R | 6-5 | 200 | 1-29-73 | 1991 | Riverside, Calif. |
| Grimm, John ............... | 2 | 1 | 2.45 | 16 | 0 | 0 | 3 | 18 | 12 | 7 | 5 | 11 | 17 | R | R | 5-10 | 175 | 9-13-70 | 1992 | Reynoldsburg, Ohio |
| Guilfoyle, Mike ........... | 0 | 0 | 0.96 | 9 | 0 | 0 | 5 | 9 | 5 | 1 | 1 | 3 | 10 | L | L | 5-11 | 187 | 4-29-68 | 1990 | Bayonne, N.J. |
| Gullickson, Bill ........... | 1 | 0 | 6.87 | 5 | 5 | 0 | 0 | 18 | 24 | 14 | 14 | 4 | 9 | R | R | 6-3 | 200 | 2-20-59 | 1977 | Brentwood, Tenn. |
| Henry, Jim................. | 1 | 1 | 5.12 | 4 | 3 | 0 | 0 | 19 | 24 | 13 | 11 | 5 | 14 | L | L | 6-3 | 195 | 10-25-70 | 1990 | Forest Hill, Calif. |
| Kelley, Rich............... | 4 | 5 | 3.05 | 26 | 9 | 0 | 2 | 86 | 78 | 31 | 29 | 31 | 45 | L | L | 6-3 | 200 | 5-27-70 | 1991 | Scituate, Mass. |
| Kosenski, John ........... | 3 | 3 | 2.74 | 35 | 2 | 0 | 3 | 66 | 45 | 24 | 20 | 43 | 42 | R | R | 6-5 | 195 | 1-28-69 | 1991 | Boulder, Colo. |
| Kostich, Bill .............. | 0 | 1 | 2.57 | 11 | 0 | 0 | 0 | 21 | 29 | 14 | 6 | 6 | 18 | L | L | 6-0 | 170 | 2-1-71 | 1989 | Taylor, Mich. |
| Mendenhall, Casey........ | 9 | 5 | 3.59 | 15 | 15 | 1 | 0 | 78 | 88 | 38 | 31 | 20 | 49 | R | R | 6-2 | 175 | 9-2-70 | 1992 | Denver, Colo. |
| Mysel, David .............. | 4 | 5 | 3.60 | 12 | 12 | 1 | 0 | 70 | 59 | 36 | 28 | 28 | 46 | R | R | 6-5 | 210 | 4-13-71 | 1992 | Hummelstown, Pa. |
| Pettiford, Cecil ........... | 2 | 1 | 2.32 | 32 | 2 | 0 | 1 | 74 | 58 | 25 | 19 | 32 | 71 | R | R | 6-3 | 176 | 6-26-68 | 1988 | Chicago, Ill. |
| Raffo, Greg ............... | 3 | 2 | 1.73 | 35 | 0 | 0 | 2 | 52 | 36 | 13 | 10 | 19 | 39 | R | R | 6-5 | 190 | 9-1-68 | 1991 | Jasper, Tenn. |
| Stidham, Phil.............. | 2 | 1 | 1.52 | 25 | 0 | 0 | 9 | 30 | 22 | 6 | 5 | 9 | 24 | R | R | 6-0 | 170 | 11-13-68 | 1991 | Tulsa, Okla. |
| Thompson, Justin ......... | 4 | 4 | 3.56 | 11 | 11 | 0 | 0 | 56 | 65 | 25 | 22 | 16 | 46 | L | L | 6-3 | 175 | 3-8-73 | 1991 | Spring, Texas |
| Walsh, Dennis ............ | 0 | 0 | 5.56 | 7 | 0 | 0 | 0 | 11 | 11 | 9 | 7 | 4 | 3 | L | L | 6-2 | 185 | 4-5-69 | 1991 | Baltimore, Md. |
| Withem, Shannon ......... | 10 | 2 | 3.42 | 16 | 16 | 2 | 0 | 113 | 108 | 47 | 43 | 24 | 62 | R | R | 6-3 | 190 | 9-21-72 | 1990 | Ypsilanti, Mich. |

# SOUTH ATLANTIC LEAGUE

| BATTING | AVG | G | AB | R | H | 2B | 3B | HR | RBI | BB | SO | SB | CS | B | T | HT | WT | DOB | 1st Yr | Resides |
|---|---|---|---|---|---|---|---|---|---|---|---|---|---|---|---|---|---|---|---|---|
| Bell, Curt, c................. | .143 | 4 | 14 | 0 | 2 | 0 | 0 | 0 | 1 | 1 | 5 | 0 | 0 | R | R | 5-11 | 185 | 3-4-72 | 1992 | West Palm Beach, Fla. |
| Brock, Tarrik, of............ | .215 | 116 | 427 | 60 | 92 | 8 | 4 | 3 | 47 | 54 | 108 | 25 | 16 | L | L | 6-3 | 170 | 12-25-73 | 1991 | Hawthorne, Calif. |
| Burguillos, Carlos of ..... | .292 | 68 | 240 | 45 | 70 | 11 | 6 | 3 | 40 | 30 | 26 | 13 | 6 | R | R | 6-0 | 180 | 10-23-71 | 1991 | Caracas, Venez. |
| DeJesus, Malvin, 2b....... | .119 | 17 | 59 | 8 | 7 | 0 | 0 | 0 | 2 | 7 | 8 | 2 | 1 | R | R | 5-9 | 160 | 9-16-71 | 1992 | Carolina, P.R. |
| Dietz, Steve, 2b-ss ....... | .181 | 36 | 105 | 14 | 19 | 3 | 1 | 0 | 13 | 18 | 17 | 2 | 4 | S | R | 5-10 | 155 | 8-1-70 | 1993 | La Mesa, Calif. |
| Evans, Matt, dh-1b ....... | .266 | 138 | 515 | 76 | 137 | 28 | 6 | 17 | 94 | 88 | 125 | 5 | 3 | L | L | 6-4 | 230 | 7-30-71 | 1992 | Scottsdale, Ariz. |
| Feeley, Peter, 3b-of....... | .251 | 98 | 323 | 33 | 81 | 18 | 3 | 2 | 36 | 49 | 76 | 6 | 5 | R | R | 6-2 | 175 | 11-4-69 | 1991 | North Reading, Mass. |
| Killen, Brent, 3b .......... | .269 | 88 | 223 | 42 | 60 | 15 | 2 | 6 | 41 | 45 | 45 | 1 | 4 | L | R | 6-1 | 225 | 5-25-70 | 1992 | St. Paul, Minn. |
| Kimsey, Keith, of .......... | .245 | 120 | 469 | 79 | 115 | 19 | 6 | 19 | 85 | 50 | 168 | 2 | 0 | R | R | 6-7 | 205 | 8-15-72 | 1991 | Lakeland, Fla. |
| Lidle, Kevin, c ............ | .213 | 58 | 197 | 29 | 42 | 14 | 1 | 5 | 25 | 34 | 42 | 2 | 0 | R | R | 5-11 | 170 | 3-22-72 | 1992 | West Covina, Calif. |
| Marine, Del, c-3b.......... | .280 | 25 | 75 | 4 | 21 | 7 | 0 | 0 | 4 | 16 | 25 | 1 | 0 | R | R | 6-0 | 195 | 10-18-71 | 1992 | Woodland Hills, Calif. |

# TIGERS: MOST COMMON LINEUPS

| | Detroit | Toledo | London | Lakeland | Fayetteville |
|---|---|---|---|---|---|
| | Majors | AAA | AA | A | A |
| C | Chad Kreuter (119) | Rich Rowland (88) | Joe Perona (70) | Pedro Gonzalez (60) | Kevin Lidle (57) |
| 1B | Cecil Fielder (119) | Rico Brogna (116) | Mike Rendina (132) | Brian Dubose (122) | Corey Parker (81) |
| 2B | Lou Whitaker (110) | Johnny Paredes (132) | Shannon Penn (110) | Kelley O'Neal (114) | Tim Thomas (104) |
| 3B | Travis Fryman (69) | Rod Robertson (90) | Evan Pratte (74) | Carlos Fermin (52) | Peter Feeley (74) |
| SS | Travis Fryman (81) | Chris Gomez (87) | Jim Givens (79) | Kevin Morgan (110) | Yuri Sanchez (110) |
| OF | Tony Phillips (108) | John Cangelosi (112) | Rudy Pemberton (115) | Justin Mashore (118) | Roberto Rojas (119) |
| | Rob Deer (86) | Shawn Hare (105) | Danny Bautista (108) | Johnny Lamar (74) | Tarrik Brock (114) |
| | Dan Gladden (86) | Riccardo Ingram (101) | Brian Saltzgaber (72) | Dan Ruff (67) | Keith Kimsey (108) |
| DH | Kirk Gibson (76) | Ivan Cruz (83) | Dean Decillis (29) | Tim McConnell (27) | Matt Evans (79) |
| SP | Mike Moore (36) | John DeSilva (24) | Jose Lima (27) | Pat Ahearne (24) | Trever Miller (28) |
| RP | Bob MacDonald (68) | Wally Ritchie (62) | Mike Guilfoyle (49) | Greg Raffo (35) | Rick Navarro (41) |
| | Full-season farm clubs only | No. of games at position in parenthesis | | | |

# TIGERS TOP 10 PROSPECTS

How the Tigers Top 10 prospects, as judged by Baseball America prior to the 1993 season, fared in 1993:

| Player, Pos. | Club (Class) | AVG | AB | H | HR | RBI | SB |
|---|---|---|---|---|---|---|---|
| 2. Rico Brogna, 1b | Toledo (AAA) | .273 | 483 | 132 | 11 | 59 | 7 |
| 5. Ivan Cruz, 1b | Toledo (AAA) | .226 | 402 | 91 | 13 | 50 | 1 |
| 9. Chris Gomez, ss | Toledo (AAA) | .245 | 277 | 68 | 0 | 20 | 6 |
|  | Detroit | .250 | 128 | 32 | 0 | 11 | 2 |
| 10. Daniel Bautista, of | London (AA) | .285 | 424 | 121 | 6 | 48 | 28 |
|  | Detroit | .311 | 61 | 19 | 1 | 9 | 3 |

| Player, Pos. | Club (Class) | W | L | ERA | IP | H | BB | SO |
|---|---|---|---|---|---|---|---|---|
| 1. Greg Gohr, rhp | Toledo (AAA) | 3 | 10 | 5.80 | 107 | 127 | 38 | 77 |
|  | Detroit | 0 | 0 | 5.96 | 23 | 26 | 14 | 23 |
| 3. J. Thompson, lhp | Lakeland (A) | 4 | 4 | 3.56 | 56 | 65 | 16 | 46 |
|  | London (AA) | 4 | 4 | 4.09 | 84 | 96 | 37 | 72 |
| 4. Sean Bergman, rhp | Toledo (AAA) | 8 | 9 | 4.38 | 117 | 124 | 53 | 91 |
|  | Detroit | 1 | 4 | 5.67 | 40 | 47 | 23 | 19 |
| 6. Rick Greene, rhp | Lakeland (A) | 2 | 3 | 6.20 | 41 | 57 | 16 | 32 |
|  | London (AA) | 2 | 2 | 6.52 | 29 | 31 | 20 | 19 |
| 7. Ben Blomdahl, rhp | London (AA) | 6 | 3 | 3.71 | 119 | 108 | 42 | 72 |
|  | Toledo (AAA) | 3 | 4 | 4.88 | 63 | 67 | 19 | 27 |
| 8. Ken Carlyle, rhp | London (AA) | 4 | 6 | 3.69 | 78 | 72 | 35 | 50 |
|  | Toledo (AAA) | 2 | 10 | 6.42 | 76 | 88 | 36 | 43 |

**Greg Gohr**
3-10 at Toledo

| BATTING | AVG | G | AB | R | H | 2B | 3B | HR | RBI | BB | SO | SB | CS | B | T | HT | WT | DOB | 1st Yr | Resides |
|---|---|---|---|---|---|---|---|---|---|---|---|---|---|---|---|---|---|---|---|---|
| Moreno, Jorge, of | .227 | 17 | 66 | 7 | 15 | 0 | 0 | 1 | 8 | 3 | 18 | 1 | 2 | S | R | 6-2 | 150 | 8-19-72 | 1989 | Santo Domingo, D.R. |
| Parker, Corey, 1b | .225 | 110 | 377 | 48 | 85 | 20 | 2 | 4 | 52 | 66 | 70 | 3 | 6 | L | L | 6-3 | 180 | 4-17-71 | 1992 | Tustin, Calif. |
| Rea, Clarke, c | .168 | 27 | 95 | 9 | 16 | 2 | 0 | 1 | 8 | 14 | 18 | 1 | 0 | L | R | 6-2 | 190 | 1-9-70 | 1991 | Scottsdale, Ariz. |
| Rojas, Roberto, of | .254 | 120 | 492 | 68 | 125 | 17 | 6 | 1 | 29 | 41 | 118 | 30 | 16 | L | L | 6-0 | 185 | 11-23-70 | 1991 | Santo Domingo, D.R. |
| Roman, Mark, c-dh | .125 | 14 | 24 | 4 | 3 | 0 | 0 | 0 | 2 | 8 | 11 | 0 | 0 | R | R | 6-0 | 190 | 8-26-69 | 1993 | Redding, Conn. |
| Sanchez, Yuri, ss | .203 | 111 | 340 | 53 | 69 | 7 | 6 | 0 | 30 | 73 | 125 | 20 | 9 | L | R | 6-0 | 160 | 11-11-73 | 1992 | Lynn, Mass. |
| Thomas, Tim, 2b | .303 | 104 | 380 | 80 | 115 | 31 | 3 | 4 | 48 | 82 | 85 | 5 | 1 | R | R | 6-2 | 185 | 7-21-69 | 1992 | St. Paul, Minn. |
| Thompson, Billy, c | .275 | 42 | 142 | 14 | 39 | 6 | 1 | 1 | 19 | 20 | 28 | 2 | 2 | R | R | 5-11 | 185 | 11-5-70 | 1993 | Wayne, W.Va. |
| Velandia, Jorge, ss-3b | .160 | 37 | 106 | 15 | 17 | 4 | 0 | 0 | 11 | 13 | 21 | 5 | 0 | R | R | 5-9 | 160 | 1-12-75 | 1992 | Caracas, Venez. |
| Wooten, Sean, 1b-3b | .250 | 5 | 16 | 2 | 4 | 0 | 0 | 1 | 5 | 3 | 3 | 0 | 0 | R | R | 5-10 | 205 | 7-24-72 | 1993 | LaVerne, Calif. |

| PITCHING | W | L | ERA | G | GS | CG | SV | IP | H | R | ER | BB | SO | B | T | HT | WT | DOB | 1st Yr | Resides |
|---|---|---|---|---|---|---|---|---|---|---|---|---|---|---|---|---|---|---|---|---|
| Adams, Art | 0 | 1 | 3.52 | 3 | 0 | 0 | 0 | 8 | 8 | 3 | 3 | 4 | 6 | S | R | 6-1 | 185 | 7-29-70 | 1991 | Richmond, Calif. |
| Arguto, Sam | 2 | 3 | 2.92 | 23 | 0 | 0 | 6 | 25 | 19 | 8 | 8 | 15 | 22 | R | R | 6-0 | 165 | 3-11-71 | 1993 | Stamford, Conn. |
| Bauer, Matt | 6 | 5 | 2.90 | 40 | 0 | 0 | 5 | 62 | 57 | 30 | 20 | 23 | 81 | L | L | 6-1 | 195 | 3-25-70 | 1991 | Saginaw, Mich. |
| Berlin, Mike | 4 | 2 | 3.24 | 18 | 5 | 1 | 2 | 58 | 50 | 29 | 21 | 28 | 44 | R | R | 6-1 | 185 | 2-14-71 | 1992 | Moundsville, W.Va. |
| Bussa, Todd | 4 | 3 | 3.65 | 39 | 0 | 0 | 7 | 79 | 70 | 33 | 32 | 36 | 92 | R | R | 5-11 | 165 | 12-13-72 | 1991 | Palm Beach Gardens, Fla. |
| Cedeno, Blas | 6 | 6 | 3.15 | 28 | 22 | 1 | 0 | 149 | 145 | 64 | 52 | 55 | 103 | R | R | 6-0 | 165 | 11-15-72 | 1991 | Campo Carabobo, Venez. |
| Crombie, Kevin | 2 | 1 | 4.57 | 28 | 0 | 0 | 0 | 41 | 46 | 23 | 21 | 14 | 25 | R | R | 6-4 | 190 | 10-3-70 | 1992 | Staten Island, N.Y. |
| Gaillard, Eddie | 5 | 2 | 4.09 | 11 | 11 | 0 | 0 | 62 | 64 | 30 | 28 | 20 | 41 | R | R | 6-2 | 220 | 6-11-71 | 1993 | West Palm Beach, Fla. |
| Grimm, John | 0 | 2 | 1.45 | 23 | 0 | 0 | 10 | 37 | 18 | 7 | 6 | 14 | 58 | R | R | 5-10 | 175 | 9-13-70 | 1992 | Reynoldsburg, Ohio |
| Maxcy, Brian | 12 | 4 | 2.93 | 39 | 12 | 1 | 9 | 114 | 111 | 51 | 37 | 42 | 101 | R | R | 6-1 | 170 | 5-4-71 | 1992 | Amory, Miss. |
| Miller, Trever | 8 | 13 | 4.19 | 28 | 28 | 2 | 0 | 161 | 151 | 99 | 75 | 67 | 116 | R | L | 6-3 | 175 | 5-29-73 | 1991 | Louisville, Ky. |
| Mysel, David | 5 | 2 | 2.61 | 12 | 12 | 1 | 0 | 72 | 69 | 25 | 21 | 16 | 46 | R | R | 6-5 | 215 | 4-13-71 | 1992 | Hummelstown, Pa. |
| Navarro, Rick | 1 | 5 | 2.85 | 41 | 0 | 0 | 5 | 76 | 59 | 27 | 24 | 23 | 96 | S | L | 5-10 | 175 | 1-22-70 | 1992 | La Mesa, Calif. |
| Santos, Henry | 3 | 2 | 4.70 | 8 | 8 | 0 | 0 | 44 | 43 | 25 | 23 | 30 | 29 | L | L | 6-1 | 175 | 1-17-73 | 1990 | Santiago, D.R. |
| Sodowsky, Clint | 14 | 10 | 5.09 | 27 | 27 | 1 | 0 | 156 | 177 | 101 | 88 | 51 | 80 | S | R | 6-3 | 190 | 7-13-72 | 1991 | Ponca City, Okla. |
| Whiteside, Sean | 3 | 5 | 4.65 | 24 | 16 | 0 | 0 | 101 | 113 | 68 | 52 | 41 | 85 | L | L | 6-4 | 190 | 4-19-71 | 1992 | Cordele, Ga. |

# NIAGARA FALLS
## NEW YORK-PENN LEAGUE

**A**

| BATTING | AVG | G | AB | R | H | 2B | 3B | HR | RBI | BB | SO | SB | CS | B | T | HT | WT | DOB | 1st Yr | Resides |
|---|---|---|---|---|---|---|---|---|---|---|---|---|---|---|---|---|---|---|---|---|
| Barker, Glen, of | .217 | 72 | 253 | 49 | 55 | 11 | 4 | 5 | 23 | 24 | 71 | 37 | 12 | R | R | 5-10 | 175 | 5-10-71 | 1993 | Albany, N.Y. |
| Broome, Corey, c | .219 | 47 | 137 | 17 | 30 | 4 | 1 | 2 | 20 | 6 | 36 | 6 | 3 | L | L | 5-10 | 175 | 7-18-71 | 1993 | Belmont, N.C. |
| Brown, Shawn, 2b-3b | .291 | 71 | 247 | 37 | 72 | 6 | 4 | 0 | 21 | 16 | 40 | 29 | 6 | R | R | 6-1 | 176 | 4-16-71 | 1993 | Tabernacle, N.J. |
| Conant, Scott, 2b-3b | .000 | 3 | 5 | 0 | 0 | 0 | 0 | 0 | 0 | 0 | 2 | 0 | 0 | R | R | 6-0 | 178 | 12-28-70 | 1993 | Oak Forest, Ill. |
| Danapilis, Eric, of-dh | .341 | 65 | 208 | 35 | 71 | 9 | 1 | 3 | 28 | 33 | 36 | 8 | 4 | R | R | 6-2 | 220 | 6-11-71 | 1993 | St. Joseph, Mich. |
| DeJesus, Malvin, 3b-2b | .254 | 54 | 142 | 26 | 36 | 7 | 3 | 0 | 15 | 19 | 29 | 20 | 10 | R | R | 5-9 | 160 | 9-16-71 | 1992 | Carolina, P.R. |
| Dickerson, Robert, of-dh | .228 | 56 | 171 | 29 | 39 | 8 | 3 | 3 | 23 | 15 | 44 | 14 | 4 | L | L | 6-2 | 188 | 8-1-71 | 1992 | Gulfport, Miss. |
| Dixon, Tyrone, of-3b | .272 | 50 | 147 | 24 | 40 | 4 | 2 | 0 | 13 | 18 | 25 | 16 | 8 | R | R | 5-9 | 174 | 3-13-70 | 1993 | Grand Bay, Ala. |
| Kinnon, Duane, 1b | .253 | 66 | 229 | 20 | 58 | 14 | 2 | 3 | 32 | 12 | 40 | 2 | 10 | L | L | 6-2 | 225 | 12-22-68 | 1993 | Brooklyn, N.Y. |
| Marine, Del, c | .264 | 55 | 182 | 24 | 48 | 12 | 0 | 7 | 32 | 20 | 48 | 5 | 5 | R | R | 6-0 | 195 | 10-18-71 | 1992 | Woodland Hills, Calif. |
| Marrero, Kenny, c-dh | .221 | 31 | 77 | 9 | 17 | 7 | 0 | 1 | 11 | 8 | 17 | 0 | 0 | R | R | 6-3 | 205 | 5-13-70 | 1991 | Dorado, P.R. |
| Martinez, Dalvis, 3b | .220 | 31 | 100 | 8 | 22 | 4 | 0 | 0 | 12 | 9 | 28 | 1 | 1 | R | R | 5-10 | 185 | 5-17-73 | 1993 | Santo Domingo, D.R. |
| Moreno, Jorge, of | .188 | 55 | 101 | 16 | 19 | 4 | 0 | 0 | 7 | 14 | 36 | 4 | 6 | S | R | 6-2 | 150 | 8-19-72 | 1989 | Santo Domingo, D.R. |
| Ordway, Kirk, 3b-dh | .181 | 40 | 116 | 17 | 21 | 9 | 0 | 1 | 11 | 7 | 35 | 3 | 2 | R | R | 6-0 | 180 | 3-2-70 | 1993 | Cottage Grove, Ore. |
| Pagano, Scott, ph | .167 | 5 | 6 | 1 | 1 | 0 | 0 | 1 | 3 | 1 | 0 | 1 | 0 | S | R | 5-11 | 175 | 4-26-71 | 1992 | Dania, Fla. |
| Velandia, Jorge, ss | .193 | 72 | 212 | 30 | 41 | 1 | 0 | 1 | 22 | 19 | 48 | 22 | 4 | R | R | 5-9 | 160 | 1-12-75 | 1992 | Caracas, Venez. |
| Wiseley, Mike, of | .321 | 73 | 287 | 46 | 92 | 19 | 1 | 0 | 28 | 35 | 27 | 8 | 5 | R | R | 5-11 | 172 | 6-29-71 | 1993 | Brighton, Mich. |

| PITCHING | W | L | ERA | G | GS | CG | SV | IP | H | R | ER | BB | SO | B | T | HT | WT | DOB | 1st Yr | Resides |
|---|---|---|---|---|---|---|---|---|---|---|---|---|---|---|---|---|---|---|---|---|
| Arguto, Samuel | 0 | 0 | 0.00 | 7 | 0 | 0 | 6 | 8 | 1 | 0 | 0 | 4 | 14 | R | R | 6-0 | 165 | 3-11-71 | 1993 | Stamford, Conn. |
| Gaillard, Eddie | 1 | 2 | 3.68 | 3 | 3 | 0 | 0 | 15 | 15 | 6 | 6 | 4 | 12 | R | R | 6-2 | 220 | 6-11-71 | 1993 | West Palm Beach, Fla. |
| Goldsmith, Gary | 4 | 2 | 2.30 | 21 | 0 | 0 | 0 | 55 | 43 | 21 | 14 | 20 | 64 | R | R | 6-2 | 205 | 7-4-71 | 1993 | Alamogordo, N.M. |
| Hunt, Will | 2 | 1 | 2.20 | 14 | 0 | 0 | 0 | 16 | 11 | 6 | 4 | 8 | 16 | L | L | 6-2 | 215 | 3-3-71 | 1993 | Byars, Okla. |
| Jackson, Roderick | 1 | 3 | 3.91 | 15 | 8 | 0 | 1 | 53 | 51 | 26 | 23 | 36 | 34 | R | R | 6-1 | 200 | 7-12-70 | 1993 | Rockledge, Fla. |
| Magrini, Paul | 0 | 0 | 3.38 | 2 | 0 | 0 | 0 | 3 | 1 | 1 | 1 | 2 | 0 | R | R | 6-4 | 200 | 3-27-73 | 1991 | Wallington, N.J. |
| McFarland, Toby | 2 | 0 | 1.16 | 25 | 1 | 0 | 2 | 39 | 28 | 11 | 5 | 19 | 22 | L | L | 6-2 | 185 | 1-27-72 | 1993 | Petoskey, Mich. |
| Moehler, Brian | 6 | 5 | 3.22 | 12 | 11 | 0 | 0 | 59 | 51 | 33 | 21 | 27 | 38 | R | R | 6-3 | 195 | 12-31-71 | 1993 | Rockingham, N.C. |

| PITCHING | W | L | ERA | G | GS | CG | SV | IP | H | R | ER | BB | SO | B | T | HT | WT | DOB | 1st Yr | Resides |
|---|---|---|---|---|---|---|---|---|---|---|---|---|---|---|---|---|---|---|---|---|
| Neese, Joshua | 12 | 3 | 2.54 | 21 | 8 | 0 | 0 | 71 | 44 | 24 | 20 | 34 | 73 | L | R | 6-1 | 180 | 4-22-71 | 1993 | Freedom, Okla. |
| Nowak, Steve | 0 | 0 | 8.44 | 2 | 0 | 0 | 0 | 5 | 10 | 5 | 5 | 4 | 8 | R | R | 6-1 | 195 | 12-22-70 | 1992 | Gaylord, Mich. |
| Reincke, Corey | 1 | 1 | 7.02 | 20 | 1 | 0 | 1 | 33 | 35 | 29 | 26 | 23 | 26 | R | R | 6-6 | 210 | 7-9-72 | 1991 | Athens, Mich. |
| Richardson, Mike | 3 | 4 | 4.58 | 24 | 2 | 0 | 0 | 53 | 56 | 29 | 27 | 29 | 37 | R | R | 6-3 | 215 | 12-31-71 | 1993 | San Diego, Calif. |
| Rodriguez, David | 0 | 1 | 2.25 | 25 | 0 | 0 | 1 | 44 | 31 | 15 | 11 | 36 | 45 | R | R | 6-5 | 210 | 10-29-70 | 1992 | Westbury, N.Y. |
| Rosengren, John | 7 | 3 | 2.41 | 15 | 15 | 0 | 0 | 82 | 52 | 32 | 22 | 38 | 91 | L | L | 6-4 | 190 | 8-10-72 | 1992 | Rye, N.Y. |
| Salazar, Mike | 3 | 4 | 3.17 | 15 | 15 | 0 | 0 | 82 | 80 | 36 | 29 | 24 | 68 | L | L | 6-4 | 200 | 4-16-71 | 1993 | Clovis, Calif. |
| Santos, Henry | 2 | 1 | 2.34 | 7 | 7 | 0 | 0 | 42 | 29 | 15 | 11 | 17 | 50 | L | L | 6-1 | 175 | 1-17-73 | 1990 | Santiago, D.R. |
| Smith, Cameron | 0 | 0 | 18.00 | 2 | 2 | 0 | 0 | 5 | 12 | 11 | 10 | 6 | 0 | R | R | 6-3 | 185 | 9-20-73 | 1993 | Selkirk, N.Y. |
| Sollecito, Gabe | 2 | 1 | 0.34 | 23 | 0 | 0 | 14 | 27 | 18 | 4 | 1 | 10 | 23 | S | R | 6-1 | 190 | 3-3-72 | 1993 | Monterey, Calif. |

# BRISTOL

## APPALACHIAN LEAGUE

| BATTING | AVG | G | AB | R | H | 2B | 3B | HR | RBI | BB | SO | SB | CS | B | T | HT | WT | DOB | 1st Yr | Resides |
|---|---|---|---|---|---|---|---|---|---|---|---|---|---|---|---|---|---|---|---|---|
| Arano, Eloy, 3b-ss | .217 | 31 | 83 | 11 | 18 | 5 | 1 | 0 | 9 | 1 | 22 | 1 | 0 | S | R | 5-11 | 170 | 3-5-74 | 1993 | Veracruz, Mexico |
| Ayala, Moises, c | .000 | 8 | 22 | 0 | 0 | 0 | 0 | 0 | 0 | 0 | 8 | 0 | 0 | R | R | 6-2 | 195 | 12-28-73 | 1992 | Sabana Grande, P.R. |
| Bass, Jason, of | .210 | 35 | 119 | 21 | 25 | 6 | 2 | 4 | 13 | 14 | 42 | 2 | 2 | L | L | 6-3 | 205 | 6-22-74 | 1993 | Seattle, Wash. |
| Catalanotto, Frank, 2b | .307 | 55 | 199 | 37 | 61 | 9 | 5 | 3 | 22 | 15 | 19 | 3 | 6 | L | R | 5-11 | 180 | 4-27-74 | 1993 | Smithtown, N.Y. |
| Christmon, Drew, of-dh | .208 | 33 | 101 | 12 | 21 | 4 | 2 | 3 | 13 | 15 | 32 | 5 | 0 | L | R | 5-10 | 190 | 6-8-72 | 1993 | Midwest City, Okla. |
| Cordero, Ed, ss | .000 | 1 | 1 | 0 | 0 | 0 | 0 | 0 | 0 | 0 | 0 | 0 | 0 | R | R | 6-0 | 155 | 6-6-75 | 1992 | Santo Domingo, D.R. |
| Corey, Bryan, ss-2b | .105 | 39 | 95 | 14 | 10 | 3 | 0 | 0 | 3 | 26 | 35 | 2 | 3 | R | R | 6-1 | 170 | 10-21-73 | 1993 | Thousand Oaks, Calif. |
| Crafton, David, dh | .000 | 1 | 2 | 1 | 0 | 0 | 0 | 0 | 0 | 1 | 2 | 0 | 0 | L | R | 5-11 | 175 | 2-5-75 | 1993 | LaGrange Park, Ill. |
| Facione, Chris, of | .289 | 48 | 173 | 27 | 50 | 10 | 2 | 2 | 16 | 16 | 26 | 15 | 2 | R | R | 6-3 | 190 | 9-21-70 | 1993 | Millbrae, Calif. |
| Garcia, Luis, 2b-ss | .211 | 24 | 57 | 7 | 12 | 1 | 0 | 1 | 7 | 3 | 11 | 3 | 1 | R | R | 6-0 | 174 | 5-20-75 | 1993 | San Fran. de Macoris, D.R. |
| Guzman, Ismael, of | .303 | 33 | 109 | 15 | 33 | 6 | 0 | 4 | 21 | 4 | 16 | 2 | 3 | R | R | 6-0 | 170 | 2-6-73 | 1991 | Santo Domingo, D.R. |
| Hamilton, Jason, 1b | .249 | 56 | 173 | 30 | 43 | 11 | 0 | 6 | 29 | 31 | 44 | 5 | 2 | L | L | 6-4 | 225 | 2-7-71 | 1993 | Hemet, Calif. |
| Jones, Bobby, of | .278 | 47 | 144 | 27 | 40 | 10 | 2 | 6 | 24 | 22 | 38 | 4 | 4 | R | R | 5-11 | 190 | 1-7-73 | 1993 | Riverside, Calif. |
| Keenan, Chris, of-dh | .141 | 28 | 78 | 10 | 11 | 3 | 2 | 1 | 4 | 6 | 46 | 2 | 2 | R | R | 6-3 | 198 | 10-8-72 | 1991 | Lantana, Fla. |
| Landry, Lonny, of | .232 | 41 | 142 | 20 | 33 | 6 | 2 | 3 | 7 | 16 | 52 | 14 | 9 | R | R | 5-11 | 185 | 11-2-72 | 1993 | Broussard, La. |
| Martinez, Dalvis, 3b-2b | .229 | 9 | 35 | 3 | 8 | 4 | 1 | 0 | 4 | 3 | 6 | 0 | 1 | R | R | 5-10 | 185 | 5-17-73 | 1993 | Santo Domingo, D.R. |
| Rodriguez, Adam, c | .221 | 42 | 131 | 19 | 29 | 4 | 2 | 5 | 19 | 13 | 36 | 5 | 1 | R | R | 5-10 | 190 | 3-16-71 | 1993 | Tucson, Ariz. |
| Sanjurjo, Jose, of-dh | .308 | 26 | 91 | 8 | 28 | 3 | 0 | 2 | 18 | 3 | 23 | 2 | 2 | R | R | 6-1 | 158 | 3-26-73 | 1991 | Canovanas, P.R. |
| Tupper, Craig, c | .176 | 27 | 85 | 7 | 15 | 3 | 0 | 2 | 7 | 10 | 24 | 1 | 0 | R | R | 6-2 | 190 | 11-6-70 | 1993 | Woodacre, Calif. |
| Valdez, Ken, 3b | .211 | 24 | 71 | 8 | 15 | 1 | 1 | 2 | 7 | 6 | 31 | 2 | 1 | R | R | 6-0 | 170 | 10-4-74 | 1992 | Tampa, Fla. |
| Wooten, Sean, 1b-3b | .350 | 52 | 177 | 26 | 62 | 12 | 2 | 8 | 39 | 24 | 20 | 1 | 2 | R | R | 5-10 | 205 | 7-24-72 | 1993 | LaVerne, Calif. |
| Wyrick, Chris, ss-3b | .221 | 33 | 113 | 11 | 25 | 5 | 0 | 2 | 12 | 6 | 25 | 5 | 1 | R | R | 6-0 | 185 | 7-12-71 | 1993 | Jefferson City, Mo. |

| PITCHING | W | L | ERA | G | GS | CG | SV | IP | H | R | ER | BB | SO | B | T | HT | WT | DOB | 1st Yr | Resides |
|---|---|---|---|---|---|---|---|---|---|---|---|---|---|---|---|---|---|---|---|---|
| Brazoban, Candy | 0 | 2 | 9.43 | 15 | 0 | 0 | 0 | 21 | 33 | 28 | 22 | 20 | 16 | R | R | 6-2 | 150 | 2-14-75 | 1993 | Santo Domingo, D.R. |
| Brown, Alvin | 2 | 2 | 6.23 | 15 | 6 | 0 | 1 | 39 | 27 | 30 | 27 | 47 | 30 | R | R | 6-1 | 200 | 9-2-70 | 1993 | Los Angeles, Calif. |
| Fuduric, Tony | 1 | 6 | 7.38 | 13 | 13 | 0 | 0 | 54 | 52 | 54 | 44 | 52 | 40 | R | R | 5-11 | 182 | 4-9-72 | 1993 | Mishinomiyo, Japan |
| • Furusato, Yasu | 1 | 1 | 8.36 | 11 | 0 | 0 | 0 | 14 | 16 | 15 | 13 | 9 | 16 | R | R | 6-2 | 215 | 3-3-71 | 1993 | Byars, Okla. |
| Granger, Greg | 3 | 3 | 4.28 | 13 | 13 | 0 | 0 | 74 | 74 | 40 | 35 | 27 | 62 | R | R | 6-6 | 190 | 3-7-73 | 1993 | Ellettsville, Ind. |
| Hunt, Will | 0 | 1 | 2.03 | 12 | 0 | 0 | 8 | 13 | 7 | 4 | 3 | 8 | 14 | L | L | 6-2 | 215 | 3-3-71 | 1993 | Byars, Okla. |
| Meredith, Ryan | 4 | 0 | 4.85 | 19 | 0 | 0 | 2 | 30 | 27 | 17 | 16 | 16 | 38 | R | R | 6-3 | 200 | 2-9-72 | 1993 | Mission Viejo, Calif. |
| • Nakagawa, Shinya | 2 | 2 | 3.34 | 24 | 0 | 0 | 4 | 30 | 35 | 13 | 11 | 7 | 40 | L | L | 5-11 | 155 | 6-30-72 | 1993 | Mishinomiyo, Japan |
| Norman, Scott | 3 | 6 | 5.26 | 13 | 13 | 1 | 0 | 77 | 100 | 54 | 45 | 18 | 43 | R | R | 6-1 | 195 | 12-22-70 | 1992 | Gaylord, Mich. |
| Nowak, Steve | 1 | 1 | 5.03 | 16 | 0 | 0 | 0 | 34 | 39 | 20 | 19 | 16 | 28 | R | R | 6-3 | 170 | 6-19-75 | 1992 | San Cristobal, D.R. |
| Roberts, Willis | 2 | 3 | 1.38 | 10 | 2 | 0 | 1 | 26 | 24 | 16 | 4 | 11 | 23 | R | R | 6-3 | 140 | 11-24-73 | 1991 | Santo Domingo, D.R. |
| Severino, Jose | 0 | 0 | 35.10 | 4 | 0 | 0 | 0 | 3 | 12 | 13 | 13 | 6 | 2 | R | R | 6-4 | 205 | 11-6-72 | 1993 | Satellite Beach, Fla. |
| Skrmetta, Matthew | 2 | 3 | 4.89 | 8 | 5 | 0 | 0 | 35 | 30 | 23 | 19 | 22 | 29 | R | R | 6-6 | 225 | 7-2-74 | 1993 | Satellite Beach, Fla. |
| Smith, Cameron | 3 | 1 | 3.58 | 9 | 7 | 1 | 0 | 38 | 25 | 22 | 15 | 22 | 33 | R | R | 6-3 | 185 | 9-20-73 | 1993 | Selkirk, N.Y. |
| Timko, John | 0 | 1 | 7.13 | 13 | 0 | 0 | 0 | 24 | 27 | 19 | 19 | 24 | 16 | R | R | 6-2 | 185 | 11-4-71 | 1992 | Clearwater, Fla. |
| Weber, Eric | 2 | 4 | 4.87 | 16 | 5 | 0 | 0 | 44 | 43 | 33 | 24 | 33 | 24 | R | R | 6-3 | 185 | 10-3-74 | 1993 | Saginaw, Mich. |
| Wilson, Michael | 1 | 3 | 6.50 | 7 | 3 | 0 | 0 | 18 | 22 | 13 | 13 | 10 | 15 | R | R | 6-5 | 220 | 4-4-73 | 1993 | Dallas, Texas |

• Property of Hanshin Tigers (Japan)

# FLORIDA MARLINS

**Manager:** Rene Lachemann.        **1993 Record:** 64-98, .395 (6th, NL East)

| BATTING | AVG | G | AB | R | H | 2B | 3B | HR | RBI | BB | SO | SB | CS | B | T | HT | WT | DOB | 1st Yr | Resides |
|---|---|---|---|---|---|---|---|---|---|---|---|---|---|---|---|---|---|---|---|---|
| Arias, Alex | .269 | 96 | 249 | 27 | 67 | 5 | 1 | 2 | 20 | 27 | 18 | 1 | 1 | R | R | 6-3 | 185 | 11-20-67 | 1987 | New York, N.Y. |
| Barberie, Bret | .277 | 99 | 375 | 45 | 104 | 16 | 2 | 5 | 33 | 33 | 58 | 2 | 4 | S | R | 5-11 | 185 | 8-16-67 | 1989 | Cerritos, Calif. |
| Berroa, Geronimo | .118 | 14 | 34 | 3 | 4 | 1 | 0 | 0 | 0 | 2 | 7 | 0 | 0 | R | R | 6-0 | 165 | 3-18-65 | 1984 | Santo Domingo, D.R. |
| Briley, Greg | .194 | 120 | 170 | 17 | 33 | 6 | 0 | 3 | 12 | 12 | 42 | 6 | 2 | L | R | 5-8 | 180 | 5-24-65 | 1986 | Greenville, N.C. |
| Carr, Chuck | .267 | 142 | 551 | 75 | 147 | 19 | 2 | 4 | 41 | 49 | 74 | 58 | 22 | S | R | 5-10 | 165 | 8-10-68 | 1986 | Fontana, Calif. |
| Carrillo, Matias | .255 | 24 | 55 | 4 | 14 | 6 | 0 | 0 | 3 | 1 | 7 | 0 | 0 | L | L | 5-11 | 190 | 2-24-63 | 1982 | Guaymas, Mexico |
| Conine, Jeff | .292 | 162 | 595 | 75 | 174 | 24 | 3 | 12 | 79 | 52 | 135 | 2 | 2 | R | R | 6-1 | 220 | 6-27-66 | 1988 | Rialto, Calif. |
| Cotto, Henry | .296 | 54 | 135 | 15 | 40 | 7 | 0 | 3 | 14 | 3 | 18 | 11 | 1 | R | R | 6-2 | 180 | 1-5-61 | 1980 | Renton, Wash. |
| Decker, Steve | .000 | 8 | 15 | 0 | 0 | 0 | 0 | 0 | 1 | 3 | 3 | 0 | 0 | R | R | 6-3 | 205 | 10-25-65 | 1988 | Salem, Ore. |
| Destrade, Orestes | .255 | 153 | 569 | 61 | 145 | 20 | 3 | 20 | 87 | 58 | 130 | 0 | 2 | S | R | 6-4 | 230 | 5-8-62 | 1981 | St. Petersburg, Fla. |
| Everett, Carl | .105 | 11 | 19 | 0 | 2 | 0 | 0 | 0 | 1 | 9 | 1 | 0 | 0 | S | R | 6-0 | 181 | 6-3-70 | 1990 | Tampa, Fla. |
| Fariss, Monty | .172 | 18 | 29 | 3 | 5 | 2 | 1 | 0 | 2 | 5 | 13 | 0 | 0 | R | R | 6-4 | 205 | 10-13-67 | 1988 | Leedey, Okla. |
| Felix, Junior | .238 | 57 | 214 | 25 | 51 | 11 | 1 | 7 | 22 | 10 | 50 | 2 | 1 | S | R | 5-11 | 165 | 10-3-67 | 1986 | Yamasa, D.R. |
| Lyden, Mitch | .300 | 6 | 10 | 2 | 3 | 0 | 0 | 1 | 1 | 0 | 3 | 0 | 0 | R | R | 6-3 | 225 | 12-14-64 | 1983 | Fort Lauderdale, Fla. |
| Magadan, Dave | .286 | 66 | 227 | 22 | 65 | 12 | 0 | 4 | 29 | 44 | 30 | 0 | 1 | L | R | 6-3 | 200 | 9-30-62 | 1983 | Tampa, Fla. |
| McGriff, Terry | .000 | 3 | 7 | 0 | 0 | 0 | 0 | 0 | 0 | 0 | 1 | 0 | 0 | R | R | 6-2 | 180 | 9-23-63 | 1981 | Fort Pierce, Fla. |
| Natal, Rob | .214 | 41 | 117 | 3 | 25 | 4 | 1 | 1 | 6 | 6 | 22 | 1 | 0 | R | R | 5-11 | 190 | 11-13-65 | 1987 | Chula Vista, Calif. |
| Polidor, Gus | .167 | 7 | 6 | 0 | 1 | 1 | 0 | 0 | 0 | 0 | 2 | 0 | 0 | R | R | 6-0 | 180 | 10-26-61 | 1981 | Caracas, Venez. |
| Pose, Scott | .195 | 15 | 41 | 0 | 8 | 2 | 0 | 0 | 3 | 2 | 4 | 0 | 2 | L | R | 5-11 | 165 | 2-11-67 | 1989 | West Des Moines, Iowa |
| Renteria, Rich | .255 | 103 | 263 | 27 | 67 | 9 | 2 | 2 | 30 | 21 | 31 | 0 | 2 | R | R | 5-9 | 172 | 12-25-61 | 1980 | Las Vegas, Nev. |
| Santiago, Benito | .230 | 139 | 469 | 49 | 108 | 19 | 6 | 13 | 50 | 37 | 88 | 10 | 7 | R | R | 6-1 | 182 | 3-9-65 | 1983 | Chula Vista, Calif. |
| Sheffield, Gary | .292 | 72 | 236 | 33 | 69 | 8 | 3 | 10 | 37 | 29 | 34 | 12 | 4 | R | R | 5-11 | 190 | 11-18-68 | 1986 | St. Petersburg, Fla. |
| 2-team (68 S.D.) | .294 | 140 | 494 | 67 | 145 | 20 | 5 | 20 | 73 | 47 | 64 | 17 | 5 | | | | | | | |
| Weiss, Walt | .266 | 158 | 500 | 50 | 133 | 14 | 2 | 1 | 39 | 79 | 73 | 7 | 3 | S | R | 6-0 | 178 | 11-28-63 | 1985 | Suffern, N.Y. |
| Whitmore, Darrell | .204 | 76 | 250 | 24 | 51 | 8 | 2 | 4 | 19 | 10 | 72 | 4 | 2 | L | R | 6-1 | 210 | 11-18-68 | 1990 | Front Royal, Va. |
| Wilson, Nigel | .000 | 7 | 16 | 0 | 0 | 0 | 0 | 0 | 0 | 1 | 11 | 0 | 0 | L | L | 6-1 | 170 | 1-12-70 | 1988 | Ajax, Ontario |

| PITCHING | W | L | ERA | G | GS | CG | SV | IP | H | R | ER | BB | SO | B | T | HT | WT | DOB | 1st Yr | Resides |
|---|---|---|---|---|---|---|---|---|---|---|---|---|---|---|---|---|---|---|---|---|
| Aquino, Luis | 6 | 8 | 3.42 | 38 | 13 | 0 | 0 | 111 | 115 | 43 | 42 | 40 | 67 | R | R | 6-1 | 190 | 5-19-65 | 1982 | Caguas, P.R. |
| Armstrong, Jack | 9 | 17 | 4.49 | 36 | 33 | 0 | 0 | 196 | 210 | 105 | 98 | 78 | 118 | R | R | 6-5 | 215 | 3-7-65 | 1987 | Neptune, N.J. |
| Bowen, Ryan | 8 | 12 | 4.42 | 27 | 27 | 2 | 0 | 157 | 156 | 83 | 77 | 87 | 98 | R | R | 6-0 | 185 | 2-10-68 | 1987 | Hanford, Calif. |
| Carpenter, Cris | 0 | 1 | 2.89 | 29 | 0 | 0 | 0 | 37 | 29 | 15 | 12 | 13 | 26 | R | R | 6-2 | 195 | 4-5-65 | 1988 | Gainesville, Ga. |
| Corsi, Jim | 0 | 2 | 6.64 | 15 | 0 | 0 | 0 | 20 | 28 | 15 | 15 | 10 | 7 | R | R | 6-1 | 220 | 9-9-61 | 1982 | Newtonville, Mass. |
| Hammond, Chris | 11 | 12 | 4.66 | 32 | 32 | 1 | 0 | 191 | 207 | 106 | 99 | 66 | 108 | L | L | 6-1 | 195 | 1-21-66 | 1986 | Birmingham, Ala. |
| Harvey, Bryan | 1 | 5 | 1.70 | 59 | 0 | 0 | 45 | 69 | 45 | 14 | 13 | 13 | 73 | R | R | 6-2 | 212 | 6-2-63 | 1985 | Maiden, N.C. |
| Hoffman, Trevor | 2 | 2 | 3.28 | 28 | 0 | 0 | 2 | 36 | 24 | 13 | 13 | 19 | 26 | R | R | 6-0 | 195 | 10-13-67 | 1989 | Anaheim, Calif. |
| Hough, Charlie | 9 | 16 | 4.27 | 34 | 34 | 0 | 0 | 204 | 202 | 109 | 97 | 71 | 126 | R | R | 6-2 | 190 | 1-5-48 | 1966 | Brea, Calif. |
| Johnstone, John | 2 | 2 | 5.91 | 7 | 0 | 0 | 0 | 11 | 16 | 8 | 7 | 7 | 5 | R | R | 6-3 | 195 | 11-25-68 | 1987 | Liverpool, N.Y. |
| Klink, Joe | 0 | 2 | 5.02 | 59 | 0 | 0 | 0 | 38 | 37 | 22 | 21 | 24 | 22 | L | L | 5-11 | 170 | 2-3-62 | 1983 | Hollywood, Fla. |
| Lewis, Richie | 6 | 3 | 3.26 | 57 | 0 | 0 | 0 | 77 | 68 | 37 | 28 | 43 | 65 | R | R | 5-10 | 175 | 1-25-66 | 1987 | Losantville, Ind. |
| McClure, Bob | 1 | 1 | 7.11 | 14 | 0 | 0 | 0 | 6 | 13 | 5 | 5 | 5 | 6 | R | L | 5-11 | 188 | 4-29-53 | 1973 | Los Altos, Calif. |
| Nen, Robb | 1 | 0 | 7.02 | 15 | 1 | 0 | 0 | 33 | 35 | 28 | 26 | 20 | 27 | R | R | 6-4 | 190 | 11-28-69 | 1987 | Seal Beach, Calif. |
| Rapp, Pat | 4 | 6 | 4.02 | 16 | 16 | 1 | 0 | 94 | 101 | 49 | 42 | 39 | 57 | R | R | 6-3 | 210 | 7-13-67 | 1989 | Sulphur, La. |
| Rodriguez, Rich | 0 | 1 | 4.11 | 36 | 0 | 0 | 1 | 46 | 39 | 23 | 21 | 24 | 21 | R | L | 5-11 | 200 | 3-1-63 | 1984 | Knoxville, Tenn. |
| 2-team (34 S.D.) | 2 | 4 | 3.79 | 70 | 0 | 0 | 3 | 76 | 73 | 38 | 32 | 33 | 43 | | | | | | | |
| Turner, Matt | 4 | 5 | 2.91 | 55 | 0 | 0 | 0 | 68 | 55 | 23 | 22 | 26 | 59 | R | R | 6-5 | 215 | 2-18-67 | 1986 | Lexington, Ky. |
| Weathers, David | 2 | 3 | 5.12 | 14 | 6 | 0 | 0 | 46 | 57 | 26 | 26 | 13 | 34 | R | R | 6-3 | 205 | 9-25-69 | 1988 | Leoma, Tenn. |

## FIELDING

| Catcher | PCT | G | PO | A | E | DP |
|---|---|---|---|---|---|---|
| Decker | .968 | 5 | 28 | 2 | 1 | 0 |
| Lyden | 1.000 | 2 | 4 | 0 | 0 | 0 |
| McGriff | 1.000 | 3 | 12 | 0 | 0 | 0 |
| Natal | 1.000 | 38 | 196 | 18 | 0 | 2 |
| Santiago | .987 | 136 | 740 | 64 | 11 | 4 |

| First Base | PCT | G | PO | A | E | DP |
|---|---|---|---|---|---|---|
| Conine | 1.000 | 43 | 151 | 14 | 0 | 11 |
| Destrade | .987 | 152 | 1313 | 90 | 19 | 109 |
| Magadan | 1.000 | 2 | 5 | 1 | 0 | 0 |

| Second Base | PCT | G | PO | A | E | DP |
|---|---|---|---|---|---|---|
| Arias | .987 | 30 | 59 | 88 | 2 | 15 |
| Barberie | .982 | 97 | 201 | 303 | 9 | 62 |
| Polidor | .000 | 1 | 0 | 0 | 0 | 0 |

| | PCT | G | PO | A | E | DP |
|---|---|---|---|---|---|---|
| Renteria | .989 | 45 | 70 | 116 | 2 | 16 |
| **Third Base** | PCT | G | PO | A | E | DP |
| Arias | .975 | 22 | 13 | 26 | 1 | 2 |
| Magadan | .961 | 63 | 50 | 121 | 7 | 12 |
| Polidor | 1.000 | 1 | 1 | 0 | 0 | 0 |
| Renteria | 1.000 | 25 | 14 | 35 | 0 | 4 |
| Sheffield | .894 | 66 | 38 | 123 | 19 | 4 |
| **Shortstop** | PCT | G | PO | A | E | DP |
| Arias | .945 | 18 | 22 | 30 | 3 | 8 |
| Weiss | .977 | 153 | 229 | 406 | 15 | 80 |
| **Outfield** | PCT | G | PO | A | E | DP |
| Berroa | .833 | 9 | 9 | 1 | 2 | 0 |

| | PCT | G | PO | A | E | DP |
|---|---|---|---|---|---|---|
| Briley | .986 | 67 | 71 | 2 | 1 | 0 |
| Carr | .985 | 139 | 393 | 7 | 6 | 2 |
| Carrillo | 1.000 | 16 | 21 | 0 | 0 | 0 |
| Conine | .992 | 147 | 252 | 11 | 2 | 0 |
| Cotto | .977 | 46 | 85 | 1 | 2 | 0 |
| Everett | .857 | 8 | 6 | 0 | 1 | 0 |
| Fariss | 1.000 | 10 | 14 | 0 | 0 | 0 |
| Felix | .940 | 52 | 91 | 3 | 6 | 0 |
| Pose | 1.000 | 10 | 14 | 0 | 0 | 0 |
| Renteria | .000 | 1 | 0 | 0 | 0 | 0 |
| Santiago | .000 | 1 | 0 | 0 | 0 | 0 |
| Whitmore | .979 | 69 | 140 | 3 | 3 | 1 |
| Wilson | 1.000 | 3 | 4 | 0 | 0 | 0 |

# MARLINS FARM SYSTEM

| Class | Club | League | W | L | Pct. | Finish* | Manager | First Year |
|---|---|---|---|---|---|---|---|---|
| AAA | Edmonton (Alta.) Trappers | Pacific Coast | 72 | 69 | .511 | 4th (10) | Sal Rende | 1993 |
| A# | High Desert (Calif.) Mavericks | California | 85 | 52 | .620 | 1st†† (10) | Fredi Gonzalez | 1993 |
| A | Kane County (Ill.) Cougars | Midwest | 75 | 62 | .547 | 6th (14) | Carlos Tosca | 1993 |
| A | Elmira (N.Y.) Pioneers | New York-Penn | 31 | 44 | .413 | 12th (14) | Lynn Jones | 1993 |

DAN ARNOLD

MORRIS FOSTOFF

**Expansion Rookies.** Outfielders Jeff Conine, left, and Chuck Carr made impressive debuts for the expansion Marlins. Conine hit a team-best .292 while Carr led the National League with 58 stolen bases.

| Class | Club | League | W | L | Pct. | Finish* | Manager | First Year |
|---|---|---|---|---|---|---|---|---|
| Rookie | Kissimmee (Fla.) Marlins | Gulf Coast | 32 | 28 | .533 | T-6th (15) | Jim Hendry | 1992 |

*Finish in overall standings (No. of teams in league)   #Advanced level   †Won league championship

# EDMONTON AAA
## PACIFIC COAST LEAGUE

| BATTING | AVG | G | AB | R | H | 2B | 3B | HR | RBI | BB | SO | SB | CS | B | T | HT | WT | DOB | 1st Yr | Resides |
|---|---|---|---|---|---|---|---|---|---|---|---|---|---|---|---|---|---|---|---|---|
| Barberie, Bret | .421 | 4 | 19 | 3 | 8 | 2 | 0 | 1 | 8 | 0 | 2 | 0 | 1 | S | R | 5-11 | 185 | 8-16-67 | 1989 | Cerritos, Calif. |
| Berroa, Geronimo | .327 | 90 | 327 | 64 | 107 | 33 | 4 | 16 | 68 | 36 | 71 | 1 | 2 | R | R | 6-0 | 165 | 3-18-65 | 1984 | Santo Domingo, D.R. |
| Capra, Nick | .278 | 106 | 389 | 71 | 108 | 19 | 4 | 7 | 44 | 58 | 42 | 20 | 13 | R | R | 5-8 | 165 | 3-8-58 | 1979 | Oklahoma City, Okla. |
| De los Santos, Luis | .311 | 125 | 425 | 49 | 132 | 25 | 2 | 2 | 66 | 25 | 56 | 0 | 3 | R | R | 6-5 | 225 | 12-29-66 | 1984 | New York, N.Y. |
| Everett, Carl | .309 | 35 | 136 | 28 | 42 | 13 | 4 | 6 | 16 | 19 | 45 | 12 | 1 | S | R | 6-0 | 181 | 6-3-70 | 1990 | Tampa, Fla. |
| Fariss, Monty | .256 | 74 | 254 | 32 | 65 | 11 | 4 | 6 | 37 | 43 | 74 | 1 | 5 | R | R | 6-4 | 205 | 10-13-67 | 1988 | Leedey, Okla. |
| Felix, Junior | .355 | 7 | 31 | 7 | 11 | 2 | 0 | 0 | 5 | 4 | 8 | 0 | 0 | S | R | 5-11 | 165 | 10-3-67 | 1986 | Yamasa, D.R. |
| Jackson, Chuck | .279 | 36 | 129 | 23 | 36 | 4 | 3 | 5 | 11 | 9 | 30 | 0 | 1 | R | R | 6-0 | 190 | 3-19-63 | 1984 | Scottsdale, Ariz. |
| Lyden, Mitch | .306 | 50 | 160 | 34 | 49 | 15 | 1 | 8 | 31 | 5 | 34 | 1 | 1 | R | R | 6-3 | 225 | 12-14-64 | 1983 | Fort Lauderdale, Fla. |
| McGriff, Terry | .345 | 105 | 339 | 62 | 117 | 29 | 2 | 7 | 55 | 49 | 29 | 2 | 1 | R | R | 6-2 | 180 | 9-23-63 | 1981 | Fort Pierce, Fla. |
| Natal, Bob | .318 | 17 | 66 | 16 | 21 | 6 | 1 | 3 | 16 | 8 | 10 | 0 | 0 | R | R | 5-11 | 190 | 11-13-65 | 1987 | Chula Vista, Calif. |
| Pedrique, Al | .305 | 121 | 403 | 54 | 123 | 14 | 1 | 2 | 42 | 44 | 43 | 5 | 6 | R | R | 6-0 | 155 | 8-11-60 | 1978 | Ciudad Alianza, Venez. |
| Polidor, Gus | .285 | 72 | 249 | 26 | 71 | 16 | 2 | 3 | 40 | 17 | 17 | 1 | 1 | R | R | 6-0 | 180 | 10-26-61 | 1981 | Caracas, Venez. |
| Pose, Scott | .284 | 109 | 398 | 61 | 113 | 8 | 6 | 0 | 27 | 42 | 36 | 19 | 9 | L | R | 5-11 | 165 | 2-11-67 | 1989 | West Des Moines, Iowa |
| Renteria, Edinson | .265 | 24 | 68 | 6 | 18 | 0 | 0 | 1 | 8 | 7 | 12 | 0 | 1 | R | R | 5-11 | 160 | 4-7-68 | 1985 | Barranquilla, Columbia |
| Santana, Andres | .228 | 61 | 171 | 20 | 39 | 3 | 1 | 0 | 11 | 12 | 15 | 5 | 3 | S | R | 5-9 | 150 | 3-19-68 | 1986 | San Pedro de Macoris, D.R. |
| Small, Jeff | .271 | 92 | 328 | 29 | 89 | 19 | 6 | 2 | 39 | 10 | 56 | 3 | 3 | R | R | 6-0 | 175 | 8-12-65 | 1985 | Kingman, Ariz. |
| Snyder, Randy | .266 | 38 | 94 | 12 | 25 | 6 | 0 | 1 | 10 | 7 | 28 | 0 | 1 | S | R | 6-2 | 210 | 3-28-67 | 1988 | Yakima, Wash. |
| Whitmore, Darrell | .355 | 73 | 273 | 52 | 97 | 24 | 2 | 9 | 62 | 22 | 53 | 11 | 8 | L | R | 6-1 | 210 | 11-18-68 | 1990 | Front Royal, Va. |
| Wilson, Nigel | .292 | 96 | 370 | 66 | 108 | 26 | 7 | 17 | 68 | 25 | 108 | 8 | 3 | L | L | 6-1 | 170 | 1-12-70 | 1988 | Ajax, Ontario |

| PITCHING | W | L | ERA | G | GS | CG | SV | IP | H | R | ER | BB | SO | B | T | HT | WT | DOB | 1st Yr | Resides |
|---|---|---|---|---|---|---|---|---|---|---|---|---|---|---|---|---|---|---|---|---|
| Adamson, Joel | 1 | 2 | 6.92 | 5 | 5 | 0 | 0 | 26 | 39 | 21 | 20 | 13 | 7 | L | L | 6-4 | 180 | 7-2-71 | 1990 | Lakewood, Calif. |
| Anderson, Scott | 5 | 4 | 3.53 | 44 | 1 | 0 | 4 | 66 | 74 | 30 | 26 | 15 | 52 | R | R | 6-6 | 185 | 5-1-62 | 1984 | Bellevue, Wash. |
| Darwin, Jeff | 2 | 2 | 8.51 | 25 | 0 | 0 | 2 | 31 | 50 | 34 | 29 | 10 | 22 | R | R | 6-3 | 180 | 7-6-69 | 1989 | Bonham, Texas |
| Gleaton, Jerry Don | 3 | 1 | 3.99 | 46 | 0 | 0 | 7 | 65 | 73 | 30 | 29 | 26 | 46 | L | L | 6-3 | 210 | 9-14-57 | 1979 | Brownwood, Texas |
| Jeffcoat, Mike | 4 | 3 | 4.14 | 33 | 0 | 0 | 3 | 54 | 58 | 25 | 25 | 6 | 32 | L | L | 6-2 | 190 | 8-3-59 | 1980 | Arlington, Texas |
| Johnstone, John | 4 | 15 | 5.18 | 30 | 21 | 1 | 4 | 144 | 167 | 95 | 83 | 59 | 126 | R | R | 6-3 | 195 | 11-25-68 | 1987 | Liverpool, N.Y. |
| Kramer, Randy | 5 | 4 | 5.52 | 46 | 0 | 0 | 5 | 62 | 76 | 45 | 38 | 24 | 44 | R | R | 6-2 | 180 | 9-20-60 | 1982 | Oakley, Calif. |
| Lemon, Don | 3 | 3 | 5.21 | 21 | 11 | 0 | 0 | 74 | 89 | 48 | 43 | 20 | 52 | R | R | 6-4 | 195 | 6-2-67 | 1989 | Locust Grove, Ga. |
| Martinez, Jose | 6 | 4 | 4.28 | 13 | 13 | 3 | 0 | 80 | 92 | 49 | 38 | 24 | 29 | R | R | 6-2 | 155 | 4-1-71 | 1989 | Santiago, D.R. |
| McGraw, Tom | 2 | 0 | 5.59 | 5 | 2 | 0 | 0 | 10 | 12 | 7 | 6 | 4 | 8 | L | L | 6-2 | 195 | 12-8-67 | 1990 | Yacolt, Wash. |
| Miller, Kurt | 3 | 3 | 4.50 | 9 | 9 | 0 | 0 | 48 | 42 | 24 | 24 | 34 | 19 | R | R | 6-5 | 200 | 8-24-72 | 1990 | Bakersfield, Calif. |
| Myers, Mike | 7 | 14 | 5.18 | 27 | 27 | 3 | 0 | 162 | 195 | 109 | 93 | 52 | 112 | L | L | 6-3 | 197 | 6-26-69 | 1990 | Wheeling, Ill. |
| Newlin, Jim | 0 | 0 | 13.50 | 4 | 0 | 0 | 0 | 6 | 11 | 9 | 9 | 4 | 3 | R | R | 6-2 | 205 | 9-11-66 | 1989 | Leawood, Kan. |
| Rapp, Pat | 8 | 3 | 3.43 | 17 | 17 | 4 | 0 | 108 | 89 | 45 | 41 | 34 | 93 | R | R | 6-3 | 210 | 7-13-67 | 1989 | Sulphur, La. |

# MARLINS: ORGANIZATION LEADERS

### MAJOR LEAGUERS

**BATTING**

| | | |
|---|---|---|
| *AVG | Jeff Conine | .292 |
| R | Two tied at | 75 |
| H | Jeff Conine | 174 |
| TB | Jeff Conine | 240 |
| 2B | Jeff Conine | 24 |
| 3B | Benito Santiago | 6 |
| HR | Orestes Destrade | 20 |
| RBI | Orestes Destrade | 87 |
| BB | Walt Weiss | 79 |
| SO | Jeff Conine | 135 |
| SB | Chuck Carr | 58 |

**PITCHING**

| | | |
|---|---|---|
| W | Chris Hammond | 11 |
| L | Jack Armstrong | 17 |
| #ERA | Richie Lewis | 3.26 |
| G | Two tied at | 59 |
| CG | Ryan Bowen | 2 |
| SV | Brian Harvey | 45 |
| IP | Charlie Hough | 204 |
| BB | Ryan Bowen | 87 |
| SO | Charlie Hough | 126 |

GEORGE GOJKOVICH

**Orestes Destrade**

Returns to majors with 20 homers

### MINOR LEAGUERS

**BATTING**

| | | |
|---|---|---|
| *AVG | Tim Clark, High Desert | .363 |
| R | Kerwin Moore, High Desert | 120 |
| H | Tim Clark, High Desert | 185 |
| TB | Tim Clark, High Desert | 298 |
| 2B | Tim Clark, High Desert | 42 |
| 3B | Two tied at | 10 |
| HR | John Toale, High Desert | 28 |
| RBI | Tim Clark, High Desert | 126 |
| BB | Kerwin Moore, High Desert | 114 |
| SO | Todd Pridy, Kane County | 129 |
| SB | Kerwin Moore, High Desert | 71 |

**PITCHING**

| | | |
|---|---|---|
| W | Two tied at | 12 |
| L | John Johnstone, Edmonton | 15 |
| #ERA | Tony Saunders, Kane County | 2.27 |
| G | Doug Pettit, Kane County | 52 |
| CG | Joel Adamson, High Desert-Edmonton | 6 |
| SV | Doug Pettit, Kane County | 17 |
| IP | Robert Person, High Desert | 169 |
| BB | Hector Carrasco, Kane County | 76 |
| SO | Reynol Mendoza, Kane County | 153 |

*Minimum 250 At-Bats #Minimum 75 Innings

| PITCHING | W | L | ERA | G | GS | CG | SV | IP | H | R | ER | BB | SO | B | T | HT | WT | DOB | 1st Yr | Resides |
|---|---|---|---|---|---|---|---|---|---|---|---|---|---|---|---|---|---|---|---|---|
| McGraw, Tom | 2 | 0 | 5.59 | 5 | 2 | 0 | 0 | 10 | 12 | 7 | 6 | 4 | 8 | L | L | 6-2 | 195 | 12-8-67 | 1990 | Yacolt, Wash. |
| Miller, Kurt | 3 | 3 | 4.50 | 9 | 9 | 0 | 0 | 48 | 42 | 24 | 24 | 34 | 19 | R | R | 6-5 | 200 | 8-24-72 | 1990 | Bakersfield, Calif. |
| Myers, Mike | 7 | 14 | 5.18 | 27 | 27 | 3 | 0 | 162 | 195 | 109 | 93 | 52 | 112 | L | L | 6-3 | 197 | 6-26-69 | 1990 | Wheeling, Ill. |
| Newlin, Jim | 0 | 0 | 13.50 | 4 | 0 | 0 | 0 | 6 | 11 | 9 | 9 | 4 | 3 | R | R | 6-2 | 205 | 9-11-66 | 1989 | Leawood, Kan. |
| Rapp, Pat | 8 | 3 | 3.43 | 17 | 17 | 4 | 0 | 108 | 89 | 45 | 41 | 34 | 93 | R | R | 6-3 | 210 | 7-13-67 | 1989 | Sulphur, La. |
| Scheid, Rich | 5 | 7 | 5.07 | 38 | 12 | 0 | 0 | 110 | 130 | 68 | 62 | 38 | 84 | L | L | 6-3 | 185 | 2-3-65 | 1986 | Summit, N.J. |
| Turner, Matt | 0 | 0 | 0.66 | 12 | 0 | 0 | 10 | 14 | 9 | 1 | 1 | 2 | 15 | R | R | 6-5 | 215 | 2-18-67 | 1986 | Lexington, Ky. |
| Walter, Gene | 2 | 0 | 7.88 | 6 | 0 | 0 | 0 | 8 | 13 | 7 | 7 | 3 | 4 | L | L | 6-4 | 200 | 11-22-60 | 1982 | LaGrange, Ky. |
| Weathers, Dave | 11 | 4 | 3.83 | 22 | 22 | 3 | 0 | 141 | 150 | 77 | 60 | 47 | 117 | R | R | 6-3 | 205 | 9-25-69 | 1988 | Leoma, Tenn. |
| Yaughn, Kip | 1 | 0 | 0.00 | 1 | 1 | 0 | 0 | 5 | 6 | 0 | 0 | 1 | 2 | R | R | 6-1 | 180 | 7-20-69 | 1990 | Concord, Calif. |

**FIELDING**

| Catcher | PCT | G | PO | A | E | DP |
|---|---|---|---|---|---|---|
| Lyden | .993 | 22 | 129 | 12 | 1 | 1 |
| McGriff | .996 | 83 | 505 | 38 | 2 | 1 |
| Natal | .986 | 17 | 119 | 19 | 2 | 0 |
| Snyder | .957 | 27 | 144 | 10 | 7 | 4 |

| First Base | PCT | G | PO | A | E | DP |
|---|---|---|---|---|---|---|
| Berroa | .947 | 13 | 84 | 6 | 5 | 8 |
| Delo Santos | .986 | 112 | 850 | 63 | 13 | 81 |
| Fariss | .990 | 24 | 190 | 18 | 2 | 23 |
| Lyden | .982 | 7 | 52 | 4 | 1 | 4 |
| Snyder | 1.000 | 3 | 5 | 0 | 0 | 2 |

| Second Base | PCT | G | PO | A | E | DP |
|---|---|---|---|---|---|---|
| Barberie | .952 | 4 | 8 | 12 | 1 | 0 |
| Capra | .000 | 1 | 0 | 0 | 0 | 0 |
| Jackson | .895 | 5 | 8 | 9 | 2 | 4 |
| Pedrique | .946 | 16 | 34 | 36 | 4 | 12 |
| Polidor | 1.000 | 11 | 32 | 30 | 0 | 6 |
| Renteria | .948 | 14 | 31 | 42 | 4 | 12 |
| Santana | .939 | 36 | 89 | 96 | 12 | 20 |
| Small | .974 | 64 | 121 | 180 | 8 | 43 |

| Third Base | PCT | G | PO | A | E | DP |
|---|---|---|---|---|---|---|
| Capra | .944 | 70 | 58 | 144 | 12 | 7 |
| Delo Santos | 1.000 | 4 | 1 | 5 | 0 | 2 |
| Jackson | .923 | 26 | 25 | 59 | 7 | 11 |
| Pedrique | 1.000 | 23 | 14 | 46 | 0 | 5 |
| Polidor | 1.000 | 2 | 1 | 1 | 0 | 0 |
| Renteria | .824 | 5 | 2 | 12 | 3 | 1 |
| Small | .964 | 25 | 18 | 62 | 3 | 8 |

| Shortstop | PCT | G | PO | A | E | DP |
|---|---|---|---|---|---|---|
| Pedrique | .931 | 85 | 118 | 233 | 26 | 44 |
| Polidor | .969 | 60 | 75 | 179 | 8 | 35 |
| Santana | 1.000 | 2 | 1 | 3 | 0 | 1 |
| Small | 1.000 | 2 | 0 | 1 | 0 | 0 |

| Outfield | PCT | G | PO | A | E | DP |
|---|---|---|---|---|---|---|
| Berroa | .985 | 53 | 126 | 4 | 2 | 2 |
| Capra | .985 | 36 | 62 | 3 | 1 | 0 |
| Everett | .976 | 34 | 69 | 12 | 2 | 0 |
| Fariss | .990 | 56 | 95 | 2 | 1 | 1 |
| Felix | 1.000 | 7 | 18 | 1 | 0 | 0 |
| Jackson | .667 | 3 | 1 | 1 | 1 | 0 |
| Pose | .970 | 99 | 192 | 4 | 6 | 1 |
| Renteria | 1.000 | 2 | 5 | 0 | 0 | 0 |
| Whitmore | .978 | 72 | 171 | 7 | 4 | 3 |
| Wilson | .985 | 85 | 121 | 13 | 2 | 1 |

# HIGH DESERT — A

## CALIFORNIA LEAGUE

| BATTING | AVG | G | AB | R | H | 2B | 3B | HR | RBI | BB | SO | SB | CS | B | T | HT | WT | DOB | 1st Yr | Resides |
|---|---|---|---|---|---|---|---|---|---|---|---|---|---|---|---|---|---|---|---|---|
| Clark, Tim, of-dh | .363 | 128 | 510 | 109 | 185 | 42 | 10 | 17 | 126 | 56 | 65 | 2 | 5 | L | L | 6-3 | 210 | 2-10-69 | 1990 | Philadelphia, Pa. |
| Everett, Carl, of | .289 | 59 | 253 | 48 | 73 | 12 | 6 | 10 | 52 | 22 | 73 | 24 | 9 | S | R | 6-0 | 181 | 6-3-70 | 1990 | Tampa, Fla. |
| Gousha, Sean, c | .183 | 45 | 126 | 22 | 23 | 2 | 0 | 0 | 11 | 26 | 47 | 0 | 1 | R | R | 6-4 | 200 | 9-19-70 | 1992 | Escondido, Calif. |
| Kosco, Bryn, 3b-1b | .307 | 121 | 450 | 96 | 138 | 25 | 3 | 27 | 121 | 62 | 97 | 1 | 6 | L | R | 6-1 | 185 | 3-9-67 | 1988 | West Palm Beach, Fla. |
| Malinoski, Chris, 2b-3b | .304 | 111 | 368 | 62 | 112 | 24 | 3 | 3 | 72 | 81 | 54 | 7 | 7 | R | R | 5-9 | 185 | 4-7-68 | 1990 | Chandler, Ariz. |
| Martinez, Ramon, ss | .265 | 118 | 412 | 73 | 109 | 10 | 6 | 2 | 46 | 49 | 79 | 46 | 11 | S | R | 6-2 | 165 | 9-8-69 | 1990 | Villa Gonzalez, D.R. |
| Moore, Kerwin, of | .269 | 132 | 510 | 120 | 137 | 20 | 9 | 6 | 52 | 114 | 95 | 71 | 16 | S | R | 6-1 | 190 | 10-29-70 | 1988 | Detroit, Mich. |
| North, Tim, ss | .000 | 9 | 4 | 4 | 0 | 0 | 0 | 0 | 0 | 1 | 0 | 1 | 1 | S | R | 5-10 | 170 | 3-13-69 | 1992 | Whitehouse, N.J. |
| Prater, Andrew, c | .125 | 2 | 8 | 1 | 1 | 0 | 0 | 0 | 0 | 0 | 2 | 0 | 0 | R | R | 6-1 | 195 | 7-4-72 | 1990 | Austin, Texas |
| Renteria, Edinson, ss-3b | .314 | 56 | 207 | 43 | 65 | 12 | 0 | 2 | 27 | 22 | 33 | 1 | 4 | R | R | 5-11 | 160 | 4-7-68 | 1985 | Barranquilla, Colombia |
| Samuels, Scott, of | .297 | 76 | 219 | 43 | 65 | 10 | 4 | 6 | 40 | 45 | 55 | 12 | 4 | L | R | 5-11 | 190 | 5-19-71 | 1992 | San Jose, Calif. |
| Skeels, Mark, c | .277 | 91 | 300 | 48 | 83 | 16 | 4 | 6 | 56 | 69 | 62 | 3 | 1 | S | R | 5-11 | 195 | 2-20-70 | 1992 | Thousand Oaks, Calif. |
| Snyder, Randy, c | .294 | 20 | 68 | 13 | 20 | 5 | 1 | 3 | 17 | 9 | 11 | 0 | 0 | S | R | 6-2 | 210 | 3-28-67 | 1988 | Yakima, Wash. |
| Tavarez, Jesus, of | .293 | 109 | 444 | 104 | 130 | 21 | 8 | 7 | 71 | 57 | 66 | 47 | 14 | S | R | 6-0 | 170 | 3-26-71 | 1990 | Santo Domingo, D.R. |
| Toale, John, 1b | .286 | 134 | 517 | 108 | 148 | 30 | 3 | 28 | 125 | 84 | 101 | 1 | 3 | L | R | 6-0 | 190 | 1-11-65 | 1983 | Coral Springs, Fla. |
| Torres, Tony, 2b | .230 | 89 | 287 | 45 | 66 | 9 | 3 | 1 | 25 | 24 | 69 | 14 | 8 | R | R | 5-9 | 165 | 6-1-70 | 1992 | San Pablo, Calif. |

| PITCHING | W | L | ERA | G | GS | CG | SV | IP | H | R | ER | BB | SO | B | T | HT | WT | DOB | 1st Yr | Resides |
|---|---|---|---|---|---|---|---|---|---|---|---|---|---|---|---|---|---|---|---|---|
| Adamson, Joel | 5 | 5 | 4.58 | 22 | 20 | 6 | 0 | 130 | 160 | 83 | 66 | 30 | 72 | L | L | 6-4 | 180 | 7-2-71 | 1990 | Lakewood, Calif. |
| Berumen, Andres | 9 | 2 | 3.62 | 14 | 13 | 1 | 0 | 92 | 85 | 45 | 37 | 36 | 74 | R | R | 6-2 | 195 | 4-5-71 | 1989 | Banning, Calif. |
| Corsi, Jim | 0 | 1 | 3.00 | 3 | 3 | 0 | 0 | 9 | 11 | 3 | 3 | 2 | 6 | R | R | 6-1 | 220 | 9-9-61 | 1982 | Newtonville, Mass. |
| Darensbourg, Victor | 0 | 0 | 0.00 | 1 | 0 | 0 | 0 | 1 | 1 | 0 | 0 | 0 | 1 | L | L | 5-10 | 165 | 11-13-70 | 1992 | Los Angeles, Calif. |
| Juelsgaard, Jarod | 6 | 5 | 5.56 | 17 | 16 | 0 | 0 | 79 | 81 | 57 | 49 | 58 | 58 | R | R | 6-3 | 190 | 6-27-68 | 1991 | Elk Horn, Iowa |

| PITCHING | W | L | ERA | G | GS | CG | SV | IP | H | R | ER | BB | SO | B | T | HT | WT | DOB | 1st Yr | Resides |
|---|---|---|---|---|---|---|---|---|---|---|---|---|---|---|---|---|---|---|---|---|
| Kendrena, Ken | 6 | 0 | 6.62 | 40 | 0 | 0 | 2 | 67 | 78 | 50 | 49 | 26 | 63 | R | R | 5-11 | 170 | 10-29-70 | 1992 | Rancho Cucamonga, Calif. |
| Kerfut, George | 3 | 0 | 5.85 | 28 | 2 | 0 | 4 | 68 | 86 | 60 | 44 | 23 | 35 | R | R | 6-1 | 200 | 8-20-67 | 1989 | Croton, N.Y. |
| Lemon, Don | 0 | 1 | 3.70 | 5 | 5 | 0 | 0 | 24 | 35 | 17 | 10 | 2 | 17 | R | R | 6-4 | 195 | 6-2-67 | 1989 | Locust Grove, Ga. |
| MaGill, Jim | 1 | 0 | 6.65 | 14 | 0 | 0 | 0 | 23 | 26 | 21 | 17 | 23 | 18 | R | R | 6-10 | 225 | 3-11-69 | 1988 | Staten Island, N.Y. |
| McGraw, Tom | 2 | 3 | 3.55 | 6 | 6 | 1 | 0 | 38 | 38 | 17 | 15 | 7 | 31 | L | L | 6-2 | 195 | 12-8-67 | 1990 | La Center, Wash. |
| Newlin, Jim | 3 | 0 | 2.86 | 17 | 0 | 0 | 3 | 28 | 30 | 15 | 9 | 9 | 23 | R | R | 6-2 | 205 | 9-11-66 | 1989 | Leawood, Kan. |
| Parisotto, Barry | 6 | 5 | 4.03 | 32 | 14 | 1 | 3 | 118 | 137 | 71 | 53 | 34 | 92 | L | R | 6-2 | 190 | 11-23-67 | 1989 | White Rock, B.C. |
| Patterson, Jim | 7 | 6 | 5.10 | 33 | 1 | 0 | 1 | 67 | 71 | 49 | 38 | 44 | 51 | R | R | 6-2 | 190 | 9-17-70 | 1992 | Riverside, Calif. |
| Person, Robert | 12 | 10 | 4.69 | 28 | 26 | 4 | 0 | 169 | 184 | 115 | 88 | 48 | 107 | R | R | 5-11 | 180 | 10-6-69 | 1989 | St. Louis, Mo. |
| Spencer, Stan | 4 | 4 | 4.09 | 13 | 13 | 0 | 0 | 62 | 67 | 33 | 28 | 18 | 38 | R | R | 6-3 | 195 | 8-2-68 | 1991 | Vancouver, Wash. |
| Stafford, Gerry | 7 | 4 | 4.93 | 27 | 7 | 1 | 2 | 80 | 85 | 55 | 44 | 42 | 45 | S | L | 6-4 | 210 | 4-7-70 | 1992 | Oceanside, Calif. |
| Whitman, Ryan | 8 | 2 | 3.73 | 12 | 5 | 0 | 0 | 51 | 49 | 26 | 21 | 21 | 31 | R | R | 6-2 | 180 | 1-4-70 | 1990 | Lake Park, Fla. |
| Whitten, Mike | 5 | 2 | 2.22 | 43 | 0 | 0 | 13 | 53 | 44 | 20 | 13 | 30 | 26 | L | L | 6-4 | 200 | 12-27-68 | 1992 | Raleigh, N.C. |
| Wiley, Skip | 1 | 2 | 7.23 | 11 | 0 | 0 | 0 | 19 | 25 | 15 | 15 | 3 | 13 | L | R | 6-3 | 215 | 6-6-67 | 1989 | Olathe, Kan. |
| Yaughn, Kip | 0 | 0 | 6.86 | 6 | 6 | 0 | 0 | 21 | 25 | 17 | 16 | 13 | 13 | R | R | 6-1 | 180 | 7-20-69 | 1990 | Concord, Calif. |

# KANE COUNTY      A
## MIDWEST LEAGUE

| BATTING | AVG | G | AB | R | H | 2B | 3B | HR | RBI | BB | SO | SB | CS | B | T | HT | WT | DOB | 1st Yr | Resides |
|---|---|---|---|---|---|---|---|---|---|---|---|---|---|---|---|---|---|---|---|---|
| Christian, Eddie, of | .268 | 112 | 366 | 49 | 98 | 21 | 5 | 3 | 46 | 58 | 77 | 9 | 11 | S | L | 5-11 | 180 | 8-26-71 | 1992 | Richmond, Calif. |
| Clapinski, Chris, 2b | .210 | 82 | 214 | 22 | 45 | 12 | 1 | 0 | 27 | 31 | 55 | 3 | 8 | S | R | 6-0 | 165 | 8-20-71 | 1992 | Rancho Mirage, Calif. |
| Gamble, Freddie, 2b | .242 | 58 | 99 | 17 | 24 | 3 | 3 | 0 | 10 | 6 | 9 | 5 | 3 | L | R | 5-9 | 160 | 11-25-70 | 1989 | Manning, S.C. |
| Johnson, Charles, c | .275 | 135 | 488 | 74 | 134 | 29 | 5 | 19 | 94 | 62 | 111 | 9 | 1 | R | R | 6-2 | 215 | 7-20-71 | 1992 | Fort Pierce, Fla. |
| Lucca, Lou, 3b | .277 | 127 | 419 | 52 | 116 | 25 | 2 | 6 | 53 | 60 | 58 | 4 | 10 | R | R | 5-11 | 210 | 10-13-71 | 1992 | So. San Francisco, Calif. |
| Pridy, Todd, 1b | .272 | 132 | 475 | 63 | 129 | 38 | 5 | 13 | 75 | 55 | 129 | 5 | 2 | L | L | 5-11 | 215 | 2-28-71 | 1992 | Napa, Calif. |
| Redmond, Mike, c | .200 | 43 | 100 | 10 | 20 | 2 | 0 | 0 | 6 | 17 | 2 | 0 | 0 | R | R | 6-0 | 190 | 5-5-71 | 1993 | Spokane, Wash. |
| Renteria, Edgar, ss | .203 | 116 | 384 | 40 | 78 | 8 | 0 | 1 | 35 | 35 | 94 | 7 | 8 | R | R | 6-1 | 172 | 8-7-75 | 1992 | Barranquilla, Colombia |
| Robinson, Dan, of-1b | .242 | 105 | 363 | 60 | 88 | 23 | 2 | 2 | 34 | 50 | 90 | 5 | 7 | L | R | 6-1 | 195 | 8-19-70 | 1992 | Shreveport, La. |
| Sheff, Chris, of | .272 | 129 | 456 | 79 | 124 | 22 | 5 | 5 | 50 | 58 | 100 | 33 | 10 | R | R | 6-3 | 210 | 2-4-71 | 1992 | Laguna Hills, Calif. |
| Sylvestri, Tony, 2b-ss | .259 | 106 | 367 | 40 | 95 | 13 | 3 | 0 | 31 | 36 | 37 | 9 | 9 | S | R | 5-9 | 165 | 10-11-70 | 1992 | San Bruno, Calif. |
| Wilson, Pookie, of | .249 | 129 | 469 | 74 | 117 | 8 | 2 | 0 | 27 | 52 | 55 | 34 | 15 | L | L | 5-10 | 180 | 10-24-70 | 1992 | Sylacauga, Ala. |
| Wulf, Eric, dh | .261 | 82 | 272 | 22 | 71 | 15 | 0 | 1 | 35 | 19 | 60 | 2 | 1 | L | R | 6-2 | 210 | 1-5-70 | 1993 | Wenatchee, Wash. |

| PITCHING | W | L | ERA | G | GS | CG | SV | IP | H | R | ER | BB | SO | B | T | HT | WT | DOB | 1st Yr | Resides |
|---|---|---|---|---|---|---|---|---|---|---|---|---|---|---|---|---|---|---|---|---|
| Carrasco, Hector | 6 | 12 | 4.11 | 28 | 28 | 0 | 0 | 149 | 153 | 90 | 68 | 76 | 127 | R | R | 6-2 | 175 | 10-22-69 | 1988 | San Pedro de Macoris, D.R. |
| Darensbourg, Victor | 9 | 1 | 2.14 | 46 | 0 | 0 | 16 | 71 | 58 | 17 | 17 | 28 | 89 | L | L | 5-10 | 165 | 11-13-70 | 1992 | Los Angeles, Calif. |
| Donahue, Matt | 3 | 2 | 4.70 | 31 | 3 | 0 | 2 | 67 | 66 | 39 | 35 | 31 | 70 | R | R | 6-1 | 210 | 8-14-70 | 1992 | McCormick, S.C. |
| Frazier, Brad | 5 | 0 | 5.93 | 39 | 0 | 0 | 1 | 30 | 35 | 24 | 20 | 26 | 23 | L | L | 6-0 | 185 | 8-19-70 | 1992 | Clarion, Pa. |
| Juelsgaard, Jarod | 3 | 0 | 3.81 | 11 | 2 | 1 | 0 | 26 | 21 | 11 | 11 | 7 | 18 | R | R | 6-3 | 190 | 6-27-68 | 1991 | Elk Horn, Iowa |
| Leahy, Pat | 8 | 11 | 3.22 | 25 | 25 | 2 | 0 | 140 | 124 | 68 | 50 | 43 | 106 | R | R | 6-6 | 245 | 10-31-70 | 1992 | Yakima, Wash. |
| Lynch, John | 1 | 0 | 3.00 | 2 | 2 | 0 | 0 | 9 | 4 | 4 | 3 | 12 | 3 | R | R | 6-2 | 215 | 9-25-71 | 1992 | Solana Beach, Calif. |
| Mendoza, Reynol | 12 | 5 | 2.86 | 26 | 23 | 3 | 2 | 164 | 129 | 59 | 52 | 45 | 153 | R | R | 6-1 | 205 | 10-27-70 | 1992 | San Antonio, Texas |
| Petersen, Matt | 9 | 11 | 4.89 | 30 | 22 | 1 | 3 | 142 | 139 | 85 | 77 | 46 | 118 | R | R | 6-4 | 190 | 5-21-70 | 1992 | Omaha, Neb. |
| Pettit, Doug | 5 | 10 | 2.45 | 52 | 0 | 0 | 17 | 77 | 67 | 26 | 21 | 16 | 63 | L | R | 6-1 | 220 | 4-10-70 | 1992 | Deer Park, Texas |
| Saunders, Tony | 6 | 1 | 2.27 | 23 | 10 | 2 | 1 | 83 | 72 | 23 | 21 | 32 | 87 | L | L | 6-1 | 189 | 4-29-74 | 1992 | Ellicott City, Md. |
| Tidwell, Jason | 3 | 1 | 3.22 | 25 | 7 | 0 | 2 | 81 | 68 | 34 | 29 | 38 | 78 | R | R | 6-3 | 190 | 8-2-71 | 1992 | Cartersville, Ga. |
| Vlcek, Jim | 3 | 1 | 3.65 | 33 | 0 | 0 | 1 | 62 | 64 | 33 | 25 | 35 | 54 | R | R | 6-4 | 190 | 12-17-66 | 1985 | Palos Hills, Ill. |
| Whisenant, Matt | 2 | 6 | 4.69 | 15 | 15 | 0 | 0 | 71 | 68 | 45 | 37 | 56 | 74 | S | L | 6-3 | 215 | 6-8-71 | 1990 | La Canada, Calif. |
| Wiley, Skip | 0 | 1 | 1.50 | 7 | 0 | 0 | 0 | 12 | 11 | 2 | 2 | 0 | 9 | L | R | 6-3 | 215 | 6-6-67 | 1989 | Olathe, Kan. |

# ELMIRA      A
## NEW YORK-PENN LEAGUE

| BATTING | AVG | G | AB | R | H | 2B | 3B | HR | RBI | BB | SO | SB | CS | B | T | HT | WT | DOB | 1st Yr | Resides |
|---|---|---|---|---|---|---|---|---|---|---|---|---|---|---|---|---|---|---|---|---|
| Berg, Dave, 3b-2b | .263 | 75 | 281 | 37 | 74 | 13 | 1 | 4 | 28 | 34 | 37 | 7 | 4 | R | R | 5-11 | 185 | 9-3-70 | 1993 | Roseville, Calif. |
| Bonifazio, Anthony, of | .207 | 22 | 82 | 10 | 17 | 0 | 0 | 1 | 10 | 2 | 24 | 1 | 2 | R | R | 6-2 | 205 | 6-15-71 | 1992 | Las Vegas, Nev. |
| Brown, Ronnie, of | .284 | 75 | 285 | 52 | 81 | 22 | 1 | 9 | 54 | 37 | 60 | 4 | 2 | R | R | 6-3 | 185 | 1-17-70 | 1993 | Tampa, Fla. |
| Gross, William, dh-c | .231 | 4 | 13 | 1 | 3 | 0 | 0 | 0 | 0 | 1 | 5 | 0 | 0 | R | R | 6-0 | 190 | 8-29-70 | 1993 | Glendora, N.J. |
| Martinez, Matt, 2b | .225 | 64 | 218 | 43 | 49 | 5 | 0 | 1 | 19 | 27 | 39 | 14 | 4 | R | R | 5-9 | 185 | 1-25-71 | 1993 | Elverta, Calif. |
| McMillon, Bill, of | .305 | 57 | 226 | 38 | 69 | 14 | 2 | 6 | 35 | 31 | 43 | 5 | 4 | L | L | 5-11 | 172 | 11-17-71 | 1993 | Sumter, S.C. |
| Moen, Robbie, of-2b | .286 | 49 | 182 | 16 | 52 | 10 | 0 | 2 | 16 | 15 | 28 | 2 | 4 | R | R | 5-10 | 180 | 3-27-71 | 1993 | Tucson, Ariz. |
| Prater, Andrew, c | .199 | 45 | 156 | 19 | 31 | 7 | 0 | 3 | 15 | 17 | 30 | 1 | 4 | R | R | 6-1 | 195 | 7-4-72 | 1990 | Austin, Texas |
| Sanchez, Sergio, 2b | .133 | 17 | 45 | 3 | 6 | 0 | 0 | 0 | 3 | 9 | 13 | 0 | 0 | R | R | 5-10 | 168 | 1-1-71 | 1993 | Watsonville, Calif. |
| Seminoff, Rich, 1b | .211 | 67 | 218 | 34 | 46 | 8 | 0 | 11 | 40 | 35 | 72 | 3 | 0 | L | L | 6-4 | 225 | 12-11-70 | 1993 | Phoenix, Ariz. |

# MARLINS: MOST COMMON LINEUPS

| | Florida | Edmonton | High Desert | Kane County |
|---|---|---|---|---|
| | Majors | AAA | A | A |
| C | Benito Santiago (136) | Terry McGriff (83) | Mark Skeels (80) | Charles Johnson (118) |
| 1B | Orestes Destrade (152) | Luis De los Santos (112) | John Toale (101) | Todd Pridy (107) |
| 2B | Bret Barberie (97) | Jeff Small (64) | Tony Torres (80) | Chris Clapinski (66) |
| 3B | Gary Sheffield (66) | Nick Capra (70) | Bryn Kosco (87) | Lou Lucca (122) |
| SS | Walt Weiss (153) | Al Pedrique (85) | Ramon Martinez (107) | Edgar Renteria (114) |
| OF | Jeff Conine (147) | Scott Pose (101) | Kerwin Moore (128) | Pookie Wilson (126) |
| | Chuck Carr (139) | Nigel Wilson (85) | Jesus Tavarez (108) | Chris Sheff (125) |
| | Darrell Whitmore (69) | Darrell Whitmore (72) | Tim Clark (101) | Eddie Christian (104) |
| DH | N/A | Geronimo Berroa (22) | Tim Clark (35) | Eric Wulf (73) |
| SP | Charlie Hough (34) | Mike Myers (27) | Robert Person (26) | Hector Carrasco (28) |
| RP | Harvey/Klink (59) | Gleaton/Kramer (46) | Mike Whitten (43) | Doug Pettit (52) |
| | Full-season farm clubs only | No. of games at position in parenthesis | | |

# MARLINS TOP 10 PROSPECTS

How the Marlins Top 10 prospects, as judged by Baseball America prior to the 1993 season, fared in 1993:

| Player, Pos. | Club (Class) | AVG | AB | H | HR | RBI | SB |
|---|---|---|---|---|---|---|---|
| 1. Nigel Wilson, of | Edmonton (AAA) | .292 | 370 | 108 | 17 | 68 | 8 |
| | Florida | .000 | 16 | 0 | 0 | 0 | 0 |
| 2. Edgar Renteria, ss | Kane County (A) | .203 | 384 | 78 | 1 | 35 | 7 |
| 5. Carl Everett, of | High Desert (A) | .289 | 253 | 73 | 10 | 52 | 24 |
| | Edmonton (AAA) | .309 | 136 | 42 | 6 | 16 | 12 |
| | Florida | .105 | 19 | 2 | 0 | 0 | 1 |
| 7. Charles Johnson, c | Kane County (A) | .275 | 488 | 134 | 19 | 94 | 9 |
| 8. Darrell Whitmore, of | Edmonton (AAA) | .355 | 273 | 97 | 9 | 62 | 11 |
| | Florida | .204 | 250 | 51 | 4 | 19 | 4 |

| Player, Pos. | Club (Class) | W | L | ERA | IP | H | BB | SO |
|---|---|---|---|---|---|---|---|---|
| 3. Jose Martinez, rhp* | Edmonton (AAA) | 6 | 4 | 4.28 | 80 | 92 | 24 | 29 |
| | Las Vegas (AAA) | 2 | 3 | 9.93 | 35 | 56 | 15 | 16 |
| 4. Matt Whisenant, lhp | Kane County (A) | 2 | 6 | 4.69 | 71 | 68 | 56 | 74 |
| 6. Pat Rapp, rhp | Edmonton (AAA) | 8 | 3 | 3.43 | 108 | 89 | 34 | 93 |
| | Florida | 4 | 6 | 4.02 | 94 | 101 | 39 | 57 |
| 9. Hector Carrasco, rhp | Kane County (A) | 6 | 12 | 4.11 | 149 | 153 | 76 | 127 |
| 10. John Lynch, rhp | Kane County (A) | 1 | 0 | 3.00 | 9 | 4 | 12 | 3 |

*Traded to San Diego Padres

**Nigel Wilson**
.292 at Edmonton

## BATTING

| | AVG | G | AB | R | H | 2B | 3B | HR | RBI | BB | SO | SB | CS | B | T | HT | WT | DOB | 1st Yr | Resides |
|---|---|---|---|---|---|---|---|---|---|---|---|---|---|---|---|---|---|---|---|---|
| Sims, Mike, c | .176 | 24 | 85 | 6 | 15 | 3 | 0 | 0 | 7 | 1 | 18 | 0 | 0 | R | R | 5-11 | 185 | 2-23-71 | 1993 | Lancaster, Calif. |
| Small, Andy, dh-1b | .216 | 56 | 176 | 25 | 38 | 8 | 1 | 1 | 16 | 34 | 72 | 2 | 1 | R | R | 6-3 | 200 | 2-19-70 | 1993 | Riverside, Calif. |
| Southard, Scott, ss | .238 | 74 | 281 | 34 | 67 | 11 | 0 | 1 | 20 | 24 | 41 | 3 | 4 | R | R | 5-10 | 165 | 10-14-71 | 1993 | Pensacola, Fla. |
| Strickland, Erick, of | .259 | 59 | 212 | 30 | 55 | 11 | 3 | 4 | 34 | 35 | 32 | 8 | 4 | L | R | 6-3 | 205 | 11-25-73 | 1992 | Bellevue, Neb. |
| Turnbull, Tony, c-dh | .103 | 9 | 29 | 3 | 3 | 0 | 0 | 0 | 2 | 2 | 10 | 0 | 0 | R | R | 6-0 | 200 | 8-22-71 | 1993 | San Jose, Calif. |

## PITCHING

| | W | L | ERA | G | GS | CG | SV | IP | H | R | ER | BB | SO | B | T | HT | WT | DOB | 1st Yr | Resides |
|---|---|---|---|---|---|---|---|---|---|---|---|---|---|---|---|---|---|---|---|---|
| Bowen, Mitch | 1 | 2 | 4.70 | 18 | 0 | 0 | 2 | 46 | 55 | 37 | 24 | 14 | 45 | R | R | 6-5 | 225 | 10-24-72 | 1993 | La Crescenta, Calif. |
| Chergey, Dan | 3 | 5 | 3.50 | 15 | 10 | 1 | 0 | 80 | 85 | 34 | 31 | 14 | 53 | R | R | 6-2 | 195 | 1-29-71 | 1993 | Thousand Oaks, Calif. |
| Dominguez, Johnny | 0 | 2 | 10.00 | 6 | 0 | 0 | 0 | 9 | 7 | 12 | 10 | 11 | 8 | L | L | 5-10 | 175 | 9-25-69 | 1992 | Miami, Fla. |
| Filbeck, Ryan | 4 | 3 | 4.71 | 13 | 13 | 0 | 0 | 57 | 70 | 35 | 30 | 24 | 42 | R | R | 6-2 | 200 | 12-23-72 | 1993 | El Toro, Calif. |
| Gomez, Phil | 2 | 2 | 4.35 | 12 | 7 | 0 | 1 | 41 | 45 | 29 | 20 | 14 | 17 | R | R | 6-0 | 190 | 8-21-73 | 1993 | Watsonville, Calif. |
| Larkin, Andy | 5 | 7 | 2.97 | 14 | 14 | 4 | 0 | 88 | 74 | 43 | 29 | 23 | 89 | R | R | 6-4 | 181 | 6-27-74 | 1992 | Medford, Ore. |
| Minyard, Sam | 0 | 0 | 2.35 | 3 | 0 | 0 | 0 | 8 | 6 | 3 | 2 | 4 | 7 | L | L | 6-3 | 195 | 10-30-71 | 1993 | Newhall, Calif. |
| Mix, Greg | 3 | 3 | 4.17 | 17 | 1 | 0 | 2 | 45 | 51 | 26 | 21 | 17 | 38 | R | R | 6-4 | 210 | 8-21-71 | 1993 | Albuquerque, N.M. |
| Nunez, Clemente | 4 | 3 | 3.98 | 14 | 9 | 0 | 0 | 63 | 66 | 31 | 28 | 17 | 34 | R | R | 5-11 | 181 | 2-10-75 | 1993 | Bonao, D.R. |
| Thornton, Paul | 3 | 5 | 2.26 | 16 | 7 | 1 | 2 | 64 | 51 | 29 | 16 | 27 | 59 | R | R | 6-2 | 210 | 6-21-70 | 1993 | Callahan, Fla. |
| Valdes, Marc | 0 | 2 | 5.59 | 3 | 3 | 0 | 0 | 16 | 8 | 9 | 6 | 7 | 15 | R | R | 6-0 | 170 | 12-20-71 | 1993 | Tampa, Fla. |
| Van Zandt, Jon | 1 | 2 | 6.52 | 17 | 0 | 0 | 4 | 29 | 42 | 22 | 21 | 5 | 28 | R | R | 6-2 | 190 | 11-12-70 | 1993 | Imperial, Calif. |
| Walania, Al | 3 | 3 | 3.07 | 22 | 0 | 0 | 4 | 44 | 43 | 21 | 15 | 13 | 47 | S | R | 6-2 | 175 | 1-14-71 | 1993 | Derby, Conn. |
| Ward, Bryan | 2 | 5 | 4.99 | 14 | 11 | 0 | 0 | 61 | 82 | 41 | 34 | 26 | 63 | L | L | 6-2 | 210 | 1-28-72 | 1993 | Mt. Holly, N.J. |

## KISSIMMEE
## GULF COAST LEAGUE

R

### BATTING

| | AVG | G | AB | R | H | 2B | 3B | HR | RBI | BB | SO | SB | CS | B | T | HT | WT | DOB | 1st Yr | Resides |
|---|---|---|---|---|---|---|---|---|---|---|---|---|---|---|---|---|---|---|---|---|
| Aranzamendi, Alex, 3b | .309 | 42 | 149 | 13 | 46 | 8 | 0 | 2 | 31 | 13 | 17 | 1 | 1 | R | R | 6-2 | 189 | 5-1-74 | 1992 | Rio Piedras, P.R. |
| Babin, Brady, ss | .237 | 54 | 186 | 29 | 44 | 2 | 1 | 0 | 21 | 18 | 25 | 3 | 3 | R | R | 6-0 | 170 | 9-17-75 | 1993 | Gonzales, La. |
| Barberie, Bret, 2b | .250 | 2 | 8 | 0 | 2 | 0 | 0 | 0 | 1 | 1 | 1 | 0 | 0 | S | R | 5-11 | 185 | 8-16-67 | 1989 | Cerritos, Calif. |
| Carr, Chuck, cf | .417 | 3 | 12 | 4 | 5 | 1 | 0 | 1 | 3 | 0 | 2 | 3 | 0 | S | R | 5-10 | 165 | 8-10-68 | 1986 | Fontana, Calif. |
| Dunwoody, Todd, of | .193 | 31 | 109 | 13 | 21 | 2 | 2 | 0 | 7 | 7 | 28 | 5 | 0 | L | L | 6-2 | 185 | 4-11-75 | 1993 | West Lafayette, Ind. |
| Fantauzzi, Hiram, 1b-of | .264 | 37 | 121 | 22 | 32 | 9 | 1 | 2 | 15 | 12 | 39 | 5 | 2 | R | R | 6-4 | 177 | 4-19-74 | 1993 | Arroyo, P.R. |
| Frazier, Jason, 2b-ss | .111 | 12 | 18 | 3 | 2 | 0 | 0 | 0 | 2 | 2 | 2 | 0 | 0 | S | R | 5-10 | 180 | 12-4-72 | 1992 | Bluffton, S.C. |
| Genden, Eric, of-dh | .232 | 40 | 112 | 21 | 26 | 3 | 0 | 2 | 21 | 17 | 41 | 0 | 0 | R | R | 6-3 | 215 | 4-17-75 | 1993 | Coral Springs, Fla. |
| Gross, William, c | .220 | 23 | 59 | 4 | 13 | 3 | 1 | 0 | 9 | 6 | 11 | 0 | 0 | R | R | 6-0 | 190 | 8-29-70 | 1993 | Glendora, N.J. |
| Hubley, Greg, of | .296 | 48 | 142 | 27 | 42 | 5 | 2 | 0 | 21 | 19 | 28 | 11 | 3 | R | R | 6-3 | 180 | 11-22-72 | 1993 | San Mateo, Calif. |
| Jefferson, David, of | .263 | 15 | 38 | 4 | 10 | 1 | 0 | 1 | 6 | 2 | 3 | 0 | 0 | R | R | 6-2 | 190 | 6-18-75 | 1993 | Palo Alto, Calif. |
| Johnson, Damon, dh-3b | .276 | 39 | 127 | 12 | 35 | 4 | 0 | 0 | 7 | 5 | 34 | 4 | 0 | R | R | 6-1 | 195 | 8-22-75 | 1993 | Crossett, Ark. |
| Kingman, Brendan, 1b-3b | .251 | 57 | 203 | 34 | 51 | 14 | 1 | 2 | 37 | 25 | 36 | 0 | 0 | R | R | 6-1 | 195 | 5-22-73 | 1992 | Sydney, Australia |
| Lewis, Jeffrey, of | .231 | 40 | 78 | 14 | 18 | 0 | 0 | 0 | 8 | 9 | 29 | 7 | 5 | R | R | 5-11 | 175 | 12-29-72 | 1993 | Bedford, Va. |
| Milliard, Ralph, 2b | .234 | 53 | 192 | 35 | 45 | 15 | 0 | 0 | 25 | 30 | 17 | 11 | 5 | R | R | 5-10 | 160 | 12-30-73 | 1993 | Curacao, Neth. Antilles |
| Nolte, Bruce, 3b-2b | .271 | 36 | 70 | 11 | 19 | 3 | 1 | 1 | 12 | 10 | 10 | 0 | 1 | R | R | 6-0 | 160 | 4-4-74 | 1993 | Pennsauken, N.J. |
| Reeves, Glenn, of | .282 | 48 | 177 | 36 | 50 | 6 | 2 | 0 | 19 | 22 | 29 | 6 | 3 | R | R | 6-0 | 175 | 1-19-74 | 1993 | Victoria, Australia |
| Rodriguez, Maximo, c | .326 | 48 | 187 | 30 | 61 | 8 | 5 | 0 | 29 | 10 | 26 | 3 | 2 | R | R | 6-0 | 170 | 11-18-73 | 1993 | La Romana, D.R. |
| Roskos, John, dh-c | .175 | 11 | 40 | 6 | 7 | 1 | 0 | 3 | 5 | 11 | 1 | 1 | | R | R | 5-11 | 198 | 11-19-74 | 1993 | Rio Rancho, N.M. |

### PITCHING

| | W | L | ERA | G | GS | CG | SV | IP | H | R | ER | BB | SO | B | T | HT | WT | DOB | 1st Yr | Resides |
|---|---|---|---|---|---|---|---|---|---|---|---|---|---|---|---|---|---|---|---|---|
| Bavousett, Brian | 4 | 0 | 2.33 | 11 | 0 | 0 | 0 | 27 | 24 | 8 | 7 | 5 | 10 | R | R | 6-2 | 200 | 8-20-74 | 1992 | Odessa, Texas |
| Carl, Todd | 1 | 2 | 6.00 | 10 | 0 | 0 | 1 | 18 | 23 | 12 | 12 | 17 | 20 | R | R | 6-5 | 220 | 1-3-73 | 1993 | Stitzer, Wis. |
| Cunnane, Will | 3 | 3 | 2.70 | 16 | 9 | 0 | 2 | 67 | 75 | 32 | 20 | 8 | 64 | R | R | 6-2 | 165 | 4-24-74 | 1993 | Congers, N.Y. |
| Delgado, Ernesto | 4 | 3 | 3.08 | 11 | 11 | 0 | 0 | 61 | 61 | 27 | 21 | 19 | 46 | R | R | 6-2 | 190 | 7-21-75 | 1993 | Tucson, Ariz. |
| Ehler, Dan | 2 | 3 | 4.73 | 10 | 7 | 0 | 0 | 40 | 45 | 25 | 21 | 15 | 38 | R | R | 6-3 | 180 | 2-17-75 | 1993 | Covina, Calif. |
| Foshie, Josh | 0 | 0 | 0.00 | 1 | 0 | 0 | 2 | 2 | 2 | 0 | 0 | 3 | 2 | R | R | 6-3 | 200 | 12-25-72 | 1993 | Tempe, Ariz. |
| Harms, Mike | 2 | 3 | 3.66 | 18 | 0 | 0 | 3 | 39 | 41 | 20 | 16 | 10 | 22 | R | R | 6-2 | 205 | 8-22-73 | 1993 | Sparks, Nev. |
| Heredia, Felix | 5 | 1 | 2.47 | 12 | 12 | 0 | 0 | 62 | 50 | 18 | 17 | 11 | 53 | L | L | 6-0 | 160 | 6-18-76 | 1993 | Barahona, D.R. |
| Howard, Thomas | 2 | 4 | 3.18 | 8 | 6 | 1 | 0 | 34 | 35 | 16 | 12 | 20 | 31 | R | L | 6-4 | 170 | 7-29-75 | 1993 | Cocoa Beach, Fla. |
| Ireland, Rich | 1 | 2 | 3.12 | 8 | 4 | 0 | 0 | 26 | 12 | 11 | 9 | 23 | 19 | L | L | 6-0 | 198 | 11-11-74 | 1993 | Central Point, Ore. |
| Johnson, Scott | 2 | 2 | 2.82 | 19 | 0 | 0 | 2 | 38 | 41 | 16 | 12 | 12 | 30 | R | R | 6-4 | 205 | 7-28-74 | 1992 | Greeley, Colo. |
| Matthews, Fred | 3 | 3 | 3.46 | 17 | 0 | 0 | 0 | 26 | 17 | 13 | 10 | 23 | 15 | R | R | 6-2 | 200 | 12-8-73 | 1993 | Longview, Wash. |
| Mays, Marcus | 4 | 5 | 3.79 | 12 | 11 | 0 | 0 | 62 | 66 | 34 | 26 | 19 | 47 | L | L | 6-4 | 175 | 5-4-74 | 1993 | DeKalb, Ga. |
| Touchet, Sean | 2 | 0 | 3.71 | 13 | 0 | 0 | 3 | 17 | 14 | 7 | 7 | 11 | 25 | R | R | 5-11 | 200 | 11-25-72 | 1993 | Chalmette, La. |

# HOUSTON ASTROS

**Manager:** Art Howe.　　　**1993 Record:** 85-77, .525 (3rd, NL West).

| BATTING | AVG | G | AB | R | H | 2B | 3B | HR | RBI | BB | SO | SB | CS | B | T | HT | WT | DOB | 1st Yr | Resides |
|---|---|---|---|---|---|---|---|---|---|---|---|---|---|---|---|---|---|---|---|---|
| Anthony, Eric | .249 | 145 | 486 | 70 | 121 | 19 | 4 | 15 | 66 | 49 | 88 | 3 | 5 | L | L | 6-2 | 195 | 11-8-67 | 1986 | Houston, Texas |
| Bagwell, Jeff | .320 | 142 | 535 | 76 | 171 | 37 | 4 | 20 | 88 | 62 | 73 | 13 | 4 | R | R | 6-0 | 195 | 5-27-68 | 1989 | Houston, Texas |
| Bass, Kevin | .284 | 111 | 229 | 31 | 65 | 18 | 0 | 3 | 37 | 26 | 31 | 7 | 1 | S | R | 6-0 | 190 | 5-12-59 | 1977 | Sugar Land, Texas |
| Biggio, Craig | .287 | 155 | 610 | 98 | 175 | 41 | 5 | 21 | 64 | 77 | 93 | 15 | 17 | R | R | 5-11 | 180 | 12-14-65 | 1987 | Houston, Texas |
| Brumley, Mike | .300 | 8 | 10 | 1 | 3 | 0 | 0 | 0 | 2 | 1 | 3 | 0 | 1 | S | R | 5-10 | 155 | 4-9-63 | 1983 | Broken Arrow, Okla. |
| Caminiti, Ken | .262 | 143 | 543 | 75 | 142 | 31 | 0 | 13 | 75 | 49 | 88 | 8 | 5 | S | R | 6-0 | 200 | 4-21-63 | 1985 | Richmond, Texas |
| Candaele, Casey | .240 | 75 | 121 | 18 | 29 | 8 | 0 | 1 | 7 | 10 | 14 | 2 | 3 | S | R | 5-9 | 165 | 1-12-61 | 1983 | San Luis Obispo, Calif. |
| Cedeno, Andujar | .283 | 149 | 505 | 69 | 143 | 24 | 4 | 11 | 56 | 48 | 97 | 9 | 7 | R | R | 6-1 | 168 | 8-21-69 | 1987 | La Romana, D.R. |
| Daugherty, Jack | .333 | 4 | 3 | 0 | 1 | 0 | 0 | 0 | 0 | 0 | 0 | 0 | 0 | S | L | 6-0 | 190 | 7-3-60 | 1983 | San Diego, Calif. |
| Donnels, Chris | .257 | 88 | 179 | 18 | 46 | 14 | 2 | 2 | 24 | 19 | 33 | 2 | 0 | L | R | 6-0 | 185 | 4-21-66 | 1987 | Torrance, Calif. |
| Finley, Steve | .266 | 142 | 545 | 69 | 145 | 15 | 13 | 8 | 44 | 28 | 65 | 19 | 6 | L | L | 6-2 | 180 | 3-12-65 | 1987 | Houston, Texas |
| Gonzalez, Luis | .300 | 154 | 540 | 82 | 162 | 34 | 3 | 15 | 72 | 47 | 83 | 20 | 9 | L | R | 6-2 | 180 | 9-3-67 | 1988 | Houston, Texas |
| James, Chris | .256 | 65 | 129 | 19 | 33 | 10 | 1 | 6 | 19 | 15 | 34 | 2 | 0 | R | R | 6-1 | 202 | 10-4-62 | 1982 | Alto, Texas |
| Lindeman, Jim | .348 | 9 | 23 | 2 | 8 | 3 | 0 | 0 | 0 | 0 | 7 | 0 | 0 | R | R | 6-1 | 200 | 1-10-62 | 1983 | Des Plaines, Ill. |
| Parker, Rick | .333 | 45 | 45 | 11 | 15 | 3 | 0 | 0 | 4 | 3 | 8 | 1 | 2 | R | R | 6-0 | 185 | 3-20-63 | 1985 | Independence, Mo. |
| Rhodes, Karl | .000 | 5 | 2 | 0 | 0 | 0 | 0 | 0 | 0 | 0 | 0 | 0 | 0 | L | L | 5-11 | 170 | 8-21-68 | 1986 | Cincinnati, Ohio |
| Servais, Scott | .244 | 85 | 258 | 24 | 63 | 11 | 0 | 11 | 32 | 22 | 45 | 0 | 0 | R | R | 6-2 | 195 | 6-4-67 | 1989 | Coon Valley, Wis. |
| Taubensee, Eddie | .250 | 94 | 288 | 26 | 72 | 11 | 1 | 9 | 42 | 21 | 44 | 1 | 0 | L | R | 6-4 | 205 | 10-31-68 | 1986 | Longwood, Fla. |
| Tucker, Scooter | .192 | 9 | 26 | 1 | 5 | 1 | 0 | 0 | 3 | 2 | 3 | 0 | 0 | R | R | 6-2 | 205 | 11-18-66 | 1988 | Pensacola, Fla. |
| Uribe, Jose | .245 | 45 | 53 | 4 | 13 | 1 | 0 | 0 | 3 | 8 | 5 | 1 | 0 | S | R | 5-10 | 165 | 1-21-60 | 1981 | Santo Domingo, D.R. |

| PITCHING | W | L | ERA | G | GS | CG | SV | IP | H | R | ER | BB | SO | B | T | HT | WT | DOB | 1st Yr | Resides |
|---|---|---|---|---|---|---|---|---|---|---|---|---|---|---|---|---|---|---|---|---|
| Agosto, Juan | 0 | 0 | 6.00 | 6 | 0 | 0 | 0 | 6 | 8 | 4 | 4 | 0 | 3 | L | L | 6-2 | 190 | 2-23-58 | 1975 | Sarasota, Fla. |
| Bell, Eric | 0 | 1 | 6.14 | 10 | 0 | 0 | 0 | 7 | 10 | 5 | 5 | 2 | 2 | L | L | 6-0 | 165 | 10-27-63 | 1982 | Modesto, Calif. |
| Drabek, Doug | 9 | 18 | 3.79 | 34 | 34 | 7 | 0 | 238 | 242 | 108 | 100 | 60 | 157 | R | R | 6-1 | 185 | 7-25-62 | 1983 | The Woodlands, Texas |
| Edens, Tom | 1 | 1 | 3.12 | 38 | 0 | 0 | 0 | 49 | 47 | 17 | 17 | 19 | 21 | R | R | 6-2 | 185 | 6-9-61 | 1983 | Asotin, Wash. |
| Grant, Mark | 0 | 0 | 0.82 | 6 | 0 | 0 | 0 | 11 | 11 | 4 | 1 | 5 | 6 | R | R | 6-2 | 215 | 10-24-63 | 1981 | Alpine, Calif. |
| 2-team (14 Colo.) | 0 | 0 | 7.46 | 20 | 0 | 0 | 1 | 25 | 34 | 24 | 21 | 11 | 14 | | | | | | | |
| Harnisch, Pete | 16 | 9 | 2.98 | 33 | 33 | 5 | 0 | 218 | 171 | 84 | 72 | 79 | 185 | R | R | 6-0 | 207 | 9-23-66 | 1987 | Freehold, N.J. |
| Hernandez, Xavier | 4 | 5 | 2.61 | 72 | 0 | 0 | 9 | 97 | 75 | 37 | 28 | 28 | 101 | L | R | 6-2 | 185 | 8-16-65 | 1986 | Missouri City, Texas |
| Jones, Doug | 4 | 10 | 4.54 | 71 | 0 | 0 | 26 | 85 | 102 | 46 | 43 | 21 | 66 | R | R | 6-2 | 195 | 6-24-57 | 1978 | Tucson, Ariz. |
| Jones, Todd | 1 | 2 | 3.13 | 27 | 0 | 0 | 2 | 37 | 28 | 14 | 13 | 15 | 25 | L | R | 6-3 | 200 | 4-24-68 | 1989 | Pell City, Ala. |
| Juden, Jeff | 0 | 1 | 5.40 | 2 | 0 | 0 | 0 | 5 | 4 | 3 | 3 | 4 | 7 | R | R | 6-7 | 245 | 1-19-71 | 1989 | Salem, Mass. |
| Kile, Darryl | 15 | 8 | 3.51 | 32 | 26 | 4 | 0 | 172 | 152 | 73 | 67 | 69 | 141 | R | R | 6-5 | 185 | 12-2-68 | 1988 | Corona, Calif. |
| Osuna, Al | 1 | 1 | 3.20 | 44 | 0 | 0 | 2 | 25 | 17 | 10 | 9 | 13 | 21 | R | L | 6-3 | 200 | 8-10-65 | 1987 | Houston, Texas |
| Portugal, Mark | 18 | 4 | 2.77 | 33 | 33 | 1 | 0 | 208 | 194 | 75 | 64 | 77 | 131 | R | R | 6-0 | 190 | 10-30-62 | 1981 | Missouri City, Texas |
| Reynolds, Shane | 0 | 0 | 0.82 | 5 | 1 | 0 | 0 | 11 | 11 | 4 | 1 | 6 | 10 | R | R | 6-3 | 210 | 3-26-68 | 1989 | Monroe, La. |
| Swindell, Greg | 12 | 13 | 4.16 | 31 | 30 | 1 | 0 | 190 | 215 | 98 | 88 | 40 | 124 | R | L | 6-3 | 225 | 1-2-65 | 1986 | Sugar Land, Texas |
| Williams, Brian | 4 | 4 | 4.83 | 42 | 5 | 0 | 3 | 82 | 76 | 48 | 44 | 38 | 56 | R | R | 6-2 | 195 | 2-15-69 | 1990 | Columbia, S.C. |

## FIELDING

| Catcher | PCT | G | PO | A | E | DP |
|---|---|---|---|---|---|---|
| Servais | .996 | 82 | 493 | 40 | 2 | 9 |
| Taubensee | .992 | 90 | 551 | 41 | 5 | 5 |
| Tucker | 1.000 | 8 | 56 | 3 | 0 | 0 |

| First Base | PCT | G | PO | A | E | DP |
|---|---|---|---|---|---|---|
| Bagwell | .993 | 140 | 1200 | 113 | 9 | 106 |
| Daugherty | .000 | 1 | 0 | 0 | 0 | 0 |
| Donnels | .988 | 23 | 157 | 10 | 2 | 14 |
| Lindeman | 9 | 40 | 5 | 0 | 6 | |

| Second Base | PCT | G | PO | A | E | DP |
|---|---|---|---|---|---|---|
| Biggio | .982 | 155 | 306 | 447 | 14 | 90 |
| Candaele | 1.000 | 19 | 15 | 19 | 0 | 3 |
| Donnels | 1.000 | 1 | 1 | 3 | 0 | 2 |

| | PCT | G | PO | A | E | DP |
|---|---|---|---|---|---|---|
| Parker | 1.000 | 1 | 1 | 0 | 0 | 0 |
| **Third Base** | **PCT** | **G** | **PO** | **A** | **E** | **DP** |
| Brumley | .000 | 1 | 0 | 0 | 0 | 0 |
| Caminiti | .942 | 143 | 123 | 264 | 24 | 23 |
| Candaele | 1.000 | 4 | 0 | 1 | 0 | 0 |
| Cedeno | 1.000 | 1 | 2 | 1 | 0 | 0 |
| Donnels | .898 | 31 | 11 | 42 | 6 | 5 |
| **Shortstop** | **PCT** | **G** | **PO** | **A** | **E** | **DP** |
| Brumley | 1.000 | 1 | 0 | 1 | 0 | 0 |
| Candaele | .933 | 14 | 9 | 19 | 2 | 1 |
| Cedeno | .955 | 149 | 153 | 375 | 25 | 78 |
| Parker | .000 | 1 | 0 | 0 | 0 | 0 |

| | PCT | G | PO | A | E | DP |
|---|---|---|---|---|---|---|
| Uribe | .944 | 41 | 34 | 51 | 5 | 20 |
| **Outfield** | **PCT** | **G** | **PO** | **A** | **E** | **DP** |
| Anthony | .988 | 131 | 233 | 6 | 3 | 0 |
| Bass | .989 | 64 | 83 | 3 | 1 | 0 |
| Brumley | 1.000 | 1 | 1 | 0 | 0 | 0 |
| Candaele | .958 | 17 | 22 | 1 | 1 | 0 |
| Daugherty | 1.000 | 1 | 1 | 0 | 0 | 0 |
| Finley | .988 | 140 | 329 | 12 | 4 | 4 |
| Gonzalez | .978 | 149 | 347 | 10 | 8 | 2 |
| James | .958 | 34 | 65 | 4 | 3 | 1 |
| Parker | 1.000 | 16 | 17 | 0 | 0 | 0 |
| Rhodes | 1.000 | 4 | 2 | 0 | 0 | 0 |

# ASTROS FARM SYSTEM

| Class | Club | League | W | L | Pct. | Finish* | Manager | First Year |
|---|---|---|---|---|---|---|---|---|
| AAA | Tucson (Ariz.) Toros | Pacific Coast | 83 | 60 | .580 | 2nd† (10) | Rick Sweet | 1980 |
| AA | Jackson (Miss.) Generals | Texas | 73 | 61 | .545 | 2nd† (8) | Sal Butera | 1991 |
| A# | Osceola (Fla.) Astros | Florida State | 56 | 74 | .431 | 9th (13) | Tim Tolman | 1985 |
| A | Quad City (Iowa) River Bandits | Midwest | 56 | 74 | .431 | 11th (14) | Steve Dillard | 1993 |
| A | Asheville (N.C.) Tourists | South Atlantic | 51 | 88 | .367 | 14th (14) | Bobby Ramos | 1982 |
| A | Auburn (N.Y.) Astros | New York-Penn | 30 | 46 | .395 | 14th (14) | Manny Acta | 1982 |
| Rookie | Kissimmee (Fla.) Astros | Gulf Coast | 35 | 24 | .593 | 3rd (15) | Julio Linares | 1977 |

*Finish in overall standings (No. of teams in league)　#Advanced level　†Won league championship

**Reliable Righthanders.** Pete Harnisch (16-9), left, and Mark Portugal (18-4) combined to win 34 games for Houston, which expected better results from free agents Doug Drabek and Greg Swindell, who combined for 31 losses.

# TUCSON
## PACIFIC COAST LEAGUE

AAA

| BATTING | AVG | G | AB | R | H | 2B | 3B | HR | RBI | BB | SO | SB | CS | B | T | HT | WT | DOB | 1st Yr | Resides |
|---|---|---|---|---|---|---|---|---|---|---|---|---|---|---|---|---|---|---|---|---|
| Ansley, Willie | .262 | 125 | 382 | 71 | 100 | 20 | 7 | 5 | 61 | 79 | 93 | 22 | 9 | R | R | 6-2 | 200 | 12-15-69 | 1989 | Houston, Texas |
| Barrett, Tom | .279 | 69 | 204 | 31 | 57 | 3 | 5 | 1 | 19 | 24 | 14 | 5 | 2 | S | R | 5-9 | 157 | 4-2-60 | 1982 | Las Vegas, Nev. |
| Brumley, Mike | .353 | 93 | 346 | 65 | 122 | 25 | 8 | 0 | 47 | 44 | 71 | 24 | 10 | S | R | 5-10 | 155 | 4-9-63 | 1983 | Broken Arrow, Okla. |
| Candaele, Casey | .296 | 6 | 27 | 4 | 8 | 1 | 0 | 0 | 4 | 3 | 2 | 1 | 2 | S | R | 5-9 | 165 | 1-12-61 | 1983 | San Luis Obispo, Calif. |
| Carter, Steve | .247 | 40 | 146 | 26 | 36 | 7 | 0 | 1 | 17 | 11 | 13 | 6 | 2 | L | R | 6-4 | 205 | 12-12-64 | 1987 | Charlottesville, Va. |
| Castillo, Braulio | .375 | 17 | 56 | 6 | 21 | 4 | 1 | 0 | 15 | 5 | 14 | 1 | 0 | R | R | 6-0 | 160 | 5-13-68 | 1986 | Elias Pina, D.R. |
| 2-team (39 Colo. Spr.) | .363 | 56 | 212 | 40 | 77 | 20 | 4 | 2 | 37 | 22 | 54 | 9 | 3 | | | | | | | |
| Daugherty, Jack | .390 | 42 | 141 | 23 | 55 | 9 | 2 | 2 | 29 | 26 | 12 | 1 | 0 | S | L | 6-0 | 190 | 7-3-60 | 1983 | San Diego, Calif. |
| Eusebio, Tony | .324 | 78 | 281 | 39 | 91 | 20 | 1 | 1 | 43 | 22 | 40 | 1 | 1 | R | R | 6-2 | 180 | 4-27-67 | 1985 | San Pedro de Macoris, D.R. |
| Lindeman, Jim | .362 | 101 | 390 | 72 | 141 | 28 | 7 | 12 | 88 | 41 | 68 | 5 | 0 | R | R | 6-1 | 200 | 1-10-62 | 1983 | Des Plaines, Ill. |
| Massarelli, John | .281 | 114 | 423 | 66 | 119 | 28 | 4 | 2 | 42 | 46 | 61 | 37 | 14 | R | R | 6-2 | 200 | 1-23-66 | 1987 | Canton, Ohio |
| Mikulik, Joe | .301 | 94 | 296 | 48 | 89 | 24 | 2 | 4 | 45 | 14 | 39 | 9 | 6 | R | R | 5-11 | 180 | 10-30-63 | 1984 | Asheville, N.C. |
| Miller, Orlando | .304 | 122 | 471 | 86 | 143 | 29 | 16 | 16 | 89 | 20 | 95 | 2 | 4 | R | R | 6-1 | 180 | 1-13-69 | 1988 | El Dorado, Panama |
| Montgomery, Ray | .340 | 15 | 50 | 9 | 17 | 3 | 1 | 2 | 6 | 5 | 7 | 1 | 2 | R | R | 6-3 | 195 | 8-8-69 | 1990 | Bronxville, N.Y. |
| Mota, Andy | .167 | 3 | 6 | 1 | 1 | 0 | 0 | 0 | 1 | 0 | 2 | 1 | 0 | R | R | 5-10 | 180 | 3-4-66 | 1987 | Glendale, Calif. |
| Mouton, James | .315 | 134 | 546 | 126 | 172 | 42 | 12 | 16 | 92 | 72 | 82 | 40 | 18 | R | R | 5-9 | 175 | 12-29-68 | 1991 | Sacramento, Calif. |
| Nevin, Phil | .286 | 123 | 448 | 67 | 128 | 21 | 3 | 10 | 93 | 52 | 99 | 8 | 1 | R | R | 6-2 | 185 | 1-19-71 | 1992 | Placentia, Calif. |
| Parker, Rick | .308 | 29 | 120 | 28 | 37 | 9 | 3 | 2 | 14 | 14 | 20 | 6 | 2 | R | R | 6-0 | 185 | 3-20-63 | 1985 | Independence, Mo. |
| Quinones, Luis | .221 | 64 | 136 | 14 | 30 | 10 | 1 | 0 | 18 | 25 | 23 | 0 | 1 | S | R | 5-11 | 185 | 4-28-62 | 1980 | Ponce, P.R. |
| Trafton, Todd | .250 | 8 | 20 | 3 | 5 | 1 | 1 | 0 | 2 | 2 | 4 | 0 | 1 | R | R | 6-2 | 210 | 3-16-64 | 1986 | Elk Grove, Calif. |
| Tucker, Scooter | .274 | 98 | 318 | 54 | 87 | 20 | 2 | 1 | 37 | 47 | 37 | 1 | 5 | R | R | 6-2 | 205 | 11-18-66 | 1988 | Pensacola, Fla. |

| PITCHING | W | L | ERA | G | GS | CG | SV | IP | H | R | ER | BB | SO | B | T | HT | WT | DOB | 1st Yr | Resides |
|---|---|---|---|---|---|---|---|---|---|---|---|---|---|---|---|---|---|---|---|---|
| Agosto, Juan | 5 | 3 | 6.00 | 32 | 0 | 0 | 3 | 33 | 45 | 24 | 22 | 24 | 18 | L | L | 6-2 | 190 | 2-23-58 | 1975 | Sarasota, Fla. |
| 2-team (19 Las Vegas) | 7 | 3 | 5.29 | 51 | 0 | 0 | 3 | 51 | 66 | 32 | 30 | 29 | 33 | | | | | | | |
| Bell, Eric | 4 | 6 | 4.05 | 22 | 16 | 3 | 0 | 107 | 131 | 59 | 48 | 39 | 53 | L | L | 6-0 | 165 | 10-27-63 | 1982 | Modesto, Calif. |
| Bruske, Jim | 4 | 2 | 3.78 | 12 | 9 | 0 | 1 | 67 | 77 | 36 | 28 | 18 | 42 | R | R | 6-1 | 185 | 10-7-64 | 1986 | Palmdale, Calif. |
| Capel, Mike | 0 | 4 | 7.16 | 25 | 1 | 0 | 3 | 33 | 46 | 30 | 26 | 11 | 33 | R | R | 6-1 | 175 | 10-13-61 | 1983 | Houston, Texas |
| Costello, Fred | 6 | 2 | 3.69 | 14 | 14 | 0 | 0 | 83 | 92 | 42 | 34 | 33 | 36 | R | R | 6-4 | 190 | 10-1-66 | 1986 | San Bruno, Calif. |
| Dixon, Eddie | 4 | 3 | 4.15 | 50 | 0 | 0 | 0 | 80 | 92 | 54 | 37 | 22 | 41 | R | R | 6-3 | 195 | 4-16-64 | 1985 | Sasser, Ga. |
| Edens, Tom | 1 | 0 | 6.14 | 5 | 0 | 0 | 0 | 7 | 9 | 5 | 5 | 3 | 6 | R | R | 6-2 | 185 | 6-9-61 | 1983 | Asotin, Wash. |
| Grant, Mark | 1 | 0 | 1.08 | 4 | 0 | 0 | 0 | 8 | 5 | 1 | 1 | 4 | 10 | R | R | 6-2 | 215 | 10-24-63 | 1981 | Alpine, Calif. |
| Hartgraves, Dean | 1 | 6 | 6.37 | 23 | 10 | 0 | 0 | 78 | 90 | 65 | 55 | 40 | 42 | R | L | 6-0 | 185 | 8-12-66 | 1987 | Central Point, Ore. |
| Hudek, John | 3 | 1 | 3.79 | 13 | 1 | 0 | 0 | 19 | 17 | 11 | 8 | 11 | 18 | S | R | 6-1 | 200 | 8-8-66 | 1988 | Orlando, Fla. |
| Huisman, Rick | 1 | 0 | 7.36 | 2 | 0 | 0 | 0 | 4 | 6 | 5 | 3 | 1 | 4 | R | R | 6-3 | 200 | 5-17-69 | 1990 | Bensenville, Ill. |
| 2-team (2 Phoenix) | 1 | 0 | 7.36 | 2 | 0 | 0 | 0 | 4 | 6 | 5 | 3 | 1 | 4 | | | | | | | |
| Hurta, Bob | 2 | 1 | 6.00 | 8 | 0 | 0 | 1 | 12 | 11 | 8 | 8 | 13 | 10 | L | L | 6-0 | 190 | 11-17-65 | 1987 | Freeport, Texas |
| Jones, Todd | 4 | 2 | 4.44 | 41 | 0 | 0 | 12 | 49 | 49 | 26 | 24 | 31 | 45 | L | R | 6-3 | 200 | 4-24-68 | 1989 | Pell City, Ala. |
| Juden, Jeff | 11 | 6 | 4.63 | 27 | 27 | 0 | 0 | 169 | 174 | 102 | 87 | 76 | 156 | R | R | 6-7 | 245 | 1-19-71 | 1989 | Salem, Mass. |
| Mathews, Terry | 5 | 0 | 3.55 | 16 | 4 | 0 | 2 | 33 | 40 | 14 | 13 | 11 | 34 | L | R | 6-2 | 225 | 10-5-64 | 1987 | Boyce, La. |
| Osuna, Al | 3 | 1 | 4.50 | 13 | 4 | 0 | 1 | 30 | 26 | 16 | 15 | 17 | 38 | R | L | 6-3 | 200 | 8-10-65 | 1987 | Houston, Texas |
| Reynolds, Shane | 10 | 6 | 3.62 | 25 | 20 | 2 | 1 | 139 | 147 | 74 | 56 | 21 | 106 | R | R | 6-3 | 210 | 3-26-68 | 1989 | Monroe, La. |
| Robinson, Jeff | 1 | 0 | 5.06 | 13 | 0 | 0 | 1 | 21 | 22 | 12 | 12 | 9 | 15 | R | R | 6-4 | 200 | 12-13-60 | 1983 | Mission Viejo, Calif. |

| PITCHING | W | L | ERA | G | GS | CG | SV | IP | H | R | ER | BB | SO | B | T | HT | WT | DOB | 1st Yr | Resides |
|---|---|---|---|---|---|---|---|---|---|---|---|---|---|---|---|---|---|---|---|---|
| Veres, Dave | 6 | 10 | 4.90 | 43 | 15 | 1 | 5 | 130 | 156 | 88 | 71 | 32 | 122 | R | R | 6-2 | 195 | 10-19-66 | 1986 | Gresham, Ore. |
| Wall, Donnie | 6 | 4 | 3.83 | 25 | 22 | 0 | 0 | 132 | 147 | 73 | 56 | 35 | 89 | R | R | 6-1 | 180 | 7-11-67 | 1989 | Festus, Mo. |
| Walton, Bruce | 2 | 0 | 1.80 | 13 | 0 | 0 | 7 | 15 | 12 | 4 | 3 | 3 | 14 | R | R | 6-2 | 195 | 12-25-62 | 1985 | Bakersfield, Calif. |
| Williams, Brian | 1 | 0 | .00 | 2 | 0 | 0 | 0 | 3 | 1 | 0 | 0 | 0 | 3 | R | R | 6-2 | 195 | 2-15-69 | 1990 | Columbia, S.C. |
| Windes, Rodney | 1 | 3 | 9.00 | 13 | 0 | 0 | 0 | 12 | 20 | 13 | 12 | 6 | 10 | L | L | 6-2 | 175 | 7-21-66 | 1988 | Los Alamitos, Calif. |

## FIELDING

| Catcher | PCT | G | PO | A | E | DP |
|---|---|---|---|---|---|---|
| Eusebio | .994 | 73 | 450 | 46 | 3 | 6 |
| Massarelli | 1.000 | 5 | 35 | 5 | 0 | 0 |
| Tucker | .993 | 78 | 500 | 55 | 4 | 9 |

| First Base | PCT | G | PO | A | E | DP |
|---|---|---|---|---|---|---|
| Brumley | 1.000 | 7 | 51 | 2 | 0 | 4 |
| Daugherty | .988 | 38 | 310 | 19 | 4 | 24 |
| Lindeman | .987 | 84 | 715 | 45 | 10 | 64 |
| Parker | 1.000 | 1 | 13 | 0 | 0 | 1 |
| Quinones | .989 | 11 | 85 | 7 | 1 | 6 |
| Trafton | 1.000 | 3 | 30 | 1 | 0 | 4 |
| Tucker | .993 | 17 | 121 | 12 | 1 | 12 |

| Second Base | PCT | G | PO | A | E | DP |
|---|---|---|---|---|---|---|
| Barrett | .979 | 24 | 30 | 62 | 2 | 7 |
| Candaele | .727 | 1 | 3 | 5 | 3 | 3 |
| Mouton | .936 | 126 | 277 | 354 | 43 | 75 |

| | PCT | G | PO | A | E | DP |
|---|---|---|---|---|---|---|
| Quinones | 1.000 | 1 | 1 | 3 | 0 | 1 |
| **Third Base** | **PCT** | **G** | **PO** | **A** | **E** | **DP** |
| Barrett | .940 | 39 | 24 | 55 | 5 | 5 |
| Brumley | .941 | 6 | 4 | 12 | 1 | 0 |
| Mota | .667 | 1 | 0 | 2 | 1 | 0 |
| Nevin | .891 | 96 | 50 | 186 | 29 | 11 |
| Parker | 1.000 | 2 | 0 | 1 | 0 | 0 |
| Quinones | .944 | 33 | 22 | 45 | 4 | 3 |
| Tucker | 1.000 | 2 | 0 | 2 | 0 | 0 |
| **Shortstop** | **PCT** | **G** | **PO** | **A** | **E** | **DP** |
| Barrett | .917 | 3 | 2 | 9 | 1 | 0 |
| Brumley | .914 | 22 | 26 | 59 | 8 | 8 |
| Candaele | 1.000 | 2 | 6 | 5 | 0 | 2 |
| Miller | .945 | 118 | 180 | 389 | 33 | 74 |
| Quinones | 1.000 | 14 | 10 | 27 | 0 | 6 |

| Outfield | PCT | G | PO | A | E | DP |
|---|---|---|---|---|---|---|
| Ansley | .958 | 116 | 174 | 9 | 8 | 2 |
| Barrett | 1.000 | 3 | 1 | 0 | 0 | 0 |
| Brumley | .943 | 51 | 80 | 3 | 5 | 1 |
| Candaele | 1.000 | 4 | 3 | 0 | 0 | 0 |
| Carter | .923 | 35 | 56 | 4 | 5 | 1 |
| Castillo | 1.000 | 12 | 34 | 3 | 0 | 1 |
| Daugherty | 1.000 | 2 | 3 | 0 | 0 | 0 |
| Lindeman | .938 | 26 | 28 | 2 | 2 | 0 |
| Massarelli | .932 | 94 | 129 | 8 | 10 | 3 |
| Mikulik | .970 | 79 | 156 | 5 | 5 | 1 |
| Montgomery | 1.000 | 14 | 33 | 1 | 0 | 0 |
| Nevin | 1.000 | 23 | 18 | 1 | 0 | 0 |
| Parker | .957 | 28 | 64 | 2 | 3 | 0 |
| Trafton | .000 | 1 | 0 | 0 | 0 | 0 |

# JACKSON                                                   AA
## TEXAS LEAGUE

| BATTING | AVG | G | AB | R | H | 2B | 3B | HR | RBI | BB | SO | SB | CS | B | T | HT | WT | DOB | 1st Yr | Resides |
|---|---|---|---|---|---|---|---|---|---|---|---|---|---|---|---|---|---|---|---|---|
| Gilmore, Tony, c | .172 | 47 | 145 | 14 | 25 | 4 | 0 | 2 | 7 | 7 | 29 | 1 | 0 | R | R | 6-2 | 195 | 10-15-68 | 1990 | Tulsa, Okla. |
| Groppuso, Mike, 3b | .241 | 114 | 370 | 41 | 89 | 18 | 0 | 10 | 49 | 35 | 121 | 3 | 3 | R | R | 6-3 | 195 | 3-9-70 | 1991 | Lake Katrine, N.Y. |
| Hajek, Dave, 2b-3b | .292 | 110 | 332 | 50 | 97 | 20 | 2 | 5 | 27 | 17 | 14 | 6 | 5 | R | R | 5-10 | 165 | 10-14-67 | 1990 | Colorado Springs, Colo. |
| Hatcher, Chris, of-dh | .259 | 101 | 367 | 45 | 95 | 15 | 3 | 15 | 64 | 11 | 104 | 5 | 8 | R | R | 6-3 | 220 | 1-7-69 | 1990 | Carter Lake, Iowa |
| Hunter, Brian, of | .294 | 133 | 523 | 84 | 154 | 22 | 5 | 10 | 52 | 34 | 85 | 35 | 18 | R | R | 6-2 | 170 | 3-5-71 | 1989 | Vancouver, Wash. |
| Kellner, Frank, ss | .301 | 121 | 355 | 51 | 107 | 27 | 2 | 4 | 36 | 38 | 51 | 11 | 12 | S | R | 5-11 | 175 | 1-5-67 | 1990 | Tucson, Ariz. |
| Madsen, Lance, of-3b | .221 | 116 | 353 | 58 | 78 | 19 | 1 | 23 | 65 | 43 | 136 | 2 | 6 | R | R | 6-0 | 185 | 10-14-68 | 1989 | Salt Lake City, Utah |
| Makarewicz, Scott, c | .246 | 92 | 285 | 31 | 70 | 14 | 1 | 7 | 35 | 17 | 51 | 1 | 1 | R | R | 6-0 | 200 | 3-1-67 | 1989 | Grand Rapids, Mich. |
| Montgomery, Ray, of | .281 | 100 | 338 | 50 | 95 | 16 | 3 | 10 | 59 | 36 | 54 | 12 | 6 | R | R | 6-3 | 195 | 8-8-69 | 1990 | Bronxville, N.Y. |
| Mota, Gary, of | .144 | 27 | 90 | 7 | 13 | 2 | 0 | 3 | 8 | 2 | 25 | 1 | 1 | R | R | 6-0 | 195 | 10-6-70 | 1990 | St. Cloud, Fla. |
| Nevers, Tom, ss | .272 | 55 | 184 | 21 | 50 | 8 | 2 | 1 | 10 | 16 | 36 | 7 | 2 | R | R | 6-1 | 175 | 9-13-71 | 1990 | Edina, Minn. |
| Petagine, Roberto, 1b | .334 | 128 | 437 | 73 | 146 | 36 | 2 | 15 | 90 | 84 | 89 | 6 | 5 | L | L | 6-1 | 172 | 6-7-71 | 1990 | Nueva Esparta, Venez. |
| Scott, Kevin, c-of | .284 | 50 | 109 | 11 | 31 | 4 | 0 | 1 | 13 | 3 | 26 | 2 | 1 | R | R | 6-3 | 175 | 11-23-67 | 1989 | Woodinville, Wash. |
| Thompson, Fletcher, 2b | .294 | 98 | 316 | 64 | 93 | 15 | 2 | 4 | 29 | 55 | 83 | 23 | 12 | L | R | 5-11 | 180 | 9-14-68 | 1990 | Jackson, Miss. |

| PITCHING | W | L | ERA | G | GS | CG | SV | IP | H | R | ER | BB | SO | B | T | HT | WT | DOB | 1st Yr | Resides |
|---|---|---|---|---|---|---|---|---|---|---|---|---|---|---|---|---|---|---|---|---|
| Anderson, Tom | 2 | 5 | 6.05 | 8 | 8 | 0 | 0 | 39 | 47 | 30 | 26 | 20 | 27 | R | R | 6-3 | 210 | 11-18-69 | 1991 | Carroll, Iowa |
| Bruske, Jim | 9 | 5 | 2.31 | 15 | 15 | 1 | 0 | 97 | 86 | 34 | 25 | 22 | 83 | R | R | 6-1 | 185 | 10-7-64 | 1986 | Palmdale, Calif. |
| Costello, Fred | 8 | 3 | 2.82 | 12 | 12 | 0 | 0 | 61 | 57 | 24 | 19 | 13 | 45 | R | R | 6-4 | 190 | 10-1-66 | 1986 | San Bruno, Calif. |
| Dougherty, Jim | 2 | 2 | 1.87 | 52 | 0 | 0 | 36 | 53 | 39 | 15 | 11 | 21 | 55 | R | R | 6-0 | 210 | 3-8-68 | 1991 | Brentwood, N.Y. |
| Gallaher, Kevin | 0 | 2 | 2.63 | 4 | 4 | 0 | 0 | 24 | 14 | 7 | 7 | 10 | 30 | R | R | 6-3 | 190 | 8-1-68 | 1991 | Vienna, Va. |
| Gonzales, Ben | 2 | 2 | 5.12 | 41 | 0 | 0 | 0 | 65 | 90 | 43 | 37 | 15 | 36 | R | R | 5-10 | 180 | 3-5-67 | 1988 | Lompoc, Calif. |
| Hill, Chris | 6 | 4 | 3.86 | 58 | 3 | 0 | 2 | 105 | 90 | 52 | 45 | 53 | 93 | L | L | 6-0 | 160 | 4-13-69 | 1988 | Duncanville, Texas |
| Hurta, Bob | 7 | 9 | 4.42 | 36 | 12 | 0 | 2 | 94 | 101 | 55 | 46 | 38 | 72 | L | L | 6-0 | 190 | 11-17-65 | 1987 | Freeport, Texas |
| Kent, Troy | 1 | 0 | 2.45 | 2 | 0 | 0 | 0 | 4 | 2 | 1 | 1 | 1 | 1 | R | R | 6-0 | 175 | 2-24-67 | 1988 | San Diego, Calif. |
| Ketchen, Doug | 7 | 12 | 4.11 | 27 | 27 | 3 | 0 | 160 | 160 | 91 | 73 | 50 | 104 | R | R | 6-1 | 190 | 7-9-68 | 1990 | Calgary, Alberta |
| Mathews, Terry | 6 | 5 | 3.67 | 17 | 17 | 0 | 0 | 103 | 116 | 55 | 42 | 29 | 74 | L | R | 6-2 | 225 | 10-5-64 | 1987 | Boyce, La. |

# ASTROS: ORGANIZATION LEADERS

### MAJOR LEAGUERS
**BATTING**
| | | |
|---|---|---|
| *AVG | Jeff Bagwell | .320 |
| R | Craig Biggio | 98 |
| H | Craig Biggio | 175 |
| TB | Craig Biggio | 289 |
| 2B | Craig Biggio | 41 |
| 3B | Steve Finley | 13 |
| HR | Craig Biggio | 21 |
| RBI | Jeff Bagwell | 88 |
| BB | Craig Biggio | 77 |
| SO | Andujar Cedeno | 97 |
| SB | Luis Gonzalez | 20 |

**PITCHING**
| | | |
|---|---|---|
| W | Mark Portugal | 18 |
| L | Doug Drabek | 18 |
| #ERA | Xavier Hernandez | 2.61 |
| G | Xavier Hernandez | 72 |
| CG | Doug Drabek | 7 |
| SV | Doug Jones | 26 |
| IP | Doug Drabek | 238 |
| BB | Pete Harnisch | 79 |
| SO | Pete Harnisch | 185 |

### MINOR LEAGUERS
**BATTING**
| | | |
|---|---|---|
| *AVG | Jim Lindeman, Tucson | .362 |
| R | James Mouton, Tucson | 126 |
| H | James Mouton, Tucson | 172 |
| TB | James Mouton, Tucson | 286 |
| 2B | James Mouton, Tucson | 42 |
| 3B | Bob Abreu, Osceola | 17 |
| HR | Lance Madsen, Jackson | 23 |
| RBI | Phil Nevin, Tucson | 93 |
| BB | Roberto Petagine, Jackson | 84 |
| SO | Jermaine Swinton, Asheville | 137 |
| SB | Two tied at | 40 |

**PITCHING**
| | | |
|---|---|---|
| W | Fred Costello, Tucson-Jackson | 14 |
| L | Two tied at | 14 |
| #ERA | Tim Kester, Auburn | 2.06 |
| G | Sean Fesh, Asheville | 65 |
| CG | Chris Holt, Quad City | 10 |
| SV | Jim Dougherty, Jackson | 36 |
| IP | Chris Holt, Quad City | 186 |
| BB | Danny Young, Asheville | 95 |
| SO | Chris Holt, Quad City | 176 |

**Craig Biggio**
Only 2B to lead team in homers (21)

*Minimum 250 At-Bats    #Minimum 75 Innings

# ASTROS: MOST COMMON LINEUPS

| | Houston | Tucson | Jackson | Osceola | Quad City | Asheville |
|---|---|---|---|---|---|---|
| | Majors | AAA | AA | A | A | A |
| **C** | Eddie Taubensee (90) | Scooter Tucker (78) | Scott Makarewicz (85) | Raul Chavez (57) | Alan Probst (45) | Randy Albaladejo (65) |
| **1B** | Jeff Bagwell (140) | Jim Lindeman (84) | Roberto Petagine (127) | Michael Burns (45) | Bryant Winslow (91) | Kevin Webb (57) |
| **2B** | Craig Biggio (155) | James Mouton (126) | Fletcher Thompson (86) | Al Harley (118) | Henri Centeno (96) | Donovan Mitchell (99) |
| **3B** | Ken Caminiti (143) | Phil Nevin (96) | Mike Groppuso (111) | Dennis Colon (67) | Eddie Ramos (90) | Greg Elliott (110) |
| **SS** | Andujar Cedeno (149) | Orlando Miller (118) | Frank Kellner (94) | Jose Flores (124) | Brian McGlone (81) | Jose Santana (133) |
| **OF** | Luis Gonzalez (149) | Willie Ansley (116) | Brian Hunter (129) | Bob Abreu (123) | Tim Evans (120) | Shawn Livsey (113) |
| | Steve Finley (140) | John Massarelli (111) | Ray Montgomery (98) | Jimmy White (123) | Vince Roman (73) | Richard Hidalgo (108) |
| | Eric Anthony (131) | Joe Mikulik (82) | Lance Madsen (88) | Buck McNabb (115) | Rich Schulte (50) | Mike Rennhack (101) |
| **DH** | N/A | Nevin/Massarelli (12) | Chris Hatcher (35) | Ruben Cruz (24) | Jeff Ball (35) | Mora/Swinton (28) |
| **SP** | Doug Drabek (34) | Jeff Juden (27) | Doug Ketchen (27) | Mlicki/Wheeler (23) | Evans/Holt (26) | Tyrone Narcisse (29) |
| **RP** | Xavier Hernandez (72) | Eddie Dixon (50) | Chris Hill (55) | Kevin Lane (58) | Pat Murphy (42) | Sean Fesh (65) |

Full-season farm clubs only    No. of games at position in parenthesis

| PITCHING | W | L | ERA | G | GS | CG | SV | IP | H | R | ER | BB | SO | B | T | HT | WT | DOB | 1st Yr | Resides |
|---|---|---|---|---|---|---|---|---|---|---|---|---|---|---|---|---|---|---|---|---|
| Morman, Alvin | 8 | 2 | 2.96 | 19 | 19 | 0 | 0 | 97 | 77 | 35 | 32 | 28 | 101 | L | L | 6-3 | 210 | 1-6-69 | 1991 | Rockingham, N.C. |
| Small, Mark | 7 | 2 | 3.19 | 51 | 0 | 0 | 0 | 85 | 71 | 34 | 30 | 41 | 64 | R | R | 6-3 | 205 | 11-12-67 | 1989 | Seattle, Wash. |
| White, Chris | 3 | 5 | 7.35 | 16 | 11 | 0 | 1 | 60 | 80 | 54 | 49 | 25 | 44 | R | R | 6-0 | 180 | 9-15-69 | 1991 | Greenville, Pa. |
| Windes, Rodney | 5 | 4 | 2.93 | 41 | 7 | 0 | 2 | 95 | 84 | 34 | 31 | 22 | 84 | L | L | 6-2 | 175 | 7-21-66 | 1988 | Los Alamitos, Calif. |

# OSCEOLA    A
## FLORIDA STATE LEAGUE

| BATTING | AVG | G | AB | R | H | 2B | 3B | HR | RBI | BB | SO | SB | CS | B | T | HT | WT | DOB | 1st Yr | Resides |
|---|---|---|---|---|---|---|---|---|---|---|---|---|---|---|---|---|---|---|---|---|
| Abreu, Bob, of | .283 | 129 | 474 | 62 | 134 | 21 | 17 | 5 | 55 | 51 | 90 | 10 | 9 | L | R | 6-0 | 160 | 3-11-74 | 1991 | Turmero, Venez. |
| Berry, Perry, 3b-2b | .259 | 84 | 239 | 25 | 62 | 8 | 6 | 2 | 31 | 24 | 55 | 8 | 5 | R | R | 6-1 | 190 | 4-11-69 | 1990 | Dolores, Colo. |
| Burns, Michael, 1b-c | .183 | 123 | 438 | 43 | 80 | 17 | 1 | 7 | 56 | 35 | 110 | 10 | 12 | R | R | 6-0 | 185 | 11-2-68 | 1991 | Decatur, Ala. |
| Chavez, Raul, c | .228 | 58 | 197 | 13 | 45 | 5 | 1 | 0 | 16 | 8 | 19 | 1 | 1 | R | R | 5-11 | 175 | 3-18-73 | 1990 | Valencia, Venez. |
| Colon, Dennis, 3b-1b | .316 | 118 | 469 | 51 | 148 | 20 | 6 | 2 | 59 | 17 | 41 | 10 | 4 | L | R | 5-10 | 165 | 8-4-73 | 1991 | Manati, P.R. |
| Cruz, Ruben, 1b-dh | .251 | 79 | 243 | 20 | 61 | 6 | 1 | 1 | 28 | 12 | 15 | 2 | 2 | L | L | 5-11 | 185 | 5-19-72 | 1990 | Salinas, P.R. |
| Flores, Jose, ss | .243 | 124 | 452 | 47 | 110 | 11 | 1 | 0 | 39 | 39 | 64 | 12 | 11 | S | R | 6-1 | 155 | 1-1-71 | 1990 | Cidra, P.R. |
| Harley, Al, 2b | .228 | 121 | 391 | 42 | 89 | 12 | 8 | 1 | 51 | 36 | 67 | 20 | 13 | S | R | 5-11 | 165 | 11-11-71 | 1990 | Eugene, Ore. |
| McNabb, Buck, of | .285 | 125 | 487 | 69 | 139 | 15 | 7 | 1 | 35 | 52 | 66 | 28 | 15 | L | R | 6-0 | 180 | 1-17-73 | 1991 | Fort Walton Beach, Fla. |
| Ross, Tony, of | .160 | 9 | 25 | 3 | 4 | 0 | 0 | 1 | 1 | 9 | 0 | 0 | 0 | R | R | 5-11 | 185 | 9-17-73 | 1992 | Kansas City, Mo. |
| Schulte, Rich, of | .227 | 19 | 44 | 4 | 10 | 0 | 0 | 0 | 3 | 3 | 7 | 2 | 3 | L | R | 6-0 | 180 | 7-16-70 | 1991 | Pella, Iowa |
| Scott, Kevin, 1b | .253 | 30 | 75 | 11 | 19 | 5 | 1 | 0 | 9 | 4 | 17 | 2 | 1 | R | R | 6-3 | 175 | 11-23-67 | 1989 | Woodinville, Wash. |
| Truby, Chris, 3b | .000 | 3 | 13 | 0 | 0 | 0 | 0 | 0 | 0 | 2 | 0 | 0 | 0 | R | R | 6-2 | 195 | 12-9-73 | 1993 | Mukilteo, Wash. |
| White, Jimmy, of | .275 | 125 | 447 | 80 | 123 | 9 | 12 | 7 | 37 | 54 | 120 | 24 | 17 | L | R | 6-1 | 170 | 12-1-72 | 1991 | Brandon, Fla. |
| Winston, Todd, c-of | .156 | 72 | 212 | 28 | 33 | 9 | 1 | 1 | 21 | 26 | 57 | 10 | 6 | R | R | 6-0 | 190 | 1-27-70 | 1991 | Marysville, Mich. |
| Wyngarden, Brett, dh-c | .255 | 22 | 55 | 5 | 14 | 4 | 0 | 0 | 6 | 5 | 14 | 0 | 1 | R | R | 6-2 | 200 | 10-8-70 | 1992 | St. Joseph, Mich. |

| PITCHING | W | L | ERA | G | GS | CG | SV | IP | H | R | ER | BB | SO | B | T | HT | WT | DOB | 1st Yr | Resides |
|---|---|---|---|---|---|---|---|---|---|---|---|---|---|---|---|---|---|---|---|---|
| Anderson, Tom | 2 | 8 | 3.01 | 16 | 16 | 1 | 0 | 99 | 109 | 50 | 33 | 28 | 72 | R | R | 6-3 | 210 | 11-18-69 | 1991 | Carroll, Iowa |
| Brown, Duane | 2 | 1 | 5.02 | 35 | 0 | 0 | 0 | 52 | 65 | 32 | 29 | 31 | 27 | R | R | 6-5 | 170 | 12-19-69 | 1989 | Myrtle Creek, Ore. |
| Edens, Tom | 1 | 0 | 0.00 | 3 | 1 | 0 | 0 | 4 | 5 | 0 | 0 | 4 | 4 | R | R | 6-2 | 185 | 6-9-61 | 1983 | Asotin, Wash. |
| Gallaher, Kevin | 7 | 7 | 3.80 | 21 | 21 | 1 | 0 | 135 | 132 | 68 | 57 | 57 | 93 | R | R | 6-3 | 190 | 8-1-68 | 1991 | Vienna, Va. |
| Guerry, Kyle | 1 | 2 | 3.35 | 56 | 0 | 0 | 1 | 48 | 46 | 27 | 18 | 34 | 26 | L | L | 6-1 | 195 | 12-14-69 | 1992 | Lubbock, Texas |
| Hennis, Randy | 0 | 3 | 3.31 | 14 | 14 | 0 | 0 | 35 | 21 | 13 | 13 | 15 | 26 | R | R | 6-6 | 220 | 12-16-65 | 1987 | San Diego, Calif. |
| Holliday, Brian | 0 | 0 | 2.35 | 6 | 3 | 0 | 1 | 8 | 6 | 2 | 2 | 2 | 4 | R | R | 6-1 | 185 | 9-29-69 | 1991 | Anchorage, Alaska |
| Kent, Troy | 0 | 0 | 1.93 | 24 | 0 | 0 | 15 | 23 | 21 | 10 | 5 | 11 | 21 | R | R | 6-0 | 175 | 2-24-67 | 1988 | San Diego, Calif. |
| Lane, Kevin | 3 | 10 | 2.69 | 58 | 0 | 0 | 11 | 60 | 54 | 31 | 18 | 31 | 31 | R | R | 6-1 | 180 | 1-12-67 | 1988 | Boca Raton, Fla. |
| Lewis, James | 0 | 0 | 2.35 | 4 | 4 | 0 | 0 | 8 | 8 | 4 | 2 | 2 | 3 | R | R | 6-4 | 190 | 1-31-70 | 1991 | Jacksonville, Fla. |
| Mercado, Hector | 1 | 1 | 5.19 | 2 | 2 | 0 | 0 | 9 | 9 | 7 | 5 | 6 | 5 | L | L | 6-3 | 205 | 4-29-74 | 1992 | Dorado, P.R. |
| Mlicki, Doug | 11 | 10 | 3.91 | 26 | 23 | 0 | 0 | 159 | 158 | 81 | 69 | 65 | 111 | R | R | 6-3 | 180 | 4-23-71 | 1992 | Dublin, Ohio |
| Nieto, Roy | 3 | 3 | 4.50 | 42 | 0 | 0 | 2 | 66 | 76 | 45 | 33 | 36 | 39 | R | R | 6-4 | 210 | 10-30-67 | 1991 | Georgetown, Texas |
| Padron, Oscar | 0 | 0 | 18.00 | 2 | 0 | 0 | 0 | 2 | 7 | 4 | 4 | 1 | 0 | R | R | 6-3 | 175 | 3-22-74 | 1992 | Miranda, Venez. |
| Powers, Steve | 4 | 8 | 4.32 | 36 | 11 | 0 | 0 | 94 | 105 | 62 | 45 | 41 | 66 | L | L | 6-0 | 185 | 9-16-69 | 1990 | Columbia, Mo. |
| Sewell, Joe | 4 | 3 | 5.18 | 38 | 0 | 0 | 2 | 57 | 84 | 42 | 33 | 14 | 32 | R | R | 6-0 | 180 | 4-30-69 | 1991 | Littleton, Colo. |
| Waring, James | 1 | 1 | 2.60 | 4 | 0 | 0 | 0 | 17 | 16 | 5 | 5 | 6 | 16 | L | R | 6-2 | 180 | 9-19-69 | 1991 | DeLand, Fla. |
| Wheeler, Ken | 10 | 14 | 4.35 | 26 | 23 | 3 | 0 | 159 | 196 | 101 | 77 | 38 | 70 | R | R | 6-4 | 180 | 7-3-71 | 1989 | Chillicothe, Ohio |
| White, Chris | 6 | 3 | 3.36 | 13 | 12 | 1 | 0 | 88 | 88 | 37 | 33 | 19 | 51 | R | R | 6-0 | 180 | 9-15-69 | 1991 | Greenville, Pa. |

# QUAD CITY    A
## MIDWEST LEAGUE

| BATTING | AVG | G | AB | R | H | 2B | 3B | HR | RBI | BB | SO | SB | CS | B | T | HT | WT | DOB | 1st Yr | Resides |
|---|---|---|---|---|---|---|---|---|---|---|---|---|---|---|---|---|---|---|---|---|
| Ball, Jeff, dh-of | .293 | 112 | 389 | 69 | 114 | 28 | 2 | 14 | 76 | 58 | 62 | 40 | 19 | R | R | 5-10 | 185 | 4-17-69 | 1990 | Merced, Calif. |
| Bridges, Kary, 3b-2b | .281 | 65 | 263 | 37 | 74 | 9 | 0 | 3 | 24 | 31 | 18 | 15 | 10 | L | R | 5-10 | 160 | 10-27-71 | 1993 | Hattiesburg, Miss. |
| Cacini, Ron, 2b-ss | .182 | 7 | 22 | 3 | 4 | 0 | 0 | 1 | 1 | 3 | 6 | 1 | 0 | R | R | 6-3 | 185 | 8-24-70 | 1990 | Mt. Prospect, Ill. |
| Centeno, Henri, 2b | .251 | 102 | 295 | 42 | 74 | 5 | 3 | 1 | 24 | 30 | 50 | 23 | 9 | S | R | 5-11 | 159 | 1-1-70 | 1990 | Casanay, Venez. |
| Dorencz, Mark, ss | .182 | 50 | 165 | 18 | 30 | 3 | 3 | 3 | 15 | 13 | 40 | 2 | 2 | R | R | 6-0 | 185 | 6-13-71 | 1993 | Chicago, Ill. |
| Durkin, Chris, of | .273 | 25 | 77 | 14 | 21 | 6 | 1 | 1 | 6 | 15 | 13 | 6 | 4 | L | L | 6-5 | 210 | 8-12-70 | 1991 | Youngstown, Ohio |
| Eidle, Scott, of | .258 | 56 | 194 | 34 | 50 | 12 | 2 | 3 | 24 | 33 | 60 | 4 | 0 | L | R | 6-0 | 185 | 10-3-70 | 1993 | Boyertown, Pa. |
| Evans, Tim, of | .277 | 124 | 440 | 62 | 122 | 24 | 5 | 6 | 53 | 36 | 76 | 11 | 7 | L | L | 6-0 | 195 | 6-18-69 | 1992 | Cedar Rapids, Iowa |
| Gonzalez, Jimmy, c | .227 | 47 | 154 | 20 | 35 | 9 | 1 | 0 | 15 | 14 | 36 | 2 | 2 | R | R | 6-3 | 210 | 3-8-73 | 1991 | Hartford, Conn. |
| Linares, Mario, c-dh | .256 | 57 | 199 | 18 | 51 | 10 | 0 | 3 | 22 | 10 | 22 | 1 | 0 | R | R | 6-0 | 190 | 6-7-68 | 1991 | Orlando, Fla. |
| McGlone, Brian, ss-3b | .204 | 97 | 250 | 25 | 51 | 4 | 0 | 0 | 15 | 31 | 80 | 5 | 8 | L | R | 5-11 | 170 | 10-9-70 | 1991 | Tampa, Fla. |
| Probst, Alan, c | .273 | 49 | 176 | 18 | 48 | 9 | 2 | 3 | 28 | 16 | 48 | 2 | 0 | R | R | 6-4 | 205 | 10-24-70 | 1992 | Avis, Pa. |
| Ramos, Eddie, 3b-1b | .258 | 125 | 446 | 52 | 115 | 18 | 0 | 11 | 63 | 26 | 117 | 7 | 5 | R | R | 6-2 | 195 | 12-20-72 | 1991 | Miami, Fla. |
| Rhein, Jeff, of | .208 | 53 | 149 | 15 | 33 | 5 | 2 | 2 | 16 | 14 | 49 | 14 | 7 | R | R | 6-1 | 180 | 8-3-71 | 1991 | Ann Arbor, Mich. |
| Roman, Vince, of | .282 | 81 | 291 | 52 | 82 | 10 | 2 | 4 | 28 | 28 | 75 | 29 | 15 | S | R | 5-10 | 190 | 10-21-68 | 1990 | Yonkers, N.Y. |

# ASTROS
## TOP 10 PROSPECTS

**Todd Jones**
4-2 at Tucson

How the Astros Top 10 prospects, as judged by Baseball America prior to the 1993 season, fared in 1993:

| Player, Pos. | Club (Class) | AVG | AB | H | HR | RBI | SB |
|---|---|---|---|---|---|---|---|
| 2. Phil Nevin, 3b | Tucson (AAA) | .286 | 448 | 128 | 10 | 93 | 8 |
| 3. Brian Hunter, of | Jackson (AA) | .294 | 523 | 154 | 10 | 52 | 35 |
| 4. Bob Abreu, of | Osceola (A) | .283 | 474 | 134 | 5 | 55 | 10 |
| 7. Orlando Miller, ss | Tuscon (AAA) | .304 | 471 | 143 | 16 | 89 | 2 |
| 8. James Mouton, 2b | Tuscon (AAA) | .315 | 546 | 172 | 16 | 92 | 40 |
| 9. Gary Mota, of | Jackson (AA) | .144 | 90 | 13 | 3 | 8 | 1 |
| 10. Chris Hatcher, of | Jackson (AA) | .259 | 367 | 95 | 15 | 64 | 5 |

| Player, Pos. | Club (Class) | W | L | ERA | IP | H | BB | SO |
|---|---|---|---|---|---|---|---|---|
| 1. Todd Jones, rhp | Tucson (AAA) | 4 | 2 | 4.44 | 49 | 49 | 31 | 45 |
| | Houston | 1 | 2 | 3.13 | 37 | 28 | 15 | 25 |
| 5. Alvin Morman, lhp | Jackson (AA) | 8 | 2 | 2.96 | 97 | 77 | 28 | 101 |
| 6. Jeff Juden, rhp | Tucson (AAA) | 11 | 6 | 4.63 | 169 | 174 | 76 | 156 |
| | Houston | 0 | 1 | 5.40 | 5 | 4 | 4 | 7 |

| BATTING | AVG | G | AB | R | H | 2B | 3B | HR | RBI | BB | SO | SB | CS | B | T | HT | WT | DOB | 1st Yr | Resides |
|---|---|---|---|---|---|---|---|---|---|---|---|---|---|---|---|---|---|---|---|---|
| Schulte, Rich, of | .229 | 50 | 188 | 26 | 43 | 8 | 5 | 5 | 20 | 12 | 48 | 6 | 5 | L | R | 6-0 | 180 | 7-16-70 | 1991 | Pella, Iowa |
| Torino, Damian, c-dh | .138 | 26 | 65 | 2 | 9 | 1 | 0 | 1 | 6 | 5 | 33 | 0 | 0 | R | R | 6-3 | 215 | 3-3-70 | 1993 | Sparr, Fla. |
| Winslow, Bryant, 1b | .238 | 114 | 404 | 59 | 96 | 19 | 2 | 7 | 59 | 28 | 122 | 1 | 5 | R | R | 6-4 | 200 | 11-17-68 | 1991 | Littleton, Colo. |

| PITCHING | W | L | ERA | G | GS | CG | SV | IP | H | R | ER | BB | SO | B | T | HT | WT | DOB | 1st Yr | Resides |
|---|---|---|---|---|---|---|---|---|---|---|---|---|---|---|---|---|---|---|---|---|
| Bjornson, Craig | 0 | 6 | 5.08 | 39 | 0 | 0 | 3 | 51 | 63 | 34 | 29 | 18 | 37 | L | L | 6-0 | 185 | 2-14-69 | 1991 | Tucson, Ariz. |
| Dawson, Dwayne | 0 | 5 | 5.44 | 31 | 0 | 0 | 0 | 44 | 48 | 30 | 25 | 31 | 29 | R | R | 6-2 | 208 | 9-2-69 | 1992 | Wheatley, Ontario |
| Evans, Jamie | 7 | 11 | 4.17 | 26 | 26 | 1 | 0 | 160 | 165 | 96 | 74 | 65 | 126 | R | R | 5-11 | 180 | 7-9-70 | 1991 | Burlington, Ontario |
| Gutierrez, Anthony | 1 | 0 | 4.35 | 11 | 1 | 0 | 0 | 21 | 24 | 18 | 10 | 14 | 17 | L | L | 6-0 | 180 | 3-28-69 | 1988 | Littleton, Colo. |
| Holt, Chris | 11 | 10 | 2.27 | 26 | 26 | 10 | 0 | 186 | 162 | 70 | 47 | 54 | 176 | R | R | 6-4 | 205 | 9-18-71 | 1992 | Dallas, Texas |
| Krislock, Zak | 2 | 0 | 7.94 | 7 | 0 | 0 | 0 | 11 | 15 | 14 | 10 | 8 | 17 | R | R | 6-5 | 185 | 5-17-70 | 1992 | Laguna Niguel, Calif. |
| Loughlin, Mark | 4 | 6 | 3.57 | 19 | 12 | 1 | 0 | 71 | 66 | 37 | 28 | 26 | 60 | R | L | 6-3 | 210 | 12-2-69 | 1991 | Newton, Mass. |
| Murphy, Pat | 4 | 5 | 4.81 | 42 | 0 | 0 | 1 | 64 | 59 | 38 | 34 | 32 | 52 | R | R | 6-2 | 195 | 6-3-69 | 1991 | Cincinnati, Ohio |
| Ponte, Ed | 3 | 6 | 4.01 | 39 | 0 | 0 | 17 | 52 | 48 | 27 | 23 | 18 | 67 | R | R | 6-0 | 180 | 9-20-67 | 1988 | Sarasota, Fla. |
| Rees, Rob | 7 | 3 | 3.56 | 17 | 13 | 0 | 0 | 81 | 82 | 44 | 32 | 27 | 62 | R | R | 6-5 | 180 | 9-19-70 | 1989 | Kirkland, Wash. |
| Rees, Sean | 3 | 3 | 5.19 | 12 | 9 | 0 | 0 | 52 | 60 | 34 | 30 | 17 | 45 | R | L | 5-11 | 180 | 4-9-70 | 1991 | San Diego, Calif. |
| Rose, Heath | 1 | 2 | 5.30 | 7 | 2 | 1 | 0 | 19 | 18 | 12 | 11 | 8 | 14 | L | L | 6-2 | 195 | 10-25-68 | 1991 | Jacksonville, Ill. |
| Smith, Chuck | 7 | 5 | 4.64 | 22 | 17 | 2 | 0 | 111 | 109 | 73 | 57 | 52 | 103 | R | R | 6-1 | 175 | 10-21-69 | 1991 | Cleveland, Ohio |
| Walker, Jamie | 3 | 11 | 5.13 | 25 | 24 | 1 | 0 | 132 | 140 | 92 | 75 | 48 | 121 | L | L | 6-2 | 195 | 7-1-71 | 1992 | McMinnville, Tenn. |
| Westbrook, Destry | 3 | 1 | 2.48 | 27 | 0 | 0 | 2 | 36 | 29 | 11 | 10 | 23 | 41 | R | R | 6-1 | 195 | 12-13-70 | 1991 | Montrose, Colo. |

# ASHEVILLE      A
## SOUTH ATLANTIC LEAGUE

| BATTING | AVG | G | AB | R | H | 2B | 3B | HR | RBI | BB | SO | SB | CS | B | T | HT | WT | DOB | 1st Yr | Resides |
|---|---|---|---|---|---|---|---|---|---|---|---|---|---|---|---|---|---|---|---|---|
| Albaladejo, Randy, c | .231 | 66 | 225 | 20 | 52 | 22 | 1 | 0 | 20 | 9 | 49 | 2 | 2 | R | R | 6-3 | 190 | 4-10-73 | 1991 | Rio Piedras, P.R. |
| Cedeno, Eddie, 2b-ss | .097 | 9 | 31 | 3 | 3 | 1 | 0 | 0 | 0 | 1 | 10 | 0 | 1 | R | R | 6-0 | 150 | 8-2-72 | 1990 | La Romana, D.R. |
| Elliott, Greg, 3b | .269 | 120 | 424 | 50 | 114 | 25 | 1 | 11 | 55 | 42 | 95 | 17 | 10 | L | R | 6-0 | 195 | 4-17-70 | 1992 | Delta, B.C. |
| Gonzalez, Jimmy, c | .221 | 43 | 149 | 16 | 33 | 5 | 0 | 4 | 15 | 7 | 37 | 3 | 1 | R | R | 6-3 | 210 | 3-8-73 | 1991 | Hartford, Conn. |
| Grapenthien, Dan, 1b | .204 | 28 | 98 | 7 | 20 | 6 | 1 | 0 | 6 | 8 | 31 | 1 | 3 | R | R | 6-3 | 220 | 12-11-72 | 1991 | Chicago, Ill. |
| Hidalgo, Richard, of | .270 | 111 | 403 | 49 | 109 | 23 | 3 | 10 | 55 | 30 | 76 | 21 | 13 | R | R | 6-2 | 175 | 7-2-75 | 1991 | Guarenas, Venez. |
| Hobson, Todd, of-dh | .214 | 76 | 234 | 44 | 50 | 12 | 5 | 3 | 17 | 29 | 95 | 15 | 6 | R | R | 6-1 | 195 | 3-9-70 | 1991 | Indianapolis, Ind. |
| Livsey, Shawn, of | .263 | 124 | 453 | 50 | 119 | 26 | 1 | 2 | 60 | 62 | 92 | 26 | 15 | S | R | 5-11 | 180 | 7-21-73 | 1991 | Chicago, Ill. |
| McCraw, Johnny, 1b-dh | .283 | 26 | 60 | 8 | 17 | 4 | 0 | 2 | 14 | 12 | 24 | 1 | 2 | R | R | 6-3 | 225 | 4-19-71 | 1993 | Little River, S.C. |
| Mitchell, Donovan, 2b | .291 | 113 | 453 | 67 | 132 | 20 | 3 | 3 | 45 | 33 | 52 | 28 | 18 | L | R | 5-1 | 172 | 11-27-69 | 1992 | White Plains, N.Y. |
| Mora, Melvin, 2b-of | .285 | 108 | 365 | 66 | 104 | 22 | 2 | 2 | 31 | 36 | 46 | 20 | 13 | R | R | 5-10 | 160 | 2-2-72 | 1991 | Naquanqua, Venez. |
| Probst, Alan, c | .258 | 40 | 124 | 14 | 32 | 4 | 0 | 5 | 21 | 12 | 34 | 0 | 2 | R | R | 6-4 | 205 | 10-24-70 | 1992 | Avis, Pa. |
| Rennhack, Mike, of | .272 | 118 | 441 | 57 | 120 | 30 | 3 | 10 | 52 | 37 | 90 | 16 | 10 | S | R | 6-2 | 185 | 8-25-74 | 1992 | San Jose, Calif. |
| Rodriguez, Noel, of-dh | .263 | 38 | 133 | 23 | 35 | 8 | 0 | 1 | 12 | 9 | 31 | 3 | 0 | R | R | 6-3 | 180 | 12-5-73 | 1991 | Yabucoa, P.R. |
| Santana, Jose, ss | .238 | 133 | 429 | 50 | 102 | 13 | 3 | 3 | 30 | 28 | 69 | 9 | 9 | S | R | 6-0 | 160 | 4-30-72 | 1990 | San Pedro de Macoris, D.R. |
| Swinton, Jermaine, 1b | .188 | 89 | 272 | 39 | 51 | 8 | 2 | 13 | 44 | 45 | 137 | 5 | 3 | R | R | 6-4 | 210 | 10-9-72 | 1990 | Brooklyn, N.Y. |
| Webb, Kevin, 1b-3b | .225 | 76 | 267 | 32 | 60 | 14 | 1 | 7 | 39 | 21 | 78 | 9 | 4 | R | R | 6-4 | 215 | 12-27-69 | 1991 | Yorba Linda, Calif. |
| Williams, Cliff, c | .067 | 11 | 15 | 0 | 1 | 0 | 0 | 0 | 0 | 1 | 7 | 0 | 0 | R | R | 6-0 | 185 | 1-16-69 | 1988 | Fairview Heights, Ill. |

| PITCHING | W | L | ERA | G | GS | CG | SV | IP | H | R | ER | BB | SO | B | T | HT | WT | DOB | 1st Yr | Resides |
|---|---|---|---|---|---|---|---|---|---|---|---|---|---|---|---|---|---|---|---|---|
| Billingsley, Marvin | 8 | 12 | 4.15 | 28 | 28 | 3 | 0 | 169 | 169 | 99 | 78 | 75 | 110 | L | L | 6-3 | 185 | 7-9-72 | 1992 | Jackson, N.J. |
| Bottoms, Derrick | 0 | 0 | 19.80 | 3 | 0 | 0 | 0 | 5 | 12 | 12 | 11 | 7 | 3 | L | L | 6-3 | 190 | 9-24-71 | 1991 | Nashville, Tenn. |
| Centeno, Jose | 1 | 2 | 4.19 | 43 | 0 | 0 | 1 | 67 | 79 | 41 | 31 | 20 | 29 | L | L | 6-3 | 168 | 11-9-72 | 1993 | Anzoategui, Venez. |
| Czanstkowski, Tom | 1 | 1 | 4.70 | 10 | 0 | 0 | 0 | 23 | 32 | 18 | 12 | 7 | 17 | R | R | 6-2 | 195 | 9-8-72 | 1993 | Midway, Ark. |
| Fesh, Sean | 10 | 6 | 3.61 | 65 | 0 | 0 | 20 | 82 | 75 | 39 | 33 | 37 | 49 | L | L | 6-2 | 165 | 11-3-72 | 1991 | Bethel, Conn. |
| Henriquez, Oscar | 9 | 10 | 4.44 | 27 | 26 | 2 | 0 | 150 | 154 | 95 | 74 | 70 | 117 | R | R | 6-4 | 175 | 1-28-74 | 1991 | La Guaira, Venez. |
| Krislock, Zak | 4 | 6 | 4.09 | 48 | 4 | 0 | 5 | 99 | 91 | 55 | 45 | 56 | 90 | R | R | 6-5 | 185 | 5-17-70 | 1992 | Laguna Niguel, Calif. |
| Lewis, Eddie | 0 | 2 | 7.91 | 12 | 0 | 0 | 1 | 19 | 24 | 18 | 17 | 15 | 15 | S | R | 6-0 | 190 | 8-4-71 | 1993 | Kansas City, Mo. |
| Madrigal, Victor | 1 | 5 | 3.92 | 31 | 9 | 0 | 0 | 87 | 73 | 47 | 38 | 37 | 85 | R | R | 6-1 | 185 | 6-2-72 | 1989 | San Cristobal, D.R. |
| McCutchen, Jim | 1 | 2 | 7.30 | 16 | 0 | 0 | 1 | 25 | 24 | 22 | 20 | 23 | 23 | R | R | 6-5 | 220 | 8-19-68 | 1986 | Clovis, Calif. |
| Narcisse, Tyrone | 6 | 12 | 4.38 | 29 | 29 | 2 | 0 | 160 | 173 | 95 | 78 | 66 | 114 | R | R | 6-2 | 185 | 2-4-72 | 1990 | Port Arthur, Texas |
| Tenbarge, Jeff | 5 | 10 | 6.58 | 36 | 12 | 1 | 0 | 104 | 135 | 89 | 76 | 64 | 54 | R | R | 6-2 | 200 | 8-12-70 | 1992 | Evansville, Ind. |
| Valdez, Victor | 0 | 6 | 6.15 | 30 | 7 | 0 | 0 | 60 | 72 | 49 | 41 | 30 | 23 | R | R | 6-2 | 155 | 3-20-73 | 1991 | La Romana, D.R. |
| Young, Danny | 5 | 14 | 6.12 | 32 | 24 | 2 | 0 | 143 | 174 | 114 | 97 | 95 | 101 | R | L | 6-5 | 180 | 11-3-71 | 1991 | Woodbury, Tenn. |

# AUBURN      A
## NEW YORK-PENN LEAGUE

| BATTING | AVG | G | AB | R | H | 2B | 3B | HR | RBI | BB | SO | SB | CS | B | T | HT | WT | DOB | 1st Yr | Resides |
|---|---|---|---|---|---|---|---|---|---|---|---|---|---|---|---|---|---|---|---|---|
| Basey, Marsalis, 2b | .232 | 39 | 142 | 20 | 33 | 6 | 0 | 1 | 8 | 10 | 15 | 6 | 4 | R | R | 5-8 | 175 | 12-10-71 | 1990 | Martinsburg, W.Va. |
| Callan, Brett, c | .264 | 42 | 129 | 16 | 34 | 6 | 1 | 1 | 15 | 25 | 35 | 8 | 0 | R | R | 6-1 | 203 | 8-12-71 | 1993 | San Diego, Calif. |

## BATTING

| BATTING | AVG | G | AB | R | H | 2B | 3B | HR | RBI | BB | SO | SB | CS | B | T | HT | WT | DOB | 1st Yr | Resides |
|---|---|---|---|---|---|---|---|---|---|---|---|---|---|---|---|---|---|---|---|---|
| Cedeno, Eddie, 2b | .287 | 39 | 150 | 27 | 43 | 8 | 1 | 3 | 16 | 4 | 36 | 2 | 2 | R | R | 6-0 | 150 | 8-2-72 | 1990 | La Romana, D.R. |
| Crispin, Carlos, ss-2b | .188 | 32 | 85 | 10 | 16 | 1 | 0 | 0 | 8 | 10 | 21 | 1 | 2 | S | R | 6-0 | 160 | 11-5-72 | 1991 | San Pedro de Macoris, D.R. |
| Forkner, Tim, 3b | .285 | 72 | 267 | 32 | 76 | 14 | 9 | 0 | 39 | 38 | 29 | 3 | 3 | L | R | 5-11 | 180 | 3-28-73 | 1993 | Greeley, Colo. |
| Froschauer, Trevor, c | .190 | 45 | 137 | 22 | 26 | 3 | 1 | 10 | 20 | 27 | 54 | 0 | 0 | R | R | 6-6 | 235 | 9-21-72 | 1993 | Springfield, Ill. |
| Grapenthien, Dan, 1b | .237 | 47 | 173 | 16 | 41 | 7 | 0 | 0 | 20 | 16 | 54 | 0 | 0 | R | R | 6-3 | 220 | 12-11-72 | 1991 | Chicago, Ill. |
| Klaas, Klint, dh-of | .204 | 35 | 113 | 12 | 23 | 4 | 0 | 3 | 18 | 19 | 41 | 1 | 2 | R | R | 6-0 | 195 | 12-1-72 | 1993 | Bloomington, Minn. |
| Peterson, Nate, of-dh | .260 | 69 | 277 | 35 | 72 | 17 | 1 | 2 | 29 | 17 | 34 | 5 | 2 | L | R | 6-2 | 185 | 7-12-71 | 1993 | Melbourne, Australia |
| Rodriguez, Noel, of | .300 | 69 | 273 | 41 | 82 | 12 | 4 | 6 | 54 | 12 | 52 | 0 | 2 | R | R | 6-3 | 180 | 12-5-73 | 1991 | Yabucoa, P.R. |
| Verduzco, Steve, ss | .222 | 64 | 239 | 30 | 53 | 7 | 1 | 1 | 19 | 19 | 48 | 8 | 1 | R | R | 6-2 | 185 | 9-10-72 | 1993 | San Jose, Calif. |
| Vindivich, John, of | .255 | 66 | 220 | 36 | 56 | 12 | 0 | 2 | 19 | 22 | 58 | 13 | 3 | L | R | 6-3 | 195 | 10-24-71 | 1993 | Tacoma, Wash. |
| White, Chad, of | .291 | 66 | 247 | 47 | 72 | 12 | 2 | 2 | 29 | 34 | 33 | 15 | 8 | S | R | 6-2 | 180 | 5-26-71 | 1993 | Brewer, Maine |
| Wieczorek, Ted, 1b | .160 | 34 | 100 | 7 | 16 | 2 | 1 | 0 | 6 | 4 | 29 | 0 | 0 | R | R | 6-0 | 190 | 5-16-72 | 1993 | Springfield, Ore. |

## PITCHING

| PITCHING | W | L | ERA | G | GS | CG | SV | IP | H | R | ER | BB | SO | B | T | HT | WT | DOB | 1st Yr | Resides |
|---|---|---|---|---|---|---|---|---|---|---|---|---|---|---|---|---|---|---|---|---|
| Czanstkowski, Tom | 5 | 1 | 2.50 | 10 | 8 | 2 | 0 | 58 | 56 | 30 | 16 | 19 | 29 | R | R | 6-2 | 195 | 9-8-72 | 1993 | Midway, Ark. |
| Dault, Donnie | 0 | 3 | 4.00 | 20 | 0 | 0 | 0 | 36 | 38 | 32 | 16 | 21 | 51 | R | R | 6-6 | 185 | 4-15-72 | 1991 | Austin, Texas |
| Diorio, Michael | 3 | 7 | 5.13 | 15 | 15 | 0 | 0 | 79 | 98 | 57 | 45 | 27 | 57 | R | R | 6-2 | 175 | 3-1-73 | 1993 | Pueblo, Colo. |
| Grzanich, Mike | 5 | 8 | 4.82 | 16 | 14 | 4 | 0 | 93 | 106 | 63 | 50 | 27 | 71 | R | R | 6-1 | 175 | 8-24-72 | 1992 | Champaign, Ill. |
| Hartnett, William | 2 | 5 | 4.30 | 12 | 9 | 1 | 0 | 61 | 49 | 34 | 29 | 31 | 69 | R | R | 6-4 | 200 | 3-2-71 | 1993 | South Weymouth, Mass. |
| Humphrey, Richard | 4 | 3 | 2.50 | 29 | 0 | 0 | 9 | 40 | 34 | 18 | 11 | 10 | 49 | R | R | 6-1 | 185 | 6-24-71 | 1993 | Lakeland, Fla. |
| Kester, Tim | 4 | 6 | 2.06 | 15 | 13 | 4 | 0 | 96 | 78 | 40 | 22 | 19 | 83 | R | R | 6-4 | 185 | 12-1-71 | 1993 | Coral Springs, Fla. |
| Lugo, Arquimedes | 1 | 2 | 3.64 | 22 | 0 | 0 | 0 | 47 | 38 | 20 | 19 | 21 | 39 | R | R | 5-10 | 150 | 4-29-72 | 1990 | Santo Domingo, D.R. |
| Rhine, Kendall | 0 | 2 | 9.82 | 16 | 10 | 0 | 0 | 48 | 61 | 62 | 52 | 48 | 36 | R | R | 6-7 | 215 | 11-27-70 | 1992 | Lilburn, Ga. |
| Schulte, Troy | 2 | 1 | 5.00 | 8 | 0 | 0 | 1 | 9 | 9 | 5 | 5 | 4 | 11 | R | R | 6-2 | 205 | 7-15-71 | 1993 | Westphalia, Iowa |
| Smith, Kevin | 0 | 1 | 7.63 | 13 | 0 | 0 | 0 | 15 | 14 | 16 | 13 | 14 | 12 | L | L | 6-1 | 170 | 1-1-73 | 1991 | Columbus, Ga. |
| Spring, Josh | 3 | 4 | 3.57 | 26 | 0 | 0 | 0 | 40 | 34 | 27 | 16 | 25 | 35 | R | R | 6-1 | 210 | 11-26-72 | 1991 | Lebanon, Ohio |
| Wagner, Billy | 1 | 3 | 4.08 | 7 | 7 | 0 | 0 | 29 | 25 | 19 | 13 | 25 | 31 | L | L | 5-10 | 180 | 7-25-71 | 1993 | Tannersville, Va. |

# KISSIMMEE   R
## GULF COAST LEAGUE

## BATTING

| BATTING | AVG | G | AB | R | H | 2B | 3B | HR | RBI | BB | SO | SB | CS | B | T | HT | WT | DOB | 1st Yr | Resides |
|---|---|---|---|---|---|---|---|---|---|---|---|---|---|---|---|---|---|---|---|---|
| Amezcua, Adan, c | .297 | 48 | 145 | 14 | 43 | 13 | 3 | 0 | 24 | 12 | 19 | 1 | 0 | R | R | 6-1 | 180 | 3-9-74 | 1993 | Sinaloa, Mexico |
| Beyna, Terry, c-3b | .275 | 41 | 120 | 24 | 33 | 6 | 2 | 0 | 23 | 16 | 13 | 2 | 1 | R | R | 6-1 | 195 | 8-1-72 | 1993 | Mt. Prospect, Ill. |
| Bowers, Ray, of | .274 | 55 | 208 | 24 | 57 | 13 | 0 | 1 | 21 | 4 | 43 | 10 | 2 | R | R | 6-1 | 175 | 2-10-74 | 1992 | West Middlesex, Pa. |
| Dolney, Dan, c | .316 | 26 | 57 | 12 | 18 | 7 | 1 | 1 | 8 | 15 | 9 | 1 | 0 | L | R | 5-10 | 190 | 7-22-75 | 1993 | Wilmette, Ill. |
| Gosch, Grant, of | .154 | 12 | 26 | 3 | 4 | 0 | 0 | 0 | 3 | 2 | 8 | 0 | 0 | L | L | 6-2 | 180 | 6-3-75 | 1993 | Belmont, Calif. |
| Hammer, Ben, of | .250 | 44 | 108 | 19 | 27 | 4 | 0 | 0 | 12 | 18 | 19 | 4 | 1 | L | R | 5-10 | 174 | 2-11-74 | 1993 | Churchill, Australia |
| Landaker, David, dh-ss | .500 | 10 | 32 | 12 | 16 | 5 | 0 | 0 | 4 | 6 | 6 | 2 | 0 | R | R | 6-0 | 185 | 2-20-74 | 1992 | Simi Valley, Calif. |
| Larson, Kirk, 2b | .200 | 3 | 5 | 0 | 1 | 0 | 0 | 0 | 0 | 0 | 2 | 0 | 0 | R | R | 5-11 | 175 | 9-21-72 | 1992 | Sunnyvale, Calif. |
| Lee, Angelo, of | .248 | 46 | 145 | 21 | 36 | 7 | 2 | 3 | 25 | 11 | 36 | 8 | 1 | R | R | 6-2 | 195 | 2-21-73 | 1991 | Calumet, Ill. |
| Lopez, Yamil, 2b | .143 | 23 | 42 | 5 | 6 | 0 | 0 | 0 | 2 | 2 | 13 | 0 | 1 | R | R | 6-0 | 169 | 9-13-74 | 1993 | Puerto Nuevo, P.R. |
| Ramos, Juan, of | .221 | 50 | 140 | 14 | 31 | 3 | 4 | 0 | 17 | 9 | 33 | 4 | 4 | R | R | 6-0 | 165 | 7-8-73 | 1993 | San Pedro de Macoris, D.R. |
| Root, Derek, 1b | .282 | 41 | 131 | 12 | 37 | 8 | 0 | 0 | 16 | 12 | 21 | 1 | 2 | L | L | 6-4 | 175 | 5-26-75 | 1993 | Lakewood, Ohio |
| Ross, Tony, of | .316 | 37 | 133 | 29 | 42 | 4 | 2 | 1 | 9 | 8 | 19 | 11 | 1 | R | R | 5-11 | 185 | 9-17-73 | 1992 | Kansas City, Mo. |
| Saylor, Jamie, ss | .235 | 51 | 162 | 29 | 38 | 5 | 2 | 0 | 14 | 23 | 28 | 5 | 3 | L | R | 5-11 | 185 | 9-11-74 | 1993 | Garland, Texas |
| Trammell, Gary, 2b | .288 | 59 | 215 | 25 | 62 | 5 | 5 | 0 | 19 | 14 | 38 | 11 | 3 | L | R | 6-0 | 180 | 10-16-72 | 1993 | Garland, Texas |
| Truby, Chris, 3b-ss | .228 | 57 | 215 | 30 | 49 | 10 | 2 | 1 | 24 | 22 | 30 | 16 | 1 | R | R | 6-2 | 195 | 12-9-73 | 1993 | Mukilteo, Wash. |
| Witt, Joe, 1b | .189 | 39 | 106 | 13 | 20 | 5 | 1 | 0 | 8 | 9 | 13 | 3 | 0 | L | R | 6-2 | 215 | 12-29-73 | 1993 | Richfield, Minn. |

## PITCHING

| PITCHING | W | L | ERA | G | GS | CG | SV | IP | H | R | ER | BB | SO | B | T | HT | WT | DOB | 1st Yr | Resides |
|---|---|---|---|---|---|---|---|---|---|---|---|---|---|---|---|---|---|---|---|---|
| Baptist, Brett | 2 | 0 | 5.02 | 19 | 0 | 0 | 1 | 38 | 49 | 32 | 21 | 22 | 22 | L | R | 6-3 | 170 | 7-5-73 | 1993 | Jacksonville, Ill. |
| Blanco, Alberto | 0 | 1 | 2.00 | 9 | 1 | 0 | 1 | 18 | 15 | 4 | 4 | 11 | 32 | L | L | 6-1 | 170 | 6-27-76 | 1993 | Miranda, Venez. |
| Creek, Ryan | 7 | 3 | 2.34 | 12 | 11 | 2 | 1 | 69 | 53 | 22 | 18 | 30 | 62 | R | R | 6-1 | 175 | 9-24-72 | 1993 | Martinsburg, W.Va. |
| Crossley, Chad | 2 | 1 | 5.22 | 17 | 0 | 0 | 2 | 29 | 27 | 19 | 17 | 10 | 21 | S | R | 6-5 | 215 | 6-22-72 | 1993 | Seffner, Fla. |
| Linehan, Andrew | 2 | 1 | 5.12 | 12 | 0 | 0 | 0 | 19 | 26 | 12 | 11 | 6 | 13 | L | L | 6-2 | 170 | 10-11-75 | 1992 | Yarrambat, Australia |
| Mercado, Hector | 5 | 4 | 2.42 | 11 | 11 | 1 | 0 | 67 | 49 | 26 | 18 | 29 | 59 | L | L | 6-3 | 205 | 4-29-74 | 1993 | Dorado, P.R. |
| Padron, Oscar | 3 | 2 | 3.09 | 15 | 0 | 0 | 2 | 23 | 24 | 9 | 8 | 7 | 22 | R | R | 6-3 | 175 | 3-22-74 | 1992 | Miranda, Venez. |
| Phillips, Jon | 0 | 1 | 3.38 | 3 | 0 | 0 | 0 | 3 | 1 | 5 | 1 | 3 | 6 | L | L | 6-0 | 190 | 6-29-72 | 1993 | Collins, N.Y. |
| Ramos, Edgar | 5 | 2 | 2.16 | 14 | 12 | 0 | 0 | 75 | 59 | 23 | 18 | 13 | 70 | R | R | 6-4 | 190 | 3-6-75 | 1992 | Cumana, Venez. |
| Runyan, Sean | 4 | 3 | 2.98 | 12 | 12 | 0 | 0 | 66 | 66 | 35 | 22 | 24 | 52 | L | L | 6-3 | 180 | 6-21-74 | 1992 | Urbandale, Iowa |
| Steinke, Brock | 3 | 2 | 4.73 | 15 | 2 | 0 | 0 | 27 | 33 | 19 | 14 | 16 | 22 | R | R | 6-2 | 180 | 6-27-75 | 1993 | Cedar Rapids, Iowa |
| Tucker, Julien | 2 | 3 | 3.95 | 11 | 10 | 1 | 0 | 55 | 55 | 36 | 24 | 22 | 33 | L | R | 6-7 | 200 | 4-19-73 | 1993 | Chateauguay, Quebec |
| Walter, Michael | 0 | 1 | 2.79 | 17 | 0 | 0 | 8 | 19 | 15 | 10 | 6 | 12 | 16 | R | R | 6-1 | 195 | 9-23-74 | 1993 | San Diego, Calif. |

# KANSAS CITY
## ROYALS

**Manager:** Hal McRae.   **1993 Record:** 84-78, .519 (3rd, AL West).

| BATTING | AVG | G | AB | R | H | 2B | 3B | HR | RBI | BB | SO | SB | CS | B | T | HT | WT | DOB | 1st Yr | Resides |
|---|---|---|---|---|---|---|---|---|---|---|---|---|---|---|---|---|---|---|---|---|
| Brett, George | .266 | 145 | 560 | 69 | 149 | 31 | 3 | 19 | 75 | 39 | 67 | 7 | 5 | L | R | 6-0 | 205 | 5-15-53 | 1971 | Mission Hills, Kan. |
| Brooks, Hubie | .286 | 75 | 168 | 14 | 48 | 12 | 0 | 1 | 24 | 11 | 27 | 0 | 1 | R | R | 6-0 | 205 | 9-24-56 | 1978 | Chatsworth, Calif. |
| Gaetti, Gary | .256 | 82 | 281 | 37 | 72 | 18 | 1 | 14 | 46 | 16 | 75 | 0 | 3 | R | R | 6-0 | 200 | 8-19-58 | 1979 | Eden Prairie, Minn. |
| 2-team (20 Calif.) | .245 | 102 | 331 | 40 | 81 | 20 | 1 | 14 | 50 | 21 | 87 | 1 | 3 | | | | | | | |
| Gagne, Greg | .280 | 159 | 540 | 66 | 151 | 32 | 3 | 10 | 57 | 33 | 93 | 10 | 12 | R | R | 5-11 | 180 | 11-12-61 | 1979 | Rehoboth, Mass. |
| Gwynn, Chris | .300 | 103 | 287 | 36 | 86 | 14 | 4 | 1 | 25 | 24 | 34 | 0 | 1 | L | L | 6-0 | 220 | 10-13-64 | 1985 | Alta Loma, Calif. |
| Hamelin, Bob | .224 | 16 | 49 | 2 | 11 | 3 | 0 | 2 | 5 | 6 | 15 | 0 | 0 | L | L | 6-0 | 235 | 11-29-67 | 1988 | Charlotte, N.C. |
| Hiatt, Phil | .218 | 81 | 238 | 30 | 52 | 12 | 1 | 7 | 36 | 16 | 82 | 6 | 3 | R | R | 6-3 | 200 | 5-1-69 | 1990 | Pensacola, Fla. |
| Howard, Dave | .333 | 15 | 24 | 5 | 8 | 0 | 1 | 0 | 2 | 2 | 5 | 1 | 0 | S | R | 6-0 | 175 | 2-26-67 | 1987 | Sarasota, Fla. |
| Jose, Felix | .253 | 149 | 499 | 64 | 126 | 24 | 3 | 6 | 43 | 36 | 95 | 31 | 13 | S | R | 6-1 | 220 | 5-8-65 | 1984 | Santo Domingo, D.R. |
| Joyner, Wally | .292 | 141 | 497 | 83 | 145 | 36 | 3 | 15 | 65 | 66 | 67 | 5 | 9 | L | L | 6-2 | 200 | 6-16-62 | 1983 | Lee's Summitt, Mo. |
| Koslofski, Kevin | .269 | 15 | 26 | 4 | 7 | 0 | 0 | 1 | 2 | 4 | 5 | 0 | 1 | L | R | 5-8 | 175 | 9-24-66 | 1984 | Decatur, Ill. |
| Lind, Jose | .248 | 136 | 431 | 33 | 107 | 13 | 2 | 0 | 37 | 13 | 36 | 3 | 2 | R | R | 5-11 | 180 | 5-1-64 | 1983 | Dorado, P.R. |
| Macfarlane, Mike | .273 | 117 | 388 | 55 | 106 | 27 | 0 | 20 | 67 | 40 | 83 | 2 | 5 | R | R | 6-1 | 205 | 4-12-64 | 1985 | Overland Park, Kan. |
| Mayne, Brent | .254 | 71 | 205 | 22 | 52 | 9 | 1 | 2 | 22 | 18 | 31 | 3 | 2 | L | R | 6-1 | 190 | 4-19-68 | 1989 | Costa Mesa, Calif. |
| McRae, Brian | .282 | 153 | 627 | 78 | 177 | 28 | 9 | 12 | 69 | 37 | 105 | 23 | 14 | S | R | 6-0 | 185 | 8-27-67 | 1985 | Leawood, Kan. |
| McReynolds, Kevin | .245 | 110 | 351 | 44 | 86 | 22 | 4 | 11 | 42 | 37 | 56 | 2 | 2 | R | R | 6-1 | 225 | 10-16-59 | 1982 | Little Rock, Ark. |
| Miller, Keith | .167 | 37 | 108 | 9 | 18 | 3 | 0 | 0 | 3 | 8 | 19 | 3 | 1 | R | R | 5-11 | 185 | 6-12-63 | 1985 | Frankenmuth, Mich. |
| Pulliam, Harvey | .258 | 27 | 62 | 7 | 16 | 5 | 0 | 1 | 6 | 2 | 14 | 0 | 0 | R | R | 6-0 | 205 | 10-20-67 | 1986 | San Francisco, Calif. |
| Rossy, Rico | .221 | 46 | 86 | 10 | 19 | 4 | 0 | 2 | 12 | 9 | 11 | 0 | 0 | R | R | 5-10 | 165 | 2-16-64 | 1985 | Bayamon, P.R. |
| Santovenia, Nelson | .125 | 4 | 8 | 0 | 1 | 0 | 0 | 0 | 1 | 2 | 0 | 0 | 0 | R | R | 6-3 | 210 | 7-27-61 | 1982 | Miami, Fla. |
| Shumpert, Terry | .100 | 8 | 10 | 0 | 1 | 0 | 0 | 0 | 0 | 2 | 2 | 1 | 0 | R | R | 5-11 | 185 | 8-16-66 | 1987 | Paducah, Ky. |
| Wilkerson, Curtis | .143 | 12 | 28 | 1 | 4 | 0 | 0 | 0 | 0 | 1 | 6 | 2 | 0 | S | R | 5-9 | 175 | 4-26-61 | 1980 | Arlington, Texas |
| Wilson, Craig | .265 | 21 | 49 | 6 | 13 | 1 | 0 | 1 | 3 | 7 | 6 | 1 | 1 | R | R | 5-11 | 210 | 11-28-64 | 1984 | Annapolis, Md. |

| PITCHING | W | L | ERA | G | GS | CG | SV | IP | H | R | ER | BB | SO | B | T | HT | WT | DOB | 1st Yr | Resides |
|---|---|---|---|---|---|---|---|---|---|---|---|---|---|---|---|---|---|---|---|---|
| Appier, Kevin | 18 | 8 | 2.56 | 34 | 34 | 5 | 0 | 239 | 183 | 74 | 68 | 81 | 186 | R | R | 6-2 | 195 | 12-6-67 | 1987 | Overland Park, Kan. |
| Belinda, Stan | 1 | 1 | 4.28 | 23 | 0 | 0 | 0 | 27 | 30 | 13 | 13 | 6 | 25 | R | R | 6-3 | 185 | 8-6-66 | 1985 | Alexandria, Pa. |
| Brewer, Billy | 2 | 2 | 3.46 | 46 | 0 | 0 | 0 | 39 | 31 | 16 | 15 | 20 | 28 | L | L | 6-1 | 175 | 4-15-68 | 1990 | Longview, Texas |
| Burgos, Enrique | 0 | 1 | 9.00 | 5 | 0 | 0 | 0 | 5 | 5 | 5 | 5 | 6 | 6 | S | L | 5-10 | 145 | 10-21-67 | 1985 | Bayamon, P.R. |
| Cadaret, Greg | 1 | 1 | 2.93 | 13 | 0 | 0 | 0 | 15 | 14 | 5 | 5 | 7 | 12 | L | L | 6-3 | 215 | 2-27-62 | 1983 | Mesa, Ariz. |
| Cone, David | 11 | 14 | 3.33 | 34 | 34 | 6 | 0 | 254 | 205 | 102 | 94 | 114 | 191 | L | R | 6-1 | 190 | 1-2-63 | 1981 | Leawood, Kan. |
| DiPino, Frank | 1 | 1 | 6.89 | 11 | 0 | 0 | 0 | 16 | 21 | 12 | 12 | 6 | 5 | L | L | 6-0 | 180 | 10-22-56 | 1977 | Manlius, N.Y. |
| Gardner, Mark | 4 | 6 | 6.19 | 17 | 16 | 0 | 0 | 92 | 92 | 65 | 63 | 36 | 54 | R | R | 6-1 | 190 | 3-1-62 | 1985 | Fresno, Calif. |
| Gordon, Tom | 12 | 6 | 3.58 | 48 | 14 | 2 | 1 | 156 | 125 | 65 | 62 | 77 | 143 | R | R | 5-9 | 180 | 11-18-67 | 1986 | Avon Park, Fla. |
| Granger, Jeff | 0 | 0 | 27.00 | 1 | 0 | 0 | 0 | 1 | 3 | 3 | 3 | 2 | 1 | R | L | 6-4 | 200 | 12-16-71 | 1993 | Orange, Texas |
| Gubicza, Mark | 5 | 8 | 4.66 | 49 | 6 | 0 | 2 | 104 | 128 | 61 | 54 | 43 | 80 | R | R | 6-5 | 230 | 8-14-62 | 1981 | Northridge, Calif. |
| Habyan, John | 0 | 0 | 4.50 | 12 | 0 | 0 | 0 | 14 | 14 | 7 | 7 | 4 | 10 | R | R | 6-2 | 195 | 1-29-64 | 1982 | Bel Air, Md. |
| 2-team (36 N.Y.) | 2 | 1 | 4.15 | 48 | 0 | 0 | 1 | 56 | 59 | 27 | 26 | 20 | 39 | | | | | | | |
| Haney, Chris | 9 | 9 | 6.02 | 23 | 23 | 1 | 0 | 124 | 141 | 87 | 83 | 53 | 65 | L | L | 6-3 | 195 | 11-16-68 | 1990 | Barboursville, Va. |
| Magnante, Mike | 1 | 2 | 4.08 | 7 | 6 | 0 | 0 | 35 | 37 | 16 | 16 | 11 | 16 | L | L | 6-1 | 190 | 6-17-65 | 1988 | Burbank, Calif. |
| Meacham, Rusty | 2 | 2 | 5.57 | 15 | 0 | 0 | 0 | 21 | 31 | 15 | 13 | 5 | 13 | R | R | 6-2 | 175 | 1-27-68 | 1988 | Palm City, Fla. |
| Montgomery, Jeff | 7 | 5 | 2.27 | 69 | 0 | 0 | 45 | 87 | 65 | 22 | 22 | 23 | 66 | R | R | 5-11 | 180 | 1-7-62 | 1983 | Cincinnati, Ohio |
| Pichardo, Hipolito | 7 | 8 | 4.04 | 30 | 25 | 2 | 0 | 165 | 183 | 85 | 74 | 53 | 70 | R | R | 6-1 | 160 | 8-22-69 | 1988 | Esperanza, D.R. |
| Rasmussen, Dennis | 1 | 2 | 7.45 | 9 | 4 | 0 | 0 | 29 | 40 | 25 | 24 | 14 | 12 | L | L | 6-7 | 240 | 4-18-59 | 1980 | Omaha, Neb. |
| Reed, Rick | 0 | 0 | 9.82 | 1 | 0 | 0 | 0 | 4 | 6 | 4 | 4 | 1 | 3 | R | R | 6-0 | 200 | 8-16-64 | 1986 | Huntington, W.Va. |
| Sampen, Bill | 2 | 2 | 5.89 | 18 | 0 | 0 | 0 | 18 | 25 | 12 | 12 | 9 | 9 | R | R | 6-2 | 200 | 1-18-63 | 1985 | Havana, Ill. |

### FIELDING

| Catcher | PCT | G | PO | A | E | DP |
|---|---|---|---|---|---|---|
| Macfarlane | .985 | 114 | 647 | 68 | 11 | 11 |
| Mayne | .995 | 68 | 356 | 27 | 2 | 1 |
| Santovenia | 1.000 | 4 | 14 | 1 | 0 | 1 |

| First Base | PCT | G | PO | A | E | DP |
|---|---|---|---|---|---|---|
| Brooks | 1.000 | 3 | 19 | 3 | 0 | 1 |
| Gaetti | .991 | 18 | 97 | 10 | 1 | 11 |
| Gwynn | 1.000 | 1 | 12 | 1 | 0 | 1 |
| Hamelin | .986 | 15 | 129 | 9 | 2 | 10 |
| Joyner | .994 | 140 | 1116 | 145 | 7 | 116 |

| Second Base | PCT | G | PO | A | E | DP |
|---|---|---|---|---|---|---|
| Howard | .927 | 7 | 15 | 23 | 3 | 2 |
| Lind | .994 | 136 | 269 | 362 | 4 | 75 |
| Miller | .900 | 3 | 3 | 6 | 1 | 1 |
| Rossy | .987 | 24 | 29 | 48 | 1 | 11 |

| | PCT | G | PO | A | E | DP |
|---|---|---|---|---|---|---|
| Shumpert | 1.000 | 8 | 11 | 11 | 0 | 3 |
| Wilkerson | 1.000 | 10 | 5 | 16 | 0 | 3 |
| Wilson | .800 | 1 | 1 | 3 | 1 | 0 |

| Third Base | PCT | G | PO | A | E | DP |
|---|---|---|---|---|---|---|
| Gaetti | .974 | 72 | 50 | 136 | 5 | 15 |
| Hiatt | .909 | 70 | 45 | 114 | 16 | 6 |
| Howard | 1.000 | 2 | 1 | 0 | 0 | 0 |
| Miller | .889 | 21 | 11 | 29 | 5 | 2 |
| Rossy | 1.000 | 16 | 2 | 7 | 0 | 0 |
| Wilson | 1.000 | 15 | 7 | 19 | 0 | 4 |

| Shortstop | PCT | G | PO | A | E | DP |
|---|---|---|---|---|---|---|
| Gagne | .986 | 159 | 266 | 451 | 10 | 93 |
| Howard | 1.000 | 3 | 1 | 5 | 0 | 0 |
| Rossy | 1.000 | 11 | 11 | 21 | 0 | 7 |

| | PCT | G | PO | A | E | DP |
|---|---|---|---|---|---|---|
| Wilkerson | 1.000 | 4 | 3 | 9 | 0 | 0 |

| Outfield | PCT | G | PO | A | E | DP |
|---|---|---|---|---|---|---|
| Brooks | .966 | 40 | 53 | 3 | 2 | 1 |
| Gwynn | .994 | 83 | 149 | 6 | 1 | 0 |
| Howard | .000 | 1 | 0 | 0 | 0 | 0 |
| Jose | .972 | 144 | 237 | 6 | 7 | 3 |
| Koslofski | 1.000 | 13 | 20 | 2 | 0 | 2 |
| McRae | .983 | 153 | 394 | 4 | 7 | 3 |
| McReynolds | .990 | 104 | 191 | 5 | 2 | 0 |
| Miller | 1.000 | 4 | 4 | 0 | 0 | 0 |
| Pulliam | .971 | 26 | 33 | 0 | 1 | 0 |
| Wilson | .000 | 1 | 0 | 0 | 0 | 0 |

# ROYALS FARM SYSTEM

| Class | Club | League | W | L | Pct. | Finish* | Manager | First Year |
|---|---|---|---|---|---|---|---|---|
| AAA | Omaha (Neb.) Royals | American Assoc. | 70 | 74 | .486 | 5th (8) | Jeff Cox | 1969 |
| AA | Memphis (Tenn.) Chicks | Southern | 63 | 77 | .450 | 9th (10) | Tom Poquette | 1984 |
| A# | Wilmington (Del.) Blue Rocks | Carolina | 74 | 65 | .532 | 2nd (8) | Ron Johnson | 1993 |

TOM DiPACE

**Kevin Appier.** Royals righthander went 18-8 and led American League with a 2.56 ERA.

R&R SPORTS GROUP

**Brian McRae.** Son of Royals manager Hal McRae hit .282 and led team in hits (177) and total bases (259).

| Class | Club | League | W | L | Pct. | Finish* | Manager | First Year |
|---|---|---|---|---|---|---|---|---|
| A | Rockford (Ill.) Royals | Midwest | 78 | 54 | .591 | 2nd (14) | Mike Jirschele | 1993 |
| A | Eugene (Ore.) Emeralds | Northwest | 40 | 36 | .526 | 4th (8) | John Mizerock | 1984 |
| Rookie | Fort Myers (Fla.) Royals | Gulf Coast | 29 | 30 | .492 | 10th (15) | Bob Herold | 1993 |

*Finish in overall standings (No. of teams in league)  #Advanced level

## OMAHA        AAA
### AMERICAN ASSOCIATION

| BATTING | AVG | G | AB | R | H | 2B | 3B | HR | RBI | BB | SO | SB | CS | B | T | HT | WT | DOB | 1st Yr | Resides |
|---|---|---|---|---|---|---|---|---|---|---|---|---|---|---|---|---|---|---|---|---|
| Abner, Shawn | .246 | 37 | 134 | 14 | 33 | 6 | 2 | 2 | 16 | 8 | 20 | 2 | 2 | R | R | 6-1 | 194 | 6-17-66 | 1984 | San Diego, Calif. |
| Diaz, Kiki | .273 | 57 | 154 | 21 | 42 | 5 | 2 | 0 | 14 | 8 | 15 | 0 | 0 | R | R | 6-1 | 175 | 2-8-64 | 1982 | San Juan, P.R. |
| Hamelin, Bob | .259 | 137 | 479 | 77 | 124 | 19 | 3 | 29 | 84 | 82 | 94 | 8 | 3 | L | L | 6-0 | 235 | 11-29-67 | 1988 | Charlotte, N.C. |
| Hiatt, Phil | .235 | 12 | 51 | 8 | 12 | 2 | 0 | 3 | 10 | 4 | 20 | 0 | 0 | R | R | 6-3 | 200 | 5-1-69 | 1990 | Pensacola, Fla. |
| Howard, David | .255 | 47 | 157 | 15 | 40 | 8 | 2 | 0 | 18 | 7 | 20 | 3 | 1 | S | R | 6-0 | 175 | 2-26-67 | 1987 | Sarasota, Fla. |
| Kingery, Mike | .263 | 116 | 399 | 61 | 105 | 19 | 5 | 10 | 41 | 36 | 24 | 9 | 3 | L | L | 6-0 | 185 | 3-29-61 | 1980 | Atwater, Minn. |
| Knapp, Mike | .290 | 70 | 200 | 22 | 58 | 7 | 0 | 2 | 19 | 34 | 32 | 2 | 4 | R | R | 6-0 | 195 | 10-6-64 | 1986 | Sacramento, Calif. |
| Koslofski, Kevin | .276 | 111 | 395 | 58 | 109 | 22 | 5 | 7 | 45 | 43 | 73 | 15 | 7 | L | R | 5-8 | 175 | 9-24-66 | 1984 | Decatur, Ill. |
| Long, Kevin | .255 | 17 | 51 | 7 | 13 | 2 | 0 | 0 | 4 | 2 | 13 | 3 | 0 | L | L | 5-9 | 165 | 12-30-66 | 1989 | Phoenix, Ariz. |
| McGinnis, Russ | .291 | 78 | 275 | 53 | 80 | 20 | 2 | 16 | 54 | 42 | 44 | 1 | 0 | R | R | 6-3 | 225 | 6-18-63 | 1985 | Phoenix, Ariz. |
| Miller, Keith | .292 | 6 | 24 | 2 | 7 | 1 | 1 | 0 | 2 | 0 | 2 | 1 | 0 | R | R | 5-11 | 185 | 6-12-63 | 1985 | Frankenmuth, Mich. |
| Mota, Jose | .282 | 105 | 330 | 46 | 93 | 11 | 2 | 3 | 35 | 34 | 34 | 29 | 13 | S | R | 5-9 | 155 | 3-16-65 | 1985 | Glendale, Calif. |
| Ortiz, Javier | .286 | 3 | 7 | 0 | 2 | 0 | 0 | 0 | 2 | 1 | 1 | 0 | 1 | R | R | 6-4 | 210 | 1-22-63 | 1983 | Hialeah, Fla. |
| Pulliam, Harvey | .264 | 54 | 208 | 28 | 55 | 10 | 0 | 5 | 26 | 17 | 36 | 1 | 0 | R | R | 6-0 | 205 | 10-20-67 | 1986 | San Francisco, Calif. |
| Rhodes, Karl | .318 | 88 | 365 | 81 | 116 | 31 | 2 | 23 | 64 | 38 | 60 | 10 | 5 | L | L | 5-11 | 170 | 8-21-68 | 1986 | Cincinnati, Ohio |
| Rohrmeier, Dan | .248 | 118 | 432 | 51 | 107 | 23 | 3 | 17 | 70 | 23 | 59 | 2 | 1 | R | R | 6-0 | 185 | 9-27-65 | 1987 | Woodridge, Ill. |
| Rossy, Rico | .298 | 37 | 131 | 25 | 39 | 10 | 1 | 5 | 21 | 20 | 19 | 3 | 2 | R | R | 5-10 | 165 | 2-16-64 | 1985 | Bayamon, P.R. |
| Santovenia, Nelson | .237 | 81 | 274 | 33 | 65 | 13 | 0 | 11 | 42 | 12 | 50 | 0 | 1 | R | R | 6-3 | 210 | 7-27-61 | 1982 | Miami, Fla. |
| Shumpert, Terry | .300 | 111 | 413 | 70 | 124 | 29 | 1 | 14 | 59 | 41 | 62 | 36 | 8 | R | R | 5-11 | 185 | 8-16-66 | 1987 | Paducah, Ky. |
| Stephenson, Phil | .306 | 20 | 72 | 12 | 22 | 7 | 1 | 4 | 8 | 5 | 12 | 0 | 0 | L | L | 6-1 | 201 | 9-19-60 | 1982 | Wichita, Kan. |
| Vindivich, Paul | .000 | 2 | 2 | 0 | 0 | 0 | 0 | 0 | 0 | 0 | 1 | 0 | 0 | R | R | 6-2 | 215 | 12-13-73 | 1992 | Tacoma, Wash. |
| Wilson, Craig | .278 | 65 | 234 | 26 | 65 | 13 | 1 | 3 | 28 | 20 | 24 | 7 | 4 | R | R | 5-11 | 210 | 11-28-64 | 1984 | Annapolis, Md. |

| PITCHING | W | L | ERA | G | GS | CG | SV | IP | H | R | ER | BB | SO | B | T | HT | WT | DOB | 1st Yr | Resides |
|---|---|---|---|---|---|---|---|---|---|---|---|---|---|---|---|---|---|---|---|---|
| Ahern, Brian | 1 | 2 | 5.68 | 6 | 5 | 0 | 0 | 19 | 18 | 17 | 12 | 13 | 16 | R | R | 6-0 | 205 | 5-18-68 | 1989 | Glenwood, Ill. |
| Boddicker, Mike | 0 | 2 | 4.60 | 3 | 3 | 0 | 0 | 16 | 18 | 9 | 8 | 4 | 12 | R | R | 5-11 | 190 | 8-23-57 | 1978 | Overland Park, Kan. |
| Brown, Keith | 13 | 8 | 4.84 | 26 | 25 | 1 | 0 | 149 | 166 | 85 | 80 | 36 | 98 | S | R | 6-4 | 215 | 2-14-64 | 1986 | Antioch, Tenn. |
| Burgos, Enrique | 2 | 4 | 3.16 | 48 | 0 | 0 | 9 | 63 | 36 | 26 | 22 | 37 | 91 | L | L | 6-4 | 195 | 10-7-65 | 1983 | Chorrera, Panama |
| Campbell, Jim | 3 | 5 | 5.04 | 27 | 4 | 0 | 0 | 55 | 72 | 33 | 31 | 17 | 33 | L | L | 5-11 | 190 | 5-19-66 | 1987 | Oroville, Calif. |
| Clark, Dera | 4 | 4 | 4.37 | 51 | 0 | 0 | 5 | 82 | 86 | 43 | 40 | 30 | 53 | R | R | 6-1 | 200 | 4-14-65 | 1987 | Lindsay, Texas |
| Curry, Steve | 6 | 7 | 4.88 | 33 | 21 | 1 | 0 | 146 | 141 | 86 | 79 | 56 | 91 | R | R | 6-6 | 217 | 9-13-65 | 1984 | Perrysburg, Ohio |
| DiPino, Frank | 1 | 2 | 2.78 | 15 | 0 | 0 | 1 | 23 | 21 | 9 | 7 | 4 | 9 | L | L | 6-0 | 180 | 10-22-56 | 1977 | Manlius, N.Y. |
| Gardner, Mark | 4 | 2 | 2.79 | 8 | 8 | 1 | 0 | 48 | 34 | 17 | 15 | 19 | 41 | R | R | 6-1 | 190 | 3-1-62 | 1985 | Fresno, Calif. |
| Haney, Chris | 6 | 1 | 2.27 | 8 | 7 | 2 | 0 | 48 | 43 | 13 | 12 | 14 | 32 | L | L | 6-3 | 195 | 11-16-68 | 1990 | Baboursville, Va. |

| PITCHING | W | L | ERA | G | GS | CG | SV | IP | H | R | ER | BB | SO | B | T | HT | WT | DOB | 1st Yr | Resides |
|---|---|---|---|---|---|---|---|---|---|---|---|---|---|---|---|---|---|---|---|---|
| Magnante, Mike | 2 | 6 | 3.67 | 33 | 13 | 0 | 2 | 105 | 97 | 46 | 43 | 29 | 74 | L | L | 6-1 | 190 | 6-17-65 | 1988 | Burbank, Calif. |
| Meacham, Rusty | 0 | 0 | 4.82 | 7 | 0 | 0 | 0 | 9 | 10 | 5 | 5 | 1 | 10 | R | R | 6-2 | 175 | 1-27-68 | 1988 | Palm City, Fla. |
| Pierce, Eddie | 0 | 2 | 5.45 | 12 | 2 | 0 | 0 | 35 | 40 | 24 | 21 | 13 | 20 | L | L | 6-1 | 190 | 10-6-68 | 1989 | San Dimas, Calif. |
| Rasmussen, Dennis | 7 | 8 | 5.03 | 17 | 17 | 3 | 0 | 106 | 124 | 68 | 59 | 27 | 59 | L | L | 6-7 | 240 | 4-18-59 | 1980 | Omaha, Neb. |
| Reed, Rick | 11 | 4 | 3.09 | 19 | 19 | 3 | 0 | 128 | 116 | 48 | 44 | 14 | 58 | R | R | 6-0 | 200 | 8-16-64 | 1986 | Huntington, W.Va. |
| Roesler, Mike | 1 | 1 | 6.16 | 4 | 3 | 0 | 0 | 19 | 21 | 14 | 13 | 10 | 6 | R | R | 6-5 | 210 | 9-12-63 | 1985 | Fort Wayne, Ind. |
| Sampen, Bill | 1 | 2 | 3.41 | 33 | 0 | 0 | 8 | 37 | 37 | 16 | 14 | 13 | 34 | R | R | 6-2 | 200 | 1-18-63 | 1985 | Havana, Ill. |
| Sanchez, Alex | 2 | 8 | 8.12 | 16 | 9 | 1 | 0 | 51 | 62 | 46 | 46 | 28 | 31 | R | R | 6-2 | 200 | 4-8-66 | 1987 | Antioch, Calif. |
| Shifflett, Steve | 3 | 3 | 4.98 | 43 | 0 | 0 | 5 | 56 | 78 | 34 | 31 | 15 | 31 | R | R | 6-1 | 200 | 1-5-66 | 1989 | Pleasant Hill, Mo. |
| Stieb, Dave | 3 | 3 | 6.42 | 9 | 8 | 1 | 0 | 48 | 63 | 37 | 34 | 12 | 18 | R | R | 6-0 | 195 | 7-22-57 | 1978 | Gilroy, Calif. |
| 2-team (1 Nashville) | 3 | 4 | 6.09 | 10 | 9 | 1 | 0 | 55 | 71 | 40 | 37 | 14 | 21 | | | | | | | |

### FIELDING

| Catcher | PCT | G | PO | A | E | DP |
|---|---|---|---|---|---|---|
| Knapp | .988 | 67 | 357 | 43 | 5 | 9 |
| McGinnis | 1.000 | 8 | 59 | 6 | 0 | 0 |
| Santovenia | .990 | 77 | 446 | 44 | 5 | 7 |

| First Base | PCT | G | PO | A | E | DP |
|---|---|---|---|---|---|---|
| Hamelin | .991 | 127 | 1104 | 90 | 11 | 116 |
| Knapp | 1.000 | 1 | 3 | 0 | 0 | 0 |
| McGinnis | .979 | 14 | 87 | 8 | 2 | 11 |
| Rohrmeier | 1.000 | 1 | 1 | 0 | 0 | 0 |
| Stephenson | .983 | 7 | 49 | 10 | 1 | 5 |
| Wilson | .909 | 1 | 10 | 0 | 1 | 1 |

| Second Base | PCT | G | PO | A | E | DP |
|---|---|---|---|---|---|---|
| Diaz | .931 | 10 | 11 | 16 | 2 | 5 |
| Mota | .971 | 32 | 52 | 83 | 4 | 23 |

| | PCT | G | PO | A | E | DP |
|---|---|---|---|---|---|---|
| Shumpert | .972 | 108 | 190 | 303 | 14 | 73 |

| Third Base | PCT | G | PO | A | E | DP |
|---|---|---|---|---|---|---|
| Diaz | .931 | 16 | 12 | 15 | 2 | 1 |
| Hiatt | .946 | 12 | 11 | 24 | 2 | 3 |
| McGinnis | .959 | 45 | 28 | 88 | 5 | 7 |
| Miller | .909 | 6 | 2 | 8 | 1 | 0 |
| Mota | .600 | 4 | 0 | 3 | 2 | 1 |
| Rossy | .976 | 16 | 10 | 31 | 1 | 5 |
| Wilson | .951 | 60 | 40 | 115 | 8 | 14 |

| Shortstop | PCT | G | PO | A | E | DP |
|---|---|---|---|---|---|---|
| Diaz | .947 | 29 | 41 | 66 | 6 | 14 |
| Howard | .964 | 46 | 76 | 137 | 8 | 34 |
| Mota | .966 | 56 | 75 | 125 | 7 | 29 |

| | PCT | G | PO | A | E | DP |
|---|---|---|---|---|---|---|
| Rossy | .958 | 27 | 44 | 93 | 6 | 25 |

| Outfield | PCT | G | PO | A | E | DP |
|---|---|---|---|---|---|---|
| Abner | .988 | 34 | 75 | 4 | 1 | 2 |
| Kingery | .996 | 105 | 212 | 15 | 1 | 5 |
| Kioslofski | .983 | 109 | 285 | 13 | 5 | 4 |
| Long | 1.000 | 15 | 33 | 4 | 0 | 1 |
| Mota | .000 | 1 | 0 | 0 | 0 | 0 |
| Ortiz | 1.000 | 3 | 5 | 0 | 0 | 0 |
| Pulliam | .948 | 43 | 102 | 7 | 6 | 2 |
| Rhodes | .961 | 84 | 135 | 13 | 6 | 2 |
| Rohmeier | 1.000 | 39 | 70 | 2 | 0 | 0 |
| Stephenson | 1.000 | 8 | 24 | 0 | 0 | 0 |

# MEMPHIS                                                                AA
## SOUTHERN LEAGUE

| BATTING | AVG | G | AB | R | H | 2B | 3B | HR | RBI | BB | SO | SB | CS | B | T | HT | WT | DOB | 1st Yr | Resides |
|---|---|---|---|---|---|---|---|---|---|---|---|---|---|---|---|---|---|---|---|---|
| Casillas, Adam, of-1b | .304 | 126 | 450 | 53 | 137 | 33 | 6 | 4 | 50 | 59 | 18 | 3 | 3 | L | L | 5-10 | 170 | 7-30-65 | 1987 | Stockton, Calif. |
| Cole, Butch, of | .257 | 80 | 292 | 33 | 75 | 16 | 0 | 2 | 36 | 13 | 39 | 5 | 3 | R | R | 6-1 | 180 | 5-14-69 | 1990 | Kansas City, Mo. |
| Colvard, Benny, dh-of | .236 | 56 | 182 | 20 | 43 | 10 | 0 | 4 | 25 | 8 | 39 | 0 | 1 | R | R | 6-1 | 205 | 8-17-66 | 1988 | Hartshorne, Okla. |
| Dempsey, John, c | .250 | 1 | 4 | 0 | 1 | 0 | 0 | 0 | 0 | 1 | 2 | 0 | 0 | L | R | 6-1 | 200 | 8-18-71 | 1989 | Westlake, Calif. |
| Diaz, Carlos, c | .215 | 54 | 163 | 13 | 35 | 3 | 0 | 3 | 25 | 3 | 33 | 1 | 0 | R | R | 6-3 | 200 | 12-24-64 | 1986 | Palm Harbor, Fla. |
| Diaz, Kiki, ss | .282 | 21 | 78 | 12 | 22 | 2 | 0 | 0 | 5 | 13 | 7 | 1 | 1 | R | R | 6-1 | 175 | 2-8-64 | 1982 | San Juan, P.R. |
| Garber, Jeff, inf-of | .281 | 81 | 253 | 40 | 71 | 13 | 0 | 12 | 32 | 26 | 61 | 1 | 3 | R | R | 5-11 | 180 | 9-27-66 | 1988 | Valdosta, Ga. |
| Guerrero, Mike, ss | .265 | 24 | 68 | 7 | 18 | 6 | 0 | 0 | 4 | 4 | 7 | 0 | 2 | R | R | 5-11 | 155 | 1-8-68 | 1987 | Santo Domingo, D.R. |
| Halter, Shane, ss | .258 | 81 | 306 | 50 | 79 | 7 | 0 | 4 | 20 | 30 | 74 | 4 | 7 | R | R | 5-10 | 160 | 11-8-69 | 1991 | Papillion, Neb. |
| Jaster, Scott, of | .251 | 55 | 183 | 24 | 46 | 11 | 1 | 6 | 24 | 19 | 41 | 6 | 2 | R | R | 6-5 | 220 | 8-29-65 | 1985 | Midland, Mich. |
| Jennings, Lance, c | .205 | 98 | 327 | 27 | 67 | 11 | 0 | 4 | 33 | 21 | 83 | 0 | 1 | R | R | 6-0 | 195 | 10-3-71 | 1989 | Modesto, Calif. |
| Johnson, Mark, of-dh | .197 | 61 | 213 | 24 | 42 | 4 | 3 | 5 | 22 | 14 | 24 | 6 | 2 | L | R | 5-9 | 165 | 8-19-69 | 1991 | Gladstone, Mo. |
| Long, Kevin, of | .272 | 79 | 301 | 47 | 82 | 14 | 6 | 1 | 20 | 37 | 56 | 7 | 11 | L | L | 5-9 | 165 | 12-30-66 | 1989 | Phoenix, Ariz. |
| May, Lee, of | .205 | 14 | 39 | 3 | 8 | 0 | 0 | 3 | 0 | 16 | 2 | 0 | 3 | S | R | 6-1 | 177 | 5-30-68 | 1986 | Cincinnati, Ohio |
| Mota, Domingo, 2b | .214 | 56 | 196 | 22 | 42 | 7 | 3 | 1 | 16 | 11 | 48 | 10 | 9 | R | R | 5-8 | 180 | 8-4-69 | 1990 | La Crescenta, Calif. |
| Norman, Les, of | .291 | 133 | 484 | 78 | 141 | 32 | 5 | 17 | 81 | 50 | 88 | 11 | 9 | R | R | 6-0 | 185 | 2-25-69 | 1991 | Braidwood, Ill. |
| Randa, Joe, 3b | .295 | 131 | 505 | 74 | 149 | 31 | 5 | 11 | 72 | 39 | 64 | 8 | 7 | R | R | 5-10 | 190 | 12-18-69 | 1991 | Delafield, Wis. |
| Tucker, Michael, 2b | .279 | 72 | 244 | 38 | 68 | 7 | 4 | 9 | 35 | 42 | 51 | 12 | 5 | L | R | 6-2 | 185 | 6-25-71 | 1992 | Chase City, Va. |
| Vitiello, Joe, 1b | .288 | 117 | 413 | 62 | 119 | 25 | 2 | 15 | 66 | 57 | 95 | 2 | 0 | R | R | 6-3 | 215 | 4-11-70 | 1991 | Stoneham, Mass. |

| PITCHING | W | L | ERA | G | GS | CG | SV | IP | H | R | ER | BB | SO | B | T | HT | WT | DOB | 1st Yr | Resides |
|---|---|---|---|---|---|---|---|---|---|---|---|---|---|---|---|---|---|---|---|---|
| Ahern, Brian | 4 | 9 | 5.34 | 18 | 18 | 0 | 0 | 98 | 113 | 69 | 58 | 46 | 63 | R | R | 6-0 | 205 | 5-18-68 | 1989 | Glenwood, Ill. |
| Bevil, Brian | 3 | 3 | 4.36 | 6 | 6 | 0 | 0 | 33 | 36 | 17 | 16 | 14 | 26 | R | R | 6-3 | 190 | 9-5-71 | 1991 | Houston, Texas |

# ROYALS: ORGANIZATION LEADERS

**David Cone**
Lost 14 despite good numbers

### MAJOR LEAGUERS

**BATTING**

| | | |
|---|---|---|
| *AVG | Chris Gwynn | .300 |
| R | Wally Joyner | 83 |
| H | Brian McRae | 177 |
| TB | Brian McRae | 259 |
| 2B | Wally Joyner | 36 |
| 3B | Brian McRae | 9 |
| HR | Mike Macfarlane | 20 |
| RBI | George Brett | 75 |
| BB | Wally Joyner | 66 |
| SO | Brian McRae | 105 |
| SB | Felix Jose | 31 |

**PITCHING**

| | | |
|---|---|---|
| W | Kevin Appier | 18 |
| L | David Cone | 14 |
| #ERA | Jeff Montgomery | 2.27 |
| G | Jeff Montgomery | 69 |
| CG | David Cone | 6 |
| SV | Jeff Montgomery | 45 |
| IP | David Cone | 254 |
| BB | David Cone | 114 |
| SO | David Cone | 191 |

### MINOR LEAGUERS

**BATTING**

| | | |
|---|---|---|
| *AVG | Karl Rhodes, Omaha | .318 |
| R | Shane Halter, Memphis-Wilmington | 94 |
| H | Darren Burton, Wilmington | 152 |
| TB | Bob Hamelin, Omaha | 236 |
| 2B | Ramy Brooks, Rockford | 34 |
| 3B | Johnny Damon, Rockford | 13 |
| HR | Bob Hamelin, Omaha | 29 |
| RBI | Bob Hamelin, Omaha | 84 |
| BB | Larry Sutton, Rockford | 95 |
| SO | Shane Halter, Memphis-Wilmington | 129 |
| SB | Johnny Damon, Rockford | 59 |

**PITCHING**

| | | |
|---|---|---|
| W | Mike Fyhrie, Memphis-Wilmington | 14 |
| L | Alex Sanchez, Omaha-Memphis | 12 |
| #ERA | Kevin Hodges, GCL Royals-Wilm. | 1.90 |
| G | Chris Eddy, Wilmington | 55 |
| CG | Rodney Myers, Memphis-Rockford | 6 |
| SV | Jeff Smith, Wilmington | 24 |
| IP | John Gross, Wilmington | 175 |
| BB | Sherard, Clinkscales, Rockford | 83 |
| SO | Robert Toth, Wilmington | 129 |

*Minimum 250 At-Bats   #Minimum 75 Innings

# ROYALS: MOST COMMON LINEUPS

| | Kansas City<br>Majors | Omaha<br>AAA | Memphis<br>AA | Wilmington<br>A | Rockford<br>A |
|---|---|---|---|---|---|
| C | Mike Macfarlane (114) | Nelson Santovenia (77) | Lance Jennings (98) | Chad Strickland (110) | Ramy Brooks (100) |
| 1B | Wally Joyner (140) | Bob Hamelin (127) | Joe Vitiello (100) | Steve Hiinton (81) | Larry Sutton (107) |
| 2B | Jose Lind (136) | Terry Shumpert (108) | Michael Tucker (72) | Michael Tucker (61) | Steve Sisco (124) |
| 3B | Gary Gaetti (79) | Craig Wilson (60) | Joe Randa (125) | Jason Marshall (60) | Ryan Long (99) |
| SS | Greg Gagne (159) | Jose Mota (56) | Shane Halter (81) | Shane Halter (53) | Julio Montilla (79) |
| OF | Brian McRae (153) | Kevin Koslofski (109) | Les Norman (123) | Darren Burton (128) | Johnny Damon (127) |
| | Felix Jose (144) | Mike Kingery (103) | Butch Cole (79) | Raul Gonzalez (125) | Rod Myers (123) |
| | Kevin McReynolds (104) | Karl Rhodes (84) | Kevin Long (77) | Hugh Walker (105) | Steve Murphy (103) |
| DH | George Brett (140) | Dan Rohrmeier (74) | Benny Colvard (38) | Pat Dando (43) | Andre Newhouse (54) |
| SP | Appier/Cone (34) | Keith Brown (25) | Mike Fyhrie (22) | John Gross (28) | Mike Bovee (20) |
| RP | Jeff Montgomery (69) | Dera Clark (51) | Danny Miceli (40) | Chris Eddy (55) | Chris Connolly (34) |
| | Full-season farm clubs only | No. of games at position in parenthesis | | | |

| PITCHING | W | L | ERA | G | GS | CG | SV | IP | H | R | ER | BB | SO | B | T | HT | WT | DOB | 1st Yr | Resides |
|---|---|---|---|---|---|---|---|---|---|---|---|---|---|---|---|---|---|---|---|---|
| Bittiger, Jeff | 1 | 0 | 1.59 | 2 | 2 | 0 | 0 | 11 | 6 | 2 | 2 | 3 | 11 | R | R | 5-10 | 175 | 4-13-62 | 1980 | Colonia, N.J. |
| Campbell, Jim | 1 | 1 | 5.82 | 11 | 0 | 0 | 1 | 22 | 23 | 14 | 14 | 10 | 11 | L | L | 5-11 | 190 | 5-19-66 | 1987 | Oroville, Calif. |
| Chrisman, Jim | 0 | 0 | 4.66 | 8 | 0 | 0 | 0 | 19 | 20 | 11 | 10 | 5 | 15 | R | R | 6-1 | 195 | 11-14-70 | 1989 | Charleston, W.Va. |
| Fyhrie, Mike | 11 | 4 | 3.56 | 22 | 22 | 3 | 0 | 131 | 143 | 59 | 52 | 59 | 59 | R | R | 6-2 | 190 | 12-9-69 | 1991 | Westminster, Calif. |
| Givens, Brian | 1 | 3 | 4.58 | 14 | 4 | 0 | 2 | 35 | 37 | 22 | 18 | 11 | 29 | R | L | 6-6 | 220 | 11-6-65 | 1984 | Aurora, Colo. |
| Harris, Doug | 3 | 6 | 4.67 | 22 | 12 | 1 | 0 | 87 | 99 | 52 | 45 | 13 | 38 | R | R | 6-4 | 205 | 9-27-69 | 1990 | Carlisle, Pa. |
| Karchner, Matt | 3 | 2 | 4.20 | 6 | 5 | 0 | 0 | 30 | 34 | 16 | 14 | 4 | 14 | R | R | 6-4 | 245 | 6-28-67 | 1989 | Berwick, Pa. |
| Landress, Roger | 3 | 4 | 3.14 | 26 | 0 | 0 | 2 | 52 | 55 | 21 | 18 | 15 | 25 | R | R | 6-2 | 188 | 8-3-68 | 1991 | Lawrenceville, Ga. |
| Lieber, Jon | 2 | 1 | 6.86 | 4 | 4 | 0 | 0 | 21 | 32 | 16 | 16 | 6 | 17 | L | R | 6-3 | 205 | 4-2-70 | 1992 | Council Bluffs, Iowa |
| Limbach, Chris | 3 | 4 | 2.73 | 42 | 5 | 0 | 6 | 92 | 85 | 34 | 28 | 22 | 82 | L | L | 6-3 | 200 | 5-23-68 | 1986 | Indianapolis, Ind. |
| Mason, Mike | 1 | 0 | 0.00 | 1 | 0 | 0 | 0 | 2 | 0 | 0 | 0 | 1 | 0 | L | L | 6-2 | 195 | 11-21-58 | 1980 | Greenwood, Minn. |
| Miceli, Danny | 6 | 4 | 4.60 | 40 | 0 | 0 | 7 | 59 | 54 | 30 | 30 | 39 | 68 | R | R | 5-11 | 205 | 9-9-70 | 1990 | Orlando, Fla. |
| Morton, Kevin | 3 | 6 | 4.81 | 20 | 9 | 1 | 1 | 73 | 88 | 48 | 39 | 29 | 59 | R | L | 6-2 | 185 | 8-3-68 | 1989 | Norwalk, Conn. |
| Myers, Rodney | 3 | 6 | 5.62 | 12 | 12 | 1 | 0 | 66 | 73 | 46 | 41 | 32 | 42 | R | R | 6-1 | 190 | 6-26-69 | 1990 | Rockford, Ill. |
| Perez, Vladimir | 1 | 0 | 3.00 | 18 | 1 | 1 | 3 | 42 | 37 | 15 | 14 | 11 | 35 | R | R | 6-1 | 180 | 3-8-69 | 1986 | Nigua, D.R. |
| Peters, Doug | 1 | 2 | 5.87 | 6 | 6 | 0 | 0 | 23 | 32 | 16 | 15 | 10 | 14 | R | R | 6-1 | 200 | 2-14-68 | 1990 | New Castle, Pa. |
| Piatt, Doug | 0 | 1 | 8.78 | 11 | 0 | 0 | 0 | 13 | 19 | 13 | 13 | 6 | 8 | L | R | 6-1 | 190 | 9-26-65 | 1988 | Beaver, Pa. |
| Pierce, Ed | 6 | 5 | 3.74 | 37 | 2 | 0 | 1 | 67 | 65 | 35 | 28 | 34 | 53 | L | L | 6-1 | 190 | 10-6-68 | 1989 | San Dimas, Calif. |
| Richards, Dave | 0 | 1 | 3.68 | 7 | 3 | 0 | 1 | 22 | 12 | 9 | 9 | 12 | 24 | L | L | 6-3 | 215 | 9-18-67 | 1987 | San Diego, Calif. |
| Roesler, Mike | 2 | 1 | 2.38 | 3 | 3 | 2 | 0 | 23 | 11 | 7 | 6 | 4 | 16 | R | R | 6-5 | 210 | 9-12-63 | 1985 | Fort Wayne, Ind. |
| Sanchez, Alex | 1 | 4 | 4.37 | 15 | 10 | 0 | 0 | 70 | 64 | 36 | 34 | 35 | 47 | R | R | 6-2 | 200 | 4-8-66 | 1987 | Antioch, Calif. |
| Ventura, Jose | 2 | 5 | 3.94 | 20 | 12 | 0 | 0 | 82 | 88 | 40 | 36 | 45 | 61 | R | R | 6-2 | 195 | 6-14-69 | 1988 | La Romana, D.R. |
| Wagner, Hector | 2 | 4 | 4.50 | 10 | 4 | 0 | 0 | 36 | 38 | 19 | 18 | 4 | 19 | R | R | 6-3 | 200 | 11-26-68 | 1987 | Santo Domingo, D.R. |

# WILMINGTON                                                                 A

## CAROLINA LEAGUE

| BATTING | AVG | G | AB | R | H | 2B | 3B | HR | RBI | BB | SO | SB | CS | B | T | HT | WT | DOB | 1st Yr | Resides |
|---|---|---|---|---|---|---|---|---|---|---|---|---|---|---|---|---|---|---|---|---|
| Burton, Darren, of | .277 | 134 | 549 | 82 | 152 | 23 | 5 | 10 | 45 | 48 | 111 | 30 | 10 | S | R | 6-0 | 175 | 9-16-72 | 1990 | Somerset, Ky. |
| Caraballo, Gary, 3b | .303 | 39 | 145 | 20 | 44 | 8 | 3 | 2 | 26 | 20 | 25 | 3 | 0 | R | R | 5-11 | 205 | 7-11-71 | 1989 | Yauco, P.R. |
| Dando, Pat, dh-1b | .237 | 82 | 253 | 25 | 60 | 11 | 1 | 6 | 29 | 13 | 74 | 1 | 1 | L | L | 6-1 | 210 | 12-3-68 | 1990 | Pearland, Texas |
| Dempsey, John, c-3b | .176 | 18 | 34 | 3 | 6 | 2 | 0 | 0 | 4 | 2 | 5 | 0 | 0 | L | R | 6-1 | 200 | 8-8-71 | 1989 | Westlake, Calif. |
| Gonzalez, Raul, of | .269 | 127 | 461 | 59 | 124 | 30 | 3 | 11 | 55 | 54 | 58 | 13 | 5 | R | R | 5-8 | 175 | 12-27-73 | 1991 | Carolina, P.R. |
| Guerrero, Mike, ss | .273 | 44 | 150 | 24 | 41 | 4 | 1 | 0 | 7 | 32 | 20 | 4 | 12 | R | R | 5-11 | 155 | 1-8-68 | 1987 | Santo Domingo, D.R. |
| Halter, Shane, ss | .299 | 54 | 211 | 44 | 63 | 8 | 5 | 5 | 32 | 27 | 55 | 5 | 4 | R | R | 5-10 | 160 | 11-8-69 | 1991 | Papillion, Neb. |
| Hinton, Steve, 1b-of | .247 | 104 | 344 | 43 | 85 | 11 | 1 | 8 | 42 | 46 | 79 | 4 | 5 | L | L | 6-2 | 200 | 9-5-69 | 1991 | Elgin, Ill. |
| Marshall, Jason, 3b-ss | .240 | 92 | 279 | 34 | 67 | 13 | 2 | 1 | 27 | 18 | 49 | 0 | 2 | R | R | 6-0 | 175 | 6-27-70 | 1992 | Abilene, Texas |
| Martinez, Ramon, 2b | .253 | 24 | 75 | 8 | 19 | 4 | 0 | 0 | 6 | 11 | 9 | 1 | 4 | R | R | 5-11 | 170 | 10-10-72 | 1993 | Toa Alta, P.R. |
| Mendoza, Francisco, 3b | .236 | 42 | 123 | 12 | 29 | 9 | 1 | 1 | 15 | 12 | 31 | 0 | 1 | R | R | 6-0 | 180 | 10-4-72 | 1992 | Santo Domingo, D.R. |
| Mota, Domingo, 2b | .194 | 14 | 36 | 1 | 7 | 1 | 1 | 0 | 6 | 2 | 6 | 0 | 1 | R | R | 5-8 | 180 | 8-4-69 | 1990 | La Crescenta, Calif. |
| Smith, Tom, of-dh | .213 | 92 | 296 | 33 | 63 | 11 | 2 | 5 | 32 | 27 | 92 | 5 | 5 | S | R | 6-2 | 200 | 1-0-70 | 1990 | Avon Park, Fla. |
| Stewart, Andy, 1b-c | .277 | 110 | 361 | 54 | 100 | 20 | 3 | 8 | 42 | 26 | 88 | 7 | 1 | R | R | 5-11 | 205 | 12-5-70 | 1990 | Oshawa, Ontario |
| Stewart, Brady, 2b-ss | .217 | 87 | 258 | 22 | 56 | 6 | 0 | 0 | 21 | 14 | 61 | 7 | 8 | R | R | 5-11 | 180 | 5-4-69 | 1990 | Cincinnati, Ohio |
| Strickland, Chad, c | .249 | 122 | 409 | 51 | 102 | 16 | 6 | 2 | 46 | 23 | 46 | 4 | 3 | R | R | 6-1 | 185 | 3-16-72 | 1990 | Oklahoma City, Okla. |
| Tucker, Michael, 2b | .305 | 61 | 239 | 42 | 73 | 14 | 2 | 6 | 44 | 34 | 49 | 12 | 2 | L | R | 6-2 | 185 | 6-25-71 | 1992 | Chase City, Va. |
| Walker, Hugh, of | .258 | 126 | 450 | 66 | 116 | 20 | 3 | 21 | 71 | 35 | 106 | 14 | 14 | L | R | 5-11 | 210 | 2-9-70 | 1988 | Jacksonville, Ark. |

| PITCHING | W | L | ERA | G | GS | CG | SV | IP | H | R | ER | BB | SO | B | T | HT | WT | DOB | 1st Yr | Resides |
|---|---|---|---|---|---|---|---|---|---|---|---|---|---|---|---|---|---|---|---|---|
| Baez, Francisco | 2 | 5 | 5.05 | 28 | 0 | 0 | 1 | 36 | 38 | 22 | 20 | 12 | 29 | L | L | 5-11 | 190 | 12-17-69 | 1988 | San Cristobal, D.R. |
| Bevil, Brian | 7 | 1 | 2.30 | 12 | 12 | 2 | 0 | 74 | 46 | 21 | 19 | 23 | 61 | R | R | 6-3 | 190 | 9-5-71 | 1991 | Houston, Texas |
| Bladow, David | 3 | 2 | 4.83 | 30 | 0 | 0 | 1 | 50 | 45 | 29 | 27 | 24 | 33 | R | R | 6-2 | 205 | 10-14-69 | 1992 | Orange, Calif. |
| Bunch, Melvin | 5 | 3 | 2.33 | 10 | 10 | 1 | 0 | 66 | 52 | 22 | 17 | 14 | 54 | R | R | 6-1 | 165 | 11-4-71 | 1990 | Texarkana, Texas |
| Chrisman, Jim | 3 | 0 | 2.16 | 24 | 1 | 0 | 0 | 42 | 35 | 11 | 10 | 17 | 33 | R | R | 6-1 | 195 | 11-14-70 | 1989 | Charleston, W.Va. |
| Eddy, Chris | 2 | 2 | 2.83 | 55 | 0 | 0 | 14 | 54 | 39 | 23 | 17 | 37 | 67 | L | L | 6-3 | 200 | 11-27-69 | 1992 | Duncanville, Texas |
| Fyhrie, Mike | 3 | 2 | 3.68 | 5 | 5 | 0 | 0 | 29 | 32 | 15 | 12 | 18 | 19 | R | R | 6-2 | 190 | 12-9-69 | 1991 | Westminster, Calif. |
| Gross, John | 11 | 10 | 3.60 | 28 | 28 | 2 | 0 | 175 | 180 | 91 | 70 | 55 | 100 | R | R | 6-0 | 165 | 6-26-70 | 1989 | Clovis, Calif. |
| Harrison, Brian | 13 | 6 | 3.28 | 26 | 26 | 1 | 0 | 173 | 168 | 76 | 63 | 38 | 98 | R | R | 6-1 | 175 | 12-18-68 | 1992 | Bryan, Texas |
| Hodges, Kevin | 0 | 0 | 0.00 | 3 | 0 | 0 | 0 | 5 | 2 | 0 | 0 | 3 | 1 | R | R | 6-4 | 200 | 6-24-73 | 1991 | Spring, Texas |
| Huffman, Jason | 0 | 0 | 3.38 | 4 | 0 | 0 | 0 | 5 | 7 | 6 | 2 | 0 | 1 | L | R | 6-1 | 190 | 9-30-72 | 1993 | Raeford, N.C. |
| Landress, Roger | 2 | 2 | 3.86 | 20 | 0 | 0 | 2 | 28 | 23 | 16 | 12 | 11 | 18 | R | R | 6-2 | 188 | 8-3-68 | 1991 | Lawrenceville, Ga. |
| Lieber, Jon | 3 | 2 | 2.67 | 17 | 16 | 2 | 0 | 115 | 123 | 47 | 34 | 9 | 89 | L | R | 6-3 | 205 | 4-2-70 | 1992 | Council Bluffs, Iowa |
| Perez, Dario | 3 | 9 | 4.06 | 33 | 3 | 0 | 1 | 69 | 77 | 41 | 31 | 14 | 56 | R | R | 6-1 | 190 | 6-27-70 | 1988 | Nigua, D.R. |
| Rea, Shayne | 0 | 2 | 6.64 | 11 | 1 | 0 | 0 | 20 | 23 | 18 | 15 | 13 | 11 | R | R | 6-3 | 220 | 2-13-71 | 1990 | Waterford, Mich. |
| Smith, Dan | 3 | 4 | 3.94 | 51 | 0 | 0 | 24 | 64 | 66 | 35 | 28 | 24 | 60 | R | R | 6-0 | 195 | 5-30-70 | 1991 | Pasco, Wash. |
| Toth, Robert | 8 | 7 | 2.91 | 25 | 24 | 0 | 0 | 152 | 129 | 57 | 49 | 40 | 129 | R | R | 6-2 | 185 | 7-30-72 | 1991 | Cypress, Calif. |
| Wagner, Hector | 1 | 7 | 3.38 | 13 | 13 | 0 | 0 | 69 | 71 | 30 | 26 | 10 | 37 | R | R | 6-3 | 200 | 11-26-68 | 1987 | Santo Domingo, D.R. |

## MIDWEST LEAGUE

| BATTING | AVG | G | AB | R | H | 2B | 3B | HR | RBI | BB | SO | SB | CS | B | T | HT | WT | DOB | 1st Yr | Resides |
|---|---|---|---|---|---|---|---|---|---|---|---|---|---|---|---|---|---|---|---|---|
| Antoon, Jeff, dh-1b........ | .278 | 60 | 205 | 27 | 57 | 13 | 1 | 2 | 35 | 12 | 41 | 3 | 0 | R | R | 6-0 | 210 | 12-31-69 | 1992 | Sherman Oaks, Calif. |
| Brooks, Ramy, c............ | .255 | 120 | 415 | 74 | 106 | 34 | 2 | 15 | 65 | 60 | 91 | 14 | 5 | R | R | 6-2 | 180 | 4-12-70 | 1990 | Blanchard, Okla. |
| Damon, Johnny, of......... | .290 | 127 | 511 | 82 | 148 | 25 | 13 | 5 | 50 | 52 | 83 | 59 | 18 | L | L | 6-0 | 175 | 11-5-73 | 1992 | Orlando, Fla. |
| Delaney, Sean, c.......... | .178 | 20 | 45 | 7 | 8 | 0 | 0 | 0 | 2 | 2 | 15 | 1 | 0 | R | R | 5-11 | 190 | 5-22-70 | 1992 | Berwyn, Ill. |
| Good, Thomathan, of...... | .188 | 9 | 32 | 3 | 6 | 0 | 0 | 0 | 2 | 3 | 7 | 3 | 1 | L | L | 6-1 | 180 | 9-5-72 | 1991 | Clute, Texas |
| Hauswirth, Trenton, c..... | .171 | 37 | 105 | 6 | 18 | 3 | 0 | 0 | 14 | 15 | 42 | 0 | 0 | R | R | 6-2 | 250 | 10-20-72 | 1992 | Palm Springs, Calif. |
| Long, Ryan, 3b............. | .290 | 107 | 396 | 46 | 115 | 27 | 6 | 8 | 68 | 16 | 76 | 16 | 6 | R | R | 6-2 | 185 | 2-3-73 | 1991 | Houston, Texas |
| Montilla, Julio, ss......... | .273 | 84 | 289 | 34 | 79 | 13 | 3 | 2 | 27 | 17 | 38 | 6 | 10 | S | R | 5-10 | 170 | 6-9-73 | 1992 | Caracas, Venez. |
| Morillo, Cesar, ss-3b..... | .260 | 101 | 327 | 47 | 85 | 13 | 3 | 3 | 36 | 30 | 65 | 4 | 1 | S | R | 5-9 | 175 | 7-21-73 | 1990 | Caracas, Venez. |
| Murphy, Steve, of......... | .292 | 110 | 349 | 56 | 102 | 17 | 5 | 2 | 49 | 48 | 69 | 29 | 14 | L | R | 5-8 | 165 | 4-13-71 | 1992 | Germantown, Tenn. |
| Myers, Rod, of............. | .259 | 129 | 474 | 69 | 123 | 24 | 5 | 9 | 68 | 58 | 117 | 49 | 16 | L | L | 6-0 | 190 | 1-14-73 | 1991 | Conroe, Texas |
| Newhouse, Andre, dh-of | .240 | 94 | 271 | 42 | 65 | 18 | 0 | 2 | 28 | 26 | 68 | 24 | 8 | R | R | 6-0 | 190 | 6-30-72 | 1990 | Houston, Texas |
| Sisco, Steve, 2b .......... | .287 | 124 | 460 | 62 | 132 | 22 | 4 | 2 | 57 | 42 | 65 | 25 | 10 | R | R | 5-9 | 180 | 12-2-69 | 1992 | Thousand Oaks, Calif. |
| Sutton, Larry, 1b.......... | .269 | 113 | 361 | 67 | 97 | 24 | 1 | 7 | 50 | 95 | 65 | 3 | 5 | L | L | 5-11 | 175 | 5-14-70 | 1992 | Temecula, Calif. |
| Walls, Eric, of ............. | .219 | 15 | 32 | 8 | 7 | 1 | 0 | 0 | 1 | 4 | 9 | 3 | 2 | L | L | 6-0 | 155 | 9-13-72 | 1992 | Centralia, Ill. |

| PITCHING | W | L | ERA | G | GS | CG | SV | IP | H | R | ER | BB | SO | B | T | HT | WT | DOB | 1st Yr | Resides |
|---|---|---|---|---|---|---|---|---|---|---|---|---|---|---|---|---|---|---|---|---|
| Bovee, Mike ................. | 5 | 9 | 4.21 | 20 | 20 | 2 | 0 | 109 | 118 | 58 | 51 | 30 | 111 | R | R | 5-10 | 200 | 8-21-73 | 1991 | San Diego, Calif. |
| Bunch, Melvin ............... | 6 | 4 | 2.12 | 19 | 11 | 1 | 4 | 85 | 79 | 24 | 20 | 18 | 71 | R | R | 6-2 | 180 | 11-4-71 | 1992 | Texarkana, Texas |
| Burley, Rick ............... | 4 | 2 | 5.26 | 9 | 6 | 0 | 0 | 38 | 43 | 26 | 22 | 26 | 15 | S | L | 5-10 | 170 | 8-7-72 | 1991 | Corriganville, Md. |
| Clinkscales, Sherard....... | 5 | 3 | 6.75 | 20 | 13 | 0 | 0 | 61 | 57 | 58 | 46 | 83 | 46 | R | R | 6-2 | 210 | 4-15-70 | 1992 | Indianapolis, Ind. |
| Connolly, Chris ............. | 6 | 3 | 3.98 | 34 | 0 | 0 | 3 | 75 | 83 | 37 | 33 | 31 | 50 | L | L | 6-2 | 192 | 12-4-70 | 1991 | Lynchburg, Va. |
| Dickens, John .............. | 2 | 0 | 3.94 | 32 | 0 | 0 | 2 | 62 | 57 | 28 | 27 | 34 | 60 | L | L | 6-3 | 195 | 6-25-71 | 1992 | Fort Worth, Texas |
| Dorlarque, Aaron .......... | 2 | 3 | 1.46 | 28 | 0 | 0 | 16 | 49 | 37 | 12 | 8 | 12 | 51 | R | R | 6-3 | 180 | 2-16-70 | 1992 | Vancouver, Wash. |
| Downs, John ............... | 1 | 3 | 5.46 | 5 | 5 | 0 | 0 | 28 | 36 | 22 | 17 | 11 | 21 | R | R | 6-2 | 185 | 9-15-70 | 1991 | Englewood, Ohio |
| Evans, Bart ............... | 10 | 4 | 4.36 | 27 | 16 | 0 | 0 | 99 | 95 | 52 | 48 | 60 | 120 | R | R | 6-1 | 190 | 12-30-70 | 1992 | Mansfield, Mo. |
| Haas, Jeff.................... | 4 | 2 | 3.90 | 24 | 4 | 1 | 2 | 67 | 67 | 37 | 29 | 21 | 37 | L | L | 6-1 | 200 | 2-28-71 | 1992 | Springfield, Ind. |
| Myers, Rodney ............. | 7 | 3 | 1.79 | 12 | 12 | 5 | 0 | 85 | 65 | 22 | 17 | 18 | 65 | R | R | 6-1 | 190 | 6-26-69 | 1990 | Rockford, Ill. |
| Page, Duane ............... | 2 | 0 | 5.87 | 16 | 0 | 0 | 2 | 23 | 27 | 18 | 15 | 13 | 16 | R | R | 6-3 | 215 | 3-10-72 | 1993 | Westminister, Calif. |
| Peters, Doug................ | 2 | 2 | 3.11 | 11 | 7 | 0 | 0 | 46 | 46 | 25 | 16 | 13 | 34 | R | R | 6-1 | 200 | 2-14-68 | 1990 | New Castle, Pa. |
| Pittsley, Jim ................ | 5 | 5 | 4.26 | 15 | 15 | 2 | 0 | 80 | 76 | 43 | 38 | 32 | 87 | R | R | 6-7 | 215 | 4-3-74 | 1992 | Dubois, Pa. |
| Rawitzer, Kevin ............ | 3 | 0 | 1.50 | 5 | 5 | 0 | 0 | 30 | 23 | 7 | 5 | 11 | 34 | L | L | 5-10 | 185 | 2-28-71 | 1993 | Danville, Calif. |
| Rusch, Glendon ............ | 0 | 1 | 3.38 | 2 | 2 | 0 | 0 | 8 | 10 | 6 | 3 | 7 | 8 | L | L | 6-2 | 175 | 11-7-74 | 1993 | Seattle, Wash. |
| Sheehan, Chris............. | 9 | 5 | 2.83 | 31 | 12 | 2 | 6 | 118 | 97 | 40 | 37 | 22 | 101 | R | R | 6-4 | 205 | 1-5-69 | 1992 | Kirkland, Wash. |
| Weglarz, John................ | 5 | 5 | 2.87 | 23 | 4 | 0 | 3 | 63 | 47 | 22 | 20 | 23 | 72 | R | R | 6-1 | 180 | 11-12-70 | 1992 | Franklin Square, N.Y. |

## NORTHWEST LEAGUE

| BATTING | AVG | G | AB | R | H | 2B | 3B | HR | RBI | BB | SO | SB | CS | B | T | HT | WT | DOB | 1st Yr | Resides |
|---|---|---|---|---|---|---|---|---|---|---|---|---|---|---|---|---|---|---|---|---|
| Byington, Jimmie, of...... | .259 | 53 | 170 | 23 | 44 | 5 | 0 | 8 | 32 | 14 | 45 | 9 | 1 | R | R | 6-0 | 175 | 8-22-73 | 1993 | Tulsa, Okla. |
| Carr, Jeremy, 2b .......... | .228 | 42 | 136 | 33 | 31 | 2 | 5 | 0 | 12 | 20 | 18 | 30 | 3 | R | R | 5-10 | 170 | 3-30-71 | 1993 | Boise, Idaho |
| Cepeda, Malcolm, 1b-dh | .091 | 4 | 11 | 1 | 1 | 0 | 0 | 0 | 2 | 2 | 4 | 0 | 0 | R | R | 6-1 | 190 | 11-3-72 | 1993 | Suisun City, Calif. |
| Diaz, Lino, 3b-2b .......... | .251 | 53 | 183 | 19 | 46 | 7 | 1 | 1 | 23 | 13 | 25 | 6 | 2 | R | R | 5-11 | 182 | 7-22-70 | 1993 | Altoona, Pa. |
| Dunn, Bill, 2b .............. | .187 | 40 | 123 | 13 | 23 | 2 | 0 | 1 | 6 | 22 | 21 | 8 | 4 | R | R | 6-2 | 186 | 3-25-72 | 1993 | Ellicott City, Md. |
| Evans, Mike, of-dh ........ | .207 | 56 | 193 | 25 | 40 | 6 | 1 | 7 | 25 | 19 | 55 | 4 | 3 | L | R | 6-0 | 190 | 8-7-72 | 1993 | Houston, Texas |
| Fasano, Sal, c .............. | .267 | 49 | 176 | 25 | 47 | 11 | 1 | 10 | 36 | 19 | 49 | 4 | 3 | R | R | 6-2 | 220 | 8-10-71 | 1993 | Hanover Park, Ill. |
| Gerald, Dwayne, 3b-ss . | .206 | 55 | 170 | 16 | 35 | 1 | 2 | 2 | 13 | 9 | 57 | 10 | 2 | R | R | 6-3 | 189 | 12-27-72 | 1991 | St. Pauls, N.C. |
| Good, Thomathan, of...... | .244 | 44 | 123 | 22 | 30 | 4 | 1 | 0 | 13 | 15 | 26 | 19 | 5 | L | L | 6-1 | 180 | 9-5-72 | 1991 | Clute, Texas |
| Hickman, Braxton, 1b.... | .299 | 67 | 234 | 30 | 70 | 16 | 1 | 5 | 30 | 27 | 48 | 1 | 3 | L | L | 6-3 | 210 | 9-3-70 | 1993 | Houston, Texas |
| Jimenez, Oscar, of........ | .266 | 62 | 184 | 34 | 49 | 15 | 2 | 5 | 18 | 40 | 65 | 16 | 4 | R | R | 6-0 | 190 | 12-18-74 | 1991 | Panama City, Panama |
| Oglesby, Luke, of......... | .204 | 45 | 147 | 19 | 30 | 5 | 1 | 0 | 10 | 22 | 42 | 26 | 5 | L | R | 5-7 | 155 | 6-27-71 | 1993 | Fort Collins, Colo. |
| Rhone, O.J., of ............ | .272 | 48 | 125 | 12 | 34 | 9 | 0 | 0 | 8 | 4 | 29 | 7 | 3 | R | R | 6-3 | 180 | 7-2-71 | 1993 | McAlester, Okla. |
| Smith, Toby, p-dh.......... | .111 | 28 | 45 | 5 | 3 | 0 | 1 | 4 | 9 | 24 | 0 | 0 | | R | R | 6-2 | 196 | 11-16-71 | 1993 | Guthrie, Okla. |
| Subero, Carlos, ss........ | .243 | 68 | 251 | 23 | 61 | 5 | 0 | 1 | 21 | 18 | 50 | 6 | 3 | S | R | 6-0 | 155 | 6-15-72 | 1991 | Caracas, Venez. |
| Sweeney, Mike, c .......... | .240 | 53 | 175 | 32 | 42 | 10 | 2 | 6 | 29 | 30 | 41 | 1 | 0 | R | R | 6-2 | 200 | 7-22-73 | 1991 | Ontario, Calif. |
| Wojtkowski, Steve, 3b... | .238 | 6 | 21 | 1 | 5 | 1 | 0 | 0 | 2 | 0 | 4 | 1 | 1 | L | R | 6-2 | 185 | 4-10-73 | 1993 | Middletown, N.Y. |

## ROYALS TOP 10 PROSPECTS

How the Royals Top 10 prospects, as judged by Baseball America prior to the 1993 season, fared in 1993:

| Player, Pos. | Club (Class) | AVG | AB | H | HR | RBI | SB |
|---|---|---|---|---|---|---|---|
| 1. Johnny Damon, of | Rockford (A) | .290 | 511 | 148 | 5 | 50 | 59 |
| 3. Michael Tucker, 2b | Wilmington (A) | .305 | 239 | 73 | 6 | 44 | 12 |
| | Memphis (AA) | .279 | 244 | 68 | 9 | 35 | 12 |
| 4. Joe Vitiello, 1b-of | Memphis (AA) | .288 | 413 | 119 | 15 | 66 | 2 |
| 5. Phil Hiatt, 3b | Omaha (AAA) | .235 | 51 | 12 | 3 | 10 | 0 |
| | Kansas City | .218 | 238 | 52 | 7 | 36 | 6 |
| 7. Darren Burton, of | Wilmington (A) | .277 | 549 | 152 | 10 | 45 | 30 |
| 8. Joe Randa, 3b | Memphis (AA) | .295 | 505 | 149 | 11 | 72 | 8 |

| | | W | L | ERA | IP | H | BB | SO |
|---|---|---|---|---|---|---|---|---|
| 2. Jim Pittsley, rhp | Rockford (A) | 5 | 5 | 4.26 | 80 | 76 | 32 | 87 |
| 6. Brian Bevil, rhp | Wilmington (A) | 4 | 1 | 2.30 | 74 | 46 | 23 | 61 |
| | Memphis (AA) | 3 | 3 | 4.36 | 33 | 36 | 14 | 26 |
| 9. Danny Miceli, rhp* | Memphis (AA) | 6 | 4 | 4.60 | 59 | 54 | 39 | 68 |
| | Carolina (AA) | 2 | 2 | 5.11 | 12 | 11 | 4 | 19 |
| | Pittsburgh | 0 | 0 | 5.06 | 5 | 6 | 3 | 4 |
| 10. Chris Eddy, lhp | Wilmington (A) | 2 | 2 | 3.00 | 54 | 39 | 37 | 67 |

*Traded to Pittsburgh Pirates

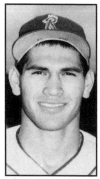

**Johnny Damon**
.290 at Class A

| PITCHING | W | L | ERA | G | GS | CG | SV | IP | H | R | ER | BB | SO | B | T | HT | WT | DOB | 1st Yr | Resides |
|---|---|---|---|---|---|---|---|---|---|---|---|---|---|---|---|---|---|---|---|---|
| Aminoff, Matt | 0 | 1 | 3.60 | 17 | 0 | 0 | 2 | 40 | 41 | 19 | 16 | 17 | 42 | R | R | 6-1 | 185 | 12-29-71 | 1993 | Santa Monica, Calif. |
| Atkinson, Neil | 2 | 3 | 4.34 | 23 | 4 | 0 | 3 | 48 | 50 | 28 | 23 | 26 | 43 | L | L | 6-0 | 190 | 1-14-71 | 1993 | San Antonio, Texas |
| Bacon, Rick | 2 | 3 | 7.28 | 16 | 0 | 0 | 0 | 30 | 33 | 27 | 24 | 26 | 29 | R | R | 6-2 | 185 | 11-8-70 | 1992 | Mt. Shasta, Calif. |
| Brassington, Phil | 1 | 3 | 2.42 | 11 | 8 | 0 | 1 | 48 | 35 | 14 | 13 | 19 | 32 | R | R | 6-2 | 180 | 4-19-70 | 1993 | Wanniassa, Australia |
| Brewer, Nevin | 3 | 0 | 0.97 | 10 | 8 | 0 | 0 | 37 | 26 | 7 | 4 | 17 | 31 | R | R | 6-4 | 195 | 8-1-71 | 1993 | Wilmington, N.C. |
| Burley, Rick | 3 | 3 | 3.00 | 22 | 2 | 0 | 2 | 45 | 30 | 18 | 15 | 24 | 42 | S | L | 5-10 | 170 | 8-7-72 | 1991 | Corriganville, Md. |
| Flury, Pat | 2 | 2 | 3.27 | 27 | 0 | 0 | 7 | 33 | 25 | 15 | 12 | 22 | 34 | R | R | 6-2 | 205 | 3-14-73 | 1993 | Sparks, Nev. |
| Granger, Jeff | 3 | 3 | 3.00 | 8 | 7 | 0 | 0 | 36 | 28 | 17 | 12 | 10 | 56 | R | L | 6-4 | 200 | 12-16-71 | 1993 | Orange, Texas |
| Grundy, Phil | 3 | 5 | 3.26 | 15 | 13 | 0 | 0 | 69 | 68 | 31 | 25 | 37 | 61 | R | R | 6-2 | 195 | 9-8-72 | 1993 | Somerset, Ky. |
| Hogue, Jay | 3 | 2 | 5.83 | 21 | 0 | 0 | 1 | 29 | 35 | 22 | 19 | 10 | 27 | L | L | 6-3 | 220 | 8-24-72 | 1993 | Montgomery, Texas |
| Kosman, Cody | 3 | 2 | 3.00 | 16 | 0 | 0 | 2 | 30 | 27 | 11 | 10 | 22 | 29 | R | R | 6-0 | 180 | 9-13-71 | 1993 | Idaho Falls, Idaho |
| Lopez, Andres | 2 | 0 | 2.41 | 9 | 0 | 0 | 0 | 19 | 15 | 6 | 5 | 8 | 15 | L | L | 6-0 | 150 | 11-10-72 | 1992 | Santo Domingo, D.R. |
| Ralston, Kris | 7 | 3 | 2.74 | 15 | 15 | 1 | 0 | 82 | 52 | 29 | 25 | 36 | 75 | R | R | 6-2 | 205 | 8-8-71 | 1993 | Carthage, Mo. |
| Rawitzer, Kevin | 1 | 0 | 0.50 | 6 | 4 | 0 | 0 | 18 | 13 | 1 | 1 | 5 | 20 | R | L | 5-10 | 185 | 2-28-71 | 1993 | Danville, Calif. |
| Santos, Juan | 0 | 2 | 11.66 | 9 | 0 | 0 | 0 | 15 | 18 | 20 | 19 | 14 | 12 | L | L | 5-11 | 155 | 9-3-71 | 1990 | La Vega, D.R. |
| Smith, Toby | 1 | 1 | 2.35 | 14 | 0 | 0 | 4 | 23 | 14 | 8 | 6 | 7 | 31 | R | R | 6-2 | 196 | 11-16-71 | 1993 | Guthrie, Okla. |
| Towns, Ryan | 4 | 3 | 3.46 | 15 | 15 | 0 | 0 | 68 | 59 | 33 | 26 | 36 | 43 | R | R | 6-2 | 210 | 6-26-72 | 1991 | Gonzales, Texas |

# FORT MYERS      R
## GULF COAST LEAGUE

| BATTING | AVG | G | AB | R | H | 2B | 3B | HR | RBI | BB | SO | SB | CS | B | T | HT | WT | DOB | 1st Yr | Resides |
|---|---|---|---|---|---|---|---|---|---|---|---|---|---|---|---|---|---|---|---|---|
| Brandon, Jelani, of | .238 | 53 | 151 | 18 | 36 | 5 | 5 | 1 | 18 | 23 | 36 | 4 | 2 | R | R | 6-0 | 190 | 3-21-74 | 1992 | Erlanger, Ky. |
| Burgos, Carlos, c | .333 | 3 | 3 | 0 | 1 | 0 | 0 | 0 | 2 | 0 | 0 | 0 | 0 | R | R | 6-2 | 225 | 6-13-72 | 1991 | Luquillo, P.R. |
| Cepeda, Malcolm, 1b | .265 | 48 | 155 | 15 | 41 | 4 | 2 | 2 | 20 | 11 | 37 | 4 | 1 | R | R | 6-1 | 190 | 11-3-72 | 1993 | Suisun City, Calif. |
| Dondero, Daron, ss-3b | .127 | 35 | 71 | 4 | 9 | 2 | 1 | 0 | 7 | 11 | 34 | 0 | 0 | R | R | 6-4 | 178 | 8-3-73 | 1993 | San Jacinto, Calif. |
| Frazier, Tyrone, of | .200 | 39 | 90 | 11 | 18 | 1 | 0 | 0 | 4 | 13 | 27 | 7 | 2 | R | R | 5-11 | 178 | 10-26-74 | 1993 | Shreveport, La. |
| Kern, Mike, of | .169 | 39 | 89 | 7 | 15 | 4 | 1 | 1 | 6 | 5 | 24 | 1 | 3 | R | R | 6-3 | 200 | 1-17-74 | 1992 | Hawthorne, Calif. |
| Lopez, Miguel, 3b | .200 | 47 | 145 | 15 | 29 | 5 | 0 | 0 | 12 | 10 | 23 | 0 | 2 | R | R | 5-10 | 165 | 1-15-72 | 1992 | Cartagena, Colombia |
| Martinez, Felix, ss-2b | .255 | 57 | 165 | 23 | 42 | 5 | 1 | 0 | 12 | 17 | 26 | 22 | 5 | R | R | 6-0 | 168 | 5-18-74 | 1993 | Nagua, D.R. |
| Martinez, Ramon, 2b | .237 | 37 | 97 | 16 | 23 | 5 | 0 | 0 | 9 | 8 | 6 | 3 | 0 | R | R | 6-1 | 170 | 10-10-72 | 1993 | Toa Alta, P.R. |
| McCoy, Justin, ss | .148 | 39 | 81 | 3 | 12 | 2 | 1 | 0 | 7 | 3 | 22 | 0 | 1 | R | R | 5-11 | 170 | 8-16-74 | 1993 | South Jordan, Utah |
| Mendez, Carlos, c | .313 | 50 | 163 | 18 | 51 | 10 | 0 | 4 | 27 | 4 | 15 | 6 | 1 | R | R | 6-1 | 195 | 8-18-74 | 1991 | Caracas, Venez. |
| Mendoza, Francisco, 3b | .545 | 11 | 44 | 12 | 24 | 7 | 1 | 1 | 11 | 3 | 7 | 0 | 0 | R | R | 6-0 | 190 | 10-4-72 | 1992 | Santo Domingo, D.R. |
| Payano, Adolfo, of | .325 | 40 | 114 | 23 | 37 | 7 | 1 | 0 | 8 | 8 | 16 | 15 | 5 | R | R | 5-11 | 170 | 4-10-73 | 1992 | Santo Domingo, D.R. |
| Prieto, Alejandro, ss-2b | .246 | 43 | 114 | 14 | 28 | 3 | 0 | 0 | 6 | 9 | 13 | 4 | 2 | R | R | 5-11 | 150 | 6-19-76 | 1993 | Caracas, Venez. |
| Smith, Larry, of | .169 | 31 | 71 | 7 | 12 | 2 | 0 | 0 | 4 | 5 | 23 | 3 | 0 | R | R | 6-0 | 195 | 8-18-74 | 1993 | Broomfield, Colo. |
| Vindivich, Paul, dh-1b | .291 | 52 | 175 | 24 | 51 | 9 | 4 | 3 | 26 | 4 | 33 | 1 | 1 | R | R | 6-2 | 215 | 12-13-73 | 1992 | Tacoma, Wash. |
| Walls, Eric, of | .282 | 24 | 71 | 10 | 20 | 2 | 5 | 0 | 9 | 5 | 12 | 5 | 4 | L | L | 6-0 | 155 | 9-13-72 | 1992 | Centralia, Ill. |
| Weathersby, Len, of | .158 | 33 | 76 | 6 | 12 | 1 | 0 | 0 | 7 | 3 | 26 | 0 | 1 | R | R | 6-0 | 180 | 5-13-75 | 1993 | Los Angeles, Calif. |
| Wojtkowski, Steve, 3b | .143 | 26 | 70 | 9 | 10 | 3 | 0 | 0 | 1 | 13 | 12 | 3 | 1 | L | R | 6-2 | 185 | 4-10-73 | 1993 | Middletown, N.Y. |

| PITCHING | W | L | ERA | G | GS | CG | SV | IP | H | R | ER | BB | SO | B | T | HT | WT | DOB | 1st Yr | Resides |
|---|---|---|---|---|---|---|---|---|---|---|---|---|---|---|---|---|---|---|---|---|
| Acevedo, Milton | 4 | 6 | 2.90 | 15 | 0 | 0 | 0 | 40 | 34 | 20 | 13 | 16 | 22 | L | L | 5-8 | 155 | 8-29-73 | 1991 | Villa Altagracia, D.R. |
| Anderson, Eric | 1 | 4 | 4.03 | 12 | 7 | 1 | 0 | 45 | 47 | 34 | 20 | 19 | 18 | R | R | 6-0 | 185 | 10-20-74 | 1993 | Blue Springs, Mo. |
| Bennett, Matt | 0 | 2 | 4.76 | 11 | 3 | 0 | 1 | 34 | 35 | 29 | 18 | 27 | 25 | S | R | 6-3 | 215 | 9-13-73 | 1991 | Modesto, Calif. |
| Brixey, Dustin | 2 | 1 | 4.65 | 14 | 1 | 0 | 2 | 31 | 30 | 22 | 16 | 17 | 11 | R | R | 6-2 | 190 | 10-16-73 | 1993 | Jay, Okla. |
| Campusano, Anibal | 1 | 0 | 4.67 | 15 | 0 | 0 | 2 | 27 | 35 | 21 | 14 | 13 | 10 | R | R | 6-2 | 160 | 4-15-73 | 1990 | San Cristobal, D.R. |
| Downs, John | 0 | 0 | 1.50 | 3 | 3 | 0 | 0 | 12 | 12 | 3 | 2 | 2 | 11 | R | R | 6-2 | 185 | 9-15-70 | 1991 | Englewood. Ohio |
| Fitzpatrick, Kenny | 4 | 3 | 2.57 | 12 | 10 | 1 | 1 | 58 | 58 | 25 | 16 | 20 | 35 | R | R | 6-6 | 230 | 8-25-74 | 1992 | Bell Gardens, Calif. |
| Givens, Brian | 0 | 1 | 3.38 | 4 | 4 | 0 | 0 | 8 | 7 | 3 | 3 | 1 | 11 | R | L | 6-6 | 220 | 11-6-65 | 1984 | Aurora, Colo. |
| Hodges, Kevin | 7 | 2 | 2.03 | 12 | 10 | 0 | 0 | 71 | 52 | 25 | 16 | 25 | 40 | R | R | 6-4 | 200 | 6-24-73 | 1991 | Spring, Texas |
| Huffman, Jason | 2 | 0 | 0.79 | 13 | 0 | 0 | 5 | 23 | 14 | 8 | 2 | 13 | 21 | R | R | 6-1 | 195 | 9-30-72 | 1993 | Raeford, N.C. |
| Lopez, Andres | 2 | 1 | 1.76 | 7 | 0 | 0 | 2 | 15 | 9 | 4 | 3 | 2 | 18 | L | L | 6-0 | 150 | 11-10-72 | 1992 | Santo Domingo, D.R. |
| Page, Duane | 0 | 0 | 0.00 | 2 | 0 | 0 | 0 | 4 | 2 | 0 | 0 | 3 | 2 | R | R | 6-3 | 215 | 3-10-72 | 1993 | Westminster, Calif. |
| Ray, Ken | 2 | 3 | 2.28 | 13 | 7 | 0 | 0 | 47 | 44 | 21 | 12 | 17 | 45 | R | R | 6-2 | 160 | 11-27-74 | 1993 | Roswell, Ga. |
| Rea, Shayne | 0 | 0 | 0.00 | 6 | 0 | 0 | 3 | 11 | 5 | 2 | 0 | 0 | 10 | R | R | 6-3 | 220 | 2-13-71 | 1990 | Waterford, Mich. |
| Rusch, Glendon | 4 | 2 | 1.60 | 11 | 10 | 0 | 0 | 62 | 43 | 14 | 11 | 11 | 48 | L | L | 6-2 | 175 | 11-7-74 | 1993 | Seattle, Wash. |
| Smith, Jarred | 0 | 5 | 3.22 | 12 | 1 | 0 | 0 | 22 | 19 | 13 | 8 | 16 | 16 | L | R | 6-0 | 200 | 7-28-71 | 1992 | Winter Haven, Fla. |

# LOS ANGELES
# DODGERS

**Manager:** Tommy Lasorda.    **1993 Record:** 81-81, .500 (4th, NL West).

| BATTING | AVG | G | AB | R | H | 2B | 3B | HR | RBI | BB | SO | SB | CS | B | T | HT | WT | DOB | 1st Yr | Resides |
|---|---|---|---|---|---|---|---|---|---|---|---|---|---|---|---|---|---|---|---|---|
| Ashley, Billy | .243 | 14 | 37 | 0 | 9 | 0 | 0 | 0 | 0 | 2 | 11 | 0 | 0 | R | R | 6-7 | 220 | 7-11-70 | 1988 | Belleville, Mich. |
| Bournigal, Rafael | .500 | 8 | 18 | 0 | 9 | 1 | 0 | 0 | 3 | 0 | 2 | 0 | 0 | R | R | 5-11 | 160 | 5-12-66 | 1987 | Santo Domingo, D.R. |
| Brooks, Jerry | .222 | 9 | 9 | 2 | 2 | 1 | 0 | 1 | 1 | 0 | 2 | 0 | 0 | R | R | 6-0 | 195 | 3-23-67 | 1988 | Syracuse, N.Y. |
| Butler, Brett | .298 | 156 | 607 | 80 | 181 | 21 | 10 | 1 | 42 | 86 | 69 | 39 | 19 | L | L | 5-10 | 160 | 6-15-57 | 1979 | Atlanta, Ga. |
| Davis, Eric | .234 | 108 | 376 | 57 | 88 | 17 | 0 | 14 | 53 | 41 | 88 | 33 | 5 | R | R | 6-3 | 185 | 5-29-62 | 1980 | Cincinnati, Ohio |
| Goodwin, Tom | .294 | 30 | 17 | 6 | 5 | 1 | 0 | 0 | 1 | 1 | 4 | 1 | 2 | L | R | 6-1 | 165 | 7-27-68 | 1989 | Fresno, Calif. |
| Hansen, Dave | .362 | 84 | 105 | 13 | 38 | 3 | 0 | 4 | 30 | 21 | 13 | 0 | 1 | L | R | 6-0 | 180 | 11-24-68 | 1986 | Long Beach, Calif. |
| Harris, Lenny | .238 | 107 | 160 | 20 | 38 | 6 | 1 | 2 | 11 | 15 | 15 | 3 | 1 | L | R | 5-10 | 205 | 10-28-64 | 1983 | Miami, Fla. |
| Hernandez, Carlos | .253 | 50 | 99 | 6 | 25 | 5 | 0 | 2 | 7 | 2 | 11 | 0 | 0 | R | R | 5-11 | 185 | 5-24-67 | 1985 | Bolivar, Venez. |
| Karros, Eric | .247 | 158 | 619 | 74 | 153 | 27 | 2 | 23 | 80 | 34 | 82 | 0 | 1 | R | R | 6-4 | 205 | 11-4-67 | 1988 | San Diego, Calif. |
| Mondesi, Raul | .291 | 42 | 86 | 13 | 25 | 3 | 1 | 4 | 10 | 4 | 16 | 4 | 1 | R | R | 5-11 | 150 | 3-12-71 | 1988 | San Cristobal, D.R. |
| Offerman, Jose | .269 | 158 | 590 | 77 | 159 | 21 | 6 | 1 | 62 | 71 | 75 | 30 | 13 | S | R | 6-0 | 160 | 11-8-68 | 1988 | San Pedro de Macoris, D.R. |
| Piazza, Mike | .318 | 149 | 547 | 81 | 174 | 24 | 2 | 35 | 112 | 46 | 86 | 3 | 4 | R | R | 6-3 | 200 | 9-4-68 | 1989 | Valley Forge, Pa. |
| Reed, Jody, | .276 | 132 | 445 | 48 | 123 | 21 | 2 | 2 | 31 | 38 | 40 | 1 | 3 | R | R | 5-9 | 160 | 7-26-62 | 1984 | Tampa, Fla. |
| Rodriguez, Henry | .222 | 76 | 176 | 20 | 39 | 10 | 0 | 8 | 23 | 11 | 39 | 1 | 0 | L | L | 6-1 | 180 | 11-8-67 | 1986 | New York, N.Y. |
| Sharperson, Mike | .256 | 73 | 90 | 13 | 23 | 4 | 0 | 2 | 10 | 5 | 17 | 2 | 0 | R | R | 6-3 | 190 | 10-4-61 | 1982 | Stone Mountain, Ga. |
| Snyder, Cory | .266 | 143 | 516 | 61 | 137 | 33 | 1 | 11 | 56 | 47 | 147 | 4 | 1 | R | R | 6-3 | 175 | 11-11-62 | 1985 | Laguna Hills, Calif. |
| Strawberry, Darryl | .140 | 32 | 100 | 12 | 14 | 2 | 0 | 5 | 12 | 16 | 19 | 1 | 0 | L | L | 6-6 | 200 | 3-12-62 | 1980 | Los Angeles, Calif. |
| Wallach, Tim | .222 | 133 | 477 | 42 | 106 | 19 | 1 | 12 | 62 | 32 | 70 | 0 | 2 | R | R | 6-3 | 200 | 9-14-57 | 1979 | Tustin, Calif. |
| Webster, Mitch | .244 | 88 | 172 | 26 | 42 | 6 | 2 | 2 | 14 | 11 | 24 | 4 | 6 | S | L | 6-1 | 185 | 5-16-59 | 1977 | Great Bend, Kan. |

| PITCHING | W | L | ERA | G | GS | CG | SV | IP | H | R | ER | BB | SO | B | T | HT | WT | DOB | 1st Yr | Resides |
|---|---|---|---|---|---|---|---|---|---|---|---|---|---|---|---|---|---|---|---|---|
| Astacio, Pedro | 14 | 9 | 3.57 | 31 | 31 | 3 | 0 | 186 | 165 | 80 | 74 | 68 | 122 | R | R | 6-2 | 174 | 11-28-69 | 1988 | Hato Mayor, D.R. |
| Candiotti, Tom | 8 | 10 | 3.12 | 33 | 32 | 2 | 0 | 214 | 192 | 86 | 74 | 71 | 155 | R | R | 6-2 | 200 | 8-31-57 | 1979 | Danville, Calif. |
| Daal, Omar | 2 | 3 | 5.09 | 47 | 0 | 0 | 0 | 35 | 36 | 20 | 20 | 21 | 19 | L | L | 6-3 | 160 | 3-1-72 | 1990 | Valencia, Venez. |
| DeSilva, John | 0 | 0 | 6.75 | 3 | 0 | 0 | 0 | 5 | 6 | 4 | 4 | 1 | 6 | R | R | 6-0 | 193 | 9-30-67 | 1989 | Fort Bragg, Calif. |
| Gott, Jim | 4 | 8 | 2.32 | 62 | 0 | 0 | 25 | 78 | 71 | 23 | 20 | 17 | 67 | R | R | 6-4 | 220 | 8-3-59 | 1977 | Pasadena, Calif. |
| Gross, Kevin | 13 | 13 | 4.14 | 33 | 32 | 3 | 0 | 202 | 224 | 110 | 93 | 74 | 150 | R | R | 6-5 | 215 | 6-8-61 | 1981 | Chino, Calif. |
| Gross, Kip | 0 | 0 | 0.60 | 10 | 0 | 0 | 0 | 15 | 13 | 1 | 1 | 4 | 12 | R | R | 6-2 | 190 | 8-24-64 | 1987 | Gering, Neb. |
| Hershiser, Orel | 12 | 14 | 3.59 | 33 | 33 | 5 | 0 | 216 | 201 | 106 | 86 | 72 | 141 | R | R | 6-3 | 193 | 9-16-58 | 1979 | Pasadena, Calif. |
| Martinez, Pedro | 10 | 5 | 2.61 | 65 | 2 | 0 | 2 | 107 | 76 | 34 | 31 | 57 | 119 | R | R | 5-11 | 150 | 10-25-71 | 1988 | Santo Domingo, D.R. |
| Martinez, Ramon | 10 | 12 | 3.44 | 32 | 32 | 4 | 0 | 212 | 202 | 88 | 81 | 104 | 127 | R | R | 6-4 | 173 | 3-22-68 | 1985 | Santo Domingo, D.R. |
| McDowell, Roger | 5 | 3 | 2.25 | 54 | 0 | 0 | 2 | 68 | 76 | 32 | 17 | 30 | 27 | R | R | 6-1 | 175 | 12-21-60 | 1982 | Jackson, Miss. |
| Nichols, Rod | 0 | 1 | 5.68 | 4 | 0 | 0 | 0 | 6 | 9 | 5 | 4 | 2 | 3 | R | R | 6-2 | 190 | 12-29-64 | 1985 | Columbus, Ga. |
| Trlicek, Ricky | 1 | 2 | 4.08 | 41 | 0 | 0 | 1 | 64 | 59 | 32 | 29 | 21 | 41 | R | R | 6-3 | 200 | 4-26-69 | 1987 | Houston, Texas |
| Wilson, Steve | 1 | 0 | 4.56 | 25 | 0 | 0 | 1 | 26 | 30 | 13 | 13 | 14 | 23 | L | L | 6-3 | 190 | 12-13-64 | 1985 | Tempe, Ariz. |
| Worrell, Todd | 1 | 1 | 6.05 | 35 | 0 | 0 | 5 | 39 | 46 | 28 | 26 | 11 | 31 | R | R | 6-5 | 200 | 9-28-59 | 1982 | Temple City, Calif. |

## FIELDING

| Catcher | PCT | G | PO | A | E | DP |
|---|---|---|---|---|---|---|
| Hernandez | .966 | 43 | 181 | 15 | 7 | 0 |
| Piazza | .989 | 146 | 899 | 98 | 11 | 10 |

| First Base | PCT | G | PO | A | E | DP |
|---|---|---|---|---|---|---|
| Karros | .992 | 157 | 1335 | 147 | 12 | 118 |
| Piazza | 1.000 | 1 | 2 | 0 | 0 | 1 |
| Rodriguez | 1.000 | 13 | 70 | 6 | 0 | 2 |
| Sharperson | .000 | 1 | 0 | 0 | 0 | 0 |
| Snyder | 1.000 | 12 | 22 | 3 | 0 | 1 |
| Wallach | 1.000 | 1 | 9 | 1 | 0 | 1 |

| Second Base | PCT | G | PO | A | E | DP |
|---|---|---|---|---|---|---|
| Bournigal | 1.000 | 4 | 0 | 1 | 0 | 0 |
| Harris | .987 | 35 | 56 | 92 | 2 | 11 |
| Reed | .993 | 132 | 280 | 413 | 5 | 76 |

| | PCT | G | PO | A | E | DP |
|---|---|---|---|---|---|---|
| Sharperson | .945 | 17 | 24 | 28 | 3 | 8 |

| Third Base | PCT | G | PO | A | E | DP |
|---|---|---|---|---|---|---|
| Hansen | .927 | 18 | 11 | 27 | 3 | 1 |
| Harris | .889 | 17 | 2 | 6 | 1 | 0 |
| Sharperson | .833 | 6 | 3 | 2 | 1 | 0 |
| Snyder | .884 | 23 | 12 | 26 | 5 | 3 |
| Wallach | .958 | 130 | 112 | 228 | 15 | 14 |

| Shortstop | PCT | G | PO | A | E | DP |
|---|---|---|---|---|---|---|
| Bournigal | 1.000 | 4 | 5 | 13 | 0 | 3 |
| Harris | 1.000 | 3 | 2 | 1 | 0 | 0 |
| Offerman | .950 | 158 | 250 | 454 | 37 | 95 |
| Sharperson | .909 | 3 | 2 | 8 | 1 | 1 |
| Snyder | 1.000 | 2 | 4 | 3 | 0 | 3 |

| Outfield | PCT | G | PO | A | E | DP |
|---|---|---|---|---|---|---|
| Ashley | 1.000 | 11 | 11 | 3 | 0 | 0 |
| Brooks | .000 | 2 | 0 | 0 | 0 | 0 |
| Butler | 1.000 | 155 | 369 | 6 | 0 | 0 |
| Davis | .991 | 103 | 221 | 7 | 2 | 2 |
| Goodwin | 1.000 | 12 | 8 | 0 | 0 | 0 |
| Harris | 1.000 | 2 | 1 | 0 | 0 | 0 |
| Mondesi | .951 | 40 | 55 | 3 | 3 | 1 |
| Rodriguez | .984 | 48 | 57 | 3 | 1 | 0 |
| Sharperson | .000 | 1 | 0 | 0 | 0 | 0 |
| Snyder | .979 | 115 | 172 | 14 | 4 | 1 |
| Strawberry | .905 | 29 | 37 | 1 | 4 | 0 |
| Webster | .950 | 56 | 75 | 1 | 4 | 0 |

# DODGERS FARM SYSTEM

| Class | Club | League | W | L | Pct. | Finish* | Manager | First Year |
|---|---|---|---|---|---|---|---|---|
| AAA | Albuquerque (N.M.) Dukes | Pacific Coast | 71 | 72 | .497 | 5th (10) | Bill Russell | 1972 |
| AA | San Antonio (Texas) Missions | Texas | 58 | 75 | .436 | 8th (8) | Glenn Hoffman | 1977 |
| A# | Bakersfield (Calif.) Dodgers | California | 42 | 94 | .309 | 10th (10) | Rick Dempsey | 1984 |
| A# | Vero Beach (Fla.) Dodgers | Florida State | 56 | 77 | .421 | 11th (13) | Joe Vavra | 1980 |
| A | Yakima (Wash.) Bears | Northwest | 30 | 46 | .395 | 8th (8) | John Shoemaker | 1988 |
| Rookie# | Great Falls (Mont.) Dodgers | Pioneer | 37 | 35 | .514 | 4th (8) | Jon Debus | 1984 |

*Finish in overall standings (No. of teams in league)   #Advanced level

## PACIFIC COAST LEAGUE

| BATTING | AVG | G | AB | R | H | 2B | 3B | HR | RBI | BB | SO | SB | CS | B | T | HT | WT | DOB | 1st Yr | Resides |
|---|---|---|---|---|---|---|---|---|---|---|---|---|---|---|---|---|---|---|---|---|
| Ashley, Billy | .297 | 125 | 482 | 88 | 143 | 31 | 4 | 26 | 100 | 35 | 143 | 6 | 4 | R | R | 6-7 | 220 | 7-11-70 | 1988 | Belleville, Mich. |
| Barron, Tony | .290 | 107 | 259 | 42 | 75 | 22 | 1 | 8 | 36 | 27 | 59 | 6 | 5 | R | R | 6-0 | 185 | 8-17-66 | 1987 | Tacoma, Wash. |
| Bournigal, Rafael | .277 | 134 | 465 | 75 | 129 | 25 | 0 | 4 | 55 | 29 | 18 | 3 | 5 | R | R | 5-11 | 160 | 5-12-66 | 1987 | Santo Domingo, D.R. |
| Brooks, Jerry | .344 | 116 | 421 | 67 | 145 | 28 | 4 | 11 | 71 | 21 | 44 | 3 | 4 | R | R | 6-0 | 195 | 3-23-67 | 1988 | Syracuse, N.Y. |
| Busch, Mike | .283 | 122 | 431 | 87 | 122 | 32 | 4 | 22 | 70 | 53 | 89 | 1 | 2 | R | R | 6-5 | 243 | 7-7-68 | 1990 | Donahue, Iowa |
| Cedeno, Roger | .222 | 6 | 18 | 1 | 4 | 1 | 0 | 4 | 3 | 3 | 0 | 1 | | S | R | 6-2 | 190 | 8-16-74 | 1992 | Carabobo, Venez. |
| Goodwin, Tom | .260 | 85 | 289 | 48 | 75 | 5 | 5 | 1 | 28 | 30 | 51 | 21 | 6 | L | R | 6-1 | 165 | 7-27-68 | 1989 | Fresno, Calif. |
| Howard, Matt | .154 | 18 | 26 | 3 | 4 | 0 | 1 | 0 | 4 | 3 | 2 | 1 | 1 | R | R | 5-10 | 165 | 9-22-67 | 1989 | Irvine, Calif. |
| Maurer, Ron | .293 | 58 | 116 | 19 | 34 | 7 | 0 | 3 | 14 | 11 | 17 | 1 | 1 | R | R | 6-1 | 195 | 6-10-68 | 1990 | Beachwood, N.J. |
| Mondesi, Raul | .280 | 110 | 425 | 65 | 119 | 22 | 7 | 12 | 65 | 18 | 85 | 13 | 10 | R | R | 5-11 | 150 | 3-12-71 | 1988 | San Cristobal, D.R. |
| Munoz, Jose | .288 | 127 | 438 | 66 | 126 | 21 | 5 | 1 | 54 | 29 | 46 | 6 | 3 | S | R | 5-11 | 165 | 11-11-67 | 1987 | Yabucoa, P.R. |
| Ortiz, Hector | .182 | 18 | 44 | 0 | 8 | 1 | 1 | 0 | 3 | 0 | 6 | 0 | 0 | R | R | 6-0 | 200 | 10-14-69 | 1988 | Canovanas, P.R. |
| Parrish, Lance | .273 | 11 | 33 | 4 | 9 | 2 | 0 | 0 | 1 | 5 | 4 | 0 | 0 | R | R | 6-3 | 220 | 6-15-56 | 1974 | Yorba Linda, Calif. |
| Pye, Eddie | .329 | 101 | 365 | 53 | 120 | 21 | 7 | 7 | 66 | 32 | 43 | 5 | 9 | R | R | 5-10 | 170 | 2-13-67 | 1988 | Murfreesboro, Tenn. |
| Rodriguez, Henry | .296 | 46 | 179 | 26 | 53 | 13 | 5 | 4 | 30 | 14 | 37 | 1 | 2 | L | L | 6-1 | 180 | 11-8-67 | 1986 | New York, N.Y. |
| Spearman, Vernon | .254 | 62 | 185 | 31 | 47 | 6 | 5 | 0 | 15 | 17 | 28 | 11 | 4 | L | L | 5-9 | 160 | 12-17-69 | 1991 | Union City, Calif. |
| Strawberry, Darryl | .316 | 5 | 19 | 3 | 6 | 2 | 0 | 1 | 2 | 2 | 5 | 1 | 0 | L | L | 6-6 | 200 | 3-12-62 | 1980 | Los Angeles, Calif. |
| Traxler, Brian | .333 | 127 | 441 | 81 | 147 | 36 | 3 | 16 | 83 | 46 | 38 | 0 | 2 | L | L | 5-10 | 200 | 9-26-67 | 1988 | San Antonio, Texas |
| Wakamatsu, Don | .337 | 54 | 181 | 30 | 61 | 11 | 1 | 7 | 31 | 15 | 31 | 0 | 1 | R | R | 6-2 | 200 | 2-22-63 | 1985 | Hayward, Calif. |

| PITCHING | W | L | ERA | G | GS | CG | SV | IP | H | R | ER | BB | SO | B | T | HT | WT | DOB | 1st Yr | Resides |
|---|---|---|---|---|---|---|---|---|---|---|---|---|---|---|---|---|---|---|---|---|
| Allen, Steve | 1 | 0 | 10.80 | 2 | 0 | 0 | 0 | 2 | 3 | 2 | 2 | 2 | 1 | R | R | 6-3 | 210 | 7-27-66 | 1988 | Nashua, N.H. |
| Ayrault, Bob | 2 | 2 | 6.14 | 11 | 0 | 0 | 0 | 15 | 21 | 10 | 10 | 7 | 13 | R | R | 6-4 | 235 | 4-27-66 | 1989 | Carson City, Nev. |
| 2-team (3 Calgary) | 2 | 2 | 7.11 | 14 | 0 | 0 | 1 | 19 | 29 | 15 | 15 | 9 | 16 | | | | | | | |
| Bustillos, Albert | 2 | 1 | 4.45 | 20 | 0 | 0 | 2 | 30 | 37 | 15 | 15 | 13 | 17 | R | R | 6-2 | 225 | 4-8-68 | 1988 | Gilroy, Calif. |
| Daal, Omar | 1 | 1 | 3.38 | 6 | 0 | 0 | 2 | 5 | 5 | 2 | 2 | 3 | 2 | L | L | 6-3 | 160 | 3-1-72 | 1990 | Valencia, Venez. |
| Dayley, Ken | 0 | 0 | 12.19 | 9 | 1 | 0 | 0 | 14 | 15 | 14 | 12 | 9 | 13 | L | L | 6-0 | 180 | 2-25-59 | 1980 | Chesterfield, Mo. |
| Gross, Kip | 13 | 7 | 4.05 | 59 | 7 | 0 | 13 | 124 | 115 | 58 | 56 | 41 | 96 | R | R | 6-2 | 190 | 8-24-64 | 1987 | Gering, Neb. |
| Hansell, Greg | 5 | 10 | 6.93 | 26 | 20 | 0 | 0 | 101 | 131 | 86 | 78 | 60 | 60 | R | R | 6-5 | 215 | 3-12-71 | 1989 | La Palma, Calif. |
| Hurst, Jonathan | 7 | 2 | 4.15 | 18 | 15 | 0 | 0 | 87 | 101 | 47 | 40 | 29 | 62 | R | R | 6-2 | 175 | 10-20-66 | 1987 | Spartanburg, S.C. |
| James, Mike | 1 | 0 | 7.47 | 16 | 0 | 0 | 2 | 31 | 38 | 28 | 26 | 19 | 32 | R | R | 6-3 | 180 | 8-15-67 | 1988 | Mary Esther, Fla. |
| Kutzler, Jerry | 5 | 6 | 5.58 | 35 | 11 | 0 | 1 | 100 | 124 | 70 | 62 | 31 | 50 | L | R | 6-1 | 175 | 3-25-65 | 1987 | Zion, Ill. |
| Marquez, Isidrio | 1 | 0 | 1.50 | 9 | 0 | 0 | 2 | 12 | 7 | 2 | 2 | 3 | 10 | R | R | 6-3 | 190 | 5-15-65 | 1985 | Navojoa, Mexico |
| Martinez, Fili | 0 | 2 | 4.32 | 4 | 1 | 0 | 0 | 8 | 11 | 8 | 4 | 1 | 2 | L | L | 6-2 | 180 | 1-15-67 | 1989 | Los Angeles, Calif. |
| Martinez, Pedro | 0 | 0 | 3.00 | 1 | 1 | 0 | 0 | 3 | 1 | 1 | 1 | 4 | 1 | R | R | 5-11 | 150 | 10-25-71 | 1988 | Santo Domingo, D.R. |
| Mimbs, Mark | 0 | 1 | 10.13 | 19 | 1 | 0 | 1 | 19 | 20 | 21 | 21 | 16 | 12 | L | L | 6-2 | 180 | 2-13-69 | 1990 | Macon, Ga. |
| Nichols, Rod | 6 | 5 | 4.30 | 21 | 21 | 3 | 0 | 128 | 132 | 68 | 61 | 50 | 79 | R | R | 6-2 | 190 | 12-29-64 | 1985 | Columbus, Ga. |
| Nolte, Eric | 2 | 3 | 5.11 | 23 | 4 | 0 | 0 | 49 | 63 | 36 | 28 | 18 | 40 | L | L | 6-3 | 210 | 4-28-64 | 1985 | Hemet, Calif. |
| 2-team (10 Calgary) | 3 | 5 | 6.34 | 33 | 7 | 0 | 1 | 71 | 101 | 60 | 50 | 30 | 63 | | | | | | | |
| Perschke, Greg | 7 | 4 | 6.36 | 33 | 13 | 0 | 0 | 105 | 146 | 76 | 74 | 24 | 63 | R | R | 6-3 | 180 | 8-3-67 | 1989 | LaPorte, Ind. |
| Springer, Dennis | 3 | 8 | 5.99 | 35 | 18 | 0 | 0 | 131 | 173 | 104 | 87 | 39 | 69 | R | R | 5-10 | 185 | 2-12-65 | 1987 | Fresno, Calif. |
| Treadwell, Jody | 5 | 4 | 4.70 | 39 | 10 | 0 | 0 | 105 | 119 | 58 | 55 | 52 | 102 | R | R | 6-0 | 190 | 12-14-68 | 1990 | Jacksonville, Fla. |
| VanRyn, Ben | 1 | 4 | 10.73 | 6 | 6 | 0 | 0 | 24 | 35 | 30 | 29 | 17 | 9 | L | L | 6-5 | 195 | 8-19-71 | 1990 | Kendallville, Ind. |
| Vierra, Joey | 0 | 4 | 4.91 | 29 | 0 | 0 | 1 | 33 | 38 | 22 | 18 | 18 | 24 | L | L | 5-7 | 170 | 1-31-66 | 1987 | Honolulu, Hawaii |
| Williams, Todd | 5 | 5 | 4.99 | 65 | 0 | 0 | 21 | 70 | 87 | 44 | 39 | 31 | 56 | R | R | 6-3 | 185 | 2-13-71 | 1991 | Syracuse, N.Y. |
| Wilson, Steve | 0 | 3 | 4.38 | 13 | 12 | 0 | 0 | 51 | 57 | 29 | 25 | 14 | 44 | L | L | 6-2 | 190 | 12-13-64 | 1985 | Tempe, Ariz. |
| Worrell, Todd | 1 | 0 | 1.04 | 7 | 2 | 0 | 0 | 9 | 7 | 2 | 1 | 2 | 13 | R | R | 6-5 | 200 | 9-28-59 | 1982 | Temple City, Calif. |

### FIELDING

| Catcher | PCT | G | PO | A | E | DP |
|---|---|---|---|---|---|---|
| Barron | 1.000 | 5 | 6 | 2 | 0 | 0 |
| Brooks | .976 | 75 | 414 | 42 | 11 | 3 |
| Ortiz | .978 | 18 | 78 | 11 | 2 | 0 |
| Parrish | 1.000 | 11 | 67 | 7 | 0 | 0 |
| Wakamatsu | .989 | 53 | 329 | 35 | 4 | 0 |

| First Base | PCT | G | PO | A | E | DP |
|---|---|---|---|---|---|---|
| Busch | .977 | 17 | 112 | 13 | 3 | 11 |
| Rodriguez | .982 | 28 | 254 | 17 | 5 | 28 |
| Traxler | .995 | 115 | 969 | 89 | 5 | 98 |

| Second Base | PCT | G | PO | A | E | DP |
|---|---|---|---|---|---|---|
| Howard | .969 | 12 | 9 | 22 | 1 | 5 |

| | PCT | G | PO | A | E | DP |
|---|---|---|---|---|---|---|
| Maurer | 1.000 | 2 | 1 | 0 | 0 | 0 |
| Munoz | .982 | 68 | 126 | 207 | 6 | 48 |
| Pye | .973 | 82 | 181 | 245 | 12 | 53 |

| Third Base | PCT | G | PO | A | E | DP |
|---|---|---|---|---|---|---|
| Busch | .881 | 108 | 57 | 218 | 37 | 17 |
| Maurer | .957 | 14 | 7 | 15 | 1 | 3 |
| Munoz | .908 | 40 | 18 | 61 | 8 | 1 |
| Pye | 1.000 | 2 | 0 | 4 | 0 | 0 |

| Shortstop | PCT | G | PO | A | E | DP |
|---|---|---|---|---|---|---|
| Bournigal | .980 | 133 | 196 | 427 | 13 | 97 |
| Maurer | .931 | 25 | 18 | 63 | 6 | 9 |

| | PCT | G | PO | A | E | DP |
|---|---|---|---|---|---|---|
| Pye | 1.000 | 4 | 1 | 5 | 0 | 0 |

| Outfield | PCT | G | PO | A | E | DP |
|---|---|---|---|---|---|---|
| Ashley | .952 | 116 | 211 | 7 | 11 | 0 |
| Barron | .967 | 77 | 82 | 5 | 3 | 2 |
| Brooks | 1.000 | 20 | 19 | 2 | 0 | 1 |
| Cedeno | .923 | 5 | 12 | 0 | 1 | 0 |
| Goodwin | .986 | 77 | 145 | 1 | 2 | 0 |
| Mondesi | .957 | 105 | 211 | 10 | 10 | 2 |
| Munoz | 1.000 | 5 | 3 | 0 | 0 | 0 |
| Rodriguez | 1.000 | 24 | 23 | 1 | 0 | 0 |
| Spearman | .985 | 56 | 130 | 5 | 2 | 1 |
| Strawberry | 1.000 | 5 | 7 | 0 | 0 | 0 |

## TEXAS LEAGUE

| BATTING | AVG | G | AB | R | H | 2B | 3B | HR | RBI | BB | SO | SB | CS | B | T | HT | WT | DOB | 1st Yr | Resides |
|---|---|---|---|---|---|---|---|---|---|---|---|---|---|---|---|---|---|---|---|---|
| Abbe, Chris, c | .205 | 82 | 254 | 32 | 52 | 7 | 1 | 13 | 36 | 35 | 61 | 0 | 3 | R | R | 6-4 | 215 | 2-6-71 | 1992 | Sherman, Texas |
| Alvarez, Jorge, 2b-3b | .271 | 93 | 251 | 26 | 68 | 24 | 0 | 4 | 34 | 20 | 34 | 9 | 8 | R | R | 5-10 | 155 | 10-30-68 | 1988 | Las Terrenas Sanchez, D.R. |
| Blanco, Henry, 3b | .195 | 117 | 374 | 33 | 73 | 19 | 1 | 10 | 42 | 29 | 80 | 3 | 3 | R | R | 5-11 | 195 | 8-29-71 | 1990 | Guarenas, Venez. |
| Castro, Juan, ss | .276 | 118 | 424 | 55 | 117 | 23 | 8 | 7 | 41 | 30 | 40 | 12 | 11 | R | R | 5-11 | 172 | 6-20-72 | 1991 | Los Mochis, Mexico |
| Cedeno, Roger, of | .288 | 122 | 465 | 70 | 134 | 12 | 8 | 4 | 30 | 45 | 90 | 28 | 20 | S | R | 6-2 | 190 | 8-16-74 | 1992 | Carabobo, Venez. |
| Collier, Anthony, of | .207 | 83 | 193 | 21 | 40 | 8 | 0 | 4 | 15 | 10 | 43 | 2 | 4 | L | L | 5-11 | 180 | 11-10-70 | 1988 | Pasadena, Calif. |
| Doffek, Scott, 2b-3b | .259 | 26 | 85 | 5 | 22 | 7 | 0 | 0 | 8 | 2 | 6 | 1 | 1 | R | R | 5-9 | 170 | 7-31-68 | 1989 | Hartland, Wis. |
| Elster, Kevin, ss | .282 | 10 | 39 | 5 | 11 | 2 | 1 | 0 | 7 | 4 | 4 | 0 | 0 | R | R | 6-2 | 200 | 8-3-64 | 1984 | Huntington Beach, Calif. |
| Hollandsworth, Todd, of | .251 | 126 | 474 | 57 | 119 | 24 | 9 | 17 | 63 | 29 | 101 | 24 | 12 | L | L | 6-2 | 193 | 4-20-73 | 1991 | Bellevue, Wash. |
| Howard, Matt, 2b | .287 | 41 | 122 | 12 | 35 | 5 | 1 | 0 | 5 | 16 | 14 | 4 | 5 | R | R | 5-10 | 165 | 9-22-67 | 1989 | Irvine, Calif. |
| Huckaby, Ken, c | .220 | 28 | 82 | 4 | 18 | 1 | 0 | 0 | 5 | 2 | 7 | 0 | 0 | R | R | 6-1 | 205 | 1-27-71 | 1991 | Manteca, Calif. |
| Ingram, Garey, 2b | .269 | 84 | 305 | 43 | 82 | 14 | 5 | 6 | 33 | 31 | 50 | 19 | 6 | R | R | 5-11 | 178 | 7-25-70 | 1990 | Columbus, Ga. |
| Kirkpatrick, Jay, 1b | .320 | 97 | 97 | 17 | 31 | 6 | 1 | 6 | 17 | 14 | 15 | 0 | 1 | L | R | 6-4 | 220 | 7-10-69 | 1991 | Tallahassee, Fla. |

MEL BIAILEY

DAN ARNOLD

**Pedro Power.** Los Angeles pitching staff got a big boost in 1993 from Dominican righthanders Pedro Astacio, left, who won 14 games, and Pedro Martinez, who went 10-5 and struck out 119 in 107 innings.

| BATTING | AVG | G | AB | R | H | 2B | 3B | HR | RBI | BB | SO | SB | CS | B | T | HT | WT | DOB | 1st Yr | Resides |
|---|---|---|---|---|---|---|---|---|---|---|---|---|---|---|---|---|---|---|---|---|
| Kliafas, Steve, ss | .143 | 6 | 14 | 2 | 2 | 0 | 0 | 0 | 0 | 2 | 6 | 0 | 0 | R | R | 5-10 | 185 | 11-4-68 | 1990 | Houston, Texas |
| Lott, Billy, of | .254 | 114 | 418 | 49 | 106 | 17 | 2 | 15 | 49 | 23 | 111 | 5 | 11 | R | R | 6-4 | 210 | 8-16-70 | 1989 | Petal, Miss. |
| Magnusson, Brett, c | .111 | 13 | 9 | 1 | 1 | 1 | 0 | 0 | 4 | 3 | 0 | 0 | 0 | R | R | 5-10 | 210 | 8-20-67 | 1988 | Hollister, Calif. |
| Maurer, Ron, 3b-ss | .189 | 11 | 37 | 6 | 7 | 1 | 0 | 1 | 4 | 7 | 12 | 0 | 1 | R | R | 6-1 | 195 | 6-10-68 | 1990 | Beachwood, N.J. |
| Melendez, Dan, 1b | .241 | 47 | 158 | 25 | 38 | 11 | 0 | 7 | 30 | 11 | 29 | 0 | 0 | L | L | 6-4 | 195 | 1-4-71 | 1992 | Los Angeles, Calif. |
| Ortiz, Hector, c | .214 | 49 | 131 | 6 | 28 | 5 | 0 | 1 | 6 | 9 | 17 | 0 | 2 | R | R | 6-0 | 200 | 10-14-69 | 1988 | Canovanas, P.R. |
| Proctor, Murph, 1b | .252 | 91 | 294 | 38 | 74 | 10 | 0 | 5 | 42 | 45 | 45 | 1 | 4 | S | L | 6-1 | 185 | 6-12-69 | 1991 | Altadena, Calif. |
| Spearman, Vernon, of | .259 | 56 | 162 | 22 | 42 | 4 | 2 | 0 | 13 | 11 | 21 | 13 | 4 | L | L | 5-9 | 160 | 12-17-69 | 1991 | Union City, Calif. |

| PITCHING | W | L | ERA | G | GS | CG | SV | IP | H | R | ER | BB | SO | B | T | HT | WT | DOB | 1st Yr | Resides |
|---|---|---|---|---|---|---|---|---|---|---|---|---|---|---|---|---|---|---|---|---|
| Bene, Bill | 5 | 6 | 4.84 | 46 | 0 | 0 | 1 | 71 | 50 | 43 | 38 | 53 | 82 | R | R | 6-4 | 205 | 11-21-67 | 1988 | Long Beach, Calif. |
| Brosnan, Jason | 0 | 2 | 4.43 | 3 | 3 | 0 | 0 | 20 | 21 | 11 | 10 | 7 | 10 | L | L | 6-1 | 190 | 1-26-68 | 1989 | San Leandro, Calif. |
| Castro, Nelson | 2 | 1 | 4.94 | 5 | 5 | 0 | 0 | 27 | 35 | 16 | 15 | 4 | 15 | R | R | 6-1 | 190 | 12-10-71 | 1990 | Los Angeles, Calif. |
| Correa, Edwin | 0 | 2 | 8.00 | 2 | 2 | 0 | 0 | 9 | 17 | 8 | 8 | 8 | 8 | R | R | 6-2 | 215 | 4-29-66 | 1993 | Fort Worth, Texas |
| Daspit, Jimmy | 3 | 8 | 4.43 | 15 | 15 | 0 | 0 | 81 | 92 | 48 | 40 | 33 | 58 | R | R | 6-7 | 210 | 8-10-69 | 1990 | Sacramento, Calif. |
| Delahoya, Javier | 8 | 10 | 3.66 | 21 | 21 | 1 | 0 | 125 | 122 | 61 | 51 | 42 | 107 | R | R | 6-2 | 160 | 2-21-70 | 1989 | North Hollywood, Calif. |
| Gorecki, Rick | 6 | 9 | 3.35 | 26 | 26 | 1 | 0 | 156 | 136 | 76 | 58 | 62 | 118 | R | R | 6-3 | 180 | 8-27-73 | 1991 | Oak Forest, Ill. |
| Henderson, Ryan | 0 | 0 | 2.52 | 23 | 0 | 0 | 5 | 25 | 19 | 10 | 7 | 16 | 22 | R | R | 6-0 | 180 | 9-30-69 | 1992 | Dana Point, Calif. |
| Jones, Kiki | 0 | 1 | 4.50 | 3 | 3 | 0 | 0 | 14 | 14 | 9 | 7 | 8 | 7 | R | R | 5-11 | 175 | 6-8-70 | 1989 | Tampa, Fla. |
| Kutzler, Jerry | 1 | 0 | 1.59 | 2 | 0 | 0 | 0 | 6 | 3 | 1 | 1 | 0 | 3 | L | R | 6-1 | 175 | 3-25-65 | 1987 | Zion, Ill. |
| Marquez, Isidrio | 1 | 4 | 2.84 | 30 | 0 | 0 | 12 | 32 | 34 | 13 | 10 | 8 | 25 | R | R | 6-3 | 190 | 5-15-65 | 1985 | Navojoa, Mexico |
| McFarlin, Terry | 4 | 7 | 2.83 | 52 | 0 | 0 | 4 | 95 | 87 | 37 | 30 | 37 | 77 | S | R | 6-0 | 160 | 4-6-69 | 1991 | Brooklyn, N.Y. |
| Mimbs, Mark | 3 | 3 | 1.60 | 49 | 0 | 0 | 10 | 68 | 49 | 21 | 12 | 18 | 77 | L | L | 6-2 | 180 | 2-13-69 | 1990 | Macon, Ga. |
| Parra, Jose | 1 | 8 | 3.15 | 17 | 17 | 0 | 0 | 111 | 103 | 46 | 39 | 12 | 87 | R | R | 5-11 | 160 | 11-28-72 | 1990 | Santiago, D.R. |
| Piotrowicz, Brian | 0 | 0 | 4.66 | 6 | 2 | 0 | 0 | 19 | 31 | 18 | 10 | 7 | 12 | R | R | 6-1 | 185 | 12-10-67 | 1990 | North Liberty, Ind. |
| Snedeker, Sean | 4 | 5 | 4.35 | 12 | 12 | 0 | 0 | 70 | 92 | 42 | 34 | 17 | 36 | R | R | 6-3 | 180 | 6-18-65 | 1988 | The Woodlands, Texas |
| Thomas, Royal | 4 | 6 | 3.94 | 47 | 6 | 0 | 2 | 110 | 116 | 58 | 48 | 44 | 52 | R | R | 6-2 | 187 | 9-3-69 | 1987 | Beaumont, Texas |
| Valdez, Ismael | 1 | 0 | 1.38 | 3 | 2 | 0 | 0 | 13 | 12 | 2 | 2 | 0 | 11 | R | R | 6-3 | 183 | 8-21-73 | 1991 | Victoria, Mexico |
| VanRyn, Ben | 14 | 4 | 2.21 | 21 | 21 | 1 | 0 | 134 | 118 | 43 | 33 | 37 | 144 | L | L | 6-5 | 195 | 8-19-71 | 1990 | Kendallville, Ind. |
| Vierra, Joey | 1 | 0 | 5.40 | 9 | 0 | 0 | 1 | 12 | 14 | 7 | 7 | 4 | 6 | L | L | 5-7 | 170 | 1-31-66 | 1987 | Honolulu, Hawaii |

## BAKERSFIELD A
### CALIFORNIA LEAGUE

| BATTING | AVG | G | AB | R | H | 2B | 3B | HR | RBI | BB | SO | SB | CS | B | T | HT | WT | DOB | 1st Yr | Resides |
|---|---|---|---|---|---|---|---|---|---|---|---|---|---|---|---|---|---|---|---|---|
| Anderson, Cliff, 2b-ss | .139 | 12 | 36 | 4 | 5 | 3 | 0 | 0 | 3 | 1 | 13 | 0 | 1 | L | R | 5-8 | 165 | 7-9-70 | 1992 | Kodiak, Alaska |
| Dunn, Nathan, 3b | .214 | 4 | 14 | 1 | 3 | 0 | 0 | 0 | 1 | 3 | 2 | 0 | 0 | R | R | 5-11 | 175 | 8-1-70 | 1992 | Harriman, Tenn. |
| Ebel, Dino, 2b-3b | .280 | 19 | 50 | 7 | 14 | 5 | 0 | 0 | 4 | 4 | 9 | 0 | 1 | R | R | 5-10 | 178 | 3-20-66 | 1988 | Barstow, Calif. |
| Edmondson, Gavin, c | .185 | 45 | 119 | 14 | 22 | 3 | 0 | 0 | 8 | 7 | 31 | 2 | 1 | R | R | 6-1 | 185 | 6-19-72 | 1992 | Morley, Australia |
| Filson, Matt, dh-of | .233 | 98 | 283 | 33 | 66 | 16 | 4 | 8 | 37 | 36 | 84 | 1 | 3 | L | R | 5-10 | 190 | 2-12-69 | 1992 | El Segundo, Calif. |

# DODGERS TOP 10 PROSPECTS

How the Dodgers Top 10 prospects, as judged by Baseball America prior to the 1993 season, fared in 1993:

| Player, Pos. | Club (Class) | AVG | AB | H | HR | RBI | SB |
|---|---|---|---|---|---|---|---|
| 1. Mike Piazza, c | Los Angeles | .318 | 547 | 174 | 35 | 112 | 3 |
| 2. Raul Mondesi, of | Albuq. (AAA) | .280 | 425 | 119 | 12 | 65 | 13 |
| | Los Angeles | .291 | 86 | 25 | 4 | 10 | 4 |
| 3. Roger Cedeno, of | San Antonio (AA) | .288 | 465 | 134 | 4 | 30 | 28 |
| | Albuq. (AAA) | .222 | 18 | 4 | 0 | 4 | 0 |
| 7. Billy Ashley, of | Albuq. (AAA) | .297 | 482 | 143 | 26 | 100 | 6 |
| | Los Angeles | .243 | 37 | 9 | 0 | 0 | 0 |
| 9. T. Hollandsworth, of | San Antonio (AA) | .251 | 474 | 119 | 17 | 63 | 23 |

| Player, Pos. | Club (Class) | W | L | ERA | IP | H | BB | SO |
|---|---|---|---|---|---|---|---|---|
| 4. Greg Hansell, rhp | Albuq. (AAA) | 5 | 10 | 6.93 | 101 | 131 | 60 | 60 |
| 5. Pedro Martinez, rhp | Albuq. (AAA) | 0 | 0 | 3.00 | 3 | 1 | 1 | 4 |
| | Los Angeles | 10 | 5 | 2.61 | 107 | 76 | 57 | 119 |
| 6. Todd Williams, rhp | Albuq. (AAA) | 5 | 4 | 4.99 | 70 | 87 | 31 | 56 |
| 8. Omar Daal, lhp | Albuq. (AAA) | 1 | 1 | 3.38 | 5 | 5 | 3 | 2 |
| | Los Angeles | 2 | 3 | 5.09 | 35 | 36 | 21 | 19 |
| 10. Rick Gorecki, rhp | San Antonio (AA) | 6 | 9 | 3.35 | 156 | 136 | 62 | 118 |

**Mike Piazza**
NL Rookie of Year
DAN ARNOLD

## BATTING

| | AVG | G | AB | R | H | 2B | 3B | HR | RBI | BB | SO | SB | CS | B | T | HT | WT | DOB | 1st Yr | Resides |
|---|---|---|---|---|---|---|---|---|---|---|---|---|---|---|---|---|---|---|---|---|
| Garcia, Karim, of | .241 | 123 | 460 | 61 | 111 | 20 | 9 | 19 | 54 | 37 | 109 | 5 | 4 | L | L | 6-0 | 200 | 10-29-75 | 1993 | Obregon, Mexico |
| Jaime, Angel, ss | .230 | 46 | 152 | 21 | 35 | 5 | 0 | 0 | 8 | 18 | 34 | 14 | 6 | R | R | 6-0 | 175 | 3-6-73 | 1992 | Santo Domingo, D.R. |
| Kirkpatrick, Jay, 1b | .288 | 103 | 375 | 42 | 108 | 21 | 0 | 8 | 63 | 35 | 78 | 1 | 4 | L | R | 6-4 | 220 | 7-10-69 | 1991 | Tallahassee, Fla. |
| Kliafas, Steve, ss | .235 | 88 | 328 | 40 | 77 | 13 | 0 | 1 | 24 | 13 | 37 | 4 | 1 | R | R | 5-10 | 185 | 11-4-68 | 1990 | Houston, Texas |
| Latham, Chris, of | .185 | 6 | 27 | 1 | 5 | 1 | 0 | 0 | 3 | 4 | 5 | 2 | 2 | S | R | 6-0 | 185 | 5-26-73 | 1991 | Las Vegas, Nev. |
| Lewis, Tyrone, 2b | .232 | 83 | 332 | 31 | 77 | 8 | 3 | 0 | 23 | 16 | 67 | 4 | 6 | R | R | 5-10 | 192 | 1-22-74 | 1992 | Waco, Texas |
| Lund, Ed, c-1b | .261 | 66 | 203 | 20 | 53 | 4 | 0 | 2 | 21 | 21 | 25 | 2 | 1 | R | R | 6-3 | 215 | 12-3-67 | 1990 | Pasadena, Calif. |
| Luzinski, Ryan, c | .279 | 48 | 147 | 18 | 41 | 10 | 1 | 3 | 9 | 13 | 24 | 2 | 2 | R | R | 6-1 | 225 | 8-22-73 | 1992 | Medford, N.J. |
| Martin, James, of | .259 | 118 | 441 | 60 | 114 | 17 | 3 | 12 | 50 | 45 | 131 | 27 | 12 | R | L | 6-1 | 215 | 12-10-70 | 1992 | Eufaula, Okla. |
| McKamie, Sean, inf | .328 | 21 | 67 | 15 | 22 | 4 | 0 | 2 | 12 | 7 | 6 | 4 | 3 | R | R | 6-2 | 180 | 9-27-69 | 1989 | New Brighton, Minn. |
| Moore, Michael, of | .288 | 100 | 403 | 61 | 116 | 25 | 1 | 13 | 58 | 29 | 103 | 23 | 10 | R | R | 6-4 | 215 | 3-7-71 | 1992 | Beverly Hills, Calif. |
| Otanez, Willis, 3b | .262 | 95 | 325 | 34 | 85 | 11 | 2 | 10 | 39 | 29 | 63 | 1 | 4 | R | R | 5-11 | 150 | 4-19-73 | 1990 | Las Matas De Cotui, D.R. |
| Rios, Eduardo, 2b | .283 | 29 | 113 | 19 | 32 | 4 | 0 | 7 | 17 | 8 | 17 | 2 | 3 | R | R | 5-10 | 175 | 10-13-72 | 1991 | Charallave, Venez. |
| Romero, Wilfredo, of | .351 | 20 | 77 | 8 | 27 | 5 | 0 | 1 | 12 | 5 | 16 | 4 | 2 | R | R | 5-8 | 185 | 8-5-74 | 1991 | Candelaria, Venez. |
| Schwenke, Matt, c-dh | .220 | 13 | 41 | 2 | 9 | 0 | 0 | 4 | 3 | 12 | 0 | 0 | 1 | S | R | 6-2 | 200 | 8-12-72 | 1993 | Poway, Calif. |
| Smith, Frank, of | .258 | 102 | 299 | 36 | 77 | 11 | 3 | 5 | 30 | 32 | 91 | 1 | 7 | R | R | 6-2 | 200 | 8-11-72 | 1990 | Riverside, Calif. |
| Watts, Craig, 1b | .144 | 34 | 118 | 5 | 17 | 0 | 0 | 1 | 5 | 7 | 38 | 0 | 0 | R | R | 6-2 | 220 | 3-5-74 | 1991 | Glenside, Calif. |
| Williams, Leroy, 3b | .240 | 62 | 192 | 18 | 46 | 8 | 0 | 1 | 17 | 25 | 43 | 0 | 1 | R | R | 6-0 | 180 | 4-13-72 | 1992 | Garyville, La. |
| Wittig, Paul, c | .129 | 23 | 62 | 7 | 8 | 1 | 0 | 1 | 2 | 7 | 27 | 1 | 1 | R | R | 6-1 | 190 | 7-31-73 | 1992 | Bremerton, Wash. |

## PITCHING

| | W | L | ERA | G | GS | CG | SV | IP | H | R | ER | BB | SO | B | T | HT | WT | DOB | 1st Yr | Resides |
|---|---|---|---|---|---|---|---|---|---|---|---|---|---|---|---|---|---|---|---|---|
| Brosnan, Jason | 4 | 1 | 3.47 | 9 | 6 | 0 | 0 | 36 | 36 | 20 | 14 | 15 | 34 | L | L | 6-1 | 190 | 1-26-68 | 1993 | San Leandro, Calif. |
| Castro, Nelson | 4 | 7 | 4.27 | 20 | 20 | 0 | 0 | 86 | 100 | 47 | 41 | 37 | 54 | R | R | 6-1 | 190 | 12-10-71 | 1990 | Los Angeles, Calif. |
| Colson, Brent | 2 | 4 | 5.60 | 39 | 1 | 0 | 1 | 55 | 64 | 37 | 34 | 39 | 37 | R | L | 6-0 | 180 | 2-1-71 | 1992 | Stone Mountain, Ga. |
| Costello, Chris | 3 | 3 | 6.89 | 16 | 7 | 0 | 0 | 50 | 54 | 44 | 38 | 35 | 34 | R | R | 6-4 | 240 | 9-20-72 | 1991 | Walpole, Mass. |
| Garcia, Jose | 0 | 3 | 6.83 | 27 | 0 | 0 | 4 | 29 | 47 | 23 | 22 | 12 | 25 | R | R | 6-3 | 175 | 6-12-72 | 1991 | Monte Cristi, D.R. |
| Herges, Matt | 2 | 6 | 3.69 | 51 | 0 | 0 | 2 | 90 | 70 | 49 | 37 | 56 | 84 | L | R | 6-0 | 200 | 4-1-70 | 1992 | Champaign, Ill. |
| Hubbs, Dan | 2 | 1 | 1.81 | 19 | 1 | 0 | 1 | 45 | 36 | 12 | 9 | 15 | 44 | R | R | 6-2 | 206 | 1-23-71 | 1993 | Renton, Wash. |
| Iglesias, Mike | 1 | 2 | 5.59 | 6 | 3 | 0 | 0 | 19 | 26 | 16 | 12 | 12 | 10 | R | R | 6-5 | 215 | 11-9-72 | 1991 | Castro Valley, Calif. |
| Jacobsen, Joe | 1 | 0 | 4.58 | 6 | 0 | 0 | 2 | 20 | 22 | 16 | 10 | 8 | 23 | R | R | 6-4 | 230 | 12-26-71 | 1992 | Clovis, Calif. |
| Kenady, Jason | 0 | 4 | 6.15 | 8 | 6 | 0 | 0 | 26 | 26 | 27 | 18 | 28 | 17 | L | L | 6-4 | 205 | 9-21-73 | 1991 | Apple Valley, Minn. |
| Martinez, Jesus | 4 | 13 | 4.14 | 30 | 21 | 0 | 0 | 146 | 144 | 95 | 67 | 75 | 108 | L | L | 6-2 | 162 | 3-13-74 | 1991 | Santo Domingo, D.R. |
| Miran, Tory | 2 | 5 | 3.45 | 32 | 7 | 0 | 0 | 76 | 83 | 40 | 29 | 27 | 48 | L | L | 5-9 | 175 | 9-5-70 | 1992 | Boise, Idaho |
| Osuna, Antonio | 0 | 2 | 4.91 | 14 | 2 | 0 | 2 | 18 | 19 | 10 | 10 | 5 | 20 | R | R | 6-2 | 185 | 4-12-73 | 1991 | Sinaloa, Mexico |
| Pincavitch, Kevin | 1 | 2 | 1.99 | 6 | 5 | 0 | 0 | 32 | 27 | 11 | 7 | 25 | 32 | R | R | 5-11 | 180 | 7-5-70 | 1992 | Greensboro, Pa. |
| Salcedo, Jose | 1 | 0 | 7.27 | 16 | 0 | 0 | 0 | 26 | 35 | 26 | 21 | 19 | 23 | R | R | 6-0 | 162 | 2-26-73 | 1990 | Santo Domingo, D.R. |
| Sinacori, Chris | 2 | 6 | 5.54 | 31 | 3 | 0 | 6 | 39 | 42 | 29 | 24 | 37 | 39 | R | R | 6-4 | 215 | 8-19-70 | 1991 | Wantagh, N.Y. |
| Snedeker, Sean | 1 | 5 | 5.58 | 13 | 5 | 0 | 0 | 40 | 51 | 31 | 25 | 16 | 20 | R | R | 6-3 | 180 | 6-18-65 | 1988 | The Woodlands, Texas |
| Thomas, Carlos | 5 | 9 | 4.33 | 38 | 8 | 0 | 1 | 98 | 89 | 51 | 47 | 75 | 82 | R | R | 6-4 | 215 | 8-6-68 | 1991 | Memphis, Tenn. |
| Veras, Dario | 1 | 0 | 7.43 | 7 | 0 | 0 | 0 | 13 | 13 | 11 | 11 | 6 | 11 | R | R | 6-1 | 155 | 3-13-73 | 1991 | Villa Vasquez, D.R. |
| Watts, Burgess | 0 | 0 | 6.35 | 10 | 0 | 0 | 0 | 23 | 30 | 19 | 16 | 9 | 9 | R | R | 6-2 | 190 | 11-22-68 | 1990 | Warrenville, Ill. |
| Weaver, Eric | 6 | 11 | 4.28 | 28 | 27 | 0 | 0 | 158 | 135 | 89 | 75 | 118 | 110 | R | R | 6-5 | 230 | 8-4-73 | 1991 | Illiopolis, Ill. |
| White, Brandon | 0 | 0 | 27.00 | 1 | 0 | 0 | 0 | 1 | 2 | 3 | 3 | 3 | 2 | R | R | 1 | 192 | 9-28-70 | 1992 | Saline, Mich. |
| Worrell, Todd | 0 | 0 | 0.00 | 2 | 2 | 0 | 0 | 2 | 1 | 0 | 0 | 0 | 5 | R | R | 6-5 | 200 | 9-28-59 | 1982 | Temple City, Calif. |
| Zerbe, Chad | 0 | 10 | 5.91 | 14 | 12 | 1 | 0 | 67 | 83 | 60 | 44 | 47 | 41 | L | L | 6-0 | 180 | 4-27-72 | 1991 | Tampa, Fla. |

# VERO BEACH                                                                A

## FLORIDA STATE LEAGUE

### BATTING

| | AVG | G | AB | R | H | 2B | 3B | HR | RBI | BB | SO | SB | CS | B | T | HT | WT | DOB | 1st Yr | Resides |
|---|---|---|---|---|---|---|---|---|---|---|---|---|---|---|---|---|---|---|---|---|
| Adams, Bill, of | .133 | 18 | 45 | 8 | 6 | 1 | 0 | 1 | 7 | 7 | 16 | 3 | 3 | L | L | 5-11 | 180 | 12-15-68 | 1993 | Camp Hill, Pa. |
| Brown, Mike, c | .174 | 39 | 86 | 9 | 15 | 0 | 0 | 0 | 9 | 8 | 14 | 0 | 0 | R | R | 5-11 | 190 | 3-7-70 | 1991 | Lexington, Ill. |
| Cairo, Miguel, 2b-ss | .315 | 90 | 346 | 50 | 109 | 10 | 1 | 1 | 23 | 28 | 22 | 23 | 16 | R | R | 6-0 | 160 | 5-4-74 | 1991 | Anaco, Venez. |
| Demetral, Chris, 2b | .325 | 122 | 437 | 63 | 142 | 22 | 3 | 5 | 48 | 69 | 47 | 6 | 6 | L | R | 5-10 | 175 | 12-8-69 | 1991 | Sterling Heights, Mich. |
| Dotel, Angel, 1b-of | .221 | 88 | 263 | 33 | 58 | 9 | 2 | 4 | 15 | 35 | 56 | 2 | 5 | L | L | 6-1 | 185 | 3-14-71 | 1989 | Santo Domingo, D.R. |
| Gray, Dan, c | .200 | 1 | 5 | 1 | 1 | 0 | 0 | 0 | 1 | 0 | 0 | 1 | 0 | R | R | 6-2 | 200 | 8-17-69 | 1990 | Thornwood, N.Y. |
| Green, Steve, of | .188 | 15 | 48 | 5 | 9 | 1 | 0 | 0 | 3 | 11 | 11 | 0 | 1 | R | R | 6-3 | 195 | 8-8-66 | 1987 | Lilburn, Ga. |
| Huckaby, Ken, c | .267 | 79 | 281 | 22 | 75 | 14 | 1 | 4 | 41 | 11 | 35 | 2 | 1 | R | R | 6-1 | 205 | 1-27-71 | 1991 | Manteca, Calif. |
| Johnson, Keith, ss | .238 | 111 | 404 | 37 | 96 | 22 | 0 | 4 | 48 | 18 | 71 | 13 | 13 | R | R | 5-11 | 190 | 4-17-71 | 1992 | Hanford, Calif. |
| Johnson, Reggie, 1b-3b | .263 | 84 | 270 | 27 | 71 | 16 | 1 | 2 | 29 | 17 | 73 | 5 | 6 | R | R | 6-1 | 190 | 3-15-71 | 1992 | Columbus, Ga. |
| Landrum, Tito, 3b | .232 | 116 | 396 | 50 | 92 | 13 | 2 | 9 | 42 | 41 | 95 | 8 | 6 | R | R | 6-3 | 185 | 8-26-70 | 1991 | Sweetwater, Ala. |
| Lantigua, Ed, 3b | .271 | 119 | 439 | 70 | 119 | 16 | 4 | 10 | 79 | 31 | 107 | 10 | 2 | R | R | 6-0 | 178 | 9-4-73 | 1991 | Moca, D.R. |

| BATTING | AVG | G | AB | R | H | 2B | 3B | HR | RBI | BB | SO | SB | CS | B | T | HT | WT | DOB | 1st Yr | Resides |
|---|---|---|---|---|---|---|---|---|---|---|---|---|---|---|---|---|---|---|---|---|
| LoDuca, Paul, c-dh | .313 | 39 | 134 | 17 | 42 | 6 | 0 | 0 | 13 | 13 | 22 | 0 | 0 | R | R | 5-10 | 193 | 4-12-72 | 1993 | Phoenix, Ariz. |
| Maness, Dwight, of | .259 | 118 | 409 | 57 | 106 | 21 | 4 | 6 | 42 | 32 | 105 | 22 | 13 | R | R | 6-3 | 180 | 4-3-74 | 1992 | New Castle, Del. |
| Morrow, Chris, dh-of | .310 | 88 | 316 | 47 | 98 | 18 | 3 | 13 | 66 | 21 | 40 | 7 | 3 | L | L | 6-1 | 190 | 11-8-69 | 1988 | Pacifica, Calif. |
| Pinkney, Alton, dh-of | .239 | 14 | 46 | 8 | 11 | 0 | 0 | 1 | 4 | 9 | 7 | 4 | 2 | L | R | 5-11 | 175 | 1-13-71 | 1990 | Brunswick, Ga. |
| Puchales, Javier, of | .337 | 77 | 279 | 46 | 94 | 6 | 0 | 0 | 27 | 17 | 44 | 4 | 5 | L | L | 6-0 | 190 | 3-29-72 | 1989 | Caguas, P.R. |
| Teel, Garrett, c | .000 | 5 | 9 | 0 | 0 | 0 | 0 | 0 | 0 | 2 | 0 | 0 | 0 | R | R | 5-9 | 170 | 11-20-67 | 1989 | Ridgefield Park, N.J. |
| Vorbeck, Eric, of | .194 | 51 | 129 | 17 | 25 | 4 | 0 | 0 | 12 | 16 | 27 | 5 | 2 | R | R | 6-1 | 205 | 11-9-68 | 1991 | Butte Falls, Ore. |
| Webb, Lonnie, dh | .258 | 31 | 97 | 15 | 25 | 5 | 1 | 2 | 8 | 9 | 23 | 2 | 2 | R | R | 5-11 | 180 | 4-25-70 | 1990 | Sparta, Ga. |

| PITCHING | W | L | ERA | G | GS | CG | SV | IP | H | R | ER | BB | SO | B | T | HT | WT | DOB | 1st Yr | Resides |
|---|---|---|---|---|---|---|---|---|---|---|---|---|---|---|---|---|---|---|---|---|
| Brosnan, Jason | 0 | 2 | 4.56 | | | | 1 | 26 | 30 | 22 | 13 | 19 | 32 | L | L | 6-1 | 190 | 1-26-68 | 1989 | San Leandro, Calif. |
| Correa, Edwin | 3 | 4 | 4.45 | 10 | 10 | 0 | 0 | 55 | 61 | 34 | 27 | 22 | 56 | R | R | 6-2 | 215 | 4-29-66 | 1993 | Fort Worth, Texas |
| Daspit, Jimmy | 0 | 0 | 0.00 | 1 | 1 | 0 | 0 | 3 | 4 | 0 | 0 | 2 | 2 | R | R | 6-7 | 210 | 8-10-69 | 1990 | Sacramento, Calif. |
| Duran, Roberto | 1 | 1 | 3.72 | 8 | 0 | 0 | 0 | 10 | 10 | 4 | 4 | 8 | 9 | L | L | 6-0 | 167 | 3-23-73 | 1990 | Moca, D.R. |
| Gutierrez, Rafael | 1 | 4 | 7.20 | 15 | 6 | 0 | 0 | 40 | 42 | 38 | 32 | 33 | 22 | R | R | 6-3 | 202 | 9-20-70 | 1990 | Monteballo, Calif. |
| Hamilton, Ken | 6 | 6 | 4.54 | 32 | 12 | 0 | 1 | 105 | 113 | 55 | 53 | 45 | 70 | R | R | 6-2 | 190 | 12-27-70 | 1990 | Jackson, Ala. |
| Henderson, Ryan | 0 | 3 | 3.97 | 30 | 0 | 0 | 0 | 34 | 29 | 24 | 15 | 28 | 34 | R | R | 6-0 | 180 | 9-30-69 | 1992 | Dana Point, Calif. |
| James, Mike | 2 | 3 | 4.92 | 30 | 1 | 0 | 5 | 60 | 54 | 37 | 33 | 33 | 60 | R | R | 6-3 | 180 | 8-15-67 | 1988 | Mary Esther, Fla. |
| Jones, Kiki | 4 | 7 | 5.32 | 15 | 15 | 0 | 0 | 69 | 63 | 46 | 41 | 45 | 44 | R | R | 5-11 | 175 | 6-8-70 | 1989 | Tampa, Fla. |
| Lavigne, Martin | 7 | 8 | 5.56 | 22 | 19 | 0 | 0 | 91 | 104 | 65 | 56 | 45 | 76 | R | L | 6-2 | 200 | 5-11-71 | 1991 | Loretteville, Quebec |
| Licursi, Richard | 3 | 0 | 5.09 | 25 | 0 | 0 | 0 | 46 | 38 | 30 | 26 | 31 | 36 | R | R | 6-3 | 200 | 12-26-70 | 1992 | Trumbull, Conn. |
| Linares, Rich | 4 | 1 | 1.81 | 45 | 7 | 0 | 13 | 109 | 97 | 36 | 22 | 28 | 80 | R | R | 5-10 | 185 | 8-31-72 | 1992 | Long Beach, Calif. |
| Nichting, Chris | 0 | 0 | 4.15 | 4 | 4 | 0 | 0 | 17 | 18 | 9 | 8 | 6 | 18 | R | R | 6-1 | 205 | 5-13-66 | 1988 | Cincinnati, Ohio |
| Pincavitch, Kevin | 0 | 0 | 4.66 | 6 | 0 | 0 | 0 | 10 | 11 | 10 | 5 | 10 | 3 | R | R | 5-11 | 180 | 7-5-70 | 1992 | Greensboro, Pa. |
| Prado, Jose | 3 | 4 | 4.37 | 12 | 9 | 0 | 0 | 56 | 45 | 31 | 27 | 29 | 31 | R | R | 6-2 | 195 | 5-9-72 | 1993 | Miami, Fla. |
| Pyc, Dave | 7 | 8 | 2.38 | 23 | 15 | 1 | 0 | 113 | 97 | 41 | 30 | 47 | 78 | L | L | 6-3 | 230 | 2-11-71 | 1992 | Depew, N.Y. |
| Rodriguez, Felix | 8 | 8 | 3.75 | 32 | 20 | 2 | 0 | 132 | 109 | 71 | 55 | 71 | 80 | R | R | 6-1 | 190 | 12-5-72 | 1990 | Monte Cristi, D.R. |
| Salcedo, Jose | 0 | 0 | 3.65 | 8 | 0 | 0 | 0 | 12 | 9 | 6 | 5 | 6 | 10 | R | R | 6-0 | 162 | 2-26-73 | 1990 | Santo Domingo, D.R. |
| Sinacori, Chris | 3 | 5 | 4.15 | 16 | 5 | 0 | 1 | 48 | 63 | 27 | 22 | 16 | 29 | R | R | 6-4 | 215 | 8-19-70 | 1991 | Wantagh, N.Y. |
| Veras, Dario | 2 | 2 | 2.80 | 24 | 0 | 0 | 2 | 55 | 59 | 23 | 17 | 14 | 31 | R | R | 6-1 | 155 | 3-13-73 | 1991 | Villa Vasquez, D.R. |
| Walden, Ron | 1 | 1 | 4.00 | 3 | 3 | 0 | 0 | 9 | 9 | 5 | 4 | 7 | 2 | L | L | 6-2 | 170 | 9-28-72 | 1990 | Blanchard, Okla. |
| Watts, Brandon | 0 | 1 | 4.08 | 8 | 0 | 0 | 0 | 18 | 14 | 11 | 8 | 16 | 12 | L | L | 6-3 | 190 | 9-13-72 | 1991 | Ruston, La. |
| White, Brandon | 0 | 5 | 8.45 | 8 | 6 | 0 | 0 | 33 | 43 | 35 | 31 | 18 | 20 | R | R | 6-1 | 192 | 9-28-70 | 1992 | Saline, Mich. |
| Zerbe, Chad | 1 | 0 | 6.57 | 10 | 0 | 0 | 0 | 12 | 12 | 10 | 9 | 13 | 11 | L | L | 6-0 | 180 | 4-27-72 | 1991 | Tampa, Fla. |

# YAKIMA    A
## NORTHWEST LEAGUE

| BATTING | AVG | G | AB | R | H | 2B | 3B | HR | RBI | BB | SO | SB | CS | B | T | HT | WT | DOB | 1st Yr | Resides |
|---|---|---|---|---|---|---|---|---|---|---|---|---|---|---|---|---|---|---|---|---|
| Anderson, Cliff, ss | .222 | 23 | 81 | 7 | 18 | 4 | 0 | 1 | 7 | 7 | 19 | 1 | 0 | L | R | 5-8 | 165 | 7-9-70 | 1992 | Kodiak, Alaska |
| Compton, Scott, of | .148 | 19 | 27 | 4 | 4 | 1 | 0 | 0 | 2 | 6 | 8 | 1 | 0 | S | R | 6-0 | 180 | 11-3-70 | 1993 | Tampa, Fla. |
| Dunn, Nathan, 2b-3b | .308 | 4 | 13 | 1 | 4 | 1 | 0 | 0 | 1 | 2 | 1 | 0 | 0 | R | R | 5-11 | 175 | 8-1-70 | 1993 | Harriman, Tenn. |
| Haley, Rick, 1b | .264 | 63 | 220 | 28 | 58 | 14 | 0 | 8 | 50 | 28 | 83 | 2 | 1 | L | L | 6-4 | 215 | 12-29-71 | 1992 | Rancho Cordova, Calif. |
| Harris, John, of | .135 | 47 | 89 | 12 | 12 | 0 | 0 | 1 | 5 | 22 | 44 | 7 | 7 | R | R | 6-0 | 175 | 12-9-73 | 1993 | Mobile, Ala. |
| Hawkins, Richard, of | .266 | 55 | 207 | 30 | 55 | 8 | 1 | 3 | 27 | 24 | 41 | 5 | 3 | R | R | 6-0 | 192 | 10-30-70 | 1993 | Boonsboro, Md. |
| Jackson, Vince, of-dh | .237 | 22 | 59 | 11 | 14 | 2 | 0 | 1 | 6 | 7 | 13 | 1 | 2 | S | L | 6-1 | 185 | 10-9-72 | 1991 | Davenport, Iowa |
| Jaime, Angel, ss | .262 | 50 | 168 | 29 | 44 | 8 | 3 | 2 | 25 | 18 | 27 | 9 | 4 | R | R | 6-0 | 175 | 3-6-73 | 1992 | Santo Domingo, D.R. |
| Latham, Chris, of | .260 | 54 | 192 | 46 | 50 | 2 | 6 | 4 | 17 | 39 | 53 | 25 | 9 | S | R | 6-0 | 185 | 5-26-73 | 1991 | Las Vegas, Nev. |
| Luzinski, Ryan, c-dh | .257 | 69 | 237 | 32 | 61 | 10 | 3 | 4 | 46 | 41 | 44 | 6 | 1 | R | R | 6-1 | 225 | 8-22-73 | 1992 | Medford, N.J. |
| Newstrom, Doug, 3b | .297 | 75 | 279 | 51 | 83 | 17 | 2 | 2 | 36 | 53 | 44 | 11 | 1 | L | R | 6-2 | 195 | 9-18-71 | 1993 | Fairfax Station, Va. |
| Pitts, Kevin, of | .235 | 60 | 226 | 23 | 53 | 13 | 2 | 6 | 32 | 13 | 69 | 2 | 4 | R | L | 6-3 | 195 | 11-23-72 | 1993 | East St. Louis, Ill. |
| Post, David, 2b | .252 | 60 | 210 | 34 | 53 | 8 | 1 | 1 | 22 | 35 | 27 | 7 | 4 | R | R | 5-11 | 175 | 9-3-73 | 1992 | Kingston, N.Y. |
| Ravitz, David, 2b | .185 | 28 | 92 | 12 | 17 | 4 | 0 | 1 | 4 | 6 | 8 | 1 | 1 | R | R | 5-9 | 170 | 9-24-70 | 1993 | Los Angeles, Calif. |
| Romero, Wilfredo, of | .255 | 13 | 51 | 8 | 13 | 0 | 0 | 0 | 1 | 1 | 12 | 3 | 0 | R | R | 5-8 | 185 | 8-5-74 | 1991 | Candelaria, Venez. |
| Uribe, Dilone, c | .188 | 16 | 32 | 2 | 6 | 0 | 0 | 1 | 3 | 3 | 7 | 0 | 0 | L | R | 6-0 | 175 | 9-18-72 | 1988 | San Cristobal, D.R. |

# DODGERS: ORGANIZATION LEADERS

## MAJOR LEAGUERS

### BATTING
| | | |
|---|---|---|
| *AVG | Mike Piazza | .318 |
| R | Mike Piazza | 81 |
| H | Brett Butler | 181 |
| TB | Mike Piazza | 307 |
| 2B | Cory Snyder | 33 |
| 3B | Brett Butler | 10 |
| HR | Mike Piazza | 35 |
| RBI | Mike Piazza | 112 |
| BB | Brett Butler | 86 |
| SO | Cory Snyder | 147 |
| SB | Brett Butler | 39 |

### PITCHING
| | | |
|---|---|---|
| W | Pedro Astacio | 14 |
| L | Orel Hershiser | 14 |
| #ERA | Jim Gott | 2.32 |
| G | Pedro Martinez | 65 |
| CG | Orel Hershiser | 5 |
| SV | Jim Gott | 25 |
| IP | Orel Hershiser | 216 |
| BB | Ramon Martinez | 104 |
| SO | Tom Candiotti | 155 |

**Jim Gott**
Career-best 2.32 ERA

MORRIS FOSTOFF

## MINOR LEAGUERS

### BATTING
| | | |
|---|---|---|
| *AVG | Jerry Brooks, Albuquerque | .344 |
| R | Billy Ashley, Albuquerque | 88 |
| H | Brian Traxler, Albuquerque | 147 |
| TB | Billy Ashley, Albuquerque | 260 |
| 2B | Brian Traxler, Albuquerque | 36 |
| 3B | Two tied at | 9 |
| HR | Billy Ashley, Albuquerque | 26 |
| RBI | Billy Ashley, Albuquerque | 100 |
| BB | Chris Demetral, Vero Beach | 69 |
| SO | Billy Ashley, Albuquerque | 143 |
| SB | Roger Cedeno, San Antonio-Albu. | 28 |

### PITCHING
| | | |
|---|---|---|
| W | Ben VanRyn, San Antonio-Albuquerque | 15 |
| L | Jesus Martinez, Bakersfield | 11 |
| #ERA | Rich Linares, Vero Beach | 1.81 |
| G | Mark Mimbs, San Antonio-Albuquerque | 68 |
| CG | Rod Nichols, Albuquerque | 3 |
| SV | Todd Williams, Albuquerque | 21 |
| IP | Ben VanRyn, San Antonio-Albu. | 159 |
| BB | Eric Weaver, Bakersfield | 118 |
| SO | Ben VanRyn, San Antonio-Albu. | 153 |

*Minimum 250 At-Bats   #Minimum 75 Innings

# DODGERS: MOST COMMON LINEUPS

| | Los Angeles<br>Majors | Albuquerque<br>AAA | San Antonio<br>AA | Bakersfield<br>A | Vero Beach<br>A |
|---|---|---|---|---|---|
| C | Mike Piazza (146) | Jerry Brooks (75) | Chris Abbe (74) | Ed Lund (42) | Ken Huckaby (79) |
| 1B | Eric Karros (157) | Brian Traxler (115) | Murph Proctor (66) | Jay Kirkpatrick (102) | Angel Dotel (70) |
| 2B | Jody Reed (132) | Eddie Pye (82) | Garey Ingram (66) | Tyrone Lewis (81) | Chris Demetral (83) |
| 3B | Tim Wallach (130) | Mike Busch (108) | Henry Blanco (111) | Willis Otanez (87) | Ed Lantigua (104) |
| SS | Jose Offerman (158) | Rafael Bournigal (133) | Juan Castro (110) | Stephen Kliafas (85) | Keith Johnson (111) |
| OF | Brett Butler (155) | Billy Ashley (116) | Todd Hollandsworth (117) | Karim Garcia (114) | Dwight Maness (118) |
| | Cory Snyder (115) | Raul Mondesi (110) | Roger Cedeno (111) | James Martin (98) | Tito Landrum (115) |
| | Eric Davis (103) | Tom Goodwin (83) | Billy Lott (104) | Michael Moore (97) | Javier Puchales (62) |
| DH | N/A | Jerry Brooks (17) | Murph Proctor (17) | Matt Filson (60) | Chris Demetral (33) |
| SP | Orel Hershiser (33) | Rod Nichols (21) | Rick Gorecki (26) | Eric Weaver (27) | Felix Rodriguez (20) |
| RP | Pedro Martinez (63) | Todd Williams (65) | Terry McFarlin (52) | Matt Herges (51) | Rich Linares (38) |

Full-season farm clubs only   No. of games at position in parenthesis

| BATTING | AVG | G | AB | R | H | 2B | 3B | HR | RBI | BB | SO | SB | CS | B | T | HT | WT | DOB | 1st Yr | Resides |
|---|---|---|---|---|---|---|---|---|---|---|---|---|---|---|---|---|---|---|---|---|
| Williams, Leroy, 1b | .241 | 39 | 141 | 17 | 34 | 5 | 1 | 3 | 23 | 16 | 33 | 1 | 0 | R | R | 6-0 | 200 | 4-13-72 | 1990 | Garyville, La. |
| Yard, Bruce, ss-3b | .225 | 44 | 129 | 18 | 29 | 5 | 1 | 0 | 12 | 22 | 12 | 0 | 1 | L | R | 6-0 | 170 | 10-17-71 | 1993 | McIntyre, Pa. |
| Zahner, Kevin, c | .218 | 33 | 110 | 11 | 24 | 4 | 1 | 0 | 4 | 14 | 18 | 0 | 2 | R | R | 6-1 | 187 | 9-13-72 | 1991 | Rockville, Conn. |

| PITCHING | W | L | ERA | G | GS | CG | SV | IP | H | R | ER | BB | SO | B | T | HT | WT | DOB | 1st Yr | Resides |
|---|---|---|---|---|---|---|---|---|---|---|---|---|---|---|---|---|---|---|---|---|
| Baxter, Herbert | 4 | 1 | 3.44 | 25 | 0 | 0 | 0 | 50 | 41 | 35 | 19 | 38 | 54 | L | L | 6-1 | 159 | 8-25-71 | 1992 | Pinewood, S.C. |
| Binkley, Preston | 1 | 1 | 5.93 | 14 | 0 | 0 | 2 | 14 | 15 | 10 | 9 | 7 | 14 | L | L | 5-10 | 180 | 9-28-71 | 1993 | Lilburn, Ga. |
| Bland, Nathan | 4 | 6 | 2.84 | 16 | 13 | 0 | 0 | 63 | 54 | 34 | 20 | 29 | 43 | L | L | 6-4 | 186 | 12-27-74 | 1993 | Birmingham, Ala. |
| Botts, Jake | 1 | 6 | 6.80 | 13 | 9 | 0 | 0 | 48 | 56 | 48 | 36 | 45 | 40 | L | R | 6-2 | 215 | 8-5-72 | 1990 | Salinas, Calif. |
| Cook, Jim | 3 | 1 | 6.28 | 24 | 0 | 0 | 0 | 43 | 39 | 38 | 30 | 44 | 33 | R | R | 6-5 | 215 | 10-22-72 | 1992 | Pickens, S.C. |
| Duran, Roberto | 2 | 2 | 6.98 | 20 | 3 | 0 | 0 | 40 | 37 | 34 | 31 | 42 | 50 | L | L | 6-0 | 167 | 3-23-73 | 1990 | Moca, D.R. |
| Garcia, Jose | 2 | 2 | 2.42 | 36 | 0 | 0 | 5 | 45 | 40 | 14 | 12 | 19 | 19 | R | R | 6-3 | 175 | 6-12-72 | 1991 | Monte Cristi, D.R. |
| Groot, Franz | 2 | 6 | 7.56 | 12 | 7 | 0 | 0 | 42 | 48 | 42 | 35 | 37 | 27 | R | R | 6-6 | 187 | 11-3-70 | 1991 | Uithoorn, Holland |
| Iglesias, Mike | 0 | 3 | 7.63 | 10 | 5 | 0 | 0 | 31 | 42 | 29 | 26 | 21 | 24 | R | R | 6-5 | 215 | 11-9-72 | 1991 | Castro Valley, Calif. |
| Jacobsen, Joe | 1 | 0 | 2.39 | 25 | 0 | 0 | 3 | 38 | 27 | 16 | 10 | 28 | 55 | R | R | 6-4 | 230 | 12-26-71 | 1992 | Clovis, Calif. |
| Lagarde, Joe | 5 | 4 | 3.31 | 15 | 12 | 0 | 2 | 71 | 69 | 28 | 26 | 28 | 45 | R | R | 5-8 | 175 | 1-17-75 | 1993 | Winston-Salem, N.C. |
| Perez, Jayson | 0 | 0 | 4.13 | 17 | 0 | 0 | 0 | 28 | 26 | 16 | 13 | 19 | 14 | R | R | 6-2 | 152 | 6-27-74 | 1992 | Mayaguez, P.R. |
| Pincavitch, Kevin | 3 | 4 | 1.89 | 9 | 9 | 0 | 0 | 57 | 40 | 22 | 12 | 29 | 43 | R | R | 5-11 | 180 | 7-5-70 | 1992 | Greensboro, Pa. |
| Spykstra, David | 2 | 6 | 5.20 | 13 | 12 | 0 | 0 | 55 | 65 | 43 | 32 | 36 | 39 | R | R | 6-2 | 186 | 8-26-73 | 1992 | Denver, Colo. |
| Watts, Brandon | 0 | 2 | 8.00 | 2 | 2 | 0 | 0 | 9 | 8 | 8 | 8 | 7 | 12 | L | L | 6-3 | 190 | 9-13-72 | 1991 | Ruston, La. |
| Winslett, Dax | 0 | 2 | 5.51 | 8 | 4 | 0 | 1 | 33 | 46 | 23 | 20 | 10 | 25 | R | R | 6-2 | 212 | 1-1-72 | 1993 | Houston, Texas |

# GREAT FALLS

R

## PIONEER LEAGUE

| BATTING | AVG | G | AB | R | H | 2B | 3B | HR | RBI | BB | SO | SB | CS | B | T | HT | WT | DOB | 1st Yr | Resides |
|---|---|---|---|---|---|---|---|---|---|---|---|---|---|---|---|---|---|---|---|---|
| Anderson, Cliff, 2b-ss | .298 | 37 | 141 | 19 | 42 | 9 | 2 | 1 | 22 | 5 | 27 | 1 | 3 | L | R | 5-8 | 165 | 7-9-70 | 1992 | Kodiak, Ak |
| Biltimier, Mike, 1b | .240 | 69 | 250 | 35 | 60 | 12 | 0 | 3 | 29 | 35 | 62 | 1 | 4 | L | L | 6-1 | 215 | 10-30-70 | 1993 | Aurora, Colo. |
| Bostic, Dwaine, ss | .143 | 4 | 14 | 0 | 2 | 0 | 0 | 0 | 0 | 1 | 2 | 0 | 1 | R | R | 6-0 | 180 | 10-29-74 | 1992 | San Diego, Calif. |
| Breuer, Jim, of | .178 | 40 | 118 | 16 | 21 | 4 | 0 | 0 | 8 | 6 | 49 | 3 | 0 | R | R | 6-4 | 175 | 8-15-73 | 1993 | Bismarck, N.D. |
| Clark, Brian, dh | .182 | 9 | 11 | 0 | 2 | 1 | 0 | 0 | 4 | 5 | 1 | 1 | 0 | L | R | 6-3 | 195 | 4-15-73 | 1993 | Las Vegas, Nev. |
| Davis, Eddie, of | .224 | 60 | 205 | 32 | 46 | 8 | 1 | 8 | 44 | 28 | 54 | 11 | 10 | R | R | 6-0 | 185 | 12-22-70 | 1993 | New Orleans, La. |
| Dunn, Nathan, 2b-dh | .313 | 22 | 83 | 11 | 26 | 5 | 0 | 3 | 12 | 7 | 8 | 1 | 1 | R | R | 5-11 | 175 | 8-1-70 | 1992 | Harriman, Tenn. |
| Guerrero, Wilton, ss | .297 | 66 | 256 | 44 | 76 | 5 | 1 | 0 | 21 | 24 | 33 | 20 | 8 | R | R | 5-11 | 160 | 10-24-74 | 1992 | Santo Domingo, D.R. |
| Hernaiz, Juan, of | .349 | 52 | 186 | 24 | 65 | 7 | 2 | 3 | 19 | 3 | 42 | 8 | 5 | R | R | 5-11 | 168 | 2-15-75 | 1992 | Carolina, P.R. |
| Kinney, Mike, of | .232 | 50 | 164 | 23 | 38 | 6 | 3 | 0 | 16 | 13 | 44 | 10 | 3 | R | R | 5-11 | 200 | 8-25-71 | 1993 | Plano, Texas |
| Rash, Josh, of | .277 | 54 | 177 | 38 | 49 | 6 | 4 | 0 | 20 | 24 | 49 | 6 | 3 | R | R | 6-3 | 180 | 6-4-74 | 1993 | Arlington, Texas |
| Richardson, Brian, 3b | .225 | 54 | 178 | 16 | 40 | 11 | 0 | 0 | 13 | 14 | 47 | 1 | 2 | R | R | 6-2 | 186 | 8-31-75 | 1992 | Walnut, Calif. |
| Rios, Eduardo, 2b | .261 | 26 | 107 | 18 | 29 | 4 | 3 | 2 | 13 | 9 | 11 | 2 | 4 | R | R | 5-11 | 175 | 10-13-72 | 1991 | Charallave, Venez. |
| Romero, Wilfredo, of | .276 | 15 | 58 | 12 | 16 | 5 | 0 | 0 | 9 | 2 | 9 | 2 | 1 | R | R | 5-8 | 185 | 8-5-74 | 1993 | Candelaria, Venez. |
| Schwenke, Matt, c | .228 | 29 | 79 | 6 | 18 | 4 | 0 | 0 | 4 | 10 | 21 | 0 | 0 | S | R | 6-2 | 210 | 8-12-72 | 1993 | Poway, Calif. |
| Steed, Dave, c | .200 | 42 | 120 | 13 | 24 | 4 | 2 | 0 | 16 | 27 | 28 | 1 | 0 | R | R | 6-1 | 205 | 2-25-73 | 1993 | Starkville, Miss. |
| Watts, Craig, 1b-dh | .325 | 26 | 83 | 15 | 27 | 4 | 0 | 5 | 15 | 7 | 19 | 0 | 0 | R | R | 6-2 | 220 | 3-5-74 | 1991 | Glenside, Australia |
| Wingate, Ervan, 3b-2b | .198 | 38 | 126 | 13 | 25 | 12 | 1 | 0 | 18 | 15 | 21 | 0 | 0 | R | R | 6-0 | 175 | 2-4-74 | 1992 | Redlands, Calif. |
| Wittig, Paul, c | .273 | 15 | 44 | 4 | 12 | 1 | 0 | 0 | 5 | 6 | 17 | 1 | 0 | R | R | 6-1 | 190 | 7-31-73 | 1992 | Bremerton, Wash. |

| PITCHING | W | L | ERA | G | GS | CG | SV | IP | H | R | ER | BB | SO | B | T | HT | WT | DOB | 1st Yr | Resides |
|---|---|---|---|---|---|---|---|---|---|---|---|---|---|---|---|---|---|---|---|---|
| Ashworth, Kym | 3 | 3 | 2.44 | 11 | 11 | 0 | 0 | 59 | 43 | 25 | 16 | 14 | 52 | L | L | 6-2 | 185 | 7-31-76 | 1993 | Para Hills West, Australia |
| Camacho, Daniel | 5 | 2 | 1.38 | 28 | 0 | 0 | 5 | 65 | 38 | 14 | 10 | 18 | 79 | R | R | 5-11 | 197 | 11-11-73 | 1992 | San Diego, Calif. |
| Carpenter, Brian | 4 | 2 | 4.99 | 14 | 1 | 0 | 0 | 31 | 28 | 18 | 17 | 22 | 38 | R | R | 6-5 | 190 | 7-20-71 | 1993 | Texarkana, Texas |
| Costello, Chris | 4 | 2 | 3.21 | 12 | 12 | 0 | 0 | 70 | 61 | 30 | 25 | 26 | 59 | R | R | 6-5 | 240 | 9-20-72 | 1991 | Walpole, Mass. |
| Hubbs, Dan | 1 | 1 | 1.17 | 3 | 0 | 0 | 0 | 8 | 3 | 1 | 1 | 2 | 12 | R | R | 6-2 | 206 | 1-23-71 | 1993 | Renton, Wash. |
| Kenady, Jason | 5 | 5 | 3.79 | 17 | 10 | 0 | 0 | 59 | 52 | 27 | 25 | 30 | 54 | L | L | 6-4 | 205 | 9-21-73 | 1991 | Apple Valley, Minn. |
| Markham, Dan | 1 | 5 | 6.26 | 18 | 6 | 0 | 0 | 42 | 50 | 44 | 29 | 36 | 29 | L | L | 6-6 | 230 | 8-31-72 | 1992 | Concord, Calif. |
| Perez, George | 1 | 0 | 7.17 | 22 | 0 | 0 | 0 | 38 | 42 | 35 | 30 | 30 | 29 | R | L | 6-1 | 170 | 6-16-74 | 1993 | Rosemead, Calif. |
| Rolocut, Brian | 4 | 2 | 5.03 | 17 | 8 | 0 | 0 | 48 | 45 | 34 | 27 | 44 | 30 | R | R | 6-1 | 190 | 4-8-74 | 1993 | Gambrills, Md. |
| Rosario, Juan | 0 | 1 | 21.94 | 2 | 2 | 0 | 0 | 5 | 11 | 13 | 13 | 6 | 4 | R | R | 6-4 | 195 | 11-3-75 | 1993 | Perth Amboy, N.J. |
| Sarmiento, Dan | 2 | 3 | 6.35 | 6 | 4 | 0 | 0 | 23 | 20 | 18 | 16 | 14 | 15 | L | L | 6-0 | 200 | 3-28-74 | 1992 | Tempe, Ariz. |
| Scheffler, Craig | 5 | 3 | 5.75 | 15 | 10 | 1 | 1 | 61 | 68 | 46 | 39 | 27 | 56 | S | L | 6-2 | 195 | 9-13-71 | 1993 | Wausau, Wis. |
| Sikes, Ken | 1 | 1 | 7.01 | 16 | 4 | 0 | 1 | 44 | 52 | 40 | 34 | 39 | 37 | R | R | 6-5 | 245 | 1-25-73 | 1993 | Perry, Ga. |
| Troutman, Keith | 1 | 1 | 1.71 | 27 | 0 | 0 | 16 | 42 | 26 | 12 | 8 | 12 | 48 | R | R | 5-11 | 205 | 5-29-73 | 1992 | Candor, N.C. |
| Vukson, John | 0 | 4 | 9.10 | 16 | 4 | 0 | 0 | 30 | 37 | 42 | 30 | 45 | 24 | R | R | 6-3 | 190 | 10-27-75 | 1993 | Fresno, Calif. |

# MILWAUKEE BREWERS

**Manager:** Phil Garner.  **1993 Record:** 69-93, .426 (7th, AL East).

| BATTING | AVG | G | AB | R | H | 2B | 3B | HR | RBI | BB | SO | SB | CS | B | T | HT | WT | DOB | 1st Yr | Resides |
|---|---|---|---|---|---|---|---|---|---|---|---|---|---|---|---|---|---|---|---|---|
| Bell, Juan | .234 | 91 | 286 | 42 | 67 | 6 | 2 | 5 | 29 | 36 | 64 | 6 | 6 | S | R | 5-11 | 170 | 3-29-68 | 1985 | San Pedro de Macoris, D.R. |
| Brunansky, Tom | .183 | 80 | 224 | 20 | 41 | 7 | 3 | 6 | 29 | 25 | 59 | 3 | 4 | R | R | 6-4 | 220 | 8-20-60 | 1978 | San Diego, Calif. |
| Diaz, Alex | .319 | 32 | 69 | 9 | 22 | 2 | 0 | 0 | 1 | 0 | 12 | 5 | 3 | S | R | 5-11 | 175 | 10-5-68 | 1987 | San Sebastian, P.R. |
| Doran, Bill | .217 | 28 | 60 | 7 | 13 | 4 | 0 | 0 | 6 | 6 | 3 | 1 | 0 | S | R | 6-0 | 180 | 5-28-58 | 1979 | Cincinnati, Ohio |
| Hamilton, Darryl | .310 | 135 | 520 | 74 | 161 | 21 | 1 | 9 | 48 | 45 | 62 | 21 | 13 | L | R | 6-1 | 180 | 12-3-64 | 1986 | Houston, Texas |
| Jaha, John | .264 | 153 | 515 | 78 | 136 | 21 | 0 | 19 | 70 | 51 | 109 | 13 | 9 | R | R | 6-1 | 195 | 5-27-66 | 1985 | Portland, Ore. |
| Kmak, Joe | .218 | 51 | 110 | 9 | 24 | 5 | 0 | 0 | 7 | 14 | 13 | 6 | 2 | R | R | 6-0 | 185 | 5-3-63 | 1985 | Foster City, Calif. |
| Lampkin, Tom | .198 | 73 | 162 | 22 | 32 | 8 | 0 | 4 | 25 | 20 | 26 | 7 | 3 | L | R | 5-11 | 183 | 3-4-64 | 1986 | Boring, Ore. |
| Listach, Pat | .244 | 98 | 356 | 50 | 87 | 15 | 1 | 3 | 30 | 37 | 70 | 18 | 9 | S | R | 5-9 | 170 | 9-12-67 | 1988 | Waco, Texas |
| McIntosh, Tim | .000 | 1 | 0 | 0 | 0 | 0 | 0 | 0 | 0 | 0 | 0 | 0 | 0 | R | R | 5-11 | 195 | 3-21-65 | 1986 | Herald, Calif. |
| Mieske, Matt | .241 | 23 | 58 | 9 | 14 | 0 | 0 | 3 | 7 | 4 | 14 | 0 | 2 | R | R | 6-0 | 185 | 2-13-68 | 1990 | Auburn, Mich. |
| Nilsson, Dave | .257 | 100 | 296 | 35 | 76 | 10 | 2 | 7 | 40 | 37 | 36 | 3 | 6 | L | R | 6-3 | 185 | 12-14-69 | 1987 | Deagon, Australia |
| O'Leary, Troy | .293 | 19 | 41 | 3 | 12 | 3 | 0 | 0 | 3 | 5 | 9 | 0 | 0 | L | L | 6-0 | 175 | 8-4-69 | 1987 | Cypress, Calif. |
| Reimer, Kevin | .249 | 125 | 437 | 53 | 109 | 22 | 1 | 13 | 60 | 30 | 72 | 5 | 4 | L | R | 6-2 | 230 | 6-28-64 | 1985 | Enderby, B.C. |
| Seitzer, Kevin | .290 | 47 | 162 | 21 | 47 | 6 | 0 | 7 | 30 | 17 | 15 | 3 | 0 | R | R | 5-11 | 190 | 3-26-62 | 1983 | Overland Park, Kan. |
|  2-team (73 Oak.) | .269 | 120 | 417 | 45 | 112 | 16 | 2 | 11 | 57 | 44 | 48 | 7 | 7 | | | | | | | |
| Spiers, Bill | .238 | 113 | 340 | 43 | 81 | 8 | 4 | 2 | 36 | 29 | 51 | 9 | 8 | L | R | 6-2 | 190 | 6-5-66 | 1987 | Elloree, S.C. |
| Suero, William | .286 | 15 | 14 | 0 | 4 | 0 | 0 | 0 | 0 | 1 | 3 | 0 | 1 | R | R | 5-9 | 175 | 11-7-66 | 1985 | Santo Domingo, D.R. |
| Surhoff, B.J. | .274 | 148 | 552 | 66 | 151 | 38 | 3 | 7 | 79 | 36 | 47 | 12 | 9 | L | R | 6-1 | 200 | 8-4-65 | 1985 | Franklin, Wis. |
| Thon, Dickie | .269 | 85 | 245 | 23 | 66 | 10 | 1 | 1 | 33 | 22 | 39 | 6 | 5 | R | R | 5-11 | 178 | 6-20-58 | 1976 | Sugar Land, Texas |
| Valentin, Jose | .245 | 19 | 53 | 10 | 13 | 1 | 2 | 1 | 7 | 7 | 16 | 1 | 0 | S | R | 5-10 | 175 | 10-12-69 | 1987 | Manati, P.R. |
| Vaughn, Greg | .267 | 154 | 569 | 97 | 152 | 28 | 2 | 30 | 97 | 89 | 118 | 10 | 7 | R | R | 6-0 | 193 | 7-3-65 | 1986 | Elk Grove, Calif. |
| Yount, Robin | .258 | 127 | 454 | 62 | 117 | 25 | 3 | 8 | 51 | 44 | 93 | 9 | 2 | R | R | 6-0 | 180 | 9-16-55 | 1973 | Paradise Valley, Ariz. |

| PITCHING | W | L | ERA | G | GS | CG | SV | IP | H | R | ER | BB | SO | B | T | HT | WT | DOB | 1st Yr | Resides |
|---|---|---|---|---|---|---|---|---|---|---|---|---|---|---|---|---|---|---|---|---|
| Austin, Jim | 1 | 2 | 3.82 | 31 | 0 | 0 | 0 | 33 | 28 | 15 | 14 | 13 | 15 | R | R | 6-2 | 200 | 12-7-63 | 1986 | Richmond, Va. |
| Boddicker, Mike | 3 | 5 | 5.67 | 10 | 10 | 1 | 0 | 54 | 77 | 35 | 34 | 15 | 24 | R | R | 5-11 | 190 | 8-23-57 | 1978 | Overland Park, Kan. |
| Bones, Ricky | 11 | 11 | 4.86 | 32 | 31 | 3 | 0 | 204 | 222 | 122 | 110 | 63 | 63 | R | R | 6-0 | 190 | 4-7-69 | 1986 | Guayama, P.R. |
| Eldred, Cal | 16 | 16 | 4.01 | 36 | 36 | 8 | 0 | 258 | 232 | 120 | 115 | 91 | 180 | R | R | 6-4 | 215 | 11-24-67 | 1989 | Iowa City, Iowa |
| Fetters, Mike | 3 | 3 | 3.34 | 45 | 0 | 0 | 0 | 59 | 59 | 29 | 22 | 22 | 23 | R | R | 6-4 | 212 | 12-19-64 | 1986 | Kailua, Hawaii |
| Henry, Doug | 4 | 4 | 5.56 | 54 | 0 | 0 | 17 | 55 | 67 | 37 | 34 | 25 | 38 | R | R | 6-4 | 185 | 12-10-63 | 1986 | Hartland, Wis. |
| Higuera, Ted | 1 | 3 | 7.20 | 8 | 8 | 0 | 0 | 30 | 43 | 24 | 24 | 16 | 27 | S | L | 5-10 | 178 | 11-9-58 | 1979 | Chandler, Ariz. |
| Ignasiak, Mike | 1 | 1 | 3.65 | 27 | 0 | 0 | 0 | 37 | 32 | 17 | 15 | 21 | 28 | S | R | 5-10 | 180 | 3-12-66 | 1988 | Anchorville, Mich. |
| Kiefer, Mark | 0 | 0 | 0.00 | 6 | 0 | 0 | 1 | 9 | 3 | 0 | 0 | 5 | 7 | R | R | 6-3 | 185 | 11-13-68 | 1988 | Garden Grove, Calif. |
| Lloyd, Graeme | 3 | 4 | 2.83 | 55 | 0 | 0 | 0 | 64 | 64 | 24 | 20 | 13 | 31 | L | L | 6-7 | 215 | 4-9-67 | 1988 | Victoria, Australia |
| Maldonado, Carlos | 2 | 2 | 4.58 | 29 | 0 | 0 | 1 | 37 | 40 | 20 | 19 | 17 | 18 | R | R | 6-1 | 215 | 10-18-66 | 1986 | Chepo, Panama |
| Manzanillo, Josias | 1 | 1 | 9.53 | 10 | 1 | 0 | 1 | 17 | 22 | 20 | 18 | 10 | 10 | R | R | 6-0 | 190 | 10-16-67 | 1983 | San Pedro de Macoris, D.R. |
| Maysey, Matt | 1 | 2 | 5.73 | 23 | 0 | 0 | 1 | 22 | 28 | 14 | 14 | 13 | 10 | R | R | 6-4 | 225 | 1-8-67 | 1985 | Yuma, Ariz. |
| Miranda, Angel | 4 | 5 | 3.30 | 22 | 17 | 2 | 0 | 120 | 100 | 53 | 44 | 52 | 88 | L | L | 6-1 | 160 | 11-9-69 | 1987 | Bajadero, P.R. |
| Navarro, Jaime | 11 | 12 | 5.33 | 35 | 34 | 5 | 0 | 214 | 254 | 135 | 127 | 73 | 114 | R | R | 6-4 | 210 | 3-27-67 | 1987 | Orlando, Fla. |
| Novoa, Rafael | 0 | 3 | 4.50 | 15 | 7 | 2 | 0 | 56 | 58 | 32 | 28 | 22 | 17 | L | L | 6-1 | 180 | 10-26-67 | 1989 | Phoenix, Ariz. |
| Orosco, Jesse | 3 | 5 | 3.18 | 57 | 0 | 0 | 8 | 57 | 47 | 25 | 20 | 17 | 67 | R | L | 6-2 | 185 | 4-21-57 | 1978 | Poway, Calif. |
| Wegman, Bill | 4 | 14 | 4.48 | 20 | 18 | 5 | 0 | 121 | 135 | 70 | 60 | 34 | 50 | R | R | 6-5 | 220 | 12-19-62 | 1981 | Cincinnati, Ohio |

## FIELDING

| Catcher | PCT | G | PO | A | E | DP |
|---|---|---|---|---|---|---|
| Kmak | 1.000 | 50 | 172 | 23 | 0 | 4 |
| Lampkin | .978 | 60 | 242 | 24 | 6 | 2 |
| McIntosh | .000 | 1 | 0 | 0 | 0 | 0 |
| Nilsson | .981 | 91 | 430 | 30 | 9 | 3 |
| Surhoff | 1.000 | 3 | 9 | 0 | 0 | 0 |

| First Base | PCT | G | PO | A | E | DP |
|---|---|---|---|---|---|---|
| Doran | 1.000 | 4 | 16 | 2 | 0 | 2 |
| Jaha | .992 | 150 | 1186 | 128 | 10 | 116 |
| Nilsson | 1.000 | 4 | 27 | 3 | 0 | 3 |
| Seitzer | 1.000 | 7 | 43 | 1 | 0 | 4 |
| Surhoff | 1.000 | 8 | 28 | 2 | 0 | 2 |
| Yount | 1.000 | 7 | 43 | 1 | 0 | 7 |

| Second Base | PCT | G | PO | A | E | DP |
|---|---|---|---|---|---|---|
| Bell | .983 | 47 | 115 | 114 | 4 | 33 |
| Doran | .964 | 17 | 28 | 26 | 2 | 5 |
| Jaha | 1.000 | 1 | 1 | 0 | 0 | 0 |

| | PCT | G | PO | A | E | DP |
|---|---|---|---|---|---|---|
| Seitzer | 1.000 | 1 | 1 | 1 | 0 | 1 |
| Spiers | .971 | 104 | 209 | 226 | 13 | 53 |
| Suero | .944 | 8 | 5 | 12 | 1 | 1 |
| Thon | .960 | 22 | 40 | 32 | 3 | 9 |

| Third Base | PCT | G | PO | A | E | DP |
|---|---|---|---|---|---|---|
| Jaha | .000 | 1 | 0 | 0 | 0 | 0 |
| Seitzer | .942 | 33 | 22 | 59 | 5 | 7 |
| Suero | 1.000 | 1 | 1 | 1 | 0 | 1 |
| Surhoff | .949 | 121 | 101 | 216 | 17 | 19 |
| Thon | .977 | 25 | 12 | 30 | 1 | 2 |

| Shortstop | PCT | G | PO | A | E | DP |
|---|---|---|---|---|---|---|
| Bell | .962 | 40 | 67 | 110 | 7 | 20 |
| Listach | .975 | 95 | 127 | 267 | 10 | 53 |
| Seitzer | 1.000 | 1 | 1 | 1 | 0 | 0 |
| Spiers | 1.000 | 4 | 1 | 4 | 0 | 2 |
| Thon | .966 | 28 | 28 | 57 | 3 | 8 |

| | PCT | G | PO | A | E | DP |
|---|---|---|---|---|---|---|
| Valentin | .922 | 19 | 20 | 51 | 6 | 9 |

| Outfield | PCT | G | PO | A | E | DP |
|---|---|---|---|---|---|---|
| Bell | .750 | 3 | 3 | 0 | 1 | 0 |
| Bones | .000 | 1 | 0 | 0 | 0 | 0 |
| Brunansky | .987 | 71 | 146 | 4 | 2 | 0 |
| Diaz | .979 | 28 | 46 | 1 | 1 | 0 |
| Hamilton | .992 | 129 | 340 | 10 | 3 | 1 |
| Lampkin | .000 | 3 | 0 | 0 | 0 | 0 |
| Listach | 1.000 | 6 | 8 | 0 | 0 | 0 |
| Mieske | .936 | 22 | 43 | 1 | 3 | 0 |
| O'Leary | 1.000 | 19 | 32 | 1 | 0 | 0 |
| Reimer | .962 | 37 | 75 | 1 | 3 | 0 |
| Seitzer | 1.000 | 1 | 4 | 0 | 0 | 0 |
| Spiers | 1.000 | 7 | 3 | 1 | 0 | 0 |
| Surhoff | .975 | 24 | 37 | 2 | 1 | 0 |
| Vaughn | .986 | 94 | 214 | 1 | 3 | 1 |
| Yount | .997 | 114 | 299 | 6 | 1 | 1 |

# BREWERS FARM SYSTEM

| Class | Club | League | W | L | Pct. | Finish* | Manager(s) | First Year |
|---|---|---|---|---|---|---|---|---|
| AAA | New Orleans (La.) Zephyrs | American Assoc. | 80 | 64 | .556 | 3rd (8) | Chris Bando | 1993 |
| AA | El Paso (Texas) Diablos | Texas | 75 | 59 | .560 | 1st (8) | Tim Ireland | 1981 |
| A# | Stockton (Calif.) Ports | California | 79 | 57 | .581 | T-2nd (10) | Lamar Johnson | 1979 |

**Cal Eldred.** Brewers righthander proved to be a workhorse in 1993, pitching an American League-high 258 innings.

**B.J. Surhoff.** Moving from catcher to third base, Surhoff hit .274 and led the Brewers with 38 doubles.

R&R SPORTS GROUP

| Class | Club | League | W | L | Pct. | Finish* | Manager(s) | First Year |
|---|---|---|---|---|---|---|---|---|
| A | Beloit (Wis.) Brewers | Midwest | 60 | 74 | .448 | 10th (14) | Wayne Krenchicki | 1982 |
| Rookie# | Helena (Mont.) Brewers | Pioneer | 43 | 30 | .589 | 2nd (8) | M. Epstein, H. Dunlop | 1985 |
| Rookie | Chandler (Ariz.) Brewers | Arizona | 29 | 27 | .518 | 5th (8) | Ralph Dickenson | 1988 |

*Finish in overall standings (No. of teams in league)   #Advanced level

# NEW ORLEANS                                                          AAA
## AMERICAN ASSOCIATION

| BATTING | AVG | G | AB | R | H | 2B | 3B | HR | RBI | BB | SO | SB | CS | B | T | HT | WT | DOB | 1st Yr | Resides |
|---|---|---|---|---|---|---|---|---|---|---|---|---|---|---|---|---|---|---|---|---|
| Barbara, Don | .294 | 84 | 255 | 34 | 75 | 10 | 1 | 4 | 38 | 42 | 38 | 1 | 3 | L | L | 6-2 | 215 | 10-27-68 | 1990 | Long Beach, Calif. |
| Byington, John | .280 | 123 | 436 | 58 | 122 | 33 | 2 | 11 | 63 | 35 | 32 | 3 | 2 | R | R | 5-8 | 165 | 11-4-67 | 1989 | Baytown, Tenn. |
| Caceres, Edgar | .317 | 114 | 420 | 73 | 133 | 20 | 2 | 5 | 45 | 35 | 39 | 7 | 4 | S | R | 6-1 | 170 | 6-6-64 | 1984 | Barquisimeto, Venez. |
| Carter, Michael | .276 | 104 | 369 | 49 | 102 | 18 | 5 | 3 | 31 | 17 | 52 | 20 | 11 | R | R | 5-9 | 170 | 5-5-69 | 1990 | Vicksburg, Miss. |
| Cirillo, Jeff | .293 | 58 | 215 | 31 | 63 | 13 | 2 | 3 | 32 | 29 | 33 | 2 | 1 | R | R | 6-2 | 190 | 9-23-69 | 1991 | Van Nuys, Calif. |
| Davis, Mark | .174 | 10 | 23 | 4 | 4 | 1 | 1 | 1 | 2 | 3 | 11 | 0 | 1 | R | R | 6-0 | 190 | 11-25-64 | 1986 | Lemon Grove, Calif. |
| Diaz, Alex | .291 | 16 | 55 | 8 | 16 | 2 | 0 | 0 | 5 | 3 | 6 | 7 | 0 | S | R | 5-11 | 175 | 10-5-68 | 1987 | San Sebastian, P.R. |
| Diggs, Tony | .259 | 11 | 27 | 4 | 7 | 3 | 0 | 0 | 1 | 3 | 6 | 4 | 2 | S | R | 6-0 | 175 | 4-20-67 | 1989 | Starke, Fla. |
| Finn, John | .281 | 117 | 335 | 47 | 94 | 13 | 2 | 1 | 37 | 33 | 36 | 27 | 9 | R | R | 5-8 | 168 | 10-18-67 | 1989 | Oakland, Calif. |
| Fitzgerald, Mike | .259 | 102 | 297 | 35 | 77 | 21 | 0 | 7 | 35 | 35 | 45 | 3 | 2 | R | R | 6-0 | 185 | 7-13-60 | 1978 | Lakewood, Calif. |
| Housie, Wayne | .274 | 64 | 113 | 22 | 31 | 6 | 1 | 0 | 7 | 18 | 21 | 6 | 2 | S | R | 5-9 | 165 | 5-20-65 | 1986 | Riverside, Calif. |
| Kappesser, Bob | .091 | 4 | 11 | 0 | 1 | 1 | 0 | 0 | 2 | 1 | 4 | 0 | 0 | R | R | 5-9 | 185 | 2-14-67 | 1989 | Auburn, N.Y. |
| Kmak, Joe | .303 | 24 | 76 | 9 | 23 | 3 | 2 | 1 | 13 | 8 | 14 | 1 | 0 | R | R | 6-0 | 185 | 5-3-63 | 1985 | Foster City, Calif. |
| Kremers, Jimmy | .265 | 51 | 155 | 29 | 41 | 10 | 0 | 9 | 26 | 21 | 44 | 0 | 0 | L | R | 6-3 | 200 | 10-8-65 | 1988 | North Little Rock, Ark. |
| Lampkin, Tom | .325 | 25 | 80 | 18 | 26 | 5 | 0 | 2 | 10 | 18 | 4 | 5 | 4 | L | R | 5-11 | 183 | 3-4-64 | 1986 | Boring, Ore. |
| Lukachyk, Rob | .167 | 8 | 24 | 5 | 4 | 1 | 0 | 0 | 4 | 3 | 6 | 0 | 0 | L | R | 6-0 | 185 | 7-24-68 | 1987 | Highlands, N.J. |
| Mieske, Matt | .260 | 60 | 219 | 36 | 57 | 14 | 2 | 8 | 22 | 27 | 46 | 6 | 4 | R | R | 6-0 | 185 | 2-13-68 | 1990 | Auburn, Mich. |
| Nilsson, Dave | .344 | 17 | 61 | 9 | 21 | 6 | 1 | 1 | 9 | 5 | 6 | 0 | 1 | L | R | 6-3 | 185 | 12-14-69 | 1987 | Deagon, Australia |
| O'Leary, Troy | .273 | 111 | 388 | 65 | 106 | 32 | 1 | 7 | 59 | 43 | 61 | 6 | 3 | L | L | 6-0 | 175 | 8-4-69 | 1987 | Cypress, Calif. |
| Riesgo, Nikco | .291 | 27 | 79 | 9 | 23 | 5 | 3 | 1 | 12 | 3 | 16 | 0 | 1 | R | R | 6-2 | 185 | 1-11-67 | 1988 | Clarinda, Iowa |
| Sheets, Larry | .280 | 127 | 457 | 60 | 128 | 28 | 1 | 18 | 98 | 31 | 52 | 3 | 6 | L | R | 6-3 | 230 | 12-6-59 | 1978 | Lutherville, Md. |
| Suero, William | .226 | 46 | 124 | 14 | 28 | 4 | 1 | 1 | 13 | 21 | 17 | 8 | 7 | R | R | 5-9 | 175 | 11-7-66 | 1985 | Santo Domingo, D.R. |
| Valentin, Jose | .247 | 122 | 389 | 56 | 96 | 22 | 5 | 9 | 53 | 47 | 87 | 9 | 10 | S | R | 5-10 | 175 | 10-12-69 | 1987 | Manati, P.R. |
| Williams, Eddie | .259 | 8 | 27 | 2 | 7 | 0 | 1 | 1 | 4 | 7 | 4 | 0 | 0 | R | R | 6-0 | 175 | 11-1-64 | 1983 | La Mesa, Calif. |
| Yacopino, Ed | .203 | 23 | 69 | 7 | 14 | 3 | 1 | 0 | 0 | 11 | 9 | 0 | 1 | S | L | 6-0 | 170 | 9-19-65 | 1987 | Aliquippa, Pa. |

| PITCHING | W | L | ERA | G | GS | CG | SV | IP | H | R | ER | BB | SO | B | T | HT | WT | DOB | 1st Yr | Resides |
|---|---|---|---|---|---|---|---|---|---|---|---|---|---|---|---|---|---|---|---|---|
| Austin, Jim | 1 | 2 | 5.06 | 8 | 3 | 0 | 0 | 16 | 17 | 11 | 9 | 7 | 7 | R | R | 6-2 | 200 | 12-7-63 | 1986 | Richmond, Va. |
| Cole, Victor | 0 | 2 | 10.50 | 6 | 1 | 0 | 0 | 6 | 9 | 7 | 7 | 7 | 5 | S | R | 5-10 | 160 | 1-23-68 | 1988 | Monterey, Calif. |
| 2-team (6 Buffalo) | 1 | 5 | 8.91 | 12 | 7 | 0 | 0 | 33 | 44 | 32 | 32 | 31 | 19 | | | | | | | |
| Farmer, Howard | 4 | 3 | 5.73 | 20 | 13 | 1 | 0 | 75 | 93 | 52 | 48 | 24 | 55 | R | R | 6-2 | 184 | 1-18-66 | 1987 | Gary, Ind. |
| Farrell, Mike | 9 | 9 | 4.86 | 26 | 26 | 3 | 0 | 152 | 164 | 92 | 82 | 32 | 63 | L | L | 6-2 | 184 | 1-28-69 | 1991 | Logansport, Ind. |
| Higuera, Ted | 0 | 1 | 9.00 | 3 | 3 | 0 | 0 | 8 | 11 | 11 | 8 | 7 | 7 | S | L | 5-10 | 178 | 11-9-58 | 1979 | Chandler, Ariz. |
| Hunter, Jim | 5 | 2 | 4.19 | 39 | 3 | 0 | 1 | 69 | 82 | 40 | 32 | 25 | 35 | R | R | 6-3 | 205 | 6-22-64 | 1985 | Middletown, N.J. |
| Ignasiak, Mike | 6 | 0 | 1.09 | 35 | 0 | 0 | 9 | 58 | 26 | 10 | 7 | 20 | 61 | S | R | 5-10 | 180 | 3-12-66 | 1988 | Anchorville, Mich. |
| Johnson, Dane | 0 | 0 | 2.40 | 13 | 0 | 0 | 6 | 15 | 11 | 4 | 4 | 4 | 10 | R | R | 6-5 | 205 | 2-10-63 | 1993 | Miami, Fla. |
| Kiefer, Mark | 3 | 2 | 5.08 | 5 | 5 | 0 | 0 | 28 | 28 | 20 | 16 | 17 | 23 | R | R | 6-3 | 185 | 11-13-68 | 1988 | Garden Grove, Calif. |

## PITCHING

| PITCHING | W | L | ERA | G | GS | CG | SV | IP | H | R | ER | BB | SO | B | T | HT | WT | DOB | 1st Yr | Resides |
|---|---|---|---|---|---|---|---|---|---|---|---|---|---|---|---|---|---|---|---|---|
| Kiser, Garland | 5 | 4 | 5.40 | 50 | 4 | 0 | 1 | 67 | 69 | 43 | 40 | 24 | 42 | L | L | 6-3 | 190 | 7-8-68 | 1986 | Blountville, Tenn. |
| Maldonado, Carlos | 1 | 0 | 0.47 | 12 | 0 | 0 | 7 | 19 | 13 | 1 | 1 | 7 | 14 | R | R | 6-1 | 215 | 10-18-66 | 1986 | Chepo, Panama |
| Manzanillo, Josias | 0 | 1 | 9.00 | 1 | 0 | 0 | 0 | 1 | 1 | 1 | 1 | 1 | 3 | R | R | 6-0 | 190 | 10-16-67 | 1983 | San Pedro de Macoris, D.R. |
| Maysey, Matt | 0 | 3 | 4.13 | 29 | 5 | 0 | 2 | 52 | 48 | 25 | 24 | 14 | 40 | R | R | 6-4 | 225 | 1-8-67 | 1985 | Yuma, Ariz. |
| McAndrew, Jamie | 11 | 6 | 3.94 | 27 | 25 | 5 | 0 | 167 | 172 | 78 | 73 | 45 | 97 | R | R | 6-1 | 200 | 9-2-67 | 1989 | Paducah, Ky. |
| Miranda, Angel | 0 | 1 | 3.44 | 9 | 2 | 0 | 0 | 18 | 11 | 8 | 7 | 10 | 24 | L | L | 6-1 | 160 | 11-9-69 | 1987 | Bajadero, P.R. |
| Nolte, Eric | 0 | 0 | 6.35 | 7 | 0 | 0 | 0 | 6 | 7 | 4 | 4 | 2 | 3 | L | L | 6-3 | 210 | 4-28-64 | 1985 | Hemet, Calif. |
| Novoa, Rafael | 10 | 5 | 3.42 | 20 | 18 | 2 | 0 | 113 | 105 | 55 | 43 | 38 | 74 | L | L | 6-1 | 180 | 10-26-67 | 1989 | Phoenix, Ariz. |
| Rightnowar, Ron | 0 | 0 | 10.38 | 4 | 0 | 0 | 0 | 9 | 19 | 10 | 10 | 2 | 8 | R | R | 5-9 | 180 | 9-5-64 | 1987 | Toledo, Ohio |
| Sparks, Steve | 9 | 13 | 3.84 | 29 | 28 | 7 | 0 | 180 | 174 | 89 | 77 | 80 | 104 | R | R | 6-0 | 180 | 7-2-65 | 1987 | Tulsa, Okla. |
| Tabaka, Jeff | 6 | 6 | 3.24 | 53 | 0 | 0 | 1 | 58 | 50 | 26 | 21 | 30 | 63 | R | L | 6-0 | 190 | 1-17-64 | 1986 | Akron, Ohio |
| Taylor, Scott | 5 | 1 | 2.31 | 12 | 8 | 1 | 0 | 62 | 48 | 17 | 16 | 21 | 47 | R | R | 6-3 | 200 | 10-3-66 | 1989 | Wichita, Kan. |
| Wishnevski, Rob | 5 | 3 | 4.09 | 52 | 0 | 0 | 10 | 70 | 68 | 34 | 32 | 17 | 72 | R | R | 6-1 | 215 | 1-2-67 | 1987 | Valparaiso, Ind. |

## FIELDING

| Catcher | PCT | G | PO | A | E | DP |
|---|---|---|---|---|---|---|
| Fitzgerald | .990 | 65 | 362 | 26 | 4 | 8 |
| Kappesser | .964 | 4 | 22 | 5 | 1 | 0 |
| Kmak | .984 | 20 | 106 | 18 | 2 | 1 |
| Kremers | .978 | 38 | 202 | 19 | 5 | 2 |
| Lampkin | .982 | 20 | 150 | 12 | 3 | 1 |
| Nilsson | .984 | 11 | 55 | 7 | 1 | 1 |

| First Base | PCT | G | PO | A | E | DP |
|---|---|---|---|---|---|---|
| Barbara | .994 | 81 | 676 | 44 | 4 | 61 |
| Byington | 1.000 | 19 | 129 | 11 | 0 | 15 |
| Caceres | .993 | 26 | 134 | 13 | 1 | 18 |
| Fitzgerald | .941 | 5 | 26 | 6 | 2 | 3 |
| Kiser | 1.000 | 1 | 1 | 0 | 0 | 0 |
| Kremers | .983 | 5 | 52 | 5 | 1 | 12 |
| O'Leary | 1.000 | 1 | 2 | 0 | 0 | 0 |
| Riesgo | 1.000 | 3 | 22 | 1 | 0 | 3 |
| Sheets | .994 | 24 | 155 | 9 | 1 | 14 |
| Suero | 1.000 | 2 | 10 | 0 | 0 | 0 |
| Valentin | 1.000 | 1 | 1 | 0 | 0 | 0 |
| Williams | 1.000 | 1 | 6 | 1 | 0 | 0 |

| Second Base | PCT | G | PO | A | E | DP |
|---|---|---|---|---|---|---|
| Byington | .914 | 7 | 13 | 19 | 3 | 6 |

| | PCT | G | PO | A | E | DP |
|---|---|---|---|---|---|---|
| Caceres | .983 | 63 | 115 | 175 | 5 | 42 |
| Carter | 1.000 | 1 | 1 | 1 | 0 | 0 |
| Cirillo | 1.000 | 4 | 4 | 13 | 0 | 5 |
| Finn | .968 | 56 | 97 | 116 | 7 | 29 |
| Suero | .953 | 36 | 70 | 72 | 7 | 19 |

| Third Base | PCT | G | PO | A | E | DP |
|---|---|---|---|---|---|---|
| Byington | .971 | 82 | 67 | 165 | 7 | 16 |
| Caceres | 1.000 | 9 | 7 | 15 | 0 | 2 |
| Cirillo | .972 | 53 | 42 | 129 | 5 | 18 |
| Finn | 1.000 | 4 | 2 | 3 | 0 | 0 |
| Fitzgerald | .000 | 1 | 0 | 0 | 0 | 0 |
| Riesgo | .000 | 1 | 0 | 0 | 0 | 0 |
| Williams | .952 | 6 | 8 | 12 | 1 | 1 |

| Shortstop | PCT | G | PO | A | E | DP |
|---|---|---|---|---|---|---|
| Caceres | .976 | 27 | 25 | 55 | 2 | 11 |
| Carter | 1.000 | 1 | 0 | 1 | 0 | 1 |
| Cirillo | 1.000 | 1 | 0 | 3 | 0 | 0 |
| Finn | .958 | 9 | 10 | 13 | 1 | 3 |
| Riesgo | .714 | 2 | 0 | 5 | 2 | 0 |
| Valentin | .951 | 119 | 211 | 351 | 29 | 80 |

| Outfield | PCT | G | PO | A | E | DP |
|---|---|---|---|---|---|---|
| Caceres | 1.000 | 1 | 1 | 1 | 0 | 1 |
| Carter | .977 | 100 | 243 | 9 | 6 | 1 |
| Davis | 1.000 | 6 | 15 | 1 | 0 | 0 |
| Diaz | 1.000 | 13 | 38 | 1 | 0 | 0 |
| Diggs | 1.000 | 10 | 25 | 1 | 0 | 0 |
| Farrell | .000 | 1 | 0 | 0 | 0 | 0 |
| Finn | .960 | 52 | 66 | 6 | 3 | 0 |
| Fitzgerald | 1.000 | 3 | 1 | 0 | 0 | 0 |
| Housie | 1.000 | 59 | 86 | 3 | 0 | 1 |
| Kremers | 1.000 | 1 | 0 | 0 | 0 | 0 |
| Lampkin | 1.000 | 2 | 2 | 0 | 0 | 0 |
| Lukachyk | 1.000 | 8 | 14 | 0 | 0 | 0 |
| McAndrew | 1.000 | 1 | 1 | 0 | 0 | 0 |
| Mieske | .983 | 57 | 114 | 4 | 2 | 0 |
| O'Leary | .970 | 110 | 187 | 8 | 6 | 1 |
| Riesgo | 1.000 | 1 | 26 | 0 | 0 | 0 |
| Sheets | 1.000 | 32 | 38 | 4 | 0 | 1 |
| Sparks | 1.000 | 1 | 1 | 0 | 0 | 0 |
| Suero | 1.000 | 1 | 3 | 0 | 0 | 0 |
| Valentin | .000 | 1 | 0 | 0 | 0 | 0 |
| Yacopino | .978 | 23 | 44 | 1 | 1 | 0 |

# EL PASO — AA

## TEXAS LEAGUE

| BATTING | AVG | G | AB | R | H | 2B | 3B | HR | RBI | BB | SO | SB | CS | B | T | HT | WT | DOB | 1st Yr | Resides |
|---|---|---|---|---|---|---|---|---|---|---|---|---|---|---|---|---|---|---|---|---|
| Basse, Mike, of | .267 | 108 | 386 | 65 | 103 | 14 | 5 | 1 | 36 | 51 | 72 | 26 | 13 | L | L | 6-0 | 180 | 3-7-70 | 1991 | San Juan Capistrano, Calif. |
| Campillo, Rob, c | .000 | 4 | 11 | 0 | 0 | 0 | 0 | 0 | 0 | 0 | 3 | 0 | 0 | R | R | 5-11 | 195 | 11-2-70 | 1992 | Tucson, Ariz. |
| Carter, Michael, of | .370 | 17 | 73 | 16 | 27 | 4 | 1 | 2 | 16 | 3 | 7 | 6 | 4 | R | R | 5-9 | 170 | 5-5-69 | 1990 | Vicksburg, Miss. |
| Castleberry, Kevin, 2b | .300 | 98 | 327 | 46 | 98 | 9 | 5 | 2 | 49 | 26 | 38 | 13 | 3 | L | R | 5-9 | 160 | 4-22-68 | 1989 | Norman, Okla. |
| Cirillo, Jeff, 2b-3b | .341 | 67 | 249 | 53 | 85 | 16 | 2 | 9 | 41 | 26 | 37 | 2 | 3 | R | R | 6-2 | 190 | 9-23-69 | 1991 | Van Nuys, Calif. |
| Cole, Mark, 2b-3b | .313 | 5 | 16 | 3 | 5 | 1 | 0 | 0 | 1 | 2 | 5 | 1 | 0 | S | R | 5-9 | 175 | 4-18-67 | 1989 | Sacramento, Calif. |
| Couture, Mike, of | .000 | 4 | 0 | 0 | 0 | 0 | 0 | 0 | 0 | 0 | 0 | 0 | 0 | R | R | 6-2 | 185 | 3-23-68 | 1990 | Surfside Beach, S.C. |
| Diggs, Tony, of | .143 | 18 | 63 | 5 | 9 | 1 | 0 | 1 | 3 | 1 | 14 | 3 | 0 | S | R | 6-0 | 175 | 4-20-67 | 1988 | Starke, Fla. |
| Dodson, Bill, 1b | .312 | 101 | 330 | 58 | 103 | 27 | 4 | 9 | 59 | 42 | 69 | 1 | 6 | L | L | 6-3 | 200 | 12-7-70 | 1989 | West Sacramento, Calif. |
| Doran, Bill, 2b | .364 | 5 | 11 | 3 | 4 | 1 | 0 | 0 | 3 | 2 | 0 | 0 | 0 | S | R | 6-0 | 180 | 5-28-58 | 1979 | Cincinnati, Ohio |
| Gill, Steve, of-1b | .249 | 70 | 229 | 35 | 57 | 13 | 4 | 2 | 30 | 21 | 40 | 8 | 7 | L | L | 6-1 | 170 | 11-17-68 | 1990 | Anaheim, Calif. |
|   2-team (39 Wichita) | .246 | 109 | 329 | 50 | 81 | 18 | 4 | 5 | 43 | 28 | 67 | 14 | 12 | | | | | | | |
| Kappesser, Bob, c | .249 | 67 | 173 | 25 | 43 | 9 | 1 | 2 | 23 | 20 | 29 | 7 | 3 | R | R | 5-9 | 180 | 2-14-67 | 1989 | Auburn, N.Y. |
| Lewis, Alan, 3b | .258 | 113 | 380 | 53 | 98 | 22 | 5 | 4 | 48 | 57 | 58 | 4 | 3 | L | R | 5-11 | 180 | 8-3-66 | 1987 | Charlotte, N.C. |
| Lofton, Rodney, 2b-3b | .265 | 67 | 200 | 39 | 53 | 8 | 5 | 2 | 21 | 13 | 40 | 16 | 1 | R | R | 6-0 | 175 | 10-7-67 | 1988 | East St. Louis, Ill. |
| Lukachyk, Rob, of | .265 | 113 | 362 | 58 | 96 | 24 | 7 | 9 | 63 | 52 | 75 | 8 | 10 | L | R | 6-0 | 185 | 7-24-68 | 1987 | Highlands, N.J. |
| Matheny, Mike, c | .254 | 107 | 339 | 39 | 86 | 21 | 2 | 2 | 28 | 17 | 73 | 1 | 4 | S | R | 6-3 | 205 | 9-22-70 | 1991 | Reynoldsburg, Ohio |

**BREWERS TOP 10 PROSPECTS**

How the Brewers Top 10 prospects, as judged by Baseball America prior to the 1993 season, fared in 1993:

| Player, Pos. | Club (Class) | AVG | AB | H | HR | RBI | SB |
|---|---|---|---|---|---|---|---|
| 2. Matt Mieske, of | New Orl. (AAA) | .260 | 219 | 57 | 8 | 22 | 6 |
| | Milwaukee | .241 | 58 | 14 | 3 | 7 | 0 |
| 5. Troy O'Leary, of | New Orl. (AAA) | .273 | 388 | 106 | 7 | 59 | 6 |
| | Milwaukee | .293 | 41 | 12 | 0 | 3 | 0 |
| 6. Jose Valentin, ss | New Orl. (AAA) | .247 | 389 | 96 | 9 | 53 | 9 |
| | Milwaukee | .245 | 53 | 13 | 1 | 7 | 1 |
| 7. Kenny Felder, of | Beloit (A) | .182 | 99 | 18 | 3 | 8 | 1 |
| 8. Duane Singleton, of | El Paso (AA) | .230 | 456 | 105 | 2 | 61 | 23 |

| | | W | L | ERA | IP | H | BB | SO |
|---|---|---|---|---|---|---|---|---|
| 1. Tyrone Hill, lhp | Stockton (A) | 1 | 3 | 4.50 | 66 | 43 | 60 | 65 |
| 3. Mark Kiefer, rhp | El Paso (AA) | 3 | 4 | 4.01 | 52 | 48 | 19 | 44 |
| | New Orl. (AAA) | 3 | 2 | 5.08 | 28 | 28 | 17 | 32 |
| | Milwaukee | 0 | 0 | 0.00 | 9 | 3 | 5 | 7 |
| 4. Mike Farrell, lhp | New Orl. (AAA) | 9 | 4 | 4.86 | 152 | 164 | 32 | 63 |
| 9. Marshall Boze, rhp | Stockton (A) | 7 | 2 | 2.65 | 88 | 82 | 41 | 54 |
| | El Paso (AA) | 10 | 3 | 2.71 | 86 | 78 | 32 | 48 |
| 10. Angel Miranda, lhp | New Orl. (AAA) | 0 | 1 | 3.44 | 18 | 11 | 10 | 24 |
| | Milwaukee | 4 | 5 | 3.30 | 120 | 100 | 52 | 88 |

**Tyrone Hill**
1-3 at Class A

# BREWERS: MOST COMMON LINEUPS

| | Milwaukee | New Orleans | El Paso | Stockton | Beloit |
|---|---|---|---|---|---|
| | **Majors** | AAA | AA | A | A |
| **C** | Dave Nilsson (91) | Mike Fitzgerald (65) | Mike Matheny (102) | Mike Stefanski (80) | Bobby Hughes (76) |
| **1B** | John Jaha (150) | Don Barbara (81) | Bo Dodson (88) | Andy Fairman (90) | Scott Talanoa (73) |
| **2B** | Bill Spiers (104) | Edgar Caceres (63) | Kevin Castleberry (64) | Kevin Riggs (87) | Scott Richardson (94) |
| **3B** | B.J. Surhoff (121) | John Byington (82) | Alan Lewis (83) | Tim Unroe (104) | Mike Boyzuick (95) |
| **SS** | Pat Listach (95) | Jose Valentin (119) | Wes Weger (122) | Mike Huyler (75) | Gabby Martinez (92) |
| **OF** | Darryl Hamilton (129) | Troy O'Leary (99) | Duane Singleton (122) | Todd Samples (124) | Jackie Ross (114) |
| | Robin Yount (114) | Michael Carter (97) | Rob Lukachyk (97) | Mike Harris (109) | Cecil Rodrigues (102) |
| | Greg Vaughn (94) | Matt Mieske (57) | Mike Basse (93) | Tony Diggs (82) | Danny Perez (96) |
| **DH** | Kevin Reimer (93) | Larry Sheets (71) | Ed Smith (39) | Derek Wachter (51) | Gordon Powell (38) |
| **SP** | Cal Eldred (36) | Steve Sparks (28) | Scott Karl (27) | Byron Browne (27) | Robert Jones (25) |
| **RP** | Jesse Orosco (57) | Jeff Tabaka (53) | Kurt Archer (49) | Billy Hardwick (61) | Kirk Demyan (40) |
| | Full-season farm clubs only | No. of games at position in parenthesis | | | |

## BATTING

| | AVG | G | AB | R | H | 2B | 3B | HR | RBI | BB | SO | SB | CS | B | T | HT | WT | DOB | 1st Yr | Resides |
|---|---|---|---|---|---|---|---|---|---|---|---|---|---|---|---|---|---|---|---|---|
| Nilsson, Dave, c | .471 | 5 | 17 | 5 | 8 | 1 | 0 | 1 | 7 | 2 | 4 | 1 | 1 | L | R | 6-3 | 185 | 12-14-69 | 1987 | Deagon, Australia |
| Riesgo, Nikco, dh-1b | .280 | 30 | 93 | 15 | 26 | 6 | 1 | 7 | 21 | 9 | 23 | 2 | 0 | R | R | 6-2 | 185 | 1-11-67 | 1988 | Clarinda, Iowa |
| Singleton, Duane, of | .230 | 125 | 456 | 52 | 105 | 21 | 6 | 2 | 61 | 34 | 90 | 23 | 19 | L | R | 6-1 | 170 | 8-6-72 | 1990 | Staten Island, N.Y. |
| Smith, Ed, 1b-dh | .294 | 118 | 419 | 64 | 123 | 23 | 6 | 8 | 69 | 38 | 97 | 13 | 5 | R | R | 6-4 | 220 | 6-5-69 | 1987 | Browns Mills, N.J. |
| Weger, Wes, ss | .291 | 123 | 471 | 69 | 137 | 24 | 5 | 5 | 53 | 31 | 44 | 9 | 9 | R | R | 6-1 | 170 | 10-3-70 | 1992 | Longwood, Fla. |

## PITCHING

| | W | L | ERA | G | GS | CG | SV | IP | H | R | ER | BB | SO | B | T | HT | WT | DOB | 1st Yr | Resides |
|---|---|---|---|---|---|---|---|---|---|---|---|---|---|---|---|---|---|---|---|---|
| Archer, Kurt | 9 | 8 | 4.90 | 54 | 5 | 0 | 11 | 105 | 129 | 63 | 57 | 38 | 50 | R | R | 6-4 | 215 | 4-27-69 | 1990 | Burlington, Wash. |
| Boze, Marshall | 10 | 3 | 2.71 | 13 | 13 | 1 | 0 | 86 | 78 | 36 | 26 | 32 | 48 | R | R | 6-1 | 212 | 5-23-71 | 1990 | Soldotna, Alaska |
| Carter, Glenn | 3 | 5 | 5.12 | 18 | 9 | 1 | 0 | 63 | 65 | 44 | 36 | 22 | 47 | R | R | 6-0 | 175 | 11-29-67 | 1988 | Melrose Park, Ill. |
| Correa, Ramser | 1 | 0 | 5.06 | 5 | 1 | 0 | 0 | 11 | 15 | 15 | 6 | 7 | 5 | R | R | 6-5 | 225 | 11-13-70 | 1987 | Carolina, P.R. |
| Dell, Tim | 4 | 2 | 5.13 | 48 | 3 | 0 | 1 | 105 | 151 | 71 | 60 | 32 | 56 | R | R | 6-5 | 205 | 4-8-67 | 1988 | Indianapolis, Ind. |
| Farmer, Howard | 2 | 1 | 3.33 | 4 | 4 | 1 | 0 | 24 | 14 | 9 | 9 | 10 | 16 | R | R | 6-2 | 184 | 1-18-66 | 1987 | Gary, Ind. |
| Felix, Nick | 0 | 0 | 2.45 | 5 | 0 | 0 | 1 | 18 | 12 | 6 | 5 | 8 | 15 | L | L | 6-0 | 205 | 2-21-67 | 1988 | Mesa, Ariz. |
| 2-team (27 Wichita) | 2 | 1 | 4.32 | 42 | 0 | 0 | 4 | 67 | 61 | 36 | 32 | 32 | 69 | | | | | | | |
| Gamez, Francisco | 2 | 8 | 5.40 | 15 | 14 | 1 | 0 | 68 | 92 | 45 | 41 | 25 | 26 | R | R | 6-2 | 185 | 4-2-70 | 1990 | Hermosillo, Mexico |
| Hancock, Brian | 1 | 0 | 7.04 | 10 | 6 | 0 | 0 | 31 | 40 | 26 | 24 | 30 | 15 | L | L | 6-2 | 190 | 3-10-71 | 1991 | Nashville, Tenn. |
| Hunter, Jim | 3 | 1 | 2.45 | 14 | 0 | 0 | 1 | 22 | 20 | 8 | 6 | 6 | 10 | R | R | 6-3 | 205 | 6-22-64 | 1985 | Middletown, N.J. |
| Johnson, Dane | 2 | 2 | 3.91 | 15 | 1 | 0 | 1 | 25 | 23 | 12 | 11 | 10 | 26 | R | R | 6-5 | 205 | 2-10-63 | 1993 | Miami, Fla. |
| Karl, Scott | 13 | 8 | 2.45 | 27 | 27 | 4 | 0 | 180 | 172 | 67 | 49 | 35 | 95 | L | L | 6-3 | 197 | 8-9-71 | 1992 | Carlsbad, Calif. |
| Kiefer, Mark | 3 | 4 | 4.01 | 11 | 11 | 0 | 0 | 52 | 48 | 29 | 23 | 19 | 44 | R | R | 6-3 | 185 | 11-13-68 | 1988 | Garden Grove, Calif. |
| Kloek, Kevin | 9 | 6 | 4.11 | 23 | 23 | 1 | 0 | 136 | 148 | 75 | 62 | 53 | 97 | R | R | 6-3 | 175 | 8-15-70 | 1992 | Santa Barbara, Calif. |
| Lewis, Mark | 0 | 0 | 1.59 | 2 | 0 | 0 | 0 | 6 | 3 | 1 | 1 | 0 | 2 | L | R | 5-11 | 180 | 8-3-66 | 1987 | Charlotte, N.C. |
| Pitcher, Scott | 2 | 0 | 8.24 | 13 | 0 | 0 | 1 | 20 | 32 | 24 | 18 | 10 | 12 | R | R | 6-1 | 180 | 3-29-68 | 1988 | Tampa, Fla. |
| Richards, Dave | 2 | 2 | 3.80 | 35 | 0 | 0 | 1 | 64 | 66 | 31 | 27 | 26 | 54 | L | L | 6-3 | 215 | 9-18-67 | 1987 | San Diego, Calif. |
| Rogers, Charlie | 4 | 3 | 1.74 | 48 | 2 | 0 | 23 | 72 | 50 | 17 | 14 | 23 | 55 | L | L | 6-0 | 180 | 8-21-68 | 1990 | Bremen, Ala. |
| Taylor, Scott | 6 | 6 | 3.80 | 17 | 16 | 1 | 0 | 104 | 105 | 53 | 44 | 31 | 76 | R | R | 6-3 | 200 | 10-3-66 | 1989 | Wichita, Kan. |

# STOCKTON
## CALIFORNIA LEAGUE

**A**

### BATTING

| | AVG | G | AB | R | H | 2B | 3B | HR | RBI | BB | SO | SB | CS | B | T | HT | WT | DOB | 1st Yr | Resides |
|---|---|---|---|---|---|---|---|---|---|---|---|---|---|---|---|---|---|---|---|---|
| Carmona, Greg, ss-2b | .170 | 20 | 47 | 9 | 8 | 1 | 0 | 0 | 7 | 18 | 11 | 5 | 5 | S | R | 6-0 | 150 | 5-9-68 | 1987 | Bani, D.R. |
| Cole, Mark, 2b-3b | .240 | 79 | 242 | 30 | 58 | 8 | 1 | 3 | 34 | 17 | 40 | 7 | 3 | S | R | 5-9 | 175 | 4-18-67 | 1989 | Sacramento, Calif. |
| Couture, Mike, c | .241 | 32 | 87 | 22 | 21 | 6 | 0 | 2 | 9 | 17 | 28 | 14 | 2 | R | R | 6-2 | 185 | 3-23-68 | 1990 | Surfside Beach, S.C. |
| Diggs, Tony, of | .295 | 81 | 285 | 48 | 84 | 14 | 3 | 1 | 31 | 43 | 34 | 31 | 11 | S | R | 6-0 | 175 | 4-20-67 | 1989 | Starke, Fla. |
| Dobrolsky, Bill, c | .211 | 67 | 190 | 18 | 40 | 2 | 0 | 1 | 21 | 16 | 43 | 2 | 1 | R | R | 6-2 | 190 | 3-16-70 | 1991 | Orwigsburg, Pa. |
| Doran, Bill, 2b | .500 | 1 | 2 | 0 | 1 | 0 | 0 | 0 | 0 | 1 | 0 | 1 | 0 | S | R | 6-0 | 180 | 5-28-58 | 1979 | Cincinnati, Ohio |
| Fairman, Andy, 1b-dh | .265 | 122 | 456 | 59 | 121 | 20 | 2 | 15 | 70 | 39 | 51 | 4 | 8 | L | L | 6-2 | 215 | 4-9-70 | 1991 | Huntington Woods, Mich. |
| Glenn, Leon, 1b-of | .276 | 114 | 431 | 77 | 119 | 27 | 3 | 15 | 76 | 49 | 110 | 35 | 15 | L | R | 6-2 | 215 | 9-16-69 | 1988 | Louisville, Miss. |
| Harris, Mike, of | .309 | 104 | 363 | 64 | 112 | 17 | 3 | 9 | 65 | 63 | 56 | 19 | 7 | L | L | 5-11 | 205 | 4-30-70 | 1991 | Lexington, Ky. |
| Hostetler, Brian, c | .423 | 11 | 26 | 5 | 11 | 2 | 0 | 0 | 4 | 7 | 2 | 1 | 0 | L | R | 6-1 | 205 | 3-21-70 | 1992 | Edwardsburg, Mich. |
| Huyler, Mike, ss-2b | .281 | 92 | 338 | 66 | 95 | 19 | 3 | 3 | 34 | 43 | 48 | 16 | 5 | R | R | 6-2 | 180 | 7-21-68 | 1988 | Sun City, Calif. |
| Loretta, Mark, ss | .363 | 53 | 201 | 36 | 73 | 4 | 1 | 4 | 31 | 22 | 17 | 8 | 2 | R | R | 6-0 | 175 | 8-14-71 | 1993 | Arcadia, Calif. |
| Perez, Danny, of | .292 | 10 | 24 | 4 | 7 | 3 | 1 | 0 | 2 | 5 | 2 | 1 | 1 | R | R | 5-10 | 188 | 2-25-71 | 1992 | El Paso, Texas |
| Riggs, Kevin, 2b | .347 | 108 | 377 | 84 | 131 | 18 | 3 | 3 | 45 | 101 | 46 | 12 | 15 | L | R | 6-0 | 190 | 2-3-69 | 1990 | East Hartford, Conn. |
| Samples, Todd, of | .264 | 122 | 401 | 63 | 106 | 21 | 3 | 6 | 48 | 28 | 63 | 36 | 12 | R | R | 6-2 | 180 | 8-1-69 | 1990 | Springfield, Mo. |
| Stefanski, Mike, c-3b | .322 | 97 | 345 | 58 | 111 | 22 | 2 | 10 | 57 | 49 | 45 | 6 | 1 | R | R | 6-2 | 190 | 9-12-69 | 1991 | Redford, Mich. |
| Unroe, Tim, 3b | .251 | 108 | 382 | 57 | 96 | 21 | 6 | 12 | 63 | 36 | 96 | 9 | 10 | R | R | 6-3 | 210 | 10-7-70 | 1992 | Round Lake Beach, Ill. |
| Wachter, Derek, of-dh | .293 | 115 | 420 | 75 | 123 | 20 | 4 | 22 | 108 | 64 | 93 | 3 | 3 | R | R | 6-1 | 195 | 8-28-70 | 1991 | Miller Place, N.Y. |
| Whitford, Eric, 2b-ss | .188 | 8 | 16 | 1 | 3 | 0 | 0 | 0 | 2 | 3 | 1 | 1 | 1 | R | R | 6-0 | 170 | 12-30-68 | 1991 | Kingston, N.Y. |

### PITCHING

| | W | L | ERA | G | GS | CG | SV | IP | H | R | ER | BB | SO | B | T | HT | WT | DOB | 1st Yr | Resides |
|---|---|---|---|---|---|---|---|---|---|---|---|---|---|---|---|---|---|---|---|---|
| Allen, Chad | 1 | 3 | 1.78 | 26 | 0 | 0 | 8 | 30 | 39 | 10 | 6 | 10 | 17 | S | R | 6-4 | 200 | 8-15-68 | 1989 | Richland, Wash. |
| Blair, Donnie | 2 | 2 | 3.95 | 4 | 2 | 0 | 0 | 14 | 19 | 8 | 6 | 3 | 4 | R | R | 6-3 | 170 | 10-19-70 | 1991 | Wabash, Ind. |
| Boze, Marshall | 7 | 2 | 2.65 | 14 | 14 | 0 | 0 | 88 | 82 | 36 | 26 | 41 | 54 | R | R | 6-1 | 212 | 5-23-71 | 1990 | Soldotna, Alaska |
| Browne, Byron | 10 | 5 | 4.07 | 29 | 27 | 0 | 0 | 144 | 117 | 73 | 65 | 117 | 110 | R | R | 6-7 | 200 | 8-8-70 | 1991 | Phoenix, Ariz. |
| Correa, Ramser | 4 | 3 | 4.52 | 21 | 10 | 0 | 3 | 68 | 78 | 38 | 34 | 30 | 32 | R | R | 6-5 | 225 | 11-13-70 | 1987 | Carolina, P.R. |
| Criminger, John | 5 | 5 | 4.47 | 29 | 0 | 0 | 4 | 58 | 61 | 35 | 29 | 30 | 50 | R | R | 6-2 | 195 | 8-21-69 | 1991 | Lancaster, S.C. |
| Dorn, Chris | 3 | 2 | 4.06 | 22 | 0 | 0 | 4 | 38 | 43 | 21 | 17 | 16 | 31 | R | R | 6-1 | 195 | 3-22-68 | 1988 | Spring, Texas |
| Duda, Steve | 1 | 0 | 4.50 | 2 | 2 | 0 | 0 | 10 | 10 | 6 | 5 | 4 | 7 | R | R | 5-11 | 170 | 4-27-71 | 1993 | Whittier, Calif. |
| Fetty, Pat | 4 | 7 | 4.40 | 32 | 0 | 0 | 1 | 43 | 41 | 29 | 21 | 26 | 27 | R | R | 6-0 | 175 | 4-27-68 | 1991 | Sun River, Ore. |
| Gerstein, Ron | 8 | 4 | 5.32 | 36 | 7 | 1 | 0 | 86 | 103 | 59 | 51 | 63 | 49 | L | L | 6-3 | 200 | 1-1-69 | 1990 | Santa Cruz, Calif. |
| Hampton, Mark | 2 | 1 | 5.51 | 19 | 3 | 0 | 1 | 33 | 41 | 25 | 20 | 25 | 21 | R | R | 6-3 | 196 | 9-20-69 | 1990 | Hammond, La. |
| Hancock, Brian | 2 | 4 | 4.69 | 13 | 9 | 0 | 0 | 56 | 57 | 39 | 29 | 29 | 42 | L | L | 6-2 | 190 | 3-10-71 | 1991 | Nashville, Tenn. |
| Hardwick, Billy | 6 | 2 | 2.90 | 61 | 0 | 0 | 14 | 84 | 95 | 32 | 27 | 30 | 59 | L | L | 5-10 | 170 | 1-18-72 | 1992 | Eaton Park, Fla. |
| Hill, Tyrone | 1 | 3 | 4.50 | 19 | 17 | 0 | 1 | 66 | 43 | 45 | 33 | 60 | 65 | L | L | 6-7 | 210 | 3-7-72 | 1991 | Yucaipa, Calif. |

| PITCHING | W | L | ERA | G | GS | CG | SV | IP | H | R | ER | BB | SO | B | T | HT | WT | DOB | 1st Yr | Resides |
|---|---|---|---|---|---|---|---|---|---|---|---|---|---|---|---|---|---|---|---|---|
| McKeon, Brian | 4 | 2 | 4.80 | 27 | 5 | 0 | 2 | 60 | 69 | 37 | 32 | 23 | 32 | R | R | 6-5 | 210 | 12-24-68 | 1989 | Blanchardville, Wis. |
| Murphy, Matt | 0 | 0 | 1.50 | 2 | 2 | 0 | 0 | 12 | 11 | 3 | 2 | 2 | 11 | L | L | 6-2 | 200 | 7-28-70 | 1993 | Woodstock, Vt. |
| Pruitt, Don | 2 | 3 | 5.99 | 16 | 12 | 0 | 0 | 68 | 84 | 48 | 45 | 21 | 40 | R | R | 6-2 | 200 | 9-3-68 | 1990 | Phoenix, Ariz. |
| Roberson, Sid | 12 | 8 | 2.60 | 24 | 23 | 6 | 0 | 166 | 157 | 68 | 48 | 34 | 87 | L | L | 5-9 | 170 | 9-7-71 | 1992 | Orange Park, Fla. |
| Steinmetz, Earl | 4 | 1 | 3.92 | 28 | 3 | 0 | 0 | 60 | 73 | 36 | 26 | 22 | 41 | R | R | 6-4 | 205 | 5-17-71 | 1989 | San Antonio, Texas |
| Thibault, Ryan | 0 | 0 | 0.00 | 1 | 0 | 0 | 0 | 1 | 0 | 0 | 0 | 0 | 1 | L | L | 6-1 | 185 | 12-15-68 | 1990 | Fountain Valley, Calif. |

# BELOIT     A
## MIDWEST LEAGUE

| BATTING | AVG | G | AB | R | H | 2B | 3B | HR | RBI | BB | SO | SB | CS | B | T | HT | WT | DOB | 1st Yr | Resides |
|---|---|---|---|---|---|---|---|---|---|---|---|---|---|---|---|---|---|---|---|---|
| Banks, Brian, of | .245 | 38 | 147 | 21 | 36 | 5 | 1 | 4 | 19 | 7 | 34 | 1 | 2 | S | R | 6-3 | 200 | 9-28-70 | 1993 | Mesa, Ariz. |
| Boyzuick, Mike, 3b | .266 | 108 | 346 | 50 | 92 | 18 | 2 | 7 | 43 | 57 | 70 | 2 | 4 | R | R | 6-0 | 210 | 10-1-68 | 1991 | Oswego, N.Y. |
| Dumas, Brian-ss | .230 | 76 | 174 | 28 | 40 | 3 | 0 | 0 | 9 | 27 | 30 | 13 | 11 | R | R | 5-9 | 163 | 5-28-71 | 1992 | Hattiesburg, Miss. |
| Felder, Ken, of | .182 | 32 | 99 | 12 | 18 | 4 | 2 | 3 | 8 | 10 | 40 | 1 | 1 | R | R | 6-3 | 220 | 2-9-71 | 1992 | Niceville, Fla. |
| Gay, Brad, c | .194 | 36 | 98 | 12 | 19 | 5 | 0 | 2 | 15 | 13 | 31 | 1 | 0 | R | R | 5-11 | 198 | 8-9-72 | 1992 | St. Petersburg, Fla. |
| Gorman, Paul, 3b | .237 | 22 | 59 | 13 | 14 | 4 | 0 | 1 | 3 | 14 | 6 | 0 | 3 | R | R | 6-0 | 180 | 11-20-70 | 1992 | Burpengary, Australia |
| Hostetler, Brian, c | .197 | 73 | 218 | 20 | 43 | 7 | 1 | 4 | 17 | 34 | 44 | 2 | 1 | L | R | 6-1 | 205 | 3-21-70 | 1992 | Edwardsburg, Mich. |
| Hughes, Bobby, c-1b | .277 | 98 | 321 | 42 | 89 | 11 | 3 | 17 | 56 | 23 | 76 | 1 | 3 | R | R | 6-4 | 210 | 3-10-71 | 1992 | North Hollywood, Calif. |
| Imperial, Jason, 3b-1b | .120 | 15 | 50 | 4 | 6 | 2 | 0 | 0 | 2 | 1 | 19 | 0 | 0 | R | R | 6-1 | 210 | 12-14-69 | 1991 | Caldwell, N.J. |
| Landry, Todd, 1b | .302 | 38 | 149 | 26 | 45 | 6 | 0 | 4 | 24 | 4 | 36 | 4 | 4 | R | L | 6-4 | 210 | 8-21-72 | 1993 | Donaldsonville, La. |
| Listach, Pat, ss-dh | .250 | 4 | 12 | 2 | 3 | 0 | 0 | 0 | 1 | 1 | 2 | 2 | 0 | S | R | 5-9 | 170 | 9-12-67 | 1988 | Waco, Texas |
| Martinez, Gabby, ss | .242 | 94 | 285 | 40 | 69 | 14 | 5 | 0 | 24 | 14 | 52 | 22 | 10 | R | R | 6-2 | 170 | 1-7-74 | 1992 | Santurce, P.R. |
| Mendoza, Francisco, ss | .061 | 27 | 49 | 3 | 3 | 0 | 0 | 1 | 5 | 3 | 18 | 2 | 0 | S | R | 5-11 | 160 | 6-4-72 | 1989 | Santo Domingo, D.R. |
| Perez, Danny, of | .300 | 106 | 377 | 70 | 113 | 17 | 6 | 10 | 59 | 56 | 64 | 23 | 8 | R | R | 5-10 | 188 | 2-25-71 | 1992 | El Paso, Texas |
| Powell, Gordon, dh-2b | .273 | 47 | 172 | 27 | 47 | 16 | 1 | 4 | 19 | 6 | 51 | 8 | 3 | R | R | 6-2 | 202 | 9-27-70 | 1989 | Cincinnati, Ohio |
| Richardson, Scott, 2b-of | .276 | 125 | 475 | 76 | 131 | 26 | 7 | 3 | 64 | 42 | 85 | 50 | 12 | R | R | 6-1 | 175 | 2-19-71 | 1992 | Rialto, Calif. |
| Riesgo, Nikco, of-1b | .194 | 9 | 31 | 7 | 6 | 0 | 0 | 2 | 6 | 9 | 8 | 1 | 2 | R | R | 6-2 | 185 | 1-11-67 | 1988 | Clarinda, Iowa |
| Rodriques, Cecil, of | .238 | 104 | 349 | 50 | 83 | 21 | 4 | 8 | 49 | 43 | 94 | 18 | 12 | R | R | 6-0 | 175 | 9-3-71 | 1991 | Fort Pierce, Fla. |
| Ross, Jackie, of | .243 | 122 | 415 | 64 | 101 | 7 | 4 | 2 | 41 | 63 | 101 | 23 | 14 | S | R | 5-8 | 158 | 12-28-71 | 1991 | Hollywood, Fla. |
| Schmidt, Keith, of | .085 | 15 | 47 | 3 | 4 | 2 | 0 | 0 | 2 | 3 | 18 | 0 | 0 | L | R | 6-4 | 195 | 2-25-71 | 1989 | Burton, Texas |
| Smith, Craig, ss | .218 | 53 | 147 | 16 | 32 | 11 | 1 | 1 | 15 | 13 | 38 | 3 | 1 | R | R | 6-0 | 175 | 9-19-71 | 1992 | Tucson, Ariz. |
| Talanoa, Scott, 1b | .287 | 87 | 258 | 55 | 74 | 12 | 0 | 25 | 66 | 71 | 86 | 5 | 3 | R | R | 6-5 | 240 | 11-12-69 | 1991 | Lawndale, Calif. |

| PITCHING | W | L | ERA | G | GS | CG | SV | IP | H | R | ER | BB | SO | B | T | HT | WT | DOB | 1st Yr | Resides |
|---|---|---|---|---|---|---|---|---|---|---|---|---|---|---|---|---|---|---|---|---|
| Aronetz, Cam | 1 | 1 | 3.29 | 30 | 0 | 0 | 5 | 38 | 39 | 19 | 14 | 16 | 38 | L | L | 6-9 | 260 | 9-19-69 | 1991 | Coquitlam, B.C. |
| Blair, Donnie | 9 | 6 | 3.40 | 21 | 21 | 6 | 0 | 135 | 130 | 60 | 51 | 11 | 126 | R | R | 6-3 | 170 | 10-19-71 | 1990 | Wabash, Ind. |
| Boddicker, Mike | 0 | 0 | 2.25 | 1 | 1 | 0 | 0 | 4 | 3 | 1 | 1 | 1 | 4 | R | R | 5-11 | 190 | 8-23-57 | 1978 | Overland Park, Kan. |
| Demyan, Kirk | 8 | 7 | 3.38 | 50 | 0 | 0 | 4 | 91 | 94 | 49 | 34 | 44 | 70 | R | R | 6-0 | 185 | 8-28-71 | 1992 | Bethlehem, Pa. |
| Droll, Jeff | 0 | 3 | 7.64 | 4 | 4 | 0 | 0 | 18 | 32 | 20 | 15 | 8 | 5 | R | R | 6-5 | 205 | 2-2-71 | 1992 | Bigler, Pa. |
| Duda, Steve | 2 | 1 | 4.46 | 6 | 6 | 0 | 0 | 36 | 45 | 18 | 18 | 11 | 30 | R | R | 5-11 | 170 | 6-27-71 | 1993 | Whittier, Calif. |
| Fetty, Pat | 0 | 0 | 9.00 | 2 | 0 | 0 | 0 | 3 | 5 | 4 | 3 | 1 | 1 | R | R | 6-0 | 175 | 4-27-68 | 1991 | Sun River, Ore. |
| Froning, Tom | 0 | 1 | 10.29 | 4 | 1 | 0 | 0 | 7 | 15 | 12 | 8 | 7 | 4 | L | L | 6-2 | 195 | 6-1-71 | 1992 | Sidney, Ohio |
| Hampton, Mark | 1 | 4 | 6.43 | 11 | 7 | 0 | 0 | 42 | 53 | 36 | 30 | 24 | 19 | R | R | 6-3 | 196 | 9-20-69 | 1989 | Hammond, La. |
| Jones, Robert | 10 | 10 | 4.11 | 25 | 25 | 4 | 0 | 145 | 159 | 82 | 66 | 65 | 115 | R | L | 6-0 | 175 | 4-11-72 | 1992 | Rutherford, N.J. |
| Kyslinger, Dan | 4 | 5 | 3.60 | 35 | 0 | 0 | 15 | 40 | 24 | 19 | 16 | 21 | 52 | R | R | 6-4 | 234 | 7-17-71 | 1992 | Winston-Salem, N.C. |
| Meek, Darryl | 5 | 10 | 5.19 | 24 | 17 | 1 | 0 | 109 | 108 | 81 | 63 | 52 | 64 | L | R | 6-2 | 190 | 3-12-71 | 1990 | St. Louis, Mo. |
| O'Laughlin, Chad | 0 | 0 | 0.00 | 2 | 0 | 0 | 0 | 3 | 4 | 1 | 0 | 0 | 1 | L | L | 6-5 | 220 | 1-7-72 | 1991 | Lake Havasu, Ariz. |
| Paul, Andy | 1 | 3 | 2.96 | 8 | 8 | 1 | 0 | 55 | 53 | 22 | 18 | 30 | 52 | R | R | 6-4 | 200 | 9-4-71 | 1992 | Whitehouse Station, N.Y. |
| Pike, Dave | 2 | 3 | 4.84 | 35 | 0 | 0 | 3 | 58 | 57 | 42 | 31 | 41 | 72 | R | R | 6-4 | 200 | 1-24-71 | 1990 | Sarasota, Fla. |
| Sadler, Aldren | 6 | 6 | 4.11 | 20 | 20 | 1 | 0 | 116 | 126 | 67 | 53 | 47 | 87 | R | R | 6-6 | 180 | 2-10-72 | 1992 | Conyers, Ga. |
| Schenbeck, Tom | 6 | 4 | 6.13 | 38 | 10 | 1 | 3 | 94 | 117 | 72 | 64 | 39 | 78 | R | R | 6-0 | 200 | 6-21-72 | 1992 | Aurora, Colo. |
| Thibault, Ryan | 4 | 5 | 4.59 | 40 | 2 | 0 | 2 | 65 | 64 | 44 | 33 | 44 | 65 | L | L | 6-1 | 185 | 12-15-68 | 1990 | Fountain Valley, Calif. |
| Torrez, Rafael | 0 | 0 | 7.71 | 10 | 0 | 0 | 0 | 16 | 21 | 18 | 14 | 10 | 13 | R | R | 6-0 | 175 | 11-15-67 | 1989 | Santo Domingo, D.R. |
| Wunsch, Kelly | 1 | 5 | 4.83 | 12 | 12 | 0 | 0 | 63 | 58 | 39 | 34 | 39 | 61 | L | L | 6-5 | 192 | 7-12-72 | 1993 | Houston, Texas |

# BREWERS: ORGANIZATION LEADERS

## MAJOR LEAGUERS

**BATTING**

| | | |
|---|---|---|
| *AVG | Darryl Hamilton | .310 |
| R | Greg Vaughn | 97 |
| H | Darryl Hamilton | 161 |
| TB | Greg Vaughn | 274 |
| 2B | B.J. Surhoff | 38 |
| 3B | Bill Spiers | 4 |
| HR | Greg Vaughn | 30 |
| RBI | Greg Vaughn | 97 |
| BB | Greg Vaughn | 89 |
| SO | Greg Vaughn | 118 |
| SB | Darryl Hamilton | 21 |

**PITCHING**

| | | |
|---|---|---|
| W | Cal Eldred | 16 |
| L | Cal Eldred | 16 |
| #ERA | Angel Miranda | 3.30 |
| G | Jesse Orosco | 57 |
| CG | Cal Eldred | 8 |
| SV | Doug Henry | 17 |
| IP | Cal Eldred | 258 |
| BB | Cal Eldred | 91 |
| SO | Cal Eldred | 180 |

**Greg Vaughn**
30 home runs, 97 RBIs

## MINOR LEAGUERS

**BATTING**

| | | |
|---|---|---|
| *AVG | Kevin Riggs, Stockton | .347 |
| R | Two tied at | 84 |
| H | Jeff Cirillo, El Paso-New Orleans | 148 |
| TB | Jeff Cirillo, El Paso-New Orleans | 221 |
| 2B | John Byington, New Orleans | 33 |
| 3B | Two tied at | 7 |
| HR | Scott Talanoa, Beloit | 25 |
| RBI | Derek Wachter, Stockton | 108 |
| BB | Kevin Riggs, Stockton | 101 |
| SO | Leon Glenn, Stockton | 110 |
| SB | Scott Richardson, Beloit | 50 |

**PITCHING**

| | | |
|---|---|---|
| W | Marshall Boze, Stockton-El Paso | 17 |
| L | Steve Sparks, New Orleans | 13 |
| #ERA | Andy Paul, Beloit-Chandler | 2.28 |
| G | Billy Hardwick, Stockton | 61 |
| CG | Steve Sparks, New Orleans | 7 |
| SV | Charlie Rogers, El Paso | 23 |
| IP | Steve Sparks, New Orleans | 180 |
| BB | Byron Browne, Stockton | 117 |
| SO | Donnie Blair, Beloit-Stockton | 130 |

*Minimum 250 At-Bats    #Minimum 75 Innings

## PIONEER LEAGUE

| BATTING | AVG | G | AB | R | H | 2B | 3B | HR | RBI | BB | SO | SB | CS | B | T | HT | WT | DOB | 1st Yr | Resides |
|---|---|---|---|---|---|---|---|---|---|---|---|---|---|---|---|---|---|---|---|---|
| Acosta, Eduardo, ss-of | .209 | 30 | 43 | 10 | 9 | 0 | 0 | 0 | 2 | 1 | 13 | 0 | 1 | S | R | 6-1 | 155 | 12-5-71 | 1993 | Rock Falls, Ill. |
| Banks, Brian, of | .396 | 12 | 48 | 8 | 19 | 1 | 1 | 2 | 8 | 11 | 8 | 1 | 2 | S | R | 6-3 | 200 | 9-28-70 | 1993 | Mesa, Ariz. |
| Campillo, Rob, c | .250 | 33 | 92 | 13 | 23 | 3 | 0 | 2 | 19 | 17 | 22 | 3 | 3 | R | R | 5-11 | 195 | 11-2-70 | 1992 | Tucson, Ariz. |
| Carter, Chris, c-1b | .234 | 32 | 94 | 13 | 22 | 7 | 0 | 1 | 14 | 15 | 28 | 2 | 2 | R | R | 6-1 | 195 | 5-25-71 | 1993 | Orlando, Fla. |
| Cephas, Ruben, of | .230 | 60 | 191 | 33 | 44 | 3 | 1 | 0 | 19 | 25 | 38 | 26 | 6 | S | L | 5-11 | 195 | 6-11-73 | 1992 | Seaford, Del. |
| Dunn, Todd, of | .307 | 43 | 150 | 33 | 46 | 11 | 2 | 10 | 42 | 22 | 52 | 5 | 2 | R | R | 6-5 | 225 | 7-29-70 | 1993 | Jacksonville, Fla. |
| Gay, Brad, c | .272 | 29 | 92 | 15 | 25 | 5 | 1 | 5 | 23 | 10 | 28 | 2 | 1 | R | R | 5-11 | 198 | 8-9-72 | 1992 | St. Petersburg, Fla. |
| Hardy, Hayland, dh | .277 | 66 | 235 | 43 | 65 | 9 | 1 | 13 | 52 | 39 | 85 | 3 | 2 | R | R | 5-11 | 210 | 8-3-69 | 1993 | Quitman, Texas |
| Hill, Clay, of | .234 | 53 | 158 | 23 | 37 | 10 | 1 | 4 | 27 | 28 | 46 | 3 | 1 | R | R | 6-2 | 195 | 1-10-73 | 1993 | Grand Prairie, Texas |
| Hughes, Danan, of | .233 | 10 | 30 | 8 | 7 | 1 | 1 | 1 | 4 | 8 | 11 | 0 | 1 | R | R | 6-2 | 205 | 12-11-70 | 1992 | Bayonne, N.J. |
| Klassen, Danny, ss | .200 | 18 | 45 | 8 | 9 | 1 | 0 | 0 | 3 | 7 | 11 | 2 | 1 | R | R | 6-0 | 175 | 9-22-75 | 1993 | Port St. Lucie, Fla. |
| Landry, Todd, 1b-of | .315 | 29 | 124 | 27 | 39 | 10 | 1 | 5 | 24 | 8 | 20 | 4 | 1 | R | L | 6-4 | 210 | 8-21-72 | 1993 | Donaldsonville, La. |
| Loretta, Mark, ss | .321 | 6 | 28 | 5 | 9 | 1 | 0 | 1 | 8 | 1 | 4 | 0 | 0 | R | R | 6-0 | 175 | 8-14-71 | 1993 | Arcadia, Calif. |
| Mackie, Ed, 3b | .190 | 36 | 105 | 8 | 20 | 1 | 1 | 2 | 12 | 9 | 45 | 0 | 2 | R | R | 6-1 | 200 | 4-1-72 | 1993 | Cooper City, Fla. |
| Martinez, Greg, of | .290 | 52 | 183 | 45 | 53 | 4 | 2 | 0 | 19 | 30 | 26 | 29 | 6 | S | R | 5-10 | 168 | 1-27-72 | 1993 | Las Vegas, Nev. |
| McInnes, Chris, 2b | .312 | 64 | 218 | 49 | 68 | 14 | 5 | 1 | 37 | 45 | 42 | 29 | 4 | S | R | 5-9 | 160 | 6-18-71 | 1993 | South Jordan, Utah |
| Olexa, Mike, ss-3b | .252 | 59 | 214 | 35 | 54 | 14 | 1 | 5 | 34 | 32 | 42 | 4 | 7 | R | R | 5-10 | 185 | 11-12-70 | 1993 | Milford, Ohio |
| Powers, Robert, 3b-2b | .274 | 41 | 106 | 30 | 29 | 3 | 1 | 0 | 8 | 36 | 29 | 4 | 2 | R | R | 5-7 | 165 | 6-23-73 | 1992 | Bayonne, N.J. |
| Salzano, Jerry, 1b-3b | .260 | 66 | 227 | 30 | 59 | 12 | 2 | 1 | 18 | 25 | 39 | 6 | 3 | R | R | 6-1 | 195 | 10-27-74 | 1992 | Trenton, N.J. |
| Smith, Craig, 2b-ss | .321 | 7 | 28 | 6 | 9 | 2 | 0 | 1 | 4 | 1 | 2 | 0 | 1 | R | R | 6-0 | 175 | 9-19-71 | 1992 | Tucson, Ariz. |
| Thomas, Chris, 1b | .250 | 8 | 16 | 6 | 4 | 1 | 0 | 0 | 4 | 9 | 1 | 0 | 0 | R | R | 6-3 | 220 | 6-28-71 | 1992 | Colchester, Conn. |

| PITCHING | W | L | ERA | G | GS | CG | SV | IP | H | R | ER | BB | SO | B | T | HT | WT | DOB | 1st Yr | Resides |
|---|---|---|---|---|---|---|---|---|---|---|---|---|---|---|---|---|---|---|---|---|
| Arias, Wagner | 4 | 3 | 5.89 | 17 | 6 | 0 | 1 | 47 | 46 | 32 | 31 | 28 | 36 | R | R | 6-1 | 180 | 11-22-74 | 1992 | Bani, D.R. |
| Cole, James | 1 | 0 | 2.82 | 18 | 1 | 0 | 8 | 54 | 57 | 24 | 17 | 20 | 53 | R | R | 6-2 | 195 | 2-19-73 | 1993 | Augusta, Ga. |
| Droll, Jeff | 0 | 2 | 2.16 | 4 | 2 | 0 | 0 | 8 | 9 | 5 | 2 | 2 | 11 | R | R | 6-5 | 205 | 2-2-71 | 1992 | Bigler, Pa. |
| Duda, Steve | 3 | 1 | 5.18 | 5 | 4 | 0 | 0 | 24 | 24 | 15 | 14 | 8 | 21 | R | R | 5-11 | 170 | 6-27-71 | 1993 | Whittier, Calif. |
| England, Dave | 0 | 2 | 10.80 | 2 | 2 | 0 | 0 | 5 | 7 | 6 | 6 | 1 | 8 | R | R | 6-3 | 195 | 8-21-69 | 1992 | Flowery Branch, Ga. |
| Kopitzke, Chad | 4 | 1 | 4.30 | 18 | 1 | 0 | 1 | 29 | 31 | 20 | 14 | 8 | 21 | R | R | 6-1 | 185 | 6-28-72 | 1993 | Greenleaf, Wis. |
| Maloney, Sean | 2 | 2 | 4.34 | 17 | 3 | 0 | 4 | 48 | 55 | 31 | 23 | 11 | 35 | R | R | 6-7 | 205 | 5-25-71 | 1993 | North Kingston, R.I. |
| Mercado, Gabe | 1 | 0 | 8.31 | 3 | 1 | 0 | 0 | 9 | 9 | 8 | 8 | 3 | 2 | R | R | 5-11 | 175 | 11-26-72 | 1993 | Luquillo, P.R. |
| Murphy, Matt | 4 | 0 | 1.41 | 5 | 5 | 0 | 0 | 32 | 21 | 5 | 5 | 9 | 33 | L | L | 6-2 | 200 | 7-28-70 | 1993 | Woodstock, Vt. |
| Rhoda, Gary | 4 | 3 | 4.20 | 14 | 14 | 2 | 0 | 79 | 79 | 40 | 37 | 32 | 82 | R | L | 6-2 | 179 | 10-20-73 | 1992 | Elizabethtown, N.C. |
| Rodriguez, Frankie | 2 | 1 | 2.41 | 18 | 1 | 0 | 5 | 41 | 31 | 19 | 11 | 17 | 63 | R | R | 5-9 | 160 | 1-6-73 | 1992 | Rowland Heights, Calif. |
| Salmon, Fabian | 8 | 3 | 2.64 | 13 | 13 | 1 | 0 | 82 | 84 | 37 | 24 | 25 | 62 | S | R | 6-1 | 180 | 10-4-71 | 1992 | Miami, Fla. |
| Schmitt, Chris | 3 | 3 | 1.62 | 23 | 2 | 0 | 7 | 44 | 32 | 12 | 8 | 26 | 48 | L | L | 5-11 | 180 | 1-1-71 | 1993 | Sarasota, Fla. |
| Wagner, Joe | 3 | 2 | 2.61 | 8 | 7 | 0 | 0 | 41 | 39 | 17 | 12 | 20 | 30 | R | R | 6-1 | 190 | 12-8-71 | 1993 | Janesville, Wis. |
| Werner, Rick | 1 | 2 | 5.19 | 14 | 1 | 0 | 0 | 43 | 70 | 40 | 25 | 14 | 31 | R | R | 6-2 | 175 | 1-12-74 | 1992 | Oviedo, Fla. |
| Wilstead, Judd | 1 | 5 | 8.50 | 11 | 10 | 0 | 0 | 42 | 55 | 46 | 40 | 36 | 17 | L | R | 6-4 | 185 | 3-14-73 | 1991 | St. George, Utah |

## ARIZONA LEAGUE

| BATTING | AVG | G | AB | R | H | 2B | 3B | HR | RBI | BB | SO | SB | CS | B | T | HT | WT | DOB | 1st Yr | Resides |
|---|---|---|---|---|---|---|---|---|---|---|---|---|---|---|---|---|---|---|---|---|
| Acosta, Eduardo, ss | .320 | 8 | 25 | 6 | 8 | 1 | 0 | 0 | 4 | 6 | 7 | 3 | 0 | S | R | 6-1 | 155 | 12-5-71 | 1993 | Rock Falls, Ill. |
| Cantrell, Derrick, of | .247 | 49 | 154 | 31 | 38 | 4 | 1 | 0 | 21 | 16 | 35 | 30 | 5 | R | R | 6-3 | 160 | 6-27-73 | 1992 | Lithia Springs, Ga. |
| Feliz-Nova, Jose, 3b | .267 | 44 | 120 | 20 | 32 | 4 | 5 | 0 | 15 | 12 | 36 | 2 | 1 | R | R | 6-1 | 180 | 5-23-75 | 1993 | Santo Domingo, D.R. |
| Figueroa, Walter, of-dh | .240 | 35 | 104 | 17 | 25 | 6 | 3 | 0 | 10 | 2 | 28 | 3 | 0 | L | L | 6-3 | 185 | 3-13-74 | 1992 | Caguas, P.R. |
| Fryman, Jarod, 3b-1b | .103 | 31 | 58 | 8 | 6 | 0 | 0 | 1 | 2 | 15 | 23 | 0 | 0 | R | R | 6-2 | 175 | 1-17-73 | 1993 | Pensacola, Fla. |
| Fuertes, Derrick, 3b | .203 | 33 | 69 | 9 | 14 | 1 | 0 | 0 | 4 | 8 | 18 | 2 | 1 | R | R | 5-11 | 188 | 6-28-75 | 1993 | Carolina, P.R. |
| Garcia, Francisco, c | .171 | 19 | 35 | 2 | 6 | 1 | 0 | 0 | 1 | 1 | 8 | 1 | 0 | R | R | 6-0 | 200 | 3-7-75 | 1993 | Levittown, P.R. |
| Garcia, Franklin, 2b | .314 | 56 | 236 | 43 | 74 | 5 | 3 | 1 | 32 | 25 | 31 | 36 | 10 | R | R | 5-11 | 150 | 5-4-75 | 1992 | Ochoa, D.R. |
| Hodge, Jim, of | .233 | 46 | 133 | 18 | 31 | 6 | 1 | 3 | 20 | 11 | 37 | 1 | 0 | R | R | 6-2 | 195 | 8-17-72 | 1993 | Trenton, N.J. |
| Klassen, Danny, ss | .222 | 38 | 117 | 26 | 26 | 5 | 0 | 2 | 20 | 24 | 28 | 14 | 3 | R | R | 6-0 | 175 | 9-22-75 | 1993 | Port St. Lucie, Fla. |
| Martinez, Greg, of | .632 | 5 | 19 | 6 | 12 | 0 | 0 | 0 | 3 | 4 | 0 | 7 | 1 | S | R | 5-10 | 168 | 1-27-72 | 1993 | Las Vegas, Nev. |
| Mealing, Allen, of | .256 | 48 | 121 | 23 | 31 | 1 | 1 | 0 | 12 | 12 | 31 | 12 | 5 | L | R | 6-1 | 190 | 12-30-73 | 1993 | Edgefield, S.C. |
| Millsitz, John, c | .212 | 21 | 33 | 3 | 7 | 2 | 0 | 0 | 7 | 7 | 13 | 1 | 0 | R | R | 6-1 | 185 | 10-10-73 | 1993 | Severna Park, Md. |
| Nunez, Francisco, 1b | .252 | 52 | 163 | 21 | 41 | 2 | 5 | 0 | 24 | 23 | 32 | 2 | 1 | R | R | 6-0 | 180 | 6-26-74 | 1991 | Moca, D.R. |
| Rodriguez, Miguel, c | .308 | 27 | 65 | 8 | 20 | 1 | 1 | 0 | 9 | 2 | 12 | 1 | 1 | R | R | 6-2 | 195 | 5-14-75 | 1993 | El Seibo, D.R. |
| Sanchez, Cecilio, of-1b | .302 | 44 | 149 | 22 | 45 | 6 | 2 | 0 | 23 | 7 | 29 | 6 | 2 | L | L | 6-1 | 180 | 2-24-73 | 1993 | Brooklyn, N.Y. |
| Soto, Wilson, ss-dh | .301 | 41 | 123 | 31 | 37 | 6 | 2 | 1 | 19 | 12 | 30 | 20 | 5 | R | R | 6-0 | 155 | 11-30-74 | 1992 | Bani, D.R. |
| Torres, Derrick, of | .253 | 38 | 99 | 19 | 25 | 3 | 1 | 2 | 11 | 7 | 30 | 1 | 2 | R | R | 6-1 | 175 | 3-2-74 | 1993 | Guanica, P.R. |
| Zwisler, Josh, c | .337 | 35 | 89 | 13 | 30 | 4 | 1 | 0 | 15 | 10 | 10 | 6 | 0 | R | R | 5-9 | 180 | 9-30-74 | 1993 | Cuyahoga Falls, Ohio |

| PITCHING | W | L | ERA | G | GS | CG | SV | IP | H | R | ER | BB | SO | B | T | HT | WT | DOB | 1st Yr | Resides |
|---|---|---|---|---|---|---|---|---|---|---|---|---|---|---|---|---|---|---|---|---|
| Benny, Pete | 1 | 3 | 7.21 | 14 | 8 | 0 | 0 | 44 | 56 | 44 | 35 | 37 | 29 | R | R | 6-2 | 196 | 11-9-75 | 1993 | Carson City, Nev. |
| Calderon, Jose | 0 | 0 | 2.77 | 12 | 0 | 0 | 0 | 13 | 15 | 9 | 4 | 13 | 8 | R | R | 6-3 | 180 | 12-19-74 | 1993 | San Juan, P.R. |
| Gaskill, Derek | 2 | 0 | 3.12 | 13 | 1 | 0 | 1 | 26 | 22 | 10 | 9 | 14 | 19 | R | R | 6-6 | 180 | 5-6-74 | 1992 | Portsmouth, Va. |
| Gold, Steve | 2 | 1 | 5.29 | 19 | 0 | 0 | 2 | 34 | 36 | 24 | 20 | 15 | 29 | R | R | 6-4 | 180 | 5-20-74 | 1993 | Shelby, N.C. |
| Hillis, Jon | 2 | 3 | 4.03 | 16 | 0 | 0 | 1 | 22 | 23 | 13 | 10 | 12 | 24 | R | R | 6-2 | 180 | 1-25-72 | 1993 | Wharton, Texas |
| Jaen, Juan | 0 | 1 | 9.35 | 13 | 1 | 0 | 0 | 17 | 23 | 21 | 18 | 14 | 8 | R | R | 6-2 | 180 | 1-19-76 | 1993 | Guarenas, Venez. |
| Krause, Kevin | 4 | 4 | 4.50 | 12 | 12 | 0 | 0 | 64 | 72 | 38 | 32 | 34 | 36 | R | R | 6-0 | 165 | 8-27-73 | 1992 | Syracuse, N.Y. |
| Mercado, Gabe | 1 | 4 | 4.93 | 17 | 1 | 0 | 3 | 35 | 34 | 24 | 19 | 16 | 35 | R | R | 5-11 | 175 | 11-26-72 | 1993 | Luquillo, P.R. |
| Paul, Andy | 4 | 1 | 1.25 | 5 | 5 | 2 | 0 | 36 | 18 | 7 | 5 | 9 | 55 | R | R | 6-4 | 200 | 9-4-71 | 1992 | Whitehouse Station, N.Y. |
| Perkins, Scott | 0 | 0 | 20.25 | 7 | 0 | 0 | 0 | 4 | 5 | 10 | 9 | 9 | 4 | R | R | 6-1 | 185 | 5-26-72 | 1993 | Missouri City, Texas |
| Prempas, Lyle | 2 | 3 | 5.35 | 10 | 9 | 0 | 0 | 39 | 37 | 28 | 23 | 14 | 19 | L | L | 6-2 | 205 | 12-3-74 | 1993 | Westchester, Ill. |
| Preston, George | 2 | 5 | 3.66 | 9 | 9 | 0 | 0 | 47 | 33 | 23 | 19 | 28 | 48 | R | R | 5-11 | 175 | 9-22-73 | 1993 | Brenham, Texas |
| Sheldon, Shane | 0 | 0 | 12.54 | 11 | 0 | 0 | 0 | 9 | 12 | 16 | 13 | 15 | 9 | R | R | 6-3 | 215 | 10-22-72 | 1993 | Portage, Mich. |
| Snure, Jeremy | 3 | 1 | 4.70 | 16 | 0 | 0 | 2 | 38 | 36 | 21 | 20 | 13 | 22 | L | L | 6-4 | 205 | 11-21-73 | 1992 | Cleveland, Ohio |
| Tijerina, Tano | 6 | 1 | 2.94 | 10 | 10 | 1 | 0 | 64 | 51 | 34 | 21 | 24 | 55 | R | R | 6-3 | 220 | 6-23-71 | 1993 | Laredo, Texas |

# MINNESOTA TWINS

**Manager:** Tom Kelly.      **1993 Record:** 71-91, .438 (T-5th, AL West).

| BATTING | AVG | G | AB | R | H | 2B | 3B | HR | RBI | BB | SO | SB | CS | B | T | HT | WT | DOB | 1st Yr | Resides |
|---|---|---|---|---|---|---|---|---|---|---|---|---|---|---|---|---|---|---|---|---|
| Becker, Rich | .286 | 3 | 7 | 3 | 2 | 2 | 0 | 0 | 0 | 5 | 4 | 1 | 1 | S | L | 5-10 | 190 | 2-1-72 | 1990 | Aurora, Ill. |
| Brito, Bernardo | .241 | 27 | 54 | 8 | 13 | 2 | 0 | 4 | 9 | 1 | 20 | 0 | 0 | R | R | 6-1 | 190 | 12-4-63 | 1981 | Santo Domingo, D.R. |
| Bruett, J.T. | .250 | 17 | 20 | 2 | 5 | 2 | 0 | 0 | 1 | 1 | 4 | 0 | 0 | L | L | 5-11 | 175 | 10-8-67 | 1988 | Oconomowoc, Wis. |
| Bush, Randy | .156 | 35 | 45 | 1 | 7 | 2 | 0 | 0 | 3 | 7 | 13 | 0 | 0 | L | L | 6-1 | 186 | 10-5-58 | 1979 | Longwood, Fla. |
| Hale, Chip | .333 | 69 | 186 | 25 | 62 | 6 | 1 | 3 | 27 | 18 | 17 | 2 | 1 | L | R | 5-10 | 175 | 12-64 | 1987 | Hermosa Beach, Calif. |
| Harper, Brian | .304 | 147 | 530 | 52 | 161 | 26 | 1 | 12 | 73 | 29 | 29 | 1 | 3 | R | R | 6-2 | 193 | 10-16-59 | 1977 | Rolling Hills, Calif. |
| Hocking, Denny | .139 | 15 | 36 | 7 | 5 | 1 | 0 | 0 | 0 | 6 | 8 | 1 | 0 | S | R | 5-10 | 180 | 4-2-70 | 1990 | Torrance, Calif. |
| Hrbek, Kent | .242 | 123 | 392 | 60 | 95 | 11 | 1 | 25 | 83 | 71 | 57 | 4 | 2 | L | R | 6-4 | 229 | 5-21-60 | 1979 | Excelsior, Minn. |
| Jorgensen, Terry | .224 | 59 | 152 | 15 | 34 | 7 | 0 | 1 | 12 | 10 | 21 | 1 | 0 | R | R | 6-4 | 210 | 9-2-66 | 1987 | Luxemburg, Wis. |
| Knoblauch, Chuck | .277 | 153 | 602 | 82 | 167 | 27 | 4 | 2 | 41 | 65 | 44 | 29 | 11 | R | R | 5-9 | 170 | 7-7-68 | 1989 | Houston, Texas |
| Larkin, Gene | .264 | 56 | 144 | 17 | 38 | 7 | 1 | 1 | 19 | 21 | 16 | 0 | 1 | S | R | 6-3 | 195 | 10-24-62 | 1984 | North Bellmore, N.Y. |
| Lee, Derek | .152 | 15 | 33 | 3 | 5 | 1 | 0 | 0 | 4 | 1 | 4 | 0 | 0 | L | R | 6-0 | 195 | 7-28-66 | 1988 | Reston, Va. |
| Leius, Scott | .167 | 10 | 18 | 4 | 3 | 0 | 0 | 0 | 2 | 2 | 4 | 0 | 0 | R | R | 6-3 | 180 | 9-24-65 | 1986 | Mamaroneck, N.Y. |
| Mack, Shane | .276 | 128 | 503 | 66 | 139 | 30 | 4 | 10 | 61 | 41 | 76 | 15 | 5 | R | R | 6-0 | 185 | 12-7-63 | 1985 | Cerritos, Calif. |
| Maksudian, Mike | .167 | 5 | 12 | 2 | 2 | 1 | 0 | 0 | 2 | 4 | 2 | 0 | 0 | L | R | 5-11 | 220 | 5-28-66 | 1987 | Libertyville, Ill. |
| McCarty, Dave | .214 | 98 | 350 | 36 | 75 | 15 | 2 | 2 | 21 | 19 | 80 | 2 | 6 | R | L | 6-5 | 210 | 11-23-69 | 1991 | Houston, Texas |
| Meares, Pat | .251 | 111 | 346 | 33 | 87 | 14 | 3 | 0 | 33 | 7 | 52 | 4 | 5 | R | R | 5-11 | 180 | 9-6-68 | 1990 | Salina, Kan. |
| Munoz, Pedro | .233 | 104 | 326 | 34 | 76 | 11 | 1 | 13 | 38 | 25 | 97 | 1 | 2 | R | R | 5-11 | 170 | 9-19-68 | 1985 | Ponce, P.R. |
| Pagliarulo, Mike | .292 | 83 | 253 | 31 | 74 | 16 | 4 | 3 | 23 | 18 | 34 | 6 | 6 | L | R | 6-2 | 195 | 3-15-60 | 1981 | Melrose, Mass. |
| Parks, Derek | .200 | 7 | 20 | 3 | 4 | 0 | 0 | 1 | 1 | 2 | 0 | 0 | 0 | R | R | 6-0 | 195 | 9-29-68 | 1986 | Upland, Calif. |
| Puckett, Kirby | .296 | 156 | 622 | 89 | 184 | 39 | 3 | 22 | 89 | 47 | 93 | 8 | 6 | R | R | 5-8 | 210 | 3-14-61 | 1982 | Chicago, Ill. |
| Reboulet, Jeff | .258 | 109 | 240 | 33 | 62 | 8 | 0 | 1 | 15 | 35 | 37 | 5 | 5 | R | R | 6-0 | 168 | 4-20-64 | 1986 | Kettering, Ohio |
| Stahoviak, Scott | .193 | 20 | 57 | 1 | 11 | 4 | 0 | 0 | 1 | 3 | 22 | 0 | 2 | L | R | 6-5 | 225 | 3-6-70 | 1991 | Grays Lake, Ill. |
| Webster, Lenny | .198 | 49 | 106 | 14 | 21 | 2 | 0 | 1 | 8 | 11 | 8 | 1 | 0 | R | R | 5-9 | 187 | 2-10-65 | 1986 | Lutcher, La. |
| Winfield, Dave | .271 | 143 | 547 | 72 | 148 | 27 | 2 | 21 | 76 | 45 | 106 | 2 | 3 | R | R | 6-6 | 246 | 10-3-51 | 1973 | Teaneck, N.J. |

| PITCHING | W | L | ERA | G | GS | CG | SV | IP | H | R | ER | BB | SO | B | T | HT | WT | DOB | 1st Yr | Resides |
|---|---|---|---|---|---|---|---|---|---|---|---|---|---|---|---|---|---|---|---|---|
| Aguilera, Rick | 4 | 3 | 3.11 | 65 | 0 | 0 | 34 | 72 | 60 | 25 | 25 | 14 | 59 | R | R | 6-4 | 200 | 12-31-61 | 1983 | West Covina, Calif. |
| Banks, Willie | 11 | 12 | 4.04 | 31 | 30 | 0 | 0 | 171 | 186 | 91 | 77 | 78 | 138 | R | R | 6-1 | 185 | 2-27-69 | 1987 | Jersey City, N.J. |
| Brummett, Greg | 2 | 1 | 5.74 | 5 | 5 | 0 | 0 | 27 | 29 | 17 | 17 | 15 | 10 | R | R | 6-0 | 180 | 4-20-67 | 1989 | Wichita, Kan. |
| Casian, Larry | 5 | 3 | 3.02 | 54 | 0 | 0 | 1 | 57 | 59 | 23 | 19 | 14 | 31 | R | L | 6-0 | 170 | 10-28-65 | 1987 | Lakewood, Calif. |
| Deshaies, Jim | 11 | 13 | 4.41 | 27 | 27 | 1 | 0 | 167 | 159 | 85 | 82 | 51 | 80 | L | L | 6-4 | 225 | 6-23-60 | 1982 | Massena, N.Y. |
| Erickson, Scott | 8 | 19 | 5.19 | 34 | 34 | 1 | 0 | 219 | 266 | 138 | 126 | 71 | 116 | R | R | 6-4 | 225 | 2-2-68 | 1989 | Sunnyvale, Calif. |
| Garces, Rich | 0 | 0 | 0.00 | 3 | 0 | 0 | 0 | 4 | 4 | 2 | 0 | 2 | 3 | R | R | 6-0 | 200 | 5-18-70 | 1988 | Maracay, Venez. |
| Guardado, Eddie | 3 | 8 | 6.18 | 19 | 16 | 0 | 0 | 95 | 123 | 68 | 65 | 36 | 46 | R | L | 6-0 | 187 | 10-2-70 | 1991 | Stockton, Calif. |
| Guthrie, Mark | 2 | 1 | 4.71 | 22 | 0 | 0 | 0 | 21 | 20 | 11 | 11 | 16 | 15 | S | L | 6-4 | 205 | 9-22-65 | 1987 | Venice, Fla. |
| Hartley, Mike | 1 | 2 | 4.00 | 53 | 0 | 0 | 1 | 81 | 86 | 38 | 36 | 36 | 57 | R | R | 6-1 | 197 | 8-31-61 | 1982 | El Cajon, Calif. |
| Mahomes, Pat | 1 | 5 | 7.71 | 12 | 5 | 0 | 0 | 37 | 47 | 34 | 32 | 16 | 23 | R | R | 6-3 | 198 | 8-9-70 | 1988 | Lindale, Texas |
| Merriman, Brett | 1 | 1 | 9.67 | 19 | 0 | 0 | 0 | 27 | 36 | 29 | 29 | 23 | 14 | R | R | 6-2 | 180 | 7-15-66 | 1988 | Chandler, Ariz. |
| Tapani, Kevin | 12 | 15 | 4.43 | 36 | 35 | 3 | 0 | 226 | 243 | 123 | 111 | 57 | 150 | R | R | 6-0 | 175 | 2-18-64 | 1986 | Wells, Mich. |
| Trombley, Mike | 6 | 6 | 4.88 | 44 | 10 | 0 | 2 | 114 | 131 | 72 | 62 | 41 | 85 | R | R | 6-2 | 200 | 4-14-67 | 1989 | Wilbraham, Mass. |
| Tsamis, George | 1 | 2 | 6.19 | 41 | 0 | 0 | 1 | 68 | 86 | 51 | 47 | 27 | 30 | R | L | 6-2 | 175 | 6-14-67 | 1989 | Clearwater, Fla. |
| Willis, Carl | 3 | 0 | 3.10 | 53 | 0 | 0 | 5 | 58 | 56 | 23 | 20 | 17 | 44 | L | R | 6-4 | 210 | 12-28-60 | 1983 | Yanceyville, N.C. |

## FIELDING

| Catcher | PCT | G | PO | A | E | DP |
|---|---|---|---|---|---|---|
| Harper | .988 | 134 | 736 | 64 | 10 | 6 |
| Parks | .970 | 7 | 28 | 4 | 1 | 1 |
| Webster | 1.000 | 45 | 177 | 13 | 0 | 1 |

| First Base | PCT | G | PO | A | E | DP |
|---|---|---|---|---|---|---|
| Bush | 1.000 | 4 | 13 | 0 | 0 | 2 |
| Hale | 1.000 | 1 | 5 | 1 | 0 | 1 |
| Hrbek | .995 | 115 | 940 | 81 | 5 | 98 |
| Jorgensen | .977 | 9 | 36 | 6 | 1 | 5 |
| Larkin | .985 | 18 | 123 | 6 | 2 | 10 |
| Maksudian | 1.000 | 4 | 28 | 6 | 0 | 3 |
| McCarty | .994 | 36 | 278 | 30 | 2 | 24 |
| Winfield | 1.000 | 5 | 29 | 1 | 0 | 3 |

| Second Base | PCT | G | PO | A | E | DP |
|---|---|---|---|---|---|---|
| Hale | .952 | 21 | 23 | 36 | 3 | 8 |
| Hocking | 1.000 | 1 | 4 | 4 | 0 | 2 |
| Knoblauch | .988 | 148 | 298 | 425 | 9 | 98 |

| | PCT | G | PO | A | E | DP |
|---|---|---|---|---|---|---|
| Reboulet | 1.000 | 11 | 14 | 16 | 0 | 6 |

| Third Base | PCT | G | PO | A | E | DP |
|---|---|---|---|---|---|---|
| Hale | .974 | 19 | 11 | 26 | 1 | 2 |
| Jorgensen | .982 | 45 | 27 | 85 | 2 | 8 |
| Larkin | .000 | 2 | 0 | 0 | 0 | 0 |
| Maksudian | .000 | 1 | 0 | 0 | 0 | 0 |
| Pagliarulo | .984 | 79 | 42 | 137 | 3 | 11 |
| Reboulet | .978 | 35 | 22 | 65 | 2 | 7 |
| Stahoviak | .922 | 19 | 9 | 38 | 4 | 1 |

| Shortstop | PCT | G | PO | A | E | DP |
|---|---|---|---|---|---|---|
| Hale | .000 | 1 | 0 | 0 | 0 | 0 |
| Hocking | .971 | 12 | 15 | 19 | 1 | 9 |
| Jorgensen | 1.000 | 6 | 2 | 4 | 0 | 0 |
| Knoblauch | 1.000 | 6 | 2 | 6 | 0 | 1 |
| Leius | .947 | 9 | 10 | 26 | 2 | 7 |
| Meares | .961 | 111 | 165 | 304 | 19 | 70 |

| | PCT | G | PO | A | E | DP |
|---|---|---|---|---|---|---|
| Reboulet | .982 | 62 | 85 | 134 | 4 | 27 |

| Outfield | PCT | G | PO | A | E | DP |
|---|---|---|---|---|---|---|
| Becker | .875 | 3 | 7 | 0 | 1 | 0 |
| Brito | 1.000 | 10 | 12 | 1 | 0 | 0 |
| Bruett | .857 | 13 | 12 | 0 | 2 | 0 |
| Bush | .000 | 1 | 0 | 0 | 0 | 0 |
| Knoblauch | 1.000 | 1 | 2 | 0 | 0 | 0 |
| Larkin | 1.000 | 28 | 33 | 1 | 0 | 1 |
| Lee | 1.000 | 13 | 15 | 0 | 0 | 0 |
| Mack | .986 | 128 | 347 | 8 | 5 | 1 |
| McCarty | .959 | 67 | 134 | 8 | 6 | 1 |
| Munoz | .983 | 102 | 172 | 5 | 3 | 2 |
| Puckett | .994 | 139 | 312 | 13 | 2 | 2 |
| Reboulet | 1.000 | 3 | 1 | 0 | 0 | 0 |
| Winfield | 1.000 | 31 | 62 | 2 | 0 | 0 |

# TWINS FARM SYSTEM

| Class | Club | League | W | L | Pct. | Finish* | Manager | First Year |
|---|---|---|---|---|---|---|---|---|
| AAA | Portland (Ore.) Beavers | Pacific Coast | 87 | 56 | .608 | 1st (10) | Scott Ullger | 1987 |
| AA | Nashville (Tenn.) Xpress | Southern | 72 | 70 | .507 | 5th (10) | Phil Roof | 1993 |
| A# | Fort Myers (Fla.) Miracle | Florida State | 55 | 79 | .410 | 12th (13) | Steve Liddle | 1993 |
| A | Fort Wayne (Ind.) Wizards | Midwest | 68 | 67 | .504 | 7th (14) | Jim Dwyer | 1993 |

BERNARD TRONCALE

MICHAEL VELMAN

**Kirby Puckett.** Twins sparkplug center fielder hit .296 and led team with 39 doubles and 89 RBIs.

**Kent Hrbek.** Powerful Twins first baseman led team with 25 home runs, but his average slipped to .242.

| Class | Club | League | W | L | Pct. | Finish* | Manager | First Year |
|---|---|---|---|---|---|---|---|---|
| Rookie# | Elizabethton (Tenn.) Twins | Appalachian | 37 | 30 | .552 | 4th (10) | Roy Smith | 1974 |
| Rookie | Fort Myers (Fla.) Twins | Gulf Coast | 23 | 36 | .390 | 12th (15) | Jose Marzan | 1989 |

*Finish in overall standings (No. of teams in league)   #Advanced level

# PORTLAND                                                                              AAA
## PACIFIC COAST LEAGUE

| BATTING | AVG | G | AB | R | H | 2B | 3B | HR | RBI | BB | SO | SB | CS | B | T | HT | WT | DOB | 1st Yr | Resides |
|---|---|---|---|---|---|---|---|---|---|---|---|---|---|---|---|---|---|---|---|---|
| Brito, Bernardo | .339 | 85 | 319 | 64 | 108 | 18 | 3 | 20 | 72 | 26 | 65 | 0 | 2 | R | R | 6-1 | 190 | 12-4-63 | 1981 | Santo Domingo, D.R. |
| Bruett, J.T. | .322 | 90 | 320 | 70 | 103 | 17 | 6 | 2 | 40 | 55 | 38 | 12 | 11 | L | L | 5-11 | 175 | 10-8-67 | 1988 | Oconomowoc, Wis. |
| Carter, Jeff | .325 | 101 | 381 | 73 | 124 | 21 | 7 | 0 | 48 | 63 | 53 | 17 | 12 | S | R | 5-10 | 160 | 10-20-63 | 1985 | Evanston, Ill. |
| Grifol, Pedro | .330 | 28 | 94 | 14 | 31 | 4 | 2 | 2 | 17 | 4 | 14 | 0 | 0 | R | R | 6-1 | 195 | 11-28-69 | 1991 | Miami, Fla. |
| Grotewold, Jeff | .252 | 52 | 151 | 27 | 38 | 6 | 3 | 6 | 30 | 27 | 41 | 2 | 1 | L | R | 6-0 | 215 | 12-8-65 | 1987 | Lake Arrowhead, Calif. |
| Hale, Chip | .280 | 55 | 211 | 37 | 59 | 15 | 3 | 1 | 24 | 21 | 13 | 2 | 1 | L | R | 5-10 | 175 | 2-12-64 | 1987 | Hermosa Beach, Calif. |
| Howell, Pat | .209 | 114 | 369 | 57 | 77 | 11 | 3 | 2 | 29 | 12 | 77 | 36 | 10 | S | R | 5-11 | 155 | 8-31-68 | 1987 | Prichard, Ala. |
| Jorgensen, Terry | .307 | 61 | 238 | 37 | 73 | 18 | 2 | 4 | 44 | 19 | 28 | 1 | 0 | R | R | 6-4 | 210 | 9-2-66 | 1985 | Luxemburg, Wis. |
| Landrum, Ced | .000 | 4 | 4 | 0 | 0 | 0 | 0 | 0 | 0 | 0 | 1 | 0 | 1 | L | R | 5-8 | 170 | 9-3-63 | 1986 | Sweetwater, Ala. |
| Lee, Derek | .315 | 106 | 381 | 79 | 120 | 30 | 7 | 10 | 80 | 60 | 51 | 16 | 5 | L | R | 6-0 | 195 | 7-28-66 | 1988 | Reston, Va. |
| Maksudian, Mike | .314 | 76 | 264 | 57 | 83 | 16 | 7 | 10 | 49 | 45 | 51 | 5 | 1 | L | R | 5-11 | 220 | 5-28-66 | 1987 | Libertyville, Ill. |
| Masteller, Dan | .322 | 61 | 211 | 35 | 68 | 13 | 4 | 7 | 47 | 24 | 25 | 3 | 4 | L | L | 6-0 | 185 | 3-17-68 | 1989 | Lyndhurst, Ohio |
| McCarty, Dave | .385 | 40 | 143 | 42 | 55 | 11 | 0 | 8 | 31 | 27 | 25 | 5 | 2 | R | L | 6-5 | 210 | 11-23-69 | 1991 | Houston, Texas |
| Meares, Pat | .296 | 18 | 54 | 6 | 16 | 5 | 0 | 0 | 3 | 3 | 11 | 0 | 0 | R | R | 5-11 | 180 | 9-6-68 | 1990 | Salina, Kan. |
| Ortiz, Ray | .283 | 111 | 357 | 42 | 101 | 18 | 2 | 5 | 53 | 14 | 58 | 2 | 1 | L | L | 6-2 | 215 | 4-27-68 | 1989 | San Francisco, Calif. |
| Parks, Derek | .311 | 107 | 363 | 63 | 113 | 23 | 1 | 17 | 71 | 48 | 57 | 0 | 0 | R | R | 6-0 | 195 | 9-29-68 | 1986 | Upland, Calif. |
| Russo, Paul | .281 | 83 | 288 | 43 | 81 | 24 | 2 | 10 | 47 | 29 | 69 | 0 | 1 | R | R | 6-0 | 210 | 8-26-69 | 1990 | Tampa, Fla. |
| Schunk, Jerry | .270 | 118 | 397 | 53 | 107 | 28 | 1 | 2 | 47 | 18 | 23 | 5 | 3 | R | R | 5-11 | 180 | 10-5-65 | 1986 | Cincinnati, Ohio |
| Scott, Gary | .291 | 54 | 189 | 26 | 55 | 8 | 4 | 1 | 28 | 27 | 33 | 3 | 1 | R | R | 6-0 | 175 | 8-22-68 | 1989 | Pelham, N.Y. |
| Wade, Scott | .324 | 11 | 37 | 6 | 12 | 3 | 1 | 0 | 4 | 2 | 10 | 0 | 1 | R | R | 6-2 | 200 | 4-26-63 | 1984 | Seabrook, Md. |

## PITCHING

| PITCHING | W | L | ERA | G | GS | CG | SV | IP | H | R | ER | BB | SO | B | T | HT | WT | DOB | 1st Yr | Resides |
|---|---|---|---|---|---|---|---|---|---|---|---|---|---|---|---|---|---|---|---|---|
| Casian, Larry | 1 | 0 | 0.00 | 7 | 0 | 0 | 2 | 8 | 9 | 0 | 0 | 2 | 2 | R | L | 6-0 | 170 | 10-28-65 | 1987 | Lakewood, Calif. |
| Chapin, Darrin | 5 | 2 | 4.31 | 47 | 0 | 0 | 14 | 56 | 58 | 28 | 27 | 24 | 43 | R | R | 6-0 | 170 | 2-1-66 | 1986 | Cortland, Ohio |
| Drees, Tom | 15 | 10 | 6.22 | 31 | 24 | 3 | 0 | 153 | 183 | 112 | 106 | 62 | 83 | S | L | 6-6 | 210 | 6-17-63 | 1985 | Edina, Minn. |
| Garces, Rich | 1 | 3 | 8.33 | 35 | 7 | 0 | 0 | 54 | 70 | 55 | 50 | 64 | 48 | R | R | 6-0 | 200 | 5-18-70 | 1988 | Maracay, Venez. |
| Henry, Jon | 6 | 5 | 5.70 | 26 | 13 | 0 | 1 | 95 | 122 | 68 | 60 | 30 | 62 | R | R | 6-5 | 215 | 8-1-68 | 1990 | Jamestown, N.Y. |
| LaPoint, Dave | 6 | 4 | 6.09 | 13 | 13 | 0 | 0 | 75 | 99 | 60 | 51 | 29 | 40 | L | L | 6-3 | 224 | 7-29-59 | 1977 | Glens Falls, N.Y. |
| Mahomes, Pat | 11 | 4 | 3.03 | 17 | 16 | 3 | 0 | 116 | 89 | 47 | 39 | 54 | 94 | R | R | 6-3 | 198 | 8-9-70 | 1988 | Lindale, Texas |
| Merriman, Brett | 5 | 0 | 3.00 | 39 | 0 | 0 | 15 | 48 | 46 | 19 | 16 | 18 | 29 | R | R | 6-2 | 180 | 7-15-66 | 1988 | Chandler, Ariz. |
| Munoz, Oscar | 2 | 2 | 4.31 | 5 | 5 | 0 | 0 | 31 | 29 | 18 | 15 | 17 | 29 | R | R | 6-2 | 205 | 9-25-69 | 1990 | Hialeah, Fla. |
| Neidlinger, Jim | 9 | 8 | 5.19 | 29 | 24 | 3 | 0 | 158 | 175 | 106 | 91 | 54 | 112 | R | R | 6-4 | 191 | 9-24-64 | 1984 | Burlington, Vt. |
| Ontiveros, Steve | 7 | 6 | 2.87 | 20 | 16 | 2 | 0 | 103 | 90 | 40 | 33 | 20 | 73 | R | R | 6-0 | 180 | 3-5-61 | 1982 | Stafford, Texas |
| Pulido, Carlos | 10 | 6 | 4.19 | 33 | 22 | 1 | 0 | 146 | 169 | 74 | 68 | 45 | 79 | L | L | 6-0 | 182 | 8-5-71 | 1989 | Caracas, Venez. |
| Sims, Mark | 3 | 1 | 3.41 | 50 | 0 | 0 | 3 | 66 | 69 | 33 | 25 | 36 | 32 | S | L | 6-1 | 170 | 4-7-68 | 1986 | Monroe, La. |
| Stevens, Matt | 5 | 3 | 1.98 | 53 | 0 | 0 | 2 | 82 | 75 | 27 | 18 | 35 | 60 | R | R | 6-1 | 200 | 1-20-67 | 1989 | Glens Falls, N.Y. |
| Tsamis, George | 1 | 2 | 8.36 | 3 | 3 | 0 | 0 | 14 | 27 | 15 | 13 | 5 | 10 | R | L | 6-2 | 175 | 6-14-67 | 1989 | Clearwater, Fla. |
| Willis, Carl | 0 | 0 | 2.25 | 2 | 0 | 0 | 0 | 4 | 6 | 2 | 1 | 1 | 2 | L | R | 6-4 | 210 | 12-28-60 | 1983 | Yanceyville, N.C. |

## FIELDING

| Catcher | PCT | G | PO | A | E | DP |
|---|---|---|---|---|---|---|
| Grifol | .978 | 28 | 171 | 10 | 4 | 2 |
| Grotewold | .941 | 31 | 149 | 11 | 10 | 1 |
| Maksudian | .981 | 28 | 146 | 12 | 3 | 2 |
| Parks | .993 | 69 | 376 | 47 | 3 | 5 |

| First Base | PCT | G | PO | A | E | DP |
|---|---|---|---|---|---|---|
| Grotewald | .889 | 2 | 7 | 1 | 1 | 2 |
| Jorgensen | 1.000 | 3 | 101 | 10 | 0 | 6 |
| Maksudian | .996 | 32 | 246 | 23 | 1 | 21 |
| Masteller | .988 | 39 | 303 | 28 | 4 | 28 |
| McCarty | .994 | 21 | 143 | 20 | 1 | 8 |
| Ortiz | .968 | 22 | 166 | 13 | 6 | 20 |
| Russo | .976 | 23 | 187 | 17 | 5 | 20 |
| Schunk | 1.000 | 1 | 1 | 0 | 0 | 0 |

| Second Base | PCT | G | PO | A | E | DP |
|---|---|---|---|---|---|---|
| Carter | .970 | 91 | 207 | 208 | 13 | 46 |

| | PCT | G | PO | A | E | DP |
|---|---|---|---|---|---|---|
| Hale | .946 | 35 | 69 | 89 | 9 | 18 |
| Schunk | 1.000 | 11 | 20 | 20 | 0 | 5 |
| Scott | 1.000 | 12 | 21 | 36 | 0 | 8 |

| Third Base | PCT | G | PO | A | E | DP |
|---|---|---|---|---|---|---|
| Grotewold | 1.000 | 1 | 1 | 0 | 0 | 0 |
| Hale | .951 | 16 | 5 | 34 | 2 | 3 |
| Jorgensen | .966 | 43 | 34 | 79 | 4 | 4 |
| Maksudian | .857 | 10 | 5 | 13 | 3 | 0 |
| Parks | 1.000 | 2 | 0 | 2 | 0 | 0 |
| Russo | .939 | 54 | 24 | 115 | 9 | 4 |
| Schunk | 1.000 | 2 | 2 | 5 | 0 | 0 |
| Scott | .928 | 23 | 18 | 46 | 5 | 4 |

| Shortstop | PCT | G | PO | A | E | DP |
|---|---|---|---|---|---|---|
| Hale | 1.000 | 4 | 5 | 11 | 0 | 1 |
| Jorgensen | .944 | 5 | 7 | 10 | 1 | 4 |

| Third Base | PCT | G | PO | A | E | DP |
|---|---|---|---|---|---|---|
| Meares | .938 | 18 | 28 | 48 | 5 | 9 |
| Schunk | .959 | 105 | 160 | 309 | 20 | 54 |
| Scott | .927 | 18 | 33 | 56 | 7 | 16 |

| Outfield | PCT | G | PO | A | E | DP |
|---|---|---|---|---|---|---|
| Brito | .951 | 36 | 37 | 2 | 2 | 0 |
| Bruett | .991 | 87 | 213 | 11 | 2 | 2 |
| Carter | 1.000 | 3 | 4 | 0 | 0 | 0 |
| Howell | .993 | 110 | 270 | 14 | 2 | 1 |
| Landrum | 1.000 | 2 | 1 | 0 | 0 | 0 |
| Lee | .971 | 102 | 188 | 10 | 6 | 4 |
| Masteller | .975 | 19 | 38 | 1 | 1 | 0 |
| McCarty | .977 | 22 | 42 | 1 | 1 | 0 |
| Ortiz | .946 | 74 | 114 | 8 | 7 | 0 |
| Wade | 1.000 | 6 | 6 | 1 | 0 | 0 |

# NASHVILLE    AA
## SOUTHERN LEAGUE

| BATTING | AVG | G | AB | R | H | 2B | 3B | HR | RBI | BB | SO | SB | CS | B | T | HT | WT | DOB | 1st Yr | Resides |
|---|---|---|---|---|---|---|---|---|---|---|---|---|---|---|---|---|---|---|---|---|
| Becker, Rich, of | .287 | 138 | 516 | 93 | 148 | 25 | 7 | 15 | 66 | 94 | 117 | 29 | 7 | S | L | 5-10 | 190 | 2-1-72 | 1990 | Aurora, Ill. |
| Corbin, Ted, ss | .333 | 5 | 15 | 2 | 5 | 1 | 0 | 0 | 1 | 2 | 2 | 0 | 0 | S | R | 5-9 | 150 | 4-27-71 | 1992 | Naples, Fla. |
| Cordova, Marty, of | .250 | 138 | 508 | 83 | 127 | 30 | 5 | 19 | 77 | 64 | 153 | 10 | 5 | R | R | 6-0 | 190 | 7-10-69 | 1989 | Las Vegas, Nev. |
| Delanuez, Rex, of | .236 | 115 | 352 | 71 | 83 | 20 | 3 | 8 | 43 | 93 | 80 | 23 | 4 | R | R | 5-10 | 175 | 1-7-68 | 1989 | Glendale, Calif. |
| Dunn, Steve, 1b | .262 | 97 | 366 | 48 | 96 | 20 | 2 | 14 | 60 | 35 | 88 | 1 | 2 | L | L | 6-4 | 220 | 4-18-70 | 1988 | Fairfax, Va. |
| Durant, Mike, c-dh | .243 | 123 | 437 | 58 | 106 | 23 | 1 | 8 | 57 | 44 | 68 | 17 | 3 | R | R | 6-2 | 205 | 9-14-69 | 1991 | Columbus, Ohio |
| Grifol, Pedro, c | .203 | 58 | 197 | 22 | 40 | 13 | 0 | 5 | 29 | 11 | 38 | 0 | 1 | R | R | 6-1 | 195 | 11-28-69 | 1991 | Miami, Fla. |
| Hocking, Denny, ss | .267 | 107 | 409 | 54 | 109 | 9 | 4 | 8 | 50 | 34 | 66 | 15 | 5 | S | R | 5-10 | 180 | 4-2-70 | 1990 | Torrance, Calif. |
| Houk, Tom, inf | .229 | 48 | 131 | 17 | 30 | 3 | 1 | 1 | 16 | 26 | 28 | 2 | 2 | R | R | 6-0 | 165 | 6-14-69 | 1989 | Bloomington, Ill. |
| Masteller, Dan, 1b-of | .273 | 36 | 121 | 19 | 33 | 3 | 0 | 3 | 16 | 11 | 19 | 2 | 1 | L | L | 6-1 | 185 | 3-17-68 | 1989 | Lyndhurst, Ohio |
| McDonald, Mike, of | .257 | 82 | 268 | 28 | 69 | 12 | 1 | 7 | 31 | 30 | 63 | 1 | 3 | L | R | 6-1 | 173 | 7-30-68 | 1986 | Douglasville, Ga. |
| Miller, Damian, c-dh | .231 | 4 | 13 | 0 | 3 | 0 | 0 | 0 | 2 | 4 | 0 | 0 | 0 | R | R | 6-2 | 190 | 10-13-69 | 1990 | West Salem, Wis. |
| Mota, Willie, 1b-3b | .234 | 64 | 201 | 16 | 47 | 10 | 2 | 2 | 26 | 9 | 33 | 1 | 1 | S | R | 6-2 | 192 | 5-29-71 | 1988 | Aragua, Venez. |
| Raabe, Brian, 2b-3b | .286 | 134 | 524 | 80 | 150 | 23 | 2 | 6 | 52 | 56 | 28 | 18 | 8 | R | R | 5-9 | 170 | 11-5-67 | 1990 | New Ulm, Minn. |
| Rivera, David, 2b | .237 | 105 | 325 | 41 | 77 | 7 | 2 | 3 | 33 | 17 | 42 | 35 | 9 | R | R | 5-10 | 165 | 8-26-69 | 1988 | Coamo, P.R. |
| Stahoviak, Scott, 3b | .272 | 93 | 331 | 40 | 90 | 25 | 1 | 12 | 56 | 56 | 95 | 10 | 2 | L | R | 6-5 | 225 | 3-6-70 | 1991 | Grays Lake, Ill. |

| PITCHING | W | L | ERA | G | GS | CG | SV | IP | H | R | ER | BB | SO | B | T | HT | WT | DOB | 1st Yr | Resides |
|---|---|---|---|---|---|---|---|---|---|---|---|---|---|---|---|---|---|---|---|---|
| Barcelo, Marc | 1 | 0 | 3.86 | 2 | 2 | 0 | 0 | 9 | 9 | 5 | 4 | 5 | 5 | R | R | 6-3 | 220 | 1-10-72 | 1993 | Tucson, Ariz. |
| Best, Jayson | 1 | 0 | 11.81 | 3 | 0 | 0 | 1 | 5 | 11 | 7 | 7 | 4 | 7 | R | R | 6-0 | 190 | 9-9-68 | 1989 | Otterbein, Ind. |
| Gavaghan, Sean | 4 | 0 | 0.49 | 20 | 1 | 0 | 7 | 37 | 21 | 3 | 2 | 12 | 30 | R | R | 6-1 | 185 | 12-19-69 | 1992 | Fort Washington, Pa. |
| Guardado, Eddie | 4 | 0 | 1.24 | 10 | 10 | 2 | 0 | 65 | 53 | 10 | 9 | 10 | 57 | R | L | 6-0 | 187 | 10-2-70 | 1991 | Stockton, Calif. |
| Henry, Jon | 4 | 2 | 2.74 | 6 | 6 | 1 | 0 | 43 | 41 | 14 | 13 | 7 | 20 | R | R | 6-5 | 215 | 8-1-68 | 1990 | Jamestown, N.Y. |
| Johnson, Greg | 3 | 1 | 2.80 | 31 | 0 | 0 | 13 | 35 | 30 | 12 | 11 | 10 | 54 | R | R | 6-2 | 190 | 5-29-66 | 1987 | Hixson, Tenn. |
| Klonoski, Jason | 4 | 6 | 3.16 | 56 | 0 | 0 | 3 | 77 | 69 | 33 | 27 | 34 | 56 | L | L | 6-2 | 195 | 3-24-67 | 1990 | River Forest, Ill. |
| Konieczki, Dom | 2 | 6 | 6.66 | 42 | 0 | 0 | 4 | 49 | 65 | 47 | 36 | 16 | 39 | R | L | 6-1 | 170 | 6-16-69 | 1991 | Erie, Pa. |
| Mansur, Jeff | 10 | 8 | 4.25 | 33 | 19 | 4 | 0 | 159 | 180 | 82 | 75 | 38 | 89 | L | L | 6-0 | 185 | 8-2-70 | 1991 | Hood River, Ore. |

# TWINS: MOST COMMON LINEUPS

| | Minnesota | Portland | Nashville | Fort Myers | Fort Wayne |
|---|---|---|---|---|---|
| | Majors | AAA | AA | A | A |
| C | Brian Harper (134) | Derek Parks (69) | Mike Durant (95) | Damian Miller (78) | Rene Lopez (69) |
| 1B | Kent Hrbek (115) | Dan Masteller (39) | Steve Dunn (81) | Andrew Kontorinis (102) | Ken Tirpack (125) |
| 2B | Chuck Knoblauch (148) | Jeff Carter (91) | David Rivera (98) | Chris Phillips (54) | Marlo Nava (64) |
| 3B | Mike Pagliarulo (79) | Paul Russo (54) | Scott Stahoviak (80) | Chad Roper (125) | Tom Knauss (53) |
| SS | Pat Meares (111) | Jerry Schunk (105) | Denny Hocking (99) | David Garrow (81) | Ramon Vallette (111) |
| OF | Kirby Puckett (139) | Pat Howell (110) | Rich Becker (131) | Jamie Ogden (106) | Anthony Byrd (117) |
| | Shane Mack (128) | Derek Lee (98) | Marty Cordova (130) | Kenny Norman (78) | Tim Costic (54) |
| | Pedro Munoz (102) | J.T. Bruett (98) | Rex Delanuez (97) | Tim Moore (66) | Ryan Radmanovich (51) |
| DH | Dave Winfield (105) | Bernardo Brito (49) | Mike Durant (28) | Mike Fernandez (54) | Matt Lawton (54) |
| SP | Kevin Tapani (35) | Drees/Neidlinger (24) | Bill Wissler (28) | Brett Roberts (28) | Caridad/Serafini (27) |
| RP | Rick Aguilera (65) | Matt Stevens (53) | Jason Klonoski (56) | Bigham/Garcia (53) | Gus Gandarillas (52) |
| | Full-season farm clubs only | No. of games at position in parenthesis | | | |

## TWINS TOP 10 PROSPECTS

**How the Twins Top 10 prospects, as judged by Baseball America prior to the 1993 season, fared in 1993:**

| Player, Pos. | Club (Class) | AVG | AB | H | HR | RBI | SB |
|---|---|---|---|---|---|---|---|
| 1. David McCarty, of | Portland (AAA) | .385 | 143 | 55 | 8 | 31 | 5 |
| | Minnesota | .214 | 350 | 75 | 2 | 21 | 2 |
| 3. Rich Becker, of | Nashville (AA) | .287 | 516 | 148 | 15 | 66 | 29 |
| | Minnesota | .286 | 7 | 2 | 0 | 0 | 1 |
| 5. Marty Cordova, of | Nashville (AA) | .250 | 508 | 127 | 19 | 77 | 10 |
| 6. Denny Hocking, ss | Nashville (AA) | .267 | 409 | 109 | 8 | 50 | 15 |
| | Minnesota | .139 | 36 | 5 | 0 | 0 | 1 |
| 8. Scott Stahoviak, 3b | Nashville (AA) | .272 | 331 | 90 | 12 | 56 | 10 |
| | Minnesota | .193 | 57 | 11 | 0 | 1 | 0 |
| 9. Edgar Herrera, of | Elizabethton (R) | .286 | 266 | 76 | 8 | 48 | 1 |
| | Ft. Wayne (A) | .195 | 113 | 22 | 1 | 13 | 0 |

| | | W | L | ERA | IP | H | BB | SO |
|---|---|---|---|---|---|---|---|---|
| 2. Mike Trombley, rhp | Minnesota | 6 | 6 | 4.88 | 114 | 131 | 41 | 85 |
| 4. Todd Ritchie, rhp | Nashville (AA) | 3 | 2 | 3.66 | 47 | 46 | 15 | 41 |
| 7. Alan Newman, lhp* | Nashville (AA) | 1 | 6 | 6.03 | 66 | 75 | 40 | 35 |
| | Indy (AAA) | 1 | 3 | 8.55 | 20 | 24 | 27 | 15 |
| 10. Dan Serafini, lhp | Ft. Wayne (A) | 10 | 8 | 3.65 | 141 | 117 | 83 | 147 |

*Traded to Cincinnati Reds

**David McCarty**
.214 at Minnesota

MEL BAILEY

### PITCHING

| | W | L | ERA | G | GS | CG | SV | IP | H | R | ER | BB | SO | B | T | HT | WT | DOB | 1st Yr | Resides |
|---|---|---|---|---|---|---|---|---|---|---|---|---|---|---|---|---|---|---|---|---|
| McCreary, Bob | 3 | 8 | 5.31 | 38 | 5 | 1 | 1 | 78 | 111 | 55 | 46 | 20 | 42 | S | R | 6-2 | 175 | 8-28-67 | 1989 | Dresher, Pa. |
| Misuraca, Mike | 6 | 6 | 3.82 | 25 | 17 | 2 | 0 | 113 | 103 | 57 | 48 | 40 | 80 | R | R | 6-1 | 185 | 8-21-68 | 1989 | Glendora, Calif. |
| Munoz, Oscar | 11 | 4 | 3.08 | 20 | 20 | 1 | 0 | 132 | 123 | 56 | 45 | 51 | 139 | R | R | 6-2 | 205 | 9-25-69 | 1990 | Hialeah, Fla. |
| Newman, Alan | 1 | 6 | 6.03 | 14 | 11 | 1 | 0 | 66 | 75 | 52 | 44 | 40 | 35 | L | L | 6-6 | 225 | 10-2-69 | 1988 | La Habra, Calif. |
| Radke, Brad | 2 | 6 | 4.62 | 13 | 13 | 1 | 0 | 76 | 81 | 42 | 39 | 16 | 76 | R | R | 6-2 | 180 | 10-27-72 | 1991 | Tampa, Fla. |
| Ritchie, Todd | 3 | 2 | 3.66 | 12 | 10 | 0 | 0 | 47 | 46 | 21 | 19 | 15 | 41 | R | R | 6-3 | 185 | 11-7-71 | 1990 | Duncanville, Texas |
| Robinson, Bob | 2 | 4 | 5.16 | 35 | 0 | 0 | 3 | 45 | 64 | 34 | 26 | 15 | 26 | R | R | 6-0 | 185 | 12-12-69 | 1991 | Circleville, Ohio |
| Schullstrom, Erik | 1 | 0 | 4.85 | 4 | 3 | 0 | 0 | 13 | 16 | 7 | 7 | 6 | 11 | R | R | 6-5 | 220 | 3-25-69 | 1990 | San Leandro, Calif. |
| Watkins, Scott | 0 | 1 | 5.94 | 13 | 0 | 0 | 0 | 17 | 19 | 15 | 11 | 7 | 17 | L | L | 6-3 | 180 | 5-15-70 | 1992 | Sand Springs, Okla. |
| Wissler, Bill | 10 | 10 | 3.95 | 29 | 25 | 2 | 0 | 175 | 169 | 88 | 77 | 48 | 115 | R | R | 6-3 | 205 | 8-27-70 | 1991 | Harrisburg, Pa. |

# FORT MYERS — A
## FLORIDA STATE LEAGUE

### BATTING

| | AVG | G | AB | R | H | 2B | 3B | HR | RBI | BB | SO | SB | CS | B | T | HT | WT | DOB | 1st Yr | Resides |
|---|---|---|---|---|---|---|---|---|---|---|---|---|---|---|---|---|---|---|---|---|
| Brede, Brent, of | .330 | 53 | 182 | 27 | 60 | 10 | 1 | 0 | 27 | 32 | 19 | 8 | 4 | L | L | 6-4 | 175 | 9-13-71 | 1990 | New Baden, Ill. |
| Brown, Matt, c | .164 | 60 | 201 | 8 | 33 | 2 | 0 | 0 | 17 | 11 | 41 | 1 | 2 | R | R | 6-0 | 195 | 4-4-69 | 1990 | Foster City, Calif. |
| Burrough, Butch, of-dh | .210 | 77 | 248 | 28 | 52 | 12 | 3 | 8 | 30 | 35 | 75 | 8 | 4 | R | R | 6-1 | 192 | 5-7-71 | 1992 | Eastchester, N.Y. |
| Corbin, Ted, ss-2b | .236 | 91 | 339 | 46 | 80 | 11 | 2 | 0 | 22 | 36 | 47 | 22 | 8 | S | R | 5-9 | 150 | 4-27-71 | 1992 | Naples, Fla. |
| Duncan, Andres, ss | .364 | 5 | 22 | 3 | 8 | 0 | 0 | 1 | 1 | 3 | 6 | 4 | 2 | S | R | 5-11 | 155 | 11-30-71 | 1989 | San Pedro de Macoris, D.R. |
| Fernandez, Mike, dh-of | .267 | 107 | 375 | 47 | 100 | 29 | 3 | 1 | 37 | 45 | 73 | 14 | 2 | R | R | 5-10 | 170 | 8-21-69 | 1991 | Elmhurst, N.Y. |
| Garrow, David, ss-of | .208 | 109 | 351 | 33 | 73 | 15 | 0 | 2 | 25 | 25 | 62 | 11 | 4 | R | R | 6-3 | 190 | 9-26-70 | 1991 | Mesa, Ariz. |
| Hazlett, Steve, of | .339 | 29 | 115 | 19 | 39 | 5 | 2 | 0 | 6 | 15 | 21 | 12 | 5 | R | R | 5-11 | 170 | 3-30-70 | 1991 | Longmont, Colo. |
| Horincewich, Tom, 2b | .217 | 45 | 161 | 19 | 35 | 9 | 1 | 0 | 12 | 19 | 19 | 1 | 1 | L | R | 5-11 | 188 | 7-26-70 | 1992 | Gillette, N.J. |
| Kontorinis, Andrew, 1b | .255 | 114 | 408 | 44 | 104 | 24 | 3 | 3 | 59 | 40 | 42 | 4 | 5 | L | R | 6-0 | 198 | 11-18-69 | 1992 | Astoria, N.Y. |
| Miller, Damian, c | .212 | 87 | 325 | 31 | 69 | 12 | 1 | 1 | 26 | 31 | 44 | 6 | 3 | R | R | 6-2 | 190 | 10-13-69 | 1990 | West Salem, Wis. |
| Moore, Tim, of | .252 | 69 | 222 | 32 | 56 | 15 | 3 | 6 | 32 | 28 | 52 | 17 | 3 | S | L | 5-9 | 215 | 8-27-71 | 1989 | Greenville, N.C. |
| Mota, Willie, 1b-dh | .235 | 39 | 149 | 13 | 35 | 6 | 0 | 2 | 5 | 8 | 21 | 1 | 1 | S | R | 6-2 | 192 | 5-29-71 | 1988 | Aragua, Venez. |
| Norman, Kenny, of | .207 | 84 | 237 | 27 | 49 | 9 | 0 | 1 | 8 | 11 | 67 | 12 | 7 | S | R | 5-10 | 180 | 7-13-71 | 1989 | Sweetwater, Texas |
| Ogden, Jamie, of | .242 | 118 | 396 | 37 | 96 | 22 | 4 | 8 | 46 | 34 | 89 | 7 | 1 | L | L | 6-5 | 205 | 1-19-72 | 1990 | White Bear Lake, Minn. |
| Phillips, Chris, 2b | .264 | 54 | 197 | 32 | 52 | 9 | 1 | 0 | 15 | 26 | 34 | 9 | 9 | R | R | 6-0 | 175 | 9-27-71 | 1993 | Louisville, Ky. |
| Roper, Chad, 3b | .248 | 125 | 452 | 46 | 112 | 17 | 3 | 9 | 65 | 43 | 96 | 1 | 2 | R | R | 6-1 | 212 | 3-29-74 | 1992 | Belton, S.C. |
| Shockey, Greg, of-dh | .259 | 16 | 54 | 8 | 14 | 3 | 0 | 0 | 5 | 12 | 7 | 4 | 2 | L | L | 6-1 | 195 | 4-11-70 | 1992 | Boise, Idaho |

### PITCHING

| | W | L | ERA | G | GS | CG | SV | IP | H | R | ER | BB | SO | B | T | HT | WT | DOB | 1st Yr | Resides |
|---|---|---|---|---|---|---|---|---|---|---|---|---|---|---|---|---|---|---|---|---|
| Barcelo, Marc | 1 | 1 | 2.74 | 7 | 3 | 0 | 0 | 23 | 18 | 10 | 7 | 4 | 24 | R | R | 6-3 | 220 | 1-10-72 | 1993 | Tucson, Ariz. |
| Bigham, Dave | 8 | 3 | 3.40 | 53 | 0 | 0 | 5 | 85 | 87 | 37 | 32 | 22 | 60 | L | L | 6-0 | 190 | 9-20-70 | 1989 | Mankato, Minn. |
| Dixon, Dickie | 4 | 12 | 4.21 | 25 | 25 | 1 | 0 | 152 | 168 | 87 | 71 | 32 | 109 | L | L | 6-4 | 205 | 1-6-69 | 1990 | Nashville, Tenn. |
| Garcia, Luis | 4 | 1 | 4.04 | 55 | 2 | 0 | 10 | 89 | 105 | 53 | 40 | 31 | 54 | R | R | 5-11 | 185 | 6-18-70 | 1991 | Miami Beach, Fla. |
| Gavaghan, Sean | 1 | 3 | 2.61 | 19 | 0 | 0 | 4 | 31 | 37 | 10 | 9 | 8 | 24 | R | R | 6-1 | 185 | 12-19-69 | 1992 | Fort Washington, Pa. |
| Johnson, Greg | 0 | 0 | 0.00 | 2 | 0 | 0 | 1 | 2 | 1 | 0 | 0 | 1 | 4 | R | R | 6-2 | 190 | 5-29-66 | 1987 | Hixson, Tenn. |
| Kohl, Jim | 1 | 1 | 5.13 | 17 | 0 | 0 | 0 | 26 | 35 | 20 | 15 | 11 | 10 | R | L | 6-1 | 175 | 5-31-69 | 1991 | South Plainfield, N.J. |
| Konieczki, Dom | 0 | 2 | 3.78 | 12 | 0 | 0 | 2 | 17 | 18 | 7 | 7 | 16 | 15 | R | L | 6-1 | 170 | 6-16-69 | 1991 | Erie, Pa. |
| Legault, Kevin | 3 | 9 | 5.71 | 18 | 18 | 3 | 0 | 110 | 142 | 80 | 70 | 33 | 60 | R | R | 6-1 | 196 | 3-5-71 | 1992 | Watervliet, N.Y. |
| Naulty, Dan | 0 | 3 | 5.70 | 7 | 6 | 0 | 0 | 30 | 41 | 22 | 19 | 14 | 20 | R | R | 6-5 | 190 | 1-6-70 | 1992 | Huntington Beach, Calif. |
| Radke, Brad | 3 | 5 | 3.82 | 14 | 14 | 0 | 0 | 92 | 85 | 42 | 39 | 21 | 69 | R | R | 6-2 | 180 | 10-27-72 | 1991 | Tampa, Fla. |
| Roberts, Brett | 9 | 16 | 4.35 | 28 | 28 | 3 | 0 | 174 | 184 | 93 | 84 | 86 | 108 | R | R | 6-7 | 225 | 3-24-70 | 1991 | South Webster, Ohio |
| Robinson, Bob | 0 | 1 | 3.26 | 15 | 0 | 0 | 4 | 19 | 28 | 9 | 7 | 3 | 15 | R | R | 6-0 | 185 | 12-12-69 | 1991 | Circleville, Ohio |
| Saccavino, Craig | 5 | 8 | 4.70 | 23 | 19 | 2 | 0 | 105 | 122 | 63 | 55 | 49 | 55 | R | R | 6-1 | 200 | 10-1-69 | 1992 | Stewart, Pa. |
| Sweeney, Dennis | 8 | 7 | 3.92 | 39 | 13 | 1 | 0 | 115 | 110 | 56 | 50 | 55 | 77 | L | L | 6-0 | 190 | 8-6-69 | 1991 | Danville, Pa. |
| Swope, Mark | 3 | 4 | 4.99 | 26 | 4 | 0 | 1 | 58 | 74 | 42 | 32 | 23 | 32 | R | R | 6-1 | 180 | 1-18-69 | 1990 | Spring Hill, Kan. |
| Thelen, Jeff | 3 | 1 | 6.75 | 10 | 2 | 0 | 0 | 24 | 33 | 18 | 18 | 7 | 14 | R | R | 6-2 | 180 | 12-8-70 | 1990 | Janesville, Wis. |
| Watkins, Scott | 2 | 2 | 2.93 | 20 | 0 | 0 | 3 | 28 | 27 | 14 | 9 | 12 | 41 | L | L | 6-3 | 180 | 5-15-70 | 1992 | Sand Springs, Okla. |

# FORT WAYNE — A
## MIDWEST LEAGUE

### BATTING

| | AVG | G | AB | R | H | 2B | 3B | HR | RBI | BB | SO | SB | CS | B | T | HT | WT | DOB | 1st Yr | Resides |
|---|---|---|---|---|---|---|---|---|---|---|---|---|---|---|---|---|---|---|---|---|
| Brown, Armann, of | .194 | 41 | 124 | 11 | 24 | 3 | 0 | 0 | 10 | 18 | 27 | 13 | 1 | R | R | 6-1 | 165 | 9-10-72 | 1992 | Austin, Texas |

| BATTING | AVG | G | AB | R | H | 2B | 3B | HR | RBI | BB | SO | SB | CS | B | T | HT | WT | DOB | 1st Yr | Resides |
|---|---|---|---|---|---|---|---|---|---|---|---|---|---|---|---|---|---|---|---|---|
| Byrd, Anthony, of | .292 | 123 | 479 | 84 | 140 | 19 | 10 | 16 | 79 | 58 | 79 | 24 | 11 | R | R | 5-11 | 185 | 11-13-70 | 1992 | La Grange, Ga. |
| Claus, Marc, 2b-ss | .206 | 81 | 248 | 29 | 51 | 7 | 1 | 0 | 9 | 24 | 60 | 7 | 4 | R | R | 6-0 | 175 | 4-4-71 | 1992 | Oakland Park, Fla. |
| Costic, Tim, of-1b | .238 | 85 | 273 | 28 | 65 | 14 | 3 | 4 | 29 | 26 | 75 | 5 | 7 | L | L | 6-2 | 176 | 3-4-71 | 1992 | Sepulveda, Calif. |
| Herrera, Edgar, of | .195 | 37 | 113 | 8 | 22 | 4 | 0 | 1 | 13 | 12 | 28 | 0 | 0 | R | R | 6-3 | 185 | 2-12-73 | 1992 | Caracas, Venez. |
| Horn, Jeff, c | .195 | 66 | 200 | 19 | 39 | 7 | 0 | 5 | 23 | 18 | 51 | 1 | 2 | R | R | 6-1 | 188 | 8-23-70 | 1992 | Riverside, Calif. |
| Knauss, Tom, 3b | .188 | 55 | 186 | 26 | 35 | 3 | 2 | 5 | 22 | 21 | 44 | 5 | 3 | R | R | 6-2 | 205 | 6-16-74 | 1992 | Arlington Heights, Ill. |
| Lawton, Matt, dh-of | .285 | 111 | 340 | 50 | 97 | 21 | 3 | 9 | 38 | 65 | 42 | 23 | 15 | L | R | 5-9 | 180 | 11-30-71 | 1991 | Saucier, Miss. |
| Legree, Keith, of | .242 | 49 | 178 | 28 | 43 | 6 | 2 | 3 | 14 | 21 | 51 | 1 | 2 | L | R | 6-2 | 200 | 12-26-71 | 1991 | Statesboro, Ga. |
| Lopez, Rene, c | .250 | 92 | 340 | 26 | 85 | 12 | 1 | 3 | 44 | 45 | 57 | 0 | 1 | R | R | 6-1 | 195 | 12-10-71 | 1992 | Downey, Calif. |
| Miller, Joey, of | .243 | 67 | 169 | 30 | 41 | 8 | 3 | 1 | 9 | 25 | 60 | 20 | 7 | R | R | 6-1 | 190 | 5-21-71 | 1992 | San Pedro, Calif. |
| Nava, Marlon, 2b-3b | .259 | 115 | 455 | 48 | 118 | 25 | 2 | 2 | 47 | 23 | 61 | 9 | 3 | R | R | 5-11 | 170 | 6-18-73 | 1991 | LaGunillas, Venez. |
| Radmanovich, Ryan, of. | .289 | 62 | 204 | 36 | 59 | 7 | 5 | 8 | 38 | 30 | 60 | 8 | 2 | L | R | 6-2 | 185 | 8-9-71 | 1993 | Calgary, Alberta |
| Santini, Aaron, 2b-ss | .194 | 46 | 139 | 17 | 27 | 3 | 1 | 1 | 7 | 17 | 31 | 7 | 1 | R | R | 5-11 | 178 | 12-17-71 | 1993 | Tucson, Ariz. |
| Stricklin, Scott, c | .065 | 9 | 31 | 1 | 2 | 0 | 0 | 0 | 0 | 4 | 7 | 0 | 0 | L | R | 6-0 | 180 | 2-17-72 | 1993 | The Plains, Ohio |
| Tirpack, Ken, 1b | .294 | 127 | 473 | 71 | 139 | 34 | 3 | 9 | 70 | 68 | 103 | 1 | 4 | R | R | 6-0 | 186 | 10-3-69 | 1992 | Campbell, Ohio |
| Tomberlin, Justin, 3b | .258 | 45 | 151 | 20 | 39 | 10 | 1 | 1 | 16 | 7 | 21 | 0 | 0 | R | R | 6-1 | 185 | 11-15-70 | 1993 | Coleraine, Minn. |
| Valette, Ramon, ss | .238 | 112 | 382 | 46 | 91 | 20 | 0 | 6 | 38 | 23 | 89 | 12 | 7 | R | R | 6-1 | 150 | 1-20-72 | 1990 | Sabana Gr. Palenque, D.R. |

| PITCHING | W | L | ERA | G | GS | CG | SV | IP | H | R | ER | BB | SO | B | T | HT | WT | DOB | 1st Yr | Resides |
|---|---|---|---|---|---|---|---|---|---|---|---|---|---|---|---|---|---|---|---|---|
| Caridad, Ron | 6 | 8 | 3.51 | 27 | 27 | 0 | 0 | 144 | 138 | 68 | 56 | 91 | 124 | R | R | 5-10 | 180 | 3-22-72 | 1990 | Miami, Fla. |
| Correa, Jose | 4 | 5 | 2.63 | 41 | 0 | 0 | 9 | 96 | 81 | 33 | 28 | 36 | 107 | R | R | 6-2 | 175 | 6-21-72 | 1992 | Guarenas, Venez. |
| Fultz, Aaron | 0 | 0 | 9.00 | 1 | 1 | 0 | 0 | 4 | 10 | 4 | 4 | 0 | 3 | L | L | 5-11 | 195 | 9-4-73 | 1992 | Munford, Tenn. |
| 2-team (26 Clinton) | 14 | 8 | 3.55 | 27 | 26 | 2 | 0 | 152 | 142 | 67 | 60 | 64 | 147 | | | | | | | |
| Gandarillas, Gus | 5 | 5 | 3.26 | 52 | 0 | 0 | 25 | 66 | 66 | 37 | 24 | 22 | 59 | R | R | 6-0 | 178 | 7-19-71 | 1992 | Hialeah, Fla. |
| Gavaghan, Sean | 3 | 1 | 1.23 | 11 | 0 | 0 | 1 | 22 | 14 | 5 | 3 | 7 | 25 | R | R | 6-1 | 185 | 12-19-69 | 1992 | Fort Washington, Pa. |
| Hawkins, LaTroy | 15 | 5 | 2.06 | 26 | 23 | 4 | 0 | 157 | 110 | 53 | 36 | 41 | 179 | R | R | 6-5 | 195 | 12-21-72 | 1991 | Gary, Ind. |
| Legault, Kevin | 1 | 1 | 3.38 | 12 | 0 | 0 | 2 | 27 | 28 | 13 | 10 | 12 | 28 | R | R | 6-1 | 196 | 3-5-71 | 1992 | Watervliet, N.Y. |
| Linebarger, Keith | 5 | 7 | 4.25 | 35 | 11 | 1 | 0 | 97 | 113 | 60 | 46 | 43 | 76 | R | R | 6-6 | 220 | 5-11-71 | 1992 | Ringgold, Ga. |
| Miller, Shawn | 0 | 0 | 5.81 | 8 | 2 | 0 | 1 | 26 | 32 | 28 | 17 | 14 | 18 | R | R | 6-3 | 190 | 4-27-73 | 1991 | Modesto, Calif. |
| Moten, Scott | 7 | 11 | 5.05 | 30 | 22 | 0 | 1 | 141 | 152 | 99 | 79 | 63 | 141 | R | R | 6-1 | 192 | 4-12-72 | 1992 | Bellflower, Calif. |
| Naulty, Dan | 6 | 8 | 3.26 | 18 | 18 | 3 | 0 | 116 | 101 | 45 | 42 | 48 | 96 | R | R | 6-5 | 190 | 1-6-70 | 1992 | Huntington Beach, Calif. |
| Ohme, Kevin | 3 | 2 | 2.53 | 15 | 4 | 0 | 0 | 46 | 38 | 19 | 13 | 15 | 45 | L | L | 6-1 | 175 | 4-13-71 | 1993 | West Palm Beach, Fla. |
| Sartain, David | 1 | 1 | 2.57 | 5 | 0 | 0 | 1 | 7 | 3 | 2 | 2 | 2 | 7 | L | L | 6-2 | 190 | 2-7-70 | 1991 | Virginia Beach, Va. |
| Serafini, Dan | 10 | 8 | 3.65 | 27 | 27 | 1 | 0 | 141 | 117 | 72 | 57 | 83 | 147 | S | L | 6-2 | 175 | 1-25-74 | 1992 | San Bruno, Calif. |
| Tatar, Jason | 0 | 0 | 2.57 | 2 | 0 | 0 | 0 | 7 | 4 | 2 | 2 | 2 | 7 | R | R | 6-0 | 175 | 8-15-74 | 1992 | Rantoul, Ill. |
| Taylor, Todd | 0 | 5 | 5.14 | 25 | 0 | 0 | 0 | 49 | 54 | 32 | 28 | 23 | 40 | L | L | 5-9 | 157 | 5-25-71 | 1992 | Long Beach, Calif. |
| Watkins, Scott | 2 | 0 | 3.26 | 15 | 0 | 0 | 1 | 30 | 26 | 13 | 11 | 9 | 31 | L | L | 6-3 | 180 | 5-15-70 | 1992 | Sand Springs, Okla. |

# ELIZABETHTON     R
## APPALACHIAN LEAGUE

| BATTING | AVG | G | AB | R | H | 2B | 3B | HR | RBI | BB | SO | SB | CS | B | T | HT | WT | DOB | 1st Yr | Resides |
|---|---|---|---|---|---|---|---|---|---|---|---|---|---|---|---|---|---|---|---|---|
| Acevedo, Jesus, c-dh | .105 | 5 | 19 | 1 | 2 | 0 | 0 | 0 | 1 | 0 | 5 | 0 | 0 | R | R | 6-0 | 170 | 4-26-74 | 1991 | Maracaibo, Venez. |
| Baker, Jason, of | .298 | 60 | 248 | 45 | 74 | 19 | 4 | 3 | 26 | 20 | 27 | 16 | 2 | L | L | 5-10 | 180 | 7-31-72 | 1992 | Shelbyville, Tenn. |
| Baucom, Chad, c | .204 | 21 | 49 | 9 | 10 | 2 | 0 | 1 | 5 | 13 | 14 | 0 | 0 | R | R | 6-2 | 210 | 2-12-73 | 1991 | Hibbing, Minn. |
| Blanco, Pedro, 3b-2b | .202 | 38 | 129 | 14 | 26 | 3 | 1 | 1 | 12 | 8 | 22 | 8 | 1 | S | R | 5-10 | 165 | 7-16-73 | 1990 | Furmero Aragua, Venez. |
| Brown, Armann, of | .269 | 50 | 182 | 31 | 49 | 8 | 2 | 3 | 21 | 19 | 41 | 7 | 3 | R | R | 6-1 | 165 | 9-10-72 | 1992 | Austin, Texas |
| Ferrante, Steve, c-dh | .217 | 18 | 46 | 9 | 10 | 4 | 0 | 1 | 8 | 7 | 16 | 0 | 0 | R | R | 6-2 | 210 | 10-12-71 | 1993 | Bernardsville, N.J. |
| Herrera, Edgar, of | .286 | 67 | 266 | 48 | 76 | 15 | 1 | 8 | 48 | 22 | 52 | 1 | 2 | R | R | 6-3 | 185 | 2-12-73 | 1992 | Caracas, Venez. |
| Jones, Ben, of | .273 | 40 | 139 | 26 | 38 | 12 | 0 | 0 | 19 | 8 | 15 | 7 | 4 | R | R | 5-10 | 175 | 9-15-73 | 1992 | Alexandria, La. |
| Knauss, Tom, 3b | .243 | 54 | 206 | 36 | 50 | 15 | 3 | 5 | 34 | 26 | 37 | 2 | 1 | R | R | 6-2 | 205 | 6-16-74 | 1992 | Arlington Heights, Ill. |
| Motte, James, dh-ss | .288 | 45 | 153 | 32 | 44 | 7 | 1 | 10 | 27 | 15 | 29 | 3 | 2 | R | R | 6-2 | 175 | 5-4-72 | 1993 | Pueblo, Colo. |
| Rupp, Chad, 1b | .246 | 67 | 228 | 54 | 56 | 14 | 1 | 10 | 36 | 44 | 79 | 0 | 1 | R | R | 6-2 | 215 | 9-30-71 | 1993 | Tampa, Fla. |
| Stricklin, Scott, c | .224 | 38 | 125 | 18 | 28 | 2 | 0 | 1 | 15 | 16 | 17 | 1 | 0 | L | R | 6-0 | 180 | 2-17-72 | 1993 | The Plains, Ohio |
| Valentin, Jose, c | .208 | 9 | 24 | 3 | 5 | 1 | 0 | 0 | 3 | 4 | 2 | 0 | 0 | S | R | 5-10 | 190 | 9-19-75 | 1993 | Manati, P.R. |

# TWINS: ORGANIZATION LEADERS

**Kevin Tapani**
Led '93 Twins with 12 wins

### MAJOR LEAGUERS
**BATTING**
| | | |
|---|---|---|
| *AVG | Brian Harper | .304 |
| R | Kirby Puckett | 89 |
| H | Kirby Puckett | 184 |
| TB | Kirby Puckett | 295 |
| 2B | Kirby Puckett | 39 |
| 3B | Two tied at | 4 |
| HR | Kent Hrbek | 25 |
| RBI | Kirby Puckett | 89 |
| BB | Kent Hrbek | 71 |
| SO | Dave Winfield | 106 |
| SB | Chuck Knoblauch | 29 |

**PITCHING**
| | | |
|---|---|---|
| W | Kevin Tapani | 12 |
| L | Scott Erickson | 19 |
| #ERA | Mike Hartley | 4.00 |
| G | Rick Aguilera | 65 |
| CG | Kevin Tapani | 3 |
| SV | Rick Aguilera | 34 |
| IP | Kevin Tapani | 226 |
| BB | Willie Banks | 78 |
| SO | Kevin Tapani | 150 |

### MINOR LEAGUERS
**BATTING**
| | | |
|---|---|---|
| *AVG | Bernardo Brito, Portland | .339 |
| R | Rich Becker, Nashville | 93 |
| H | Brian Raabe, Nashville | 150 |
| TB | Rich Becker, Nashville | 232 |
| 2B | Ken Tirpack, Fort Wayne | 34 |
| 3B | Anthony Byrd, Fort Wayne | 10 |
| HR | Bernardo Brito, Portland | 20 |
| RBI | Derek Lee, Portland | 80 |
| BB | Rich Becker, Nashville | 94 |
| SO | Marty Cordova, Nashville | 153 |
| SB | Pat Howell, Portland | 36 |

**PITCHING**
| | | |
|---|---|---|
| W | Two tied at | 15 |
| L | Brett Roberts, Fort Myers | 16 |
| #ERA | Sean Gavaghan, Nash.-Ft.M.-Ft.W. | 1.41 |
| G | Jason Klonoski, Nashville | 56 |
| CG | Two tied at | 4 |
| SV | Gus Gandarillas, Fort Wayne | 25 |
| IP | Bill Wissler, Nashville | 175 |
| BB | Ron Caridad, Fort Wayne | 91 |
| SO | LaTroy Hawkins, Fort Wayne | 179 |

*Minimum 250 At-Bats    #Minimum 75 Innings

| BATTING | AVG | G | AB | R | H | 2B | 3B | HR | RBI | BB | SO | SB | CS | B | T | HT | WT | DOB | 1st Yr | Resides |
|---|---|---|---|---|---|---|---|---|---|---|---|---|---|---|---|---|---|---|---|---|
| Venezia, Danny, 2b | .310 | 62 | 258 | 47 | 80 | 9 | 1 | 2 | 36 | 18 | 34 | 21 | 8 | R | R | 6-1 | 180 | 11-4-71 | 1993 | Brooklyn, N.Y. |
| Wilson, Enrique, ss | .289 | 58 | 197 | 42 | 57 | 8 | 4 | 13 | 50 | 14 | 18 | 5 | 4 | S | R | 5-11 | 158 | 7-27-75 | 1992 | Santo Domingo, D.R. |

| PITCHING | W | L | ERA | G | GS | CG | SV | IP | H | R | ER | BB | SO | B | T | HT | WT | DOB | 1st Yr | Resides |
|---|---|---|---|---|---|---|---|---|---|---|---|---|---|---|---|---|---|---|---|---|
| Bowers, Shane | 2 | 0 | 4.76 | 7 | 1 | 0 | 0 | 11 | 13 | 7 | 6 | 1 | 13 | R | R | 6-6 | 215 | 7-27-71 | 1993 | Covina, Calif. |
| Carrasco, Troy | 2 | 4 | 3.20 | 14 | 10 | 0 | 2 | 70 | 46 | 32 | 25 | 39 | 75 | S | L | 5-11 | 172 | 1-27-75 | 1993 | Tampa, Fla. |
| Cobb, Trevor | 5 | 4 | 3.92 | 13 | 13 | 1 | 0 | 83 | 71 | 48 | 36 | 40 | 53 | L | L | 6-2 | 182 | 7-13-73 | 1992 | Marysville, Wash. |
| DeJesus, Javier | 9 | 0 | 2.99 | 12 | 12 | 0 | 0 | 78 | 55 | 27 | 26 | 36 | 79 | L | L | 5-11 | 175 | 3-4-71 | 1992 | Beaumont, Texas |
| Dowhower, Deron | 0 | 2 | 3.69 | 20 | 0 | 0 | 1 | 32 | 11 | 17 | 13 | 30 | 40 | R | R | 6-2 | 195 | 2-14-72 | 1993 | Ashburn, Va. |
| Lehoisky, Russel | 2 | 8 | 5.79 | 23 | 2 | 0 | 4 | 47 | 48 | 37 | 30 | 23 | 55 | R | R | 6-5 | 207 | 1-30-71 | 1993 | Comstock, N.J. |
| Miller, Shawn | 5 | 0 | 2.63 | 13 | 11 | 1 | 0 | 68 | 60 | 26 | 20 | 23 | 35 | R | R | 6-3 | 190 | 4-27-73 | 1991 | Modesto, Calif. |
| O'Brien, Brian | 1 | 5 | 3.64 | 14 | 0 | 0 | 1 | 30 | 36 | 21 | 12 | 17 | 39 | L | L | 6-4 | 173 | 7-4-71 | 1993 | Bellevue, Neb. |
| Oiler, David | 2 | 2 | 3.47 | 19 | 1 | 0 | 4 | 36 | 37 | 24 | 14 | 16 | 32 | L | L | 6-0 | 187 | 6-10-71 | 1993 | Elizabethton, Tenn. |
| Perkins, Dan | 3 | 3 | 5.00 | 10 | 10 | 0 | 0 | 45 | 46 | 33 | 25 | 25 | 30 | R | R | 6-2 | 182 | 3-15-75 | 1993 | Miami, Fla. |
| Sampson, Benj | 4 | 1 | 1.91 | 11 | 6 | 0 | 1 | 42 | 33 | 12 | 9 | 15 | 34 | R | L | 6-1 | 190 | 4-27-75 | 1993 | Bondurant, Iowa |
| Schooler, Aaron | 2 | 1 | 3.86 | 17 | 1 | 0 | 2 | 28 | 28 | 17 | 12 | 17 | 26 | R | R | 6-2 | 210 | 6-14-73 | 1993 | Malaga, Wash. |

# FORT MYERS R

## GULF COAST LEAGUE

| BATTING | AVG | G | AB | R | H | 2B | 3B | HR | RBI | BB | SO | SB | CS | B | T | HT | WT | DOB | 1st Yr | Resides |
|---|---|---|---|---|---|---|---|---|---|---|---|---|---|---|---|---|---|---|---|---|
| Abreu, Guillermo, ss | .200 | 25 | 60 | 9 | 12 | 2 | 0 | 0 | 9 | 4 | 10 | 1 | 0 | R | R | 5-10 | 150 | 11-20-75 | 1993 | San Cristobal, D.R. |
| Baucom, Chad, c-1b | .057 | 11 | 35 | 1 | 2 | 1 | 0 | 0 | 1 | 1 | 9 | 0 | 0 | R | R | 6-2 | 210 | 2-12-73 | 1991 | Hibbing, Minn. |
| Casique, Willie, ss | .241 | 10 | 29 | 4 | 7 | 1 | 0 | 0 | 2 | 3 | 4 | 0 | 1 | R | R | 6-0 | 175 | 10-15-75 | 1993 | Caracas, Venez. |
| Castro, Ruben, 2b-3b | .267 | 40 | 135 | 19 | 36 | 8 | 2 | 0 | 12 | 21 | 18 | 3 | 2 | R | R | 5-11 | 180 | 4-16-76 | 1993 | Maracaibo, Venez. |
| Crick, Jeff, 1b-3b | .127 | 24 | 71 | 7 | 9 | 1 | 0 | 0 | 5 | 7 | 29 | 0 | 0 | R | R | 6-3 | 180 | 2-18-74 | 1993 | Jacksonville, Fla. |
| Cruz, Hiram, 2b | .215 | 39 | 107 | 21 | 23 | 4 | 0 | 2 | 11 | 18 | 38 | 8 | 2 | R | R | 5-10 | 175 | 6-19-73 | 1992 | Miami, Fla. |
| Doezie, David, c | .126 | 31 | 87 | 11 | 11 | 2 | 0 | 0 | 8 | 9 | 25 | 1 | 0 | R | R | 6-2 | 190 | 9-6-73 | 1992 | Sandy, Utah |
| Fortin, Troy, c-dh | .257 | 30 | 101 | 6 | 26 | 3 | 0 | 2 | 15 | 8 | 11 | 3 | 0 | R | R | 5-11 | 200 | 2-24-75 | 1993 | Lundar, Manitoba |
| Garcia, Carlos, 2b | .240 | 16 | 50 | 7 | 12 | 3 | 1 | 0 | 6 | 4 | 14 | 3 | 2 | R | R | 5-11 | 165 | 5-21-74 | 1993 | Vargas, Venez. |
| Gordon, Adrian, of | .241 | 37 | 112 | 11 | 27 | 2 | 1 | 0 | 8 | 17 | 29 | 5 | 3 | R | R | 6-3 | 231 | 3-8-74 | 1992 | Alexandria, La. |
| Hunter, Torii, of | .190 | 28 | 100 | 6 | 19 | 3 | 0 | 0 | 8 | 4 | 23 | 4 | 2 | S | R | 6-1 | 180 | 7-18-75 | 1993 | Pine Bluff, Ark. |
| Johnson, Mike, of | .379 | 7 | 29 | 4 | 11 | 2 | 1 | 0 | 6 | 4 | 4 | 0 | 0 | R | R | 6-1 | 180 | 8-11-73 | 1993 | Quitman, Ga. |
| Lane, Ryan, ss | .145 | 43 | 138 | 15 | 20 | 3 | 2 | 0 | 5 | 15 | 38 | 3 | 1 | R | R | 6-1 | 180 | 7-6-74 | 1993 | Bellefontaine, Ohio |
| Mucker, Kelcey, dh | .138 | 9 | 29 | 6 | 4 | 0 | 0 | 0 | 2 | 4 | 10 | 2 | 0 | L | R | 6-1 | 220 | 2-17-75 | 1993 | Lawrenceburg, Ind. |
| Patterson, Jacob, 1b | .207 | 44 | 140 | 14 | 29 | 6 | 1 | 2 | 16 | 13 | 34 | 1 | 0 | L | L | 6-1 | 235 | 8-1-73 | 1993 | Golden, Colo. |
| Pearson, Kevin, of-1b | .142 | 42 | 120 | 13 | 17 | 1 | 0 | 1 | 6 | 20 | 21 | 5 | 2 | R | R | 6-5 | 195 | 2-20-73 | 1992 | Fergus Falls, Minn. |
| Perez, Luis, of | .250 | 43 | 144 | 31 | 36 | 5 | 0 | 0 | 14 | 22 | 28 | 12 | 2 | R | R | 6-1 | 180 | 7-9-73 | 1991 | Layurillas, Venez. |
| Valentin, Jose, c-dh | .262 | 32 | 103 | 18 | 27 | 6 | 1 | 1 | 19 | 14 | 19 | 0 | 2 | S | R | 5-10 | 190 | 9-19-75 | 1993 | Manati, P.R. |
| Vizcaino, Romulo, of | .279 | 47 | 179 | 26 | 50 | 9 | 4 | 2 | 27 | 11 | 14 | 14 | 3 | S | R | 6-2 | 160 | 1-20-74 | 1991 | Santo Domingo, D.R. |
| Zorrilla, Miguel, 3b | .259 | 41 | 116 | 19 | 30 | 3 | 1 | 2 | 16 | 19 | 25 | 1 | 3 | R | R | 6-2 | 194 | 12-2-74 | 1993 | Seccion Santana, D.R. |

| PITCHING | W | L | ERA | G | GS | CG | SV | IP | H | R | ER | BB | SO | B | T | HT | WT | DOB | 1st Yr | Resides |
|---|---|---|---|---|---|---|---|---|---|---|---|---|---|---|---|---|---|---|---|---|
| Alvarado, Luis | 3 | 5 | 3.39 | 13 | 10 | 1 | 0 | 58 | 65 | 34 | 22 | 21 | 40 | R | R | 6-0 | 163 | 8-28-74 | 1992 | Cayey, P.R. |
| Anderson, Eric | 2 | 8 | 5.36 | 12 | 9 | 1 | 0 | 45 | 49 | 44 | 27 | 36 | 35 | R | L | 6-2 | 185 | 2-25-73 | 1993 | Downers Grove, Ill. |
| Belcher, James | 1 | 0 | 0.00 | 1 | 0 | 0 | 0 | 1 | 1 | 0 | 0 | 0 | 1 | L | R | 6-4 | 210 | 3-1-72 | 1991 | Olathe, Kan. |
| DeBrino, Robert | 1 | 4 | 3.48 | 25 | 0 | 0 | 11 | 41 | 34 | 19 | 16 | 27 | 47 | R | R | 6-2 | 205 | 9-25-73 | 1992 | Northvale, N.J. |
| Fidge, Darren | 1 | 8 | 4.19 | 12 | 12 | 1 | 0 | 67 | 72 | 48 | 31 | 27 | 31 | R | R | 6-2 | 180 | 11-12-74 | 1992 | Adelaide, Australia |
| Gourdin, Thomas | 1 | 2 | 4.59 | 24 | 4 | 0 | 3 | 51 | 53 | 34 | 26 | 17 | 33 | R | R | 6-3 | 190 | 5-24-73 | 1992 | Murray, Utah |
| Herrera, Raul | 5 | 4 | 2.81 | 11 | 11 | 0 | 0 | 64 | 59 | 28 | 20 | 21 | 41 | R | R | 6-2 | 170 | 7-7-74 | 1992 | Cocorote, Venez. |
| Johnson, Greg | 0 | 0 | 0.00 | 1 | 0 | 0 | 0 | 1 | 0 | 0 | 0 | 2 | 2 | R | R | 6-2 | 190 | 5-29-66 | 1987 | Hixson, Tenn. |
| Pina, Pedro | 3 | 1 | 3.72 | 17 | 0 | 0 | 0 | 36 | 41 | 21 | 15 | 24 | 23 | R | R | 6-3 | 188 | 3-30-75 | 1992 | Carabobo, Venez. |
| Sartain, David | 1 | 0 | 6.43 | 5 | 0 | 0 | 0 | 7 | 9 | 6 | 5 | 7 | 6 | L | L | 6-2 | 190 | 2-7-70 | 1991 | Virginia Beach, Va. |
| Sosa, Alexander | 0 | 0 | 18.00 | 3 | 0 | 0 | 0 | 3 | 6 | 7 | 6 | 6 | 1 | R | R | 6-3 | 165 | 5-23-75 | 1991 | Valencia, Venez. |
| Stadelhofer, Mike | 0 | 1 | 5.40 | 5 | 2 | 0 | 0 | 10 | 9 | 7 | 6 | 8 | 13 | R | R | 6-3 | 195 | 6-4-74 | 1993 | Calistoga, Calif. |
| Tatar, Jason | 5 | 1 | 2.57 | 12 | 11 | 1 | 0 | 67 | 52 | 26 | 19 | 29 | 73 | R | R | 6-0 | 175 | 8-15-74 | 1992 | Rantoul, Ill. |
| Wilson, Ricardo | 0 | 1 | 8.05 | 15 | 0 | 0 | 0 | 19 | 24 | 24 | 17 | 24 | 9 | R | R | 6-0 | 160 | 7-22-70 | 1993 | Santo Domingo, D.R. |
| Woodman, Hank | 0 | 1 | 1.37 | 13 | 0 | 0 | 0 | 26 | 14 | 7 | 4 | 23 | 19 | S | R | 6-1 | 185 | 11-16-72 | 1993 | Fort Myers, Fla. |

# MONTREAL
## EXPOS

**Manager:** Felipe Alou.          **1993 Record:** 94-68, .580 (2nd, NL East).

| BATTING | AVG | G | AB | R | H | 2B | 3B | HR | RBI | BB | SO | SB | CS | B | T | HT | WT | DOB | 1st Yr | Resides |
|---|---|---|---|---|---|---|---|---|---|---|---|---|---|---|---|---|---|---|---|---|
| Alou, Moises | .286 | 136 | 482 | 70 | 138 | 29 | 6 | 18 | 85 | 38 | 53 | 17 | 6 | R | R | 6-3 | 175 | 7-3-66 | 1986 | Redwood City, Calif. |
| Berry, Sean | .261 | 122 | 299 | 50 | 78 | 15 | 2 | 14 | 49 | 41 | 70 | 12 | 2 | R | R | 5-11 | 210 | 3-22-66 | 1986 | Rolling Hills Estates, Calif. |
| Bolick, Frank | .211 | 95 | 213 | 25 | 45 | 13 | 0 | 4 | 24 | 23 | 37 | 1 | 0 | S | R | 5-10 | 177 | 6-28-66 | 1987 | Smyrna, Ga. |
| Cianfrocco, Archi | .235 | 12 | 17 | 3 | 4 | 1 | 0 | 1 | 1 | 0 | 5 | 0 | 0 | R | R | 6-5 | 200 | 10-6-66 | 1987 | Rome, N.Y. |
| Colbrunn, Greg | .255 | 70 | 153 | 15 | 39 | 9 | 0 | 4 | 23 | 6 | 33 | 4 | 2 | R | R | 6-0 | 200 | 7-26-69 | 1988 | Fontana, Calif. |
| Cordero, Wil | .248 | 138 | 475 | 56 | 118 | 32 | 2 | 10 | 58 | 34 | 60 | 12 | 3 | R | R | 6-2 | 185 | 10-3-71 | 1988 | Mayaguez, P.R. |
| DeShields, Delino | .295 | 123 | 481 | 75 | 142 | 17 | 7 | 2 | 29 | 72 | 64 | 43 | 10 | L | R | 6-1 | 170 | 1-15-65 | 1987 | Seaford, Del. |
| Fletcher, Darrin | .255 | 133 | 396 | 33 | 101 | 20 | 1 | 9 | 60 | 34 | 40 | 0 | 0 | L | R | 6-2 | 195 | 10-3-66 | 1987 | Oakwood, Ill. |
| Floyd, Cliff | .226 | 10 | 31 | 3 | 7 | 0 | 0 | 1 | 2 | 0 | 9 | 0 | 0 | L | L | 6-4 | 220 | 12-5-72 | 1991 | Markham, Ill. |
| Frazier, Lou | .286 | 112 | 189 | 27 | 54 | 7 | 1 | 1 | 16 | 16 | 24 | 17 | 2 | S | R | 6-2 | 175 | 1-26-65 | 1986 | St. Louis, Mo. |
| Grissom, Marquis | .298 | 157 | 630 | 104 | 188 | 27 | 2 | 19 | 95 | 52 | 76 | 53 | 10 | R | R | 5-11 | 192 | 4-17-67 | 1988 | Red Oak, Ga. |
| Laker, Tim | .198 | 43 | 86 | 3 | 17 | 2 | 1 | 0 | 7 | 2 | 16 | 2 | 0 | R | R | 6-2 | 175 | 11-27-69 | 1988 | Simi Valley, Calif. |
| Lansing, Mike | .287 | 141 | 491 | 64 | 141 | 29 | 1 | 3 | 45 | 46 | 56 | 23 | 5 | R | R | 6-0 | 175 | 4-3-68 | 1990 | Casper, Wyo. |
| Marrero, Oreste | .210 | 32 | 81 | 10 | 17 | 5 | 1 | 1 | 4 | 14 | 16 | 1 | 3 | L | L | 6-0 | 205 | 10-31-69 | 1987 | Bayamon, P.R. |
| McIntosh, Tim | .095 | 20 | 21 | 2 | 2 | 1 | 0 | 0 | 2 | 0 | 7 | 0 | 0 | R | R | 5-11 | 195 | 3-21-65 | 1986 | Herald, Calif. |
| Montoyo, Charlie | .400 | 4 | 5 | 1 | 2 | 1 | 0 | 0 | 3 | 0 | 0 | 0 | 0 | R | R | 5-10 | 170 | 10-17-65 | 1987 | Florida, P.R. |
| Pride, Curtis | .444 | 10 | 9 | 3 | 4 | 1 | 1 | 1 | 5 | 0 | 3 | 1 | 0 | L | R | 5-11 | 195 | 12-17-68 | 1986 | Silver Spring, Md. |
| Ready, Randy | .254 | 40 | 134 | 22 | 34 | 8 | 1 | 1 | 10 | 23 | 8 | 2 | 1 | R | R | 5-11 | 180 | 1-8-60 | 1980 | Cardiff, Calif. |
| Siddall, Joe | .100 | 19 | 20 | 0 | 2 | 1 | 0 | 0 | 1 | 1 | 5 | 0 | 0 | L | R | 6-1 | 197 | 10-25-67 | 1988 | Windsor, Ontario |
| Spehr, Tim | .230 | 53 | 87 | 14 | 20 | 6 | 0 | 2 | 10 | 6 | 20 | 2 | 0 | R | R | 6-2 | 205 | 7-2-66 | 1988 | Waco, Texas |
| Stairs, Matt | .375 | 6 | 8 | 1 | 3 | 1 | 0 | 0 | 2 | 0 | 1 | 0 | 0 | R | R | 5-9 | 175 | 2-27-69 | 1989 | Stanley, New Brunswick |
| VanderWal, John | .233 | 106 | 215 | 34 | 50 | 7 | 4 | 5 | 30 | 27 | 30 | 6 | 3 | L | L | 6-1 | 180 | 4-29-66 | 1987 | Hudsonville, Mich. |
| Walker, Larry | .265 | 138 | 490 | 85 | 130 | 24 | 5 | 22 | 86 | 80 | 76 | 29 | 7 | L | R | 6-2 | 185 | 12-1-66 | 1985 | Maple Ridge, B.C. |
| White, Derrick | .224 | 17 | 49 | 6 | 11 | 3 | 0 | 2 | 4 | 2 | 12 | 2 | 0 | R | R | 6-1 | 215 | 10-12-69 | 1991 | San Rafael, Calif. |
| White, Rondell | .260 | 23 | 73 | 9 | 19 | 3 | 1 | 2 | 15 | 7 | 16 | 1 | 2 | R | R | 6-1 | 193 | 2-23-72 | 1990 | Gray, Ga. |
| Wood, Ted | .192 | 13 | 26 | 4 | 5 | 1 | 0 | 0 | 3 | 3 | 3 | 0 | 0 | L | L | 6-2 | 187 | 1-4-67 | 1989 | New Orleans, La. |

| PITCHING | W | L | ERA | G | GS | CG | SV | IP | H | R | ER | BB | SO | B | T | HT | WT | DOB | 1st Yr | Resides |
|---|---|---|---|---|---|---|---|---|---|---|---|---|---|---|---|---|---|---|---|---|
| Aldred, Scott | 1 | 0 | 6.75 | 3 | 0 | 0 | 0 | 5 | 9 | 4 | 4 | 1 | 4 | L | L | 6-4 | 195 | 6-12-68 | 1987 | Lakeland, Fla. |
| 2-team (5 Colo.) | 1 | 0 | 9.00 | 8 | 0 | 0 | 0 | 12 | 19 | 14 | 12 | 10 | 9 | | | | | | | |
| Barnes, Brian | 2 | 6 | 4.41 | 52 | 8 | 0 | 3 | 100 | 105 | 53 | 49 | 48 | 60 | L | L | 5-9 | 170 | 3-25-67 | 1989 | Roanoke Rapids, N.C. |
| Bottenfield, Kent | 5 | 4 | 4.12 | 23 | 11 | 0 | 0 | 83 | 93 | 49 | 38 | 33 | 33 | S | R | 6-3 | 215 | 11-14-68 | 1986 | Portland, Ore. |
| Boucher, Denis | 3 | 1 | 1.91 | 5 | 5 | 0 | 0 | 28 | 24 | 7 | 6 | 3 | 14 | R | L | 6-1 | 195 | 3-7-68 | 1988 | Lachine, Quebec |
| Fassero, Jeff | 12 | 5 | 2.29 | 56 | 15 | 1 | 1 | 150 | 119 | 50 | 38 | 54 | 140 | L | L | 6-1 | 180 | 1-5-63 | 1984 | Springfield, Ill. |
| Gardiner, Mike | 2 | 3 | 5.21 | 24 | 2 | 0 | 0 | 38 | 40 | 28 | 22 | 19 | 21 | R | R | 6-0 | 185 | 10-19-65 | 1987 | Sarnia, Ontario |
| Henry, Butch | 1 | 1 | 3.93 | 10 | 1 | 0 | 0 | 18 | 18 | 10 | 8 | 4 | 8 | L | L | 6-1 | 195 | 10-7-68 | 1987 | El Paso, Texas |
| 2-team (20 Colo.) | 3 | 9 | 6.12 | 30 | 16 | 1 | 0 | 103 | 135 | 76 | 70 | 28 | 47 | | | | | | | |
| Heredia, Gil | 4 | 2 | 3.92 | 20 | 9 | 1 | 2 | 57 | 66 | 28 | 25 | 14 | 40 | R | R | 6-1 | 190 | 10-26-65 | 1987 | Tucson, Ariz. |
| Hill, Ken | 9 | 7 | 3.23 | 28 | 28 | 2 | 0 | 184 | 163 | 84 | 66 | 74 | 90 | R | R | 6-2 | 175 | 12-14-65 | 1985 | Lynn, Mass. |
| Jones, Jimmy | 4 | 1 | 6.35 | 12 | 6 | 0 | 0 | 40 | 47 | 34 | 28 | 9 | 21 | R | R | 6-2 | 190 | 4-20-64 | 1982 | Highland Village, Texas |
| Looney, Brian | 0 | 0 | 3.00 | 3 | 1 | 0 | 0 | 6 | 8 | 2 | 2 | 7 | 2 | L | L | 5-10 | 190 | 9-26-69 | 1991 | Cheshire, Conn. |
| Martinez, Dennis | 15 | 9 | 3.85 | 35 | 34 | 2 | 1 | 225 | 211 | 110 | 96 | 64 | 138 | R | R | 6-1 | 183 | 5-14-55 | 1974 | Randallstown, Md. |
| Nabholz, Chris | 9 | 8 | 4.09 | 26 | 21 | 1 | 0 | 117 | 100 | 57 | 53 | 63 | 74 | L | L | 6-5 | 210 | 1-5-67 | 1989 | Pottsville, Pa. |
| Risley, Bill | 0 | 0 | 6.00 | 2 | 0 | 0 | 0 | 3 | 2 | 3 | 2 | 2 | 2 | R | R | 6-2 | 210 | 5-29-67 | 1987 | Chicago, Ill. |
| Rojas, Mel | 5 | 8 | 2.95 | 66 | 0 | 0 | 10 | 88 | 80 | 39 | 29 | 30 | 48 | R | R | 5-11 | 165 | 12-10-66 | 1986 | Santo Domingo, D.R. |
| Rueter, Kirk | 8 | 0 | 2.73 | 14 | 14 | 1 | 0 | 86 | 85 | 33 | 26 | 18 | 31 | L | L | 6-3 | 190 | 12-1-70 | 1991 | Hoyleton, Ill. |
| Scott, Tim | 5 | 2 | 3.71 | 32 | 0 | 0 | 1 | 34 | 31 | 15 | 14 | 19 | 35 | R | R | 6-2 | 205 | 11-16-66 | 1984 | Hanford, Calif. |
| 2-team (24 S.D.) | 7 | 2 | 3.01 | 56 | 0 | 0 | 1 | 72 | 69 | 28 | 24 | 34 | 65 | | | | | | | |
| Shaw, Jeff | 2 | 7 | 4.14 | 55 | 8 | 0 | 0 | 96 | 91 | 47 | 44 | 32 | 50 | R | R | 6-2 | 185 | 7-7-66 | 1986 | Wash. Courthouse, Ohio |
| Valdez, Sergio | 0 | 0 | 9.00 | 4 | 0 | 0 | 0 | 3 | 4 | 4 | 3 | 1 | 2 | R | R | 6-1 | 190 | 9-7-65 | 1983 | Santo Domingo, D.R. |
| Walton, Bruce | 0 | 0 | 9.53 | 4 | 0 | 0 | 0 | 6 | 11 | 6 | 6 | 3 | 0 | R | R | 6-2 | 195 | 12-25-62 | 1985 | Bakersfield, Calif. |
| Wetteland, John | 9 | 3 | 1.37 | 70 | 0 | 0 | 43 | 85 | 58 | 17 | 13 | 28 | 113 | R | R | 6-2 | 195 | 8-21-66 | 1985 | Monroe, La. |
| Young, Pete | 1 | 0 | 3.38 | 4 | 0 | 0 | 0 | 5 | 4 | 2 | 2 | 0 | 3 | R | R | 6-0 | 225 | 3-19-68 | 1989 | Summit, Miss. |

## FIELDING

| Catcher | PCT | G | PO | A | E | DP |
|---|---|---|---|---|---|---|
| Fletcher | .988 | 127 | 620 | 41 | 8 | 3 |
| Laker | .987 | 43 | 136 | 18 | 2 | 2 |
| McIntosh | 1.000 | 5 | 5 | 1 | 0 | 0 |
| Siddall | 1.000 | 15 | 33 | 5 | 0 | 0 |
| Spehr | .954 | 49 | 166 | 22 | 9 | 3 |

| First Base | PCT | G | PO | A | E | DP |
|---|---|---|---|---|---|---|
| Bolick | .992 | 51 | 333 | 33 | 3 | 28 |
| Cianfrocco | 1.000 | 11 | 45 | 2 | 0 | 6 |
| Colbrunn | .995 | 61 | 372 | 27 | 2 | 31 |
| Floyd | 1.000 | 10 | 80 | 4 | 0 | 5 |
| Frazier | .970 | 8 | 27 | 5 | 1 | 1 |
| Marrero | .991 | 32 | 194 | 15 | 2 | 21 |
| Ready | .960 | 13 | 87 | 8 | 4 | 5 |
| Siddall | .000 | 1 | 0 | 0 | 0 | 0 |
| VanderWal | .988 | 42 | 237 | 13 | 3 | 17 |

| Walker | 1.000 | 4 | 43 | 3 | 0 | 2 |
| D. White | .993 | 17 | 129 | 8 | 1 | 16 |

| Second Base | PCT | G | PO | A | E | DP |
|---|---|---|---|---|---|---|
| DeShields | .983 | 123 | 242 | 381 | 11 | 74 |
| Frazier | 1.000 | 1 | 1 | 1 | 0 | 0 |
| Lansing | .956 | 25 | 35 | 52 | 4 | 11 |
| Montoyo | .000 | 3 | 0 | 0 | 0 | 0 |
| Ready | .968 | 28 | 46 | 75 | 4 | 17 |

| Third Base | PCT | G | PO | A | E | DP |
|---|---|---|---|---|---|---|
| Berry | .936 | 96 | 66 | 153 | 15 | 13 |
| Bolick | .875 | 24 | 5 | 30 | 5 | 3 |
| Cordero | .625 | 2 | 2 | 3 | 3 | 0 |
| Lansing | .942 | 81 | 50 | 162 | 13 | 19 |
| Ready | 1.000 | 3 | 2 | 9 | 0 | 0 |

| Shortstop | PCT | G | PO | A | E | DP |
|---|---|---|---|---|---|---|
| Cordero | .941 | 134 | 161 | 370 | 33 | 61 |
| Lansing | .961 | 51 | 51 | 122 | 7 | 23 |

| Outfield | PCT | G | PO | A | E | DP |
|---|---|---|---|---|---|---|
| Alou | .985 | 136 | 254 | 11 | 4 | 2 |
| Frazier | .986 | 60 | 70 | 3 | 1 | 0 |
| Grissom | .984 | 157 | 416 | 8 | 7 | 3 |
| McIntosh | 1.000 | 7 | 3 | 0 | 0 | 0 |
| Pride | 1.000 | 2 | 2 | 0 | 0 | 0 |
| Siddall | .000 | 1 | 0 | 0 | 0 | 0 |
| Stairs | 1.000 | 1 | 1 | 0 | 0 | 0 |
| VanderWal | .972 | 38 | 34 | 1 | 1 | 0 |
| Walker | .979 | 132 | 273 | 13 | 6 | 2 |
| R. White | 1.000 | 21 | 33 | 0 | 0 | 0 |
| Wood | 1.000 | 8 | 16 | 0 | 0 | 0 |

MORRIS FOSTOFF

DAN ARNOLD

**Marquis Grissom.** Expos center fielder led team in batting (.298), runs (104), hits (188) and RBIs (95).

**John Wetteland.** Expos all-star reliever went 9-3 with a 1.37 ERA, 43 saves and 113 strikeouts in 85 innings.

# EXPOS FARM SYSTEM

| Class | Club | League | W | L | Pct. | Finish* | Manager | First Year |
|---|---|---|---|---|---|---|---|---|
| AAA | Ottawa (Ont.) Lynx | International | 73 | 69 | .514 | 5th (10) | Mike Quade | 1993 |
| AA | Harrisburg (Pa.) Senators | Eastern | 94 | 44 | .681 | 1st† (8) | Jim Tracy | 1991 |
| A# | West Palm Beach (Fla.) Expos | Florida State | 69 | 67 | .507 | 8th (13) | Rob Leary | 1969 |
| A | Burlington (Iowa) Bees | Midwest | 64 | 71 | .474 | 8th (14) | Lorenzo Bundy | 1993 |
| A | Jamestown (N.Y.) Expos | New York-Penn | 31 | 46 | .403 | 13th (14) | Tim Torricelli | 1977 |
| Rookie | West Palm Beach (Fla.) Expos | Gulf Coast | 27 | 31 | .466 | 11th (15) | Nelson Norman | 1986 |

*Finish in overall standings (No. of teams in league)   #Advanced level   †Won league championship

## OTTAWA                                                                              AAA

### INTERNATIONAL LEAGUE

| BATTING | AVG | G | AB | R | H | 2B | 3B | HR | RBI | BB | SO | SB | CS | B | T | HT | WT | DOB | 1st Yr | Resides |
|---|---|---|---|---|---|---|---|---|---|---|---|---|---|---|---|---|---|---|---|---|
| Barker, Tim | .228 | 51 | 167 | 25 | 38 | 5 | 1 | 2 | 14 | 26 | 42 | 5 | 3 | R | R | 6-0 | 175 | 6-30-68 | 1989 | Salisbury, Md. |
| Bolick, Frank | .125 | 2 | 8 | 0 | 1 | 0 | 0 | 0 | 0 | 0 | 0 | 0 | 0 | S | R | 5-10 | 177 | 6-28-66 | 1987 | Smyrna, Ga. |
| Bryant, Scott | .283 | 112 | 364 | 48 | 103 | 19 | 1 | 12 | 65 | 53 | 90 | 1 | 2 | R | R | 6-2 | 215 | 10-31-67 | 1989 | San Antonio, Texas |
| Castaldo, Vince | .241 | 77 | 241 | 22 | 58 | 9 | 1 | 2 | 45 | 29 | 49 | 0 | 4 | L | R | 6-0 | 185 | 7-19-67 | 1990 | Ballwin, Mo. |
| Cianfrocco, Archi | .298 | 50 | 188 | 21 | 56 | 14 | 2 | 4 | 27 | 7 | 33 | 4 | 2 | R | R | 6-5 | 200 | 10-6-66 | 1987 | Rome, N.Y. |
| Colbrunn, Greg | .273 | 6 | 22 | 4 | 6 | 1 | 0 | 0 | 8 | 1 | 2 | 1 | 0 | R | R | 6-0 | 200 | 7-26-69 | 1988 | Fontana, Calif. |
| Floyd, Cliff | .240 | 32 | 125 | 12 | 30 | 2 | 2 | 2 | 18 | 16 | 34 | 2 | 2 | L | L | 6-4 | 220 | 12-5-72 | 1991 | Markham, Ill. |
| Garner, Kevin | .273 | 36 | 99 | 15 | 27 | 9 | 0 | 7 | 28 | 15 | 31 | 0 | 0 | L | R | 6-2 | 200 | 10-21-65 | 1987 | Austin, Texas |
| Haney, Todd | .291 | 136 | 506 | 69 | 147 | 30 | 4 | 3 | 46 | 36 | 56 | 11 | 8 | R | R | 5-9 | 165 | 7-30-65 | 1987 | Waco, Texas |
| Hansen, Terrel | .230 | 108 | 352 | 45 | 81 | 19 | 0 | 10 | 39 | 18 | 103 | 1 | 1 | R | R | 6-3 | 210 | 9-25-66 | 1987 | Bremerton, Wash. |
| Hirtensteiner, Rick | .214 | 10 | 14 | 1 | 3 | 0 | 0 | 0 | 2 | 3 | 1 | 1 | 0 | L | L | 5-11 | 185 | 10-9-67 | 1989 | Ventura, Calif. |
| Hymel, Gary | .000 | 3 | 3 | 0 | 0 | 0 | 0 | 0 | 0 | 0 | 2 | 0 | 0 | R | R | 6-2 | 195 | 5-21-68 | 1991 | Cypress, Texas |
| Kremers, Jimmy | .200 | 4 | 15 | 1 | 3 | 0 | 0 | 1 | 2 | 1 | 2 | 0 | 0 | L | R | 6-3 | 200 | 10-8-65 | 1988 | North Little Rock, Ark. |
| Laker, Tim | .230 | 56 | 204 | 26 | 47 | 10 | 0 | 4 | 23 | 21 | 41 | 3 | 2 | R | R | 6-2 | 175 | 11-27-69 | 1988 | Simi Valley, Calif. |
| Mack, Quinn | .095 | 8 | 21 | 1 | 2 | 0 | 0 | 0 | 0 | 1 | 3 | 0 | 0 | L | L | 5-10 | 180 | 9-11-65 | 1987 | Cerritos, Calif. |
| McIntosh, Tim | .292 | 27 | 106 | 15 | 31 | 7 | 1 | 6 | 21 | 10 | 22 | 1 | 0 | R | R | 5-11 | 195 | 3-21-65 | 1986 | Herald, Calif. |
| Montoyo, Charlie | .279 | 99 | 319 | 43 | 89 | 18 | 2 | 1 | 43 | 71 | 37 | 0 | 9 | R | R | 5-10 | 170 | 10-17-65 | 1987 | Florida, P.R. |
| Pride, Curtis | .302 | 69 | 262 | 55 | 79 | 11 | 4 | 6 | 22 | 34 | 61 | 29 | 12 | L | R | 5-11 | 195 | 12-17-68 | 1986 | Silver Spring, Md. |
| Santangelo, F.P. | .274 | 131 | 453 | 86 | 124 | 21 | 2 | 4 | 45 | 59 | 52 | 18 | 8 | S | R | 5-10 | 165 | 10-24-67 | 1989 | El Dorado Hills, Calif. |
| Siddall, Joe | .213 | 48 | 136 | 14 | 29 | 6 | 0 | 1 | 16 | 19 | 33 | 2 | 2 | L | R | 6-1 | 197 | 10-25-67 | 1988 | Windsor, Ontario |
| Spehr, Tim | .199 | 46 | 141 | 15 | 28 | 6 | 1 | 4 | 13 | 14 | 35 | 2 | 1 | R | R | 6-2 | 205 | 7-2-66 | 1988 | Waco, Texas |
| Stairs, Matt | .280 | 34 | 125 | 18 | 35 | 4 | 2 | 3 | 20 | 11 | 15 | 4 | 1 | R | R | 5-9 | 175 | 2-27-69 | 1989 | Stanley, New Brunswick |
| Vargas, Hector | .183 | 36 | 93 | 10 | 17 | 3 | 1 | 0 | 6 | 15 | 25 | 3 | 3 | R | R | 5-11 | 155 | 6-3-66 | 1986 | Arecibo, P.R. |
| White, Derrick | .281 | 67 | 249 | 32 | 70 | 15 | 1 | 4 | 29 | 20 | 52 | 10 | 7 | R | R | 6-1 | 215 | 10-12-69 | 1991 | San Rafael, Calif. |
| White, Rondell | .380 | 37 | 150 | 28 | 57 | 8 | 2 | 7 | 32 | 12 | 20 | 10 | 1 | R | R | 6-1 | 193 | 2-23-72 | 1990 | Gray, Ga. |
| Wood, Ted | .255 | 83 | 231 | 39 | 59 | 11 | 4 | 1 | 21 | 38 | 54 | 12 | 2 | L | L | 6-2 | 187 | 1-4-67 | 1989 | New Orleans, La. |

| PITCHING | W | L | ERA | G | GS | CG | SV | IP | H | R | ER | BB | SO | B | T | HT | WT | DOB | 1st Yr | Resides |
|---|---|---|---|---|---|---|---|---|---|---|---|---|---|---|---|---|---|---|---|---|
| Alvarez, Tavo | 7 | 10 | 4.22 | 25 | 25 | 1 | 0 | 141 | 163 | 80 | 66 | 55 | 77 | R | R | 6-3 | 183 | 11-25-71 | 1990 | Tucson, Ariz. |
| Boucher, Denis | 6 | 0 | 2.72 | 11 | 6 | 0 | 0 | 43 | 36 | 13 | 13 | 11 | 22 | R | L | 6-1 | 195 | 3-7-68 | 1988 | Lachine, Quebec |
| Brantley, Cliff | 1 | 5 | 7.67 | 6 | 6 | 0 | 0 | 27 | 50 | 23 | 23 | 9 | 20 | R | R | 6-2 | 215 | 4-12-68 | 1986 | Staten Island, N.Y. |
| 2-team (7 Scranton) | 2 | 8 | 6.50 | 13 | 11 | 0 | 0 | 54 | 81 | 44 | 39 | 37 | 37 | | | | | | | |

## PITCHING

| PITCHING | W | L | ERA | G | GS | CG | SV | IP | H | R | ER | BB | SO | B | T | HT | WT | DOB | 1st Yr | Resides |
|---|---|---|---|---|---|---|---|---|---|---|---|---|---|---|---|---|---|---|---|---|
| Brito, Mario | 2 | 0 | 1.32 | 23 | 0 | 0 | 2 | 34 | 25 | 6 | 5 | 17 | 29 | R | R | 6-3 | 179 | 4-9-66 | 1985 | Bonao, D.R. |
| Eischen, Joey | 2 | 2 | 3.54 | 6 | 6 | 0 | 0 | 41 | 34 | 18 | 16 | 15 | 29 | L | L | 6-1 | 190 | 5-25-70 | 1989 | West Covina, Calif. |
| Farmer, Howard | 0 | 1 | 11.25 | 2 | 0 | 0 | 0 | 4 | 7 | 5 | 5 | 0 | 1 | R | R | 6-2 | 184 | 1-18-66 | 1987 | Gary, Ind. |
| Fortugno, Tim | 2 | 1 | 3.60 | 28 | 4 | 0 | 1 | 40 | 28 | 17 | 16 | 31 | 42 | L | L | 6-0 | 185 | 4-11-62 | 1986 | Huntington Beach, Calif. |
| Gardiner, Mike | 1 | 1 | 2.16 | 5 | 5 | 0 | 0 | 25 | 17 | 8 | 6 | 9 | 25 | R | R | 6-0 | 185 | 10-19-65 | 1987 | Sarnia, Ontario |
| Henry, Butch | 3 | 1 | 3.73 | 5 | 5 | 1 | 0 | 31 | 34 | 15 | 13 | 1 | 25 | L | L | 6-1 | 195 | 10-7-68 | 1987 | El Paso, Texas |
| Heredia, Gil | 8 | 4 | 2.98 | 16 | 16 | 1 | 0 | 103 | 97 | 46 | 34 | 26 | 66 | R | R | 6-1 | 190 | 10-26-65 | 1987 | Tucson, Ariz. |
| Hill, Ken | 0 | 0 | 0.00 | 1 | 0 | 0 | 0 | 4 | 1 | 0 | 0 | 1 | 0 | R | R | 6-2 | 175 | 12-14-65 | 1985 | Lynn, Mass. |
| Hurst, Jonathan | 1 | 5 | 6.63 | 8 | 8 | 0 | 0 | 37 | 44 | 31 | 27 | 17 | 28 | R | R | 6-2 | 175 | 10-20-66 | 1987 | Spartanburg, S.C. |
| Jones, Jimmy | 1 | 0 | 1.20 | 3 | 3 | 0 | 0 | 15 | 10 | 2 | 2 | 5 | 12 | R | R | 6-2 | 190 | 4-20-64 | 1982 | Highland Village, Texas |
| Mathile, Mike | 9 | 9 | 4.17 | 31 | 21 | 2 | 1 | 140 | 147 | 74 | 65 | 41 | 56 | R | R | 6-4 | 220 | 11-24-68 | 1990 | Brookville, Ohio |
| Nabholz, Chris | 1 | 1 | 4.39 | 5 | 5 | 0 | 0 | 27 | 24 | 15 | 13 | 7 | 20 | L | L | 6-5 | 210 | 1-5-67 | 1989 | Pottsville, Pa. |
| Perez, Yorkis | 0 | 1 | 3.60 | 20 | 0 | 0 | 5 | 20 | 14 | 12 | 8 | 7 | 17 | L | L | 6-0 | 160 | 9-30-67 | 1983 | Bajos De Haina, D.R. |
| Picota, Len | 0 | 1 | 7.36 | 8 | 0 | 0 | 5 | 7 | 12 | 6 | 6 | 5 | 3 | R | R | 6-1 | 185 | 7-23-66 | 1984 | Panama City, Panama |
| Risley, Bill | 2 | 4 | 2.69 | 41 | 0 | 0 | 1 | 64 | 51 | 26 | 19 | 34 | 74 | R | R | 6-2 | 210 | 5-29-67 | 1987 | Chicago, Ill. |
| Rosario, Dave | 1 | 1 | 3.58 | 22 | 0 | 0 | 0 | 28 | 22 | 12 | 11 | 21 | 28 | L | L | 6-2 | 175 | 6-4-66 | 1986 | Manati, P.R. |
| Rueter, Kirk | 4 | 2 | 2.70 | 7 | 7 | 1 | 0 | 43 | 46 | 20 | 13 | 3 | 27 | L | L | 6-3 | 190 | 12-1-70 | 1991 | Hoyleton, Ill. |
| Shaw, Jeff | 0 | 0 | 0.00 | 2 | 1 | 0 | 0 | 4 | 5 | 0 | 0 | 2 | 1 | R | R | 6-2 | 185 | 7-7-66 | 1986 | Wash. Courthouse, Ohio |
| Simons, Doug | 7 | 7 | 4.75 | 34 | 13 | 1 | 0 | 116 | 134 | 67 | 61 | 16 | 75 | L | L | 6-0 | 160 | 9-15-66 | 1988 | Orlando, Fla. |
| Valdez, Sergio | 5 | 3 | 3.12 | 30 | 4 | 0 | 1 | 84 | 77 | 31 | 29 | 22 | 53 | R | R | 6-1 | 190 | 9-7-65 | 1983 | Santo Domingo, D.R. |
| Walton, Bruce | 4 | 4 | 1.05 | 40 | 0 | 0 | 16 | 43 | 32 | 12 | 5 | 8 | 40 | R | R | 6-2 | 195 | 12-25-62 | 1985 | Bakersfield, Calif. |
| White, Gabe | 2 | 1 | 3.12 | 6 | 6 | 1 | 0 | 40 | 38 | 15 | 14 | 6 | 28 | L | L | 6-2 | 200 | 11-20-71 | 1990 | Sebring, Fla. |
| Young, Pete | 4 | 5 | 3.72 | 48 | 0 | 0 | 1 | 73 | 63 | 32 | 30 | 33 | 46 | R | R | 6-0 | 225 | 3-19-68 | 1989 | Summit, Miss. |

## FIELDING

| Catcher | PCT | G | PO | A | E | DP |
|---|---|---|---|---|---|---|
| Hymel | 1.000 | 3 | 5 | 0 | 0 | 0 |
| Kremers | 1.000 | 2 | 6 | 1 | 0 | 0 |
| Laker | .971 | 53 | 332 | 37 | 11 | 4 |
| McIntosh | .988 | 11 | 71 | 10 | 1 | 1 |
| Siddall | .983 | 41 | 206 | 32 | 4 | 3 |
| Spehr | .978 | 43 | 248 | 24 | 6 | 0 |

| First Base | PCT | G | PO | A | E | DP |
|---|---|---|---|---|---|---|
| Cianfrocco | .994 | 18 | 147 | 12 | 1 | 15 |
| Colbrunn | 1.000 | 6 | 50 | 1 | 0 | 3 |
| Floyd | .983 | 31 | 272 | 23 | 5 | 23 |
| Garner | .923 | 1 | 11 | 1 | 1 | 0 |
| Hansen | .978 | 20 | 171 | 11 | 4 | 7 |
| Laker | 1.000 | 1 | 9 | 0 | 0 | 2 |
| McIntosh | 1.000 | 1 | 6 | 1 | 0 | 0 |
| Montoyo | 1.000 | 1 | 8 | 2 | 0 | 1 |
| Siddall | .929 | 3 | 12 | 1 | 1 | 9 |
| D. White | .988 | 67 | 632 | 49 | 8 | 57 |

| Second Base | PCT | G | PO | A | E | DP |
|---|---|---|---|---|---|---|
| Haney | .976 | 125 | 235 | 388 | 15 | 76 |
| Montoyo | .984 | 12 | 21 | 39 | 1 | 6 |
| Santangelo | .967 | 5 | 16 | 13 | 1 | 3 |
| Vargas | 1.000 | 5 | 7 | 12 | 0 | 2 |

| Third Base | PCT | G | PO | A | E | DP |
|---|---|---|---|---|---|---|
| Bolick | 1.000 | 2 | 0 | 4 | 0 | 0 |
| Castaldo | .922 | 56 | 23 | 96 | 10 | 5 |
| Cianfrocco | .895 | 10 | 5 | 12 | 2 | 2 |
| Hansen | .714 | 3 | 0 | 5 | 2 | 1 |
| Montoyo | .930 | 51 | 29 | 90 | 9 | 14 |
| Santangelo | .848 | 15 | 7 | 21 | 5 | 2 |
| Siddall | .000 | 1 | 0 | 0 | 0 | 0 |
| Vargas | .929 | 21 | 13 | 39 | 4 | 1 |

| Shortstop | PCT | G | PO | A | E | DP |
|---|---|---|---|---|---|---|
| Barker | .955 | 51 | 85 | 148 | 11 | 27 |
| Haney | 1.000 | 7 | 10 | 13 | 0 | 2 |

| | PCT | G | PO | A | E | DP |
|---|---|---|---|---|---|---|
| Montoyo | .966 | 37 | 43 | 99 | 5 | 19 |
| Santangelo | .979 | 54 | 84 | 149 | 5 | 32 |
| Vargas | .833 | 1 | 2 | 3 | 1 | 0 |

| Outfield | PCT | G | PO | A | E | DP |
|---|---|---|---|---|---|---|
| Bryant | .978 | 73 | 126 | 5 | 3 | 1 |
| Castaldo | .800 | 2 | 3 | 1 | 1 | 0 |
| Cianfrocco | 1.000 | 25 | 36 | 2 | 0 | 0 |
| Hansen | .976 | 72 | 120 | 2 | 3 | 0 |
| Hirtensteiner | 1.000 | 8 | 6 | 1 | 0 | 0 |
| Mack | 1.000 | 4 | 11 | 1 | 0 | 0 |
| McIntosh | .964 | 14 | 26 | 1 | 1 | 0 |
| Pride | .986 | 68 | 136 | 3 | 2 | 1 |
| Santangelo | .979 | 59 | 139 | 3 | 3 | 1 |
| Siddall | 1.000 | 3 | 3 | 0 | 0 | 0 |
| Stairs | 1.000 | 29 | 49 | 4 | 0 | 1 |
| R. White | .988 | 35 | 79 | 0 | 1 | 0 |
| Wood | 1.000 | 70 | 108 | 6 | 0 | 0 |

# HARRISBURG · AA
## EASTERN LEAGUE

| BATTING | AVG | G | AB | R | H | 2B | 3B | HR | RBI | BB | SO | SB | CS | B | T | HT | WT | DOB | 1st Yr | Resides |
|---|---|---|---|---|---|---|---|---|---|---|---|---|---|---|---|---|---|---|---|---|
| Andrews, Shane, 3b | .260 | 124 | 442 | 77 | 115 | 29 | 2 | 18 | 70 | 64 | 118 | 10 | 6 | R | R | 6-1 | 205 | 8-28-71 | 1990 | Carlsbad, N.M. |
| Barker, Tim, ss | .308 | 49 | 185 | 40 | 57 | 10 | 1 | 4 | 16 | 30 | 32 | 7 | 4 | R | R | 6-0 | 175 | 6-30-68 | 1989 | Salisbury, Md. |
| Bradbury, Miah, c-dh | .313 | 9 | 32 | 4 | 10 | 5 | 0 | 1 | 6 | 0 | 1 | 0 | 0 | R | R | 6-4 | 210 | 1-30-68 | 1990 | San Diego, Calif. |
| Daniel, Mike, dh-1b | .333 | 3 | 6 | 1 | 2 | 0 | 1 | 0 | 3 | 0 | 3 | 0 | 0 | R | R | 6-1 | 195 | 9-21-69 | 1991 | Weatherford, Okla. |
| Fitzpatrick, Rob, c | .226 | 99 | 341 | 44 | 77 | 10 | 1 | 11 | 46 | 36 | 82 | 6 | 8 | R | R | 6-0 | 190 | 9-14-68 | 1990 | Midland Park, N.J. |
| Floyd, Cliff, 1b-of | .329 | 101 | 380 | 82 | 125 | 17 | 4 | 26 | 101 | 54 | 71 | 31 | 10 | L | L | 6-4 | 220 | 12-5-72 | 1991 | Markham, Ill. |
| Fulton, Greg, c | .000 | 1 | 4 | 0 | 0 | 0 | 0 | 0 | 0 | 0 | 3 | 0 | 0 | S | R | 6-4 | 200 | 2-20-63 | 1985 | Braintree, Mass. |
| Griffin, Marc, of | .151 | 24 | 53 | 5 | 8 | 2 | 0 | 0 | 6 | 7 | 9 | 5 | 1 | L | R | 6-0 | 170 | 9-15-68 | 1989 | Ste-Foy, Quebec |
| Hardge, Michael, 2b | .244 | 99 | 386 | 70 | 94 | 15 | 10 | 6 | 35 | 37 | 97 | 27 | 8 | R | R | 5-11 | 183 | 1-27-72 | 1990 | Killeen, Texas |
| Horne, Tyrone, of | .359 | 35 | 128 | 22 | 46 | 8 | 1 | 4 | 22 | 22 | 37 | 3 | 2 | L | R | 5-10 | 185 | 11-2-70 | 1989 | Troy, N.C. |
| Krause, Ron, 2b-ss | .288 | 17 | 59 | 12 | 17 | 5 | 1 | 1 | 8 | 8 | 14 | 2 | 0 | L | R | 6-1 | 175 | 12-27-70 | 1989 | Willowick, Ohio |

# EXPOS
## TOP 10 PROSPECTS

### How the Expos Top 10 prospects, as judged by Baseball America prior to the 1993 season, fared in 1993:

| Player, Pos. | Club (Class) | AVG | AB | H | HR | RBI | SB |
|---|---|---|---|---|---|---|---|
| 1. Cliff Floyd, of-1b | Harrisburg (AA) | .329 | 380 | 125 | 26 | 101 | 31 |
| | Ottawa (AAA) | .240 | 125 | 30 | 2 | 18 | 2 |
| | Montreal | .226 | 31 | 7 | 1 | 2 | 0 |
| 2. Wil Cordero, ss | Montreal | .248 | 475 | 118 | 10 | 56 | 12 |
| 4. Rondell White, of | Harrisburg (AA) | .328 | 372 | 122 | 12 | 52 | 21 |
| | Ottawa (AAA) | .380 | 150 | 57 | 7 | 32 | 10 |
| | Montreal | .260 | 73 | 19 | 2 | 15 | 1 |
| 5. Tim Laker, c | Ottawa (AAA) | .230 | 204 | 47 | 4 | 23 | 3 |
| | Montreal | .198 | 86 | 17 | 0 | 7 | 2 |
| 8. Mike Lansing, ss | Montreal | .287 | 491 | 141 | 3 | 45 | 23 |
| 10. Jose Vidro, 2b | Burlington (A) | .240 | 287 | 69 | 2 | 34 | 3 |

| Player, Pos. | Club (Class) | W | L | ERA | IP | H | BB | SO |
|---|---|---|---|---|---|---|---|---|
| 3. Tavo Alvarez, rhp | Ottawa (AAA) | 7 | 10 | 4.22 | 141 | 163 | 55 | 77 |
| 6. Gabe White, lhp | Harrisburg (AA) | 7 | 2 | 2.16 | 100 | 80 | 28 | 80 |
| | Ottawa (AAA) | 2 | 1 | 3.12 | 40 | 38 | 6 | 28 |
| 7. B.J. Wallace, lhp | West Palm (A) | 11 | 8 | 3.28 | 137 | 112 | 65 | 126 |
| 9. Joey Eischen, lhp | Harrisburg (AA) | 14 | 4 | 3.62 | 119 | 122 | 60 | 110 |
| | Ottawa (AAA) | 2 | 2 | 3.54 | 41 | 34 | 15 | 29 |

**Cliff Floyd**
.329 at Double-A

## MAJOR LEAGUERS

**BATTING**

| | | |
|---|---|---|
| *AVG | Marquis Grissom.... | .298 |
| R | Marquis Grissom..... | 104 |
| H | Marquis Grissom..... | 188 |
| TB | Marquis Grissom..... | 276 |
| 2B | Wil Cordero............... | 32 |
| 3B | Delino DeShields ....... | 7 |
| HR | Larry Walker ............. | 22 |
| RBI | Marquis Grissom ..... | 95 |
| BB | Larry Walker ............. | 80 |
| SO | Two tied at ............... | 76 |
| SB | Marquis Grissom ..... | 53 |

**PITCHING**

| | | |
|---|---|---|
| W | Dennis Martinez........ | 15 |
| L | Dennis Martinez......... | 9 |
| #ERA | John Wetteland...... | 1.37 |
| G | John Wetteland......... | 70 |
| CG | Two tied at ................. | 2 |
| SV | John Wetteland......... | 43 |
| IP | Dennis Martinez........ | 225 |
| BB | Ken Hill .................... | 74 |
| SO | Jeff Fassero ............. | 140 |

**Dennis Martinez**
Sixth straight 200-inning season

R&R SPORTS GROUP

## MINOR LEAGUERS

**BATTING**

| | | |
|---|---|---|
| *AVG | Rondell White, Harrisburg-Ottawa........ | .343 |
| R | Curtis Pride, Ottawa-Harrisburg ............ | 106 |
| H | Rondell White, Harrisburg-Ottawa........ | 179 |
| TB | Rondell White, Harrisburg-Ottawa........ | 284 |
| 2B | Todd Haney, Ottawa ............................... | 30 |
| 3B | Rondell White, Harrisburg-Ottawa......... | 12 |
| HR | Cliff Floyd, Harrisburg-Ottawa............. | 28 |
| RBI | Cliff Floyd, Harrisburg-Ottawa............. | 119 |
| BB | Chris Hmielewski, Burlington................. | 74 |
| SO | Isreal Alcantara, Burlington ................. | 125 |
| SB | Curtis Pride, Harrisburg-Ottawa ........... | 50 |

**PITCHING**

| | | |
|---|---|---|
| W | Rod Henderson, WPB-Harrisburg .......... | 17 |
| L | Two tied at................................................. | 12 |
| #ERA | Kirk Rueter, Harrisburg-Ottawa ............ | 1.92 |
| G | Mario Brito, Harrisburg-Ottawa.............. | 59 |
| CG | Ugueth Urbina, Burlington-Harrisburg ....... | 7 |
| SV | Mark LaRosa, West Palm Beach ........... | 19 |
| IP | Ugueth Urbina, Burlington-Harrisburg ... | 178 |
| BB | Miguel Batista, Harrisburg ....................... | 86 |
| SO | Brian Looney, WPB-Harrisburg ............. | 185 |

*Minimum 250 At-Bats   #Minimum 75 Innings

| BATTING | AVG | G | AB | R | H | 2B | 3B | HR | RBI | BB | SO | SB | CS | B | T | HT | WT | DOB | 1st Yr | Resides |
|---|---|---|---|---|---|---|---|---|---|---|---|---|---|---|---|---|---|---|---|---|
| Marrero, Oreste, 1b-dh ..333 | | 85 | 255 | 39 | 85 | 18 | 1 | 10 | 49 | 22 | 46 | 3 | 3 | L | L | 6-0 | 205 | 10-31-69 | 1987 | Bayamon, P.R. |
| Martin, Chris, ss-2b ....... | .294 | 116 | 395 | 68 | 116 | 23 | 1 | 7 | 54 | 40 | 48 | 16 | 7 | R | R | 6-1 | 170 | 1-25-68 | 1990 | Los Angeles, Calif. |
| Murray, Glenn, of ......... | .253 | 127 | 475 | 82 | 120 | 21 | 4 | 26 | 96 | 56 | 111 | 16 | 7 | R | R | 6-2 | 200 | 11-23-70 | 1989 | Manning, S.C. |
| Pride, Curtis, of............... | .356 | 50 | 180 | 51 | 64 | 6 | 3 | 15 | 39 | 12 | 36 | 21 | 5 | L | R | 5-11 | 195 | 12-17-68 | 1986 | Silver Spring, Md. |
| Rice, Lance, c ............... | .235 | 46 | 136 | 12 | 32 | 10 | 0 | 1 | 20 | 16 | 22 | 0 | 1 | S | R | 6-1 | 195 | 10-19-66 | 1988 | Salem, Ore. |
| Rundels, Matt, of-3b....... | .342 | 34 | 117 | 27 | 40 | 5 | 0 | 6 | 17 | 14 | 31 | 8 | 2 | R | R | 5-11 | 180 | 4-26-70 | 1992 | Pataskala, Ohio |
| Simons, Mitch, dh-3b ...... | .234 | 29 | 77 | 5 | 18 | 1 | 1 | 0 | 5 | 7 | 14 | 2 | 0 | R | R | 5-9 | 170 | 12-13-68 | 1991 | Midwest City, Okla. |
| Tovar, Edgar, ss........... | .262 | 12 | 42 | 5 | 11 | 0 | 0 | 0 | 3 | 1 | 4 | 0 | 1 | R | R | 6-1 | 170 | 11-28-73 | 1992 | Aragua, Venez. |
| White, Derrick, 1b........... | .228 | 21 | 79 | 14 | 18 | 1 | 0 | 2 | 12 | 5 | 17 | 2 | 0 | R | R | 6-1 | 215 | 10-12-69 | 1991 | San Rafael, Calif. |
| White, Rondell, of......... | .328 | 90 | 372 | 72 | 122 | 16 | 10 | 12 | 52 | 22 | 72 | 21 | 6 | R | R | 6-1 | 193 | 2-3-72 | 1990 | Gray, Ga. |
| Wilstead, Randy, 1b-dh.. | .259 | 45 | 108 | 10 | 28 | 7 | 0 | 4 | 15 | 12 | 21 | 1 | 1 | L | L | 6-4 | 200 | 4-5-68 | 1990 | Provo, Utah |
| Woods, Tyrone, of-1b ... | .252 | 106 | 318 | 51 | 80 | 15 | 1 | 16 | 59 | 35 | 77 | 4 | 1 | R | R | 6-1 | 190 | 8-19-69 | 1988 | Brooksville, Fla. |

| PITCHING | W | L | ERA | G | GS | CG | SV | IP | H | R | ER | BB | SO | B | T | HT | WT | DOB | 1st Yr | Resides |
|---|---|---|---|---|---|---|---|---|---|---|---|---|---|---|---|---|---|---|---|---|
| Ausanio, Joe .................. | 2 | 0 | 1.21 | 19 | 0 | 0 | 6 | 22 | 16 | 3 | 3 | 4 | 30 | R | R | 6-1 | 195 | 12-9-65 | 1988 | Kingston, N.Y. |
| Batista, Miguel ............. | 13 | 5 | 4.34 | 26 | 26 | 0 | 0 | 141 | 139 | 79 | 68 | 86 | 91 | R | R | 6-0 | 160 | 2-19-71 | 1988 | San Pedro de Macoris, D.R. |
| Brito, Mario .................... | 4 | 3 | 2.68 | 36 | 0 | 0 | 10 | 50 | 41 | 17 | 15 | 11 | 51 | R | R | 6-3 | 179 | 4-9-66 | 1985 | Bonao, D.R. |
| Corbin, Archie ............... | 5 | 3 | 3.68 | 42 | 2 | 0 | 4 | 73 | 43 | 31 | 30 | 59 | 91 | R | R | 6-4 | 187 | 12-30-67 | 1986 | Beaumont, Texas |
| Cornelius, Reid ............. | 10 | 7 | 4.17 | 27 | 27 | 1 | 0 | 158 | 146 | 95 | 73 | 82 | 119 | R | R | 6-0 | 190 | 6-2-70 | 1989 | Thomasville, Ala. |
| DeHart, Rick ................. | 2 | 4 | 7.68 | 12 | 7 | 0 | 0 | 34 | 45 | 31 | 29 | 19 | 18 | L | R | 6-1 | 180 | 3-21-70 | 1992 | Topeka, Kan. |
| Diaz, Rafael ................... | 5 | 4 | 3.56 | 31 | 8 | 0 | 0 | 91 | 86 | 46 | 36 | 31 | 62 | R | R | 6-1 | 175 | 12-12-69 | 1988 | Maywood, Calif. |
| Eischen, Joey ............... | 14 | 4 | 3.62 | 20 | 20 | 0 | 0 | 119 | 122 | 62 | 48 | 60 | 110 | L | L | 6-1 | 190 | 5-25-70 | 1989 | West Covina, Calif. |
| Haynes, Heath .............. | 8 | 0 | 2.59 | 57 | 0 | 0 | 5 | 66 | 46 | 27 | 19 | 19 | 78 | R | R | 6-2 | 175 | 11-30-68 | 1991 | Wheeling, W.Va. |
| Henderson, Rod ............ | 5 | 0 | 1.82 | 5 | 5 | 0 | 0 | 30 | 20 | 10 | 6 | 15 | 25 | R | R | 6-4 | 195 | 3-11-71 | 1992 | Glasgow, Ky. |
| Johnson, Chris................ | 0 | 0 | 13.50 | 1 | 0 | 0 | 0 | 1 | 1 | 2 | 2 | 3 | 0 | R | R | 6-8 | 215 | 12-7-68 | 1987 | Hixson, Tenn. |
| Looney, Brian ................. | 3 | 2 | 2.38 | 8 | 8 | 1 | 0 | 57 | 36 | 15 | 15 | 17 | 76 | L | L | 5-10 | 180 | 9-26-69 | 1989 | Cheshire, Conn. |
| Perez, Yorkis ................. | 4 | 2 | 3.45 | 34 | 0 | 0 | 3 | 44 | 49 | 26 | 17 | 20 | 58 | L | L | 6-0 | 160 | 9-30-67 | 1983 | Bajos de Haina, D.R. |
| Puig, Benny .................... | 0 | 1 | 2.45 | 14 | 0 | 0 | 1 | 18 | 16 | 5 | 5 | 7 | 10 | L | L | 5-10 | 183 | 10-16-65 | 1985 | Arecibo, P.R. |
| Rueter, Kirk ................... | 5 | 0 | 1.36 | 9 | 8 | 1 | 0 | 60 | 47 | 10 | 9 | 7 | 36 | L | L | 6-3 | 190 | 12-1-70 | 1991 | Hoyleton, Ill. |
| Thomas, Mike ............... | 2 | 2 | 4.73 | 25 | 0 | 0 | 6 | 32 | 34 | 18 | 17 | 19 | 40 | L | L | 6-1 | 175 | 9-2-69 | 1989 | Cabot, Ark. |
| Urbina, Ugueth .............. | 4 | 5 | 3.99 | 11 | 11 | 3 | 0 | 70 | 66 | 32 | 31 | 32 | 45 | R | R | 6-2 | 170 | 2-15-74 | 1991 | Caracas, Venez. |
| White, Gabe.................... | 7 | 2 | 2.16 | 16 | 16 | 2 | 0 | 100 | 80 | 30 | 24 | 28 | 80 | L | L | 6-2 | 200 | 11-20-71 | 1990 | Sebring, Fla. |
| Winston, Darrin .............. | 1 | 0 | 4.63 | 24 | 0 | 0 | 1 | 45 | 53 | 30 | 23 | 19 | 36 | R | L | 6-0 | 195 | 7-6-66 | 1988 | Fords, N.J. |

## WEST PALM BEACH                                                                 A

### FLORIDA STATE LEAGUE

| BATTING | AVG | G | AB | R | H | 2B | 3B | HR | RBI | BB | SO | SB | CS | B | T | HT | WT | DOB | 1st Yr | Resides |
|---|---|---|---|---|---|---|---|---|---|---|---|---|---|---|---|---|---|---|---|---|
| Allen, Matt, c................. | .211 | 57 | 152 | 10 | 32 | 10 | 0 | 0 | 8 | 13 | 41 | 4 | 0 | R | R | 6-2 | 190 | 12-25-69 | 1991 | Tampa, Fla. |
| Austin, Jim, dh-of .......... | .236 | 39 | 89 | 2 | 21 | 3 | 1 | 0 | 9 | 6 | 20 | 2 | 2 | R | R | 6-0 | 175 | 12-26-69 | 1991 | Coto de Caza, Calif. |
| Civit, Xavier, of-p ......... | .100 | 11 | 30 | 1 | 3 | 0 | 0 | 0 | 1 | 0 | 11 | 0 | 0 | R | R | 6-2 | 175 | 5-17-73 | 1993 | Barcelona, Spain |
| Colbrunn, Greg, 1b........ | .387 | 8 | 31 | 6 | 12 | 2 | 1 | 1 | 5 | 4 | 1 | 0 | 0 | R | R | 6-0 | 200 | 7-26-69 | 1988 | Fontana, Calif. |
| Coquillette, Trace, 2b.... | .278 | 6 | 18 | 2 | 5 | 3 | 0 | 0 | 3 | 2 | 5 | 0 | 0 | R | R | 5-11 | 165 | 6-4-74 | 1993 | Orangevale, Calif. |
| Daniel, Mike, 1b-c......... | .245 | 106 | 359 | 39 | 88 | 27 | 1 | 5 | 48 | 43 | 71 | 2 | 1 | R | R | 6-1 | 195 | 9-21-69 | 1991 | Weatherford, Okla. |
| Griffin, Marc, of ............ | .319 | 69 | 226 | 34 | 72 | 6 | 2 | 2 | 18 | 29 | 34 | 23 | 8 | L | R | 6-0 | 170 | 9-15-68 | 1989 | Ste-Foy, Quebec |
| Grissom, Antonio, of..... | .225 | 40 | 138 | 16 | 31 | 3 | 1 | 2 | 7 | 19 | 29 | 7 | 1 | R | R | 6-1 | 195 | 1-11-70 | 1990 | Red Oak, Ga. |
| Grudzielanek, Mark, inf. | .267 | 86 | 300 | 41 | 80 | 11 | 6 | 1 | 34 | 14 | 42 | 17 | 10 | R | R | 6-1 | 170 | 6-30-70 | 1991 | El Paso, Texas |
| Hardge, Michael, 2b...... | .228 | 27 | 92 | 14 | 21 | 2 | 1 | 1 | 12 | 14 | 16 | 5 | 6 | R | R | 5-11 | 183 | 1-27-72 | 1990 | Killeen, Texas |
| Horne, Tyrone, of........... | .295 | 82 | 288 | 43 | 85 | 19 | 2 | 10 | 44 | 40 | 72 | 11 | 10 | L | R | 5-10 | 185 | 11-2-70 | 1989 | Troy, N.C. |
| Hymel, Gary, c-dh......... | .259 | 37 | 112 | 15 | 29 | 9 | 1 | 3 | 10 | 7 | 31 | 2 | 2 | R | R | 6-2 | 195 | 5-21-68 | 1991 | Cypress, Texas |
| Koeyers, Ramsey, c....... | .167 | 4 | 12 | 0 | 2 | 0 | 0 | 0 | 3 | 0 | 3 | 0 | 0 | R | R | 6-1 | 187 | 8-7-74 | 1991 | Curacao, Neth. Antilles |
| Lane, Dan, 3b-2b........... | .228 | 66 | 193 | 25 | 44 | 9 | 2 | 2 | 24 | 26 | 31 | 2 | 2 | R | R | 6-2 | 180 | 12-5-69 | 1992 | Laguna Beach, Calif. |
| Manahan, Austin, 3b...... | .237 | 77 | 274 | 34 | 65 | 14 | 2 | 4 | 29 | 26 | 78 | 7 | 3 | S | R | 6-1 | 185 | 4-12-70 | 1988 | Scottsdale, Ariz. |
| Matos, Domingo, 1b....... | .251 | 46 | 171 | 23 | 43 | 10 | 1 | 3 | 20 | 6 | 34 | 4 | 0 | R | R | 6-1 | 200 | 3-3-72 | 1988 | Barahona, D.R. |
| Northrup, Kevin, of ........ | .296 | 131 | 459 | 65 | 136 | 29 | 0 | 6 | 63 | 70 | 76 | 10 | 7 | R | R | 6-1 | 190 | 1-27-70 | 1992 | Sanford, N.C. |

# EXPOS: MOST COMMON LINEUPS

| | Montreal | Ottawa | Harrisburg | West Palm Beach | Burlington |
|---|---|---|---|---|---|
| | Majors | AAA | AA | A | A |
| C | Darrin Fletcher (127) | Tim Laker (53) | Rob Fitzpatrick (94) | Matt Allen (53) | Javier Pages (89) |
| 1B | Greg Colbrunn (61) | Derrick White (67) | Cliff Floyd (61) | Mike Daniel (55) | Chris Hmielewski (115) |
| 2B | Delino DeShields (123) | Todd Haney (125) | Michael Hardge (98) | Mike Tosar (32) | Jose Vidro (74) |
| 3B | Sean Berry (96) | Vince Castaldo (56) | Shane Andrews (123) | Austin Manahan (75) | Isreal Alcantara (125) |
| SS | Wil Cordero (134) | F.P. Santangelo (54) | Chris Martin (74) | Edgar Tovar (116) | Jolbert Cabrera (126) |
| OF | Marquis Grissom (157) | Scott Bryant (75) | Glenn Murray (130) | Kevin Northrup (128) | Yamil Benitez (104) |
| | Moises Alou (136) | Ted Wood (74) | Rondell White (90) | Claudio Ozoria (72) | Antonio Grissom (64) |
| | Larry Walker (132) | Terrel Hansen (72) | Tyrone Woods (73) | Tyrone Horne (69) | Charles Lee (64) |
| DH | N/A | Scott Bryant (33) | Oreste Marrero (35) | Raul Santana (32) | Corey Powell (44) |
| SP | Dennis Martinez (34) | Tavo Alvarez (25) | Reid Cornelius (27) | Scott Gentile (25) | Scott Pisciotta (24) |
| RP | John Wetteland (70) | Pete Young (48) | Heath Haynes (57) | Mark LaRosa (54) | Alberto Reyes (53) |

Full-season farm clubs only    No. of games at position in parenthesis

| BATTING | AVG | G | AB | R | H | 2B | 3B | HR | RBI | BB | SO | SB | CS | B | T | HT | WT | DOB | 1st Yr | Resides |
|---|---|---|---|---|---|---|---|---|---|---|---|---|---|---|---|---|---|---|---|---|
| Ozoria, Claudio, of | .199 | 81 | 226 | 28 | 45 | 5 | 3 | 2 | 18 | 9 | 57 | 8 | 3 | R | R | 5-9 | 165 | 8-22-71 | 1989 | Santo Domingo, D.R. |
| Reyes, Roberto, of-3b | .140 | 16 | 43 | 4 | 6 | 0 | 0 | 0 | 3 | 6 | 8 | 1 | 0 | R | R | 5-11 | 160 | 12-2-72 | 1990 | Mao Valverde, D.R. |
| Rundels, Matt, 2b-3b | .115 | 8 | 26 | 2 | 3 | 0 | 1 | 0 | 2 | 3 | 4 | 3 | 1 | R | R | 5-11 | 180 | 4-26-70 | 1992 | Pataskala, Ohio |
| Saffer, Jon, of | .208 | 7 | 24 | 3 | 5 | 0 | 0 | 0 | 2 | 2 | 5 | 1 | 3 | L | R | 6-2 | 200 | 7-6-73 | 1992 | Tucson, Ariz. |
| Santana, Raul, c-dh | .230 | 74 | 256 | 23 | 59 | 11 | 2 | 5 | 27 | 14 | 47 | 1 | 3 | R | R | 5-10 | 150 | 2-9-72 | 1989 | Santo Domingo, D.R. |
| Simons, Mitch, 2b-of | .256 | 45 | 156 | 24 | 40 | 4 | 1 | 1 | 13 | 19 | 9 | 14 | 8 | R | R | 5-9 | 170 | 12-13-68 | 1991 | Midwest City, Okla. |
| Tosar, Mike, 2b | .267 | 33 | 101 | 9 | 27 | 3 | 0 | 0 | 11 | 7 | 17 | 4 | 0 | L | R | 5-10 | 175 | 6-25-69 | 1991 | Miami, Fla. |
| Tovar, Edgar, ss | .229 | 116 | 467 | 52 | 107 | 21 | 2 | 2 | 32 | 16 | 33 | 4 | 5 | R | R | 6-1 | 170 | 11-28-73 | 1992 | Aragua, Venez. |
| White, Derrick, 1b-dh | .200 | 6 | 25 | 1 | 5 | 0 | 0 | 1 | 1 | 2 | 2 | 0 | R | R | 6-1 | 215 | 10-12-69 | 1991 | San Rafael, Calif. |
| Wilstead, Randy, 1b-dh | .333 | 60 | 201 | 33 | 67 | 19 | 3 | 3 | 35 | 39 | 39 | 3 | 1 | L | L | 6-4 | 200 | 4-5-68 | 1990 | Provo, Utah |

| PITCHING | W | L | ERA | G | GS | CG | SV | IP | H | R | ER | BB | SO | B | T | HT | WT | DOB | 1st Yr | Resides |
|---|---|---|---|---|---|---|---|---|---|---|---|---|---|---|---|---|---|---|---|---|
| Arteaga, Ivan | 0 | 3 | 8.04 | 4 | 4 | 0 | 0 | 16 | 23 | 15 | 14 | 9 | 10 | L | R | 6-2 | 186 | 7-20-72 | 1989 | Cabello, Venez. |
| Aucoin, Derek | 4 | 4 | 4.23 | 38 | 6 | 0 | 1 | 87 | 89 | 48 | 41 | 44 | 62 | R | R | 6-7 | 226 | 3-27-70 | 1989 | Montreal, Quebec |
| Baxter, Bob | 2 | 2 | 2.28 | 33 | 0 | 0 | 6 | 59 | 55 | 20 | 15 | 5 | 29 | R | L | 6-1 | 180 | 2-17-69 | 1990 | Norwood, Mass. |
| Civit, Xavier | 0 | 0 | 4.50 | 2 | 0 | 0 | 0 | 2 | 1 | 1 | 1 | 4 | 1 | R | R | 6-2 | 175 | 5-17-73 | 1993 | Barcelona, Spain |
| Connolly, Matt | 1 | 1 | 4.91 | 6 | 0 | 0 | 0 | 15 | 14 | 9 | 8 | 9 | 8 | R | R | 6-8 | 230 | 10-1-68 | 1991 | Richmond Hill, N.Y. |
| DeHart, Rick | 1 | 3 | 3.00 | 7 | 7 | 1 | 0 | 42 | 42 | 14 | 14 | 17 | 33 | L | R | 6-1 | 180 | 3-21-70 | 1992 | Topeka, Kan. |
| Gentile, Scott | 8 | 9 | 4.03 | 25 | 25 | 0 | 0 | 138 | 132 | 72 | 62 | 54 | 108 | R | R | 5-11 | 210 | 12-21-70 | 1992 | Berlin, Conn. |
| Henderson, Rod | 12 | 7 | 2.90 | 22 | 22 | 1 | 0 | 143 | 110 | 50 | 46 | 44 | 127 | R | R | 6-4 | 195 | 3-11-71 | 1992 | Glasgow, Ky. |
| LaRosa, Mark | 3 | 3 | 2.57 | 54 | 0 | 0 | 19 | 70 | 59 | 28 | 20 | 21 | 79 | L | L | 6-1 | 195 | 2-17-69 | 1991 | Southington, Conn. |
| Looney, Brian | 4 | 6 | 3.14 | 18 | 16 | 0 | 0 | 106 | 108 | 48 | 37 | 29 | 109 | L | L | 5-10 | 180 | 9-26-69 | 1991 | Cheshire, Conn. |
| McDonald, Kevin | 2 | 3 | 5.65 | 15 | 0 | 0 | 1 | 29 | 34 | 19 | 18 | 22 | 18 | L | R | 6-2 | 205 | 1-3-69 | 1990 | Houston, Texas |
| Norris, Joe | 7 | 4 | 2.67 | 26 | 13 | 0 | 0 | 81 | 62 | 27 | 24 | 29 | 81 | R | R | 6-4 | 200 | 11-29-70 | 1989 | Inyokern, Calif. |
| Powers, Terry | 6 | 3 | 4.25 | 24 | 13 | 0 | 0 | 91 | 89 | 52 | 43 | 45 | 57 | R | R | 6-1 | 175 | 2-14-71 | 1990 | Goodlettsville, Tenn. |
| Rushworth, Jim | 1 | 1 | 3.91 | 24 | 0 | 0 | 1 | 46 | 43 | 24 | 20 | 19 | 23 | R | R | 6-0 | 180 | 7-3-71 | 1992 | West Monroe, La. |
| Schmidt, Curt | 4 | 6 | 3.17 | 44 | 2 | 0 | 5 | 65 | 63 | 32 | 23 | 25 | 51 | R | R | 6-6 | 223 | 3-16-70 | 1992 | Miles City, Mont. |
| Thomas, Mike | 1 | 3 | 3.29 | 25 | 0 | 0 | 9 | 27 | 19 | 13 | 10 | 23 | 28 | L | L | 6-1 | 175 | 9-2-69 | 1989 | Cabot, Ark. |
| Wallace, B.J. | 11 | 8 | 3.28 | 25 | 24 | 0 | 0 | 137 | 112 | 61 | 50 | 65 | 126 | R | L | 6-4 | 195 | 5-18-71 | 1992 | Monroeville, Ala. |
| Wetteland, John | 0 | 0 | 0.00 | 2 | 2 | 0 | 0 | 3 | 0 | 0 | 0 | 4 | 6 | R | R | 6-2 | 195 | 8-21-66 | 1985 | Monroe, La. |
| Winston, Darrin | 2 | 0 | 1.46 | 8 | 2 | 1 | 0 | 25 | 18 | 6 | 4 | 3 | 21 | R | L | 6-0 | 195 | 7-6-66 | 1988 | Fords, N.J. |
| Woodring, Jason | 0 | 1 | 4.32 | 4 | 0 | 0 | 0 | 8 | 9 | 5 | 4 | 5 | 4 | R | R | 6-3 | 190 | 4-2-74 | 1993 | Trinidad, Colo. |

# BURLINGTON                                                                 A

## MIDWEST LEAGUE

| BATTING | AVG | G | AB | R | H | 2B | 3B | HR | RBI | BB | SO | SB | CS | B | T | HT | WT | DOB | 1st Yr | Resides |
|---|---|---|---|---|---|---|---|---|---|---|---|---|---|---|---|---|---|---|---|---|
| Alcantara, Isreal, 3b | .245 | 126 | 470 | 65 | 115 | 26 | 3 | 18 | 73 | 20 | 125 | 6 | 7 | R | R | 6-2 | 165 | 5-6-73 | 1991 | Santo Domingo, D.R. |
| Benitez, Yamil, of | .273 | 111 | 411 | 70 | 112 | 21 | 5 | 15 | 61 | 29 | 99 | 18 | 7 | R | R | 6-2 | 180 | 10-5-72 | 1990 | San Juan, P.R. |
| Berry, Mike, 2b | .239 | 31 | 92 | 15 | 22 | 2 | 0 | 1 | 6 | 20 | 22 | 0 | 1 | R | R | 5-10 | 175 | 8-12-70 | 1993 | Rolling Hills Estate, Calif. |
| Cabrera, Jolbert, ss | .254 | 128 | 507 | 62 | 129 | 24 | 2 | 0 | 38 | 39 | 93 | 31 | 11 | R | R | 6-0 | 177 | 12-8-72 | 1991 | Cartagena, Colombia |
| Doyle, Tom, dh-1b | .079 | 13 | 38 | 3 | 3 | 2 | 0 | 0 | 4 | 0 | 13 | 0 | 1 | L | R | 6-4 | 220 | 9-25-70 | 1992 | Rapid City, S.D. |
| Grissom, Antonio, of | .251 | 73 | 271 | 40 | 68 | 13 | 5 | 5 | 27 | 35 | 60 | 22 | 11 | R | R | 6-1 | 195 | 1-11-70 | 1990 | Red Oak, Ga. |
| Haar, Rich, 2b | .211 | 24 | 71 | 9 | 15 | 3 | 0 | 0 | 8 | 14 | 16 | 2 | 2 | R | R | 6-0 | 180 | 9-14-70 | 1993 | La Mesa, Calif. |
| Hmielewski, Chris, 1b | .274 | 125 | 412 | 69 | 113 | 25 | 2 | 14 | 70 | 74 | 99 | 4 | 2 | L | L | 6-4 | 210 | 7-18-70 | 1991 | Franklin Park, Ill. |
| Hymel, Gary, dh-c | .275 | 50 | 182 | 28 | 50 | 14 | 1 | 11 | 41 | 3 | 60 | 1 | 0 | R | R | 6-2 | 195 | 5-21-68 | 1991 | Cypress, Texas |
| LaChance, Vince, of | .164 | 19 | 61 | 6 | 10 | 1 | 0 | 3 | 12 | 5 | 18 | 0 | 0 | L | R | 5-11 | 195 | 2-4-72 | 1992 | Montreal, Quebec |
| Lee, Charles, of | .219 | 68 | 228 | 33 | 50 | 12 | 1 | 4 | 21 | 32 | 65 | 16 | 5 | R | R | 6-1 | 200 | 12-7-71 | 1991 | Poplar Branch, N.C. |
| Marabella, Tony, 2b | .286 | 17 | 42 | 7 | 12 | 6 | 0 | 2 | 11 | 6 | 6 | 0 | 0 | R | R | 5-11 | 179 | 4-25-73 | 1989 | Montreal, Quebec |
| McCubbin, Shane, c | .149 | 40 | 121 | 12 | 18 | 4 | 0 | 2 | 6 | 11 | 45 | 1 | 0 | R | R | 6-1 | 200 | 9-18-72 | 1992 | Rock Island, Ill. |
| O'Neill, Doug, of | .212 | 67 | 203 | 26 | 43 | 6 | 3 | 3 | 20 | 33 | 69 | 3 | 1 | R | R | 5-10 | 190 | 6-29-70 | 1991 | Campbell, Calif. |
| Pages, Javier, c | .261 | 96 | 295 | 35 | 77 | 20 | 0 | 7 | 47 | 44 | 74 | 2 | 2 | R | R | 6-0 | 190 | 7-27-71 | 1990 | Fort Lauderdale, Fla. |
| Powell, Corey, of | .279 | 115 | 433 | 55 | 121 | 18 | 5 | 13 | 62 | 29 | 97 | 2 | 1 | R | R | 6-3 | 210 | 9-3-70 | 1990 | San Diego, Calif. |
| Rundels, Matt, of-inf | .271 | 64 | 203 | 36 | 55 | 7 | 4 | 4 | 17 | 38 | 36 | 14 | 7 | R | R | 5-11 | 180 | 4-26-70 | 1992 | Pataskala, Ohio |
| Tosone, Joe, of | .151 | 28 | 73 | 6 | 11 | 1 | 0 | 0 | 4 | 13 | 28 | 0 | 2 | R | L | 5-11 | 170 | 7-21-73 | 1993 | Hanover, N.H. |
| Vidro, Jose, 2b | .240 | 76 | 287 | 39 | 69 | 14 | 3 | 2 | 26 | 28 | 54 | 3 | 2 | S | R | 5-11 | 175 | 8-27-74 | 1992 | Sabana Grande, P.R. |

| PITCHING | W | L | ERA | G | GS | CG | SV | IP | H | R | ER | BB | SO | B | T | HT | WT | DOB | 1st Yr | Resides |
|---|---|---|---|---|---|---|---|---|---|---|---|---|---|---|---|---|---|---|---|---|
| Arteaga, Ivan | 6 | 5 | 2.83 | 20 | 20 | 2 | 0 | 127 | 114 | 57 | 40 | 47 | 111 | L | R | 6-2 | 186 | 7-20-72 | 1989 | Cabello, Venez. |
| Clelland, Ricky | 5 | 7 | 3.71 | 30 | 12 | 0 | 1 | 97 | 94 | 57 | 40 | 61 | 86 | R | R | 6-4 | 205 | 10-1-71 | 1990 | Brilliant, Ohio |
| DaSilva, Fernando | 4 | 4 | 4.75 | 11 | 10 | 0 | 0 | 61 | 66 | 38 | 32 | 18 | 50 | R | R | 6-2 | 194 | 9-6-71 | 1991 | Brossard, Quebec |
| Eggert, David | 5 | 4 | 2.83 | 51 | 0 | 0 | 8 | 60 | 59 | 22 | 19 | 24 | 83 | R | L | 6-1 | 200 | 5-20-70 | 1992 | Ventura, Calif. |
| Falteisek, Steve | 3 | 5 | 5.90 | 14 | 14 | 0 | 0 | 76 | 86 | 59 | 50 | 35 | 63 | R | R | 6-2 | 200 | 1-28-72 | 1992 | Floral Park, N.Y. |
| Hostetler, Jeff | 1 | 6 | 6.56 | 32 | 5 | 0 | 1 | 59 | 59 | 49 | 43 | 51 | 56 | L | L | 6-4 | 195 | 6-17-71 | 1991 | Johnson City, Tenn. |
| Kermode, Al | 0 | 0 | 3.67 | 19 | 0 | 0 | 3 | 27 | 29 | 11 | 11 | 9 | 32 | R | R | 6-4 | 185 | 12-10-70 | 1992 | Chandler, Ariz. |
| Maloney, Ryan | 0 | 1 | 3.00 | 11 | 0 | 0 | 0 | 15 | 16 | 11 | 5 | 6 | 8 | L | L | 6-3 | 190 | 1-24-72 | 1990 | Lancaster, Ohio |
| Martinez, Williams | 0 | 0 | 0.00 | 2 | 0 | 0 | 0 | 3 | 3 | 0 | 1 | 1 | 1 | R | R | 5-11 | 165 | 1-4-70 | 1989 | Caracas, Venez. |

| PITCHING | W | L | ERA | G | GS | CG | SV | IP | H | R | ER | BB | SO | B | T | HT | WT | DOB | 1st Yr | Resides |
|---|---|---|---|---|---|---|---|---|---|---|---|---|---|---|---|---|---|---|---|---|
| Pacheco, Alex.............. | 3 | 5 | 4.19 | 13 | 7 | 0 | 1 | 43 | 47 | 31 | 20 | 12 | 24 | R | R | 6-3 | 170 | 7-19-73 | 1990 | Caracas, Venez. |
| Paxton, Darrin.............. | 6 | 1 | 2.88 | 41 | 3 | 0 | 1 | 75 | 57 | 28 | 24 | 34 | 110 | R | L | 6-4 | 220 | 4-17-70 | 1991 | Wichita, Kan. |
| Perez, Carlos............... | 1 | 0 | 3.24 | 12 | 1 | 0 | 0 | 17 | 13 | 6 | 6 | 9 | 21 | L | L | 6-3 | 200 | 4-14-71 | 1990 | San Cristobal, D.R. |
| Phelps, Tom................. | 2 | 4 | 3.73 | 8 | 8 | 0 | 0 | 41 | 36 | 18 | 17 | 13 | 33 | L | L | 6-3 | 192 | 3-4-74 | 1993 | Tampa, Fla. |
| Pisciotta, Scott............ | 9 | 12 | 4.06 | 24 | 24 | 1 | 0 | 135 | 129 | 85 | 61 | 79 | 112 | R | R | 6-7 | 225 | 6-8-73 | 1991 | Marietta, Ga. |
| Reyes, Alberto............. | 7 | 6 | 2.68 | 53 | 0 | 0 | 11 | 74 | 52 | 33 | 22 | 26 | 80 | R | R | 6-0 | 165 | 4-10-71 | 1988 | Santo Domingo, D.R. |
| Rushworth, Jim............ | 2 | 0 | 0.83 | 24 | 0 | 0 | 0 | 33 | 16 | 7 | 3 | 11 | 40 | R | R | 6-0 | 180 | 7-3-71 | 1992 | West Monroe, La. |
| Stull, Everett ............... | 4 | 9 | 3.83 | 15 | 15 | 1 | 0 | 82 | 68 | 44 | 35 | 59 | 85 | R | R | 6-3 | 195 | 8-24-71 | 1992 | Stone Mountain, Ga. |
| Urbina, Ugueth ........... | 10 | 1 | 1.99 | 16 | 16 | 4 | 0 | 108 | 78 | 30 | 24 | 36 | 107 | R | R | 6-2 | 170 | 2-15-74 | 1991 | Caracas, Venez. |

# JAMESTOWN       A
## NEW YORK-PENN LEAGUE

| BATTING | AVG | G | AB | R | H | 2B | 3B | HR | RBI | BB | SO | SB | CS | B | T | HT | WT | DOB | 1st Yr | Resides |
|---|---|---|---|---|---|---|---|---|---|---|---|---|---|---|---|---|---|---|---|---|
| Batista, Juan, 3b .......... | .239 | 75 | 280 | 45 | 67 | 10 | 3 | 9 | 32 | 21 | 97 | 4 | 6 | R | R | 5-11 | 160 | 7-8-72 | 1993 | Santo Domingo, D.R. |
| Campos, Jesus, of ........ | .242 | 70 | 285 | 43 | 69 | 6 | 6 | 1 | 22 | 18 | 39 | 9 | 9 | R | R | 5-9 | 145 | 10-12-73 | 1991 | San Pedro de Macoris, D.R. |
| Foster, Jeff, ss............. | .231 | 28 | 91 | 15 | 21 | 1 | 2 | 2 | 13 | 10 | 30 | 1 | 1 | L | R | 6-2 | 175 | 2-25-72 | 1993 | Knoxville, Tenn. |
| Grubb, Chris, 2b-of ...... | .220 | 53 | 132 | 14 | 29 | 4 | 2 | 1 | 14 | 24 | 22 | 6 | 0 | S | R | 5-11 | 165 | 10-6-71 | 1993 | Ellicott City, Md. |
| Haar, Rich, ss-2b ......... | .351 | 21 | 57 | 10 | 20 | 5 | 2 | 0 | 6 | 10 | 13 | 3 | 0 | R | R | 6-0 | 180 | 9-14-70 | 1993 | La Mesa, Calif. |
| Harrell, Matt, c-dh ........ | .200 | 25 | 55 | 9 | 11 | 3 | 0 | 0 | 6 | 7 | 13 | 0 | 0 | R | R | 6-3 | 205 | 1-14-71 | 1993 | Chevy Chase, Md. |
| Henley, Robert, dh-c ..... | .257 | 60 | 206 | 25 | 53 | 10 | 4 | 7 | 29 | 20 | 60 | 0 | 1 | R | R | 6-2 | 190 | 1-30-73 | 1993 | Grand Bay, Ala. |
| Koeyers, Ramsey, c....... | .223 | 65 | 233 | 25 | 52 | 9 | 2 | 4 | 29 | 10 | 69 | 1 | 1 | R | R | 6-1 | 187 | 8-7-74 | 1991 | Curacao, Neth. Antilles |
| LaChance, Vince, of...... | .288 | 39 | 139 | 16 | 40 | 9 | 2 | 5 | 18 | 10 | 32 | 4 | 3 | L | R | 6-1 | 195 | 2-4-72 | 1992 | Montreal, Quebec |
| Marabella, Tony, 2b ...... | .243 | 52 | 185 | 25 | 45 | 13 | 1 | 6 | 24 | 16 | 32 | 1 | 0 | R | R | 5-11 | 179 | 4-25-73 | 1989 | Montreal, Quebec |
| Quade, Scott, ss........... | .140 | 47 | 121 | 6 | 17 | 0 | 4 | 0 | 4 | 20 | 31 | 1 | 1 | R | R | 6-1 | 185 | 3-9-71 | 1993 | Mt. Prospect, Ill. |
| Raleigh, Matt, 1b .......... | .236 | 77 | 263 | 51 | 62 | 17 | 0 | 15 | 42 | 39 | 99 | 5 | 2 | R | R | 5-11 | 205 | 7-18-70 | 1992 | Swanton, Vt. |
| Saffer, Jon, of .............. | .258 | 61 | 225 | 31 | 58 | 17 | 5 | 0 | 18 | 31 | 46 | 11 | 5 | L | R | 6-2 | 200 | 7-6-73 | 1992 | Tucson, Ariz. |
| Thompson, Angelo, of.... | .223 | 66 | 215 | 20 | 48 | 10 | 2 | 2 | 28 | 28 | 70 | 5 | 3 | R | R | 6-0 | 215 | 1-1-72 | 1993 | Raleigh, N.C. |
| Tosone, Joe, of ............ | .174 | 10 | 23 | 2 | 4 | 0 | 1 | 0 | 4 | 1 | 5 | 0 | 0 | R | L | 5-11 | 170 | 7-21-71 | 1993 | Hanover, N.H. |

| PITCHING | W | L | ERA | G | GS | CG | SV | IP | H | R | ER | BB | SO | B | T | HT | WT | DOB | 1st Yr | Resides |
|---|---|---|---|---|---|---|---|---|---|---|---|---|---|---|---|---|---|---|---|---|
| Alfonseca, Antonio........ | 2 | 2 | 6.15 | 15 | 4 | 0 | 1 | 34 | 31 | 26 | 23 | 22 | 29 | R | R | 6-4 | 160 | 4-16-72 | 1990 | La Romana, D.R. |
| Brown, Nate................. | 0 | 1 | 3.00 | 2 | 2 | 0 | 0 | 3 | 1 | 1 | 1 | 4 | 6 | L | L | 6-5 | 225 | 2-3-71 | 1993 | Berkeley, Calif. |
| Bullock, Joshua ........... | 5 | 3 | 2.97 | 23 | 0 | 0 | 6 | 36 | 25 | 14 | 12 | 14 | 35 | L | L | 6-0 | 192 | 10-24-70 | 1993 | Grasonville, Md. |
| DaSilva, Fernando......... | 3 | 8 | 4.19 | 15 | 14 | 0 | 0 | 92 | 107 | 58 | 43 | 25 | 59 | R | R | 6-2 | 194 | 9-6-71 | 1991 | Brossard, Quebec |
| Harrison, Scott............. | 1 | 4 | 3.38 | 24 | 0 | 0 | 6 | 27 | 27 | 16 | 10 | 9 | 25 | R | R | 6-4 | 215 | 12-19-68 | 1992 | Houston, Texas |
| Knieper, Aaron............. | 4 | 5 | 4.42 | 15 | 11 | 0 | 1 | 79 | 83 | 47 | 39 | 27 | 40 | R | R | 6-5 | 205 | 6-15-72 | 1993 | Saginaw, Mich. |
| Leon, Michael ............... | 0 | 2 | 3.23 | 20 | 0 | 0 | 0 | 31 | 34 | 14 | 11 | 12 | 17 | R | L | 5-10 | 170 | 10-15-71 | 1993 | Tucson, Ariz. |
| Pacheco, Alex............... | 0 | 1 | 3.21 | 6 | 1 | 0 | 0 | 14 | 11 | 7 | 5 | 4 | 15 | R | R | 6-3 | 170 | 7-19-73 | 1990 | Caracas, Venez. |
| Phelps, Tom................. | 3 | 8 | 4.58 | 16 | 15 | 1 | 0 | 92 | 102 | 62 | 47 | 37 | 74 | L | L | 6-3 | 192 | 3-4-74 | 1993 | Tampa, Fla. |
| Respondek, Mark .......... | 1 | 1 | 6.19 | 18 | 0 | 0 | 1 | 32 | 48 | 28 | 22 | 11 | 26 | L | L | 6-0 | 180 | 6-15-71 | 1991 | Emerald, Australia |
| Schneider, Tom ............ | 6 | 5 | 3.93 | 14 | 14 | 2 | 0 | 87 | 102 | 50 | 38 | 23 | 44 | R | L | 6-4 | 205 | 9-27-72 | 1993 | Shreveport, La. |
| Stutts, Dennis .............. | 0 | 1 | 3.34 | 26 | 0 | 0 | 2 | 35 | 29 | 17 | 13 | 7 | 31 | R | R | 6-0 | 190 | 4-20-70 | 1993 | Durham, N.C. |
| Weber, Neil ................. | 6 | 5 | 2.77 | 16 | 16 | 2 | 0 | 94 | 84 | 46 | 29 | 36 | 80 | L | L | 6-5 | 205 | 12-6-72 | 1993 | Irvine, Calif. |

# WEST PALM BEACH       R
## GULF COAST LEAGUE

| BATTING | AVG | G | AB | R | H | 2B | 3B | HR | RBI | BB | SO | SB | CS | B | T | HT | WT | DOB | 1st Yr | Resides |
|---|---|---|---|---|---|---|---|---|---|---|---|---|---|---|---|---|---|---|---|---|
| Brinkley, Joshua, 2b-dh | .270 | 16 | 63 | 6 | 17 | 2 | 0 | 0 | 4 | 2 | 8 | 0 | 1 | R | R | 5-10 | 175 | 8-5-73 | 1993 | Raleigh, N.C. |
| Campos, Jesus, dh-of ... | .125 | 2 | 8 | 1 | 1 | 0 | 0 | 0 | 1 | 2 | 1 | 0 | 0 | R | R | 5-9 | 145 | 10-12-73 | 1991 | San Pedro de Macoris, D.R. |
| Civit, Xavier, dh-of ......... | .304 | 33 | 102 | 16 | 31 | 4 | 1 | 0 | 15 | 6 | 22 | 0 | 0 | R | R | 6-2 | 175 | 5-17-73 | 1993 | Barcelona, Spain |
| Coquillette, Trace, 2b..... | .252 | 44 | 159 | 27 | 40 | 4 | 3 | 2 | 11 | 37 | 28 | 16 | 3 | R | R | 5-11 | 165 | 6-4-74 | 1993 | Orangevale, Calif. |
| Culp, Randy, 3b-c ......... | .271 | 55 | 210 | 31 | 57 | 14 | 1 | 5 | 23 | 18 | 56 | 0 | 0 | R | R | 6-1 | 195 | 8-18-74 | 1993 | Killeen, Texas |
| Estrada, Josue, of ......... | .243 | 55 | 214 | 24 | 52 | 5 | 3 | 1 | 32 | 20 | 48 | 2 | 1 | R | R | 6-0 | 185 | 1-21-75 | 1993 | Rio Piedras, P.R. |
| Foster, Jeff, dh-ss ......... | .179 | 8 | 28 | 4 | 5 | 1 | 0 | 0 | 1 | 5 | 7 | 0 | 0 | L | R | 6-2 | 175 | 2-25-72 | 1993 | Knoxville, Tenn. |
| Gonzalez, Carlos, 1b ..... | .272 | 22 | 81 | 6 | 22 | 4 | 1 | 0 | 8 | 3 | 21 | 0 | 0 | R | R | 6-3 | 195 | 7-13-73 | 1992 | Caracas, Venez. |
| Hall, Ronnie, of............. | .226 | 49 | 177 | 21 | 40 | 6 | 0 | 1 | 13 | 19 | 32 | 4 | 3 | R | R | 6-3 | 195 | 10-14-75 | 1993 | Tustin, Calif. |
| Martinez, Luis, c ........... | .230 | 19 | 61 | 8 | 14 | 2 | 0 | 0 | 3 | 7 | 13 | 0 | 0 | R | R | 6-2 | 165 | 12-11-74 | 1992 | Santa Isabel, P.R. |
| Meran, Jorge, of-dh ....... | .153 | 17 | 59 | 6 | 9 | 1 | 0 | 0 | 2 | 7 | 19 | 1 | 0 | R | R | 6-0 | 165 | 2-14-75 | 1991 | Santo Domingo, D.R. |
| Niethammer, Marc, 1b .. | .197 | 49 | 157 | 21 | 31 | 4 | 0 | 6 | 18 | 26 | 55 | 0 | 1 | L | R | 6-5 | 230 | 9-28-73 | 1992 | Lake Wales, Fla. |
| Pachot, John, c ............ | .306 | 35 | 121 | 13 | 37 | 4 | 1 | 0 | 16 | 2 | 7 | 0 | 1 | R | R | 6-2 | 168 | 11-11-74 | 1993 | Ponce, P.R. |
| Perez, Tomas, ss .......... | .243 | 52 | 189 | 27 | 46 | 3 | 1 | 2 | 21 | 23 | 25 | 8 | 3 | S | R | 5-11 | 160 | 12-29-73 | 1991 | Santo Domingo, D.R. |
| Reyes, Roberto, 3b-2b.. | .304 | 30 | 112 | 17 | 34 | 6 | 3 | 1 | 15 | 9 | 18 | 9 | 3 | R | R | 5-11 | 160 | 12-2-72 | 1990 | Mao Valverde, D.R. |
| Schwab, Chris, of ......... | .220 | 56 | 218 | 21 | 48 | 12 | 1 | 0 | 20 | 22 | 53 | 0 | 2 | L | R | 6-3 | 215 | 7-25-74 | 1993 | Eagan, Minn. |

| PITCHING | W | L | ERA | G | GS | CG | SV | IP | H | R | ER | BB | SO | B | T | HT | WT | DOB | 1st Yr | Resides |
|---|---|---|---|---|---|---|---|---|---|---|---|---|---|---|---|---|---|---|---|---|
| Ausanio, Joe................. | 0 | 0 | 0.00 | 5 | 0 | 0 | 0 | 5 | 3 | 1 | 0 | 1 | 6 | R | R | 6-1 | 195 | 12-9-65 | 1988 | Kingston, N.Y. |
| Baker, Jason................. | 1 | 1 | 2.25 | 7 | 7 | 0 | 0 | 32 | 26 | 14 | 8 | 11 | 24 | R | R | 6-4 | 195 | 11-21-74 | 1993 | Midland, Texas |
| Brown, Nate................. | 0 | 0 | 0.00 | 1 | 0 | 0 | 1 | 0 | 0 | 0 | 0 | 0 | 1 | L | L | 6-5 | 225 | 2-3-71 | 1993 | Berkeley, Calif. |
| Detwiler, Brian.............. | 1 | 2 | 4.97 | 17 | 0 | 0 | 3 | 42 | 48 | 25 | 23 | 21 | 26 | R | R | 6-5 | 235 | 4-13-71 | 1993 | Wyomissing, Pa. |
| Durocher, Jayson .......... | 2 | 3 | 3.46 | 7 | 7 | 3 | 0 | 39 | 32 | 23 | 15 | 13 | 21 | R | R | 6-3 | 195 | 8-18-74 | 1993 | Scottsdale, Ariz. |
| Foster, Kris .................. | 1 | 6 | 3.43 | 17 | 3 | 0 | 1 | 45 | 44 | 26 | 17 | 16 | 30 | R | R | 6-0 | 180 | 8-30-74 | 1993 | Lehigh Acres, Fla. |
| Handy, Russell .............. | 1 | 2 | 3.42 | 11 | 10 | 0 | 0 | 47 | 33 | 25 | 18 | 39 | 23 | R | R | 6-4 | 200 | 8-4-74 | 1993 | Bakersfield, Calif. |
| Hylton, Jim .................. | 3 | 3 | 3.23 | 11 | 3 | 0 | 0 | 31 | 32 | 18 | 11 | 17 | 16 | R | R | 6-0 | 180 | 4-26-73 | 1992 | Concord, Calif. |
| Kermode, Al ................. | 0 | 0 | 3.00 | 4 | 0 | 0 | 1 | 6 | 5 | 2 | 2 | 1 | 5 | R | R | 6-4 | 185 | 12-10-70 | 1992 | Chandler, Ariz. |
| Mainville, Martin .......... | 1 | 2 | 5.25 | 6 | 5 | 0 | 0 | 24 | 26 | 15 | 14 | 4 | 12 | R | R | 6-4 | 160 | 7-18-65 | 1993 | Montreal, Quebec |
| Markham, Andy ............ | 5 | 4 | 3.13 | 11 | 10 | 2 | 0 | 72 | 59 | 31 | 25 | 21 | 45 | R | R | 6-3 | 205 | 11-12-72 | 1993 | Phoenix, Ariz. |
| Paniagua, Jose ............ | 3 | 0 | 0.67 | 4 | 4 | 1 | 0 | 27 | 13 | 2 | 2 | 5 | 25 | R | R | 6-1 | 160 | 8-20-73 | 1991 | Santo Domingo, D.R. |
| Schmidt, Curt ............... | 1 | 0 | 0.00 | 1 | 1 | 0 | 0 | 5 | 1 | 0 | 0 | 0 | 7 | R | R | 6-6 | 203 | 3-16-70 | 1992 | Miles City, Mont. |
| Taveras, Roberto........... | 2 | 4 | 1.48 | 17 | 5 | 0 | 3 | 55 | 52 | 21 | 9 | 18 | 37 | R | R | 6-1 | 162 | 4-10-72 | 1990 | Monte Christi, D.R. |
| Vializ, Arce ................. | 3 | 3 | 3.92 | 15 | 2 | 0 | 0 | 44 | 37 | 25 | 19 | 43 | 32 | R | R | 6-4 | 185 | 9-25-74 | 1992 | Aguada, P.R. |
| Woodring, Jason ........... | 2 | 1 | 0.76 | 14 | 0 | 0 | 3 | 36 | 19 | 5 | 3 | 9 | 20 | R | R | 6-3 | 190 | 4-2-74 | 1993 | Trinidad, Colo. |

# NEW YORK YANKEES

**Manager:** Buck Showalter.  **1993 Record:** 88-74, .543 (2nd, AL East).

| BATTING | AVG | G | AB | R | H | 2B | 3B | HR | RBI | BB | SO | SB | CS | B | T | HT | WT | DOB | 1st Yr | Resides |
|---|---|---|---|---|---|---|---|---|---|---|---|---|---|---|---|---|---|---|---|---|
| Boggs, Wade | .302 | 143 | 560 | 83 | 169 | 26 | 1 | 2 | 59 | 74 | 49 | 0 | 1 | L | R | 6-2 | 197 | 6-15-58 | 1976 | Tampa, Fla. |
| Gallego, Mike | .283 | 119 | 403 | 63 | 114 | 20 | 1 | 10 | 54 | 50 | 65 | 3 | 2 | R | R | 5-8 | 160 | 10-31-60 | 1981 | Yorba Linda, Calif. |
| Humphreys, Mike | .171 | 25 | 35 | 6 | 6 | 2 | 1 | 1 | 6 | 4 | 11 | 2 | 1 | R | R | 6-0 | 185 | 4-10-67 | 1988 | De Soto, Texas |
| James, Dion | .332 | 115 | 343 | 62 | 114 | 21 | 2 | 7 | 36 | 31 | 31 | 0 | 0 | L | L | 6-1 | 175 | 11-9-62 | 1980 | Sacramento, Calif. |
| Kelly, Pat | .273 | 127 | 406 | 49 | 111 | 24 | 1 | 7 | 51 | 24 | 68 | 14 | 11 | R | R | 6-0 | 180 | 10-14-67 | 1988 | Bangor, Pa. |
| Leyritz, Jim | .309 | 95 | 259 | 43 | 80 | 14 | 0 | 14 | 53 | 37 | 59 | 0 | 0 | R | R | 6-0 | 190 | 12-27-63 | 1986 | Plantation, Fla. |
| Maas, Kevin | .205 | 59 | 151 | 20 | 31 | 4 | 0 | 9 | 25 | 24 | 32 | 1 | 1 | L | L | 6-3 | 205 | 1-20-65 | 1986 | Castro Valley, Calif. |
| Mattingly, Don | .291 | 134 | 530 | 78 | 154 | 27 | 2 | 17 | 86 | 61 | 42 | 0 | 0 | L | L | 6-0 | 175 | 4-20-61 | 1979 | Evansville, Ind. |
| Meulens, Hensley | .170 | 30 | 53 | 8 | 9 | 1 | 1 | 2 | 5 | 8 | 19 | 0 | 1 | R | R | 6-3 | 212 | 6-23-67 | 1986 | Curacao, Neth. Antilles |
| Nokes, Matt | .249 | 76 | 217 | 25 | 54 | 8 | 0 | 10 | 35 | 16 | 31 | 0 | 0 | L | R | 6-1 | 195 | 10-31-63 | 1981 | San Diego, Calif. |
| O'Neill, Paul | .311 | 141 | 498 | 71 | 155 | 34 | 1 | 20 | 75 | 44 | 69 | 2 | 4 | L | L | 6-4 | 215 | 2-25-63 | 1981 | Cincinnati, Ohio |
| Owen, Spike | .234 | 103 | 334 | 41 | 78 | 16 | 2 | 2 | 20 | 29 | 30 | 3 | 2 | S | R | 5-9 | 165 | 4-19-61 | 1982 | Cleburne, Texas |
| Silvestri, Dave | .286 | 7 | 21 | 4 | 6 | 1 | 0 | 1 | 4 | 5 | 3 | 0 | 0 | R | R | 6-0 | 180 | 9-29-67 | 1989 | St. Louis, Mo. |
| Stankiewicz, Andy | .000 | 16 | 9 | 5 | 0 | 0 | 0 | 0 | 1 | 1 | 0 | 0 | 0 | R | R | 5-9 | 165 | 8-10-64 | 1986 | Los Alamitos, Calif. |
| Stanley, Mike | .305 | 130 | 423 | 70 | 129 | 17 | 1 | 26 | 84 | 57 | 85 | 1 | 1 | R | R | 6-0 | 190 | 6-25-63 | 1985 | Oviedo, Fla. |
| Tartabull, Danny | .250 | 138 | 513 | 87 | 128 | 33 | 2 | 31 | 102 | 92 | 156 | 0 | 0 | R | R | 6-1 | 210 | 10-30-62 | 1980 | Malibu, Calif. |
| Velarde, Randy | .301 | 85 | 226 | 28 | 68 | 13 | 2 | 7 | 24 | 18 | 39 | 2 | 2 | R | R | 6-0 | 185 | 11-24-62 | 1985 | Midland, Texas |
| Williams, Bernie | .268 | 139 | 567 | 67 | 152 | 31 | 4 | 12 | 68 | 53 | 106 | 9 | 9 | S | R | 6-2 | 196 | 9-13-68 | 1986 | Vega Alta, P.R. |
| Williams, Gerald | .149 | 42 | 67 | 11 | 10 | 2 | 3 | 0 | 6 | 1 | 14 | 2 | 0 | R | R | 6-2 | 185 | 8-10-66 | 1987 | LaPlace, La. |

| PITCHING | W | L | ERA | G | GS | CG | SV | IP | H | R | ER | BB | SO | B | T | HT | WT | DOB | 1st Yr | Resides |
|---|---|---|---|---|---|---|---|---|---|---|---|---|---|---|---|---|---|---|---|---|
| Abbott, Jim | 11 | 14 | 4.37 | 32 | 32 | 4 | 0 | 214 | 221 | 115 | 104 | 73 | 95 | L | L | 6-3 | 210 | 9-19-67 | 1989 | Newport Beach, Calif. |
| Assenmacher, Paul | 2 | 2 | 3.12 | 26 | 0 | 0 | 0 | 17 | 10 | 6 | 6 | 9 | 11 | L | L | 6-3 | 195 | 12-10-60 | 1983 | Stone Mountain, Ga. |
| Cook, Andy | 0 | 1 | 5.06 | 4 | 0 | 0 | 0 | 5 | 4 | 3 | 3 | 7 | 4 | R | R | 6-5 | 205 | 8-30-67 | 1988 | Memphis, Tenn. |
| Farr, Steve | 2 | 2 | 4.21 | 49 | 0 | 0 | 25 | 47 | 44 | 22 | 22 | 28 | 39 | R | R | 5-11 | 204 | 12-12-56 | 1977 | Corolla, N.C. |
| Gibson, Paul | 2 | 0 | 3.06 | 20 | 0 | 0 | 0 | 35 | 31 | 15 | 12 | 9 | 25 | R | L | 6-0 | 185 | 1-4-60 | 1978 | Center Moriches, N.Y. |
| Habyan, John | 2 | 1 | 4.04 | 36 | 0 | 0 | 1 | 42 | 45 | 20 | 19 | 16 | 29 | R | R | 6-2 | 195 | 1-29-64 | 1982 | Bel Air, Md. |
| Heaton, Neal | 1 | 0 | 6.00 | 18 | 0 | 0 | 0 | 27 | 34 | 19 | 18 | 11 | 15 | L | L | 6-3 | 200 | 3-3-60 | 1981 | East Patchogue, N.Y. |
| Hitchcock, Sterling | 1 | 2 | 4.65 | 6 | 6 | 0 | 0 | 31 | 32 | 18 | 16 | 14 | 26 | L | L | 6-1 | 195 | 4-29-71 | 1989 | Seffner, Fla. |
| Howe, Steve | 3 | 5 | 4.97 | 51 | 0 | 0 | 4 | 51 | 58 | 31 | 28 | 10 | 19 | L | L | 5-11 | 195 | 3-10-58 | 1979 | Whitefish, Mont. |
| Hutton, Mark | 1 | 1 | 5.73 | 7 | 4 | 0 | 0 | 22 | 24 | 17 | 14 | 17 | 12 | R | R | 6-6 | 225 | 2-6-70 | 1989 | West Lakes, Australia |
| Jean, Domingo | 1 | 1 | 4.46 | 10 | 6 | 0 | 0 | 40 | 37 | 20 | 20 | 19 | 20 | R | R | 6-2 | 175 | 1-9-69 | 1989 | San Pedro de Macoris, D.R. |
| Johnson, Jeff | 0 | 2 | 30.38 | 2 | 2 | 0 | 0 | 3 | 12 | 10 | 9 | 2 | 0 | R | L | 6-3 | 200 | 8-4-66 | 1988 | Charlotte, N.C. |
| Kamieniecki, Scott | 10 | 7 | 4.08 | 30 | 20 | 2 | 1 | 154 | 163 | 73 | 70 | 59 | 72 | R | R | 6-0 | 190 | 4-19-64 | 1987 | Flint, Mich. |
| Key, Jimmy | 18 | 6 | 3.00 | 34 | 34 | 4 | 0 | 237 | 219 | 84 | 79 | 43 | 173 | R | L | 6-1 | 185 | 4-22-61 | 1982 | Tarpon Springs, Fla. |
| Militello, Sam | 1 | 1 | 6.75 | 3 | 2 | 0 | 0 | 9 | 10 | 8 | 7 | 7 | 5 | R | R | 6-3 | 200 | 11-26-69 | 1990 | Tampa, Fla. |
| Monteleone, Rich | 7 | 4 | 4.94 | 42 | 0 | 0 | 0 | 86 | 85 | 52 | 47 | 35 | 50 | R | R | 6-2 | 217 | 3-22-63 | 1982 | Tampa, Fla. |
| Munoz, Bobby | 3 | 3 | 5.32 | 38 | 0 | 0 | 0 | 46 | 48 | 27 | 27 | 26 | 33 | R | R | 6-7 | 237 | 3-3-68 | 1989 | Hialeah, Fla. |
| Perez, Melido | 6 | 14 | 5.19 | 25 | 25 | 0 | 0 | 163 | 173 | 103 | 94 | 64 | 148 | R | R | 6-4 | 180 | 2-15-66 | 1984 | San Cristobal, D.R. |
| Smith, Lee | 0 | 0 | 0.00 | 8 | 0 | 0 | 3 | 8 | 4 | 0 | 0 | 5 | 11 | R | R | 6-6 | 250 | 12-4-57 | 1975 | Castor, La. |
| Tanana, Frank | 0 | 2 | 3.20 | 3 | 3 | 0 | 0 | 20 | 18 | 10 | 7 | 7 | 12 | L | L | 6-3 | 195 | 7-3-53 | 1971 | Farmington Hills, Mich. |
| Wickman, Bob | 14 | 4 | 4.63 | 41 | 19 | 1 | 4 | 140 | 156 | 82 | 72 | 69 | 70 | R | R | 6-1 | 220 | 2-6-69 | 1990 | Abrams, Wis. |
| Witt, Mike | 3 | 2 | 5.27 | 9 | 9 | 0 | 0 | 41 | 39 | 26 | 24 | 22 | 30 | R | R | 6-7 | 203 | 7-20-60 | 1978 | Laguna Hills, Calif. |

## FIELDING

| Catcher | PCT | G | PO | A | E | DP |
|---|---|---|---|---|---|---|
| Leyritz | 1.000 | 12 | 31 | 1 | 0 | 0 |
| Nokes | .992 | 56 | 245 | 19 | 2 | 0 |
| Stanley | .996 | 122 | 652 | 46 | 3 | 5 |

| First Base | PCT | G | PO | A | E | DP |
|---|---|---|---|---|---|---|
| James | 1.000 | 1 | 1 | 0 | 0 | 0 |
| Leyritz | .993 | 29 | 260 | 13 | 2 | 22 |
| Maas | .984 | 17 | 115 | 5 | 2 | 13 |
| Mattingly | .998 | 130 | 1258 | 84 | 3 | 123 |
| Meulens | 1.000 | 3 | 5 | 0 | 0 | 0 |

| Second Base | PCT | G | PO | A | E | DP |
|---|---|---|---|---|---|---|
| Gallego | .978 | 52 | 83 | 143 | 5 | 36 |
| Kelly | .978 | 125 | 245 | 369 | 14 | 84 |

| | PCT | G | PO | A | E | DP |
|---|---|---|---|---|---|---|
| Stankiewicz | 1.000 | 6 | 7 | 10 | 0 | 4 |

| Third Base | PCT | G | PO | A | E | DP |
|---|---|---|---|---|---|---|
| Boggs | .970 | 134 | 75 | 311 | 12 | 29 |
| Gallego | .973 | 27 | 18 | 53 | 2 | 5 |
| Meulens | .000 | 1 | 0 | 0 | 0 | 0 |
| Silvestri | .800 | 3 | 0 | 8 | 2 | 0 |
| Stankiewicz | 1.000 | 4 | 0 | 5 | 0 | 0 |
| Velarde | .955 | 16 | 5 | 16 | 1 | 2 |

| Shortstop | PCT | G | PO | A | E | DP |
|---|---|---|---|---|---|---|
| Gallego | .976 | 55 | 68 | 172 | 6 | 35 |
| Owen | .968 | 96 | 116 | 312 | 14 | 44 |
| Silvestri | .955 | 4 | 9 | 12 | 1 | 4 |

| | PCT | G | PO | A | E | DP |
|---|---|---|---|---|---|---|
| Stankiewicz | .000 | 1 | 0 | 0 | 0 | 0 |
| Velarde | .972 | 26 | 31 | 74 | 3 | 18 |

| Outfield | PCT | G | PO | A | E | DP |
|---|---|---|---|---|---|---|
| Humphreys | 1.000 | 21 | 14 | 0 | 0 | 0 |
| James | .966 | 103 | 140 | 4 | 5 | 1 |
| Leyritz | 1.000 | 28 | 42 | 1 | 0 | 0 |
| Meulens | 1.000 | 24 | 27 | 0 | 0 | 0 |
| O'Neill | .992 | 138 | 230 | 7 | 2 | 0 |
| Tartabull | .978 | 50 | 88 | 3 | 2 | 2 |
| Velarde | .932 | 50 | 66 | 2 | 5 | 0 |
| B. Williams | .989 | 139 | 366 | 5 | 4 | 0 |
| G. Williams | .956 | 37 | 41 | 2 | 2 | 0 |

# YANKEES FARM SYSTEM

| Class | Club | League | W | L | Pct. | Finish* | Manager(s) | First Year |
|---|---|---|---|---|---|---|---|---|
| AAA | Columbus (Ohio) Clippers | International | 78 | 62 | .557 | 3rd (10) | Stump Merrill | 1979 |
| AA | Albany-Colonie (N.Y.) Yankees | Eastern | 70 | 68 | .507 | 4th (8) | M. Hart, B. Evers | 1985 |
| A# | Prince William (Va.) Cannons | Carolina | 67 | 73 | .479 | 6th (8) | Trey Hillman | 1987 |
| A | Greensboro (N.C.) Hornets | South Atlantic | 85 | 56 | .603 | 3rd (14) | B. Evers, G. Denbo | 1990 |
| A | Oneonta (N.Y.) Yankees | New York-Penn | 36 | 40 | .474 | 9th (14) | Ken Dominguez | 1967 |
| Rookie | Tampa (Fla.) Yankees | Gulf Coast | 30 | 29 | .508 | 9th (15) | Glenn Sherlock | 1980 |

*Finish in overall standings (No. of teams in league)   #Advanced level

**Danny Tartabull.** DH-outfielder led club with 31 home runs and 102 RBIs.

**Jimmy Key.** A free agent signee, Key led Yankees pitchers with 18 wins, a 3.00 ERA and 173 strikeouts.

# COLUMBUS

## INTERNATIONAL LEAGUE

**AAA**

| BATTING | AVG | G | AB | R | H | 2B | 3B | HR | RBI | BB | SO | SB | CS | B | T | HT | WT | DOB | 1st Yr | Resides |
|---|---|---|---|---|---|---|---|---|---|---|---|---|---|---|---|---|---|---|---|---|
| Carpenter, Bubba | .266 | 70 | 199 | 29 | 53 | 9 | 0 | 5 | 17 | 29 | 35 | 2 | 2 | L | L | 6-1 | 185 | 7-23-68 | 1991 | Winslow, Ark. |
| Davis, Russ | .255 | 113 | 424 | 63 | 108 | 24 | 1 | 26 | 83 | 40 | 118 | 1 | 1 | R | R | 6-0 | 170 | 9-13-69 | 1988 | Hueytown, Ala. |
| DeJardin, Bobby | .275 | 103 | 360 | 45 | 99 | 17 | 7 | 5 | 37 | 34 | 44 | 10 | 8 | S | R | 5-11 | 180 | 1-8-67 | 1988 | Huntington Beach, Calif. |
| Gedman, Rich | .262 | 89 | 275 | 30 | 72 | 15 | 0 | 12 | 35 | 35 | 63 | 0 | 4 | L | R | 6-0 | 215 | 9-26-59 | 1978 | Framingham, Mass. |
| Hernandez, Kiki | .241 | 22 | 54 | 8 | 13 | 4 | 0 | 1 | 8 | 6 | 12 | 0 | 0 | R | R | 5-11 | 195 | 4-16-69 | 1988 | Florida, P.R. |
| Humphreys, Mike | .288 | 92 | 330 | 59 | 95 | 16 | 2 | 6 | 42 | 52 | 57 | 18 | 15 | R | R | 6-0 | 185 | 4-10-67 | 1988 | DeSoto, Texas |
| Knoblauh, Jay | .187 | 56 | 171 | 23 | 32 | 13 | 0 | 4 | 21 | 9 | 46 | 1 | 1 | R | R | 6-0 | 185 | 11-3-65 | 1988 | Houston, Texas |
| Livesey, Jeff | .247 | 34 | 89 | 9 | 22 | 5 | 0 | 2 | 8 | 2 | 19 | 0 | 0 | R | R | 6-0 | 185 | 5-24-66 | 1988 | Spring Hill, Fla. |
| Maas, Kevin | .279 | 28 | 104 | 14 | 29 | 6 | 0 | 4 | 18 | 19 | 22 | 0 | 1 | L | L | 6-3 | 205 | 1-20-65 | 1986 | Castro Valley, Calif. |
| Masse, Billy | .316 | 117 | 402 | 81 | 127 | 35 | 3 | 19 | 91 | 82 | 68 | 17 | 7 | R | R | 6-1 | 190 | 7-6-66 | 1989 | Wethersfield, Conn. |
| Meulens, Hensley | .204 | 75 | 279 | 39 | 57 | 14 | 0 | 14 | 45 | 32 | 92 | 6 | 2 | R | R | 6-3 | 212 | 6-23-67 | 1986 | Curacao, Neth. Antilles |
| Ramos, John | .259 | 49 | 158 | 17 | 41 | 7 | 0 | 1 | 18 | 19 | 32 | 1 | 2 | R | R | 6-0 | 190 | 8-6-65 | 1986 | Tampa, Fla. |
| Rodriguez, Carlos | .253 | 57 | 154 | 25 | 39 | 9 | 1 | 1 | 11 | 20 | 10 | 2 | 1 | S | R | 5-9 | 160 | 11-1-67 | 1987 | Mexico City, Mexico |
| Sanchez, Gordon | .173 | 25 | 75 | 12 | 13 | 2 | 2 | 0 | 6 | 8 | 21 | 0 | 2 | L | R | 6-2 | 195 | 12-23-70 | 1992 | Romana, Calif. |
| Silvestri, Dave | .269 | 120 | 428 | 76 | 115 | 26 | 4 | 20 | 65 | 68 | 127 | 6 | 9 | R | R | 6-0 | 180 | 9-29-67 | 1989 | St. Louis, Mo. |
| Sparks, Don | .284 | 128 | 475 | 63 | 135 | 33 | 7 | 11 | 72 | 29 | 83 | 0 | 3 | R | R | 6-2 | 185 | 6-19-66 | 1988 | Long Beach, Calif. |
| Stankiewicz, Andy | .242 | 90 | 331 | 45 | 80 | 12 | 5 | 0 | 32 | 29 | 46 | 12 | 8 | R | R | 5-9 | 165 | 8-10-64 | 1986 | Los Alamitos, Calif. |
| Viera, John | .500 | 3 | 6 | 2 | 3 | 1 | 0 | 0 | 1 | 3 | 0 | 0 | 0 | L | L | 6-1 | 170 | 11-30-67 | 1990 | Miami, Fla. |
| Williams, Gerald | .283 | 87 | 336 | 53 | 95 | 19 | 6 | 8 | 38 | 20 | 66 | 29 | 12 | R | R | 6-2 | 185 | 8-10-66 | 1987 | LaPlace, La. |

| PITCHING | W | L | ERA | G | GS | CG | SV | IP | H | R | ER | BB | SO | B | T | HT | WT | DOB | 1st Yr | Resides |
|---|---|---|---|---|---|---|---|---|---|---|---|---|---|---|---|---|---|---|---|---|
| Batchelor, Richard | 1 | 1 | 2.76 | 15 | 0 | 0 | 6 | 16 | 14 | 5 | 5 | 8 | 17 | R | R | 6-1 | 195 | 4-8-67 | 1990 | Hartsville, S.C. |
| Clayton, Royal | 7 | 6 | 3.54 | 47 | 11 | 0 | 8 | 117 | 119 | 56 | 46 | 31 | 66 | R | R | 6-2 | 210 | 11-25-65 | 1987 | Inglewood, Calif. |
| Cook, Andy | 6 | 7 | 6.54 | 21 | 20 | 0 | 0 | 118 | 149 | 91 | 86 | 49 | 47 | R | R | 6-5 | 205 | 8-30-67 | 1988 | Memphis, Tenn. |
| De la Rosa, Francisco | 1 | 1 | 6.45 | 31 | 0 | 0 | 1 | 45 | 45 | 34 | 32 | 31 | 31 | R | R | 5-11 | 185 | 3-3-66 | 1985 | La Romana, D.R. |
| Gibson, Paul | 1 | 0 | 0.00 | 3 | 1 | 0 | 1 | 7 | 4 | 0 | 0 | 1 | 7 | R | L | 6-0 | 185 | 1-4-60 | 1978 | Center Moriches, N.Y. |
| 2-team (14 Norfolk) | 2 | 1 | 0.64 | 17 | 1 | 0 | 8 | 28 | 14 | 2 | 2 | 6 | 36 | | | | | | | |
| Gogolewski, Doug | 5 | 3 | 4.38 | 28 | 0 | 0 | 3 | 51 | 63 | 32 | 25 | 14 | 32 | R | R | 6-2 | 190 | 6-8-65 | 1987 | Brighton, Mich. |
| Greer, Ken | 9 | 4 | 4.42 | 46 | 0 | 0 | 6 | 79 | 78 | 41 | 39 | 36 | 50 | R | R | 6-2 | 215 | 5-12-67 | 1988 | Hull, Mass. |
| Hines, Rich | 2 | 5 | 4.02 | 43 | 0 | 0 | 4 | 56 | 50 | 28 | 25 | 34 | 40 | L | L | 6-1 | 185 | 5-20-69 | 1990 | Milton, Fla. |
| Hitchcock, Sterling | 3 | 5 | 4.81 | 16 | 16 | 0 | 0 | 77 | 80 | 43 | 41 | 28 | 85 | L | L | 6-1 | 195 | 4-29-71 | 1989 | Seffner, Fla. |
| Howe, Steve | 0 | 1 | 10.13 | 2 | 2 | 0 | 0 | 3 | 6 | 3 | 3 | 1 | 1 | L | L | 5-11 | 195 | 3-10-58 | 1979 | Whitefish, Mont. |
| Hutton, Mark | 10 | 4 | 3.18 | 21 | 21 | 0 | 0 | 133 | 98 | 52 | 47 | 53 | 112 | R | R | 6-6 | 225 | 2-6-70 | 1989 | West Lakes, Australia |
| Jean, Domingo | 2 | 2 | 2.82 | 7 | 7 | 1 | 0 | 45 | 40 | 15 | 14 | 13 | 39 | R | R | 6-2 | 175 | 1-9-69 | 1988 | San Pedro de Macoris, D.R. |
| Johnson, Jeff | 7 | 6 | 3.45 | 19 | 17 | 3 | 0 | 115 | 125 | 55 | 44 | 47 | 59 | R | L | 6-3 | 200 | 8-4-66 | 1988 | Charlotte, N.C. |
| Kamieniecki, Scott | 1 | 0 | 1.50 | 1 | 1 | 0 | 0 | 6 | 5 | 1 | 1 | 0 | 4 | R | R | 6-0 | 190 | 4-19-64 | 1987 | Flint, Mich. |
| Militello, Sam | 1 | 3 | 5.73 | 7 | 7 | 0 | 0 | 33 | 36 | 22 | 21 | 20 | 39 | R | R | 6-3 | 200 | 11-26-69 | 1990 | Tampa, Fla. |
| Munoz, Bobby | 3 | 1 | 1.44 | 22 | 1 | 0 | 10 | 31 | 24 | 6 | 5 | 8 | 16 | R | R | 6-7 | 237 | 3-3-68 | 1988 | Hialeah, Fla. |
| Ojala, Kirt | 8 | 9 | 5.50 | 31 | 20 | 0 | 0 | 126 | 145 | 85 | 77 | 71 | 83 | L | L | 6-2 | 200 | 12-24-68 | 1990 | Portage, Mich. |
| Popplewell, Tom | 0 | 0 | 4.50 | 1 | 0 | 0 | 0 | 2 | 2 | 1 | 1 | 1 | 2 | R | R | 6-3 | 225 | 8-14-67 | 1988 | Fairfield, Ohio |
| Quirico, Rafael | 2 | 0 | 7.36 | 5 | 2 | 0 | 0 | 11 | 12 | 10 | 9 | 7 | 16 | L | L | 6-3 | 170 | 9-7-69 | 1987 | Santo Domingo, D.R. |
| Seiler, Keith | 0 | 0 | 13.50 | 1 | 0 | 0 | 0 | 2 | 2 | 3 | 3 | 2 | 1 | L | L | 6-1 | 180 | 11-17-67 | 1990 | Richmond, Va. |
| Stanford, Don | 5 | 3 | 5.04 | 36 | 7 | 0 | 0 | 104 | 119 | 65 | 58 | 56 | 44 | R | R | 6-4 | 220 | 10-16-67 | 1987 | Syracuse, N.Y. |
| Taylor, Wade | 3 | 1 | 4.45 | 7 | 5 | 0 | 0 | 30 | 31 | 17 | 15 | 11 | 16 | R | R | 6-1 | 180 | 10-19-65 | 1987 | Longwood, Fla. |
| Witt, Mike | 1 | 0 | 1.98 | 3 | 3 | 0 | 0 | 14 | 11 | 3 | 3 | 5 | 11 | R | R | 6-7 | 203 | 7-20-60 | 1978 | Laguna Hills, Calif. |

## FIELDING

| Catcher | PCT | G | PO | A | E | DP |
|---|---|---|---|---|---|---|
| Gedman | .991 | 84 | 495 | 47 | 5 | 3 |
| Hernandez | .976 | 22 | 76 | 7 | 2 | 0 |
| Livesey | .986 | 33 | 132 | 13 | 2 | 1 |
| Sanchez | .982 | 25 | 145 | 16 | 3 | 5 |

| First Base | PCT | G | PO | A | E | DP |
|---|---|---|---|---|---|---|
| DeJardin | .000 | 1 | 0 | 0 | 0 | 0 |
| Gedman | .750 | 1 | 3 | 0 | 1 | 0 |
| Maas | .976 | 27 | 270 | 20 | 7 | 27 |
| Meulens | .958 | 18 | 164 | 17 | 8 | 24 |
| Ramos | 1.000 | 6 | 48 | 2 | 0 | 7 |
| Rodriguez | 1.000 | 4 | 6 | 0 | 0 | 1 |
| Sparks | .993 | 91 | 795 | 61 | 6 | 91 |

| Second Base | PCT | G | PO | A | E | DP |
|---|---|---|---|---|---|---|
| DeJardin | .980 | 63 | 118 | 182 | 6 | 41 |
| Rodriguez | 1.000 | 11 | 20 | 40 | 0 | 13 |

| | PCT | G | PO | A | E | DP |
|---|---|---|---|---|---|---|
| Sparks | 1.000 | 1 | 0 | 1 | 0 | 0 |
| Stankiewicz | .989 | 72 | 129 | 236 | 4 | 51 |

| Third Base | PCT | G | PO | A | E | DP |
|---|---|---|---|---|---|---|
| Davis | .922 | 109 | 71 | 225 | 25 | 24 |
| DeJardin | .750 | 2 | 0 | 6 | 2 | 2 |
| Humphreys | .786 | 6 | 2 | 9 | 3 | 1 |
| Meulens | .000 | 1 | 0 | 0 | 3 | 0 |
| Rodriguez | 1.000 | 1 | 1 | 2 | 0 | 0 |
| Silvestri | 1.000 | 8 | 9 | 16 | 0 | 0 |
| Sparks | .875 | 6 | 3 | 11 | 2 | 3 |
| Stankiewicz | .971 | 15 | 7 | 27 | 1 | 2 |

| Shortstop | PCT | G | PO | A | E | DP |
|---|---|---|---|---|---|---|
| Davis | .971 | 5 | 14 | 20 | 1 | 7 |
| DeJardin | 1.000 | 9 | 11 | 21 | 0 | 5 |
| Rodriguez | .992 | 36 | 51 | 72 | 1 | 17 |

| | PCT | G | PO | A | E | DP |
|---|---|---|---|---|---|---|
| Silvestri | .966 | 105 | 171 | 283 | 16 | 73 |
| Stankiewicz | .800 | 1 | 2 | 2 | 1 | 1 |

| Outfield | PCT | G | PO | A | E | DP |
|---|---|---|---|---|---|---|
| Carpenter | .969 | 56 | 91 | 3 | 3 | 1 |
| Clayton | .000 | 1 | 0 | 0 | 0 | 0 |
| DeJardin | .971 | 18 | 33 | 1 | 1 | 0 |
| Hernandez | 1.000 | 1 | 1 | 0 | 0 | 0 |
| Humphreys | .983 | 80 | 170 | 7 | 3 | 1 |
| Knoblauh | .992 | 52 | 123 | 3 | 1 | 0 |
| Masse | .976 | 99 | 154 | 10 | 4 | 3 |
| Meulens | .928 | 56 | 100 | 3 | 8 | 1 |
| Silvestri | 1.000 | 1 | 3 | 0 | 0 | 0 |
| Viera | .750 | 3 | 2 | 1 | 1 | 0 |
| Williams | .985 | 79 | 191 | 6 | 3 | 1 |

# ALBANY                                                                 AA
## EASTERN LEAGUE

| BATTING | AVG | G | AB | R | H | 2B | 3B | HR | RBI | BB | SO | SB | CS | B | T | HT | WT | DOB | 1st Yr | Resides |
|---|---|---|---|---|---|---|---|---|---|---|---|---|---|---|---|---|---|---|---|---|
| Barnwell, Richard, dh-of | .298 | 131 | 463 | 98 | 138 | 24 | 7 | 11 | 50 | 77 | 101 | 33 | 13 | R | R | 6-0 | 190 | 4-8-71 | 1989 | Hawthorne, Calif. |
| Carpenter, Bubba, of-dh | .321 | 14 | 53 | 8 | 17 | 4 | 0 | 2 | 14 | 7 | 4 | 2 | 2 | L | L | 6-1 | 185 | 7-23-68 | 1991 | Winslow, Ark. |
| DeBerry, Joe, 1b | .256 | 125 | 446 | 58 | 114 | 19 | 7 | 12 | 63 | 24 | 111 | 3 | 7 | L | L | 6-2 | 195 | 6-30-70 | 1991 | Colorado Springs, Colo. |
| Eenhoorn, Robert, ss | .280 | 82 | 314 | 48 | 88 | 24 | 3 | 6 | 46 | 21 | 39 | 3 | 5 | R | R | 6-3 | 175 | 2-9-68 | 1990 | Rotterdam, Holland |
| Erickson, Greg, 3b | .100 | 3 | 10 | 2 | 1 | 0 | 0 | 0 | 0 | 2 | 1 | 0 | 0 | S | R | 5-11 | 175 | 10-26-69 | 1991 | Valencia, Calif. |
| Figga, Mike, c | .227 | 6 | 22 | 3 | 5 | 0 | 0 | 0 | 2 | 2 | 9 | 1 | 0 | R | R | 6-0 | 200 | 7-31-70 | 1990 | Tampa, Fla. |
| Flannelly, Tim, 3b | .272 | 53 | 184 | 21 | 50 | 9 | 2 | 2 | 18 | 10 | 30 | 5 | 1 | L | R | 6-2 | 198 | 7-25-70 | 1991 | Ocean, N.J. |
| Fox, Andy, 3b | .275 | 65 | 236 | 44 | 65 | 16 | 1 | 3 | 24 | 32 | 54 | 12 | 6 | L | R | 6-4 | 185 | 1-12-71 | 1989 | Sacramento, Calif. |
| Hankins, Mike, 3b-ss | .223 | 63 | 175 | 16 | 39 | 2 | 0 | 0 | 12 | 29 | 27 | 2 | 2 | S | R | 5-11 | 175 | 4-10-68 | 1990 | Simi Valley, Calif. |
| Jordan, Kevin, 2b | .283 | 135 | 513 | 87 | 145 | 33 | 4 | 16 | 87 | 41 | 53 | 8 | 4 | R | R | 6-1 | 185 | 10-9-69 | 1990 | San Francisco, Calif. |
| Leach, Jalal, of | .282 | 125 | 457 | 64 | 129 | 19 | 9 | 14 | 79 | 47 | 113 | 15 | 12 | L | L | 6-2 | 200 | 3-14-69 | 1990 | Novato, Calif. |
| Leshnock, Donnie, c | .000 | 1 | 3 | 0 | 0 | 0 | 0 | 0 | 0 | 0 | 2 | 0 | 0 | L | R | 6-4 | 220 | 4-20-71 | 1992 | Columbus, Ohio |
| Livesey, Jeff, c | .154 | 32 | 104 | 6 | 16 | 4 | 0 | 0 | 9 | 7 | 22 | 0 | 0 | R | R | 6-0 | 185 | 5-24-66 | 1988 | Spring Hill, Fla. |
| Mouton, Lyle, of | .255 | 135 | 491 | 74 | 125 | 22 | 3 | 16 | 76 | 50 | 125 | 18 | 14 | R | R | 6-4 | 240 | 5-13-69 | 1991 | Lafayette, La. |
| Oster, Paul, 1b-of | .208 | 39 | 106 | 11 | 22 | 7 | 1 | 0 | 8 | 6 | 27 | 1 | 0 | S | L | 6-0 | 172 | 3-31-67 | 1989 | Hamburg, Mich. |
| Pineda, Jose, c | .150 | 38 | 107 | 12 | 16 | 2 | 0 | 2 | 12 | 11 | 40 | 0 | 0 | R | R | 6-2 | 168 | 3-15-71 | 1990 | Bocas Del Toro, Panama |
| Posada, Jorge, c | .280 | 7 | 25 | 3 | 7 | 0 | 0 | 0 | 2 | 7 | 0 | 0 | 0 | S | R | 6-0 | 167 | 8-17-71 | 1991 | Rio Piedras, P.R. |
| Robertson, Jason, of | .228 | 130 | 483 | 65 | 110 | 30 | 4 | 6 | 41 | 43 | 126 | 35 | 12 | L | L | 6-2 | 200 | 3-24-71 | 1989 | Country Club Hills, Ill. |
| Rodriguez, Carlos, ss | .368 | 38 | 152 | 16 | 56 | 14 | 1 | 0 | 30 | 12 | 9 | 2 | 4 | S | R | 5-9 | 160 | 11-1-67 | 1987 | Mexico City, Mexico |
| Sanchez, Gordon, c | .215 | 65 | 195 | 23 | 42 | 11 | 0 | 1 | 21 | 19 | 34 | 3 | 1 | L | R | 6-2 | 195 | 12-23-70 | 1992 | Romana, Calif. |
| Velarde, Randy, ss-dh | .235 | 5 | 17 | 2 | 4 | 0 | 0 | 1 | 2 | 2 | 2 | 0 | 0 | R | R | 6-0 | 185 | 11-24-62 | 1985 | Midland, Texas |

| PITCHING | W | L | ERA | G | GS | CG | SV | IP | H | R | ER | BB | SO | B | T | HT | WT | DOB | 1st Yr | Resides |
|---|---|---|---|---|---|---|---|---|---|---|---|---|---|---|---|---|---|---|---|---|
| Batchelor, Richard | 1 | 3 | 0.89 | 36 | 0 | 0 | 19 | 40 | 27 | 9 | 4 | 12 | 40 | R | R | 6-1 | 195 | 4-8-67 | 1990 | Hartsville, S.C. |
| Carper, Mark | 7 | 10 | 4.52 | 25 | 25 | 0 | 0 | 155 | 148 | 96 | 78 | 70 | 98 | R | R | 6-2 | 200 | 9-29-68 | 1991 | Highland, Md. |
| Dunbar, Matt | 1 | 0 | 2.66 | 15 | 0 | 0 | 0 | 24 | 23 | 8 | 7 | 6 | 18 | L | L | 6-0 | 160 | 10-15-68 | 1990 | Tallahassee, Fla. |
| Faw, Brian | 9 | 5 | 5.23 | 45 | 5 | 1 | 4 | 86 | 95 | 61 | 50 | 36 | 52 | R | R | 6-0 | 185 | 3-19-68 | 1990 | Roswell, Ga. |
| Frazier, Ron | 4 | 3 | 3.84 | 12 | 12 | 0 | 0 | 80 | 93 | 43 | 34 | 16 | 65 | R | R | 6-2 | 185 | 6-13-69 | 1990 | Otis, Mass. |
| Garagozzo, Keith | 4 | 6 | 4.48 | 17 | 14 | 1 | 0 | 86 | 88 | 49 | 43 | 24 | 71 | L | L | 6-0 | 170 | 10-25-69 | 1991 | Maple Shade, N.J. |
| Gogolewski, Doug | 4 | 1 | 2.21 | 13 | 0 | 0 | 1 | 20 | 20 | 7 | 5 | 4 | 10 | R | R | 6-2 | 190 | 6-8-65 | 1987 | Brighton, Mich. |
| Haller, Jim | 2 | 2 | 3.99 | 41 | 0 | 0 | 0 | 68 | 66 | 37 | 30 | 29 | 53 | L | L | 6-0 | 180 | 12-28-66 | 1989 | Shawnee, Kan. |
| Hines, Richard | 0 | 1 | 2.08 | 14 | 0 | 0 | 0 | 26 | 17 | 9 | 6 | 11 | 27 | L | L | 6-1 | 185 | 5-20-69 | 1990 | Milton, Fla. |
| Hodges, Darren | 10 | 10 | 4.72 | 30 | 24 | 2 | 0 | 153 | 161 | 89 | 80 | 61 | 96 | R | R | 6-1 | 190 | 11-3-69 | 1990 | Rocky Mount, Va. |
| Jean, Domingo | 5 | 3 | 2.51 | 11 | 11 | 1 | 0 | 61 | 42 | 24 | 17 | 33 | 41 | R | R | 6-2 | 175 | 1-9-69 | 1989 | San Pedro de Macoris, D.R. |

# YANKEES: ORGANIZATION LEADERS

**Paul O'Neill**
Former Red belted 34 doubles

## MAJOR LEAGUERS
**BATTING**

| | | |
|---|---|---|
| *AVG | Dion James | .332 |
| R | Danny Tartabull | 87 |
| H | Wade Boggs | 169 |
| TB | Danny Tartabull | 258 |
| 2B | Paul O'Neill | 34 |
| 3B | Bernie Williams | 4 |
| HR | Danny Tartabull | 31 |
| RBI | Danny Tartabull | 102 |
| BB | Danny Tartabull | 92 |
| SO | Danny Tartabull | 156 |
| SB | Pat Kelly | 14 |

**PITCHING**

| | | |
|---|---|---|
| W | Jimmy Key | 18 |
| L | Jim Abbott | 14 |
| #ERA | Jimmy Key | 3.00 |
| G | Steve Howe | 51 |
| CG | Two tied at | 4 |
| SV | Steve Farr | 25 |
| IP | Jimmy Key | 237 |
| BB | Jim Abbott | 73 |
| SO | Jimmy Key | 173 |

## MINOR LEAGUERS
**BATTING**

| | | |
|---|---|---|
| *AVG | Billy Masse, Columbus | .316 |
| R | Richard Barnwell, Albany | 98 |
| H | Matt Luke, Greensboro | 157 |
| TB | Matt Luke, Greensboro | 267 |
| 2B | Matt Luke, Greensboro | 37 |
| 3B | Derek Jeter, Greensboro | 11 |
| HR | Russ Davis, Columbus | 26 |
| RBI | Two tied at | 91 |
| BB | Tom Wilson, Greensboro | 91 |
| SO | Nick Delvecchio, Greensboro | 156 |
| SB | Kraig Hawkins, Greensboro | 67 |

**PITCHING**

| | | |
|---|---|---|
| W | Ryan Karp, Greensboro-Pr.Will.-Albany.. | 16 |
| L | Andy Croghan, Prince William | 11 |
| #ERA | Keith Heberling, Greensboro-Oneonta. | 1.76 |
| G | Matt Dunbar, Prince William-Albany | 64 |
| CG | Jeff Johnson, Columbus | 3 |
| SV | Rich Batchelor, Albany-Columbus | 25 |
| IP | Ron Frazier, Prince William-Albany | 181 |
| BB | Brien Taylor, Albany | 102 |
| SO | Ryan Karp, Greensboro-Pr.Will.-Albany | 176 |

*Minimum 250 At-Bats   #Minimum 75 Innings

# YANKEES: MOST COMMON LINEUPS

| | New York<br>Majors | Columbus<br>AAA | Albany<br>AA | Prince William<br>A | Greensboro<br>A |
|---|---|---|---|---|---|
| C | Mike Stanley (122) | Rich Gedman (84) | Gordon Sanchez (63) | Jorge Posada (107) | Tom Wilson (113) |
| 1B | Don Mattingly (130) | Don Sparks (91) | Joe DeBerry (125) | Tate Seefried (119) | Nick Delvecchio (127) |
| 2B | Pat Kelly (125) | Andy Stankiewicz (72) | Kevin Jordan (133) | Carlton Fleming (116) | Robert Hinds (124) |
| 3B | Wade Boggs (134) | Russ Davis (109) | Andy Fox (64) | Tim Flannelly (59) | Scott Romano (111) |
| SS | Spike Owen (96) | Dave Silvestri (105) | Robert Eenhoorn (82) | Eric Knowles (103) | Derek Jeter (126) |
| OF | Bernie Williams (139) | Billy Masse (104) | Jason Robertson (129) | Jovino Carvajal (119) | Matt Luke (134) |
| | Paul O'Neill (138) | Mike Humphreys (81) | Lyle Mouton (114) | Lew Hill (106) | Kraig Hawkins (126) |
| | Dion James (103) | Gerald Williams (79) | Jalal Leach (111) | Mark Hubbard (91) | Shane Spencer (81) |
| DH | Danny Tartabull (88) | John Ramos (38) | Richard Barnwell (87) | Bo Gilliam (24) | Shane Spencer (38) |
| SP | Jimmy Key (34) | Mark Hutton (21) | Brien Taylor (27) | Carter/Pettitte (26) | Mike Buddie (26) |
| RP | Steve Howe (51) | Ken Greer (46) | Jim Haller (41) | Scott Gully (59) | Billy Coleman (59) |

Full-season farm clubs only    No. of games at position in parenthesis

| PITCHING | W | L | ERA | G | GS | CG | SV | IP | H | R | ER | BB | SO | B | T | HT | WT | DOB | 1st Yr | Resides |
|---|---|---|---|---|---|---|---|---|---|---|---|---|---|---|---|---|---|---|---|---|
| Karp, Ryan | 0 | 0 | 4.15 | 3 | 3 | 0 | 0 | 13 | 13 | 7 | 6 | 9 | 10 | L | L | 6-4 | 205 | 4-5-70 | 1992 | Coral Gables, Fla. |
| Ojala, Kirt | 1 | 0 | 0.00 | 1 | 1 | 0 | 0 | 6 | 5 | 0 | 0 | 2 | 6 | L | L | 6-2 | 200 | 12-24-68 | 1990 | Portage, Mich. |
| Pettitte, Andy | 1 | 0 | 3.60 | 1 | 1 | 0 | 0 | 5 | 5 | 4 | 2 | 2 | 6 | L | L | 6-5 | 220 | 6-15-72 | 1991 | Deer Park, Texas |
| Polak, Rich | 3 | 4 | 4.55 | 21 | 0 | 0 | 5 | 28 | 34 | 18 | 14 | 10 | 16 | R | R | 5-11 | 190 | 3-24-67 | 1989 | Chicago, Ill. |
| Popplewell, Tom | 1 | 3 | 5.88 | 34 | 4 | 1 | 1 | 64 | 60 | 45 | 42 | 48 | 59 | R | R | 6-3 | 225 | 8-3-67 | 1987 | Fairfield, Ohio |
| Prybylinski, Bruce | 0 | 0 | 1.93 | 2 | 0 | 0 | 0 | 5 | 4 | 1 | 1 | 1 | 1 | R | R | 5-11 | 185 | 2-18-67 | 1988 | LaSalle, Ill. |
| Quirico, Rafael | 4 | 10 | 3.52 | 36 | 11 | 0 | 7 | 95 | 92 | 46 | 37 | 33 | 79 | L | L | 6-3 | 170 | 9-7-69 | 1987 | Santo Domingo, D.R. |
| Taylor, Brien | 13 | 7 | 3.48 | 27 | 27 | 1 | 0 | 163 | 127 | 83 | 63 | 102 | 150 | L | L | 6-3 | 195 | 12-26-71 | 1991 | Beaufort, N.C. |
| Witt, Mike | 0 | 0 | 0.00 | 1 | 0 | 0 | 0 | 2 | 2 | 0 | 0 | 0 | 2 | R | R | 6-7 | 203 | 7-20-60 | 1978 | Laguna Hills, Calif. |

# PRINCE WILLIAM                                                                                    A
## CAROLINA LEAGUE

| BATTING | AVG | G | AB | R | H | 2B | 3B | HR | RBI | BB | SO | SB | CS | B | T | HT | WT | DOB | 1st Yr | Resides |
|---|---|---|---|---|---|---|---|---|---|---|---|---|---|---|---|---|---|---|---|---|
| Burnett, Roger, ss-dh | .189 | 18 | 53 | 3 | 10 | 1 | 0 | 2 | 7 | 6 | 7 | 1 | 0 | R | R | 6-1 | 185 | 11-14-69 | 1991 | Broken Arrow, Okla. |
| Carvajal, Jovino, of | .265 | 120 | 445 | 52 | 118 | 20 | 9 | 1 | 42 | 21 | 69 | 17 | 13 | S | R | 6-1 | 160 | 9-2-68 | 1987 | La Romana, D.R. |
| Cooper, Tim, 3b | .301 | 58 | 193 | 33 | 58 | 9 | 2 | 4 | 29 | 30 | 49 | 2 | 5 | R | R | 6-3 | 190 | 3-10-71 | 1989 | Sacramento, Calif. |
| Deller, Bob, of | .265 | 53 | 166 | 30 | 44 | 8 | 2 | 3 | 22 | 19 | 45 | 6 | 1 | L | R | 6-2 | 190 | 6-6-68 | 1990 | Arlington, Texas |
| Epps, Scott, dh-c | .196 | 34 | 92 | 12 | 18 | 4 | 0 | 1 | 17 | 9 | 24 | 0 | 0 | R | R | 5-11 | 180 | 12-8-69 | 1992 | Jenks, Okla. |
| Erickson, Greg, ss-2b | .274 | 80 | 288 | 44 | 79 | 11 | 3 | 0 | 21 | 25 | 54 | 10 | 5 | S | R | 5-11 | 175 | 10-26-69 | 1991 | Valencia, Calif. |
| Flannelly, Tim, 3b | .281 | 73 | 274 | 45 | 77 | 18 | 3 | 7 | 40 | 42 | 39 | 7 | 3 | L | R | 6-2 | 198 | 7-25-70 | 1991 | Ocean, N.J. |
| Fleming, Carlton, 2b | .299 | 120 | 442 | 72 | 132 | 14 | 2 | 0 | 25 | 80 | 23 | 21 | 10 | S | R | 5-11 | 175 | 8-25-71 | 1992 | Freeport, N.Y. |
| Gilliam, Bo, of | .250 | 86 | 340 | 37 | 85 | 13 | 3 | 10 | 55 | 11 | 84 | 4 | 3 | R | R | 6-0 | 215 | 9-14-68 | 1989 | Tallahassee, Fla. |
| Hill, Lew, of | .250 | 116 | 460 | 66 | 115 | 22 | 3 | 13 | 57 | 29 | 124 | 12 | 7 | S | R | 5-10 | 190 | 4-16-69 | 1987 | Cleveland, Ohio |
| Hubbard, Mark, of-1b | .218 | 114 | 376 | 41 | 82 | 17 | 2 | 2 | 26 | 37 | 101 | 5 | 11 | L | L | 6-2 | 190 | 2-2-70 | 1991 | Dover, Fla. |
| Knowles, Eric, ss | .193 | 105 | 353 | 33 | 68 | 16 | 0 | 4 | 37 | 30 | 96 | 2 | 5 | R | R | 5-11 | 157 | 10-21-73 | 1991 | Miami, Fla. |
| Lohry, Adin, c | .000 | 1 | 2 | 0 | 0 | 0 | 0 | 0 | 0 | 1 | 2 | 0 | 0 | L | R | 6-1 | 180 | 1-12-71 | 1989 | Maitland, Fla. |
| Motuzas, Jeff, c | .208 | 16 | 53 | 5 | 11 | 4 | 1 | 0 | 3 | 1 | 20 | 0 | 1 | R | R | 6-2 | 205 | 10-1-71 | 1990 | Nashua, N.H. |
| Pineda, Jose, c | .143 | 6 | 21 | 5 | 3 | 0 | 0 | 0 | 3 | 4 | 9 | 0 | 0 | R | R | 6-2 | 190 | 3-15-71 | 1990 | Bocas Del Toro, Panama |
| Posada, Jorge, c | .259 | 118 | 410 | 71 | 106 | 27 | 2 | 17 | 61 | 67 | 90 | 17 | 5 | S | R | 6-0 | 167 | 8-17-71 | 1991 | Rio Piedras, P.R. |
| Salcedo, Edwin, dh-c | .163 | 23 | 80 | 8 | 13 | 4 | 0 | 2 | 6 | 3 | 22 | 0 | 2 | R | R | 6-0 | 214 | 7-8-70 | 1990 | Yauco, P.R. |
| Seefried, Tate, 1b | .265 | 125 | 464 | 63 | 123 | 25 | 4 | 21 | 89 | 50 | 150 | 8 | 8 | L | R | 6-4 | 180 | 4-22-72 | 1990 | El Segundo, Calif. |
| Twitty, Sean, dh-of | .192 | 36 | 125 | 13 | 24 | 9 | 1 | 1 | 15 | 13 | 50 | 1 | 2 | R | R | 6-3 | 190 | 10-23-70 | 1989 | Astoria, N.Y. |

| PITCHING | W | L | ERA | G | GS | CG | SV | IP | H | R | ER | BB | SO | B | T | HT | WT | DOB | 1st Yr | Resides |
|---|---|---|---|---|---|---|---|---|---|---|---|---|---|---|---|---|---|---|---|---|
| Brown, Charles | 0 | 0 | 5.40 | 2 | 1 | 0 | 0 | 7 | 5 | 4 | 4 | 6 | 4 | R | R | 6-3 | 178 | 9-13-73 | 1992 | Fort Pierce, Fla. |
| Carter, Tommy | 8 | 10 | 4.39 | 26 | 26 | 1 | 0 | 146 | 160 | 87 | 71 | 53 | 105 | L | L | 6-3 | 215 | 4-30-70 | 1991 | Anniston, Ala. |
| Croghan, Andy | 5 | 11 | 4.80 | 39 | 14 | 1 | 11 | 105 | 117 | 66 | 56 | 27 | 80 | R | R | 6-5 | 205 | 10-26-69 | 1991 | Yorba Linda, Calif. |
| Dunbar, Matt | 6 | 2 | 1.73 | 49 | 0 | 0 | 4 | 73 | 50 | 21 | 14 | 30 | 66 | L | L | 6-0 | 160 | 10-15-68 | 1990 | Tallahassee, Fla. |
| Frazier, Ron | 8 | 3 | 2.14 | 15 | 15 | 1 | 0 | 101 | 79 | 34 | 24 | 23 | 108 | R | R | 6-2 | 185 | 6-13-69 | 1990 | Otis, Mass. |
| Garagozzo, Keith | 5 | 4 | 2.59 | 11 | 11 | 1 | 0 | 66 | 44 | 23 | 19 | 21 | 52 | L | L | 6-0 | 170 | 10-25-69 | 1991 | Maple Shade, N.J. |
| Gully, Scott | 5 | 6 | 4.52 | 59 | 0 | 0 | 1 | 88 | 76 | 56 | 44 | 50 | 72 | R | R | 5-11 | 180 | 4-5-70 | 1991 | Hammonton, N.J. |
| Jean, Domingo | 0 | 0 | 0.00 | 1 | 0 | 0 | 0 | 2 | 1 | 0 | 0 | 1 | 0 | R | R | 6-2 | 175 | 1-9-69 | 1989 | San Pedro de Macoris, D.R. |
| Karp, Ryan | 3 | 2 | 2.20 | 8 | 8 | 1 | 0 | 49 | 35 | 17 | 12 | 12 | 34 | L | L | 6-4 | 205 | 4-5-70 | 1992 | Coral Gables, Fla. |
| Munda, Steve | 1 | 1 | 3.68 | 37 | 1 | 0 | 0 | 66 | 69 | 36 | 27 | 33 | 48 | R | R | 6-3 | 195 | 11-7-69 | 1991 | Calumet City, Ill. |
| Pettitte, Andy | 11 | 9 | 3.04 | 26 | 26 | 2 | 0 | 160 | 146 | 68 | 54 | 47 | 129 | L | L | 6-5 | 220 | 6-15-72 | 1991 | Deer Park, Texas |
| Prybylinski, Bruce | 4 | 3 | 4.71 | 11 | 11 | 0 | 0 | 65 | 74 | 42 | 34 | 13 | 40 | R | R | 5-11 | 185 | 2-18-67 | 1988 | LaSalle, Ill. |
| Ralph, Curtis | 3 | 3 | 5.11 | 32 | 0 | 0 | 15 | 37 | 39 | 23 | 21 | 11 | 41 | R | R | 6-0 | 205 | 8-6-68 | 1988 | Sacramento, Calif. |
| Seiler, Keith | 3 | 3 | 3.92 | 31 | 0 | 0 | 1 | 44 | 47 | 26 | 19 | 9 | 21 | L | L | 6-1 | 180 | 11-17-67 | 1990 | Richmond, Va. |
| Short, Ben | 0 | 0 | 3.79 | 11 | 0 | 0 | 0 | 19 | 23 | 10 | 8 | 9 | 20 | R | R | 6-3 | 210 | 5-21-69 | 1991 | Hueytown, Ala. |
| Sullivan, Grant | 3 | 8 | 5.89 | 34 | 15 | 0 | 1 | 96 | 122 | 74 | 63 | 44 | 35 | L | L | 6-5 | 210 | 3-19-70 | 1991 | Signal Mountain, Tenn. |
| Wiley, Jim | 2 | 8 | 4.73 | 36 | 12 | 0 | 1 | 91 | 114 | 69 | 48 | 39 | 54 | L | R | 6-3 | 195 | 12-25-68 | 1989 | Des Moines, Iowa |

# GREENSBORO                                                                                    A
## SOUTH ATLANTIC LEAGUE

| BATTING | AVG | G | AB | R | H | 2B | 3B | HR | RBI | BB | SO | SB | CS | B | T | HT | WT | DOB | 1st Yr | Resides |
|---|---|---|---|---|---|---|---|---|---|---|---|---|---|---|---|---|---|---|---|---|
| Ashby, Chris, c | .750 | 1 | 4 | 2 | 3 | 0 | 0 | 0 | 0 | 0 | 0 | 0 | 0 | R | R | 6-3 | 185 | 12-15-74 | 1993 | Boca Raton, Fla. |
| Delvecchio, Nick, 1b | .270 | 137 | 485 | 90 | 131 | 30 | 3 | 21 | 80 | 80 | 156 | 4 | 3 | L | R | 6-5 | 203 | 1-23-70 | 1992 | Natick, Mass. |
| Hansen, Elston, dh-3b | .239 | 48 | 155 | 29 | 37 | 4 | 2 | 7 | 30 | 19 | 43 | 0 | 1 | R | R | 5-11 | 165 | 11-16-71 | 1990 | Curacao, Neth. Antilles |
| Hawkins, Kraig, of | .254 | 131 | 418 | 66 | 106 | 13 | 1 | 0 | 45 | 67 | 112 | 67 | 18 | S | R | 6-2 | 170 | 12-4-71 | 1992 | Lake Charles, La. |
| Hinds, Robert, 2b | .227 | 126 | 503 | 80 | 114 | 15 | 5 | 0 | 50 | 72 | 101 | 50 | 22 | R | R | 6-1 | 185 | 4-26-71 | 1992 | Cerritos, Calif. |
| Jeter, Derek, ss | .295 | 128 | 515 | 85 | 152 | 14 | 11 | 5 | 71 | 58 | 95 | 18 | 9 | R | R | 6-3 | 175 | 6-26-74 | 1992 | Kalamazoo, Mich. |
| Long, R.D., ss-2b | .241 | 58 | 170 | 21 | 41 | 4 | 4 | 3 | 20 | 33 | 45 | 6 | 4 | S | R | 6-1 | 183 | 4-2-71 | 1992 | Penfield, N.Y. |
| Luke, Matt, of | .286 | 135 | 549 | 83 | 157 | 37 | 5 | 21 | 91 | 47 | 79 | 11 | 3 | L | L | 6-5 | 225 | 2-26-71 | 1992 | Brea, Calif. |
| Pineda, Jose, c | .000 | 4 | 6 | 0 | 0 | 0 | 0 | 0 | 0 | 0 | 2 | 0 | 0 | R | R | 6-2 | 168 | 3-15-71 | 1990 | Bocas Del Toro, Panama |

| BATTING | AVG | G | AB | R | H | 2B | 3B | HR | RBI | BB | SO | SB | CS | B | T | HT | WT | DOB | 1st Yr | Resides |
|---|---|---|---|---|---|---|---|---|---|---|---|---|---|---|---|---|---|---|---|---|
| Romano, Scott, 3b ........ | .282 | 121 | 418 | 75 | 118 | 33 | 4 | 7 | 62 | 63 | 69 | 14 | 7 | R | R | 6-1 | 185 | 8-3-71 | 1989 | Tampa, Fla. |
| Shelton, Derek, c........... | .291 | 23 | 55 | 7 | 16 | 4 | 0 | 1 | 6 | 6 | 4 | 0 | 0 | R | R | 6-0 | 190 | 7-30-70 | 1992 | Gurnee, Ill. |
| Spencer, Shane, of-dh .. | .269 | 122 | 431 | 89 | 116 | 35 | 2 | 12 | 80 | 52 | 62 | 14 | 2 | R | R | 5-11 | 182 | 2-20-72 | 1990 | El Cajon, Calif. |
| Suplee, Ray, of.............. | .280 | 90 | 353 | 54 | 99 | 30 | 2 | 5 | 46 | 30 | 72 | 1 | 3 | R | R | 6-3 | 200 | 12-15-70 | 1992 | Sarasota, Fla. |
| Torres, Jaime, c-dh ....... | .283 | 25 | 92 | 9 | 26 | 5 | 0 | 1 | 12 | 7 | 7 | 1 | 0 | R | R | 6-0 | 176 | 3-12-73 | 1992 | Aragua, Venez. |
| Wilson, Tom, c ............. | .249 | 120 | 394 | 55 | 98 | 20 | 1 | 10 | 63 | 91 | 112 | 2 | 5 | R | R | 6-3 | 185 | 12-19-70 | 1991 | Yorba Linda, Calif. |
| Wuerch, Jason, 1b-of.... | .232 | 51 | 151 | 18 | 35 | 5 | 1 | 1 | 9 | 19 | 35 | 2 | 1 | L | R | 6-2 | 190 | 7-14-71 | 1991 | Leamington, Ontario |

| PITCHING | W | L | ERA | G | GS | CG | SV | IP | H | R | ER | BB | SO | B | T | HT | WT | DOB | 1st Yr | Resides |
|---|---|---|---|---|---|---|---|---|---|---|---|---|---|---|---|---|---|---|---|---|
| Antolick, Jeff .................. | 6 | 2 | 2.96 | 13 | 13 | 1 | 0 | 73 | 63 | 32 | 24 | 24 | 57 | R | R | 6-6 | 205 | 3-3-71 | 1992 | Drums, Pa. |
| Buddie, Mike ................ | 13 | 10 | 4.87 | 27 | 26 | 0 | 0 | 155 | 138 | 104 | 84 | 89 | 143 | R | R | 6-3 | 210 | 12-12-70 | 1992 | Berea, Ohio |
| Cindrich, Jeff ................. | 6 | 7 | 3.82 | 35 | 9 | 0 | 0 | 111 | 97 | 64 | 47 | 62 | 88 | R | R | 6-6 | 230 | 2-22-71 | 1991 | Cape Coral, Fla. |
| Coleman, Billy ............... | 5 | 3 | 2.57 | 59 | 0 | 0 | 14 | 70 | 54 | 24 | 20 | 23 | 82 | R | R | 6-1 | 185 | 1-18-69 | 1991 | Roanoke, Texas |
| DeJean, Mike................. | 2 | 3 | 5.00 | 20 | 0 | 0 | 9 | 18 | 22 | 12 | 10 | 8 | 16 | R | R | 6-2 | 205 | 9-28-70 | 1992 | Denham Springs, La. |
| Heberling, Keith ............. | 8 | 1 | 2.07 | 11 | 11 | 0 | 0 | 70 | 47 | 18 | 16 | 18 | 74 | L | L | 6-3 | 190 | 9-21-72 | 1993 | Vero Beach, Fla. |
| Inman, Bert ................... | 7 | 10 | 5.20 | 26 | 23 | 0 | 0 | 126 | 147 | 99 | 73 | 61 | 90 | R | R | 6-2 | 195 | 6-9-71 | 1991 | Belton, Texas |
| Karp, Ryan.................... | 13 | 1 | 1.81 | 17 | 17 | 0 | 0 | 109 | 73 | 26 | 22 | 40 | 132 | L | L | 6-4 | 205 | 4-5-70 | 1992 | Coral Gables, Fla. |
| Long, Joe .................... | 6 | 4 | 3.95 | 36 | 7 | 0 | 4 | 100 | 96 | 56 | 44 | 33 | 63 | R | R | 6-4 | 200 | 6-23-71 | 1991 | Glendora, Calif. |
| Mendoza, Ramiro .......... | 0 | 1 | 2.45 | 2 | 0 | 0 | 0 | 4 | 3 | 1 | 1 | 5 | 3 | R | R | 6-2 | 154 | 6-15-72 | 1992 | Los Santos, Panama |
| Musselwhite, Jim .......... | 5 | 3 | 2.79 | 11 | 10 | 0 | 0 | 68 | 60 | 29 | 21 | 24 | 60 | R | R | 6-1 | 190 | 10-25-71 | 1993 | Apopka, Fla. |
| Pool, Bruce .................. | 2 | 6 | 4.79 | 55 | 0 | 0 | 3 | 68 | 68 | 39 | 36 | 33 | 73 | R | L | 6-3 | 190 | 8-26-70 | 1992 | Nederland, Texas |
| Prybylinski, Bruce ......... | 2 | 0 | 2.01 | 6 | 2 | 0 | 1 | 22 | 17 | 5 | 5 | 2 | 20 | R | R | 5-11 | 185 | 2-18-67 | 1988 | LaSalle, Ill. |
| Rivera, Mariano ............ | 1 | 0 | 2.06 | 10 | 10 | 0 | 0 | 39 | 31 | 12 | 9 | 15 | 32 | R | R | 6-4 | 168 | 11-29-69 | 1990 | Puerto Caimito, Panama |
| Santiago, Sandi ............ | 1 | 1 | 6.42 | 29 | 0 | 0 | 0 | 48 | 54 | 44 | 34 | 26 | 36 | R | R | 5-11 | 160 | 3-16-70 | 1989 | Nizao De Bani, D.R. |
| Short, Ben .................... | 0 | 0 | 2.53 | 6 | 0 | 0 | 0 | 11 | 11 | 3 | 3 | 5 | 17 | R | R | 6-3 | 210 | 5-21-69 | 1991 | Hueytown, Ala. |
| Underwood, Bill ............ | 3 | 1 | 3.83 | 22 | 3 | 0 | 3 | 47 | 45 | 25 | 20 | 27 | 36 | R | R | 6-2 | 195 | 3-25-71 | 1992 | Tallmadge, Ohio |
| Wallace, Kent................ | 4 | 2 | 3.00 | 13 | 10 | 2 | 2 | 66 | 63 | 31 | 22 | 12 | 48 | L | R | 6-3 | 192 | 8-22-70 | 1992 | Paducah, Ky. |
| Wharton, Joe ................ | 1 | 1 | 3.15 | 16 | 0 | 0 | 0 | 20 | 14 | 7 | 7 | 9 | 21 | R | R | 6-1 | 175 | 4-11-71 | 1993 | Dallas, Texas |

## ONEONTA A

### NEW YORK-PENN LEAGUE

| BATTING | AVG | G | AB | R | H | 2B | 3B | HR | RBI | BB | SO | SB | CS | B | T | HT | WT | DOB | 1st Yr | Resides |
|---|---|---|---|---|---|---|---|---|---|---|---|---|---|---|---|---|---|---|---|---|
| Aldridge, Steve, c .......... | .313 | 34 | 112 | 21 | 35 | 5 | 1 | 0 | 12 | 12 | 18 | 2 | 2 | L | R | 6-4 | 180 | 10-13-71 | 1993 | Jefferson City, Mo. |
| Bierek, Kurt, 3b-1b ... | .234 | 70 | 274 | 36 | 64 | 6 | 6 | 5 | 37 | 19 | 49 | 4 | 4 | L | R | 6-4 | 200 | 9-13-72 | 1993 | Hillsboro, Ore. |
| Cumberbatch, Abdiel, of | .289 | 45 | 142 | 30 | 41 | 3 | 6 | 0 | 18 | 33 | 28 | 20 | 5 | S | R | 5-10 | 164 | 11-10-71 | 1990 | Calodonia, Panama |
| Gipner, Marcus, ph........ | .000 | 3 | 3 | 0 | 0 | 0 | 0 | 0 | 0 | 0 | 2 | 0 | 0 | S | R | 6-3 | 190 | 9-1-73 | 1991 | Dunedin, Fla. |
| Hansen, Elston, 2b-3b .. | .272 | 67 | 239 | 45 | 65 | 16 | 3 | 7 | 32 | 35 | 46 | 2 | 3 | R | R | 5-11 | 165 | 11-16-71 | 1990 | Curacao, Neth. Antilles |
| Josepher, Rick, 1b ........ | .000 | 4 | 1 | 0 | 0 | 0 | 0 | 0 | 1 | 2 | 0 | 0 | 0 | L | R | 6-1 | 190 | 8-1-71 | 1993 | Chicago, Ill. |
| Ledee, Ricky, of .......... | .255 | 52 | 192 | 32 | 49 | 7 | 6 | 8 | 20 | 25 | 46 | 7 | 5 | L | L | 6-2 | 160 | 11-22-73 | 1990 | Salinas, P.R. |
| Lewis, Brian, of ............ | .208 | 30 | 72 | 11 | 15 | 2 | 1 | 1 | 4 | 11 | 17 | 1 | 2 | L | R | 6-1 | 176 | 3-3-72 | 1991 | Bristol, Va. |
| McLamb, Brian, ss ........ | .227 | 54 | 194 | 20 | 44 | 7 | 2 | 0 | 18 | 19 | 61 | 4 | 3 | S | R | 6-3 | 185 | 12-13-72 | 1993 | Jacksonville, Fla. |
| Navas, Silverio, 2b ........ | .270 | 55 | 189 | 21 | 51 | 5 | 2 | 0 | 15 | 14 | 30 | 1 | 3 | S | R | 5-10 | 155 | 5-4-74 | 1992 | Aragua, Venez. |
| Renteria, David, ss ........ | .233 | 43 | 129 | 19 | 30 | 7 | 0 | 0 | 16 | 14 | 25 | 1 | 3 | R | R | 6-0 | 175 | 12-1-72 | 1992 | Redlands, Calif. |
| Rivera, Ruben, of .......... | .276 | 55 | 199 | 45 | 55 | 7 | 6 | 13 | 47 | 32 | 66 | 12 | 5 | R | R | 6-3 | 190 | 11-14-73 | 1992 | Chorrera, Panama |
| Schmitz, Mike, 1b.......... | .180 | 69 | 245 | 22 | 44 | 7 | 3 | 2 | 32 | 17 | 65 | 0 | 3 | R | R | 6-3 | 215 | 4-22-71 | 1993 | Coconut Creek, Fla. |
| Smith, Sloan, of ............ | .198 | 34 | 116 | 14 | 23 | 5 | 1 | 1 | 10 | 15 | 33 | 3 | 2 | S | R | 6-4 | 215 | 11-29-72 | 1993 | Evanston, Ill. |
| Torres, Jaime, c ............ | .260 | 28 | 104 | 13 | 27 | 6 | 0 | 1 | 8 | 9 | 9 | 2 | 0 | R | R | 6-0 | 176 | 3-12-73 | 1992 | Aragua, Venez. |
| Trimble, Rob, c ............. | .219 | 43 | 160 | 13 | 35 | 3 | 1 | 0 | 12 | 9 | 36 | 0 | 2 | L | R | 6-1 | 195 | 6-2-72 | 1993 | Carthage, Texas |
| Wuerch, Jason, of-1b..... | .103 | 13 | 39 | 4 | 4 | 0 | 0 | 0 | 2 | 7 | 10 | 1 | 2 | L | R | 6-2 | 190 | 7-14-71 | 1991 | Leamington, Ontario |
| Yaroshuk, Ernie, of........ | .300 | 29 | 100 | 15 | 30 | 3 | 5 | 2 | 18 | 12 | 13 | 1 | 0 | L | R | 6-1 | 190 | 10-20-70 | 1992 | Miami, Fla. |

| PITCHING | W | L | ERA | G | GS | CG | SV | IP | H | R | ER | BB | SO | B | T | HT | WT | DOB | 1st Yr | Resides |
|---|---|---|---|---|---|---|---|---|---|---|---|---|---|---|---|---|---|---|---|---|
| Alazaus, Shawn .............. | 2 | 1 | 0.98 | 28 | 0 | 0 | 6 | 37 | 23 | 5 | 4 | 21 | 37 | L | L | 6-4 | 195 | 3-20-72 | 1993 | Carrolton, Ohio |
| Cumberland, Chris......... | 4 | 4 | 3.34 | 15 | 15 | 0 | 0 | 89 | 109 | 43 | 33 | 28 | 62 | R | L | 6-1 | 185 | 1-15-73 | 1993 | Safety Harbor, Fla. |
| Drumheller, Al ................ | 3 | 1 | 5.04 | 16 | 0 | 0 | 0 | 30 | 28 | 18 | 17 | 11 | 28 | R | L | 6-0 | 185 | 7-31-71 | 1993 | Shenandoah, Pa. |
| Gordon, Mike ................. | 0 | 3 | 6.91 | 3 | 3 | 1 | 0 | 14 | 13 | 12 | 11 | 11 | 15 | L | R | 6-2 | 195 | 11-30-72 | 1992 | Quincy, Fla. |
| Heberling, Keith ............. | 2 | 1 | 0.99 | 4 | 3 | 0 | 0 | 27 | 20 | 4 | 3 | 8 | 27 | L | L | 6-3 | 190 | 9-21-72 | 1993 | Vero Beach, Fla. |

# YANKEES
## TOP
## 10
### PROSPECTS

How the Yankees Top 10 prospects, as judged by Baseball America prior to the 1993 season, fared in 1993:

| Player, Pos. | Club (Class) | AVG | AB | H | HR | RBI | SB |
|---|---|---|---|---|---|---|---|
| 2. Derek Jeter, ss | Greensboro (A) | .295 | 515 | 152 | 5 | 71 | 18 |
| 3. Gerald Williams, of | Columbus (AAA) | .283 | 336 | 95 | 8 | 38 | 29 |
| | New York | .149 | 67 | 10 | 0 | 6 | 2 |
| 4. Russ Davis, 3b | Columbus (AAA) | .255 | 424 | 108 | 26 | 83 | 1 |
| 7. Robert Eenhoorn, ss | Albany (AA) | .280 | 314 | 88 | 6 | 46 | 3 |
| 10. Dave Silvestri, ss | Columbus (AAA) | .269 | 428 | 115 | 20 | 65 | 6 |
| | New York | .286 | 21 | 6 | 1 | 4 | 0 |

| | | W | L | ERA | IP | H | BB | SO |
|---|---|---|---|---|---|---|---|---|
| 1. Brien Taylor, lhp | Albany (AA) | 13 | 7 | 3.48 | 163 | 127 | 102 | 150 |
| 5. S. Hitchcock, lhp | Oneonta (A) | 0 | 0 | 0.00 | 1 | 1 | 0 | 1 |
| | Columbus (AAA) | 3 | 5 | 4.81 | 77 | 80 | 28 | 85 |
| | New York | 1 | 2 | 4.65 | 31 | 32 | 14 | 26 |
| 6. Domingo Jean, rhp | Pr. William (A) | 0 | 0 | 0.00 | 2 | 1 | 0 | 1 |
| | Albany (AA) | 5 | 3 | 2.51 | 61 | 42 | 33 | 41 |
| | Columbus (AAA) | 2 | 2 | 2.82 | 45 | 40 | 13 | 39 |
| | New York | 1 | 1 | 4.46 | 40 | 37 | 19 | 20 |
| 8. Mark Hutton, rhp | Columbus (AAA) | 10 | 4 | 3.18 | 133 | 98 | 53 | 112 |
| | New York | 1 | 1 | 5.73 | 22 | 24 | 17 | 12 |
| 9. Mariano Rivera, rhp | GCL Yanks (R) | 0 | 1 | 2.25 | 4 | 2 | 1 | 6 |
| | Greensboro (A) | 1 | 0 | 2.06 | 39 | 31 | 15 | 32 |

**Brien Taylor**
13-7 at Double-A

STAN DENNY

| PITCHING | W | L | ERA | G | GS | CG | SV | IP | H | R | ER | BB | SO | B | T | HT | WT | DOB | 1st Yr | Resides |
|---|---|---|---|---|---|---|---|---|---|---|---|---|---|---|---|---|---|---|---|---|
| Hitchcock, Sterling | 0 | 0 | 0.00 | 1 | 0 | 0 | 0 | 1 | 0 | 0 | 0 | 0 | 0 | L | L | 6-1 | 195 | 4-29-71 | 1989 | Seffner, Fla. |
| Jerzembeck, Mike | 8 | 4 | 2.68 | 14 | 14 | 0 | 0 | 77 | 70 | 25 | 23 | 26 | 76 | R | R | 6-1 | 185 | 5-18-72 | 1993 | Queens Village, N.Y. |
| Kozeniewski, Blaise | 2 | 1 | 4.86 | 24 | 0 | 0 | 1 | 37 | 45 | 29 | 20 | 17 | 21 | R | R | 6-3 | 185 | 11-2-69 | 1992 | Somerdale, N.J. |
| Lankford, Frank | 4 | 5 | 3.34 | 16 | 7 | 0 | 0 | 65 | 60 | 41 | 24 | 22 | 61 | R | R | 6-2 | 190 | 3-26-71 | 1993 | Atlanta, Ga. |
| Leshnock, Donnie | 0 | 5 | 5.50 | 10 | 0 | 0 | 0 | 18 | 23 | 15 | 11 | 8 | 12 | L | R | 6-4 | 220 | 4-20-71 | 1992 | Columbus, Ohio |
| Musselwhite, Jim | 1 | 1 | 2.25 | 5 | 4 | 0 | 0 | 20 | 15 | 7 | 5 | 8 | 18 | R | R | 6-1 | 190 | 10-25-71 | 1993 | Apopka, Fla. |
| Rathbun, Jason | 2 | 0 | 2.67 | 7 | 6 | 1 | 0 | 30 | 27 | 9 | 9 | 15 | 26 | R | R | 6-2 | 220 | 8-29-72 | 1993 | Houston, Texas |
| Resz, Greg | 3 | 0 | 3.76 | 24 | 0 | 0 | 9 | 26 | 18 | 14 | 11 | 16 | 16 | L | R | 6-5 | 215 | 12-25-71 | 1993 | Springfield, Mo. |
| Shelby, Anthony | 0 | 0 | 17.47 | 3 | 0 | 0 | 0 | 6 | 14 | 12 | 11 | 6 | 0 | L | L | 6-3 | 195 | 12-11-73 | 1993 | Willow Springs, Ill. |
| Standish, Scott | 2 | 3 | 4.35 | 20 | 3 | 0 | 1 | 50 | 58 | 33 | 24 | 22 | 45 | R | R | 6-5 | 225 | 10-5-72 | 1993 | Omaha, Neb. |
| Thomforde, Jim | 2 | 7 | 5.14 | 15 | 15 | 0 | 0 | 75 | 73 | 52 | 43 | 34 | 64 | R | R | 6-6 | 205 | 11-2-70 | 1992 | Centerville, Mass. |
| Wharton, Joe | 0 | 1 | 1.45 | 13 | 0 | 0 | 4 | 19 | 13 | 8 | 3 | 5 | 30 | R | R | 6-1 | 175 | 4-11-71 | 1993 | Dallas, Texas |
| Whitworth, Clint | 1 | 2 | 7.07 | 10 | 6 | 0 | 0 | 36 | 48 | 36 | 28 | 17 | 20 | R | R | 6-7 | 210 | 9-11-71 | 1993 | Frederick, Okla. |

# TAMPA     R
## GULF COAST LEAGUE

| BATTING | AVG | G | AB | R | H | 2B | 3B | HR | RBI | BB | SO | SB | CS | B | T | HT | WT | DOB | 1st Yr | Resides |
|---|---|---|---|---|---|---|---|---|---|---|---|---|---|---|---|---|---|---|---|---|
| Ashby, Chris, c-dh | .211 | 49 | 175 | 24 | 37 | 12 | 0 | 0 | 23 | 32 | 45 | 5 | 3 | R | R | 6-3 | 185 | 12-15-74 | 1993 | Boca Raton, Fla. |
| Beaumont, Hamil, of | .208 | 39 | 125 | 14 | 26 | 5 | 1 | 1 | 11 | 18 | 56 | 2 | 3 | R | R | 6-3 | 200 | 1-3-75 | 1993 | Panama City, Panama |
| Brown, Vick, ss-2b | .245 | 52 | 212 | 31 | 52 | 7 | 1 | 0 | 15 | 19 | 44 | 18 | 2 | R | R | 6-1 | 165 | 11-14-72 | 1993 | Cypress, Fla. |
| Gipner, Marcus, dh-c | .207 | 47 | 174 | 17 | 36 | 2 | 0 | 0 | 19 | 20 | 39 | 3 | 0 | S | R | 6-3 | 190 | 9-1-73 | 1991 | Dunedin, Fla. |
| Lobaton, Jose, ss-2b | .345 | 44 | 165 | 30 | 57 | 8 | 6 | 1 | 16 | 19 | 28 | 24 | 2 | R | R | 5-11 | 154 | 3-29-74 | 1992 | Acarigua, Venez. |
| Lopez, Orangel, 2b-ss | .224 | 32 | 116 | 13 | 26 | 4 | 2 | 1 | 12 | 13 | 15 | 2 | 3 | R | R | 5-11 | 170 | 3-6-73 | 1993 | Maracay, Venez. |
| Nelson, Travion, of | .179 | 57 | 195 | 24 | 35 | 10 | 1 | 4 | 22 | 21 | 54 | 3 | 3 | R | R | 6-3 | 210 | 10-15-74 | 1992 | Covina, Calif. |
| Palmer, Jim, 3b | .217 | 50 | 175 | 22 | 38 | 6 | 3 | 2 | 23 | 17 | 48 | 7 | 2 | R | R | 6-3 | 195 | 9-11-74 | 1993 | Coral Springs, Fla. |
| Perez, Pablo, c-3b | .227 | 19 | 44 | 7 | 10 | 1 | 4 | 0 | 4 | 9 | 8 | 2 | 2 | R | R | 6-0 | 170 | 8-27-73 | 1991 | Santo Domingo, D.R. |
| Samuel, Quvia, 1b | .252 | 57 | 202 | 22 | 51 | 9 | 0 | 3 | 21 | 28 | 65 | 4 | 2 | R | R | 6-1 | 210 | 4-10-74 | 1992 | Redondo Beach, Calif. |
| Seguignol, Fernando, of | .217 | 45 | 161 | 16 | 35 | 3 | 3 | 2 | 20 | 9 | 37 | 2 | 0 | S | R | 6-5 | 179 | 1-19-75 | 1993 | Panama City, Panama |
| Shumpert, Derek, of | .153 | 43 | 131 | 9 | 20 | 1 | 0 | 0 | 5 | 16 | 57 | 7 | 2 | S | R | 6-2 | 185 | 9-30-75 | 1993 | St. Louis, Mo. |
| Torres, Denny, 1b-3b | .236 | 20 | 55 | 8 | 13 | 3 | 1 | 0 | 4 | 10 | 11 | 0 | 3 | R | R | 6-2 | 185 | 5-3-74 | 1993 | Araure, Venez. |

| PITCHING | W | L | ERA | G | GS | CG | SV | IP | H | R | ER | BB | SO | B | T | HT | WT | DOB | 1st Yr | Resides |
|---|---|---|---|---|---|---|---|---|---|---|---|---|---|---|---|---|---|---|---|---|
| Berry, Jason | 1 | 2 | 0.85 | 15 | 0 | 0 | 0 | 32 | 20 | 10 | 3 | 12 | 20 | R | R | 6-3 | 210 | 4-2-74 | 1993 | Brockton, Mass. |
| Brown, Charlie | 3 | 3 | 3.59 | 16 | 6 | 0 | 1 | 53 | 51 | 28 | 21 | 13 | 54 | R | R | 6-3 | 178 | 9-13-73 | 1992 | Fort Pierce, Fla. |
| Estrella, Alejandro | 0 | 1 | 30.38 | 1 | 1 | 0 | 0 | 3 | 12 | 9 | 9 | 0 | 4 | R | R | 6-4 | 178 | 8-8-73 | 1991 | Haina, D.R. |
| Ferguson, Howie | 0 | 6 | 4.57 | 10 | 7 | 0 | 1 | 43 | 49 | 40 | 22 | 18 | 32 | R | R | 6-4 | 210 | 2-14-71 | 1992 | Hamilton, Ontario |
| Gordon, Mike | 4 | 2 | 1.67 | 11 | 9 | 0 | 0 | 65 | 43 | 23 | 12 | 27 | 61 | L | R | 6-2 | 195 | 11-30-72 | 1992 | Quincy, Fla. |
| Janzen, Marty | 0 | 1 | 1.21 | 5 | 5 | 0 | 0 | 22 | 20 | 5 | 3 | 3 | 19 | R | R | 6-3 | 197 | 5-31-73 | 1991 | Gainesville, Fla. |
| Leshnock, Donnie | 0 | 0 | 1.35 | 3 | 0 | 0 | 0 | 7 | 4 | 1 | 1 | 2 | 7 | L | R | 6-4 | 220 | 4-20-71 | 1992 | Columbus, Ohio |
| Medina, Rafael | 2 | 0 | 0.66 | 5 | 5 | 0 | 0 | 27 | 16 | 6 | 2 | 12 | 21 | R | R | 6-3 | 194 | 2-15-75 | 1993 | Panama City, Panama |
| Mendoza, Ramiro | 4 | 5 | 2.79 | 15 | 9 | 0 | 1 | 68 | 59 | 26 | 21 | 7 | 61 | R | R | 6-2 | 154 | 6-15-72 | 1992 | Los Santos, Panama |
| Mittauer, Casey | 6 | 1 | 2.68 | 21 | 0 | 0 | 3 | 40 | 34 | 17 | 12 | 4 | 34 | R | R | 6-5 | 225 | 9-1-72 | 1993 | Cooper City, Fla. |
| Rios, Dan | 2 | 1 | 3.52 | 24 | 0 | 0 | 6 | 38 | 34 | 18 | 15 | 16 | 29 | R | R | 6-2 | 200 | 11-11-72 | 1993 | Hialeah, Fla. |
| Rivera, Mariano | 0 | 1 | 2.25 | 2 | 2 | 0 | 0 | 4 | 2 | 1 | 1 | 1 | 6 | R | R | 6-4 | 168 | 11-29-69 | 1990 | Puerto Caimito, Panama |
| Rush, Tony | 0 | 0 | 12.60 | 8 | 0 | 0 | 0 | 10 | 21 | 16 | 14 | 10 | 7 | L | L | 6-2 | 175 | 11-12-72 | 1993 | West Helena, Ark. |
| Santaella, Alexis | 3 | 5 | 3.24 | 17 | 4 | 1 | 1 | 42 | 35 | 22 | 15 | 21 | 42 | R | R | 6-4 | 175 | 12-16-71 | 1990 | Caracas, Venez. |
| Santiago, Sandi | 0 | 0 | 4.50 | 1 | 0 | 0 | 0 | 2 | 3 | 2 | 1 | 0 | 1 | R | R | 5-11 | 160 | 3-16-70 | 1989 | Nizao De Bani, D.R. |
| Shelby, Anthony | 4 | 1 | 2.67 | 10 | 10 | 1 | 0 | 54 | 46 | 25 | 16 | 22 | 48 | L | L | 6-3 | 195 | 12-11-73 | 1993 | Willow Springs, Ill. |
| Short, Ben | 1 | 0 | 0.00 | 2 | 1 | 0 | 0 | 3 | 2 | 0 | 0 | 0 | 3 | R | R | 6-3 | 210 | 5-21-69 | 1991 | Hueytown, Ala. |

# NEW YORK METS

**Managers:** Jeff Torborg, Dallas Green.    **1993 Record:** 59-103, .364 (7th, NL East).

| BATTING | AVG | G | AB | R | H | 2B | 3B | HR | RBI | BB | SO | SB | CS | B | T | HT | WT | DOB | 1st Yr | Resides |
|---|---|---|---|---|---|---|---|---|---|---|---|---|---|---|---|---|---|---|---|---|
| Baez, Kevin | .183 | 52 | 126 | 10 | 23 | 9 | 0 | 0 | 7 | 13 | 17 | 0 | 0 | R | R | 6-0 | 170 | 1-10-67 | 1988 | Brooklyn, N.Y. |
| Bogar, Tim | .244 | 78 | 205 | 19 | 50 | 13 | 0 | 3 | 25 | 14 | 29 | 0 | 1 | R | R | 6-1 | 190 | 10-28-66 | 1987 | Kankakee, Ill. |
| Bonilla, Bobby | .265 | 139 | 502 | 81 | 133 | 21 | 3 | 34 | 87 | 72 | 96 | 3 | 3 | S | R | 6-3 | 240 | 2-23-63 | 1981 | Bradenton, Fla. |
| Burnitz, Jeromy | .243 | 86 | 263 | 49 | 64 | 10 | 6 | 13 | 38 | 38 | 66 | 3 | 6 | L | R | 6-0 | 190 | 4-14-69 | 1990 | Key Largo, Fla. |
| Coleman, Vince | .279 | 92 | 373 | 64 | 104 | 14 | 8 | 2 | 25 | 21 | 58 | 38 | 13 | S | R | 6-1 | 185 | 9-22-61 | 1982 | St. Louis, Mo. |
| Fernandez, Tony | .225 | 48 | 173 | 20 | 39 | 5 | 2 | 1 | 14 | 25 | 19 | 6 | 2 | S | R | 6-2 | 175 | 6-30-62 | 1980 | Santo Domingo, D.R. |
| Gallagher, Dave | .274 | 99 | 201 | 34 | 55 | 12 | 2 | 6 | 28 | 20 | 18 | 1 | 1 | R | R | 6-0 | 184 | 9-20-60 | 1980 | Trenton, N.J. |
| Housie, Wayne | .188 | 18 | 16 | 2 | 3 | 1 | 0 | 0 | 1 | 1 | 1 | 0 | 0 | S | R | 5-9 | 165 | 5-20-65 | 1986 | Riverside, Calif. |
| Hundley, Todd | .228 | 130 | 417 | 40 | 95 | 17 | 2 | 11 | 53 | 23 | 62 | 1 | 1 | S | R | 5-11 | 185 | 5-27-69 | 1987 | Palatine, Ill. |
| Huskey, Butch | .146 | 13 | 41 | 2 | 6 | 1 | 0 | 0 | 3 | 1 | 13 | 0 | 0 | R | R | 6-3 | 240 | 11-10-71 | 1989 | Lawton, Okla. |
| Jackson, Darrin | .195 | 31 | 87 | 4 | 17 | 1 | 0 | 1 | 7 | 2 | 22 | 0 | 0 | R | R | 6-0 | 186 | 8-22-63 | 1981 | Mesa, Ariz. |
| Johnson, Howard | .238 | 72 | 235 | 32 | 56 | 8 | 2 | 7 | 26 | 43 | 43 | 6 | 4 | S | R | 5-10 | 195 | 11-29-60 | 1979 | Poway, Calif. |
| Kent, Jeff | .270 | 140 | 496 | 65 | 134 | 24 | 0 | 21 | 80 | 30 | 88 | 4 | 4 | R | R | 6-1 | 185 | 3-7-68 | 1989 | Huntington Beach, Calif. |
| Landrum, Ced | .263 | 22 | 19 | 2 | 5 | 1 | 0 | 0 | 1 | 0 | 5 | 0 | 0 | L | R | 5-8 | 170 | 9-3-63 | 1986 | Sweetwater, Ala. |
| McKnight, Jeff | .256 | 105 | 164 | 19 | 42 | 3 | 1 | 2 | 13 | 13 | 31 | 0 | 0 | S | R | 6-0 | 175 | 2-18-63 | 1983 | Bee Branch, Ark. |
| Murray, Eddie | .285 | 154 | 610 | 77 | 174 | 28 | 1 | 27 | 100 | 40 | 61 | 2 | 2 | S | R | 6-2 | 222 | 2-24-56 | 1973 | Canyon Country, Calif. |
| Navarro, Tito | .059 | 12 | 17 | 1 | 1 | 0 | 0 | 0 | 1 | 0 | 4 | 0 | 0 | S | R | 5-10 | 155 | 9-12-70 | 1988 | Hato Rey, P.R. |
| O'Brien, Charlie | .255 | 67 | 188 | 15 | 48 | 11 | 0 | 4 | 23 | 14 | 14 | 1 | 1 | R | R | 6-2 | 195 | 5-1-61 | 1982 | Tulsa, Okla. |
| Orsulak, Joe | .284 | 134 | 409 | 59 | 116 | 15 | 4 | 8 | 35 | 28 | 25 | 5 | 4 | L | L | 6-1 | 203 | 5-31-62 | 1981 | Cockeysville, Md. |
| Saunders, Doug | .209 | 28 | 67 | 8 | 14 | 2 | 0 | 0 | 3 | 4 | 0 | 0 | 0 | R | R | 6-0 | 172 | 12-13-69 | 1988 | Yorba Linda, Calif. |
| Thompson, Ryan | .250 | 80 | 288 | 34 | 72 | 19 | 2 | 11 | 26 | 19 | 81 | 2 | 7 | R | R | 6-3 | 205 | 11-4-67 | 1987 | Edesville, Md. |
| Walker, Chico | .225 | 115 | 213 | 18 | 48 | 7 | 1 | 5 | 19 | 14 | 29 | 7 | 0 | S | R | 5-9 | 185 | 11-25-58 | 1976 | Chicago, Ill. |

| PITCHING | W | L | ERA | G | GS | CG | SV | IP | H | R | ER | BB | SO | B | T | HT | WT | DOB | 1st Yr | Resides |
|---|---|---|---|---|---|---|---|---|---|---|---|---|---|---|---|---|---|---|---|---|
| Draper, Mike | 1 | 1 | 4.25 | 29 | 1 | 0 | 0 | 42 | 53 | 22 | 20 | 14 | 16 | R | R | 6-2 | 175 | 9-14-66 | 1988 | Boonsboro, Md. |
| Fernandez, Sid | 5 | 6 | 2.93 | 18 | 18 | 1 | 0 | 120 | 82 | 42 | 39 | 36 | 81 | L | L | 6-1 | 220 | 10-12-62 | 1981 | Hawaii Kai, Hawaii |
| Franco, John | 4 | 3 | 5.20 | 35 | 0 | 0 | 10 | 36 | 46 | 24 | 21 | 19 | 29 | L | L | 5-10 | 185 | 9-17-60 | 1981 | Staten Island, N.Y. |
| Gibson, Paul | 1 | 1 | 5.19 | 8 | 0 | 0 | 0 | 9 | 14 | 6 | 5 | 2 | 12 | R | L | 6-0 | 185 | 1-4-60 | 1978 | Center Moriches, N.Y. |
| Gooden, Dwight | 12 | 15 | 3.45 | 29 | 29 | 7 | 0 | 209 | 188 | 89 | 80 | 61 | 149 | R | R | 6-2 | 210 | 11-16-64 | 1982 | St. Petersburg, Fla. |
| Gozzo, Mauro | 0 | 1 | 2.57 | 10 | 0 | 0 | 1 | 14 | 11 | 5 | 4 | 5 | 6 | R | R | 6-3 | 212 | 3-7-66 | 1984 | Kensington, Conn. |
| Greer, Ken | 1 | 0 | 0.00 | 1 | 0 | 0 | 0 | 1 | 0 | 0 | 0 | 2 | R | R | 6-2 | 215 | 5-12-67 | 1988 | Hull, Mass. |
| Hillman, Eric | 2 | 9 | 3.97 | 27 | 22 | 3 | 0 | 145 | 173 | 83 | 64 | 24 | 60 | L | L | 6-10 | 225 | 4-27-66 | 1987 | Citrus Heights, Calif. |
| Innis, Jeff | 2 | 3 | 4.11 | 67 | 0 | 0 | 3 | 77 | 81 | 39 | 35 | 38 | 36 | R | R | 6-1 | 180 | 7-5-62 | 1983 | Jupiter, Fla. |
| Jones, Bobby | 2 | 4 | 3.65 | 9 | 9 | 0 | 0 | 62 | 61 | 35 | 25 | 22 | 35 | R | R | 6-4 | 210 | 2-10-70 | 1991 | Kerman, Calif. |
| Kaiser, Jeff | 0 | 0 | 11.57 | 6 | 0 | 0 | 0 | 5 | 6 | 6 | 6 | 5 | 3 | R | L | 6-3 | 205 | 7-24-60 | 1982 | Trenton, Mich. |
| 2-team (3 Cinc.) | 0 | 0 | 7.88 | 9 | 0 | 0 | 0 | 8 | 10 | 7 | 7 | 5 | 9 | | | | | | | |
| Maddux, Mike | 3 | 8 | 3.60 | 58 | 0 | 0 | 5 | 75 | 67 | 34 | 30 | 27 | 57 | L | R | 6-2 | 180 | 8-27-61 | 1982 | Las Vegas, Nev. |
| Manzanillo, Josias | 0 | 0 | 3.00 | 6 | 0 | 0 | 0 | 12 | 8 | 7 | 4 | 5 | 9 | R | R | 6-0 | 190 | 10-16-67 | 1983 | San Pedro de Macoris, D.R. |
| Saberhagen, Bret | 7 | 7 | 3.29 | 19 | 19 | 4 | 0 | 139 | 131 | 55 | 51 | 17 | 93 | R | R | 6-1 | 200 | 4-11-64 | 1983 | Thousand Oaks, Calif. |
| Schourek, Pete | 5 | 12 | 5.96 | 41 | 18 | 0 | 0 | 128 | 168 | 90 | 85 | 45 | 72 | L | L | 6-5 | 195 | 5-10-69 | 1987 | Falls Church, Va. |
| Tanana, Frank | 7 | 15 | 4.48 | 29 | 29 | 0 | 0 | 183 | 198 | 101 | 91 | 48 | 104 | L | L | 6-3 | 195 | 7-3-53 | 1971 | Farmington Hills, Mich. |
| Telgheder, Dave | 6 | 2 | 4.76 | 24 | 7 | 0 | 0 | 76 | 82 | 40 | 40 | 21 | 35 | R | R | 6-2 | 212 | 11-11-66 | 1989 | Slate Hill, N.Y. |
| Weston, Mickey | 0 | 0 | 7.94 | 4 | 0 | 0 | 0 | 6 | 11 | 5 | 5 | 1 | 2 | R | R | 6-1 | 180 | 3-26-61 | 1982 | Fenton, Mich. |
| Young, Anthony | 1 | 16 | 3.77 | 39 | 10 | 1 | 3 | 100 | 103 | 52 | 42 | 42 | 62 | R | R | 6-2 | 200 | 1-19-66 | 1987 | Houston, Texas |

## FIELDING

| Catcher | PCT | G | PO | A | E | DP |
|---|---|---|---|---|---|---|
| Hundley | .988 | 123 | 592 | 63 | 8 | 6 |
| McKnight | .000 | 1 | 0 | 0 | 0 | 0 |
| O'Brien | .986 | 65 | 325 | 39 | 5 | 5 |

| First Base | PCT | G | PO | A | E | DP |
|---|---|---|---|---|---|---|
| Bonilla | .981 | 6 | 50 | 1 | 1 | 4 |
| Gallagher | 1.000 | 9 | 22 | 1 | 0 | 0 |
| McKnight | 1.000 | 10 | 35 | 5 | 0 | 5 |
| Murray | .988 | 154 | 1319 | 111 | 18 | 118 |
| Orsulak | 1.000 | 4 | 16 | 1 | 0 | 0 |

| Second Base | PCT | G | PO | A | E | DP |
|---|---|---|---|---|---|---|
| Bogar | .963 | 6 | 13 | 13 | 1 | 6 |
| Kent | .969 | 127 | 250 | 311 | 18 | 68 |
| McKnight | .930 | 15 | 17 | 23 | 3 | 3 |
| Saunders | .956 | 22 | 36 | 50 | 4 | 18 |

| | PCT | G | PO | A | E | DP |
|---|---|---|---|---|---|---|
| Walker | .976 | 24 | 40 | 43 | 2 | 8 |

| Third Base | PCT | G | PO | A | E | DP |
|---|---|---|---|---|---|---|
| Bogar | 1.000 | 7 | 4 | 11 | 0 | 2 |
| Bonilla | .929 | 52 | 40 | 103 | 11 | 6 |
| Huskey | .923 | 13 | 9 | 27 | 3 | 2 |
| Johnson | .944 | 67 | 52 | 135 | 11 | 11 |
| Kent | .925 | 12 | 9 | 28 | 3 | 5 |
| McKnight | .846 | 9 | 3 | 8 | 2 | 0 |
| Saunders | 1.000 | 4 | 1 | 2 | 0 | 1 |
| Walker | .907 | 23 | 12 | 37 | 5 | 3 |

| Shortstop | PCT | G | PO | A | E | DP |
|---|---|---|---|---|---|---|
| Baez | .967 | 52 | 57 | 117 | 6 | 24 |
| Bogar | .972 | 66 | 88 | 193 | 8 | 34 |
| T. Fernandez | .975 | 48 | 83 | 150 | 6 | 28 |

| | PCT | G | PO | A | E | DP |
|---|---|---|---|---|---|---|
| Kent | .800 | 2 | 2 | 2 | 1 | 0 |
| McKnight | .943 | 29 | 31 | 52 | 5 | 11 |
| Navarro | 1.000 | 2 | 8 | 7 | 0 | 0 |
| Saunders | .000 | 1 | 0 | 0 | 0 | 0 |

| Outfield | PCT | G | PO | A | E | DP |
|---|---|---|---|---|---|---|
| Bonilla | .969 | 85 | 148 | 8 | 5 | 1 |
| Burnitz | .977 | 79 | 165 | 6 | 4 | 2 |
| Coleman | .982 | 90 | 162 | 5 | 3 | 0 |
| Gallagher | 1.000 | 72 | 117 | 6 | 0 | 1 |
| Housie | .000 | 2 | 0 | 0 | 0 | 0 |
| Jackson | 1.000 | 26 | 51 | 4 | 0 | 2 |
| Landrum | .000 | 3 | 0 | 0 | 0 | 0 |
| Orsulak | .978 | 114 | 215 | 9 | 5 | 1 |
| Thompson | .987 | 76 | 228 | 4 | 3 | 0 |
| Walker | .947 | 15 | 16 | 2 | 1 | 0 |

# METS FARM SYSTEM

| Class | Club | League | W | L | Pct. | Finish* | Manager | First Year |
|---|---|---|---|---|---|---|---|---|
| AAA | Norfolk (Va.) Tides | International | 70 | 71 | .496 | 6th (10) | Clint Hurdle | 1969 |
| AA | Binghamton (N.Y.) Mets | Eastern | 68 | 72 | .486 | 5th (8) | Steve Swisher | 1992 |
| A# | St. Lucie (Fla.) Mets | Florida State | 78 | 52 | .600 | 2nd (13) | John Tamargo | 1988 |
| A | Capital City (S.C.) Bombers | South Atlantic | 64 | 77 | .454 | 10th (14) | Ron Washington | 1983 |
| A | Pittsfield (Mass.) Mets | New York-Penn | 40 | 35 | .533 | 5th (14) | Howie Freiling | 1989 |

| Class | Club | League | W | L | Pct. | Finish* | Manager | First Year |
|---|---|---|---|---|---|---|---|---|
| Rookie# | Kingsport (Tenn.) Mets | Appalachian | 30 | 38 | .441 | 7th (10) | Ron Gideon | 1980 |
| Rookie | St. Lucie (Fla.) Mets | Gulf Coast | 39 | 20 | .661 | 2nd (15) | Junior Roman | 1988 |

*Finish in overall standings (No. of teams in league)   #Advanced level

## NORFOLK — AAA
### INTERNATIONAL LEAGUE

| BATTING | AVG | G | AB | R | H | 2B | 3B | HR | RBI | BB | SO | SB | CS | B | T | HT | WT | DOB | 1st Yr | Resides |
|---|---|---|---|---|---|---|---|---|---|---|---|---|---|---|---|---|---|---|---|---|
| Allison, Tom | .235 | 13 | 34 | 9 | 8 | 0 | 0 | 0 | 3 | 8 | 7 | 0 | 0 | S | R | 5-10 | 165 | 9-13-67 | 1990 | Encinitas, Calif. |
| Baez, Kevin | .258 | 63 | 209 | 23 | 54 | 11 | 1 | 2 | 21 | 20 | 29 | 0 | 2 | R | R | 6-0 | 170 | 1-10-67 | 1988 | Brooklyn, N.Y. |
| Bilardello, Dann | .241 | 48 | 145 | 13 | 35 | 6 | 1 | 3 | 15 | 9 | 22 | 1 | 0 | R | R | 6-0 | 190 | 5-26-59 | 1978 | West Palm Beach, Fla. |
| Bullock, Eric | .254 | 117 | 437 | 55 | 111 | 26 | 8 | 4 | 48 | 52 | 56 | 45 | 15 | L | L | 5-11 | 185 | 2-16-60 | 1981 | Carson, Calif. |
| Burnitz, Jeromy | .227 | 65 | 255 | 33 | 58 | 15 | 3 | 8 | 44 | 25 | 53 | 10 | 7 | L | R | 6-0 | 190 | 4-14-69 | 1990 | Key Largo, Fla. |
| Delli Carri, Joe | .077 | 7 | 13 | 0 | 1 | 0 | 0 | 0 | 1 | 2 | 5 | 1 | 0 | R | R | 6-1 | 178 | 1-16-67 | 1989 | River Vale, N.J. |
| Fordyce, Brook | .259 | 116 | 409 | 33 | 106 | 21 | 2 | 2 | 41 | 26 | 62 | 2 | 2 | R | R | 6-1 | 185 | 5-7-70 | 1989 | Old Lyme, Conn. |
| Housie, Wayne | .209 | 16 | 67 | 5 | 14 | 0 | 0 | 1 | 5 | 3 | 13 | 7 | 2 | S | R | 5-9 | 165 | 5-20-65 | 1986 | Riverside, Calif. |
| Howard, Tim | .264 | 64 | 197 | 18 | 52 | 7 | 2 | 3 | 16 | 10 | 13 | 2 | 1 | L | R | 5-10 | 155 | 6-2-69 | 1988 | Brawley, Calif. |
| Hunter, Bert | .170 | 23 | 53 | 7 | 9 | 2 | 0 | 0 | 1 | 10 | 14 | 2 | 1 | R | R | 6-4 | 200 | 8-23-67 | 1985 | Riverside, Calif. |
| Landrum, Ced | .291 | 69 | 275 | 39 | 80 | 13 | 5 | 5 | 29 | 19 | 30 | 16 | 6 | L | R | 5-8 | 170 | 9-3-63 | 1986 | Sweetwater, Ala. |
| Martinez, Luis | .248 | 66 | 202 | 18 | 50 | 3 | 1 | 4 | 22 | 10 | 28 | 0 | 0 | R | R | 6-1 | 165 | 3-8-66 | 1987 | Roseland, Fla. |
| Navarro, Tito | .282 | 96 | 273 | 35 | 77 | 11 | 1 | 0 | 16 | 33 | 39 | 19 | 3 | S | R | 5-10 | 155 | 9-12-70 | 1988 | Hato Rey, P.R. |
| Robinson, Dwight | .143 | 3 | 7 | 0 | 1 | 0 | 0 | 0 | 0 | 0 | 0 | 0 | 0 | L | R | 6-0 | 190 | 12-15-69 | 1991 | Lewisburg, Tenn. |
| Sandy, Tim | .250 | 6 | 16 | 1 | 4 | 1 | 0 | 0 | 1 | 0 | 3 | 0 | 1 | L | R | 6-0 | 175 | 1-28-71 | 1990 | Fargo, N.D. |
| Saunders, Doug | .247 | 105 | 356 | 37 | 88 | 12 | 6 | 2 | 24 | 44 | 63 | 6 | 5 | R | R | 6-0 | 172 | 12-13-69 | 1988 | Yorba Linda, Calif. |
| Springer, Steve | .267 | 131 | 484 | 52 | 129 | 22 | 4 | 13 | 69 | 31 | 85 | 5 | 6 | R | R | 6-0 | 190 | 2-11-61 | 1982 | Huntington Beach, Calif. |
| Thompson, Ryan | .259 | 60 | 224 | 39 | 58 | 11 | 2 | 12 | 34 | 24 | 81 | 6 | 3 | R | R | 6-3 | 200 | 11-4-67 | 1987 | Edesville, Md. |
| Twardoski, Mike | .281 | 131 | 427 | 66 | 120 | 15 | 2 | 9 | 38 | 69 | 65 | 9 | 11 | L | L | 5-11 | 185 | 7-13-64 | 1986 | Lockport, N.Y. |
| Vina, Fernando | .230 | 73 | 287 | 24 | 66 | 6 | 4 | 4 | 27 | 7 | 17 | 16 | 11 | L | R | 5-9 | 160 | 4-16-69 | 1990 | Sacramento, Calif. |
| Wade, Scott | .190 | 23 | 79 | 10 | 15 | 3 | 1 | 6 | 13 | 5 | 32 | 0 | 0 | R | R | 6-2 | 200 | 4-26-63 | 1984 | Seabrook, Md. |
| Winningham, Herm | .250 | 36 | 124 | 15 | 31 | 4 | 3 | 2 | 9 | 5 | 21 | 7 | 4 | L | R | 5-11 | 190 | 12-1-61 | 1981 | Orangeburg, S.C. |
| 2-team (59 Paw.) | .254 | 95 | 338 | 46 | 86 | 10 | 4 | 7 | 33 | 37 | 73 | 15 | 6 | | | | | | | |

| PITCHING | W | L | ERA | G | GS | CG | SV | IP | H | R | ER | BB | SO | B | T | HT | WT | DOB | 1st Yr | Resides |
|---|---|---|---|---|---|---|---|---|---|---|---|---|---|---|---|---|---|---|---|---|
| Filer, Tom | 2 | 10 | 3.79 | 22 | 20 | 0 | 0 | 123 | 132 | 64 | 52 | 34 | 65 | R | R | 6-1 | 198 | 12-1-56 | 1978 | Langhorne, Pa. |
| Gibson, Paul | 1 | 1 | 0.86 | 14 | 0 | 0 | 7 | 21 | 10 | 2 | 2 | 5 | 29 | L | R | 6-0 | 185 | 1-4-60 | 1978 | Center Moriches, N.Y. |
| Gozzo, Mauro | 8 | 11 | 3.45 | 28 | 28 | 2 | 0 | 190 | 208 | 88 | 73 | 49 | 97 | R | R | 6-3 | 212 | 3-7-66 | 1984 | Kensington, Conn. |
| Gunderson, Eric | 3 | 2 | 3.71 | 6 | 5 | 1 | 0 | 34 | 41 | 16 | 14 | 9 | 26 | L | R | 6-0 | 175 | 3-29-66 | 1987 | Portland, Ore. |
| Hillman, Eric | 6 | 2 | 2.21 | 10 | 9 | 3 | 0 | 61 | 52 | 18 | 15 | 12 | 27 | L | L | 6-10 | 225 | 4-27-66 | 1987 | Citrus Heights, Calif. |
| Jones, Bobby | 12 | 10 | 3.63 | 24 | 24 | 6 | 0 | 166 | 149 | 72 | 67 | 32 | 126 | R | R | 6-4 | 210 | 2-10-70 | 1991 | Kerman, Calif. |
| Kaiser, Jeff | 1 | 1 | 5.64 | 21 | 0 | 0 | 9 | 22 | 23 | 15 | 14 | 6 | 23 | R | L | 6-3 | 205 | 7-24-60 | 1982 | Trenton, Mich. |
| Langbehn, Greg | 2 | 2 | 5.43 | 49 | 0 | 0 | 2 | 70 | 76 | 46 | 42 | 34 | 58 | R | L | 5-11 | 170 | 11-14-69 | 1988 | Schofield, Wis. |
| Lazorko, Jack | 0 | 0 | 3.38 | 2 | 0 | 0 | 0 | 3 | 4 | 1 | 1 | 1 | 2 | R | R | 5-11 | 218 | 3-30-56 | 1978 | Rowlett, Texas |
| Manzanillo, Josias | 1 | 5 | 3.11 | 14 | 12 | 2 | 0 | 84 | 82 | 40 | 29 | 25 | 79 | R | R | 6-0 | 190 | 10-16-67 | 1983 | San Pedro de Macoris, D.R. |
| Marshall, Randy | 0 | 2 | 19.64 | 4 | 1 | 0 | 0 | 7 | 18 | 16 | 16 | 4 | 3 | L | L | 6-3 | 170 | 10-12-66 | 1989 | Ypsilanti, Mich. |
| Plummer, Dale | 7 | 3 | 5.16 | 47 | 2 | 0 | 4 | 75 | 93 | 47 | 43 | 26 | 47 | R | R | 6-0 | 190 | 1-26-65 | 1988 | Bath, Maine |
| Smith, Ottis | 0 | 2 | 6.38 | 5 | 3 | 0 | 0 | 18 | 22 | 14 | 13 | 10 | 11 | R | L | 6-1 | 160 | 1-28-71 | 1990 | Fond du Lac, Wis. |
| Telgheder, Dave | 7 | 3 | 2.95 | 13 | 12 | 0 | 1 | 76 | 81 | 29 | 25 | 19 | 52 | R | R | 6-3 | 212 | 11-11-66 | 1989 | Slate Hill, N.Y. |
| Vann, Brandy | 4 | 4 | 3.22 | 53 | 0 | 0 | 11 | 64 | 53 | 28 | 23 | 33 | 52 | R | R | 6-0 | 205 | 12-9-66 | 1986 | Oklahoma City, Okla. |
| Wegmann, Tom | 5 | 3 | 3.23 | 44 | 2 | 0 | 2 | 86 | 68 | 33 | 31 | 34 | 99 | R | R | 6-0 | 190 | 8-29-68 | 1990 | Dyersville, Iowa |
| Weston, Mickey | 10 | 9 | 4.24 | 21 | 20 | 3 | 0 | 127 | 149 | 77 | 60 | 18 | 41 | R | R | 6-1 | 180 | 3-26-61 | 1982 | Fenton, Mich. |
| Young, Anthony | 1 | 1 | 1.13 | 3 | 3 | 0 | 0 | 16 | 14 | 2 | 2 | 5 | 8 | R | R | 6-2 | 200 | 1-19-66 | 1987 | Houston, Texas |

### FIELDING

| Catcher | PCT | G | PO | A | E | DP |
|---|---|---|---|---|---|---|
| Billardello | .967 | 30 | 150 | 25 | 6 | 3 |
| Fordyce | .990 | 114 | 735 | 67 | 8 | 11 |

| First Base | PCT | G | PO | A | E | DP |
|---|---|---|---|---|---|---|
| Bilardello | 1.000 | 11 | 89 | 6 | 0 | 11 |
| Springer | .993 | 14 | 125 | 11 | 1 | 14 |
| Twardoski | .992 | 124 | 1087 | 80 | 9 | 126 |

| Second Base | PCT | G | PO | A | E | DP |
|---|---|---|---|---|---|---|
| Allison | .964 | 6 | 12 | 15 | 1 | 2 |
| Dellicarri | 1.000 | 1 | 0 | 0 | 0 | 0 |
| Howard | 1.000 | 2 | 4 | 5 | 0 | 1 |
| Martinez | .900 | 2 | 5 | 4 | 1 | 1 |
| Saunders | .973 | 101 | 209 | 322 | 15 | 78 |
| Springer | 1.000 | 1 | 2 | 2 | 0 | 1 |
| Vina | .974 | 33 | 83 | 101 | 5 | 28 |

| Third Base | PCT | G | PO | A | E | DP |
|---|---|---|---|---|---|---|
| Allison | .889 | 3 | 2 | 6 | 1 | 1 |
| Dellicarri | 1.000 | 1 | 0 | 2 | 0 | 0 |
| Howard | .818 | 16 | 6 | 12 | 4 | 3 |
| Martinez | .955 | 19 | 8 | 34 | 2 | 1 |
| Robinson | 1.000 | 2 | 4 | 2 | 0 | 1 |
| Springer | .945 | 113 | 70 | 241 | 18 | 37 |
| Twardoski | 1.000 | 1 | 0 | 4 | 0 | 0 |

| Shortstop | PCT | G | PO | A | E | DP |
|---|---|---|---|---|---|---|
| Allison | 1.000 | 1 | 0 | 1 | 0 | 0 |
| Baez | .950 | 63 | 94 | 193 | 15 | 40 |
| Dellicarri | .824 | 4 | 7 | 7 | 3 | 3 |
| Martinez | .952 | 37 | 61 | 97 | 8 | 29 |
| Navarro | .861 | 8 | 14 | 17 | 5 | 6 |
| Vina | .955 | 37 | 60 | 131 | 9 | 26 |

| Outfield | PCT | G | PO | A | E | DP |
|---|---|---|---|---|---|---|
| Bullock | .980 | 115 | 195 | 6 | 4 | 1 |
| Burnitz | .993 | 65 | 133 | 9 | 1 | 2 |
| Housie | .977 | 16 | 40 | 2 | 1 | 0 |
| Howard | .953 | 27 | 35 | 6 | 2 | 3 |
| Hunter | .931 | 19 | 27 | 0 | 2 | 0 |
| Landrum | .972 | 64 | 134 | 3 | 4 | 1 |
| Martinez | 1.000 | 7 | 6 | 2 | 0 | 0 |
| Sandy | 1.000 | 6 | 5 | 0 | 0 | 0 |
| Thompson | .973 | 59 | 138 | 4 | 4 | 0 |
| Twardoski | 1.000 | 5 | 9 | 1 | 0 | 0 |
| Vina | 1.000 | 1 | 3 | 0 | 0 | 0 |
| Wade | .882 | 21 | 30 | 0 | 4 | 0 |
| Wegmann | 1.000 | 2 | 1 | 0 | 0 | 0 |
| Winningham | .967 | 34 | 85 | 2 | 3 | 0 |

## BINGHAMTON — AA
### EASTERN LEAGUE

| BATTING | AVG | G | AB | R | H | 2B | 3B | HR | RBI | BB | SO | SB | CS | B | T | HT | WT | DOB | 1st Yr | Resides |
|---|---|---|---|---|---|---|---|---|---|---|---|---|---|---|---|---|---|---|---|---|
| Allison, Tom, ss-2b | .200 | 63 | 130 | 16 | 26 | 7 | 2 | 0 | 5 | 20 | 34 | 5 | 0 | S | R | 5-10 | 165 | 9-13-67 | 1990 | Encinitas, Calif. |
| Butterfield, Chris, of-ss | .211 | 77 | 237 | 32 | 50 | 10 | 5 | 9 | 37 | 24 | 72 | 0 | 4 | S | R | 6-2 | 190 | 8-27-67 | 1989 | Modesto, Calif. |
| Davis, Jay, of | .279 | 119 | 409 | 52 | 114 | 15 | 4 | 1 | 35 | 21 | 71 | 5 | 7 | L | L | 6-0 | 190 | 10-3-70 | 1989 | Chicago, Ill. |
| Delli Carri, Joe, ss | .250 | 85 | 252 | 37 | 63 | 15 | 1 | 1 | 19 | 30 | 49 | 2 | 1 | R | R | 6-1 | 178 | 1-16-67 | 1989 | River Vale, N.J. |
| Dziadkowiec, Andy, c | .210 | 67 | 176 | 19 | 37 | 12 | 1 | 1 | 18 | 18 | 38 | 0 | 1 | L | R | 6-2 | 188 | 9-12-66 | 1986 | Chicago, Ill. |
| Gonzalez, Javier, c | .230 | 94 | 257 | 30 | 59 | 7 | 0 | 10 | 36 | 24 | 53 | 0 | 1 | R | R | 5-11 | 180 | 10-3-68 | 1986 | Carolina, P.R. |
| Howard, Tim, of | .300 | 28 | 100 | 13 | 30 | 6 | 1 | 2 | 15 | 23 | 8 | 2 | 0 | L | R | 5-10 | 155 | 6-2-69 | 1988 | Brawley, Calif. |
| Hunter, Bert, of | .224 | 92 | 308 | 38 | 69 | 10 | 3 | 5 | 30 | 24 | 85 | 9 | 7 | R | R | 6-4 | 200 | 8-23-67 | 1985 | Riverside, Calif. |
| Huskey, Butch, 3b | .251 | 139 | 526 | 72 | 132 | 23 | 1 | 25 | 98 | 48 | 102 | 11 | 2 | R | R | 6-3 | 240 | 11-10-71 | 1989 | Lawton, Okla. |
| Jacobs, Frank, 1b-dh | .269 | 109 | 346 | 50 | 93 | 17 | 3 | 9 | 46 | 42 | 72 | 2 | 3 | L | L | 6-4 | 245 | 5-22-68 | 1991 | Highland Heights, Ky. |

**Mets Plundered.** The Mets suffered an almost total collapse in 1993, save for the efforts of Bobby Bonilla, left, who slammed 34 home runs, and Eddie Murray, who drove in 100 runs.

| BATTING | AVG | G | AB | R | H | 2B | 3B | HR | RBI | BB | SO | SB | CS | B | T | HT | WT | DOB | 1st Yr | Resides |
|---|---|---|---|---|---|---|---|---|---|---|---|---|---|---|---|---|---|---|---|---|
| Ledesma, Aaron, dh-ss | .267 | 66 | 206 | 23 | 55 | 12 | 0 | 5 | 22 | 14 | 43 | 2 | 1 | R | R | 6-2 | 195 | 6-3-71 | 1990 | Union City, Calif. |
| Lowery, David, inf | .050 | 12 | 20 | 0 | 1 | 0 | 1 | 0 | 0 | 0 | 5 | 0 | 0 | S | R | 5-10 | 185 | 6-13-68 | 1990 | Vidor, Texas |
| Otero, Ricky, of | .264 | 124 | 503 | 63 | 133 | 21 | 10 | 2 | 54 | 38 | 57 | 29 | 15 | S | R | 5-7 | 150 | 4-15-72 | 1991 | Vega Baja, P.R. |
| Sandy, Tim, of | .242 | 70 | 157 | 29 | 38 | 8 | 2 | 5 | 26 | 30 | 26 | 0 | 1 | L | R | 6-0 | 185 | 1-28-71 | 1990 | Fargo, N.D. |
| Veras, Quilvio, 2b | .306 | 128 | 444 | 87 | 136 | 19 | 7 | 2 | 51 | 91 | 62 | 52 | 19 | S | R | 5-9 | 165 | 4-3-71 | 1990 | Santo Domingo, D.R. |
| Zinter, Alan, 1b-dh | .262 | 134 | 432 | 68 | 113 | 24 | 4 | 24 | 87 | 90 | 105 | 1 | 0 | S | R | 6-2 | 190 | 5-19-68 | 1989 | El Paso, Texas |

| PITCHING | W | L | ERA | G | GS | CG | SV | IP | H | R | ER | BB | SO | B | T | HT | WT | DOB | 1st Yr | Resides |
|---|---|---|---|---|---|---|---|---|---|---|---|---|---|---|---|---|---|---|---|---|
| Castillo, Juan | 7 | 11 | 4.56 | 26 | 26 | 2 | 0 | 166 | 167 | 93 | 84 | 55 | 118 | R | R | 6-5 | 205 | 6-23-70 | 1988 | La Boyera, Venez. |
| Dorn, Chris | 2 | 1 | 5.44 | 23 | 1 | 0 | 0 | 41 | 48 | 27 | 25 | 17 | 22 | R | R | 6-1 | 195 | 3-22-68 | 1988 | Spring, Texas |
| Douma, Todd | 0 | 3 | 6.90 | 15 | 4 | 0 | 0 | 30 | 46 | 26 | 23 | 16 | 23 | L | L | 6-0 | 165 | 2-5-69 | 1990 | Enid, Okla. |
| Fernandez, Sid | 0 | 1 | 1.80 | 2 | 2 | 0 | 0 | 10 | 6 | 2 | 2 | 3 | 11 | L | L | 6-1 | 220 | 10-12-62 | 1981 | Hawaii Kai, Hawaii |
| Gunderson, Eric | 2 | 1 | 5.24 | 20 | 1 | 0 | 1 | 22 | 20 | 14 | 13 | 14 | 26 | R | L | 6-0 | 175 | 3-29-66 | 1987 | Portland, Ore. |
| Guzik, Robbie | 1 | 1 | 8.06 | 15 | 0 | 0 | 0 | 22 | 36 | 20 | 20 | 7 | 12 | R | R | 6-3 | 190 | 7-1-69 | 1989 | Latrobe, Pa. |
| Harriger, Denny | 13 | 10 | 2.95 | 35 | 24 | 4 | 1 | 171 | 174 | 69 | 56 | 40 | 89 | R | R | 5-11 | 185 | 7-21-69 | 1987 | Ford City, Pa. |
| Jacome, Jason | 8 | 4 | 3.21 | 14 | 14 | 0 | 0 | 87 | 85 | 36 | 31 | 38 | 56 | L | L | 6-1 | 150 | 11-24-70 | 1991 | Tucson, Ariz. |
| Knackert, Brent | 1 | 3 | 5.56 | 15 | 6 | 0 | 0 | 44 | 59 | 30 | 27 | 13 | 27 | R | R | 6-3 | 195 | 8-1-69 | 1987 | Huntington Beach, Calif. |
| Long, Steve | 12 | 8 | 3.96 | 38 | 19 | 4 | 1 | 157 | 165 | 87 | 69 | 58 | 70 | R | R | 6-4 | 220 | 7-17-69 | 1990 | Worth, Ill. |
| Marshall, Randy | 0 | 3 | 8.49 | 7 | 7 | 0 | 0 | 35 | 61 | 39 | 33 | 8 | 21 | L | L | 6-3 | 170 | 10-12-66 | 1989 | Ypsilanti, Mich. |
| McCready, Jim | 1 | 1 | 3.44 | 14 | 0 | 0 | 0 | 18 | 18 | 7 | 7 | 4 | 12 | R | R | 6-1 | 177 | 11-25-69 | 1991 | Norwood, Mass. |
| Miller, Pat | 0 | 0 | 9.00 | 2 | 0 | 0 | 0 | 2 | 3 | 2 | 2 | 1 | 2 | R | R | 6-3 | 185 | 5-29-68 | 1990 | Redford, Mich. |
| Reich, Andy | 0 | 4 | 3.34 | 24 | 0 | 0 | 4 | 35 | 38 | 15 | 13 | 9 | 16 | R | R | 6-3 | 185 | 1-25-69 | 1988 | Raleigh, N.C. |
| Roa, Joe | 12 | 7 | 3.87 | 32 | 23 | 2 | 0 | 167 | 190 | 80 | 72 | 24 | 73 | R | R | 6-2 | 180 | 10-11-71 | 1989 | Hazel Park, Mich. |
| Rogers, Bryan | 5 | 4 | 2.34 | 62 | 0 | 0 | 8 | 85 | 80 | 29 | 22 | 25 | 42 | R | R | 6-1 | 170 | 10-30-67 | 1988 | Hollister, Calif. |
| Silcox, Rusty | 0 | 1 | 6.97 | 3 | 3 | 0 | 0 | 10 | 10 | 9 | 8 | 9 | 8 | R | R | 6-0 | 190 | 3-11-69 | 1990 | Winnie, Texas |
| Walker, Pete | 4 | 9 | 3.44 | 45 | 10 | 0 | 19 | 99 | 89 | 45 | 38 | 46 | 89 | R | R | 6-2 | 195 | 4-8-69 | 1990 | East Lyme, Conn. |

## ST. LUCIE     A
### FLORIDA STATE LEAGUE

| BATTING | AVG | G | AB | R | H | 2B | 3B | HR | RBI | BB | SO | SB | CS | B | T | HT | WT | DOB | 1st Yr | Resides |
|---|---|---|---|---|---|---|---|---|---|---|---|---|---|---|---|---|---|---|---|---|
| Alfonzo, Edgardo, ss | .294 | 128 | 494 | 75 | 145 | 18 | 3 | 11 | 86 | 57 | 51 | 26 | 16 | R | R | 5-11 | 178 | 8-11-73 | 1991 | Caracas, Venez. |
| Barry, Jeff, of | .257 | 114 | 420 | 68 | 108 | 17 | 5 | 4 | 50 | 49 | 37 | 17 | 14 | S | R | 6-1 | 192 | 9-22-68 | 1990 | San Diego, Calif. |
| Beals, Greg, c-dh | .233 | 22 | 60 | 6 | 14 | 2 | 1 | 1 | 8 | 9 | 11 | 0 | 0 | R | R | 5-10 | 185 | 2-9-70 | 1991 | Springfield, Ohio |
| Castillo, Alberto, c | .258 | 105 | 333 | 37 | 86 | 21 | 0 | 5 | 42 | 28 | 46 | 0 | 2 | R | R | 6-0 | 170 | 2-10-70 | 1987 | Las Matas de Far Fan, D.R. |
| Curtis, Randy, of | .319 | 126 | 467 | 91 | 149 | 30 | 12 | 2 | 38 | 93 | 72 | 52 | 17 | L | L | 5-10 | 180 | 1-16-71 | 1991 | Norco, Calif. |
| Fully, Ed, of | .239 | 117 | 393 | 49 | 94 | 12 | 5 | 2 | 29 | 17 | 66 | 15 | 9 | R | R | 5-11 | 175 | 7-14-71 | 1989 | La Romana, D.R. |
| Garcia, Omar, 1b | .322 | 129 | 485 | 73 | 156 | 17 | 7 | 3 | 76 | 57 | 47 | 25 | 8 | R | R | 6-0 | 188 | 11-16-71 | 1989 | Carolina, P.R. |
| Graham, Greg, 2b-ss | .196 | 26 | 56 | 10 | 11 | 1 | 0 | 0 | 4 | 13 | 10 | 1 | 2 | S | R | 6-0 | 175 | 1-30-69 | 1990 | Bowling Green, Ky. |
| Keister, Tripp, pr | .500 | 3 | 4 | 0 | 2 | 0 | 0 | 0 | 0 | 1 | 1 | 0 | 1 | L | L | 5-9 | 165 | 9-27-70 | 1992 | Newark, Del. |
| King, Jason, 2b-ss | .294 | 12 | 34 | 11 | 10 | 1 | 0 | 0 | 5 | 7 | 4 | 0 | 2 | S | R | 5-10 | 170 | 3-5-69 | 1990 | San Mateo, Calif. |
| McClinton, Tim, dh-of | .211 | 49 | 161 | 22 | 34 | 7 | 1 | 2 | 17 | 9 | 37 | 6 | 1 | R | R | 5-10 | 190 | 2-8-71 | 1989 | Woodridge, Ill. |
| Millan, Bernie, 2b | .270 | 122 | 459 | 33 | 124 | 12 | 0 | 0 | 54 | 22 | 28 | 2 | 9 | S | R | 6-1 | 202 | 12-27-70 | 1990 | Trujillo Alto, P.R. |
| Rudolph, Mason, c | .188 | 22 | 64 | 7 | 12 | 2 | 1 | 0 | 5 | 2 | 19 | 0 | 0 | R | R | 6-1 | 204 | 1-28-70 | 1988 | Mesa, Ariz. |
| Sandy, Tim, dh-of | .067 | 4 | 15 | 0 | 1 | 1 | 0 | 0 | 1 | 1 | 3 | 0 | 0 | L | R | 6-0 | 185 | 1-28-70 | 1990 | Fargo, N.D. |
| Saunders, Chris, 3b | .252 | 123 | 456 | 45 | 115 | 14 | 4 | 4 | 64 | 40 | 89 | 6 | 7 | R | R | 6-2 | 200 | 7-19-70 | 1992 | Clovis, Calif. |
| Smith, John, dh-of | .268 | 110 | 365 | 66 | 98 | 19 | 8 | 11 | 56 | 48 | 86 | 22 | 13 | R | R | 5-9 | 175 | 7-7-69 | 1992 | Indianapolis, Ind. |

# METS: ORGANIZATION LEADERS

## MAJOR LEAGUERS

**BATTING**

| | | |
|---|---|---|
| *AVG | Eddie Murray | .285 |
| R | Bobby Bonilla | 81 |
| H | Eddie Murray | 174 |
| TB | Eddie Murray | 285 |
| 2B | Eddie Murray | 28 |
| 3B | Vince Coleman | 8 |
| HR | Bobby Bonilla | 34 |
| RBI | Eddie Murray | 100 |
| BB | Bobby Bonilla | 72 |
| SO | Bobby Bonilla | 96 |
| SB | Vince Coleman | 38 |

**PITCHING**

| | | |
|---|---|---|
| W | Dwight Gooden | 12 |
| L | Anthony Young | 16 |
| #ERA | Sid Fernandez | 2.93 |
| G | Jeff Innis | 67 |
| CG | Dwight Gooden | 7 |
| SV | John Franco | 10 |
| IP | Dwight Gooden | 209 |
| BB | Dwight Gooden | 61 |
| SO | Dwight Gooden | 149 |

**Dwight Gooden**
Tenth straight 100-strikeout season

R&R SPORTS GROUP

## MINOR LEAGUERS

**BATTING**

| | | |
|---|---|---|
| *AVG | Omar Garcia, St. Lucie | .322 |
| R | Randy Curtis, St. Lucie | 91 |
| H | Omar Garcia, St. Lucie | 156 |
| TB | Butch Huskey, Binghamton | 232 |
| 2B | Dwight Robinson, Capital City-Norfolk | 34 |
| 3B | Randy Curtis, St. Lucie | 12 |
| HR | Butch Huskey, Binghamton | 25 |
| RBI | Butch Huskey, Binghamton | 98 |
| BB | Randy Curtis, St. Lucie | 93 |
| SO | Al Shirley, Capital City-Kingsport | 178 |
| SB | Quilvio Veras, Binghamton | 52 |

**PITCHING**

| | | |
|---|---|---|
| W | Jason Jacome, Binghamton-St. Lucie | 14 |
| L | Steve Lyons, Capital City | 16 |
| #ERA | Jim McCready, St. Lucie-Binghamton | 2.15 |
| G | Bryan Rogers, Binghamton | 62 |
| CG | Bobby Jones, Norfolk | 6 |
| SV | Andy Beckerman, Capital City-St. Lucie | 24 |
| IP | Mauro Gozzo, Norfolk | 190 |
| BB | Erik Hiljus, Capital City | 111 |
| SO | Erik Hiljus, Capital City | 157 |

*Minimum 250 At-Bats    #Minimum 75 Innings

| PITCHING | W | L | ERA | G | GS | CG | SV | IP | H | R | ER | BB | SO | B | T | HT | WT | DOB | 1st Yr | Resides |
|---|---|---|---|---|---|---|---|---|---|---|---|---|---|---|---|---|---|---|---|---|
| Beckerman, Andy | 2 | 0 | 0.38 | 20 | 0 | 0 | 14 | 24 | 16 | 3 | 1 | 2 | 28 | L | R | 6-1 | 185 | 12-21-69 | 1992 | Plano, Texas |
| Carpentier, Rob | 2 | 1 | 3.50 | 23 | 1 | 0 | 0 | 36 | 39 | 19 | 14 | 12 | 12 | L | R | 6-1 | 205 | 7-24-68 | 1990 | Windham, N.H. |
| Crawford, Joe | 3 | 3 | 3.65 | 34 | 0 | 0 | 5 | 37 | 38 | 15 | 15 | 14 | 24 | L | L | 6-4 | 215 | 5-2-70 | 1991 | Hillsboro, Ohio |
| Fernandez, Sid | 0 | 0 | 4.50 | 1 | 1 | 0 | 0 | 4 | 3 | 2 | 2 | 1 | 7 | L | L | 6-1 | 220 | 10-12-62 | 1981 | Hawaii Kai, Hawaii |
| Fiegel, Todd | 10 | 7 | 3.39 | 25 | 16 | 0 | 0 | 117 | 122 | 60 | 44 | 42 | 71 | L | L | 6-3 | 190 | 10-16-69 | 1991 | Springfield, Va. |
| Fuller, Mark | 4 | 3 | 1.90 | 40 | 0 | 0 | 2 | 47 | 53 | 13 | 10 | 12 | 31 | L | R | 6-6 | 212 | 8-5-70 | 1992 | Melbourne, Fla. |
| Guzik, Robbie | 0 | 3 | 3.70 | 19 | 5 | 1 | 6 | 49 | 52 | 26 | 20 | 7 | 26 | R | R | 6-3 | 190 | 7-1-69 | 1989 | Latrobe, Pa. |
| Jacome, Jason | 6 | 3 | 3.08 | 14 | 14 | 2 | 0 | 99 | 106 | 37 | 34 | 23 | 66 | L | L | 6-1 | 150 | 11-24-70 | 1991 | Tucson, Ariz. |
| Kindell, Scott | 0 | 1 | 0.00 | 1 | 0 | 0 | 0 | 1 | 2 | 1 | 0 | 0 | 1 | L | L | 6-1 | 190 | 11-18-72 | 1990 | Fort Pierce, Fla. |
| McCready, Jim | 6 | 4 | 1.76 | 40 | 0 | 0 | 16 | 61 | 51 | 18 | 12 | 22 | 40 | R | R | 6-1 | 177 | 11-25-69 | 1991 | Norwood, Mass. |
| Miller, Pat | 4 | 1 | 3.15 | 21 | 4 | 0 | 0 | 46 | 54 | 17 | 16 | 9 | 30 | R | R | 6-3 | 185 | 5-29-68 | 1990 | Redford, Mich. |
| Petcka, Joe | 0 | 1 | 7.82 | 3 | 2 | 0 | 0 | 13 | 18 | 12 | 11 | 4 | 7 | R | R | 6-3 | 190 | 10-20-70 | 1992 | Clintonville, Wis. |
| Pulsipher, Bill | 7 | 3 | 2.24 | 13 | 13 | 3 | 0 | 96 | 63 | 27 | 24 | 39 | 102 | L | L | 6-4 | 195 | 10-9-73 | 1991 | Clifton, Va. |
| Roberts, Chris | 13 | 5 | 2.75 | 25 | 25 | 3 | 0 | 173 | 162 | 64 | 53 | 36 | 111 | R | L | 6-0 | 180 | 6-25-71 | 1992 | Middleburg, Fla. |
| Schorr, Brad | 11 | 10 | 3.72 | 27 | 26 | 4 | 0 | 182 | 192 | 87 | 75 | 52 | 75 | R | R | 6-3 | 189 | 1-21-72 | 1990 | Columbus, Ga. |
| Smith, Ottis | 10 | 7 | 3.57 | 22 | 21 | 0 | 0 | 134 | 140 | 65 | 53 | 48 | 83 | R | L | 6-1 | 160 | 1-28-71 | 1990 | Fond du Lac, Wis. |
| Vitko, Joe | 0 | 0 | 1.29 | 2 | 2 | 0 | 0 | 7 | 4 | 1 | 1 | 1 | 5 | R | R | 6-8 | 210 | 2-2-70 | 1989 | Ebensburg, Pa. |

# CAPITAL CITY                                                                   A

## SOUTH ATLANTIC LEAGUE

| BATTING | AVG | G | AB | R | H | 2B | 3B | HR | RBI | BB | SO | SB | CS | B | T | HT | WT | DOB | 1st Yr | Resides |
|---|---|---|---|---|---|---|---|---|---|---|---|---|---|---|---|---|---|---|---|---|
| Adams, Jason, of | .175 | 31 | 80 | 18 | 14 | 2 | 0 | 0 | 5 | 13 | 33 | 3 | 1 | S | R | 6-0 | 170 | 7-26-71 | 1993 | Montgomery, Ala. |
| Childers, Terry, dh | .250 | 3 | 8 | 2 | 2 | 1 | 0 | 0 | 0 | 1 | 3 | 0 | 0 | R | R | 6-3 | 215 | 10-25-69 | 1993 | Augusta, Ga. |
| Daubach, Brian, dh-1b | .280 | 102 | 379 | 50 | 106 | 19 | 3 | 7 | 72 | 52 | 84 | 6 | 1 | L | R | 6-1 | 205 | 2-11-72 | 1990 | Belleville, Ill. |
| Farmer, Randy, ss-2b | .230 | 16 | 61 | 5 | 14 | 2 | 0 | 0 | 1 | 1 | 9 | 1 | 1 | R | R | 5-10 | 175 | 7-26-71 | 1991 | Wetumpka, Ala. |
| Flores, Joe, ss | .167 | 34 | 96 | 12 | 16 | 2 | 0 | 2 | 9 | 18 | 28 | 3 | 1 | R | R | 6-0 | 185 | 4-22-70 | 1992 | San Antonio, Texas |
| Garcia, Guillermo, c-3b | .289 | 119 | 429 | 64 | 124 | 28 | 2 | 3 | 72 | 49 | 60 | 10 | 8 | R | R | 6-3 | 190 | 4-4-72 | 1990 | Santo Domingo, D.R. |
| Hammell, Al, of | .174 | 11 | 23 | 0 | 4 | 1 | 0 | 0 | 3 | 3 | 6 | 0 | 0 | R | R | 5-11 | 190 | 7-23-71 | 1992 | Pleasant Valley, N.Y. |
| Keister, Tripp, of | .274 | 101 | 314 | 60 | 86 | 11 | 2 | 1 | 39 | 91 | 60 | 33 | 17 | L | L | 5-9 | 165 | 9-27-70 | 1992 | Newark, Del. |
| King, Jason, ss | .207 | 94 | 304 | 34 | 63 | 12 | 3 | 0 | 37 | 54 | 49 | 7 | 4 | S | R | 5-10 | 170 | 3-5-69 | 1990 | San Mateo, Calif. |
| Kiraly, Jeff, 1b | .214 | 132 | 491 | 60 | 105 | 20 | 2 | 9 | 58 | 44 | 131 | 3 | 2 | L | L | 6-3 | 205 | 5-16-73 | 1991 | Albuquerque, N.M. |
| Martinez, Jacen, 2b | .221 | 35 | 104 | 15 | 23 | 2 | 0 | 0 | 6 | 12 | 34 | 4 | 3 | S | R | 5-9 | 160 | 8-2-70 | 1992 | Towson, Md. |
| Mompres, Danilo, ss | .133 | 5 | 15 | 2 | 2 | 0 | 0 | 0 | 1 | 0 | 4 | 0 | 0 | R | R | 6-2 | 155 | 1-13-71 | 1989 | San Pedro de Macoris, D.R. |
| Moreno, Juan, dh-of | .159 | 31 | 107 | 10 | 17 | 1 | 3 | 0 | 9 | 10 | 36 | 6 | 2 | R | R | 6-2 | 162 | 2-19-72 | 1990 | San Pedro de Macoris, D.R. |
| Osentowski, Jared, 2b | .203 | 86 | 300 | 38 | 61 | 13 | 1 | 0 | 25 | 24 | 99 | 18 | 3 | R | R | 6-0 | 175 | 10-2-72 | 1991 | Kearney, Neb. |
| Patrizi, Mike, c | .200 | 2 | 5 | 1 | 1 | 0 | 1 | 0 | 0 | 1 | 0 | 0 | 1 | R | R | 6-1 | 190 | 11-1-71 | 1990 | Pennsauken, N.J. |
| Robinson, Dwight, 3b | .292 | 116 | 407 | 59 | 119 | 34 | 3 | 4 | 51 | 53 | 74 | 5 | 4 | L | R | 6-0 | 190 | 12-15-69 | 1991 | Lewisburg, Tenn. |
| Shirley, Al, of | .146 | 72 | 240 | 32 | 35 | 9 | 4 | 4 | 22 | 50 | 121 | 12 | 2 | R | R | 6-2 | 208 | 10-18-73 | 1991 | Danville, Va. |
| Smith, Demond, of | .000 | 1 | 2 | 0 | 0 | 0 | 0 | 0 | 0 | 1 | 0 | 2 | 0 | S | R | 5-11 | 170 | 11-6-72 | 1990 | Rialto, Calif. |
| Tijerina, Tony, c | .309 | 53 | 175 | 15 | 54 | 9 | 3 | 0 | 21 | 14 | 25 | 3 | 5 | S | R | 6-0 | 185 | 12-19-69 | 1991 | Georgetown, Texas |
| Tooch, Chuck, 2b-3b | .186 | 42 | 118 | 10 | 22 | 7 | 0 | 1 | 11 | 9 | 47 | 2 | 0 | R | R | 5-11 | 175 | 11-14-71 | 1990 | Lake Clarke Shores, Fla. |
| 2-team (17 Augusta) | .219 | 59 | 160 | 19 | 35 | 10 | 0 | 1 | 14 | 14 | 60 | 2 | 0 | | | | | | | |
| White, Don, of | .304 | 114 | 441 | 86 | 134 | 18 | 6 | 3 | 41 | 54 | 75 | 43 | 14 | R | R | 6-0 | 170 | 3-13-72 | 1991 | Rock Island, Ill. |
| Wipf, Mark, of | .210 | 127 | 471 | 51 | 99 | 15 | 2 | 5 | 58 | 36 | 107 | 17 | 7 | S | R | 6-4 | 180 | 1-11-73 | 1991 | Santa Barbara, Calif. |

| PITCHING | W | L | ERA | G | GS | CG | SV | IP | H | R | ER | BB | SO | B | T | HT | WT | DOB | 1st Yr | Resides |
|---|---|---|---|---|---|---|---|---|---|---|---|---|---|---|---|---|---|---|---|---|
| Beckerman, Andy | 5 | 1 | 0.90 | 25 | 0 | 0 | 10 | 30 | 19 | 5 | 3 | 10 | 41 | L | R | 6-1 | 185 | 12-21-69 | 1992 | Plano, Texas |
| Bellman, Bill | 1 | 1 | 9.56 | 11 | 0 | 0 | 0 | 16 | 30 | 20 | 17 | 13 | 8 | R | R | 6-2 | 195 | 12-30-69 | 1991 | Taylor, Mich. |
| Bullock, Craig | 7 | 6 | 4.13 | 30 | 21 | 2 | 1 | 144 | 158 | 78 | 66 | 45 | 57 | R | R | 6-3 | 210 | 2-11-72 | 1990 | Houston, Texas |
| Cotner, Andy | 3 | 2 | 4.71 | 27 | 0 | 0 | 1 | 29 | 24 | 15 | 15 | 18 | 32 | L | L | 6-0 | 190 | 9-6-69 | 1991 | Decatur, Ill. |
| Engle, Tom | 0 | 2 | 5.40 | 15 | 3 | 0 | 1 | 30 | 30 | 19 | 18 | 20 | 38 | R | R | 6-3 | 220 | 2-14-71 | 1989 | Lancaster, Ohio |
| Hiljus, Erik | 7 | 10 | 4.32 | 27 | 27 | 1 | 0 | 146 | 114 | 76 | 70 | 111 | 157 | R | R | 6-5 | 225 | 12-25-72 | 1991 | Santa Clarita, Calif. |
| Hokanson, Mark | 4 | 3 | 6.15 | 44 | 0 | 0 | 0 | 67 | 86 | 55 | 46 | 33 | 41 | R | R | 6-4 | 185 | 5-12-70 | 1991 | Lockport, Ill. |
| Kohl, Jim | 1 | 2 | 5.79 | 20 | 0 | 0 | 2 | 28 | 42 | 26 | 18 | 7 | 17 | R | R | 6-1 | 175 | 5-31-69 | 1991 | South Plainfield, N.J. |

MORRIS FOSTOFF

| PITCHING | W | L | ERA | G | GS | CG | SV | IP | H | R | ER | BB | SO | B | T | HT | WT | DOB | 1st Yr | Resides |
|---|---|---|---|---|---|---|---|---|---|---|---|---|---|---|---|---|---|---|---|---|
| Kroon, Marc | 2 | 11 | 3.47 | 29 | 19 | 0 | 2 | 124 | 123 | 65 | 48 | 70 | 122 | S | R | 6-2 | 165 | 4-2-73 | 1991 | Phoenix, Ariz. |
| Lyons, Steve | 8 | 16 | 3.69 | 27 | 25 | 4 | 0 | 163 | 165 | 97 | 67 | 75 | 91 | R | R | 6-6 | 220 | 5-18-71 | 1992 | Springfield, Va. |
| Petcka, Joe | 12 | 6 | 3.77 | 25 | 25 | 1 | 0 | 155 | 141 | 81 | 65 | 58 | 101 | R | R | 6-3 | 195 | 10-20-70 | 1992 | Clintonville, Wis. |
| Pulsipher, Bill | 2 | 3 | 2.08 | 6 | 6 | 1 | 0 | 43 | 34 | 17 | 10 | 12 | 29 | L | L | 6-4 | 195 | 10-9-73 | 1991 | Clifton, Va. |
| Ramirez, Hector | 4 | 6 | 5.34 | 14 | 14 | 0 | 0 | 64 | 86 | 51 | 38 | 23 | 42 | R | R | 6-3 | 200 | 12-15-72 | 1988 | El Seibo, D.R. |
| Reichenbach, Eric | 6 | 4 | 3.96 | 56 | 0 | 0 | 12 | 77 | 77 | 39 | 34 | 30 | 58 | R | R | 6-4 | 210 | 10-12-70 | 1991 | Farmingville, N.Y. |
| Shanahan, Chris | 1 | 1 | 2.93 | 13 | 0 | 0 | 0 | 15 | 17 | 5 | 5 | 4 | 16 | L | L | 6-2 | 182 | 2-26-68 | 1991 | Omaha, Neb. |
| Stark, Greg | 1 | 3 | 4.15 | 41 | 1 | 0 | 1 | 87 | 99 | 60 | 40 | 27 | 41 | R | R | 6-5 | 205 | 12-30-69 | 1992 | Fort Worth, Texas |

## PITTSFIELD    A
### NEW YORK-PENN LEAGUE

| BATTING | AVG | G | AB | R | H | 2B | 3B | HR | RBI | BB | SO | SB | CS | B | T | HT | WT | DOB | 1st Yr | Resides |
|---|---|---|---|---|---|---|---|---|---|---|---|---|---|---|---|---|---|---|---|---|
| Agbayani, Benny, of | .251 | 51 | 167 | 26 | 42 | 6 | 3 | 2 | 22 | 20 | 43 | 7 | 2 | R | R | 5-11 | 175 | 12-28-71 | 1993 | Aiea, Hawaii |
| Childers, Terry, c | .121 | 21 | 66 | 4 | 8 | 2 | 0 | 0 | 2 | 4 | 24 | 0 | 0 | R | R | 6-3 | 215 | 10-25-69 | 1993 | Augusta, Ga. |
| Collum, Gary, of | .275 | 54 | 211 | 32 | 58 | 9 | 0 | 0 | 17 | 9 | 33 | 15 | 4 | R | L | 5-11 | 185 | 7-14-71 | 1993 | Pitman, N.J. |
| Diaz, Cesar, c | .188 | 14 | 48 | 6 | 9 | 1 | 0 | 0 | 8 | 3 | 11 | 4 | 0 | R | R | 6-3 | 185 | 7-12-74 | 1990 | Maracay, Venez. |
| Guerrero, Rafael, of | .269 | 8 | 26 | 8 | 7 | 1 | 0 | 0 | 1 | 4 | 5 | 1 | 1 | R | R | 6-2 | 175 | 12-3-74 | 1991 | Santo Domingo, D.R. |
| Haggas, Josh, 3b | .182 | 45 | 143 | 11 | 26 | 5 | 1 | 0 | 20 | 11 | 33 | 0 | 1 | R | R | 6-1 | 195 | 1-29-71 | 1992 | Whitesboro, N.Y. |
| Harris, Eric, 1b | .222 | 52 | 185 | 18 | 41 | 7 | 0 | 7 | 35 | 16 | 68 | 2 | 3 | R | R | 6-4 | 215 | 11-5-71 | 1992 | Oakland, Calif. |
| Hernandez, Rafael, 3b | .220 | 49 | 159 | 17 | 35 | 8 | 0 | 0 | 11 | 7 | 39 | 4 | 1 | R | R | 6-1 | 183 | 6-21-73 | 1990 | Caracas, Venez. |
| Lewis, Kevin, c | .203 | 54 | 187 | 22 | 38 | 8 | 0 | 5 | 22 | 21 | 50 | 1 | 1 | R | R | 5-11 | 192 | 9-1-71 | 1993 | West Palm Beach, Fla. |
| Maize, Dave, c-3b | .400 | 16 | 25 | 2 | 10 | 0 | 0 | 0 | 2 | 1 | 3 | 2 | 1 | S | R | 5-11 | 205 | 7-15-71 | 1991 | Chicago, Ill. |
| Mazion, Rodney, of | .266 | 46 | 184 | 25 | 49 | 5 | 2 | 0 | 18 | 10 | 39 | 16 | 6 | R | R | 5-8 | 165 | 2-4-71 | 1993 | Tampa, Fla. |
| Petrulis, Paul, ss-dh | .283 | 69 | 237 | 33 | 67 | 9 | 2 | 1 | 30 | 40 | 52 | 6 | 9 | R | R | 5-10 | 160 | 1-25-72 | 1993 | River Forest, Ill. |
| Smith, Tad, 1b | .278 | 37 | 115 | 12 | 32 | 6 | 1 | 0 | 7 | 8 | 28 | 2 | 2 | L | R | 6-2 | 200 | 5-23-71 | 1993 | Belleville, Ill. |
| Sullivan, Charlie, 2b | .269 | 55 | 156 | 20 | 42 | 11 | 4 | 0 | 17 | 22 | 26 | 3 | 1 | L | R | 6-0 | 175 | 12-7-70 | 1991 | Nashville, Tenn. |
| Terrell, Matt, of | .270 | 65 | 226 | 37 | 61 | 9 | 2 | 2 | 25 | 37 | 59 | 17 | 3 | R | R | 6-2 | 195 | 6-2-72 | 1993 | Sturgis, Mich. |
| Warner, Randy, of | .215 | 19 | 65 | 10 | 14 | 3 | 1 | 2 | 8 | 4 | 21 | 1 | 1 | R | R | 6-2 | 200 | 8-5-73 | 1991 | Seattle, Wash. |
| Wilson, Preston, 3b | .552 | 8 | 29 | 6 | 16 | 5 | 1 | 1 | 12 | 2 | 7 | 1 | 0 | R | R | 6-3 | 190 | 7-19-74 | 1992 | Eastover, S.C. |
| Zuniga, David, ss-2b | .268 | 61 | 205 | 33 | 55 | 3 | 1 | 0 | 14 | 17 | 29 | 7 | 2 | R | R | 5-8 | 150 | 4-19-71 | 1993 | Los Banos, Calif. |

| PITCHING | W | L | ERA | G | GS | CG | SV | IP | H | R | ER | BB | SO | B | T | HT | WT | DOB | 1st Yr | Resides |
|---|---|---|---|---|---|---|---|---|---|---|---|---|---|---|---|---|---|---|---|---|
| Bellman, Bill | 0 | 1 | 1.93 | 4 | 0 | 0 | 0 | 9 | 8 | 6 | 2 | 4 | 3 | R | R | 6-2 | 195 | 12-30-69 | 1992 | Taylor, Mich. |
| Cosman, Jeff | 2 | 7 | 4.19 | 14 | 14 | 1 | 0 | 82 | 84 | 49 | 38 | 31 | 46 | R | R | 6-4 | 205 | 2-8-71 | 1993 | Memphis, Tenn. |
| Engle, Tom | 7 | 7 | 3.21 | 15 | 14 | 3 | 0 | 84 | 57 | 35 | 30 | 35 | 100 | R | R | 6-3 | 220 | 2-14-71 | 1989 | Lancaster, Ohio |
| Grennan, Steve | 3 | 0 | 1.85 | 21 | 0 | 0 | 6 | 39 | 17 | 8 | 8 | 20 | 44 | L | L | 5-10 | 165 | 7-3-70 | 1991 | Salina, Kan. |
| Isringhausen, Jason | 7 | 4 | 3.29 | 15 | 15 | 2 | 0 | 90 | 68 | 45 | 33 | 28 | 104 | R | R | 6-3 | 188 | 9-7-72 | 1992 | Brighton, Ill. |
| Jones, Scott | 0 | 1 | 7.71 | 12 | 1 | 0 | 2 | 21 | 17 | 23 | 18 | 31 | 15 | R | R | 6-3 | 192 | 11-26-70 | 1993 | Chamblee, Ga. |
| Kenny, Sean | 0 | 0 | 1.50 | 7 | 0 | 0 | 1 | 12 | 11 | 2 | 2 | 4 | 9 | R | R | 6-2 | 205 | 8-3-72 | 1993 | Ann Arbor, Mich. |
| Ludwick, Eric | 4 | 4 | 3.18 | 10 | 10 | 1 | 0 | 51 | 51 | 27 | 18 | 18 | 40 | R | R | 6-5 | 205 | 12-14-71 | 1993 | Las Vegas, Nev. |
| McDill, Allen | 2 | 3 | 5.40 | 5 | 5 | 0 | 0 | 28 | 31 | 22 | 17 | 15 | 24 | L | L | 6-0 | 155 | 8-23-71 | 1992 | Hot Springs, Ark. |
| Newell, Brandon | 2 | 0 | 3.54 | 16 | 2 | 0 | 2 | 48 | 54 | 25 | 19 | 13 | 32 | R | R | 6-0 | 190 | 1-1-72 | 1993 | Blaine, Wash. |
| Shaffer, Travis | 1 | 1 | 2.89 | 7 | 0 | 0 | 1 | 19 | 17 | 10 | 6 | 7 | 21 | R | R | 6-0 | 200 | 2-22-69 | 1992 | Pittsburg, Kan. |
| Swanson, David | 6 | 3 | 2.99 | 15 | 13 | 2 | 0 | 81 | 60 | 34 | 27 | 28 | 63 | L | L | 6-0 | 184 | 10-19-72 | 1991 | Kensington, Conn. |
| Tam, Jeff | 3 | 3 | 3.35 | 21 | 1 | 0 | 0 | 40 | 50 | 21 | 15 | 7 | 31 | R | R | 6-1 | 185 | 8-19-70 | 1993 | Tallahassee, Fla. |
| Welch, Mike | 3 | 1 | 1.45 | 17 | 0 | 0 | 9 | 31 | 23 | 9 | 5 | 6 | 34 | L | R | 6-2 | 195 | 8-25-72 | 1993 | Nashua, N.H. |

## KINGSPORT    R
### APPALACHIAN LEAGUE

| BATTING | AVG | G | AB | R | H | 2B | 3B | HR | RBI | BB | SO | SB | CS | B | T | HT | WT | DOB | 1st Yr | Resides |
|---|---|---|---|---|---|---|---|---|---|---|---|---|---|---|---|---|---|---|---|---|
| Adams, Jason, of | .216 | 14 | 51 | 6 | 11 | 2 | 0 | 0 | 0 | 11 | 15 | 2 | 2 | S | R | 6-0 | 170 | 7-26-71 | 1993 | Montgomery, Ala. |
| Daly, Rob, 1b | .303 | 62 | 238 | 47 | 72 | 16 | 2 | 6 | 32 | 24 | 23 | 1 | 2 | R | R | 6-2 | 220 | 10-8-72 | 1992 | Downers Grove, Ill. |
| Diaz, Cesar, c | .327 | 55 | 211 | 36 | 69 | 12 | 1 | 11 | 37 | 15 | 41 | 0 | 1 | R | R | 6-3 | 185 | 7-12-74 | 1990 | Maracay, Venez. |
| Dorsey, James, of | .256 | 43 | 129 | 14 | 33 | 9 | 0 | 4 | 19 | 13 | 21 | 0 | 2 | R | R | 6-2 | 195 | 12-29-72 | 1993 | Columbia, S.C. |
| Epperson, Chad, dh-c | .342 | 38 | 117 | 15 | 40 | 7 | 0 | 6 | 26 | 18 | 24 | 3 | 1 | S | R | 6-2 | 215 | 3-26-72 | 1992 | Fort Myers, Fla. |
| Farrell, Mike, ss-2b | .205 | 44 | 112 | 18 | 23 | 5 | 1 | 0 | 10 | 21 | 31 | 2 | 1 | R | R | 6-0 | 170 | 4-1-72 | 1992 | Lakeside, Calif. |

## METS TOP 10 PROSPECTS

How the Mets Top 10 prospects, as judged by Baseball America prior to the 1993 season, fared in 1993:

| Player, Pos. | Club (Class) | AVG | AB | H | HR | RBI | SB |
|---|---|---|---|---|---|---|---|
| 2. Jeromy Burnitz, of | Norfolk (AAA) | .227 | 255 | 58 | 8 | 44 | 10 |
| | New York | .243 | 263 | 64 | 13 | 38 | 3 |
| 3. Brook Fordyce, c | Norfolk (AAA) | .259 | 409 | 106 | 2 | 40 | 2 |
| 4. Al Shirley, of | Kingsport (R) | .180 | 133 | 24 | 0 | 11 | 6 |
| | Capital City (A) | .146 | 240 | 35 | 4 | 22 | 12 |
| 5. Butch Huskey, 3b | Binghamton (AA) | .251 | 526 | 132 | 25 | 98 | 11 |
| | New York | .146 | 41 | 6 | 0 | 3 | 0 |
| 6. Preston Wilson, 3b | Kingsport (R) | .232 | 259 | 60 | 16 | 48 | 6 |
| | Pittsfield (A) | .552 | 29 | 16 | 1 | 12 | 1 |
| 7. Ryan Thompson, of | Norfolk (AAA) | .259 | 224 | 58 | 12 | 34 | 6 |
| | New York | .250 | 288 | 72 | 11 | 26 | 2 |
| 9. Edgar Alfonzo, ss | St. Lucie (A) | .294 | 494 | 145 | 11 | 86 | 26 |
| 10. Rafael Guerrero, of | Kingsport (R) | .234 | 188 | 44 | 1 | 18 | 4 |
| | Pittsfield (A) | .269 | 26 | 7 | 0 | 1 | 1 |

| | | W | L | ERA | IP | H | BB | SO |
|---|---|---|---|---|---|---|---|---|
| 1. Bobby Jones, rhp | Norfolk (AAA) | 12 | 10 | 3.63 | 166 | 149 | 32 | 126 |
| | New York | 2 | 4 | 3.65 | 62 | 61 | 22 | 35 |
| 8. Bill Pulsipher, lhp | Capital City (A) | 2 | 3 | 2.08 | 43 | 34 | 12 | 29 |
| | St. Lucie (A) | 7 | 3 | 2.24 | 96 | 63 | 39 | 102 |

**Bobby Jones**
12-10 at Triple-A

# METS: MOST COMMON LINEUPS

| | New York<br>Majors | Norfolk<br>AAA | Binghamton<br>AA | St. Lucie<br>A | Capital City<br>A |
|---|---|---|---|---|---|
| **C** | Todd Hundley (123) | Brook Fordyce (114) | Javier Gonzalez (93) | Alberto Castillo (105) | Guillermo Garcia (96) |
| **1B** | Eddie Murray (154) | Mike Twardoski (124) | Jacobs/Zinter (72) | Omar Garcia (129) | Jeff Kiraly (97) |
| **2B** | Jeff Kent (127) | Doug Saunders (101) | Quilvio Veras (127) | Bernie Millan (117) | Jared Osentowski (83) |
| **3B** | Howard Johnson (67) | Steve Springer (113) | Butch Huskey (138) | Chris Saunders (123) | Dwight Robinson (113) |
| **SS** | Tim Bogar (66) | Kevin Baez (63) | Joe Dellicarri (84) | Edgardo Alfonzo (124) | Jason King (94) |
| **OF** | Joe Orsulak (114) | Eric Bullock (115) | Ricky Otero (124) | Randy Curtis (123) | Mark Wipf (120) |
| | Vince Coleman (90) | Jeromy Burnitz (65) | Jay Davis (95) | Ed Fully (112) | Don White (113) |
| | Bobby Bonilla (85) | Ced Landrum (64) | Bert Hunter (90) | Jeff Barry (98) | Tripp Keister (90) |
| **DH** | N/A | Tito Navarro (57) | Alan Zinter (33) | John Smith (62) | Brian Daubach (55) |
| **SP** | Gooden/Tanana (29) | Mauro Gozzo (28) | Juan Castillo (26) | Brad Schorr (26) | Erik Hiljus (27) |
| **RP** | Jeff Innis (67) | Brandy Vann (53) | Bryan Rogers (62) | Fuller/McCready (40) | Eric Reichenbach (56) |

Full-season farm clubs only    No. of games at position in parenthesis

## BATTING

| | AVG | G | AB | R | H | 2B | 3B | HR | RBI | BB | SO | SB | CS | B | T | HT | WT | DOB | 1st Yr | Resides |
|---|---|---|---|---|---|---|---|---|---|---|---|---|---|---|---|---|---|---|---|---|
| Guerrero, Rafael, of ...... | .234 | 51 | 188 | 25 | 44 | 10 | 1 | 1 | 18 | 15 | 23 | 4 | 4 | R | R | 6-2 | 175 | 12-3-74 | 1991 | Santo Domingo, D.R. |
| Johnson, Michael, 2b ..... | .255 | 19 | 51 | 6 | 13 | 2 | 0 | 0 | 3 | 3 | 19 | 0 | 0 | R | R | 6-0 | 180 | 1-20-71 | 1993 | Newington, Conn. |
| Lackey, Steve, ss ......... | .146 | 53 | 171 | 14 | 25 | 4 | 0 | 0 | 9 | 14 | 30 | 3 | 4 | R | R | 6-0 | 160 | 9-25-74 | 1992 | Riverside, Calif. |
| Palmer, Travis, of .......... | .067 | 8 | 15 | 0 | 1 | 0 | 0 | 0 | 0 | 2 | 10 | 0 | 0 | R | R | 6-1 | 180 | 11-28-73 | 1992 | Camp Verde, Ariz. |
| Pichardo, Sandy, 2b ...... | .302 | 51 | 192 | 25 | 58 | 6 | 2 | 1 | 15 | 22 | 25 | 12 | 10 | L | R | 5-11 | 167 | 11-26-74 | 1991 | Santiago, D.R. |
| Rojas, Freddy, 1b-dh ..... | .297 | 41 | 128 | 22 | 38 | 8 | 1 | 3 | 14 | 28 | 50 | 4 | 2 | R | R | 6-2 | 170 | 5-22-72 | 1991 | Santo Domingo, D.R. |
| Shirley, Al, of .............. | .180 | 43 | 133 | 22 | 24 | 5 | 1 | 0 | 11 | 42 | 57 | 6 | 5 | R | R | 6-2 | 208 | 10-18-73 | 1991 | Danville, Va. |
| Warner, Randy, of ......... | .305 | 58 | 223 | 37 | 68 | 12 | 0 | 15 | 37 | 13 | 55 | 1 | 0 | R | R | 6-2 | 200 | 8-5-73 | 1991 | Seattle, Wash. |
| Wilson, Preston, 3b ........ | .232 | 54 | 259 | 44 | 60 | 10 | 0 | 16 | 48 | 24 | 75 | 6 | 2 | R | R | 6-3 | 190 | 7-19-74 | 1992 | Eastover, S.C. |
| Winterlee, Scott, c ......... | .278 | 12 | 36 | 6 | 10 | 4 | 0 | 0 | 2 | 4 | 0 | 0 | 0 | R | R | 6-0 | 195 | 12-22-70 | 1993 | Mt. Morris, Mich. |

## PITCHING

| | W | L | ERA | G | GS | CG | SV | IP | H | R | ER | BB | SO | B | T | HT | WT | DOB | 1st Yr | Resides |
|---|---|---|---|---|---|---|---|---|---|---|---|---|---|---|---|---|---|---|---|---|
| Baker, Derek............. | 5 | 6 | 4.19 | 14 | 14 | 2 | 0 | 82 | 92 | 47 | 38 | 31 | 45 | S | R | 6-4 | 205 | 6-19-73 | 1992 | Phoenix, Ariz. |
| Carr, Robert ................. | 1 | 2 | 4.45 | 19 | 0 | 0 | 4 | 28 | 26 | 14 | 14 | 4 | 23 | R | L | 6-0 | 180 | 1-26-72 | 1992 | Millbrook, Ala. |
| Collier, Ervin ............... | 1 | 4 | 6.39 | 16 | 3 | 0 | 2 | 44 | 51 | 40 | 31 | 19 | 27 | R | R | 6-2 | 169 | 3-10-72 | 1991 | New Madrid, Mo. |
| Cotner, Andy ............... | 4 | 0 | 1.26 | 6 | 0 | 0 | 0 | 14 | 10 | 6 | 2 | 7 | 18 | L | L | 6-0 | 190 | 9-6-69 | 1991 | Decatur, Ill. |
| Gontkosky, Robert......... | 7 | 3 | 3.54 | 14 | 11 | 2 | 0 | 76 | 82 | 42 | 30 | 18 | 56 | L | L | 6-2 | 180 | 2-21-72 | 1993 | Cresco, Pa. |
| Kenny, Sean ............... | 1 | 2 | 1.77 | 13 | 0 | 0 | 4 | 20 | 9 | 4 | 4 | 6 | 16 | R | R | 6-2 | 205 | 8-3-72 | 1993 | Ann Arbor, Mich. |
| Krablin, Justin ............ | 1 | 0 | 4.76 | 4 | 1 | 0 | 0 | 11 | 13 | 9 | 6 | 4 | 9 | R | R | 6-0 | 193 | 5-12-74 | 1992 | Hot Springs, Ark. |
| Mast, Brian ................. | 2 | 4 | 4.83 | 13 | 9 | 0 | 1 | 60 | 63 | 39 | 32 | 24 | 60 | R | R | 6-7 | 200 | 2-10-71 | 1993 | Bremen, Ohio |
| McDill, Allen ............... | 5 | 2 | 2.19 | 9 | 9 | 0 | 0 | 53 | 52 | 19 | 13 | 14 | 42 | L | L | 6-0 | 155 | 8-23-71 | 1992 | Hot Springs, Ark. |
| Moreno, Juan ............... | 1 | 4 | 3.86 | 20 | 0 | 0 | 5 | 42 | 37 | 23 | 18 | 10 | 37 | R | R | 6-2 | 162 | 2-19-72 | 1990 | San Pedro de Macoris, D.R. |
| Roque, Rafael ............... | 1 | 3 | 6.15 | 14 | 7 | 0 | 0 | 45 | 58 | 44 | 31 | 26 | 36 | L | L | 6-2 | 152 | 1-1-72 | 1991 | Santo Domingo, D.R. |
| Sutton, Derek................. | 0 | 4 | 7.99 | 11 | 8 | 1 | 0 | 42 | 51 | 45 | 37 | 19 | 31 | R | L | 6-0 | 185 | 2-2-73 | 1993 | Laval, Quebec |
| Tatis, Ramon ............... | 0 | 2 | 6.12 | 13 | 3 | 0 | 1 | 43 | 51 | 42 | 29 | 23 | 25 | L | L | 6-2 | 180 | 1-5-73 | 1991 | Guayubin, D.R. |
| Wolff, Tom ................... | 1 | 2 | 10.95 | 3 | 3 | 0 | 0 | 12 | 21 | 22 | 15 | 13 | 5 | R | R | 6-3 | 185 | 7-29-73 | 1993 | Hillsdale, Mich. |

# ST. LUCIE      R

## GULF COAST LEAGUE

### BATTING

| | AVG | G | AB | R | H | 2B | 3B | HR | RBI | BB | SO | SB | CS | B | T | HT | WT | DOB | 1st Yr | Resides |
|---|---|---|---|---|---|---|---|---|---|---|---|---|---|---|---|---|---|---|---|---|
| Alfonzo, Robert, 2b ........ | .261 | 40 | 134 | 13 | 35 | 2 | 0 | 0 | 19 | 12 | 11 | 9 | 3 | S | R | 5-11 | 169 | 12-9-72 | 1993 | Caracas, Venez. |
| Arvelo, Tomas, ss ........ | .227 | 56 | 207 | 50 | 47 | 6 | 0 | 1 | 17 | 40 | 49 | 25 | 2 | R | R | 6-1 | 170 | 12-11-73 | 1991 | Santo Domingo, D.R. |
| Bradley, Ken, of............. | .269 | 36 | 130 | 16 | 35 | 9 | 1 | 1 | 15 | 9 | 26 | 4 | 4 | R | R | 6-0 | 170 | 12-12-72 | 1992 | Pine Bluff, Ark. |
| Brea, Juan, of .............. | .383 | 19 | 60 | 12 | 23 | 3 | 4 | 1 | 10 | 6 | 10 | 0 | 3 | R | R | 5-11 | 170 | 5-30-74 | 1992 | Santo Domingo, D.R. |
| Fellhauer, David, 1b ...... | .288 | 30 | 104 | 19 | 30 | 7 | 2 | 1 | 15 | 11 | 16 | 2 | 0 | L | L | 6-1 | 205 | 11-22-75 | 1993 | Tampa, Fla. |
| Ferrier, Ross, of............. | .277 | 43 | 155 | 23 | 43 | 10 | 1 | 2 | 21 | 20 | 27 | 1 | 2 | R | R | 6-5 | 225 | 8-10-71 | 1993 | Waterloo, Ontario |
| Gomez, Paul, c............... | .150 | 10 | 20 | 2 | 3 | 0 | 1 | 0 | 3 | 9 | 3 | 2 | 0 | R | R | 5-11 | 190 | 3-8-73 | 1993 | Miami, Fla. |
| Hiraldo, Jerry, dh-of ...... | .221 | 32 | 104 | 15 | 23 | 6 | 2 | 0 | 12 | 17 | 20 | 2 | 1 | R | R | 6-2 | 170 | 8-4-74 | 1992 | Carolina, P.R. |
| Maize, Dave, c .............. | .100 | 3 | 10 | 0 | 1 | 0 | 0 | 0 | 1 | 0 | 3 | 0 | 0 | S | R | 5-11 | 205 | 7-15-71 | 1991 | Chicago, Ill. |
| Morales, Hery, c............. | .215 | 40 | 130 | 26 | 28 | 7 | 1 | 0 | 14 | 30 | 25 | 1 | 0 | S | R | 6-0 | 180 | 9-26-73 | 1992 | Moca, P.R. |
| Morales, Jesus, 2b-3b-.. | .167 | 35 | 114 | 10 | 19 | 4 | 0 | 0 | 7 | 19 | 21 | 2 | 3 | R | R | 6-2 | 180 | 11-21-72 | 1993 | Alhambra, Calif. |
| Mota, Guillermo, 3b........ | .249 | 43 | 169 | 23 | 42 | 7 | 2 | 1 | 22 | 7 | 37 | 1 | 0 | R | R | 6-3 | 147 | 7-25-73 | 1991 | San Pedro de Macoris, D.R. |
| Navarro, Tito, ss-dh........ | .286 | 4 | 14 | 2 | 4 | 1 | 1 | 0 | 5 | 3 | 1 | 1 | 0 | S | R | 5-10 | 155 | 9-12-70 | 1988 | Hato Rey, P.R. |
| Osentowski, Jared, 3b-.. | .118 | 4 | 17 | 0 | 2 | 0 | 0 | 0 | 0 | 2 | 1 | 0 | 0 | R | R | 6-0 | 175 | 10-2-72 | 1991 | Kearney, Neb. |
| Ozario, Yudith, of ......... | .230 | 55 | 213 | 38 | 49 | 7 | 2 | 0 | 13 | 33 | 35 | 39 | 11 | R | R | 5-11 | 148 | 1-1-75 | 1991 | La Romana, D.R. |
| Patterson, Jarrod, 1b...... | .241 | 46 | 166 | 27 | 40 | 9 | 1 | 2 | 25 | 24 | 28 | 1 | 3 | L | R | 6-0 | 190 | 9-7-73 | 1993 | Clanton, Ala. |
| Ramirez, Juan, of .......... | .304 | 52 | 204 | 37 | 62 | 4 | 3 | 2 | 31 | 15 | 45 | 10 | 3 | R | R | 6-0 | 165 | 2-3-73 | 1991 | San Pedro de Macoris, D.R. |
| Winterlee, Scott, dh-c ..... | .455 | 4 | 11 | 1 | 5 | 3 | 0 | 0 | 2 | 1 | 0 | 0 | 0 | R | R | 6-0 | 195 | 12-22-70 | 1993 | Mt. Morris, Mich. |

### PITCHING

| | W | L | ERA | G | GS | CG | SV | IP | H | R | ER | BB | SO | B | T | HT | WT | DOB | 1st Yr | Resides |
|---|---|---|---|---|---|---|---|---|---|---|---|---|---|---|---|---|---|---|---|---|
| Adair, Scott .................. | 3 | 2 | 4.59 | 11 | 9 | 0 | 0 | 51 | 66 | 30 | 26 | 13 | 29 | R | R | 6-0 | 175 | 11-10-75 | 1993 | Riverside, Calif. |
| Atwater, Joe.................. | 7 | 1 | 0.93 | 11 | 10 | 0 | 0 | 58 | 44 | 9 | 6 | 6 | 44 | L | L | 6-3 | 155 | 2-12-75 | 1993 | Graham, N.C. |
| Bowman, Paul .............. | 2 | 3 | 5.02 | 10 | 2 | 0 | 4 | 29 | 28 | 19 | 16 | 18 | 18 | R | R | 6-4 | 180 | 3-27-73 | 1993 | Stubenville, Ohio |
| Coronado, Osvaldo........ | 3 | 3 | 5.36 | 12 | 6 | 0 | 1 | 44 | 54 | 26 | 26 | 20 | 19 | R | R | 6-2 | 156 | 12-30-73 | 1992 | Puerta Plata, D.R. |
| Grennan, Steve ............ | 0 | 0 | 0.00 | 1 | 1 | 0 | 0 | 4 | 1 | 1 | 0 | 1 | 3 | L | L | 5-10 | 165 | 7-3-70 | 1991 | Salina, Kan. |
| Kindell, Scott................ | 1 | 0 | 1.48 | 14 | 0 | 0 | 1 | 24 | 16 | 6 | 4 | 6 | 21 | L | L | 6-1 | 180 | 11-18-72 | 1990 | Fort Pierce, Fla. |
| Krablin, Justin .............. | 3 | 0 | 3.76 | 10 | 5 | 0 | 1 | 38 | 40 | 23 | 16 | 14 | 43 | R | R | 6-0 | 193 | 5-12-74 | 1992 | Hot Springs, Ark. |
| McEntire, Ethan ............ | 4 | 1 | 2.53 | 10 | 7 | 0 | 0 | 43 | 36 | 12 | 12 | 14 | 41 | L | L | 6-2 | 180 | 7-19-75 | 1993 | Clarkesville, Ga. |
| McGinn, Mark .............. | 1 | 1 | 5.06 | 9 | 1 | 0 | 0 | 16 | 10 | 11 | 9 | 16 | 9 | R | R | 6-0 | 168 | 4-4-74 | 1992 | Omaha, Neb. |
| Pack, Steve .................. | 5 | 3 | 4.19 | 12 | 11 | 0 | 0 | 58 | 52 | 34 | 27 | 18 | 41 | R | R | 6-4 | 180 | 8-6-73 | 1993 | Fallbrook, Calif. |
| Pena, Moises ................ | 1 | 2 | 2.83 | 18 | 0 | 0 | 2 | 41 | 32 | 22 | 13 | 16 | 40 | R | R | 6-3 | 170 | 9-2-74 | 1992 | Puerto Plata, D.R. |
| Quillin, Ty .................... | 3 | 1 | 2.70 | 17 | 0 | 0 | 6 | 27 | 18 | 8 | 8 | 15 | 27 | L | R | 6-4 | 210 | 1-23-72 | 1990 | Buhler, Kan. |
| Ramirez, Hector ............ | 1 | 0 | 0.00 | 1 | 1 | 0 | 0 | 7 | 5 | 1 | 0 | 1 | 6 | R | R | 200 | 12-15-72 | 1988 | El Seibo, D.R. |
| Spang, R.J................... | 1 | 0 | 2.70 | 4 | 2 | 0 | 1 | 10 | 9 | 3 | 3 | 1 | 2 | R | R | 6-1 | 170 | 10-19-74 | 1993 | Racine, Wis. |
| Vitko, Joe .................... | 0 | 0 | 0.00 | 1 | 1 | 0 | 0 | 3 | 1 | 0 | 0 | 1 | 2 | R | R | 6-8 | 210 | 2-2-70 | 1989 | Ebensburg, Pa. |
| Wolff, Tom ................... | 2 | 2 | 2.73 | 10 | 3 | 0 | 1 | 33 | 26 | 16 | 10 | 13 | 29 | R | R | 6-3 | 185 | 7-29-73 | 1993 | Hillsdale, Mich. |
| Young, Ty .................... | 3 | 3 | 3.34 | 17 | 0 | 0 | 3 | 35 | 38 | 13 | 16 | 18 | 18 | L | R | 6-4 | 190 | 6-11-73 | 1991 | Kountz, Texas |

# OAKLAND
## ATHLETICS

**Manager:** Tony La Russa.      **1993 Record:** 68-94, .420 (7th, AL West).

| BATTING | AVG | G | AB | R | H | 2B | 3B | HR | RBI | BB | SO | SB | CS | B | T | HT | WT | DOB | 1st Yr | Resides |
|---|---|---|---|---|---|---|---|---|---|---|---|---|---|---|---|---|---|---|---|---|
| Abbott, Kurt | .246 | 20 | 61 | 10 | 15 | 1 | 0 | 3 | 9 | 3 | 20 | 2 | 0 | R | R | 6-0 | 170 | 6-2-69 | 1989 | St. Petersburg, Fla. |
| Aldrete, Mike | .267 | 95 | 255 | 40 | 68 | 13 | 1 | 10 | 33 | 34 | 45 | 1 | 1 | L | L | 5-11 | 180 | 1-29-61 | 1983 | Monterey, Calif. |
| Armas, Marcos | .194 | 15 | 31 | 7 | 6 | 2 | 0 | 1 | 1 | 1 | 12 | 1 | 0 | R | R | 6-5 | 195 | 8-5-69 | 1988 | Puerto Piritu, Venez. |
| Blankenship, Lance | .190 | 94 | 252 | 43 | 48 | 8 | 1 | 2 | 23 | 67 | 64 | 13 | 5 | R | R | 6-0 | 180 | 12-3-63 | 1986 | Concord, Calif. |
| Bordick, Mike | .249 | 159 | 546 | 60 | 136 | 21 | 2 | 3 | 48 | 60 | 58 | 10 | 10 | R | R | 5-11 | 170 | 7-21-65 | 1986 | Winterport, Maine |
| Brosius, Scott | .249 | 70 | 213 | 26 | 53 | 10 | 1 | 6 | 25 | 14 | 37 | 6 | 0 | R | R | 6-1 | 190 | 8-15-66 | 1987 | McMinnville, Ore. |
| Browne, Jerry | .250 | 76 | 260 | 27 | 65 | 13 | 0 | 2 | 19 | 22 | 17 | 4 | 0 | S | R | 5-10 | 170 | 2-13-66 | 1983 | Arlington, Texas |
| Fox, Eric | .143 | 29 | 56 | 5 | 8 | 1 | 0 | 1 | 5 | 2 | 7 | 0 | 2 | S | L | 5-10 | 185 | 8-15-63 | 1986 | Paso Robles, Calif. |
| Gates, Brent | .290 | 139 | 535 | 64 | 155 | 29 | 2 | 7 | 69 | 56 | 75 | 7 | 3 | S | R | 6-1 | 180 | 3-14-70 | 1991 | Grandville, Mich. |
| Helfand, Eric | .231 | 8 | 13 | 1 | 3 | 0 | 0 | 1 | 0 | 1 | 0 | 0 | 1 | L | R | 6-0 | 210 | 3-25-69 | 1990 | San Diego, Calif. |
| Hemond, Scott | .256 | 91 | 215 | 31 | 55 | 16 | 0 | 6 | 26 | 32 | 55 | 14 | 5 | R | R | 6-0 | 215 | 11-18-65 | 1986 | Dunedin, Fla. |
| Henderson, Dave | .220 | 107 | 382 | 37 | 84 | 19 | 0 | 20 | 53 | 32 | 113 | 0 | 3 | R | R | 6-2 | 210 | 7-21-58 | 1977 | Bellevue, Wash. |
| Henderson, Rickey | .327 | 90 | 318 | 77 | 104 | 19 | 1 | 17 | 47 | 85 | 46 | 31 | 6 | R | L | 5-10 | 195 | 12-25-58 | 1976 | Oakland, Calif. |
| Lydy, Scott | .225 | 41 | 102 | 11 | 23 | 5 | 0 | 2 | 7 | 8 | 39 | 2 | 0 | R | R | 6-5 | 205 | 10-26-68 | 1989 | Mesa, Ariz. |
| McGwire, Mark | .333 | 27 | 84 | 16 | 28 | 6 | 0 | 9 | 24 | 21 | 19 | 0 | 1 | R | R | 6-5 | 225 | 10-1-63 | 1984 | Claremont, Calif. |
| Mercedes, Henry | .213 | 20 | 47 | 5 | 10 | 2 | 0 | 0 | 3 | 2 | 15 | 1 | 1 | R | R | 5-11 | 185 | 7-23-69 | 1988 | Santo Domingo, D.R. |
| Neel, Troy | .290 | 123 | 427 | 59 | 124 | 21 | 0 | 19 | 63 | 49 | 101 | 3 | 5 | L | R | 6-4 | 210 | 9-14-65 | 1986 | El Campo, Texas |
| Paquette, Craig | .219 | 105 | 393 | 35 | 86 | 20 | 4 | 12 | 46 | 14 | 108 | 4 | 2 | R | R | 6-0 | 190 | 3-28-69 | 1989 | Garden Grove, Calif. |
| Seitzer, Kevin | .255 | 73 | 255 | 24 | 65 | 10 | 2 | 4 | 27 | 27 | 33 | 4 | 7 | R | R | 5-11 | 190 | 3-26-62 | 1983 | Overland Park, Kan. |
| Sierra, Ruben | .233 | 158 | 630 | 77 | 147 | 23 | 5 | 22 | 101 | 52 | 97 | 25 | 5 | S | R | 6-1 | 200 | 10-6-65 | 1983 | Carolina, P.R. |
| Steinbach, Terry | .285 | 104 | 389 | 47 | 111 | 19 | 1 | 10 | 43 | 25 | 65 | 3 | 3 | R | R | 6-1 | 195 | 3-2-62 | 1983 | Plymouth, Minn. |
| Sveum, Dale | .177 | 30 | 79 | 12 | 14 | 2 | 1 | 2 | 6 | 16 | 21 | 0 | 0 | S | R | 6-3 | 185 | 11-23-63 | 1982 | Glendale, Ariz. |

| PITCHING | W | L | ERA | G | GS | CG | SV | IP | H | R | ER | BB | SO | B | T | HT | WT | DOB | 1st Yr | Resides |
|---|---|---|---|---|---|---|---|---|---|---|---|---|---|---|---|---|---|---|---|---|
| Boever, Joe | 4 | 2 | 3.86 | 42 | 0 | 0 | 0 | 79 | 87 | 40 | 34 | 33 | 49 | R | R | 6-1 | 200 | 10-4-60 | 1982 | Palm Harbor, Fla. |
| Briscoe, John | 1 | 0 | 8.03 | 17 | 0 | 0 | 0 | 25 | 26 | 25 | 22 | 26 | 24 | R | R | 6-3 | 195 | 9-22-67 | 1988 | Richardson, Texas |
| Campbell, Kevin | 0 | 0 | 7.31 | 11 | 0 | 0 | 0 | 16 | 20 | 13 | 13 | 11 | 9 | R | R | 6-4 | 225 | 12-6-64 | 1986 | Des Arc, Ark. |
| Darling, Ron | 5 | 9 | 5.16 | 31 | 29 | 3 | 0 | 178 | 198 | 107 | 102 | 72 | 95 | R | R | 6-3 | 195 | 8-19-60 | 1981 | New York, N.Y. |
| Davis, Storm | 2 | 6 | 6.18 | 19 | 8 | 0 | 0 | 63 | 68 | 45 | 43 | 33 | 37 | R | R | 6-4 | 225 | 12-26-61 | 1979 | Atlantic Beach, Fla. |
| Downs, Kelly | 5 | 10 | 5.64 | 42 | 12 | 0 | 0 | 120 | 135 | 80 | 75 | 60 | 66 | R | R | 6-4 | 205 | 10-25-60 | 1980 | Centerville, Utah |
| Eckersley, Dennis | 2 | 4 | 4.16 | 64 | 0 | 0 | 36 | 67 | 67 | 32 | 31 | 13 | 80 | R | R | 6-2 | 195 | 10-3-54 | 1972 | Sudbury, Mass. |
| Gossage, Goose | 4 | 5 | 4.53 | 39 | 0 | 0 | 1 | 48 | 49 | 24 | 24 | 26 | 40 | R | R | 6-3 | 225 | 7-5-51 | 1970 | Colorado Springs, Colo. |
| Hillegas, Shawn | 3 | 6 | 6.97 | 18 | 11 | 0 | 0 | 61 | 78 | 48 | 47 | 33 | 29 | R | R | 6-2 | 223 | 8-21-64 | 1984 | Phoenix, Ariz. |
| Honeycutt, Rick | 1 | 4 | 2.81 | 52 | 0 | 0 | 1 | 42 | 30 | 13 | 13 | 20 | 21 | L | L | 6-1 | 192 | 6-29-54 | 1976 | La Habra Heights, Calif. |
| Horsman, Vince | 2 | 0 | 5.40 | 40 | 0 | 0 | 0 | 25 | 25 | 15 | 15 | 15 | 17 | R | L | 6-2 | 175 | 3-9-67 | 1985 | Dartmouth, N.S. |
| Jimenez, Miguel | 1 | 0 | 4.00 | 5 | 4 | 0 | 0 | 27 | 27 | 12 | 12 | 16 | 13 | R | R | 6-2 | 205 | 8-19-69 | 1991 | New York, N.Y. |
| Karsay, Steve | 3 | 3 | 4.04 | 8 | 8 | 0 | 0 | 49 | 49 | 23 | 22 | 16 | 33 | R | R | 6-3 | 180 | 3-24-72 | 1990 | College Point, N.Y. |
| Mohler, Mike | 1 | 6 | 5.60 | 42 | 9 | 0 | 0 | 64 | 57 | 45 | 40 | 44 | 42 | R | L | 6-2 | 195 | 7-26-68 | 1990 | Gonzales, La. |
| Nunez, Edwin | 3 | 6 | 3.81 | 56 | 0 | 0 | 1 | 76 | 89 | 36 | 32 | 29 | 58 | R | R | 6-5 | 240 | 5-27-63 | 1979 | Tempe, Ariz. |
| Slusarski, Joe | 0 | 0 | 5.19 | 2 | 1 | 0 | 0 | 9 | 9 | 5 | 5 | 11 | 1 | R | R | 6-4 | 195 | 12-19-66 | 1989 | Springfield, Ill. |
| Smithberg, Roger | 1 | 2 | 2.75 | 13 | 0 | 0 | 3 | 20 | 13 | 7 | 6 | 7 | 4 | R | R | 6-3 | 210 | 3-21-66 | 1988 | Elgin, Ill. |
| Van Poppel, Todd | 6 | 6 | 5.04 | 16 | 16 | 0 | 0 | 84 | 76 | 50 | 47 | 62 | 47 | R | R | 6-5 | 210 | 12-9-71 | 1990 | Arlington, Texas |
| Welch, Bob | 9 | 11 | 5.29 | 30 | 28 | 0 | 0 | 167 | 208 | 102 | 98 | 56 | 63 | R | R | 6-3 | 190 | 11-3-56 | 1977 | Huntington Beach, Calif. |
| Witt, Bobby | 14 | 13 | 4.21 | 35 | 33 | 5 | 0 | 220 | 226 | 112 | 103 | 91 | 131 | R | R | 6-2 | 205 | 5-11-64 | 1985 | Colleyville, Texas |
| Young, Curt | 1 | 1 | 4.30 | 3 | 3 | 0 | 0 | 15 | 14 | 7 | 7 | 6 | 4 | R | L | 6-1 | 175 | 4-16-60 | 1981 | Saginaw, Mich. |

## FIELDING

| Catcher | PCT | G | PO | A | E | DP |
|---|---|---|---|---|---|---|
| Helfand | 1.000 | 5 | 25 | 5 | 0 | 1 |
| Hemond | .991 | 75 | 395 | 38 | 4 | 5 |
| Mercedes | .987 | 18 | 66 | 10 | 1 | 1 |
| Steinbach | .989 | 86 | 422 | 38 | 5 | 9 |

| First Base | PCT | G | PO | A | E | DP |
|---|---|---|---|---|---|---|
| Aldrete | .995 | 59 | 370 | 28 | 2 | 39 |
| Armas | 1.000 | 12 | 74 | 4 | 0 | 4 |
| Blankenship | 1.000 | 6 | 12 | 0 | 0 | 1 |
| Brosius | 1.000 | 11 | 68 | 2 | 0 | 7 |
| Browne | .909 | 2 | 8 | 2 | 1 | 3 |
| Hemond | 1.000 | 1 | 5 | 0 | 0 | 0 |
| McGwire | 1.000 | 25 | 197 | 14 | 0 | 20 |
| Neel | .981 | 34 | 236 | 22 | 5 | 25 |
| Seitzer | 1.000 | 24 | 168 | 17 | 0 | 24 |
| Steinbach | .982 | 15 | 102 | 9 | 2 | 9 |
| Sveum | .976 | 14 | 116 | 5 | 3 | 11 |

| Second Base | PCT | G | PO | A | E | DP |
|---|---|---|---|---|---|---|
| Abbott | .000 | 2 | 0 | 0 | 0 | 0 |

| | PCT | G | PO | A | E | DP |
|---|---|---|---|---|---|---|
| Blankenship | .957 | 19 | 32 | 56 | 4 | 13 |
| Bordick | 1.000 | 1 | 5 | 2 | 0 | 2 |
| Browne | 1.000 | 3 | 5 | 9 | 0 | 1 |
| Gates | .981 | 139 | 281 | 432 | 14 | 88 |
| Hemond | 1.000 | 1 | 2 | 1 | 0 | 1 |
| Seitzer | 1.000 | 2 | 2 | 6 | 0 | 1 |
| Sveum | 1.000 | 4 | 4 | 7 | 0 | 1 |

| Third Base | PCT | G | PO | A | E | DP |
|---|---|---|---|---|---|---|
| Brosius | 1.000 | 10 | 2 | 19 | 0 | 2 |
| Browne | .880 | 13 | 6 | 16 | 3 | 2 |
| Paquette | .950 | 104 | 81 | 165 | 13 | 17 |
| Seitzer | .933 | 46 | 31 | 66 | 7 | 6 |
| Sveum | 1.000 | 7 | 5 | 4 | 0 | 1 |

| Shortstop | PCT | G | PO | A | E | DP |
|---|---|---|---|---|---|---|
| Abbott | .938 | 6 | 3 | 12 | 1 | 2 |
| Blankenship | 1.000 | 2 | 1 | 8 | 0 | 1 |
| Bordick | .982 | 159 | 280 | 418 | 13 | 108 |
| Brosius | .857 | 6 | 0 | 6 | 1 | 2 |

| | PCT | G | PO | A | E | DP |
|---|---|---|---|---|---|---|
| Sveum | 1.000 | 1 | 3 | 1 | 0 | 0 |

| Outfield | PCT | G | PO | A | E | DP |
|---|---|---|---|---|---|---|
| Abbott | .971 | 13 | 33 | 1 | 1 | 0 |
| Aldrete | 1.000 | 20 | 37 | 0 | 0 | 0 |
| Armas | 1.000 | 1 | 3 | 0 | 0 | 0 |
| Blankenship | .994 | 66 | 162 | 1 | 1 | 0 |
| Brosius | .991 | 46 | 103 | 2 | 1 | 0 |
| Browne | .985 | 56 | 130 | 1 | 2 | 0 |
| Fox | 1.000 | 26 | 47 | 0 | 0 | 1 |
| Hemond | 1.000 | 6 | 2 | 0 | 0 | 0 |
| D. Henderson | .991 | 76 | 205 | 7 | 2 | 4 |
| R. Henderson | .974 | 74 | 182 | 5 | 5 | 1 |
| Lydy | .958 | 38 | 67 | 2 | 3 | 0 |
| Paquette | 1.000 | 1 | 1 | 0 | 0 | 0 |
| Seitzer | 1.000 | 3 | 4 | 0 | 0 | 0 |
| Sierra | .977 | 133 | 291 | 9 | 7 | 3 |
| Sveum | .000 | 1 | 0 | 0 | 0 | 0 |

MICHAEL PONZINI

FRANK RAGSDALE

**How Mighty Have Fallen.** American League West champions in 1992, Oakland finished last in 1993 despite the efforts of closer Dennis Eckersley (36 saves) and rookie second baseman Brent Gates (.290-7-69).

# ATHLETICS FARM SYSTEM

| Class | Club | League | W | L | Pct. | Finish* | Manager | First Year |
|-------|------|--------|---|---|------|---------|---------|-----------|
| AAA | Tacoma (Wash.) Tigers | Pacific Coast | 69 | 74 | .483 | 7th (10) | Bob Boone | 1981 |
| AA | Huntsville (Ala.) Stars | Southern | 71 | 70 | .504 | T-6th (10) | Casey Parsons | 1985 |
| A# | Modesto (Calif.) A's | California | 72 | 64 | .529 | 5th (10) | Ted Kubiak | 1975 |
| A | Madison (Wis.) Muskies | Midwest | 77 | 58 | .570 | 4th (14) | Gary Jones | 1982 |
| A | Southern Oregon A's | Northwest | 37 | 39 | .487 | 5th (8) | Dickie Scott | 1979 |
| Rookie | Scottsdale (Ariz.) Athletics | Arizona | 35 | 20 | .636 | 1st (8) | Bruce Hines | 1988 |

*Finish in overall standings (No. of teams in league)    #Advanced level

# TACOMA                                                                   AAA
## PACIFIC COAST LEAGUE

| BATTING | AVG | G | AB | R | H | 2B | 3B | HR | RBI | BB | SO | SB | CS | B | T | HT | WT | DOB | 1st Yr | Resides |
|---------|-----|---|----|----|----|----|----|----|-----|----|----|----|----|---|---|----|----|----|--------|---------|
| Abbott, Kurt | .319 | 133 | 480 | 75 | 153 | 36 | 11 | 12 | 79 | 33 | 123 | 19 | 9 | R | R | 6-0 | 170 | 6-2-69 | 1989 | St. Petersburg, Fla. |
| Aldrete, Mike | .320 | 37 | 122 | 20 | 39 | 11 | 2 | 7 | 21 | 26 | 22 | 2 | 2 | L | L | 5-11 | 180 | 1-29-61 | 1983 | Monterey, Calif. |
| Armas, Marcos | .290 | 117 | 434 | 69 | 126 | 27 | 8 | 15 | 89 | 35 | 113 | 4 | 0 | R | R | 6-5 | 195 | 8-5-69 | 1988 | Puerto Piritu, Venez. |
| Batista, Tony | .167 | 4 | 12 | 1 | 2 | 1 | 0 | 0 | 1 | 1 | 4 | 0 | 0 | R | R | 6-0 | 167 | 12-9-73 | 1992 | Mao Valverde, D.R. |
| Beard, Garrett | .143 | 19 | 49 | 3 | 7 | 4 | 0 | 0 | 2 | 4 | 8 | 1 | 1 | R | R | 6-1 | 190 | 2-1-69 | 1989 | Irwin, Pa. |
| Borrelli, Dean | .243 | 76 | 210 | 29 | 51 | 7 | 2 | 1 | 19 | 18 | 37 | 1 | 0 | R | R | 6-2 | 210 | 10-20-66 | 1988 | Salem, N.H. |
| Brosius, Scott | .297 | 56 | 209 | 38 | 62 | 13 | 2 | 8 | 41 | 21 | 50 | 8 | 5 | R | R | 6-1 | 190 | 8-15-66 | 1987 | McMinnville, Ore. |
| Browne, Jerry | .240 | 6 | 25 | 3 | 6 | 0 | 0 | 0 | 2 | 0 | 4 | 1 | 0 | S | R | 5-10 | 170 | 2-13-66 | 1983 | Arlington, Texas |
| Buccheri, Jim | .276 | 90 | 293 | 45 | 81 | 9 | 3 | 2 | 40 | 39 | 46 | 12 | 9 | R | R | 5-11 | 165 | 11-12-68 | 1988 | Fountain Valley, Calif. |
| Cruz, Fausto | .243 | 21 | 74 | 13 | 18 | 2 | 1 | 0 | 6 | 5 | 16 | 3 | 3 | R | R | 5-11 | 155 | 1-5-72 | 1990 | Villa Vasquez, D.R. |
| Dattola, Kevin | .193 | 25 | 57 | 6 | 11 | 1 | 0 | 0 | 2 | 4 | 12 | 1 | 1 | S | R | 6-2 | 180 | 11-23-67 | 1990 | La Grange, Ill. |
| Fox, Eric | .312 | 92 | 317 | 49 | 99 | 14 | 5 | 11 | 52 | 41 | 48 | 18 | 8 | S | L | 5-10 | 185 | 8-15-63 | 1986 | Paso Robles, Calif. |
| Garrison, Webster | .303 | 138 | 544 | 91 | 165 | 29 | 5 | 7 | 73 | 58 | 64 | 17 | 9 | R | R | 5-10 | 160 | 8-24-65 | 1984 | Marrero, La. |
| Gates, Brent | .341 | 12 | 44 | 7 | 15 | 7 | 0 | 1 | 4 | 4 | 6 | 2 | 0 | S | R | 6-1 | 180 | 3-14-70 | 1991 | Grandville, Mich. |
| Gomez, Fabio | .282 | 67 | 252 | 28 | 71 | 10 | 1 | 2 | 29 | 20 | 47 | 5 | 9 | R | R | 6-0 | 185 | 5-12-68 | 1987 | Tucson, Ariz. |
| Henderson, Dave | .182 | 3 | 11 | 1 | 2 | 1 | 0 | 0 | 2 | 0 | 2 | 0 | 0 | R | R | 6-2 | 210 | 7-21-58 | 1977 | Bellevue, Wash. |
| Killeen, Tim | .444 | 3 | 9 | 4 | 4 | 0 | 0 | 0 | 0 | 1 | 4 | 0 | 1 | L | R | 6-0 | 195 | 7-26-70 | 1992 | Phoenix, Ariz. |
| Lydy, Scott | .293 | 95 | 341 | 70 | 100 | 22 | 6 | 9 | 41 | 50 | 87 | 12 | 4 | R | R | 6-5 | 205 | 10-26-68 | 1989 | Mesa, Ariz. |
| Martinez, Manuel | .305 | 20 | 59 | 9 | 18 | 2 | 0 | 1 | 6 | 4 | 12 | 2 | 3 | R | R | 6-2 | 169 | 10-3-70 | 1988 | San Pedro de Macoris, D.R. |
| Mercedes, Henry | .238 | 85 | 256 | 37 | 61 | 13 | 1 | 4 | 32 | 31 | 53 | 1 | 2 | R | R | 5-11 | 185 | 7-23-69 | 1988 | Santo Domingo, D.R. |
| Morales, Willie | .000 | 2 | 3 | 0 | 0 | 0 | 0 | 0 | 0 | 1 | 1 | 0 | 0 | R | R | 5-10 | 182 | 9-7-72 | 1993 | Tucson, Ariz. |
| Neel, Troy | .360 | 13 | 50 | 11 | 18 | 4 | 0 | 1 | 9 | 6 | 9 | 2 | 1 | L | R | 6-4 | 210 | 9-14-65 | 1986 | El Campo, Texas |
| Paquette, Craig | .268 | 50 | 183 | 29 | 49 | 8 | 0 | 8 | 29 | 14 | 54 | 3 | 3 | R | R | 6-0 | 190 | 3-28-69 | 1989 | Garden Grove, Calif. |
| Pettis, Gary | .237 | 26 | 76 | 16 | 18 | 4 | 0 | 0 | 6 | 22 | 24 | 5 | 2 | S | R | 6-1 | 160 | 4-3-58 | 1979 | Laguna Hills, Calif. |
| Robbins, Doug | .226 | 57 | 164 | 23 | 37 | 9 | 1 | 3 | 18 | 20 | 37 | 1 | 0 | R | R | 6-1 | 210 | 7-6-66 | 1989 | Moraga, Calif. |
| Shockey, Scott | .254 | 21 | 71 | 2 | 18 | 5 | 0 | 1 | 12 | 8 | 17 | 1 | 0 | L | L | 6-2 | 230 | 7-4-67 | 1989 | Boise, Idaho |
| Soriano, Fred | .167 | 2 | 6 | 3 | 1 | 1 | 0 | 0 | 3 | 2 | 3 | 0 | 0 | R | R | 5-8 | 160 | 8-5-74 | 1992 | Bani, D.R. |

| BATTING | AVG | G | AB | R | H | 2B | 3B | HR | RBI | BB | SO | SB | CS | B | T | HT | WT | DOB | 1st Yr | Resides |
|---|---|---|---|---|---|---|---|---|---|---|---|---|---|---|---|---|---|---|---|---|
| Sveum, Dale | .349 | 12 | 43 | 10 | 15 | 1 | 0 | 2 | 6 | 6 | 7 | 2 | 1 | S | R | 6-3 | 185 | 11-23-63 | 1982 | Glendale, Ariz. |
| Witmyer, Ron | .254 | 132 | 452 | 52 | 115 | 22 | 4 | 3 | 52 | 57 | 96 | 7 | 3 | L | L | 6-3 | 215 | 6-28-67 | 1989 | West Bayshore, N.Y. |

| PITCHING | W | L | ERA | G | GS | CG | SV | IP | H | R | ER | BB | SO | B | T | HT | WT | DOB | 1st Yr | Resides |
|---|---|---|---|---|---|---|---|---|---|---|---|---|---|---|---|---|---|---|---|---|
| Allison, Dana | 3 | 3 | 4.48 | 23 | 5 | 0 | 0 | 62 | 75 | 35 | 31 | 19 | 30 | R | L | 6-3 | 210 | 8-14-66 | 1989 | Front Royal, Va. |
| Arnsberg, Brad | 3 | 2 | 7.48 | 21 | 0 | 0 | 1 | 28 | 31 | 25 | 23 | 21 | 12 | R | R | 6-4 | 210 | 8-20-63 | 1984 | Arlington, Texas |
| Briscoe, John | 1 | 1 | 2.92 | 9 | 0 | 0 | 6 | 12 | 13 | 5 | 4 | 9 | 16 | R | R | 6-3 | 195 | 9-22-67 | 1988 | Richardson, Texas |
| Campbell, Kevin | 3 | 5 | 2.75 | 40 | 0 | 0 | 12 | 56 | 42 | 19 | 17 | 19 | 46 | R | R | 6-4 | 225 | 12-6-64 | 1986 | Des Arc, Ark. |
| Chitren, Steve | 1 | 0 | 3.00 | 14 | 0 | 0 | 1 | 24 | 21 | 9 | 8 | 14 | 27 | R | R | 6-0 | 180 | 6-8-67 | 1989 | Las Vegas, Nev. |
| Guzman, Johnny | 2 | 7 | 7.32 | 20 | 16 | 0 | 0 | 87 | 130 | 87 | 71 | 44 | 50 | R | L | 5-10 | 150 | 1-21-71 | 1988 | Monte Christi, D.R. |
| Hillegas, Shawn | 2 | 3 | 5.48 | 9 | 9 | 0 | 0 | 48 | 62 | 31 | 29 | 13 | 29 | R | R | 6-2 | 223 | 8-21-64 | 1984 | Phoenix, Ariz. |
| Horsman, Vince | 1 | 2 | 4.28 | 26 | 0 | 0 | 3 | 34 | 37 | 25 | 16 | 9 | 23 | R | L | 6-2 | 175 | 3-9-67 | 1985 | Dartmouth, N.S. |
| Jimenez, Miguel | 2 | 3 | 4.78 | 8 | 8 | 0 | 0 | 38 | 32 | 23 | 20 | 24 | 34 | R | R | 6-2 | 205 | 8-19-69 | 1991 | New York, N.Y. |
| Osteen, Dave | 7 | 7 | 5.08 | 16 | 15 | 0 | 0 | 83 | 89 | 51 | 47 | 31 | 46 | R | L | 6-0 | 195 | 11-27-69 | 1989 | Bethany Beach, Del. |
| Patrick, Bronswell | 3 | 8 | 7.05 | 35 | 13 | 1 | 1 | 105 | 156 | 87 | 82 | 42 | 56 | R | R | 6-1 | 205 | 9-16-70 | 1988 | Greenville, N.C. |
| Peek, Tim | 9 | 6 | 3.95 | 60 | 0 | 0 | 5 | 87 | 103 | 46 | 38 | 28 | 63 | R | R | 6-2 | 195 | 1-23-68 | 1987 | Elkhart, Ind. |
| Phoenix, Steve | 0 | 2 | 6.97 | 11 | 5 | 0 | 0 | 31 | 42 | 27 | 24 | 27 | 21 | R | R | 6-3 | 183 | 1-31-68 | 1990 | El Cajon, Calif. |
| Raczka, Mike | 2 | 1 | 5.37 | 55 | 0 | 0 | 0 | 60 | 65 | 39 | 36 | 30 | 40 | L | L | 6-2 | 180 | 11-16-62 | 1984 | Southington, Conn. |
| Shikles, Larry | 7 | 7 | 4.49 | 38 | 21 | 1 | 2 | 148 | 179 | 85 | 74 | 34 | 68 | R | R | 5-10 | 175 | 7-13-63 | 1986 | Ballwin, Mo. |
| Slusarski, Joe | 7 | 5 | 4.76 | 24 | 21 | 1 | 0 | 113 | 133 | 67 | 60 | 40 | 61 | R | R | 6-4 | 195 | 12-19-66 | 1989 | Springfield, Ill. |
| Smith, Tim | 3 | 0 | 7.15 | 6 | 4 | 0 | 0 | 23 | 31 | 18 | 18 | 11 | 16 | R | R | 6-2 | 185 | 10-24-69 | 1991 | Westerville, Ohio |
| Smithberg, Roger | 3 | 3 | 1.78 | 28 | 0 | 0 | 4 | 51 | 50 | 14 | 10 | 11 | 25 | R | R | 6-3 | 210 | 3-21-66 | 1988 | Elgin, Ill. |
| Van Poppel, Todd | 4 | 8 | 5.83 | 16 | 16 | 0 | 0 | 79 | 67 | 53 | 51 | 54 | 71 | R | R | 6-5 | 210 | 12-9-71 | 1990 | Arlington, Texas |
| Young, Curt | 6 | 1 | 1.93 | 10 | 10 | 1 | 0 | 65 | 53 | 23 | 14 | 16 | 31 | R | L | 6-1 | 175 | 4-16-60 | 1981 | Saginaw, Mich. |

### FIELDING

| Catcher | PCT | G | PO | A | E | DP |
|---|---|---|---|---|---|---|
| Beard | .955 | 6 | 21 | 0 | 1 | 0 |
| Borrelli | .980 | 71 | 359 | 37 | 8 | 3 |
| Mercedes | .969 | 72 | 328 | 50 | 12 | 10 |
| Morales | 1.000 | 1 | 4 | 1 | 0 | 0 |
| Robbins | 1.000 | 22 | 87 | 8 | 0 | 1 |

| First Base | PCT | G | PO | A | E | DP |
|---|---|---|---|---|---|---|
| Aldrete | .970 | 4 | 30 | 2 | 1 | 5 |
| Armas | .983 | 67 | 537 | 32 | 10 | 53 |
| Beard | 1.000 | 3 | 14 | 1 | 0 | 3 |
| Borrelli | 1.000 | 1 | 6 | 1 | 0 | 1 |
| Brosius | .966 | 4 | 25 | 3 | 1 | 3 |
| Robbins | .976 | 5 | 39 | 1 | 1 | 2 |
| Shockey | .994 | 19 | 146 | 9 | 1 | 16 |
| Sveum | 1.000 | 1 | 5 | 0 | 0 | 0 |
| Witmyer | .991 | 62 | 404 | 30 | 4 | 35 |

| Second Base | PCT | G | PO | A | E | DP |
|---|---|---|---|---|---|---|
| Brosius | .923 | 8 | 31 | 17 | 4 | 4 |
| Browne | .778 | 1 | 3 | 4 | 2 | 2 |
| Buccheri | 1.000 | 3 | 1 | 0 | 0 | 0 |
| Cruz | .818 | 2 | 6 | 3 | 2 | 1 |

| | PCT | G | PO | A | E | DP |
|---|---|---|---|---|---|---|
| Garrison | .972 | 112 | 225 | 333 | 16 | 64 |
| Gates | .984 | 12 | 27 | 36 | 1 | 9 |
| Paquette | 1.000 | 1 | 1 | 1 | 0 | 1 |
| Sveum | 1.000 | 11 | 23 | 19 | 0 | 5 |

| Third Base | PCT | G | PO | A | E | DP |
|---|---|---|---|---|---|---|
| Armas | 1.000 | 4 | 0 | 10 | 0 | 0 |
| Beard | .900 | 9 | 3 | 15 | 2 | 1 |
| Brosius | .935 | 30 | 15 | 85 | 7 | 7 |
| Browne | 1.000 | 3 | 0 | 8 | 0 | 0 |
| Cruz | .976 | 12 | 18 | 22 | 1 | 5 |
| Garrison | .000 | 1 | 0 | 0 | 0 | 0 |
| Gomez | .872 | 32 | 26 | 49 | 11 | 3 |
| Mercedes | .813 | 13 | 2 | 24 | 6 | 6 |
| Paquette | .911 | 50 | 31 | 113 | 14 | 9 |

| Shortstop | PCT | G | PO | A | E | DP |
|---|---|---|---|---|---|---|
| Abbott | .951 | 129 | 210 | 367 | 30 | 76 |
| Batista | 1.000 | 4 | 6 | 9 | 0 | 2 |
| Brosius | 1.000 | 2 | 3 | 4 | 0 | 1 |
| Cruz | 1.000 | 6 | 9 | 18 | 0 | 4 |
| Garrison | 1.000 | 5 | 4 | 10 | 0 | 1 |

| | PCT | G | PO | A | E | DP |
|---|---|---|---|---|---|---|
| Paquette | .667 | 1 | 0 | 2 | 1 | 0 |
| Soriano | 1.000 | 2 | 3 | 5 | 0 | 0 |
| Sveum | 1.000 | 1 | 1 | 2 | 0 | 0 |

| Outfield | PCT | G | PO | A | E | DP |
|---|---|---|---|---|---|---|
| Aldrete | 1.000 | 23 | 45 | 3 | 0 | 2 |
| Armas | 1.000 | 2 | 1 | 0 | 0 | 0 |
| Brosius | .964 | 16 | 27 | 0 | 1 | 0 |
| Browne | 1.000 | 1 | 4 | 0 | 0 | 0 |
| Buccheri | .989 | 85 | 181 | 7 | 2 | 2 |
| Cruz | 1.000 | 1 | 1 | 0 | 0 | 0 |
| Dattola | .909 | 19 | 28 | 2 | 3 | 1 |
| Fox | .981 | 77 | 198 | 6 | 4 | 2 |
| Garrison | .973 | 21 | 34 | 2 | 1 | 1 |
| Gomez | .974 | 30 | 71 | 3 | 2 | 0 |
| Henderson | 1.000 | 3 | 7 | 0 | 0 | 0 |
| Lydy | .970 | 88 | 182 | 9 | 6 | 3 |
| Martinez | 1.000 | 19 | 33 | 6 | 0 | 1 |
| Mercedes | 1.000 | 1 | 2 | 0 | 0 | 0 |
| Pettis | .963 | 25 | 76 | 3 | 3 | 0 |
| Witmyer | .968 | 64 | 89 | 2 | 3 | 0 |

# HUNTSVILLE   AA
## SOUTHERN LEAGUE

| BATTING | AVG | G | AB | R | H | 2B | 3B | HR | RBI | BB | SO | SB | CS | B | T | HT | WT | DOB | 1st Yr | Resides |
|---|---|---|---|---|---|---|---|---|---|---|---|---|---|---|---|---|---|---|---|---|
| Beard, Garrett, 3b | .262 | 18 | 61 | 8 | 16 | 3 | 1 | 0 | 6 | 6 | 13 | 1 | 1 | R | R | 6-1 | 190 | 2-1-69 | 1989 | Irwin, Pa. |
| Bowie, Jim, 1b | .333 | 138 | 501 | 77 | 167 | 33 | 1 | 14 | 101 | 56 | 52 | 8 | 3 | L | L | 6-0 | 200 | 2-17-65 | 1986 | Suisun City, Calif. |
| Brito, Jorge, dh | .278 | 18 | 36 | 6 | 10 | 3 | 0 | 4 | 11 | 10 | 10 | 0 | 0 | R | R | 6-1 | 188 | 6-22-66 | 1986 | Huntsville, Ala. |
| Cruz, Fausto, ss-3b | .335 | 63 | 251 | 45 | 84 | 15 | 2 | 3 | 31 | 20 | 42 | 2 | 4 | R | R | 5-11 | 155 | 1-5-72 | 1990 | Villa Vasquez, D.R. |
| Dattola, Kevin, of | .253 | 91 | 296 | 43 | 75 | 17 | 1 | 10 | 32 | 32 | 70 | 12 | 6 | S | R | 6-2 | 180 | 11-23-67 | 1990 | La Grange, Ill. |
| Gates, Brent, 2b | .333 | 12 | 45 | 7 | 15 | 4 | 0 | 1 | 11 | 7 | 9 | 0 | 0 | S | R | 6-1 | 180 | 3-14-70 | 1991 | Grandville, Mich. |
| Gomez, Fabio, 3b-2b | .259 | 60 | 220 | 26 | 57 | 10 | 1 | 7 | 33 | 17 | 43 | 5 | 3 | R | R | 6-0 | 185 | 5-12-68 | 1987 | Tucson, Ariz. |
| Hart, Chris, of | .256 | 103 | 301 | 39 | 77 | 7 | 3 | 6 | 42 | 10 | 82 | 12 | 9 | R | R | 6-0 | 190 | 5-2-69 | 1990 | Harrisonburg, Va. |
| Helfand, Eric, c | .228 | 100 | 302 | 38 | 69 | 15 | 2 | 10 | 48 | 43 | 78 | 1 | 1 | L | R | 6-0 | 210 | 3-25-69 | 1990 | San Diego, Calif. |
| Johnson, Herman, dh | .333 | 2 | 3 | 0 | 1 | 0 | 0 | 0 | 0 | 0 | 2 | 1 | 0 | R | R | 6-2 | 209 | 8-11-69 | 1992 | DeSoto, Texas |
| Kuehl, John, dh-3b | .240 | 111 | 379 | 49 | 91 | 28 | 2 | 11 | 67 | 36 | 107 | 3 | 0 | S | R | 6-4 | 202 | 8-15-67 | 1988 | Fountain Hills, Ariz. |
| Mashore, Damon, of | .233 | 70 | 253 | 35 | 59 | 7 | 2 | 3 | 20 | 25 | 64 | 18 | 4 | S | R | 5-11 | 195 | 10-31-69 | 1991 | Concord, Calif. |
| Matos, Francisco, 2b | .275 | 123 | 461 | 69 | 127 | 12 | 3 | 1 | 32 | 22 | 54 | 16 | 6 | R | R | 6-1 | 160 | 4-8-70 | 1988 | Azua, D.R. |
| Neill, Mike, of | .246 | 54 | 179 | 30 | 44 | 8 | 0 | 1 | 15 | 34 | 45 | 3 | 4 | L | L | 6-2 | 189 | 4-27-70 | 1991 | Langhorne, Pa. |
| Simmons, Enoch, of | .229 | 43 | 140 | 24 | 32 | 7 | 0 | 3 | 20 | 17 | 39 | 5 | 2 | R | R | 6-4 | 215 | 9-28-67 | 1988 | Sunnymead, Calif. |
| Waggoner, Jim, 2b-3b | .140 | 57 | 129 | 12 | 18 | 3 | 0 | 1 | 8 | 29 | 38 | 2 | 2 | L | R | 5-11 | 185 | 4-17-67 | 1989 | Hermitage, Tenn. |
| Williams, George, c-of | .295 | 124 | 434 | 80 | 128 | 26 | 2 | 14 | 77 | 67 | 66 | 6 | 3 | S | R | 5-10 | 190 | 4-22-69 | 1991 | LaCrosse, Wis. |
| Wolfe, Joel, of | .299 | 36 | 134 | 20 | 40 | 6 | 0 | 3 | 18 | 13 | 24 | 6 | 3 | R | R | 6-2 | 205 | 6-18-70 | 1991 | Northridge, Calif. |
| Wood, Jason, ss | .230 | 103 | 370 | 44 | 85 | 21 | 2 | 5 | 36 | 33 | 97 | 2 | 4 | R | R | 6-1 | 170 | 12-16-69 | 1991 | Fresno, Calif. |
| Young, Ernie, of | .208 | 45 | 120 | 26 | 25 | 5 | 3 | 5 | 16 | 20 | 36 | 5 | 5 | R | R | 6-1 | 190 | 7-8-69 | 1990 | Chicago, Ill. |

| PITCHING | W | L | ERA | G | GS | CG | SV | IP | H | R | ER | BB | SO | B | T | HT | WT | DOB | 1st Yr | Resides |
|---|---|---|---|---|---|---|---|---|---|---|---|---|---|---|---|---|---|---|---|---|
| Acre, Mark | 1 | 1 | 2.42 | 19 | 0 | 0 | 10 | 22 | 22 | 10 | 6 | 3 | 21 | R | R | 6-8 | 230 | 9-16-68 | 1991 | Corning, Calif. |
| Allison, Dana | 2 | 3 | 1.80 | 19 | 0 | 0 | 0 | 40 | 40 | 9 | 8 | 4 | 18 | R | L | 6-3 | 210 | 8-14-66 | 1989 | Front Royal, Va. |
| Baker, Scott | 10 | 4 | 4.14 | 25 | 25 | 1 | 0 | 130 | 141 | 73 | 60 | 84 | 97 | L | L | 6-3 | 210 | 5-18-70 | 1990 | Henderson, Nev. |
| Briscoe, John | 4 | 0 | 3.03 | 30 | 0 | 0 | 16 | 39 | 28 | 14 | 13 | 16 | 62 | R | R | 6-3 | 195 | 9-22-67 | 1988 | Richardson, Texas |
| Chitren, Steve | 2 | 1 | 5.17 | 32 | 0 | 0 | 1 | 56 | 53 | 38 | 32 | 35 | 39 | R | R | 6-0 | 180 | 6-8-67 | 1989 | Las Vegas, Nev. |
| Connolly, Craig | 1 | 1 | 5.59 | 20 | 0 | 0 | 1 | 37 | 37 | 23 | 23 | 12 | 13 | R | R | 6-1 | 195 | 2-16-68 | 1990 | Ridgeland, S.C. |
| Garland, Chaon | 3 | 3 | 7.26 | 23 | 3 | 0 | 0 | 48 | 58 | 40 | 39 | 35 | 37 | R | R | 6-5 | 190 | 10-29-69 | 1990 | Odessa, Fla. |
| Jimenez, Miguel | 10 | 6 | 2.94 | 20 | 19 | 0 | 0 | 107 | 92 | 49 | 35 | 64 | 105 | R | R | 6-2 | 205 | 8-19-69 | 1991 | New York, N.Y. |
| Johns, Doug | 7 | 5 | 2.97 | 40 | 6 | 0 | 1 | 91 | 82 | 41 | 30 | 22 | 53 | R | L | 6-2 | 185 | 12-19-67 | 1990 | Plantation, Fla. |
| Karsay, Steve | 0 | 0 | 5.14 | 2 | 2 | 0 | 0 | 14 | 13 | 8 | 8 | 3 | 22 | R | R | 6-3 | 180 | 3-24-72 | 1991 | College Point, N.Y. |
|   2-team (19 Knoxville) | 8 | 4 | 3.58 | 21 | 20 | 1 | 0 | 118 | 111 | 50 | 47 | 35 | 122 | | | | | | | |

| PITCHING | W | L | ERA | G | GS | CG | SV | IP | H | R | ER | BB | SO | B | T | HT | WT | DOB | 1st Yr | Resides |
|---|---|---|---|---|---|---|---|---|---|---|---|---|---|---|---|---|---|---|---|---|
| Latter, Dave | 0 | 0 | 15.00 | 6 | 0 | 0 | 0 | 9 | 19 | 15 | 15 | 7 | 5 | R | R | 6-3 | 195 | 10-14-66 | 1989 | Shorewood, Minn. |
| Osteen, Gavin | 7 | 3 | 2.30 | 11 | 11 | 2 | 0 | 70 | 56 | 21 | 18 | 25 | 46 | R | L | 6-0 | 195 | 11-27-69 | 1989 | Bethany Beach, Del. |
| Phoenix, Steve | 2 | 2 | 1.40 | 11 | 0 | 0 | 1 | 19 | 13 | 5 | 3 | 5 | 15 | R | R | 6-3 | 183 | 1-31-68 | 1990 | El Cajon, Calif. |
| Shaw, Curtis | 6 | 16 | 4.93 | 28 | 28 | 2 | 0 | 152 | 141 | 98 | 83 | 89 | 132 | L | L | 6-2 | 190 | 8-16-69 | 1990 | Bartlesville, Okla. |
| Smith, Tim | 1 | 3 | 3.35 | 9 | 6 | 1 | 0 | 43 | 46 | 22 | 16 | 18 | 31 | R | R | 6-2 | 185 | 10-24-69 | 1991 | Westerville, Ohio |
| Smithberg, Roger | 4 | 2 | 2.21 | 27 | 0 | 0 | 0 | 37 | 34 | 15 | 9 | 16 | 36 | R | R | 6-3 | 210 | 3-21-66 | 1988 | Elgin, Ill. |
| Strebeck, Rick | 2 | 2 | 5.18 | 23 | 0 | 0 | 0 | 49 | 54 | 38 | 28 | 22 | 29 | R | R | 6-4 | 215 | 9-16-66 | 1989 | Houston, Texas |
| Sturtze, Tanyon | 5 | 12 | 4.78 | 28 | 28 | 1 | 0 | 166 | 169 | 102 | 88 | 85 | 112 | R | R | 6-5 | 190 | 10-12-70 | 1990 | Worcester, Mass. |
| Wojciechowski, Steve | 4 | 6 | 5.32 | 13 | 13 | 1 | 0 | 68 | 91 | 50 | 40 | 30 | 52 | L | L | 6-2 | 185 | 7-29-70 | 1991 | Calumet City, Ill. |

# MODESTO    A
## CALIFORNIA LEAGUE

| BATTING | AVG | G | AB | R | H | 2B | 3B | HR | RBI | BB | SO | SB | CS | B | T | HT | WT | DOB | 1st Yr | Resides |
|---|---|---|---|---|---|---|---|---|---|---|---|---|---|---|---|---|---|---|---|---|
| Barns, Jeff, 1b-3b | .308 | 53 | 143 | 17 | 44 | 8 | 0 | 0 | 14 | 24 | 9 | 1 | 1 | S | R | 6-0 | 185 | 11-18-63 | 1987 | Fairview, Pa. |
| Beard, Garrett, 1b | .268 | 83 | 284 | 46 | 76 | 17 | 2 | 6 | 33 | 63 | 55 | 3 | 2 | R | R | 6-1 | 190 | 2-1-69 | 1989 | Irwin, Pa. |
| Buccheri, Jim, of | .286 | 2 | 7 | 3 | 2 | 0 | 0 | 0 | 1 | 2 | 0 | 0 | | R | R | 5-11 | 165 | 11-12-68 | 1988 | Fountain Valley, Calif. |
| Cruz, Fausto, ss | .236 | 43 | 165 | 21 | 39 | 3 | 0 | 1 | 20 | 25 | 34 | 6 | 4 | R | R | 5-11 | 155 | 1-5-72 | 1990 | Villa Vasquez, D.R. |
| Felix, Lauro, ss | .205 | 102 | 302 | 55 | 62 | 6 | 2 | 2 | 35 | 69 | 70 | 7 | 4 | R | R | 5-9 | 150 | 6-24-70 | 1992 | El Paso, Texas |
| Frazier, Terance, of | .276 | 96 | 340 | 48 | 94 | 9 | 2 | 0 | 29 | 25 | 57 | 22 | 8 | R | R | 5-10 | 196 | 12-20-68 | 1992 | Oakland, Calif. |
| Giambi, Jason, 3b | .291 | 89 | 313 | 72 | 91 | 16 | 2 | 12 | 60 | 73 | 47 | 2 | 3 | L | R | 6-2 | 200 | 1-8-71 | 1992 | Covina, Calif. |
| Johnson, Herman, c | .000 | 5 | 6 | 1 | 0 | 0 | 0 | 0 | 1 | 1 | 2 | 0 | 0 | R | R | 6-0 | 209 | 8-11-69 | 1992 | DeSoto, Texas |
| Molina, Izzy, c | .261 | 125 | 444 | 61 | 116 | 26 | 5 | 6 | 69 | 44 | 85 | 2 | 8 | R | R | 6-0 | 200 | 6-3-71 | 1990 | Miami, Fla. |
| Neill, Mike, of | .194 | 17 | 62 | 4 | 12 | 3 | 0 | 0 | 4 | 12 | 12 | 0 | 1 | L | L | 6-2 | 189 | 4-27-70 | 1991 | Langhorne, Pa. |
| Norton, Rick, c-1b | .200 | 44 | 120 | 14 | 24 | 0 | 0 | 1 | 9 | 20 | 37 | 1 | 2 | L | R | 6-1 | 195 | 12-24-68 | 1991 | Lexington, Ky. |
| Ramirez, Roberto, of | .257 | 41 | 140 | 17 | 36 | 8 | 0 | 3 | 14 | 17 | 36 | 2 | 5 | R | R | 6-2 | 180 | 3-18-70 | 1989 | Tempe, Ariz. |
| Salvador, Felix, 3b-ss | .125 | 11 | 16 | 2 | 2 | 1 | 0 | 0 | 0 | 1 | 4 | 0 | 0 | R | R | 5-10 | 145 | 2-21-73 | 1992 | Puerto Plata, D.R. |
| Shockey, Scott, dh-1b | .303 | 97 | 350 | 62 | 106 | 20 | 1 | 20 | 87 | 64 | 70 | 1 | 1 | L | L | 6-2 | 230 | 7-4-67 | 1989 | Boise, Idaho |
| Simmons, Enoch, of-dh | .209 | 26 | 86 | 12 | 18 | 2 | 0 | 2 | 14 | 17 | 16 | 2 | 2 | R | R | 6-4 | 215 | 9-28-67 | 1988 | Sunnymead, Calif. |
| Sobolewski, Mark, 2b | .229 | 130 | 507 | 66 | 116 | 23 | 3 | 5 | 60 | 42 | 100 | 1 | 0 | R | R | 5-11 | 185 | 2-10-70 | 1992 | Southington, Conn. |
| Soriano, Fred, ss | .250 | 11 | 40 | 6 | 10 | 2 | 1 | 0 | 5 | 1 | 12 | 1 | 0 | R | R | 5-8 | 160 | 8-5-74 | 1992 | Bani, D.R. |
| Spiezio, Scott, 3b-1b | .255 | 32 | 110 | 12 | 28 | 9 | 1 | 1 | 13 | 23 | 19 | 1 | 5 | S | R | 6-2 | 195 | 9-21-72 | 1993 | Morris, Ill. |
| Walker, Dane, of | .296 | 122 | 443 | 94 | 131 | 22 | 1 | 9 | 67 | 94 | 55 | 16 | 16 | L | R | 5-10 | 180 | 11-16-69 | 1991 | Lake Oswego, Ore. |
| Wolfe, Joel, of | .350 | 87 | 300 | 54 | 105 | 29 | 1 | 6 | 56 | 51 | 42 | 18 | 14 | R | R | 6-3 | 205 | 6-18-70 | 1991 | Northridge, Calif. |
| Young, Ernie, of | .306 | 85 | 301 | 83 | 92 | 18 | 6 | 23 | 71 | 72 | 92 | 23 | 7 | R | R | 6-1 | 190 | 7-8-69 | 1990 | Chicago, Ill. |

| PITCHING | W | L | ERA | G | GS | CG | SV | IP | H | R | ER | BB | SO | B | T | HT | WT | DOB | 1st Yr | Resides |
|---|---|---|---|---|---|---|---|---|---|---|---|---|---|---|---|---|---|---|---|---|
| Brock, Russ | 12 | 4 | 3.81 | 27 | 26 | 1 | 0 | 139 | 137 | 69 | 59 | 44 | 121 | R | R | 6-5 | 210 | 10-13-69 | 1991 | Lockland, Ohio |
| Chouinard, Bobby | 8 | 10 | 4.26 | 24 | 24 | 1 | 0 | 146 | 154 | 75 | 69 | 56 | 82 | R | R | 6-1 | 188 | 5-1-72 | 1990 | Forest Grove, Ore. |
| Connolly, Craig | 5 | 0 | 3.60 | 22 | 1 | 0 | 0 | 55 | 45 | 22 | 22 | 22 | 45 | R | R | 6-3 | 215 | 2-16-68 | 1990 | Ridgeland, S.C. |
| Dressendorfer, Kirk | 0 | 0 | 3.97 | 5 | 5 | 0 | 0 | 11 | 14 | 5 | 5 | 5 | 15 | R | R | 5-11 | 180 | 4-8-69 | 1990 | Pearland, Texas |
| Fermin, Ramon | 4 | 6 | 6.15 | 31 | 5 | 0 | 1 | 67 | 78 | 56 | 46 | 37 | 47 | R | R | 6-3 | 180 | 11-25-72 | 1990 | San Fran. de Macoris, D.R. |
| Grigsby, Benji | 5 | 6 | 4.78 | 39 | 10 | 0 | 6 | 90 | 90 | 49 | 48 | 42 | 72 | R | R | 6-1 | 190 | 12-2-70 | 1992 | Lafayette, La. |
| Haught, Gary | 0 | 1 | 5.09 | 12 | 0 | 0 | 0 | 23 | 25 | 14 | 13 | 17 | 15 | S | R | 6-1 | 180 | 9-29-70 | 1992 | Choctaw, Okla. |
| Ingram, Todd | 5 | 7 | 5.48 | 32 | 0 | 0 | 9 | 43 | 49 | 30 | 26 | 18 | 39 | R | R | 6-4 | 200 | 4-1-68 | 1991 | Bellevue, Wash. |
| Mejia, Delfino | 1 | 1 | 6.35 | 12 | 0 | 0 | 0 | 23 | 30 | 18 | 16 | 14 | 18 | R | R | 5-9 | 150 | 12-24-71 | 1989 | Los Arroces, D.R. |
| Myers, Tom | 5 | 1 | 3.72 | 44 | 0 | 0 | 3 | 58 | 55 | 30 | 24 | 40 | 43 | L | L | 5-11 | 175 | 8-12-69 | 1991 | San Jose, Calif. |
| Pierce, Rob | 1 | 1 | 1.87 | 36 | 0 | 0 | 14 | 53 | 41 | 11 | 11 | 28 | 44 | R | R | 6-2 | 200 | 12-17-70 | 1991 | Mapleton, Utah |
| Plaster, Allen | 4 | 4 | 4.70 | 21 | 18 | 0 | 0 | 96 | 89 | 55 | 50 | 61 | 89 | R | R | 6-3 | 210 | 8-13-70 | 1991 | Kernersville, N.C. |
| Rossiter, Mike | 8 | 6 | 4.34 | 20 | 17 | 2 | 0 | 112 | 120 | 62 | 54 | 45 | 96 | R | R | 6-6 | 217 | 6-20-73 | 1991 | Burbank, Calif. |
| Smock, Greg | 0 | 0 | 5.11 | 7 | 0 | 0 | 0 | 12 | 7 | 10 | 7 | 7 | 14 | L | L | 6-2 | 185 | 10-9-70 | 1991 | Abingdon, Ill. |
| Strebeck, Ricky | 1 | 0 | 3.86 | 11 | 0 | 0 | 6 | 14 | 11 | 6 | 6 | 11 | 12 | R | R | 6-4 | 215 | 9-16-66 | 1989 | Houston, Texas |
| Sudbury, Craig | 2 | 6 | 8.27 | 42 | 1 | 0 | 4 | 70 | 105 | 74 | 64 | 50 | 39 | R | R | 6-6 | 235 | 5-18-68 | 1990 | Salt Lake City, Utah |
| Wasdin, John | 0 | 3 | 3.86 | 3 | 3 | 0 | 0 | 16 | 17 | 9 | 7 | 4 | 11 | R | R | 6-2 | 195 | 8-5-72 | 1993 | Tallahassee, Fla. |
| Wengert, Don | 3 | 6 | 4.73 | 12 | 12 | 0 | 0 | 70 | 75 | 42 | 37 | 29 | 43 | R | R | 6-3 | 205 | 11-6-69 | 1992 | Sioux City, Iowa |

# ATHLETICS: ORGANIZATION LEADERS

## MAJOR LEAGUERS

**BATTING**

| | | |
|---|---|---|
| *AVG | Rickey Henderson | .327 |
| R | Two tied at | 77 |
| H | Brent Gates | 155 |
| TB | Ruben Sierra | 246 |
| 2B | Brent Gates | 29 |
| 3B | Ruben Sierra | 5 |
| HR | Ruben Sierra | 22 |
| RBI | Ruben Sierra | 101 |
| BB | Rickey Henderson | 85 |
| SO | Dave Henderson | 113 |
| SB | Rickey Henderson | 31 |

**PITCHING**

| | | |
|---|---|---|
| W | Bobby Witt | 14 |
| L | Bobby Witt | 13 |
| #ERA | Edwin Nunez | 3.81 |
| G | Dennis Eckersley | 64 |
| CG | Bobby Witt | 5 |
| SV | Dennis Eckersley | 36 |
| IP | Bobby Witt | 220 |
| BB | Bobby Witt | 91 |
| SO | Bobby Witt | 131 |

**Ruben Sierra**
22 homers, 101 RBIs

MEL BAILEY

## MINOR LEAGUERS

**BATTING**

| | | |
|---|---|---|
| *AVG | Joel Wolfe, Modesto-Huntsville | .334 |
| R | Ernie Young, Modesto-Huntsville | 109 |
| H | Jim Bowie, Huntsville | 167 |
| TB | Kurt Abbott, Tacoma | 247 |
| 2B | Kurt Abbott, Tacoma | 36 |
| 3B | Kurt Abbott, Tacoma | 11 |
| HR | Ernie Young, Modesto-Huntsville | 28 |
| RBI | Jim Bowie, Huntsville | 101 |
| BB | Ernie Young, Modesto-Huntsville | 96 |
| SO | Gary Hust, Madison | 141 |
| SB | Ernie Young, Modesto-Huntsville | 31 |

**PITCHING**

| | | |
|---|---|---|
| W | Gavin Osteen, Tacoma-Huntsville | 14 |
| L | Curtis Shaw, Huntsville | 16 |
| #ERA | Roger Smithberg, Tacoma-Huntsville | 1.96 |
| G | Tim Peek, Tacoma | 60 |
| CG | Seven tied at | 2 |
| SV | Mark Acre, Madison-Huntsville | 30 |
| IP | Tanyon Sturtze, Huntsville | 166 |
| BB | Cliff Foster, Madison | 92 |
| SO | Cliff Foster, Madison | 146 |

*Minimum 250 At-Bats   #Minimum 75 Innings

# ATHLETICS: MOST COMMON LINEUPS

| | Oakland<br>Majors | Tacoma<br>AAA | Huntsville<br>AA | Modesto<br>A | Madison<br>A |
|---|---|---|---|---|---|
| C | Terry Steinbach (86) | Henry Mercedes (72) | Eric Helfand (93) | Izzy Molina (118) | Creighton Gubanich (86) |
| 1B | Mike Aldrete (59) | Marcos Armas (67) | Jim Bowie (136) | Garrett Beard (71) | Jason White (116) |
| 2B | Brent Gates (139) | Webster Garrison (112) | Francisco Matos (113) | Mark Sobolewski (128) | Jose Guillen (81) |
| 3B | Craig Paquette (104) | Craig Paquette (50) | Fabio Gomez (52) | Jason Giambi (88) | Scott Sheldon (119) |
| SS | Mike Bordick (159) | Kurt Abbott (129) | Jason Wood (99) | Lauro Felix (83) | Vincente Francisco (114) |
| OF | Ruben Sierra (133) | Jim Buccheri (91) | Chris Hart (97) | Dane Walker (107) | David Francisco (129) |
| | Dave Henderson (76) | Scott Lydy (89) | Kevin Dattola (82) | Ernie Young (84) | Brian Lesher (117) |
| | Rickey Henderson (74) | Eric Fox (81) | Damon Mashore (68) | Joel Wolfe (78) | Gary Hust (111) |
| DH | Troy Neel (85) | Marcos Armas (43) | John Kuehl (65) | Scott Shockey (61) | Troy Penix (64) |
| SP | Bobby Witt (33) | Shikles/Slusarski (21) | Shaw/Sturtze (28) | Russ Brock (26) | Foster/Hollins (26) |
| RP | Dennis Eckersley (64) | Tim Peek (60) | Doug Johns (34) | Tom Myers (44) | Jim Banks (44) |
| | Full-season farm clubs only | No. of games at position in parenthesis | | | |

| PITCHING | W | L | ERA | G | GS | CG | SV | IP | H | R | ER | BB | SO | B | T | HT | WT | DOB | 1st Yr | Resides |
|---|---|---|---|---|---|---|---|---|---|---|---|---|---|---|---|---|---|---|---|---|
| Wojciechowski, Steve | 8 | 2 | 2.55 | 14 | 14 | 1 | 0 | 85 | 64 | 29 | 24 | 36 | 52 | L | L | 6-2 | 185 | 7-29-70 | 1991 | Calumet City, Ill. |

# MADISON     A
## MIDWEST LEAGUE

| BATTING | AVG | G | AB | R | H | 2B | 3B | HR | RBI | BB | SO | SB | CS | B | T | HT | WT | DOB | 1st Yr | Resides |
|---|---|---|---|---|---|---|---|---|---|---|---|---|---|---|---|---|---|---|---|---|
| Aracena, Luinis, of-dh | .270 | 42 | 89 | 7 | 24 | 3 | 0 | 0 | 6 | 5 | 20 | 2 | 3 | R | R | 6-0 | 165 | 5-8-70 | 1990 | Mao, D.R. |
| Cromer, D.T., of-1b | .262 | 98 | 321 | 37 | 84 | 20 | 4 | 4 | 41 | 22 | 72 | 8 | 6 | L | L | 6-2 | 195 | 3-19-71 | 1992 | Lexington, S.C. |
| Eldridge, Brian, 2b-3b | .245 | 85 | 253 | 37 | 62 | 12 | 1 | 1 | 22 | 27 | 48 | 5 | 4 | R | R | 5-10 | 180 | 3-5-70 | 1992 | North Hills, Calif. |
| Francisco, David, of | .277 | 129 | 484 | 87 | 134 | 24 | 8 | 2 | 50 | 50 | 108 | 27 | 16 | R | R | 6-0 | 165 | 2-27-72 | 1991 | Santiago, D.R. |
| Francisco, Vincente, ss | .249 | 116 | 325 | 36 | 81 | 10 | 4 | 0 | 29 | 21 | 61 | 4 | 4 | S | R | 6-2 | 150 | 7-5-72 | 1990 | Mao Valverde, D.R. |
| Gubanich, Creighton, c | .268 | 119 | 373 | 65 | 100 | 19 | 2 | 19 | 78 | 63 | 105 | 3 | 3 | R | R | 6-3 | 190 | 3-27-72 | 1991 | Phoenixville, Pa. |
| Guillen, Jose, 2b-ss | .268 | 104 | 332 | 44 | 89 | 17 | 4 | 0 | 25 | 52 | 69 | 16 | 11 | S | R | 5-11 | 150 | 6-1-73 | 1991 | Santo Domingo, D.R. |
| Herrera, Jose, of | .214 | 4 | 14 | 1 | 3 | 0 | 0 | 0 | 0 | 0 | 6 | 1 | 1 | L | L | 6-0 | 164 | 8-30-72 | 1991 | Santo Domingo, D.R. |
| Hust, Gary, of | .223 | 118 | 364 | 52 | 81 | 20 | 2 | 14 | 54 | 51 | 141 | 7 | 4 | R | R | 6-4 | 205 | 3-15-72 | 1990 | Petal, Miss. |
| Killeen, Tim, c | .202 | 76 | 243 | 33 | 49 | 15 | 0 | 10 | 36 | 39 | 70 | 0 | 0 | L | R | 6-0 | 195 | 7-26-70 | 1992 | Phoenix, Ariz. |
| Leary, Rob, 1b | .143 | 8 | 28 | 2 | 4 | 0 | 0 | 0 | 2 | 10 | 0 | 0 | 1 | L | L | 6-3 | 195 | 7-9-71 | 1992 | Floral Park, N.Y. |
| Lesher, Brian, of | .274 | 119 | 394 | 63 | 108 | 13 | 5 | 5 | 47 | 46 | 102 | 20 | 9 | R | L | 6-5 | 205 | 3-5-71 | 1992 | Newark, Del. |
| Moore, Mark, c | .158 | 12 | 19 | 0 | 3 | 1 | 0 | 0 | 5 | 2 | 4 | 0 | 0 | R | R | 6-2 | 205 | 7-22-70 | 1992 | Overland Park, Kan. |
| Penix, Troy, dh | .254 | 66 | 236 | 35 | 60 | 10 | 3 | 10 | 45 | 20 | 39 | 1 | 1 | L | L | 6-4 | 230 | 8-25-71 | 1992 | Stockton, Calif. |
| Ramirez, Roberto, of-dh | .309 | 14 | 55 | 9 | 17 | 4 | 0 | 1 | 7 | 3 | 10 | 2 | 2 | R | R | 6-2 | 180 | 3-18-70 | 1989 | Tempe, Ariz. |
| Sheldon, Scott, 3b-ss | .213 | 131 | 428 | 67 | 91 | 22 | 1 | 8 | 67 | 49 | 121 | 8 | 7 | R | R | 6-3 | 185 | 11-28-68 | 1991 | Houston, Texas |
| White, Jason, 1b | .267 | 119 | 382 | 61 | 102 | 24 | 0 | 14 | 55 | 36 | 100 | 1 | 4 | R | L | 6-2 | 200 | 2-26-70 | 1992 | Midwest City, Okla. |

| PITCHING | W | L | ERA | G | GS | CG | SV | IP | H | R | ER | BB | SO | B | T | HT | WT | DOB | 1st Yr | Resides |
|---|---|---|---|---|---|---|---|---|---|---|---|---|---|---|---|---|---|---|---|---|
| Acre, Mark | 0 | 0 | 0.29 | 28 | 0 | 0 | 20 | 31 | 9 | 1 | 1 | 13 | 41 | R | R | 6-8 | 230 | 9-16-68 | 1991 | Corning, Calif. |
| Adams, Willie | 0 | 2 | 3.38 | 5 | 5 | 0 | 0 | 19 | 21 | 10 | 7 | 8 | 22 | R | R | 6-7 | 215 | 10-8-72 | 1993 | La Mirada, Calif. |
| Banks, Jim | 4 | 1 | 2.62 | 44 | 0 | 0 | 4 | 55 | 39 | 24 | 16 | 46 | 66 | R | R | 6-0 | 200 | 1-3-70 | 1992 | Olive Branch, Miss. |
| Belliard, Carlos | 5 | 3 | 3.63 | 26 | 11 | 0 | 0 | 87 | 81 | 44 | 35 | 54 | 64 | L | L | 6-1 | 150 | 11-4-72 | 1991 | Monte Christi, D.R. |
| Bennett, Bob | 7 | 8 | 3.28 | 26 | 17 | 0 | 1 | 107 | 103 | 63 | 39 | 23 | 102 | R | R | 6-4 | 205 | 12-30-70 | 1992 | Rapid City, S.D. |
| Bojan, Tim | 8 | 5 | 3.70 | 43 | 5 | 0 | 2 | 92 | 78 | 45 | 38 | 43 | 78 | R | R | 6-3 | 195 | 5-28-70 | 1992 | New Lenox, Ill. |
| Foster, Cliff | 10 | 8 | 3.14 | 26 | 26 | 1 | 0 | 140 | 106 | 62 | 49 | 92 | 64 | R | R | 6-0 | 182 | 12-24-71 | 1992 | Texarkana, Texas |
| Gienger, Craig | 0 | 1 | 2.54 | 15 | 0 | 0 | 0 | 28 | 28 | 10 | 8 | 10 | 20 | R | R | 6-3 | 215 | 4-25-70 | 1992 | Castle Rock, Colo. |
| Haught, Gary | 7 | 1 | 2.58 | 17 | 12 | 2 | 0 | 84 | 62 | 27 | 24 | 29 | 75 | S | R | 6-1 | 180 | 9-29-70 | 1992 | Choctaw, Okla. |
| Hollins, Stacy | 10 | 11 | 5.14 | 26 | 26 | 2 | 0 | 151 | 145 | 100 | 86 | 52 | 105 | R | R | 6-3 | 175 | 7-31-72 | 1992 | Willis, Texas |
| Lemke, Steve | 7 | 0 | 3.50 | 16 | 0 | 0 | 0 | 36 | 41 | 17 | 14 | 6 | 22 | R | R | 6-0 | 185 | 1-4-70 | 1992 | Lincolnshire, Ill. |
| Martinez, Julio | 1 | 0 | 4.58 | 10 | 1 | 0 | 1 | 20 | 18 | 11 | 10 | 15 | 13 | R | R | 6-1 | 160 | 10-6-72 | 1990 | Santo Domingo, D.R. |
| Mejia, Delfino | 2 | 1 | 2.79 | 5 | 0 | 0 | 1 | 10 | 9 | 4 | 3 | 2 | 8 | R | R | 5-9 | 150 | 12-24-71 | 1989 | Los Arroces, D.R. |
| Moncion, Manuel | 0 | 0 | 0.00 | 3 | 0 | 0 | 0 | 6 | 1 | 0 | 0 | 2 | 8 | R | R | 6-2 | 190 | 3-26-72 | 1991 | Santo Domingo, D.R. |
| Sawyer, Zack | 3 | 6 | 3.83 | 25 | 2 | 0 | 0 | 49 | 50 | 28 | 21 | 20 | 25 | R | R | 6-3 | 215 | 3-19-73 | 1991 | Clinton, Mass. |
| Smock, Greg | 2 | 0 | 2.45 | 40 | 0 | 0 | 7 | 48 | 32 | 15 | 13 | 22 | 41 | L | L | 6-2 | 185 | 10-9-70 | 1991 | Abingdon, Ill. |
| Urbina, William | 2 | 3 | 4.50 | 10 | 8 | 0 | 0 | 46 | 41 | 31 | 23 | 22 | 30 | R | R | 6-4 | 210 | 2-9-74 | 1992 | Tucson, Ariz. |
| Wasdin, John | 2 | 3 | 1.86 | 9 | 9 | 0 | 0 | 48 | 32 | 11 | 10 | 9 | 40 | R | R | 6-2 | 195 | 8-5-72 | 1993 | Tallahassee, Fla. |
| Wengert, Don | 6 | 5 | 3.32 | 13 | 13 | 2 | 0 | 79 | 79 | 30 | 29 | 18 | 46 | R | R | 6-3 | 205 | 11-6-69 | 1992 | Sioux City, Iowa |

# SOUTHERN OREGON     A
## NORTHWEST LEAGUE

| BATTING | AVG | G | AB | R | H | 2B | 3B | HR | RBI | BB | SO | SB | CS | B | T | HT | WT | DOB | 1st Yr | Resides |
|---|---|---|---|---|---|---|---|---|---|---|---|---|---|---|---|---|---|---|---|---|
| Aracena, Luinis, of | .213 | 28 | 80 | 6 | 17 | 1 | 0 | 0 | 4 | 9 | 22 | 2 | 1 | R | R | 6-0 | 165 | 5-8-70 | 1990 | Mao, D.R. |
| Banks, Tony, of | .250 | 49 | 172 | 29 | 43 | 11 | 1 | 4 | 22 | 32 | 25 | 9 | 4 | L | L | 5-11 | 190 | 9-21-71 | 1993 | Oakland, Calif. |
| Bengoechea, Brandy, 3b | .292 | 31 | 72 | 11 | 21 | 1 | 1 | 0 | 11 | 8 | 16 | 2 | 1 | R | R | 5-10 | 162 | 8-2-71 | 1993 | Lewiston, Idaho |
| Cox, Steve, 1b | .316 | 15 | 57 | 10 | 18 | 4 | 1 | 2 | 16 | 5 | 15 | 0 | 0 | L | L | 6-4 | 200 | 10-31-74 | 1992 | Strathmore, Calif. |
| D'Amico, Jeff, ss-3b | .263 | 33 | 114 | 12 | 30 | 9 | 0 | 3 | 15 | 9 | 21 | 1 | 2 | R | R | 6-3 | 190 | 11-9-74 | 1993 | Redmond, Wash. |
| Dilone, Juan, 2b-of | .211 | 54 | 152 | 19 | 32 | 6 | 1 | 1 | 19 | 22 | 52 | 7 | 5 | S | R | 6-1 | 165 | 5-10-73 | 1990 | Higuey, D.R. |
| Galligani, Marcel, 1b-ss | .287 | 63 | 223 | 44 | 64 | 11 | 1 | 6 | 32 | 40 | 65 | 12 | 5 | R | R | 6-1 | 185 | 3-30-71 | 1992 | Mamaroneck, N.Y. |
| Harris, Eric, of | .245 | 50 | 155 | 27 | 38 | 9 | 0 | 7 | 26 | 23 | 55 | 5 | 4 | R | R | 6-1 | 205 | 2-9-73 | 1993 | Columbia, Tenn. |
| Johnson, Herman, c | .500 | 1 | 2 | 0 | 1 | 0 | 0 | 0 | 2 | 0 | 0 | 0 | 0 | R | R | 6-0 | 209 | 8-11-69 | 1992 | DeSoto, Texas |
| Keel, David, of | .267 | 61 | 195 | 38 | 52 | 9 | 0 | 1 | 18 | 47 | 31 | 12 | 1 | L | R | 6-3 | 205 | 7-23-72 | 1992 | Toney, Ala. |
| Loomis, Geoff, of | .247 | 55 | 255 | 33 | 63 | 15 | 1 | 3 | 50 | 26 | 57 | 4 | 5 | R | R | 6-0 | 185 | 12-22-70 | 1992 | Oregon City, Ore. |
| McDonald, Jason, 2b | .295 | 35 | 112 | 26 | 33 | 5 | 2 | 0 | 8 | 31 | 17 | 22 | 4 | S | R | 5-8 | 175 | 3-20-72 | 1993 | Elk Grove, Calif. |
| Moore, Mark, c | .242 | 48 | 153 | 24 | 37 | 12 | 2 | 2 | 24 | 31 | 36 | 2 | 3 | R | R | 6-2 | 205 | 7-22-70 | 1992 | Overland Park, Kan. |
| Morales, Willie, c | .269 | 60 | 208 | 34 | 56 | 10 | 1 | 0 | 27 | 19 | 36 | 0 | 3 | R | R | 5-10 | 180 | 9-7-72 | 1993 | Tucson, Ariz. |
| Reese, Mat, of | .244 | 47 | 123 | 25 | 30 | 5 | 1 | 2 | 23 | 27 | 36 | 6 | 2 | L | L | 6-0 | 190 | 5-3-71 | 1993 | Maricopa, Ariz. |
| Richardson, Jeff, of | .227 | 37 | 110 | 11 | 25 | 2 | 1 | 0 | 10 | 15 | 31 | 9 | 2 | R | R | 6-1 | 180 | 2-6-73 | 1993 | Walnut, Calif. |
| Salvador, Felix, ss | .172 | 30 | 87 | 16 | 15 | 1 | 0 | 0 | 5 | 18 | 16 | 4 | 0 | R | R | 5-10 | 145 | 2-21-73 | 1992 | Puerto Plata, D.R. |

# ATHLETICS
## TOP 10 PROSPECTS

How the Athletics Top 10 prospects, as judged by Baseball America prior to the 1993 season, fared in 1993:

| Player, Pos. | Club (Class) | AVG | AB | H | HR | RBI | SB |
|---|---|---|---|---|---|---|---|
| 2. Brent Gates, 2b | Huntsville (AA) | .333 | 45 | 15 | 1 | 11 | 0 |
| | Tacoma (AAA) | .341 | 44 | 15 | 1 | 4 | 2 |
| | Oakland | .290 | 535 | 155 | 7 | 69 | 7 |
| 4. Scott Lydy, of | Tacoma (AAA) | .293 | 341 | 100 | 9 | 41 | 12 |
| | Oakland | .225 | 102 | 23 | 2 | 7 | 2 |
| 5. Damon Mashore, of | Huntsville (AA) | .233 | 253 | 59 | 3 | 20 | 18 |
| 7. Craig Paquette, 3b | Tacoma (AAA) | .268 | 183 | 49 | 8 | 29 | 3 |
| | Oakland | .219 | 393 | 86 | 12 | 46 | 4 |
| 10. Mike Neill, of | Modesto (A) | .194 | 62 | 12 | 0 | 4 | 0 |
| | Huntsville (AA) | .246 | 179 | 44 | 1 | 15 | 3 |

| | | W | L | ERA | IP | H | BB | SO |
|---|---|---|---|---|---|---|---|---|
| 1. Todd Van Poppel, rhp | Tacoma (AAA) | 4 | 8 | 5.83 | 79 | 67 | 54 | 71 |
| | Oakland | 6 | 6 | 5.04 | 84 | 76 | 62 | 47 |
| 3. Curtis Shaw, lhp | Huntsville (AA) | 6 | 16 | 4.93 | 152 | 141 | 89 | 132 |
| 6. Miguel Jimenez, rhp | Huntsville (AA) | 10 | 6 | 2.94 | 107 | 92 | 64 | 105 |
| | Tacoma (AAA) | 2 | 3 | 4.78 | 38 | 32 | 24 | 34 |
| | Oakland | 1 | 0 | 4.00 | 27 | 27 | 16 | 13 |
| 8. Johnny Guzman, lhp | Tacoma (AAA) | 2 | 7 | 7.32 | 87 | 130 | 44 | 50 |
| 9. David Zancanaro, lhp | Injured—Did Not Play | | | | | | | |

**Todd Van Poppel**
6-6 at Oakland

MEL BAILEY

| BATTING | AVG | G | AB | R | H | 2B | 3B | HR | RBI | BB | SO | SB | CS | B | T | HT | WT | DOB | 1st Yr | Resides |
|---|---|---|---|---|---|---|---|---|---|---|---|---|---|---|---|---|---|---|---|---|
| Sanders, Pat, 1b | .214 | 45 | 126 | 10 | 27 | 6 | 2 | 2 | 12 | 15 | 39 | 2 | 0 | L | L | 6-0 | 195 | 8-28-71 | 1993 | Huntsville, Ala. |
| Spiezio, Scott, 3b-1b | .328 | 31 | 125 | 32 | 41 | 10 | 2 | 3 | 19 | 16 | 18 | 0 | 1 | S | R | 6-2 | 195 | 9-21-72 | 1993 | Morris, Ill. |

| PITCHING | W | L | ERA | G | GS | CG | SV | IP | H | R | ER | BB | SO | B | T | HT | WT | DOB | 1st Yr | Resides |
|---|---|---|---|---|---|---|---|---|---|---|---|---|---|---|---|---|---|---|---|---|
| Baldwin, Scott | 3 | 3 | 6.11 | 15 | 10 | 0 | 0 | 56 | 70 | 47 | 38 | 26 | 40 | L | L | 6-2 | 205 | 3-27-70 | 1993 | Lewiston, Idaho |
| Conte, Mike | 2 | 4 | 8.41 | 18 | 7 | 0 | 0 | 56 | 71 | 55 | 52 | 31 | 31 | R | R | 6-2 | 210 | 8-11-67 | 1989 | Brownsville, Pa. |
| Gienger, Craig | 3 | 0 | 2.19 | 4 | 4 | 0 | 0 | 25 | 20 | 9 | 6 | 6 | 11 | R | R | 6-3 | 215 | 4-25-70 | 1992 | Castle Rock, Colo. |
| King, Richard | 1 | 2 | 3.40 | 22 | 2 | 0 | 3 | 56 | 63 | 32 | 21 | 14 | 49 | R | R | 6-4 | 205 | 12-30-69 | 1992 | Stone Mountain, Ga. |
| Kubinski, Tim | 5 | 5 | 2.83 | 12 | 12 | 1 | 0 | 70 | 67 | 36 | 22 | 18 | 51 | L | L | 6-4 | 205 | 1-20-72 | 1993 | San Luis Obispo, Calif. |
| Lemke, Steve | 1 | 0 | 4.40 | 8 | 0 | 1 | 0 | 14 | 13 | 11 | 7 | 6 | 11 | R | R | 6-0 | 185 | 1-4-70 | 1993 | Lincolnshire, Ill. |
| Lowe, Jason | 0 | 4 | 6.98 | 22 | 1 | 0 | 0 | 30 | 31 | 32 | 23 | 42 | 29 | R | R | 5-11 | 185 | 12-27-72 | 1993 | Pensacola, Fla. |
| MacCauley, John | 2 | 1 | 4.21 | 25 | 3 | 0 | 4 | 51 | 54 | 29 | 24 | 20 | 32 | R | R | 6-4 | 215 | 3-4-70 | 1992 | Evansville, Ind. |
| Manning, Derek | 5 | 4 | 3.63 | 15 | 13 | 2 | 0 | 79 | 71 | 35 | 32 | 21 | 63 | L | L | 6-3 | 220 | 7-21-70 | 1993 | Wilmington, N.C. |
| Michalak, Chris | 7 | 3 | 2.85 | 16 | 15 | 0 | 0 | 79 | 77 | 41 | 25 | 36 | 57 | L | L | 6-2 | 195 | 1-4-71 | 1993 | Lemont, Ill. |
| Rajotte, Jason | 0 | 1 | 6.28 | 9 | 0 | 0 | 0 | 14 | 15 | 11 | 10 | 9 | 14 | L | L | 6-0 | 175 | 12-15-73 | 1993 | West Warwick, R.I. |
| Urbina, William | 3 | 5 | 5.36 | 13 | 9 | 0 | 0 | 49 | 58 | 41 | 29 | 22 | 28 | R | R | 6-4 | 210 | 2-9-74 | 1993 | Tucson, Ariz. |
| Walsh, Matt | 1 | 0 | 2.08 | 3 | 0 | 0 | 0 | 4 | 4 | 1 | 1 | 3 | 1 | R | R | 6-1 | 185 | 12-12-72 | 1993 | Melrose, Mass. |
| Whitaker, Ryan | 2 | 3 | 4.40 | 27 | 0 | 0 | 7 | 45 | 39 | 25 | 22 | 21 | 42 | R | R | 6-0 | 175 | 2-3-72 | 1993 | Broken Arrow, Okla. |
| Zongor, Steve | 2 | 4 | 3.90 | 27 | 0 | 0 | 3 | 28 | 24 | 17 | 12 | 19 | 33 | R | L | 5-11 | 185 | 6-30-70 | 1993 | Franklin, Tenn. |

# SCOTTSDALE
## ARIZONA LEAGUE
R

| BATTING | AVG | G | AB | R | H | 2B | 3B | HR | RBI | BB | SO | SB | CS | B | T | HT | WT | DOB | 1st Yr | Resides |
|---|---|---|---|---|---|---|---|---|---|---|---|---|---|---|---|---|---|---|---|---|
| Batista, Tony, 3b-2b | .327 | 24 | 104 | 21 | 34 | 6 | 2 | 2 | 17 | 6 | 14 | 6 | 2 | R | R | 6-0 | 167 | 12-9-73 | 1992 | Mao Valverde, D.R. |
| Carr, Jeffrey, c-1b | .139 | 26 | 36 | 4 | 5 | 2 | 0 | 0 | 4 | 7 | 4 | 1 | 0 | R | R | 6-1 | 188 | 5-24-74 | 1993 | Mission Viejo, Calif. |
| Darwin, Brian, of | .235 | 29 | 68 | 12 | 16 | 2 | 0 | 0 | 7 | 10 | 25 | 7 | 2 | R | R | 6-3 | 185 | 10-17-73 | 1992 | Cerritos, Calif. |
| German, Juan, of | .227 | 36 | 97 | 13 | 22 | 3 | 1 | 1 | 13 | 12 | 25 | 2 | 1 | R | R | 6-2 | 166 | 10-26-74 | 1992 | San Pedro de Macoris, D.R. |
| Griffin, Chad, 2b | .155 | 26 | 58 | 7 | 9 | 2 | 1 | 1 | 3 | 5 | 18 | 2 | 0 | L | R | 5-9 | 165 | 4-28-74 | 1993 | Charlotte, N.C. |
| Hamburg, Leon, of | .279 | 48 | 165 | 38 | 46 | 14 | 1 | 5 | 27 | 35 | 42 | 9 | 3 | R | R | 6-0 | 195 | 1-4-75 | 1993 | Orangevale, Calif. |
| Hause, Brendan, of-1b | .667 | 1 | 3 | 0 | 2 | 0 | 0 | 0 | 2 | 1 | 1 | 0 | 0 | L | L | 6-1 | 185 | 10-21-74 | 1992 | San Diego, Calif. |
| Jones, John, 3b-1b | .341 | 50 | 170 | 38 | 58 | 9 | 3 | 5 | 39 | 28 | 33 | 1 | 3 | R | R | 6-3 | 195 | 9-14-72 | 1992 | Oakland, Calif. |
| McLeod, Mike, of | .257 | 51 | 175 | 34 | 45 | 7 | 2 | 1 | 26 | 24 | 24 | 10 | 3 | L | R | 6-3 | 230 | 8-7-73 | 1993 | Wheeling, W.Va. |
| Moschetti, Mike, dh-2b | .263 | 30 | 99 | 26 | 26 | 4 | 1 | 2 | 19 | 11 | 16 | 4 | 2 | R | R | 6-0 | 175 | 3-14-73 | 1993 | La Mirada, Calif. |
| Ortega, Randy, c | .250 | 36 | 88 | 14 | 22 | 5 | 0 | 1 | 12 | 20 | 13 | 2 | 2 | R | R | 6-1 | 205 | 7-5-72 | 1993 | Stockton, Calif. |
| Quintana, Eddy, 1b | .224 | 47 | 170 | 18 | 38 | 7 | 1 | 0 | 19 | 16 | 44 | 3 | 0 | R | R | 6-0 | 170 | 7-7-72 | 1993 | Buroz, Venez. |
| Salvador, Felix, ss | .387 | 9 | 31 | 5 | 12 | 0 | 0 | 4 | 4 | 4 | 1 | 1 | R | R | 5-10 | 145 | 2-21-73 | 1992 | Puerto Plata, D.R. |
| Simmons, Enoch, of-dh | .538 | 4 | 13 | 4 | 7 | 1 | 0 | 1 | 3 | 3 | 2 | 1 | 0 | R | R | 6-4 | 215 | 9-28-67 | 1988 | Sunnymead, Calif. |
| Soriano, Fred, ss-2b | .260 | 41 | 131 | 34 | 34 | 5 | 4 | 5 | 19 | 21 | 41 | 7 | 2 | R | R | 5-8 | 160 | 8-5-74 | 1992 | Bani, D.R. |
| Soriano, Jose, of | .265 | 48 | 181 | 30 | 48 | 7 | 5 | 3 | 31 | 12 | 51 | 8 | 3 | R | R | 6-0 | 175 | 4-20-74 | 1992 | Escondido, Calif. |
| Vargas, Julio, ss-3b | .287 | 50 | 195 | 46 | 56 | 6 | 6 | 0 | 25 | 15 | 37 | 12 | 6 | R | R | 5-10 | 150 | 9-10-74 | 1992 | San Pedro de Macoris, D.R. |
| Ventura, Leonardo, c | .192 | 35 | 73 | 9 | 14 | 3 | 0 | 0 | 7 | 6 | 19 | 0 | 1 | R | R | 6-2 | 215 | 7-16-73 | 1992 | Santo Domingo, D.R. |

| PITCHING | W | L | ERA | G | GS | CG | SV | IP | H | R | ER | BB | SO | B | T | HT | WT | DOB | 1st Yr | Resides |
|---|---|---|---|---|---|---|---|---|---|---|---|---|---|---|---|---|---|---|---|---|
| Chambers, Shawn | 1 | 1 | 4.09 | 13 | 8 | 0 | 1 | 44 | 43 | 23 | 20 | 14 | 36 | S | L | 6-4 | 205 | 12-9-73 | 1993 | Vernon Hills, Ill. |
| Domenico, Brian | 4 | 1 | 3.17 | 15 | 11 | 0 | 1 | 60 | 47 | 27 | 21 | 39 | 59 | R | R | 6-2 | 190 | 2-10-73 | 1993 | Lincoln, R.I. |
| Gil, Gustavo | 7 | 1 | 4.52 | 14 | 13 | 0 | 0 | 76 | 63 | 43 | 38 | 31 | 63 | R | R | 6-2 | 188 | 9-22-70 | 1991 | Anzoate, Venez. |
| Huber, Aaron | 1 | 2 | 5.81 | 12 | 2 | 0 | 1 | 31 | 45 | 29 | 20 | 12 | 21 | R | R | 6-2 | 190 | 8-24-72 | 1993 | Humble, Texas |
| Kubinski, Tim | 1 | 0 | 6.00 | 1 | 1 | 0 | 0 | 3 | 5 | 2 | 2 | 0 | 3 | L | L | 6-4 | 205 | 1-20-72 | 1993 | San Luis Obispo, Calif. |
| Leibee, Skye | 4 | 4 | 0.99 | 14 | 2 | 0 | 3 | 27 | 27 | 10 | 3 | 10 | 20 | L | L | 5-9 | 180 | 10-29-73 | 1993 | Taft, Calif. |
| Luft, Thomas | 1 | 1 | 6.32 | 17 | 0 | 0 | 3 | 31 | 35 | 36 | 22 | 21 | 26 | R | R | 6-2 | 185 | 9-14-70 | 1993 | Bellevue, Wash. |
| Mojica, Francis | 6 | 2 | 4.15 | 24 | 0 | 0 | 5 | 30 | 31 | 19 | 14 | 8 | 33 | R | R | 5-9 | 154 | 11-30-73 | 1992 | Santo Domingo, D.R. |
| Moncion, Manuel | 0 | 0 | 10.80 | 1 | 1 | 0 | 0 | 3 | 7 | 5 | 4 | 1 | 0 | R | R | 6-2 | 190 | 3-26-72 | 1991 | Santo Domingo, D.R. |
| Montgomery, Trent | 4 | 3 | 3.12 | 15 | 7 | 0 | 0 | 58 | 51 | 30 | 20 | 19 | 41 | R | R | 6-2 | 195 | 3-23-72 | 1993 | Mobile, Ala. |
| Newman, Damon | 0 | 4 | 4.08 | 9 | 2 | 0 | 0 | 18 | 17 | 12 | 8 | 8 | 10 | R | R | 6-3 | 210 | 7-17-73 | 1993 | Greensboro, N.C. |
| Perez, Juan | 4 | 1 | 2.31 | 12 | 0 | 0 | 0 | 35 | 34 | 12 | 9 | 9 | 31 | L | L | 6-0 | 155 | 3-28-73 | 1992 | La Romana, D.R. |
| Smith, Andy | 1 | 2 | 9.00 | 8 | 2 | 0 | 0 | 19 | 32 | 24 | 19 | 6 | 10 | R | R | 6-5 | 220 | 1-29-75 | 1993 | Kannapolis, N.C. |
| Vargas, Julio | 0 | 1 | 5.40 | 5 | 0 | 0 | 1 | 5 | 7 | 6 | 3 | 4 | 1 | R | R | 5-10 | 150 | 9-10-74 | 1992 | San Pedro de Macoris, D.R. |
| Walsh, Matt | 2 | 0 | 1.62 | 9 | 5 | 0 | 0 | 33 | 29 | 9 | 6 | 6 | 33 | R | R | 6-1 | 185 | 12-12-72 | 1993 | Melrose, Mass. |
| Wasdin, John | 0 | 0 | 3.00 | 1 | 1 | 0 | 0 | 3 | 3 | 1 | 1 | 0 | 1 | R | R | 6-2 | 195 | 8-5-72 | 1993 | Tallahassee, Fla. |

# PHILADELPHIA PHILLIES

**Manager:** Jim Fregosi.     **1993 Record:** 97-65, .599 (1st, NL East).

| BATTING | AVG | G | AB | R | H | 2B | 3B | HR | RBI | BB | SO | SB | CS | B | T | HT | WT | DOB | 1st Yr | Resides |
|---|---|---|---|---|---|---|---|---|---|---|---|---|---|---|---|---|---|---|---|---|
| Amaro, Ruben | .333 | 25 | 48 | 7 | 16 | 2 | 2 | 1 | 6 | 6 | 5 | 0 | 0 | S | R | 5-10 | 175 | 2-12-65 | 1987 | Philadelphia, Pa. |
| Batiste, Kim | .282 | 79 | 156 | 14 | 44 | 7 | 1 | 5 | 29 | 3 | 29 | 0 | 1 | R | R | 6-0 | 193 | 3-15-68 | 1987 | Prairieville, La. |
| Bell, Juan | .200 | 24 | 65 | 5 | 13 | 6 | 1 | 0 | 7 | 5 | 12 | 0 | 1 | S | R | 5-11 | 170 | 3-29-68 | 1985 | San Pedro de Macoris, D.R. |
| Chamberlain, Wes | .282 | 96 | 284 | 34 | 80 | 20 | 2 | 12 | 45 | 17 | 51 | 2 | 1 | R | R | 6-2 | 219 | 4-13-66 | 1987 | Chicago, Ill. |
| Daulton, Darren | .257 | 147 | 510 | 90 | 131 | 35 | 4 | 24 | 105 | 117 | 111 | 5 | 0 | L | R | 6-2 | 201 | 1-3-62 | 1980 | Safety Harbor, Fla. |
| Duncan, Mariano | .282 | 124 | 496 | 68 | 140 | 26 | 4 | 11 | 73 | 12 | 88 | 6 | 5 | R | R | 6-0 | 185 | 3-13-63 | 1982 | Cherry Hill, N.J. |
| Dykstra, Lenny | .305 | 161 | 637 | 143 | 194 | 44 | 6 | 19 | 66 | 129 | 64 | 37 | 12 | L | L | 5-10 | 160 | 2-10-63 | 1981 | Philadelphia, Pa. |
| Eisenreich, Jim | .318 | 153 | 362 | 51 | 115 | 17 | 4 | 7 | 54 | 26 | 36 | 5 | 0 | L | L | 5-11 | 200 | 4-18-59 | 1980 | Blue Springs, Mo. |
| Hollins, Dave | .273 | 143 | 543 | 104 | 148 | 30 | 4 | 18 | 93 | 85 | 109 | 2 | 3 | S | R | 6-1 | 207 | 5-25-66 | 1987 | Orchard Park, N.Y. |
| Incaviglia, Pete | .274 | 116 | 368 | 60 | 101 | 16 | 3 | 24 | 89 | 21 | 82 | 1 | 1 | R | R | 6-1 | 225 | 4-2-64 | 1986 | Collegeville, Texas |
| Jordan, Ricky | .289 | 90 | 159 | 21 | 46 | 4 | 1 | 5 | 18 | 8 | 32 | 0 | 0 | R | R | 6-3 | 205 | 5-26-65 | 1983 | Gold River, Calif. |
| Kruk, John | .316 | 150 | 535 | 100 | 169 | 33 | 5 | 14 | 85 | 111 | 87 | 6 | 2 | L | L | 5-10 | 214 | 2-9-61 | 1981 | Burlington, W.Va. |
| Lindsey, Doug | .500 | 2 | 2 | 0 | 1 | 0 | 0 | 0 | 0 | 0 | 1 | 0 | 0 | R | R | 6-2 | 232 | 9-22-67 | 1987 | Austin, Texas |
| Longmire, Tony | .231 | 11 | 13 | 1 | 3 | 0 | 0 | 1 | 0 | 1 | 0 | 0 | 1 | L | R | 6-1 | 180 | 8-12-68 | 1986 | Vallejo, Calif. |
| Manto, Jeff | .056 | 8 | 18 | 0 | 1 | 0 | 0 | 0 | 0 | 0 | 3 | 0 | 0 | R | R | 6-3 | 210 | 8-23-64 | 1985 | Bristol, Pa. |
| Millette, Joe | .200 | 10 | 10 | 3 | 2 | 0 | 0 | 0 | 2 | 1 | 2 | 0 | 0 | R | R | 6-1 | 175 | 8-12-66 | 1989 | Lafayette, Calif. |
| Morandini, Mickey | .247 | 120 | 425 | 57 | 105 | 19 | 9 | 3 | 33 | 34 | 73 | 13 | 2 | L | R | 5-11 | 171 | 4-22-66 | 1989 | Valparaiso, Ind. |
| Pratt, Todd | .287 | 33 | 87 | 8 | 25 | 6 | 0 | 5 | 13 | 5 | 19 | 0 | 0 | R | R | 6-3 | 195 | 2-9-67 | 1985 | Boca Raton, Fla. |
| Stocker, Kevin | .324 | 70 | 259 | 46 | 84 | 12 | 3 | 2 | 31 | 30 | 43 | 5 | 0 | S | R | 6-1 | 175 | 2-13-70 | 1991 | Spokane, Wash. |
| Thompson, Milt | .262 | 129 | 340 | 42 | 89 | 14 | 2 | 4 | 44 | 40 | 57 | 9 | 4 | L | R | 5-11 | 170 | 1-5-59 | 1979 | Ballwin, Mo. |

| PITCHING | W | L | ERA | G | GS | CG | SV | IP | H | R | ER | BB | SO | B | T | HT | WT | DOB | 1st Yr | Resides |
|---|---|---|---|---|---|---|---|---|---|---|---|---|---|---|---|---|---|---|---|---|
| Andersen, Larry | 3 | 2 | 2.92 | 64 | 0 | 0 | 0 | 62 | 54 | 22 | 20 | 21 | 67 | R | R | 6-3 | 205 | 5-6-53 | 1971 | Bellevue, Wash. |
| Ayrault, Bob | 2 | 0 | 9.58 | 10 | 0 | 0 | 0 | 10 | 18 | 11 | 11 | 10 | 8 | R | R | 6-4 | 235 | 4-27-66 | 1989 | Carson City, Nev. |
| Brink, Brad | 0 | 0 | 3.00 | 2 | 0 | 0 | 0 | 6 | 3 | 2 | 2 | 3 | 8 | R | R | 6-2 | 203 | 1-20-65 | 1986 | Modesto, Calif. |
| Davis, Mark | 1 | 2 | 5.17 | 25 | 0 | 0 | 0 | 31 | 35 | 22 | 18 | 24 | 28 | L | L | 6-4 | 210 | 10-19-60 | 1979 | Marietta, Ga. |
| DeLeon, Jose | 3 | 0 | 3.26 | 24 | 3 | 0 | 0 | 47 | 39 | 25 | 17 | 27 | 34 | R | R | 6-3 | 215 | 12-20-60 | 1979 | Boca Raton, Fla. |
| Fletcher, Paul | 0 | 0 | 0.00 | 1 | 0 | 0 | 0 | 0 | 0 | 0 | 0 | 0 | 0 | R | R | 6-1 | 185 | 1-14-67 | 1988 | Ravenswood, W.Va. |
| Foster, Kevin | 0 | 1 | 14.85 | 2 | 1 | 0 | 0 | 7 | 13 | 11 | 11 | 7 | 6 | R | R | 6-1 | 160 | 1-13-69 | 1988 | Evanston, Ill. |
| Green, Tyler | 0 | 0 | 7.36 | 3 | 2 | 0 | 0 | 7 | 16 | 9 | 6 | 5 | 7 | R | R | 6-5 | 185 | 2-18-70 | 1991 | Englewood, Colo. |
| Greene, Tommy | 16 | 4 | 3.42 | 31 | 30 | 7 | 0 | 200 | 175 | 84 | 76 | 62 | 167 | R | R | 6-5 | 225 | 4-6-67 | 1985 | Richmond, Va. |
| Jackson, Danny | 12 | 11 | 3.77 | 32 | 32 | 2 | 0 | 210 | 214 | 105 | 88 | 80 | 120 | R | L | 6-0 | 205 | 1-5-62 | 1982 | Overland Park, Kan. |
| Mason, Roger | 5 | 5 | 4.89 | 34 | 0 | 0 | 0 | 50 | 47 | 28 | 27 | 16 | 32 | R | R | 6-6 | 220 | 9-18-58 | 1981 | Bellaire, Mich. |
| 2-team (34 S.D.) | 5 | 12 | 4.06 | 68 | 0 | 0 | 0 | 100 | 90 | 48 | 45 | 34 | 71 | | | | | | | |
| Mauser, Tim | 0 | 0 | 4.96 | 8 | 0 | 0 | 0 | 16 | 15 | 9 | 9 | 7 | 14 | R | R | 6-0 | 185 | 10-4-66 | 1988 | Fort Worth, Texas |
| Mulholland, Terry | 12 | 9 | 3.25 | 29 | 28 | 7 | 0 | 191 | 177 | 80 | 69 | 40 | 116 | R | L | 6-3 | 200 | 3-9-63 | 1984 | Scottsdale, Ariz. |
| Pall, Donn | 1 | 0 | 2.55 | 8 | 0 | 0 | 0 | 18 | 15 | 7 | 5 | 3 | 11 | R | R | 6-1 | 180 | 1-11-62 | 1985 | Bloomingdale, Ill. |
| Rivera, Ben | 13 | 9 | 5.02 | 30 | 28 | 1 | 0 | 163 | 175 | 99 | 91 | 85 | 123 | R | R | 6-6 | 230 | 1-11-69 | 1986 | San Pedro de Macoris, D.R. |
| Schilling, Curt | 16 | 7 | 4.02 | 34 | 34 | 7 | 0 | 235 | 234 | 114 | 105 | 57 | 186 | R | R | 6-4 | 215 | 11-14-66 | 1986 | Marlton, N.J. |
| Thigpen, Bobby | 3 | 1 | 6.05 | 17 | 0 | 0 | 0 | 19 | 23 | 13 | 13 | 9 | 10 | R | R | 6-3 | 195 | 7-17-63 | 1985 | St. Petersburg, Fla. |
| West, David | 6 | 4 | 2.92 | 76 | 0 | 0 | 3 | 86 | 60 | 37 | 28 | 51 | 87 | L | L | 6-6 | 225 | 9-1-64 | 1983 | Stuart, Fla. |
| Williams, Mike | 1 | 3 | 5.29 | 17 | 4 | 0 | 0 | 51 | 50 | 32 | 30 | 22 | 33 | R | R | 6-2 | 190 | 7-29-68 | 1990 | Newport, Va. |
| Williams, Mitch | 3 | 7 | 3.34 | 65 | 0 | 0 | 43 | 62 | 56 | 30 | 23 | 44 | 60 | L | L | 6-4 | 200 | 11-17-64 | 1982 | Arlington, Texas |

## FIELDING

| Catcher | PCT | G | PO | A | E | DP |
|---|---|---|---|---|---|---|
| Daulton | .991 | 146 | 981 | 67 | 9 | 19 |
| Lindsey | 1.000 | 2 | 3 | 0 | 0 | 0 |
| Pratt | .989 | 26 | 169 | 7 | 2 | 3 |

| First Base | PCT | G | PO | A | E | DP |
|---|---|---|---|---|---|---|
| Eisenreich | 1.000 | 1 | 5 | 0 | 0 | 0 |
| Jordan | .990 | 33 | 201 | 4 | 2 | 20 |
| Kruk | .993 | 144 | 1149 | 69 | 8 | 79 |

| Second Base | PCT | G | PO | A | E | DP |
|---|---|---|---|---|---|---|
| Duncan | .969 | 65 | 109 | 168 | 9 | 29 |
| Morandini | .990 | 111 | 208 | 288 | 5 | 48 |

| Third Base | PCT | G | PO | A | E | DP |
|---|---|---|---|---|---|---|
| Batiste | .956 | 58 | 24 | 41 | 3 | 2 |
| Hollins | .914 | 143 | 73 | 215 | 27 | 9 |
| Manto | 1.000 | 6 | 2 | 7 | 0 | 0 |
| Millette | 1.000 | 3 | 0 | 4 | 0 | 0 |

| Shortstop | PCT | G | PO | A | E | DP |
|---|---|---|---|---|---|---|
| Batiste | .943 | 24 | 48 | 67 | 7 | 13 |
| Bell | .909 | 22 | 33 | 57 | 9 | 11 |
| Duncan | .945 | 59 | 71 | 136 | 12 | 21 |
| Manto | 1.000 | 1 | 0 | 1 | 0 | 0 |
| Millette | 1.000 | 7 | 3 | 14 | 0 | 1 |

| | PCT | G | PO | A | E | DP |
|---|---|---|---|---|---|---|
| Stocker | .958 | 70 | 118 | 202 | 14 | 44 |

| Outfield | PCT | G | PO | A | E | DP |
|---|---|---|---|---|---|---|
| Amaro | .963 | 16 | 25 | 1 | 1 | 1 |
| Chamberlain | .993 | 76 | 131 | 10 | 1 | 3 |
| Dykstra | .979 | 160 | 469 | 2 | 10 | 0 |
| Eisenreich | .996 | 137 | 218 | 6 | 1 | 0 |
| Incaviglia | .971 | 97 | 164 | 4 | 5 | 1 |
| Longmire | 1.000 | 2 | 4 | 0 | 0 | 0 |
| Thompson | .994 | 106 | 162 | 6 | 1 | 1 |

# PHILLIES FARM SYSTEM

| Class Club | League | W | L | Pct. | Finish* | Manager | First Year |
|---|---|---|---|---|---|---|---|
| AAA Scranton/WB (Pa.) Red Barons | International | 62 | 80 | .437 | 8th (10) | George Culver | 1989 |
| AA Reading (Pa.) Phillies | Eastern | 62 | 78 | .443 | 7th (8) | Don McCormack | 1967 |
| A# Clearwater (Fla.) Phillies | Florida State | 75 | 60 | .556 | 5th† (13) | Bill Dancy | 1985 |
| A Spartanburg (S.C.) Phillies | South Atlantic | 62 | 80 | .437 | 11th (14) | Roy Majtyka | 1963 |
| A Batavia (N.Y.) Clippers | New York-Penn | 38 | 39 | .494 | 7th (14) | Al LeBoeuf | 1988 |
| Rookie# Martinsville (Va.) Phillies | Appalachian | 22 | 46 | .324 | 10th (10) | Ramon Henderson | 1988 |

*Finish in overall standings (No. of teams in league)   #Advanced level   †Won league championship

MORRIS FOSTOFF

TOM DiPACE

**Phillies Heavyweights.** Catcher Darren Daulton, left, drove in 105 runs while first baseman John Kruk hit .316 to lead Philadelphia to its first National League pennant in 10 years.

## SCRANTON/WILKES-BARRE
### INTERNATIONAL LEAGUE

AAA

| BATTING | AVG | G | AB | R | H | 2B | 3B | HR | RBI | BB | SO | SB | CS | B | T | HT | WT | DOB | 1st Yr | Resides |
|---|---|---|---|---|---|---|---|---|---|---|---|---|---|---|---|---|---|---|---|---|
| Amaro, Ruben | .291 | 101 | 412 | 76 | 120 | 30 | 5 | 9 | 37 | 31 | 44 | 25 | 4 | S | R | 5-10 | 175 | 2-12-65 | 1987 | Philadelphia, Pa. |
| Bieser, Steve | .253 | 26 | 83 | 3 | 21 | 4 | 0 | 0 | 4 | 2 | 14 | 3 | 0 | S | R | 5-10 | 170 | 8-4-67 | 1989 | St. Genevieve, Mo. |
| Brady, Pat | .228 | 63 | 189 | 28 | 43 | 10 | 4 | 8 | 26 | 49 | 40 | 1 | 4 | L | R | 6-0 | 180 | 3-25-66 | 1988 | Lafayette, Calif. |
| Dostal, Bruce | .231 | 6 | 13 | 0 | 3 | 0 | 0 | 0 | 1 | 2 | 5 | 1 | 1 | L | L | 6-0 | 195 | 3-10-65 | 1987 | Towaco, N.J. |
| Fernandez, Jose | .188 | 16 | 32 | 2 | 6 | 1 | 0 | 0 | 1 | 4 | 11 | 0 | 0 | L | R | 6-3 | 210 | 8-24-67 | 1989 | Jupiter, Fla. |
| Hyde, Mickey | .167 | 2 | 6 | 1 | 1 | 0 | 0 | 0 | 0 | 0 | 1 | 0 | 0 | R | R | 6-1 | 175 | 7-9-66 | 1988 | East Bethany, N.Y. |
| Legg, Greg | .280 | 73 | 225 | 27 | 63 | 13 | 3 | 0 | 25 | 19 | 23 | 2 | 2 | R | R | 6-1 | 185 | 4-21-60 | 1982 | Vista, Calif. |
| Lieberthal, Mike | .262 | 112 | 382 | 35 | 100 | 17 | 0 | 7 | 40 | 24 | 32 | 2 | 0 | R | R | 6-0 | 170 | 1-18-72 | 1990 | Westlake Village, Calif. |
| Lindsey, Doug | .174 | 38 | 121 | 9 | 21 | 4 | 1 | 2 | 7 | 5 | 24 | 0 | 0 | R | R | 6-2 | 232 | 9-22-67 | 1987 | Austin, Texas |
| Longmire, Tony | .304 | 120 | 447 | 63 | 136 | 36 | 4 | 6 | 67 | 41 | 71 | 12 | 4 | L | R | 6-1 | 180 | 8-12-68 | 1986 | Vallejo, Calif. |
| Manto, Jeff | .289 | 106 | 388 | 62 | 112 | 30 | 1 | 17 | 88 | 55 | 58 | 4 | 1 | R | R | 6-3 | 210 | 8-23-64 | 1985 | Bristol, Pa. |
| Marsh, Tom | .286 | 78 | 315 | 45 | 90 | 16 | 8 | 12 | 57 | 14 | 47 | 10 | 4 | R | R | 6-2 | 180 | 12-27-65 | 1988 | Toledo, Ohio |
| Millette, Joe | .224 | 107 | 343 | 27 | 77 | 15 | 2 | 1 | 24 | 19 | 56 | 5 | 4 | R | R | 6-1 | 175 | 8-12-66 | 1989 | Lafayette, Calif. |
| Pratt, Todd | .222 | 3 | 9 | 1 | 2 | 1 | 0 | 0 | 1 | 3 | 1 | 0 | 0 | R | R | 6-3 | 195 | 2-9-67 | 1985 | Boca Raton, Fla. |
| Rodriguez, Victor | .305 | 118 | 442 | 59 | 135 | 24 | 3 | 12 | 64 | 17 | 40 | 2 | 4 | R | R | 5-11 | 173 | 7-14-61 | 1977 | Villa Carolina, P.R. |
| Ryan, Sean | .221 | 66 | 208 | 14 | 46 | 9 | 0 | 1 | 16 | 26 | 39 | 0 | 0 | S | R | 6-3 | 215 | 1-29-69 | 1990 | Bound Brook, N.J. |
| Schall, Gene | .237 | 40 | 139 | 16 | 33 | 6 | 1 | 4 | 16 | 19 | 38 | 4 | 2 | R | R | 6-3 | 190 | 6-5-70 | 1991 | Willow Grove, Pa. |
| Stocker, Kevin | .233 | 83 | 313 | 54 | 73 | 14 | 1 | 3 | 17 | 29 | 56 | 17 | 6 | S | R | 6-1 | 175 | 2-13-70 | 1991 | Spokane, Wash. |
| Taylor, Sam | .241 | 67 | 191 | 24 | 46 | 7 | 1 | 6 | 25 | 20 | 36 | 4 | 2 | L | L | 5-11 | 185 | 8-6-68 | 1989 | Murray, Ky. |
| Waller, Casey | .176 | 58 | 160 | 19 | 30 | 7 | 1 | 1 | 13 | 10 | 20 | 2 | 0 | S | R | 5-11 | 180 | 12-15-67 | 1989 | South Boston, Va. |
| Williams, Cary | .216 | 78 | 232 | 27 | 50 | 15 | 2 | 0 | 14 | 23 | 27 | 3 | 4 | R | R | 6-3 | 175 | 6-14-67 | 1989 | Florence, Ala. |

| PITCHING | W | L | ERA | G | GS | CG | SV | IP | H | R | ER | BB | SO | B | T | HT | WT | DOB | 1st Yr | Resides |
|---|---|---|---|---|---|---|---|---|---|---|---|---|---|---|---|---|---|---|---|---|
| Abbott, Kyle | 12 | 10 | 3.95 | 27 | 27 | 2 | 0 | 173 | 163 | 85 | 76 | 62 | 109 | L | L | 6-4 | 195 | 2-18-68 | 1989 | Cherry Hill, N.J. |
| Allen, Ronnie | 0 | 2 | 5.18 | 5 | 5 | 0 | 0 | 24 | 30 | 15 | 14 | 8 | 12 | R | R | 5-11 | 185 | 5-10-70 | 1991 | Kirkland, Wash. |
| Ayrault, Bob | 0 | 1 | 1.23 | 5 | 1 | 0 | 0 | 7 | 8 | 2 | 1 | 3 | 9 | R | R | 6-4 | 235 | 4-27-66 | 1989 | Carson City, Nev. |
| Borland, Toby | 2 | 4 | 5.76 | 26 | 0 | 0 | 1 | 30 | 31 | 20 | 19 | 20 | 26 | R | R | 6-7 | 175 | 5-29-69 | 1989 | Quitman, La. |
| Brantley, Cliff | 1 | 3 | 5.33 | 7 | 5 | 0 | 0 | 27 | 31 | 21 | 16 | 28 | 17 | R | R | 6-2 | 215 | 4-12-68 | 1986 | Staten Island, N.Y. |
| Brink, Brad | 7 | 7 | 4.22 | 18 | 18 | 2 | 0 | 107 | 104 | 53 | 50 | 27 | 89 | R | R | 6-2 | 203 | 1-20-65 | 1986 | Modesto, Calif. |
| Carter, Andy | 7 | 7 | 4.54 | 30 | 13 | 0 | 1 | 109 | 104 | 59 | 55 | 35 | 68 | L | L | 6-5 | 190 | 11-9-68 | 1987 | Erdenheim, Pa. |
| Combs, Pat | 0 | 9 | 4.84 | 15 | 15 | 1 | 0 | 84 | 97 | 57 | 45 | 27 | 60 | L | L | 6-4 | 213 | 10-29-66 | 1989 | Houston, Texas |
| Fletcher, Paul | 4 | 12 | 5.66 | 34 | 19 | 2 | 0 | 140 | 146 | 99 | 88 | 60 | 116 | R | R | 6-1 | 185 | 1-14-67 | 1988 | Ravenswood, W.Va. |
| Foster, Kevin | 1 | 1 | 3.93 | 17 | 9 | 1 | 0 | 71 | 63 | 32 | 31 | 29 | 59 | R | R | 6-1 | 160 | 1-13-69 | 1988 | Evanston, Ill. |
| Gaddy, Bob | 1 | 4 | 5.59 | 23 | 3 | 0 | 0 | 48 | 54 | 35 | 30 | 29 | 40 | R | L | 6-1 | 202 | 1-11-67 | 1989 | Pensacola, Fla. |
| Green, Tyler | 6 | 10 | 3.95 | 28 | 14 | 4 | 0 | 118 | 102 | 62 | 52 | 43 | 87 | R | R | 6-5 | 185 | 2-18-70 | 1991 | Englewood, Colo. |
| Hall, Drew | 2 | 2 | 2.76 | 61 | 0 | 0 | 7 | 65 | 56 | 25 | 20 | 23 | 62 | L | L | 6-5 | 220 | 3-27-63 | 1984 | Colleyville, Texas |
| Mauser, Tim | 2 | 0 | 0.87 | 19 | 0 | 0 | 10 | 21 | 10 | 2 | 2 | 5 | 25 | R | R | 6-0 | 185 | 10-4-66 | 1988 | Fort Worth, Texas |
| Parris, Steve | 0 | 0 | 12.71 | 3 | 0 | 0 | 0 | 6 | 9 | 9 | 8 | 3 | 4 | R | R | 6-0 | 190 | 12-17-67 | 1989 | Joliet, Ill. |
| Patterson, Jeff | 7 | 5 | 2.69 | 62 | 0 | 0 | 8 | 94 | 79 | 32 | 28 | 42 | 68 | R | R | 6-2 | 200 | 10-1-68 | 1989 | Anaheim, Calif. |
| Wells, Bob | 1 | 1 | 2.79 | 11 | 0 | 0 | 0 | 19 | 19 | 7 | 6 | 5 | 8 | R | R | 6-0 | 180 | 11-1-66 | 1989 | Yakima, Wash. |
| Williams, Mike | 9 | 2 | 2.87 | 14 | 13 | 1 | 0 | 97 | 93 | 34 | 31 | 16 | 53 | R | R | 6-2 | 190 | 7-29-68 | 1990 | Newport, Va. |

## FIELDING

| Catcher | PCT | G | PO | A | E | DP |
|---|---|---|---|---|---|---|
| Bieser | 1.000 | 6 | 41 | 3 | 0 | 1 |
| Fernandez | 1.000 | 4 | 12 | 2 | 0 | 0 |
| Lieberthal | .985 | 106 | 659 | 75 | 11 | 5 |
| Lindsey | .983 | 31 | 202 | 30 | 4 | 2 |
| Manto | 1.000 | 2 | 4 | 1 | 0 | 0 |
| Pratt | 1.000 | 2 | 11 | 0 | 0 | 0 |

| First Base | PCT | G | PO | A | E | DP |
|---|---|---|---|---|---|---|
| Bieser | 1.000 | 1 | 5 | 0 | 0 | 0 |
| Brady | .969 | 18 | 118 | 6 | 4 | 10 |
| Fernandez | 1.000 | 2 | 12 | 0 | 0 | 1 |
| Lindsey | 1.000 | 2 | 12 | 1 | 0 | 0 |
| Manto | .995 | 53 | 347 | 35 | 2 | 27 |
| Rodriguez | 1.000 | 2 | 5 | 0 | 0 | 0 |
| Ryan | .992 | 45 | 335 | 24 | 3 | 32 |
| Schall | .991 | 39 | 287 | 28 | 3 | 22 |

| Second Base | PCT | G | PO | A | E | DP |
|---|---|---|---|---|---|---|
| Amaro | .000 | 1 | 0 | 0 | 0 | 0 |
| Legg | .976 | 55 | 83 | 124 | 5 | 20 |
| Millette | .967 | 49 | 92 | 114 | 7 | 26 |
| Rodriguez | .989 | 39 | 80 | 96 | 2 | 22 |
| Waller | .983 | 15 | 26 | 31 | 1 | 13 |

| Third Base | PCT | G | PO | A | E | DP |
|---|---|---|---|---|---|---|
| Brady | 1.000 | 4 | 0 | 12 | 0 | 1 |
| Legg | .750 | 4 | 3 | 6 | 3 | 0 |
| Manto | .961 | 54 | 50 | 98 | 6 | 14 |
| Millette | 1.000 | 1 | 1 | 3 | 0 | 0 |
| Rodriguez | .963 | 64 | 44 | 86 | 5 | 8 |
| Waller | .840 | 32 | 16 | 47 | 12 | 3 |

| Shortstop | PCT | G | PO | A | E | DP |
|---|---|---|---|---|---|---|
| Legg | 1.000 | 1 | 0 | 2 | 0 | 0 |
| Millette | .939 | 58 | 75 | 140 | 14 | 18 |
| Rodriguez | .939 | 12 | 11 | 20 | 2 | 3 |
| Stocker | .961 | 81 | 122 | 248 | 15 | 47 |

| Outfield | PCT | G | PO | A | E | DP |
|---|---|---|---|---|---|---|
| Amaro | .982 | 99 | 272 | 8 | 5 | 2 |
| Bieser | .978 | 18 | 44 | 0 | 1 | 0 |
| Brady | 1.000 | 30 | 63 | 1 | 0 | 0 |
| Dostal | .750 | 4 | 3 | 0 | 1 | 0 |
| Hyde | 1.000 | 2 | 2 | 0 | 0 | 0 |
| Longmire | .976 | 107 | 195 | 5 | 5 | 1 |
| Marsh | .957 | 64 | 145 | 10 | 7 | 5 |
| Taylor | .979 | 53 | 92 | 3 | 2 | 1 |
| Williams | .983 | 72 | 168 | 4 | 3 | 2 |

# READING — AA

## EASTERN LEAGUE

| BATTING | AVG | G | AB | R | H | 2B | 3B | HR | RBI | BB | SO | SB | CS | B | T | HT | WT | DOB | 1st Yr | Resides |
|---|---|---|---|---|---|---|---|---|---|---|---|---|---|---|---|---|---|---|---|---|
| Bieser, Steve, c-of | .312 | 53 | 170 | 21 | 53 | 6 | 3 | 1 | 19 | 15 | 24 | 9 | 5 | S | R | 5-10 | 170 | 8-4-67 | 1989 | St. Genevieve, Mo. |
| Brady, Pat, of-1b | .236 | 46 | 140 | 23 | 33 | 8 | 0 | 5 | 14 | 30 | 28 | 1 | 3 | L | R | 6-0 | 180 | 3-25-66 | 1988 | Lafayette, Calif. |
| Colombino, Carlo, 3b | .228 | 86 | 325 | 31 | 74 | 8 | 1 | 2 | 22 | 19 | 48 | 4 | 5 | R | R | 5-10 | 180 | 9-28-64 | 1985 | Point Pleasant, N.J. |
| Escobar, John, 2b-3b | .193 | 65 | 202 | 15 | 39 | 4 | 0 | 3 | 17 | 16 | 42 | 0 | 1 | R | R | 6-1 | 162 | 11-22-69 | 1987 | La Guaira, Venez. |
| Fernandez, Jose, c | .248 | 38 | 129 | 8 | 32 | 5 | 0 | 3 | 18 | 12 | 37 | 0 | 0 | L | R | 6-3 | 210 | 8-24-67 | 1989 | Jupiter, Fla. |
| Geisler, Phil, of | .270 | 48 | 178 | 25 | 48 | 14 | 1 | 3 | 14 | 17 | 50 | 4 | 2 | L | L | 6-3 | 200 | 10-23-69 | 1991 | Springfield, Ore. |
| Grable, Rob, 3b | .233 | 37 | 120 | 10 | 28 | 4 | 1 | 1 | 10 | 18 | 27 | 2 | 1 | R | R | 6-2 | 200 | 1-20-70 | 1991 | Bohemia, N.Y. |
| Hyde, Mickey, of | .285 | 94 | 277 | 32 | 79 | 6 | 2 | 5 | 30 | 14 | 43 | 3 | 4 | R | R | 6-1 | 175 | 7-9-66 | 1988 | East Bethany, N.Y. |
| Jackson, Jeff, of | .238 | 113 | 374 | 45 | 89 | 14 | 3 | 9 | 51 | 30 | 117 | 20 | 8 | R | R | 6-2 | 180 | 1-2-72 | 1989 | Chicago, Ill. |
| Kimberlin, Keith, ss | .264 | 137 | 504 | 56 | 133 | 13 | 3 | 2 | 29 | 57 | 70 | 19 | 7 | S | R | 6-1 | 170 | 7-25-66 | 1989 | St. Louis, Mo. |
| Lewis, Mica, 2b-of | .189 | 74 | 243 | 29 | 46 | 12 | 2 | 0 | 16 | 32 | 47 | 13 | 2 | R | R | 5-11 | 170 | 1-12-67 | 1988 | Los Angeles, Calif. |
| Lockett, Ron, 1b | .242 | 105 | 368 | 53 | 89 | 18 | 5 | 11 | 53 | 27 | 79 | 12 | 2 | L | L | 6-1 | 190 | 9-5-69 | 1990 | Chicago, Ill. |
| Moler, Jason, c | .283 | 38 | 138 | 15 | 39 | 11 | 0 | 2 | 19 | 12 | 31 | 1 | 1 | R | R | 6-1 | 195 | 10-29-69 | 1992 | Yorba Linda, Calif. |
| Nuneviller, Tom, of-dh | .230 | 71 | 226 | 24 | 52 | 11 | 0 | 2 | 32 | 16 | 23 | 3 | 0 | R | R | 6-3 | 210 | 5-15-69 | 1990 | Ottsville, Pa. |
| Rosado, Ed, c | .171 | 31 | 76 | 6 | 13 | 3 | 0 | 0 | 0 | 4 | 12 | 0 | 1 | S | R | 5-9 | 170 | 1-25-69 | 1988 | Bristol, Pa. |
| Rusk, Troy, dh-c | .243 | 41 | 144 | 14 | 35 | 6 | 1 | 6 | 26 | 11 | 45 | 0 | 0 | L | R | 6-3 | 225 | 9-24-67 | 1990 | Seattle, Wash. |
| Schall, Gene, 1b-dh | .326 | 82 | 285 | 51 | 93 | 12 | 4 | 15 | 60 | 24 | 56 | 2 | 1 | R | R | 6-3 | 190 | 6-5-70 | 1991 | Willow Grove, Pa. |
| Taylor, Sam, of | .277 | 49 | 173 | 31 | 48 | 12 | 0 | 5 | 27 | 30 | 24 | 9 | 3 | L | L | 5-11 | 185 | 8-6-68 | 1989 | Murray, Ky. |
| Tokheim, David, of | .292 | 65 | 257 | 30 | 75 | 11 | 6 | 2 | 25 | 12 | 36 | 9 | 6 | L | L | 6-1 | 185 | 5-25-69 | 1991 | Menlo Park, Calif. |
| Waller, Casey, 2b | .260 | 53 | 169 | 25 | 44 | 8 | 4 | 2 | 18 | 15 | 20 | 1 | 0 | S | R | 5-11 | 180 | 12-15-67 | 1989 | South Boston, Va. |

| PITCHING | W | L | ERA | G | GS | CG | SV | IP | H | R | ER | BB | SO | B | T | HT | WT | DOB | 1st Yr | Resides |
|---|---|---|---|---|---|---|---|---|---|---|---|---|---|---|---|---|---|---|---|---|
| Allen, Ron | 4 | 5 | 4.45 | 15 | 15 | 0 | 0 | 85 | 82 | 45 | 42 | 35 | 63 | R | R | 5-11 | 185 | 5-10-70 | 1991 | Kirkland, Wash. |
| Borland, Toby | 2 | 2 | 2.52 | 44 | 0 | 0 | 13 | 54 | 38 | 17 | 15 | 20 | 74 | R | R | 6-7 | 175 | 5-29-69 | 1989 | Quitman, La. |
| Bottalico, Ricky | 3 | 3 | 2.25 | 49 | 0 | 0 | 20 | 72 | 63 | 22 | 18 | 26 | 65 | L | R | 6-1 | 190 | 8-26-69 | 1991 | Newington, Conn. |
| Brown, Greg | 5 | 6 | 5.72 | 18 | 17 | 1 | 0 | 94 | 119 | 72 | 60 | 29 | 42 | R | R | 6-2 | 200 | 3-28-70 | 1991 | Marietta, Ga. |
| Carter, Andy | 1 | 1 | 2.82 | 4 | 4 | 0 | 0 | 22 | 15 | 8 | 7 | 12 | 16 | L | L | 6-5 | 190 | 11-9-68 | 1987 | Erdenheim, Pa. |
| Doolan, Blake | 7 | 8 | 5.09 | 27 | 15 | 1 | 0 | 110 | 135 | 70 | 62 | 36 | 61 | R | R | 6-0 | 178 | 2-11-69 | 1992 | Pasadena, Texas |
| Farmer, Mike | 5 | 10 | 5.03 | 22 | 18 | 0 | 0 | 102 | 125 | 62 | 57 | 34 | 64 | S | L | 6-1 | 175 | 7-3-68 | 1990 | Gary, Ind. |
| Gaddy, Bob | 6 | 4 | 2.51 | 22 | 8 | 1 | 0 | 75 | 64 | 22 | 21 | 29 | 55 | R | L | 6-1 | 202 | 1-11-67 | 1989 | Pensacola, Fla. |
| Goedhart, Darrell | 9 | 12 | 5.20 | 27 | 26 | 1 | 0 | 152 | 160 | 94 | 88 | 54 | 110 | R | R | 6-3 | 210 | 7-18-70 | 1989 | San Jacinto, Calif. |
| Goergen, Todd | 2 | 1 | 3.06 | 3 | 3 | 0 | 0 | 18 | 14 | 7 | 6 | 4 | 10 | S | R | 6-2 | 190 | 6-22-68 | 1988 | Lakewood, Colo. |
| Hassinger, Brad | 0 | 0 | 9.00 | 1 | 0 | 0 | 0 | 2 | 4 | 2 | 2 | 0 | 0 | R | R | 6-0 | 195 | 11-29-67 | 1990 | Berrysburg, Pa. |
| Hill, Eric | 2 | 3 | 4.59 | 21 | 7 | 0 | 0 | 69 | 72 | 44 | 35 | 30 | 37 | R | R | 6-2 | 190 | 11-19-67 | 1990 | Corryton, Tenn. |
| Holman, Craig | 8 | 13 | 4.14 | 24 | 24 | 4 | 0 | 139 | 134 | 73 | 64 | 43 | 86 | S | R | 6-2 | 200 | 3-13-69 | 1991 | Attalla, Ala. |

# PHILLIES: ORGANIZATION LEADERS

### MAJOR LEAGUERS

**BATTING**

| | | |
|---|---|---|
| *AVG | Kevin Stocker | .324 |
| R | Len Dykstra | 143 |
| H | Len Dykstra | 194 |
| TB | Len Dykstra | 307 |
| 2B | Len Dykstra | 44 |
| 3B | Mickey Morandini | 9 |
| HR | Two tied at | 24 |
| RBI | Darren Daulton | 105 |
| BB | Len Dykstra | 129 |
| SO | Darren Daulton | 111 |
| SB | Len Dykstra | 37 |

**PITCHING**

| | | |
|---|---|---|
| W | Tommy Greene | 16 |
| L | Danny Jackson | 11 |
| #ERA | David West | 2.92 |
| G | David West | 76 |
| CG | Three tied at | 7 |
| SV | Mitch Williams | 43 |
| IP | Curt Schilling | 235 |
| BB | Ben Rivera | 85 |
| SO | Curt Schilling | 186 |

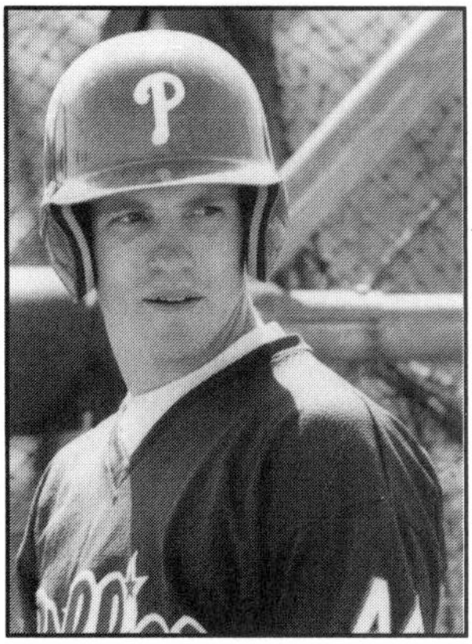

MEL BAILEY

**Kevin Stocker**
Rookie shortstop hit .324

### MINOR LEAGUERS

**BATTING**

| | | |
|---|---|---|
| *AVG | Luis Brito, Spartanburg | .313 |
| R | Phil Geisler, Clearwater-Reading | 97 |
| H | Phil Geisler, Clearwater-Reading | 153 |
| TB | Phil Geisler, Clearwater-Reading | 254 |
| 2B | Two tied at | 37 |
| 3B | Two tied at | 8 |
| HR | Gene Schall, Reading | 19 |
| RBI | Alan Burke, Spartanburg-Clearwater | 99 |
| BB | Pat Brady, Scranton-Reading | 79 |
| SO | Phil Geisler, Clearwater | 120 |
| SB | Mike Murphy, Spartanburg | 33 |

**PITCHING**

| | | |
|---|---|---|
| W | Mark Tranberg, Clearwater-Spartanburg | 15 |
| L | Chad Anderson, Spartanburg | 14 |
| #ERA | Mark Tranberg, Clearwater-Spart | 2.23 |
| G | Toby Borland, Reading-Scranton | 70 |
| CG | Mark Tranberg, Clearwater-Spartanburg | 6 |
| SV | Ricky Bottalico, Reading-Clearwater | 24 |
| IP | Chad Anderson, Spartanburg | 191 |
| BB | Larry Mitchell, Spartanburg-Clearwater | 75 |
| SO | Larry Mitchell, Spartanburg-Clearwater | 159 |

*Minimum 250 At-Bats #Minimum 75 Innings

## PHILLIES: MOST COMMON LINEUPS

| | Philadelphia<br>Majors | Scranton/WB<br>AAA | Reading<br>AA | Clearwater<br>A | Spartanburg<br>A |
|---|---|---|---|---|---|
| C | Darren Daulton (146) | Mike Lieberthal (106) | Jose Fernandez (38) | Jason Moler (73) | Scott Haws (69) |
| 1B | John Kruk (144) | Jeff Manto (53) | Ron Lockett (98) | Jon Zuber (117) | Alan Burke (73) |
| 2B | Mickey Morandini (111) | Greg Legg (55) | Mica Lewis (59) | Mike Gomez (118) | David Doster (60) |
| 3B | Dave Hollins (143) | Victor Rodriguez (64) | Carlo Colombino (85) | Rob Grable (95) | Andy Sallee (63) |
| SS | Kevin Stocker (70) | Kevin Stocker (81) | Keith Kimberlin (134) | David Fisher (113) | Luis Brito (127) |
| OF | Lenny Dykstra (160) | Tony Longmire (107) | Jeff Jackson (96) | Jay Edwards (119) | Mike Murphy (125) |
| | Jim Eisenreich (137) | Ruben Amaro (100) | Mickey Hyde (69) | Chad McConnell (87) | Shawn Wills (105) |
| | Milt Thompson (106) | Cary Williams (73) | David Tokheim (64) | Phil Geisler (85) | Stan Evans (77) |
| DH | N/A | Sean Ryan (15) | Gene Schall (29) | Troy Rusk (38) | Steve Solomon (27) |
| SP | Curt Schilling (34) | Kyle Abbott (27) | Darrell Goedhart (26) | Jamie Sepeda (26) | Chad Anderson (29) |
| RP | David West (76) | Jeff Patterson (62) | Scott Wiegandt (56) | J.J. Munoz (56) | Steve Nutt (46) |

Full-season farm clubs only    No. of games at position in parenthesis

| PITCHING | W | L | ERA | G | GS | CG | SV | IP | H | R | ER | BB | SO | B | T | HT | WT | DOB | 1st Yr | Resides |
|---|---|---|---|---|---|---|---|---|---|---|---|---|---|---|---|---|---|---|---|---|
| Marchok, Chris | 2 | 5 | 5.59 | 40 | 3 | 0 | 0 | 77 | 82 | 52 | 48 | 19 | 50 | L | L | 6-2 | 190 | 12-25-64 | 1987 | Morrisville, Pa. |
| Sullivan, Mike | 0 | 3 | 3.38 | 31 | 0 | 0 | 4 | 45 | 42 | 20 | 17 | 13 | 29 | R | R | 6-3 | 195 | 1-27-68 | 1989 | Dallas, Texas |
| Wiegandt, Scott | 6 | 2 | 3.56 | 56 | 0 | 0 | 0 | 73 | 75 | 41 | 29 | 44 | 60 | L | L | 5-11 | 180 | 12-9-67 | 1989 | Louisville, Ky. |

## CLEARWATER     A
### FLORIDA STATE LEAGUE

| BATTING | AVG | G | AB | R | H | 2B | 3B | HR | RBI | BB | SO | SB | CS | B | T | HT | WT | DOB | 1st Yr | Resides |
|---|---|---|---|---|---|---|---|---|---|---|---|---|---|---|---|---|---|---|---|---|
| Bennett, Gary, c-dh | .327 | 17 | 55 | 5 | 18 | 0 | 0 | 1 | 6 | 3 | 10 | 0 | 1 | R | R | 6-0 | 190 | 4-17-72 | 1990 | Waukegan, Ill. |
| Burke, Alan, of-dh | .111 | 8 | 27 | 2 | 3 | 0 | 0 | 1 | 3 | 2 | 7 | 0 | 0 | R | R | 6-0 | 190 | 11-28-70 | 1992 | Anaheim, Calif. |
| Doster, David, 2b-3b | .357 | 9 | 28 | 4 | 10 | 3 | 1 | 0 | 2 | 2 | 2 | 0 | 0 | R | R | 5-10 | 185 | 10-8-70 | 1993 | New Haven, Ind. |
| Edwards, Jay, of | .253 | 124 | 430 | 57 | 109 | 23 | 4 | 0 | 53 | 48 | 64 | 21 | 11 | R | R | 6-2 | 180 | 1-16-69 | 1990 | Crawford, Miss. |
| Estalella, Robert, c | .229 | 11 | 35 | 4 | 8 | 0 | 0 | 4 | 2 | 3 | 0 | 0 | 0 | R | R | 6-1 | 200 | 8-23-74 | 1993 | Pembroke Pines, Fla. |
| Evans, Stan, of | .271 | 39 | 133 | 13 | 36 | 5 | 1 | 0 | 12 | 14 | 12 | 4 | 3 | L | R | 5-11 | 175 | 12-17-70 | 1992 | Oak Hill, Fla. |
| Fisher, David, ss | .240 | 126 | 430 | 54 | 103 | 25 | 2 | 6 | 54 | 52 | 42 | 11 | 17 | R | R | 6-0 | 160 | 2-26-70 | 1992 | Joplin, Mo. |
| Geisler, Phil, of | .305 | 87 | 344 | 72 | 105 | 23 | 4 | 15 | 62 | 29 | 70 | 4 | 5 | L | L | 6-3 | 200 | 10-23-69 | 1991 | Springfield, Ore. |
| Gomez, Mike, 2b | .286 | 124 | 496 | 63 | 142 | 21 | 2 | 1 | 44 | 26 | 23 | 7 | 11 | R | R | 5-11 | 170 | 11-25-70 | 1992 | Northeast, Md. |
| Grable, Rob, 3b | .313 | 98 | 351 | 60 | 110 | 27 | 5 | 5 | 55 | 49 | 72 | 16 | 9 | R | R | 6-2 | 200 | 1-20-70 | 1991 | Bohemia, N.Y. |
| Hayden, David, 3b-ss | .310 | 97 | 290 | 42 | 90 | 13 | 0 | 0 | 27 | 39 | 38 | 8 | 9 | R | R | 5-11 | 170 | 12-1-69 | 1991 | Okahumpka, Fla. |
| Hopp, Dean, c | .098 | 26 | 51 | 5 | 5 | 1 | 0 | 1 | 4 | 4 | 16 | 0 | 1 | R | R | 6-3 | 185 | 3-20-70 | 1991 | Tulsa, Okla. |
| Larson, Danny, of-dh | .248 | 47 | 129 | 14 | 32 | 5 | 1 | 0 | 16 | 8 | 38 | 3 | 2 | L | L | 6-2 | 195 | 1-24-72 | 1990 | Van Nuys, Calif. |
| McConnell, Chad, of | .240 | 90 | 300 | 43 | 72 | 17 | 3 | 6 | 37 | 51 | 98 | 9 | 5 | R | R | 6-1 | 180 | 10-13-70 | 1992 | Sioux Falls, S.D. |
| Moler, Jason, c | .289 | 97 | 350 | 59 | 101 | 17 | 2 | 15 | 64 | 46 | 40 | 5 | 7 | R | R | 6-1 | 195 | 10-29-69 | 1991 | Yorba Linda, Calif. |
| Rosado, Edwin, c-1b | .204 | 39 | 137 | 22 | 28 | 7 | 2 | 2 | 12 | 9 | 18 | 4 | 1 | S | R | 5-9 | 170 | 1-25-69 | 1988 | Bristol, Pa. |
| Rusk, Troy, dh-c | .296 | 61 | 199 | 30 | 59 | 8 | 1 | 10 | 40 | 23 | 55 | 0 | 3 | L | R | 6-3 | 225 | 9-24-67 | 1990 | Seattle, Wash. |
| Sirak, Ken, inf | .196 | 25 | 51 | 8 | 10 | 3 | 0 | 1 | 5 | 6 | 16 | 1 | 0 | L | R | 6-1 | 185 | 11-8-68 | 1989 | Camarillo, Calif. |
| Tokheim, David, of | .329 | 41 | 155 | 27 | 51 | 8 | 2 | 0 | 11 | 14 | 17 | 7 | 5 | L | L | 6-1 | 185 | 5-25-69 | 1991 | Menlo Park, Calif. |
| Vilet, Tom, of | .185 | 18 | 27 | 4 | 5 | 0 | 0 | 0 | 4 | 3 | 11 | 0 | 0 | R | R | 6-0 | 175 | 1-25-70 | 1991 | Cortland, Ill. |
| Zuber, Jon, 1b-of | .308 | 129 | 494 | 70 | 152 | 37 | 5 | 5 | 69 | 49 | 47 | 6 | 6 | L | L | 6-1 | 175 | 12-10-69 | 1992 | Moraga, Calif. |

| PITCHING | W | L | ERA | G | GS | CG | SV | IP | H | R | ER | BB | SO | B | T | HT | WT | DOB | 1st Yr | Resides |
|---|---|---|---|---|---|---|---|---|---|---|---|---|---|---|---|---|---|---|---|---|
| Blazier, Ron | 9 | 8 | 3.94 | 27 | 23 | 1 | 0 | 155 | 171 | 80 | 68 | 40 | 86 | R | R | 6-6 | 215 | 7-30-71 | 1990 | Bellwood, Pa. |
| Boldt, Sean | 0 | 0 | 9.00 | 2 | 0 | 0 | 0 | 3 | 7 | 5 | 3 | 1 | 2 | R | R | 6-2 | 180 | 10-12-72 | 1991 | West Hills, Calif. |
| Bottalico, Ricky | 1 | 0 | 2.75 | 13 | 0 | 0 | 4 | 20 | 19 | 6 | 6 | 5 | 19 | L | R | 6-1 | 190 | 8-26-69 | 1991 | Newington, Conn. |
| Brown, Greg | 8 | 3 | 2.94 | 11 | 11 | 1 | 0 | 67 | 76 | 29 | 22 | 11 | 21 | R | R | 6-2 | 200 | 3-28-70 | 1991 | Marietta, Ga. |
| Corry, Steve | 0 | 0 | 1.50 | 1 | 1 | 0 | 0 | 6 | 4 | 3 | 1 | 2 | 5 | S | R | 6-2 | 180 | 4-23-70 | 1988 | Cedar City, Utah |
| DeJesus, Jose | 3 | 6 | 4.07 | 11 | 10 | 1 | 0 | 55 | 65 | 32 | 25 | 19 | 33 | R | R | 6-5 | 195 | 1-6-65 | 1983 | Cidra, P.R. |
| DeSantis, Dom | 1 | 3 | 3.45 | 49 | 1 | 0 | 3 | 89 | 92 | 43 | 34 | 27 | 42 | R | R | 6-3 | 225 | 5-14-69 | 1991 | Pembroke Pines, Fla. |
| Gilmore, Joel | 5 | 0 | 3.30 | 7 | 7 | 0 | 0 | 44 | 45 | 18 | 16 | 7 | 22 | R | R | 6-6 | 230 | 12-16-69 | 1991 | Conroe, Texas |
| Gomes, Wayne | 0 | 0 | 1.17 | 9 | 0 | 0 | 4 | 8 | 4 | 1 | 1 | 9 | 13 | R | R | 6-0 | 215 | 1-15-73 | 1993 | Hampton, Va. |
| Heisler, Laurence | 1 | 3 | 3.26 | 19 | 2 | 0 | 0 | 50 | 49 | 18 | 18 | 19 | 27 | R | R | 6-0 | 185 | 2-17-70 | 1991 | St. Cloud, Fla. |
| Holman, Craig | 0 | 0 | 2.50 | 7 | 1 | 0 | 0 | 18 | 17 | 7 | 5 | 1 | 7 | S | R | 6-2 | 200 | 3-13-69 | 1991 | Attalla, Ala. |
| Humphry, Trevor | 0 | 1 | 6.75 | 9 | 0 | 0 | 0 | 13 | 18 | 11 | 10 | 13 | 7 | R | R | 6-2 | 210 | 10-31-71 | 1992 | Delight, Ark. |
| Juhl, Mike | 2 | 1 | 0.96 | 21 | 0 | 0 | 4 | 28 | 23 | 6 | 3 | 3 | 24 | L | L | 5-9 | 180 | 8-10-69 | 1991 | Lake Katrine, N.Y. |
| Kirkland, Kris | 0 | 1 | 15.00 | 2 | 0 | 0 | 0 | 3 | 7 | 5 | 5 | 3 | 0 | R | R | 6-0 | 200 | 5-3-70 | 1992 | West Columbia, S.C. |
| Mitchell, Larry | 4 | 4 | 3.00 | 9 | 9 | 1 | 0 | 57 | 50 | 23 | 19 | 21 | 45 | R | R | 6-1 | 200 | 10-16-71 | 1992 | Charlottesville, Va. |
| Munoz, J.J. | 5 | 2 | 2.45 | 56 | 0 | 0 | 9 | 77 | 59 | 22 | 21 | 26 | 81 | L | L | 5-9 | 170 | 11-1-67 | 1990 | Mesquite, Texas |
| Rama, Shelby | 3 | 2 | 4.26 | 7 | 6 | 2 | 0 | 38 | 35 | 19 | 18 | 18 | 12 | S | R | 6-6 | 210 | 1-22-72 | 1993 | Phoenix, Ariz. |
| Randall, Mark | 6 | 8 | 5.11 | 52 | 2 | 0 | 8 | 76 | 99 | 47 | 43 | 26 | 41 | R | R | 6-1 | 175 | 5-17-70 | 1989 | Sherwood Park, Alberta |
| Sepeda, Jamie | 9 | 9 | 3.60 | 26 | 26 | 2 | 0 | 160 | 165 | 81 | 64 | 63 | 97 | R | R | 6-2 | 200 | 12-8-70 | 1992 | Sinton, Texas |
| Tranberg, Mark | 7 | 3 | 2.50 | 14 | 13 | 2 | 0 | 76 | 78 | 26 | 21 | 18 | 59 | R | R | 6-4 | 210 | 2-28-69 | 1992 | Buena Park, Calif. |
| Trisler, John | 10 | 6 | 4.69 | 27 | 22 | 0 | 0 | 117 | 138 | 74 | 61 | 49 | 71 | R | R | 6-4 | 235 | 3-19-70 | 1991 | Indianapolis, Ind. |
| Wells, Robert | 1 | 0 | 0.98 | 12 | 1 | 0 | 2 | 28 | 23 | 5 | 3 | 6 | 24 | R | R | 6-0 | 180 | 11-1-66 | 1989 | Yakima, Wash. |

## SPARTANBURG     A
### SOUTH ATLANTIC LEAGUE

| BATTING | AVG | G | AB | R | H | 2B | 3B | HR | RBI | BB | SO | SB | CS | B | T | HT | WT | DOB | 1st Yr | Resides |
|---|---|---|---|---|---|---|---|---|---|---|---|---|---|---|---|---|---|---|---|---|
| Bennett, Gary, c | .254 | 42 | 126 | 18 | 32 | 4 | 1 | 0 | 15 | 12 | 22 | 0 | 2 | R | R | 6-0 | 190 | 4-17-72 | 1990 | Waukegan, Ill. |
| Bigler, Jeff, 1b | .260 | 66 | 231 | 26 | 60 | 23 | 1 | 1 | 35 | 23 | 43 | 0 | 0 | L | L | 6-0 | 190 | 9-13-69 | 1991 | Mequon, Wis. |
| Brito, Luis, ss | .313 | 127 | 467 | 56 | 146 | 16 | 4 | 0 | 33 | 11 | 47 | 9 | 12 | S | R | 6-0 | 155 | 4-12-71 | 1989 | San Pedro de Macoris, D.R. |
| Brophy, E.J., c | .185 | 51 | 162 | 12 | 30 | 4 | 0 | 2 | 11 | 6 | 48 | 1 | 0 | R | R | 6-3 | 210 | 4-17-70 | 1992 | Montgomery, Ala. |
| Burke, Alan, 1b-of | .281 | 129 | 481 | 62 | 135 | 29 | 0 | 17 | 96 | 49 | 92 | 1 | 1 | R | R | 6-0 | 190 | 11-28-70 | 1992 | Anaheim, Calif. |
| Carmona, William, 1b | .200 | 4 | 10 | 2 | 2 | 0 | 0 | 0 | 3 | 2 | 1 | 0 | 0 | R | R | 6-2 | 198 | 6-20-72 | 1990 | San Mateo, Venez. |
| De los Santos, Rey, dh | .231 | 37 | 104 | 12 | 24 | 2 | 2 | 1 | 11 | 9 | 31 | 1 | 1 | L | R | 6-2 | 190 | 11-31-70 | 1988 | San Pedro de Macoris, D.R. |
| Doster, David, 2b | .274 | 60 | 223 | 34 | 61 | 15 | 0 | 3 | 20 | 25 | 36 | 1 | 0 | R | R | 5-10 | 185 | 10-8-70 | 1993 | New Haven, Ind. |

| BATTING | AVG | G | AB | R | H | 2B | 3B | HR | RBI | BB | SO | SB | CS | B | T | HT | WT | DOB | 1st Yr | Resides |
|---|---|---|---|---|---|---|---|---|---|---|---|---|---|---|---|---|---|---|---|---|
| Evans, Stan, of | .273 | 83 | 275 | 52 | 75 | 13 | 2 | 1 | 24 | 46 | 48 | 17 | 12 | L | R | 5-11 | 175 | 12-17-70 | 1992 | Oak Hill, Fla. |
| Haws, Scott, c | .244 | 73 | 234 | 23 | 57 | 7 | 0 | 1 | 21 | 37 | 44 | 2 | 3 | L | R | 6-0 | 190 | 1-11-72 | 1992 | Fairless Hills, Pa. |
| Hernandez, Ramon, 3b | .176 | 7 | 17 | 0 | 3 | 1 | 0 | 0 | 1 | 0 | 5 | 0 | 0 | R | R | 6-0 | 160 | 6-25-72 | 1990 | San Pedro de Macoris, D.R. |
| Kratz, Ron, 3b | .184 | 28 | 87 | 4 | 16 | 0 | 0 | 1 | 8 | 4 | 29 | 0 | 0 | L | R | 5-11 | 183 | 11-20-69 | 1992 | Schwenksville, Pa. |
| Kupsey, John, 3b-dh | .271 | 35 | 118 | 18 | 32 | 10 | 1 | 3 | 20 | 8 | 23 | 4 | 0 | R | R | 6-1 | 185 | 9-21-69 | 1988 | Gibbstown, N.J. |
| Larson, Danny, of | .250 | 34 | 112 | 16 | 28 | 4 | 2 | 1 | 10 | 19 | 29 | 1 | 3 | L | L | 6-2 | 195 | 1-24-72 | 1990 | Van Nuys, Calif. |
| Lawler, Brian, dh-1b | .185 | 18 | 54 | 5 | 10 | 3 | 0 | 0 | 2 | 3 | 19 | 0 | 0 | R | R | 6-0 | 215 | 11-22-69 | 1993 | Columbia, S.C. |
| Martinez, Ben, 2b | .000 | 1 | 0 | 0 | 0 | 0 | 0 | 0 | 0 | 0 | 0 | 0 | 0 | R | R | 5-10 | 185 | 3-19-74 | 1992 | St. Paul, Minn. |
| Murphy, Mike, of | .289 | 133 | 509 | 70 | 147 | 29 | 6 | 3 | 60 | 35 | 91 | 33 | 14 | R | R | 6-2 | 185 | 1-23-72 | 1990 | Albuquerque, N.M. |
| Ollison, Ron, 3b-2b | .267 | 100 | 322 | 43 | 86 | 8 | 2 | 3 | 35 | 30 | 51 | 10 | 7 | R | R | 5-9 | 170 | 7-7-71 | 1991 | Malvern, Ark. |
| Petillo, Bruce, c | .250 | 2 | 8 | 3 | 2 | 1 | 0 | 0 | 1 | 2 | 0 | 0 | 0 | R | R | 6-1 | 200 | 11-21-70 | 1993 | Yorba Linda, Calif. |
| Romero, Phil, 2b | .213 | 45 | 141 | 17 | 30 | 6 | 1 | 0 | 14 | 15 | 10 | 5 | 4 | R | R | 5-8 | 160 | 5-24-69 | 1992 | Fresno, Calif. |
| Ruth, Pat, dh-of | .286 | 4 | 14 | 1 | 4 | 1 | 0 | 0 | 1 | 0 | 4 | 0 | 0 | R | R | 6-1 | 200 | 3-17-69 | 1991 | Clovis, Calif. |
| Sallee, Andy, 3b-1b | .239 | 93 | 305 | 37 | 73 | 10 | 4 | 5 | 38 | 18 | 58 | 5 | 2 | L | R | 6-5 | 210 | 3-13-69 | 1991 | Sonoma, Calif. |
| Solomon, Steve, of-dh | .288 | 81 | 306 | 59 | 88 | 16 | 4 | 1 | 33 | 39 | 49 | 14 | 3 | L | L | 6-0 | 180 | 4-9-70 | 1992 | Los Angeles, Calif. |
| Wills, Shawn, of | .223 | 116 | 403 | 60 | 90 | 17 | 1 | 4 | 53 | 44 | 86 | 21 | 17 | R | R | 5-11 | 188 | 6-22-70 | 1992 | Hanford, Calif. |

| PITCHING | W | L | ERA | G | GS | CG | SV | IP | H | R | ER | BB | SO | B | T | HT | WT | DOB | 1st Yr | Resides |
|---|---|---|---|---|---|---|---|---|---|---|---|---|---|---|---|---|---|---|---|---|
| Agostinelli, Peter | 0 | 0 | 5.79 | 6 | 0 | 0 | 0 | 9 | 13 | 9 | 6 | 3 | 8 | L | L | 6-3 | 195 | 11-7-68 | 1992 | Spenceport, N.Y. |
| Alger, Kevin | 1 | 3 | 3.55 | 38 | 1 | 0 | 1 | 63 | 48 | 34 | 25 | 42 | 86 | L | L | 6-1 | 175 | 5-26-70 | 1993 | Harrisonburg, Va. |
| Anderson, Chad | 7 | 14 | 4.42 | 29 | 29 | 5 | 0 | 191 | 216 | 111 | 94 | 65 | 129 | R | R | 6-3 | 205 | 4-9-72 | 1990 | Roseburg, Ore. |
| Boldt, Sean | 0 | 0 | 5.84 | 17 | 0 | 0 | 4 | 25 | 34 | 17 | 16 | 12 | 24 | R | R | 6-2 | 180 | 10-12-72 | 1991 | West Hills, Calif. |
| Brown, Dan | 6 | 6 | 2.95 | 39 | 0 | 0 | 3 | 61 | 53 | 25 | 20 | 14 | 43 | R | R | 6-5 | 210 | 12-26-68 | 1991 | Vinita, Okla. |
| Corry, Steve | 0 | 2 | 6.75 | 15 | 4 | 0 | 0 | 29 | 28 | 23 | 22 | 21 | 22 | S | R | 6-2 | 180 | 4-23-70 | 1988 | Cedar City, Utah |
| Doolan, Blake | 2 | 2 | 1.70 | 8 | 8 | 1 | 0 | 58 | 50 | 16 | 11 | 9 | 34 | R | R | 6-0 | 178 | 2-11-69 | 1992 | Pasadena, Texas |
| Edwards, Sam | 3 | 6 | 4.38 | 15 | 15 | 3 | 0 | 99 | 105 | 49 | 48 | 25 | 63 | R | R | 6-3 | 160 | 12-20-71 | 1990 | Kissimmee, Fla. |
| Herrmann, Gary | 7 | 3 | 3.13 | 13 | 13 | 0 | 0 | 83 | 74 | 40 | 29 | 31 | 76 | R | L | 6-4 | 205 | 10-15-69 | 1992 | Houston, Texas |
| Humphry, Trevor | 1 | 7 | 11.78 | 10 | 9 | 0 | 0 | 37 | 57 | 54 | 48 | 29 | 29 | R | R | 6-2 | 210 | 10-31-71 | 1992 | Delight, Ark. |
| Irwin, Tom | 2 | 3 | 5.75 | 20 | 0 | 0 | 1 | 36 | 44 | 30 | 23 | 15 | 20 | R | R | 6-1 | 195 | 1-5-70 | 1992 | Victorville, Calif. |
| Lundberg, Bryan | 1 | 0 | 1.15 | 2 | 2 | 1 | 0 | 16 | 13 | 2 | 2 | 6 | 13 | R | R | 6-0 | 185 | 7-27-71 | 1993 | Glendale, Ariz. |
| Mitchell, Larry | 6 | 6 | 4.10 | 19 | 19 | 4 | 0 | 116 | 113 | 55 | 53 | 54 | 114 | R | R | 6-1 | 200 | 10-16-71 | 1992 | Charlottesville, Va. |
| Mitchell, Rob | 6 | 9 | 4.53 | 32 | 20 | 1 | 0 | 129 | 134 | 83 | 65 | 62 | 83 | R | R | 6-5 | 165 | 10-21-69 | 1991 | Phoenixville, Pa. |
| Nutt, Steve | 6 | 5 | 3.12 | 46 | 0 | 0 | 3 | 69 | 59 | 30 | 24 | 31 | 41 | L | L | 6-4 | 180 | 8-25-71 | 1992 | Ponca City, Okla. |
| Rama, Shelby | 4 | 6 | 3.21 | 10 | 10 | 1 | 0 | 70 | 62 | 28 | 25 | 36 | 32 | S | R | 6-6 | 210 | 1-22-72 | 1993 | Phoenix, Ariz. |
| Smith, Eric | 2 | 7 | 2.62 | 35 | 1 | 0 | 8 | 55 | 51 | 19 | 16 | 30 | 52 | R | R | 6-3 | 200 | 12-9-69 | 1992 | Salem, Utah |
| Tranberg, Mark | 8 | 1 | 1.98 | 11 | 11 | 4 | 0 | 82 | 54 | 24 | 18 | 21 | 83 | R | R | 6-4 | 210 | 2-28-69 | 1992 | Buena Park, Calif. |

## BATATIA A

### NEW YORK-PENN LEAGUE

| BATTING | AVG | G | AB | R | H | 2B | 3B | HR | RBI | BB | SO | SB | CS | B | T | HT | WT | DOB | 1st Yr | Resides |
|---|---|---|---|---|---|---|---|---|---|---|---|---|---|---|---|---|---|---|---|---|
| Angeli, Doug, ss | .218 | 75 | 252 | 20 | 55 | 7 | 3 | 0 | 15 | 18 | 33 | 5 | 6 | R | R | 5-10 | 180 | 1-7-71 | 1993 | Springfield, Ill. |
| Bell, Brent, of | .240 | 41 | 154 | 14 | 37 | 6 | 3 | 0 | 15 | 13 | 37 | 3 | 0 | R | R | 6-0 | 180 | 5-12-73 | 1991 | Downey, Calif. |
| Brainard, Matt, 3b-c | .212 | 63 | 226 | 23 | 48 | 13 | 3 | 1 | 16 | 22 | 51 | 7 | 5 | R | R | 6-1 | 195 | 1-3-71 | 1993 | New Castle, Del. |
| Gyselman, Jeff, c | .192 | 36 | 120 | 7 | 23 | 5 | 2 | 0 | 8 | 8 | 33 | 1 | 1 | R | R | 6-3 | 193 | 7-10-70 | 1993 | Bothell, Wash. |
| Held, Dan, 1b | .205 | 45 | 151 | 18 | 31 | 8 | 1 | 3 | 16 | 16 | 40 | 2 | 3 | R | R | 6-0 | 200 | 10-7-70 | 1993 | Neosho, Mo. |
| Hernandez, Ramon, ss | .229 | 10 | 35 | 3 | 8 | 1 | 0 | 0 | 4 | 0 | 7 | 1 | 0 | R | R | 6-0 | 160 | 6-25-72 | 1990 | San Pedro de Macoris, D.R. |
| Kendall, Jeremy, of | .280 | 73 | 275 | 48 | 77 | 17 | 4 | 1 | 23 | 27 | 60 | 31 | 13 | R | R | 5-9 | 170 | 9-3-71 | 1992 | East Troy, Wis. |
| Madden, Joe, of | .235 | 62 | 230 | 24 | 54 | 6 | 3 | 2 | 27 | 17 | 55 | 3 | 2 | R | R | 6-4 | 190 | 2-1-71 | 1993 | Richmond, Calif. |
| Mayfield, Chris, of | .095 | 8 | 21 | 3 | 2 | 0 | 0 | 0 | 1 | 5 | 7 | 1 | 1 | R | R | 6-0 | 200 | 8-1-71 | 1993 | Crowley, La. |
| McDonald, Dan, of-dh | .238 | 35 | 122 | 16 | 29 | 6 | 0 | 1 | 5 | 17 | 22 | 1 | 3 | R | R | 5-10 | 185 | 10-13-73 | 1993 | Sarasota, Fla. |
| McGinn, Shaun, 3b | .000 | 3 | 6 | 0 | 0 | 0 | 0 | 0 | 0 | 1 | 1 | 1 | 0 | R | R | 6-2 | 175 | 10-7-71 | 1993 | Omaha, Neb. |
| McMullen, Jon, dh-1b | .293 | 65 | 249 | 31 | 73 | 13 | 2 | 6 | 37 | 21 | 58 | 2 | 1 | L | R | 6-0 | 240 | 11-30-73 | 1992 | Ventura, Calif. |
| Moore, Charlton, of | .122 | 16 | 49 | 0 | 6 | 1 | 1 | 0 | 4 | 2 | 20 | 0 | 0 | R | R | 6-3 | 210 | 8-29-71 | 1993 | Hazel Crest, Ill. |
| Murphy, Neal, 1b-c | .167 | 39 | 150 | 11 | 25 | 5 | 0 | 1 | 10 | 5 | 26 | 1 | 0 | R | R | 6-0 | 205 | 6-7-71 | 1993 | Wappingers Falls, N.Y. |
| Petillo, Bruce, c | .228 | 19 | 57 | 12 | 13 | 5 | 0 | 1 | 5 | 12 | 15 | 0 | 0 | R | R | 6-1 | 200 | 11-21-70 | 1993 | Yorba Linda, Calif. |
| Sefcik, Kevin, 2b | .299 | 74 | 281 | 49 | 84 | 24 | 4 | 2 | 28 | 27 | 22 | 20 | 6 | R | R | 5-1 | 175 | 2-10-71 | 1993 | Tinley Park, Ill. |
| Thompson, Mike, of-dh | .239 | 30 | 92 | 11 | 22 | 4 | 1 | 1 | 11 | 11 | 36 | 1 | 1 | R | L | 6-4 | 212 | 10-25-71 | 1992 | Panama City, Fla. |
| Wiegandt, Bryan, 3b-2b | .281 | 27 | 96 | 6 | 27 | 1 | 1 | 0 | 10 | 7 | 18 | 2 | 1 | R | R | 6-1 | 185 | 3-25-71 | 1993 | Louisville, Ky. |

| PITCHING | W | L | ERA | G | GS | CG | SV | IP | H | R | ER | BB | SO | B | T | HT | WT | DOB | 1st Yr | Resides |
|---|---|---|---|---|---|---|---|---|---|---|---|---|---|---|---|---|---|---|---|---|
| Agostinelli, Peter | 3 | 2 | 2.59 | 24 | 1 | 1 | 4 | 42 | 31 | 12 | 12 | 13 | 36 | L | L | 6-3 | 195 | 11-7-68 | 1992 | Spenceport, N.Y. |
| Barstad, Scott | 0 | 2 | 5.02 | 8 | 0 | 0 | 0 | 14 | 14 | 8 | 8 | 15 | 9 | R | R | 6-3 | 200 | 8-4-71 | 1993 | Casper, Wyo. |

# PHILLIES TOP 10 PROSPECTS

How the Phillies Top 10 prospects, as judged by Baseball America prior to the 1993 season, fared in 1993:

| Player, Pos. | Club (Class) | AVG | AB | H | HR | RBI | SB |
|---|---|---|---|---|---|---|---|
| 2. Mike Lieberthal, c | Scranton (AAA) | .262 | 382 | 100 | 7 | 40 | 2 |
| 3. Kevin Stocker, ss | Scranton (AAA) | .233 | 313 | 73 | 3 | 17 | 17 |
| | Philadelphia | .324 | 259 | 84 | 2 | 31 | 5 |
| 4. Chad McConnell, of | Clearwater (A) | .240 | 300 | 72 | 6 | 37 | 9 |
| 5. Tom Nuneviller, of | Reading (AA) | .230 | 226 | 52 | 2 | 32 | 3 |
| 8. Tony Longmire, of | Scranton (AAA) | .304 | 447 | 136 | 6 | 67 | 12 |
| | Philadelphia | .231 | 13 | 3 | 0 | 1 | 0 |

| Player, Pos. | Club (Class) | W | L | ERA | IP | H | BB | SO |
|---|---|---|---|---|---|---|---|---|
| 1. Tyler Green, rhp | Scranton (AAA) | 6 | 10 | 3.95 | 118 | 102 | 43 | 87 |
| | Philadelphia | 0 | 0 | 7.36 | 7 | 16 | 5 | 7 |
| 6. Ron Blazier, rhp | Clearwater (A) | 9 | 8 | 3.94 | 155 | 171 | 40 | 86 |
| 7. Mike Williams, rhp | Scranton (AAA) | 9 | 2 | 2.87 | 97 | 93 | 16 | 53 |
| | Philadelphia | 1 | 3 | 5.29 | 51 | 50 | 22 | 33 |
| 9. Mike Farmer, lhp | Reading (AA) | 5 | 10 | 5.03 | 102 | 125 | 34 | 64 |
| 10. Paul Fletcher, rhp | Scranton (AAA) | 4 | 12 | 5.66 | 140 | 146 | 60 | 116 |
| | Philadelphia | 0 | 0 | 0.00 | 0 | 0 | 0 | 0 |

**Tyler Green**
6-10 at Triple-A

| PITCHING | W | L | ERA | G | GS | CG | SV | IP | H | R | ER | BB | SO | B | T | HT | WT | DOB | 1st Yr | Resides |
|---|---|---|---|---|---|---|---|---|---|---|---|---|---|---|---|---|---|---|---|---|
| Censale, Silvio | 5 | 2 | 2.08 | 9 | 9 | 1 | 0 | 52 | 39 | 20 | 12 | 19 | 54 | L | L | 6-2 | 195 | 11-21-71 | 1993 | Lodi, N.J. |
| Costa, Tony | 3 | 4 | 4.94 | 10 | 9 | 0 | 0 | 51 | 56 | 32 | 28 | 19 | 37 | R | R | 6-4 | 210 | 12-19-70 | 1992 | LeMoore, Calif. |
| Eggleston, Scott | 5 | 1 | 2.03 | 15 | 3 | 0 | 1 | 44 | 42 | 21 | 10 | 23 | 37 | R | R | 6-0 | 210 | 8-20-70 | 1991 | Liberty, Mo. |
| Fiore, Tony | 2 | 8 | 3.05 | 16 | 16 | 1 | 0 | 97 | 82 | 51 | 33 | 40 | 55 | R | R | 6-4 | 200 | 10-12-71 | 1992 | Chicago, Ill. |
| Franek, Tom | 3 | 5 | 3.34 | 15 | 15 | 0 | 0 | 86 | 86 | 39 | 32 | 21 | 40 | R | R | 6-3 | 200 | 11-16-70 | 1993 | Fort Collins, Colo. |
| Genke, Todd | 2 | 3 | 6.03 | 18 | 2 | 0 | 1 | 37 | 51 | 26 | 25 | 7 | 22 | R | R | 6-1 | 190 | 4-8-71 | 1993 | Greenfield, Wis. |
| Gomes, Wayne | 1 | 0 | 1.23 | 5 | 0 | 0 | 0 | 7 | 1 | 1 | 1 | 8 | 11 | R | R | 6-0 | 215 | 1-15-73 | 1993 | Hampton, Va. |
| Irwin, Tom | 1 | 3 | 2.72 | 26 | 0 | 0 | 8 | 43 | 40 | 16 | 13 | 11 | 43 | R | R | 6-1 | 195 | 1-5-70 | 1992 | Victorville, Calif. |
| Kirkland, Kris | 2 | 0 | 0.64 | 11 | 0 | 0 | 2 | 14 | 9 | 2 | 1 | 3 | 17 | R | R | 6-0 | 200 | 5-3-70 | 1992 | West Columbia, S.C. |
| Metheney, Nelson | 3 | 0 | 2.96 | 7 | 7 | 0 | 0 | 27 | 24 | 10 | 9 | 7 | 16 | R | R | 6-3 | 205 | 6-14-71 | 1993 | Salem, Va. |
| Pugh, Tim | 1 | 2 | 4.36 | 22 | 0 | 0 | 1 | 33 | 41 | 21 | 16 | 16 | 25 | L | L | 6-0 | 195 | 3-14-71 | 1992 | Baltimore, Md. |
| Swan, Tyrone | 5 | 4 | 3.19 | 15 | 15 | 1 | 0 | 87 | 83 | 43 | 31 | 34 | 86 | R | R | 6-7 | 195 | 5-7-69 | 1993 | Sparks, Nev. |
| Wood, Mike | 2 | 3 | 3.38 | 22 | 0 | 0 | 1 | 37 | 24 | 17 | 14 | 19 | 39 | R | R | 6-1 | 185 | 12-5-70 | 1993 | Chino Hills, Calif. |

# MARTINSVILLE R
## APPALACHIAN LEAGUE

| BATTING | AVG | G | AB | R | H | 2B | 3B | HR | RBI | BB | SO | SB | CS | B | T | HT | WT | DOB | 1st Yr | Resides |
|---|---|---|---|---|---|---|---|---|---|---|---|---|---|---|---|---|---|---|---|---|
| Allen, Dell, dh | .192 | 12 | 26 | 3 | 5 | 1 | 0 | 0 | 2 | 6 | 11 | 0 | 0 | R | R | 6-3 | 205 | 8-21-72 | 1992 | Davenport, Iowa |
| Amador, Manny, ss | .235 | 61 | 234 | 38 | 55 | 7 | 1 | 9 | 35 | 26 | 49 | 5 | 1 | S | R | 6-0 | 165 | 11-21-75 | 1993 | Santo Domingo, D.R. |
| Cornish, Tim, 3b-of | .194 | 19 | 62 | 10 | 12 | 3 | 1 | 1 | 4 | 7 | 19 | 4 | 2 | R | R | 6-1 | 175 | 10-16-72 | 1993 | Somis, Calif. |
| Costello, Brian, of | .254 | 60 | 209 | 28 | 53 | 8 | 1 | 5 | 19 | 37 | 52 | 6 | 3 | R | R | 6-1 | 195 | 10-4-74 | 1993 | Orlando, Fla. |
| Diaz, Linardo, of | .221 | 35 | 68 | 12 | 15 | 1 | 0 | 3 | 12 | 12 | 28 | 3 | 2 | R | R | 6-1 | 165 | 12-30-74 | 1993 | Berabona, D.R. |
| Estalella, Robert, c | .295 | 35 | 122 | 14 | 36 | 11 | 0 | 3 | 19 | 14 | 24 | 0 | 1 | R | R | 6-1 | 200 | 8-23-74 | 1993 | Pembroke Pines, Fla. |
| Fitzgerald, Barry, 1b | .192 | 26 | 78 | 8 | 15 | 3 | 0 | 3 | 7 | 5 | 29 | 0 | 0 | L | R | 5-11 | 180 | 8-6-74 | 1993 | Santee, Calif. |
| Hobbs, Shane, 1b-c | .193 | 44 | 135 | 14 | 26 | 7 | 1 | 0 | 14 | 8 | 23 | 0 | 1 | R | R | 6-2 | 195 | 4-9-74 | 1992 | Santee, Calif. |
| Key, Jeffrey, of | .251 | 61 | 219 | 37 | 55 | 8 | 1 | 10 | 35 | 26 | 69 | 8 | 5 | L | R | 6-1 | 200 | 11-22-74 | 1993 | Covington, Ga. |
| McGlawn, Tom, 2b | .159 | 23 | 63 | 7 | 10 | 1 | 0 | 0 | 1 | 8 | 12 | 4 | 1 | R | R | 5-8 | 160 | 3-18-70 | 1993 | Philadelphia, Pa. |
| Pierre-Louis, Danton, 1b | .261 | 35 | 115 | 14 | 30 | 5 | 1 | 3 | 17 | 8 | 35 | 5 | 3 | L | L | 6-1 | 200 | 2-6-75 | 1993 | New York, N.Y. |
| Rodriguez, Nate, 2b-ss | .245 | 57 | 208 | 22 | 51 | 1 | 0 | 0 | 16 | 10 | 15 | 4 | 6 | R | R | 5-8 | 165 | 1-7-70 | 1993 | Oakland, Calif. |
| Rolen, Scott, 3b | .313 | 25 | 80 | 8 | 25 | 5 | 0 | 0 | 12 | 10 | 15 | 3 | 4 | R | R | 6-4 | 210 | 4-4-75 | 1993 | Jasper, Ind. |
| Shipman, Mike, c | .238 | 45 | 160 | 20 | 38 | 8 | 0 | 2 | 11 | 9 | 49 | 1 | 1 | R | R | 6-0 | 195 | 3-29-74 | 1992 | Dexter, Mo. |
| Stingley, Derek, of | .254 | 34 | 126 | 32 | 32 | 9 | 4 | 2 | 20 | 17 | 31 | 18 | 5 | R | R | 6-0 | 185 | 4-9-71 | 1993 | Chicago, Ill. |
| Tinsley, Charles, of-dh | .100 | 22 | 50 | 9 | 5 | 1 | 0 | 1 | 4 | 9 | 29 | 2 | 1 | R | R | 6-2 | 195 | 1-4-75 | 1993 | Lynch, Ky. |
| Watts, Josh, of | .245 | 58 | 216 | 31 | 53 | 9 | 1 | 4 | 38 | 20 | 56 | 10 | 3 | L | R | 6-1 | 205 | 3-24-75 | 1993 | Glendale, Ariz. |
| Wiegandt, Bryan, 3b-2b | .255 | 29 | 98 | 12 | 25 | 6 | 0 | 1 | 10 | 12 | 29 | 1 | 1 | R | R | 6-1 | 185 | 3-25-71 | 1993 | Louisville, Ky. |

| PITCHING | W | L | ERA | G | GS | CG | SV | IP | H | R | ER | BB | SO | B | T | HT | WT | DOB | 1st Yr | Resides |
|---|---|---|---|---|---|---|---|---|---|---|---|---|---|---|---|---|---|---|---|---|
| Barstad, Scott | 1 | 1 | 9.37 | 9 | 0 | 0 | 0 | 16 | 18 | 17 | 17 | 10 | 15 | R | R | 6-3 | 200 | 8-4-71 | 1993 | Casper, Wyo. |
| Dabalack, Darin | 2 | 1 | 5.13 | 19 | 0 | 0 | 0 | 40 | 45 | 29 | 23 | 16 | 25 | R | R | 6-3 | 220 | 11-21-72 | 1993 | Garden Grove, Calif. |
| Foster, Mark | 1 | 9 | 4.93 | 13 | 13 | 0 | 0 | 69 | 77 | 55 | 38 | 42 | 50 | L | L | 6-1 | 200 | 12-24-71 | 1993 | Severn, Md. |
| Genke, Matt | 0 | 1 | 9.00 | 2 | 2 | 0 | 0 | 8 | 14 | 10 | 8 | 2 | 4 | R | R | 6-1 | 190 | 4-8-71 | 1993 | Greenfield, Wis. |
| Hamilton, Paul | 1 | 1 | 14.18 | 7 | 1 | 0 | 0 | 13 | 29 | 22 | 21 | 13 | 2 | R | R | 6-4 | 185 | 10-31-71 | 1993 | Cleveland, Texas |
| Humphry, Trevor | 1 | 3 | 1.64 | 18 | 0 | 0 | 3 | 33 | 25 | 8 | 6 | 13 | 40 | R | R | 6-2 | 210 | 10-31-71 | 1992 | Delight, Ark. |
| Hunter, Rich | 0 | 6 | 9.55 | 13 | 9 | 0 | 0 | 49 | 82 | 61 | 52 | 27 | 36 | R | R | 6-1 | 180 | 9-25-74 | 1993 | Temecula, Calif. |
| Lundberg, Bryan | 3 | 4 | 2.78 | 13 | 12 | 0 | 0 | 71 | 71 | 30 | 22 | 21 | 60 | R | R | 6-0 | 185 | 7-27-71 | 1993 | Glendale, Ariz. |
| McClurg, Clint | 1 | 1 | 4.71 | 11 | 0 | 0 | 0 | 21 | 17 | 19 | 11 | 14 | 18 | R | R | 6-5 | 195 | 11-29-73 | 1993 | Arvada, Colo. |
| Mejias, Fernando | 1 | 0 | 6.32 | 8 | 0 | 0 | 0 | 16 | 22 | 11 | 11 | 3 | 11 | R | R | 6-3 | 215 | 3-15-72 | 1991 | Maracay, Venez. |
| O'Connor, Brian | 3 | 2 | 4.28 | 8 | 7 | 0 | 0 | 40 | 48 | 23 | 19 | 11 | 34 | R | R | 6-1 | 190 | 4-21-71 | 1993 | Council Bluffs, Iowa |
| Olson, Chris | 2 | 3 | 5.26 | 11 | 9 | 1 | 0 | 53 | 64 | 33 | 31 | 23 | 27 | R | R | 6-3 | 215 | 9-27-71 | 1993 | Hastings, Neb. |
| Phipps, Chris | 0 | 6 | 8.84 | 14 | 6 | 0 | 2 | 39 | 63 | 63 | 38 | 26 | 28 | R | R | 6-3 | 200 | 2-27-74 | 1992 | Bristol, Tenn. |
| Rife, Jackie | 0 | 2 | 5.87 | 13 | 2 | 0 | 0 | 31 | 26 | 24 | 20 | 20 | 19 | S | R | 6-0 | 165 | 6-26-75 | 1993 | Richlands, Va. |
| Sanders, Lance | 2 | 3 | 4.50 | 12 | 7 | 1 | 0 | 50 | 55 | 43 | 25 | 18 | 40 | R | R | 6-0 | 185 | 4-25-71 | 1993 | Cypress, Texas |
| Szarko, Andy | 2 | 5 | 3.58 | 25 | 0 | 0 | 2 | 33 | 37 | 28 | 13 | 22 | 32 | S | R | 6-0 | 178 | 11-9-70 | 1993 | Yardley, Pa. |

# PITTSBURGH
## PIRATES

**Manager:** Jim Leyland.     **1993 Record:** 75-87, .463 (5th, NL East).

| BATTING | AVG | G | AB | R | H | 2B | 3B | HR | RBI | BB | SO | SB | CS | B | T | HT | WT | DOB | 1st Yr | Resides |
|---|---|---|---|---|---|---|---|---|---|---|---|---|---|---|---|---|---|---|---|---|
| Aude, Rich | .115 | 13 | 26 | 1 | 3 | 1 | 0 | 0 | 4 | 1 | 7 | 0 | 0 | R | R | 6-5 | 220 | 7-13-71 | 1989 | Chatsworth, Calif. |
| Bell, Jay | .310 | 154 | 604 | 102 | 187 | 32 | 9 | 9 | 51 | 77 | 122 | 16 | 10 | R | R | 6-1 | 175 | 12-11-65 | 1984 | Valrico, Fla. |
| Bullett, Scott | .200 | 23 | 55 | 2 | 11 | 0 | 2 | 0 | 4 | 3 | 15 | 3 | 2 | L | L | 6-2 | 190 | 12-25-68 | 1988 | Martinsburg, W.Va. |
| Clark, Dave | .271 | 110 | 277 | 43 | 75 | 11 | 2 | 11 | 46 | 38 | 58 | 1 | 0 | L | R | 6-2 | 210 | 9-3-62 | 1983 | Tupelo, Miss. |
| Cummings, Midre | .111 | 13 | 36 | 5 | 4 | 1 | 0 | 0 | 3 | 4 | 9 | 0 | 0 | L | R | 6-1 | 190 | 10-14-71 | 1990 | Miami, Fla. |
| Foley, Tom | .253 | 86 | 194 | 18 | 49 | 11 | 1 | 3 | 22 | 11 | 26 | 0 | 0 | L | R | 6-1 | 175 | 9-9-59 | 1977 | Miami, Fla. |
| Garcia, Carlos | .269 | 141 | 546 | 77 | 147 | 25 | 5 | 12 | 47 | 31 | 67 | 18 | 11 | R | R | 6-2 | 160 | 10-15-67 | 1987 | Bolivar, Venez. |
| Goff, Jerry | .297 | 14 | 37 | 5 | 11 | 2 | 0 | 2 | 6 | 8 | 9 | 0 | 0 | L | R | 6-3 | 200 | 4-12-64 | 1986 | San Rafael, Calif. |
| King, Jeff | .295 | 158 | 611 | 82 | 180 | 35 | 3 | 9 | 98 | 59 | 54 | 8 | 6 | R | R | 6-1 | 180 | 12-16-64 | 1986 | Wexford, Pa. |
| LaValliere, Mike | .200 | 1 | 5 | 0 | 1 | 0 | 0 | 0 | 0 | 0 | 0 | 0 | 0 | L | R | 5-10 | 210 | 8-18-60 | 1981 | Bradenton, Fla. |
| Martin, Al | .281 | 143 | 480 | 85 | 135 | 26 | 8 | 18 | 64 | 42 | 122 | 16 | 9 | L | L | 6-2 | 220 | 11-24-67 | 1985 | West Covina, Calif. |
| McClendon, Lloyd | .221 | 88 | 181 | 21 | 40 | 11 | 1 | 2 | 19 | 23 | 17 | 0 | 3 | R | R | 5-10 | 195 | 1-11-59 | 1980 | Merrillville, Ind. |
| Merced, Orlando | .313 | 137 | 447 | 68 | 140 | 26 | 4 | 8 | 70 | 77 | 64 | 3 | 3 | S | R | 5-11 | 170 | 11-2-66 | 1985 | Orlando, Fla. |
| Pennyfeather, Will | .206 | 21 | 34 | 4 | 7 | 1 | 0 | 0 | 2 | 0 | 6 | 0 | 1 | R | R | 6-2 | 215 | 5-25-68 | 1988 | Perth Amboy, N.J. |
| Prince, Tom | .196 | 66 | 179 | 14 | 35 | 14 | 0 | 2 | 24 | 13 | 38 | 1 | 1 | R | R | 5-11 | 185 | 8-13-64 | 1984 | Bradenton, Fla. |
| Shelton, Ben | .250 | 15 | 24 | 3 | 6 | 1 | 0 | 2 | 7 | 3 | 3 | 0 | 0 | R | L | 6-3 | 210 | 9-21-69 | 1987 | Oak Park, Ill. |
| Slaught, Don | .300 | 116 | 377 | 34 | 113 | 19 | 2 | 10 | 55 | 29 | 56 | 2 | 1 | R | R | 6-1 | 190 | 9-11-58 | 1980 | Arlington, Texas |
| Smith, Lonnie | .286 | 94 | 199 | 35 | 57 | 5 | 4 | 6 | 24 | 43 | 42 | 9 | 4 | R | R | 5-9 | 195 | 12-22-55 | 1974 | Atlanta, Ga. |
| Tomberlin, Andy | .286 | 27 | 42 | 4 | 12 | 0 | 1 | 1 | 5 | 2 | 14 | 0 | 0 | L | L | 5-11 | 160 | 11-7-66 | 1986 | Monroe, N.C. |
| Van Slyke, Andy | .310 | 83 | 323 | 42 | 100 | 13 | 4 | 8 | 50 | 24 | 40 | 11 | 2 | L | R | 6-2 | 195 | 12-21-60 | 1980 | Chesterfield, Mo. |
| Wehner, John | .143 | 29 | 35 | 3 | 5 | 0 | 0 | 0 | 6 | 1 | 0 | 0 | 0 | R | R | 6-3 | 205 | 6-29-67 | 1988 | Pittsburgh, Pa. |
| Wilson, Glenn | .143 | 10 | 14 | 0 | 2 | 0 | 0 | 0 | 0 | 0 | 9 | 0 | 0 | R | R | 6-1 | 190 | 12-22-58 | 1980 | Montgomery, Texas |
| Womack, Tony | .083 | 15 | 24 | 5 | 2 | 0 | 0 | 0 | 0 | 3 | 3 | 2 | 0 | L | R | 5-9 | 160 | 9-25-69 | 1991 | Chatham, Va. |
| Young, Kevin | .236 | 141 | 449 | 38 | 106 | 24 | 3 | 6 | 47 | 36 | 82 | 2 | 2 | R | R | 6-3 | 210 | 6-16-69 | 1990 | Kansas City, Kan. |

| PITCHING | W | L | ERA | G | GS | CG | SV | IP | H | R | ER | BB | SO | B | T | HT | WT | DOB | 1st Yr | Resides |
|---|---|---|---|---|---|---|---|---|---|---|---|---|---|---|---|---|---|---|---|---|
| Ballard, Jeff | 4 | 1 | 4.86 | 25 | 5 | 0 | 0 | 54 | 70 | 31 | 29 | 15 | 16 | L | L | 6-3 | 203 | 8-13-63 | 1985 | Billings, Mont. |
| Belinda, Stan | 3 | 1 | 3.61 | 40 | 0 | 0 | 19 | 42 | 35 | 18 | 17 | 11 | 30 | R | R | 6-3 | 185 | 8-6-66 | 1985 | Alexandria, Pa. |
| Candelaria, John | 0 | 3 | 8.24 | 24 | 0 | 0 | 1 | 20 | 25 | 19 | 18 | 9 | 17 | S | L | 6-6 | 225 | 11-6-53 | 1973 | Laguna Hills, Calif. |
| Cooke, Steve | 10 | 10 | 3.89 | 32 | 32 | 3 | 0 | 211 | 207 | 101 | 91 | 59 | 132 | R | L | 6-6 | 220 | 1-14-70 | 1990 | Tigard, Ore. |
| Dewey, Mark | 1 | 2 | 2.36 | 21 | 0 | 0 | 7 | 27 | 14 | 8 | 7 | 5 | 10 | R | R | 6-0 | 205 | 1-3-65 | 1987 | Jenison, Mich. |
| Hope, John | 0 | 2 | 4.03 | 7 | 7 | 0 | 0 | 38 | 47 | 19 | 17 | 8 | 8 | R | R | 6-3 | 195 | 12-21-70 | 1989 | Fort Lauderdale, Fla. |
| Johnston, Joel | 2 | 4 | 3.38 | 33 | 0 | 0 | 2 | 53 | 38 | 20 | 20 | 19 | 31 | R | R | 6-4 | 220 | 3-8-67 | 1988 | West Chester, Pa. |
| Menendez, Tony | 2 | 0 | 3.00 | 14 | 0 | 0 | 0 | 21 | 20 | 8 | 7 | 4 | 13 | R | R | 6-2 | 195 | 2-20-65 | 1984 | Carol City, Fla. |
| Miceli, Danny | 0 | 0 | 5.06 | 9 | 0 | 0 | 0 | 5 | 6 | 3 | 3 | 3 | 4 | R | R | 5-11 | 205 | 9-9-70 | 1990 | Orlando, Fla. |
| Miller, Paul | 0 | 0 | 5.40 | 3 | 2 | 0 | 0 | 10 | 15 | 6 | 6 | 2 | 2 | R | R | 6-5 | 215 | 4-27-65 | 1987 | Palatine, Ill. |
| Minor, Blas | 8 | 6 | 4.10 | 65 | 0 | 0 | 2 | 94 | 94 | 43 | 43 | 26 | 84 | R | R | 6-3 | 200 | 3-20-66 | 1988 | Gilbert, Ariz. |
| Moeller, Dennis | 1 | 0 | 9.92 | 10 | 0 | 0 | 0 | 16 | 26 | 20 | 18 | 7 | 13 | R | L | 6-2 | 195 | 9-15-67 | 1986 | Granada Hills, Calif. |
| Neagle, Denny | 3 | 5 | 5.31 | 50 | 7 | 0 | 1 | 81 | 82 | 49 | 48 | 37 | 73 | L | L | 6-2 | 215 | 9-13-68 | 1989 | Gambrills, Md. |
| Otto, Dave | 3 | 4 | 5.03 | 28 | 8 | 0 | 0 | 68 | 85 | 40 | 38 | 28 | 30 | L | L | 6-7 | 210 | 11-12-64 | 1985 | Elk Grove, Ill. |
| Petkovsek, Mark | 3 | 0 | 6.96 | 26 | 0 | 0 | 0 | 32 | 43 | 25 | 25 | 9 | 14 | R | R | 6-0 | 185 | 11-18-65 | 1987 | Beaumont, Texas |
| Robertson, Rich | 0 | 1 | 6.00 | 9 | 0 | 0 | 0 | 9 | 15 | 6 | 6 | 4 | 5 | L | L | 6-4 | 175 | 9-15-68 | 1990 | Waller, Texas |
| Shouse, Brian | 0 | 0 | 9.00 | 6 | 0 | 0 | 0 | 4 | 7 | 4 | 4 | 2 | 3 | L | L | 5-11 | 180 | 9-26-68 | 1990 | Effingham, Ill. |
| Smith, Zane | 3 | 7 | 4.55 | 14 | 14 | 1 | 0 | 83 | 97 | 43 | 42 | 22 | 32 | L | L | 6-2 | 195 | 12-28-60 | 1982 | Stone Mountain, Ga. |
| Toliver, Fred | 1 | 0 | 3.74 | 12 | 0 | 0 | 0 | 22 | 20 | 10 | 9 | 8 | 14 | R | R | 6-1 | 170 | 2-3-61 | 1979 | Highland, Calif. |
| Tomlin, Randy | 4 | 8 | 4.85 | 18 | 18 | 1 | 0 | 98 | 109 | 57 | 53 | 15 | 44 | L | L | 5-10 | 170 | 6-14-66 | 1988 | Mars, Pa. |
| Wagner, Paul | 8 | 8 | 4.27 | 44 | 17 | 1 | 2 | 141 | 143 | 72 | 67 | 42 | 114 | R | R | 6-3 | 205 | 11-14-67 | 1989 | Germantown, Wis. |
| Wakefield, Tim | 6 | 11 | 5.61 | 24 | 20 | 3 | 0 | 128 | 145 | 83 | 80 | 75 | 59 | R | R | 6-2 | 200 | 8-2-66 | 1988 | Melbourne, Fla. |
| Walk, Bob | 13 | 14 | 5.68 | 32 | 32 | 3 | 0 | 187 | 214 | 121 | 118 | 70 | 80 | R | R | 6-4 | 212 | 11-26-56 | 1977 | Frazier Park, Calif. |

## FIELDING

| Catcher | PCT | G | PO | A | E | DP |
|---|---|---|---|---|---|---|
| Goff | .984 | 14 | 54 | 7 | 1 | 1 |
| LaValliere | 1.000 | 1 | 12 | 0 | 0 | 0 |
| Prince | .984 | 59 | 271 | 31 | 5 | 6 |
| Slaught | .993 | 105 | 539 | 51 | 4 | 10 |

| First Base | PCT | G | PO | A | E | DP |
|---|---|---|---|---|---|---|
| Aude | 1.000 | 7 | 47 | 3 | 0 | 6 |
| Foley | .972 | 12 | 31 | 4 | 1 | 3 |
| McClendon | 1.000 | 6 | 14 | 2 | 0 | 1 |
| Merced | .993 | 42 | 276 | 20 | 2 | 23 |
| Shelton | 1.000 | 2 | 10 | 1 | 0 | 1 |
| Young | .998 | 135 | 1116 | 101 | 3 | 108 |

| Second Base | PCT | G | PO | A | E | DP |
|---|---|---|---|---|---|---|
| Foley | .993 | 35 | 70 | 64 | 1 | 19 |
| Garcia | .983 | 140 | 297 | 343 | 11 | 84 |

| | PCT | G | PO | A | E | DP |
|---|---|---|---|---|---|---|
| King | .900 | 2 | 3 | 6 | 1 | 2 |
| Wehner | 1.000 | 3 | 1 | 4 | 0 | 2 |

| Third Base | PCT | G | PO | A | E | DP |
|---|---|---|---|---|---|---|
| Foley | .958 | 7 | 4 | 19 | 1 | 1 |
| King | .964 | 156 | 105 | 353 | 17 | 28 |
| Wehner | 1.000 | 3 | 0 | 3 | 0 | 1 |
| Young | 1.000 | 6 | 6 | 11 | 0 | 0 |

| Shortstop | PCT | G | PO | A | E | DP |
|---|---|---|---|---|---|---|
| Bell | .986 | 154 | 255 | 527 | 11 | 100 |
| Foley | .935 | 6 | 11 | 18 | 2 | 6 |
| Garcia | 1.000 | 3 | 3 | 4 | 0 | 3 |
| King | 1.000 | 2 | 0 | 3 | 0 | 0 |
| Womack | .971 | 6 | 11 | 22 | 1 | 6 |

| Outfield | PCT | G | PO | A | E | DP |
|---|---|---|---|---|---|---|
| Aude | .000 | 1 | 0 | 0 | 1 | 0 |
| Bullett | 1.000 | 19 | 35 | 1 | 0 | 0 |
| Clark | .957 | 91 | 132 | 3 | 6 | 1 |
| Cummings | 1.000 | 11 | 21 | 0 | 0 | 0 |
| Martin | .975 | 136 | 268 | 6 | 7 | 0 |
| McClendon | .967 | 61 | 84 | 3 | 3 | 1 |
| Merced | .965 | 109 | 209 | 11 | 8 | 5 |
| Pennyfeather | 1.000 | 17 | 21 | 0 | 0 | 0 |
| Shelton | .889 | 6 | 7 | 1 | 1 | 0 |
| L. Smith | .981 | 60 | 104 | 1 | 2 | 0 |
| Tomberlin | 1.000 | 7 | 9 | 1 | 0 | 0 |
| Van Slyke | .995 | 78 | 205 | 2 | 1 | 1 |
| Wehner | 1.000 | 13 | 16 | 1 | 0 | 0 |
| Wilson | .875 | 5 | 5 | 2 | 1 | 0 |

# PIRATES FARM SYSTEM

| Class | Club | League | W | L | Pct. | Finish* | Manager | First Year |
|---|---|---|---|---|---|---|---|---|
| AAA | Buffalo (N.Y.) Bisons | American Assoc. | 71 | 73 | .493 | 4th (8) | Doc Edwards | 1988 |

| Class | Club | League | W | L | Pct. | Finish* | Manager | First Year |
|---|---|---|---|---|---|---|---|---|
| AA | Carolina (N.C.) Mudcats | Southern | 74 | 67 | .525 | 3rd (10) | John Wockenfuss | 1991 |
| A# | Salem (Va.) Buccaneers | Carolina | 61 | 79 | .436 | 8th (8) | Scott Little | 1987 |
| A | Augusta (Ga.) Pirates | South Atlantic | 59 | 82 | .418 | 12th (14) | Trent Jewett | 1988 |
| A | Welland (Ont.) Pirates | New York-Penn | 35 | 42 | .455 | 11th (14) | Larry Smith | 1989 |
| Rookie | Bradenton (Fla.) Pirates | Gulf Coast | 21 | 38 | .356 | 14th (15) | Woody Huyke | 1967 |

*Finish in overall standings (No. of teams in league)  #Advanced level

# BUFFALO   AAA
## AMERICAN ASSOCIATION

| BATTING | AVG | G | AB | R | H | 2B | 3B | HR | RBI | BB | SO | SB | CS | B | T | HT | WT | DOB | 1st Yr | Resides |
|---|---|---|---|---|---|---|---|---|---|---|---|---|---|---|---|---|---|---|---|---|
| Aude, Rich | .375 | 21 | 64 | 17 | 24 | 9 | 0 | 4 | 16 | 10 | 15 | 0 | 0 | R | R | 6-5 | 220 | 7-13-71 | 1989 | Chatsworth, Calif. |
| Beasley, Tony | .189 | 30 | 95 | 9 | 18 | 3 | 0 | 0 | 8 | 4 | 17 | 1 | 0 | R | R | 5-8 | 165 | 12-5-66 | 1989 | Bowling Green, Va. |
| Bell, Mike | .155 | 32 | 97 | 12 | 15 | 4 | 1 | 4 | 13 | 9 | 28 | 0 | 0 | L | L | 6-1 | 180 | 4-22-68 | 1987 | Andover, N.J. |
| Bullett, Scott | .287 | 110 | 408 | 62 | 117 | 13 | 6 | 1 | 30 | 39 | 67 | 28 | 17 | L | L | 6-2 | 190 | 12-25-68 | 1988 | Martinsburg, W.Va. |
| Cooper, Gary | .269 | 102 | 349 | 66 | 94 | 27 | 2 | 16 | 63 | 52 | 88 | 2 | 3 | R | R | 6-1 | 200 | 8-13-64 | 1986 | Orem, Utah |
| Cummings, Midre | .276 | 60 | 232 | 36 | 64 | 12 | 1 | 9 | 21 | 22 | 45 | 5 | 1 | L | R | 6-1 | 190 | 10-14-71 | 1990 | Miami, Fla. |
| Edge, Tim | .000 | 1 | 2 | 0 | 0 | 0 | 0 | 0 | 0 | 0 | 0 | 0 | 0 | R | R | 6-0 | 210 | 10-26-68 | 1990 | Auburn, Ala. |
| Encarnacion, Angelo | .333 | 3 | 9 | 1 | 3 | 0 | 0 | 0 | 2 | 0 | 0 | 0 | 0 | R | R | 5-9 | 175 | 4-18-73 | 1990 | Santo Domingo, D.R. |
| Goff, Jerry | .251 | 104 | 362 | 52 | 91 | 27 | 3 | 14 | 69 | 55 | 82 | 1 | 1 | L | R | 6-3 | 200 | 4-12-64 | 1986 | San Rafael, Calif. |
| Green, Tom | .346 | 8 | 26 | 3 | 9 | 2 | 0 | 0 | 9 | 2 | 7 | 0 | 0 | R | R | 6-2 | 173 | 5-19-68 | 1990 | Murrayville, Ga. |
| Leiper, Tim | .327 | 75 | 208 | 21 | 68 | 15 | 5 | 2 | 33 | 11 | 18 | 1 | 3 | L | R | 5-11 | 175 | 7-19-66 | 1985 | Cary, N.C. |
| Marx, Tim | .143 | 4 | 14 | 1 | 2 | 1 | 0 | 0 | 0 | 2 | 4 | 0 | 0 | R | R | 6-2 | 190 | 11-27-68 | 1991 | Evansville, Ind. |
| Morman, Russ | .320 | 119 | 409 | 79 | 131 | 34 | 2 | 22 | 77 | 48 | 59 | 0 | 3 | R | R | 6-4 | 215 | 4-28-62 | 1983 | Blue Springs, Mo. |
| Munoz, Omer | .217 | 40 | 129 | 7 | 28 | 4 | 1 | 2 | 16 | 3 | 11 | 0 | 0 | R | R | 5-9 | 156 | 3-6-66 | 1985 | Oshkosh, Wis. |
| Pennyfeather, William | .249 | 112 | 457 | 54 | 114 | 18 | 3 | 14 | 41 | 18 | 92 | 10 | 12 | R | R | 6-2 | 215 | 5-25-68 | 1988 | Perth Amboy, N.J. |
| Rohde, Dave | .244 | 131 | 464 | 64 | 113 | 22 | 2 | 11 | 48 | 50 | 46 | 4 | 5 | S | R | 6-2 | 182 | 5-8-64 | 1986 | Newport Beach, Calif. |
| Romero, Mandy | .228 | 42 | 136 | 11 | 31 | 6 | 1 | 2 | 14 | 6 | 12 | 1 | 0 | R | S | 5-11 | 196 | 10-19-67 | 1988 | Miami, Fla. |
| Sandoval, Jim | .230 | 65 | 209 | 23 | 48 | 7 | 2 | 5 | 21 | 13 | 37 | 1 | 0 | R | R | 5-11 | 170 | 8-25-69 | 1990 | Ahoeme, Mexico |
| Schreiber, Bruce | .200 | 15 | 40 | 8 | 8 | 1 | 0 | 0 | 2 | 2 | 11 | 0 | 0 | R | R | 6-0 | 185 | 5-4-67 | 1989 | Appleton, Wis. |
| Shelton, Ben | .277 | 65 | 173 | 25 | 48 | 8 | 1 | 5 | 22 | 24 | 44 | 0 | 0 | R | L | 6-3 | 210 | 9-21-69 | 1987 | Oak Park, Ill. |
| Tomberlin, Andy | .285 | 68 | 221 | 41 | 63 | 11 | 6 | 12 | 45 | 18 | 43 | 3 | 0 | L | L | 5-11 | 160 | 11-7-66 | 1986 | Monroe, N.C. |
| Wehner, John | .252 | 89 | 330 | 61 | 83 | 22 | 2 | 7 | 34 | 40 | 53 | 17 | 3 | R | R | 6-3 | 205 | 6-29-67 | 1988 | Pittsburgh, Pa. |
| Wilson, Glenn | .279 | 61 | 201 | 32 | 56 | 14 | 1 | 12 | 43 | 16 | 38 | 0 | 1 | R | R | 6-1 | 190 | 12-22-58 | 1980 | Montgomery, Texas |

| PITCHING | W | L | ERA | G | GS | CG | SV | IP | H | R | ER | BB | SO | B | T | HT | WT | DOB | 1st Yr | Resides |
|---|---|---|---|---|---|---|---|---|---|---|---|---|---|---|---|---|---|---|---|---|
| Backlund, Brett | 0 | 4 | 10.55 | 5 | 5 | 0 | 0 | 21 | 30 | 25 | 25 | 14 | 10 | R | R | 6-0 | 195 | 12-16-69 | 1992 | Salem, Ore. |
| Ballard, Jeff | 6 | 1 | 2.29 | 12 | 12 | 1 | 0 | 75 | 79 | 22 | 19 | 17 | 40 | L | L | 6-3 | 203 | 8-13-63 | 1985 | Billings, Mont. |
| Beatty, Blaine | 2 | 3 | 5.50 | 20 | 4 | 0 | 1 | 36 | 51 | 25 | 22 | 8 | 14 | L | L | 6-2 | 190 | 4-25-64 | 1986 | Victoria, Texas |
| Cecena, Jose | 0 | 1 | 4.91 | 6 | 0 | 0 | 0 | 7 | 12 | 10 | 4 | 8 | 7 | R | R | 5-9 | 180 | 8-20-63 | 1983 | Obregon, Mexico |
| Cole, Victor | 1 | 3 | 8.54 | 6 | 6 | 0 | 0 | 26 | 35 | 25 | 25 | 24 | 14 | S | R | 5-10 | 160 | 1-23-68 | 1988 | Monterey, Calif. |
| Dalton, Mike | 3 | 1 | 4.11 | 25 | 0 | 0 | 2 | 35 | 37 | 16 | 16 | 12 | 16 | R | L | 6-0 | 200 | 3-27-63 | 1983 | Mountain View, Calif. |
| Dewey, Mark | 2 | 0 | 1.23 | 22 | 0 | 0 | 6 | 29 | 21 | 9 | 4 | 5 | 17 | R | R | 6-0 | 205 | 1-3-65 | 1987 | Jenison, Mich. |
| Hancock, Lee | 2 | 6 | 4.91 | 11 | 11 | 0 | 0 | 66 | 73 | 38 | 36 | 14 | 30 | L | L | 6-4 | 215 | 6-27-67 | 1988 | Saratoga, Calif. |
| Hope, John | 2 | 1 | 6.33 | 4 | 4 | 0 | 0 | 21 | 30 | 16 | 15 | 2 | 6 | R | R | 6-3 | 195 | 12-21-70 | 1989 | Fort Lauderdale, Fla. |
| Hunter, Bobby | 0 | 1 | 9.64 | 11 | 0 | 0 | 0 | 14 | 18 | 15 | 15 | 10 | 8 | S | R | 6-1 | 187 | 8-29-68 | 1989 | Allandale, Fla. |
| Irvine, Daryl | 1 | 3 | 4.30 | 37 | 0 | 0 | 0 | 46 | 41 | 24 | 22 | 26 | 19 | R | R | 6-3 | 195 | 11-15-64 | 1985 | McGaheysville, Va. |
| Johnston, Joel | 1 | 3 | 7.76 | 26 | 0 | 0 | 1 | 31 | 30 | 28 | 27 | 25 | 26 | R | R | 6-4 | 220 | 3-8-67 | 1988 | West Chester, Pa. |
| McMurtry, Craig | 6 | 4 | 3.44 | 30 | 13 | 1 | 1 | 97 | 102 | 44 | 37 | 38 | 63 | R | R | 6-5 | 215 | 11-5-59 | 1980 | Troy, Texas |
| Menendez, Tony | 4 | 5 | 2.42 | 54 | 0 | 0 | 24 | 63 | 50 | 20 | 17 | 21 | 48 | R | R | 6-2 | 195 | 2-20-65 | 1984 | Carol City, Fla. |
| Miller, Paul | 3 | 1 | 4.47 | 10 | 10 | 0 | 0 | 52 | 57 | 28 | 26 | 14 | 25 | R | R | 6-5 | 215 | 4-27-65 | 1987 | Palatine, Ill. |
| Moeller, Dennis | 3 | 4 | 4.34 | 24 | 11 | 0 | 0 | 77 | 85 | 43 | 37 | 21 | 33 | R | L | 6-2 | 195 | 9-15-67 | 1986 | Granada Hills, Calif. |
| Neagle, Denny | 0 | 0 | 0.00 | 3 | 0 | 0 | 0 | 3 | 3 | 0 | 0 | 2 | 6 | L | L | 6-2 | 215 | 9-13-68 | 1989 | Gambrills, Md. |
| Petkovsek, Mark | 3 | 4 | 4.33 | 14 | 11 | 1 | 0 | 71 | 74 | 38 | 34 | 16 | 27 | R | R | 6-0 | 185 | 11-18-65 | 1987 | Beaumont, Texas |
| Piatt, Doug | 1 | 0 | 27.00 | 2 | 0 | 0 | 0 | 1 | 3 | 3 | 3 | 1 | 2 | L | R | 6-1 | 190 | 9-26-65 | 1988 | Beaver, Pa. |
| Robertson, Rich | 9 | 8 | 4.28 | 23 | 23 | 2 | 0 | 132 | 141 | 67 | 63 | 52 | 71 | L | L | 6-4 | 175 | 9-15-68 | 1990 | Waller, Texas |
| Shouse, Brian | 1 | 0 | 3.83 | 48 | 0 | 0 | 2 | 52 | 54 | 24 | 22 | 17 | 25 | L | L | 5-11 | 180 | 9-26-68 | 1990 | Effingham, Ill. |
| Smith, Roy | 15 | 11 | 4.13 | 28 | 28 | 4 | 0 | 168 | 178 | 87 | 77 | 38 | 87 | R | R | 6-3 | 212 | 9-6-61 | 1979 | New Rochelle, N.Y. |
| Toliver, Fred | 1 | 3 | 3.65 | 13 | 0 | 0 | 0 | 12 | 13 | 5 | 5 | 9 | 11 | R | R | 6-1 | 179 | 1-24-61 | 1979 | Highland, Calif. |
| Tracy, Jim | 2 | 2 | 4.33 | 15 | 5 | 0 | 0 | 35 | 35 | 19 | 17 | 10 | 20 | R | R | 6-3 | 180 | 11-30-65 | 1985 | Lynn, Mass. |
| White, Rick | 0 | 3 | 3.54 | 7 | 3 | 0 | 0 | 28 | 25 | 13 | 11 | 8 | 16 | R | R | 6-3 | 210 | 12-23-68 | 1990 | Paducah, Ky. |
| Zimmerman, Mike | 3 | 1 | 4.08 | 33 | 0 | 0 | 1 | 46 | 45 | 23 | 21 | 28 | 32 | R | R | 6-1 | 180 | 2-6-69 | 1990 | Brooklyn, N.Y. |

### FIELDING

| Catcher | PCT | G | PO | A | E | DP |
|---|---|---|---|---|---|---|
| Edge | 1.000 | 1 | 2 | 1 | 0 | 1 |
| Encamacion | 1.000 | 3 | 14 | 1 | 0 | 0 |
| Goff | .987 | 100 | 499 | 48 | 7 | 2 |
| Marx | 1.000 | 4 | 21 | 1 | 0 | 0 |
| Romero | .973 | 36 | 168 | 13 | 5 | 2 |

| First Base | PCT | G | PO | A | E | DP |
|---|---|---|---|---|---|---|
| Aude | .995 | 18 | 174 | 13 | 1 | 17 |
| Bell | .995 | 21 | 174 | 16 | 1 | 23 |
| Leiper | 1.000 | 5 | 55 | 1 | 0 | 7 |
| Morman | .991 | 89 | 814 | 60 | 8 | 97 |
| Shelton | .979 | 24 | 170 | 13 | 4 | 27 |

| Second Base | PCT | G | PO | A | E | DP |
|---|---|---|---|---|---|---|
| Beasley | .959 | 28 | 68 | 74 | 6 | 23 |
| Munoz | .962 | 23 | 37 | 64 | 4 | 21 |
| Rohde | .974 | 53 | 104 | 160 | 7 | 49 |

| | PCT | G | PO | A | E | DP |
|---|---|---|---|---|---|---|
| Schreiber | 1.000 | 1 | 3 | 3 | 0 | 2 |
| Wehner | .968 | 44 | 106 | 139 | 8 | 37 |

| Third Base | PCT | G | PO | A | E | DP |
|---|---|---|---|---|---|---|
| Cooper | .932 | 73 | 38 | 153 | 14 | 23 |
| Goff | 1.000 | 2 | 1 | 5 | 0 | 1 |
| Leiper | .938 | 22 | 16 | 44 | 4 | 7 |
| Rohde | .833 | 7 | 1 | 14 | 3 | 1 |
| Schreiber | .833 | 7 | 4 | 11 | 3 | 4 |
| Wehner | .941 | 47 | 27 | 117 | 9 | 17 |

| Shortstop | PCT | G | PO | A | E | DP |
|---|---|---|---|---|---|---|
| Cooper | 1.000 | 1 | 2 | 1 | 0 | 2 |
| Leiper | 1.000 | 1 | 0 | 1 | 0 | 0 |
| Munoz | .954 | 15 | 20 | 42 | 3 | 6 |
| Rohde | .972 | 64 | 101 | 211 | 9 | 51 |
| Sandoval | .966 | 60 | 86 | 200 | 10 | 50 |

| | PCT | G | PO | A | E | DP |
|---|---|---|---|---|---|---|
| Schreiber | .976 | 7 | 16 | 24 | 1 | 2 |

| Outfield | PCT | G | PO | A | E | DP |
|---|---|---|---|---|---|---|
| Bell | 1.000 | 10 | 12 | 0 | 0 | 0 |
| Bullett | .970 | 102 | 222 | 6 | 7 | 1 |
| Cooper | 1.000 | 30 | 49 | 1 | 0 | 0 |
| Cummings | .978 | 58 | 90 | 1 | 2 | 1 |
| Green | 1.000 | 7 | 18 | 0 | 0 | 0 |
| Leiper | 1.000 | 33 | 57 | 3 | 0 | 1 |
| Pennyfeather | .987 | 111 | 293 | 21 | 4 | 4 |
| Rohde | 1.000 | 7 | 11 | 0 | 0 | 0 |
| Shelton | .964 | 17 | 25 | 2 | 1 | 2 |
| Tomberlin | .957 | 60 | 104 | 7 | 5 | 1 |
| Wehner | .000 | 1 | 0 | 0 | 0 | 0 |
| Wilson | .984 | 25 | 59 | 4 | 1 | 0 |

**Promising Rookies.** Three first-year players who made an impact with the Pirates in 1993, from left: lefthander Steve Cooke (10-10, 3.89), outfielder Al Martin (.281-18-64) and second baseman Carlos Garcia (.269-12-47).

# CAROLINA                                                                                 AA
## SOUTHERN LEAGUE

| BATTING | AVG | G | AB | R | H | 2B | 3B | HR | RBI | BB | SO | SB | CS | B | T | HT | WT | DOB | 1st Yr | Resides |
|---|---|---|---|---|---|---|---|---|---|---|---|---|---|---|---|---|---|---|---|---|
| Aude, Rich, 1b | .289 | 120 | 422 | 66 | 122 | 25 | 3 | 18 | 73 | 50 | 79 | 8 | 4 | R | R | 6-5 | 220 | 7-13-71 | 1989 | Chatsworth, Calif. |
| Banister, Jeff, c-1b | .333 | 8 | 15 | 2 | 5 | 1 | 0 | 0 | 4 | 1 | 0 | 0 | 0 | R | R | 6-2 | 200 | 1-15-65 | 1986 | La Porte, Texas |
| Beasley, Tony, 2b | .202 | 82 | 252 | 39 | 51 | 7 | 3 | 4 | 13 | 23 | 52 | 11 | 6 | R | R | 5-8 | 165 | 12-5-66 | 1989 | Bowling Green, Va. |
| Cummings, Midre, of | .295 | 63 | 237 | 33 | 70 | 17 | 2 | 6 | 26 | 14 | 23 | 5 | 3 | L | R | 6-1 | 190 | 10-14-71 | 1990 | Miami, Fla. |
| De los Santos, Alberto, of | .223 | 47 | 148 | 17 | 33 | 5 | 3 | 0 | 10 | 5 | 18 | 4 | 3 | R | R | 5-11 | 160 | 12-16-69 | 1988 | San Pedro de Macoris, D.R. |
| Edge, Tim, c | .219 | 46 | 160 | 12 | 35 | 8 | 0 | 3 | 16 | 11 | 41 | 1 | 2 | R | R | 6-0 | 210 | 10-26-68 | 1990 | Auburn, Ala. |
| Green, Tom, of | .238 | 98 | 311 | 42 | 74 | 14 | 4 | 5 | 48 | 32 | 66 | 4 | 7 | R | R | 6-2 | 173 | 5-19-68 | 1990 | Murrayville, Ga. |
| Johnson, Mark, 1b-of | .233 | 125 | 399 | 48 | 93 | 18 | 4 | 14 | 52 | 66 | 93 | 6 | 2 | L | L | 6-4 | 220 | 10-17-67 | 1990 | Worcester, Mass. |
| Krevokuch, Jim, 3b | .253 | 125 | 395 | 58 | 100 | 15 | 3 | 4 | 30 | 53 | 38 | 4 | 3 | R | R | 5-11 | 175 | 5-13-69 | 1991 | West Newton, Pa. |
| Leiper, Tim, 3b-of | .258 | 44 | 132 | 11 | 34 | 4 | 0 | 1 | 11 | 10 | 6 | 0 | 1 | L | R | 5-11 | 175 | 7-19-66 | 1985 | Cary, N.C. |
| Neff, Marty, of | .222 | 20 | 63 | 2 | 14 | 3 | 0 | 0 | 5 | 0 | 18 | 0 | 1 | R | R | 6-2 | 185 | 2-12-70 | 1991 | Anaheim, Calif. |
| Ortiz, Javier, of | .339 | 33 | 109 | 17 | 37 | 10 | 1 | 5 | 24 | 15 | 18 | 1 | 1 | R | R | 6-4 | 210 | 1-22-63 | 1983 | Hialeah, Fla. |
| Osik, Keith, c | .280 | 103 | 371 | 47 | 104 | 21 | 2 | 10 | 47 | 30 | 46 | 0 | 2 | R | R | 6-0 | 195 | 10-22-68 | 1990 | Rocky Point, N.Y. |
| Polcovich, Kevin, 2b | .273 | 4 | 11 | 1 | 3 | 0 | 0 | 0 | 1 | 1 | 1 | 0 | 0 | R | R | 5-9 | 165 | 6-28-70 | 1992 | Auburn, N.Y. |
| Purdy, Alan, 2b-ss | .268 | 18 | 56 | 9 | 15 | 3 | 1 | 0 | 9 | 3 | 11 | 0 | 0 | R | R | 6-2 | 170 | 11-6-70 | 1993 | Nashville, Tenn. |
| Ratliff, Daryl, of | .284 | 121 | 454 | 59 | 129 | 15 | 4 | 0 | 47 | 35 | 58 | 29 | 13 | R | R | 6-1 | 180 | 10-15-69 | 1989 | Santa Cruz, Calif. |
| Rodriguez, Roman, ss | .182 | 4 | 11 | 0 | 2 | 0 | 0 | 0 | 0 | 3 | 3 | 0 | 0 | R | R | 6-1 | 162 | 3-30-69 | 1988 | Aragua, Venez. |
| Schreiber, Bruce, ss-3b | .260 | 94 | 296 | 42 | 77 | 11 | 3 | 2 | 28 | 20 | 50 | 1 | 2 | R | R | 6-0 | 185 | 5-4-67 | 1989 | Appleton, Wis. |
| Sondrini, Joe, 2b | .222 | 60 | 185 | 21 | 41 | 8 | 0 | 0 | 13 | 13 | 33 | 2 | 3 | R | R | 6-1 | 180 | 3-28-68 | 1990 | Pittsfield, Mass. |
| Thomas, Keith, of | .238 | 94 | 336 | 40 | 80 | 9 | 2 | 15 | 52 | 22 | 110 | 12 | 8 | R | R | 6-1 | 180 | 9-12-68 | 1986 | Chicago, Ill. |
| Van Slyke, Andy, of | .000 | 2 | 4 | 0 | 0 | 0 | 0 | 0 | 1 | 1 | 3 | 0 | 0 | L | R | 6-2 | 195 | 12-21-60 | 1980 | Chesterfield, Mo. |
| Womack, Tony, ss | .304 | 60 | 247 | 41 | 75 | 7 | 2 | 0 | 23 | 17 | 34 | 21 | 6 | L | R | 5-9 | 160 | 9-25-69 | 1991 | Chatham, Va. |

| PITCHING | W | L | ERA | G | GS | CG | SV | IP | H | R | ER | BB | SO | B | T | HT | WT | DOB | 1st Yr | Resides |
|---|---|---|---|---|---|---|---|---|---|---|---|---|---|---|---|---|---|---|---|---|
| Backlund, Brett | 7 | 5 | 4.58 | 20 | 20 | 0 | 0 | 106 | 115 | 66 | 54 | 28 | 94 | R | R | 6-0 | 195 | 12-16-69 | 1992 | Salem, Ore. |
| Beatty, Blaine | 7 | 3 | 2.85 | 18 | 13 | 2 | 0 | 95 | 68 | 42 | 30 | 35 | 67 | L | L | 6-2 | 190 | 4-25-64 | 1986 | Victoria, Texas |
| Cecena, Jose | 3 | 3 | 2.20 | 14 | 0 | 0 | 0 | 16 | 10 | 4 | 4 | 6 | 21 | R | R | 5-9 | 180 | 8-20-63 | 1983 | Obregon, Mexico |
| Christiansen, Jason | 0 | 0 | 0.00 | 2 | 0 | 0 | 0 | 3 | 3 | 0 | 0 | 1 | 2 | R | L | 6-5 | 235 | 9-21-69 | 1991 | Elkhorn, Neb. |
| Cole, Victor | 0 | 4 | 5.93 | 27 | 0 | 0 | 8 | 41 | 39 | 30 | 27 | 31 | 35 | S | R | 5-10 | 160 | 1-23-68 | 1988 | Monterey, Calif. |
| De los Santos, Mariano | 1 | 2 | 4.73 | 8 | 8 | 0 | 0 | 40 | 49 | 24 | 21 | 15 | 34 | L | R | 5-11 | 200 | 7-13-70 | 1989 | Santo Domingo, D.R. |
| Garza, Alex | 4 | 3 | 3.69 | 35 | 4 | 0 | 1 | 68 | 63 | 34 | 28 | 24 | 45 | R | R | 6-6 | 215 | 5-21-66 | 1989 | Monterrey, Mexico |
| Hancock, Lee | 7 | 3 | 2.53 | 25 | 11 | 0 | 0 | 100 | 87 | 42 | 28 | 32 | 85 | L | L | 6-4 | 215 | 6-27-67 | 1988 | Saratoga, Calif. |

# PIRATES: ORGANIZATION LEADERS

## MAJOR LEAGUERS

**BATTING**

| | | |
|---|---|---|
| *AVG | Orlando Merced | .313 |
| R | Jay Bell | 102 |
| H | Jay Bell | 187 |
| TB | Jay Bell | 264 |
| 2B | Jeff King | 35 |
| 3B | Jay Bell | 9 |
| HR | Al Martin | 18 |
| RBI | Jeff King | 98 |
| BB | Two tied at | 77 |
| SO | Two tied at | 122 |
| SB | Carlos Garcia | 18 |

**PITCHING**

| | | |
|---|---|---|
| W | Bob Walk | 13 |
| L | Bob Walk | 14 |
| #ERA | Steve Cooke | 3.89 |
| G | Blas Minor | 65 |
| CG | Three tied at | 3 |
| SV | Stan Belinda | 19 |
| IP | Steve Cooke | 211 |
| BB | Tim Wakefield | 75 |
| SO | Steve Cooke | 132 |

**Jay Bell**
Steady shortstop scored 102 runs

## MINOR LEAGUERS

**BATTING**

| | | |
|---|---|---|
| *AVG | Russ Morman, Buffalo | .320 |
| R | Rich Aude, Carolina-Buffalo | 83 |
| H | Tony Womack, Salem-Carolina | 166 |
| TB | Rich Aude, Carolina-Buffalo | 252 |
| 2B | Two tied at | 34 |
| 3B | Scott Bullett, Buffalo | 6 |
| HR | Two tied at | 22 |
| RBI | Rich Aude, Carolina-Buffalo | 89 |
| BB | Mark Johnson, Carolina | 66 |
| SO | Keith Thomas, Carolina-Salem | 140 |
| SB | Tony Womack, Salem-Carolina | 49 |

**PITCHING**

| | | |
|---|---|---|
| W | Roy Smith, Buffalo | 15 |
| L | Dave Doorneweerd, Salem-Augusta | 13 |
| #ERA | Jeff Ballard, Buffalo | 2.29 |
| G | Mike Zimmerman, Buffalo-Carolina | 66 |
| CG | Roy Smith, Buffalo | 4 |
| SV | Two tied at | 24 |
| IP | Roy Smith, Buffalo | 168 |
| BB | Dave Doorneweerd, Salem-Augusta | 74 |
| SO | Michel LaPlante, Buffalo-Salem | 124 |

*Minimum 250 At-Bats   #Minimum 75 Innings

BERNARD TRONCALE

| PITCHING | W | L | ERA | G | GS | CG | SV | IP | H | R | ER | BB | SO | B | T | HT | WT | DOB | 1st Yr | Resides |
|---|---|---|---|---|---|---|---|---|---|---|---|---|---|---|---|---|---|---|---|---|
| Harrah, Doug | 1 | 4 | 9.47 | 6 | 6 | 1 | 0 | 26 | 40 | 28 | 27 | 9 | 17 | R | R | 6-0 | 175 | 4-23-69 | 1991 | Newton Falls, Ohio |
| Hope, John | 9 | 4 | 4.37 | 21 | 20 | 0 | 0 | 111 | 123 | 69 | 54 | 29 | 66 | R | R | 6-3 | 195 | 12-21-70 | 1989 | Fort Lauderdale, Fla. |
| Hunter, Bobby | 5 | 3 | 1.01 | 46 | 0 | 0 | 7 | 71 | 54 | 11 | 8 | 35 | 53 | S | R | 6-4 | 187 | 8-29-68 | 1989 | Allandale, Fla. |
| Jones, Dan | 0 | 5 | 4.82 | 11 | 9 | 0 | 1 | 52 | 63 | 30 | 28 | 21 | 34 | R | R | 6-2 | 210 | 11-15-69 | 1991 | Cedar Falls, Iowa |
| Leiper, Dave | 2 | 1 | 1.48 | 8 | 4 | 2 | 0 | 30 | 26 | 6 | 5 | 5 | 16 | L | L | 6-1 | 160 | 6-18-62 | 1982 | Plano, Texas |
| Lieber, Jon | 4 | 2 | 3.97 | 6 | 6 | 0 | 0 | 34 | 39 | 15 | 15 | 10 | 28 | L | R | 6-3 | 205 | 4-2-70 | 1992 | Council Bluffs, Iowa |
| 2-team (4 Memphis).... | 6 | 3 | 5.07 | 10 | 10 | 0 | 0 | 55 | 71 | 31 | 31 | 16 | 48 | | | | | | | |
| Loaiza, Steve | 2 | 1 | 3.77 | 7 | 7 | 1 | 0 | 43 | 39 | 18 | 18 | 12 | 40 | R | R | 6-2 | 172 | 12-31-71 | 1991 | Imperial Beach, Calif. |
| McCurry, Jeff | 2 | 1 | 2.79 | 23 | 0 | 0 | 0 | 29 | 24 | 11 | 9 | 14 | 14 | R | R | 6-6 | 220 | 1-21-70 | 1991 | Houston, Texas |
| Miceli, Dan | 0 | 2 | 5.11 | 13 | 0 | 0 | 10 | 12 | 11 | 8 | 7 | 4 | 19 | R | R | 5-11 | 205 | 9-9-70 | 1990 | Orlando, Fla. |
| 2-team (40 Memphis).. | 0 | 0 | 4.69 | 53 | 0 | 0 | 17 | 71 | 65 | 38 | 37 | 43 | 87 | | | | | | | |
| Miller, Paul | 2 | 2 | 2.82 | 6 | 6 | 0 | 0 | 38 | 31 | 15 | 12 | 12 | 33 | R | R | 6-5 | 215 | 4-27-65 | 1987 | Palatine, Ill. |
| Parkinson, Eric | 0 | 0 | 2.08 | 2 | 0 | 0 | 0 | 4 | 4 | 2 | 1 | 1 | 2 | R | R | 6-3 | 175 | 3-3-69 | 1989 | Adrian, Mich. |
| Piatt, Doug | 0 | 0 | 14.73 | 3 | 0 | 0 | 0 | 4 | 10 | 6 | 6 | 1 | 3 | L | R | 6-1 | 190 | 9-26-65 | 1988 | Beaver, Pa. |
| 2-team (11 Memphis).. | 0 | 1 | 10.06 | 14 | 0 | 0 | 0 | 17 | 29 | 19 | 19 | 7 | 11 | | | | | | | |
| Smith, Zane | 1 | 2 | 3.05 | 4 | 4 | 0 | 0 | 21 | 20 | 10 | 7 | 5 | 13 | L | L | 6-2 | 195 | 12-28-60 | 1982 | Stone Mountain, Ga. |
| Tafoya, Dennis | 5 | 4 | 3.09 | 49 | 0 | 0 | 0 | 82 | 87 | 35 | 28 | 21 | 55 | R | R | 6-3 | 195 | 7-20-64 | 1987 | Stockton, Calif. |
| Toliver, Fred | 2 | 2 | 3.15 | 33 | 0 | 0 | 12 | 40 | 32 | 16 | 14 | 24 | 48 | R | R | 6-1 | 170 | 2-3-61 | 1979 | Highland, Calif. |
| Tomlin, Randy | 1 | 0 | 0.75 | 2 | 2 | 0 | 0 | 12 | 7 | 1 | 1 | 9 | 5 | L | L | 5-10 | 170 | 6-14-66 | 1988 | Mars, Pa. |
| Wakefield, Tim | 3 | 5 | 6.99 | 9 | 9 | 1 | 0 | 57 | 68 | 48 | 44 | 22 | 36 | R | R | 6-2 | 200 | 8-2-66 | 1988 | Melbourne, Fla. |
| White, Rick | 4 | 3 | 3.50 | 12 | 12 | 1 | 0 | 69 | 59 | 29 | 27 | 12 | 52 | R | R | 6-3 | 210 | 12-23-68 | 1990 | Paducah, Ky. |
| Zimmerman, Mike | 2 | 3 | 3.60 | 33 | 0 | 0 | 9 | 45 | 40 | 26 | 18 | 21 | 30 | R | R | 6-1 | 180 | 2-6-69 | 1990 | Brooklyn, N.Y. |

## SALEM A

## CAROLINA LEAGUE

| BATTING | AVG | G | AB | R | H | 2B | 3B | HR | RBI | BB | SO | SB | CS | B | T | HT | WT | DOB | 1st Yr | Resides |
|---|---|---|---|---|---|---|---|---|---|---|---|---|---|---|---|---|---|---|---|---|
| Bonifay, Ken, 3b-1b | .277 | 100 | 361 | 59 | 100 | 19 | 1 | 18 | 60 | 42 | 63 | 12 | 2 | L | R | 6-0 | 185 | 9-1-70 | 1991 | Kingsport, Tenn. |
| Brown, Mike, 1b | .271 | 126 | 436 | 71 | 118 | 25 | 3 | 21 | 70 | 61 | 109 | 6 | 4 | L | L | 6-7 | 245 | 11-4-71 | 1989 | Vacaville, Calif. |
| Calder, Joe, dh-1b | .231 | 13 | 39 | 4 | 9 | 2 | 0 | 1 | 6 | 3 | 15 | 1 | 0 | R | R | 6-2 | 210 | 12-9-72 | 1990 | San Sebastian, P.R. |
| Conger, Jeff, of | .230 | 110 | 391 | 40 | 90 | 12 | 1 | 4 | 31 | 31 | 125 | 24 | 10 | L | L | 6-0 | 185 | 8-6-71 | 1990 | Charlotte, N.C. |
| Encarnacion, Angelo, c | .256 | 70 | 238 | 20 | 61 | 12 | 1 | 3 | 24 | 13 | 27 | 1 | 4 | R | R | 5-9 | 175 | 4-18-73 | 1990 | Santo Domingo, D.R. |
| Espinosa, Ramon, of | .269 | 54 | 208 | 30 | 56 | 8 | 2 | 8 | 25 | 6 | 36 | 11 | 6 | R | R | 6-1 | 165 | 2-7-72 | 1990 | San Pedro de Macoris, D.R. |
| Farrell, Jon, of-dh | .238 | 105 | 386 | 58 | 92 | 9 | 1 | 20 | 51 | 40 | 103 | 5 | 6 | R | R | 6-2 | 180 | 7-30-71 | 1991 | Jacksonville, Fla. |
| Garvey, Dan, 3b-2b | .204 | 54 | 152 | 19 | 31 | 6 | 0 | 3 | 12 | 10 | 22 | 4 | 6 | R | R | 6-0 | 180 | 9-9-70 | 1991 | Appleton, Wis. |
| Hanel, Marcus, c | .185 | 69 | 195 | 18 | 36 | 6 | 2 | 2 | 16 | 18 | 65 | 5 | 3 | R | R | 6-4 | 205 | 10-19-71 | 1989 | Racine, Wis. |
| Juday, Rick, 3b | .133 | 9 | 30 | 1 | 4 | 2 | 0 | 0 | 3 | 0 | 8 | 0 | 1 | R | R | 5-10 | 180 | 5-31-69 | 1991 | Midland, Mich. |
| Marx, Tim, c | .233 | 14 | 30 | 2 | 10 | 0 | 0 | 0 | 5 | 7 | 9 | 1 | 1 | R | R | 6-2 | 190 | 11-27-68 | 1991 | Evansville, Ind. |
| Neff, Marty, of-3b | .227 | 89 | 344 | 39 | 78 | 12 | 1 | 18 | 50 | 14 | 87 | 5 | 7 | R | R | 6-2 | 185 | 2-12-70 | 1991 | Anaheim, Calif. |
| Polcovich, Kevin, ss-2b | .255 | 94 | 282 | 44 | 72 | 10 | 3 | 1 | 25 | 49 | 42 | 13 | 6 | R | R | 5-9 | 165 | 6-28-70 | 1992 | Auburn, N.Y. |
| Ponder, Marcus, of | .230 | 39 | 126 | 17 | 29 | 4 | 0 | 2 | 12 | 8 | 24 | 10 | 3 | R | R | 5-9 | 184 | 10-19-70 | 1991 | Moultrie, Ga. |
| Purdy, Alan, 3b-2b | .234 | 15 | 47 | 9 | 11 | 4 | 0 | 0 | 0 | 4 | 12 | 0 | 0 | R | R | 6-2 | 170 | 11-6-70 | 1993 | Nashville, Tenn. |
| Ragland, Trace, of-dh | .237 | 91 | 278 | 35 | 66 | 13 | 0 | 9 | 32 | 32 | 77 | 1 | 3 | L | R | 6-0 | 185 | 7-3-69 | 1991 | Madison, Tenn. |
| Ronca, Joe, of-3b | .286 | 92 | 290 | 41 | 83 | 13 | 2 | 12 | 51 | 26 | 60 | 5 | 7 | R | R | 6-2 | 169 | 7-3-71 | 1989 | Cantonment, Fla. |
| Sanford, Chance, 2b | .255 | 115 | 428 | 54 | 109 | 21 | 5 | 10 | 37 | 33 | 80 | 11 | 10 | L | R | 5-10 | 165 | 6-2-72 | 1992 | Houston, Texas |
| Thomas, Keith, of | .266 | 25 | 94 | 17 | 25 | 8 | 0 | 4 | 11 | 7 | 30 | 8 | 1 | R | R | 6-1 | 180 | 9-12-68 | 1986 | Chicago, Ill. |
| Womack, Tony, ss | .299 | 72 | 304 | 41 | 91 | 11 | 3 | 2 | 18 | 13 | 34 | 28 | 14 | L | R | 5-9 | 160 | 9-25-69 | 1991 | Chatham, Va. |

| PITCHING | W | L | ERA | G | GS | CG | SV | IP | H | R | ER | BB | SO | B | T | HT | WT | DOB | 1st Yr | Resides |
|---|---|---|---|---|---|---|---|---|---|---|---|---|---|---|---|---|---|---|---|---|
| Christiansen, Jason | 1 | 1 | 3.15 | 57 | 0 | 0 | 4 | 71 | 48 | 30 | 25 | 24 | 70 | R | L | 6-5 | 235 | 9-21-69 | 1991 | Elkhorn, Neb. |
| De los Santos, Mariano | 9 | 5 | 3.36 | 18 | 18 | 2 | 0 | 99 | 90 | 46 | 37 | 41 | 80 | L | R | 5-11 | 200 | 7-13-70 | 1989 | Santo Domingo, D.R. |
| Doorneweerd, Dave | 2 | 8 | 5.48 | 15 | 15 | 1 | 0 | 71 | 70 | 54 | 43 | 44 | 47 | R | R | 6-1 | 185 | 9-29-72 | 1991 | New Port Richey, Fla. |
| Evans, Sean | 1 | 4 | 5.56 | 45 | 3 | 0 | 0 | 66 | 67 | 50 | 41 | 33 | 70 | R | R | 6-1 | 185 | 11-6-70 | 1991 | Buffalo, N.Y. |
| Harrah, Doug | 8 | 5 | 4.23 | 24 | 19 | 0 | 0 | 115 | 125 | 61 | 54 | 26 | 85 | R | R | 6-0 | 175 | 4-23-69 | 1991 | Newton Falls, Ohio |
| Jones, Dan | 3 | 3 | 3.96 | 11 | 11 | 0 | 0 | 61 | 61 | 36 | 27 | 21 | 50 | R | R | 6-2 | 210 | 11-15-69 | 1991 | Cedar Falls, Iowa |
| Konuszewski, Dennis | 4 | 10 | 4.63 | 39 | 13 | 0 | 1 | 103 | 121 | 66 | 53 | 43 | 81 | R | R | 6-3 | 220 | 2-4-71 | 1992 | Bridgeport, Mich. |
| LaPlante, Michel | 3 | 2 | 3.44 | 11 | 11 | 0 | 0 | 65 | 71 | 35 | 25 | 19 | 44 | R | R | 6-2 | 180 | 12-9-69 | 1992 | East Montreal, Quebec |
| Lawrence, Sean | 1 | 3 | 10.20 | 4 | 4 | 0 | 0 | 15 | 25 | 19 | 17 | 9 | 14 | L | L | 6-4 | 215 | 9-2-70 | 1992 | Ephraim, Ill. |
| Loaiza, Esteban | 6 | 7 | 3.39 | 17 | 17 | 3 | 0 | 109 | 113 | 53 | 41 | 30 | 61 | R | R | 6-2 | 172 | 12-31-71 | 1991 | Imperial Beach, Calif. |
| Martin, Jim | 2 | 0 | 6.95 | 17 | 0 | 0 | 0 | 22 | 25 | 19 | 17 | 12 | 18 | L | L | 6-2 | 200 | 7-16-70 | 1991 | Trenton, Mich. |
| McCurry, Jeff | 1 | 4 | 3.89 | 41 | 0 | 0 | 22 | 44 | 41 | 21 | 19 | 15 | 32 | R | R | 6-6 | 220 | 1-21-70 | 1991 | Houston, Texas |
| Mesewicz, Mark | 4 | 4 | 2.76 | 48 | 0 | 0 | 1 | 65 | 57 | 24 | 20 | 15 | 75 | L | L | 6-3 | 195 | 10-13-69 | 1992 | Newark, Ohio |
| Mooney, Troy | 0 | 2 | 6.29 | 15 | 2 | 0 | 1 | 34 | 47 | 30 | 24 | 19 | 13 | R | R | 6-3 | 190 | 6-12-68 | 1989 | Westerville, Ohio |
| Parkinson, Eric | 2 | 8 | 5.85 | 17 | 9 | 0 | 0 | 68 | 96 | 52 | 44 | 25 | 43 | R | R | 6-3 | 175 | 3-3-69 | 1989 | Adrian, Mich. |
| Pisciotta, Marc | 0 | 0 | 2.95 | 20 | 0 | 0 | 12 | 18 | 23 | 13 | 6 | 13 | 13 | R | R | 6-5 | 240 | 8-7-70 | 1991 | Marietta, Ga. |
| Ruebel, Matt | 1 | 4 | 5.94 | 19 | 1 | 0 | 0 | 33 | 34 | 31 | 22 | 32 | 29 | L | L | 6-2 | 180 | 10-16-69 | 1991 | Ames, Iowa |

## PIRATES: MOST COMMON LINEUPS

| | Pittsburgh Majors | Buffalo AAA | Carolina AA | Salem A | Augusta A |
|---|---|---|---|---|---|
| C | Don Slaught (105) | Jerry Goff (100) | Keith Osik (99) | Angelo Encarnacion (67) | Jason Kendall (62) |
| 1B | Kevin Young (135) | Russ Morman (89) | Rich Aude (90) | Mike Brown (115) | Rico Gholston (116) |
| 2B | Carlos Garcia (140) | Dave Rohde (53) | Tony Beasley (69) | Chance Sanford (108) | Ramon Zapata (77) |
| 3B | Jeff King (156) | Gary Cooper (73) | Jim Krevokuch (123) | Ken Bonifay (67) | Jake Austin (117) |
| SS | Jay Bell (154) | Dave Rohde (64) | Bruce Schreiber (76) | Tony Womack (72) | Jay Cranford (118) |
| OF | Al Martin (136) | Wm. Pennyfeather (110) | Daryl Ratliff (113) | Jeff Conger (107) | Danny Clyburn (101) |
| | Orlando Merced (109) | Scott Bullett (102) | Tom Green (92) | Jon Farrell (71) | Trey Beamon (81) |
| | Dave Clark (91) | Cummings/Tomberlin (58) | Keith Thomas (79) | Marty Neff (54) | Dario Tena (80) |
| DH | N/A | Glenn Wilson (27) | Mark Johnson (32) | Jon Farrell (33) | Jason Kendall (33) |
| SP | Cooke/Walk (32) | Roy Smith (28) | Backlund/Hope (20) | Doug Harrah (19) | Ted Klamm (25) |
| RP | Blas Minor (65) | Tony Menendez (54) | Dennis Tafoya (49) | Jason Christiansen (57) | Richard Townsend (53) |
| | Full-season farm clubs only | No. of games at position in parenthesis | | | |

# PIRATES TOP 10 PROSPECTS

How the Pirates Top 10 prospects, as judged by Baseball America prior to the 1993 season, fared in 1993:

| Player, Pos. | Club (Class) | AVG | AB | H | HR | RBI | SB |
|---|---|---|---|---|---|---|---|
| 1. Kevin Young, 1b | Pittsburgh | .236 | 449 | 106 | 6 | 47 | 2 |
| 2. Carlos Garcia, 2b | Pittsburgh | .269 | 546 | 147 | 12 | 47 | 11 |
| 3. Midre Cummings, of | Carolina (AA) | .295 | 237 | 70 | 6 | 26 | 5 |
|  | Buffalo (AAA) | .276 | 232 | 64 | 9 | 21 | 5 |
|  | Pittsburgh | .111 | 36 | 4 | 0 | 3 | 0 |
| 4. Danny Clyburn, of | Augusta (A) | .265 | 457 | 121 | 9 | 66 | 5 |
| 5. Al Martin, of | Pittsburgh | .281 | 480 | 135 | 18 | 64 | 16 |
| 7. Trey Beamon, of | Augusta (A) | .271 | 373 | 101 | 0 | 45 | 19 |
| 8. Jason Kendall, c | Augusta (A) | .276 | 366 | 101 | 1 | 40 | 8 |
| 10. Scott Bullett, of | Buffalo (AAA) | .287 | 408 | 117 | 1 | 30 | 28 |
|  | Pittsburgh | .200 | 55 | 11 | 0 | 4 | 3 |

| | | W | L | ERA | IP | H | BB | SO |
|---|---|---|---|---|---|---|---|---|
| 6. Steve Cooke, lhp | Pittsburgh | 10 | 10 | 3.89 | 211 | 207 | 59 | 132 |
| 9. Brett Backlund, rhp | Carolina (AA) | 7 | 5 | 4.58 | 106 | 115 | 28 | 94 |
|  | Buffalo (AAA) | 0 | 4 | 10.55 | 21 | 30 | 14 | 10 |

**Kevin Young**
.236 at Pittsburgh

**PITCHING**

| | W | L | ERA | G | GS | CG | SV | IP | H | R | ER | BB | SO | B | T | HT | WT | DOB | 1st Yr | Resides |
|---|---|---|---|---|---|---|---|---|---|---|---|---|---|---|---|---|---|---|---|---|
| Rychel, Kevin | 5 | 4 | 3.95 | 53 | 2 | 0 | 0 | 73 | 68 | 41 | 32 | 44 | 86 | R | R | 5-9 | 176 | 9-24-71 | 1989 | Midland, Texas |
| Teich, Michael | 1 | 0 | 3.50 | 12 | 0 | 0 | 0 | 18 | 18 | 17 | 7 | 3 | 12 | L | L | 6-1 | 195 | 11-1-69 | 1991 | West Hills, Calif. |
| Wilson, Gary | 5 | 5 | 5.74 | 15 | 15 | 0 | 0 | 78 | 102 | 58 | 50 | 25 | 54 | R | R | 6-3 | 180 | 1-1-70 | 1992 | Arcata, Calif. |

# AUGUSTA                                                                     A
## SOUTH ATLANTIC LEAGUE

**BATTING**

| | AVG | G | AB | R | H | 2B | 3B | HR | RBI | BB | SO | SB | CS | B | T | HT | WT | DOB | 1st Yr | Resides |
|---|---|---|---|---|---|---|---|---|---|---|---|---|---|---|---|---|---|---|---|---|
| Austin, Jake, 3b | .294 | 123 | 449 | 71 | 132 | 24 | 4 | 7 | 54 | 32 | 85 | 14 | 7 | S | R | 6-0 | 205 | 4-30-70 | 1992 | Atlanta, Ga. |
| Beamon, Trey, of | .271 | 104 | 373 | 64 | 101 | 18 | 6 | 0 | 45 | 48 | 60 | 19 | 6 | L | R | 6-3 | 195 | 2-11-74 | 1992 | Dallas, Texas |
| Calder, Joe, dh-1b | .205 | 12 | 39 | 6 | 8 | 1 | 0 | 0 | 3 | 1 | 18 | 0 | 0 | R | R | 6-2 | 210 | 12-9-72 | 1990 | San Sebastian, P.R. |
| Clyburn, Danny, of | .265 | 127 | 457 | 55 | 121 | 21 | 4 | 9 | 66 | 37 | 97 | 5 | 5 | R | R | 6-3 | 217 | 4-6-74 | 1992 | Lancaster, S.C. |
| Cranford, Jay, ss | .267 | 128 | 469 | 55 | 125 | 31 | 0 | 6 | 72 | 32 | 101 | 17 | 2 | R | R | 6-3 | 175 | 4-7-71 | 1992 | Macon, Ga. |
| Espinosa, Ramon, of | .297 | 70 | 266 | 32 | 79 | 9 | 3 | 2 | 27 | 12 | 51 | 17 | 5 | R | R | 6-1 | 185 | 2-7-72 | 1990 | San Pedro de Macoris, D.R. |
| Garvey, Don, 2b-ss | .169 | 43 | 124 | 12 | 21 | 3 | 0 | 2 | 6 | 10 | 18 | 2 | 2 | R | R | 6-0 | 180 | 9-9-70 | 1991 | Appleton, Wis. |
| Gholston, Rico, 1b | .231 | 120 | 415 | 52 | 96 | 20 | 3 | 9 | 46 | 26 | 130 | 2 | 1 | R | R | 6-3 | 225 | 1-4-70 | 1992 | Kansas City, Kan. |
| Harris, G.G., dh | .288 | 15 | 52 | 7 | 15 | 4 | 1 | 0 | 3 | 5 | 10 | 0 | 1 | R | R | 6-2 | 215 | 5-14-73 | 1992 | Lancaster, S.C. |
| Kendall, Jason, c-dh | .276 | 102 | 366 | 43 | 101 | 17 | 4 | 1 | 40 | 22 | 30 | 8 | 5 | R | R | 6-0 | 170 | 6-26-74 | 1992 | Torrance, Calif. |
| Marx, Tim, c | .278 | 53 | 162 | 28 | 45 | 8 | 0 | 3 | 21 | 34 | 18 | 3 | 4 | R | R | 6-2 | 190 | 11-27-68 | 1991 | Evansville, Ind. |
| Polcovich, Kevin, ss | .271 | 14 | 48 | 9 | 13 | 2 | 0 | 0 | 4 | 7 | 8 | 2 | 1 | R | R | 5-9 | 165 | 6-28-70 | 1992 | Auburn, N.Y. |
| Ponder, Marcus, of | .225 | 47 | 138 | 18 | 31 | 1 | 2 | 2 | 5 | 12 | 36 | 4 | 5 | R | R | 5-9 | 184 | 10-19-70 | 1991 | Moultrie, Ga. |
| Purdy, Alan, ss-2b | .107 | 12 | 28 | 3 | 3 | 2 | 0 | 0 | 1 | 0 | 4 | 0 | 0 | R | R | 6-2 | 170 | 11-6-70 | 1993 | Nashville, Tenn. |
| Rivera, Maximo, 2b | .273 | 5 | 11 | 1 | 3 | 0 | 0 | 0 | 0 | 0 | 3 | 1 | 1 | S | R | 6-2 | 175 | 4-8-73 | 1990 | Santo Domingo, D.R. |
| Secrist, Reed, 3b-of | .267 | 90 | 266 | 38 | 71 | 16 | 3 | 6 | 47 | 27 | 43 | 4 | 1 | L | R | 6-1 | 205 | 5-7-70 | 1992 | Farmington, Utah |
| Stahlhoefer, Larry, c-2b | .245 | 77 | 220 | 22 | 54 | 9 | 0 | 1 | 25 | 15 | 35 | 4 | 6 | R | R | 6-0 | 175 | 6-21-70 | 1992 | Chino, Calif. |
| Tena, Dario, of | .263 | 87 | 308 | 45 | 81 | 9 | 1 | 0 | 19 | 31 | 56 | 39 | 16 | S | R | 5-10 | 160 | 12-19-72 | 1990 | San Cristobal, D.R. |
| Tooch, Chuck, 2b-ss | .310 | 17 | 42 | 9 | 13 | 3 | 0 | 0 | 3 | 5 | 13 | 0 | 0 | R | R | 5-11 | 175 | 11-14-71 | 1990 | Lake Clarke Shores, Fla. |
| Walker, Shon, of | .208 | 64 | 226 | 26 | 47 | 11 | 0 | 3 | 26 | 19 | 85 | 2 | 5 | L | L | 6-1 | 182 | 6-9-74 | 1992 | Cynthiana, Ky. |
| Zapata, Ramon, 2b | .247 | 81 | 235 | 31 | 58 | 10 | 3 | 2 | 32 | 37 | 47 | 6 | 7 | R | R | 5-8 | 155 | 1-14-71 | 1990 | Santo Domingo, D.R. |

**PITCHING**

| | W | L | ERA | G | GS | CG | SV | IP | H | R | ER | BB | SO | B | T | HT | WT | DOB | 1st Yr | Resides |
|---|---|---|---|---|---|---|---|---|---|---|---|---|---|---|---|---|---|---|---|---|
| Bonilla, Miguel | 1 | 0 | 7.16 | 15 | 0 | 0 | 0 | 28 | 43 | 30 | 22 | 10 | 23 | R | R | 6-2 | 195 | 8-23-73 | 1990 | Santo Domingo, D.R. |
| Chamberlain, Matt | 2 | 4 | 2.25 | 6 | 6 | 2 | 0 | 36 | 35 | 16 | 9 | 7 | 29 | R | R | 6-4 | 205 | 9-16-71 | 1993 | Baton Rouge, La. |
| Doorneweerd, Dave | 1 | 5 | 1.98 | 13 | 13 | 0 | 0 | 77 | 60 | 30 | 17 | 30 | 70 | R | R | 6-1 | 185 | 9-29-72 | 1991 | New Port Richey, Fla. |
| Fairfax, Ken | 3 | 2 | 4.32 | 5 | 5 | 0 | 0 | 25 | 29 | 14 | 12 | 9 | 17 | R | R | 6-2 | 180 | 8-9-73 | 1991 | Uniontown, Pa. |
| Ford, John | 1 | 1 | 2.49 | 31 | 0 | 0 | 2 | 43 | 42 | 17 | 12 | 11 | 40 | L | L | 6-0 | 170 | 11-30-71 | 1992 | Paris, Texas |
| Garcia-Luna, Francisco | 3 | 1 | 4.26 | 7 | 7 | 0 | 0 | 32 | 34 | 15 | 15 | 3 | 29 | R | R | 6-3 | 190 | 4-6-73 | 1991 | Mexico City, Mexico |
| Klamm, Ted | 10 | 10 | 3.94 | 26 | 25 | 3 | 0 | 132 | 122 | 71 | 58 | 53 | 113 | L | L | 5-10 | 170 | 4-8-70 | 1992 | Syracuse, N.Y. |
| Lawrence, Sean | 6 | 8 | 3.12 | 22 | 22 | 0 | 0 | 121 | 108 | 59 | 42 | 50 | 96 | L | L | 6-4 | 215 | 9-2-70 | 1992 | Ephraim, Ill. |
| LaPlante, Michel | 5 | 5 | 3.46 | 14 | 14 | 0 | 0 | 83 | 89 | 37 | 32 | 10 | 80 | R | R | 6-2 | 180 | 12-9-69 | 1992 | East Montreal, Quebec |
| Martin, Jim | 0 | 0 | 5.87 | 5 | 0 | 0 | 0 | 8 | 6 | 6 | 5 | 3 | 5 | L | L | 6-2 | 200 | 7-16-70 | 1991 | Trenton, Mich. |
| Mesewicz, Mark | 0 | 2 | 4.11 | 12 | 0 | 0 | 0 | 15 | 14 | 9 | 7 | 3 | 17 | L | L | 6-3 | 195 | 10-13-69 | 1992 | Newark, Ohio |
| Nuttle, Jamison | 1 | 2 | 6.35 | 12 | 0 | 0 | 4 | 11 | 6 | 11 | 8 | 1 | 11 | R | R | 6-5 | 205 | 2-2-72 | 1992 | Spencerville, Ind. |
| Pisciotta, Marc | 5 | 2 | 2.68 | 34 | 0 | 0 | 12 | 44 | 31 | 18 | 13 | 17 | 49 | R | R | 6-5 | 240 | 8-7-70 | 1991 | Marietta, Ga. |
| Pontbriant, Matt | 0 | 2 | 3.27 | 3 | 3 | 0 | 0 | 11 | 13 | 13 | 4 | 6 | 12 | L | L | 6-4 | 200 | 5-20-72 | 1991 | Norwich, Conn. |
| Ruebel, Matt | 5 | 5 | 2.42 | 23 | 7 | 1 | 0 | 63 | 51 | 28 | 17 | 34 | 50 | L | L | 6-2 | 180 | 10-16-69 | 1991 | Ames, Iowa |
| Salamon, John | 1 | 2 | 3.54 | 47 | 0 | 0 | 1 | 61 | 43 | 37 | 24 | 42 | 59 | R | R | 6-2 | 205 | 3-30-72 | 1991 | McKees Rocks, Pa. |
| Santana, Manuel | 3 | 6 | 3.35 | 38 | 13 | 0 | 0 | 110 | 113 | 65 | 41 | 35 | 85 | R | R | 6-2 | 185 | 4-29-73 | 1991 | San Pedro de Macoris, D.R. |
| Sosa, Jose | 3 | 9 | 5.92 | 33 | 15 | 0 | 0 | 106 | 125 | 88 | 70 | 32 | 62 | R | R | 6-2 | 185 | 9-2-72 | 1990 | Santo Domingo, D.R. |
| Townsend, Rich | 1 | 3 | 5.30 | 53 | 0 | 0 | 2 | 70 | 79 | 53 | 41 | 23 | 79 | L | L | 6-0 | 180 | 9-10-70 | 1992 | Clearwater, Fla. |
| Wilkins, Marc | 5 | 6 | 4.21 | 48 | 5 | 0 | 1 | 77 | 83 | 52 | 36 | 31 | 73 | R | R | 5-11 | 215 | 10-21-70 | 1992 | Mansfield, Ohio |
| Wilson, Gary | 3 | 7 | 5.47 | 20 | 6 | 0 | 0 | 51 | 66 | 35 | 31 | 11 | 42 | R | R | 6-3 | 180 | 1-1-70 | 1992 | Arcata, Calif. |

# WELLAND                                                                     A
## NEW YORK-PENN LEAGUE

**BATTING**

| | AVG | G | AB | R | H | 2B | 3B | HR | RBI | BB | SO | SB | CS | B | T | HT | WT | DOB | 1st Yr | Resides |
|---|---|---|---|---|---|---|---|---|---|---|---|---|---|---|---|---|---|---|---|---|
| Allensworth, Jermaine, of | .308 | 67 | 263 | 44 | 81 | 16 | 4 | 1 | 32 | 24 | 38 | 18 | 3 | R | R | 6-0 | 188 | 1-11-72 | 1993 | Anderson, Ind. |
| Cannaday, Aaron, c-dh | .221 | 47 | 163 | 23 | 36 | 8 | 0 | 6 | 33 | 24 | 66 | 2 | 1 | R | R | 6-3 | 215 | 9-13-71 | 1992 | Richmond, Va. |
| Collier, Louis, ss | .303 | 50 | 201 | 35 | 61 | 6 | 2 | 1 | 19 | 12 | 31 | 8 | 7 | R | R | 5-10 | 170 | 8-21-73 | 1993 | Chicago, Ill. |
| Gosselin, Patrick, 2b | .284 | 33 | 109 | 21 | 31 | 7 | 1 | 0 | 10 | 12 | 19 | 1 | 2 | R | R | 5-11 | 180 | 11-2-72 | 1993 | Sherbrooke, Quebec |
| Harris, G.G., 1b | .295 | 31 | 112 | 16 | 33 | 6 | 2 | 2 | 21 | 8 | 21 | 2 | 0 | R | R | 6-2 | 215 | 5-14-73 | 1992 | Lancaster, S.C. |

| BATTING | AVG | G | AB | R | H | 2B | 3B | HR | RBI | BB | SO | SB | CS | B | T | HT | WT | DOB | 1st Yr | Resides |
|---|---|---|---|---|---|---|---|---|---|---|---|---|---|---|---|---|---|---|---|---|
| House, Mitch, 3b-dh | .247 | 62 | 227 | 39 | 56 | 13 | 2 | 9 | 41 | 27 | 48 | 2 | 2 | R | R | 6-2 | 205 | 5-28-72 | 1990 | Dante, Va. |
| Hunt, Riegal, of | .154 | 8 | 26 | 3 | 4 | 0 | 0 | 1 | 2 | 2 | 12 | 0 | 0 | L | R | 6-3 | 185 | 1-11-71 | 1992 | Hampton, Va. |
| Johnston, Tom, 2b-ss | .156 | 10 | 32 | 0 | 5 | 0 | 0 | 1 | 1 | 10 | 0 | 0 | 0 | R | R | 6-0 | 180 | 2-28-73 | 1991 | Indianapolis, Ind. |
| Kelley, Erskine, of | .264 | 42 | 159 | 21 | 42 | 7 | 2 | 5 | 20 | 7 | 41 | 3 | 2 | R | R | 6-5 | 210 | 2-27-71 | 1992 | Freeport, N.Y. |
| Luna, Richard, 2b-ss | .220 | 33 | 91 | 9 | 20 | 1 | 2 | 0 | 6 | 12 | 16 | 5 | 3 | R | R | 6-0 | 180 | 10-6-73 | 1993 | Sacramento, Calif. |
| Mendez, Sergio, c | .248 | 32 | 121 | 12 | 30 | 4 | 1 | 0 | 10 | 0 | 28 | 0 | 1 | R | R | 6-2 | 180 | 10-12-73 | 1992 | Santo Domingo, D.R. |
| Mitchell, John, of | .219 | 50 | 178 | 24 | 39 | 7 | 2 | 1 | 19 | 14 | 21 | 1 | 2 | R | R | 6-4 | 215 | 8-21-71 | 1993 | Marietta, Ga. |
| Paez, Raul, 1b | .236 | 39 | 148 | 10 | 35 | 3 | 0 | 2 | 14 | 10 | 25 | 1 | 0 | S | L | 6-1 | 185 | 1-26-74 | 1993 | Tijuana, Mexico |
| Purdy, Alan, 2b-ss | .167 | 7 | 24 | 2 | 4 | 0 | 0 | 0 | 0 | 1 | 2 | 0 | 0 | R | R | 6-2 | 170 | 11-6-70 | 1993 | Nashville, Tenn. |
| Reed, Patrick, of | .253 | 46 | 158 | 22 | 40 | 10 | 1 | 2 | 24 | 12 | 48 | 10 | 6 | R | R | 6-3 | 195 | 12-9-71 | 1991 | San Leandro, Calif. |
| Rivera, Maximo, ss-2b | .243 | 32 | 115 | 17 | 28 | 5 | 1 | 0 | 11 | 4 | 27 | 4 | 8 | S | R | 6-2 | 175 | 4-8-73 | 1990 | Santo Domingo, D.R. |
| Walker, Shon, of | .195 | 35 | 118 | 15 | 23 | 3 | 1 | 2 | 9 | 14 | 52 | 4 | 0 | L | L | 6-1 | 182 | 6-9-74 | 1992 | Cynthiana, Ky. |
| Williamson, Joel, c | .207 | 23 | 82 | 9 | 17 | 3 | 0 | 1 | 9 | 3 | 16 | 1 | 0 | R | R | 5-11 | 180 | 10-18-69 | 1993 | Winnetka, Ill. |
| Wiltz, Stan, 3b | .255 | 51 | 184 | 24 | 47 | 11 | 0 | 2 | 14 | 5 | 25 | 1 | 1 | R | R | 6-2 | 210 | 11-1-71 | 1992 | New Orleans, La. |
| Yselsian, John, 1b-dh | .148 | 16 | 54 | 3 | 8 | 2 | 0 | 1 | 8 | 8 | 16 | 0 | 1 | R | R | 6-2 | 210 | 8-18-71 | 1993 | Margate, Fla. |

| PITCHING | W | L | ERA | G | GS | CG | SV | IP | H | R | ER | BB | SO | B | T | HT | WT | DOB | 1st Yr | Resides |
|---|---|---|---|---|---|---|---|---|---|---|---|---|---|---|---|---|---|---|---|---|
| Abramavicius, Jason | 2 | 4 | 3.12 | 14 | 7 | 1 | 1 | 52 | 44 | 22 | 18 | 10 | 43 | L | L | 6-4 | 190 | 12-14-69 | 1993 | Marengo, Ill. |
| Beck, Brian | 3 | 1 | 4.08 | 22 | 0 | 0 | 0 | 35 | 34 | 21 | 16 | 25 | 25 | L | L | 6-3 | 195 | 4-30-71 | 1989 | Grants Pass, Ore. |
| Chamberlain, Matt | 2 | 3 | 3.86 | 8 | 7 | 0 | 0 | 37 | 41 | 19 | 16 | 9 | 28 | R | R | 6-4 | 205 | 9-16-71 | 1993 | Baton Rouge, La. |
| Fairfax, Ken | 1 | 3 | 5.85 | 11 | 8 | 0 | 0 | 32 | 33 | 30 | 21 | 21 | 22 | R | R | 6-2 | 180 | 8-9-73 | 1993 | Uniontown, Pa. |
| Garcia, Ramon | 0 | 2 | 12.60 | 2 | 2 | 0 | 0 | 5 | 10 | 11 | 7 | 5 | 1 | R | R | 6-0 | 175 | 9-19-73 | 1991 | San Cristobal, D.R. |
| Isom, Jeff | 1 | 1 | 5.83 | 22 | 0 | 0 | 2 | 29 | 35 | 23 | 19 | 9 | 28 | L | L | 6-0 | 175 | 9-22-72 | 1993 | West Lafayette, Ind. |
| Johnson, Jason | 1 | 5 | 4.63 | 6 | 6 | 1 | 0 | 35 | 33 | 24 | 18 | 9 | 19 | R | R | 6-6 | 220 | 10-27-73 | 1992 | Burlington, Ky. |
| Lutt, Jeff | 0 | 2 | 5.86 | 26 | 0 | 0 | 2 | 28 | 24 | 21 | 18 | 16 | 16 | R | R | 6-4 | 225 | 5-8-72 | 1993 | Wayne, Neb. |
| Mattson, Craig | 2 | 1 | 2.12 | 18 | 0 | 0 | 1 | 30 | 25 | 13 | 7 | 5 | 32 | R | R | 6-4 | 205 | 11-25-73 | 1993 | Belvedere, Ill. |
| Morel, Ramon | 7 | 8 | 4.21 | 16 | 16 | 0 | 0 | 77 | 90 | 45 | 36 | 21 | 51 | R | R | 6-2 | 170 | 8-15-74 | 1991 | Villa Gonzalez, D.R. |
| Nuttle, Jamison | 0 | 0 | 0.65 | 21 | 0 | 0 | 10 | 28 | 13 | 2 | 2 | 10 | 43 | R | R | 6-5 | 205 | 2-2-72 | 1992 | Spencerville, Ind. |
| Pelka, Brian | 8 | 4 | 3.59 | 15 | 15 | 0 | 0 | 85 | 87 | 40 | 34 | 24 | 71 | R | R | 6-6 | 185 | 3-14-72 | 1992 | Philipsburg, Pa. |
| Perez, Gil | 1 | 0 | 3.86 | 14 | 0 | 0 | 0 | 19 | 14 | 11 | 8 | 16 | 14 | R | R | 6-1 | 160 | 9-1-72 | 1990 | San Cristobal, D.R. |
| Peters, Chris | 1 | 0 | 4.55 | 16 | 0 | 0 | 0 | 28 | 33 | 16 | 14 | 20 | 25 | L | L | 6-1 | 170 | 1-28-72 | 1993 | McMurray, Pa. |
| Phillips, Jason | 4 | 6 | 3.53 | 14 | 14 | 0 | 0 | 71 | 60 | 44 | 28 | 36 | 66 | R | R | 6-6 | 215 | 3-22-74 | 1992 | Muncy, Pa. |
| Pickich, Jeff | 2 | 1 | 4.37 | 21 | 2 | 0 | 0 | 47 | 35 | 27 | 23 | 19 | 54 | R | R | 6-1 | 180 | 9-4-71 | 1993 | Biloxi, Miss. |
| Ryan, Matt | 0 | 1 | 2.08 | 16 | 0 | 0 | 5 | 17 | 11 | 10 | 4 | 12 | 25 | R | R | 6-5 | 190 | 3-20-72 | 1993 | Memphis, Tenn. |

# BRADENTON

## GULF COAST LEAGUE

| BATTING | AVG | G | AB | R | H | 2B | 3B | HR | RBI | BB | SO | SB | CS | B | T | HT | WT | DOB | 1st Yr | Resides |
|---|---|---|---|---|---|---|---|---|---|---|---|---|---|---|---|---|---|---|---|---|
| Borges, Mariano, of | .225 | 29 | 102 | 8 | 23 | 6 | 2 | 0 | 7 | 1 | 20 | 1 | 3 | R | R | 6-0 | 170 | 12-7-72 | 1993 | Arecibo, P.R. |
| Cunningham, Ryan, 3b | .167 | 25 | 78 | 5 | 13 | 3 | 0 | 0 | 7 | 8 | 12 | 0 | 0 | R | R | 6-1 | 185 | 2-17-75 | 1993 | Lancaster, S.C. |
| Delgado, Jose, ss | .254 | 33 | 118 | 15 | 30 | 6 | 2 | 0 | 9 | 17 | 16 | 10 | 2 | S | R | 5-11 | 155 | 3-20-75 | 1993 | Carolina, P.R. |
| Galarza, Eduardo, 3b | .256 | 38 | 121 | 9 | 31 | 5 | 0 | 0 | 15 | 6 | 12 | 0 | 0 | S | R | 6-2 | 180 | 5-3-74 | 1993 | Guallama, P.R. |
| Hagen, Sean, ss | .189 | 32 | 106 | 11 | 20 | 4 | 1 | 0 | 8 | 10 | 26 | 1 | 0 | S | R | 5-11 | 170 | 11-28-74 | 1993 | Sandy, Utah |
| Hairston, Jeff, of | .202 | 29 | 99 | 5 | 20 | 2 | 2 | 2 | 12 | 3 | 29 | 2 | 6 | R | R | 6-2 | 175 | 8-16-74 | 1992 | Portland, Ore. |
| Keefe, Jamie, 2b | .500 | 5 | 14 | 3 | 7 | 0 | 0 | 0 | 2 | 2 | 3 | 1 | 1 | R | R | 5-11 | 180 | 8-29-73 | 1992 | Rochester, N.H. |
| Leger, Tim, of | .190 | 31 | 105 | 12 | 20 | 3 | 0 | 0 | 10 | 17 | 19 | 4 | 1 | R | R | 6-3 | 189 | 11-15-73 | 1992 | Lafayette, La. |
| Lyde, Alfredo, dh-of | .154 | 20 | 52 | 4 | 8 | 0 | 1 | 0 | 2 | 6 | 22 | 1 | 0 | R | R | 6-1 | 193 | 1-23-75 | 1993 | Timmonsville, S.C. |
| Mackert, Jamie, 3b | .353 | 5 | 14 | 6 | 1 | 0 | 1 | 4 | 1 | 4 | 0 | 0 | 0 | R | R | 6-1 | 190 | 5-2-74 | 1992 | West Chicago, Ill. |
| Ojeda, Miguel, c | .278 | 27 | 97 | 9 | 27 | 3 | 1 | 3 | 11 | 10 | 18 | 2 | 0 | R | R | 6-1 | 190 | 1-29-75 | 1993 | Guaymas, Mexico |
| Ortiz, Javier, dh-of | .304 | 8 | 23 | 5 | 7 | 3 | 0 | 0 | 6 | 8 | 7 | 0 | 0 | R | R | 6-4 | 210 | 1-22-63 | 1983 | Hialeah, Fla. |
| Palmer, Travis, 1b-dh | .222 | 6 | 18 | 2 | 4 | 0 | 0 | 1 | 1 | 5 | 1 | 1 | 1 | R | R | 6-1 | 185 | 11-28-73 | 1992 | Camp Verde, Ariz. |
| Peterson, Charles, of | .303 | 49 | 188 | 28 | 57 | 11 | 3 | 1 | 23 | 22 | 22 | 8 | 6 | R | R | 6-3 | 200 | 5-8-74 | 1993 | Laurens, S.C. |
| Polanco, Felipe, 2b-3b | .293 | 38 | 133 | 16 | 39 | 4 | 2 | 0 | 13 | 8 | 20 | 13 | 7 | R | R | 5-11 | 170 | 8-25-75 | 1992 | San Pedro de Macoris, D.R. |
| Rice, Andy, 1b | .206 | 41 | 126 | 17 | 26 | 2 | 2 | 3 | 14 | 26 | 46 | 1 | 1 | S | R | 6-2 | 220 | 8-31-75 | 1993 | Birmingham, Ala. |
| Smith, Akili, of | .200 | 29 | 95 | 13 | 19 | 3 | 2 | 1 | 9 | 10 | 18 | 1 | 1 | R | R | 6-3 | 200 | 8-21-75 | 1993 | San Diego, Calif. |
| Staton, Tarrence, of | .357 | 32 | 115 | 23 | 41 | 9 | 2 | 1 | 18 | 8 | 14 | 10 | 3 | L | L | 6-3 | 200 | 2-17-75 | 1993 | Elyria, Ohio |
| Swafford, Derek, 2b | .190 | 32 | 121 | 10 | 23 | 1 | 2 | 0 | 5 | 4 | 15 | 5 | 1 | L | R | 5-10 | 175 | 1-21-75 | 1993 | Ventura, Calif. |
| Torres, Matt, c | .174 | 18 | 46 | 5 | 8 | 2 | 0 | 0 | 5 | 6 | 8 | 0 | 0 | R | R | 5-11 | 180 | 12-24-72 | 1993 | Rancho Cordova, Calif. |
| Turlais, John, c | .227 | 25 | 75 | 10 | 17 | 4 | 0 | 0 | 4 | 2 | 15 | 1 | 0 | L | R | 6-3 | 200 | 12-30-73 | 1992 | Flora, Ill. |
| Wolf, Brian, 1b | .150 | 26 | 80 | 4 | 12 | 0 | 2 | 0 | 2 | 11 | 28 | 2 | 1 | L | L | 6-6 | 225 | 11-7-73 | 1993 | Minster, Ohio |

| PITCHING | W | L | ERA | G | GS | CG | SV | IP | H | R | ER | BB | SO | B | T | HT | WT | DOB | 1st Yr | Resides |
|---|---|---|---|---|---|---|---|---|---|---|---|---|---|---|---|---|---|---|---|---|
| Bullard, Jason | 0 | 1 | 3.86 | 4 | 0 | 0 | 0 | 7 | 11 | 3 | 3 | 2 | 8 | R | R | 6-2 | 185 | 10-23-68 | 1991 | Sweeney, Texas |
| Davis, Kane | 0 | 4 | 7.07 | 11 | 4 | 0 | 0 | 28 | 34 | 30 | 22 | 19 | 24 | R | R | 6-3 | 180 | 6-25-75 | 1993 | Reedy, W.Va. |
| Duer, Doug | 0 | 1 | 11.25 | 4 | 0 | 0 | 0 | 4 | 6 | 5 | 5 | 6 | 3 | R | R | 6-6 | 240 | 4-16-72 | 1993 | Stony Point, N.Y. |
| Ford, John | 0 | 0 | 0.00 | 6 | 0 | 0 | 1 | 7 | 2 | 0 | 0 | 3 | 9 | L | L | 6-0 | 170 | 11-30-71 | 1992 | Paris, Texas |
| Galarza, Eduardo | 0 | 1 | 2.30 | 7 | 0 | 0 | 0 | 11 | 11 | 6 | 3 | 4 | 3 | S | R | 6-2 | 180 | 5-3-74 | 1993 | Guallama, P.R. |
| Garcia, Ramon | 2 | 3 | 3.93 | 14 | 4 | 0 | 3 | 37 | 38 | 19 | 16 | 9 | 26 | R | R | 6-0 | 175 | 9-19-73 | 1991 | San Cristobal, D.R. |
| Goldman, Ben | 1 | 1 | 5.91 | 12 | 0 | 0 | 0 | 21 | 22 | 19 | 14 | 25 | 11 | R | R | 6-3 | 190 | 10-10-74 | 1993 | San Luis Obispo, Calif. |
| Johnson, Jason | 1 | 4 | 2.33 | 9 | 9 | 0 | 0 | 54 | 48 | 22 | 14 | 14 | 39 | R | R | 6-6 | 220 | 10-27-73 | 1992 | Burlington, Ky. |
| Keener, Kevin | 1 | 0 | 6.08 | 7 | 0 | 0 | 0 | 13 | 17 | 11 | 9 | 15 | 12 | R | L | 6-1 | 190 | 6-17-75 | 1993 | Texarkana, Ark. |
| Leiper, Dave | 0 | 0 | 1.69 | 7 | 4 | 0 | 0 | 21 | 17 | 4 | 4 | 0 | 24 | L | L | 6-1 | 160 | 6-18-62 | 1982 | Plano, Texas |
| Mooney, Troy | 2 | 2 | 1.75 | 5 | 5 | 0 | 0 | 26 | 20 | 13 | 5 | 13 | 16 | R | R | 6-3 | 190 | 6-12-68 | 1989 | Westerville, Ohio |
| Pickford, Kevin | 0 | 4 | 3.41 | 9 | 7 | 0 | 0 | 34 | 24 | 19 | 13 | 20 | 28 | L | L | 6-3 | 200 | 3-12-75 | 1993 | Fresno, Calif. |
| Reid, Rayon | 4 | 3 | 1.74 | 13 | 8 | 0 | 1 | 62 | 50 | 16 | 12 | 15 | 39 | R | R | 6-0 | 185 | 7-25-73 | 1993 | North Miami Beach, Fla. |
| Ryan, Matt | 1 | 1 | 2.33 | 9 | 0 | 0 | 2 | 19 | 17 | 8 | 5 | 9 | 20 | R | R | 6-5 | 190 | 3-20-72 | 1993 | Memphis, Tenn. |
| Serna, Jason | 0 | 0 | 0.00 | 7 | 0 | 0 | 3 | 9 | 2 | 0 | 0 | 7 | 15 | S | R | 6-1 | 230 | 12-18-73 | 1993 | Valinda, Calif. |
| Sharer, Anthony | 0 | 1 | 7.71 | 7 | 0 | 0 | 0 | 9 | 15 | 10 | 8 | 6 | 5 | R | R | 6-1 | 185 | 7-22-75 | 1993 | Tyrone, Pa. |
| Skjerpen, Trevor | 4 | 0 | 1.77 | 14 | 0 | 0 | 2 | 36 | 23 | 16 | 7 | 13 | 31 | R | R | 6-0 | 190 | 12-11-72 | 1993 | Saskatoon, Sask. |
| Temple, Jason | 2 | 2 | 5.08 | 10 | 0 | 0 | 0 | 39 | 35 | 35 | 22 | 32 | 36 | R | R | 6-1 | 185 | 11-8-74 | 1993 | Woodhaven, Mich. |
| Ward, Kerry | 1 | 7 | 4.26 | 11 | 9 | 0 | 0 | 51 | 53 | 36 | 24 | 20 | 35 | R | R | 6-3 | 185 | 10-2-74 | 1993 | Tallevast, Fla. |
| Whitehead, Steve | 0 | 3 | 2.51 | 6 | 2 | 0 | 0 | 14 | 12 | 11 | 4 | 6 | 14 | R | R | 6-1 | 165 | 6-27-70 | 1988 | Brawley, Calif. |

# ST. LOUIS CARDINALS

**Manager:** Joe Torre.  **1993 Record:** 87-75, .537 (3rd, NL East).

| BATTING | AVG | G | AB | R | H | 2B | 3B | HR | RBI | BB | SO | SB | CS | B | T | HT | WT | DOB | 1st Yr | Resides |
|---|---|---|---|---|---|---|---|---|---|---|---|---|---|---|---|---|---|---|---|---|
| Alicea, Luis | .279 | 115 | 362 | 50 | 101 | 19 | 3 | 3 | 46 | 47 | 54 | 11 | 1 | S | R | 5-9 | 165 | 7-29-65 | 1986 | Guaynabo, P.R. |
| Brewer, Rod | .286 | 110 | 147 | 15 | 42 | 8 | 0 | 2 | 20 | 17 | 26 | 1 | 0 | L | L | 6-3 | 208 | 2-24-66 | 1987 | Zellwood, Fla. |
| Canseco, Ozzie | .176 | 6 | 17 | 0 | 3 | 0 | 0 | 0 | 0 | 1 | 3 | 0 | 0 | R | R | 6-3 | 220 | 7-2-64 | 1983 | Miami, Fla. |
| Cromer, Tripp | .087 | 10 | 23 | 1 | 2 | 0 | 0 | 0 | 0 | 1 | 6 | 0 | 0 | R | R | 6-2 | 160 | 11-21-67 | 1989 | Lexington, S.C. |
| Gilkey, Bernard | .305 | 137 | 557 | 99 | 170 | 40 | 5 | 16 | 70 | 56 | 66 | 15 | 10 | R | R | 6-0 | 170 | 9-24-66 | 1985 | St. Louis, Mo. |
| Jefferies, Gregg | .342 | 142 | 544 | 89 | 186 | 24 | 3 | 16 | 83 | 62 | 32 | 46 | 9 | S | R | 5-10 | 185 | 8-1-67 | 1985 | Millbrae, Calif. |
| Jones, Tim | .262 | 29 | 61 | 13 | 16 | 6 | 0 | 0 | 1 | 9 | 8 | 2 | 2 | L | R | 5-10 | 172 | 12-1-62 | 1985 | Sumter, S.C. |
| Jordan, Brian | .309 | 67 | 223 | 33 | 69 | 10 | 6 | 10 | 44 | 12 | 35 | 6 | 6 | R | R | 6-1 | 205 | 3-29-67 | 1988 | Baltimore, Md. |
| Lankford, Ray | .238 | 127 | 407 | 64 | 97 | 17 | 3 | 7 | 45 | 81 | 111 | 14 | 14 | L | L | 5-11 | 180 | 6-5-67 | 1987 | Modesto, Calif. |
| Maclin, Lonnie | .077 | 12 | 13 | 2 | 1 | 0 | 0 | 0 | 1 | 0 | 5 | 1 | 0 | L | L | 5-11 | 180 | 2-17-67 | 1987 | St. Louis, Mo. |
| Oquendo, Jose | .205 | 46 | 73 | 7 | 15 | 0 | 0 | 0 | 4 | 12 | 8 | 0 | 0 | S | R | 5-10 | 156 | 7-4-63 | 1979 | Rio Piedras, P.R. |
| Pagnozzi, Tom | .258 | 92 | 330 | 31 | 85 | 15 | 1 | 7 | 41 | 19 | 30 | 1 | 0 | R | R | 6-1 | 190 | 7-30-62 | 1983 | Tucson, Ariz. |
| Pappas, Erik | .276 | 82 | 228 | 25 | 63 | 12 | 0 | 1 | 28 | 35 | 35 | 1 | 3 | R | R | 6-0 | 195 | 4-25-66 | 1984 | Chicago, Ill. |
| Pena, Geronimo | .256 | 74 | 254 | 34 | 65 | 19 | 2 | 5 | 30 | 25 | 71 | 13 | 5 | S | R | 6-1 | 170 | 3-29-67 | 1985 | Los Alcarrizos, D.R. |
| Perry, Gerald | .337 | 96 | 98 | 21 | 33 | 5 | 0 | 4 | 16 | 18 | 23 | 1 | 1 | L | R | 5-11 | 180 | 10-30-60 | 1978 | Smyrna, Ga. |
| Ronan, Marc | .083 | 6 | 12 | 0 | 1 | 0 | 0 | 0 | 0 | 0 | 5 | 0 | 0 | L | R | 6-2 | 190 | 9-19-69 | 1990 | Tallahassee, Fla. |
| Royer, Stan | .304 | 24 | 46 | 4 | 14 | 2 | 0 | 1 | 8 | 2 | 14 | 0 | 1 | R | R | 6-3 | 195 | 8-31-67 | 1988 | Springfield, Ill. |
| Smith, Ozzie | .288 | 141 | 545 | 75 | 157 | 22 | 6 | 1 | 53 | 43 | 18 | 21 | 8 | S | R | 5-10 | 150 | 12-26-54 | 1977 | Ladue, Mo. |
| Villanueva, Hector | .145 | 17 | 55 | 7 | 8 | 1 | 0 | 3 | 9 | 4 | 17 | 0 | 0 | R | R | 6-1 | 220 | 10-2-64 | 1985 | Rio Piedras, P.R. |
| Whiten, Mark | .253 | 152 | 562 | 81 | 142 | 13 | 4 | 25 | 99 | 58 | 110 | 15 | 8 | S | R | 6-3 | 215 | 11-25-66 | 1986 | Pensacola, Fla. |
| Woodson, Tracy | .208 | 62 | 77 | 4 | 16 | 2 | 0 | 0 | 2 | 1 | 14 | 0 | 0 | R | R | 6-3 | 215 | 10-5-62 | 1984 | Mechanicsville, Va. |
| Zeile, Todd | .277 | 157 | 571 | 82 | 158 | 36 | 1 | 17 | 103 | 70 | 76 | 5 | 4 | R | R | 6-1 | 185 | 9-9-65 | 1986 | Valencia, Calif. |

| PITCHING | W | L | ERA | G | GS | CG | SV | IP | H | R | ER | BB | SO | B | T | HT | WT | DOB | 1st Yr | Resides |
|---|---|---|---|---|---|---|---|---|---|---|---|---|---|---|---|---|---|---|---|---|
| Arocha, Rene | 11 | 8 | 3.78 | 32 | 29 | 1 | 0 | 188 | 197 | 89 | 79 | 31 | 96 | R | R | 6-0 | 180 | 2-24-66 | 1992 | Miami, Fla. |
| Batchelor, Rich | 0 | 0 | 8.10 | 9 | 0 | 0 | 0 | 10 | 14 | 12 | 9 | 3 | 4 | R | R | 6-1 | 195 | 4-8-67 | 1990 | Hartsville, S.C. |
| Burns, Todd | 0 | 4 | 6.16 | 24 | 0 | 0 | 0 | 31 | 32 | 21 | 21 | 9 | 10 | R | R | 6-1 | 185 | 7-6-63 | 1984 | Huntsville, Ala. |
| Cormier, Rheal | 7 | 6 | 4.33 | 38 | 21 | 1 | 0 | 145 | 163 | 80 | 70 | 27 | 75 | L | L | 5-10 | 185 | 4-23-67 | 1989 | Moncton, N.B. |
| Dixon, Steve | 0 | 0 | 33.75 | 4 | 0 | 0 | 0 | 3 | 7 | 10 | 10 | 5 | 2 | L | L | 6-0 | 195 | 8-3-69 | 1989 | Louisville, Ky. |
| Guetterman, Lee | 3 | 3 | 2.93 | 40 | 0 | 0 | 1 | 46 | 41 | 18 | 15 | 16 | 19 | L | L | 6-8 | 225 | 11-22-58 | 1981 | Lenoir City, Tenn. |
| Kilgus, Paul | 1 | 0 | 0.63 | 22 | 1 | 0 | 1 | 29 | 18 | 2 | 2 | 8 | 21 | L | L | 6-1 | 175 | 2-2-62 | 1984 | Bowling Green, Ky. |
| Lancaster, Les | 4 | 1 | 2.93 | 50 | 0 | 0 | 0 | 61 | 56 | 24 | 20 | 21 | 36 | R | R | 6-2 | 205 | 4-21-65 | 1985 | Irving, Texas |
| Magrane, Joe | 8 | 10 | 4.97 | 22 | 20 | 0 | 0 | 116 | 127 | 68 | 64 | 37 | 38 | R | L | 6-6 | 225 | 7-2-64 | 1985 | Morehead, Ky. |
| Murphy, Rob | 5 | 7 | 4.87 | 73 | 0 | 0 | 1 | 65 | 73 | 37 | 35 | 20 | 41 | L | L | 6-2 | 215 | 5-26-60 | 1981 | Miami, Fla. |
| Olivares, Omar | 5 | 3 | 4.17 | 58 | 9 | 0 | 1 | 119 | 134 | 60 | 55 | 54 | 63 | R | R | 6-1 | 183 | 7-6-67 | 1987 | San German, P.R. |
| Perez, Mike | 7 | 2 | 2.48 | 65 | 0 | 0 | 7 | 73 | 65 | 24 | 20 | 20 | 58 | R | R | 6-0 | 187 | 10-19-64 | 1986 | Yauco, P.R. |
| Smith, Lee | 2 | 4 | 4.50 | 55 | 0 | 0 | 43 | 50 | 49 | 25 | 25 | 9 | 49 | R | R | 6-6 | 250 | 12-4-57 | 1975 | Castor, La. |
| Tewksbury, Bob | 17 | 10 | 3.83 | 32 | 32 | 2 | 0 | 214 | 258 | 99 | 91 | 20 | 97 | R | R | 6-4 | 200 | 11-30-60 | 1981 | Concord, N.H. |
| Urbani, Tom | 1 | 3 | 4.65 | 18 | 9 | 0 | 0 | 62 | 73 | 44 | 32 | 26 | 33 | L | L | 6-1 | 190 | 1-21-68 | 1990 | Santa Cruz, Calif. |
| Watson, Allen | 6 | 7 | 4.60 | 16 | 15 | 0 | 0 | 86 | 90 | 53 | 44 | 28 | 49 | L | L | 6-3 | 195 | 11-18-70 | 1991 | Middle Village, N.Y. |

## FIELDING

| Catcher | PCT | G | PO | A | E | DP |
|---|---|---|---|---|---|---|
| Pagnozzi | .991 | 92 | 421 | 44 | 4 | 4 |
| Pappas | .982 | 63 | 294 | 32 | 6 | 5 |
| Ronan | 1.000 | 6 | 29 | 0 | 0 | 0 |
| Villanueva | 1.000 | 17 | 86 | 3 | 0 | 0 |

| First Base | PCT | G | PO | A | E | DP |
|---|---|---|---|---|---|---|
| Brewer | .991 | 32 | 101 | 5 | 1 | 13 |
| Gilkey | 1.000 | 3 | 24 | 1 | 0 | 2 |
| Jefferies | .993 | 140 | 1279 | 76 | 9 | 114 |
| Pappas | 1.000 | 2 | 6 | 0 | 0 | 1 |
| Perry | .976 | 15 | 77 | 3 | 2 | 5 |
| Royer | 1.000 | 2 | 19 | 1 | 0 | 0 |
| Woodson | .981 | 11 | 49 | 2 | 1 | 7 |

| Second Base | PCT | G | PO | A | E | DP |
|---|---|---|---|---|---|---|
| Alicea | .978 | 96 | 202 | 280 | 11 | 61 |
| Jefferies | 1.000 | 1 | 2 | 1 | 0 | 1 |
| Jones | 1.000 | 7 | 8 | 9 | 0 | 1 |
| Oquendo | 1.000 | 16 | 25 | 24 | 0 | 6 |
| Pena | .966 | 64 | 140 | 200 | 12 | 47 |

| Third Base | PCT | G | PO | A | E | DP |
|---|---|---|---|---|---|---|
| Alicea | .000 | 1 | 0 | 0 | 0 | 0 |
| Royer | .857 | 10 | 3 | 15 | 3 | 1 |
| Woodson | .909 | 28 | 7 | 23 | 3 | 3 |
| Zeile | .923 | 153 | 83 | 310 | 33 | 26 |

| Shortstop | PCT | G | PO | A | E | DP |
|---|---|---|---|---|---|---|
| Cromer | .912 | 9 | 13 | 18 | 3 | 3 |
| Jones | .976 | 21 | 26 | 54 | 2 | 8 |

| | PCT | G | PO | A | E | DP |
|---|---|---|---|---|---|---|
| Oquendo | .988 | 22 | 27 | 58 | 1 | 9 |
| O. Smith | .974 | 134 | 251 | 451 | 19 | 98 |

| Outfield | PCT | G | PO | A | E | DP |
|---|---|---|---|---|---|---|
| Alicea | 1.000 | 4 | 8 | 1 | 0 | 0 |
| Brewer | .960 | 33 | 47 | 1 | 2 | 0 |
| Canseco | .500 | 5 | 1 | 0 | 1 | 0 |
| Gilkey | .969 | 134 | 227 | 19 | 8 | 2 |
| Jordan | .973 | 65 | 140 | 4 | 4 | 0 |
| Lankford | .978 | 121 | 312 | 6 | 7 | 0 |
| Maclin | 1.000 | 5 | 3 | 0 | 0 | 0 |
| Pappas | 1.000 | 16 | 37 | 0 | 0 | 0 |
| Perry | 1.000 | 1 | 2 | 0 | 0 | 0 |
| Whiten | .971 | 148 | 329 | 9 | 10 | 1 |

# CARDINALS FARM SYSTEM

| Class | Club | League | W | L | Pct. | Finish* | Manager | First Year |
|---|---|---|---|---|---|---|---|---|
| AAA | Louisville (Ky.) Redbirds | American Assoc. | 68 | 76 | .472 | 6th (8) | Jack Krol | 1982 |
| AA | Arkansas Travelers | Texas | 66 | 69 | .489 | T-5th (8) | Joe Pettini | 1966 |
| A# | St. Petersburg (Fla.) Cardinals | Florida State | 75 | 58 | .564 | 4th (13) | Terry Kennedy | 1966 |
| A | Springfield (Ill.) Cardinals | Midwest | 78 | 58 | .574 | 3rd (14) | Mike Ramsey | 1982 |
| A | Savannah (Ga.) Cardinals | South Atlantic | 94 | 48 | .662 | 1st† (14) | Chris Maloney | 1984 |
| A | Glens Falls (N.Y.) Redbirds | New York-Penn | 37 | 40 | .481 | 8th (14) | Steve Turco | 1993 |
| Rookie# | Johnson City (Tenn.) Cardinals | Appalachian | 37 | 31 | .544 | 5th (10) | Joe Cunningham | 1975 |
| Rookie | Chandler (Ariz.) Cardinals | Arizona | 31 | 22 | .585 | 2nd (8) | Roy Silver | 1989 |

*Finish in overall standings (No. of teams in league)   #Advanced level   †Won league championship

## AMERICAN ASSOCIATION

| BATTING | AVG | G | AB | R | H | 2B | 3B | HR | RBI | BB | SO | SB | CS | B | T | HT | WT | DOB | 1st Yr | Resides |
|---|---|---|---|---|---|---|---|---|---|---|---|---|---|---|---|---|---|---|---|---|
| Canseco, Ozzie | .240 | 44 | 154 | 20 | 37 | 6 | 1 | 13 | 33 | 15 | 59 | 1 | 2 | R | R | 6-3 | 220 | 7-2-64 | 1983 | Miami, Fla. |
| Cromer, Tripp | .275 | 85 | 309 | 39 | 85 | 8 | 4 | 11 | 33 | 15 | 60 | 1 | 3 | R | R | 6-2 | 160 | 11-21-67 | 1989 | Lexington, S.C. |
| Dozier, D.J. | .230 | 45 | 139 | 24 | 32 | 10 | 1 | 6 | 15 | 18 | 43 | 0 | 4 | R | R | 6-1 | 204 | 9-21-65 | 1990 | Eden Prarie, Minn. |
| Ellis, Paul | .200 | 50 | 125 | 12 | 25 | 6 | 0 | 0 | 8 | 13 | 16 | 0 | 0 | L | R | 6-1 | 205 | 11-28-68 | 1990 | San Ramon, Calif. |
| Figueroa, Bien | .239 | 93 | 272 | 44 | 65 | 17 | 1 | 0 | 15 | 16 | 27 | 1 | 1 | R | R | 5-10 | 167 | 2-7-64 | 1986 | Tallahassee, Fla. |
| Fulton, Ed | .211 | 61 | 147 | 13 | 31 | 5 | 0 | 3 | 18 | 11 | 27 | 0 | 0 | L | R | 6-0 | 195 | 1-7-66 | 1987 | Danville, Va. |
| Jones, Tim | .289 | 101 | 408 | 72 | 118 | 22 | 10 | 5 | 46 | 44 | 67 | 13 | 8 | L | R | 5-10 | 172 | 12-1-62 | 1985 | Sumter, S.C. |
| Jordan, Brian | .375 | 38 | 144 | 24 | 54 | 13 | 2 | 5 | 35 | 16 | 17 | 9 | 4 | R | R | 6-1 | 205 | 3-29-67 | 1988 | Baltimore, Md. |
| Lockhart, Keith | .300 | 132 | 467 | 66 | 140 | 24 | 3 | 13 | 68 | 60 | 43 | 3 | 3 | L | R | 5-10 | 170 | 11-10-64 | 1986 | Largo, Fla. |
| Lyons, Barry | .269 | 107 | 401 | 36 | 108 | 19 | 0 | 18 | 65 | 15 | 64 | 0 | 1 | R | R | 6-1 | 200 | 6-3-60 | 1982 | Biloxi, Miss. |
| Mabry, John | .143 | 4 | 7 | 0 | 1 | 0 | 0 | 0 | 1 | 0 | 1 | 0 | 0 | L | R | 6-4 | 195 | 10-17-70 | 1991 | Warwick, Md. |
| Maclin, Lonnie | .277 | 62 | 220 | 29 | 61 | 10 | 3 | 4 | 18 | 16 | 48 | 4 | 4 | L | L | 5-11 | 160 | 2-17-67 | 1987 | St. Louis, Mo. |
| Morris, Jim | .239 | 20 | 71 | 13 | 17 | 5 | 0 | 2 | 9 | 7 | 14 | 1 | 2 | L | L | 6-1 | 185 | 2-23-61 | 1982 | Gulfport, Fla. |
| Pagnozzi, Tom | .279 | 12 | 43 | 5 | 12 | 3 | 0 | 1 | 1 | 2 | 3 | 0 | 0 | R | R | 6-1 | 190 | 7-30-62 | 1983 | Tucson, Ariz. |
| Pappas, Erik | .338 | 21 | 71 | 19 | 24 | 6 | 1 | 4 | 13 | 11 | 12 | 0 | 2 | R | R | 6-0 | 175 | 4-25-66 | 1984 | Chicago, Ill. |
| Patterson, Dave | .278 | 80 | 180 | 26 | 50 | 6 | 0 | 5 | 16 | 27 | 27 | 0 | 0 | R | R | 5-11 | 175 | 6-15-64 | 1986 | Ventura, Calif. |
| Pena, Geronimo | .174 | 7 | 23 | 4 | 4 | 1 | 0 | 0 | 0 | 1 | 4 | 1 | 0 | S | R | 6-1 | 170 | 3-29-67 | 1985 | Los Alcarrizos, D.R. |
| Prager, Howard | .263 | 63 | 209 | 27 | 55 | 17 | 0 | 4 | 28 | 24 | 37 | 0 | 0 | L | L | 6-2 | 190 | 4-6-67 | 1989 | Dallas, Texas |
| Royer, Stan | .280 | 98 | 368 | 46 | 103 | 19 | 0 | 16 | 54 | 33 | 74 | 2 | 0 | R | R | 6-3 | 195 | 8-31-67 | 1988 | Springfield, Ill. |
| Savinon, Odalis | .203 | 35 | 59 | 10 | 12 | 1 | 1 | 0 | 2 | 4 | 13 | 0 | 2 | R | R | 6-1 | 170 | 5-8-70 | 1988 | Bani, D.R. |
| Snider, Van | .265 | 118 | 423 | 54 | 112 | 29 | 4 | 14 | 56 | 24 | 98 | 3 | 1 | L | R | 6-3 | 200 | 8-11-63 | 1982 | Birmingham, Ala. |
| Thomas, Skeets | .276 | 108 | 377 | 30 | 104 | 15 | 1 | 9 | 40 | 15 | 75 | 1 | 0 | L | R | 5-11 | 195 | 9-9-68 | 1990 | Hamlet, N.C. |
| Villanueva, Hector | .242 | 40 | 124 | 13 | 30 | 9 | 0 | 5 | 20 | 16 | 18 | 0 | 0 | R | R | 6-1 | 220 | 10-2-64 | 1985 | Rio Piedras, P.R. |

| PITCHING | W | L | ERA | G | GS | CG | SV | IP | H | R | ER | BB | SO | B | T | HT | WT | DOB | 1st Yr | Resides |
|---|---|---|---|---|---|---|---|---|---|---|---|---|---|---|---|---|---|---|---|---|
| Anderson, Paul | 3 | 5 | 4.89 | 11 | 11 | 2 | 0 | 70 | 74 | 41 | 38 | 14 | 32 | R | R | 6-4 | 215 | 12-19-68 | 1990 | San Diego, Calif. |
| Arnsberg, Brad | 0 | 2 | 4.11 | 23 | 0 | 0 | 0 | 31 | 30 | 14 | 14 | 25 | 17 | R | R | 6-4 | 210 | 8-20-63 | 1984 | Arlington, Texas |
| 2-team (6 Indy) | 0 | 2 | 5.31 | 29 | 0 | 0 | 0 | 41 | 47 | 24 | 24 | 27 | 19 | | | | | | | |
| Barber, Brian | 0 | 1 | 4.76 | 1 | 1 | 0 | 0 | 6 | 4 | 3 | 3 | 4 | 5 | R | R | 6-1 | 172 | 3-4-73 | 1991 | Orlando, Fla. |
| Buckels, Gary | 4 | 2 | 5.42 | 40 | 0 | 1 | | 88 | 116 | 58 | 53 | 25 | 64 | R | R | 6-0 | 185 | 7-22-65 | 1987 | Huntington Beach, Calif. |
| Cimorelli, Frank | 2 | 1 | 2.72 | 27 | 0 | 0 | 2 | 43 | 34 | 15 | 13 | 25 | 24 | R | R | 6-0 | 175 | 8-2-68 | 1989 | Hyde Park, N.Y. |
| Compres, Fidel | 3 | 5 | 6.91 | 21 | 0 | 0 | 0 | 27 | 41 | 26 | 21 | 19 | 18 | R | R | 6-0 | 165 | 5-10-65 | 1984 | La Vega, D.R. |
| Creek, Doug | 0 | 0 | 3.21 | 2 | 2 | 0 | 0 | 14 | 10 | 5 | 5 | 9 | 9 | L | L | 5-10 | 205 | 3-1-69 | 1991 | Martinsburg, W.Va. |
| Dixon, Steve | 5 | 7 | 5.05 | 57 | 0 | 0 | 20 | 68 | 57 | 39 | 38 | 33 | 61 | L | L | 6-0 | 195 | 8-3-69 | 1989 | Louisville, Ky. |
| Guetterman, Lee | 2 | 1 | 2.94 | 25 | 0 | 0 | 2 | 34 | 35 | 11 | 11 | 12 | 20 | L | L | 6-8 | 225 | 11-22-58 | 1981 | Lenoir City, Tenn. |
| Kilgus, Paul | 7 | 1 | 2.65 | 9 | 9 | 4 | 0 | 68 | 59 | 21 | 20 | 19 | 54 | L | L | 6-1 | 175 | 2-2-62 | 1984 | Bowling Green, Ky. |
| Knox, Kerry | 1 | 4 | 4.50 | 7 | 7 | 1 | 0 | 44 | 48 | 25 | 22 | 10 | 24 | L | L | 6-0 | 188 | 4-10-67 | 1989 | Fort Worth, Texas |
| Meier, Kevin | 8 | 6 | 5.80 | 27 | 24 | 1 | 0 | 135 | 156 | 95 | 87 | 44 | 98 | R | R | 6-4 | 200 | 2-20-66 | 1987 | Southington, Conn. |
| Milchin, Mike | 7 | 3 | 3.95 | 32 | 17 | 1 | 0 | 112 | 108 | 56 | 49 | 43 | 72 | L | L | 6-1 | 190 | 2-28-68 | 1989 | Richmond, Va. |
| Ozuna, Gab | 0 | 4 | 2.93 | 35 | 0 | 0 | 4 | 40 | 32 | 16 | 13 | 14 | 61 | R | R | 6-1 | 160 | 4-10-69 | 1988 | San Pedro de Macoris, D.R. |
| Sebra, Bob | 9 | 12 | 4.90 | 27 | 26 | 1 | 0 | 145 | 173 | 91 | 79 | 52 | 83 | R | R | 6-2 | 215 | 12-11-61 | 1983 | Medford Lakes, N.J. |
| Urbani, Tom | 9 | 5 | 2.47 | 18 | 13 | 0 | 1 | 95 | 86 | 29 | 26 | 23 | 65 | L | L | 6-1 | 190 | 1-21-68 | 1990 | Santa Cruz, Calif. |
| Watson, Allen | 5 | 4 | 2.91 | 17 | 17 | 2 | 0 | 121 | 101 | 46 | 39 | 16 | 87 | L | L | 6-3 | 195 | 11-18-70 | 1991 | Middle Village, N.Y. |
| Wiseman, Denny | 7 | 9 | 5.06 | 33 | 13 | 1 | 1 | 112 | 144 | 79 | 63 | 23 | 39 | R | R | 6-4 | 200 | 6-27-67 | 1989 | Baltimore, Md. |

### FIELDING

| Catcher | PCT | G | PO | A | E | DP |
|---|---|---|---|---|---|---|
| Ellis | 1.000 | 45 | 192 | 14 | 0 | 0 |
| Fulton | .990 | 43 | 182 | 18 | 2 | 1 |
| Lyons | .995 | 39 | 192 | 21 | 1 | 5 |
| Pagnozzi | .966 | 12 | 51 | 6 | 2 | 1 |
| Pappas | .978 | 21 | 131 | 5 | 3 | 0 |
| Villanueva | .992 | 18 | 117 | 11 | 1 | 1 |

| First Base | PCT | G | PO | A | E | DP |
|---|---|---|---|---|---|---|
| Canseco | .979 | 14 | 85 | 8 | 2 | 4 |
| Fulton | 1.000 | 1 | 11 | 0 | 0 | 2 |
| Lockhart | 1.000 | 1 | 0 | 1 | 0 | 0 |
| Lyons | .986 | 51 | 449 | 32 | 7 | 44 |
| Patterson | .992 | 46 | 339 | 23 | 3 | 36 |
| Prager | .984 | 43 | 344 | 22 | 6 | 33 |
| Royer | 1.000 | 6 | 48 | 1 | 0 | 6 |
| Villanueva | .987 | 9 | 71 | 3 | 1 | 8 |

| Second Base | PCT | G | PO | A | E | DP |
|---|---|---|---|---|---|---|
| Figueroa | .988 | 16 | 40 | 44 | 1 | 9 |
| Jones | .988 | 86 | 176 | 250 | 5 | 58 |
| Lockhart | .980 | 45 | 74 | 127 | 4 | 31 |
| Patterson | .667 | 2 | 0 | 2 | 1 | 0 |
| Pena | 1.000 | 6 | 10 | 18 | 0 | 2 |

| Third Base | PCT | G | PO | A | E | DP |
|---|---|---|---|---|---|---|
| Figueroa | .966 | 14 | 13 | 15 | 1 | 2 |
| Lockhart | .950 | 48 | 27 | 107 | 7 | 5 |
| Patterson | 1.000 | 7 | 4 | 11 | 0 | 0 |
| Royer | .960 | 85 | 61 | 201 | 11 | 18 |

| Shortstop | PCT | G | PO | A | E | DP |
|---|---|---|---|---|---|---|
| Cromer | .969 | 85 | 123 | 253 | 12 | 59 |
| Figueroa | .971 | 51 | 77 | 156 | 7 | 38 |
| Jones | .962 | 15 | 11 | 39 | 2 | 5 |

| Outfield | PCT | G | PO | A | E | DP |
|---|---|---|---|---|---|---|
| Canseco | .967 | 25 | 28 | 1 | 1 | 0 |
| Dozier | .940 | 40 | 60 | 3 | 4 | 1 |
| Figueroa | .000 | 1 | 0 | 0 | 0 | 0 |
| Jordan | 1.000 | 37 | 75 | 2 | 0 | 0 |
| Lockhart | .984 | 31 | 56 | 5 | 1 | 0 |
| Mabry | 1.000 | 1 | 3 | 0 | 0 | 0 |
| Maclin | 1.000 | 59 | 100 | 2 | 0 | 0 |
| Morris | .980 | 20 | 46 | 2 | 1 | 0 |
| Patterson | 1.000 | 7 | 4 | 0 | 0 | 0 |
| Prager | .969 | 23 | 29 | 2 | 1 | 0 |
| Savinon | 1.000 | 31 | 51 | 3 | 0 | 0 |
| Snider | .969 | 103 | 212 | 8 | 7 | 2 |
| Thomas | .957 | 97 | 191 | 7 | 9 | 1 |

## TEXAS LEAGUE

| BATTING | AVG | G | AB | R | H | 2B | 3B | HR | RBI | BB | SO | SB | CS | B | T | HT | WT | DOB | 1st Yr | Resides |
|---|---|---|---|---|---|---|---|---|---|---|---|---|---|---|---|---|---|---|---|---|
| Aversa, Joe, 3b-2b | .181 | 95 | 199 | 23 | 36 | 4 | 2 | 0 | 5 | 17 | 34 | 3 | 1 | S | R | 5-10 | 150 | 5-20-68 | 1990 | Huntington Beach, Calif. |
| Battle, Allen, of | .274 | 108 | 390 | 71 | 107 | 24 | 12 | 3 | 40 | 45 | 75 | 20 | 12 | R | R | 6-0 | 170 | 11-29-68 | 1991 | Mobile, Ala. |
| Cholowsky, Dan, 3b | .217 | 68 | 212 | 31 | 46 | 10 | 2 | 3 | 16 | 38 | 54 | 10 | 2 | R | R | 6-0 | 195 | 10-30-70 | 1991 | San Jose, Calif. |
| Coleman, Paul, of | .244 | 123 | 401 | 44 | 98 | 24 | 3 | 7 | 30 | 32 | 97 | 8 | 6 | R | R | 5-11 | 200 | 12-9-70 | 1989 | Frankston, Texas |
| Deak, Darrel, 2b | .242 | 121 | 414 | 63 | 100 | 22 | 1 | 19 | 73 | 58 | 103 | 4 | 8 | S | R | 6-0 | 180 | 7-5-69 | 1991 | Scottsdale, Ariz. |
| Ellis, Paul, c | .333 | 24 | 78 | 5 | 26 | 3 | 0 | 1 | 11 | 16 | 2 | 0 | 2 | L | R | 6-1 | 205 | 11-28-68 | 1990 | San Ramon, Calif. |
| Fanning, Steve, ss-3b | .213 | 97 | 249 | 28 | 53 | 14 | 0 | 3 | 20 | 26 | 71 | 5 | 3 | R | R | 6-3 | 180 | 5-16-67 | 1988 | Conyers, Ga. |
| Faulkner, Craig, 1b-c | .237 | 104 | 299 | 34 | 71 | 18 | 0 | 15 | 55 | 26 | 78 | 1 | 0 | R | R | 6-5 | 235 | 10-18-65 | 1987 | Venice, Fla. |
| Lewis, Anthony, of-dh | .264 | 112 | 326 | 48 | 86 | 28 | 2 | 13 | 50 | 25 | 98 | 3 | 4 | L | L | 6-0 | 185 | 2-2-71 | 1989 | North Las Vegas. Nev. |
| Mabry, John, of | .290 | 136 | 528 | 68 | 153 | 32 | 2 | 16 | 72 | 27 | 68 | 7 | 15 | L | R | 6-4 | 195 | 10-17-70 | 1991 | Warwick, Md. |
| Pimentel, Wander, ss-2b | .204 | 27 | 49 | 3 | 10 | 0 | 0 | | 5 | 1 | 7 | 0 | 0 | R | R | 5-11 | 150 | 9-18-72 | 1993 | Bani, D.R. |
| Prager, Howard, 1b | .316 | 59 | 158 | 31 | 50 | 8 | 1 | 7 | 21 | 28 | 34 | 4 | 2 | L | L | 6-2 | 190 | 4-6-67 | 1989 | Dallas, Texas |
| Ronan, Marc, c | .214 | 96 | 281 | 33 | 60 | 16 | 1 | 7 | 34 | 26 | 47 | 1 | 3 | L | R | 6-2 | 190 | 9-19-69 | 1990 | Tallahassee. Fla. |

BOB ROSATO

**Todd Zeile.** Cardinals third baseman drove in a career-high 103 runs in 1993.

**Bob Tewksbury.** Righthander led Cardinals pitchers with 17 wins, while walking 20 in 214 innings.

| BATTING | AVG | G | AB | R | H | 2B | 3B | HR | RBI | BB | SO | SB | CS | B | T | HT | WT | DOB | 1st Yr | Resides |
|---|---|---|---|---|---|---|---|---|---|---|---|---|---|---|---|---|---|---|---|---|
| Savinon, Odalis, of | .200 | 15 | 20 | 3 | 4 | 1 | 0 | 0 | 1 | 1 | 3 | 0 | 1 | R | R | 6-1 | 170 | 5-8-70 | 1988 | Bani, D.R. |
| Shireman, Jeff, ss | .285 | 107 | 333 | 32 | 95 | 20 | 0 | 2 | 32 | 25 | 43 | 3 | 7 | S | R | 5-8 | 165 | 3-20-66 | 1988 | Gainesville, Fla. |
| Tahan, Kevin, c | .154 | 35 | 65 | 5 | 10 | 1 | 1 | 1 | 5 | 4 | 16 | 1 | 0 | R | R | 6-0 | 190 | 8-11-66 | 1989 | San Diego, Calif. |
| Young, Dmitri, 1b | .247 | 45 | 166 | 13 | 41 | 11 | 2 | 3 | 21 | 9 | 29 | 4 | 4 | S | R | 6-2 | 215 | 10-11-73 | 1991 | Camarillo, Calif. |

| PITCHING | W | L | ERA | G | GS | CG | SV | IP | H | R | ER | BB | SO | B | T | HT | WT | DOB | 1st Yr | Resides |
|---|---|---|---|---|---|---|---|---|---|---|---|---|---|---|---|---|---|---|---|---|
| Anderson, Paul | 6 | 9 | 3.76 | 17 | 17 | 4 | 0 | 108 | 102 | 52 | 45 | 24 | 81 | R | R | 6-4 | 215 | 12-19-68 | 1990 | San Diego, Calif. |
| Barber, Brian | 9 | 8 | 4.02 | 24 | 24 | 1 | 0 | 143 | 154 | 70 | 64 | 56 | 126 | R | R | 6-1 | 172 | 3-4-73 | 1991 | Orlando, Fla. |
| Beltran, Rigo | 5 | 5 | 3.25 | 18 | 16 | 0 | 0 | 89 | 74 | 39 | 32 | 38 | 82 | L | L | 5-11 | 185 | 11-13-69 | 1991 | San Diego, Calif. |
| Brumley, Duff | 4 | 5 | 3.50 | 12 | 12 | 2 | 0 | 69 | 57 | 30 | 27 | 26 | 79 | R | R | 6-4 | 195 | 8-25-70 | 1990 | Cleveland, Tenn. |
| Cimorelli, Frank | 1 | 1 | 2.54 | 37 | 0 | 0 | 1 | 57 | 44 | 20 | 16 | 23 | 36 | R | R | 6-0 | 175 | 8-2-68 | 1989 | Hyde Park, N.Y. |
| Creek, Doug | 11 | 10 | 4.02 | 25 | 25 | 1 | 0 | 148 | 142 | 75 | 66 | 48 | 128 | L | L | 5-10 | 205 | 3-1-69 | 1991 | Martinsburg, W.Va. |
| Davis, Clint | 2 | 0 | 1.95 | 28 | 0 | 0 | 1 | 37 | 22 | 10 | 8 | 10 | 37 | R | R | 6-3 | 205 | 9-26-69 | 1991 | Irving, Texas |
| Eversgerd, Bryan | 4 | 4 | 2.18 | 62 | 0 | 0 | 0 | 66 | 60 | 24 | 16 | 19 | 68 | R | L | 6-1 | 185 | 2-11-69 | 1989 | Centralia, Ill. |
| Faccio, Luis | 0 | 3 | 8.37 | 8 | 4 | 0 | 0 | 24 | 33 | 23 | 22 | 7 | 20 | R | R | 6-5 | 220 | 11-3-67 | 1985 | Rio Piedras, P.R. |
| Johnson, Steve | 2 | 2 | 4.33 | 11 | 3 | 0 | 0 | 27 | 30 | 18 | 13 | 7 | 18 | R | R | 6-1 | 190 | 3-13-70 | 1991 | Salisbury, Mo. |
| Kelly, John | 2 | 4 | 3.55 | 51 | 0 | 0 | 27 | 58 | 53 | 28 | 23 | 12 | 40 | R | R | 6-4 | 185 | 7-3-67 | 1990 | Buford, Ga. |
| Knox, Kerry | 4 | 4 | 2.78 | 22 | 11 | 0 | 0 | 81 | 78 | 30 | 25 | 14 | 61 | L | L | 6-0 | 188 | 4-10-67 | 1988 | Fort Worth, Texas |
| Martinez, Francisco | 0 | 1 | 6.43 | 2 | 2 | 0 | 0 | 7 | 8 | 5 | 5 | 1 | 3 | R | R | 6-2 | 187 | 4-24-68 | 1987 | Santo Domingo, D.R. |
| Montgomery, Steve | 3 | 3 | 3.94 | 6 | 6 | 0 | 0 | 32 | 34 | 17 | 14 | 12 | 19 | R | R | 6-4 | 200 | 12-25-70 | 1992 | Corona Del Mar, Calif. |
| Perez, Mike | 0 | 0 | 7.36 | 4 | 0 | 0 | 0 | 4 | 7 | 3 | 3 | 0 | 4 | R | R | 6-0 | 187 | 10-19-64 | 1986 | Yauco, P.R. |
| Santos, Gerald | 3 | 6 | 2.63 | 57 | 0 | 0 | 3 | 82 | 80 | 36 | 24 | 41 | 65 | R | R | 5-10 | 175 | 7-9-69 | 1991 | Miami, Fla. |
| Shackle, Rick | 4 | 1 | 4.57 | 10 | 6 | 0 | 0 | 41 | 48 | 24 | 21 | 12 | 19 | R | R | 6-3 | 215 | 1-20-67 | 1989 | Bagdad, Fla. |
| Simmons, Scott | 6 | 3 | 2.70 | 13 | 10 | 0 | 0 | 77 | 68 | 26 | 23 | 18 | 35 | R | L | 6-2 | 205 | 8-15-69 | 1991 | St. Charles, Mo. |

## ST. PETERSBURG
### FLORIDA STATE LEAGUE

**A**

| BATTING | AVG | G | AB | R | H | 2B | 3B | HR | RBI | BB | SO | SB | CS | B | T | HT | WT | DOB | 1st Yr | Resides |
|---|---|---|---|---|---|---|---|---|---|---|---|---|---|---|---|---|---|---|---|---|
| Beasley, Andy, c | .143 | 13 | 35 | 1 | 5 | 0 | 0 | 0 | 3 | 7 | 10 | 0 | 0 | L | R | 6-4 | 220 | 7-1-68 | 1990 | Newport News, Va. |
| Berblinger, Jeff, 2b | .186 | 19 | 70 | 7 | 13 | 1 | 0 | 0 | 5 | 5 | 10 | 3 | 1 | R | R | 6-0 | 185 | 11-14-70 | 1993 | Goddard, Kan. |
| Bradshaw, Terry, of | .291 | 125 | 461 | 84 | 134 | 25 | 6 | 5 | 51 | 82 | 60 | 43 | 17 | L | R | 6-0 | 180 | 2-3-69 | 1990 | Zuni, Va. |
| Cantu, Mike, dh-1b | .289 | 127 | 463 | 54 | 134 | 28 | 1 | 10 | 75 | 40 | 81 | 2 | 6 | R | R | 6-3 | 220 | 11-8-68 | 1991 | Corpus Christi, Texas |
| Cerio, Steve, of | .301 | 52 | 176 | 20 | 53 | 14 | 1 | 3 | 29 | 12 | 33 | 1 | 2 | R | R | 6-0 | 200 | 8-29-69 | 1991 | Las Vegas, Nev. |
| Cholowsky, Dan, 2b-3b | .288 | 54 | 208 | 30 | 60 | 12 | 0 | 2 | 22 | 20 | 54 | 6 | 8 | R | R | 6-0 | 195 | 10-30-70 | 1991 | San Jose, Calif. |
| DiFelice, Mike, c | .227 | 30 | 97 | 5 | 22 | 2 | 0 | 0 | 8 | 11 | 13 | 1 | 0 | R | R | 6-2 | 205 | 5-28-69 | 1991 | Knoxville, Tenn. |
| Gerald, Ed, of | .199 | 52 | 176 | 17 | 35 | 12 | 4 | 0 | 17 | 17 | 58 | 2 | 1 | S | R | 6-3 | 185 | 7-18-70 | 1989 | St. Pauls, N.C. |
| Holbert, Aaron, ss | .265 | 121 | 460 | 60 | 121 | 18 | 3 | 2 | 31 | 28 | 61 | 45 | 22 | R | R | 6-0 | 160 | 1-9-73 | 1990 | Long Beach, Calif. |
| Jones, Keith, of | .244 | 102 | 324 | 40 | 79 | 12 | 4 | 0 | 25 | 14 | 40 | 21 | 9 | L | L | 5-10 | 150 | 1-28-71 | 1991 | Paducah, Ky. |
| Mediavilla, Ricky, of-dh | .205 | 30 | 83 | 5 | 17 | 1 | 0 | 0 | 8 | 7 | 13 | 7 | 0 | R | R | 5-10 | 165 | 12-21-69 | 1991 | Colorado Springs, Colo. |
| Meza, Larry, 2b-3b | .272 | 86 | 257 | 31 | 70 | 11 | 1 | 0 | 22 | 37 | 41 | 3 | 6 | L | R | 6-0 | 175 | 9-28-72 | 1990 | National City, Calif. |
| Morel, Plinio, c | .000 | 3 | 3 | 1 | 0 | 0 | 0 | 0 | 0 | 1 | 0 | 0 | 0 | R | R | 5-11 | 185 | 5-7-71 | 1990 | Villa Vasquez, D.R. |
| O'Brien, John, 1b | .320 | 9 | 25 | 2 | 8 | 1 | 0 | 1 | 5 | 2 | 3 | 0 | 0 | R | R | 6-4 | 220 | 3-15-69 | 1991 | Tulsa, Okla. |
| Pimentel, Wander, 2b-ss | .190 | 23 | 58 | 3 | 11 | 0 | 0 | 0 | 4 | 3 | 8 | 0 | 0 | R | R | 5-11 | 150 | 9-18-72 | 1993 | Bani, D.R. |

# CARDINALS: ORGANIZATION LEADERS

**Bernard Gilkey**
40 doubles, 268 total bases

## MAJOR LEAGUERS

### BATTING
| | | |
|---|---|---|
| *AVG | Gregg Jefferies | .342 |
| R | Bernard Gilkey | 99 |
| H | Gregg Jefferies | 186 |
| TB | Bernard Gilkey | 268 |
| 2B | Bernard Gilkey | 40 |
| 3B | Two tied at | 6 |
| HR | Mark Whiten | 25 |
| RBI | Todd Zeile | 103 |
| BB | Ray Lankford | 81 |
| SO | Ray Lankford | 111 |
| SB | Gregg Jefferies | 46 |

### PITCHING
| | | |
|---|---|---|
| W | Bob Tewksbury | 17 |
| L | Two tied at | 10 |
| #ERA | Donovan Osborne | 3.76 |
| G | Rob Murphy | 73 |
| CG | Bob Tewksbury | 2 |
| SV | Lee Smith | 43 |
| IP | Bob Tewksbury | 214 |
| BB | Omar Olivares | 54 |
| SO | Bob Tewksbury | 97 |

## MINOR LEAGUERS

### BATTING
| | | |
|---|---|---|
| *AVG | Doug Radziewicz, St. Petersburg | .342 |
| R | Joe McEwing, Savannah | 94 |
| H | Aldo Pecorilli, Savannah | 157 |
| TB | Aldo Pecorilli, Savannah | 243 |
| 2B | Doug Radziewicz, St. Petersburg | 36 |
| 3B | Allen Battle, Arkansas | 12 |
| HR | Joe Biasucci, Springfield | 26 |
| RBI | Aldo Pecorilli, Savannah | 93 |
| BB | Joe McEwing, Savannah | 89 |
| SO | Darond Stovall, Springfield | 143 |
| SB | Aaron Holbert, St. Petersburg | 45 |

### PITCHING
| | | |
|---|---|---|
| W | Two tied at | 15 |
| L | Paul Anderson, Arkansas-Louisville | 14 |
| #ERA | Jeff Matranga, Savannah-St. Pete. | 1.64 |
| G | Frank Cimorelli, Arkansas-Louisville | 64 |
| CG | Paul Anderson, Arkansas-Louisville | 6 |
| SV | Jamie Cochran, Savannah | 46 |
| IP | Paul Anderson, Arkansas-Louisville | 178 |
| BB | Jeff Alkire, Savannah | 68 |
| SO | Jeff Alkire, Savannah | 175 |

*Minimum 250 At-Bats   #Minimum 75 Innings

| BATTING | AVG | G | AB | R | H | 2B | 3B | HR | RBI | BB | SO | SB | CS | B | T | HT | WT | DOB | 1st Yr | Resides |
|---|---|---|---|---|---|---|---|---|---|---|---|---|---|---|---|---|---|---|---|---|
| Prybylinski, Don, c | .191 | 67 | 209 | 27 | 40 | 11 | 0 | 0 | 10 | 16 | 39 | 2 | 0 | R | R | 6-0 | 175 | 4-11-68 | 1990 | LaSalle, Ill. |
| Radziewicz, Doug, 1b | .342 | 123 | 439 | 66 | 150 | 36 | 2 | 4 | 72 | 73 | 58 | 6 | 8 | L | L | 6-1 | 195 | 4-24-69 | 1991 | Somerville, N.J. |
| Ronan, Marc, c | .310 | 25 | 87 | 13 | 27 | 5 | 0 | 0 | 6 | 6 | 10 | 0 | 0 | L | R | 6-2 | 190 | 9-19-69 | 1991 | Tallahassee, Fla. |
| Turvey, Joe, c | .259 | 18 | 27 | 1 | 7 | 1 | 0 | 0 | 3 | 2 | 15 | 0 | 0 | L | R | 6-1 | 182 | 10-27-69 | 1989 | Philadelphia, Pa. |
| Vazquez, Jose, of | .254 | 29 | 71 | 10 | 18 | 2 | 0 | 0 | 3 | 6 | 18 | 5 | 0 | R | R | 6-0 | 190 | 5-28-70 | 1992 | Miami, Fla. |
| Velez, Jose, of | .236 | 81 | 178 | 12 | 42 | 3 | 2 | 0 | 15 | 6 | 32 | 0 | 1 | S | L | 6-2 | 165 | 3-6-73 | 1990 | Mayaguez, P.R. |
| Warner, Ron, 3b-2b | .289 | 103 | 311 | 42 | 90 | 8 | 3 | 4 | 37 | 31 | 39 | 5 | 1 | R | R | 6-3 | 185 | 12-2-68 | 1991 | Redlands, Calif. |
| Young, Dmitri, 3b-1b | .315 | 69 | 270 | 31 | 85 | 13 | 3 | 5 | 43 | 24 | 28 | 3 | 4 | S | R | 6-2 | 215 | 10-11-73 | 1991 | Camarillo, Calif. |

| PITCHING | W | L | ERA | G | GS | CG | SV | IP | H | R | ER | BB | SO | B | T | HT | WT | DOB | 1st Yr | Resides |
|---|---|---|---|---|---|---|---|---|---|---|---|---|---|---|---|---|---|---|---|---|
| Arrandale, Matt | 1 | 0 | 1.29 | 2 | 2 | 0 | 0 | 14 | 8 | 2 | 2 | 3 | 11 | R | R | 6-0 | 170 | 12-14-70 | 1993 | Webster Groves, Mo. |
| Badorek, Mike | 15 | 7 | 3.44 | 29 | 28 | 2 | 0 | 170 | 170 | 76 | 65 | 53 | 60 | R | R | 6-5 | 230 | 5-15-69 | 1991 | Mt. Zion, Ill. |
| Bailey, Roy | 2 | 3 | 3.89 | 31 | 0 | 0 | 1 | 44 | 34 | 22 | 19 | 17 | 29 | R | R | 6-0 | 185 | 1-16-67 | 1990 | Shelbyville, Ky. |
| Botkin, Alan | 3 | 3 | 3.17 | 49 | 0 | 0 | 0 | 48 | 45 | 21 | 17 | 25 | 24 | L | L | 6-3 | 204 | 10-6-67 | 1988 | West Palm Beach, Fla. |
| Brumley, Duff | 5 | 1 | 0.64 | 8 | 8 | 0 | 0 | 56 | 26 | 5 | 4 | 13 | 67 | R | R | 6-4 | 195 | 8-25-70 | 1990 | Cleveland, Ohio |
| Corona, John | 3 | 4 | 2.82 | 59 | 0 | 0 | 16 | 61 | 52 | 26 | 19 | 22 | 51 | L | L | 6-0 | 185 | 5-28-69 | 1989 | Santa Fe Springs, Calif. |
| Corrigan, Cory | 0 | 1 | 9.00 | 4 | 0 | 0 | 0 | 5 | 8 | 5 | 5 | 2 | 2 | R | R | 6-0 | 170 | 9-14-71 | 1993 | Athens, Ohio |
| Davis, Clint | 1 | 0 | 1.93 | 29 | 0 | 0 | 19 | 28 | 26 | 8 | 6 | 10 | 44 | R | R | 6-3 | 205 | 9-26-69 | 1991 | Irving, Texas |
| Hisey, Jason | 6 | 6 | 3.54 | 17 | 17 | 0 | 0 | 97 | 75 | 50 | 38 | 38 | 70 | R | R | 6-2 | 230 | 9-30-69 | 1991 | Klamath Falls, Ore. |
| Johnson, Steve | 6 | 2 | 2.80 | 21 | 3 | 0 | 0 | 55 | 56 | 18 | 17 | 22 | 40 | R | R | 6-1 | 190 | 3-13-70 | 1991 | Salisbury, Mo. |
| Jolley, Mike | 2 | 0 | 0.35 | 11 | 2 | 0 | 1 | 26 | 14 | 3 | 1 | 5 | 12 | R | R | 6-1 | 225 | 12-3-70 | 1990 | St. George, Utah |
| Lowe, Sean | 6 | 11 | 4.27 | 25 | 25 | 0 | 0 | 133 | 152 | 80 | 63 | 62 | 87 | R | R | 6-2 | 200 | 3-29-71 | 1992 | Mesquite, Texas |
| Martinez, Francisco | 3 | 2 | 1.37 | 13 | 7 | 1 | 0 | 66 | 55 | 13 | 10 | 22 | 38 | R | R | 6-2 | 187 | 4-24-68 | 1987 | Santo Domingo, D.R. |
| Matranga, Jeff | 2 | 0 | 2.22 | 5 | 3 | 0 | 0 | 28 | 23 | 10 | 7 | 6 | 21 | R | R | 6-2 | 170 | 12-14-70 | 1992 | Temecula, Calif. |
| McGarity, Jeremy | 9 | 7 | 3.88 | 34 | 7 | 0 | 0 | 93 | 102 | 48 | 40 | 47 | 48 | R | R | 6-5 | 195 | 3-22-71 | 1989 | Lakeside, Calif. |
| Miller, Eric | 1 | 1 | 1.15 | 26 | 0 | 0 | 1 | 31 | 19 | 6 | 4 | 18 | 35 | R | R | 6-2 | 195 | 5-27-71 | 1993 | Heyburn, Idaho |
| Montgomery, Steve | 2 | 1 | 2.66 | 14 | 5 | 0 | 3 | 41 | 33 | 14 | 12 | 9 | 34 | R | R | 6-4 | 200 | 12-25-70 | 1992 | Corona Del Mar, Calif. |
| Romanoli, Paul | 0 | 0 | 4.29 | 17 | 0 | 0 | 0 | 21 | 21 | 14 | 10 | 21 | 17 | L | L | 6-2 | 182 | 9-22-69 | 1991 | Germantown, Tenn. |
| Simmons, Scott | 4 | 5 | 3.43 | 13 | 12 | 1 | 0 | 79 | 70 | 38 | 30 | 31 | 54 | R | L | 6-2 | 205 | 8-15-69 | 1991 | St. Charles, Mo. |
| Slininger, Dennis | 3 | 3 | 4.42 | 12 | 12 | 2 | 0 | 71 | 75 | 40 | 35 | 25 | 40 | R | R | 6-2 | 190 | 6-29-72 | 1991 | Largo, Fla. |
| Wiseman, Denny | 1 | 1 | 1.59 | 2 | 2 | 0 | 0 | 17 | 10 | 3 | 3 | 2 | 9 | R | R | 6-4 | 200 | 6-27-67 | 1989 | Baltimore, Md. |

# SPRINGFIELD    A

## MIDWEST LEAGUE

| BATTING | AVG | G | AB | R | H | 2B | 3B | HR | RBI | BB | SO | SB | CS | B | T | HT | WT | DOB | 1st Yr | Resides |
|---|---|---|---|---|---|---|---|---|---|---|---|---|---|---|---|---|---|---|---|---|
| Ballara, Juan, c | .246 | 60 | 195 | 24 | 48 | 8 | 1 | 5 | 29 | 12 | 42 | 1 | 1 | R | R | 6-2 | 150 | 3-30-72 | 1990 | Santo Domingo, D.R. |
| Biasucci, Joe, 2b | .289 | 119 | 398 | 76 | 115 | 30 | 3 | 26 | 86 | 62 | 110 | 15 | 6 | R | R | 5-11 | 180 | 4-28-70 | 1990 | Hollywood, Fla. |
| Biermann, Steve, ss-3b | .091 | 3 | 11 | 0 | 1 | 0 | 0 | 0 | 0 | 0 | 6 | 0 | 1 | S | R | 6-0 | 175 | 9-30-71 | 1993 | St. Louis, Mo. |
| Bruce, Andy, 1b-dh | .255 | 105 | 364 | 61 | 93 | 13 | 1 | 21 | 70 | 44 | 136 | 1 | 2 | R | R | 6-0 | 220 | 4-15-69 | 1991 | Marietta, Ga. |
| DiFelice, Mike, c | .350 | 8 | 20 | 5 | 7 | 1 | 0 | 0 | 3 | 2 | 3 | 0 | 1 | R | R | 6-2 | 205 | 5-28-69 | 1991 | Knoxville, Tenn. |
| Eicher, Mike, of | .172 | 38 | 87 | 10 | 15 | 3 | 0 | 1 | 11 | 16 | 28 | 1 | 0 | R | R | 6-4 | 210 | 9-10-69 | 1991 | San Diego, Calif. |
| Ellsworth, Ben, 2b-3b | .189 | 29 | 74 | 6 | 14 | 3 | 0 | 0 | 8 | 5 | 13 | 0 | 2 | S | R | 5-10 | 160 | 1-8-71 | 1989 | Las Vegas, Nev. |
| Gerteisen, Aaron, of | .333 | 4 | 6 | 1 | 2 | 0 | 0 | 0 | 1 | 3 | 2 | 1 | 0 | S | R | 6-0 | 165 | 10-26-72 | 1993 | Tallahassee, Fla. |
| Gulan, Mike, 3b | .259 | 132 | 455 | 81 | 118 | 28 | 4 | 23 | 76 | 34 | 135 | 8 | 4 | R | R | 6-1 | 190 | 12-18-70 | 1992 | Steubenville, Ohio |
| Hamlin, Jonas, 1b-dh | .217 | 121 | 428 | 57 | 93 | 19 | 2 | 17 | 62 | 40 | 119 | 3 | 2 | R | R | 6-4 | 200 | 4-18-70 | 1990 | West Valley City, Utah |
| Henry, Antoine, of | .273 | 18 | 66 | 12 | 18 | 4 | 0 | 1 | 11 | 11 | 13 | 5 | 1 | R | R | 6-0 | 180 | 5-29-73 | 1991 | San Diego, Calif. |
| Johns, Keith, ss | .259 | 132 | 467 | 74 | 121 | 24 | 1 | 2 | 40 | 70 | 68 | 40 | 20 | R | R | 6-0 | 170 | 7-19-71 | 1992 | Jacksonville, Fla. |
| Jordan, Tim, of | .100 | 3 | 10 | 2 | 1 | 0 | 0 | 0 | 1 | 0 | 5 | 0 | 0 | L | R | 6-1 | 195 | 9-23-70 | 1989 | Yulee, Fla. |
| Landinez, Carlos, 2b-of | .214 | 47 | 126 | 18 | 27 | 7 | 0 | 0 | 3 | 6 | 19 | 5 | 4 | R | R | 6-1 | 170 | 7-20-70 | 1989 | Palmarejo, Venez. |
| Morel, Plinio, c | .227 | 26 | 75 | 3 | 17 | 2 | 0 | 0 | 3 | 4 | 17 | 0 | 0 | R | R | 5-11 | 185 | 5-7-71 | 1990 | Villa Vasquez, D.R. |
| Rudolph, Greg, of | .242 | 90 | 277 | 35 | 67 | 11 | 2 | 2 | 24 | 36 | 63 | 9 | 5 | R | R | 5-9 | 175 | 11-30-69 | 1992 | Gadsden, Ala. |
| Shabazz, Basil, of | .297 | 64 | 239 | 44 | 71 | 12 | 2 | 4 | 18 | 29 | 66 | 29 | 16 | R | R | 6-0 | 190 | 1-31-72 | 1991 | Pine Bluff, Ark. |
| Stovall, Darond, of | .257 | 135 | 460 | 73 | 118 | 19 | 4 | 20 | 81 | 53 | 143 | 18 | 12 | S | L | 6-1 | 185 | 1-3-73 | 1991 | East St. Louis, Ill. |
| Taylor, Gary, of-dh | .274 | 100 | 307 | 42 | 84 | 15 | 3 | 1 | 37 | 54 | 89 | 0 | 1 | L | R | 6-2 | 205 | 5-6-69 | 1991 | Hyannis, Mass. |

| BATTING | AVG | G | AB | R | H | 2B | 3B | HR | RBI | BB | SO | SB | CS | B | T | HT | WT | DOB | 1st Yr | Resides |
|---|---|---|---|---|---|---|---|---|---|---|---|---|---|---|---|---|---|---|---|---|
| Vazquez, Jose, of | .257 | 37 | 70 | 13 | 18 | 1 | 0 | 0 | 6 | 18 | 18 | 5 | 4 | R | R | 6-0 | 190 | 5-28-70 | 1992 | Miami, Fla. |
| Williams, Eddie, c | .236 | 53 | 182 | 25 | 43 | 6 | 3 | 1 | 19 | 18 | 36 | 2 | 1 | S | R | 6-3 | 220 | 1-22-72 | 1991 | Hialeah, Fla. |

| PITCHING | W | L | ERA | G | GS | CG | SV | IP | H | R | ER | BB | SO | B | T | HT | WT | DOB | 1st Yr | Resides |
|---|---|---|---|---|---|---|---|---|---|---|---|---|---|---|---|---|---|---|---|---|
| Bailey, Roy | 1 | 2 | 5.25 | 9 | 0 | 0 | 1 | 12 | 19 | 7 | 7 | 2 | 7 | R | R | 6-0 | 185 | 1-16-67 | 1990 | Shelbyville, Ky. |
| Blake, Todd | 9 | 6 | 4.31 | 24 | 18 | 1 | 0 | 117 | 125 | 61 | 56 | 25 | 98 | L | L | 6-2 | 205 | 9-22-70 | 1992 | Durham, N.C. |
| Bullinger, Kirk | 1 | 3 | 2.28 | 50 | 0 | 0 | 33 | 51 | 26 | 19 | 13 | 21 | 72 | R | R | 6-1 | 170 | 10-28-69 | 1992 | Hammond, La. |
| Carrillo, Joe | 0 | 1 | 5.04 | 15 | 1 | 0 | 1 | 30 | 34 | 19 | 17 | 14 | 21 | L | L | 6-0 | 200 | 12-20-70 | 1992 | Chula Vista, Calif. |
| DeGrasse, Tim | 4 | 3 | 2.20 | 49 | 0 | 0 | 1 | 78 | 56 | 28 | 19 | 32 | 90 | R | R | 6-1 | 195 | 7-14-69 | 1991 | Woodland Hills, Calif. |
| Frascatore, John | 7 | 12 | 3.78 | 27 | 26 | 2 | 0 | 157 | 157 | 84 | 66 | 33 | 126 | R | R | 6-1 | 200 | 2-4-70 | 1991 | Oceanside, N.Y. |
| Hammond, Allan | 0 | 0 | 27.00 | 1 | 0 | 0 | 0 | 1 | 2 | 3 | 3 | 2 | 1 | R | R | 6-5 | 180 | 1-26-71 | 1989 | Wellston, Ohio |
| Johnson, Steve | 1 | 3 | 5.91 | 5 | 5 | 0 | 0 | 21 | 26 | 17 | 14 | 7 | 16 | R | R | 6-1 | 190 | 3-13-70 | 1991 | Salisbury, Mo. |
| Jolley, Mike | 2 | 1 | 3.52 | 5 | 5 | 0 | 0 | 31 | 27 | 13 | 12 | 9 | 26 | R | R | 6-1 | 225 | 12-3-70 | 1990 | St. George, Utah |
| Knowles, Greg | 11 | 4 | 2.58 | 54 | 0 | 0 | 3 | 73 | 62 | 25 | 21 | 22 | 59 | R | R | 6-3 | 196 | 1-9-69 | 1991 | Plantation, Fla. |
| Lucchetti, Larry | 10 | 5 | 3.16 | 20 | 20 | 1 | 0 | 111 | 98 | 50 | 39 | 51 | 88 | R | R | 6-3 | 207 | 4-6-69 | 1991 | Linden, Calif. |
| Mathews, T.J. | 12 | 9 | 2.71 | 25 | 25 | 5 | 0 | 159 | 121 | 59 | 48 | 29 | 144 | R | R | 6-1 | 200 | 1-19-70 | 1992 | Columbia, Ill. |
| Miller, Eric | 2 | 1 | 0.91 | 24 | 0 | 0 | 2 | 30 | 22 | 4 | 3 | 9 | 32 | R | R | 6-2 | 195 | 5-27-71 | 1991 | Heyburn, Idaho |
| Oehrlein, David | 3 | 4 | 4.92 | 13 | 13 | 0 | 0 | 60 | 70 | 38 | 33 | 21 | 52 | L | L | 6-0 | 190 | 9-1-69 | 1992 | Rockville, Minn. |
| Ruiz, Diego | 1 | 0 | 0.00 | 1 | 1 | 0 | 0 | 6 | 2 | 1 | 0 | 1 | 2 | R | L | 6-0 | 175 | 10-26-70 | 1992 | Miami, Fla. |
| Slininger, Dennis | 8 | 1 | 2.96 | 13 | 13 | 1 | 0 | 76 | 69 | 34 | 25 | 21 | 57 | R | R | 6-2 | 190 | 6-29-72 | 1991 | Largo, Fla. |
| Smith, Chad | 1 | 3 | 7.20 | 13 | 5 | 0 | 0 | 35 | 48 | 36 | 28 | 9 | 33 | R | R | 6-2 | 175 | 8-29-69 | 1991 | Lynchburg, Va. |
| Smith, Mike | 4 | 0 | 6.80 | 14 | 4 | 0 | 0 | 42 | 50 | 36 | 32 | 18 | 32 | R | R | 6-3 | 210 | 6-17-70 | 1992 | San Diego, Calif. |
| Spiller, Derron | 1 | 0 | 2.25 | 31 | 0 | 0 | 0 | 44 | 44 | 14 | 11 | 10 | 39 | R | L | 6-5 | 220 | 12-20-69 | 1989 | Camarillo, Calif. |

## SAVANNAH A

### SOUTH ATLANTIC LEAGUE

| BATTING | AVG | G | AB | R | H | 2B | 3B | HR | RBI | BB | SO | SB | CS | B | T | HT | WT | DOB | 1st Yr | Resides |
|---|---|---|---|---|---|---|---|---|---|---|---|---|---|---|---|---|---|---|---|---|
| Anderson, Charlie, 3b-2b | .247 | 46 | 146 | 17 | 36 | 7 | 2 | 4 | 20 | 10 | 37 | 3 | 1 | R | R | 6-0 | 190 | 3-18-70 | 1992 | Jacksonville, Fla. |
| Black, Keith, 2b | .238 | 125 | 442 | 68 | 105 | 11 | 1 | 5 | 59 | 76 | 80 | 22 | 11 | R | R | 5-10 | 170 | 7-8-69 | 1991 | Florence, Ala. |
| Blanton, Garrett, of | .178 | 84 | 241 | 34 | 43 | 10 | 4 | 2 | 22 | 37 | 64 | 3 | 2 | R | R | 6-0 | 175 | 12-9-69 | 1991 | Tallahassee, Fla. |
| Colon, Hector, of | .231 | 100 | 295 | 39 | 68 | 5 | 1 | 0 | 18 | 30 | 33 | 13 | 5 | R | R | 6-2 | 155 | 11-3-71 | 1990 | Arroyo, P.R. |
| Doucette, Darren, 1b-dh | .249 | 91 | 225 | 22 | 56 | 12 | 3 | 4 | 21 | 53 | 87 | 0 | 1 | L | L | 6-4 | 225 | 6-10-71 | 1992 | Dartmouth, N.S. |
| Dudek, Steve, of | .174 | 23 | 46 | 1 | 8 | 1 | 0 | 0 | 2 | 3 | 11 | 0 | 0 | L | L | 5-11 | 175 | 1-15-72 | 1990 | Las Vegas, Nev. |
| French, Ronnie, of | .197 | 70 | 152 | 30 | 30 | 4 | 0 | 4 | 12 | 22 | 44 | 4 | 1 | R | R | 5-11 | 175 | 12-6-70 | 1989 | Yulee, Fla. |
| Martin, Andy, 1b | .235 | 54 | 149 | 17 | 35 | 5 | 1 | 1 | 16 | 23 | 42 | 1 | 0 | L | R | 6-0 | 190 | 11-22-70 | 1992 | Escondido, Calif. |
| McEwing, Joe, of | .249 | 138 | 511 | 94 | 127 | 35 | 1 | 0 | 43 | 89 | 73 | 22 | 9 | R | R | 5-10 | 170 | 10-19-72 | 1992 | Bristol, Pa. |
| Milne, Blaine, c | .219 | 11 | 32 | 0 | 7 | 1 | 0 | 0 | 1 | 1 | 4 | 0 | 0 | R | R | 6-3 | 195 | 12-18-68 | 1991 | Washington, Utah |
| Mota, Santo, ss | .248 | 62 | 202 | 32 | 50 | 3 | 2 | 2 | 25 | 29 | 41 | 14 | 10 | S | R | 5-9 | 150 | 4-12-72 | 1991 | San Pedro de Macoris, D.R. |
| Murphy, Jeff, c | .226 | 98 | 345 | 40 | 78 | 21 | 1 | 7 | 47 | 49 | 105 | 2 | 1 | S | R | 6-2 | 210 | 12-27-70 | 1992 | Las Vegas, Nev. |
| O'Brien, John, 1b | .249 | 68 | 265 | 31 | 66 | 11 | 0 | 14 | 66 | 13 | 62 | 0 | 0 | R | R | 6-4 | 220 | 3-15-69 | 1991 | Tulsa, Okla. |
| Pecorilli, Aldo, dh-c | .305 | 141 | 515 | 75 | 157 | 30 | 7 | 14 | 93 | 81 | 86 | 16 | 11 | R | R | 5-11 | 185 | 9-12-70 | 1992 | Sterling Heights, Mich. |
| Rupp, Brian, ss-3b | .320 | 122 | 472 | 80 | 151 | 31 | 7 | 4 | 81 | 48 | 70 | 3 | 2 | R | R | 6-4 | 190 | 9-20-71 | 1992 | Florissant, Mo. |
| Sumner, Chad, 3b | .212 | 89 | 297 | 37 | 63 | 10 | 2 | 2 | 22 | 18 | 56 | 2 | 1 | R | R | 6-1 | 190 | 7-27-69 | 1991 | Ocilla, Ga. |
| Ugueto, Jesus, ss-2b | .228 | 47 | 127 | 17 | 29 | 6 | 0 | 1 | 12 | 13 | 25 | 1 | 0 | R | R | 6-0 | 145 | 12-29-72 | 1990 | Catia La Mar, Venez. |
| Vlasis, Chris, of | .211 | 71 | 199 | 36 | 42 | 6 | 1 | 0 | 19 | 45 | 39 | 21 | 8 | L | R | 6-1 | 175 | 8-26-69 | 1991 | Charlottesville, Va. |

| PITCHING | W | L | ERA | G | GS | CG | SV | IP | H | R | ER | BB | SO | B | T | HT | WT | DOB | 1st Yr | Resides |
|---|---|---|---|---|---|---|---|---|---|---|---|---|---|---|---|---|---|---|---|---|
| Alkire, Jeff | 15 | 6 | 2.46 | 28 | 28 | 0 | 0 | 172 | 143 | 56 | 47 | 68 | 175 | R | L | 6-0 | 200 | 11-15-69 | 1992 | San Jose, Calif. |
| Busby, Mike | 12 | 2 | 2.44 | 23 | 21 | 1 | 0 | 144 | 116 | 49 | 39 | 31 | 125 | R | R | 6-4 | 215 | 12-27-72 | 1991 | Wilmington, Calif. |
| Carpenter, Brian | 10 | 8 | 2.86 | 28 | 28 | 0 | 0 | 154 | 145 | 55 | 49 | 41 | 147 | R | R | 6-0 | 220 | 3-3-71 | 1992 | Marble Falls, Texas |
| Carrillo, Joe | 0 | 0 | 5.23 | 6 | 0 | 0 | 0 | 10 | 9 | 6 | 6 | 10 | 11 | L | L | 6-0 | 200 | 12-20-70 | 1992 | Chula Vista, Calif. |
| Cochran, Jamie | 4 | 1 | 1.55 | 58 | 0 | 0 | 46 | 64 | 51 | 14 | 11 | 22 | 62 | R | R | 6-0 | 196 | 10-14-68 | 1991 | Flint, Mich. |
| Davis, Ray | 9 | 7 | 3.63 | 26 | 26 | 1 | 0 | 131 | 141 | 73 | 53 | 53 | 120 | R | R | 6-1 | 170 | 2-6-73 | 1991 | Palatka, Fla. |
| Goodman, Doug | 5 | 3 | 3.26 | 60 | 0 | 0 | 0 | 77 | 66 | 33 | 28 | 29 | 45 | R | R | 6-0 | 175 | 6-8-68 | 1992 | Oklahoma City, Okla. |
| Jones, Steve | 6 | 5 | 2.51 | 56 | 0 | 0 | 4 | 68 | 61 | 30 | 19 | 26 | 69 | R | R | 6-0 | 180 | 8-1-68 | 1991 | Cordova, Tenn. |
| Lucchetti, Larry | 2 | 1 | 2.86 | 9 | 1 | 0 | 0 | 22 | 16 | 8 | 7 | 6 | 29 | R | R | 6-3 | 207 | 4-6-69 | 1991 | Linden, Calif. |
| Martinez, Frankie | 7 | 3 | 1.89 | 14 | 14 | 2 | 0 | 95 | 70 | 28 | 20 | 23 | 79 | R | R | 6-2 | 187 | 4-24-68 | 1987 | Santo Domingo, D.R. |
| Matranga, Jeff | 11 | 3 | 1.49 | 15 | 15 | 3 | 0 | 103 | 74 | 24 | 17 | 13 | 90 | R | R | 6-2 | 170 | 12-14-70 | 1992 | Temecula, Calif. |
| Matulevich, Jeff | 4 | 4 | 4.80 | 34 | 1 | 0 | 0 | 51 | 61 | 31 | 27 | 14 | 42 | R | R | 6-3 | 200 | 4-15-70 | 1992 | Haddam, Conn. |
| Ottmers, Marc | 2 | 2 | 4.29 | 4 | 4 | 0 | 0 | 21 | 20 | 12 | 10 | 12 | 13 | R | R | 6-0 | 185 | 12-31-71 | 1993 | San Antonio, Texas |
| Smith, Chad | 1 | 0 | 2.27 | 20 | 2 | 0 | 1 | 44 | 33 | 15 | 11 | 14 | 47 | R | R | 6-2 | 175 | 8-29-69 | 1991 | Lynchburg, Va. |
| Stanley, Karl | 0 | 1 | 2.33 | 22 | 0 | 0 | 1 | 27 | 13 | 7 | 7 | 14 | 36 | R | R | 6-2 | 200 | 6-13-68 | 1990 | Orange, Va. |
| Tranbarger, Mark | 5 | 2 | 3.14 | 56 | 1 | 0 | 1 | 66 | 56 | 25 | 23 | 29 | 50 | L | L | 6-2 | 205 | 9-17-69 | 1991 | Cincinnati, Ohio |
| Witasick, Jay | 1 | 0 | 4.50 | 1 | 1 | 0 | 0 | 6 | 7 | 3 | 3 | 2 | 8 | R | R | 6-4 | 205 | 8-28-72 | 1993 | Bel Air, Md. |

## CARDINALS: MOST COMMON LINEUPS

| | St. Louis Majors | Louisville AAA | Arkansas AA | St. Petersburg A | Springfield A | Savannah A |
|---|---|---|---|---|---|---|
| C | Tom Pagnozzi (92) | Paul Ellis (45) | Marc Ronan (93) | Don Prybylinski (66) | Juan Ballara (56) | Jeff Murphy (89) |
| 1B | Gregg Jefferies (140) | Barry Lyons (51) | Howard Prager (56) | Doug Radziewicz (99) | Andy Bruce (70) | John O'Brien (68) |
| 2B | Luis Alicea (96) | Tim Jones (86) | Darrel Deak (119) | Larry Meza (40) | Joe Biasucci (108) | Keith Black (123) |
| 3B | Todd Zeile (153) | Stan Royer (85) | Dan Cholowsky (65) | Dmitri Young (48) | Mike Gulan (129) | Chad Sumner (86) |
| SS | Ozzie Smith (134) | Tripp Cromer (85) | Jeff Shireman (99) | Aaron Holbert (119) | Keith Johns (132) | Brian Rupp (66) |
| OF | Mark Whiten (148) | Van Snider (103) | John Mabry (136) | Terry Bradshaw (125) | Darond Stovall (137) | Joe McEwing (138) |
| | Bernard Gilkey (134) | Skeets Thomas (94) | Paul Coleman (111) | Keith Jones (93) | Greg Rudolph (82) | Hector Colon (95) |
| | Ray Lankford (121) | Lonnie Maclin (57) | Allen Battle (105) | Jose Velez (77) | Gary Taylor (65) | Garrett Blanton (80) |
| DH | N/A | Barry Lyons (19) | Anthony Lewis (28) | Mike Cantu (106) | Jonas Hamlin (51) | Aldo Pecorilli (61) |
| SP | Bob Tewksbury (32) | Bob Sebra (26) | Doug Creek (25) | Mike Badorek (28) | John Frascatore (26) | Alkire/Carpenter (28) |
| RP | Rob Murphy (73) | Steve Dixon (57) | Bryan Eversgerd (62) | John Corona (59) | Greg Knowles (54) | Doug Goodman (60) |

Full-season farm clubs only No. of games at position in parenthesis

# CARDINALS TOP 10 PROSPECTS

How the Cardinals Top 10 prospects, as judged by Baseball America prior to the 1993 season, fared in 1993:

| Player, Pos. | Club (Class) | AVG | AB | H | HR | RBI | SB |
|---|---|---|---|---|---|---|---|
| 2. Dmitri Young, 3b | St. Petersburg (A) | .315 | 270 | 85 | 5 | 43 | 3 |
| | Arkansas (AA) | .247 | 166 | 41 | 3 | 21 | 4 |
| 5. Aaron Holbert, ss | St. Petersburg (A) | .265 | 457 | 121 | 2 | 31 | 45 |
| 8. Basil Shabazz, of | Springfield (A) | .297 | 239 | 71 | 4 | 18 | 29 |
| 10. Mike Gulan, 3b | Springfield (A) | .259 | 455 | 118 | 23 | 76 | 8 |

| Player, Pos. | Club (Class) | W | L | ERA | IP | H | BB | SO |
|---|---|---|---|---|---|---|---|---|
| 1. Allen Watson, lhp | Louisville (AAA) | 5 | 4 | 2.91 | 121 | 101 | 31 | 86 |
| | St. Louis | 6 | 7 | 4.60 | 86 | 90 | 28 | 49 |
| 3. Brian Barber, rhp | Arkansas (AA) | 9 | 8 | 4.02 | 143 | 154 | 56 | 126 |
| | Louisville (AAA) | 0 | 1 | 4.76 | 6 | 4 | 4 | 5 |
| 4. Rene Arocha, rhp | St. Louis | 11 | 8 | 3.78 | 188 | 197 | 31 | 96 |
| 6. Mike Milchin, lhp | Louisville (AAA) | 3 | 7 | 3.95 | 112 | 108 | 43 | 72 |
| 7. Sean Lowe, rhp | St. Petersburg (A) | 6 | 11 | 4.27 | 133 | 152 | 62 | 87 |
| 9. Steve Dixon, lhp | Louisville (AAA) | 5 | 7 | 4.92 | 68 | 57 | 33 | 61 |

**Allen Watson**
6-7 at St. Louis

LARRY KINKER

# GLENS FALLS · A
## NEW YORK-PENN LEAGUE

| BATTING | AVG | G | AB | R | H | 2B | 3B | HR | RBI | BB | SO | SB | CS | B | T | HT | WT | DOB | 1st Yr | Resides |
|---|---|---|---|---|---|---|---|---|---|---|---|---|---|---|---|---|---|---|---|---|
| Almond, Greg, c-dh | .255 | 68 | 239 | 33 | 61 | 17 | 1 | 2 | 30 | 31 | 47 | 4 | 5 | R | R | 6-0 | 195 | 4-14-71 | 1993 | Panama City, Fla. |
| Bando, Sal, dh-1b | .188 | 27 | 69 | 4 | 13 | 5 | 0 | 0 | 7 | 7 | 24 | 0 | 0 | L | R | 6-3 | 220 | 7-11-70 | 1993 | Mequon, Wis. |
| Berblinger, Jeff, 2b | .312 | 38 | 138 | 26 | 43 | 9 | 0 | 2 | 21 | 11 | 14 | 9 | 4 | R | R | 6-0 | 185 | 11-14-70 | 1993 | Goddard, Kan. |
| Borzello, Mike, c | .111 | 13 | 18 | 1 | 2 | 0 | 0 | 0 | 0 | 3 | 7 | 0 | 0 | R | R | 6-2 | 180 | 8-14-70 | 1991 | Tarzana, Calif. |
| Dean, Mark, ss | .231 | 52 | 156 | 21 | 36 | 3 | 1 | 0 | 10 | 16 | 31 | 7 | 6 | S | R | 6-0 | 160 | 5-4-71 | 1993 | Wadsworth, Ohio |
| Deares, Greg, of | .248 | 69 | 250 | 28 | 62 | 12 | 0 | 2 | 31 | 25 | 42 | 6 | 4 | L | R | 6-2 | 190 | 4-22-71 | 1993 | Baltimore, Md. |
| Garcia, Osmel, of | .214 | 57 | 168 | 27 | 36 | 6 | 0 | 0 | 13 | 7 | 38 | 7 | 4 | R | R | 6-1 | 180 | 10-14-73 | 1993 | Hialeah, Fla. |
| Henry, Antoine, of | .296 | 51 | 186 | 38 | 55 | 15 | 1 | 0 | 7 | 29 | 31 | 18 | 5 | R | R | 6-0 | 180 | 5-29-73 | 1991 | San Diego, Calif. |
| Henson, Joe, 1b | .191 | 18 | 47 | 4 | 9 | 1 | 0 | 0 | 2 | 8 | 2 | 0 | 0 | L | L | 6-2 | 195 | 3-24-71 | 1993 | Pinson, Ala. |
| Jumonville, Joe, 3b | .219 | 60 | 224 | 19 | 49 | 12 | 0 | 3 | 22 | 4 | 28 | 1 | 1 | R | R | 6-1 | 205 | 8-18-70 | 1993 | New Iberia, La. |
| Llanos, Victor, 1b-3b | .258 | 46 | 132 | 18 | 34 | 8 | 0 | 2 | 19 | 9 | 31 | 1 | 3 | R | R | 6-2 | 195 | 6-26-73 | 1991 | Carolina, P.R. |
| Matvey, Michael, ss-2b | .289 | 70 | 239 | 37 | 69 | 11 | 5 | 3 | 42 | 29 | 43 | 7 | 4 | R | R | 6-0 | 180 | 10-10-71 | 1993 | Charlotte, N.C. |
| Mota, Santo, ss | .289 | 10 | 38 | 6 | 11 | 2 | 0 | 0 | 7 | 6 | 6 | 9 | 2 | S | R | 5-9 | 150 | 4-12-72 | 1991 | San Pedro de Macoris, D.R. |
| Ritz, Trey, 2b | .209 | 31 | 86 | 7 | 18 | 1 | 2 | 0 | 7 | 5 | 15 | 3 | 4 | L | R | 6-1 | 175 | 8-17-69 | 1992 | Hot Springs, Ark. |
| Santucci, Steven, of | .254 | 68 | 209 | 21 | 53 | 5 | 1 | 5 | 23 | 27 | 58 | 9 | 7 | R | R | 6-0 | 190 | 12-16-71 | 1993 | Leominster, Mass. |
| Stutz, John, 1b-3b | .203 | 54 | 182 | 7 | 37 | 6 | 1 | 0 | 14 | 13 | 51 | 1 | 3 | R | R | 6-4 | 205 | 6-16-70 | 1992 | Wilmette, Ill. |
| Taylor, Mike, 1b-dh | .233 | 35 | 86 | 5 | 20 | 3 | 1 | 0 | 6 | 13 | 7 | 0 | 0 | L | L | 6-0 | 195 | 9-17-70 | 1993 | Girard, Ohio |
| Williams, Mark, c | .137 | 38 | 95 | 10 | 13 | 1 | 0 | 0 | 5 | 23 | 37 | 0 | 0 | R | R | 6-0 | 180 | 11-17-70 | 1992 | Coral Springs, Fla. |

| PITCHING | W | L | ERA | G | GS | CG | SV | IP | H | R | ER | BB | SO | B | T | HT | WT | DOB | 1st Yr | Resides |
|---|---|---|---|---|---|---|---|---|---|---|---|---|---|---|---|---|---|---|---|---|
| Alexander, Eric | 5 | 5 | 3.21 | 15 | 15 | 1 | 0 | 87 | 86 | 35 | 31 | 32 | 55 | R | R | 6-4 | 195 | 9-6-70 | 1993 | Gilbert, Ariz. |
| Arrandale, Matt | 3 | 4 | 4.59 | 12 | 12 | 0 | 0 | 69 | 77 | 42 | 35 | 14 | 53 | R | R | 6-5 | 220 | 12-14-70 | 1993 | Webster Groves, Mo. |
| Benes, Alan | 0 | 4 | 3.65 | 7 | 7 | 0 | 0 | 37 | 39 | 20 | 15 | 14 | 29 | R | R | 6-5 | 220 | 1-21-72 | 1993 | Lake Forest, Ill. |
| Britt, Ken | 2 | 4 | 5.62 | 35 | 0 | 0 | 1 | 42 | 49 | 30 | 26 | 10 | 32 | L | R | 6-3 | 195 | 4-7-70 | 1992 | Blythewood, S.C. |
| Cain, Sheldon | 5 | 2 | 2.45 | 24 | 4 | 0 | 0 | 51 | 48 | 19 | 14 | 15 | 55 | R | R | 6-3 | 195 | 2-4-71 | 1993 | Canton, Ga. |
| Croushore, Rich | 4 | 1 | 3.05 | 31 | 0 | 0 | 1 | 41 | 38 | 16 | 14 | 22 | 36 | R | R | 6-4 | 210 | 8-7-70 | 1993 | Houston, Texas |
| Grasser, Craig | 2 | 1 | 2.06 | 36 | 0 | 0 | 19 | 39 | 30 | 13 | 9 | 14 | 39 | R | R | 6-3 | 190 | 4-24-70 | 1992 | Baltimore, Md. |
| Jolley, Mike | 0 | 0 | 0.00 | 2 | 0 | 0 | 0 | 5 | 4 | 2 | 0 | 3 | 5 | R | R | 6-1 | 225 | 12-3-70 | 1990 | St. George, Utah |
| Kehrli, Ed | 0 | 2 | 11.52 | 16 | 0 | 0 | 0 | 27 | 45 | 37 | 35 | 16 | 18 | L | R | 6-4 | 225 | 1-4-71 | 1993 | Monsey, N.Y. |
| Larson, Joe | 3 | 4 | 5.65 | 18 | 11 | 0 | 0 | 64 | 77 | 51 | 40 | 17 | 41 | R | L | 6-2 | 200 | 3-4-70 | 1992 | Lanesboro, Mass. |
| Magnelli, Tony | 3 | 2 | 5.72 | 27 | 1 | 0 | 0 | 39 | 53 | 34 | 25 | 15 | 34 | R | R | 5-11 | 180 | 9-8-70 | 1993 | Nanuet, N.Y. |
| Ottmers, Marc | 4 | 3 | 2.30 | 9 | 9 | 0 | 0 | 47 | 35 | 17 | 12 | 30 | 48 | R | R | 6-0 | 185 | 12-31-71 | 1993 | San Antonio, Texas |
| Pontes, Daniel | 2 | 3 | 3.83 | 20 | 6 | 0 | 0 | 45 | 49 | 26 | 19 | 18 | 40 | R | R | 6-3 | 205 | 4-27-71 | 1993 | Geneva, N.Y. |
| Redovian, Dan | 0 | 0 | 4.05 | 8 | 1 | 0 | 0 | 13 | 13 | 6 | 6 | 6 | 9 | R | R | 6-2 | 180 | 1-8-71 | 1993 | Dunwoody, Ga. |
| Ritz, Trey | 0 | 0 | 7.71 | 3 | 0 | 0 | 0 | 7 | 9 | 7 | 6 | 3 | 6 | L | R | 6-1 | 175 | 8-17-69 | 1992 | Hot Springs, Ark. |
| Windham, Mike | 4 | 5 | 2.65 | 11 | 11 | 0 | 0 | 58 | 55 | 24 | 17 | 16 | 44 | R | R | 6-1 | 185 | 3-8-72 | 1993 | Jacksonville, Fla. |

# JOHNSON CITY · R
## APPALACHIAN LEAGUE

| BATTING | AVG | G | AB | R | H | 2B | 3B | HR | RBI | BB | SO | SB | CS | B | T | HT | WT | DOB | 1st Yr | Resides |
|---|---|---|---|---|---|---|---|---|---|---|---|---|---|---|---|---|---|---|---|---|
| Bautista, Juan, of | .156 | 29 | 77 | 10 | 12 | 1 | 1 | 0 | 4 | 5 | 16 | 4 | 0 | R | R | 6-1 | 175 | 6-12-73 | 1991 | Boca Chica, D.R. |
| Biermann, Steve, 3b-2b | .284 | 33 | 116 | 10 | 33 | 5 | 0 | 0 | 17 | 6 | 16 | 2 | 3 | S | R | 6-0 | 175 | 9-30-71 | 1993 | St. Louis, Mo. |
| Christopher, Chris, of | .299 | 55 | 204 | 34 | 61 | 5 | 3 | 3 | 28 | 35 | 21 | 18 | 5 | S | R | 5-11 | 175 | 11-16-71 | 1993 | Greenville, N.C. |
| Dalton, Dee, ss-3b | .271 | 68 | 240 | 36 | 65 | 13 | 2 | 11 | 46 | 30 | 56 | 5 | 4 | R | R | 5-11 | 170 | 6-17-72 | 1993 | Roanoke, Va. |
| Dicken, Rongie, 2b | .203 | 31 | 74 | 12 | 15 | 1 | 2 | 0 | 3 | 6 | 23 | 10 | 1 | R | R | 6-1 | 170 | 8-28-72 | 1992 | Campbellsville, Ky. |
| Dishington, Nate, of | .157 | 36 | 121 | 13 | 19 | 5 | 1 | 1 | 7 | 16 | 52 | 3 | 1 | L | R | 6-3 | 210 | 1-8-75 | 1993 | Glendale, Calif. |
| Donohue, Pat, 3b | .198 | 36 | 101 | 15 | 20 | 1 | 1 | 3 | 12 | 19 | 23 | 1 | 1 | L | R | 6-0 | 165 | 9-22-72 | 1992 | St. Louis, Mo. |
| Gerteisen, Aaron, of | .252 | 63 | 222 | 49 | 56 | 8 | 1 | 2 | 28 | 55 | 35 | 19 | 3 | S | R | 6-0 | 165 | 10-26-72 | 1993 | Tallahassee, Fla. |
| Herde, Kevin, c | .264 | 22 | 53 | 5 | 14 | 5 | 0 | 0 | 7 | 7 | 11 | 0 | 3 | R | R | 6-0 | 200 | 7-13-71 | 1993 | Escondido, Calif. |
| Lopez, Richard, of-dh | .276 | 52 | 210 | 39 | 58 | 7 | 2 | 2 | 17 | 35 | 41 | 12 | 7 | R | R | 6-2 | 200 | 8-19-73 | 1993 | Chino Hills, Calif. |
| Marrero, Elieser, c | .361 | 18 | 61 | 10 | 22 | 8 | 0 | 2 | 14 | 12 | 9 | 2 | 2 | R | R | 6-1 | 180 | 11-17-73 | 1993 | Miami, Fla. |
| McKinnon, Tom, 1b | .301 | 68 | 256 | 42 | 77 | 13 | 6 | 10 | 53 | 25 | 51 | 4 | 2 | L | R | 6-5 | 220 | 5-16-73 | 1991 | Lakewood, Calif. |
| Minton, Rusty, of | .000 | 3 | 3 | 0 | 0 | 0 | 0 | 0 | 0 | 0 | 1 | 0 | 0 | R | R | 5-10 | 170 | 1-7-72 | 1992 | Richland, Miss. |
| Pellot, Victor, of | .143 | 14 | 28 | 2 | 4 | 1 | 0 | 0 | 1 | 1 | 7 | 0 | 1 | R | R | 5-11 | 165 | 9-30-72 | 1992 | Guaynabo, P.R. |
| Robinson, Darek, 2b | .192 | 47 | 146 | 18 | 28 | 5 | 0 | 0 | 6 | 13 | 29 | 4 | 0 | S | R | 5-11 | 180 | 2-14-73 | 1993 | Pleasant Grove, Utah |
| Strehlow, Rob, of | .250 | 8 | 4 | 1 | 1 | 0 | 0 | 0 | 1 | 0 | 3 | 0 | 0 | R | R | 5-10 | 175 | 12-22-72 | 1991 | Henderson, Nev. |
| Strus, George, dh-c | .278 | 15 | 36 | 3 | 10 | 1 | 0 | 1 | 6 | 2 | 13 | 0 | 0 | S | R | 6-2 | 220 | 12-5-71 | 1993 | North Caldwell, N.J. |
| Ugueto, Hector, 3b-of | .250 | 36 | 100 | 14 | 25 | 3 | 1 | 0 | 8 | 12 | 19 | 3 | 1 | R | R | 6-1 | 175 | 12-16-73 | 1991 | Catia La Mar, Venez. |
| Wallace, Joe, c-3b | .227 | 51 | 154 | 31 | 35 | 9 | 0 | 7 | 32 | 36 | 40 | 2 | 2 | R | R | 6-0 | 205 | 2-17-72 | 1993 | Staunton, Ill. |

| PITCHING | W | L | ERA | G | GS | CG | SV | IP | H | R | ER | BB | SO | B | T | HT | WT | DOB | 1st Yr | Resides |
|---|---|---|---|---|---|---|---|---|---|---|---|---|---|---|---|---|---|---|---|---|
| Almanza, Armando | 1 | 1 | 4.15 | 3 | 0 | 0 | 0 | 4 | 6 | 2 | 2 | 3 | 4 | L | L | 6-3 | 205 | 10-26-72 | 1993 | El Paso, Texas |
| Battles, Jeff | 5 | 4 | 3.20 | 13 | 13 | 0 | 0 | 82 | 82 | 38 | 29 | 15 | 69 | R | R | 6-0 | 175 | 8-8-71 | 1993 | Douglasville, Ga. |
| Bledsoe, Randy | 1 | 1 | 5.81 | 5 | 5 | 0 | 0 | 26 | 34 | 20 | 17 | 8 | 17 | L | R | 6-3 | 195 | 1-25-72 | 1992 | Huntington, Texas |
| Carroll, David | 4 | 1 | 1.83 | 6 | 6 | 1 | 0 | 34 | 27 | 8 | 7 | 10 | 22 | S | L | 6-2 | 200 | 7-23-72 | 1993 | Fairfax, Va. |
| Charles, Domingo | 1 | 4 | 7.20 | 9 | 8 | 0 | 0 | 35 | 52 | 33 | 28 | 10 | 17 | R | R | 6-5 | 184 | 7-25-72 | 1991 | San Pedro de Macoris, D.R. |
| Corrigan, Cory | 3 | 0 | 1.86 | 11 | 6 | 0 | 1 | 48 | 26 | 15 | 10 | 8 | 46 | R | R | 6-0 | 170 | 9-14-71 | 1993 | Athens, Ohio |
| Marchesi, Jimmy | 3 | 2 | 5.24 | 20 | 3 | 0 | 1 | 34 | 40 | 28 | 20 | 17 | 27 | S | R | 6-3 | 200 | 8-30-72 | 1990 | Spokane, Wash. |
| Marquardt, Scott | 0 | 0 | 3.60 | 4 | 2 | 0 | 0 | 10 | 11 | 4 | 4 | 4 | 11 | R | R | 6-2 | 190 | 8-25-72 | 1993 | Baytown, Texas |
| Sailors, Jim | 0 | 6 | 4.42 | 14 | 13 | 0 | 0 | 77 | 72 | 44 | 38 | 31 | 81 | R | L | 5-11 | 170 | 9-12-72 | 1992 | Brookston, Ind. |
| Scott, Ron | 2 | 1 | 3.70 | 21 | 0 | 0 | 9 | 24 | 18 | 11 | 10 | 17 | 22 | L | L | 5-10 | 190 | 7-24-71 | 1993 | Sarasota, Fla. |
| Stanton, Duane | 5 | 2 | 3.90 | 24 | 0 | 0 | 2 | 32 | 25 | 19 | 14 | 20 | 36 | R | R | 6-0 | 190 | 10-18-71 | 1992 | Woodbury, N.J. |
| Stewart, Chris | 2 | 1 | 2.93 | 29 | 0 | 0 | 7 | 43 | 21 | 18 | 14 | 25 | 49 | R | R | 6-2 | 205 | 7-20-71 | 1993 | Memphis, Tenn. |
| Stoppello, Jason | 0 | 0 | 11.81 | 4 | 0 | 0 | 0 | 5 | 9 | 7 | 7 | 5 | 6 | L | L | 6-1 | 200 | 10-1-72 | 1992 | Boise, Idaho |
| Surratt, Jamie | 5 | 2 | 4.29 | 29 | 0 | 0 | 1 | 36 | 41 | 28 | 17 | 17 | 43 | R | R | 5-10 | 175 | 12-17-70 | 1993 | Midland, Texas |
| Tatrow, Dan | 0 | 0 | 7.71 | 3 | 0 | 0 | 0 | 2 | 5 | 2 | 2 | 2 | 3 | R | R | 6-3 | 180 | 12-29-72 | 1992 | Arlington, Texas |
| Wagner, Dale | 1 | 3 | 9.00 | 16 | 0 | 0 | 0 | 24 | 30 | 32 | 24 | 24 | 30 | R | R | 6-0 | 183 | 8-17-72 | 1992 | Gold Hill, N.C. |
| Witasick, Jay | 4 | 3 | 4.12 | 12 | 12 | 0 | 0 | 68 | 65 | 42 | 31 | 19 | 74 | R | R | 6-4 | 205 | 8-28-72 | 1993 | Bel Air, Md. |

# CHANDLER R

## ARIZONA LEAGUE

| BATTING | AVG | G | AB | R | H | 2B | 3B | HR | RBI | BB | SO | SB | CS | B | T | HT | WT | DOB | 1st Yr | Resides |
|---|---|---|---|---|---|---|---|---|---|---|---|---|---|---|---|---|---|---|---|---|
| Bowen, Glenn, c | .190 | 32 | 79 | 12 | 15 | 1 | 1 | 0 | 11 | 14 | 27 | 2 | 0 | R | R | 6-2 | 175 | 11-18-73 | 1992 | Mayo, S.C. |
| Cardona, Alex, c | .339 | 19 | 56 | 9 | 19 | 2 | 2 | 0 | 10 | 4 | 7 | 0 | 0 | R | R | 5-11 | 190 | 10-19-74 | 1993 | Kissimmee, Fla. |
| Colon, Marlon, 1b-dh | .111 | 19 | 45 | 5 | 5 | 1 | 0 | 0 | 4 | 4 | 7 | 0 | 0 | R | R | 5-11 | 185 | 7-19-72 | 1993 | Carolina, P.R. |
| Current, Jeremy, of | .178 | 25 | 73 | 6 | 13 | 1 | 0 | 0 | 3 | 5 | 24 | 4 | 1 | R | R | 6-5 | 175 | 9-15-73 | 1993 | Mt. Zion, Ill. |
| Fernandez, Randy, of | .256 | 31 | 90 | 17 | 23 | 2 | 2 | 1 | 10 | 8 | 22 | 9 | 0 | L | L | 6-0 | 170 | 3-17-74 | 1992 | Villa Mella, D.R. |
| French, Anton, of | .274 | 34 | 106 | 19 | 29 | 3 | 2 | 1 | 17 | 10 | 22 | 15 | 5 | S | R | 5-10 | 163 | 7-25-75 | 1993 | St. Louis, Mo. |
| Green, Bert, ss | .221 | 33 | 95 | 16 | 21 | 3 | 1 | 0 | 11 | 7 | 13 | 4 | 2 | R | R | 5-10 | 170 | 6-9-74 | 1993 | Ballwin, Mo. |
| Harper, Rantie, of | .220 | 29 | 91 | 14 | 20 | 1 | 4 | 0 | 11 | 10 | 29 | 4 | 2 | S | R | 6-2 | 185 | 5-20-75 | 1993 | San Diego, Calif. |
| Iverson, Eric, of | .176 | 10 | 17 | 0 | 3 | 1 | 0 | 0 | 0 | 1 | 4 | 0 | 0 | L | R | 6-0 | 175 | 2-17-74 | 1993 | Fargo, N.D. |
| Jimenez, Ruben, 2b | .237 | 43 | 135 | 21 | 32 | 2 | 2 | 0 | 7 | 25 | 30 | 9 | 8 | R | R | 5-11 | 155 | 8-18-75 | 1993 | San Pedro de Macoris, D.R. |
| Lopez, Richard, of | .429 | 4 | 14 | 1 | 6 | 0 | 0 | 0 | 1 | 2 | 0 | 2 | 0 | R | R | 6-2 | 200 | 8-19-73 | 1993 | Chino Hills, Calif. |
| Lugo, Jesus, of | .292 | 38 | 137 | 18 | 40 | 7 | 1 | 0 | 23 | 2 | 10 | 2 | 1 | R | R | 6-2 | 170 | 5-8-75 | 1993 | Puerto La Cruz, Venez. |
| Madsen, Dave, 3b | .287 | 53 | 181 | 32 | 52 | 12 | 4 | 4 | 38 | 37 | 38 | 4 | 2 | R | R | 6-2 | 195 | 6-14-72 | 1993 | Murray, Utah |
| McMillan, Thomas, of | .267 | 25 | 60 | 16 | 16 | 5 | 0 | 0 | 5 | 17 | 15 | 4 | 3 | R | R | 6-0 | 170 | 9-6-75 | 1993 | Guaynabo, P.R. |
| Millan, Jorge, 2b-3b | .247 | 29 | 93 | 15 | 23 | 5 | 1 | 0 | 10 | 6 | 16 | 3 | 2 | R | R | 5-9 | 160 | 12-25-73 | 1992 | Bonita, Calif. |
| Norton, Chris, dh-c | .229 | 27 | 83 | 10 | 19 | 5 | 3 | 0 | 11 | 11 | 23 | 0 | 0 | R | R | 6-2 | 215 | 9-21-70 | 1992 | Maitland, Fla. |
| Nunez, Isaias, 1b | .234 | 51 | 184 | 27 | 43 | 3 | 2 | 0 | 22 | 18 | 33 | 2 | 1 | L | L | 6-4 | 170 | 4-10-74 | 1992 | Bajos de Haina, D.R. |
| Robles, Rafael, ss | .270 | 42 | 126 | 19 | 34 | 4 | 2 | 0 | 18 | 21 | 34 | 5 | 6 | S | R | 6-1 | 175 | 5-8-73 | 1991 | Villa Mella, D.R. |
| Williams, Curtis, of | .200 | 34 | 75 | 14 | 15 | 0 | 1 | 0 | 14 | 18 | 49 | 2 | 1 | L | L | 6-1 | 175 | 9-27-72 | 1993 | Lewisville, Ark. |

| PITCHING | W | L | ERA | G | GS | CG | SV | IP | H | R | ER | BB | SO | B | T | HT | WT | DOB | 1st Yr | Resides |
|---|---|---|---|---|---|---|---|---|---|---|---|---|---|---|---|---|---|---|---|---|
| Alexis, Julio | 1 | 2 | 6.50 | 14 | 7 | 0 | 0 | 46 | 63 | 46 | 33 | 13 | 30 | R | R | 6-3 | 170 | 7-12-73 | 1991 | San Pedro de Macoris, D.R. |
| Almanza, Armando | 4 | 1 | 3.21 | 20 | 4 | 0 | 0 | 42 | 38 | 19 | 15 | 14 | 56 | L | L | 6-3 | 205 | 10-26-72 | 1993 | El Paso, Texas |
| Barrick, Troy | 3 | 0 | 1.01 | 24 | 0 | 0 | 12 | 27 | 18 | 3 | 3 | 4 | 23 | R | R | 6-5 | 185 | 10-18-72 | 1993 | Walkersville, Md. |
| Bledsoe, Randy | 4 | 0 | 0.72 | 4 | 4 | 0 | 0 | 25 | 11 | 3 | 2 | 8 | 26 | L | R | 6-3 | 195 | 1-25-72 | 1992 | Huntington, Texas |
| Conway, Keith | 1 | 1 | 2.97 | 28 | 0 | 0 | 0 | 39 | 31 | 13 | 13 | 21 | 47 | R | L | 6-2 | 185 | 5-8-73 | 1993 | Philadelphia, Pa. |
| Cruise, Mark | 3 | 2 | 1.60 | 23 | 0 | 0 | 2 | 34 | 25 | 10 | 6 | 7 | 28 | R | R | 6-5 | 230 | 10-1-72 | 1993 | San Pablo, Calif. |
| Curran, Tighe | 2 | 1 | 3.69 | 27 | 0 | 0 | 0 | 32 | 37 | 17 | 13 | 9 | 38 | L | L | 6-0 | 180 | 12-28-73 | 1993 | Newbury Park, Calif. |
| Lair, Scott | 1 | 3 | 5.92 | 6 | 6 | 0 | 0 | 24 | 26 | 22 | 16 | 16 | 23 | R | R | 6-3 | 195 | 11-15-73 | 1992 | Chesterfield, Mo. |
| Manon, Julio | 2 | 3 | 5.13 | 15 | 4 | 0 | 0 | 33 | 44 | 21 | 19 | 12 | 22 | R | R | 6-1 | 183 | 7-10-73 | 1992 | Boca Chica, D.R. |
| Martin, Mike | 1 | 5 | 5.54 | 11 | 9 | 0 | 0 | 39 | 53 | 30 | 24 | 11 | 44 | R | R | 6-3 | 185 | 7-25-73 | 1993 | Kingsport, Tenn. |
| Parker, Freddie | 0 | 1 | 5.17 | 8 | 0 | 0 | 0 | 16 | 17 | 18 | 9 | 16 | 18 | R | R | 5-11 | 163 | 10-31-73 | 1993 | Clarksville, Tenn. |
| Ramirez, Rafael | 2 | 2 | 2.34 | 9 | 9 | 0 | 0 | 50 | 49 | 18 | 13 | 16 | 41 | R | R | 6-2 | 178 | 10-20-74 | 1992 | San Pedro de Macons, D.R. |
| Welch, Travis | 7 | 1 | 2.04 | 10 | 10 | 0 | 0 | 57 | 44 | 14 | 13 | 12 | 67 | R | R | 6-0 | 202 | 1-30-74 | 1993 | Loomis, Calif. |

# SAN DIEGO PADRES

**Manager:** Jim Riggleman.  **1993 Record:** 61-101, .377 (7th, NL West).

| BATTING | AVG | G | AB | R | H | 2B | 3B | HR | RBI | BB | SO | SB | CS | B | T | HT | WT | DOB | 1st Yr | Resides |
|---|---|---|---|---|---|---|---|---|---|---|---|---|---|---|---|---|---|---|---|---|
| Ausmus, Brad | .256 | 49 | 160 | 18 | 41 | 8 | 1 | 5 | 12 | 6 | 28 | 2 | 0 | R | R | 5-11 | 185 | 4-14-69 | 1988 | Cheshire, Conn. |
| Bean, Billy | .260 | 88 | 177 | 19 | 46 | 9 | 0 | 5 | 32 | 6 | 29 | 2 | 4 | L | L | 6-1 | 185 | 5-11-64 | 1986 | Hollywood, Calif. |
| Bell, Derek | .262 | 150 | 542 | 73 | 142 | 19 | 1 | 21 | 72 | 23 | 122 | 26 | 5 | R | R | 6-2 | 200 | 12-11-68 | 1987 | Tampa, Fla. |
| Brown, Jarvis | .233 | 47 | 133 | 21 | 31 | 9 | 2 | 0 | 8 | 15 | 26 | 3 | 3 | R | R | 5-7 | 170 | 3-26-67 | 1986 | Waukegan, Ill. |
| Cianfrocco, Archi | .244 | 84 | 279 | 27 | 68 | 10 | 2 | 11 | 47 | 17 | 64 | 2 | 0 | R | R | 6-5 | 200 | 10-6-66 | 1987 | Rome, N.Y. |
| 2-team (12 Mtl.) | .243 | 96 | 296 | 30 | 72 | 11 | 2 | 12 | 48 | 17 | 69 | 2 | 0 | | | | | | | |
| Clark, Phil | .313 | 102 | 240 | 33 | 75 | 17 | 0 | 9 | 33 | 8 | 31 | 2 | 0 | R | R | 6-0 | 180 | 5-6-68 | 1986 | Toledo, Ohio |
| Gardner, Jeff | .262 | 140 | 404 | 53 | 106 | 21 | 7 | 1 | 24 | 45 | 69 | 2 | 6 | L | R | 5-11 | 165 | 2-4-64 | 1985 | Costa Mesa, Calif. |
| Geren, Bob | .214 | 58 | 145 | 8 | 31 | 6 | 0 | 3 | 6 | 13 | 28 | 0 | 0 | R | R | 6-3 | 228 | 9-22-61 | 1979 | San Diego, Calif. |
| Gutierrez, Ricky | .251 | 133 | 438 | 76 | 110 | 10 | 5 | 5 | 26 | 50 | 97 | 4 | 3 | R | R | 6-1 | 175 | 5-23-70 | 1988 | Miami, Fla. |
| Gwynn, Tony | .358 | 122 | 489 | 70 | 175 | 41 | 3 | 7 | 59 | 36 | 19 | 14 | 1 | L | L | 5-11 | 210 | 5-9-60 | 1981 | Poway, Calif. |
| Higgins, Kevin | .221 | 71 | 181 | 17 | 40 | 4 | 1 | 0 | 13 | 16 | 17 | 0 | 1 | L | R | 5-11 | 185 | 1-22-67 | 1989 | Torrance, Calif. |
| Lopez, Luis | .116 | 17 | 43 | 1 | 5 | 1 | 0 | 0 | 1 | 0 | 17 | 0 | 0 | S | R | 5-11 | 175 | 9-4-70 | 1988 | Cidra, P.R. |
| McGriff, Fred | .275 | 83 | 302 | 52 | 83 | 11 | 1 | 18 | 46 | 42 | 55 | 4 | 3 | L | L | 6-3 | 215 | 10-31-63 | 1981 | Tampa, Fla. |
| Nieves, Melvin | .191 | 19 | 47 | 4 | 9 | 0 | 0 | 2 | 3 | 3 | 21 | 0 | 0 | S | R | 6-2 | 185 | 12-28-71 | 1988 | Bayamon, P.R. |
| Plantier, Phil | .240 | 138 | 462 | 67 | 111 | 20 | 1 | 34 | 100 | 61 | 124 | 4 | 5 | L | R | 5-11 | 195 | 1-27-69 | 1987 | San Diego, Calif. |
| Sheffield, Gary | .295 | 68 | 258 | 34 | 76 | 12 | 2 | 10 | 36 | 18 | 30 | 5 | 1 | R | R | 5-11 | 190 | 11-18-68 | 1986 | St. Petersburg, Fla. |
| Sherman, Darrell | .222 | 37 | 63 | 8 | 14 | 1 | 0 | 0 | 2 | 6 | 8 | 2 | 1 | L | L | 5-9 | 160 | 12-4-67 | 1989 | Lynwood, Calif. |
| Shipley, Craig | .235 | 105 | 230 | 25 | 54 | 9 | 0 | 4 | 22 | 10 | 31 | 12 | 3 | R | R | 6-0 | 168 | 1-7-63 | 1984 | Jupiter, Fla. |
| Staton, Dave | .262 | 17 | 42 | 7 | 11 | 3 | 0 | 5 | 9 | 3 | 12 | 0 | 0 | R | R | 6-5 | 215 | 4-12-68 | 1989 | Auburn, Calif. |
| Stillwell, Kurt | .215 | 57 | 121 | 9 | 26 | 4 | 0 | 1 | 11 | 11 | 24 | 4 | 3 | S | R | 5-11 | 185 | 6-4-65 | 1983 | Poway, Calif. |
| Teufel, Tim | .250 | 96 | 200 | 26 | 50 | 11 | 2 | 7 | 31 | 27 | 39 | 2 | 2 | R | R | 6-0 | 175 | 7-7-58 | 1980 | Escondido, Calif. |
| Velasquez, Guillermo | .210 | 79 | 143 | 7 | 30 | 2 | 0 | 3 | 20 | 13 | 35 | 0 | 0 | L | R | 6-0 | 170 | 4-23-68 | 1986 | Calexico, Mexico |
| Walters, Dan | .202 | 27 | 94 | 6 | 19 | 3 | 0 | 1 | 10 | 7 | 13 | 0 | 0 | R | R | 6-2 | 190 | 8-15-66 | 1985 | Santee, Calif. |

| PITCHING | W | L | ERA | G | GS | CG | SV | IP | H | R | ER | BB | SO | B | T | HT | WT | DOB | 1st Yr | Resides |
|---|---|---|---|---|---|---|---|---|---|---|---|---|---|---|---|---|---|---|---|---|
| Ashby, Andy | 3 | 6 | 5.48 | 12 | 12 | 0 | 0 | 69 | 79 | 46 | 42 | 24 | 44 | R | R | 6-5 | 180 | 7-11-67 | 1986 | Kansas City, Mo. |
| 2-team (20 Colo.) | 3 | 10 | 6.80 | 32 | 21 | 0 | 1 | 123 | 168 | 100 | 93 | 56 | 77 | | | | | | | |
| Benes, Andy | 15 | 15 | 3.78 | 34 | 34 | 4 | 0 | 231 | 200 | 111 | 97 | 86 | 179 | R | R | 6-6 | 238 | 8-20-67 | 1989 | Poway, Calif. |
| Brocail, Doug | 4 | 13 | 4.56 | 24 | 24 | 0 | 0 | 128 | 143 | 75 | 65 | 42 | 70 | L | R | 6-5 | 190 | 5-16-67 | 1986 | Lamar, Colo. |
| Davis, Mark | 0 | 3 | 3.52 | 35 | 0 | 0 | 4 | 38 | 44 | 15 | 15 | 20 | 42 | L | L | 6-4 | 210 | 10-19-60 | 1979 | Marietta, Ga. |
| 2-team (25 Phil.) | 1 | 5 | 4.26 | 60 | 0 | 0 | 4 | 70 | 79 | 37 | 33 | 44 | 70 | | | | | | | |
| Eiland, Dave | 0 | 3 | 5.21 | 10 | 9 | 0 | 0 | 48 | 58 | 33 | 28 | 17 | 14 | R | R | 6-3 | 205 | 7-5-66 | 1987 | Dade City, Fla. |
| Ettles, Mark | 1 | 0 | 6.50 | 14 | 0 | 0 | 0 | 18 | 23 | 16 | 13 | 4 | 9 | R | R | 6-0 | 178 | 10-30-66 | 1989 | South Perth, Australia |
| Gomez, Pat | 1 | 2 | 5.12 | 27 | 1 | 0 | 0 | 32 | 35 | 19 | 18 | 19 | 26 | L | L | 5-11 | 185 | 3-17-68 | 1986 | Citrus Heights, Calif. |
| Harris, Gene | 6 | 6 | 3.03 | 59 | 0 | 0 | 23 | 59 | 57 | 27 | 20 | 37 | 39 | R | R | 5-11 | 190 | 12-5-64 | 1986 | Okeechobee, Fla. |
| Harris, Greg W. | 10 | 9 | 3.67 | 22 | 22 | 4 | 0 | 152 | 151 | 65 | 62 | 39 | 83 | R | R | 6-2 | 195 | 12-1-63 | 1985 | Cary, N.C. |
| Hernandez, Jeremy | 0 | 2 | 4.72 | 10 | 0 | 0 | 0 | 34 | 41 | 19 | 18 | 7 | 26 | R | R | 6-5 | 195 | 7-6-66 | 1987 | Yuma, Ariz. |
| Hoffman, Trevor | 2 | 4 | 4.31 | 39 | 0 | 0 | 3 | 54 | 56 | 30 | 26 | 20 | 53 | R | R | 6-0 | 195 | 10-13-67 | 1989 | Anaheim, Calif. |
| 2-team (28 Florida) | 4 | 6 | 3.90 | 67 | 0 | 0 | 5 | 90 | 80 | 43 | 39 | 39 | 79 | | | | | | | |
| Hurst, Bruce | 0 | 1 | 12.46 | 2 | 2 | 0 | 0 | 4 | 9 | 7 | 6 | 3 | 3 | L | L | 6-3 | 219 | 3-24-58 | 1976 | Rancho Sante Fe, Calif. |
| Martinez, Pedro A. | 3 | 1 | 2.43 | 32 | 0 | 0 | 0 | 37 | 23 | 11 | 10 | 13 | 32 | L | L | 6-2 | 155 | 11-29-68 | 1987 | Villa Mella, D.R. |
| Mason, Roger | 0 | 7 | 3.24 | 34 | 0 | 0 | 0 | 50 | 43 | 20 | 18 | 18 | 39 | R | R | 6-6 | 220 | 9-18-58 | 1981 | Bellaire, Mich. |
| Mauser, Tim | 1 | 0 | 3.58 | 28 | 0 | 0 | 0 | 38 | 36 | 19 | 15 | 17 | 32 | R | R | 6-0 | 185 | 10-4-66 | 1988 | Fort Worth, Texas |
| 2-team (8 Phil.) | 0 | 1 | 4.00 | 36 | 0 | 0 | 0 | 54 | 51 | 28 | 24 | 24 | 46 | | | | | | | |
| Rodriguez, Rich | 2 | 3 | 3.30 | 34 | 0 | 0 | 2 | 36 | 34 | 15 | 11 | 9 | 22 | R | L | 5-11 | 200 | 3-1-63 | 1984 | Knoxville, Tenn. |
| Sanders, Scott | 3 | 3 | 4.13 | 9 | 9 | 0 | 0 | 52 | 54 | 32 | 24 | 23 | 37 | R | R | 6-4 | 220 | 3-25-69 | 1990 | Thibodaux, La. |
| Scott, Tim | 2 | 0 | 2.39 | 24 | 0 | 0 | 0 | 38 | 38 | 13 | 10 | 15 | 30 | R | R | 6-2 | 205 | 11-16-66 | 1984 | Hanford, Calif. |
| Seanez, Rudy | 0 | 0 | 13.50 | 3 | 0 | 0 | 0 | 3 | 8 | 6 | 5 | 2 | 1 | R | R | 5-10 | 185 | 10-20-68 | 1986 | El Centro, Calif. |
| Seminara, Frank | 3 | 3 | 4.47 | 18 | 7 | 0 | 0 | 46 | 53 | 30 | 23 | 21 | 22 | R | R | 6-2 | 195 | 5-16-67 | 1988 | Brooklyn, N.Y. |
| Taylor, Kerry | 0 | 5 | 6.45 | 36 | 7 | 0 | 0 | 68 | 72 | 53 | 49 | 49 | 45 | R | R | 6-3 | 200 | 1-25-71 | 1989 | Roseau, Minn. |
| Whitehurst, Wally | 4 | 7 | 3.83 | 21 | 19 | 0 | 0 | 106 | 109 | 47 | 45 | 30 | 57 | R | R | 6-3 | 185 | 4-11-64 | 1985 | Madisonville, La. |
| Worrell, Tim | 2 | 7 | 4.92 | 21 | 16 | 0 | 0 | 101 | 104 | 63 | 55 | 43 | 52 | R | R | 6-4 | 215 | 7-5-67 | 1990 | Arcadia, Calif. |

## FIELDING

| Catcher | PCT | G | PO | A | E | DP |
|---|---|---|---|---|---|---|
| Ausmus | .975 | 49 | 272 | 34 | 8 | 5 |
| Clark | .964 | 11 | 23 | 4 | 1 | 1 |
| Geren | .993 | 49 | 251 | 26 | 2 | 6 |
| Higgins | .983 | 59 | 308 | 31 | 6 | 1 |
| Walters | .970 | 26 | 138 | 21 | 5 | 1 |

| First Base | PCT | G | PO | A | E | DP |
|---|---|---|---|---|---|---|
| Bean | 1.000 | 12 | 51 | 3 | 0 | 5 |
| Cianfrocco | .994 | 31 | 150 | 19 | 1 | 15 |
| Clark | .976 | 24 | 144 | 20 | 4 | 12 |
| Geren | 1.000 | 1 | 1 | 0 | 0 | 0 |
| Higgins | 1.000 | 3 | 5 | 0 | 0 | 1 |
| McGriff | .983 | 83 | 640 | 47 | 12 | 50 |
| Staton | 1.000 | 12 | 66 | 14 | 0 | 10 |
| Teufel | .958 | 8 | 21 | 1 | 0 | 5 |
| Velasquez | .984 | 38 | 221 | 21 | 4 | 20 |

| Second Base | PCT | G | PO | A | E | DP |
|---|---|---|---|---|---|---|
| Gardner | .983 | 133 | 213 | 294 | 9 | 48 |

| | PCT | G | PO | A | E | DP |
|---|---|---|---|---|---|---|
| Gutierrez | 1.000 | 6 | 1 | 14 | 0 | 0 |
| Higgins | .000 | 1 | 0 | 0 | 0 | 0 |
| Lopez | .983 | 15 | 23 | 34 | 1 | 5 |
| Shipley | .968 | 12 | 11 | 19 | 1 | 1 |
| Teufel | .990 | 52 | 85 | 117 | 2 | 22 |

| Third Base | PCT | G | PO | A | E | DP |
|---|---|---|---|---|---|---|
| Bell | .820 | 19 | 12 | 29 | 9 | 3 |
| Cianfrocco | .932 | 64 | 48 | 76 | 9 | 8 |
| Clark | 1.000 | 5 | 2 | 6 | 0 | 1 |
| Gardner | .000 | 1 | 0 | 0 | 1 | 0 |
| Geren | 1.000 | 1 | 0 | 3 | 0 | 0 |
| Gutierrez | 1.000 | 4 | 2 | 5 | 0 | 0 |
| Higgins | 1.000 | 4 | 1 | 1 | 0 | 0 |
| Sheffield | .905 | 67 | 41 | 102 | 15 | 11 |
| Shipley | .974 | 37 | 17 | 20 | 1 | 4 |
| Stillwell | 1.000 | 3 | 2 | 3 | 0 | 0 |
| Teufel | 1.000 | 9 | 3 | 5 | 0 | 1 |

| Shortstop | PCT | G | PO | A | E | DP |
|---|---|---|---|---|---|---|
| Gardner | 1.000 | 1 | 1 | 0 | 0 | 0 |
| Gutierrez | .971 | 117 | 190 | 286 | 14 | 55 |
| Shipley | .964 | 38 | 50 | 82 | 5 | 10 |
| Stillwell | .921 | 30 | 45 | 60 | 9 | 12 |

| Outfield | PCT | G | PO | A | E | DP |
|---|---|---|---|---|---|---|
| Bean | .987 | 54 | 71 | 6 | 1 | 0 |
| Bell | .976 | 125 | 322 | 8 | 8 | 4 |
| Brown | .982 | 43 | 109 | 2 | 2 | 0 |
| Clark | .963 | 36 | 74 | 5 | 3 | 0 |
| Gutierrez | 1.000 | 5 | 1 | 0 | 0 | 0 |
| Gwynn | .981 | 121 | 244 | 8 | 5 | 2 |
| Higgins | 1.000 | 3 | 0 | 0 | 0 | 0 |
| Nieves | .931 | 15 | 27 | 0 | 2 | 0 |
| Plantier | .990 | 134 | 272 | 14 | 3 | 3 |
| Sherman | 1.000 | 26 | 47 | 0 | 0 | 0 |
| Shipley | 1.000 | 5 | 5 | 0 | 0 | 0 |
| Velasquez | 1.000 | 6 | 4 | 0 | 0 | 0 |

MICHAEL PONZINI

DAN ARNOLD

**Padres Leftovers.** San Diego cleaned house in 1993, purging the organization of several big name players. Among the holdovers, from left: Tony Gwynn (.358), Phil Plantier (34 homers) and Andy Benes (15-15, 3.78).

# PADRES FARM SYSTEM

| Class | Club | League | W | L | Pct. | Finish* | Manager | First Year |
|---|---|---|---|---|---|---|---|---|
| AAA | Las Vegas (Nev.) Stars | Pacific Coast | 58 | 85 | .406 | 10th (10) | Russ Nixon | 1983 |
| AA | Wichita (Kan.) Wranglers | Texas | 67 | 68 | .496 | 4th (8) | Dave Trembley | 1987 |
| A# | Rancho Cuca. (Calif.) Quakes | California | 64 | 72 | .471 | 6th (10) | Keith Champion | 1993 |
| A | Waterloo (Iowa) Diamonds | Midwest | 54 | 79 | .406 | 13th (14) | Ed Romero | 1989 |
| A | Spokane (Wash.) Indians | Northwest | 35 | 41 | .461 | T-6th (8) | Tim Flannery | 1983 |
| Rookie | Peoria (Ariz.) Padres | Arizona | 24 | 31 | .436 | 6th (8) | Ken Berry | 1988 |

*Finish in overall standings (No. of teams in league)    #Advanced level

## LAS VEGAS                                                                        AAA

### PACIFIC COAST LEAGUE

| BATTING | AVG | G | AB | R | H | 2B | 3B | HR | RBI | BB | SO | SB | CS | B | T | HT | WT | DOB | 1st Yr | Resides |
|---|---|---|---|---|---|---|---|---|---|---|---|---|---|---|---|---|---|---|---|---|
| Basso, Mike | .253 | 34 | 91 | 12 | 23 | 6 | 0 | 4 | 17 | 9 | 25 | 1 | 0 | R | R | 6-2 | 195 | 7-18-64 | 1986 | Pearland, Texas |
| Bean, Billy | .353 | 53 | 167 | 31 | 59 | 11 | 2 | 7 | 40 | 32 | 14 | 3 | 1 | L | L | 6-1 | 185 | 5-11-64 | 1986 | Hollywood, Calif. |
| Bethea, Steve | .180 | 39 | 61 | 7 | 11 | 2 | 0 | 0 | 2 | 14 | 22 | 0 | 1 | S | R | 5-10 | 172 | 6-20-67 | 1989 | Austin, Texas |
| Brown, Jarvis | .308 | 100 | 402 | 74 | 124 | 27 | 9 | 3 | 47 | 41 | 55 | 22 | 5 | R | R | 5-7 | 170 | 3-26-67 | 1986 | Waukegan, Ill. |
| Dozier, D.J. | .270 | 43 | 122 | 25 | 33 | 10 | 3 | 2 | 13 | 25 | 34 | 6 | 4 | R | R | 6-1 | 204 | 9-21-65 | 1990 | Eden Prairie, Minn. |
| Gonzalez, Paul | .240 | 75 | 267 | 36 | 64 | 11 | 4 | 7 | 34 | 21 | 64 | 3 | 2 | L | R | 6-0 | 185 | 4-22-69 | 1990 | Fort Worth, Texas |
| Gutierrez, Ricky | .417 | 5 | 24 | 4 | 10 | 4 | 0 | 0 | 4 | 0 | 4 | 0 | 0 | R | R | 6-1 | 175 | 5-23-70 | 1988 | Miami, Fla. |
| Higgins, Kevin | .359 | 40 | 142 | 22 | 51 | 8 | 0 | 1 | 22 | 18 | 8 | 1 | 1 | L | R | 5-11 | 185 | 1-22-67 | 1989 | Torrance, Calif. |
| Hosey, Dwayne | .264 | 32 | 110 | 21 | 29 | 4 | 4 | 3 | 12 | 11 | 17 | 7 | 4 | S | R | 5-10 | 170 | 3-11-67 | 1987 | Altadena, Calif. |
| Jelic, Chris | .208 | 46 | 130 | 16 | 27 | 4 | 2 | 2 | 14 | 18 | 22 | 2 | 0 | R | R | 5-11 | 180 | 12-16-63 | 1985 | Pittsburgh, Pa. |
| Johnson, Brian | .339 | 115 | 416 | 58 | 141 | 35 | 6 | 10 | 71 | 41 | 53 | 0 | 0 | R | R | 6-2 | 210 | 1-8-68 | 1989 | Oakland, Calif. |
| Lopez, Luis | .305 | 131 | 491 | 52 | 150 | 36 | 6 | 6 | 58 | 27 | 62 | 8 | 0 | S | R | 5-11 | 175 | 9-4-70 | 1988 | Cidra, P.R. |
| Martinez, Pablo | .231 | 76 | 251 | 24 | 58 | 4 | 1 | 2 | 20 | 18 | 46 | 3 | 3 | S | R | 5-10 | 155 | 6-29-69 | 1989 | San Juan Baron, D.R. |
| Nieves, Melvin | .308 | 43 | 159 | 31 | 49 | 10 | 1 | 7 | 24 | 18 | 42 | 2 | 2 | S | R | 6-2 | 186 | 12-28-71 | 1988 | Bayamon, P.R. |
| Pegues, Steve | .352 | 68 | 270 | 52 | 95 | 20 | 5 | 9 | 50 | 7 | 43 | 12 | 6 | R | R | 6-2 | 190 | 5-21-68 | 1987 | Pontotoc, Miss. |
| Sherman, Darrell | .265 | 82 | 272 | 52 | 72 | 8 | 2 | 0 | 11 | 38 | 27 | 20 | 10 | L | L | 5-9 | 160 | 12-4-67 | 1989 | Lynwood, Calif. |
| Simms, Mike | .268 | 129 | 414 | 74 | 111 | 25 | 2 | 24 | 80 | 67 | 114 | 1 | 1 | R | R | 6-4 | 185 | 1-12-67 | 1985 | Houston, Texas |
| Staton, Dave | .270 | 11 | 37 | 8 | 10 | 0 | 0 | 7 | 11 | 3 | 9 | 0 | 0 | R | R | 6-5 | 215 | 4-12-68 | 1989 | Auburn, Calif. |
| Vatcher, Jim | .317 | 103 | 293 | 36 | 93 | 17 | 2 | 7 | 45 | 35 | 46 | 3 | 4 | R | R | 5-9 | 165 | 5-27-65 | 1987 | Pacific Palisades, Calif. |
| Velasquez, Guillermo | .333 | 30 | 129 | 23 | 43 | 6 | 1 | 5 | 24 | 10 | 19 | 0 | 0 | L | R | 6-0 | 170 | 4-23-68 | 1986 | Calexico, Mexico |
| Walters, Dan | .287 | 66 | 223 | 24 | 64 | 14 | 0 | 5 | 39 | 14 | 21 | 1 | 2 | R | R | 6-2 | 190 | 8-15-66 | 1985 | Santee, Calif. |
| Witkowski, Mat | .283 | 91 | 286 | 49 | 81 | 6 | 3 | 1 | 35 | 33 | 42 | 10 | 2 | R | R | 6-0 | 175 | 2-5-70 | 1988 | Glendale, Calif. |

| PITCHING | W | L | ERA | G | GS | CG | SV | IP | H | R | ER | BB | SO | B | T | HT | WT | DOB | 1st Yr | Resides |
|---|---|---|---|---|---|---|---|---|---|---|---|---|---|---|---|---|---|---|---|---|
| Agosto, Juan | 2 | 0 | 4.00 | 19 | 0 | 0 | 0 | 18 | 21 | 8 | 8 | 5 | 15 | L | L | 6-2 | 190 | 2-23-58 | 1975 | Sarasota, Fla. |
| Bochtler, Doug | 0 | 5 | 5.22 | 7 | 7 | 1 | 0 | 40 | 52 | 26 | 23 | 11 | 30 | R | R | 6-3 | 200 | 7-5-70 | 1989 | West Palm Beach, Fla. |
| 2-team (12 Colo. Spr.) | 1 | 9 | 6.18 | 19 | 18 | 1 | 0 | 90 | 123 | 67 | 62 | 37 | 68 | | | | | | | |
| Boucher, Denis | 4 | 7 | 6.43 | 24 | 7 | 1 | 1 | 70 | 101 | 59 | 50 | 27 | 46 | R | L | 6-1 | 195 | 3-7-68 | 1988 | Lachine, Quebec |
| Brocail, Doug | 4 | 2 | 3.68 | 10 | 8 | 0 | 1 | 51 | 51 | 26 | 21 | 14 | 32 | L | R | 6-5 | 190 | 5-16-67 | 1986 | Lamar, Colo. |
| Brown, Jeff | 0 | 0 | 9.00 | 1 | 0 | 0 | 0 | 5 | 9 | 5 | 5 | 0 | 4 | L | L | 6-0 | 165 | 9-8-70 | 1990 | Grand Prairie, Texas |
| Campbell, Mike | 2 | 1 | 5.40 | 21 | 0 | 0 | 1 | 32 | 39 | 20 | 19 | 9 | 24 | R | R | 6-3 | 210 | 2-17-64 | 1985 | Kirkland, Wash. |
| Compres, Fidel | 1 | 1 | 5.54 | 24 | 0 | 0 | 4 | 26 | 33 | 16 | 16 | 10 | 7 | R | R | 6-0 | 165 | 5-10-65 | 1984 | La Vega, D.R. |
| Davis, Rick | 1 | 8 | 7.14 | 34 | 4 | 0 | 3 | 52 | 94 | 54 | 41 | 20 | 27 | R | R | 6-2 | 175 | 9-2-66 | 1989 | La Verne, Calif. |
| Elliott, Donnie | 2 | 5 | 6.37 | 8 | 7 | 0 | 0 | 41 | 48 | 32 | 29 | 24 | 44 | R | R | 6-4 | 190 | 9-20-68 | 1988 | Deer Park, Texas |
| Ettles, Mark | 3 | 6 | 4.71 | 47 | 0 | 0 | 15 | 50 | 58 | 28 | 26 | 22 | 29 | R | R | 6-0 | 178 | 10-30-66 | 1989 | Perth, Australia |
| Garrelts, Scott | 0 | 0 | 21.00 | 1 | 1 | 0 | 0 | 3 | 10 | 7 | 7 | 2 | 1 | R | R | 6-4 | 205 | 10-30-61 | 1979 | Shreveport, La. |
| Hamilton, Joey | 3 | 2 | 4.40 | 8 | 8 | 0 | 0 | 47 | 49 | 25 | 23 | 22 | 33 | R | R | 6-4 | 220 | 9-9-70 | 1991 | Statesboro, Ga. |

# PADRES TOP 10 PROSPECTS

How the Padres Top 10 prospects, as judged by Baseball America prior to the 1993 season, fared in 1993:

| Player, Pos. | Club (Class) | AVG | AB | H | HR | RBI | SB |
|---|---|---|---|---|---|---|---|
| 1. Ray McDavid, of | Wichita (AA) | .270 | 441 | 119 | 11 | 55 | 33 |
| 5. Ray Holbert, ss | Wichita (AA) | .260 | 388 | 101 | 5 | 48 | 30 |
| 6. Luis Lopez, ss | Las Vegas (AAA) | .305 | 491 | 150 | 6 | 58 | 8 |
|  | San Diego | .116 | 43 | 5 | 0 | 1 | 0 |
| 7. Billy Hall, 2b | Wichita (AA) | .270 | 486 | 131 | 4 | 46 | 29 |
| 9. Julio Bruno, 3b | Rancho Cuc. (A) | .308 | 201 | 62 | 3 | 16 | 15 |
|  | Wichita (AA) | .285 | 246 | 70 | 3 | 24 | 3 |
| 10. Darrell Sherman, of | Las Vegas (AAA) | .265 | 272 | 72 | 0 | 11 | 20 |
|  | San Diego | .222 | 63 | 14 | 0 | 2 | 2 |

| Player, Pos. | Club (Class) | W | L | ERA | IP | H | BB | SO |
|---|---|---|---|---|---|---|---|---|
| 2. Joey Hamilton, rhp | Rancho Cuc. (A) | 1 | 0 | 4.09 | 11 | 11 | 2 | 6 |
|  | Wichita (AA) | 4 | 9 | 3.97 | 91 | 101 | 36 | 50 |
|  | Las Vegas (AAA) | 3 | 2 | 4.40 | 47 | 49 | 22 | 33 |
| 3. Scott Sanders, rhp | Las Vegas (AAA) | 5 | 10 | 4.96 | 152 | 170 | 62 | 161 |
|  | San Diego | 3 | 3 | 4.13 | 52 | 54 | 23 | 37 |
| 4. Tim Worrell, rhp | Las Vegas (AAA) | 5 | 6 | 5.48 | 87 | 102 | 26 | 89 |
|  | San Diego | 2 | 7 | 4.92 | 101 | 104 | 43 | 52 |
| 8. Robbie Beckett, lhp | Rancho Cuc. (A) | 2 | 4 | 6.02 | 84 | 75 | 93 | 88 |

**Ray McDavid**
.270 at Double-A

MEL BAILEY

## PITCHING

| | W | L | ERA | G | GS | CG | SV | IP | H | R | ER | BB | SO | | | | DOB | 1st Yr | Resides |
|---|---|---|---|---|---|---|---|---|---|---|---|---|---|---|---|---|---|---|---|
| Hurst, Bruce | 0 | 1 | 9.00 | 1 | 1 | 0 | 0 | 5 | 8 | 6 | 5 | 0 | 7 | L L | 6-3 | 219 | 3-24-58 | 1976 | Rancho Sante Fe, Calif. |
| Linskey, Mike | 4 | 5 | 4.68 | 30 | 13 | 0 | 1 | 108 | 130 | 68 | 56 | 46 | 77 | L L | 6-5 | 220 | 6-18-66 | 1988 | New Port Richey, Fla. |
| Martinez, Jose | 2 | 3 | 9.93 | 14 | 5 | 0 | 0 | 35 | 56 | 39 | 39 | 15 | 16 | R R | 6-2 | 155 | 4-1-71 | 1989 | Santiago, D.R. |
| 2-team (13 Edm.) | 8 | 7 | 6.01 | 27 | 18 | 3 | 0 | 115 | 148 | 88 | 77 | 39 | 43 | | | | | | |
| Martinez, Pedro | 3 | 5 | 4.72 | 15 | 14 | 1 | 0 | 88 | 94 | 49 | 46 | 40 | 65 | L L | 6-2 | 155 | 11-29-68 | 1987 | Villa Mella, D.R. |
| Pena, Jim | 1 | 2 | 6.10 | 39 | 0 | 0 | 1 | 52 | 69 | 41 | 35 | 16 | 31 | L L | 6-1 | 185 | 9-17-64 | 1986 | Phoenix, Ariz. |
| Sager, A.J. | 6 | 5 | 3.70 | 21 | 11 | 2 | 1 | 90 | 91 | 49 | 37 | 18 | 58 | R R | 6-4 | 220 | 3-3-65 | 1988 | Kirkersville, Ohio |
| Sanders, Scott | 5 | 10 | 4.96 | 24 | 24 | 4 | 0 | 152 | 170 | 101 | 84 | 62 | 161 | R R | 6-4 | 220 | 3-25-69 | 1990 | Thibodaux, La. |
| Seanez, Rudy | 0 | 1 | 6.41 | 14 | 0 | 0 | 0 | 20 | 24 | 15 | 14 | 11 | 14 | R R | 5-10 | 185 | 10-20-68 | 1986 | El Centro, Calif. |
| 2-team (3 Colo. Spr.) | 0 | 1 | 6.75 | 17 | 0 | 0 | 0 | 23 | 27 | 18 | 17 | 12 | 19 | | | | | | |
| Seminara, Frank | 8 | 5 | 5.43 | 21 | 19 | 0 | 1 | 114 | 136 | 79 | 69 | 52 | 99 | R R | 6-2 | 195 | 5-16-67 | 1988 | Brooklyn, N.Y. |
| Strong, Joe | 1 | 3 | 5.67 | 21 | 0 | 0 | 0 | 27 | 37 | 23 | 17 | 10 | 18 | S R | 6-0 | 180 | 9-9-62 | 1984 | Vallejo, Calif. |
| Worrell, Tim | 5 | 6 | 5.48 | 15 | 14 | 2 | 0 | 87 | 102 | 61 | 53 | 26 | 89 | R R | 6-4 | 215 | 7-5-67 | 1990 | Arcadia, Calif. |
| Young, Ray | 1 | 2 | 6.10 | 14 | 0 | 0 | 2 | 21 | 29 | 15 | 14 | 8 | 20 | R R | 6-3 | 180 | 5-27-64 | 1984 | Tempe, Ariz. |

## FIELDING

### Catcher
| | PCT | G | PO | A | E | DP |
|---|---|---|---|---|---|---|
| Basso | .981 | 33 | 200 | 12 | 4 | 2 |
| Higgins | 1.000 | 9 | 48 | 4 | 0 | 1 |
| Johnson | .987 | 78 | 498 | 39 | 7 | 2 |
| Walters | .992 | 41 | 245 | 14 | 2 | 3 |

### First Base
| | PCT | G | PO | A | E | DP |
|---|---|---|---|---|---|---|
| Bean | 1.000 | 13 | 103 | 13 | 0 | 12 |
| Higgins | 1.000 | 1 | 2 | 0 | 0 | 0 |
| Jelic | .950 | 5 | 19 | 0 | 1 | 0 |
| Simms | .987 | 92 | 762 | 45 | 11 | 57 |
| Staton | .969 | 10 | 88 | 5 | 3 | 13 |
| Velasquez | .990 | 30 | 278 | 28 | 3 | 29 |
| Witkowski | 1.000 | 2 | 4 | 0 | 0 | 0 |

### Second Base
| | PCT | G | PO | A | E | DP |
|---|---|---|---|---|---|---|
| Bethea | 1.000 | 19 | 19 | 25 | 0 | 3 |
| Gutierrez | .900 | 5 | 9 | 9 | 2 | 4 |

| | PCT | G | PO | A | E | DP |
|---|---|---|---|---|---|---|
| Higgins | 1.000 | 3 | 4 | 6 | 0 | 2 |
| Lopez | .982 | 60 | 141 | 189 | 6 | 50 |
| Martinez | .857 | 2 | 6 | 6 | 2 | 0 |
| Witkowski | .974 | 76 | 122 | 179 | 8 | 35 |

### Third Base
| | PCT | G | PO | A | E | DP |
|---|---|---|---|---|---|---|
| Bethea | 1.000 | 4 | 1 | 0 | 0 | 0 |
| Gonzalez | .933 | 70 | 31 | 137 | 12 | 16 |
| Higgins | .944 | 30 | 20 | 48 | 4 | 7 |
| Jelic | .887 | 30 | 11 | 52 | 8 | 2 |
| Johnson | .956 | 19 | 15 | 28 | 2 | 2 |
| Simms | 1.000 | 2 | 1 | 0 | 0 | 0 |
| Witkowski | 1.000 | 6 | 2 | 7 | 0 | 1 |

### Shortstop
| | PCT | G | PO | A | E | DP |
|---|---|---|---|---|---|---|
| Bethea | .867 | 6 | 5 | 8 | 2 | 0 |
| Gutierrez | 1.000 | 1 | 2 | 5 | 0 | 2 |

| | PCT | G | PO | A | E | DP |
|---|---|---|---|---|---|---|
| Lopez | .924 | 69 | 89 | 191 | 23 | 33 |
| Martinez | .941 | 74 | 91 | 259 | 22 | 38 |
| Witkowski | .000 | 1 | 0 | 0 | 0 | 0 |

### Outfield
| | PCT | G | PO | A | E | DP |
|---|---|---|---|---|---|---|
| Bean | .981 | 36 | 46 | 7 | 1 | 0 |
| Brown | .963 | 97 | 217 | 16 | 9 | 1 |
| Dozier | .897 | 31 | 24 | 2 | 3 | 1 |
| Higgins | .000 | 2 | 0 | 0 | 0 | 0 |
| Hosey | .957 | 27 | 43 | 1 | 2 | 0 |
| Johnson | .000 | 1 | 0 | 0 | 0 | 0 |
| Nieves | .988 | 41 | 79 | 4 | 1 | 1 |
| Pegues | .982 | 64 | 103 | 5 | 2 | 2 |
| Sherman | .981 | 73 | 152 | 6 | 3 | 1 |
| Simms | .857 | 10 | 11 | 1 | 2 | 0 |
| Vatcher | .968 | 79 | 139 | 11 | 5 | 3 |

# WICHITA                                                                 AA

## TEXAS LEAGUE

| BATTING | AVG | G | AB | R | H | 2B | 3B | HR | RBI | BB | SO | SB | CS | B | T | HT | WT | DOB | 1st Yr | Resides |
|---|---|---|---|---|---|---|---|---|---|---|---|---|---|---|---|---|---|---|---|---|
| Abercrombie, John, 1b | .254 | 71 | 181 | 21 | 46 | 7 | 0 | 7 | 31 | 8 | 44 | 6 | 5 | R R | 5-9 | 185 | 7-31-69 | 1990 | Houston, Texas |
| Bethea, Steve, 3b-ss | .265 | 15 | 49 | 2 | 13 | 0 | 0 | 1 | 4 | 16 | 0 | 1 | | S R | 5-10 | 172 | 6-20-67 | 1989 | Austin, Texas |
| Bish, Brent, 2b-ss | .266 | 24 | 64 | 12 | 17 | 2 | 1 | 0 | 6 | 6 | 19 | 2 | 2 | R R | 6-0 | 180 | 11-3-68 | 1990 | Yorba Linda, Calif. |
| Bruno, Julio, 3b | .285 | 70 | 246 | 34 | 70 | 17 | 1 | 3 | 24 | 11 | 46 | 3 | 5 | R R | 5-11 | 190 | 10-15-72 | 1990 | Puerto Plata, D.R. |
| Gash, Darius, of | .269 | 91 | 271 | 34 | 73 | 9 | 4 | 5 | 37 | 20 | 58 | 15 | 6 | S R | 6-0 | 175 | 6-15-67 | 1990 | Cleveland, Tenn. |
| Gieseke, Mark, 1b | .244 | 15 | 41 | 5 | 10 | 3 | 0 | 0 | 4 | 4 | 9 | 0 | 0 | S L | 6-1 | 200 | 12-22-67 | 1989 | Westlake Village, Calif. |
| Gill, Steve, of | .240 | 39 | 100 | 15 | 24 | 5 | 0 | 3 | 13 | 7 | 27 | 6 | 5 | L L | 6-1 | 170 | 11-17-68 | 1990 | Anaheim, Calif. |
| Gonzalez, Paul, 3b | .270 | 59 | 215 | 36 | 58 | 7 | 3 | 7 | 33 | 25 | 55 | 5 | 5 | L R | 6-0 | 185 | 4-22-69 | 1990 | Fort Worth, Texas |
| Hall, Billy, 2b | .270 | 124 | 486 | 80 | 131 | 27 | 7 | 4 | 46 | 36 | 88 | 29 | 19 | S R | 5-9 | 180 | 6-17-69 | 1991 | Wichita, Kan. |
| Harris, Vince, of | .274 | 112 | 350 | 55 | 96 | 13 | 2 | 0 | 36 | 45 | 45 | 27 | 16 | S R | 5-8 | 160 | 8-9-67 | 1986 | Elgin, Ill. |
| Henderson, Lee, c | .176 | 31 | 74 | 7 | 13 | 0 | 0 | 0 | 3 | 7 | 18 | 1 | 2 | R R | 6-3 | 210 | 4-21-71 | 1989 | West Covina, Calif. |
| Holbert, Ray, ss | .260 | 112 | 388 | 56 | 101 | 13 | 5 | 5 | 48 | 54 | 87 | 30 | 17 | R R | 6-0 | 165 | 9-25-70 | 1988 | Moreno Valley, Calif. |
| Hosey, Dwayne, of-dh | .291 | 86 | 326 | 52 | 95 | 19 | 2 | 18 | 61 | 25 | 44 | 13 | 4 | S R | 5-10 | 170 | 3-11-67 | 1987 | Altadena, Calif. |
| Lopez, Pedro, c | .204 | 50 | 142 | 12 | 29 | 7 | 0 | 4 | 14 | 22 | 24 | 3 | 0 | R R | 6-0 | 160 | 3-29-69 | 1988 | Vega Baja, P.R. |
| Martinez, Pablo, ss-2b | .277 | 45 | 130 | 19 | 36 | 5 | 1 | 2 | 14 | 11 | 24 | 8 | 5 | S R | 5-10 | 155 | 6-29-69 | 1989 | San Juan Baron, D.R. |
| McDavid, Ray, of | .270 | 126 | 441 | 65 | 119 | 18 | 5 | 11 | 55 | 70 | 104 | 33 | 17 | L R | 6-3 | 195 | 7-20-71 | 1989 | San Diego, Calif. |
| Pugh, Scott, 1b | .316 | 26 | 79 | 15 | 25 | 1 | 0 | 4 | 11 | 4 | 7 | 0 | 1 | L L | 5-11 | 180 | 6-16-71 | 1989 | Abilene, Texas |
| Sanders, Tracy, of | .323 | 77 | 266 | 44 | 86 | 13 | 4 | 13 | 47 | 34 | 67 | 6 | 5 | L R | 6-2 | 200 | 7-26-69 | 1990 | Dallas, N.C. |
| Smith, Ira, of-dh | .231 | 13 | 39 | 7 | 9 | 0 | 1 | 0 | 4 | 4 | 9 | 0 | 2 | R R | 5-11 | 185 | 8-4-67 | 1990 | Chestertown, Md. |
| Spann, Tookie, 1b | .274 | 79 | 281 | 30 | 77 | 17 | 1 | 8 | 42 | 15 | 64 | 6 | 1 | R R | 6-2 | 200 | 2-18-67 | 1988 | New Orleans, La. |
| Staton, Dave, dh | .417 | 5 | 12 | 2 | 5 | 3 | 0 | 0 | 2 | 3 | 0 | 0 | 1 | R R | 6-5 | 215 | 4-12-68 | 1989 | Auburn, Calif. |
| Thurston, Jerrey, c | .244 | 78 | 197 | 22 | 48 | 10 | 0 | 2 | 22 | 14 | 62 | 2 | 0 | R R | 6-4 | 200 | 4-17-72 | 1990 | Longwood, Fla. |

| PITCHING | W | L | ERA | G | GS | CG | SV | IP | H | R | ER | BB | SO | B | T | HT | WT | DOB | 1st Yr | Resides |
|---|---|---|---|---|---|---|---|---|---|---|---|---|---|---|---|---|---|---|---|---|
| Berumen, Andres........... | 3 | 1 | 5.74 | 7 | 7 | 0 | 0 | 27 | 35 | 17 | 17 | 11 | 17 | R | R | 6-2 | 195 | 4-5-71 | 1989 | Banning, Calif. |
| Bryand, Renay............... | 3 | 5 | 2.41 | 52 | 0 | 0 | 2 | 71 | 67 | 29 | 19 | 32 | 63 | L | L | 5-10 | 170 | 9-22-66 | 1988 | Isla Vista, Calif. |
| Clark, Terry ................... | 3 | 0 | 2.43 | 19 | 0 | 0 | 0 | 30 | 27 | 10 | 8 | 7 | 30 | R | R | 6-2 | 196 | 10-10-60 | 1979 | LaPuente, Calif. |
| Cromwell, Nate .............. | 3 | 5 | 4.13 | 21 | 11 | 1 | 0 | 89 | 90 | 49 | 41 | 38 | 86 | L | L | 6-1 | 185 | 8-23-68 | 1987 | Las Vegas, Nev. |
| Felix, Nick ..................... | 2 | 1 | 5.03 | 27 | 0 | 0 | 3 | 48 | 49 | 30 | 27 | 24 | 54 | L | L | 6-0 | 205 | 2-21-67 | 1988 | Mesa, Ariz. |
| Florie, Bryce.................. | 11 | 8 | 3.96 | 27 | 27 | 0 | 0 | 155 | 128 | 80 | 68 | 100 | 133 | R | R | 6-0 | 170 | 5-21-70 | 1988 | Hanahan, S.C. |
| Freitas, Mike ................. | 0 | 2 | 10.57 | 8 | 0 | 0 | 0 | 8 | 13 | 14 | 9 | 2 | 4 | R | R | 6-1 | 160 | 9-22-69 | 1989 | Sacramento, Calif. |
| Hamilton, Joey .............. | 4 | 9 | 3.97 | 15 | 15 | 0 | 0 | 91 | 101 | 55 | 40 | 36 | 50 | R | R | 6-4 | 220 | 9-9-70 | 1991 | Statesboro, Ga. |
| Heinkel, Don ................. | 2 | 5 | 5.47 | 33 | 0 | 0 | 5 | 49 | 59 | 33 | 30 | 6 | 41 | L | R | 6-0 | 185 | 10-20-59 | 1982 | Racine, Wis. |
| Hoeme, Steve................ | 2 | 3 | 2.42 | 44 | 0 | 0 | 19 | 48 | 41 | 17 | 13 | 16 | 47 | R | R | 6-6 | 230 | 11-2-67 | 1987 | Preston, Kan. |
| Huber, Jeff .................... | 3 | 1 | 3.26 | 15 | 0 | 0 | 3 | 19 | 16 | 9 | 7 | 9 | 18 | R | L | 6-4 | 220 | 12-17-70 | 1990 | Scottsdale, Ariz. |
| Kellogg, Geoff ............... | 7 | 11 | 5.37 | 22 | 21 | 2 | 0 | 124 | 137 | 83 | 74 | 45 | 71 | R | R | 6-3 | 165 | 4-30-71 | 1989 | Spokane, Wash. |
| •Leskanic, Curtis ........... | 3 | 2 | 3.45 | 7 | 7 | 0 | 0 | 44 | 37 | 20 | 17 | 17 | 42 | R | R | 6-0 | 180 | 4-2-68 | 1990 | Pineville, La. |
| Lifgren, Kelly ................ | 5 | 3 | 5.35 | 37 | 4 | 0 | 2 | 74 | 88 | 47 | 44 | 28 | 45 | L | R | 6-6 | 230 | 2-1-68 | 1988 | Peoria, Ariz. |
| Paskievitch, Tom ........... | 1 | 2 | 7.00 | 7 | 0 | 0 | 0 | 9 | 11 | 8 | 7 | 8 | 5 | R | R | 6-3 | 210 | 7-19-68 | 1991 | Erie, Pa. |
| Pena, Jim...................... | 2 | 0 | 1.69 | 10 | 1 | 0 | 0 | 16 | 10 | 5 | 3 | 2 | 12 | L | L | 6-1 | 185 | 9-17-64 | 1986 | Phoenix, Ariz. |
| Sager, A.J..................... | 5 | 3 | 3.19 | 11 | 11 | 2 | 0 | 73 | 69 | 30 | 26 | 16 | 49 | R | R | 6-4 | 220 | 3-3-65 | 1988 | Kirkersville, Ohio |
| Strong, Joe ................... | 1 | 0 | 6.75 | 4 | 3 | 0 | 0 | 15 | 13 | 13 | 11 | 11 | 13 | S | R | 6-0 | 180 | 9-9-62 | 1984 | Vallejo, Calif. |
| Wengert, Bill ................. | 7 | 7 | 4.10 | 28 | 25 | 3 | 0 | 162 | 167 | 86 | 74 | 43 | 106 | R | R | 6-5 | 210 | 1-4-67 | 1988 | Sioux City, Iowa |
| Whitehurst, Wally........... | 1 | 0 | 1.27 | 4 | 4 | 0 | 0 | 21 | 11 | 4 | 3 | 5 | 14 | R | R | 6-3 | 185 | 4-11-64 | 1989 | Madisonville, La. |

•Property of Colorado Rockies

# RANCHO CUCAMONGA     A
## CALIFORNIA LEAGUE

| BATTING | AVG | G | AB | R | H | 2B | 3B | HR | RBI | BB | SO | SB | CS | B | T | HT | WT | DOB | 1st Yr | Resides |
|---|---|---|---|---|---|---|---|---|---|---|---|---|---|---|---|---|---|---|---|---|
| Baber, Larue, of ............ | .333 | 3 | 3 | 1 | 1 | 0 | 0 | 0 | 1 | 1 | 1 | 1 | 0 | R | R | 6-1 | 188 | 5-15-72 | 1990 | Sacramento, Calif. |
| Bish, Brent, 3b-2b ......... | .210 | 52 | 143 | 22 | 30 | 8 | 2 | 0 | 13 | 11 | 21 | 4 | 4 | R | R | 6-0 | 180 | 11-3-68 | 1990 | Yorba Linda, Calif. |
| Bream, Scott, of-ss........ | .281 | 113 | 405 | 70 | 114 | 15 | 6 | 4 | 52 | 74 | 85 | 30 | 14 | S | R | 6-1 | 170 | 11-4-70 | 1989 | Omaha, Neb. |
| Bruno, Julio, 3b ............. | .308 | 54 | 201 | 37 | 62 | 11 | 2 | 3 | 16 | 19 | 56 | 15 | 6 | R | R | 5-11 | 190 | 10-15-72 | 1990 | Puerto Plata, D.R. |
| Drinkwater, Sean, ss-3b | .270 | 121 | 486 | 69 | 131 | 29 | 1 | 10 | 84 | 35 | 78 | 2 | 0 | R | R | 6-3 | 195 | 6-22-71 | 1992 | El Toro, Calif. |
| Encarnacion, Anito, 1b... | .194 | 22 | 62 | 5 | 12 | 4 | 0 | 1 | 6 | 5 | 10 | 0 | 0 | R | R | 6-2 | 185 | 8-26-72 | 1991 | Sabana Perdida, D.R. |
| Gennaro, Brad, of........... | .285 | 127 | 481 | 77 | 137 | 23 | 7 | 13 | 70 | 30 | 88 | 3 | 9 | L | L | 6-1 | 175 | 8-2-71 | 1992 | La Mesa, Calif. |
| Gieseke, Mark, 1b ......... | .353 | 5 | 17 | 4 | 6 | 2 | 0 | 0 | 3 | 5 | 0 | 0 | 0 | S | L | 6-1 | 200 | 12-22-67 | 1989 | Westlake Village, Calif. |
| Hardtke, Jason, 2b-3b... | .319 | 130 | 523 | 98 | 167 | 38 | 7 | 11 | 85 | 61 | 54 | 7 | 8 | S | R | 5-10 | 175 | 9-15-71 | 1990 | San Jose, Calif. |
| Henderson, Lee, c.......... | .266 | 56 | 177 | 28 | 47 | 11 | 0 | 1 | 23 | 16 | 36 | 0 | 1 | R | R | 6-3 | 210 | 4-21-71 | 1989 | West Covina, Calif. |
| Lee, Derrek, 1b-dh ........ | .274 | 20 | 73 | 13 | 20 | 5 | 1 | 1 | 10 | 10 | 20 | 0 | 2 | R | R | 6-5 | 205 | 9-6-75 | 1993 | Fair Oaks, Calif. |
| Lopez, Pedro, c.............. | .252 | 37 | 103 | 25 | 26 | 10 | 0 | 1 | 9 | 24 | 19 | 0 | 1 | R | R | 6-0 | 160 | 3-29-69 | 1988 | Vega Baja, P.R. |
| Manahan, Austin, 3b-2b | .290 | 43 | 145 | 17 | 42 | 8 | 4 | 2 | 22 | 11 | 38 | 7 | 2 | S | R | 6-1 | 185 | 4-12-70 | 1988 | Scottsdale, Ariz. |
| Moore, Vince, of ............ | .258 | 39 | 159 | 33 | 41 | 8 | 0 | 6 | 23 | 15 | 52 | 9 | 7 | L | L | 6-1 | 177 | 9-22-71 | 1991 | Houston, Texas |
| Mowry, David, dh-1b ...... | .243 | 22 | 74 | 9 | 18 | 0 | 0 | 7 | 23 | 6 | 24 | 0 | 0 | L | L | 6-4 | 225 | 10-22-71 | 1990 | Glendora, Calif. |
| Mulligan, Sean, c-dh ...... | .280 | 79 | 268 | 29 | 75 | 10 | 3 | 6 | 36 | 34 | 33 | 1 | 3 | R | R | 6-2 | 205 | 4-25-70 | 1991 | Diamond Bar, Calif. |
| Pearce, Jeff, of ............. | .281 | 101 | 324 | 51 | 91 | 17 | 0 | 7 | 55 | 30 | 52 | 12 | 9 | L | L | 6-2 | 205 | 7-14-69 | 1990 | Sebastopol, Calif. |
| Powell, Ken, of .............. | .268 | 22 | 41 | 10 | 11 | 1 | 1 | 1 | 7 | 7 | 12 | 1 | 0 | R | R | 6-6 | 218 | 12-6-70 | 1989 | Long Beach, Calif. |
| Pugh, Scott, 1b.............. | .294 | 96 | 327 | 39 | 96 | 19 | 2 | 5 | 43 | 26 | 52 | 3 | 2 | L | L | 5-11 | 180 | 6-18-70 | 1991 | Abilene, Texas |
| Robbs, Bill, of ............... | .258 | 47 | 120 | 19 | 31 | 4 | 1 | 2 | 16 | 18 | 29 | 0 | 1 | R | R | 6-3 | 220 | 7-1-69 | 1992 | Sandy, Utah |
| Skeels, Andy, c ............. | .318 | 32 | 66 | 11 | 21 | 9 | 0 | 0 | 10 | 15 | 14 | 0 | 0 | L | R | 5-11 | 175 | 7-25-65 | 1987 | Thousand Oaks, Calif. |
| Smith, Ira, of ................ | .346 | 92 | 347 | 71 | 120 | 30 | 6 | 7 | 47 | 55 | 41 | 32 | 16 | R | R | 5-11 | 185 | 8-4-67 | 1990 | Chestertown, Md. |
| Staton, Dave, dh-1b ...... | .317 | 58 | 221 | 37 | 70 | 21 | 0 | 18 | 58 | 30 | 52 | 0 | 0 | R | R | 6-5 | 215 | 4-12-68 | 1989 | Auburn, Calif. |

| PITCHING | W | L | ERA | G | GS | CG | SV | IP | H | R | ER | BB | SO | B | T | HT | WT | DOB | 1st Yr | Resides |
|---|---|---|---|---|---|---|---|---|---|---|---|---|---|---|---|---|---|---|---|---|
| Baker, Jared .................. | 1 | 5 | 7.29 | 9 | 9 | 0 | 0 | 42 | 57 | 44 | 34 | 30 | 21 | L | R | 6-4 | 220 | 3-25-71 | 1992 | Goose Creek, S.C. |
| Barnes, Jon................... | 5 | 5 | 5.67 | 14 | 13 | 0 | 0 | 79 | 88 | 60 | 50 | 54 | 59 | R | R | 6-1 | 175 | 4-11-73 | 1991 | Lancaster, S.C. |
| Beckett, Robbie ............. | 2 | 4 | 6.02 | 37 | 10 | 0 | 4 | 84 | 75 | 62 | 56 | 93 | 88 | R | L | 6-5 | 235 | 7-16-72 | 1990 | Austin, Texas |
| Brown, Jeff.................... | 6 | 6 | 5.68 | 38 | 8 | 1 | 0 | 95 | 137 | 75 | 60 | 28 | 63 | L | L | 6-0 | 165 | 9-8-70 | 1990 | Grand Prairie, Texas |
| Cairncross, Cam............. | 10 | 11 | 5.12 | 29 | 26 | 0 | 0 | 155 | 182 | 112 | 88 | 81 | 122 | R | L | 6-2 | 212 | 5-11-72 | 1991 | Cairns, Australia |
| Campbell, Mike............... | 1 | 0 | 1.93 | 2 | 0 | 0 | 0 | 5 | 1 | 1 | 1 | 4 | 4 | R | R | 6-3 | 210 | 2-17-64 | 1985 | Kirkland, Wash. |
| Clark, Terry ................... | 0 | 2 | 4.66 | 8 | 0 | 0 | 0 | 10 | 7 | 5 | 5 | 4 | 7 | R | R | 6-2 | 196 | 10-10-60 | 1979 | LaPuente, Calif. |
| Compton, Clint ............... | 3 | 3 | 4.62 | 39 | 1 | 0 | 0 | 74 | 82 | 50 | 38 | 50 | 59 | R | R | 6-3 | 175 | 4-23-71 | 1991 | Texarkana, Texas |
| Dale, Ron...................... | 0 | 0 | 10.13 | 8 | 0 | 0 | 0 | 13 | 20 | 19 | 15 | 13 | 8 | R | R | 6-3 | 210 | 8-9-70 | 1992 | Boulder City, Nev. |
| Davis, Ricky .................. | 0 | 2 | 8.00 | 8 | 0 | 0 | 1 | 9 | 13 | 9 | 8 | 4 | 10 | R | R | 6-3 | 210 | 9-2-66 | 1989 | La Verne, Calif. |
| Dishman, Glenn .............. | 0 | 1 | 7.15 | 2 | 2 | 0 | 0 | 11 | 14 | 9 | 9 | 5 | 6 | R | L | 6-1 | 195 | 11-5-70 | 1993 | Fremont, Calif. |
| Garrelts, Scott............... | 0 | 5 | 5.16 | 9 | 8 | 0 | 1 | 30 | 39 | 23 | 17 | 17 | 32 | R | R | 6-4 | 205 | 10-30-61 | 1979 | Shreveport, La. |
| Grzelaczyk, Ken ............. | 12 | 7 | 4.30 | 33 | 24 | 1 | 1 | 165 | 180 | 93 | 79 | 51 | 100 | R | R | 6-4 | 200 | 1-11-71 | 1992 | Howard Beach, N.Y. |
| Hamilton, Joey ............... | 1 | 0 | 4.09 | 2 | 0 | 0 | 0 | 11 | 11 | 5 | 5 | 2 | 6 | R | R | 6-4 | 220 | 9-9-70 | 1991 | Statesboro, Ga. |
| Hernandez, Fernando .... | 7 | 5 | 4.15 | 17 | 17 | 1 | 0 | 100 | 90 | 54 | 46 | 67 | 121 | R | R | 6-2 | 185 | 6-16-71 | 1990 | Santiago, D.R. |

# PADRES: MOST COMMON LINEUPS

|  | San Diego<br>Majors | Las Vegas<br>AAA | Wichita<br>AA | Rancho Cucamonga<br>A | Waterloo<br>A |
|---|---|---|---|---|---|
| C | Kevin Higgins (59) | Brian Johnson (78) | Jerrey Thurston (78) | Lee Henderson (55) | Charlie Greene (77) |
| 1B | Fred McGriff (83) | Mike Simms (92) | Tookie Spann (75) | Scott Pugh (93) | John Fantauzzi (106) |
| 2B | Jeff Gardner (133) | Mat Witkowski (76) | Billy Hall (117) | Jason Hardtke (112) | Homer Bush (127) |
| 3B | Gary Sheffield (67) | Paul Gonzalez (70) | Julio Bruno (69) | Julio Bruno (54) | Iggy Duran (82) |
| SS | Ricky Gutierrez (117) | Pablo Martinez (74) | Ray Holbert (102) | Sean Drinkwater (93) | Roberto DeLeon (101) |
| OF | Phil Plantier (134) | Jarvis Brown (99) | Ray McDavid (121) | Brad Gennaro (127) | Stoney Briggs (122) |
|  | Derek Bell (125) | Jim Vatcher (83) | Vince Harris (85) | Ira Smith (92) | John Roberts (114) |
|  | Tony Gwynn (121) | Darrell Sherman (74) | Darius Gash (68) | Jeff Pearce (73) | Bobby Bonds (93) |
| DH | N/A | Johnson/Walters (17) | Dwayne Hosey (29) | Dave Staton (50) | Dave Mowry (22) |
| SP | Andy Benes (34) | Scott Sanders (24) | Bryce Florie (27) | Cam Cairncross (26) | Mike Hermanson (18) |
| RP | Gene Harris (59) | Mark Ettles (47) | Renay Bryand (52) | Tom Martin (46) | Todd Schmitt (51) |
|  | Full-season farm clubs only | No. of games at position in parenthesis |  |  |  |

# PADRES: ORGANIZATION LEADERS

## MAJOR LEAGUERS

**BATTING**

| | | |
|---|---|---|
| *AVG | Tony Gwynn | .358 |
| R | Ricky Gutierrez | 76 |
| H | Tony Gwynn | 175 |
| TB | Tony Gwynn | 243 |
| 2B | Tony Gwynn | 41 |
| 3B | Jeff Gardner | 7 |
| HR | Phil Plantier | 34 |
| RBI | Phil Plantier | 100 |
| BB | Phil Plantier | 61 |
| SO | Phil Plantier | 124 |
| SB | Derek Bell | 26 |

**PITCHING**

| | | |
|---|---|---|
| W | Andy Benes | 15 |
| L | Andy Benes | 15 |
| #ERA | Andy Benes | 3.78 |
| G | Gene Harris | 59 |
| CG | Andy Benes | 4 |
| SV | Gene Harris | 23 |
| IP | Andy Benes | 231 |
| BB | Andy Benes | 86 |
| SO | Andy Benes | 179 |

MORRIS FOSTOFF

**Gene Harris**
59 appearances, 23 saves

## MINOR LEAGUERS

**BATTING**

| | | |
|---|---|---|
| *AVG | Steve Pegues, Las Vegas | .352 |
| R | Jason Hardtke, Rancho Cucamonga | 98 |
| H | Jason Hardtke, Rancho Cucamonga | 167 |
| TB | Jason Hardtke, Rancho Cucamonga | 252 |
| 2B | Jason Hardtke, Rancho Cucamonga | 38 |
| 3B | Jarvis Brown, Las Vegas | 9 |
| HR | Dave Staton, R.C.-Wichita-Las Vegas | 25 |
| RBI | Jason Hardtke, Rancho Cucamonga | 85 |
| BB | Scott Bream, Rancho Cucamonga | 74 |
| SO | Bobby Bonds Jr., Waterloo | 124 |
| SB | Homer Bush, Waterloo | 39 |

**PITCHING**

| | | |
|---|---|---|
| W | Ken Grzelaczyk, Rancho Cucamonga | 12 |
| L | Todd Erdos, Spokane-Waterloo | 15 |
| #ERA | Glenn Dishman, Spokane-R.C. | 2.83 |
| G | Jeff Huber, Rancho Cuca.-Wichita | 57 |
| CG | Two tied at | 4 |
| SV | Todd Schmitt, Waterloo | 25 |
| IP | Ken Grzelaczyk, Rancho Cucamonga | 165 |
| BB | Bryce Florie, Wichita | 100 |
| SO | Scott Sanders, Las Vegas | 161 |

*Minimum 250 At-Bats   #Minimum 75 Innings

| PITCHING | W | L | ERA | G | GS | CG | SV | IP | H | R | ER | BB | SO | B | T | HT | WT | DOB | 1st Yr | Resides |
|---|---|---|---|---|---|---|---|---|---|---|---|---|---|---|---|---|---|---|---|---|
| Hoeme, Steve | 1 | 0 | 6.48 | 8 | 0 | 0 | 0 | 8 | 8 | 9 | 6 | 5 | 4 | R | R | 6-6 | 230 | 11-2-67 | 1987 | Preston, Kan. |
| Huber, Jeff | 4 | 1 | 3.14 | 42 | 0 | 0 | 18 | 49 | 43 | 22 | 17 | 18 | 43 | R | L | 6-4 | 220 | 12-17-70 | 1990 | Scottsdale, Ariz. |
| Hurst, Bruce | 0 | 0 | 8.31 | 1 | 1 | 0 | 0 | 4 | 4 | 5 | 4 | 1 | 6 | L | L | 6-3 | 219 | 3-24-58 | 1976 | Rancho Sante Fe, Calif. |
| Kerr, Jason | 0 | 1 | 11.57 | 6 | 0 | 0 | 0 | 12 | 17 | 15 | 15 | 8 | 7 | R | L | 6-4 | 215 | 9-14-69 | 1991 | Temple City, Calif. |
| Loiselle, Rich | 5 | 8 | 5.77 | 14 | 14 | 1 | 0 | 83 | 109 | 64 | 53 | 34 | 53 | R | R | 6-5 | 225 | 1-12-72 | 1991 | Oshkosh, Wis. |
| Martin, Tom | 1 | 4 | 5.61 | 47 | 1 | 0 | 0 | 59 | 72 | 41 | 37 | 39 | 53 | L | L | 6-1 | 185 | 5-21-70 | 1989 | Panama City, Fla. |
| Paskievitch, Tom | 3 | 0 | 1.19 | 31 | 0 | 0 | 1 | 45 | 26 | 9 | 6 | 18 | 45 | R | R | 6-3 | 210 | 7-19-68 | 1991 | Erie, Pa. |
| Strong, Joe | 1 | 0 | 2.70 | 7 | 0 | 0 | 1 | 10 | 10 | 3 | 3 | 2 | 13 | S | R | 6-0 | 180 | 9-9-62 | 1984 | Vallejo, Calif. |
| Waldron, Joe | 1 | 2 | 5.91 | 30 | 0 | 0 | 0 | 35 | 43 | 28 | 23 | 11 | 31 | L | L | 6-0 | 180 | 7-4-69 | 1990 | McAlester, Okla. |
| White, Darell | 0 | 0 | 1.35 | 2 | 0 | 0 | 1 | 7 | 5 | 2 | 1 | 1 | 6 | R | R | 6-1 | 190 | 4-16-72 | 1992 | Alexandria, La. |

# WATERLOO   A

## MIDWEST LEAGUE

| BATTING | AVG | G | AB | R | H | 2B | 3B | HR | RBI | BB | SO | SB | CS | B | T | HT | WT | DOB | 1st Yr | Resides |
|---|---|---|---|---|---|---|---|---|---|---|---|---|---|---|---|---|---|---|---|---|
| Baber, Larue, of | .272 | 90 | 254 | 31 | 69 | 15 | 0 | 2 | 19 | 19 | 71 | 13 | 8 | R | R | 6-1 | 188 | 5-15-72 | 1990 | Sacramento, Calif. |
| Bonds, Bobby Jr., of | .248 | 102 | 359 | 44 | 89 | 12 | 3 | 4 | 35 | 30 | 124 | 30 | 11 | R | R | 6-4 | 180 | 3-7-70 | 1992 | San Carlos, Calif. |
| Briggs, Stoney, of | .257 | 125 | 421 | 57 | 108 | 15 | 5 | 9 | 55 | 30 | 103 | 21 | 8 | R | R | 6-2 | 215 | 12-26-71 | 1991 | Seaford, Del. |
| Bush, Homer, 2b | .322 | 130 | 472 | 63 | 152 | 19 | 3 | 5 | 51 | 19 | 87 | 39 | 14 | R | R | 5-11 | 180 | 11-11-72 | 1991 | East St. Louis, Ill. |
| Carrion, German, ss-3b | .218 | 48 | 110 | 11 | 24 | 3 | 0 | 0 | 7 | 4 | 18 | 1 | 2 | S | R | 5-10 | 165 | 8-26-72 | 1990 | Gurabo, P.R. |
| Casanova, Raul, c | .256 | 76 | 227 | 32 | 58 | 12 | 0 | 6 | 30 | 21 | 46 | 0 | 1 | R | R | 5-11 | 192 | 8-23-72 | 1990 | Ponce, P.R. |
| Cora, Manny, ss | .329 | 22 | 73 | 8 | 24 | 4 | 0 | 1 | 11 | 5 | 6 | 1 | 1 | S | R | 5-11 | 165 | 12-20-73 | 1991 | Levittown, P.R. |
| DeLeon, Roberto, ss-3b | .266 | 118 | 391 | 51 | 104 | 20 | 5 | 11 | 59 | 19 | 67 | 6 | 2 | R | R | 5-10 | 175 | 3-29-71 | 1992 | Missouri City, Texas |
| Duran, Iggy, 3b | .196 | 88 | 240 | 21 | 47 | 7 | 2 | 3 | 18 | 17 | 62 | 1 | 1 | R | R | 6-0 | 180 | 3-21-71 | 1989 | La Vega, D.R. |
| Ellstrom, Rich, 3b | .224 | 44 | 116 | 19 | 26 | 10 | 1 | 0 | 5 | 21 | 38 | 5 | 0 | R | R | 5-9 | 175 | 3-26-71 | 1993 | Houston, Texas |
| Encarnacion, Anito, dh | .091 | 20 | 44 | 1 | 4 | 1 | 0 | 0 | 5 | 2 | 9 | 0 | 0 | R | R | 6-2 | 185 | 8-26-72 | 1991 | Sabana Perdida, D.R. |
| Fantauzzi, John, 1b | .226 | 119 | 367 | 57 | 83 | 10 | 1 | 14 | 41 | 48 | 115 | 0 | 0 | L | L | 6-6 | 220 | 11-26-71 | 1992 | Lakeland, Fla. |
| Greene, Charlie, c | .178 | 84 | 213 | 19 | 38 | 8 | 0 | 2 | 20 | 13 | 33 | 0 | 0 | R | R | 6-3 | 170 | 1-23-71 | 1991 | Miami, Fla. |
| Minchk, Kevin, dh-1b | .205 | 33 | 73 | 7 | 15 | 2 | 0 | 0 | 6 | 10 | 21 | 0 | 0 | L | L | 6-3 | 210 | 5-26-71 | 1992 | Barrington, Ill. |
| Mowry, Dave, dh-1b | .239 | 46 | 142 | 16 | 34 | 4 | 1 | 7 | 25 | 28 | 41 | 1 | 0 | L | L | 6-4 | 225 | 10-22-71 | 1990 | Glendora, Calif. |
| Perez, Ralph, of | .125 | 4 | 8 | 1 | 0 | 0 | 0 | 0 | 0 | 0 | 2 | 0 | 0 | L | R | 5-10 | 160 | 4-19-73 | 1991 | Miami, Fla. |
| Robbs, Bill, dh-of | .273 | 6 | 22 | 1 | 6 | 2 | 1 | 0 | 2 | 1 | 6 | 0 | 0 | R | R | 6-3 | 220 | 7-1-69 | 1992 | Sandy, Utah |
| Roberts, John, of | .249 | 126 | 390 | 65 | 97 | 20 | 5 | 10 | 46 | 65 | 90 | 33 | 10 | R | R | 5-9 | 165 | 9-30-73 | 1991 | Pine Bluff, Ark. |
| Rosario, Mel, dh-c | .210 | 32 | 105 | 15 | 22 | 6 | 2 | 5 | 15 | 7 | 37 | 5 | 2 | S | R | 6-0 | 191 | 3-25-72 | 1992 | Miami, Fla. |
| Stewart, Reggie, of | .212 | 28 | 33 | 7 | 7 | 2 | 0 | 3 | 1 | 11 | 2 | 5 | R | R | 6-1 | 175 | 8-23-72 | 1991 | Yulee, Fla. |

| PITCHING | W | L | ERA | G | GS | CG | SV | IP | H | R | ER | BB | SO | B | T | HT | WT | DOB | 1st Yr | Resides |
|---|---|---|---|---|---|---|---|---|---|---|---|---|---|---|---|---|---|---|---|---|
| Anthony, Pepper | 1 | 2 | 6.66 | 7 | 7 | 0 | 0 | 26 | 29 | 21 | 19 | 10 | 11 | L | R | 6-3 | 215 | 11-9-71 | 1991 | Tavares, Fla. |
| Arroyo, Luis | 5 | 7 | 4.52 | 17 | 16 | 1 | 0 | 96 | 99 | 59 | 48 | 46 | 59 | L | L | 6-0 | 165 | 9-29-73 | 1992 | Bajadero, P.R. |
| Baker, Jared | 6 | 7 | 5.64 | 15 | 15 | 2 | 0 | 81 | 82 | 60 | 51 | 54 | 62 | L | R | 6-4 | 203 | 3-25-71 | 1992 | Goose Creek, S.C. |
| Barnes, Jon | 5 | 3 | 2.86 | 10 | 10 | 0 | 0 | 57 | 51 | 27 | 18 | 23 | 46 | R | R | 6-1 | 175 | 4-11-73 | 1991 | Lancaster, S.C. |
| Burns, J.J. | 5 | 4 | 5.09 | 19 | 7 | 0 | 1 | 64 | 68 | 44 | 36 | 33 | 37 | L | R | 6-5 | 212 | 7-25-70 | 1991 | Fairfield, Calif. |
| D'Amato, Brian | 1 | 0 | 5.11 | 21 | 0 | 0 | 0 | 25 | 31 | 19 | 14 | 7 | 17 | R | R | 6-0 | 200 | 3-20-72 | 1991 | Warwick, R.I. |
| Doyle, Tom | 0 | 0 | 6.75 | 4 | 0 | 0 | 0 | 7 | 7 | 6 | 5 | 6 | 7 | L | L | 6-3 | 205 | 1-20-70 | 1988 | Redondo Beach, Calif. |
| Dunckel, Keith | 2 | 6 | 6.96 | 30 | 3 | 0 | 0 | 53 | 74 | 56 | 41 | 41 | 32 | R | R | 6-1 | 190 | 12-15-69 | 1992 | Des Moines, Iowa |
| Duran, Iggy | 1 | 0 | 1.42 | 5 | 0 | 0 | 0 | 6 | 2 | 1 | 1 | 4 | 7 | R | R | 6-0 | 180 | 3-21-71 | 1989 | La Vega, D.R. |
| Erdos, Todd | 1 | 9 | 8.31 | 11 | 11 | 0 | 0 | 48 | 64 | 51 | 44 | 31 | 27 | R | R | 6-1 | 185 | 11-21-73 | 1992 | Meadville, Pa. |
| Hanson, Craig | 7 | 14 | 4.90 | 28 | 16 | 1 | 0 | 112 | 120 | 78 | 61 | 62 | 90 | R | R | 6-3 | 180 | 9-30-70 | 1991 | Roseville, Minn. |
| Hermanson, Mike | 3 | 6 | 4.74 | 18 | 18 | 0 | 0 | 82 | 79 | 51 | 43 | 52 | 57 | R | R | 6-3 | 195 | 11-26-71 | 1992 | Chicago, Ill. |
| Hollinger, Adrian | 8 | 3 | 2.54 | 44 | 0 | 0 | 5 | 60 | 44 | 23 | 17 | 40 | 67 | L | R | 6-0 | 172 | 9-23-70 | 1991 | Mira Loma, Calif. |
| Kindler, Tom | 0 | 7 | 6.55 | 20 | 11 | 0 | 0 | 69 | 80 | 64 | 52 | 49 | 48 | R | R | 6-6 | 230 | 11-18-70 | 1992 | North Canton, Ohio |
| Loiselle, Richard | 1 | 5 | 3.94 | 10 | 10 | 1 | 0 | 59 | 55 | 28 | 26 | 29 | 47 | R | R | 6-5 | 225 | 1-12-72 | 1991 | Oshkosh, Wis. |
| Long, Joey | 4 | 3 | 4.86 | 33 | 7 | 0 | 0 | 96 | 96 | 56 | 52 | 36 | 90 | R | L | 6-2 | 195 | 7-15-70 | 1991 | Quincy, Ohio |
| Sandt, Tom | 2 | 6 | 5.86 | 17 | 1 | 0 | 1 | 29 | 27 | 12 | 12 | 14 | 23 | R | R | 6-3 | 220 | 8-23-71 | 1993 | Evanston, Ill. |
| Schmitt, Todd | 1 | 4 | 1.99 | 51 | 0 | 0 | 25 | 59 | 41 | 15 | 13 | 33 | 76 | R | R | 6-2 | 170 | 2-12-70 | 1992 | Fraser, Mich. |
| Waldron, Joe | 3 | 3 | 2.53 | 16 | 1 | 1 | 1 | 32 | 19 | 11 | 9 | 13 | 30 | L | L | 6-0 | 180 | 7-4-69 | 1990 | McAlester, Okla. |

# SPOKANE

## NORTHWEST LEAGUE

| BATTING | AVG | G | AB | R | H | 2B | 3B | HR | RBI | BB | SO | SB | CS | B | T | HT | WT | DOB | 1st Yr | Resides |
|---|---|---|---|---|---|---|---|---|---|---|---|---|---|---|---|---|---|---|---|---|
| Bostock, Jim, ss-2b | .237 | 57 | 169 | 28 | 40 | 5 | 1 | 0 | 21 | 16 | 36 | 7 | 1 | L | R | 6-0 | 170 | 6-30-71 | 1993 | Howell, Mich. |
| Corps, Erick, ss | .000 | 4 | 7 | 1 | 0 | 0 | 0 | 0 | 1 | 0 | 3 | 0 | 0 | S | R | 6-0 | 155 | 9-6-74 | 1992 | Carolina, P.R. |
| Cuevas, Eduardo, 2b | .250 | 2 | 8 | 0 | 2 | 0 | 0 | 0 | 1 | 0 | 0 | 0 | 1 | R | R | 5-10 | 155 | 12-1-73 | 1992 | Santo Domingo, D.R. |
| Dandridge, Brad, of-c | .238 | 64 | 248 | 26 | 59 | 8 | 2 | 4 | 41 | 16 | 38 | 2 | 0 | R | R | 6-0 | 190 | 11-29-71 | 1993 | Santa Maria, Calif. |
| Duke, Darrick, of | .286 | 49 | 147 | 26 | 42 | 6 | 1 | 2 | 25 | 21 | 29 | 5 | 2 | R | R | 6-2 | 206 | 3-31-71 | 1993 | Houston, Texas |
| Gillis, Troy, dh-of | .118 | 7 | 17 | 0 | 2 | 0 | 0 | 0 | 1 | 1 | 8 | 0 | 0 | R | R | 5-11 | 175 | 4-13-74 | 1992 | Tacoma, Wash. |
| Johnson, Earl, of | .246 | 63 | 199 | 33 | 49 | 3 | 1 | 0 | 14 | 16 | 49 | 19 | 3 | S | R | 5-9 | 163 | 10-3-71 | 1991 | Detroit, Mich. |
| McKinnis, Roy, c-1b | .241 | 58 | 191 | 35 | 46 | 8 | 0 | 3 | 27 | 25 | 45 | 2 | 3 | R | R | 6-1 | 185 | 11-14-72 | 1993 | Macon, Ga. |
| Powell, Kenny, of | .000 | 5 | 14 | 1 | 0 | 0 | 0 | 0 | 0 | 2 | 7 | 0 | 0 | R | R | 6-6 | 218 | 12-6-70 | 1989 | Long Beach, Calif. |
| Prieto, Chris, of | .289 | 73 | 280 | 64 | 81 | 17 | 5 | 1 | 28 | 47 | 30 | 36 | 3 | L | L | 5-10 | 170 | 8-24-72 | 1993 | Carmel, Calif. |
| Rivera, Alex, of | .000 | 1 | 1 | 0 | 0 | 0 | 0 | 0 | 0 | 0 | 0 | 0 | 0 | R | R | 6-1 | 160 | 3-9-73 | 1991 | Cayey, P.R. |
| Rivera, Santiago, ss | .210 | 49 | 119 | 13 | 25 | 7 | 0 | 0 | 14 | 22 | 33 | 3 | 1 | S | R | 5-11 | 180 | 12-15-72 | 1993 | Rio Piedras, P.R. |
| Rosario, Melvin, dh-c | .229 | 41 | 140 | 17 | 32 | 5 | 0 | 4 | 19 | 8 | 36 | 2 | 1 | S | R | 6-0 | 191 | 5-25-73 | 1992 | Miami, Fla. |
| Scheibe, Britton, of | .182 | 46 | 99 | 11 | 18 | 2 | 0 | 0 | 11 | 13 | 39 | 0 | 2 | S | R | 6-2 | 185 | 1-4-72 | 1992 | Rancho Santa Fe, Calif. |
| Stadler, Mike, c | .000 | 1 | 1 | 0 | 0 | 0 | 0 | 0 | 0 | 0 | 1 | 0 | 0 | R | R | 6-2 | 190 | 7-5-74 | 1992 | El Cajon, Calif. |
| Thompson, Jason, 1b | .300 | 66 | 240 | 36 | 72 | 25 | 1 | 7 | 38 | 37 | 47 | 3 | 2 | L | L | 6-4 | 200 | 6-13-71 | 1993 | Laguna Hills, Calif. |
| West, Chris, dh-3b | .265 | 68 | 226 | 37 | 60 | 14 | 1 | 4 | 37 | 26 | 57 | 1 | 2 | L | R | 6-4 | 210 | 5-27-72 | 1993 | La Grange, N.C. |
| Woodridge, Dickie, 2b | .264 | 70 | 250 | 42 | 66 | 13 | 5 | 1 | 34 | 49 | 21 | 16 | 5 | L | R | 5-9 | 170 | 1-24-71 | 1993 | Jordan, N.Y. |
| Zanolla, Dan, 3b-ss | .216 | 57 | 194 | 31 | 42 | 10 | 2 | 2 | 21 | 23 | 16 | 3 | 2 | R | R | 6-0 | 175 | 9-18-70 | 1993 | Hobart, Ind. |

| PITCHING | W | L | ERA | G | GS | CG | SV | IP | H | R | ER | BB | SO | B | T | HT | WT | DOB | 1st Yr | Resides |
|---|---|---|---|---|---|---|---|---|---|---|---|---|---|---|---|---|---|---|---|---|
| Clark, Byron | 0 | 0 | 14.66 | 13 | 0 | 0 | 0 | 12 | 20 | 22 | 19 | 12 | 8 | L | L | 6-2 | 180 | 1-3-72 | 1993 | Tucson, Ariz. |
| Dishman, Glenn | 6 | 3 | 2.20 | 12 | 12 | 2 | 0 | 78 | 59 | 25 | 19 | 13 | 79 | R | L | 6-1 | 195 | 11-5-70 | 1993 | Fremont, Calif. |
| Doyle, Tom | 0 | 0 | 13.50 | 6 | 0 | 0 | 0 | 6 | 12 | 9 | 9 | 6 | 5 | L | L | 6-3 | 205 | 1-20-70 | 1988 | Redondo Beach, Calif. |
| Drewien, Dan | 1 | 0 | 5.28 | 23 | 0 | 0 | 0 | 29 | 28 | 21 | 17 | 21 | 31 | R | R | 6-1 | 185 | 8-29-72 | 1993 | Medford, Ore. |
| Erdos, Todd | 5 | 6 | 3.19 | 16 | 15 | 0 | 0 | 90 | 73 | 39 | 32 | 53 | 64 | R | R | 6-1 | 185 | 11-21-73 | 1992 | Meadville, Pa. |
| Fargas, Hector | 2 | 2 | 5.93 | 21 | 0 | 0 | 0 | 41 | 49 | 34 | 27 | 24 | 28 | R | R | 6-0 | 185 | 10-16-73 | 1992 | Rio Piedras, P.R. |
| Kaufman, Brad | 5 | 4 | 6.88 | 25 | 8 | 1 | 4 | 54 | 56 | 56 | 41 | 41 | 48 | R | R | 6-2 | 210 | 4-26-72 | 1993 | Traer, Iowa |
| Keagle, Greg | 3 | 3 | 3.25 | 15 | 15 | 1 | 0 | 83 | 80 | 37 | 30 | 40 | 77 | R | R | 6-2 | 185 | 6-28-71 | 1993 | Horseheads, N.Y. |
| Matos, Alberto | 0 | 0 | 7.11 | 5 | 0 | 0 | 0 | 6 | 9 | 7 | 5 | 10 | 6 | R | R | 6-3 | 185 | 12-2-72 | 1990 | Mesa, Ariz. |
| McLain, Brian | 1 | 6 | 5.87 | 14 | 9 | 0 | 0 | 38 | 37 | 28 | 25 | 23 | 30 | R | R | 6-3 | 205 | 12-13-72 | 1992 | Vancouver, Wash. |
| Mix, Derek | 2 | 1 | 7.13 | 24 | 1 | 0 | 0 | 42 | 42 | 38 | 33 | 46 | 41 | R | R | 6-4 | 195 | 5-11-74 | 1993 | Moreno Valley, Calif. |
| Schlutt, Jason | 5 | 4 | 3.38 | 35 | 0 | 0 | 5 | 48 | 45 | 25 | 18 | 23 | 40 | R | L | 6-0 | 175 | 1-21-72 | 1993 | Baroda, Mich. |
| White, Kyle | 1 | 0 | 3.35 | 23 | 4 | 0 | 0 | 40 | 43 | 17 | 15 | 23 | 33 | R | R | 6-5 | 210 | 2-13-71 | 1992 | Alameda, Calif. |
| Winchester, Marty | 1 | 3 | 7.41 | 17 | 4 | 0 | 0 | 34 | 39 | 32 | 28 | 37 | 31 | L | L | 6-5 | 220 | 7-25-72 | 1992 | Whittier, Calif. |
| Wolff, Bryan | 3 | 9 | 5.53 | 25 | 8 | 0 | 1 | 57 | 52 | 50 | 35 | 44 | 48 | R | R | 6-0 | 185 | 3-16-72 | 1993 | Herrin, Ill. |

# PEORIA

## ARIZONA LEAGUE

| BATTING | AVG | G | AB | R | H | 2B | 3B | HR | RBI | BB | SO | SB | CS | B | T | HT | WT | DOB | 1st Yr | Resides |
|---|---|---|---|---|---|---|---|---|---|---|---|---|---|---|---|---|---|---|---|---|
| Bowden, Joe, of | .143 | 20 | 56 | 10 | 8 | 2 | 1 | 0 | 2 | 7 | 21 | 6 | 2 | R | R | 6-2 | 176 | 1-24-74 | 1992 | Chicago, Ill. |
| Cartaya, Luis, 2b-ss | .222 | 22 | 81 | 5 | 18 | 2 | 0 | 0 | 5 | 5 | 12 | 4 | 0 | R | R | 5-10 | 160 | 4-8-75 | 1992 | La Guaira, Venez. |
| Corps, Erick, ss-2b | .281 | 43 | 153 | 28 | 43 | 8 | 4 | 0 | 18 | 33 | 23 | 4 | 6 | S | R | 6-0 | 155 | 9-6-74 | 1992 | Carolina, P.R. |
| Cruz, Francisco, of | .161 | 37 | 112 | 16 | 18 | 2 | 3 | 0 | 7 | 12 | 58 | 6 | 1 | R | R | 6-2 | 183 | 12-9-74 | 1993 | Bani, D.R. |
| Cuevas, Eduardo, 2b | .295 | 35 | 139 | 17 | 41 | 6 | 1 | 0 | 13 | 4 | 12 | 9 | 3 | R | R | 5-10 | 155 | 12-1-73 | 1992 | Santo Domingo, D.R. |
| Derotal, Francisco, 1b | .239 | 45 | 163 | 21 | 39 | 8 | 2 | 4 | 24 | 10 | 47 | 6 | 1 | R | R | 5-11 | 175 | 4-15-74 | 1993 | Puerto Cabello, Venez. |
| Espinal, Juan, 3b | .301 | 37 | 136 | 23 | 41 | 11 | 1 | 2 | 19 | 15 | 40 | 3 | 3 | R | R | 6-0 | 185 | 4-15-75 | 1992 | La Vega, D.R. |
| Gillis, Troy, 2b-dh | .283 | 26 | 92 | 14 | 26 | 2 | 0 | 0 | 7 | 12 | 29 | 8 | 1 | R | R | 5-11 | 175 | 4-13-74 | 1992 | Tacoma, Wash. |
| Lee, Derrek, 1b | .327 | 15 | 52 | 11 | 17 | 1 | 1 | 2 | 5 | 6 | 7 | 4 | 0 | R | R | 6-5 | 205 | 9-6-75 | 1993 | Fair Oaks, Calif. |
| Luckett, Zaven, of | .227 | 33 | 97 | 15 | 22 | 3 | 1 | 0 | 11 | 18 | 41 | 7 | 5 | R | R | 6-0 | 160 | 12-19-73 | 1992 | Houston, Texas |
| Malekovic, Brett, 1b | .153 | 19 | 59 | 3 | 9 | 0 | 1 | 0 | 2 | 8 | 21 | 2 | 0 | R | R | 6-0 | 195 | 3-9-74 | 1992 | Palos Hills, Ill. |
| Martinez, Gabby, c-1b | .224 | 29 | 76 | 11 | 17 | 5 | 0 | 0 | 10 | 2 | 30 | 3 | 2 | R | R | 6-1 | 175 | 4-16-74 | 1992 | Levittown, P.R. |
| Rivera, Alex, of | .297 | 46 | 165 | 22 | 49 | 8 | 1 | 0 | 14 | 13 | 28 | 10 | 5 | R | R | 6-1 | 160 | 3-9-73 | 1991 | Cayey, P.R. |
| Rodriguez, Nelson, ss | .188 | 30 | 101 | 10 | 19 | 4 | 0 | 0 | 6 | 9 | 20 | 4 | 2 | R | R | 6-1 | 157 | 7-14-74 | 1992 | Tunapui, Venez. |
| Roques, Juan, 3b | .165 | 32 | 103 | 10 | 17 | 3 | 1 | 0 | 14 | 12 | 40 | 7 | 4 | R | R | 6-0 | 175 | 8-22-74 | 1992 | Moreno Valley, Calif. |
| Sanchez, Marcos, c-3b | .195 | 36 | 118 | 17 | 23 | 2 | 0 | 0 | 15 | 16 | 30 | 5 | 6 | S | R | 6-0 | 175 | 9-25-74 | 1992 | San Cristobal, D.R. |
| Sanders, Mike, of | .188 | 4 | 16 | 1 | 3 | 0 | 0 | 0 | 0 | 0 | 6 | 1 | 0 | R | R | 6-1 | 195 | 2-16-70 | 1993 | Palm Bay, Fla. |
| Stadler, Mike, c | .107 | 21 | 56 | 6 | 6 | 2 | 0 | 1 | 5 | 11 | 20 | 3 | 1 | R | R | 6-2 | 190 | 7-5-74 | 1992 | El Cajon, Calif. |
| Talbott, Ricky, c-dh | .029 | 17 | 35 | 3 | 1 | 0 | 1 | 0 | 2 | 12 | 22 | 2 | 0 | R | R | 6-1 | 190 | 12-29-73 | 1993 | Covina, Calif. |

| PITCHING | W | L | ERA | G | GS | CG | SV | IP | H | R | ER | BB | SO | B | T | HT | WT | DOB | 1st Yr | Resides |
|---|---|---|---|---|---|---|---|---|---|---|---|---|---|---|---|---|---|---|---|---|
| Baron, Jimmy | 1 | 3 | 4.44 | 13 | 8 | 1 | 1 | 49 | 38 | 33 | 24 | 38 | 36 | L | L | 6-3 | 200 | 2-22-74 | 1992 | Humble, Texas |
| Burgos, Ali | 0 | 0 | 0.00 | 1 | 0 | 0 | 0 | 2 | 1 | 1 | 0 | 2 | 2 | R | R | 6-2 | 156 | 8-14-74 | 1993 | La Guaira, Venez. |
| Clark, Byron | 1 | 2 | 6.00 | 5 | 5 | 0 | 0 | 24 | 26 | 20 | 16 | 10 | 26 | L | L | 6-2 | 180 | 1-3-72 | 1993 | Tucson, Ariz. |
| Duncan, DeVohn | 3 | 3 | 1.96 | 13 | 7 | 1 | 3 | 46 | 37 | 18 | 10 | 28 | 39 | R | R | 6-3 | 195 | 4-1-75 | 1993 | Jersey City, N.J. |
| Estrella, Alejandro | 0 | 0 | 9.00 | 3 | 0 | 0 | 0 | 4 | 6 | 5 | 4 | 2 | 4 | R | R | 6-4 | 178 | 8-8-73 | 1991 | Haina, D.R. |
| Garrett, Hal | 6 | 5 | 3.24 | 14 | 14 | 0 | 0 | 72 | 64 | 40 | 26 | 31 | 83 | R | R | 6-1 | 160 | 4-27-75 | 1993 | Mt. Juliet, Tenn. |
| Harpe, Dan | 1 | 0 | 2.61 | 6 | 0 | 0 | 0 | 10 | 5 | 5 | 3 | 5 | 5 | R | R | 6-3 | 180 | 12-29-74 | 1993 | San Diego, Calif. |
| Johnson, Byron | 0 | 0 | 0.00 | 3 | 0 | 0 | 0 | 5 | 1 | 0 | 0 | 2 | 5 | L | L | 5-11 | 170 | 4-9-71 | 1993 | San Diego, Calif. |
| Jones, Jeff | 3 | 5 | 3.80 | 12 | 9 | 0 | 0 | 47 | 39 | 27 | 20 | 24 | 35 | R | R | 6-6 | 205 | 8-1-73 | 1992 | Windsor, Ontario |
| LaChappa, Matt | 2 | 4 | 4.18 | 12 | 10 | 0 | 0 | 56 | 59 | 37 | 26 | 25 | 73 | L | L | 6-2 | 175 | 6-29-75 | 1993 | Lakeside, Calif. |
| Matos, Alberto | 0 | 2 | 6.28 | 11 | 0 | 0 | 0 | 14 | 14 | 15 | 10 | 13 | 11 | R | R | 6-3 | 185 | 12-2-72 | 1990 | Mesa, Ariz. |
| Meyer, Alan | 0 | 0 | 8.10 | 8 | 0 | 0 | 0 | 10 | 11 | 17 | 9 | 14 | 8 | R | R | 6-1 | 190 | 4-9-75 | 1993 | Huntington Beach, Calif. |
| Paniagua, Feliz | 1 | 2 | 4.50 | 16 | 2 | 0 | 0 | 36 | 40 | 25 | 18 | 12 | 19 | L | L | 6-1 | 165 | 11-20-74 | 1993 | Boca Canasta, D.R. |
| Sandt, Tom | 0 | 0 | 0.00 | 1 | 0 | 0 | 0 | 2 | 2 | 1 | 0 | 0 | 0 | R | R | 6-3 | 220 | 8-23-71 | 1993 | Evanston, Ill. |
| Singleton, Scott | 0 | 1 | 1.88 | 15 | 0 | 0 | 2 | 29 | 24 | 9 | 6 | 9 | 28 | R | R | 6-6 | 175 | 7-24-74 | 1992 | Thousand Oaks, Calif. |
| Talbott, Ricky | 1 | 0 | 0.00 | 3 | 0 | 0 | 0 | 5 | 2 | 0 | 0 | 0 | 5 | R | R | 6-1 | 190 | 12-29-73 | 1993 | Covina, Calif. |
| White, Darell | 2 | 2 | 3.63 | 19 | 0 | 0 | 2 | 40 | 28 | 20 | 16 | 22 | 33 | R | R | 6-1 | 190 | 4-16-72 | 1992 | Alexandria, La. |
| Willis, Marcus | 3 | 2 | 3.24 | 17 | 0 | 0 | 1 | 25 | 24 | 19 | 9 | 14 | 27 | R | R | 6-1 | 185 | 3-25-74 | 1993 | Dallas, Texas |

# SAN FRANCISCO GIANTS

**Manager:** Dusty Baker.  **1993 Record:** 103-59, .636 (2nd, NL West).

| BATTING | AVG | G | AB | R | H | 2B | 3B | HR | RBI | BB | SO | SB | CS | B | T | HT | WT | DOB | 1st Yr | Resides |
|---|---|---|---|---|---|---|---|---|---|---|---|---|---|---|---|---|---|---|---|---|
| Allanson, Andy | .167 | 13 | 24 | 3 | 4 | 1 | 0 | 0 | 2 | 1 | 2 | 0 | 0 | R | R | 6-5 | 225 | 12-22-61 | 1983 | Cleveland, Ohio |
| Benjamin, Mike | .199 | 63 | 146 | 22 | 29 | 7 | 0 | 4 | 16 | 9 | 23 | 0 | 0 | R | R | 6-0 | 169 | 11-22-65 | 1987 | Chandler, Ariz. |
| Benzinger, Todd | .288 | 86 | 177 | 25 | 51 | 7 | 2 | 6 | 26 | 13 | 35 | 0 | 0 | S | R | 6-1 | 195 | 2-11-63 | 1981 | Cincinnati, Ohio |
| Bonds, Barry | .336 | 159 | 539 | 129 | 181 | 38 | 4 | 46 | 123 | 126 | 79 | 29 | 12 | L | L | 6-1 | 185 | 7-24-64 | 1985 | Murietta, Calif. |
| Carreon, Mark | .327 | 78 | 150 | 22 | 49 | 9 | 1 | 7 | 33 | 13 | 16 | 1 | 0 | R | L | 6-0 | 195 | 7-9-63 | 1981 | Tucson, Ariz. |
| Clark, Will | .283 | 132 | 491 | 82 | 139 | 27 | 2 | 14 | 73 | 63 | 68 | 2 | 2 | L | L | 6-1 | 196 | 3-13-64 | 1985 | New Orleans, La. |
| Clayton, Royce | .282 | 153 | 549 | 54 | 155 | 21 | 5 | 6 | 70 | 38 | 91 | 11 | 10 | R | R | 6-0 | 183 | 1-2-70 | 1988 | Inglewood, Calif. |
| Colbert, Craig | .162 | 23 | 37 | 2 | 6 | 2 | 0 | 1 | 5 | 3 | 13 | 0 | 0 | R | R | 6-0 | 214 | 2-13-65 | 1986 | Pearland, Texas |
| Faneyte, Rikkert | .133 | 7 | 15 | 2 | 2 | 0 | 0 | 0 | 2 | 4 | 0 | 0 | 0 | R | R | 6-1 | 170 | 5-31-69 | 1991 | Amsterdam, Holland |
| Faries, Paul | .222 | 15 | 36 | 6 | 8 | 2 | 1 | 0 | 4 | 1 | 4 | 2 | 0 | R | R | 5-10 | 170 | 2-20-65 | 1987 | San Diego, Calif. |
| Hosey, Steve | .500 | 3 | 2 | 0 | 1 | 1 | 0 | 0 | 1 | 1 | 1 | 0 | 0 | R | R | 6-3 | 225 | 4-2-69 | 1989 | Inglewood, Calif. |
| Johnson, Erik | .400 | 4 | 5 | 1 | 2 | 0 | 0 | 0 | 0 | 1 | 0 | 0 | 0 | R | R | 5-11 | 175 | 10-11-65 | 1987 | San Ramon, Calif. |
| Lewis, Darren | .253 | 136 | 522 | 84 | 132 | 17 | 7 | 2 | 48 | 30 | 40 | 46 | 15 | R | R | 6-0 | 180 | 8-28-67 | 1988 | San Mateo, Calif. |
| Manwaring, Kirt | .275 | 130 | 432 | 48 | 119 | 15 | 1 | 5 | 49 | 41 | 76 | 1 | 3 | R | R | 5-11 | 203 | 7-15-65 | 1986 | Scottsdale, Ariz. |
| Martinez, Dave | .241 | 91 | 241 | 28 | 58 | 12 | 1 | 5 | 27 | 27 | 39 | 6 | 3 | L | L | 5-10 | 175 | 9-26-64 | 1983 | Safety Harbor, Fla. |
| McGee, Willie | .301 | 130 | 475 | 53 | 143 | 28 | 1 | 4 | 46 | 38 | 67 | 10 | 9 | S | R | 6-1 | 185 | 11-2-58 | 1977 | Hercules, Calif. |
| McNamara, Jim | .143 | 4 | 7 | 0 | 1 | 0 | 0 | 0 | 1 | 0 | 1 | 0 | 0 | L | R | 6-4 | 220 | 6-10-65 | 1986 | Vienna, Va. |
| Mercedes, Luis | .160 | 18 | 25 | 1 | 4 | 0 | 1 | 0 | 3 | 1 | 3 | 0 | 1 | R | R | 6-3 | 183 | 2-20-68 | 1987 | San Pedro de Macoris, D.R. |
| Patterson, John | .188 | 16 | 16 | 1 | 3 | 0 | 0 | 1 | 2 | 0 | 5 | 0 | 1 | S | R | 5-9 | 165 | 2-11-67 | 1988 | Phoenix, Ariz. |
| Phillips, J.R. | .313 | 11 | 16 | 1 | 5 | 1 | 1 | 1 | 4 | 0 | 5 | 0 | 0 | L | L | 6-1 | 185 | 4-29-70 | 1988 | Moreno Valley, Calif. |
| Reed, Jeff | .261 | 66 | 119 | 10 | 31 | 3 | 0 | 6 | 12 | 16 | 22 | 0 | 1 | L | R | 6-2 | 190 | 11-12-62 | 1980 | Elizabethton, Tenn. |
| Scarsone, Steve | .252 | 44 | 103 | 16 | 26 | 9 | 0 | 2 | 15 | 4 | 32 | 0 | 1 | R | R | 6-2 | 170 | 4-11-66 | 1986 | Anaheim, Calif. |
| Thompson, Robby | .312 | 128 | 494 | 85 | 154 | 30 | 2 | 19 | 65 | 45 | 97 | 10 | 4 | R | R | 5-11 | 173 | 5-10-62 | 1983 | Tequesta, Fla. |
| Williams, Matt | .294 | 145 | 579 | 105 | 170 | 33 | 4 | 38 | 110 | 27 | 80 | 1 | 3 | R | R | 6-2 | 205 | 11-28-65 | 1986 | Scottsdale, Ariz. |

| PITCHING | W | L | ERA | G | GS | CG | SV | IP | H | R | ER | BB | SO | B | T | HT | WT | DOB | 1st Yr | Resides |
|---|---|---|---|---|---|---|---|---|---|---|---|---|---|---|---|---|---|---|---|---|
| Beck, Rod | 3 | 1 | 2.16 | 76 | 0 | 0 | 48 | 79 | 57 | 20 | 19 | 13 | 86 | R | R | 6-1 | 236 | 8-3-68 | 1986 | Scottsdale, Ariz. |
| Black, Bud | 8 | 2 | 3.56 | 16 | 16 | 0 | 0 | 94 | 89 | 44 | 37 | 33 | 45 | L | L | 6-2 | 185 | 6-30-57 | 1979 | San Diego, Calif. |
| Brantley, Jeff | 5 | 6 | 4.28 | 53 | 12 | 0 | 0 | 114 | 112 | 60 | 54 | 46 | 76 | R | R | 5-10 | 189 | 9-5-63 | 1985 | Clinton, Miss. |
| Bross, Terry | 0 | 0 | 9.00 | 2 | 0 | 0 | 0 | 2 | 3 | 2 | 2 | 1 | 1 | R | R | 6-9 | 263 | 3-30-66 | 1987 | Commack, N.Y. |
| Brummett, Greg | 2 | 3 | 4.70 | 8 | 8 | 0 | 0 | 46 | 53 | 25 | 24 | 13 | 20 | R | R | 6-0 | 180 | 4-20-67 | 1989 | Wichita, Kan. |
| Burba, Dave | 10 | 3 | 4.25 | 54 | 5 | 0 | 0 | 95 | 95 | 49 | 45 | 37 | 88 | R | R | 6-4 | 240 | 7-7-66 | 1987 | Springfield, Ohio |
| Burkett, John | 22 | 7 | 3.65 | 34 | 34 | 2 | 0 | 232 | 224 | 100 | 94 | 40 | 145 | R | R | 6-3 | 205 | 11-28-64 | 1983 | Scottsdale, Ariz. |
| Deshaies, Jim | 2 | 2 | 4.24 | 5 | 4 | 0 | 0 | 17 | 24 | 9 | 8 | 6 | 5 | L | L | 6-4 | 225 | 6-23-60 | 1982 | Massena, N.Y. |
| Hickerson, Bryan | 7 | 5 | 4.26 | 47 | 15 | 0 | 0 | 120 | 137 | 58 | 57 | 39 | 69 | L | L | 6-2 | 203 | 10-13-63 | 1986 | Scottsdale, Ariz. |
| Jackson, Mike | 6 | 6 | 3.03 | 81 | 0 | 0 | 1 | 77 | 58 | 28 | 26 | 24 | 70 | R | R | 6-2 | 223 | 12-22-64 | 1984 | Spring, Texas |
| Layana, Tim | 0 | 0 | 22.50 | 1 | 0 | 0 | 0 | 2 | 7 | 5 | 5 | 1 | 1 | R | R | 6-2 | 190 | 3-2-64 | 1986 | Florence, Ky. |
| Minutelli, Gino | 0 | 1 | 3.77 | 9 | 0 | 0 | 0 | 14 | 7 | 9 | 6 | 15 | 10 | L | L | 6-0 | 190 | 5-23-64 | 1985 | Nashville, Tenn. |
| Righetti, Dave | 1 | 1 | 5.70 | 51 | 0 | 0 | 1 | 47 | 58 | 31 | 30 | 17 | 31 | L | L | 6-4 | 219 | 11-28-58 | 1977 | Los Altos, Calif. |
| Rogers, Kevin | 2 | 2 | 2.68 | 64 | 0 | 0 | 0 | 81 | 71 | 28 | 24 | 28 | 62 | S | L | 6-1 | 198 | 8-20-68 | 1988 | Parchman, Miss. |
| Sanderson, Scott | 4 | 2 | 3.51 | 11 | 8 | 0 | 0 | 49 | 48 | 20 | 19 | 7 | 36 | R | R | 6-5 | 192 | 7-22-56 | 1977 | Northbrook, Ill. |
| Swift, Bill | 21 | 8 | 2.82 | 34 | 34 | 1 | 0 | 233 | 195 | 82 | 73 | 55 | 157 | R | R | 6-0 | 191 | 10-27-61 | 1985 | South Portland, Maine |
| Torres, Salomon | 3 | 5 | 4.03 | 8 | 8 | 0 | 0 | 45 | 37 | 21 | 20 | 27 | 23 | R | R | 5-11 | 150 | 3-11-72 | 1990 | San Pedro de Macoris, D.R. |
| Wilson, Trevor | 7 | 5 | 3.60 | 22 | 18 | 1 | 0 | 110 | 110 | 45 | 44 | 40 | 57 | L | L | 6-0 | 204 | 6-7-66 | 1985 | Scottsdale, Ariz. |

## FIELDING

| Catcher | PCT | G | PO | A | E | DP |
|---|---|---|---|---|---|---|
| Allanson | 1.000 | 8 | 30 | 0 | 0 | 0 |
| Colbert | .982 | 10 | 51 | 3 | 1 | 0 |
| Manwaring | .998 | 130 | 739 | 70 | 2 | 12 |
| McNamara | 1.000 | 4 | 12 | 0 | 0 | 0 |
| Reed | 1.000 | 37 | 180 | 14 | 0 | 4 |

| First Base | PCT | G | PO | A | E | DP |
|---|---|---|---|---|---|---|
| Allanson | 1.000 | 2 | 8 | 0 | 0 | 0 |
| Benzinger | 1.000 | 40 | 289 | 15 | 0 | 27 |
| Carreon | 1.000 | 3 | 6 | 2 | 0 | 1 |
| Clark | .988 | 129 | 1078 | 88 | 14 | 113 |
| Phillips | .971 | 5 | 32 | 2 | 1 | 1 |
| Scarsone | 1.000 | 6 | 9 | 0 | 0 | 0 |

| Second Base | PCT | G | PO | A | E | DP |
|---|---|---|---|---|---|---|
| Benjamin | .991 | 23 | 54 | 54 | 1 | 23 |

| | PCT | G | PO | A | E | DP |
|---|---|---|---|---|---|---|
| Colbert | 1.000 | 2 | 0 | 1 | 0 | 0 |
| Faries | 1.000 | 7 | 12 | 18 | 0 | 3 |
| Johnson | 1.000 | 2 | 1 | 0 | 0 | 0 |
| Scarsone | 1.000 | 20 | 40 | 35 | 0 | 10 |
| Thompson | .988 | 128 | 273 | 384 | 8 | 95 |

| Third Base | PCT | G | PO | A | E | DP |
|---|---|---|---|---|---|---|
| Benjamin | .936 | 16 | 10 | 34 | 3 | 3 |
| Benzinger | .000 | 1 | 0 | 0 | 0 | 0 |
| Colbert | 1.000 | 1 | 1 | 0 | 1 |  |
| Faries | .000 | 1 | 0 | 0 | 1 | 0 |
| Johnson | 1.000 | 1 | 0 | 1 | 0 | 0 |
| Scarsone | .929 | 8 | 4 | 9 | 1 | 1 |
| Williams | .970 | 144 | 117 | 266 | 12 | 34 |

| Shortstop | PCT | G | PO | A | E | DP |
|---|---|---|---|---|---|---|
| Benjamin | .982 | 23 | 10 | 45 | 1 | 7 |
| Clayton | .963 | 153 | 251 | 449 | 27 | 103 |
| Faries | 1.000 | 4 | 3 | 5 | 0 | 0 |
| Johnson | .000 | 1 | 0 | 0 | 0 | 0 |

| Outfield | PCT | G | PO | A | E | DP |
|---|---|---|---|---|---|---|
| Benzinger | 1.000 | 7 | 10 | 0 | 0 | 0 |
| Bonds | .984 | 157 | 310 | 7 | 5 | 0 |
| Carreon | .943 | 41 | 48 | 2 | 3 | 0 |
| Faneyte | 1.000 | 6 | 10 | 0 | 0 | 0 |
| Hosey | .000 | 1 | 0 | 0 | 0 | 0 |
| Lewis | 1.000 | 131 | 344 | 4 | 0 | 3 |
| Martinez | .993 | 73 | 131 | 6 | 1 | 2 |
| McGee | .979 | 126 | 224 | 9 | 5 | 1 |
| Mercedes | 1.000 | 5 | 5 | 0 | 0 | 0 |

# GIANTS FARM SYSTEM

| Class | Club | League | W | L | Pct. | Finish* | Manager | First Year |
|---|---|---|---|---|---|---|---|---|
| AAA | Phoenix (Ariz.) Firebirds | Pacific Coast | 64 | 79 | .448 | 9th (10) | Carlos Alfonso | 1966 |
| AA | Shreveport (La.) Captains | Texas | 66 | 69 | .489 | T-5th (8) | Ron Wotus | 1979 |
| A# | San Jose (Calif.) Giants | California | 79 | 57 | .581 | T-2nd (10) | Dick Dietz | 1988 |
| A | Clinton (Iowa) Giants | Midwest | 80 | 54 | .597 | 1st (14) | Jack Mull | 1980 |

MICHAEL PONZINI

DAN ARNOLD

**Robby Thompson.** Veteran Giants second baseman had his best season, hitting .312 with 19 home runs.

**John Burkett.** Giants righthander teamed with Billy Swift to give team pair of 20-game winners.

| Class | Club | League | W | L | Pct. | Finish* | Manager | First Year |
|---|---|---|---|---|---|---|---|---|
| A | Everett (Wash.) Giants | Northwest | 42 | 34 | .553 | 2nd (8) | Norm Sherry | 1984 |
| Rookie | Scottsdale (Ariz.) Giants | Arizona | 31 | 24 | .564 | 3rd (8) | Alan Bannister | 1991 |

*Finish in overall standings (No. of teams in league)    #Advanced level

# PHOENIX                                                                    AAA
## PACIFIC COAST LEAGUE

| BATTING | AVG | G | AB | R | H | 2B | 3B | HR | RBI | BB | SO | SB | CS | B | T | HT | WT | DOB | 1st Yr | Resides |
|---|---|---|---|---|---|---|---|---|---|---|---|---|---|---|---|---|---|---|---|---|
| Allanson, Andy | .354 | 50 | 161 | 31 | 57 | 15 | 2 | 6 | 23 | 10 | 18 | 7 | 4 | R | R | 6-5 | 225 | 12-22-61 | 1983 | Cleveland, Ohio |
| Bellinger, Clay | .256 | 122 | 407 | 50 | 104 | 20 | 3 | 6 | 49 | 38 | 81 | 7 | 7 | R | R | 6-3 | 195 | 11-18-68 | 1989 | Oneonta, N.Y. |
| Brantley, Mickey | .364 | 65 | 247 | 45 | 90 | 23 | 6 | 8 | 49 | 22 | 22 | 2 | 1 | R | R | 5-10 | 180 | 6-17-61 | 1983 | Port St. Lucie, Fla. |
| Calcagno, Danny | .206 | 16 | 34 | 4 | 7 | 1 | 0 | 0 | 2 | 8 | 8 | 1 | 0 | R | R | 5-9 | 165 | 3-12-68 | 1991 | San Leandro, Calif. |
| Chimelis, Joel | .309 | 80 | 262 | 40 | 81 | 14 | 3 | 13 | 46 | 22 | 41 | 4 | 3 | R | R | 6-0 | 165 | 7-27-67 | 1988 | Brooklyn, N.Y. |
| Colbert, Craig | .222 | 13 | 45 | 5 | 10 | 2 | 1 | 1 | 7 | 0 | 11 | 0 | 0 | R | R | 6-0 | 214 | 2-13-65 | 1986 | Pearland, Texas |
| Davenport, Adell | .300 | 14 | 40 | 5 | 12 | 1 | 0 | 2 | 8 | 3 | 10 | 0 | 1 | R | R | 5-11 | 195 | 7-16-67 | 1988 | Greenville, Miss. |
| Duncan, Andres | .500 | 5 | 4 | 1 | 2 | 0 | 0 | 0 | 0 | 1 | 0 | 0 | 0 | S | R | 5-11 | 155 | 11-30-71 | 1989 | San Pedro de Macoris, D.R. |
| Faneyte, Rikkert | .312 | 115 | 426 | 71 | 133 | 23 | 2 | 11 | 71 | 40 | 72 | 15 | 9 | R | R | 6-1 | 170 | 5-31-69 | 1991 | Amsterdam, Holland |
| Faries, Paul | .303 | 78 | 327 | 56 | 99 | 14 | 5 | 2 | 32 | 22 | 30 | 18 | 11 | R | R | 5-10 | 170 | 2-20-65 | 1987 | San Diego, Calif. |
| Fernandez, Danny | .263 | 42 | 118 | 17 | 31 | 3 | 1 | 0 | 7 | 17 | 24 | 1 | 2 | R | R | 5-11 | 180 | 6-6-66 | 1988 | San Lorenzo, Calif. |
| Hecht, Steve | .314 | 48 | 169 | 27 | 53 | 8 | 1 | 2 | 20 | 20 | 23 | 9 | 1 | L | R | 5-9 | 165 | 11-12-65 | 1988 | Broken Arrow, Okla. |
| Heffernan, Bert | .286 | 16 | 49 | 7 | 14 | 1 | 1 | 0 | 6 | 9 | 11 | 2 | 2 | L | R | 5-10 | 185 | 3-3-65 | 1988 | Stony Brook, N.Y. |
| Hosey, Steve | .292 | 129 | 455 | 70 | 133 | 40 | 4 | 16 | 85 | 66 | 129 | 16 | 10 | R | R | 6-3 | 225 | 4-2-69 | 1989 | Inglewood, Calif. |
| Johnson, Erik | .248 | 101 | 363 | 33 | 90 | 8 | 5 | 0 | 33 | 29 | 51 | 3 | 9 | R | R | 5-11 | 175 | 10-11-65 | 1987 | San Ramon, Calif. |
| Johnson, Juan | .000 | 1 | 4 | 0 | 0 | 0 | 0 | 0 | 0 | 0 | 1 | 0 | 0 | S | R | 5-10 | 167 | 2-1-73 | 1992 | Waldorf, Md. |
| Katzaroff, Robbie | .154 | 9 | 26 | 2 | 4 | 0 | 0 | 0 | 3 | 1 | 4 | 0 | 0 | R | R | 5-8 | 190 | 7-29-68 | 1990 | West Hills, Calif. |
| Martinez, Dave | .467 | 3 | 15 | 4 | 7 | 0 | 0 | 0 | 2 | 1 | 1 | 1 | 0 | L | L | 5-10 | 175 | 9-26-64 | 1983 | Safety Harbor, Fla. |
| McNamara, Jim | .196 | 50 | 158 | 10 | 31 | 5 | 0 | 1 | 23 | 12 | 29 | 1 | 0 | L | R | 6-4 | 220 | 6-10-65 | 1986 | Vienna, Va. |
| Mercedes, Luis | .291 | 70 | 244 | 28 | 71 | 5 | 3 | 0 | 15 | 36 | 30 | 14 | 6 | R | R | 6-3 | 183 | 2-20-68 | 1987 | San Pedro de Macoris, D.R. |
| Mota, Andy | .169 | 29 | 77 | 9 | 13 | 6 | 0 | 0 | 10 | 8 | 17 | 1 | 2 | R | R | 5-10 | 180 | 3-4-66 | 1987 | Glendale, Calif. |
| Murray, Calvin | .316 | 5 | 19 | 4 | 6 | 1 | 1 | 0 | 0 | 2 | 5 | 1 | 1 | R | R | 5-11 | 185 | 7-30-71 | 1992 | Dallas, Texas |
| Peters, Reed | .300 | 96 | 240 | 43 | 72 | 16 | 4 | 5 | 31 | 41 | 18 | 8 | 3 | R | R | 6-1 | 180 | 8-16-65 | 1987 | Las Vegas, Nev. |
| Phillips, J.R. | .263 | 134 | 506 | 80 | 133 | 35 | 2 | 27 | 94 | 53 | 127 | 7 | 5 | L | L | 6-1 | 185 | 4-29-70 | 1988 | Moreno Valley, Calif. |
| Scarsone, Steve | .257 | 19 | 70 | 13 | 18 | 1 | 2 | 3 | 9 | 8 | 21 | 2 | 0 | R | R | 6-2 | 170 | 4-11-66 | 1986 | Anaheim, Calif. |
| Smiley, Reuben | .300 | 99 | 313 | 58 | 94 | 16 | 7 | 7 | 37 | 15 | 67 | 24 | 3 | L | L | 6-4 | 195 | 8-27-68 | 1988 | Los Angeles, Calif. |

| PITCHING | W | L | ERA | G | GS | CG | SV | IP | H | R | ER | BB | SO | B | T | HT | WT | DOB | 1st Yr | Resides |
|---|---|---|---|---|---|---|---|---|---|---|---|---|---|---|---|---|---|---|---|---|
| Bross, Terry | 4 | 4 | 3.97 | 54 | 0 | 0 | 5 | 79 | 76 | 37 | 35 | 37 | 69 | R | R | 6-9 | 230 | 3-30-66 | 1987 | Commack, N.Y. |
| Brown, Kevin | 6 | 10 | 4.94 | 23 | 20 | 0 | 0 | 120 | 134 | 74 | 66 | 60 | 75 | L | L | 6-1 | 185 | 3-5-66 | 1986 | Broderick, Calif. |
| Brummett, Greg | 7 | 7 | 3.62 | 18 | 18 | 1 | 0 | 107 | 114 | 56 | 43 | 27 | 84 | R | R | 6-0 | 180 | 4-20-67 | 1989 | Wichita, Kan. |
| Carlson, Dan | 5 | 6 | 6.56 | 13 | 12 | 0 | 0 | 70 | 79 | 54 | 51 | 32 | 48 | R | R | 6-1 | 185 | 1-26-70 | 1990 | Portland, Ore. |
| Carter, Larry | 3 | 1 | 2.88 | 7 | 7 | 0 | 0 | 34 | 28 | 14 | 11 | 15 | 31 | R | R | 6-5 | 198 | 5-22-65 | 1986 | Haughton, La. |
| Fisher, Brian | 3 | 4 | 8.08 | 14 | 9 | 0 | 0 | 49 | 75 | 52 | 44 | 15 | 25 | R | R | 6-4 | 225 | 3-18-62 | 1980 | Aurora, Colo. |

| PITCHING | W | L | ERA | G | GS | CG | SV | IP | H | R | ER | BB | SO | B | T | HT | WT | DOB | 1st Yr | Resides |
|---|---|---|---|---|---|---|---|---|---|---|---|---|---|---|---|---|---|---|---|---|
| Hanselman, Carl | 2 | 6 | 5.98 | 21 | 13 | 0 | 0 | 87 | 115 | 66 | 58 | 35 | 45 | L | R | 6-5 | 190 | 5-23-70 | 1988 | Shreveport, La. |
| Hartsock, Jeff | 2 | 5 | 5.53 | 12 | 7 | 0 | 0 | 55 | 83 | 36 | 34 | 20 | 35 | R | R | 6-0 | 190 | 11-19-66 | 1988 | Greensboro, N.C. |
| Huisman, Rick | 3 | 4 | 5.97 | 14 | 14 | 0 | 0 | 72 | 78 | 54 | 48 | 45 | 59 | R | R | 6-3 | 200 | 5-17-69 | 1990 | Bensenville, Ill. |
| Layana, Tim | 3 | 2 | 4.81 | 55 | 0 | 0 | 9 | 67 | 80 | 42 | 36 | 24 | 55 | R | R | 6-2 | 190 | 3-2-64 | 1986 | Florence, Ky. |
| McGehee, Kevin | 0 | 3 | 4.91 | 4 | 4 | 0 | 0 | 22 | 28 | 16 | 12 | 8 | 16 | R | R | 6-0 | 190 | 1-18-69 | 1990 | Pineville, La. |
| Minutelli, Gino | 2 | 2 | 4.02 | 49 | 0 | 0 | 11 | 54 | 55 | 28 | 24 | 26 | 57 | L | L | 6-0 | 190 | 5-23-64 | 1985 | Nashville, Tenn. |
| Myers, Jimmy | 2 | 5 | 3.68 | 31 | 3 | 0 | 0 | 59 | 69 | 35 | 24 | 22 | 20 | R | R | 6-1 | 185 | 4-28-69 | 1987 | Crowder, Okla. |
| Peltzer, Kurt | 2 | 0 | 6.75 | 12 | 0 | 0 | 2 | 16 | 16 | 13 | 12 | 7 | 16 | R | L | 6-3 | 190 | 1-13-69 | 1990 | New Berlin, Wis. |
| Rambo, Dan | 1 | 3 | 7.14 | 18 | 5 | 0 | 0 | 52 | 77 | 44 | 41 | 33 | 31 | R | R | 6-0 | 190 | 10-7-66 | 1989 | Sault Ste. Marie, Mich. |
| Taylor, Rob | 10 | 8 | 4.24 | 49 | 12 | 0 | 2 | 144 | 166 | 85 | 68 | 49 | 110 | R | R | 6-3 | 225 | 3-25-66 | 1984 | Dunkirk, Md. |
| Torres, Salomon | 7 | 4 | 3.50 | 14 | 14 | 4 | 0 | 105 | 105 | 43 | 41 | 27 | 99 | R | R | 5-11 | 150 | 3-11-72 | 1990 | San Pedro de Macoris, D.R. |
| Vanlandingham, Bill | 0 | 1 | 6.43 | 1 | 1 | 0 | 0 | 7 | 8 | 6 | 5 | 0 | 2 | R | R | 6-2 | 210 | 7-16-70 | 1991 | Franklin, Tenn. |
| Wassenaar, Rob | 2 | 4 | 5.10 | 21 | 4 | 0 | 1 | 55 | 85 | 33 | 31 | 14 | 41 | R | R | 6-2 | 200 | 4-28-65 | 1987 | Orinda, Calif. |
| 2-team (13 Colo. Spr.) | 2 | 4 | 6.56 | 34 | 4 | 0 | 2 | 70 | 117 | 54 | 51 | 24 | 50 | | | | | | | |

## FIELDING

| Catcher | PCT | G | PO | A | E | DP |
|---|---|---|---|---|---|---|
| Allanson | .983 | 39 | 213 | 20 | 4 | 1 |
| Calcagno | .970 | 15 | 84 | 14 | 3 | 0 |
| Colbert | .982 | 9 | 51 | 5 | 1 | 0 |
| Fernandez | .978 | 41 | 230 | 35 | 6 | 0 |
| Heffernan | .992 | 16 | 112 | 8 | 1 | 2 |
| McNamaara | .976 | 44 | 251 | 30 | 7 | 3 |
| Peters | 1.000 | 1 | 2 | 0 | 0 | 0 |

| First Base | PCT | G | PO | A | E | DP |
|---|---|---|---|---|---|---|
| Allanson | .968 | 3 | 26 | 4 | 1 | 5 |
| Bellinger | 1.000 | 1 | 8 | 1 | 0 | 2 |
| Chimelis | 1.000 | 6 | 32 | 2 | 0 | 6 |
| Colbert | 1.000 | 2 | 20 | 1 | 0 | 6 |
| Davenport | 1.000 | 1 | 12 | 0 | 0 | 3 |
| Hosey | 1.000 | 9 | 62 | 4 | 0 | 7 |
| Peters | .000 | 1 | 0 | 0 | 0 | 0 |
| Phillips | .978 | 129 | 1135 | 93 | 28 | 117 |
| Scarsone | 1.000 | 1 | 7 | 0 | 0 | 1 |

| Second Base | PCT | G | PO | A | E | DP |
|---|---|---|---|---|---|---|
| Chimelis | .978 | 29 | 59 | 72 | 3 | 28 |
| Faries | 1.000 | 21 | 50 | 66 | 0 | 21 |
| Hecht | .976 | 41 | 83 | 123 | 5 | 31 |

| | PCT | G | PO | A | E | DP |
|---|---|---|---|---|---|---|
| E. Johnson | .984 | 45 | 82 | 100 | 3 | 28 |
| Mota | .938 | 21 | 28 | 32 | 4 | 3 |
| Peters | .000 | 1 | 0 | 0 | 0 | 0 |
| Scarsone | .966 | 12 | 22 | 34 | 2 | 5 |

| Third Base | PCT | G | PO | A | E | DP |
|---|---|---|---|---|---|---|
| Allanson | .667 | 1 | 1 | 1 | 1 | 0 |
| Bellinger | .910 | 78 | 43 | 128 | 17 | 18 |
| Calcagno | .000 | 1 | 0 | 0 | 1 | 0 |
| Chimelis | .940 | 46 | 16 | 94 | 7 | 10 |
| Colbert | .833 | 2 | 2 | 3 | 1 | 0 |
| Davenport | .788 | 9 | 10 | 16 | 7 | 1 |
| Faries | 1.000 | 4 | 0 | 14 | 0 | 4 |
| Hecht | 1.000 | 2 | 0 | 1 | 0 | 0 |
| E. Johnson | .885 | 9 | 4 | 193 | 0 | 0 |
| Mota | .333 | 1 | 0 | 1 | 2 | 0 |
| Peters | .875 | 14 | 4 | 24 | 4 | 3 |
| Scarsone | .923 | 4 | 5 | 7 | 1 | 1 |

| Shortstop | PCT | G | PO | A | E | DP |
|---|---|---|---|---|---|---|
| Bellinger | .951 | 53 | 72 | 143 | 11 | 34 |
| Duncan | .500 | 4 | 1 | 0 | 1 | 0 |
| Faries | .987 | 53 | 62 | 164 | 3 | 32 |

| | PCT | G | PO | A | E | DP |
|---|---|---|---|---|---|---|
| E. Johnson | .965 | 52 | 77 | 144 | 8 | 31 |
| J. Johnson | .900 | 1 | 2 | 7 | 1 | 2 |
| Peters | .000 | 1 | 0 | 0 | 0 | 0 |
| Scarsone | 1.000 | 2 | 2 | 7 | 0 | 1 |

| Outfield | PCT | G | PO | A | E | DP |
|---|---|---|---|---|---|---|
| Allanson | .667 | 2 | 3 | 1 | 2 | 0 |
| Brantley | 1.000 | 44 | 72 | 1 | 0 | 0 |
| Chimelis | .500 | 2 | 1 | 0 | 1 | 0 |
| Faneyte | .987 | 104 | 223 | 11 | 3 | 2 |
| Faries | 1.000 | 5 | 9 | 0 | 0 | 0 |
| Hecht | 1.000 | 6 | 8 | 0 | 0 | 0 |
| Hosey | .961 | 107 | 166 | 5 | 7 | 0 |
| Katzaroff | 1.000 | 8 | 16 | 1 | 0 | 1 |
| Martinez | 1.000 | 3 | 5 | 1 | 0 | 0 |
| Mercedes | .924 | 58 | 104 | 6 | 9 | 1 |
| Mota | 1.000 | 6 | 8 | 0 | 0 | 0 |
| Murray | .867 | 5 | 13 | 0 | 2 | 0 |
| Peters | .982 | 72 | 107 | 4 | 2 | 1 |
| Phillips | .750 | 1 | 3 | 0 | 1 | 0 |
| Smiley | .918 | 67 | 88 | 1 | 8 | 0 |

# SHREVEPORT                                           AA
## TEXAS LEAGUE

| BATTING | AVG | G | AB | R | H | 2B | 3B | HR | RBI | BB | SO | SB | CS | B | T | HT | WT | DOB | 1st Yr | Resides |
|---|---|---|---|---|---|---|---|---|---|---|---|---|---|---|---|---|---|---|---|---|
| Bellomo, Kevin, of | .083 | 10 | 12 | 0 | 1 | 0 | 0 | 0 | 1 | 2 | 7 | 0 | 0 | R | L | 6-0 | 195 | 5-21-69 | 1991 | Rutland, Vt. |
| Calcagno, Dan, c | .500 | 3 | 4 | 1 | 2 | 0 | 0 | 0 | 0 | 1 | 1 | 0 | 0 | R | R | 5-9 | 165 | 3-12-68 | 1991 | San Leandro, Calif. |
| Cavanagh, Mike, c | .571 | 4 | 7 | 3 | 4 | 1 | 0 | 1 | 3 | 1 | 2 | 0 | 0 | R | R | 6-0 | 205 | 6-20-70 | 1992 | Baker City, Ore. |
| Chimelis, Joel, 2b-3b | .202 | 36 | 114 | 10 | 23 | 5 | 0 | 6 | 18 | 8 | 14 | 3 | 0 | R | R | 6-0 | 165 | 7-27-67 | 1988 | Brooklyn, N.Y. |
| Christopherson, Eric, c | .152 | 15 | 46 | 5 | 7 | 2 | 0 | 0 | 2 | 9 | 10 | 1 | 1 | R | R | 6-1 | 190 | 4-25-69 | 1990 | Westminster, Calif. |
| Davenport, Adell, 3b-1b | .262 | 103 | 370 | 43 | 97 | 21 | 0 | 15 | 62 | 29 | 73 | 4 | 2 | R | R | 5-11 | 195 | 7-16-67 | 1988 | Greenville, Miss. |
| Davis, Matt, ss-3b | .270 | 131 | 423 | 44 | 114 | 25 | 0 | 4 | 42 | 52 | 64 | 3 | 5 | S | R | 5-8 | 185 | 5-28-68 | 1990 | Chico, Calif. |
| Decillis, Dean, ss | .200 | 2 | 5 | 0 | 1 | 0 | 0 | 0 | 1 | 0 | 0 | 0 | 0 | R | R | 5-11 | 180 | 7-9-67 | 1987 | Pembroke Pines, Fla. |
| Duncan, Andres, ss | .147 | 35 | 75 | 4 | 11 | 2 | 1 | 1 | 9 | 5 | 25 | 2 | 0 | S | R | 5-11 | 155 | 11-30-71 | 1989 | San Pedro de Macoris, D.R. |
| Fernandez, Dan, c | .188 | 48 | 128 | 12 | 24 | 5 | 1 | 1 | 13 | 14 | 32 | 1 | 2 | R | R | 5-11 | 180 | 6-6-66 | 1988 | San Lorenzo, Calif. |
| Florez, Tim, 2b | .255 | 106 | 318 | 33 | 81 | 17 | 2 | 1 | 26 | 16 | 43 | 3 | 5 | R | R | 5-10 | 170 | 7-23-69 | 1991 | Goleta, Calif. |
| Hecht, Steve, 2b-of | .298 | 49 | 168 | 25 | 50 | 8 | 6 | 3 | 11 | 11 | 25 | 5 | 3 | L | R | 5-9 | 165 | 11-12-65 | 1988 | Broken Arrow, Okla. |
| Heffernan, Bert, c | .235 | 33 | 98 | 8 | 23 | 2 | 0 | 0 | 7 | 10 | 14 | 1 | 1 | L | R | 5-10 | 185 | 3-3-65 | 1988 | Stony Brook, N.Y. |
| Hyzdu, Adam, of | .202 | 86 | 302 | 30 | 61 | 17 | 0 | 6 | 25 | 20 | 82 | 0 | 5 | R | R | 6-2 | 210 | 12-6-71 | 1990 | Cincinnati, Ohio |
| Jones, Dax, of | .284 | 118 | 436 | 59 | 124 | 19 | 5 | 4 | 36 | 26 | 53 | 13 | 8 | R | R | 6-0 | 170 | 8-4-70 | 1991 | Waukegan, Ill. |
| Kasper, Kevin, 3b-ss | .215 | 65 | 121 | 13 | 26 | 5 | 0 | 0 | 11 | 14 | 23 | 4 | 2 | R | R | 6-0 | 175 | 7-6-67 | 1989 | Costa Mesa, Calif. |
| Katzaroff, Robbie, of | .300 | 104 | 406 | 52 | 122 | 22 | 4 | 0 | 30 | 35 | 33 | 15 | 13 | R | R | 5-8 | 190 | 7-29-68 | 1990 | West Hills, Calif. |
| McFarlin, Jason, of | .186 | 21 | 59 | 12 | 11 | 2 | 1 | 0 | 1 | 4 | 12 | 4 | 1 | L | L | 6-0 | 175 | 6-28-70 | 1989 | Pensacola, Fla. |

# GIANTS
# TOP
# 10
## PROSPECTS

How the Giants Top 10 prospects, as judged by Baseball America prior to the 1993 season, fared in 1993:

| Player, Pos. | Club (Class) | AVG | AB | H | HR | RBI | SB |
|---|---|---|---|---|---|---|---|
| 1. Calvin Murray, of | San Jose (A) | .281 | 345 | 97 | 9 | 42 | 42 |
| | Shreveport (AA) | .188 | 138 | 26 | 0 | 6 | 12 |
| | Phoenix (AAA) | .316 | 19 | 6 | 0 | 0 | 1 |
| 3. Steve Hosey, of | Phoenix (AAA) | .292 | 455 | 133 | 16 | 85 | 16 |
| | San Francisco | .500 | 2 | 1 | 0 | 1 | 0 |
| 6. Andre Keene, dh | Injured—Did Not Play | | | | | | |
| 8. D.J. Thielen, 3b | Clinton (A) | .231 | 446 | 103 | 15 | 68 | 21 |
| 10. Benji Simonton, of | Clinton (A) | .255 | 310 | 79 | 12 | 49 | 8 |

| | | W | L | ERA | IP | H | BB | SO |
|---|---|---|---|---|---|---|---|---|
| 2. Kevin Rogers, lhp | San Francisco | 2 | 2 | 2.68 | 81 | 71 | 28 | 62 |
| 4. Joe Rosselli, lhp | Shreveport (AA) | 0 | 1 | 3.13 | 23 | 22 | 7 | 19 |
| 5. Salomon Torres, rhp | Shreveport (AA) | 7 | 4 | 2.70 | 83 | 67 | 12 | 67 |
| | Phoenix (AAA) | 7 | 4 | 3.50 | 105 | 105 | 27 | 99 |
| | San Francisco | 3 | 5 | 4.03 | 45 | 37 | 27 | 23 |
| 7. Chris Gambs, rhp | Clinton (A) | 9 | 5 | 4.02 | 112 | 100 | 76 | 82 |
| 9. B. Vanlandingham, rhp | San Jose (A) | 14 | 8 | 5.12 | 163 | 167 | 87 | 171 |

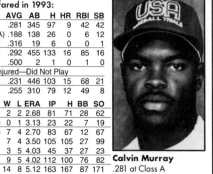

**Calvin Murray**
.281 at Class A

| | San Francisco<br>Majors | Phoenix<br>AAA | Shreveport<br>AA | San Jose<br>A | Clinton<br>A |
|---|---|---|---|---|---|
| C | Kirt Manwaring (130) | Jim McNamara (44) | Roger Miller (58) | Doug Mirabelli (113) | Marcus Jensen (90) |
| 1B | Will Clark (129) | J.R. Phillips (129) | Barry Miller (126) | Troy Clemens (88) | Charles Alimena (100) |
| 2B | Robby Thompson (128) | Erik Johnson (45) | Tim Florez (94) | Chris Wimmer (119) | Tom O'Neill (75) |
| 3B | Matt Williams (144) | Clay Bellinger (78) | Adell Davenport (83) | C.L. Dotolo (49) | D.J. Thielen (116) |
| SS | Royce Clayton (153) | Bellinger/Faries (53) | Matt Davis (113) | Kurt Ehmann (112) | Chad Fonville (119) |
| OF | Barry Bonds (157) | Rikkert Faneyte (109) | Dax Jones (105) | Jason McFarlin (97) | Marvin Benard (111) |
| | Darren Lewis (131) | Steve Hosey (109) | Robbie Katzaroff (103) | Calvin Murray (85) | Tracey Ealy (105) |
| | Willie McGee (126) | Reed Peters (74) | Adam Hyzdu (80) | Ron Pezzoni (79) | Kenny Woods (89) |
| DH | N/A | Michael Brantley (20) | Adell Davenport (11) | Andy Albrecht (40) | Craig Mayes (48) |
| SP | Burkett/Swift (34) | Kevin Brown (20) | Griffiths/Hancock (23) | Bill Vanlandingham (27) | Brewington/Fultz (25) |
| RP | Mike Jackson (81) | Tim Layana (55) | Rich Simon (52) | Charlie Hicks (36) | Castillo/Richey (40) |
| | Full-season farm clubs only | No. of games at position in parenthesis | | | |

| BATTING | AVG | G | AB | R | H | 2B | 3B | HR | RBI | BB | SO | SB | CS | B | T | HT | WT | DOB | 1st Yr | Resides |
|---|---|---|---|---|---|---|---|---|---|---|---|---|---|---|---|---|---|---|---|---|
| Miller, Barry, 1b ............ | .288 | 129 | 452 | 59 | 130 | 30 | 2 | 13 | 82 | 49 | 91 | 5 | 4 | L | L | 6-5 | 210 | 7-10-68 | 1990 | Hampton, Va. |
| Miller, Roger, c ............. | .247 | 61 | 194 | 19 | 48 | 10 | 0 | 2 | 12 | 14 | 24 | 0 | 2 | R | R | 6-0 | 190 | 4-4-67 | 1989 | Sarasota, Fla. |
| Murray, Calvin, of ......... | .188 | 37 | 138 | 15 | 26 | 6 | 0 | 0 | 6 | 14 | 29 | 12 | 6 | R | R | 5-11 | 185 | 7-30-71 | 1992 | Dallas, Texas |
| Ward, Ricky, 3b-2b........ | .256 | 33 | 90 | 8 | 23 | 8 | 0 | 0 | 5 | 7 | 8 | 0 | 1 | R | R | 5-11 | 180 | 8-30-70 | 1990 | Portland, Ore. |
| Weber, Pete, of ............. | .194 | 105 | 278 | 33 | 54 | 14 | 0 | 6 | 27 | 26 | 84 | 7 | 5 | L | L | 5-11 | 165 | 12-15-68 | 1990 | Anaheim, Calif. |

| PITCHING | W | L | ERA | G | GS | CG | SV | IP | H | R | ER | BB | SO | B | T | HT | WT | DOB | 1st Yr | Resides |
|---|---|---|---|---|---|---|---|---|---|---|---|---|---|---|---|---|---|---|---|---|
| Ard, Johnny.................. | 0 | 0 | 0.00 | 3 | 0 | 0 | 0 | 5 | 1 | 0 | 0 | 4 | 0 | R | R | 6-5 | 220 | 6-1-67 | 1988 | Sarasota, Fla. |
| Carlson, Dan................. | 7 | 4 | 2.24 | 15 | 15 | 2 | 0 | 100 | 86 | 30 | 25 | 26 | 81 | R | R | 6-1 | 185 | 1-26-70 | 1990 | Portland, Ore. |
| Gardella, Mike............... | 0 | 0 | 1.04 | 5 | 0 | 0 | 1 | 9 | 4 | 1 | 1 | 3 | 11 | L | L | 5-10 | 195 | 1-18-67 | 1989 | Sapulpa, Okla. |
| Griffiths, Brian.............. | 5 | 11 | 4.85 | 24 | 23 | 1 | 0 | 134 | 152 | 85 | 72 | 68 | 83 | R | R | 6-2 | 190 | 5-29-68 | 1988 | Milwaukie, Ore. |
| Hancock, Chris ............. | 8 | 8 | 4.06 | 23 | 23 | 0 | 0 | 124 | 126 | 71 | 56 | 52 | 93 | L | L | 6-3 | 205 | 9-12-69 | 1988 | Riverside, Calif. |
| Hanselman, Carl.......... | 1 | 5 | 2.91 | 15 | 6 | 0 | 2 | 56 | 54 | 23 | 18 | 13 | 36 | L | R | 6-5 | 190 | 5-23-70 | 1988 | Shreveport, La. |
| Hyde, Rich ................... | 1 | 1 | 7.78 | 6 | 3 | 0 | 0 | 20 | 33 | 17 | 17 | 2 | 14 | R | R | 6-0 | 175 | 12-24-68 | 1991 | Champaign, Ill. |
| Jones, Stacy ............... | 4 | 1 | 3.58 | 24 | 2 | 0 | 1 | 50 | 53 | 21 | 20 | 19 | 28 | R | R | 6-6 | 225 | 5-26-67 | 1988 | Attalla, Ala. |
| Masters, Dave ............. | 0 | 2 | 1.07 | 14 | 0 | 0 | 2 | 25 | 21 | 8 | 3 | 15 | 25 | R | R | 6-9 | 225 | 8-13-64 | 1985 | Honolulu, Hawaii |
| Myers, Jim .................. | 2 | 2 | 2.01 | 29 | 0 | 0 | 1 | 49 | 50 | 14 | 11 | 19 | 23 | R | R | 6-1 | 185 | 4-28-69 | 1987 | Crowder, Okla. |
| Peltzer, Kurt ............... | 4 | 3 | 3.19 | 30 | 0 | 0 | 1 | 42 | 33 | 16 | 15 | 9 | 28 | R | L | 6-3 | 190 | 1-13-69 | 1990 | New Berlin, Wis. |
| Pote, Lou .................... | 8 | 7 | 4.07 | 19 | 19 | 0 | 0 | 108 | 111 | 53 | 49 | 45 | 81 | R | R | 6-3 | 190 | 8-27-71 | 1991 | Chicago, Ill. |
| Rambo, Dan ................ | 7 | 5 | 3.18 | 15 | 15 | 1 | 0 | 102 | 98 | 46 | 36 | 27 | 61 | R | R | 6-0 | 190 | 10-7-66 | 1989 | Sault Ste. Marie, Mich. |
| Rosselli, Joe ............... | 0 | 1 | 3.13 | 4 | 4 | 0 | 0 | 23 | 22 | 9 | 8 | 7 | 19 | R | L | 6-1 | 170 | 5-28-72 | 1990 | Woodland Hills, Calif. |
| Simon, Rich ................ | 2 | 7 | 4.33 | 52 | 0 | 0 | 26 | 54 | 56 | 32 | 26 | 24 | 38 | R | R | 6-2 | 200 | 11-29-65 | 1986 | Brooklyn, N.Y. |
| Smith, Shad ................ | 6 | 3 | 3.76 | 24 | 13 | 0 | 0 | 96 | 95 | 43 | 40 | 37 | 65 | R | R | 6-4 | 220 | 5-21-67 | 1990 | League City, Texas |
| Torres, Salomon ........... | 7 | 4 | 2.70 | 12 | 12 | 2 | 0 | 83 | 67 | 27 | 25 | 12 | 67 | R | R | 5-11 | 150 | 3-11-72 | 1990 | San Pedro de Macoris, D.R. |
| Vanderweele, Doug.... | 0 | 0 | 0.00 | 1 | 0 | 0 | 0 | 2 | 0 | 0 | 0 | 0 | 1 | R | R | 6-3 | 200 | 3-18-70 | 1991 | Las Vegas, Nev. |
| Whitaker, Steve .......... | 1 | 0 | 1.08 | 4 | 1 | 0 | 0 | 8 | 5 | 1 | 1 | 7 | 12 | L | L | 6-6 | 225 | 4-15-70 | 1991 | Atwater, Calif. |
| Yockey, Mark ................ | 3 | 6 | 2.13 | 48 | 0 | 0 | 4 | 72 | 60 | 23 | 17 | 20 | 60 | L | L | 6-3 | 200 | 5-25-68 | 1990 | Woodinville, Wash. |

# SAN JOSE     A

## CALIFORNIA LEAGUE

| BATTING | AVG | G | AB | R | H | 2B | 3B | HR | RBI | BB | SO | SB | CS | B | T | HT | WT | DOB | 1st Yr | Resides |
|---|---|---|---|---|---|---|---|---|---|---|---|---|---|---|---|---|---|---|---|---|
| Albrecht, Andy, dh-of.... | .259 | 76 | 239 | 33 | 62 | 13 | 4 | 2 | 32 | 29 | 42 | 6 | 7 | L | R | 6-1 | 195 | 10-13-68 | 1991 | Cherry Hill, N.J. |
| Bellomo, Kevin, of ........ | .235 | 33 | 102 | 7 | 24 | 2 | 2 | 1 | 15 | 12 | 22 | 1 | 1 | R | L | 6-0 | 195 | 5-21-69 | 1991 | Rutland, Vt. |
| Benjamin, Mike, ss-2b.. | .000 | 2 | 8 | 1 | 0 | 0 | 0 | 0 | 0 | 1 | 0 | 0 | 0 | R | R | 6-0 | 169 | 11-22-65 | 1987 | Chandler, Ariz. |
| Calcagno, Dan, c.......... | .250 | 25 | 64 | 10 | 16 | 1 | 0 | 0 | 6 | 11 | 8 | 1 | 1 | R | R | 5-9 | 165 | 3-12-68 | 1991 | San Leandro, Calif. |
| Casper, Tim, 2b............ | .143 | 13 | 21 | 3 | 3 | 0 | 1 | 0 | 5 | 10 | 0 | 3 | S | R | 5-8 | 160 | 12-8-68 | 1991 | Pittsburg, Kan. |
| Clemens, Troy, 1b........ | .291 | 96 | 306 | 36 | 89 | 15 | 1 | 0 | 31 | 35 | 34 | 1 | 1 | L | R | 6-1 | 195 | 1-12-68 | 1988 | Boulder City, Nev. |
| Cookson, Brent, of ....... | .256 | 67 | 234 | 43 | 60 | 10 | 1 | 17 | 50 | 43 | 73 | 14 | 6 | R | R | 5-11 | 200 | 9-7-69 | 1991 | Santa Paula, Calif. |
| Dotolo, C.L., 3b ........... | .197 | 58 | 157 | 17 | 31 | 9 | 0 | 0 | 22 | 23 | 36 | 1 | 3 | R | R | 5-11 | 175 | 10-1-68 | 1991 | Norfolk, Va. |
| Duncan, Andres, ss-3b . | .225 | 36 | 111 | 17 | 25 | 1 | 2 | 1 | 12 | 12 | 28 | 14 | 3 | S | R | 5-11 | 155 | 11-30-71 | 1989 | San Pedro de Macoris, D.R. |
| Ehmann, Kurt, ss.......... | .262 | 123 | 439 | 81 | 115 | 20 | 1 | 5 | 57 | 75 | 69 | 12 | 9 | R | R | 6-1 | 185 | 8-18-70 | 1992 | Ukiah, Calif. |
| Hyzdu, Adam, of........... | .291 | 44 | 165 | 35 | 48 | 11 | 3 | 13 | 38 | 29 | 53 | 1 | 1 | R | R | 6-2 | 210 | 12-6-71 | 1990 | Cincinnati, Ohio |
| Jenkins, Brett, dh-3b .... | .233 | 52 | 189 | 25 | 44 | 11 | 0 | 7 | 25 | 16 | 25 | 1 | 0 | R | R | 6-1 | 195 | 4-5-70 | 1991 | Rancho Cordova, Calif. |
| King, Clay, 1b-3b.......... | .303 | 51 | 188 | 27 | 57 | 9 | 0 | 5 | 33 | 20 | 34 | 0 | 1 | R | R | 6-1 | 190 | 6-15-70 | 1992 | Houston, Texas |
| McFarlin, Jason, of ........ | .311 | 97 | 395 | 71 | 123 | 20 | 4 | 7 | 53 | 29 | 67 | 49 | 10 | L | L | 6-0 | 175 | 6-28-70 | 1989 | Pensacola, Fla. |
| Mirabelli, Doug, c ......... | .270 | 113 | 371 | 58 | 100 | 19 | 2 | 1 | 48 | 72 | 55 | 0 | 4 | R | R | 6-1 | 205 | 10-18-70 | 1992 | Las Vegas, Nev. |
| Montgomery, Don, 1b .... | .167 | 34 | 96 | 8 | 16 | 2 | 0 | 1 | 9 | 10 | 38 | 0 | 0 | R | R | 6-2 | 195 | 8-27-69 | 1991 | Seattle, Wash. |
| Murray, Calvin, of ........ | .281 | 85 | 345 | 61 | 97 | 24 | 1 | 9 | 42 | 40 | 63 | 42 | 10 | R | R | 5-11 | 185 | 7-30-71 | 1992 | Dallas, Texas |
| O'Neill, Tom, 3b-2b ....... | .000 | 2 | 5 | 0 | 0 | 0 | 0 | 0 | 0 | 0 | 2 | 0 | 0 | R | R | 5-11 | 170 | 6-14-70 | 1992 | Tinley Park, Ill. |
| Patterson, John, dh-2b.. | .235 | 16 | 68 | 8 | 16 | 7 | 0 | 1 | 14 | 7 | 12 | 6 | 5 | S | R | 5-9 | 180 | 2-11-67 | 1988 | Phoenix, Ariz. |
| Pezzoni, Ron, of........... | .256 | 100 | 340 | 51 | 87 | 18 | 0 | 5 | 53 | 50 | 42 | 11 | 5 | R | R | 6-0 | 180 | 8-22-67 | 1990 | Ypsilanti, Mich. |
| Reed, Jeff, c ................ | .500 | 4 | 10 | 2 | 5 | 1 | 0 | 0 | 2 | 1 | 0 | 0 | 0 | L | R | 6-2 | 190 | 11-12-62 | 1980 | Elizabethton, Tenn. |
| Reid, Derek, dh-of........ | .188 | 29 | 80 | 9 | 15 | 1 | 1 | 0 | 8 | 6 | 16 | 5 | 2 | R | R | 6-3 | 195 | 2-4-70 | 1990 | Cincinnati, Ohio |
| Ward, Ricky, 3b-2b........ | .182 | 41 | 143 | 17 | 26 | 4 | 0 | 0 | 12 | 13 | 14 | 2 | 2 | R | R | 5-11 | 180 | 8-30-70 | 1990 | Portland, Ore. |
| Wimmer, Chris, 2b ........ | .264 | 123 | 493 | 76 | 130 | 21 | 4 | 3 | 53 | 42 | 72 | 49 | 12 | R | R | 5-11 | 170 | 9-25-70 | 1992 | Wichita, Kan. |

| PITCHING | W | L | ERA | G | GS | CG | SV | IP | H | R | ER | BB | SO | B | T | HT | WT | DOB | 1st Yr | Resides |
|---|---|---|---|---|---|---|---|---|---|---|---|---|---|---|---|---|---|---|---|---|
| Alvarez, Ivan ............... | 3 | 4 | 5.32 | 10 | 9 | 0 | 0 | 44 | 34 | 28 | 26 | 42 | 32 | L | L | 6-3 | 220 | 5-19-70 | 1993 | Canoga Park, Calif. |
| Black, Bud.................... | 0 | 0 | 9.00 | 1 | 1 | 0 | 0 | 3 | 2 | 1 | 1 | 0 | 2 | L | L | 6-2 | 185 | 6-30-57 | 1979 | San Diego, Calif. |
| Crowe, Ron.................. | 2 | 0 | 1.84 | 8 | 0 | 0 | 0 | 15 | 11 | 5 | 3 | 5 | 8 | R | R | 6-0 | 175 | 7-6-68 | 1989 | Caldwell, Idaho |
| Dour, Brian.................. | 4 | 0 | 1.52 | 18 | 0 | 0 | 10 | 30 | 21 | 5 | 5 | 6 | 16 | R | R | 6-3 | 205 | 1-8-67 | 1989 | Virginia, Ill. |
| Heckman, Andy ............ | 5 | 1 | 2.44 | 30 | 0 | 0 | 7 | 59 | 45 | 20 | 16 | 23 | 40 | R | L | 6-3 | 185 | 10-17-71 | 1992 | Pine Bush, N.Y. |
| Hicks, Charlie .............. | 5 | 4 | 5.27 | 36 | 0 | 0 | 7 | 68 | 63 | 48 | 40 | 42 | 48 | R | R | 6-7 | 230 | 6-20-69 | 1992 | Gadsden, Ala. |
| Huisman, Rich ............. | 2 | 1 | 2.31 | 4 | 4 | 1 | 0 | 23 | 19 | 6 | 6 | 9 | 18 | R | R | 6-3 | 190 | 5-17-69 | 1990 | Bensenville, Ill. |
| Hyde, Rich .................. | 2 | 0 | 4.79 | 23 | 1 | 0 | 2 | 47 | 59 | 31 | 25 | 14 | 34 | R | R | 6-0 | 175 | 12-24-68 | 1991 | Champaign, Ill. |
| McLeod, Brian .............. | 0 | 2 | 7.23 | 12 | 0 | 0 | 0 | 19 | 12 | 16 | 15 | 27 | 14 | R | R | 6-0 | 190 | 8-1-69 | 1990 | Huntington Beach, Calif. |

# GIANTS: ORGANIZATION LEADERS

Darren Lewis
Swiped 46 bases

DAN ARNOLD

## MAJOR LEAGUERS

**BATTING**
| | | |
|---|---|---|
| *AVG | Barry Bonds | .336 |
| R | Barry Bonds | 129 |
| H | Barry Bonds | 181 |
| TB | Barry Bonds | 365 |
| 2B | Barry Bonds | 38 |
| 3B | Darren Lewis | 7 |
| HR | Barry Bonds | 46 |
| RBI | Barry Bonds | 123 |
| BB | Barry Bonds | 126 |
| SO | Robby Thompson | 97 |
| SB | Darren Lewis | 46 |

**PITCHING**
| | | |
|---|---|---|
| W | John Burkett | 22 |
| L | Billy Swift | 8 |
| #ERA | Rod Beck | 2.16 |
| G | Mike Jackson | 81 |
| CG | John Burkett | 2 |
| SV | Rod Beck | 48 |
| IP | Billy Swift | 233 |
| BB | Billy Swift | 55 |
| SO | Billy Swift | 157 |

## MINOR LEAGUERS

**BATTING**
| | | |
|---|---|---|
| *AVG | Rikkert Faneyte, Phoenix | .312 |
| R | Marvin Benard, Clinton | 84 |
| H | Chad Fonville, Clinton | 137 |
| TB | J.R. Phillips, Phoenix | 253 |
| 2B | Steve Hosey, Phoenix | 40 |
| 3B | Chad Fonville, Clinton | 10 |
| HR | J.R. Phillips, Phoenix | 27 |
| RBI | J.R. Phillips, Phoenix | 94 |
| BB | Kurt Ehmann, San Jose | 75 |
| SO | Adam Hyzdu, Shreveport-San Jose | 135 |
| SB | Calvin Murray, San Jose-Shreve.-Phx. | 55 |

**PITCHING**
| | | |
|---|---|---|
| W | Two tied at | 14 |
| L | Brian Griffiths, Shreveport | 11 |
| #ERA | Kris Franko, Everett | 1.47 |
| G | Jeff Richey, Clinton-San Jose | 61 |
| CG | Salomon Torres, Phoenix-Shreveport | 6 |
| SV | Jeff Richey, Clinton-San Jose | 32 |
| IP | Salomon Torres, Phoenix-Shreveport | 189 |
| BB | Steve Whitaker, San Jose-Shreveport | 121 |
| SO | Bill Vanlandingham, San Jose-Phoenix | 173 |

*Minimum 250 At-Bats   #Minimum 75 Innings

| PITCHING | W | L | ERA | G | GS | CG | SV | IP | H | R | ER | BB | SO | B | T | HT | WT | DOB | 1st Yr | Resides |
|---|---|---|---|---|---|---|---|---|---|---|---|---|---|---|---|---|---|---|---|---|
| Myers, Jeff | 3 | 2 | 5.17 | 5 | 5 | 0 | 0 | 31 | 38 | 21 | 18 | 19 | 16 | R | L | 6-0 | 190 | 11-13-71 | 1992 | Carlsbad, Calif. |
| Peltzer, Kurt | 2 | 3 | 2.93 | 17 | 0 | 0 | 3 | 28 | 28 | 16 | 9 | 8 | 20 | R | L | 6-3 | 190 | 1-13-69 | 1990 | New Berlin, Wis. |
| Peterson, Mark | 4 | 1 | 3.43 | 37 | 7 | 1 | 0 | 81 | 95 | 36 | 31 | 15 | 45 | L | L | 5-11 | 195 | 11-27-70 | 1992 | Clinton, Wash. |
| Richey, Jeff | 3 | 1 | 3.41 | 21 | 0 | 0 | 4 | 29 | 34 | 13 | 11 | 11 | 30 | R | R | 6-0 | 175 | 9-30-69 | 1992 | Monroe, La. |
| Stonecipher, Eric | 5 | 7 | 5.91 | 26 | 15 | 0 | 0 | 116 | 146 | 94 | 76 | 71 | 69 | R | R | 6-5 | 195 | 12-10-69 | 1991 | Rapid City, S.D. |
| Vanderweele, Doug | 10 | 6 | 3.89 | 25 | 24 | 3 | 0 | 171 | 188 | 78 | 74 | 55 | 106 | R | R | 6-3 | 200 | 3-18-70 | 1991 | Las Vegas, Nev. |
| Vanlandingham, Bill | 14 | 8 | 5.12 | 27 | 27 | 1 | 0 | 163 | 167 | 103 | 93 | 87 | 171 | R | R | 6-2 | 210 | 7-16-70 | 1991 | Franklin, Tenn. |
| Wanke, Chuck | 6 | 7 | 5.08 | 27 | 20 | 0 | 2 | 131 | 137 | 91 | 74 | 75 | 98 | R | L | 6-5 | 200 | 2-2-71 | 1990 | Beaverton, Ore. |
| Whitaker, Steve | 8 | 10 | 3.82 | 22 | 21 | 1 | 0 | 127 | 106 | 70 | 54 | 114 | 94 | L | L | 6-6 | 225 | 4-15-70 | 1991 | Atwater, Calif. |
| Wilson, Trevor | 1 | 0 | 0.00 | 2 | 2 | 0 | 0 | 10 | 4 | 0 | 0 | 3 | 8 | L | L | 6-0 | 204 | 6-7-66 | 1985 | Scottsdale, Ariz. |

# CLINTON                                                                                                      A

## MIDWEST LEAGUE

| BATTING | AVG | G | AB | R | H | 2B | 3B | HR | RBI | BB | SO | SB | CS | B | T | HT | WT | DOB | 1st Yr | Resides |
|---|---|---|---|---|---|---|---|---|---|---|---|---|---|---|---|---|---|---|---|---|
| Alimena, Charles, 1b | .249 | 110 | 309 | 36 | 77 | 12 | 0 | 7 | 44 | 38 | 77 | 2 | 5 | L | L | 6-3 | 195 | 1-21-72 | 1990 | Sacramento, Calif. |
| Bellomo, Kevin, of | .254 | 24 | 67 | 10 | 17 | 3 | 0 | 0 | 5 | 10 | 6 | 3 | 0 | R | L | 6-0 | 195 | 5-21-69 | 1991 | Rutland, Vt. |
| Benard, Marvin, of | .301 | 112 | 349 | 84 | 105 | 14 | 2 | 5 | 50 | 56 | 66 | 42 | 10 | L | L | 5-10 | 180 | 1-20-71 | 1992 | Cudahy, Calif. |
| Cavanah, Mike, c | .241 | 39 | 87 | 13 | 21 | 5 | 0 | 4 | 16 | 15 | 30 | 0 | 1 | R | R | 6-0 | 205 | 6-20-70 | 1992 | Baker City, Ore. |
| Ealy, Tracey, of | .253 | 122 | 396 | 60 | 100 | 13 | 5 | 8 | 65 | 36 | 93 | 24 | 12 | S | R | 5-11 | 180 | 7-8-71 | 1989 | Las Vegas, Nev. |
| Fonville, Chad, ss | .306 | 120 | 447 | 80 | 137 | 16 | 10 | 1 | 44 | 40 | 48 | 52 | 16 | S | R | 5-6 | 155 | 3-5-71 | 1992 | Midway Park, N.C. |
| Jensen, Marcus, c | .262 | 104 | 324 | 53 | 85 | 24 | 2 | 11 | 56 | 66 | 98 | 1 | 2 | S | R | 6-4 | 195 | 12-14-72 | 1990 | Oakland, Calif. |
| King, Clay, 1b-3b | .214 | 39 | 126 | 14 | 27 | 5 | 0 | 1 | 16 | 7 | 19 | 0 | 0 | R | R | 6-1 | 190 | 6-15-70 | 1992 | Houston, Texas |
| Mayes, Craig, dh-c | .296 | 75 | 226 | 25 | 67 | 12 | 1 | 3 | 37 | 10 | 52 | 1 | 0 | L | R | 5-10 | 195 | 5-8-70 | 1992 | Rochester Hills, Mich. |
| Miller, Roger, c | .192 | 10 | 26 | 1 | 5 | 0 | 0 | 1 | 4 | 2 | 3 | 0 | 0 | R | R | 6-0 | 190 | 4-4-67 | 1989 | Sarasota, Fla. |
| O'Neill, Tom, 2b-3b | .247 | 88 | 215 | 41 | 53 | 13 | 3 | 4 | 34 | 40 | 46 | 6 | 3 | R | R | 5-11 | 170 | 6-14-70 | 1992 | Tinley Park, Ill. |
| Petering, Todd, of | .146 | 27 | 48 | 9 | 7 | 0 | 0 | 0 | 2 | 8 | 17 | 1 | 1 | L | R | 6-0 | 180 | 6-23-71 | 1993 | Elizabethtown, Kan. |
| Ramos, Papo, of-dh | .308 | 3 | 13 | 2 | 4 | 0 | 0 | 0 | 0 | 3 | 0 | 0 | 0 | R | R | 5-11 | 185 | 12-27-69 | 1992 | Carencro, La. |
| Reid, Derek, dh-of | .298 | 15 | 57 | 5 | 17 | 2 | 0 | 0 | 7 | 1 | 6 | 3 | 2 | R | R | 6-3 | 195 | 2-4-70 | 1990 | Cincinnati, Ohio |
| Roach, Petie, of-1b | .174 | 28 | 92 | 8 | 16 | 3 | 0 | 1 | 7 | 13 | 26 | 0 | 1 | L | L | 6-2 | 170 | 9-19-70 | 1992 | Redding, Calif. |
| Saugstad, Mark, 3b-dh | .111 | 5 | 9 | 0 | 1 | 0 | 0 | 0 | 0 | 4 | 0 | 0 | 0 | R | R | 6-4 | 210 | 11-6-70 | 1992 | Apple Valley, Calif. |
| Sbrocco, Jon, 2b | .268 | 56 | 179 | 28 | 48 | 6 | 2 | 0 | 17 | 29 | 31 | 8 | 6 | L | R | 5-10 | 165 | 1-5-71 | 1993 | Willoughby Hills, Ohio |
| Simonton, Benji, of | .255 | 100 | 310 | 52 | 79 | 18 | 4 | 12 | 49 | 40 | 112 | 8 | 7 | R | R | 6-1 | 225 | 5-5-72 | 1992 | Pittsburg, Calif. |
| Stasio, Chris, 1b | .188 | 31 | 69 | 8 | 13 | 0 | 0 | 1 | 5 | 2 | 31 | 0 | 2 | R | R | 6-2 | 200 | 6-21-71 | 1993 | Lauderhill, Fla. |
| Thielen, D.J., 3b | .231 | 124 | 446 | 72 | 103 | 18 | 3 | 15 | 68 | 29 | 125 | 21 | 6 | R | R | 6-2 | 185 | 8-5-71 | 1991 | Portland, Ore. |
| Thomas, Gene, of | .203 | 28 | 59 | 12 | 12 | 1 | 0 | 1 | 9 | 13 | 10 | 2 | 1 | S | R | 5-11 | 175 | 8-18-70 | 1993 | Columbia, Md. |
| Wong, Kevin, 2b | .156 | 30 | 77 | 10 | 12 | 4 | 1 | 0 | 3 | 6 | 13 | 0 | 2 | R | R | 5-10 | 175 | 8-24-69 | 1991 | Honolulu, Hawaii |
| Woods, Kenny, of-ss | .281 | 108 | 320 | 56 | 90 | 10 | 1 | 4 | 44 | 41 | 55 | 30 | 5 | R | R | 5-9 | 173 | 8-2-70 | 1992 | Los Angeles, Calif. |

| PITCHING | W | L | ERA | G | GS | CG | SV | IP | H | R | ER | BB | SO | B | T | HT | WT | DOB | 1st Yr | Resides |
|---|---|---|---|---|---|---|---|---|---|---|---|---|---|---|---|---|---|---|---|---|
| Baine, David | 0 | 1 | 10.97 | 3 | 3 | 0 | 0 | 11 | 16 | 13 | 13 | 9 | 6 | S | L | 6-5 | 200 | 12-24-69 | 1992 | Novato, Calif. |
| Brewington, Jamie | 8 | 9 | 4.78 | 26 | 25 | 1 | 0 | 134 | 126 | 78 | 71 | 61 | 111 | R | R | 6-4 | 180 | 9-28-71 | 1992 | Greenville, N.C. |
| Castillo, Mariano | 4 | 2 | 3.39 | 40 | 0 | 0 | 6 | 69 | 64 | 31 | 26 | 19 | 59 | R | R | 6-0 | 168 | 3-17-71 | 1990 | Boca Chica, D.R. |
| Crowe, Ron | 4 | 3 | 3.13 | 33 | 1 | 0 | 8 | 60 | 56 | 34 | 21 | 17 | 52 | R | R | 6-0 | 175 | 7-6-68 | 1989 | Caldwell, Idaho |
| Fultz, Aaron | 14 | 8 | 3.41 | 26 | 25 | 2 | 0 | 148 | 132 | 63 | 56 | 64 | 144 | L | L | 5-11 | 195 | 9-4-73 | 1992 | Munford, Tenn. |
| Gambs, Chris | 9 | 5 | 4.02 | 21 | 21 | 0 | 0 | 112 | 100 | 56 | 50 | 76 | 82 | R | R | 6-2 | 210 | 10-26-73 | 1991 | Richmond, Calif. |
| Grande, Marc | 0 | 0 | 7.71 | 2 | 0 | 0 | 0 | 2 | 3 | 4 | 2 | 3 | 1 | R | R | 5-10 | 180 | 1-30-71 | 1993 | Rome, N.Y. |
| Heckman, Andy | 2 | 1 | 1.74 | 11 | 1 | 0 | 0 | 21 | 18 | 6 | 4 | 4 | 24 | R | L | 6-3 | 185 | 10-17-71 | 1992 | Pine Bush, N.Y. |
| Henrikson, Dan | 3 | 2 | 2.65 | 12 | 4 | 0 | 0 | 34 | 27 | 14 | 10 | 17 | 27 | L | L | 6-0 | 180 | 9-12-68 | 1989 | Everett, Wash. |
| Locklear, Jeff | 7 | 2 | 3.07 | 28 | 10 | 0 | 0 | 108 | 103 | 51 | 37 | 44 | 90 | L | L | 6-4 | 210 | 2-6-70 | 1991 | Glen Burnie, Md. |
| McLain, Mike | 4 | 3 | 2.93 | 36 | 1 | 0 | 7 | 74 | 66 | 36 | 24 | 23 | 78 | R | R | 6-2 | 190 | 3-18-70 | 1992 | Elk Grove, Calif. |
| Myers, Jason | 0 | 0 | .00 | 1 | 0 | 0 | 0 | 3 | 0 | 0 | 0 | 2 | 5 | L | L | 6-4 | 210 | 9-19-73 | 1993 | Fontana, Calif. |
| Myers, Jeff | 8 | 6 | 2.71 | 18 | 18 | 2 | 0 | 100 | 83 | 41 | 30 | 57 | 91 | R | L | 6-0 | 190 | 11-13-71 | 1992 | Carlsbad, Calif. |
| Richey, Jeff | 2 | 1 | 1.03 | 40 | 0 | 0 | 8 | 52 | 19 | 7 | 6 | 17 | 75 | R | R | 6-0 | 175 | 9-30-69 | 1992 | Monroe, La. |
| Rosenbohm, Jim | 6 | 8 | 4.89 | 23 | 23 | 1 | 0 | 107 | 98 | 74 | 58 | 86 | 91 | R | R | 6-1 | 190 | 9-19-73 | 1992 | Omaha, Neb. |
| Valdez, Carlos | 4 | 7 | 3.99 | 35 | 2 | 0 | 3 | 90 | 74 | 47 | 40 | 44 | 85 | R | R | 5-11 | 165 | 12-26-71 | 1990 | Bani, D.R. |

## NORTHWEST LEAGUE

| BATTING | AVG | G | AB | R | H | 2B | 3B | HR | RBI | BB | SO | SB | CS | B | T | HT | WT | DOB | 1st Yr | Resides |
|---|---|---|---|---|---|---|---|---|---|---|---|---|---|---|---|---|---|---|---|---|
| Barrett, Scott, c | .259 | 35 | 108 | 14 | 28 | 6 | 1 | 2 | 21 | 10 | 20 | 0 | 0 | R | R | 6-1 | 210 | 11-15-70 | 1993 | Oregon, Ohio |
| Cecere, Michael, c | .218 | 47 | 133 | 19 | 29 | 3 | 1 | 4 | 18 | 41 | 27 | 2 | 0 | R | R | 6-0 | 195 | 12-5-70 | 1993 | Lakeland, Fla. |
| Davis, Melvin, of | .146 | 26 | 96 | 12 | 14 | 1 | 0 | 2 | 9 | 12 | 29 | 9 | 3 | R | R | 5-10 | 165 | 10-15-71 | 1991 | San Pedro de Macoris, D.R. |
| Gulseth, Mark, dh-1b | .240 | 60 | 196 | 29 | 47 | 10 | 0 | 7 | 35 | 36 | 50 | 0 | 1 | L | R | 6-4 | 200 | 11-12-71 | 1993 | Callaway, Minn. |
| Gump, Chris, 2b | .253 | 21 | 75 | 4 | 19 | 3 | 0 | 0 | 4 | 4 | 18 | 0 | 4 | R | R | 5-11 | 195 | 10-14-70 | 1993 | Phoenix, Ariz. |
| Hartwell, Ed, of | .226 | 32 | 93 | 17 | 21 | 5 | 1 | 3 | 14 | 26 | 18 | 2 | 1 | L | R | 6-0 | 200 | 8-14-71 | 1993 | Fort Worth, Texas |
| King, Brett, ss | .226 | 69 | 243 | 43 | 55 | 10 | 0 | 2 | 24 | 40 | 63 | 26 | 11 | R | R | 6-1 | 180 | 7-20-72 | 1993 | Apopka, Fla. |
| Lootens, Brian, of | .216 | 40 | 125 | 17 | 27 | 5 | 0 | 1 | 11 | 11 | 35 | 4 | 3 | L | R | 6-0 | 185 | 1-19-71 | 1993 | Phoenix, Ariz. |
| Mason, Andy, of | .143 | 7 | 7 | 3 | 1 | 0 | 0 | 0 | 0 | 0 | 5 | 0 | 0 | R | R | 6-2 | 235 | 8-31-71 | 1993 | Longview, Wash. |
| Mueller, Bill, 2b | .300 | 58 | 200 | 31 | 60 | 8 | 2 | 1 | 24 | 42 | 17 | 13 | 6 | S | R | 5-11 | 173 | 3-17-71 | 1993 | Maryland Heights, Mo. |
| Phillips, Gary, 3b-dh | .239 | 54 | 180 | 24 | 43 | 8 | 0 | 7 | 31 | 25 | 45 | 4 | 4 | R | R | 5-11 | 165 | 9-25-71 | 1992 | Tullahoma, Tenn. |
| Reynolds, Chance, c | .231 | 12 | 26 | 3 | 6 | 0 | 0 | 1 | 2 | 10 | 0 | 0 | 5 | S | R | 5-10 | 185 | 9-16-71 | 1993 | Byromville, Ga. |
| Roach, Petie, 1b-of | .264 | 76 | 284 | 37 | 75 | 10 | 2 | 2 | 32 | 54 | 76 | 3 | 2 | L | L | 6-2 | 170 | 9-19-70 | 1992 | Redding, Calif. |
| Sbrocco, Jon, 2b | .333 | 2 | 3 | 0 | 1 | 0 | 0 | 0 | 0 | 0 | 0 | 0 | 0 | L | R | 5-10 | 165 | 1-5-71 | 1993 | Willoughby Hills, Ohio |
| Singleton, Chris, of | .265 | 58 | 219 | 39 | 58 | 14 | 4 | 3 | 18 | 18 | 46 | 14 | 3 | L | L | 6-2 | 195 | 8-15-72 | 1993 | Hercules, Calif. |
| Stafford, Mitch, 2b | .176 | 16 | 34 | 6 | 6 | 0 | 0 | 0 | 3 | 4 | 12 | 1 | 0 | L | R | 5-11 | 170 | 1-7-72 | 1992 | Swainsboro, Ga. |
| Stasio, Chris, 1b | .000 | 1 | 3 | 0 | 0 | 0 | 0 | 0 | 0 | 0 | 1 | 0 | 0 | R | R | 6-2 | 200 | 6-21-71 | 1993 | Lauderhill, Fla. |
| Tessicini, David, ss-dh | .292 | 27 | 65 | 13 | 19 | 3 | 0 | 1 | 7 | 9 | 13 | 3 | 3 | L | R | 6-0 | 185 | 8-21-72 | 1993 | Milford, Mass. |
| Thomas, Gene, dh | .170 | 17 | 53 | 6 | 9 | 1 | 0 | 1 | 3 | 10 | 16 | 6 | 4 | S | R | 5-11 | 175 | 8-18-70 | 1993 | Columbia, Md. |
| Williams, Keith, of | .302 | 85 | 288 | 57 | 87 | 21 | 5 | 12 | 48 | 73 | 21 | 7 | | R | R | 6-0 | 190 | 4-21-72 | 1993 | Bedford, Pa. |
| Zaletel, Brian, 3b | .293 | 54 | 184 | 29 | 54 | 11 | 2 | 5 | 27 | 23 | 48 | 5 | 2 | R | R | 6-1 | 185 | 1-9-71 | 1993 | Largo, Fla. |

| PITCHING | W | L | ERA | G | GS | CG | SV | IP | H | R | ER | BB | SO | B | T | HT | WT | DOB | 1st Yr | Resides |
|---|---|---|---|---|---|---|---|---|---|---|---|---|---|---|---|---|---|---|---|---|
| Altman, Heath | 2 | 5 | 5.42 | 15 | 15 | 0 | 0 | 73 | 69 | 62 | 44 | 53 | 64 | S | R | 6-5 | 200 | 6-2-71 | 1993 | Hamlet, N.C. |
| Anderson, Clark | 2 | 1 | 5.27 | 17 | 1 | 0 | 2 | 41 | 49 | 30 | 24 | 7 | 24 | R | R | 6-2 | 175 | 3-28-71 | 1993 | Portland, Ore. |
| Baine, David | 0 | 0 | 0.00 | 1 | 1 | 0 | 0 | 4 | 2 | 0 | 0 | 3 | 7 | S | L | 6-5 | 200 | 12-24-69 | 1992 | Novato, Calif. |
| Baumann, Matt | 2 | 2 | 6.04 | 14 | 0 | 0 | 0 | 22 | 13 | 19 | 15 | 27 | 20 | R | R | 6-5 | 200 | 6-19-71 | 1993 | Silver Spring, Md. |
| Bourgeois, Steve | 5 | 3 | 4.21 | 15 | 15 | 0 | 0 | 77 | 62 | 44 | 36 | 44 | 77 | R | R | 6-1 | 220 | 8-4-72 | 1993 | Paulina, La. |
| Day, Steve | 9 | 2 | 1.79 | 30 | 0 | 0 | 7 | 45 | 35 | 14 | 9 | 21 | 47 | L | L | 6-0 | 185 | 7-31-70 | 1993 | Grand Junction, Colo. |
| Drumm, Doug | 1 | 0 | 8.22 | 20 | 4 | 0 | 0 | 38 | 48 | 44 | 35 | 36 | 39 | R | R | 6-2 | 190 | 5-25-71 | 1993 | Albany, N.Y. |
| Franko, Kris | 5 | 0 | 1.47 | 13 | 12 | 0 | 0 | 79 | 59 | 15 | 13 | 25 | 72 | L | L | 6-0 | 185 | 9-26-70 | 1993 | Cumberland, Ohio |
| Grande, Marc | 3 | 3 | 3.88 | 21 | 1 | 0 | 0 | 49 | 43 | 27 | 21 | 38 | 59 | R | R | 5-10 | 180 | 1-30-71 | 1993 | Rome, N.Y. |
| Hanneman, Blair | 0 | 2 | 6.57 | 19 | 1 | 0 | 1 | 25 | 22 | 20 | 18 | 33 | 21 | R | R | 6-0 | 190 | 9-22-69 | 1992 | Denver, Colo. |
| Martin, Jeff | 5 | 5 | 3.00 | 25 | 0 | 0 | 4 | 54 | 38 | 22 | 18 | 20 | 44 | R | R | 6-2 | 180 | 3-28-73 | 1991 | Renton, Wash. |
| Saugstad, Mark | 1 | 1 | 5.86 | 12 | 0 | 0 | 0 | 28 | 30 | 18 | 18 | 19 | 17 | R | R | 6-4 | 210 | 11-6-70 | 1992 | Apple Valley, Calif. |
| Smith, Brent | 1 | 7 | 6.55 | 9 | 9 | 0 | 0 | 34 | 41 | 26 | 25 | 24 | 19 | R | R | 6-3 | 190 | 4-13-72 | 1993 | Fullerton, Calif. |
| Smith, Brook | 5 | 3 | 4.40 | 17 | 17 | 1 | 0 | 92 | 83 | 51 | 45 | 47 | 79 | L | L | 6-0 | 180 | 11-4-71 | 1993 | Waukesha, Wis. |
| Soult, David | 1 | 0 | 1.05 | 12 | 0 | 0 | 4 | 26 | 20 | 7 | 3 | 7 | 21 | R | R | 6-1 | 200 | 1-6-71 | 1993 | Cincinnati, Ohio |

## ARIZONA LEAGUE

| BATTING | AVG | G | AB | R | H | 2B | 3B | HR | RBI | BB | SO | SB | CS | B | T | HT | WT | DOB | 1st Yr | Resides |
|---|---|---|---|---|---|---|---|---|---|---|---|---|---|---|---|---|---|---|---|---|
| Alguacil, Jose, 3b-1b | .241 | 42 | 145 | 28 | 35 | 6 | 1 | 1 | 13 | 6 | 23 | 8 | 1 | L | R | 6-2 | 175 | 8-9-72 | 1993 | Caracas, Venez. |
| Benner, Brian, of | .245 | 32 | 110 | 11 | 27 | 3 | 2 | 2 | 14 | 18 | 36 | 2 | 1 | R | R | 6-0 | 205 | 8-22-75 | 1993 | Mission Viejo, Calif. |
| Canizaro, Jay, 2b | .261 | 49 | 180 | 34 | 47 | 10 | 6 | 3 | 41 | 22 | 40 | 12 | 3 | R | R | 5-10 | 175 | 7-4-73 | 1993 | Orange, Texas |
| Christopherson, Eric, c | .409 | 8 | 22 | 7 | 9 | 1 | 0 | 4 | 9 | 1 | 0 | 0 | 0 | R | R | 6-1 | 190 | 4-25-69 | 1990 | Westminster, Calif. |
| Cordero, Pablo, of | .290 | 29 | 107 | 10 | 31 | 2 | 3 | 0 | 14 | 2 | 18 | 4 | 0 | R | R | 6-0 | 189 | 6-24-73 | 1991 | El Seibo, D.R. |
| Cruz, Devei, 3b-ss | .341 | 29 | 82 | 8 | 28 | 3 | 0 | 0 | 15 | 4 | 5 | 3 | 0 | R | R | 5-11 | 160 | 6-11-75 | 1993 | Bani, D.R. |
| Davis, Melvin, dh | .259 | 23 | 85 | 12 | 22 | 1 | 3 | 0 | 8 | 5 | 14 | 6 | 0 | R | R | 5-10 | 165 | 10-15-71 | 1991 | San Pedro de Macoris, D.R. |
| Denbow, Don, of | .200 | 39 | 130 | 27 | 26 | 7 | 1 | 2 | 17 | 24 | 57 | 4 | 0 | R | R | 6-4 | 215 | 4-30-73 | 1993 | Corsicana, Texas |
| Galarza, Joel, c | .326 | 42 | 132 | 26 | 43 | 12 | 3 | 3 | 26 | 17 | 26 | 4 | 4 | R | R | 5-11 | 214 | 10-14-73 | 1993 | Yabucoa, P.R. |
| Gonzalez, Jesus, 3b | .053 | 7 | 19 | 2 | 1 | 0 | 0 | 0 | 1 | 1 | 5 | 1 | 0 | R | R | 6-1 | 179 | 6-2-73 | 1992 | El Seibo, D.R. |
| Hartwell, Ed, dh-of | .382 | 19 | 68 | 17 | 26 | 4 | 2 | 0 | 4 | 16 | 10 | 2 | 5 | L | R | 6-0 | 200 | 8-14-71 | 1993 | Fort Worth, Texas |
| Heffernan, Bert, c-dh | .320 | 7 | 25 | 3 | 8 | 0 | 0 | 0 | 4 | 6 | 2 | 2 | 1 | L | R | 5-10 | 185 | 3-3-65 | 1988 | Stony Brook, N.Y. |
| Johnson, Juan, ss | .241 | 43 | 158 | 36 | 38 | 8 | 1 | 0 | 18 | 26 | 34 | 22 | 6 | S | R | 5-10 | 167 | 2-1-73 | 1992 | Waldorf, Md. |
| Martinez, Pablo, 2b | .286 | 13 | 35 | 4 | 10 | 0 | 0 | 0 | 4 | 1 | 5 | 2 | 0 | R | R | 5-11 | 165 | 1-7-76 | 1993 | Bani, D.R. |
| Marval, Raul, ss | .234 | 19 | 47 | 8 | 11 | 2 | 0 | 0 | 3 | 3 | 4 | 3 | 1 | R | R | 6-0 | 170 | 12-13-75 | 1993 | Lara, Venez. |
| Peguero, Juan, of | .289 | 30 | 90 | 11 | 26 | 3 | 2 | 0 | 13 | 1 | 31 | 0 | 4 | R | R | 6-1 | 193 | 7-20-74 | 1993 | Azua, D.R. |
| Perez, Sergio, 2b | .100 | 12 | 20 | 3 | 2 | 0 | 1 | 0 | 2 | 5 | 7 | 0 | 0 | S | R | 6-0 | 180 | 10-26-74 | 1993 | Barquisimeto, Venez. |
| Pooschke, Mark, of | .212 | 38 | 113 | 23 | 24 | 5 | 4 | 0 | 15 | 20 | 44 | 6 | 3 | R | R | 6-2 | 190 | 7-3-74 | 1992 | Portland, Ore. |
| Ramirez, Hiram, 1b-c | .294 | 54 | 201 | 31 | 59 | 14 | 1 | 3 | 34 | 26 | 40 | 3 | 2 | R | R | 6-2 | 200 | 9-10-72 | 1991 | Ensenada, P.R. |
| Reynolds, Paul, c | .200 | 7 | 20 | 1 | 4 | 2 | 0 | 0 | 4 | 5 | 2 | 0 | 0 | S | R | 5-10 | 185 | 9-16-71 | 1993 | Byromville, Ga. |
| Sterling, Henry, c | .094 | 23 | 32 | 3 | 3 | 0 | 0 | 0 | 2 | 3 | 11 | 0 | 0 | R | R | 6-1 | 185 | 2-22-76 | 1993 | San Pedro de Macoris, D.R. |
| Urena, Santiago, ss | .222 | 10 | 18 | 3 | 4 | 0 | 0 | 0 | 1 | 5 | 5 | 0 | 1 | R | R | 6-1 | 155 | 12-31-75 | 1993 | San Pedro de Macoris, D.R. |
| Vega, Ramon, of | .279 | 32 | 68 | 13 | 19 | 3 | 0 | 0 | 8 | 5 | 19 | 1 | 1 | R | R | 6-0 | 170 | 2-12-74 | 1993 | Arroyo, P.R. |

| PITCHING | W | L | ERA | G | GS | CG | SV | IP | H | R | ER | BB | SO | B | T | HT | WT | DOB | 1st Yr | Resides |
|---|---|---|---|---|---|---|---|---|---|---|---|---|---|---|---|---|---|---|---|---|
| Abreu, Jose | 1 | 1 | 4.58 | 22 | 0 | 0 | 0 | 35 | 39 | 24 | 18 | 27 | 20 | R | R | 6-2 | 184 | 2-4-75 | 1993 | Puerto Plata, D.R. |
| Abreu, Juan | 7 | 0 | 4.11 | 12 | 12 | 0 | 0 | 61 | 54 | 30 | 28 | 46 | 46 | L | L | 6-0 | 207 | 10-26-75 | 1993 | Quibor, Venez. |
| Brown, Kevin | 0 | 0 | 0.00 | 1 | 0 | 0 | 1 | 3 | 0 | 0 | 0 | 0 | 6 | R | R | 6-3 | 195 | 2-14-72 | 1991 | Brampton, Ontario |
| Carrasco, Joel | 0 | 0 | 11.66 | 12 | 0 | 0 | 0 | 15 | 23 | 25 | 19 | 14 | 12 | R | R | 6-2 | 170 | 3-23-76 | 1993 | Santo Domingo, D.R. |
| Grundt, Ken | 0 | 0 | 2.25 | 4 | 0 | 0 | 0 | 4 | 5 | 1 | 1 | 0 | 2 | L | L | 6-4 | 195 | 8-26-69 | 1991 | Chicago, Ill. |
| McMullen, Mike | 1 | 6 | 6.33 | 14 | 14 | 0 | 0 | 64 | 70 | 60 | 45 | 53 | 44 | R | R | 6-6 | 210 | 10-13-73 | 1993 | Granada Hills, Calif. |
| Mercedes, Manuel | 1 | 0 | 5.40 | 10 | 0 | 0 | 0 | 13 | 10 | 9 | 8 | 14 | 9 | L | L | 6-2 | 194 | 6-30-73 | 1993 | San Pedro de Macoris, D.R. |
| Mitchell, Kendrick | 0 | 2 | 1.77 | 14 | 0 | 0 | 0 | 20 | 15 | 7 | 4 | 12 | 25 | R | L | 6-4 | 215 | 12-6-73 | 1992 | Portland, Ore. |
| Morfin, Bret | 4 | 3 | 3.40 | 21 | 3 | 0 | 3 | 42 | 41 | 19 | 16 | 24 | 37 | L | L | 6-0 | 160 | 8-15-73 | 1993 | Beaverton, Ore. |
| Murray, Jim | 5 | 4 | 3.30 | 15 | 12 | 0 | 0 | 71 | 58 | 36 | 26 | 23 | 72 | L | L | 6-0 | 175 | 10-9-74 | 1992 | Martinsburg, W.Va. |
| Myers, Jason | 8 | 1 | 1.69 | 13 | 13 | 0 | 0 | 75 | 50 | 19 | 14 | 16 | 105 | L | L | 6-2 | 165 | 9-19-73 | 1993 | Fontana, Calif. |
| Pinder, Chris | 1 | 1 | 5.72 | 22 | 0 | 0 | 0 | 39 | 41 | 33 | 25 | 39 | 30 | R | R | 6-2 | 165 | 8-17-74 | 1993 | Woodbridge, Va. |
| Vasquez, Jorge | 3 | 6 | 3.55 | 26 | 1 | 0 | 8 | 46 | 47 | 25 | 18 | 27 | 38 | R | R | 6-1 | 185 | 11-20-73 | 1992 | Comerio, P.R. |

# SEATTLE MARINERS

**Manager:** Lou Piniella.  **1993 Record:** 82-80, .506 (4th, AL West).

| BATTING | AVG | G | AB | R | H | 2B | 3B | HR | RBI | BB | SO | SB | CS | B | T | HT | WT | DOB | 1st Yr | Resides |
|---|---|---|---|---|---|---|---|---|---|---|---|---|---|---|---|---|---|---|---|---|
| Amaral, Rich | .290 | 110 | 373 | 53 | 108 | 24 | 1 | 1 | 44 | 33 | 54 | 19 | 11 | R | R | 6-0 | 175 | 4-1-62 | 1983 | Orange, Calif. |
| Backman, Wally | .138 | 10 | 29 | 2 | 4 | 0 | 0 | 0 | 1 | 8 | 0 | 0 | 0 | S | R | 5-9 | 160 | 9-22-59 | 1977 | Kailua, Hawaii |
| Blowers, Mike | .280 | 127 | 379 | 55 | 106 | 23 | 3 | 15 | 57 | 44 | 98 | 1 | 5 | R | R | 6-2 | 210 | 4-24-65 | 1986 | Tacoma, Wash. |
| Boone, Bret | .251 | 76 | 271 | 31 | 68 | 12 | 2 | 12 | 38 | 17 | 52 | 2 | 3 | R | R | 5-10 | 180 | 4-6-69 | 1990 | Villa Park, Calif. |
| Buhner, Jay | .272 | 158 | 563 | 91 | 153 | 28 | 3 | 27 | 98 | 100 | 144 | 2 | 5 | R | R | 6-3 | 210 | 8-13-64 | 1984 | League City, Texas |
| Cotto, Henry | .190 | 54 | 105 | 10 | 20 | 1 | 0 | 2 | 7 | 2 | 22 | 5 | 4 | R | R | 6-2 | 180 | 1-5-61 | 1980 | Renton, Wash. |
| Felder, Mike | .211 | 109 | 342 | 31 | 72 | 7 | 5 | 1 | 20 | 22 | 34 | 15 | 9 | S | R | 5-9 | 175 | 11-18-62 | 1981 | Richmond, Calif. |
| Griffey, Ken Jr. | .309 | 156 | 582 | 113 | 180 | 38 | 3 | 45 | 109 | 96 | 91 | 17 | 9 | L | L | 6-3 | 205 | 11-21-69 | 1987 | Renton, Wash. |
| Haselman, Bill | .255 | 58 | 137 | 21 | 35 | 8 | 0 | 5 | 16 | 12 | 19 | 2 | 1 | R | R | 6-3 | 215 | 5-25-66 | 1987 | Saratoga, Calif. |
| Howard, Chris | .000 | 4 | 1 | 0 | 0 | 0 | 0 | 0 | 0 | 0 | 0 | 0 | 0 | R | R | 6-2 | 200 | 2-27-66 | 1988 | Houston, Texas |
| Howitt, Dann | .211 | 32 | 76 | 6 | 16 | 3 | 1 | 2 | 8 | 4 | 18 | 0 | 0 | L | R | 6-5 | 205 | 2-13-64 | 1986 | Medford, Ore. |
| Litton, Greg | .299 | 72 | 174 | 25 | 52 | 17 | 0 | 3 | 25 | 18 | 30 | 0 | 1 | R | R | 6-0 | 175 | 7-13-64 | 1984 | Pensacola, Fla. |
| Magadan, Dave | .259 | 71 | 228 | 27 | 59 | 11 | 0 | 1 | 21 | 36 | 33 | 2 | 0 | L | R | 6-3 | 200 | 9-30-62 | 1983 | Tampa, Fla. |
| Martinez, Edgar | .237 | 42 | 135 | 20 | 32 | 7 | 0 | 4 | 13 | 28 | 19 | 0 | 0 | R | R | 5-11 | 190 | 1-2-63 | 1983 | Kirkland, Wash. |
| Martinez, Tino | .265 | 109 | 408 | 48 | 108 | 25 | 1 | 17 | 60 | 45 | 56 | 0 | 3 | L | R | 6-2 | 210 | 12-7-67 | 1989 | Tampa, Fla. |
| Newfield, Marc | .227 | 22 | 66 | 5 | 15 | 3 | 0 | 1 | 7 | 2 | 8 | 0 | 1 | R | R | 6-4 | 205 | 10-19-72 | 1990 | Huntington Beach, Calif. |
| O'Brien, Pete | .257 | 72 | 210 | 30 | 54 | 7 | 0 | 7 | 27 | 26 | 21 | 0 | 0 | L | L | 6-2 | 205 | 2-9-58 | 1979 | Arlington, Texas |
| Pirkl, Greg | .174 | 7 | 23 | 1 | 4 | 0 | 0 | 1 | 4 | 0 | 4 | 0 | 0 | R | R | 6-5 | 225 | 8-7-70 | 1988 | Los Alamitos, Calif. |
| Sasser, Mackey | .218 | 83 | 188 | 18 | 41 | 10 | 2 | 1 | 21 | 15 | 30 | 1 | 0 | L | R | 6-1 | 210 | 8-3-62 | 1984 | Lynn Haven, Fla. |
| Sheets, Larry | .118 | 11 | 17 | 0 | 2 | 1 | 0 | 0 | 1 | 2 | 1 | 0 | 0 | L | R | 6-3 | 230 | 12-6-59 | 1978 | Lutherville, Md. |
| Tinsley, Lee | .158 | 11 | 19 | 2 | 3 | 1 | 0 | 1 | 2 | 2 | 9 | 0 | 0 | S | R | 5-10 | 180 | 3-4-69 | 1987 | Shelbyville, Ky. |
| Turang, Brian | .250 | 40 | 140 | 22 | 35 | 11 | 1 | 0 | 7 | 17 | 20 | 6 | 2 | R | R | 5-10 | 170 | 6-14-67 | 1989 | Long Beach, Calif. |
| Valle, Dave | .258 | 135 | 423 | 48 | 109 | 19 | 0 | 13 | 63 | 48 | 56 | 1 | 0 | R | R | 6-2 | 200 | 10-30-60 | 1978 | Renton, Wash. |
| Vina, Fernando | .222 | 24 | 45 | 5 | 10 | 2 | 0 | 0 | 2 | 4 | 3 | 6 | 0 | L | R | 5-9 | 165 | 4-16-69 | 1990 | Sacramento, Calif. |
| Vizquel, Omar | .255 | 158 | 560 | 68 | 143 | 14 | 2 | 2 | 31 | 50 | 71 | 12 | 14 | S | R | 5-9 | 165 | 4-24-67 | 1984 | Caracas, Venez. |

| PITCHING | W | L | ERA | G | GS | CG | SV | IP | H | R | ER | BB | SO | B | T | HT | WT | DOB | 1st Yr | Resides |
|---|---|---|---|---|---|---|---|---|---|---|---|---|---|---|---|---|---|---|---|---|
| Ayrault, Bob | 1 | 1 | 3.20 | 14 | 0 | 0 | 0 | 20 | 18 | 8 | 7 | 6 | 7 | R | R | 6-4 | 235 | 4-27-66 | 1989 | Carson City, Nev. |
| Bosio, Chris | 9 | 9 | 3.45 | 29 | 24 | 3 | 1 | 164 | 138 | 75 | 63 | 59 | 119 | R | R | 6-3 | 205 | 4-3-63 | 1982 | Shingle Springs, Calif. |
| Charlton, Norm | 1 | 3 | 2.34 | 34 | 0 | 0 | 18 | 35 | 22 | 12 | 9 | 17 | 48 | S | L | 6-3 | 205 | 1-6-63 | 1984 | Jamaica Beach, Texas |
| Converse, Jim | 1 | 3 | 5.31 | 4 | 4 | 0 | 0 | 20 | 23 | 12 | 12 | 14 | 10 | L | R | 5-9 | 180 | 8-17-71 | 1990 | Citrus Heights, Calif. |
| Cummings, John | 0 | 6 | 6.02 | 10 | 8 | 1 | 0 | 46 | 59 | 34 | 31 | 16 | 19 | L | L | 6-3 | 200 | 5-10-69 | 1990 | Laguna Niguel, Calif. |
| DeLucia, Rich | 3 | 6 | 4.64 | 30 | 1 | 0 | 0 | 43 | 46 | 24 | 22 | 23 | 48 | R | R | 6-0 | 185 | 10-7-64 | 1986 | Columbia, S.C. |
| Fleming, Dave | 12 | 5 | 4.36 | 26 | 26 | 1 | 0 | 167 | 189 | 84 | 81 | 67 | 75 | L | L | 6-3 | 200 | 11-7-69 | 1990 | Mahopac, N.Y. |
| Hampton, Mike | 1 | 3 | 9.53 | 13 | 3 | 0 | 1 | 17 | 28 | 20 | 18 | 17 | 8 | R | L | 5-10 | 180 | 9-9-72 | 1990 | Homosassa, Fla. |
| Hanson, Erik | 11 | 12 | 3.47 | 31 | 30 | 7 | 0 | 215 | 215 | 91 | 83 | 60 | 163 | R | R | 6-6 | 215 | 5-18-65 | 1986 | Kirkland, Wash. |
| Henry, Dwayne | 2 | 1 | 6.67 | 31 | 1 | 0 | 2 | 54 | 56 | 40 | 40 | 35 | 35 | R | R | 6-3 | 205 | 2-16-62 | 1980 | Glen Allen, Va. |
| Holman, Brad | 1 | 3 | 3.72 | 19 | 0 | 0 | 3 | 36 | 27 | 17 | 15 | 16 | 17 | R | R | 6-5 | 200 | 2-9-68 | 1990 | Wichita, Kan. |
| Johnson, Randy | 19 | 8 | 3.24 | 35 | 34 | 10 | 1 | 255 | 185 | 97 | 92 | 99 | 308 | R | L | 6-10 | 225 | 9-10-63 | 1985 | Bellevue, Wash. |
| King, Kevin | 0 | 1 | 6.17 | 13 | 0 | 0 | 0 | 12 | 9 | 8 | 8 | 8 | 4 | L | L | 6-4 | 200 | 2-11-69 | 1990 | Tulsa, Okla. |
| Leary, Tim | 11 | 9 | 5.05 | 33 | 27 | 0 | 0 | 169 | 202 | 104 | 95 | 58 | 68 | R | R | 6-3 | 220 | 12-23-58 | 1979 | Pacific Palisades, Calif. |
| Nelson, Jeff | 5 | 3 | 4.35 | 71 | 0 | 0 | 1 | 60 | 57 | 30 | 29 | 34 | 61 | R | R | 6-8 | 225 | 11-17-66 | 1984 | Baltimore, Md. |
| Ontiveros, Steve | 0 | 2 | 1.00 | 14 | 0 | 0 | 0 | 18 | 18 | 3 | 2 | 6 | 13 | R | R | 6-0 | 180 | 3-5-61 | 1982 | Stafford, Texas |
| Plantenberg, Eric | 0 | 0 | 6.52 | 20 | 0 | 0 | 1 | 10 | 11 | 7 | 7 | 12 | 3 | S | L | 6-1 | 180 | 10-30-68 | 1990 | Bellevue, Wash. |
| Powell, Dennis | 0 | 0 | 4.15 | 33 | 2 | 0 | 0 | 48 | 42 | 22 | 22 | 24 | 32 | R | L | 6-3 | 227 | 8-13-63 | 1983 | Norman Park, Ga. |
| Power, Ted | 2 | 2 | 3.91 | 25 | 0 | 0 | 13 | 25 | 27 | 11 | 11 | 9 | 16 | R | R | 6-4 | 215 | 1-31-55 | 1976 | Cincinnati, Ohio |
| 2-team (20 Cleve.) | 2 | 4 | 5.36 | 45 | 0 | 0 | 13 | 45 | 57 | 28 | 27 | 17 | 27 | | | | | | | |
| Salkeld, Roger | 0 | 0 | 2.51 | 3 | 2 | 0 | 0 | 14 | 13 | 4 | 4 | 4 | 13 | R | R | 6-5 | 215 | 3-6-71 | 1989 | Saugus, Calif. |
| Shinall, Zak | 0 | 0 | 3.38 | 1 | 0 | 0 | 0 | 3 | 4 | 1 | 1 | 2 | 0 | R | R | 6-3 | 215 | 10-14-68 | 1987 | Vero Beach, Fla. |
| Swan, Russ | 3 | 3 | 9.15 | 23 | 0 | 0 | 0 | 20 | 25 | 20 | 20 | 18 | 10 | L | L | 6-4 | 210 | 1-3-64 | 1986 | Kent, Wash. |
| Wainhouse, David | 0 | 0 | 27.00 | 3 | 0 | 0 | 0 | 2 | 7 | 7 | 7 | 5 | 2 | L | R | 6-2 | 185 | 11-7-67 | 1989 | Mercer Island, Wash. |

## FIELDING

### Catcher
| Catcher | PCT | G | PO | A | E | DP |
|---|---|---|---|---|---|---|
| Blowers | 1.000 | 1 | 1 | 0 | 0 | 0 |
| Haselman | .992 | 49 | 236 | 17 | 2 | 2 |
| Howard | 1.000 | 4 | 5 | 0 | 0 | 0 |
| Sasser | 1.000 | 4 | 8 | 1 | 0 | 0 |
| Valle | .995 | 135 | 881 | 71 | 5 | 13 |

### First Base
| First Base | PCT | G | PO | A | E | DP |
|---|---|---|---|---|---|---|
| Amaral | 1.000 | 3 | 4 | 0 | 0 | 2 |
| Blowers | 1.000 | 1 | 1 | 0 | 0 | 0 |
| Griffey | 1.000 | 1 | 1 | 0 | 0 | 0 |
| Litton | 1.000 | 13 | 86 | 8 | 0 | 15 |
| Magadan | .991 | 41 | 308 | 19 | 3 | 33 |
| T. Martinez | .997 | 103 | 932 | 60 | 3 | 89 |
| O'Brien | .988 | 9 | 76 | 8 | 1 | 10 |
| Pirkl | 1.000 | 5 | 42 | 5 | 0 | 8 |
| Sasser | 1.000 | 1 | 2 | 0 | 0 | 0 |

### Second Base
| Second Base | PCT | G | PO | A | E | DP |
|---|---|---|---|---|---|---|
| Amaral | .975 | 77 | 151 | 206 | 9 | 48 |
| Backman | 1.000 | 1 | 0 | 1 | 0 | 0 |

### (Outfield continued)
| | PCT | G | PO | A | E | DP |
|---|---|---|---|---|---|---|
| Boone | .991 | 74 | 140 | 177 | 3 | 55 |
| Litton | 1.000 | 17 | 22 | 27 | 0 | 9 |
| Turang | 1.000 | 1 | 1 | 0 | 0 | 0 |
| Vina | 1.000 | 16 | 25 | 38 | 0 | 12 |

### Third Base
| Third Base | PCT | G | PO | A | E | DP |
|---|---|---|---|---|---|---|
| Amaral | .972 | 19 | 5 | 30 | 1 | 7 |
| Backman | .857 | 9 | 4 | 14 | 3 | 0 |
| Blowers | .951 | 117 | 66 | 225 | 15 | 14 |
| Felder | 1.000 | 2 | 0 | 3 | 0 | 1 |
| Litton | 1.000 | 7 | 1 | 6 | 0 | 1 |
| Magadan | .972 | 27 | 17 | 53 | 2 | 5 |
| E. Martinez | .889 | 16 | 5 | 11 | 2 | 1 |
| Turang | .000 | 2 | 0 | 0 | 0 | 0 |

### Shortstop
| Shortstop | PCT | G | PO | A | E | DP |
|---|---|---|---|---|---|---|
| Amaral | 1.000 | 14 | 20 | 34 | 0 | 14 |
| Litton | 1.000 | 5 | 2 | 8 | 0 | 0 |
| Vina | 1.000 | 4 | 3 | 2 | 0 | 0 |
| Vizquel | .980 | 155 | 244 | 475 | 15 | 108 |

### Outfield
| Outfield | PCT | G | PO | A | E | DP |
|---|---|---|---|---|---|---|
| Blowers | 1.000 | 2 | 2 | 0 | 0 | 0 |
| Buhner | .978 | 148 | 263 | 8 | 6 | 2 |
| Cotto | .983 | 34 | 59 | 0 | 1 | 0 |
| Felder | .987 | 95 | 143 | 9 | 2 | 0 |
| Griffey | .991 | 139 | 316 | 8 | 3 | 3 |
| Haselman | .000 | 2 | 0 | 0 | 0 | 0 |
| Howitt | 1.000 | 29 | 42 | 1 | 0 | 0 |
| Johnson | .000 | 1 | 0 | 0 | 0 | 0 |
| Litton | 1.000 | 22 | 25 | 3 | 0 | 1 |
| Nelson | .000 | 1 | 0 | 0 | 0 | 0 |
| Newfield | .000 | 5 | 0 | 0 | 0 | 0 |
| O'Brien | 1.000 | 1 | 1 | 0 | 0 | 0 |
| Sasser | .946 | 37 | 50 | 3 | 3 | 0 |
| Sheets | 1.000 | 1 | 1 | 0 | 0 | 0 |
| Tinsley | .900 | 6 | 9 | 0 | 1 | 0 |
| Turang | .986 | 38 | 71 | 2 | 1 | 0 |

**Supporting Roles.** Ken Griffey and Randy Johnson took center stage for Seattle, but Jay Buhner (.272-27-98), Omar Vizquel (.255-2-31) and Dave Fleming (12-5, 4.36) all played key roles in the team's second-ever .500-plus finish.

# MARINERS FARM SYSTEM

| Class | Club | League | W | L | Pct. | Finish* | Manager | First Year |
|---|---|---|---|---|---|---|---|---|
| AAA | Calgary (Alta.) Cannons | Pacific Coast | 68 | 72 | .486 | 6th (10) | Keith Bodie | 1985 |
| AA | Jacksonville (Fla.) Suns | Southern | 59 | 81 | .421 | 10th (10) | Marc Hill | 1991 |
| A# | Riverside (Calif.) Pilots | California | 76 | 61 | .555 | 4th (10) | Dave Myers | 1993 |
| A | Appleton (Wis.) Foxes | Midwest | 62 | 73 | .459 | 9th (14) | Carlos Lezcano | 1993 |
| A | Bellingham (Wash.) Mariners | Northwest | 44 | 32 | .579 | 1st (8) | Mike Goff | 1977 |
| Rookie | Peoria (Ariz.) Mariners | Arizona | 18 | 36 | .333 | 8th (8) | Marty Martinez | 1988 |

*Finish in overall standings (No. of teams in league)    #Advanced level

## CALGARY                                                    AAA
### PACIFIC COAST LEAGUE

| BATTING | AVG | G | AB | R | H | 2B | 3B | HR | RBI | BB | SO | SB | CS | B | T | HT | WT | DOB | 1st Yr | Resides |
|---|---|---|---|---|---|---|---|---|---|---|---|---|---|---|---|---|---|---|---|---|
| Boone, Bret | .332 | 71 | 274 | 48 | 91 | 18 | 3 | 8 | 56 | 28 | 58 | 3 | 8 | R | R | 5-10 | 180 | 4-6-69 | 1990 | Villa Park, Calif. |
| Brundage, Dave | .000 | 5 | 1 | 0 | 0 | 0 | 0 | 0 | 0 | 0 | 1 | 0 | 0 | L | L | 6-3 | 190 | 10-6-64 | 1986 | Salem, Ore. |
| Deak, Brian | .247 | 80 | 235 | 43 | 58 | 12 | 0 | 11 | 41 | 41 | 65 | 5 | 1 | R | R | 6-0 | 185 | 10-25-67 | 1986 | Scottsdale, Ariz. |
| Furtado, Tim | .188 | 6 | 16 | 1 | 3 | 1 | 0 | 0 | 1 | 2 | 3 | 0 | 0 | R | R | 6-1 | 200 | 10-29-71 | 1991 | Fall River, Mass. |
| Holley, Bobby | .263 | 12 | 38 | 8 | 10 | 2 | 2 | 2 | 9 | 2 | 8 | 1 | 0 | R | R | 6-2 | 190 | 9-27-67 | 1988 | Long Beach, Calif. |
| Howard, Chris | .320 | 94 | 331 | 40 | 106 | 23 | 0 | 6 | 55 | 23 | 62 | 1 | 5 | R | R | 6-2 | 200 | 2-27-66 | 1988 | Houston, Texas |
| Howitt, Dann | .279 | 95 | 333 | 57 | 93 | 20 | 1 | 21 | 77 | 39 | 67 | 7 | 5 | L | R | 6-5 | 205 | 2-13-64 | 1986 | Medford, Ore. |
| Jeter, Shawn | .156 | 11 | 32 | 3 | 5 | 2 | 0 | 0 | 3 | 4 | 10 | 3 | 0 | L | R | 6-2 | 185 | 6-28-66 | 1985 | New York, N.Y. |
| Litton, Greg | .318 | 49 | 170 | 35 | 54 | 16 | 3 | 6 | 27 | 25 | 36 | 3 | 1 | R | R | 6-0 | 175 | 7-13-64 | 1984 | Pensacola, Fla. |
| Mack, Quinn | .308 | 84 | 325 | 48 | 100 | 25 | 1 | 6 | 39 | 17 | 41 | 9 | 6 | L | L | 5-10 | 180 | 9-11-65 | 1987 | Cerritos, Calif. |
| Manahan, Anthony | .302 | 117 | 451 | 70 | 136 | 31 | 4 | 3 | 62 | 38 | 48 | 19 | 4 | R | R | 6-0 | 190 | 12-15-68 | 1990 | Scottsdale, Ariz. |
| Martinez, Carmelo | .255 | 42 | 149 | 21 | 38 | 5 | 0 | 4 | 18 | 22 | 25 | 4 | 0 | R | R | 6-2 | 220 | 7-28-60 | 1979 | Dorado, P.R. |
| Maynard, Dave | .143 | 9 | 21 | 7 | 3 | 0 | 0 | 0 | 0 | 5 | 7 | 4 | 1 | R | R | 5-10 | 170 | 2-23-66 | 1988 | North Miami, Fla. |
| Pirkl, Greg | .308 | 115 | 445 | 67 | 137 | 24 | 1 | 21 | 94 | 13 | 50 | 3 | 3 | R | R | 6-5 | 225 | 8-7-70 | 1988 | Los Alamitos, Calif. |
| Quinones, Luis | .385 | 12 | 39 | 7 | 15 | 3 | 2 | 3 | 7 | 9 | 10 | 0 | 2 | S | R | 5-11 | 185 | 4-28-62 | 1980 | Ponce, P.R. |
| 2-team (64 Tucson) | .257 | 76 | 175 | 21 | 45 | 13 | 3 | 3 | 25 | 34 | 33 | 0 | 3 | | | | | | | |
| Smith, Jack | .286 | 128 | 458 | 61 | 131 | 30 | 3 | 8 | 57 | 37 | 73 | 5 | 9 | R | R | 6-2 | 180 | 11-9-64 | 1985 | Tavares, Fla. |
| Sveum, Dale | .300 | 33 | 120 | 31 | 36 | 11 | 1 | 6 | 26 | 24 | 32 | 0 | 1 | S | R | 6-3 | 185 | 11-23-63 | 1982 | Glendale, Ariz. |
| 2-team (12 Tacoma) | .313 | 45 | 163 | 41 | 51 | 12 | 1 | 8 | 32 | 30 | 39 | 2 | 2 | | | | | | | |
| Tinsley, Lee | .302 | 111 | 450 | 95 | 136 | 25 | 18 | 10 | 63 | 50 | 98 | 34 | 11 | S | R | 5-10 | 180 | 3-4-69 | 1987 | Shelbyville, Ky. |
| Turang, Brian | .324 | 110 | 423 | 83 | 137 | 20 | 11 | 8 | 54 | 40 | 48 | 24 | 8 | R | R | 5-10 | 170 | 6-14-67 | 1989 | Long Beach, Calif. |
| Turner, Shane | .303 | 86 | 323 | 46 | 98 | 22 | 1 | 0 | 38 | 32 | 57 | 6 | 5 | L | R | 5-10 | 190 | 1-8-63 | 1986 | Chino Hills, Calif. |
| Waggoner, Aubrey | .263 | 13 | 38 | 9 | 10 | 2 | 1 | 2 | 4 | 15 | 17 | 3 | 0 | L | R | 5-11 | 185 | 12-6-66 | 1985 | San Bernardino, Calif. |
| Wilson, Jim | .254 | 18 | 63 | 10 | 16 | 3 | 0 | 1 | 9 | 6 | 13 | 0 | 0 | R | R | 6-3 | 225 | 12-29-60 | 1980 | Corvallis, Ore. |
| Young, Gerald | .298 | 26 | 104 | 19 | 31 | 8 | 2 | 1 | 10 | 20 | 16 | 7 | 9 | S | R | 6-2 | 185 | 10-22-64 | 1982 | Santa Ana, Calif. |

| PITCHING | W | L | ERA | G | GS | CG | SV | IP | H | R | ER | BB | SO | B | T | HT | WT | DOB | 1st Yr | Resides |
|---|---|---|---|---|---|---|---|---|---|---|---|---|---|---|---|---|---|---|---|---|
| Ayrault, Bob | 0 | 0 | 10.38 | 3 | 0 | 0 | 1 | 4 | 8 | 5 | 5 | 2 | 3 | R | R | 6-4 | 235 | 4-27-66 | 1989 | Carson City, Nev. |
| Barton, Shawn | 3 | 1 | 3.56 | 51 | 0 | 0 | 4 | 61 | 64 | 29 | 24 | 27 | 29 | R | L | 6-3 | 195 | 5-14-63 | 1984 | Reading, Pa. |
| Brundage, Dave | 0 | 1 | 2.25 | 4 | 1 | 0 | 0 | 8 | 8 | 4 | 2 | 4 | 4 | L | L | 6-3 | 190 | 10-6-64 | 1986 | Salem, Ore. |
| Carman, Don | 1 | 0 | 3.55 | 6 | 0 | 0 | 0 | 13 | 12 | 6 | 5 | 2 | 6 | L | L | 6-3 | 201 | 8-14-59 | 1979 | Cherry Hill, N.J. |
| Converse, Jim | 7 | 8 | 5.40 | 23 | 22 | 4 | 0 | 122 | 144 | 86 | 73 | 64 | 78 | L | R | 5-9 | 180 | 8-17-71 | 1990 | Citrus Heights, Calif. |
| Cummings, John | 1 | 4 | 4.13 | 11 | 10 | 0 | 0 | 65 | 69 | 40 | 30 | 21 | 42 | L | L | 6-3 | 200 | 5-10-69 | 1990 | Laguna Niguel, Calif. |
| Czarkowski, Mark | 1 | 4 | 7.61 | 9 | 8 | 0 | 0 | 37 | 62 | 33 | 31 | 11 | 11 | R | R | 6-3 | 195 | 3-14-67 | 1989 | Newington, Conn. |
| DeLucia, Rich | 1 | 5 | 5.73 | 8 | 7 | 0 | 1 | 44 | 45 | 30 | 28 | 20 | 38 | R | R | 6-0 | 185 | 10-7-64 | 1986 | Columbia, S.C. |
| Grater, Mark | 0 | 1 | 7.71 | 9 | 0 | 0 | 0 | 12 | 19 | 10 | 10 | 6 | 4 | R | R | 5-10 | 205 | 1-19-64 | 1986 | Monaca, Pa. |
| Gunderson, Eric | 0 | 1 | 18.90 | 5 | 0 | 0 | 0 | 7 | 14 | 15 | 14 | 8 | 3 | R | L | 6-0 | 175 | 3-29-66 | 1987 | Portland, Ore. |
| Harris, Reggie | 8 | 6 | 5.20 | 17 | 15 | 1 | 0 | 88 | 74 | 55 | 51 | 61 | 75 | R | R | 6-1 | 190 | 8-12-68 | 1987 | Waynesboro, Va. |
| Holman, Brad | 8 | 4 | 4.74 | 21 | 13 | 1 | 0 | 99 | 109 | 59 | 52 | 42 | 54 | R | R | 6-5 | 200 | 2-9-68 | 1990 | Wichita, Kan. |
| Kent, Troy | 0 | 1 | 11.45 | 9 | 0 | 0 | 0 | 11 | 21 | 16 | 14 | 8 | 10 | R | R | 6-0 | 175 | 2-24-67 | 1988 | San Diego, Calif. |
| McCullers, Lance | 4 | 5 | 5.67 | 33 | 10 | 0 | 1 | 87 | 106 | 62 | 55 | 40 | 42 | S | R | 6-1 | 218 | 3-8-64 | 1982 | Lutz, Fla. |
| Nelson, Jeff | 1 | 0 | 1.17 | 5 | 0 | 0 | 1 | 8 | 6 | 1 | 1 | 2 | 6 | R | R | 6-8 | 225 | 11-17-66 | 1984 | Baltimore, Md. |
| Nolte, Eric | 1 | 2 | 9.14 | 10 | 3 | 0 | 1 | 22 | 38 | 24 | 22 | 12 | 23 | L | L | 6-3 | 210 | 4-28-64 | 1985 | Hemet, Calif. |

| PITCHING | W | L | ERA | G | GS | CG | SV | IP | H | R | ER | BB | SO | B | T | HT | WT | DOB | 1st Yr | Resides |
|---|---|---|---|---|---|---|---|---|---|---|---|---|---|---|---|---|---|---|---|---|
| Parkins, Rob | 0 | 0 | 10.13 | 3 | 0 | 0 | 0 | 3 | 6 | 3 | 3 | 0 | 3 | S | R | 6-2 | 195 | 4-29-64 | 1982 | Downey, Calif. |
| Picota, Len | 1 | 2 | 6.14 | 22 | 0 | 0 | 5 | 29 | 32 | 22 | 20 | 16 | 10 | R | R | 6-1 | 185 | 7-23-66 | 1984 | Panama City, Panama |
| Powell, Dennis | 3 | 2 | 3.60 | 12 | 4 | 0 | 1 | 40 | 37 | 16 | 16 | 19 | 30 | R | L | 6-3 | 227 | 8-13-63 | 1983 | Norman Park, Ga. |
| Remlinger, Mike | 4 | 3 | 5.53 | 19 | 18 | 0 | 0 | 85 | 100 | 57 | 52 | 52 | 51 | L | L | 6-0 | 195 | 3-23-66 | 1987 | Plymouth, Mass. |
| Shinall, Zak | 2 | 1 | 5.01 | 33 | 0 | 0 | 5 | 47 | 55 | 29 | 26 | 18 | 25 | R | R | 6-3 | 215 | 10-14-68 | 1987 | Vero Beach, Fla. |
| St.Claire, Randy | 4 | 6 | 6.79 | 27 | 0 | 0 | 3 | 52 | 70 | 40 | 39 | 13 | 45 | R | R | 6-3 | 190 | 8-23-60 | 1979 | Whitehall, N.Y. |
| Swan, Russ | 2 | 1 | 8.44 | 9 | 0 | 0 | 0 | 11 | 14 | 11 | 10 | 8 | 7 | L | L | 6-4 | 210 | 1-3-64 | 1986 | Kent, Wash. |
| Wainhouse, David | 0 | 1 | 4.02 | 13 | 0 | 0 | 5 | 16 | 10 | 7 | 7 | 7 | 7 | L | R | 6-2 | 185 | 11-7-67 | 1989 | Mercer Island, Wash. |
| Walker, Mike | 13 | 8 | 4.03 | 28 | 27 | 3 | 0 | 170 | 197 | 91 | 76 | 47 | 131 | R | R | 6-3 | 205 | 6-23-65 | 1986 | Splendora, Texas |
| Wapnick, Steve | 1 | 5 | 4.96 | 32 | 2 | 0 | 2 | 62 | 74 | 39 | 34 | 24 | 26 | R | R | 6-2 | 200 | 9-25-65 | 1987 | Sepulveda, Calif. |

## FIELDING

| Catcher | PCT | G | PO | A | E | DP |
|---|---|---|---|---|---|---|
| Deak | .972 | 53 | 266 | 47 | 9 | 4 |
| Howard | .988 | 89 | 506 | 65 | 7 | 8 |

| First Base | PCT | G | PO | A | E | DP |
|---|---|---|---|---|---|---|
| Deak | 1.000 | 1 | 9 | 0 | 0 | 0 |
| Furtado | .833 | 1 | 5 | 0 | 1 | 0 |
| Holley | .952 | 2 | 16 | 4 | 1 | 0 |
| Martinez | 1.000 | 13 | 96 | 12 | 0 | 9 |
| Pirkl | .986 | 108 | 918 | 71 | 14 | 121 |
| Quinones | 1.000 | 5 | 37 | 1 | 0 | 3 |
| Smith | 1.000 | 1 | 2 | 0 | 0 | 1 |
| Sveum | .983 | 6 | 53 | 4 | 1 | 7 |
| Turner | 1.000 | 1 | 5 | 2 | 0 | 0 |
| Wilson | .991 | 11 | 106 | 2 | 1 | 15 |

| Second Base | PCT | G | PO | A | E | DP |
|---|---|---|---|---|---|---|
| Boone | .976 | 64 | 146 | 180 | 8 | 51 |
| Litton | 1.000 | 9 | 31 | 25 | 0 | 13 |
| Manahan | .983 | 41 | 95 | 132 | 4 | 28 |
| Quinones | .962 | 5 | 14 | 11 | 1 | 3 |

| | PCT | G | PO | A | E | DP |
|---|---|---|---|---|---|---|
| Smith | 1.000 | 4 | 7 | 17 | 0 | 4 |
| Turang | .978 | 17 | 33 | 58 | 2 | 15 |
| Turner | .912 | 5 | 13 | 18 | 3 | 7 |

| Third Base | PCT | G | PO | A | E | DP |
|---|---|---|---|---|---|---|
| Holley | .905 | 6 | 8 | 11 | 2 | 0 |
| Litton | .988 | 24 | 21 | 59 | 1 | 6 |
| Manahan | .899 | 43 | 12 | 77 | 10 | 9 |
| Pirkl | 1.000 | 1 | 2 | 1 | 0 | 1 |
| Quinones | 1.000 | 3 | 0 | 5 | 0 | 0 |
| Smith | 1.000 | 4 | 1 | 7 | 0 | 0 |
| Sveum | .944 | 11 | 9 | 25 | 2 | 2 |
| Turang | .786 | 7 | 3 | 8 | 3 | 1 |
| Turner | .951 | 59 | 23 | 112 | 7 | 13 |

| Shortstop | PCT | G | PO | A | E | DP |
|---|---|---|---|---|---|---|
| Litton | .909 | 2 | 6 | 4 | 1 | 0 |
| Manahan | .930 | 28 | 53 | 93 | 11 | 23 |
| Smith | .948 | 113 | 156 | 351 | 28 | 90 |
| Turang | .750 | 1 | 0 | 3 | 1 | 0 |

| | PCT | G | PO | A | E | DP |
|---|---|---|---|---|---|---|
| Turner | 1.000 | 1 | 1 | 6 | 0 | 0 |

| Outfield | PCT | G | PO | A | E | DP |
|---|---|---|---|---|---|---|
| Brundage | .000 | 1 | 0 | 0 | 0 | 0 |
| Deak | 1.000 | 2 | 2 | 0 | 0 | 0 |
| Furtado | .833 | 3 | 5 | 0 | 1 | 0 |
| Holley | .000 | 1 | 0 | 0 | 0 | 0 |
| Howard | .000 | 1 | 0 | 0 | 0 | 0 |
| Howitt | .984 | 88 | 174 | 5 | 3 | 3 |
| Jeter | 1.000 | 9 | 15 | 0 | 0 | 0 |
| Litton | 1.000 | 5 | 7 | 0 | 0 | 0 |
| Mack | .983 | 63 | 113 | 3 | 2 | 0 |
| Manahan | 1.000 | 1 | 2 | 0 | 0 | 0 |
| Martinez | 1.000 | 13 | 18 | 2 | 0 | 0 |
| Maynard | 1.000 | 8 | 13 | 0 | 0 | 0 |
| Tinsley | .988 | 108 | 241 | 4 | 3 | 0 |
| Turang | .965 | 88 | 185 | 6 | 7 | 1 |
| Turner | 1.000 | 19 | 30 | 2 | 0 | 0 |
| Waggoner | 1.000 | 9 | 7 | 0 | 0 | 0 |
| Young | .937 | 26 | 58 | 1 | 4 | 0 |

# JACKSONVILLE                                          AA
## SOUTHERN LEAGUE

| BATTING | AVG | G | AB | R | H | 2B | 3B | HR | RBI | BB | SO | SB | CS | B | T | HT | WT | DOB | 1st Yr | Resides |
|---|---|---|---|---|---|---|---|---|---|---|---|---|---|---|---|---|---|---|---|---|
| Adams, Tommy, of | .276 | 61 | 232 | 19 | 64 | 12 | 2 | 4 | 20 | 14 | 34 | 4 | 0 | R | R | 6-1 | 205 | 11-26-69 | 1991 | Mission Viejo, Calif. |
| Beeler, Pete, c | .207 | 18 | 58 | 6 | 12 | 3 | 0 | 1 | 6 | 6 | 5 | 1 | 0 | R | R | 6-2 | 215 | 2-24-67 | 1985 | Cedar Rapids, Iowa |
| Bragg, Darren, of | .264 | 131 | 451 | 74 | 119 | 26 | 3 | 11 | 46 | 81 | 82 | 19 | 11 | L | R | 5-9 | 180 | 9-7-69 | 1991 | Wolcott, Conn. |
| Campanis, Jim, c | .245 | 70 | 212 | 16 | 52 | 7 | 0 | 3 | 22 | 23 | 43 | 0 | 2 | R | R | 6-1 | 200 | 8-27-67 | 1989 | Yorba Linda, Calif. |
| Clayton, Craig, 3b-of | .298 | 59 | 215 | 23 | 64 | 8 | 2 | 1 | 23 | 17 | 29 | 10 | 5 | R | R | 6-0 | 185 | 11-29-70 | 1991 | Anaheim, Calif. |
| Cornelius, Brian, of-1b | .286 | 48 | 168 | 28 | 48 | 11 | 0 | 3 | 17 | 8 | 28 | 5 | 5 | L | R | 6-0 | 170 | 2-16-67 | 1989 | Homestead, Fla. |
| Diaz, Eddy, of-2b | .251 | 77 | 259 | 36 | 65 | 16 | 0 | 6 | 26 | 17 | 31 | 6 | 3 | R | R | 5-10 | 160 | 9-29-71 | 1990 | Barquisimeto, Venez. |
| Holley, Bobby, 1b-3b | .247 | 108 | 388 | 59 | 96 | 22 | 1 | 13 | 66 | 43 | 50 | 7 | 5 | R | R | 6-2 | 190 | 9-27-67 | 1988 | Long Beach, Calif. |
| Jackson, Kenny, of | .000 | 4 | 10 | 1 | 0 | 0 | 0 | 0 | 1 | 1 | 4 | 0 | 0 | R | R | 5-11 | 175 | 9-15-64 | 1986 | Iselin, N.J. |
| Kounas, Tony, c-1b | .278 | 49 | 158 | 22 | 44 | 14 | 0 | 4 | 22 | 14 | 24 | 2 | 1 | R | R | 6-2 | 210 | 11-6-67 | 1990 | Highland, Calif. |
| Marquez, Jesus, of | .313 | 11 | 32 | 7 | 10 | 0 | 0 | 2 | 5 | 9 | 9 | 3 | 2 | L | L | 6-1 | 160 | 3-12-73 | 1990 | Caracas, Venez. |
| Martinez, Edgar, dh | .357 | 4 | 14 | 2 | 5 | 0 | 0 | 1 | 3 | 2 | 0 | 0 | 0 | R | R | 5-11 | 190 | 1-2-63 | 1983 | Kirkland, Wash. |
| Maynard, Tow, of | .215 | 60 | 195 | 21 | 42 | 5 | 1 | 2 | 8 | 15 | 50 | 17 | 7 | R | R | 5-10 | 170 | 2-23-66 | 1988 | North Miami, Fla. |
| Morales, Jorge, c-1b | .282 | 55 | 170 | 15 | 48 | 9 | 0 | 3 | 25 | 9 | 39 | 9 | 5 | R | R | 5-11 | 185 | 11-2-70 | 1990 | Caguas, P.R. |
| Nava, Lipso, 3b-2b | .254 | 114 | 397 | 52 | 101 | 20 | 0 | 7 | 41 | 31 | 43 | 5 | 6 | R | R | 6-2 | 175 | 11-28-68 | 1990 | Maracaibo, Venez. |
| Newfield, Marc, 1b-of | .307 | 91 | 336 | 48 | 103 | 18 | 0 | 19 | 51 | 33 | 35 | 1 | 1 | R | R | 6-4 | 205 | 10-19-72 | 1990 | Huntington Beach, Calif. |
| Relaford, Desi, ss | .244 | 133 | 472 | 49 | 115 | 16 | 4 | 8 | 47 | 50 | 103 | 16 | 12 | S | R | 5-8 | 155 | 9-16-73 | 1991 | Jacksonville, Fla. |
| Santana, Ruben, 2b | .301 | 128 | 499 | 79 | 150 | 21 | 2 | 21 | 84 | 38 | 101 | 13 | 8 | R | R | 6-2 | 175 | 3-7-70 | 1990 | Santo Domingo, D.R. |
| Scruggs, Tony, of | .241 | 61 | 224 | 26 | 54 | 11 | 1 | 7 | 38 | 13 | 53 | 5 | 4 | R | R | 6-1 | 210 | 3-19-66 | 1987 | Mountain View, Calif. |
| Smith, Bubba, 1b | .219 | 37 | 137 | 12 | 30 | 8 | 0 | 6 | 21 | 7 | 52 | 0 | 2 | R | R | 6-2 | 225 | 12-18-69 | 1991 | Riverside, Calif. |
| Waggoner, Aubrey, of | .245 | 34 | 102 | 29 | 25 | 8 | 2 | 3 | 7 | 40 | 34 | 7 | 3 | L | R | 5-11 | 185 | 12-6-66 | 1985 | San Bernardino, Calif. |

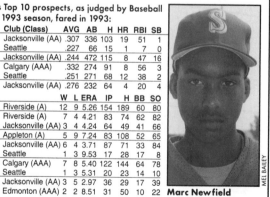

# MARINERS
# TOP
# 10
## PROSPECTS

How the Mariners Top 10 prospects, as judged by Baseball America prior to the 1993 season, fared in 1993:

| Player, Pos. | Club (Class) | AVG | AB | H | HR | RBI | SB |
|---|---|---|---|---|---|---|---|
| 1. Marc Newfield, of | Jacksonville (AA) | .307 | 336 | 103 | 19 | 51 | 1 |
| | Seattle | .227 | 66 | 15 | 1 | 7 | 0 |
| 4. Desi Relaford, ss | Jacksonville (AA) | .244 | 472 | 115 | 8 | 47 | 16 |
| 5. Bret Boone, 2b | Calgary (AAA) | .332 | 274 | 91 | 8 | 56 | 3 |
| | Seattle | .251 | 271 | 68 | 12 | 38 | 2 |
| 10. Tommy Adams, of | Jacksonville (AA) | .276 | 232 | 64 | 4 | 20 | 4 |

| | | W | L | ERA | IP | H | BB | SO |
|---|---|---|---|---|---|---|---|---|
| 2. Derek Lowe, rhp | Riverside (A) | 12 | 9 | 5.26 | 154 | 189 | 60 | 80 |
| 3. Ron Villone, lhp | Riverside (A) | 7 | 4 | 4.21 | 83 | 74 | 62 | 82 |
| | Jacksonville (AA) | 3 | 4 | 4.24 | 64 | 49 | 41 | 66 |
| 6. Shawn Estes, lhp | Appleton (A) | 5 | 9 | 7.24 | 83 | 108 | 52 | 65 |
| 7. Mike Hampton, lhp | Jacksonville (AA) | 6 | 4 | 3.71 | 87 | 71 | 33 | 84 |
| | Seattle | 1 | 3 | 9.53 | 17 | 28 | 17 | 8 |
| 8. Jim Converse, rhp | Calgary (AAA) | 7 | 8 | 5.40 | 122 | 144 | 64 | 78 |
| | | 1 | 3 | 5.31 | 20 | 23 | 14 | 10 |
| 9. Jeff Darwin, rhp* | Jacksonville (AA) | 3 | 5 | 2.97 | 36 | 29 | 17 | 39 |
| | Edmonton (AAA) | 2 | 2 | 8.51 | 31 | 50 | 10 | 22 |

*Traded to Florida Marlins

**Marc Newfield**
.307-19-51 in Double-A

MEL BAILEY

# MARINERS: MOST COMMON LINEUPS

| | Seattle<br>Majors | Calgary<br>AAA | Jacksonville<br>AA | Riverside<br>A | Appleton<br>A |
|---|---|---|---|---|---|
| C | Dave Valle (135) | Chris Howard (89) | Jim Campanis (50) | Chris Widger (80) | Alex Sutherland (97) |
| 1B | Tino Martinez (103) | Greg Pirkl (108) | Bobby Holley (49) | Fred McNair (104) | Jim Koehler (101) |
| 2B | Rich Amaral (77) | Bret Boone (64) | Ruben Santana (101) | Arquimedez Pozo (123) | Charles Gipson (48) |
| 3B | Mike Blowers (117) | Shane Turner (59) | Lipso Nava (71) | Dave Waldenberger (63) | Brian Wallace (115) |
| SS | Omar Vizquel (155) | Jack Smith (113) | Desi Relaford (124) | Craig Bryant (55) | Andy Sheets (65) |
| OF | Jay Buhner (148) | Lee Tinsley (108) | Darren Bragg (129) | Tommy Robertson (92) | David Lawson (103) |
| | Ken Griffey (139) | Brian Turang (91) | Tommy Adams (55) | Greg Shockey (92) | Enrique Atencio (75) |
| | Mike Felder (95) | Dann Howitt (90) | Tow Maynard (50) | John Tejcek (59) | Jesus Marquez (60) |
| DH | Pete O'Brien (52) | Martinez/Mack (19) | Marc Newfield (22) | Raul Rodarte (32) | Robbie Robertson (38) |
| SP | Randy Johnson (34) | Mike Walker (27) | Lagrande Russell (17) | Adam/Gutierrez (27) | Jose Sanchez (25) |
| RP | Jeff Nelson (71) | Shawn Barton (51) | Scott Schanz (46) | Jeff Borski (47) | Robert Worley (45) |

Full-season farm clubs only       No. of games at position in parenthesis

| PITCHING | W | L | ERA | G | GS | CG | SV | IP | H | R | ER | BB | SO | B | T | HT | WT | DOB | 1st Yr | Resides |
|---|---|---|---|---|---|---|---|---|---|---|---|---|---|---|---|---|---|---|---|---|
| Bicknell, Greg .............. | 6 | 6 | 4.31 | 24 | 12 | 2 | 1 | 94 | 96 | 59 | 45 | 28 | 45 | R | R | 6-1 | 185 | 6-1-69 | 1989 | Fresno, Calif. |
| Buckley, Travis .............. | 2 | 3 | 6.14 | 10 | 9 | 0 | 0 | 48 | 57 | 35 | 33 | 18 | 38 | R | R | 6-4 | 208 | 6-15-70 | 1989 | Overland Park, Kan. |
| 2-team (2 Chatt.)........ | 2 | 4 | 5.75 | 12 | 11 | 0 | 0 | 56 | 64 | 41 | 36 | 22 | 44 | | | | | | | |
| Clayton, Craig .............. | 0 | 0 | 0.00 | 3 | 0 | 0 | 0 | 4 | 3 | 0 | 0 | 1 | 1 | R | R | 6-0 | 185 | 11-29-70 | 1991 | Anaheim, Calif. |
| Coffman, Kevin .............. | 1 | 7 | 5.40 | 10 | 10 | 0 | 0 | 50 | 33 | 33 | 30 | 47 | 45 | R | R | 6-3 | 205 | 1-19-65 | 1983 | Victoria, Texas |
| Cummings, John .......... | 2 | 2 | 3.15 | 7 | 7 | 1 | 0 | 46 | 50 | 24 | 16 | 9 | 35 | L | L | 6-3 | 200 | 5-10-69 | 1990 | Laguna Niguel, Calif. |
| Czarkowski, Mark .......... | 0 | 3 | 4.19 | 25 | 4 | 0 | 1 | 58 | 68 | 36 | 27 | 16 | 26 | R | R | 6-3 | 195 | 3-14-67 | 1989 | Newington, Conn. |
| Darwin, Jeff.................. | 3 | 5 | 2.97 | 27 | 0 | 0 | 7 | 36 | 29 | 17 | 12 | 17 | 39 | R | R | 6-3 | 180 | 7-6-69 | 1989 | Bonham, Texas |
| Fleming, Dave .............. | 0 | 2 | 4.41 | 4 | 4 | 0 | 0 | 16 | 16 | 9 | 8 | 7 | 10 | L | L | 6-3 | 200 | 11-7-69 | 1990 | Mahopac, N.Y. |
| Foster, Kevin .............. | 4 | 4 | 3.97 | 12 | 12 | 1 | 0 | 66 | 53 | 32 | 29 | 29 | 72 | R | R | 6-1 | 160 | 1-13-69 | 1988 | Evanston, Ill. |
| Glinatsis, George .......... | 5 | 2 | 6.75 | 9 | 5 | 0 | 0 | 35 | 39 | 26 | 26 | 15 | 25 | R | R | 6-4 | 195 | 6-29-69 | 1991 | Youngstown, Ohio |
| Hampton, Mike .......... | 6 | 4 | 3.71 | 15 | 14 | 1 | 0 | 87 | 71 | 43 | 36 | 33 | 84 | R | L | 5-10 | 180 | 9-9-72 | 1990 | Homosassa, Fla. |
| Harris, Reggie .............. | 1 | 4 | 4.78 | 9 | 8 | 0 | 0 | 38 | 33 | 24 | 20 | 22 | 30 | R | R | 6-1 | 190 | 8-12-68 | 1987 | Waynesboro, Va. |
| Kent, Troy .................. | 0 | 0 | 5.21 | 14 | 0 | 0 | 1 | 19 | 26 | 14 | 11 | 5 | 17 | R | R | 6-0 | 175 | 2-24-67 | 1988 | San Diego, Calif. |
| King, Kevin .................. | 2 | 0 | 3.14 | 16 | 0 | 0 | 1 | 29 | 25 | 10 | 10 | 7 | 13 | L | L | 6-4 | 200 | 2-11-69 | 1990 | Tulsa, Okla. |
| Knackert, Brent .......... | 0 | 1 | 2.57 | 4 | 2 | 0 | 1 | 14 | 6 | 4 | 4 | 4 | 10 | R | R | 6-3 | 195 | 8-1-69 | 1987 | Huntington Beach, Calif. |
| Newlin, Jim .................. | 1 | 1 | 4.67 | 8 | 0 | 0 | 0 | 17 | 22 | 12 | 9 | 3 | 11 | R | R | 6-2 | 205 | 9-11-66 | 1989 | Leawood, Kan. |
| Parris, Steve .............. | 0 | 1 | 5.93 | 7 | 1 | 0 | 0 | 14 | 15 | 9 | 9 | 6 | 5 | R | R | 6-0 | 190 | 12-17-67 | 1989 | Joliet, Ill. |
| Perkins, Paul .............. | 2 | 4 | 5.40 | 36 | 1 | 0 | 1 | 60 | 69 | 40 | 36 | 23 | 34 | R | R | 6-4 | 210 | 8-4-70 | 1990 | Fairfield, Calif. |
| Phillips, Tony .............. | 1 | 3 | 1.72 | 27 | 0 | 0 | 5 | 31 | 34 | 6 | 6 | 5 | 26 | R | R | 6-4 | 195 | 6-9-69 | 1991 | Hattiesburg, Miss. |
| Picota, Len .................. | 0 | 4 | 4.87 | 11 | 0 | 0 | 0 | 20 | 26 | 20 | 11 | 12 | 7 | R | R | 6-1 | 180 | 7-23-66 | 1984 | Panama City, Panama |
| Plantenberg, Erik .......... | 2 | 1 | 2.01 | 34 | 0 | 0 | 1 | 45 | 38 | 11 | 10 | 14 | 49 | S | L | 6-1 | 180 | 10-30-68 | 1990 | Bellevue, Wash. |
| Remlinger, Mike.......... | 1 | 3 | 6.58 | 7 | 7 | 0 | 0 | 40 | 40 | 30 | 29 | 19 | 23 | L | L | 6-0 | 195 | 3-23-66 | 1987 | Plymouth, Mass. |
| Russell, Lagrande .......... | 4 | 9 | 5.52 | 17 | 17 | 0 | 0 | 90 | 115 | 67 | 55 | 32 | 52 | R | R | 6-2 | 195 | 8-20-70 | 1990 | Hallsboro, N.C. |
| Salkeld, Roger .............. | 4 | 3 | 3.27 | 14 | 14 | 0 | 0 | 77 | 71 | 39 | 28 | 29 | 56 | R | R | 6-5 | 215 | 3-6-71 | 1989 | Saugus, Calif. |
| Schanz, Scott.............. | 7 | 4 | 2.56 | 49 | 3 | 0 | 1 | 102 | 77 | 38 | 29 | 51 | 81 | R | R | 6-2 | 190 | 4-2-69 | 1990 | Riverside, Calif. |
| Villone, Ron .............. | 3 | 4 | 4.38 | 11 | 11 | 0 | 0 | 64 | 49 | 34 | 31 | 41 | 66 | L | L | 6-3 | 230 | 1-16-70 | 1992 | Bergenfield, N.J. |
| Weber, Weston.............. | 2 | 1 | 1.69 | 17 | 0 | 0 | 1 | 27 | 25 | 6 | 5 | 7 | 12 | R | R | 6-0 | 175 | 1-5-64 | 1986 | Dodge Center, Minn. |

# RIVERSIDE      A
## CALIFORNIA LEAGUE

| BATTING | AVG | G | AB | R | H | 2B | 3B | HR | RBI | BB | SO | SB | CS | B | T | HT | WT | DOB | 1st Yr | Resides |
|---|---|---|---|---|---|---|---|---|---|---|---|---|---|---|---|---|---|---|---|---|
| Bonnici, James, c-1b..... | .307 | 104 | 375 | 69 | 115 | 21 | 1 | 9 | 58 | 58 | 72 | 0 | 0 | R | R | 6-4 | 220 | 1-21-72 | 1991 | Ortonville, Mich. |
| Bryant, Craig ss........ | .258 | 61 | 236 | 38 | 61 | 15 | 4 | 3 | 28 | 36 | 39 | 8 | 4 | R | R | 6-2 | 180 | 4-15-70 | 1991 | Birmingham, Ala. |
| Cervantes, Manny, dh..... | .333 | 2 | 3 | 0 | 1 | 0 | 0 | 0 | 0 | 0 | 1 | 0 | 0 | L | L | 6-2 | 205 | 2-12-69 | 1991 | Whittier, Calif. |
| Clayton, Craig, 3b ........ | .328 | 60 | 235 | 37 | 77 | 13 | 2 | 1 | 32 | 30 | 30 | 4 | 4 | R | R | 6-0 | 185 | 11-29-70 | 1991 | Anaheim, Calif. |
| Furtado, Jeff, c-1b....... | .161 | 43 | 112 | 7 | 18 | 2 | 0 | 1 | 10 | 8 | 22 | 1 | 1 | R | R | 6-1 | 200 | 10-29-71 | 1991 | Fall River, Mass. |
| Griffey, Craig, of ........ | .241 | 58 | 191 | 30 | 46 | 4 | 4 | 3 | 25 | 17 | 25 | 10 | 2 | R | R | 5-11 | 175 | 6-3-71 | 1991 | West Chester, Ohio |
| Koehler, Jim, of-dh........ | .190 | 12 | 42 | 7 | 8 | 1 | 1 | 2 | 12 | 5 | 11 | 1 | 1 | L | L | 6-3 | 215 | 11-5-70 | 1991 | Pleasanton, Calif. |
| Marquez, Jesus of........ | .308 | 12 | 39 | 3 | 12 | 2 | 0 | 0 | 6 | 6 | 9 | 2 | 2 | L | L | 6-1 | 180 | 3-12-73 | 1990 | Caracas, Venez. |
| Maxwell, Trent, c .......... | .500 | 4 | 2 | 1 | 0 | 0 | 0 | 0 | 1 | 1 | 0 | 0 | 0 | R | R | 6-2 | 190 | 11-9-73 | 1992 | Cotton Valley, La. |
| Maynard, Tow, of .......... | .228 | 36 | 136 | 19 | 31 | 10 | 2 | 0 | 19 | 16 | 28 | 16 | 2 | R | R | 5-10 | 170 | 2-23-66 | 1988 | North Miami, Fla. |
| McNair, Fred, 1b........ | .270 | 112 | 400 | 70 | 108 | 21 | 1 | 14 | 65 | 41 | 91 | 6 | 7 | R | R | 6-4 | 215 | 1-31-70 | 1989 | Mesa, Ariz. |
| Pozo, Arquimedez, 2b..... | .342 | 127 | 515 | 98 | 176 | 46 | 6 | 13 | 83 | 56 | 56 | 10 | 10 | R | R | 5-10 | 180 | 8-24-71 | 1991 | Santo Domingo, D.R. |
| Robertson, Tommy, of .. | .251 | 96 | 339 | 50 | 85 | 9 | 5 | 6 | 51 | 43 | 53 | 10 | 2 | L | R | 6-1 | 195 | 12-27-71 | 1990 | Ridgeway, S.C. |
| Rodarte, Raul, inf....... | .289 | 106 | 402 | 79 | 116 | 19 | 1 | 5 | 49 | 46 | 53 | 7 | 4 | R | R | 5-11 | 190 | 4-9-70 | 1991 | Diamond Bar, Calif. |
| Sheets, Andy, ss ......... | .193 | 52 | 176 | 23 | 34 | 9 | 1 | 1 | 12 | 17 | 51 | 2 | 2 | R | R | 6-2 | 180 | 11-19-71 | 1992 | St. Amant, La. |
| Shockey, Greg, of ........ | .311 | 95 | 354 | 61 | 110 | 10 | 0 | 6 | 63 | 50 | 50 | 2 | 2 | L | L | 6-1 | 195 | 4-11-70 | 1992 | Boise, Idaho |
| Smith, Bubba, 1b-dh ..... | .421 | 5 | 19 | 5 | 8 | 3 | 0 | 0 | 3 | 7 | 3 | 0 | 0 | R | R | 6-2 | 225 | 12-18-69 | 1991 | Riverside, Calif. |
| Tejcek, John, of........ | .286 | 64 | 241 | 42 | 69 | 12 | 2 | 4 | 36 | 28 | 46 | 4 | 4 | R | R | 5-10 | 185 | 7-16-71 | 1993 | San Diego, Calif. |
| Triessl, Mike, c .............. | .333 | 3 | 3 | 1 | 1 | 0 | 0 | 0 | 0 | 0 | 0 | 0 | 0 | R | R | 6-1 | 215 | 2-27-71 | 1993 | Malverne, N.Y. |
| Waldenberger, Dave, 3b | .247 | 96 | 336 | 40 | 83 | 20 | 1 | 6 | 52 | 43 | 87 | 4 | 3 | S | R | 6-1 | 215 | 2-24-71 | 1988 | Rowland Heights, Calif. |
| Widger, Chris, c........ | .264 | 97 | 360 | 44 | 95 | 28 | 2 | 9 | 58 | 19 | 64 | 5 | 4 | R | R | 6-3 | 195 | 5-21-71 | 1992 | Pennsville, N.J. |
| Wilder, Willie, of............ | .275 | 63 | 200 | 37 | 55 | 16 | 1 | 1 | 19 | 35 | 47 | 11 | 6 | R | R | 6-3 | 190 | 4-24-69 | 1990 | Boonville, Ind. |

| PITCHING | W | L | ERA | G | GS | CG | SV | IP | H | R | ER | BB | SO | B | T | HT | WT | DOB | 1st Yr | Resides |
|---|---|---|---|---|---|---|---|---|---|---|---|---|---|---|---|---|---|---|---|---|
| Adam, Dave ................ | 12 | 8 | 4.05 | 27 | 27 | 1 | 0 | 169 | 180 | 91 | 76 | 51 | 98 | R | R | 6-3 | 202 | 2-14-69 | 1990 | Shelton, Conn. |
| Borski, Jeff.................. | 3 | 4 | 2.58 | 47 | 0 | 0 | 8 | 77 | 71 | 39 | 22 | 37 | 46 | R | R | 6-0 | 190 | 8-26-69 | 1991 | Springfield, Ill. |
| Davis, Tim.................. | 3 | 0 | 1.76 | 18 | 0 | 0 | 7 | 31 | 14 | 6 | 6 | 9 | 56 | L | L | 5-11 | 165 | 7-14-70 | 1992 | Bristol, Fla. |
| Evans, Dave .................. | 3 | 2 | 4.54 | 8 | 8 | 1 | 0 | 42 | 41 | 22 | 21 | 23 | 42 | R | R | 6-3 | 185 | 1-1-68 | 1990 | Houston, Texas |
| Glinatsis, George .......... | 1 | 0 | 4.54 | 14 | 3 | 0 | 2 | 36 | 40 | 24 | 18 | 9 | 30 | R | R | 6-4 | 195 | 6-29-69 | 1991 | Youngstown, Ohio |
| Gutierrez, Jim .............. | 12 | 9 | 3.78 | 27 | 27 | 2 | 0 | 171 | 182 | 95 | 72 | 53 | 84 | R | R | 6-2 | 190 | 11-28-69 | 1989 | Burlington, Wash. |
| King, Kevin .................. | 12 | 9 | 1.57 | 25 | 0 | 0 | 5 | 46 | 37 | 10 | 8 | 35 | 62 | L | L | 6-4 | 205 | 2-11-69 | 1990 | Tulsa, Okla. |
| Lowe, Derek .................. | 12 | 9 | 5.26 | 27 | 26 | 3 | 0 | 154 | 189 | 104 | 90 | 60 | 80 | R | R | 6-6 | 185 | 6-1-73 | 1991 | Dearborn, Mich. |
| Mecir, Jim .................. | 9 | 11 | 4.33 | 26 | 26 | 1 | 0 | 145 | 160 | 89 | 70 | 58 | 85 | S | R | 6-1 | 195 | 5-16-70 | 1991 | St. James, N.Y. |

# MARINERS: ORGANIZATION LEADERS

## MAJOR LEAGUERS

**Rich Amaral**
19 stolen bases

### BATTING
| | | |
|---|---|---|
| *AVG | Ken Griffey | .309 |
| R | Ken Griffey | 113 |
| H | Ken Griffey | 180 |
| TB | Ken Griffey | 359 |
| 2B | Ken Griffey | 38 |
| 3B | Mike Felder | 5 |
| HR | Ken Griffey | 45 |
| RBI | Ken Griffey | 109 |
| BB | Jay Buhner | 100 |
| SO | Jay Buhner | 144 |
| SB | Rich Amaral | 19 |

### PITCHING
| | | |
|---|---|---|
| W | Randy Johnson | 19 |
| L | Erik Hanson | 12 |
| #ERA | Randy Johnson | 3.24 |
| G | Jeff Nelson | 71 |
| CG | Randy Johnson | 10 |
| SV | Norm Charlton | 18 |
| IP | Randy Johnson | 255 |
| BB | Randy Johnson | 99 |
| SO | Randy Johnson | 308 |

## MINOR LEAGUERS

### BATTING
| | | |
|---|---|---|
| *AVG | Arquimedez Pozo, Riverside | .342 |
| R | Arquimedez Pozo, Riverside | 98 |
| H | Arquimedez Pozo, Riverside | 176 |
| TB | Arquimedez Pozo, Riverside | 271 |
| 2B | Arquimedez Pozo, Riverside | 44 |
| 3B | Lee Tinsley, Calgary | 18 |
| HR | Two tied at | 21 |
| RBI | Greg Pirkl, Calgary | 94 |
| BB | Darren Bragg, Jacksonville | 81 |
| SO | Brian Wallace, Appleton | 145 |
| SB | Tow Maynard, Riverside-Jack.-Calgary | 37 |

### PITCHING
| | | |
|---|---|---|
| W | Two tied at | 13 |
| L | Two tied at | 11 |
| #ERA | Tim Davis, Riverside-Appleton | 1.83 |
| G | Tony Phillips, Riverside-Jacksonville | 52 |
| CG | Jim Converse, Calgary | 4 |
| SV | Robert Worley, Appleton | 22 |
| IP | Jim Gutierrez, Riverside | 171 |
| BB | Ron Villone, Riverside-Jacksonville | 103 |
| SO | Jackie Nickell, Appleton | 151 |

*Minimum 250 At-Bats   #Minimum 75 Innings

| PITCHING | W | L | ERA | G | GS | CG | SV | IP | H | R | ER | BB | SO | B | T | HT | WT | DOB | 1st Yr | Resides |
|---|---|---|---|---|---|---|---|---|---|---|---|---|---|---|---|---|---|---|---|---|
| Perkins, Paul | 1 | 0 | 4.80 | 11 | 0 | 0 | 0 | 15 | 18 | 11 | 8 | 7 | 10 | R | R | 6-4 | 210 | 8-4-70 | 1990 | Fairfield, Calif. |
| Phillips, Tony | 3 | 1 | 1.80 | 25 | 0 | 0 | 15 | 30 | 22 | 8 | 6 | 4 | 19 | R | R | 6-4 | 195 | 6-9-69 | 1991 | Hattiesburg, Miss. |
| Rees, Sean | 0 | 1 | 6.19 | 18 | 1 | 0 | 1 | 32 | 52 | 27 | 22 | 11 | 27 | R | L | 5-11 | 180 | 4-9-70 | 1991 | San Diego, Calif. |
| Rosenberg, Steve | 0 | 0 | 1.17 | 6 | 0 | 0 | 1 | 8 | 5 | 1 | 1 | 1 | 13 | L | L | 6-0 | 190 | 10-31-64 | 1986 | Coral Gables, Fla. |
| Sullivan, Dan | 2 | 3 | 6.99 | 34 | 0 | 0 | 1 | 55 | 72 | 49 | 43 | 31 | 27 | R | R | 6-4 | 195 | 2-5-70 | 1991 | Pittsburgh, Pa. |
| Villone, Ron | 7 | 4 | 4.21 | 16 | 16 | 0 | 0 | 83 | 74 | 47 | 39 | 62 | 82 | L | L | 6-3 | 230 | 1-16-70 | 1992 | Bergenfield, N.J. |
| Wiley, Chuck | 3 | 2 | 4.61 | 31 | 0 | 0 | 2 | 55 | 65 | 44 | 28 | 25 | 49 | R | R | 6-0 | 180 | 11-20-70 | 1990 | Lenexa, Kan. |
| Youngblood, Todd | 2 | 5 | 6.10 | 26 | 3 | 0 | 0 | 59 | 64 | 44 | 40 | 30 | 55 | R | R | 6-1 | 210 | 7-23-70 | 1990 | Farmington, N.M. |

# APPLETON                                                                   A

## MIDWEST LEAGUE

| BATTING | AVG | G | AB | R | H | 2B | 3B | HR | RBI | BB | SO | SB | CS | B | T | HT | WT | DOB | 1st Yr | Resides |
|---|---|---|---|---|---|---|---|---|---|---|---|---|---|---|---|---|---|---|---|---|
| Atencio, Enrique, of-2b | .232 | 101 | 358 | 45 | 83 | 9 | 6 | 5 | 49 | 9 | 77 | 6 | 3 | R | R | 5-11 | 170 | 12-21-71 | 1990 | Maracaibo, Venez. |
| Bryant, Craig, ss | .300 | 51 | 170 | 33 | 51 | 11 | 3 | 5 | 29 | 18 | 32 | 12 | 2 | R | R | 6-2 | 180 | 4-15-70 | 1991 | Birmingham, Ala. |
| Diaz, Eddy, 2b-ss | .333 | 46 | 189 | 28 | 63 | 14 | 2 | 3 | 33 | 15 | 13 | 13 | 9 | R | R | 5-10 | 160 | 9-29-71 | 1990 | Barquisimeto, Venez. |
| Gipson, Charles, 2b-of | .256 | 109 | 348 | 63 | 89 | 13 | 1 | 0 | 20 | 61 | 76 | 21 | 16 | R | R | 6-2 | 180 | 12-16-72 | 1992 | Orange, Calif. |
| Griffey, Craig, of | .255 | 37 | 102 | 14 | 26 | 7 | 0 | 2 | 20 | 12 | 18 | 9 | 3 | R | R | 5-11 | 175 | 6-3-71 | 1991 | West Chester, Ohio |
| Hickey, Mike, of-2b | .286 | 69 | 255 | 35 | 73 | 14 | 3 | 2 | 41 | 38 | 49 | 14 | 7 | S | R | 6-2 | 180 | 6-22-70 | 1992 | Honolulu, Hawaii |
| Ibanez, Raul, dh-1b | .274 | 52 | 157 | 26 | 43 | 9 | 0 | 5 | 21 | 24 | 31 | 0 | 2 | L | R | 6-2 | 200 | 6-2-72 | 1992 | Miami, Fla. |
| Koehler, Jim, 1b-of | .242 | 115 | 372 | 52 | 90 | 28 | 5 | 17 | 60 | 55 | 95 | 4 | 6 | L | L | 6-3 | 215 | 11-5-70 | 1991 | Pleasanton, Calif. |
| Lawson, David, of | .252 | 113 | 333 | 59 | 84 | 26 | 3 | 11 | 38 | 65 | 129 | 6 | 14 | L | L | 6-1 | 190 | 11-11-72 | 1990 | West Covina, Calif. |
| Llanos, Aurelio, dh-1b | .252 | 81 | 246 | 35 | 62 | 15 | 4 | 6 | 30 | 15 | 67 | 6 | 6 | S | R | 6-4 | 215 | 10-14-70 | 1988 | Carolina, P.R. |
| Marquez, Jesus, of | .273 | 61 | 216 | 23 | 59 | 7 | 1 | 4 | 27 | 13 | 47 | 5 | 4 | L | L | 6-1 | 160 | 3-12-73 | 1990 | Caracas, Venez. |
| Martinez, Eduard, 3b | .152 | 10 | 33 | 3 | 5 | 0 | 1 | 0 | 0 | 0 | 8 | 0 | 0 | R | R | 6-1 | 175 | 4-13-73 | 1991 | Moca, D.R. |
| Morales, Jorge, c | .194 | 38 | 103 | 8 | 20 | 6 | 0 | 4 | 9 | 6 | 26 | 1 | 1 | R | R | 5-11 | 185 | 11-2-70 | 1991 | Caguas, P.R. |
| Robertson, Robbie, of | .285 | 105 | 340 | 49 | 97 | 16 | 7 | 4 | 46 | 42 | 63 | 7 | 7 | L | L | 6-4 | 190 | 9-11-71 | 1993 | Mobile, Ala. |
| Serrano, Nestor, of-3b | .085 | 19 | 47 | 4 | 4 | 0 | 1 | 0 | 2 | 3 | 10 | 0 | 2 | R | R | 5-9 | 165 | 6-1-72 | 1991 | Guarenas, Venez. |
| Sheets, Andy, ss | .263 | 69 | 259 | 32 | 68 | 10 | 4 | 1 | 25 | 20 | 59 | 7 | 7 | R | R | 6-2 | 180 | 11-19-71 | 1992 | St. Amant, La. |
| Sutherland, Alex, c | .240 | 103 | 325 | 40 | 78 | 20 | 0 | 6 | 31 | 20 | 62 | 5 | 4 | R | R | 5-11 | 170 | 3-13-71 | 1991 | Maracaibo, Venez. |
| Triessl, Mike, c | .185 | 34 | 81 | 9 | 15 | 5 | 0 | 1 | 8 | 14 | 32 | 0 | 0 | R | R | 6-1 | 215 | 2-27-71 | 1993 | Malverne, N.Y. |
| Wallace, Brian, 3b | .215 | 117 | 396 | 46 | 85 | 17 | 2 | 5 | 42 | 37 | 145 | 15 | 9 | R | R | 6-2 | 200 | 9-10-71 | 1992 | Newark, Del. |

| PITCHING | W | L | ERA | G | GS | CG | SV | IP | H | R | ER | BB | SO | B | T | HT | WT | DOB | 1st Yr | Resides |
|---|---|---|---|---|---|---|---|---|---|---|---|---|---|---|---|---|---|---|---|---|
| Aschoff, Jerry | 3 | 4 | 6.10 | 9 | 6 | 0 | 0 | 38 | 45 | 28 | 26 | 29 | 26 | L | L | 6-0 | 175 | 5-11-70 | 1992 | Villa Park, Calif. |
| Bruce, Tim | 2 | 1 | 1.29 | 12 | 0 | 0 | 3 | 21 | 12 | 8 | 3 | 5 | 25 | L | R | 6-4 | 205 | 8-29-72 | 1993 | Detroit, Mich. |
| Cody, Ron | 5 | 7 | 5.56 | 26 | 10 | 0 | 0 | 91 | 98 | 67 | 56 | 26 | 52 | R | R | 6-3 | 185 | 7-4-70 | 1992 | Citrus Heights, Calif. |
| Cope, Robin | 0 | 0 | 6.19 | 3 | 2 | 0 | 0 | 16 | 17 | 12 | 11 | 11 | 5 | L | R | 6-5 | 230 | 4-26-73 | 1991 | Okeechobee, Fla. |
| Davis, Tim | 10 | 2 | 1.85 | 16 | 10 | 3 | 2 | 78 | 54 | 20 | 16 | 33 | 89 | L | L | 5-11 | 165 | 7-14-70 | 1992 | Bristol, Fla. |
| Deal, Jamon | 0 | 1 | 12.32 | 11 | 1 | 0 | 0 | 19 | 31 | 38 | 26 | 25 | 15 | R | R | 6-0 | 200 | 5-4-70 | 1992 | Conover, N.C. |
| Estes, Shawn | 5 | 9 | 7.24 | 19 | 18 | 0 | 0 | 83 | 108 | 85 | 67 | 52 | 65 | R | L | 6-2 | 185 | 2-18-73 | 1991 | Gardnerville, Nev. |
| Evans, David | 2 | 1 | 2.28 | 5 | 5 | 0 | 0 | 28 | 21 | 9 | 7 | 15 | 23 | R | R | 6-3 | 185 | 1-1-68 | 1990 | Houston, Texas |
| Graham, Richard | 2 | 3 | 4.46 | 43 | 0 | 0 | 2 | 77 | 75 | 48 | 38 | 31 | 59 | S | R | 6-1 | 175 | 2-26-70 | 1992 | Northboro, Mass. |
| Harikkala, Tim | 3 | 3 | 6.52 | 15 | 4 | 0 | 0 | 39 | 50 | 30 | 28 | 12 | 33 | R | R | 6-2 | 185 | 7-15-71 | 1992 | Lake Worth, Fla. |
| Kostich, Bill | 0 | 2 | 0.91 | 20 | 0 | 0 | 3 | 30 | 28 | 7 | 3 | 8 | 33 | L | L | 6-0 | 170 | 2-1-71 | 1989 | Taylor, Mich. |
| Kovach, Tim | 1 | 0 | 7.27 | 3 | 1 | 0 | 0 | 9 | 10 | 7 | 7 | 6 | 5 | L | R | 6-7 | 185 | 11-17-68 | 1989 | Medina, Ohio |
| Lisiecki, David | 2 | 3 | 3.22 | 20 | 0 | 0 | 1 | 36 | 22 | 15 | 13 | 20 | 58 | R | R | 6-4 | 250 | 9-15-71 | 1991 | Clinton Township, Mich. |
| Nickell, Jackie | 7 | 7 | 3.06 | 24 | 23 | 2 | 0 | 150 | 135 | 54 | 51 | 41 | 151 | R | R | 5-10 | 175 | 4-20-70 | 1992 | Tiburon, Calif. |
| O'Donnell, Erik | 0 | 1 | 4.00 | 6 | 2 | 0 | 0 | 18 | 18 | 11 | 8 | 4 | 11 | R | R | 6-6 | 205 | 3-14-70 | 1991 | Portland, Ore. |
| Rivera, Oscar | 2 | 2 | 3.53 | 13 | 13 | 0 | 0 | 71 | 70 | 33 | 28 | 22 | 33 | R | R | 6-2 | 200 | 10-2-71 | 1992 | Arecibo, P.R. |
| Sanchez, Jose | 8 | 11 | 4.56 | 26 | 25 | 2 | 0 | 130 | 132 | 80 | 66 | 79 | 133 | R | R | 6-1 | 170 | 4-14-73 | 1991 | Cartagena, Colombia |
| Urso, Sal | 4 | 4 | 3.35 | 36 | 1 | 0 | 2 | 54 | 57 | 24 | 20 | 24 | 50 | R | L | 5-11 | 175 | 1-19-72 | 1990 | Tampa, Fla. |
| Witte, Trey | 3 | 9 | 4.28 | 28 | 14 | 1 | 0 | 101 | 111 | 57 | 48 | 22 | 62 | R | R | 6-1 | 192 | 1-15-70 | 1991 | Houston, Texas |
| Worley, Robert | 3 | 3 | 2.21 | 45 | 0 | 0 | 22 | 53 | 48 | 23 | 13 | 23 | 37 | R | R | 6-3 | 185 | 2-15-71 | 1992 | Waterville, Ohio |

## NORTHWEST LEAGUE

| BATTING | AVG | G | AB | R | H | 2B | 3B | HR | RBI | BB | SO | SB | CS | B | T | HT | WT | DOB | 1st Yr | Resides |
|---|---|---|---|---|---|---|---|---|---|---|---|---|---|---|---|---|---|---|---|---|
| Augustine, Andy, c | .200 | 7 | 20 | 5 | 4 | 0 | 0 | 1 | 5 | 6 | 8 | 0 | 0 | R | R | 5-10 | 180 | 11-13-72 | 1993 | Rothschild, Wis. |
| Barger, Michael, of | .261 | 68 | 203 | 30 | 53 | 7 | 3 | 0 | 21 | 26 | 26 | 15 | 6 | R | R | 6-0 | 165 | 4-6-71 | 1993 | Ballwin, Mo. |
| Berube, Joe, of-dh | .252 | 44 | 139 | 17 | 35 | 6 | 1 | 2 | 28 | 23 | 38 | 4 | 1 | L | R | 6-1 | 190 | 6-26-72 | 1993 | Northboro, Mass. |
| Cabrera, Antonio, 3b | .220 | 48 | 123 | 22 | 27 | 3 | 0 | 3 | 15 | 14 | 42 | 4 | 2 | R | R | 6-2 | 180 | 9-2-71 | 1989 | Santo Domingo, D.R. |
| Cardenas, Johnny, c | .204 | 47 | 157 | 17 | 32 | 5 | 1 | 2 | 24 | 17 | 34 | 1 | 0 | R | R | 6-3 | 210 | 7-23-70 | 1993 | Fort Worth, Texas |
| Clifford, James, 1b-dh | .269 | 62 | 193 | 39 | 52 | 14 | 0 | 9 | 40 | 36 | 63 | 8 | 6 | L | L | 6-2 | 225 | 3-23-70 | 1992 | Seattle, Wash. |
| Dunavan, Chad, of | .223 | 48 | 130 | 18 | 29 | 11 | 1 | 1 | 12 | 11 | 48 | 3 | 2 | R | R | 6-0 | 195 | 10-31-72 | 1993 | Fort Worth, Texas |
| Guevara, Giomar, ss | .227 | 62 | 211 | 31 | 48 | 8 | 3 | 1 | 23 | 34 | 46 | 4 | 7 | R | R | 5-8 | 150 | 10-23-72 | 1991 | Guarenas, Venez. |
| Heath, Jason, c-of | .146 | 22 | 41 | 4 | 6 | 0 | 0 | 0 | 1 | 4 | 12 | 3 | 0 | R | R | 6-2 | 195 | 2-5-71 | 1993 | Shawnee, Okla. |
| Ibanez, Raul, c-dh | .284 | 43 | 134 | 16 | 38 | 5 | 2 | 0 | 15 | 21 | 23 | 0 | 3 | L | R | 6-2 | 200 | 6-2-72 | 1992 | Miami, Fla. |
| Jorgensen, Randy, 1b-of | .263 | 67 | 228 | 42 | 60 | 13 | 0 | 5 | 22 | 37 | 33 | 7 | 4 | L | L | 6-2 | 190 | 4-3-72 | 1993 | Everett, Wash. |
| Martinez, Eduard, 3b-dh | .193 | 45 | 119 | 14 | 23 | 7 | 0 | 2 | 9 | 10 | 35 | 2 | 0 | R | R | 6-1 | 175 | 4-13-73 | 1991 | Moca, D.R. |
| Miller, Roy, 3b-ss | .224 | 55 | 165 | 26 | 37 | 3 | 0 | 2 | 15 | 28 | 42 | 4 | 7 | R | R | 5-10 | 180 | 12-22-71 | 1993 | Newberg, Ore. |
| Patel, Manny, 2b | .233 | 66 | 227 | 41 | 53 | 8 | 0 | 3 | 38 | 54 | 43 | 12 | 9 | L | R | 5-10 | 165 | 4-22-72 | 1993 | Tampa, Fla. |
| Rackley, Keifer, of | .246 | 33 | 114 | 21 | 28 | 4 | 0 | 2 | 15 | 12 | 16 | 3 | 1 | L | R | 6-1 | 200 | 2-27-71 | 1993 | Butler, Ala. |
| Serrano, Nestor, of-3b | .204 | 29 | 93 | 8 | 19 | 3 | 0 | 0 | 12 | 12 | 11 | 3 | 3 | R | R | 5-9 | 165 | 6-1-72 | 1991 | Guarenas, Venez. |
| Sturdivant, Marcus, of | .256 | 64 | 238 | 34 | 61 | 8 | 3 | 4 | 32 | 22 | 28 | 8 | 5 | L | L | 5-10 | 150 | 10-29-73 | 1992 | Oakboro, N.C. |

| PITCHING | W | L | ERA | G | GS | CG | SV | IP | H | R | ER | BB | SO | B | T | HT | WT | DOB | 1st Yr | Resides |
|---|---|---|---|---|---|---|---|---|---|---|---|---|---|---|---|---|---|---|---|---|
| Apana, Matt | 5 | 3 | 4.43 | 14 | 14 | 0 | 0 | 61 | 50 | 38 | 30 | 43 | 59 | R | R | 6-0 | 195 | 1-16-71 | 1993 | Honolulu, Hawaii |
| Bruce, Tim | 3 | 0 | 4.97 | 8 | 0 | 0 | 0 | 13 | 10 | 8 | 7 | 9 | 14 | L | R | 6-4 | 205 | 8-29-72 | 1993 | Detroit, Mich. |
| Carmona, Rafael | 2 | 3 | 3.79 | 23 | 0 | 0 | 2 | 36 | 33 | 19 | 15 | 14 | 30 | L | R | 6-2 | 175 | 10-2-72 | 1993 | Comerio, P.R. |
| Collett, Mike | 0 | 0 | 0.00 | 1 | 0 | 0 | 0 | 1 | 1 | 0 | 0 | 0 | 0 | R | R | 6-1 | 185 | 11-19-71 | 1993 | Glendora, Calif. |
| Crow, Dean | 5 | 3 | 1.89 | 25 | 0 | 0 | 4 | 48 | 31 | 14 | 10 | 21 | 38 | L | R | 6-5 | 212 | 8-21-72 | 1993 | Houston, Texas |
| Doughty, Brian | 5 | 4 | 2.49 | 14 | 14 | 1 | 0 | 76 | 65 | 30 | 21 | 42 | 39 | R | R | 6-5 | 210 | 9-21-74 | 1992 | Bothell, Wash. |
| Franklin, Ryan | 5 | 3 | 2.92 | 15 | 14 | 1 | 0 | 74 | 72 | 38 | 24 | 27 | 55 | R | R | 6-3 | 160 | 3-5-73 | 1993 | Spiro, Okla. |
| Harikkala, Tim | 1 | 0 | 1.13 | 4 | 0 | 0 | 0 | 8 | 3 | 1 | 1 | 2 | 12 | R | R | 6-2 | 185 | 7-15-71 | 1992 | Lake Worth, Fla. |
| Krueger, Robert | 2 | 0 | 3.58 | 13 | 3 | 0 | 0 | 28 | 25 | 13 | 11 | 11 | 17 | L | L | 6-2 | 185 | 10-19-71 | 1993 | Oak Forest, Ill. |
| Mantei, Matt | 1 | 1 | 5.96 | 26 | 0 | 0 | 12 | 26 | 26 | 19 | 17 | 15 | 34 | R | R | 6-1 | 181 | 7-7-73 | 1991 | Sawyer, Mich. |
| Montane, Ivan | 5 | 4 | 3.93 | 15 | 15 | 1 | 0 | 73 | 55 | 36 | 32 | 37 | 53 | R | R | 6-2 | 195 | 6-3-73 | 1992 | Miami, Fla. |
| Santana, Marino | 0 | 1 | 5.82 | 15 | 0 | 0 | 0 | 22 | 27 | 19 | 14 | 22 | 24 | R | R | 6-1 | 175 | 5-10-72 | 1990 | Santo Domingo, D.R. |
| Sosa, Brian | 1 | 3 | 2.83 | 18 | 0 | 0 | 0 | 35 | 26 | 13 | 11 | 17 | 30 | S | R | 5-11 | 185 | 4-4-73 | 1993 | Fontana, Calif. |
| Theron, Greg | 1 | 1 | 3.25 | 23 | 0 | 0 | 2 | 53 | 46 | 25 | 19 | 19 | 47 | R | R | 6-6 | 210 | 9-20-73 | 1992 | Mesa, Ariz. |
| Thompson, John | 0 | 2 | 4.24 | 17 | 1 | 0 | 0 | 34 | 31 | 23 | 16 | 33 | 28 | R | R | 6-2 | 200 | 1-18-73 | 1992 | Spokane, Wash. |
| Wolcott, Bob | 8 | 4 | 2.64 | 15 | 15 | 1 | 0 | 95 | 70 | 31 | 28 | 26 | 79 | R | R | 6-0 | 190 | 9-8-73 | 1992 | Medford, Ore. |

## ARIZONA LEAGUE

| BATTING | AVG | G | AB | R | H | 2B | 3B | HR | RBI | BB | SO | SB | CS | B | T | HT | WT | DOB | 1st Yr | Resides |
|---|---|---|---|---|---|---|---|---|---|---|---|---|---|---|---|---|---|---|---|---|
| Aquino, Pedro, 1b | .292 | 34 | 120 | 18 | 35 | 9 | 0 | 1 | 23 | 9 | 8 | 1 | 0 | R | R | 6-2 | 175 | 12-11-73 | 1991 | Santo Domingo, D.R. |
| Augustine, Andy, c | .125 | 3 | 8 | 0 | 1 | 0 | 0 | 1 | 1 | 5 | 0 | 0 | 0 | R | R | 5-10 | 180 | 11-13-72 | 1993 | Rothschild, Wis. |
| Batista, Dario, of | .265 | 30 | 102 | 22 | 27 | 4 | 0 | 0 | 7 | 14 | 18 | 8 | 1 | S | R | 6-3 | 175 | 2-5-73 | 1990 | Moca, D.R. |
| Brady, Michael, of | .169 | 26 | 83 | 15 | 14 | 1 | 0 | 1 | 5 | 11 | 29 | 1 | 2 | R | R | 6-3 | 190 | 5-17-74 | 1993 | Newark, Del. |
| Brannon, Paul, dh | .368 | 5 | 19 | 2 | 7 | 2 | 1 | 0 | 2 | 1 | 6 | 0 | 0 | R | R | 6-0 | 215 | 5-19-72 | 1993 | Kings Mountain, N.C. |
| Cook, Jason, ss-3b | .319 | 45 | 160 | 31 | 51 | 10 | 4 | 2 | 24 | 16 | 20 | 9 | 1 | R | R | 6-0 | 180 | 12-9-71 | 1993 | Fairfax, Va. |
| Davis, Stacey, 1b-of | .172 | 36 | 122 | 18 | 21 | 2 | 3 | 1 | 12 | 13 | 47 | 2 | 1 | L | R | 6-3 | 195 | 12-21-73 | 1992 | Decatur, Ga. |
| DeLeon, Jose, of | .238 | 25 | 84 | 8 | 20 | 1 | 0 | 0 | 9 | 5 | 22 | 5 | 1 | R | R | 6-2 | 175 | 8-30-73 | 1993 | La Vega, D.R. |
| DeLeon, Santo, of-2b | .309 | 43 | 152 | 31 | 47 | 5 | 4 | 1 | 15 | 16 | 32 | 19 | 2 | S | R | 5-11 | 170 | 10-18-73 | 1992 | Washington, D.C. |
| Domingo, Tyrone, 2b | .200 | 13 | 35 | 4 | 7 | 1 | 0 | 0 | 2 | 5 | 6 | 1 | 2 | R | R | 5-8 | 169 | 10-22-74 | 1991 | Los Angeles, Calif. |
| Dumas, Chris, of | .245 | 32 | 106 | 15 | 26 | 3 | 3 | 1 | 11 | 9 | 29 | 4 | 2 | R | R | 6-1 | 190 | 9-30-74 | 1993 | Sweetwater, Ala. |
| Lopez, Carlos, 2b | .245 | 36 | 110 | 13 | 27 | 2 | 1 | 0 | 10 | 12 | 43 | 1 | 3 | S | R | 6-1 | 165 | 8-17-74 | 1993 | Caracas, Venez. |
| Martinez, Victor, c | .212 | 16 | 52 | 8 | 11 | 0 | 1 | 1 | 6 | 1 | 8 | 1 | 0 | R | R | 6-1 | 185 | 12-22-74 | 1992 | Santiago, D.R. |
| Mathis, Joe, of | .250 | 36 | 84 | 14 | 21 | 4 | 1 | 0 | 9 | 5 | 26 | 7 | 1 | L | R | 5-10 | 173 | 8-10-74 | 1993 | Johnston, S.C. |
| Maxwell, Trent, c | .159 | 19 | 44 | 6 | 7 | 0 | 0 | 0 | 5 | 4 | 16 | 1 | 0 | R | R | 6-2 | 190 | 11-9-73 | 1992 | Cotton Valley, La. |
| Molina, Luis, ss-2b | .214 | 39 | 112 | 19 | 24 | 3 | 1 | 0 | 6 | 30 | 13 | 7 | 4 | R | R | 6-1 | 170 | 3-22-74 | 1993 | Panama City, Panama |
| Pomierski, Joe, 3b | .225 | 48 | 173 | 19 | 39 | 8 | 4 | 2 | 29 | 19 | 39 | 4 | 1 | L | R | 6-2 | 180 | 4-15-74 | 1992 | Biloxi, Miss. |
| Randolph, Ed, c-dh | .269 | 19 | 52 | 6 | 14 | 4 | 0 | 1 | 12 | 6 | 13 | 2 | 1 | S | R | 6-2 | 202 | 10-17-74 | 1993 | Dallas, Texas |
| Tinoco, Luis, of | .259 | 39 | 112 | 20 | 29 | 4 | 2 | 1 | 20 | 31 | 41 | 4 | 1 | R | R | 6-2 | 170 | 7-24-74 | 1992 | Maracaibo, Venez. |
| Valentino, Rob, c | .211 | 23 | 71 | 6 | 15 | 1 | 0 | 2 | 9 | 9 | 12 | 2 | 0 | R | R | 6-3 | 190 | 6-22-74 | 1993 | Dearborn Heights, Mich. |

| PITCHING | W | L | ERA | G | GS | CG | SV | IP | H | R | ER | BB | SO | B | T | HT | WT | DOB | 1st Yr | Resides |
|---|---|---|---|---|---|---|---|---|---|---|---|---|---|---|---|---|---|---|---|---|
| Bieniasz, Derek | 3 | 0 | 4.85 | 6 | 0 | 0 | 0 | 13 | 11 | 8 | 7 | 4 | 15 | R | R | 6-4 | 175 | 4-19-74 | 1993 | Toronto, Ontario |
| Coffman, Kevin | 0 | 1 | 1.29 | 4 | 0 | 0 | 0 | 7 | 3 | 4 | 1 | 5 | 6 | R | R | 6-3 | 205 | 1-19-65 | 1983 | Victoria, Texas |
| Cope, Robin | 3 | 4 | 5.08 | 11 | 11 | 0 | 0 | 62 | 66 | 42 | 35 | 20 | 62 | L | R | 6-5 | 230 | 4-26-73 | 1993 | Okeechobee, Fla. |
| Craig, Casey | 0 | 1 | 8.03 | 9 | 1 | 0 | 1 | 12 | 15 | 13 | 11 | 9 | 5 | R | R | 6-4 | 160 | 10-8-75 | 1993 | Jackson, Mich. |
| Daniels, John | 3 | 4 | 3.40 | 13 | 8 | 0 | 0 | 53 | 46 | 30 | 20 | 13 | 50 | S | R | 6-3 | 185 | 2-7-74 | 1993 | Valinda, Calif. |
| Dessellier, Chris | 1 | 5 | 6.56 | 12 | 10 | 0 | 0 | 48 | 62 | 50 | 35 | 36 | 32 | R | R | 6-5 | 220 | 6-29-74 | 1992 | Ypsilanti, Mich. |
| Golden, Stan | 2 | 1 | 6.12 | 14 | 6 | 0 | 0 | 50 | 52 | 50 | 34 | 37 | 46 | R | R | 6-4 | 200 | 2-7-74 | 1992 | Opelika, Ala. |
| Green, Chris | 2 | 5 | 3.72 | 24 | 0 | 0 | 6 | 36 | 29 | 21 | 15 | 16 | 31 | L | R | 6-0 | 180 | 8-13-74 | 1993 | La Mesa, Calif. |
| Hinchliffe, Brett | 0 | 0 | 5.08 | 10 | 9 | 0 | 0 | 44 | 55 | 32 | 25 | 5 | 29 | S | R | 6-4 | 188 | 7-21-74 | 1992 | Detroit, Mich. |
| Mitchell, Kelvin | 0 | 0 | 2.70 | 3 | 0 | 0 | 0 | 3 | 4 | 1 | 1 | 2 | 2 | R | L | 6-2 | 225 | 10-17-74 | 1993 | Butler, Ala. |
| Newton, Geronimo | 1 | 4 | 2.23 | 21 | 1 | 0 | 1 | 40 | 31 | 27 | 10 | 23 | 39 | L | L | 6-0 | 150 | 12-31-73 | 1992 | St. Croix, V.I. |
| Updike, Jon | 1 | 3 | 5.97 | 21 | 0 | 0 | 0 | 35 | 36 | 27 | 23 | 22 | 32 | S | R | 6-5 | 175 | 1-26-73 | 1993 | Deltona, Fla. |
| Vallejo, Julio | 0 | 1 | 121.50 | 2 | 1 | 0 | 0 | 1 | 4 | 10 | 9 | 8 | 0 | L | L | 6-1 | 170 | 2-12-73 | 1991 | Pedernales, D.R. |
| Vanhof, John | 0 | 0 | 1.64 | 5 | 2 | 0 | 0 | 11 | 7 | 2 | 2 | 4 | 12 | L | L | 6-3 | 180 | 12-4-73 | 1992 | Southgate, Mich. |
| Williams, Brian | 2 | 3 | 3.35 | 16 | 5 | 0 | 1 | 43 | 37 | 21 | 16 | 24 | 44 | R | R | 6-3 | 180 | 6-29-72 | 1993 | Phoenix, Ariz. |

# TEXAS RANGERS

**Manager:** Kevin Kennedy.          **1993 Record:** 86-76, .531 (2nd, AL West).

| BATTING | AVG | G | AB | R | H | 2B | 3B | HR | RBI | BB | SO | SB | CS | B | T | HT | WT | DOB | 1st Yr | Resides |
|---|---|---|---|---|---|---|---|---|---|---|---|---|---|---|---|---|---|---|---|---|
| Balboni, Steve | .600 | 2 | 5 | 0 | 3 | 0 | 0 | 0 | 0 | 0 | 2 | 0 | 0 | R | R | 6-3 | 225 | 1-16-57 | 1978 | Lee's Summit, Mo. |
| Canseco, Jose | .255 | 60 | 231 | 30 | 59 | 14 | 1 | 10 | 46 | 16 | 62 | 6 | 6 | R | R | 6-3 | 185 | 7-2-64 | 1982 | Miami, Fla. |
| Dascenzo, Doug | .199 | 76 | 146 | 20 | 29 | 5 | 1 | 2 | 10 | 8 | 22 | 2 | 0 | S | L | 5-8 | 160 | 6-30-64 | 1985 | LaBelle, Pa. |
| Davis, Butch | .245 | 62 | 159 | 24 | 39 | 10 | 4 | 3 | 20 | 5 | 28 | 3 | 1 | R | R | 6-0 | 185 | 6-19-58 | 1980 | Garner, N.C. |
| Diaz, Mario | .273 | 71 | 205 | 24 | 56 | 10 | 1 | 2 | 24 | 8 | 13 | 1 | 0 | R | R | 5-10 | 160 | 1-10-62 | 1979 | Yabucoa, P.R. |
| Ducey, Rob | .282 | 27 | 85 | 15 | 24 | 6 | 3 | 2 | 9 | 10 | 17 | 2 | 3 | L | R | 6-2 | 180 | 5-24-65 | 1984 | Palm Harbor, Fla. |
| Franco, Julio | .289 | 144 | 532 | 85 | 154 | 31 | 3 | 14 | 84 | 62 | 95 | 9 | 3 | R | R | 6-1 | 188 | 8-23-61 | 1978 | Arlington, Texas |
| Gil, Benji | .123 | 22 | 57 | 3 | 7 | 0 | 0 | 0 | 2 | 5 | 22 | 1 | 2 | R | R | 6-2 | 180 | 10-6-72 | 1991 | San Diego, Calif. |
| Gonzalez, Juan | .310 | 140 | 536 | 105 | 166 | 33 | 1 | 46 | 118 | 37 | 99 | 4 | 1 | R | R | 6-3 | 210 | 10-16-69 | 1986 | Vega Baja, P.R. |
| Harris, Donald | .197 | 40 | 76 | 10 | 15 | 2 | 0 | 1 | 8 | 5 | 18 | 0 | 1 | R | R | 6-1 | 185 | 11-12-67 | 1989 | Waco, Texas |
| Hulse, David | .290 | 114 | 407 | 71 | 118 | 9 | 10 | 1 | 29 | 26 | 57 | 29 | 9 | L | L | 5-11 | 170 | 2-25-68 | 1990 | San Angelo, Texas |
| Huson, Jeff | .133 | 23 | 45 | 3 | 6 | 1 | 1 | 0 | 2 | 0 | 10 | 0 | 0 | L | R | 6-3 | 180 | 8-15-64 | 1986 | Bedford, Texas |
| James, Chris | .355 | 8 | 31 | 5 | 11 | 1 | 0 | 3 | 7 | 3 | 6 | 0 | 0 | R | R | 6-1 | 202 | 10-4-62 | 1982 | Alto, Texas |
| Lee, Manuel | .220 | 73 | 205 | 31 | 45 | 3 | 1 | 1 | 12 | 22 | 39 | 2 | 4 | S | R | 5-9 | 161 | 6-17-65 | 1982 | San Pedro de Macoris, D.R. |
| Palmeiro, Rafael | .295 | 160 | 597 | 124 | 176 | 40 | 2 | 37 | 105 | 73 | 85 | 22 | 3 | L | L | 6-0 | 188 | 9-24-64 | 1985 | Arlington, Texas |
| Palmer, Dean | .245 | 148 | 519 | 88 | 127 | 31 | 2 | 33 | 96 | 53 | 154 | 11 | 10 | R | R | 6-2 | 195 | 12-27-68 | 1986 | Tallahassee, Fla. |
| Peltier, Dan | .269 | 65 | 160 | 23 | 43 | 7 | 1 | 1 | 17 | 20 | 27 | 0 | 4 | L | L | 6-1 | 200 | 6-30-68 | 1989 | Eden Prairie, Minn. |
| Petralli, Geno | .241 | 59 | 133 | 16 | 32 | 5 | 0 | 1 | 13 | 22 | 17 | 2 | 0 | S | R | 6-1 | 190 | 9-25-59 | 1978 | Arlington, Texas |
| Redus, Gary | .288 | 77 | 222 | 28 | 64 | 12 | 4 | 6 | 31 | 23 | 35 | 4 | 4 | R | R | 6-1 | 180 | 11-1-56 | 1978 | Decatur, Ala. |
| Ripken, Billy | .189 | 50 | 132 | 12 | 25 | 4 | 0 | 0 | 11 | 11 | 19 | 0 | 2 | R | R | 6-1 | 188 | 12-16-64 | 1982 | Cockeysville, Md. |
| Rodriguez, Ivan | .273 | 137 | 473 | 56 | 129 | 28 | 4 | 10 | 66 | 29 | 70 | 8 | 7 | R | R | 5-9 | 205 | 11-30-71 | 1989 | Vega Baja, P.R. |
| Russell, John | .227 | 18 | 22 | 1 | 5 | 1 | 0 | 1 | 3 | 2 | 10 | 0 | 0 | R | R | 6-0 | 195 | 1-5-61 | 1982 | Wyndmoor, Pa. |
| Shave, Jon | .319 | 17 | 47 | 3 | 15 | 2 | 0 | 0 | 7 | 0 | 8 | 1 | 3 | R | R | 6-0 | 180 | 11-4-67 | 1990 | Fernandina Beach, Fla. |
| Strange, Doug | .256 | 145 | 484 | 58 | 124 | 29 | 0 | 7 | 60 | 43 | 69 | 6 | 4 | S | R | 6-2 | 170 | 4-13-64 | 1985 | Scottsdale, Ariz. |

| PITCHING | W | L | ERA | G | GS | CG | SV | IP | H | R | ER | BB | SO | B | T | HT | WT | DOB | 1st Yr | Resides |
|---|---|---|---|---|---|---|---|---|---|---|---|---|---|---|---|---|---|---|---|---|
| Bohanon, Brian | 4 | 4 | 4.76 | 36 | 8 | 0 | 0 | 93 | 107 | 54 | 49 | 46 | 45 | L | L | 6-3 | 220 | 8-1-68 | 1987 | Houston, Texas |
| Bronkey, Jeff | 1 | 1 | 4.00 | 21 | 0 | 0 | 1 | 36 | 39 | 20 | 16 | 11 | 18 | R | R | 6-3 | 210 | 9-18-65 | 1986 | Klamath Falls, Ore. |
| Brown, Kevin | 15 | 12 | 3.59 | 34 | 34 | 12 | 0 | 233 | 228 | 105 | 93 | 74 | 142 | R | R | 6-4 | 195 | 3-14-65 | 1986 | Macon, Ga. |
| Burns, Todd | 0 | 4 | 4.57 | 25 | 5 | 0 | 0 | 65 | 63 | 36 | 33 | 32 | 35 | R | R | 6-1 | 185 | 7-6-63 | 1984 | Huntsville, Ala. |
| Carpenter, Cris | 4 | 1 | 4.22 | 27 | 0 | 0 | 1 | 32 | 35 | 15 | 15 | 12 | 27 | R | R | 6-2 | 195 | 4-5-65 | 1988 | Gainesville, Ga. |
| Dreyer, Steve | 3 | 3 | 5.71 | 10 | 6 | 0 | 0 | 41 | 48 | 26 | 26 | 20 | 23 | R | R | 6-3 | 180 | 11-19-69 | 1990 | Cedar Falls, Iowa |
| Fajardo, Hector | 0 | 0 | 0.00 | 1 | 0 | 0 | 0 | 1 | 0 | 0 | 0 | 1 | 1 | R | R | 6-4 | 200 | 11-6-70 | 1989 | Michoacan, Mexico |
| Henke, Tom | 5 | 5 | 2.91 | 66 | 0 | 0 | 40 | 74 | 55 | 25 | 24 | 27 | 79 | R | R | 6-5 | 225 | 12-21-57 | 1980 | Jefferson City, Mo. |
| Lefferts, Craig | 3 | 9 | 6.05 | 52 | 8 | 0 | 0 | 83 | 102 | 57 | 56 | 28 | 58 | L | L | 6-1 | 200 | 9-29-57 | 1980 | Poway, Calif. |
| Leibrandt, Charlie | 9 | 10 | 4.55 | 26 | 26 | 1 | 0 | 150 | 169 | 84 | 76 | 45 | 89 | R | L | 6-4 | 200 | 10-4-56 | 1978 | Alpharetta, Ga. |
| Nelson, Gene | 0 | 0 | 3.38 | 6 | 0 | 0 | 1 | 8 | 10 | 3 | 3 | 1 | 4 | R | R | 6-0 | 174 | 12-3-60 | 1978 | Dade City, Fla. |
| 2-team (46 Calif.) | 0 | 0 | 3.12 | 52 | 0 | 0 | 5 | 61 | 60 | 28 | 21 | 24 | 35 |  |  |  |  |  |  |  |
| Nen, Robb | 1 | 1 | 6.35 | 9 | 3 | 0 | 0 | 23 | 28 | 17 | 16 | 26 | 12 | R | R | 6-4 | 190 | 11-28-69 | 1987 | Seal Beach, Calif. |
| Oliver, Darren | 0 | 0 | 2.70 | 2 | 0 | 0 | 0 | 3 | 2 | 1 | 1 | 1 | 4 | R | L | 6-0 | 170 | 10-6-70 | 1988 | Rio Linda, Calif. |
| Patterson, Bob | 2 | 4 | 4.78 | 52 | 0 | 0 | 1 | 53 | 59 | 28 | 28 | 11 | 46 | R | L | 6-2 | 185 | 5-16-59 | 1982 | Hickory, N.C. |
| Pavlik, Roger | 12 | 6 | 3.41 | 26 | 26 | 2 | 0 | 166 | 151 | 67 | 63 | 80 | 131 | R | R | 6-2 | 220 | 10-4-67 | 1987 | Houston, Texas |
| Reed, Rick | 1 | 0 | 2.25 | 2 | 0 | 0 | 0 | 4 | 6 | 1 | 1 | 1 | 2 | R | R | 6-0 | 200 | 8-16-64 | 1986 | Huntington, W.Va. |
| 2-team (1 K.C.) | 1 | 0 | 5.87 | 3 | 0 | 0 | 0 | 8 | 12 | 5 | 5 | 2 | 5 |  |  |  |  |  |  |  |
| Rogers, Kenny | 16 | 10 | 4.10 | 35 | 33 | 5 | 0 | 208 | 210 | 108 | 95 | 71 | 140 | L | L | 6-1 | 205 | 11-10-64 | 1982 | Arlington, Texas |
| Ryan, Nolan | 5 | 5 | 4.88 | 13 | 13 | 0 | 0 | 66 | 54 | 47 | 36 | 40 | 46 | R | R | 6-2 | 212 | 1-31-47 | 1965 | Alvin, Texas |
| Schooler, Mike | 3 | 0 | 5.55 | 17 | 0 | 0 | 0 | 24 | 30 | 17 | 15 | 10 | 16 | R | R | 6-3 | 210 | 8-10-62 | 1985 | Renton, Wash. |
| Whiteside, Matt | 2 | 1 | 4.32 | 60 | 0 | 0 | 1 | 73 | 78 | 37 | 35 | 23 | 39 | R | R | 6-0 | 185 | 8-8-67 | 1990 | Charleston, Mo. |

## FIELDING

| Catcher | PCT | G | PO | A | E | DP |
|---|---|---|---|---|---|---|
| Petralli | .990 | 39 | 178 | 11 | 2 | 4 |
| Rodriguez | .991 | 134 | 801 | 76 | 8 | 7 |
| Russell | 1.000 | 11 | 21 | 0 | 0 | 0 |

| First Base | PCT | G | PO | A | E | DP |
|---|---|---|---|---|---|---|
| Diaz | 1.000 | 1 | 1 | 0 | 0 | 0 |
| Palmeiro | .997 | 160 | 1389 | 146 | 5 | 133 |
| Peltier | 1.000 | 5 | 8 | 0 | 0 | 0 |
| Redus | .957 | 5 | 21 | 1 | 1 | 5 |
| Russell | 1.000 | 1 | 9 | 0 | 0 | 0 |

| Second Base | PCT | G | PO | A | E | DP |
|---|---|---|---|---|---|---|
| Huson | 1.000 | 5 | 8 | 6 | 0 | 2 |
| Petralli | 1.000 | 1 | 1 | 0 | 0 | 0 |
| Redus | .000 | 1 | 0 | 0 | 0 | 0 |
| Ripken | .992 | 34 | 52 | 73 | 1 | 16 |
| Shave | 1.000 | 8 | 9 | 17 | 0 | 3 |

| | PCT | G | PO | A | E | DP |
|---|---|---|---|---|---|---|
| Strange | .980 | 135 | 272 | 362 | 13 | 81 |
| Third Base | PCT | G | PO | A | E | DP |
| Diaz | 1.000 | 12 | 8 | 19 | 0 | 2 |
| Huson | .750 | 2 | 1 | 2 | 1 | 0 |
| Palmer | .922 | 148 | 85 | 258 | 29 | 21 |
| Petralli | .000 | 1 | 0 | 0 | 0 | 0 |
| Ripken | .667 | 1 | 1 | 1 | 1 | 0 |
| Russell | .000 | 1 | 0 | 0 | 0 | 0 |
| Strange | 1.000 | 9 | 4 | 12 | 0 | 2 |

| Shortstop | PCT | G | PO | A | E | DP |
|---|---|---|---|---|---|---|
| Diaz | .986 | 57 | 81 | 134 | 3 | 27 |
| Gil | .954 | 22 | 27 | 76 | 5 | 10 |
| Huson | .909 | 12 | 16 | 34 | 5 | 8 |
| Lee | .968 | 72 | 96 | 205 | 10 | 35 |
| Palmer | 1.000 | 1 | 1 | 0 | 0 | 0 |

| | PCT | G | PO | A | E | DP |
|---|---|---|---|---|---|---|
| Ripken | 1.000 | 18 | 27 | 49 | 0 | 12 |
| Shave | .917 | 9 | 13 | 20 | 3 | 6 |
| Strange | .000 | 1 | 0 | 0 | 0 | 0 |

| Outfield | PCT | G | PO | A | E | DP |
|---|---|---|---|---|---|---|
| Canseco | .970 | 59 | 94 | 4 | 3 | 2 |
| Dascenzo | .990 | 68 | 91 | 5 | 1 | 2 |
| Davis | .960 | 44 | 94 | 2 | 4 | 1 |
| Ducey | 1.000 | 26 | 51 | 1 | 0 | 0 |
| Gonzalez | .985 | 129 | 265 | 5 | 4 | 0 |
| Harris | .943 | 38 | 47 | 3 | 3 | 0 |
| Hulse | .988 | 112 | 244 | 3 | 3 | 0 |
| James | 1.000 | 7 | 14 | 0 | 0 | 0 |
| Peltier | .950 | 55 | 72 | 4 | 4 | 2 |
| Redus | .981 | 61 | 103 | 3 | 2 | 0 |
| Russell | .000 | 1 | 0 | 0 | 0 | 0 |

BERNARD TONCALE

LARRY KINKER

**Rafael Palmeiro.** Rangers first baseman had the best season of his career in 1993, hitting 37 home runs and driving in 105.

**Dean Palmer.** One of three Rangers to hit more than 30 home runs, Palmer launched a career-best 33.

# RANGERS FARM SYSTEM

| Class | Club | League | W | L | Pct. | Finish* | Manager | First Year |
|---|---|---|---|---|---|---|---|---|
| AAA | Oklahoma City 89ers | American Assoc. | 54 | 90 | .375 | 8th (8) | Bobby Jones | 1983 |
| AA | Tulsa (Okla.) Drillers | Texas | 65 | 69 | .485 | 7th (8) | Stan Cliburn | 1977 |
| A# | Charlotte (Fla.) Rangers | Florida State | 84 | 49 | .632 | 1st (13) | Tommy Thompson | 1987 |
| A | Charleston (S.C.) Rainbows | South Atlantic | 65 | 77 | .458 | 9th (14) | Walt Williams | 1993 |
| A | Erie (Pa.) Sailors | New York-Penn | 36 | 41 | .468 | 10th (14) | Doug Sisson | 1993 |
| Rookie | Port Charlotte (Fla.) Rangers | Gulf Coast | 40 | 20 | .667 | 1st† (15) | Chino Cadahia | 1973 |

*Finish in overall standings (No. of teams in league)   #Advanced level   †Won league championship

## OKLAHOMA CITY                                                    AAA
### AMERICAN ASSOCIATION

| BATTING | AVG | G | AB | R | H | 2B | 3B | HR | RBI | BB | SO | SB | CS | B | T | HT | WT | DOB | 1st Yr | Resides |
|---|---|---|---|---|---|---|---|---|---|---|---|---|---|---|---|---|---|---|---|---|
| Balboni, Steve | .244 | 126 | 471 | 67 | 115 | 22 | 0 | 36 | 108 | 51 | 98 | 0 | 1 | R | R | 6-3 | 225 | 1-16-57 | 1978 | Lee's Summit, Mo. |
| Berger, Mike | .286 | 6 | 14 | 2 | 4 | 0 | 0 | 1 | 1 | 3 | 0 | 0 | R | R | 6-1 | 205 | 9-24-62 | 1980 | Pittsburgh, Pa. |
| Dascenzo, Doug | .248 | 38 | 157 | 21 | 39 | 8 | 2 | 1 | 13 | 16 | 16 | 6 | 5 | S | L | 5-8 | 160 | 6-30-64 | 1985 | LaBelle, Pa. |
| Davis, Doug | .207 | 83 | 241 | 34 | 50 | 10 | 2 | 4 | 21 | 43 | 48 | 2 | 1 | R | R | 6-0 | 180 | 9-24-62 | 1984 | Bloomsburg, Pa. |
| Diaz, Mario | .328 | 48 | 177 | 24 | 58 | 12 | 2 | 3 | 20 | 7 | 15 | 3 | 1 | R | R | 5-10 | 160 | 1-10-62 | 1979 | Yabucoa, P.R. |
| Distefano, Benny | .222 | 116 | 414 | 51 | 92 | 17 | 5 | 6 | 34 | 31 | 64 | 2 | 1 | L | L | 6-1 | 195 | 1-23-62 | 1982 | Thiells, N.Y. |
| Ducey, Rob | .303 | 105 | 389 | 68 | 118 | 17 | 10 | 17 | 56 | 46 | 97 | 17 | 9 | L | R | 6-2 | 180 | 5-24-65 | 1984 | Palm Harbor, Fla. |
| Greer, Rusty | .222 | 8 | 27 | 6 | 6 | 2 | 0 | 1 | 4 | 6 | 7 | 0 | 0 | L | L | 6-0 | 190 | 1-21-69 | 1990 | Albertville, Ala. |
| Hanlon, Lawrence | .223 | 121 | 376 | 45 | 84 | 16 | 0 | 4 | 37 | 41 | 71 | 5 | 6 | R | R | 6-0 | 165 | 1-23-70 | 1991 | Richland Hills, Texas |
| Harris, Donald | .253 | 96 | 367 | 48 | 93 | 13 | 9 | 6 | 40 | 23 | 89 | 4 | 4 | R | R | 6-1 | 185 | 11-12-67 | 1989 | Waco, Texas |
| Huson, Jeff | .289 | 24 | 76 | 11 | 22 | 5 | 0 | 1 | 10 | 13 | 10 | 1 | 3 | L | R | 6-3 | 180 | 8-15-64 | 1986 | Bedford, Texas |
| Jackson, Chuck | .316 | 85 | 316 | 51 | 100 | 24 | 4 | 6 | 43 | 34 | 53 | 0 | 2 | R | R | 6-0 | 190 | 3-19-63 | 1984 | Scottsdale, Ariz. |
| Kennedy, Darryl | .063 | 6 | 16 | 2 | 1 | 0 | 0 | 0 | 0 | 3 | 4 | 0 | 0 | R | R | 5-10 | 170 | 1-23-69 | 1991 | Davenport, Fla. |
| Magallanes, Ever | .310 | 33 | 116 | 16 | 36 | 6 | 1 | 0 | 18 | 10 | 17 | 0 | 3 | L | R | 5-10 | 165 | 11-6-65 | 1987 | Downey, Calif. |
| McCoy, Trey | .250 | 8 | 28 | 6 | 7 | 1 | 1 | 3 | 11 | 5 | 5 | 0 | 0 | R | R | 6-3 | 215 | 10-12-66 | 1988 | Virginia Beach, Va. |
| Miller, Keith | .285 | 95 | 316 | 37 | 90 | 19 | 0 | 5 | 45 | 50 | 65 | 2 | 1 | S | R | 5-11 | 165 | 3-7-63 | 1984 | Kaufman, Texas |
| Morris, Rod | .212 | 12 | 33 | 4 | 7 | 2 | 0 | 0 | 1 | 0 | 7 | 0 | 0 | L | L | 5-9 | 163 | 5-5-66 | 1988 | Hammond, La. |
| Morrow, Timmie | .259 | 7 | 27 | 2 | 7 | 2 | 0 | 0 | 5 | 1 | 6 | 0 | 0 | R | R | 6-3 | 180 | 2-7-70 | 1988 | Graham, N.C. |
| Peltier, Dan | .321 | 48 | 187 | 28 | 60 | 15 | 4 | 5 | 33 | 19 | 27 | 2 | 2 | L | L | 6-1 | 200 | 6-30-68 | 1989 | Eden Prairie, Minn. |
| Petralli, Geno | .200 | 6 | 20 | 2 | 4 | 1 | 0 | 1 | 1 | 3 | 3 | 0 | 0 | S | R | 6-1 | 190 | 9-25-59 | 1978 | Arlington, Texas |
| Sable, Luke | .207 | 94 | 295 | 42 | 61 | 11 | 0 | 0 | 17 | 28 | 47 | 3 | 3 | R | R | 5-11 | 175 | 9-1-65 | 1987 | Alexandria, Va. |
| Shave, Jon | .263 | 100 | 399 | 58 | 105 | 17 | 3 | 4 | 41 | 20 | 60 | 4 | 3 | R | R | 6-0 | 180 | 11-4-67 | 1990 | Fernandina Beach, Fla. |
| Stephens, Ray | .228 | 97 | 333 | 29 | 76 | 15 | 2 | 7 | 49 | 32 | 78 | 0 | 2 | R | R | 6-0 | 190 | 9-22-62 | 1985 | Charleston, Tenn. |

# RANGERS TOP 10 PROSPECTS

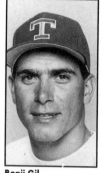

How the Rangers Top 10 prospects, as judged by Baseball America prior to the 1993 season, fared in 1993:

| Player, Pos. | Club (Class) | AVG | AB | H | HR | RBI | SB |
|---|---|---|---|---|---|---|---|
| 1. Benji Gil, ss | Tulsa (AA) | .275 | 342 | 94 | 17 | 59 | 20 |
| | Texas | .123 | 57 | 7 | 0 | 2 | 1 |
| 8. David Hulse, of | Texas | .290 | 407 | 118 | 1 | 29 | 29 |
| 10. Desi Wilson, 1b | Charlotte (A) | .305 | 511 | 156 | 3 | 70 | 29 |

| Player, Pos. | Club (Class) | W | L | ERA | IP | H | BB | SO |
|---|---|---|---|---|---|---|---|---|
| 2. Kurt Miller, rhp* | Tulsa (AA) | 6 | 8 | 5.06 | 96 | 102 | 45 | 68 |
| | Edmonton (AAA) | 3 | 3 | 4.50 | 48 | 42 | 34 | 19 |
| 3. Dan Smith, lhp | Charlotte (A) | 1 | 0 | 0.00 | 7 | 3 | 0 | 5 |
| | Okla. City (AAA) | 1 | 2 | 4.70 | 15 | 16 | 5 | 12 |
| 4. Scott Eyre, lhp | Charleston (A) | 11 | 7 | 3.45 | 144 | 115 | 59 | 154 |
| 5. Terry Burrows, lhp | Okla. City (AAA) | 7 | 15 | 6.39 | 138 | 171 | 76 | 74 |
| 6. Rick Helling, rhp | Tulsa (AA) | 12 | 8 | 3.60 | 177 | 150 | 46 | 188 |
| | Okla. City (AAA) | 1 | 1 | 1.64 | 11 | 5 | 3 | 17 |
| 7. Ritchie Moody, lhp | Tulsa (AA) | 3 | 2 | 2.18 | 66 | 58 | 34 | 60 |
| 9. Matt Whiteside, rhp | Okla. City (AAA) | 2 | 1 | 5.56 | 11 | 17 | 8 | 10 |
| | Texas | 2 | 1 | 4.32 | 73 | 78 | 23 | 39 |

*Traded to Florida Marlins

**Benji Gil**
*.275 at Double-A*

## PITCHING

| | W | L | ERA | G | GS | CG | SV | IP | H | R | ER | BB | SO | B | T | HT | WT | DOB | 1st Yr | Resides |
|---|---|---|---|---|---|---|---|---|---|---|---|---|---|---|---|---|---|---|---|---|
| Acker, Jim | 0 | 1 | 8.31 | 6 | 0 | 0 | 0 | 4 | 7 | 4 | 4 | 4 | 2 | R | R | 6-2 | 215 | 9-24-58 | 1980 | Freer, Texas |
| Alberro, Jose | 0 | 0 | 6.88 | 12 | 0 | 0 | 0 | 17 | 25 | 15 | 13 | 11 | 14 | R | R | 6-2 | 190 | 6-29-69 | 1991 | San Juan, P.R. |
| Alexander, Gerald | 1 | 2 | 9.25 | 10 | 3 | 0 | 0 | 24 | 40 | 27 | 25 | 9 | 13 | R | R | 5-11 | 200 | 3-26-68 | 1989 | Donaldsonville, La. |
| Anderson, Allan | 2 | 8 | 5.32 | 19 | 18 | 0 | 1 | 115 | 137 | 72 | 68 | 37 | 52 | L | L | 6-0 | 180 | 1-7-64 | 1983 | Lancaster, Ohio |
| Bohanon, Brian | 0 | 1 | 6.43 | 2 | 2 | 0 | 0 | 7 | 7 | 6 | 5 | 3 | 7 | L | L | 6-3 | 220 | 8-1-68 | 1987 | Houston, Texas |
| Bronkey, Jeff | 2 | 2 | 2.65 | 29 | 2 | 0 | 0 | 14 | 37 | 29 | 11 | 11 | 7 | 19 | R | R | 6-3 | 210 | 9-18-65 | 1986 | Klamath Falls, Ore. |
| Brown, Rob | 5 | 8 | 6.09 | 30 | 16 | 0 | 1 | 99 | 134 | 83 | 67 | 41 | 60 | R | R | 6-5 | 220 | 1-13-67 | 1989 | Seattle, Wash. |
| Burrows, Terry | 7 | 15 | 6.39 | 27 | 25 | 1 | 0 | 138 | 171 | 107 | 98 | 76 | 74 | L | L | 6-1 | 185 | 11-28-68 | 1990 | Lake Charles, La. |
| Dreyer, Steve | 4 | 6 | 3.03 | 16 | 16 | 1 | 0 | 107 | 108 | 39 | 36 | 31 | 59 | R | R | 6-3 | 180 | 11-19-69 | 1990 | Cedar Falls, Iowa |
| Eiland, Dave | 3 | 1 | 4.29 | 7 | 7 | 1 | 0 | 36 | 39 | 18 | 17 | 9 | 15 | R | R | 6-3 | 205 | 7-5-66 | 1987 | Dade City, Fla. |
| Fireovid, Steve | 1 | 1 | 7.59 | 7 | 4 | 0 | 0 | 21 | 35 | 24 | 18 | 4 | 14 | S | R | 6-2 | 210 | 6-6-58 | 1978 | Bryan, Ohio |
| Helling, Rick | 1 | 1 | 1.64 | 2 | 2 | 1 | 0 | 11 | 5 | 3 | 2 | 3 | 17 | R | R | 6-3 | 215 | 12-15-70 | 1992 | West Fargo, N.D. |
| Hurst, James | 4 | 6 | 4.53 | 16 | 14 | 2 | 0 | 91 | 106 | 50 | 46 | 29 | 60 | L | L | 6-0 | 165 | 6-1-67 | 1990 | Sebring, Fla. |
| Lee, Mark | 5 | 3 | 4.34 | 52 | 1 | 0 | 4 | 102 | 112 | 61 | 49 | 43 | 61 | L | L | 6-3 | 195 | 7-20-64 | 1985 | Colorado Springs, Colo. |
| Lefferts, Craig | 0 | 1 | 7.50 | 1 | 1 | 0 | 0 | 6 | 9 | 5 | 5 | 2 | 1 | L | L | 6-1 | 209 | 9-29-57 | 1980 | Poway, Calif. |
| Leon, Danilo | 2 | 2 | 5.52 | 13 | 1 | 0 | 0 | 31 | 28 | 21 | 19 | 26 | 33 | R | R | 6-1 | 175 | 4-3-67 | 1986 | La Canada, Venez. |
| Manuel, Barry | 2 | 2 | 7.99 | 21 | 0 | 0 | 2 | 24 | 29 | 21 | 21 | 16 | 19 | R | R | 5-11 | 185 | 8-12-65 | 1987 | Mamou, La. |
| Nen, Robb | 0 | 2 | 6.67 | 6 | 5 | 0 | 0 | 28 | 45 | 22 | 21 | 18 | 12 | R | R | 6-4 | 190 | 11-28-69 | 1987 | Seal Beach, Calif. |
| Oliveras, Francisco | 4 | 8 | 5.68 | 44 | 7 | 0 | 2 | 124 | 146 | 81 | 78 | 52 | 77 | R | R | 5-10 | 170 | 1-31-63 | 1981 | Caguas, P.R. |
| Pavlik, Roger | 3 | 2 | 1.70 | 6 | 6 | 0 | 0 | 37 | 26 | 12 | 7 | 14 | 32 | R | R | 6-2 | 220 | 10-4-67 | 1987 | Houston, Texas |
| Perez, David | 1 | 0 | 12.27 | 2 | 1 | 0 | 0 | 7 | 8 | 10 | 10 | 4 | 3 | R | R | 5-11 | 170 | 5-23-68 | 1989 | San Antonio, Texas |
| Reed, Rick | 1 | 3 | 4.19 | 5 | 5 | 1 | 0 | 34 | 43 | 20 | 16 | 2 | 21 | R | R | 6-0 | 200 | 8-16-64 | 1986 | Huntington, W.Va. |
| 2-team (19 Omaha) | 12 | 7 | 3.32 | 24 | 24 | 4 | 0 | 163 | 159 | 68 | 60 | 16 | 79 | | | | | | | |
| Sadecki, Steve | 0 | 3 | 7.08 | 12 | 2 | 1 | 0 | 20 | 22 | 17 | 16 | 15 | 13 | R | R | 6-1 | 190 | 5-14-70 | 1991 | Kansas City, Kan. |
| Schooler, Mike | 1 | 3 | 5.91 | 28 | 0 | 0 | 5 | 46 | 59 | 33 | 30 | 11 | 31 | R | R | 6-3 | 210 | 8-10-62 | 1985 | Renton, Wash. |
| Shaw, Cedric | 2 | 6 | 7.91 | 28 | 5 | 0 | 0 | 52 | 78 | 47 | 46 | 36 | 28 | L | L | 5-11 | 175 | 5-28-67 | 1988 | Brusly, La. |
| Smith, Dan | 1 | 2 | 4.70 | 3 | 3 | 0 | 0 | 15 | 16 | 11 | 8 | 5 | 12 | L | L | 6-5 | 190 | 8-20-69 | 1990 | Apple Valley, Minn. |
| Whiteside, Matt | 2 | 1 | 5.56 | 8 | 0 | 0 | 1 | 11 | 17 | 7 | 7 | 8 | 10 | R | R | 6-0 | 185 | 8-8-67 | 1990 | Charleston, Mo. |

## FIELDING

| Catcher | PCT | G | PO | A | E | DP |
|---|---|---|---|---|---|---|
| Davis | .994 | 57 | 326 | 23 | 2 | 5 |
| Distefano | .923 | 2 | 12 | 0 | 1 | 0 |
| Kennedy | .973 | 6 | 35 | 1 | 1 | 0 |
| Petralli | .857 | 1 | 5 | 1 | 1 | 0 |
| Stephens | .977 | 81 | 419 | 50 | 11 | 6 |

| First Base | PCT | G | PO | A | E | DP |
|---|---|---|---|---|---|---|
| Balboni | 1.000 | 7 | 59 | 10 | 0 | 2 |
| Berger | 1.000 | 1 | 2 | 0 | 0 | 0 |
| Davis | 1.000 | 2 | 11 | 1 | 0 | 3 |
| Distefano | .987 | 42 | 364 | 23 | 5 | 43 |
| Jackson | .000 | 1 | 0 | 0 | 0 | 0 |
| Miller | .995 | 48 | 400 | 25 | 2 | 44 |
| Peltier | .986 | 37 | 328 | 21 | 5 | 30 |
| Sable | 1.000 | 1 | 1 | 0 | 0 | 0 |
| Stephens | .991 | 16 | 107 | 8 | 1 | 11 |

| Second Base | PCT | G | PO | A | E | DP |
|---|---|---|---|---|---|---|
| Diaz | .984 | 15 | 21 | 41 | 1 | 4 |
| Huson | .962 | 6 | 11 | 14 | 1 | 5 |

| | PCT | G | PO | A | E | DP |
|---|---|---|---|---|---|---|
| Jackson | 1.000 | 1 | 1 | 4 | 0 | 1 |
| Magallanes | .986 | 24 | 56 | 82 | 2 | 27 |
| Miller | .000 | 1 | 0 | 0 | 0 | 0 |
| Sable | .975 | 22 | 55 | 64 | 3 | 18 |
| Shave | .973 | 86 | 164 | 232 | 11 | 55 |

| Third Base | PCT | G | PO | A | E | DP |
|---|---|---|---|---|---|---|
| Davis | .944 | 20 | 7 | 27 | 2 | 1 |
| Diaz | 1.000 | 26 | 17 | 46 | 0 | 6 |
| Hanlon | .000 | 1 | 0 | 0 | 0 | 0 |
| Huson | .976 | 14 | 17 | 23 | 1 | 2 |
| Jackson | .966 | 41 | 16 | 99 | 4 | 11 |
| Magallanes | .960 | 9 | 8 | 16 | 1 | 2 |
| Miller | .941 | 5 | 1 | 15 | 1 | 0 |
| Sable | .941 | 41 | 25 | 71 | 6 | 12 |

| Shortstop | PCT | G | PO | A | E | DP |
|---|---|---|---|---|---|---|
| Diaz | .943 | 7 | 15 | 18 | 2 | 4 |
| Hanlon | .961 | 117 | 198 | 337 | 22 | 71 |
| Huson | .955 | 6 | 6 | 15 | 1 | 4 |

| | PCT | G | PO | A | E | DP |
|---|---|---|---|---|---|---|
| Jackson | 1.000 | 1 | 1 | 4 | 0 | 1 |
| Sable | .909 | 5 | 9 | 11 | 2 | 4 |
| Shave | .973 | 15 | 26 | 45 | 2 | 12 |

| Outfield | PCT | G | PO | A | E | DP |
|---|---|---|---|---|---|---|
| Berger | .000 | 2 | 0 | 0 | 0 | 0 |
| Dascenzo | .984 | 38 | 118 | 4 | 2 | 3 |
| Davis | 1.000 | 2 | 6 | 0 | 0 | 0 |
| Distefano | .954 | 72 | 119 | 5 | 6 | 1 |
| Ducey | .973 | 100 | 244 | 8 | 7 | 1 |
| Greer | 1.000 | 8 | 16 | 0 | 0 | 0 |
| Harris | .976 | 94 | 241 | 5 | 6 | 2 |
| Huson | 1.000 | 3 | 5 | 0 | 0 | 0 |
| Jackson | .973 | 41 | 66 | 5 | 2 | 0 |
| Miller | .966 | 39 | 55 | 2 | 2 | 0 |
| Morris | 1.000 | 12 | 18 | 1 | 0 | 0 |
| Morrow | 1.000 | 7 | 17 | 0 | 0 | 0 |
| Peltier | 1.000 | 11 | 18 | 1 | 0 | 0 |
| Sable | .980 | 23 | 48 | 0 | 1 | 0 |

# TULSA
## TEXAS LEAGUE                                                                    AA

### BATTING

| | AVG | G | AB | R | H | 2B | 3B | HR | RBI | BB | SO | SB | CS | B | T | HT | WT | DOB | 1st Yr | Resides |
|---|---|---|---|---|---|---|---|---|---|---|---|---|---|---|---|---|---|---|---|---|
| Castellanos, Miguel, 3b | .169 | 49 | 142 | 10 | 24 | 4 | 1 | 1 | 13 | 12 | 29 | 1 | 1 | R | R | 6-1 | 185 | 7-19-69 | 1989 | Maracaibo, Venez. |
| Castillo, Ben, of | .228 | 86 | 272 | 34 | 62 | 12 | 1 | 5 | 14 | 20 | 53 | 6 | 3 | R | R | 6-1 | 192 | 7-15-66 | 1988 | Baltimore, Md. |
| Clinton, Jim, ss-3b | .083 | 6 | 12 | 0 | 1 | 0 | 0 | 0 | 2 | 1 | 3 | 0 | 0 | R | R | 6-2 | 185 | 6-17-67 | 1989 | Lewistown, Mont. |
| Colon, Cris, 3b-ss | .300 | 124 | 490 | 63 | 147 | 27 | 3 | 11 | 47 | 13 | 76 | 6 | 3 | S | R | 6-2 | 180 | 1-3-69 | 1987 | La Guaira, Venez. |
| Epley, Daren, of | .151 | 20 | 53 | 4 | 8 | 0 | 0 | 1 | 2 | 2 | 5 | 0 | 0 | L | L | 6-2 | 190 | 6-15-67 | 1988 | Washington, Ill. |
| Gil, Benji, ss | .275 | 101 | 342 | 45 | 94 | 9 | 1 | 17 | 59 | 35 | 89 | 20 | 12 | R | R | 6-2 | 180 | 10-6-72 | 1991 | San Diego, Calif. |

| BATTING | AVG | G | AB | R | H | 2B | 3B | HR | RBI | BB | SO | SB | CS | B | T | HT | WT | DOB | 1st Yr | Resides |
|---|---|---|---|---|---|---|---|---|---|---|---|---|---|---|---|---|---|---|---|---|
| Greer, Rusty, 1b | .291 | 129 | 474 | 76 | 138 | 25 | 6 | 15 | 59 | 53 | 79 | 10 | 5 | L | L | 6-0 | 190 | 1-21-69 | 1990 | Albertville, Ala. |
| List, Paul, of | .200 | 40 | 125 | 8 | 25 | 3 | 1 | 0 | 6 | 10 | 30 | 2 | 6 | R | R | 6-3 | 200 | 11-17-65 | 1987 | North Hollywood, Calif. |
| Lowery, Terrell, of | .240 | 66 | 258 | 29 | 62 | 5 | 1 | 3 | 14 | 28 | 50 | 10 | 12 | R | R | 6-3 | 175 | 10-25-70 | 1991 | Oakland, Calif. |
| Luce, Roger, c | .193 | 101 | 321 | 35 | 62 | 14 | 2 | 8 | 29 | 17 | 107 | 2 | 1 | R | R | 6-4 | 215 | 5-7-69 | 1991 | Houston, Texas |
| Magallanes, Ever, 2b | .326 | 55 | 184 | 20 | 60 | 12 | 2 | 1 | 14 | 16 | 22 | 0 | 4 | L | R | 5-10 | 165 | 11-6-65 | 1987 | Downey, Calif. |
| McCoy, Trey, dh | .293 | 125 | 420 | 72 | 123 | 27 | 3 | 29 | 95 | 65 | 79 | 3 | 2 | R | R | 6-3 | 215 | 10-12-66 | 1988 | Virginia Beach, Va. |
| McDowell, Oddibe, of | .342 | 34 | 114 | 26 | 39 | 7 | 1 | 8 | 31 | 19 | 24 | 3 | 3 | L | L | 5-9 | 180 | 8-25-62 | 1985 | Arlington, Texas |
| Morrow, Timmie, of | .246 | 108 | 390 | 46 | 96 | 25 | 2 | 9 | 45 | 19 | 98 | 11 | 14 | R | R | 6-3 | 180 | 2-7-70 | 1988 | Graham, N.C. |
| Rolls, David, c-3b | .240 | 72 | 221 | 23 | 53 | 9 | 0 | 5 | 23 | 22 | 51 | 1 | 2 | R | R | 6-0 | 195 | 10-1-66 | 1988 | Tucson, Ariz. |
| Simonson, Bob, of | .237 | 34 | 118 | 11 | 28 | 4 | 0 | 4 | 14 | 6 | 27 | 3 | 1 | R | R | 6-2 | 220 | 5-30-64 | 1984 | Grand Rapids, Mich. |
| Turco, Frank, 2b-of | .267 | 118 | 423 | 45 | 113 | 13 | 2 | 8 | 39 | 27 | 86 | 13 | 8 | R | R | 5-11 | 165 | 7-3-68 | 1990 | Cooper City, Fla. |

| PITCHING | W | L | ERA | G | GS | CG | SV | IP | H | R | ER | BB | SO | B | T | HT | WT | DOB | 1st Yr | Resides |
|---|---|---|---|---|---|---|---|---|---|---|---|---|---|---|---|---|---|---|---|---|
| Alberro, Jose | 0 | 0 | 0.95 | 17 | 0 | 0 | 5 | 19 | 11 | 2 | 2 | 8 | 24 | R | R | 6-2 | 190 | 6-29-69 | 1991 | San Juan, P.R. |
| Arner, Mike | 1 | 0 | 4.53 | 27 | 0 | 0 | 0 | 58 | 58 | 33 | 29 | 14 | 37 | R | R | 6-4 | 185 | 11-3-70 | 1989 | Clearwater, Fla. |
| Brumley, Duff | 3 | 2 | 1.96 | 6 | 6 | 0 | 0 | 41 | 30 | 13 | 9 | 9 | 42 | R | R | 6-4 | 195 | 8-25-70 | 1990 | Cleveland, Tenn. |
| 2-team (12 Arkansas) | .7 | 7 | 2.93 | 18 | 18 | 2 | 0 | 111 | 87 | 43 | 36 | 35 | 121 | | | | | | | |
| Dreyer, Steve | 2 | 2 | 3.73 | 5 | 5 | 1 | 0 | 31 | 26 | 13 | 13 | 8 | 27 | R | R | 6-3 | 180 | 11-19-69 | 1990 | Cedar Falls, Iowa |
| Gies, Chris | 1 | 5 | 5.02 | 26 | 8 | 0 | 1 | 66 | 67 | 42 | 37 | 24 | 28 | R | R | 6-3 | 190 | 10-8-68 | 1990 | Philadelphia, Pa. |
| Goetz, Barry | 2 | 3 | 6.55 | 38 | 0 | 0 | 1 | 56 | 70 | 51 | 41 | 44 | 57 | R | R | 6-2 | 195 | 8-28-68 | 1990 | Arlington, Texas |
| Helling, Rick | 12 | 8 | 3.60 | 26 | 26 | 2 | 0 | 177 | 150 | 76 | 71 | 46 | 188 | R | R | 6-3 | 215 | 12-15-70 | 1992 | West Fargo, N.D. |
| Hurst, James | 2 | 3 | 3.26 | 11 | 7 | 0 | 1 | 50 | 41 | 21 | 18 | 12 | 44 | L | L | 6-0 | 165 | 6-1-67 | 1990 | Sebring, Fla. |
| Miller, Kurt | 6 | 8 | 5.06 | 18 | 18 | 0 | 0 | 96 | 102 | 69 | 54 | 45 | 68 | R | R | 6-5 | 200 | 8-24-72 | 1990 | Bakersfield, Calif. |
| Moody, Ritchie | 3 | 2 | 2.15 | 47 | 0 | 0 | 16 | 67 | 58 | 27 | 16 | 34 | 61 | R | L | 6-1 | 185 | 2-22-71 | 1992 | Brookville, Ohio |
| Oliver, Darren | 7 | 5 | 1.96 | 46 | 0 | 0 | 6 | 73 | 51 | 18 | 16 | 41 | 77 | R | L | 6-0 | 170 | 10-6-70 | 1988 | Rio Linda, Calif. |
| Perez, David | 9 | 10 | 4.02 | 33 | 14 | 1 | 2 | 125 | 119 | 64 | 56 | 34 | 111 | R | R | 5-11 | 170 | 5-23-68 | 1989 | San Antonio, Texas |
| Reed, Bobby | 5 | 7 | 4.32 | 14 | 14 | 0 | 0 | 75 | 88 | 45 | 36 | 22 | 34 | R | R | 6-5 | 210 | 10-3-67 | 1990 | Long Beach, Miss. |
| Romero, Brian | 5 | 6 | 3.91 | 21 | 18 | 1 | 0 | 94 | 98 | 47 | 41 | 34 | 72 | R | L | 6-1 | 185 | 11-3-68 | 1989 | South El Monte, Calif. |
| Rowley, Steve | 8 | 7 | 6.04 | 20 | 19 | 0 | 0 | 92 | 103 | 71 | 62 | 33 | 63 | R | R | 6-0 | 175 | 5-25-68 | 1989 | Baton Rouge, La. |
| Sadecki, Steve | 0 | 1 | 3.94 | 9 | 0 | 0 | 1 | 16 | 16 | 10 | 7 | 4 | 12 | R | R | 6-1 | 190 | 5-14-70 | 1991 | Kansas City, Kan. |

# CHARLOTTE                                                                A
## FLORIDA STATE LEAGUE

| BATTING | AVG | G | AB | R | H | 2B | 3B | HR | RBI | BB | SO | SB | CS | B | T | HT | WT | DOB | 1st Yr | Resides |
|---|---|---|---|---|---|---|---|---|---|---|---|---|---|---|---|---|---|---|---|---|
| Aurilia, Rich, ss | .309 | 122 | 440 | 80 | 136 | 16 | 5 | 5 | 56 | 75 | 57 | 15 | 18 | R | R | 6-0 | 170 | 9-2-71 | 1992 | Hazlet, N.J. |
| Bethke, Jamie, c | .000 | 1 | 1 | 0 | 0 | 0 | 0 | 0 | 0 | 0 | 0 | 0 | 0 | S | R | 6-2 | 185 | 2-11-73 | 1991 | Kansas City, Mo. |
| Cairo, Sergio, of | .369 | 34 | 122 | 15 | 45 | 4 | 1 | 5 | 25 | 15 | 11 | 3 | 4 | R | R | 6-1 | 165 | 10-22-70 | 1988 | San Pedro de Macoris, D.R. |
| Clinton, Jim, of-2b | .175 | 86 | 285 | 26 | 50 | 9 | 0 | 1 | 23 | 18 | 72 | 4 | 3 | R | R | 6-2 | 185 | 6-17-67 | 1989 | Lewistown, Mont. |
| Crespo, Mike, c | .131 | 30 | 99 | 5 | 13 | 4 | 0 | 0 | 6 | 5 | 30 | 1 | 1 | S | R | 5-10 | 175 | 11-18-70 | 1990 | Vega Alta, P.R. |
| Edwards, Mike, 3b-1b | .279 | 130 | 458 | 73 | 128 | 26 | 2 | 12 | 79 | 82 | 70 | 11 | 6 | R | R | 6-1 | 205 | 3-9-70 | 1991 | Placentia, Calif. |
| Evangelista, George, 3b | .231 | 98 | 321 | 39 | 74 | 12 | 1 | 1 | 18 | 41 | 62 | 6 | 6 | R | R | 5-9 | 180 | 12-22-68 | 1990 | Georgetown, Mass. |
| Guggiana, Todd, dh | .286 | 134 | 514 | 53 | 147 | 34 | 0 | 4 | 79 | 41 | 62 | 7 | 4 | L | R | 6-0 | 180 | 8-6-68 | 1990 | Cerritos, Calif. |
| Kennedy, Darryl, c | .280 | 106 | 347 | 47 | 97 | 23 | 0 | 1 | 30 | 47 | 38 | 5 | 7 | R | R | 5-10 | 170 | 1-23-69 | 1991 | Davenport, Fla. |
| Lowery, Terrell, of | .300 | 65 | 257 | 46 | 77 | 7 | 9 | 3 | 36 | 46 | 47 | 14 | 15 | R | R | 6-3 | 175 | 10-25-70 | 1991 | Oakland, Calif. |
| Morris, Rod, of | .206 | 33 | 107 | 11 | 22 | 0 | 2 | 0 | 6 | 7 | 24 | 2 | 3 | L | L | 5-9 | 163 | 5-5-66 | 1988 | Hammond, La. |
| Powell, Ken, of | .302 | 31 | 116 | 15 | 35 | 1 | 0 | 1 | 20 | 13 | 32 | 3 | 2 | R | R | 6-6 | 190 | 12-6-70 | 1989 | Long Beach, Calif. |
| Smith, Mike, 2b | .235 | 86 | 327 | 33 | 77 | 16 | 4 | 3 | 43 | 37 | 55 | 3 | 6 | R | R | 6-0 | 180 | 12-1-69 | 1992 | Piqua, Ohio |
| Texidor, Jose, of | .319 | 19 | 72 | 14 | 23 | 4 | 0 | 0 | 4 | 5 | 11 | 2 | 0 | R | R | 6-0 | 150 | 12-14-71 | 1990 | Juana Diaz, P.R. |
| Thomas, Brian, of | .289 | 34 | 135 | 26 | 39 | 3 | 2 | 2 | 11 | 18 | 29 | 4 | 1 | L | R | 6-0 | 185 | 5-6-71 | 1993 | Portland, Ore. |
| Welch, Mike, of | .231 | 50 | 173 | 15 | 40 | 7 | 1 | 0 | 10 | 13 | 45 | 4 | 2 | L | L | 6-1 | 210 | 1-13-70 | 1992 | Central Islip, N.Y. |
| Williams, Lanny, of | .229 | 58 | 175 | 15 | 40 | 5 | 0 | 3 | 18 | 12 | 59 | 5 | 3 | R | R | 5-11 | 215 | 8-23-69 | 1991 | Mineola, Texas |
| Wilson, Desi, 1b-of | .305 | 131 | 511 | 83 | 156 | 21 | 7 | 3 | 70 | 50 | 90 | 29 | 11 | L | L | 6-7 | 230 | 5-9-68 | 1991 | Glen Cove, N.Y. |

| PITCHING | W | L | ERA | G | GS | CG | SV | IP | H | R | ER | BB | SO | B | T | HT | WT | DOB | 1st Yr | Resides |
|---|---|---|---|---|---|---|---|---|---|---|---|---|---|---|---|---|---|---|---|---|
| Brownholtz, Joe | 4 | 0 | 1.56 | 24 | 5 | 0 | 2 | 69 | 62 | 15 | 12 | 19 | 48 | R | L | 6-1 | 195 | 12-6-69 | 1991 | San Diego, Calif. |
| Curtis, Chris | 8 | 8 | 3.99 | 27 | 26 | 1 | 0 | 151 | 159 | 76 | 67 | 19 | 50 | R | R | 6-2 | 185 | 5-8-71 | 1991 | Duncanville, Texas |
| Dettmer, John | 16 | 3 | 2.15 | 27 | 27 | 5 | 0 | 163 | 132 | 44 | 39 | 33 | 128 | R | R | 6-0 | 185 | 3-4-70 | 1992 | Glencoe, Mo. |
| Fajardo, Hector | 0 | 0 | 1.80 | 2 | 1 | 0 | 0 | 5 | 5 | 1 | 1 | 1 | 3 | R | R | 6-4 | 200 | 11-6-70 | 1989 | Michoacan, Mexico |
| Gandolph, Dave | 4 | 2 | 3.92 | 34 | 0 | 0 | 2 | 44 | 49 | 23 | 19 | 29 | 24 | L | L | 6-4 | 220 | 3-20-70 | 1991 | Greenwood, Ind. |
| Geeve, Dave | 11 | 8 | 2.85 | 24 | 23 | 1 | 0 | 133 | 141 | 52 | 42 | 19 | 80 | R | R | 6-3 | 190 | 10-19-69 | 1991 | Niles, Ill. |
| Giberti, David | 11 | 4 | 3.70 | 31 | 20 | 2 | 1 | 141 | 132 | 63 | 58 | 52 | 85 | R | L | 6-2 | 175 | 11-20-70 | 1989 | Martinez, Calif. |
| Henderson, Daryl | 7 | 2 | 2.64 | 16 | 16 | 0 | 0 | 92 | 71 | 32 | 27 | 33 | 81 | L | L | 6-0 | 160 | 9-24-72 | 1991 | Elgin, Ill. |
| Heredia, Wilson | 1 | 5 | 3.72 | 34 | 0 | 0 | 15 | 39 | 30 | 17 | 16 | 20 | 36 | R | R | 6-0 | 185 | 3-30-72 | 1990 | San Pedro de Macoris, D.R. |
| Lacy, Kerry | 0 | 0 | 1.93 | 4 | 0 | 0 | 2 | 5 | 2 | 2 | 1 | 3 | 3 | R | R | 6-2 | 195 | 8-7-72 | 1991 | Higdon, Ala. |
| Magee, Bo | 6 | 3 | 4.15 | 30 | 14 | 0 | 0 | 89 | 76 | 44 | 41 | 51 | 64 | R | L | 6-4 | 180 | 4-9-68 | 1991 | Jackson, Miss. |
| Manuel, Barry | 0 | 0 | 0.00 | 3 | 0 | 0 | 0 | 5 | 6 | 0 | 0 | 2 | 4 | R | R | 5-11 | 185 | 8-12-65 | 1987 | Mamou, La. |

# RANGERS: MOST COMMON LINEUPS

| | Texas<br>Majors | Oklahoma City<br>AAA | Tulsa<br>AA | Charlotte<br>A | Charleston<br>A |
|---|---|---|---|---|---|
| C | Ivan Rodriguez (134) | Ray Stephens (81) | Roger Luce (97) | Darryl Kennedy (105) | Jamie Bethke (97) |
| 1B | Rafael Palmeiro (160) | Keith Miller (48) | Rusty Greer (129) | Desi Wilson (77) | Steve Burton (99) |
| 2B | Doug Strange (135) | Jon Shave (46) | Frank Turco (75) | Mike Smith (86) | Hanley Frias (106) |
| 3B | Dean Palmer (148) | Jackson/Sable (41) | Cris Colon (96) | Mike Edwards (79) | Jack Stanczak (77) |
| SS | Manuel Lee (72) | Larry Hanlon (117) | Benji Gil (101) | Rich Aurilia (122) | Guillermo Mercedes (127) |
| OF | Juan Gonzalez (129) | Rob Ducey (100) | Timmie Morrow (108) | Terrell Lowery (65) | Scott Malone (127) |
| | David Hulse (112) | Donald Harris (94) | Ben Castillo (83) | Jim Clinton (55) | Malvin Matos (104) |
| | Doug Dascenzo (68) | Benny Distefano (70) | Terrell Lowery (66) | Desi Wilson (55) | Mike Welch (64) |
| DH | Juan Gonzalez (140) | Steve Balboni (119) | Trey McCoy (115) | Todd Guggiana (121) | Chris Burr (81) |
| SP | Kevin Brown (34) | Terry Burrows (25) | Rick Helling (26) | John Dettmer (27) | Jerry Martin (28) |
| RP | Tom Henke (66) | Mark Lee (51) | Moody/Oliver (46) | Danny Patterson (47) | Kerry Lacy (56) |

Full-season farm clubs only | No. of games at position in parenthesis

# RANGERS: ORGANIZATION LEADERS

## MAJOR LEAGUERS

**BATTING**

| | | |
|---|---|---|
| *AVG | Juan Gonzalez | .310 |
| R | Rafael Palmeiro | 124 |
| H | Rafael Palmeiro | 176 |
| TB | Juan Gonzalez | 339 |
| 2B | Rafael Palmeiro | 40 |
| 3B | David Hulse | 10 |
| HR | Juan Gonzalez | 46 |
| RBI | Juan Gonzalez | 118 |
| BB | Rafael Palmeiro | 73 |
| SO | Dean Palmer | 154 |
| SB | David Hulse | 29 |

**PITCHING**

| | | |
|---|---|---|
| W | Kenny Rogers | 16 |
| L | Kevin Brown | 12 |
| #ERA | Roger Pavlik | 3.41 |
| G | Tom Henke | 66 |
| CG | Kevin Brown | 12 |
| SV | Tom Henke | 40 |
| IP | Kevin Brown | 233 |
| BB | Roger Pavlik | 80 |
| SO | Kevin Brown | 142 |

**Kevin Brown**
Career-high 233 innings

MEL BAILEY

## MINOR LEAGUERS

**BATTING**

| | | |
|---|---|---|
| *AVG | Wes Shook, Erie | .321 |
| R | Desi Wilson, Charlotte | 83 |
| H | Desi Wilson, Charlotte | 156 |
| TB | Trey McCoy, Tulsa-Oklahoma City | 262 |
| 2B | Two tied at | 34 |
| 3B | Two tied at | 10 |
| HR | Steve Balboni, Oklahoma City | 36 |
| RBI | Steve Balboni, Oklahoma City | 108 |
| BB | Mike Edwards, Charlotte | 82 |
| SO | Malvin Matos, Charleston | 114 |
| SB | Guillermo Mercedes, Charleston | 41 |

**PITCHING**

| | | |
|---|---|---|
| W | John Dettmer, Charlotte | 16 |
| L | Terry Burrows, Oklahoma City | 15 |
| #ERA | John Dettmer, Charlotte | 2.15 |
| G | Kerry Lacy, Charleston-Charlotte | 62 |
| CG | John Dettmer, Charlotte | 5 |
| SV | Kerry Lacy, Charleston-Charlotte | 38 |
| IP | Rick Helling, Tulsa-Oklahoma City | 188 |
| BB | Ramiro Martinez, Charleston | 90 |
| SO | Rick Helling, Tulsa-Oklahoma City | 205 |

*Minimum 250 At-Bats   #Minimum 75 Innings

| PITCHING | W | L | ERA | G | GS | CG | SV | IP | H | R | ER | BB | SO | B | T | HT | WT | DOB | 1st Yr | Resides |
|---|---|---|---|---|---|---|---|---|---|---|---|---|---|---|---|---|---|---|---|---|
| Newcomb, Chris | 4 | 0 | 2.00 | 21 | 0 | 0 | 1 | 36 | 35 | 11 | 8 | 10 | 26 | R | R | 6-1 | 185 | 1-6-71 | 1992 | Indianapolis, Ind. |
| Patterson, Danny | 5 | 6 | 2.51 | 47 | 0 | 0 | 7 | 68 | 55 | 22 | 19 | 28 | 41 | R | R | 6-0 | 168 | 2-17-71 | 1990 | Rosemead, Calif. |
| Reed, Bobby | 1 | 0 | 0.00 | 1 | 1 | 0 | 0 | 6 | 2 | 0 | 0 | 1 | 4 | R | R | 6-5 | 210 | 10-3-67 | 1990 | Long Beach, Miss. |
| Sadecki, Steve | 3 | 2 | 2.01 | 24 | 0 | 0 | 1 | 40 | 40 | 9 | 9 | 11 | 37 | R | R | 6-1 | 190 | 5-14-70 | 1991 | Kansas City, Kan. |
| Schuermann, Lance | 1 | 4 | 2.07 | 46 | 0 | 0 | 16 | 65 | 40 | 20 | 15 | 28 | 59 | L | L | 6-2 | 200 | 2-7-70 | 1991 | St. Louis, Mo. |
| Smith, Dan | 1 | 0 | 0.00 | 1 | 1 | 0 | 0 | 7 | 3 | 0 | 0 | 0 | 5 | L | L | 6-5 | 190 | 8-20-69 | 1990 | Apple Valley, Minn. |
| Washington, Tyrone | 1 | 2 | 5.14 | 23 | 0 | 0 | 0 | 35 | 40 | 28 | 20 | 24 | 16 | R | R | 6-6 | 190 | 7-3-67 | 1989 | Chicago, Ill. |

# CHARLESTON                                          A

## SOUTH ATLANTIC LEAGUE

| BATTING | AVG | G | AB | R | H | 2B | 3B | HR | RBI | BB | SO | SB | CS | B | T | HT | WT | DOB | 1st Yr | Resides |
|---|---|---|---|---|---|---|---|---|---|---|---|---|---|---|---|---|---|---|---|---|
| Bethke, Jamie, c | .247 | 103 | 352 | 31 | 87 | 19 | 0 | 1 | 31 | 30 | 54 | 3 | 10 | S | R | 6-2 | 185 | 2-11-73 | 1991 | Kansas City, Mo. |
| Burr, Chris, dh-1b | .235 | 118 | 409 | 36 | 96 | 18 | 3 | 10 | 65 | 48 | 95 | 0 | 4 | R | R | 6-2 | 187 | 5-27-70 | 1992 | Vienna, Va. |
| Burton, Steve, 1b | .237 | 118 | 354 | 39 | 84 | 16 | 0 | 9 | 44 | 47 | 101 | 1 | 4 | L | R | 6-6 | 200 | 1-16-69 | 1991 | Paoli, Pa. |
| Campusano, Gen., dh | .174 | 29 | 69 | 3 | 12 | 2 | 0 | 3 | 11 | 6 | 40 | 0 | 0 | R | R | 6-0 | 220 | 7-17-69 | 1988 | Manoguayabo, D.R. |
| Cossins, Tim, c | .146 | 27 | 89 | 8 | 13 | 2 | 0 | 0 | 10 | 7 | 21 | 0 | 1 | R | R | 6-1 | 190 | 1-31-70 | 1993 | Windsor, Calif. |
| Eggleston, Wayne, 2b | .227 | 91 | 216 | 34 | 49 | 13 | 4 | 1 | 10 | 23 | 54 | 7 | 5 | R | S | 5-10 | 170 | 8-6-69 | 1992 | Martinsville, Va. |
| Frias, Hanley, 2b-of | .230 | 132 | 473 | 61 | 109 | 20 | 4 | 4 | 37 | 40 | 108 | 27 | 14 | R | R | 6-0 | 160 | 12-5-73 | 1991 | Villa Altagracia, D.R. |
| Hieb, Dave, c | .231 | 5 | 13 | 1 | 3 | 2 | 0 | 0 | 1 | 1 | 2 | 0 | 0 | R | R | 6-0 | 195 | 1-25-71 | 1992 | Cherry Hill, N.J. |
| Malone, Scott, of | .288 | 130 | 458 | 70 | 132 | 34 | 4 | 12 | 71 | 59 | 75 | 20 | 9 | L | R | 6-3 | 215 | 4-16-71 | 1992 | Aledo, Texas |
| Matos, Malvin, of | .223 | 105 | 359 | 40 | 80 | 17 | 2 | 9 | 32 | 24 | 114 | 6 | 9 | R | R | 6-2 | 175 | 6-18-72 | 1989 | Bobures, Venez. |
| Mercedes, Guillermo, ss | .239 | 127 | 457 | 55 | 109 | 12 | 2 | 0 | 30 | 47 | 60 | 41 | 17 | R | R | 5-11 | 155 | 1-17-74 | 1991 | La Romana, D.R. |
| Morris, Rod, of | .235 | 17 | 51 | 8 | 12 | 0 | 2 | 0 | 3 | 4 | 13 | 3 | 0 | L | L | 5-9 | 163 | 5-5-66 | 1988 | Hammond, La. |
| Parra, Franklin, 3b-of | .213 | 125 | 446 | 52 | 95 | 13 | 6 | 5 | 25 | 37 | 99 | 18 | 13 | S | R | 6-0 | 165 | 7-8-71 | 1989 | Puerto Plata, D.R. |
| Sagmoen, Marc, of | .295 | 63 | 234 | 44 | 69 | 13 | 4 | 6 | 34 | 23 | 39 | 16 | 4 | L | L | 5-11 | 180 | 4-6-71 | 1993 | Seattle, Wash. |
| Sealy, Scot, c | .143 | 2 | 7 | 0 | 1 | 0 | 0 | 0 | 0 | 0 | 4 | 0 | 0 | R | R | 6-2 | 200 | 2-10-71 | 1992 | Satsuma, Ala. |
| Seesz, Brian, c | .200 | 20 | 55 | 6 | 11 | 1 | 0 | 0 | 5 | 9 | 8 | 0 | 1 | L | R | 6-4 | 212 | 8-23-70 | 1992 | Worthington, Minn. |
| Simonson, Bob, of | .250 | 11 | 32 | 4 | 8 | 3 | 1 | 1 | 6 | 0 | 8 | 2 | 0 | R | R | 6-2 | 220 | 5-30-64 | 1984 | Grand Rapids, Mich. |
| Stanczak, Jack, 3b | .256 | 79 | 281 | 34 | 72 | 14 | 5 | 3 | 30 | 41 | 50 | 9 | 5 | R | R | 6-1 | 200 | 1-8-71 | 1993 | Philadelphia, Pa. |
| Welch, Mike, of | .303 | 67 | 238 | 33 | 72 | 20 | 3 | 1 | 37 | 41 | 43 | 6 | 2 | L | L | 6-1 | 210 | 1-13-70 | 1992 | Central Islip, N.Y. |
| Wells, Beck, dh-c | .216 | 22 | 74 | 9 | 16 | 4 | 0 | 1 | 7 | 4 | 21 | 0 | 2 | R | R | 6-0 | 170 | 7-25-70 | 1993 | Brownwood, Texas |
| Woodall, Kevin, of | .244 | 24 | 45 | 7 | 11 | 0 | 1 | 0 | 2 | 2 | 12 | 3 | 0 | R | R | 6-2 | 170 | 10-17-71 | 1990 | Georgetown, S.C. |

| PITCHING | W | L | ERA | G | GS | CG | SV | IP | H | R | ER | BB | SO | B | T | HT | WT | DOB | 1st Yr | Resides |
|---|---|---|---|---|---|---|---|---|---|---|---|---|---|---|---|---|---|---|---|---|
| Anderson, Mike | 3 | 1 | 3.42 | 30 | 0 | 0 | 0 | 50 | 44 | 24 | 19 | 30 | 26 | R | R | 6-0 | 170 | 8-15-71 | 1992 | Bethlehem, Pa. |
| Brandenburg, Mark | 6 | 3 | 1.46 | 44 | 0 | 0 | 4 | 80 | 62 | 23 | 13 | 22 | 67 | R | R | 6-0 | 170 | 7-14-70 | 1992 | Humble, Texas |
| Eyre, Scott | 11 | 7 | 3.45 | 26 | 26 | 0 | 0 | 144 | 115 | 74 | 55 | 59 | 154 | L | L | 6-1 | 160 | 5-30-72 | 1991 | Magna, Utah |
| Kimel, Jack | 9 | 7 | 3.97 | 36 | 11 | 1 | 0 | 118 | 121 | 70 | 52 | 34 | 98 | L | L | 6-1 | 175 | 12-24-69 | 1992 | Clemmons, N.C. |
| Lacy, Kerry | 0 | 6 | 3.15 | 58 | 0 | 0 | 36 | 60 | 49 | 25 | 21 | 32 | 54 | R | R | 6-2 | 195 | 8-7-72 | 1991 | Higdon, Ala. |
| Manning, David | 6 | 7 | 3.03 | 37 | 10 | 0 | 2 | 116 | 112 | 54 | 39 | 39 | 83 | R | R | 6-3 | 205 | 8-14-71 | 1992 | Lantana, Fla. |
| Martin, Jerry | 8 | 10 | 4.18 | 28 | 28 | 1 | 0 | 162 | 157 | 83 | 75 | 61 | 109 | R | R | 6-3 | 175 | 3-15-72 | 1992 | McMinnville, Tenn. |
| Martinez, Ramiro | 6 | 10 | 5.85 | 27 | 27 | 2 | 0 | 125 | 129 | 91 | 81 | 90 | 129 | L | L | 6-2 | 185 | 1-28-72 | 1992 | Los Angeles, Calif. |
| Perez, Paulino | 4 | 4 | 4.29 | 37 | 2 | 0 | 0 | 78 | 78 | 40 | 37 | 34 | 60 | R | R | 6-0 | 160 | 9-18-73 | 1991 | San Pedro de Macoris, D.R. |
| Reynoso, Querbin | 3 | 3 | 5.38 | 15 | 15 | 0 | 0 | 75 | 102 | 56 | 45 | 23 | 29 | R | R | 6-2 | 162 | 1-6-74 | 1992 | Bani, D.R. |
| Runion, Jeff | 2 | 7 | 8.40 | 15 | 15 | 0 | 0 | 60 | 73 | 60 | 56 | 49 | 32 | R | R | 6-5 | 185 | 8-29-74 | 1992 | Riverdale, Ga. |
| Vaughn, Heath | 3 | 1 | 3.81 | 32 | 0 | 0 | 0 | 52 | 40 | 28 | 22 | 38 | 79 | S | R | 6-3 | 185 | 1-12-71 | 1991 | Oklahoma City, Okla. |
| Wheeler, Earl | 3 | 3 | 2.06 | 11 | 6 | 0 | 0 | 48 | 46 | 14 | 11 | 14 | 19 | R | R | 6-2 | 205 | 12-3-69 | 1993 | Stillwater, Okla. |
| Wiley, Chad | 3 | 2 | 3.84 | 14 | 2 | 0 | 2 | 80 | 60 | 42 | 34 | 54 | 72 | R | R | 5-11 | 175 | 11-20-71 | 1992 | Lenexa, Kan. |

# ERIE                                          A

## NEW YORK-PENN LEAGUE

| BATTING | AVG | G | AB | R | H | 2B | 3B | HR | RBI | BB | SO | SB | CS | B | T | HT | WT | DOB | 1st Yr | Resides |
|---|---|---|---|---|---|---|---|---|---|---|---|---|---|---|---|---|---|---|---|---|
| Cabreja, Alexis, of-dh | .226 | 46 | 159 | 23 | 36 | 9 | 2 | 1 | 27 | 9 | 36 | 5 | 2 | R | R | 6-1 | 205 | 3-22-69 | 1993 | Canoga Park, Calif. |
| Clark, Brian, of | .249 | 65 | 233 | 33 | 58 | 11 | 2 | 5 | 26 | 24 | 47 | 11 | 4 | L | L | 6-0 | 180 | 4-9-72 | 1993 | Belton, Texas |

## BATTING

| BATTING | AVG | G | AB | R | H | 2B | 3B | HR | RBI | BB | SO | SB | CS | B | T | HT | WT | DOB | 1st Yr | Resides |
|---|---|---|---|---|---|---|---|---|---|---|---|---|---|---|---|---|---|---|---|---|
| Cossins, Tim, c | .400 | 4 | 10 | 1 | 4 | 1 | 0 | 0 | 3 | 2 | 0 | 0 | 1 | R R | 6-1 | 192 | 3-31-70 | 1993 | Windsor, Calif. |
| DeSimone, Ray, of-3b | .241 | 65 | 249 | 35 | 60 | 6 | 6 | 1 | 19 | 23 | 41 | 18 | 6 | L R | 6-0 | 185 | 8-1-71 | 1993 | Matawan, N.J. |
| Dominow, Eric, 1b | .216 | 62 | 204 | 23 | 44 | 6 | 1 | 2 | 17 | 18 | 34 | 4 | 1 | L L | 6-3 | 210 | 1-25-72 | 1993 | Madison, Ill. |
| Estrada, Osmani, ss-2b | .267 | 60 | 225 | 24 | 60 | 11 | 0 | 4 | 22 | 17 | 26 | 1 | 7 | R R | 5-8 | 180 | 1-23-69 | 1993 | Canoga Park, Calif. |
| Goldberg, Lonnie, 2b-3b | .254 | 72 | 283 | 39 | 72 | 11 | 1 | 1 | 37 | 32 | 40 | 22 | 10 | R R | 5-10 | 170 | 8-1-70 | 1993 | Falls Church, Va. |
| Hill, Michael, 1b-of | .251 | 63 | 203 | 30 | 51 | 10 | 1 | 4 | 28 | 31 | 49 | 3 | 2 | L L | 6-2 | 205 | 3-25-71 | 1993 | Cincinnati, Ohio |
| Melendez, Jorge, c | .128 | 14 | 47 | 6 | 6 | 0 | 0 | 1 | 5 | 8 | 11 | 0 | 0 | R R | 6-0 | 170 | 3-18-74 | 1992 | Cementerio, Venez. |
| Pearson, Cory, of | .209 | 69 | 230 | 27 | 48 | 9 | 1 | 4 | 24 | 14 | 74 | 13 | 8 | R R | 6-0 | 170 | 7-30-74 | 1992 | Logan, W.Va. |
| Pyle, John, c | .125 | 13 | 32 | 5 | 4 | 0 | 0 | 1 | 4 | 5 | 7 | 0 | 0 | R R | 5-11 | 180 | 5-27-72 | 1993 | Winnebago, Ill. |
| Sagmoen, Marc, of | .304 | 6 | 23 | 6 | 7 | 1 | 1 | 0 | 2 | 3 | 7 | 0 | 0 | L L | 5-11 | 180 | 4-6-71 | 1993 | Seattle, Wash. |
| Shook, Wes, dh-c | .321 | 68 | 268 | 48 | 86 | 12 | 2 | 17 | 52 | 18 | 43 | 1 | 2 | R R | 5-10 | 175 | 1-24-70 | 1992 | Lamesa, Texas |
| Sims, Wesley, ss-2b | .239 | 74 | 284 | 38 | 68 | 8 | 0 | 7 | 22 | 31 | 49 | 2 | 5 | S R | 6-0 | 175 | 11-7-71 | 1993 | Charlotte, Tenn. |
| Triplett, Al, 3b-of | .215 | 37 | 93 | 16 | 20 | 2 | 0 | 2 | 14 | 14 | 12 | 5 | 3 | R R | 5-10 | 175 | 6-26-69 | 1992 | Louisville, Miss. |
| Unrat, Chris, c-dh | .290 | 36 | 124 | 25 | 36 | 8 | 1 | 8 | 22 | 11 | 27 | 1 | 1 | L R | 6-1 | 205 | 3-28-71 | 1993 | Kirkland, Quebec |
| Woodall, Kevin, of | .000 | 3 | 3 | 0 | 0 | 0 | 0 | 0 | 1 | 0 | 2 | 0 | 0 | R R | 6-2 | 170 | 10-17-71 | 1990 | Georgetown, S.C. |

## PITCHING

| PITCHING | W | L | ERA | G | GS | CG | SV | IP | H | R | ER | BB | SO | B | T | HT | WT | DOB | 1st Yr | Resides |
|---|---|---|---|---|---|---|---|---|---|---|---|---|---|---|---|---|---|---|---|---|
| Davis, Jeffrey | 0 | 5 | 3.65 | 27 | 0 | 0 | 13 | 37 | 32 | 18 | 15 | 10 | 41 | R R | 6-0 | 170 | 9-20-72 | 1993 | Brockton, Mass. |
| Franklin, Jim | 1 | 4 | 6.16 | 17 | 2 | 0 | 1 | 31 | 38 | 29 | 21 | 12 | 34 | R R | 6-6 | 190 | 1-18-72 | 1993 | Jefferson City, Tenn. |
| Gerhart, Bert | 6 | 4 | 2.88 | 15 | 15 | 2 | 0 | 97 | 82 | 42 | 31 | 13 | 68 | R R | 6-3 | 190 | 12-27-72 | 1991 | Columbus, Miss. |
| Hartman, Pete | 6 | 7 | 4.18 | 15 | 15 | 1 | 0 | 88 | 74 | 51 | 41 | 43 | 98 | L L | 6-2 | 200 | 5-13-71 | 1993 | Ennis, Texas |
| Kell, Robert | 2 | 0 | 1.87 | 18 | 1 | 0 | 1 | 34 | 16 | 8 | 7 | 18 | 44 | R L | 6-2 | 200 | 9-21-70 | 1993 | Hatfield, Pa. |
| Kunz, Devin | 0 | 2 | 7.43 | 5 | 4 | 0 | 0 | 13 | 23 | 19 | 11 | 5 | 9 | L L | 6-4 | 215 | 2-24-68 | 1990 | Sandy, Utah |
| Lesch, J.R. | 1 | 2 | 5.33 | 19 | 0 | 0 | 0 | 25 | 31 | 21 | 15 | 10 | 19 | R R | 6-6 | 205 | 3-19-72 | 1992 | Milwaukie, Ore. |
| Moody, Eric | 3 | 3 | 3.83 | 17 | 7 | 0 | 0 | 54 | 54 | 30 | 23 | 13 | 33 | R R | 6-6 | 185 | 1-6-71 | 1993 | Williamston, S.C. |
| Morvay, Joe | 2 | 3 | 2.82 | 18 | 2 | 0 | 2 | 38 | 32 | 18 | 12 | 14 | 42 | L R | 6-4 | 200 | 2-8-71 | 1993 | Boardman, Ohio |
| O'Brien, Mark | 2 | 3 | 2.86 | 20 | 6 | 1 | 0 | 66 | 57 | 32 | 21 | 21 | 63 | R L | 6-0 | 170 | 3-2-73 | 1991 | Portland, Maine |
| Seip, Rod | 8 | 2 | 3.17 | 16 | 16 | 1 | 0 | 94 | 76 | 41 | 33 | 19 | 82 | R R | 6-2 | 190 | 3-12-74 | 1992 | Thebes, Ill. |
| Smith, Scotty | 1 | 1 | 8.10 | 3 | 1 | 0 | 0 | 7 | 9 | 6 | 6 | 4 | 2 | R R | 6-3 | 200 | 3-8-71 | 1993 | Chattanooga, Tenn. |
| Tipton, Shawn | 3 | 1 | 1.88 | 10 | 0 | 0 | 0 | 14 | 16 | 6 | 3 | 7 | 15 | S L | 5-11 | 173 | 8-5-73 | 1993 | Davidsonville, Md. |
| Willming, Greg | 1 | 4 | 4.18 | 18 | 8 | 0 | 0 | 75 | 64 | 47 | 35 | 22 | 55 | R R | 6-2 | 190 | 12-16-70 | 1993 | Dowagiac, Mich. |
| Wozney, Kevin | 0 | 0 | 6.17 | 7 | 0 | 0 | 0 | 12 | 15 | 8 | 8 | 7 | 8 | R R | 6-3 | 205 | 7-30-70 | 1993 | Arcadia, Wis. |

# PORT CHARLOTTE    R
## GULF COAST LEAGUE

| BATTING | AVG | G | AB | R | H | 2B | 3B | HR | RBI | BB | SO | SB | CS | B | T | HT | WT | DOB | 1st Yr | Resides |
|---|---|---|---|---|---|---|---|---|---|---|---|---|---|---|---|---|---|---|---|---|
| Bell, Mike, 3b | .317 | 60 | 230 | 48 | 73 | 13 | 6 | 3 | 34 | 27 | 23 | 9 | 2 | R R | 6-2 | 185 | 12-7-74 | 1993 | Cincinnati, Ohio |
| Deno, Ariel, c-dh | .200 | 14 | 25 | 4 | 5 | 0 | 0 | 0 | 4 | 1 | 7 | 0 | 0 | R R | 6-2 | 210 | 2-23-74 | 1993 | New York, N.Y. |
| Diaz, Edwin, 2b | .305 | 43 | 154 | 27 | 47 | 10 | 5 | 1 | 23 | 19 | 21 | 12 | 5 | R R | 5-11 | 170 | 1-15-75 | 1993 | Vega Alta, P.R. |
| Ephan, Larry, c-1b | .350 | 56 | 180 | 42 | 63 | 16 | 2 | 1 | 38 | 41 | 30 | 0 | 1 | R R | 6-0 | 210 | 2-12-71 | 1993 | Kalaheo, Hawaii |
| Garcia, Luis, of | .182 | 41 | 99 | 9 | 18 | 1 | 0 | 0 | 5 | 8 | 25 | 10 | 7 | S R | 6-1 | 150 | 8-3-73 | 1990 | San Pedro de Macorís, D.R. |
| Gonzalez, Mario, ss-2b | .284 | 53 | 183 | 33 | 52 | 10 | 0 | 0 | 15 | 32 | 19 | 21 | 5 | S R | 5-11 | 155 | 2-21-74 | 1992 | La Guaira, Venez. |
| Lewis, Andreaus, of | .261 | 56 | 203 | 44 | 53 | 3 | 5 | 2 | 15 | 35 | 50 | 25 | 9 | R R | 6-2 | 215 | 1-22-74 | 1993 | Decatur, Ga. |
| Lewis, Greg, dh-of | .000 | 3 | 9 | 1 | 0 | 0 | 0 | 0 | 0 | 1 | 2 | 2 | 0 | R R | 6-1 | 200 | 6-29-71 | 1993 | Newburgh, N.Y. |
| Macon, Leland, of | .264 | 56 | 193 | 35 | 51 | 1 | 7 | 2 | 27 | 14 | 25 | 29 | 5 | R R | 6-2 | 205 | 5-4-73 | 1993 | Kirkwood, Mo. |
| Ouimet, Steve, 1b | .227 | 34 | 97 | 9 | 22 | 3 | 2 | 1 | 16 | 15 | 15 | 0 | 1 | R R | 6-0 | 200 | 2-21-75 | 1993 | Glenwood Landing, N.Y. |
| Shanklin, Whitney, dh | .197 | 29 | 71 | 8 | 14 | 1 | 0 | 1 | 7 | 16 | 26 | 4 | 5 | R R | 6-3 | 175 | 4-3-74 | 1993 | Los Angeles, Calif. |
| Shows, Travis, c | .063 | 11 | 16 | 1 | 1 | 0 | 0 | 0 | 1 | 2 | 8 | 0 | 0 | R R | 6-1 | 175 | 5-24-73 | 1993 | Menifee, Calif. |
| Unrat, Chris, c | .258 | 12 | 31 | 3 | 8 | 2 | 0 | 0 | 5 | 4 | 4 | 1 | 0 | L R | 6-1 | 205 | 3-28-71 | 1993 | Kirkland, Quebec |
| Vessel, Andrew, of | .219 | 51 | 192 | 23 | 42 | 10 | 2 | 1 | 31 | 8 | 28 | 6 | 2 | R R | 6-3 | 205 | 3-11-75 | 1993 | Richmond, Calif. |
| Walker, Roderic, ss | .152 | 27 | 79 | 7 | 12 | 1 | 0 | 0 | 8 | 9 | 23 | 6 | 2 | R R | 6-1 | 167 | 2-8-76 | 1993 | Chicago, Ill. |
| Williams, Ray, 1b-ss | .185 | 57 | 162 | 19 | 30 | 4 | 0 | 0 | 20 | 26 | 44 | 8 | 6 | R R | 6-1 | 160 | 1-26-74 | 1992 | Dallas, Texas |

| PITCHING | W | L | ERA | G | GS | CG | SV | IP | H | R | ER | BB | SO | B | T | HT | WT | DOB | 1st Yr | Resides |
|---|---|---|---|---|---|---|---|---|---|---|---|---|---|---|---|---|---|---|---|---|
| Cather, Mike | 1 | 1 | 1.76 | 25 | 0 | 0 | 4 | 31 | 20 | 7 | 6 | 9 | 30 | R R | 6-2 | 180 | 12-7-70 | 1993 | Folsom, Calif. |
| Delzine, Domingo | 5 | 0 | 1.82 | 20 | 1 | 0 | 1 | 40 | 39 | 10 | 8 | 5 | 17 | R R | 6-2 | 175 | 4-14-73 | 1992 | LaGuaira, Venez. |
| Evans, Brent | 0 | 0 | 36.00 | 2 | 0 | 0 | 0 | 1 | 4 | 5 | 4 | 2 | 1 | L L | 6-2 | 185 | 7-18-70 | 1993 | Mansfield, Mo. |
| Fajardo, Hector | 3 | 1 | 1.80 | 6 | 6 | 0 | 0 | 30 | 21 | 8 | 6 | 5 | 27 | R R | 6-4 | 200 | 11-6-70 | 1989 | Michoacan, Mexico |
| Falmier, Ryan | 1 | 0 | 3.90 | 14 | 0 | 0 | 1 | 28 | 18 | 12 | 12 | 10 | 17 | R R | 6-3 | 180 | 2-10-75 | 1993 | Tunnel Hill, Ill. |
| Farmer, Jason | 0 | 1 | 18.00 | 2 | 0 | 0 | 0 | 2 | 3 | 5 | 4 | 3 | 2 | R R | 6-5 | 190 | 5-11-72 | 1993 | Oklahoma City, Okla. |
| Howell, Ken | 1 | 0 | 2.08 | 6 | 4 | 0 | 0 | 13 | 8 | 3 | 3 | 5 | 17 | R R | 6-3 | 230 | 11-28-60 | 1982 | Farmington, Mich. |
| Jackson, Michael | 1 | 4 | 5.88 | 15 | 5 | 0 | 0 | 26 | 33 | 25 | 17 | 9 | 12 | R R | 6-4 | 198 | 4-24-75 | 1993 | Texarkana, Texas |
| Knighton, Toure | 3 | 1 | 2.31 | 8 | 7 | 0 | 0 | 35 | 33 | 12 | 9 | 12 | 25 | R R | 6-3 | 180 | 7-4-75 | 1993 | Tucson, Ariz. |
| O'Flynn, Gardner | 4 | 3 | 0.67 | 18 | 0 | 0 | 0 | 27 | 23 | 7 | 2 | 5 | 15 | S L | 6-2 | 205 | 7-5-71 | 1993 | Ipswich, Mass. |
| Ocasio, Mark | 3 | 1 | 3.88 | 12 | 9 | 0 | 1 | 46 | 46 | 24 | 20 | 32 | 38 | R R | 6-3 | 180 | 1-26-75 | 1993 | Carolina, P.R. |
| Oropeza, Igor | 6 | 0 | 2.73 | 12 | 10 | 1 | 0 | 56 | 48 | 23 | 17 | 22 | 43 | R R | 6-0 | 160 | 7-11-72 | 1992 | La Guaira, Venez. |
| Perez, Leo | 1 | 4 | 3.99 | 19 | 0 | 0 | 2 | 29 | 37 | 23 | 13 | 13 | 23 | R R | 6-1 | 165 | 7-31-74 | 1991 | Sabana Palenque, D.R. |
| Reynoso, Querbin | 3 | 1 | 1.97 | 6 | 5 | 1 | 0 | 32 | 29 | 15 | 7 | 5 | 15 | R R | 6-2 | 162 | 1-6-74 | 1992 | Bani, D.R. |
| Rosenkranz, Terry | 0 | 0 | 9.58 | 6 | 0 | 0 | 0 | 10 | 16 | 12 | 11 | 4 | 6 | L L | 6-4 | 205 | 11-5-70 | 1992 | Chicago, Ill. |
| Runion, Jeff | 1 | 0 | 7.02 | 6 | 3 | 0 | 0 | 17 | 15 | 15 | 13 | 22 | 13 | R R | 6-5 | 185 | 8-29-74 | 1992 | Riverdale, Ga. |
| Santana, Julio | 4 | 1 | 1.38 | 26 | 0 | 0 | 7 | 39 | 31 | 9 | 6 | 7 | 50 | R R | 6-0 | 175 | 1-20-73 | 1990 | San Pedro de Macorís, D.R. |
| Smith, Daniel | 3 | 2 | 2.87 | 12 | 10 | 1 | 0 | 53 | 50 | 19 | 17 | 8 | 27 | R R | 6-2 | 175 | 9-15-75 | 1993 | Girard, Kan. |

# TORONTO BLUE JAYS

**Manager:** Cito Gaston.　　　　**1993 Record:** 95-67, .586 (1st, AL East).

| BATTING | AVG | G | AB | R | H | 2B | 3B | HR | RBI | BB | SO | SB | CS | B | T | HT | WT | DOB | 1st Yr | Resides |
|---|---|---|---|---|---|---|---|---|---|---|---|---|---|---|---|---|---|---|---|---|
| Alomar, Roberto | .326 | 153 | 589 | 109 | 192 | 35 | 6 | 17 | 93 | 80 | 67 | 55 | 15 | S | R | 6-0 | 175 | 2-5-68 | 1985 | Salinas, P.R. |
| Borders, Pat | .254 | 138 | 488 | 38 | 124 | 30 | 0 | 9 | 55 | 20 | 66 | 2 | 2 | R | R | 6-2 | 195 | 5-14-63 | 1982 | Lake Wales, Fla. |
| Butler, Rob | .271 | 17 | 48 | 8 | 13 | 4 | 0 | 0 | 2 | 7 | 12 | 2 | 2 | L | L | 5-11 | 185 | 4-10-70 | 1991 | Toronto, Ontario |
| Canate, Willie | .213 | 38 | 47 | 12 | 10 | 0 | 0 | 1 | 3 | 6 | 15 | 1 | 1 | R | R | 6-0 | 170 | 12-11-71 | 1990 | Maracaibo, Venez. |
| Carter, Joe | .254 | 155 | 603 | 92 | 153 | 33 | 5 | 33 | 121 | 47 | 113 | 8 | 3 | R | R | 6-3 | 215 | 3-7-60 | 1981 | Leawood, Kan. |
| Cedeno, Domingo | .174 | 15 | 46 | 5 | 8 | 0 | 0 | 0 | 7 | 1 | 10 | 1 | 0 | S | R | 6-1 | 170 | 11-4-68 | 1988 | La Romana, D.R. |
| Coles, Darnell | .253 | 64 | 194 | 26 | 49 | 9 | 1 | 4 | 26 | 16 | 29 | 1 | 1 | R | R | 6-1 | 185 | 6-2-62 | 1991 | Safety Harbor, Fla. |
| Delgado, Carlos | .000 | 2 | 1 | 0 | 0 | 0 | 0 | 0 | 0 | 1 | 0 | 0 | 0 | L | R | 6-3 | 206 | 6-25-72 | 1989 | Aguadilla, P.R. |
| Fernandez, Tony | .306 | 94 | 353 | 45 | 108 | 18 | 9 | 4 | 50 | 31 | 26 | 15 | 8 | S | R | 6-2 | 175 | 8-30-80 | 1980 | Santo Domingo, D.R. |
| Green, Shawn | .000 | 3 | 6 | 0 | 0 | 0 | 0 | 0 | 0 | 0 | 1 | 0 | 0 | L | L | 6-4 | 180 | 11-10-72 | 1992 | Santa Ana, Calif. |
| Griffin, Alfredo | .211 | 46 | 95 | 15 | 20 | 3 | 0 | 0 | 3 | 3 | 13 | 0 | 0 | S | R | 5-11 | 165 | 3-6-57 | 1974 | San Pedro de Macoris, D.R. |
| Henderson, Rickey | .215 | 44 | 163 | 37 | 35 | 3 | 1 | 4 | 12 | 35 | 19 | 22 | 2 | R | L | 5-10 | 195 | 12-25-58 | 1976 | Oakland, Calif. |
| 2-team (90 Oak.) | .289 | 134 | 481 | 114 | 139 | 22 | 2 | 21 | 59 | 120 | 65 | 8 | 9 | | | | | | | |
| Jackson, Darrin | .216 | 46 | 176 | 13 | 38 | 8 | 0 | 5 | 19 | 8 | 53 | 0 | 2 | R | R | 6-0 | 186 | 8-22-63 | 1981 | Mesa, Ariz. |
| Knorr, Randy | .248 | 39 | 101 | 11 | 25 | 3 | 2 | 4 | 20 | 9 | 29 | 0 | 0 | R | R | 6-2 | 212 | 11-12-68 | 1986 | Covina, Calif. |
| Martinez, Domingo | .286 | 8 | 14 | 2 | 4 | 0 | 0 | 1 | 3 | 1 | 7 | 0 | 0 | R | R | 6-2 | 185 | 8-4-67 | 1985 | Santo Domingo, D.R. |
| Molitor, Paul | .332 | 160 | 636 | 121 | 211 | 37 | 5 | 22 | 111 | 77 | 71 | 22 | 4 | R | R | 6-0 | 185 | 8-22-56 | 1977 | Mequon, Wis. |
| Olerud, John | .363 | 158 | 551 | 109 | 200 | 54 | 2 | 24 | 107 | 114 | 65 | 0 | 2 | L | L | 6-5 | 218 | 8-5-68 | 1989 | Bellevue, Wash. |
| Schofield, Dick | .191 | 36 | 110 | 11 | 21 | 1 | 2 | 0 | 5 | 16 | 25 | 3 | 0 | R | R | 5-10 | 178 | 11-21-62 | 1981 | Laguna Hills, Calif. |
| Sojo, Luis | .170 | 19 | 47 | 5 | 8 | 2 | 0 | 0 | 6 | 4 | 2 | 0 | 0 | R | R | 5-11 | 174 | 1-3-66 | 1987 | Barquisimeto, Venez. |
| Sprague, Ed | .260 | 150 | 546 | 50 | 142 | 31 | 1 | 12 | 73 | 32 | 85 | 1 | 0 | R | R | 6-2 | 215 | 7-25-67 | 1989 | Lodi, Calif. |
| Ward, Turner | .192 | 72 | 167 | 20 | 32 | 4 | 2 | 4 | 28 | 23 | 26 | 3 | 3 | S | R | 6-2 | 185 | 4-11-65 | 1986 | Saraland, Ala. |
| White, Devon | .273 | 146 | 598 | 116 | 163 | 42 | 6 | 15 | 52 | 57 | 127 | 34 | 4 | S | R | 6-2 | 178 | 12-29-62 | 1981 | Mesa, Ariz. |

| PITCHING | W | L | ERA | G | GS | CG | SV | IP | H | R | ER | BB | SO | B | T | HT | WT | DOB | 1st Yr | Resides |
|---|---|---|---|---|---|---|---|---|---|---|---|---|---|---|---|---|---|---|---|---|
| Brow, Scott | 1 | 1 | 6.00 | 6 | 3 | 0 | 0 | 18 | 19 | 15 | 12 | 10 | 7 | R | R | 6-3 | 200 | 3-17-69 | 1990 | Hillsboro, Ore. |
| Castillo, Tony | 3 | 2 | 3.38 | 51 | 0 | 0 | 0 | 51 | 44 | 19 | 19 | 22 | 28 | L | L | 5-10 | 190 | 3-1-63 | 1983 | Lara, Venez. |
| Cox, Danny | 7 | 6 | 3.12 | 44 | 0 | 0 | 2 | 84 | 73 | 31 | 29 | 29 | 84 | R | R | 6-4 | 225 | 9-21-59 | 1981 | Freeburg, Ill. |
| Dayley, Ken | 0 | 0 | 0.00 | 2 | 0 | 0 | 0 | 1 | 1 | 2 | 0 | 4 | 2 | L | L | 6-0 | 180 | 2-25-59 | 1980 | Chesterfield, Mo. |
| Eichhorn, Mark | 3 | 1 | 2.72 | 54 | 0 | 0 | 0 | 73 | 76 | 26 | 22 | 22 | 47 | R | R | 6-3 | 210 | 11-21-60 | 1979 | Naples, Fla. |
| Flener, Huck | 0 | 0 | 4.05 | 6 | 0 | 0 | 0 | 7 | 7 | 3 | 3 | 4 | 4 | S | L | 5-11 | 180 | 2-25-69 | 1990 | Fairfield, Calif. |
| Guzman, Juan | 14 | 3 | 3.99 | 33 | 33 | 2 | 0 | 221 | 211 | 107 | 98 | 110 | 194 | R | R | 5-11 | 190 | 10-28-66 | 1985 | Manoguayabo, D.R. |
| Hentgen, Pat | 19 | 9 | 3.87 | 34 | 32 | 3 | 0 | 216 | 215 | 103 | 93 | 74 | 122 | R | R | 6-2 | 200 | 11-13-68 | 1986 | Fraser, Mich. |
| Leiter, Al | 9 | 6 | 4.11 | 34 | 12 | 1 | 2 | 105 | 93 | 52 | 48 | 56 | 66 | L | L | 6-1 | 190 | 10-23-65 | 1984 | Plantation, Fla. |
| Linton, Doug | 0 | 1 | 6.55 | 4 | 1 | 0 | 0 | 11 | 11 | 8 | 8 | 9 | 4 | R | R | 6-1 | 190 | 9-2-65 | 1987 | Kingsport, Tenn. |
| Morris, Jack | 7 | 12 | 6.19 | 27 | 27 | 4 | 0 | 153 | 189 | 116 | 105 | 65 | 103 | R | R | 6-3 | 200 | 5-16-55 | 1976 | Great Falls, Mont. |
| Stewart, Dave | 12 | 8 | 4.44 | 26 | 26 | 0 | 0 | 162 | 146 | 86 | 80 | 72 | 96 | R | R | 6-2 | 200 | 2-19-57 | 1975 | Emeryville, Calif. |
| Stottlemyre, Todd | 11 | 12 | 4.84 | 30 | 28 | 1 | 0 | 177 | 204 | 107 | 95 | 69 | 98 | L | R | 6-3 | 195 | 5-20-65 | 1986 | Yakima, Wash. |
| Timlin, Mike | 4 | 2 | 4.69 | 54 | 0 | 0 | 1 | 56 | 63 | 32 | 29 | 27 | 49 | R | R | 6-4 | 210 | 3-10-66 | 1987 | Oldsmar, Fla. |
| Ward, Duane | 2 | 3 | 2.13 | 71 | 0 | 0 | 45 | 72 | 49 | 17 | 17 | 25 | 97 | R | R | 6-4 | 210 | 5-28-64 | 1982 | Las Vegas, Nev. |
| Williams, Woody | 3 | 1 | 4.38 | 30 | 0 | 0 | 0 | 37 | 40 | 18 | 18 | 22 | 24 | R | R | 6-0 | 190 | 8-19-66 | 1988 | Houston, Texas |

## FIELDING

| Catcher | PCT | G | PO | A | E | DP |
|---|---|---|---|---|---|---|
| Borders | .986 | 138 | 869 | 80 | 13 | 12 |
| Delgado | 1.000 | 1 | 2 | 0 | 0 | 0 |
| Knorr | 1.000 | 39 | 168 | 20 | 0 | 4 |

| First Base | PCT | G | PO | A | E | DP |
|---|---|---|---|---|---|---|
| Coles | 1.000 | 1 | 1 | 0 | 0 | 0 |
| Martinez | 1.000 | 7 | 25 | 4 | 0 | 2 |
| Molitor | .985 | 23 | 178 | 14 | 3 | 16 |
| Olerud | .992 | 137 | 1160 | 97 | 10 | 107 |
| T. Ward | 1.000 | 1 | 3 | 0 | 0 | 0 |

| Second Base | PCT | G | PO | A | E | DP |
|---|---|---|---|---|---|---|
| Alomar | .980 | 150 | 254 | 439 | 14 | 92 |
| Cedeno | 1.000 | 5 | 2 | 11 | 0 | 1 |

| | PCT | G | PO | A | E | DP |
|---|---|---|---|---|---|---|
| Griffin | .978 | 11 | 22 | 23 | 1 | 6 |
| Sojo | 1.000 | 8 | 9 | 11 | 0 | 2 |

| Third Base | PCT | G | PO | A | E | DP |
|---|---|---|---|---|---|---|
| Coles | .882 | 16 | 11 | 19 | 4 | 0 |
| Griffin | 1.000 | 6 | 3 | 5 | 0 | 0 |
| Martinez | .000 | 1 | 0 | 0 | 0 | 0 |
| Sojo | .667 | 3 | 1 | 1 | 1 | 0 |
| Sprague | .955 | 150 | 127 | 232 | 17 | 21 |

| Shortstop | PCT | G | PO | A | E | DP |
|---|---|---|---|---|---|---|
| Cedeno | .973 | 10 | 8 | 28 | 1 | 4 |
| Fernandez | .985 | 94 | 196 | 260 | 7 | 62 |
| Griffin | .960 | 20 | 34 | 38 | 3 | 9 |

| | PCT | G | PO | A | E | DP |
|---|---|---|---|---|---|---|
| Schofield | .977 | 36 | 61 | 106 | 4 | 23 |
| Sojo | .974 | 8 | 14 | 23 | 1 | 6 |

| Outfield | PCT | G | PO | A | E | DP |
|---|---|---|---|---|---|---|
| Butler | .970 | 16 | 32 | 0 | 1 | 0 |
| Canate | 1.000 | 31 | 38 | 2 | 0 | 1 |
| Carter | .974 | 151 | 289 | 7 | 8 | 0 |
| Coles | .957 | 44 | 65 | 1 | 3 | 0 |
| Green | 1.000 | 2 | 1 | 0 | 0 | 0 |
| Henderson | .975 | 44 | 76 | 1 | 2 | 0 |
| Jackson | .989 | 46 | 86 | 2 | 1 | 0 |
| T. Ward | .990 | 65 | 94 | 2 | 1 | 0 |
| White | .993 | 145 | 399 | 6 | 3 | 2 |

# BLUE JAYS FARM SYSTEM

| Class | Club | League | W | L | Pct. | Finish* | Manager(s) | First Year |
|---|---|---|---|---|---|---|---|---|
| AAA | Syracuse (N.Y.) Chiefs | International | 59 | 82 | .418 | 10th (10) | N. Leyva, B. Didier | 1978 |
| AA | Knoxville (Tenn.) Smokies | Southern | 71 | 71 | .500 | 8th (10) | Garth Iorg | 1980 |
| A# | Dunedin (Fla.) Blue Jays | Florida State | 68 | 64 | .515 | 6th (13) | Dennis Holmberg | 1987 |
| A | Hagerstown (Md.) Suns | South Atlantic | 74 | 68 | .521 | 7th (14) | Jim Nettles | 1993 |
| A | St. Catharines (Ont.) Blue Jays | New York-Penn | 49 | 29 | .628 | 1st (14) | J.J. Cannon | 1986 |
| Rookie | Medicine Hat (Alta.) Blue Jays | Pioneer | 39 | 34 | .534 | 3rd (8) | Omar Malave | 1978 |
| Rookie | Dunedin (Fla.) Blue Jays | Gulf Coast | 22 | 38 | .367 | 13th (15) | Hector Torres | 1993 |

*Finish in overall standings (No. of teams in league)　#Advanced level

BRUCE SCHWARTZMANN

**Key Contributors.** Second baseman Roberto Alomar, left, and righthander Pat Hentgen played major roles in Toronto repeating as World Series champions. Alomar hit .326 with 93 RBIs and 55 stolen bases; Hentgen led the pitching staff with 19 wins.

# SYRACUSE        AAA
## INTERNATIONAL LEAGUE

| BATTING | AVG | G | AB | R | H | 2B | 3B | HR | RBI | BB | SO | SB | CS | B | T | HT | WT | DOB | 1st Yr | Resides |
|---|---|---|---|---|---|---|---|---|---|---|---|---|---|---|---|---|---|---|---|---|
| Butler, Rob | .284 | 55 | 208 | 30 | 59 | 11 | 2 | 1 | 14 | 15 | 29 | 7 | 5 | L | L | 5-11 | 185 | 4-10-70 | 1991 | Toronto, Ontario |
| Canate, William | .250 | 7 | 24 | 3 | 6 | 0 | 0 | 2 | 5 | 5 | 3 | 0 | 2 | R | R | 6-0 | 170 | 12-11-71 | 1989 | Maracaibo, Venez. |
| Cedeno, Domingo | .272 | 103 | 382 | 58 | 104 | 16 | 10 | 2 | 28 | 33 | 67 | 15 | 10 | S | R | 6-1 | 170 | 11-4-68 | 1988 | La Romana, D.R. |
| De la Rosa, Juan | .227 | 60 | 198 | 17 | 45 | 10 | 2 | 4 | 15 | 7 | 41 | 4 | 4 | R | R | 6-1 | 190 | 12-1-68 | 1986 | La Romana, D.R. |
| Giannelli, Ray | .253 | 127 | 411 | 51 | 104 | 18 | 4 | 11 | 42 | 38 | 79 | 1 | 6 | L | R | 6-0 | 195 | 2-5-66 | 1988 | Lindenhurst, N.Y. |
| Henderson, Derek | .370 | 14 | 27 | 2 | 10 | 1 | 0 | 0 | 3 | 3 | 7 | 0 | 2 | R | R | 6-1 | 180 | 6-2-68 | 1989 | Indianapolis, Ind. |
| Martinez, Domingo | .273 | 127 | 465 | 50 | 127 | 24 | 2 | 24 | 79 | 31 | 115 | 4 | 5 | R | R | 6-2 | 185 | 8-4-67 | 1985 | Santo Domingo, D.R. |
| Montalvo, Rob | .214 | 85 | 234 | 25 | 50 | 6 | 1 | 0 | 16 | 21 | 47 | 1 | 1 | R | R | 6-1 | 165 | 3-25-70 | 1988 | West New York, N.J. |
| Monzon, Jose | .239 | 71 | 197 | 14 | 47 | 7 | 0 | 3 | 21 | 11 | 37 | 0 | 1 | R | R | 6-1 | 178 | 11-8-68 | 1987 | Munkipio Vargas, Venez. |
| O'Halloran, Greg | .267 | 109 | 322 | 32 | 86 | 14 | 3 | 3 | 35 | 13 | 54 | 2 | 1 | L | R | 6-2 | 200 | 5-21-68 | 1989 | Mississauga, Ontario |
| Perez, Robert | .294 | 138 | 524 | 72 | 154 | 26 | 10 | 12 | 64 | 24 | 65 | 13 | 15 | R | R | 6-3 | 195 | 6-4-69 | 1990 | Bolivar, Venez. |
| Quinlan, Tom | .236 | 141 | 461 | 63 | 109 | 20 | 5 | 16 | 53 | 56 | 156 | 6 | 1 | R | R | 6-3 | 210 | 3-27-68 | 1987 | Maplewood, Minn. |
| Scott, Shawn | .210 | 103 | 290 | 30 | 61 | 9 | 1 | 0 | 18 | 23 | 60 | 7 | 5 | S | R | 5-10 | 160 | 1-9-69 | 1988 | Pacifica, Calif. |
| Sojo, Luis | .218 | 43 | 142 | 17 | 31 | 7 | 2 | 1 | 12 | 8 | 12 | 2 | 1 | R | R | 5-11 | 174 | 1-3-66 | 1987 | Barquisimeto, Venez. |
| Stevens, Lee | .264 | 116 | 401 | 61 | 106 | 30 | 1 | 14 | 66 | 39 | 85 | 2 | 4 | L | L | 6-4 | 205 | 7-10-67 | 1986 | Wichita, Kan. |
| Yan, Julian | .266 | 91 | 278 | 30 | 74 | 9 | 5 | 7 | 36 | 14 | 91 | 3 | 2 | R | R | 6-4 | 190 | 7-24-65 | 1985 | El Seibo, D.R. |
| Zosky, Eddie | .215 | 28 | 93 | 9 | 20 | 5 | 0 | 0 | 8 | 1 | 20 | 0 | 1 | R | R | 6-0 | 175 | 2-10-68 | 1989 | Whittier, Calif. |

| PITCHING | W | L | ERA | G | GS | CG | SV | IP | H | R | ER | BB | SO | B | T | HT | WT | DOB | 1st Yr | Resides |
|---|---|---|---|---|---|---|---|---|---|---|---|---|---|---|---|---|---|---|---|---|
| Adkins, Steve | 0 | 0 | 4.91 | 5 | 0 | 0 | 0 | 4 | 4 | 2 | 2 | 3 | 0 | R | L | 6-6 | 215 | 10-26-64 | 1986 | Devon, Pa. |
| Akerfelds, Darrel | 3 | 4 | 4.36 | 40 | 1 | 0 | 0 | 64 | 68 | 36 | 31 | 30 | 34 | R | R | 6-2 | 210 | 6-12-61 | 1983 | Denver, Colo. |
| Bailes, Scott | 0 | 1 | 2.21 | 19 | 0 | 0 | 2 | 20 | 19 | 10 | 5 | 3 | 22 | L | L | 6-2 | 171 | 12-18-62 | 1982 | Springfield, Mo. |
| Blohm, Pete | 2 | 6 | 5.44 | 30 | 9 | 0 | 0 | 103 | 122 | 67 | 62 | 52 | 57 | R | R | 6-5 | 200 | 8-19-65 | 1987 | Lynbrook, N.Y. |
| Brow, Scott | 6 | 8 | 4.38 | 20 | 19 | 2 | 0 | 121 | 119 | 63 | 59 | 37 | 64 | R | R | 6-3 | 200 | 3-17-69 | 1990 | Hillsboro, Ore. |
| Brown, Tim | 5 | 13 | 4.47 | 28 | 25 | 3 | 0 | 151 | 159 | 85 | 75 | 35 | 87 | R | R | 6-3 | 185 | 9-16-68 | 1988 | Brandon, Fla. |
| Castillo, Tony | 0 | 0 | 0.00 | 1 | 1 | 0 | 0 | 6 | 4 | 2 | 0 | 0 | 2 | L | L | 5-10 | 190 | 3-1-63 | 1983 | Lara, Venez. |
| Cross, Jesse | 8 | 6 | 3.16 | 29 | 25 | 0 | 0 | 151 | 137 | 68 | 53 | 53 | 127 | R | R | 5-10 | 195 | 1-15-68 | 1989 | Tunnel Hill, Ga. |
| Duey, Kyle | 2 | 1 | 4.05 | 11 | 0 | 0 | 1 | 20 | 19 | 10 | 9 | 7 | 13 | R | R | 6-2 | 215 | 11-8-67 | 1990 | Vancouver, Wash. |
| Hall, Darren | 6 | 7 | 5.33 | 60 | 0 | 0 | 13 | 79 | 75 | 51 | 47 | 31 | 68 | R | R | 6-3 | 190 | 7-14-64 | 1986 | Irving, Texas |
| Linton, Doug | 2 | 6 | 5.32 | 13 | 7 | 0 | 2 | 47 | 48 | 29 | 28 | 14 | 42 | R | R | 6-1 | 190 | 9-2-65 | 1987 | Kingsport, Tenn. |
| Menhart, Paul | 9 | 10 | 3.64 | 25 | 25 | 4 | 0 | 151 | 143 | 74 | 61 | 67 | 108 | R | R | 6-2 | 190 | 3-25-69 | 1990 | Conyers, Ga. |
| Ohlms, Mark | 3 | 6 | 7.05 | 47 | 0 | 0 | 5 | 60 | 85 | 50 | 47 | 42 | 37 | R | R | 6-1 | 175 | 1-15-67 | 1988 | St. Charles, Mo. |
| Spoljaric, Paul | 8 | 7 | 5.29 | 18 | 18 | 1 | 0 | 95 | 97 | 63 | 56 | 52 | 88 | R | L | 6-3 | 205 | 9-24-70 | 1990 | Kelowna, B.C. |
| St.Claire, Randy | 1 | 2 | 3.00 | 14 | 0 | 0 | 0 | 21 | 20 | 8 | 7 | 4 | 13 | R | R | 6-3 | 190 | 8-23-60 | 1979 | Whitehall, N.Y. |
| 2-team (6 Richmond) | 1 | 2 | 2.93 | 20 | 0 | 0 | 0 | 31 | 34 | 14 | 10 | 6 | 16 | | | | | | | |
| Terrell, Walt | 0 | 1 | 5.30 | 8 | 6 | 0 | 0 | 36 | 41 | 25 | 21 | 11 | 20 | R | R | 6-2 | 205 | 5-11-58 | 1980 | Grosse Point Park, Mich. |
| Ward, Anthony | 1 | 2 | 3.70 | 35 | 1 | 0 | 1 | 41 | 37 | 22 | 17 | 25 | 45 | L | L | 6-1 | 190 | 6-9-67 | 1988 | Bartlesville, Okla. |
| Williams, Woody | 1 | 1 | 2.20 | 12 | 0 | 0 | 3 | 16 | 15 | 5 | 4 | 5 | 6 | R | R | 6-0 | 190 | 8-19-66 | 1988 | Houston, Texas |
| Young, Matt | 2 | 1 | 2.27 | 7 | 5 | 0 | 0 | 32 | 22 | 10 | 8 | 14 | 38 | L | L | 6-3 | 205 | 8-9-58 | 1980 | La Canada, Calif. |
| 2-team (3 Charlotte) | 5 | 1 | 2.37 | 10 | 8 | 1 | 0 | 49 | 33 | 15 | 13 | 19 | 55 | | | | | | | |

# BLUE JAYS: ORGANIZATION LEADERS

## MAJOR LEAGUERS

### BATTING

| | | |
|---|---|---|
| *AVG | John Olerud | .363 |
| R | Paul Molitor | 121 |
| H | Paul Moltior | 211 |
| TB | John Olerud | 330 |
| 2B | John Olerud | 54 |
| 3B | Tony Fernandez | 9 |
| HR | Joe Carter | 33 |
| RBI | Joe Carter | 121 |
| BB | John Olerud | 114 |
| SO | Devon White | 127 |
| SB | Roberto Alomar | 55 |

### PITCHING

| | | |
|---|---|---|
| W | Pat Hentgen | 19 |
| L | Two tied with | 12 |
| #ERA | Danny Cox | 3.12 |
| G | Duane Ward | 71 |
| CG | Jack Morris | 4 |
| SV | Duane Ward | 45 |
| IP | Juan Guzman | 221 |
| BB | Juan Guzman | 110 |
| SO | Juan Guzman | 194 |

**Duane Ward**
Team-high 45 saves

## MINOR LEAGUERS

### BATTING

| | | |
|---|---|---|
| *AVG | Jose Herrera, Hagerstown | .317 |
| R | Alex Gonzalez, Knoxville | 93 |
| H | Alex Gonzalez, Knoxville | 162 |
| TB | Alex Gonzalez, Knoxville | 253 |
| 2B | D.J. Boston, Hagerstown | 35 |
| 3B | Two tied at | 12 |
| HR | Carlos Delgado, Knoxville | 25 |
| RBI | Carlos Delgado, Knoxville | 102 |
| BB | Carlos Delgado, Knoxville | 102 |
| SO | Tom Quinlan, Syracuse | 156 |
| SB | Lonell Roberts, Hagerstown | 54 |

### PITCHING

| | | |
|---|---|---|
| W | Paul Spoljaric, Syr.-Knoxville-Dunedin | 15 |
| L | Tim Crabtree, Knoxville | 14 |
| #ERA | Alonso Beltran, St. Catharines | 2.36 |
| G | Darren Hall, Syracuse | 60 |
| CG | Two tied at | 4 |
| SV | Aaron Small, Knoxville | 16 |
| IP | Brad Cornett, Hagerstown | 172 |
| BB | Dennis Gray, Dunedin | 97 |
| SO | Paul Spoljaric, Syr.-Knoxville-Dunedin | 168 |

*Minimum 250 At-Bats   #Minimum 75 Innings

## FIELDING

### Catcher

| | PCT | G | PO | A | E | DP |
|---|---|---|---|---|---|---|
| Montalvo | 1.000 | 1 | 2 | 0 | 0 | 0 |
| Monzon | .983 | 70 | 359 | 56 | 7 | 5 |
| O'Halloran | .983 | 95 | 535 | 49 | 10 | 6 |

### First Base

| | PCT | G | PO | A | E | DP |
|---|---|---|---|---|---|---|
| Giannelli | 1.000 | 3 | 19 | 1 | 0 | 1 |
| Martinez | .986 | 121 | 991 | 104 | 16 | 94 |
| O'Haloran | 1.000 | 1 | 8 | 0 | 0 | 0 |
| Sojo | 1.000 | 1 | 2 | 0 | 0 | 0 |
| Stevens | 1.000 | 8 | 56 | 4 | 0 | 7 |
| Yan | .987 | 21 | 143 | 12 | 2 | 13 |

### Second Base

| | PCT | G | PO | A | E | DP |
|---|---|---|---|---|---|---|
| Cedeno | .957 | 28 | 42 | 68 | 5 | 13 |
| Giannelli | .970 | 82 | 113 | 207 | 10 | 39 |

| | PCT | G | PO | A | E | DP |
|---|---|---|---|---|---|---|
| Henderson | 1.000 | 2 | 1 | 5 | 0 | 1 |
| Montalvo | .982 | 40 | 46 | 66 | 2 | 20 |
| Sojo | .953 | 19 | 27 | 55 | 4 | 13 |

### Third Base

| | PCT | G | PO | A | E | DP |
|---|---|---|---|---|---|---|
| Giannelli | 1.000 | 4 | 0 | 3 | 0 | 0 |
| Martinez | .714 | 3 | 1 | 4 | 2 | 0 |
| Montalvo | .000 | 1 | 0 | 0 | 0 | 0 |
| Quinlan | .957 | 140 | 128 | 273 | 18 | 25 |
| Sojo | 1.000 | 2 | 2 | 3 | 0 | 1 |

### Shortstop

| | PCT | G | PO | A | E | DP |
|---|---|---|---|---|---|---|
| Cedeno | .946 | 78 | 108 | 174 | 16 | 43 |
| Henderson | .914 | 11 | 10 | 22 | 3 | 5 |
| Montalvo | .940 | 39 | 45 | 97 | 9 | 13 |

| | PCT | G | PO | A | E | DP |
|---|---|---|---|---|---|---|
| Quinlan | 1.000 | 1 | 2 | 2 | 0 | 2 |
| Sojo | 1.000 | 1 | 1 | 2 | 0 | 0 |
| Zosky | .960 | 27 | 48 | 71 | 5 | 18 |

### Outfield

| | PCT | G | PO | A | E | DP |
|---|---|---|---|---|---|---|
| Butler | .989 | 55 | 93 | 1 | 1 | 0 |
| Canate | 1.000 | 6 | 9 | 2 | 0 | 1 |
| De la Rosa | .984 | 54 | 122 | 1 | 2 | 0 |
| Hall | .000 | 1 | 0 | 0 | 0 | 0 |
| Martinez | 1.000 | 2 | 4 | 0 | 0 | 0 |
| Montalvo | 1.000 | 9 | 18 | 1 | 0 | 1 |
| Perez | .960 | 137 | 278 | 13 | 12 | 3 |
| Scott | .985 | 91 | 193 | 4 | 3 | 3 |
| Sojo | 1.000 | 13 | 14 | 0 | 0 | 0 |
| Stevens | .981 | 85 | 145 | 8 | 3 | 0 |

# KNOXVILLE
## SOUTHERN LEAGUE                                                                    AA

### BATTING

| | AVG | G | AB | R | H | 2B | 3B | HR | RBI | BB | SO | SB | CS | B | T | HT | WT | DOB | 1st Yr | Resides |
|---|---|---|---|---|---|---|---|---|---|---|---|---|---|---|---|---|---|---|---|---|
| Adriana, Sharnol, 2b | .215 | 64 | 177 | 19 | 38 | 3 | 1 | 0 | 18 | 24 | 59 | 9 | 8 | R | R | 6-1 | 185 | 11-13-70 | 1991 | Curacao, Neth. Antilles |
| Battle, Howard, 3b | .278 | 141 | 521 | 66 | 145 | 21 | 5 | 7 | 70 | 45 | 94 | 12 | 9 | R | R | 6-0 | 197 | 3-25-72 | 1990 | Ocean Springs, Miss. |
| Bowers, Brent, of | .248 | 141 | 577 | 63 | 143 | 23 | 4 | 5 | 43 | 21 | 121 | 36 | 19 | L | R | 6-3 | 200 | 5-2-71 | 1989 | Bridgeview, Ill. |
| Butler, Rich, of-dh | .095 | 6 | 21 | 3 | 2 | 0 | 1 | 0 | 0 | 3 | 5 | 0 | 0 | L | R | 6-1 | 180 | 5-1-73 | 1991 | Toronto, Ontario |
| Canate, William, of | .270 | 9 | 37 | 8 | 10 | 2 | 0 | 1 | 4 | 5 | 2 | 2 | 1 | R | R | 6-0 | 170 | 12-11-71 | 1989 | Maracaibo, Venez. |
| Delgado, Carlos, c | .303 | 140 | 468 | 91 | 142 | 28 | 0 | 25 | 102 | 102 | 98 | 10 | 3 | L | R | 6-3 | 206 | 6-25-72 | 1989 | Aguadilla, P.R. |
| Gonzalez, Alex, ss | .289 | 142 | 561 | 93 | 162 | 29 | 7 | 16 | 69 | 39 | 110 | 38 | 13 | R | R | 6-0 | 182 | 4-8-73 | 1991 | Miami, Fla. |
| Green, Shawn, of | .283 | 99 | 360 | 40 | 102 | 14 | 2 | 4 | 34 | 26 | 72 | 4 | 9 | L | L | 6-4 | 180 | 11-10-72 | 1992 | Santa Ana, Calif. |
| Henderson, Derek, dh | .241 | 13 | 29 | 4 | 7 | 0 | 0 | 1 | 3 | 7 | 1 | 1 | R | R | 6-1 | 180 | 6-2-68 | 1989 | Indianapolis, Ind. |
| Hodge, Tim, dh-of | .242 | 102 | 289 | 21 | 70 | 18 | 0 | 1 | 31 | 34 | 79 | 5 | 1 | R | R | 6-1 | 195 | 8-2-70 | 1988 | Jackson, Miss. |
| Hyers, Tim, 1b | .306 | 140 | 487 | 72 | 149 | 26 | 3 | 3 | 61 | 53 | 51 | 12 | 3 | L | L | 6-1 | 180 | 10-3-71 | 1990 | Covington, Ga. |
| Lis, Joe, 2b | .290 | 129 | 448 | 66 | 130 | 29 | 3 | 8 | 64 | 42 | 58 | 6 | 9 | R | R | 5-10 | 170 | 11-3-68 | 1991 | Newburgh, Ind. |
| Morland, Mike, c | .232 | 45 | 112 | 7 | 26 | 4 | 1 | 0 | 15 | 10 | 31 | 1 | 1 | R | R | 6-0 | 180 | 8-17-69 | 1991 | Cascade Locks, Ore. |
| Reams, Ron, of | .227 | 96 | 299 | 39 | 68 | 14 | 1 | 6 | 33 | 11 | 69 | 16 | 3 | R | R | 6-1 | 175 | 6-24-70 | 1990 | Oakland, Calif. |
| Rosario, Gabriel, 2b | .500 | 4 | 2 | 0 | 0 | 0 | 0 | 1 | 0 | 1 | 0 | 1 | R | R | 6-0 | 150 | 10-19-70 | 1990 | Santo Domingo, D.R. |
| Sheppard, Don, of | .281 | 72 | 249 | 32 | 70 | 11 | 1 | 2 | 27 | 14 | 70 | 5 | 5 | R | R | 6-2 | 180 | 5-2-71 | 1989 | Pittsburg, Calif. |
| Ward, Turner, of | .261 | 7 | 23 | 6 | 6 | 2 | 0 | 2 | 7 | 3 | 3 | 0 | S | R | 6-2 | 185 | 4-11-65 | 1986 | Saraland, Ala. |

### PITCHING

| | W | L | ERA | G | GS | CG | SV | IP | H | R | ER | BB | SO | B | T | HT | WT | DOB | 1st Yr | Resides |
|---|---|---|---|---|---|---|---|---|---|---|---|---|---|---|---|---|---|---|---|---|
| Baptist, Travis | 1 | 3 | 4.09 | 7 | 7 | 0 | 0 | 33 | 37 | 17 | 15 | 7 | 24 | S | L | 6-0 | 190 | 12-30-71 | 1990 | Aloha, Ore. |
| Brow, Scott | 1 | 2 | 3.32 | 3 | 3 | 1 | 0 | 19 | 13 | 8 | 7 | 9 | 12 | R | R | 6-3 | 200 | 3-17-69 | 1990 | Hillsboro, Ore. |
| Brown, Daren | 4 | 5 | 5.00 | 46 | 2 | 0 | 10 | 72 | 72 | 44 | 40 | 32 | 67 | S | R | 6-4 | 185 | 6-13-67 | 1989 | Holdenville, Okla. |
| Crabtree, Tim | 9 | 14 | 4.08 | 27 | 27 | 2 | 0 | 159 | 178 | 93 | 72 | 59 | 67 | R | R | 6-4 | 205 | 10-13-69 | 1992 | Jackson, Mich. |
| Cromwell, Nate | 0 | 1 | 11.00 | 6 | 1 | 0 | 0 | 9 | 15 | 13 | 11 | 10 | 11 | L | L | 6-1 | 185 | 8-23-68 | 1987 | Las Vegas, Nev. |
| Duey, Kyle | 2 | 3 | 6.88 | 37 | 1 | 0 | 0 | 68 | 92 | 57 | 52 | 27 | 40 | R | R | 6-2 | 215 | 11-8-67 | 1990 | Vancouver, Wash. |
| Flener, Huck | 13 | 6 | 3.30 | 38 | 16 | 2 | 4 | 136 | 130 | 56 | 50 | 39 | 114 | S | L | 5-11 | 180 | 2-25-69 | 1990 | Fairfield, Calif. |
| Ganote, Joe | 8 | 6 | 4.15 | 33 | 19 | 1 | 1 | 139 | 149 | 70 | 64 | 52 | 87 | R | R | 6-1 | 180 | 1-22-68 | 1990 | Lake Wylie, S.C. |
| Grove, Scott | 0 | 2 | 7.16 | 10 | 0 | 0 | 0 | 16 | 18 | 13 | 13 | 9 | 10 | R | R | 6-0 | 180 | 9-24-68 | 1988 | Littleton, Colo. |
| Heble, Kurt | 1 | 3 | 3.72 | 6 | 0 | 0 | 0 | 10 | 12 | 5 | 4 | 4 | 13 | R | R | 6-3 | 205 | 2-9-69 | 1991 | West Columbia, Texas |
| Jordan, Ricardo | 1 | 4 | 2.45 | 25 | 0 | 0 | 2 | 37 | 33 | 17 | 10 | 18 | 35 | L | L | 5-11 | 165 | 6-27-70 | 1990 | Delray Beach, Fla. |
| Karsay, Steve | 8 | 4 | 3.38 | 19 | 18 | 1 | 0 | 104 | 98 | 42 | 39 | 32 | 100 | R | R | 6-3 | 180 | 3-24-72 | 1990 | College Point, N.Y. |
| Kizziah, Daren | 3 | 0 | 2.83 | 27 | 1 | 0 | 0 | 54 | 47 | 25 | 17 | 18 | 33 | R | R | 6-4 | 220 | 4-26-67 | 1989 | Peterson, Ala. |
| Montoya, Al | 0 | 5 | 5.14 | 5 | 0 | 0 | 0 | 7 | 8 | 4 | 4 | 3 | 5 | L | L | 6-2 | 168 | 6-10-69 | 1991 | Roswell, N.M. |
| Newlin, Jim | 0 | 2 | 8.89 | 13 | 2 | 0 | 0 | 26 | 41 | 28 | 26 | 13 | 19 | R | R | 6-2 | 205 | 9-11-66 | 1989 | Leawood, Kan. |
| 2-team (21 Jacksonv.) | 1 | 3 | 7.21 | 21 | 2 | 0 | 0 | 44 | 63 | 40 | 35 | 16 | 30 | | | | | | | |

| PITCHING | W | L | ERA | G | GS | CG | SV | IP | H | R | ER | BB | SO | B | T | HT | WT | DOB | 1st Yr | Resides |
|---|---|---|---|---|---|---|---|---|---|---|---|---|---|---|---|---|---|---|---|---|
| Ohlms, Mark .................. | 1 | 0 | 2.70 | 7 | 0 | 0 | 1 | 7 | 6 | 2 | 2 | 3 | 4 | R | R | 6-1 | 175 | 1-15-67 | 1988 | St. Charles, Mo. |
| Phillips, Randy .............. | 2 | 2 | 6.12 | 5 | 5 | 0 | 0 | 25 | 32 | 20 | 17 | 12 | 12 | R | R | 6-3 | 210 | 3-18-71 | 1992 | Pine Bluff, Ark. |
| Renko, Steve ................ | 1 | 3 | 3.63 | 12 | 5 | 0 | 0 | 35 | 38 | 21 | 14 | 8 | 30 | R | R | 6-3 | 205 | 8-1-67 | 1990 | Overland Park, Kan. |
| Rogers, Jimmy .............. | 7 | 7 | 4.04 | 19 | 19 | 0 | 0 | 100 | 107 | 54 | 45 | 33 | 80 | R | R | 6-2 | 190 | 1-3-67 | 1987 | Tulsa, Okla. |
| Small, Aaron ................. | 4 | 4 | 3.39 | 48 | 9 | 0 | 16 | 93 | 99 | 44 | 35 | 40 | 44 | R | R | 6-5 | 200 | 11-23-71 | 1989 | Victorville, Calif. |
| Spoljaric, Paul.............. | 4 | 1 | 2.28 | 7 | 7 | 0 | 0 | 43 | 30 | 12 | 11 | 22 | 51 | R | L | 6-3 | 205 | 9-24-70 | 1990 | Kelowna, B.C. |
| Ward, Anthony.............. | 1 | 1 | 1.71 | 11 | 0 | 0 | 3 | 21 | 17 | 5 | 4 | 10 | 23 | L | L | 6-1 | 190 | 6-9-67 | 1988 | Bartlesville, Okla. |

# DUNEDIN    A
## FLORIDA STATE LEAGUE

| BATTING | AVG | G | AB | R | H | 2B | 3B | HR | RBI | BB | SO | SB | CS | B | T | HT | WT | DOB | 1st Yr | Resides |
|---|---|---|---|---|---|---|---|---|---|---|---|---|---|---|---|---|---|---|---|---|
| Anthony, Mark, of .......... | .250 | 2 | 4 | 1 | 1 | 0 | 0 | 0 | 1 | 1 | 0 | 0 | 0 | R | R | 6-0 | 185 | 12-6-70 | 1990 | Lancaster, S.C. |
| Brito, Tilson, ss.............. | .269 | 126 | 465 | 80 | 125 | 21 | 3 | 6 | 44 | 59 | 60 | 27 | 16 | R | R | 6-0 | 170 | 5-28-72 | 1990 | Los Trinitarios, D.R. |
| Brooks, Eric, c .............. | .197 | 43 | 142 | 18 | 28 | 4 | 0 | 1 | 10 | 17 | 21 | 1 | 2 | R | R | 6-2 | 195 | 5-18-69 | 1988 | La Mirada, Calif. |
| Butler, Rich, of.............. | .306 | 110 | 444 | 68 | 136 | 19 | 8 | 11 | 65 | 48 | 64 | 11 | 13 | L | R | 6-1 | 180 | 5-1-73 | 1991 | Toronto, Ontario |
| Cabrera, Carlos, 2b........ | .200 | 4 | 15 | 1 | 3 | 0 | 0 | 0 | 1 | 0 | 2 | 0 | 1 | S | R | 5-11 | 160 | 11-4-73 | 1991 | Mao Valverde, D.R. |
| Colmenares, Carlos, 2b | .000 | 4 | 2 | 1 | 0 | 0 | 0 | 0 | 0 | 0 | 0 | 0 | 0 | R | R | 5-10 | 160 | 11-17-70 | 1991 | Caracas, Venez. |
| Crespo, Felipe, 2b........ | .299 | 96 | 345 | 51 | 103 | 16 | 8 | 6 | 39 | 47 | 40 | 18 | 5 | S | R | 5-11 | 190 | 3-5-73 | 1991 | Caguas, P.R. |
| Helsel, Ron, of-dh ........ | .333 | 9 | 30 | 4 | 10 | 2 | 0 | 0 | 1 | 4 | 1 | 0 | 0 | R | R | 6-0 | 185 | 6-6-71 | 1993 | Duncansville, Pa. |
| Hines, Keith, of............. | .230 | 45 | 152 | 21 | 35 | 6 | 2 | 4 | 28 | 14 | 28 | 8 | 0 | R | R | 6-6 | 200 | 9-16-69 | 1990 | Lucama, N.C. |
| Holifield, Rick, of........... | .275 | 127 | 407 | 84 | 112 | 18 | 12 | 20 | 68 | 56 | 129 | 30 | 13 | L | L | 6-2 | 165 | 3-25-70 | 1988 | Montclair, Calif. |
| Johnson, Matt, dh-.... | .209 | 148 | 19 | 31 | 5 | 0 | 3 | 18 | 18 | 31 | 3 | 2 | R | R | 5-10 | 175 | 5-5-70 | 1992 | Arvada, Colo. |
| Loeb, Marc, c-dh ........... | .238 | 75 | 248 | 20 | 59 | 10 | 0 | 2 | 27 | 29 | 57 | 4 | 4 | R | R | 6-3 | 210 | 11-14-69 | 1989 | Rialto, Calif. |
| Lutz, Brent, c-of ........... | .264 | 84 | 246 | 38 | 65 | 12 | 3 | 4 | 33 | 31 | 60 | 16 | 8 | R | R | 6-1 | 185 | 5-7-70 | 1991 | Issaquah, Wash. |
| Rosario, Gabriel, 2b-ss | .224 | 72 | 219 | 19 | 49 | 3 | 3 | 0 | 18 | 7 | 24 | 12 | 6 | R | R | 6-0 | 150 | 10-19-70 | 1990 | Santo Domingo, D.R. |
| Schofield, Dick, ss........ | .200 | 11 | 30 | 4 | 6 | 2 | 0 | 0 | 4 | 3 | 7 | 0 | 1 | R | R | 5-10 | 178 | 11-21-62 | 1981 | Laguna Hills, Calif. |
| Sheppard, Don, of ........ | .310 | 39 | 116 | 12 | 36 | 4 | 2 | 0 | 10 | 17 | 26 | 6 | 4 | R | R | 6-2 | 180 | 5-2-71 | 1989 | Pittsburg, Calif. |
| Steverson, Todd, of-dh . | .271 | 106 | 413 | 68 | 112 | 32 | 4 | 11 | 54 | 44 | 118 | 15 | 12 | R | R | 6-2 | 185 | 11-15-71 | 1992 | Inglewood, Calif. |
| Stynes, Chris, 3b.......... | .304 | 123 | 496 | 72 | 151 | 28 | 5 | 7 | 48 | 25 | 40 | 19 | 9 | R | R | 5-9 | 170 | 1-19-73 | 1991 | Boca Raton, Fla. |
| Townley, Jason, c ......... | .500 | 2 | 4 | 1 | 2 | 0 | 0 | 1 | 0 | 0 | 0 | 0 | 0 | R | R | 6-2 | 220 | 6-18-69 | 1987 | Pensacola, Fla. |
| Weinke, Chris, 1b.......... | .284 | 128 | 476 | 68 | 135 | 16 | 2 | 17 | 98 | 66 | 78 | 8 | 6 | L | L | 6-3 | 205 | 7-31-72 | 1991 | St. Paul, Minn. |

| PITCHING | W | L | ERA | G | GS | CG | SV | IP | H | R | ER | BB | SO | B | T | HT | WT | DOB | 1st Yr | Resides |
|---|---|---|---|---|---|---|---|---|---|---|---|---|---|---|---|---|---|---|---|---|
| Arias, Alfredo ................ | 0 | 0 | 8.10 | 3 | 0 | 0 | 0 | 3 | 6 | 3 | 3 | 0 | 2 | R | R | 6-2 | 160 | 11-5-72 | 1991 | San Pedro de Macoris, D.R. |
| Carrara, Giovanni .......... | 6 | 11 | 3.45 | 27 | 24 | 1 | 0 | 141 | 136 | 69 | 54 | 59 | 108 | R | R | 6-2 | 210 | 3-4-68 | 1990 | Anzoategui, Venez. |
| Daniels, Lee................... | 0 | 1 | 6.23 | 2 | 1 | 0 | 0 | 4 | 6 | 4 | 3 | 2 | 5 | R | R | 6-4 | 180 | 3-31-71 | 1990 | Rochelle, Ga. |
| Darley, Ned.................... | 2 | 0 | 2.59 | 5 | 4 | 0 | 0 | 24 | 18 | 8 | 7 | 12 | 12 | L | R | 6-4 | 205 | 2-27-71 | 1990 | Alcolu, S.C. |
| Gray, Dennis.................. | 8 | 10 | 3.57 | 26 | 26 | 0 | 0 | 141 | 115 | 71 | 56 | 97 | 108 | L | L | 6-6 | 225 | 12-24-69 | 1991 | Banning, Calif. |
| Grove, Scott .................. | 3 | 2 | 2.40 | 30 | 0 | 0 | 4 | 45 | 34 | 20 | 12 | 23 | 32 | R | R | 6-0 | 180 | 9-24-68 | 1988 | Littleton, Colo. |
| Heble, Kurt.................... | 6 | 1 | 2.49 | 41 | 0 | 0 | 4 | 51 | 35 | 16 | 14 | 34 | 66 | R | R | 6-3 | 205 | 2-9-69 | 1991 | West Columbia, Texas |
| Hotchkiss, Tom .............. | 0 | 3 | 5.40 | 43 | 0 | 0 | 6 | 67 | 76 | 48 | 40 | 28 | 52 | R | R | 5-9 | 205 | 9-30-68 | 1990 | Carmichael, Calif. |
| Jordan, Ricardo ............ | 2 | 0 | 4.38 | 15 | 0 | 0 | 1 | 25 | 20 | 13 | 12 | 15 | 24 | L | L | 5-11 | 165 | 6-27-70 | 1990 | Delray Beach, Fla. |
| Kotes, Chris .................. | 2 | 2 | 2.57 | 10 | 8 | 0 | 0 | 42 | 37 | 17 | 12 | 12 | 41 | R | R | 6-3 | 195 | 5-11-69 | 1991 | Hopewell Junction, N.Y. |
| Lindsay, Tim .................. | 1 | 1 | 2.55 | 22 | 1 | 0 | 0 | 42 | 52 | 16 | 12 | 14 | 17 | R | R | 6-4 | 200 | 1-12-68 | 1991 | Arcadia, Calif. |
| Montoya, Al.................... | 7 | 4 | 3.59 | 50 | 1 | 0 | 5 | 80 | 78 | 37 | 32 | 26 | 35 | L | L | 6-2 | 168 | 6-10-69 | 1991 | Roswell, N.M. |
| Phillips, Randy............... | 7 | 6 | 3.83 | 17 | 17 | 0 | 0 | 110 | 99 | 51 | 47 | 30 | 87 | R | R | 6-3 | 210 | 3-18-71 | 1992 | Pine Bluff, Ark. |
| Singer, Tom .................. | 9 | 11 | 4.01 | 26 | 26 | 0 | 0 | 137 | 139 | 75 | 61 | 71 | 90 | L | L | 6-4 | 190 | 4-27-69 | 1990 | College Point, N.Y. |
| Spoljaric, Paul............... | 3 | 0 | 1.38 | 4 | 4 | 0 | 0 | 26 | 16 | 5 | 4 | 12 | 29 | R | L | 6-3 | 205 | 9-24-70 | 1990 | Kelowna, B.C. |
| Steed, Rick ................... | 4 | 9 | 5.03 | 22 | 20 | 2 | 0 | 111 | 120 | 81 | 62 | 62 | 66 | R | R | 6-2 | 185 | 9-8-70 | 1989 | West Covina, Calif. |
| Timlin, Mike.................... | 0 | 0 | 1.00 | 4 | 0 | 0 | 1 | 9 | 4 | 1 | 1 | 0 | 8 | R | R | 6-4 | 210 | 3-10-66 | 1987 | Oldsmar, Fla. |
| Weber, Ben.................... | 8 | 3 | 2.92 | 55 | 0 | 0 | 12 | 83 | 87 | 36 | 27 | 25 | 45 | R | R | 6-4 | 180 | 11-17-69 | 1991 | Groves, Texas |
| Williams, Woody ............ | 0 | 0 | 0.00 | 2 | 0 | 0 | 0 | 4 | 0 | 0 | 0 | 2 | 2 | R | R | 6-0 | 190 | 8-19-66 | 1988 | Houston, Texas |

# HAGERSTOWN    A
## SOUTH ATLANTIC LEAGUE

| BATTING | AVG | G | AB | R | H | 2B | 3B | HR | RBI | BB | SO | SB | CS | B | T | HT | WT | DOB | 1st Yr | Resides |
|---|---|---|---|---|---|---|---|---|---|---|---|---|---|---|---|---|---|---|---|---|
| Anthony, Mark, dh-of..... | .176 | 11 | 34 | 6 | 6 | 0 | 0 | 2 | 5 | 7 | 13 | 0 | 0 | R | R | 6-0 | 185 | 12-6-70 | 1990 | Lancaster, S.C. |
| Benbow, Lou, ss............ | .166 | 71 | 193 | 22 | 32 | 5 | 2 | 1 | 12 | 13 | 47 | 2 | 1 | R | R | 6-0 | 160 | 1-12-71 | 1991 | Laguna Hills, Calif. |
| Boston, D.J., 1b............ | .315 | 127 | 464 | 77 | 146 | 35 | 4 | 13 | 93 | 54 | 77 | 31 | 11 | L | L | 6-7 | 230 | 9-6-71 | 1991 | Cincinnati, Ohio |
| Coolbaugh, Mike, 2b-3b | .244 | 112 | 389 | 58 | 95 | 23 | 1 | 16 | 62 | 32 | 94 | 4 | 3 | R | R | 6-1 | 190 | 6-5-72 | 1990 | San Antonio, Texas |
| Cradle, Rickey, of.......... | .254 | 129 | 441 | 72 | 112 | 26 | 4 | 13 | 62 | 68 | 125 | 19 | 14 | R | R | 6-2 | 180 | 6-20-73 | 1991 | Cerritos, Calif. |
| Dotel, Mariano, ss ......... | .207 | 99 | 270 | 31 | 56 | 10 | 4 | 0 | 16 | 20 | 91 | 6 | 9 | S | R | 6-1 | 130 | 4-3-71 | 1989 | San Pedro de Macoris, D.R. |
| Durso, Joe, c ................ | .171 | 15 | 41 | 3 | 7 | 2 | 0 | 0 | 5 | 4 | 9 | 0 | 0 | R | R | 6-2 | 210 | 1-3-71 | 1992 | Glendale, N.Y. |

## BLUE JAYS: MOST COMMON LINEUPS

| | Toronto | Syracuse | Knoxville | Dunedin | Hagerstown |
|---|---|---|---|---|---|
| | Majors | AAA | AA | A | A |
| C | Pat Borders (138) | Greg O'Halloran (95) | Carlos Delgado (107) | Brent Lutz (50) | Angel Martinez (69) |
| 1B | John Olerud (137) | Domingo Martinez (121) | Tim Hyers (140) | Chris Weinke (128) | D.J. Boston (123) |
| 2B | Roberto Alomar (150) | Ray Giannelli (82) | Joe Lis (111) | Felipe Crespo (88) | Santiago Henry (108) |
| 3B | Ed Sprague (150) | Tom Quinlan (140) | Howard Battle (141) | Chris Stynes (115) | Tom Evans (104) |
| SS | Tony Fernandez (94) | Domingo Cedeno (78) | Alex Gonzalez (142) | Tilson Brito (117) | Mariano Dotel (91) |
| OF | Joe Carter (151) | Robert Perez (135) | Brent Bowers (141) | Rick Holifield (122) | Lonell Roberts (128) |
| | Devon White (145) | Shawn Scott (89) | Shawn Green (100) | Rich Butler (103) | Rickey Cradle (125) |
| | Turner Ward (65) | Lee Stevens (83) | Ron Reams (84) | Todd Steverson (68) | Jose Herrera (88) |
| DH | Paul Molitor (99) | Julian Yan (63) | Tim Hodge (64) | Todd Steverson (37) | Kris Harmes (59) |
| SP | Juan Guzman (33) | 3 tied at 25 | Tim Crabtree (27) | Gray/Singer (26) | Doman/Mallory (26) |
| RP | Duane Ward (71) | Darren Hall (60) | Daren Brown (44) | Ben Weber (55) | Aaron Jersild (44) |
| | Full-season farm clubs only | No. of games at position in parenthesis | | | |

# BLUE JAYS
## TOP
# 10
## PROSPECTS

**Carlos Delgado**
.303-25-102 at Double-A

How the Blue Jays Top 10 prospects, as judged by Baseball America prior to the 1993 season, fared in 1993:

| Player, Pos. | Club (Class) | AVG | AB | H | HR | RBI | SB |
|---|---|---|---|---|---|---|---|
| 1. Carlos Delgado, c | Knoxville (AA) | .303 | 468 | 142 | 25 | 102 | 10 |
| | Toronto | .000 | 1 | 0 | 0 | 0 | 0 |
| 2. Alex Gonzalez, ss | Knoxville (AA) | .289 | 561 | 162 | 16 | 69 | 38 |
| 3. Shawn Green, of | Knoxville (AA) | .283 | 360 | 102 | 4 | 34 | 4 |
| | Toronto | .000 | 6 | 0 | 0 | 0 | 0 |
| 6. Howard Battle, 3b | Knoxville (AA) | .278 | 521 | 145 | 7 | 70 | 12 |
| 9. Brent Bowers, of | Knoxville (AA) | .248 | 577 | 143 | 5 | 43 | 36 |
| 10. Rob Butler, of | Syracuse (AAA) | .284 | 208 | 59 | 1 | 14 | 7 |
| | Toronto | .271 | 48 | 13 | 0 | 2 | 2 |

| | | W | L | ERA | IP | H | BB | SO |
|---|---|---|---|---|---|---|---|---|
| 4. Steve Karsay, rhp* | Knoxville (AA) | 8 | 4 | 3.38 | 104 | 98 | 32 | 100 |
| | Huntsville (AA) | 0 | 0 | 5.14 | 14 | 13 | 3 | 22 |
| | Oakland | 3 | 3 | 4.04 | 49 | 49 | 16 | 33 |
| 5. Jose Pett, rhp | GCL Jays (R) | 1 | 1 | 3.60 | 10 | 10 | 3 | 7 |
| 7. Paul Spoljaric, lhp | Dunedin (A) | 3 | 0 | 1.38 | 26 | 16 | 12 | 29 |
| | Knoxville (AA) | 4 | 1 | 2.28 | 43 | 30 | 22 | 51 |
| | Syracuse (AAA) | 8 | 7 | 5.29 | 95 | 97 | 52 | 88 |
| 8. Aaron Small, rhp | Knoxville (AA) | 4 | 4 | 3.39 | 93 | 99 | 40 | 44 |

*Traded to Oakland Athletics

## BATTING

| | AVG | G | AB | R | H | 2B | 3B | HR | RBI | BB | SO | SB | CS | B | T | HT | WT | DOB | 1st Yr | Resides |
|---|---|---|---|---|---|---|---|---|---|---|---|---|---|---|---|---|---|---|---|---|
| Evans, Tom, 3b | .257 | 119 | 389 | 47 | 100 | 25 | 1 | 7 | 54 | 53 | 61 | 9 | 2 | R | R | 6-1 | 180 | 7-9-74 | 1992 | Kirkland, Wash. |
| Harmes, Kris, dh-c | .276 | 130 | 482 | 68 | 133 | 29 | 1 | 14 | 73 | 69 | 86 | 3 | 4 | L | R | 6-2 | 190 | 6-13-71 | 1990 | Mount Joy, Pa. |
| Hearn, Sean, of | .279 | 24 | 86 | 12 | 24 | 3 | 0 | 3 | 9 | 6 | 22 | 2 | 0 | L | L | 6-3 | 197 | 8-8-70 | 1990 | Houston, Texas |
| Henry, Santiago, 2b | .275 | 115 | 404 | 64 | 111 | 30 | 12 | 8 | 54 | 20 | 110 | 13 | 4 | R | R | 5-11 | 156 | 7-27-72 | 1991 | San Pedro de Macoris, D.R. |
| Herrera, Jose, of | .317 | 95 | 388 | 60 | 123 | 22 | 5 | 5 | 42 | 26 | 63 | 36 | 20 | L | L | 6-0 | 164 | 8-30-72 | 1991 | Santo Domingo, D.R. |
| Hines, Keith, of | .222 | 59 | 189 | 26 | 42 | 7 | 3 | 2 | 17 | 12 | 37 | 7 | 4 | R | R | 6-6 | 200 | 9-16-69 | 1990 | Lucama, N.C. |
| Ladd, Jeff, c-dh | .211 | 22 | 57 | 8 | 12 | 4 | 0 | 3 | 11 | 12 | 25 | 2 | 1 | R | R | 6-3 | 200 | 7-10-70 | 1992 | Oregon, Ohio |
| Lombardi, John, c-dh | .238 | 8 | 21 | 2 | 5 | 0 | 0 | 0 | 1 | 1 | 4 | 0 | 0 | R | R | 5-10 | 190 | 12-25-69 | 1991 | Worcester, Mass. |
| Lutz, Brent, c | .000 | 1 | 0 | 0 | 0 | 0 | 0 | 0 | 0 | 0 | 0 | 0 | 0 | R | R | 6-1 | 185 | 5-7-71 | 1991 | Issaquah, Wash. |
| Martinez, Angel, c | .263 | 94 | 338 | 41 | 89 | 16 | 1 | 9 | 46 | 19 | 71 | 1 | 1 | L | R | 6-2 | 200 | 10-3-72 | 1990 | Villa Mella, D.R. |
| McCloughan, Scot, dh-of | .231 | 12 | 26 | 4 | 6 | 0 | 0 | 0 | 5 | 3 | 10 | 0 | 0 | L | R | 6-0 | 190 | 3-1-71 | 1992 | Loveland, Colo. |
| Roberts, Lonell, of | .240 | 131 | 501 | 78 | 120 | 21 | 4 | 3 | 46 | 53 | 123 | 54 | 15 | S | R | 6-0 | 172 | 6-7-71 | 1989 | Bloomington, Calif. |
| Zosky, Eddie, ss | .100 | 5 | 20 | 2 | 2 | 0 | 0 | 0 | 1 | 2 | 1 | 0 | 0 | R | R | 6-0 | 175 | 2-10-68 | 1988 | Whittier, Calif. |

## PITCHING

| | W | L | ERA | G | GS | CG | SV | IP | H | R | ER | BB | SO | B | T | HT | WT | DOB | 1st Yr | Resides |
|---|---|---|---|---|---|---|---|---|---|---|---|---|---|---|---|---|---|---|---|---|
| Brandow, Derek | 4 | 5 | 3.66 | 40 | 1 | 0 | 6 | 76 | 76 | 38 | 31 | 34 | 62 | R | R | 6-1 | 200 | 1-25-70 | 1992 | London, Ontario |
| Cornett, Brad | 10 | 8 | 2.40 | 31 | 21 | 3 | 3 | 172 | 164 | 77 | 46 | 31 | 161 | R | R | 6-3 | 190 | 2-4-69 | 1992 | Odessa, Texas |
| Daniels, Lee | 2 | 4 | 3.43 | 33 | 0 | 0 | 12 | 39 | 31 | 20 | 15 | 26 | 38 | R | R | 6-4 | 180 | 3-31-71 | 1990 | Rochelle, Ga. |
| Darley, Ned | 5 | 3 | 5.01 | 24 | 6 | 0 | 0 | 56 | 48 | 38 | 31 | 39 | 40 | L | R | 6-4 | 205 | 2-27-71 | 1990 | Alcolu, S.C. |
| Dolson, Andy | 10 | 11 | 3.64 | 29 | 25 | 4 | 0 | 163 | 148 | 74 | 66 | 58 | 143 | L | L | 6-4 | 205 | 10-31-69 | 1991 | Lakeland, Fla. |
| Doman, Roger | 8 | 6 | 4.11 | 26 | 26 | 0 | 0 | 147 | 153 | 78 | 67 | 73 | 102 | R | R | 6-5 | 185 | 1-26-73 | 1991 | Joplin, Mo. |
| Jersild, Aaron | 3 | 2 | 3.68 | 44 | 0 | 0 | 3 | 71 | 74 | 39 | 29 | 25 | 59 | L | L | 6-0 | 180 | 6-28-69 | 1992 | Columbia, S.C. |
| Largusa, Levon | 3 | 1 | 2.17 | 6 | 6 | 0 | 0 | 29 | 16 | 10 | 7 | 16 | 33 | L | L | 5-11 | 180 | 5-21-71 | 1992 | Hayward, Calif. |
| Lindsay, Tim | 1 | 1 | 6.43 | 16 | 1 | 0 | 0 | 35 | 49 | 27 | 25 | 10 | 23 | R | R | 6-4 | 200 | 1-12-68 | 1991 | Arcadia, Calif. |
| Maldonado, Jay | 1 | 0 | 3.00 | 8 | 0 | 0 | 0 | 12 | 11 | 4 | 4 | 6 | 9 | R | R | 6-0 | 195 | 3-24-73 | 1992 | San Antonio, Texas |
| Mallory, Trevor | 7 | 10 | 4.06 | 26 | 26 | 3 | 0 | 149 | 145 | 81 | 67 | 49 | 92 | R | R | 6-4 | 180 | 5-31-72 | 1991 | St. Petersburg, Fla. |
| Meinershagen, Adam | 0 | 3 | 7.36 | 5 | 5 | 0 | 0 | 26 | 37 | 22 | 21 | 11 | 16 | R | R | 6-4 | 190 | 7-25-73 | 1991 | St. Louis, Mo. |
| Renko, Steve | 4 | 2 | 3.40 | 23 | 1 | 0 | 5 | 42 | 35 | 20 | 16 | 11 | 45 | R | R | 6-3 | 205 | 8-1-67 | 1990 | Overland Park, Kan. |
| Robinson, Ken | 4 | 7 | 4.65 | 40 | 0 | 0 | 7 | 72 | 74 | 43 | 37 | 31 | 65 | R | R | 5-9 | 175 | 11-3-69 | 1991 | Akron, Ohio |
| Silva, Jose | 12 | 5 | 2.52 | 24 | 24 | 0 | 0 | 143 | 103 | 50 | 40 | 62 | 161 | R | R | 6-6 | 180 | 12-19-73 | 1991 | San Diego, Calif. |

## ST. CATHARINES
### NEW YORK-PENN LEAGUE
A

## BATTING

| | AVG | G | AB | R | H | 2B | 3B | HR | RBI | BB | SO | SB | CS | B | T | HT | WT | DOB | 1st Yr | Resides |
|---|---|---|---|---|---|---|---|---|---|---|---|---|---|---|---|---|---|---|---|---|
| Cromer, Brandon, ss | .230 | 75 | 278 | 29 | 64 | 9 | 2 | 5 | 20 | 21 | 64 | 2 | 4 | L | R | 6-2 | 175 | 1-25-74 | 1992 | Lexington, S.C. |
| Debrand, Rafael, of | .218 | 66 | 229 | 43 | 50 | 7 | 0 | 0 | 19 | 35 | 41 | 9 | 12 | L | L | 5-10 | 160 | 10-24-71 | 1991 | Santo Domingo, D.R. |
| De la Cruz, Lorenzo, of | .000 | 6 | 16 | 2 | 0 | 0 | 0 | 0 | 0 | 3 | 5 | 0 | 0 | R | R | 6-1 | 199 | 9-5-71 | 1991 | Santo Domingo, D.R. |
| Durso, Joe, c | .324 | 43 | 145 | 20 | 47 | 6 | 1 | 8 | 30 | 14 | 21 | 1 | 1 | R | R | 6-2 | 210 | 1-3-71 | 1992 | Glendale, N.Y. |
| Hayes, Emanuel, of | .136 | 27 | 66 | 5 | 9 | 1 | 0 | 0 | 2 | 13 | 30 | 4 | 2 | R | R | 6-2 | 181 | 1-14-72 | 1992 | Houston, Texas |
| Hearn, Sean, of | .299 | 44 | 174 | 33 | 52 | 7 | 1 | 8 | 45 | 7 | 45 | 13 | 2 | L | L | 6-3 | 197 | 8-8-70 | 1990 | Houston, Texas |
| Lombardi, John, c | .333 | 4 | 12 | 1 | 4 | 0 | 0 | 1 | 4 | 0 | 3 | 0 | 0 | R | R | 5-10 | 190 | 12-25-69 | 1991 | Worcester, Mass. |
| Melhuse, Adam, 3b | .256 | 73 | 266 | 40 | 68 | 14 | 2 | 5 | 32 | 45 | 61 | 4 | 0 | S | R | 6-2 | 185 | 3-27-72 | 1993 | Stockton, Calif. |
| Moultrie, Pat, of | .269 | 73 | 264 | 29 | 71 | 6 | 3 | 1 | 19 | 16 | 46 | 18 | 13 | L | L | 5-11 | 180 | 4-27-73 | 1992 | Fresno, Calif. |
| Mummau, Rob, 2b | .241 | 75 | 257 | 35 | 62 | 9 | 3 | 3 | 21 | 23 | 44 | 7 | 12 | R | R | 5-11 | 180 | 8-21-71 | 1993 | Manheim, Pa. |
| Querecuto, Juan, c-of | .274 | 57 | 223 | 29 | 61 | 8 | 3 | 8 | 39 | 10 | 47 | 0 | 4 | R | R | 6-0 | 175 | 12-3-69 | 1989 | Anzuategui, Venez. |
| Ramirez, Angel, of | .273 | 6 | 22 | 2 | 6 | 1 | 0 | 0 | 2 | 0 | 7 | 0 | 2 | R | R | 5-10 | 166 | 1-24-73 | 1991 | Azua, D.R. |
| Roggendorf, Kristian, 1b | .296 | 58 | 179 | 19 | 53 | 8 | 2 | 6 | 21 | 20 | 46 | 2 | 1 | L | L | 6-6 | 220 | 8-20-71 | 1993 | Hollbrook, N.Y. |
| Stewart, Shannon, dh-of | .279 | 75 | 301 | 53 | 84 | 15 | 2 | 3 | 29 | 33 | 43 | 25 | 5 | R | R | 6-1 | 185 | 2-25-74 | 1992 | Miami, Fla. |
| Vaught, Craig, 1b-dh | .237 | 47 | 156 | 17 | 37 | 5 | 1 | 3 | 13 | 7 | 57 | 4 | 3 | R | R | 6-0 | 180 | 1-11-73 | 1991 | Tallassee, Ala. |

## PITCHING

| | W | L | ERA | G | GS | CG | SV | IP | H | R | ER | BB | SO | B | T | HT | WT | DOB | 1st Yr | Resides |
|---|---|---|---|---|---|---|---|---|---|---|---|---|---|---|---|---|---|---|---|---|
| Adkins, Tim | 5 | 6 | 3.54 | 16 | 15 | 1 | 0 | 97 | 80 | 43 | 38 | 45 | 91 | L | L | 6-0 | 195 | 5-12-74 | 1992 | Huntington, W.Va. |
| Beltran, Alonso | 11 | 2 | 2.36 | 15 | 15 | 1 | 0 | 99 | 63 | 36 | 26 | 28 | 101 | R | R | 6-3 | 180 | 3-4-72 | 1991 | El Paso, Texas |
| Brown, Chad | 2 | 0 | 1.74 | 18 | 0 | 0 | 10 | 21 | 7 | 4 | 4 | 5 | 23 | L | L | 6-0 | 195 | 12-9-71 | 1993 | Gastonia, N.C. |
| Cheek, Jeff | 2 | 3 | 5.04 | 18 | 0 | 0 | 2 | 30 | 34 | 20 | 17 | 8 | 25 | R | R | 6-0 | 195 | 6-26-70 | 1992 | Oldsmar, Fla. |
| Hurtado, Edwin | 10 | 2 | 2.50 | 15 | 15 | 3 | 0 | 101 | 69 | 34 | 28 | 34 | 98 | R | R | 6-2 | 215 | 2-1-70 | 1991 | Carabobo, Venez. |
| Maldonado, Jay | 1 | 1 | 0.99 | 13 | 0 | 0 | 1 | 36 | 16 | 7 | 4 | 15 | 38 | R | R | 6-0 | 195 | 3-24-73 | 1992 | San Antonio, Texas |
| Meiners, Doug | 5 | 6 | 3.96 | 15 | 15 | 1 | 0 | 91 | 89 | 52 | 40 | 32 | 56 | R | R | 6-8 | 190 | 5-16-74 | 1992 | Staten Island, N.Y. |

| PITCHING | W | L | ERA | G | GS | CG | SV | IP | H | R | ER | BB | SO | B | T | HT | WT | DOB | 1st Yr | Resides |
|---|---|---|---|---|---|---|---|---|---|---|---|---|---|---|---|---|---|---|---|---|
| Meinershagen, Adam ..... | 8 | 1 | 1.88 | 13 | 13 | 1 | 0 | 86 | 53 | 19 | 18 | 26 | 87 | R | R | 6-4 | 190 | 7-25-73 | 1991 | St. Louis, Mo. |
| Muir, Harry ..................... | 4 | 1 | 2.30 | 21 | 2 | 0 | 2 | 47 | 44 | 26 | 12 | 14 | 29 | R | R | 6-2 | 168 | 7-14-72 | 1991 | Delaware, Ontario |
| Pearlman, Dave............. | 0 | 1 | 5.52 | 18 | 0 | 0 | 1 | 31 | 39 | 20 | 19 | 14 | 25 | R | R | 6-3 | 220 | 11-18-71 | 1991 | Fountain Valley, Calif. |
| Steinert, Rob ................ | 0 | 2 | 1.50 | 8 | 3 | 0 | 2 | 18 | 10 | 5 | 3 | 8 | 24 | R | R | 6-2 | 195 | 9-29-71 | 1993 | Greenlawn, N.Y. |
| Torres, Dilson ............. | 1 | 4 | 3.13 | 17 | 0 | 0 | 3 | 23 | 21 | 13 | 8 | 6 | 23 | R | R | 6-1 | 215 | 5-31-70 | 1991 | Suredo, Venez. |

## MEDICINE HAT    R
## PIONEER LEAGUE

| BATTING | AVG | G | AB | R | H | 2B | 3B | HR | RBI | BB | SO | SB | CS | B | T | HT | WT | DOB | 1st Yr | Resides |
|---|---|---|---|---|---|---|---|---|---|---|---|---|---|---|---|---|---|---|---|---|
| Candelaria, Ben, of-dh .. | .264 | 62 | 208 | 24 | 55 | 7 | 1 | 5 | 34 | 27 | 49 | 3 | 3 | L | R | 5-11 | 167 | 1-29-75 | 1992 | Hatillo, P.R. |
| Colmenares, Carlos, ss . | .154 | 10 | 26 | 8 | 4 | 2 | 0 | 0 | 3 | 5 | 10 | 0 | 0 | R | R | 5-10 | 160 | 11-17-70 | 1991 | Caracas, Venez. |
| Daunic, Willie, 1b-dh ..... | .252 | 46 | 143 | 20 | 36 | 4 | 0 | 1 | 17 | 29 | 20 | 0 | 3 | L | L | 6-3 | 180 | 2-9-71 | 1993 | Orlando, Fla. |
| De la Cruz, Lorenzo, of . | .298 | 62 | 208 | 44 | 62 | 11 | 6 | 11 | 43 | 23 | 59 | 5 | 1 | R | R | 6-1 | 199 | 9-5-71 | 1991 | Santo Domingo, D.R. |
| Garcia, Freddy, 3b ......... | .239 | 72 | 264 | 47 | 63 | 8 | 2 | 11 | 42 | 31 | 71 | 4 | 5 | R | R | 6-2 | 186 | 8-1-72 | 1991 | La Romana, D.R. |
| Jones, Ryan, 1b ............ | .246 | 47 | 171 | 20 | 42 | 5 | 0 | 3 | 27 | 12 | 46 | 1 | 1 | R | R | 6-3 | 220 | 11-5-74 | 1993 | Irvine, Calif. |
| Lutz, Rck, dh ................ | .000 | 1 | 4 | 0 | 0 | 0 | 0 | 0 | 0 | 0 | 1 | 0 | 0 | R | R | 6-3 | 205 | 2-11-71 | 1993 | Ridgefield Park, N.J. |
| Martinez, Hector, c ........ | .307 | 26 | 101 | 15 | 31 | 11 | 0 | 2 | 15 | 5 | 14 | 0 | 0 | R | R | 6-1 | 198 | 6-2-72 | 1990 | Dunedin, Fla. |
| Morgan, David, c........... | .238 | 62 | 210 | 35 | 50 | 9 | 0 | 5 | 34 | 36 | 57 | 2 | 1 | R | R | 6-4 | 215 | 11-19-71 | 1993 | Needham, Mass. |
| Patzke, Jeff, ss ............ | .293 | 71 | 273 | 45 | 80 | 11 | 2 | 1 | 22 | 34 | 31 | 5 | 7 | S | R | 6-0 | 170 | 11-19-73 | 1992 | Klamath Falls, Ore. |
| Polis, Peter, c ................ | .118 | 11 | 34 | 0 | 4 | 1 | 0 | 0 | 1 | 2 | 13 | 0 | 0 | R | R | 6-4 | 200 | 11-21-70 | 1991 | Levittown, N.Y. |
| Ramirez, Angel, of......... | .352 | 62 | 227 | 40 | 80 | 8 | 5 | 4 | 30 | 8 | 43 | 15 | 9 | R | R | 5-10 | 166 | 1-24-73 | 1991 | Azua, D.R. |
| Sanders, Tony, of........... | .262 | 63 | 225 | 44 | 59 | 9 | 3 | 4 | 33 | 20 | 49 | 6 | 5 | R | R | 6-2 | 180 | 3-2-74 | 1993 | Tucson, Ariz. |
| Vasquez, Eddy, 2b........ | .221 | 71 | 281 | 45 | 62 | 9 | 1 | 5 | 27 | 7 | 74 | 4 | 12 | R | R | 6-1 | 172 | 8-16-72 | 1991 | New York, N.Y. |

| PITCHING | W | L | ERA | G | GS | CG | SV | IP | H | R | ER | BB | SO | B | T | HT | WT | DOB | 1st Yr | Resides |
|---|---|---|---|---|---|---|---|---|---|---|---|---|---|---|---|---|---|---|---|---|
| Adkins, Rob .................. | 3 | 3 | 4.74 | 14 | 11 | 0 | 0 | 49 | 51 | 39 | 26 | 37 | 25 | R | R | 6-4 | 200 | 9-17-71 | 1991 | Bradenton, Fla. |
| Grant, Brian ................. | 5 | 4 | 2.84 | 14 | 13 | 0 | 0 | 73 | 61 | 33 | 23 | 34 | 49 | L | L | 6-3 | 200 | 11-1-72 | 1993 | Novato, Calif. |
| Jeffery, Scott................. | 1 | 4 | 4.18 | 16 | 0 | 0 | 2 | 28 | 29 | 14 | 13 | 3 | 21 | L | L | 6-1 | 210 | 5-6-74 | 1991 | Yarmouth, N.S. |
| Kennedy, Scott ............ | 3 | 2 | 3.09 | 19 | 0 | 0 | 0 | 32 | 20 | 13 | 11 | 21 | 31 | R | R | 6-3 | 216 | 11-8-72 | 1992 | Plymouth, Mich. |
| Leystra, Jeff ................. | 3 | 2 | 2.51 | 28 | 0 | 0 | 11 | 47 | 37 | 17 | 13 | 15 | 56 | R | R | 6-3 | 185 | 5-30-73 | 1991 | Corunna, Ontario |
| Patterson, Rob.............. | 3 | 4 | 2.35 | 26 | 0 | 0 | 1 | 54 | 51 | 29 | 14 | 18 | 38 | L | L | 6-1 | 175 | 2-14-73 | 1991 | Toronto, Ontario |
| Romano, Michael........... | 4 | 1 | 2.63 | 9 | 8 | 0 | 0 | 41 | 34 | 20 | 12 | 11 | 28 | S | R | 6-2 | 195 | 3-3-72 | 1993 | Chalmette, La. |
| Sievert, Mark................ | 6 | 3 | 5.00 | 15 | 15 | 0 | 0 | 63 | 63 | 40 | 35 | 30 | 52 | L | R | 6-4 | 180 | 2-16-73 | 1991 | Janesville, Wis. |
| Sinclair, Steve.............. | 5 | 2 | 3.33 | 15 | 12 | 0 | 0 | 78 | 87 | 41 | 29 | 16 | 45 | L | L | 6-2 | 172 | 8-2-71 | 1991 | Victoria, B.C. |
| Sinnes, David................ | 3 | 4 | 2.20 | 19 | 4 | 0 | 2 | 45 | 37 | 20 | 11 | 25 | 45 | R | R | 5-11 | 185 | 5-12-71 | 1993 | Miami, Fla. |
| Smith, Keilan ............... | 1 | 1 | 2.84 | 15 | 4 | 0 | 1 | 38 | 28 | 14 | 12 | 11 | 37 | R | R | 6-4 | 175 | 12-20-73 | 1992 | Memphis, Tenn. |
| Toney, Mike .................. | 0 | 2 | 0.38 | 11 | 0 | 0 | 0 | 24 | 13 | 4 | 1 | 13 | 12 | R | R | 6-3 | 200 | 7-31-73 | 1993 | Sierra Vista, Ariz. |
| Vogelgesang, Joe.......... | 2 | 1 | 5.46 | 12 | 4 | 0 | 3 | 30 | 37 | 21 | 18 | 6 | 19 | R | R | 6-2 | 210 | 9-24-70 | 1992 | Cleves, Ohio |
| Young, Joe .................... | 0 | 1 | 2.38 | 2 | 2 | 0 | 0 | 11 | 6 | 3 | 3 | 6 | 7 | R | R | 6-4 | 205 | 4-28-75 | 1993 | Fort McMurray, Alberta |

## DUNEDIN    R
## GULF COAST LEAGUE

| BATTING | AVG | G | AB | R | H | 2B | 3B | HR | RBI | BB | SO | SB | CS | B | T | HT | WT | DOB | 1st Yr | Resides |
|---|---|---|---|---|---|---|---|---|---|---|---|---|---|---|---|---|---|---|---|---|
| Becker, David, c ........... | .209 | 38 | 110 | 14 | 23 | 7 | 1 | 0 | 8 | 20 | 37 | 8 | 1 | R | R | 6-2 | 200 | 8-30-74 | 1992 | Cincinnati, Ohio |
| Bourne, Tim, of-dh ........ | .244 | 44 | 160 | 26 | 39 | 6 | 0 | 0 | 11 | 17 | 57 | 10 | 2 | R | R | 6-2 | 180 | 5-21-75 | 1993 | Altadena, Calif. |
| Cabrera, Carlos, 2b-ss .. | .303 | 52 | 201 | 35 | 61 | 14 | 4 | 2 | 23 | 14 | 23 | 12 | 6 | S | R | 5-11 | 160 | 11-4-73 | 1991 | Mao Valverde, D.R. |
| Cormenares, Carlos, ss | .233 | 9 | 30 | 3 | 7 | 1 | 0 | 0 | 1 | 1 | 8 | 0 | 1 | R | R | 5-11 | 160 | 11-17-70 | 1991 | Caracas, Venez. |
| Davila, Vic, 3b-2b ......... | .302 | 50 | 182 | 23 | 55 | 10 | 3 | 2 | 20 | 13 | 42 | 4 | 3 | L | R | 6-0 | 185 | 10-27-72 | 1993 | New York, N.Y. |
| Farner, Matt, of............. | .181 | 27 | 94 | 12 | 17 | 2 | 0 | 0 | 6 | 19 | 22 | 6 | 3 | L | L | 6-4 | 185 | 10-15-74 | 1993 | Enola, Pa. |
| Halbruner, Rich, 1b ....... | .230 | 41 | 126 | 20 | 29 | 9 | 2 | 3 | 19 | 17 | 32 | 0 | 2 | L | L | 6-3 | 190 | 5-17-74 | 1992 | Matthews, N.C. |
| Helsel, Ron, c............... | .286 | 5 | 14 | 2 | 4 | 2 | 0 | 0 | 1 | 3 | 2 | 0 | 0 | R | R | 6-0 | 185 | 6-6-71 | 1993 | Duncansville, Pa. |
| Hightower, Aaron, of ..... | .257 | 54 | 202 | 25 | 52 | 9 | 6 | 1 | 37 | 11 | 40 | 13 | 3 | R | R | 6-3 | 210 | 4-2-74 | 1992 | Opp, Ala. |
| King, Kevin, of .............. | .115 | 17 | 52 | 5 | 6 | 0 | 0 | 0 | 2 | 4 | 21 | 3 | 2 | R | R | 6-1 | 175 | 4-7-74 | 1993 | St. Croix, V.I. |
| Medrano, Anthony, ss .... | .266 | 39 | 158 | 20 | 42 | 9 | 0 | 0 | 9 | 10 | 9 | 6 | 2 | R | R | 5-11 | 155 | 12-8-74 | 1993 | Long Beach, Calif. |
| Mosquera, Julio, c......... | .259 | 35 | 108 | 9 | 28 | 3 | 2 | 0 | 15 | 8 | 16 | 3 | 3 | R | R | 6-0 | 165 | 1-29-72 | 1991 | Panama City, Panama |
| Rivers, Jon, of .............. | .191 | 51 | 178 | 13 | 34 | 5 | 2 | 0 | 19 | 16 | 31 | 7 | 2 | R | R | 6-2 | 200 | 8-17-74 | 1992 | Tallassee, Ala. |
| Santiago, Carlos, of....... | .277 | 38 | 119 | 12 | 33 | 2 | 0 | 0 | 9 | 10 | 21 | 3 | 1 | R | R | 6-3 | 175 | 10-2-73 | 1993 | Comerio, P.R. |
| Stone, Craig, 1b ........... | .160 | 30 | 94 | 5 | 15 | 3 | 0 | 0 | 3 | 7 | 36 | 0 | 1 | R | R | 6-2 | 185 | 7-12-75 | 1993 | Quaker Hill, Australia |
| Vaninetti, Gene, 3b ....... | .162 | 43 | 148 | 11 | 24 | 5 | 1 | 0 | 12 | 8 | 41 | 1 | 0 | R | R | 6-3 | 187 | 2-20-75 | 1992 | Morphett Vale, Australia |

| PITCHING | W | L | ERA | G | GS | CG | SV | IP | H | R | ER | BB | SO | B | T | HT | WT | DOB | 1st Yr | Resides |
|---|---|---|---|---|---|---|---|---|---|---|---|---|---|---|---|---|---|---|---|---|
| Arias, Alfredo ................ | 2 | 3 | 2.92 | 22 | 4 | 0 | 6 | 49 | 46 | 23 | 16 | 16 | 44 | R | R | 6-2 | 160 | 11-5-72 | 1991 | San Pedro de Macoris, D.R. |
| Ashley, Scott................. | 0 | 2 | 6.86 | 12 | 0 | 0 | 0 | 20 | 19 | 19 | 15 | 19 | 15 | L | R | 6-6 | 220 | 5-2-72 | 1992 | Wesson, Miss. |
| Coe, Brent..................... | 0 | 0 | 13.50 | 1 | 0 | 0 | 0 | 1 | 1 | 2 | 2 | 3 | 2 | R | L | 6-4 | 187 | 10-22-74 | 1993 | Indianapolis, Ind. |
| Corral, Ruben ............... | 3 | 5 | 5.92 | 20 | 3 | 0 | 0 | 49 | 53 | 40 | 32 | 26 | 32 | L | R | 6-6 | 185 | 1-1-76 | 1993 | El Monte, Calif. |
| Geraldo, Antonio........... | 2 | 5 | 4.17 | 16 | 11 | 0 | 0 | 73 | 81 | 47 | 34 | 34 | 46 | R | R | 6-2 | 156 | 3-13-75 | 1992 | Azula, D.R. |
| Hartshorn, Tyson ........... | 0 | 4 | 6.08 | 9 | 4 | 0 | 1 | 27 | 36 | 26 | 18 | 7 | 18 | R | R | 6-5 | 190 | 8-3-74 | 1993 | Lamar, Colo. |
| Johnson, Michael........... | 0 | 2 | 4.87 | 16 | 1 | 0 | 1 | 44 | 51 | 40 | 24 | 22 | 31 | L | L | 6-2 | 175 | 10-3-75 | 1993 | Edmonton, Alberta |
| Lee, Jeremy .................. | 1 | 4 | 4.71 | 9 | 7 | 0 | 0 | 29 | 29 | 15 | 15 | 8 | 22 | R | R | 6-7 | 205 | 10-20-74 | 1993 | Galesburg, Ill. |
| Pett, Jose ..................... | 1 | 1 | 3.60 | 4 | 4 | 0 | 0 | 10 | 10 | 4 | 4 | 3 | 7 | R | R | 6-6 | 190 | 1-8-76 | 1992 | Sao Paulo, Brazil |
| Sinnes, David................ | 1 | 0 | 0.00 | 6 | 0 | 0 | 2 | 10 | 3 | 0 | 0 | 1 | 11 | R | R | 5-11 | 185 | 5-12-71 | 1993 | Miami, Fla. |
| Smith, Keilan ............... | 0 | 0 | 2.45 | 1 | 0 | 0 | 0 | 4 | 4 | 1 | 1 | 1 | 4 | R | R | 6-4 | 175 | 12-20-73 | 1992 | Memphis, Tenn. |
| Stefanoff, Mike.............. | 1 | 2 | 16.69 | 11 | 1 | 0 | 0 | 18 | 21 | 34 | 34 | 36 | 12 | R | R | 6-2 | 190 | 3-13-74 | 1992 | Rowland Heights, Calif. |
| Stone, Matt ................... | 5 | 2 | 3.22 | 15 | 10 | 0 | 1 | 64 | 52 | 28 | 23 | 27 | 56 | L | L | 6-4 | 220 | 2-7-75 | 1993 | Vista, Calif. |
| Volkert, Oreste .............. | 2 | 3 | 3.38 | 14 | 3 | 1 | 2 | 48 | 54 | 24 | 18 | 6 | 34 | R | R | 6-6 | 187 | 1-16-75 | 1993 | La Habra, Calif. |
| Young, Joe.................... | 4 | 5 | 3.90 | 14 | 12 | 1 | 0 | 62 | 59 | 30 | 27 | 31 | 61 | R | R | 6-4 | 205 | 4-28-75 | 1993 | Fort McMurray, Alberta |

# INDEPENDENT
## TEAMS

**Note:** In some cases, players on independently operated clubs were provided by major league organizations. Where applicable, the organization has been noted in parentheses.

## SAN BERNARDINO                A
### CALIFORNIA LEAGUE

| BATTING | AVG | G | AB | R | H | 2B | 3B | HR | RBI | BB | SO | SB | CS | B | T | HT | WT | DOB | 1st Yr | Resides |
|---|---|---|---|---|---|---|---|---|---|---|---|---|---|---|---|---|---|---|---|---|
| Anderson, Steve, 2b (NY-A)... | .274 | 113 | 405 | 61 | 111 | 21 | 0 | 16 | 76 | 33 | 74 | 3 | 4 | L | R | 6-2 | 180 | 1-31-69 | 1991 | San Jose, Calif. |
| Bates, Tommy, ss-2b (Cle) ... | .159 | 15 | 44 | 8 | 7 | 1 | 0 | 1 | 5 | 10 | 10 | 2 | 0 | R | R | 6-1 | 175 | 9-2-68 | 1991 | Arlington, Texas |
| Buchanan, Shawn, of (Chi-A) | .258 | 53 | 182 | 39 | 47 | 11 | 2 | 2 | 29 | 50 | 38 | 11 | 7 | R | R | 6-0 | 190 | 2-1-69 | 1991 | Gary, Ind. |
| Burnett, Roger, ss (NY-A) .... | .286 | 72 | 245 | 34 | 70 | 15 | 0 | 6 | 33 | 25 | 39 | 3 | 2 | R | R | 6-1 | 185 | 11-14-69 | 1991 | Broken Arrow, Okla. |
| Cervantes, Ray, 2b-ss ......... | .209 | 82 | 244 | 37 | 51 | 5 | 0 | 4 | 19 | 43 | 52 | 3 | 5 | R | R | 5-10 | 160 | 10-30-70 | 1992 | San Bernardino, Calif. |
| Cooper, Tim, ss-3b (NY-A).... | .281 | 60 | 217 | 32 | 61 | 13 | 2 | 10 | 44 | 40 | 49 | 4 | 4 | R | R | 6-3 | 190 | 3-10-71 | 1989 | Sacramento, Calif. |
| Demerson, Tim, of (NY-A)..... | .261 | 115 | 426 | 73 | 111 | 21 | 3 | 7 | 46 | 39 | 89 | 24 | 4 | R | R | 6-1 | 193 | 10-29-69 | 1990 | Midland, Texas |
| Figga, Mike, c (NY-A) .......... | .266 | 83 | 308 | 48 | 82 | 17 | 1 | 25 | 71 | 17 | 84 | 2 | 3 | R | R | 6-0 | 200 | 7-31-70 | 1990 | Tampa, Fla. |
| Freeburg, Ryan, dh-1b (Cal) | .241 | 120 | 432 | 57 | 104 | 19 | 3 | 9 | 57 | 47 | 121 | 5 | 7 | L | R | 6-1 | 190 | 10-16-70 | 1992 | Scottsdale, Ariz. |
| Freehling, Rick, dh (Balt)...... | .091 | 3 | 11 | 3 | 1 | 0 | 0 | 0 | 0 | 3 | 3 | 0 | 0 | S | L | 5-10 | 175 | 4-1-70 | 1992 | Denver, Colo. |
| Gilliam, Bo, of (NY-A) .......... | .280 | 39 | 157 | 19 | 44 | 8 | 1 | 5 | 28 | 8 | 34 | 3 | 2 | R | R | 6-0 | 215 | 9-14-68 | 1991 | Tallahassee, Fla. |
| Livesey, Steve, dh-3b (NY-A) | .308 | 4 | 13 | 2 | 4 | 1 | 0 | 0 | 3 | 1 | 5 | 0 | 0 | R | R | 6-3 | 205 | 7-27-68 | 1991 | Spring Hill, Fla. |
| Lohry, Adin, c (NY-A) ........... | .250 | 28 | 84 | 13 | 21 | 3 | 0 | 0 | 7 | 13 | 17 | 2 | 1 | L | R | 6-1 | 180 | 1-12-71 | 1989 | Maitland, Fla. |
| Martinez, Manny, of (Oak)..... | .322 | 109 | 459 | 88 | 148 | 26 | 3 | 11 | 52 | 41 | 60 | 28 | 21 | R | R | 6-2 | 169 | 10-3-70 | 1988 | San Pedro, D.R. |
| Motuzas, Jeff, c (NY-A) ....... | .156 | 52 | 154 | 16 | 24 | 7 | 0 | 2 | 13 | 13 | 45 | 2 | 3 | R | R | 6-2 | 205 | 10-1-71 | 1990 | Nashua, N.H. |
| Ostermeyer, Bill, dh-1b ........ | .194 | 16 | 36 | 3 | 7 | 1 | 0 | 0 | 6 | 6 | 10 | 0 | 1 | R | R | 6-7 | 235 | 9-4-66 | 1990 | Santa Clara, Calif. |
| Phillips, Steve, of (NY-A) ..... | .274 | 57 | 208 | 29 | 57 | 11 | 1 | 9 | 38 | 37 | 71 | 3 | 4 | L | L | 6-2 | 205 | 1-12-68 | 1991 | Fairfield, Ohio |
| Scott, Tim, 3b (Colo.) .......... | .219 | 98 | 356 | 46 | 78 | 11 | 1 | 11 | 35 | 24 | 64 | 3 | 5 | R | R | 6-3 | 205 | 11-16-68 | 1992 | Ellsworth, Maine |
| Turner, Brian, 1b (NY-A)....... | .325 | 109 | 406 | 69 | 132 | 23 | 3 | 21 | 68 | 49 | 75 | 4 | 2 | L | L | 6-2 | 210 | 6-9-71 | 1989 | Orwell, Ohio |
| Twitty, Sean, of (NY-A)......... | .301 | 78 | 289 | 54 | 87 | 18 | 1 | 8 | 38 | 45 | 90 | 13 | 2 | R | R | 6-3 | 190 | 10-23-70 | 1989 | Astoria, N.Y. |

| PITCHING | W | L | ERA | G | GS | CG | SV | IP | H | R | ER | BB | SO | B | T | HT | WT | DOB | 1st Yr | Resides |
|---|---|---|---|---|---|---|---|---|---|---|---|---|---|---|---|---|---|---|---|---|
| Conte, Mike (Oak) .................. | 0 | 1 | 12.27 | 6 | 0 | 0 | 0 | 7 | 10 | 15 | 10 | 12 | 2 | R | R | 6-2 | 210 | 8-11-67 | 1989 | Brownsville, Pa. |
| DeHart, Rick (Mtl) .................. | 4 | 3 | 3.04 | 9 | 9 | 0 | 0 | 53 | 56 | 28 | 18 | 25 | 44 | L | R | 6-1 | 180 | 3-21-70 | 1992 | Topeka, Kan. |
| Edwards, Todd ...................... | 0 | 1 | 16.20 | 7 | 0 | 0 | 0 | 7 | 13 | 16 | 12 | 10 | 6 | L | L | 6-3 | 185 | 11-17-68 | 1990 | Casa Grande, Ariz. |
| 2-team (11 Palm Sprs.) ......... | 3 | 4 | 5.23 | 34 | 1 | | 2 | 43 | 39 | 31 | 25 | 37 | 30 | | | | | | | |
| Ferguson, Jim (Cal)................ | 3 | 2 | 4.26 | 23 | 0 | 0 | 2 | 32 | 30 | 21 | 15 | 21 | 23 | R | R | 6-6 | 240 | 6-22-69 | 1991 | Anaheim, Calif. |
| Grimes, Mike (Colo.) .............. | 0 | 0 | 11.81 | 4 | 0 | 0 | 0 | 5 | 12 | 7 | 7 | 3 | 4 | R | R | 6-2 | 195 | 6-29-68 | 1989 | Dallas, Texas |
| 2-team (26 C.V.) .................... | 1 | 3 | 5.55 | 30 | 0 | | 1 | 58 | 64 | 40 | 36 | 25 | 56 | | | | | | | |
| Hovey, James (Colo) .............. | 1 | 3 | 10.43 | 22 | 1 | 0 | 1 | 29 | 62 | 47 | 34 | 26 | 21 | S | L | 6-1 | 210 | 4-18-71 | 1992 | Eau Claire, Wis. |
| 2-team (23 C.V.) .................... | 2 | 7 | 9.09 | 45 | 1 | | 0 | 69 | 124 | 92 | 70 | 53 | 44 | | | | | | | |
| Malone, Todd (NY-A) .............. | 3 | 9 | 7.03 | 38 | 11 | 0 | 2 | 88 | 91 | 76 | 69 | 89 | 75 | S | L | 6-2 | 195 | 5-16-69 | 1988 | Citrus Heights, Calif. |
| Pedraza, Rod (Mtl) ................. | 9 | 7 | 3.18 | 24 | 23 | 2 | 0 | 142 | 145 | 74 | 50 | 33 | 95 | R | R | 6-2 | 210 | 12-28-69 | 1991 | Cuero, Texas |
| Perez, Carlos (Mtl) ................ | 8 | 7 | 3.44 | 20 | 18 | 3 | 0 | 131 | 120 | 57 | 50 | 44 | 98 | L | L | 6-3 | 200 | 4-14-71 | 1990 | San Cristobal, D.R. |
| Rose, Scott (Oak)................... | 9 | 10 | 4.26 | 28 | 25 | 1 | 0 | 173 | 184 | 110 | 82 | 63 | 73 | R | R | 6-3 | 205 | 5-12-70 | 1990 | Tampa, Fla. |
| Shoemaker, Steve (Oak) ........ | 9 | 6 | 5.40 | 24 | 23 | 1 | 0 | 127 | 146 | 92 | 76 | 56 | 116 | R | R | 6-3 | 195 | 2-24-70 | 1991 | Columbus, Ohio |
| Smith, Tim (Oak) .................... | 4 | 4 | 4.38 | 16 | 15 | 2 | 0 | 88 | 84 | 47 | 43 | 45 | 72 | R | R | 6-2 | 185 | 10-24-69 | 1991 | Westerville, Ohio |
| Sutch, Ray (Oak).................... | 1 | 5 | 4.64 | 51 | 6 | 0 | 6 | 114 | 123 | 72 | 59 | 64 | 88 | R | R | 6-0 | 183 | 9-12-69 | 1991 | Annapolis, Md. |
| Sutherland, John (NY-A) ........ | 3 | 7 | 4.99 | 43 | 1 | 0 | 4 | 70 | 73 | 46 | 39 | 37 | 59 | R | R | 6-1 | 185 | 10-11-68 | 1991 | Walnut Creek, Calif. |
| Suzuki, Makoto ...................... | 4 | 4 | 3.68 | 48 | 1 | 0 | 12 | 81 | 59 | 37 | 33 | 56 | 87 | R | R | 6-4 | 195 | 5-31-75 | 1992 | Kobe, Japan |
| Tajima, Toshio ....................... | 1 | 3 | 5.46 | 13 | 3 | 0 | 0 | 30 | 28 | 24 | 18 | 17 | 22 | R | R | 6-0 | 175 | 10-1-67 | 1993 | Tokyo, Japan |
| Wilkins, Dean ....................... | 1 | 2 | 7.50 | 20 | 0 | 0 | 4 | 24 | 25 | 24 | 20 | 23 | 26 | R | R | 6-1 | 170 | 8-24-66 | 1986 | San Diego, Calif. |

## BUTTE                R
### PIONEER LEAGUE

| BATTING | AVG | G | AB | R | H | 2B | 3B | HR | RBI | BB | SO | SB | CS | B | T | HT | WT | DOB | 1st Yr | Resides |
|---|---|---|---|---|---|---|---|---|---|---|---|---|---|---|---|---|---|---|---|---|
| Cook, Steve, 2b ..................... | .254 | 37 | 138 | 19 | 35 | 4 | 0 | 2 | 15 | 19 | 20 | 4 | 2 | R | R | 6-1 | 175 | 12-7-71 | 1993 | Buffalo, N.Y. |
| DeRosa, Jeff, 2b (Tex.) ......... | .251 | 46 | 175 | 31 | 44 | 6 | 0 | 0 | 20 | 22 | 32 | 2 | 3 | R | R | 6-1 | 185 | 3-16-72 | 1993 | Trail, B.C. |
| Gatti, Dom, of (Texas)........... | .289 | 64 | 239 | 44 | 69 | 7 | 7 | 4 | 35 | 40 | 34 | 17 | 9 | R | R | 5-10 | 175 | 11-2-71 | 1993 | New Hyde Park, N.Y. |
| Holland, Rod, of (Cle.) .......... | .326 | 36 | 129 | 26 | 42 | 10 | 1 | 1 | 18 | 22 | 29 | 11 | 1 | R | L | 5-10 | 165 | 5-1-71 | 1993 | New Braunfels, Tex. |
| Huff, Matt, of (Texas)............ | .276 | 63 | 232 | 40 | 64 | 11 | 6 | 8 | 46 | 26 | 52 | 7 | 2 | R | R | 6-2 | 185 | 11-9-70 | 1993 | Wilmette, Ill. |
| Ignash, Reggie, of (Cle.) ...... | .242 | 52 | 124 | 14 | 30 | 3 | 1 | 3 | 25 | 23 | 50 | 16 | 5 | R | R | 6-1 | 215 | 10-19-75 | 1992 | Pigeon, Mich. |
| King, Tiger, ss-2b (Cle.) ....... | .259 | 71 | 232 | 34 | 60 | 10 | 3 | 4 | 25 | 21 | 58 | 2 | 3 | R | R | 6-0 | 175 | 8-5-71 | 1993 | Norton, Mass. |
| Mahalik, John, 3b ................. | .271 | 74 | 258 | 25 | 70 | 15 | 0 | 1 | 27 | 21 | 52 | 10 | 0 | R | R | 6-2 | 190 | 7-28-71 | 1993 | Irving, Texas |
| McCubbin, Shane, c (Mtl)....... | .340 | 47 | 10 | 16 | 1 | 1 | 3 | 9 | 4 | 14 | 1 | 1 | R | R | 6-1 | 200 | 9-18-72 | 1992 | Rock Island, Ill. |
| Pitts, Jon, c (Texas) ............. | .349 | 41 | 149 | 19 | 52 | 9 | 1 | 2 | 26 | 5 | 19 | 0 | 0 | R | R | 6-3 | 175 | 6-22-72 | 1991 | Anaheim, Calif. |
| Sievers, Jason, c (SF) .......... | .310 | 36 | 113 | 21 | 35 | 7 | 0 | 0 | 20 | 26 | 30 | 1 | 1 | R | R | 6-0 | 190 | 10-29-71 | 1990 | Marysville, Wash. |
| Tomaselo, John, 1b (Cle.) ..... | .240 | 49 | 154 | 29 | 37 | 43 | 12 | 1 | 9 | 31 | 15 | 60 | 1 | 1 | L | L | 6-2 | 210 | 2-24-70 | 1992 | Pacifica, Calif. |
| Watson, Marty, of (Tex.) ....... | .303 | 62 | 218 | 46 | 66 | 12 | 5 | 11 | 41 | 34 | 62 | 10 | 7 | R | R | 6-1 | 195 | 12-3-70 | 1993 | Chandler, Ind. |
| Winget, Jeremy, 1b (Balt) ...... | .303 | 44 | 142 | 22 | 43 | 5 | 1 | 0 | 18 | 29 | 20 | 2 | 3 | L | L | 6-1 | 212 | 6-5-73 | 1991 | Murray, Utah |

| PITCHING | W | L | ERA | G | GS | CG | SV | IP | H | R | ER | BB | SO | B | T | HT | WT | DOB | 1st Yr | Resides |
|---|---|---|---|---|---|---|---|---|---|---|---|---|---|---|---|---|---|---|---|---|
| Beard, Richie ....................... | 2 | 4 | 6.32 | 20 | 1 | 0 | 3 | 31 | 40 | 25 | 22 | 14 | 28 | R | R | 6-0 | 185 | 8-11-70 | 1993 | Texas City, Texas |
| Bobb, Jason ........................ | 2 | 9 | 8.65 | 15 | 10 | 0 | 1 | 52 | 87 | 58 | 50 | 32 | 38 | R | R | 6-2 | 180 | 11-3-72 | 1991 | Chippewa Falls, Wis. |
| Carew, Jeff (Texas) .............. | 2 | 6 | 7.45 | 13 | 11 | 1 | 0 | 54 | 83 | 55 | 45 | 19 | 35 | R | R | 6-4 | 190 | 11-28-72 | 1991 | Kimberly, Wis. |
| Harris, John ....................... | 1 | 3 | 6.85 | 14 | 4 | 0 | 0 | 47 | 50 | 43 | 36 | 35 | 43 | R | R | 6-1 | 195 | 8-8-69 | 1991 | Morrilton, Ark. |
| Hendricks, Kacy ................... | 1 | 1 | 6.15 | 17 | 1 | 0 | 1 | 53 | 67 | 43 | 36 | 30 | 30 | L | L | 6-0 | 172 | 1-29-74 | 1992 | St. Thomas, V.I. |
| Kelley, Chris (Texas) ............ | 3 | 2 | 5.69 | 23 | 6 | 0 | 6 | 62 | 88 | 50 | 39 | 21 | 47 | R | R | 6-3 | 195 | 9-14-70 | 1992 | Simpsonville, S.C. |
| LaPoint, Jason ..................... | 5 | 3 | 4.81 | 12 | 10 | 2 | 0 | 67 | 93 | 52 | 36 | 19 | 37 | L | L | 6-4 | 180 | 8-1-70 | 1993 | LaPorte, Texas |

| PITCHING | W | L | ERA | G | GS | CG | SV | IP | H | R | ER | BB | SO | B | T | HT | WT | DOB | 1st Yr | Resides |
|---|---|---|---|---|---|---|---|---|---|---|---|---|---|---|---|---|---|---|---|---|
| Minear, Clint | 3 | 5 | 6.43 | 16 | 14 | 2 | 0 | 78 | 94 | 59 | 56 | 24 | 53 | R | L | 6-5 | 185 | 7-18-71 | 1991 | Tuscaloosa, Ala. |
| Morrill, Craig (Texas) | 2 | 3 | 10.43 | 15 | 4 | 0 | 1 | 34 | 53 | 49 | 39 | 35 | 20 | R | R | 6-6 | 215 | 3-17-71 | 1993 | Grand Junction, Colo. |
| Seaton, Billy Jo (Texas) | 2 | 4 | 8.65 | 6 | 6 | 0 | 0 | 26 | 39 | 25 | 25 | 9 | 7 | S | R | 6-2 | 185 | 8-8-73 | 1991 | Riviera, Ariz. |
| Starr, Chris (Texas) | 3 | 5 | 6.53 | 8 | 7 | 2 | 0 | 40 | 53 | 35 | 29 | 10 | 29 | R | R | 6-2 | 200 | 8-4-68 | 1991 | Salesville, Ohio |
| Week, Ben | 0 | 2 | 7.98 | 9 | 0 | 0 | 3 | 15 | 22 | 13 | 13 | 13 | 18 | R | R | 6-2 | 210 | 11-30-70 | 1991 | Sonoma, Calif. |
| Williams, Juan | 0 | 2 | 6.00 | 19 | 1 | 0 | 2 | 33 | 38 | 34 | 22 | 30 | 26 | R | L | 6-0 | 175 | 12-24-73 | 1993 | Irvington, N.J. |

## LETHBRIDGE R
### PIONEER LEAGUE

| BATTING | AVG | G | AB | R | H | 2B | 3B | HR | RBI | BB | SO | SB | CS | B | T | HT | WT | DOB | 1st Yr | Resides |
|---|---|---|---|---|---|---|---|---|---|---|---|---|---|---|---|---|---|---|---|---|
| Allen, John, 2b (Pitt) | .050 | 8 | 20 | 0 | 1 | 0 | 0 | 0 | 1 | 1 | 11 | 0 | 1 | R | R | 5-10 | 155 | 12-16-73 | 1992 | Randleman, N.C. |
| Baugh, Gavin, 3b (Fla) | .245 | 70 | 249 | 40 | 61 | 12 | 3 | 4 | 29 | 24 | 60 | 11 | 1 | R | R | 6-3 | 197 | 7-26-73 | 1992 | San Mateo, Calif. |
| Boka, Ben, c (Pitt) | .165 | 35 | 109 | 7 | 18 | 3 | 0 | 1 | 7 | 10 | 40 | 2 | 1 | R | R | 6-4 | 215 | 1-9-73 | 1991 | Dowingtown, Pa. |
| Bonifazio, Anthony, of (Fla) | .169 | 25 | 77 | 6 | 13 | 3 | 0 | 2 | 10 | 8 | 24 | 0 | 2 | R | R | 6-2 | 205 | 6-15-71 | 1992 | Las Vegas, Nev. |
| Brown, Adrian, of (Pitt) | .266 | 69 | 282 | 47 | 75 | 12 | 9 | 3 | 27 | 17 | 34 | 22 | 7 | R | R | 6-0 | 185 | 2-7-74 | 1992 | Summit, Miss. |
| Brown, Willie, of (Fla) | .244 | 65 | 213 | 43 | 52 | 6 | 2 | 16 | 44 | 40 | 86 | 11 | 6 | L | R | 6-2 | 197 | 8-31-70 | 1992 | Edison, Ga. |
| Cordova, Luis, of (Fla.) | .279 | 68 | 251 | 28 | 70 | 10 | 3 | 2 | 38 | 29 | 33 | 9 | 4 | L | L | 5-11 | 170 | 7-22-70 | 1992 | Vega Baja, P.R. |
| Haddock, Doug, p-3b | .214 | 26 | 42 | 5 | 9 | 1 | 0 | 0 | 1 | 3 | 13 | 3 | 0 | R | R | 5-11 | 195 | 4-14-71 | 1993 | Watts, Okla. |
| Jones, Matt, 1b (Pitt) | .247 | 28 | 97 | 16 | 24 | 5 | 0 | 2 | 11 | 5 | 15 | 1 | 2 | L | L | 6-3 | 210 | 9-9-69 | 1992 | Buffalo Grove, Ill. |
| Keefe, Jamie, 2b (Pitt) | .204 | 46 | 137 | 27 | 28 | 2 | 1 | 0 | 9 | 26 | 27 | 11 | 5 | R | R | 5-11 | 180 | 8-29-73 | 1993 | Rochester, N.H. |
| Lea, Corey, of (Pitt) | .272 | 39 | 114 | 15 | 31 | 5 | 1 | 0 | 7 | 10 | 34 | 11 | 8 | R | R | 6-1 | 175 | 10-10-70 | 1993 | Greensboro, N.C. |
| Lussier, Pat, dh-of (Pitt) | .293 | 51 | 167 | 16 | 49 | 10 | 0 | 5 | 26 | 11 | 33 | 1 | 6 | R | R | 6-2 | 205 | 2-28-71 | 1992 | LaSalle, Quebec |
| Marshall, Jason, c (Cle) | .222 | 8 | 18 | 4 | 4 | 0 | 0 | 1 | 4 | 2 | 2 | 1 | 0 | R | R | 5-11 | 195 | 8-28-70 | 1993 | Leonard, Texas |
| Mills, Tony, 2b | .193 | 38 | 88 | 13 | 17 | 0 | 0 | 0 | 6 | 13 | 18 | 11 | 3 | R | R | 5-9 | 160 | 2-20-70 | 1993 | Wichita, Kan. |
| Reiber, Lee, c (Pitt) | .183 | 42 | 109 | 10 | 20 | 5 | 0 | 1 | 12 | 18 | 37 | 1 | 2 | R | R | 6-0 | 195 | 8-17-71 | 1993 | Meridian, Idaho |
| Segura, Juan, ss (Pitt) | .306 | 66 | 242 | 33 | 74 | 13 | 0 | 0 | 25 | 13 | 53 | 4 | 2 | R | R | 6-1 | 160 | 1-27-74 | 1992 | Mao Valverde, D.R. |
| Yselonia, John, 1b (Pitt) | .244 | 36 | 119 | 18 | 29 | 7 | 1 | 6 | 23 | 14 | 23 | 2 | 2 | L | R | 6-2 | 210 | 8-18-71 | 1993 | Margate, Fla. |

| PITCHING | W | L | ERA | G | GS | CG | SV | IP | H | R | ER | BB | SO | B | T | HT | WT | DOB | 1st Yr | Resides |
|---|---|---|---|---|---|---|---|---|---|---|---|---|---|---|---|---|---|---|---|---|
| Ballance, Dale | 4 | 2 | 3.88 | 20 | 3 | 0 | 2 | 51 | 44 | 29 | 22 | 25 | 32 | L | L | 6-2 | 175 | 12-11-72 | 1992 | Nanaimo, B.C. |
| Bonilla, Miguel (Pitt) | 4 | 8 | 2.87 | 16 | 15 | 5 | 0 | 107 | 105 | 46 | 34 | 24 | 59 | R | R | 6-2 | 195 | 8-23-73 | 1990 | Santo Domingo, D.R. |
| Davidson, Rodney (Pitt) | 1 | 5 | 11.44 | 17 | 4 | 0 | 0 | 28 | 45 | 46 | 36 | 20 | 25 | L | L | 6-2 | 225 | 2-11-74 | 1992 | Rustburg, Va. |
| DeLeon, Elcilio (Pitt) | 2 | 4 | 4.07 | 19 | 2 | 1 | 1 | 42 | 38 | 24 | 19 | 29 | 49 | R | R | 6-1 | 170 | 4-14-72 | 1990 | La Romana, D.R. |
| Dillinger, John (Pitt) | 3 | 10 | 3.92 | 15 | 15 | 3 | 0 | 80 | 65 | 51 | 35 | 60 | 94 | R | R | 6-6 | 230 | 8-28-73 | 1992 | Connellsville, Pa. |
| Haddock, Doug | 1 | 2 | 5.75 | 13 | 0 | 0 | 2 | 20 | 21 | 17 | 13 | 13 | 13 | R | R | 5-11 | 195 | 4-14-71 | 1993 | Watts, Okla. |
| Hyman, Terrance | 0 | 0 | 18.00 | 3 | 0 | 0 | 0 | 2 | 1 | 4 | 4 | 6 | 1 | R | R | 6-5 | 197 | 10-31-73 | 1993 | Middletown, Conn. |
| Kath, Merlin | 1 | 1 | 5.08 | 17 | 0 | 0 | 1 | 34 | 43 | 25 | 19 | 11 | 15 | R | R | 6-2 | 205 | 1-28-71 | 1993 | Owatonna, Minn. |
| Musso, Samuel | 1 | 0 | 5.40 | 15 | 0 | 0 | 10 | 17 | 16 | 10 | 10 | 8 | 12 | R | R | 6-1 | 200 | 11-24-71 | 1993 | Metairie, La. |
| Ohman, Shawn | 3 | 4 | 4.46 | 16 | 13 | 1 | 0 | 79 | 91 | 56 | 39 | 29 | 68 | L | L | 6-4 | 203 | 6-29-71 | 1993 | Detroit Lakes, Minn. |
| Roman, Dan (Fla) | 3 | 5 | 5.80 | 15 | 15 | 0 | 0 | 76 | 74 | 67 | 49 | 62 | 65 | L | L | 6-5 | 220 | 3-22-71 | 1992 | Staten Island, N.Y. |
| Solomon, Ray | 2 | 2 | 3.60 | 23 | 0 | 0 | 3 | 30 | 31 | 15 | 12 | 8 | 23 | R | R | 5-10 | 195 | 2-18-71 | 1992 | Windsor, Ontario |
| Terminie, Chad | 4 | 1 | 3.67 | 9 | 6 | 1 | 0 | 49 | 49 | 26 | 20 | 9 | 30 | R | R | 6-1 | 170 | 10-20-71 | 1993 | Chalmette, La. |

## POCATELLO R
### PIONEER LEAGUE

| BATTING | AVG | G | AB | R | H | 2B | 3B | HR | RBI | BB | SO | SB | CS | B | T | HT | WT | DOB | 1st Yr | Resides |
|---|---|---|---|---|---|---|---|---|---|---|---|---|---|---|---|---|---|---|---|---|
| Bingham, David, of-2b | .348 | 55 | 178 | 42 | 62 | 8 | 3 | 5 | 30 | 28 | 45 | 8 | 2 | R | R | 5-11 | 180 | 1-22-71 | 1992 | Walla Walla, Wash. |
| Boyle, Jeff, ss-2b | .208 | 60 | 159 | 24 | 33 | 6 | 1 | 0 | 15 | 13 | 43 | 5 | 4 | R | R | 5-9 | 170 | 9-11-68 | 1993 | Palo Cedro, Calif. |
| Carranza, Pedro, 3b | .273 | 64 | 227 | 44 | 62 | 12 | 4 | 8 | 48 | 43 | 42 | 3 | 6 | R | R | 5-9 | 185 | 9-29-71 | 1993 | El Centro, Calif. |
| Fitzpatrick, Will, 1b | .330 | 57 | 194 | 33 | 64 | 14 | 0 | 9 | 58 | 38 | 52 | 0 | 2 | L | R | 6-5 | 230 | 11-17-70 | 1993 | San Mateo, Calif. |
| Garcia, Orlando, ss | .233 | 50 | 150 | 13 | 35 | 3 | 0 | 0 | 16 | 4 | 25 | 22 | 7 | R | R | 6-0 | 165 | 4-11-72 | 1989 | Levittown, P.R. |
| Greenlee, Darren, dh | .143 | 9 | 21 | 1 | 3 | 0 | 0 | 0 | 2 | 3 | 5 | 0 | 0 | R | R | 5-9 | 200 | 8-24-69 | 1993 | Santa Maria, Calif. |
| Harris, D.J., of-2b | .271 | 59 | 155 | 30 | 42 | 8 | 2 | 5 | 28 | 23 | 39 | 9 | 5 | R | R | 5-10 | 190 | 4-11-71 | 1993 | Las Vegas, Nev. |
| Hunt, Chris, c-of | .282 | 66 | 195 | 26 | 55 | 7 | 1 | 0 | 18 | 36 | 24 | 1 | 1 | L | R | 6-0 | 205 | 9-8-69 | 1992 | Yorba Linda, Calif. |
| Mendoza, Alonso, of | .276 | 55 | 170 | 32 | 47 | 9 | 1 | 2 | 24 | 18 | 18 | 9 | 4 | S | R | 6-3 | 200 | 10-10-70 | 1993 | El Monte, Calif. |
| Pollock, Jason, of | .248 | 59 | 129 | 27 | 32 | 3 | 1 | 0 | 7 | 16 | 47 | 8 | 1 | R | R | 5-11 | 190 | 5-30-71 | 1993 | Lompoc, Calif. |
| Postiff, J.P., c-of | .277 | 62 | 191 | 34 | 53 | 6 | 0 | 1 | 21 | 33 | 42 | 6 | 2 | R | R | 6-0 | 190 | 9-30-68 | 1990 | Casmalia, Calif. |
| Salazar, Julian, 2b | .293 | 52 | 174 | 42 | 51 | 7 | 2 | 4 | 21 | 31 | 37 | 5 | 4 | R | R | 5-11 | 170 | 6-29-69 | 1990 | Rosemead, Calif. |
| Takayoshi, Todd, dh-c | .358 | 69 | 243 | 38 | 87 | 9 | 1 | 5 | 40 | 50 | 25 | 3 | 1 | L | R | 6-1 | 190 | 10-4-70 | 1993 | Honolulu, Hawaii |
| Vaughn, Derek, of | .311 | 72 | 299 | 60 | 93 | 14 | 3 | 5 | 43 | 24 | 52 | 40 | 13 | R | R | 6-3 | 180 | 1-11-70 | 1991 | Los Angeles, Calif. |

| PITCHING | W | L | ERA | G | GS | CG | SV | IP | H | R | ER | BB | SO | B | T | HT | WT | DOB | 1st Yr | Resides |
|---|---|---|---|---|---|---|---|---|---|---|---|---|---|---|---|---|---|---|---|---|
| Atwood, Jason | 1 | 5 | 8.31 | 12 | 7 | 0 | 0 | 43 | 61 | 42 | 40 | 29 | 20 | R | R | 6-5 | 205 | 3-10-70 | 1993 | Salem, Ore. |
| Birdt, Lou | 1 | 2 | 9.69 | 8 | 0 | 0 | 0 | 13 | 25 | 18 | 14 | 4 | 11 | R | R | 6-1 | 180 | 8-13-69 | 1993 | Westhills, Calif. |
| Caruso, Gene | 7 | 5 | 3.17 | 16 | 14 | 7 | 0 | 111 | 83 | 52 | 39 | 58 | 163 | S | L | 5-11 | 180 | 7-20-69 | 1992 | Las Vegas, Nev. |
| Dempsey, Steve | 0 | 0 | 9.00 | 4 | 0 | 0 | 0 | 8 | 15 | 9 | 8 | 1 | 6 | R | R | 5-11 | 180 | 5-7-70 | 1992 | Burbank, Calif. |
| Diaz, Rafael | 2 | 3 | 4.38 | 15 | 4 | 0 | 0 | 49 | 56 | 34 | 24 | 30 | 31 | S | L | 6-3 | 205 | 8-20-71 | 1988 | Bayamon, P.R. |
| Evenhus, Jason | 6 | 2 | 4.85 | 14 | 6 | 1 | 0 | 59 | 69 | 40 | 32 | 22 | 44 | R | R | 6-1 | 195 | 9-30-70 | 1993 | E. Wenatchee, Wash. |
| Graham, Mark | 0 | 0 | 9.45 | 4 | 0 | 0 | 0 | 7 | 10 | 7 | 7 | 4 | 7 | L | L | 6-2 | 200 | 12-2-69 | 1993 | Los Angeles, Calif. |
| Harris, D.J. | 0 | 0 | 6.43 | 5 | 0 | 0 | 1 | 7 | 14 | 10 | 5 | 3 | 10 | R | R | 5-10 | 190 | 4-11-71 | 1993 | Las Vegas, Nev. |
| Ishii, Galen | 3 | 2 | 6.37 | 19 | 0 | 0 | 0 | 30 | 32 | 25 | 21 | 17 | 40 | L | L | 5-8 | 165 | 7-30-71 | 1993 | San Diego, Calif. |
| Lidle, Cory | 8 | 4 | 4.13 | 17 | 16 | 3 | 1 | 107 | 104 | 59 | 49 | 54 | 91 | R | R | 5-11 | 165 | 3-22-72 | 1991 | West Covina, Calif. |
| Lymberopoulos, Nick | 0 | 1 | 16.50 | 5 | 2 | 0 | 0 | 14 | 18 | 11 | 8 | 5 | 5 | R | R | 6-5 | 225 | 7-16-70 | 1993 | Las Vegas, Nev. |
| Matthews, Ron | 0 | 0 | 12.00 | 2 | 1 | 0 | 0 | 3 | 5 | 7 | 4 | 6 | 4 | R | R | 6-2 | 190 | 12-6-70 | 1993 | Lethbridge, Alberta |
| May, Steve | 1 | 1 | 2.57 | 14 | 0 | 0 | 3 | 21 | 27 | 8 | 6 | 3 | 20 | R | R | 6-0 | 189 | 1-29-73 | 1993 | Westchester, Calif. |
| Orta, Edgar | 0 | 0 | 13.89 | 6 | 2 | 0 | 0 | 12 | 25 | 20 | 18 | 10 | 9 | L | L | 6-2 | 180 | 1-1-73 | 1993 | Alhambra, Calif. |
| Ploeger, Tim | 4 | 7 | 5.63 | 14 | 12 | 4 | 0 | 78 | 101 | 63 | 49 | 29 | 82 | R | R | 6-1 | 185 | 2-16-72 | 1990 | Las Vegas, Nev. |
| Post, Jeff | 3 | 8 | 8.68 | 6 | 0 | 0 | 0 | 9 | 23 | 14 | 9 | 1 | 9 | R | R | 5-10 | 170 | 8-21-70 | 1992 | Beaverton, Ore. |
| Pruitt, Don | 1 | 4 | 9.58 | 5 | 5 | 0 | 0 | 21 | 35 | 25 | 22 | 10 | 14 | R | R | 6-2 | 200 | 9-3-68 | 1993 | Phoenix, Ariz. |
| Woods, Barry | 3 | 1 | 4.66 | 17 | 2 | 0 | 2 | 37 | 37 | 25 | 19 | 16 | 31 | R | R | 6-0 | 180 | 7-13-70 | 1993 | Sacramento, Calif. |
| Wright, Scott | 0 | 0 | 6.94 | 9 | 0 | 0 | 0 | 12 | 11 | 9 | 9 | 14 | 5 | R | R | 6-2 | 190 | 8-7-69 | 1993 | Bryan, Texas |

# MINOR LEAGUES

# Record Attendance Highlights NA Season

**By MIKE BERARDINO**

Business was booming in 1993.

For the ninth straight year, the National Association posted an increase in attendance. More than 30 million fans attended minor league baseball games in 1993, the highest aggregate total since 1950, when 33 million paid admissions supported 446 clubs in 58 different leagues.

Free from contentious negotiations with the major leagues and with most every club locked into two-year player-development contracts, minor league operators were able to kick back and enjoy the prosperity for the first time in several seasons.

**Mike Moore**

Still, it wouldn't be a minor league baseball season without at least some controversy. Sure enough, danders were raised several times in 1993.

There was the midwinter territorial flap over New Orleans, with the Triple-A Denver Zephyrs and Double-A Charlotte Knights warring over who could play in a town that hadn't seen minor league ball since 1977. The Zephyrs, displaced by the expansion Colorado Rockies, used their higher classification to draft the New Orleans territory and, thanks to National Association president Mike Moore's Winter Meetings ruling, sent their Double-A competitors packing.

The former Knights eventually landed in Nashville. More on that later.

In season, there was the minor league tobacco ban, an extension of former Commissioner Fay Vincent's 1991 prohibition of the stuff at the Rookie and short-season levels. This time the ban applied to virtually everyone in the minors, from the freshest-faced 17-year-old from the islands to the most grizzled 35-year-old veteran.

From the moment the ban went into effect on June 15, everyone bristled. Longtime coach Rocky Bridges, the Pirates roving minor league infield instructor, spoke for many when he said, "They're making a sneak chewer out of me. They haven't run me out of baseball. They haven't run me out of Red Man either."

Columbus Clippers (International) shortstop Dave Silvestri became one of the higher-profile players caught violating the ban. Afterwards, Silvestri blasted the rule.

"This might be bad for me, but it's my body," he said. "I'm not hurting anyone but myself. I don't know what baseball is trying to prove with this rule. It's ridiculous.

"Look, I can inject heroin into my body or any other deadly drug, but that's OK because I don't have to take a drug test. What kind of sense does that make?"

Even those charged with enforcing the ban didn't like it very much. John Levenda, in his first year as Eastern League president, questioned the wisdom and legality of the ban, which carried a $300 fine for first offenders.

"From a health standpoint, it's an excellent idea," Levenda said. "But we're dealing with adults here, and I think they should be free to live their lives as they choose. It's not our place to prohibit them from their own vices . . . "

Balancing these criticisms was the sad case of Louisville Redbirds (American Association) manager Jack Krol, a longtime tobacco chewer, who underwent outpatient surgery to remove a cancerous growth from the right side of his tongue.

"There's no doubt in my mind this is from dipping and chewing," said Krol, who added that he didn't mind being an example for his players, but said, "This is not the way I wanted to do it."

Ironically, Krol's surgery came on June 15.

## Standards Can Wait

Another potential source of conflict was removed in early August, when Major League Baseball agreed to a one-year extension of the ballpark standards compliance deadline.

Instead of scrambling to complete renovations by April 1, 1994, the original deadline, minor league clubs were given until April 1, 1995 to bring their facilities up to the standards outlined in Sections 11-13 of the Professional Baseball Agreement.

**Rocky Bridges**

In exchange for the extension, the National Association voted to defer a final decision on reopening PBA negotiations until Sept. 30, 1994. The current PBA, achieved after months of tense discussions in 1990, runs through the 1997 season.

"We're trying to be reasonable," said Jimmie Lee Solomon, MLB director of minor league relations. "A lot of communities are financially strapped to the point that achieving compliance by next April would be difficult. A one-year extension would work to everybody's best interests."

Midwest League president George Spelius was among many minor league executives who hailed the agreement. In the Midwest League alone, the specter of new ballpark standards have chased teams from Kenosha, Madison and Waterloo, although the latter may remain through

# PLAYER OF THE YEAR

## Indians' Ramirez Earns 1993 Honor

**Player of Year.** Cleveland's Manny Ramirez, flanked on his left by Baseball America associate editor John Royster and on his right by Indians GM John Hart.

The amazing Manny Ramirez Hitting Show made it all the way up to the major leagues in 1993, but not before setting the Eastern and International leagues ablaze in an offensive maelstrom that had eyewitnesses summoning references to the game's greatest batters.

"He reminds me of Roberto Clemente," Cleveland Indians hitting coach Jose Morales said. "Manny's a front-foot hitter just like Clemente was. He has extremely quick hands. The first time I saw him hit, I told him, 'You can hit anywhere.' "

At age 21, in just his third pro-

### PREVIOUS WINNERS

- 1981—Mike Marshall, 1b Albuquerque (Dodgers)
- 1982—Ron Kittle, of Edmonton (White Sox)
- 1983—Dwight Gooden, rhp Lynchburg (Mets)
- 1984—Mike Bielecki, rhp Hawaii (Pirates)
- 1985—Jose Canseco, of Huntsville/Tacoma (Athletics)
- 1986—Gregg Jefferies, ss Columbia/Lynchburg (Mets)
- 1987—Gregg Jefferies, ss Jackson (Mets)
- 1988—Tom Gordon, rhp Appleton/Mem./Omaha (Royals)
- 1989—Sandy Alomar Jr., c Las Vegas (Padres)
- 1990—Frank Thomas, 1b Birmingham (White Sox)
- 1991—Derek Bell, of Syracuse (Blue Jays)
- 1992—Tim Salmon, of Edmonton (Angels)

fessional season, Ramirez hit .340 with 17 home runs and 79 RBIs at Double-A Canton-Akron to win the Eastern League batting crown. He also finished second in slugging (.581) and doubles (32) while playing in a pitcher's park.

On July 19 Ramirez was promoted to Triple-A Charlotte and really started hitting. In just 145 at-bats, Ramirez hit .317 with 14 homers and 36 RBIs to earn a September callup to Cleveland. He batted just .178 in 45 big league at-bats, but the damage was done.

Ramirez, a 6-foot, 190-pound right fielder, was named Baseball America's Minor League Player of the Year. In batting a combined .333 with 31 homers, 115 RBIs and 44 doubles, Ramirez edged out Expos hitting prospects Cliff Floyd and Rondell White, Richmond Braves shortstop Chipper Jones and Charlotte Knights teammate Jim Thome for the award.

"Hitting is hard," says Ramirez, whose family moved from the Dominican Republic to the Washington Heights section of New York City when he was 13. "(But) I don't put any pressure on me. I don't think about that, you know? I just go and play, and if I do good, I do good."

Good is a pitiful understatement for Ramirez' performance since he was drafted 13th overall by the Indians in the 1991 draft. Signed for a $285,000 bonus, Ramirez reported to Rookie-level Burlington (Appalachian) and batted .326 with 19 homers and 63 RBIs in just 215 at-bats.

He followed that up with a .278-13-63 year at Class A Kinston (Carolina). His season essentially ended on July 4, when he severely bruised the hamate bone in his left hand.

His huge 1993 brought Ramirez' career minor league totals to .316-63-241. Indians officials said Ramirez would compete for the starting right field job in spring training, but that he would probably return to Triple-A for more seasoning in 1994.

Bad news, indeed, for International League pitchers.

---

the 1994 season before moving to suburban Chicago.

"This is the right road to take," Spelius said. "Some leagues and cities have had problems getting financing for facility updates. If the major leagues feel comfortable giving us the extra year, then we do, too. It's a win-win situation."

From the moment the standards were passed, observers wondered how they would be enforced. Would teams that didn't comply be fined or shut down? Would extensions be granted for minor violations? Would there be instances of forced relocation or unilaterally terminated player-development contracts?

The whole thing seemed to be a mess waiting to happen. Then came the one-year extension, and operators in most cases were left to soothe their nerves with the warm sounds of cash registers ringing up record revenue totals.

Ahhhhhhhh.

## Then The Floods Came

Nature wreaked havoc with the minors as well. As July flooding reached epic proportions in America's heartland, the Iowa Cubs (American Association) and Quad City River Bandits (Midwest) found themselves without a home.

In Des Moines, the Cubs saw flood waters from the Raccoon and Des Moines rivers cover the parking lot and part of the outfield at Sec Taylor Stadium. Fortunately, the team was out of town from July 9-22, and by the time the Cubs returned home, the water had receded.

Still, that didn't stop I-Cubs righthander Turk Wendell from finding a fish in his glove upon returning to the home clubhouse.

Across the state in Davenport, the River Bandits were set adrift for several weeks after John O'Donnell Stadium was flooded. The team played home games at North Scott High in nearby Eldridge, Iowa.

"We were kind of like the Bingo Long Traveling All-Stars," said Quad City manager Steve Dillard. "It seemed like a new crisis every day. It was too late to build an ark."

Such a sense of humor prevailed in the area, where local entrepreneurs peddled "Field of Streams" T-shirts to commemorate the ordeal. But Jim Wehmeier, Quad City's general manager, wasn't laughing. Wehmeier estimated the club's combined losses from flood damage and lost revenue at $500,000.

Fortunately, none of Iowa's five other minor

**Natural Disaster.** Excessive flooding of the Mississippi River wreaked havoc at Quad City (Midwest) in 1993, forcing postponement or relocation of a number of games.

league clubs—Burlington, Cedar Rapids, Clinton and Waterloo of the Midwest League; and Sioux City of the independent Northern League—were affected by the flooding.

## Double Your Pleasure

We promised you more on the New Orleans fallout, so here it is. Months of wrangling finally ended in February, when Nashville Sounds (American Association) president Larry Schmittou offered to bring the wandering Southern League club to Herschel

Greer Stadium for at least one season.

Owner George Shinn, who already had an expansion International League franchise on his hands in Charlotte, agreed to the plan, provided he retain ownership of the Double-A club and Schmittou assume all financial responsibility for the team.

Ironically, Charlotte was the last city to have two minor league teams, fielding Minnesota Twins affiliates from the Southern and Western Carolinas leagues at Griffith Park in 1972. The Twins again were involved in the latest two-team venture, supplying the newly named Xpress with players while the Chicago White Sox served their first season as parent organization of the Sounds.

So it came to pass that Nashville's 17-person front-office staff tackled the significant challenge of a 143-game home schedule. With only eight off days all season, the already hazy days of summer became that much crazier for the Tour de Nashville gang.

"We all thought about it and said, 'This is crazy,' but we have a big enough staff to pull it off," said Ron Schmittou, Larry's son and Sounds director of administration and concessions. "As far as days off, we'll work something out. Krystal's and Shoney's stay open 365 days a year, 24 hours a day, and they get by."

Combined attendance for the Sounds and the newly named Xpress was 617,482. That figure was somewhat disappointing for Schmittou, whose Sounds alone had drawn 490,000 in 1992. Nevertheless, Southern League directors voted in August to accept Schmittou's offer to field two teams again in 1994.

Dennis Bastien, owner of the Charleston (W.Va.) Wheelers (South Atlantic), had purchased an option to buy the Xpress from Shinn. Bastien planned to move the club to a new stadium in Lexington, Ky., by 1995.

Meanwhile, down in New Orleans, the Zephyrs drew just 2,452 fans per game at tiny Privateer Park. The Triple-A club expected to

### ORGANIZATION STANDINGS

| | —1993— | | | 1992 | 1991 | 1990 |
|---|---|---|---|---|---|---|
| | W | L | Pct. | Pct. | Pct. | Pct. |
| Cleveland (6) | 408 | 297 | .579 | .543 | .525 | .541 |
| St. Louis (8) | 487 | 402 | .548 | .511 | .417 | .461 |
| Milwaukee (6) | 367 | 311 | .541 | .567 | .555 | .551 |
| Florida (5) | 295 | 255 | .536 | .533 | — | — |
| Baltimore (6) | 369 | 320 | .536 | .478 | .517 | .507 |
| San Francisco (6) | 362 | 318 | .532 | .506 | .552 | .502 |
| Atlanta (7) | 404 | 361 | .528 | .490 | .563 | .504 |
| Chicago-AL (6) | 397 | 357 | .527 | .552 | .496 | .491 |
| New York-AL (6) | 366 | 328 | .527 | .523 | .523 | .515 |
| Oakland (6) | 361 | 325 | .526 | .501 | .504 | .510 |
| Montreal (6) | 358 | 328 | .522 | .534 | .552 | .536 |
| New York-NL (7) | 389 | 365 | .516 | .509 | .538 | .554 |
| Kansas City (6) | 354 | 336 | .513 | .519 | .471 | .480 |
| Cincinnati (6) | 361 | 346 | .511 | .570 | .491 | .552 |
| Minnesota (6) | 342 | 338 | .503 | .530 | .489 | .543 |
| Texas (6) | 345 | 346 | .499 | .512 | .439 | .529 |
| Toronto (7) | 382 | 386 | .497 | .463 | .457 | .479 |
| Detroit (6) | 343 | 351 | .494 | .496 | .467 | .506 |
| Chicago-NL (7) | 367 | 393 | .483 | .456 | .502 | .518 |
| California (6) | 324 | 352 | .479 | .540 | .523 | .507 |
| Seattle (6) | 327 | 355 | .479 | .478 | .458 | .479 |
| Houston (7) | 384 | 428 | .473 | .466 | .491 | .481 |
| Pittsburgh (6) | 321 | 381 | .457 | .459 | .481 | .485 |
| Philadelphia (6) | 321 | 383 | .456 | .507 | .505 | .428 |
| Colorado (4) | 183 | 223 | .451 | .462 | — | — |
| San Diego (6) | 303 | 376 | .446 | .462 | .494 | .437 |
| Independents (3) | 154 | 205 | .429 | .382 | .453 | .417 |
| Boston (6) | 293 | 395 | .426 | .444 | .460 | .428 |
| Los Angeles (6) | 294 | 400 | .424 | .467 | .568 | .592 |

Number of farm teams in parentheses

# DEPARTMENT LEADERS
## MINOR LEAGUES
Full-Season Teams Only

## TEAM

### WINS
Harrisburg (Eastern) .................... 94
Savannah (South Atlantic) .................... 94
Portland (Pacific Coast) .................... 87
Charlotte (International) .................... 86
Columbus (South Atlantic) .................... 86

### LONGEST WINNING STREAK
Tucson (Pacific Coast) .................... 15
Bluefield (Appalachian) .................... 14
Modesto (California) .................... 12
Harrisburg (Eastern) .................... 12
Omaha (American Association) .................... 11
San Jose (California) .................... 11
Savannah (South Atlantic) .................... 11

### LOSSES
Bakersfield (California) .................... 94
Oklahoma City (American Association).. 90
Asheville (South Atlantic) .................... 88
Hickory (South Atlantic) .................... 88
New Britain (Eastern) .................... 88

### LONGEST LOSING STREAK
Oneonta (New York-Penn) .................... 16
New Britain (Eastern) .................... 12
Edmonton (Pacific Coast) .................... 12
Rancho Cucamonga (California) .................... 11
Martinsville (Appalachian) .................... 11

### BATTING AVERAGE
Calgary (Pacific Coast) .................... .298
Portland (Pacific Coast) .................... .298
Tucson (Pacific Coast) .................... .297
Colorado Springs (Pacific Coast) .................... .295
Albuquerque (Pacific Coast) .................... .293

### HOME RUNS
Charlotte (International) .................... 185
Harrisburg (Eastern) .................... 170
Richmond (International) .................... 161
Winston-Salem (Carolina) .................... 160
Omaha (American Association) .................... 154

### STOLEN BASES
Rockford (Midwest) .................... 239
High Desert (California) .................... 230
San Jose (California) .................... 216
Clinton (Midwest) .................... 214
Stockton (California) .................... 211

### EARNED RUN AVERAGE
Savannah (South Atlantic) .................... 2.73
Charlotte (Florida State) .................... 2.97
Macon (South Atlantic) .................... 3.03
St. Lucie (Florida State) .................... 3.08
St. Petersburg (Florida State) .................... 3.11

### STRIKEOUTS
Frederick (Carolina) .................... 1161
Savannah (South Atlantic) .................... 1150
Macon (South Atlantic) .................... 1138
Fort Wayne (Midwest) .................... 1136
Burlington (Midwest) .................... 1107

### FIELDING AVERAGE
Iowa (American Association) .................... .980
Louisville (American Association) .................... .979
New Orleans (American Association).. .978
Omaha (American Association) .................... .976
Buffalo (American Association) .................... .976

## INDIVIDUAL BATTING

### BATTING AVERAGE
(Minimum 350 At-Bats)
Tim Clark, High Desert .................... .363
Jim Lindeman, Tucson .................... .362
Nelson Liriano, Cent. Valley-Colo. Spr. .359
Mark Sweeney, Palm Springs-Midland .356
Mike Brumley, Tucson .................... .353

---

DON ALLEN

**High Desert's Tim Clark**
.363 average, 126 RBIs

Kevin Riggs, Stockton .................... .347
Terry McGriff, Edmonton .................... .345
Jerry Brooks, Albuquerque .................... .344
Rondell White, Harrisburg-Ottawa .................... .343
Arquimedez Pozo, Riverside .................... .342

### RUNS
James Mouton, Tucson .................... 126
Kerwin Moore, High Desert .................... 120
Omar Ramirez, Canton .................... 116
Karl Rhodes, Omaha-Iowa .................... 112
Tim Clark, High Desert .................... 109
Ernie Young, Modesto-Huntsville .................... 109

### HITS
Tim Clark, High Desert .................... 185
Norberto Martin, Nashville (AAA) .................... 179
Rondell White, Ottawa-Harrisburg .................... 179
Arquimedez Pozo, Riverside .................... 176
Chipper Jones, Richmond .................... 174

### TOP HITTING STREAKS
Trey McCoy, Tulsa .................... 26
Rondell White, Harrisburg .................... 24
T.J. O'Donnell, Utica .................... 24
Tony Eusebio, Tucson .................... 24

### MOST HITS, ONE GAME
Lee Tinsley, Calgary vs. Las Vegas .................... 7
Jim Edmonds, Vancouver vs. Calgary .................... 6

### TOTAL BASES
Manny Ramirez, Canton-Char. (AAA) . 300
Tim Clark, High Desert .................... 298
Karl Rhodes, Omaha-Iowa .................... 295
James Mouton, Tucson .................... 286
Rondell White, Harrisburg-Ottaw. .................... 284

### EXTRA-BASE HITS
Karl Rhodes, Omaha-Iowa .................... 76
Manny Ramirez, Canton-Char. (AAA) .... 75
James Mouton, Tucson .................... 70
Tim Clark, High Desert .................... 69
J.R. Phillips, Phoenix .................... 64
Trey McCoy, Tulsa-Okla. City .................... 64

### DOUBLES
Manny Ramirez, Canton-Char. (AAA) .... 44
Arquimedez Pozo, Riverside .................... 44
Karl Rhodes, Omaha-Iowa .................... 43
Tim Clark, High Desert .................... 42
James Mouton, Tucson .................... 42

### TRIPLES
Lee Tinsley, Calgary .................... 18

---

Brad Tyler, Bowie .................... 17
Bob Abreu, Osceola .................... 17
Orlando Miller, Tucson .................... 16
Johnny Damon, Rockford .................... 13

### HOME RUNS
Sam Horn, Charlotte (AAA) .................... 38
Steve Balboni, Oklahoma City .................... 36
Bubba Smith, W-S/Jax/Riverside .................... 33
Trey McCoy, Tulsa-Okla. City .................... 32
Eddie Zambrano, Iowa .................... 32

### RUNS BATTED IN
Tim Clark, High Desert .................... 126
John Toale, High Desert .................... 125
Bryn Kosco, High Desert .................... 121
Cliff Floyd, Harrisburg-Ottawa .................... 119
Manny Ramirez, Canton-Char. (AAA).. 115
Eddie Zambrano, Iowa .................... 115

### MOST RBIs, ONE GAME
Izzy Molina, Modesto vs. Stockton .................... 8
Tom Knauss, Fort Wayne vs. Appleton ... 8
John Kuehl, Huntsville vs. Nashville .................... 8
Scott Talanoa, Beloit vs. Appleton. .................... 8
Trey McCoy, Tulsa vs. Jackson. .................... 8
Jeff Garber, Memphis vs. Nashville. .................... 8
Franklin Stubbs, Pawtucket vs. Toledo .... 8
Jim Edmonds, Vanc. vs. Albuquerque .... 8

### STOLEN BASES
Essex Burton, South Bend .................... 74
Kerwin Moore, High Desert .................... 71
Marquis Riley, Palm Springs .................... 69
Kraig Hawkins, Greensboro .................... 67
Curtis Goodwin, Frederick .................... 61

### BASE ON BALLS
Kerwin Moore, High Desert .................... 114
Carlos Delgado, Knoxville .................... 102
Kevin Riggs, Stockton .................... 101
Ernie Young, Modesto-Huntsville .................... 96
Craig Counsell, Central Valley .................... 95
Larry Sutton, Rockford .................... 95

### STRIKEOUTS
Al Shirley, Capital City-Kingsport .................... 178
Keith Kimsey, Fayetteville .................... 168
Bubba Smith, Riverside/Win.-Salem .... 164
Nick Delvecchio, Greensboro .................... 156
Tom Quinlan, Syracuse .................... 156

### SLUGGING PERCENTAGE
Manny Ramirez, Canton-Char. (AAA) . .613

MEL BAILEY

**Tucson's James Mouton**
126 runs, 42 doubles

Bernardo Brito, Portland ...................... .602
Karl Rhodes, Omaha-Iowa ................. .602
Sam Horn, Charlotte (AAA) ................ .600
Geronimo Berroa, Edmonton ............. .599

## ON-BASE PERCENTAGE

Kevin Riggs, Stockton .......................... .482
Mark Sweeney, Midland-Palm Springs .447
Roberto Petagine, Jackson ................. .442
Jim Thome, Charlotte (AAA) ............... .441
Chris Malinoski, High Desert .............. .439

## BATTING AVERAGE
### By Position
(Minimum 350 At-Bats)

### CATCHER

Terry McGriff, Edmonton ...................... .345
Jerry Brooks, Albuquerque ................. .344
Brian Johnson, Las Vegas ................. .339
Matt Merullo, Nashville (AAA)............. .332
Mike Stefanski, Stockton ..................... .322

### FIRST BASEMEN

Jim Lindeman, Tucson ........................ .362
Doug Radziewicz, St. Petersburg........ .342
Brant Brown, Daytona-Orlando .......... .334
Roberto Petagine, Jackson ................. .334
Jim Bowie, Huntsville.......................... .333
Brian Traxler, Albuquerque................. .333

### SECOND BASEMEN

Kevin Riggs, Stockton ........................ .347
Arquimedez Pozo, Riverside .............. .342
Eddie Pye, Albuquerque ..................... .329
Chris Demetral, Vero Beach................ .325
Jeff Carter, Portland........................... .325

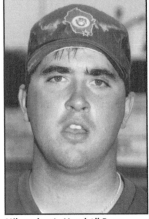

**Savannah's Jamie Cochran**
46 saves

### THIRD BASEMEN

Jim Thome, Charlotte (AAA) .............. .332
Jeff Cirillo, El Paso-New Orleans ........ .319
Ron Coomer, Birm.-Nashville (AAA) ... .319
Olmedo Saenz, Birm.-Sar.-So. Bend .. .317
Dennis Colon, Osceola ...................... .316

### SHORTSTOPS

Chipper Jones, Richmond .................. .325
Brian Rupp, Savannah ....................... .320
Kurt Abbott, Tacoma........................... .319
Luis Brito, Spartanburg....................... .313
Rich Aurilia, Charlotte (A) ................... .309

### OUTFIELDERS

Tim Clark, High Desert ....................... .363
Mark Sweeney, Midland-Palm Springs .356
Mike Brumley, Tucson ........................ .353
Rondell White, Harrisburg-Ottawa....... .343
Ira Smith, Rancho Cuca.-Wichita ........ .334

**Cleveland's Manny Ramirez**
300 total bases, 115 RBIs

## INDIVIDUAL PITCHING

### EARNED RUN AVERAGE
(Minimum 106 Innings)

Jeff Matranga, Savannah-St. Pete ...... 1.64
Rich Linares, Vero Beach ................... 1.81
Tim Davis, Riverside-Appleton ............ 1.83
Francisco Martinez, Sav.-St. Pete-Ark. 1.88
Luis Andujar, Birmingham-Sarasota.... 1.93
LaTroy Hawkins, Fort Wayne ............. 2.06
J.J. Thobe, Columbus (A)-Kinston....... 2.09
Ryan Karp, G'boro-Pr. Will.-Alb. (AA).. 2.10
John Dettmer, Charlotte (A)................. 2.15
Duff Brumley, St. Pete-Ark.-Tulsa ....... 2.16

### WINS

Marshall Boze, Stockton-El Paso .......... 17
Rod Henderson, West Palm-H'burg ...... 17
John Carter, Columbus (A) ................... 17
Garrett Stephenson, Albany (A) ............ 16
Ryan Karp, G'boro-Pr. Will.-Alb. (AA) ... 16
Joey Eischen, Harrisburg-Ottawa.......... 16
John Dettmer, Charlotte (A)................... 16

### LOSSES

Brent Hansen, New Brit.-Ft. Lauderdale 17
Kenny Carlyle, London-Toledo .............. 16
Steve Lyons, Capital City ...................... 16
Brett Roberts, Fort Myers ..................... 16
Curtis Shaw, Huntsville ......................... 16

### GAMES

Toby Borland, Reading-Scranton .......... 70
Mark Mimbs, San Antonio-Alb. ............. 68
Mike Zimmerman, Buffalo-Carolina........ 66
Sean Fesh, Asheville ............................ 65
Todd Williams, Albuquerque.................. 65

### COMPLETE GAMES

Robert Ellis, Birmingham-Sarasota ........ 10
Chris Holt, Quad City ............................ 10
Matt Jarvis, Albany (A) ........................... 8
Mark Ratekin, Midland-Palm Springs ....... 8
Rob Henkel, Lynchburg ........................... 7
Steve Sparks, New Orleans ..................... 7
Nate Minchey, Pawtucket ........................ 7
Ugueth Urbina, Burlington-Harrisburg ...... 7

### SAVES

Jamie Cochran, Savannah ..................... 46
Kerry Lacy, Charleston, S.C.-Char. (A) .. 38
Jim Dougherty, Jackson ......................... 36
Cesar Perez, Columbus (A)-Kinston ...... 35
Kirk Bullinger, Springfield....................... 33

### INNINGS PITCHED

Brent Hansen, New Brit.-Ft. Lauderdale 196
Nate Minchey, Pawtucket ..................... 195
Chad Anderson, Spartanburg.............. 191
Tim Vanegmond, New Britain .............. 190
Mauro Gozzo, Norfolk ......................... 190

### BASE ON BALLS

Steve Whitaker, San Jose-Shreveport . 121

Eric Weaver, Bakersfield ...................... 118
Byron Browne, Stockton ...................... 117
Erik Hiljus, Capital City......................... 111
Ron Villone, Riverside-Jacksonville...... 103

### STRIKEOUTS

Joel Bennett, Lynchburg ...................... 221
Terrell Wade, Macon-Durham-G'ville ... 208
Rick Helling, Tulsa-Okla. City .............. 205
Duff Brumley, St. Pete-Arkansas-Tulsa 188
Mike Bertotti, South Bend-Hickory........ 185
Scott Ruffcorn, Birm.-Nashville (AAA).. 185
Brian Looney, West Palm-Harrisburg... 185

### STRIKEOUTS/9 INNINGS
(Starters)

Terrell Wade, Macon-Durham-G'ville 11.82
Joel Bennett, Lynchburg................... 10.99
Charles York, Columbus (A) ............. 10.37
Fernando Hemandez, Kin.-Cant.-R. Cuca. 10.35
Mike D'Andrea, Macon ..................... 10.30

### STRIKEOUTS/9 INNINGS
(Relievers)

Armando Benitez, Frederick-Alb. (A). 15.04
Ricky Pickett, Charleston, W.Va. ....... 13.40
Enrique Burgos, Omaha ................... 13.07
Tony Chavez, Midland-Cedar Rapids 12.71
Kirk Bullinger, Springfield.................. 12.62

### BATTING AVERAGE AGAINST
(Starters)

Duff Brumley, St. Pete-Ark.-Tulsa ....... .189
LaTroy Hawkins, Fort Wayne .............. .195
Jason Fronio, Kinston .......................... .196
Ryan Karp, G'boro-Pr. Will.-Alb. (AA).. .197
Bill Pulsipher, St. Lucie-Capital City .... .198

### BATTING AVERAGE AGAINST
(Relievers)

Cesar Perez, Columbus (A)-Kinston .... .138
Kirk Bullinger, Springfield..................... .144
Enrique Burgos, Omaha ...................... .164
Armando Benitez, Albany (A)-Fred....... .165
Mark Acre, Huntsville-Madison ............ .168

### MOST STRIKEOUTS IN ONE GAME

Terrell Wade, Macon vs. Albany............. 18
Duff Brumley, St. Pete. vs. Ft. Laud. ...... 16
Kevin Foster, Jax vs. Chattanooga......... 16

## INDIVIDUAL FIELDING

### MOST ERRORS

Jay Cranford, ss, Augusta ..................... 68
Israel Alcantara, 3b, Burlington.............. 57
Derek Jeter, ss, Greensboro ................. 56
Damian Jackson, ss, Columbus ............. 52
Tim Cooper, 3b-ss, San Bern.-Pr. Wm... 49
Eric Knowles, ss, Prince William............ 49
Ricky Magdaleno, ss, Charl., W.Va. ...... 49
Eddie Ramos, 3b, Quad City ................. 49

**Milwaukee's Marshall Boze**
17 wins

# CLASSIFICATION ALL-STARS
Selected by Baseball America

## TRIPLE-A

| Pos. Player, Club | B-T | Ht. | Wt. | Age | AVG | AB | R | H | 2B | 3B | HR | RBI | BB | SO | SB |
|---|---|---|---|---|---|---|---|---|---|---|---|---|---|---|---|
| C Javy Lopez, Richmond (International) | R-R | 6-3 | 185 | 22 | .305 | 380 | 56 | 116 | 23 | 2 | 17 | 74 | 47 | 69 | 4 |
| 1B Jim Lindeman, Tucson (Pacific Coast) | R-R | 6-1 | 200 | 31 | .362 | 390 | 72 | 141 | 28 | 7 | 12 | 88 | 41 | 68 | 5 |
| 2B James Mouton, Tucson (Pacific Coast) | R-R | 5-9 | 175 | 24 | .315 | 546 | 126 | 172 | 42 | 12 | 16 | 92 | 72 | 82 | 40 |
| 3B Jim Thome, Charlotte (International) | L-R | 6-4 | 200 | 23 | .332 | 410 | 85 | 136 | 21 | 4 | 25 | 102 | 76 | 94 | 1 |
| SS Chipper Jones, Richmond (International) | B-R | 6-3 | 185 | 21 | .325 | 536 | 97 | 174 | 31 | 12 | 13 | 89 | 57 | 70 | 23 |
| OF Billy Ashley, Albuquerque (Pacific Coast) | R-R | 6-7 | 220 | 23 | .297 | 482 | 88 | 143 | 31 | 4 | 26 | 100 | 35 | 143 | 6 |
| Karl Rhodes, Omaha/Iowa (American Assoc.) | L-L | 5-11 | 170 | 25 | .318 | 490 | 112 | 156 | 43 | 3 | 30 | 89 | 58 | 82 | 16 |
| Eddie Zambrano, Iowa (American Assoc.) | R-R | 6-2 | 175 | 27 | .303 | 469 | 95 | 142 | 29 | 2 | 32 | 115 | 54 | 93 | 10 |
| DH Sam Horn, Charlotte (International) | L-L | 6-5 | 250 | 29 | .269 | 402 | 62 | 108 | 17 | 1 | 38 | 96 | 60 | 131 | 1 |

| P | | | | | | | | | W | L | ERA | G | GS | CG | SV | IP | H | BB | SO |
|---|---|---|---|---|---|---|---|---|---|---|---|---|---|---|---|---|---|---|---|
| Rod Bolton, Nashville (American Assoc.) | R-R | 6-2 | 190 | 24 | | | | | 10 | 1 | 2.88 | 18 | 16 | 1 | 1 | 116 | 108 | 37 | 75 |
| Mark Hutton, Columbus (International) | R-R | 6-6 | 225 | 23 | | | | | 10 | 4 | 3.18 | 21 | 21 | 0 | 0 | 133 | 98 | 53 | 112 |
| Pat Mahomes, Portland (Pacific Coast) | R-R | 6-3 | 198 | 23 | | | | | 11 | 4 | 3.03 | 17 | 16 | 3 | 0 | 116 | 89 | 54 | 94 |
| Aaron Sele, Pawtucket (International) | R-R | 6-5 | 205 | 23 | | | | | 8 | 2 | 2.19 | 14 | 14 | 2 | 0 | 94 | 74 | 23 | 87 |
| Bill Taylor, Richmond (International) | R-R | 6-8 | 200 | 31 | | | | | 2 | 4 | 1.98 | 59 | 0 | 0 | 26 | 68 | 56 | 26 | 81 |

**Player of the Year:** Jim Thome, 3b, Charlotte (International).   **Manager of the Year:** Scott Ullger, Portland (Pacific Coast).

## DOUBLE-A

| Pos. Player, Club | B-T | Ht. | Wt. | Age | AVG | AB | R | H | 2B | 3B | HR | RBI | BB | SO | SB |
|---|---|---|---|---|---|---|---|---|---|---|---|---|---|---|---|
| C Carlos Delgado, Knoxville (Southern) | L-R | 6-3 | 206 | 21 | .303 | 468 | 91 | 142 | 28 | 0 | 25 | 102 | 102 | 98 | 10 |
| 1B Roberto Petagine, Jackson (Texas) | L-L | 6-1 | 172 | 22 | .334 | 437 | 73 | 146 | 36 | 2 | 15 | 90 | 84 | 89 | 6 |
| 2B Ruben Santana, Jacksonville (Southern) | R-R | 6-2 | 175 | 23 | .301 | 499 | 79 | 150 | 21 | 2 | 21 | 84 | 38 | 101 | 13 |
| 3B Butch Huskey, Binghamton (Eastern) | R-R | 6-3 | 240 | 21 | .251 | 526 | 72 | 132 | 23 | 1 | 25 | 98 | 48 | 102 | 11 |
| SS Alex Gonzalez, Knoxville (Southern) | R-R | 6-0 | 182 | 20 | .289 | 561 | 93 | 162 | 29 | 7 | 16 | 69 | 39 | 110 | 38 |
| OF Brian Hunter, Jackson (Texas) | R-R | 6-2 | 170 | 22 | .294 | 523 | 84 | 154 | 22 | 5 | 10 | 52 | 34 | 85 | 35 |
| Manny Ramirez, Canton (Eastern) | R-R | 6-0 | 190 | 21 | .340 | 344 | 67 | 117 | 32 | 0 | 17 | 79 | 45 | 68 | 2 |
| Rondell White, Harrisburg (Eastern) | R-R | 6-1 | 193 | 21 | .328 | 372 | 72 | 122 | 16 | 10 | 12 | 52 | 22 | 72 | 21 |
| DH Cliff Floyd, Harrisburg (Eastern) | L-L | 6-4 | 220 | 20 | .329 | 380 | 82 | 125 | 17 | 4 | 26 | 101 | 54 | 71 | 31 |

| P | | | | | | | | | W | L | ERA | G | GS | CG | SV | IP | H | BB | SO |
|---|---|---|---|---|---|---|---|---|---|---|---|---|---|---|---|---|---|---|---|
| Jim Dougherty, Jackson (Texas) | R-R | 6-0 | 210 | 25 | | | | | 2 | 2 | 1.87 | 52 | 0 | 0 | 36 | 53 | 39 | 21 | 55 |
| Joey Eischen, Harrisburg (Eastern) | L-L | 6-1 | 190 | 23 | | | | | 14 | 4 | 3.62 | 20 | 20 | 0 | 0 | 119 | 122 | 60 | 110 |
| Oscar Munoz, Nashville (Southern) | R-R | 6-2 | 205 | 23 | | | | | 11 | 4 | 3.08 | 20 | 20 | 1 | 0 | 132 | 123 | 51 | 139 |
| Scott Ruffcorn, Birmingham (Southern) | R-R | 6-4 | 215 | 23 | | | | | 9 | 4 | 2.73 | 20 | 20 | 3 | 0 | 135 | 108 | 52 | 141 |
| Ben VanRyn, San Antonio (Texas) | L-L | 6-5 | 195 | 22 | | | | | 14 | 4 | 2.21 | 21 | 21 | 1 | 0 | 134 | 118 | 38 | 144 |

**Player of the Year:** Cliff Floyd, 1b-of, Harrisburg (Eastern).   **Manager of the Year:** Terry Francona, Birmingham (Southern).

## CLASS A

| Pos. Player, Club | B-T | Ht. | Wt. | Age | AVG | AB | R | H | 2B | 3B | HR | RBI | BB | SO | SB |
|---|---|---|---|---|---|---|---|---|---|---|---|---|---|---|---|
| C Charles Johnson, Kane County (Midwest) | R-R | 6-2 | 215 | 22 | .275 | 488 | 74 | 134 | 29 | 5 | 19 | 94 | 62 | 111 | 9 |
| 1B D.J. Boston, Hagerstown (South Atlantic) | L-L | 6-7 | 230 | 21 | .315 | 464 | 76 | 146 | 35 | 4 | 13 | 92 | 54 | 77 | 31 |
| 2B Arquimedez Pozo, Riverside (California) | R-R | 5-10 | 160 | 20 | .342 | 515 | 98 | 176 | 44 | 6 | 13 | 81 | 56 | 56 | 10 |
| 3B Brian Rupp, Savannah (South Atlantic) | R-R | 6-4 | 190 | 21 | .320 | 472 | 80 | 151 | 31 | 7 | 4 | 81 | 48 | 70 | 3 |
| SS Edgardo Alfonzo, St. Lucie (Florida State) | R-R | 5-11 | 178 | 20 | .294 | 494 | 75 | 145 | 18 | 3 | 11 | 86 | 57 | 51 | 26 |
| OF Tim Clark, High Desert (California) | L-L | 6-4 | 220 | 24 | .363 | 510 | 109 | 185 | 42 | 10 | 17 | 126 | 56 | 65 | 2 |
| Randy Curtis, St. Lucie (Florida State) | L-L | 5-10 | 180 | 22 | .319 | 467 | 91 | 149 | 30 | 12 | 2 | 38 | 93 | 72 | 52 |
| Chad Mottola, Winston-Salem (Carolina) | R-R | 6-3 | 215 | 21 | .280 | 493 | 76 | 138 | 25 | 3 | 21 | 91 | 62 | 109 | 13 |
| DH Bubba Smith, Riverside (Cal)/Win.-Salem (Car.) | R-R | 6-2 | 225 | 23 | .335 | 361 | 60 | 121 | 19 | 0 | 27 | 84 | 42 | 112 | 2 |

| P | | | | | | | | | W | L | ERA | G | GS | CG | SV | IP | H | BB | SO |
|---|---|---|---|---|---|---|---|---|---|---|---|---|---|---|---|---|---|---|---|
| Jamie Cochran, Savannah (South Atlantic) | R-R | 6-0 | 196 | 24 | | | | | 4 | 1 | 1.55 | 58 | 0 | 0 | 46 | 64 | 51 | 22 | 62 |
| Tim Davis, Appleton (MWL)/Riverside (Cal) | L-L | 5-11 | 165 | 23 | | | | | 13 | 2 | 1.82 | 34 | 10 | 3 | 9 | 109 | 68 | 42 | 145 |
| John Dettmer, Charlotte (Florida State) | R-R | 6-0 | 185 | 23 | | | | | 16 | 3 | 2.15 | 27 | 27 | 5 | 0 | 163 | 132 | 33 | 126 |
| LaTroy Hawkins, Fort Wayne (Midwest) | R-R | 6-5 | 195 | 20 | | | | | 15 | 5 | 2.06 | 26 | 23 | 4 | 0 | 157 | 110 | 41 | 179 |
| Ryan Karp, G'boro (SAL)/Prince William (Car.) | L-L | 6-4 | 205 | 23 | | | | | 16 | 3 | 1.93 | 25 | 25 | 1 | 0 | 158 | 108 | 52 | 186 |

**Player of the Year:** Tim Clark, of, High Desert (California).   **Manager of the Year:** Chris Maloney, Savannah (South Atlantic).

## SHORT SEASON

| Pos. Player, Club | B-T | Ht. | Wt. | Age | AVG | AB | R | H | 2B | 3B | HR | RBI | BB | SO | SB |
|---|---|---|---|---|---|---|---|---|---|---|---|---|---|---|---|
| C Cesar Diaz, Kingsport (Appy)/Pittsfield (NY-P) | R-R | 6-3 | 185 | 19 | .301 | 259 | 42 | 78 | 13 | 1 | 11 | 45 | 18 | 52 | 4 |
| 1B Bryan Link, Bluefield (Appalachian) | L-L | 6-1 | 185 | 22 | .338 | 266 | 64 | 90 | 17 | 1 | 14 | 60 | 42 | 38 | 9 |
| 2B T.J. O'Donnell, Utica (New York-Penn) | R-R | 6-0 | 180 | 22 | .329 | 255 | 47 | 84 | 22 | 1 | 4 | 33 | 18 | 24 | 5 |
| 3B Mike Bell, Rangers (Gulf Coast) | R-R | 6-2 | 185 | 18 | .317 | 230 | 48 | 73 | 13 | 6 | 3 | 34 | 27 | 23 | 9 |
| SS Enrique Wilson, Elizabethton (Appalachian) | B-R | 5-11 | 158 | 18 | .289 | 197 | 42 | 57 | 8 | 4 | 13 | 50 | 14 | 18 | 5 |
| OF Todd Greene, Boise (Northwest) | R-R | 5-10 | 195 | 22 | .269 | 305 | 55 | 82 | 15 | 3 | 15 | 71 | 34 | 44 | 4 |
| Damon Hollins, Danville (Appalachian) | R-L | 5-11 | 187 | 19 | .321 | 240 | 37 | 77 | 15 | 2 | 7 | 51 | 19 | 30 | 10 |
| Keith Williams, Everett (Northwest) | R-R | 6-0 | 190 | 21 | .302 | 288 | 57 | 87 | 21 | 5 | 12 | 49 | 48 | 73 | 21 |
| DH Wes Shook, Erie (New York-Penn) | R-R | 5-10 | 175 | 23 | .321 | 268 | 48 | 86 | 12 | 2 | 17 | 52 | 18 | 43 | 1 |

| P | | | | | | | | | W | L | ERA | G | GS | CG | SV | IP | H | BB | SO |
|---|---|---|---|---|---|---|---|---|---|---|---|---|---|---|---|---|---|---|---|
| Alonso Beltran, St. Catharines (NY-P) | R-R | 6-3 | 180 | 21 | | | | | 11 | 2 | 2.36 | 15 | 15 | 1 | 0 | 99 | 63 | 28 | 101 |
| Glenn Dishman, Spokane (Northwest) | R-L | 6-1 | 195 | 22 | | | | | 6 | 3 | 2.20 | 12 | 12 | 2 | 0 | 78 | 59 | 13 | 79 |
| Adam Meinershagen, St. Catharines (NY-P) | R-R | 6-4 | 190 | 20 | | | | | 8 | 1 | 1.88 | 13 | 13 | 1 | 0 | 86 | 53 | 26 | 87 |
| Jason Myers, Giants (Arizona) | L-L | 6-4 | 210 | 19 | | | | | 8 | 1 | 1.69 | 13 | 13 | 0 | 0 | 75 | 50 | 16 | 105 |
| Joshua Neese, Niagara Falls (NY-P) | R-R | 6-1 | 180 | 22 | | | | | 12 | 3 | 2.54 | 21 | 8 | 0 | 0 | 71 | 44 | 34 | 73 |

**Player of the Year:** Todd Greene, of, Boise (Northwest).   **Manager of the Year:** Donnie Scott, Billings (Pioneer).

play one more season at the University of New Orleans site before moving to Jefferson Parish and a new facility in 1995.

## Cute Name

The recent trend toward esoteric team names in the minor leagues continued in 1993. Besides the two Eastern League expansion teams, the Portland Sea Dogs and the New Haven Ravens, 1994 will also feature the debut of the Greensboro Bats (nee Hornets), Charleston, S.C., RiverDogs (nee Rainbows) and the Augusta Green Jackets (nee Pirates).

These names came on the heels of 1993 debuts by the Nashville Xpress, Pocatello Posse, Wilmington Blue Rocks, Rancho Cucamonga Quakes, Fort Wayne Wizards et al.

In each case, the potential for seven-figure merchandise sales played a role in the odd selections. The stranger the team name, it seems, the more desirable its memorabilia.

In Charleston, for instance, RiverDogs wasn't even among the 3,000-plus entries in a name-the-team contest. A local newspaper call-in poll yielded a 20-to-1 disapproval rating.

That didn't faze Charleston GM Rob Dlugozima, who said of the RiverDogs name, "It's something that has identity to Charleston and gives us something we can market."

## Strange Year For Bulls

Speaking of marketability, Dlugozima's former team, the Durham Bulls (South Atlantic), staged several Turn Back the Clock nights to commemorate their last season at 54-year-old Durham Athletic Park.

They even had Hall of Fame second baseman and former Bulls player Joe Morgan come to town. Bulls management retired Morgan's No. 18 in a pregame ceremony on June 17.

Trouble was, Morgan apparently wore No. 8 while with the Bulls in 1963. This was brought to the team's attention by Hubert Deans, a longtime Bulls fan who produced two yellowing scorecards with Morgan's correct number.

"This is an embarrassment to a certain extent," said Al Mangum, Bulls vice president and then general manager. "But we were told by Joe's dad and it was verified by Joe, although not emphatically . . . Maybe Joe wore No. 18 and it was too big for him and you couldn't see the one when he stood up at the plate."

Mangum was reassigned at season's end, but not until the much-ballyhooed DAP finale was washed

# MANAGER OF THE YEAR

## Barons' Francona Earns Top Honor

Terry Francona hasn't been at this managing thing very long, but it's already abundantly clear he's quite good at it.

Francona, 34, led the Double-A Birmingham Barons to the Southern League's best record (78-64) and postseason title in 1993. For his efforts, the former 10-year major league outfielder/first baseman was named Baseball America's Minor League Manager of the Year.

Francona managed Birmingham to the title despite significant turnover in his pitching staff. Eight members of the Opening Day staff had moved up by the end of July. The team also lost its top hitter, third baseman Ron Coomer, early in the second half.

Nevertheless, the Barons maintained a high level of play all season, capping it off with playoff victories over Nashville and Knoxville. Birmingham swept Nashville in three games, then downed Knoxville in four games to win the best-of-5 final.

Francona joined the White Sox organization as a Rookie-level coach in 1991. In 1992, he led Class A South Bend to a 73-64 mark, then served as a coach with Grand Canyon of the Arizona Fall League.

In his brief time calling the

**Terry Francona**

shots, Francona has already earned a reputation as a player's manager. His time with the Expos, Cubs, Reds, Indians and Brewers helps in that regard.

"I don't hide the fact that I like the players," said the son of former major leaguer Tito Francona. "The guys are young and need supervision, but they're great to be around. This is the best part of their lives, trying to get to the big leagues."

Francona himself is considered a strong prospect to return to the big leagues. The White Sox have made no secret of their plans to fast-track their impressive young manager. That's fine with Francona, but he contends he has no grand scheme for his career.

"To be honest, I don't even know if I want to be a big league manager," he said. "I don't know if I'm good enough, if somebody wants me or if I want the aggravation.

"Really, I'm happy doing what I do. I love baseball, probably more than most people. So if they come back next year and tell me I'm coming back to Birmingham, that's fine. It's probably what I would expect."

### PREVIOUS WINNERS

1981—Ed Nottle, Tacoma (Athletics)
1982—Eddie Haas, Richmond (Braves)
1983—Bill Dancy, Reading (Phillies)
1984—Sam Perlozzo, Jackson (Mets)
1985—Jim Lefebvre, Phoenix (Giants)
1986—Brad Fischer, Huntsville (Athletics)
1987—Dave Trembley, Harrisburg (Pirates)
1988—Joe Sparks, Indianapolis (Expos)
1989—Buck Showalter, Albany (Yankees)
1990—Kevin Kennedy, Albuquerque (Dodgers)
1991—Butch Hobson, Pawtucket (Red Sox)
1992—Grady Little, Greenville (Braves)

out with the Bulls leading Kinston 1-0 in the first inning. "It's like someone upstairs was trying to tell us something," Bulls pitcher Chris Seelbach said.

Meanwhile, construction lagged at the Bulls' new $12 million crosstown stadium, and the team conceded that it would spend at least another half-season at DAP.

On a more positive note, the Bulls topped 300,000 in season attendance for the fourth straight year.

# ORGANIZATION OF THE YEAR

## World Series Champions Honored By Baseball America

What more can you say about the Toronto Blue Jays, Baseball America's 1993 Organization of the Year?

They parlayed prudent free-agent signings and a stacked farm system into back-to-back World Series championships. In the process, they became the first team to repeat since the 1977-78 New York Yankees.

Not bad, considering the Jays entered 1993 with 11 new faces on their 25-man big league roster, the most turnover on a defending champion since the 1915 Philadelphia Athletics.

Sure, by the time they added Rickey Henderson in late August, they had the highest payroll in the game, more than $51 million. But the Blue Jays, with the exceptions of righthander Jack Morris ($5.4 million) and perhaps

**Pat Gillick**

rent-a-headache Henderson, spent that money wisely.

See Paul Molitor.

With executive vice president Pat Gillick leading the way, the Jays maintained a strong commitment to player development and scouting, as they have since their inception in 1977. That commitment knows no boundaries, as the Jays' influence extends across the globe and back.

Their minor league winning percentage of .497 ranked just 17th overall, but as usual there was no shortage of prospects. Shortstop Alex Gonzalez and catcher Carlos Delgado, both of whom played at Double-A Knoxville in 1993, led the way.

Amazingly, for all their achievements and model comportment over the past decade, this is the first time BA has bestowed its organizational honor on the Blue Jays. It was always a question of when.

### PREVIOUS WINNERS

| | |
|---|---|
| 1992—Cleveland Indians | 1986—Milwaukee Brewers |
| 1991—Atlanta Braves | 1985—Milwaukee Brewers |
| 1990—Montreal Expos | 1984—New York Mets |
| 1989—Texas Rangers | 1983—New York Mets |
| 1988—Montreal Expos | 1982—Oakland Athletics |
| 1987—Milwaukee Brewers | |

---

**The Diamond.** Home of the Richmond Braves, The Diamond attracted more than 533,000 fans in 1993, a franchise record.

### PREVIOUS WINNERS

**Triple-A**
1992—Iowa (American Association)
1991—Buffalo (American Association)
1990—Pawtucket (International)
1989—Columbus (International)

**Double-A**
1992—Tulsa (Texas)
1991—Reading (Eastern)
1990—Arkansas (Texas)
1989—El Paso (Texas)

**Class A**
1992—Springfield (Midwest)
1991—Asheville (South Atlantic)
1990—San Jose (California)
1989—Durham (Carolina)

**Short-Season**
1992—Boise (Northwest)
1991—Spokane (Northwest)
1990—Salt Lake City (Pioneer)
1989—Eugene (Northwest)

# BOB FREITAS AWARDS

## Richmond Wins Triple-A Honor

The Baseball America/Bob Freitas Awards, named after a longtime operator, promoter and minor league ambassador who died in 1989, recognize long-term success and stability in minor league operations.

Attendance records caused by a relocation or a new stadium catch the eye, but Freitas Award winners have proven themselves over time.

One team is selected annually by Baseball America at each classification. The 1993 winners: Richmond (Triple-A), Harrisburg (Double-A), South Bend (Class A) and Billings (short-season).

All have been strong members of their local communities since at least 1988 (South Bend). While Harrisburg (1987) is another relative newcomer, Richmond (1966) and Billings (1969) are practically graybeards in terms of International and Pioneer League longevity, respectively.

## Kiddie Corps

The younger generation gained prominence with a pair of odd episodes. First, there was the curious case of Tommy McCoy, the 14-year-old Savannah Cardinals (South Atlantic) batboy who was fired May 20 because of federal child-labor laws.

McCoy went back to work May 28 and even threw out the first pitch before a game against the Augusta Pirates. In the wake of a national flap over the intent of the law, U.S. Labor Secretary Robert Reich suspended the law as it pertained to batboys and batgirls.

According to federal law, children ages 14 and 15 can't work past 7 p.m. on a school night or past 9 p.m. in the summer. Mc-Coy's batboy gig frequently kept him at Grayson Stadium until well past 10 p.m.

A feature story in the Savannah News-Press brought McCoy's work schedule to the attention of local labor department officials. Following his dismissal, national press ranging from CBS and CNN to Paul Harvey and "The Maury Povich Show" swooped in for follow-up stories.

"It started out as just a simple little job for Tommy," said Marcia McCoy, the boy's mother. "Then all of a sudden: Boom!"

Look for Macaulay Culkin to play McCoy in a summer blockbuster coming to a theater near you.

Later in the summer, 4-year-old Kyle Carnaroli came within eight hours of starting in right field for the Pocatello Posse (Pioneer). Carnaroli supplied the team with its new name in a contest, for which first prize was a one-time spot in the team's lineup.

The independent club actually signed Carnaroli (3-foot-6, 50 pounds) and announced plans to use him in a game against Medicine Hat. But the National Association stepped in and quashed the idea that afternoon.

Carnaroli, who would have become the youngest person ever to play professional baseball, instead had to settle for a Posse jacket and hat, season tickets and a color-analyst slot on a Posse radio broadcast.

## Around The Minors

Former major league righthander Bert Blyleven led a contingent of minor leaguers that represented the

# TEAM OF THE YEAR

### Harrisburg Takes Award

Really, now, who else could have been Baseball America's first Minor League Team of the Year besides the Double-A Harrisburg Senators?

All manager Jim Tracy's bunch did was win 100 games (counting playoffs) and the Eastern League championship. The bulk of these feats were accomplished without the benefit of such early-season standouts as first baseman Cliff Floyd, outfielder Rondell White and the nasty lefthanded trio of Joey Eischen, Kirk Rueter and Gabe White.

The Senators, who started 35-9 and never slowed down, were the most dominant team in the Eastern League since Reading won 96 games in 1983.

"We started out kicking butt, and basically kicked butt all season long," outfielder Glenn Murray said.

# TRIPLE-A ALL-STAR GAME

It was the Richmond Braves Show at the sixth annual Triple-A all-star game in Albuquerque, where fans braved a two-hour rain delay before the first pitch.

Richmond first baseman Ryan Klesko went 4-for-4 with two home runs and three RBIs to lead the National League all-stars to a 14-3 victory.

### ROSTERS

#### AMERICAN LEAGUE AFFILIATES

**Manager:** Charlie Manuel (Charlotte).

**Coaches:** Jeff Cox (Omaha), Scott Ullger (Portland).

**Pitchers:** Keith Brown (Omaha), Jerry DiPoto (Charlotte), Brian Drahman (Nashville), Don Florence (Pawtucket), John O'Donoghue (Rochester), Rick Reed (Omaha), Wally Ritchie (Toledo), Darryl Scott (Vancouver).

**Catchers:** Derek Parks (Portland), Rich Rowland (Toledo).

**Infielders:** Kurt Abbott, Kurt (Tacoma), Drew Denson (Nashville), Webster Garrison (Portland), Tommy Hinzo (Rochester), Anthony Manahan (Calgary), Eduardo Perez (Vancouver), Terry Shumpert (Omaha), Jim Thome (Charl.).

**Outfielders:** Rob Ducey (Oklahoma City), Billy Masse (Columbus), Troy O'Leary (New Orleans), Karl Rhodes (Omaha), Mark Smith (Rochester), Lee Stevens (Syracuse).

#### NATIONAL LEAGUE AFFILIATES

**Manager:** Bill Russell (Albuquerque).

**Coaches:** Marc Bombard (Indianapolis), George Culver (Scranton/Wilkes-Barre).

**Pitchers:** Steve Dixon (Louisville), Kip Gross (Albuquerque), Scott Ruskin (Indianapolis), Roy Smith (Buffalo), Bill Taylor (Richmond), Steve Trachsel (Iowa), Dave Weathers (Edmonton), Todd Williams (Albuquerque).

**Catchers:** Jerry Brooks (Albuquerque), Javy Lopez (Richmond).

**Infielders:** Rafael Bournigal (Albuquerque), Todd Haney (Ottawa), Chipper Jones (Richmond), Ryan Klesko (Richmond), Keith Lockhart (Louisville), Roberto Mejia (Colorado Springs), James Mouton (Tucson), J.R. Phillips (Phoenix).

**Outfielders:** Billy Ashley (Albuquerque), Tony Longmire (Scranton/Wilkes-Barre), Steve Pegues (Las Vegas), Scott Pose (Edmonton), Kevin Roberson (Iowa), Ryan Thompson (Norfolk), Eddie Zambrano (Iowa).

### BOX SCORE

| AMERICAN | ab | r | h | bi | NATIONAL | ab | r | h | bi |
|---|---|---|---|---|---|---|---|---|---|
| Rhodes cf | 3 | 0 | 0 | 1 | Jones ss | 3 | 0 | 1 | 1 |
| Ducey cf | 1 | 0 | 0 | 0 | Bournigal ss | 1 | 0 | 1 | 1 |
| Shumpert 2b | 3 | 0 | 0 | 0 | Lockhart 3b | 3 | 1 | 1 | 0 |
| Garrison 2b | 2 | 0 | 0 | 0 | Haney 3b | 2 | 0 | 0 | 0 |
| Thome 3b | 1 | 0 | 0 | 0 | Klesko 1b | 4 | 4 | 4 | 3 |
| Perez 3b | 2 | 0 | 0 | 0 | Ashley rf | 3 | 0 | 2 | 1 |
| Denson 1b | 4 | 1 | 1 | 1 | Pegues rf | 2 | 1 | 1 | 2 |
| Masse lf | 2 | 0 | 1 | 0 | Phillips dh | 3 | 1 | 1 | 0 |
| O'Leary lf | 2 | 0 | 1 | 0 | Thompson dh | 2 | 1 | 1 | 1 |
| Smith rf | 2 | 0 | 0 | 0 | Roberson lf | 3 | 1 | 1 | 2 |
| Stevens rf | 2 | 1 | 1 | 1 | Longmire lf | 2 | 0 | 0 | 0 |
| Parks c | 2 | 0 | 0 | 0 | Zambrano cf | 3 | 2 | 1 | 0 |
| Rowland c | 2 | 0 | 0 | 0 | Pose cf | 2 | 0 | 0 | 0 |
| Abbott ss | 2 | 1 | 1 | 0 | Lopez c | 3 | 1 | 2 | 1 |
| Manahan ss | 2 | 0 | 2 | 0 | Brooks c | 1 | 1 | 0 | 0 |
| Hinzo dh | 4 | 0 | 1 | 0 | Mouton 2b | 3 | 1 | 1 | 1 |
| | | | | | Mejia 2b | 1 | 0 | 0 | 0 |
| **Totals** | **36** | **3** | **8** | **3** | **Totals** | **41** | **14** | **17** | **13** |

| | |
|---|---|
| **American** | **001 000 110— 3** |
| **National** | **141 304 10x—14** |

E—Thome, Perez, Klesko. LOB—American 8, National 6. 2B—Klesko, Lopez. HR—Denson, Stevens, Klesko 2, Pegues, Thompson, Roberson. SB—Rhodes, Mouton.

| American | ip | h | r | er | bb | so | National | ip | h | r | er | bb | so |
|---|---|---|---|---|---|---|---|---|---|---|---|---|---|
| O'Donoghue L | 1⅔ | 7 | 5 | 3 | 0 | 3 | Smith W | 2 | 1 | 0 | 0 | 0 | 0 |
| Reed | 2⅓ | 6 | 4 | 4 | 0 | 3 | Trachsel | 1 | 2 | 1 | 1 | 1 | 2 |
| Brown | 1 | 0 | 0 | 0 | 1 | 1 | Taylor | 2 | 0 | 0 | 0 | 0 | 3 |
| Florence | 1 | 3 | 4 | 3 | 2 | 1 | Gross | 2 | 2 | 1 | 1 | 1 | 0 |
| Scott | 1 | 1 | 1 | 1 | 0 | 3 | Dixon | 1 | 2 | 1 | 1 | 0 | 1 |
| Ritchie | 1 | 0 | 0 | 0 | 0 | 0 | Williams | 1 | 1 | 0 | 0 | 0 | 1 |

T—2:42. A—10,541.

# MINOR LEAGUES
## BEST TOOLS

| | American Association AAA | International League AAA | Pacific Coast League AAA | Eastern League AA | Southern League AA | Texas League AA | California League A | Carolina League A | Florida State League A | Midwest League A | South Atlantic League A |
|---|---|---|---|---|---|---|---|---|---|---|---|
| **Best Batting Prospect** | Karl Rhodes, Omaha | Jim Thome, Charlotte | Darrell Whitmore, Edmonton | Manny Ramirez, Canton-Akron | Carlos Delgado, Knoxville | Roberto Petagine, Jackson | Tim Clark, High Desert | Jose Malave, Lynchburg | Doug Radziewicz, St. Petersburg | Ken Tirpack, Fort Wayne | Jose Herrera, Hagerstown |
| **Best Power Prospect** | Eddie Zambrano, Iowa | Ryan Klesko, Richmond | Billy Ashley, Albuquerque | Cliff Floyd, Harrisburg | Carlos Delgado, Knoxville | Trey McCoy, Tulsa | Dave Staton, Rancho Cuca. | Tate Seefried, Prince William | Chris Weinke, Dunedin | Scott Talanoa, Beloit | Nick Delvecchio, Greensboro |
| **Best Baserunner** | Terry Shumpert, Omaha | Eric Bullock, Norfolk | John Massarelli, Tucson | Shannon Penn, London | Ray Durham, Birmingham | Brian Hunter, Jackson | Kerwin Moore, High Desert | Curtis Goodwin, Frederick | Randy Curtis, St. Petersburg | Essex Burton, South Bend | Lonell Roberts, Hagerstown |
| **Fastest Baserunner** | Scott Bullett, Buffalo | Ted Williams, Toledo | Pat Howell, Portland | Danny Bautista, London | Ray Durham, Birmingham | Brian Hunter, Jackson | Kerwin Moore, High Desert | Curtis Goodwin, Frederick | Terry Bradshaw, St. Lucie | Essex Burton, South Bend | Kraig Hawkins, Greensboro |
| **Best Pitching Prospect** | Jason Bere, Nashville | Aaron Sele, Pawtucket | Pat Rapp, Edmonton | Brien Taylor, Albany | James Baldwin, Birmingham | Rick Gorecki, San Antonio | Mark Thompson, Central Valley | Julian Tavarez, Kinston | Rod Henderson, West Palm Beach | Ugueth Urbina, Burlington | Terrell Wade, Macon |
| **Best Fastball** | Enrique Burgos, Omaha | Mark Wohlers, Richmond | Todd Van Poppel, Tacoma | Brien Taylor, Albany | Scott Ruffcorn, Birmingham | Ben VanRyn, San Antonio | Andres Berumen, High Desert | Julian Tavarez, Kinston | Felix Rodriguez, Vero Beach | Ugueth Urbina, Burlington | Terrell Wade, Macon |
| **Best Breaking Pitch** | John Roper, Indianapolis | Aaron Sele, Pawtucket | Greg Brummett, Phoenix | Rick Krivda, Bowie | Steve Karsay, Knoxville | Rick Gorecki, San Antonio | John Burke, Central Valley | Joel Bennett, Lynchburg | Robert Ellis, Sarasota | Tim Davis, Appleton | Ryan Karp, Greensboro |
| **Best Control** | Rick Reed, Omaha | Mike Williams, Scranton/WB | Pat Rapp, Edmonton | Denny Harriger, Binghamton | Steve Karsay, Knoxville | A.J. Sager, Wichita | Mark Thompson, Central Valley | Jon Lieber, Wilmington | Kennie Steenstra, Daytona | Hector Trinidad, Peoria | Ryan Karp, Greensboro |
| **Best Reliever** | Tony Menendez, Buffalo | Bill Taylor, Richmond | Todd Williams, Albuquerque | Rich Batchelor, Albany | Don Strange, Greenville | Jim Dougherty, Jackson | John Pricher, Palm Springs | Jeff McCurry, Salem | Clint Davis, St. Petersburg | Mark Acre, Madison | Kerry Lacy, Charleston, S.C. |
| **Best Defensive C** | Matt Walbeck, Iowa | John Flaherty, Pawtucket | Brad Ausmus, Colorado Springs | Greg Zaun, Bowie | Darron Cox, Chattanooga | Mike Matheny, El Paso | Izzy Molina, Modesto | Scott Stricklin, Wilmington | Ken Huckaby, Vero Beach | Charles Johnson, Kane County | Jason Kendall, Augusta |
| **Best Defensive 1B** | Dan Peltier, Oklahoma City | Rico Brogna, Toledo | J.R. Phillips, Phoenix | Willie Tatum, New Britain | Tim Hyers, Knoxville | Barry Miller, Shreveport | Jay Kirkpatrick, Bakersfield | Tim Belk, Winston-Salem | Jon Zuber, Clearwater | Larry Sutton, Rockford | D.J. Boston, Hagerstown |
| **Best Defensive 2B** | Norberto Martin, Nashville | Doug Saunders, Norfolk | Roberto Mejia, Colorado Springs | Miguel Flores, Canton-Akron | Jose Olmeda, Greenville | Darrel Deak, Arkansas | Jason Hardtke, Rancho Cuca. | Pat Maxwell, Kinston | Bernie Millan, Clearwater | Steve Sisco, Rockford | Dee Jenkins, Charleston, W.Va. |
| **Best Defensive 3B** | John Byington, New Orleans | Russ Davis, Columbus | Craig Paquette, Tacoma | David Bell, Canton-Akron | Howard Battle, Knoxville | Henry Blanco, San Antonio | Jason Giambi, Modesto | Scott McClain, Frederick | Rob Grable, Clearwater | D.J. Thielen, Clinton | Eric Chavez, Albany |
| **Best Defensive SS** | Tripp Cromer, Louisville | Mark Lewis, Charlotte | Rafael Bournigal, Albuquerque | Robert Eenhoorn, Albany | Alex Gonzalez, Knoxville | Benji Gil, Tulsa | Kurt Ehmann, San Jose | Shane Halter, Wilmington | Chris Peterson, Daytona | Keith Johns, Springfield | Derek Jeter, Greensboro |
| **Best Infield Arm** | Esteban Beltre, Nashville | Manny Alexander, Rochester | Craig Paquette, Tacoma | Robert Eenhoorn, Albany | Howard Battle, Knoxville | Benji Gil, Tulsa | Willie Otanez, Bakersfield | Scott McClain, Frederick | Chad Roper, Fort Myers | Gabby Martinez, Beloit | Derek Jeter, Greensboro |
| **Best Defensive OF** | Kevin Koslofski, Omaha | Gerald Williams, Columbus | Pat Howell, Portland | Omar Ramirez, Canton-Akron | Rich Becker, Nashville | Brian Hunter, Jackson | Carl Everett, High Desert | Curtis Goodwin, Frederick | Randy Curtis, St. Lucie | David Francisco, Madison | Kraig Hawkins, Greensboro |
| **Best Outfield Arm** | Cesar Hernandez, Indianapolis | Tony Tarasco, Richmond | Raul Mondesi, Albuquerque | Danny Bautista, London | Rich Becker, Nashville | Duane Singleton, El Paso | Michael Moore, Bakersfield | Alex Ochoa, Frederick | Justin Mashore, Lakeland | David Francisco, Madison | Jose Herrera, Hagerstown |
| **Most Exciting Player** | Brian Jordan, Louisville | Ryan Klesko, Richmond | Darrell Whitmore, Edmonton | Cliff Floyd, Harrisburg | Alex Gonzalez, Knoxville | Brian Hunter, Jackson | Carl Everett, High Desert | Curtis Goodwin, Frederick | Rich Butler, Dunedin | Johnny Damon, Rockford | Derek Jeter, Greensboro |

Selected at midpoint of 1993 season by minor league managers in consultation with Baseball America    Full-season leagues only

**Bull!** Durham Athletic Park, where the hit movie "Bull Durham" was filmed, was supposed to be put to pasture in 1993.

United States at the World Port Tournament in Rotterdam, The Netherlands. The U.S. team beat Aruba 7-0 in the three-inning final to close out a 6-2 showing. Outfielder Ryan Turner (Rockies) was named tournament MVP after batting .433 (13-for-30) with one home run and nine RBIs . . . The Norfolk Tides (International) were fined $8,000 by the Federal Communications Commission for operating an unlicensed radar gun. The team used the gun in its "Speedball" promotion, where fans get three pitches for $1 to see how fast they can throw a baseball. "We're pioneers—$8,000 pioneers" said Tides GM Dave Rosenfield, who added no one in the National Association office had ever heard of needing a license for a radar gun . . . The Kinston Indians (Carolina) invited comedian Jerry Seinfeld to play right field for them in what became a season-long promotional gag. Seinfeld, who refused to respond for fear that he would then be deluged with similar offers, apparently bears a striking resemblance to Indians right fielder Marc Marini. The team even went so far as to have Marini and three others—manager Dave Keller, pitching coach Greg Booker and closer Ian Doyle—spend three hours in a photo studio recreating the Rolling Stone cover that featured the cast of NBC's "Seinfeld." All that and still no word from Jerry . . . Jericho the Miracle Dog retired after four years as mascot of the Fort Myers Miracle (Florida State). Jericho, an 11-year-old golden retriever, was slowed by an arthritic hip in his final year. Next up is Jericho's son, Jake the Diamond Dog.

## QUOTES OF THE YEAR

**TERRELL BUCKLEY,** Macon (South Atlantic) outfielder, who once called himself the Jim Thorpe of the second half-century, on questions about his hitting:

"A lot of uneducated people really bug me when they say, 'You hit .118 or .120.' A lot of guys made a lot of great catches. Can I hit? Yeah, I can hit."

**LARRY KING,** celebrity American League manager for the Double-A all-star game, on the experience:

"Minor league baseball? It's a hoot."

**MIKE BIRKBECK,** Richmond (International) pitcher, on the minor league tobacco ban:

"You don't really think I'll quit, do you? It's kind of like a spitball. It's only illegal if you get caught."

# DOUBLE-A ALL-STAR GAME

Wichita outfielder Dwayne Hosey, a late addition to the roster, went 3-for-4 with four runs scored and a near cycle to lead the National League to a 12-7 win in the third Double-A all-star game at Tim McCarver Stadium in Memphis.

## ROSTERS
### NATIONAL LEAGUE AFFILIATES
**Manager:** Jim Tracy (Harrisburg).
**Coach:** Sal Butera (Jackson).
**Pitchers:** Brian Barber (Arkansas), Juan Castillo (Binghamton), Jim Dougherty (Jackson), Joey Eischen (Harrisburg), Rick Gorecki (San Antonio), Steve Hoeme (Wichita), Carlos Reyes (Greenville), Ben VanRyn (San Antonio), Travis Willis (Orlando).
**Catchers:** Tyler Houston (Greenville), Keith Osik (Carolina).
**Infielders:** Rich Aude (Carolina), Juan Castro (San Antonio), Darrel Deak (Arkansas), Cliff Floyd (Harrisburg), Butch Huskey (Binghamton), Keith Kimberlin (Reading), Brian Lane (Chattanooga), Roberto Petagine (Jackson), Jeff Shireman (Arkansas).
**Outfielders:** Dwayne Hosey (Wichita), Brian Hunter (Jackson), Dax Jones (Shreveport), Rondell White (Harrisburg).

### AMERICAN LEAGUE AFFILIATES
**Manager:** Don Buford (Bowie).
**Coach:** Tom Poquette (Memphis).
**Pitchers:** Richard Batchelor (Albany), John Fritz (Midland), Steve Karsay (Knoxville), Rick Krivda (Bowie), Felipe Lira (London), Albie Lopez (Canton-Akron), Ritchie Moody (Tulsa), Oscar Munoz (Nashville), Frank Rodriguez (New Britain), Scott Ruffcorn (Birmingham).
**Catchers:** Carlos Delgado (Knoxville), George Williams (Huntsville).
**Infielders:** Cris Colon (Tulsa), Robert Eenhoorn (Albany), P.J. Forbes (Midland), Tim Hyers (Knoxville), Shannon Penn (London), Joe Randa (Memphis), Ruben Santana (Jacksonville).
**Outfielders:** Rich Becker (Nashville), John Jackson (Midland), Rob Lukachyk (El Paso), Trey McCoy (Tulsa), Les Norman (Memphis), Manny Ramirez (Canton-Akron).

## BOX SCORE

| NATIONAL | ab | r | h | bi | AMERICAN | ab | r | h | bi |
|---|---|---|---|---|---|---|---|---|---|
| Hunter rf | 3 | 1 | 1 | 0 | Santana 2b | 2 | 1 | 1 | 0 |
| Jones rf | 1 | 0 | 0 | 0 | Penn 2b | 3 | 0 | 0 | 0 |
| Hosey lf | 4 | 4 | 3 | 2 | Hyers 1b | 4 | 1 | 0 | 0 |
| White cf | 5 | 2 | 2 | 2 | Ramirez cf | 2 | 1 | 1 | 1 |
| Floyd 1b | 3 | 0 | 0 | 0 | Williams c | 2 | 0 | 0 | 0 |
| Aude 1b | 1 | 1 | 1 | 2 | McCoy dh | 3 | 0 | 2 | 0 |
| Petagine dh | 3 | 1 | 0 | 1 | Becker dh | 2 | 0 | 0 | 0 |
| Huskey 3b | 2 | 0 | 0 | 0 | Norman rf | 5 | 2 | 1 | 2 |
| Lane 3b | 3 | 0 | 0 | 0 | Colon 3b | 2 | 0 | 0 | 0 |
| Deak 2b | 2 | 1 | 1 | 0 | Randa 3b | 2 | 1 | 1 | 0 |
| Castro 2b | 2 | 1 | 1 | 3 | Delgado c | 3 | 0 | 0 | 0 |
| Houston c | 2 | 0 | 1 | 0 | Jackson cf | 0 | 1 | 0 | 0 |
| Osik c | 3 | 0 | 1 | 0 | Lukachyk lf | 4 | 0 | 1 | 0 |
| Shireman ss | 2 | 0 | 0 | 1 | Eenhoorn ss | 3 | 0 | 0 | 0 |
| Kimberlin ss | 2 | 0 | 0 | 0 | Forbes ph | 1 | 0 | 1 | 2 |
| **Totals** | **38** | **12** | **11** | **11** | **Totals** | **38** | **7** | **8** | **5** |

| | | |
|---|---|---|
| National | 201 120 330— | 12 |
| American | 400 000 030— | 7 |

E—Houston, Castro, Floyd, Santana, Norman, Eenhoorn. LOB—National 6, American 7. 2B—White, Houston. 3B—Hosey. HR—Castro, Hosey, Norman. SB—Hosey. SF—Shireman.

| National | ip | h | r | er | bb | so | American | ip | h | r | er | bb | so |
|---|---|---|---|---|---|---|---|---|---|---|---|---|---|
| Eischen | 1 | 3 | 4 | 1 | 0 | 1 | Krivda | 2 | 2 | 2 | 2 | 0 | 2 |
| Barber | 1 | 0 | 0 | 0 | 1 | 2 | Lira | 2 | 3 | 2 | 2 | 0 | 2 |
| VanRyn | 1 | 0 | 0 | 0 | 0 | 1 | Fritz L | 1 | 1 | 2 | 2 | 2 | 0 |
| Castillo W | 1 | 0 | 0 | 0 | 0 | 0 | Rodriguez | 2 | 2 | 3 | 3 | 2 | 1 |
| Gorecki | 1 | 1 | 0 | 0 | 1 | 1 | Moody | ⅔ | 3 | 3 | 3 | 1 | 0 |
| Hoeme | 1 | 1 | 0 | 0 | 0 | 0 | Chaves | ⅓ | 0 | 0 | 0 | 0 | 0 |
| Willis | 1 | 0 | 0 | 0 | 0 | 1 | Batchelor | 1 | 0 | 0 | 0 | 0 | 0 |
| Reyes | 1 | 3 | 3 | 3 | 0 | 1 | | | | | | | |
| Dougherty | 1 | 0 | 0 | 0 | 0 | 2 | | | | | | | |

WP—Eischen, Fritz, Lira. HBP—Petagine (by Krivda), Jackson (by Reyes). T—2:42. A—6,335.

# SIX-YEAR FREE AGENTS

A record 368 players were granted free agency under baseball's six-year plan, which provides free agency to players who signed in 1987 or earlier who weren't placed on major league 40-man rosters by Oct. 15, 1993.

A list of free agents and their 1993 organization:

## ATLANTA (12)

| | |
|---|---|
| Jay Baller, rhp | Bobby Moore, of |
| Scott Bradley, c | Dale Polley, lhp |
| Ron Jones, of | Boi Rodriguez, 1b |
| Orlando Lind, rhp | Billy Taylor, rhp |
| Mike Loynd, rhp | Marcos Vazquez, rhp |
| Keith Mitchell, of | Gerry Willard, c |

## BALTIMORE (10)

| | |
|---|---|
| Edgar Alfonzo, 3b | Sam Ferretti, 3b |
| Rafael Chaves, rhp | Tommy Hinzo, 2b |
| Bobby Dickerson, ss | Tim Holland, ss |
| Bruce Dostal, of | Chuck Ricci, rhp |
| Brian DuBois, lhp | Don Schulze, rhp |

## BOSTON (17)

| | |
|---|---|
| Mike Beams, of | John Mitchell, rhp |
| Luis Dorante, c | Anthony Mosley, lhp |
| Marty Durkin, of | Jeff Plympton, rhp |
| Dan Gakeler, rhp | Jeff Richardson, ss |
| Jeff Gray, rhp | Ruben Rodriguez, c |
| Danny Johnston, rhp | John Shea, lhp |
| Derek Livernois, rhp | Franklin Stubbs, 1b |
| Dave Milstien, 2b | Paul Thoutsis, of |
| Steve Mintz, rhp | |

## CALIFORNIA (13)

| | |
|---|---|
| Tim Burcham, rhp | Jeff Pico, rhp |
| Kevin Davis, ss | Guillermo Sandoval, rhp |
| Wayne Edwards, lhp | Nelson Simmons, of |
| Mark Grant, rhp | Ty Van Burkleo, 1b |
| Otis Green, lhp | Jim Walewander, 2b |
| Dom Johnson, rhp | Mark Wasinger, 3b |
| Ray Martinez, ss | |

## CHICAGO-NL (14)

| | |
|---|---|
| Tony Chance, of | Fernando Ramsey, of |
| Sherman Corbett, lhp | Greg Smith, 2b |
| Jim Czajkowski, rhp | Ed Vosberg, lhp |
| Chris Johnson, rhp | Mike Walker, rhp |
| Greg Lonigro, ss | Billy White, 2b |
| Bill Melvin, rhp | Jimmy Williams, lhp |
| Jorge Pedre, c | Craig Worthington, 3b |

## CHICAGO-AL (11)

| | |
|---|---|
| Steve Adkins, lhp | John Gardner, rhp |
| Geronimo Aquino, of | Shawn Gilbert, 3b |
| Kevin Belcher, of | Brad Komminsk, of |
| Frank Campos, rhp | Kinnis Pledger, of |
| Jeff Carter, rhp | Dan Sanchez, ss |
| Chris Cron, 1b | |

## CINCINNATI (7)

| | |
|---|---|
| Kash Beauchamp, of | Junior Noboa, 2b |
| John Burgos, rhp | Rich Sauveur, lhp |
| Motorboat Jones, of | Razor Shines, 1b |
| Bo Kennedy, rhp | |

## CLEVELAND (24)

| | |
|---|---|
| Beau Allred, of | Bob Milacki, rhp |
| Allan Anderson, lhp | Carlos Mota, c |
| Don August, rhp | Donell Nixon, of |
| Alan Cockrell, of | Julio Peguero, of |
| Mark Davidson, of | Nap Robinson, rhp |
| Mike Dyer, rhp | Paul Romanoli, lhp |
| Apolinar Garcia, rhp | Jeff Schaefer, 2b |
| Calvin Jones, rhp | Julio Solano, rhp |
| Jeff Kunkel, ss | Greg Sparks, 1b |
| Patrick Lennon, of | Hector Vargas, ss |
| Luis Lopez, 1b | Randy Veres, rhp |
| Tom McCarthy, rhp | Cliff Young, lhp |

## COLORADO (9)

| | |
|---|---|
| Edwin Alicea, of | Jim Olander, of |
| George Canale, 1b | Dana Ridenour, rhp |
| Trent Hubbard, of | Sean Ross, of |
| Randy Marshall, lhp | Terry Wells, lhp |
| Andy Mota, 2b | |

## DETROIT (7)

| | |
|---|---|
| John Cangelosi, of | Wally Ritchie, lhp |
| Dean Decillis, ss | Rod Robertson, 2b |
| Johnny Paredes, 2b | Ted Williams, of |
| Marty Pevey, c | |

## FLORIDA (16)

| | |
|---|---|
| Scott Anderson, rhp | Jim Newlin, rhp |
| Nick Capra, 3b | Roberto Ramos, rhp |
| Jim Corsi, rhp | Ed Renteria, 2b |
| Luis de los Santos, 1b | Luis Reyes, lhp |
| Jerry Don Gleaton, lhp | Jeff Small, 2b |
| Mike Jeffcoat, rhp | Randy Snyder, c |
| Bryn Kosco, 3b | John Toale, 1b |
| Randy Kramer, rhp | Jim Vlcek, rhp |

## HOUSTON (14)

| | |
|---|---|
| Jesus Alvarez, 3b | Bob Hurta, lhp |
| Tom Barrett, 2b | John Massarelli, of |
| Steve Carter, of | Terry Mathews, rhp |
| Fred Costello, rhp | Joe Mikulik, of |
| Eddie Dixon, rhp | Matt Rambo, rhp |
| Dean Hartgraves, lhp | James Steels, of |
| Randy Hennis, rhp | Dave Veres, rhp |

## KANSAS CITY (19)

| | |
|---|---|
| Shawn Abner, of | Scott Jaster, of |
| Keith Brown, rhp | Mike Kingery, of |
| Jim Campbell, lhp | Russ McGinnis, 3b |
| Adam Casillas, 1b | Jose Mota, 2b |
| Dera Clark, rhp | Harvey Pulliam, of |
| Steve Curry, rhp | Mike Roesler, rhp |
| Carlos Diaz, c | Dan Rohrmeier, of |
| Kiki Diaz, ss | Alex Sanchez, rhp |
| Brian Givens, lhp | Phil Stephenson, 1b |
| Mike Guerrero, rhp | |

## LOS ANGELES (7)

| | |
|---|---|
| Jorge Alvarez, 2b | Eric Nolte, lhp |
| Tony Barron, of | Dennis Springer, rhp |
| Edwin Correa, rhp | Royal Thomas, rhp |
| Jose Munoz, 2b | |

## MILWAUKEE (12)

| | |
|---|---|
| Edgar Caceres, 2b | Garland Kiser, lhp |
| Ramser Correa, rhp | Alan Lewis, 3b |
| Howard Farmer, rhp | Rob Lukachyk, of |
| Mike Fitzgerald, c | Ed Smith, 3b |
| Jim Hunter, rhp | Steve Sparks, rhp |
| Dane Johnson, rhp | Jeff Tabaka, lhp |

## MINNESOTA (10)

| | |
|---|---|
| Bernardo Brito, of | Pat Howell, of |
| Darrin Chapin, rhp | Greg Johnson, rhp |
| Tom Drees, rhp | Mike Maksudian, 1b |
| Jeff Grotewold, c | Jim Neidlinger, rhp |
| Mike Hartley, rhp | Jerry Schunk, ss |

## MONTREAL (7)

| | |
|---|---|
| Archie Corbin, rhp | Yorkis Perez, lhp |
| Todd Haney, 2b | David Rosario, lhp |
| Terrel Hansen, of | Mike Tosar, 2b |
| Tim McIntosh, c | |

## NEW YORK-NL (17)

| | |
|---|---|
| Dann Bilardello, c | Luis Martinez, ss |
| Eric Bullock, of | Steve Springer, 3b |
| Tom Filer, rhp | Charlie Sullivan, 2b |
| Javier Gonzalez, c | Mike Twardoski, 1b |
| Eric Gunderson, lhp | Brandy Vann, rhp |
| Denny Harriger, rhp | Scott Wade, of |
| Bert Hunter, rhp | Mickey Weston, rhp |
| Brent Knackert, rhp | Herm Winningham, of |
| Jacen Martinez, 2b | |

## NEW YORK-AL (15)

| | |
|---|---|
| Jovino Carvajal, of | Rich Monteleone, rhp |
| Royal Clayton, rhp | Tom Popplewell, rhp |

| | |
|---|---|
| Francisco de la Rosa, rhp | Rafael Quirico, lhp |
| Andy Dziadkowiec, c | John Ramos, c |
| Rich Gedman, c | Carlos Rodriguez, ss |
| Doug Gogolewski, rhp | Don Stanford, rhp |
| Lew Hill, of | Wade Taylor, rhp |
| Ed Martel, rhp | |

## OAKLAND (9)

| | |
|---|---|
| Jim Bowie, 1b | Fabio Gomez, 3b |
| Jorge Brito, c | Tim Peek, rhp |
| Kevin Campbell, rhp | Mike Raczka, lhp |
| Eric Fox, of | Larry Shikles, rhp |
| Webster Garrison, 2b | |

## PHILADELPHIA (6)

| | |
|---|---|
| Andy Carter, lhp | Jeff Manto, 3b |
| Drew Hall, lhp | Chris Marchok, lhp |
| Greg Legg, 2b | Victor Rodriguez, 3b |

## PITTSBURGH (27)

| | |
|---|---|
| Blaine Beatty, lhp | Javier Ortiz, of |
| Jose Cecena, rhp | Dave Pavlas, rhp |
| Gary Cooper, 3b | Mark Petkovsek, rhp |
| Mike Dalton, rhp | Doug Piatt, rhp |
| Stan Fansler, rhp | Tom Prince, c |
| Daryl Irvine, rhp | Dave Rohde, ss |
| Dave Leiper, lhp | Roy Smith, rhp |
| Tim Leiper, of | Matt Stark, c |
| Craig McMurtry, rhp | Dennis Tafoya, rhp |
| Tony Menendez, rhp | Keith Thomas, of |
| Paul Miller, rhp | Andy Tomberlin, of |
| Johnny Monell, of | Todd Trafton, 1b |
| Russ Morman, 1b | Glenn Wilson, of |
| Omer Munoz, 2b | |

## ST. LOUIS (11)

| | |
|---|---|
| Brad Arnsberg, rhp | Kevin Meier, rhp |
| Craig Faulkner, c | David Patterson, 1b |
| Bien Figueroa, ss | Bob Sebra, rhp |
| Ed Fulton, c | Van Snider, of |
| Keith Lockhart, 3b | Tracy Woodson, 3b |
| Lonnie Maclin, of | |

## SAN DIEGO (11)

| | |
|---|---|
| Mike Basso, c | Dwayne Hosey, of |
| Terry Clark, rhp | Jim Pena, lhp |
| Tom Doyle, rhp | Mike Simms, 1b |
| Pat Gomez, lhp | Andy Skeels, c |
| Vince Harris, of | Jim Vatcher, of |
| Steve Hoeme, rhp | |

## SAN FRANCISCO (9)

| | |
|---|---|
| Andy Allanson, c | Reed Peters, of |
| Kevin Brown, lhp | Rich Simon, rhp |
| Erik Johnson, ss | Rob Taylor, rhp |
| Tim Layana, rhp | Rob Wassenaar, rhp |
| Jim Myers, rhp | |

## SEATTLE (19)

| | |
|---|---|
| Shawn Barton, lhp | Mike Remlinger, lhp |
| Pete Beeler, c | Steve Rosenberg, lhp |
| Don Carman, lhp | Jack Smith, ss |
| Tyrone Domingo, 2b | Shane Turner, 3b |
| Mark Grater, rhp | Aubrey Waggoner, of |
| Shawn Jeter, of | Mike Walker, rhp |
| Quinn Mack, of | Steve Wapnick, rhp |
| Lance McCullers, rhp | Jim Wilson, 1b |
| Leni Montano, rhp | Gerald Young, of |
| Len Picota, rhp | |

## TEXAS (14)

| | |
|---|---|
| Mike Berger, 1b | Chuck Jackson, 3b |
| Cris Colon, ss | Mark Lee, lhp |
| Doug Davis, c | Oddibe McDowell, of |
| Mario Diaz, ss | Keith Miller, 1b |
| Benny Distefano, 1b | Francisco Oliveras, rhp |
| David Eiland, rhp | Luke Sable, 3b |
| Steve Fireovid, rhp | Willie Smith, of |

## TORONTO (9)

| | |
|---|---|
| Darrel Akerfelds, rhp | Jimmy Rogers, rhp |
| Pete Blohm, rhp | Randy St. Claire, rhp |
| Darren Hall, rhp | Lee Stevens, of |
| Jose Monzon, c | Julian Yan, 1b |
| Tom Quinlan, 3b | |

*Refused minor league assignment.

# Rule V Draft Again Has Little Impact

The 1992 Rule V draft of players off Triple-A reserve lists saw the unusually high number of 18 players selected, but as usual, few made an impact in the major leagues in 1993.

Of the 18 selected at the 1992 Winter Meetings, only four—outfielder Sherman Obando (Orioles), left-hander Billy Brewer (Royals) and righthanders Mike Draper (Mets) and Kerry Taylor (Padres)—spent the entire 1993 season in the big leagues with the club that drafted them.

Outfielder Willie Canate spent most of 1993 with Toronto. He was actually drafted by Cincinnati, but failed to clear waivers when the Reds attempted to send him to the minors and he was claimed by the Blue Jays. Canate got only 47 at-bats for Toronto, spending part of the year in the minor leagues on an injury rehabilitation assignment.

Lefthander Graeme Lloyd also spent 1993 in the big leagues, but he was acquired by Milwaukee in trade with Philadelphia after the draft. The Phillies had drafted him from Toronto.

Los Angeles opened the proceedings by selecting righthander Dera Clark off Kansas City's Triple-A Omaha roster for the $50,000 draft price. But Clark, a six-year minor league veteran, failed to earn a spot on the Dodgers Opening Day roster and was offered back to Kansas City for $25,000.

The expansion Florida Marlins and Colorado Rockies took part in the proceedings, but their selec-

MORRIS FOSTOFF

**Dera Clark**

MORRIS FOSTOFF

**RULE V DRAFT**
**Last 25 Years**

| Year | Club | Player, Pos. | From |
|------|------|--------------|------|
| 1968 | Astros | Gary Geiger, of | Cardinals |
| 1969 | Indians | Larry Staab, lhp | Dodgers |
| 1970 | Padres | Bill Laxton, lhp | Phillies |
| 1971 | Indians | Jim Moyer, rhp | Giants |
| 1972 | Phillies | Mike Bruhert, rhp | Mets |
| 1973 | Phillies | Ed Crosby, ss | Reds |
| 1974 | Cubs | Tim Hosley, c | Athletics |
| 1975 | Tigers | Bruce Taylor, rhp | Reds |
| 1976 | Expos | Tom Carroll, rhp | Reds |
| 1977 | Blue Jays | Willie Upshaw, 1b | Yankees |
| 1978 | Mets | Bobby Brown, of | Yankees |
| 1979 | Blue Jays | Mike Macha, 3b-of | Braves |
| 1980 | Cubs | Jody Davis, c | Cardinals |
| 1981 | Blue Jays | Jim Gott, rhp | Cardinals |
| 1982 | Reds | Dann Bilardello, c | Dodgers |
| 1983 | Mariners | Dave Geisel, lhp | Blue Jays |
| 1984 | Giants | Doug Gwosdz, c | Padres |
| 1985 | Indians | Eddie Williams, 3b | Reds |
| 1986 | Mariners | Tony Ferreira, lhp | Mets |
| 1987 | Indians | Todd Pratt, c | Red Sox |
| 1988 | Braves | Ben Rivera, rhp | Braves |
| 1989 | Tigers | Steve Wapnick, rhp | Blue Jays |
| 1990 | Twins | Pat Howell, of | Mets |
| 1991 | Indians | Mike Thomas, lhp | Expos |
| 1992 | Dodgers | Dera Clark, rhp | Royals |

tions were limited to players off National League reserve lists. However, the Marlins and Rockies were permitted to send all their selections to the minors for additional seasoning without penalty of first having to offer the player back to his original club.

Normally, a Rule V draft pick must remain on the selecting club's big league roster all of the following season or be offered back to the original team for half the $50,000 draft price. Players are subject to selection in the Rule V draft if they have not been protected on a major league club's 40-man winter roster after either his third or fourth professional season.

The Rule V draft extends to the Triple-A and Double-A levels, but does not provide that selecting clubs must keep a player on its roster the following season.

## 1992 RULE V DRAFT

**WINTER MEETINGS, 1992**

### MAJOR LEAGUE DRAFT
Selection Price: $50,000

**ROUND ONE**
Selecting Club. Player, Pos., From
Dodgers. Dera Clark, rhp (Royals)
Mariners. Reggie Harris, rhp (Athletics)
Phillies. Graeme Lloyd, lhp (Blue Jays)
Giants. Jim McNamara, c (Marlins)
Royals. Billy Brewer, lhp (Expos)
Mets. Mike Draper, rhp (Yankees)
Tigers. John Hudek, rhp (White Sox)
Padres. Kerry Taylor, rhp (Twins)
Reds. Willie Canate, of (Indians)
Orioles. Sherman Obando, of (Yankees)
Pirates. Mike Bell, 1b (Braves)
Brewers. Larry Stanford, rhp (Yankees)
Athletics. Kirt Ojala, lhp (Yankees)
Blue Jays. Bill Taylor, rhp (Braves)

**ROUND TWO**
Selecting Club. Player, Pos., From
Mariners. Fernando Vina, ss (Mets)
Marlins. Mike Myers, lhp (Giants)

**SUPPLEMENTAL**
Selecting Club. Player, Pos., From
Marlins. Scott Pose, of (Reds)

### TRIPLE-A DRAFT
Selection Price: $12,000

**ROUND ONE**
Selecting Club. Player, Pos., From
Dodgers. Doug Fitzer, lhp (Mariners)
Mariners. Ricky Rhodes, rhp (Yankees)
Phillies. Keith Kimberlin, ss (Tigers)
Giants. Tracey Ealy, of (Royals)
Cubs. Ron Stephens, rhp (White Sox)
Tigers. Billy White, ss (Cubs)
Astros. Rob Rees, rhp (Mets)
Indians. Cesar Perez, rhp (Yankees)
Padres. Ira Smith, of (Dodgers)
Expos. Vince Castaldo, of (Brewers)
Reds. Dave Proctor, rhp (Mets)
Pirates. Dave Otto, lhp (Indians)
Twins. Matt Stevens, rhp (Phillies)
Brewers. Darryl Meek, rhp (Cardinals)
Blue Jays. Steve Renko, rhp (Red Sox)

**ROUND TWO**
Selecting Club. Player, Pos., From
Phillies. James Grimes, rhp (Athletics)
Cubs. Darryl Vice, 2b (Athletics)
Indians. Rafael Mercado, 1b (Athletics)
Padres. Andy Rush, rhp (Red Sox)
Expos. Dave Brundage, lhp (Mariners)
Reds. Mateo Ozuna, 2b (Cardinals)
Pirates. Steve Whitehead, rhp (Expos)
Brewers. David Pike, rhp (Braves)
Blue Jays. Don Sheppard, of (White Sox)

### ROUND THREE
Selecting Club. Player, Pos., From
Cubs. Earnie Johnson, lhp (White Sox)
Reds. Troy Buckley, c (Twins)
Pirates. Jose Garza, rhp (Angels)
Brewers. Ryan Thibault, lhp (Padres)

**ROUND FOUR**
Selecting Club. Player, Pos., From
Reds. Kevin Shaw, rhp (Royals)

### DOUBLE-A DRAFT
Selection Price: $4,000

**ROUND ONE**
Selecting Club. Player, Pos., From
Mariners. Erik Plantenberg, lhp (Red Sox)
Mets. Rusty Silcox, rhp (Padres)
Red Sox. Ed Perozo, of (Mets)
Cubs. Jay Franklin, rhp (Rangers)
Astros. Victor Madrigal, rhp (Rangers)
Padres. Jason Kerr, lhp (Dodgers)
Cardinals. Larry Carter, rhp (Brewers)

**ROUND TWO**
Selecting Club. Player, Pos., From
Padres. Matt Kluge, c (Mariners)
Cardinals. Kerry Knox, lhp (Brewers)

**ROUND THREE**
Selecting Club. Player, Pos., From
Padres. Iggy Duran, 3b (Cardinals)
Cardinals. Craig Faulkner, c (Brewers)

# Late-Inning Homer Ends 25-Year Drought

**By GEORGE RORRER**

At the end of a season of turmoil in the American Association, the Iowa Cubs stood tall by winning the 1993 championship, their first in 25 years of trying.

Iowa and the Nashville Sounds took a thrilling best-of-7 championship series past the limit, with the Cubs winning the seventh game, 3-2, on a dramatic 11th-inning leadoff home run by outfielder Karl Rhodes.

Rhodes' shot, off Sounds righthander James Baldwin, gave series MVP Jim Bullinger the victory to go with two earlier saves. He pitched three scoreless innings in the deciding game.

It also gave the Chicago Cubs' top farm club the title and Windy City bragging rights against their White Sox counterparts. The parent clubs last met in a meaningful game in the 1906 World Series.

Iowa made the biggest turnaround in Association history, going from worst in 1992 (51-92) to first in the Western Division at 85-59. The I-Cubs finished five games ahead of fast-closing New Orleans to earn their first division title since 1973.

DAN ARNOLD

**Eddie Zambrano**

Slugging outfielder Eddie Zambrano (.303-32-115) became the first I-Cub to win the Mickey Mantle Award as the Association's regular season MVP.

Rhodes, who came to Iowa from Omaha in a July 29 trade involving Kansas City, the Chicago Cubs and New York Yankees, had a career year: .318-30-89. In the playoff against Nashville, he went 10-for-28 with three home runs.

Rhodes spent the first seven years of his career in the Houston Astros organization and had never hit more than four homers in a season. He signed with Kansas City as a free agent after Houston dropped him from its 40-man roster just prior to the 1993 season.

Manager of the Year Rick Renick's Nashville club won the Eastern Division crown in their first season of

STAN DENNY

**Karl Rhodes.** Iowa outfielder capped a heroic season with an 11th-inning home run.

affiliation with the White Sox, who switched from Vancouver of the Pacific Coast League after the 1992 season. The Sounds beat runner-up Buffalo by 10½ games.

Nashville led the league in team batting (.281) and pitching (3.88 ERA). Catcher Matt Merullo won the batting title at .332, while Rod Bolton had the top ERA (2.88), the highest winner since Pascual Perez's all-time league high of 3.79 in 1987.

Exciting prospects such as Nashville pitcher Jason Bere, Louisville outfielder Brian Jordan, Indianapolis third baseman Willie Greene, Iowa outfielder Kevin Roberson and Louisville pitcher Allen Watson passed through quickly on their way to the big leagues. In

## STANDINGS

| Page | EAST | W | L | PCT | GB | Manager | Attendance/Dates | Last Pennant |
|---|---|---|---|---|---|---|---|---|
| 73 | **Nashville Sounds (White Sox)** | 81 | 62 | .566 | — | Rick Renick | 438,745 (68) | None |
| 174 | **Buffalo Bisons (Pirates)** | 71 | 73 | .493 | 10 ½ | Doc Edwards | 1,058,620 (70) | None |
| 180 | **Louisville Redbirds (Cardinals)** | 68 | 76 | .472 | 13 ½ | Jack Krol | 643,833 (69) | 1985 |
| 86 | **Indianapolis Indians (Reds)** | 66 | 77 | .462 | 15 | Marc Bombard | 300,397 (68) | 1989 |

| Page | WEST | W | L | PCT | GB | Manager | Attendance/Dates | Last Pennant |
|---|---|---|---|---|---|---|---|---|
| 79 | **Iowa Cubs (Cubs)** | 85 | 59 | .590 | — | Marv Foley | 446,860 (68) | 1993 |
| 132 | **New Orleans Zephyrs (Brewers)** | 80 | 64 | .556 | 5 | Chris Bando | 161,846 (66) | None |
| 120 | **Omaha Royals (Royals)** | 70 | 74 | .486 | 15 | Jeff Cox | 384,972 (63) | 1990 |
| 205 | **Oklahoma City 89ers (Rangers)** | 54 | 90 | .375 | 31 | Bobby Jones | 364,673 (68) | 1992 |

**PLAYOFFS:** Iowa defeated Nashville, 4-3, in best-of-7 final.
**NOTE:** Team's individual batting, pitching and fielding statistics can be found on page indicated in lefthand column.

Baseball America polls, Jordan was named the league's Most Exciting Player and Best Prospect. Greene was named Rookie of the Year.

## Attendance Down Slightly

Off the field, there was turmoil. The I-Cubs kept going despite one of the most devastating floods in history, and other Association cities endured a summer of sweltering heat.

For the first time in four seasons, the Association failed to set a record for minor league attendance. The smallest of the three Triple-A leagues drew 3,799,946, led by Buffalo's 1,058,620. Overall, that's the fourth-highest league total of all time, exceeded only by the Association's 4,158,394 in 1992, 4,147,777 in 1991 and 4,061,717 in 1990.

A major factor in the decrease was the switch of the Milwaukee Brewers' top farm club, the Zephyrs, from Denver to New Orleans to make way for the National League expansion Colorado Rockies. Denver drew 347,615 in 1992, while New Orleans, playing temporarily in 5,000-seat Privateer Park on the University of New Orleans campus, attracted just 161,846.

Zephyrs owner John Dikeou searched high and low for a site to relocate his Triple-A franchise and didn't officially settle on New Orleans until little more than two months before the 1993 season began. He had to

**Matt Merullo.** Nashville catcher won American Association batting title with a .332 average.

get a special ruling from the National Association to move the franchise to New Orleans, whose territory already had been claimed by the Double-A Southern League.

Attendance was down in every Association city but Oklahoma City, which drew a club-record 364,673 although the defending champion 89ers struggled to a last-place 54-90 record.

For Buffalo, the attendance total was an unprecedented sixth straight one million-plus, but it was the Bisons' lowest total since their move to Pilot Field in 1988. It came in the year when Buffalo had hoped to be a National League expansion city, only to see franchises awarded to Miami and Denver.

Attendance should be back to normal by 1995 when New Orleans' new stadium is expected to be completed. New stadia also are in the planning phases for Indianapolis, Nashville and Oklahoma City.

## Pennant Fever

In the East, Buffalo and Louisville hung in the race with Nashville until August only to see the Sounds pull away. The Bisons' Russ Morman led league hitters most of the year, finishing fourth at .320. Buffalo righthander Roy Smith topped pitchers in victories with 15.

Louisville was within 2½ games of the Sounds as late as Aug. 5, but went 9-22 in August and had to beat Indianapolis on the final day of the season to avoid finishing last.

Indianapolis was not a factor in the race from June 1 on, finishing 15 games off the pace despite the hitting of Tim Costo (.326) and the relief pitching of lefthander Scott Ruskin (league-high 28 saves).

In the West, Omaha was 2½ games off **Steve Balboni**

Iowa's pace when Rhodes went to the I-Cubs. Omaha skidded to third place, 15 games behind.

New Orleans trailed by 14 games on June 3, and drew within three on Aug. 24 only to finish five back. Oklahoma City fell 10 games behind by May 11 and was no factor thereafter. Steve Balboni, 36, gave the 89ers their fourth consecutive home run title with his second straight, belting 36. His 108 RBIs were second to Zambrano's 115.

## LEAGUE CHAMPIONS

### Last 25 Years

| Year | Regular Season* | Pct. | Playoff |
|------|-----------------|------|---------|
| 1969 | Omaha (Royals) | .607 | None |
| 1970 | Omaha (Royals) | .529 | Omaha (Royals) |
| 1971 | Indianapolis (Reds) | .604 | Denver (Senators) |
| 1972 | Wichita (Cubs) | .621 | Evansville (Brewers) |
| 1973 | Iowa (White Sox) | .610 | Tulsa (Cardinals) |
| 1974 | Indianapolis (Reds) | .578 | Tulsa (Cardinals) |
| 1975 | Denver (White Sox) | .596 | Evansville (Tigers) |
| 1976 | Denver (Expos) | .632 | Denver (Expos) |
| 1977 | Omaha (Royals) | .563 | Denver (Expos) |
| 1978 | Indianapolis (Reds) | .578 | Omaha (Royals) |
| 1979 | Evansville (Tigers) | .574 | Evansville (Tigers) |
| 1980 | Denver (Expos) | .676 | Springfield (Cardinals) |
| 1981 | Omaha (Royals) | .581 | Denver (Expos) |
| 1982 | Indianapolis (Reds) | .551 | Indianapolis (Reds) |
| 1983 | Louisville (Cardinals) | .578 | Denver (White Sox) |
| 1984 | Indianapolis (Expos) | .591 | Louisville (Cardinals) |
| 1985 | Oklahoma City (Rangers) | .556 | Louisville (Cardinals) |
| 1986 | Indianapolis (Expos) | .563 | Indianapolis (Expos) |
| 1987 | Denver (Brewers) | .564 | Indianapolis (Expos) |
| 1988 | Indianapolis (Expos) | .627 | Indianapolis (Expos) |
| 1989 | Indianapolis (Expos) | .596 | Indianapolis (Expos) |
| 1990 | Omaha (Royals) | .589 | Omaha (Royals) |
| 1991 | Buffalo (Pirates) | .566 | Denver (Brewers) |
| 1992 | Buffalo (Pirates) | .604 | Oklahoma City (Rangers) |
| 1993 | Iowa (Cubs) | .590 | Iowa (Cubs) |

*Best overall record

# AMERICAN ASSOCIATION
## 1993 BATTING, PITCHING STATISTICS

### CLUB BATTING

| | AVG | G | AB | R | H | 2B | 3B | HR | BB | SO | SB |
|---|---|---|---|---|---|---|---|---|---|---|---|
| Nashville | .281 | 143 | 4841 | 731 | 1362 | 270 | 31 | 141 | 475 | 863 | 108 |
| New Orleans | .276 | 144 | 4712 | 685 | 1300 | 274 | 33 | 95 | 500 | 694 | 118 |
| Omaha | .274 | 144 | 4787 | 710 | 1311 | 258 | 33 | 154 | 477 | 715 | 130 |
| Iowa | .270 | 144 | 4864 | 706 | 1312 | 291 | 22 | 148 | 445 | 895 | 100 |
| Louisville | .268 | 144 | 4884 | 639 | 1308 | 256 | 32 | 139 | 412 | 878 | 40 |
| Indianapolis | .267 | 143 | 4761 | 644 | 1270 | 295 | 31 | 127 | 440 | 845 | 77 |
| Buffalo | .261 | 144 | 4781 | 684 | 1246 | 263 | 39 | 142 | 450 | 869 | 75 |
| Oklahoma City | .257 | 144 | 4797 | 656 | 1235 | 235 | 45 | 110 | 483 | 891 | 51 |

### CLUB PITCHING

| | ERA | G | CG | SHO | SV | IP | H | R | ER | BB | SO |
|---|---|---|---|---|---|---|---|---|---|---|---|
| Nashville | 3.88 | 143 | 10 | 4 | 40 | 1250 | 1182 | 631 | 539 | 448 | 910 |
| New Orleans | 4.05 | 144 | 19 | 6 | 37 | 1250 | 1226 | 638 | 562 | 433 | 857 |
| Louisville | 4.25 | 144 | 13 | 5 | 31 | 1256 | 1311 | 671 | 593 | 432 | 815 |
| Iowa | 4.27 | 144 | 7 | 10 | 42 | 1278 | 1285 | 656 | 607 | 482 | 930 |
| Buffalo | 4.32 | 144 | 9 | 7 | 39 | 1248 | 1322 | 667 | 599 | 443 | 677 |
| Indianapolis | 4.34 | 143 | 8 | 5 | 37 | 1231 | 1248 | 686 | 594 | 534 | 880 |
| Omaha | 4.47 | 144 | 13 | 11 | 30 | 1244 | 1289 | 679 | 618 | 392 | 817 |
| Oklahoma City | 5.33 | 144 | 8 | 1 | 30 | 1249 | 1481 | 827 | 740 | 518 | 764 |

### CLUB FIELDING

| | PCT | PO | A | E | DP | | PCT | PO | A | E | DP |
|---|---|---|---|---|---|---|---|---|---|---|---|
| Iowa | .980 | 3835 | 1648 | 114 | 166 | Buffalo | .976 | 3745 | 1668 | 134 | 186 |
| Louisville | .979 | 3769 | 1603 | 115 | 141 | Oklahoma City | .975 | 3748 | 1568 | 135 | 145 |
| New Orleans | .978 | 3750 | 1538 | 121 | 143 | Nashville | .973 | 3751 | 1621 | 148 | 126 |
| Omaha | .977 | 3732 | 1572 | 127 | 159 | Indianapolis | .971 | 3692 | 1432 | 152 | 117 |

**Brian Jordan**
No. 1 Prospect

STAN DENNY

**Roy Smith**
15-11, 4.13

### INDIVIDUAL BATTING LEADERS
(Minimum 389 Plate Appearances)

| | AVG | G | AB | R | H | 2B | 3B | HR | RBI | BB | SO | SB |
|---|---|---|---|---|---|---|---|---|---|---|---|---|
| Merullo, Matt, Nashville | .332 | 103 | 352 | 50 | 117 | 30 | 1 | 12 | 65 | 28 | 47 | 0 |
| Costo, Tim, Indianapolis | .326 | 106 | 362 | 49 | 118 | 30 | 2 | 11 | 57 | 22 | 60 | 3 |
| Morman, Russ, Buffalo | .320 | 119 | 409 | 79 | 131 | 34 | 2 | 22 | 77 | 48 | 59 | 0 |
| Rhodes, Karl, Omaha-Iowa | .318 | 123 | 490 | 112 | 156 | 43 | 3 | 30 | 89 | 58 | 82 | 16 |
| Caceres, Edgar, NO | .317 | 114 | 420 | 73 | 133 | 20 | 2 | 5 | 45 | 35 | 39 | 7 |
| Martin, Norberto, Nash | .309 | 137 | 580 | 87 | 179 | 21 | 6 | 9 | 74 | 26 | 59 | 31 |
| Ducey, Rob, Okla. City | .303 | 105 | 389 | 68 | 118 | 17 | 10 | 17 | 56 | 46 | 97 | 17 |
| Zambrano, Eddie, Iowa | .303 | 133 | 469 | 95 | 142 | 29 | 2 | 32 | 115 | 54 | 93 | 10 |
| Shumpert, Terry, Omaha | .300 | 111 | 413 | 70 | 124 | 29 | 1 | 14 | 59 | 41 | 62 | 36 |
| Lockhart, Keith, Louisville | .300 | 132 | 467 | 66 | 140 | 24 | 3 | 13 | 68 | 60 | 43 | 3 |

### INDIVIDUAL PITCHING LEADERS
(Minimum 115 Innings)

| | W | L | ERA | G | GS | CG | SV | IP | H | R | ER | BB | SO |
|---|---|---|---|---|---|---|---|---|---|---|---|---|---|
| Bolton, Rod, Nashville | 10 | 1 | 2.88 | 18 | 16 | 1 | 1 | 116 | 108 | 40 | 37 | 37 | 75 |
| Watson, Allen, Louisville | 5 | 4 | 2.91 | 17 | 17 | 2 | 0 | 121 | 101 | 46 | 39 | 31 | 86 |
| Reed, Rick, Omaha-Okla. City | 12 | 7 | 3.32 | 24 | 24 | 4 | 0 | 163 | 159 | 68 | 60 | 16 | 79 |
| Campos, Frank, Nashville | 7 | 5 | 3.55 | 19 | 19 | 2 | 0 | 117 | 104 | 60 | 46 | 58 | 86 |
| Anderson, Mike, Indianapolis | 10 | 6 | 3.75 | 23 | 23 | 2 | 0 | 151 | 150 | 73 | 63 | 56 | 111 |
| Sparks, Steve, New Orleans | 9 | 13 | 3.84 | 29 | 28 | 7 | 0 | 180 | 174 | 89 | 77 | 80 | 104 |
| Schrenk, Steve, Nashville | 6 | 8 | 3.90 | 21 | 20 | 0 | 0 | 122 | 117 | 61 | 53 | 47 | 78 |
| McAndrew, Jamie, NO | 11 | 6 | 3.94 | 27 | 25 | 5 | 0 | 167 | 172 | 78 | 73 | 45 | 97 |
| Ilsley, Blaise, Iowa | 12 | 7 | 3.94 | 48 | 16 | 0 | 4 | 135 | 147 | 61 | 59 | 32 | 78 |
| Trachsel, Steve, Iowa | 13 | 6 | 3.96 | 27 | 26 | 1 | 0 | 171 | 170 | 78 | 75 | 45 | 135 |

## DEPARTMENT LEADERS

### BATTING
| | | |
|---|---|---|
| R | Karl Rhodes, Omaha-Iowa | 112 |
| H | Norberto Martin, Nashville | 179 |
| TB | Karl Rhodes, Omaha-Iowa | 295 |
| 2B | Karl Rhodes, Omaha-Iowa | 43 |
| 3B | 2 tied at | 10 |
| HR | Steve Balboni, Ok.la City | 36 |
| RBI | Eddie Zambrano, Iowa | 115 |
| SH | Terry Shumpert, Omaha | 21 |
| SF | Larry Sheets, New Orleans | 10 |
| BB | Bob Hamelin, Omaha | 82 |
| IBB | Eddie Zambrano, Iowa | 11 |
| HBP | Drew Denson, Nashville | 23 |
| SO | Chris Cron, Nashville | 114 |
| SB | Terry Shumpert, Omaha | 36 |
| CS | Scott Bullett, Buffalo | 17 |
| GIDP | Drew Denson, Nashville | 22 |
| OB% | Mike Huff, Nashville | .411 |
| SL% | Karl Rhodes, Omaha-Iowa | .602 |

### PITCHING
| | | |
|---|---|---|
| G | David Lynch, Indianapolis | 59 |
| GS | 3 tied at | 28 |
| CG | Steve Sparks, New Orleans | 7 |
| ShO | Rick Reed, Oklahoma City | 2 |
| GF | Brian Drahman, Nashville | 50 |
| Sv | Scott Ruskin, Indianapolis | 28 |
| W | Roy Smith, Buffalo | 15 |
| L | Terry Burrows, Okla. City | 15 |
| IP | Steve Sparks, New Orleans | 180 |
| H | Bill Brennan, Iowa | 180 |
| R | Terry Burrows, Okla. City | 107 |
| ER | Terry Burrows, Okla. City | 98 |
| HR | Ross Powell, Indianapolis | 27 |
| BB | Steve Sparks, New Orleans | 80 |
| HB | Bill Brennan, Iowa | 15 |
| SO | Bill Brennan, Iowa | 143 |
| WP | Bill Brennan, Iowa | 23 |
| Bk | 2 tied at | 5 |

### FIELDING
| | | |
|---|---|---|
| C AVG | Matt Walbeck, Iowa | .998 |
| E | Ray Stephens, Okla. City | 11 |
| 1B AVG | Bob Hamelin, Omaha | .991 |
| E | 2 tied at | 11 |
| 2B AVG | Greg Smith, Iowa | .983 |
| E | Norberto Martin, Nash. | 18 |
| 3B AVG | Craig Worthington, Iowa | .940 |
| E | Willie Greene, Indy. | 23 |
| SS AVG | Lawrence Hanlon, Okla. City | .961 |
| E | Esteban Beltre, Nashville | 30 |
| OF AVG | Mike Kingery, Omaha | .996 |
| E | Skeets Thomas, Louisville | 9 |

## HONOR ROLL

### OFFICIAL ALL-STAR TEAM
| | |
|---|---|
| C | Matt Walbeck, Iowa |
| 1B | Bob Hamelin, Omaha |
| 2B | Norberto Martin, Nashville |
| 3B | Keith Lockhart, Louisville |
| SS | Esteban Beltre, Nashville |
| OF | Rob Ducey, Oklahoma City |
| | Karl Rhodes, Omaha-Iowa |
| | Eddie Zambrano, Iowa |
| DH | Steve Balboni, Oklahoma City |
| RHP | Roy Smith, Buffalo |
| LHP | Blaise Ilsley, Iowa |
| RP | Tony Menendez, Buffalo |

**MVP:** Eddie Zambrano, Iowa
**Manager:** Rick Renick, Nashville

### TOP 10 PROSPECTS
(Selected by league managers)
1. Brian Jordan, of, Louisville
2. Jason Bere, rhp, Nashville
3. Allen Watson, lhp, Louisville
4. Willie Greene, 3b, Indianapolis
5. Karl Rhodes, of, Omaha-Iowa
6. Kevin Roberson, of, Iowa
7. Matt Walbeck, c, Iowa
8. Midre Cummings, of, Buffalo
9. John Roper, rhp, Indianapolis
10. Steve Trachsel, rhp, Iowa

# YEAR-BY-YEAR LEADERS: 1946-93

## AMERICAN ASSOCIATION

| Year | Batting Average | | Home Runs | | RBIs | | Wins | | ERA | | Strikeouts | |
|---|---|---|---|---|---|---|---|---|---|---|---|---|
| 1946 | Sibby Sisti, Ind. | .343 | Jerome Witte, Toledo | 46 | John McCarthy, Minn. | 122 | 3 tied at | 15 | Al Widmar, Lou. | 2.43 | Fred Sanford, Toledo | 154 |
| 1947 | Heinz Becker, Milw. | .363 | Carden Gillenwater, Milw. | 23 | Cliff Mapes, K.C. | 117 | Clem Dreisewerd, Lou. | 18 | Clem Dreiseward, Lou. | 2.15 | Phil Haugstad, St. Paul | 145 |
| 1948 | Glenn McQuillen, Tol. | .329 | Mike Natisin, Columbus | 30 | Les Fleming, Ind. | 143 | Bob Malloy, Ind. | 21 | Glenn Elliott, Milw. | 3.76 | John McCall, St. Paul | 149 |
| 1949 | Tom Wright, Lou. | .368 | Charles Workman, Ind. | 41 | Froilan Fernandez, Ind. | 128 | 2 tied at | 22 | Mel Queen, Ind. | 2.57 | Mel Queen, Ind. | 178 |
| 1950 | Bob Addis, Milw. | .323 | Lou Limmer, St. Paul | 29 | Lou Limmer, St. Paul | 111 | Harvey Haddix, Columbus | 18 | Harvey Haddix, Columbus | 2.70 | Harvey Haddix, Col. | 160 |
| 1951 | Harry Walker, Columbus | .393 | Harold Gilbert, Minn. | 29 | George Crowe, Milw. | 119 | Jim Atkins, Louisville | 18 | Ernie Johnson, Milw. | 2.62 | Bob Weisler, K.C. | 162 |
| 1952 | Dave Pope, Ind. | .352 | Bill Skowron, K.C. | 31 | Bill Skowron, K.C. | 134 | Ed Erautt, K.C. | 21 | Don Liddle, Milw. | 2.70 | Don Liddle, Milw. | 159 |
| 1953 | Vic Power, K.C. | .349 | George Wilson, Minn. | 34 | Wally Post, Ind. | 120 | Gene Conley, Toledo | 23 | Gene Conley, Toledo | 2.90 | Gene Conley, Toledo | 211 |
| 1954 | Hal Smith, Columbus | .350 | Rocky Colavito, Ind. | 38 | George Crowe, Toledo | 128 | Herb Score, Ind. | 22 | Herb Score, Ind. | 2.62 | Herb Score, Ind. | 330 |
| 1955 | Rance Pless, Minn. | .337 | Marv Throneberry, Den. | 36 | Marv Throneberry, Den. | 117 | Al Worthington, Minn. | 19 | Willard Schmidt, Omaha | 2.56 | Jerry Casale, Lou. | 186 |
| 1956 | Charlie Peete, Omaha | .350 | Marv Throneberry, Den. | 42 | Marv Throneberry, Den. | 145 | 2 tied at | 15 | John Gray, Ind. | 2.72 | Ted Abernathy, Lou. | 212 |
| 1957 | Norm Siebern, Denver | .349 | Marv Throneberry, Den. | 40 | Marv Throneberry, Den. | 124 | Carlton Willey, Wichita | 21 | Frank Barnes, Omaha | 2.41 | Stan Williams, St. Paul | 223 |
| 1958 | Gordon Windhorn, Den. | .328 | John Callison, Ind. | 29 | Earl Hersh, Wichita | 98 | John Gabler, Denver | 19 | Jerry Davie, Charleston | 2.45 | Bob Blaylock, Omaha | 193 |
| 1959 | Luis Marquez, Dallas | .345 | Ron Jackson, Ind. | 30 | Ron Jackson, Ind. | 119 | 2 tied at | 18 | Marion Fricano, Dallas | 2.02 | Bob Bruce, Charleston | 177 |
| 1960 | Larry Osborne, Denver | .342 | Larry Osborne, Denver | 34 | 2 tied at | 119 | Jim Golden, St.Paul | 20 | Jim Golden, St.Paul | 2.32 | Dick Tomanek, Dall.-Ft.W. | 172 |
| 1961 | Don Wert, Denver | .328 | Cliff Cook, Ind. | 32 | Cliff Cook, Ind. | 119 | Don Rudolph, Ind. | 18 | Federico Olivo, Lou. | 2.66 | Charley Spell, Omaha | 164 |
| 1962 | Tom McCraw, Ind. | .326 | Leo Burke, Dall.-Ft.W. | 27 | Jim Koranda, Ind. | 103 | Nick Willhite, Omaha | 18 | Connie Grob, Louis. | 2.86 | Federico Olivo, Lou. | 151 |
| 1963 | DID NOT OPERATE | | | | | | | | | | | |
| 1964 | DID NOT OPERATE | | | | | | | | | | | |
| 1965 | DID NOT OPERATE | | | | | | | | | | | |
| 1966 | DID NOT OPERATE | | | | | | | | | | | |
| 1967 | DID NOT OPERATE | | | | | | | | | | | |
| 1968 | DID NOT OPERATE | | | | | | | | | | | |
| 1969 | Bernie Carbo, Ind. | .359 | Danny Walton, Okla. City | 25 | Danny Walton, Okla. City | 110 | 2 tied at | 13 | Ron Cook, Okla. City | 3.11 | Jerry Reuss, Tulsa | 151 |
| 1970 | Chris Chambliss, Wich. | .342 | Cotton Nash, Denver | 33 | Richie Scheinblum, Wich. | 84 | Francisco Carlos, Den. | 13 | Ross Grimsley, Ind. | 2.73 | Vida Blue, Iowa | 165 |
| 1971 | Richie Scheinblum, Den. | .388 | Bill McNulty, Iowa | 27 | Richie Scheinblum, Den. | 108 | Dick Estelle, Evans. | 13 | J.R. Richard, Okla. City | 2.45 | J.R. Richard, Okla. City | 202 |
| 1972 | Gene Locklear, Ind. | .325 | Bob Hansen, Evans. | 25 | Roe Skidmore, Ind. | 89 | Lloyd Gladden, Evans. | 15 | Joe Decker, Wichita | 2.27 | Steve Busby, Omaha | 221 |
| 1973 | Jim Dwyer, Tulsa | .387 | Cliff Johnson, Denver | 33 | Cliff Johnson, Denver | 117 | Mark Littell, Omaha | 16 | Mark Littell, Omaha | 2.51 | Lowell Palmer, Okla. City | 203 |
| 1974 | Keith Hernandez, Tulsa | .351 | Adrian Garrett, Wich. | 26 | Lamar Johnson, Iowa | 96 | Jim Kern, Okla. City | 17 | Ray Bare, Tulsa | 2.34 | Jim Kern, Okla. City | 220 |
| 1975 | Lamar Johnson, Denver | .336 | Hector Cruz, Tulsa | 29 | Hector Cruz, Tulsa | 116 | Steve Dunning, Denver | 15 | Pat Zachny, Ind. | 2.44 | Steve Dunning, Denver | 139 |
| 1976 | Mike Easler, Tulsa | .352 | Roger Freed, Denver | 42 | Roger Freed, Denver | 102 | 2 tied at | 14 | Joe Henderson, Ind. | 2.31 | Randy Lerch, OklaCity | 152 |
| 1977 | Jim Dwyer, Wichita | .332 | Frank Ortenzio, Den. | 40 | Frank Ortenzio, Den. | 126 | Gary Lance, Omaha | 16 | Jack Kucek, Iowa | 2.54 | Larry Landreth, Den. | 134 |
| 1978 | Dane Iorg, Spring. | .371 | Champ Summers, Ind. | 34 | Champ Summers, Ind. | 124 | 2 tied at | 14 | Jack Kucek, Iowa | 2.47 | Dan Warthen, Okla. City | 144 |
| 1979 | Keith Smith, Spring. | .350 | Karl Pagel, Wichita | 39 | Karl Pagel, Wichita | 123 | Dewey Robinson, Iowa | 13 | Bruce Berenyi, Ind. | 2.82 | Bruce Berenyi, Ind. | 136 |
| 1980 | Tim Raines, Denver | .354 | Randy Bass, Denver | 37 | Randy Bass, Denver | 143 | Steve Ratzer, Denver | 15 | Alan Olmstead, Spring. | 2.77 | Bruce Berenyi, Ind. | 121 |
| 1981 | Mike Richardt, Wich. | .354 | George Bjorkman, Spring. | 28 | Dan Briggs, Denver | 110 | Bryn Smith, Denver | 15 | Larry Pashnick, Evans. | 2.89 | Dave LaPoint, Spring. | 129 |
| 1982 | Roy Johnson, Wichita | .367 | Ken Phelps, Wichita | 46 | Ken Phelps, Wichita | 141 | Ralph Citarella, Lou. | 15 | Jay Howell, Iowa | 2.36 | Mike Smithson, Den. | 144 |
| 1983 | Mike Stenhouse, Wich. | .355 | Carmelo Martinez, Iowa | 31 | Jim Adduci, Lou. | 101 | Fernando Arroyo, Denver | 14 | Craig Eaton, Evans. | 2.64 | Greg Harris, Ind. | 146 |
| 1984 | Tom Dunbar, Okla. City | .337 | Joe Hicks, Iowa | 37 | Alan Knicely, Wich. | 126 | Reggie Patterson, Iowa | 14 | Chris Welsh, Ind. | 3.01 | Tom Browning, Wich. | 160 |
| 1985 | Scotty Madison, Nash. | .341 | Dave Hostetler, Ind.-Iowa | 29 | Dave Hostetler, Ind.-Iowa | 89 | Bill Long, Buffalo | 13 | Steve Farr, Omaha | 2.02 | Todd Worrell, Lou. | 126 |
| 1986 | Bruce Fields, Nash. | .368 | Lloyd McClendon, Den. | 24 | Jim Lindeman, Louis. | 96 | Pete Filson, Buffalo | 14 | Pete Filson, Buffalo | 2.27 | Jack Lazorko, Nash. | 119 |
| 1987 | Dallas Williams, Ind. | .357 | Brad Komminsk, Den. | 22 | Wade Rowdon, Iowa | 113 | Bill Taylor, Okla. City | 15 | Pascual Perez, Ind. | 3.79 | Sergio Valdez, Ind. | 128 |
| 1988 | LaVel Freeman, Denver | .318 | Van Snider, Nash. | 23 | 2 tied at | 87 | Dave Johnson, Buffalo | 15 | Dom Taylor, Buffalo | 2.14 | Norm Charlton, Nash. | 161 |
| 1989 | Junior Noboa, Ind. | .340 | Greg Vaughn, Denver | 26 | Greg Vaughn, Denver | 92 | 4 tied at | 13 | Rich Thompson, Ind. | 2.06 | Mark Gardner, Ind. | 175 |
| 1990 | Mark Ryal, Buffalo | .334 | Juan Gonzalez, Okla. City | 29 | Juan Gonzalez, Okla. City | 101 | Chris Hammond, Nash. | 15 | Chris Hammond, Nash. | 2.17 | Chris Hammond, Nash. | 149 |
| 1991 | Jim Olander, Den. | .325 | Dean Palmer, Okla. City | 22 | Tim McIntosh, Denver | 91 | Rick Reed, Buffalo | 14 | Rick Reed, Buffalo | 2.15 | Cal Eldred, Denver | 168 |
| 1992 | Jim Tatum, Denver | .329 | Steve Balboni, Okla. City | 30 | Steve Balboni, Okla. City | 104 | 5 tied at | 12 | Dennis Moeller, Omaha | 2.46 | Mark Kiefer, Denver | 145 |
| 1993 | Matt Merullo, Nash. | .332 | Steve Balboni, Okla. City | 36 | Eddie Zambrano, Iowa | 115 | Roy Smith, Buffalo | 15 | Rod Bolton, Nashville | 2.88 | Bill Brennan, Iowa | 143 |

# Charlotte Wins Battle of Expansion Clubs

**By TIM PEARRELL**

The Charlotte Knights and Ottawa Lynx injected a lot of cold air into the theory of expansion.

The Knights and Lynx were the International League's two expansion teams in 1993, but their balloons were anything but tethered to the bottom of the standings. Both made the playoffs, with Charlotte sweeping the Western Division title and Governors' Cup.

Charlotte, stocked with a combination of outstanding Cleveland Indians prospects and a corps of veterans, outdueled Richmond and Columbus in the ultra-competitive West and finished with the top record (86-55) in the league.

It was the second straight Triple-A championship for Cleveland, whose top farm club never had won a postseason title prior to 1992. Indians farm teams posted a .579 winning percentage, the highest in professional baseball in 1993.

The West boasted the league's three best teams. Richmond's "Great Eight," trumpeted as one of the finest collections of prospects ever assembled, slugged it out with the Knights before a late-season collapse on a road trip left the Braves in a chase mode.

Richmond finished 80-62 but had to get some help from Toledo in the final two games of the season to even make the playoffs. Columbus, with several of the same players who helped the Clippers to a 95-win season in 1992, finished just out of the playoff picture at 78-61.

Charlotte and Richmond dominated most statistical categories.

## Thome Wins Batting Crown

Charlotte third baseman Jim Thome, re-establishing himself after a disappointing 1992 campaign that led to his demotion from Cleveland, won the batting title with a .332 average. Richmond's Tony Tarasco was second at .330, and R-Braves shortstop Chipper Jones, the league's top rookie, was third at .325.

Thome, named the league's top prospect in a poll of

**Jim Thome.** Charlotte third baseman led IL in batting (.332) and RBIs (102).

managers, took two-thirds of the Triple Crown by also claiming the RBI title (102). He was third in home runs (25), despite missing the last month of the season when he was recalled by Cleveland.

Charlotte DH Sam Horn amassed the highest tater total in the minors since 1987 by blasting 38. He smacked four more in the playoffs.

Richmond pitcher Mike Birkbeck nearly won pitching's Triple Crown. The veteran righthander tied with Charlotte's Chad Ogea as the top winner (13) and tied with Toledo's John DeSilva as the top strikeout artist (136). Birkbeck (3.11) was second to Rochester's Kevin McGehee (2.96) for the ERA title.

Ottawa, with professional baseball for the first time since 1954, provided its fans with a lot of "Eh?" mate-

R&R SPORTS GROUP

## STANDINGS

| Page | EAST | W | L | PCT | GB | Manager(s) | Attendance/Dates | Last Pennant |
|---|---|---|---|---|---|---|---|---|
| 55 | Rochester Red Wings (Orioles) | 74 | 67 | .525 | — | Bob Miscik | 361,676 (69) | 1990 |
| 144 | Ottawa Lynx (Expos) | 73 | 69 | .514 | 1½ | Mike Quade | 663,926 (68) | None |
| 168 | Scranton/W-B Red Barons (Phils) | 62 | 80 | .437 | 12½ | George Culver | 531,620 (67) | None |
| 61 | Pawtucket Red Sox (Red Sox) | 60 | 82 | .423 | 14½ | Buddy Bailey | 466,428 (71) | 1984 |
| 211 | Syracuse Chiefs (Blue Jays) | 59 | 82 | .418 | 15 | Nick Leyva, Bob Didier | 262,760 (64) | 1976 |

| Page | WEST | W | L | PCT | GB | Manager | Attendance/Dates | Last Pennant |
|---|---|---|---|---|---|---|---|---|
| 92 | Charlotte Knights (Indians) | 86 | 55 | .610 | — | Charlie Manuel | 403,029 (68) | 1993 |
| 49 | Richmond Braves (Braves) | 80 | 62 | .563 | 6½ | Grady Little | 533,076 (68) | 1989 |
| 150 | Columbus Clippers (Yankees) | 78 | 62 | .557 | 7½ | Stump Merrill | 580,570 (70) | 1992 |
| 156 | Norfolk Tides (Mets) | 70 | 71 | .496 | 16 | Clint Hurdle | 529,708 (67) | 1985 |
| 103 | Toledo Mud Hens (Tigers) | 65 | 77 | .458 | 21½ | Joe Sparks | 274,047 (67) | 1967 |

**PLAYOFFS—Division:** Rochester defeated Ottawa, 3-2, and Charlotte defeated Richmond, 3-1, in best-of-5 series. **Finals:** Charlotte defeated Rochester, 3-2, in best-of-5 series.

**NOTE:** Team's individual batting, pitching and fielding statistics can be found on page indicated in lefthand column.

rial by nearly overtaking Rochester at the wire in the Eastern Division. The Red Wings, however, held on by winning the last two games of the season against the Lynx, then took their semifinal series, three games to two. Charlotte eliminated Richmond in four games in the other semifinal.

The Knights went on to beat the Red Wings, 3-2, in the best-of-5 Governors' Cup final. Charlotte won the deciding game 6-1 at Rochester in a game that was twice delayed by rain. Ogea, who absorbed a 7-3 loss in Game One, rebounded with six strong innings, allowing just one run on five hits in the finale. Horn provided most of the offensive support with a three-run homer in the fourth inning. Horn also had a three-run blast in the Knights' 8-2 victory in Game Three.

With two new teams and two new stadiums—Norfolk unveiled picturesque Harbor Park on the Elizabeth River, and Ottawa opened Stade d'Ottawa — the league attracted a record 4,723,236 fans, obliterating the old mark of 3,055,012 set in 1992.

Ottawa led the way with an average of 9,761, including 45 sellouts in 71 openings. Five clubs—Ottawa, Columbus, Scranton/Wilkes-Barre, Norfolk and Richmond—drew more than 500,000 through the turnstiles.

TOM DiPACE

**Chipper Jones** and **Javy Lopez.** Richmond's twosome hit .325 and .305, respectively, to headline an impressive Richmond lineup.

## Three No-Hitters

Other highlights of the 1993 season:

■ Syracuse's Tim Brown threw a seven-inning perfect game against Toledo. Brown was 1-4, 5.02 at the time and had allowed 14 runs in his previous 11 innings.

■ Scranton/Wilkes-Barre's Tyler Green fired a seven-inning no-hitter against Ottawa.

■ Ottawa's Chris Nabholz combined with Bruce Walton to no-hit Richmond. Nabholz, pitching on three days' rest, left after eight innings after reaching his 80-pitch limit.

■ Norfolk's Tides were caught on "radar" by the Federal Communications Commission and tagged with an $8,000 fine for operating a radar gun without a license.

■ Even the stingiest ballparks couldn't contain a significant number of sluggers throughout the league. The 10 teams, led by Charlotte's 185 and Richmond's 161, averaged more than 118 home runs, up from 104 in 1992. The league also averaged 33 more runs per team.

DAN ARNOLD

**Aaron Sele.** Pawtucket righthander's stay was brief (14 starts) but he left his mark: 8-2, 2.19.

## LEAGUE CHAMPIONS

### Last 25 Years

| Year | Regular Season* | Pct. | Playoff |
|------|-----------------|------|---------|
| 1969 | Tidewater (Mets) | .563 | Syracuse (Yankees) |
| 1970 | Syracuse (Yankees) | .600 | Syracuse (Yankees) |
| 1971 | Rochester (Orioles) | .614 | Rochester (Orioles) |
| 1972 | Louisville (Red Sox) | .563 | Tidewater (Mets) |
| 1973 | Charleston (Pirates) | .586 | Pawtucket (Red Sox) |
| 1974 | Memphis (Expos) | .613 | Rochester (Orioles) |
| 1975 | Tidewater (Mets) | .607 | Tidewater (Mets) |
| 1976 | Rochester (Orioles) | .638 | Syracuse (Yankees) |
| 1977 | Pawtucket (Red Sox) | .571 | Charleston (Astros) |
| 1978 | Charleston (Astros) | .607 | Richmond (Braves) |
| 1979 | Columbus (Yankees) | .612 | Columbus (Yankees) |
| 1980 | Columbus (Yankees) | .593 | Columbus (Yankees) |
| 1981 | Columbus (Yankees) | .633 | Columbus (Yankees) |
| 1982 | Richmond (Braves) | .590 | Tidewater (Mets) |
| 1983 | Columbus (Yankees) | .593 | Tidewater (Mets) |
| 1984 | Columbus (Yankees) | .590 | Pawtucket (Red Sox) |
| 1985 | Syracuse (Blue Jays) | .564 | Tidewater (Mets) |
| 1986 | Richmond (Braves) | .571 | Richmond (Braves) |
| 1987 | Tidewater (Mets) | .579 | Columbus (Yankees) |
| 1988 | Tidewater (Mets) | .546 | Rochester (Orioles) |
|      | Rochester (Orioles) | .546 | |
| 1989 | Syracuse (Blue Jays) | .572 | Richmond (Braves) |
| 1990 | Rochester (Orioles) | .614 | Rochester (Orioles) |
| 1991 | Columbus (Yankees) | .590 | Columbus (Yankees) |
| 1992 | Columbus (Yankees) | .660 | Columbus (Yankees) |
| 1993 | Charlotte (Indians) | .610 | Charlotte (Indians) |

*Best overall record

# INTERNATIONAL LEAGUE
## 1993 BATTING, PITCHING STATISTICS

### CLUB BATTING

| | AVG | G | AB | R | H | 2B | 3B | HR | BB | SO | SB |
|---|---|---|---|---|---|---|---|---|---|---|---|
| Charlotte | .283 | 141 | 4852 | 769 | 1371 | 245 | 40 | 185 | 456 | 886 | 58 |
| Richmond | .277 | 142 | 4827 | 746 | 1335 | 236 | 49 | 161 | 467 | 966 | 112 |
| Rochester | .265 | 142 | 4844 | 718 | 1283 | 258 | 41 | 130 | 500 | 994 | 92 |
| Ottawa | .264 | 142 | 4679 | 649 | 1233 | 229 | 32 | 84 | 531 | 925 | 120 |
| Columbus | .264 | 141 | 4651 | 693 | 1228 | 267 | 38 | 139 | 536 | 962 | 105 |
| Toledo | .258 | 142 | 4677 | 611 | 1205 | 225 | 37 | 111 | 410 | 816 | 158 |
| Scranton/W-B. | .256 | 142 | 4758 | 603 | 1218 | 260 | 37 | 89 | 417 | 727 | 97 |
| Syracuse | .256 | 142 | 4660 | 564 | 1194 | 213 | 48 | 100 | 342 | 970 | 67 |
| Norfolk | .253 | 141 | 4680 | 537 | 1182 | 190 | 49 | 80 | 426 | 772 | 154 |
| Pawtucket | .249 | 142 | 4766 | 566 | 1188 | 200 | 21 | 108 | 404 | 952 | 81 |

### CLUB PITCHING

| | ERA | G | CG | SHO | SV | IP | H | R | ER | BB | SO |
|---|---|---|---|---|---|---|---|---|---|---|---|
| Ottawa | 3.65 | 142 | 8 | 10 | 33 | 1232 | 1211 | 586 | 500 | 402 | 844 |
| Richmond | 3.74 | 142 | 4 | 8 | 33 | 1235 | 1209 | 606 | 513 | 456 | 1024 |
| Norfolk | 3.77 | 141 | 17 | 9 | 36 | 1247 | 1276 | 610 | 522 | 357 | 845 |
| Charlotte | 3.94 | 141 | 13 | 5 | 41 | 1239 | 1228 | 635 | 543 | 368 | 861 |
| Rochester | 4.04 | 141 | 9 | 8 | 37 | 1249 | 1249 | 633 | 560 | 496 | 965 |
| Scranton/W-B. | 4.14 | 142 | 13 | 7 | 27 | 1240 | 1198 | 649 | 571 | 465 | 912 |
| Columbus | 4.37 | 141 | 4 | 9 | 39 | 1227 | 1263 | 668 | 595 | 527 | 819 |
| Syracuse | 4.39 | 142 | 10 | 6 | 27 | 1221 | 1238 | 684 | 595 | 485 | 882 |
| Pawtucket | 4.43 | 142 | 13 | 9 | 34 | 1244 | 1285 | 699 | 612 | 479 | 911 |
| Toledo | 4.53 | 142 | 10 | 2 | 28 | 1219 | 1280 | 686 | 613 | 454 | 907 |

### CLUB FIELDING

| | PCT | PO | A | E | DP | | PCT | PO | A | E | DP |
|---|---|---|---|---|---|---|---|---|---|---|---|
| Charlotte | .975 | 3718 | 1558 | 136 | 130 | Ottawa | .973 | 3696 | 1575 | 147 | 120 |
| Columbus | .975 | 3680 | 1556 | 134 | 158 | Scranton/W-B. | .972 | 3721 | 1393 | 147 | 107 |
| Norfolk | .974 | 3742 | 1605 | 144 | 167 | Syracuse | .971 | 3663 | 1503 | 153 | 130 |
| Rochester | .974 | 3746 | 1440 | 137 | 124 | Richmond | .970 | 3706 | 1515 | 164 | 133 |
| Toledo | .974 | 3656 | 1484 | 137 | 136 | Pawtucket | .968 | 3733 | 1453 | 174 | 145 |

**Sam Horn**
38 homers

**Mike Birkbeck**
13 wins

**Bill Taylor**
26 saves

MEL BAILEY

### INDIVIDUAL BATTING LEADERS
(Minimum 383 Plate Appearances)

| | AVG | G | AB | R | H | 2B | 3B | HR | RBI | BB | SO | SB |
|---|---|---|---|---|---|---|---|---|---|---|---|---|
| Thome, Jim, Charlotte | .332 | 115 | 410 | 85 | 136 | 21 | 4 | 25 | 102 | 76 | 94 | 1 |
| Tarasco, Tony, Richmond | .330 | 93 | 370 | 73 | 122 | 15 | 7 | 15 | 53 | 36 | 54 | 19 |
| Jones, Chipper, Richmond | .325 | 139 | 536 | 97 | 174 | 31 | 12 | 13 | 89 | 57 | 70 | 23 |
| Masse, Billy, Columbus | .316 | 117 | 402 | 81 | 127 | 35 | 3 | 19 | 91 | 82 | 68 | 17 |
| Carey, Paul, Rochester | .311 | 96 | 325 | 63 | 101 | 20 | 4 | 12 | 50 | 65 | 92 | 0 |
| Rodriguez, Victor, Scranton | .305 | 118 | 442 | 59 | 135 | 24 | 3 | 12 | 64 | 17 | 40 | 2 |
| Lopez, Javy, Richmond | .305 | 100 | 380 | 56 | 116 | 23 | 2 | 17 | 74 | 12 | 53 | 1 |
| Longmire, Tony, Scranton | .304 | 120 | 447 | 63 | 136 | 36 | 4 | 6 | 67 | 41 | 71 | 12 |
| Perez, Robert, Syracuse | .294 | 138 | 524 | 72 | 154 | 26 | 10 | 12 | 64 | 24 | 65 | 13 |
| Ortiz, Luis, Pawtucket | .294 | 102 | 402 | 45 | 118 | 28 | 1 | 18 | 81 | 13 | 74 | 1 |

### INDIVIDUAL PITCHING LEADERS
(Minimum 114 Innings)

| | W | L | ERA | G | GS | CG | SV | IP | H | R | ER | BB | SO |
|---|---|---|---|---|---|---|---|---|---|---|---|---|---|
| McGehee, Kevin, Rochester | 7 | 6 | 2.96 | 20 | 20 | 2 | 0 | 134 | 124 | 53 | 44 | 37 | 92 |
| Birkbeck, Mike, Richmond | 13 | 8 | 3.01 | 27 | 26 | 1 | 0 | 159 | 143 | 67 | 55 | 41 | 136 |
| Cross, Jesse, Syracuse | 8 | 6 | 3.06 | 29 | 25 | 0 | 0 | 151 | 137 | 68 | 53 | 53 | 127 |
| Hutton, Mark, Columbus | 10 | 4 | 3.08 | 21 | 21 | 0 | 0 | 133 | 98 | 52 | 47 | 53 | 112 |
| Grimsley, Jason, Charlotte | 6 | 6 | 3.39 | 28 | 19 | 3 | 0 | 135 | 138 | 64 | 51 | 49 | 102 |
| Gozzo, Mauro, Norfolk | 8 | 11 | 3.45 | 28 | 28 | 2 | 0 | 190 | 208 | 88 | 73 | 49 | 97 |
| Johnson, Jeff, Columbus | 7 | 6 | 3.45 | 19 | 17 | 3 | 0 | 115 | 125 | 55 | 44 | 47 | 59 |
| Oquist, Mike, Rochester | 9 | 8 | 3.50 | 28 | 21 | 2 | 0 | 149 | 144 | 62 | 58 | 41 | 128 |
| Clayton, Royal, Columbus | 7 | 6 | 3.54 | 47 | 11 | 0 | 8 | 117 | 119 | 56 | 46 | 31 | 66 |
| Jones, Bobby, Norfolk | 12 | 10 | 3.63 | 24 | 24 | 6 | 0 | 166 | 149 | 72 | 67 | 32 | 126 |

## DEPARTMENT LEADERS

### BATTING
| | | |
|---|---|---|
| R | Chipper Jones, Richmond | 97 |
| H | Chipper Jones, Richmond | 174 |
| TB | Chipper Jones, Richmond | 268 |
| 2B | Tony Longmire, Scranton/W-B | 36 |
| 3B | Chipper Jones, Richmond | 12 |
| HR | Sam Horn, Charlotte | 38 |
| RBI | Jim Thome, Charlotte | 102 |
| SH | Johnny Paredes, Toledo | 11 |
| SF | Beau Allred, Charlotte | 8 |
| BB | Billy Masse, Columbus | 82 |
| IBB | Paul Carey, Rochester | 11 |
| HBP | Terrel Hansen, Ottawa | 27 |
| SO | Tom Quinlan, Syracuse | 156 |
| SB | Eric Bullock, Norfolk | 45 |
| CS | John Cangelosi, Toledo | 18 |
| GIDP | 2 tied at | 19 |
| OB% | Jim Thome, Charlotte | .441 |
| SL% | Sam Horn, Charlotte | .600 |

### PITCHING
| | | |
|---|---|---|
| G | 2 tied at | 62 |
| GS | 2 tied at | 29 |
| CG | Nate Minchey, Pawtucket | 7 |
| ShO | Bobby Jones, Norfolk | 3 |
| GF | Billy Taylor, Richmond | 55 |
| Sv | Billy Taylor, Richmond | 26 |
| W | 2 tied at | 13 |
| L | Nate Minchey, Pawtucket | 14 |
| IP | Nate Minchey, Pawtucket | 195 |
| H | Mauro Gozzo, Norfolk | 208 |
| R | Nate Minchey, Pawtucket | 103 |
| ER | Paul Fletcher, Scranton/W-B | 88 |
| HR | Chad Ogea, Charlotte | 26 |
| BB | Brian Bark, Richmond | 72 |
| HB | Bobby Jones, Norfolk | 11 |
| SO | 2 tied at | 136 |
| WP | Paul Fletcher, Scranton/W-B | 21 |
| Bk | Chad Ogea, Charlotte | 4 |

### FIELDING
| | | |
|---|---|---|
| C AVG | Mark Parent, Rochester | .995 |
| E | 2 tied at | 11 |
| 1B AVG | Rico Brogna, Toledo | .992 |
| E | Domingo Martinez, Syracuse | 16 |
| 2B AVG | Johnny Paredes, Toledo | .980 |
| E | Tommy Hinzo, Rochester | 24 |
| 3B AVG | Tom Quinlan, Syracuse | .957 |
| E | Russ Davis, Columbus | 25 |
| SS AVG | Manny Alexander, Roch. | .966 |
| E | Chipper Jones, Richmond | 43 |
| OF AVG | Mike Kelly, Richmond | .993 |
| E | Robert Perez, Syracuse | 12 |

## HONOR ROLL
### OFFICIAL ALL-STAR TEAM
- **C** Javy Lopez, Richmond
- **1B** Ryan Klesko, Richmond
- **2B** Tommy Hinzo, Rochester
- **3B** Jim Thome, Charlotte
- **SS** Chipper Jones, Richmond
- **OF** Tony Longmire, Scranton
- Billy Masse, Columbus
- Tony Tarasco, Richmond
- **DH** Sam Horn, Charlotte
- **SP** Aaron Sele, Pawtucket
- **RP** Billy Taylor, Richmond

**MVP:** Jim Thome, Charlotte
**MV Pitcher:** Aaron Sele, Pawtucket
**Manager:** Mike Quade, Ottawa

### TOP 10 PROSPECTS
(Selected by league managers)
1. Jim Thome, 3b, Charlotte
2. Chipper Jones, ss, Richmond
3. Aaron Sele, rhp, Pawtucket
4. Ryan Klesko, 1b, Richmond
5. Javy Lopez, c, Richmond
6. Tony Tarasco, of, Richmond
7. Russ Davis, 3b, Columbus
8. Jeffrey Hammonds, of, Rochester
9. Mark Lewis, ss, Charlotte
10. Mark Hutton, rhp, Columbus

# YEAR-BY-YEAR LEADERS: 1946-93 — INTERNATIONAL LEAGUE

| Year | Batting Average | Home Runs | RBIs | Wins | ERA | Strikeouts |
|---|---|---|---|---|---|---|
| 1946 | Jackie Robinson, Mtl. .349 | Howard Moss, Balt. 38 | Eddie Robinson, Balt. 123 | 2 tied at 17 | Herb Karpel, Newark 2.41 | Art Houtteman, Buff. 147 |
| 1947 | Vernal Jones, Roch. .337 | Howard Moss, Balt. 53 | Hank Sauer, Syracuse 141 | Jim Pendergrast, Syr. 20 | Luke Hamlin, Toronto 2.22 | John Banta, Montreal 199 |
| 1948 | Coaker Triplett, Buff. .353 | Howard Moss, Balt. 33 | Ed Sanicki, Toronto 107 | 2 tied at 19 | Bob Porterfield, New. 2.17 | John Banta, Montreal 193 |
| 1949 | Bobby Morgan, Mtl. .337 | Russ Derry, Rochester 42 | Steve Bilko, Roch. 125 | Al Widmar, Baltimore 22 | Bubba Church, Tor. 2.35 | Dan Bankhead, Mtl. 176 |
| 1950 | Don Richmond, Roch. .333 | 2 tied at 30 | Russ Derry, Rochester 102 | Tom Poholsky, Roch. 18 | Tom Poholsky, Roch. 2.17 | Roger Bowman, Jersey City 181 |
| 1951 | Don Richmond, Roch. .350 | Marv Richert, Baltimore 35 | Archie Wilson, Buff. 112 | John Hetki, Toronto 19 | Alex Konikowski, Ottawa 2.59 | Bill Miller, Syracuse 131 |
| 1952 | Frank Carswell, Buff. .344 | Frank Carswell, Buffalo 30 | Ed Stevens, Toronto 113 | 2 tied at 20 | Marion Fricano, Ottawa 2.26 | Duke Markell, Toronto 120 |
| 1953 | Sandy Amoros, Mtl. .353 | John Wallaesa, Spring.-Buff. 36 | Rocky Nelson, Mtl. 136 | Bob Trice, Ottawa 21 | Don Johnson, Toronto 2.67 | Don Johnson, Toronto 156 |
| 1954 | Bill Virdon, Roch. .333 | Rocky Nelson, Mtl. 31 | Elston Howard, Toronto 109 | 3 tied at 18 | Jim Owens, Syracuse 2.87 | Bob Meyer, Syracuse 173 |
| 1955 | Rocky Nelson, Mtl. .364 | Rocky Nelson, Mtl. 37 | Rocky Nelson, Montreal 130 | Lynn Lovenguth, Tor. 24 | Jack Crimian, Toronto 2.10 | Jim Owens, Syracuse 161 |
| 1956 | Clyde Parris, Mtl. .321 | Luke Easter, Buffalo 35 | Luke Easter, Buffalo 106 | Lynn Lovenguth, Tor. 18 | Ed Blake, Toronto 2.61 | Seth Morehead, Miami 168 |
| 1957 | Joe Caffie, Buffalo .330 | Luke Easter, Buffalo 40 | Luke Easter, Buffalo 128 | Tom Lasorda, Montreal 18 | Mike Cuellar, Havana 2.44 | Jim Coates, Roch. 161 |
| 1958 | Rocky Nelson, Tor. .326 | Rocky Nelson, Tor. 43 | Rocky Nelson, Tor. 120 | Bob Keegan, Roch. 16 | Bob Tiefanauer, Tor. 1.89 | Cal Browning, Roch. 173 |
| 1959 | Pancho Herrera, Buff. .329 | Pancho Herrera, Buff. 37 | Pancho Herrera, Buff. 105 | 2 tied at 16 | Artie Kay, Miami 2.08 | Joe Gibbon, Col. 152 |
| 1960 | Jim Frey, Rochester .317 | Joe Altobelli, Mtl. 31 | Joe Altobelli, Mtl. 98 | 3 tied at 18 | Al Cicotte, Toronto 1.79 | Al Cicotte, Toronto 158 |
| 1961 | Ted Savage, Buffalo .325 | Boog Powell, Roch. 32 | Frank Leja, Rich.-Syr. 98 | Ray Washburn, Char 18 | Ray Washburn, Char 2.34 | Bob Veale, Columbus 208 |
| 1962 | Vic Davalillo, Jax. .346 | Pancho Herrera, Buff. 32 | 2 tied at 108 | Joe Schaffernoth, Jax. 18 | Jim Constable, Tor. 2.56 | Harry Fanok, Atlanta 192 |
| 1963 | Don Buford, Ind. .336 | Richie Allen, Arkansas 33 | Richie Allen, Arkansas 97 | Fritz Ackley, Ind. 16 | Fritz Ackley, Ind. 2.76 | Frank Kreutzer, Ind. 157 |
| 1964 | Sandy Valdespino, Atl. .337 | Mack Jones, Syracuse 39 | Mack Jones, Syracuse 102 | Bruce Brubaker, Syr. 16 | Bruce Brubaker, Syr. 2.63 | Jim Merritt, Atlanta 174 |
| 1965 | Joe Foy, Toronto .302 | Pancho Herrera, Buff. 21 | Steve Demeter, Roch. 70 | Dick LeMay, Jax. 17 | Jack Hamilton, Syr. 2.42 | Frank Bertaina, Roch. 188 |
| 1966 | Reggie Smith, Toronto .320 | Mike Epstein, Roch. 29 | Mike Epstein, Roch. 86 | Gary Waslewski, Tor. 18 | Wilbur Wood, Col. 2.41 | Tom Phoebus, Roch. 208 |
| 1967 | Elvio Jimenez, Col. .340 | Jim Beauchamp, Rich. 25 | Curt Motton, Roch. 92 | Dave Leonhard, Roch. 15 | Tug McGraw, Jax. 1.99 | Jerry Koosman, Jax. 183 |
| 1968 | Merv Rettenmund, Roch. .331 | Dave Nicholson, Rich. 34 | Dave Nicholson, Rich. 130 | Dave Roberts, Columbus 18 | Galen Cisco, Lou. 2.21 | Jim Rooker, Toledo 206 |
| 1969 | Ralph Garr, Richmond .329 | Bob Robertson, Col. 34 | Roy Foster, Tide. 109 | 3 tied at 16 | Ron Klimkowski, Syr. 2.18 | Mike Adamson, Roch. 133 |
| 1970 | Ralph Garr, Richmond .386 | Hal Breeden, Rich. 37 | Roger Freed, Roch. 95 | Rick Gardner, Syr. 15 | Rick Gardner, Syr. 2.53 | Ernie McAnally, Winn. 178 |
| 1971 | Bobby Grich, Roch. .336 | Bobby Grich, Roch. 32 | Richie Zisk, Charleston 108 | 2 tied at 15 | Buzz Capra, Tide. 2.19 | Roric Harrison, Roch. 182 |
| 1972 | Al Bumbry, Roch. .345 | Richie Zisk, Charleston 26 | Dwight Evans, Louisville 93 | Craig Skok, Louisville 15 | Gene Garber, Char. 2.26 | Jim McKee, Charleston 159 |
| 1973 | Juan Beniquez, Paw. .298 | Jim Fuller, Roch. 39 | Jim Fuller, Roch. 81 | Ed Montague, Peninsula 15 | Dick Pole, Pawtucket 2.03 | Dick Pole, Pawtucket 158 |
| 1974 | Jim Rice, Pawtucket .337 | Jim Rice, Pawtucket 25 | Jim Rice, Pawtucket 101 | Bill Kirkpatrick, Roch. 15 | Larry Gura, Syracuse 2.14 | Jim Burton, Pawtucket 165 |
| 1975 | Mike Vail, Tidewater .342 | Bill Nahorodny, Tide. 28 | Roy Staiger, Tidewater 90 | 2 tied at 14 | Pablo Torrealba, Rich. 1.45 | Odell Jones, Char. 157 |
| 1976 | Rich Dauer, Rochester .336 | Jack Baker, Pawtucket 36 | Joe Lis, Toledo 101 | Dennis Martinez, Roch. 14 | Dennis Martinez, Roch. 2.50 | Dennis Martinez, Roch. 140 |
| 1977 | Wayne Harer, Pawtucket .350 | Terry Crowley, Roch. 30 | Dale Murphy, Rich. 75 | Larry McCall, Syracuse 16 | Tom Dixon, Charleston 2.25 | Mike Parrott, Roch. 146 |
| 1978 | Mike Easler, Col. .330 | Hank Small, Richmond 33 | Hank Small, Richmond 92 | 2 tied at 16 | Frank Riccelli, Char. 2.78 | Odell Jones, Columbus 169 |
| 1979 | Garry Hancock, Paw. .325 | Sam Bowen, Pawtucket 28 | 2 tied at 98 | Bob Kammeyer, Columbus 15 | Dennis Holman, Tide. 1.99 | Tommy Boggs, Rich. 138 |
| 1980 | Dave Engle, Toledo .307 | Marshall Brant, Col. 23 | Marshall Brant, Col. 107 | Bob Kammeyer, Columbus 16 | Ken Clay, Columbus 1.96 | Juan Berenguer, Tide. 178 |
| 1981 | Wade Boggs, Pawtucket .335 | Steve Balboni, Col. 33 | Steve Balboni, Col. 84 | 2 tied at 14 | Bob Ojeda, Maine 2.13 | Ken Dayley, Richmond 162 |
| 1982 | Boomer Wells, Toledo .336 | Steve Balboni, Col. 32 | Boomer Wells, Toledo 101 | Craig McMurty, Richmond 17 | Jim Lewis, Columbus 2.60 | Don Cooper, Toledo 125 |
| 1983 | Jack Perconte, Char. .346 | Brian Dayett, Col. 35 | Brian Dayett, Col. 108 | 2 tied at 13 | Tom Brennan, Char. 3.31 | Dennis Rasmussen, Col. 187 |
| 1984 | Scott Bradley, Col. .335 | Jerry Keller, Syracuse 26 | 2 tied at 102 | Jerry Ujdur, Maine 14 | Jim Deshaies, Col. 2.39 | Brad Havens, Toledo 169 |
| 1985 | Juan Bonilla, Col. .330 | Jim Wilson, Maine 26 | Jim Wilson, Maine 101 | 2 tied at 14 | Don Gordon, Syracuse 2.07 | Brad Havens, Roch. 129 |
| 1986 | Andre David, Toledo .328 | Ken Gerhart, Roch. 28 | Pat Dodson, Paw. 103 | Charlie Puleo, Richmond 14 | Doug Jones, Maine 2.09 | 2 tied at 124 |
| 1987 | Randy Milligan, Tide. .326 | Jay Buhner, Columbus 31 | Randy Milligan, Tide. 102 | Paul Gibson, Toledo 13 | DeWayne Vaughn, Tide. 2.66 | Odell Jones, Syracuse 147 |
| 1988 | Steve Finley, Roch. .314 | Dave Griffin, Richmond 21 | Ron Jones, Maine 75 | 2 tied at 13 | David West, Tidewater 1.80 | Steve Searcy, Toledo 176 |
| 1989 | Hal Morris, Columbus .326 | Glenalien Hill, Syr. 21 | Leo Gomez, Rochester 97 | 3 tied at 13 | Jose Nunez, Syracuse 2.21 | Kent Mercker, Richmond 144 |
| 1990 | Jim Eppard, Syracuse .310 | Phil Plantier, Paw. 33 | 2 tied at 84 | Dave Eiland, Columbus 16 | Paul Marak, Richmond 2.49 | Manny Hernandez, Tide. 157 |
| 1991 | Derek Bell, Syracuse .346 | Rick Lancellotti, Paw. 21 | Derek Bell, Syracuse 93 | 6 tied at 12 | Armando Reynoso, Rich. 2.61 | Pat Hentgen, Syr. 155 |
| 1992 | J.T. Snow, Columbus .313 | Hensley Meulens, Col. 26 | Hensley Meulens, Col. 100 | David Nied, Richmond 14 | Sam Militello, Col. 2.29 | David Nied, Richmond 159 |
| 1993 | Jim Thome, Charlotte .332 | Sam Horn, Charlotte 38 | Jim Thome, Charlotte 102 | 2 tied at 13 | Kevin McGehee, Roch. 2.96 | 2 tied at 136 |

# PACIFIC COAST
## LEAGUE

## Fast Finish Lifts Tucson Toros To Title

**By KEVIN IOLE**

The Tucson Toros played great baseball for most of 1993, but when it mattered most, the Toros played their best.

Tucson, Triple-A affiliate of the Houston Astros, won 28 of its final 34 games, including a minor league high 15 in a row to start the streak and three straight to end it. The final victory clinched a four games to two series win over Portland for the Pacific Coast League championship, Tucson's second in three years.

Both Portland and Tucson won both halves of their respective split-season schedules, marking the first time since the league went to a split-season format in 1979 that the same two teams won both halves. Normally a best-of-5 format, the championship series was expanded to seven games. Tucson won the title at home.

Toros catcher Scooter Tucker was selected MVP of the series, going 9-for-23 with five RBIs.

The core of the Tucson team remained intact as the parent Astros rarely had need for any reinforcements.

"Really, the only guy we ever lost was Rick Parker," Tucson manager Rick Sweet said. "Other than that, we had everybody the entire time."

**Scooter Tucker**

### Mouton Shines

Second baseman James Mouton, who made the jump from Class A, won the league's MVP award in a rout. Mouton batted .315 with 16 home runs and 40 stolen bases and finished among league leaders in virtually every offensive category.

He led the league with 126 runs and 70 extra-base hits. He also had 42 doubles and 12 triples.

Making a switch from the outfield, Mouton was shaky at second base in the early part of the season, but by season's end, he had convinced Sweet he was ready for the big-time.

"The only negative for James was his errors (43),

**Jim Lindeman.** Veteran first baseman's .362 average was best in Triple-A in 1993.

but if you look closely, you see that about 75 percent of them came in the first half," Sweet said. "Nobody had better range at second and offensively, he just jumps out at you. I don't know how much the organization believed in him before 1993, but I know they do now.

"He'll hit wherever he goes. He's as close to a Rickey Henderson at this age as you're going to see. There's no limit to how good he can be."

Mouton wasn't Tucson's only highly regarded prospect. Third baseman Phil Nevin, who was the No. 1 pick in the 1992 draft out of Cal State Fullerton, had a strong season and finished fourth in the league with 93 RBIs. Shortstop Orlando Miller batted .304, with 16

## STANDINGS: OVERALL

| Page | | W | L | PCT | GB | Manager | Attendance/Dates | Last Pennant |
|------|------|----|----|------|------|---------|------------------|--------------|
| 138 | Portland Beavers (Twins) | 87 | 56 | .608 | — | Scott Ullger | 186,010 (64) | 1983 |
| 114 | Tucson Toros (Astros) | 83 | 60 | .580 | 4 | Rick Sweet | 307,791 (69) | 1993 |
| 67 | Vancouver Canadians (Angels) | 72 | 68 | .514 | 13½ | Max Olivares | 349,726 (66) | 1989 |
| 109 | Edmonton Trappers (Marlins) | 72 | 69 | .511 | 14 | Sal Rende | 261,361 (60) | 1984 |
| 126 | Albuquerque Dukes (Dodgers) | 71 | 72 | .497 | 16 | Bill Russell | 390,652 (72) | 1990 |
| 199 | Calgary Cannons (Mariners) | 68 | 72 | .486 | 17½ | Keith Bodie | 278,140 (62) | None |
| 162 | Tacoma Tigers (Athletics) | 69 | 74 | .483 | 18 | Bob Boone | 316,475 (65) | 1978 |
| 98 | Colorado Springs Sky Sox (Rockies) | 66 | 75 | .468 | 20 | Brad Mills | 189,293 (67) | 1992 |
| 193 | Phoenix Firebirds (Giants) | 64 | 79 | .448 | 23 | Carlos Alfonso | 246,414 (72) | 1977 |
| 187 | Las Vegas Stars (Padres) | 58 | 85 | .406 | 29 | Russ Nixon | 386,310 (71) | 1988 |

**NOTE:** Team's individual batting, pitching and fielding statistics can be found on page indicated in lefthand column.

homers, 89 RBIs and a league-high 16 triples.

It was a pair of Tucson veterans, though, who finished on top of the PCL. Jim Lindeman had a huge finish and caught teammate Mike Brumley for the batting title in the final week. Lindeman batted .362, Brumley .353.

Portland had a better overall record than Tucson, but failed to preserve a 2-1 playoff advantage in its final season in the Oregon city. The Beavers announced before the 1993 season that they planned to move to Salt Lake City for 1994.

## Expansion Clubs Impress

An unusually high number of the league's top prospects played for the National League's two expansion teams. The Florida Marlins and Colorado Rockies made their debuts in the PCL and each supplied exciting players.

The Marlins' team played in Edmonton and the Trappers were the talk of the PCL for the first half because of their outfield combination of Darrell Whitmore and Nigel Wilson, both first-round picks in the expansion draft.

Whitmore was among league leaders in all major offensive categories when he was promoted to Florida in July. A severe hamstring injury cost Wilson a shot at an in-season callup, but he was summoned to Florida when rosters expanded in September.

The Rockies' Triple-A team was only a few miles down the road in Colorado Springs. Second baseman Roberto Mejia, who was drafted out of the Dodgers' organization, impressed all before finding out after the PCL all-star game he was going to the big leagues.

Calgary led the PCL in hitting with a .298 team average and was third in runs with 810, but those numbers were helped considerably by a four-game series in Las Vegas in June. The Cannons lost the first game of the series 9-6,

### STANDINGS: SPLIT SEASON

| FIRST HALF | | | | | SECOND HALF | | | | |
|---|---|---|---|---|---|---|---|---|---|
| **NORTH** | W | L | PCT | GB | **NORTH** | W | L | PCT | GB |
| Portland | 42 | 29 | .592 | — | Portland | 45 | 27 | .625 | — |
| Edmonton | 39 | 32 | .549 | 3 | Vancouver | 38 | 32 | .543 | 6 |
| Vancouver | 34 | 36 | .486 | 7½ | Tacoma | 37 | 35 | .514 | 8 |
| Calgary | 34 | 36 | .486 | 7½ | Calgary | 34 | 36 | .486 | 10 |
| Tacoma | 32 | 39 | .451 | 10 | Edmonton | 33 | 37 | .471 | 11 |
| **SOUTH** | W | L | PCT | GB | **SOUTH** | W | L | PCT | GB |
| Tucson | 38 | 33 | .535 | — | Tucson | 45 | 27 | .625 | — |
| Colo. Springs | 35 | 34 | .507 | 2 | Albuquerque | 37 | 34 | .521 | 7½ |
| Phoenix | 34 | 37 | .479 | 4 | Colo. Springs | 31 | 41 | .431 | 14 |
| Albuquerque | 34 | 38 | .472 | 4½ | Phoenix | 30 | 42 | .417 | 15 |
| Las Vegas | 32 | 40 | .444 | 6½ | Las Vegas | 26 | 45 | .366 | 18½ |

**PLAYOFFS:** Tucson defeated Portland, 4-2, in best-of-7 series.

**Darrell Whitmore**

but rallied to post three straight victories—23-12, 18-3 and 11-1. The Cannons finished the series with 58 runs and 89 hits.

In the 23-12 victory, the Cannons pounded out 35 hits, including nine in a row, and outfielder Lee Tinsley went 7-for-8. Tinsley had two homers, a triple and four singles in that game. He drove in five runs and scored four.

"I never had seven hits in a game," Tinsley said. "Not even in Little League."

Unfortunately, the Cannons didn't fare as well against the rest of the league and manager Keith Bodie was told at the end of the season he would not be offered a job in the Seattle organization for 1994.

## Veteran League

The PCL was characterized by veterans, with an unusual collection of players who were 30-plus, headed by 35-year-old Nick Capra of Edmonton. Veteran Tom Drees of Portland led the league with 15 wins.

The league did not have a 30-home run man and had just one player with 100 RBIs. Phoenix first baseman J.R. Phillips led the loop with 27 homers, while Albuquerque outfielder Billy Ashley finished with 100 RBIs exactly.

Tucson had the league's best pitching, finishing with a 4.42 ERA. Colorado Springs

**Billy Ashley**

led the league with 10 shutouts and was tied for second with 12 complete games.

### LEAGUE CHAMPIONS

**Last 25 Years**

| Year | Regular Season* | Pct. | Playoff |
|---|---|---|---|
| 1969 | Eugene (Phillies) | .603 | Tacoma (Cubs) |
| 1970 | Hawaii (Angels) | .671 | Spokane (Dodgers) |
| 1971 | Tacoma (Cubs) | .545 | Salt Lake City (Angels) |
| 1972 | Albuquerque (Dodgers) | .622 | Albuquerque (Dodgers) |
| 1973 | Tucson (Athletics) | .583 | Spokane (Rangers) |
| 1974 | Spokane (Rangers) | .549 | Spokane (Rangers) |
| 1975 | Hawaii (Padres) | .611 | Hawaii (Padres) |
| 1976 | Salt Lake City (Angels) | .625 | Hawaii (Padres) |
| 1977 | Phoenix (Giants) | .579 | Phoenix (Giants) |
| 1978 | Tacoma (Yankees) | .584 | Tacoma (Yankees)# |
| | | | Albuquerque (Dodgers)# |
| 1979 | Albuquerque (Dodgers) | .581 | Salt Lake City (Angels) |
| 1980 | Tucson (Astros) | .595 | Albuquerque (Dodgers) |
| 1981 | Albuquerque (Dodgers) | .712 | Albuquerque (Dodgers) |
| 1982 | Albuquerque (Dodgers) | .594 | Albuquerque (Dodgers) |
| 1983 | Albuquerque (Dodgers) | .594 | Portland (Phillies) |
| 1984 | Hawaii (Pirates) | .621 | Edmonton (Angels) |
| 1985 | Hawaii (Pirates) | .587 | Vancouver (Brewers) |
| 1986 | Vancouver (Brewers) | .616 | Las Vegas (Padres) |
| 1987 | Calgary (Mariners) | .596 | Albuquerque (Dodgers) |
| 1988 | Albuquerque (Dodgers) | .605 | Las Vegas (Padres) |
| 1989 | Albuquerque (Dodgers) | .563 | Vancouver (White Sox) |
| 1990 | Albuquerque (Dodgers) | .641 | Albuquerque (Dodgers) |
| 1991 | Albuquerque (Dodgers) | .580 | Tucson (Astros) |
| 1992 | Colo. Springs (Indians) | .596 | Colo. Springs (Indians) |
| 1993 | Portland (Twins) | .608 | Tucson (Astros) |

*Best overall record  #Co-champions

# PACIFIC COAST LEAGUE
## 1993 BATTING, PITCHING STATISTICS

### CLUB BATTING

| | AVG | G | AB | R | H | 2B | 3B | HR | BB | SO | SB |
|---|---|---|---|---|---|---|---|---|---|---|---|
| Calgary | .298 | 140 | 4848 | 810 | 1446 | 304 | 54 | 127 | 492 | 849 | 141 |
| Portland | .298 | 143 | 4778 | 831 | 1425 | 289 | 58 | 107 | 524 | 745 | 110 |
| Tucson | .297 | 143 | 4995 | 851 | 1486 | 311 | 76 | 78 | 558 | 876 | 171 |
| Colorado Springs | .295 | 141 | 4730 | 795 | 1397 | 280 | 63 | 127 | 461 | 905 | 134 |
| Albuquerque | .293 | 143 | 4995 | 806 | 1463 | 291 | 55 | 126 | 398 | 802 | 79 |
| Edmonton | .292 | 141 | 4824 | 728 | 1408 | 281 | 51 | 96 | 451 | 837 | 89 |
| Las Vegas | .288 | 143 | 4929 | 739 | 1419 | 271 | 53 | 112 | 506 | 867 | 114 |
| Vancouver | .286 | 140 | 4636 | 746 | 1326 | 250 | 41 | 68 | 512 | 858 | 183 |
| Phoenix | .281 | 143 | 4940 | 726 | 1389 | 260 | 53 | 110 | 496 | 933 | 145 |
| Tacoma | .281 | 143 | 4850 | 744 | 1362 | 263 | 52 | 98 | 531 | 1007 | 130 |

### CLUB PITCHING

| | ERA | G | CG | SHO | SV | IP | H | R | ER | BB | SO |
|---|---|---|---|---|---|---|---|---|---|---|---|
| Tucson | 4.42 | 143 | 6 | 6 | 37 | 1268 | 1418 | 762 | 623 | 461 | 946 |
| Portland | 4.58 | 143 | 12 | 4 | 37 | 1212 | 1322 | 708 | 617 | 498 | 800 |
| Vancouver | 4.68 | 140 | 9 | 7 | 36 | 1199 | 1293 | 731 | 623 | 503 | 899 |
| Edmonton | 4.73 | 141 | 14 | 5 | 35 | 1216 | 1382 | 729 | 639 | 417 | 869 |
| Tacoma | 4.85 | 143 | 4 | 6 | 35 | 1235 | 1414 | 772 | 666 | 498 | 765 |
| Phoenix | 4.91 | 143 | 5 | 3 | 30 | 1258 | 1475 | 792 | 686 | 498 | 920 |
| Colorado Springs | 5.04 | 141 | 12 | 10 | 34 | 1192 | 1413 | 800 | 667 | 545 | 895 |
| Calgary | 5.21 | 140 | 9 | 3 | 30 | 1201 | 1397 | 790 | 695 | 534 | 765 |
| Albuquerque | 5.39 | 143 | 3 | 2 | 45 | 1257 | 1488 | 837 | 753 | 505 | 870 |
| Las Vegas | 5.39 | 143 | 11 | 1 | 31 | 1236 | 1519 | 855 | 740 | 470 | 950 |

### CLUB FIELDING

| | PCT | PO | A | E | DP | | PCT | PO | A | E | DP |
|---|---|---|---|---|---|---|---|---|---|---|---|
| Albuquerque | .972 | 3772 | 1702 | 155 | 144 | Las Vegas | .969 | 3708 | 1526 | 169 | 125 |
| Portland | .972 | 3636 | 1503 | 146 | 117 | Tacoma | .969 | 3706 | 1566 | 171 | 136 |
| Vancouver | .972 | 3596 | 1469 | 147 | 123 | Colo. Springs | .967 | 3576 | 1558 | 175 | 135 |
| Calgary | .971 | 3603 | 1611 | 156 | 168 | Phoenix | .967 | 3773 | 1625 | 184 | 158 |
| Edmonton | .971 | 3648 | 1532 | 152 | 132 | Tucson | .962 | 3803 | 1653 | 217 | 137 |

**Pat Mahomes**
ERA leader

**J.R. Phillips**
HR leader

**Orlando Miller**
.304-16-89

MEL BAILEY

### INDIVIDUAL BATTING LEADERS
(Minimum 383 Plate Appearances)

| | AVG | G | AB | R | H | 2B | 3B | HR | RBI | BB | SO | SB |
|---|---|---|---|---|---|---|---|---|---|---|---|---|
| Lindeman, Jim, Tucson | .362 | 101 | 390 | 72 | 141 | 28 | 7 | 12 | 88 | 41 | 68 | 5 |
| Brumley, Mike, Tucson | .353 | 93 | 346 | 65 | 122 | 25 | 8 | 0 | 47 | 44 | 71 | 24 |
| McGriff, Terry, Edmonton | .345 | 105 | 339 | 62 | 117 | 29 | 2 | 7 | 55 | 49 | 29 | 2 |
| Brooks, Jerry, Albuquerque | .344 | 116 | 421 | 67 | 145 | 28 | 4 | 11 | 71 | 21 | 44 | 3 |
| Johnson, Brian, Las Vegas | .339 | 115 | 416 | 58 | 141 | 35 | 6 | 10 | 71 | 41 | 53 | 0 |
| Traxler, Brian, Albuquerque | .333 | 127 | 441 | 81 | 147 | 36 | 3 | 16 | 83 | 46 | 38 | 0 |
| Pye, Eddie, Albuquerque | .329 | 101 | 365 | 53 | 120 | 21 | 7 | 6 | 66 | 32 | 43 | 5 |
| Carter, Jeff, Portland | .325 | 101 | 381 | 73 | 124 | 21 | 7 | 0 | 48 | 63 | 53 | 17 |
| Turang, Brian, Calgary | .324 | 110 | 423 | 83 | 137 | 20 | 11 | 8 | 54 | 40 | 48 | 24 |
| Bruett, J.T., Portland | .322 | 90 | 320 | 70 | 103 | 17 | 6 | 2 | 40 | 55 | 38 | 12 |

### INDIVIDUAL PITCHING LEADERS
(Minimum 114 Innings)

| | W | L | ERA | G | GS | CG | SV | IP | H | R | ER | BB | SO |
|---|---|---|---|---|---|---|---|---|---|---|---|---|---|
| Mahomes, Pat, Portland | 11 | 4 | 3.03 | 17 | 16 | 3 | 0 | 116 | 89 | 47 | 39 | 54 | 94 |
| Reynolds, Shane, Tucson | 10 | 6 | 3.62 | 25 | 20 | 2 | 1 | 139 | 147 | 74 | 56 | 21 | 106 |
| Wall, Donnie, Tucson | 10 | 4 | 3.83 | 25 | 22 | 0 | 0 | 132 | 147 | 73 | 56 | 35 | 89 |
| Weathers, Dave, Edmonton | 11 | 4 | 3.83 | 22 | 22 | 3 | 0 | 141 | 150 | 77 | 60 | 47 | 117 |
| Walker, Mike, Calgary | 13 | 8 | 4.03 | 28 | 27 | 3 | 0 | 170 | 197 | 91 | 76 | 47 | 131 |
| Gross, Kip, Albuquerque | 13 | 7 | 4.15 | 59 | 7 | 0 | 13 | 124 | 115 | 58 | 56 | 41 | 96 |
| Pulido, Carlos, Portland | 10 | 6 | 4.19 | 33 | 22 | 1 | 0 | 146 | 169 | 74 | 68 | 45 | 79 |
| Taylor, Rob, Phoenix | 10 | 8 | 4.24 | 49 | 12 | 0 | 2 | 144 | 166 | 85 | 68 | 49 | 110 |
| Nichols, Rod, Albuquerque | 8 | 5 | 4.30 | 21 | 21 | 3 | 0 | 128 | 132 | 68 | 61 | 50 | 79 |
| Painter, Lance, Colo. Springs | 9 | 7 | 4.30 | 23 | 22 | 4 | 0 | 138 | 165 | 90 | 66 | 44 | 91 |

## DEPARTMENT LEADERS

### BATTING
| | | |
|---|---|---|
| R | James Mouton, Tucson | 126 |
| H | James Mouton, Tucson | 172 |
| TB | James Mouton, Tucson | 286 |
| 2B | James Mouton, Tucson | 42 |
| 3B | Lee Tinsley, Calgary | 18 |
| HR | J.R. Phillips, Phoenix | 27 |
| RBI | Billy Ashley, Albuquerque | 100 |
| SH | 2 tied at | 13 |
| SF | Greg Pirkl, Calgary | 10 |
| BB | Reggie Williams, Vancouver | 88 |
| IBB | Brian Traxler, Albuquerque | 14 |
| HBP | Jason Bates, Colorado Springs | 10 |
| SO | Billy Ashley, Albuquerque | 143 |
| SB | Reggie Williams, Vancouver | 50 |
| CS | 2 tied at | 18 |
| GIDP | Jose Munoz, Albuquerque | 19 |
| OB% | Terry McGriff, Edmonton | .426 |
| SL% | Jim Lindeman, Tucson | .562 |

### PITCHING
| | | |
|---|---|---|
| G | Todd Williams, Albuquerque | 65 |
| GS | Ryan Hawblitzel, Colorado Springs | 28 |
| CG | 5 tied at | 4 |
| ShO | Tom Drees, Portland | 2 |
| GF | Todd Williams, Albuquerque | 50 |
| Sv | Todd Williams, Albuquerque | 21 |
| W | Tom Drees, Portland | 15 |
| L | John Johnstone, Edmonton | 15 |
| IP | Mike Walker, Calgary | 170 |
| H | Ryan Hawblitzel, Colorado Springs | 221 |
| R | Ryan Hawblitzel, Colorado Springs | 129 |
| ER | Ryan Hawblitzel, Colorado Springs | 113 |
| HR | Tom Drees, Portland | 23 |
| BB | Jeff Juden, Tucson | 76 |
| HB | Mike Myers, Edmonton | 10 |
| SO | Scott Sanders, Las Vegas | 161 |
| WP | Dana Ridenour, Colorado Springs | 16 |
| Bk | Mike Linskey, Las Vegas | 6 |

### FIELDING
| | | |
|---|---|---|
| C AVG | Terry McGriff, Edmonton | .996 |
| E | Henry Mercedes, Tacoma | 12 |
| 1B AVG | Brian Traxler, Albuquerque | .995 |
| E | J.R. Phillips, Phoenix | 28 |
| 2B AVG | Webster Garrison, Tacoma | .972 |
| E | James Mouton, Tucson | 43 |
| 3B AVG | Phil Nevin, Tucson | .891 |
| E | Mike Busch, Albuquerque | 37 |
| SS AVG | Rafael Bournigal, Alb. | .980 |
| E | Orlando Miller, Tucson | 33 |
| OF AVG | Pat Howell, Portland | .993 |
| E | Billy Ashley, Albuquerque | 11 |

## HONOR ROLL

### OFFICIAL ALL-STAR TEAM
| | |
|---|---|
| C | Brian Johnson, Las Vegas |
| 1B | J.R. Phillips, Phoenix |
| 2B | James Mouton, Tucson |
| 3B | Eduardo Perez, Vancouver |
| SS | Kurt Abbott, Tacoma |
| OF | Billy Ashley, Albuquerque |
| | Rikkert Faneyte, Phoenix |
| | Nigel Wilson, Edmonton |
| DH | Bernardo Brito, Portland |
| RHP | Dave Weathers, Edmonton |
| LHP | Carlos Pulido, Portland |
| RP | Todd Williams, Albuqurque |

**MVP:** James Mouton, Tucson
**Manager:** Scott Ullger, Portland

### TOP 10 PROSPECTS
(Selected by league managers)
1. Darrell Whitmore, of, Edmonton
2. Pat Mahomes, rhp, Portland
3. Todd Van Poppel, rhp, Tacoma
4. Nigel Wilson, of, Edmonton
5. Eduardo Perez, 3b, Vancouver
6. Garret Anderson, of, Vancouver
7. Phil Nevin, 3b, Tucson
8. Salomon Torres, rhp, Phoenix
9. Kurt Abbott, ss, Tacoma
10. Orlando Miller, ss, Tucson

# YEAR-BY-YEAR LEADERS: 1946-93

## PACIFIC COAST LEAGUE

| Year | Batting Average | Home Runs | RBIs | Wins | ERA | Strikeouts |
|---|---|---|---|---|---|---|
| 1946 | Harvey Storey, L.A.-Port. .326 | Loyd Christopher, L.A.-Port. 26 | Ferris Fain, S.F. 112 | Larry Jansen, S.F. 30 | Larry Jansen, S.F. 1.57 | Ed Erautt, Hollywood 234 |
| 1947 | Hillis Layne, Seattle .367 | Max West, San Diego 43 | Max West, San Diego 124 | Cliff Chambers, L.A. 24 | Bob Chesnes, S.F. 2.32 | Cliff Chambers, L.A. 175 |
| 1948 | Gene Wooding, S.F. .385 | Jack Graham, S.D. 48 | Gus Zernial, Hollywood 156 | Red Lynn, L.A. 19 | Con Dempsey, S.F. 2.10 | Con Dempsey, S.F. 171 |
| 1949 | Artie Wilson, S.D.-Oak. .348 | Max West, San Diego 48 | Max West, San Diego 166 | 3 tied at... 23 | Willard Ramsdell, Holly. 2.60 | Con Dempsey, S.F. 164 |
| 1950 | Frank Baumholtz, L.A. .379 | Francis Kelleher, Holly. 40 | Harry Simpson, S.D. 156 | Jim Wilson, Seattle 24 | Jack Salveson, Holly. 2.84 | Jim Wilson, Seattle 228 |
| 1951 | Jim Rivera, Seattle .352 | Joe Gordon, Sac. 43 | Joe Gordon, Sac. 136 | 2 tied at... 20 | James Davis, Seattle 2.44 | Sam Jones, S.D. 246 |
| 1952 | Bob Boyd, Seattle .320 | Max West, L.A. 35 | Harold Gilbert, Oakland 118 | Johnny Lindell, Hollywood 24 | Red Adams, Portland 2.17 | Johnny Lindell, Holly. 190 |
| 1953 | Bob Elliott, Sac. .366 | Dale Long, Hollywood 35 | Dale Long, Hollywood 116 | Allen Gettel, Oakland 22 | Memo Luna, S.D. 2.67 | Joe Hatten, L.A. 152 |
| 1954 | Harry Elliott, S.D. .350 | Jim Marshall, Oakland 31 | Jim Marshall, Oakland 116 | Roger Bowman, Holly. 22 | Bill Wight, S.D. 1.93 | Tommy Byrne, Seattle 199 |
| 1955 | George Metkovich .335 | Steve Bilko, L.A. 37 | Earl Rapp, San Diego 133 | Red Munger, Hollywood 23 | Red Munger, Hollywood 1.85 | Bob Garber, Holly. 199 |
| 1956 | Steve Bilko, L.A. .360 | Steve Bilko, L.A. 55 | Steve Bilko, L.A. 164 | Rene Valdes, Portland 22 | Elmer Singleton, Sea. 2.55 | Dick Drott, L.A. 184 |
| 1957 | Ken Aspromonte, S.F. .334 | Steve Bilko, L.A. 56 | Steve Bilko, L.A. 140 | Leo Kiely, S.F. 21 | Morrie Martin, Van. 1.90 | Mudcat Grant, S.D. 178 |
| 1958 | Andre Rodgers, Phoenix .354 | Jim McDaniel, Salt Lake 37 | 2 tied at... 100 | 2 tied at... 16 | George Bamberger, Van. 2.45 | Marshall Bridges, Sac. 205 |
| 1959 | Tommy Davis, Spokane .345 | Willie McCovey, Phoe. 29 | Dick Hall, Salt Lake 92 | Dick Hall, Salt Lake 18 | Dick Hall, Salt Lake 1.87 | Dick Stigman, S.D. 181 |
| 1960 | Willie Davis, Spokane .346 | R.C. Stevens, Spokane 37 | Harry Bright, Salt Lake 119 | Chet Nichols, Van. 18 | Don Rudolph, Seattle 2.42 | Noel Mickelson, Port. 156 |
| 1961 | Carlos Bernier, Haw. .351 | Gene Oliver, Portland 36 | Harry Simpson, S.D. 105 | 2 tied at... 16 | Ron Piche, Vancouver. 2.26 | Sam McDowell, Salt Lake 156 |
| 1962 | Jesse Gonder, S.D. .342 | Stan Palys, Hawaii. 33 | Jesse Gonder, S.D. 116 | Dick Egan, Hawaii 17 | Gaylord Perry, Tacoma 2.48 | Dick Egan, Hawaii. 201 |
| 1963 | Chico Salmon, Denver. .325 | Deron Johnson, Denver. 33 | Billy Cowan, Salt Lake 120 | Howie Reed, Spokane 16 | Sammy Ellis, S.D. 2.62 | Bill Spanswick, Sea. 209 |
| 1964 | Lou Klimchock, Denver .334 | Costen Shockley, Ark. 36 | 2 tied at... 112 | 2 tied at... 16 | Bruce Howard, Ind. 2.20 | Al Stanek, Tacoma 220 |
| 1965 | Ted Uhlaender, Denver. .340 | Dave Roberts, Okla. City. 38 | Andy Kosco, Denver 116 | Jim Ollom, Denver. 17 | Bill Hands, Tacoma 2.19 | Tom Kelley, Portland 190 |
| 1966 | Walt Williams, Tulsa .330 | Tommy Murray, Okla. City 30 | 2 tied at... 94 | Howie Reed, Ok. City 20 | Bill Fischer, Ind. 2.35 | Bill Singer, Spokane 217 |
| 1967 | Cesar Gutierrez, Phoe. .322 | Willie Kirkland, Hawaii 34 | Willie Kirkland, Hawaii 97 | 3 tied at... 19 | Bobby Locke, Seattle 2.22 | Rich Robertson, Phoe. 184 |
| 1968 | Jim Hicks, Tulsa .366 | Clarence Jones, Tacoma. 24 | Coco Laboy, Tulsa 100 | 3 tied at... 18 | Pete Mikkelson, Tulsa 1.91 | Rich Robertson, Phoe. 216 |
| 1969 | Angel Bravo, Tucson. .342 | Russ Nagelson, Portland. 34 | John Werhas, Hawaii. 90 | 5 tied at... 18 | Jim Colburn, Tacoma. 2.28 | Jeff James, Eugene 155 |
| 1970 | Bobby Valentine, Spo. .340 | Joe Lis, Eugene 36 | Winston Llenas, Haw. 108 | 2 tied at... 18 | Jerry Stephenson, Spo. 2.82 | Darrell Brandon, Tac. 167 |
| 1971 | Tommy Hutton, Spokane .352 | Adrian Garrett, Tacoma 43 | Ron Cey, Spokane 123 | Dick Woodson, Spokane 16 | Dick Woodson, Portland. 3.29 | Dick Woodson, Port. 163 |
| 1972 | Von Joshua, Alb. .337 | Tom Paciorek, Alb. 27 | Doug Howard, Salt Lake 109 | Mike Wallace, Eugene. 16 | Dick Lane, Salt Lake 2.97 | Steve Luebber, Alb. 199 |
| 1973 | Steve Ontiveros, Phoe. .357 | Gene Martin, Eug.-Haw. 31 | Gene Martin, Eug.-Haw. 106 | Glenn Abbott, Tucson 18 | Dave Freisleben, Haw. 2.82 | Dave Freisleben, Haw. 206 |
| 1974 | Glenn Adams, Phoenix. .352 | Bill McNulty, Sac. 55 | Bill McNulty, Sac. 135 | Rex Hudson, Alb. 16 | Butch Metzger, Phoe. 3.67 | Butch Metzger, Phoe. 148 |
| 1975 | Jerry Royster, Alb. .333 | Bob Hansen, Sac. 29 | Bob Hansen, Sac. 102 | Gary Ross, Hawaii 16 | Greg Shanahan, Alb. 2.39 | Greg Shanahan, Alb. 147 |
| 1976 | Paul Dade, Salt Lake .352 | Bob Gorinski, Tacoma. 28 | Bob Gorinski, Tacoma. 110 | 3 tied at... 15 | Gary Wheelock, Salt Lake 3.18 | Gary Wheelock, Salt Lake 138 |
| 1977 | Don Cardoza, Alb. .356 | Danny Walton, Alb. 42 | Danny Walton, Alb. 116 | Mark Wiley, Hawaii 16 | Frank Riccelli, Phoe. 4.14 | Frank Riccelli, Phoe. 135 |
| 1978 | Jeff Leonard, Alb. .365 | Willie Aikens, Salt Lake 29 | Pedro Guerrero, Alb. 118 | Eric Wilkins, Portland 19 | Steve Mura, Hawaii. 2.93 | Steve Mura, Hawaii. 158 |
| 1979 | Mickey Hatcher, Alb. .371 | Ike Hampton, Salt Lake 30 | Pedro Guerrero, Alb. 103 | Mark Bombach, Van. 22 | Juan Berenguer, Tac. 2.56 | Juan Berenguer, Tac. 220 |
| 1980 | Danny Heep, Tucson .343 | Tim Hosley, Ogden 26 | Alan Knicely, Tucson 105 | 4 tied at... 15 | Mickey Mahler, Port. 2.13 | Mickey Mahler, Port. 140 |
| 1981 | Mike Marshall, Alb. .373 | Mike Marshall, Alb. 34 | Mike Marshall, Alb. 137 | Ted Power, Alb. 18 | Bob Stoddard, Spo. 2.90 | Odell Jones, Portland. 135 |
| 1982 | Tack Wilson, Alb. .378 | Ron Kittle, Edmonton. 50 | Ron Kittle, Edmonton. 144 | Odell Jones, Portland 16 | Chris Codiroli, Tacoma 1.90 | Odell Jones, Portland. 172 |
| 1983 | Chris Smith, Phoenix .379 | 2 tied at... 32 | Sid Bream, Alb. 118 | Rick Rodas, Alb. 16 | Jose DeLeon, Haw. 3.04 | Rick Rodas, Alb. 157 |
| 1984 | Tony Brewer, Alb. .357 | Rob Deer, Phoenix 28 | Rick Lancelotti, L.V. 131 | Bob Walk, Hawaii 19 | Bob Walk, Hawaii 2.26 | Mike Bielecki, Hawaii 162 |
| 1985 | John Kruk, Las Vegas .351 | Danny Tartabull, Cal. 43 | Danny Tartabull, Cal. 109 | Bob Walk, Hawaii 16 | Jeff Bittiger, Alb. 2.12 | Jose Rijo, Tacoma 179 |
| 1986 | Ty Gainey, Tucson. .353 | Rick Lancelotti, Phoe. 31 | Tim Pyznarski, L.V. 119 | Mark Grant, Phoenix 14 | Dave Johnson, Haw. 3.17 | Bob Patterson, Hawaii 137 |
| 1987 | Jim Eppard, Edmonton. .346 | Dave Hengel, Calgary 23 | Dave Hengel, Calgary 103 | Mike Campbell, Calgary 15 | Vicente Palacios, Van. 2.58 | Tim Belcher, Tacoma 133 |
| 1988 | Edgar Martinez, Cal. .363 | Luis Medina, Colo. Spr. 28 | Rod Allen, Colo. Spr. 100 | Bill Krueger, Alb. 15 | Bill Krueger, Alb. 3.01 | Erik Hanson, Calgary 154 |
| 1989 | Bruce Fields, Calgary .351 | Denny Gonzalez, C.S. 27 | Jim Wilson, Calgary 133 | Bryan Clark, Tacoma. 15 | Jeff Bittiger, Van. 2.12 | Mike Fetters, Edm. 144 |
| 1990 | Luis Lopez, Alb. .353 | Bernardo Brito, Portland 25 | Tom Dodd, Tacoma. 114 | Jeff Bittiger, Alb. 14 | Mike Cook, Portland. 3.20 | Ray Young, Tacoma. 137 |
| 1991 | Rich Amaral, Calgary .346 | 2 tied at... 27 | Ted Wood, Phoenix. 109 | 2 tied at... 14 | Gil Heredia, Phoenix 2.82 | Jeff Hartsock, Alb. 123 |
| 1992 | Troy Neel, Tacoma. .351 | Tim Salmon, Edmonton. 29 | Tim Salmon, Edmonton. 105 | 2 tied at... 13 | Mike Dunne, Van. 2.78 | Mike Trombley, Port. 138 |
| 1993 | Jim Lindeman, Tucson. .362 | J.R. Phillips, Phoenix. 27 | Billy Ashley, Alb. 100 | Tom Drees, Portland 15 | Pat Mahomes, Portland. 3.03 | Scott Sanders, Las Vegas 161 |

# EASTERN LEAGUE

## No Slowing Down Harrisburg Express

**By BILL PALMER**

Critics who bemoan the lack of action by legislative bodies obviously didn't get a chance to see a group of Senators at work in the Eastern League in 1993.

From Day One, the Harrisburg Senators were the consensus choice to win the league's regular season title. They did—by 19 games. But it was the manner in which the Senators won their second title in three years which made them one of the best EL teams ever and Baseball America's 1993 Minor League Team of the Year.

By the time Harrisburg capped a 94-44 regular season—the best mark in the league since Reading went 96-44 in 1983 and the fourth-best win total in league history—the Senators were playing with a lineup retooled by the promotion of 11 members of the Opening Day roster.

That revamped roster also claimed the league's playoff title, winning three straight games in Canton after dropping the first two of the best-of-5 series at home. The Senators won the clincher 8-0 as Reid Cornelius pitched seven scoreless innings and outfielder Glenn Murray drove in three runs.

"It's been a bunch of dedicated guys," said Harrisburg manager Jim Tracy, who was named the league's top manager. "Like I said when they gave us the regular season championship trophy, this wasn't just for the guys here, but the others who have been promoted."

The promotions began when lefthander Kirk Rueter (5-0, 1.36) and outfielder Curtis Pride (.350-15-39) were sent to Triple-A. By the time Montreal had finished reshaping its minor league rosters, megaprospects such as Gabe White, Rondell White, Cliff Floyd and Joey Eischen also had left Harrisburg.

Even with the constant flux of the roster, Tracy got his team to play well.

"We've created an atmosphere here where these guys come to the ballpark and don't want to lose," Tracy said. "We've had the talent all year, but we've lost 11 players off this team.

"I think what we've done is create a foundation for 1994. These guys have not come up and been put in a situation of, 'Just go up and do the best you can.' They've come into a situation where not just the

**Cliff Floyd.** Expos megaprospect left his mark on the Eastern League in 1993, leading in home runs (26) and RBIs (101).

Eastern League, but all of baseball, was looking at the Harrisburg Senators, to see how they'd react. Well, when we started losing those guys, we were 35 games over .500. We finished 50 games over."

Harrisburg hitters led the league in batting average, runs scored, hits and home runs while the pitching staff finished first in ERA and strikeouts.

### Talent Abounds

The Eastern League was a scout's dream in 1993.

Floyd, 20, was named the league's MVP and rookie

## STANDINGS

| Page | | W | L | PCT | GB | Manager(s) | Attendance/Dates | Last Pennant |
|------|---|---|---|-----|----|-----------|-----------------|-------------|
| 145 | **Harrisburg Senators (Expos)** | 94 | 44 | .681 | — | Jim Tracy | 250,476 (69) | 1993 |
| 93 | **Canton-Akron Indians (Indians)** | 75 | 63 | .543 | 19 | Brian Graham | 273,639 (61) | None |
| 56 | **Bowie Baysox (Orioles)** | 72 | 68 | .514 | 23 | Don Buford | 254,861 (61) | None |
| 151 | **Albany-Colonie Yankees (Yankees)** | 70 | 68 | .507 | 24 | Mike Hart, Bill Evers | 137,541 (61) | 1991 |
| 156 | **Binghamton Mets (Mets)** | 68 | 72 | .486 | 27 | Steve Swisher | 225,467 (65) | 1992 |
| 104 | **London Tigers (Tigers)** | 63 | 75 | .457 | 31 | Tom Runnells | 103,840 (69) | 1990 |
| 169 | **Reading Phillies (Phillies)** | 62 | 78 | .443 | 33 | Don McCormack | 313,083 (65) | 1973 |
| 62 | **New Britain Red Sox (Red Sox)** | 52 | 88 | .371 | 43 | Jim Pankovits | 140,915 (66) | 1983 |

**PLAYOFFS—Semifinals:** Harrisburg defeated Albany, 3-1, and Canton-Akron defeated Bowie, 3-2, in best-of-5 series. **Finals:** Harrisburg defeated Canton, 3-2, in best-of-5 series.

**NOTE:** Team's individual batting and pitching statistics can be found on page indicated in lefthand column.

**Ramirez Boys.** Canton-Akron's Manny (left) and Omar Ramirez both hit in excess of .300 to lead Indians to second-place finish.

of the year. He led the league with 26 homers and 101 RBIs, and finished second in the batting race with a .329 mark in 101 games. He also had a .600 slugging percentage before being promoted to Triple-A Ottawa.

Canton-Akron's Manny Ramirez won the batting title at .340 despite taking his considerable talents to Triple-A with a month left in the season. Teammates Brian Giles, Omar Ramirez, Miguel Flores and David Bell also finished in the top 12 in batting to help Canton-Akron to its distant second-place showing.

Albany's Brien Taylor, the top pick in the 1991 draft, finished strong, completing his second full pro season with a 13-7 record, 3.48 ERA and 150 strikeouts in 163 innings. He still showed there's room for improvement by reaching triple figures (102) in walks and allowing opponents to steal 37 bases in 49 attempts.

It was also the Year of the Brawl in the EL, high-lighted by a two-day battle royal in London between the Tigers and Albany in mid-June. Ten players received suspensions after the main event, and Yankee reliever Rich Polak suffered hand and facial injuries that sidelined him for two months.

The Tigers also skirmished with the Senators during the season.

There was a managerial change in the league as well. Albany's Mike Hart was replaced in late June by Bill Evers, who opened the season at Class A Greensboro. The Yankees cited philosophical differences with his approach. Under Hart, the Yankees were 31-30.

The 1994 season will bring several changes to the Eastern League.

With the addition of the Portland Sea Dogs (Florida Marlins) and New Haven Ravens (Colorado Rockies), the 1994 season will see the 10-team league split into two divisions with an unbalanced schedule.

The Detroit Tigers also announced following the 1993 season that they planned to move their London team out of Ontario and into a new facility in Trenton, N.J. New Jersey last had professional baseball in 1977-78, when Jersey City played in the EL.

The Tigers spent five years in London, but were plagued by a substandard facility and poor attendance. The Tigers finished last in the EL in attendance each of their final two seasons.

## LEAGUE CHAMPIONS

### Last 25 Years

| Year | Regular Season* | Pct. | Playoff |
|------|-----------------|------|---------|
| 1969 | York (Pirates) | .640 | None |
| 1970 | Waterbury (Pirates) | .560 | None |
| 1971 | Three Rivers (Reds) | .569 | Elmira (Royals) |
| 1972 | West Haven (Yankees) | .600 | West Haven (Yankees) |
| 1973 | Reading (Phillies) | .551 | Reading (Phillies) |
|  | Pittsfield (Rangers) | .551 |  |
| 1974 | Bristol (Red Sox) | .548 | Thetford Mines (Pirates) |
| 1975 | Reading (Phillies) | .613 | Bristol (Red Sox) |
| 1976 | Three Rivers (Reds) | .601 | West Haven (Yankees) |
| 1977 | West Haven (Yankees) | .623 | West Haven (Yankees) |
| 1978 | West Haven (Yankees) | .589 | Bristol (Red Sox) |
| 1979 | West Haven (Yankees) | .597 | None |
| 1980 | Bristol (Red Sox) | .568 | Holyoke (Brewers) |
| 1981 | Glens Falls (White Sox) | .615 | Bristol (Red Sox) |
| 1982 | West Haven (Athletics) | .614 | West Haven (Athletics) |
| 1983 | Reading (Phillies) | .686 | New Britain (Red Sox) |
| 1984 | Albany (Athletics) | .586 | Vermont (Reds) |
| 1985 | Albany (Yankees) | .589 | Vermont (Reds) |
| 1986 | Reading (Phillies) | .566 | Vermont (Reds) |
| 1987 | Pittsfield (Cubs) | .630 | Harrisburg (Pirates) |
| 1988 | Glens Falls (Tigers) | .583 | Albany (Yankees) |
| 1989 | Albany (Yankees) | .657 | Albany (Yankees) |
| 1990 | Albany (Yankees) | .568 | London (Tigers) |
| 1991 | Harrisburg (Expos) | .621 | Albany (Yankees) |
| 1992 | Canton-Akron (Indians) | .580 | Binghamton (Mets) |
| 1993 | Harrisburg (Expos) | .681 | Harrisburg (Expos) |
| | *Best overall record | | |

**Rondell White.** Outfielder contributed a .328 average to Harrisburg's 94-win season.

# EASTERN LEAGUE
## 1993 BATTING, PITCHING STATISTICS

### CLUB BATTING

| | AVG | G | AB | R | H | 2B | 3B | HR | BB | SO | SB |
|---|---|---|---|---|---|---|---|---|---|---|---|
| Harrisburg | .278 | 138 | 4672 | 802 | 1301 | 230 | 42 | 170 | 507 | 1006 | 187 |
| Canton-Akron | .273 | 138 | 4667 | 713 | 1276 | 234 | 36 | 93 | 511 | 738 | 131 |
| Bowie | .264 | 140 | 4609 | 600 | 1219 | 213 | 44 | 88 | 463 | 832 | 156 |
| Albany | .261 | 138 | 4556 | 661 | 1189 | 240 | 42 | 92 | 444 | 936 | 143 |
| London | .259 | 138 | 4626 | 570 | 1197 | 217 | 26 | 64 | 473 | 854 | 183 |
| Binghamton | .253 | 140 | 4573 | 634 | 1159 | 206 | 45 | 101 | 541 | 914 | 120 |
| Reading | .253 | 140 | 4569 | 551 | 1157 | 186 | 37 | 80 | 417 | 881 | 113 |
| New Britain | .234 | 140 | 4569 | 502 | 1069 | 200 | 25 | 60 | 455 | 967 | 60 |

### CLUB PITCHING

| | ERA | G | CG | SHO | SV | IP | H | R | ER | BB | SO |
|---|---|---|---|---|---|---|---|---|---|---|---|
| Harrisburg | 3.48 | 138 | 8 | 10 | 36 | 1212 | 1086 | 569 | 469 | 538 | 1056 |
| Bowie | 3.67 | 140 | 12 | 9 | 35 | 1215 | 1179 | 594 | 495 | 453 | 887 |
| New Britain | 3.94 | 140 | 12 | 7 | 26 | 1235 | 1228 | 630 | 541 | 454 | 863 |
| Albany | 3.95 | 138 | 7 | 6 | 37 | 1182 | 1124 | 636 | 519 | 509 | 902 |
| Binghamton | 4.08 | 140 | 12 | 12 | 34 | 1202 | 1295 | 630 | 545 | 387 | 717 |
| Canton-Akron | 4.27 | 138 | 4 | 6 | 43 | 1203 | 1176 | 639 | 571 | 536 | 966 |
| Reading | 4.31 | 140 | 8 | 12 | 33 | 1197 | 1224 | 651 | 571 | 429 | 823 |
| London | 4.32 | 138 | 12 | 5 | 30 | 1219 | 1255 | 684 | 585 | 505 | 914 |

### CLUB FIELDING

| | PCT | PO | A | E | DP | | PCT | PO | A | E | DP |
|---|---|---|---|---|---|---|---|---|---|---|---|
| Reading | .975 | 3573 | 1511 | 133 | 112 | Binghamton | .968 | 3605 | 1575 | 170 | 140 |
| Canton-Akron | .973 | 3608 | 1469 | 143 | 127 | Bowie | .968 | 3646 | 1484 | 170 | 117 |
| Harrisburg | .971 | 3636 | 1310 | 147 | 108 | New Britain | .966 | 3706 | 1502 | 182 | 127 |
| London | .969 | 3656 | 1453 | 161 | 102 | Albany | .965 | 3545 | 1416 | 181 | 130 |

**Brien Taylor**
13-7, 3.48

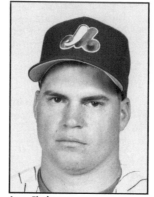

**Joey Eischen**
14-4, 3.62

### INDIVIDUAL BATTING LEADERS
(Minimum 375 Plate Appearances)

| | AVG | G | AB | R | H | 2B | 3B | HR | RBI | BB | SO | SB |
|---|---|---|---|---|---|---|---|---|---|---|---|---|
| Ramirez, Manny, Canton | .340 | 89 | 344 | 67 | 117 | 32 | 0 | 17 | 79 | 45 | 68 | 2 |
| Floyd, Cliff, Harrisburg | .329 | 101 | 380 | 82 | 125 | 17 | 4 | 26 | 101 | 54 | 71 | 31 |
| White, Rondell, Harrisburg | .328 | 90 | 372 | 72 | 122 | 16 | 10 | 12 | 52 | 22 | 72 | 21 |
| Giles, Brian, Canton | .327 | 123 | 425 | 64 | 139 | 17 | 6 | 8 | 64 | 57 | 43 | 18 |
| Ramirez, Omar, Canton | .314 | 125 | 516 | 116 | 162 | 24 | 6 | 7 | 53 | 53 | 49 | 24 |
| Veras, Quilvio, Binghamton | .306 | 128 | 444 | 87 | 136 | 19 | 7 | 2 | 51 | 91 | 62 | 52 |
| Lewis, T.R., Bowie | .304 | 127 | 480 | 73 | 146 | 26 | 2 | 5 | 64 | 36 | 80 | 22 |
| Barnwell, Richard, Albany | .298 | 131 | 463 | 98 | 138 | 24 | 7 | 11 | 50 | 77 | 101 | 33 |
| Wawruck, Jim, Bowie | .297 | 128 | 475 | 59 | 141 | 21 | 5 | 4 | 44 | 43 | 66 | 28 |
| Martin, Chris, Harrisburg | .294 | 116 | 395 | 68 | 116 | 23 | 1 | 7 | 54 | 40 | 48 | 16 |

### INDIVIDUAL PITCHING LEADERS
(Minimum 111 Innings)

| | W | L | ERA | G | GS | CG | SV | IP | H | R | ER | BB | SO |
|---|---|---|---|---|---|---|---|---|---|---|---|---|---|
| Harriger, Denny, Bing. | 13 | 10 | 2.95 | 35 | 24 | 4 | 1 | 171 | 174 | 69 | 56 | 40 | 89 |
| Krivda, Rick, Bowie | 7 | 5 | 3.08 | 22 | 22 | 0 | 0 | 126 | 114 | 46 | 43 | 50 | 108 |
| Lira, Felipe, London | 10 | 4 | 3.38 | 22 | 22 | 2 | 0 | 152 | 157 | 63 | 57 | 39 | 122 |
| Taylor, Brien, Albany | 13 | 7 | 3.48 | 27 | 27 | 1 | 0 | 163 | 127 | 83 | 63 | 102 | 150 |
| Farrar, Terry, Bowie | 7 | 7 | 3.49 | 24 | 21 | 2 | 0 | 116 | 114 | 51 | 45 | 40 | 85 |
| Eischen, Joey, Harrisburg | 14 | 4 | 3.62 | 20 | 20 | 0 | 0 | 119 | 122 | 62 | 48 | 60 | 110 |
| Blomdahl, Ben, London | 6 | 6 | 3.71 | 17 | 17 | 3 | 0 | 119 | 108 | 58 | 49 | 42 | 72 |
| Bryant, Shawn, Canton | 10 | 5 | 3.72 | 27 | 27 | 0 | 0 | 172 | 159 | 80 | 71 | 61 | 111 |
| Rodriguez, Frank, NB | 7 | 11 | 3.74 | 28 | 26 | 4 | 0 | 171 | 147 | 79 | 71 | 78 | 151 |
| Smith, Tim, New Britain | 7 | 13 | 3.79 | 28 | 28 | 3 | 0 | 180 | 192 | 91 | 76 | 44 | 81 |

## DEPARTMENT LEADERS

**BATTING**
| | | |
|---|---|---|
| R | Omar Ramirez, Canton-Akron | 116 |
| H | Omar Ramirez, Canton-Akron | 162 |
| TB | Kevin Jordan, Albany | 234 |
| 2B | Kevin Jordan, Albany | 33 |
| 3B | Brad Tyler, Bowie | 17 |
| HR | 2 tied at | 26 |
| RBI | Cliff Floyd, Harrisburg | 101 |
| SH | Keith Kimberlin, Reading | 11 |
| SF | Edgar Alfonzo, Bowie | 11 |
| BB | Quilvio Veras, Binghamton | 91 |
| IBB | Cliff Floyd, Harrisburg | 12 |
| HBP | Herbert Perry, Canton-Akron | 15 |
| SO | Jason Robertson, Albany | 126 |
| SB | Shannon Penn, London | 53 |
| CS | Quilvio Veras, Binghamton | 23 |
| GIDP | Brent Miller, Bowie | 17 |
| OB% | Quilvio Veras, Binghamton | .430 |
| SL% | Cliff Floyd, Harrisburg | .600 |

**PITCHING**
| | | |
|---|---|---|
| G | Bryan Rogers, Binghamton | 62 |
| GS | Tim Vanegmond, New Britain | 29 |
| CG | 4 tied at | 4 |
| ShO | Denny Harriger, Binghamton | 3 |
| GF | Tom Schwarber, London | 42 |
| Sv | Calvin Jones, Canton-Akron | 22 |
| W | Joey Eischen, Harrisburg | 14 |
| L | 3 tied at | 13 |
| IP | Tim Vanegmond, New Britain | 190 |
| H | Tim Smith, New Britain | 192 |
| R | Tim Vanegmond, New Britain | 99 |
| ER | Darrell Goedhart, Reading | 88 |
| HR | Juan Castillo, Binghamton | 27 |
| BB | Brien Taylor, Albany | 102 |
| HB | Tim Vanegmond, New Britain | 14 |
| SO | Tim Vanegmond, New Britain | 163 |
| WP | Mark Carper, Albany | 17 |
| Bk | Jose Lima, London | 13 |

**FIELDING**
| | | | |
|---|---|---|---|
| C | AVG | Javier Gonzalez, Bing. | .992 |
| | E | Rob Fitzpatrick, Harrisburg | 18 |
| 1B | AVG | Mike Rendina, London | .992 |
| | E | Joe DeBerry, Albany | 19 |
| 2B | AVG | Miguel Flores, Canton-Akron | .975 |
| | E | Jim Crowley, New Britain | 26 |
| 3B | AVG | Edgar Alfonzo, Bowie | .967 |
| | E | Butch Huskey, Binghamton | 34 |
| SS | AVG | Keith Kimberlin, Reading | .962 |
| | E | Tim Holland, Bowie | 39 |
| OF | AVG | Jim Wawruck, Bowie | .991 |
| | E | 3 tied at | 11 |

## HONOR ROLL

**OFFICIAL ALL-STAR TEAM**
- C Greg Zaun, Bowie
- 1B Cliff Floyd, Harrisburg
- 2B Quilvio Veras, Binghamton
- 3B Butch Huskey, Binghamton
- SS Robert Eenhoorn, Albany
- OF Manny Ramirez, Canton-Akron
  Omar Ramirez, Canton-Akron
  Rondell White, Harrisburg
- DH Lewis, Bowie; Zinter, Binghamton
- P Lopez, Canton-Akron; Lira, London; G. White, Harrisburg

**MVP:** Cliff Floyd, Harrisburg
**MV Pitcher:** Joey Eischen, Harrisburg
**Manager:** Jim Tracy, Harrisburg

**TOP 10 PROSPECTS**
(Selected by league managers)
1. Cliff Floyd, 1b-of, Harrisburg
2. Manny Ramirez, of, Canton-Akron
3. Rondell White, of, Harrisburg
4. Brien Taylor, lhp, Albany
5. Butch Huskey, 3b, Binghamton
6. Albie Lopez, rhp, Canton-Akron
7. Gabe White, lhp, Harrisburg
8. Kevin Jordan, 2b, Albany
9. Frank Rodriguez, rhp, New Britain
10. David Bell, 3b, Canton-Akron

| Year | Batting Average | Home Runs | RBIs | Wins | ERA | Strikeouts |
|---|---|---|---|---|---|---|
| 1946 | Sam Mele, Scranton .342 | 2 tied at.... 12 | Don Manno, Hartford 97 | Tom Fine, Scranton 23 | Mel Parnell, Scran. 1.30 | Bob Kuzava, W-B. 207 |
| 1947 | Joe Tipton, W-Barre .375 | Bud Heslet, Bing. 24 | Frank Heller, Wpt. 98 | Bill Kennedy, Scranton 17 | Mickey McDermott, Scr. 2.62 | Bill Kennedy, Scranton 136 |
| 1948 | Bruce Blanchard, Hart. .327 | Homer Moore, Hart. 20 | Jim Piersall, Scranton 92 | Lou Kretlow, Wpt. 21 | Max Peterson, Utica 2.03 | Lou Kretlow, Wpt. 219 |
| 1949 | Bill Reed, Hartford .333 | Harry Simpson, W-B. 31 | Harry Simpson, W-B. 120 | Orrie Arntzen, Albany 25 | Whitey Ford, Bing. 1.61 | Bob Rainey, Elmira. 191 |
| 1950 | George Crowe, Hart. .353 | Dale Long, Bing. 27 | Dale Long, Bing. 130 | William Freese, Bing. 19 | Bob Chakales, W-B. 2.04 | Sam Jones, W-B. 169 |
| 1951 | Bob Verrier, Hart. .323 | 2 tied at.... 24 | Eulas Hutson, W-Barre 117 | Jose Santiago, W-B. 21 | Jose Santiago, W-B. 1.59 | Paul Stuffel, Schnec. 183 |
| 1952 | Mike Lutz, Reading .321 | Rufus Crawford, Scran. 27 | 2 tied at.... 93 | 2 tied at.... 18 | George Uhaze, Albany 2.13 | Ron Mrozinski, Schnec. 148 |
| 1953 | Danny Schell, Scran. .333 | Rocky Colavito, Read. 28 | Rocky Colavito, Read. 121 | Wally Burnette, Bing. 23 | Steve Kraly, Bing. 2.08 | John Meyer, Schnec. 226 |
| 1954 | Clyde Parris, Elmira .313 | George Wopinek, Wpt. 16 | Clyde Parris, Elmira 90 | Al Schroll, Albany 16 | Al Schroll, Albany 2.07 | Seth Morehead, Schnec. 207 |
| 1955 | Zeke Bella, Bing. .371 | John Blanchard, Bing. 34 | Neal Hertwick, Albany 112 | Don Minick, Reading 20 | Jim Singleton, Johns./W-B. 2.42 | Jim Coates, Bing. 186 |
| 1956 | Tony Bartirome, Wpt. .305 | Andy Rellick, Read.-Schnec. 22 | Dick Sanders, Bing. 95 | Larry Locke, Reading 20 | Vic Lapiner, Reading 1.96 | Gary Bell, Reading 192 |
| 1957 | Dick McCarthy, Alb. .327 | Deron Johnson, Bing. 26 | Frank Leja, Bing. 117 | Ed Dick, Binghamton 18 | Bill Slack, Albany 2.24 | Ed Dick, Binghamton 204 |
| 1958 | John Easton, Wpt. .321 | Don Gile, Albany 23 | Dale Bennetch, Wpt. 102 | Gordon Seyfried, Lan. 17 | Bill Stafford, Bing. 2.25 | Julio Navarro, Spring. 142 |
| 1959 | Lou Jackson, Lancaster .339 | Jackie Davis, Wpt. 33 | Fred Hopke, Wpt. 130 | Juan Marichal, Spring. 18 | Juan Marichal, Spring. 2.39 | Juan Marichal, Spring. 208 |
| 1960 | Pedro Gonzalez, Bing. .327 | Don Lock, Binghamton 35 | Don Lock, Binghamton 117 | Jim Duffalo, Spring. 16 | Jim Duffalo, Spring. 2.63 | Clark Johnson, Spring. 169 |
| 1961 | Charley Keller, Bing. .349 | George Banks, Bing. 30 | George Banks, Bing. 108 | Gerry Thomas, Spring. 20 | Gerry Thomas, Spring. 2.40 | Gerry Thomas, Spring. 214 |
| 1962 | Jim Ray Hart, Spring. .337 | Ken Harrelson, Bing. 38 | Ken Harrelson, Bing. 138 | Paul Seitz, Bing. 16 | Frank Hamner, Bing. 2.03 | Bob Heffner, York. 234 |
| 1963 | Bob Chance, Charleston .343 | Bob Chance, Charleston 26 | Bob Chance, Charleston 114 | 2 tied at.... 16 | Frank Linzy, Spring. 1.55 | Fred Norman, Bing. 258 |
| 1964 | Paul Blair, Elmira .311 | Bobby Sanders, Wpt. 15 | Jose Calero, Spring. 86 | Joe Overton, Spring. 16 | Joe Overton, Spring. 1.72 | Tom Arruda, Spring. 178 |
| 1965 | George Scott, Pitts. .319 | George Scott, Pitts. 25 | George Scott, Pitts. 94 | Dave Leonhard, Elmira 20 | Dave Leonhard, Elmira 1.88 | Dave Leonhard, Elmira 209 |
| 1966 | Howie Bedell, York .322 | Hank McGraw, Wpt.-Elm. 12 | Tony Torchia, Pitts. 83 | Jerry Hudgins, Pitts. 15 | Tom Fisher, Elmira 1.88 | Tom Fisher, Elm. 142 |
| 1967 | Bernie Smith, Wpt. .306 | Bill Schlesinger, Pitts. 21 | Bill Schlesinger, Pitts. 81 | Gary Girouard, Bing. 14 | Jim McAndrew, Wpt. 1.47 | Alan Schmelz, Wpt. 181 |
| 1968 | Tony Torchia, Pitts. .294 | Carmen Fanzone, Pitts. 17 | Carmen Fanzone, Pitts. 98 | 2 tied at.... 14 | Silvano Quezada, York 1.34 | Mike Hedlund, Water. 149 |
| 1969 | Bob Kelly, Reading .323 | Pepe Mangual, Read. 26 | Pepe Mangual, Read. 102 | 2 tied at.... 16 | Lyn Fizer, York 2.03 | Ken Reynolds, Reading 180 |
| 1970 | Greg Luzinski, Read. .325 | Richie Zisk, Waterbury 34 | Greg Luzinski, Read. 120 | 2 tied at.... 14 | Dave Bennett, Water. 2.22 | Bill Gogolewski, Pitts. 146 |
| 1971 | Gene Locklear, Three Riv. .323 | Al Thompson, Pitts. 27 | Al Thompson, Pitts. 92 | Steve Blateric, Three Riv. 14 | Bob Terlecky, Read. 2.30 | Mike Ruddell, Three Riv. 186 |
| 1972 | Fernando Gonzalez, Sher. .333 | Al Thompson, Pitts. 31 | Al Thompson, Pitts. 110 | Pete Hamm, Three Rivers 17 | Pete Hamm, Three Rivers 2.30 | Brad Meyring, Sher. 181 |
| 1973 | Jim Rice, Bristol .317 | Tom Robson, Pitts. 38 | Tom Robson, Pitts. 126 | 5 tied at.... 12 | Joe Pactwa, West Haven. 3.18 | Greg Heydeman, Water... 179 |
| 1974 | Ken Macha, Thet. Mines. .345 | Jack Baker, Bristol 27 | Jack Baker, Bristol 105 | Steve Barr, Bristol 16 | Denis McSween, Que. City 1.89 | Roy Thomas, Reading... 168 |
| 1975 | Dave Bergman, Bristol .311 | Dick Davis, Thet. Mines. 16 | Gary Roenicke, Que. City. 74 | Randy Lerch, Reading 16 | Tom Farias, Bristol 1.55 | Rick Anderson, W.Haven. 138 |
| 1976 | Danny Thomas, Pitts. .325 | Danny Thomas, Pitts. 29 | Danny Thomas, Pitts. 83 | Gerald Hannahs, Que. City 20 | Paul Moskau, Three Riv. 1.55 | Gerald Hannahs, Que. City. 126 |
| 1977 | Harry Spilman, Three Riv. .373 | Ike Blessitt, Holyoke 30 | Ike Blessitt, Holyoke 104 | Mike Armstrong, Three Riv. 16 | Roger Slagle, West Haven 2.81 | Alan Wirth, Water. 149 |
| 1978 | Mike Henderson, Holy. .325 | Jeff Yurak, Holyoke 21 | Rick Stenholm, W.Haven 102 | Paul Semall, W.Haven. 16 | Steve Schneck, Bris. 2.15 | Steve Schneck, Bristol. 180 |
| 1979 | Dave Schmidt, Bristol .322 | Rick Lancelotti, Buffalo 41 | 2 tied at.... 107 | 2 tied at.... 14 | Bob Walk, Reading 2.24 | Bob Walk, Reading 135 |
| 1980 | Junior Ortiz, Buffalo .346 | Nick Esasky, Water. 30 | Ozzie Virgil, Reading 104 | Mark Davis, Reading 19 | Mark Davis, Reading 2.47 | Mark Davis, Reading 185 |
| 1981 | Ed Jurak, Bristol .340 | Ron Kittle, Gl. Falls. 40 | Ron Kittle, Gl. Falls. 103 | 4 tied at.... 15 | Brian Denman, Bristol 2.44 | Jerome King, Bristol. 168 |
| 1982 | Phil Klimas, Glens Falls .311 | Jim Bennett, West Haven. 29 | Jim Bennett, West Haven. 115 | John Lackey, Gl. Falls 16 | Jay Baller, Reading 2.68 | Oil Can Boyd, Bris. 191 |
| 1983 | Dave Gallagher, Buff. .338 | Willie Darkis, Reading 31 | Jim Wilson, Buffalo 105 | 2 tied at.... 15 | Steve Farr, Buffalo 1.61 | Mike Bielecki, Lynn 143 |
| 1984 | Thad Reece, Albany .331 | Pat Adams, Glens Falls. 24 | Pat Adams, Glens Falls. 102 | Tim Lambert, Albany 17 | Scott Terry, Vermont. 1.50 | Bob Bastian, Water. 119 |
| 1985 | Andy Allanson, Water. .312 | Cory Snyder, Water. 28 | Cory Snyder, Water. 94 | 2 tied at.... 14 | Brad Arnsberg, Alb. 1.59 | Doug Drabek, Albany 153 |
| 1986 | Jim Olander, Read. .325 | Bernardo Brito, Water. 18 | Rafael Palmeiro, Pitts. 95 | Jeff Gray, Vermont. 14 | Jim Neidlinger, Nashua 2.42 | Steve Searcy, Gl. Falls. 139 |
| 1987 | Tommy Gregg, Harris. .371 | Bernardo Brito, Wpt. 24 | Mark Grace, Pittsfield. 101 | Bob Scanlan, Read. 15 | Rob Lopez, Vermont. 2.40 | Rich Sauveur, Harris. 160 |
| 1988 | Jerome Walton, Pitts. .331 | 2 tied at.... 17 | Rob Richie, Glens Falls. 82 | Mike Walker, Wpt. 15 | Paul Wenson, Glens Falls. 2.04 | Mike Walker, Wpt. 144 |
| 1989 | Jim Leyritz, Albany .315 | Rob Sepanek, Alb. 22 | Wes Chamberlain, Harris. 87 | Rodney Imes, Albany 17 | Steve Adkins, Albany 2.07 | Scott Kamieniecki, Alb. 140 |
| 1990 | Luis Mercedes, Hagers. .334 | Rico Brogna, London 21 | 2 tied at.... 77 | Rusty Meacham, London 15 | Mike Gardiner, Wpt. 1.90 | Mike Gardiner, Wpt. 149 |
| 1991 | Matt Stairs, Harrisburg .333 | Jeromy Burnitz, Wpt. 31 | 2 tied at.... 85 | 2 tied at.... 13 | Jeff Mutis, Canton 1.80 | Ed Martel, Albany 141 |
| 1992 | Ken Ramos, Canton .339 | Greg Sparks, London 25 | Ivan Cruz, London 104 | Paul Byrd, Canton 104 | Bobby Jones, Bing. 1.88 | Sterling Hitchcock, Alb. 156 |
| 1993 | Manny Ramirez, Canton .340 | 2 tied at.... 26 | Cliff Floyd, Harrisburg 101 | Joey Eischen, Harrisburg 14 | Denny Harriger, Bing. 2.95 | Tim Vanegmond, N.B. 163 |

# Pitching Depth Spurs Birmingham To Title

**By RUBIN GRANT**

During the long, hot summer of 1993, it figured that the team that could keep its cool would wind up winning the Southern League championship.

Despite seeing eight members of their 10-man Opening Day pitching staff, including ERA champ James Baldwin and strikeout leader Scott Ruffcorn, move on and losing their top hitter (Ron Coomer) at midseason, the Birmingham Barons calmly went about their business and captured the league title.

"The reason we won is because of these guys," Birmingham manager Terry Francona said of the players who finished the season with the Barons. "The way they persevered, I've never been so proud of people in my life."

The Barons, who had the league's best overall record (78-64), lost only once in seven postseason games. They swept Nashville 3-0 in the divisional playoffs, then beat Knoxville in four games in the championship series.

MEL BAILEY

**Scott Ruffcorn**

Birmingham, which led the league in pitching during the regular season, dominated the playoffs with its hitting. The Barons had a .359 team batting average and scored 30 runs in sweeping Nashville, then hit .301 and averaged 5.8 runs a game in the four games against Knoxville.

Second baseman Ray Durham went 7-for-13 in the championship series and drove in five runs from the leadoff spot. In the title clincher, Durham scored the winning run on first baseman Mike Robertson's single in the top of the 10th in the Barons' 7-6 victory.

Birmingham relievers, led by veteran Jeff Carter, allowed only two runs in 24 innings in the playoffs. Carter had two saves and was the winner in the clincher against Knoxville.

TOM DiPACE

**Carlos Delgado.** Blue Jays catching prospect led Southern League in home runs (25) and RBIs (102).

The championship was Birmingham's first in the 1990s after leading the league with three in the '80s.

## Smokies Stacked

It was only fitting that Birmingham would have to beat Knoxville in the championship series. With the most talent-laden team in the league, the Smokies overcame a 6-17 April to reach the playoffs.

The Smokies also showed some cool. They got to the championship series by eliminating defending champion Greenville in five games, bouncing back from a no-hitter thrown by the Braves' Mike Hostetler in Game One.

Knoxville led the league in hitting with four of the

## STANDINGS: OVERALL

| Page | | W | L | PCT | GB | Manager | Attendance/Dates | Last Pennant |
|------|---|---|---|-----|-----|---------|------------------|--------------|
| 73 | Birmingham Barons (White Sox) | 78 | 64 | .549 | — | Terry Francona | 277,096 (67) | 1993 |
| 50 | Greenville Braves (Braves) | 75 | 67 | .528 | 3 | Bruce Kimm | 232,369 (68) | 1992 |
| 175 | Carolina Mudcats (Pirates) | 74 | 67 | .525 | 3½ | John Wockenfuss | 328,207 (67) | None |
| 87 | Chattanooga Lookouts (Reds) | 72 | 69 | .511 | 5½ | Pat Kelly | 270,671 (66) | 1988 |
| 139 | Nashville Xpress (Twins) | 72 | 70 | .507 | 6 | Phil Roof | 178,737 (67) | None |
| 163 | Huntsville Stars (Athletics) | 71 | 70 | .504 | 6½ | Casey Parsons | 282,731 (69) | 1985 |
| 80 | Orlando Cubs (Cubs) | 71 | 70 | .504 | 6½ | Tommy Jones | 217,716 (66) | 1991 |
| 212 | Knoxville Smokies (Blue Jays) | 71 | 71 | .500 | 7 | Garth Iorg | 140,868 (64) | 1978 |
| 121 | Memphis Chicks (Royals) | 63 | 77 | .450 | 14 | Tom Poquette | 230,181 (61) | 1990 |
| 200 | Jacksonville Suns (Mariners) | 59 | 81 | .421 | 18 | Marc Hill | 250,002 (68) | None |

**NOTE:** Team's individual batting and pitching statistics can be found on page indicated in lefthand column.

SL's top 15 hitters: first baseman Tim Hyers (.306), catcher Carlos Delgado (.303), second baseman Joe Lis (.290) and shortstop Alex Gonzalez (.289).

Delgado was named the league's MVP after leading the league in home runs (25), RBIs (102), walks (102), on-base percentage (.430) and slugging percentage (.524). He became the first player in the league to drive in more than 100 runs since 1990.

But Delgado was not tabbed as the league's top major league prospect. That honor went to teammate Gonzalez, who led the league in total bases (253) and tied for the lead in runs (93). He also finished second in hits (162) and triples (7), and third in steals (38).

## Bowie, Bowie, Bowie

Huntsville first baseman Jim Bowie won his second league batting title in three years with a .333 average and also finished second in RBIs (101), one behind Delgado. Bowie won his first title with Jacksonville, batting .310 in 1991.

While Bowie might have won the batting title, the biggest offensive explosion in the league occurred on Aug. 1, when Memphis set a league record for runs in a 25-5 rout of Nashville. The Chicks had a league-record 32 hits in the game with Adam Casillas, Benny Colvard and Jeff Garber collecting five apiece. Garber had a double, two home runs and eight RBIs, one shy of the league record.

Nashville righthander Oscar Munoz missed the final seven weeks of the season after being called up to Triple-A Portland, but still won the league's most outstanding pitcher award. He was leading the league in wins with an 11-4 record, was third in ERA (3.08) and second in strikeouts (139) when he was promoted.

Huntsville lefthander Curtis Shaw had the dubious distinction of setting a league record with 13 straight losses. He went into his final start of the season one loss shy of the league record for losses (17) in a season, but pitched a three-hit shutout against Birmingham to finish 6-16.

Birmingham's Ruffcorn and reliever Jeff Pierce combined for 20 strikeouts (15 by Ruffcorn) in a game against Chattanooga April 28, to set a league record for strikeouts in a nine-inning game. Pierce later joined Chattanooga in a trade between the White Sox and Cincinnati involving Tim Belcher.

For the third straight year, the Southern League set a league attendance record, drawing 2,408,578 fans during the regular season. Orlando, Jacksonville and Knoxville all set franchise records.

The league also voted to return to Nashville for the 1994 season, meaning that city again will field two teams—the Triple-A Sounds and Double-A Xpress.

That unwieldy situation developed just weeks prior to the start of the 1993 season when Charlotte's Southern League franchise was left without a home after Charlotte was granted a Triple-A expansion franchise and the National Association later ruled against New Orleans as a new site for the Double-A club.

With nowhere else to go and time running short, Nashville Sounds owner Larry Schmittou agreed to take on the wayward franchise as a second tenant, ostensibly for one season.

**Alex Gonzalez.** Knoxville shortstop was selected league's best prospect

**Oscar Munoz**

## STANDINGS: SPLIT SEASON

### FIRST HALF

| EAST | W | L | PCT | GB |
|---|---|---|---|---|
| Greenville | 39 | 32 | .549 | — |
| Orlando | 38 | 33 | .535 | 1 |
| Carolina | 37 | 33 | .529 | 1½ |
| Knoxville | 33 | 38 | .465 | 6 |
| Jacksonville | 32 | 39 | .451 | 7 |

| WEST | W | L | PCT | GB |
|---|---|---|---|---|
| Nashville | 40 | 31 | .563 | — |
| Birmingham | 35 | 36 | .493 | 5 |
| Huntsville | 34 | 37 | .479 | 6 |
| Chattanooga | 34 | 38 | .472 | 6½ |
| Memphis | 33 | 38 | .465 | 7 |

### SECOND HALF

| EAST | W | L | PCT | GB |
|---|---|---|---|---|
| Knoxville | 38 | 33 | .535 | — |
| Carolina | 37 | 34 | .521 | 1 |
| Greenville | 36 | 35 | .507 | 2 |
| Orlando | 33 | 37 | .471 | 4½ |
| Jacksonville | 27 | 42 | .391 | 10 |

| WEST | W | L | PCT | GB |
|---|---|---|---|---|
| Birmingham | 43 | 28 | .606 | — |
| Chattanooga | 38 | 31 | .551 | 4 |
| Huntsville | 37 | 33 | .529 | 5½ |
| Nashville | 32 | 39 | .451 | 11 |
| Memphis | 30 | 39 | .435 | 12 |

**PLAYOFFS—Division:** Knoxville defeated Greenville, 3-2, and Birmingham defeated Nashville, 3-0, in best-of-5 series. **Finals:** Birmingham defeated Knoxville, 3-1, in best-of-5 series.

## LEAGUE CHAMPIONS

**Last 25 Years**

| Year | Regular Season* | Pct. | Playoff |
|---|---|---|---|
| 1969 | Charlotte (Twins) | .579 | None |
| 1970 | Columbus (Astros) | .569 | None |
| 1971 | Charlotte (Twins) | .647 | Charlotte (Twins) |
| 1972 | Asheville (Orioles) | .583 | Montgomery (Tigers) |
| 1973 | Montgomery (Tigers) | .579 | Montgomery (Tigers) |
| 1974 | Jacksonville (Royals) | .565 | Knoxville (White Sox) |
| 1975 | Orlando (Twins) | .586 | Montgomery (Tigers) |
| 1976 | Montgomery (Tigers) | .591 | Montgomery (Tigers) |
| 1977 | Montgomery (Tigers) | .627 | Montgomery (Tigers) |
| 1978 | Knoxville (White Sox) | .611 | Knoxville (White Sox) |
| 1979 | Columbus (Astros) | .587 | Nashville (Reds) |
| 1980 | Nashville (Yankees) | .678 | Charlotte (Orioles) |
| 1981 | Nashville (Yankees) | .566 | Orlando (Twins) |
| 1982 | Jacksonville (Royals) | .576 | Nashville (Yankees) |
| 1983 | Birmingham (Tigers) | .627 | Birmingham (Tigers) |
| 1984 | Greenville (Braves) | .567 | Charlotte (Orioles) |
| 1985 | Knoxville (Blue Jays) | .552 | Huntsville (Athletics) |
| 1986 | Huntsville (Athletics) | .553 | Columbus (Astros) |
| 1987 | Jacksonville (Expos) | .590 | Birmingham (White Sox) |
| 1988 | Greenville (Braves) | .604 | Chattanooga (Reds) |
| 1989 | Birmingham (White Sox) | .615 | Birmingham (White Sox) |
| 1990 | Orlando (Twins) | .590 | Memphis (Royals) |
| 1991 | Greenville (Braves) | .611 | Orlando (Twins) |
| 1992 | Greenville (Braves) | .699 | Greenville (Braves) |
| 1993 | Birmingham (White Sox) | .549 | Birmingham (White Sox) |

*Best overall record

# SOUTHERN LEAGUE
## 1993 BATTING, PITCHING STATISTICS

### CLUB BATTING

| | AVG | G | AB | R | H | 2B | 3B | HR | BB | SO | SB |
|---|---|---|---|---|---|---|---|---|---|---|---|
| Knoxville | .273 | 142 | 4663 | 630 | 1273 | 224 | 29 | 78 | 439 | 930 | 160 |
| Orlando | .266 | 142 | 4737 | 686 | 1262 | 256 | 27 | 122 | 516 | 928 | 96 |
| Memphis | .265 | 140 | 4701 | 627 | 1245 | 232 | 35 | 98 | 447 | 846 | 79 |
| Jacksonville | .264 | 141 | 4735 | 624 | 1248 | 235 | 18 | 125 | 471 | 850 | 130 |
| Huntsville | .264 | 141 | 4620 | 678 | 1221 | 230 | 22 | 100 | 502 | 972 | 111 |
| Birmingham | .260 | 142 | 4598 | 630 | 1196 | 211 | 40 | 86 | 453 | 926 | 159 |
| Chattanooga | .259 | 141 | 4663 | 628 | 1207 | 216 | 35 | 108 | 415 | 1122 | 114 |
| Nashville | .257 | 142 | 4717 | 672 | 1213 | 224 | 31 | 111 | 584 | 925 | 164 |
| Carolina | .256 | 141 | 4733 | 615 | 1213 | 202 | 38 | 88 | 427 | 842 | 109 |
| Greenville | .254 | 142 | 4665 | 602 | 1184 | 233 | 38 | 89 | 476 | 852 | 97 |

### CLUB PITCHING

| | ERA | G | CG | SHO | SV | IP | H | R | ER | BB | SO |
|---|---|---|---|---|---|---|---|---|---|---|---|
| Birmingham | 3.36 | 142 | 17 | 12 | 39 | 1223 | 1104 | 564 | 456 | 446 | 1022 |
| Chattanooga | 3.56 | 141 | 10 | 4 | 43 | 1228 | 1185 | 583 | 486 | 422 | 857 |
| Carolina | 3.75 | 141 | 8 | 6 | 48 | 1249 | 1211 | 626 | 521 | 431 | 951 |
| Greenville | 3.84 | 142 | 7 | 6 | 36 | 1248 | 1203 | 631 | 533 | 572 | 967 |
| Nashville | 4.01 | 142 | 15 | 8 | 26 | 1246 | 1303 | 651 | 556 | 396 | 943 |
| Knoxville | 4.11 | 142 | 7 | 11 | 37 | 1215 | 1277 | 653 | 555 | 461 | 885 |
| Jacksonville | 4.15 | 141 | 5 | 5 | 21 | 1227 | 1189 | 679 | 565 | 500 | 912 |
| Huntsville | 4.15 | 141 | 8 | 14 | 30 | 1207 | 1198 | 676 | 557 | 588 | 949 |
| Orlando | 4.22 | 142 | 10 | 6 | 31 | 1243 | 1317 | 673 | 583 | 440 | 869 |
| Memphis | 4.32 | 140 | 9 | 10 | 24 | 1214 | 1275 | 656 | 583 | 474 | 838 |

### CLUB FIELDING

| | PCT | PO | A | E | DP | | PCT | PO | A | E | DP |
|---|---|---|---|---|---|---|---|---|---|---|---|
| Orlando | .973 | 3730 | 1609 | 148 | 139 | Carolina | .969 | 3748 | 1555 | 167 | 140 |
| Knoxville | .972 | 3644 | 1603 | 151 | 125 | Nashville | .969 | 3739 | 1547 | 167 | 112 |
| Greenville | .971 | 3745 | 1665 | 163 | 152 | Birmingham | .966 | 3668 | 1405 | 179 | 108 |
| Chattanooga | .970 | 3684 | 1488 | 160 | 115 | Jacksonville | .966 | 3680 | 1465 | 183 | 102 |
| Memphis | .970 | 3641 | 1505 | 160 | 120 | Huntsville | .964 | 3622 | 1451 | 190 | 126 |

**Jim Bowie**
Batting Champ

KEN BABBITT

**James Baldwin**
ERA leader

**Rich Becker**
.287-15-66

### INDIVIDUAL BATTING LEADERS
(Minimum 381 Plate Appearances)

| | AVG | G | AB | R | H | 2B | 3B | HR | RBI | BB | SO | SB |
|---|---|---|---|---|---|---|---|---|---|---|---|---|
| Bowie, Jim, Huntsville | .333 | 138 | 501 | 77 | 167 | 33 | 1 | 14 | 101 | 56 | 52 | 8 |
| Hyers, Tim, Knoxville | .306 | 140 | 487 | 72 | 149 | 26 | 3 | 3 | 61 | 53 | 51 | 12 |
| Dismuke, Jamie, Chatt. | .306 | 136 | 497 | 69 | 152 | 22 | 1 | 20 | 91 | 48 | 60 | 4 |
| Wolak, Jerry, Birmingham | .305 | 137 | 525 | 78 | 160 | 35 | 4 | 9 | 64 | 26 | 95 | 16 |
| Casillas, Adam, Memphis | .304 | 126 | 450 | 53 | 137 | 33 | 6 | 4 | 50 | 59 | 18 | 3 |
| Delgado, Carlos, Knoxville | .303 | 140 | 468 | 91 | 142 | 28 | 0 | 25 | 102 | 102 | 98 | 10 |
| Santana, Ruben, Jack. | .301 | 128 | 499 | 79 | 150 | 21 | 2 | 21 | 84 | 38 | 101 | 13 |
| Merchant, Mark, Chatt. | .301 | 109 | 336 | 56 | 101 | 16 | 0 | 17 | 61 | 50 | 79 | 3 |
| Randa, Joe, Memphis | .295 | 131 | 505 | 74 | 149 | 31 | 5 | 11 | 72 | 39 | 64 | 8 |
| Williams, George, Huntsville | .295 | 124 | 434 | 80 | 128 | 26 | 2 | 14 | 77 | 67 | 66 | 6 |

### INDIVIDUAL PITCHING LEADERS
(Minimum 113 Innings)

| | W | L | ERA | G | GS | CG | SV | IP | H | R | ER | BB | SO |
|---|---|---|---|---|---|---|---|---|---|---|---|---|---|
| Baldwin, James, Birm. | 8 | 5 | 2.25 | 17 | 17 | 4 | 0 | 120 | 94 | 48 | 30 | 43 | 107 |
| Hostetler, Mike, Greenville | 8 | 5 | 2.72 | 19 | 19 | 2 | 0 | 136 | 122 | 48 | 41 | 36 | 105 |
| Ruffcorn, Scott, Birm. | 9 | 4 | 2.73 | 20 | 20 | 3 | 0 | 135 | 108 | 47 | 41 | 52 | 141 |
| Munoz, Oscar, Nashville | 11 | 4 | 3.08 | 20 | 20 | 1 | 0 | 132 | 123 | 56 | 45 | 51 | 139 |
| Upshaw, Lee, Greenville | 9 | 9 | 3.29 | 34 | 4 | 0 | 2 | 120 | 109 | 49 | 44 | 56 | 99 |
| Flener, Huck, Knoxville | 13 | 6 | 3.30 | 38 | 16 | 2 | 4 | 136 | 130 | 56 | 50 | 39 | 114 |
| Ferry, Mike, Chattanooga | 13 | 4 | 3.42 | 28 | 28 | 4 | 0 | 187 | 176 | 85 | 71 | 30 | 110 |
| Courtright, John, Chatt. | 5 | 11 | 3.50 | 27 | 27 | 1 | 0 | 175 | 179 | 81 | 68 | 70 | 96 |
| Fyhrie, Mike, Memphis | 11 | 4 | 3.56 | 22 | 22 | 3 | 0 | 131 | 143 | 59 | 52 | 59 | 59 |
| Karsay, Steve, Knox.-Hunt. | 8 | 4 | 3.58 | 21 | 20 | 1 | 0 | 118 | 111 | 50 | 47 | 35 | 122 |

**DEPARTMENT LEADERS**

**BATTING**
| | | |
|---|---|---|
| R | 2 tied at | 93 |
| H | Jim Bowie, Huntsville | 167 |
| TB | Alex Gonzalez, Knoxville | 253 |
| 2B | Jerry Wolak, Birmingham | 35 |
| 3B | Ray Durham, Birmingham | 10 |
| HR | Carlos Delgado, Knoxville | 25 |
| RBI | Carlos Delgado, Knoxville | 102 |
| SH | Daryl Ratliff, Carolina | 14 |
| SF | Joe Randa, Memphis | 10 |
| BB | Carlos Delgado, Knoxville | 102 |
| IBB | Carlos Delgado, Knoxville | 18 |
| HBP | Joe Lis, Knoxville | 16 |
| SO | Marty Cordova, Nashville | 153 |
| SB | Brandon Wilson, Birmingham | 43 |
| CS | Ray Durham, Birmingham | 25 |
| GIDP | Jim Bowie, Huntsville | 17 |
| OB% | Carlos Delgado, Knoxville | .430 |
| SL% | Carlos Delgado, Knoxville | .524 |

**PITCHING**
| | | |
|---|---|---|
| G | 2 tied at | 61 |
| GS | 4 tied at | 28 |
| CG | 3 tied at | 4 |
| ShO | Scott Ruffcorn, Birmingham | 3 |
| GF | Travis Willis, Orlando | 57 |
| Sv | Chris Bushing, Chattanooga | 29 |
| W | 2 tied at | 13 |
| L | Curtis Shaw, Huntsville | 16 |
| IP | Mike Ferry, Chattanooga | 187 |
| H | John Salles, Orlando | 203 |
| R | John Salles, Orlando | 103 |
| ER | Tanyon Sturtze, Huntsville | 88 |
| HR | Bill Wissler, Nashville | 23 |
| BB | Curtis Shaw, Huntsville | 89 |
| HB | Curtis Shaw, Huntsville | 14 |
| SO | Scott Ruffcorn, Birmingham | 141 |
| WP | 2 tied at | 19 |
| Bk | Huck Flener, Knoxville | 8 |

**FIELDING**
| | | |
|---|---|---|
| C AVG | Mike Durant, Nashville | .992 |
| E | Carlos Delgado, Knoxville | 14 |
| 1B AVG | Tim Hyers, Knoxville | .996 |
| E | 2 tied at | 17 |
| 2B AVG | Jose Olmeda, Greenville | .977 |
| E | Ray Durham, Birmingham | 30 |
| 3B AVG | Ed Giovanola, Greenville | .963 |
| E | Howard Battle, Knoxville | 29 |
| SS AVG | Alex Gonzalez, Knoxville | .956 |
| E | 2 tied at | 35 |
| OF AVG | Marty Cordova, Nashville | .991 |
| E | Darren Bragg, Jacksonville | 10 |

## HONOR ROLL
**OFFICIAL ALL-STAR TEAM**
- C Delgado, Knoxville; Williams, Hunt.
- 1B Jim Bowie, Huntsville
- 2B Ruben Santana, Jacksonville
- 3B Joe Randa, Memphis
- SS Alex Gonzalez, Knoxville
- OF Becker, Nashville; Newfield, Jax; Norman, Memphis; Wolak, Birm.
- DH Jamie Dismuke, Chattanooga
- RHP Scott Ruffcorn, Birmingham
- LHP Huck Flener, Knoxville
- RP Chris Bushing, Chattanooga

**MVP:** Carlos Delgado, Knoxville
**MV Pitcher:** Oscar Munoz, Nashville
**Manager:** Terry Francona, Birmingham

**TOP 10 PROSPECTS**
(Selected by league managers)
1. Alex Gonzalez, ss, Knoxville
2. Carlos Delgado, c, Knoxville
3. James Baldwin, rhp, Birmingham
4. Steve Karsay, rhp, Knoxville-Huntsville
5. Scott Ruffcorn, rhp, Birmingham
6. Richie Becker, of, Nashville
7. Marc Newfield, of, Jacksonville
8. Rich Aude, 1b, Carolina
9. Joe Randa, 3b, Memphis
10. Shawn Green, of, Knoxville

# YEAR-BY-YEAR LEADERS: 1946–93 — SOUTHERN LEAGUE

| Year | Batting Average | Home Runs | RBIs | Wins | ERA | Strikeouts |
|---|---|---|---|---|---|---|
| 1946 | Tom Neill, Birm. .374 | Ted Pawelek, Nash. 15 | Tom Neill, Birm. 124 | Earl McGowan, Atlanta 22 | Bill Ayers, Atlanta 1.95 | Bob McCall, Nash. 179 |
| 1947 | Ted Kluszewski, Mem. .377 | Albert Flair, N.O. 24 | Albert Flair, N.O. 128 | Bill Kennedy, Chatt. 20 | Bob Hall, Mobile 2.80 | Ben Wade, Nashville. 145 |
| 1948 | Smoky Burgess, Nash. .384 | Chuck Workman, Nash. 52 | Chuck Workman, Nash. 182 | Norman Brown, Atlanta. 22 | Mike Palm, Birm. 2.20 | John Perkovich, Mem. 153 |
| 1949 | Bob Borkowski, Nash. .376 | Carl Sawatski, Nash. 45 | Carl Sawatski, Nash. 153 | Pete Mallory, Nash. 20 | Jim Suchecki, Birm. 2.77 | Bobo Newsom, Chatt. 141 |
| 1950 | Pat Haggarty, Lit. Rock .346 | Bill Wilson, Memphis 36 | Bill Wilson, Mem. 125 | Robert Schultz, Nash. 25 | Marvin Rotblatt, Mem. 2.67 | Marvin Rotblatt, Mem. 203 |
| 1951 | Babe Barna, Nash. .358 | Jack Harshman, Nash. 47 | Walt Moryn, Mobile 148 | 5 tied at 16 | Frank Biscan, Mem. 2.55 | Dick Littlefield, Mem. 195 |
| 1952 | Rance Pless, Nash. .364 | Frank Thomas, N.O. 35 | Frank Thomas, N.O. 131 | Al Sima, Chattanooga 24 | Wade Browning, Mob. 2.90 | Al Worthington, Nash. 152 |
| 1953 | Bill Taylor, Nashville .350 | Bill Wilson, Memphis 34 | Bill Sinovic, Atlanta 126 | Jack Harshman, Nash. 23 | Art Fowler, Atlanta 3.03 | Dick Strahs, Mem. 153 |
| 1954 | Bob Lennon, Nashville. .345 | Bob Lennon, Nash. 64 | Bob Lennon, Nash. 161 | Leo Cristante, Atlanta 24 | Nellie King, N.O. 2.25 | Joe Marganeri, Nash. 184 |
| 1955 | Charles Williams, Nash. .368 | Bob Hazle, Nashville 29 | 2 tied at 109 | Jerry Dahlke, Mem. 19 | Ralph Mauriello, Mob. 2.76 | Gene Host, Lit. Rock. 184 |
| 1956 | Stan Roseboro, Chatt. .340 | Johnny Powers, N.O. 39 | Gordy Coleman, Mobile 118 | Al Papai, Memphis 20 | Bill Dailey, Mobile 3.18 | Bob Kelly, Nash. 180 |
| 1957 | Stan Palys, Nashville .340 | Stan Palys, Nashville 29 | Jess Levan, Chatt. 114 | Bob Kelly, Nashville 20 | Hy Cohen, Memphis 2.72 | George Brunet, Lit. Rock. 235 |
| 1958 | Marv Staehle, Nash. .359 | Harmon Killebrew, Chatt. 29 | Charles Coles, Nash. 107 | 3 tied at 18 | Bob Davis, Lit. Rock 2.17 | 2 tied at 189 |
| 1959 | Jim Fridley, Nashville .348 | Kent Hadley, Lit. Rock. 34 | Gordy Coleman, Mobile. 110 | Don Bradley, N.O. 19 | Bill Dailey, Mobile 2.41 | Carl Mathias, Mobile 183 |
| 1960 | Gordy Coleman, Mobile .353 | Gordy Coleman, Mobile. 30 | Leo Posada, Shreve. 110 | Pete Richert, Atlanta 19 | Ron Nischwitz, Birm. 2.31 | Pete Richert, Atl. 251 |
| 1961 | Stan Reimer, Birm. .370 | Bill Gabler, Macon 30 | Stan Palys, Birm. 114 | Howie Koplitz, Birm. 23 | Jack Smith, Atlanta 2.00 | Bo Belinsky, Lit. Rock. 182 |
| 1962 | Don Saner, Lit. Rock. .349 | 2 tied at 36 | Deacon Jones, Savannah. 101 | Camilo Estevis, Green. 18 | Dick Lines, Ashe. 2.11 | Leo Marenette, Knox. 205 |
| 1963 | Elmo Plaskett, Ashe. .349 | Wayne Redmond, Mont. 21 | Jim Hicks, Macon-Lynch. 83 | 2 tied at 20 | Tom Richards, Lynch. 2.22 | Troy Giles, Asheville 159 |
| 1964 | Arlie Burge, Asheville .337 | Dick Kenworthy, Lynch. 29 | Lee May, Macon 110 | Manly Johnston, Lynch. 18 | Manly Johnston, Lynch. 2.46 | David Galligan, Macon 168 |
| 1965 | Gerry Reimer, Knox. .310 | Orlando McFarlane, Ashe. 22 | Charles Leonard, Ashe. 78 | 2 tied at 17 | Luke Walker, Ashe. 2.26 | Luke Walker, Ashe. 197 |
| 1966 | John Fenderson, Knox. .324 | Bob Robertson, Ashe. 32 | Bob Robertson, Ashe. 99 | Bill Edgerton, Mobile 15 | Dave Roberts, Ashe. 2.61 | George Korince, Mont. 183 |
| 1967 | Minnie Mendoza, Char. .297 | 2 tied at 19 | Barry Morgan, Mont. 87 | Dick Drago, Mont. 15 | George Lauzerique, Birm. 2.29 | Dick Drago, Mont. 134 |
| 1968 | Arlie Burge, Asheville .317 | Wayne Redmond, Mont. 26 | Barry Morgan, Mont. 91 | Grover Powell, Ashe. 17 | Grover Powell, Ashe. 2.54 | George Korince, Mont. 146 |
| 1969 | Don Anderson, Ashe. .307 | Bobby Brooks, Ashe. 23 | 2 tied at 73 | 2 tied at 13 | LaDon Boyd, Birm. 2.19 | Paul Coleman, Ashe. 153 |
| 1970 | Steve Brye, Charlotte .324 | Jim Covington, Jax. 21 | Ken Hotman, Ashe. 116 | Ken Hotman, Ashe. 16 | David Hartman, Jax. 2.01 | Bill Gilbreth, Mont. 192 |
| 1971 | Minnie Mendoza, Char. .316 | Ken Hotman, Ashe. 37 | Mike Reinbach, Ashe. 109 | Paul Mitchell, Ashe. 16 | Dick Rusteck, Char. 2.40 | Chris Floethe, Birm. 225 |
| 1972 | Mike Reinbach, Ashe. .346 | Mike Reinbach, Ashe. 30 | Terry Clapp, Ashe. 98 | Joe Henderson, Knox. 17 | Dan Vossler, Char. 2.11 | Bill Campbell, Char. 204 |
| 1973 | Rob Andrews, Ashe. .309 | Terry Clapp, Ashe. 35 | Bob Gorinski, Orl. 100 | 2 tied at 14 | Russ Rothermel, Col. 1.81 | Doug Konieczny, Col. 222 |
| 1974 | Nyls Nyman, Knoxville .325 | 2 tied at 23 | Jim O'Bradovich, Orl. 74 | 3 tied at 17 | Mike Beard, Savannah 2.40 | Mike Stanton, Col. 146 |
| 1975 | Chuck Heil, Asheville .322 | Jim O'Bradovich, Orl. 27 | Jim O'Bradovich, Orl. 68 | Dave Ford, Charlotte 15 | Dan Larson, Columbus 2.18 | Joe Sambito, Columbus. 140 |
| 1976 | Larry Foster, Knox. .311 | Jim O'Bradovich, Orl. 21 | Jerry Keller, Savannah 86 | Bryn Smith, Charlotte 17 | Dave Rozema, Mont. 1.57 | Dave Ford, Charlotte. 121 |
| 1977 | Mark Corey, Charlotte .310 | Eddie Gates, Memphis 25 | Sal Rende, Chatt. 87 | Terry Sheehan, Col. 17 | Sammy Stewart, Char. 2.08 | Matt Keough, Chatt. 153 |
| 1978 | Joe Gates, Knoxville .332 | Alan Knicely, Col. 33 | Dave Hostetler, Mem. 114 | Del Leatherwood, Col. 15 | Roger Alexander, Sav. 1.84 | Jay Howell, Nash. 173 |
| 1979 | Joe Charboneau, Chatt. .352 | Dan Pasqua, Nash. 33 | Steve Balboni, Nash. 122 | Jim MacDonald, Col. 17 | Scott Brown, Ont. 2.40 | Bob Veselic, Orl. 151 |
| 1980 | Chris Bando, Chatt. .341 | Tim Laudner, Orlando 42 | Tim Laudner, Orlando 107 | Craig McMurtry, Sav. 15 | Andy McGaffigan, Nash. 2.38 | Steve Bedrosian, Sav. 161 |
| 1981 | Kevin Rhomberg, Chatt. .366 | Mark Funderburk, Orl. 34 | Mike Fuentes, Memphis 115 | 2 tied at 16 | Mark Ross, Columbus 2.25 | Jamie Werly, Nashville. 193 |
| 1982 | Kenny Baker, Birm. .342 | Glenallen Hill, Knox. 31 | Miguel Sosa, Savannah 93 | Don Heinkel, Birm. 16 | Stefan Wever, Nash. 2.78 | Stefan Wever, Nash. 191 |
| 1983 | Ivan Calderon, Chatt. .311 | Rondal Rollin, Birm. 39 | Stan Holmes, Orlando 101 | 2 tied at 16 | Roger Mason, Birm. 2.06 | Mark Gubicza, Knox. 146 |
| 1984 | Doc Estes, Greenville. .303 | 2 tied at 25 | Mark Funderburk, Orl. 116 | Steve Davis, Knoxville 17 | Mark Williams, Jax. 2.49 | Alex Sanchez, Knox. 164 |
| 1985 | Bruce Fields, Chatt. .341 | Matt Winters, Memphis 25 | Terry Steinbach, Hunts. 132 | Anthony Kelley, Col. 14 | Steve Davis, Knox. 2.45 | Ken Dixon, Charlotte. 211 |
| 1986 | Brick Smith, Chatt. .344 | Eric Anthony, Col. 28 | Tom Dodd, Charlotte 127 | John Trautwein, Jax. 15 | Eric Bell, Charlotte 3.05 | Terry Taylor, Chatt. 164 |
| 1987 | Dave Myers, Charlotte .328 | Matt Stark, Birm. 24 | Matt Winters, Memphis 91 | Chris Hammond, Chatt. 16 | Brian Holman, Jax. 2.50 | Randy Johnson, Jax. 163 |
| 1988 | Butch Davis, Charlotte .301 | Elvin Paulino, Char. 24 | Paul Sorrento, Orl. 112 | Laddie Renfroe, Char. 16 | Chris Hammond, Chatt. 1.72 | Alex Sanchez, Knox. 166 |
| 1989 | Scott Leius, Orlando .303 | Eric Anthony, Col. 28 | Paul Sorrento, Orl. 112 | Doug Simons, Orlando. 17 | Pete Delkus, Orlando 1.87 | Shawn Boskie, Charlotte 164 |
| 1990 | Adam Casillas, Chatt. .336 | Matt Stark, Birm. 24 | Matt Stark, Birm. 109 | Nap Robinson, Green. 16 | Jeff Carter, Jax. 2.45 | Brian Barnes, Jax. 213 |
| 1991 | Jim Bowie, Jax. .310 | Elvin Paulino, Char. 24 | Elvin Paulino, Char. 81 | 4 tied at 13 | Pat Mahomes, Orl. 1.78 | Mike Trombley, Orl. 175 |
| 1992 | Scott Pose, Chatt. .342 | Tim Costo, Chatt. 28 | Scott Cepicky, Birm. 87 | 2 tied at 13 | Larry Thomas, Birm. 1.94 | Jim Converse, Jax. 157 |
| 1993 | Jim Bowie, Huntsville. .333 | Carlos Delgado, Knox. 25 | Carlos Delgado, Knox. 102 | 2 tied at 13 | James Baldwin, Birm. 2.25 | Scott Ruffcorn, Birm. 141 |

NOTE: Southern Association from 1946-61; South Atlantic League from 1962-63; Southern League 1964-present.

# TEXAS
## LEAGUE

# Petagine Leads Generals To TL Title

**By MIKE BERARDINO**

Paced by the bat of league MVP Roberto Petagine, the Jackson Generals won their first Texas League playoff championship since 1985 and their first title as an Astros affiliate.

Jackson lost seven of 10 regular-season meetings with El Paso, but summoned the strength to sweep the Diablos in the best-of-5 final. Jackson took the first two games of the series in El Paso, winning 6-4 and 3-2, before returning home for the clincher.

Reserve third baseman Mike Groppuso drove in three runs to lead the Generals to an 8-1 win in Game Three.

In the best-of-5 semifinals, Jackson downed Shreveport and El Paso bested Wichita in four games apiece.

Petagine, 22, punished opposing pitchers all season. The lefthanded-hitting first baseman batted .336 to lead the league in hitting and finish second in RBIs (90). Petagine also smacked 36 doubles and 15 home runs, and drew 84 walks.

"As disciplined a hitter as I've ever seen at this level," Jackson manager Sal Butera said of Petagine, a native of Venezuela. "He did a great job all season of adjusting to how he was being pitched. You just didn't get him out the same way twice in a row."

**Roberto Petagine**

Butera, named TL manager of the year, had more weapons than just Petagine in his arsenal. Other Generals included:

■ Center fielder Brian Hunter, who batted .294 with 35 stolen bases and ran down everything in sight;

■ Submarining closer Jim Dougherty, who went 2-2 with a 1.87 ERA and 36 saves in 39 save opportunities to earn a spot on Baseball America's year-end Double-A All-Star team. Dougherty broke by two a 15-year-old TL record for saves.

"One of the steadiest pitching jobs I've ever seen," Butera said of Dougherty. "He was money in the bank for us all year long."

**Ben VanRyn.** Texas League's top prospect went 14-4 with a 2.21 ERA for San Antonio

STAN DENNY

The Generals won the first half with a strong showing, then tapered off to three games under .500 in the second. Losing shortstop Tom Nevers for the year after thumb surgery in early July didn't help.

## Prospects Galore

While Hunter (No. 2), Petagine (No. 4) and Morman (No. 8) left Jackson well-represented on the list of Top 10 Prospects, as selected by managers, the San Antonio Missions matched the league champions with three players of their own.

Lefthander Ben VanRyn went 14-4 with a 2.21 ERA in 21 San Antonio starts before earning a late-July callup to Triple-A Albuquerque. VanRyn, acquired in a trade from the Expos organization after the 1991 sea-

## STANDINGS: OVERALL

| Page | | W | L | PCT | GB | Manager | Attendance/Dates | Last Pennant |
|------|------|---|---|-----|-----|---------|------------------|--------------|
| 133 | El Paso Diablos (Brewers) | 75 | 59 | .560 | — | Tim Ireland | 306,948 (67) | 1986 |
| 115 | Jackson Generals (Astros) | 73 | 61 | .545 | 2 | Sal Butera | 148,230 (60) | 1993 |
| 68 | Midland Angels (Angels) | 67 | 67 | .500 | 8 | Don Long | 196,464 (67) | 1975 |
| 188 | Wichita Wranglers (Padres) | 67 | 68 | .496 | 8 ½ | Dave Trembley | 236,378 (67) | 1992 |
| 180 | Arkansas Travelers (Cardinals) | 66 | 69 | .489 | 9 ½ | Joe Pettini | 285,757 (56) | 1989 |
| 194 | Shreveport Captains (Giants) | 66 | 69 | .489 | 9 ½ | Ron Wotus | 203,479 (61) | 1991 |
| 206 | Tulsa Drillers (Rangers) | 65 | 69 | .485 | 10 | Stan Cliburn | 325,135 (64) | 1988 |
| 126 | San Antonio Missions (Dodgers) | 58 | 75 | .436 | 16 ½ | Glenn Hoffman | 189,251 (64) | None |

**NOTE:** Team's individual batting and pitching statistics can be found on page indicated in lefthand column.

son, struck out 144 in 134 Double-A innings to earn the No. 1 prospect label.

No. 6 prospect Roger Cedeno also earned high marks. At the tender age of 18, the Missions outfielder batted .288 with 28 stolen bases. Outfielder Todd Hollandsworth (No. 9) hit .251 with 17 homers at age 20 to round out San Antonio's presence on the list.

Cedeno, who like Petagine is from Venezuela, was the youngest player in the league. He didn't turn 19 until August.

Two other Texas Leaguers spent part of 1993 in the major leagues. Tulsa shortstop Benji Gil had two stints with the injury-riddled Texas Rangers, including one at the start of the season. Once Gil, 20, returned to his rightful place, he batted .275 with 17 home runs and 20 stolen bases for Tulsa.

Righthander Salomon Torres was the other TL member to reach the bigs. Torres went 7-4 with a 2.20 ERA in 12 starts for Shreveport before earning a September callup to the San Francisco Giants. Torres made eight starts for the Giants in the heat of the pennant race, including the season-ending loss to the Dodgers. He went 3-5, 4.03.

## All-Star Showing

Wichita outfielder Dwayne Hosey played in two all-star games in 1993, and stood out in both.

In the Double-A game in Memphis, he went 3-for-4 with a double, a home run and two RBIs. Hosey was a last-minute replacement in that game.

In the TL game in Wichita, the score was tied 3-3

## STANDINGS: SPLIT SEASON

| FIRST HALF | | | | | SECOND HALF | | | | |
|---|---|---|---|---|---|---|---|---|---|
| EAST | W | L | PCT | GB | EAST | W | L | PCT | GB |
| Jackson | 41 | 26 | .612 | — | Shreveport | 37 | 31 | .544 | — |
| Arkansas | 36 | 31 | .537 | 5 | Tulsa | 35 | 32 | .522 | 1½ |
| Tulsa | 30 | 37 | .448 | 11 | Jackson | 32 | 35 | .478 | 4½ |
| Shreveport | 29 | 38 | .433 | 12 | Arkansas | 30 | 38 | .441 | 7 |
| **WEST** | **W** | **L** | **PCT** | **GB** | **WEST** | **W** | **L** | **PCT** | **GB** |
| El Paso | 35 | 31 | .530 | — | El Paso | 40 | 28 | .588 | — |
| San Antonio | 33 | 33 | .500 | 2 | Wichita | 37 | 31 | .544 | 3 |
| Midland | 33 | 34 | .493 | 2½ | Midland | 34 | 33 | .507 | 5½ |
| Wichita | 30 | 37 | .448 | 5½ | San Antonio | 25 | 42 | .373 | 14½ |

**PLAYOFFS—Division:** Jackson defeated Shreveport, 3-1, and El Paso defeated Wichita, 3-1, in best-of-5 series. **Finals:** Jackson defeated El Paso, 3-0, in best-of-5 series.

**Trey McCoy.** Tulsa slugger led TL with 29 homers, 95 RBIs.

after nine innings and neither team had any pitchers left. It was decided that Arkansas Travelers second baseman Darrel Deak and Hosey would face off in a home run contest to decide the outcome.

Hosey already had two homers in the game, but both he and Deak missed with their first two attempts. On the third try, Deak homered just inside the right-field foul pole. Hosey followed with another shot to right, but his went just foul.

The game was the last East-West all-star game for the league. Beginning in 1994, Texas League all-stars will meet the Mexican League all-stars in a two-game series. The first game is set for San Antonio.

## Speed Demons

Before the 1993 season, TL president Tom Kayser sent a memo to clubs urging them to follow specific rules to speed up games. That reminder paid off with an average game time of 2:35, easily the fastest in Double-A, Triple-A or the majors.

"I'm very much pleased with it," Kayser said. "That's a dramatic improvement. We're shooting for 2:20 next season."

The league was so serious about enforcing Rule 8.04, which requires a pitch be thrown every 20 seconds, it discussed putting in a pitch clock at its midseason meetings. If future games continue at the 1993 pace, the clock won't be necessary.

Perhaps not unrelated to the faster games was an increase in league attendance. Tulsa again led the way at a club-record 325,135. El Paso, after a 4 percent dip in 1992, rebounded with a club-record 306,948.

**Rick Helling.** Tulsa righthander had league-best 188 strikeouts.

## LEAGUE CHAMPIONS

**Last 25 Years**

| Year | Regular Season* | Pct. | Playoff |
|---|---|---|---|
| 1969 | Amarillo (Giants) | .593 | Memphis (Mets) |
| 1970 | Albuquerque (Dodgers) | .615 | Albuquerque (Dodgers) |
| 1971 | Amarillo (Giants) | .620 | Arkansas (Cardinals) |
| 1972 | Alexandria (Padres) | .600 | El Paso (Dodgers) |
| 1973 | San Antonio (Indians) | .589 | Memphis (Mets) |
| 1974 | Victoria (Mets) | .580 | Victoria (Mets) |
| 1975 | Midland (Cubs) | .604 | Midland (Cubs)# |
| | | | Lafayette (Giants)# |
| 1976 | Amarillo (Padres) | .600 | Amarillo (Padres) |
| 1977 | El Paso (Angels) | .600 | Arkansas (Cardinals) |
| 1978 | El Paso (Angels) | .592 | El Paso (Angels) |
| 1979 | Arkansas (Cardinals) | .571 | Arkansas (Cardinals) |
| 1980 | Arkansas (Cardinals) | .595 | Arkansas (Cardinals) |
| 1981 | San Antonio (Dodgers) | .571 | Jackson (Mets) |
| 1982 | El Paso (Brewers) | .568 | Tulsa (Rangers) |
| 1983 | El Paso (Brewers) | .544 | Beaumont (Padres) |
| 1984 | Beaumont (Padres) | .654 | Jackson (Mets) |
| 1985 | El Paso (Brewers) | .632 | Jackson (Mets) |
| 1986 | El Paso (Brewers) | .629 | El Paso (Brewers) |
| 1987 | Shreveport (Giants) | .577 | Wichita (Padres) |
| 1988 | El Paso (Brewers) | .552 | Tulsa (Rangers) |
| 1989 | Arkansas (Cardinals) | .585 | Arkansas (Cardinals) |
| 1990 | San Antonio (Dodgers) | .582 | Shreveport (Giants) |
| 1991 | Shreveport (Giants) | .632 | Shreveport (Giants) |
| 1992 | Shreveport (Giants) | .566 | Wichita (Padres) |
| | Tulsa (Rangers) | .566 | |
| 1993 | El Paso (Brewers) | .560 | Jackson (Astros) |
| *Best overall record | | #Co-champions | |

# TEXAS LEAGUE
## 1993 BATTING, PITCHING STATISTICS

### CLUB BATTING

| | AVG | G | AB | R | H | 2B | 3B | HR | BB | SO | SB |
|---|---|---|---|---|---|---|---|---|---|---|---|
| Midland | .285 | 136 | 4639 | 729 | 1322 | 229 | 39 | 84 | 471 | 799 | 68 |
| El Paso | .275 | 135 | 4610 | 703 | 1266 | 245 | 59 | 68 | 448 | 824 | 144 |
| Wichita | .267 | 136 | 4502 | 631 | 1200 | 198 | 37 | 97 | 435 | 980 | 196 |
| Jackson | .267 | 135 | 4387 | 615 | 1171 | 224 | 23 | 113 | 409 | 975 | 115 |
| Tulsa | .260 | 135 | 4360 | 547 | 1135 | 196 | 26 | 125 | 365 | 908 | 91 |
| San Antonio | .247 | 135 | 4504 | 533 | 1114 | 204 | 39 | 100 | 385 | 843 | 121 |
| Shreveport | .247 | 136 | 4420 | 497 | 1090 | 222 | 22 | 64 | 374 | 824 | 83 |
| Arkansas | .247 | 136 | 4330 | 550 | 1069 | 239 | 30 | 100 | 415 | 918 | 74 |

### CLUB PITCHING

| | ERA | G | CG | SHO | SV | IP | H | R | ER | BB | SO |
|---|---|---|---|---|---|---|---|---|---|---|---|
| San Antonio | 3.45 | 135 | 5 | 9 | 35 | 1199 | 1165 | 570 | 460 | 417 | 957 |
| Shreveport | 3.46 | 136 | 6 | 7 | 38 | 1166 | 1137 | 528 | 448 | 412 | 828 |
| Arkansas | 3.49 | 136 | 8 | 13 | 32 | 1154 | 1098 | 531 | 448 | 369 | 921 |
| Jackson | 3.77 | 135 | 4 | 10 | 43 | 1143 | 1118 | 570 | 479 | 389 | 915 |
| El Paso | 3.88 | 135 | 9 | 11 | 40 | 1201 | 1268 | 635 | 518 | 427 | 753 |
| Tulsa | 4.01 | 135 | 5 | 12 | 33 | 1138 | 1088 | 602 | 507 | 412 | 945 |
| Wichita | 4.12 | 136 | 8 | 7 | 34 | 1177 | 1171 | 640 | 539 | 457 | 901 |
| Midland | 4.78 | 136 | 10 | 3 | 29 | 1198 | 1322 | 729 | 636 | 419 | 851 |

### CLUB FIELDING

| | PCT | PO | A | E | DP | | PCT | PO | A | E | DP |
|---|---|---|---|---|---|---|---|---|---|---|---|
| Shreveport | .972 | 3498 | 1404 | 143 | 164 | San Antonio | .966 | 3597 | 1487 | 181 | 97 |
| Arkansas | .971 | 3462 | 1363 | 143 | 89 | Wichita | .966 | 3530 | 1490 | 174 | 110 |
| Midland | .968 | 3593 | 1421 | 167 | 126 | Tulsa | .965 | 3415 | 1310 | 172 | 103 |
| El Paso | .967 | 3603 | 1601 | 177 | 160 | Jackson | .962 | 3429 | 1486 | 192 | 135 |

**Jim Dougherty**
36 saves

**Brian Hunter**
35 stolen bases

MEL BAILEY

### INDIVIDUAL BATTING LEADERS
(Minimum 367 Plate Appearances)

| | AVG | G | AB | R | H | 2B | 3B | HR | RBI | BB | SO | SB |
|---|---|---|---|---|---|---|---|---|---|---|---|---|
| Petagine, Roberto, Jackson | .334 | 128 | 437 | 73 | 146 | 36 | 2 | 15 | 90 | 84 | 89 | 6 |
| Forbes, P.J., Midland | .319 | 126 | 498 | 90 | 159 | 23 | 2 | 15 | 64 | 26 | 50 | 6 |
| Dodson, Bo, El Paso | .312 | 101 | 330 | 58 | 103 | 27 | 4 | 9 | 59 | 42 | 69 | 1 |
| Pritchett, Chris, Midland | .308 | 127 | 464 | 61 | 143 | 30 | 6 | 2 | 66 | 61 | 72 | 3 |
| Palmeiro, Orlando, Midland | .305 | 131 | 535 | 85 | 163 | 19 | 5 | 0 | 64 | 42 | 35 | 18 |
| Kellner, Frank, Jackson | .301 | 121 | 355 | 51 | 107 | 27 | 2 | 4 | 36 | 38 | 51 | 11 |
| Katzaroff, Robbie, Shreve. | .300 | 104 | 406 | 52 | 122 | 22 | 4 | 0 | 30 | 35 | 33 | 15 |
| Colon, Cris, Tulsa | .300 | 124 | 490 | 63 | 147 | 27 | 3 | 11 | 47 | 13 | 76 | 6 |
| Hunter, Brian, Jackson | .294 | 133 | 523 | 84 | 154 | 22 | 5 | 10 | 52 | 34 | 85 | 35 |
| Thompson, Fletcher, Jackson | .294 | 98 | 316 | 64 | 93 | 15 | 2 | 4 | 29 | 55 | 83 | 23 |

### INDIVIDUAL PITCHING LEADERS
(Minimum 109 Innings)

| | W | L | ERA | G | GS | CG | SV | IP | H | R | ER | BB | SO |
|---|---|---|---|---|---|---|---|---|---|---|---|---|---|
| VanRyn, Ben, San Antonio | 14 | 4 | 2.21 | 21 | 21 | 1 | 0 | 134 | 118 | 43 | 33 | 37 | 144 |
| Karl, Scott, El Paso | 13 | 8 | 2.45 | 27 | 27 | 4 | 0 | 180 | 172 | 67 | 49 | 35 | 95 |
| Brumley, Duff, Ark.-Tulsa | 7 | 7 | 2.93 | 18 | 18 | 2 | 0 | 111 | 87 | 43 | 36 | 35 | 121 |
| Parra, Jose, San Antonio | 1 | 8 | 3.05 | 17 | 17 | 0 | 0 | 111 | 103 | 46 | 39 | 12 | 87 |
| Gorecki, Rick, San Antonio | 6 | 9 | 3.35 | 26 | 26 | 1 | 0 | 156 | 136 | 76 | 58 | 62 | 118 |
| Helling, Rick, Tulsa | 12 | 8 | 3.60 | 26 | 26 | 2 | 0 | 177 | 150 | 76 | 71 | 46 | 188 |
| Fritz, John, Midland | 9 | 5 | 3.61 | 20 | 20 | 2 | 0 | 130 | 125 | 61 | 52 | 42 | 85 |
| Delahoya, Javier, SA | 8 | 10 | 3.66 | 21 | 21 | 1 | 0 | 125 | 122 | 61 | 51 | 42 | 107 |
| Thomas, Royal, SA | 4 | 6 | 3.94 | 47 | 6 | 0 | 2 | 110 | 116 | 58 | 48 | 44 | 52 |
| Florie, Bryce, Wichita | 11 | 8 | 3.96 | 27 | 27 | 0 | 0 | 155 | 128 | 80 | 68 | 100 | 133 |

### DEPARTMENT LEADERS

**BATTING**
| | | |
|---|---|---|
| R | P.J. Forbes, Midland | 90 |
| H | Orlando Palmeiro, Midland | 163 |
| TB | Trey McCoy, Tulsa | 243 |
| 2B | Roberto Petagine, Jackson | 36 |
| 3B | Allen Battle, Arkansas | 12 |
| HR | Trey McCoy, Tulsa | 29 |
| RBI | Trey McCoy, Tulsa | 95 |
| SH | Orlando Palmeiro, Midland | 18 |
| SF | Ray Holbert, Wichita | 9 |
| BB | Roberto Petagine, Jackson | 84 |
| IBB | Roberto Petagine, Jackson | 14 |
| HBP | Trey McCoy, Tulsa | 19 |
| SO | Lance Madsen, Jackson | 136 |
| SB | Brian Hunter, Jackson | 35 |
| CS | Roger Cedeno, San Antonio | 20 |
| GIDP | 2 tied at | 17 |
| OB% | Roberto Petagine, Jackson | .442 |
| SL% | Trey McCoy, Tulsa | .579 |

**PITCHING**
| | | |
|---|---|---|
| G | Bryan Eversgerd, Arkansas | 62 |
| GS | 5 tied at | 27 |
| CG | 2 tied at | 4 |
| ShO | 3 tied at | 2 |
| GF | 2 tied at | 50 |
| Sv | Jim Dougherty, Jackson | 36 |
| W | Ben Vanryn, San Antonio | 14 |
| L | Doug Ketchen, Jackson | 12 |
| IP | Scott Karl, El Paso | 180 |
| H | David Holdridge, Midland | 202 |
| R | David Holdridge, Midland | 117 |
| ER | David Holdridge, Midland | 102 |
| HR | Brian Barber, Arkansas | 19 |
| BB | Bryce Florie, Wichita | 100 |
| HB | 2 tied at | 11 |
| SO | Rick Helling, Tulsa | 188 |
| WP | Bryce Florie, Wichita | 24 |
| Bk | 2 tied at | 7 |

**FIELDING**
| | | |
|---|---|---|
| C AVG | Marc Ronan, Arkansas | .994 |
| E | 2 tied at | 11 |
| 1B AVG | Barry Miller, Shreveport | .996 |
| E | Chris Pritchett, Midland | 19 |
| 2B AVG | P.J. Forbes, Midland | .970 |
| E | Fletcher Thompson, Jackson | 27 |
| 3B AVG | Henry Blanco, San Antonio | .944 |
| E | Mike Groppuso, Jackson | 33 |
| SS AVG | Jeff Shireman, Arkansas | .971 |
| E | Wes Weger, El Paso | 36 |
| OF AVG | John Mabry, Arkansas | .989 |
| E | Brian Hunter, Jackson | 14 |

### HONOR ROLL

**OFFICIAL ALL-STAR TEAM**
C Jorge Fabregas, Midland
1B Roberto Petagine, Jackson
2B P.J. Forbes, Midland
3B Cris Colon, Tulsa
SS Wes Weger, El Paso
OF Dwayne Hosey, Wichita
　　Brian Hunter, Jackson
　　John Mabry, Arkansas
DH Trey McCoy, Tulsa
P Dougherty, Jackson; Florie, Wichita; Gorecki, SA; Helling, Tulsa; Karl, El Paso; VanRyn, SA

**MVP:** Roberto Petagine, Jackson
**Manager:** Sal Butera, Jackson

**TOP 10 PROSPECTS**
(Selected by league managers)
1. Ben VanRyn, lhp, San Antonio
2. Brian Hunter, of, Jackson
3. Salomon Torres, rhp, Shreveport
4. Roberto Petagine, 1b, Jackson
5. Benji Gil, ss, Tulsa
6. Roger Cedeno, of, San Antonio
7. Rick Helling, rhp, Tulsa
8. Alvin Morman, lhp, Jackson
9. Todd Hollandsworth, of, San Antonio
10. Calvin Murray, of, Shreveport

# YEAR-BY-YEAR LEADERS: 1946-93 — TEXAS LEAGUE

| Year | Batting Average | Home Runs | RBIs | Wins | ERA | Strikeouts |
|---|---|---|---|---|---|---|
| 1946 | Dale Mitchell, Okla. City .337 | Bob Moyer, Dallas 24 | Bob Moyer, Dallas 102 | Henry Oana, Dallas 24 | John Van Cuyk, Ft. Worth 1.42 | John Van Cuyk, Ft. Worth 207 |
| 1947 | Al Rosen, Okla. City .349 | Nick Gregory, Shreve. 28 | Al Rosen, Okla. City 141 | Clarence Beers, Hous. 25 | Dwain Sloat, Ft. Worth 1.99 | Dwain Sloat, Ft. Worth 162 |
| 1948 | Tom Tatum, Tulsa .333 | Russ Burns, Tulsa 26 | Russ Burns, Tulsa 113 | Harry Perkowski, Tulsa 22 | Bud Byerly, Tulsa 2.21 | Cloyd Boyer, Houston 188 |
| 1949 | Herb Conyers, Okla. City .355 | Jerry Witte, Dallas 50 | Russ Witte, Dallas 153 | Joe Landrum, Ft. Worth 19 | Carl Erskine, Ft. Worth 2.07 | Dick Rozek, Okla. City 145 |
| 1950 | Frank Saucier, S.A. .343 | Bob Lemon, Okla. City 39 | Bob Lemon, Okla. City 119 | 3 tied at 21 | Carl Rutherford, Ft. Worth 2.21 | Joe Presko, Houston 165 |
| 1951 | Bob Nieman, Okla. City .324 | Jerry Witte, Houston 38 | Al Papai, Houston 127 | Tom Gorman, Beau. 23 | Tom Gorman, Beau. 1.94 | Wilmer Mizell, Hous. 257 |
| 1952 | Grant Dunlap, Shreve. .333 | Bud Heslet, S.A. 31 | Al Dyck, San Antonio 120 | Dave Hoskins, Dallas 22 | Joe Landrum, Ft. Worth 1.94 | John Gray, Beaumont 152 |
| 1953 | Joe Frazier, Okla. City .332 | Bud Heslet, Shreve. 41 | Russ Burns, Okla. City 120 | Red Murff, Dallas 17 | Floyd Woolridge, Hous. 2.46 | Ryne Duren, San Antonio 212 |
| 1954 | Les Fleming, Beau.-Dall. .358 | Buzz Clarkson, Dallas 42 | Frank Kellert, S.A. 146 | 2 tied at 21 | Bob Smith, Shreve. 2.89 | Karl Spooner, Ft. Worth 262 |
| 1955 | Eddie Knoblauch, Beau.-Dall. .327 | Pidge Browne, Shreve. 33 | Jim Pisoni, S.A. 118 | Red Murff, Dallas 27 | Red Murff, Dallas 1.99 | Pete Burnside, Dallas 235 |
| 1956 | Albie Pearson, Okla. City .371 | Ken Guettler, Shreve. 62 | Ken Guettler, Shreve. 143 | Tom Bowers, Dallas 21 | Bob Mabe, Houston 2.33 | Bob Mabe, Houston 195 |
| 1957 | Jim Frey, Tulsa .336 | Keith Little, Houston 30 | Spence Robbins, Okla. City 95 | Joe Kotrany, Dallas 20 | Larry Sherry, Ft. Worth 1.79 | Larry Sherry, Ft. Worth 146 |
| 1958 | Eric Roden, Cor. Christi .320 | Mike Lutz, Cor. Christi 39 | Mike Lutz, Cor. Christi. 111 | Carroll Beringer, Vic. 19 | Jim Tugerson, Dallas 2.96 | Jim Tugerson, Dallas 195 |
| 1959 | Al Nagel, Amarillo .344 | Carl Warwick, Victoria 35 | Al Nagel, Amarillo 123 | Jack Curtis, S.A. 19 | Don Erickson, Tulsa 2.96 | Charles Gorin, Austin 173 |
| 1960 | Chuck Hiller, Rio Grande .334 | Layton Ducote, Tulsa 32 | Harry Watts, Tulsa 99 | Paul Toth, Tulsa 18 | Charles Gorin, Austin 2.83 | Denny Lemaster, Austin 181 |
| 1961 | Phil Linz, Amarillo .349 | Craig Sorenson, S.A. 27 | Dick Berardino, Amarillo 93 | John Santiago, Alb. 16 | Denny Lemaster, Austin 2.08 | Harry Fanok, Tulsa 158 |
| 1962 | Charlie Dees, El Paso .348 | Jerry Robinson, El Paso 36 | Cap Peterson, El Paso 130 | Camilo Estevis, Alb. 16 | Harry Fanok, Tulsa 3.18 | G. Richardson, Tulsa 116 |
| 1963 | Dick Dietz, El Paso .354 | Arlo Engel, El Paso 41 | Arlo Engel, El Paso 126 | Jim Ward, Albuquerque 16 | Harvey Branch, S.A. 3.00 | Camilo Estevis, Alb. 196 |
| 1964 | Mel Corbo, Alb. .339 | Chuck Harrison, S.A. 40 | Moose Stubing, El Paso 120 | Ken Nixon, Austin 17 | Sterling Slaughter, Amar. 2.55 | Sterling Slaughter, Amar. 224 |
| 1965 | Dave Pavlesic, Tulsa .344 | Leo Posada, Amarillo 26 | Leo Posada, Amarillo 107 | Bill Larkin, Albuquerque 19 | Dick Burwell, Ft. Worth 2.18 | Dick Burwell, Ft. Worth 219 |
| 1966 | Tommy Hutton, Alb. .340 | Tommy Hutton, Alb. 25 | Tommy Hutton, Alb. 81 | John Duffie, Alb. 20 | Fred Norman, Dall.-Ft.W. 2.13 | Chuck Hartenstein, Dall.-Ft.W 198 |
| 1967 | Luis Alcaraz, Alb. .328 | Nate Colbert, Amarillo 28 | Joe Hague, Ark. 95 | 6 tied at 16 | Ed Everett, Albuque. 2.40 | Pat House, Austin 200 |
| 1968 | Bob Taylor, Amarillo .321 | Jim Spencer, El Paso 28 | Jim Spencer, El Paso 96 | Jim Flynn, Albuquerque 13 | Paul Doyle, Dall.-Ft.Worth 2.17 | Sal Campisi, Ark. 149 |
| 1969 | Larry Johnson, Dall.-Ft.W. .337 | Adrian Garrett, Shreve. 24 | Carlos Trevino, El Paso. 92 | Dave Freisleben, Alex. 16 | Jim Strickland, Alb. 2.40 | Joe DiFabio, Ark. 137 |
| 1970 | Mickey Rivers, El Paso .343 | Adrian Garrett, S.A. 29 | Arsenio Diaz, Memphis 102 | Rick Sawyer, S.A. 19 | Randy Cohen, Dall.-Ft.W. 1.99 | Ramon Hernandez, Ark. 151 |
| 1971 | Enos Cabell, Dall.-Ft.W .311 | Larry Fritz, Memphis 20 | Gary Matthews, Amar. 86 | Tim Jones, Shreveport 19 | Tommy Moore, Memphis 1.71 | George Manz, Dall.-Ft.W. 160 |
| 1972 | Randy Elliott, Alex. .335 | Gorman Thomas, S.A. 26 | Randy Elliott, Alex. 85 | 2 tied at 17 | Frank Riccelli, Amar. 2.32 | Wayne Garland, Dall.-Ft.W. 183 |
| 1973 | Morris Nettles, El Paso .332 | Hector Cruz, Ark. 30 | Hector Cruz, Ark. 105 | Mike Scott, Jackson 18 | Frank Tanana, El Paso 2.32 | Dave Freisleben, Amar. 197 |
| 1974 | Dave Collins, El Paso .352 | 2 tied at 29 | John Balaz, El Paso 111 | Jeff Reardon, Jackson 14 | Dennis Eckersley, S.A. 2.56 | Dan Corder, Midland 163 |
| 1975 | Butch Alberts, El Paso .342 | 3 tied at 23 | Mitchell Page, Shreve. 90 | Bob Tufts, Shreveport 16 | Frank Panik, El Paso 2.62 | Dennis Willis, Ark. 126 |
| 1976 | Fred Frazier, El Paso .363 | Willie Aikens, El Paso 30 | Willie Aikens, El Paso 117 | 2 tied at 15 | Bill Caudill, Ark. 2.31 | Mike Bruhert, Jackson 140 |
| 1977 | Tom Smith, El Paso .366 | Karl Pagel, Midland 28 | Steve Stroughter, El Paso 116 | 3 tied at 13 | Juan Berenguer, Jackson 2.47 | Rick Honeycutt, Shreve 126 |
| 1978 | Danny Goodwin, El Paso .360 | Bob Clark, El Paso 31 | Bob Clark, El Paso. 111 | 3 tied at 17 | Dick Sander, S.A. 2.09 | Neil Allen, Jackson 159 |
| 1979 | Jim Tracy, Midland .355 | Mark Brouhard, El Paso 28 | Mark Brouhard, El Paso 107 | 3 tied at 14 | 2 tied at 2.26 | Greg Harris, Jackson 110 |
| 1980 | Daryl Sconiers, El Paso .370 | Mike Bishop, El Paso 33 | Mike Bishop, El Paso 104 | George Ferran, Shreve. 15 | Fernando Valenzuela, S.A. 2.62 | Joe Edelen, Ark. 162 |
| 1981 | Steve Sax, S.A. .346 | Greg Brock, S.A. 32 | Stan Davis, El Paso 109 | 2 tied at 13 | Alan Fowlkes, Shreve. 2.27 | Tim Hamm, Amarillo 152 |
| 1982 | Randy Ready, El Paso .375 | Darryl Strawberry, Jack. 34 | Bill Foley, El Paso 106 | Blaine Beatty, Jackson 13 | Jeff Bittiger, Jackson 2.67 | Doug Sisk, Jackson 190 |
| 1983 | Ernie Riles, El Paso .349 | Rob Deer, Shreve. 35 | Mark Gillaspie, Beau. 122 | Dave Osteen, Ark. 14 | Sid Fernandez, S.A. 2.82 | Sid Fernandez, S.A. 209 |
| 1984 | James Steels, Beau. .340 | Ralph Bryant, S.A. 31 | Mark Gillaspie, Beau. 87 | 2 tied at 14 | John Young, Ark. 2.60 | John Young, Ark. 136 |
| 1985 | Billy Joe Robidoux, E.P. .342 | Joey Meyer, El Paso 37 | Billy Joe Robidoux, E.P. 132 | 3 tied at 16 | Chris Bosio, El Paso 2.73 | Randy Bockus, Shreve 155 |
| 1986 | Steve Stanicek, El Paso .343 | Kevin King, Midland 30 | Jason Felice, Jackson 97 | 2 tied at 14 | George Ferran, Shreve. 2.29 | George Ferran, Shreve. 147 |
| 1987 | LaVel Freeman, El Paso .395 | 3 tied at 30 | 3 tied at 108 | 3 tied at 16 | David West, Jackson 2.85 | Chuck McGrath, Ark. 186 |
| 1988 | Jim McCollom, Mid. .343 | Greg Vaughn, El Paso 28 | Greg Vaughn, El Paso 105 | 2 tied at 15 | Brian Givens, Jackson 2.23 | Mickey Weston, Jackson 156 |
| 1989 | Bob Rose, Midland .359 | Dean Palmer, Tulsa 25 | Chris Cron, Midland 103 | 2 tied at 15 | Julio Valera, Jackson 2.49 | Julio Valera, Jackson 136 |
| 1990 | Eric Karros, S.A. .352 | Henry Rodriguez, S.A. 28 | Henry Rodriguez, S.A. 109 | Anthony Young, Jackson 14 | Tom Hostetler, Shreve 1.65 | Anthony Young, Jackson 112 |
| 1991 | Mark H. Midland .364 | John Jaha, El Paso 30 | John Jaha, El Paso 134 | Frank Seminara, Wich. 15 | Dennis Springer, S.A. 2.95 | Larry Carter, Shreve 138 |
| 1992 | Troy OLeary, El Paso .334 | Billy Ashley, S.A. 24 | Adell Davenport, Shreve. 88 | Dan Carlson, Shreve 15 | Dan Carlson, Shreve 2.52 | Dan Smith, Tulsa 157 |
| 1993 | Roberto Petagine, Jack. .334 | Trey McCoy, Tulsa 29 | Trey McCoy, Tulsa 95 | Ben VanRyn, S.A. 14 | Ben VanRyn, S.A. 2.21 | Rick Helling, Tulsa 188 |

# CALIFORNIA LEAGUE

## Champ Mavericks Achieve A Marlins First

**By MAUREEN DELANY**

While the Florida Marlins struggled through their inaugural season in the National League, their California League affiliate, the High Desert Mavericks, ran away with the best record during the regular season and the league's postseason championship in 1993.

The Mavericks (85-52) defeated the Modesto A's, three games to two, in the Cal League finals to win their second title in the team's three-year existence. The championship was the first-ever for the Marlins organization.

High Desert jumped out to a 2-0 lead in the championship series, but Modesto won the next two games at home. The Marlins' heavy-hitting trio of John Toale, Tim Clark and Bryn Kosco, who went 1-2-3 in RBIs in the minor leagues, then combined to drive in six runs in the fifth and deciding game at Modesto, leading the Mavericks to a 9-5 victory.

Clark edged out Toale for the RBI title, 126-125,

**John Toale**

and led all of minor league baseball with a .363 average, but fell short of the league's Triple Crown by hitting only 17 home runs. Toale won the home run title with 28, while Kosco had 121 RBIs and was second with 27 homers.

Clark, whom the Milwaukee Brewers tried unsuccessfully to convert into a pitcher two years earlier, was named the Marlins' organization player of the year.

Toale, 28, returned to Organized Baseball after a one-year layoff to pursue his college degree. Given the chance to play every day for the first time in his career, Toale was able to display his power at the hitter-

**Tim Clark.** High Desert outfielder led minor leagues with a .363 average and 126 RBIs.

friendly Mavericks Stadium.

A key to the Mavericks' domination in the league was the Marlins lack of a Double-A team in 1993. Many players who might have started the season at Double-A or been promoted remained at High Desert.

### Rancho Ruckus

With the addition of the immensely successful Rancho Cucamonga franchise, the Cal League broke its attendance record for the fifth straight season. The league drew 1,353,455 fans in 1993, averaging 2,029 a game. For the first time in the league's history, every team averaged more than 1,000 fans a game.

The Rancho Cucamonga Quakes, named for the club's proximity to an earthquake fault, toppled the league record with 331,005 (an average of 4,868). Quakes owner Hank Stickney had relocated from San Bernardino after the 1992 season to play in a new stadium (appropriately named the Epicenter).

Two other franchises followed Stickney's lead. Salinas moved to fill the vacancy at San Bernardino and Reno headed for Riverside,

## STANDINGS: SPLIT SEASON

### FIRST HALF

| NORTH | W | L | PCT | GB |
|---|---|---|---|---|
| Modesto | 42 | 26 | .618 | — |
| San Jose | 41 | 27 | .603 | 1 |
| Stockton | 37 | 31 | .544 | 5 |
| Central Valley | 26 | 42 | .382 | 16 |
| Bakersfield | 18 | 50 | .265 | 24 |

| SOUTH | W | L | PCT | GB |
|---|---|---|---|---|
| High Desert | 44 | 24 | .647 | — |
| Riverside | 36 | 32 | .529 | 8 |
| Rancho Cuca. | 35 | 33 | .515 | 9 |
| San Bernardino | 31 | 37 | .456 | 13 |
| Palm Springs | 30 | 38 | .441 | 14 |

### SECOND HALF

| NORTH | W | L | PCT | GB |
|---|---|---|---|---|
| Stockton | 42 | 26 | .618 | — |
| San Jose | 38 | 30 | .559 | 4 |
| Central Valley | 35 | 33 | .515 | 7 |
| Modesto | 30 | 38 | .441 | 12 |
| Bakersfield | 24 | 44 | .353 | 18 |

| SOUTH | W | L | PCT | GB |
|---|---|---|---|---|
| High Desert | 41 | 28 | .594 | — |
| Riverside | 40 | 29 | .580 | 1 |
| San Bernardino | 31 | 37 | .456 | 9½ |
| Palm Springs | 31 | 37 | .456 | 9½ |
| Rancho Cuca. | 29 | 39 | .426 | 11½ |

**PLAYOFFS—Division:** Modesto defeated Stockton, 3-1, and High Desert defeated Riverside, 3-1, in best-of-5 series. **Finals:** High Desert defeated Modesto, 3-2, in best-of-5 series.

MEL BAILEY

MEL BAILEY

| Page | | W | L | PCT | GB | Manager | Attendance/Dates | Last Pennant |
|------|---|---|---|-----|-----|---------|------------------|--------------|
| 110 | **High Desert Mavericks (Marlins)** | 85 | 52 | .620 | — | Fredi Gonzalez | 191,697 (68) | 1993 |
| 134 | **Stockton Ports (Brewers)** | 79 | 57 | .581 | 5 ½ | Lamar Johnson | 108,629 (66) | 1992 |
| 195 | **San Jose Giants (Giants)** | 79 | 57 | .581 | 5 ½ | Dick Dietz | 133,138 68) | 1979 |
| 201 | **Riverside Pilots (Mariners)** | 76 | 61 | .555 | 9 | Dave Myers | 68,821 (67) | None |
| 164 | **Modesto A's (Athletics)** | 72 | 64 | .529 | 12 ½ | Ted Kubiak | 100,016 (65) | 1984 |
| 189 | **Rancho Cucamonga Quakes (Padres)** | 64 | 72 | .471 | 20 ½ | Keith Champion | 331,005 (68) | None |
| 216 | **San Bernardino Spirit (Co-op)** | 62 | 74 | .456 | 22 ½ | Greg Mahlberg | 88,468 (66) | None |
| 69 | **Palm Springs Angels (Angels)** | 61 | 75 | .449 | 23 ½ | Mario Mendoza | 105,039 (67) | None |
| 99 | **Central Valley Rockies (Rockies)** | 61 | 75 | .449 | 23 ½ | Paul Zuvella | 77,547 (65) | 1978 |
| 127 | **Bakersfield Dodgers (Dodgers)** | 42 | 94 | .309 | 42 ½ | Rick Dempsey | 149,095 (67) | 1989 |

**NOTE:** Team's individual batting and pitching statistics can be found on page indicated in lefthand column.

despite the continued absence of a beer license at Riverside Sports Center which forced the relocation of the old Riverside franchise to High Desert after the 1990 season.

The league continued its change after the '93 season.

Stickney's son, Ken Stickney, pulled his club out of the heat in Palm Springs and relocated the California Angels' affiliate to Lake Elsinore. Recognizing the possibility of attracting a Cal League team, Lake Elsinore city officials moved forward with plans for a new stadium. Ken Stickney predicted the stadium, which was scheduled to open in time for the 1994 season, would be the "finest minor league stadium in the country."

## Connections

For the first time since 1989, all 10 Cal League

**John Burke.** Central Valley righthander named league's top prospect.

teams were either affiliated with major league clubs or operated as a co-op arrangment.

The San Bernardino Spirit was the sole co-op team, getting most of its players from the Yankees and A's. The Spirit featured some of the top pitchers in the league—notably 18-year-old Japanese righthander Mac Suzuki.

Suzuki was not under contract to any Japanese League team when he came to the United States to play for Salinas in 1992 and San Bernardino in 1993. He progressed so rapidly during the second half of 1993, finishing with 12 saves and a 3.68 ERA, that a bidding war for his services developed among U.S. major league teams. He signed with the Seattle Mariners after the season for a bonus of $750,000.

While several franchises improved on the field in 1993, Bakersfield experienced an uncharacticaly down year. The Dodgers, the youngest team in the league, slumped to the worst record in minor league baseball (42-94) and managed just one complete game, a 2-0 loss at San Jose May 10.

The Central Valley Rockies (formerly Visalia), aligned with the expansion Colorado Rockies, struggled through the first half but made a run for the Northern Division second-half title.

Outfielder Ryan Turner, the first player ever signed by the Rockies organization,

**Mac Suzuki**

was Central Valley's leading hitter, while John Burke and Mark Thompson, Colorado's first two draft picks in 1992, were selected as the league's two best pitching prospects in Baseball America's annual managers survey. Both Burke and Thompson were promoted to Triple-A Colorado Springs in the middle of the season.

## LEAGUE CHAMPIONS

**Last 25 Years**

| Year | Regular Season* | Pct. | Playoff |
|------|-----------------|------|---------|
| 1969 | Stockton (Orioles) | .579 | Stockton (Orioles) |
| 1970 | Bakersfield (Dodgers) | .669 | None |
| 1971 | Modesto (Cardinals) | .597 | Visalia (Mets) |
| 1972 | Bakersfield (Dodgers) | .629 | Modesto (Cardinals) |
| 1973 | Lodi (Orioles) | .550 | Lodi (Orioles) |
| | Salinas (Angels) | .550 | |
| 1974 | Fresno (Giants) | .607 | Fresno (Giants) |
| 1975 | Reno (Twins/Padres) | .614 | None |
| 1976 | Salinas (Angels) | .650 | Reno (Twins/Padres) |
| 1977 | Fresno (Giants) | .592 | Lodi (Dodgers) |
| 1978 | Visalia (Twins) | .697 | Visalia (Twins) |
| 1979 | San Jose (Mariners) | .636 | San Jose (Mariners) |
| 1980 | Stockton (Brewers) | .638 | Stockton (Brewers) |
| 1981 | Visalia (Twins) | .621 | Lodi (Dodgers) |
| 1982 | Modesto (Athletics) | .671 | Modesto (Athletics) |
| 1983 | Visalia (Twins) | .621 | Redwood (Angels) |
| 1984 | Redwood (Angels) | .654 | Modesto (Athletics) |
| 1985 | Salinas (Mariners) | .618 | Fresno (Giants) |
| 1986 | Palm Springs (Angels) | .612 | Stockton (Brewers) |
| 1987 | Stockton (Brewers) | .667 | Fresno (Giants) |
| 1988 | Stockton (Brewers) | .657 | Riverside (Padres) |
| 1989 | Stockton (Brewers) | .626 | Bakersfield (Dodgers) |
| 1990 | Visalia (Twins) | .638 | Stockton (Brewers) |
| 1991 | San Jose (Giants) | .676 | High Desert (Padres) |
| 1992 | Stockton (Brewers) | .604 | Stockton (Brewers) |
| 1993 | High Desert (Marlins) | .620 | High Desert (Marlins) |

*Best overall record

# CALIFORNIA LEAGUE
## 1993 BATTING, PITCHING STATISTICS

### CLUB BATTING

| | AVG | G | AB | R | H | 2B | 3B | HR | BB | SO | SB |
|---|---|---|---|---|---|---|---|---|---|---|---|
| High Desert | .289 | 137 | 4683 | 939 | 1355 | 238 | 60 | 118 | 721 | 909 | 230 |
| Rancho Cucamonga | .287 | 136 | 4766 | 775 | 1369 | 283 | 43 | 106 | 538 | 867 | 128 |
| Stockton | .285 | 136 | 4634 | 776 | 1320 | 225 | 35 | 106 | 617 | 792 | 211 |
| Riverside | .278 | 137 | 4716 | 760 | 1310 | 259 | 34 | 84 | 566 | 852 | 109 |
| Central Valley | .269 | 136 | 4640 | 666 | 1250 | 187 | 25 | 85 | 607 | 873 | 161 |
| Modesto | .269 | 136 | 4479 | 750 | 1204 | 222 | 27 | 97 | 740 | 856 | 108 |
| San Bernardino | .267 | 136 | 4679 | 732 | 1248 | 232 | 21 | 147 | 544 | 1030 | 115 |
| Palm Springs | .263 | 136 | 4611 | 656 | 1211 | 201 | 40 | 44 | 585 | 814 | 208 |
| San Jose | .260 | 136 | 4569 | 696 | 1189 | 219 | 27 | 78 | 580 | 795 | 216 |
| Bakersfield | .251 | 136 | 4664 | 558 | 1170 | 195 | 26 | 94 | 405 | 1065 | 100 |

### CLUB PITCHING

| | ERA | G | CG | SHO | SV | IP | H | R | ER | BB | SO |
|---|---|---|---|---|---|---|---|---|---|---|---|
| Stockton | 3.98 | 136 | 7 | 10 | 38 | 1202 | 1239 | 659 | 531 | 592 | 781 |
| Riverside | 4.25 | 137 | 8 | 5 | 42 | 1207 | 1286 | 711 | 570 | 491 | 831 |
| San Jose | 4.35 | 136 | 7 | 8 | 35 | 1195 | 1212 | 683 | 578 | 631 | 868 |
| Modesto | 4.47 | 136 | 5 | 7 | 43 | 1184 | 1207 | 666 | 588 | 562 | 897 |
| Palm Springs | 4.53 | 136 | 14 | 8 | 27 | 1211 | 1319 | 717 | 610 | 513 | 803 |
| Central Valley | 4.57 | 136 | 6 | 7 | 28 | 1204 | 1200 | 719 | 612 | 653 | 1063 |
| Bakersfield | 4.60 | 136 | 1 | 5 | 19 | 1194 | 1235 | 766 | 610 | 722 | 912 |
| High Desert | 4.61 | 137 | 14 | 7 | 28 | 1198 | 1318 | 769 | 614 | 469 | 814 |
| San Bernardino | 4.76 | 136 | 9 | 6 | 31 | 1209 | 1274 | 797 | 639 | 629 | 917 |
| Rancho Cucamonga | 5.10 | 136 | 4 | 3 | 28 | 1196 | 1336 | 821 | 678 | 641 | 967 |

### CLUB FIELDING

| | PCT | PO | A | E | DP |
|---|---|---|---|---|---|
| San Jose | .972 | 3586 | 1537 | 146 | 128 |
| Modesto | .967 | 3553 | 1480 | 174 | 138 |
| Stockton | .966 | 3606 | 1616 | 183 | 132 |
| Palm Springs | .964 | 3633 | 1595 | 196 | 152 |
| Central Valley | .963 | 3612 | 1460 | 197 | 100 |
| Riverside | .961 | 3622 | 1551 | 210 | 138 |
| High Desert | .960 | 3595 | 1588 | 215 | 147 |
| Bakersfield | .959 | 3583 | 1559 | 220 | 129 |
| Rancho Cuca. | .958 | 3588 | 1499 | 225 | 143 |
| San Bernardino | .956 | 3626 | 1582 | 240 | 122 |

**Sid Roberson**
ERA leader

**Arquimedez Pozo**
44 doubles

**Kevin Riggs**
.347 batting average

### INDIVIDUAL BATTING LEADERS
(Minimum 367 Plate Appearances)

| | AVG | G | AB | R | H | 2B | 3B | HR | RBI | BB | SO | SB |
|---|---|---|---|---|---|---|---|---|---|---|---|---|
| Clark, Tim, High Desert | .363 | 128 | 510 | 109 | 185 | 42 | 10 | 17 | 126 | 56 | 65 | 2 |
| Riggs, Kevin, Stockton | .347 | 108 | 377 | 84 | 131 | 18 | 3 | 3 | 45 | 101 | 46 | 12 |
| Smith, Ira, RC | .346 | 92 | 347 | 71 | 120 | 30 | 6 | 7 | 47 | 55 | 41 | 32 |
| Pozo, Arquimedez, Riverside | .342 | 127 | 515 | 98 | 176 | 44 | 6 | 13 | 83 | 56 | 56 | 10 |
| Turner, Brian, SB | .325 | 109 | 406 | 69 | 132 | 23 | 3 | 21 | 68 | 49 | 75 | 4 |
| Martinez, Manny, SB | .322 | 109 | 459 | 88 | 148 | 26 | 3 | 11 | 52 | 41 | 60 | 28 |
| Stefanski, Mike, Stock. | .322 | 97 | 345 | 58 | 111 | 22 | 2 | 10 | 57 | 49 | 45 | 6 |
| Hardtke, Jason, RC | .319 | 130 | 523 | 98 | 167 | 38 | 7 | 11 | 85 | 61 | 54 | 7 |
| McFarlin, Jason, San Jose | .311 | 97 | 395 | 71 | 123 | 20 | 4 | 7 | 53 | 29 | 67 | 49 |
| Shockey, Greg, Riverside | .311 | 95 | 354 | 61 | 110 | 10 | 0 | 6 | 63 | 50 | 50 | 2 |

### INDIVIDUAL PITCHING LEADERS
(Minimum 109 Innings)

| | W | L | ERA | G | GS | CG | SV | IP | H | R | ER | BB | SO |
|---|---|---|---|---|---|---|---|---|---|---|---|---|---|
| Roberson, Sid, Stockton | 12 | 8 | 2.60 | 24 | 23 | 6 | 0 | 166 | 157 | 68 | 48 | 34 | 87 |
| Pedraza, Rod, San Bern. | 9 | 7 | 3.18 | 24 | 23 | 2 | 0 | 142 | 145 | 74 | 50 | 33 | 95 |
| Burke, John, Central Valley | 7 | 8 | 3.18 | 20 | 20 | 2 | 0 | 119 | 104 | 62 | 42 | 64 | 114 |
| Keling, Korey, Palm Springs | 8 | 8 | 3.29 | 31 | 21 | 2 | 0 | 159 | 152 | 69 | 58 | 62 | 131 |
| Perez, Carlos, San Bern. | 8 | 7 | 3.44 | 20 | 18 | 3 | 0 | 131 | 120 | 57 | 50 | 44 | 98 |
| Gutierrez, Jim, Riverside | 12 | 9 | 3.78 | 27 | 27 | 2 | 0 | 171 | 182 | 95 | 72 | 53 | 84 |
| Brock, Russ, Modesto | 12 | 4 | 3.81 | 27 | 26 | 1 | 0 | 139 | 137 | 69 | 59 | 44 | 121 |
| Whitaker, Steve, San Jose | 8 | 10 | 3.82 | 22 | 21 | 1 | 0 | 127 | 106 | 70 | 54 | 114 | 94 |
| Ratekin, Mark, Palm Spr. | 7 | 7 | 3.89 | 21 | 21 | 6 | 0 | 143 | 151 | 78 | 62 | 46 | 66 |
| Vanderweele, Doug, San Jose | 10 | 6 | 3.89 | 25 | 24 | 0 | 0 | 171 | 188 | 78 | 74 | 55 | 106 |

## DEPARTMENT LEADERS

**BATTING**
- **R** Kerwin Moore, High Desert ......... 120
- **H** Tim Clark, High Desert .............. 185
- **TB** Tim Clark, High Desert ............ 298
- **2B** Arquimedez Pozo, Riverside ..... 44
- **3B** Tim Clark, High Desert ............. 10
- **HR** John Toale, High Desert ......... 28
- **RBI** Tim Clark, High Desert ......... 126
- **SH** Quinton McCracken, CV ......... 12
- **SF** Tim Clark, High Desert ............. 13
- **BB** Kerwin Moore, High Desert ... 114
- **IBB** Jason Giambi, Modesto ......... 7
- **HBP** James Martin, Bakersfield ... 13
- **SO** James Martin, Bakersfield ... 131
- **SB** Kerwin Moore, High Desert ..... 71
- **CS** Marquis Riley, Palm Springs ... 25
- **GIDP** Arquimedez Pozo, Riverside .... 22
- **OB%** Kevin Riggs, Stockton ........ .482
- **SL%** Ernie Young, Modesto ......... .635

**PITCHING**
- **G** Billy Hardwick, Stockton ............. 61
- **GS** 2 tied at ............................... 27
- **CG** 3 tied at ................................. 6
- **ShO** Joel Adamson, High Desert .... 3
- **GF** John Pricher, Palm Springs ...... 45
- **Sv** John Pricher, Palm Springs ...... 26
- **W** 2 tied at ................................. 14
- **L** Jesus Martinez, Bakersfield ....... 13
- **IP** Mike Butler, Palm Springs ...... 179
- **H** Keith Morrison, Palm Springs ... 200
- **R** Robert Person, High Desert ...... 115
- **ER** Bill Vanlandingham, San Jose ... 93
- **HR** Doug Vanderweele, San Jose ... 17
- **BB** Eric Weaver, Bakersfield ....... 118
- **HB** Jim Mecir, Riverside ............... 15
- **SO** Bill Vanlandingham, San Jose ... 171
- **WP** Robbie Beckett, RC ............... 25
- **Bk** 2 tied at ................................. 9

**FIELDING**
- **C AVG** Mark Skeels, High Desert ...... .992
- **E** Izzy Molina, Modesto ............... 15
- **1B AVG** Jay Kirkpatrick, Bakersfield ... .993
- **E** 3 tied at ............................... 14
- **2B AVG** Chris Wimmer, San Jose ....... .992
- **E** Steve Anderson, San Bern ...... 26
- **3B AVG** Tim Unroe, Stockton ............. .936
- **E** Tom Schmidt, Central Valley ... 34
- **SS AVG** Kurt Ehmann, San Jose ........ .944
- **E** Ramon Martinez, High Desert .. 42
- **OF AVG** Marquis Riley, Palm Springs . .984
- **E** Karim Garcia, Bakersfield ........ 13

## HONOR ROLL

**OFFICIAL ALL-STAR TEAM**
- **C** Izzy Molina, Modesto
- **1B** John Toale, High Desert
- **2B** Arquimedez Pozo, Riverside
- **3B** Bryn Kosco, High Desert
- **SS** Kurt Ehmann, San Jose
  Sean Drinkwater, Rancho Cucamonga
- **OF** Tim Clark, High Desert
  Ira Smith, Rancho Cucamonga
  Ernie Young, Modesto
- **DH** Kevin Riggs, Stockton
- **P** Roberson, Stockton; Pricher, PS;
  Brock, Modesto; Burke, CV

**MVP:** Tim Clark, High Desert
**Manager:** Fredi Gonzalez, High Desert

**TOP 10 PROSPECTS**
(Selected by league managers)
1. John Burke, rhp, Central Valley
2. Carl Everett, of, High Desert
3. Michael Moore, of, Bakersfield
4. Arquimedez Pozo, 2b, Riverside
5. Mark Thompson, rhp, Central Valley
6. Mac Suzuki, rhp, San Bernardino
7. Izzy Molina, c, Modesto
8. Calvin Murray, of, San Jose
9. Jason Giambi, 3b, Modesto
10. Tyrone Hill, lhp, Stockton

| Year | Batting Average | Home Runs | RBIs | Wins | ERA | Strikeouts |
|---|---|---|---|---|---|---|
| 1946 | Al Prieto, Bakersfield .380 | Harry Goorabian, Stock. 24 | Irv Noren, Santa Barbara 129 | Don Belton, Stockton 23 | Mike Garcia, Bakersfield 2.56 | Mike Garcia, Bakersfield 186 |
| 1947 | Lou Vezelich, Fresno .364 | Bill Enos, Modesto 30 | Lou Vezelich, Fresno 141 | Don Belton, Stockton 21 | Lloyd Hittle, Vis. 2.24 | John Hoffman, Vis. 263 |
| 1948 | Harold Cox, Bakers. .345 | Vince DiMaggio, Stock. 30 | Rip Repulski, Fresno 156 | Frank Meagher, Santa Barb. 18 | Walter Olsen, Santa Barb. 2.16 | Walter Olsen, Santa Barb. 246 |
| 1949 | Max Macon, Modesto .383 | Jess Pike, Bakersfield 37 | Jess Pike, Bakersfield 156 | Earl Escalante, Bak. 28 | Drexel Waters, Santa Barb. 2.54 | Armand Castro, Modesto. 237 |
| 1950 | James Acton, Visalia .355 | Richard Wilson, Mod. 30 | Richard Wilson, Mod. 154 | Bud Guldborg, Stockton 22 | Tony Freitas, Mod. 2.56 | Gordon Jones, Fresno 200 |
| 1951 | Richard Wilson, Mod. .371 | Richard Wilson, Mod. 40 | William Gabler, S.B. 153 | Tony Freitas, Stockton 25 | Stan McWilliams, S.J. 2.55 | Frank Dasso, Modesto 210 |
| 1952 | Alan Grandcolas, Fresno .347 | Bill Downs, Fresno 34 | Bill Downs, Fresno 154 | Larry Jackson, Fresno 28 | Jake Abbott, Santa Barb. 2.26 | Larry Jackson, Fresno 351 |
| 1953 | Jose Perez, Ventura .373 | Ray Perry, Bakersfield 36 | Ed Sobczak, San Jose 142 | Tony Freitas, Stockton 22 | Tex Clevenger, S.J. 1.51 | Clair Parkin, San Jose 192 |
| 1954 | Joe Brunacki, Fresno .344 | Ray Perry, Bakersfield 37 | Nick Ananias, Bakersfield 139 | Robert Thorpe, Stock. 28 | Robert Thorpe, Stock. 2.28 | Rick Botelho, Mod. 234 |
| 1955 | Bobby Smith, Fresno .370 | Russ Rosburg, Mod. 33 | Bobby Smith, Fresno 141 | Glen Stabelfeld, Fresno 24 | Charles Beamon, Stock. 1.36 | Tom Hughes, Fresno 273 |
| 1956 | Dick Whitman, San Jose .391 | Bud Heslet, Visalia 51 | Bud Heslet, Visalia 172 | Peter Hernandez, Vis. 24 | Alvin Spearman, Stock. 2.62 | David Jordan; Stock. 227 |
| 1957 | Fran Boniar, Reno. .436 | Richard Wilson, Bak. 27 | Fran Boniar, Reno. 138 | Peter Hernandez, Vis. 25 | Bill Dial, San Jose. 2.12 | Charles Drummond, Stock. 251 |
| 1958 | Neil Wilson, Fresno. .349 | Barton Dupon, Bak. 40 | Barton Dupon, Bak. 136 | Len Fergunson, Mod. 23 | Alvin Spearman, Stock. 2.60 | Len Fergunson, Mod. 302 |
| 1959 | Willie Davis, Reno. .365 | Rich Barry, Modesto 37 | Ron Wiley, Bakersfield 125 | Hal Reniff, Modesto 21 | George Gaffney, Stock. 2.49 | Paul Underwood, Vis. 193 |
| 1960 | Chuck Hinton, Stockton .369 | Dick Edwards, Bak. 22 | Lowell Barnhart, Reno. 109 | Thad Tillotson, Reno. 19 | John Hogg, Bakersfield 2.59 | Gary Kroll, Bak. 309 |
| 1961 | Don Williams, Reno. .363 | Dick Nen, Reno 32 | Dick Nen, Reno 144 | Bruce Gardner, Reno 20 | Bruce Gardner, Reno 2.82 | Jose Santiago, Visalia 218 |
| 1962 | Bill Haas, Reno. .368 | Larry Daniels, Bak. 44 | Bill Haas, Reno. 144 | 2 tied at 15 | Darold Knowles, Stock. 2.29 | Norm Koch, Reno 244 |
| 1963 | Jose Vidal, Reno. .340 | Jose Vidal, Reno. 40 | Jose Vidal, Reno. 162 | Bob Olson, Stockton 18 | Dick Selma, Salinas 2.58 | Dick Selma, Salinas 221 |
| 1964 | Bob Taylor, Fresno .364 | Ollie Brown, Fresno 40 | Ollie Brown, Fresno 133 | Pedro Reinoso, Fresno 18 | Ed Barnowski, Stock. 1.95 | Ed Barnowski, Stock. 321 |
| 1965 | Mike Epstein, Stockton. .338 | Mike Epstein, Stockton 30 | Bobby Etheridge, Fresno 107 | Jack Nutter, Bak. 17 | George Sherrod, S.J. 2.81 | Jack Nutter, Bak. 223 |
| 1966 | Dan Greenfield, Mod. .339 | Dave Duncan, Modesto. 46 | Larry Wilson, Modesto 117 | 3 tied at 16 | Greg Conger, Modesto 2.73 | Dick Armstrong, S.B. 186 |
| 1967 | Phil Mastagni, Stock. .308 | Joe Lis, Bakersfield 33 | Joe Lis, Bakersfield 90 | Pat Bayless, Bak. 18 | Ken Tatum, San Jose 2.12 | Pat Bayless, Bak. 217 |
| 1968 | Ted Simmons, Modesto .331 | Tom Robson, Visalia 35 | Ted Simmons, Modesto 117 | 2 tied at 18 | Tim Griffin, Stock. 2.15 | Jim Moyer, Fresno 269 |
| 1969 | Mike Carruthers, Reno. .353 | Ernie Davis, Modesto 27 | Paul Alderete, S.J. 93 | Bill Kirkpatrick, Stock. 18 | Bill Kirkpatrick, Stock. 1.96 | Ron Zuber, Reno 230 |
| 1970 | Paul Johnson, Bak. .350 | Larry Fritz, Visalia 24 | George Greer, Modesto 96 | Al Dawson, Bak. 17 | Al Dawson, Bak. 2.47 | Al Dawson, Bak. 244 |
| 1971 | Bill Bright, Modesto .340 | Frank Ortenzio, S.J. 32 | Frank Ortenzio, S.J. 113 | Doug Bird, San Jose 15 | Don Durham, Modesto 2.80 | Don Durham, Modesto 202 |
| 1972 | Glenn Monroe, Reno. .349 | Skip James, Fresno. 32 | Skip James, Fresno. 113 | Rick Nitz, Bakersfield 18 | Paul Pelz, San Jose 2.36 | John D'Acquisto, Fresno 245 |
| 1973 | Dave Cripe, San Jose .310 | John Balaz, Salinas 28 | John Balaz, Salinas 113 | Dennis Leonard, San Jose 15 | Curt Isom, San Jose 2.42 | Curt Isom, San Jose 227 |
| 1974 | Jose Baez, Bakersfield .330 | Gary Alexander, Fresno 27 | Jack Clark, Fresno 112 | Bob Knepper, Fresno 20 | Lynn McKinney, San Jose 2.23 | Bob Knepper, Fresno 247 |
| 1975 | Gene Richards, Reno. .381 | Claude Westmoreland, Bak. 29 | Claude Westmoreland, Bak. 115 | 2 tied at 17 | Eddie Plank, Fresno 2.26 | Jerry Garvin, Reno 129 |
| 1976 | Dan Argee, Modesto .356 | Dan Graham, Reno. 32 | Dan Graham, Reno. 139 | Ken Califano, Stockton 15 | Monroe Greenfield, Fresno 2.45 | Greg Heydeman, Lodi 159 |
| 1977 | Rudy Law, Lodi .386 | Kelly Snider, Lodi. 36 | Kelly Snider, Lodi. 120 | David Mendoza, Fresno 16 | John Johnson, Fresno. 3.38 | Ted Barnicle, Fresno 179 |
| 1978 | Joe Charboneau, Vis. .350 | Steve McManaman, Vis. 37 | Steve McManaman, Vis. 121 | 2 tied at 16 | Jim Lewis, Stockton 2.12 | Jim Lewis, Stockton 189 |
| 1979 | Mike Marshall, Lodi .354 | Mark Funderburk, Vis. 31 | Les Pearsey, Vis. 102 | Steve Brown, Salinas 16 | Steve Brown, Salinas 2.41 | Dave LaPoint, Stock. 208 |
| 1980 | Chris Flammang, San Jose .348 | Greg Brock, Lodi 29 | Candy Maldonado, Lodi 131 | Scott Stranski, San Jose 18 | Mike Madden, Stock. 1.95 | Brad Havens, Visalia 179 |
| 1981 | Kent Hrbek, Visalia .379 | Rob Deer, Fresno 33 | George Hinshaw, Reno. 101 | Paul Voigt, Visalia 15 | Ron Romanick, Red. 2.91 | Ron Romanick, Red. 178 |
| 1982 | Kevin McReynolds, Reno. .376 | Kevin McReynolds, Reno. 28 | Ricky Nelson, Bakers. 115 | Mike Warren, Stock.-Mod. 19 | Mark Ferguson, Modesto 1.77 | Tim Conroy, Modesto 184 |
| 1983 | David Klipstein, Stock. .341 | Stan Holmes, Visalia 37 | Stan Holmes, Visalia 92 | Bill Wegman, Stock. 16 | Bill Wegman, Stock. 1.30 | Randy Bockus, Fresno 144 |
| 1984 | Rickey Coleman, Reno. .351 | Mark Bonner, Redwood 20 | Mark Bonner, Redwood. 106 | Bob Kipper, Redwood 18 | Bob Kipper, Redwood 2.04 | Randy Newman, Salinas 169 |
| 1985 | Jim Eppard, Modesto .345 | 2 tied at 24 | 2 tied at 103 | Charlie Corbell, Fresno 17 | Jeff Parrett, Stockton 2.75 | Dennis Livingston, Bak. 166 |
| 1986 | Roberto Alomar, Reno. .346 | Brad Pounders, Reno. 35 | Ty Van Burkleo, Palm Spr. 103 | Jeff Peterek, Stock. 15 | Mike Christ, Salinas 2.69 | Dennis Cook, Fresno 173 |
| 1987 | James Lester, Reno. .331 | Bill Stevenson, Reno. 21 | Gary Sheffield, Stock. 118 | 2 tied at 16 | David Snell, Salinas 1.96 | Park Pittman, Visalia 198 |
| 1988 | Adam Brown, Bakersfield .352 | Warren Newson, Riverside. 22 | Mark Leonard, San Jose 101 | 2 tied at 17 | Rich Holsman, Riverside. 2.31 | Paul Abbott, Visalia 205 |
| 1989 | Ruben Gonzalez, San Bern. .308 | Ruben Gonzalez, San Ber. 27 | Ruben Gonzalez, San Ber. 120 | 3 tied at 13 | Steve Lienhard, San Jose. 1.79 | Willie Banks, Visalia 173 |
| 1990 | Tom Eiterman, Reno. .331 | Ken Whitfield, Reno. 24 | Frank Bolick, San Bern.-Stock. 131 | George Tsamis, Visalia 17 | Dan Rambo, San Jose 2.19 | Kevin Rogers, San Jose 186 |
| 1991 | Matt Mieske, High Des. .341 | Jay Gainer, High Des. 32 | Jay Gainer, High Des. 120 | Rich Huisman, San Jose 16 | Rich Huisman, San Jose 1.83 | Rich Huisman, San Jose 216 |
| 1992 | Billy Hall, High Desert. .356 | Marty Cordova, Visalia 28 | Marty Cordova, Visalia 131 | Brian Hancock, Stockton. 14 | Joey Rosselli, S.J. 2.41 | Curtis Shaw, Modesto 154 |
| 1993 | Tim Clark, High Desert. .363 | John Toale, High Desert 28 | Tim Toale, High Desert 126 | 2 tied at 14 | Sid Roberson, Stockton. 2.60 | Bill Vaniandingham, S.J. 171 |

# CAROLINA
## LEAGUE

## Spirited Rally Spurs Spirits To CL Title

**By ALAN SCHWARZ**

On a team with several stars having enjoyed monstrous years, a little shortstop who had been with the club less than a month stole the show.

The Winston-Salem Spirits summoned Ricky Gonzalez from the South Atlantic League Aug. 21 for the Carolina League stretch drive after starter Eric Owens was injured and lost for the balance of the season. The move paid off handsomely when Gonzalez' RBI single in the 11th inning gave the Spirits a 5-4, fourth-game victory over the Wilmington Blue Rocks in an excruciatingly close best-of-5 series for the 1993 Carolina League championship.

Gonzalez was named MVP after collecting four hits in the series, including a two-RBI single that helped break open the Spirits' 5-2 win in the third game. Winston-Salem rebounded from a first-game loss to win three straight and its third CL championship since 1985.

"Going into the series, you'd say Bubba Smith or Motorboat Jones or Chad Mottola, they're going to be the hero," Spirits manager Mark Berry said of the team's more well-known players. "But you look back at a lot of series, and it comes down to the little guy getting his knock. That's why this game is crazy. A guy comes out of nowhere and he's the MVP."

Until that point, Smith had been the story of the year in the Carolina League. The rotund and immensely popular first baseman, who had won over fans all around the league by swatting 32 homers—most in the minors—in 1992 for Peninsula, returned to the CL after being traded from the Seattle Mariners to the

**Chad Mottola.** Reds outfield prospect led Winston-Salem to Carolina League title, hitting .280 with 21 home runs.

Cincinnati Reds in June. Smith hit .301 with 27 homers and 81 RBIs the rest of the way to win his second straight CL MVP award.

Mottola, one of the top prospects in baseball, hit .280 with 21 home runs and a league-leading 91 RBIs in his first pro summer after being the Reds' first-round draft pick in 1992. Jones, a minor league veteran, hit .300 with 19 homers and spent some time in Double-A.

### Wilmington A Success

Wilmington, in its first year of operation after moving from Peninsula and switching affiliations from the Mariners to the Kansas City Royals, still enjoyed a phenomenal season.

The Blue Rocks finished second in the attendance race at 332,132, trailing only Frederick

**Bubba Smith**

## STANDINGS: SPLIT SEASON

| FIRST HALF | | | | SECOND HALF | | | |
|---|---|---|---|---|---|---|---|
| **NORTH** | **W** | **L** | **PCT** | **GB** | **NORTH** | **W** | **L** | **PCT** | **GB** |
| Wilmington | 44 | 25 | .638 | — | Frederick | 43 | 27 | .614 | — |
| Frederick | 35 | 35 | .500 | 9½ | Prince William | 37 | 33 | .529 | 6 |
| Lynchburg | 32 | 37 | .464 | 12 | Lynchburg | 33 | 37 | .471 | 10 |
| Prince William | 30 | 40 | .429 | 14½ | Wilmington | 30 | 40 | .429 | 13 |
| **SOUTH** | **W** | **L** | **PCT** | **GB** | **SOUTH** | **W** | **L** | **PCT** | **GB** |
| Kinston | 38 | 31 | .551 | — | Win.-Salem | 39 | 31 | .557 | — |
| Durham | 35 | 34 | .507 | 3 | Durham | 34 | 35 | .493 | 4½ |
| Win.-Salem | 33 | 37 | .471 | 5½ | Kinston | 33 | 36 | .478 | 5½ |
| Salem | 31 | 39 | .443 | 7½ | Salem | 30 | 40 | .429 | 9 |

**PLAYOFFS—Division:** Wilmington defeated Frederick, 2-0, and Winston-Salem defeated Kinston, 2-1, in best-of-3 series. **Finals:** Winston-Salem defeated Wilmington, 3-1, in best-of-5 series.

JIM McLEAN

JIM McLEAN

| Page | | W | L | PCT | GB | Manager | Attendance/Dates | Last Pennant |
|---|---|---|---|---|---|---|---|---|
| 57 | Frederick Keys (Orioles) | 78 | 62 | .557 | — | Pete Mackanin | 351,146 (69) | 1990 |
| 122 | Wilmington Blue Rocks (Royals) | 74 | 65 | .532 | 3½ | Ron Johnson | 332,132 (65) | None |
| 94 | Kinston Indians (Indians) | 71 | 67 | .514 | 6 | Dave Keller | 134,506 (68) | 1991 |
| 88 | Winston-Salem Spirits (Reds) | 72 | 68 | .514 | 6 | Mark Berry | 164,509 (67) | 1993 |
| 51 | Durham Bulls (Braves) | 69 | 69 | .500 | 8 | Leon Roberts | 305,692 (67) | 1967 |
| 152 | Prince William Cannons (Yankees) | 67 | 73 | .479 | 11 | Trey Hillman | 209,273 (64) | 1989 |
| 63 | Lynchburg Red Sox (Red Sox) | 65 | 74 | .468 | 12½ | Mark Meleski | 100,113 (67) | 1984 |
| 176 | Salem Buccaneers (Pirates) | 61 | 79 | .436 | 17 | Scott Little | 145,657 (68) | 1987 |

**NOTE:** Team's individual batting and pitching statistics can be found on page indicated in lefthand column.

(351,146). They romped to a 45-22 record to run away with the Northern Division's first-half championship. The club also featured the most prospects in the league, though many of them were promoted long before the playoffs.

Righthander Jon Lieber went 9-3 with a 2.67 ERA and phenomenal control before getting whisked up to Double-A Memphis (he later was shipped by the Royals to the Pirates organization in the Stan Belinda trade). Other pitchers Brian Bevil (7-1, 2.30), Chris Eddy (2-2, 3.00, 14 saves), Brian Harrison (13-6, 3.28) and Robert Toth (8-7, 2.91) also played key roles in Wilmington's success.

The Blue Rocks also boasted the league's best pure hitting prospect, second baseman Michael Tucker. He hit .305 before his late-June promotion. Center fielder Darren Burton was an offensive (.277-10-45, 30 stolen bases) and defensive force the entire season.

**Curtis Goodwin**

JIM McLEAN

## Goodwin, Ochoa Key In

One manager called Frederick's outfield the best he had ever seen in the minor leagues. The Keys boasted the CL's two top prospects in center fielder Curtis Goodwin and right fielder Alex Ochoa.

Goodwin's speed terrified opposing teams on both offense and defense. He led the league with 10 triples, 98 runs and 61 stolen bases. Ochoa, whose shotgun arm made it almost impossible for teams to run the bases effectively, finished second in the stolen-base race with 34.

Goodwin was named MVP of the midseason all-star game, hitting a home run and double in the Northern Division's 6-3 victory.

**Michael Tucker**

JIM McLEAN

"When he's at the plate, he controls the pitcher," Wilmington manager Ron Johnson said. "He controls

the infield. He has everyone on pins and needles, that son of a gun.

"He's so fast, he'll read pitchouts and go back. And he's bunting with two strikes!"

Another highlight of Goodwin's season came when he hit a home run off the wooden right field Bull at Durham Athletic Park, winning him a steak at a local restaurant.

## Sorry, Wrong Number

The Durham Bulls thought they had retired Joe Morgan's No. 18 on June 17 as they celebrated what was supposed to be their last season at historic DAP. Problem was, Morgan wore No. 8.

"This is an embarrassment to a certain extent," said general manager Al Mangum, who later was replaced in an unrelated move. "Maybe Joe wore No. 18 and it was too big for him and you couldn't see the 1 when he stood up at the plate."

The Bulls' new ballpark won't be ready for Opening Day 1994, and DAP will be used for at least the first half.

## LEAGUE CHAMPIONS

**Last 25 Years**

| Year | Regular Season* | Pct. | Playoff |
|---|---|---|---|
| 1969 | Rocky Mount (Tigers) | .569 | Raleigh-Durham (Phillies) |
| 1970 | Win.-Salem (Red Sox) | .580 | Win.-Salem (Red Sox) |
| 1971 | Peninsula (Phillies) | .616 | Peninsula (Phillies) |
| 1972 | Salem (Pirates) | .577 | Salem (Pirates) |
| 1973 | Lynchburg (Twins) | .565 | Win.-Salem (Red Sox) |
| 1974 | Salem (Pirates) | .628 | None |
| 1975 | Rocky Mount (Phillies) | .641 | None |
| 1976 | Win.-Salem (Red Sox) | .584 | None |
| 1977 | Lynchburg (Mets) | .565 | Peninsula (Phillies) |
| 1978 | Peninsula (Phillies) | .647 | Lynchburg (Mets) |
| 1979 | Win.-Salem (Red Sox) | .607 | None |
| 1980 | Peninsula (Phillies) | .714 | Peninsula (Phillies) |
| 1981 | Peninsula (Phillies) | .522 | Hagerstown (Co-op) |
| 1982 | Peninsula (Phillies) | .656 | Alexandria (Pirates) |
| 1983 | Lynchburg (Mets) | .690 | Lynchburg (Mets) |
| 1984 | Lynchburg (Mets) | .645 | Lynchburg (Mets) |
| 1985 | Lynchburg (Mets) | .678 | Winston-Salem (Cubs) |
| 1986 | Hagerstown (Orioles) | .654 | Winston-Salem (Cubs) |
| 1987 | Salem (Pirates) | .575 | Salem (Pirates) |
| 1988 | Kinston (Indians) | .628 | Kinston (Indians) |
| 1989 | Durham (Braves) | .609 | Prince William (Yankees) |
| 1990 | Kinston (Indians) | .651 | Frederick (Orioles) |
| 1991 | Kinston (Indians) | .644 | Kinston (Indians) |
| 1992 | Lynchburg (Red Sox) | .570 | Peninsula (Mariners) |
| 1993 | Frederick (Orioles) | .557 | Winston-Salem (Reds) |

*Best overall record

# CAROLINA LEAGUE
## 1993 BATTING, PITCHING STATISTICS

### CLUB BATTING

| | AVG | G | AB | R | H | 2B | 3B | HR | BB | SO | SB |
|---|---|---|---|---|---|---|---|---|---|---|---|
| Winston-Salem | .273 | 140 | 4863 | 734 | 1329 | 211 | 27 | 160 | 425 | 956 | 131 |
| Durham | .265 | 138 | 4591 | 671 | 1218 | 234 | 33 | 106 | 444 | 1060 | 151 |
| Wilmington | .258 | 139 | 4673 | 623 | 1207 | 211 | 39 | 86 | 444 | 964 | 110 |
| Kinston | .256 | 138 | 4574 | 586 | 1172 | 209 | 28 | 87 | 419 | 949 | 96 |
| Lynchburg | .255 | 139 | 4684 | 635 | 1195 | 246 | 28 | 108 | 480 | 1051 | 46 |
| Salem | .251 | 140 | 4672 | 619 | 1171 | 197 | 25 | 138 | 417 | 1028 | 151 |
| Prince William | .251 | 140 | 4639 | 633 | 1166 | 222 | 37 | 88 | 478 | 1060 | 113 |
| Frederick | .251 | 140 | 4545 | 605 | 1143 | 211 | 37 | 75 | 491 | 854 | 159 |

### CLUB PITCHING

| | ERA | G | CG | SHO | SV | IP | H | R | ER | BB | SO |
|---|---|---|---|---|---|---|---|---|---|---|---|
| Frederick | 3.20 | 140 | 8 | 12 | 45 | 1218 | 1127 | 552 | 433 | 448 | 1161 |
| Wilmington | 3.32 | 139 | 8 | 9 | 43 | 1226 | 1158 | 558 | 452 | 353 | 896 |
| Kinston | 3.62 | 138 | 11 | 7 | 35 | 1210 | 1080 | 589 | 487 | 526 | 1097 |
| Prince William | 3.84 | 140 | 7 | 7 | 34 | 1214 | 1201 | 656 | 518 | 427 | 910 |
| Durham | 4.03 | 138 | 4 | 4 | 36 | 1220 | 1182 | 628 | 546 | 465 | 1026 |
| Lynchburg | 4.11 | 139 | 18 | 9 | 25 | 1210 | 1297 | 665 | 552 | 402 | 949 |
| Winston-Salem | 4.18 | 140 | 11 | 7 | 39 | 1228 | 1251 | 700 | 571 | 482 | 906 |
| Salem | 4.43 | 140 | 6 | 2 | 41 | 1232 | 1305 | 758 | 606 | 495 | 977 |

### CLUB FIELDING

| | PCT | PO | A | E | DP | | PCT | PO | A | E | DP |
|---|---|---|---|---|---|---|---|---|---|---|---|
| Lynchburg | .970 | 3629 | 1478 | 160 | 155 | Wilmington | .961 | 3677 | 1471 | 207 | 129 |
| Durham | .969 | 3661 | 1398 | 164 | 101 | Winston-Salem | .959 | 3685 | 1491 | 220 | 108 |
| Kinston | .965 | 3630 | 1513 | 188 | 124 | Prince William | .957 | 3641 | 1633 | 235 | 107 |
| Frederick | .962 | 3654 | 1349 | 195 | 90 | Salem | .957 | 3697 | 1576 | 238 | 107 |

**Joel Bennett**
Strikeout Leader

TY SPORT PHOTOS

JIM McLEAN

**Marc Marini**
34 doubles

### INDIVIDUAL BATTING LEADERS
(Minimum 375 Plate Appearances)

| | AVG | G | AB | R | H | 2B | 3B | HR | RBI | BB | SO | SB |
|---|---|---|---|---|---|---|---|---|---|---|---|---|
| Colon, Felix, Lynchburg | .320 | 98 | 319 | 52 | 102 | 22 | 0 | 16 | 58 | 45 | 65 | 0 |
| Belk, Tim, W-S | .306 | 134 | 509 | 89 | 156 | 23 | 3 | 14 | 65 | 48 | 76 | 9 |
| Smith, Bubba, W-S | .301 | 92 | 342 | 55 | 103 | 16 | 0 | 27 | 81 | 35 | 109 | 1 |
| Marini, Marc, Kinston | .300 | 124 | 440 | 65 | 132 | 34 | 4 | 5 | 53 | 63 | 70 | 7 |
| Therrien, Dom, Durham | .300 | 117 | 387 | 53 | 116 | 26 | 3 | 6 | 55 | 49 | 40 | 10 |
| Wollenburg, Doug, Dur. | .299 | 113 | 361 | 49 | 108 | 21 | 4 | 5 | 42 | 27 | 61 | 6 |
| Fleming, Carlton, PW | .299 | 120 | 442 | 72 | 132 | 14 | 2 | 0 | 25 | 80 | 23 | 21 |
| Juday, Bob, Lynchburg | .297 | 114 | 354 | 67 | 105 | 15 | 1 | 4 | 32 | 83 | 58 | 5 |
| Maxwell, Pat, Kinston | .293 | 103 | 400 | 46 | 117 | 17 | 3 | 4 | 35 | 22 | 32 | 6 |
| Ladell, Cleveland, W-S | .284 | 132 | 531 | 90 | 151 | 15 | 7 | 20 | 66 | 16 | 95 | 24 |

### INDIVIDUAL PITCHING LEADERS
(Minimum 111 Innings)

| | W | L | ERA | G | GS | CG | SV | IP | H | R | ER | BB | SO |
|---|---|---|---|---|---|---|---|---|---|---|---|---|---|
| Fronio, Jason, Kinston | 7 | 9 | 2.41 | 32 | 20 | 2 | 0 | 138 | 95 | 46 | 37 | 66 | 147 |
| Tavarez, Julian, Kinston | 11 | 5 | 2.42 | 18 | 18 | 2 | 0 | 119 | 102 | 48 | 32 | 28 | 107 |
| Lieber, Jon, Wilmington | 9 | 3 | 2.67 | 17 | 16 | 2 | 0 | 115 | 125 | 47 | 34 | 9 | 89 |
| Forney, Rick, Frederick | 14 | 9 | 2.78 | 27 | 27 | 2 | 0 | 165 | 156 | 64 | 51 | 64 | 175 |
| Toth, Robert, Wilmington | 8 | 7 | 2.91 | 25 | 24 | 0 | 0 | 152 | 129 | 57 | 49 | 40 | 129 |
| Klingenbeck, Scott, Fred. | 13 | 4 | 2.98 | 23 | 23 | 0 | 0 | 139 | 151 | 62 | 46 | 35 | 146 |
| Haynes, Jimmy, Frederick | 12 | 8 | 3.33 | 27 | 27 | 2 | 0 | 172 | 139 | 73 | 58 | 61 | 174 |
| Pettitte, Andy, PW | 11 | 9 | 3.34 | 26 | 26 | 2 | 0 | 160 | 146 | 68 | 54 | 47 | 129 |
| Williams, Matt, Kinston | 12 | 12 | 3.37 | 27 | 27 | 2 | 0 | 153 | 125 | 65 | 54 | 100 | 134 |
| Sackinsky, Brian, Fred. | 6 | 8 | 3.40 | 18 | 18 | 1 | 0 | 121 | 117 | 55 | 43 | 37 | 112 |

## DEPARTMENT LEADERS

### BATTING

| | | |
|---|---|---|
| R | Curtis Goodwin, Frederick | 98 |
| H | 2 tied at | 156 |
| TB | Cleveland Ladell, Winston-Salem | 240 |
| 2B | Marc Marini, Kinston | 34 |
| 3B | Curtis Goodwin, Frederick | 10 |
| HR | Bubba Smith, Winston-Salem | 27 |
| RBI | Chad Mottola, Winston-Salem | 91 |
| SH | 2 tied at | 13 |
| SF | 3 tied at | 9 |
| BB | Bob Juday, Lynchburg | 83 |
| IBB | 7 tied at | 4 |
| HBP | Lew Hill, Prince William | 18 |
| SO | Tate Seefried, Prince William | 150 |
| SB | Curtis Goodwin, Frederick | 61 |
| CS | John Cotton, Kinston | 24 |
| GIDP | 3 tied at | 15 |
| OB% | Bob Juday, Lynchburg | .430 |
| SL% | Bubba Smith, Winston-Salem | .585 |

### PITCHING

| | | |
|---|---|---|
| G | Scott Gully, Prince William | 59 |
| GS | Joel Bennett, Lynchburg | 29 |
| CG | Rob Henkel, Lynchburg | 7 |
| ShO | Scott Bakkum, Lynchburg | 4 |
| GF | John Hrusovsky, Winston-Salem | 40 |
| Sv | John Hrusovsky, Winston-Salem | 25 |
| W | Rick Forney, Frederick | 14 |
| L | 3 tied at | 12 |
| IP | Joel Bennett, Lynchburg | 181 |
| H | Scott Bakkum, Lynchburg | 201 |
| R | Rod Steph, Winston-Salem | 101 |
| ER | Kevin Logsdon, Kinston | 85 |
| HR | 2 tied at | 23 |
| BB | Matt Williams, Kinston | 100 |
| HB | Jason Fronio, Kinston | 15 |
| SO | Joel Bennett, Lynchburg | 221 |
| WP | Kevin Rychel, Salem | 27 |
| Bk | Matt Williams, Kinston | 6 |

### FIELDING

| | | | |
|---|---|---|---|
| C | AVG | Joe Ayrault, Durham | .992 |
| | E | Angelo Encarnacion, Salem | 21 |
| 1B | AVG | Mike Brown, Salem | .989 |
| | E | Steve Hinton, Wilmington | 18 |
| 2B | AVG | Tony Graffanino, Durham | .968 |
| | E | Chance Sanford, Salem | 34 |
| 3B | AVG | Dom Therrien, Durham | .957 |
| | E | Bobby Perna, Winston-Salem | 37 |
| SS | AVG | Manny Jimenez, Durham | .970 |
| | E | Eric Knowles, Prince William | 49 |
| OF | AVG | Basilio Ortiz, Frederick | .989 |
| | E | Chad Mottola, Winston-Salem | 15 |

## HONOR ROLL

### OFFICIAL ALL-STAR TEAM

| | |
|---|---|
| C | Jorge Posada, Prince William |
| 1B | Tate Seefried, Prince William |
| 2B | Tony Graffanino, Durham |
| 3B | Scott McClain, Frederick |
| SS | Eric Owens, Winston-Salem |
| OF | Curtis Goodwin, Frederick |
| | Chad Mottola, Winston-Salem |
| | Alex Ochoa, Frederick |
| Util | Belk, W-S; Jones, W-S |
| DH | Bubba Smith, Winston-Salem |
| SP | Julian Tavarez, Kinston |
| RP | Ian Doyle, Kinston |

**MVP:** Bubba Smith, Winston-Salem
**Manager:** Keller, Kin.; Mackanin, Fred.

### TOP 10 PROSPECTS
(Selected by league managers)

1. Curtis Goodwin, of, Frederick
2. Alex Ochoa, of, Frederick
3. Michael Tucker, 2b, Wilmington
4. Julian Tavarez, rhp, Kinston
5. Vince Moore, of, Durham
6. Chad Mottola, of, Winston-Salem
7. Darren Burton, of, Wilmington
8. Jon Lieber, rhp, Wilmington
9. Jose Malave, of, Lynchburg
10. Brian Bevil, rhp, Wilmington

# YEAR-BY-YEAR LEADERS: 1946-93

## CAROLINA LEAGUE

| Year | Batting Average | Home Runs | RBIs | Wins | ERA | Strikeouts |
|---|---|---|---|---|---|---|
| 1946 | Tom Wright, Durham .380 | Gus Zernial, Burl. 41 | Woody Fair, Durham 161 | 2 tied at... 19 | Harold Brown, Durham 2.42 | Frank Paulin, Leaksville 220 |
| 1947 | Harry Sullivan, Ral. .391 | Gene Petty, Danville 35 | Bill Nagel, Leaksville 128 | Ken Deal, Burlington 23 | Harvey Haddix, W-S 1.90 | Ken Deal, Burlington 275 |
| 1948 | Eddie Morgan, Mart. .373 | Russ Sullivan, Dan. 35 | Russ Sullivan, Dan. 129 | Lewis Hester, Reids. 25 | Al Henencheck, Ral. 2.24 | Jack Frisinger, W-S. 234 |
| 1949 | Bill Brown, Danville .361 | Leo Shoals, Reidsville 55 | Leo Shoals, Reids. 137 | Eddie Neville, Durham 25 | Adam Twarkins, Dan. 2.07 | Adam Twarkins, Dan. 240 |
| 1950 | Bill Evans, Burlington .338 | Fred Vaughan, Greensboro 27 | Woody Fair, Danville 103 | Woody Rich, Greensboro 21 | Woody Rich, Greensboro 2.41 | Wilmer Mizell, W-S 227 |
| 1951 | Ray Jablonski, W-S .363 | 2 tied at... 28 | Ray Jablonski, W-S 127 | Mike Fortine, Reids. 21 | James Lewey, W-S 2.64 | Dennis Reeder, W-S 155 |
| 1952 | Emil Karlik, Durham .347 | Dale Powell, Danville 25 | 2 tied at... 105 | Len Matarazzo, Fay. 22 | Eddie Neville, Durham 1.72 | Ron Necciai, Burl. 172 |
| 1953 | Bill Radulovich, Dur. .349 | Jack Hussey, Raleigh 28 | Don Buddin, Greensboro 123 | Ramon Monzant, Danv. 23 | Duane Wilson, Greens. 2.21 | Ramon Monzant, Danv. 232 |
| 1954 | Guy Morton, Greens. .348 | Jim Pokel, Fay. 38 | Guy Morton, Greensboro 120 | 2 tied at... 23 | John Patula, Greens. 1.58 | Don Schultz, Burl. 178 |
| 1955 | Dan Morejon, HP-Thom. .324 | Harold Holland, Dan. 31 | Harold Holland, Danv. 121 | Woody Rich, HP-Thom. 19 | Jack Taylor, HP-Thom. 1.78 | John Fitzgerald, Danv. 233 |
| 1956 | Curt Flood, HP-Thom. .340 | Leon Wagner, Danville 51 | Leon Wagner, Danville 166 | Jack Taylor, HP-Thom. 22 | Cleo Lewright, Kins. 2.38 | Earl Hunsinger, Wilson. 232 |
| 1957 | Eddie Logan, HP-Thom. .327 | 2 tied at... 30 | Ino Rodriguez, Danv. 114 | George Moton, W-S. 18 | David Reed, Durham 2.04 | David Reed, Durham 200 |
| 1958 | Don Bosch, Kinston .319 | 2 tied at... 25 | Al Milley, Danville 109 | Jack Taylor, HP-Thom. 19 | Johnny Aehl, Durham 1.86 | Eugene Snyder, HP-Thom. 234 |
| 1959 | Carl Yastrzemski, Ral. .377 | Don Lock, Greensboro 30 | Jim Price, Kinston 97 | Don Hagen, Raleigh 19 | Bill Spanswick, Ral. 2.49 | Bob Veale, Wilson. 187 |
| 1960 | Phil Linz, Greensboro .321 | Ed Olivares, W-S 35 | Don Lock, Greensboro 100 | Lee Stange, Wilson 20 | Jim Bouton, Greensboro 2.73 | Johnny Seale, Durham 197 |
| 1961 | Gates Brown, Durham .324 | Chuck Weatherspoon, Wil. 31 | Chuck Weatherspoon, Wil. 123 | 4 tied at... 15 | Bill MacLeod, W-S. 2.31 | Bill MacLeod, W-S. 208 |
| 1962 | Cesar Tovar, Rocky Mount .329 | Bert Barth, Rocky Mount 33 | Bert Barth, Rocky Mount 136 | Frank Bork, Kinston 15 | Steve Blass, Kinston 1.97 | Steve Blass, Kinston 209 |
| 1963 | Don Bosch, Kinston .332 | Walt Matthews, Durham 28 | Tony Solaita, HP-Thom. 122 | Jim Minshall, Salem 16 | Sherman Jones, Ral. 2.10 | Luis Tiant, Burlington 207 |
| 1964 | Mike Page, W-S .344 | 2 tied at... 30 | Greg Luzinski, Ral.-Dur. 109 | John Penn, Ral.-Dur. 17 | Don Hagen, Burlington 2.47 | Don Hagen, Raleigh 202 |
| 1965 | Ed Stroud, Portsmouth .341 | Ed Chasteen, Raleigh 28 | Steve Whitaker, Greens. 100 | Lynn McGlothen, W-S. 16 | Tom Moser, Burlington 1.97 | Ernest Barron, Wilson 183 |
| 1966 | Jose Calero, Salem .330 | Barry Morgan, Kinston 28 | Barry Morgan, Kinston 104 | Robbie Snow, W-S 20 | Robbie Snow, W-S 1.75 | Wally Wolf, Peninsula 185 |
| 1967 | Van Kelly, Kinston .323 | Hal King, Asheville 30 | Ron Allen, Portsmouth 100 | 4 tied at... 15 | Harold Clem, Raleigh 1.64 | Mark Schaeffer, W-S. 226 |
| 1968 | Carlos May, Lynchburg .330 | Tony Solaita, HP-Thom. 49 | Tony Solaita, HP-Thom. 122 | Jim Minshall, Salem 15 | Billy Champion, Ports. 2.03 | Al Fitzmorris, Lynch. 214 |
| 1969 | Ken Huebner, HP-Thom. .324 | Cliff Johnson, Ral.-Dur. 27 | Greg Luzinski, Ral.-Dur. 92 | John Penn, Ral.-Dur. 15 | Gordon Knutson, Ral.-Dur. 1.90 | 2 tied at... 183 |
| 1970 | Rennie Stennett, Salem .326 | Charlie Spikes, Kinston 22 | Cliff Johnson, Ral.-Dur. 91 | Lynn McGlothen, W-S. 14 | Dan Bootcheck, R.M. 1.92 | Lynn McGlothen, W-S. 202 |
| 1971 | Art Howe, Salem .348 | Bob Gorinski, Lynch. 22 | Craig Kusick, Lynch. 91 | Richard Fusari, Penin. 16 | Richard Fusari, Penin. 2.19 | Don Schroeder, Kins. 176 |
| 1972 | Dave Parker, Salem .310 | 2 tied at... 18 | Dave Parker, Salem 101 | Dave Pagan, Kinston 16 | Dave Pagan, Kinston 2.53 | Dave Pagan, Kinston 192 |
| 1973 | Terry Whitfield, Kin. .335 | Randy Bass, Lynchburg 20 | Chuck Erickson, W-S. 101 | Roy Thomas, R.M. 15 | Roy Thomas, R.M. 2.24 | Roy Thomas, Rocky Mount 193 |
| 1974 | Frank Grundler, Lynch. .335 | Randy Bass, Lynchburg 18 | Randy Bass, Lynchburg 103 | Don Aase, W-S. 15 | Don Aase, W-S. 2.43 | Don Aase, W-S. 176 |
| 1975 | Ted Cox, Winston-Salem .305 | Jim Morrison, R.M. 30 | Luke Wrenn, Salem 112 | Fred Jones, W-S. 14 | Fred Jones, W-S. 2.11 | Burke Suter, W-S. 150 |
| 1976 | Bobby Brown, Peninsula .349 | Marshall Brant, Lynch. 23 | Marshall Brant, Lynch. 93 | Peter Manos, Peninsula 15 | Peter Manos, Peninsula 1.16 | Ed Whitson, Salem 186 |
| 1977 | Ossie Olivares, Salem .370 | John Hughes, Penin. 29 | Eugenio Cotes, Salem 102 | Jeff Schneider, Penin. 15 | Jeff Schneider, Penin. 2.50 | Neil Allen, Lynch. 126 |
| 1978 | Ron MacDonald, Lynch. .325 | Ozzie Virgil, Penin. 29 | Ozzie Virgil, Penin. 98 | Jose Martinez, Penin. 15 | Jose Martinez, Penin. 2.07 | Marty Bystrom, Penin. 159 |
| 1979 | Pat Kelly, Kinston .309 | Gary Pellant, Alex. 18 | Mike Fitzgerald, Lynch. 75 | Tom Hart, Penin. 14 | Tom Hart, Penin. 2.22 | Mike Howard, W-S. 161 |
| 1980 | Wil Culmer, Peninsula .369 | Craig Brooks, W-S. 24 | Julio Franco, Peninsula 99 | Roy Smith, Peninsula 17 | Jim Wright, Penin. 1.85 | Don Carman, Peninsula 141 |
| 1981 | Brad Komminsk, Dur. .354 | Ron Gant, Salem 34 | Brad Komminsk, Dur. 104 | Mike Brown, W-S. 14 | Mike Brown, W-S. 1.49 | Jeff Bittiger, Lynch. 168 |
| 1982 | Rich Renteria, Alex. .326 | Dave Malpeso, W-S 29 | Rich Renteria, Alex. 100 | Charles Hudson, Penin. 15 | Charles Hudson, Penin. 1.85 | Tony Ghelfi, Penin. 162 |
| 1983 | Len Dykstra, Lynch. .358 | Ken Gerhart, Hagers. 31 | Dave Cochrane, Lynch. 108 | Dwight Gooden, Lynch. 16 | Dwight Gooden, Lynch. 2.50 | Dwight Gooden, Lynch. 300 |
| 1984 | Dave Magadan, Lynch. .335 | Randy Day, Peninsula 29 | Randy Day, Peninsula 105 | Mitch Cook, Lynchburg 16 | Randy Myers, Lynch. 2.06 | Mitch Cook, Lynch. 178 |
| 1985 | David Martinez, W-S .342 | James Dickerson, W-S 28 | Shawn Abner, Lynchburg 89 | Kyle Hartshorn, Lynch. 17 | Eric Bell, Hagerstown. 1.69 | Eric Bell, Hagerstown. 162 |
| 1986 | Gregg Jefferies, Lynch. .354 | Ron Jones, Salem 26 | Craig Worthington, Hag. 105 | Marty Reed, Kinston 16 | Jeff Ballard, Hagers. 1.85 | Chris Ritter, P.W. 149 |
| 1987 | Gregg Gagne, Hagerstown .326 | Hensley Meulens, P.W. 28 | Casey Webster, Kins. 111 | David Miller, Durham 16 | Kent Mercker, Durham 2.75 | David Miller, Durham 155 |
| 1988 | Bernie Williams, P.W. .335 | Mickey Pina, Lynch. 21 | Mickey Pina, Lynch. 108 | 3 tied at... 14 | Phil Harrison, W-S. 2.32 | Phil Harrison, W-S. 169 |
| 1989 | Luis Mercedes, Fred. .309 | Phil Plantier, Lynch. 27 | Phil Plantier, Lynch. 105 | Mike Draper, P.W. 16 | Derek Livernois, Lynch. 1.90 | Derek Livernois, Lynch. 151 |
| 1990 | Ken Ramos, Kinston .345 | Greg Blosser, Lynch. 18 | Mandy Romero, Salem 90 | Frank Seminara, P.W. 16 | Frank Seminara, P.W. 1.90 | Mike Oquist, Fred. 170 |
| 1991 | Jeff McNeely, Lynch. .322 | Tracy Sanders, Kinston 18 | Pedro Castellano, W-S. 88 | 2 tied at... 15 | Tim Smith, Lynchburg 2.16 | Curtis Leskanic, Kinston 163 |
| 1992 | Corey Kapano, W-S .318 | Bubba Smith, Peninsula 32 | Andy Hartung, W-S. 94 | John Cummings, Lynchburg 14 | Joe Caruso, Lynchburg 1.98 | John Cummings, Pen. 144 |
| 1993 | Felix Colon, Lynchburg .320 | Bubba Smith, Lynchburg 27 | Chad Mottola, W-S. 91 | Rick Forney, Frederick 11 | Jason Fronio, Kinston 2.41 | Joel Bennett, Lynchburg 221 |

# Clearwater Charges Through Back Door

**By SEAN KERNAN**

The Charlotte Rangers had the Florida State League's best overall record (84-49) in 1993, the St. Lucie Mets had the most big league prospects, but the Clearwater Phillies had their first FSL championship after a stunning performance in the playoffs.

The Phillies had gone 44-24 to win the West Division in the first half, but after losing five everyday players to promotions the club struggled in the second half to a 31-36 mark. By most accounts, the FSL championship was supposed to come down to Charlotte, which was 44-22 in the second half, and St. Lucie, which was 41-22.

But manager Bill Dancy got his new Phillies to peak at the right time. Playing a hit-and-run, aggressive style of baseball, the Phillies generated enough offense and got some superb pitching to top Charlotte 2-1 in the best-of-3 semifinal series and win three straight against St. Lucie after the Mets had taken Game One of the best-of-5 championship series.

"These guys were looking forward to the playoffs because we were so far behind in the second-half standings," Dancy said. "We got the breaks when we needed them. But you've got to give our pitchers some credit for a super performance."

St. Lucie, which had been shut out just three times all year, suddenly couldn't score. Phillies hurlers tossed 21 straight shutout innings against the Mets, who had beaten the Lakeland Tigers in a three-game playoff to reach the final.

**Mark Tranberg**

Phillies starters Mark Tranberg (2-0, 0.75 in 14 playoff innings) and Ron Blazier earned the series-clinching wins in Clearwater after J.J. Munoz went 3⅓ scoreless frames in relief for an extra-inning victory in

**John Dettmer.** Righthander led Charlotte to best regular-season record by going 16-3 with a 2.15 ERA.

Game Two at St. Lucie. That setback apparently took the life out of the Mets, who were blanked 8-0 in Game Three and 7-0 in Game Four despite starting top prospects Bill Pulsipher and Chris Roberts, a pair of tough lefthanders who were a combined 20-8 in the regular season.

## Attention to Attendance

With the Florida Marlins playing their first season in the National League, general managers of several FSL clubs weren't sure how detrimental the expansion team's existence would be to their own attendance figures. The FSL fared nearly as well as ever, however.

The league, coming off an all-time record attendance of 1,099,001 in 1992, would have topped the 1 million mark for the third straight season if it had been

## STANDINGS: OVERALL

| Page | | W | L | PCT | GB | Manager | Attendance/Dates | Last Pennant |
|---|---|---|---|---|---|---|---|---|
| 207 | **Charlotte Rangers (Rangers)** | 84 | 49 | .632 | — | Tommy Thompson | 90,792 (67) | 1989 |
| 157 | **St. Lucie Mets (Mets)** | 78 | 52 | .600 | 4½ | John Tamargo | 69,078 (60) | 1988 |
| 74 | **Sarasota White Sox (White Sox)** | 77 | 57 | .575 | 7½ | Dave Huppert | 91,883 (62) | 1963 |
| 181 | **St. Petersburg Cardinals (Cardinals)** | 75 | 58 | .564 | 9 | Terry Kennedy | 123,275 (64) | 1986 |
| 170 | **Clearwater Phillies (Phillies)** | 75 | 60 | .556 | 10 | Bill Dancy | 86,508 (68) | 1993 |
| 213 | **Dunedin Blue Jays (Blue Jays)** | 68 | 64 | .515 | 15½ | Dennis Holmberg | 77,382 (62) | None |
| 105 | **Lakeland Tigers (Tigers)** | 65 | 63 | .508 | 16½ | Gerry Groninger | 25,248 (58) | 1992 |
| 146 | **West Palm Beach Expos (Expos)** | 69 | 67 | .507 | 16½ | Rob Leary | 69,289 (67) | 1991 |
| 116 | **Osceola Astros (Astros)** | 56 | 74 | .431 | 26½ | Tim Tolman | 51,527 (64) | None |
| 81 | **Daytona Cubs (Cubs)** | 57 | 76 | .429 | 27 | Bill Hayes | 95,089 (65) | None |
| 128 | **Vero Beach Dodgers (Dodgers)** | 56 | 77 | .421 | 28 | Joe Vavra | 72,861 (68) | 1990 |
| 140 | **Fort Myers Miracle (Twins)** | 55 | 79 | .410 | 29½ | Steve Liddle | 95,054 (65) | 1985 |
| 63 | **Fort Lauderdale Red Sox (Red Sox)** | 46 | 85 | .351 | 37 | DeMarlo Hale | 28,240 (59) | 1987 |

**NOTE:** Team's individual batting and pitching statistics can be found on page indicated in lefthand column.

at full strength. But with the New York Yankees leaving Fort Lauderdale and sitting out the 1993 season, reducing active membership from 14 to an awkward 13, the FSL came up just short with attendance of 983,401.

"Overall we were down, but we had a pretty good year," league president Chuck Murphy said. "We got our schedules out late because the Red Sox decided they were going to play in Fort Lauderdale at the last minute and the Marlins hurt us a little bit, but the other thing is we got some more clubs to change their philosophy about ticket giveaways."

The league's biggest success at the gate came in Daytona Beach, where the FSL returned for the first time since 1987. The Daytona Cubs finished second in total attendance with 95,089 fans.

Counting Daytona's franchise, which was moved from Baseball City (17,400 fans in '92), and the Fort Lauderdale Red Sox, which drew 28,240 fans compared to the '92 total of 16,082 in Winter Haven, the league had seven clubs show an increase in attendance. Dunedin set a franchise record at 77,382.

The 1993 season will be remembered as the year of the barbaric schedule. Because there was an uneven number of 13 teams after the Yankees decided to pull out of Fort Lauderdale and the Boston Red Sox, rebuffed in their efforts to field a team at their new spring-training base in Fort Myers, unexpectedly jumped back into play at Fort Lauderdale, the league was forced to go to an unorthodox schedule.

"It was terrible," one manager said. "You couldn't learn the players like you would if you were playing three- and four-game series. Then, by the time you played some teams again, they'd have different players."

The 1994 schedule should be better. The Yankees will get back into the loop with a team in Tampa, site of their minor league development complex. The Red Sox will try to settle up with the Miracle, which owns

## STANDINGS: SPLIT SEASON

| FIRST HALF | | | | | SECOND HALF | | | | |
|---|---|---|---|---|---|---|---|---|---|
| **EAST** | W | L | PCT | GB | **EAST** | W | L | PCT | GB |
| Lakeland | 38 | 30 | .559 | — | St. Lucie | 41 | 22 | .651 | — |
| St. Lucie | 37 | 30 | .552 | ½ | Vero Beach | 32 | 36 | .471 | 11½ |
| West Palm | 37 | 30 | .552 | ½ | West Palm | 32 | 37 | .464 | 12 |
| Osceola | 28 | 38 | .424 | 9 | Lakeland | 27 | 33 | .450 | 12½ |
| Daytona | 28 | 39 | .418 | 9½ | Daytona | 29 | 37 | .439 | 13½ |
| Vero Beach | 24 | 41 | .369 | 12½ | Osceola | 28 | 36 | .438 | 13½ |
| Ft. Lauderdale | 22 | 43 | .338 | 14½ | Ft. Lauderdale | 24 | 42 | .364 | 18½ |
| **WEST** | W | L | PCT | GB | **WEST** | W | L | PCT | GB |
| Clearwater | 44 | 24 | .647 | — | Charlotte | 44 | 22 | .667 | — |
| Charlotte | 40 | 27 | .597 | 3½ | Sarasota | 40 | 28 | .588 | 5 |
| Sarasota | 37 | 29 | .561 | 6 | St. Petersburg | 38 | 28 | .576 | 6 |
| St. Petersburg | 37 | 30 | .552 | 6½ | Dunedin | 34 | 31 | .523 | 9½ |
| Dunedin | 34 | 33 | .507 | 9½ | Clearwater | 31 | 36 | .463 | 13½ |
| Fort Myers | 27 | 39 | .409 | 16 | Fort Myers | 28 | 40 | .412 | 17 |

**PLAYOFFS—Division:** St. Lucie defeated Lakeland, 2-1, and Clearwater defeated Charlotte, 2-1, in best-of-3 series. **Finals:** Clearwater defeated St. Lucie, 3-1, in best-of-5 series.

JoANNE COLENZO

**Randy Curtis** and **Chris Weinke.** Curtis (left) was selected MVP while Weinke led league in RBIs.

territorial rights to Fort Myers, to place a second team in Fort Myers.

## Memorable Performances

Clearwater's Phil Geisler launched three home runs, and threw in a single to boot, in a game against St. Petersburg July 20. Geisler, who less than two weeks earlier had served a three-game suspension because he had used a corked bat, was promoted to Double-A Reading on July 21. The Phillies outfielder also was the only player in the league to hit for the cycle.

Vero Beach catcher-turned-pitcher Felix Rodriguez had the league's only no-hitter of '93 when he blanked Sarasota 11-0 on Aug. 28. Rodriguez reported to spring training as a catcher, but the Dodgers converted the righthander to pitcher because of his live fastball.

St. Petersburg's Doug Radziewicz, the Cardinals' 48th-round draft choice in 1991, garnered the league's batting championship with a .342 average. Dunedin's Rick Holifield claimed the home run title with 20 and his Blue Jays teammate, Chris Weinke, drove in a league-high 98 runs. St. Lucie's Randy Curtis, who was named the league's MVP, batted .319 and led the league in runs (91) and stolen bases (52).

Charlotte righthander John Dettmer went 16-3 for the best won-lost mark and most wins. But he was edged out in the ERA contest by Vero Beach righthander Rich Linares, who registered in at 1.81. He worked one-third of an inning more than the minimum of 109. Dettmer was second at 2.15.

## LEAGUE CHAMPIONS

**Last 25 Years**

| Year | Regular Season* | Pct. | Playoff |
|---|---|---|---|
| 1969 | Miami (Orioles) | .606 | Miami (Orioles) |
| | Orlando (Twins) | .606 | |
| 1970 | Miami (Orioles) | .662 | Miami (Orioles) |
| 1971 | Miami (Orioles) | .667 | Miami (Orioles) |
| 1972 | Daytona Beach (Dodgers) | .606 | Miami (Orioles) |
| 1973 | West Palm Beach (Expos) | .580 | St. Petersburg (Cardinals) |
| 1974 | Ft. Lauderdale (Yankees) | .626 | West Palm Beach (Expos) |
| 1975 | St. Petersburg (Cardinals) | .651 | St. Petersburg (Cardinals) |
| 1976 | Tampa (Reds) | .559 | Lakeland (Tigers) |
| 1977 | Lakeland (Tigers) | .616 | Lakeland (Tigers) |
| 1978 | St. Petersburg (Cardinals) | .600 | Miami (Orioles) |
| 1979 | Ft. Lauderdale (Yankees) | .643 | Winter Haven (Red Sox) |
| 1980 | Daytona Beach (Astros) | .627 | Ft. Lauderdale (Yankees) |
| 1981 | Ft. Lauderdale (Yankees) | .604 | Daytona Beach (Astros) |
| 1982 | Ft. Lauderdale (Yankees) | .621 | Ft. Lauderdale (Yankees) |
| 1983 | Daytona Beach (Astros) | .634 | Vero Beach (Dodgers) |
| 1984 | Fort Myers (Royals) | .574 | Ft. Lauderdale (Yankees) |
| 1985 | Fort Myers (Royals) | .589 | Fort Myers (Royals) |
| 1986 | St. Petersburg (Cardinals) | .647 | St. Pete (Cardinals) |
| 1987 | Ft. Lauderdale (Yankees) | .615 | Ft. Lauderdale (Yankees) |
| 1988 | Osceola (Astros) | .605 | St. Lucie (Mets) |
| 1989 | St. Lucie (Mets) | .589 | Charlotte (Rangers) |
| 1990 | West Palm Beach (Expos) | .696 | Vero Beach (Dodgers) |
| 1991 | Clearwater (Phillies) | .623 | West Palm Beach (Expos) |
| 1992 | Sarasota (White Sox) | .639 | Lakeland (Tigers) |
| 1993 | Charlotte (Rangers) | .632 | Clearwater (Phillies) |

*Best overall record

# FLORIDA STATE LEAGUE
## 1993 BATTING, PITCHING STATISTICS

### CLUB BATTING

| | AVG | G | AB | R | H | 2B | 3B | HR | BB | SO | SB |
|---|---|---|---|---|---|---|---|---|---|---|---|
| Clearwater | .276 | 135 | 4525 | 659 | 1249 | 243 | 35 | 69 | 479 | 704 | 111 |
| St. Petersburg | .272 | 133 | 4486 | 562 | 1221 | 216 | 30 | 36 | 450 | 724 | 155 |
| Dunedin | .272 | 132 | 4402 | 650 | 1199 | 198 | 52 | 92 | 484 | 789 | 179 |
| St. Lucie | .272 | 130 | 4266 | 593 | 1159 | 174 | 47 | 45 | 453 | 607 | 172 |
| Charlotte | .269 | 134 | 4460 | 595 | 1199 | 192 | 34 | 44 | 525 | 799 | 117 |
| Vero Beach | .269 | 133 | 4439 | 582 | 1194 | 184 | 22 | 62 | 395 | 815 | 117 |
| Lakeland | .261 | 129 | 4253 | 558 | 1112 | 175 | 49 | 50 | 505 | 803 | 133 |
| Daytona | .259 | 133 | 4407 | 577 | 1141 | 181 | 36 | 66 | 451 | 796 | 114 |
| West Palm Beach | .254 | 136 | 4469 | 549 | 1133 | 220 | 31 | 53 | 435 | 807 | 139 |
| Sarasota | .251 | 134 | 4436 | 579 | 1114 | 204 | 42 | 61 | 447 | 812 | 98 |
| Osceola | .251 | 130 | 4261 | 503 | 1071 | 142 | 62 | 27 | 367 | 753 | 139 |
| Fort Lauderdale | .245 | 131 | 4393 | 494 | 1075 | 157 | 30 | 42 | 417 | 827 | 94 |
| Fort Myers | .241 | 134 | 4434 | 500 | 1067 | 210 | 27 | 42 | 454 | 815 | 142 |

### CLUB PITCHING

| | ERA | G | CG | SHO | SV | IP | H | R | ER | BB | SO |
|---|---|---|---|---|---|---|---|---|---|---|---|
| Charlotte | 2.97 | 134 | 9 | 15 | 47 | 1192 | 1080 | 459 | 394 | 415 | 789 |
| St. Lucie | 3.08 | 130 | 13 | 9 | 43 | 1125 | 1115 | 467 | 385 | 324 | 718 |
| St. Petersburg | 3.09 | 133 | 8 | 16 | 41 | 1185 | 1074 | 502 | 407 | 455 | 794 |
| Sarasota | 3.14 | 134 | 29 | 11 | 29 | 1171 | 1057 | 518 | 409 | 419 | 793 |
| West Palm Beach | 3.42 | 136 | 3 | 10 | 42 | 1192 | 1082 | 544 | 453 | 473 | 963 |
| Clearwater | 3.55 | 135 | 10 | 5 | 34 | 1190 | 1253 | 566 | 469 | 389 | 738 |
| Lakeland | 3.59 | 129 | 8 | 8 | 28 | 1129 | 1121 | 527 | 450 | 406 | 697 |
| Dunedin | 3.60 | 132 | 3 | 9 | 27 | 1147 | 1079 | 571 | 459 | 524 | 829 |
| Daytona | 3.80 | 133 | 9 | 10 | 26 | 1164 | 1154 | 608 | 491 | 410 | 673 |
| Osceola | 3.85 | 130 | 6 | 9 | 32 | 1125 | 1207 | 621 | 481 | 439 | 697 |
| Vero Beach | 4.20 | 133 | 3 | 4 | 33 | 1164 | 1138 | 672 | 543 | 593 | 849 |
| Fort Myers | 4.31 | 134 | 10 | 2 | 30 | 1180 | 1317 | 664 | 565 | 479 | 792 |
| Fort Lauderdale | 4.45 | 131 | 18 | 7 | 20 | 1162 | 1257 | 682 | 575 | 536 | 719 |

### CLUB FIELDING

| | PCT | PO | A | E | DP | | PCT | PO | A | E | DP |
|---|---|---|---|---|---|---|---|---|---|---|---|
| Charlotte | .975 | 3577 | 1640 | 135 | 127 | St. Petersburg | .967 | 3556 | 1500 | 173 | 129 |
| Clearwater | .972 | 3569 | 1623 | 151 | 128 | Dunedin | .963 | 3442 | 1536 | 191 | 121 |
| St. Lucie | .972 | 3376 | 1552 | 142 | 152 | Fort Myers | .963 | 3540 | 1538 | 193 | 127 |
| West Palm | .971 | 3576 | 1520 | 151 | 85 | Daytona | .962 | 3492 | 1583 | 198 | 151 |
| Sarasota | .970 | 3513 | 1653 | 160 | 101 | Vero Beach | .961 | 3493 | 1435 | 201 | 131 |
| Lakeland | .969 | 3388 | 1596 | 157 | 124 | Osceola | .959 | 3374 | 1528 | 211 | 153 |
| Ft. Lauderdale | .968 | 3487 | 1577 | 170 | 121 | | | | | | |

### INDIVIDUAL BATTING LEADERS
(Minimum 359 Plate Appearances)

| | AVG | G | AB | R | H | 2B | 3B | HR | RBI | BB | SO | SB |
|---|---|---|---|---|---|---|---|---|---|---|---|---|
| Radziewicz, Doug, St. Pete. | .342 | 123 | 439 | 66 | 150 | 36 | 2 | 4 | 72 | 73 | 58 | 6 |
| Demetral, Chris, VB | .325 | 122 | 437 | 63 | 142 | 22 | 3 | 5 | 48 | 69 | 47 | 6 |
| Garcia, Omar, St. Lucie | .322 | 129 | 485 | 73 | 156 | 17 | 7 | 3 | 76 | 57 | 47 | 25 |
| Curtis, Randy, St. Lucie | .319 | 126 | 467 | 91 | 149 | 30 | 12 | 2 | 38 | 93 | 72 | 52 |
| Colon, Dennis, Osceola | .316 | 118 | 469 | 51 | 148 | 20 | 6 | 2 | 59 | 17 | 41 | 10 |
| Cairo, Miguel, Vero Beach | .315 | 90 | 346 | 50 | 109 | 10 | 1 | 1 | 23 | 28 | 22 | 23 |
| Grable, Rob, Clearwater | .313 | 98 | 351 | 60 | 110 | 27 | 5 | 5 | 55 | 49 | 72 | 16 |
| DuBose, Brian, Lakeland | .313 | 122 | 448 | 74 | 140 | 27 | 11 | 8 | 68 | 49 | 97 | 18 |
| Aurilia, Rich, Charlotte | .309 | 122 | 440 | 80 | 136 | 16 | 5 | 5 | 56 | 75 | 57 | 15 |
| Coughlin, Kevin, Sarasota | .308 | 112 | 415 | 53 | 128 | 19 | 2 | 2 | 32 | 42 | 51 | 4 |
| Zuber, Jon, Clearwater | .308 | 129 | 494 | 70 | 152 | 37 | 5 | 5 | 69 | 49 | 47 | 6 |

### INDIVIDUAL PITCHING LEADERS
(Minimum 106 Innings)

| | W | L | ERA | G | GS | CG | SV | IP | H | R | ER | BB | SO |
|---|---|---|---|---|---|---|---|---|---|---|---|---|---|
| Linares, Rich, Vero Beach | 4 | 4 | 1.81 | 45 | 7 | 0 | 13 | 109 | 97 | 36 | 22 | 28 | 80 |
| Dettmer, John, Charlotte | 16 | 3 | 2.05 | 27 | 27 | 5 | 0 | 163 | 132 | 44 | 39 | 33 | 128 |
| Pyc, Dave, Vero Beach | 7 | 8 | 2.38 | 23 | 15 | 1 | 0 | 113 | 97 | 41 | 30 | 47 | 78 |
| Roberts, Chris, St. Lucie | 13 | 5 | 2.75 | 25 | 25 | 3 | 0 | 173 | 162 | 64 | 53 | 36 | 111 |
| Boehringer, Brian, Sar. | 10 | 8 | 2.80 | 18 | 17 | 3 | 0 | 119 | 103 | 47 | 37 | 51 | 92 |
| Geeve, Dave, Charlotte | 11 | 8 | 2.85 | 24 | 23 | 1 | 0 | 133 | 141 | 52 | 42 | 19 | 80 |
| Henderson, Rod, WPB | 12 | 7 | 2.90 | 22 | 22 | 1 | 0 | 143 | 110 | 50 | 46 | 44 | 127 |
| Edmondson, Brian, Lake. | 8 | 5 | 2.99 | 19 | 19 | 1 | 0 | 114 | 115 | 44 | 38 | 43 | 60 |
| Looney, Brian, WPB | 4 | 6 | 3.14 | 18 | 16 | 0 | 0 | 106 | 108 | 48 | 37 | 29 | 109 |
| Wallace, B.J., WPB | 11 | 8 | 3.28 | 25 | 24 | 0 | 0 | 137 | 112 | 61 | 50 | 65 | 126 |

## DEPARTMENT LEADERS

### BATTING

| | | |
|---|---|---|
| R | Randy Curtis, St. Lucie | 91 |
| H | 2 tied at | 156 |
| TB | 2 tied at | 214 |
| 2B | Jon Zuber, Clearwater | 37 |
| 3B | Bob Abreu, Osceola | 17 |
| HR | Rick Holifield, Dunedin | 20 |
| RBI | Chris Weinke, Dunedin | 98 |
| SH | Chris Peterson, Daytona | 17 |
| SF | David Fisher, Clearwater | 10 |
| BB | Randy Curtis, St. Lucie | 93 |
| IBB | Doug Radziewicz, St. Pete. | 11 |
| HBP | Rick Holifield, Dunedin | 16 |
| SO | Rick Holifield, Dunedin | 129 |
| SB | Randy Curtis, St. Lucie | 52 |
| CS | Aaron Holbert, St. Petersburg | 22 |
| GIDP | Mike Gomez, Clearwater | 22 |
| OB% | Doug Radziewicz, St. Pete. | .437 |
| SL% | Phil Geisler, Clearwater | .526 |

### PITCHING

| | | |
|---|---|---|
| G | John Corona, St. Petersburg | 59 |
| GS | 2 tied at | 28 |
| CG | Robert Ellis, Sarasota | 8 |
| ShO | Wes Brooks, Fort Lauderdale | 3 |
| GF | Mark LaRosa, West Palm Beach | 43 |
| Sv | 2 tied at | 19 |
| W | John Dettmer, Charlotte | 16 |
| L | Brett Roberts, Fort Myers | 16 |
| IP | Brad Schorr, St. Lucie | 182 |
| H | Ken Wheeler, Osceola | 196 |
| R | Ken Wheeler, Osceola | 101 |
| ER | Brett Roberts, Fort Myers | 84 |
| HR | Doug Mlicki, Osceola | 16 |
| BB | Dennis Gray, Dunedin | 97 |
| HB | B.J. Wallace, West Palm Beach | 11 |
| SO | Alan Levine, Sarasota | 129 |
| WP | Tom Singer, Dunedin | 17 |
| Bk | Derek Wallace, Daytona | 11 |

### FIELDING

| | | |
|---|---|---|
| C AVG | Darryl Kennedy, Charlotte | .986 |
| E | Don Prybylinski, St. Pete. | 17 |
| 1B AVG | Jon Zuber, Clearwater | .996 |
| E | Chris Weinke, Dunedin | 20 |
| 2B AVG | Bernie Millan, St. Lucie | .969 |
| E | Al Harley, Osceola | 34 |
| 3B AVG | Chris Stynes, Dunedin | .938 |
| E | Chad Roper, Fort Myers | 36 |
| SS AVG | Todd Carey, Fort Lauderdale | .970 |
| E | 2 tied at | 37 |
| OF AVG | Terry Bradshaw, St. Pete. | .997 |
| E | 4 tied at | 12 |

## HONOR ROLL

**OFFICIAL ALL-STAR TEAM**

- C Moler, Clear.; Huckaby, VB
- 1B Chris Weinke, Dunedin
- 2B Chris Demetral, Vero Beach
- 3B Ed Lantiqua, Vero Beach
- SS Edgardo Alfonzo, St. Lucie
- OF Rich Butler, Dunedin
- Randy Curtis, St. Lucie
- Rick Holifield, Dunedin
- DH Doug Radziewicz, St. Petersburg
- LHP Roberts, St.L; Wallace, WPB
- RHP Henderson, WPB; Dettmer, Char.
- RP Davis, St. Pete; McCready, St. Lucie

**MVP:** Randy Curtis, St. Lucie

**Manager:** John Tamargo, St. Lucie

**TOP 10 PROSPECTS**
(Selected by league managers)

1. Rod Henderson, rhp, West Palm Beach
2. Edgardo Alfonzo, ss, St. Lucie
3. Bill Pulsipher, lhp, St. Lucie
4. Terrell Lowery, of, Charlotte
5. Dmitri Young, 1b-3b, St. Petersburg
6. Jason Moler, c, Clearwater
7. Randy Curtis, of, St. Lucie
8. Justin Thompson, lhp, Lakeland
9. Rich Butler, of, Dunedin
10. Felix Rodriguez, rhp, Vero Beach

# YEAR-BY-YEAR LEADERS: 1946-93 — FLORIDA STATE LEAGUE

| Year | Batting Average | Home Runs | RBIs | Wins | ERA | Strikeouts |
|---|---|---|---|---|---|---|
| 1946 | Myril Hoag, Palatka 342 | 3 tied at 8 | Buddy Lake, Sanford 140 | 2 tied at 22 | Jodie Howington, Sanford 2.03 | Scott Cary, Orlando 244 |
| 1947 | Myril Hoag, Gainesville 350 | Ben Thorpe, Gainesville 10 | David Bride, Sanford 99 | George Fultz, Gaines 23 | Myril Hoag, Gainesville 1.82 | Juan Perez, DeLand 244 |
| 1948 | Charles Heinbaugh, Orl. 338 | Ralph Bartolozzi, Lees. 17 | John Garrison, Orl. 133 | Elwin Stabefield, Day. Beach 28 | Myril Hoag, Gaines. 1.32 | Joe Cleary, Gaines. 257 |
| 1949 | Al Pirtle, Gaines. 383 | Louis Bevil, Day. Beach 18 | Al Pirtle, Gaines. 110 | Stan Karpinski, St. Aug. 29 | Stan Karpinski, St. Aug. 1.56 | Myril Hoag, Gainesville 280 |
| 1950 | Bruce Barnes, Orl. 372 | Ed Levy, Sanford 33 | Al Pirtle, Gaines. 124 | Charles Tedesco, Sanford 19 | Bill Glessner, Day. Beach. 1.61 | Clyde Stevens, Sanford 186 |
| 1951 | Gene Oravetz, Orl. 364 | 2 tied at 23 | Al Pirtle, DeLand-Gain. 119 | John Jansce, DeLand 26 | Walt Jasinski, DeLand 1.70 | James Coppock, Day. Beach 176 |
| 1952 | Jesse Cade, DeLand 382 | Chuck Aleno, Sanford 25 | Chuck Aleno, Sanford 131 | Thomas Mills, Jax. Beach. 27 | Perry Roberts, DeLand 1.94 | Richard Wenger, Day. Beach 203 |
| 1953 | Jack Leonard, Sanford 381 | Ed Levy, Day. Beach 14 | Carvel Rowell, Cocoa 127 | Joe Angel, Jax. Beach 28 | James Vickery, DeLand 2.23 | Bobby Locke, Day. Beach 247 |
| 1954 | Russ Nixon, Jax. Beach. 387 | Herman Niehouse, Lakeland 23 | Gail Penza, DeLand 110 | John Blodgett, DeLand 19 | Carmelo Ruiz, DeLand 2.23 | Ray Konkoleski, Jax. Beach 228 |
| 1955 | Dan Keith, San.-D.B. 400 | Ino Rodriguez, Cocoa 20 | Dan Keith, San.-D.B. 122 | 2 tied at 25 | Bill Boyette, W.P.B. 1.91 | John Ivory Smith, D.B. 320 |
| 1956 | Felipe Alou, Cocoa 380 | 2 tied at 22 | Don Dillard, Day.Beach 127 | Julio Navarro, Cocoa 24 | Julio Navarro, Cocoa 2.16 | Julio Navarro, Cocoa 216 |
| 1957 | Nesbit Wilson, St.Pete 373 | German Pizzaro, Gaines. 16 | Larry Helms, Palatka 112 | Harry Coe, Tampa 26 | Harry Coe, Tampa 1.37 | Julio Guerra, Cocoa 308 |
| 1958 | Jim Niemann, Palatka 340 | German Pizzaro, Gain.-Tampa 25 | George Banks, St.Pete. 113 | 4 tied at 18 | Jim Horsford, St.Pete 1.93 | Harry Coe, Tampa 194 |
| 1959 | Tom Hamilton, St.Pete. 387 | Don Pepper, Lakeland 20 | Hugo Moskus, Tampa 110 | Gilberto Clark, Palatka 22 | Vic Davalillo, Pal. 2.45 | Gilberto Clark, Palatka 213 |
| 1960 | Sandy Rosario, Day. Beach. 319 | 2 tied at 15 | Miles McWilliams, Pal. 113 | Ken Sanders, Sanford 19 | Ted Davidson, Palatka. 2.35 | Marcelino Lopez, Tampa. 231 |
| 1961 | Jim Livesey, Leesburg 339 | Paul Catto, Palatka 12 | Paul Catto, Palatka 93 | 2 tied at 18 | Dan Neville, Tampa 1.94 | Jim Farland, Orl. 206 |
| 1962 | Alex Johnson, Miami 313 | Jim Wynn, Tampa 14 | Terry Bartholome, Orl. 81 | Ed Stein, Tampa 16 | Nicky Curtis, Day. Beach 2.13 | John Zahn, Sar. 255 |
| 1963 | Ramon Webster, Day. Beach 333 | Rich Littleton, Sar. 12 | Terry Harmon, Orl. 84 | Henry Hardin, St.Pete. 22 | Gil Downs, Sarasota 1.38 | Rick Gardner, Orl. 178 |
| 1964 | Mike Ferraro, Ft.Laud. 317 | Don Pepper, Lakeland 11 | Mike Ferraro, Ft.Laud. 78 | Jim Smith, Ft.Laud. 17 | Jim Smith, Ft.Laud. 1.38 | Tom Frondorf, Tampa. 167 |
| 1965 | Harvey Yancey, Tampa 305 | Roy Bethell, Cocoa 9 | Bill McNulty, Leesburg 62 | Larry Whitby, Orl. 18 | Earl Willoughby, Ft.Laud. 0.90 | Gerry Nyman, Sarasota 226 |
| 1966 | Bruce Andrews, We.Haven 329 | Charles Robinson, Lees. 13 | Charles Robinson, Lees. 78 | Lloyd Fourroux, Miami. 17 | Paul Gilliford, Miami. 1.27 | Lloyd Fourroux, Miami 183 |
| 1967 | Charles Stewart, St.Pete 296 | Joe Keough, Lees. 18 | Joe Keough, Lees. 80 | 2 tied at 17 | Brian Clark, Ft.Laud. 1.50 | Charles Murray, Orl. 206 |
| 1968 | Stan Martin, Miami 303 | Nate King, Orlando 16 | Larry Johnson, Miami 74 | Reggie Cleveland, St.Pete. 15 | Joe DeLuise, Day. Beach. 1.94 | Mike Willis, Tampa 174 |
| 1969 | John Young, Lakeland 325 | Wayne Dees, St. Pete. 14 | Ron Downing, Day. Beach 78 | Larry Gowell, Ft. Laud. 16 | John Montague, Miami. 1.53 | Larry Gowell, Ft. Laud. 217 |
| 1970 | Joe Staton, Lakeland 346 | Moe Hill, Orlando 22 | Lee Robinson, Day. Beach 86 | Mike Hebert, Miami 21 | Mike Hebert, Miami 1.44 | Steve Luebber, Orl. 172 |
| 1971 | Donnie Collins, Miami 330 | Jim Fuller, Miami 33 | Jim Fuller, Miami 110 | Herbie Hutson, Miami 17 | Herbie Hutson, Miami. 1.65 | Mike Cosgrove, Cocoa 231 |
| 1972 | Thad Philyaw, Day. Beach 317 | Jack Baker, W.H. 27 | Jack Baker, W.H. 89 | 2 tied at 15 | Dale Harrington, W.P.B. 1.51 | Santo Alcala, Key West 176 |
| 1973 | Kim Andrew, Miami 336 | Wayne Cage, Key West 18 | Wayne Cage, Key West 82 | Tony Gonzalez, St. Pete. 15 | Mike Proly, St. Pete. 1.76 | Tony Gonzalez, St. Pete. 162 |
| 1974 | Ron LeFlore, Lake. 339 | Joe Wallis, Key West 16 | Gary Roenicke, W.P.B. 82 | Joe Keener, W.P.B. 16 | Tony Chavez, Miami 1.57 | Rick Anderson, Ft. Laud. 179 |
| 1975 | Jim Chism, Miami 314 | Jerry Fry, Miami 14 | Martin Parrill, Miami 75 | 3 tied at 14 | Lawrence Bashaw, St. Pete. 1.69 | Bill Caudill, St. Pete. 153 |
| 1976 | Bobby G. Smith, Miami 324 | Dave Koza, W.H. 18 | Dave Koza, W.H. 83 | Ricky Mayo, Miami 15 | Win Remmerswaal, W.H. 1.74 | Mario Soto, Tampa 124 |
| 1977 | Marshall Edwards, Miami 334 | John Scoras, W.P.B. 19 | John Scoras, W.P.B. 86 | Mike Chris, Lakeland 18 | Mike Chris, Lakeland 2.01 | John Fulgham, St.Pete. 130 |
| 1978 | Dennis Webb, Ft. Myers 324 | Fay Thompson, Dunedin 19 | Clay Westlake, Ft.Laud. 96 | Brian Denman, W.H. 16 | Scott Brown, Tampa. 1.31 | Larry Jones, Miami 143 |
| 1979 | Ray Rivas, St. Pete. 334 | Steve Balboni, Ft.Laud. 26 | Steve Balboni, Ft.Laud. 91 | 2 tied at 16 | Jeff Taylor, Ft. Laud. 1.67 | Brian Ryder, Ft. Laud. 156 |
| 1980 | Wallace Johnson, W.P.B. 334 | Mark Strucher, Day. Beach. 17 | German Rivera, Vero Beach. 80 | Gene Nelson, Ft. Laud. 20 | Greg Mathews, St. Pete. 1.68 | Chuck Wickensheimer, V.B. 162 |
| 1981 | Danny Tartabull, Tampa 310 | Wes Clements, W.H. 19 | 2 tied at 84 | Ben Callahan, Ft. Laud. 17 | Al Nipper, W.H. 1.70 | Ken Westray, W.P.B. 171 |
| 1982 | Ty Gainey, Day. Beach 341 | 2 tied at 19 | 2 tied at 85 | Bob Tewksbury, Ft. Laud. 15 | Bob Tewksbury, Ft. Laud. 1.88 | Sid Fernandez, V.B. 137 |
| 1983 | Tommy Barrett, Ft. Laud. 327 | Crestwell Pratt, Tampa 21 | Glenn Carpenter, Day. Beach 104 | Jose Rijo, Ft. Laud. 15 | Jose Rijo, Ft. Laud. 1.68 | Tim Birtsas, Ft. Laud. 160 |
| 1984 | Dana Williams, W.H. 327 | Billy Moore, W.P.B. 22 | Billy Hocutt, W.P.B. 100 | Billy Hawley, Tampa. 16 | Billy Hawley, Tampa. 1.87 | Eric Plunk, Ft. Laud. 152 |
| 1985 | Jody Reed, Winter Haven 321 | Steve DeAngelis, Clear. 16 | Jack Daugherty, W.P.B. 87 | Greg Mathews, St. Pete. 16 | Greg Mathews, St. Pete. 1.11 | Rob Mallicoat, Osceola 158 |
| 1986 | Ron Jones, Clearwater 371 | Jimmy Fortenberry, Clear. 18 | Tary Scott, W.H. 93 | Sergio Valdez, W.P.B. 16 | Rob Lopez, Tampa 1.92 | Dody Rather, Osceola 151 |
| 1987 | Charles Culberson, Ft. Myers 320 | Brian Morrison, Miami 17 | Pat Sipe, W.P.B. 81 | Jose Cano, Osceola 15 | Jose Cano, Osceola 1.94 | Dan Gabriele, W.P.B. 150 |
| 1988 | Mike White, Vero Beach 340 | Julian Yan, Dunedin 17 | Dave Hansen, Vero Beach 78 | Jerry Kutzler, Tampa 16 | Kevin Brown, St.Lucie 1.81 | Chris Nichting, Vero Beach 151 |
| 1989 | Andy Mota, Osceola 319 | Ray Giannelli, Dun. 24 | Chris Donnels, St. Lucie 94 | Wally Trice, Osceola 16 | Ron Stephens, Sara. 1.47 | Nate Cromwell, Dunedin. 161 |
| 1990 | Jacob Brumfield, BB City 336 | 2 tied at 18 | Nikco Riesgo, St. Lucie 76 | John Johnstone, St. Lucie 15 | Ron Brown, Charlotte 1.90 | Anthony Ward, Dunedin. 137 |
| 1991 | Robert Perez, Dunedin 302 | 2 tied at 14 | Scott Cepicky, Sarasota 100 | 2 tied at 12 | Bill Wengert, Vero Beach 2.06 | Tom Michno, Miami 190 |
| 1992 | Rob Butler, Dunedin 358 | Carlos Delgado, Dunedin 30 | Carlos Delgado, Dunedin 100 | Chris Hill, Osceola 16 | Tavo Alvarez, W.P.B. 1.49 | Brien Taylor, Ft. Laud. 187 |
| 1993 | Doug Radziewicz, St. Pete. 342 | Rick Holifield, Dunedin. 20 | Chris Weinke, Dunedin 98 | John Dettmer, Charlotte 16 | Rich Linares, Vero Beach. 1.81 | Alan Levine, Sarasota 129 |

# South Bend Ascends To League Throne

**By CURT RALLO**

It was a season of triumph and tragedy, a season of natural disaster and new dimensions for the Midwest League. In the end, triumph belonged to the South Bend White Sox and manager Tony Franklin in 1993.

South Bend survived a tumultuous playoff run to beat Clinton, three games to one, for the Midwest League crown. The title was South Bend's second in its six-year history, the other coming in 1989. The White Sox also own a Northern Division pennant from the 1990 season.

Franklin celebrated his first championship in 25 years in the minor leagues as a player and manager.

Manager Jack Mull guided Clinton to the Southern Division pennant with a two-game sweep of Springfield, but his club entered the playoffs without pitching ace Aaron Fultz, who was traded by the parent San Francisco Giants to the Minnesota Twins organization the day after Clinton clinched a playoff spot.

South Bend got off on the right foot by scoring a dramatic 7-6 triumph in the opening game against the

**Essex Burton**

hot Giants. D.J. Thielen hit a two-run homer in the bottom of the eighth inning to give Clinton a 6-5 lead, but Robert Machado answered with a two-run triple in the top of the ninth to give the Sox a 7-6 victory.

The White Sox wrapped up the crown with a 4-1 triumph in Game Four.

Franklin's club endured some tough personnel losses on its climb to the top. South

Bend bolted to a 9-1 start in the first half, but finished the rest of the first half 25-31.

Remarkable turnarounds by a number of players sparked the Sox title drive. Pitchers Tim Moore and Jason Pierson each reeled off seven-game winning streaks in the second half.

**Charles Johnson.** Kane County catcher was selected league's top major league prospect by managers.

Also highlighting South Bend's season was a league-high 15 victories by Mike Call. Essex Burton stole a minor league-high 74 bases, and Jimmy Hurst belted a Sox club record 20 homers.

## Disaster Strikes

Tragedy occurred when Springfield Cardinals relief pitcher Diego Ruiz lost his life in an automobile acci-

## STANDINGS: OVERALL

| Page | Team | W | L | PCT | GB | Manager(s) | Attendance/Dates | Last Pennant |
|------|------|---|---|-----|----|-----------|--------|------|
| 196 | **Clinton Giants (Giants)** | 80 | 54 | .597 | — | Jack Mull | 62,873 (56) | 1991 |
| 123 | **Rockford Royals (Royals)** | 78 | 54 | .591 | 1 | Mike Jirschele | 68,206 (63) | None |
| 182 | **Springfield Cardinals (Cardinals)** | 78 | 58 | .574 | 3 | Mike Ramsey | 110,189 (60) | None |
| 165 | **Madison Muskies (Athletics)** | 77 | 58 | .570 | 3½ | Gary Jones | 101,219 (59) | None |
| 75 | **South Bend White Sox (White Sox)** | 77 | 59 | .566 | 4 | Tony Franklin | 229,883 (61) | 1993 |
| 111 | **Kane County Cougars (Marlins)** | 75 | 62 | .547 | 6½ | Carlos Tosca | 354,327 (65) | None |
| 140 | **Fort Wayne Wizards (Twins)** | 68 | 67 | .504 | 12½ | Jim Dwyer | 318,506 (68) | None |
| 147 | **Burlington Bees (Expos)** | 64 | 71 | .474 | 16½ | Lorenzo Bundy | 77,492 (56) | 1977 |
| 202 | **Appleton Foxes (Mariners)** | 62 | 73 | .459 | 18½ | Carlos Lezcano | 56,036 (58) | 1984 |
| 135 | **Beloit Brewers (Brewers)** | 60 | 74 | .448 | 20 | Wayne Krenchicki | 65,728 (64) | None |
| 116 | **Quad City River Bandits (Astros)** | 56 | 74 | .431 | 22 | Steve Dillard | 103,797 (49) | 1990 |
| 82 | **Peoria Chiefs (Cubs)** | 59 | 79 | .428 | 23 | Steve Roadcap | 100,811 (64) | None |
| 190 | **Waterloo Diamonds (Padres)** | 54 | 79 | .406 | 25½ | Ed Romero | 51,329 (51) | 1986 |
| 70 | **Cedar Rapids Kernels (Angels)** | 54 | 80 | .403 | 26 | Mitch Seoane | 114,105 (62) | 1992 |

**NOTE:** Team's individual batting and pitching statistics can be found on page indicated in lefthand column.

**FIRST HALF**

| NORTH | W | L | PCT | GB |
|---|---|---|---|---|
| Rockford | 43 | 22 | .662 | — |
| Madison | 39 | 28 | .582 | 5 |
| Kane County | 39 | 29 | .574 | 5½ |
| Appleton | 34 | 32 | .515 | 9½ |
| South Bend | 34 | 32 | .515 | 9½ |
| Fort Wayne | 33 | 33 | .500 | 10½ |
| Beloit | 29 | 36 | .446 | 14 |

| SOUTH | W | L | PCT | GB |
|---|---|---|---|---|
| Springfield | 41 | 26 | .612 | — |
| Clinton | 36 | 29 | .554 | 4 |
| Burlington | 35 | 31 | .530 | 5½ |
| Peoria | 29 | 40 | .420 | 13 |
| Quad City | 25 | 40 | .385 | 15 |
| Cedar Rapids | 24 | 40 | .375 | 15½ |
| Waterloo | 22 | 45 | .328 | 19 |

**SECOND HALF**

| NORTH | W | L | PCT | GB |
|---|---|---|---|---|
| South Bend | 43 | 27 | .614 | — |
| Madison | 38 | 30 | .559 | 4 |
| Rockford | 35 | 32 | .522 | 6½ |
| Kane County | 36 | 33 | .522 | 6½ |
| Fort Wayne | 35 | 34 | .507 | 7½ |
| Beloit | 31 | 38 | .449 | 11½ |
| Appleton | 28 | 41 | .406 | 14½ |

| SOUTH | W | L | PCT | GB |
|---|---|---|---|---|
| Clinton | 44 | 25 | .638 | — |
| Springfield | 37 | 32 | .536 | 7 |
| Waterloo | 32 | 34 | .485 | 10½ |
| Quad City | 31 | 34 | .477 | 11 |
| Peoria | 30 | 39 | .435 | 14 |
| Cedar Rapids | 30 | 40 | .429 | 14½ |
| Burlington | 29 | 40 | .420 | 15 |

**PLAYOFFS—Division:** South Bend defeated Rockford, 2-0, and Clinton defeated Springfield, 2-0, in best-of-3 series. **Finals:** South Bend defeated Clinton, 3-1, in best-of-5 series.

dent May 22. Ruiz, 22, was a passenger in a car driven by Springfield catcher Eddie Williams.

Springfield police said that alcohol was a factor, but no charges were brought against Williams.

Natural disaster hammered John O'Donnell Stadium in Davenport, Iowa. The Mississippi River submerged the stadium, forcing the Quad City River Bandits to hit the road for the second half of the season.

Quad City played only one game at home in the second half. The River Bandits played home games at two local high schools, and a number of Quad City's home games were switched to the home fields of Midwest League opponents.

Devastation caused by the flooding in the Midwest hit the River Bandits hard. The franchise was estimated to have lost almost a half-million

**Johnny Damon.** Rockford outfielder stamped himself as a future major league star by hitting .290 with 59 stolen bases.

dollars in revenues.

## Russian Revolution

Breakthroughs in the form of new dimensions celebrated the arrival of the first Russian player in the Midwest League.

Yevgeni Puchkov became the first Russian to reach the Class A level when he took the field for the Cedar Rapids Kernels. Puchkov, a second baseman, was released by the parent California Angels after the season.

The Fort Wayne Wizards, who moved from Kenosha in the offseason, enjoyed their first season in the league with whopping attendance and a pitcher's version of the triple crown by LaTroy Hawkins.

Hawkins captured the league ERA crown with a mark of 2.06 and reigned as the league strikeout king with 179 whiffs. With 15 victories, he tied for the league high with South Bend's Call.

Madison's Stacy Hollins and Springfield's T.J. Matthews tossed no-hitters, while Waterloo's Homer Bush was a runaway winner in the batting race with a .322 average.

Springfield second baseman Joe Biasucci, signed as a free agent by St. Louis prior to the season, beat out some big boppers for the home run crown, whacking 26 homers. He was selected the league's MVP. Beloit bomber Scott Talanoa hit 25 homers but suffered a season-ending injury at midseason.

Midwest League fans said farewell to Madison. The Wisconsin capital lost its fabled Muskies to Grand Rapids, as the Midwest League expands into Michigan for 1994.

**LaTroy Hawkins**

## LEAGUE CHAMPIONS

**Last 25 Years**

| Year | Regular Season* | Pct. | Playoff |
|---|---|---|---|
| 1969 | Appleton (White Sox) | .672 | None |
| 1970 | Quincy (Cubs) | .602 | Quincy (Cubs) |
| 1971 | Appleton (White Sox) | .642 | Quad City (Angels) |
| 1972 | Appleton (White Sox) | .598 | Danville (Brewers) |
| 1973 | Clinton (Tigers) | .588 | Wisconsin Rapids (Twins) |
| 1974 | Wisconsin Rapids (Twins) | .625 | Danville (Brewers) |
| 1975 | Waterloo (Royals) | .726 | Waterloo (Royals) |
| 1976 | Waterloo (Royals) | .600 | Waterloo (Royals) |
| 1977 | Waterloo (Indians) | .579 | Burlington (Brewers) |
| 1978 | Appleton (White Sox) | .708 | Appleton (White Sox) |
| 1979 | Waterloo (Indians) | .600 | Quad City (Cubs) |
| 1980 | Waterloo (Indians) | .609 | Waterloo (Indians) |
| 1981 | Wausau (Mariners) | .636 | Wausau (Mariners) |
| 1982 | Madison (Athletics) | .625 | Appleton (White Sox) |
| 1983 | Appleton (White Sox) | .635 | Appleton (White Sox) |
| 1984 | Appleton (White Sox) | .639 | Appleton (White Sox) |
| 1985 | Appleton (White Sox) | .611 | Kenosha (Twins) |
| 1986 | Springfield (Cardinals) | .621 | Waterloo (Indians) |
| 1987 | Springfield (Cardinals) | .671 | Kenosha (Twins) |
| 1988 | Cedar Rapids (Reds) | .621 | Cedar Rapids (Reds) |
| 1989 | South Bend (White Sox) | .643 | South Bend (White Sox) |
| 1990 | Cedar Rapids (Reds) | .656 | Quad City (Angels) |
| 1991 | Clinton (Giants) | .583 | Clinton (Giants) |
| 1992 | Quad City (Angels) | .664 | Cedar Rapids (Reds) |
| 1993 | Clinton (Giants) | .597 | South Bend (White Sox) |

*Best overall record

TOM DiPACE

# MIDWEST LEAGUE
## 1993 BATTING, PITCHING STATISTICS

### CLUB BATTING

| | AVG | G | AB | R | H | 2B | 3B | HR | BB | SO | SB |
|---|---|---|---|---|---|---|---|---|---|---|---|
| South Bend | .269 | 136 | 4539 | 659 | 1222 | 216 | 44 | 65 | 455 | 952 | 155 |
| Rockford | .269 | 132 | 4272 | 630 | 1148 | 234 | 43 | 57 | 480 | 851 | 239 |
| Clinton | .258 | 134 | 4251 | 679 | 1096 | 179 | 34 | 78 | 502 | 975 | 214 |
| Kane County | .255 | 137 | 4473 | 602 | 1139 | 219 | 33 | 50 | 528 | 892 | 127 |
| Appleton | .253 | 135 | 4330 | 604 | 1095 | 227 | 43 | 77 | 467 | 1039 | 131 |
| Springfield | .253 | 136 | 4317 | 662 | 1091 | 206 | 26 | 124 | 517 | 1131 | 144 |
| Peoria | .252 | 138 | 4379 | 578 | 1103 | 218 | 21 | 53 | 469 | 914 | 81 |
| Madison | .252 | 135 | 4340 | 636 | 1092 | 214 | 34 | 88 | 488 | 1086 | 105 |
| Quad City | .252 | 130 | 4179 | 570 | 1052 | 180 | 30 | 68 | 403 | 957 | 169 |
| Beloit | .250 | 134 | 4279 | 641 | 1068 | 191 | 37 | 98 | 514 | 1004 | 182 |
| Fort Wayne | .249 | 135 | 4485 | 578 | 1117 | 203 | 37 | 74 | 505 | 946 | 136 |
| Burlington | .248 | 135 | 4400 | 616 | 1093 | 224 | 31 | 104 | 473 | 1079 | 125 |
| Waterloo | .248 | 133 | 4060 | 525 | 1008 | 172 | 29 | 79 | 360 | 987 | 158 |
| Cedar Rapids | .231 | 134 | 4220 | 580 | 976 | 167 | 26 | 79 | 565 | 1017 | 132 |

### CLUB PITCHING

| | ERA | G | CG | SHO | SV | IP | H | R | ER | BB | SO |
|---|---|---|---|---|---|---|---|---|---|---|---|
| Madison | 3.39 | 135 | 7 | 7 | 37 | 1146 | 985 | 521 | 432 | 494 | 965 |
| Fort Wayne | 3.49 | 135 | 9 | 16 | 41 | 1178 | 1089 | 585 | 457 | 511 | 1136 |
| Springfield | 3.53 | 136 | 10 | 8 | 41 | 1137 | 1058 | 548 | 446 | 336 | 995 |
| Kane County | 3.56 | 137 | 9 | 7 | 45 | 1185 | 1079 | 560 | 468 | 491 | 1074 |
| Burlington | 3.59 | 135 | 8 | 6 | 26 | 1138 | 1029 | 595 | 454 | 534 | 1107 |
| Rockford | 3.61 | 132 | 13 | 11 | 38 | 1127 | 1063 | 537 | 452 | 466 | 1001 |
| Clinton | 3.61 | 134 | 6 | 16 | 52 | 1127 | 989 | 559 | 452 | 546 | 1021 |
| South Bend | 3.79 | 136 | 18 | 14 | 40 | 1178 | 1126 | 583 | 496 | 395 | 870 |
| Peoria | 4.08 | 138 | 15 | 16 | 25 | 1174 | 1148 | 644 | 532 | 429 | 986 |
| Quad City | 4.10 | 130 | 16 | 11 | 23 | 1087 | 1088 | 630 | 495 | 441 | 967 |
| Appleton | 4.27 | 135 | 8 | 7 | 35 | 1146 | 1151 | 669 | 544 | 495 | 967 |
| Cedar Rapids | 4.48 | 134 | 11 | 3 | 26 | 1134 | 1214 | 732 | 564 | 479 | 947 |
| Beloit | 4.49 | 134 | 14 | 4 | 32 | 1139 | 1208 | 712 | 568 | 514 | 958 |
| Waterloo | 4.75 | 133 | 6 | 5 | 33 | 1066 | 1073 | 685 | 563 | 595 | 836 |

### CLUB FIELDING

| | PCT | PO | A | E | DP | | PCT | PO | A | E | DP |
|---|---|---|---|---|---|---|---|---|---|---|---|
| Madison | .969 | 3439 | 1400 | 156 | 82 | Quad City | .961 | 3262 | 1338 | 185 | 109 |
| Rockford | .968 | 3381 | 1451 | 161 | 131 | Beloit | .960 | 3417 | 1307 | 195 | 97 |
| Kane County | .966 | 3554 | 1470 | 178 | 111 | Fort Wayne | .960 | 3535 | 1341 | 204 | 116 |
| Peoria | .966 | 3523 | 1423 | 174 | 106 | Appleton | .958 | 3437 | 1498 | 215 | 112 |
| Clinton | .964 | 3380 | 1348 | 175 | 107 | Waterloo | .957 | 3199 | 1334 | 204 | 114 |
| South Bend | .964 | 3533 | 1451 | 186 | 112 | Burlington | .955 | 3414 | 1297 | 222 | 97 |
| Springfield | .964 | 3411 | 1457 | 184 | 93 | Cedar Rapids | .953 | 3401 | 1401 | 237 | 100 |

### INDIVIDUAL BATTING LEADERS
(Minimum 365 Plate Appearances)

| | AVG | G | AB | R | H | 2B | 3B | HR | RBI | BB | SO | SB |
|---|---|---|---|---|---|---|---|---|---|---|---|---|
| Bush, Homer, Waterloo | .322 | 130 | 472 | 63 | 152 | 19 | 3 | 5 | 51 | 19 | 87 | 39 |
| Jennings, Robin, Peoria | .308 | 132 | 474 | 64 | 146 | 29 | 5 | 3 | 65 | 46 | 73 | 11 |
| Fonville, Chad, Clinton | .306 | 120 | 447 | 80 | 137 | 16 | 10 | 1 | 44 | 40 | 48 | 52 |
| Cappuccio, Carmine, SB | .305 | 101 | 383 | 59 | 117 | 26 | 5 | 4 | 52 | 42 | 56 | 2 |
| Benard, Marvin, Clinton | .301 | 112 | 349 | 84 | 105 | 14 | 2 | 5 | 50 | 56 | 66 | 42 |
| Perez, Danny, Beloit | .300 | 106 | 377 | 70 | 113 | 17 | 6 | 10 | 59 | 56 | 64 | 23 |
| Tirpack, Ken, Fort Wayne | .294 | 127 | 473 | 71 | 139 | 34 | 3 | 9 | 70 | 68 | 103 | 1 |
| Ball, Jeff, Quad City | .293 | 112 | 389 | 69 | 114 | 28 | 2 | 14 | 76 | 58 | 62 | 40 |
| Byrd, Anthony, Fort Wayne | .292 | 123 | 479 | 84 | 140 | 19 | 10 | 16 | 79 | 58 | 79 | 24 |
| Murphy, Steve, Rockford | .292 | 110 | 349 | 56 | 102 | 17 | 5 | 2 | 49 | 48 | 69 | 29 |

### INDIVIDUAL PITCHING LEADERS
(Minimum 108 Innings)

| | W | L | ERA | G | GS | CG | SV | IP | H | R | ER | BB | SO |
|---|---|---|---|---|---|---|---|---|---|---|---|---|---|
| Urbina, Ugueth, Burlington | 10 | 1 | 1.99 | 16 | 16 | 4 | 0 | 108 | 78 | 30 | 24 | 36 | 107 |
| Hawkins, LaTroy, Ft. Wayne | 15 | 5 | 2.06 | 26 | 23 | 4 | 0 | 157 | 110 | 53 | 36 | 41 | 179 |
| Holt, Chris, Quad City | 11 | 10 | 2.27 | 26 | 26 | 10 | 0 | 186 | 162 | 70 | 47 | 54 | 176 |
| Trinidad, Hector, Peoria | 7 | 6 | 2.47 | 22 | 22 | 4 | 0 | 153 | 142 | 56 | 42 | 29 | 118 |
| Mathews, T.J., Springfield | 12 | 9 | 2.71 | 25 | 25 | 5 | 0 | 159 | 121 | 59 | 48 | 29 | 144 |
| Sheehan, Chris, Rockford | 9 | 5 | 2.83 | 31 | 12 | 2 | 6 | 118 | 97 | 40 | 37 | 22 | 101 |
| Arteaga, Ivan, Burlington | 6 | 5 | 2.83 | 20 | 20 | 2 | 0 | 127 | 114 | 57 | 40 | 47 | 111 |
| Mendoza, Reynol, KC | 12 | 5 | 2.86 | 26 | 23 | 3 | 2 | 164 | 129 | 59 | 52 | 45 | 153 |
| Sebach, Kyle, Cedar Rapids | 6 | 9 | 3.04 | 26 | 26 | 4 | 0 | 154 | 138 | 73 | 52 | 70 | 138 |
| Nickell, Jackie, Appleton | 7 | 7 | 3.06 | 24 | 23 | 2 | 0 | 150 | 135 | 54 | 51 | 41 | 151 |

## DEPARTMENT LEADERS

### BATTING

| | | |
|---|---|---|
| R | Essex Burton, South Bend | 95 |
| H | Homer Bush, Waterloo | 152 |
| TB | Charles Johnson, Kane County | 230 |
| 2B | Todd Pridy, Kane County | 38 |
| 3B | Johnny Damon, Rockford | 13 |
| HR | Joe Biasucci, Springfield | 26 |
| RBI | Charles Johnson, Kane County | 94 |
| SH | Richard Perez, Peoria | 29 |
| SF | Creighton Gubanich, Madison | 12 |
| BB | Larry Sutton, Rockford | 95 |
| IBB | Chris Hmielewski, Burlington | 10 |
| HBP | Charles Gipson, Appleton | 27 |
| SO | Brian Wallace, Appleton | 145 |
| SB | Essex Burton, South Bend | 74 |
| CS | Essex Burton, South Bend | 24 |
| GIDP | Brandon Markiewicz, CR | 18 |
| OB% | Larry Sutton, Rockford | .424 |
| SL% | Joe Biasucci, Springfield | .575 |

### PITCHING

| | | |
|---|---|---|
| G | Greg Knowles, Springfield | 54 |
| GS | Hector Carrasco, Kane County | 28 |
| CG | Chris Holt, Quad City | 10 |
| ShO | 2 tied at | 3 |
| GF | Gus Gandarillas, Fort Wayne | 48 |
| Sv | Kirk Bullinger, Springfield | 33 |
| W | 2 tied at | 15 |
| L | 2 tied at | 14 |
| IP | Chris Holt, Quad City | 186 |
| H | Mike Call, South Bend | 187 |
| R | Jeff Schmidt, Cedar Rapids | 105 |
| ER | Stacy Hollins, Madison | 86 |
| HR | 2 tied at | 21 |
| BB | Cliff Foster, Madison | 92 |
| HB | Pat Leahy, Kane County | 23 |
| SO | LaTroy Hawkins, Fort Wayne | 179 |
| WP | Jose Sanchez, Appleton | 27 |
| Bk | Jackie Nickell, Appleton | 12 |

### FIELDING

| | | |
|---|---|---|
| C AVG | Marcus Jensen, Clinton | .990 |
| E | Bobby Hughes, Burlington | 17 |
| 1B AVG | Ken Tirpack, Fort Wayne | .992 |
| E | Chris Hmielewski, Burlington | 18 |
| 2B AVG | Henri Centeno, Quad City | .982 |
| E | Homer Bush, Waterloo | 38 |
| 3B AVG | Lou Lucca, Kane County | .932 |
| E | Isreal Alcantara, Burlington | 57 |
| SS AVG | Craig Wilson, South Bend | .963 |
| E | Jolbert Cabrera, Burlington | 36 |
| OF AVG | Eddie Christian, KC | 1.000 |
| E | 3 tied at | 12 |

## HONOR ROLL

### OFFICIAL ALL-STAR TEAM

| | |
|---|---|
| C | Charles Johnson, Kane County |
| 1B | Ken Tirpack, Fort Wayne |
| 2B | Joe Biasucci, Springfield |
| 3B | Mike Gulan, Springfield |
| SS | Chad Fonville, Clinton |
| OF | Anthony Byrd, Fort Wayne |
| | Johnny Damon, Rockford |
| | Carmine Cappuccio, South Bend |
| DH | Scott Talanoa, Beloit |
| LHP | Ugueth Urbina, Burlington |
| RHP | Tim Davis, Appleton |
| RP | Darensbourg, KC; Bullinger, Spr. |

**MVP:** Joe Biasucci, Springfield

**Manager:** Jack Mull, Clinton

### TOP 10 PROSPECTS
(Selected by league managers)

1. Charles Johnson, c, Kane County
2. Ugueth Urbina, rhp, Burlington
3. Johnny Damon, of, Rockford
4. Anthony Byrd, of, Fort Wayne
5. LaTroy Hawkins, rhp, Fort Wayne
6. Chad Fonville, ss, Clinton
7. Jimmy Hurst, of, South Bend
8. Marcus Jensen, c, Clinton
9. Keith Johns, ss, Springfield
10. Hector Trinidad, rhp, Peoria

# YEAR-BY-YEAR LEADERS: 1946-93

## MIDWEST LEAGUE

| Year | Batting Average | | Home Runs | | RBIs | | Wins | | ERA | | Strikeouts | |
|---|---|---|---|---|---|---|---|---|---|---|---|---|
| 1946 | DID NOT OPERATE | | | | | | | | | | | |
| 1947 | Billy Klaus, Centralia | .341 | Rip Repulski, West. Frank. | 10 | Billy Klaus, Centralia | 84 | Robert Freels, Bell. | 19 | Ken Wild, West Frank. | 1.73 | Don Liddle, Mt. Vernon | 192 |
| 1948 | Dick Martz, Marion | .361 | Paul Deters, Marion | 8 | Frank Porreca, West Frank. | 94 | Floyd Melliere, W.Frank. | 21 | Floyd Melliere, W.Frank. | 1.77 | Mike Blyzka, Belleville | 192 |
| 1949 | Bunny Mick, Belleville | .354 | Art Oliver, Paducah | 17 | Dick Martz, Paducah | 100 | Joe Prucha, Centralia | 19 | Dick Loeser, West Frank. | 2.02 | Joe Mattis, Mattoon | 166 |
| 1950 | Jim Belz, West Frankfort | .349 | Ken Dickens, Vincennes | 21 | Lew Bezeka, Centralia | 120 | Gene Pisarski, Cen. | 22 | Gene Pisarski, Cen. | 2.06 | Bill Ecklund, Cen. | 174 |
| 1951 | Clint McCord, Paris | .363 | 2 tied at | 16 | Jim Given, Mt. Vernon | 119 | Lee Tunnison, Cen. | 20 | Lee Tunnison, Cen. | 3.12 | Lee Tunnison, Cen. | 170 |
| 1952 | Clint McCord, Paris | .392 | Jim Zapp, Paris | 20 | Jim Zapp, Paris | 136 | Ken Gohn, Danville | 22 | Ken Gohn, Danville | 1.58 | Amacio Ferro, Hannibal | 183 |
| 1953 | Bob Schmidt, Mt. Vernon | .358 | Ken Payne, Paris | 16 | Jim Freeman, Decatur | 106 | 2 tied at | 18 | Bill Bright, Mattoon | 2.51 | Dennis Hamilton, Mattoon | 195 |
| 1954 | John Lucadello, Decatur | .362 | J.C. Dunn, Hannibal | 26 | Joe Schmidt, Paris | 125 | John Baumgarner, Dec. | 22 | John Baumgarner, Dec. | 2.62 | Dave Jiminez, Clinton | 249 |
| 1955 | Orlando Cepeda, Kokomo | .393 | Walt Dixon, Kokomo | 24 | Jimmy Lynn, Dubuque | 121 | Allen Evans, Kokomo | 21 | David Wegerek, Laf. | 2.59 | Ben Rich, Clinton | 199 |
| 1956 | Deacon Jones, Dubuque | .409 | Carroll Gholson, Paris | 30 | Bob Lawrence, Wat. | 120 | Arturo Miro, Clinton | 22 | Charles Alsop, Mich. City | 2.64 | Charles Smith, Lafayette. | 263 |
| 1957 | Tommy Davis, Kokomo | .357 | Don Gordon, Dubuque | 22 | Tony Torchia, Keokuk | 116 | Emerson Unzicker, Kok. | 20 | Dick Lines, Clinton | 1.80 | Harold Harris, Mattoon | 202 |
| 1958 | Lou Johnson, Paris | .336 | Gus Sancimino, Kok. | 29 | 2 tied at | 88 | Ken Turner, Quad City | 18 | Juan Marichal, Mich. City | 1.87 | Hal Kolstad, Waterloo | 250 |
| 1959 | Don Branson, Keokuk | .324 | Dale Reichert, Kokomo | 30 | Fred Whitfield, Keo. | 118 | Juan Marichal, Mich. City | 21 | Galen Cisco, Waterloo | 2.23 | Joel McDaniel, Dec. | 212 |
| 1960 | Julio Linares, Quincy | .324 | Art Blunt, Dubuque | 26 | Clarence Stanley, Dec. | 116 | Joel McDaniel, Dec. | 22 | Tom Haake, Dubuque | 2.52 | Bob Sprout, Decatur | 264 |
| 1961 | Antulio Martinez, Quincy | .368 | Bob Lawrence, Wat. | 30 | John Oster, Wis. Rap. | 127 | Tom Haake, Dubuque | 19 | Dennis Ribant, Davenport. | 1.86 | David Busby, Waterloo | 237 |
| 1962 | Tony Torchia, Keokuk | .324 | John Price, Deca. | 27 | Deacon Jones, Appleton | 94 | David Busby, Waterloo | 21 | Bob DeLong, Decatur | 2.10 | Barry Shollenberger, Wat. | 226 |
| 1963 | Tommie Reynolds, Bur. | .332 | Lincoln Curtis, C.R. | 28 | 2 tied at | 88 | Paul Deem, Quincy | 18 | Tony Komisar, C.R. | 1.97 | Mark Littell, Waterloo | 237 |
| 1964 | Dave May, Appleton | .368 | Rene Lachemann, Bur. | 24 | Roe Skidmore, Decatur | 94 | Ken Turner, Quad City | 15 | Jerome Rozmus, Clinton | 1.44 | Nick DeMatteis, Dec. | 208 |
| 1965 | Dan DiPace, Wis. Rap. | .333 | Randy Schwartz, Bur. | 29 | Joe Bowen, Danville | 83 | Danny Morris, Wis. Rap. | 16 | Mike Carubia, Quad City | 1.69 | Joe McKirahan, Dec. | 274 |
| 1966 | Deacon Jones, Appleton | .353 | Graig Nettles, Wis. Rap. | 28 | Deacon Jones, Appleton | 80 | Fred Rath, Appleton | 17 | Tony Pierce, Bur. | 1.84 | Danny Morris, Wis. Rap. | 206 |
| 1967 | Charlie Manuel, Wis. Rap. | .313 | Jim Williams, Quincy | 17 | 2 tied at | 70 | 3 tied at | 15 | Vern Geishert, Quad City | 1.13 | Mickey Abarbanel, App. | 191 |
| 1968 | George Hendrick, Bur. | .327 | Roe Skidmore, Decatur | 27 | Roe Skidmore, Decatur | 94 | Alex Distaso, Quincy | 13 | Bob DeLong, Decatur | 1.97 | Bob DeLong, Decatur | 231 |
| 1969 | Ted Parks, Waterloo | .307 | 2 tied at | 18 | Joe Bowen, Danville | 83 | Don Eddy, Appleton | 18 | Steve Sibley, Dec. | 2.01 | Vida Blue, Burlington | 200 |
| 1970 | Cecil Cooper, Danville | .336 | Roger Cain, Burlington | 23 | Roger Cain, Burlington | 80 | 5 tied at | 12 | Don Eddy, Appleton | 1.81 | Bart Johnson, Appleton | 161 |
| 1971 | Randy Crews, Quincy | .323 | Gorman Thomas, Danville | 31 | Gorman Thomas, Quincy | 97 | Rich Gossage, Appleton | 18 | Doug Bird, Waterloo | 1.84 | Steve Hardin, Wis. Rap. | 244 |
| 1972 | Duane Espy, Danville | .340 | Lamar Johnson, Apple. | 26 | Lamar Johnson, Apple. | 89 | Carl Austerman, Dan. | 16 | Rich Gossage, Appleton | 1.83 | John D'Acquisto, Dec. | 199 |
| 1973 | Jerry Remy, Quad City | .335 | Chet Lemon, Burlington | 31 | Chet Lemon, Burlington | 88 | Jerry Gomez, Waterloo | 14 | Fred Bruntrager, Clin. | 1.67 | Mark Littell, Waterloo | 168 |
| 1974 | Moe Hill, Wis. Rap. | .339 | Moe Hill, Wis. Rap. | 32 | Moe Hill, Wis. Rap. | 113 | Mike Messman, Wis. Rap. | 16 | Gerald Tyler, Clinton | 2.17 | Gerald Tyler, Clinton | 184 |
| 1975 | Pedro Guerrero, Dan. | .345 | Willie Aikens, Quad City | 31 | Willie Aikens, Quad City | 91 | Mitch Bobinger, Dan. | 17 | Luis Sanchez, C.R. | 1.59 | Lafayette Currence, Dan. | 201 |
| 1976 | Don Pisker, Dubuque | .345 | Moe Hill, Wis. Rap. | 30 | Moe Hill, Wis. Rap. | 103 | 2 tied at | 14 | David Aloi, Dubuque | 1.69 | Mitch Bobinger, Dan. | 160 |
| 1977 | Elmer Cardwell, Wausau | .332 | Moe Hill, Wis. Rap. | 41 | Moe Hill, Wis. Rap. | 112 | Dave Stewart, Clinton | 17 | Ron Hodges, Ced. Rap. | 1.24 | Ted Barnicle, Ced. Rap. | 155 |
| 1978 | Bobby G. Smith, Burl. | .336 | Bill Foley, Burlington | 34 | Brian Harper, Quad City | 101 | Lamar Hoyt, Appleton | 18 | Phil Nastu, Ced. Rap. | 1.88 | Brad Havens, Quad City | 197 |
| 1979 | Mitch Webster, Clinton. | .326 | David Stockstill, Wau. | 30 | David Stockstill, Wau. | 101 | Randy Clark, Quad City | 16 | Sam Spence, Wausau | 2.38 | Tom Owens, Wausau | 136 |
| 1980 | Von Hayes, Waterloo | .329 | Gary Gaetti, Wis. Rap. | 22 | Greg Walker, Appleton | 98 | Bob Konopa, Wis. Rap. | 17 | Doug Jones, Burlington | 1.75 | Scott Garrells, Clinton | 159 |
| 1981 | Ed Saavedra, Wat. | .336 | Glen Walker, Wausau | 35 | Glen Walker, Wausau | 111 | Jose Nunez, Wausau | 16 | Bengie Biggus, Burl. | 2.27 | Jose Nunez, Wausau | 205 |
| 1982 | Dick Schofield, Dan. | .360 | Alan Hunsinger, Spring. | 42 | Alan Hunsinger, Spring. | 102 | Mark Grant, Clinton. | 16 | Ken Pryce, Quad City | 1.98 | Mark Grant, Clinton | 243 |
| 1983 | Javier Ortiz, Burl. | .352 | Curt Ford, Spring. | 27 | Joey Meyer, Beloit | 91 | Rich DeVincenzo, App. | 18 | Mike Tanzi, Appleton | 2.22 | Rich DeVincenzo, App. | 193 |
| 1984 | Joey Meyer, Beloit | .320 | Joey Meyer, Beloit | 29 | Joey Meyer, Beloit | 102 | Chris Bosio, Beloit | 17 | Barry Bass, Burlington | 1.68 | Mark Ciardi, Beloit | 166 |
| 1985 | Henry McCulla, Spring. | .317 | Jim Winters, Appleton. | 29 | Bernardo Brito, Water. | 91 | Keith Silver, Clinton | 17 | Bruce Tanner, Apple. | 1.96 | Alan Sontag, Kenosha | 213 |
| 1986 | Mark Grace, Peoria | .342 | Luis Medina, Waterloo | 35 | Greg Vaughn, Beloit | 110 | Jeff Oyster, Spring. | 17 | Keith Silver, Clinton | 2.24 | Steve Gasser, Kenosha | 225 |
| 1987 | Chip Hale, Kenosha | .345 | Todd Zeile, Spring. | 33 | 2 tied at | 106 | Bob Faron, Spring. | 19 | Greg Simpson, Ced. Rap. | 1.81 | Paul McClellan, Clin. | 209 |
| 1988 | Ruben Gonzalez, Wau. | .314 | Reggie Jefferson, Ced. Rap. | 22 | Tom Redington, Burl. | 90 | Pat Bangston, Kenosha | 17 | Keith Brown, Ced. Rap. | 1.59 | Tom Gordon, Appleton | 172 |
| 1989 | Adam Casillas, C.R. | .321 | 2 tied at | 17 | Fred Cooley, Mad. | 81 | Marcos Lopez, Peoria | 18 | Mark Dewey, Clinton | 1.43 | Glenn Carter, Quad City | 190 |
| 1990 | Scott Cepicky, So. Bend | .312 | John Byington, Beloit | 16 | John Byington, Beloit | 89 | Marcus Moore, Quad City | 16 | Jose Ventura, So. Bend. | 1.57 | Fili Martinez, Quad City | 195 |
| 1991 | Midre Cummings, Ken. | .322 | Paul Russo, Kenosha | 20 | Paul Russo, Kenosha | 100 | 2 tied at | 16 | Alan Newman, Kenosha | 1.64 | Salomon Torres, Clin. | 214 |
| 1992 | Orlando Palmeiro, QC | .317 | Steve Gibralter, Ced. Rap. | 19 | Steve Gibralter, Ced. Rap. | 99 | John Fritz, Quad City | 20 | Bobby Chouinard, K.C. | 2.08 | Gabe White, Rockford | 176 |
| 1993 | Homer Bush, Waterloo | .322 | Joe Biasucci, Springfield | 26 | Charles Johnson, Kane Cty. | 94 | 2 tied at | 15 | LaTroy Hawkins, Ft.W. | 2.06 | LaTroy Hawkins, Ft.W. | 179 |

NOTE: League known as Illinois State League from 1947-48, and Mississippi-Ohio Valley League from 1949-55.

# SOUTH ATLANTIC LEAGUE

## Batboy Upstages Savannah's Title Run

**By GENE SAPAKOFF**

Rarely does a batboy get more publicity than the players—especially on a championship team. It was an unusual season, however, for Tommy McCoy and the Savannah Cardinals.

The Cardinals made winning the 1993 South Atlantic League title look fairly easy, winning eight more games than any other team during the regular season and then defeating Greensboro, 3-2, in the SAL championship series. But McCoy, 14, got national headlines in May when Savannah labor department officials insisted he be fired because the Cardinals were in violation of child labor laws.

McCoy eventually was rehired after U.S. Labor Secretary Robert Reich suspended the law as it pertained to batboys and batgirls.

With McCoy helping out, Savannah won its first title since rejoining the SAL in 1984.

"I thought we would have a good team coming out of Florida," manager Chris Maloney said. "Then when I saw what the other teams in this league had, I knew we had a chance to win. There's a lot of desire on this team, a lot of guys who come to the park to get their work done."

**Jamie Cochran.** A hitter he's not, but Savannah reliever left his mark with minor league record 46 saves.

ROBERT GURGANUS

**Jeff Alkire**

Along the way, the Cardinals won more regular-season games (94) than any team in the minors except Harrisburg (Eastern), set a franchise attendance record (106,287) and led the SAL in defense (.968 fielding percentage). Individually, closer Jamie Cochran established a minor league record for saves with 46 and third baseman Brian Rupp won his second straight minor league batting title, hitting .320 to win the SAL crown.

Former University of Miami and 1992 U.S. Olympic team lefthander Jeff Alkire, finished at 15-6 with a 2.46 ERA and won twice in the championship series, including Savannah's 8-1 victory in Game Five.

All year long, the Cardinals' strength was pitching (minor league-leading 2.73 ERA), particularly the rotation of Alkire and righthanders Mike Busby (12-2), Jeff Matranga (11-3) and Brian Carpenter (10-8). Matranga was especially effective down the stretch.

## STANDINGS: OVERALL

| Page | | W | L | PCT | GB | Manager(s) | Attendance/Dates | Last Pennant |
|---|---|---|---|---|---|---|---|---|
| 183 | Savannah Cardinals (Cardinals) | 94 | 48 | .662 | — | Chris Maloney | 106,287 (69) | 1993 |
| 95 | Columbus RedStixx (Indians) | 86 | 56 | .606 | 8 | Mike Brown | 122,137 (71) | None |
| 152 | Greensboro Hornets (Yankees) | 85 | 56 | .603 | 8 ½ | Bill Evers, Gary Denbo | 201,222 (68) | 1982 |
| 89 | Charleston, W.Va., Wheelers (Reds) | 76 | 64 | .543 | 17 | Tom Nieto | 110,118 (66) | 1990 |
| 105 | Fayetteville Generals (Tigers) | 75 | 66 | .532 | 18 ½ | Mark Wagner | 100,321 (65) | None |
| 51 | Macon Braves (Braves) | 74 | 67 | .525 | 19 ½ | Randy Ingle | 96,450 (66) | None |
| 213 | Hagerstown Suns (Blue Jays) | 74 | 68 | .521 | 20 | Jim Nettles | 95,702 (66) | None |
| 58 | Albany Polecats (Orioles) | 71 | 71 | .500 | 23 | Mike O'Berry | 140,140 (67) | None |
| 208 | Charleston, S.C., Rainbows (Rangers) | 65 | 77 | .458 | 29 | Walt Williams | 98,670 (70) | None |
| 158 | Capital City Bombers (Mets) | 64 | 77 | .454 | 29 ½ | Ron Washington | 144,054 (65) | 1991 |
| 170 | Spartanburg Phillies (Phillies) | 62 | 80 | .437 | 32 | Roy Majtyka | 53,975 (66) | 1988 |
| 177 | Augusta Pirates (Pirates) | 59 | 82 | .418 | 34 ½ | Trent Jewett | 115,051 (68) | 1989 |
| 76 | Hickory Crawdads (White Sox) | 52 | 88 | .371 | 41 | Fred Kendall | 283,727 (70) | None |
| 117 | Asheville Tourists (Astros) | 51 | 88 | .367 | 41 ½ | Bobby Ramos | 121,573 (64) | 1984 |

NOTE: Team's individual batting and pitching statistics can be found on page indicated in lefthand column.

JIM McLEAN

**Ryan Karp**

He took the mound in a one-game playoff against Columbus to decide the Southern Division's second-half title and scattered three hits over eight innings, winning 5-0. He also stopped Greensboro, 2-0, in Game Three of the championship series, allowing two hits and striking out 12 over eight innings.

Cochran, 24, got at least one save against each SAL team in breaking Steve Reed's record of 43 set at Double-A Shreveport and Triple-A Phoenix in 1992. Cochran set a New York-Penn League save record with 24 at Hamilton in 1992.

## Hickory-Smoked Ballpark

The Hickory Crawdads set a league attendance record, drawing 278,198 fans for 70 openings. Not bad considering Hickory hadn't had a pro team in 33 years, new L.P. Frans Stadium wasn't even ready for opening day and the Crawdads finished 52-88.

"I was thinking we would probably be able to average 1,300 per game," Hickory general manager Marty Steele said. "Then I hoped we could grow from there. I don't think anyone expected this."

The Crawdads averaged 3,974 fans per game and their merchandise was a hot seller from Charleston to Charleston. The previous SAL attendance record was

**Terrell Wade**

JIM McLEAN

260,340 set by Greensboro in 1981.

## Father-Son League

When Augusta catcher Jason Kendall found out he was headed to the SAL, he phoned his father. Fred Kendall, a former major league catcher, was already committed to the circuit as manager of the Hickory Crawdads.

"I called him and said, 'Hey, I'm going to beat you,' " Jason said.

Jason, the Pirates' 1992 first-round draft pick out of Torrance (Calif.) High School, was named the SAL's best defensive catcher in a Baseball America poll and was considered one of the top prospects in the league all season.

"I'm proud of him," Fred said. "He's a young guy who has maintained a consistent level of play and kept his composure while playing against older players."

Hagerstown had the most prospects—righthander Jose Silva, outfielder Jose Herrera, first baseman D.J. Boston and catcher Angel Martinez. Boston, the younger brother of Colorado Rockies outfielder Daryl Boston, was named the SAL MVP.

Macon lefthander Terrell Wade caught the eyes of the Atlanta Braves at a tryout camp in Sumter, S.C., in 1991 and had by far his best pro season in '93. Wade, in a half-season in the SAL, was 8-2 with a 1.73 ERA and had 121 strikeouts in 83 innings, including an 18-strikeout game.

Greensboro lefthander Ryan Karp was 13-0, matching the best start in SAL history (Fayetteville's Randy Marshall was 13-0 in 1990), then lost a 2-1 game to Savannah's Alkire before getting a promotion to Prince William (Carolina).

Three SAL franchises changed their nicknames for the 1994 season. Greensboro went from the Hornets to the Bats, Augusta from the Pirates to the Green Jackets and Charleston, S.C., from the Rainbows to the RiverDogs.

Columbus RedStixx manager Mike Brown married Claudette Smith at home plate just prior to the SAL all-star game at Columbus' Golden Park. The groom wore a tuxedo jacket, black jeans and boots.

### STANDINGS: SPLIT SEASON

| FIRST HALF | | | | | SECOND HALF | | | | |
|---|---|---|---|---|---|---|---|---|---|
| **NORTH** | W | L | PCT | GB | **NORTH** | W | L | PCT | GB |
| Greensboro | 45 | 25 | .643 | — | Fayetteville | 44 | 28 | .611 | — |
| Charl., W.Va. | 38 | 32 | .543 | 7 | Greensboro | 40 | 31 | .563 | 3½ |
| Hagerstown | 34 | 36 | .486 | 11 | Hagerstown | 40 | 32 | .556 | 4 |
| Fayetteville | 31 | 38 | .449 | 13½ | Charl., W.Va. | 38 | 32 | .543 | 5 |
| Spartanburg | 28 | 42 | .400 | 17 | Spartanburg | 34 | 38 | .472 | 10 |
| Hickory | 26 | 43 | .377 | 18½ | Hickory | 26 | 45 | .366 | 17½ |
| Asheville | 26 | 43 | .377 | 18½ | Asheville | 25 | 45 | .357 | 18 |
| **SOUTH** | W | L | PCT | GB | **SOUTH** | W | L | PCT | GB |
| Savannah | 47 | 23 | .671 | — | Savannah | 47 | 25 | .653 | — |
| Macon | 41 | 29 | .586 | 6 | Columbus | 46 | 26 | .639 | 1 |
| Columbus | 40 | 30 | .571 | 7 | Capital City | 36 | 36 | .500 | 11 |
| Albany | 39 | 31 | .557 | 8 | Macon | 33 | 38 | .465 | 13½ |
| Charl., S.C. | 34 | 36 | .486 | 13 | Albany | 32 | 40 | .444 | 15 |
| Augusta | 31 | 39 | .443 | 16 | Charl., S.C. | 31 | 41 | .431 | 16 |
| Capital City | 28 | 41 | .406 | 18½ | Augusta | 28 | 43 | .394 | 18½ |

**PLAYOFFS—Division:** Greensboro defeated Fayetteville, 2-1, in best-of-3 series. **Finals:** Savannah defeated Greensboro, 3-2, in best-of-5 series.

### LEAGUE CHAMPIONS

**Last 25 Years**

| Year | Regular Season* | Pct. | Playoff |
|---|---|---|---|
| 1969 | Greenwood (Braves) | .556 | Greenwood (Braves) |
| 1970 | Greenville (Red Sox) | .597 | None |
| 1971 | Greenwood (Braves) | .691 | None |
| 1972 | Spartanburg (Phillies) | .674 | Spartanburg (Phillies) |
| 1973 | Charleston (Pirates) | .581 | Spartanburg (Phillies) |
| 1974 | Gastonia (Rangers) | .636 | None |
| 1975 | Spartanburg (Phillies) | .578 | None |
| 1976 | Asheville (Rangers) | .551 | Greenwood (Braves) |
| 1977 | Gastonia (Cardinals) | .589 | Gastonia (Cardinals) |
| 1978 | Greenwood (Braves) | .589 | None |
| 1979 | Greenwood (Braves) | .565 | Greenwood (Braves) |
| 1980 | Greensboro (Yankees) | .589 | Greensboro (Yankees) |
| 1981 | Greensboro (Yankees) | .695 | Greensboro (Yankees) |
| 1982 | Greensboro (Yankees) | .681 | Greensboro (Yankees) |
| 1983 | Columbia (Mets) | .619 | Gastonia (Expos) |
| 1984 | Columbia (Mets) | .589 | Asheville (Astros) |
| 1985 | Florence (Blue Jays) | .599 | Florence (Blue Jays) |
| 1986 | Columbia (Mets) | .681 | Columbia (Mets) |
| 1987 | Asheville (Astros) | .654 | Myrtle Beach (Blue Jays) |
| 1988 | Charleston, S.C. (Padres) | .615 | Spartanburg (Phillies) |
| 1989 | Gastonia (Rangers) | .657 | Augusta (Pirates) |
| 1990 | Columbia (Mets) | .580 | Charleston, W.Va. (Reds) |
| 1991 | Charleston, W.Va. (Reds) | .597 | Columbia (Mets) |
| 1992 | Columbia (Mets) | .572 | Myrtle Beach (Blue Jays) |
| 1993 | Savannah (Cardinals) | .662 | Savannah (Cardinals) |

*Best overall record

# SOUTH ATLANTIC LEAGUE
## 1993 BATTING, PITCHING STATISTICS

### CLUB BATTING

| | AVG | G | AB | R | H | 2B | 3B | HR | BB | SO | SB |
|---|---|---|---|---|---|---|---|---|---|---|---|
| Greensboro | .266 | 141 | 4699 | 763 | 1249 | 248 | 39 | 94 | 644 | 994 | 190 |
| Spartanburg | .261 | 142 | 4717 | 630 | 1231 | 219 | 31 | 47 | 442 | 849 | 124 |
| Augusta | .259 | 141 | 4694 | 627 | 1218 | 219 | 34 | 53 | 412 | 948 | 149 |
| Hagerstown | .258 | 142 | 4733 | 681 | 1221 | 258 | 42 | 99 | 474 | 1049 | 189 |
| Columbus | .255 | 142 | 4777 | 700 | 1218 | 224 | 30 | 111 | 414 | 1015 | 176 |
| Macon | .252 | 141 | 4630 | 611 | 1168 | 210 | 44 | 73 | 443 | 994 | 167 |
| Asheville | .252 | 139 | 4577 | 595 | 1155 | 243 | 26 | 76 | 422 | 1053 | 176 |
| Albany | .247 | 142 | 4663 | 631 | 1152 | 234 | 28 | 74 | 507 | 909 | 134 |
| Savannah | .247 | 142 | 4662 | 670 | 1151 | 209 | 33 | 64 | 640 | 959 | 127 |
| Charleston, S.C. | .242 | 142 | 4714 | 582 | 1142 | 223 | 41 | 66 | 493 | 1021 | 162 |
| Fayetteville | .242 | 141 | 4685 | 690 | 1134 | 210 | 41 | 68 | 718 | 1142 | 127 |
| Charleston, W.Va. | .242 | 140 | 4576 | 660 | 1106 | 220 | 42 | 79 | 596 | 1101 | 140 |
| Capital City | .241 | 141 | 4570 | 624 | 1101 | 206 | 35 | 39 | 590 | 1085 | 178 |
| Hickory | .224 | 140 | 4586 | 540 | 1028 | 166 | 36 | 48 | 493 | 1051 | 153 |

### CLUB PITCHING

| | ERA | G | CG | SHO | SV | IP | H | R | ER | BB | SO |
|---|---|---|---|---|---|---|---|---|---|---|---|
| Savannah | 2.72 | 142 | 7 | 19 | 53 | 1257 | 1086 | 472 | 380 | 409 | 1150 |
| Macon | 3.03 | 141 | 10 | 16 | 35 | 1232 | 1054 | 529 | 414 | 476 | 1138 |
| Columbus | 3.21 | 142 | 6 | 10 | 56 | 1246 | 1067 | 552 | 444 | 517 | 994 |
| Albany | 3.51 | 142 | 13 | 12 | 29 | 1216 | 1155 | 636 | 474 | 525 | 1010 |
| Greensboro | 3.66 | 141 | 3 | 14 | 42 | 1229 | 1108 | 633 | 499 | 518 | 1097 |
| Hagerstown | 3.67 | 142 | 10 | 5 | 36 | 1231 | 1164 | 621 | 502 | 482 | 1049 |
| Fayetteville | 3.69 | 141 | 7 | 13 | 44 | 1246 | 1205 | 627 | 511 | 479 | 1027 |
| Charleston, W.Va. | 3.83 | 140 | 2 | 5 | 44 | 1228 | 1103 | 678 | 523 | 623 | 1016 |
| Augusta | 3.84 | 141 | 6 | 8 | 22 | 1214 | 1202 | 711 | 518 | 437 | 1051 |
| Spartanburg | 3.99 | 142 | 20 | 5 | 20 | 1229 | 1208 | 649 | 545 | 506 | 955 |
| Charleston, S.C. | 4.06 | 142 | 4 | 11 | 44 | 1249 | 1191 | 690 | 563 | 586 | 1022 |
| Capital City | 4.14 | 141 | 9 | 7 | 30 | 1222 | 1251 | 713 | 562 | 559 | 894 |
| Hickory | 4.17 | 140 | 11 | 5 | 22 | 1228 | 1186 | 692 | 569 | 566 | 937 |
| Asheville | 4.96 | 139 | 10 | 2 | 28 | 1194 | 1294 | 801 | 658 | 605 | 830 |

### CLUB FIELDING

| | PCT | PO | A | E | DP | | PCT | PO | A | E | DP |
|---|---|---|---|---|---|---|---|---|---|---|---|
| Savannah | .968 | 3772 | 1479 | 172 | 110 | Greensboro | .961 | 3686 | 1463 | 210 | 106 |
| Macon | .966 | 3695 | 1464 | 181 | 104 | Hagerstown | .960 | 3694 | 1446 | 213 | 114 |
| Columbus | .965 | 3739 | 1516 | 191 | 133 | Hickory | .957 | 3685 | 1459 | 230 | 85 |
| Fayetteville | .964 | 3737 | 1623 | 201 | 112 | Albany | .953 | 3647 | 1445 | 251 | 108 |
| Spartanburg | .963 | 3687 | 1615 | 203 | 125 | Asheville | .952 | 3583 | 1654 | 263 | 137 |
| Capital City | .961 | 3665 | 1590 | 213 | 131 | Charl., W.Va. | .952 | 3683 | 1367 | 255 | 102 |
| Charleston, S.C. | .961 | 3746 | 1411 | 209 | 125 | Augusta | .945 | 3643 | 1416 | 297 | 109 |

### INDIVIDUAL BATTING LEADERS
(Minimum 381 Plate Appearances)

| | AVG | G | AB | R | H | 2B | 3B | HR | RBI | BB | SO | SB |
|---|---|---|---|---|---|---|---|---|---|---|---|---|
| Rupp, Brian, Savannah | .320 | 122 | 472 | 80 | 151 | 31 | 7 | 4 | 81 | 48 | 70 | 3 |
| Herrera, Jose, Hagerstown | .317 | 95 | 388 | 60 | 123 | 22 | 5 | 5 | 42 | 26 | 63 | 36 |
| Hacopian, Derek, Col. | .315 | 131 | 454 | 81 | 143 | 29 | 0 | 24 | 82 | 60 | 69 | 4 |
| Boston, D.J., Hagerstown | .315 | 127 | 464 | 77 | 146 | 35 | 4 | 13 | 93 | 54 | 77 | 31 |
| Brito, Luis, Spartanburg | .313 | 127 | 467 | 56 | 146 | 16 | 4 | 0 | 33 | 11 | 47 | 9 |
| Pecorilli, Aldo, Sav. | .305 | 141 | 515 | 75 | 157 | 30 | 7 | 14 | 93 | 81 | 86 | 16 |
| White, Don, Capital City | .304 | 114 | 441 | 86 | 134 | 18 | 6 | 3 | 41 | 54 | 75 | 43 |
| Thomas, Tim, Fay. | .303 | 104 | 380 | 80 | 115 | 31 | 3 | 4 | 48 | 82 | 85 | 5 |
| Owens, Billy, Albany | .297 | 120 | 458 | 64 | 136 | 23 | 2 | 11 | 66 | 49 | 70 | 3 |
| Grijak, Kevin, Macon | .296 | 120 | 389 | 50 | 115 | 26 | 5 | 7 | 58 | 37 | 37 | 9 |

### INDIVIDUAL PITCHING LEADERS
(Minimum 113 Innings)

| | W | L | ERA | G | GS | CG | SV | IP | H | R | ER | BB | SO |
|---|---|---|---|---|---|---|---|---|---|---|---|---|---|
| Thobe, J.J., Columbus | 11 | 2 | 1.91 | 19 | 19 | 2 | 0 | 132 | 105 | 36 | 28 | 25 | 106 |
| Cornett, Brad, Hag. | 10 | 8 | 2.40 | 31 | 21 | 3 | 3 | 172 | 164 | 77 | 46 | 31 | 161 |
| Busby, Mike, Savannah | 12 | 2 | 2.44 | 23 | 21 | 1 | 0 | 144 | 116 | 49 | 39 | 31 | 125 |
| Alkire, Jeff, Savannah | 15 | 6 | 2.46 | 28 | 28 | 0 | 0 | 172 | 143 | 56 | 47 | 68 | 175 |
| Silva, Jose, Hagerstown | 12 | 5 | 2.52 | 24 | 24 | 0 | 0 | 143 | 103 | 50 | 40 | 62 | 161 |
| Cabrera, Jose, Columbus | 11 | 6 | 2.67 | 26 | 26 | 1 | 0 | 155 | 122 | 54 | 46 | 53 | 160 |
| York, Charles, Columbus | 10 | 7 | 2.79 | 26 | 26 | 1 | 0 | 158 | 127 | 59 | 49 | 78 | 182 |
| Carter, John, Columbus | 17 | 7 | 2.79 | 29 | 29 | 1 | 0 | 180 | 147 | 72 | 56 | 48 | 134 |
| Stephenson, Garrett, Alb. | 16 | 7 | 2.84 | 30 | 24 | 3 | 1 | 171 | 142 | 65 | 54 | 44 | 147 |
| Carpenter, Brian, Sav. | 10 | 8 | 2.86 | 28 | 28 | 0 | 0 | 154 | 145 | 55 | 49 | 41 | 147 |

## DEPARTMENT LEADERS

**BATTING**
| | | |
|---|---|---|
| R | Joe McEwing, Savannah | 94 |
| H | 2 tied at | 157 |
| TB | Matt Luke, Greensboro | 267 |
| 2B | Eric Chavez, Albany | 38 |
| 3B | Santiago Henry, Hagerstown | 12 |
| HR | Derek Hacopian, Columbus | 24 |
| RBI | Alan Burke, Spartanburg | 96 |
| SH | Mariano Dotel, Hagerstown | 10 |
| SF | Alan Burke, Spartanburg | 14 |
| BB | 2 tied at | 91 |
| IBB | Nick Delvecchio, Greensboro | 9 |
| HBP | Nick Delvecchio, Greensboro | 23 |
| SO | Keith Kimsey, Fayetteville | 168 |
| SB | Kraig Hawkins, Greensboro | 67 |
| CS | Robert Hinds, Greensboro | 22 |
| GIDP | Dan Kopriva, Charleston, W.V. | 19 |
| OB% | Tripp Keister, Capital City | .437 |
| SL% | Derek Hacopian, Columbus | .537 |

**PITCHING**
| | | |
|---|---|---|
| G | Sean Fesh, Asheville | 65 |
| GS | 4 tied at | 29 |
| CG | Matt Jarvis, Albany | 8 |
| ShO | 4 tied at | 4 |
| GF | Sean Fesh, Asheville | 58 |
| Sv | Jamie Cochran, Savannah | 46 |
| W | John Carter, Columbus | 17 |
| L | Steve Lyons, Capital City | 16 |
| IP | Chad Anderson, Spartanburg | 191 |
| H | Chad Anderson, Spartanburg | 216 |
| R | Danny Young, Asheville | 114 |
| ER | Danny Young, Asheville | 97 |
| HR | Mike Buddie, Greensboro | 19 |
| BB | Erik Hiljus, Capital City | 111 |
| HB | Joe Petcka, Capital City | 18 |
| SO | Charles York, Columbus | 182 |
| WP | Zak Krislock, Asheville | 25 |
| Bk | Jerry Martin, Charleston, S.C. | 7 |

**FIELDING**
| | | |
|---|---|---|
| C AVG | Jeff Murphy, Savannah | .993 |
| E | Marco Manrique, Albany | 23 |
| 1B AVG | Chad Townsend, Columbus | .993 |
| E | Rico Gholston, Augusta | 23 |
| 2B AVG | Tim Thomas, Fayetteville | .983 |
| E | Donovan Mitchell, Asheville | 27 |
| 3B AVG | Dwight Robinson, Cap. City | .961 |
| E | 2 tied at | 38 |
| SS AVG | Guillermo Mercedes, C-S.C. | .962 |
| E | Jay Cranford, Augusta | 68 |
| OF AVG | Matt Luke, Greensboro | .987 |
| E | Al Shirley, Capital City | 13 |

## HONOR ROLL

**OFFICIAL ALL-STAR TEAM**
- **C** Jason Kendall, Augusta
- **1B** D.J. Boston, Hagerstown
- **2B** Donovan Mitchell, Asheville
- **3B** Eric Chavez, Albany
- **SS** Derek Jeter, Greensboro
- **OF** Herrera, Hagerstown; Luke, Greensboro; Hacopian, Columbus; Pecorilli, Savannah; White, Capital City
- **DH** Nick Delvecchio, Greensboro
- **Util** Brian Rupp, Savannah
- **LHP** Ryan Karp, Greensboro
- **RHP** J.J. Thobe, Columbus

**MVP:** D.J. Boston, Hagerstown
**Manager:** Chris Maloney, Savannah

**TOP 10 PROSPECTS**
(Selected by league managers)
1. Terrell Wade, lhp, Macon
2. Derek Jeter, ss, Greensboro
3. Jose Silva, rhp, Hagerstown
4. Trey Beamon, of, Augusta
5. D.J. Boston, 1b, Hagerstown
6. Jason Kendall, c, Augusta
7. Armando Benitez, rhp, Albany
8. Jose Herrera, of, Hagerstown
9. Richard Hidalgo, of, Asheville
10. Ryan Karp, lhp, Greensboro

# YEAR-BY-YEAR LEADERS: 1946-93

## SOUTH ATLANTIC LEAGUE

| Year | Batting Average | Home Runs | RBIs | Wins | ERA | Strikeouts |
|---|---|---|---|---|---|---|
| 1946 | DID NOT OPERATE | | | | | |
| 1947 | DID NOT OPERATE | | | | | |
| 1948 | Wes Ferrell, Marion ....425 | Ed Yount, New.-Con. ....43 | Ed Yount, New.-Con. ....140 | Ray Lindsey, New.-Con. ....21 | Bob McGimsey, Morg. ....2.76 | Ray Lindsey, New.-Con. ....255 |
| 1949 | Carl Miller, Lincolnton ...404 | Carl Miller, Lincolnton ....22 | Bob McGimsey, Morg. ....118 | Ben Jaynes, Morganton ....19 | Walter Lentz, Lenoir ....3.03 | Ben Jaynes, Morganton ....202 |
| 1950 | Russ Mincy, Marion ...421 | Bob Featherston, Lenoir ....27 | George Rose, Lincolnton ....120 | John White, New.-Con. ....21 | John White, New.-Con. ....3.05 | Carl Brown, New.-Con. ....236 |
| 1951 | Henry Miller, Shelby ...387 | Bordie Waddle, Morg. ....24 | Ed Bass, Shelby ....157 | Eurice Treece, Morg. ....25 | George Long, Ruth. Cty. ....2.12 | Eurice Treece, Morg. ....264 |
| 1952 | Charles Ballard, Shelby ...352 | Ken Paschal, Ruth. Cty. ....19 | George Rose, Lincolnton ....107 | Joe Sheppard, Shelby ....24 | Joe Sheppard, Shelby ....2.31 | Harold Griggs, Hickory ....195 |
| 1953 | DID NOT OPERATE | | | | | |
| 1954 | DID NOT OPERATE | | | | | |
| 1955 | DID NOT OPERATE | | | | | |
| 1956 | DID NOT OPERATE | | | | | |
| 1957 | DID NOT OPERATE | | | | | |
| 1958 | DID NOT OPERATE | | | | | |
| 1959 | DID NOT OPERATE | | | | | |
| 1960 | Jack Turney, Salisbury ...362 | Paul Roberts, Salisbury ....23 | Paul Roberts, Salisbury ....91 | Donny Hayling, Hickory ....22 | Bill Bethea, Lexington ....1.35 | John Isaac, New.-Conover 177 |
| 1961 | Aaron Pointer, Salisbury ...402 | Dick Simpson, Statesville ....15 | Tommy Murray, Salisbury ....83 | Phil Andress, Shelby ....13 | George Conrad, States. ....3.21 | George Conrad, States. ....172 |
| 1962 | Charles Truesdell, States. ...344 | 3 tied at ....9 | Henry Nichols, New.-Con. ....66 | Robert Kenny, Statesville ....16 | Robert Kenny, Statesville ....2.12 | Nick DeMatteis, States. ....161 |
| 1963 | John May, Greenville ...333 | Dave McDonald, Shel.-Stat. ....20 | Levi Renfroe, Greenville ....91 | Rich Licklider, Lex. ....16 | Dave Roberts, Spart. ....1.79 | Mike Szemplenski, States. ....313 |
| 1964 | Dick Schmidt, Salisbury ...306 | Bill Parlier, Salisbury ....20 | Roy Foster, Gastonia ....72 | Felix Roque, Rock Hill ....16 | Rich Licklider, Lex. ....1.52 | Herman Alvarez, Lex. ....243 |
| 1965 | Ed Moxey, Salisbury ...345 | Bob Robertson, Gas. ....32 | Bob Robertson, Gas. ....98 | Nolan Ryan, Greenville ....18 | Sal Campisi, Rock Hill ....1.95 | Richard Sommer, Thom. ....199 |
| 1966 | Gil Torres, Spart. ...365 | Luis Lagunas, Thom. ....35 | Luis Lagunas, Thom. ....106 | Nolan Ryan, Greenville ....17 | John Penn, Spartanburg ....2.21 | Nolan Ryan, Greenville ....272 |
| 1967 | Dave Cash, Gastonia ...335 | John Jeter, Gastonia ....18 | Paul Dennebaum, Lex. ....83 | 2 tied at ....17 | John Parker, Spartanburg ....1.78 | Ken Reynolds, Spart. ....215 |
| 1968 | Zelman Jack, Gastonia ...326 | Zelman Jack, Gastonia ....24 | Jim Breazeale, Greenwood ....88 | Dave Warmbrod, Gas. ....12 | Dave Warmbrod, Gas. ....2.26 | Mike Thompson, Sal. ....136 |
| 1969 | Earl Williams, Greenw. ...340 | Earl Williams, Greenw. ....33 | Dalton Renfroe, Shelby ....113 | Jimmy Blackmon, Shelby ....15 | Tom Dettore, Gas. ....1.91 | John Curtis, Greenville ....158 |
| 1970 | George Hodge, Spart. ...357 | Roy Gibson, Anderson ....18 | Lamar Davis, Anderson ....88 | Paul Sparkman, Gville. ....16 | Brad Gratz, Gastonia ....2.26 | Brad Gratz, Gastonia ....160 |
| 1971 | Steve Gardner, Sumter ...343 | 2 tied at ....25 | Bias Santana, Spart. ....93 | 2 tied at ....12 | Mike Martin, Spartanburg ....2.92 | Jim Streleski, Sumter ....132 |
| 1972 | Charles Bordes, Gville. ...352 | Ken Caldwell, Gville. ....19 | Jerry Martin, Spart. ....112 | Don Kreke, Spartanburg ....15 | Chuck Kniffin, Spart. ....2.11 | Lou Lemer, Charlotte ....194 |
| 1973 | Mike Hargrove, Gas. ...351 | Doug Ault, Gastonia ....19 | Doug Ault, Gastonia ....88 | 2 tied at ....14 | Tom Underwood, Spart. ....2.10 | Tom Underwood, Spart. ....187 |
| 1974 | Calvin Smith, Greenwood ...324 | John Guarnaccia, Spart. ....28 | Dan Duran, Gastonia ....99 | Mike Bacsik, Gastonia ....15 | Randy Sealy, Charleston ....1.97 | Willie Hernandez, Spart. ....179 |
| 1975 | Barry Bonnell, Spart.-Green ...324 | Gary Begnaud, Spart. ....25 | Gary Begnaud, Spart. ....100 | Jim Wright, Spart. ....14 | Joey McLaughlin, Greens. ....2.58 | John Gibson, Spart. ....143 |
| 1976 | Pat Putnam, Asheville ...361 | Pat Putnam, Asheville ....24 | Pat Putnam, Asheville ....142 | Harold Kelly, Asheville ....13 | Harold Kelly, Asheville ....3.02 | Paul Mirabella, Ashe. ....136 |
| 1977 | David Rivera, Ashe. ...346 | David Rivera, Ashe. ....26 | David Rivera, Ashe. ....118 | Mike Griffin, Ashe. ....17 | Mike Griffin, Shelby ....2.30 | Mike Griffin, Ashe. ....201 |
| 1978 | Steve Hammond, Greenw. ...306 | Jim Braun, Asheville ....18 | Jim Belle, Asheville ....99 | Scott Munninghoff, Spart. ....17 | Greg Hughes, Shelby ....2.14 | Chuck Lamson, Asheville ....155 |
| 1979 | Gerald Perry, Greenwood ...333 | Hedi Vargas, Shelby ....31 | Hedi Vargas, Shelby ....121 | Jim Farr, Asheville ....14 | Jerry Johnson, Gas. ....2.65 | Darren Burroughs, Spart. ....180 |
| 1980 | Don Mattingly, Greens. ...358 | Dave Kable, Ashe. ....26 | George Bell, Spart. ....102 | Byron Ballard, Greens. ....17 | Ralph Citarella, Gas. ....1.64 | Ron Krauss, Charleston ....150 |
| 1981 | Danny Murphy, Asheville ...369 | Pete Mueller, Ashe. ....28 | Brook Jacoby, Anderson ....103 | 2 tied at ....16 | Jeff Gladden, Char. ....2.09 | Tim Wheeler, Greenwood ....166 |
| 1982 | Cliff Pastornicky, Char. ...343 | Tom Dodd, Greensboro ....26 | Jeff Reynolds, Greens. ....108 | Mike Griffin, Ashe. ....18 | Dom Taylor, Greenwood ....2.30 | Devallon Harper, Flor. ....186 |
| 1983 | Vince Coleman, Macon ...350 | Randy Braun, Asheville ....23 | John Christensen, Shelby ....97 | 3 tied at ....14 | Kevin Brown, Columbia ....2.74 | Kevin Brown, Columbia ....221 |
| 1984 | Manny Lee, Columbia ...329 | Tracy Dophied, Ashe. ....27 | Chris James, Spart. ....121 | Charlie Kerfeld, Ashe. ....16 | Kyle Hartshorn, Columbia ....2.48 | Reggie Dobie, Columbia ....128 |
| 1985 | Manny Jose, Greensboro ...323 | Dave Kable, Ashe. ....31 | Angelo Cuevas, Columbia ....101 | Tim Englund, Florence ....18 | Tom Glavine, Sumter ....2.35 | Ron Krauss, Charleston ....150 |
| 1986 | Carlo Colombino, Ashe. ...339 | Cameron Drew, Ashe. ....26 | Cameron Drew, Ashe. ....117 | Kevin Armstrong, Col'bia ....17 | Blaise Ilsley, Ashe. ....1.95 | Brian Givens, Columbia ....189 |
| 1987 | Ed Whited, Asheville ...323 | Mike Simms, Asheville ....39 | Ed Whited, Asheville ....126 | Micheal York, Macon. ....16 | Doug Linton, Myr. Beach. ....1.55 | Curt Schilling, Greens. ....189 |
| 1988 | Derek Bell, Myr. Beach ...344 | Eric Anthony, Ashe. ....29 | Brant Alyea, Gastonia ....98 | Jimmy Rogers, Myr. Beach ....18 | Joe Pacholec, Augusta. ....2.06 | Jimmy Rogers, Myr. Beach ....198 |
| 1989 | Jeff Frye, Gastonia ...313 | Doug Cronk, Gastonia ....22 | Mike Mulvaney, Greens. ....112 | Francisco Valdez, Gas. ....14 | Pedro Martinez, Char.(SC) ....1.97 | John Ericks, Savannah ....211 |
| 1990 | Tim Howard, Columbia ...323 | Cliff Brannon, Sav. ....18 | Tim Pugh, Columbia ....89 | Tim Pugh, Char.(WV) ....15 | Jeff Hoffman, Greens. ....1.49 | Sterling Hitchcock, Greens. ....171 |
| 1991 | Kyle Washington, Columbus ...343 | Butch Huskey, Columbia ....26 | Butch Huskey, Columbia ....99 | Jose Martinez, Columbia ....20 | Jose Martinez, Columbia ....1.49 | John Roper, Char. (WV) ....189 |
| 1992 | Quivio Veras, Columbia ...319 | Shane Andrews, Albany ....25 | Cliff Floyd, Albany ....97 | 2 tied at ....14 | Travis Baptist, Myr. Beach. ....1.44 | Jason Hisey, Savannah ....182 |
| 1993 | Brian Rupp, Savannah ...320 | Derek Hacopian, Columbus ....24 | Alan Burke, Spart. ....96 | John Carter, Columbus ....17 | J.J. Thobe, Columbus ....1.91 | Charles York, Columbus ....182 |

NOTE: League known as Western Carolina League from 1948-62, and Western Carolinas League from 1963-79.

# NEW YORK-PENN
## LEAGUE

# Second-Place Finishers Claim League Title

**By CHRIS KRUG**

The New York-Penn League is a starting point, a place where diamonds in the rough refine their skills and learn to be professionals. It's also a place to learn how to win, something the Niagara Falls Rapids were able to do better than any other NY-P team in 1993.

Glen Barker's two-strike drag bunt off Pittsfield Mets reliever Mike Welch in the top of the 10th inning scored Mike Wiseley from third base, giving the Rapids a 1-0 win and a sweep of their best-of-3 league championship series. The Rapids edged Pittsfield 2-1 in the opener.

Gary Goldsmith started the finale for Niagara Falls and shut out the Mets on five hits over six innings. Relievers Mike Richardson and Gabe Sollecito were perfect the rest of the way, keeping Pittsfield without a hit over the final four innings. Richardson worked three innings for the win and Sollecito tossed the 10th for a save.

The victory gave the city its first league title since 1982.

The great job out of the bullpen and Barker's clutch bunt culminated a Rapids playoff run of fairy-tale proportions.

After finishing two games behind the St. Catharines Blue Jays in the Stadler Division, their 47-31 record—second-best in the entire league—earned them the wild-card playoff berth. The Rapids were paired against St. Catharines in a sudden death semifinal and won 5-2 on a three-run homer by Del Marine in the top of the 13th inning.

The Rapids won the first game of the final on a two-run home run by Wiseley, his first of the season.

## Raves for Rivera

While his team, the Oneonta Yankees, didn't make it out of the McNamara Division, outfielder Ruben Rivera made 1993 his year to bloom.

After two seasons with marginal numbers, Rivera exploded on the scene in 1993 at the expense of NY-P pitching. The 19-year-old product of Chorrera, Panama, signed as a free agent by the New York Yankees in 1991, batted .276 with 13 homers and 47 RBIs to earn league MVP honors.

The league's top pitching prospect also enjoyed a season of blossoming. St. Catharines pitcher Adam Meinershagen toiled through a 1-7, 4.47 year in 1992. Returning to the same team in '93,

**Eric Danapilis.** Notre Dame All-America outfielder won NY-P batting title and led Niagara Falls to league championship.

**Andy Larkin**

Meinershagen brought a new maturity with him.

The 19-year old Missouri native, selected by Toronto in the 11th round of the 1991 draft, mowed down the NY-P in 1993. He led the Blue Jays to the Stadler Division championship and the best record in the league. Meinershagen went 8-1 with a league-leading 1.88 ERA and 86 strikeouts in 79 innings.

Greg Twiggs and Andy Larkin each stole the league's spotlight for a night in 1993, making history with no-hitters. Twiggs authored just the third hitless game in Geneva Cubs history with a 10-strikeout effort in a blanking of the Auburn Astros June 30. Larkin's gem, a 6-0 win over the Welland Pirates July 24, was the first ever by a member of the Marlins organization.

Only one single-season record fell in 1993. Geneva outfielder Demitrius Dowler established a NY-P record with 26 doubles, erasing the previous high of 24 set by Geneva's Paul Torres in 1990.

Offensively, the NY-P leaderboard was dominated by Rapids players. Eric Danapilis, a 1993 Baseball America All-American at Notre Dame, led the league in batting average (.341) and on-base percentage (.444). Fellow Rapids outfielders Wiseley and Barker led the loop in hits (92) and stolen bases (37), respectively.

Erie catcher-DH Wes Shook paced the NY-P in three categories: home runs (17), total bases (153) and slugging percentage (.571).

| Page | McNAMARA | W | L | PCT | GB | Manager | Attendance/Dates | Last Pennant |
|---|---|---|---|---|---|---|---|---|
| 159 | Pittsfield Mets (Mets) | 40 | 35 | .533 | — | Howard Freiling | 46,682 (38) | None |
| 64 | Utica Blue Sox (Red Sox) | 38 | 38 | .500 | 2 ½ | Dave Holt | 77,645 (35) | 1983 |
| 184 | Glens Falls Redbirds (Cardinals) | 37 | 40 | .481 | 4 | Steve Turco | 78,725 (36) | None |
| 153 | Oneonta Yankees (Yankees) | 36 | 40 | .474 | 4 ½ | Ken Dominguez | 55,144 (34) | 1990 |

| Page | PINCKNEY | W | L | PCT | GB | Manager | Attendance/Dates | Last Pennant |
|---|---|---|---|---|---|---|---|---|
| 95 | Watertown Indians (Indians) | 46 | 32 | .590 | — | Mike Young | 40,082 (36) | None |
| 82 | Geneva Cubs (Cubs) | 43 | 34 | .558 | 2 ½ | Jerry Weinstein | 34,634 (36) | 1992 |
| 111 | Elmira Pioneers (Marlins) | 31 | 44 | .413 | 13 ½ | Lynn Jones | 65,106 (37) | 1976 |
| 118 | Auburn Astros (Astros) | 30 | 46 | .395 | 15 | Manny Acta | 30,325 (35) | 1973 |

| Page | STEDLER | W | L | PCT | GB | Manager | Attendance/Dates | Last Pennant |
|---|---|---|---|---|---|---|---|---|
| 214 | St. Catharines Blue Jays (Blue Jays) | 49 | 29 | .628 | — | J.J. Cannon | 46,535 (38) | 1986 |
| 106 | Niagara Falls Rapids (Tigers) | 47 | 31 | .603 | 2 | Larry Parrish | 50,190 (38) | 1993 |
| 171 | Batavia Clippers (Phillies) | 38 | 39 | .494 | 10 ½ | Al LeBoeuf | 41,539 (34) | 1963 |
| 208 | Erie Sailors (Rangers) | 36 | 41 | .468 | 12 ½ | Doug Sisson | 65,316 (36) | 1957 |
| 177 | Welland Pirates (Pirates) | 35 | 42 | .455 | 13 ½ | Larry Smith | 35,664 (35) | None |
| 148 | Jamestown Expos (Expos) | 31 | 46 | .403 | 17 ½ | Tim Torricelli | 40,588 (37) | 1991 |

**PLAYOFFS—Semifinals:** Niagara Falls defeated St. Catharines and Pittsfield defeated Watertown in one-game series. **Finals:** Niagara Falls defeated Pittsfield, 2-0, in best-of-3 series.

**NOTE:** Team's individual batting and pitching statistics can be found on page indicated in lefthand column.

A mere 5-foot-8, Shook showcased his strength in 1992 at Texas Tech by winning the NCAA's national strength and conditioning title. He bench pressed 400 pounds.

"I never dreamed of getting that strong," said Shook, 23, a 28th-round draft pick of the Texas Rangers in 1992.

"We ran every morning and stretched twice a day. It really helped with bat speed. I knew I'd need to get a wood bat through the zone. I really don't know if I'd be here today if it weren't for weights."

Niagara Falls righthander Joshua Neese came within one win of tying the NY-P record for single-season victories, leading the league with 12. Craig Grasser, who appeared in 36 of Glens Falls' 77 games, was the top fireman with 19 saves. Pittsfield's Jason Isringhausen led with 104 strikeouts.

## New Administration

While the focus of baseball is usually limited to the playing field, the NY-P also made news in the front office. Robert Julian took over as league president, succeeding Leo Pinckney, who had held the presidency since 1985.

Julian, a Utica-based attorney, became only the fourth president in the 54-year history of the league. The league's three divisions are named in honor of the three past presidents.

Of the moves Julian made in his inaugural season, the development of a minority internship program, believed to be the first of its kind in professional baseball, gave three St. John's University students a chance to experience minor league baseball on the inside.

**Wes Shook**

Glens Falls, N.Y., five years removed from fielding an Eastern League franchise, made a one-year reappearance in the New York-Penn League and drew a surprising 78,725 to lead the league in attendance.

The former Hamilton Redbirds franchise moved to temporary quarters in Glens Falls in 1993, while awaiting construction of a new stadium in Sussex County, N.J. The franchise will relocate there for 1994.

The Redbirds' move necessitated a shift in the league's division alignment. Hamilton played in the Stedler

**Bob Julian**

Division, but moved to the McNamara in Glens Falls. The rest of the chain reaction found Watertown moving from the McNamara to the Pinckney, and Batavia moving from the Pinckney to the Stedler.

## LEAGUE CHAMPIONS

**Last 25 Years**

| Year | Regular Season* | Pct. | Playoff |
|---|---|---|---|
| 1969 | Oneonta (Yankees) | .662 | None |
| 1970 | Auburn (Twins) | .623 | None |
| 1971 | Oneonta (Yankees) | .662 | None |
| 1972 | Niagara Falls (Pirates) | .686 | None |
| 1973 | Auburn (Phillies) | .667 | None |
| 1974 | Oneonta (Yankees) | .768 | None |
| 1975 | Newark (Brewers) | .701 | None |
| 1976 | Elmira (Red Sox) | .714 | None |
| 1977 | Oneonta (Yankees) | .671 | Oneonta (Yankees) |
| 1978 | Oneonta (Yankees) | .729 | Geneva (Cubs) |
| 1979 | Geneva (Cubs) | .725 | Oneonta (Yankees) |
| 1980 | Oneonta (Yankees) | .662 | Oneonta (Yankees) |
| 1981 | Oneonta (Yankees) | .658 | Oneonta (Yankees) |
| 1982 | Oneonta (Yankees) | .566 | Niagara Falls (White Sox) |
| 1983 | Utica (Independent) | .649 | Utica (Independent) |
| | Newark (Orioles) | .649 | |
| 1984 | Newark (Orioles) | .622 | Little Falls (Mets) |
| 1985 | Oneonta (Yankees) | .705 | Oneonta (Yankees) |
| 1986 | Oneonta (Yankees) | .766 | St. Cath. (Blue Jays) |
| 1987 | Geneva (Cubs) | .632 | Geneva (Cubs) |
| 1988 | Oneonta (Yankees) | .632 | Oneonta (Yankees) |
| 1989 | Pittsfield (Mets) | .697 | Jamestown (Expos) |
| 1990 | Oneonta (Yankees) | .667 | Oneonta (Yankees) |
| 1991 | Pittsfield (Mets) | .662 | Jamestown (Expos) |
| 1992 | Hamilton (Cardinals) | .737 | Geneva (Cubs) |
| 1993 | St. Catharines (Blue Jays) | .628 | Niagara Falls (Tigers) |

*Best overall record

# NEW YORK-PENN LEAGUE
## 1993 BATTING, PITCHING STATISTICS

### CLUB BATTING

| | AVG | G | AB | R | H | 2B | 3B | HR | BB | SO | SB |
|---|---|---|---|---|---|---|---|---|---|---|---|
| St. Catharines | .258 | 78 | 2588 | 357 | 668 | 96 | 20 | 51 | 247 | 560 | 89 |
| Watertown | .258 | 78 | 2567 | 442 | 662 | 120 | 23 | 31 | 342 | 605 | 97 |
| Niagara Falls | .253 | 78 | 2620 | 393 | 662 | 129 | 21 | 27 | 230 | 570 | 195 |
| Auburn | .252 | 76 | 2555 | 351 | 643 | 111 | 21 | 31 | 257 | 542 | 62 |
| Utica | .252 | 76 | 2503 | 383 | 631 | 148 | 20 | 41 | 255 | 601 | 69 |
| Pittsfield | .251 | 75 | 2434 | 322 | 610 | 98 | 18 | 20 | 236 | 570 | 89 |
| Welland | .250 | 77 | 2565 | 349 | 640 | 112 | 21 | 36 | 200 | 562 | 63 |
| Erie | .247 | 77 | 2670 | 379 | 660 | 105 | 18 | 58 | 260 | 505 | 86 |
| Geneva | .246 | 77 | 2519 | 397 | 620 | 116 | 12 | 38 | 259 | 567 | 130 |
| Oneonta | .244 | 76 | 2510 | 361 | 612 | 89 | 43 | 40 | 285 | 554 | 61 |
| Elmira | .243 | 75 | 2489 | 351 | 606 | 112 | 8 | 43 | 310 | 514 | 50 |
| Glens Falls | .242 | 77 | 2562 | 312 | 621 | 117 | 13 | 19 | 266 | 518 | 84 |
| Batavia | .239 | 77 | 2566 | 296 | 614 | 122 | 28 | 19 | 229 | 541 | 82 |
| Jamestown | .237 | 77 | 2510 | 337 | 596 | 114 | 36 | 53 | 269 | 657 | 52 |

### CLUB PITCHING

| | ERA | G | CG | SHO | SV | IP | H | R | ER | BB | SO |
|---|---|---|---|---|---|---|---|---|---|---|---|
| St. Catharines | 2.87 | 78 | 7 | 13 | 21 | 680 | 525 | 279 | 217 | 235 | 609 |
| Niagara Falls | 3.05 | 78 | 0 | 7 | 25 | 695 | 574 | 304 | 236 | 342 | 626 |
| Batavia | 3.24 | 77 | 4 | 6 | 18 | 675 | 624 | 319 | 243 | 256 | 528 |
| Pittsfield | 3.36 | 75 | 9 | 5 | 21 | 638 | 548 | 316 | 238 | 247 | 562 |
| Watertown | 3.71 | 78 | 6 | 4 | 26 | 667 | 662 | 372 | 275 | 230 | 560 |
| Erie | 3.74 | 77 | 5 | 2 | 17 | 687 | 619 | 379 | 285 | 220 | 613 |
| Geneva | 3.78 | 77 | 3 | 3 | 20 | 671 | 636 | 383 | 282 | 318 | 570 |
| Oneonta | 3.83 | 76 | 2 | 5 | 21 | 658 | 658 | 364 | 280 | 276 | 558 |
| Welland | 3.98 | 77 | 2 | 3 | 21 | 658 | 624 | 381 | 291 | 269 | 564 |
| Utica | 3.99 | 76 | 2 | 5 | 20 | 649 | 644 | 365 | 288 | 268 | 530 |
| Elmira | 4.00 | 75 | 6 | 2 | 15 | 645 | 685 | 372 | 287 | 216 | 545 |
| Jamestown | 4.02 | 77 | 5 | 3 | 17 | 657 | 684 | 386 | 293 | 231 | 481 |
| Glens Falls | 4.15 | 77 | 1 | 10 | 21 | 676 | 722 | 387 | 312 | 246 | 547 |
| Auburn | 4.25 | 76 | 11 | 3 | 10 | 651 | 640 | 423 | 307 | 291 | 573 |

### CLUB FIELDING

| | PCT | PO | A | E | DP | | PCT | PO | A | E | DP |
|---|---|---|---|---|---|---|---|---|---|---|---|
| St. Catharines | .968 | 2040 | 770 | 93 | 54 | Watertown | .953 | 2002 | 770 | 137 | 59 |
| Glens Falls | .960 | 2029 | 806 | 119 | 50 | Jamestown | .950 | 1970 | 845 | 148 | 53 |
| Oneonta | .956 | 1975 | 790 | 126 | 68 | Niagara Falls | .950 | 2086 | 811 | 154 | 67 |
| Pittsfield | .955 | 1914 | 700 | 122 | 37 | Utica | .950 | 1947 | 800 | 145 | 53 |
| Batavia | .954 | 2024 | 855 | 138 | 68 | Erie | .949 | 2060 | 833 | 154 | 64 |
| Elmira | .954 | 1936 | 895 | 137 | 69 | Welland | .943 | 1974 | 793 | 166 | 49 |
| Geneva | .954 | 2013 | 805 | 136 | 62 | Auburn | .942 | 1952 | 808 | 169 | 59 |

### INDIVIDUAL BATTING LEADERS
(Minimum 208 Plate Appearances)

| | AVG | G | AB | R | H | 2B | 3B | HR | RBI | BB | SO | SB |
|---|---|---|---|---|---|---|---|---|---|---|---|---|
| Danapilis, Eric, NF | .341 | 65 | 208 | 35 | 71 | 9 | 1 | 3 | 28 | 33 | 36 | 8 |
| O'Donnell, T.J., Utica | .329 | 68 | 255 | 47 | 84 | 22 | 1 | 4 | 33 | 18 | 24 | 5 |
| Shook, Wes, Erie | .321 | 68 | 268 | 48 | 86 | 12 | 2 | 17 | 52 | 18 | 43 | 1 |
| Wiseley, Mike, NF | .321 | 73 | 287 | 46 | 92 | 19 | 1 | 0 | 28 | 35 | 35 | 27 |
| Allensworth, Jermaine, Well. | .308 | 67 | 263 | 44 | 81 | 16 | 4 | 1 | 32 | 24 | 38 | 18 |
| Thomas, Greg, Watertown | .307 | 73 | 277 | 48 | 85 | 20 | 5 | 9 | 63 | 27 | 47 | 3 |
| McMillon, Billy, Elmira | .305 | 57 | 226 | 38 | 69 | 14 | 2 | 6 | 35 | 31 | 43 | 5 |
| Collier, Louis, Welland | .303 | 50 | 201 | 35 | 61 | 6 | 2 | 1 | 19 | 12 | 31 | 8 |
| Rodriguez, Noel, Auburn | .300 | 69 | 273 | 41 | 82 | 12 | 4 | 6 | 54 | 12 | 52 | 0 |
| Sefcik, Kevin, Batavia | .299 | 74 | 281 | 49 | 84 | 24 | 4 | 2 | 28 | 27 | 22 | 20 |

### INDIVIDUAL PITCHING LEADERS
(Minimum 62 Innings)

| | W | L | ERA | G | GS | CG | SV | IP | H | R | ER | BB | SO |
|---|---|---|---|---|---|---|---|---|---|---|---|---|---|
| Meinershagen, Adam, St.C. | 8 | 1 | 1.88 | 13 | 13 | 1 | 0 | 86 | 53 | 19 | 18 | 26 | 87 |
| Kester, Tim, Auburn | 4 | 6 | 2.26 | 15 | 13 | 4 | 0 | 96 | 78 | 40 | 22 | 19 | 83 |
| Thornton, Paul, Elmira | 3 | 5 | 2.36 | 16 | 7 | 1 | 2 | 64 | 51 | 29 | 16 | 27 | 59 |
| Beltran, Alonso, St.C. | 11 | 2 | 2.36 | 15 | 15 | 1 | 0 | 99 | 63 | 36 | 26 | 28 | 101 |
| Rosengren, John, NF | 7 | 3 | 2.41 | 15 | 15 | 0 | 0 | 82 | 52 | 32 | 22 | 38 | 91 |
| Whitten, Casey, Wat. | 6 | 3 | 2.42 | 14 | 14 | 0 | 0 | 82 | 75 | 28 | 22 | 18 | 81 |
| Hurtado, Edwin, St.C. | 10 | 2 | 2.50 | 15 | 15 | 3 | 0 | 101 | 69 | 34 | 28 | 34 | 87 |
| De la Maza, Roland, Wat. | 10 | 3 | 2.52 | 15 | 15 | 1 | 0 | 100 | 90 | 39 | 28 | 14 | 81 |
| Neese, Joshua, NF | 12 | 3 | 2.54 | 21 | 8 | 0 | 11 | 71 | 44 | 24 | 20 | 34 | 73 |
| Jerzembeck, Mike, One. | 8 | 4 | 2.68 | 14 | 14 | 0 | 0 | 77 | 70 | 25 | 23 | 26 | 76 |

## DEPARTMENT LEADERS

**BATTING**
R 3 tied at ........................................ 53
H Mike Wiseley, Niagara Falls ........ 92
TB Wes Shook, Erie ...................... 153
2B Demetrius Dowler, Geneva ........ 26
3B Tim Forkner, Auburn .................... 9
HR Wes Shook, Erie ...................... 17
RBI Greg Thomas, Watertown .......... 63
SH Osmel Garcia, Glens Falls ........ 10
SF Noel Rodriguez, Auburn .............. 7
BB Mike Neal, Watertown ................ 55
IBB 4 tied at ...................................... 4
HBP Jeremy Kendall, Batavia .......... 16
SO Matt Raleigh, Jamestown .......... 99
SB Glen Barker, Niagara Falls ........ 37
CS Joe Biernat, Geneva .................. 15
GIDP Nate Peterson, Auburn .......... 14
OB% Eric Danapilis, Niagara Falls .. .444
SL% Wes Shook, Erie .................... .571

**PITCHING**
G Craig Grasser, Glens Falls .......... 36
GS 4 tied at .................................... 16
CG 3 tied at ...................................... 4
ShO 20 tied at .................................. 1
GF Craig Grasser, Glens Falls .......... 36
Sv Craig Grasser, Glens Falls .......... 19
W Joshua Neese, Niagara Falls ...... 12
L 5 tied at ........................................ 8
IP Eric Cormier, Utica .................... 105
H Chris Cumberland, Oneonta ........ 109
R Mike Grzanich, Auburn ................ 63
ER Kendall Rhine, Auburn .............. 52
HR Mike Grzanich, Auburn .............. 11
BB Kendall Rhine, Auburn ................ 48
HB Andy Larkin, Elmira .................... 12
SO Jason Isringhausen, Pittsfield ...... 104
WP Kendall Rhine, Auburn .............. 21
Bk Bryan Ward, Elmira ...................... 5

**FIELDING**
C AVG Joe Durso, St. Catharines .... .997
    E Richie Borrero, Utica .............. 11
1B AVG Matt Raleigh, Jamestown .. .993
    E 2 tied at .............................. 14
2B AVG Rob Mummau, St.C .......... .965
    E Richard Prieto, Watertown ...... 17
3B AVG Steve Kulpa, Geneva ........ .932
    E Juan Batista, Jamestown ........ 36
SS AVG Scott Southard, Elmira ...... .927
    E Steve Verduzco, Auburn .......... 32
OF AVG Glen Barker, Niagara Falls... .993
    E Angelo Thompson, Jam .......... 14

## HONOR ROLL

**OFFICIAL ALL-STAR TEAM**
C Shook, Erie; Koeyers, Jamestown
1B Greg Thomas, Watertown
2B T.J. O'Donnell, Utica
3B Adam Melhuse, St. Catharines
SS Mike Neal, Watertown
OF Allensworth, Welland; Brown, Elmira; Rivera, Oneonta; Rodriguez, Auburn
DH Wes Shook, Erie
Util Joe Biernat, Geneva
RHP Meinershagen, St.C; Neese, NF
LHP Censale, Batavia; Whitten, Water
MVP: Ruben Rivera, Oneonta
Manager: J.J. Cannon, St. Catharines

**TOP 10 PROSPECTS**
(Selected by league managers)
1. Ruben Rivera, of, Oneonta
2. Adam Meinershagen, rhp, St. Catharines
3. Jermaine Allensworth, of, Welland
4. J.J. Johnson, of, Utica
5. Daron Kirkreit, rhp, Watertown
6. Alan Benes, rhp, Glens Falls
7. Casey Whitten, lhp, Watertown
8. Jason Isringhausen, rhp, Pittsfield
9. Andy Larkin, rhp, Elmira
10. Glen Barker, of, Niagara Falls

# Offensive-Minded Boise Streaks To Crown

**By JEFF GARRETSON**

Most of the time good pitching beats good hitting. And Northwest League managers generally agreed that pitching was above average in 1993.

But Boise was the exception to that rule. The Hawks put on an offensive show in earning their second league championship in three years, sweeping the best-of-3 championship series from Bellingham, the 1992 champion.

In 1991, Boise won the title primarily because of a top-notch pitching staff, including two relievers who dominated the league.

But in 1993 it was Boise's offense, which led the league in average (.258), runs (432) and slugging percentage (.381). Fittingly, the Hawks routed Bellingham 15-4 in Game Two to wrap up the championship series.

"Talent around the league was pretty spread out this year, except for Boise," Everett manager Norm Sherry said toward the end of the regular season. "They have too many good hitters. Normally, a team will have one or two hitters you can deal with as an opposing pitcher. But Boise was solid most of the way through its lineup."

Leading Boise's offense were infielder Mark Simmons and right fielder Todd Greene, who hit leadoff and cleanup, respectively.

Simmons, who split time almost equally between second and third base, won the batting title with a meagre .304 average, the lowest average by a batting champion in league history.

Greene, a Georgia Southern product who finished his college career No. 3 on the all-time NCAA home run list, was selected the league's MVP. He hit a mild

**Todd Greene.** Boise outfielder earned MVP honors by leading Northwest League with 15 home runs and 71 RBIs.

.269, but his power couldn't be ignored. Playing in all 76 regular-season games, Greene led in RBIs (71) and home runs (15), was second in total bases (148) and extra-base hits (33), third in hits (78) and slugging per-

## STANDINGS

| Page | NORTH | W | L | PCT | GB | Manager(s) | Attendance/Dates | Last Pennant |
|---|---|---|---|---|---|---|---|---|
| 203 | **Bellingham Mariners (Mariners)** | 44 | 32 | .579 | — | Mike Goff | 74,900 (36) | 1992 |
| 197 | **Everett Giants (Giants)** | 42 | 34 | .553 | 2 | Norm Sherry | 87,874 (38) | 1985 |
| 191 | **Spokane Indians (Padres)** | 35 | 41 | .461 | 9 | Tim Flannery | 126,028 (35) | 1990 |
| 129 | **Yakima Bears (Dodgers)** | 30 | 46 | .395 | 14 | John Shoemaker | 86,822 (38) | 1964 |

| Page | SOUTH | W | L | PCT | GB | Manager(s) | Attendance/Dates | Last Pennant |
|---|---|---|---|---|---|---|---|---|
| 71 | **Boise Hawks (Angels)** | 41 | 35 | .539 | — | Tom Kotchman | 151,080 (38) | 1993 |
| 123 | **Eugene Emeralds (Royals)** | 40 | 36 | .526 | 1 | John Mizerock | 121,283 (36) | 1980 |
| 165 | **Southern Oregon A's (Athletics)** | 37 | 39 | .487 | 4 | Dick Scott | 78,202 (37) | 1983 |
| 100 | **Bend Rockies (Rockies)** | 35 | 41 | .461 | 6 | Howie Bedell | 60,612 (37) | None |

**PLAYOFFS:** Boise defeated Bellingham, 2-0, in best-of-3 series.
**NOTE:** Team's individual batting and pitching statistics can be found on page indicated in lefthand column.

centage (.485).

Greene also homered in his first two at-bats in the second game of the league championship series, powering Boise to its 15-4 win over Bellingham. Hawks lefthander Bryan Harris pitched a four-hitter in the opener for a 1-0 win.

"He is a tough out," Yakima manager John Shoemaker said. "It seemed like every time Boise had a chance to drive in runs, Todd Greene would step to the plate. And most of the time, those runs would score."

## Pitching Prowess

Bellingham's pitching staff was nearly as impressive as Boise's offense, particularly in the early and middle parts of the season. It led the league in ERA (3.38) for the second straight year.

**Bryan Harris**

Leading the staff was righthander Bob Wolcott, Seattle's second-round draft pick in 1992 who finished his second year in the league. Wolcott made significant strides in 1993, leading his team in wins (8), innings (95) and strikeouts (79) while compiling a 2.64 ERA, second-best among the Baby M's starters.

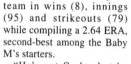

**Glenn Dishman**

"He's not flashy, but he gets people out," Eugene manager John Mizerock said. "He doesn't make many mistakes."

Wolcott made just one mistake in the league championship series opener, a fifth-inning home run to Boise's David Kennedy that gave the Hawks their 1-0 win.

Spokane's Glenn Dishman, signed out of Texas Christian by San Diego as a free agent, had one of two no-hitters, beating Yakima 1-0 on July 17. He came within one out of the first nine-inning perfect game in league history.

After retiring the first 26 Yakima Bears, Dishman induced a soft grounder to second baseman Dickie Woodridge for what appeared to be the final out. First baseman Jason Thompson reached up for the throw, but brought his glove down toward his body before he caught the ball, which glanced off the top of his glove and past the bag for an error.

Dishman, 22, rebounded by ending the game with another grounder and settled for a no-hitter, the first by a single pitcher since 1989. The league had just two perfect games in history, both in seven-inning games, and none since 1958.

"Everything went my way . . . except for that little error thing," said a grinning Dishman. "Jason made a play in the hole earlier in the game to help me out."

Three Bellingham pitchers, Matt Apana, Greg Theron and Matt Mantei, who led the league with 12 saves, combined on the other no-hitter, blanking Spokane 4-0 on June 23—just a week into the season.

Bellingham hitters, meanwhile, set a Northwest League record by scoring 17 runs in one inning

**Jeff Granger**

against Spokane. The Mariners scored 12 runs before Spokane recorded an out, and won the seven-inning game 25-2. The Mariners were one of three minor league teams to score 25 runs in a game in 1993.

Eugene lefthander Jeff Granger, the highest pick (No. 5, Royals) from the 1993 draft to play in the NWL, was selected the league's top major league prospect in a Baseball America poll of managers. He spent the month of September with the parent Kansas City Royals, but pitched only one inning.

## Record-Setting Year

Fielding the same eight clubs and major league affiliates as 1992, the Northwest League again broke the short-season record for attendance, drawing 786,801 in 295 playing dates. The previous record: 722,329 by the NWL in 1992.

Boise, Yakima, Southern Oregon, Bellingham and Bend all set franchise attendance records.

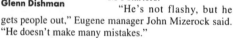

## LEAGUE CHAMPIONS

### Last 25 Years

| Year | Regular Season* | Pct. | Playoff |
|---|---|---|---|
| 1969 | Medford (Dodgers) | .633 | None |
| 1970 | Coos Bay-No. Bend (A's) | .563 | None |
| 1971 | Tri-Cities (Padres) | .625 | None |
| 1972 | Lewiston (Orioles) | .675 | None |
| 1973 | Walla Walla (Padres) | .638 | None |
| 1974 | Bellingham (Dodgers) | .619 | Eugene (Independent) |
| 1975 | Eugene (Reds) | .684 | Eugene (Reds) |
| 1976 | Walla Walla (Padres) | .639 | Walla Walla (Padres) |
| 1977 | Portland (Independent) | .667 | Bellingham (Mariners) |
| 1978 | Grays Harbor (Ind.) | .671 | Grays Harbor (Ind.) |
| 1979 | Bend (Phillies) | .606 | Bend (Phillies) |
| 1980 | Bellingham (Mariners) | .643 | Bellingham (Mariners)# |
| | | | Eugene (Reds)# |
| 1981 | Medford (Athletics) | .600 | Medford (Athletics) |
| 1982 | Medford (Athletics) | .757 | Salem (Angels) |
| 1983 | Medford (Athletics) | .735 | Medford (Athletics) |
| 1984 | Tri-Cities (Rangers) | .622 | Tri-Cities (Rangers) |
| 1985 | Everett (Giants) | .541 | Everett (Giants) |
| | Eugene (Royals) | .541 | |
| 1986 | Bellingham (Mariners) | .608 | Bellingham (Mariners) |
| | Eugene (Royals) | .608 | |
| 1987 | Spokane (Padres) | .711 | Spokane (Padres) |
| 1988 | So. Oregon (Athletics) | .605 | Spokane (Padres) |
| 1989 | So. Oregon (Athletics) | .600 | Spokane (Padres) |
| 1990 | Boise (Angels) | .697 | Spokane (Padres) |
| 1991 | Boise (Angels) | .650 | Boise (Angels) |
| 1992 | Bellingham (Mariners) | .566 | Bellingham (Mariners) |
| | Bend (Rockies) | .566 | |
| 1993 | Bellingham (Mariners) | .579 | Boise (Angels) |

*Best overall record   #Co-champions

# NORTHWEST LEAGUE
## 1993 BATTING, PITCHING STATISTICS

### CLUB BATTING

| | AVG | G | AB | R | H | 2B | 3B | HR | BB | SO | SB |
|---|---|---|---|---|---|---|---|---|---|---|---|
| Boise | .258 | 76 | 2527 | 432 | 651 | 113 | 21 | 52 | 409 | 510 | 59 |
| Southern Oregon | .255 | 76 | 2521 | 407 | 643 | 133 | 16 | 37 | 395 | 572 | 101 |
| Everett | .252 | 76 | 2615 | 403 | 659 | 118 | 18 | 53 | 415 | 622 | 113 |
| Spokane | .249 | 76 | 2550 | 401 | 636 | 123 | 19 | 28 | 322 | 495 | 99 |
| Yakima | .247 | 76 | 2563 | 376 | 632 | 106 | 21 | 38 | 357 | 563 | 82 |
| Eugene | .240 | 76 | 2467 | 333 | 593 | 102 | 17 | 47 | 283 | 603 | 148 |
| Bellingham | .239 | 76 | 2535 | 385 | 605 | 105 | 14 | 37 | 367 | 548 | 81 |
| Bend | .239 | 76 | 2519 | 360 | 602 | 95 | 21 | 62 | 308 | 616 | 115 |

### CLUB PITCHING

| | ERA | G | CG | SHO | SV | IP | H | R | ER | BB | SO |
|---|---|---|---|---|---|---|---|---|---|---|---|
| Bellingham | 3.38 | 76 | 4 | 8 | 20 | 681 | 571 | 327 | 256 | 338 | 559 |
| Eugene | 3.43 | 76 | 1 | 6 | 22 | 669 | 569 | 306 | 255 | 336 | 622 |
| Boise | 4.05 | 76 | 5 | 6 | 18 | 664 | 608 | 360 | 299 | 301 | 603 |
| Bend | 4.06 | 76 | 3 | 2 | 15 | 667 | 671 | 385 | 301 | 319 | 534 |
| Everett | 4.24 | 76 | 1 | 2 | 18 | 688 | 614 | 399 | 324 | 404 | 610 |
| Southern Oregon | 4.54 | 76 | 3 | 6 | 18 | 666 | 691 | 440 | 336 | 303 | 495 |
| Yakima | 4.59 | 76 | 0 | 2 | 13 | 665 | 653 | 440 | 339 | 439 | 537 |
| Spokane | 4.80 | 76 | 4 | 4 | 10 | 658 | 644 | 440 | 351 | 416 | 569 |

### CLUB FIELDING

| | PCT | PO | A | E | DP | | PCT | PO | A | E | DP |
|---|---|---|---|---|---|---|---|---|---|---|---|
| Eugene | .966 | 2007 | 832 | 101 | 76 | Bend | .955 | 2001 | 916 | 138 | 67 |
| Boise | .963 | 1991 | 774 | 107 | 60 | Spokane | .955 | 1974 | 742 | 127 | 58 |
| Everett | .963 | 2063 | 873 | 113 | 61 | Yakima | .947 | 1995 | 850 | 160 | 65 |
| Bellingham | .962 | 2044 | 840 | 113 | 59 | So. Oregon | .946 | 1998 | 831 | 163 | 61 |

**Keith Williams**
.302-12-49

**Jamie Burke**
.301-1-30

### INDIVIDUAL BATTING LEADERS
(Minimum 205 Plate Appearances)

| | AVG | G | AB | R | H | 2B | 3B | HR | RBI | BB | SO | SB |
|---|---|---|---|---|---|---|---|---|---|---|---|---|
| Simmons, Mark, Boise | .304 | 58 | 230 | 46 | 70 | 9 | 1 | 2 | 24 | 39 | 57 | 18 |
| Williams, Keith, Everett | .302 | 75 | 288 | 57 | 87 | 21 | 5 | 12 | 49 | 48 | 73 | 21 |
| Burke, Jamie, Boise | .301 | 66 | 226 | 32 | 68 | 11 | 1 | 1 | 30 | 29 | 22 | 2 |
| Thompson, Jason, Spokane | .300 | 66 | 240 | 36 | 72 | 25 | 1 | 7 | 38 | 37 | 47 | 3 |
| Mueller, Bill, Everett | .300 | 58 | 200 | 31 | 60 | 8 | 2 | 1 | 24 | 42 | 17 | 13 |
| Hickman, Braxton, Eugene | .299 | 67 | 234 | 30 | 70 | 16 | 1 | 5 | 30 | 27 | 48 | 1 |
| Newstrom, Doug, Yakima | .297 | 75 | 279 | 51 | 83 | 17 | 2 | 2 | 36 | 53 | 44 | 11 |
| Zaletel, Brian, Everett | .293 | 54 | 184 | 29 | 54 | 11 | 2 | 5 | 27 | 23 | 48 | 5 |
| Prieto, Chris, Spokane | .289 | 73 | 280 | 64 | 81 | 17 | 5 | 1 | 28 | 47 | 30 | 36 |
| Iatarola, Aaron, Boise | .289 | 57 | 218 | 36 | 63 | 12 | 2 | 7 | 39 | 28 | 46 | 4 |

### INDIVIDUAL PITCHING LEADERS
(Minimum 61 Innings)

| | W | L | ERA | G | GS | CG | SV | IP | H | R | ER | BB | SO |
|---|---|---|---|---|---|---|---|---|---|---|---|---|---|
| Franko, Kris, Everett | 5 | 0 | 1.47 | 13 | 12 | 0 | 0 | 79 | 59 | 15 | 13 | 25 | 72 |
| Harris, Bryan, Boise | 8 | 3 | 1.89 | 16 | 16 | 1 | 0 | 105 | 80 | 29 | 22 | 29 | 96 |
| Dishman, Glenn, Spokane | 6 | 3 | 2.30 | 12 | 12 | 2 | 0 | 78 | 59 | 25 | 19 | 13 | 79 |
| Doughty, Brian, Bellingham | 5 | 4 | 2.49 | 14 | 14 | 1 | 0 | 76 | 65 | 30 | 21 | 42 | 39 |
| Wolcott, Bob, Bellingham | 8 | 4 | 2.64 | 15 | 15 | 1 | 0 | 95 | 70 | 31 | 28 | 26 | 79 |
| Ralston, Kris, Eugene | 7 | 3 | 2.74 | 15 | 15 | 1 | 0 | 82 | 52 | 29 | 25 | 36 | 75 |
| Kubinski, Tim, SO | 5 | 4 | 2.83 | 12 | 12 | 1 | 0 | 70 | 67 | 36 | 22 | 18 | 51 |
| Bland, Nathan, Yakima | 4 | 6 | 2.84 | 16 | 13 | 0 | 0 | 63 | 54 | 34 | 20 | 29 | 43 |
| Michalak, Chris, SO | 7 | 3 | 2.85 | 16 | 15 | 0 | 0 | 79 | 77 | 41 | 25 | 36 | 57 |
| Franklin, Ryan, Bellingham | 5 | 3 | 2.92 | 15 | 14 | 1 | 0 | 74 | 72 | 38 | 24 | 27 | 55 |

## DEPARTMENT LEADERS

### BATTING

| | | |
|---|---|---|
| R | Chris Prieto, Spokane | 64 |
| H | Keith Williams, Everett | 87 |
| TB | Keith Williams, Everett | 154 |
| 2B | Jason Thompson, Spokane | 25 |
| 3B | Chris Latham, Yakima | 6 |
| HR | Todd Greene, Boise | 15 |
| RBI | Todd Greene, Boise | 71 |
| SH | Brett King, Everett | 9 |
| SF | Carlos Subero, Eugene | 6 |
| BB | David Kennedy, Boise | 65 |
| IBB | David Kennedy, Boise | 7 |
| HBP | Greg Boyd, Bend | 15 |
| SO | Rick Haley, Yakima | 83 |
| SB | Chris Prieto, Spokane | 36 |
| CS | Neifi Perez, Bend | 14 |
| GIDP | Bruce Yard, Yakima | 9 |
| OB% | Bill Mueller, Everett | .425 |
| SL% | Keith Williams, Everett | .535 |

### PITCHING

| | | |
|---|---|---|
| G | Jose Garcia, Yakima | 36 |
| GS | Brook Smith, Everett | 17 |
| CG | Andrew Lorraine, Boise | 3 |
| ShO | 2 tied at | 2 |
| GF | Jose Garcia, Yakima | 30 |
| Sv | Matt Mantei, Beloit | 12 |
| W | Steve Day, Everett | 9 |
| L | 2 tied at | 7 |
| IP | Bryan Harris, Boise | 105 |
| H | 2 tied at | 90 |
| R | Heath Altman, Everett | 62 |
| ER | Mike Conte, Southern Oregon | 52 |
| HR | Todd Erdos, Spokane | 13 |
| BB | 2 tied at | 53 |
| HB | Brook Smith, Everett | 10 |
| SO | Bryan Harris, Boise | 96 |
| WP | 2 tied at | 12 |
| Bk | Heath Altman, Everett | 5 |

### FIELDING

| | | | |
|---|---|---|---|
| C | AVG | Mike Cecere, Everett | .994 |
| | E | Mike Higgins, Bend | 10 |
| 1B | AVG | John Donati, Boise | .993 |
| | E | Rick Haley, Yakima | 16 |
| 2B | AVG | Dickie Woodridge, Spokane | .961 |
| | E | David Post, Yakima | 17 |
| 3B | AVG | Mario Munoz, Bend | .890 |
| | E | Doug Newstrom, Yakima | 29 |
| SS | AVG | Carlos Subero, Eugene | .945 |
| | E | Brett King, Everett | 27 |
| OF | AVG | Derrin Doty, Boise | 1.000 |
| | E | Kevin Pitts, Yakima | 10 |

## HONOR ROLL

### OFFICIAL ALL-STAR TEAM

| | |
|---|---|
| C | Mike Sweeney, Eugene |
| 1B | Jason Thompson, Spokane |
| 2B | Mark Simmons, Boise |
| 3B | Doug Newstrom, Yakima |
| SS | Brett King, Everett |
| OF | Todd Greene, Boise |
| | Aaron Iatarola, Boise |
| | Keith Williams, Everett |
| DH | Sal Fasano, Eugene |
| LHP | Glenn Dishman, Spokane |
| RHP | Bob Wolcott, Bellingham |
| RP | Day, Everett; Mantei, Bellingham |

**MVP:** Todd Greene, Boise

**Manager:** Dick Scott, Southern Oregon

### TOP 10 PROSPECTS
(Selected by league managers)

1. Jeff Granger, lhp, Eugene
2. Bob Wolcott, rhp, Bellingham
3. Keith Williams, of, Everett
4. Todd Greene, of, Boise
5. Chris Singleton, of, Everett
6. Scott Spiezio, 3b, Southern Oregon
7. Chris Prieto, of, Spokane
8. Glenn Dishman, lhp, Spokane
9. Matt Mantei, rhp, Bellingham
10. Neifi Perez, ss, Bend

# APPALACHIAN
## LEAGUE

# Fast-Charging Burlington Captures Title

**By DAVID HARDEE**

The Burlington Indians won their first league championship in six years by staging their own version of the Atlanta Braves' "Furious Finish," coming from 4½ games out with just two weeks remaining in the regular season.

Burlington went on an eight-game winning streak to close within a game of Bluefield, setting up a showdown, three-game series at Bluefield on the final weekend of the season to decide the Northern Division title. After splitting the first two games, Burlington's Maximo de la Rosa and Jason Mackey combined to shut out the Orioles and earn a spot opposite Southern Division champion Elizabethton for the Appy League championship.

Burlington and Bluefield, which took a commanding early lead in the Northern Division race on the strength of a 14-game winning streak, actually tied for first with identical 44-24 records, but Burlington was given the nod because it had beaten the Orioles 7-3 in head-to-head competition.

In the best-of-3 final, Burlington took the first game, 3-0, and clinched the title with a 4-3 win in Game Two when shortstop Richard Ramirez drove in Einar Diaz with a two-out double in the bottom of the 12th inning.

Bluefield first baseman Bryan Link was selected the league's MVP. He led the league in runs (64), hits (90), total bases (151) and RBIs (60), while hitting .338 (second) with 14 home runs (third). Link was Baltimore's 32nd-round draft pick out of Austin Peay State University in June.

**Bryan Link**

The league's top two position prospects, as determined by survey of the league's managers, were .300-hitting outfielders Damon Hollins (.321-7-51) and Andre King (.309-0-18), both of Danville.

Kingsport outfielder Al Shirley, voted the Appy League's top prospect in 1992, made an unexpected return to the league in 1993 and struggled mightily. He hit only .180 with 57 strikeouts in 133 at-bats. Combined with 121 strikeouts in 240 at-bats at Class A Capital City, where he started the '93 season, Shirley fanned a minor league high 178 times. He was the Mets' first draft pick in 1991.

Danville's Carey Paige (seven innings), Will Havens (one) and Matt Byrd (one) combined to throw the league's only no-hitter, a 4-0 win over Bristol.

The only offseason franchise shift proved wildly successful as Danville drew a league-record 80,539 fans. Atlanta's affiliate had been located in Pulaski, Va., where it drew just 16,993 spectators in 1992. Danville had been without professional baseball since 1958, when the city lost its Carolina League franchise.

## LEAGUE CHAMPIONS

**Last 25 Years**

| Year | Regular Season* | Pct. | Playoff |
|------|----------------|------|---------|
| 1969 | Pulaski (Phillies) | .576 | None |
| 1970 | Bluefield (Orioles) | .638 | None |
| 1971 | Bluefield (Orioles) | .609 | None |
| 1972 | Bristol (Tigers) | .588 | None |
| 1973 | Kingsport (Royals) | .757 | None |
| 1974 | Bristol (Tigers) | .754 | None |
| 1975 | Johnson City (Cards) | .603 | None |
| 1976 | Johnson City (Cards) | .714 | None |
| 1977 | Kingsport (Braves) | .623 | None |
| 1978 | Elizabethton (Twins) | .594 | None |
| 1979 | Paintsville (Yankees) | .800 | None |
| 1980 | Paintsville (Yankees) | .657 | None |
| 1981 | Paintsville (Yankees) | .657 | None |
| 1982 | Bluefield (Orioles) | .681 | None |
| 1983 | Paintsville (Brewers) | .653 | None |
| 1984 | Elizabethton (Twins) | .580 | Elizabethton (Twins) |
| 1985 | Bristol (Tigers) | .638 | None |
| 1986 | Johnson City (Cards) | .667 | Pulaski (Braves) |
| 1987 | Burlington (Indians) | .725 | Burlington (Indians) |
| 1988 | Kingsport (Mets) | .644 | Kingsport (Mets) |
| 1989 | Elizabethton (Twins) | .691 | Elizabethton (Twins) |
| 1990 | Elizabethton (Twins) | .761 | None |
| 1991 | Pulaski (Braves) | .662 | Pulaski (Braves) |
| 1992 | Elizabethton (Twins) | .742 | Bluefield (Orioles) |
| 1993 | Burlington (Indians) | .647 | Burlington (Indians) |
| | Bluefield (Orioles) | .647 | |

*Best overall record

## STANDINGS

| Page | NORTH | W | L | PCT | GB | Manager | Attendance/Dates | Last Pennant |
|------|-------|---|---|-----|-----|---------|-----------------|--------------|
| 96 | Burlington Indians (Indians) | 44 | 24 | .647 | — | Jim Gabella | 61,088 (33) | 1993 |
| 58 | Bluefield Orioles (Orioles) | 44 | 24 | .647 | — | Andy Etchebarren | 47,281 (32) | 1992 |
| 52 | Danville Braves (Braves) | 38 | 30 | .559 | 6 | Bruce Benedict | 80,539 (34) | None |
| 90 | Princeton Reds (Reds) | 26 | 42 | .382 | 18 | Tommy Dunbar | 32,606 (34) | None |
| 172 | Martinsville Phillies (Phillies) | 22 | 46 | .324 | 22 | Ramon Henderson | 58,368 (33) | None |

| Page | SOUTH | W | L | PCT | GB | Manager | Attendance/Dates | Last Pennant |
|------|-------|---|---|-----|-----|---------|-----------------|--------------|
| 141 | Elizabethton Twins (Twins) | 37 | 30 | .552 | — | Ray Smith | 18,422 (27) | 1990 |
| 184 | Johnson City Cardinals (Cardinals) | 37 | 31 | .544 | ½ | Joe Cunningham | 37,751 (31) | 1976 |
| 83 | Huntington Cubs (Cubs) | 33 | 35 | .485 | 4 ½ | Steve Kolinsky | 51,365 (33) | None |
| 159 | Kingsport Mets (Mets) | 30 | 38 | .441 | 7 ½ | Ron Gideon | 25,467 (28) | 1988 |
| 107 | Bristol Tigers (Tigers) | 28 | 39 | .418 | 9 | Ruben Amaro | 29,868 (34) | 1985 |

**PLAYOFFS:** Burlington defeated Elizabethton, 2-0, in best-of-3 series.

**NOTE:** Team's individual batting and pitching statistics can be found on page indicated in lefthand column.

# APPALACHIAN LEAGUE
## 1993 BATTING, PITCHING STATISTICS

### CLUB BATTING

| | AVG | G | AB | R | H | 2B | 3B | HR | BB | SO | SB |
|---|---|---|---|---|---|---|---|---|---|---|---|
| Bluefield | .273 | 68 | 2336 | 475 | 638 | 124 | 14 | 59 | 382 | 510 | 114 |
| Elizabethton | .267 | 67 | 2269 | 415 | 605 | 119 | 18 | 58 | 234 | 408 | 71 |
| Burlington | .265 | 68 | 2291 | 402 | 608 | 113 | 15 | 49 | 270 | 445 | 106 |
| Kingsport | .261 | 68 | 2254 | 337 | 589 | 112 | 9 | 63 | 265 | 503 | 44 |
| Danville | .257 | 68 | 2272 | 327 | 584 | 108 | 25 | 23 | 225 | 501 | 75 |
| Johnson City | .251 | 68 | 2218 | 344 | 556 | 91 | 20 | 42 | 317 | 474 | 90 |
| Huntington | .249 | 68 | 2187 | 381 | 545 | 89 | 15 | 55 | 297 | 468 | 59 |
| Bristol | .245 | 67 | 2201 | 314 | 539 | 106 | 24 | 54 | 235 | 558 | 74 |
| Princeton | .244 | 68 | 2234 | 315 | 545 | 90 | 28 | 20 | 222 | 445 | 80 |
| Martinsville | .238 | 68 | 2269 | 319 | 541 | 94 | 11 | 47 | 244 | 575 | 74 |

### CLUB PITCHING

| | ERA | G | CG | SHO | SV | IP | H | R | ER | BB | SO |
|---|---|---|---|---|---|---|---|---|---|---|---|
| Danville | 3.38 | 68 | 1 | 3 | 23 | 592 | 511 | 311 | 222 | 252 | 514 |
| Burlington | 3.57 | 68 | 4 | 6 | 19 | 595 | 523 | 287 | 236 | 301 | 508 |
| Elizabethton | 3.58 | 67 | 2 | 1 | 15 | 571 | 484 | 301 | 227 | 282 | 511 |
| Bluefield | 4.04 | 68 | 6 | 1 | 15 | 599 | 584 | 341 | 269 | 216 | 507 |
| Johnson City | 4.21 | 68 | 1 | 2 | 21 | 588 | 565 | 352 | 275 | 240 | 558 |
| Huntington | 4.42 | 68 | 3 | 2 | 15 | 573 | 594 | 361 | 281 | 232 | 465 |
| Princeton | 4.51 | 68 | 4 | 5 | 10 | 586 | 587 | 390 | 294 | 321 | 484 |
| Kingsport | 4.71 | 68 | 5 | 4 | 17 | 573 | 616 | 396 | 300 | 218 | 430 |
| Bristol | 5.37 | 67 | 2 | 3 | 16 | 573 | 593 | 414 | 342 | 348 | 469 |
| Martinsville | 5.49 | 68 | 2 | 2 | 7 | 582 | 693 | 476 | 355 | 281 | 441 |

### CLUB FIELDING

| | PCT | PO | A | E | DP | | PCT | PO | A | E | DP |
|---|---|---|---|---|---|---|---|---|---|---|---|
| Burlington | .963 | 1784 | 822 | 101 | 68 | Kingsport | .948 | 1719 | 685 | 133 | 59 |
| Bluefield | .952 | 1798 | 721 | 127 | 48 | Danville | .947 | 1775 | 652 | 136 | 41 |
| Elizabethton | .951 | 1712 | 712 | 124 | 50 | Huntington | .946 | 1718 | 739 | 140 | 52 |
| Johnson City | .951 | 1764 | 704 | 128 | 51 | Princeton | .945 | 1759 | 730 | 146 | 64 |
| Bristol | .948 | 1720 | 715 | 133 | 52 | Martinsville | .932 | 1747 | 780 | 183 | 67 |

**Preston Wilson**
16 homers

MARK McINTYRE

**Damon Hollins**
No. 1 prospect

BILL SETLIFF

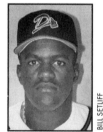

**Andre King**
All-Star OF

BILL SETLIFF

### INDIVIDUAL BATTING LEADERS
(Minimum 184 Plate Appearances)

| | AVG | G | AB | R | H | 2B | 3B | HR | RBI | BB | SO | SB |
|---|---|---|---|---|---|---|---|---|---|---|---|---|
| Wooten, Sean, Bristol | .350 | 52 | 177 | 26 | 62 | 12 | 2 | 8 | 39 | 24 | 20 | 1 |
| Link, Bryan, Bluefield | .338 | 68 | 266 | 64 | 90 | 17 | 1 | 14 | 60 | 42 | 38 | 9 |
| Diaz, Cesar, Kingsport | .327 | 55 | 211 | 36 | 69 | 12 | 1 | 11 | 37 | 15 | 41 | 0 |
| Foster, Jim, Bluefield | .326 | 61 | 218 | 59 | 71 | 21 | 1 | 10 | 45 | 42 | 34 | 3 |
| White, Eric, Bristol | .321 | 68 | 249 | 41 | 80 | 19 | 1 | 1 | 45 | 27 | 37 | 14 |
| Hollins, Damon, Danville | .321 | 62 | 240 | 37 | 77 | 15 | 2 | 7 | 51 | 19 | 30 | 10 |
| Venezia, Danny, Eliz. | .310 | 62 | 258 | 47 | 80 | 9 | 1 | 2 | 36 | 18 | 34 | 21 |
| King, Andre, Danville | .309 | 60 | 223 | 41 | 69 | 10 | 6 | 0 | 18 | 36 | 40 | 15 |
| Catalanotto, Frank, Bris. | .307 | 55 | 199 | 37 | 61 | 9 | 5 | 3 | 22 | 15 | 19 | 3 |
| Warner, Randy, King. | .305 | 58 | 223 | 37 | 68 | 12 | 0 | 15 | 37 | 13 | 55 | 1 |

### INDIVIDUAL PITCHING LEADERS
(Minimum 54 Innings)

| | W | L | ERA | G | GS | CG | SV | IP | H | R | ER | BB | SO |
|---|---|---|---|---|---|---|---|---|---|---|---|---|---|
| Etheridge, Roger, Prince. | 3 | 2 | 1.49 | 9 | 9 | 1 | 0 | 54 | 40 | 14 | 9 | 28 | 60 |
| Mackey, Jason, Burlington | 6 | 0 | 2.05 | 22 | 5 | 0 | 1 | 54 | 28 | 14 | 13 | 36 | 53 |
| Martinez, Johnny, Bur. | 6 | 1 | 2.32 | 11 | 10 | 1 | 0 | 73 | 63 | 21 | 18 | 25 | 54 |
| Miller, Shawn, Eliz. | 5 | 0 | 2.63 | 13 | 11 | 1 | 0 | 68 | 60 | 26 | 20 | 23 | 35 |
| Lundberg, Bryan, Mart. | 3 | 4 | 2.78 | 13 | 12 | 0 | 0 | 71 | 71 | 30 | 22 | 21 | 60 |
| DeJesus, Javier, Eliz. | 9 | 0 | 2.99 | 12 | 12 | 0 | 0 | 78 | 55 | 27 | 26 | 36 | 79 |
| Yan, Esteban, Danville | 4 | 7 | 3.03 | 14 | 14 | 0 | 0 | 71 | 73 | 46 | 24 | 24 | 60 |
| Hagan, Danny, Princeton | 2 | 1 | 3.07 | 17 | 6 | 0 | 1 | 60 | 44 | 23 | 21 | 35 | 63 |
| Bryant, Chris, Huntsville | 5 | 4 | 3.08 | 12 | 12 | 0 | 0 | 65 | 57 | 28 | 23 | 37 | 56 |
| Battles, Jeff, Johnson City | 5 | 4 | 3.40 | 13 | 13 | 0 | 0 | 82 | 82 | 38 | 29 | 15 | 69 |
| Carrasco, Troy, Eliz. | 2 | 4 | 3.40 | 14 | 10 | 0 | 2 | 70 | 46 | 32 | 25 | 39 | 75 |

---

## DEPARTMENT LEADERS

### BATTING
| | | |
|---|---|---|
| R | Bryan Link, Bluefield | 64 |
| H | Bryan Link, Bluefield | 90 |
| TB | Bryan Link, Bluefield | 151 |
| 2B | Jim Foster, Bluefield | 21 |
| 3B | Mike Wieser, Danville | 8 |
| HR | Preston Wilson, Kingsport | 16 |
| RBI | Bryan Link, Bluefield | 60 |
| SH | Jhonny Carvajal, Princeton | 8 |
| SF | Jeff Ramey, Princeton | 7 |
| BB | Myles Barnden, Bluefield | 58 |
| IBB | Tom McKinnon, Johnson City | 4 |
| HBP | Joe Wallace, Johnson City | 10 |
| SO | Chad Rupp, Elizabethton | 79 |
| SB | Kimera Bartee, Bluefield | 27 |
| CS | Jhonny Carvajal, Princeton | 11 |
| GIDP | 2 tied at | 9 |
| OB% | Myles Barnden, Bluefield | .442 |
| SL% | Sean Wooten, Bristol | .576 |

### PITCHING
| | | |
|---|---|---|
| G | Kevin Dinnen, Bristol | 30 |
| GS | 7 tied at | 14 |
| CG | Calvin Maduro, Bluefield | 3 |
| ShO | 4 tied at | 1 |
| GF | Cesar Ramos, Bristol | 27 |
| Sv | Cesar Ramos, Bristol | 14 |
| W | 2 tied at | 9 |
| L | 2 tied at | 9 |
| IP | Calvin Maduro, Bluefield | 91 |
| H | Scott Norman, Bristol | 100 |
| R | Chris Phipps, Martinsville | 63 |
| ER | Rich Hunter, Martinsville | 52 |
| HR | Carlos Chavez, Bluefield | 15 |
| BB | Tony Fuduric, Bristol | 52 |
| HB | 2 tied at | 7 |
| SO | Calvin Maduro, Bluefield | 83 |
| WP | 2 tied at | 14 |
| Bk | 2 tied at | 5 |

### FIELDING
| | | |
|---|---|---|
| C AVG | Adam Rodriguez, Bristol | .984 |
| E | Einar Diaz, Burlington | 9 |
| 1B AVG | Rob Daly, Kingsport | .986 |
| E | Tom McKinnon, Johnson City | 22 |
| 2B AVG | Jesus Azuaje, Burlington | .986 |
| E | Bob Morris, Huntington | 20 |
| 3B AVG | Todd Betts, Burlington | .912 |
| E | Preston Wilson, Kingsport | 25 |
| SS AVG | Richard Ramirez, Burlington | .955 |
| E | Manny Amador, Martinsville | 37 |
| OF AVG | Randy Warner, Kingsport | 1.000 |
| E | Brian Costello, Martinsville | 11 |

---

## HONOR ROLL

### OFFICIAL ALL-STAR TEAM
| | |
|---|---|
| C | Cesar Diaz, Kingsport |
| 1B | Bryan Link, Bluefield |
| 2B | Jesus Azuaje, Burlington |
| 3B | Myles Barnden, Bluefield |
| SS | Enrique Wilson, Elizabethton |
| OF | Damon Hollins, Danville |
| | Andre King, Danville |
| | Randy Warner, Kingsport |
| DH | Sean Wooten, Bristol |
| LHP | Javier DeJesus, Elizabethton |
| RHP | Calvin Maduro, Bluefield |
| RP | Cesar Ramos, Burlington |

**MVP:** Bryan Link, Bluefield
**Manager:** Joe Cunningham, JC

### TOP 10 PROSPECTS
(Selected by league managers)
1. Damon Hollins, of, Danville
2. Jay Witasick, rhp, Johnson City
3. Andre King, of, Danville
4. Cesar Diaz, c, Kingsport
5. Troy Carrasco, lhp, Elizabethton
6. Preston Wilson, 3b, Kingsport
7. Bryan Link, 1b, Bluefield
8. William Benson, rhp, Bluefield
9. Elieser Marrero, c, Johnson City
10. Einar Diaz, c, Burlington

# PIONEER
## LEAGUE

# Mustangs Romp To Second Straight Crown

**By DAVID HARDEE**

The Billings Mustangs sat back and endured a seven-year period of domination by Salt Lake City and Great Falls from 1985-91. Now, it's the Mustangs chance to enjoy the Pioneer League as their own little dynasty.

Billings, in its 20th year of affiliation with the Cincinnati Reds, won its second straight Pioneer League title in 1993, beating Helena 2-1 in a best-of-3 final. That earned Donnie Scott his second straight Baseball America short-season Manager of the Year award.

Scott again led the Mustangs to a first-place finish in the Northern Division, beating out Medicine Hat by nine games. In the championship series, Southern Division champion Helena took the first game before Billings came back to take the last two. Righthander Todd Etler pitched 6⅔ innings to earn the win in the 6-3 deciding game.

Billings last won back-to-back championships in 1972-73. More recently, Great Falls won three straight championships from 1988-90 and Salt Lake City won three in a row from 1985-87.

GAINES DuVALL

**Kym Ashworth**

Great Falls was never in contention in 1993. Salt Lake didn't even operate a team.

Prior to the 1993 season, the Pioneer League lost its flagship franchise and perennial attendance leader when the Trappers, who annually drew more than 200,000 spectators, were forced out of business because Salt Lake City officials decided to raze the Trappers' Derks Field in order to break ground on an $18 million, 12,000-seat stadium on the same site. The new park will serve as the home of the former Triple-A Portland Beavers in 1994.

League owners were forced to field an independent team in Pocatello, Idaho, in order to maintain eight teams.

The league ended up with three independent or co-

op clubs in all as both Lethbridge and Butte were forced to rely on Major League Baseball for players. Lethbridge lost its local ownership while Butte was left scrambling for players when the Texas Rangers unexpectedly broke off a working agreement after the 1992 season.

With Salt Lake no longer in the league, Billings led the circuit with 101,490 fans.

Though Etler was 8-1 in the regular season, had the league's fourth-best ERA (2.71) and played a key role in Billings' playoff win, two other Mustang pitchers, righthanders Scott Sullivan (No. 3) and Brad Tweedlie (No. 6), earned spots among the Pioneer League's top 10 prospects, as judged by managers.

Great Falls lefthander Kym Ashworth was voted the league's top prospect after going 3-3 with a 2.44 ERA. Ashworth, the youngest player in the league at 17, is a native Australian.

## LEAGUE CHAMPIONS

**Last 25 Years**

| Year | Regular Season* | Pct. | Playoff |
|---|---|---|---|
| 1969 | Ogden (Dodgers) | .620 | None |
| 1970 | Idaho Falls (Angels) | .629 | None |
| 1971 | Great Falls (Giants) | .643 | None |
| 1972 | Billings (Royals) | .694 | None |
| 1973 | Billings (Royals) | .629 | None |
| 1974 | Idaho Falls (Angels) | .569 | None |
| 1975 | Great Falls (Giants) | .577 | None |
| 1976 | Great Falls (Giants) | .577 | None |
| 1977 | Lethbridge (Dodgers) | .629 | None |
| 1978 | Billings (Reds) | .735 | Billings (Reds) |
| 1979 | Helena (Phillies) | .623 | Lethbridge (Dodgers) |
| 1980 | Lethbridge (Dodgers) | .740 | Lethbridge (Dodgers) |
| 1981 | Calgary (Expos) | .657 | Butte (Brewers) |
| 1982 | Medicine Hat (Blue Jays) | .629 | Medicine Hat (Blue Jays) |
| 1983 | Billings (Reds) | .614 | Billings (Reds) |
| 1984 | Billings (Reds) | .691 | Helena (Independent) |
| 1985 | Great Falls (Dodgers) | .771 | Salt Lake (Independent) |
| 1986 | Salt Lake (Independent) | .643 | Salt Lake (Independent) |
| 1987 | Salt Lake (Independent) | .700 | Salt Lake (Independent) |
| 1988 | Great Falls (Dodgers) | .754 | Great Falls (Dodgers) |
| 1989 | Great Falls (Dodgers) | .791 | Great Falls (Dodgers) |
| 1990 | Great Falls (Dodgers) | .706 | Great Falls (Dodgers) |
| 1991 | Salt Lake (Independent) | .700 | Salt Lake (Independent) |
| 1992 | Billings (Reds) | .697 | Billings (Reds) |
| | Salt Lake (Independent) | .697 | |
| 1993 | Billings (Reds) | .653 | Billings (Reds) |

*Best overall record

## STANDINGS

| Page | NORTH | W | L | PCT | GB | Manager | Attendance/Dates | Last Pennant |
|---|---|---|---|---|---|---|---|---|
| 90 | **Billings Mustangs (Reds)** | 49 | 26 | .653 | — | Donnie Scott | 101,490 (35) | 1992 |
| 215 | **Medicine Hat Blue Jays (Blue Jays)** | 39 | 34 | .534 | 9 | Omar Malave | 25,102 (33) | 1982 |
| 130 | **Great Falls Dodgers (Dodgers)** | 37 | 35 | .514 | 10 ½ | Jon Debus | 59,924 (31) | 1990 |
| 216 | **Lethbridge Mounties (Independent)** | 29 | 44 | .397 | 19 | Phillip Wellman | 28,053 (32) | 1980 |

| Page | SOUTH | W | L | PCT | GB | Manager(s) | Attendance/Dates | Last Pennant |
|---|---|---|---|---|---|---|---|---|
| 136 | **Helena Brewers (Brewers)** | 43 | 30 | .589 | — | M. Epstein, H. Dunlop | 39,211 (35) | 1993 |
| 217 | **Pocatello Posse (Independent)** | 37 | 38 | .493 | 7 | E. Rodriguez, J. Stein | 45,638 (36) | None |
| 53 | **Idaho Falls Braves (Braves)** | 36 | 40 | .474 | 8 ½ | Paul Runge | 37,385 (36) | 1974 |
| 216 | **Butte Copper Kings (Independent)** | 26 | 49 | .347 | 18 | John Shelby | 19,750 (28) | 1981 |

**PLAYOFFS:** Billings defeated Helena, 2-1, in best-of-3 series.
**NOTE:** Team's individual batting and pitching statistics can be found on page indicated in lefthand column.

# PIONEER LEAGUE
## 1993 BATTING, PITCHING STATISTICS

### CLUB BATTING

| | AVG | G | AB | R | H | 2B | 3B | HR | BB | SO | SB |
|---|---|---|---|---|---|---|---|---|---|---|---|
| Pocatello | .289 | 75 | 2499 | 451 | 721 | 107 | 19 | 44 | 360 | 502 | 100 |
| Idaho Falls | .286 | 76 | 2573 | 472 | 735 | 132 | 30 | 47 | 308 | 524 | 128 |
| Butte | .280 | 75 | 2414 | 398 | 677 | 112 | 27 | 48 | 307 | 536 | 84 |
| Billings | .279 | 75 | 2466 | 447 | 687 | 120 | 20 | 53 | 287 | 427 | 121 |
| Helena | .268 | 73 | 2427 | 448 | 650 | 113 | 21 | 54 | 379 | 592 | 123 |
| Medicine Hat | .265 | 73 | 2377 | 387 | 629 | 95 | 20 | 52 | 239 | 537 | 45 |
| Great Falls | .258 | 72 | 2400 | 339 | 618 | 108 | 19 | 26 | 241 | 544 | 69 |
| Lethbridge | .246 | 73 | 2334 | 328 | 575 | 94 | 20 | 43 | 244 | 543 | 101 |

### CLUB PITCHING

| | ERA | G | CG | SHO | SV | IP | H | R | ER | BB | SO |
|---|---|---|---|---|---|---|---|---|---|---|---|
| Medicine Hat | 3.24 | 73 | 0 | 3 | 20 | 614 | 554 | 308 | 221 | 246 | 467 |
| Billings | 3.30 | 75 | 10 | 6 | 17 | 638 | 574 | 299 | 234 | 287 | 546 |
| Helena | 3.90 | 73 | 4 | 5 | 22 | 633 | 653 | 358 | 274 | 260 | 562 |
| Lethbridge | 4.57 | 73 | 11 | 3 | 19 | 615 | 623 | 416 | 312 | 304 | 486 |
| Great Falls | 4.60 | 72 | 1 | 2 | 23 | 626 | 576 | 399 | 320 | 366 | 575 |
| Idaho Falls | 5.20 | 76 | 3 | 4 | 16 | 652 | 749 | 460 | 377 | 285 | 554 |
| Pocatello | 5.49 | 75 | 15 | 2 | 7 | 634 | 752 | 487 | 387 | 319 | 603 |
| Butte | 6.78 | 75 | 7 | 1 | 17 | 596 | 811 | 543 | 449 | 298 | 412 |

### CLUB FIELDING

| | PCT | PO | A | E | DP | | PCT | PO | A | E | DP |
|---|---|---|---|---|---|---|---|---|---|---|---|
| Billings | .961 | 1913 | 807 | 111 | 67 | Butte | .952 | 1789 | 792 | 131 | 65 |
| Pocatello | .958 | 1903 | 807 | 120 | 67 | Idaho Falls | .950 | 1957 | 822 | 147 | 70 |
| Great Falls | .957 | 1878 | 743 | 118 | 51 | Lethbridge | .947 | 1844 | 785 | 148 | 60 |
| Helena | .957 | 1899 | 802 | 120 | 57 | Medicine Hat | .946 | 1841 | 789 | 149 | 67 |

**Todd Takayoshi**
Batting Champ

**Paul Bako**
.314-4-30

### INDIVIDUAL BATTING LEADERS
(Minimum 200 Plate Appearances)

| | AVG | G | AB | R | H | 2B | 3B | HR | RBI | BB | SO | SB |
|---|---|---|---|---|---|---|---|---|---|---|---|---|
| Takayoshi, Todd, Poc. | .358 | 69 | 243 | 38 | 87 | 9 | 1 | 5 | 40 | 50 | 25 | 3 |
| Ramirez, Angel, MH | .352 | 62 | 227 | 40 | 80 | 8 | 5 | 4 | 30 | 8 | 43 | 15 |
| Bingham, David, Poc. | .348 | 55 | 178 | 42 | 62 | 8 | 3 | 5 | 30 | 28 | 45 | 8 |
| Sexton, Chris, Billings | .333 | 72 | 273 | 63 | 91 | 14 | 4 | 4 | 46 | 35 | 27 | 13 |
| Fitzpatrick, Will, Poc. | .330 | 57 | 194 | 33 | 64 | 14 | 0 | 9 | 58 | 38 | 52 | 0 |
| Eaglin, Michael, IF. | .326 | 66 | 236 | 50 | 77 | 5 | 4 | 2 | 35 | 29 | 48 | 28 |
| Bako, Paul, Billings | .314 | 57 | 194 | 34 | 61 | 11 | 0 | 4 | 30 | 22 | 37 | 5 |
| McInnes, Chris, Helena | .312 | 64 | 218 | 49 | 68 | 14 | 5 | 1 | 37 | 45 | 42 | 29 |
| Vaughn, Derek, Poc. | .311 | 72 | 299 | 60 | 93 | 14 | 3 | 5 | 43 | 24 | 52 | 40 |
| Segura, Juan, Leth. | .306 | 66 | 242 | 33 | 74 | 13 | 0 | 0 | 25 | 13 | 53 | 4 |

### INDIVIDUAL PITCHING LEADERS
(Minimum 59 Innings)

| | W | L | ERA | G | GS | CG | SV | IP | H | R | ER | BB | SO |
|---|---|---|---|---|---|---|---|---|---|---|---|---|---|
| Camacho, Daniel, GF | 5 | 2 | 1.38 | 28 | 0 | 0 | 5 | 65 | 38 | 14 | 10 | 18 | 79 |
| Ashworth, Kym, GF | 3 | 3 | 2.44 | 11 | 11 | 0 | 0 | 59 | 43 | 25 | 16 | 14 | 52 |
| Salmon, Fabian, Helena | 8 | 3 | 2.64 | 13 | 13 | 1 | 0 | 82 | 84 | 37 | 24 | 25 | 62 |
| Etler, Todd, Billings | 8 | 1 | 2.71 | 15 | 15 | 1 | 0 | 90 | 75 | 33 | 27 | 30 | 55 |
| Grant, Brian, MH | 5 | 4 | 2.84 | 14 | 13 | 0 | 0 | 73 | 61 | 33 | 23 | 34 | 49 |
| Bonilla, Miguel, Leth. | 4 | 8 | 2.87 | 16 | 15 | 5 | 0 | 107 | 105 | 46 | 34 | 24 | 59 |
| Lyons, Curt, Billings | 7 | 3 | 3.00 | 15 | 12 | 2 | 0 | 84 | 89 | 35 | 28 | 20 | 64 |
| Caruso, Gene, Pocatello | 7 | 5 | 3.07 | 16 | 14 | 7 | 0 | 111 | 83 | 52 | 39 | 58 | 163 |
| Costello, Chris, GF | 4 | 2 | 3.21 | 12 | 12 | 0 | 0 | 70 | 61 | 30 | 25 | 26 | 59 |
| Sinclair, Steve, MH | 5 | 2 | 3.33 | 15 | 12 | 0 | 0 | 78 | 87 | 41 | 29 | 16 | 45 |

## DEPARTMENT LEADERS

### BATTING

| | | |
|---|---|---|
| R | Chris Sexton, Billings | 63 |
| H | Derek Vaughn, Pocatello | 93 |
| TB | Derek Vaughn, Pocatello | 128 |
| 2B | 2 tied at | 17 |
| 3B | Adrian Brown, Lethbridge | 9 |
| HR | Willie Brown, Lethbridge | 16 |
| RBI | Will Fitzpatrick, Pocatello | 58 |
| SH | Ruben Cephas, Helena | 8 |
| SF | Stephen Gann, Billings | 9 |
| BB | Todd Takayoshi, Pocatello | 50 |
| IBB | John Yselonia, Lethbridge | 4 |
| HBP | 2 tied at | 10 |
| SO | Willie Brown, Lethbridge | 86 |
| SB | Derek Vaughn, Pocatello | 40 |
| CS | Derek Vaughn, Pocatello | 13 |
| GIDP | J.P. Postiff, Pocatello | 10 |
| OB% | Todd Takayoshi, Pocatello | .466 |
| SL% | Lorenzo De la Cruz, MH | .567 |

### PITCHING

| | | |
|---|---|---|
| G | 2 tied at | 28 |
| GS | Cory Lidle, Pocatello | 16 |
| CG | Gene Caruso, Pocatello | 7 |
| ShO | 3 tied at | 2 |
| GF | Jeff Leystra, Medicine Hat | 26 |
| Sv | Keith Troutman, Great Falls | 16 |
| W | 3 tied at | 8 |
| L | John Dillinger, Lethbridge | 10 |
| IP | Gene Caruso, Pocatello | 111 |
| H | Miguel Bonilla, Lethbridge | 105 |
| R | Dan Roman, Lethbridge | 67 |
| ER | Jason Bobb, Butte | 50 |
| HR | Fabian Salmon, Helena | 13 |
| BB | Dan Roman, Lethbridge | 62 |
| HB | 2 tied at | 12 |
| SO | Gene Caruso, Pocatello | 163 |
| WP | 2 tied at | 17 |
| Bk | 4 tied at | 5 |

### FIELDING

| | | |
|---|---|---|
| C AVG | Erik Moreno, Idaho Falls | .994 |
| E | 2 tied at | 11 |
| 1B AVG | Mike Biltimier, Great Falls | .989 |
| E | 2 tied at | 9 |
| 2B AVG | Michael Eaglin, Idaho Falls | .955 |
| E | Eddy Vasquez, Medicine Hat | 23 |
| 3B AVG | Pedro Carranza, Pocatello | .943 |
| E | 2 tied at | 29 |
| SS AVG | Tiger King, Butte | .927 |
| E | Juan Segura, Lethbridge | 33 |
| OF AVG | Adrian Brown, Lethbridge | .992 |
| E | Derek Vaughn, Pocatello | 9 |

## HONOR ROLL

### OFFICIAL ALL-STAR TEAM

| | |
|---|---|
| C | Paul Bako, Billings |
| 1B | Will Fitzpatrick, Pocatello |
| 2B | Michael Eaglin, Idaho Falls |
| 3B | Adam Burton, Idaho Falls |
| SS | Jeff Patzke, Medicine Hat |
| OF | Willie Brown, Lethbridge |
| | Derek Vaughn, Pocatello |
| | Marty Watson, Butte |
| DH | Todd Takayoshi, Pocatello |
| P | Daniel Camacho, Great Falls |
| | Todd Etler, Billings |
| | Fabian Salmon, Helena |

**Manager:** Harry Dunlop, Helena

### TOP 10 PROSPECTS
(Selected by league managers)

1. Kym Ashworth, lhp, Great Falls
2. Wilton Guerrero, ss, Great Falls
3. Scott Sullivan, rhp, Billings
4. Freddy Garcia, 3b, Medicine Hat
5. Todd Dunn, of, Helena
6. Brad Tweedlie, rhp, Billings
7. Brian Grant, lhp, Medicine Hat
8. Angel Ramirez, of, Medicine Hat
9. Paul Bako, c, Billings
10. Joe Wagner, rhp, Helena

# Rookie League Sees Another Hat Trick

**By DAVID HARDEE**

Like basketball's Chicago Bulls, the Arizona League Athletics pulled off their own version of a three-peat in 1993.

The Athletics earned their third straight Arizona League title by edging the Cardinals by three games in the regular-season standings. The complex-based Rookie league has no playoffs.

It was the second time in the league's six-year history that a team won three straight titles. The Brewers turned the hat trick from 1988-90.

Third baseman John Jones provided much of the offensive thrust for the Athletics, missing a triple

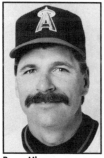

crown by two RBIs. He led the league with a .341 average and was one of three players to hit five home runs.

Brothers Fred (.260-5-19) and Jose Soriano (.265-3-31) also played a pivotal role for the Athletics. Fred's play earned him a late-season chance to play at Triple-A Tacoma while Jose was picked to the all-star team in addition to being selected the league's fourth-best prospect

**Bruce Hines**

in a managers' poll.

Bruce Hines, son of Dodgers first-base coach Ben Hines, managed the Athletics to their last two titles but was let go by parent Oakland at the end of the season. His father also was dismissed shortly thereafter.

Giants lefthander Jason Myers was the league's single most dominant performer. He earned league MVP honors and a spot on Baseball America's short-season all-star team by going 8-1 with a league-leading 1.69 ERA. In 75 innings, Myers struck out 105 while walking just 16.

The player voted the league's top prospect was Padres first baseman Derrek Lee, the 14th overall selection in the 1993 draft. He was in the league for only 15 games before earn-

**Derrek Lee.** Padres first baseman played only 15 games, but made an impression on managers.

ing a promotion to Class A Rancho Cucamonga.

Lee, an all-around athlete who had committed to playing baseball and basketball at the University of North Carolina before signing with the Padres, is the latest in a line of talented Lees. Derrek's uncle, Leron, was selected by the Cardinals in the first round of the 1967 draft. Both he and brother Leon, Derrek's father, were two of the most productive import players in Japanese League history.

### LEAGUE CHAMPIONS

| Year | Regular Season | Pct. | Playoff |
|------|----------------|------|---------|
| 1988 | Brewers | .690 | None |
| 1989 | Brewers | .727 | None |
| 1990 | Brewers | .679 | None |
| 1991 | Athletics | .650 | None |
| 1992 | Athletics | .604 | None |
| 1993 | Athletics | .636 | None |

### STANDINGS

| Page | | Complex Site | W | L | PCT | GB | Manager(s) | Last Pennant |
|------|-----------|--------------|----|----|------|------|----------------|--------------|
| 166 | **Athletics** | Scottsdale | 35 | 20 | .636 | — | Bruce Hines | 1993 |
| 185 | **Cardinals** | Chandler | 31 | 22 | .585 | 3 | Roy Silver | None |
| 198 | **Giants** | Scottsdale | 31 | 24 | .564 | 4 | Alan Bannister | None |
| 71 | **Angels** | Mesa | 29 | 26 | .527 | 6 | Bill Lachemann | None |
| 136 | **Brewers** | Chandler | 29 | 27 | .518 | 6½ | Ralph Dickenson | 1990 |
| 191 | **Padres** | Peoria | 24 | 31 | .436 | 11 | Ken Berry | None |
| 101 | **Rockies** | Mesa | 21 | 32 | .396 | 13 | P.J. Carey | None |
| 203 | **Mariners** | Peoria | 18 | 36 | .333 | 16½ | Marty Martinez | None |

**PLAYOFFS:** None.
**NOTE:** Team's individual batting and pitching statistics can be found on page indicated in lefthand column.

# ARIZONA LEAGUE
## 1993 BATTING, PITCHING STATISTICS

### CLUB BATTING

| | AVG | G | AB | R | H | 2B | 3B | HR | BB | SO | SB |
|---|---|---|---|---|---|---|---|---|---|---|---|
| Brewers | .266 | 56 | 1912 | 326 | 508 | 58 | 26 | 10 | 204 | 438 | 148 |
| Athletics | .266 | 55 | 1862 | 353 | 495 | 83 | 27 | 27 | 237 | 417 | 76 |
| Giants | .264 | 55 | 1907 | 321 | 503 | 86 | 31 | 14 | 230 | 439 | 85 |
| Mariners | .246 | 54 | 1801 | 277 | 443 | 65 | 27 | 12 | 217 | 433 | 79 |
| Angels | .246 | 56 | 1779 | 261 | 437 | 69 | 25 | 9 | 248 | 334 | 38 |
| Cardinals | .246 | 53 | 1740 | 271 | 428 | 58 | 28 | 6 | 216 | 376 | 77 |
| Padres | .230 | 55 | 1812 | 243 | 417 | 69 | 18 | 9 | 206 | 508 | 94 |
| Rockies | .221 | 54 | 1729 | 241 | 382 | 70 | 18 | 13 | 212 | 443 | 111 |

### CLUB PITCHING

| | ERA | G | CG | SHO | SV | IP | H | R | ER | BB | SO |
|---|---|---|---|---|---|---|---|---|---|---|---|
| Angels | 3.34 | 56 | 10 | 6 | 8 | 483 | 405 | 239 | 179 | 188 | 455 |
| Cardinals | 3.47 | 53 | 0 | 5 | 14 | 464 | 456 | 234 | 179 | 159 | 463 |
| Padres | 3.72 | 55 | 2 | 1 | 9 | 476 | 421 | 292 | 197 | 251 | 439 |
| Rockies | 3.92 | 54 | 2 | 1 | 8 | 457 | 468 | 291 | 199 | 176 | 350 |
| Athletics | 3.97 | 55 | 0 | 1 | 15 | 478 | 479 | 289 | 211 | 186 | 391 |
| Giants | 4.09 | 55 | 0 | 1 | 12 | 489 | 453 | 288 | 222 | 295 | 446 |
| Brewers | 4.68 | 56 | 3 | 4 | 9 | 492 | 473 | 322 | 256 | 287 | 439 |
| Mariners | 4.78 | 54 | 0 | 1 | 9 | 459 | 458 | 338 | 244 | 228 | 405 |

### CLUB FIELDING

| | PCT | PO | A | E | DP | | PCT | PO | A | E | DP |
|---|---|---|---|---|---|---|---|---|---|---|---|
| Cardinals | .958 | 1391 | 552 | 85 | 39 | Mariners | .945 | 1377 | 593 | 114 | 40 |
| Angels | .954 | 1449 | 561 | 98 | 46 | Athletics | .942 | 1434 | 572 | 123 | 43 |
| Brewers | .951 | 1477 | 663 | 111 | 45 | Padres | .940 | 1429 | 532 | 125 | 36 |
| Giants | .951 | 1467 | 644 | 109 | 62 | Rockies | .937 | 1371 | 595 | 133 | 43 |

### INDIVIDUAL BATTING LEADERS
(Minimum 149 Plate Appearances)

| | AVG | G | AB | R | H | 2B | 3B | HR | RBI | BB | SO | SB |
|---|---|---|---|---|---|---|---|---|---|---|---|---|
| Jones, John, Athletics | .341 | 50 | 170 | 38 | 58 | 9 | 3 | 5 | 39 | 28 | 33 | 1 |
| Galarza, Joel, Giants | .326 | 42 | 132 | 26 | 43 | 12 | 3 | 3 | 26 | 17 | 26 | 4 |
| Henderson, Juan, Angels | .323 | 54 | 192 | 37 | 62 | 11 | 3 | 1 | 16 | 29 | 29 | 10 |
| Cook, Jason, Mariners | .319 | 45 | 160 | 31 | 51 | 10 | 4 | 2 | 24 | 16 | 20 | 9 |
| Garcia, Franklin, Brewers | .314 | 56 | 236 | 43 | 74 | 5 | 3 | 1 | 32 | 25 | 31 | 36 |
| Deleon, Santo, Mariners | .309 | 43 | 152 | 31 | 47 | 5 | 4 | 1 | 15 | 16 | 32 | 19 |
| Sanchez, Cecilio, Brewers | .302 | 44 | 149 | 22 | 45 | 6 | 2 | 0 | 23 | 7 | 29 | 6 |
| Espinal, Juan, Padres | .301 | 37 | 136 | 23 | 41 | 11 | 1 | 2 | 19 | 15 | 40 | 3 |
| Herrick, Jason, Angels | .301 | 56 | 196 | 34 | 59 | 9 | 4 | 3 | 36 | 41 | 51 | 5 |
| Garcia, Vincente, Rockies | .299 | 38 | 137 | 13 | 41 | 10 | 0 | 0 | 13 | 18 | 27 | 12 |

### INDIVIDUAL PITCHING LEADERS
(Minimum 44 Innings)

| | W | L | ERA | G | GS | CG | SV | IP | H | R | ER | BB | SO |
|---|---|---|---|---|---|---|---|---|---|---|---|---|---|
| Myers, Jason, Giants | 8 | 1 | 1.69 | 13 | 13 | 0 | 0 | 75 | 50 | 19 | 14 | 16 | 105 |
| Duncan, DeVohn, Padres | 3 | 3 | 1.96 | 13 | 7 | 1 | 3 | 46 | 37 | 18 | 10 | 28 | 39 |
| Welch, Travis, Cardinals | 7 | 1 | 2.24 | 10 | 10 | 0 | 0 | 57 | 44 | 14 | 13 | 12 | 67 |
| Ramirez, Rafael, Cardinals | 2 | 2 | 2.34 | 9 | 9 | 0 | 0 | 50 | 49 | 18 | 13 | 16 | 41 |
| Barnes, Keith, Rockies | 5 | 4 | 2.67 | 11 | 11 | 1 | 0 | 61 | 60 | 30 | 18 | 14 | 38 |
| Aguirre, Jose, Angels | 5 | 5 | 2.75 | 11 | 11 | 5 | 0 | 72 | 51 | 29 | 22 | 18 | 62 |
| Garrett, Neil, Rockies | 1 | 1 | 2.91 | 11 | 10 | 1 | 0 | 56 | 50 | 27 | 18 | 10 | 42 |
| Tijerina, Tano, Brewers | 6 | 1 | 2.94 | 10 | 10 | 1 | 0 | 64 | 51 | 34 | 21 | 24 | 55 |
| Montgomery, Trent, A's | 4 | 3 | 3.22 | 15 | 7 | 0 | 0 | 58 | 51 | 30 | 20 | 19 | 41 |
| Domenico, Brian, A's | 4 | 1 | 3.27 | 15 | 11 | 0 | 1 | 60 | 47 | 27 | 21 | 39 | 59 |

## DEPARTMENT LEADERS

### BATTING
| | | |
|---|---|---|
| R | Julio Vargas, Athletics | 46 |
| H | Franklin Garcia, Brewers | 73 |
| TB | John Jones, Athletics | 88 |
| 2B | 2 tied at | 14 |
| 3B | 2 tied at | 6 |
| HR | 3 tied at | 5 |
| RBI | Jay Canizaro, Giants | 41 |
| SH | Orlando Rodriguez, Angels | 7 |
| SF | 4 tied at | 5 |
| BB | Jason Herrick, Angels | 41 |
| IBB | 3 tied at | 3 |
| HBP | Derrick Cantrell, Brewers | 15 |
| SO | Francisco Cruz, Padres | 58 |
| SB | Franklin Garcia, Brewers | 36 |
| CS | Franklin Garcia, Brewers | 10 |
| GIDP | Hommy Mazara, Angels | 14 |
| OB% | John Jones, Athletics | .438 |
| SL% | Joel Galarza, Giants | .530 |

### PITCHING
| | | |
|---|---|---|
| G | Keith Conway, Cardinals | 28 |
| GS | 2 tied at | 14 |
| CG | Jose Aguirre, Angels | 5 |
| ShO | Andy Paul, Brewers | 2 |
| GF | Troy Barrick, Cardinals | 23 |
| Sv | Troy Barrick, Cardinals | 12 |
| W | Jason Myers, Giants | 8 |
| L | Doug Walls, Rockies | 7 |
| IP | Gustavo Gil, Athletics | 76 |
| H | Kevin Krause, Brewers | 72 |
| R | Michael McMullen, Giants | 60 |
| ER | Michael McMullen, Giants | 45 |
| HR | Gustavo Gil, Athletics | 6 |
| BB | Michael McMullen, Giants | 53 |
| HB | Stan Golden, Mariners | 9 |
| SO | Jason Myers, Giants | 105 |
| WP | 3 tied at | 14 |
| Bk | Juan Jaen, Brewers | 5 |

### FIELDING
| | | |
|---|---|---|
| C AVG | Randy Ortega, Athletics | .990 |
| E | Mike Stadler, Padres | 10 |
| 1B AVG | Isaias Nunez, Cardinals | .991 |
| E | Jose Cedeno, Rockies | 12 |
| 2B AVG | Vincente Garcia, Rockies | .973 |
| E | Ruben Jimenez, Cardinals | 12 |
| 3B AVG | Dave Madsen, Cardinals | .966 |
| E | 2 tied at | 26 |
| SS AVG | Juan Henderson, Angels | .927 |
| E | Juan Johnson, Giants | 22 |
| OF AVG | Don Denbow, Giants | .983 |
| E | 2 tied at | 7 |

## HONOR ROLL

**OFFICIAL ALL-STAR TEAM**
| | |
|---|---|
| C | Joel Galarza, Giants |
| 1B | Harold Herdocia, Angels |
| 2B | Franklin Garcia, Brewers |
| 3B | Dave Madsen, Cardinals |
| SS | Juan Henderson, Angels |
| OF | Tony Dermendziev, Rockies |
| | Jason Herrick, Angels |
| | Alex Rivera, Padres |
| | Jose Soriano, Athletics |
| DH | John Jones, Athletics |
| LHP | Jason Myers, Giants |
| RHP | Gustavo Gil, Athletics |
| LHRP | Bret Morfin, Giants |
| RHRP | Jose Carrasco, Angels |

**MVP:** Jason Myers, Giants

**Manager:** Roy Silver, Cardinals

**TOP 5 PROSPECTS**
(Selected by league managers)
1. Derrek Lee, 1b, Padres
2. Jason Myers, lhp, Giants
3. Jose Soriano, of, Athletics
4. Matt LaChappa, lhp, Padres
5. Juan Henderson, ss, Angels

# Rangers Romp To Rookie League Crown

**By DAVID HARDEE**

The Rangers enjoyed the Gulf Coast League's best overall record in 1993 and swept the Astros in the best-of-3 championship series to win their first title since 1984.

The Rangers went 40-20 and won the Western Division by 7½ games over the White Sox. They swept the Astros in two straight games, winning 3-0 and 10-2. The Astros upset the Mets in a one-game semifinal to reach the championship round.

Rangers manager Chino Cadahia, in his eighth season as Rangers manager, earned manager-of-the-year honors after finishing sixth in the West in 1992.

Mike Bell

"Right from the start I knew this team was special," Cadahia said. "It's the best talent I've ever had, certainly the best in Rookie ball."

The parent Texas Rangers stocked their GCL affiliate with the first seven picks from the 1993 draft, none older than 18.

Top pick Mike Bell, who led the league in hits (73) and total bases (107), keyed an eighth-inning rally with a two-run single that put the deciding game out of reach.

Bell, son of former major league third baseman Buddy Bell, was voted the league's No. 2 prospect after leading the league in hitting much of the season only to finish at .317.

Bell's teammate, righthander Julio Santana, a converted outfielder, was named the league's top prospect in a managers survey. Santana was 4-1 with a 1.38

ERA and seven saves in 26 regular season appearances. He made the transition to closer after three unproductive years in the Dominican Summer League.

The league retained its same three-division, 15-team format from 1992. The Cubs replaced the Dodgers in the Eastern Division, while Kansas City's departure from its Baseball City complex and Boston's departure from its longtime spring-training home in Winter Haven for its new complex in Fort Myers forced a shakeup in the alliance of the other two divisions. The New York Yankees and Toronto moved from the Western to Central Division.

## LEAGUE CHAMPIONS

**Last 25 Years**

| Year | Regular Season* | Pct. | Playoff |
|------|------------------|------|---------|
| 1969 | Expos | .585 | None |
| 1970 | White Sox | .600 | None |
| 1971 | Royals | .755 | None |
| 1972 | Cubs | .651 | None |
|      | Royals | .651 | |
| 1973 | Rangers | .732 | None |
| 1974 | Cubs | .702 | None |
| 1975 | Rangers | .774 | None |
| 1976 | Rangers | .704 | None |
| 1977 | White Sox | .731 | None |
| 1978 | Rangers | .600 | None |
| 1979 | Astros | .635 | None |
| 1980 | Royals Blue | .635 | None |
| 1981 | Royals Gold | .688 | None |
| 1982 | Yankees | .667 | None |
| 1983 | Rangers | .645 | Dodgers |
| 1984 | White Sox | .651 | Rangers |
| 1985 | Yankees | .705 | None |
| 1986 | Reds | .548 | Dodgers |
| 1987 | Dodgers | .683 | Dodgers |
| 1988 | Yankees | .714 | Yankees |
| 1989 | Yankees | .651 | Yankees |
| 1990 | Expos | .635 | Dodgers |
| 1991 | Orioles | .593 | Expos |
| 1992 | Royals | .695 | Royals |
| 1993 | Rangers | .667 | Rangers |

*Best overall record

## STANDINGS

| Page | EAST | Complex Site | W | L | PCT | GB | Manager(s) | Last Pennant |
|------|------|--------------|---|---|-----|-----|------------|--------------|
| 160 | Mets | St. Lucie | 39 | 20 | .661 | — | Junior Roman | None |
| 53 | Braves | West Palm Beach | 32 | 26 | .552 | 6 ½ | Jim Saul | 1964 |
| 148 | Expos | West Palm Beach | 27 | 31 | .466 | 11 ½ | Nelson Norman | 1991 |
| 84 | Cubs | St. Lucie | 19 | 40 | .322 | 20 | Butch Hughes | None |

| Page | NORTH | Complex Site | W | L | PCT | GB | Manager(s) | Last Pennant |
|------|-------|--------------|---|---|-----|-----|------------|--------------|
| 118 | Astros | Kissimmee | 35 | 24 | .593 | — | Julio Linares | 1979 |
| 112 | Marlins | Kissimmee | 32 | 28 | .533 | 3 ½ | Jim Hendry | None |
| 154 | Yankees | Tampa | 30 | 29 | .508 | 5 | Glenn Sherlock | 1989 |
| 215 | Blue Jays | Dunedin | 22 | 38 | .367 | 13 ½ | Hector Torres | None |

| Page | WEST | Complex Site | W | L | PCT | GB | Manager(s) | Last Pennant |
|------|------|--------------|---|---|-----|-----|------------|--------------|
| 209 | Rangers | Port Charlotte | 40 | 20 | .667 | — | Chino Cadahia | 1993 |
| 77 | White Sox | Sarasota | 32 | 27 | .542 | 7 ½ | Mike Rojas | 1977 |
| 65 | Red Sox | Fort Myers | 32 | 28 | .533 | 8 | Felix Maldonado | None |
| 59 | Orioles | Sarasota | 30 | 28 | .517 | 9 | Oneri Fleita | None |
| 124 | Royals | Fort Myers | 29 | 30 | .492 | 10 ½ | Bob Herold | 1992 |
| 142 | Twins | Fort Myers | 23 | 36 | .390 | 16 ½ | Jose Marzan | None |
| 178 | Pirates | Bradenton | 21 | 38 | .356 | 18 ½ | Woody Huyke | None |

**PLAYOFFS—Semifinal:** Astros defeated Mets in one-game series. **Finals:** Rangers defeated Astros, 2-0, in best-of-3 series.
**NOTE:** Team's individual batting and pitching statistics can be found on page indicated in lefthand column.

# GULF COAST LEAGUE
## 1993 BATTING, PITCHING STATISTICS

### CLUB BATTING

| | AVG | G | AB | R | H | 2B | 3B | HR | BB | SO | SB |
|---|---|---|---|---|---|---|---|---|---|---|---|
| Marlins | .261 | 60 | 2028 | 318 | 529 | 85 | 16 | 12 | 213 | 389 | 60 |
| Astros | .261 | 59 | 1990 | 286 | 520 | 95 | 24 | 7 | 187 | 367 | 76 |
| Rangers | .255 | 60 | 1924 | 313 | 491 | 75 | 29 | 12 | 258 | 350 | 133 |
| Mets | .250 | 59 | 1962 | 314 | 491 | 85 | 21 | 11 | 259 | 361 | 100 |
| Expos | .247 | 58 | 1959 | 249 | 484 | 72 | 15 | 18 | 208 | 413 | 40 |
| Braves | .246 | 58 | 1921 | 275 | 472 | 74 | 19 | 12 | 178 | 348 | 66 |
| Red Sox | .244 | 60 | 1988 | 241 | 485 | 89 | 13 | 11 | 217 | 355 | 53 |
| Royals | .242 | 59 | 1945 | 235 | 471 | 77 | 22 | 12 | 155 | 392 | 78 |
| White Sox | .242 | 59 | 1910 | 281 | 463 | 87 | 24 | 13 | 293 | 389 | 115 |
| Cubs | .238 | 59 | 1848 | 243 | 440 | 54 | 14 | 8 | 222 | 364 | 92 |
| Blue Jays | .237 | 60 | 1976 | 235 | 469 | 87 | 21 | 8 | 178 | 438 | 76 |
| Pirates | .237 | 59 | 1929 | 218 | 458 | 72 | 22 | 12 | 187 | 378 | 65 |
| Yankees | .226 | 59 | 1930 | 237 | 436 | 71 | 22 | 14 | 231 | 507 | 79 |
| Twins | .216 | 59 | 1885 | 248 | 408 | 65 | 14 | 12 | 218 | 403 | 66 |
| Orioles | .207 | 58 | 1852 | 200 | 383 | 42 | 16 | 3 | 189 | 438 | 122 |

### CLUB PITCHING

| | ERA | G | CG | SHO | SV | IP | H | R | ER | BB | SO |
|---|---|---|---|---|---|---|---|---|---|---|---|
| White Sox | 2.59 | 59 | 2 | 5 | 15 | 522 | 421 | 202 | 150 | 197 | 406 |
| Red Sox | 2.65 | 60 | 4 | 5 | 12 | 527 | 426 | 212 | 155 | 203 | 479 |
| Royals | 2.72 | 59 | 2 | 4 | 16 | 509 | 446 | 244 | 154 | 202 | 343 |
| Yankees | 2.95 | 59 | 2 | 2 | 13 | 512 | 451 | 249 | 168 | 168 | 449 |
| Expos | 2.99 | 58 | 6 | 7 | 12 | 518 | 437 | 239 | 172 | 224 | 338 |
| Rangers | 3.06 | 60 | 3 | 6 | 16 | 515 | 474 | 234 | 175 | 178 | 368 |
| Braves | 3.19 | 58 | 0 | 3 | 14 | 505 | 421 | 262 | 179 | 248 | 455 |
| Astros | 3.22 | 59 | 4 | 3 | 15 | 509 | 472 | 252 | 182 | 205 | 430 |
| Mets | 3.27 | 59 | 0 | 5 | 20 | 521 | 476 | 239 | 189 | 189 | 372 |
| Marlins | 3.29 | 60 | 1 | 2 | 13 | 519 | 506 | 239 | 190 | 196 | 422 |
| Orioles | 3.39 | 58 | 2 | 5 | 16 | 505 | 440 | 251 | 190 | 227 | 337 |
| Pirates | 3.46 | 59 | 0 | 2 | 12 | 505 | 464 | 288 | 194 | 238 | 398 |
| Twins | 3.88 | 59 | 4 | 0 | 14 | 497 | 488 | 305 | 214 | 272 | 374 |
| Cubs | 4.42 | 59 | 0 | 1 | 7 | 509 | 553 | 341 | 250 | 206 | 321 |
| Blue Jays | 4.68 | 60 | 2 | 2 | 13 | 512 | 525 | 336 | 266 | 240 | 400 |

### CLUB FIELDING

| | PCT | PO | A | E | DP | | PCT | PO | A | E | DP |
|---|---|---|---|---|---|---|---|---|---|---|---|
| Marlins | .961 | 1558 | 670 | 90 | 57 | Blue Jays | .949 | 1536 | 700 | 119 | 48 |
| Expos | .960 | 1555 | 750 | 95 | 53 | Royals | .949 | 1526 | 672 | 118 | 37 |
| Rangers | .959 | 1545 | 693 | 95 | 50 | Braves | .946 | 1514 | 596 | 121 | 42 |
| White Sox | .959 | 1565 | 637 | 94 | 45 | Astros | .944 | 1526 | 660 | 130 | 48 |
| Mets | .957 | 1562 | 637 | 99 | 54 | Twins | .943 | 1491 | 574 | 125 | 31 |
| Red Sox | .956 | 1580 | 662 | 102 | 46 | Cubs | .939 | 1526 | 602 | 138 | 48 |
| Orioles | .955 | 1514 | 651 | 101 | 49 | Pirates | .938 | 1516 | 631 | 142 | 37 |
| Yankees | .950 | 1537 | 642 | 115 | 30 | | | | | | |

### INDIVIDUAL BATTING LEADERS
(Minimum 159 Plate Appearances)

| | AVG | G | AB | R | H | 2B | 3B | HR | RBI | BB | SO | SB |
|---|---|---|---|---|---|---|---|---|---|---|---|---|
| Ephan, Larry, Rangers | .350 | 56 | 180 | 42 | 63 | 16 | 2 | 1 | 38 | 41 | 30 | 0 |
| Lobaton, Jose, Yankees | .345 | 44 | 165 | 30 | 57 | 8 | 6 | 1 | 16 | 19 | 28 | 24 |
| Rodriguez, Maximo, Marlins | .326 | 48 | 187 | 30 | 61 | 8 | 5 | 0 | 29 | 10 | 26 | 3 |
| Jackson, Gavin, Red Sox | .318 | 41 | 157 | 29 | 50 | 7 | 2 | 0 | 11 | 14 | 18 | 11 |
| Bell, Mike, Rangers | .317 | 60 | 230 | 48 | 73 | 13 | 6 | 3 | 34 | 27 | 23 | 9 |
| Mendez, Carlos, Royals | .313 | 50 | 163 | 18 | 51 | 10 | 0 | 4 | 27 | 4 | 15 | 6 |
| Catlett, David, Braves | .311 | 54 | 193 | 33 | 60 | 11 | 2 | 5 | 33 | 31 | 19 | 11 |
| Aranzamendi, Alex, Marlins | .309 | 42 | 149 | 13 | 46 | 8 | 0 | 2 | 31 | 13 | 17 | 1 |
| Diaz, Edwin, Braves | .305 | 43 | 154 | 27 | 47 | 10 | 5 | 1 | 23 | 19 | 21 | 12 |
| Ramirez, Juan, Mets | .304 | 52 | 204 | 37 | 62 | 4 | 3 | 2 | 31 | 15 | 45 | 10 |

### INDIVIDUAL PITCHING LEADERS
(Minimum 47 Innings)

| | W | L | ERA | G | GS | CG | SV | IP | H | R | ER | BB | SO |
|---|---|---|---|---|---|---|---|---|---|---|---|---|---|
| Lombardi, John, Orioles | 7 | 1 | 0.92 | 10 | 10 | 0 | 0 | 59 | 32 | 10 | 6 | 27 | 45 |
| Atwater, Joe, Mets | 7 | 1 | 0.93 | 11 | 10 | 0 | 0 | 58 | 44 | 9 | 6 | 6 | 44 |
| Miller, Jerrod, Braves | 5 | 2 | 1.17 | 13 | 7 | 0 | 0 | 51 | 31 | 12 | 6 | 16 | 43 |
| Taveras, Roberto, Expos | 2 | 4 | 1.48 | 17 | 5 | 0 | 3 | 55 | 52 | 21 | 9 | 18 | 37 |
| Rusch, Glendon, Royals | 4 | 2 | 1.60 | 11 | 10 | 0 | 0 | 62 | 43 | 14 | 11 | 11 | 48 |
| Gordon, Mike, Yankees | 4 | 2 | 1.67 | 11 | 9 | 0 | 0 | 65 | 43 | 23 | 12 | 27 | 61 |
| Pinango, Simon, Red Sox | 0 | 4 | 1.73 | 13 | 7 | 0 | 1 | 52 | 36 | 17 | 10 | 17 | 58 |
| Reid, Rayon, Pirates | 4 | 3 | 1.74 | 13 | 8 | 0 | 1 | 62 | 50 | 16 | 12 | 15 | 39 |
| Cafaro, Rocco, Orioles | 2 | 2 | 1.79 | 14 | 8 | 1 | 1 | 81 | 58 | 21 | 16 | 12 | 57 |
| Hodges, Kevin, Royals | 7 | 2 | 2.23 | 12 | 10 | 0 | 0 | 71 | 52 | 25 | 16 | 25 | 40 |

## DEPARTMENT LEADERS

### BATTING
| | | |
|---|---|---|
| R | Tomas Arvelo, Mets | 50 |
| H | Mike Bell, Rangers | 73 |
| TB | Mike Bell, Rangers | 107 |
| 2B | Larry Ephan, Rangers | 16 |
| 3B | Leland Macon, Rangers | 7 |
| HR | Marc Niethammer, Expos | 6 |
| RBI | Larry Ephan, Rangers | 39 |
| SH | Joe Scopio, Cubs | 9 |
| SF | Travion Nelson, Yankees | 8 |
| BB | Larry Ephan, Rangers | 41 |
| IBB | Larry Ephan, Rangers | 3 |
| HBP | Leland Macon, Rangers | 13 |
| SO | Craig McClure, White Sox | 66 |
| SB | Yudith Ozario, Mets | 39 |
| CS | Yudith Ozario, Mets | 11 |
| GIDP | Andrew Vessel, Rangers | 10 |
| OB% | Larry Ephan, Rangers | .485 |
| SL% | Jose Lobaton, Yankees | .485 |

### PITCHING
| | | |
|---|---|---|
| G | Julio Santana, Rangers | 26 |
| GS | 5 tied at | 12 |
| CG | Jayson Durocher, Expos | 3 |
| ShO | Jayson Durocher, Expos | 2 |
| GF | Robert DeBrino, Twins | 19 |
| Sv | Robert DeBrino, Twins | 11 |
| W | 4 tied at | 7 |
| L | 2 tied at | 8 |
| IP | Rocco Cafaro, Orioles | 81 |
| H | Antonio Geraldo, Blue Jays | 81 |
| R | Mike Lane, Orioles | 49 |
| ER | Mike Lane, Orioles | 37 |
| HR | 2 tied at | 5 |
| BB | 2 tied at | 43 |
| HB | 6 tied at | 8 |
| SO | Jason Tatar, Twins | 73 |
| WP | 3 tied at | 11 |
| Bk | Alfredo Garcia, Cubs | 5 |

### FIELDING
| | | |
|---|---|---|
| C AVG | Kevin Clark, Red Sox | .983 |
| E | Pasqual Matos, Braves | 10 |
| 1B AVG | Ray Williams, Rangers | .992 |
| E | Quvia Samuel, Yankees | 14 |
| 2B AVG | Ralph Milliard, Marlins | .984 |
| E | 2 tied at | 12 |
| 3B AVG | Guillermo Mota, Mets | .943 |
| E | David Gibralter, Red Sox | 20 |
| SS AVG | Tomas Perez, Expos | .964 |
| E | Jamie Saylor, Astros | 26 |
| OF AVG | Josue Estrada, Expos | 1.000 |
| E | 6 tied at | 6 |

## HONOR ROLL

### OFFICIAL ALL-STAR TEAM
| | |
|---|---|
| C | Larry Ephan, Rangers |
| 1B | David Catlett, Braves |
| 2B | Carlos Cabrera, Blue Jays |
| 3B | Mike Bell, Rangers |
| SS | Gavin Jackson, Red Sox |
| OF | Romulo Vizcaino, Twins |
| | Charles Peterson, Pirates |
| | Juan Ramirez, Mets |
| SP | John Lombardi, Orioles |
| RP | Julio Santana, Rangers |

**Manager:** Chino Cadahia, Rangers

### TOP 10 PROSPECTS
(Selected by league managers)
1. Julio Santana, rhp, Rangers
2. Mike Bell, 3b, Rangers
3. Charles Peterson, of, Pirates
4. Jason Green, rhp, Braves
5. Jeff Suppan, rhp, Red Sox
6. Andrew Vessel, of, Rangers
7. Mike Gordon, rhp, Yankees
8. Jermaine Dye, of, Braves
9. Gavin Jackson, ss, Red Sox
10. David Gibralter, 3b, Red Sox

# DOMINICAN SUMMER LEAGUE

## Dodgers Upend Blue Jays For Second Title

The Toronto Blue Jays achieved the sweet taste of victory again in 1993, but a championship eluded their powerful Dominican Summer League farm team for the second straight year.

Toronto East, one of two Blue Jays entries in the 22-team league, compiled the best overall record for the second year in a row but were beaten by the defending-champion Dodgers II, 3-1, in a best-of-5 final. The Jays had gone 50-17 (.746) and won the Santo Domingo Eastern Division race by 12½ games.

In 1992, Toronto East posted the best record in professional baseball history, going a gaudy 68-2 (.971), but promptly lost two straight playoff games to Oakland, which in turn lost to Dodgers II.

The Blue Jays-Dodgers final marked a showdown between the two most aggressive organizations in terms of securing Dominican talent. A rival third group surfaced from an unexpected source in 1993.

Japan's Hiroshima Toyo Carp, vigorously trying to get a foothold in the Dominican Republic, entered a team in the San Pedro de Macoris Division and won by a commanding 10-game margin. The Carp's 52 wins were the most in the league, though Toronto East beat the upstart Japanese in the playoffs.

The Carp boasted the league's MVP, outfielder Charlies Pena, who hit .372 and led the league with 105 hits and 69 RBIs.

The Dominican Summer League, in its ninth year of sponsorship by major league clubs and fielding its largest-ever contingent of teams, is a feeder program for Hispanic players not ready to participate in American professional leagues. All but three clubs—Boston, Cincinnati and Minnesota—fielded clubs, some as joint entries.

### STANDINGS

| SANTO DOMINGO EAST | W | L | PCT | GB |
|---|---|---|---|---|
| Blue Jays East | 50 | 17 | .746 | — |
| Dodgers I | 39 | 31 | .537 | 12½ |
| Mariners | 34 | 34 | .500 | 16½ |
| Expos | 29 | 38 | .433 | 21 |
| Brewers | 27 | 40 | .403 | 23 |
| Marlins | 25 | 44 | .362 | 26 |
| **SANTO DOMINGO WEST** | **W** | **L** | **PCT** | **GB** |
| Athletics | 49 | 23 | .681 | — |
| Mets | 48 | 24 | .667 | 1 |
| Pirates | 39 | 29 | .574 | 6 |
| Yankees/Padres | 33 | 36 | .478 | 14½ |
| Tigers/Cardinals | 34 | 30 | .472 | 15 |
| Blue Jays West | 26 | 44 | .371 | 22 |
| Cubs/Rangers | 17 | 52 | .246 | 30½ |
| **SAN PEDRO DE MACORIS** | **W** | **L** | **PCT** | **GB** |
| Toyo Carp (Japan) | 52 | 18 | .743 | — |
| Angels | 42 | 28 | .600 | 10 |
| Orioles/White Sox | 36 | 34 | .514 | 16 |
| Astros | 35 | 35 | .500 | 17 |
| Braves | 28 | 42 | .400 | 24 |
| Giants/Phillies/Astros | 17 | 53 | .243 | 35 |
| **CIBAO** | **W** | **L** | **PCT** | **GB** |
| Dodgers II | 42 | 28 | .600 | — |
| Indians | 39 | 31 | .557 | 3 |
| Royals/Rockies | 24 | 46 | .343 | 18 |

**PLAYOFFS—Semifinals:** Blue Jays East defeated Toyo Carp, 2-0, and Dodgers II defeated Oakland, 2-0, in best-of-3 series. **Finals:** Dodgers II defeated Blue Jays, 3-1, in best-of-5 series.

**ALL-STAR TEAM: C**—Ramon Sosa, Indians. **1B**—Juan Jose Martinez, Blue Jays East. **2B**—Jose Alcantara, Toyo Carp. **3B**—Junior Abreu, Brewers. **SS**—Fausto Solano, Blue Jays East. **OF**—Charlies Pena, Toyo Carp; Kadil Villalona, Blue Jays East; Felix Rosario, Blue Jays East. **DH**—Mauro Zerpa, White Sox. **RHP**—Hernan Silva, Athletics. **LHP**—Erick Ojeda, Mets. **Manager**—Antonio Bautista, Dodgers II.

**Most Valuable Player**—Charlies Pena, Toyo Carp.
**Outstanding Pitcher**—Hernan Silva, Athletics.

### INDIVIDUAL BATTING LEADERS
(Minimum 170 Plate Appearances)

| | AVG | AB | R | H | 2B | 3B | HR | RBI | SB |
|---|---|---|---|---|---|---|---|---|---|
| Abreu, Junior, Brewers | .403 | 243 | 45 | 98 | 12 | 3 | 5 | 39 | 17 |
| Zerpa, Mauro, Orioles/WSox | .377 | 159 | 34 | 60 | 10 | 0 | 5 | 32 | 5 |
| Garcia, Miguel, Indians | .376 | 173 | 41 | 65 | 14 | 5 | 0 | 29 | 8 |
| Pena, Charlies, Toyo Carp | .372 | 282 | 74 | 105 | 22 | 7 | 10 | 69 | 13 |
| Mendoza, Jesus, Orioles/WSox | .371 | 248 | 62 | 92 | 17 | 1 | 8 | 52 | 11 |
| Cesar, Angel, Dodgers I | .367 | 240 | 54 | 88 | 14 | 6 | 2 | 46 | 9 |
| Villalona, Kadil, Blue Jays East | .361 | 249 | 52 | 90 | 8 | 6 | 5 | 45 | 17 |
| Vilomar, Henry, Mets | .355 | 242 | 47 | 86 | 13 | 3 | 6 | 38 | 12 |
| Domingo, Salomon, Braves | .353 | 215 | 32 | 76 | 23 | 2 | 0 | 26 | 8 |
| Mota, Alfonzo, Angels | .348 | 224 | 56 | 78 | 17 | 3 | 2 | 46 | 13 |
| Lara, Edward, Athletics | .343 | 198 | 24 | 68 | 7 | 4 | 1 | 34 | 5 |
| Almonte, Waddy, Orioles/WSox | .342 | 222 | 53 | 76 | 19 | 0 | 7 | 41 | 4 |
| Nunez, Sergio, Royals/Rockies | .341 | 249 | 63 | 85 | 18 | 2 | 2 | 35 | 32 |
| Faneyte, Reynaldo, BJays East | .341 | 182 | 30 | 62 | 10 | 3 | 6 | 35 | 5 |
| Brown, Alfonso, Dodgers I | .339 | 227 | 45 | 77 | 9 | 5 | 2 | 56 | 14 |
| Roche, Marlon, Astros | .338 | 204 | 46 | 69 | 13 | 3 | 1 | 37 | 7 |
| Sanchez, Omar, Blue Jays East | .333 | 225 | 66 | 75 | 8 | 4 | 0 | 30 | 40 |
| Alcantara, Jose, Toyo Carp | .332 | 283 | 74 | 94 | 11 | 6 | 2 | 41 | 46 |
| Bonilla, Ramon, Athletics | .324 | 182 | 33 | 59 | 12 | 1 | 0 | 26 | 5 |
| Pimentel, Jose, Dodgers I | .324 | 216 | 45 | 70 | 6 | 2 | 5 | 35 | 9 |
| Portes, Miguel, Yankees/Padres | .322 | 214 | 35 | 69 | 3 | 0 | 3 | 28 | 14 |
| Agnoly, Earl, Marlins | .321 | 246 | 49 | 79 | 9 | 4 | 0 | 28 | 20 |
| Ramirez, Daniel, Mets | .321 | 271 | 48 | 87 | 14 | 3 | 3 | 50 | 23 |
| Blanco, Tirso, Astros | .320 | 172 | 47 | 55 | 9 | 0 | 6 | 36 | 13 |
| Patrone, Carlos, Braves | .319 | 166 | 21 | 53 | 14 | 0 | 2 | 24 | 1 |
| Rodriguez, Miguel, Athletics | .319 | 160 | 51 | 51 | 7 | 3 | 4 | 26 | 18 |
| Fernandez, Jose M., Expos | .319 | 251 | 40 | 80 | 8 | 1 | 10 | 49 | 2 |
| Solano, Fausto, Blue Jays East | .318 | 264 | 79 | 84 | 8 | 1 | 7 | 26 | 25 |
| Castillo, Amaury, Astros | .318 | 211 | 26 | 67 | 11 | 0 | 4 | 38 | 2 |
| Henriquez, Ramon, Tigers/Card. | .317 | 205 | 30 | 65 | 10 | 2 | 9 | 50 | 3 |

### INDIVIDUAL PITCHING LEADERS
(Minimum 50 Innings)

| | W | L | ERA | G | SV | IP | H | BB | SO |
|---|---|---|---|---|---|---|---|---|---|
| Avila, Edwin, Angels | 4 | 2 | 1.09 | 18 | 4 | 83 | 54 | 28 | 78 |
| Silva, Hernan, Athletics | 7 | 2 | 1.40 | 14 | 0 | 90 | 57 | 27 | 62 |
| Duran, Juan, Toyo Carp | 5 | 1 | 1.55 | 18 | 6 | 58 | 45 | 15 | 34 |
| Aracena, Ramon, Toyo Carp | 7 | 2 | 1.59 | 13 | 0 | 85 | 66 | 25 | 54 |
| Martinez, Gustavo, Dodgers II | 8 | 4 | 1.83 | 14 | 0 | 89 | 72 | 21 | 44 |
| Ramirez, Felipe, Toyo Carp | 4 | 4 | 1.95 | 18 | 1 | 111 | 87 | 44 | 96 |
| Perez, Angel, Angels | 3 | 4 | 2.00 | 21 | 8 | 63 | 49 | 12 | 35 |
| Linares, Mario, Toyo Carp | 7 | 0 | 2.18 | 21 | 3 | 70 | 60 | 42 | 34 |
| Balbuena, Roberto, Cubs/Rangers | 3 | 6 | 2.20 | 25 | 6 | 65 | 64 | 28 | 54 |
| Lois, Newman, Astros | 3 | 2 | 2.21 | 15 | 0 | 90 | 65 | 41 | 60 |
| Acosta, Roberto, Blue Jays East | 7 | 4 | 2.25 | 19 | 4 | 76 | 74 | 19 | 42 |
| Colome, Jesus, Cubs/Rangers | 5 | 5 | 2.31 | 16 | 0 | 97 | 81 | 46 | 58 |
| Pena, Jesus, Pirates | 6 | 3 | 2.37 | 18 | 2 | 68 | 48 | 51 | 79 |
| Dore, Johnny, Blue Jays West | 4 | 5 | 2.39 | 14 | 0 | 75 | 64 | 23 | 47 |
| Sanchez, Jesus, Mets | 7 | 3 | 2.40 | 16 | 0 | 82 | 63 | 36 | 94 |
| Fuente, Joel, Yankees/Padres | 6 | 2 | 2.43 | 10 | 0 | 56 | 47 | 22 | 56 |
| Ojeda, Erick, Mets | 6 | 1 | 2.55 | 13 | 0 | 74 | 47 | 34 | 84 |
| Betancourt, Damaso, Dodgers I | 4 | 3 | 2.57 | 24 | 6 | 74 | 55 | 29 | 75 |
| Colon, Bartolo, Indians | 6 | 1 | 2.59 | 11 | 1 | 66 | 44 | 33 | 43 |
| Mesa, Rafael, Indians | 7 | 2 | 2.63 | 16 | 1 | 72 | 65 | 18 | 51 |

# FOREIGN, INDEPENDENT LEAGUES

# NORTHERN
## LEAGUE

# Triumphant Return For Old League

Year One of the Northern League's revival proved wildly successful, both on the field and at the gate.

With the St. Paul Saints leading the way, the six-team independent league packed long-dormant stadiums in the Upper Midwest in 1993 and provided second chances to dozens of players.

St. Paul, featuring the promotional wizardry of team

**Mike Veeck**

president Mike Veeck, sold 97 percent of all available tickets at 5,069-seat Municipal Stadium, finishing the season with 22 straight sellouts. The Saints then capped a second-half surge by defeating first-half champion Rochester in four games to win the best-of-5 championship series.

"I love St. Paul," Veeck said. "They've embraced the silliness, and in the process this place has already stolen a piece of my heart."

Saints first baseman-DH Leon Durham, 36, led the league with 11 home runs, then rapped eight hits in the playoffs. Durham, the former Cubs and Reds slugger, came back after 2½ years out of the game.

Durham's equal in name recognition was Pedro Guerrero, who joined the Sioux Falls Canaries several weeks into the season. Guerrero, the former Dodgers and Cardinals star, signed on after being suspended, then released by the Mexican League.

After some initial resentment, Guerrero's stay in Sioux Falls proved pleasurable, as he batted .278 with three homers and 33 RBIs and even inquired about purchasing the Thunder Bay Whiskey Jacks.

League officials liked to compare the quality of play to Double-A. They got a chance to test that theory when the Reds organization purchased Rochester outfielder Kash Beauchamp and assigned him to Double-A Chattanooga for the final few weeks of the 1993 season. Beauchamp, who batted .367 to win the Northern League batting title, hit .400 with five homers in 60 Chattanooga at-bats.

Every league club sold at least one contract to a major league organization. The Florida Marlins and Colorado Rockies proved particularly hungry for Northern League talent as they attempted to stock Double-A teams for the first time in 1994.

About the only negatives were rampant complaints about local umpiring crews and failed league experiments with a 20-second pitch clock and the limited DH.

"This is the future of minor league baseball," said Duluth manager Mal Fichman, a veteran of the independent scene. "In five years, I'll bet 50 percent of the clubs will be independent. Really. This is great. It's Rotisserie League Live."

**—MIKE BERARDINO**

## STANDINGS

| FIRST HALF | W | L | PCT | GB |
|---|---|---|---|---|
| Rochester Aces | 21 | 15 | .583 | — |
| St. Paul Saints | 19 | 16 | .543 | 1½ |
| Thunder Bay Whiskey Jacks | 19 | 16 | .543 | 1½ |
| Sioux Falls Canaries | 17 | 19 | .472 | 4 |
| Sioux City Explorers | 16 | 20 | .444 | 5 |
| Duluth-Superior Dukes | 15 | 21 | .417 | 6 |

| SECOND HALF | W | L | PCT | GB |
|---|---|---|---|---|
| St. Paul Saints | 23 | 13 | .639 | — |
| Sioux City Explorers | 18 | 18 | .500 | 5 |
| Thunder Bay Whiskey Jacks | 17 | 19 | .472 | 6 |
| Sioux Falls Canaries | 17 | 19 | .472 | 6 |
| Rochester Aces | 17 | 19 | .472 | 6 |
| Duluth-Superior Dukes | 16 | 20 | .444 | 7 |

**CHAMPIONSHIP SERIES:** St. Paul defeated Rochester, 3-1, in best-of-5 final.

**MANAGERS:** Duluth-Superior—Mal Fichman; Rochester—Doug Simunic; St. Paul—Tim Blackwell; Sioux City—Ed Nottle; Sioux Falls—Frank Verdi; Thunder Bay—John Shwan.

### INDIVIDUAL BATTING LEADERS
(Minimum 194 Plate Appearances)

| | AVG | AB | R | H | 2B | 3B | HR | RBI | SB |
|---|---|---|---|---|---|---|---|---|---|
| Beauchamp, Kash, Rochester | .367 | 166 | 32 | 61 | 8 | 1 | 9 | 33 | 2 |
| Ramirez, J.D., Sioux City | .338 | 216 | 30 | 73 | 10 | 1 | 3 | 30 | 5 |
| Todd, Theron, Sioux Falls | .337 | 288 | 49 | 97 | 26 | 1 | 3 | 45 | 13 |
| Farlow, Kevin, Sioux City | .333 | 189 | 42 | 63 | 14 | 1 | 4 | 26 | 8 |
| Aldrete, Rich, Sioux Falls | .328 | 201 | 30 | 66 | 13 | 2 | 4 | 35 | 1 |
| Sawkiw, Warren, Rochester | .327 | 272 | 42 | 89 | 21 | 2 | 9 | 45 | 14 |
| Meadows, Scott, St. Paul | .324 | 250 | 42 | 81 | 11 | 1 | 4 | 43 | 8 |
| Hood, Dennis, Thunder Bay | .322 | 261 | 36 | 84 | 13 | 7 | 7 | 34 | 30 |
| Resetar, Gary, D-S | .319 | 279 | 32 | 89 | 12 | 1 | 1 | 42 | 2 |
| Gallone, Santy, Sioux Falls | .319 | 235 | 51 | 75 | 15 | 0 | 7 | 37 | 13 |

### INDIVIDUAL PITCHING LEADERS
(Minimum 58 Innings)

| | W | L | ERA | G | SV | IP | H | BB | SO |
|---|---|---|---|---|---|---|---|---|---|
| Manfred, Jim, St. Paul | 5 | 4 | 2.06 | 18 | 2 | 74 | 59 | 27 | 52 |
| Cain, Tim, Rochester | 4 | 4 | 2.37 | 20 | 1 | 102 | 76 | 28 | 73 |
| Seo, Yoshi, Thunder Bay | 4 | 4 | 2.37 | 13 | 0 | 65 | 65 | 36 | 41 |
| Thoden, John, St. Paul | 6 | 4 | 2.76 | 16 | 0 | 108 | 103 | 22 | 76 |
| Lewis, Craig, Sioux Falls | 6 | 3 | 2.76 | 14 | 0 | 85 | 83 | 37 | 54 |
| Tilmon, Pat, Thunder Bay | 5 | 4 | 2.86 | 13 | 0 | 79 | 69 | 34 | 62 |
| Kraemer, Joe, Sioux City | 10 | 4 | 2.91 | 16 | 0 | 108 | 100 | 26 | 90 |
| Garcia, Mike, Rochester | 9 | 2 | 2.95 | 16 | 0 | 95 | 89 | 27 | 100 |
| Pollack, Chris, Thunder Bay | 7 | 5 | 3.02 | 13 | 0 | 86 | 75 | 32 | 39 |
| Winawer, Larry, Thunder Bay | 4 | 1 | 3.13 | 16 | 2 | 60 | 67 | 19 | 26 |

## DULUTH-SUPERIOR

| BATTING | AVG | AB | R | H | 2B | 3B | HR | RBI | SB |
|---|---|---|---|---|---|---|---|---|---|
| Blackwell, Juan, 3b | .285 | 137 | 12 | 39 | 4 | 2 | 2 | 15 | 0 |
| Canan, Dick, ss | .306 | 147 | 26 | 45 | 16 | 0 | 6 | 25 | 4 |
| Craddox, Ken, cf | .000 | 5 | 2 | 0 | 0 | 0 | 0 | 0 | 0 |
| Felice, Jason, dh-of (31 TB) | .264 | 220 | 34 | 58 | 16 | 0 | 9 | 44 | 4 |
| Henry, Scott, 1b-3b | .303 | 241 | 38 | 73 | 21 | 1 | 3 | 39 | 1 |
| Holtzclaw, Shawn, of | .184 | 49 | 2 | 9 | 1 | 1 | 0 | 6 | 1 |
| Hubel, Mike, c-of | .219 | 114 | 11 | 25 | 2 | 0 | 1 | 5 | 1 |
| Jackson, Paul, of | .000 | 5 | 0 | 0 | 0 | 0 | 0 | 0 | 0 |
| Kowilcik, Chris, dh-1b | .281 | 260 | 33 | 73 | 12 | 1 | 5 | 31 | 3 |
| North, Tim, 3b-of | .283 | 120 | 16 | 34 | 1 | 0 | 0 | 3 | 4 |
| Resetar, Gary, c-1b | .319 | 279 | 32 | 89 | 12 | 1 | 1 | 42 | 2 |
| Rhein, Jeff, of | .246 | 114 | 23 | 28 | 5 | 3 | 5 | 13 | 6 |
| Roebuck, Joe, of | .258 | 155 | 21 | 40 | 7 | 2 | 5 | 22 | 2 |
| Smedes, Mike, of | .222 | 108 | 9 | 24 | 6 | 0 | 0 | 9 | 1 |
| Tollison, David, 2b | .240 | 250 | 32 | 60 | 9 | 0 | 2 | 30 | 2 |
| Wallace, Tim, ss | .211 | 123 | 17 | 26 | 2 | 0 | 0 | 6 | 3 |
| Williams, Dana, of | .297 | 273 | 40 | 81 | 13 | 3 | 1 | 33 | 11 |

| PITCHER | W | L | ERA | G | SV | IP | H | BB | SO |
|---|---|---|---|---|---|---|---|---|---|
| Abugherir, Amer | 0 | 2 | 8.31 | 4 | 0 | 13 | 20 | 5 | 5 |

| | W | L | ERA | G | SV | IP | H | BB | SO |
|---|---|---|---|---|---|---|---|---|---|
| Collins, Stacey | 5 | 5 | 3.82 | 14 | 0 | 64 | 66 | 28 | 37 |
| LaValley, Todd | 4 | 4 | 3.98 | 18 | 0 | 84 | 72 | 39 | 44 |
| Magria, Javier | 3 | 4 | 3.90 | 13 | 0 | 60 | 56 | 38 | 43 |
| Mikkelsen, Linc | 2 | 6 | 4.19 | 18 | 0 | 105 | 112 | 37 | 86 |
| Powers, Jim | 1 | 1 | 9.64 | 5 | 0 | 9 | 7 | 11 | 8 |
| Rohr, Mike | 2 | 3 | 4.82 | 30 | 1 | 47 | 56 | 25 | 34 |
| Rosenthal, Wayne | 2 | 4 | 4.80 | 37 | 5 | 51 | 43 | 27 | 45 |
| Schenck, Dave | 0 | 1 | 9.53 | 7 | 0 | 11 | 16 | 11 | 10 |
| Tegtmeier, Doug | 3 | 4 | 4.54 | 22 | 0 | 77 | 93 | 30 | 34 |
| Tellers, Dave | 7 | 3 | 2.45 | 38 | 9 | 51 | 57 | 19 | 40 |

## ROCHESTER

| BATTING | AVG | AB | R | H | 2B | 3B | HR | RBI | SB |
|---|---|---|---|---|---|---|---|---|---|
| Bailey, Rob, 2b | .243 | 284 | 37 | 69 | 8 | 1 | 2 | 23 | 30 |
| Beauchamp, Kash, of-1b | .367 | 166 | 32 | 61 | 8 | 1 | 9 | 33 | 2 |
| Billmeyer, Mick, c | .262 | 210 | 23 | 55 | 6 | 2 | 8 | 35 | 0 |
| Camposano, Bo, of (4 TB) | .237 | 135 | 20 | 32 | 6 | 0 | 4 | 22 | 6 |
| Cutshall, Bill, dh-of | .275 | 167 | 27 | 46 | 9 | 2 | 5 | 27 | 5 |
| Dailey, Steve, of | .281 | 217 | 48 | 61 | 13 | 2 | 8 | 30 | 13 |
| Dreasky, Darin, ss-2b | .289 | 173 | 17 | 50 | 5 | 1 | 2 | 22 | 14 |
| Ford, Curt, of | .234 | 248 | 48 | 58 | 5 | 1 | 5 | 30 | 31 |
| Glenn, Darrin, 3b | .234 | 201 | 30 | 47 | 17 | 0 | 4 | 26 | 4 |
| Jones, Chris, of (31 SC) | .208 | 101 | 12 | 21 | 6 | 1 | 1 | 10 | 4 |
| Klavitter, Clay, c | .183 | 93 | 11 | 17 | 0 | 0 | 2 | 5 | 2 |
| Pina, Mickey, of | .270 | 37 | 7 | 10 | 1 | 0 | 3 | 8 | 3 |
| Sawkiw, Warren, 1b | .327 | 272 | 42 | 89 | 21 | 2 | 9 | 45 | 14 |
| Vollmer, Randy, ss | .219 | 178 | 22 | 39 | 12 | 0 | 1 | 25 | 3 |

| PITCHER | W | L | ERA | G | SV | IP | H | BB | SO |
|---|---|---|---|---|---|---|---|---|---|
| Bishop, Craig | 2 | 1 | 0.64 | 18 | 2 | 28 | 24 | 19 | 19 |
| Bittiger, Jeff | 5 | 4 | 4.48 | 12 | 0 | 66 | 68 | 27 | 67 |
| Brady, Mike (20 D-S) | 1 | 3 | 7.50 | 26 | 0 | 42 | 57 | 23 | 18 |
| Caccavale, Paul (2 D-S) | 1 | 0 | 7.06 | 6 | 0 | 22 | 30 | 5 | 12 |
| Cain, Tim | 4 | 4 | 2.37 | 20 | 1 | 102 | 76 | 28 | 73 |
| Cutshall, Bill | 1 | 0 | 4.68 | 12 | 1 | 25 | 25 | 17 | 19 |
| Dippold, Frank | 1 | 5 | 6.72 | 24 | 0 | 66 | 83 | 29 | 40 |
| Erazmus, Mark | 0 | 2 | 3.95 | 10 | 1 | 27 | 30 | 9 | 9 |
| Futrell, Mark | 5 | 6 | 2.81 | 32 | 12 | 48 | 42 | 22 | 41 |
| Garcia, Mike | 9 | 2 | 2.95 | 16 | 0 | 95 | 89 | 27 | 100 |
| Gay, Chris | 1 | 0 | 6.55 | 3 | 0 | 11 | 13 | 10 | 8 |
| Heather, Brian | 0 | 0 | 20.25 | 2 | 0 | 3 | 8 | 0 | 0 |
| Johnson, A.J. | 1 | 3 | 8.71 | 8 | 0 | 21 | 31 | 9 | 11 |
| Kotch, Darrin | 1 | 2 | 6.28 | 12 | 1 | 14 | 19 | 4 | 14 |
| Krahenbuhl, Ken | 3 | 1 | 4.61 | 6 | 0 | 27 | 29 | 9 | 10 |
| Lawler, Ivan | 2 | 2 | 3.90 | 6 | 0 | 28 | 27 | 13 | 11 |
| Marchitto, Jeff | 0 | 0 | 18.00 | 2 | 0 | 2 | 3 | 2 | 2 |
| Piehl, Tracy | 0 | 0 | 0.00 | 3 | 0 | 5 | 3 | 1 | 5 |
| Ryder, Scott | 2 | 2 | 7.36 | 11 | 1 | 33 | 42 | 21 | 30 |

## ST. PAUL

| BATTING | AVG | AB | R | H | 2B | 3B | HR | RBI | SB |
|---|---|---|---|---|---|---|---|---|---|
| Blasingame, Kent, of | .203 | 79 | 10 | 16 | 2 | 0 | 0 | 2 | 12 |
| Charles, Frank, c | .273 | 216 | 27 | 59 | 13 | 0 | 2 | 37 | 5 |
| D'Alexander, Greg, ss-3b | .268 | 228 | 31 | 61 | 12 | 3 | 0 | 18 | 5 |
| Dietrich, Derrick, of | .339 | 56 | 12 | 19 | 0 | 0 | 0 | 8 | 1 |
| Durham, Leon, dh-1b | .292 | 226 | 44 | 66 | 12 | 1 | 11 | 59 | 4 |
| Eppard, Jim, 1b-dh | .296 | 226 | 40 | 67 | 12 | 1 | 1 | 22 | 9 |
| Gogas, Keith, of-1b | .200 | 80 | 10 | 16 | 2 | 0 | 3 | 13 | 0 |
| Hirtensteiner, Rick, of | .310 | 271 | 52 | 84 | 10 | 3 | 4 | 35 | 8 |
| Meadows, Scott, of | .324 | 250 | 42 | 81 | 11 | 1 | 4 | 43 | 8 |
| Millar, Kevin, 3b | .260 | 227 | 33 | 59 | 11 | 1 | 5 | 30 | 2 |
| Minoso, Minnie, dh | .000 | 1 | 0 | 0 | 0 | 0 | 0 | 0 | 0 |
| Ordonez, Rey, ss-2b | .283 | 60 | 10 | 17 | 4 | 0 | 0 | 7 | 3 |
| Ortega, Eddie, 2b | .286 | 189 | 31 | 54 | 5 | 0 | 0 | 22 | 7 |
| Raffo, Tom, of | .321 | 156 | 14 | 50 | 7 | 0 | 2 | 20 | 0 |
| Smith, Willie, c | .220 | 59 | 8 | 13 | 0 | 0 | 1 | 8 | 2 |

| PITCHING | W | L | ERA | G | SV | IP | H | BB | SO |
|---|---|---|---|---|---|---|---|---|---|
| Darden, Tony | 3 | 2 | 6.05 | 24 | 2 | 39 | 44 | 21 | 17 |
| Gogas, Keith | 0 | 0 | 0.00 | 1 | 0 | 2 | 3 | 3 | 1 |
| Grewal, Ranbir | 5 | 5 | 3.86 | 19 | 0 | 100 | 115 | 50 | 79 |
| Heinkel, Don | 2 | 3 | 4.20 | 10 | 0 | 49 | 53 | 11 | 26 |
| Hoffman, Edson | 2 | 0 | 11.88 | 5 | 0 | 8 | 8 | 5 | 8 |
| Manfred, Jim | 5 | 4 | 2.06 | 18 | 2 | 74 | 59 | 27 | 52 |
| Marak, Paul | 1 | 3 | 9.77 | 11 | 0 | 16 | 23 | 7 | 7 |
| Mimbs, Mike | 8 | 2 | 3.20 | 20 | 0 | 98 | 94 | 45 | 97 |
| Moran, Eric | 3 | 1 | 4.78 | 22 | 1 | 32 | 33 | 26 | 15 |
| Oropesa, Eddie | 3 | 1 | 1.93 | 4 | 0 | 19 | 6 | 9 | 19 |
| Pollard, Damon | 2 | 2 | 2.27 | 29 | 14 | 32 | 25 | 24 | 35 |
| Stryker, Ed | 2 | 2 | 6.65 | 24 | 2 | 46 | 56 | 19 | 38 |
| Thoden, John | 6 | 4 | 2.76 | 16 | 0 | 108 | 103 | 22 | 76 |

## SIOUX CITY

| BATTING | AVG | AB | R | H | 2B | 3B | HR | RBI | SB |
|---|---|---|---|---|---|---|---|---|---|
| Booker, Eric, of | .280 | 250 | 36 | 70 | 11 | 1 | 3 | 28 | 16 |

**Familiar Face.** Former big leaguer Leon Durham resumed his career in the Northern League, hitting a league-best 11 homers.

| | | | | | | | | |
|---|---|---|---|---|---|---|---|---|
| Carcione, Tom, c | .227 | 203 | 24 | 46 | 5 | 0 | 5 | 22 | 0 |
| DiCarlo, Marc, dh | .242 | 66 | 5 | 16 | 3 | 0 | 1 | 6 | 0 |
| Farlow, Kevin, ss | .333 | 189 | 42 | 63 | 14 | 1 | 4 | 26 | 8 |
| Lane, Nolan, of | .308 | 263 | 49 | 81 | 13 | 2 | 6 | 43 | 33 |
| Leary, Rob, of-1b | .247 | 186 | 26 | 46 | 19 | 1 | 4 | 27 | 0 |
| McDonnell, Tim, 3b | .179 | 28 | 4 | 5 | 0 | 0 | 1 | 1 | 1 |
| Melancon, Troy, of-1b | .203 | 158 | 20 | 32 | 3 | 0 | 0 | 15 | 8 |
| Mora, Frankie, c (34 TB) | .168 | 113 | 14 | 19 | 2 | 0 | 0 | 7 | 4 |
| Partrick, Dave, of | .125 | 40 | 3 | 5 | 1 | 1 | 0 | 5 | 0 |
| Ramirez, J.D., 2b | .338 | 216 | 30 | 73 | 10 | 1 | 3 | 30 | 5 |
| Robbins, Lance, 2b-3b | .293 | 150 | 23 | 44 | 4 | 1 | 0 | 13 | 6 |
| Robinson, Darryl, 1b | .249 | 261 | 24 | 65 | 14 | 1 | 2 | 30 | 3 |
| Serrano, Nandy, 3b | .191 | 68 | 1 | 13 | 1 | 0 | 0 | 4 | 1 |
| Valdez, Frank, 3b-ss | .291 | 179 | 31 | 52 | 11 | 1 | 4 | 21 | 1 |

| PITCHING | W | L | ERA | G | SV | IP | H | BB | SO |
|---|---|---|---|---|---|---|---|---|---|
| Arrieta, Fadul | 1 | 2 | 3.43 | 18 | 0 | 58 | 60 | 25 | 55 |
| Burbank, Dennis | 1 | 4 | 5.53 | 23 | 1 | 55 | 76 | 23 | 40 |
| Connolly, Matt | 5 | 8 | 4.74 | 17 | 0 | 101 | 111 | 32 | 71 |
| Goldman, Barry | 2 | 4 | 4.32 | 23 | 2 | 67 | 58 | 39 | 59 |
| Harrison, Tom | 5 | 3 | 4.83 | 18 | 1 | 78 | 82 | 33 | 47 |
| Kobetitsch, Kevin | 2 | 5 | 3.09 | 30 | 1 | 35 | 36 | 13 | 30 |
| Kraemer, Joe | 10 | 4 | 2.91 | 16 | 0 | 108 | 100 | 26 | 90 |
| LeTourneau, Jeff | 5 | 4 | 3.83 | 26 | 2 | 80 | 64 | 50 | 52 |
| Quijada, Ed | 1 | 2 | 5.73 | 5 | 0 | 22 | 27 | 8 | 14 |
| Rich, Bart | 2 | 2 | 3.09 | 28 | 9 | 32 | 27 | 21 | 38 |

## SIOUX FALLS

| BATTING | AVG | AB | R | H | 2B | 3B | HR | RBI | SB |
|---|---|---|---|---|---|---|---|---|---|
| Aldrete, Rich, dh-1b | .328 | 201 | 30 | 66 | 13 | 2 | 4 | 35 | 1 |
| Burton, Mike, 1b-dh | .271 | 280 | 37 | 76 | 19 | 0 | 10 | 51 | 0 |
| Byers, James, 2b-ss | .261 | 23 | 1 | 6 | 0 | 0 | 0 | 2 | 0 |
| Casper, Tim, 2b-3b | .266 | 207 | 25 | 55 | 3 | 3 | 2 | 17 | 1 |
| Drent, Steve, c | .083 | 24 | 3 | 2 | 0 | 0 | 0 | 0 | 0 |
| Dunford, Jeremy, of | .236 | 106 | 10 | 25 | 5 | 0 | 4 | 10 | 0 |
| Gallone, Santy, 3b-2b | .319 | 235 | 51 | 75 | 15 | 0 | 7 | 37 | 13 |
| Guerrero, Pedro, of-dh | .278 | 151 | 23 | 42 | 5 | 0 | 3 | 33 | 3 |
| Hall, Lamar, ss | .182 | 44 | 6 | 8 | 0 | 1 | 0 | 4 | 2 |
| Joseph, Doug, c | .231 | 134 | 12 | 31 | 4 | 0 | 0 | 11 | 1 |
| Larson, Kirk, ss | .288 | 104 | 15 | 30 | 9 | 0 | 1 | 11 | 0 |
| Nichols, Carl, c | .254 | 173 | 25 | 44 | 11 | 0 | 5 | 31 | 1 |
| Palfalvi, Mark, of | .208 | 24 | 2 | 5 | 1 | 0 | 0 | 3 | 0 |
| Powell, Chris, of | .302 | 235 | 47 | 71 | 5 | 5 | 4 | 19 | 13 |
| Reep, William, of | .163 | 43 | 5 | 7 | 4 | 0 | 0 | 2 | 1 |
| Relaford, Winston, of | .000 | 12 | 0 | 0 | 0 | 0 | 0 | 1 | 1 |
| Sanchez, Ralph, of | .065 | 31 | 1 | 2 | 0 | 0 | 0 | 0 | 0 |

# Independent League A Bust At Gate

With poor attendance and folding franchises providing an unseemly backdrop, the independent Frontier League kicked off its inaugural season in 1993.

The league, stocked primarily with graduating college talent, began with eight franchises in cities in Ohio, Kentucky and West Virginia, but staggered home with only six as the West Virginia Coal Sox (Wayne, W. Va.), averaging 117 fans a game, and the Tri-State Tomahawks (Ashland, Ky.), averaging 170, folded along the way.

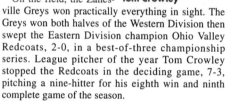

**Tom Crowley**

League founder Bud Bickel was ousted at midseason in a coup of owners.

"There are all kinds of financial problems," a league official said at the time of Bickel's dismissal. "It's a mess."

On the field, the Zanesville Greys won practically everything in sight. The Greys won both halves of the Western Division then swept the Eastern Division champion Ohio Valley Redcoats, 2-0, in a best-of-three championship series. League pitcher of the year Tom Crowley stopped the Redcoats in the deciding game, 7-3, pitching a nine-hitter for his eighth win and ninth complete game of the season.

James Wambach homered three times in the two playoff games for Zanesville, which averaged almost 1,000 fans per game—easily the league's best. Greys third baseman Kyle Shade won the batting title with a .378 average and was selected the league's MVP.

Shade was Zanesville's first-round pick in the league's preseason dispersal draft.

**—ALLAN SIMPSON**

## STANDINGS

### FIRST HALF

| EAST | W | L | PCT | GB | WEST | W | L | PCT | GB |
|---|---|---|---|---|---|---|---|---|---|
| Kentucky | 17 | 9 | .654 | — | Zanesville | 18 | 11 | .621 | — |
| Ohio Valley | 15 | 14 | .517 | 3½ | Chillicothe | 14 | 15 | .483 | 4 |
| Portsmouth | 10 | 18 | .357 | 8 | Lancaster | 14 | 16 | .467 | 4½ |
| West Virginia | 3 | 7 | .300 | 6 | Tri-State | 5 | 6 | .455 | 4 |

### SECOND HALF

| EAST | W | L | PCT | GB | WEST | W | L | PCT | GB |
|---|---|---|---|---|---|---|---|---|---|
| Ohio Valley | 14 | 8 | .636 | — | Zanesville | 17 | 6 | .739 | — |
| Portsmouth | 10 | 13 | .434 | 4½ | Chillicothe | 11 | 12 | .478 | 6 |
| Kentucky | 10 | 14 | .416 | 5 | Lancaster | 8 | 17 | .320 | 10 |

West Virginia and Tri-State franchises withdrew from league.

**CHAMPIONSHIP SERIES:** Zanesville defeated Ohio Valley, 2-0, in best-of-3 final.

## INDIVIDUAL BATTING LEADERS
### (Minimum 125 At-Bats)

| | AVG | AB | R | H | 2B | 3B | HR | RBI | SB |
|---|---|---|---|---|---|---|---|---|---|
| Shade, Kyle, Zanesville | .378 | 193 | 42 | 73 | 19 | 0 | 6 | 42 | 0 |
| O'Conner, Pat, Lancaster | .354 | 130 | 30 | 46 | 14 | 2 | 2 | 23 | 9 |
| Brice, Billy, Kentucky | .349 | 152 | 28 | 53 | 11 | 1 | 6 | 32 | 1 |
| Sutaris, Thomas, Ohio Valley | .349 | 175 | 41 | 61 | 11 | 1 | 3 | 23 | 2 |
| Cosmo, Nick, Ohio Valley | .343 | 181 | 36 | 62 | 7 | 1 | 3 | 15 | 8 |
| Rollyson, Jeff, Zanesville | .336 | 128 | 35 | 43 | 6 | 1 | 4 | 18 | 11 |
| Wambach, James, Zanesville | .335 | 170 | 28 | 57 | 8 | 1 | 10 | 35 | 3 |
| Buso, Steve, Portsmouth | .332 | 187 | 36 | 62 | 11 | 1 | 6 | 30 | 8 |
| Ramion, Shawn, Portsmouth | .331 | 136 | 19 | 45 | 10 | 0 | 4 | 25 | 1 |
| Scruggs, Ricky, Lancaster | .322 | 174 | 23 | 56 | 13 | 0 | 5 | 36 | 5 |
| Smith, Adam, Kentucky | .320 | 128 | 13 | 41 | 8 | 0 | 6 | 32 | 3 |
| Kennaw, Matt, Portsmouth | .316 | 171 | 20 | 54 | 10 | 1 | 1 | 27 | 0 |
| McGuire, Michael, Zanesville | .316 | 158 | 19 | 50 | 6 | 0 | 4 | 26 | 7 |
| Zunich, Chris, Zanesville | .311 | 167 | 40 | 52 | 7 | 2 | 6 | 24 | 1 |
| Kerns, Tim, Ohio Valley | .307 | 153 | 28 | 47 | 10 | 0 | 7 | 42 | 0 |

## INDIVIDUAL PITCHING LEADERS
### (Minimum 50 Innings)

| | W | L | ERA | G | SV | IP | H | BB | SO |
|---|---|---|---|---|---|---|---|---|---|
| Crowley, Tom, Zanesville | 7 | 1 | 2.05 | 11 | 0 | 88 | 80 | 15 | 78 |
| Newman, Jeff, Ohio Valley | 5 | 4 | 2.41 | 15 | 0 | 78 | 61 | 31 | 66 |
| Pate, Cory, Chillicothe | 5 | 3 | 3.01 | 11 | 0 | 81 | 72 | 39 | 52 |
| Lantz, Mick, Zanesville | 5 | 1 | 3.02 | 8 | 0 | 54 | 52 | 12 | 27 |
| Conkling, Bill, Ohio Valley | 7 | 3 | 3.13 | 11 | 0 | 75 | 71 | 32 | 67 |
| Brown, Jeff, Portsmouth | 7 | 5 | 3.26 | 16 | 1 | 88 | 69 | 31 | 76 |
| Puente, Upi, Zanesville | 8 | 1 | 3.31 | 13 | 0 | 68 | 66 | 23 | 39 |
| McLaury, Mike, Kentucky | 7 | 3 | 3.33 | 13 | 0 | 78 | 83 | 17 | 93 |
| Ybarra, Jamie, Kentucky | 2 | 5 | 3.34 | 11 | 0 | 65 | 71 | 37 | 44 |
| Ertel, Will, Lancaster | 5 | 4 | 3.35 | 14 | 1 | 81 | 87 | 19 | 52 |

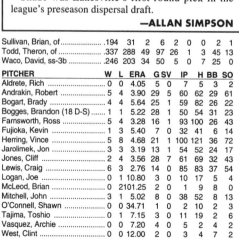

| | | | | | | | | | |
|---|---|---|---|---|---|---|---|---|---|
| Sullivan, Brian, of | .194 | 31 | 2 | 6 | 2 | 0 | 0 | 2 | 1 |
| Todd, Theron, of | .337 | 288 | 49 | 97 | 26 | 1 | 3 | 45 | 13 |
| Waco, David, ss-3b | .246 | 203 | 34 | 50 | 5 | 0 | 7 | 25 | 0 |

| PITCHER | W | L | ERA | G | SV | IP | H | BB | SO |
|---|---|---|---|---|---|---|---|---|---|
| Aldrete, Rich | 0 | 0 | 4.05 | 5 | 0 | 7 | 5 | 3 | 2 |
| Andrakin, Robert | 5 | 4 | 3.90 | 29 | 5 | 60 | 62 | 29 | 61 |
| Bogart, Brady | 4 | 4 | 5.64 | 25 | 1 | 59 | 82 | 26 | 22 |
| Bogges, Brandon (18 D-S) | 1 | 1 | 5.22 | 28 | 1 | 50 | 54 | 31 | 23 |
| Farnsworth, Ross | 5 | 4 | 3.28 | 16 | 1 | 93 | 100 | 26 | 43 |
| Fujioka, Kevin | 1 | 3 | 5.40 | 7 | 0 | 32 | 41 | 6 | 14 |
| Herring, Vince | 5 | 8 | 4.68 | 21 | 1 | 100 | 121 | 36 | 72 |
| Jarolimek, Jon | 3 | 3 | 3.19 | 13 | 1 | 54 | 52 | 24 | 17 |
| Jones, Cliff | 2 | 4 | 3.56 | 28 | 7 | 61 | 69 | 32 | 43 |
| Lewis, Craig | 6 | 3 | 2.76 | 14 | 0 | 85 | 83 | 37 | 54 |
| Logan, Joe | 0 | 1 | 10.80 | 3 | 0 | 10 | 17 | 5 | 4 |
| McLeod, Brian | 0 | 2 | 101.25 | 2 | 0 | 1 | 9 | 8 | 0 |
| Mitchell, John | 3 | 1 | 5.02 | 8 | 0 | 38 | 52 | 8 | 13 |
| O'Connell, Shawn | 0 | 0 | 34.71 | 1 | 0 | 2 | 10 | 2 | 3 |
| Tajima, Toshio | 0 | 1 | 7.15 | 3 | 0 | 11 | 19 | 2 | 6 |
| Vasquez, Archie | 0 | 0 | 7.20 | 4 | 0 | 5 | 2 | 4 | 2 |
| West, Clint | 0 | 0 | 12.00 | 2 | 0 | 3 | 4 | 7 | 2 |

### THUNDER BAY

| BATTING | AVG | AB | R | H | 2B | 3B | HR | RBI | SB |
|---|---|---|---|---|---|---|---|---|---|
| Arnold, Ken, ss-3b | .295 | 183 | 22 | 54 | 7 | 0 | 0 | 19 | 12 |
| Berry, Mike, 3b | .205 | 44 | 7 | 9 | 2 | 0 | 1 | 5 | 0 |

| | | | | | | | | | |
|---|---|---|---|---|---|---|---|---|---|
| Cox, Joey, of (4 Roch) | .130 | 23 | 1 | 3 | 1 | 0 | 0 | 2 | 0 |
| DeFabbia, Jerry, ss-3b (31 St. P) | .256 | 133 | 23 | 34 | 6 | 1 | 1 | 13 | 4 |
| Forkerway, Trey, ss | .279 | 43 | 7 | 12 | 1 | 1 | 0 | 4 | 3 |
| Gray, Dan, 3b-c | .264 | 193 | 25 | 51 | 14 | 0 | 2 | 30 | 1 |
| Griffin, Ty, 2b | .274 | 234 | 49 | 64 | 9 | 0 | 11 | 35 | 12 |
| Griffith, Tom, of-c (35 SC) | .253 | 170 | 15 | 43 | 3 | 0 | 0 | 15 | 13 |
| Hood, Dennis, of | .322 | 261 | 36 | 84 | 13 | 7 | 7 | 34 | 30 |
| Kantor, Brad, 3b | .091 | 22 | 0 | 2 | 0 | 0 | 0 | 1 | 0 |
| Kuld, Pete, c | .261 | 134 | 13 | 35 | 4 | 0 | 6 | 26 | 3 |
| Marzano, David, of | .278 | 212 | 19 | 59 | 12 | 1 | 1 | 31 | 5 |
| McCray, Rodney, of | .242 | 223 | 42 | 54 | 8 | 4 | 2 | 20 | 36 |
| Munoz, Ken, ss-2b | .182 | 88 | 12 | 16 | 5 | 0 | 0 | 5 | 3 |
| Rosenthal, Todd, 1b | .309 | 259 | 26 | 80 | 12 | 1 | 0 | 26 | 6 |
| Turley, Brent, 3b | .171 | 41 | 3 | 7 | 0 | 0 | 0 | 4 | 0 |

| PITCHING | W | L | ERA | G | SV | IP | H | BB | SO |
|---|---|---|---|---|---|---|---|---|---|
| Gilligan, John | 1 | 4 | 5.08 | 19 | 4 | 34 | 41 | 13 | 29 |
| Mammola, Mark | 0 | 2 | 2.56 | 13 | 0 | 53 | 55 | 23 | 36 |
| McDonald, Kevin | 3 | 5 | 2.77 | 18 | 4 | 39 | 37 | 14 | 44 |
| Montane, Omar | 0 | 0 | 3.09 | 8 | 0 | 12 | 15 | 7 | 8 |
| Pollack, Chris | 7 | 5 | 3.02 | 13 | 0 | 86 | 75 | 32 | 39 |
| Seo, Yoshi | 4 | 4 | 2.37 | 13 | 0 | 65 | 65 | 36 | 41 |
| Shinada, Ayahito | 3 | 1 | 3.33 | 23 | 6 | 49 | 42 | 20 | 48 |
| Souza, Brian | 4 | 3 | 4.53 | 19 | 0 | 56 | 54 | 40 | 44 |
| Stephens, Mark | 5 | 6 | 4.24 | 16 | 0 | 76 | 94 | 23 | 49 |
| Tilmon, Pat | 5 | 4 | 2.86 | 13 | 0 | 79 | 69 | 34 | 62 |
| Winawer, Larry | 4 | 1 | 3.13 | 16 | 2 | 60 | 67 | 19 | 26 |

# MEXICAN
## LEAGUE

# Tabasco Turns Tables On History

**By ALLAN SIMPSON**

The 1993 Mexican League season was payback time. For the Tabasco Olmecas. And manager Juan Navarette.

Tabasco had never won a league championship, but rallied from a third-place finish during the regular season to upset the Mexico City Tigers and Mexico City Reds in the South Zone playoffs. The Olmecas then dispatched North Zone champion Laredos in the best-of-7 championship series, winning 4-1.

The Olmecas dropped the first game to Laredos, 12-1, then reeled off four wins in a row. Tabasco won three straight one-run games and took the deciding game, 4-1, behind the four-hit pitching of playoff MVP Ricardo Osuna.

The title was particularly satisfying for Navarrete, who was abruptly dismissed in 1992 as manager of Saltillo after the Owls dropped the first two games of a playoff series to Laredos. Saltillo finished dead last in the North Zone in 1993.

**Nelson Simmons**

"Very satisfying," said Navarrete, who never played on a winning team in 16 years as a player. "This organization wanted a winner. We worked hard before and during the season."

Tabasco pitchers limited Laredos to four runs and 21 hits over the final four games. Osuna put the Olmecas on the comeback trail with a 3-2 win in Game Two.

While hitting was scarce in the championship series, there was plenty of it during the regular season—particularly in Mexico City where the Reds hit .320 as a team and Tigers outfielder Matias Carrillo led the league with 113 runs, 38 home runs and 125 RBIs. Carrillo, whose contract was bought after the season by the Florida Marlins, set a league record May 18 by hitting five home runs in a doubleheader.

Jalisco failed to make the playoffs despite possessing both the batting champion and the league's best pitcher. The Cowboys went only 61-65 as outfielder Nelson Simmons led with a .382 average and was second to Carrillo with 34 home runs. Jalisco's Urbano Lugo led the league with 17 wins and 164 strikeouts.

The switch-hitting first baseman-outfielder had brief stints with the Tigers in 1984-85 and the Orioles in 1987, but has been stymied in his bid to return to the big leagues.

"I've had my ups and downs but I'm not going to quit," said Simmons, 30. "I can't believe I've been around this long and I'm not in the majors. I believe I can play in the big leagues."

Simmons played at Class A Palm Springs of the Angels system for the final three weeks of the 1993 season, which helped facilitate his sale to a Japanese club. He is expected to play in Japan in 1994.

## Assault On Espino's Records

Jalisco first baseman Jesus Sommers, in his 24th season, set a league record for career hits with his 2,753rd, eclipsing the mark held by Hector Espino, who played from 1962-84.

Another Jalisco player made headlines in 1993 when 16-year major leaguer veteran Pedro Guerrero, who went to Mexico when he failed to hook on with a team in spring training, was suspended for 10 days by Mexican League president Pedro Treto Cisneros after Guerrero went into the stands Easter Sunday to confront a fan.

Guerrero played only six more games after he returned and was released by the Cowboys. He spent the rest of the '93 season playing in the independent Northern League.

Laredos DH Andres Mora continued his assault on Espino's lifetime record of 453 home runs. Mora, 38, hit 20 in 1993 to close to within 43 of Espino's mark. Mora plans to play three more years.

"If I play three more years and average 15 home runs, I'll get the record," figured Mora, who has never played on a championship team.

The Mexican League adopted a new playoff system in 1993 by splitting the league into two halves and awarding points (eight for first, seven for second) based on finish in each half. The Mexico City Reds, first-place finishers in both halves of the South Zone, had the maximum 16.

Tabasco finished with 13 points—seven for a second-place finish in the first half and six for a third-place finish in the second half.

## LEAGUE CHAMPIONS

### Last 25 Years

| Year | Regular Season* | | Playoff |
|------|-----------------|------|---------|
| 1969 | Reynosa | .591 | None |
| 1970 | Mexico City Reds | .607 | Aguila |
| 1971 | Saltillo | .593 | Jalisco |
| 1972 | Saltillo | .636 | Cordoba |
| 1973 | Saltillo | .656 | Mexico City Reds |
| 1974 | Jalisco | .627 | Mexico City Reds |
| 1975 | Cordoba | .649 | Tampico |
| 1976 | Cordoba | .595 | Mexico City Reds |
| 1977 | Puebla | .640 | Nuevo Laredo |
| 1978 | Cordoba | .655 | Aguascalientes |
| 1979 | Saltillo | .704 | Puebla |
| 1980 | Puebla | .716 | None |
| 1981 | Mexico City Reds | .615 | Reynosa |
| 1982 | Poza Rica | .623 | Ciudad Juarez |
| 1983 | Mexico City Reds | .667 | Campeche |
| 1984 | Mexico City Reds | .647 | Yucatan |
| 1985 | Mexico City Reds | .606 | Mexico City Reds |
| 1986 | Puebla | .682 | Puebla |
| 1987 | Mexico City Reds | .604 | Mexico City Reds |
| 1988 | Mexico City Reds | .646 | Mexico City Reds |
| 1989 | Los Dos Laredos | .621 | Los Dos Laredos |
| 1990 | Los Dos Laredos | .618 | Leon |
| 1991 | Monterrey Sultans | .683 | Monterrey Sultans |
| 1992 | Mexico City Tigers | .594 | Mexico City Tigers |
| 1993 | Mexico City Reds | .633 | Tabasco |

*Best Overall Record

## STANDINGS

### NORTH ZONE

| NORTH ZONE | W | L | PCT | GB |
|---|---|---|---|---|
| Laredos Owls (15) | 76 | 53 | .589 | — |
| Monterrey Sultans (14) | 75 | 55 | .577 | 1½ |
| Monclova Steelers (12) | 73 | 57 | .562 | 3½ |
| Aguascalientes Railroadmen (9) | 67 | 64 | .511 | 10 |
| Jalisco Cowboys (7) | 61 | 65 | .484 | 13½ |
| Monterrey Industrialists (7) | 61 | 67 | .477 | 14½ |
| Union Laguna Cotton Pickers (7) | 61 | 70 | .466 | 16 |
| Saltillo Sarape Makers (2) | 51 | 80 | .389 | 26 |

| SOUTH ZONE | W | L | PCT | GB |
|---|---|---|---|---|
| Mexico City Reds (16) | 81 | 47 | .633 | — |
| Mexico City Tigers (13) | 74 | 54 | .578 | 7 |
| Tabasco Olmecas (13) | 66 | 59 | .528 | 13½ |
| Veracruz Eagles (10) | 65 | 66 | .496 | 17½ |
| Minatitlan Oilers (7) | 60 | 66 | .476 | 20 |
| Yucatan Lions (4) | 51 | 72 | .415 | 27½ |
| Puebla Parrots (5) | 52 | 74 | .413 | 28 |
| Campeche Pirates (5) | 49 | 74 | .398 | 29½ |

**NOTE:** League played a split-season schedule. Points were awarded on basis of finish in each half (eight for first, seven for second, etc.), to determine playoff pairings.

**PLAYOFFS—North Zone:** Laredos defeated Aguascalientes, 4-1, and Monterrey Sultans defeated Monclova, 4-1, in best-of-7 series; Laredos defeated Monterrey, 4-1, in best-of-7 zone final. **South Zone:** Mexico City Reds defeated Veracruz, 4-0, and Tabasco defeated Mexico City Tigers, 4-3, in best-of-7 series; Tabasco defeated Mexico City Reds, 4-3, in best-of-7 zone final. **Finals:** Tabasco defeated Laredos, 4-1, in best-of-7 series.

**REGULAR-SEASON ATTENDANCE:** Yucatan 199,589; Mexico City Reds 183,798; Laredos 181,392; Mexico City Tigers 180,120; Tabasco 176,876; Jalisco 173,526; Monclova 170,823; Veracruz 170,213; Union Laguna 169,715; Campeche 167,937; Saltillo 164,413; Minatitlan 160,672; Aguascalientes 160,389; Monterrey Sultans 159,998; Puebla 152,905; Monterrey Industrialists 150,943.

## INDIVIDUAL BATTING LEADERS
(Minimum 250 At-Bats)

| | AVG | AB | R | H | 2B | 3B | HR | RBI | SB |
|---|---|---|---|---|---|---|---|---|---|
| SIMMONS, NELSON, Jal. | .382 | 369 | 81 | 141 | 27 | 0 | 34 | 95 | 1 |
| Mangham, Eric, Tigers | .373 | 351 | 87 | 131 | 29 | 3 | 11 | 56 | 33 |
| Garcia, Cornelio, Yucatan | .362 | 406 | 98 | 147 | 27 | 3 | 7 | 41 | 45 |
| Stark, Matt, MC Reds | .361 | 413 | 101 | 149 | 24 | 0 | 31 | 114 | 2 |
| Monell, Johnny, MC Reds | .356 | 432 | 94 | 154 | 19 | 4 | 19 | 101 | 6 |
| Gonzalez, Jose, Aguas | .349 | 398 | 76 | 139 | 21 | 10 | 7 | 48 | 22 |
| Perez-Tovar, Raul, Min. | .349 | 453 | 68 | 158 | 36 | 2 | 5 | 52 | 6 |
| Garbey, Barbaro, Tigers | .348 | 463 | 71 | 161 | 27 | 0 | 21 | 102 | 5 |
| Bellazetin, Jose, Tigers | .347 | 251 | 51 | 87 | 13 | 1 | 3 | 46 | 0 |
| Sanchez, Armando, MCR | .347 | 452 | 79 | 157 | 26 | 2 | 5 | 55 | 3 |
| Carrillo, Matias, Tigers | .345 | 414 | 113 | 143 | 36 | 0 | 38 | 125 | 28 |
| Arredondo, Luis, Jalisco | .344 | 479 | 80 | 165 | 24 | 3 | 12 | 52 | 20 |
| Brown, Todd, Tabasco | .343 | 431 | 67 | 148 | 35 | 1 | 22 | 95 | 11 |
| Moore, Bobby, Laredo | .340 | 435 | 82 | 148 | 24 | 3 | 7 | 43 | 23 |
| Fernandez, Daniel, MCR | .339 | 445 | 106 | 151 | 28 | 10 | 5 | 54 | 29 |
| Avila, Ruben, Union Lag. | .337 | 501 | 93 | 169 | 25 | 0 | 26 | 112 | 5 |
| Stockstill, David, Union Lag. | .335 | 472 | 71 | 158 | 20 | 2 | 10 | 61 | 0 |
| Steels, James, Ind. | .334 | 473 | 96 | 158 | 27 | 3 | 29 | 100 | 18 |
| Azocar, Oscar, Yucatan | .333 | 489 | 84 | 163 | 37 | 1 | 10 | 81 | 7 |
| Machiria, Pablo, Saltillo | .333 | 495 | 76 | 165 | 25 | 8 | 13 | 76 | 2 |
| Abrego, Jesus, Monclova | .332 | 286 | 49 | 95 | 15 | 4 | 3 | 29 | 1 |
| Jimenez, Eduardo, Sultans | .331 | 447 | 75 | 148 | 22 | 2 | 19 | 90 | 4 |
| Leyva, German, Monclova | .331 | 441 | 85 | 146 | 20 | 9 | 5 | 44 | 12 |
| Naveda, Edgar, Ind. | .330 | 467 | 98 | 154 | 34 | 1 | 18 | 70 | 6 |
| Leal, Guadalupe, Monclova | .328 | 338 | 53 | 111 | 17 | 1 | 10 | 51 | 4 |
| Mere, Pedro, Laredo | .328 | 461 | 87 | 151 | 22 | 3 | 18 | 84 | 8 |
| Delima, Rafael, Tabasco | .327 | 450 | 86 | 147 | 23 | 6 | 4 | 56 | 32 |
| Morones, Martin, Jalisco | .325 | 366 | 63 | 119 | 17 | 8 | 9 | 64 | 5 |
| Aganza, Ruben, Monclova | .324 | 401 | 65 | 130 | 21 | 1 | 20 | 69 | 2 |
| Yuriar, Jesus, Monclova | .324 | 358 | 50 | 116 | 18 | 3 | 4 | 59 | 10 |
| Castro, Eddie, Monclova | .323 | 390 | 88 | 126 | 29 | 0 | 18 | 92 | 8 |
| Stephenson, Phil, Aguas | .323 | 381 | 64 | 123 | 26 | 5 | 13 | 71 | 3 |
| Villaescusa, Fernando, Yuc. | .317 | 284 | 41 | 90 | 8 | 0 | 1 | 31 | 3 |
| Traber, Jim, Sultans | .316 | 487 | 73 | 154 | 20 | 0 | 17 | 118 | 3 |
| Tatis, Bernie, Puebla | .315 | 397 | 87 | 125 | 18 | 7 | 14 | 59 | 6 |
| Fentanes, Oscar, Un. Lag. | .312 | 526 | 65 | 164 | 31 | 6 | 5 | 80 | 2 |
| Diaz, Luis, Laredo | .311 | 457 | 80 | 142 | 31 | 0 | 15 | 71 | 0 |
| Tellez, Alonso, Ind | .311 | 488 | 55 | 152 | 22 | 6 | 12 | 88 | 5 |
| Valverde, Raul, Jalisco | .311 | 341 | 53 | 106 | 12 | 4 | 8 | 62 | 1 |

| | | | | | | | | | |
|---|---|---|---|---|---|---|---|---|---|
| Blocker, Terry, Minatitlan | .309 | 408 | 70 | 126 | 26 | 6 | 8 | 59 | 14 |
| Johnson, Roy, Puebla | .309 | 376 | 58 | 116 | 13 | 1 | 17 | 64 | 1 |
| Herrera, Isidro, Campeche | .308 | 402 | 66 | 124 | 22 | 2 | 4 | 48 | 10 |
| Rubio, Antonio, Saltillo | .307 | 349 | 38 | 107 | 12 | 1 | 3 | 45 | 4 |
| Romero, Oscar, Aguas | .305 | 410 | 58 | 125 | 23 | 1 | 9 | 52 | 5 |
| Cruz, Luis, Yucatan | .300 | 424 | 67 | 127 | 18 | 1 | 17 | 74 | 7 |
| Verdugo, Vicente, MCR | .299 | 442 | 69 | 132 | 26 | 1 | 2 | 48 | 2 |
| Villela, Carlos, Saltillo | .299 | 338 | 43 | 101 | 6 | 6 | 1 | 40 | 0 |
| Vizcarra, Roberto, Ind | .299 | 501 | 84 | 150 | 28 | 1 | 16 | 56 | 15 |
| Valdez, Baltazar, Aguas | .299 | 341 | 40 | 102 | 16 | 3 | 13 | 66 | 1 |
| Valenzuela, Leo, Tabasco | .299 | 363 | 58 | 108 | 17 | 2 | 5 | 47 | 1 |
| Romero, Marco, Laredo | .298 | 400 | 72 | 119 | 11 | 1 | 17 | 78 | 7 |
| Barrera, Nelson, Campeche | .298 | 389 | 53 | 116 | 19 | 0 | 26 | 75 | 3 |
| Dominguez, David, Aguas | .298 | 426 | 57 | 127 | 23 | 0 | 15 | 74 | 1 |
| Ortiz, Alejandro, Laredo | .297 | 461 | 93 | 137 | 25 | 0 | 30 | 102 | 1 |
| Ruiz, Juan, Union Laguna | .296 | 466 | 59 | 138 | 32 | 2 | 11 | 65 | 7 |
| Aguilar, Enrique, Aguas | .292 | 459 | 79 | 134 | 14 | 2 | 19 | 74 | 6 |
| Infante, Alexis, Tabasco | .291 | 461 | 77 | 134 | 14 | 4 | 0 | 49 | 13 |
| Melendez, Francisco, Agu. | .291 | 316 | 43 | 92 | 12 | 0 | 9 | 49 | 0 |
| Sanchez, Alex, Monclova | .291 | 485 | 93 | 141 | 22 | 2 | 24 | 79 | 21 |
| Lopez, Gonzalo, Monclova | .290 | 397 | 52 | 115 | 18 | 4 | 4 | 49 | 0 |
| Munoz, Noe, MC Reds | .290 | 369 | 47 | 107 | 12 | 1 | 2 | 47 | 4 |
| Sanchez, Gerardo, Laredo | .290 | 507 | 89 | 147 | 29 | 3 | 18 | 88 | 1 |
| Esquer, Ramon, Union Lag. | .289 | 470 | 97 | 136 | 24 | 5 | 10 | 47 | 18 |
| Cazarin, Manuel, Minatitlan | .288 | 375 | 32 | 108 | 10 | 5 | 54 | 2 | |
| Zazueta, Mauricio, MCR | .287 | 310 | 39 | 89 | 24 | 2 | 2 | 48 | 2 |
| Valencia, Carlos, Aguas | .287 | 407 | 57 | 117 | 27 | 1 | 8 | 61 | 5 |
| Canizales, Juan, Sultans | .287 | 352 | 58 | 101 | 13 | 4 | 13 | 54 | 5 |
| Diaz, Remigio, Sultans | .286 | 434 | 86 | 124 | 16 | 2 | 2 | 42 | 31 |
| Espinoza, Javier, Ind. | .285 | 417 | 61 | 119 | 14 | 5 | 4 | 49 | 9 |
| Gutierrez, Felipe, Monclova | .285 | 291 | 33 | 83 | 15 | 0 | 3 | 31 | 1 |
| Martinez, Raul, Union Lag. | .285 | 365 | 43 | 104 | 9 | 0 | 9 | 46 | 1 |
| Peralta, Amado, Minatitlan | .282 | 309 | 42 | 87 | 11 | 2 | 14 | 64 | 1 |
| Sommers, Jim, Aguas | .281 | 406 | 35 | 114 | 20 | 0 | 8 | 45 | 0 |
| Taylor, Dwight, Aguas | .281 | 345 | 52 | 97 | 8 | 3 | 3 | 25 | 31 |
| Abril, Ramon, Jalisco | .281 | 292 | 41 | 82 | 10 | 1 | 0 | 33 | 0 |
| Alfaro, Jesus, Yucatan | .281 | 398 | 65 | 112 | 29 | 0 | 25 | 97 | 3 |
| Jackson, Kenny, Saltillo | .281 | 413 | 82 | 116 | 26 | 4 | 23 | 69 | 3 |
| Estrada, Roberto, Puebla | .280 | 404 | 43 | 113 | 13 | 2 | 4 | 49 | 3 |
| Saenz, Ricardo, Tigers | .280 | 410 | 63 | 115 | 20 | 1 | 25 | 91 | 1 |
| Estrada, Hector, Puebla | .279 | 419 | 44 | 117 | 16 | 1 | 14 | 70 | 1 |
| Sanchez, Orlando, Aguas | .278 | 421 | 59 | 117 | 22 | 1 | 11 | 59 | 1 |
| Aguilera, Tony, Sultans | .278 | 309 | 59 | 86 | 15 | 1 | 2 | 36 | 18 |
| Robles, Javier, Union Lag. | .278 | 353 | 54 | 98 | 14 | 6 | 4 | 36 | 8 |
| Rojas, Homar, Industrialists | .278 | 356 | 35 | 99 | 11 | 2 | 3 | 50 | 3 |
| Rodriguez, Juan, Aguas | .277 | 455 | 59 | 126 | 18 | 3 | 3 | 52 | 9 |
| Valenzuela, Armando, Salt. | .277 | 415 | 51 | 115 | 5 | 3 | 1 | 27 | 8 |
| Garza, Gerardo, Tigers | .276 | 315 | 34 | 87 | 12 | 0 | 1 | 32 | 0 |
| Escalera, Ruben, Aguas | .273 | 373 | 73 | 102 | 15 | 5 | 7 | 51 | 11 |
| Valle, Jose, Minatitlan | .272 | 404 | 51 | 110 | 25 | 0 | 7 | 50 | 2 |
| Guzman, Marco, Aguas | .271 | 343 | 44 | 93 | 18 | 1 | 12 | 57 | 1 |
| Rivera, Alberto, Jalisco | .269 | 301 | 34 | 81 | 13 | 1 | 0 | 24 | 4 |
| Iturbe, Pedro, Puebla | .268 | 295 | 33 | 79 | 7 | 4 | 0 | 16 | 4 |
| Castaneda, Rafael, Tigers | .268 | 365 | 54 | 98 | 12 | 3 | 3 | 36 | 5 |
| Perez, Francisco, Minatitlan | .268 | 313 | 41 | 84 | 14 | 1 | 4 | 26 | 3 |
| Tillman, Rusty, Tabasco | .268 | 410 | 62 | 110 | 20 | 1 | 21 | 77 | 29 |
| Guerrero, Francisco, Tigers | .267 | 360 | 57 | 96 | 12 | 0 | 11 | 46 | 11 |
| Lopez, Salvador, Aguas | .267 | 300 | 38 | 80 | 11 | 2 | 5 | 39 | 8 |
| Camacho, Adulfo, Tigers | .265 | 358 | 68 | 95 | 20 | 0 | 1 | 34 | 6 |
| Pardo, Victor, Puebla | .264 | 413 | 51 | 109 | 12 | 1 | 3 | 35 | 3 |
| Saiz, Herminio, Tabasco | .263 | 304 | 29 | 80 | 11 | 0 | 0 | 23 | 0 |
| Alvarez, Hector, Union Lag. | .262 | 423 | 43 | 111 | 25 | 1 | 3 | 51 | 7 |
| Ramirez, Enrique, Laredo | .262 | 489 | 59 | 128 | 17 | 0 | 1 | 40 | 14 |
| Rivera, German, Aguas | .261 | 447 | 67 | 115 | 21 | 0 | 15 | 63 | 6 |

### (Remaining U.S. Players)

| | AVG | AB | R | H | 2B | 3B | HR | RBI | SB |
|---|---|---|---|---|---|---|---|---|---|
| Ford, Curt, MC Reds | .367 | 169 | 39 | 62 | 11 | 1 | 4 | 28 | 0 |
| Ritchie, Gregg, Ind. | .356 | 174 | 29 | 62 | 3 | 0 | 1 | 15 | 8 |
| Williams, Eddie, Sultans | .352 | 210 | 40 | 74 | 17 | 0 | 12 | 34 | 0 |
| Lennon, Patrick, Union Lag. | .351 | 97 | 18 | 34 | 5 | 0 | 5 | 15 | 0 |
| Coachman, Pete, Jalisco | .349 | 249 | 50 | 87 | 18 | 0 | 5 | 42 | 7 |
| Castaneda, Nick, Sultans | .342 | 202 | 32 | 69 | 18 | 2 | 8 | 44 | 0 |
| Trafton, Todd, MC Reds | .342 | 240 | 50 | 82 | 13 | 2 | 15 | 59 | 3 |
| Wilson, Jim, Yucatan | .329 | 155 | 22 | 51 | 10 | 0 | 4 | 34 | 0 |
| Davis, Mark, Minatitlan | .328 | 180 | 42 | 59 | 10 | 2 | 12 | 52 | 11 |
| Nelson, Jerome, Minatitlan | .321 | 134 | 28 | 43 | 4 | 3 | 0 | 7 | 6 |
| Lee, Terry, Campeche | .314 | 86 | 10 | 27 | 2 | 0 | 4 | 11 | 0 |
| Alvarez, Chris, Industrialists | .301 | 163 | 12 | 49 | 8 | 1 | 1 | 23 | 1 |
| See, Larry, Aguas | .300 | 200 | 35 | 60 | 15 | 1 | 7 | 39 | 1 |
| Guerrero, Pedro, Jalisco | .293 | 99 | 14 | 29 | 5 | 0 | 2 | 19 | 0 |
| Barry, Jones, Aguas | .291 | 206 | 27 | 60 | 5 | 3 | 6 | 29 | 3 |
| Cole, Mike, Campeche | .283 | 60 | 9 | 17 | 1 | 1 | 1 | 5 | 4 |
| Hill, Orsino, Sultans | .281 | 167 | 20 | 47 | 11 | 0 | 4 | 23 | 1 |
| Jacas, David, Union Lag. | .278 | 90 | 20 | 25 | 2 | 1 | 5 | 11 | 2 |
| Alexander, Gary, Saltillo | .273 | 55 | 5 | 15 | 2 | 1 | 3 | 15 | 0 |

## MEXICAN LEAGUE: YEAR-BY-YEAR LEADERS

### Last 25 Years

| Year | Batting | | Home Runs | | Wins | | ERA | |
|---|---|---|---|---|---|---|---|---|
| 1969 | Teo Acosta, Puebla | .354 | Hector Espino, Monterrey | 37 | Al Ortiz, MC Reds | 23 | Salvador Sanchez, Rey. | 1.84 |
| 1970 | Francisco Campos, Jalisco | .358 | Rogelio Alvarez, Aguias. | 33 | Al Mariscal, Yucatan | 21 | Al Mariscal, Yucatan | 1.85 |
| 1971 | Teo Acosta, Yucatan | .392 | Humberto Garcia, Tampico | 23 | 2 tied at | 22 | Andres Ayon, Sab.-Salt. | 1.22 |
| 1972 | Don Anderson, Jal. | .362 | Hector Espino, Tampico | 37 | Andres Ayon, Saltillo | 22 | Alfredo Meza, MC Tigers | 1.83 |
| 1973 | Hector Espino, Tampico | .377 | Romel Canada, Saltillo | 26 | Ed Bauta, Poza Rica | 23 | Miguel Lugo, Jalisco | 1.60 |
| 1974 | Teo Acosta, Puebla | .366 | Byron Browne, Tampico | 32 | Antonio Pollorena, GP | 25 | Juan Pizarro, Cordoba | 1.57 |
| 1975 | Pat Bourque, MC Reds | .372 | Andres Mora, Saltillo | 35 | Jose Pena, Villa. | 21 | Ricardo Sandate, PRica | 1.42 |
| 1976 | Larry Fritz, Aguas. | .355 | Jack Pierce, Puebla | 36 | 2 tied at | 20 | Gary Ryerson, Tampico | 1.52 |
| 1977 | Vic Davalillo, Aguas. | .384 | Ismael Oquendo, Sal. | 34 | Lupe Salinas, Un.Lag. | 22 | Horacio Pina, Aguas. | 1.70 |
| 1978 | Romel Canada, Saltillo | .366 | Hal King, Saltillo | 28 | 2 tied at | 22 | Mike Nagy, Tabasco | 1.64 |
| 1979 | Jimmie Collins, Chi. | .438 | 2 tied at | 24 | Miguel Solis, Saltillo | 25 | Ralph Garcia, Juarez | 1.70 |
| 1980 | Roberto Rodriguez, UL | .404 | Ivan Murrell, Leon | 32 | 2 tied at | 16 | Gil Rondon, Yucatan | 1.44 |
| 1981 | Willie Norwood, Reynosa | .365 | Andres Mora, Saltillo | 23 | Ralph Garcia, CJ | 20 | Jose Romo, Coat. | 1.40 |
| 1982 | Bobby G. Smith, CJ | .357 | Andres Mora, Sal.-Laredo | 25 | Ralph Garcia, CJ | 19 | Ernesto Cordova, Vera | 1.58 |
| 1983 | Ricardo Duran, CJ | .377 | Carlos Soto, Laredo | 22 | 2 tied at | 17 | Art Gonzalez, Mont. | 1.92 |
| 1984 | Jimmie Collins, MCR-Cord. | .412 | Derek Bryant, Tamaulipas | 41 | 5 tied at | 17 | Salvador Colorado, Cor. | 2.20 |
| 1985 | Ossie Olivares, Agu.-Camp. | .397 | Andres Mora, Laredo | 41 | Jesus Rios, MC Tigers | 21 | Jesus Rios, MC Tigers | 2.52 |
| 1986 | Willie Aikens, Puebla | .454 | Jack Pierce, Leon | 54 | 3 tied at | 17 | Barry Bass, Monterrey | 2.03 |
| 1987 | Orlando Sanchez, Pueb. | .415 | Nelson Barrera, MC Reds | 42 | 3 tied at | 16 | Robin Fuson, Laredo | 2.67 |
| 1988 | Nick Castaneda, Yucatan | .374 | Leo Hernandez, UL | 36 | Jesus Rios, MC Tigers | 21 | Dave Walsh, Laredo | 1.73 |
| 1989 | Willie Aikens, Leon | .395 | Leo Hernandez, Cam. | 39 | Idelfonso Velazquez, Cam. | 20 | Mercedes Esquer, Yucatan | 1.98 |
| 1990 | Nick Castaneda, Yucatan | .388 | Alex Sanchez, SL Potosi | 28 | Armando Reynoso, Sal. | 20 | Guy Normand, Mon. | 2.08 |
| 1991 | Rich Renteria, Jalisco | .442 | Roy Johnson, Campeche | 37 | Juan Palafox, UL | 17 | Odell Jones, Mont.Ind. | 2.67 |
| 1992 | Raul Perez Tovar, Mon. | .416 | Ty Gainey, MC Reds | 47 | Julio Parata, Minatitlan | 20 | Mercedes Esquer, Yuc. | 2.24 |
| 1993 | Nelson Simmons, Jalisco | .382 | Matias Carrillo, MC Tigers | 38 | 2 tied at | 17 | Manny Hernandez, Aguas. | 2.20 |

| | | | | | | | | | |
|---|---|---|---|---|---|---|---|---|---|
| Felice, Jason, Campeche | .270 | 37 | 5 | 10 | 1 | 0 | 1 | 5 | 1 |
| Shepherd, Ron, Yucatan | .251 | 171 | 23 | 43 | 6 | 0 | 9 | 23 | 1 |
| Nelson, Rob, Saltillo | .250 | 260 | 37 | 65 | 12 | 0 | 14 | 52 | 0 |
| Brown, Chris, Sultans | .250 | 24 | 4 | 6 | 1 | 0 | 0 | 1 | 0 |
| Brown, Tony, Union Laguna | .250 | 56 | 6 | 14 | 3 | 0 | 1 | 9 | 0 |
| Dean, Kevin, Minatitlan | .240 | 50 | 5 | 12 | 3 | 1 | 0 | 9 | 0 |
| Smith, Greg, Saltillo | .238 | 80 | 9 | 19 | 3 | 0 | 2 | 9 | 0 |
| Shamburg, Ken, Yucatan | .222 | 45 | 5 | 10 | 2 | 0 | 0 | 4 | 0 |
| Hinshaw, George, Aguas. | .148 | 27 | 3 | 4 | 1 | 0 | 0 | 0 | 0 |
| McCray, Rodney, Sultans | .050 | 40 | 13 | 2 | 1 | 0 | 0 | 3 | 8 |

### INDIVIDUAL PITCHING LEADERS

(Minimum 75 Innings)

| | W | L | ERA | G | SV | IP | H | BB | SO |
|---|---|---|---|---|---|---|---|---|---|
| Baller, Jay, Laredo | 7 | 3 | 2.09 | 61 | 30 | 82 | 64 | 25 | 85 |
| Edwards, Wayne, Sultans | 6 | 5 | 2.14 | 18 | 1 | 84 | 67 | 44 | 66 |
| HERNANDEZ, MANNY, Agu. | 13 | 9 | 2.20 | 24 | 0 | 180 | 139 | 67 | 126 |
| Couoh, Enrique, Laredo | 7 | 2 | 2.24 | 43 | 5 | 88 | 67 | 28 | 95 |
| Araujo, Andy, Campeche | 9 | 9 | 2.63 | 20 | 0 | 133 | 113 | 33 | 31 |
| Osuna, Ricardo, Tabasco | 8 | 3 | 2.84 | 20 | 0 | 108 | 107 | 36 | 57 |
| Lugo, Urbano, Jalisco | 17 | 5 | 2.88 | 29 | 0 | 206 | 182 | 75 | 164 |
| Lind, Orlando, Laredo | 13 | 7 | 2.95 | 23 | 0 | 159 | 142 | 64 | 121 |
| Quinones, Enrique, Sultans | 7 | 4 | 2.96 | 26 | 0 | 76 | 66 | 18 | 20 |
| Browning, Mike, Campeche | 5 | 6 | 2.96 | 50 | 22 | 82 | 80 | 23 | 35 |
| Carman, Don, Puebla | 8 | 9 | 2.98 | 22 | 1 | 142 | 129 | 59 | 85 |
| Alvarez, Juan, Laredo | 13 | 11 | 3.07 | 28 | 0 | 194 | 175 | 68 | 163 |
| Jimenez, German, Aguas | 10 | 4 | 3.09 | 20 | 0 | 140 | 134 | 46 | 55 |
| Perry, Jeff, Union Laguna | 10 | 7 | 3.11 | 50 | 14 | 98 | 99 | 34 | 61 |
| Sanchez, Hector, Aguas | 6 | 8 | 3.14 | 29 | 1 | 100 | 106 | 20 | 39 |
| Rincon, Ricardo, Union Lag. | 7 | 3 | 3.17 | 57 | 8 | 82 | 80 | 36 | 81 |
| Bennett, Chris, Puebla | 13 | 11 | 3.19 | 27 | 0 | 198 | 185 | 46 | 135 |
| Luevano, Juan, Aguas | 9 | 11 | 3.23 | 26 | 0 | 170 | 148 | 78 | 83 |
| Cordoba, Francisco, MCR | 9 | 2 | 3.23 | 43 | 4 | 106 | 96 | 47 | 71 |
| Jimenez, Isaac, Yucatan | 11 | 7 | 3.24 | 24 | 0 | 158 | 157 | 60 | 90 |
| Raygoza, Martin, Sultans | 15 | 7 | 3.28 | 26 | 0 | 186 | 198 | 44 | 81 |
| Barraza, Ernesto, Laredo | 15 | 8 | 3.40 | 28 | 0 | 177 | 185 | 86 | 115 |
| Ramirez, Roberto, MC Reds | 14 | 5 | 3.40 | 25 | 0 | 156 | 136 | 65 | 100 |
| Lopez, Emigdio, Tabasco | 13 | 10 | 3.41 | 29 | 0 | 187 | 195 | 38 | 85 |
| Montano, Francisco, Tigers | 9 | 6 | 3.43 | 23 | 0 | 152 | 139 | 56 | 81 |
| Ruiz, Cecilio, Tabasco | 9 | 9 | 3.47 | 29 | 0 | 181 | 204 | 32 | 120 |
| Valdez, Rudolfo, Tigers | 15 | 5 | 3.48 | 26 | 0 | 176 | 171 | 53 | 86 |
| Enriquez, Martin, Aguas | 9 | 6 | 3.49 | 19 | 0 | 116 | 109 | 45 | 67 |
| Veliz, Francisco, Ind. | 4 | 4 | 3.54 | 50 | 4 | 76 | 84 | 38 | 44 |
| Castillo, Luis, Tigers | 10 | 10 | 3.67 | 26 | 2 | 150 | 171 | 35 | 85 |
| Mendez, Luis, MC Reds | 10 | 9 | 3.73 | 26 | 0 | 135 | 136 | 46 | 78 |
| Aguilar, Miguel, Minatitlan | 9 | 3 | 3.79 | 29 | 0 | 133 | 120 | 64 | 82 |
| Munoz, Miguel, Aguas | 14 | 11 | 3.82 | 28 | 0 | 174 | 178 | 33 | 66 |
| Sierra, Abel, Campeche | 7 | 14 | 3.83 | 26 | 0 | 153 | 147 | 73 | 82 |
| Orozco, Jaime, Sultans | 6 | 10 | 3.89 | 25 | 0 | 146 | 172 | 33 | 61 |
| Valdez, Ismael, Tigers | 16 | 7 | 3.94 | 26 | 0 | 174 | 192 | 55 | 113 |
| Smith, Daryl, Tigers | 8 | 5 | 3.97 | 24 | 3 | 111 | 99 | 74 | 91 |
| Pulido, Alfonso, Aguas | 9 | 10 | 4.10 | 28 | 0 | 140 | 162 | 25 | 48 |
| Gonzalez, Arturo, Sultans | 13 | 8 | 4.12 | 26 | 0 | 146 | 160 | 56 | 75 |
| Puig, Benny, Saltillo | 4 | 6 | 4.13 | 15 | 1 | 85 | 87 | 46 | 26 |
| Purata, Julio, Industrialists | 7 | 11 | 4.13 | 26 | 0 | 155 | 157 | 75 | 84 |
| Soto, Fernando, Minatitlan | 13 | 14 | 4.20 | 31 | 1 | 197 | 229 | 55 | 91 |
| Villegas, Ramon, Puebla | 5 | 6 | 4.23 | 22 | 0 | 106 | 122 | 48 | 38 |
| Velazquez, Isreal, Minatitlan | 6 | 8 | 4.26 | 27 | 1 | 108 | 105 | 60 | 64 |
| Normand, Guy, Aguas | 5 | 9 | 4.26 | 20 | 1 | 120 | 134 | 68 | 49 |
| Retes, Lorenzo, Tabasco | 8 | 7 | 4.30 | 29 | 0 | 128 | 129 | 63 | 42 |
| Saldana, Edgardo, Tabasco | 2 | 9 | 4.32 | 39 | 12 | 90 | 100 | 40 | 43 |
| May, Scott, Campeche | 9 | 7 | 4.35 | 19 | 0 | 118 | 113 | 63 | 87 |
| Huerta, Luis, Industrialists | 12 | 11 | 4.36 | 28 | 0 | 163 | 188 | 61 | 77 |
| Martinez, Fili, MC Reds | 11 | 7 | 4.42 | 28 | 0 | 143 | 150 | 59 | 104 |
| Solis, Ricardo, Sultans | 7 | 11 | 4.43 | 23 | 0 | 144 | 180 | 39 | 67 |
| Rojo, Oscar, Campeche | 3 | 8 | 4.44 | 32 | 0 | 79 | 79 | 42 | 40 |
| Murillo, Felipe, Monclova | 5 | 3 | 4.48 | 29 | 0 | 94 | 114 | 37 | 37 |
| Valdez, Efrain, Puebla | 3 | 9 | 4.50 | 16 | 0 | 102 | 118 | 39 | 43 |
| Valencia, Jorge, Saltillo | 5 | 3 | 4.54 | 44 | 0 | 81 | 86 | 48 | 27 |
| Iniguez, Dario, Jalisco | 8 | 6 | 4.55 | 28 | 0 | 125 | 146 | 42 | 68 |
| Lopez, Jonas, Aguas | 3 | 6 | 4.59 | 39 | 2 | 82 | 86 | 34 | 29 |
| Cervantes, Lauro, Aguas | 11 | 6 | 4.64 | 25 | 0 | 138 | 182 | 42 | 44 |
| Watson, Preston, Laredo | 6 | 4 | 4.67 | 15 | 0 | 96 | 96 | 50 | 64 |
| Osuna, Roberto, Jalisco | 8 | 14 | 4.67 | 24 | 0 | 166 | 200 | 71 | 87 |
| Lopez, Jose, Minatitlan | 8 | 13 | 4.69 | 29 | 2 | 125 | 156 | 57 | 69 |
| Esquer, Mercedes, Yucatan | 10 | 9 | 4.74 | 23 | 0 | 148 | 166 | 49 | 114 |
| Velazquez, Ernesto, Un. Lag. | 5 | 8 | 4.74 | 29 | 0 | 106 | 113 | 60 | 63 |
| Mead, Timber, Union Lag. | 10 | 10 | 4.75 | 22 | 0 | 133 | 179 | 42 | 70 |
| Rios, Jesus, Tigers | 13 | 11 | 4.82 | 25 | 0 | 162 | 176 | 50 | 123 |
| Castaneda, Aurelio, Jalisco | 7 | 12 | 4.85 | 46 | 14 | 106 | 126 | 38 | 78 |
| Renteria, Hilario, Union Lag. | 8 | 7 | 4.86 | 22 | 0 | 113 | 129 | 34 | 52 |
| Cardenas, Benito, Aguas | 5 | 4 | 4.88 | 26 | 0 | 96 | 104 | 32 | 29 |
| Cruz, Andres, Union Laguna | 7 | 14 | 4.89 | 27 | 0 | 155 | 193 | 65 | 86 |
| Palafox, Juan, Union Laguna | 8 | 8 | 4.94 | 28 | 0 | 188 | 225 | 60 | 87 |
| Moreno, Jesus, Saltillo | 17 | 10 | 4.94 | 30 | 0 | 184 | 206 | 83 | 114 |
| Vega, Velarde, Laredo | 4 | 6 | 5.06 | 21 | 0 | 94 | 114 | 60 | 52 |
| Rodriguez, Raul, Saltillo | 7 | 11 | 5.07 | 23 | 0 | 130 | 163 | 31 | 76 |
| Smith, Mike, Tigers | 14 | 10 | 5.08 | 27 | 0 | 172 | 189 | 110 | 103 |

(Remaining U.S. Players)

| | W | L | ERA | G | SV | IP | H | BB | SO |
|---|---|---|---|---|---|---|---|---|---|
| Kraemer, Joe, MC Reds | 0 | 0 | 0.00 | 3 | 1 | 7 | 1 | 3 | 2 |
| Sinohui, David, Minatitlan | 7 | 4 | 2.79 | 36 | 19 | 58 | 45 | 22 | 38 |
| Loynd, Mike, Laredo | 6 | 1 | 3.15 | 9 | 0 | 60 | 53 | 21 | 68 |
| August, Don, Puebla | 4 | 6 | 3.21 | 11 | 0 | 73 | 90 | 17 | 31 |
| Roesler, Mike, Puebla | 6 | 4 | 3.24 | 19 | 5 | 50 | 51 | 25 | 43 |
| Sauveur, Rich, Minatitlan | 3 | 3 | 3.27 | 7 | 0 | 44 | 40 | 23 | 31 |
| Pavlas, Dave, MC Reds | 5 | 3 | 3.49 | 11 | 0 | 57 | 59 | 19 | 32 |
| Straker, Les, Saltillo | 1 | 1 | 3.52 | 4 | 0 | 15 | 16 | 11 | 7 |
| Taylor, Terry, Campeche | 1 | 1 | 3.57 | 3 | 0 | 18 | 16 | 14 | 12 |
| Stowell, Steve, Industrialists | 1 | 0 | 3.60 | 5 | 1 | 5 | 6 | 8 | 4 |
| Medvin, Scott, Aguas | 4 | 5 | 4.33 | 17 | 3 | 60 | 67 | 31 | 34 |
| Weber, Weston, Minatitlan | 0 | 2 | 4.63 | 7 | 0 | 12 | 11 | 10 | 6 |
| Boyd, Oil Can, Industrialists | 0 | 3 | 4.91 | 15 | 11 | 26 | 24 | 16 | 20 |
| McMurtry, Craig, MC Reds | 1 | 2 | 5.08 | 17 | 6 | 28 | 30 | 13 | 25 |
| Harrison, Phil, Puebla | 2 | 3 | 5.77 | 7 | 0 | 34 | 42 | 28 | 17 |
| Berenguer, Juan, Saltillo | 1 | 5 | 6.14 | 20 | 11 | 29 | 35 | 16 | 32 |
| Hansen, Mike, Tigers | 0 | 0 | 6.43 | 5 | 0 | 21 | 33 | 12 | 13 |
| Eave, Gary, Tigers | 0 | 3 | 11.12 | 3 | 0 | 11 | 22 | 7 | 6 |
| McClellan, Paul, Union Lag. | 0 | 3 | 13.97 | 3 | 0 | 10 | 16 | 8 | 7 |

# JAPANESE LEAGUES

## Yakult Ends Seibu's Three-Year Reign

**By WAYNE GRACZYK**

The Central League's Yakult Swallows won their second Japan pro baseball title, and first since 1978, as they beat the defending champion Seibu Lions 4-3 in an exciting 1993 Japan Series. The Swallows spoiled Seibu's bid for a fourth straight championship and gained revenge for the Lions' 4-3 victory over Yakult in the 1992 Series.

**Ralph Bryant**

The Tokyo-based Swallows, managed by Katsuya Nomura, won their second straight Central League crown, finishing seven games ahead of the second place Chunichi Dragons. The Lions won their fourth consecutive Pacific League pennant and 10th in the past 12 seasons, but were sluggish down the stretch, clinching the flag with just two games remaining in the regular season.

Righthander Kenjiro Kawasaki, 10-9 during the regular season, was named Japan Series MVP after winning two games, including the decider, a 4-2 win. Two Americans, second baseman Rex Hudler and third baseman Jack Howell, played for Yakult, with Howell contributing a three-run homer in the first inning of Game One to set the pace for the Swallows.

Seibu played without three-time Pacific League home run king Orestes Destrade, who left the club after the 1992 season to join the National League's expansion Florida Marlins. Destrade's potent bat was obviously missed; with him in the lineup the Lions won pennants easily and played with more confidence in the Japan Series.

Led by Kintetsu outfielder Ralph Bryant, who previously played for the Los Angeles Dodgers, American players won three offensive crowns and shared one.

With Destrade gone, Bryant easily won the 1993 Pacific League home run and RBI titles with 42 and 107, respectively. Bryant, the 1989 PL MVP, won his second home run title, beating out Nippon Ham's Matt Winters, who slammed 35.

In the Central League, former major league journeyman Tom O'Malley won the silver bat by hitting .329. O'Malley, first baseman for the Hanshin Tigers, edged Yokohama BayStars second baseman Bobby Rose, formerly of the California Angels. Rose hit .325 and tied for the league RBI lead.

Yakult catcher Atsuya Furuta (.308-17-75) was named CL MVP, while Seibu lefthander Kimiyasu Kudo won Pacific League MVP honors by going 15-3 with a league-best 2.06 ERA.

Twenty-six Americans played professionally in Japan in 1993. Other standouts included former New York Yankee outfielder Mel Hall, who hit .296 with 30 home runs and 92 RBIs for the Chiba Lotte Marines.

**Mel Hall**

The 1993 season saw the opening of Japan's second domed stadium, the first with a retractable roof. The Pacific League's Fukuoka Daiei Hawks moved into the 48,000-capacity Fukuoka Dome and set a franchise attendance record of 2,462,000.

A big change for 1994 will be the introduction of a limited free agent system for Japanese players who have played at least 10 seasons in Japan. Sixty players were eligible to declare free agency under the plan, but those signed by new teams are restricted to contracts that pay up to 150 percent of their previous season's salary.

In addition, a team gaining a free agent must compensate the team losing the free agent by paying the amount of the player's salary for the previous season and offering a player from an unprotected list established after compiling a list of 40 protected players.

## JAPAN SERIES

Last 25 Years

| Year Champion | Manager | Runner-Up | Result | MVP |
|---|---|---|---|---|
| 1969 Yomiuri (CL) | Tetsuharu Kawakami | Hankyu (PL) | 4-2 | Shigeo Nagashima, Yomiuri |
| 1970 Yomiuri (CL) | Tetsuharu Kawakami | Lotte (PL) | 4-1 | Shigeo Nagashima, Yomiuri |
| 1971 Yomiuri (CL) | Tetsuharu Kawakami | Hankyu (PL) | 4-1 | Toshimitsu Suetsugu, Yomiuri |
| 1972 Yomiuri (CL) | Tetsuharu Kawakami | Hankyu (PL) | 4-1 | Tsuneo Horiuchi, Yomiuri |
| 1973 Yomiuri (CL) | Tetsuharu Kawakami | Nankai (PL) | 4-1 | Tsuneo Horiuchi, Yomiuri |
| 1974 Lotte (PL) | Masaichi Kaneda | Chunichi (CL) | 4-2 | Sumio Hirota, Lotte |
| 1975 Hankyu (PL) | Toshiharu Veda | Hiroshima (CL) | 4-2 | Takashi Yamaguchi, Hankyu |
| 1976 Hankyu (PL) | Toshiharu Veda | Yomiuri (CL) | 4-3 | Yutaka Fukumoto, Hankyu |
| 1977 Hankyu (PL) | Toshiharu Veda | Yomiuri (CL) | 4-1 | Hisashi Yamada, Hankyu |
| 1978 Yakult (CL) | Tatsuro Hirooka | Hankyu (PL) | 4-3 | Katsuo Osugi, Yakult |
| 1979 Hiroshima (CL) | Takeshi Koba | Kintetsu (PL) | 4-3 | Yoshihiko Takahashi, Hiroshima |
| 1980 Hiroshima (CL) | Takeshi Koba | Kintetsu (PL) | 4-3 | Jim Lyttle, Hiroshima |
| 1981 Yomiuri (CL) | Motoshi Fujita | Nippon Ham (PL) | 4-2 | Takashi Nishimoto, Yomiuri |
| 1982 Seibu (PL) | Tatsuro Hirooka | Chunichi (CL) | 4-2 | Osamu Higashio, Seibu |
| 1983 Seibu (PL) | Tatsuro Hirooka | Yomiuri (CL) | 4-3 | Takuji Ota, Seibu |
| 1984 Hiroshima (CL) | Toshiharu Ueda | Hankyu (PL) | 4-3 | Kiyoyuki Nagashima, Hiroshima |
| 1985 Hanshin (CL) | Yoshio Yoshida | Seibu (PL) | 4-2 | Randy Bass, Hanshin |
| 1986 Seibu (PL) | Masaaki Mori | Hiroshima (CL) | 4-3-1 | Kimiyasu Kudo, Seibu |
| 1987 Seibu (PL) | Masaaki Mori | Yomiuri (CL) | 4-2 | Kimiyasu Kudo, Seibu |
| 1988 Seibu (PL) | Masaaki Mori | Chunichi (CL) | 4-1 | Hiromichi Ishige, Seibu |
| 1989 Yomiuri (CL) | Motoshi Fujita | Kintetsu (PL) | 4-3 | Norihiro Komada, Yomiuri |
| 1990 Seibu (PL) | Masaaki Mori | Yomiuri (CL) | 4-0 | Orestes Destrade, Seibu |
| 1991 Seibu (PL) | Masaaki Mori | Hiroshima (CL) | 4-3 | Koji Akiyama, Seibu |
| 1992 Seibu (PL) | Masaaki Mori | Yakult (CL) | 4-3 | Takehiro Ishii, Seibu |
| 1993 Yakult (CL) | Katsuya Nomura | Seibu (PL) | 4-3 | Kenjiro Kawasaki, Yakult |

# CENTRAL LEAGUE

## STANDINGS

| CENTRAL LEAGUE | W | L | T | PCT | GB |
|---|---|---|---|---|---|
| Yakult Swallows | 80 | 50 | 2 | .615 | — |
| Chunichi Dragons | 73 | 57 | 2 | .562 | 7 |
| Yomiuri Giants | 64 | 66 | 1 | .492 | 16 |
| Hanshin Tigers | 63 | 67 | 2 | .485 | 17 |
| Yokohama BayStars | 57 | 73 | 0 | .438 | 23 |
| Hiroshima Carp | 53 | 77 | 1 | .408 | 27 |

### INDIVIDUAL BATTING LEADERS
(Minimum 403 Plate Appearances)

| | AVG | AB | R | H | 2B | 3B | HR | RBI | SB |
|---|---|---|---|---|---|---|---|---|---|
| O'Malley, Tom, Tigers | .329 | 434 | 60 | 142 | 32 | 1 | 23 | 87 | 1 |
| Rose, Bobby, BayStars | .325 | 486 | 61 | 158 | 33 | 4 | 19 | 94 | 2 |
| Powell, Alonzo, Dragons | .317 | 394 | 63 | 125 | 20 | 1 | 27 | 66 | 3 |
| Maeda, Tomonori, Carp | .317 | 499 | 85 | 158 | 33 | 2 | 27 | 70 | 10 |
| Wada, Yutaka, Tigers | .315 | 511 | 63 | 161 | 22 | 2 | 0 | 36 | 4 |
| Furuta, Atsuya, Swallows | .308 | 522 | 90 | 161 | 29 | 0 | 17 | 75 | 11 |
| Hudler, Rex, Swallows | .300 | 410 | 48 | 123 | 26 | 3 | 14 | 64 | 1 |
| Howell, Jack, Swallows | .295 | 396 | 72 | 117 | 15 | 1 | 28 | 88 | 3 |
| Arai, Yukio, Swallows | .291 | 357 | 45 | 104 | 15 | 2 | 9 | 35 | 1 |
| Kawai, Masahiro, Giants | .290 | 462 | 58 | 134 | 23 | 2 | 5 | 35 | 2 |
| Hirosawa, Katsumi, Swallows | .288 | 524 | 87 | 151 | 22 | 0 | 25 | 94 | 7 |
| Tatsunami, Kazuyoshi, Dragons | .286 | 500 | 73 | 143 | 18 | 3 | 16 | 50 | 6 |
| Ochiai, Hiromitsu, Dragons | .285 | 396 | 64 | 113 | 19 | 0 | 17 | 65 | 1 |
| Eto, Akira, Carp | .282 | 482 | 88 | 136 | 15 | 1 | 34 | 82 | 7 |
| Hatayama, Hitoshi, BayStars | .281 | 452 | 41 | 127 | 27 | 2 | 14 | 72 | 0 |
| Brown, Marty, Carp | .276 | 428 | 60 | 118 | 21 | 2 | 27 | 83 | 1 |
| Takagi, Yataka, BayStars | .268 | 489 | 53 | 131 | 21 | 0 | 3 | 42 | 9 |
| Nomura, Kenjiro, Carp | .266 | 556 | 67 | 148 | 21 | 1 | 14 | 48 | 12 |
| Ishii, Takuro, BayStars | .266 | 414 | 53 | 110 | 19 | 5 | 5 | 36 | 24 |
| Taihoh, Yasuaki, Dragons | .259 | 367 | 53 | 95 | 14 | 0 | 25 | 59 | 0 |
| Shinjo, Tsuyoshi, Tigers | .257 | 408 | 50 | 105 | 13 | 1 | 23 | 62 | 19 |
| Shoda, Kozo, Carp | .257 | 443 | 60 | 114 | 13 | 0 | 7 | 24 | 4 |
| Ikeyama, Takahiro, Swallows | .256 | 390 | 63 | 100 | 15 | 1 | 24 | 71 | 10 |
| Taneda, Hitoshi, Dragons | .254 | 512 | 65 | 130 | 13 | 4 | 10 | 40 | 10 |
| Komada, Norihiro, Giants | .249 | 437 | 35 | 109 | 18 | 0 | 7 | 39 | 1 |

(Remaining U.S. Players)

| | AVG | AB | R | H | 2B | 3B | HR | RBI | SB |
|---|---|---|---|---|---|---|---|---|---|
| Braggs, Glenn, BayStars | .345 | 264 | 61 | 91 | 10 | 2 | 19 | 41 | 2 |
| Medina, Luis, Carp | .333 | 9 | 2 | 3 | 0 | 0 | 0 | 1 | 0 |
| Stairs, Matt, Dragons | .250 | 132 | 10 | 33 | 6 | 0 | 6 | 23 | 1 |
| Moseby, Lloyd, Giants | .246 | 126 | 21 | 31 | 3 | 0 | 4 | 13 | 0 |
| Paciorek, Jim, Tigers | .243 | 263 | 24 | 64 | 12 | 1 | 7 | 36 | 1 |
| Barfield, Jesse, Giants | .215 | 344 | 52 | 74 | 8 | 2 | 26 | 53 | 1 |
| Jacoby, Brook, Dragons | .183 | 60 | 4 | 11 | 4 | 0 | 2 | 6 | 0 |
| Brantley, Mickey, Giants | .182 | 44 | 3 | 8 | 1 | 1 | 0 | 4 | 0 |

### INDIVIDUAL PITCHING LEADERS
(Minimum 130 Innings)

| | W | L | ERA | G | SV | IP | H | BB | SO |
|---|---|---|---|---|---|---|---|---|---|
| Yamamoto, Masahiro, Dragons | 17 | 5 | 2.05 | 27 | 0 | 188 | 140 | 30 | 132 |
| Imanaka, Shinji, Dragons | 17 | 7 | 2.20 | 31 | 1 | 249 | 183 | 59 | 247 |
| Makihara, Hiromi, Giants | 13 | 5 | 2.28 | 28 | 0 | 174 | 149 | 53 | 175 |
| Nomura, Hiroki, BayStars | 17 | 6 | 2.51 | 28 | 0 | 179 | 148 | 41 | 137 |
| Ito, Akimitsu, Swallows | 13 | 4 | 3.11 | 26 | 2 | 174 | 162 | 45 | 94 |
| Saito, Masaki, Giants | 9 | 11 | 3.19 | 23 | 0 | 150 | 135 | 40 | 105 |
| Kida, Masao, Giants | 7 | 7 | 3.35 | 35 | 2 | 132 | 129 | 40 | 97 |
| Kawasaki, Kenjiro, Swallows | 10 | 9 | 3.48 | 27 | 0 | 140 | 120 | 61 | 108 |
| Yufune, Toshiro, Tigers | 12 | 6 | 3.52 | 23 | 0 | 161 | 158 | 61 | 131 |
| Kawaguchi, Kazuhisa, Carp | 8 | 11 | 3.54 | 25 | 0 | 163 | 167 | 74 | 128 |
| Nakagomi, Shin, Tigers | 8 | 13 | 3.71 | 28 | 0 | 199 | 175 | 62 | 153 |
| Nishimura, Tatsuji, Swallows | 11 | 6 | 3.72 | 26 | 1 | 155 | 148 | 42 | 98 |
| Saito, Takashi, BayStars | 8 | 10 | 3.81 | 29 | 0 | 149 | 127 | 61 | 125 |
| Inomata, Takashi, Tigers | 11 | 12 | 3.89 | 27 | 0 | 167 | 179 | 71 | 133 |
| Kuwata, Masumi, Giants | 8 | 15 | 3.99 | 26 | 0 | 178 | 162 | 61 | 158 |

# PACIFIC LEAGUE

## STANDINGS

| | W | L | T | PCT | GB |
|---|---|---|---|---|---|
| Seibu Lions | 74 | 53 | 3 | .583 | — |
| Nippon Ham Fighters | 71 | 52 | 7 | .577 | 1 |
| Orix Blue Wave | 70 | 56 | 4 | .556 | 3½ |
| Kintetsu Buffaloes | 66 | 59 | 5 | .528 | 7 |
| Chiba Lotte Marines | 51 | 77 | 2 | .398 | 23½ |
| Fukuoka Daiei Hawks | 45 | 80 | 5 | .360 | 28 |

**Tom O'Malley** (left) and **Bobby Rose.** Ex-major leaguers finished 1-2 in Central League batting race.

### INDIVIDUAL BATTING LEADERS
(Minimum 403 Plate Appearances)

| | AVG | AB | R | H | 2B | 3B | HR | RBI | SB |
|---|---|---|---|---|---|---|---|---|---|
| Tsuji, Hatsuhiko, Lions | .319 | 429 | 68 | 137 | 26 | 5 | 3 | 31 | 14 |
| Ishii, Hiroo, Buffaloes | .309 | 475 | 74 | 147 | 26 | 5 | 22 | 80 | 0 |
| Ishige, Hiromichi, Lions | .306 | 434 | 64 | 133 | 26 | 2 | 15 | 53 | 12 |
| Yamamoto, Kazunori, Hawks | .301 | 369 | 49 | 111 | 12 | 3 | 12 | 40 | 8 |
| Hall, Mel, Marines | .296 | 480 | 71 | 142 | 29 | 1 | 30 | 92 | 21 |
| Yoshinaga, Koichiro, Hawks | .291 | 413 | 39 | 120 | 29 | 3 | 12 | 44 | 1 |
| Kataoka, Atsushi, Buffaloes | .287 | 425 | 55 | 122 | 29 | 2 | 8 | 39 | 4 |
| Hirose, Tetsuro, Fighters | .279 | 412 | 52 | 115 | 17 | 0 | 0 | 29 | 21 |
| Sasaki, Makoto, Hawks | .277 | 444 | 38 | 123 | 24 | 1 | 7 | 41 | 23 |
| Ishimine, Kazuhiko, Wave | .273 | 495 | 56 | 135 | 21 | 2 | 24 | 77 | 4 |
| Venable, Max, Marines | .272 | 372 | 30 | 101 | 15 | 2 | 7 | 54 | 3 |
| Schu, Rick, Fighters | .270 | 482 | 74 | 130 | 30 | 4 | 24 | 79 | 6 |
| Shirai, Kazuyuki, Fighters | .270 | 497 | 67 | 134 | 20 | 2 | 7 | 54 | 27 |
| Kiyohara, Kazuhiro, Lions | .268 | 448 | 66 | 120 | 15 | 1 | 25 | 75 | 3 |
| Fukura, Junichi, Blue Wave | .267 | 453 | 63 | 121 | 16 | 1 | 2 | 30 | 20 |
| Oishi, Daijiro, Buffaloes | .257 | 470 | 69 | 121 | 10 | 2 | 10 | 49 | 31 |
| Tamura, Fujio, Fighters | .257 | 401 | 37 | 103 | 14 | 1 | 5 | 40 | 6 |
| Ogawa, Hirofuma, Wave | .256 | 414 | 36 | 106 | 18 | 2 | 8 | 36 | 8 |
| Tanaka, Yukio, Fighters | .253 | 474 | 63 | 120 | 32 | 1 | 12 | 63 | 5 |
| Bryant, Ralph, Buffaloes | .252 | 497 | 83 | 125 | 20 | 1 | 42 | 107 | 4 |
| Takahashi, Satoshi, Wave | .251 | 370 | 42 | 93 | 19 | 3 | 11 | 48 | 6 |
| Aiko, Takeshi, Marines | .251 | 398 | 42 | 100 | 27 | 2 | 8 | 33 | 3 |
| Hatsushiba, Kiyoshi, Marines | .251 | 407 | 46 | 102 | 25 | 2 | 12 | 43 | 0 |
| Fujii, Yasuo, Blue Wave | .251 | 463 | 62 | 116 | 23 | 1 | 28 | 86 | 2 |
| Nishimura, Norifumi, Marines | .250 | 352 | 43 | 88 | 10 | 6 | 1 | 28 | 21 |

(Remaining U.S. Players)

| | AVG | AB | R | H | 2B | 3B | HR | RBI | SB |
|---|---|---|---|---|---|---|---|---|---|
| Reynolds, R.J., Buffaloes | .298 | 336 | 46 | 100 | 20 | 1 | 18 | 50 | 12 |
| Gainey, Ty, Blue Wave | .290 | 310 | 58 | 90 | 14 | 1 | 23 | 43 | 9 |
| Winters, Matt, Fighters | .248 | 460 | 78 | 114 | 14 | 0 | 35 | 87 | 5 |
| Motley, Darryl, Marines | .242 | 66 | 6 | 16 | 0 | 0 | 2 | 3 | 2 |
| Wright, George, Hawks | .234 | 351 | 42 | 82 | 20 | 1 | 9 | 44 | 9 |
| Torve, Kelvin, Blue Wave | .232 | 327 | 27 | 76 | 16 | 0 | 9 | 35 | 5 |
| Tolentino, Jose, Lions | .152 | 66 | 3 | 10 | 4 | 1 | 1 | 6 | 0 |

### INDIVIDUAL PITCHING LEADERS
(Minimum 130 Innings)

| | W | L | ERA | G | SV | IP | H | BB | SO |
|---|---|---|---|---|---|---|---|---|---|
| Kudo, Kimiyasu, Lions | 15 | 3 | 2.06 | 24 | 0 | 170 | 129 | 65 | 130 |
| Nishizaki, Yukihiro, Fighters | 11 | 9 | 2.20 | 23 | 1 | 176 | 121 | 61 | 143 |
| Noda, Koki, Blue Wave | 17 | 5 | 2.56 | 26 | 0 | 225 | 187 | 62 | 209 |
| Shirai, Yasukatsu, Fighters | 10 | 3 | 2.66 | 27 | 0 | 152 | 140 | 85 | 86 |
| Hasegawa, Shietoshi, BW | 12 | 6 | 2.71 | 23 | 0 | 160 | 146 | 48 | 86 |
| Irabu, Hideki, Marines | 8 | 7 | 3.10 | 32 | 1 | 142 | 125 | 58 | 160 |
| Ishii, Takehiro, Lions | 12 | 10 | 3.19 | 26 | 0 | 192 | 173 | 28 | 144 |
| Murata, Katsuyoshi, Hawks | 10 | 12 | 3.21 | 25 | 0 | 197 | 171 | 81 | 127 |
| Takeda, Kazuhiro, Fighters | 10 | 8 | 3.33 | 27 | 0 | 170 | 181 | 53 | 125 |
| Hoshino, Nobuyuki, BW | 10 | 12 | 3.35 | 25 | 0 | 185 | 172 | 52 | 153 |
| Komiyama, Satoru, Marines | 12 | 14 | 3.44 | 27 | 0 | 204 | 193 | 71 | 160 |
| Kaku, Taigen, Lions | 8 | 8 | 3.51 | 22 | 0 | 133 | 121 | 26 | 88 |
| Sato, Yoshinori, Blue Wave | 9 | 8 | 3.55 | 21 | 0 | 142 | 123 | 55 | 99 |
| Shibata, Yasumitsu, Fighters | 7 | 11 | 3.55 | 25 | 0 | 132 | 125 | 34 | 76 |
| Nomo, Hideo, Buffaloes | 17 | 12 | 3.70 | 32 | 0 | 243 | 201 | 148 | 276 |

(Remaining U.S. Player)

| | W | L | ERA | G | SV | IP | H | BB | SO |
|---|---|---|---|---|---|---|---|---|---|
| Tunnell, Lee, Hawks | 2 | 8 | 4.82 | 20 | 0 | 75 | 83 | 37 | 28 |

# Puerto Rico Repeats As CWS Champion

**By ALLAN SIMPSON**

In the ever-changing and often turbulent world of winter baseball, the status quo was in order at the 1993 Caribbean World Series.

Defending champion Puerto Rico, represented by Santurce, won the 36th annual classic, beating Aguilas, the Dominican Republic entry, 9-5, in a one-game playoff. The four-team tournament was played in the Mexican resort city of Mazatlan.

A year earlier, in Hermosillo, Mexico, Mayaguez won the title for Puerto Rico, beating Venezuela in a winner-take-all final.

Santurce successfully kept the title in the Puerto Rican family, even though it lost twice to Aguilas in the double-round robin format. Both teams finished that segment with 4-2 records, but in the playoff Santurce blistered Aguilas behind a ringing 18-hit attack.

Shortstop Dickie Thon (Brewers) and outfielder Eric Fox (Athletics) had three hits apiece and drove in six runs for the Crabbers, who won the CWS for the first time since the series was resumed in 1970. Lefthander Kevin Brown (Mariners), who came on in the fourth

TY SPORT PHOTOS

inning of a 5-5 tie and pitched 5⅓ scoreless innings, picked up the win. Thon's two-run homer in the sixth was the game winner.

"This was important for me," said Thon, who made his first Caribbean Series appearance since 1983, when he played for the Arecibo team that won the title. "At first I didn't plan to come here, but I felt this might be the last time I would have a chance to play for Puerto Rico and wanted to be part of this."

**Hector Villaneuva**

First baseman Hector Villaneuva (Cardinals), who went 9-for-18 with two homers and nine RBIs in the preliminary phase of the tournament, won MVP honors for Santurce, while righthander Mike Cook (Orioles), a stalwart in the Crabbers bullpen all season long, won two games without allowing a run in 11 innings.

The series was not without its usual controversy.

Zulia and host Mazatlan were scheduled to play the final game of the round-robin segment immediately after Aguilas beat Santurce, 4-2, to force the one-game playoff. With national hero Fernando Valenzuela slated to make his second series start for Mazatlan, the stands at Teodoro Mariscal Stadium were packed for the final session.

Caribbean Baseball Confederation officials at first decided that the Santurce-Aguilas playoff game would

be played after the meaningless Zulia-Mazatlan encounter, about 11 p.m., to ensure the tournament would finish on the sixth day and facilitate airline flights out of Mexico the next day. But players from both Puerto Rico and the Dominican Republic voted to boycott the late start.

It was then decided that the two finalists would meet immediately after their first encounter that day, with the Zulia-Mazatlan game to follow. But Zulia owner Pepe Machada was so upset with the lack of direction from series officials that he ordered his players onto the team bus and back to the hotel while the playoff game was in progress.

After Valenzuela warmed up and it became obvious

---

# 1993 CARIBBEAN WORLD SERIES

Mazatlan, Mexico
Feb. 4-9, 1993

## CHAMPIONSHIP STANDINGS

| | W | L | PCT. | GB |
|---|---|---|---|---|
| Puerto Rico (Santurce) | 4 | 2 | .667 | — |
| Dominican Republic (Aguilas) | 4 | 2 | .667 | — |
| Venezuela (Zulia) | 2 | 4 | .333 | 2 |
| Mexico (Mazatlan) | 2 | 4 | .333 | 2 |

**CHAMPIONSHIP PLAYOFF:** Puerto Rico 9, Dominican Republic 5.

## INDIVIDUAL BATTING LEADERS
(Minimum 15 Plate Appearances)

| | AVG | AB | R | H | 2B | 3B | HR | RBI | SB |
|---|---|---|---|---|---|---|---|---|---|
| Villanueva, Hector, PRico | .500 | 18 | 5 | 9 | 1 | 0 | 2 | 9 | 0 |
| Cedeno, Andujar, Dom. Rep. | .381 | 21 | 5 | 8 | 2 | 0 | 0 | 2 | 0 |
| Ortiz, Junior, PRico | .375 | 24 | 5 | 9 | 0 | 0 | 1 | 3 | 0 |
| Bryant, Scott, Ven. | .368 | 19 | 1 | 7 | 1 | 0 | 1 | 2 | 1 |
| Pena, Tony, Dom. Rep. | .300 | 20 | 3 | 6 | 0 | 0 | 1 | 3 | 0 |
| Rivera, German, PRico | .294 | 17 | 2 | 5 | 0 | 0 | 1 | 2 | 0 |
| Alou, Moises, Dom. Rep. | .273 | 22 | 4 | 6 | 0 | 0 | 1 | 2 | 3 |
| Thon, Dickie, PRico | .273 | 22 | 3 | 6 | 2 | 0 | 0 | 2 | 0 |
| Carrillo, Matias, Mexico | .250 | 20 | 2 | 5 | 1 | 0 | 2 | 3 | 0 |
| Colon, Cris, Ven. | .250 | 20 | 2 | 5 | 1 | 0 | 1 | 5 | 0 |
| Naveda, Edgar, Ven. | .250 | 16 | 0 | 4 | 1 | 0 | 0 | 2 | 0 |
| Grotewald, Jeff, Ven. | .235 | 17 | 1 | 4 | 0 | 0 | 0 | 0 | 0 |
| Munoz, Jose, PRico | .227 | 22 | 6 | 5 | 2 | 0 | 0 | 0 | 3 |
| Canate, Willie, Ven. | .211 | 19 | 2 | 4 | 2 | 0 | 0 | 1 | 0 |
| Ramirez, Omar, Dom. Rep. | .211 | 19 | 3 | 4 | 2 | 0 | 0 | 2 | 1 |

## INDIVIDUAL PITCHING LEADERS
(Minimum 5 Innings)

| | W | L | ERA | G | SV | IP | H | BB | SO |
|---|---|---|---|---|---|---|---|---|---|
| Cook, Mike, PRico | 2 | 0 | 0.00 | 4 | 0 | 11 | 4 | 4 | 8 |
| Johnson, Earnie, Mexico | 0 | 0 | 0.00 | 2 | 0 | 8 | 6 | 1 | 7 |
| Garcia, Mike, Mexico | 0 | 0 | 0.00 | 1 | 0 | 5 | 0 | 2 | 4 |
| Scott, Darryl, PRico | 0 | 0 | 0.00 | 3 | 1 | 5 | 2 | 0 | 10 |
| Martinez, Jose, Dom. Rep. | 1 | 0 | 0.77 | 2 | 0 | 12 | 10 | 1 | 8 |
| Fraser, Willie, PRico | 0 | 1 | 0.90 | 2 | 0 | 10 | 9 | 2 | 4 |
| Gomez, Henrique, Ven. | 1 | 0 | 1.00 | 1 | 0 | 9 | 6 | 4 | 6 |
| Grimsley, Jason, Ven. | 0 | 0 | 1.13 | 1 | 0 | 8 | 4 | 5 | 7 |
| Lugo, Urbano, Ven. | 1 | 0 | 1.13 | 1 | 0 | 8 | 3 | 2 | 5 |
| Johnson, Dave, Dom. Rep. | 1 | 0 | 1.29 | 2 | 0 | 14 | 7 | 9 | 8 |

**Most Valuable Player**—Hector Villanueva, Puerto Rico.

---

that Mazatlan wouldn't have an opponent, Mexico was awarded a victory by forfeit, a decision that didn't sit well with more than 12,000 fans who had come to see Valenzuela pitch.

Valenzuela, 32, had pitched effectively during the Mexican Pacific League regular season, going 7-4 with a 2.95 ERA for Navojoa. He joined Mazatlan for the Caribbean Series when more than 10,000 fans, speaking by phone and mail, urged the Mazatlan club to add the portly lefthander to its roster.

## Ongoing Problems

Despite the resurgence of the Caribbean Series after an ill-fated attempt to move the series to Miami in 1990 and 1991, winter ball in the four competing Caribbean countries still faced problems compounded by declining attendance, political upheaval, a devalued currency and the reluctance of native major leaguers, earning large salaries, to suit up.

In response, Major League Baseball in the fall of 1992 established a winter league of its own, the Arizona Fall League, in which each major league club provided at least six of its best upper-tier prospects. The burgeoning Australian League, in its fourth season, and the Hawaiian Winter League, which began play in the fall of 1993, also further diluted the talent pool avaialable to Caribbean nations.

JULIE D. LANZILLO

**Fernando Valenzuela**

Underscoring the political unrest, the Venezuelan League season was seriously threatened Nov. 27, 1992, when about 1,300 of the nation's air force and army troops tried to overthrow its democratic government. Several major league clubs, fearing for the safety of their players, called a number home although Caracas manager Phil Regan (Dodgers) said his players never

| CARIBBEAN WORLD SERIES | | |
| --- | --- | --- |
| Year | Site | Champion |
| 1968-69 | No Series | |
| 1969-70 | Caracas, Venez. | Magallanes (Venezuela) |
| 1970-71 | San Juan, P.R. | Licey (Dominican Republic) |
| 1971-72 | Santo Domingo, D.R. | Ponce (Puerto Rico) |
| 1972-73 | Caracas, Venez. | Licey (Dominican Republic) |
| 1973-74 | Hermosillo, Mexico | Caguas (Puerto Rico) |
| 1974-75 | San Juan, P.R. | Bayamon (Puerto Rico) |
| 1975-76 | Santo Domingo, D.R. | Hermosillo (Mexico) |
| 1976-77 | Caracas, Venez. | Licey (Dominican Republic) |
| 1977-78 | Mazatlan, Mexico | Mayaguez (Puerto Rico) |
| 1978-79 | San Juan, P.R. | Magallanes (Venezuela) |
| 1979-80 | Santo Domingo, D.R. | Licey (Dominican Republic) |
| 1980-81 | No Series | |
| 1981-82 | Hermosillo, Mexico | Caracas (Venezuela) |
| 1982-83 | Caracas, Venez. | Arecibo (Puerto Rico) |
| 1983-84 | San Juan, P.R. | Zulia (Venezuela) |
| 1984-85 | Mazatlan, Mexico | Licey (Dominican Republic) |
| 1985-86 | Maracaibo, Venez. | Mexicali (Mexico) |
| 1986-87 | Hermosillo, Mexico | Caguas (Puerto Rico) |
| 1987-88 | Santo Domingo, D.R. | Escogido (Dominican Republic) |
| 1988-89 | Mazatlan, Mexico | Zulia (Venezuela) |
| 1989-90 | Miami | Escogido (Dominican Republic) |
| 1990-91 | Miami | Licey (Dominican Republic) |
| 1991-92 | Hermosillo, Mexico | Mayaguez (Puerto Rico) |
| 1992-93 | Mazatlan, Mexico | Santurce (Puerto Rico) |

were in real danger.

"I think they handled it well," Regan said. "They were under control at all times, and I think that things went well, everything considered."

Despite the trouble, Venezuela was picked as the site of the 1994 Caribbean Series—Feb. 3-8 in Puerto La Plata. Caribbean Series officials were hopeful they can resume rotating the series among the four competing countries, a practice that was abandoned in the mid-1980s.

## Carrillo Shines

Outfielder Matias Carrillo, whose slugging exploits lifted Mexicali to the Mexican Pacific League's best overall record, was selected Baseball America's 1992-93 Winter Player of the Year. He hit a league-high .404.

Carrillo, 30, had tried for several years to hook on with a major league club, but his best shot was an eight-day trial with Milwaukee in 1991, when he failed to make a single plate appearance. Tired of the minor leagues and waiting for his chance, Carrillo resigned himself to playing the rest of his career in his native country.

"I have scouts who want to sign me, but I don't want to play anymore in the minor leagues," Carrillo said. "I'd rather stay in Mexico where it's comfortable and I have a chance to play."

Matias enjoyed a big 1993 summer season for the Mexican League's Mexico City Tigers, leading the league with 38 homers and 125 RBIs, and finally was rewarded with a chance to play in the big leagues when the expansion Florida Marlins purchased his contract following the season.

# 1992-93 WINTER ALL-STAR TEAM

Selected by Baseball America

| Pos. | Player, Club (Nation) | Org. | AVG | AB | R | H | 2B | 3B | HR | RBI | SB |
| --- | --- | --- | --- | --- | --- | --- | --- | --- | --- | --- | --- |
| C | Todd Pratt, Oriente (Venezuela) | Phillies | .290 | 145 | 30 | 42 | 10 | 0 | 9 | 32 | 3 |
| 1B | Ryan Klesko, Grand Canyon (Arizona) | Braves | .270 | 126 | 29 | 34 | 4 | 0 | 11 | 26 | 7 |
| 2B | Jeff Frye, Oriente (Venezuela) | Rangers | .385 | 161 | 29 | 62 | 6 | 4 | 0 | 20 | 8 |
| 3B | Pedro Castellano, Zulia (Venezuela) | Rangers | .314 | 274 | 29 | 86 | 16 | 1 | 4 | 36 | 4 |
| SS | Carlos Garcia, Magallanes (Venezuela) | Pirates | .364 | 220 | 42 | 80 | 19 | 3 | 3 | 35 | 9 |
| OF | Matias Carrillo, Mexicali (Mexico) | None | .374 | 291 | 68 | 109 | 14 | 1 | 15 | 51 | 41 |
| | Steve Pegues, Tucson (Arizona), La Guaira (Venezuela) | Padres | .345 | 246 | 44 | 85 | 11 | 6 | 8 | 42 | 11 |
| | Willie Canate, Lara (Venezuela) | Reds | .300 | 290 | 53 | 87 | 11 | 2 | 6 | 30 | 21 |
| DH | Scott Cepicky, Oriente (Venezuela) | White Sox | .282 | 202 | 34 | 57 | 10 | 0 | 13 | 36 | 1 |

| | | | W | L | ERA | G | SV | IP | H | BB | SO |
| --- | --- | --- | --- | --- | --- | --- | --- | --- | --- | --- | --- |
| P | Mike Cook, Santurce (Puerto Rico) | Orioles | 8 | 2 | 0.60 | 29 | 3 | 82 | 54 | 18 | 65 |
| | Dave Burba, Caracas (Venezuela) | Giants | 7 | 0 | 1.23 | 11 | 0 | 73 | 60 | 24 | 63 |
| | Roberto Hernandez, Mayaguez (P.R.) | White Sox | 0 | 3 | 1.85 | 25 | 16 | 34 | 18 | 10 | 33 |
| | Kevin Rogers, Scottsdale (Arizona) | Giants | 2 | 1 | 0.49 | 25 | 3 | 37 | 13 | 9 | 38 |

**PLAYER OF THE YEAR:** Matias Carrillo, of, Mexicali (Mexico).

# PUERTO RICAN LEAGUE

## Gonzalez Sparks Santurce To Title

Attrition was the name of the game in the Puerto Rican Winter League in 1992-93.

Not only did the 54-year-old league lose a member club when Bayamon folded, reducing active membership to five, but the league sharply scaled back its playing schedule from 60 games to 48. At that, rainy weather played such havoc that Arecibo lost nine more dates and never was able to make up the 3½-game deficit between itself and the fourth and final playoff berth.

Attrition was equally pronounced on the playing field, where the league-wide batting average was a lowly .224. There were only 48 home runs hit during the regular season.

Only one player, Mayaguez shortstop Wilfredo Cordero (Expos), qualified for the batting title with an average of at least .300. Cordero hit .304—the lowest average by a batting champion since Felix Millan hit .318 in 1968-69. Mayaguez lefthander Fernando Figueroa's 0.63 ERA was the lowest in league history.

About the only spark of offensive proficiency came from outfielder Juan Gonzalez (Rangers), who sandwiched American League home run titles around seven homers he hit in only 66 at-bats for Santurce. His meager total still was good enough to lead the league, but his .333 average did not stand up because he fell well short of the required number of plate appearances.

Gonzalez didn't don a Santurce uniform until after the league's all-star game, but his play so aroused the Crabbers that he was named the league's MVP and Santurce went on to win both the league title and its first-ever Caribbean World Series title. Veteran major leaguers Dickie Thon (Brewers) and Jose Lind (Royals) also suited up down the stretch and played an instrumental role for Santurce, which rebounded from a sub-.500 record in 1991-92.

Gonzalez' first appearance in a Santurce uniform since 1989-90 also helped Santurce draw 115,945 fans, a significant figure for a league where attendance has been on a steady decline.

Still, it was pitching that lifted Santurce to the title. Led by league pitcher of the year Jose Lebron (Padres), who led with seven wins, the Crabbers compiled a 1.67 ERA in the regular season. Against San Juan in the best-of-9 championship series, Crabbers pitchers allowed only four runs in six games, leading to a 5-1 series win.

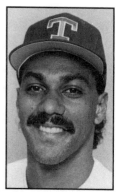

**Offensive Threats.** Wil Cordero, left, was league's only .300 hitter, while Juan Gonzalez led league with seven homers.

"We always knew we had the bats," Gonzalez said, "but the pitchers really came through for us in a big way. I've never won a championship, not even in Little League."

Gonzalez did not accompany the Crabbers to the Caribbean World Series.

Meanwhile, the league resigned itself to the loss of Bayamon when Cowboys ownership did not pay players at the end of the 1991-92 season. Its players were dispersed among the other five teams.

**—ALLAN SIMPSON**

### LEAGUE CHAMPIONS
**Last 25 Years**

| | |
|---|---|
| 1968-69 | Ponce |
| 1969-70 | Ponce |
| 1970-71 | Santurce |
| 1971-72 | Ponce |
| 1972-73 | Santurce |
| 1973-74 | Caguas |
| 1974-75 | Bayamon |
| 1975-76 | Bayamon |
| 1976-77 | Caguas |
| 1977-78 | Mayaguez |
| 1978-79 | Caguas |
| 1979-80 | Bayamon |
| 1980-81 | Mayaguez |
| 1981-82 | Ponce |
| 1982-83 | Arecibo |
| 1983-84 | Mayaguez |
| 1984-85 | San Juan |
| 1985-86 | Mayaguez |
| 1986-87 | Caguas |
| 1987-88 | Mayaguez |
| 1988-89 | Mayaguez |
| 1989-90 | San Juan |
| 1990-91 | Santurce |
| 1991-92 | Mayaguez |
| 1992-93 | Santurce |

### STANDINGS

| REGULAR SEASON | W | L | PCT | GB |
|---|---|---|---|---|
| Santurce | 29 | 18 | .617 | — |
| Mayaguez | 26 | 20 | .565 | 2½ |
| San Juan | 20 | 22 | .476 | 6½ |
| Ponce | 22 | 26 | .458 | 7½ |
| Arecibo | 14 | 25 | .359 | 11 |

### INDIVIDUAL BATTING LEADERS
(Minimum 72 Plate Appearances)

| | AVG | AB | R | H | 2B | 3B | HR | RBI | SB |
|---|---|---|---|---|---|---|---|---|---|
| Gonzalez, Juan, Santurce | .333 | 66 | 12 | 22 | 8 | 0 | 7 | 14 | 0 |
| Bolick, Frank, Mayaguez | .304 | 79 | 6 | 24 | 6 | 0 | 1 | 10 | 4 |
| CORDERO, WIL, Mayaguez | .304 | 135 | 12 | 41 | 7 | 1 | 1 | 12 | 3 |
| Sherman, Darrell, Santurce | .294 | 126 | 19 | 37 | 7 | 0 | 0 | 9 | 13 |
| Baerga, Carlos, San Juan | .293 | 82 | 10 | 24 | 2 | 0 | 3 | 9 | 4 |
| Cuevas, Angelo, Arecibo | .290 | 62 | 7 | 18 | 4 | 0 | 2 | 11 | 0 |
| Cora, Joey, Ponce | .282 | 163 | 23 | 46 | 5 | 4 | 0 | 6 | 8 |
| Rodriguez, Vic, Arecibo | .275 | 69 | 6 | 19 | 4 | 0 | 0 | 2 | 0 |
| Lopez, Luis, San Juan | .261 | 142 | 9 | 37 | 8 | 1 | 2 | 11 | 0 |
| Laboy, Carlos, San Juan | .260 | 77 | 6 | 20 | 5 | 1 | 1 | 10 | 1 |
| Lopez, Javy, San Juan | .256 | 117 | 11 | 30 | 3 | 0 | 2 | 11 | 0 |
| Monell, Johnny, Ponce | .256 | 121 | 6 | 31 | 2 | 0 | 1 | 13 | 3 |
| Thome, Jim, Ponce | .255 | 145 | 15 | 37 | 6 | 2 | 2 | 21 | 1 |
| Rivera, German, Santurce | .254 | 126 | 13 | 32 | 5 | 0 | 0 | 9 | 1 |
| Brewer, Rod, Mayaguez | .254 | 71 | 9 | 18 | 3 | 0 | 0 | 6 | 0 |
| Ortiz, Junior, Santurce | .252 | 119 | 7 | 30 | 10 | 0 | 1 | 10 | 0 |
| Cruz, Ivan, Mayaguez | .250 | 112 | 10 | 28 | 4 | 0 | 1 | 8 | 0 |
| Barron, Tony, San Juan | .250 | 104 | 12 | 26 | 4 | 0 | 0 | 6 | 7 |
| Merced, Orlando, Arecibo | .245 | 110 | 10 | 27 | 3 | 2 | 0 | 9 | 4 |
| Campanis, Jim, Mayaguez | .244 | 90 | 9 | 22 | 2 | 0 | 1 | 10 | 1 |
| Williams, Gerald, Santurce | .244 | 160 | 15 | 39 | 6 | 1 | 0 | 15 | 14 |
| Snider, Van, Mayaguez | .243 | 140 | 14 | 34 | 9 | 0 | 1 | 17 | 3 |

| | | | | | | | | | |
|---|---|---|---|---|---|---|---|---|---|
| Shields, Tommy, Arecibo | .241 | 116 | 8 | 28 | 8 | 0 | 0 | 6 | 2 |
| Delgado, Carlos, San Juan | .239 | 117 | 13 | 28 | 7 | 1 | 2 | 16 | 0 |
| Diaz, Mario, Ponce | .238 | 105 | 6 | 25 | 2 | 1 | 2 | 15 | 2 |
| Baez, Kevin, Arecibo | .238 | 101 | 9 | 24 | 5 | 0 | 0 | 8 | 0 |
| Melendez, Francisco, Santurce | .235 | 68 | 7 | 16 | 1 | 0 | 1 | 5 | 2 |
| Diaz, Alex, Mayaguez | .234 | 154 | 13 | 36 | 4 | 2 | 0 | 7 | 7 |
| Hernandez, Jose, Ponce | .227 | 88 | 10 | 20 | 3 | 0 | 0 | 3 | 6 |
| Valentin, Jose, Mayaguez | .225 | 120 | 17 | 27 | 4 | 2 | 0 | 10 | 1 |
| Olmeda, Jose, Mayaguez | .213 | 160 | 13 | 34 | 6 | 2 | 2 | 22 | 2 |
| Villanueva, Hector, Santurce | .206 | 131 | 11 | 27 | 6 | 0 | 4 | 15 | 1 |
| Quinones, Luis, Mayaguez | .205 | 112 | 14 | 23 | 4 | 0 | 0 | 3 | 1 |
| Rossy, Rico, San Juan | .202 | 124 | 15 | 25 | 5 | 0 | 1 | 10 | 1 |
| Kirby, Wayne, Ponce | .199 | 156 | 12 | 31 | 5 | 0 | 0 | 5 | 4 |
| Rosado, Edwin, Ponce | .197 | 76 | 2 | 15 | 1 | 1 | 0 | 6 | 1 |
| Martinez, Luis, Ponce | .191 | 89 | 7 | 17 | 8 | 0 | 0 | 7 | 3 |
| Martinez, Carmelo, Arecibo | .190 | 105 | 8 | 20 | 6 | 0 | 2 | 10 | 0 |
| Rodriguez, Boi, Arecibo | .190 | 100 | 6 | 19 | 2 | 0 | 0 | 3 | 1 |
| Bryant, Scott, Arecibo | .190 | 79 | 10 | 15 | 3 | 0 | 1 | 6 | 0 |
| Munoz, Jose, Santurce | .186 | 70 | 8 | 13 | 2 | 1 | 0 | 3 | 0 |
| Otero, Ricky, Arecibo | .183 | 82 | 7 | 15 | 2 | 1 | 0 | 1 | 4 |
| Escalera, Ruben, San Juan | .179 | 134 | 6 | 24 | 2 | 0 | 0 | 9 | 1 |
| Flaherty, John, Arecibo | .176 | 91 | 6 | 16 | 1 | 0 | 0 | 6 | 1 |
| Simms, Mike, Ponce | .159 | 145 | 12 | 23 | 6 | 1 | 2 | 14 | 3 |
| Fariss, Monty, San Juan | .131 | 61 | 5 | 8 | 3 | 0 | 1 | 3 | 0 |
| Alicea, Edwin, Santurce | .130 | 77 | 10 | 10 | 3 | 0 | 0 | 1 | 7 |
| Vargas, Hector, Arecibo | .121 | 58 | 3 | 7 | 3 | 0 | 0 | 5 | 1 |

### INDIVIDUAL PITCHING LEADERS
(Minimum 23 Innings)

| | W | L | ERA | G | SV | IP | H | BB | SO |
|---|---|---|---|---|---|---|---|---|---|
| Brewer, Billy, Santurce | 2 | 1 | 0.39 | 23 | 7 | 23 | 10 | 5 | 24 |
| FIGUEROA, FERNANDO, May. | 3 | 3 | 0.63 | 11 | 0 | 43 | 31 | 10 | 18 |
| Cook, Mike, Santurce | 4 | 1 | 0.70 | 16 | 3 | 38 | 25 | 8 | 25 |
| Correa, Amilcar, Mayaguez | 0 | 1 | 1.08 | 10 | 0 | 25 | 13 | 12 | 13 |
| Rivera, Roberto, Ponce | 1 | 1 | 1.19 | 14 | 2 | 23 | 16 | 2 | 5 |
| Valera, Julio, Mayaguez | 4 | 1 | 1.34 | 5 | 0 | 34 | 20 | 8 | 26 |
| McMichael, Greg, Ponce | 4 | 2 | 1.35 | 9 | 0 | 60 | 41 | 13 | 40 |
| Harris, Greg, Santurce | 4 | 1 | 1.64 | 8 | 0 | 66 | 53 | 11 | 34 |
| Smithberg, Roger, Mayaguez | 4 | 3 | 1.66 | 9 | 0 | 60 | 56 | 14 | 25 |
| Oliveras, Francisco, Santurce | 4 | 4 | 1.71 | 10 | 0 | 68 | 53 | 11 | 30 |
| Hernandez, Roberto, Mayaguez | 0 | 2 | 1.75 | 19 | 13 | 26 | 10 | 8 | 27 |
| Rambo, Dan, Arecibo | 2 | 1 | 1.76 | 7 | 0 | 46 | 30 | 17 | 17 |
| Brown, Kevin, Mayaguez | 4 | 2 | 1.77 | 9 | 0 | 56 | 49 | 15 | 27 |
| Robinson, Napoleon, Santurce | 4 | 3 | 1.78 | 10 | 0 | 56 | 34 | 14 | 27 |
| Arocha, Rene, Arecibo | 2 | 1 | 1.88 | 4 | 0 | 24 | 20 | 4 | 13 |
| Lebron, Jose, Santurce | 7 | 2 | 2.05 | 10 | 0 | 48 | 35 | 14 | 25 |
| Chaves, Rafael, Ponce | 3 | 3 | 2.08 | 17 | 1 | 30 | 18 | 9 | 12 |
| McCarthy, Tom, San Juan | 2 | 4 | 2.15 | 8 | 0 | 46 | 40 | 9 | 19 |
| Brown, Tim, Arecibo | 4 | 2 | 2.25 | 8 | 0 | 44 | 41 | 8 | 25 |
| Otto, Dave, Ponce | 3 | 4 | 2.31 | 13 | 1 | 58 | 51 | 19 | 29 |
| Montalvo, Rafael, San Juan | 4 | 1 | 2.38 | 15 | 0 | 42 | 33 | 8 | 21 |
| Boyd, Oil Can, San Juan | 2 | 3 | 2.40 | 10 | 0 | 56 | 48 | 9 | 35 |
| Springer, Dennis, San Juan | 3 | 2 | 2.41 | 8 | 0 | 52 | 40 | 16 | 29 |
| Lind, Orlando, San Juan | 1 | 4 | 2.52 | 7 | 0 | 39 | 30 | 13 | 21 |
| Alicea, Miguel, Ponce | 2 | 3 | 2.59 | 16 | 1 | 31 | 25 | 7 | 12 |

| | | | | | | | | | |
|---|---|---|---|---|---|---|---|---|---|
| Nunez, Edwin, Ponce | 2 | 1 | 2.64 | 6 | 0 | 31 | 22 | 7 | 25 |
| Correa, Ramser, Ponce | 2 | 3 | 2.66 | 10 | 1 | 47 | 35 | 25 | 19 |
| Johnson, Judd, San Juan | 2 | 1 | 2.70 | 8 | 0 | 23 | 24 | 6 | 13 |
| Lancaster, Les, Arecibo | 1 | 2 | 2.70 | 6 | 0 | 33 | 26 | 9 | 12 |
| Olivares, Omar, Mayaguez | 2 | 1 | 2.81 | 5 | 0 | 32 | 30 | 4 | 8 |
| De Leon, Luis, Mayaguez | 2 | 2 | 2.89 | 7 | 0 | 37 | 27 | 5 | 24 |
| Pacheco, Jose, Ponce | 1 | 3 | 2.93 | 9 | 1 | 28 | 30 | 10 | 11 |
| Burgos, John, Arecibo | 1 | 2 | 3.49 | 13 | 1 | 28 | 29 | 12 | 10 |
| Vasquez, Marcos, Arecibo | 2 | 2 | 3.54 | 10 | 0 | 28 | 24 | 13 | 10 |
| Grott, Matt, Mayaguez | 3 | 2 | 3.62 | 14 | 1 | 32 | 32 | 8 | 21 |
| Coffman, Kevin, Ponce | 1 | 2 | 3.75 | 6 | 0 | 24 | 19 | 31 | 12 |

| PLAYOFFS | W | L | PCT | GB |
|---|---|---|---|---|
| San Juan | 7 | 5 | .583 | — |
| Santurce | 7 | 6 | .538 | ½ |
| Mayaguez | 6 | 7 | .462 | 1½ |
| Ponce | 5 | 7 | .417 | 2 |

**Championship Series:** Santurce defeated San Juan, 5-1, in best-of-9 final.

### INDIVIDUAL BATTING LEADERS
(Minimum 24 Plate Appearances)

| | AVG | AB | R | H | 2B | 3B | HR | RBI | SB |
|---|---|---|---|---|---|---|---|---|---|
| Martinez, Luis, Ponce | .367 | 30 | 5 | 11 | 2 | 1 | 0 | 3 | 0 |
| Lopez, Javy, San Juan | .333 | 48 | 3 | 16 | 0 | 0 | 0 | 1 | 0 |
| Cora, Joey, Ponce | .327 | 49 | 3 | 16 | 1 | 0 | 0 | 4 | 2 |
| Munoz, Jose, Santurce | .308 | 39 | 4 | 12 | 1 | 0 | 0 | 0 | 1 |
| Caraballo, Gary, Ponce | .306 | 36 | 2 | 11 | 2 | 0 | 1 | 5 | 0 |
| Simms, Mike, Ponce | .302 | 43 | 5 | 13 | 6 | 0 | 0 | 3 | 0 |
| Thon, Dickie, Santurce | .302 | 53 | 4 | 16 | 2 | 0 | 1 | 2 | 3 |
| Gonzalez, Juan, Santurce | .300 | 40 | 2 | 12 | 2 | 0 | 0 | 2 | 0 |
| Harris, Donald, San Juan | .295 | 44 | 4 | 13 | 1 | 0 | 2 | 4 | 0 |
| Cruz, Ruben, San Juan | .273 | 22 | 3 | 6 | 0 | 0 | 0 | 1 | 0 |
| Williams, Gerald, Santurce | .271 | 48 | 9 | 13 | 1 | 0 | 1 | 6 | 1 |
| Rivera, German, Santurce | .268 | 41 | 1 | 11 | 1 | 0 | 1 | 4 | 0 |
| Delgado, Carlos, San Juan | .262 | 42 | 3 | 11 | 1 | 0 | 0 | 5 | 0 |
| Escalera, Ruben, San Juan | .262 | 42 | 4 | 11 | 1 | 0 | 0 | 3 | 0 |
| Cordero, Wil, Mayaguez | .259 | 54 | 6 | 14 | 3 | 2 | 0 | 8 | 1 |

### INDIVIDUAL PITCHING LEADERS
(Minimum 12 Innings)

| | W | L | ERA | G | SV | IP | H | BB | SO |
|---|---|---|---|---|---|---|---|---|---|
| Cook, Mike, Santurce | 1 | 1 | 0.40 | 6 | 0 | 22 | 18 | 5 | 20 |
| Montalvo, Rafael, San Juan | 2 | 2 | 0.59 | 6 | 0 | 15 | 12 | 4 | 8 |
| Valera, Julio, Mayaguez | 2 | 0 | 0.82 | 3 | 0 | 22 | 15 | 4 | 11 |
| Smithberg, Roger, Mayaguez | 1 | 2 | 1.15 | 4 | 0 | 31 | 22 | 6 | 10 |
| Boyd, Oil Can, San Juan | 2 | 0 | 1.29 | 3 | 0 | 14 | 8 | 3 | 7 |
| Springer, Dennis, San Juan | 2 | 0 | 1.40 | 3 | 0 | 26 | 18 | 5 | 9 |
| Fraser, Willie, Santurce | 3 | 0 | 1.40 | 3 | 0 | 19 | 10 | 3 | 11 |
| McMichael, Greg, Ponce | 1 | 1 | 1.57 | 3 | 0 | 23 | 21 | 4 | 9 |
| McCarthy, Tom, San Juan | 0 | 1 | 2.12 | 3 | 0 | 17 | 17 | 2 | 11 |
| Oliveras, Francisco, Santurce | 2 | 1 | 2.16 | 3 | 0 | 25 | 20 | 2 | 10 |
| Lebron, Jose, Santurce | 0 | 2 | 2.29 | 3 | 0 | 20 | 12 | 5 | 7 |
| Stanford, Don, Ponce | 1 | 1 | 3.00 | 3 | 0 | 18 | 19 | 7 | 4 |

# PUERTO RICAN LEAGUE: YEAR-BY-YEAR LEADERS

## Last 25 Years

| Year | Batting | Home Runs | Wins | ERA |
|---|---|---|---|---|
| 1968-69 | Felix Millan, Caguas .317 | George Scott, Santurce .. 13 | Bill Kelso, Ponce 10 | Jerry Johnson, Ponce 1.29 |
| 1969-70 | Felix Millan, Caguas .345 | Nate Colbert, Caguas 16 | Wayne Simpson, Ponce 11 | Wayne Simpson, Ponce 1.55 |
| 1970-71 | Sandy Alomar, Ponce .343 | Reggie Jackson, Sant. .. 20 | Mike Wegener, Santurce 9 | Tom Kelley, Ponce 2.04 |
| 1971-72 | Don Baylor, Santurce .324 | Willie Montanez, Caguas 15 | Roger Moret, Santurce 14 | John Strohmayer, Caguas . 1.71 |
| 1972-73 | Jose Cruz, Ponce .335 | Richie Zisk, San Juan .. 14 | 2 tied at 10 | Chris Zachary, Ponce 2.00 |
| 1973-74 | George Hendrick, Sant. .363 | 2 tied at 14 | 3 tied at 10 | Ernie McAnally, Ponce 1.72 |
| 1974-75 | Ken Griffey, Bayamon .357 | Danny Walton, Arecibo 14 | Ed Figueroa, Caguas 10 | Alan Dopfel, Ponce 1.90 |
| 1975-76 | Otto Velez, Ponce .328 | Benny Ayala, Arecibo.... 14 | Odell Jones, Bayamon. 11 | Tom Bruno, Arecibo 1.23 |
| 1976-77 | Sixto Lezcano, Caguas .366 | Roger Freed, Ponce 16 | Ed Rodriguez, Caguas 9 | Ed Rodriguez, Caguas 2.71 |
| 1977-78 | Ron LeFlore, Mayaguez .. .396 | 2 tied at 17 | Dennis Lamp, Arecibo 9 | Scott McGregor, Caguas .. 2.18 |
| 1978-79 | Jose Cruz, Caguas .370 | Jim Dwyer, Mayaguez.... 15 | 2 tied at 9 | Steve McCatty, Ponce 1.71 |
| 1979-80 | Denny Walling, Bayamon .330 | Ismael Oquendo, Sant. .. 9 | 2 tied at 9 | Darrell Jackson, Mayaguez 1.33 |
| 1980-81 | Dickie Thon, Bayamon .329 | Hector Cruz, Caguas 11 | 3 tied at 8 | Dave Smith, Bayamon 0.94 |
| 1981-82 | Dickie Thon, Bayamon .333 | Jose Cruz, Caguas 12 | Edwin Nunez, Ponce 9 | Edwin Nunez, Ponce 1.72 |
| 1982-83 | Brian Harper, Bayamon .378 | Carmelo Martinez, Bay. .. 17 | 2 tied at 9 | Ed Figueroa, Santurce 2.93 |
| 1983-84 | Don Mattingly, Caguas .368 | Candy Maldonado, Are.... 15 | Rick Mahler, Santurce 10 | Kevin Hagen, Mayaguez .... 1.92 |
| 1984-85 | Orlando Sanchez, Sant. .354 | Jerry Willard, Santurce.... 14 | Francisco Oliveras, Caguas . 8 | Jose Guzman, Mayaguez.... 1.62 |
| 1985-86 | Wally Joyner, Mayaguez .356 | Wally Joyner, Mayaguez.. 14 | 2 tied at 9 | Luis DeLeon, Mayaguez.... 1.34 |
| 1986-87 | Victor Rodriguez, Ponce.. .377 | Ivan Calderon, Ponce.... 10 | 4 tied at 6 | Scott Anderson, Caguas .... 1.47 |
| 1987-88 | Randy Milligan, Ponce..... .343 | Ivan Calderon, Ponce.... 10 | 5 tied at 6 | Miguel Alicea, Ponce 0.93 |
| 1988-89 | Lonnie Smith, San Juan .. .366 | Ricky Jordan, Mayaguez 14 | Aris Tirado, Arecibo 9 | David Rosario, San Juan .. 1.32 |
| 1989-90 | Edgar Martinez, SJ .424 | Greg Vaughn, Ponce 10 | Ricky Bones, Ponce 10 | Jeff Gray, Mayaguez 1.24 |
| 1990-91 | Hector Villanueva, SJ..... .344 | Hector Villanueva, SJ..... 12 | 2 tied at 7 | Trevor Wilson, San Juan .. 2.07 |
| 1991-92 | Alonzo Powell, Arecibo..... .354 | Mike Simms, Ponce 9 | 2 tied at 7 | Gino Minutelli, San Juan.... 0.90 |
| 1992-93 | Wil Cordero, Mayaguez.... .304 | Juan Gonzalez, Santurce.. 7 | Jose Lebron, Santurce 7 | Fernando Figueroa, May.... 0.63 |

# DOMINICAN LEAGUE

## Underdog Aguilas Rises To Championship

A changing of the guard took place in the Dominican League in 1992-93.

Traditionally strong Escogido and Licey fell to the back of the pack as Estrellas and Aguilas battled it out for first place. Aguilas, in turn, won the two-tier play-off round to become the first Dominican team other than Escogido or Licey, both based in populous Santo Domingo, to reach the Caribbean World Series in six years.

Escogido, which had won the league title four of the previous five years, finished in last place. Licey didn't survive the first round of the playoffs.

Aguilas finished the regular season one-half game behind Estrellas, but easily won the four-team round playoff and beat Azucareros 4-2 in the league's best-of-7 championship series. Outfielder Stan Javier (Angels) went 10-for-22 with five RBIs and second baseman William Suero (Brewers) went 10-for-17 to spark Aguilas offensively.

**Tom Marsh**

Javier joined Aguilas after outfielder Tom Marsh (Phillies), who became the first non-Dominican since Ken Landreaux in 1980-81 to lead the league in hitting (.318), broke his ankle two games into the round-robin playoff. Marsh also was named the league's MVP.

The Pena brothers, catcher Tony (Red Sox) and reliever Ramon, also played significant roles in Aguilas' success. Tony joined the team midway through the regular season and hit .328 the rest of the way. He then hit .434 in the round-robin. Younger brother Ramon led the league in saves (10) for the fifth year in a row, then earned four more in post-season play.

Estrellas righthander Julian Heredia (Angels), who fell eight innings shy of leading the league in ERA in 1991-92, worked the required number of innings a year later, and led at 1.18. His 1991-92 ERA: a nearly identical 1.20.

**—ALLAN SIMPSON**

### LEAGUE CHAMPIONS
**Last 25 Years**

|  |  |
|------|------|
| 1968-69 | Escogido |
| 1969-70 | Licey |
| 1970-71 | Licey |
| 1971-72 | Aguilas |
| 1972-73 | Licey |
| 1973-74 | Licey |
| 1974-75 | Aguilas |
| 1975-76 | Aguilas |
| 1976-77 | Licey |
| 1977-78 | Aguilas |
| 1978-79 | Aguilas |
| 1979-80 | Licey |
| 1980-81 | Escogido |
| 1981-82 | Escogido |
| 1982-83 | Licey |
| 1983-84 | Licey |
| 1984-85 | Licey |
| 1985-86 | Aguilas |
| 1986-87 | Aguilas |
| 1987-88 | Escogido |
| 1988-89 | Escogido |
| 1989-90 | Escogido |
| 1990-91 | Licey |
| 1991-92 | Escogido |
| 1992-93 | Aguilas |

### STANDINGS

| REGULAR SEASON | W | L | PCT | GB |
|---|---|---|---|---|
| Estrellas | 30 | 17 | .638 | — |
| Aguilas | 29 | 17 | .630 | ½ |
| Licey | 22 | 25 | .455 | 8 |
| Azucareros | 19 | 29 | .396 | 11½ |
| Escogido | 18 | 30 | .375 | 12½ |

### INDIVIDUAL BATTING LEADERS
(Minimum 72 Plate Appearances)

| | AVG | AB | R | H | 2B | 3B | HR | RBI | SB |
|---|---|---|---|---|---|---|---|---|---|
| Pena, Tony, Aguilas. | .328 | 67 | 4 | 22 | 6 | 0 | 0 | 16 | 2 |
| Santana, Miguel, Licey | .318 | 88 | 17 | 28 | 2 | 0 | 1 | 7 | 4 |
| MARSH, TOM, Aguilas. | .318 | 129 | 18 | 41 | 7 | 3 | 0 | 19 | 5 |
| Jose, Felix, Licey | .313 | 112 | 13 | 35 | 7 | 3 | 3 | 18 | 4 |
| de la Rosa, Juan, Escogido. | .308 | 65 | 9 | 20 | 2 | 1 | 0 | 3 | 2 |
| VanderWal, John, Escogido. | .304 | 115 | 19 | 35 | 5 | 2 | 3 | 17 | 9 |
| Rosario, Victor, Azucareros. | .297 | 128 | 14 | 38 | 4 | 0 | 0 | 8 | 1 |
| Eusebio, Raul, Escogido | .297 | 91 | 5 | 27 | 3 | 1 | 0 | 12 | 2 |
| Barron, Tony, Licey | .292 | 65 | 7 | 19 | 1 | 0 | 0 | 6 | 4 |
| Berroa, Geronimo, Escogido. | .290 | 124 | 19 | 36 | 11 | 0 | 2 | 16 | 0 |
| de los Santos, Luis, Esc. | .284 | 176 | 16 | 50 | 5 | 1 | 0 | 18 | 2 |
| Mercedes, Luis, Estrellas. | .282 | 156 | 23 | 44 | 1 | 2 | 2 | 14 | 7 |
| Martinez, Domingo, Escogido. | .278 | 169 | 21 | 47 | 5 | 0 | 6 | 26 | 1 |
| Nunez, Mauricio, Estrellas. | .276 | 127 | 16 | 35 | 9 | 0 | 4 | 19 | 0 |
| Suero, William, Aguilas. | .273 | 150 | 23 | 41 | 8 | 2 | 2 | 13 | 16 |
| Fermin, Felix, Aguilas. | .273 | 154 | 23 | 42 | 4 | 1 | 0 | 19 | 7 |
| Tatis, Bernie, Aguilas. | .271 | 140 | 23 | 38 | 4 | 5 | 1 | 20 | 11 |
| Mondesi, Raul, Escogido. | .271 | 129 | 16 | 35 | 2 | 1 | 2 | 15 | 7 |
| Frazier, Lou, Azucareros. | .270 | 163 | 24 | 44 | 5 | 0 | 0 | 12 | 26 |
| Alou, Moises, Aguilas | .269 | 93 | 10 | 25 | 1 | 1 | 1 | 13 | 6 |
| Bernhardt, Cesar, Estrellas. | .268 | 138 | 13 | 37 | 9 | 1 | 1 | 19 | 0 |
| Waller, Casey, Estrellas. | .266 | 94 | 12 | 25 | 6 | 2 | 0 | 6 | 1 |
| Campusano, Sil, Licey. | .265 | 166 | 25 | 44 | 10 | 1 | 3 | 24 | 8 |
| Bell, Juan, Licey. | .264 | 106 | 17 | 28 | 6 | 3 | 1 | 6 | 4 |
| Cedeno, Andujar, Azucareros. | .263 | 118 | 10 | 31 | 4 | 2 | 1 | 16 | 3 |
| McDonald, Martin, Estrellas. | .257 | 101 | 14 | 26 | 3 | 0 | 0 | 12 | 4 |
| Liriano, Nelson, Escogido. | .257 | 144 | 18 | 37 | 3 | 2 | 0 | 9 | 5 |
| Hernandez, Cesar, Estrellas. | .256 | 90 | 8 | 23 | 5 | 0 | 0 | 11 | 4 |
| Rodriguez, Ruben, Estrellas. | .254 | 114 | 13 | 29 | 5 | 0 | 0 | 9 | 1 |
| Ramirez, Omar, Estrellas. | .254 | 185 | 24 | 47 | 7 | 0 | 1 | 17 | 16 |
| Meulens, Hensley, Azu. | .254 | 63 | 7 | 16 | 2 | 1 | 2 | 11 | 2 |
| Peguero, Julio, Escogido. | .250 | 96 | 6 | 24 | 4 | 0 | 0 | 3 | 4 |
| Roa, Hector, Estrellas. | .248 | 141 | 19 | 35 | 4 | 3 | 2 | 17 | 3 |
| Noboa, Junior, Escogido. | .247 | 97 | 9 | 24 | 3 | 0 | 0 | 14 | 1 |
| Sabino, Miguel, Estrellas. | .247 | 89 | 14 | 22 | 1 | 1 | 2 | 13 | 3 |
| Cairo, Sergio, Estrellas. | .247 | 81 | 7 | 20 | 2 | 1 | 0 | 4 | 0 |
| Alvarez, Jorge, Licey. | .245 | 102 | 7 | 25 | 3 | 0 | 2 | 5 | 4 |
| Proctor, Murph, Licey. | .240 | 150 | 18 | 36 | 5 | 0 | 0 | 8 | 1 |
| Yan, Julian, Azucareros. | .231 | 156 | 11 | 36 | 4 | 2 | 1 | 13 | 1 |
| Cabrera, Francisco, Estrellas. | .229 | 109 | 15 | 25 | 4 | 1 | 4 | 15 | 0 |
| Rodriguez, Henry, Licey | .227 | 75 | 5 | 17 | 5 | 1 | 0 | 5 | 2 |
| Jose, Manny, Azucareros | .223 | 94 | 10 | 21 | 3 | 2 | 0 | 8 | 7 |
| Guerrero, Juan, Licey | .221 | 86 | 7 | 19 | 5 | 0 | 0 | 7 | 3 |
| Martinez, Julian, Estrellas. | .221 | 77 | 8 | 17 | 3 | 0 | 1 | 10 | 0 |
| Martinez, Ramon D., Aguilas. | .221 | 77 | 11 | 17 | 2 | 0 | 0 | 4 | 5 |
| Alexander, Manny, Estrellas. | .218 | 119 | 16 | 26 | 6 | 4 | 0 | 14 | 6 |
| Michel, Domingo, Azucareros. | .217 | 69 | 6 | 15 | 4 | 0 | 0 | 7 | 0 |
| Mercedes, Henry, Azu | .216 | 134 | 12 | 29 | 5 | 0 | 0 | 14 | 0 |
| Castillo, Braulio, Licey. | .215 | 79 | 6 | 17 | 3 | 0 | 0 | 11 | 0 |
| Yacopino, Ed, Azucareros | .210 | 81 | 6 | 17 | 3 | 0 | 0 | 4 | 0 |
| Castillo, Carmen, Aguilas | .200 | 70 | 9 | 14 | 4 | 0 | 2 | 9 | 0 |
| Reyes, Gilberto, Licey | .198 | 116 | 8 | 23 | 1 | 0 | 0 | 11 | 0 |
| Lee, Derek, Azucareros. | .198 | 96 | 8 | 19 | 4 | 1 | 0 | 8 | 2 |
| Mota, Jose, Azucareros. | .195 | 82 | 8 | 16 | 1 | 0 | 0 | 4 | 6 |
| Canale, George, Aguilas | .191 | 68 | 4 | 13 | 3 | 1 | 0 | 8 | 1 |
| Gonzalez, Denny, Azu. | .190 | 126 | 9 | 24 | 4 | 0 | 1 | 14 | 1 |
| Fulton, Ed, Aguilas. | .181 | 127 | 7 | 23 | 1 | 0 | 1 | 12 | 0 |

### INDIVIDUAL PITCHING LEADERS
(Minimum 24 Innings)

| | W | L | ERA | G | SV | IP | H | BB | SO |
|---|---|---|---|---|---|---|---|---|---|
| Santana, Miguel J., Licey | 1 | 0 | 0.33 | 8 | 0 | 27 | 11 | 22 | 30 |

## Last 25 Years

| Year | Batting | Home Runs | Wins | ERA |
|---|---|---|---|---|
| 1968-69 | Matty Alou, Estrellas ........ .390 | Nate Colbert, Escogido ..... 8 | Jay Ritchie, Estrellas ........... 9 | Les Scott, Estrellas ............. 1.29 |
| 1969-70 | Ralph Garr, Escogido ...... .387 | 2 tied at ............................ 9 | Gene Rounsaville, Escogido 8 | Sal Campisi, Licey .............. 0.74 |
| 1970-71 | Ralph Garr, Escogido ...... .457 | Cesar Cedeno, Escogido .. 8 | Rollie Fingers, Escogido ....... 9 | Wade Blasingame, Esc. ...... 2.22 |
| 1971-72 | Ralph Garr, Escogido ...... .388 | Charlie Sands, Aguilas.... 10 | Gene Garber, Aguilas........... 9 | Pedro Borbon, Licey .......... 1.68 |
| 1972-73 | Von Joshua, Licey ........... .358 | Adrian Garrett, Escogido... 9 | Pedro Borbon, Licey ........... 9 | Tom Dettore, Aguilas ......... 2.30 |
| 1973-74 | Dave Parker, Aguilas ....... .345 | Rico Carty, Aguilas........... 9 | Rick Waits, Aguilas ............. 8 | Charlie Hough, Licey ......... 1.29 |
| 1974-75 | Bruce Bochte, Licey ........ .352 | 2 tied at ............................ 8 | J.R. Richard, Escogido ........ 8 | J.R. Richard, Escogido ....... 1.64 |
| 1975-76 | Wilbur Howard, Escogido .341 | 7 tied at ............................ 4 | 2 tied at ............................. 8 | Kent Tekulve, Aguilas ......... 1.00 |
| 1976-77 | Mario Guerrero, Estrellas .365 | 2 tied at ............................ 6 | Angel Torres, Licey ........... 10 | Doug Bair, Aguilas ............. 1.26 |
| 1977-78 | Omar Moreno, Aguilas .... .345 | Dick Davis, Aguilas .......... 8 | 3 tied at ............................. 7 | Tom Hume, Escogido ......... 1.97 |
| 1978-79 | Ted Cox, Estrellas ........... .319 | 2 tied at ............................ 7 | 2 tied at ............................. 9 | Bo McLaughlin, Escogido ... 1.80 |
| 1979-80 | Tony Pena, Aguilas .......... .317 | 5 tied at ............................ 3 | Gerry Hannahs, Licey.......... 9 | Silvano Quesada, Esc. ...... 1.49 |
| 1980-81 | Ken Landreaux, Agu........ .394 | Tony Pena, Aguilas ........... 7 | 2 tied at ............................. 7 | Steve Ratzer, Escogido ...... 1.24 |
| 1981-82 | Pedro Hernandez, Esc. .... .408 | Dave Hostetler, Escogido .. 9 | Pascual Perez, Aguilas ...... 10 | Oscar Brito, Escogido ......... 1.85 |
| 1982-83 | Cesar Geronimo, Licey ..... .341 | Howard Johnson, Aguilas .. 8 | Pascual Perez, Aguilas ....... 8 | Pascual Perez, Aguilas ....... 2.23 |
| 1983-84 | Miguel Dilone, Aguilas ..... .343 | Reggie Whittemore, Esc. 12 | 2 tied at ............................. 8 | Orel Hershiser, Azucareros 1.34 |
| 1984-85 | Junior Noboa, Caimanes... .327 | Ralph Bryant, Caimanes.... 9 | Tom Filer, Azucareros ......... 8 | Craig Minetto, Caimanes .... 0.77 |
| 1985-86 | Tony Fernandez, Licey ..... .364 | Tony Pena, Aguilas ........... 9 | Mickey Mahler, Escogido ..... 8 | Paul Assenmacher, Est. ..... 1.22 |
| 1986-87 | Stan Javier, Azucareros .. .374 | Ralph Bryant, Escogido .. 13 | 3 tied at ............................. 8 | Gibson Alba, Aguilas ......... 1.17 |
| 1987-88 | Stan Javier, Azucareros ... .363 | Mark Parent, Estrellas ...... 9 | 2 tied at ............................. 8 | Dave Otto, Licey ................. 1.27 |
| 1988-89 | Domingo Michel, Licey ..... .310 | Domingo Michel, Licey ...... 9 | Melido Perez, Caimanes ..... 8 | Andy Araujo, Licey.............. 1.09 |
| 1989-90 | Angel Gonzalez, Aguilas . .434 | Denny Gonzalez, Aguilas.. 5 | 3 tied at ............................. 6 | Jeff Edwards, Aguilas ......... 2.17 |
| 1990-91 | Hensley Meulens, Azu...... .338 | Francisco Cabrera, Est. .... 8 | 2 tied at ............................. 7 | Juan Guzman, Licey ........... 1.69 |
| 1991-92 | Luis Mercedes, Estrellas .. .333 | 5 tied at ............................ 4 | Jose Nunez, Escogido......... 6 | Pedro Astacio, Licey .......... 1.41 |
| 1992-93 | Tom Marsh, Aguilas ........ .318 | Domingo Martinez, Esc...... 6 | 4 tied at ............................. 5 | Julian Heredia, Estrellas ..... 1.18 |

| Garcia, Apolinar, Aguilas ............ | 3 | 1 | 1.08 | 11 | 0 | 33 | 31 | 10 | 25 |
|---|---|---|---|---|---|---|---|---|---|
| HEREDIA, JULIAN, Estrellas ...... | 4 | 2 | 1.18 | 22 | 3 | 46 | 24 | 14 | 36 |
| Borbon, Pedro, Estrellas............. | 4 | 1 | 1.32 | 12 | 0 | 41 | 35 | 15 | 37 |
| Hancock, Chris, Escogido .......... | 1 | 1 | 1.38 | 9 | 0 | 26 | 25 | 17 | 13 |
| Mejia, Cesar, Aguilas.................. | 2 | 0 | 1.50 | 18 | 1 | 24 | 19 | 4 | 12 |
| Ozuna, Gabriel, Licey ................ | 2 | 0 | 1.54 | 19 | 4 | 35 | 30 | 3 | 18 |
| Rivera, Ben, Estrellas ................ | 4 | 1 | 1.69 | 5 | 0 | 27 | 23 | 16 | 16 |
| Wiseman, Denny, Aguilas .......... | 3 | 2 | 1.79 | 9 | 0 | 45 | 46 | 14 | 11 |
| Guzman, Johnny, Aguilas .......... | 4 | 1 | 1.80 | 11 | 0 | 55 | 56 | 22 | 31 |
| Valdez, Rafael, Licey ................. | 5 | 1 | 1.92 | 11 | 0 | 66 | 38 | 13 | 20 |
| Pena, Ramon, Aguilas ............... | 3 | 1 | 1.95 | 27 | 10 | 28 | 23 | 11 | 23 |
| Nunez, Jose, Escogido ............... | 0 | 2 | 2.10 | 5 | 0 | 26 | 21 | 8 | 11 |
| Perez, Vladimir, Licey ................ | 4 | 0 | 2.17 | 17 | 1 | 29 | 26 | 12 | 15 |
| Turner, Matt, Estrellas ............... | 3 | 2 | 2.33 | 23 | 5 | 39 | 35 | 13 | 20 |
| Perez, Melido, Azucareros .......... | 1 | 2 | 2.40 | 5 | 0 | 30 | 32 | 10 | 15 |
| Perez, Dario, Azucareros ........... | 2 | 3 | 2.53 | 16 | 1 | 46 | 40 | 12 | 30 |
| Dabney, Fred, Estrellas .............. | 2 | 3 | 2.56 | 8 | 0 | 39 | 44 | 15 | 12 |
| Valdez, Efrain, Licey .................. | 5 | 2 | 2.77 | 14 | 0 | 62 | 52 | 19 | 31 |
| Martinez, Jose, Aguilas .............. | 5 | 0 | 2.88 | 8 | 0 | 50 | 47 | 12 | 28 |
| Mercedes, Jose, Estrellas .......... | 2 | 3 | 3.03 | 5 | 0 | 30 | 26 | 9 | 10 |
| Araujo, Andy, Azucareros........... | 2 | 0 | 3.04 | 13 | 0 | 24 | 17 | 4 | 8 |
| Martinez, Pedro A., Azucareros ... | 4 | 5 | 3.11 | 12 | 1 | 55 | 50 | 25 | 36 |
| Farmer, Howard, Escogido .......... | 5 | 1 | 3.18 | 12 | 0 | 51 | 47 | 11 | 28 |
| Galvez, Balvino, Licey ............... | 3 | 3 | 3.25 | 11 | 0 | 61 | 55 | 14 | 32 |
| Brummett, Greg, Escogido .......... | 1 | 0 | 3.25 | 16 | 0 | 28 | 22 | 13 | 24 |
| Ventura, Jose, Azucareros .......... | 4 | 3 | 3.29 | 11 | 0 | 66 | 52 | 33 | 33 |
| Bautista, Jose, Aguilas ............... | 2 | 3 | 3.33 | 9 | 0 | 49 | 52 | 13 | 28 |
| LaPoint, Dave, Estrellas ............. | 2 | 3 | 3.35 | 10 | 0 | 48 | 51 | 15 | 24 |
| Manzanillo, Josias, Estrellas ....... | 1 | 0 | 3.38 | 6 | 0 | 29 | 23 | 12 | 31 |
| Myers, Mike, Escogido ............... | 4 | 5 | 3.52 | 13 | 0 | 61 | 59 | 18 | 27 |
| Sanchez, Alex, Azucareros ......... | 1 | 4 | 4.01 | 11 | 0 | 52 | 46 | 41 | 18 |
| Musset, Jose, Aguilas ................ | 1 | 1 | 4.03 | 18 | 2 | 29 | 23 | 15 | 21 |
| Batista, Miguel, Escogido ........... | 1 | 3 | 4.15 | 9 | 0 | 43 | 39 | 20 | 22 |
| Lima, Jose, Aguilas.................... | 4 | 5 | 4.15 | 10 | 0 | 53 | 67 | 20 | 36 |
| de la Rosa, Francisco, Est........... | 1 | 2 | 4.55 | 9 | 0 | 32 | 34 | 13 | 12 |
| Rapp, Pat, Escogido .................. | 1 | 5 | 4.71 | 9 | 0 | 36 | 44 | 13 | 17 |
| Pichardo, Hipolito, Azucareros ... | 0 | 5 | 5.15 | 7 | 0 | 37 | 40 | 17 | 15 |
| Heredia, Julian, Azucareros ...... | 0 | 2 | 6.29 | 13 | 0 | 24 | 24 | 10 | 13 |

**Leaders.** Tony Pena, left, had the Dominican League's best average (.328); Domingo Martinez led in homers (6).

| Gonzalez, Jose, Licey ........... | .343 | 67 | 9 | 23 | 6 | 1 | 0 | 10 | 3 |
|---|---|---|---|---|---|---|---|---|---|
| Castillo, Braulio, Licey ........... | .333 | 42 | 4 | 14 | 2 | 1 | 0 | 6 | 3 |
| Ramirez, Rafael, Estrellas...... | .333 | 48 | 3 | 16 | 2 | 0 | 0 | 5 | 1 |
| Cedeno, Domingo, Azucareros | .310 | 42 | 4 | 13 | 0 | 0 | 6 | 0 | |
| Jose, Felix, Licey .................. | .299 | 77 | 11 | 23 | 4 | 0 | 1 | 9 | 2 |
| Nunez, Mauricio, Estrellas..... | .290 | 31 | 3 | 9 | 5 | 0 | 0 | 4 | 0 |
| Pena, Geronimo, Licey .......... | .288 | 52 | 8 | 15 | 0 | 1 | 0 | 7 | 0 |
| Alou, Moises, Aguilas............ | .288 | 66 | 9 | 19 | 5 | 0 | 2 | 11 | 4 |
| Castillo, Carmen, Aguilas. ...... | .286 | 35 | 7 | 10 | 6 | 0 | 2 | 10 | 1 |
| Cedeno, Andujar, Azucareros . | .282 | 71 | 9 | 20 | 0 | 0 | 2 | 10 | 2 |
| Yan, Julian, Azucareros.......... | .269 | 67 | 3 | 18 | 1 | 0 | 1 | 8 | 0 |
| Frazier, Lou, Azucareros ........ | .262 | 61 | 6 | 16 | 1 | 0 | 0 | 1 | 7 |
| de los Santos, Alberto, Azu. ... | .260 | 50 | 6 | 13 | 0 | 0 | 0 | 4 | 2 |
| Alexander, Manny, Estrellas.... | .258 | 62 | 4 | 16 | 2 | 0 | 0 | 4 | 3 |
| Fermin, Felix, Aguilas. ........... | .256 | 43 | 3 | 11 | 0 | 0 | 0 | 3 | 4 |

| PLAYOFFS | W | L | PCT | GB |
|---|---|---|---|---|
| Aguilas | 12 | 6 | .667 | — |
| Azucareros | 10 | 9 | .526 | 2½ |
| Licey | 9 | 10 | .474 | 3½ |
| Estrellas | 6 | 12 | .333 | 6 |

**Championship Series:** Aguilas defeated Azucareros, 4-2, in best-of-7 final.

## INDIVIDUAL BATTING LEADERS
(Minimum 30 Plate Appearances)

| | AVG | AB | R | H | 2B | 3B | HR | RBI | SB |
|---|---|---|---|---|---|---|---|---|---|
| Pena, Tony, Aguilas. ............. | .434 | 53 | 11 | 23 | 3 | 0 | 1 | 9 | 4 |
| Campusano, Sil, Licey........... | .355 | 62 | 13 | 22 | 5 | 1 | 2 | 11 | 1 |
| Rodriguez, Henry, Licey ........ | .347 | 72 | 11 | 25 | 4 | 0 | 1 | 12 | 0 |

## INDIVIDUAL PITCHING LEADERS
(Minimum 15 Innings)

| | W | L | ERA | G | SV | IP | H | BB | SO |
|---|---|---|---|---|---|---|---|---|---|
| Johnson, Dave, Aguilas. ............. | 2 | 2 | 0.59 | 4 | 0 | 31 | 19 | 8 | 14 |
| Martinez, Pedro A., Azucareros .. | 2 | 4 | 1 | 23 | 16 | 10 | 17 | | |
| Valdez, Rafael, Licey. ............... | 2 | 1 | 1.32 | 4 | 0 | 27 | 22 | 9 | 10 |
| Kutzler, Jerry, Estrellas. ............. | 0 | 1 | 1.45 | 3 | 0 | 19 | 19 | 4 | 14 |
| Galvez, Balvino, Licey. .............. | 1 | 1 | 1.54 | 4 | 0 | 23 | 15 | 5 | 16 |
| Bautista, Jose, Aguilas. .............. | 1 | 0 | 2.35 | 5 | 0 | 15 | 19 | 6 | 7 |
| Lima, Jose, Aguilas.................... | 1 | 0 | 2.35 | 6 | 2 | 15 | 13 | 5 | 7 |
| Garcia, Apolinar, Aguilas. ........... | 1 | 0 | 2.38 | 4 | 0 | 23 | 18 | 8 | 21 |
| Valdez, Efrain, Licey. ................. | 1 | 1 | 2.42 | 5 | 0 | 26 | 20 | 10 | 22 |
| Manzanillo, Josias, Est. ............. | 1 | 0 | 2.93 | 3 | 0 | 15 | 12 | 12 | 16 |
| Perez, Dario, Azucareros .......... | 0 | 1 | 2.93 | 4 | 0 | 15 | 16 | 6 | 3 |
| Rivera, Ben, Estrellas. ............... | 0 | 2 | 2.95 | 3 | 0 | 21 | 15 | 10 | 22 |

# VENEZUELAN
## LEAGUE

## Determined Zulia Repeats As Champion

Given three chances to successfully defend their Venezuelan League championship of 1991-92, the Zulia Eagles capitulated on their final try, beating Magallanes 4-0 in the league's best-of-7 championship series.

Zulia kept its playoff hopes alive by the slimmest of margins, finishing a game ahead of extinction in both the regular season and four-team round-robin playoff. But in the final, the Eagles swept by Magallanes convincingly, winning the last two games 13-0 and 2-0, the clincher on a four-hitter by ace lefthander Wilson Alvarez (White Sox).

**Tony Castillo**

Third baseman Pedro Castellano (Rockies) was named MVP of the final series, hitting .313 with a homer and six RBIs.

But the Eagles were not successful in defending the Caribbean World Series title they won in 1992, losing four of six games. Nor did they represent Venezuela with dignity as they forfeited their final game to fall into a last-place tie with host Mexico.

Neither Alvarez nor ace relievers Jay Baller (Braves) and Julio Machado made the trip to Mexico.

Alvarez, Baseball America's 1991-92 winter league Player of the Year and 4-0, 0.71 in postseason play, was asked by the White Sox to shut it down, while Baller, who led the regular season with 11 saves and was the league's reliever of the year, simply wanted to rest up before the start of spring training.

Machado (3-0, 2.21 overall) was prohibited from leaving the country because of his alleged involvement in a December 1991 shooting death of a woman, charges for which remained unresolved.

Lara beat Zulia by two games in the Western Division, thanks to outfielder Willie Canate (Blue Jays) and lefthander Tony Castillo (Blue Jays), selected the league's MVP and pitcher of the year, respectively.

Canate hit .322 in the regular season and led the league in runs (47) and hits (73). Castillo led the league in wins (9) and strikeouts (79).

**—ALLAN SIMPSON**

### STANDINGS

| East | W | L | PCT | GB |
|---|---|---|---|---|
| Caracas | 37 | 23 | .617 | — |
| Magallanes | 34 | 26 | .567 | 3 |
| La Guaira | 27 | 32 | .458 | 9½ |
| Oriente | 27 | 33 | .450 | 10 |

| West | W | L | PCT | GB |
|---|---|---|---|---|
| Lara | 34 | 26 | .567 | — |
| Zulia | 32 | 28 | .533 | 2 |
| Aragua | 31 | 29 | .517 | 3 |
| Cabimas | 17 | 42 | .288 | 16½ |

### INDIVIDUAL BATTING LEADERS
(Minimum 90 Plate Appearances)

| | AVG | AB | R | H | 2B | 3B | HR | RBI | SB |
|---|---|---|---|---|---|---|---|---|---|
| Colon, Cris, Zulia | .431 | 102 | 14 | 44 | 8 | 0 | 0 | 15 | 2 |
| FRYE, JEFF, Oriente | .385 | 161 | 29 | 62 | 6 | 4 | 0 | 20 | 8 |
| Garcia, Carlos, Magallanes | .354 | 158 | 30 | 56 | 14 | 2 | 3 | 23 | 3 |
| Edmonds, Jim, Aragua | .333 | 132 | 19 | 44 | 11 | 0 | 3 | 22 | 4 |
| Magallanes, Willie, Magallanes | .330 | 203 | 32 | 67 | 14 | 1 | 1 | 28 | 1 |
| Sojo, Luis, Lara | .329 | 140 | 19 | 46 | 7 | 0 | 2 | 31 | 3 |
| Azocar, Oscar, Caracas | .328 | 125 | 12 | 41 | 9 | 1 | 0 | 13 | 3 |
| Delima, Rafael, Aragua | .328 | 180 | 33 | 59 | 11 | 3 | 2 | 17 | 8 |
| Armas, Marcos, Oriente | .326 | 190 | 25 | 62 | 10 | 2 | 9 | 34 | 0 |
| Hall, Joe, Oriente | .323 | 198 | 29 | 64 | 7 | 10 | 1 | 29 | 3 |
| Castellano, Pedro, Zulia | .322 | 214 | 20 | 69 | 10 | 0 | 3 | 30 | 3 |
| Canate, Willie, Lara | .322 | 227 | 47 | 73 | 6 | 2 | 6 | 27 | 17 |
| Estrada, Asdrubal, Lara | .321 | 187 | 23 | 60 | 13 | 1 | 3 | 26 | 0 |
| Naveda, Edgar, Magallanes | .316 | 196 | 23 | 62 | 13 | 0 | 0 | 21 | 3 |
| Mitchell, Jorge, Magallanes | .315 | 130 | 12 | 41 | 7 | 1 | 1 | 20 | 0 |
| Gonzalez, Luis, Magallanes | .302 | 225 | 37 | 68 | 16 | 5 | 2 | 31 | 10 |
| Zambrano, Eddie, Zulia | .302 | 159 | 28 | 48 | 14 | 1 | 3 | 27 | 4 |
| Infante, Alex, Lara | .302 | 189 | 27 | 57 | 6 | 1 | 0 | 26 | 2 |
| Perez, Robert, Lara | .298 | 225 | 37 | 67 | 8 | 3 | 4 | 31 | 4 |
| Pedrique, Al, Aragua | .295 | 95 | 17 | 28 | 4 | 1 | 0 | 14 | 2 |
| Alfonzo, Edgar, Caracas | .293 | 147 | 13 | 43 | 6 | 4 | 0 | 12 | 0 |
| Wilson, Nigel, Lara | .291 | 110 | 20 | 32 | 8 | 4 | 1 | 14 | 5 |
| Pratt, Todd, Oriente | .290 | 145 | 30 | 42 | 10 | 0 | 9 | 32 | 3 |
| Vizquel, Omar, Caracas | .288 | 104 | 15 | 30 | 7 | 2 | 0 | 12 | 9 |
| Mack, Quinn, Cabimas | .284 | 211 | 23 | 60 | 12 | 0 | 4 | 26 | 4 |
| Perez-Tovar, Raul, La Guaira | .284 | 183 | 19 | 52 | 12 | 0 | 0 | 17 | 4 |
| Zambrano, Roberto, Aragua | .283 | 145 | 18 | 41 | 7 | 2 | 0 | 12 | 0 |
| Ramsey, Fernando, Cabimas | .283 | 191 | 25 | 54 | 8 | 1 | 2 | 18 | 17 |
| Tovar, Edgar, Oriente | .282 | 85 | 8 | 24 | 2 | 0 | 0 | 4 | 3 |
| Cepicky, Scott, Oriente | .282 | 202 | 34 | 57 | 10 | 0 | 13 | 36 | 1 |
| Polidor, Gus, La Guaira | .280 | 193 | 23 | 54 | 8 | 2 | 0 | 18 | 3 |
| Wehner, John, Caracas | .279 | 122 | 24 | 34 | 8 | 0 | 1 | 14 | 3 |
| Trafton, Todd, Caracas | .276 | 199 | 21 | 55 | 9 | 3 | 6 | 23 | 2 |
| Querecuto, Juan, Lara | .276 | 181 | 22 | 50 | 7 | 1 | 1 | 21 | 1 |
| Martinez, Carlos, La Guaira | .275 | 138 | 19 | 38 | 7 | 0 | 2 | 12 | 3 |
| Rhodes, Karl, Magallanes | .275 | 229 | 28 | 63 | 9 | 3 | 1 | 23 | 13 |
| Anthony, Eric, Magallanes | .274 | 84 | 9 | 23 | 3 | 0 | 2 | 15 | 0 |
| Matos, Malvin, La Guaira | .274 | 95 | 8 | 26 | 4 | 3 | 2 | 13 | 6 |
| Mendez, Jesus, Aragua | .274 | 223 | 26 | 61 | 12 | 4 | 0 | 31 | 4 |
| O'Halloran, Greg, Lara | .273 | 143 | 20 | 39 | 7 | 2 | 0 | 17 | 3 |
| Natal, Bob, Zulia | .272 | 158 | 19 | 43 | 7 | 1 | 3 | 26 | 1 |
| Hernandez, Carlos, Caracas | .272 | 162 | 13 | 44 | 4 | 1 | 3 | 20 | 2 |
| Cedeno, Roger, Caracas | .269 | 193 | 26 | 52 | 3 | 3 | 0 | 13 | 20 |
| Pennyfeather, William, Car | .269 | 171 | 20 | 46 | 6 | 1 | 2 | 16 | 7 |
| Burguillos, Carlos, Zulia | .268 | 123 | 18 | 33 | 2 | 1 | 1 | 12 | 0 |
| Caceres, Edgar, Caracas | .268 | 153 | 14 | 41 | 6 | 0 | 0 | 9 | 5 |
| Leiva, Jose, Oriente | .267 | 161 | 14 | 43 | 2 | 2 | 1 | 13 | 12 |
| Escobar, John, Aragua | .267 | 165 | 26 | 44 | 8 | 0 | 0 | 20 | 0 |
| Armas, Julio, Oriente | .264 | 91 | 8 | 24 | 6 | 1 | 1 | 8 | 4 |
| Chavez, Pedro, Oriente | .264 | 220 | 15 | 58 | 12 | 1 | 0 | 19 | 1 |
| Abreu, Bob, Caracas | .263 | 186 | 24 | 49 | 4 | 3 | 2 | 13 | 4 |
| Obando, Sherrnan, Aragua | .262 | 84 | 14 | 22 | 6 | 1 | 3 | 18 | 0 |
| Hernandez, Rudy, Magallanes | .260 | 181 | 24 | 47 | 6 | 1 | 0 | 15 | 9 |
| Galarraga, Andres, Caracas | .259 | 135 | 18 | 35 | 10 | 0 | 4 | 25 | 4 |
| Garcia, Jose, Aragua | .258 | 186 | 25 | 48 | 10 | 1 | 1 | 19 | 5 |
| Munoz, Omer, Zulia | .255 | 157 | 27 | 40 | 6 | 1 | 0 | 7 | 4 |
| Marquez, Edwin, La Guaira | .253 | 99 | 8 | 25 | 3 | 1 | 0 | 6 | 2 |

### LEAGUE CHAMPIONS

**Last 25 Years**

| | |
|---|---|
| 1968-69 | La Guaira |
| 1969-70 | Magallanes |
| 1970-71 | La Guaira |
| 1971-72 | Aragua |
| 1972-73 | Caracas |
| 1973-74 | None |
| 1974-75 | Aragua |
| 1975-76 | Aragua |
| 1976-77 | Magallanes |
| 1977-78 | Caracas |
| 1978-79 | Magallanes |
| 1979-80 | Caracas |
| 1980-81 | Caracas |
| 1981-82 | Caracas |
| 1982-83 | La Guaira |
| 1983-84 | Zulia |
| 1984-85 | La Guaira |
| 1985-86 | La Guaira |
| 1986-87 | Caracas |
| 1987-88 | Caracas |
| 1988-89 | Zulia |
| 1989-90 | Caracas |
| 1990-91 | Lara |
| 1991-92 | Zulia |
| 1992-93 | Zulia |

| | | | | | | | | | |
|---|---|---|---|---|---|---|---|---|---|
| Salazar, Luis, La Guaira | .252 | 111 | 5 | 28 | 3 | 0 | 0 | 9 | 1 |
| Nava, Marlo, Cabimas | .252 | 143 | 14 | 36 | 3 | 1 | 0 | 3 | 1 |
| Soto, Fernando, Aragua | .250 | 120 | 18 | 30 | 3 | 1 | 0 | 14 | 2 |
| Jordan, Adrian, Zulia | .248 | 153 | 18 | 38 | 8 | 2 | 0 | 17 | 0 |
| Perez, Eduardo, Aragua | .248 | 202 | 28 | 50 | 15 | 1 | 5 | 35 | 0 |
| Strange, Doug, Lara | .239 | 113 | 19 | 27 | 6 | 3 | 1 | 20 | 3 |
| Monzon, Jose, La Guaira | .238 | 80 | 5 | 19 | 5 | 0 | 0 | 6 | 0 |
| Pedre, Jorge, Cabimas | .230 | 100 | 7 | 23 | 4 | 0 | 4 | 19 | 0 |
| Alfaro, Jesus, Caracas | .226 | 133 | 13 | 30 | 7 | 0 | 0 | 11 | 0 |
| Voigt, Jack, Zulia | .223 | 206 | 27 | 46 | 9 | 3 | 1 | 21 | 9 |
| Odor, Rouglas, Zulia | .222 | 144 | 20 | 32 | 4 | 2 | 0 | 8 | 3 |
| Harris, Donald, La Guaira | .218 | 206 | 18 | 45 | 8 | 1 | 4 | 30 | 7 |
| Traxler, Brian, Caracas | .218 | 87 | 7 | 19 | 3 | 0 | 0 | 8 | 0 |
| Salazar, Argenis, Aragua | .213 | 94 | 9 | 20 | 3 | 1 | 0 | 4 | 2 |
| Zambrano, Jose, Cabimas | .212 | 104 | 10 | 22 | 3 | 1 | 2 | 13 | 0 |
| Castellano, Miguel, La Guaira | .209 | 91 | 7 | 19 | 6 | 1 | 0 | 7 | 1 |
| Olivares, Ossie, Cabimas | .205 | 112 | 12 | 23 | 2 | 0 | 0 | 3 | 1 |
| Petagine, Roberto, Caracas | .204 | 98 | 8 | 20 | 5 | 0 | 1 | 11 | 1 |

### INDIVIDUAL PITCHING LEADERS
(Minimum 29 Innings)

| | W | L | ERA | G | SV | IP | H | BB | SO |
|---|---|---|---|---|---|---|---|---|---|
| Villa, Jose, Magallanes | 3 | 1 | 0.79 | 31 | 1 | 34 | 28 | 17 | 22 |
| ROBERTSON, RICH, La Guaira | 2 | 4 | 1.10 | 9 | 1 | 57 | 41 | 11 | 36 |
| Ohlms, Mark, Lara | 7 | 1 | 1.14 | 24 | 1 | 32 | 23 | 15 | 14 |
| Burba, Dave, Caracas | 7 | 0 | 1.23 | 11 | 0 | 73 | 60 | 24 | 63 |
| Hartgraves, Dean, Caracas | 4 | 0 | 1.30 | 6 | 0 | 42 | 31 | 14 | 20 |
| Castillo, Juan, Magallanes | 6 | 1 | 1.54 | 12 | 0 | 76 | 50 | 23 | 51 |
| Garcia, Ramon, Magallanes | 7 | 2 | 1.64 | 9 | 0 | 60 | 52 | 15 | 35 |
| Kile, Darryl, Magallanes | 3 | 3 | 1.83 | 8 | 0 | 54 | 44 | 17 | 41 |
| Bencomo, Omer, Oriente | 2 | 3 | 1.88 | 24 | 2 | 43 | 39 | 13 | 22 |
| Gomez, Henry, Zulia | 6 | 4 | 1.90 | 13 | 0 | 90 | 68 | 24 | 55 |
| Strange, Don, Caracas | 5 | 2 | 1.93 | 28 | 9 | 47 | 40 | 16 | 38 |
| Munoz, Francisco, Caracas | 2 | 2 | 1.97 | 16 | 0 | 50 | 45 | 15 | 22 |
| Machado, Julio, Zulia | 3 | 0 | 2.01 | 23 | 1 | 40 | 26 | 11 | 36 |
| Stephan, Todd, Zulia | 7 | 3 | 2.15 | 15 | 0 | 88 | 83 | 15 | 64 |
| Baller, Jay, Zulia | 4 | 1 | 2.16 | 28 | 11 | 33 | 28 | 7 | 27 |
| Castillo, Tony, Lara | 9 | 4 | 2.22 | 15 | 0 | 101 | 95 | 15 | 79 |
| Picota, Len, Aragua | 0 | 3 | 2.30 | 22 | 5 | 31 | 39 | 23 | 14 |
| Kutzler, Jerry, Oriente | 5 | 5 | 2.39 | 12 | 0 | 79 | 88 | 11 | 44 |
| Hurtado, Edwin, Lara | 1 | 3 | 2.44 | 19 | 2 | 44 | 38 | 22 | 29 |
| Daal, Omar, Caracas | 2 | 1 | 2.49 | 29 | 7 | 43 | 28 | 17 | 36 |
| Jones, Todd, Magallanes | 3 | 2 | 2.56 | 29 | 5 | 32 | 23 | 27 | 29 |
| Castillo, Roberto, Aragua | 1 | 2 | 2.56 | 25 | 6 | 39 | 39 | 12 | 11 |
| Pulido, Carlos, Magallanes | 2 | 3 | 2.57 | 14 | 0 | 42 | 43 | 19 | 22 |
| Mosquera, David, Cabimas | 2 | 7 | 2.67 | 16 | 0 | 94 | 78 | 36 | 48 |
| Aldred, Scott, Caracas | 3 | 4 | 2.78 | 12 | 0 | 65 | 60 | 39 | 32 |
| Rumer, Tim, Aragua | 0 | 1 | 2.81 | 7 | 0 | 32 | 27 | 10 | 24 |
| Portillo, Luis, Zulia | 3 | 2 | 2.82 | 16 | 0 | 45 | 40 | 17 | 23 |
| Lugo, Urbano, Caracas | 7 | 5 | 2.84 | 13 | 0 | 82 | 63 | 27 | 39 |
| Vasquez, Luis, La Guaira | 2 | 3 | 2.95 | 13 | 0 | 61 | 74 | 20 | 19 |
| Campos, Frank, La Guaira | 6 | 2 | 3.10 | 16 | 1 | 73 | 60 | 30 | 43 |
| Keyser, Brian, Oriente | 8 | 2 | 3.11 | 13 | 0 | 84 | 86 | 15 | 39 |
| Lira, Felipe, La Guaira | 4 | 5 | 3.16 | 15 | 0 | 68 | 73 | 17 | 37 |
| Taylor, Rob, Cabimas | 1 | 4 | 3.19 | 26 | 4 | 42 | 39 | 15 | 19 |

| | | | | | | | | | |
|---|---|---|---|---|---|---|---|---|---|
| Polak, Rich, Aragua | 3 | 3 | 3.38 | 21 | 1 | 35 | 36 | 17 | 19 |
| Clayton, Royal, Aragua | 4 | 1 | 3.39 | 11 | 0 | 61 | 70 | 10 | 18 |
| Draper, Mike, Aragua | 7 | 3 | 3.47 | 13 | 0 | 70 | 72 | 14 | 41 |
| Grimsley, Jason, Magallanes | 1 | 1 | 3.52 | 5 | 0 | 31 | 32 | 7 | 29 |
| Peraza, Oswald, Lara | 5 | 3 | 3.75 | 14 | 0 | 82 | 84 | 34 | 49 |
| Bowen, Ryan, Magallanes | 1 | 3 | 3.82 | 6 | 0 | 33 | 29 | 27 | 26 |
| Blohm, Pete, Lara | 1 | 5 | 3.83 | 10 | 0 | 56 | 60 | 25 | 26 |
| Straker, Les, Aragua | 7 | 4 | 4.04 | 12 | 0 | 62 | 63 | 19 | 32 |
| Alvarez, Wilson, Zulia | 3 | 3 | 4.08 | 6 | 0 | 29 | 34 | 7 | 22 |
| Williams, Woody, Lara | 6 | 4 | 4.09 | 15 | 0 | 77 | 83 | 27 | 37 |
| Conde, Argenis, Aragua | 4 | 3 | 4.13 | 13 | 0 | 61 | 63 | 23 | 39 |

### PLAYOFFS

| PLAYOFFS | W | L | PCT | GB |
|---|---|---|---|---|
| Magallanes | 8 | 4 | .667 | — |
| Zulia | 7 | 5 | .583 | 1 |
| Caracas | 6 | 6 | .500 | 2 |
| Lara | 3 | 9 | .250 | 5 |

**Championship Series:** Zulia defeated Magallanes, 4-0, in best-of-7 final.

### INDIVIDUAL BATTING LEADERS
(Minimum 20 Plate Appearances)

| | AVG | AB | R | H | 2B | 3B | HR | RBI | SB |
|---|---|---|---|---|---|---|---|---|---|
| Garcia, Carlos, Magallanes | .444 | 45 | 10 | 20 | 5 | 1 | 0 | 11 | 5 |
| Espinoza, Alvaro, Magallanes | .379 | 29 | 3 | 11 | 3 | 0 | 0 | 2 | 0 |
| Burguillos, Carlos, Zulia | .368 | 19 | 2 | 7 | 1 | 1 | 0 | 4 | 1 |
| Escobar, Oscar, Lara | .344 | 32 | 3 | 11 | 2 | 0 | 0 | 4 | 0 |
| Anthony, Eric, Magallanes | .343 | 35 | 5 | 12 | 1 | 1 | 1 | 9 | 2 |
| O'Leary, Troy, Lara | .341 | 44 | 3 | 15 | 3 | 0 | 0 | 2 | 1 |
| Carrasquel, Domingo, Lara | .333 | 21 | 1 | 7 | 0 | 2 | 0 | 3 | 0 |
| Moreno, Jose, Lara | .333 | 30 | 4 | 10 | 2 | 1 | 0 | 1 | 0 |
| Vizquel, Omar, Caracas | .318 | 44 | 6 | 14 | 1 | 0 | 0 | 4 | 5 |
| Maksudian, Mike, Lara | .316 | 38 | 5 | 12 | 2 | 0 | 0 | 3 | 1 |
| Cedeno, Roger, Caracas | .314 | 51 | 8 | 16 | 2 | 0 | 0 | 6 | 2 |
| Gonzalez, Luis, Magallanes | .313 | 32 | 3 | 10 | 0 | 1 | 0 | 4 | 2 |
| Battle, Howard, Lara | .297 | 37 | 4 | 11 | 1 | 0 | 0 | 2 | 0 |
| Bryant, Scott, Zulia | .289 | 38 | 4 | 11 | 6 | 1 | 0 | 4 | 0 |
| Alfaro, Jesus, Caracas | .289 | 45 | 5 | 13 | 4 | 0 | 1 | 6 | 0 |
| Hernandez, Carlos, Caracas | .289 | 45 | 3 | 13 | 5 | 2 | 0 | 4 | 0 |

### INDIVIDUAL PITCHING LEADERS
(Minimum 10 Innings)

| | W | L | ERA | G | SV | IP | H | BB | SO |
|---|---|---|---|---|---|---|---|---|---|
| Jones, Todd, Magallanes | 1 | 0 | 0.00 | 7 | 0 | 11 | 7 | 3 | 13 |
| Strange, Don, Caracas | 1 | 0 | 0.00 | 7 | 2 | 12 | 11 | 4 | 5 |
| Holman, Brad, Caracas | 2 | 0 | 0.66 | 4 | 0 | 27 | 21 | 7 | 13 |
| Marak, Paul, Caracas | 1 | 0 | 0.73 | 2 | 0 | 12 | 11 | 4 | 2 |
| Baller, Jay, Zulia | 1 | 0 | 0.87 | 2 | 6 | 10 | 6 | 1 | 9 |
| Alvarez, Wilson, Zulia | 3 | 1 | 0.94 | 4 | 0 | 29 | 23 | 6 | 25 |
| Grimsley, Jason, Magallanes | 2 | 0 | 1.08 | 3 | 0 | 25 | 18 | 8 | 17 |
| Rambo, Dan, Zulia | 1 | 2 | 1.71 | 3 | 0 | 21 | 14 | 6 | 8 |
| Linton, Doug, Lara | 1 | 0 | 2.08 | 3 | 0 | 22 | 21 | 4 | 17 |
| Castillo, Juan, Magallanes | 2 | 0 | 2.45 | 2 | 0 | 11 | 10 | 2 | 8 |
| Machado, Julio, Zulia | 0 | 0 | 2.51 | 8 | 2 | 14 | 12 | 4 | 17 |

## VENEZUELAN LEAGUE: YEAR-BY-YEAR LEADERS

### Last 25 Years

| Year | Batting | Home Runs | Wins | ERA |
|---|---|---|---|---|
| 1968-69 | Cito Gaston, Magallanes . .383 | Brant Alyea, Lara ............ 17 | George Lauzerique, Arag... 12 | Diego Segui, Caracas......... 1.85 |
| 1969-70 | Cito Gaston, Magallanes . .360 | John Bateman, Aragua ..... 9 | Mike Corkins, Aragua ........ 11 | Mike Hedlund, La Guaira.. 0.75 |
| 1970-71 | Vic Davalillo, Caracas........ .379 | Larry Howard, Caracas .... 12 | Bart Johnson, Chicago .......... 12 | Bart Johnson, Zulia.............. 1.39 |
| 1971-72 | Rod Carew, Aragua ........... .355 | Brant Alyea, Aragua ........ 12 | Bill Kirkpatrick, Zulia ........ 10 | Bill Kirkpatrick, Zulia......... 1.55 |
| 1972-73 | Enos Cabell, Aragua ....... .371 | Bobby Darwin, Mag......... 19 | Jim Rooker, La Guaira ........ 13 | Pete Broberg, Zulia............. 1.78 |
| 1973-74 | Al Bumbry, LaGuaira ...... .367 | Pete Koegel, Caracas ...... 18 | Jim Todd, Aragua ............... 10 | Carlos Alfonso, Zulia........... 1.05 |
| 1974-75 | Al Bumbry, La Guaira ...... .354 | Dave Parker, Magallanes.. 8 | Tom House, La Guaira ....... 10 | Tippy Martinez, Lara........... 1.71 |
| 1975-76 | Duane Kuiper, Aragua ..... .357 | Cliff Johnson, Port........... 11 | Scott McGregor, Lara ......... 8 | Stan Perzanowski, Zulia..... 1.55 |
| 1976-77 | Dave Parker, Magallanes .401 | Mitchell Page, Mag ......... 14 | 2 tied at ............................. 8 | Steve Luebber, La Guaira .. 2.59 |
| 1977-78 | J.J. Cannon, Magallanes.. .381 | Clint Hurdle, La Guaira ... 18 | Jerry Cram, Aragua ........... 13 | Scott Sanderson, Zulia ...... 1.41 |
| 1978-79 | Orlando Gonzalez, Lara ... .355 | Tom Grieve, Aragua ........ 14 | Tom Brennan, Zulia ........... 10 | Darrell Jackson, Caracas .... 1.16 |
| 1979-80 | Eddie Miller, Caracas ....... .368 | Bo Diaz, Caracas ............. 20 | Odell Jones, La Guaira ....... 11 | Mike Stanton, Caracas ...... 1.25 |
| 1980-81 | Tim Corcoran, Aragua ...... .379 | 3 tied at............................. 9 | Porfirio Altamirano, Zulia.... 8 | Luis Aponte, Lara............... 1.20 |
| 1981-82 | Lloyd Moseby, Lara ......... .362 | Bo Diaz, Caracas ............. 13 | Tom Dixon, Caracas........... 9 | Kelly Downs, Zulia ............. 1.61 |
| 1982-83 | Tito Landrum, Caracas ..... .345 | Darryl Strawberry, LaG .... 12 | Luis Leal, Lara .................... 9 | Luis Leal, Lara..................... 1.84 |
| 1983-84 | Alvin Davis, Caracas ........ .352 | 2 tied at.............................. 8 | Derek Botelho, Zulia........... 8 | Chris Green, Magallanes.... 1.46 |
| 1984-85 | Ossie Olivares, Aragua ... .352 | Ron Shepherd, Lara.......... 9 | Bill Landrum, Aragua ......... 8 | Tony Castillo, Lara.............. 2.06 |
| 1985-86 | Joe Orsulak, Zulia............ .331 | Andres Galarraga, Caracas 14 | Ubaldo Heredia, Caracas .... 8 | Bill Long, Caracas............... 1.85 |
| 1986-87 | Terry Francona, Zulia ....... .350 | Cecil Fielder, Lara ........... 19 | Stan Clarke, Lara ............... 8 | Ubaldo Heredia, Caracas ... 1.08 |
| 1987-88 | Cecil Fielder, Lara ........... .389 | Leo Hernandez, Aragua.. 11 | Jose Villa, Magallanes ....... 9 | Oswald Peraza, Lara.......... 1.16 |
| 1988-89 | Carlos Martinez, La Guaira .345 | Phil Stephenson, Zulia ..... 8 | Julio Strauss, Caracas ....... 9 | Urbano Lugo, Caracas......... 1.47 |
| 1989-90 | Luis Sojo, Lara................. .351 | Willie Magallanes, Mag.... 8 | Jim Neidlinger, Caracas ..... 8 | Luis Aponte, Lara............... 1.99 |
| 1990-91 | Luis Sojo, Lara................. .362 | Eddie Zambrano, Zul.-Ara. 11 | Joe Ausanio, Aragua .......... 8 | Brent Knackert, Caracas .... 0.92 |
| 1991-92 | Chad Curtis, La Guaira ..... .338 | 3 tied at............................. 5 | 2 tied at................................8 | Wilson Alvarez, Zulia ......... 1.47 |
| 1992-93 | Jeff Frye, Oriente............. .385 | Scott Cepicky, Oriente ..... 13 | Tony Castillo, Lara............. 9 | Jose Villa, Magallanes........ 0.79 |

# MEXICAN PACIFIC
## LEAGUE

# Carrillo Puts Up Espino-Like Numbers

Matias Carrillo cemented his reputation as Mexico's most celebrated offensive player since the legendary Hector Espino by making the Mexican Pacific League his own personal showcase in 1992-93.

The Mexicali outfielder led the league with a .404 average—a 71-point bulge over his closest rival—and also led in runs (57), hits (88), stolen bases (36), on-base percentage (.506) and slugging percentage (.638). He finished second with 13 home runs.

Carrillo became the first native Mexican to win a batting title since Espino won the last of his 13 crowns in 1982-83. He also was the first player to hit over .400 since Espino hit a league record .415 in 1972-73. For his achieve-

**Matias Carrillo**

ment, Carrillo was named Baseball America's 1992-93 Winter League Player of the Year.

Carrillo tried for seven years to reach the big leagues with Milwaukee, but his only opportunity came in 1991 when he played in three games but never got a chance to bat. Disillusioned, he returned to Mexico full time in 1992 and put up two big offensive seasons with the Mexico City Tigers, leading the Mexican League in homers and RBIs in 1993.

Finally, his contract was purchased by the Florida Marlins and Carrillo earned his first real big league exposure, spending September with the National League expansion team.

Carrillo's slugging exploits led Mexicali to the league's best overall record for the second year in a row, but Mexicali again was beaten in the playoffs by the team that represented Mexico in the Caribbean World Series, Mazatlan. Hermosillo eliminated Mexicali in 1991-92.

Mazatlan overcame a 3-1 deficit in the league's best-of-7 championship series to squeeze past Mexicali.

Angel Moreno and Isidro Marquez combined to shut out Mexicali 3-0 in the deciding game, while Chris Butterfield (Mets) and Pablo Machiria each homered.

Carrillo aside, the league's biggest drawing card in 1992-93 was Navojoa lefthander Fernando Valenzuela, who packed people in wherever he pitched. Valenzuela, who hails from a small village outside Navojoa, had not pitched effectively in four seasons in the major leagues and was hoping to use winter ball as a springboard to a return to the big leagues.

Valenzuela went 7-4 with a 2.95 ERA for Navojoa, pitched effectively as a pickup player for Mazatlan in the Caribbean World Series and eventually was signed by the Baltimore Orioles.

**—ALLAN SIMPSON**

## STANDINGS

| FIRST HALF | W | L | PCT | GB |
|---|---|---|---|---|
| Obregon | 20 | 15 | .571 | — |
| Mexicali | 19 | 16 | .543 | 1 |
| Culiacan | 19 | 16 | .543 | 1 |
| Navojoa | 18 | 16 | .529 | 1½ |
| Mazatlan | 17 | 17 | .500 | 2½ |
| Los Mochis | 16 | 19 | .457 | 4 |
| Hermosillo | 16 | 19 | .457 | 4 |
| Guasave | 14 | 21 | .400 | 6 |

| SECOND HALF | W | L | PCT | GB |
|---|---|---|---|---|
| Mexicali | 19 | 10 | .655 | — |
| Los Mochis | 20 | 12 | .625 | ½ |
| Mazatlan | 19 | 12 | .613 | 1 |
| Hermosillo | 19 | 13 | .594 | 1½ |
| Navojoa | 16 | 15 | .516 | 4 |
| Obregon | 13 | 20 | .394 | 8 |
| Culiacan | 13 | 20 | .394 | 8 |
| Guasave | 8 | 25 | .242 | 13 |

**Semifinals:** Mazatlan defeated Obregon, 5-0, and Mexicali defeated Los Mochis, 5-2, in best-of-9 series.

**Championship Series:** Mazatlan defeated Mexicali, 4-3, in best-of-7 final.

### INDIVIDUAL BATTING LEADERS
(Minimum 102 Plate Appearances)

| | AVG | AB | R | H | 2B | 3B | HR | RBI | SB |
|---|---|---|---|---|---|---|---|---|---|
| CARRILLO, MATIAS, Mexicali | .404 | 218 | 57 | 88 | 10 | 1 | 13 | 41 | 36 |
| Neel, Troy, Navojoa | .345 | 142 | 30 | 49 | 10 | 0 | 12 | 49 | 1 |
| Simmons, Nelson, LM | .333 | 231 | 43 | 77 | 17 | 0 | 16 | 52 | 0 |
| Tolentino, Jose, Mexicali | .322 | 143 | 27 | 46 | 10 | 0 | 6 | 29 | 4 |
| Brooks, Jerry, Mexicali | .317 | 224 | 30 | 71 | 14 | 0 | 8 | 35 | 6 |
| Haney, Todd, Mexicali | .312 | 231 | 43 | 72 | 13 | 4 | 3 | 23 | 12 |
| Fernandez, Daniel, Mazatlan | .301 | 229 | 45 | 69 | 3 | 3 | 1 | 18 | 20 |
| Mangham, Erick, Culiacan | .301 | 196 | 37 | 59 | 10 | 1 | 6 | 19 | 20 |
| Pacho, Juan, Mazatlan | .301 | 206 | 23 | 62 | 6 | 0 | 0 | 21 | 2 |
| Stairs, Matt, Navojoa | .298 | 178 | 42 | 53 | 10 | 1 | 7 | 44 | 6 |
| Jimenez, Eduardo, Herm. | .297 | 192 | 33 | 57 | 11 | 0 | 10 | 43 | 0 |
| Coachman, Pete, Mazatlan | .296 | 243 | 43 | 75 | 20 | 2 | 8 | 41 | 6 |
| Castaneda, Nick, Culiacan | .296 | 186 | 29 | 55 | 5 | 0 | 9 | 35 | 1 |
| Sanchez, Orlando, Guasave | .292 | 130 | 10 | 38 | 9 | 0 | 0 | 13 | 0 |
| Bullett, Scott, Guasave | .286 | 119 | 15 | 34 | 2 | 1 | 2 | 14 | 8 |
| Wearing, Mel, Mexicali | .280 | 207 | 32 | 58 | 6 | 0 | 9 | 39 | 7 |
| Tellez, Alonso, Hermosillo | .280 | 268 | 37 | 75 | 19 | 4 | 2 | 36 | 0 |
| Renteria, Rich, Guasave | .279 | 233 | 32 | 65 | 12 | 1 | 7 | 39 | 5 |
| Stark, Matt, Obregon | .279 | 201 | 40 | 56 | 7 | 0 | 13 | 41 | 2 |
| Hinzo, Tommy, Navojoa | .278 | 230 | 39 | 64 | 16 | 1 | 2 | 17 | 12 |
| Brantley, Mickey, Los Mochis | .275 | 120 | 8 | 33 | 5 | 2 | 2 | 23 | 1 |
| Brown, Jarvis, Guasave | .274 | 106 | 10 | 29 | 8 | 0 | 2 | 8 | 2 |
| Castilla, Vinny, Obregon | .273 | 183 | 27 | 50 | 6 | 1 | 6 | 22 | 4 |
| Jimenez, Houston, Mexicali | .272 | 232 | 39 | 63 | 7 | 0 | 5 | 13 | 4 |
| Lewis, Dan, Culiacan | .270 | 211 | 27 | 57 | 13 | 1 | 6 | 26 | 4 |
| Garcia, Cornelio, Hermosillo | .269 | 182 | 37 | 49 | 5 | 0 | 3 | 17 | 8 |
| Distefano, Benny, Mexicali | .269 | 104 | 14 | 28 | 5 | 1 | 2 | 14 | 1 |
| Rendina, Mike, Mazatlan | .269 | 104 | 9 | 28 | 4 | 0 | 2 | 7 | 0 |
| Guzman, Marco, Mexicali | .268 | 138 | 12 | 37 | 3 | 0 | 1 | 17 | 0 |
| Jimenez, Alfonso, Mexicali | .267 | 236 | 39 | 63 | 7 | 0 | 5 | 13 | 4 |

## MEXICAN PACIFIC LEAGUE: YEAR-BY-YEAR LEADERS

### Last 25 Years

| Year | Batting | Home Runs | Winning Percentage* | ERA |
|---|---|---|---|---|
| 1968-69 | Gabriel Lugo, Los Mochis .309 | Rogelio Alvarez, Cul. ...... 20 | Don Secrist, Los Mochis . 15-3 | Vicente Romo, Guaymas ... 1.54 |
| 1969-70 | Minnie Minoso, Mazatlan. .359 | 2 tied at.......................... 19 | Salvador Sanchez, LM.... 11-2 | Rene Paredes, Los Mochis 1.20 |
| 1970-71 | Hector Espino, Herm. ...... .348 | Hector Espino, Herm....... 22 | Maximino Leon, Herm. ..... 7-1 | Vicente Romo, Obregon ..... 1.60 |
| 1971-72 | Hector Espino, Herm. ...... .372 | Bobby Darwin, Herm. ...... 27 | Eduardo Acosta, Herm. ...... 7-2 | Mark Ballinger, Los Mochis 2.13 |
| 1972-73 | Hector Espino, Herm. ...... .415 | Hector Espino, Herm,...... 26 | Saul Montoya, Hermosillo . 8-2 | Saul Montoya, Hermosillo... 1.89 |
| 1973-74 | Jorge Orta, Navojoa ........ .370 | Roger Freed, Culiacan.... 20 | Francisco Maytorena, Nav. 8-1 | Eduardo Acosta, Herm. ...... 1.51 |
| 1974-75 | Jerry Hairston, Herm. ...... .311 | Jack Pierce, Mazatlan..... 14 | Enrique Romo, Obregon . 12-2 | Cesar Diaz, Culiacan.......... 1.40 |
| 1975-76 | Hector Espino, Herm. ...... .319 | Andres Mora, LM ........... 18 | Enrique Romo, Obregon . 12-2 | Carlos Carrazco, Mazatlan . 1.45 |
| 1976-77 | Nick Vazquez, Guay. ....... .345 | Charlie Sands, Mexicali .. 13 | Three tied at ..................... 9-3 | Max Leon, Hermosillo......... 1.47 |
| 1977-78 | Mike Easler, Los Mochis . .341 | Willie Aikens, Obregon.... 14 | Jose Pena, Navojoa........ 14-1 | Jose Pena, Navojoa .......... 1.33 |
| 1978-79 | Hector Espino, Herm. ...... .344 | 2 tied at.......................... 15 | Angel Moreno, Navojoa .... 7-1 | Byron McLaughlin, Guaymas. 1.05 |
| 1979-80 | Neil Fiala, Guasave ......... .364 | 3 tied at..........................11 | Jose Pena, Hermosillo ...... 6-1 | Max Leon, Hermosillo......... 0.87 |
| 1980-81 | David Green, Obregon .... .321 | 3 tied at.......................... 14 | Eleno Cuen, Guaymas.... 14-4 | Alejo Ahumada, Guasave... 1.42 |
| 1981-82 | Junior Moore, LM............ .325 | Mark Funderburk, Guasave 17 | Jaime Orozco, Tijuana .... 14-2 | Mike Paul, Tijuana ............. 1.32 |
| 1982-83 | Hector Espino, Herm. ...... .316 | Enrique Aguilar, Nav.-Obr. 8 | Salvador Colorado, Tij..... 11-3 | Salvador Colorado, Tijuana 0.53 |
| 1983-84 | Jimmy Collins, Mazatlan.. .314 | Chuckie Canady, LM.......... 14 | Alfonso Pulido, LM ........... 7-1 | Ramon Villegas, Navojoa ... 1.10 |
| 1984-85 | Roy Johnson, Herm.......... .337 | 3 tied at.......................... 15 | Arturo Gonzalez, Nav....... 12-2 | Teddy Higuera, Guasave.... 1.24 |
| 1985-86 | Eddie Brunson, Obregon. .335 | Carlos Soto, Guasave..... 17 | Guillermo Valenzuela, LM 13-3 | Felix Tejada, Guasave........ 1.25 |
| 1986-87 | John Kruk, Mexicali ......... .385 | Willie Aikens, Mazatlan ... 24 | Alfonso Pulido, Mexicali .... 6-1 | Vicente Palacios, Mexicali .. 2.31 |
| 1987-88 | Darrell Brown, LM............ .360 | Nelson Barrera, Culiacan 16 | Tim Leary, Tijuana ........... 9-0 | Tim Leary, Tijuana............. 1.30 |
| 1988-89 | Nelson Simmons, Maz .... .353 | Willie Aikens, Mazatlan ... 22 | Mercedes Esquer, Mex. .. 13-3 | Hector Heredia, Navojoa .... 1.43 |
| 1989-90 | Dave Hollins, Mexicali ..... .327 | Alejandro Ortiz, Obregon .16 | Arturo Gonzalez, Nav....... 10-1 | Narciso Elvira, Hermosillo .. 1.41 |
| 1990-91 | Matt Stairs, Navojoa ........ .330 | Ty Gainey, Los Mochis ... 13 | Rosario Rodriguez, Guay.. 7-1 | Derek Livernois, Culiacan... 1.21 |
| 1991-92 | Ty Gainey, Los Mochis.... .353 | Ty Gainey, Los Mochis ... 20 | Alfonso Pulido, Navojoa .... 7-2 | Tim Burcham, Obregon ...... 1.63 |
| 1992-93 | Matias Carrillo, Mexicali... .404 | Nelson Simmons, LM......... 16 | Esequiel Cano, Mexicali.... 9-1 | Blaise Ilsley, Hermosillo...... 1.88 |

*Wins leaders not available.

| | | | | | | | | | |
|---|---|---|---|---|---|---|---|---|---|
| Brumfield, Jacob, Culiacan | .267 | 150 | 28 | 40 | 6 | 2 | 4 | 25 | 14 |
| Diaz, Luis, Mazatlan | .267 | 105 | 21 | 28 | 8 | 0 | 6 | 13 | 5 |
| Cruz, Luis, Navojoa | .266 | 241 | 24 | 64 | 14 | 1 | 4 | 33 | 0 |
| Barbara, Don, Obregon | .263 | 133 | 17 | 35 | 6 | 0 | 5 | 23 | 0 |
| Velasquez, Guillermo, Mex. | .257 | 214 | 36 | 55 | 16 | 0 | 11 | 51 | 2 |
| Machiria, Pablo, Mazatlan | .257 | 226 | 29 | 58 | 13 | 2 | 4 | 28 | 7 |
| Flores, Miguel, Hermosillo | .256 | 199 | 28 | 51 | 14 | 1 | 1 | 16 | 18 |
| Phillips, J.R., Culiacan | .256 | 203 | 22 | 52 | 8 | 0 | 8 | 35 | 0 |
| Vizcarra, Roberto, Obregon | .256 | 250 | 39 | 64 | 6 | 0 | 7 | 23 | 3 |
| Valencia, Carlos, Mazatlan | .255 | 102 | 13 | 26 | 7 | 0 | 0 | 6 | 0 |
| Steels, James, Obregon | .253 | 237 | 34 | 60 | 10 | 0 | 13 | 40 | 10 |
| Martinez, Raul, Culiacan | .253 | 87 | 8 | 22 | 5 | 0 | 1 | 9 | 0 |
| Smith, Greg, Mexicali | .253 | 91 | 9 | 23 | 4 | 0 | 2 | 10 | 5 |
| Esquer, Ramon, Obregon | .252 | 107 | 14 | 27 | 3 | 2 | 0 | 11 | 0 |
| Jones, Ron, Maz.-Navojoa | .246 | 224 | 30 | 55 | 12 | 1 | 3 | 37 | 3 |
| Rodriguez, Juan, LM | .242 | 227 | 34 | 55 | 5 | 0 | 0 | 18 | 4 |
| Zazueta, Mauricio, Culiacan | .242 | 91 | 16 | 22 | 9 | 0 | 0 | 3 | 9 |
| Morones, Martin, LM | .241 | 137 | 21 | 33 | 3 | 2 | 0 | 12 | 4 |
| Pena, Luis, Los Mochis | .241 | 137 | 8 | 33 | 5 | 0 | 2 | 16 | 0 |
| Wright, George, Los Mochis | .240 | 246 | 36 | 59 | 13 | 2 | 10 | 36 | 4 |
| Valdez, Baltazar, Guasave | .239 | 142 | 12 | 34 | 5 | 0 | 4 | 24 | 1 |
| Wilson, Jim, Mazatlan | .239 | 142 | 15 | 34 | 4 | 0 | 6 | 28 | 3 |
| Lopez, Gonzalo, Guasave | .238 | 206 | 18 | 49 | 6 | 0 | 2 | 17 | 3 |
| Sanchez, Gerardo, Obregon | .236 | 237 | 34 | 56 | 13 | 1 | 1 | 20 | 2 |
| Romero, Marco, Los Mochis | .233 | 206 | 29 | 48 | 9 | 0 | 2 | 17 | 3 |
| Romero, Oscar, Culiacan | .232 | 228 | 25 | 53 | 7 | 0 | 6 | 18 | 6 |
| Cole, Mike, Guasave | .231 | 108 | 15 | 25 | 2 | 0 | 1 | 4 | 5 |
| Martinez, Grimaldo, Guasave | .231 | 225 | 33 | 52 | 4 | 0 | 0 | 13 | 3 |
| Ortiz, Alejandro, Obregon-LM | .230 | 217 | 31 | 50 | 10 | 1 | 8 | 25 | 1 |
| Paquette, Craig, Hermosillo | .229 | 157 | 17 | 36 | 5 | 3 | 5 | 27 | 0 |
| Castro, Juan, Los Mochis | .229 | 140 | 8 | 32 | 6 | 1 | 0 | 6 | 4 |
| Aguilera, Tony, Navojoa | .228 | 171 | 22 | 39 | 5 | 0 | 6 | 22 | 4 |
| Arredondo, Luis, Herm. | .225 | 151 | 24 | 34 | 6 | 1 | 1 | 14 | 7 |
| Garza, Gerardo, Navojoa | .225 | 200 | 20 | 45 | 12 | 0 | 0 | 26 | 1 |
| Samaniego, Manuel, Guasave | .225 | 160 | 15 | 36 | 2 | 0 | 0 | 4 | 0 |
| Garner, Kevin, Hermosillo | .225 | 89 | 20 | 20 | 3 | 0 | 7 | 17 | 0 |
| Quiroz, Jose, Guasave | .224 | 98 | 8 | 22 | 0 | 0 | 0 | 7 | 1 |
| Torres, Ray, Culiacan | .221 | 131 | 22 | 29 | 5 | 0 | 8 | 26 | 0 |
| Alvarez, Hector, Obregon | .219 | 137 | 12 | 30 | 4 | 0 | 0 | 7 | 0 |
| Herrera, Isidro, Mexicali | .216 | 88 | 12 | 19 | 4 | 0 | 0 | 8 | 6 |
| Leyva, German, Guasave | .206 | 97 | 11 | 20 | 5 | 1 | 0 | 3 | 2 |
| Sandoval, Jose, Hermosillo | .205 | 224 | 28 | 46 | 7 | 1 | 4 | 34 | 2 |
| Ramirez, Enrique, Culiacan | .203 | 177 | 21 | 36 | 2 | 0 | 1 | 15 | 1 |
| Hirtensteiner, Rick, Navojoa | .198 | 101 | 12 | 20 | 2 | 0 | 0 | 11 | 3 |
| Cruz, Marco, Mazatlan | .198 | 96 | 7 | 19 | 4 | 0 | 0 | 9 | 0 |
| Munoz, Noe, Los Mochis | .197 | 137 | 7 | 27 | 4 | 2 | 1 | 16 | 1 |
| Barrera, Jesus, Culiacan | .197 | 132 | 17 | 26 | 1 | 0 | 0 | 5 | 1 |
| Verdugo, Vicente, Obregon | .195 | 200 | 23 | 39 | 4 | 3 | 1 | 16 | 1 |
| Abrego, Jesus, Los Mochis | .194 | 93 | 7 | 18 | 4 | 0 | 1 | 6 | 1 |
| Saenz, Ricardo, Hermosillo | .194 | 93 | 10 | 18 | 2 | 0 | 3 | 8 | 1 |

### INDIVIDUAL PITCHING LEADERS

(Minimum 34 Innings)

| | W | L | ERA | G | SV | IP | H | BB | SO |
|---|---|---|---|---|---|---|---|---|---|
| Caruso, Joe, Hermosillo | 4 | 3 | 1.78 | 27 | 5 | 35 | 20 | 26 | 36 |
| Cabrales, Gabriel, Obregon | 4 | 2 | 1.85 | 28 | 4 | 44 | 31 | 11 | 22 |
| ILSLEY, BLAISE, Hermosillo | 7 | 3 | 1.88 | 14 | 0 | 91 | 86 | 25 | 38 |
| Gonzalez, Arturo, Navojoa | 4 | 3 | 2.14 | 10 | 0 | 59 | 51 | 27 | 21 |
| Marquez, Isidro, Mazatlan | 4 | 4 | 2.30 | 34 | 8 | 47 | 41 | 38 | 34 |
| Lopez, Emigdio, Mexicali | 6 | 3 | 2.31 | 21 | 0 | 51 | 43 | 23 | 33 |
| Johnson, Earnie, Mexicali | 6 | 0 | 2.34 | 28 | 5 | 42 | 37 | 23 | 36 |
| Lumley, Mike, Mazatlan | 5 | 2 | 2.35 | 21 | 2 | 73 | 64 | 35 | 45 |
| Green, Otis, Obregon | 2 | 4 | 2.45 | 11 | 0 | 62 | 41 | 40 | 76 |
| Vazquez, Adrian, Mexicali | 2 | 1 | 2.47 | 11 | 1 | 51 | 38 | 30 | 25 |
| Sinohui, David, Navojoa | 4 | 1 | 2.50 | 23 | 3 | 58 | 48 | 26 | 39 |
| Renteria, Hilario, Culiacan | 3 | 2 | 2.54 | 21 | 3 | 64 | 46 | 12 | 24 |
| Rios, Jesus, Culiacan | 8 | 3 | 2.58 | 16 | 0 | 91 | 71 | 48 | 90 |
| Burcham, Tim, Obregon | 7 | 4 | 2.59 | 14 | 0 | 90 | 75 | 39 | 62 |
| Mendez, Luis, Los Mochis | 8 | 1 | 2.65 | 14 | 0 | 58 | 43 | 43 | 46 |
| Zappelli, Mark, Obregon | 3 | 2 | 2.70 | 25 | 11 | 40 | 31 | 15 | 34 |
| Moreno, Jesus, Hermosillo | 2 | 2 | 2.72 | 30 | 1 | 40 | 26 | 15 | 29 |
| Rincon, Ricardo, Guasave | 1 | 3 | 2.75 | 25 | 6 | 36 | 22 | 27 | 38 |
| Meza, Leobardo, Obregon | 1 | 1 | 2.80 | 18 | 1 | 45 | 40 | 24 | 24 |
| Heredia, Hector, Navojoa | 2 | 3 | 2.83 | 23 | 10 | 35 | 27 | 18 | 32 |
| Couoh, Enrique, Mexicali | 2 | 2 | 2.91 | 17 | 1 | 34 | 11 | 19 | 33 |
| Cano, Esequiel, Mexicali | 9 | 1 | 2.92 | 12 | 0 | 77 | 63 | 25 | 34 |
| Valenzuela, Fernando, Navojoa | 7 | 4 | 2.95 | 15 | 0 | 107 | 81 | 45 | 58 |
| Castillo, Luis, Culiacan | 2 | 5 | 2.98 | 16 | 0 | 57 | 42 | 38 | 37 |
| Montano, Francisco, Mazatlan | 2 | 2 | 3.00 | 19 | 0 | 42 | 42 | 24 | 25 |
| Latter, Dave, Los Mochis | 7 | 4 | 3.01 | 16 | 0 | 99 | 82 | 56 | 47 |
| Miranda, Julio, Culiacan | 3 | 4 | 3.04 | 37 | 1 | 56 | 42 | 29 | 43 |
| Cruz, Andres, Mazatlan | 6 | 3 | 3.10 | 14 | 0 | 81 | 72 | 33 | 61 |
| Gamez, Francisco, Hermosillo | 2 | 0 | 3.19 | 12 | 0 | 59 | 58 | 37 | 22 |
| Vierra, Joey, Culiacan | 1 | 2 | 3.19 | 13 | 2 | 42 | 36 | 18 | 29 |
| Mead, Timber, Guasave | 5 | 7 | 3.20 | 14 | 0 | 90 | 77 | 56 | 53 |
| Rogers, Charlie, Los Mochis | 5 | 4 | 3.28 | 13 | 0 | 82 | 81 | 35 | 40 |
| Osuna, Antonio, Guasave | 2 | 6 | 3.34 | 22 | 7 | 67 | 45 | 57 | 72 |
| Barraza, Ernesto, Culiacan | 7 | 5 | 3.34 | 20 | 0 | 70 | 50 | 55 | 41 |
| Osuna, Ricardo, Mexicali | 1 | 5 | 3.48 | 17 | 5 | 52 | 51 | 20 | 27 |
| Palafox, Juan, Mazatlan | 2 | 6 | 3.52 | 21 | 5 | 61 | 50 | 31 | 17 |
| Solis, Ricardo, Hermosillo | 3 | 6 | 3.61 | 13 | 0 | 77 | 67 | 31 | 26 |
| Garcia, Mike, Mazatlan | 5 | 6 | 3.63 | 15 | 0 | 87 | 79 | 36 | 61 |
| Reynoso, Armando, Obregon | 3 | 3 | 3.76 | 10 | 0 | 55 | 51 | 27 | 46 |
| Moreno, Angel, Mazatlan | 8 | 2 | 4.02 | 15 | 0 | 87 | 78 | 44 | 66 |
| Upshaw, Lee, Mexicali | 1 | 3 | 4.06 | 11 | 0 | 51 | 41 | 42 | 36 |
| Delahoya, Javier, Mexicali | 4 | 2 | 4.11 | 9 | 0 | 46 | 42 | 29 | 40 |
| Rodriguez, Raul, Obregon | 3 | 3 | 4.14 | 27 | 0 | 41 | 52 | 16 | 16 |
| Herrera, Enrique, Guasave | 2 | 6 | 4.33 | 18 | 0 | 54 | 57 | 21 | 27 |
| Munoz, Miguel, Hermosillo | 5 | 4 | 4.36 | 13 | 0 | 66 | 73 | 16 | 33 |
| Valdez, Armando, Guasave | 4 | 6 | 4.39 | 15 | 0 | 82 | 73 | 54 | 52 |
| Huerta, Luis, Los Mochis | 4 | 6 | 4.39 | 15 | 1 | 70 | 79 | 38 | 32 |
| Sanchez, Hector, Guasave | 2 | 5 | 4.41 | 23 | 2 | 51 | 58 | 10 | 15 |
| Hurst, Jonathan, Hermosillo | 6 | 4 | 4.44 | 14 | 0 | 75 | 61 | 35 | 61 |
| Acosta, Aaron, Obregon | 3 | 4 | 4.46 | 22 | 1 | 42 | 44 | 25 | 24 |
| Diaz, Rafael, Navojoa | 6 | 2 | 4.46 | 12 | 0 | 67 | 53 | 42 | 42 |
| Enriquez, Martin, Navojoa | 2 | 6 | 4.52 | 14 | 0 | 72 | 74 | 42 | 59 |
| Neri, Braulio, Guasave | 1 | 1 | 4.75 | 20 | 0 | 42 | 47 | 38 | 24 |
| Ruiz, Cecilio, Obregon | 3 | 3 | 4.99 | 15 | 0 | 61 | 66 | 31 | 26 |
| Hernandez, Martin, Guasave | 3 | 6 | 5.03 | 14 | 0 | 79 | 75 | 58 | 37 |

# AUSTRALIAN
## LEAGUE

# Perth Stunned Again In Down Under Final

The Melbourne Monarchs, who didn't field a team the previous two seasons, were surprise winners of the 1992-1993 Australian Baseball League's Grand Final. The Monarchs won the best-of-3 championship series in two straight games, beating the heavily favored Perth Heat, 14-2 and 1-0.

Melbourne finished second to Perth in the regular season, but received outstanding pitching from two Florida Marlins prospects, Don Lemon and Barry Parisotto, to subdue Perth, which also finished first the previous year only to fall in the final round of the playoffs.

"Nobody in the world but the guys on our roster thought we could do it," Melbourne manager Jon Deeble said. "The guys went out and did a job. We showed our confidence with actions rather than words."

Lemon won the clinching game for the Monarchs, no-hitting Perth for seven innings before getting ninth-inning relief help from Ross Jones. The pair combined on a three-hitter. Parisotto struck out an ABL-record 11 batters in winning the opener.

The Monarchs were awarded a franchise in the league only after the Sydney Wave took a leave of absence to find a suitable venue for home games.

## Interest On Rise

Interest in Australian baseball continues to increase at a rapid rate, both in terms of the number of teenage Australian prospects being signed by major league clubs—notably Atlanta's signing in August of 16-year-old shortstop Glenn Williams to an $800,000 bonus—and their willingness to provide players to the fledgling ABL.

ABL clubs are permitted to field four American players and major league clubs that have established partial working agreements provided the full complement of players for the 1992-93 season. Those affiliations: Adelaide (Dodgers); Brisbane (Yankees); Gold Coast (Brewers); Melbourne Bushrangers (Astros); Melbourne Monarchs (Marlins); Perth (Orioles); Sydney (Blue Jays); Waverley (Braves).

Brisbane second baseman Kevin Jordan, a rising prospect in the New York Yankees organization, was named the league's MVP. He led the league with a .390 average and twice hit for the cycle—a feat never previously achieved in the ABL's four-year history.

Waverley Reds righthander Carlos Reyes (Braves) was named pitcher of the year. Reyes went 9-1 with a 2.02 ERA and led the league with 74 strikeouts.

Jones, who had 13 saves in addition to his save in the title-clinching game, was named reliever of the year. Phil Dale, a pitching coach in the Braves organization, was named the league's manager of the year. He led Waverley to a fourth place finish and also contributed seven saves as a reliever.

Perth lefthander Graeme Lloyd led the ABL with a 1.48 ERA and later in the 1993 season teamed with Milwaukee Brewers catcher David Nilsson to become the first all-Australian battery in Major League Baseball history.

**—ALLAN SIMPSON**

Kevin Jordan

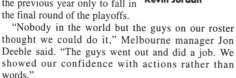
MEL BAILEY
Graeme Lloyd

### STANDINGS

| REGULAR SEASON | W | L | PCT | GB |
|---|---|---|---|---|
| Perth Heat | 30 | 18 | .625 | — |
| Melbourne Monarchs | 28 | 19 | .597 | 1½ |
| Sydney Blues | 25 | 19 | .568 | 3 |
| Waverley Reds | 26 | 21 | .553 | 3½ |
| Brisbane Bandits | 25 | 21 | .545 | 4 |
| Gold Coast Dolphins | 19 | 26 | .422 | 9½ |
| Adelaide Giants | 19 | 27 | .413 | 10 |
| Melbourne Bushrangers | 13 | 34 | .276 | 16½ |

**Semifinals:** Perth defeated Waverley, 2-0, and Melbourne Monarchs defeated Sydney, 2-1, in best-of-3 series.

**Grand Final:** Melbourne Monarchs defeated Perth, 2-0, in best-of-3 final.

### INDIVIDUAL BATTING LEADERS
(Minimum 114 Plate Appearances)

| | AVG | AB | R | H | 2B | 3B | HR | RBI | SB |
|---|---|---|---|---|---|---|---|---|---|
| Jordan, Kevin, Brisbane | .390 | 154 | 28 | 60 | 15 | 3 | 5 | 34 | 3 |
| Jelks, Greg, Perth | .378 | 164 | 42 | 62 | 11 | 3 | 12 | 41 | 4 |
| Harris, Mike, Gold Coast | .362 | 149 | 33 | 54 | 5 | 6 | 3 | 22 | 17 |
| Holland, Tim, Perth | .331 | 163 | 29 | 54 | 8 | 2 | 6 | 31 | 4 |
| Scott, Kevin, Bushrangers | .327 | 159 | 24 | 52 | 9 | 2 | 3 | 27 | 11 |
| Steed, Scott, Perth | .325 | 151 | 31 | 49 | 7 | 2 | 5 | 27 | 10 |
| Edwards, Brendan, Bushrangers | .325 | 114 | 13 | 37 | 6 | 3 | 0 | 15 | 3 |
| Singleton, Duane, Gold Coast | .321 | 159 | 27 | 51 | 10 | 3 | 2 | 21 | 18 |
| Carothers, Ron, Monarchs | .315 | 130 | 22 | 41 | 5 | 1 | 3 | 27 | 3 |
| Davison, Nathan, Adelaide | .312 | 138 | 23 | 43 | 12 | 1 | 0 | 15 | 9 |

### INDIVIDUAL PITCHING LEADERS
(Minimum 28 Innings)

| | W | L | ERA | G | SV | IP | H | BB | SO |
|---|---|---|---|---|---|---|---|---|---|
| Lloyd, Graeme, Perth | 8 | 1 | 1.48 | 10 | 0 | 61 | 52 | 4 | 57 |
| Dedrick, Jim, Perth | 6 | 4 | 1.90 | 12 | 0 | 71 | 64 | 15 | 59 |
| Reyes, Carlos, Waverley | 9 | 1 | 2.02 | 14 | 0 | 98 | 80 | 10 | 74 |
| Parisotto, Barry, Monarchs | 8 | 4 | 2.05 | 13 | 0 | 84 | 60 | 25 | 68 |
| Collins, Sheldon, Waverley | 8 | 4 | 2.25 | 15 | 0 | 80 | 60 | 15 | 40 |
| Lemon, Don, Monarchs | 6 | 4 | 2.26 | 12 | 0 | 80 | 61 | 26 | 59 |
| Krivda, Rick, Perth | 8 | 1 | 2.32 | 12 | 0 | 74 | 47 | 38 | 68 |
| Respondek, Mark, Waverley | 5 | 2 | 2.40 | 10 | 0 | 53 | 68 | 17 | 17 |
| Dale, Phil, Waverley | 3 | 5 | 2.47 | 22 | 7 | 58 | 52 | 11 | 39 |
| Nilsson, Gary, Brisbane | 3 | 0 | 2.50 | 7 | 0 | 40 | 31 | 11 | 22 |

# ARIZONA FALL LEAGUE

## New League A Hit For Scouts, Not Fans

"A League Of Their Own" was one of 1992's hit movies. It also aptly described Major League Baseball's latest play toy, the Arizona Fall League, which debuted in 1992.

Disgruntled by deteriorating conditions in the game's traditional winter leagues, MLB and its 28 member clubs sanctioned a new fall/winter league of their own, designed to enhance the offseason development of some of the game's top prospects without having to expose them to the pitfalls of playing in a foreign environment.

A six-team league was created in and around the Arizona metropolitan areas of Phoenix (five clubs) and Tucson with every major league club providing at least six prospects, almost all with at least Double-A experience. Though attendance was sparse, the AFL provided an excellent on-field opportunity for players, more than 50 of whom played in the major leagues in 1993.

**Ryan Klesko**

Phoenix (33-18) had easily the league's best overall record, but Sun Cities won a playoff doubleheader on the final day to capture the league title, two games to one. Both games were scheduled for seven innings and were decided at the wire.

Sun Cities won the opener of the twinbill, 3-2, on Mike Piazza's (Dodgers) game-tying, two-run homer and Rod Robertson's (Tigers) run-scoring single in the seventh. In the clincher, Robertson's infield single in the eighth triggered a two-run outburst which enabled the Solar Sox to win, 7-5.

Braves first base prospect Ryan Klesko, who led the league with 11 home runs while playing for Grand Canyon, was selected the league's top prospect in a managers poll.

**—ALLAN SIMPSON**

Klesko, 1b, Grand Canyon. **2.** Rondell White, of, Grand Canyon. **3.** Brad Pennington, lhp, Scottsdale. **4.** Troy Percival, rhp, Scottsdale. **5.** Kevin Young, 3b, Phoenix. **6.** Jessie Hollins, rhp, Grand Canyon. **7.** Aaron Small, rhp, Tucson. **8.** Kevin Rogers, lhp, Scottsdale. **9.** Mike Piazza, c, Sun Cities. **10.** Mike Kelly, of, Grand Canyon.

### INDIVIDUAL BATTING LEADERS
(Minimum 146 Plate Appearances)

| | AVG | AB | R | H | 2B | 3B | HR | RBI | SB |
|---|---|---|---|---|---|---|---|---|---|
| Pegues, Steve, Tucson | .347 | 196 | 34 | 68 | 11 | 4 | 7 | 34 | 7 |
| Zosky, Eddie, Tucson | .326 | 135 | 17 | 44 | 7 | 4 | 0 | 15 | 1 |
| Hamelin, Bob, Scottsdale | .325 | 160 | 24 | 52 | 7 | 4 | 7 | 37 | 0 |
| Mouton, James, Tucson | .318 | 173 | 27 | 55 | 7 | 7 | 1 | 21 | 10 |
| Martin, Al, Phoenix | .312 | 141 | 27 | 44 | 7 | 3 | 5 | 23 | 6 |
| Massarelli, John, Sun Cities | .312 | 154 | 19 | 48 | 8 | 2 | 0 | 12 | 20 |
| Peltier, Dan, Phoenix | .312 | 138 | 24 | 43 | 9 | 2 | 1 | 18 | 2 |
| Pose, Scott, Chandler | .305 | 174 | 29 | 53 | 7 | 2 | 0 | 13 | 11 |
| Hale, Chip, Grand Canyon | .297 | 175 | 20 | 52 | 3 | 2 | 1 | 21 | 1 |
| Lansing, Mike, Grand Canyon | .296 | 142 | 27 | 42 | 9 | 4 | 1 | 19 | 6 |

### INDIVIDUAL PITCHING LEADERS
(Minimum 43 Innings)

| | W | L | ERA | G | SV | IP | H | BB | SO |
|---|---|---|---|---|---|---|---|---|---|
| Kramer, Tom, Tucson | 5 | 2 | 1.93 | 17 | 0 | 51 | 40 | 20 | 55 |
| Minor, Blas, Phoenix | 2 | 0 | 2.06 | 19 | 1 | 44 | 32 | 6 | 30 |
| O'Donoghue, John, Scottsdale | 3 | 2 | 2.40 | 9 | 0 | 49 | 39 | 21 | 43 |
| Cook, Andy, Phoenix | 6 | 2 | 2.48 | 10 | 0 | 58 | 50 | 26 | 44 |
| McGehee, Kevin, Scottsdale | 3 | 6 | 2.58 | 11 | 0 | 59 | 48 | 19 | 38 |
| DeSilva, John, Sun Cities | 3 | 5 | 2.80 | 11 | 0 | 64 | 57 | 19 | 61 |
| Powell, Ross, Chandler | 2 | 2 | 2.80 | 13 | 0 | 45 | 45 | 11 | 41 |
| Zancanaro, David, Phoenix | 6 | 3 | 3.10 | 11 | 0 | 61 | 62 | 22 | 36 |
| Henry, John, Phoenix | 5 | 3 | 3.21 | 13 | 1 | 53 | 54 | 15 | 29 |
| Taylor, Scott, Chandler | 4 | 5 | 3.43 | 11 | 0 | 60 | 61 | 21 | 38 |

## CHANDLER

| BATTING | AVG | AB | R | H | 2B | 3B | HR | RBI | SB |
|---|---|---|---|---|---|---|---|---|---|
| 3 Adams, Tommy, of | .317 | 60 | 8 | 19 | 4 | 1 | 1 | 6 | 1 |
| 4 Bieser, Steve, of | .202 | 104 | 15 | 21 | 4 | 1 | 0 | 10 | 2 |
| 4 Brady, Pat, of-1b | .156 | 141 | 11 | 22 | 4 | 2 | 1 | 16 | 1 |
| 2 Dodson, Bo, 1b | .210 | 100 | 10 | 21 | 3 | 1 | 1 | 9 | 0 |
| 2 Felder, Kenny, of | .194 | 124 | 9 | 24 | 5 | 3 | 0 | 12 | 3 |
| 2 Finn, John, 2b-3b | .265 | 102 | 16 | 27 | 2 | 0 | 1 | 7 | 6 |
| 3 Howard, Chris, c | .261 | 88 | 7 | 23 | 5 | 0 | 0 | 10 | 0 |
| 4 Lieberthal, Mike, dh-c | .277 | 119 | 11 | 33 | 6 | 1 | 0 | 13 | 1 |
| 1 Mota, Andy, 3b | .214 | 159 | 12 | 34 | 8 | 0 | 3 | 19 | 1 |
| 3 Pirkl, Greg, 1b | .195 | 41 | 5 | 8 | 2 | 0 | 0 | 3 | 0 |
| 5 Pose, Scott, of | .305 | 174 | 29 | 53 | 7 | 2 | 0 | 13 | 11 |
| 5 Riggs, Kevin, 2b | .198 | 101 | 16 | 20 | 2 | 1 | 0 | 6 | 3 |
| 4 Stocker, Kevin, ss | .280 | 182 | 20 | 51 | 10 | 5 | 0 | 23 | 8 |
| 5 Sutko, Glenn, c | .190 | 63 | 5 | 12 | 2 | 1 | 0 | 4 | 0 |
| 3 Turang, Brian, 2b-of | .217 | 129 | 11 | 28 | 5 | 1 | 0 | 9 | 3 |

| PITCHING | W | L | ERA | G | SV | IP | H | BB | SO |
|---|---|---|---|---|---|---|---|---|---|
| 4 Adamson, Joel | 3 | 1 | 3.72 | 8 | 0 | 39 | 43 | 7 | 24 |
| 3 Gutierrez, Jim | 0 | 1 | 1.13 | 5 | 0 | 16 | 14 | 5 | 9 |
| 3 Holman, Brad | 3 | 0 | 3.72 | 22 | 0 | 46 | 52 | 16 | 36 |
| 1 Lewis, Jim | 2 | 3 | 3.30 | 6 | 0 | 30 | 29 | 7 | 19 |
| 5 Lynch, David | 0 | 2 | 6.60 | 22 | 1 | 30 | 36 | 8 | 23 |
| 3 Masters, Dave | 0 | 3 | 3.34 | 19 | 0 | 32 | 35 | 16 | 24 |
| 2 McGraw, Tom | 0 | 6 | 6.63 | 9 | 0 | 37 | 47 | 18 | 19 |
| 4 Patterson, Jeff | 2 | 5 | 5.03 | 21 | 0 | 34 | 40 | 16 | 22 |
| 5 Powell, Ross | 2 | 2 | 2.80 | 13 | 0 | 45 | 45 | 11 | 41 |
| 5 Satre, Jason | 1 | 4 | 6.94 | 13 | 0 | 36 | 46 | 24 | 25 |
| 6 Scheid, Rich | 0 | 0 | 0.00 | 5 | 0 | 7 | 1 | 5 | 8 |
| 2 Taylor, Scott | 4 | 5 | 3.43 | 11 | 0 | 60 | 61 | 21 | 38 |
| 3 Walker, Mike | 0 | 2 | 7.41 | 5 | 0 | 17 | 20 | 12 | 11 |
| 2 Wishnevski, Rob | 1 | 2 | 3.58 | 22 | 12 | 28 | 24 | 14 | 21 |

Property of Astros (1), Brewers (2), Mariners (3), Phillies (4), Reds (5), Padres (6).

### STANDINGS

| NORTH | W | L | PCT | GB |
|---|---|---|---|---|
| Sun Cities Solar Sox | 28 | 25 | .528 | — |
| Grand Canyon Rafters | 26 | 27 | .491 | 2 |
| Scottsdale Scorpions | 25 | 28 | .472 | 3 |

| SOUTH | W | L | PCT | GB |
|---|---|---|---|---|
| Phoenix Saguaros | 33 | 18 | .647 | — |
| Tucson Javelinas | 25 | 26 | .490 | 8 |
| Chandler Diamondbacks | 20 | 33 | .377 | 14 |

**Championship Series:** Sun Cities defeated Phoenix, 2-1, in best-of-3 final.

**MANAGERS: Chandler**—Roy Majtyka (Phillies). **Grand Canyon**—Grady Little (Braves). **Phoenix**—Scott Ullger (Twins). **Scottsdale**—Dusty Baker (Giants). **Sun Cities**—Jerry Royster (Dodgers). **Tucson**—Bob Didier (Blue Jays).

**TOP 10 PROSPECTS** (Selected by league managers): **1.** Ryan

## GRAND CANYON

| BATTING | AVG | AB | R | H | 2B | 3B | HR | RBI | SB |
|---|---|---|---|---|---|---|---|---|---|
| 5 Campbell, Darrin, c | .287 | 94 | 11 | 27 | 4 | 1 | 3 | 13 | 2 |

| | AVG | AB | R | H | 2B | 3B | HR | RBI | SB |
|---|---|---|---|---|---|---|---|---|---|
| 5 Cron, Chris, 1b-dh | .255 | 137 | 17 | 35 | 9 | 1 | 0 | 17 | 0 |
| 4 Delanuez, Rex, of | .279 | 111 | 18 | 31 | 5 | 0 | 1 | 8 | 3 |
| 3 Fitzpatrick, Rob, c | .268 | 56 | 5 | 15 | 3 | 0 | 1 | 7 | 1 |
| 2 Grace, Mike, 3b | .250 | 156 | 21 | 39 | 16 | 2 | 4 | 22 | 0 |
| 4 Hale, Chip, 2b | .297 | 175 | 20 | 52 | 3 | 2 | 1 | 21 | 1 |
| 5 Jeter, Shawn, of | .236 | 148 | 16 | 35 | 5 | 2 | 2 | 12 | 13 |
| 1 Kelly, Mike, of | .278 | 144 | 18 | 40 | 3 | 2 | 3 | 17 | 5 |
| 1 Klesko, Ryan, 1b | .270 | 126 | 29 | 34 | 4 | 0 | 11 | 26 | 7 |
| 3 Lansing, Mike, ss | .296 | 142 | 27 | 42 | 9 | 4 | 1 | 19 | 6 |
| 1 Mordecai, Mike, inf | .250 | 148 | 13 | 37 | 5 | 1 | 0 | 17 | 2 |
| 2 Robinson, Jim, c | .250 | 72 | 7 | 18 | 2 | 1 | 0 | 6 | 1 |
| 1 Tarasco, Tony, of | .248 | 129 | 12 | 32 | 8 | 3 | 1 | 17 | 3 |
| 3 White, Rondell, of-dh | .201 | 149 | 19 | 30 | 5 | 2 | 1 | 18 | 9 |

| PITCHING | W | L | ERA | G | SV | IP | H | BB | SO |
|---|---|---|---|---|---|---|---|---|---|
| 1 Bark, Brian | 3 | 4 | 3.99 | 13 | 0 | 59 | 53 | 17 | 41 |
| 1 Burlingame, Dennis | 2 | 2 | 5.71 | 11 | 0 | 41 | 46 | 27 | 19 |
| 3 Eischen, Joey | 0 | 4 | 4.78 | 10 | 0 | 26 | 30 | 22 | 23 |
| 1 Elliott, Donnie | 1 | 2 | 4.18 | 8 | 0 | 28 | 25 | 13 | 20 |
| 2 Gardner, John | 3 | 2 | 2.50 | 22 | 0 | 40 | 35 | 22 | 34 |
| 2 Hartsock, Jeff | 3 | 5 | 5.56 | 9 | 0 | 34 | 39 | 17 | 18 |
| 2 Hollins, Jessie | 2 | 1 | 0.84 | 24 | 4 | 32 | 19 | 12 | 38 |
| 2 Hudek, John | 2 | 2 | 2.38 | 13 | 0 | 42 | 32 | 20 | 32 |
| 5 Mongiello, Mike | 4 | 3 | 3.56 | 14 | 0 | 56 | 61 | 12 | 46 |
| 3 Risley, Bill | 1 | 1 | 3.03 | 8 | 0 | 36 | 31 | 17 | 23 |
| 3 Schwarz, Jeff | 3 | 0 | 2.83 | 22 | 7 | 29 | 19 | 22 | 30 |
| 2 Swartzbaugh, Dave | 2 | 4 | 3.48 | 21 | 0 | 41 | 53 | 13 | 34 |

Property of Braves (1), Cubs (2), Expos (3), Twins (4), White Sox (5).

## PHOENIX

| BATTING | AVG | AB | R | H | 2B | 3B | HR | RBI | SB |
|---|---|---|---|---|---|---|---|---|---|
| 1 Abbott, Kurt, ss | .212 | 132 | 19 | 28 | 6 | 2 | 1 | 19 | 1 |
| 5 DeJardin, Bobby, ss-2b | .284 | 148 | 25 | 42 | 2 | 4 | 2 | 11 | 8 |
| 5 Everett, Carl, of | .230 | 139 | 21 | 32 | 9 | 1 | 2 | 12 | 9 |
| 1 Helfand, Eric, c | .218 | 101 | 7 | 22 | 5 | 0 | 1 | 12 | 0 |
| 2 Luce, Roger, c | .221 | 86 | 8 | 19 | 3 | 3 | 2 | 8 | 0 |
| 1 Lydy, Scott, of | .240 | 129 | 15 | 31 | 8 | 1 | 3 | 23 | 4 |
| 2 Martin, Al, of-dh | .312 | 141 | 27 | 44 | 7 | 3 | 5 | 23 | 6 |
| 4 Ortiz, Ray, 1b-of | .354 | 65 | 10 | 23 | 5 | 0 | 0 | 8 | 1 |
| 2 Osik, Keith, c | .267 | 86 | 8 | 23 | 2 | 0 | 1 | 10 | 1 |
| 3 Peltier, Dan, of | .312 | 138 | 24 | 43 | 9 | 2 | 1 | 18 | 2 |
| 5 Redfield, Joe, 1b | .194 | 139 | 17 | 27 | 3 | 0 | 1 | 11 | 4 |
| 5 Robertson, Jason, of | .230 | 122 | 12 | 28 | 2 | 4 | 1 | 10 | 2 |
| 2 Shave, Jon, 2b | .250 | 136 | 17 | 34 | 5 | 2 | 1 | 17 | 2 |
| 2 Young, Kevin, 3b | .271 | 144 | 21 | 39 | 12 | 2 | 1 | 23 | 2 |

| PITCHING | W | L | ERA | G | SV | IP | H | BB | SO |
|---|---|---|---|---|---|---|---|---|---|
| 3 Bronkey, Jeff | 0 | 1 | 0.77 | 11 | 3 | 12 | 7 | 4 | 6 |
| 3 Brown, Rob | 4 | 2 | 2.68 | 8 | 0 | 40 | 42 | 14 | 37 |
| 5 Cook, Andy | 2 | 2 | 0.48 | 10 | 0 | 58 | 50 | 26 | 44 |
| 4 Henry, John | 5 | 3 | 3.21 | 13 | 1 | 53 | 54 | 15 | 29 |
| 3 Miller, Kurt | 3 | 2 | 3.24 | 5 | 0 | 25 | 20 | 11 | 22 |
| 3 Minor, Blas | 2 | 0 | 2.06 | 19 | 1 | 44 | 32 | 6 | 30 |
| 1 Mohler, Mike | 0 | 1 | 1.93 | 18 | 3 | 37 | 28 | 10 | 27 |
| 5 Nielsen, Jerry | 0 | 2 | 2.63 | 19 | 6 | 27 | 14 | 9 | 30 |
| 1 Revenig, Todd | 0 | 0 | 0.00 | 2 | 0 | 2 | 1 | 0 | 1 |
| 2 Shouse, Brian | 2 | 1 | 4.71 | 21 | 1 | 29 | 33 | 10 | 24 |
| 5 Springer, Russ | 3 | 1 | 3.21 | 20 | 2 | 28 | 30 | 11 | 27 |
| 1 Zancanaro, David | 6 | 3 | 3.10 | 11 | 0 | 61 | 62 | 22 | 36 |

Property of Athletics (1), Pirates (2), Rangers (3), Twins (4), Yankees (5).

## SCOTTSDALE

| BATTING | AVG | AB | R | H | 2B | 3B | HR | RBI | SB |
|---|---|---|---|---|---|---|---|---|---|
| 1 Anderson, Garret, of | .171 | 105 | 6 | 18 | 3 | 0 | 0 | 7 | 0 |
| 2 Bellinger, Clay, ss | .237 | 59 | 4 | 14 | 3 | 0 | 1 | 7 | 1 |
| 3 Buford, Damon, of | .251 | 167 | 27 | 42 | 8 | 3 | 0 | 6 | 9 |
| 4 Byrd, Jim, ss | .181 | 127 | 11 | 23 | 3 | 0 | 0 | 9 | 5 |
| 4 Chick, Bruce, of | .191 | 131 | 14 | 25 | 2 | 1 | 1 | 9 | 2 |
| 2 Christoperson, Eric, dh-c | .171 | 35 | 4 | 6 | 1 | 1 | 0 | 6 | 0 |
| 1 Easley, Damion, 3b | .308 | 26 | 6 | 8 | 1 | 0 | 0 | 1 | 2 |
| 1 Fabregas, Jorge, c | .225 | 111 | 8 | 25 | 2 | 0 | 0 | 4 | 0 |
| 6 Gilbert, Shawn, 2b | .274 | 179 | 27 | 49 | 5 | 3 | 1 | 13 | 10 |
| 1 Hamelin, Bob, 1b | .325 | 160 | 24 | 52 | 7 | 4 | 7 | 37 | 0 |
| 4 Hatteberg, Scott, c | .394 | 94 | 13 | 37 | 7 | 1 | 3 | 18 | 1 |
| 2 Hosey, Steve, of | .210 | 162 | 21 | 34 | 9 | 0 | 2 | 14 | 4 |
| 2 Patterson, John, 2b | .238 | 21 | 3 | 5 | 0 | 0 | 0 | 4 | 0 |
| 1 Perez, Eduardo, 3b-1b | .205 | 117 | 9 | 24 | 0 | 2 | 0 | 15 | 5 |
| 3 Scarsone, Steve, 3b-2b | .221 | 131 | 11 | 29 | 5 | 1 | 2 | 12 | 1 |
| 3 Smith, Mark, of | .206 | 131 | 13 | 27 | 7 | 2 | 1 | 15 | 1 |

| PITCHING | W | L | ERA | G | SV | IP | H | BB | SO |
|---|---|---|---|---|---|---|---|---|---|
| 2 Carlson, Dan | 4 | 5 | 3.68 | 11 | 0 | 59 | 54 | 19 | 53 |

| | W | L | ERA | G | SV | IP | H | BB | SO |
|---|---|---|---|---|---|---|---|---|---|
| 4 Conroy, Brian | 3 | 4 | 3.98 | 11 | 0 | 54 | 53 | 11 | 53 |
| 4 Fischer, Tom | 0 | 0 | 5.09 | 17 | 0 | 23 | 30 | 9 | 19 |
| 2 McGehee, Kevin | 3 | 6 | 2.58 | 11 | 0 | 59 | 48 | 19 | 38 |
| 1 Merriman, Brett | 2 | 2 | 1.19 | 24 | 0 | 38 | 22 | 7 | 24 |
| 3 O'Donoghue, John | 3 | 2 | 2.40 | 9 | 0 | 49 | 39 | 21 | 43 |
| 3 Pennington, Brad | 1 | 2 | 3.83 | 22 | 3 | 40 | 28 | 20 | 45 |
| 1 Percival, Troy | 1 | 0 | 4.24 | 13 | 1 | 17 | 14 | 7 | 23 |
| 2 Rogers, Kevin | 2 | 1 | 0.49 | 25 | 3 | 37 | 13 | 9 | 38 |
| 4 Ryan, Ken | 0 | 3 | 1.39 | 21 | 3 | 32 | 21 | 16 | 43 |
| 1 Swingle, Paul | 2 | 1 | 2.81 | 6 | 0 | 32 | 31 | 13 | 18 |
| 3 Williams, Jeff | 4 | 2 | 2.97 | 18 | 0 | 36 | 28 | 23 | 17 |

Property of Angels (1), Giants (2), Orioles (3), Red Sox (4), Royals (5), White Sox (6).

## SUN CITIES

| BATTING | AVG | AB | R | H | 2B | 3B | HR | RBI | SB |
|---|---|---|---|---|---|---|---|---|---|
| 1 Ansley, Willie, of | .295 | 105 | 21 | 31 | 5 | 2 | 1 | 11 | 8 |
| 4 Ashley, Billy, of | .189 | 132 | 11 | 25 | 7 | 1 | 2 | 5 | 1 |
| 3 Berry, Sean, ss | .348 | 23 | 3 | 8 | 2 | 0 | 0 | 1 | 0 |
| 4 Bogar, Tim, ss | .229 | 153 | 10 | 35 | 8 | 0 | 0 | 13 | 0 |
| 3 Brogna, Rico, 1b | .234 | 124 | 14 | 29 | 6 | 1 | 0 | 12 | 1 |
| 5 Burnitz, Jeromy, of | .267 | 116 | 18 | 31 | 9 | 1 | 6 | 25 | 3 |
| 3 Busch, Mike, 3b | .200 | 150 | 18 | 30 | 9 | 0 | 7 | 19 | 0 |
| 4 Fordyce, Brook, c-dh | .265 | 132 | 16 | 35 | 6 | 1 | 3 | 14 | 0 |
| 1 Hurst, Jody, of | .262 | 145 | 14 | 38 | 7 | 1 | 2 | 18 | 2 |
| 1 Massarelli, John, of | .312 | 154 | 19 | 48 | 8 | 2 | 0 | 12 | 20 |
| 4 Mota, Domingo, 2b | .270 | 163 | 25 | 44 | 5 | 0 | 0 | 10 | 9 |
| 7 Parks, Derek, c-dh | .301 | 103 | 11 | 31 | 9 | 1 | 2 | 6 | 0 |
| 2 Piazza, Mike, 1b-c | .291 | 134 | 15 | 39 | 9 | 1 | 3 | 23 | 2 |
| 6 Robertson, Rod, 2b-3b | .192 | 125 | 7 | 24 | 3 | 0 | 1 | 10 | 5 |

| PITCHING | W | L | ERA | G | SV | IP | H | BB | SO |
|---|---|---|---|---|---|---|---|---|---|
| 5 Clark, Dera | 3 | 1 | 1.13 | 18 | 1 | 40 | 25 | 5 | 37 |
| 4 DeSilva, John | 3 | 5 | 2.80 | 11 | 0 | 64 | 57 | 19 | 61 |
| 1 Gonzales, Frank | 1 | 1 | 2.85 | 17 | 2 | 41 | 38 | 10 | 24 |
| 3 Hansell, Greg | 1 | 3 | 3.48 | 9 | 0 | 44 | 48 | 13 | 25 |
| 4 Hillman, Eric | 2 | 0 | 1.57 | 4 | 0 | 23 | 19 | 4 | 15 |
| 1 Johnstone, John | 1 | 3 | 6.47 | 6 | 0 | 32 | 34 | 14 | 21 |
| 4 Langbehn, Greg | 1 | 0 | 2.66 | 19 | 3 | 20 | 17 | 6 | 16 |
| 2 McAndrew, Jamie | 0 | 3 | 3.48 | 17 | 0 | 34 | 37 | 9 | 28 |
| 1 Miceli, Dan | 1 | 1 | 3.63 | 16 | 3 | 17 | 15 | 10 | 12 |
| 5 Moeller, Dennis | 3 | 5 | 4.13 | 11 | 0 | 57 | 65 | 16 | 29 |
| 6 Schwarber, Tom | 4 | 0 | 0.33 | 18 | 1 | 27 | 26 | 8 | 14 |
| 4 Telgheder, Dave | 4 | 2 | 4.20 | 14 | 0 | 45 | 44 | 9 | 37 |
| 2 Williams, Todd | 4 | 1 | 0.40 | 20 | 7 | 22 | 14 | 7 | 19 |

Property of Astros (1), Dodgers (2), Expos (3), Mets (4), Royals (5), Tigers (6), Twins (7).

## TUCSON

| BATTING | AVG | AB | R | H | 2B | 3B | HR | RBI | SB |
|---|---|---|---|---|---|---|---|---|---|
| 3 Fernandez, Jose, c | .217 | 60 | 4 | 13 | 3 | 0 | 2 | 14 | 0 |
| 3 Figueroa, Bien, 2b | .240 | 129 | 11 | 31 | 5 | 1 | 0 | 8 | 1 |
| 6 Gonzalez, Paul, 3b | .152 | 112 | 12 | 17 | 2 | 2 | 3 | 7 | 0 |
| 4 Levis, Jesse, c | .302 | 86 | 9 | 26 | 5 | 0 | 1 | 10 | 1 |
| 3 Maclin, Lonnie, of | .306 | 111 | 14 | 34 | 2 | 2 | 0 | 11 | 4 |
| 1 Makarewicz, Scott, c | .214 | 84 | 5 | 18 | 1 | 1 | 0 | 6 | 0 |
| 5 McDavid, Ray, of | .204 | 152 | 22 | 31 | 8 | 0 | 2 | 10 | 6 |
| 1 Mouton, James, 2b-dh | .318 | 173 | 27 | 55 | 7 | 7 | 1 | 21 | 10 |
| 2 Pegues, Steve, of | .347 | 196 | 34 | 68 | 11 | 4 | 7 | 34 | 7 |
| 3 Ramos, Ken, of | .372 | 78 | 14 | 29 | 1 | 2 | 1 | 14 | 4 |
| 4 Sanders, Tracy, of | .178 | 73 | 7 | 13 | 2 | 1 | 2 | 9 | 0 |
| 4 Thomas, Skeets, 1b | .278 | 187 | 19 | 52 | 8 | 6 | 1 | 18 | 1 |
| 5 Thompson, Ryan, of | .220 | 50 | 6 | 11 | 2 | 1 | 1 | 5 | 2 |
| 6 Witkowski, Mat, 3b-2b | .191 | 110 | 15 | 21 | 4 | 0 | 0 | 6 | 1 |
| 3 Zosky, Eddie, ss | .326 | 135 | 17 | 44 | 7 | 4 | 0 | 15 | 1 |

| PITCHING | W | L | ERA | G | SV | IP | H | BB | SO |
|---|---|---|---|---|---|---|---|---|---|
| 5 Bross, Terry | 6 | 0 | 3.13 | 20 | 2 | 32 | 30 | 13 | 31 |
| 4 DiPoto, Jerry | 1 | 1 | 1.66 | 23 | 9 | 22 | 19 | 8 | 12 |
| 4 Kramer, Tom | 5 | 2 | 1.93 | 17 | 0 | 51 | 40 | 20 | 55 |
| 3 Meier, Kevin | 3 | 2 | 3.98 | 10 | 0 | 54 | 55 | 11 | 31 |
| 2 Milchin, Mike | 0 | 3 | 2.77 | 19 | 1 | 26 | 22 | 15 | 21 |
| 2 Moore, Marcus | 2 | 2 | 4.03 | 17 | 1 | 29 | 30 | 22 | 23 |
| 4 Mutis, Jeff | 0 | 1 | 1.00 | 2 | 0 | 9 | 6 | 4 | 5 |
| 4 Shuey, Paul | 0 | 0 | 3.38 | 10 | 0 | 16 | 10 | 10 | 8 |
| 2 Small, Aaron | 1 | 3 | 3.44 | 10 | 0 | 55 | 59 | 18 | 39 |
| 2 Thomas, Royal | 2 | 3 | 6.10 | 10 | 0 | 38 | 55 | 11 | 21 |
| 2 Ward, Anthony | 2 | 4 | 2.37 | 23 | 3 | 38 | 30 | 17 | 40 |
| 2 Weathers, David | 1 | 3 | 6.14 | 12 | 1 | 48 | 62 | 22 | 24 |
| 4 Wertz, Bill | 2 | 3 | 4.74 | 22 | 0 | 38 | 45 | 13 | 37 |

Property of Astros (1), Blue Jays (2), Cardinals (3), Indians (4), Mets (5), Padres (6).

# COLLEGE BASEBALL

**CWS Champs.** Victorious Louisiana State players celebrate their school's second NCAA baseball title in three years, an 8-0 win over Wichita State. Freshman righthander Brett Laxton stopped the Shockers on three hits, striking out 16.

# LSU Shocks Wichita State In CWS Final

**By JIM CALLIS**

College World Series? No, this was the Cardiac World Series.

"If I have a heart attack before I get home," Louisiana State second baseman Todd Walker said, "I wouldn't be surprised."

Walker made those comments before his heart endured the exhilaration of the Tigers' second national title in three seasons. LSU beat Wichita State 8-0 in a June 12 championship-game rematch of the 1991 CWS final, when the Tigers beat the Shockers 6-3.

What the finale lacked in drama, the rest of the 1993 Series more than made up for. There were so many comebacks, you half expected to see Rocky Balboa in uniform at Omaha's Rosenblatt Stadium. Only twice in 14 games did a team score first and hold its lead throughout the game.

"This has been the greatest comeback **Skip Bertman** Series I can ever recall all the times I've been here," said Skip Bertman, who has made 11 trips to Omaha, five as Miami pitching coach and six as LSU head coach. "Especially the low-percentage types of come-

**Skip Bertman**

backs."

There were two game-winning rallies in the seventh inning, four in the eighth, two in the ninth and one in the 11th, all against some of college baseball's best pitching. All-Americans Marc Barcelo (Arizona State), Daniel Choi (Long Beach State) and Brooks Kieschnick (Texas) were among the victims. Series relievers blew all five save opportunities they were handed.

All in all, there were more resurrections than a George Romero film festival. LSU rose from the dead twice after scoring seven runs in its last three innings to beat Long Beach State 7-1 and snap Choi's 14-game winning streak in its opener.

The Tigers mounted a sudden six-run rally in the bottom of the eighth to topple top seed Texas A&M 13-8 in the second round. Center fielder Armando Rios singled in the go-ahead run and Walker iced the game with a grand slam.

LSU then blew a three-run lead against Long Beach State to set up a third showdown, in which the 49ers scored two unearned runs in the top of the ninth to take a 5-3 lead. With one out, Rios doubled to left-center to

**Timely Hitter.** LSU second baseman Todd Walker drove in 12 runs and was named College World Series MVP.

plate the tying runs, and two batters later Walker hit a smash off first baseman John Swanson's glove to complete a 6-5 miracle. Walker's single completed a 4-for-5 day that also included a homer and muffled talk of his 1-for-11 CWS start.

Walker and Rios continued to hit in the championship game. While standing in the batter's box in the bottom of the first, Walker tried to call time. Umpire Jim Garman denied the request, so Walker swung away and hit a two-run homer on his way to a 2-for-4, three-RBI day and Most Outstanding Player honors. Rios contributed four RBIs and helped dump a container of ice water on Bertman during the postgame celebration.

Righthander Brett Laxton, Baseball America's Freshman of the Year, provided the only drama in an otherwise ho-hum CWS final that saw the Tigers grab a 7-0 lead after three innings. Overpowering the Shockers mainly with fastballs, he set a championship-game record with 16 strikeouts, tied another mark by allowing just three hits and became the first pitcher in 32 years to spin a shutout in the finale.

## Back To The Future

Beyond winning the national championship, LSU established itself as the closest thing to a college baseball dynasty.

Since Southern California won the last of five consecutive national titles in 1974, the 1987-88 Stanford teams are the only others to win two national championships in a three-year period. The Tigers have made six trips to Omaha in the last eight seasons, the best record in the nation, and have captured an unprecedented four straight titles in the Southeastern Conference, which has accounted for three of the last four CWS winners.

LSU finished 53-17, the fifth consecutive season it reached 50 wins. The Tigers have established a standard of excellence that leaves fans expecting them to live up to their past each season.

# COLLEGE WORLD SERIES

**Omaha, Nebraska**
June 4-12, 1993

## STANDINGS
Double-Elimination

| WEST BRACKET | W | L | RF | RA |
|---|---|---|---|---|
| Louisiana State | 3 | 1 | 34 | 24 |
| Long Beach State | 3 | 2 | 28 | 24 |
| Texas A&M | 1 | 2 | 15 | 20 |
| Kansas | 0 | 2 | 2 | 11 |

**West Bracket Final:** Louisiana St. 6, Long Beach St. 5.

| EAST BRACKET | W | L | RF | RA |
|---|---|---|---|---|
| Wichita State | 3 | 0 | 21 | 13 |
| Oklahoma State | 2 | 2 | 21 | 26 |
| Texas | 1 | 2 | 18 | 19 |
| Arizona State | 0 | 2 | 7 | 9 |

**East Bracket Final:** Wichita St. 10, Oklahoma St. 4.
**CHAMPIONSHIP GAME:** Louisiana St. 8, Wichita St. 0.

### INDIVIDUAL BATTING LEADERS
(Minimum 12 At-Bats)

| | AVG | AB | R | H | 2B | 3B | HR | RBI | SB |
|---|---|---|---|---|---|---|---|---|---|
| Jeff Liefer, Long Beach St. | .500 | 18 | 5 | 9 | 0 | 0 | 2 | 4 | 2 |
| Jim Greely, LSU | .471 | 17 | 5 | 8 | 1 | 1 | 2 | 7 | 1 |
| Jason Heath, Okla. St. | .462 | 13 | 3 | 6 | 2 | 0 | 0 | 3 | 0 |
| Hunter Triplett, Okla. St. | .462 | 13 | 2 | 6 | 1 | 0 | 0 | 4 | 0 |
| Steve Heinrich, Texas | .417 | 12 | 5 | 5 | 0 | 0 | 0 | 0 | 1 |
| Brian Thomas, Texas A&M | .417 | 12 | 2 | 5 | 0 | 0 | 1 | 2 | 1 |
| Armando Rios, LSU | .400 | 20 | 7 | 8 | 2 | 0 | 0 | 10 | 2 |
| Russ Johnson, LSU | .389 | 18 | 5 | 7 | 0 | 0 | 1 | 2 | 1 |
| Jason Adams, Wichita State | .375 | 16 | 2 | 6 | 1 | 0 | 0 | 0 | 0 |

### INDIVIDUAL PITCHING LEADERS
(Minimum 9 Innings)

| | W | L | ERA | G | SV | IP | H | BB | SO |
|---|---|---|---|---|---|---|---|---|---|
| Marc Barcelo, Arizona State | 0 | 1 | 0.82 | 1 | 0 | 11 | 9 | 0 | 8 |
| Mike Fontana, Long Beach St. | 1 | 0 | 2.30 | 2 | 0 | 16 | 12 | 4 | 7 |
| Mike Sirotka, LSU | 2 | 1 | 2.37 | 3 | 0 | 19 | 16 | 6 | 17 |
| Brett Laxton, LSU | 1 | 0 | 2.70 | 2 | 0 | 13 | 10 | 8 | 20 |
| Mike Brandley, Wichita State | 1 | 0 | 3.00 | 2 | 0 | 12 | 13 | 2 | 9 |

### ALL-TOURNAMENT TEAM

**C**—Adrian Antonini, Louisiana State. **1B**—Hunter Triplett, Oklahoma State. **2B**—Todd Walker, Louisiana State. **3B**—Casey Blake, Wichita State. **SS**—Jason Adams, Wichita State. **OF**—Jim Greely, Louisiana State; Jason Heath, Oklahoma State; Armando Rios, Louisiana State. **DH**—Jeff Liefer, Long Beach State. **P**—Brett Laxton, Louisiana State; Mike Sirotka, Louisiana State.
**Outstanding Player**—Todd Walker, 2b, Louisiana State.

## CHAMPIONSHIP GAME

### Tigers 8, Shockers 0

| WICHITA ST. | ab | r | h | bi | LOUISIANA ST. | ab | r | h | bi |
|---|---|---|---|---|---|---|---|---|---|
| Hall rf | 5 | 0 | 0 | 0 | Williams 3b | 3 | 1 | 1 | 1 |
| Adams ss | 4 | 0 | 1 | 0 | Rios cf | 3 | 0 | 1 | 4 |
| Taylor cf | 2 | 0 | 0 | 0 | Johnson ss | 3 | 1 | 1 | 0 |
| Smith 1b | 4 | 0 | 0 | 0 | Walker 2b | 4 | 1 | 2 | 3 |
| Dreifort dh-p | 3 | 0 | 1 | 0 | Berrios rf | 4 | 0 | 0 | 0 |
| JJackson 2b | 4 | 0 | 0 | 0 | Neal dh | 4 | 1 | 1 | 0 |
| Blake 3b | 3 | 0 | 0 | 0 | Greely lf | 2 | 2 | 1 | 0 |
| Tilma lf | 3 | 0 | 1 | 0 | Huffman lf | 0 | 0 | 0 | 0 |
| McCollough c | 2 | 0 | 0 | 0 | Antonini c | 2 | 1 | 0 | 0 |
| Lewallen ph | 1 | 0 | 0 | 0 | KJackson 1b | 3 | 1 | 1 | 0 |
| Wheeler c | 0 | 0 | 0 | 0 | | | | | |
| Mills ph | 1 | 0 | 0 | 0 | | | | | |
| Totals | 32 | 0 | 3 | 0 | Totals | 28 | 8 | 10 | 8 |

| | | | |
|---|---|---|---|
| Wichita State | 000 | 000 | 000—0 |
| Louisiana State | 232 | 000 | 01x—8 |

E—Greely, KJackson. DP—Wichita State 2. LOB—Wichita State 10, Louisiana State 7. 2B—KJackson (18). HR—Walker (22). SB—Greely (3), Johnson (19). S—KJackson, Williams. SF—Rios 2.

| WSU | ip | h | r | er | bb | so | LSU | ip | h | r | er | bb | so |
|---|---|---|---|---|---|---|---|---|---|---|---|---|---|
| Wyckoff L | 1⅓ | 3 | 5 | 5 | 3 | 0 | Laxton W | 9 | 3 | 0 | 0 | 5 | 16 |
| Dreifort | 1⅔ | 4 | 2 | 2 | 2 | 2 | | | | | | | |
| Baird | 5 | 3 | 1 | 1 | 1 | 4 | | | | | | | |

HBP—Antonini (by Dreifort). T—2:52. A—20,286.

"If we don't get to Omaha," Bertman said, "it appears we've had a bad year."

When LSU was ranked the preseason No. 1 team in all three college polls, Bertman had T-shirts made up that read "Wire To Wire" and planned to distribute them to his players. After they sputtered to a 3-3 start, he decided they could do without the reminder and stashed the shirts away.

But these Tigers thrived on pressure. Though they at times tormented Bertman by committing a school-record 125 errors, they emerged from the losers' bracket in both the SEC Western Division and the NCAA South Regional tournaments. For whatever reason, they didn't play at their best until they faced elimination, a trait that carried over to the CWS.

"That's the trademark of this team," Walker said. "We have to think we have to play to play. If something is given to us, we won't take it."

## Song Remains The Same

As expected, the status quo reigned over Division I baseball at the 1993 NCAA convention. For all the hope of changing the starting date or gaining even the smallest of concessions regarding cutbacks instituted in 1991, nothing happened.

Of the six Division I baseball-related measures on the NCAA agenda Jan. 12-16 at the Loews Anatole in Dallas, only two even came to a vote of university presidents and officials. Proposal 23, which would have allowed volunteer coaches to travel with their teams, lost 229-84. Proposal 34, which would have increased the time allotted for games and practice from 22 weeks to 24, lost 272-42.

After witnessing those lopsided margins, American Baseball Coaches Association executive director Dick Bergquist and ABCA president Jerry Kindall decided not to have their allies move for votes on proposals to increase assistant coaches from one per staff to two; scholarships from 11.7 per team to 13; and hours for team activities per week from 20 to 24.

"We had people ready to move them," Bergquist said, "but we decided it was just as good to go 0-for-2 rather than 0-for-5, even though that's still an .000 average."

The sixth proposal was pulled, ironically enough, because of fear it might pass. Proposals 97 and 97-1 called for moving the starting date from Jan. 25 to March 1 and directed the NCAA executive and scheduling committees to address a minimum 14-weekend schedule for regular-season play.

Baseball supporters feared the starting date would be changed without the allowance for a 14-week season. In effect, the season could start March 1 and still end with the College World Series in early June, which wasn't the proposal's intent.

Southern Mississippi coach Hill Denson, who led the push to get the schedule shift on the NCAA agenda, said resistance from lower-profile schools in the Northeast has led to preliminary discussions about trying to follow football's lead and splitting Division I into I-A and I-AA. The schedule shift may be rewritten to apply only to schools that declare an intention of competing for the national championship.

One thing is for certain. Denson burned himself out working on the proposal.

# COLLEGE WORLD SERIES

## CHAMPIONS, 1947-93

Series played at Kalamazoo, Mich., in 1947-48; at Wichita in 1949; at Omaha from 1950-93.

| Year | Champion | Coach | Record | Runner-Up | MVP |
|------|----------|-------|--------|-----------|-----|
| 1947 | California* | Clint Evans | 31-10 | Yale | None selected |
| 1948 | Southern Cal | Sam Barry | 40-12 | Yale | None selected |
| 1949 | Texas* | Bibb Falk | 23- 7 | Wake Forest | Charles Teague, 2b, Wake Forest |
| 1950 | Texas | Bibb Falk | 27- 6 | Washington St. | Ray VanCleef, of, Rutgers |
| 1951 | Oklahoma* | Jack Baer | 19- 9 | Tennessee | Sid Hatfield, 1b-p, Tennessee |
| 1952 | Holy Cross | Jack Berry | 21- 3 | Missouri | Jim O'Neill, p, Holy Cross |
| 1953 | Michigan | Ray Fisher | 21- 9 | Texas | J.L. Smith, p, Texas |
| 1954 | Missouri | Hi Simmons | 22- 4 | Rollins | Tom Yewcic, c, Michigan St. |
| 1955 | Wake Forest | Taylor Sanford | 29- 7 | W. Michigan | Tom Borland, p, Oklahoma St. |
| 1956 | Minnesota | Dick Siebert | 33- 9 | Arizona | Jerry Thomas, p, Minnesota |
| 1957 | California* | George Wolfman | 35-10 | Penn State | Cal Emery, 1b-p, Penn State |
| 1958 | Southern Cal | Rod Dedeaux | 35- 7 | Missouri | Bill Thom, p, Southern Cal |
| 1959 | Oklahoma St. | Toby Greene | 27- 5 | Arizona | Jim Dobson, 3b, Oklahoma St. |
| 1960 | Minnesota | Dick Siebert | 34- 7 | Southern Cal | John Erickson, 2b, Minnesota |
| 1961 | Southern Cal* | Rod Dedeaux | 43- 9 | Oklahoma St. | Littleton Fowler, p, Oklahoma St. |
| 1962 | Michigan | Don Lund | 31-13 | Santa Clara | Bob Garibaldi, p, Santa Clara |
| 1963 | Southern Cal | Rod Dedeaux | 37-16 | Arizona | Bud Hollowell, c, Southern Cal |
| 1964 | Minnesota | Dick Siebert | 31-12 | Missouri | Joe Ferris, p, Maine |
| 1965 | Arizona State | Bobby Winkles | 54- 8 | Ohio State | Sal Bando, 3b, Arizona State |
| 1966 | Ohio State | Marty Karow | 27- 6 | Oklahoma St. | Steve Arlin, p, Ohio State |
| 1967 | Arizona State | Bobby Winkles | 53-12 | Houston | Ron Davini, c, Arizona State |
| 1968 | Southern Cal* | Rod Dedeaux | 45-14 | S. Illinois | Bill Seinsoth, 1b, Southern Cal |
| 1969 | Arizona State | Bobby Winkles | 56-11 | Tulsa | John Dolinsek, of, Arizona State |
| 1970 | Southern Cal | Rod Dedeaux | 51-13 | Florida State | Gene Ammann, p, Florida St. |
| 1971 | Southern Cal | Rod Dedeaux | 53-13 | S. Illinois | Jerry Tabb, 1b, Tulsa |
| 1972 | Southern Cal | Rod Dedeaux | 50-13 | Arizona State | Russ McQueen, p, Southern Cal |
| 1973 | Southern Cal* | Rod Dedeaux | 51-11 | Arizona State | Dave Winfield, of-p, Minnesota |
| 1974 | Southern Cal | Rod Dedeaux | 50-20 | Miami (Fla.) | George Milke, p, Southern Cal |
| 1975 | Texas | Cliff Gustafson | 56- 6 | South Carolina | Mickey Reichenbach, 1b, Texas |
| 1976 | Arizona | Jerry Kindall | 56-17 | E. Michigan | Steve Powers, dh-p, Arizona |
| 1977 | Arizona State | Jim Brock | 57-12 | South Carolina | Bob Horner, 3b, Arizona State |
| 1978 | Southern Cal* | Rod Dedeaux | 54- 9 | Arizona State | Rod Boxberger, p, Southern Cal |
| 1979 | CS Fullerton | Augie Garrido | 60-14 | Arkansas | Tony Hudson, p, CS Fullerton |
| 1980 | Arizona | Jerry Kindall | 45-21 | Hawaii | Terry Francona, of, Arizona |
| 1981 | Arizona State | Jim Brock | 55-13 | Oklahoma St. | Stan Holmes, of, Arizona State |
| 1982 | Miami (Fla.)* | Ron Fraser | 57-18 | Wichita State | Dan Smith, p, Miami (Fla.) |
| 1983 | Texas* | Cliff Gustafson | 66-14 | Alabama | Calvin Schiraldi, p, Texas |
| 1984 | CS Fullerton | Augie Garrido | 66-20 | Texas | John Fishel, of, CS Fullerton |
| 1985 | Miami (Fla.)* | Ron Fraser | 64-16 | Texas | Greg Ellena, dh, Miami (Fla.) |
| 1986 | Arizona | Jerry Kindall | 49-19 | Florida State | Mike Senne, of, Arizona |
| 1987 | Stanford | Mark Marquess | 53-17 | Oklahoma St. | Paul Carey, of, Stanford |
| 1988 | Stanford | Mark Marquess | 46-23 | Arizona State | Lee Plemel, p, Stanford |
| 1989 | Wichita State | Gene Stephenson | 68-16 | Texas | Greg Brummett, p, Wichita St. |
| 1990 | Georgia | Steve Webber | 52-19 | Oklahoma St. | Mike Rebhan, p, Georgia |
| 1991 | Louisiana St.* | Skip Bertman | 55-18 | Wichita State | Gary Hymel, c, Louisiana St. |
| 1992 | Pepperdine* | Andy Lopez | 48-11 | CS Fullerton | Phil Nevin, 3b, CS Fullerton |
| 1993 | Louisiana St. | Skip Bertman | 53-17 | Wichita State | Todd Walker, 2b, Louisiana St. |

*Undefeated

# COLLEGE PLAYER OF THE YEAR

## Top Honor For Two-Way Star

There was little doubt Texas DH-righthander Brooks Kieschnick was the nation's best college player in 1993. And even that statement doesn't do him justice.

At the plate, he batted .374 with 27 doubles, 19 home runs and 81 RBIs. On the mound, he went 16-4, 3.25 with 126 strikeouts in 150 innings. His excellence in both areas was nearly unparalleled, as he finished one home run short of John Olerud's 1988 feat of 20 homers and 15 wins in the same season.

But Kieshnick, Baseball America's 1993 College Player of the Year, doesn't stand out solely for what he accomplished in one season. Considering his three-year career, he was one of the best college players ever.

In 176 games, he hit .360 with 67 doubles, a Texas-record 43 home runs, 215 RBIs and a .676 slugging percentage, another school record. In 63 mound appearances, he went 34-8, 3.05

**Two-Way Deal.** Baseball America managing editor Jim Callis and the publication's '93 College Player of the Year: Texas pitcher-DH Brooks Kieschnick.

with 268 whiffs in 345 innings. He was named Southwest Conference player of the year three times in three seasons.

Rice coach Wayne Graham says Kieschnick and Frank Thomas are the best college hitters he ever has seen. Baylor coach Mickey Sullivan said Kieschnick was the best hitter he had seen in the last 40 years, then revised that appraisal after watching Kieschnick smack a ball 470 feet for the longest homer in Ferrell Field history.

"He may be the best in the last 50 years," said Sullivan, who still holds the SWC record with a .519 average in 1954.

Texas has produced 72 major league players, and Cliff Gustafson has had his share of greats since becoming head coach in 1968. None better, he says, than Kieschnick.

"I wouldn't call him the best pure hitter, but I'd call him the best power hitter, and I think the record shows that," Gustafson said. "I won't call him the best pitcher, but he's among the best. But in terms of doing both, he's the best we've had."

Despite Kieschnick's nonstop success at Texas, scouts continued to point out his lack of speed and a position. The Cubs focused on his hitting ability and made him the 10th overall pick in the 1993 draft, and Kieschnick looked forward to the next level.

"I've got to prove to the Chicago Cubs that I'm worthy of the 10th pick," Kieschnick said. "I've got to prove to everyone that I was worthy of being selected in the first round. And I've got to prove to myself I can play in the big leagues and play well."

**—JIM CALLIS**

### PREVIOUS WINNERS

1981—Mike Sodders, 3b, Arizona State
1982—Jeff Ledbetter, of-lhp, Florida State
1983—Dave Magadan, 1b, Alabama
1984—Oddibe McDowell, of, Arizona St.
1985—Pete Incaviglia, of, Oklahoma St.
1986—Casey Close, of, Michigan
1987—Robin Ventura, 3b, Oklahoma St.
1988—John Olerud, 1b-lhp, Washington St.
1989—Ben McDonald, rhp, Louisiana St.
1990—Mike Kelly, of, Arizona State
1991—David McCarty, 1b, Stanford
1992—Phil Nevin, 3b, Cal State Fullerton

---

"I'm hoping somebody else will take the torch for us," he said. "Maybe some athletic director or somebody with the ABCA, somebody who's not a coach. I felt like I punished our team all last season working on this."

Like Denson, Bergquist also burned out. In March he announced his resignation, effective in June 1994, when he'll be replaced by Central Michigan athletic director and NCAA Division I baseball committee chairman Dave Keilitz. Though he said he resigned to spend more time with his family after a nonstop 35-year baseball career, he admitted it was frustrating trying to fight for change.

"The people making the decisions will not listen," Bergquist said. "They don't want to admit they made a mistake."

**Augie Garrido**

## Garrido Wins 1,000, Wilhelm Retires

Cal State Fullerton's Augie Garrido became the 10th Division I coach and 17th overall to win 1,000 college baseball games with a 12-1 victory over San Jose State May 7. It was the latest milestone in a 25-year career that includes two College World Series championships and 16 conference titles, but Garrido wasn't impressed.

"One thousand wins is a milestone that is identified by others," Garrido said. "It's not that important to me because it's not what we're about. It's the process that's important.

"I'm in a role in which I get credit for the efforts of a lot of people. This job is about giving to other people and helping them help themselves. We've never really

# 1993 COLLEGE ALL-AMERICA TEAM

## Selected by Baseball America

**Ryan McGuire**
UCLA first baseman

**Mark Loretta**
Northwestern shortstop

**Eric Danapilis**
Notre Dame outfielder

### FIRST TEAM

| Pos. | Player, School | Yr. | B-T | Ht. | Wt. | Hometown | AVG | AB | R | H | 2B | 3B | HR | RBI | SB |
|---|---|---|---|---|---|---|---|---|---|---|---|---|---|---|---|
| C | Jason Varitek, Georgia Tech | Jr. | B-R | 6-2 | 207 | Alt. Springs, Fla. | .404 | 228 | 78 | 92 | 20 | 2 | 22 | 72 | 5 |
| 1B | Ryan McGuire, UCLA | Jr. | L-L | 6-2 | 200 | Woodland Hills, Calif. | .376 | 221 | 71 | 83 | 11 | 0 | 26 | 91 | 14 |
| 2B | Todd Walker, Louisiana State | So. | L-R | 6-0 | 175 | Bossier City, La. | .395 | 276 | 85 | 109 | 17 | 11 | 22 | 102 | 14 |
| 3B | Antone Williamson, Arizona St. | So. | L-R | 6-1 | 192 | Torrance, Calif. | .378 | 275 | 71 | 104 | 29 | 1 | 14 | 85 | 2 |
| SS | Mark Loretta, Northwestern | Sr. | R-R | 6-0 | 175 | Arcadia, Calif. | .408 | 184 | 38 | 75 | 12 | 6 | 3 | 34 | 20 |
| OF | Eric Danapilis, Notre Dame | Sr. | R-R | 6-2 | 220 | St. Joseph, Mich. | .438 | 219 | 71 | 96 | 24 | 0 | 13 | 85 | 13 |
| OF | Brooks Kieschnick, Texas | Jr. | L-R | 6-4 | 228 | Corpus Christi, Texas | .374 | 257 | 76 | 96 | 27 | 1 | 19 | 81 | 3 |
| OF | Pat Watkins, East Carolina | Jr. | B-R | 6-1 | 180 | Garner, N.C. | .445 | 220 | 63 | 98 | 7 | 3 | 19 | 57 | 29 |
| DH | Paul LoDuca, Arizona State | Jr. | R-R | 5-10 | 185 | Phoenix | .446 | 289 | 63 | 129 | 24 | 2 | 14 | 88 | 0 |

| Pos. | Player, School | Yr. | B-T | Ht. | Wt. | Hometown | W | L | ERA | G | SV | IP | H | BB | SO |
|---|---|---|---|---|---|---|---|---|---|---|---|---|---|---|---|
| P | Brian Anderson, Wright State | Jr. | B-L | 6-1 | 195 | Geneva, Ohio | 10 | 1 | 1.14 | 14 | 1 | 95 | 62 | 6 | 98 |
| P | Daniel Choi, Long Beach St. | So. | R-R | 6-1 | 185 | Los Angeles | 17 | 2 | 2.57 | 20 | 0 | 147 | 116 | 52 | 116 |
| P | Darren Dreifort, Wichita State | Jr. | R-R | 6-2 | 205 | Wichita | 11 | 1 | 2.48 | 30 | 4 | 102 | 67 | 34 | 120 |
| P | Jeff Granger, Texas A&M | Jr. | L-L | 6-4 | 193 | Orange, Texas | 15 | 3 | 2.62 | 20 | 0 | 127 | 87 | 54 | 150 |
| P | John Powell, Auburn | Jr. | R-R | 5-10 | 160 | Snellville, Ga. | 15 | 5 | 2.81 | 24 | 0 | 141 | 102 | 41 | 191 |

### SECOND TEAM

| Pos. | Player, School | Yr. | B-T | Ht. | Wt. | Hometown | AVG | AB | R | H | 2B | 3B | HR | RBI | SB |
|---|---|---|---|---|---|---|---|---|---|---|---|---|---|---|---|
| C | Casey Burrill, Southern Cal | Sr. | R-R | 6-3 | 231 | Newhall, Calif. | .408 | 238 | 54 | 97 | 18 | 1 | 13 | 52 | 6 |
| 1B | Braxton Hickman, Texas | Sr. | L-L | 6-2 | 208 | Houston | .385 | 252 | 55 | 97 | 16 | 4 | 9 | 74 | 1 |
| 2B | Mark Merila, Minnesota | Jr. | B-R | 5-9 | 175 | Plymouth, Minn. | .408 | 184 | 61 | 75 | 14 | 2 | 2 | 55 | 14 |
| 3B | George Arias, Arizona | Jr. | R-R | 5-11 | 185 | Tucson | .345 | 255 | 70 | 88 | 14 | 1 | 23 | 75 | 1 |
| SS | Gabe Alvarez, Southern Cal | Fr. | R-R | 6-1 | 180 | El Monte, Calif. | .326 | 258 | 46 | 84 | 26 | 0 | 8 | 53 | 1 |
| OF | Brian Banks, Brigham Young | So. | B-R | 6-3 | 200 | Mesa, Ariz. | .389 | 216 | 67 | 84 | 11 | 2 | 20 | 73 | 21 |
| OF | Vee Hightower, Vanderbilt | Jr. | B-R | 6-5 | 193 | Mt. Lebanon, Pa. | .346 | 185 | 69 | 64 | 9 | 1 | 11 | 26 | 46 |
| OF | Dante Powell, CS Fullerton | So. | R-R | 6-2 | 180 | Long Beach | .335 | 233 | 60 | 78 | 17 | 3 | 12 | 57 | 42 |
| DH | Jason Thompson, Arizona | Jr. | L-L | 6-4 | 205 | Laguna Hills, Calif. | .353 | 255 | 68 | 90 | 15 | 4 | 20 | 74 | 3 |

| Pos. | Player, School | Yr. | B-T | Ht. | Wt. | Hometown | W | L | ERA | G | GS | IP | H | BB | SO |
|---|---|---|---|---|---|---|---|---|---|---|---|---|---|---|---|
| P | Scott Christman, Oregon St. | Jr. | L-L | 6-3 | 190 | Tualatin, Ore. | 14 | 1 | 2.20 | 17 | 14 | 111 | 84 | 38 | 119 |
| P | Steve Duda, Pepperdine | Sr. | R-R | 5-11 | 170 | Whittier, Calif. | 12 | 3 | 1.64 | 18 | 18 | 137 | 108 | 20 | 114 |
| P | Brooks Kieschnick, Texas | Jr. | L-R | 6-4 | 228 | Corpus Christi, Texas | 16 | 4 | 3.25 | 26 | 19 | 150 | 155 | 49 | 126 |
| P | Brett Laxton, Louisiana State | Fr. | R-R | 6-2 | 200 | Audubon, N.J. | 12 | 1 | 1.98 | 19 | 17 | 109 | 67 | 47 | 98 |
| P | Brad Rigby, Georgia Tech | So. | R-R | 6-7 | 194 | Longwood, Fla. | 13 | 1 | 2.46 | 17 | 17 | 99 | 57 | 56 | 132 |

### THIRD TEAM

**C**—Willie Morales, Jr., Arizona. **1B**—Todd Helton, Fr., Tennessee. **2B**—Jeff Berblinger, Sr., Kansas. **3B**—Gerad Cawhorn, Sr., San Jose State. **SS**—David Smith, Jr., LeMoyne. **OF**—Todd Greene, Sr., Georgia Southern; Marc Sagmoen, Sr., Nebraska; Brian Thomas, Sr., Texas A&M. **DH**—Pat Clougherty, Jr., North Carolina State. **P**—Marc Barcelo, Jr., Arizona State; Troy Brohawn, So., Nebraska; Dan Hubbs, Sr., Southern California; Trey Moore, So., Texas A&M; Jimmy Walker, Sr., Kansas.

focused on the winning of the games."

One member of the 1,000-win club retired after the 1993 season. Clemson's Bill Wilhelm, who ranks fourth on the Division I victories list, decided to step down a year earlier than planned because he wanted no part of a farewell tour in 1994. He also cited the recent NCAA cutbacks.

"I've always said to my players as I'd stand here and think we'd become a little complacent, 'Fellas, when the dealing's done then we can count,' " Wilhelm said at a July 2 press conference. "Well, the dealing's done for me and we can count up, and I think it was a little bit better than average job."

Wilhelm, who spent 36 years at Clemson, had been tied for the longest run of continuous service at a Division I school. Murray State coach Johnny Reagan retired in May after going 776-508 in 36 seasons. Both men were replaced by one of their assistants: Wilhelm by Jack Leggett, Reagan by Mike Thieke.

## Stormy Year For Hurricanes

Miami knew Ron Fraser's act as Hurricanes head coach would be difficult to follow. After all, the Wizard of College Baseball won two College World Series titles, ranks third on the all-time Division I victories list and made Mark Light Stadium the hottest spot in college baseball.

While Miami expected difficult, it didn't expect disappointing. And that's what it got in 1993, its first year without Fraser, who retired after coaching Team USA to a fourth-place finish at the 1992 Summer Olympics.

Battling the aftereffects of Hurricane Andrew and competition from the National League's expansion Florida Marlins, Miami's attendance fell drastically during a disappointing 36-22 season. Miami bowed out in two straight games at the South Regional and for the first time in the 13-year history of the Baseball America Top 25, the Hurricanes weren't ranked in the postseason.

Things got worse after the season. Hurricanes coach Brad Kelley, who got the job after serving as a Fraser assistant for eight years, resigned Sept. 3. His departure came after a three-month investigation by Miami's athletic department into allegations that Kelley drank with Hurricanes player Chad Rupp in an airport lounge May 23 after a loss to Wake Forest.

Kelley didn't comment on the investigation. On the day he resigned, he released a statement: "I've enjoyed

# COACH OF THE YEAR
## Stephenson Cops Second Award

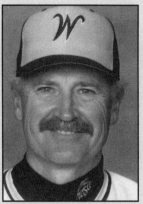

**Gene Stephenson**

For all that he has accomplished at Wichita State, Gene Stephenson still remembers his humble beginnings.

He gave up his job as an Oklahoma assistant in March 1977 to revive a Shockers baseball program that had been dormant for seven years, and took an $8,000 pay cut for the privilege. He had no players, not much of a field and a tiny office.

"It was in the football film room," Stephenson said with a laugh. "Whenever the football team wanted to use it, they came in, took my sign off the door and took over. It was underneath the football stadium, and every time it rained it flooded the office."

Stephenson's prize possession was a desk that Sooners coach Enos Semore allowed him to take from Oklahoma. He still has that desk today, but now when he sits behind it he gets a nice view of Eck Stadium at Tyler Field, a 5,665-seat gem with the largest on-campus scoreboard in the nation.

Yes, times have changed. And Stephenson, Baseball America's 1993 College Coach of the Year, is the man responsible. He joins Long Beach State's Dave Snow as the only two-time recipients of the

award, having first won in 1982, when Wichita State finished second in its first College World Series appearance.

The Shockers have made five trips to Omaha in the last six years, winning the national title in 1989, and have led Division I in wins four of the last five seasons. His 1993 edition went 58-17.

Anyone who knows Stephenson knows success hasn't made him complacent. He has been one of college baseball's most outspoken voices and most creative minds, lobbying for causes such as a summer schedule and a 20-second pitch clock.

Stephenson isn't afraid to roll up his sleeves. He's proud to note that Eck Stadium-Tyler Field was built entirely through private fundraising efforts, even if that meant constructing it in multiple phases.

Stephenson has built it, and the players indeed have come. When he sits behind his favorite desk in his office on the first-base side of Eck Stadium-Tyler Field, he doesn't have to worry about anyone kicking him out to show some film. He's firmly established at Wichita State and besides, the football program disbanded in 1986.

**—JIM CALLIS**

### PREVIOUS WINNERS

1981—Ron Fraser, Miami
1982—Gene Stephenson, Wichita State
1983—Barry Shollenberger, Alabama
1984—Augie Garrido, Cal State Fullerton
1985—Ron Polk, Mississippi State
1986—Skip Bertman, Louisiana State
      Dave Snow, Loyola Marymount
1987—Mark Marquess, Stanford
1988—Jim Brock, Arizona State
1989—Dave Snow, Long Beach State
1990—Steve Webber, Georgia
1991—Jim Hendry, Creighton
1992—Andy Lopez, Pepperdine

my nine years at the University of Miami, and feel good knowing my effort contributed to the success of the program."

The program may have trouble recapturing its previous sizzle. The Marlins have become south Florida's favorite baseball team, and Hurricanes attendance

# FRESHMAN OF THE YEAR

## Ex-Big Leaguer Steers Son To LSU

Father knows best, as far as Brett Laxton and Louisiana State are concerned.

Though the San Diego Padres selected Laxton in the fourth round of the 1992 draft and offered him $150,000 to sign, his father Bill steered him to college.

"He wants me to live a better life than he did," Brett said.

And it doesn't get any better than this: Laxton shut out Wichita State 8-0 on a three-hitter to win the 1993 College World Series, striking out a championship game-record 16 in the process. Baseball America's Freshman of the Year finished the season 12-1, 1.98 with 98 strikeouts in 109 innings.

If not for his father, Laxton might have signed with the Padres. Bill Laxton went from Audubon (N.J.) High to the Pittsburgh organization as a seventh-round pick in 1966, and spent parts of five seasons in the majors.

Since leaving baseball, Bill has held a number of jobs, including

**Father Knows Best.** LSU's Brett Laxton followed the advice of his dad, ex-big leaguer Bill, in attending school.

RICHARD LEWIS

stints as a boilermaker and real-estate agent. He currently is employed by the Audubon department of public works, mainly driving trucks. He says it's not the most glamorous life, and wants more for his son.

"I wanted him to go to college basically for an education to fall back on if things don't work out," said Bill, who earned the first win in Seattle Mariners history in 1977. "Maybe if I had more education, I'd have a better job."

LSU coach Skip Bertman thought about using Laxton as a closer in 1993 to replace departed All-American Rick Greene, but quickly shelved that idea when Laxton won his first two

starts. Laxton didn't lose until Mississippi State beat him in the Southeastern Conference Western Division tournament.

Baseball America's complete Freshman All-America first team:

**C**—A.J. Hinch, Stanford (.350-4-38). **1B**—Todd Helton, Tennessee (.348-11-66). **2B**—Mike Lowell, Florida International (.371-3-33, 12 SB). **3B**—Casey Blake, Wichita State (.366-4-57). **SS**—Gabe Alvarez, Southern California (.326-8-53). **OF**—Jose Cruz, Rice (.351-13-59); Kevin Gibbs, Old Dominion (.385-4-22, 45 SB); Shane Monahan, Clemson (.372-9-64, 17 SB). **DH**—Jeff Liefer, Long Beach State (.356-12-54). **P**—Jonathan Johnson, Florida State (10-1, 1.68, 107 IP, 124 SO); Brett Laxton, Louisiana State (12-1, 1.98, 109 IP, 98 SO); Andrew McNally, Hawaii (9-5, 3.15, 137 IP, 103 SO); Brian Powell, Georgia (6-2, 2.77, 81 IP, 74 SO); Scott Schoeneweis, Duke (12-3, 3.12, 107 IP, 110 SO).

### PREVIOUS WINNERS

1982—Cory Snyder, 3b, Brigham Young
1983—Rafael Palmeiro, of, Mississippi St.
1984—Greg Swindell, lhp, Texas
1985—Jack McDowell, rhp, Stanford
       Ron Wenrich, of, Georgia
1986—Robin Ventura, 3b, Oklahoma St.
1987—Paul Carey, of, Stanford
1988—Kirk Dressendorfer, rhp, Texas
1989—Alex Fernandez, rhp, Miami
1990—Jeffrey Hammonds, of, Stanford
1991—Brooks Kieschnick, rhp-dh, Texas
1992—Todd Walker, 2b, Louisiana State

---

dropped from 3,160 per game in 1992 to 1,502 in 1993.

At Colgate, the athletic department decided in February to terminate a baseball program dating to 1886. A month later, the school decided to field its final team in 1994.

There had been talk of dropping baseball at Colgate for several years, and the decision was recommended by the university's committee on athletics and the athletic department's long-range planning committee. Reasons given were the school's academic calendar, central New York's inclement weather and a need for gender equity in the athletic department.

## Around The Nation

■ In response to a request from the NCAA execu-

tive committee, the Division I baseball committee devised a play-in system for the regional tournaments that lead to the College World Series.

The executive committee wanted conferences that weren't granted automatic bids to be given a chance to play for the national championship. The baseball committee met July 11-14 in Monterey, Calif., and came up with a plan that did just that for the 30 conferences that meet the NCAA requirement of at least six teams.

Eighteen conference champions will receive automatic bids: Atlantic Coast, Big East, Big Eight, Big South, Big Ten, Big West, Colonial Athletic Association, Metro, Mid-American, Midwestern Collegiate, Missouri Valley, North Atlantic, Pacific-10, Southeastern, Southland, Southwest, Sun Belt and

Western Athletic.

Twelve additional conference champions will meet in best-of-three series to gain entry into the 48-team regional field: Ivy Group at Northeast, Metro Atlantic Athletic at Atlantic-10, Mid-Eastern Athletic at Trans America Athletic, Ohio Valley at Southern, Patriot League at Mid-Continent and Southwestern Athletic at West Coast.

The end result will be that 24 conference champions will advance to regional play, the same number that did so in 1993. Only two conferences, the five-team Diamond and four-team Great Midwest, won't be part of the system.

"There are some pluses and minuses," Keilitz said. "If you're from a conference which normally is not strongly considered for an at-large bid, then of course this works to your advantage. If you're a Pepperdine, this works to your disadvantage.

"The good thing is it provides an opportunity for every conference. The bad thing is that if you come from a conference that doesn't receive an automatic and you normally get strong consideration as an at-large team like Pepperdine, now you're going to have to play your way in."

Pepperdine, the 1991 CWS champion, plays in the West Coast Conference.

■ Harvard sophomore Jamie Irving became the first pitcher on record to earn wins on consecutive days while pitching from both sides.

He pitched 5⅓ innings righthanded against Yale April 17, winning a 16-7 decision. He started against the Bulldogs the next day, too, as a lefthander. He won again in a 4-3 complete game, handing the Bulldogs their first two losses of the season after 10 straight wins. In 1992, Irving pitched both lefty and righty against Boston College in the same game.

"In my mind, he's like having two pitchers," Crimson coach Leigh Hogan said. "He's Irving-R and Irving-L."

■ Alabama and Auburn put aside their rivalry long enough to let Crimson Tide infielder Jerry Shelton set the NCAA career hit-by-pitch record May 20. In the next-to-last game of his career and with Alabama losing 10-2, Shelton and the Auburn battery of John Powell and Mitch Duke conspired to put him over the top.

"Their catcher said, 'Here it comes, so get ready,' " said Shelton, better known as Stitch. "It was a situation where they could bring one inside because the game wasn't close. They helped me out, which was pretty nice of them.

"It doesn't take a lot of talent to get hit by a pitch. As far as being a great accomplishment, it's probably not. But after I got so close, I figured it would be a shame if I didn't go ahead and do it."

Powell hit Shelton to give him 52 plunkings, one more than Pete Schramka, who played for Coastal Carolina from 1989-92. Shelton almost was overtaken down the stretch by Missouri's John "Bump" Hay, who got hit 18 times in 1993 to tie Schramka.

■ Southern Utah beat Utah 10-3 Feb. 13 to end the nation's longest Division I losing streak at 32 games. Eleven days later, Georgia State beat Division II power South Carolina-Aiken 4-3 in 12 innings to snap a 29-game drought.

# NCAA REGIONALS

## ATLANTIC
**Site:** Atlanta (Georgia Tech).
**Participants:** No. 1 Georgia Tech (45-12, at-large), No. 2 South Carolina (38-18, at-large), No. 3 Wichita State (51-15, Missouri Valley), No. 4 Ohio State (41-17, at-large), No. 5 East Carolina (40-17, Colonial), No. 6 Liberty (23-23, Big South).
**Champion:** Wichita State (4-1).
**Runner-Up:** Ohio State (3-2).
**Outstanding Player:** Darren Dreifort, rhp-dh, Wichita State.
**Attendance:** 11, 356.

## CENTRAL I
**Site:** College Station, Texas (Texas A&M).
**Participants:** No. 1 Texas A&M (48-9, at-large), No. 2 North Carolina (40-18, at-large), No. 3 UCLA (35-21, at-large), No. 4 Lamar (44-16, Sun Belt), No. 5 Hawaii (33-23, at-large), No. 6 Yale (33-9, Ivy).
**Champion:** Texas A&M (4-0).
**Runner-Up:** North Carolina (3-2).
**Outstanding Player:** Jeff Granger, lhp, Texas A&M.
**Attendance:** 36,359.

## CENTRAL II
**Site:** Austin, Texas (Texas).
**Participants:** No. 1 Texas (46-14, at-large), No. 2 Cal State Fullerton (33-17, at-large), No. 3 Kentucky (38-21, at-large), No. 4 Southern California (32-27, at-large), No. 5 Maine (33-25, North Atlantic), No. 6 McNeese State (37-21, Southland).
**Champion:** Texas (4-0).
**Runner-Up:** Southern California (3-2).
**Outstanding Player:** Brooks Kieschnick, rhp-dh, Texas.
**Attendance:** 46,224.

## EAST
**Site:** Tallahassee, Fla. (Florida State).
**Participants:** No. 1 Long Beach State (39-17, Big West), No. 2 Florida State (44-17, at-large), No. 3 Mississippi State (41-19, at-large), No. 4 Notre Dame (43-14, Midwestern Collegiate), No. 5 South Florida (40-18, at-large), No. 6 Central Florida (30-29, Trans America).
**Champion:** Long Beach State (4-0).
**Runner-Up:** Notre Dame (3-2).
**Outstanding Player:** John Swanson, of, Long Beach State.
**Attendance:** 16,175.

## MIDEAST
**Site:** Knoxville (Tennessee).
**Participants:** No. 1 Tennessee (44-18, at-large), No. 2 Clemson (43-18, Atlantic Coast), No. 3 Kansas (41-15, at-large), No. 4 Fresno State (38-20, Western Athletic), No. 5 Rutgers (37-15, Atlantic-10), No. 6 North Carolina-Charlotte (26-30, Metro).
**Champion:** Kansas (4-1).
**Runner-Up:** Fresno State (3-2).
**Outstanding Player:** Bill Thrasher, of, Fresno State.
**Attendance:** 15,146.

## MIDWEST
**Site:** Stillwater, Okla. (Oklahoma State).
**Participants:** No. 1 North Carolina State (47-15, at-large), No. 2 Oklahoma State (39-14, Big Eight), No. 3 Arizona (32-24, at-large), No. 4 Auburn (39-21, at-large), No. 5 Connecticut (27-17, at-large), No. 6 Fordham (31-25, ECAC).
**Champion:** Oklahoma State (4-1).
**Runner-Up:** Arizona (3-2).
**Outstanding Player:** Jason Heath, of, Oklahoma State.
**Attendance:** 31,155.

## SOUTH
**Site:** Baton Rouge, La. (Louisiana State).
**Participants:** No. 1 Louisiana State (45-15, Southeastern), No. 2 Miami (36-20, at-large), No. 3 Kent State (39-13, Mid-American), No. 4 Baylor (40-17, Southwest), No. 5 South Alabama (34-19, at-large), No. 6 Western Carolina (33-26, Southern).
**Champion:** Louisiana State (4-1).
**Runner-Up:** South Alabama (3-2).
**Outstanding Player:** Mike Sirotka, lhp, Louisiana State.
**Attendance:** 33,935.

## WEST
**Site:** Tempe, Ariz. (Arizona State).
**Participants:** No.1 Arizona State (42-18, Pacific-10 South), No. 2 Cal State Northridge (34-18, at-large), No. 3 Pepperdine (40-15, West Coast), No. 4 Minnesota (43-16, at-large), No. 5 St. John's (25-18, Big East), No. 6 George Mason (33-13, at-large).
**Champion:** Arizona State (4-0).
**Runner-Up:** St. John's (3-2).
**Outstanding Player:** Todd Cady, dh, Arizona State.
**Attendance:** 24,020.

# COLLEGE BASEBALL

## YEAR-BY-YEAR LEADERS

Since 1965

Bob Horner, HR leader, 1977-78

Robin Ventura, RBI leader, 1986-87

Andy Benes, 188 strikeouts in 1988

Eddie Bane, SO leader, 1972-73

| Year | *Batting Average | Home Runs | RBIs | Wins | #ERA | Strikeouts |
|---|---|---|---|---|---|---|
| 1965 | Rusty Adkins, Clemson .444 | Terry Craven, CS Northridge 12 | Luis Lagunas, Arizona State 68 | Jim Merrick, Arizona State 13 | Bruce Aitken, Fla. Southern 0.63 | Steve Arlin, Ohio State 165 |
| 1966 | Jimmy Yawn, Mississippi .408 | Dale Ford, Washington St. 17 | Eddie Leon, Arizona 75 | John Stewart, USC 16 | Bill Stoneman, Idaho 0.52 | Bill Frost, California 169 |
| 1967 | Tom Paciorek, Houston .435 | Greg Riddoch, Colorado St. 17 | Dennis Lamb, Brigham Young 51 | Gary Gentry, Arizona State 17 | Jim Johnson, W. Michigan 0.51 | Gary Gentry, Arizona St. 229 |
| 1968 | Ken Lohnes, Cal St. L.A. .440 | Larry Romney, Brig. Young 13 | John Schroeder, UCSB 60 | John Schroeder, UCSB 12 | Argo Meza, Loyola (La.) 0.39 | Jeff Pryor, Fla. Southern 141 |
| 1969 | Larry Pyle, Miami .431 | Chris Chambliss, UCLA 15 | Paul Ray Powell, Arizona St. 73 | Larry Gura, Arizona St. 19 | Stan Babieracki, St. John's 0.55 | Larry Gura, Arizona St. 195 |
| 1970 | Bob Prokopowicz, UTEP .471 | Dan Stoligrosz, USC 14 | Paul Page, Idaho 58 | Gene Ammann, Florida St. 15 | Ron Hastings, East Carolina 0.56 | Pat Osburn, Florida St. 154 |
| 1971 | Glenn Borgmann, So. Alabama .471 | Roger Schmuck, Arizona St. 15 | Roger Schmuck, Arizona St. 80 | Jay Smith, Fla. Southern 15 | Brian Herosian, Connecticut 0.63 | Burt Hooton, Texas 153 |
| 1972 | Doug Ault, Texas Tech .473 | Fred Lynn, USC 14 | Alan Bannister, Arizona St. 90 | Craig Swan, Arizona St. 16 | Tom Farias, Amer. Int. 0.30 | Eddie Bane, Arizona St. 213 |
| 1973 | Mike Campbell, So. Florida .439 | John Stearns, Colorado 15 | Dick Harris, Arizona St. 72 | Eddie Bane, Arizona St. 15 | Roger Hatcher, Richmond 0.47 | Eddie Bane, Arizona St. 192 |
| 1974 | Ron Hassey, Arizona .421 | Gene Delyon, Santa Clara 19 | Rich Dauer, USC 92 | Jim Gideon, Texas 17 | Steve Ratzer, St. John's 0.84 | Rich Wortham, Texas 135 |
| 1975 | Randy Diaz-Gonzalez, N.M. St. .449 | Jerry Maddox, Arizona St. 20 | Jerry Maddox, Arizona St. 86 | Floyd Bannister, Arizona St. 19 | Al Holland, N.C. A&T 0.26 | Floyd Bannister, Arizona St. 217 |
| 1976 | Ron McNeely, Memphis State .462 | Bill Ewing, Wyoming 23 | Ken Landreaux, Arizona St. 93 | Don Kainer, Texas 15 | Jack Taylor, Connecticut 0.44 | Floyd Bannister, Arizona St. 213 |
| 1977 | Glenn Goya, Colorado St. .485 | Bob Horner, Arizona State 22 | Chris Bando, Arizona State 87 | Ron Meridith, Oral Roberts 14 | Mark Nipp, Oklahoma 0.72 | Derek Tatsuno, Hawaii 146 |
| 1978 | Mike Groh, SUNY Buffalo .464 | Bob Horner, Arizona State 25 | Bob Horner, Arizona State 102 | Derek Tatsuno, Hawaii 20 | Larry Brown, Harvard 0.95 | Derek Tatsuno, Hawaii 161 |
| 1979 | Jack Upton, Colorado St. .506 | Jim Auten, UCLA 29 | Tim Wallach, CS Fullerton 102 | Neal Heaton, Miami 18 | Dan Siler, Washington 0.94 | Derek Tatsuno, Hawaii 234 |
| 1980 | Keith Hagman, New Mexico .551 | Rick Siriano, Louisville 24 | Mike Davis, Wichita State 98 | Kendall Carter, Wichita State 19 | Kevin Quirk, St. Joseph's 1.26 | Ken Dayley, Portland 138 |
| 1981 | Derrell Baker, Ga. Southern .462 | 2 tied at 29 | Joe Carter, Wichita State 120 | Jeff Keener, Kentucky 19 | Jeff Keener, Kentucky 0.51 | Neal Heaton, Miami 172 |
| 1982 | Bill White, The Citadel .474 | Jeff Ledbetter, Florida St. 42 | Russ Morman, Wichita St. 130 | Kirk Killingsworth, Texas 18 | Kirk Killingsworth, Texas 0.80 | Bryan Oelkers, Wichita St. 166 |
| 1983 | Dave Magadan, Alabama .525 | 2 tied at 24 | Jim Hickey, Texas-Pan Am 105 | David Mills, The Citadel 16 | David Mills, The Citadel 1.13 | Dennis Livingston, Okla. St. 180 |
| 1984 | Steve Iannini, Georgetown .470 | Mark McGwire, USC 32 | Pete Incaviglia, Okla. St. 103 | John Hoover, Fresno St. 18 | Greg Brake, West. Michigan 0.95 | John Hoover, Fresno St. 205 |
| 1985 | Glen McElroy, Iona .472 | Pete Incaviglia, Okla. St. 48 | Pete Incaviglia, Okla. St. 143 | Greg Swindell, Texas 19 | Richard Lacko, Long Island 1.30 | Greg Swindell, Texas 204 |
| 1986 | Joe Kesselmark, Pace .487 | George Canale, Va. Tech. 29 | Robin Ventura, Oklahoma St. 96 | Mike Loynd, Florida State 20 | Mike Remlinger, Dartmouth 1.59 | Mike Loynd, Florida St. 223 |
| 1987 | Marteese Robinson, Seton Hall .529 | Mike Willes, Brigham Young 31 | Robin Ventura, Oklahoma St. 110 | 3 tied at 15 | Gregg Olson, Auburn 1.26 | Richie Lewis, Florida St. 196 |
| 1988 | Scott Baerns, Tenn. Tech. .476 | Mike Willes, Brigham Young 35 | Monty Fariss, Oklahoma St. 114 | 3 tied at 17 | Brian Evans, Jacksonville 1.19 | Andy Benes, Evansville 188 |
| 1989 | Mike Pisacreta, Pace .476 | Kevin Lofthus, UNLV 26 | Scott Bryant, Texas 112 | 3 tied at 18 | Jim Newlin, Wichita St. 1.08 | Brian Barnes, Clemson 208 |
| 1990 | Don Barbara, Long Beach St. .474 | Paul Ellis, UCLA 29 | Mike Daniel, Oklahoma St. 92 | David Sinnes, Notre Dame 18 | David Sinnes, Notre Dame 1.05 | Steve Wolf, Fresno St. 171 |
| 1991 | Gene Schall, Villanova .484 | Mike Daniel, Oklahoma St. 27 | Kennie Steenstra, Wichita St. 107 | Kirk Rueter, Murray St. 18 | Kirk Rueter, Murray St. 1.20 | 2 tied at 166 |
| 1992 | Mike Smith, Indiana .490 | Mike Smith, Indiana 27 | Mike Romano, Tulane 95 | Mike Romano, Tulane 17 | David Hawkins, Nicholls St. 1.38 | Kenny Kendrena, CS North. 176 |
| 1993 | Dickie Woodridge, LeMoyne .476 | Ryan McGuire, UCLA 26 | Todd Walker, LSU 102 | Daniel Choi, Long Beach St. 17 | Brian Anderson, Wright St. 1.14 | John Powell, Auburn 191 |

*Minimum 125 at-bats.  #Minimum 60 Innings.

# COLLEGE BASEBALL
## NCAA DIVISION I LEADERS

**Paul LoDuca**
.446-14-88 for Arizona State

### TEAM BATTING

**BATTING AVERAGE**

| | G | AVG |
|---|---|---|
| Brigham Young | 57 | .362 |
| New Mexico | 56 | .344 |
| Arizona | 61 | .343 |
| Old Dominion | 42 | .340 |
| Notre Dame | 62 | .334 |
| New Mexico State | 54 | .333 |
| Arizona State | 66 | .333 |
| Pittsburgh | 43 | .333 |
| LeMoyne | 40 | .330 |
| Delaware | 49 | .330 |

**RUNS SCORED**

| | G | R |
|---|---|---|
| Wichita State | 75 | 611 |
| Louisiana State | 71 | 603 |
| Arizona | 61 | 583 |
| Arizona State | 66 | 581 |
| Oklahoma State | 62 | 560 |
| Notre Dame | 62 | 550 |
| Texas | 67 | 545 |
| Kansas | 63 | 533 |
| Brigham Young | 57 | 524 |
| New Mexico | 56 | 517 |

**HOME RUNS**

| | G | HR |
|---|---|---|
| Arizona | 61 | 115 |
| Brigham Young | 57 | 99 |
| Oklahoma State | 62 | 98 |
| Arizona State | 66 | 97 |
| Louisiana State | 71 | 85 |
| Kentucky | 62 | 79 |
| New Mexico State | 54 | 78 |
| UCLA | 60 | 77 |
| Texas A&M | 64 | 75 |
| South Florida | 60 | 73 |

**STOLEN BASES**

| | G | SB | ATT |
|---|---|---|---|
| Pittsburgh | 43 | 164 | 210 |
| Yale | 44 | 160 | 195 |
| McNeese State | 61 | 154 | 203 |
| Illinois-Chicago | 57 | 153 | 195 |
| Alabama State | 45 | 143 | 174 |
| Miami (Fla.) | 58 | 143 | 191 |
| South Carolina | 60 | 141 | 177 |
| South Alabama | 59 | 134 | 177 |
| Jackson State | 45 | 131 | 151 |
| Florida A&M | 46 | 127 | 137 |

### TEAM PITCHING

**WON-LOSS PERCENTAGE**

| | W | L | PCT |
|---|---|---|---|
| LeMoyne | 34 | 6 | .850 |
| Texas A&M | 53 | 11 | .828 |
| Wichita State | 58 | 17 | .773 |
| Georgia Tech | 47 | 14 | .770 |
| Texas | 51 | 16 | .761 |
| Louisiana State | 53 | 17 | .757 |
| Yale | 33 | 11 | .750 |
| North Carolina State | 49 | 17 | .742 |
| Notre Dame | 46 | 16 | .742 |
| Texas Tech | 43 | 15 | .741 |

**EARNED RUN AVERAGE**

| | G | ERA |
|---|---|---|
| Kent State | 56 | 2.37 |
| Pepperdine | 58 | 2.65 |
| LeMoyne | 40 | 2.65 |
| Florida State | 65 | 2.90 |
| East Carolina | 60 | 2.99 |
| Lamar | 62 | 3.03 |
| Memphis State | 57 | 3.10 |
| Georgia Tech | 61 | 3.13 |
| Sam Houston State | 56 | 3.23 |
| Old Dominion | 42 | 3.25 |

### TEAM FIELDING

| | G | AVG |
|---|---|---|
| Tennessee | 65 | .975 |
| Northeastern | 36 | .974 |
| Virginia Military | 49 | .973 |
| Texas-Arlington | 54 | .972 |
| Kent State | 56 | .972 |
| Rutgers | 55 | .972 |
| Wright State | 54 | .971 |
| Miami | 58 | .971 |
| Santa Clara | 57 | .970 |
| Jacksonville | 59 | .970 |

### INDIVIDUAL BATTING

**BATTING AVERAGE**
(Minimum 125 At-Bats)

| | AVG | G | AB | R | H | 2B | 3B | HR | RBI | BB | SO | SB |
|---|---|---|---|---|---|---|---|---|---|---|---|---|
| Dickie Woodridge, LeMoyne | .476 | 34 | 126 | 56 | 60 | 14 | 2 | 2 | 28 | 27 | 4 | 21 |
| Mark Winston, Chicago State | .465 | 42 | 129 | 36 | 60 | 13 | 7 | 5 | 30 | 30 | 13 | 12 |
| Mike Martin, Boston College | .462 | 35 | 130 | 32 | 60 | 10 | 3 | 3 | 27 | 14 | 3 | 7 |
| Mike Barger, Saint Louis | .460 | 45 | 176 | 49 | 81 | 14 | 1 | 4 | 31 | 24 | 17 | 37 |
| Marc Sagmoen, Nebraska | .454 | 58 | 205 | 75 | 93 | 19 | 5 | 18 | 79 | 59 | 25 | 26 |
| Kyle Shade, Northwestern (La.) | .453 | 54 | 181 | 44 | 82 | 24 | 2 | 3 | 48 | 33 | 23 | 3 |
| Edwin Hartwell, Notre Dame | .447 | 56 | 199 | 72 | 89 | 13 | 1 | 13 | 68 | 39 | 32 | 11 |
| Paul LoDuca, Arizona State | .446 | 66 | 289 | 63 | 129 | 24 | 2 | 14 | 88 | 25 | 30 | 0 |
| Pat Watkins, East Carolina | .445 | 60 | 220 | 63 | 98 | 7 | 3 | 19 | 57 | 17 | 24 | 29 |
| David Smith, LeMoyne | .441 | 40 | 136 | 64 | 60 | 15 | 1 | 14 | 65 | 35 | 18 | 14 |
| Eric Danapilis, Notre Dame | .438 | 61 | 219 | 71 | 96 | 24 | 0 | 13 | 85 | 34 | 15 | 13 |
| Mickey Houston, Southern Utah | .436 | 45 | 165 | 27 | 72 | 15 | 4 | 6 | 36 | 18 | 18 | 2 |
| Mike Wiseley, Eastern Michigan | .435 | 54 | 177 | 43 | 77 | 14 | 4 | 1 | 33 | 27 | 16 | 19 |
| Antonio Fernandez, New Mexico | .430 | 56 | 221 | 56 | 95 | 16 | 4 | 6 | 71 | 18 | 20 | 4 |
| Chris Sexton, Miami (Ohio) | .429 | 53 | 161 | 47 | 69 | 19 | 5 | 5 | 44 | 32 | 12 | 15 |
| Jack Stanczak, Villanova | .426 | 43 | 148 | 56 | 63 | 10 | 0 | 13 | 43 | 39 | 30 | 8 |
| Dennis Dwyer, Connecticut | .425 | 44 | 167 | 40 | 71 | 17 | 2 | 0 | 21 | 27 | 18 | 40 |
| Bo Durkac, Virginia Tech | .423 | 47 | 182 | 43 | 77 | 13 | 0 | 6 | 29 | 15 | 11 | 3 |
| Bill Weyers, Western Kentucky | .422 | 51 | 192 | 59 | 81 | 16 | 0 | 7 | 46 | 32 | 25 | 4 |
| Derrick Calvin, Southern | .420 | 38 | 131 | 40 | 55 | 13 | 2 | 7 | 38 | 35 | 11 | 11 |
| Rob Mummau, James Madison | .416 | 47 | 178 | 47 | 74 | 18 | 5 | 4 | 36 | 18 | 20 | 19 |
| Mark Gabbard, Cincinnati | .416 | 44 | 166 | 39 | 69 | 9 | 2 | 13 | 46 | 15 | 24 | 3 |
| Dave Madsen, Brigham Young | .415 | 57 | 205 | 62 | 85 | 16 | 2 | 15 | 64 | 51 | 25 | 5 |
| Chuck Kulle, LeMoyne | .414 | 40 | 140 | 40 | 58 | 10 | 0 | 13 | 67 | 22 | 18 | 5 |
| Greg Elliott, Mary.-Balt. Cty. | .412 | 43 | 182 | 50 | 75 | 23 | 2 | 7 | 48 | 26 | 13 | 9 |
| Clint Straub, Detroit Mercy | .412 | 47 | 153 | 42 | 63 | 12 | 3 | 7 | 32 | 25 | 15 | 2 |
| Pat Conreaux, Saint Louis | .411 | 44 | 180 | 33 | 74 | 13 | 6 | 3 | 51 | 12 | 21 | 17 |
| Pat Schulz, Evansville | .410 | 61 | 212 | 59 | 87 | 18 | 9 | 7 | 46 | 44 | 22 | 13 |
| Mark Little, Memphis State | .409 | 56 | 181 | 53 | 74 | 20 | 7 | 7 | 49 | 38 | 29 | 15 |
| Mark Loretta, Northwestern | .408 | 53 | 184 | 38 | 75 | 12 | 6 | 3 | 34 | 28 | 7 | 20 |
| Mark Merila, Minnesota | .408 | 61 | 184 | 61 | 75 | 14 | 2 | 2 | 55 | 59 | 15 | 14 |
| Casey Burrill, Southern Cal | .408 | 64 | 238 | 54 | 97 | 18 | 1 | 13 | 52 | 26 | 17 | 6 |
| Joe Carillo, Fairfield | .405 | 40 | 148 | 27 | 60 | 15 | 1 | 5 | 40 | 15 | 16 | 1 |
| Gerad Cawhorn, San Jose State | .405 | 53 | 200 | 54 | 81 | 13 | 3 | 10 | 57 | 20 | 24 | 6 |
| Corey Boudreaux, SE Louisiana | .404 | 53 | 188 | 56 | 76 | 14 | 2 | 4 | 60 | 47 | 15 | 9 |
| Steve Abbs, Wyoming | .404 | 50 | 171 | 48 | 69 | 13 | 2 | 5 | 33 | 14 | 22 | 11 |
| Jason Varitek, Georgia Tech | .404 | 61 | 228 | 78 | 92 | 20 | 2 | 22 | 72 | 41 | 41 | 5 |
| Joe Biernat, South Carolina | .403 | 60 | 233 | 46 | 94 | 16 | 2 | 5 | 52 | 23 | 24 | 15 |
| Richard Lemons, Arizona | .403 | 51 | 129 | 33 | 52 | 10 | 3 | 8 | 39 | 14 | 28 | 2 |
| Kevin Blackhurst, Delaware | .403 | 43 | 134 | 28 | 54 | 7 | 3 | 2 | 30 | 16 | 12 | 14 |
| Derrin Doty, Washington | .402 | 57 | 194 | 53 | 78 | 13 | 3 | 6 | 50 | 36 | 17 | 19 |
| Geoffrey Clark, Brigham Young | .402 | 57 | 214 | 53 | 86 | 13 | 2 | 12 | 66 | 19 | 37 | 11 |
| Duane Filchner, Radford | .401 | 47 | 172 | 45 | 69 | 15 | 1 | 8 | 57 | 12 | 17 | 8 |
| Eric Dalton, New Mexico State | .400 | 50 | 185 | 52 | 74 | 12 | 4 | 4 | 20 | 31 | 34 | 10 |
| Darrin Forster, Grand Canyon | .400 | 54 | 200 | 57 | 80 | 21 | 2 | 15 | 64 | 39 | 24 | 1 |
| Larry Hisle, Dayton | .400 | 46 | 145 | 38 | 58 | 11 | 0 | 9 | 47 | 23 | 29 | 0 |
| Erick Sauve, Va. Commonwealth | .400 | 57 | 210 | 54 | 84 | 15 | 6 | 11 | 65 | 21 | 16 | 7 |
| Demetrius Dowler, Indiana State | .398 | 58 | 236 | 56 | 94 | 19 | 5 | 10 | 48 | 19 | 31 | 15 |
| Elgin Jeppesen, Jackson State | .397 | 44 | 131 | 43 | 52 | 10 | 2 | 5 | 28 | 38 | 21 | 35 |
| Clay Gould, Texas-Arlington | .396 | 52 | 192 | 44 | 76 | 14 | 7 | 7 | 54 | 18 | 18 | 5 |
| Chris Zonca, West Chester | .396 | 41 | 139 | 37 | 55 | 12 | 0 | 6 | 29 | 20 | 19 | 7 |
| David Morgan, Harvard | .395 | 38 | 129 | 29 | 51 | 9 | 0 | 8 | 36 | 17 | 18 | 4 |
| Todd Walker, Louisiana State | .395 | 71 | 276 | 85 | 109 | 17 | 11 | 22 | 102 | 49 | 35 | 14 |
| Jon Sbrocco, Wright State | .395 | 54 | 190 | 64 | 75 | 16 | 7 | 5 | 42 | 44 | 19 | 15 |
| Tommy Barnes, Louisiana State | .395 | 59 | 256 | 53 | 101 | 21 | 3 | 9 | 54 | 24 | 23 | 8 |
| Mark Linkletter, Ill.-Chicago | .394 | 56 | 198 | 42 | 78 | 11 | 2 | 12 | 64 | 20 | 27 | 9 |
| Justin Howard, Massachusetts | .394 | 39 | 155 | 42 | 61 | 16 | 1 | 7 | 40 | 7 | 22 | 11 |
| Artis Johnson, Florida A&M | .394 | 45 | 155 | 43 | 61 | 8 | 6 | 7 | 47 | 13 | 14 | 20 |
| Jeff Hoekstra, Memphis State | .393 | 57 | 201 | 41 | 79 | 19 | 0 | 4 | 39 | 30 | 16 | 4 |
| John Vindivich, SE Louisiana | .393 | 54 | 191 | 68 | 75 | 7 | 9 | 7 | 33 | 41 | 36 | 20 |

## RUNS SCORED

| | G | R |
|---|---|---|
| Doug Newstrom, Arizona State | 65 | 91 |
| Carl Hall, Wichita State | 74 | 89 |
| Richie Taylor, Wichita State | 73 | 87 |
| John Tejcek, Arizona | 61 | 85 |
| Todd Walker, Louisiana State | 71 | 85 |
| Russ Johnson, Louisiana State | 71 | 83 |
| Luke Oglesby, New Mexico | 55 | 82 |
| Ernesto Rivera, Okla. State | 62 | 78 |
| Jason Varitek, Georgia Tech | 61 | 78 |
| Brooks Kieschnick, Texas | 67 | 76 |
| Marc Sagmoen, Nebraska | 58 | 75 |
| Toby Smith, Wichita State | 73 | 75 |
| Edwin Hartwell, Notre Dame | 56 | 72 |
| Sean Hugo, Okla. State | 62 | 72 |
| Eric Danapilis, Notre Dame | 61 | 71 |
| Ryan McGuire, UCLA | 60 | 71 |
| Armando Rios, Louisiana State | 70 | 71 |
| Antone Williamson, Arizona State | 66 | 71 |
| George Arias, Arizona | 60 | 70 |
| Mark Gulseth, New Mexico | 56 | 70 |

## HITS

| | G | H |
|---|---|---|
| Paul LoDuca, Arizona State | 66 | 129 |
| Todd Walker, Louisiana State | 71 | 109 |
| Joey Jackson, Wichita State | 73 | 105 |
| Antone Williamson, Arizona State | 66 | 104 |
| Robbie Moen, Arizona | 61 | 102 |
| Tommy Barnes, Louisville | 59 | 101 |
| Pat Watkins, East Carolina | 60 | 98 |
| Casey Burrill, Southern Cal | 64 | 97 |
| Carl Hall, Wichita State | 74 | 97 |
| Braxton Hickman, Texas | 65 | 97 |

## TOTAL BASES

| | G | TB |
|---|---|---|
| Todd Walker, Louisiana State | 71 | 214 |
| Paul LoDuca, Arizona State | 66 | 199 |
| Jason Varitek, Georgia Tech | 61 | 182 |
| Brooks Kieschnick, Texas | 67 | 182 |
| Antone Williamson, Arizona State | 66 | 177 |
| Marc Sagmoen, Nebraska | 58 | 176 |
| Keith Williams, Clemson | 65 | 176 |
| Jason Thompson, Arizona | 60 | 173 |
| George Arias, Arizona | 60 | 173 |
| Ryan McGuire, UCLA | 60 | 172 |
| Pat Clougherty, N.C. State | 66 | 169 |
| Toby Smith, Wichita State | 73 | 169 |
| Pat Watkins, East Carolina | 60 | 168 |

## DOUBLES

| | G | 2B |
|---|---|---|
| Antone Williamson, Arizona State | 66 | 29 |
| Brooks Kieschnick, Texas | 67 | 27 |
| Gabe Alvarez, Southern Cal | 64 | 26 |
| Kevin Brunstad, Wash. State | 57 | 26 |
| Willie Morales, Arizona | 60 | 26 |
| Eric Danapilis, Notre Dame | 61 | 24 |
| Paul LoDuca, Arizona State | 66 | 24 |
| Doug Newstrom, Arizona State | 65 | 24 |
| Kyle Shade, Northwestern (La.) | 54 | 24 |
| Greg Elliott, Md.-Balt. Cty. | 43 | 23 |
| Harry Berrios, Louisiana State | 71 | 22 |
| Mike Dunnett, Ala.-Birmingham | 58 | 22 |
| Todd Helton, Tennessee | 65 | 22 |
| Jeff Niemeier, Kansas | 58 | 22 |
| Mike Simmons, St. Bonaventure | 40 | 22 |

## TRIPLES

| | G | 3B |
|---|---|---|
| Chip Glass, Oklahoma | 53 | 12 |
| Jay Payton, Georgia Tech | 61 | 12 |
| Brian Duva, Florida | 58 | 11 |
| John Tejcek, Arizona | 61 | 11 |
| Todd Walker, Louisiana State | 71 | 11 |
| Ray DeSimone, Long Island | 35 | 10 |
| Chris Hannum, Stetson | 53 | 10 |

## HOME RUNS

| | G | HR |
|---|---|---|
| Ryan McGuire, UCLA | 60 | 26 |
| George Arias, Arizona | 60 | 23 |
| Darren Dreifort, Wichita State | 55 | 22 |
| Jason Varitek, Georgia Tech | 61 | 22 |
| Todd Walker, Louisiana State | 71 | 22 |
| Pat Clougherty, N.C. State | 66 | 21 |

| | | |
|---|---|---|
| Brian Banks, Brigham Young | 57 | 20 |
| Todd Greene, Ga. Southern | 59 | 20 |
| Andy Small, Cal State Northridge | 56 | 20 |
| Jason Thompson, Arizona | 60 | 20 |
| Charlie Allen, Louisville | 59 | 19 |
| Todd Cady, Arizona State | 65 | 19 |
| Rich Dimel, Dayton | 61 | 19 |
| Hayland Hardy, Stephen F. Austin | 53 | 19 |
| Brooks Kieschnick, Texas | 67 | 19 |
| Kevin Taylor, SW Missouri St. | 55 | 19 |
| Pat Watkins, East Carolina | 60 | 19 |
| Keith Williams, Clemson | 65 | 19 |

## RUNS BATTED IN

| | G | RBI |
|---|---|---|
| Todd Walker, Louisiana State | 71 | 102 |
| Ryan McGuire, UCLA | 60 | 91 |
| Paul LoDuca, Arizona State | 66 | 88 |
| Eric Danapilis, Notre Dame | 61 | 85 |
| Antone Williamson, Arizona State | 66 | 85 |
| Harry Berrios, Louisiana State | 71 | 82 |
| Mark Gulseth, New Mexico | 56 | 82 |
| Toby Smith, Wichita State | 73 | 82 |
| Brooks Kieschnick, Texas | 67 | 81 |
| Pat Clougherty, N.C. State | 66 | 80 |
| Marc Sagmoen, Nebraska | 58 | 79 |
| Keith Williams, Clemson | 65 | 79 |
| Darren Stumberger, South Florida | 59 | 76 |
| George Arias, Arizona | 60 | 75 |
| Mike Biltimier, Purdue | 58 | 74 |
| Braxton Hickman, Texas | 65 | 74 |
| Jason Thompson, Arizona | 60 | 74 |
| Brian Banks, Brigham Young | 57 | 73 |
| Jason Varitek, Georgia Tech | 61 | 72 |
| Antonio Fernandez, New Mexico | 56 | 71 |

## BASES ON BALLS

| | G | BB |
|---|---|---|
| Ernesto Rivera, Oklahoma State | 62 | 79 |
| Doug Newstrom, Arizona State | 65 | 71 |
| Russ Johnson, Louisiana State | 71 | 67 |
| Sean Hugo, Oklahoma State | 62 | 65 |
| Brooks Kieschnick, Texas | 67 | 64 |
| Armando Rios, Louisiana State | 70 | 64 |
| Vee Hightower, Vanderbilt | 56 | 63 |
| Clint Gould, McNeese State | 56 | 62 |
| Joe Sturtz, Indiana | 58 | 62 |
| Ryan McGuire, UCLA | 60 | 62 |

## STRIKEOUTS

| | G | SO |
|---|---|---|
| Jeff Parnell, South Carolina | 58 | 80 |
| Chris Cox, North Carolina | 58 | 72 |
| Pookie Jones, Kentucky | 57 | 70 |
| Matt McKay, Nebraska | 46 | 69 |
| Andy Small, Cal State Northridge | 56 | 68 |

## TOUGHEST TO STRIKE OUT
(Minimum 120 At-Bats)

| | AB | SO | Ratio |
|---|---|---|---|
| Kris Doiron, Drexel | 141 | 2 | 70.5 |
| Mike Martin, Boston Coll. | 130 | 3 | 43.3 |

**Antone Williamson**
29 doubles

| | | | |
|---|---|---|---|
| Lou Vernagallo, Long Island | 129 | 3 | 43.0 |
| Dickie Woodridge, LeMoyne | 126 | 4 | 31.5 |
| Ryan Gorecki, Seton Hall | 156 | 5 | 31.2 |
| Lino Diaz, UNLV | 200 | 7 | 28.6 |

## STOLEN BASES

| | G | SB | ATT |
|---|---|---|---|
| Luke Oglesby, New Mexico | 55 | 56 | 63 |
| Ricky Farley, Md.-ES | 59 | 47 | 56 |
| Vee Hightower, Vanderbilt | 56 | 46 | 56 |
| Shawn Harris, Fordham | 58 | 45 | 50 |
| Kevin Gibbs, Old Dominion | 42 | 45 | 51 |
| Tyrone Dixon, S. Alabama | 56 | 45 | 54 |
| Edward Bady, Alabama St. | 44 | 44 | 53 |
| Dante Powell, CS Fullerton | 54 | 42 | 48 |
| Ben Ortman, Portland | 49 | 42 | 51 |
| Jeremy Carr, CS Fullerton | 54 | 41 | 49 |
| Mark Gugino, S. Carolina | 59 | 41 | 49 |
| Dennis Dwyer, Connecticut | 44 | 40 | 48 |
| Rob Grimes, VCU | 57 | 40 | 51 |
| Chad Holbrook, N. Carolina | 62 | 40 | 54 |
| Randall Pannell, Florida A&M | 44 | 40 | 41 |
| Doug Alongi, Rutgers | 55 | 39 | 51 |
| Carl Hall, Wichita State | 74 | 39 | 47 |
| Tom Hutchison, Yale | 42 | 39 | 46 |
| Shawn Knight, Wm. & Mary | 41 | 38 | 45 |
| Mike Kinney, Texas Tech | 58 | 37 | 42 |
| Mike Barger, Saint Louis | 45 | 37 | 47 |

## HIT BY PITCH

| | G | HBP |
|---|---|---|
| Derek Alferman, Arkansas State | 50 | 22 |
| Lou Donati, Santa Clara | 57 | 22 |
| Joe Wallace, Oklahoma State | 47 | 20 |
| Mark Palfalvi, California | 57 | 20 |
| Sean Davisson, Long Beach St. | 57 | 19 |

# INDIVIDUAL PITCHING

## EARNED RUN AVERAGE
(Minimum 60 Innings)

| | W | L | ERA | G | GS | CG | SV | IP | H | R | ER | BB | SO |
|---|---|---|---|---|---|---|---|---|---|---|---|---|---|
| Brian Anderson, Wright State | 10 | 1 | 1.14 | 14 | 13 | 8 | 1 | 95 | 62 | 15 | 12 | 6 | 98 |
| Joe Hughes, Towson State | 7 | 3 | 1.36 | 14 | 8 | 8 | 1 | 73 | 67 | 24 | 11 | 11 | 61 |
| Jaime Bluma, Wichita State | 8 | 2 | 1.39 | 33 | 0 | 0 | 12 | 65 | 40 | 17 | 10 | 9 | 76 |
| Steve Duda, Pepperdine | 12 | 3 | 1.64 | 18 | 18 | 8 | 0 | 137 | 108 | 39 | 25 | 20 | 114 |
| Jonathan Johnson, Florida State | 10 | 1 | 1.68 | 17 | 13 | 3 | 0 | 107 | 80 | 26 | 20 | 52 | 124 |
| Rod Jackson, Jackson State | 8 | 0 | 1.74 | 13 | 11 | 5 | 0 | 72 | 45 | 26 | 14 | 40 | 75 |
| Mike Nartker, Kent State | 9 | 1 | 1.85 | 16 | 10 | 6 | 0 | 73 | 56 | 15 | 15 | 11 | 58 |
| Brian Woods, Fairleigh Dickinson | 7 | 2 | 1.89 | 10 | 10 | 4 | 0 | 67 | 45 | 37 | 14 | 41 | 68 |
| Chris Myers, Georgia Tech | 4 | 0 | 1.90 | 39 | 1 | 0 | 2 | 81 | 73 | 25 | 17 | 15 | 70 |
| Dustin Hermanson, Kent State | 7 | 5 | 1.90 | 14 | 13 | 9 | 1 | 90 | 51 | 23 | 19 | 28 | 102 |
| Paul Wilson, Florida State | 11 | 5 | 1.94 | 17 | 16 | 6 | 0 | 116 | 95 | 31 | 25 | 32 | 99 |
| Brian Tutkovics, Kent State | 7 | 2 | 1.97 | 14 | 8 | 5 | 1 | 69 | 49 | 23 | 19 | 8 | 56 |
| Brett Laxton, Louisiana State | 12 | 1 | 1.98 | 19 | 17 | 5 | 0 | 109 | 67 | 32 | 24 | 47 | 98 |
| Mike Sirotka, Louisiana State | 12 | 6 | 1.99 | 23 | 16 | 10 | 0 | 145 | 121 | 42 | 32 | 35 | 105 |
| Hector Hermanson, Southern | 6 | 3 | 1.99 | 12 | 9 | 4 | 0 | 63 | 54 | 24 | 14 | 20 | 44 |
| Shawn Hill, Nicholls State | 10 | 4 | 2.02 | 19 | 14 | 8 | 3 | 111 | 94 | 34 | 25 | 25 | 108 |
| Greg Smith, Memphis State | 10 | 2 | 2.04 | 18 | 7 | 2 | 2 | 71 | 67 | 27 | 16 | 18 | 57 |
| Jon Ratliff, LeMoyne | 10 | 1 | 2.04 | 13 | 11 | 6 | 1 | 84 | 87 | 34 | 19 | 17 | 64 |
| Trey Marik, McNeese State | 5 | 2 | 2.15 | 30 | 4 | 0 | 0 | 84 | 79 | 23 | 20 | 17 | 62 |
| Bob Scafa, Indiana | 7 | 3 | 2.15 | 14 | 13 | 5 | 0 | 84 | 68 | 23 | 20 | 26 | 78 |

| | W | L | ERA | G | GS | CG | SV | IP | H | R | ER | BB | SO |
|---|---|---|---|---|---|---|---|---|---|---|---|---|---|
| Scott Christman, Oregon State ....... | 14 | 1 | 2.20 | 17 | 14 | 9 | 0 | 111 | 84 | 32 | 27 | 38 | 119 |
| Mike Jenkins, Lamar ... | 5 | 3 | 2.25 | 30 | 3 | 0 | 2 | 64 | 48 | 20 | 18 | 21 | 55 |
| Mike Sanburn, East Carolina ... | 10 | 2 | 2.26 | 15 | 15 | 6 | 0 | 112 | 98 | 41 | 28 | 13 | 78 |
| Henry DelValle, Western Michigan ... | 9 | 2 | 2.27 | 14 | 13 | 8 | 1 | 87 | 76 | 26 | 22 | 26 | 63 |
| Tony Ramsdell, Wright State ... | 10 | 2 | 2.31 | 13 | 12 | 7 | 0 | 93 | 75 | 32 | 24 | 18 | 54 |
| Kevin Loewe, Mary.-Balt. Cty. ... | 8 | 1 | 2.34 | 14 | 9 | 7 | 1 | 73 | 57 | 26 | 19 | 18 | 46 |
| Rich Humphrey, Liberty ... | 8 | 5 | 2.35 | 16 | 14 | 10 | 1 | 111 | 89 | 39 | 29 | 28 | 73 |
| Cory Corrigan, Ohio ... | 7 | 3 | 2.37 | 11 | 11 | 9 | 0 | 80 | 76 | 27 | 21 | 14 | 66 |
| Travis Miller, Kent State ... | 8 | 3 | 2.37 | 13 | 13 | 5 | 0 | 80 | 62 | 23 | 21 | 33 | 83 |
| Chad Hartvigson, Washington ... | 7 | 3 | 2.38 | 11 | 11 | 5 | 0 | 76 | 64 | 24 | 20 | 20 | 50 |
| Jimmy Walker, Kansas ... | 9 | 2 | 2.39 | 33 | 3 | 1 | 11 | 98 | 89 | 33 | 26 | 27 | 104 |
| Heath Altman, UNC-Wilmington ... | 3 | 3 | 2.39 | 21 | 6 | 1 | 8 | 64 | 42 | 21 | 17 | 32 | 80 |
| Buck Hall, Georgia Tech ... | 8 | 2 | 2.42 | 12 | 12 | 1 | 0 | 67 | 46 | 24 | 18 | 27 | 83 |
| Nick Rizzo, Drexel ... | 5 | 3 | 2.43 | 12 | 10 | 3 | 0 | 63 | 62 | 28 | 17 | 31 | 36 |
| John Smith, Old Dominion ... | 7 | 2 | 2.44 | 15 | 13 | 3 | 0 | 89 | 75 | 29 | 24 | 23 | 72 |
| Steve Prihoda, Sam Houston State .. | 6 | 4 | 2.44 | 16 | 14 | 3 | 1 | 65 | 71 | 28 | 23 | 20 | 67 |
| Chris Stewart, Memphis State ... | 10 | 2 | 2.44 | 15 | 15 | 5 | 0 | 85 | 49 | 32 | 23 | 41 | 82 |
| Bryan Rekar, Bradley ... | 8 | 2 | 2.45 | 12 | 12 | 7 | 0 | 92 | 76 | 29 | 25 | 21 | 67 |
| Matt Murphy, Vermont ... | 6 | 4 | 2.45 | 12 | 10 | 7 | 1 | 73 | 65 | 28 | 20 | 20 | 54 |
| Brad Rigby, Georgia Tech ... | 13 | 1 | 2.46 | 17 | 17 | 0 | 0 | 99 | 57 | 33 | 27 | 56 | 132 |
| Steve Reich, Army ... | 6 | 3 | 2.48 | 11 | 10 | 8 | 0 | 76 | 68 | 35 | 21 | 19 | 88 |
| Darren Dreifort, Wichita State ... | 11 | 1 | 2.48 | 30 | 0 | 0 | 4 | 102 | 67 | 36 | 28 | 34 | 120 |
| Keith Reichert, St. Francis (N.Y.) ... | 5 | 2 | 2.54 | 11 | 8 | 5 | 1 | 60 | 51 | 32 | 17 | 15 | 19 |
| Joe Wharton, Baylor ... | 10 | 3 | 2.54 | 21 | 9 | 5 | 3 | 85 | 69 | 30 | 24 | 29 | 85 |
| Scott Sullivan, Auburn ... | 4 | 3 | 2.55 | 22 | 2 | 0 | 5 | 60 | 48 | 23 | 17 | 19 | 71 |
| Basil Clausen, Eastern Illinois ... | 6 | 4 | 2.56 | 14 | 13 | 5 | 0 | 81 | 61 | 32 | 23 | 34 | 49 |
| Daniel Choi, Long Beach State... | 17 | 2 | 2.57 | 20 | 20 | 7 | 0 | 147 | 116 | 54 | 42 | 52 | 116 |
| David Hutcheson, South Florida ... | 9 | 6 | 2.59 | 19 | 19 | 3 | 0 | 132 | 131 | 53 | 38 | 45 | 97 |
| Mike McLaury, Middle Tennessee ... | 7 | 7 | 2.59 | 22 | 15 | 6 | 1 | 111 | 100 | 48 | 32 | 33 | 75 |
| Jason Schlutt, Central Florida ... | 9 | 2 | 2.62 | 34 | 2 | 0 | 8 | 76 | 72 | 33 | 22 | 29 | 75 |
| Jeff Granger, Texas A&M ... | 15 | 3 | 2.62 | 20 | 18 | 8 | 0 | 127 | 87 | 47 | 37 | 54 | 150 |
| Jamie Wilson, Delaware ... | 9 | 1 | 2.63 | 15 | 11 | 6 | 1 | 82 | 75 | 34 | 24 | 23 | 47 |
| Greg Gregory, Pepperdine ... | 7 | 3 | 2.65 | 15 | 15 | 3 | 0 | 76 | 71 | 30 | 23 | 25 | 47 |
| Mark Ballard, Maine ... | 8 | 3 | 2.67 | 14 | 13 | 6 | 0 | 91 | 60 | 32 | 27 | 37 | 95 |
| Jason Haynie, South Carolina ... | 8 | 2 | 2.68 | 18 | 14 | 0 | 0 | 77 | 52 | 43 | 23 | 46 | 86 |
| Kevin Alarie, Mary.-Balt. Cty. ... | 3 | 3 | 2.69 | 13 | 8 | 2 | 1 | 60 | 75 | 18 | 33 | 4 | 33 |
| Steve Weimer, Iowa ... | 3 | 2 | 2.70 | 14 | 13 | 4 | 0 | 73 | 65 | 24 | 22 | 28 | 53 |
| Greg Willming, Evansville ... | 10 | 3 | 2.71 | 21 | 17 | 7 | 2 | 126 | 111 | 50 | 38 | 23 | 96 |
| C.J. Nitkowski, St. John's ... | 6 | 3 | 2.71 | 16 | 9 | 3 | 2 | 80 | 79 | 37 | 24 | 28 | 65 |
| Stephen Hoppel, Temple ... | 7 | 3 | 2.71 | 12 | 10 | 7 | 1 | 76 | 53 | 32 | 23 | 37 | 72 |

**John Powell**
191 strikeouts

### INNINGS PITCHED

| | G | IP |
|---|---|---|
| Brooks Kieschnick, Texas ... | 26 | 150 |
| Daniel Choi, Long Beach St. ... | 20 | 147 |
| Mike Salazar, Fresno State ... | 20 | 147 |
| Mike Sirotka, Louisiana State ... | 23 | 145 |
| Marc Barcelo, Arizona State ... | 19 | 142 |
| John Powell, Auburn ... | 24 | 141 |
| Steve Duda, Pepperdine ... | 18 | 137 |
| Andrew McNally, Hawaii ... | 18 | 137 |
| David Hutcheson, South Florida ... | 19 | 132 |
| Sam Arguto, Jacksonville ... | 22 | 131 |

### BASES ON BALLS

| | IP | BB |
|---|---|---|
| Mike Romano, Tulane ... | 123 | 79 |
| Courtney Mitchell, Grambling St. ... | 80 | 78 |
| Sean Touchet, New Orleans ... | 87 | 76 |
| Darius Solomon, Mercer ... | 65 | 76 |
| Sean Powell, Cleveland State ... | 89 | 73 |

### STRIKEOUTS

| | IP | SO |
|---|---|---|
| John Powell, Auburn ... | 141 | 191 |
| Jeff Granger, Texas A&M ... | 127 | 150 |
| John Wasdin, Florida State ... | 114 | 138 |
| Brad Rigby, Georgia Tech ... | 99 | 132 |
| Gregg Kennedy, Southern Miss . | 113 | 129 |
| Mike Romano, Tulane ... | 123 | 128 |
| Brooks Kieschnick, Texas ... | 150 | 126 |
| Jonathan Johnson, Florida State. | 107 | 124 |
| Troy Brohawn, Nebraska ... | 111 | 123 |
| Alan Benes, Creighton ... | 105 | 122 |
| Darren Dreifort, Wichita State ... | 102 | 120 |
| Shawn Senior, N.C. State ... | 102 | 120 |
| Travis Driskill, Texas Tech ... | 121 | 120 |
| Scott Christman, Oregon State... | 111 | 119 |
| Marc Valdes, Florida ... | 123 | 119 |
| Daniel Choi, Long Beach State ... | 147 | 116 |
| Jason Meyhoff, Missouri ... | 101 | 114 |
| Steve Soderstrom, Fresno State . | 107 | 114 |
| Casey Whitten, Indiana State ... | 107 | 114 |
| Willie Adams, Stanford ... | 121 | 114 |
| Steve Duda, Pepperdine ... | 137 | 114 |

### STRIKEOUTS/9 INNINGS
(Minimum 50 Innings)

| | IP | SO | AVG |
|---|---|---|---|
| Nate Brown, California... | 66 | 99 | 13.5 |
| Jay Witasick, UMBC ... | 57 | 78 | 12.3 |
| John Powell, Auburn ... | 141 | 191 | 12.2 |
| Willard Brown, Stetson ... | 81 | 109 | 12.2 |
| Brad Rigby, Georgia Tech ... | 99 | 132 | 12.0 |
| Brian Reed, Kentucky... | 85 | 112 | 11.9 |
| Marc Ottmers, Texas-Pan Am. . | 72 | 94 | 11.8 |
| Kelly Wunsch, Texas A&M ... | 87 | 110 | 11.4 |
| Heath Altman, UNC Wilmington .. | 64 | 80 | 11.3 |
| David Goldstein, Long Beach St. | 67 | 84 | 11.2 |
| Marc Grande, Fla. Int'l ... | 55 | 68 | 11.2 |
| Buck Hall, Georgia Tech ... | 67 | 83 | 11.2 |
| Dan Wheeler, Brigham Young.. | 56 | 69 | 11.0 |
| John Wasdin, Florida State .. | 114 | 138 | 10.9 |

### WINS

| | W | L |
|---|---|---|
| Daniel Choi, Long Beach St. ... | 17 | 2 |
| Brooks Kieschnick, Texas ... | 16 | 4 |
| Jeff Granger, Texas A&M ... | 15 | 3 |
| John Powell, Auburn ... | 15 | 5 |
| Scott Christman, Oregon State ... | 14 | 1 |
| Troy Brohawn, Nebraska ... | 13 | 0 |
| Brad Rigby, Georgia Tech ... | 13 | 1 |
| Mike Salazar, Fresno State ... | 13 | 3 |
| Trey Moore, Texas A&M ... | 12 | 0 |
| Bobby Kahlon, California ... | 12 | 1 |
| Brett Laxton, Louisiana State ... | 12 | 1 |
| Jason Beverlin, Western Carolina ... | 12 | 2 |
| Chris Freeman, Tennessee ... | 12 | 2 |
| Chad Phillips, Clemson ... | 12 | 2 |
| Tom Price, Notre Dame ... | 12 | 2 |
| Steve Duda, Pepperdine ... | 12 | 3 |
| Scott Schoeneweis, Duke ... | 12 | 3 |
| Marc Barcelo, Arizona State ... | 12 | 4 |
| Joey Chavez, San Jose State ... | 12 | 6 |
| Mike Sirotka, Louisiana State ... | 12 | 6 |

### LOSSES

| | W | L |
|---|---|---|
| Ahmed Smith, Howard ... | 1 | 12 |
| Rick Miller, Mercer ... | 4 | 12 |
| Jason Flurry, Georgia State . ... | 1 | 11 |
| Jason Routt, Prairie View ... | 2 | 11 |
| Shane Wilde, Southern Utah ... | 2 | 11 |
| Shea Fleck, Gonzaga ... | 4 | 11 |
| William Parks, Chicago State ... | 4 | 11 |

### APPEARANCES

| | G |
|---|---|
| Brett Binkley, Georgia Tech ... | 39 |
| Chris Myers, Georgia Tech ... | 39 |
| Thad Chrismon, North Carolina ... | 38 |
| Joe Barbao, Vanderbilt ... | 36 |
| Tod Brown, Arizona ... | 35 |
| Paul Thornton, Georgia Southern ... | 35 |

### COMPLETE GAMES

| | GS | CG |
|---|---|---|
| Keven Kempton, CS Northridge ... | 15 | 13 |
| Andrew McNally, Hawaii ... | 18 | 12 |
| John Henrickson, Texas-Arlington | 14 | 11 |
| Rich Humphrey, Liberty ... | 14 | 10 |
| Scott Metzinger, Butler ... | 14 | 10 |
| Gary Goldsmith, New Mexico St. .. | 15 | 10 |
| Chris Michalak, Notre Dame ... | 15 | 10 |
| Mike Sirotka, Louisiana State ... | 16 | 10 |
| Marc Barcelo, Arizona State ... | 17 | 10 |
| Corey Giuliano, Chapman ... | 17 | 10 |
| Mike Salazar, Fresno State ... | 19 | 10 |

### SAVES

| | G | Sv |
|---|---|---|
| Thad Chrismon, North Carolina..... | 38 | 18 |
| Dan Hubbs, Southern California .... | 33 | 18 |
| Paul Thornton, Georgia Southern . | 35 | 17 |
| Jay Cole, Alabama-Birmingham ... | 28 | 15 |
| Alex Barylak, Georgia ... | 27 | 15 |
| Brett Binkley, Georgia Tech ... | 39 | 14 |
| Gabe Gonzalez, Long Beach St. ... | 34 | 13 |
| Jaime Bluma, Wichita State ... | 33 | 13 |
| David Allen, N.C. State ... | 33 | 12 |
| Adam Bryant, Va. Commonwealth | 23 | 12 |

**Daniel Choi**
17 wins

# Baseball America's
# COLLEGE TOP 25

**BATTERS:** 10 or more at-bats
**PITCHERS:** 5 or more innings

**Boldface** indicates selected in 1993 draft

## 1  LOUISIANA STATE

**Coach:** Skip Bertman  **Record:** 53-17

| BATTING | AVG | AB | R | H | 2B | 3B | HR | RBI | SB |
|---|---|---|---|---|---|---|---|---|---|
| Walker, Todd, 2b | .395 | 276 | 85 | 109 | 17 | 11 | 22 | 102 | 14 |
| Johnson, Russ, ss | .355 | 259 | 83 | 92 | 18 | 3 | 8 | 58 | 19 |
| Williams, Jason, 3b | .329 | 228 | 61 | 75 | 10 | 3 | 2 | 34 | 12 |
| **Berrios, Harry, of** | .326 | 270 | 69 | 88 | 22 | 2 | 17 | 82 | 21 |
| **Neal, Mike, dh-3b** | .319 | 213 | 61 | 68 | 19 | 6 | 5 | 27 | 16 |
| Rios, Armando, of | .319 | 235 | 71 | 75 | 13 | 4 | 9 | 61 | 20 |
| Stocco, Mark, of | .292 | 130 | 25 | 38 | 4 | 2 | 4 | 26 | 3 |
| Lanier, Tim, c | .286 | 14 | 3 | 4 | 0 | 0 | 0 | 0 | 1 |
| Greely, Jim, of-dh | .280 | 150 | 19 | 42 | 9 | 1 | 5 | 32 | 3 |
| Jackson, Kenny, 1b | .279 | 226 | 53 | 63 | 18 | 2 | 4 | 42 | 5 |
| **Hunt, Will, p-1b** | .244 | 41 | 9 | 10 | 4 | 1 | 2 | 12 | 0 |
| Berardi, Scott, c | .229 | 35 | 4 | 8 | 2 | 1 | 0 | 5 | 0 |
| Antonini, Adrian, c | .226 | 221 | 35 | 50 | 13 | 0 | 6 | 35 | 1 |
| Huffman, Ryan, of | .211 | 19 | 13 | 4 | 0 | 0 | 1 | 4 | 3 |
| Cooley, Chad, of | .161 | 56 | 8 | 9 | 3 | 1 | 0 | 5 | 4 |

| PITCHING | W | L | ERA | G | Sv | IP | H | BB | SO |
|---|---|---|---|---|---|---|---|---|---|
| Laxton, Brett | 12 | 1 | 1.98 | 19 | 0 | 109 | 67 | 47 | 98 |
| Sirotka, Mike | 12 | 6 | 1.99 | 23 | 0 | 145 | 121 | 35 | 105 |
| **Hunt, Will** | 9 | 1 | 3.38 | 29 | 1 | 77 | 77 | 27 | 63 |
| Winders, Brian | 1 | 0 | 3.65 | 9 | 1 | 12 | 8 | 3 | 7 |
| **Chamberlain, Matt** | 6 | 3 | 4.58 | 20 | 0 | 90 | 105 | 31 | 69 |
| Schultz, Scott | 7 | 3 | 4.91 | 23 | 3 | 66 | 76 | 33 | 52 |
| Malejke, Matt | 1 | 0 | 5.66 | 21 | 0 | 41 | 41 | 20 | 39 |
| **Rutledge, Trey** | 4 | 2 | 5.70 | 22 | 2 | 54 | 58 | 22 | 50 |
| McCabe, Bhrett | 1 | 0 | 6.30 | 10 | 0 | 10 | 11 | 6 | 11 |
| Rantz, Ronnie | 0 | 1 | 11.12 | 7 | 0 | 11 | 19 | 15 | 11 |

## 2  TEXAS A&M

**Coach:** Mark Johnson  **Record:** 53-11

| BATTING | AVG | AB | R | H | 2B | 3B | HR | RBI | SB |
|---|---|---|---|---|---|---|---|---|---|
| **Thomas, Brian, of** | .383 | 206 | 68 | 79 | 16 | 9 | 15 | 55 | 21 |
| **Trimble, Rob, c** | .355 | 141 | 29 | 50 | 10 | 1 | 2 | 28 | 2 |
| **Lewis, Robert, c-3b** | .343 | 137 | 31 | 47 | 7 | 0 | 5 | 31 | 3 |
| Fedora, Lee, 3b | .342 | 184 | 50 | 63 | 5 | 2 | 8 | 48 | 12 |
| Harris, Robert, ss | .325 | 237 | 63 | 77 | 9 | 3 | 12 | 55 | 5 |
| Moore, Trey, p-dh | .314 | 118 | 14 | 37 | 6 | 0 | 4 | 24 | 3 |
| Gonzalez, Eric, 2b | .313 | 211 | 52 | 66 | 13 | 3 | 8 | 49 | 13 |
| Minor, David, of | .304 | 46 | 21 | 14 | 1 | 1 | 3 | 19 | 0 |
| Harlan, Billy, 1b-of | .300 | 263 | 50 | 79 | 12 | 4 | 4 | 37 | 27 |
| Curl, John, 1b | .297 | 128 | 26 | 38 | 5 | 1 | 7 | 30 | 3 |
| Martin, David, ss | .292 | 24 | 6 | 7 | 0 | 0 | 0 | 3 | 1 |
| **Smith, Scott, of** | .290 | 124 | 29 | 36 | 6 | 1 | 2 | 22 | 4 |
| Claybrook, Stephen, of | .273 | 139 | 38 | 38 | 6 | 2 | 2 | 15 | 22 |
| Bittiker, Brian, 1b | .250 | 60 | 6 | 15 | 4 | 0 | 0 | 7 | 2 |
| Alexander, Chad, of-dh | .220 | 82 | 14 | 18 | 1 | 0 | 3 | 18 | 1 |
| Johnson, Brian, c | .100 | 10 | 1 | 1 | 0 | 0 | 0 | 0 | 0 |

| PITCHING | W | L | ERA | G | Sv | IP | H | BB | SO |
|---|---|---|---|---|---|---|---|---|---|
| Parker, Brian | 5 | 3 | 1.93 | 23 | 5 | 42 | 39 | 11 | 29 |
| **Granger, Jeff** | 15 | 3 | 2.62 | 20 | 0 | 127 | 87 | 54 | 150 |
| Moore, Trey | 12 | 0 | 2.77 | 18 | 1 | 101 | 84 | 54 | 91 |
| **McIntyre, Spencer** | 2 | 0 | 2.79 | 12 | 0 | 19 | 14 | 19 | 20 |
| Chesson, Jason | 1 | 1 | 3.38 | 12 | 0 | 24 | 18 | 6 | 11 |
| Clemons, Chris | 6 | 2 | 3.79 | 19 | 2 | 71 | 75 | 23 | 67 |
| Wunsch, Kelly | 7 | 2 | 4.45 | 17 | 0 | 87 | 65 | 54 | 110 |
| Codrington, John | 4 | 0 | 5.23 | 19 | 1 | 53 | 53 | 24 | 39 |
| Jansky, Jeff | 1 | 0 | 6.23 | 7 | 0 | 13 | 14 | 5 | 11 |

**Jeff Granger.** Texas A&M lefthander won 15 games for Aggies and was Kansas City's first-round draft pick.

## 3  ARIZONA STATE

**Coach:** Jim Brock  **Record:** 46-20

| BATTING | AVG | AB | R | H | 2B | 3B | HR | RBI | SB |
|---|---|---|---|---|---|---|---|---|---|
| **LoDuca, Paul, c-dh** | .446 | 289 | 63 | 129 | 24 | 2 | 14 | 88 | 0 |
| Williamson, Antone, 3b | .378 | 275 | 71 | 104 | 29 | 1 | 14 | 85 | 2 |
| **Newstrom, Doug, 1b-p** | .356 | 247 | 91 | 88 | 24 | 1 | 12 | 68 | 3 |
| Lootens, Brian, of | .354 | 237 | 51 | 84 | 16 | 4 | 7 | 39 | 9 |
| **Dunn, Bill, 2b** | .346 | 254 | 58 | 88 | 14 | 1 | 4 | 28 | 20 |
| Cruz, Jacob, of | .342 | 202 | 51 | 69 | 15 | 2 | 10 | 37 | 5 |
| Cardinale, Sal, 2b | .316 | 57 | 16 | 18 | 5 | 0 | 1 | 8 | 1 |
| Cady, Todd, c-1b | .316 | 244 | 60 | 77 | 11 | 0 | 19 | 68 | 2 |
| McKay, Cody, ss | .276 | 170 | 22 | 47 | 13 | 1 | 3 | 36 | 0 |
| **Rivera, Santiago, ss** | .264 | 91 | 23 | 24 | 3 | 1 | 0 | 9 | 4 |
| **Shores, Scott, of** | .255 | 141 | 21 | 36 | 6 | 1 | 5 | 28 | 12 |
| Delnoce, Todd, of | .237 | 118 | 17 | 28 | 6 | 0 | 5 | 19 | 1 |
| McGonigle, Billy, of | .233 | 43 | 11 | 10 | 2 | 0 | 1 | 4 | 1 |
| Tyler, Sean, of | .198 | 91 | 23 | 18 | 4 | 0 | 2 | 11 | 4 |

| PITCHING | W | L | ERA | G | Sv | IP | H | BB | SO |
|---|---|---|---|---|---|---|---|---|---|
| **Barcelo, Marc** | 12 | 4 | 2.72 | 19 | 0 | 142 | 133 | 35 | 113 |
| Rawitzer, Kevin | 5 | 3 | 3.66 | 16 | 0 | 71 | 57 | 41 | 83 |
| Fenton, Mike | 3 | 3 | 4.35 | 30 | 3 | 62 | 69 | 18 | 43 |
| Newstrom, Doug | 3 | 0 | 4.37 | 12 | 2 | 45 | 48 | 19 | 41 |
| **Winslett, Dax** | 10 | 5 | 4.46 | 22 | 0 | 125 | 127 | 65 | 98 |
| Perry, Noah | 6 | 2 | 5.66 | 29 | 6 | 62 | 65 | 55 | 66 |
| Rensmeyer, Mike | 1 | 2 | 6.32 | 8 | 1 | 16 | 15 | 10 | 10 |
| Corominas, Mike | 0 | 0 | 6.88 | 6 | 1 | 17 | 21 | 10 | 13 |
| **Smith, Brent** | 5 | 1 | 6.91 | 12 | 0 | 57 | 59 | 41 | 43 |

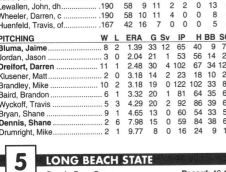

## 4 — WICHITA STATE

**Coach:** Gene Stephenson  **Record:** 58-17

| BATTING | AVG | AB | R | H | 2B | 3B | HR | RBI | SB |
|---|---|---|---|---|---|---|---|---|---|
| Blake, Casey, 3b | .366 | 232 | 42 | 85 | 9 | 3 | 4 | 57 | 7 |
| Jackson, Joey, 2b | .361 | 291 | 50 | 105 | 17 | 2 | 5 | 62 | 3 |
| **Smith, Toby, 1b** | .351 | 268 | 75 | 94 | 17 | 2 | 18 | 82 | 4 |
| Ficken, Jason, ss-2b | .333 | 36 | 8 | 12 | 1 | 0 | 0 | 9 | 0 |
| **Dreifort, Darren, dh-p** | .327 | 199 | 51 | 65 | 6 | 2 | 22 | 61 | 3 |
| Adams, Jason, ss | .318 | 274 | 61 | 87 | 18 | 3 | 2 | 49 | 6 |
| Hall, Carl, of | .316 | 307 | 89 | 97 | 18 | 7 | 3 | 36 | 39 |
| Taylor, Richie, of | .316 | 282 | 87 | 89 | 15 | 4 | 7 | 66 | 23 |
| Tilma, Tommy, of | .301 | 173 | 38 | 52 | 8 | 3 | 1 | 18 | 6 |
| Anderson, Spike, c | .277 | 47 | 11 | 13 | 3 | 0 | 0 | 7 | 1 |
| McCollough, Adam, c | .262 | 160 | 16 | 42 | 9 | 1 | 1 | 29 | 1 |
| Mills, Tony, of | .262 | 122 | 25 | 32 | 6 | 1 | 0 | 17 | 20 |
| Babcock, Trent, 3b | .246 | 57 | 11 | 14 | 0 | 0 | 1 | 17 | 2 |
| Bauer, Chris, ss-2b | .231 | 26 | 9 | 6 | 0 | 0 | 0 | 1 | 2 |
| Lewallen, John, dh | .190 | 58 | 9 | 11 | 2 | 2 | 0 | 13 | 0 |
| Wheeler, Darren, c | .190 | 58 | 10 | 11 | 4 | 0 | 0 | 8 | 0 |
| Huenfeld, Travis, of | .167 | 42 | 16 | 7 | 0 | 0 | 0 | 5 | 6 |

| PITCHING | W | L | ERA | G | Sv | IP | H | BB | SO |
|---|---|---|---|---|---|---|---|---|---|
| **Bluma, Jaime** | 8 | 2 | 1.39 | 33 | 12 | 65 | 40 | 9 | 76 |
| Jordan, Jason | 3 | 0 | 2.04 | 21 | 1 | 53 | 56 | 14 | 29 |
| **Dreifort, Darren** | 11 | 1 | 2.48 | 30 | 4 | 102 | 67 | 34 | 120 |
| Klusener, Matt | 2 | 0 | 3.18 | 14 | 2 | 23 | 18 | 10 | 26 |
| Brandley, Mike | 10 | 2 | 3.18 | 19 | 0 | 122 | 102 | 33 | 83 |
| Baird, Brandon | 6 | 1 | 3.32 | 20 | 1 | 81 | 64 | 35 | 62 |
| Wyckoff, Travis | 5 | 3 | 4.29 | 20 | 2 | 92 | 86 | 39 | 62 |
| Bryan, Shane | 9 | 1 | 4.65 | 13 | 0 | 60 | 54 | 33 | 52 |
| **Dennis, Shane** | 2 | 6 | 7.98 | 15 | 0 | 59 | 84 | 38 | 64 |
| Drumright, Mike | 2 | 1 | 9.77 | 8 | 0 | 16 | 24 | 9 | 16 |

## 5 — LONG BEACH STATE

**Coach:** Dave Snow  **Record:** 46-19

| BATTING | AVG | AB | R | H | 2B | 3B | HR | RBI | SB |
|---|---|---|---|---|---|---|---|---|---|
| **Curtis, Kevin, of** | .368 | 220 | 46 | 81 | 13 | 2 | 12 | 57 | 5 |
| Liefer, Jeff, dh-1b | .356 | 236 | 57 | 84 | 17 | 2 | 12 | 54 | 8 |
| Swanson, John, 1b-of | .341 | 176 | 48 | 60 | 2 | 3 | 5 | 38 | 16 |
| **Richardson, Jeff, of** | .310 | 71 | 18 | 22 | 3 | 0 | 0 | 13 | 2 |
| **Cradle, Cobi, of** | .302 | 242 | 62 | 73 | 14 | 2 | 5 | 38 | 35 |
| Rodriguez, Rudy, ss | .285 | 228 | 39 | 65 | 15 | 0 | 1 | 39 | 4 |
| **Whatley, Brian, c** | .270 | 174 | 34 | 47 | 8 | 1 | 2 | 22 | 2 |
| Smith, Brian, 1b | .268 | 97 | 16 | 26 | 10 | 0 | 2 | 20 | 0 |
| **Davisson, Sean, 3b-of** | .267 | 187 | 36 | 50 | 10 | 1 | 3 | 25 | 13 |
| Falsken, Tim, 3b | .266 | 139 | 23 | 37 | 5 | 2 | 1 | 28 | 4 |
| Martins, Eric, 2b | .257 | 214 | 40 | 55 | 4 | 4 | 0 | 35 | 13 |
| Pierce, Kirk, c-dh | .250 | 84 | 18 | 21 | 4 | 0 | 2 | 18 | 2 |
| **Davis, Eddie, of** | .233 | 116 | 23 | 27 | 3 | 0 | 6 | 20 | 11 |
| Strauss, Jon, c | .222 | 27 | 4 | 6 | 2 | 0 | 0 | 1 | 0 |

| PITCHING | W | L | ERA | G | Sv | IP | H | BB | SO |
|---|---|---|---|---|---|---|---|---|---|
| Gonzalez, Gabe | 4 | 3 | 1.54 | 34 | 13 | 53 | 31 | 20 | 50 |
| **Choi, Daniel** | 17 | 2 | 2.57 | 20 | 0 | 147 | 116 | 52 | 116 |
| Fontana, Mike | 9 | 3 | 2.94 | 20 | 0 | 119 | 104 | 45 | 104 |
| Goldstein, David | 3 | 2 | 3.07 | 22 | 6 | 67 | 61 | 32 | 84 |
| Aragon, Angel | 1 | 0 | 3.97 | 12 | 0 | 23 | 27 | 9 | 17 |
| Thomas, Gary | 3 | 3 | 4.87 | 14 | 0 | 44 | 60 | 21 | 27 |
| Mosebrook, Mike | 3 | 2 | 5.07 | 19 | 0 | 50 | 59 | 28 | 35 |
| Wise, Andy | 2 | 1 | 5.09 | 17 | 0 | 18 | 16 | 10 | 16 |
| **Colon, Julio** | 2 | 3 | 6.75 | 15 | 0 | 36 | 45 | 15 | 19 |
| Fontes, Brian | 2 | 0 | 6.94 | 10 | 0 | 23 | 25 | 19 | 25 |

## 6 — OKLAHOMA STATE

**Coach:** Gary Ward  **Record:** 45-17

| BATTING | AVG | AB | R | H | 2B | 3B | HR | RBI | SB |
|---|---|---|---|---|---|---|---|---|---|
| Hugo, Sean, of | .347 | 202 | 72 | 70 | 16 | 2 | 13 | 53 | 0 |
| Rivera, Ernesto, 3b-2b | .338 | 225 | 78 | 76 | 18 | 5 | 12 | 61 | 14 |
| Childers, Chabon, dh | .336 | 146 | 33 | 49 | 9 | 1 | 7 | 45 | 0 |
| Prodanov, Peter, of | .335 | 215 | 56 | 72 | 13 | 0 | 8 | 46 | 19 |
| Bando, Sal, 1b | .329 | 152 | 32 | 50 | 6 | 0 | 12 | 42 | 1 |
| Chaddrick, Thad, of | .327 | 171 | 37 | 56 | 14 | 3 | 9 | 46 | 3 |
| Triplett, Hunter, 1b-of | .308 | 159 | 29 | 49 | 12 | 3 | 12 | 55 | 4 |
| Ocasio, Fred, ss | .307 | 225 | 42 | 69 | 10 | 1 | 1 | 29 | 0 |
| Wallace, Joe, c | .303 | 109 | 37 | 33 | 5 | 0 | 7 | 29 | 0 |
| Heath, Jason, of-c | .303 | 185 | 40 | 56 | 17 | 2 | 13 | 62 | 2 |
| Sharp, Skip, c | .292 | 24 | 3 | 7 | 0 | 0 | 0 | 4 | 0 |
| Benz, Jake, of | .275 | 40 | 10 | 11 | 0 | 1 | 0 | 5 | 2 |
| Lopez, Roberto, 2b | .272 | 136 | 48 | 37 | 6 | 1 | 2 | 23 | 23 |
| Pruett, David, 3b | .237 | 59 | 22 | 14 | 5 | 1 | 1 | 13 | 2 |

**Braxton Hickman.** Senior first baseman led Texas to College World Series berth, hitting team-high .385.

| | AVG | AB | R | H | 2B | 3B | HR | RBI | SB |
|---|---|---|---|---|---|---|---|---|---|
| Grinstead, Carl, c | .196 | 92 | 15 | 18 | 1 | 0 | 0 | 10 | 0 |

| PITCHING | W | L | ERA | G | Sv | IP | H | BB | SO |
|---|---|---|---|---|---|---|---|---|---|
| Cuper, Marcus | 0 | 0 | 3.00 | 10 | 0 | 9 | 7 | 3 | 7 |
| Hogue, Jay | 8 | 0 | 3.38 | 29 | 3 | 75 | 54 | 43 | 59 |
| Benz, Jake | 9 | 2 | 3.68 | 16 | 0 | 86 | 73 | 42 | 73 |
| Gaiko, Rob | 3 | 0 | 3.88 | 27 | 1 | 46 | 37 | 20 | 48 |
| Wheeler, Earl | 6 | 1 | 4.42 | 15 | 0 | 73 | 78 | 33 | 55 |
| Linfante, Rob | 3 | 4 | 4.70 | 22 | 4 | 38 | 38 | 20 | 51 |
| Dean, Greg | 2 | 2 | 5.67 | 19 | 4 | 27 | 24 | 23 | 31 |
| Bell, Jason | 5 | 2 | 5.68 | 14 | 0 | 52 | 54 | 31 | 39 |
| **Gore, Brad** | 7 | 3 | 5.83 | 15 | 0 | 83 | 85 | 41 | 63 |
| Nichols, Brent | 0 | 0 | 6.08 | 11 | 1 | 13 | 14 | 10 | 14 |
| Kanwisher, Billy | 2 | 3 | 9.34 | 11 | 0 | 36 | 53 | 19 | 29 |

## 7 — TEXAS

**Coach:** Cliff Gustafson  **Record:** 51-16

| BATTING | AVG | AB | R | H | 2B | 3B | HR | RBI | SB |
|---|---|---|---|---|---|---|---|---|---|
| **Hickman, Braxton, 1b** | .385 | 252 | 55 | 97 | 16 | 4 | 9 | 74 | 1 |
| **Kieschnick, Brooks, dh-p** | .374 | 257 | 76 | 96 | 27 | 1 | 19 | 81 | 3 |
| Heinrich, Steve, 2b-3b | .326 | 132 | 41 | 43 | 8 | 4 | 1 | 29 | 7 |
| Williamson, Joel, c | .318 | 151 | 29 | 48 | 11 | 1 | 5 | 33 | 1 |
| Larkin, Stephen, of | .312 | 199 | 42 | 62 | 17 | 5 | 5 | 44 | 1 |
| Vasut, Tony, 2b | .308 | 146 | 48 | 45 | 13 | 2 | 0 | 13 | 6 |
| **Harkrider, Tim, ss** | .299 | 244 | 56 | 73 | 13 | 4 | 4 | 44 | 6 |
| Blessing, Chad, 3b | .291 | 141 | 35 | 41 | 12 | 1 | 0 | 27 | 4 |
| Taylor, Jerry, of | .291 | 141 | 31 | 41 | 7 | 1 | 7 | 37 | 3 |
| **Duke, Darrick, of** | .284 | 88 | 24 | 25 | 6 | 1 | 0 | 15 | 8 |
| Hendry, Marcus, 3b-ss | .243 | 37 | 5 | 9 | 1 | 0 | 1 | 5 | 0 |
| Gardere, Peter, of-dh | .238 | 105 | 28 | 25 | 6 | 0 | 3 | 18 | 3 |
| Conway, Jeff, of | .234 | 94 | 29 | 22 | 6 | 1 | 0 | 16 | 4 |
| Prather, Mark, of | .230 | 113 | 23 | 26 | 1 | 2 | 0 | 16 | 5 |
| Webb, J.P., c | .205 | 44 | 11 | 9 | 1 | 0 | 3 | 18 | 0 |
| Morenz, Shea, of | .143 | 49 | 7 | 7 | 2 | 0 | 2 | 11 | 0 |
| Merrell, Greg, 2b-3b | .143 | 21 | 3 | 3 | 0 | 0 | 0 | 4 | 0 |
| Tipton, Kenny, of | .083 | 12 | 2 | 1 | 1 | 0 | 0 | 2 | 1 |

| PITCHING | W | L | ERA | G | Sv | IP | H | BB | SO |
|---|---|---|---|---|---|---|---|---|---|
| Spurck, Todd | 5 | 0 | 1.96 | 10 | 1 | 37 | 27 | 7 | 17 |
| **Kieschnick, Brooks** | 16 | 4 | 3.25 | 26 | 3 | 150 | 155 | 49 | 126 |
| Senterfitt, Mark | 1 | 0 | 3.57 | 15 | 0 | 35 | 40 | 15 | 26 |
| Smith, Chad | 8 | 2 | 3.98 | 27 | 2 | 54 | 45 | 27 | 48 |
| Lummus, Mark | 3 | 2 | 4.33 | 17 | 0 | 27 | 35 | 10 | 17 |
| Smart, J.D. | 6 | 1 | 4.40 | 23 | 2 | 78 | 74 | 35 | 63 |
| Kjos, Ryan | 3 | 3 | 4.88 | 21 | 2 | 83 | 88 | 44 | 85 |
| Montgomery, Josh | 0 | 0 | 5.40 | 3 | 1 | 7 | 5 | 5 | 9 |
| Hinojosa, Jo Jo | 1 | 0 | 5.59 | 10 | 0 | 10 | 9 | 5 | 9 |
| Cravey, Brian | 1 | 0 | 6.52 | 7 | 0 | 19 | 24 | 12 | 13 |
| **Vaught, Jay** | 7 | 3 | 6.66 | 26 | 2 | 76 | 99 | 33 | 55 |
| **Hillman, Greg** | 1 | 0 | 11.81 | 7 | 0 | 5 | 13 | 9 | 2 |

## 8

## GEORGIA TECH

Coach: Jim Morris — Record: 47-14

| BATTING | AVG | AB | R | H | 2B | 3B | HR | RBI | SB |
|---|---|---|---|---|---|---|---|---|---|
| **Varitek, Jason, c** | .404 | 228 | 78 | 92 | 20 | 2 | 22 | 72 | 5 |
| Payton, Jay, of | .346 | 240 | 61 | 83 | 12 | 12 | 14 | 64 | 23 |
| Ritter, Ryan, of-2b | .330 | 200 | 41 | 66 | 8 | 4 | 6 | 37 | 5 |
| Smith, Michael, of | .318 | 223 | 51 | 71 | 5 | 3 | 3 | 28 | 24 |
| Newhan, David, 1b | .303 | 178 | 54 | 54 | 13 | 2 | 9 | 44 | 4 |
| Hensley, Brandon, 3b-1b | .303 | 221 | 35 | 67 | 11 | 1 | 4 | 37 | 2 |
| Garciaparra, Nomar, ss | .297 | 172 | 39 | 51 | 14 | 1 | 4 | 42 | 8 |
| Barr, Matt, dh-of | .284 | 74 | 9 | 21 | 4 | 1 | 2 | 16 | 0 |
| Buffington, Mark, of | .275 | 131 | 25 | 36 | 4 | 1 | 0 | 14 | 3 |
| McIntyre, Scott, 2b | .268 | 198 | 36 | 53 | 6 | 1 | 2 | 17 | 10 |
| Byers, Scott, 1b | .261 | 69 | 8 | 18 | 8 | 0 | 1 | 11 | 0 |
| Sorrow, Michael, 3b-ss | .258 | 120 | 21 | 31 | 7 | 1 | 3 | 22 | 3 |
| Bearden, Blake, of | .136 | 22 | 2 | 3 | 0 | 0 | 1 | 3 | 0 |
| Lucas, Tim, ss | .045 | 22 | 0 | 1 | 0 | 0 | 0 | 1 | 0 |

| PITCHING | W | L | ERA | G | Sv | IP | H | BB | SO |
|---|---|---|---|---|---|---|---|---|---|
| Myers, Chris | 4 | 0 | 1.90 | 39 | 2 | 81 | 73 | 15 | 70 |
| Hall, Buck | 8 | 2 | 2.42 | 12 | 0 | 67 | 46 | 27 | 83 |
| Rigby, Brad | 13 | 1 | 2.46 | 17 | 0 | 99 | 57 | 56 | 132 |
| **Binkley, Brett** | 3 | 3 | 2.48 | 39 | 14 | 58 | 47 | 19 | 69 |
| Gogolin, Al | 8 | 1 | 2.75 | 16 | 0 | 88 | 69 | 31 | 77 |
| Martin, Mike | 2 | 0 | 4.15 | 15 | 0 | 30 | 23 | 10 | 39 |
| Cason, Carlos | 0 | 0 | 4.15 | 11 | 0 | 17 | 13 | 7 | 10 |
| Albert, David | 9 | 7 | 5.19 | 17 | 0 | 95 | 106 | 24 | 67 |
| Somoza, Andy | 0 | 0 | 12.60 | 5 | 0 | 5 | 11 | 2 | 0 |

## 9

## ARIZONA

Coach: Jerry Kindall — Record: 35-26

| BATTING | AVG | AB | R | H | 2B | 3B | HR | RBI | SB |
|---|---|---|---|---|---|---|---|---|---|
| Lemons, Richard, dh | .403 | 129 | 33 | 52 | 10 | 3 | 8 | 39 | 2 |
| Moen, Robbie, of | .388 | 263 | 66 | 102 | 21 | 0 | 10 | 66 | 8 |
| **Morales, Willie, c** | .356 | 247 | 65 | 88 | 26 | 1 | 13 | 62 | 1 |
| Wells, Greg, of | .356 | 59 | 13 | 21 | 5 | 2 | 1 | 13 | 0 |
| **Thompson, Jason, dh-1b** | .353 | 255 | 68 | 90 | 15 | 4 | 20 | 74 | 3 |
| Tejcek, John, of | .350 | 260 | 85 | 91 | 14 | 11 | 8 | 60 | 12 |
| **Landry, Todd, 1b** | .348 | 253 | 55 | 88 | 18 | 2 | 17 | 70 | 4 |
| Arias, George, 3b | .345 | 255 | 70 | 88 | 14 | 1 | 23 | 75 | 1 |
| Gump, Chris, 2b | .329 | 228 | 56 | 75 | 20 | 5 | 4 | 22 | 12 |
| **Motte, James, ss** | .312 | 154 | 36 | 48 | 6 | 3 | 9 | 39 | 1 |
| Frisbee, Rob, c | .300 | 10 | 3 | 3 | 0 | 0 | 0 | 0 | 0 |
| Peruzzaro, Dave, of | .300 | 20 | 5 | 6 | 1 | 0 | 0 | 1 | 1 |
| Bouie, Tony, ss | .259 | 58 | 13 | 15 | 2 | 1 | 0 | 7 | 5 |
| Wickey, Menno, of | .250 | 36 | 6 | 9 | 3 | 0 | 2 | 9 | 0 |
| Oelschlager, Ron, of | .135 | 52 | 7 | 7 | 2 | 1 | 0 | 3 | 1 |

| PITCHING | W | L | ERA | G | Sv | IP | H | BB | SO |
|---|---|---|---|---|---|---|---|---|---|
| Schiefelbein, Mike | 0 | 0 | 3.60 | 1 | 0 | 5 | 1 | 5 | 1 |
| **Landry, Todd** | 1 | 1 | 4.50 | 6 | 0 | 8 | 7 | 8 | 4 |
| Brown, Tod | 6 | 7 | 4.90 | 35 | 8 | 79 | 87 | 38 | 42 |
| White, Ben | 1 | 1 | 5.28 | 21 | 2 | 46 | 64 | 22 | 18 |
| Pringle, Zachary | 3 | 1 | 5.62 | 11 | 0 | 42 | 49 | 22 | 21 |
| Frace, Ryan | 5 | 3 | 5.78 | 19 | 1 | 81 | 102 | 36 | 48 |
| **Schweitzer, Tim** | 1 | 1 | 6.52 | 3 | 0 | 10 | 11 | 2 | 7 |
| Kishita, Kirt | 3 | 2 | 6.54 | 18 | 0 | 52 | 69 | 32 | 25 |
| Arffa, Steve | 6 | 2 | 7.00 | 17 | 0 | 71 | 91 | 48 | 40 |
| Singelyn, Todd | 5 | 3 | 7.06 | 19 | 1 | 73 | 106 | 33 | 35 |
| **Ippolito, Rob** | 3 | 3 | 7.74 | 13 | 0 | 55 | 79 | 31 | 37 |
| Grajeda, Billy | 1 | 0 | 11.14 | 16 | 1 | 21 | 36 | 7 | 10 |

## 10

## KANSAS

Coach: Dave Bingham — Record: 45-18

| BATTING | AVG | AB | R | H | 2B | 3B | HR | RBI | SB |
|---|---|---|---|---|---|---|---|---|---|
| Benninghoff, Joel, of-dh | .389 | 72 | 27 | 28 | 3 | 3 | 11 | 34 | 0 |
| **Niemeier, Jeff, c** | .378 | 230 | 56 | 87 | 22 | 2 | 10 | 63 | 5 |
| Igou, Josh, of | .345 | 203 | 46 | 70 | 21 | 1 | 7 | 54 | 7 |
| **Berblinger, Jeff, 2b** | .339 | 227 | 66 | 77 | 20 | 3 | 9 | 52 | 33 |
| **Monroe, Darryl, of** | .330 | 212 | 43 | 70 | 16 | 5 | 3 | 39 | 23 |
| Wuycheck, John, 1b | .328 | 244 | 61 | 80 | 19 | 9 | 5 | 56 | 8 |
| Wilmot, Jack, c | .305 | 59 | 15 | 18 | 2 | 1 | 2 | 12 | 1 |
| Wilhelm, Brent, 3b | .304 | 191 | 53 | 58 | 14 | 4 | 5 | 39 | 6 |
| King, Alex, of | .286 | 56 | 12 | 16 | 2 | 0 | 0 | 10 | 0 |
| Tarquinio, Rory, of | .279 | 208 | 48 | 58 | 14 | 1 | 5 | 45 | 5 |
| Stickelman, Torrey, of | .273 | 44 | 10 | 12 | 1 | 0 | 0 | 8 | 1 |
| Soult, David, ss-3b-p | .269 | 78 | 13 | 21 | 1 | 3 | 1 | 13 | 0 |
| Mahon, Kent, c-dh | .267 | 90 | 13 | 24 | 5 | 1 | 0 | 13 | 1 |
| Turney, Brian, 2b | .266 | 64 | 17 | 17 | 2 | 0 | 1 | 8 | 1 |
| Rude, Dan, ss-p | .253 | 217 | 50 | 55 | 11 | 5 | 4 | 41 | 13 |

**Jason Varitek.** All-America catcher led Georgia Tech to No. 8 ranking, hitting .404 with 22 home runs.

DAVID L. GREENE

| PITCHING | W | L | ERA | G | Sv | IP | H | BB | SO |
|---|---|---|---|---|---|---|---|---|---|
| **Walker, Jimmy** | 9 | 2 | 2.39 | 33 | 11 | 98 | 89 | 27 | 104 |
| Tittrington, Scott | 0 | 0 | 2.61 | 15 | 0 | 21 | 17 | 13 | 15 |
| Baird, Clay | 1 | 0 | 2.63 | 10 | 0 | 24 | 16 | 15 | 20 |
| Rude, Dan | 2 | 1 | 3.46 | 12 | 2 | 26 | 21 | 17 | 36 |
| Splittorff, Jamie | 7 | 2 | 3.61 | 18 | 0 | 85 | 76 | 41 | 71 |
| **Corn, Chris** | 9 | 4 | 3.66 | 19 | 0 | 98 | 82 | 58 | 92 |
| Soult, David | 7 | 3 | 4.79 | 16 | 0 | 73 | 91 | 21 | 39 |
| **Meyer, David** | 3 | 1 | 5.32 | 15 | 0 | 44 | 48 | 27 | 35 |
| Stewart, Tom | 6 | 4 | 5.93 | 16 | 0 | 68 | 92 | 25 | 40 |
| Greene, Mike | 1 | 1 | 8.66 | 13 | 0 | 18 | 14 | 22 | 18 |

## NORTH CAROLINA STATE

Coach: Ray Tanner — Record: 49-17

| BATTING | AVG | AB | R | H | 2B | 3B | HR | RBI | SB |
|---|---|---|---|---|---|---|---|---|---|
| Clougherty, Pat, of | .368 | 239 | 55 | 88 | 16 | 1 | 21 | 80 | 8 |
| Giannamore, Gregg, dh | .364 | 11 | 2 | 4 | 1 | 0 | 0 | 3 | 0 |
| Tracey, Tim, 3b | .357 | 238 | 57 | 85 | 13 | 3 | 8 | 47 | 6 |
| Barkett, Andy, 1b | .343 | 207 | 50 | 71 | 16 | 3 | 8 | 49 | 4 |
| Shaw, Aubrey, dh | .326 | 92 | 19 | 30 | 7 | 1 | 3 | 21 | 3 |
| **Almond, Greg, c** | .315 | 162 | 29 | 51 | 12 | 0 | 5 | 31 | 2 |
| Bark, Robbie, of | .315 | 213 | 47 | 67 | 16 | 3 | 2 | 33 | 5 |
| Schiff, Todd, rhp-3b | .308 | 13 | 3 | 4 | 1 | 0 | 1 | 2 | 0 |
| Ferby, Ryan, of | .300 | 150 | 25 | 45 | 8 | 1 | 1 | 17 | 6 |
| Meszar, Jeff, 2b | .294 | 221 | 46 | 65 | 4 | 4 | 0 | 24 | 19 |
| Ross, Kevin, of | .283 | 145 | 34 | 41 | 4 | 1 | 2 | 21 | 5 |
| Lasater, Robbie, c | .275 | 109 | 17 | 30 | 7 | 0 | 6 | 20 | 3 |
| Carswell, Karl, of | .267 | 191 | 36 | 51 | 3 | 2 | 3 | 26 | 13 |
| Barbee, Bobby, 1b | .250 | 16 | 1 | 4 | 1 | 0 | 0 | 2 | 0 |
| Lawler, Scott, dh | .211 | 19 | 5 | 4 | 0 | 1 | 0 | 4 | 0 |
| Edens, Larry, of | .208 | 72 | 10 | 15 | 4 | 1 | 1 | 8 | 4 |
| Watkinson, Jeff, ss | .185 | 65 | 9 | 12 | 1 | 1 | 0 | 5 | 1 |
| Bryan, Kip, of | .133 | 30 | 7 | 4 | 0 | 0 | 0 | 1 | 1 |

| PITCHING | W | L | ERA | G | Sv | IP | H | BB | SO |
|---|---|---|---|---|---|---|---|---|---|
| Lucas, Jason | 0 | 0 | 1.83 | 12 | 1 | 20 | 18 | 8 | 25 |
| Flowers, Ryan | 2 | 0 | 2.49 | 13 | 0 | 22 | 19 | 14 | 21 |
| **Senior, Shawn** | 10 | 5 | 2.73 | 18 | 0 | 102 | 71 | 58 | 120 |
| **Steinert, Rob** | 6 | 3 | 2.87 | 16 | 0 | 88 | 76 | 24 | 85 |
| Harvey, Terry | 10 | 3 | 3.26 | 15 | 0 | 108 | 100 | 31 | 82 |
| Schiff, Todd | 3 | 2 | 3.41 | 10 | 0 | 29 | 18 | 13 | 29 |
| Sports, Tommy | 6 | 2 | 3.76 | 14 | 0 | 77 | 73 | 27 | 49 |

| | W | L | ERA | G | Sv | IP | H | BB | SO |
|---|---|---|---|---|---|---|---|---|---|
| Winkler, Rob | 4 | 2 | 3.92 | 17 | 1 | 44 | 32 | 24 | 38 |
| Raabusch, Mike | 1 | 0 | 4.05 | 10 | 0 | 13 | 15 | 4 | 13 |
| Allen, David | 1 | 0 | 4.15 | 23 | 12 | 30 | 21 | 16 | 41 |
| Bogle, Mark | 4 | 0 | 6.75 | 15 | 0 | 20 | 20 | 14 | 22 |
| McLamb, Chad | 2 | 0 | 7.11 | 13 | 0 | 19 | 19 | 11 | 25 |

## 12 PEPPERDINE

**Coach:** Andy Lopez  **Record:** 41-17

| BATTING | AVG | AB | R | H | 2B | 3B | HR | RBI | SB |
|---|---|---|---|---|---|---|---|---|---|
| Sacchi, John, 1b | .369 | 84 | 19 | 31 | 8 | 1 | 2 | 18 | 2 |
| **Ekdahl, Eric, ss** | .324 | 207 | 42 | 67 | 10 | 2 | 3 | 34 | 16 |
| Dell'Amico, Keven, of | .313 | 179 | 30 | 56 | 8 | 3 | 2 | 31 | 11 |
| **Wasikowski, Mark, 3b** | .313 | 224 | 37 | 70 | 12 | 0 | 6 | 38 | 4 |
| Paz, Jorge, dh-of | .309 | 110 | 23 | 34 | 6 | 1 | 3 | 16 | 3 |
| **Radmanovich, Ryan, of** | .305 | 167 | 41 | 51 | 5 | 3 | 13 | 41 | 17 |
| Lovell, David, 2b | .301 | 193 | 30 | 58 | 14 | 2 | 1 | 26 | 12 |
| **Vollmer, Scott, c** | .295 | 200 | 45 | 59 | 10 | 1 | 8 | 33 | 3 |
| Milton, Chris, inf | .278 | 36 | 10 | 10 | 2 | 0 | 0 | 1 | 2 |
| O'Hara, Pat, dh | .262 | 103 | 20 | 27 | 8 | 0 | 3 | 20 | 0 |
| Martinez, Erik, of | .258 | 62 | 15 | 16 | 5 | 0 | 1 | 11 | 3 |
| McElreath, Matt, of | .251 | 175 | 37 | 44 | 9 | 2 | 11 | 39 | 8 |
| **Welles, Robby, 1b** | .243 | 111 | 18 | 27 | 7 | 0 | 5 | 17 | 3 |
| Christenson, Ryan, of | .217 | 23 | 8 | 5 | 1 | 0 | 2 | 6 | 0 |
| Gamboa, Ruben, 1b | .129 | 31 | 4 | 4 | 0 | 0 | 0 | 3 | 1 |

| PITCHING | W | L | ERA | G | Sv | IP | H | BB | SO |
|---|---|---|---|---|---|---|---|---|---|
| **Duda, Steve** | 12 | 3 | 1.64 | 18 | 0 | 137 | 108 | 20 | 114 |
| **Housley, Adam** | 4 | 4 | 1.93 | 31 | 4 | 47 | 32 | 18 | 48 |
| Schulz, Josh | 4 | 0 | 2.10 | 17 | 0 | 34 | 31 | 11 | 25 |
| Gregory, Greg | 7 | 3 | 2.65 | 15 | 0 | 76 | 71 | 25 | 47 |
| LeBlanc, Jason | 7 | 4 | 2.63 | 15 | 0 | 86 | 77 | 20 | 55 |
| **Estavil, Mauricio** | 5 | 0 | 2.64 | 26 | 5 | 44 | 47 | 16 | 55 |
| Nichols, Chad | 2 | 0 | 3.45 | 18 | 0 | 31 | 30 | 13 | 29 |
| Brubaker, Eric | 0 | 0 | 5.81 | 4 | 0 | 9 | 9 | 6 | 7 |
| Gibbons, Jeff | 0 | 1 | 6.73 | 7 | 0 | 15 | 26 | 4 | 10 |
| Kennedy, Shawn | 0 | 2 | 7.00 | 5 | 0 | 9 | 14 | 6 | 2 |

## 13 CAL STATE FULLERTON

**Coach:** Augie Garrido  **Record:** 35-19

| BATTING | AVG | AB | R | H | 2B | 3B | HR | RBI | SB |
|---|---|---|---|---|---|---|---|---|---|
| Millan, Adam, dh-c | .354 | 212 | 43 | 75 | 18 | 1 | 7 | 57 | 0 |
| **Carr, Jeremy, 2b** | .351 | 228 | 58 | 80 | 7 | 1 | 3 | 27 | 41 |
| Powell, Dante, of | .335 | 233 | 60 | 78 | 17 | 3 | 12 | 57 | 42 |
| Allen, Scott, of | .333 | 18 | 10 | 6 | 0 | 0 | 0 | 3 | 1 |
| Ferguson, Jeff, 3b | .318 | 192 | 49 | 61 | 14 | 1 | 2 | 36 | 13 |
| Evans, Kyle, of | .317 | 63 | 16 | 20 | 4 | 0 | 3 | 17 | 0 |
| Betzsold, Jim, of-dh | .310 | 184 | 39 | 57 | 16 | 0 | 8 | 33 | 7 |
| **Rodriquez, Nate, ss** | .280 | 200 | 26 | 56 | 4 | 1 | 1 | 28 | 4 |
| **Banks, Tony, of** | .268 | 194 | 52 | 52 | 14 | 3 | 14 | 49 | 3 |
| Olsen, D.C., ss | .268 | 183 | 28 | 49 | 11 | 0 | 7 | 35 | 0 |
| **Hemphill, Bret, c** | .268 | 157 | 29 | 42 | 15 | 1 | 4 | 29 | 1 |
| Skyberg, Craig, 3b | .200 | 15 | 3 | 3 | 0 | 1 | 0 | 2 | 1 |

| PITCHING | W | L | ERA | G | Sv | IP | H | BB | SO |
|---|---|---|---|---|---|---|---|---|---|
| Rolish, Chad | | 2 | 0 | 2.74 | 28 | 0 | 46 | 39 | 17 | 45 |
| Ricabal, Dan | 11 | 3 | 3.48 | 20 | 0 | 127 | 101 | 58 | 106 |
| Silva, Ted | 4 | 2 | 3.79 | 32 | 7 | 57 | 43 | 17 | 60 |
| Parisi, Mike | 10 | 3 | 4.71 | 18 | 0 | 109 | 115 | 41 | 63 |
| Hollibaugh, Kimson | 3 | 5 | 5.40 | 27 | 1 | 53 | 52 | 19 | 36 |
| Holiday, Mark | 1 | 0 | 5.79 | 11 | 1 | 14 | 21 | 3 | 13 |
| Fahs, Derek | 3 | 3 | 6.17 | 15 | 0 | 54 | 81 | 15 | 41 |
| Ward, Jon | 1 | 3 | 7.31 | 11 | 0 | 32 | 36 | 28 | 21 |

## 14 FRESNO STATE

**Coach:** Bob Bennett  **Record:** 41-22

| BATTING | AVG | AB | R | H | 2B | 3B | HR | RBI | SB |
|---|---|---|---|---|---|---|---|---|---|
| Thrasher, Bill, of | .364 | 206 | 52 | 75 | 21 | 2 | 3 | 35 | 8 |
| **Johnson, Todd, c** | .357 | 258 | 47 | 92 | 10 | 4 | 3 | 46 | 8 |
| Roe, Mike, 1b | .345 | 194 | 49 | 67 | 16 | 2 | 6 | 39 | 1 |
| Dandridge, Brad, of | .339 | 274 | 63 | 93 | 15 | 3 | 14 | 59 | 7 |
| McNamara, Gary, of | .338 | 237 | 54 | 80 | 14 | 3 | 10 | 56 | 0 |
| Renteria, Javier, 1b-dh | .337 | 92 | 12 | 31 | 8 | 0 | 1 | 23 | 0 |
| Vigil, Scott, c | .333 | 15 | 4 | 5 | 2 | 0 | 0 | 3 | 0 |
| Greene, Eric, 2b | .291 | 182 | 42 | 53 | 10 | 3 | 5 | 33 | 5 |
| Fjelstad, Kyle, dh | .284 | 116 | 31 | 33 | 4 | 6 | 6 | 27 | 0 |
| Minor, Tommy, 3b-p | .270 | 137 | 13 | 37 | 5 | 0 | 1 | 19 | 2 |
| Reynoso, Ben, ss | .254 | 205 | 35 | 52 | 5 | 1 | 1 | 18 | 6 |
| Curtis, Matt, 3b | .254 | 71 | 13 | 18 | 2 | 1 | 2 | 14 | 0 |
| Judice, Bryan, of | .242 | 91 | 11 | 22 | 5 | 1 | 0 | 12 | 2 |
| Zepeda, Jesse, 2b | .176 | 85 | 9 | 15 | 2 | 1 | 0 | 7 | 3 |

**Steve Duda.** Senior righthander posted 12-3 record and 1.64 ERA for defending College World Series champion Pepperdine.

| | | | | | | | | | |
|---|---|---|---|---|---|---|---|---|---|
| Taglione, Lance, ss | .147 | 34 | 9 | 5 | 1 | 0 | 0 | 4 | 1 |
| Ramos, Sean, dh | .143 | 14 | 2 | 2 | 0 | 0 | 0 | 2 | 0 |

| PITCHING | W | L | ERA | G | Sv | IP | H | BB | SO |
|---|---|---|---|---|---|---|---|---|---|
| Fernandez, Jared | 7 | 3 | 3.54 | 19 | 0 | 81 | 94 | 14 | 57 |
| **Salazar, Mike** | 13 | 3 | 3.60 | 20 | 0 | 147 | 159 | 43 | 131 |
| **Soderstrom, Steve** | 6 | 5 | 3.80 | 19 | 0 | 107 | 100 | 49 | 114 |
| **Cruise, Mark** | 7 | 6 | 3.82 | 16 | 0 | 106 | 115 | 24 | 70 |
| Minor, Tommy | 7 | 1 | 4.92 | 18 | 3 | 64 | 82 | 14 | 60 |
| Gonzalez, Raul | 0 | 1 | 6.75 | 8 | 2 | 11 | 9 | 10 | 13 |
| Mercado, Victor | 1 | 0 | 6.75 | 6 | 0 | 9 | 7 | 6 | 12 |
| Enard, Tony | 0 | 1 | 8.31 | 8 | 0 | 9 | 18 | 8 | 8 |
| Newman, Eric | 0 | 2 | 9.92 | 11 | 1 | 16 | 32 | 11 | 14 |

## 15 FLORIDA STATE

**Coach:** Mike Martin  **Record:** 46-19

| BATTING | AVG | AB | R | H | 2B | 3B | HR | RBI | SB |
|---|---|---|---|---|---|---|---|---|---|
| Reams, Derek, c | .429 | 14 | 2 | 6 | 1 | 0 | 0 | 5 | 0 |
| Hendry, Clint, of | .364 | 22 | 9 | 8 | 1 | 0 | 1 | 7 | 2 |
| Mientkiewicz, Doug, 1b | .327 | 205 | 40 | 67 | 13 | 1 | 4 | 47 | 2 |
| Schroeffel, Scott, of | .309 | 123 | 24 | 38 | 8 | 0 | 0 | 14 | 9 |
| **Schmitz, Mike, dh** | .307 | 192 | 39 | 59 | 8 | 1 | 13 | 43 | 5 |
| Martin, Mike, c-3b | .307 | 212 | 44 | 65 | 12 | 0 | 5 | 43 | 10 |
| Hodges, Randy, of | .295 | 183 | 31 | 54 | 8 | 0 | 3 | 30 | 6 |
| Jordan, Grady, of | .285 | 151 | 41 | 43 | 6 | 2 | 2 | 15 | 26 |
| Weaver, Colby, c | .279 | 61 | 12 | 17 | 4 | 0 | 1 | 10 | 1 |
| Lopez, Mickey, 3b-2b | .273 | 187 | 43 | 51 | 7 | 6 | 1 | 24 | 21 |
| Mueller, Ty, of | .267 | 187 | 29 | 50 | 13 | 0 | 8 | 40 | 9 |
| McCray, Kevin, 1b | .261 | 46 | 13 | 12 | 2 | 1 | 3 | 9 | 1 |
| Marcinczyk, T.R., of | .259 | 54 | 11 | 14 | 4 | 0 | 3 | 15 | 1 |
| Jarrett, Link, ss | .242 | 248 | 38 | 60 | 12 | 0 | 0 | 22 | 4 |
| Niles, Jack, ss | .238 | 63 | 13 | 15 | 2 | 0 | 1 | 13 | 4 |
| Sheffer, Chad, 2b | .213 | 169 | 33 | 36 | 10 | 2 | 2 | 26 | 19 |
| Kanell, Danny, 3b | .182 | 22 | 2 | 4 | 0 | 0 | 1 | 3 | 0 |

| PITCHING | W | L | ERA | G | Sv | IP | H | BB | SO |
|---|---|---|---|---|---|---|---|---|---|
| Johnson, Jonathan | 10 | 1 | 1.68 | 17 | 0 | 107 | 80 | 52 | 124 |
| Nedeau, John | 3 | 3 | 1.88 | 23 | 3 | 43 | 24 | 15 | 35 |
| Wilson, Paul | 11 | 5 | 1.94 | 17 | 0 | 116 | 95 | 32 | 99 |
| Morgan, Steven | 2 | 0 | 2.18 | 9 | 1 | 21 | 21 | 8 | 22 |
| **Wasdin, John** | 10 | 1 | 3.15 | 18 | 0 | 114 | 104 | 34 | 138 |
| Cruz, Charlie | 0 | 1 | 3.27 | 20 | 2 | 22 | 22 | 18 | 28 |
| Tam, Jeff | 0 | 2 | 4.03 | 22 | 1 | 29 | 24 | 16 | 29 |
| **Harris, Bryan** | 6 | 5 | 4.06 | 21 | 0 | 78 | 77 | 40 | 82 |
| Olson, Phil | 4 | 1 | 5.09 | 29 | 4 | 53 | 53 | 37 | 57 |

## 16 NOTRE DAME

**Coach:** Pat Murphy  **Record:** 46-16

| BATTING | AVG | AB | R | H | 2B | 3B | HR | RBI | SB |
|---|---|---|---|---|---|---|---|---|---|
| Hartwell, Edwin, of-dh | .447 | 199 | 72 | 89 | 13 | 1 | 13 | 68 | 11 |
| **Danapilis, Eric, of-p** | .438 | 219 | 71 | 96 | 24 | 0 | 13 | 85 | 13 |
| Mapes, Mark, c | .392 | 51 | 10 | 20 | 3 | 0 | 1 | 15 | 5 |
| Layson, Greg, 2b-ss | .363 | 168 | 60 | 61 | 10 | 5 | 3 | 34 | 15 |
| **Michalak, Chris, of-p** | .353 | 51 | 19 | 18 | 2 | 2 | 0 | 14 | 3 |

| | AVG | AB | R | H | 2B | 3B | HR | RBI | SB |
|---|---|---|---|---|---|---|---|---|---|
| Failla, Paul, ss-3b | .346 | 208 | 55 | 72 | 15 | 3 | 5 | 45 | 8 |
| Haas, Matt, 3b-c | .345 | 197 | 49 | 68 | 10 | 3 | 4 | 61 | 28 |
| DeSensi, Craig, dh-3b | .305 | 164 | 40 | 50 | 6 | 2 | 9 | 43 | 10 |
| Topham, Ryan, of-1b | .302 | 169 | 41 | 51 | 12 | 3 | 6 | 31 | 7 |
| Kent, Robbie, 2b | .291 | 110 | 27 | 32 | 6 | 0 | 2 | 18 | 2 |
| Richards, Rowan, of | .280 | 125 | 27 | 35 | 8 | 0 | 3 | 25 | 10 |
| Lisanti, Bob, c | .237 | 160 | 36 | 38 | 12 | 3 | 1 | 28 | 5 |
| Wrobleski, Korey, dh | .186 | 59 | 8 | 11 | 3 | 0 | 4 | 10 | 1 |
| Birk, Robby, 2b | .184 | 49 | 24 | 9 | 1 | 0 | 0 | 7 | 7 |
| Clevenger, Kasey, of | .000 | 11 | 5 | 0 | 0 | 0 | 0 | 0 | 1 |

| PITCHING | W | L | ERA | G | Sv | IP | H | BB | SO |
|---|---|---|---|---|---|---|---|---|---|
| Jones, A.J. | 3 | 0 | 1.79 | 21 | 3 | 40 | 38 | 13 | 22 |
| **Sinnes, Dave** | 10 | 3 | 2.98 | 15 | 0 | 85 | 63 | 31 | 90 |
| Price, Tom | 12 | 2 | 3.53 | 18 | 1 | 94 | 82 | 19 | 69 |
| **Michalak, Chris** | 11 | 5 | 4.76 | 22 | 3 | 117 | 130 | 48 | 83 |
| Walania, Al | 5 | 3 | 4.92 | 15 | 3 | 75 | 83 | 13 | 73 |
| Degraff, Marty | 4 | 1 | 5.95 | 8 | 0 | 20 | 16 | 11 | 13 |
| Rittgers, Colin | 0 | 0 | 6.43 | 2 | 0 | 7 | 8 | 4 | 4 |
| Adams, Dan | 1 | 0 | 6.52 | 4 | 0 | 10 | 12 | 7 | 4 |
| **Danapilis, Eric** | 0 | 0 | 7.50 | 5 | 0 | 12 | 18 | 4 | 8 |
| Carlson, Garret | 0 | 0 | 8.10 | 3 | 1 | 7 | 6 | 10 | 5 |
| Kraus, Tim | 0 | 2 | 9.48 | 13 | 0 | 31 | 45 | 25 | 19 |
| Allen, Craig | 0 | 0 | 9.64 | 2 | 0 | 5 | 5 | 3 | 2 |

## 17 CLEMSON

**Coach: Bill Wilhelm**    **Record: 45-20**

| BATTING | AVG | AB | R | H | 2B | 3B | HR | RBI | SB |
|---|---|---|---|---|---|---|---|---|---|
| McMillon, Billy, of | .377 | 212 | 64 | 80 | 21 | 1 | 5 | 30 | 11 |
| Monahan, Shane, 1b-of | .372 | 253 | 56 | 94 | 15 | 7 | 9 | 64 | 17 |
| **Williams, Keith, of** | .365 | 255 | 60 | 93 | 18 | 4 | 19 | 79 | 7 |
| Morris, Jeff, 2b | .356 | 239 | 60 | 85 | 12 | 2 | 2 | 32 | 5 |
| **Carter, Chris, c** | .333 | 42 | 9 | 14 | 2 | 0 | 2 | 7 | 2 |
| Monin, Andy, c | .309 | 97 | 21 | 30 | 6 | 1 | 0 | 15 | 0 |
| Melzer, Scott, dh | .304 | 23 | 7 | 7 | 1 | 0 | 0 | 2 | 0 |
| McCleon, Dexter, of | .299 | 107 | 25 | 32 | 4 | 3 | 0 | 16 | 6 |
| **Phillips, Chad, p-dh** | .286 | 42 | 5 | 12 | 3 | 0 | 1 | 5 | 0 |
| Taylor, Joe, ss | .277 | 213 | 43 | 59 | 9 | 4 | 2 | 31 | 9 |
| Satterfield, Shawn, of | .277 | 112 | 16 | 31 | 7 | 1 | 2 | 18 | 2 |
| Mork, Hoby, ss | .276 | 56 | 12 | 16 | 1 | 0 | 1 | 6 | 0 |
| Miller, David, 1b-dh | .271 | 85 | 12 | 23 | 3 | 1 | 0 | 12 | 1 |
| Eydenberg, Mike, c | .265 | 83 | 12 | 22 | 9 | 2 | 0 | 17 | 2 |
| Galloway, Paul, dh-3b | .262 | 42 | 6 | 11 | 6 | 0 | 0 | 10 | 0 |
| Hampton, Mike, dh-1b | .254 | 130 | 29 | 33 | 13 | 2 | 3 | 22 | 3 |
| Miller, Jeff, 3b | .250 | 192 | 29 | 48 | 10 | 1 | 6 | 36 | 1 |
| Brizek, Seth, ss-of | .248 | 105 | 15 | 26 | 3 | 0 | 2 | 16 | 3 |

| PITCHING | W | L | ERA | G | Sv | IP | H | BB | SO |
|---|---|---|---|---|---|---|---|---|---|
| Winchester, Scott | 4 | 1 | 2.61 | 26 | 10 | 48 | 36 | 16 | 42 |
| Sturgeon, Chris | 2 | 0 | 2.63 | 11 | 0 | 24 | 20 | 17 | 13 |
| **Phillips, Chad** | 12 | 2 | 2.96 | 16 | 0 | 91 | 93 | 24 | 69 |
| Taulbee, Mark | 10 | 2 | 3.24 | 30 | 3 | 98 | 96 | 29 | 85 |
| Eggleston, Jamie | 0 | 0 | 3.86 | 8 | 0 | 12 | 13 | 7 | 7 |
| Dawsey, Jason | 5 | 2 | 4.06 | 27 | 1 | 78 | 85 | 21 | 70 |
| Sauve, Jeff | 6 | 5 | 4.76 | 17 | 1 | 85 | 98 | 27 | 43 |
| Williams, Rodney | 0 | 0 | 5.60 | 15 | 0 | 18 | 15 | 10 | 20 |
| Keppen, Jeff | 3 | 4 | 5.65 | 21 | 0 | 43 | 44 | 35 | 33 |
| Holtz, Mike | 3 | 4 | 6.13 | 16 | 0 | 62 | 78 | 27 | 54 |
| Miller, David | 0 | 0 | 7.15 | 6 | 0 | 11 | 15 | 5 | 9 |
| Brizek, Seth | 0 | 0 | 9.00 | 4 | 0 | 5 | 9 | 5 | 4 |

## 18 TENNESSEE

**Coach: Rod Delmonico**    **Record: 45-20**

| BATTING | AVG | AB | R | H | 2B | 3B | HR | RBI | SB |
|---|---|---|---|---|---|---|---|---|---|
| Trammell, Bubba, of | .383 | 193 | 45 | 74 | 19 | 1 | 12 | 52 | 5 |
| McDowell, Seth, of | .353 | 17 | 1 | 6 | 0 | 0 | 1 | 6 | 1 |
| Helton, Todd, 1b-p | .348 | 247 | 48 | 86 | 22 | 3 | 11 | 66 | 6 |
| Vance, David, of | .299 | 174 | 39 | 52 | 11 | 1 | 6 | 33 | 11 |
| Priest, Adam, of | .293 | 41 | 11 | 12 | 0 | 2 | 2 | 10 | 3 |
| Wyman, Richie, of | .292 | 226 | 50 | 66 | 6 | 4 | 5 | 38 | 13 |
| Carr, Fred, 2b | .289 | 159 | 39 | 46 | 5 | 2 | 0 | 19 | 4 |
| **Foster, Jeff, 3b** | .281 | 228 | 52 | 64 | 17 | 3 | 10 | 43 | 21 |
| Northeimer, James, c | .280 | 211 | 40 | 59 | 20 | 1 | 2 | 30 | 7 |
| Parker, Allen, ss | .279 | 233 | 41 | 65 | 11 | 2 | 1 | 33 | 19 |
| Sanmiguel, Alex, dh-2b | .245 | 163 | 33 | 40 | 8 | 0 | 1 | 15 | 21 |
| Curry, Rob, dh | .228 | 101 | 20 | 23 | 4 | 1 | 1 | 17 | 5 |
| Pantages, Jason, 1b | .194 | 62 | 16 | 12 | 1 | 0 | 0 | 4 | 4 |
| Lewis, Ed, 1b-3b | .153 | 59 | 6 | 9 | 1 | 0 | 0 | 7 | 1 |

| PITCHING | W | L | ERA | G | Sv | IP | H | BB | SO |
|---|---|---|---|---|---|---|---|---|---|
| Sayle, Harry | 0 | 2 | 3.10 | 11 | 1 | 20 | 20 | 17 | 9 |
| Meyers, Ryan | 5 | 4 | 3.50 | 14 | 1 | 72 | 63 | 27 | 51 |
| Freeman, Chris | 12 | 2 | 3.51 | 18 | 0 | 118 | 94 | 51 | 94 |

**Casey Burrill.** USC catcher closed out his college career, hitting .408 with 13 homers for the Trojans.

SIMON GRIFFITHS

| | W | L | ERA | G | Sv | IP | H | BB | SO |
|---|---|---|---|---|---|---|---|---|---|
| Harvell, Pete | 6 | 2 | 3.52 | 20 | 3 | 54 | 36 | 42 | 38 |
| Woods, Barry | 1 | 1 | 3.54 | 22 | 4 | 28 | 17 | 24 | 29 |
| Helton, Todd | 6 | 3 | 3.92 | 14 | 0 | 67 | 68 | 19 | 47 |
| Heflin, Bronson | 8 | 4 | 4.17 | 18 | 1 | 104 | 90 | 46 | 87 |
| Rosenbaum, Geoff | 0 | 0 | 5.40 | 5 | 0 | 8 | 9 | 1 | 8 |
| Carruth, Jason | 3 | 1 | 5.93 | 11 | 0 | 41 | 53 | 24 | 33 |
| Miller, Brandon | 4 | 1 | 7.32 | 13 | 0 | 36 | 46 | 16 | 30 |

## 19 SOUTHERN CALIFORNIA

**Coach: Mike Gillespie**    **Record: 35-29**

| BATTING | AVG | AB | R | H | 2B | 3B | HR | RBI | SB |
|---|---|---|---|---|---|---|---|---|---|
| **Burrill, Casey, c** | .408 | 238 | 54 | 97 | 18 | 1 | 13 | 52 | 6 |
| Mancuso, Mike, c | .333 | 18 | 4 | 6 | 1 | 0 | 0 | 2 | 0 |
| Alvarez, Gabe, ss | .326 | 258 | 46 | 84 | 26 | 0 | 8 | 53 | 1 |
| Jenkins, Geoff, of | .323 | 198 | 41 | 64 | 15 | 3 | 7 | 50 | 8 |
| Roberge, J.P., of-1b | .320 | 259 | 55 | 83 | 12 | 2 | 11 | 40 | 14 |
| Nieto, Tony, p-c | .313 | 32 | 9 | 10 | 4 | 0 | 1 | 9 | 1 |
| Gardocki, Ray, dh-1b | .311 | 61 | 6 | 19 | 3 | 0 | 1 | 9 | 1 |
| Donnelly, Kent, dh-1b | .308 | 26 | 0 | 8 | 0 | 0 | 0 | 2 | 0 |
| Malani, Shon, dh-of | .296 | 213 | 38 | 63 | 13 | 1 | 2 | 20 | 11 |
| Hastings, Lionel, 2b | .294 | 201 | 34 | 59 | 16 | 1 | 5 | 35 | 4 |
| Dawkins, Walter, of | .291 | 199 | 45 | 58 | 12 | 3 | 3 | 22 | 7 |
| Boone, Aaron, 3b | .286 | 220 | 43 | 63 | 19 | 4 | 5 | 39 | 8 |
| Salmon, Mike, of | .280 | 50 | 4 | 14 | 0 | 0 | 0 | 7 | 1 |
| **Bierek, Kurt, 1b** | .272 | 195 | 42 | 53 | 16 | 1 | 12 | 49 | 4 |
| Tsukashima, Darin, 3b | .235 | 51 | 11 | 12 | 0 | 0 | 0 | 4 | 5 |
| **Collett, Mike, p-dh** | .217 | 23 | 2 | 5 | 1 | 0 | 1 | 3 | 0 |

| PITCHING | W | L | ERA | G | Sv | IP | H | BB | SO |
|---|---|---|---|---|---|---|---|---|---|
| **Hubbs, Dan** | 5 | 5 | 2.96 | 33 | 18 | 76 | 67 | 24 | 90 |
| Nieto, Tony | 8 | 5 | 3.52 | 21 | 0 | 100 | 106 | 48 | 40 |
| **Collett, Mike** | 9 | 4 | 4.18 | 17 | 0 | 90 | 103 | 29 | 56 |
| Parle, Justin | 3 | 0 | 4.57 | 25 | 0 | 41 | 44 | 13 | 20 |
| Tucker, Ben | 2 | 7 | 5.37 | 16 | 0 | 59 | 63 | 39 | 23 |
| Epstein, Ian | 0 | 1 | 5.47 | 19 | 0 | 25 | 28 | 12 | 15 |
| Vermillion, Grant | 3 | 2 | 5.67 | 25 | 0 | 54 | 68 | 32 | 35 |
| Burchit, Jimmy | 2 | 3 | 6.11 | 28 | 0 | 53 | 51 | 53 | 44 |
| Casillas, German | 3 | 2 | 6.62 | 25 | 0 | 52 | 64 | 43 | 41 |
| Garner, Jason | 0 | 0 | 7.71 | 11 | 0 | 14 | 22 | 5 | 6 |

## 20 UCLA

**Coach: Gary Adams**    **Record: 37-23**

| BATTING | AVG | AB | R | H | 2B | 3B | HR | RBI | SB |
|---|---|---|---|---|---|---|---|---|---|
| **McGuire, Ryan, 1b** | .376 | 221 | 71 | 83 | 11 | 0 | 26 | 91 | 14 |
| Lohman, Chris, of | .358 | 120 | 18 | 43 | 8 | 0 | 7 | 32 | 1 |
| **Melhuse, Adam, 3b** | .344 | 250 | 64 | 86 | 19 | 2 | 10 | 50 | 5 |
| Myrow, John, of | .325 | 249 | 50 | 81 | 12 | 7 | 5 | 40 | 11 |
| Ravitz, David, 2b | .324 | 225 | 45 | 73 | 19 | 0 | 6 | 32 | 2 |
| **Boyd, Travis, ss** | .316 | 19 | 3 | 6 | 1 | 0 | 1 | 5 | 0 |
| Mitchell, Mike, dh | .314 | 207 | 34 | 65 | 15 | 0 | 12 | 53 | 0 |
| Dieter, Dave, c | .302 | 43 | 7 | 13 | 1 | 0 | 1 | 8 | 0 |
| **Roberts, David, of** | .296 | 247 | 65 | 73 | 12 | 0 | 3 | 28 | 28 |
| Schafer, Brett, of-1b | .264 | 129 | 31 | 34 | 4 | 1 | 2 | 16 | 12 |
| Carrasco, Tony, 2b | .227 | 22 | 3 | 5 | 0 | 1 | 0 | 3 | 4 |
| Vallone, Gar, ss | .224 | 192 | 34 | 43 | 9 | 1 | 1 | 29 | 2 |
| **Schwenke, Matt, c** | .223 | 184 | 26 | 41 | 9 | 0 | 2 | 32 | 1 |
| **Kubinski, Tim, p** | .167 | 12 | 2 | 2 | 0 | 0 | 0 | 0 | 0 |
| Ammirato, Zak, 3b | .100 | 20 | 3 | 2 | 1 | 0 | 0 | 2 | 1 |

| PITCHING | W | L | ERA | G | Sv | IP | H | BB | SO |
|---|---|---|---|---|---|---|---|---|---|
| McGuire, Ryan | 3 | 0 | 1.73 | 13 | 2 | 26 | 15 | 12 | 29 |
| Sollecito, Gabe | 4 | 3 | 3.94 | 24 | 9 | 62 | 59 | 25 | 34 |
| Kubinski, Tim | 11 | 3 | 4.03 | 17 | 0 | 125 | 126 | 35 | 86 |
| Kramer, Dan | 4 | 1 | 4.47 | 25 | 0 | 48 | 56 | 16 | 30 |
| Howatt, Jeffrey | 0 | 0 | 5.66 | 13 | 1 | 21 | 25 | 8 | 14 |
| Van Zandt, Jon | 7 | 7 | 5.70 | 20 | 1 | 114 | 128 | 40 | 70 |
| Adcock, Gary | 3 | 4 | 5.75 | 16 | 1 | 67 | 71 | 50 | 40 |
| Caravelli, Michael | 0 | 1 | 6.23 | 3 | 0 | 9 | 16 | 4 | 5 |
| Mitchell, John | 1 | 3 | 6.49 | 25 | 0 | 43 | 45 | 24 | 25 |
| Schwengel, Kris | 1 | 1 | 9.72 | 5 | 0 | 8 | 13 | 2 | 5 |
| Ellis, John | 0 | 0 | 9.82 | 8 | 0 | 11 | 12 | 9 | 13 |
| Heinemann, Rick | 2 | 0 | 19.06 | 6 | 0 | 6 | 14 | 8 | 4 |

## 21 NORTH CAROLINA
Coach: Mike Roberts  Record: 43-20

| BATTING | AVG | AB | R | H | 2B | 3B | HR | RBI | SB |
|---|---|---|---|---|---|---|---|---|---|
| Holbrook, Chad, of | .353 | 249 | 56 | 88 | 11 | 7 | 2 | 28 | 40 |
| DaSilva, Manny, of-1b | .339 | 224 | 45 | 76 | 12 | 3 | 15 | 66 | 10 |
| Boone, David, of-1c | .328 | 177 | 29 | 58 | 10 | 1 | 0 | 16 | 8 |
| Madonna, Chris, c | .292 | 185 | 43 | 54 | 17 | 2 | 10 | 47 | 7 |
| Cox, Chris, 3b | .288 | 215 | 47 | 62 | 10 | 0 | 17 | 57 | 6 |
| Jones, Mitch, 2b | .285 | 200 | 31 | 57 | 5 | 0 | 0 | 20 | 9 |
| Massey, Cookie, dh | .283 | 223 | 44 | 63 | 12 | 0 | 18 | 50 | 5 |
| Schaefer, Kip, of | .280 | 93 | 6 | 26 | 7 | 0 | 0 | 10 | 4 |
| Grunewald, Keith, ss | .267 | 232 | 41 | 62 | 8 | 0 | 2 | 26 | 20 |
| McIver, Robby, 2b | .250 | 36 | 6 | 9 | 1 | 1 | 0 | 7 | 3 |
| Hamrick, Chris, dh-of | .250 | 12 | 6 | 3 | 1 | 0 | 0 | 2 | 2 |
| Coltrane, Crandel, 1b | .242 | 124 | 15 | 30 | 3 | 0 | 4 | 21 | 0 |
| Hoch, Casey, 1b-3b | .233 | 90 | 16 | 21 | 7 | 0 | 1 | 9 | 5 |
| Merritt, Doug, of | .122 | 41 | 9 | 5 | 1 | 0 | 1 | 7 | 1 |

| PITCHING | W | L | ERA | G | Sv | IP | H | BB | SO |
|---|---|---|---|---|---|---|---|---|---|
| Wissel, Scott | 4 | 1 | 2.60 | 25 | 3 | 45 | 47 | 13 | 46 |
| Chrismon, Thad | 5 | 3 | 2.93 | 38 | 18 | 89 | 66 | 25 | 95 |
| Manning, Derek | 11 | 5 | 3.06 | 17 | 0 | 118 | 104 | 33 | 105 |
| Jerzembeck, Mike | 9 | 3 | 3.15 | 17 | 0 | 94 | 87 | 44 | 99 |
| Willman, Brian | 2 | 2 | 3.86 | 13 | 0 | 28 | 31 | 7 | 27 |
| Miller, David | 2 | 1 | 4.61 | 12 | 0 | 53 | 61 | 20 | 33 |
| Maney, Frank | 5 | 4 | 4.72 | 17 | 2 | 69 | 77 | 25 | 67 |
| MacMillan, Jay | 1 | 1 | 4.82 | 11 | 0 | 9 | 11 | 10 | 4 |
| Johnson, Jay | 2 | 0 | 7.66 | 11 | 0 | 22 | 32 | 10 | 14 |
| Potter, Josh | 2 | 0 | 8.24 | 10 | 0 | 20 | 29 | 9 | 6 |

## 22 OHIO STATE
Coach: Bob Todd  Record: 44-19

| BATTING | AVG | AB | R | H | 2B | 3B | HR | RBI | SB |
|---|---|---|---|---|---|---|---|---|---|
| Robinson, Joe, of | .500 | 10 | 4 | 5 | 0 | 0 | 0 | 2 | 1 |
| Meyer, Travis, 3b | .357 | 42 | 5 | 15 | 1 | 1 | 1 | 11 | 2 |
| Young, Brad, 2b | .355 | 121 | 25 | 43 | 9 | 2 | 1 | 16 | 8 |
| Chonko, Mark, dh | .350 | 80 | 15 | 28 | 6 | 0 | 6 | 22 | 4 |
| Repasky, Mike, of | .342 | 187 | 40 | 64 | 13 | 1 | 8 | 47 | 3 |
| Mannino, Brian, dh-1b | .341 | 208 | 51 | 71 | 16 | 0 | 12 | 49 | 2 |
| Sweet, Jonathan, 1b-c | .341 | 223 | 56 | 76 | 21 | 1 | 5 | 51 | 1 |
| Jones, Gary, 3b | .313 | 192 | 42 | 60 | 10 | 4 | 8 | 49 | 10 |
| Ellis, Chris, of | .297 | 37 | 6 | 11 | 4 | 0 | 0 | 8 | 1 |
| Kaczmar, Scott, of | .296 | 186 | 33 | 55 | 9 | 5 | 3 | 28 | 7 |
| Marsh, Roy, of | .289 | 211 | 56 | 61 | 10 | 1 | 7 | 31 | 32 |
| Todd, Scott, 2b | .286 | 28 | 7 | 8 | 0 | 0 | 0 | 0 | 0 |
| Estep, Mike, 2b-ss | .269 | 67 | 18 | 18 | 1 | 0 | 1 | 10 | 1 |
| Williams, Chris, ss | .254 | 177 | 33 | 45 | 3 | 0 | 2 | 17 | 5 |
| Khoury, Tony, c | .247 | 154 | 25 | 38 | 8 | 2 | 7 | 33 | 6 |
| Furrey, Matt, of | .173 | 52 | 6 | 9 | 1 | 1 | 2 | 4 | 1 |

| PITCHING | W | L | ERA | G | Sv | IP | H | BB | SO |
|---|---|---|---|---|---|---|---|---|---|
| Hale, Chad | 8 | 0 | 2.04 | 25 | 4 | 40 | 39 | 13 | 41 |
| Beaumont, Matt | 8 | 4 | 3.24 | 13 | 0 | 83 | 59 | 51 | 80 |
| Walker, Scott | 3 | 1 | 3.40 | 11 | 1 | 45 | 41 | 18 | 32 |
| Granata, Chris | 7 | 4 | 3.71 | 13 | 0 | 85 | 85 | 34 | 64 |
| Biehle, Mike | 4 | 1 | 4.02 | 11 | 0 | 54 | 50 | 33 | 47 |
| Fragle, Gary | 0 | 1 | 4.40 | 13 | 0 | 14 | 17 | 10 | 16 |
| Cannon, Kevan | 5 | 5 | 4.89 | 16 | 0 | 70 | 78 | 33 | 68 |
| Pachner, Dennis | 5 | 2 | 5.77 | 28 | 4 | 48 | 58 | 23 | 40 |
| Gussler, Steve | 2 | 0 | 6.35 | 4 | 0 | 11 | 17 | 5 | 3 |
| Noffke, Andy | 2 | 1 | 7.41 | 9 | 0 | 34 | 41 | 17 | 14 |
| Spears, Bob | 0 | 0 | 12.86 | 5 | 0 | 7 | 9 | 2 | 3 |

## 23 BAYLOR
Coach: Mickey Sullivan  Record: 41-19

| BATTING | AVG | AB | R | H | 2B | 3B | HR | RBI | SB |
|---|---|---|---|---|---|---|---|---|---|
| Crawford, Marty, of-c | .350 | 234 | 49 | 82 | 13 | 4 | 1 | 29 | 0 |

| BATTING | AVG | AB | R | H | 2B | 3B | HR | RBI | SB |
|---|---|---|---|---|---|---|---|---|---|
| Wharton, Joe, p-ss-1b | .345 | 194 | 42 | 67 | 12 | 5 | 4 | 35 | 9 |
| Marshall, Jason, c | .335 | 194 | 46 | 65 | 13 | 3 | 11 | 59 | 1 |
| Trozzo, Matt, of | .316 | 171 | 39 | 54 | 12 | 2 | 1 | 32 | 28 |
| Walton, Jason, 3b | .313 | 16 | 3 | 5 | 0 | 0 | 0 | 2 | 1 |
| Reitmeier, Traynor, 1b | .308 | 65 | 12 | 20 | 1 | 1 | 0 | 10 | 0 |
| Martin, Mark, of-1b | .307 | 166 | 50 | 51 | 8 | 4 | 4 | 21 | 11 |
| Bohny, Mike, 3b | .284 | 218 | 34 | 62 | 12 | 2 | 4 | 46 | 13 |
| Jones, Mac, of | .265 | 49 | 5 | 13 | 1 | 3 | 0 | 10 | 2 |
| Black, Brian, 2b | .259 | 143 | 28 | 37 | 5 | 0 | 3 | 24 | 5 |
| Shepherd, Brent, ss-2b | .258 | 155 | 24 | 40 | 7 | 1 | 0 | 21 | 1 |
| Stubbs, Jack, of | .241 | 108 | 16 | 26 | 4 | 2 | 0 | 13 | 18 |
| Walker, Rob, 1b | .240 | 75 | 11 | 18 | 3 | 0 | 0 | 13 | 0 |
| Murphy, Mark, of | .228 | 57 | 12 | 13 | 2 | 0 | 2 | 9 | 1 |
| Jett, Mark, of | .100 | 10 | 9 | 1 | 0 | 0 | 0 | 0 | 1 |

| PITCHING | W | L | ERA | G | Sv | IP | H | BB | SO |
|---|---|---|---|---|---|---|---|---|---|
| Martin, Jeff | 1 | 0 | 2.48 | 15 | 2 | 29 | 23 | 11 | 15 |
| Wharton, Joe | 10 | 3 | 2.54 | 21 | 3 | 85 | 69 | 29 | 85 |
| Rathbun, Jason | 7 | 5 | 3.15 | 18 | 2 | 91 | 81 | 51 | 74 |
| Lineweaver, Aaron | 9 | 5 | 3.27 | 17 | 1 | 105 | 83 | 56 | 82 |
| Richards, Aaron | 2 | 0 | 4.10 | 12 | 2 | 26 | 23 | 9 | 17 |
| Bearden, Brent | 6 | 2 | 4.70 | 21 | 5 | 61 | 51 | 41 | 43 |
| Crow, Dean | 3 | 3 | 4.81 | 20 | 2 | 64 | 62 | 44 | 45 |
| Thomas, Jeff | 3 | 1 | 7.12 | 16 | 0 | 30 | 43 | 23 | 27 |

## 24 AUBURN
Coach: Hal Baird  Record: 40-23

| BATTING | AVG | AB | R | H | 2B | 3B | HR | RBI | SB |
|---|---|---|---|---|---|---|---|---|---|
| Shanks, Cliff, dh-1b | .391 | 215 | 49 | 84 | 18 | 0 | 3 | 46 | 0 |
| Lewis, Robert, c | .382 | 34 | 7 | 13 | 2 | 2 | 1 | 7 | 1 |
| Moore, Brandon, ss | .365 | 230 | 47 | 84 | 12 | 1 | 5 | 42 | 6 |
| Duke, Mitch, c | .341 | 211 | 38 | 72 | 14 | 1 | 2 | 40 | 3 |
| Dean, Jake, of | .326 | 86 | 17 | 28 | 4 | 0 | 1 | 13 | 5 |
| Christopher, Chris, of | .325 | 228 | 50 | 74 | 12 | 5 | 3 | 29 | 19 |
| Waggoner, Jay, 3b | .320 | 247 | 54 | 79 | 9 | 2 | 0 | 33 | 2 |
| Alyea, Brian, 1b | .310 | 210 | 40 | 65 | 15 | 1 | 8 | 47 | 0 |
| Chabot, Kevin, of | .288 | 125 | 29 | 36 | 6 | 0 | 5 | 25 | 0 |
| Bellhorn, Mark, 2b | .266 | 233 | 51 | 62 | 11 | 0 | 8 | 39 | 16 |
| Whittenburg, Russ, of | .253 | 87 | 10 | 22 | 3 | 0 | 0 | 7 | 3 |
| Killimett, Mike, of | .249 | 177 | 22 | 44 | 8 | 1 | 2 | 40 | 1 |
| Key, Ken, 3b | .193 | 57 | 8 | 11 | 1 | 0 | 1 | 11 | 3 |

| PITCHING | W | L | ERA | G | Sv | IP | H | BB | SO |
|---|---|---|---|---|---|---|---|---|---|
| Sullivan, Scott | 4 | 3 | 2.53 | 22 | 5 | 60 | 48 | 19 | 71 |
| Warren, Rob | 0 | 0 | 2.77 | 8 | 1 | 13 | 18 | 4 | 12 |
| Powell, John | 15 | 5 | 2.81 | 24 | 0 | 141 | 102 | 41 | 191 |
| Halla, Ryan | 9 | 4 | 3.59 | 19 | 0 | 90 | 83 | 40 | 73 |
| Gober, Todd | 0 | 0 | 4.22 | 7 | 0 | 11 | 10 | 9 | 11 |
| Johnson, Jason | 9 | 6 | 4.53 | 21 | 0 | 105 | 129 | 42 | 89 |
| LeBoeuf, Jason | 2 | 1 | 4.56 | 19 | 1 | 47 | 48 | 19 | 39 |
| Newi, Alec | 1 | 0 | 5.40 | 12 | 1 | 20 | 19 | 9 | 19 |
| Hebel, Jon | 0 | 4 | 6.00 | 22 | 3 | 48 | 53 | 41 | 52 |

## 25 SOUTH CAROLINA
Coach: June Raines  Record: 39-20

| BATTING | AVG | AB | R | H | 2B | 3B | HR | RBI | SB |
|---|---|---|---|---|---|---|---|---|---|
| Biernat, Joe, ss | .403 | 233 | 46 | 94 | 16 | 2 | 5 | 52 | 15 |
| White, Mac, of | .355 | 220 | 50 | 78 | 16 | 4 | 7 | 59 | 21 |
| Dezenzo, Mike, of-3b | .308 | 121 | 51 | 68 | 10 | 1 | 5 | 36 | 21 |
| DeBoer, Rob, c-of | .302 | 192 | 35 | 58 | 9 | 0 | 6 | 41 | 14 |
| Stokes, Stacy, 2b | .301 | 193 | 51 | 58 | 8 | 1 | 0 | 33 | 9 |
| Gugino, Mark, of | .281 | 210 | 56 | 59 | 8 | 2 | 4 | 29 | 41 |
| Tarter, Mike, c-dh | .275 | 180 | 32 | 50 | 10 | 0 | 6 | 34 | 5 |
| Rose, Ted, dh | .275 | 80 | 15 | 22 | 6 | 1 | 2 | 14 | 4 |
| McGuire, Mike, 3b-1b | .268 | 209 | 46 | 56 | 12 | 1 | 4 | 37 | 7 |
| Parnell, Jeff, 1b | .248 | 206 | 39 | 51 | 11 | 1 | 10 | 44 | 4 |
| Galloway, Bennett, of | .231 | 13 | 1 | 3 | 0 | 0 | 0 | 3 | 0 |
| Baksh, Ray, 1b | .150 | 40 | 7 | 6 | 1 | 0 | 1 | 3 | 0 |

| PITCHING | W | L | ERA | G | Sv | IP | H | BB | SO |
|---|---|---|---|---|---|---|---|---|---|
| Mosser, Rob | 2 | 3 | 2.65 | 29 | 11 | 34 | 31 | 10 | 32 |
| Haynie, Jason | 8 | 2 | 2.68 | 18 | 0 | 77 | 52 | 46 | 86 |
| Stoops, Jim | 3 | 1 | 2.73 | 4 | 0 | 30 | 20 | 7 | 29 |
| Pace, Scott | 3 | 3 | 2.82 | 19 | 1 | 51 | 50 | 24 | 45 |
| Pratt, Rich | 11 | 3 | 2.83 | 18 | 0 | 114 | 107 | 24 | 101 |
| Kolbert, Steve | 0 | 1 | 3.63 | 10 | 0 | 17 | 20 | 6 | 8 |
| Threehouse, Matt | 7 | 4 | 3.66 | 14 | 0 | 79 | 71 | 40 | 87 |
| Ross, Craig | 2 | 0 | 3.98 | 15 | 1 | 32 | 34 | 7 | 15 |
| Pearsall, J.J. | 2 | 1 | 5.45 | 21 | 0 | 33 | 31 | 29 | 45 |
| Maynard, Wally | 1 | 1 | 5.74 | 17 | 0 | 42 | 46 | 26 | 43 |
| Rose, Ted | 0 | 0 | 6.52 | 9 | 0 | 10 | 15 | 3 | 9 |

# CONFERENCE STANDINGS, LEADERS

## NCAA Division I Conferences

*Won conference tournament
**Boldface:** NCAA regional participant

### ATLANTIC COAST CONFERENCE

| | Conference W | L | Overall W | L |
|---|---|---|---|---|
| **Georgia Tech** | 16 | 6 | 47 | 14 |
| **North Carolina State** | 15 | 7 | 49 | 17 |
| **Florida State** | 14 | 9 | 46 | 19 |
| **North Carolina** | 13 | 10 | 43 | 20 |
| *Clemson | 11 | 11 | 45 | 20 |
| Duke | 11 | 13 | 39 | 19 |
| Wake Forest | 9 | 13 | 31 | 22 |
| Virginia | 7 | 15 | 21 | 30 |
| Maryland | 5 | 17 | 24 | 29 |

**ALL-CONFERENCE TEAM: C**—Jason Varitek, Jr., Georgia Tech. **1B**—Scott Pinoni, So., Duke. **2B**—Tom Crowley, Sr., Virginia. **3B**—Tim Tracey, Jr., North Carolina State. **SS**—Nomar Garciaparra, So., Georgia Tech. **OF**—Billy McMillon, Jr., Clemson; Keith Williams, Jr., Clemson; Pat Clougherty, Jr., North Carolina State. **DH**—Cookie Massey, Sr., North Carolina. **Util**—Ryan Jackson, Jr., Duke. **SP**—Brad Rigby, So., Georgia Tech. **RP**—Brett Binkley, Jr., Georgia Tech.

**Player of the Year**—Jason Varitek, Georgia Tech.

#### INDIVIDUAL BATTING LEADERS
(Minimum 125 At-Bats)

| | AVG | AB | R | H | 2B | 3B | HR | RBI | SB |
|---|---|---|---|---|---|---|---|---|---|
| Varitek, Jason, Ga. Tech | .404 | 228 | 78 | 92 | 20 | 2 | 22 | 72 | 5 |
| McMillon, Billy, Clemson | .377 | 212 | 64 | 80 | 21 | 1 | 5 | 30 | 11 |
| Monahan, Shane, Clemson | .372 | 253 | 56 | 94 | 15 | 7 | 9 | 64 | 17 |
| Clougherty, Pat, NCS | .368 | 239 | 55 | 8 | 16 | 1 | 21 | 80 | 8 |
| Williams, Keith, Clemson | .365 | 255 | 60 | 93 | 18 | 4 | 19 | 79 | 7 |
| Tracey, Tim, NCS | .357 | 238 | 57 | 85 | 13 | 3 | 8 | 47 | 6 |
| Morris, Jeff, Clemson | .356 | 239 | 60 | 85 | 12 | 2 | 2 | 32 | 5 |
| Crowley, Tom, Virginia | .356 | 180 | 32 | 64 | 12 | 5 | 1 | 32 | 13 |
| Holbrook, Chad, NC | .353 | 249 | 56 | 88 | 11 | 7 | 2 | 28 | 40 |
| Pinoni, Scott, Duke | .352 | 210 | 49 | 74 | 20 | 3 | 7 | 50 | 8 |
| Payton, Jay, Ga. Tech | .346 | 240 | 61 | 83 | 12 | 12 | 14 | 64 | 23 |
| Barkett, Andy, NCS | .343 | 207 | 50 | 71 | 16 | 3 | 8 | 49 | 4 |
| DaSilva, Manny, NC | .339 | 224 | 45 | 76 | 12 | 3 | 15 | 66 | 10 |
| Ritter, Ryan, Ga. Tech | .330 | 200 | 41 | 66 | 8 | 4 | 6 | 37 | 5 |
| Boone, David, NC | .328 | 177 | 29 | 58 | 10 | 1 | 0 | 16 | 8 |
| Mientkiewicz, Doug, Fla. State | .327 | 205 | 40 | 67 | 13 | 1 | 4 | 47 | 2 |
| Pryce, Brad, WF | .324 | 179 | 33 | 58 | 9 | 0 | 8 | 38 | 7 |
| Buchanan, Brian, Virginia | .322 | 202 | 37 | 65 | 14 | 6 | 6 | 37 | 12 |
| Smith, Michael, Ga. Tech | .318 | 223 | 51 | 71 | 5 | 3 | 3 | 28 | 24 |
| Almond, Greg, NCS | .315 | 162 | 29 | 51 | 12 | 0 | 5 | 31 | 2 |
| Bark, Robbie, NCS | .315 | 213 | 47 | 67 | 16 | 3 | 2 | 33 | 5 |
| Cook, Jason, Virginia | .314 | 172 | 40 | 54 | 9 | 3 | 2 | 29 | 11 |
| Neuberger, Steve, Maryland | .311 | 183 | 29 | 57 | 6 | 0 | 5 | 21 | 13 |
| Jackson, Ryan, Duke | .310 | 232 | 59 | 72 | 18 | 5 | 12 | 41 | 5 |
| McNally, Sean, Duke | .309 | 223 | 52 | 69 | 13 | 3 | 5 | 50 | 8 |
| Mitchell, Shawn, Virginia | .309 | 162 | 21 | 50 | 8 | 3 | 2 | 18 | 7 |
| Schmitz, Mike, Fla. State | .307 | 192 | 39 | 59 | 8 | 1 | 13 | 43 | 5 |
| Shore, Casey, Virginia | .307 | 192 | 30 | 59 | 7 | 4 | 0 | 17 | 4 |
| Hedgecoe, David, WF | .307 | 215 | 45 | 66 | 19 | 2 | 5 | 41 | 11 |
| Martin, Mike, Fla. State | .307 | 212 | 44 | 65 | 12 | 0 | 5 | 43 | 10 |
| Wagner, Bret, WF | .306 | 186 | 45 | 57 | 9 | 3 | 9 | 28 | 7 |
| Wagner, Kyle, WF | .304 | 138 | 29 | 42 | 9 | 1 | 1 | 11 | 11 |
| Newhan, David, Ga. Tech | .303 | 178 | 54 | 54 | 13 | 2 | 9 | 44 | 4 |
| Hensley, Brandon, Ga. Tech | .303 | 221 | 35 | 67 | 11 | 1 | 4 | 37 | 2 |
| Smith, Chris, WF | .303 | 165 | 31 | 50 | 9 | 1 | 11 | 37 | 3 |

#### INDIVIDUAL PITCHING LEADERS
(Minimum 50 Innings)

| | W | L | ERA | G | Sv | IP | H | BB | SO |
|---|---|---|---|---|---|---|---|---|---|
| Johnson, Jonathan, Fla. State | 10 | 1 | 1.68 | 17 | 0 | 107 | 80 | 52 | 124 |
| Myers, Chris, Ga. Tech | 4 | 0 | 1.90 | 39 | 2 | 81 | 73 | 15 | 70 |
| Wilson, Paul, Fla. State | 11 | 5 | 1.94 | 17 | 0 | 116 | 95 | 32 | 99 |
| Hall, Buck, Ga. Tech | 8 | 2 | 2.42 | 12 | 0 | 67 | 46 | 27 | 83 |
| Rigby, Brad, Ga. Tech | 13 | 1 | 2.46 | 17 | 0 | 99 | 57 | 56 | 132 |
| Binkley, Brett, Ga. Tech | 3 | 2 | 2.48 | 39 | 14 | 58 | 47 | 19 | 69 |
| Senior, Shawn, NCS | 10 | 5 | 2.73 | 18 | 0 | 102 | 71 | 58 | 120 |

| | | | | | | | | | |
|---|---|---|---|---|---|---|---|---|---|
| Gogolin, Al, Ga. Tech | 8 | 1 | 2.75 | 16 | 0 | 88 | 69 | 31 | 77 |
| Steinert, Rob, NCS | 6 | 3 | 2.87 | 16 | 0 | 88 | 76 | 24 | 85 |
| Chrismon, Thad, NC | 5 | 3 | 2.93 | 38 | 18 | 89 | 66 | 25 | 95 |
| Phillips, Chad, Clemson | 12 | 2 | 2.96 | 16 | 0 | 91 | 93 | 24 | 69 |
| Starman, Craig, Duke | 5 | 3 | 3.02 | 20 | 2 | 63 | 74 | 13 | 25 |
| Manning, Derek, NC | 11 | 5 | 3.06 | 17 | 0 | 118 | 104 | 33 | 105 |
| Schoeneweis, Scott, Duke | 12 | 3 | 3.12 | 18 | 0 | 107 | 101 | 29 | 110 |
| Jerzembeck, Mike, NC | 9 | 3 | 3.15 | 17 | 0 | 94 | 87 | 44 | 99 |
| Wasdin, John, Fla. State | 10 | 1 | 3.15 | 18 | 0 | 114 | 104 | 34 | 138 |
| Darwin, David, Duke | 6 | 3 | 3.21 | 20 | 1 | 87 | 81 | 26 | 54 |
| Taulbee, Andy, Clemson | 10 | 2 | 3.24 | 30 | 3 | 98 | 96 | 29 | 85 |
| Harvey, Terry, NCS | 10 | 3 | 3.26 | 15 | 0 | 108 | 100 | 31 | 82 |
| Harrell, Phil, Duke | 4 | 6 | 3.31 | 16 | 0 | 87 | 75 | 26 | 60 |
| Crowley, Tom, Virginia | 5 | 5 | 3.36 | 14 | 1 | 60 | 71 | 30 | 63 |

### ATLANTIC-10 CONFERENCE

| | Conference W | L | Overall W | L |
|---|---|---|---|---|
| *Rutgers | 14 | 6 | 38 | 17 |
| West Virginia | 13 | 8 | 29 | 25 |
| Temple | 11 | 9 | 18 | 21 |
| George Washington | 10 | 10 | 19 | 26 |
| St. Joseph's | 10 | 10 | 20 | 19 |
| Massachusetts | 9 | 11 | 18 | 21 |
| St. Bonaventure | 8 | 12 | 18 | 22 |
| Rhode Island | 5 | 14 | 12 | 26 |

**ALL-CONFERENCE TEAM: C**—Mike Higgins, Jr., Rutgers. **1B**—John Bujnowski, Sr., Temple. **2B**—Mike Bennett, Sr., St. Bonaventure. **3B**—Scott Sharp, Jr., George Washington. **SS**—Bob Windows, So., Rutgers. **OF**—Doug Alongi, Jr., Rutgers; Hiram Barber, Sr., Rhode Island; Justin Howard, Jr., Massachusetts. **DH**—Dan Vasalani, Sr., West Virginia. **RHP**—Steve Hoppel, So., Temple. **LHP**—Steve Kline, Jr., West Virginia.

**Player of the Year**—Doug Alongi, Rutgers. **Pitcher of the Year**—Steve Kline, West Virginia.

#### INDIVIDUAL BATTING LEADERS
(Minimum 100 At-Bats)

| | AVG | AB | R | H | 2B | 3B | HR | RBI | SB |
|---|---|---|---|---|---|---|---|---|---|
| Howard, Justin, Mass | .394 | 155 | 42 | 61 | 16 | 1 | 7 | 40 | 11 |
| Corradi, Steve, Mass | .379 | 140 | 46 | 53 | 12 | 1 | 4 | 25 | 12 |
| Barber, Hiram, RI | .377 | 130 | 32 | 49 | 10 | 1 | 9 | 32 | 20 |
| Landers, Mark, WV | .376 | 181 | 40 | 68 | 16 | 0 | 10 | 59 | 1 |
| Alongi, Doug, Rutgers | .371 | 232 | 62 | 86 | 18 | 6 | 9 | 45 | 39 |
| Higgins, Mike, Rutgers | .370 | 189 | 45 | 70 | 20 | 1 | 9 | 56 | 4 |
| Bennett, Mike, SB | .368 | 136 | 28 | 50 | 8 | 0 | 7 | 33 | 5 |
| Knight, Bill, Mass | .352 | 128 | 33 | 45 | 4 | 1 | 10 | 35 | 6 |
| Sauro, Jim, RI | .339 | 127 | 15 | 43 | 5 | 0 | 1 | 20 | 13 |
| Winchock, Mike, Rutgers | .338 | 204 | 38 | 69 | 17 | 1 | 5 | 46 | 4 |
| Sharkey, Mike, St. Joseph's | .338 | 154 | 38 | 52 | 8 | 5 | 4 | 21 | 10 |
| Tegeler, Tom, SB | .329 | 140 | 25 | 46 | 4 | 1 | 6 | 38 | 1 |
| Bujnowski, John, Temple | .329 | 146 | 24 | 48 | 3 | 0 | 6 | 28 | 6 |
| Obermeier, Ron, St. Joseph's | .329 | 146 | 37 | 48 | 19 | 2 | 1 | 33 | 8 |
| Lucibello, Gaeton, Temple | .328 | 125 | 30 | 41 | 7 | 1 | 5 | 19 | 10 |
| Urda, Bryan, GW | .323 | 133 | 19 | 43 | 9 | 1 | 4 | 19 | 0 |
| Weingartner, Bill, St. Joseph's | .321 | 162 | 33 | 52 | 9 | 2 | 4 | 32 | 4 |
| Kassan, Scott, Rutgers | .317 | 205 | 40 | 65 | 8 | 3 | 4 | 27 | 4 |

#### INDIVIDUAL PITCHING LEADERS
(Minimum 40 Innings)

| | W | L | ERA | G | Sv | IP | H | BB | SO |
|---|---|---|---|---|---|---|---|---|---|
| Hoppel, Steve, Temple | 7 | 3 | 2.71 | 12 | 1 | 76 | 53 | 37 | 72 |
| Barckley, Mike, Rutgers | 7 | 3 | 2.89 | 13 | 0 | 90 | 89 | 16 | 50 |
| Kline, Steve, WV | 6 | 6 | 3.05 | 15 | 0 | 79 | 61 | 32 | 82 |
| Simpson, Scott, Rutgers | 5 | 3 | 3.12 | 22 | 6 | 43 | 42 | 12 | 33 |
| Clark, Ryan, GW | 1 | 2 | 3.19 | 16 | 0 | 42 | 37 | 15 | 32 |
| Barry, Dan, WV | 4 | 2 | 3.23 | 9 | 0 | 56 | 52 | 21 | 46 |
| Schneider, Phil, Rutgers | 6 | 3 | 3.58 | 12 | 0 | 83 | 75 | 37 | 68 |
| Titus, Brian, SB | 5 | 5 | 3.60 | 12 | 0 | 75 | 73 | 48 | 56 |
| Healy, Dennis, GW | 4 | 4 | 3.73 | 12 | 0 | 63 | 61 | 17 | 46 |
| Toothaker, Jeff, Mass | 6 | 6 | 3.99 | 15 | 1 | 77 | 90 | 25 | 50 |
| Cochrane, Chris, Rutgers | 7 | 4 | 4.17 | 18 | 1 | 69 | 79 | 20 | 49 |

# BIG EAST CONFERENCE

| | Conference | | Overall | |
|---|---|---|---|---|
| | W | L | W | L |
| Villanova | 14 | 7 | 27 | 15 |
| Seton Hall | 12 | 8 | 30 | 18 |
| Connecticut | 12 | 9 | 27 | 19 |
| *St. John's | 11 | 10 | 28 | 20 |
| Boston College | 11 | 10 | 22 | 14 |
| Pittsburgh | 10 | 11 | 30 | 13 |
| Providence | 8 | 12 | 21 | 24 |
| Georgetown | 5 | 16 | 7 | 22 |

ALL-CONFERENCE TEAM: C—Alex Andreopoulos, So., Seton Hall. 1B—Mike Bellagamba, Sr., St. John's. 2B—Mike Martin, Jr., Boston College; Brad Reese, Sr., Pittsburgh. 3B—Jack Stanczak, Jr., Villanova. SS—Lou Merloni, Sr., Providence. OF—Ed Deal, Sr., Villanova; Dennis Dwyer, Jr., Connecticut; Al Lardo, Sr., Pittsburgh. DH—Kevin Armstrong, Sr., Villanova. Util—Jim Foster, Sr., Providence. P—Steve Hayward, Sr., Seton Hall; David Herr, Sr., Villanova; John Kelly, So., Connecticut; C.J. Nitkowski, So., St. John's.

Co-Players of the Year—Jack Stanczak, Villanova; Lou Merloni, Providence. Pitcher of the Year—David Herr, Villanova.

## INDIVIDUAL BATTING LEADERS
(Minimum 100 At-Bats)

| | AVG | AB | R | H | 2B | 3B | HR | RBI | SB |
|---|---|---|---|---|---|---|---|---|---|
| Martin, Mike, BC | .462 | 130 | 32 | 60 | 10 | 3 | 3 | 27 | 7 |
| Stanczak, Jack, Villanova | .426 | 148 | 56 | 63 | 10 | 0 | 13 | 43 | 8 |
| Dwyer, Dennis, Conn. | .425 | 167 | 40 | 71 | 17 | 2 | 0 | 21 | 40 |
| Gonzalez, Danny, Pitt | .413 | 121 | 36 | 50 | 6 | 0 | 0 | 33 | 12 |
| Foster, Jim, Providence | .386 | 158 | 40 | 61 | 14 | 0 | 7 | 38 | 8 |
| Merloni, Lou, Providence | .378 | 164 | 48 | 62 | 16 | 3 | 10 | 43 | 6 |
| Roth, Jason, Pitt | .362 | 127 | 30 | 46 | 12 | 1 | 5 | 32 | 12 |
| Armstrong, Kevin, Villanova | .360 | 114 | 25 | 41 | 12 | 0 | 7 | 37 | 2 |
| Cosmo, Nick, St. John's | .351 | 168 | 37 | 59 | 9 | 3 | 3 | 38 | 8 |
| Mariniello, Dan, Villanova | .350 | 157 | 49 | 55 | 10 | 0 | 8 | 33 | 7 |
| Reese, Brad, Pitt | .350 | 140 | 43 | 49 | 13 | 1 | 5 | 40 | 19 |
| Ottavinia, Paul, Seton Hall | .350 | 183 | 34 | 64 | 12 | 2 | 4 | 45 | 16 |
| Walsh, Pat, Pitt | .350 | 103 | 26 | 36 | 11 | 0 | 6 | 33 | 5 |
| Young, Steve, Villanova | .348 | 178 | 39 | 62 | 8 | 3 | 2 | 25 | 4 |
| Bellagamba, Mike, St. John's | .347 | 170 | 32 | 59 | 12 | 2 | 4 | 40 | 0 |
| Evangelista, Mike, Villanova | .338 | 145 | 29 | 49 | 4 | 0 | 8 | 35 | 1 |
| Loscalzo, Jason, St. John's | .331 | 169 | 42 | 56 | 10 | 2 | 4 | 21 | 11 |
| Gorecki, Ryan, Seton Hall | .327 | 156 | 36 | 51 | 7 | 1 | 0 | 28 | 16 |
| Tomey, Mark, Providence | .325 | 117 | 21 | 38 | 8 | 1 | 3 | 21 | 2 |
| Deal, Ed, Villanova | .322 | 152 | 34 | 49 | 14 | 0 | 8 | 46 | 2 |

## INDIVIDUAL PITCHING LEADERS
(Minimum 40 Innings)

| | W | L | ERA | G | Sv | IP | H | BB | SO |
|---|---|---|---|---|---|---|---|---|---|
| Sawicki, David, Seton Hall | 5 | 1 | 1.89 | 10 | 1 | 48 | 39 | 16 | 25 |
| Nitkowski, C.J., St. John's | 6 | 3 | 2.71 | 16 | 2 | 80 | 79 | 28 | 65 |
| Herr, David, Villanova | 9 | 3 | 2.78 | 15 | 1 | 87 | 69 | 39 | 63 |
| Frontera, Chad, Seton Hall | 5 | 5 | 3.04 | 12 | 0 | 71 | 81 | 37 | 53 |
| Maerten, Mike, St. John's | 3 | 1 | 3.36 | 11 | 2 | 59 | 62 | 12 | 25 |
| Hayward, Steve, Seton Hall | 6 | 2 | 3.47 | 14 | 1 | 80 | 80 | 38 | 78 |
| Kress, Mike, St. John's | 3 | 2 | 3.72 | 8 | 0 | 46 | 47 | 17 | 24 |
| Hayes, Chris, Conn. | 1 | 1 | 3.77 | 24 | 5 | 57 | 53 | 11 | 25 |
| McKenna, Alex, BC | 3 | 3 | 3.86 | 12 | 0 | 61 | 54 | 19 | 22 |
| Maloney, Sean, Georgetown | 1 | 5 | 3.86 | 10 | 2 | 42 | 51 | 12 | 27 |
| Junker, Bill, Pitt | 5 | 5 | 3.94 | 10 | 0 | 62 | 57 | 30 | 57 |
| Kusters, Dan, Villanova | 6 | 1 | 4.11 | 9 | 0 | 50 | 51 | 24 | 29 |
| Quinn, Aaron, Conn | 5 | 3 | 4.14 | 10 | 0 | 41 | 51 | 12 | 26 |

# BIG EIGHT CONFERENCE

| | Conference | | Overall | |
|---|---|---|---|---|
| | W | L | W | L |
| *Oklahoma State | 16 | 8 | 45 | 17 |
| Kansas | 17 | 9 | 45 | 18 |
| Missouri | 15 | 10 | 30 | 19 |
| Nebraska | 16 | 12 | 35 | 23 |
| Oklahoma | 13 | 14 | 31 | 24 |
| Kansas State | 6 | 17 | 15 | 34 |
| Iowa State | 5 | 18 | 17 | 28 |

ALL-CONFERENCE TEAM: C—Jeff Niemeier, Sr., Kansas. 1B—John Wuycheck, Sr., Kansas. 2B—Rick Gutierrez, Jr., Oklahoma. 3B—Ernesto Rivera, Sr., Oklahoma State. SS—Rich Hills, So., Oklahoma. OF—Chopper Littrell, Sr., Missouri; Marc Sagmoen, Sr., Nebraska; Thad Chaddrick, Jr., Oklahoma State. DH—Troy Brohawn, So., Nebraska. Util—Brian Culp, Sr., Kansas State. SP—Jason Meyhoff, So., Missouri; Troy Brohawn, So.,

Nebraska; Jake Benz, Jr., Oklahoma State; Chris Corn, Jr., Kansas. RP—Jimmy Walker, Sr., Kansas; Steve Boyd, Sr., Nebraska.

Player of the Year—Marc Sagmoen, Nebraska.

## INDIVIDUAL BATTING LEADERS
(Minimum 125 At-Bats)

| | AVG | AB | R | H | 2B | 3B | HR | RBI | SB |
|---|---|---|---|---|---|---|---|---|---|
| Sagmoen, Marc, Nebraska | .454 | 205 | 75 | 93 | 19 | 5 | 18 | 79 | 26 |
| Niemeier, Jeff, Kansas | .378 | 230 | 56 | 87 | 22 | 2 | 10 | 63 | 5 |
| Littrell, Chopper, Missouri | .374 | 179 | 50 | 67 | 16 | 2 | 2 | 32 | 3 |
| Norton, Greg, Oklahoma | .370 | 227 | 58 | 84 | 20 | 4 | 5 | 60 | 5 |
| Gutierrez, Rick, Oklahoma | .366 | 194 | 54 | 71 | 14 | 4 | 6 | 32 | 22 |
| Hills, Rich, Oklahoma | .361 | 205 | 43 | 74 | 13 | 2 | 2 | 53 | 4 |
| Culp, Brian, Kansas State | .351 | 171 | 46 | 60 | 13 | 1 | 12 | 52 | 8 |
| Berry, Mike, Oklahoma | .350 | 163 | 34 | 57 | 15 | 2 | 1 | 36 | 4 |
| Hugo, Sean, Okla. St. | .347 | 202 | 72 | 70 | 16 | 2 | 13 | 53 | 0 |
| Igou, Josh, Kansas | .345 | 203 | 46 | 70 | 21 | 1 | 7 | 54 | 7 |
| Berblinger, Jeff, Kansas | .339 | 227 | 66 | 77 | 20 | 3 | 9 | 52 | 33 |
| Erstad, Darren, Nebraska | .339 | 239 | 52 | 81 | 16 | 1 | 10 | 54 | 14 |
| Rivera, Ernesto, Okla. St. | .338 | 225 | 78 | 76 | 18 | 5 | 12 | 61 | 14 |
| Childers, Chabon, Okla. St. | .336 | 146 | 33 | 49 | 9 | 1 | 7 | 45 | 0 |
| Prodanov, Peter, Okla. St. | .335 | 215 | 56 | 72 | 13 | 0 | 8 | 46 | 19 |
| Monroe, Darryl, Kansas | .330 | 212 | 43 | 70 | 16 | 5 | 3 | 39 | 23 |
| Bando, Sal, Okla. St. | .329 | 152 | 32 | 50 | 6 | 0 | 12 | 42 | 1 |
| Brohawn, Troy, Nebraska | .329 | 219 | 45 | 72 | 15 | 1 | 3 | 34 | 6 |
| Wuycheck, John, Kansas | .328 | 244 | 61 | 80 | 19 | 9 | 5 | 56 | 8 |
| Ball, Steve, Missouri | .328 | 180 | 49 | 59 | 8 | 2 | 7 | 26 | 12 |
| Chaddrick, Thad, Okla. St. | .327 | 171 | 37 | 56 | 14 | 3 | 9 | 46 | 3 |
| Ingram, Grant, Missouri | .326 | 175 | 34 | 57 | 15 | 1 | 2 | 33 | 5 |
| Traylor, Darvin, Oklahoma | .325 | 209 | 53 | 68 | 10 | 5 | 4 | 31 | 9 |
| Glass, Chip, Oklahoma | .323 | 220 | 53 | 71 | 10 | 12 | 2 | 28 | 23 |
| Peterson, Darin, Nebraska | .320 | 222 | 51 | 71 | 9 | 0 | 0 | 34 | 9 |
| Kopriva, Jay, Kansas State | .318 | 129 | 26 | 41 | 6 | 2 | 1 | 21 | 2 |
| Garcia, James, Nebraska | .313 | 134 | 21 | 42 | 12 | 0 | 2 | 24 | 9 |
| Monroe, Kevin, Iowa State | .312 | 138 | 31 | 43 | 8 | 3 | 0 | 13 | 14 |
| Elsinger, Mark, Iowa State | .311 | 177 | 35 | 55 | 10 | 1 | 2 | 20 | 20 |
| Triplett, Hunter, Okla. St. | .308 | 159 | 29 | 49 | 12 | 3 | 12 | 55 | 4 |
| Ocasio, Fred, Okla. St. | .307 | 225 | 42 | 69 | 11 | 1 | 1 | 29 | 0 |
| Dukart, Derek, Nebraska | .305 | 213 | 48 | 65 | 7 | 3 | 14 | 46 | 6 |
| Wilhelm, Brent, Kansas | .304 | 191 | 53 | 58 | 14 | 4 | 5 | 39 | 6 |
| Heath, Jason, Okla. St. | .303 | 185 | 40 | 56 | 17 | 2 | 13 | 62 | 2 |
| Swift, Scott, Missouri | .299 | 204 | 45 | 61 | 7 | 4 | 0 | 26 | 4 |

## INDIVIDUAL PITCHING LEADERS
(Minimum 50 Innings)

| | W | L | ERA | G | Sv | IP | H | BB | SO |
|---|---|---|---|---|---|---|---|---|---|
| Walker, Jimmy, Kansas | 9 | 2 | 2.39 | 33 | 11 | 98 | 89 | 27 | 104 |
| Brohawn, Troy, Nebraska | 13 | 0 | 3.16 | 15 | 0 | 111 | 90 | 56 | 123 |
| Hogue, Jay, Okla. St. | 8 | 0 | 3.38 | 29 | 3 | 75 | 54 | 43 | 59 |
| Splittorff, Jamie, Kansas | 7 | 2 | 3.61 | 18 | 0 | 85 | 76 | 41 | 71 |
| Corn, Chris, Kansas | 9 | 4 | 3.66 | 19 | 0 | 98 | 82 | 58 | 92 |
| Benz, Jake, Okla. St. | 9 | 2 | 3.68 | 16 | 0 | 86 | 73 | 42 | 73 |
| Chambliss, John, Missouri | 2 | 2 | 4.10 | 15 | 1 | 64 | 61 | 19 | 47 |
| Meyhoff, Jason, Missouri | 9 | 3 | 4.17 | 16 | 0 | 101 | 85 | 58 | 114 |
| Wheeler, Earl, Okla. St. | 6 | 1 | 4.42 | 15 | 0 | 73 | 78 | 33 | 55 |
| Boyd, Steve, Nebraska | 5 | 5 | 4.45 | 28 | 5 | 55 | 49 | 31 | 61 |
| Robertson, Chris, Missouri | 4 | 5 | 4.69 | 15 | 0 | 94 | 98 | 49 | 74 |
| Soult, David, Kansas | 7 | 3 | 4.79 | 16 | 0 | 73 | 91 | 21 | 39 |
| Lovingier, Kevin, Oklahoma | 6 | 2 | 5.02 | 17 | 0 | 75 | 73 | 53 | 61 |
| Merriman, Rob, Kansas State | 3 | 8 | 5.09 | 13 | 0 | 87 | 89 | 58 | 52 |
| Martin, Brian, Nebraska | 9 | 4 | 5.20 | 16 | 0 | 99 | 112 | 48 | 49 |
| Bell, Jason, Okla. St. | 5 | 2 | 5.68 | 14 | 0 | 52 | 54 | 31 | 39 |
| Gore, Brad, Okla. St. | 7 | 3 | 5.83 | 15 | 0 | 83 | 85 | 41 | 63 |
| Driskill, Dan, Kansas State | 3 | 7 | 5.88 | 14 | 0 | 90 | 107 | 32 | 64 |
| Stewart, Tom, Kansas | 6 | 4 | 5.93 | 16 | 0 | 68 | 92 | 25 | 40 |
| Connelly, Steve, Oklahoma | 6 | 4 | 5.98 | 19 | 0 | 81 | 106 | 41 | 49 |

# BIG SOUTH CONFERENCE

| | Conference | | Overall | |
|---|---|---|---|---|
| | W | L | W | L |
| Coastal Carolina | 15 | 8 | 28 | 28 |
| Maryland-Balt. County | 14 | 8 | 26 | 17 |
| Towson State | 14 | 9 | 20 | 25 |
| Winthrop | 12 | 10 | 27 | 31 |
| Radford | 10 | 10 | 29 | 19 |
| *Liberty | 10 | 11 | 23 | 25 |
| Campbell | 8 | 11 | 17 | 33 |
| Charleston Southern | 7 | 15 | 19 | 22 |
| UNC Asheville | 6 | 14 | 19 | 27 |

ALL-CONFERENCE TEAM: C—Tommy Lark, Sr., Charleston Southern. 1B—Shawn Shugars, Jr., Maryland-Baltimore County. 2B—Ed Stanley, Sr., Campbell. 3B—Heyward Bracey, Sr., Winthrop. SS—Tom Curran, Sr., Radford. OF—Charlie Kim, Jr.,

Liberty; Greg Elliott, Sr., Maryland-Baltimore County; Trevor Moore, Sr., UNC Asheville; Duane Filchner, So., Radford; Jay Logwood, Sr., Towson State. **DH**—Brian Pardue, So., Radford. **Util**—Denny Van Pelt, Jr., Radford. **P**—Rich Humphrey, Sr., Liberty; Kevin Loewe, So., Maryland-Baltimore County; Joe Hughes, Jr., Towson State.

**Player of the Year**—Kevin Loewe, Maryland-Baltimore County.

### INDIVIDUAL BATTING LEADERS
(Minimum 100 At-Bats)

| | AVG | AB | R | H | 2B | 3B | HR | RBI | SB |
|---|---|---|---|---|---|---|---|---|---|
| Elliott, Greg, UMBC | .412 | 182 | 50 | 75 | 23 | 2 | 7 | 48 | 9 |
| Filchner, Duane, Radford | .401 | 172 | 45 | 69 | 15 | 1 | 8 | 57 | 8 |
| Lark, Tommy, CS | .392 | 130 | 28 | 51 | 15 | 1 | 5 | 36 | 6 |
| Cox, Kent, Campbell | .384 | 146 | 35 | 56 | 6 | 3 | 2 | 21 | 4 |
| Shugars, Shawn, UMBC | .383 | 162 | 37 | 62 | 16 | 0 | 11 | 49 | 4 |
| Nickles, Brent, UMBC | .382 | 170 | 40 | 65 | 12 | 1 | 3 | 41 | 7 |
| Logwood, Jay, Towson St. | .377 | 146 | 49 | 55 | 7 | 2 | 17 | 50 | 5 |
| Stanley, Ed, Campbell | .374 | 171 | 36 | 64 | 11 | 6 | 3 | 38 | 8 |
| Swaim, Matt, UNCA | .360 | 150 | 37 | 54 | 13 | 0 | 1 | 16 | 1 |
| Pardue, Brian, Radford | .359 | 128 | 29 | 46 | 12 | 1 | 6 | 30 | 0 |
| Moore, Trevor, UNCA | .358 | 162 | 36 | 58 | 13 | 1 | 13 | 48 | 1 |
| Ballard, Chad, UNCA | .350 | 120 | 20 | 42 | 5 | 1 | 3 | 23 | 3 |
| Van Pelt, Denny, Radford | .349 | 149 | 40 | 52 | 14 | 1 | 7 | 41 | 13 |
| Vaxmonsky, Alex, Radford | .348 | 115 | 26 | 40 | 5 | 1 | 2 | 12 | 8 |
| Kim, Charlie, Liberty | .347 | 173 | 35 | 60 | 9 | 1 | 8 | 30 | 10 |
| Maddocks, Josh, Campbell | .345 | 171 | 42 | 59 | 6 | 4 | 2 | 13 | 7 |
| Gegg, John, Radford | .340 | 106 | 24 | 36 | 7 | 2 | 3 | 24 | 3 |
| Schilling, Matt, Coast. Car. | .337 | 169 | 37 | 57 | 12 | 3 | 3 | 30 | 6 |

### INDIVIDUAL PITCHING LEADERS
(Minimum 40 Innings)

| | W | L | ERA | G | Sv | IP | H | BB | SO |
|---|---|---|---|---|---|---|---|---|---|
| Hughes, Joe, Towson St. | 7 | 3 | 1.36 | 14 | 1 | 73 | 67 | 11 | 61 |
| Loewe, Kevin, UMBC | 8 | 1 | 2.34 | 14 | 1 | 73 | 57 | 18 | 46 |
| Humphrey, Rich, Liberty | 8 | 5 | 2.35 | 16 | 1 | 111 | 89 | 28 | 73 |
| Alarie, Kevin, UMBC | 3 | 3 | 2.69 | 13 | 1 | 60 | 75 | 4 | 33 |
| Walker, Mark, Radford | 5 | 1 | 3.32 | 11 | 1 | 43 | 46 | 12 | 13 |
| Link, Bryan, Winthrop | 5 | 5 | 3.39 | 18 | 0 | 74 | 69 | 28 | 68 |
| Abbott, Jim, Radford | 5 | 4 | 3.41 | 11 | 0 | 69 | 64 | 33 | 57 |
| Witasick, Jay, UMBC | 4 | 1 | 3.47 | 15 | 0 | 57 | 38 | 29 | 78 |
| Harris, Eric, Radford | 6 | 0 | 3.86 | 9 | 0 | 42 | 39 | 11 | 21 |
| Dale, Carl, Winthrop | 5 | 7 | 4.18 | 15 | 0 | 97 | 103 | 47 | 78 |

## BIG TEN CONFERENCE

| | Conference W | L | Overall W | L |
|---|---|---|---|---|
| **Ohio State** | 19 | 9 | 44 | 19 |
| **Minnesota** | 17 | 9 | 43 | 18 |
| Purdue | 16 | 12 | 36 | 22 |
| Indiana | 15 | 12 | 38 | 21 |
| Northwestern | 15 | 13 | 27 | 27 |
| Iowa | 13 | 13 | 32 | 20 |
| Michigan | 13 | 14 | 25 | 30 |
| Illinois | 12 | 16 | 32 | 23 |
| Michigan State | 12 | 16 | 31 | 23 |
| Penn State | 5 | 23 | 15 | 28 |

**ALL-CONFERENCE TEAM: C**—Darren Grass, So., Minnesota. **1B**—Sloan Smith, Jr., Northwestern. **2B**—Mark Merila, Jr., Minnesota. **3B**—Matt Copp, Sr., Michigan. **SS**—Mark Loretta, Sr., Northwestern. **OF**—Ryan Lefebvre, Sr., Minnesota; Matt Huff, Sr., Northwestern; Jermaine Allensworth, Jr., Purdue. **DH**—Brian Mannino, So., Ohio State. **SP**—Andy Hammerschmidt, So., Minnesota; Bob Scafa, Jr., Indiana; Jeff Isom, Jr., Purdue; Matt Beaumont, So., Ohio State. **RP**—Todd Marion, Sr., Michigan.

**Player of the Year**—Mark Loretta, Northwestern.

### INDIVIDUAL BATTING LEADERS
(Minimum 125 At-Bats)

| | AVG | AB | R | H | 2B | 3B | HR | RBI | SB |
|---|---|---|---|---|---|---|---|---|---|
| Loretta, Mark, Northwestern | .408 | 184 | 38 | 75 | 12 | 6 | 3 | 34 | 20 |
| Merila, Mark, Minnesota | .408 | 184 | 61 | 75 | 14 | 2 | 2 | 55 | 14 |
| Wells, Forry, Illinois | .385 | 179 | 46 | 69 | 11 | 7 | 12 | 54 | 7 |
| Larsen, Cory, Iowa | .380 | 163 | 30 | 62 | 14 | 0 | 0 | 20 | 9 |
| Weaver, Scott, Michigan | .378 | 143 | 17 | 54 | 11 | 3 | 6 | 42 | 5 |
| Zanella, Dan, Purdue | .365 | 197 | 50 | 72 | 12 | 4 | 1 | 32 | 7 |
| Orie, Kevin, Indiana | .358 | 201 | 62 | 72 | 21 | 2 | 9 | 59 | 6 |
| Rojas, Ron, Northwestern | .358 | 176 | 37 | 63 | 7 | 2 | 5 | 38 | 4 |
| Lefebvre, Ryan, Minnesota | .353 | 218 | 51 | 77 | 15 | 1 | 5 | 36 | 14 |
| Cotton, Jason, Indiana | .353 | 139 | 27 | 49 | 9 | 1 | 5 | 34 | 1 |
| Johnson, Steve, Mich. St. | .346 | 179 | 40 | 62 | 14 | 0 | 2 | 37 | 13 |
| Goble, Rodney, Michigan | .344 | 160 | 40 | 55 | 9 | 1 | 2 | 17 | 15 |
| Repasky, Mike, Ohio State | .342 | 187 | 40 | 64 | 13 | 1 | 8 | 47 | 3 |
| Mannino, Brian, Ohio State | .341 | 208 | 51 | 71 | 16 | 0 | 12 | 49 | 2 |

---

| | AVG | AB | R | H | 2B | 3B | HR | RBI | SB |
|---|---|---|---|---|---|---|---|---|---|
| Sweet, Jonathan, Ohio State | .341 | 223 | 56 | 76 | 21 | 1 | 5 | 51 | 1 |
| Wheeler, Ryan, Penn State | .338 | 133 | 26 | 45 | 5 | 1 | 0 | 10 | 11 |
| Biltimier, Mike, Purdue | .338 | 207 | 38 | 70 | 13 | 2 | 13 | 74 | 5 |
| Kraus, Matt, Iowa | .333 | 183 | 41 | 61 | 5 | 1 | 5 | 41 | 14 |
| Nelson, Charlie, Minnesota | .332 | 229 | 64 | 76 | 15 | 1 | 10 | 41 | 19 |
| Copp, Matt, Michigan | .331 | 151 | 27 | 50 | 5 | 2 | 7 | 23 | 4 |
| Spiezio, Scott, Illinois | .330 | 188 | 40 | 62 | 10 | 0 | 16 | 49 | 8 |
| Snedden, Dave, Indiana | .326 | 193 | 51 | 63 | 13 | 2 | 5 | 38 | 13 |
| Mobilia, Bill, Minnesota | .325 | 160 | 34 | 52 | 10 | 0 | 2 | 32 | 5 |
| Polson, Jay, Iowa | .323 | 164 | 46 | 53 | 8 | 3 | 13 | 42 | 6 |
| Grass, Darren, Minnesota | .323 | 186 | 40 | 60 | 12 | 0 | 12 | 54 | 1 |
| Money, Steve, Mich. St. | .322 | 177 | 39 | 57 | 8 | 0 | 1 | 23 | 14 |
| Gunderson, Shane, Minn. | .321 | 140 | 39 | 45 | 11 | 0 | 2 | 20 | 3 |
| Gates, Eric, Penn State | .320 | 125 | 17 | 40 | 7 | 1 | 7 | 27 | 0 |
| Huff, Matt, Northwestern | .319 | 163 | 29 | 52 | 8 | 1 | 11 | 35 | 14 |
| Porter, Marquis, Iowa | .318 | 157 | 35 | 50 | 8 | 0 | 4 | 33 | 9 |
| Suarez, Alfredo, Purdue | .318 | 151 | 29 | 48 | 8 | 0 | 11 | 44 | 2 |
| Timmerman, Scott, Michigan | .316 | 158 | 31 | 50 | 9 | 1 | 0 | 26 | 25 |
| Wohlwand, Dave, Illinois | .314 | 175 | 27 | 55 | 5 | 0 | 1 | 22 | 13 |
| Jones, Gary, Ohio State | .313 | 192 | 42 | 60 | 14 | 8 | 4 | 49 | 10 |
| Lockwood, Matt, Mich. St. | .311 | 167 | 35 | 52 | 13 | 2 | 5 | 46 | 4 |
| Bender, Tony, Minnesota | .311 | 206 | 40 | 64 | 16 | 0 | 1 | 40 | 6 |

### INDIVIDUAL PITCHING LEADERS
(Minimum 50 Innings)

| | W | L | ERA | G | Sv | IP | H | BB | SO |
|---|---|---|---|---|---|---|---|---|---|
| Scafa, Bob, Indiana | 7 | 3 | 2.15 | 14 | 0 | 84 | 68 | 26 | 78 |
| Weimer, Steve, Iowa | 7 | 2 | 2.70 | 14 | 0 | 73 | 65 | 28 | 53 |
| Craig, Justin, Penn State | 3 | 4 | 2.78 | 11 | 0 | 55 | 39 | 30 | 42 |
| Hirschman, Stu, Mich. St. | 6 | 4 | 3.00 | 11 | 0 | 69 | 70 | 24 | 44 |
| Mattiace, Colin, Iowa | 7 | 4 | 3.21 | 15 | 0 | 76 | 88 | 16 | 25 |
| Beaumont, Matt, Ohio State | 8 | 4 | 3.24 | 13 | 0 | 83 | 59 | 51 | 80 |
| Ligtenberg, Kerry, Minnesota | 7 | 6 | 3.51 | 20 | 0 | 92 | 95 | 24 | 63 |
| Hammerschmidt, Andy, Minn. | 8 | 2 | 3.52 | 21 | 0 | 84 | 87 | 24 | 59 |
| Isom, Jeff, Purdue | 10 | 3 | 3.61 | 15 | 0 | 82 | 69 | 29 | 70 |
| Granata, Chris, Ohio State | 7 | 4 | 3.71 | 13 | 0 | 85 | 85 | 34 | 64 |
| Peters, Chris, Indiana | 6 | 3 | 3.77 | 13 | 0 | 62 | 58 | 36 | 50 |
| Smith, Jason, Purdue | 6 | 3 | 3.92 | 13 | 0 | 83 | 76 | 37 | 74 |
| Garman, Dan, Mich. St. | 6 | 2 | 3.95 | 12 | 0 | 66 | 55 | 29 | 60 |
| Biehle, Mike, Ohio State | 4 | 1 | 4.02 | 11 | 0 | 54 | 50 | 33 | 47 |
| Smith, Sloan, Northwestern | 4 | 3 | 4.14 | 11 | 0 | 50 | 41 | 34 | 26 |
| Whipple, Rick, Northwestern | 6 | 6 | 4.15 | 16 | 0 | 85 | 80 | 30 | 60 |
| Arrandale, Matt, Illinois | 7 | 5 | 4.32 | 16 | 1 | 90 | 103 | 28 | 47 |
| Zanolla, Dan, Purdue | 4 | 5 | 4.44 | 11 | 1 | 51 | 49 | 18 | 45 |
| Murray, Heath, Michigan | 5 | 4 | 4.50 | 14 | 0 | 72 | 64 | 30 | 36 |
| Burris, Jeff, Penn State | 4 | 6 | 4.55 | 12 | 0 | 57 | 54 | 34 | 28 |

## BIG WEST CONFERENCE

| | Conference W | L | Overall W | L |
|---|---|---|---|---|
| **Long Beach State** | 17 | 4 | 46 | 19 |
| **Cal State Fullerton** | 16 | 5 | 35 | 19 |
| San Jose State | 11 | 10 | 34 | 19 |
| New Mexico State | 9 | 12 | 31 | 23 |
| Nevada-Las Vegas | 9 | 12 | 24 | 25 |
| UC Santa Barbara | 8 | 13 | 24 | 30 |
| Nevada | 7 | 14 | 28 | 19 |
| Pacific | 7 | 14 | 28 | 25 |

**ALL-CONFERENCE TEAM: C**—Erik Moreno, Sr., Nevada. **1B**—Doug Bame, Sr., Pacific. **2B**—Jeremy Carr, Sr., Cal State Fullerton. **3B**—Gerad Cawhorn, Sr., San Jose State. **SS**—David Zuniga, Sr., San Jose State. **OF**—Dante Powell, So., Cal State Fullerton; Cobi Cradle, Sr., Long Beach State; Efrain Lara, Sr., New Mexico State. **DH**—Adam Millan, Jr., Cal State Fullerton. **Util**—Jared Janke, Fr., UC Santa Barbara. **SP**—Dan Ricabal, Jr., Cal State Fullerton; Daniel Choi, So., Long Beach State; Mike Fontana, Jr., Long Beach State. **RP**—Gabe Gonzalez, So., Long Beach State.

**Player of the Year**—Gerad Cawhorn, San Jose State. **Pitcher of the Year**—Daniel Choi, Long Beach State.

### INDIVIDUAL BATTING LEADERS
(Minimum 125 At-Bats)

| | AVG | AB | R | H | 2B | 3B | HR | RBI | SB |
|---|---|---|---|---|---|---|---|---|---|
| Cawhorn, Gerad, SJ St. | .405 | 200 | 54 | 81 | 13 | 3 | 10 | 57 | 6 |
| Dalton, Eric, NMS | .400 | 185 | 52 | 74 | 12 | 4 | 4 | 20 | 10 |
| Sell, Chip, Pacific | .388 | 214 | 58 | 83 | 17 | 3 | 4 | 46 | 11 |
| Coats, John, UNLV | .374 | 203 | 44 | 76 | 19 | 3 | 14 | 59 | 3 |
| Zuniga, David, San Jose St. | .372 | 215 | 48 | 80 | 11 | 1 | 0 | 23 | 27 |
| Diaz, Leno, UNLV | .370 | 200 | 48 | 74 | 17 | 0 | 3 | 30 | 7 |
| Curtis, Kevin, Long Beach St. | .368 | 220 | 46 | 81 | 13 | 2 | 12 | 57 | 5 |
| Sanderson, Al, NMS | .364 | 220 | 48 | 80 | 12 | 3 | 14 | 64 | 3 |
| Wolger, Mike, UCSB | .364 | 165 | 25 | 60 | 17 | 3 | 1 | 24 | 3 |
| Bame, Doug, Pacific | .363 | 212 | 52 | 77 | 18 | 3 | 13 | 58 | 4 |

**Two-Way Talent.** Cal State Fullerton sophomore outfielder Dante Powell earned second team All-America honors, hitting .335 with 12 home runs and 42 stolen bases.

JOE MIXAN

| | | | | | | | | | |
|---|---|---|---|---|---|---|---|---|---|
| Wadsworth, Jim, NMS | .361 | 208 | 57 | 75 | 5 | 5 | 4 | 37 | 11 |
| Sanchez, Victor, Pacific | .360 | 189 | 37 | 68 | 17 | 1 | 5 | 40 | 8 |
| Liefer, Jeff, Long Beach St. | .356 | 236 | 57 | 84 | 17 | 2 | 12 | 54 | 8 |
| Millan, Adam, CS Fullerton | .354 | 212 | 43 | 75 | 18 | 1 | 7 | 57 | 0 |
| Prieto, Chris, Nevada | .353 | 190 | 61 | 67 | 10 | 9 | 4 | 27 | 35 |
| Carr, Jeremy, CS Fullerton | .351 | 228 | 58 | 80 | 7 | 1 | 3 | 27 | 41 |
| Singleton, Chris, Nevada | .348 | 184 | 40 | 64 | 10 | 4 | 2 | 34 | 21 |
| Duncan, David, NMS | .346 | 179 | 59 | 62 | 20 | 5 | 8 | 50 | 1 |
| Carrigg, Mike, San Jose St. | .344 | 160 | 36 | 55 | 8 | 4 | 1 | 21 | 10 |
| Lara, Efrain, NMS | .343 | 198 | 44 | 68 | 9 | 5 | 13 | 53 | 7 |
| Pitt, Eric, San Jose St. | .343 | 181 | 35 | 62 | 10 | 3 | 3 | 38 | 5 |
| Bokemeier, Matt, UCSB | .342 | 196 | 42 | 67 | 7 | 1 | 2 | 23 | 5 |
| Swanson, John, LB St. | .341 | 176 | 48 | 60 | 2 | 3 | 5 | 38 | 16 |
| Polson, Jon, UNLV | .339 | 192 | 63 | 65 | 9 | 3 | 14 | 42 | 27 |
| Powell, Dante, CS Fullerton | .335 | 233 | 60 | 78 | 17 | 3 | 12 | 57 | 42 |
| Janke, Jared, UCSB | .330 | 203 | 39 | 67 | 19 | 1 | 13 | 49 | 0 |
| Anthony, Brian, UNLV | .327 | 150 | 21 | 49 | 6 | 1 | 3 | 22 | 1 |
| Lewis, Mark, Nevada | .325 | 157 | 34 | 51 | 11 | 3 | 3 | 42 | 4 |
| Licon, Carlos, NMS | .323 | 130 | 24 | 42 | 6 | 2 | 3 | 21 | 2 |
| Ferguson, Jeff, UCSB | .318 | 192 | 49 | 61 | 14 | 1 | 2 | 36 | 13 |
| Phoenix, Wynter, UCSB | .315 | 200 | 45 | 63 | 8 | 6 | 4 | 28 | 13 |
| Leber, Angelo, San Jose St. | .315 | 181 | 42 | 57 | 8 | 2 | 3 | 29 | 13 |
| Mylett, Eddie, Pacific | .311 | 190 | 37 | 59 | 7 | 2 | 0 | 22 | 22 |

### INDIVIDUAL PITCHING LEADERS
(Minimum 50 Innings)

| | W | L | ERA | G | Sv | IP | H | BB | SO |
|---|---|---|---|---|---|---|---|---|---|
| Gonzalez, Gabe, LB St. | 4 | 3 | 1.54 | 34 | 13 | 53 | 31 | 20 | 50 |
| Choi, Daniel, LB St. | 17 | 2 | 2.57 | 20 | 0 | 147 | 116 | 52 | 116 |
| Fontana, Mike, LB St. | 9 | 3 | 2.94 | 20 | 0 | 119 | 104 | 45 | 104 |
| Goldstein, David, LB St. | 3 | 2 | 3.07 | 32 | 6 | 67 | 61 | 32 | 84 |
| Chavez, Joey, San Jose St. | 12 | 6 | 3.37 | 19 | 0 | 115 | 107 | 17 | 73 |
| Ricabal, Dan, CS Fullerton | 11 | 3 | 3.48 | 20 | 0 | 127 | 101 | 58 | 106 |
| Sick, Dave, San Jose St. | 7 | 5 | 3.53 | 17 | 0 | 110 | 91 | 36 | 85 |
| Carley, Shane, San Jose St. | 1 | 1 | 3.78 | 14 | 0 | 50 | 47 | 21 | 37 |
| Silva, Ted, CS Fullerton | 4 | 2 | 3.79 | 32 | 7 | 57 | 43 | 17 | 60 |
| Lake, Kevin, Nevada | 5 | 3 | 3.80 | 13 | 0 | 64 | 64 | 36 | 32 |
| Bennett, Pat, UCSB | 3 | 2 | 3.94 | 17 | 0 | 59 | 53 | 18 | 23 |
| McGowen, Bill, Pacific | 2 | 1 | 4.19 | 16 | 1 | 62 | 70 | 13 | 22 |
| Grenert, Geoff, Nevada | 4 | 7 | 4.42 | 15 | 0 | 98 | 114 | 23 | 84 |
| Miller, Dan, Pacific | 4 | 6 | 4.44 | 12 | 0 | 81 | 98 | 18 | 51 |
| Patton, John, Nevada | 7 | 5 | 4.45 | 16 | 1 | 87 | 88 | 33 | 77 |
| Rinderknecht, Bob, Pacific | 5 | 5 | 4.70 | 13 | 2 | 61 | 63 | 27 | 48 |
| Parisi, Mike, CS Fullerton | 10 | 3 | 4.71 | 18 | 0 | 109 | 115 | 41 | 63 |
| Stephenson, Brian, UCSB | 5 | 4 | 4.85 | 25 | 4 | 52 | 45 | 35 | 45 |
| Hidalgo, Lorenzo, Pacific | 6 | 4 | 4.93 | 13 | 0 | 66 | 70 | 33 | 39 |

## COLONIAL ATHLETIC CONFERENCE

| | Conference | | Overall | |
|---|---|---|---|---|
| | W | L | W | L |
| **George Mason** | 10 | 1 | 33 | 15 |
| Old Dominion | 9 | 3 | 31 | 11 |
| *East Carolina | 11 | 7 | 41 | 19 |
| UNC Wilmington | 6 | 8 | 26 | 29 |
| James Madison | 5 | 9 | 24 | 24 |
| Richmond | 3 | 8 | 29 | 18 |
| William & Mary | 3 | 11 | 24 | 19 |

**ALL-CONFERENCE TEAM: C**—Corey Broome, Sr., UNC Wilmington. **1B**—Geoff Edsell, Jr., Old Dominion. **2B**—Lonnie Goldberg, Sr., George Mason. **3B**—Alex Creighton, Sr., William & Mary. **SS**—Rob Mummau, Sr., James Madison. **OF**—Greg Deares, Sr., George Mason; Kevin Gibbs, Fr., Old Dominion; Pat Watkins, Jr., East Carolina. **DH**—Steven Pitt, So., East Carolina. **RHP**—Geoff Edsell, Jr., Old Dominion. **LHP**—John Smith, Jr., Old Dominion. **RP**—Wayne Gomes, Jr., Old Dominion.

**Player of the Year**—Pat Watkins, East Carolina.

### INDIVIDUAL BATTING LEADERS
(Minimum 125 At-Bats)

| | AVG | AB | R | H | 2B | 3B | HR | RBI | SB |
|---|---|---|---|---|---|---|---|---|---|
| Watkins, Pat, East Carolina | .445 | 220 | 63 | 98 | 7 | 3 | 19 | 57 | 29 |
| Mummau, Rob, JMU | .416 | 178 | 47 | 74 | 18 | 5 | 4 | 36 | 19 |
| Casey, Sean, Richmond | .386 | 171 | 30 | 66 | 18 | 0 | 2 | 31 | 0 |
| Gibbs, Kevin, Old Dominion | .385 | 148 | 49 | 57 | 2 | 4 | 2 | 22 | 45 |
| Baron, Mark, Old Dominion | .365 | 137 | 38 | 50 | 5 | 2 | 0 | 22 | 14 |
| Edsell, Geoff, Old Dominion | .364 | 154 | 39 | 56 | 12 | 2 | 8 | 55 | 6 |
| Kushner, Lee, East Carolina | .361 | 205 | 58 | 74 | 17 | 1 | 14 | 57 | 0 |
| Donato, Jude, Old Dominion | .344 | 160 | 33 | 55 | 16 | 2 | 1 | 36 | 11 |
| Deares, Greg, George Mason | .343 | 204 | 40 | 70 | 11 | 1 | 6 | 53 | 2 |
| Goldberg, Lonnie, GMU | .333 | 192 | 43 | 64 | 11 | 2 | 5 | 29 | 25 |
| Edsell, Brad, JMU | .331 | 160 | 30 | 53 | 10 | 0 | 1 | 19 | 7 |
| Nehring, Kevin, JMU | .331 | 154 | 36 | 51 | 11 | 0 | 4 | 36 | 18 |
| Dausch, Jeff, Richmond | .327 | 168 | 44 | 55 | 11 | 5 | 6 | 35 | 2 |
| Broome, Corey, UNCW | .324 | 216 | 38 | 70 | 21 | 1 | 11 | 35 | 10 |
| Munoz, Ken, George Mason | .323 | 198 | 46 | 64 | 15 | 4 | 4 | 41 | 15 |
| Scioscia, Tom, Richmond | .323 | 158 | 31 | 51 | 9 | 2 | 4 | 37 | 9 |
| Ruberti, Mike, W&M | .322 | 152 | 37 | 49 | 11 | 1 | 9 | 46 | 4 |
| Knight, Shawn, W&M | .316 | 152 | 42 | 48 | 6 | 3 | 1 | 23 | 38 |
| Picollo, J.J., George Mason | .314 | 175 | 44 | 55 | 14 | 1 | 10 | 38 | 1 |
| Creighton, Alex, W&M | .313 | 144 | 30 | 45 | 17 | 3 | 2 | 21 | 3 |

## INDIVIDUAL PITCHING LEADERS
(Minimum 50 Innings)

| | W | L | ERA | G | Sv | IP | H | BB | SO |
|---|---|---|---|---|---|---|---|---|---|
| Walker, Bobby, George Mason. | 4 | 1 | 1.65 | 8 | 0 | 55 | 49 | 13 | 23 |
| Sanburn, Mike, East Carolina. | 10 | 2 | 2.26 | 15 | 0 | 112 | 98 | 13 | 78 |
| Altman, Heath, UNCW | 3 | 3 | 2.39 | 21 | 8 | 64 | 42 | 32 | 80 |
| Smith, John, Old Dominion | 7 | 2 | 2.44 | 15 | 0 | 89 | 75 | 23 | 72 |
| Blackwell, Richie, ECU | 6 | 2 | 2.66 | 11 | 0 | 51 | 41 | 23 | 60 |
| Whitfield, Howard, ECU | 4 | 2 | 2.90 | 16 | 0 | 50 | 39 | 15 | 28 |
| Edsell, Geoff, Old Dominion | 7 | 2 | 2.97 | 11 | 0 | 58 | 47 | 26 | 64 |
| Beck, Johnny, East Carolina. | 8 | 5 | 3.02 | 19 | 2 | 110 | 114 | 40 | 88 |
| Slonaker, Chris, JMU | 4 | 5 | 3.17 | 11 | 0 | 60 | 53 | 19 | 36 |
| Hoy, Wayne, Richmond | 5 | 3 | 3.17 | 12 | 1 | 65 | 55 | 21 | 44 |
| Hennessy, Sean, Old Dominion. | 8 | 3 | 3.28 | 15 | 0 | 85 | 73 | 15 | 55 |
| Whiteman, Greg, JMU | 2 | 3 | 3.41 | 9 | 0 | 58 | 57 | 27 | 48 |
| Hartgrove, Lyle, ECU | 11 | 3 | 3.50 | 20 | 1 | 108 | 113 | 7 | 48 |

## ECAC

| DIAMOND | Conference W | L | Overall W | L |
|---|---|---|---|---|
| C.W. Post | 14 | 6 | 23 | 20 |
| Hofstra | 12 | 8 | 20 | 21 |
| West Chester | 12 | 8 | 21 | 20 |
| New York Tech | 8 | 12 | 13 | 31 |
| Central Connecticut State | 7 | 13 | 11 | 27 |
| Pace | 7 | 13 | 17 | 28 |

**ALL-CONFERENCE TEAM: C**—Rob Zachmann, So., Pace. **1B**—Ken Auer, Sr., C.W. Post. **2B**—Robert Kline, Sr., West Chester. **3B**—Mike Dieguez, Sr., Pace. **SS**—Gary Giersbach, Jr., New York Tech. **OF**—James Apicella, So., C.W. Post; Gary Collum, Sr., Pace; Jeff Vallillo, So., Hofstra. **DH**—Rick Casazza, So., C.W. Post. **P**—Brad Babson, So., Central Connecticut State; Chuck Fritz, Jr., West Chester; Chris McCoy, Jr., New York Tech; Bob O'Brien, Sr., C.W. Post.

**Player of the Year**—Gary Collum, Pace.

## INDIVIDUAL BATTING LEADERS
(Minimum 100 At-Bats)

| | AVG | AB | R | H | 2B | 3B | HR | RBI | SB |
|---|---|---|---|---|---|---|---|---|---|
| Zonca, Chris, West Chester | .396 | 139 | 37 | 55 | 12 | 0 | 6 | 29 | 7 |
| Collum, Gary, Pace | .389 | 167 | 44 | 65 | 13 | 3 | 7 | 40 | 27 |
| Gawitt, Nate, CCS | .377 | 106 | 17 | 40 | 9 | 1 | 2 | 19 | 2 |
| Apicella, James, C.W. Post | .363 | 146 | 32 | 53 | 8 | 0 | 5 | 42 | 1 |
| Sweeney, Craig, WC | .359 | 145 | 24 | 52 | 14 | 2 | 1 | 39 | 3 |
| Dieguez, Mike, Pace | .354 | 164 | 32 | 58 | 16 | 0 | 5 | 31 | 10 |
| Duffy, Rob, C.W. Post | .347 | 118 | 24 | 41 | 10 | 0 | 4 | 28 | 2 |
| Lipani, John, C.W. Post | .345 | 116 | 28 | 40 | 1 | 1 | 6 | 22 | 11 |
| Zachmann, Rob, Pace | .344 | 151 | 38 | 52 | 14 | 1 | 4 | 30 | 4 |
| Vallillo, Jeff, Hofstra | .340 | 144 | 27 | 49 | 7 | 0 | 5 | 40 | 5 |

## INDIVIDUAL PITCHING LEADERS
(Minimum 40 Innings)

| | W | L | ERA | G | Sv | IP | H | BB | SO |
|---|---|---|---|---|---|---|---|---|---|
| Babson, Brad, CCS | 5 | 5 | 2.81 | 12 | 0 | 67 | 57 | 37 | 60 |
| Fasano, Frank, Pace | 4 | 3 | 2.98 | 9 | 0 | 42 | 40 | 19 | 32 |
| McCoy, Chris, New York Tech. | 7 | 1 | 3.25 | 14 | 1 | 53 | 45 | 15 | 41 |
| O'Brien, Bob, C.W. Post | 5 | 3 | 3.53 | 15 | 0 | 56 | 54 | 16 | 26 |
| Peterman, Jamus, WC | 6 | 4 | 3.95 | 15 | 2 | 43 | 40 | 21 | 15 |
| Miller, Greg, CCS | 2 | 6 | 4.32 | 12 | 1 | 42 | 44 | 27 | 30 |
| Fritz, Chuck, West Chester | 4 | 0 | 4.37 | 14 | 1 | 58 | 68 | 10 | 45 |
| Kaiser, Chris, West Chester | 4 | 4 | 4.50 | 14 | 0 | 44 | 54 | 20 | 33 |

| | Conference W | L | Overall W | L |
|---|---|---|---|---|
| **MAAC NORTH** | | | | |
| LeMoyne | 16 | 2 | 34 | 6 |
| Canisius | 7 | 11 | 13 | 25 |
| Siena | 7 | 11 | 11 | 24 |
| Niagara | 6 | 12 | 12 | 19 |
| **MAAC SOUTH** | | | | |
| Fairfield | 13 | 5 | 21 | 19 |
| Iona | 11 | 7 | 19 | 19 |
| St. Peter's | 9 | 9 | 17 | 18 |
| Manhattan | 3 | 15 | 3 | 33 |

**ALL-NORTHERN DIVISION TEAM: C**—Keith Applegate, Jr., Canisius; Dan DeMonte, Jr., Niagara. **1B**—Jason Rausch, Sr., Canisius. **2B**—Dave Penafeather, Jr., Canisius; Dickie Woodridge, Sr., LeMoyne. **3B**—Ryan Diodati, Jr., Niagara. **SS**—David Smith, Jr., LeMoyne. **OF**—Chuck Kulle, So., LeMoyne; Jeff Gambitta, Sr., Niagara; Steve DeWolfe, Sr., Canisius. **DH**—Paul Feltman, Jr., Canisius; Dave Bunn, Fr., Niagara. **P**—Jon Ratliff, Jr., LeMoyne;

Scott Moody, Sr., LeMoyne; Mike Ciszewski, Sr., Niagara.
**Player of the Year**—David Smith, LeMoyne.

**ALL-SOUTHERN DIVISION TEAM: C**—Joe Carillo, Sr., Fairfield. **1B**—Drew Brown, Jr., St. Peter's. **2B**—Sean Paine, Sr., Iona. **3B**—Lou Garcia, Sr., Fairfield. **SS**—Matt Guiliano Jr., Iona. **OF**—Dave Filipkowski, So., Iona; Mike Pike, Fr., Fairfield; Bill McMahon, Jr., Fairfield. **DH**—Neil Murphy, Sr., Iona. **P**—Ralph Bonelli, Jr., Iona; Scott Larkin, Sr., Fairfield; Lou Vigliotti, Jr., Fairfield.

**Player of the Year**—Neil Murphy, Iona.

## INDIVIDUAL BATTING LEADERS
(Minimum 100 At-Bats)

| | AVG | AB | R | H | 2B | 3B | HR | RBI | SB |
|---|---|---|---|---|---|---|---|---|---|
| Woodridge, Dickie, LeMoyne... | .476 | 126 | 56 | 60 | 14 | 2 | 2 | 28 | 21 |
| Smith, David, LeMoyne | .441 | 136 | 64 | 60 | 15 | 1 | 14 | 65 | 14 |
| Kulle, Chuck, LeMoyne | .414 | 140 | 40 | 58 | 10 | 0 | 13 | 67 | 5 |
| Carillo, Joe, Fairfield | .405 | 148 | 27 | 60 | 15 | 1 | 5 | 40 | 1 |
| Brown, Drew, St. Peter's | .391 | 133 | 28 | 52 | 12 | 1 | 2 | 28 | 2 |
| Rausch, Jason, Canisius | .389 | 113 | 22 | 44 | 8 | 0 | 9 | 20 | 0 |
| Murphy, Neil, Iona | .385 | 135 | 38 | 52 | 16 | 2 | 15 | 49 | 4 |
| Nocera, Chris, St. Peter's | .383 | 115 | 35 | 44 | 7 | 3 | 1 | 11 | 12 |
| Boryczewski, Marty, St. Peter's | .381 | 126 | 17 | 48 | 8 | 2 | 2 | 30 | 3 |
| Filipkowski, Dave, Iona | .369 | 111 | 33 | 41 | 9 | 1 | 4 | 21 | 12 |
| Foit, Rick, Canisius | .356 | 135 | 27 | 48 | 12 | 2 | 2 | 13 | 6 |
| Welch, Kevin, Fairfield | .352 | 125 | 22 | 44 | 8 | 0 | 3 | 29 | 3 |

## INDIVIDUAL PITCHING LEADERS
(Minimum 40 Innings)

| | W | L | ERA | G | Sv | IP | H | BB | SO |
|---|---|---|---|---|---|---|---|---|---|
| Ratliff, Jon, LeMoyne | 10 | 1 | 2.04 | 13 | 1 | 84 | 67 | 17 | 64 |
| Kurtz, Dan, LeMoyne | 5 | 2 | 3.16 | 11 | 1 | 57 | 44 | 38 | 40 |
| Vigliotti, Lou, Fairfield | 6 | 2 | 3.22 | 11 | 1 | 64 | 64 | 16 | 31 |
| Micciulli, Bill, Fairfield | 4 | 0 | 3.55 | 8 | 0 | 46 | 36 | 21 | 22 |
| Holecek, Scott, Iona | 4 | 1 | 4.06 | 10 | 0 | 44 | 48 | 18 | 21 |
| Bonelli, Ralph, Iona | 4 | 3 | 4.09 | 11 | 0 | 62 | 76 | 13 | 32 |
| Moody, Scott, LeMoyne | 9 | 4 | 4.14 | 10 | 0 | 54 | 48 | 26 | 43 |

| NORTHEAST | Conference W | L | Overall W | L |
|---|---|---|---|---|
| Fairleigh Dickinson | 15 | 6 | 28 | 16 |
| Long Island | 14 | 6 | 17 | 18 |
| St. Francis (N.Y.) | 13 | 8 | 24 | 15 |
| Monmouth | 13 | 8 | 17 | 20 |
| Rider | 12 | 9 | 21 | 18 |
| Wagner | 6 | 14 | 9 | 23 |
| Marist | 5 | 13 | 9 | 24 |
| Mount St. Mary's | 1 | 15 | 6 | 24 |

**ALL-CONFERENCE TEAM: C**—Brett Rackett, Jr., Monmouth. **1B**—Mike Policastro, Sr., Fairleigh Dickinson; Chris DeDomenico, Sr., Wagner. **2B**—Shawn Brown, Sr., Rider. **3B**—Derek Pukash, Jr., Fairleigh Dickinson; Lou Vernagallo, Sr., Long Island. **SS**—Ray DeSimone, Sr., Long Island. **OF**—Mark D'Ambrosio, So., Fairleigh Dickinson; Sal Racobaldo, Jr., Fairleigh Dickinson; Jack Scholz, Sr., Wagner. **DH**—John Manuelian, Fr., Long Island. **P**—Randy Chirumbolo, Jr., Wagner; Rob Gontkosky, Jr., Rider.

**Player of the Year**—Ray DeSimone, Long Island. **Pitcher of the Year**—Brian Woods, Fairleigh Dickinson.

## INDIVIDUAL BATTING LEADERS
(Minimum 100 At-Bats)

| | AVG | AB | R | H | 2B | 3B | HR | RBI | SB |
|---|---|---|---|---|---|---|---|---|---|
| Rackett, Brett, Monmouth | .385 | 130 | 41 | 50 | 6 | 1 | 6 | 30 | 10 |
| Pukash, Derek, FDU | .376 | 133 | 34 | 50 | 13 | 0 | 2 | 34 | 6 |
| DeSimone, Ray, Long Island | .375 | 136 | 37 | 51 | 10 | 10 | 1 | 14 | 13 |
| Lanzaro, Jeff, St. Francis | .371 | 143 | 33 | 53 | 17 | 2 | 0 | 20 | 13 |
| Vernagallo, Lou, Long Island | .349 | 129 | 26 | 45 | 10 | 0 | 7 | 29 | 2 |
| Gola, Mark, Rider | .343 | 102 | 20 | 35 | 8 | 0 | 1 | 18 | 4 |
| Mirasola, Steve, St. Francis | .341 | 132 | 34 | 45 | 12 | 3 | 3 | 24 | 9 |
| Brown, Shawn, Rider | .340 | 147 | 38 | 50 | 7 | 3 | 6 | 35 | 11 |
| Scher, Dave, FDU | .337 | 104 | 26 | 35 | 8 | 0 | 3 | 17 | 4 |
| Wisdom, Boyd, FDU | .335 | 167 | 37 | 56 | 6 | 2 | 1 | 28 | 32 |
| D'Ambrosio, Mark, FDU | .333 | 132 | 30 | 44 | 11 | 0 | 6 | 37 | 6 |

## INDIVIDUAL PITCHING LEADERS
(Minimum 40 Innings)

| | W | L | ERA | G | Sv | IP | H | BB | SO |
|---|---|---|---|---|---|---|---|---|---|
| Halama, John, St. Francis | 5 | 0 | 1.60 | 9 | 0 | 56 | 22 | 28 | 40 |
| Woods, Brian, FDU | 7 | 2 | 1.90 | 10 | 0 | 67 | 45 | 41 | 68 |
| Chirumbolo, Randy, Wagner | 3 | 4 | 2.22 | 7 | 0 | 49 | 47 | 11 | 34 |
| Reichert, Keith, St. Francis | 5 | 2 | 2.53 | 11 | 1 | 60 | 51 | 15 | 19 |
| Torres, Jeremy, FDU | 5 | 3 | 2.67 | 9 | 0 | 57 | 49 | 22 | 42 |
| Klonis, Jason, Rider | 5 | 3 | 3.38 | 11 | 0 | 59 | 54 | 21 | 25 |
| Goodin, Jeff, Marist | 2 | 5 | 3.63 | 11 | 0 | 57 | 56 | 14 | 23 |

| PATRIOT NORTH | Conference W | L | Overall W | L |
|---|---|---|---|---|
| *Fordham | 13 | 7 | 32 | 27 |
| Army | 11 | 9 | 17 | 22 |
| Holy Cross | 9 | 11 | 12 | 20 |
| Colgate | 6 | 14 | 8 | 20 |
| PATRIOT SOUTH | W | L | W | L |
| Navy | 11 | 9 | 21 | 18 |
| Lehigh | 10 | 10 | 15 | 19 |
| Bucknell | 10 | 10 | 15 | 25 |
| Lafayette | 10 | 10 | 12 | 21 |

**ALL-CONFERENCE TEAM: C**—Doug Bohrer, Sr., Army. **1B**—Marcus Lee, Jr., Navy. **2B**—Jim Larkin, Sr., Holy Cross. **3B**—Jon Lehberger, Jr., Lehigh. **SS**—Todd Butler, Sr., Navy. **OF**—Lance Boyce, Sr., Army; Mike Butler, Jr., Fordham; Steve Mauro, So., Navy; Arthur O'Neal, So., Army. **DH**—Joe Schultz, Jr., Fordham. **Util**—Mike Mabardy, Sr., Colgate. **SP**—Steve Reich, Sr., Army; Bill Conkling, Sr., Fordham. **RP**—Joe Mackey, Fr., Fordham; Paul Perry, Sr., Army.

**Player of the Year**—Marcus Lee, Navy. **Pitcher of the Year**—Steve Reich, Army.

### INDIVIDUAL BATTING LEADERS
(Minimum 100 At-Bats)

| | AVG | AB | R | H | 2B | 3B | HR | RBI | SB |
|---|---|---|---|---|---|---|---|---|---|
| Lee, Marcus, Navy | .375 | 128 | 37 | 48 | 10 | 2 | 12 | 60 | 4 |
| Schultz, Joe, Fordham | .367 | 180 | 38 | 66 | 14 | 4 | 4 | 44 | 6 |
| Mauro, Steve, Navy | .366 | 131 | 36 | 48 | 8 | 0 | 2 | 25 | 9 |
| O'Neal, Arthur, Army | .364 | 143 | 24 | 52 | 3 | 2 | 7 | 29 | 18 |
| Houston, Mark, Army | .358 | 120 | 33 | 43 | 9 | 3 | 5 | 27 | 7 |
| Butler, Todd, Navy | .353 | 119 | 42 | 42 | 10 | 1 | 5 | 23 | 7 |
| Miltenberger, Scott, Lafayette | .349 | 109 | 26 | 38 | 6 | 2 | 0 | 15 | 6 |
| Lehberger, Jon, Lehigh | .330 | 112 | 17 | 37 | 8 | 1 | 3 | 22 | 14 |
| Boyce, Lance, Army | .324 | 139 | 39 | 45 | 10 | 2 | 9 | 30 | 17 |
| Mancia, Mike, Lafayette | .321 | 112 | 22 | 36 | 11 | 0 | 2 | 19 | 4 |
| Larkin, Jim, Holy Cross | .321 | 109 | 12 | 35 | 5 | 1 | 3 | 17 | 5 |
| Butler, Mike, Fordham | .320 | 203 | 44 | 65 | 11 | 7 | 4 | 50 | 7 |
| Beach, Brent, Navy | .319 | 113 | 37 | 36 | 4 | 3 | 0 | 14 | 2 |
| McArthur, Tom, Lafayette | .313 | 115 | 15 | 36 | 11 | 0 | 1 | 19 | 2 |

### INDIVIDUAL PITCHING LEADERS
(Minimum 40 Innings)

| | W | L | ERA | G | Sv | IP | H | BB | SO |
|---|---|---|---|---|---|---|---|---|---|
| Reich, Steve, Army | 6 | 3 | 2.48 | 11 | 0 | 76 | 68 | 19 | 88 |
| King, Dan, Lafayette | 5 | 3 | 2.56 | 10 | 0 | 53 | 41 | 16 | 20 |
| Mackey, Joe, Fordham | 6 | 2 | 2.89 | 19 | 1 | 65 | 50 | 44 | 56 |
| Moore, Toby, Navy | 5 | 3 | 2.91 | 12 | 0 | 68 | 62 | 19 | 45 |
| Boyce, Lance, Army | 2 | 5 | 2.91 | 8 | 0 | 46 | 39 | 19 | 37 |
| Werkhoven, Scott, Lafayette | 4 | 5 | 3.07 | 12 | 0 | 59 | 49 | 28 | 41 |
| Conkling, Bill, Fordham | 8 | 3 | 3.16 | 21 | 5 | 77 | 81 | 33 | 46 |
| Hernandez, Ramon, Fordham | 4 | 5 | 3.41 | 14 | 0 | 74 | 73 | 32 | 51 |
| Toolan, Henry, Fordham | 5 | 3 | 3.54 | 15 | 1 | 69 | 84 | 18 | 38 |
| Norwood, Mike, Lehigh | 3 | 4 | 3.72 | 7 | 0 | 46 | 37 | 16 | 27 |

# GREAT MIDWEST CONFERENCE

| | Conference W | L | Overall W | L |
|---|---|---|---|---|
| *Memphis State | 15 | 3 | 42 | 15 |
| Alabama-Birmingham | 12 | 6 | 35 | 23 |
| Saint Louis | 6 | 12 | 22 | 23 |
| Cincinnati | 3 | 15 | 16 | 29 |

**ALL-CONFERENCE TEAM: C**—Rob Domino, Sr., Memphis State. **INF**—Mike Dunnett, Jr., Alabama-Birmingham; Carey Fenton, Jr., Memphis State; Chris Gabbart, Jr., Alabama-Birmingham; Jeff Hoekstra, Jr., Memphis State; Steve Moss, Sr., Memphis State. **OF**—Mike Barger, Sr., Saint Louis; Pat Conreaux, Jr., Saint Louis; Mark Little, Jr., Memphis State; Keifer Rackley, Sr., Alabama-Birmingham. **DH**—Mark Gabbard, Sr., Cincinnati. **SP**—Greg Smith, Sr., Memphis State; Chris Stewart, Sr., Memphis State. **RP**—Jay Cole, Jr., Alabama-Birmingham.

**Player of the Year**—Mike Barger, Saint Louis.

### INDIVIDUAL BATTING LEADERS
(Minimum 125 At-Bats)

| | AVG | AB | R | H | 2B | 3B | HR | RBI | SB |
|---|---|---|---|---|---|---|---|---|---|
| Barger, Mike, Saint Louis | .460 | 176 | 49 | 81 | 14 | 4 | 4 | 31 | 37 |
| Gabbard, Mark, Cincinnati | .416 | 166 | 39 | 69 | 9 | 2 | 13 | 46 | 3 |
| Conreaux, Pat, Saint Louis | .411 | 180 | 33 | 74 | 13 | 6 | 3 | 51 | 15 |
| Little, Mark, Memphis State | .409 | 181 | 53 | 74 | 20 | 7 | 7 | 49 | 15 |
| Hoekstra, Jeff, Memphis State | .393 | 201 | 41 | 79 | 19 | 0 | 4 | 39 | 4 |

---

| | AVG | AB | R | H | 2B | 3B | HR | RBI | SB |
|---|---|---|---|---|---|---|---|---|---|
| Dunnett, Mike, UAB | .344 | 221 | 44 | 76 | 22 | 2 | 2 | 32 | 2 |
| Rackley, Keifer, UAB | .336 | 220 | 55 | 74 | 16 | 4 | 9 | 44 | 9 |
| Jersey, Brian, UAB | .325 | 126 | 23 | 41 | 5 | 1 | 7 | 34 | 2 |
| Cortez, Cort, UAB | .316 | 152 | 15 | 48 | 2 | 1 | 2 | 23 | 2 |
| Gabbart, Chris, UAB | .312 | 221 | 53 | 69 | 10 | 3 | 11 | 47 | 5 |
| Domino, Rob, Memphis State | .310 | 171 | 34 | 53 | 12 | 1 | 3 | 35 | 12 |
| Muckerheide, Troy, Cincinnati | .293 | 164 | 37 | 48 | 11 | 2 | 6 | 36 | 14 |
| Sullins, Sean, Cincinnati | .292 | 161 | 25 | 47 | 11 | 1 | 2 | 28 | 6 |

### INDIVIDUAL PITCHING LEADERS
(Minimum 50 Innings)

| | W | L | ERA | G | Sv | IP | H | BB | SO |
|---|---|---|---|---|---|---|---|---|---|
| Smith, Greg, Memphis State | 10 | 2 | 2.04 | 18 | 2 | 71 | 67 | 18 | 57 |
| Stewart, Chris, Memphis St. | 10 | 0 | 2.44 | 15 | 0 | 85 | 49 | 41 | 82 |
| Menard, Jeff, UAB | 8 | 1 | 3.03 | 22 | 1 | 77 | 80 | 33 | 40 |
| McCommon, Jason, Memphis St. | 6 | 5 | 3.12 | 16 | 1 | 95 | 78 | 36 | 70 |
| Glass, Lonnie, Memphis State | 7 | 3 | 3.19 | 16 | 1 | 87 | 80 | 31 | 74 |
| Blomberg, Tim, Saint Louis | 5 | 4 | 4.08 | 13 | 0 | 75 | 79 | 23 | 38 |
| Tucker, Ronnie, UAB | 7 | 7 | 4.20 | 22 | 0 | 94 | 106 | 53 | 71 |
| Wetzel, Dan, Saint Louis | 4 | 6 | 4.83 | 15 | 1 | 82 | 103 | 34 | 68 |
| Gray, Mark, UAB | 6 | 4 | 5.45 | 18 | 0 | 74 | 83 | 45 | 56 |
| Blackwell, Slade, UAB | 5 | 5 | 6.15 | 17 | 1 | 72 | 93 | 26 | 43 |

# IVY LEAGUE

| GEHRIG | Conference W | L | Overall W | L |
|---|---|---|---|---|
| Columbia | 11 | 9 | 19 | 21 |
| Pennsylvania | 10 | 10 | 17 | 19 |
| Princeton | 10 | 10 | 16 | 25 |
| Cornell | 3 | 17 | 6 | 29 |
| ROLFE | W | L | W | L |
| *Yale | 16 | 4 | 33 | 11 |
| Harvard | 12 | 8 | 18 | 20 |
| Brown | 10 | 10 | 12 | 27 |
| Dartmouth | 8 | 12 | 14 | 19 |

**ALL-CONFERENCE TEAM: C**—John Clifford, So., Dartmouth. **1B**—David Morgan, Jr., Harvard. **2B**—Manny Patel, Jr., Yale. **3B**—Rob Naddelman, So., Pennsylvania. **SS**—Mike Giardi, Jr., Harvard. **OF**—Joe Tosone, Sr., Dartmouth; Garrett Neubart, So., Columbia; Glenn Miller, Sr., Pennsylvania. **DH**—Michael Green, So., Pennsylvania. **Util**—Dan Puskas, Sr., Princeton; Chip DeLorenzo, Sr., Cornell. **P**—Keith Pelatowski, Jr., Yale; Dan Block, Sr., Pennsylvania. **RP**—Steve Ceterko, Fr., Columbia; Russell Peltz, Jr., Yale.

**Player of the Year**—David Morgan, Harvard.

### INDIVIDUAL BATTING LEADERS
(Minimum 100 At-Bats)

| | AVG | AB | R | H | 2B | 3B | HR | RBI | SB |
|---|---|---|---|---|---|---|---|---|---|
| Puskas, Dan, Princeton | .405 | 111 | 18 | 45 | 11 | 1 | 0 | 23 | 6 |
| Morgan, David, Harvard | .395 | 129 | 29 | 51 | 9 | 0 | 8 | 36 | 4 |
| Miller, Glenn, Penn | .386 | 101 | 23 | 39 | 4 | 3 | 5 | 30 | 4 |
| Tosone, Joe, Dartmouth | .379 | 116 | 34 | 44 | 7 | 6 | 1 | 14 | 15 |
| Neubart, Garrett, Columbia | .377 | 138 | 37 | 52 | 9 | 5 | 1 | 22 | 31 |
| Giardi, Mike, Harvard | .375 | 120 | 26 | 45 | 9 | 1 | 2 | 26 | 4 |
| Teal, Bart, Columbia | .360 | 139 | 26 | 50 | 12 | 2 | 3 | 29 | 3 |
| Clifford, John, Dartmouth | .357 | 112 | 22 | 40 | 3 | 0 | 3 | 18 | 6 |
| Hodson, Blair, Yale | .349 | 146 | 36 | 51 | 16 | 2 | 8 | 37 | 18 |
| Eidle, Scott, Yale | .336 | 140 | 34 | 47 | 8 | 1 | 10 | 33 | 5 |
| DeLorenzo, Chip, Cornell | .316 | 114 | 16 | 36 | 1 | 2 | 0 | 7 | 6 |
| Perry, Zack, Princeton | .314 | 102 | 13 | 32 | 5 | 0 | 1 | 24 | 1 |
| Schweitzer, Jeff, Princeton | .310 | 145 | 28 | 45 | 10 | 2 | 2 | 18 | 11 |
| Naddelman, Rob, Penn | .299 | 107 | 22 | 32 | 8 | 1 | 1 | 16 | 8 |
| Kreuscher, John, Columbia | .299 | 134 | 17 | 40 | 7 | 0 | 3 | 27 | 0 |
| Schettino, Frank, Brown | .293 | 123 | 30 | 36 | 7 | 2 | 2 | 17 | 8 |
| Shannon, Tim, Penn | .291 | 110 | 20 | 32 | 4 | 1 | 1 | 16 | 9 |
| Patel, Manny, Yale | .290 | 138 | 36 | 40 | 7 | 1 | 5 | 34 | 21 |
| Hill, Mike, Harvard | .289 | 128 | 27 | 37 | 15 | 0 | 5 | 22 | 5 |

### INDIVIDUAL PITCHING LEADERS
(Minimum 40 Innings)

| | W | L | ERA | G | Sv | IP | H | BB | SO |
|---|---|---|---|---|---|---|---|---|---|
| Bohannon, Jason, Yale | 5 | 1 | 2.15 | 12 | 0 | 50 | 38 | 16 | 28 |
| Block, Dan, Penn | 5 | 1 | 2.23 | 9 | 0 | 44 | 34 | 15 | 29 |
| Gutheil, Harry, Princeton | 5 | 2 | 2.28 | 10 | 0 | 55 | 45 | 16 | 38 |
| Ceterko, Steve, Columbia | 5 | 2 | 2.32 | 12 | 0 | 43 | 29 | 23 | 49 |
| Desrocher, Ray, Harvard | 5 | 3 | 3.04 | 9 | 0 | 50 | 45 | 26 | 30 |
| Haughey, Edmund, Penn | 3 | 3 | 3.12 | 9 | 0 | 49 | 46 | 17 | 37 |
| Thompson, Dan, Yale | 4 | 0 | 3.15 | 7 | 0 | 40 | 38 | 9 | 28 |
| Khayat, Clark, Yale | 4 | 3 | 3.25 | 14 | 1 | 61 | 61 | 31 | 29 |
| Pelatowski, Keith, Yale | 7 | 3 | 3.34 | 11 | 0 | 70 | 65 | 17 | 48 |
| Tallman, Mike, Dartmouth | 4 | 2 | 3.42 | 9 | 0 | 47 | 36 | 26 | 24 |

# METRO CONFERENCE

| | Conference | | Overall | |
|---|---|---|---|---|
| | W | L | W | L |
| **South Florida** | 13 | 5 | 40 | 20 |
| Southern Mississippi | 11 | 6 | 33 | 26 |
| Virginia Tech | 11 | 6 | 34 | 15 |
| Tulane | 8 | 7 | 23 | 31 |
| *UNC Charlotte | 6 | 11 | 26 | 32 |
| Virginia Commonwealth | 4 | 10 | 30 | 27 |
| Louisville | 3 | 11 | 18 | 41 |

**ALL-CONFERENCE TEAM: C**—Larry Schneider, Jr., Tulane. **1B**—Darren Stumberger, Jr., South Florida. **2B**—Ryan Kritscher, So., Southern Mississippi. **3B**—Erik Sauve, Jr., VCU. **SS**—Brett King, Jr., South Florida. **OF**—Cam Browder, Sr., UNC Charlotte; Doug Carroll, So., South Florida; J.R. Hawkins, Sr., Virginia Tech. **DH**—Jim Felch, Jr., South Florida. **Util**—Darren Oppel, Sr., Louisville. **P**—Mark Reed, Sr., South Florida; David Hutcheson, Sr., South Florida.

**Player of the Year**—Darren Stumberger, South Florida.

## INDIVIDUAL BATTING LEADERS
(Minimum 125 At-Bats)

| | AVG | AB | R | H | 2B | 3B | HR | RBI | SB |
|---|---|---|---|---|---|---|---|---|---|
| Durkac, Bo, Va. Tech | .423 | 182 | 43 | 77 | 13 | 0 | 6 | 29 | 3 |
| Sauve, Erik, VCU | .400 | 210 | 54 | 84 | 15 | 6 | 11 | 65 | 7 |
| Barnes, Tommy, Louisville | .395 | 256 | 53 | 101 | 21 | 3 | 9 | 54 | 8 |
| Stumberger, Darren, USF | .385 | 213 | 56 | 82 | 14 | 2 | 14 | 76 | 1 |
| Browder, Cam, UNCC | .380 | 208 | 45 | 79 | 19 | 2 | 14 | 53 | 5 |
| Carroll, Doug, USF | .370 | 227 | 63 | 84 | 20 | 5 | 7 | 59 | 14 |
| Meyers, Glenn, Louisville | .358 | 176 | 30 | 63 | 11 | 2 | 5 | 31 | 0 |
| Schneider, Larry, Tulane | .352 | 176 | 43 | 62 | 8 | 2 | 9 | 40 | 1 |
| Oppel, Darren, Louisville | .349 | 209 | 53 | 73 | 16 | 1 | 11 | 51 | 2 |
| Davis, Tommy, USM | .343 | 245 | 50 | 84 | 17 | 4 | 16 | 69 | 11 |
| Dalton, Dee, Va. Tech | .341 | 173 | 49 | 59 | 8 | 3 | 14 | 42 | 4 |
| Woodard, Andy, USM | .338 | 219 | 54 | 74 | 13 | 1 | 11 | 30 | 22 |
| Hawkins, J.R., Va. Tech | .337 | 184 | 44 | 62 | 15 | 1 | 10 | 46 | 3 |
| Kritscher, Ryan, USM | .333 | 225 | 47 | 75 | 11 | 1 | 2 | 33 | 5 |
| Lewentowicz, Jim, VCU | .332 | 214 | 34 | 71 | 13 | 0 | 6 | 49 | 2 |
| Owens, Clint, Louisville | .329 | 152 | 30 | 50 | 8 | 1 | 7 | 22 | 8 |
| Garcia, Jason, USF | .329 | 207 | 69 | 68 | 14 | 0 | 5 | 32 | 22 |
| Grimes, Rob, VCU | .324 | 219 | 53 | 71 | 15 | 2 | 1 | 23 | 40 |
| Howard, Tucker, Louisville | .317 | 202 | 36 | 64 | 13 | 1 | 8 | 34 | 0 |
| Simpson, Jason, USM | .313 | 217 | 40 | 68 | 9 | 0 | 5 | 33 | 5 |
| Allen, Charlie, Louisville | .311 | 222 | 56 | 69 | 9 | 0 | 19 | 57 | 7 |
| Felch, Jim, USF | .309 | 236 | 46 | 73 | 15 | 2 | 12 | 66 | 11 |
| Skeens, Kelly, UNCC | .307 | 225 | 39 | 69 | 18 | 2 | 3 | 41 | 2 |
| Reedy, Mike, Va. Tech | .306 | 147 | 38 | 45 | 10 | 1 | 2 | 19 | 2 |
| Yarbrough, Jeff, VCU | .305 | 190 | 26 | 58 | 9 | 4 | 4 | 34 | 1 |

## INDIVIDUAL PITCHING LEADERS
(Minimum 45 Innings)

| | W | L | ERA | G | Sv | IP | H | BB | SO |
|---|---|---|---|---|---|---|---|---|---|
| Hutcheson, David, USF | 9 | 6 | 2.59 | 19 | 0 | 132 | 131 | 45 | 97 |
| Danner, Adam, USF | 6 | 2 | 2.94 | 10 | 0 | 49 | 46 | 16 | 40 |
| Hastings, Bryan, Va. Tech | 2 | 4 | 3.06 | 10 | 0 | 62 | 58 | 17 | 53 |
| Reed, Mark, USF | 10 | 7 | 3.53 | 21 | 0 | 122 | 112 | 48 | 95 |
| Pickich, Jeff, USM | 7 | 3 | 3.61 | 19 | 1 | 117 | 115 | 45 | 105 |
| Patteson, Jamie, Va. Tech | 8 | 0 | 3.65 | 22 | 3 | 62 | 68 | 20 | 39 |
| Kennedy, Gregg, USM | 6 | 6 | 3.75 | 19 | 0 | 113 | 103 | 61 | 129 |
| Romano, Mike, Tulane | 6 | 8 | 3.82 | 17 | 0 | 123 | 118 | 79 | 128 |
| Gibbs, Brian, Tulane | 4 | 4 | 3.97 | 23 | 0 | 68 | 66 | 24 | 53 |
| Bounds, Jeff, VCU | 5 | 4 | 4.06 | 15 | 0 | 71 | 76 | 27 | 56 |
| Meyers, Glenn, Louisville | 6 | 5 | 4.06 | 15 | 0 | 93 | 94 | 31 | 72 |
| McCormack, Andrew, USF | 5 | 2 | 4.15 | 21 | 0 | 82 | 84 | 33 | 85 |
| Dyess, Todd, Tulane | 4 | 3 | 4.23 | 18 | 0 | 77 | 71 | 58 | 67 |
| Nuckols, Tommy, VCU | 5 | 0 | 4.27 | 23 | 1 | 46 | 49 | 17 | 33 |

# MID-AMERICAN CONFERENCE

| | Conference | | Overall | |
|---|---|---|---|---|
| | W | L | W | L |
| *Kent State | 22 | 10 | 41 | 15 |
| Central Michigan | 22 | 10 | 39 | 19 |
| Western Michigan | 20 | 10 | 35 | 21 |
| Ball State | 17 | 13 | 32 | 24 |
| Ohio | 13 | 15 | 21 | 26 |
| Toledo | 13 | 17 | 24 | 31 |
| Eastern Michigan | 13 | 17 | 30 | 24 |
| Miami (Ohio) | 12 | 18 | 26 | 27 |
| Bowling Green | 11 | 17 | 19 | 27 |
| Akron | 7 | 23 | 22 | 33 |

**ALL-CONFERENCE TEAM: C**—Sean Flynn, So., Miami. **1B**—Kenny Reed, Jr., Ball State. **2B**—Brian Smith, Jr., Toledo. **3B**—Tim Spahr, Sr., Central Michigan. **SS**—Scott Doyle, Sr., Central Michigan. **OF**—Dan Lehrman, Jr., Ball State; Chris Sexton, Sr., Miami; Mike Wiseley, Sr., Eastern Michigan. **DH**—Greg Vatter, Jr., Miami. **P**—Henry DelValle, Jr., Western Michigan; Dustin Hermanson, So., Kent; Rob Krueger, Sr., Western Michigan; Mike Nartker, Jr., Kent. **RP**—Steve Herbst, So., Eastern Michigan.

**Player of the Year**—Chris Sexton, Miami.

## INDIVIDUAL BATTING LEADERS
(Minimum 125 At-Bats)

| | AVG | AB | R | H | 2B | 3B | HR | RBI | SB |
|---|---|---|---|---|---|---|---|---|---|
| Wiseley, Mike, Eastern Mich. | .435 | 177 | 43 | 77 | 14 | 4 | 1 | 33 | 19 |
| Sexton, Chris, Miami | .429 | 161 | 47 | 69 | 19 | 5 | 5 | 44 | 15 |
| Kruger, Andy, Central Mich. | .365 | 167 | 42 | 61 | 15 | 4 | 1 | 27 | 11 |
| Bostock, Jim, Eastern Mich. | .364 | 162 | 37 | 59 | 12 | 2 | 2 | 40 | 16 |
| Montry, Corey, Western Mich. | .355 | 138 | 28 | 49 | 13 | 2 | 3 | 26 | 4 |
| Sims, Marc, Ohio | .355 | 172 | 37 | 61 | 12 | 3 | 3 | 18 | 8 |
| Stover, Greg, Ohio | .353 | 156 | 28 | 55 | 6 | 1 | 0 | 21 | 6 |
| Taylor, Mike, Akron | .346 | 185 | 36 | 64 | 20 | 2 | 1 | 30 | 5 |
| Petri, Ernie, Miami | .346 | 162 | 40 | 56 | 6 | 4 | 2 | 9 | 9 |
| Doyle, Scott, Central Mich. | .342 | 161 | 30 | 55 | 13 | 1 | 2 | 27 | 13 |
| Przeniczny, Joe, Toledo | .341 | 126 | 17 | 43 | 6 | 1 | 3 | 19 | 3 |
| Corey, Jeff, Bowling Green | .341 | 138 | 24 | 47 | 6 | 2 | 7 | 22 | 3 |
| Deak, Dan, Eastern Mich. | .338 | 133 | 28 | 45 | 10 | 0 | 3 | 22 | 9 |
| Lehrman, Dan, Ball State | .338 | 157 | 34 | 53 | 12 | 2 | 10 | 39 | 0 |
| Schneider, Ray, Central Mich. | .338 | 160 | 27 | 54 | 5 | 1 | 2 | 23 | 3 |
| Thompson, Michael, Ball State | .331 | 169 | 37 | 56 | 10 | 1 | 2 | 28 | 24 |
| Fails, Tim, Kent | .331 | 142 | 22 | 47 | 7 | 1 | 2 | 16 | 2 |
| Vatter, Greg, Miami | .327 | 156 | 29 | 51 | 10 | 0 | 5 | 30 | 4 |
| Staehle, Todd, Western Mich. | .325 | 160 | 35 | 52 | 10 | 3 | 2 | 36 | 4 |
| Carroll, Tony, Central Mich. | .324 | 142 | 36 | 46 | 6 | 1 | 0 | 12 | 23 |
| Flynn, Sean, Miami | .324 | 142 | 24 | 46 | 5 | 0 | 6 | 37 | 2 |
| Torok, John, Toledo | .323 | 164 | 33 | 53 | 7 | 1 | 7 | 29 | 15 |
| McDonald, Jason, Eastern Mich. | .323 | 155 | 25 | 50 | 7 | 1 | 2 | 35 | 5 |
| Smith, Brian, Toledo | .322 | 183 | 39 | 59 | 9 | 2 | 10 | 31 | 19 |

## INDIVIDUAL PITCHING LEADERS
(Minimum 50 Innings)

| | W | L | ERA | G | Sv | IP | H | BB | SO |
|---|---|---|---|---|---|---|---|---|---|
| Krueger, Rob, West. Mich. | 6 | 1 | 1.05 | 10 | 0 | 51 | 35 | 26 | 47 |
| Nartker, Mike, Kent | 9 | 1 | 1.85 | 16 | 0 | 73 | 56 | 11 | 58 |
| Hermanson, Dustin, Kent | 7 | 5 | 1.90 | 14 | 1 | 90 | 51 | 28 | 102 |
| Tutkovics, Brian, Kent | 7 | 2 | 1.97 | 14 | 1 | 69 | 49 | 8 | 56 |
| DelValle, Henry, Western Mich. | 9 | 2 | 2.27 | 14 | 1 | 87 | 76 | 26 | 63 |
| Cook, Scott, Central Mich. | 4 | 2 | 2.30 | 11 | 1 | 55 | 56 | 22 | 42 |
| Corrigan, Cory, Ohio | 7 | 3 | 2.37 | 11 | 0 | 80 | 76 | 14 | 66 |
| Miller, Travis, Kent | 8 | 3 | 2.37 | 13 | 0 | 80 | 62 | 33 | 83 |
| Morvay, Joe, Ohio | 4 | 7 | 3.62 | 12 | 0 | 55 | 64 | 20 | 34 |
| Knieper, Aaron, Central Mich. | 9 | 6 | 3.64 | 15 | 0 | 94 | 92 | 34 | 67 |
| Christopher, Tony, Ball State | 7 | 3 | 3.70 | 17 | 0 | 66 | 73 | 23 | 38 |
| Deanna, Aaron, Akron | 4 | 3 | 3.70 | 11 | 1 | 66 | 58 | 36 | 33 |
| Holmes, Thurman, Western Mich. | 4 | 6 | 3.89 | 13 | 0 | 69 | 64 | 38 | 51 |
| Siler, Jeff, Central Mich. | 2 | 3 | 3.93 | 11 | 1 | 53 | 63 | 17 | 40 |
| Ferguson, Jeff, Western Mich. | 4 | 3 | 4.17 | 11 | 0 | 54 | 55 | 16 | 47 |
| Conley, Curt, Ball State | 5 | 4 | 4.36 | 16 | 0 | 89 | 87 | 34 | 56 |
| Poppe, Jerry, Miami | 8 | 4 | 4.39 | 13 | 0 | 70 | 83 | 26 | 42 |
| Rago, Vince, Ball State | 5 | 4 | 4.45 | 14 | 0 | 63 | 76 | 23 | 30 |
| Archibald, Scott, Ball State | 3 | 4 | 4.47 | 13 | 0 | 52 | 58 | 20 | 27 |
| Griffin, Ed, Toledo | 3 | 7 | 4.69 | 14 | 0 | 63 | 76 | 21 | 44 |

# MID-CONTINENT CONFERENCE

| | Conference | | Overall | |
|---|---|---|---|---|
| | W | L | W | L |
| Wright State | 17 | 3 | 39 | 15 |
| *Illinois-Chicago | 13 | 8 | 31 | 26 |
| Eastern Illinois | 9 | 6 | 23 | 23 |
| Cleveland State | 10 | 10 | 23 | 36 |
| Valparaiso | 8 | 12 | 12 | 39 |
| Western Illinois | 7 | 12 | 12 | 28 |
| Northern Illinois | 6 | 13 | 16 | 34 |
| Youngstown State | 5 | 11 | 20 | 26 |

**ALL-CONFERENCE TEAM: C**—Shawn Ramion, Sr., Cleveland State. **1B**—Mark Linkletter, Sr., Illinois-Chicago. **2B**—Jon Sbrocco, Sr., Wright State. **3B**—Rick Short, So., Western Illinois. **SS**—Jody Brown, So., Illinois-Chicago. **OF**—Mike Birsa, Jr., Northern Illinois; Michael Petak, Jr., Illinois-Chicago; Dennis Skoda, So., Illinois-Chicago. **DH**—Greg Gargani, Sr., Northern Illinois. **P**—Brian Anderson, Jr., Wright State; Jon Piazza, So., Illinois-Chicago; Tony Ramsdell, Sr., Wright State.

**Player of the Year**—Jon Sbrocco, Wright State. **Pitcher of the Year**—Brian Anderson, Wright State.

**ERA Leader.** Wright State lefthander Brian Anderson, drafted third overall, led the nation with a 1.14 ERA.

### INDIVIDUAL BATTING LEADERS
(Minimum 100 At-Bats)

| | AVG | AB | R | H | 2B | 3B | HR | RBI | SB |
|---|---|---|---|---|---|---|---|---|---|
| Sbrocco, Jon, Wright State | .395 | 190 | 64 | 75 | 16 | 7 | 5 | 42 | 15 |
| Linkletter, Mark, Ill.-Chicago | .394 | 198 | 42 | 78 | 11 | 2 | 12 | 64 | 9 |
| Guest, Jeff, Eastern Ill. | .387 | 160 | 30 | 62 | 13 | 1 | 3 | 24 | 10 |
| Ramion, Shawn, Cleve. St. | .361 | 183 | 50 | 66 | 21 | 1 | 13 | 45 | 7 |
| Birsa, Mike, Northern Ill. | .360 | 161 | 36 | 58 | 6 | 4 | 6 | 32 | 10 |
| Long, Phil, Wright State | .355 | 124 | 31 | 44 | 7 | 5 | 1 | 39 | 7 |
| Pyle, John, Ill.-Chicago | .343 | 175 | 38 | 60 | 10 | 0 | 8 | 44 | 11 |
| Petak, Mike, Ill.-Chicago | .335 | 197 | 49 | 66 | 8 | 3 | 11 | 47 | 20 |
| Short, Rick, Western Ill. | .333 | 150 | 28 | 50 | 14 | 2 | 3 | 17 | 3 |
| Brown, Jody, Ill.-Chicago | .323 | 192 | 53 | 62 | 10 | 2 | 5 | 37 | 20 |
| Patena, Mark, Cleveland St. | .321 | 137 | 21 | 44 | 8 | 0 | 2 | 17 | 9 |
| Buck, Brian, Wright State | .319 | 163 | 30 | 52 | 9 | 5 | 3 | 35 | 10 |
| Warden, Brian, Wright State | .316 | 114 | 17 | 36 | 6 | 1 | 4 | 26 | 1 |
| Myers, Brian, Youngstown St. | .313 | 131 | 18 | 41 | 10 | 1 | 2 | 23 | 1 |
| Gargani, Greg, Northern Ill. | .312 | 157 | 32 | 49 | 8 | 1 | 4 | 22 | 5 |
| Bobe, Ramon, Cleveland St. | .311 | 135 | 22 | 42 | 6 | 1 | 4 | 18 | 3 |
| Zavac, Zach, Northern Ill. | .305 | 151 | 12 | 46 | 1 | 3 | 0 | 38 | 7 |

### INDIVIDUAL PITCHING LEADERS
(Minimum 40 Innings)

| | W | L | ERA | G | Sv | IP | H | BB | SO |
|---|---|---|---|---|---|---|---|---|---|
| Anderson, Brian, Wright St. | 10 | 1 | 1.14 | 14 | 1 | 95 | 62 | 6 | 98 |
| Morgan, Marc, Youngstown St. | 4 | 4 | 2.09 | 15 | 1 | 47 | 26 | 22 | 26 |
| Ramsdell, Tony, Wright St. | 10 | 2 | 2.31 | 13 | 0 | 93 | 75 | 18 | 54 |
| Clausen, Basil, Eastern Ill. | 6 | 4 | 2.56 | 14 | 0 | 81 | 61 | 34 | 49 |
| Piazza, Jon, Ill.-Chicago | 9 | 4 | 2.95 | 16 | 0 | 101 | 88 | 34 | 75 |
| Dahlem, Mark, Western Ill. | 5 | 2 | 3.09 | 15 | 1 | 64 | 71 | 21 | 21 |
| Schmitt, Jeff, Northern Ill. | 5 | 4 | 3.45 | 13 | 0 | 63 | 64 | 39 | 59 |
| Brooks, Jeff, Valparaiso | 4 | 7 | 3.46 | 14 | 0 | 91 | 97 | 34 | 33 |
| Kitchen, Ron, Youngstown St. | 5 | 5 | 3.50 | 14 | 0 | 75 | 71 | 27 | 48 |
| Fahey, Mike, Eastern Ill. | 4 | 3 | 3.56 | 14 | 0 | 66 | 62 | 27 | 29 |
| Host, Joseph, Ill.-Chicago | 3 | 3 | 3.86 | 13 | 1 | 49 | 33 | 33 | 42 |
| Wesley, John, Ill.-Chicago | 7 | 5 | 3.89 | 18 | 1 | 90 | 93 | 32 | 44 |

## MID-EASTERN CONFERENCE

| | Conference | | Overall | |
|---|---|---|---|---|
| **NORTH** | W | L | W | L |
| Delaware State | 9 | 3 | 16 | 19 |
| Maryland-E. Shore | 5 | 7 | 12 | 27 |
| Coppin State | 4 | 6 | 6 | 28 |
| Howard | 4 | 6 | 5 | 35 |
| **SOUTH** | W | L | W | L |
| Florida A&M | 7 | 3 | 22 | 24 |
| *North Carolina A&T | 4 | 6 | 12 | 22 |
| Bethune-Cookman | 3 | 7 | 8 | 28 |
| South Carolina State | 3 | 7 | 7 | 23 |

### INDIVIDUAL BATTING LEADERS
(Minimum 100 At-Bats)

| | AVG | AB | R | H | 2B | 3B | HR | RBI | SB |
|---|---|---|---|---|---|---|---|---|---|
| Cruz, Miguel, NC A&T | .439 | 114 | 24 | 50 | 9 | 0 | 14 | 39 | 2 |
| Johnson, Artis, Florida A&M | .393 | 155 | 43 | 61 | 8 | 6 | 7 | 47 | 20 |
| Dill, David, Del. State | .387 | 111 | 28 | 43 | 9 | 0 | 2 | 31 | 0 |
| Pannell, Randall, Florida A&M | .368 | 144 | 51 | 53 | 7 | 3 | 1 | 38 | 40 |
| Price, Adrian, Coppin State | .353 | 116 | 14 | 41 | 8 | 0 | 7 | 24 | 2 |
| Watkins, David, Florida A&M | .334 | 134 | 28 | 45 | 8 | 4 | 2 | 38 | 8 |
| Farley, Ricky, UMES | .328 | 119 | 37 | 39 | 7 | 2 | 0 | 16 | 47 |
| Lillard, Marcus, SCSU | .327 | 104 | 28 | 34 | 5 | 3 | 7 | 22 | 10 |
| O'Neal, Dwight, Florida A&M | .322 | 143 | 33 | 46 | 8 | 5 | 2 | 27 | 7 |
| Shuler, Herb, SCSU | .315 | 111 | 26 | 35 | 4 | 0 | 5 | 27 | 7 |
| Cunningham, Jamil, B-C | .309 | 123 | 24 | 38 | 7 | 3 | 0 | 20 | 18 |
| Archambault, Randy, Del. St. | .298 | 131 | 26 | 39 | 9 | 0 | 1 | 23 | 3 |

### INDIVIDUAL PITCHING LEADERS
(Minimum 40 Innings)

| | W | L | ERA | G | Sv | IP | H | BB | SO |
|---|---|---|---|---|---|---|---|---|---|
| Lorntzen, Rich, Del. State | 4 | 4 | 3.97 | 10 | 0 | 57 | 51 | 22 | 30 |
| Williams, Billy, UMES | 3 | 9 | 4.98 | 15 | 0 | 65 | 88 | 35 | 34 |
| Sartin, Matt, Del. State | 4 | 3 | 5.04 | 8 | 0 | 50 | 50 | 31 | 30 |
| Brannon, Gerald, NC A&T | 5 | 4 | 5.21 | 12 | 1 | 48 | 50 | 21 | 35 |
| Stokes, Roddrick, Coppin State | 1 | 7 | 5.30 | 11 | 2 | 50 | 63 | 54 | 31 |
| Boyd, Harvest, Coppin State | 1 | 6 | 5.39 | 18 | 0 | 55 | 77 | 44 | 37 |
| Polk, Lynott, Florida A&M | 3 | 3 | 5.60 | 13 | 1 | 53 | 45 | 41 | 43 |
| Strain, B.J., UMES | 3 | 7 | 5.63 | 14 | 2 | 68 | 99 | 35 | 50 |

## MIDWESTERN CONFERENCE

| | Conference | | Overall | |
|---|---|---|---|---|
| | W | L | W | L |
| *Notre Dame | 23 | 4 | 46 | 16 |
| Detroit Mercy | 20 | 8 | 29 | 21 |
| Evansville | 19 | 8 | 43 | 18 |
| Butler | 14 | 14 | 27 | 27 |
| Xavier | 12 | 16 | 19 | 40 |
| Dayton | 10 | 18 | 22 | 39 |
| LaSalle | 8 | 20 | 13 | 31 |
| Duquesne | 5 | 23 | 9 | 32 |

**ALL-CONFERENCE TEAM: C**—Sal Fasano, Jr., Evansville. **1B**—Pat Schulz, Sr., Evansville. **2B**—Ben Ernst, Jr., Dayton. **3B**—Kevin Harpring, Sr., Dayton. **SS**—Paul Failla, So., Notre Dame. **OF**—Eric Danapilis, Sr., Notre Dame; Edwin Hartwell, Sr., Notre Dame; Marty Watson, Sr., Evansville. **DH**—Clint Straub, Sr., Detroit Mercy. **Util**—Rich Dimel, Sr., Dayton. **P**—Chris Helfrich, Jr., Evansville; Chris Michalak, Sr., Notre Dame.

**Player of the Year**—Eric Danapilis, Notre Dame.

### INDIVIDUAL BATTING LEADERS
(Minimum 125 At-Bats)

| | AVG | AB | R | H | 2B | 3B | HR | RBI | SB |
|---|---|---|---|---|---|---|---|---|---|
| Hartwell, Edwin, Notre Dame | .447 | 199 | 72 | 89 | 13 | 1 | 13 | 68 | 11 |
| Danapilis, Eric, Notre Dame | .438 | 219 | 71 | 96 | 24 | 0 | 13 | 85 | 13 |
| Straub, Clint, Detroit | .412 | 153 | 42 | 63 | 13 | 3 | 7 | 32 | 2 |
| Schulz, Pat, Evansville | .410 | 212 | 59 | 87 | 18 | 9 | 7 | 46 | 13 |
| Hisle, Larry, Dayton | .400 | 145 | 38 | 58 | 11 | 0 | 9 | 47 | 0 |
| Certher, Keith, Xavier | .382 | 212 | 49 | 81 | 17 | 2 | 7 | 46 | 4 |
| Watson, Marty, Evansville | .382 | 228 | 58 | 87 | 15 | 2 | 18 | 66 | 16 |
| Layson, Greg, Notre Dame | .363 | 168 | 60 | 61 | 10 | 5 | 3 | 34 | 15 |
| Hribar, Mark, Detroit | .357 | 168 | 31 | 60 | 15 | 1 | 3 | 33 | 3 |
| Zeigler, Chris, Duquesne | .354 | 130 | 23 | 46 | 8 | 6 | 2 | 28 | 4 |
| Dimel, Rich, Dayton | .350 | 226 | 66 | 79 | 18 | 3 | 19 | 69 | 0 |
| Failla, Paul, Notre Dame | .346 | 208 | 55 | 72 | 15 | 3 | 5 | 45 | 8 |
| Haas, Matt, Notre Dame | .345 | 197 | 49 | 68 | 10 | 3 | 4 | 61 | 28 |
| Ernst, Ben, Dayton | .339 | 230 | 54 | 78 | 20 | 1 | 5 | 36 | 7 |
| Harpring, Kevin, Dayton | .336 | 226 | 55 | 76 | 18 | 6 | 9 | 59 | 20 |
| Merica, David, Butler | .331 | 166 | 31 | 55 | 8 | 0 | 1 | 28 | 8 |

### INDIVIDUAL PITCHING LEADERS
(Minimum 50 Innings)

| | W | L | ERA | G | Sv | IP | H | BB | SO |
|---|---|---|---|---|---|---|---|---|---|
| Willming, Greg, Evansville | 10 | 3 | 2.71 | 21 | 2 | 126 | 111 | 23 | 96 |
| Metzinger, Scott, Butler | 10 | 3 | 2.76 | 16 | 0 | 101 | 96 | 23 | 57 |
| Sinnes, Dave, Notre Dame | 10 | 3 | 2.98 | 15 | 0 | 85 | 63 | 31 | 90 |
| Helfrich, Chris, Evansville | 9 | 1 | 3.21 | 11 | 0 | 70 | 68 | 12 | 45 |
| Bruce, Tim, Detroit | 6 | 4 | 3.32 | 13 | 0 | 76 | 71 | 23 | 79 |
| Hoblitt, Andy, Evansville | 8 | 1 | 3.52 | 22 | 3 | 72 | 70 | 13 | 62 |
| Price, Tom, Notre Dame | 12 | 2 | 3.53 | 18 | 1 | 94 | 82 | 19 | 69 |
| Straub, Clint, Detroit | 4 | 3 | 3.61 | 12 | 0 | 57 | 54 | 22 | 36 |
| Elpers, Matt, Evansville | 7 | 3 | 3.63 | 17 | 1 | 72 | 71 | 41 | 44 |
| Foley, Tim, LaSalle | 6 | 4 | 4.39 | 16 | 0 | 53 | 62 | 19 | 31 |
| Michalak, Chris, Notre Dame | 11 | 5 | 4.76 | 22 | 3 | 117 | 130 | 48 | 83 |
| Ambrosius, Jim, LaSalle | 3 | 7 | 4.83 | 13 | 0 | 60 | 59 | 47 | 30 |

## MISSOURI VALLEY CONFERENCE

| | Conference | | Overall | |
|---|---|---|---|---|
| | W | L | W | L |
| *Wichita State | 17 | 3 | 58 | 17 |
| Southwest Missouri State | 14 | 6 | 32 | 23 |
| Bradley | 13 | 7 | 40 | 16 |
| Indiana State | 12 | 9 | 35 | 23 |
| Creighton | 10 | 11 | 32 | 25 |
| Illinois State | 10 | 11 | 28 | 31 |
| Southern Illinois | 5 | 15 | 22 | 29 |
| Northern Iowa | 1 | 20 | 12 | 39 |

**ALL-CONFERENCE TEAM: C**—Stoney Burke, Sr., Indiana State. **1B**—Toby Smith, Jr., Wichita State. **2B**—Dave Doster, Sr., Indiana State. **3B**—Casey Blake, Fr., Wichita State. **SS**—Jason Adams, So., Wichita State. **OF**—Demetrius Dowler, Sr., Indiana State; Mat Reese, Sr., Indiana State; Kimera Bartee, Jr., Creighton. **DH**—Darren Dreifort, Jr., Wichita State. **Util**—J.J. Gottsch, Jr., Creighton. **P**—Jaime Bluma, Jr., Wichita State; Darren Dreifort, Jr., Wichita State.

**Player of the Year**—Darren Dreifort, Jr., Wichita State.

### INDIVIDUAL BATTING LEADERS
(Minimum 125 At-Bats)

| | AVG | AB | R | H | 2B | 3B | HR | RBI | SB |
|---|---|---|---|---|---|---|---|---|---|
| Dowler, Demetrius, Ind. State | .398 | 236 | 56 | 94 | 19 | 5 | 10 | 48 | 15 |
| Allison, Chris, Bradley | .373 | 193 | 50 | 72 | 7 | 2 | 2 | 19 | 17 |
| Mueller, Bill, SW Missouri St. | .371 | 213 | 63 | 79 | 18 | 3 | 11 | 38 | 19 |
| Watkins, Sean, Bradley | .370 | 135 | 30 | 50 | 15 | 3 | 5 | 45 | 2 |
| Blake, Casey, Wichita State | .366 | 232 | 42 | 85 | 9 | 3 | 4 | 57 | 7 |
| Jackson, Joey, Wichita State | .361 | 291 | 50 | 105 | 17 | 2 | 5 | 62 | 3 |
| Doster, Dave, Ind. State | .355 | 151 | 32 | 53 | 11 | 3 | 6 | 27 | 6 |
| Smith, Toby, Wichita State | .351 | 268 | 75 | 94 | 17 | 2 | 18 | 82 | 4 |
| Burke, Stoney, Ind. State | .348 | 198 | 34 | 69 | 4 | 0 | 3 | 23 | 2 |
| Huebner, Chad, Creighton | .346 | 208 | 38 | 72 | 16 | 7 | 5 | 40 | 18 |
| Markert, Josh, Bradley | .338 | 136 | 28 | 46 | 7 | 0 | 3 | 26 | 4 |
| Aldridge, Steve, SW Missouri St. | .337 | 205 | 47 | 69 | 7 | 1 | 7 | 36 | 2 |
| Hacker, Steve, SW Missouri St. | .337 | 205 | 29 | 69 | 18 | 1 | 7 | 39 | 5 |
| Sauer, Jeff, SW Missouri St. | .335 | 170 | 37 | 57 | 6 | 3 | 3 | 28 | 11 |
| Dreifort, Darren, Wichita State | .327 | 199 | 51 | 65 | 6 | 2 | 22 | 61 | 3 |
| Gottsch, J.J., Creighton | .325 | 194 | 29 | 63 | 17 | 3 | 0 | 20 | 8 |
| Reese, Mat, Ind. State | .323 | 201 | 41 | 65 | 6 | 2 | 15 | 51 | 2 |
| Latka, Dan, Ill. State | .320 | 175 | 37 | 56 | 12 | 1 | 2 | 20 | 7 |
| Graham, Pat, Bradley | .319 | 166 | 46 | 53 | 10 | 3 | 8 | 39 | 4 |
| Adams, Jason, Wichita State | .318 | 274 | 61 | 87 | 18 | 3 | 2 | 49 | 6 |
| Hall, Carl, Wichita State | .316 | 307 | 89 | 97 | 18 | 7 | 3 | 36 | 39 |
| Taylor, Richie, Wichita State | .316 | 282 | 87 | 89 | 15 | 4 | 7 | 66 | 23 |
| Smothers, Clint, S. Illinois | .315 | 162 | 27 | 51 | 11 | 3 | 1 | 19 | 7 |

### INDIVIDUAL PITCHING LEADERS
(Minimum 50 Innings)

| | W | L | ERA | G | Sv | IP | H | BB | SO |
|---|---|---|---|---|---|---|---|---|---|
| Bluma, Jaime, Wichita State | 8 | 2 | 1.39 | 33 | 12 | 65 | 40 | 9 | 76 |
| Blang, Mike, S. Illinois | 5 | 2 | 2.04 | 7 | 0 | 53 | 45 | 20 | 33 |
| Jordan, Jason, Wichita State | 3 | 0 | 2.04 | 21 | 1 | 53 | 56 | 14 | 29 |
| Rekar, Bryan, Bradley | 8 | 2 | 2.45 | 12 | 0 | 92 | 76 | 21 | 67 |
| Dreifort, Darren, Wichita State | 11 | 1 | 2.48 | 30 | 4 | 102 | 67 | 34 | 120 |
| Benes, Alan, Creighton | 7 | 5 | 2.73 | 14 | 0 | 105 | 88 | 45 | 122 |
| Whitten, Casey, Ind. State | 9 | 2 | 2.94 | 17 | 1 | 107 | 74 | 47 | 114 |
| Brandley, Mike, Wichita State | 10 | 2 | 3.18 | 19 | 0 | 122 | 102 | 33 | 83 |
| Baird, Brandon, Wichita State | 6 | 1 | 3.32 | 20 | 1 | 81 | 64 | 35 | 62 |
| O'Malley, Paul, Ill. State | 4 | 3 | 3.68 | 18 | 0 | 88 | 95 | 37 | 62 |
| Smith, Brook, Bradley | 4 | 1 | 3.74 | 11 | 0 | 53 | 54 | 36 | 40 |
| O'Connor, Brian, Creighton | 6 | 5 | 3.98 | 19 | 1 | 81 | 96 | 25 | 57 |
| O'Brien, Brian, Creighton | 4 | 6 | 4.13 | 19 | 1 | 81 | 85 | 30 | 60 |
| Moore, Joel, Bradley | 8 | 4 | 4.14 | 13 | 0 | 87 | 85 | 34 | 89 |
| Keaffaber, Randy, Ind. State | 8 | 5 | 4.28 | 17 | 0 | 95 | 107 | 19 | 56 |
| Wyckoff, Travis, Wichita State | 5 | 3 | 4.29 | 20 | 2 | 92 | 86 | 39 | 62 |
| Weisbruch, Matt, Bradley | 6 | 3 | 4.33 | 15 | 2 | 60 | 76 | 24 | 22 |

## NORTH ATLANTIC CONFERENCE

| | Conference | | Overall | |
|---|---|---|---|---|
| | W | L | W | L |
| *Maine | 22 | 4 | 33 | 27 |
| New Hampshire | 15 | 10 | 23 | 20 |
| Delaware | 14 | 12 | 28 | 21 |
| Vermont | 15 | 13 | 25 | 18 |
| Drexel | 12 | 11 | 24 | 24 |
| Hartford | 9 | 15 | 20 | 27 |
| Northeastern | 7 | 14 | 17 | 19 |
| Boston University | 2 | 17 | 5 | 27 |

**ALL-CONFERENCE TEAM: C**—Shawn Tobin, Sr., Maine. **1B**—Gabe Duross, Jr., Maine. **2B**—Deron Brown, Jr., Delaware. **3B**—Marc Choiniere, Sr., Vermont. **SS**—Dan Hammer, So., Delaware. **OF**—Chad White, Sr., Maine; Tom Lafferty, Jr., Delaware; Paul Francesconi, Sr., Hartford. **DH**—Mike Mora, Jr., Vermont. **P**—Mark Ballard, Jr., Maine; Steve Leonard, Sr., Northeastern.

**Player of the Year**—Chad White, Maine.

### INDIVIDUAL BATTING LEADERS
(Minimum 100 At-Bats)

| | AVG | AB | R | H | 2B | 3B | HR | RBI | SB |
|---|---|---|---|---|---|---|---|---|---|
| Blackhurst, Kevin, Delaware | .403 | 134 | 28 | 54 | 7 | 3 | 2 | 30 | 14 |
| Hopkins, Mark, Northeastern | .365 | 115 | 24 | 42 | 8 | 1 | 1 | 13 | 9 |
| Choiniere, Marc, Vermont | .361 | 155 | 35 | 56 | 12 | 1 | 3 | 31 | 11 |
| Mora, Mike, Vermont | .358 | 148 | 37 | 53 | 13 | 1 | 2 | 31 | 11 |
| White, Chad, Maine | .354 | 209 | 49 | 74 | 11 | 3 | 2 | 38 | 35 |
| Duross, Gabe, Maine | .352 | 216 | 36 | 76 | 14 | 3 | 7 | 47 | 3 |
| Dilenno, Bill, Delaware | .346 | 179 | 42 | 62 | 13 | 6 | 2 | 46 | 18 |
| Brown, Deron, Delaware | .344 | 195 | 53 | 67 | 7 | 3 | 1 | 32 | 24 |
| Puscian, Tim, Boston Univ. | .343 | 105 | 14 | 36 | 8 | 1 | 1 | 9 | 2 |
| Ivens, Scott, New Hampshire | .339 | 127 | 27 | 43 | 8 | 5 | 0 | 29 | 10 |
| Caballero, Bryan, Drexel | .338 | 136 | 21 | 46 | 7 | 0 | 1 | 22 | 6 |
| Hammer, Dan, Delaware | .337 | 178 | 46 | 60 | 12 | 2 | 5 | 25 | 10 |
| Aufiero, Chris, Boston Univ. | .333 | 108 | 15 | 36 | 6 | 3 | 1 | 6 | 2 |
| Benoit, Sean, Vermont | .333 | 132 | 31 | 44 | 15 | 1 | 0 | 29 | 0 |
| Lafferty, Tom, Delaware | .333 | 168 | 41 | 56 | 15 | 1 | 1 | 30 | 6 |
| Tomberlin, Justin, Maine | .333 | 129 | 22 | 43 | 11 | 1 | 3 | 17 | 2 |
| Wallace, Jay, Hartford | .329 | 149 | 17 | 49 | 4 | 0 | 0 | 13 | 3 |
| Janasiewicz, Jack, Boston U. | .321 | 109 | 15 | 35 | 6 | 4 | 3 | 20 | 0 |
| Tobin, Shawn, Maine | .320 | 200 | 36 | 64 | 9 | 1 | 7 | 54 | 5 |
| Doiron, Kris, Drexel | .319 | 141 | 24 | 45 | 10 | 0 | 1 | 25 | 2 |

### INDIVIDUAL PITCHING LEADERS
(Minimum 40 Innings)

| | W | L | ERA | G | Sv | IP | H | BB | SO |
|---|---|---|---|---|---|---|---|---|---|
| Leonard, Steve, Northeastern | 4 | 3 | 2.05 | 4 | 0 | 53 | 41 | 16 | 36 |
| Doiron, Kris, Drexel | 5 | 2 | 2.16 | 10 | 0 | 50 | 41 | 22 | 44 |
| Rizzo, Nick, Drexel | 5 | 3 | 2.43 | 12 | 0 | 63 | 62 | 31 | 36 |
| Murphy, Matt, Vermont | 6 | 4 | 2.46 | 12 | 1 | 73 | 65 | 20 | 54 |
| Wilson, Jamie, Delaware | 9 | 1 | 2.63 | 15 | 1 | 82 | 75 | 23 | 47 |
| Ballard, Mark, Maine | 8 | 3 | 2.67 | 14 | 0 | 91 | 60 | 37 | 95 |
| Grashaw, Kurt, Hartford | 5 | 4 | 3.05 | 17 | 3 | 59 | 54 | 14 | 38 |
| O'Flynn, Gardner, New Hamp. | 7 | 2 | 3.20 | 18 | 2 | 84 | 73 | 32 | 48 |
| Barone, Ralph, Northeastern | 2 | 4 | 3.30 | 7 | 0 | 46 | 53 | 10 | 46 |
| Merrill, Ethan, Vermont | 4 | 2 | 3.35 | 9 | 0 | 40 | 38 | 22 | 25 |
| Frost, Brady, Vermont | 9 | 1 | 3.38 | 11 | 0 | 72 | 59 | 15 | 49 |
| Rajotte, Jason, Maine | 6 | 3 | 3.43 | 14 | 0 | 89 | 67 | 48 | 70 |
| Hewes, Ron, Maine | 8 | 2 | 3.53 | 15 | 0 | 87 | 80 | 35 | 72 |
| Benson, Jeremy, Delaware | 3 | 4 | 3.62 | 13 | 2 | 60 | 58 | 23 | 58 |
| Messineo, Joe, Drexel | 3 | 4 | 3.64 | 14 | 0 | 47 | 49 | 30 | 31 |

## OHIO VALLEY CONFERENCE

| | Conference | | Overall | |
|---|---|---|---|---|
| | W | L | W | L |
| Middle Tennessee State | 15 | 6 | 25 | 26 |
| Tennessee Tech | 14 | 7 | 19 | 29 |
| Eastern Kentucky | 13 | 7 | 31 | 19 |
| *Morehead State | 13 | 7 | 31 | 19 |
| Austin Peay | 13 | 8 | 30 | 22 |
| Southeast Missouri State | 9 | 10 | 13 | 27 |
| Tennessee-Martin | 7 | 13 | 13 | 28 |
| Murray State | 6 | 16 | 9 | 31 |
| Tennessee State | 1 | 17 | 9 | 32 |

**ALL-CONFERENCE TEAM: C**—Rex Crosnoe, So., Southeast Missouri. **1B**—Kevin Smith, Jr., Austin Peay. **2B**—Wes Sims, Jr., Austin Peay. **3B**—Chris Godwin, Jr., Murray State. **SS**—Jason Maxwell, Jr., Middle Tennessee State. **OF**—Buford Brewer, Jr., Middle Tennessee State; Jay Bradford, Sr., Morehead State; Bryan Link, Sr., Austin Peay. **DH**—Mark Ostby, Sr., Tennessee-Martin. **Util**—Scott Pruneau, Sr., Southeast Missouri. **P**—Mike McLaury, Sr., Middle Tennessee State; Russell Stoops, So., Tennessee Tech.

**Player of the Year**—Buford Brewer, Middle Tennessee State.
**Pitcher of the Year**—Mike McLaury, Middle Tennessee State.

### INDIVIDUAL BATTING LEADERS
(Minimum 100 At-Bats)

| | AVG | AB | R | H | 2B | 3B | HR | RBI | SB |
|---|---|---|---|---|---|---|---|---|---|
| Stein, Jason, EKU | .378 | 143 | 30 | 54 | 10 | 3 | 0 | 14 | 9 |
| Quade, Scott, Austin Peay | .359 | 184 | 44 | 66 | 11 | 1 | 3 | 26 | 14 |
| Sims, Wes, Austin Peay | .353 | 187 | 45 | 66 | 13 | 2 | 8 | 29 | 23 |
| Smith, Kevin, Austin Peay | .352 | 159 | 24 | 56 | 10 | 1 | 2 | 34 | 5 |

Pruneau, Scott, SE Missouri.... .350 143 29 50 13 2 1 20 9
Allison, Brad, Morehead State. .345 142 25 49 10 0 3 21 2
Robinson, Kerry, SE Missouri.. .336 128 23 43 3 0 0 8 11
Godwin, Chris, Murray State ... .331 133 22 44 6 2 4 25 4
Brewer, Buford, MTSU ............ .330 206 45 68 18 1 10 48 7
Greer, Brent, MTSU................ .328 186 21 61 9 0 0 31 1
Bradford, Jay, Morehead St.... .323 189 53 61 17 1 13 36 14
Ostby, Mark, UT-Martin .......... .313 144 22 45 7 0 8 27 3
Crosnoe, Rex, SE Missouri ..... .312 125 16 39 7 0 7 32 1
Vandermeeden, Brett, UT-Martin .. .311 132 24 41 4 1 6 24 1
Maxwell, Jason, MTSU............ .310 187 34 58 18 2 9 42 10
Hewitt, Greg, Morehead State.. .306 108 20 33 4 0 2 16 3

### INDIVIDUAL PITCHING LEADERS
(Minimum 40 Innings)

| | W | L | ERA | G | Sv | IP | H | BB | SO |
|---|---|---|---|---|---|---|---|---|---|
| Barner, Doug, MTSU | 6 | 2 | 2.40 | 16 | 1 | 49 | 55 | 7 | 22 |
| McLaury, Mike, MTSU | 7 | 7 | 2.59 | 22 | 1 | 111 | 100 | 33 | 75 |
| Chandler, Jason, Morehead St. | 8 | 1 | 2.99 | 14 | 0 | 84 | 71 | 36 | 49 |
| Stoops, Russell, Tenn. Tech. | 6 | 2 | 3.03 | 12 | 1 | 74 | 85 | 37 | 32 |
| Hogan, Sean, Morehead State | 6 | 4 | 3.44 | 13 | 0 | 73 | 64 | 37 | 78 |
| Dannenmueler, Darrell, SE Mo. | 4 | 4 | 3.50 | 14 | 0 | 62 | 51 | 26 | 54 |
| Dortch, Shane, Austin Peay | 5 | 1 | 3.63 | 15 | 0 | 40 | 40 | 18 | 35 |
| Koger, Glenn, Morehead State | 2 | 5 | 3.74 | 24 | 8 | 53 | 49 | 23 | 44 |
| Streeter, Rod, Austin Peay | 5 | 4 | 3.78 | 17 | 0 | 69 | 58 | 26 | 37 |
| Albright, Gerald, Austin Peay | 3 | 2 | 3.79 | 17 | 2 | 57 | 55 | 23 | 43 |
| Strange, David, UT-Martin | 8 | 3 | 4.09 | 13 | 0 | 84 | 87 | 36 | 64 |

## PACIFIC-10 CONFERENCE

| | Conference | | Overall | |
|---|---|---|---|---|
| **NORTH** | W | L | W | L |
| Oregon State | 15 | 6 | 32 | 18 |
| Washington | 16 | 7 | 39 | 19 |
| Washington State | 13 | 10 | 34 | 24 |
| Portland State | 9 | 11 | 31 | 27 |
| Gonzaga | 8 | 15 | 17 | 36 |
| Portland | 5 | 17 | 16 | 33 |

**ALL-NORTHERN DIVISION TEAM: C**—Christian Shewey, Fr., Washington; Randy Hunter, Jr., Oregon State; Jeff Gyselman, Sr., Portland State. **1B**—Randy Jorgensen, Jr., Washington. **2B**—Kevin Hooker, Jr., Oregon State. **3B**—Jason Porter, Sr., Portland State; Jamie Burke, So., Oregon State. **SS**—Roy Miller, Jr., Washington State; Shannon Hinkle, Sr., Portland State. **OF**—Derrin Doty, Sr., Washington; A.J. Marquardt, Fr., Oregon State; Kirk Ordway, Sr., Portland State; Ben Ortman, Sr., Portland. **DH**—Mike Kinkade, So., Washington State. **Util**—Jerrod Wong, Fr., Gonzaga. **P**—Scott Christman, Jr., Oregon State; Jason Evenhus, Sr., Washington State; Jason Wack, Jr., Portland State. **RP**—Brandon Newell, Jr., Washington.

**Player of the Year**—Scott Christman, Oregon State.

### INDIVIDUAL BATTING LEADERS
(Minimum 100 At-Bats)

| | AVG | AB | R | H | 2B | 3B | HR | RBI | SB |
|---|---|---|---|---|---|---|---|---|---|
| Doty, Derrin, Washington | .402 | 194 | 53 | 78 | 13 | 3 | 6 | 50 | 19 |
| Marquardt, A.J., Oregon St. | .376 | 194 | 41 | 73 | 19 | 3 | 6 | 40 | 3 |
| Jorgensen, Randy, Wash. | .374 | 206 | 48 | 77 | 13 | 2 | 9 | 61 | 9 |
| Brunstad, Kevin, Wash. State | .373 | 204 | 45 | 76 | 26 | 0 | 8 | 67 | 1 |
| Kinkade, Mike, Wash. State. | .364 | 209 | 64 | 76 | 18 | 4 | 7 | 47 | 2 |
| Akina, Jason, Oregon St. | .355 | 121 | 31 | 43 | 7 | 3 | 2 | 21 | 6 |
| Hooker, Kevin, Oregon St. | .351 | 171 | 39 | 60 | 5 | 3 | 0 | 31 | 4 |
| Burke, Jamie, Oregon St. | .346 | 182 | 38 | 63 | 7 | 2 | 0 | 31 | 5 |
| Porter, Jason, Portland State | .342 | 193 | 28 | 66 | 13 | 0 | 3 | 32 | 7 |
| Foss, Dirk, Portland State | .336 | 211 | 52 | 71 | 19 | 7 | 3 | 41 | 25 |
| Hanson, Erik, Gonzaga | .333 | 192 | 36 | 64 | 13 | 1 | 10 | 41 | 0 |
| Ordway, Kirk, Portland State | .333 | 177 | 42 | 59 | 10 | 4 | 5 | 19 | 29 |
| Ortman, Ben, Portland | .333 | 198 | 43 | 66 | 7 | 3 | 9 | 32 | 42 |
| Norton, Andy, Gonzaga | .328 | 116 | 20 | 38 | 3 | 1 | 1 | 15 | 4 |
| Wong, Jerrod, Gonzaga | .326 | 187 | 32 | 61 | 13 | 3 | 9 | 53 | 1 |
| Winner, Matt, Washington | .325 | 191 | 42 | 62 | 13 | 0 | 1 | 30 | 33 |
| Dewald, Chris, Portland State | .320 | 200 | 38 | 64 | 14 | 1 | 4 | 51 | 4 |
| Yonemitsu, Jon, Oregon St. | .319 | 166 | 41 | 53 | 9 | 0 | 0 | 33 | 15 |
| Miller, Roy, Wash. State | .317 | 208 | 57 | 66 | 15 | 2 | 4 | 42 | 9 |
| Jones, Kevin, Portland | .310 | 171 | 31 | 53 | 8 | 1 | 7 | 31 | 13 |

### INDIVIDUAL PITCHING LEADERS
(Minimum 40 Innings)

| | W | L | ERA | G | Sv | IP | H | BB | SO |
|---|---|---|---|---|---|---|---|---|---|
| Christman, Scott, Oregon St. | 14 | 1 | 2.20 | 17 | 0 | 111 | 84 | 38 | 119 |
| Hartvigson, Chad, Washington | 7 | 3 | 2.38 | 11 | 0 | 76 | 64 | 20 | 50 |
| Post, Josh, Portland State | 8 | 4 | 2.89 | 15 | 1 | 75 | 77 | 29 | 43 |
| Campbell, Tim, Washington | 6 | 3 | 3.59 | 11 | 0 | 58 | 52 | 33 | 31 |
| Lake, Dan, Portland State | 3 | 3 | 3.79 | 23 | 3 | 59 | 66 | 20 | 45 |
| Day, Jamie, Washington | 7 | 4 | 3.94 | 16 | 0 | 96 | 90 | 18 | 41 |

**Pac-10's Best.** Oregon State lefty Scott Christman led the Pacific-10 Conference in wins (14) and ERA (2.20).

| | W | L | ERA | G | Sv | IP | H | BB | SO |
|---|---|---|---|---|---|---|---|---|---|
| Wack, Jason, Portland State | 9 | 7 | 3.96 | 18 | 0 | 109 | 104 | 54 | 62 |
| Evenhus, Jason, Wash. State. | 10 | 3 | 3.97 | 15 | 0 | 93 | 95 | 19 | 45 |
| Greene, Jeremy, Port. State | 3 | 4 | 4.14 | 10 | 0 | 46 | 52 | 21 | 25 |
| Schultz, John, Oregon St. | 2 | 1 | 4.17 | 10 | 0 | 41 | 49 | 14 | 21 |
| Merrick, Brett, Washington | 4 | 1 | 4.24 | 17 | 1 | 47 | 38 | 30 | 30 |

| | Conference | | Overall | |
|---|---|---|---|---|
| **SOUTH** | W | L | W | L |
| **Arizona State** | 19 | 11 | 46 | 20 |
| **UCLA** | 17 | 13 | 37 | 23 |
| **Arizona** | 16 | 14 | 35 | 26 |
| **Southern California** | 15 | 15 | 35 | 29 |
| California | 13 | 17 | 27 | 30 |
| Stanford | 10 | 20 | 27 | 28 |

**ALL-SOUTHERN DIVISION TEAM: C**—Casey Burrill, Sr., Southern Cal; Paul LoDuca, Jr., Arizona State; Willie Morales, Jr., Arizona. **INF**—Gabe Alvarez, Fr., Southern Cal; George Arias, Jr., Arizona; Todd Landry, Jr., Arizona; Ryan McGuire, Jr., UCLA; Adam Melhuse, Jr., UCLA; David Ravitz, Sr., UCLA; Antone Williamson, So., Arizona State. **OF**—Robbie Moen, Sr., Arizona; J.P. Roberge, So., Southern Cal; John Tejcek, Sr., Arizona. **DH**—Jason Thompson, Jr., Arizona. **Util**—Doug Newstrom, Jr., Arizona State. **SP**—Marc Barcelo, Jr., Arizona State; Andrew Lorraine, So., Stanford. **RP**—Dan Hubbs, Sr., Southern Cal; Bobby Kahlon, Jr., California.

**Players of the Year**—Paul LoDuca, Arizona State; Ryan McGuire, UCLA. **Pitchers of the Year**—Marc Barcelo, Arizona State; Bobby Kahlon, California.

### INDIVIDUAL BATTING LEADERS
(Minimum 125 At-Bats)

| | AVG | AB | R | H | 2B | 3B | HR | RBI | SB |
|---|---|---|---|---|---|---|---|---|---|
| LoDuca, Paul, Arizona State | .446 | 289 | 63 | 129 | 24 | 2 | 14 | 88 | 0 |
| Burrill, Casey, USC | .408 | 238 | 54 | 97 | 18 | 1 | 13 | 52 | 6 |
| Lemons, Richard, Arizona | .403 | 129 | 33 | 52 | 10 | 3 | 8 | 39 | 2 |
| Moen, Robbie, Arizona | .388 | 263 | 66 | 102 | 21 | 0 | 10 | 66 | 8 |
| Williamson, Antone, ASU | .378 | 275 | 71 | 104 | 29 | 1 | 14 | 85 | 2 |
| McGuire, Ryan, UCLA | .376 | 221 | 71 | 83 | 11 | 0 | 26 | 91 | 14 |
| Morales, Willie, Arizona | .356 | 247 | 65 | 88 | 21 | 1 | 13 | 62 | 1 |
| Newstrom, Doug, ASU | .356 | 247 | 91 | 88 | 24 | 1 | 12 | 68 | 3 |
| Lootens, Brian, Arizona State. | .354 | 237 | 51 | 84 | 16 | 4 | 7 | 39 | 9 |
| Thompson, Jason, Arizona | .353 | 255 | 68 | 90 | 15 | 4 | 20 | 74 | 3 |
| Tejcek, John, Arizona | .350 | 260 | 85 | 91 | 14 | 11 | 8 | 60 | 12 |

| Hinch, A.J., Stanford | .350 | 203 | 42 | 71 | 7 | 5 | 4 | 38 | 10 |
|---|---|---|---|---|---|---|---|---|---|
| Landry, Todd, Arizona | .348 | 253 | 55 | 88 | 18 | 2 | 17 | 70 | 4 |
| Dunn, Bill, Arizona State | .346 | 254 | 58 | 88 | 14 | 1 | 4 | 28 | 20 |
| Arias, George, Arizona | .345 | 255 | 70 | 88 | 14 | 1 | 23 | 75 | 1 |
| Melhuse, Adam, UCLA | .344 | 250 | 64 | 86 | 19 | 2 | 10 | 50 | 5 |
| Dallimore, Brian, Stanford | .344 | 160 | 35 | 55 | 11 | 0 | 2 | 22 | 14 |
| Cruz, Jacob, Arizona State | .342 | 202 | 51 | 69 | 15 | 2 | 10 | 37 | 5 |
| Gump, Chris, Arizona | .329 | 228 | 56 | 75 | 20 | 5 | 4 | 22 | 12 |
| Alvarez, Gabe, USC | .326 | 258 | 46 | 84 | 26 | 0 | 8 | 53 | 1 |
| Myrow, John, UCLA | .325 | 249 | 50 | 81 | 12 | 7 | 5 | 40 | 11 |
| Ravitz, David, UCLA | .324 | 225 | 45 | 73 | 19 | 0 | 6 | 32 | 2 |
| Jenkins, Geoff, USC | .323 | 198 | 41 | 64 | 15 | 3 | 7 | 50 | 8 |
| Roberge, J.P., USC | .320 | 259 | 55 | 83 | 12 | 2 | 11 | 40 | 14 |
| Cady, Todd, Arizona State | .316 | 244 | 60 | 77 | 11 | 0 | 19 | 68 | 2 |
| Mitchell, Mike, UCLA | .314 | 207 | 34 | 65 | 15 | 0 | 12 | 53 | 0 |
| Carter, Cale, Stanford | .313 | 144 | 34 | 45 | 3 | 1 | 0 | 12 | 9 |
| Motte, James, Arizona | .312 | 154 | 36 | 48 | 6 | 3 | 9 | 39 | 1 |
| Carver, Steve, Stanford | .311 | 190 | 30 | 59 | 13 | 0 | 5 | 36 | 5 |
| Palfalvi, Mark, Cal | .306 | 209 | 40 | 64 | 18 | 1 | 12 | 36 | 9 |
| Malani, Shon, USC | .296 | 213 | 38 | 63 | 13 | 1 | 2 | 20 | 11 |
| Roberts, David, UCLA | .296 | 247 | 65 | 73 | 12 | 0 | 3 | 28 | 28 |
| LaRocca, Todd, Stanford | .295 | 193 | 34 | 57 | 12 | 0 | 5 | 27 | 14 |
| Hastings, Lionel, USC | .294 | 201 | 34 | 59 | 16 | 1 | 5 | 35 | 4 |
| Dawkins, Walter, USC | .291 | 199 | 45 | 58 | 12 | 3 | 3 | 22 | 7 |
| Hansen, Jed, Stanford | .290 | 221 | 47 | 64 | 7 | 8 | 9 | 47 | 6 |
| Petke, Jonathan, Cal | .288 | 125 | 22 | 36 | 4 | 1 | 4 | 13 | 2 |
| Boone, Aaron, USC | .286 | 220 | 43 | 63 | 19 | 4 | 5 | 39 | 8 |
| Fuller, Aaron, Cal | .277 | 148 | 29 | 41 | 5 | 3 | 1 | 17 | 19 |
| McKay, Cody, Arizona State | .276 | 170 | 22 | 47 | 13 | 1 | 3 | 36 | 0 |
| Aljian, Reed, Cal | .275 | 160 | 19 | 44 | 11 | 1 | 2 | 25 | 2 |
| Bierek, Kurt, USC | .272 | 195 | 42 | 53 | 16 | 1 | 12 | 49 | 4 |
| Comeaux, Eddie, Cal | .266 | 192 | 28 | 51 | 2 | 5 | 1 | 23 | 15 |
| Schafer, Brett, UCLA | .264 | 129 | 31 | 34 | 4 | 1 | 2 | 16 | 12 |
| Blum, Geoff, Cal | .263 | 209 | 29 | 55 | 6 | 4 | 0 | 26 | 13 |
| Brown, Nate, Cal | .258 | 190 | 39 | 49 | 9 | 4 | 8 | 28 | 23 |
| Shores, Scott, Arizona State | .255 | 141 | 21 | 36 | 6 | 1 | 5 | 28 | 12 |
| Allen, Dusty, Stanford | .247 | 215 | 30 | 53 | 8 | 2 | 8 | 50 | 3 |

**First-Year Phenom.** Tennessee's Todd Helton hit .348 and won six games to earn Freshman All-America honors.

## INDIVIDUAL PITCHING LEADERS
(Minimum 50 Innings)

| | W | L | ERA | G | Sv | IP | H | BB | SO |
|---|---|---|---|---|---|---|---|---|---|
| Barcelo, Marc, Arizona State | 12 | 4 | 2.72 | 19 | 0 | 142 | 133 | 35 | 113 |
| Hubbs, Dan, USC | 5 | 5 | 2.96 | 33 | 18 | 76 | 67 | 24 | 90 |
| Kahlon, Bobby, Cal | 12 | 1 | 3.28 | 29 | 9 | 69 | 69 | 35 | 49 |
| Nieto, Tony, USC | 8 | 5 | 3.52 | 21 | 0 | 100 | 106 | 48 | 40 |
| Rawitzer, Kevin, Arizona State | 5 | 3 | 3.66 | 16 | 0 | 71 | 57 | 41 | 83 |
| Sollecito, Gabe, UCLA | 4 | 3 | 3.94 | 24 | 9 | 62 | 59 | 25 | 34 |
| Kubinski, Tim, UCLA | 11 | 3 | 4.03 | 17 | 0 | 126 | 126 | 35 | 86 |
| Lorraine, Andrew, Stanford | 8 | 6 | 4.15 | 16 | 0 | 124 | 143 | 32 | 97 |
| Collett, Mike, USC | 9 | 4 | 4.18 | 17 | 0 | 90 | 103 | 29 | 56 |
| Adams, Willie, Stanford | 8 | 5 | 4.23 | 17 | 0 | 121 | 132 | 26 | 114 |
| Fenton, Mike, Arizona State | 3 | 3 | 4.35 | 30 | 3 | 62 | 69 | 18 | 43 |
| Winslett, Dax, Arizona State | 10 | 5 | 4.46 | 22 | 0 | 125 | 127 | 65 | 98 |
| Brown, Tod, Arizona | 6 | 7 | 4.90 | 35 | 8 | 79 | 87 | 38 | 42 |
| Reed, Dan, Stanford | 4 | 5 | 4.95 | 17 | 1 | 67 | 81 | 28 | 44 |
| White, Ben, Arizona | 1 | 1 | 5.28 | 21 | 2 | 46 | 64 | 22 | 18 |
| Tucker, Ben, USC | 2 | 7 | 5.37 | 16 | 0 | 59 | 63 | 39 | 23 |
| Toomey, Matt, Cal | 0 | 5 | 5.61 | 20 | 0 | 77 | 91 | 40 | 52 |
| Peery, Noah, Arizona State | 6 | 2 | 5.66 | 29 | 6 | 62 | 65 | 55 | 66 |
| Vermillion, Grant, USC | 3 | 2 | 5.67 | 25 | 0 | 54 | 68 | 32 | 35 |
| Bartels, Todd, Stanford | 0 | 3 | 5.68 | 17 | 0 | 59 | 71 | 20 | 26 |
| Van Zandt, Jon, UCLA | 7 | 7 | 5.70 | 20 | 1 | 114 | 128 | 40 | 70 |
| Adcock, Gary, UCLA | 3 | 4 | 5.75 | 16 | 1 | 67 | 71 | 50 | 40 |
| Frace, Ryan, Arizona | 5 | 3 | 5.78 | 19 | 1 | 81 | 102 | 36 | 48 |

## SOUTHEASTERN CONFERENCE

| EAST | Conference W | L | Overall W | L |
|---|---|---|---|---|
| *Tennessee | 20 | 10 | 45 | 20 |
| South Carolina | 15 | 10 | 39 | 20 |
| Kentucky | 14 | 14 | 38 | 23 |
| Florida | 12 | 14 | 33 | 25 |
| Vanderbilt | 11 | 15 | 32 | 23 |
| Georgia | 10 | 18 | 30 | 29 |
| WEST | | | | |
| *Louisiana State | 18 | 8 | 53 | 17 |
| Auburn | 17 | 11 | 40 | 23 |
| Mississippi State | 17 | 12 | 41 | 21 |
| Arkansas | 11 | 16 | 33 | 26 |
| Alabama | 9 | 15 | 27 | 25 |
| Mississippi | 8 | 19 | 31 | 25 |

**ALL-CONFERENCE TEAM: C**—Mitch Duke, Sr., Auburn. **1B**—Todd Helton, Fr., Tennessee. **2B**—Todd Walker, So., Louisiana State. **3B**—Boomer Whipple, So., Vanderbilt. **SS**—Joe Biernat, Sr., South Carolina. **OF**—Vee Hightower, Jr., Vanderbilt; Mac White, Jr., South Carolina; Bubba Trammell, Jr., Tennessee. **DH**—Brad Hindersman, Jr., Kentucky. **P**—John Powell, Jr., Auburn; Brett Laxton, Fr., Louisiana State; Rich Pratt, Sr., South Carolina.

**Player of the Year**—Todd Walker, Louisiana State.

## INDIVIDUAL BATTING LEADERS
(Minimum 125 At-Bats)

| | AVG | AB | R | H | 2B | 3B | HR | RBI | SB |
|---|---|---|---|---|---|---|---|---|---|
| Biernat, Joe, So. Carolina | .403 | 233 | 46 | 94 | 16 | 2 | 5 | 52 | 15 |
| Walker, Todd, LSU | .395 | 276 | 85 | 109 | 17 | 11 | 22 | 102 | 14 |
| Shanks, Cliff, Auburn | .391 | 215 | 49 | 84 | 18 | 0 | 3 | 46 | 0 |
| Trammell, Bubba, Tennessee | .383 | 193 | 45 | 74 | 19 | 1 | 12 | 52 | 5 |
| Whipple, Boomer, Vanderbilt | .374 | 211 | 43 | 79 | 14 | 1 | 7 | 57 | 3 |
| Hindersman, Brad, Kentucky | .366 | 235 | 44 | 86 | 15 | 2 | 9 | 56 | 2 |
| Moore, Brandon, Auburn | .365 | 230 | 47 | 84 | 12 | 1 | 5 | 42 | 6 |
| Bridges, Kary, Mississippi | .362 | 224 | 47 | 81 | 14 | 5 | 3 | 31 | 24 |
| Johnson, Russ, LSU | .355 | 259 | 83 | 92 | 18 | 3 | 8 | 58 | 19 |
| White, Mac, So. Carolina | .355 | 220 | 50 | 78 | 16 | 4 | 7 | 59 | 21 |
| Buckner, Rex, Miss. State | .349 | 241 | 52 | 84 | 19 | 2 | 7 | 38 | 3 |
| Helton, Todd, Tennessee | .348 | 247 | 48 | 86 | 22 | 3 | 11 | 66 | 6 |
| Hightower, Vee, Vanderbilt | .346 | 185 | 69 | 64 | 9 | 1 | 11 | 26 | 46 |
| Michael, Jeff, Kentucky | .345 | 235 | 68 | 81 | 17 | 2 | 9 | 34 | 28 |
| Brooks, Eddie, Kentucky | .342 | 237 | 49 | 81 | 19 | 0 | 14 | 50 | 11 |
| Brown, Ron, Miss. State | .342 | 237 | 49 | 81 | 15 | 3 | 11 | 44 | 2 |
| Gonzalez, Chris, Kentucky | .341 | 208 | 48 | 71 | 13 | 1 | 10 | 43 | 1 |
| Duke, Mitch, Auburn | .341 | 211 | 38 | 72 | 14 | 1 | 2 | 40 | 3 |
| Hegan, Steve, Miss. State | .335 | 158 | 40 | 53 | 11 | 3 | 5 | 29 | 3 |
| Williams, Allen, Arkansas | .335 | 212 | 59 | 71 | 21 | 6 | 7 | 39 | 18 |
| Purdy, Alan, Vanderbilt | .331 | 176 | 32 | 59 | 19 | 0 | 9 | 34 | 7 |
| Harrelson, Richy, Mississippi | .329 | 173 | 29 | 57 | 6 | 1 | 3 | 20 | 2 |
| Bragga, Matt, Kentucky | .329 | 240 | 49 | 79 | 14 | 1 | 11 | 46 | 8 |
| Williams, Jason, LSU | .329 | 228 | 61 | 75 | 10 | 3 | 2 | 51 | 12 |

| Player | AVG | AB | R | H | 2B | 3B | HR | RBI | SB |
|---|---|---|---|---|---|---|---|---|---|
| Whatley, Gabe, Vanderbilt | .328 | 204 | 48 | 67 | 16 | 0 | 12 | 41 | 7 |
| Berrios, Harry, LSU | .326 | 270 | 69 | 88 | 22 | 2 | 17 | 82 | 21 |
| Camposano, Bo, Florida | .326 | 175 | 39 | 57 | 13 | 0 | 12 | 53 | 5 |
| Christopher, Chris, Auburn | .325 | 228 | 50 | 74 | 12 | 5 | 3 | 29 | 19 |
| Drumheller, Al, Alabama | .323 | 189 | 43 | 61 | 8 | 1 | 8 | 38 | 0 |
| Waggoner, Jay, Auburn | .320 | 247 | 54 | 79 | 9 | 2 | 0 | 33 | 2 |
| Smelley, Chris, Alabama | .319 | 191 | 30 | 61 | 10 | 0 | 6 | 32 | 2 |
| Neal, Mike, LSU | .319 | 213 | 61 | 68 | 19 | 6 | 5 | 27 | 16 |
| Rios, Armando, LSU | .319 | 235 | 71 | 75 | 13 | 4 | 9 | 61 | 20 |
| Perry, Chan, Florida | .319 | 160 | 40 | 51 | 16 | 0 | 7 | 39 | 6 |
| Williams, Drew, Miss. State | .319 | 204 | 36 | 65 | 17 | 3 | 8 | 52 | 1 |
| Thomas, Greg, Vanderbilt | .318 | 211 | 38 | 67 | 17 | 0 | 9 | 43 | 5 |
| Redd, Ricky Joe, Miss. State | .315 | 222 | 43 | 70 | 10 | 1 | 13 | 50 | 2 |
| Alyea, Brian, Auburn | .310 | 210 | 40 | 65 | 15 | 1 | 8 | 47 | 0 |
| Nielsen, Bart, Vanderbilt | .309 | 136 | 35 | 42 | 11 | 0 | 1 | 9 | 11 |
| Yselonia, John, Georgia | .308 | 208 | 42 | 64 | 17 | 0 | 15 | 51 | 1 |
| Dezenzo, Mike, So. Carolina | .308 | 221 | 51 | 68 | 10 | 1 | 5 | 36 | 21 |
| Harris, Kyle, Arkansas | .307 | 150 | 32 | 46 | 12 | 4 | 4 | 38 | 4 |
| Dellucci, David, Mississippi | .306 | 206 | 31 | 63 | 15 | 1 | 11 | 43 | 14 |
| Stowers, Chris, Georgia | .304 | 125 | 27 | 38 | 7 | 0 | 2 | 14 | 13 |
| Stall, Carl, Arkansas | .303 | 145 | 29 | 44 | 6 | 1 | 1 | 20 | 11 |
| DeBoer, Rob, So. Carolina | .302 | 192 | 35 | 58 | 9 | 0 | 6 | 41 | 14 |
| Stokes, Stacy, So. Carolina | .301 | 193 | 51 | 58 | 8 | 1 | 0 | 33 | 9 |
| Vance, David, Tennessee | .299 | 174 | 39 | 52 | 11 | 1 | 6 | 33 | 11 |
| Menechino, Frank, Alabama | .298 | 188 | 39 | 56 | 5 | 2 | 6 | 23 | 14 |
| Houck, Jeff, Arkansas | .298 | 168 | 33 | 50 | 10 | 3 | 1 | 21 | 16 |
| Duva, Brian, Florida | .297 | 222 | 53 | 66 | 8 | 11 | 1 | 29 | 34 |
| Petrulis, Paul, Miss. State | .296 | 247 | 47 | 73 | 20 | 0 | 3 | 33 | 4 |
| Carpenter, Matt, Miss. State | .295 | 173 | 15 | 51 | 5 | 3 | 2 | 31 | 0 |
| Ingram, Reggie, Georgia | .294 | 197 | 21 | 58 | 7 | 1 | 3 | 29 | 4 |
| Stocco, Mark, LSU | .292 | 130 | 25 | 38 | 4 | 2 | 4 | 26 | 3 |
| Wyman, Richie, Tennessee | .292 | 226 | 50 | 66 | 6 | 4 | 5 | 38 | 13 |
| Moore, Kenderick, Arkansas | .290 | 155 | 29 | 45 | 6 | 1 | 2 | 15 | 14 |
| Hughes, Bob, Arkansas | .290 | 169 | 29 | 49 | 11 | 2 | 4 | 43 | 6 |
| Laubenthal, Jeff, Alabama | .289 | 187 | 33 | 54 | 7 | 1 | 6 | 30 | 6 |

## INDIVIDUAL PITCHING LEADERS
### (Minimum 50 Innings)

| | W | L | ERA | G | Sv | IP | H | BB | SO |
|---|---|---|---|---|---|---|---|---|---|
| Laxton, Brett, LSU | 12 | 1 | 1.98 | 19 | 0 | 109 | 67 | 47 | 98 |
| Sirotka, Mike, LSU | 12 | 6 | 1.99 | 23 | 0 | 145 | 121 | 35 | 105 |
| Sullivan, Scott, Auburn | 4 | 3 | 2.55 | 22 | 5 | 60 | 48 | 19 | 71 |
| Haynie, Jason, So. Carolina | 8 | 2 | 2.68 | 18 | 0 | 77 | 52 | 46 | 86 |
| Powell, Brian, Georgia | 6 | 2 | 2.77 | 14 | 0 | 81 | 82 | 23 | 74 |
| Powell, John, Auburn | 15 | 5 | 2.81 | 24 | 0 | 141 | 102 | 41 | 191 |
| Pace, Scott, So. Carolina | 3 | 3 | 2.82 | 19 | 1 | 51 | 50 | 24 | 45 |
| Pratt, Rich, So. Carolina | 11 | 3 | 2.83 | 18 | 0 | 114 | 107 | 24 | 101 |
| Ryan, Matt, Mississippi | 7 | 3 | 2.84 | 16 | 0 | 86 | 84 | 43 | 73 |
| Cook, Brian, Arkansas | 9 | 3 | 2.88 | 14 | 0 | 72 | 53 | 22 | 62 |
| Rath, Gary, Miss. State | 7 | 5 | 2.97 | 17 | 0 | 76 | 77 | 40 | 62 |
| Tanksley, Scott, Miss. State | 5 | 0 | 3.06 | 20 | 4 | 65 | 71 | 19 | 47 |
| Loewer, Carlton, Miss. State | 9 | 3 | 3.07 | 17 | 0 | 100 | 93 | 44 | 101 |
| Lowe, Jason, Mississippi | 2 | 3 | 3.28 | 28 | 7 | 74 | 55 | 37 | 60 |
| Hunt, Will, LSU | 9 | 1 | 3.38 | 29 | 1 | 77 | 77 | 27 | 63 |
| Birch, Brent, Arkansas | 7 | 7 | 3.43 | 15 | 0 | 97 | 96 | 30 | 84 |
| Trumbo, Troy, Kentucky | 4 | 0 | 3.45 | 21 | 1 | 63 | 55 | 45 | 56 |
| Bonanno, Rob, Florida | 9 | 5 | 3.49 | 19 | 1 | 98 | 83 | 47 | 110 |
| Meyers, Ryan, Tennessee | 5 | 4 | 3.50 | 14 | 1 | 72 | 63 | 27 | 51 |
| Freeman, Chris, Tennessee | 12 | 2 | 3.51 | 18 | 0 | 118 | 94 | 51 | 79 |
| Harvell, Pete, Tennessee | 6 | 2 | 3.52 | 20 | 3 | 54 | 36 | 42 | 38 |
| Powell, Jay, Miss. State | 3 | 8 | 3.55 | 26 | 7 | 73 | 58 | 36 | 73 |
| Halla, Ryan, Auburn | 9 | 4 | 3.59 | 19 | 0 | 90 | 83 | 40 | 73 |
| Threehouse, Matt, So. Car. | 7 | 4 | 3.66 | 14 | 0 | 79 | 71 | 40 | 87 |
| Valdes, Marc, Florida | 8 | 6 | 3.67 | 18 | 0 | 123 | 113 | 59 | 119 |
| McNeese, John, Mississippi | 6 | 6 | 3.67 | 15 | 0 | 76 | 66 | 44 | 49 |
| Whitaker, Ryan, Arkansas | 5 | 2 | 3.72 | 29 | 5 | 56 | 51 | 24 | 46 |
| Smith, Scott, Kentucky | 6 | 9 | 3.73 | 16 | 0 | 101 | 118 | 19 | 89 |
| Bellard, Bernie, Alabama | 3 | 6 | 3.82 | 12 | 0 | 71 | 76 | 28 | 48 |
| Reed, Brian, Kentucky | 6 | 2 | 3.83 | 30 | 2 | 85 | 75 | 32 | 112 |

## SOUTHERN CONFERENCE

| | Conference | | Overall | |
|---|---|---|---|---|
| | W | L | W | L |
| Georgia Southern | 18 | 5 | 38 | 18 |
| *Western Carolina | 15 | 6 | 34 | 28 |
| The Citadel | 13 | 9 | 32 | 25 |
| East Tennessee State | 11 | 8 | 21 | 17 |
| Davidson | 11 | 9 | 20 | 28 |
| Appalachian State | 8 | 12 | 15 | 27 |
| Marshall | 9 | 14 | 13 | 27 |
| Va. Military Institute | 5 | 15 | 20 | 29 |
| Furman | 4 | 16 | 17 | 22 |

**ALL-CONFERENCE TEAM: C**—Brett Boretti, Jr., Davidson. **1B**—Chris Lemonis, Sr., Western Carolina. **2B**—Rodney Hennon, Sr., Western Carolina. **3B**—Kevin Hallman, Jr., Georgia Southern. **SS**—Rick Bender, Sr., Davidson. **OF**—Todd Greene, Sr., Georgia Southern; Scott Lyman, Sr., Western Carolina; Dallas Monday, Sr., East Tennessee State. **DH**—Phillip Grundy, Jr., Western Carolina. **P**—Paul Thornton, Sr., Georgia Southern; Jason Beverlin, So., Western Carolina.
**Player of the Year**—Todd Greene, Georgia Southern.

## INDIVIDUAL BATTING LEADERS
### (Minimum 100 At-Bats)

| | AVG | AB | R | H | 2B | 3B | HR | RBI | SB |
|---|---|---|---|---|---|---|---|---|---|
| Hooks, Mike, ETSU | .398 | 118 | 31 | 47 | 7 | 0 | 8 | 40 | 4 |
| Boretti, Brett, Davidson | .386 | 176 | 39 | 68 | 17 | 0 | 13 | 48 | 0 |
| Roper, Russ, Furman | .385 | 109 | 11 | 42 | 8 | 0 | 1 | 25 | 4 |
| Greene, Todd, Ga. Southern | .374 | 203 | 53 | 76 | 16 | 0 | 20 | 62 | 9 |
| Kerns, Tim, Davidson | .373 | 177 | 45 | 66 | 18 | 0 | 17 | 61 | 0 |
| Lemonis, Chris, Davidson | .367 | 221 | 52 | 81 | 19 | 1 | 10 | 66 | 5 |
| Lyman, Scott, West Car. | .361 | 205 | 62 | 74 | 10 | 2 | 8 | 38 | 9 |
| Chapman, Mac, Davidson | .360 | 150 | 33 | 54 | 13 | 2 | 7 | 30 | 0 |
| Sistare, Dale, Citadel | .359 | 167 | 22 | 60 | 6 | 1 | 4 | 33 | 3 |
| Doherty, Rob, West Car. | .358 | 123 | 22 | 44 | 7 | 0 | 5 | 28 | 5 |
| Tidick, Mike, West Car. | .352 | 227 | 53 | 80 | 19 | 1 | 13 | 47 | 17 |
| Bender, Rick, Davidson | .350 | 197 | 51 | 69 | 17 | 2 | 7 | 33 | 8 |
| Henson, Jody, West Car. | .350 | 140 | 25 | 49 | 5 | 0 | 0 | 19 | 6 |
| Ficklin, Willando, Ga. South. | .346 | 228 | 33 | 79 | 8 | 3 | 5 | 35 | 5 |

## INDIVIDUAL PITCHING LEADERS
### (Minimum 40 Innings)

| | W | L | ERA | G | Sv | IP | H | BB | SO |
|---|---|---|---|---|---|---|---|---|---|
| Thornton, Paul, Ga. Southern | 3 | 1 | 1.19 | 35 | 17 | 45 | 29 | 29 | 57 |
| Morillo, Donald, Citadel | 3 | 1 | 1.60 | 22 | 3 | 45 | 40 | 17 | 36 |
| Price, John, Citadel | 3 | 2 | 2.20 | 14 | 1 | 57 | 48 | 19 | 37 |
| Grundy, Phillip, West Car. | 4 | 7 | 3.12 | 16 | 1 | 84 | 71 | 37 | 83 |
| Banks, Andrew, Furman | 1 | 0 | 3.30 | 10 | 0 | 44 | 41 | 20 | 24 |
| Basch, Steve, Citadel | 6 | 4 | 3.48 | 12 | 0 | 72 | 56 | 26 | 59 |
| Fair, Clint, Ga. Southern | 7 | 5 | 3.49 | 16 | 0 | 101 | 98 | 27 | 81 |
| Spade, Matt, Marshall | 4 | 7 | 3.49 | 13 | 0 | 77 | 73 | 30 | 71 |
| Davis, Gary, ASU | 2 | 6 | 3.73 | 10 | 0 | 60 | 56 | 8 | 27 |
| Ikenberry, Merlin, VMI | 0 | 0 | 3.79 | 27 | 6 | 40 | 51 | 11 | 23 |
| Callahan, Brian, Citadel | 5 | 4 | 3.88 | 11 | 0 | 49 | 46 | 22 | 41 |
| Beverlin, Jason, West Car. | 12 | 2 | 3.93 | 18 | 0 | 105 | 105 | 55 | 106 |

## SOUTHLAND CONFERENCE

| | Conference | | Overall | |
|---|---|---|---|---|
| | W | L | W | L |
| Northwestern State | 18 | 6 | 40 | 14 |
| Texas-Arlington | 17 | 6 | 34 | 20 |
| Sam Houston State | 13 | 9 | 30 | 26 |
| *McNeese State | 14 | 10 | 38 | 23 |
| Nicholls State | 11 | 12 | 31 | 19 |
| Stephen F. Austin State | 10 | 14 | 21 | 32 |
| Texas-San Antonio | 9 | 15 | 21 | 34 |
| Southwest Texas State | 8 | 15 | 26 | 29 |
| Northeast Louisiana | 5 | 18 | 13 | 26 |

**ALL-CONFERENCE TEAM: C**—Jared Snyder, Sr., Nicholls State. **1B**—Clint Gould, Jr., McNeese State. **2B**—Karl Heckendorn, Sr., Texas-Arlington. **3B**—Kyle Shade, Sr., Northwestern State. **SS**—Troy Conkle, Sr., Northwestern State. **OF**—Clay Gould, Sr., Texas-Arlington; Terry Joseph, So, Northwestern State; Mike McCreary, So., Sam Houston State. **DH**—Hayland Hardy, Jr., Stephen F. Austin. **P**—Shawn Hill, Sr., Nicholls State; Reggie Gatewood, Sr., Northwestern State; John Henrickson, Jr., Texas-Arlington.
**Players of the Year**—Clay Gould, Texas-Arlington; Kyle Shade, Northwestern State.

## INDIVIDUAL BATTING LEADERS
### (Minimum 125 At-Bats)

| | AVG | AB | R | H | 2B | 3B | HR | RBI | SB |
|---|---|---|---|---|---|---|---|---|---|
| Shade, Kyle, NW State | .453 | 181 | 44 | 82 | 24 | 2 | 3 | 48 | 3 |
| Gould, Clay, UT-Arlington | .396 | 192 | 44 | 76 | 14 | 7 | 7 | 54 | 5 |
| Joseph, Terry, NW State | .373 | 177 | 59 | 66 | 18 | 4 | 3 | 30 | 28 |
| Snyder, Jared, Nicholls St. | .372 | 145 | 33 | 54 | 14 | 3 | 7 | 40 | 8 |
| Stephens, Jeff, UT-Arlington | .359 | 184 | 36 | 66 | 11 | 4 | 2 | 23 | 1 |
| Olson, Brent, UT-San Antonio | .354 | 127 | 25 | 45 | 5 | 1 | 3 | 23 | 4 |
| Jensen, Jeff, Sam Houston | .351 | 171 | 34 | 60 | 12 | 1 | 8 | 36 | 6 |
| McCreary, Mike, Sam Houston | .348 | 144 | 37 | 50 | 8 | 3 | 8 | 44 | 5 |
| Hardy, Hayland, SF Austin | .345 | 168 | 39 | 58 | 9 | 0 | 19 | 55 | 0 |
| Gray, Todd, NE La. | .344 | 131 | 25 | 45 | 12 | 1 | 6 | 31 | 1 |
| Conkle, Troy, NW State | .343 | 181 | 46 | 62 | 14 | 8 | 3 | 38 | 16 |
| Hofstetter, Deron, McN. St. | .341 | 208 | 52 | 71 | 11 | 2 | 2 | 30 | 26 |

Heckendorn, Karl, UTA........... .337 193 44 65 12 2 13 50 2
McCarter, Christian, NE La..... .331 142 27 47 10 1 5 19 2
Gould, Clint, McNeese St....... .327 153 40 50 11 0 10 54 5
Guajardo, Marco, NW State .... .326 196 44 59 17 1 7 43 8
Mixon, Shawn, SF Austin ....... .317 145 22 46 13 1 2 28 2

## INDIVIDUAL PITCHING LEADERS
### (Minimum 50 Innings)

| | W | L | ERA | G | Sv | IP | H | BB | SO |
|---|---|---|---|---|---|---|---|---|---|
| Hill, Shawn, Nicholls St. | 10 | 4 | 2.02 | 19 | 3 | 111 | 94 | 25 | 108 |
| Marik, Trey, McNeese St. | 5 | 2 | 2.15 | 30 | 0 | 84 | 79 | 17 | 62 |
| Prihoda, Steve, Sam Houston | 6 | 4 | 2.45 | 16 | 1 | 65 | 71 | 20 | 67 |
| Garza, Raymundo, SHS | 5 | 6 | 2.87 | 14 | 1 | 78 | 78 | 10 | 38 |
| Henrickson, John, UTA | 9 | 4 | 2.88 | 19 | 2 | 106 | 97 | 21 | 84 |
| Schandua, Peter, SHS | 6 | 3 | 3.00 | 13 | 0 | 75 | 74 | 28 | 42 |
| Gatewood, Reggie, NW State. | 10 | 2 | 3.07 | 17 | 0 | 86 | 78 | 40 | 57 |
| Viola, Dom, NW State | 7 | 3 | 3.09 | 19 | 1 | 79 | 61 | 37 | 72 |
| Cook, Rodney, SF Austin | 7 | 5 | 3.38 | 17 | 0 | 85 | 82 | 33 | 53 |
| Garner, Greg, McNeese St. | 10 | 5 | 3.43 | 17 | 0 | 94 | 84 | 38 | 78 |
| Williams, Geoff, NW State | 5 | 2 | 3.48 | 16 | 1 | 68 | 71 | 29 | 37 |
| Sexton, Scott, UT-Arlington | 8 | 5 | 3.58 | 15 | 0 | 103 | 96 | 38 | 51 |

## SOUTHWEST CONFERENCE

| | Conference | | Overall | |
|---|---|---|---|---|
| | W | L | W | L |
| Texas A&M | 15 | 3 | 53 | 11 |
| *Baylor | 11 | 7 | 41 | 19 |
| Texas | 11 | 7 | 51 | 16 |
| Texas Tech | 11 | 7 | 43 | 15 |
| Rice | 7 | 11 | 36 | 18 |
| Texas Christian | 5 | 13 | 34 | 22 |
| Houston | 3 | 15 | 31 | 24 |

**ALL-CONFERENCE TEAM: C**—Jason Marshall, Sr., Baylor. **1B**—Braxton Hickman, Sr., Texas. **2B**—Trey Forkerway, Sr., Texas Tech. **3B**—Saul Bustos, Jr., Texas Tech. **SS**—Robert Harris, So., Texas A&M; Clint Bryant, Fr., Texas Tech; Brian Thomas, Sr., Texas A&M; Phil Lewis, Sr., Houston. **DH**—Brooks Kieschnick, Jr., Texas. **Util**—Joe Wharton, Sr., Baylor; Ricky Freeman, Jr., Houston. **SP**—Jeff Granger, Jr., Texas A&M; Trey Moore, So., Texas A&M; Travis Driskill, Jr., Texas Tech; Brooks Kieschnick, Jr., Texas. **RP**—Brian Parker, So., Texas A&M; Travis Gage, Sr., Texas A&M.

**Player of the Year**—Brooks Kieschnick, Texas.

## INDIVIDUAL BATTING LEADERS
### (Minimum 125 At-Bats)

| | AVG | AB | R | H | 2B | 3B | HR | RBI | SB |
|---|---|---|---|---|---|---|---|---|---|
| Hickman, Braxton, Texas | .385 | 252 | 55 | 97 | 16 | 4 | 9 | 74 | 1 |
| Freeman, Ricky, Houston | .384 | 172 | 39 | 66 | 12 | 2 | 6 | 47 | 9 |
| Thomas, Brian, Texas A&M.. | .383 | 206 | 68 | 79 | 16 | 9 | 15 | 55 | 21 |
| Robson, Adam, TCU | .378 | 180 | 45 | 68 | 10 | 2 | 12 | 47 | 3 |
| Kieschnick, Brooks, Texas | .374 | 257 | 76 | 96 | 27 | 1 | 19 | 81 | 3 |
| Kinney, Mike, Texas Tech | .373 | 193 | 53 | 72 | 13 | 5 | 3 | 40 | 37 |
| Bryant, Clint, Texas Tech | .366 | 191 | 47 | 70 | 15 | 6 | 5 | 44 | 7 |
| Davis, Dana, Rice | .364 | 151 | 27 | 55 | 8 | 1 | 3 | 37 | 0 |
| Blair, Brian, Houston | .359 | 181 | 48 | 65 | 8 | 2 | 4 | 40 | 17 |
| Trimble, Rob, Texas A&M | .355 | 141 | 29 | 50 | 10 | 1 | 2 | 28 | 2 |
| Cruz, Jose, Rice | .351 | 191 | 50 | 67 | 7 | 1 | 13 | 59 | 6 |
| Crawford, Marty, Baylor | .350 | 234 | 49 | 82 | 13 | 4 | 1 | 29 | 0 |
| Lewis, Phil, Houston | .349 | 189 | 44 | 66 | 7 | 8 | 9 | 45 | 21 |
| Bustos, Saul, Texas Tech | .348 | 196 | 59 | 69 | 11 | 2 | 12 | 55 | 2 |
| Wharton, Joe, Baylor | .345 | 194 | 42 | 67 | 12 | 5 | 4 | 35 | 9 |
| Lewis, Robert, Texas A&M | .343 | 137 | 31 | 47 | 7 | 0 | 5 | 31 | 3 |
| Fedora, Lee, Texas A&M | .342 | 184 | 50 | 63 | 5 | 2 | 8 | 48 | 12 |
| Marshall, Jason, Baylor | .335 | 194 | 46 | 65 | 13 | 3 | 11 | 59 | 1 |
| Forkerway, Trey, Texas Tech.. | .332 | 193 | 45 | 64 | 9 | 2 | 4 | 40 | 13 |
| Boni, Chris, Rice | .331 | 178 | 46 | 59 | 5 | 2 | 1 | 18 | 13 |
| Cardenas, Johnny, TCU | .329 | 173 | 36 | 57 | 8 | 4 | 7 | 42 | 1 |
| Garza-Gongora, Beto, TCU | .327 | 165 | 45 | 54 | 16 | 4 | 6 | 33 | 4 |
| Heinrich, Steve, Texas | .326 | 132 | 41 | 43 | 8 | 4 | 1 | 29 | 7 |
| Harris, Robert, Texas A&M.. | .325 | 237 | 63 | 77 | 9 | 3 | 12 | 55 | 5 |
| Buteaux, Shane, Houston | .325 | 157 | 31 | 51 | 6 | 1 | 1 | 26 | 24 |
| Glasscock, Kennedy, Rice | .319 | 163 | 44 | 52 | 6 | 3 | 6 | 39 | 9 |
| Williamson, Joel, Texas | .318 | 151 | 29 | 48 | 11 | 1 | 5 | 33 | 1 |
| Trozzo, Matt, Baylor | .316 | 171 | 39 | 54 | 12 | 2 | 1 | 32 | 28 |
| Kilford, George, Texas Tech.... | .315 | 165 | 60 | 52 | 8 | 2 | 4 | 44 | 9 |
| Gonzalez, Eric, Texas A&M.... | .313 | 211 | 52 | 66 | 13 | 3 | 8 | 49 | 13 |
| Larkin, Stephen, Texas | .312 | 199 | 42 | 62 | 17 | 5 | 5 | 44 | 1 |
| Vasut, Tony, Texas | .308 | 146 | 48 | 45 | 13 | 2 | 0 | 13 | 6 |
| Turner, John, TCU | .308 | 172 | 34 | 53 | 6 | 0 | 5 | 25 | 8 |
| Martin, Mark, Baylor | .307 | 166 | 50 | 51 | 8 | 4 | 4 | 21 | 11 |
| Millay, Gavin, TCU | .304 | 125 | 25 | 38 | 7 | 2 | 12 | 38 | 2 |
| Aslaksen, Donald, Rice | .303 | 185 | 55 | 56 | 16 | 2 | 7 | 46 | 11 |
| Gregg, Brody, Texas Tech | .300 | 203 | 42 | 61 | 11 | 2 | 2 | 28 | 17 |

## INDIVIDUAL PITCHING LEADERS
### (Minimum 50 Innings)

| | W | L | ERA | G | Sv | IP | H | BB | SO |
|---|---|---|---|---|---|---|---|---|---|
| Wharton, Joe, Baylor | 10 | 3 | 2.54 | 21 | 3 | 85 | 69 | 29 | 85 |
| Granger, Jeff, Texas A&M | 15 | 3 | 2.62 | 20 | 0 | 127 | 87 | 54 | 150 |
| Moore, Trey, Texas A&M | 12 | 0 | 2.77 | 18 | 1 | 101 | 84 | 54 | 91 |
| Driskill, Travis, Texas Tech | 10 | 4 | 2.83 | 17 | 0 | 121 | 112 | 42 | 120 |
| Dishman, Glenn, TCU | 5 | 3 | 3.15 | 16 | 0 | 66 | 66 | 22 | 63 |
| Rathbun, Jason, Baylor | 7 | 5 | 3.15 | 18 | 2 | 91 | 81 | 51 | 74 |
| Kieschnick, Brooks, Texas | 16 | 4 | 3.25 | 26 | 3 | 150 | 155 | 49 | 126 |
| Lineweaver, Aaron, Baylor | 9 | 5 | 3.27 | 17 | 1 | 105 | 83 | 56 | 82 |
| Madrid, James, Rice | 8 | 3 | 3.50 | 21 | 3 | 64 | 57 | 34 | 66 |
| Macatee, John, Texas Tech | 7 | 4 | 3.67 | 15 | 0 | 88 | 80 | 36 | 85 |
| Johns, Kelly, TCU | 4 | 4 | 3.76 | 17 | 1 | 91 | 85 | 51 | 88 |
| Clemons, Chris, Texas A&M | 6 | 2 | 3.79 | 19 | 2 | 71 | 75 | 23 | 67 |
| Hannah, Kevin, Texas Tech | 7 | 2 | 3.96 | 17 | 2 | 75 | 77 | 27 | 51 |
| Smith, Chad, Texas | 8 | 2 | 3.98 | 27 | 2 | 54 | 45 | 27 | 48 |
| Vamey, J.J., Texas Tech | 6 | 3 | 4.09 | 14 | 1 | 77 | 58 | 37 | 61 |
| Zimmerman, Jeff, TCU | 8 | 4 | 4.30 | 15 | 0 | 73 | 84 | 22 | 65 |
| Hamilton, Brian, Houston | 8 | 4 | 4.38 | 22 | 0 | 64 | 64 | 47 | 34 |
| Smart, J.D., Texas | 6 | 1 | 4.40 | 23 | 2 | 78 | 74 | 35 | 83 |
| Wunsch, Kelly, Texas A&M | 7 | 2 | 4.45 | 17 | 0 | 87 | 65 | 54 | 110 |
| Ryan, Reid, TCU | 6 | 4 | 4.52 | 17 | 0 | 72 | 68 | 25 | 62 |
| Bearden, Brent, Baylor | 6 | 2 | 4.70 | 21 | 5 | 61 | 51 | 41 | 43 |
| Nalepa, Marcus, Rice | 4 | 2 | 4.73 | 15 | 1 | 65 | 59 | 28 | 59 |
| Crow, Dean, Baylor | 3 | 3 | 4.81 | 20 | 2 | 64 | 62 | 44 | 45 |
| Kjos, Ryan, Texas | 3 | 3 | 4.88 | 21 | 2 | 83 | 88 | 44 | 65 |
| Wright, Jeff, Houston | 4 | 5 | 4.95 | 16 | 0 | 76 | 77 | 33 | 50 |
| Richardson, Darrell, Rice | 10 | 5 | 5.11 | 18 | 0 | 88 | 88 | 57 | 103 |
| Johnson, Bo, Rice | 6 | 3 | 5.13 | 16 | 0 | 67 | 80 | 34 | 60 |
| Codrington, John, Texas A&M.. | 4 | 0 | 5.23 | 19 | 1 | 53 | 53 | 24 | 39 |
| Beech, Matt, Houston | 4 | 5 | 5.23 | 16 | 0 | 76 | 67 | 67 | 73 |

## SWAC

| | Conference | | Overall | |
|---|---|---|---|---|
| EAST | W | L | W | L |
| Jackson State | 15 | 3 | 27 | 18 |
| Alcorn State | 8 | 11 | 10 | 22 |
| Alabama State | 7 | 12 | 18 | 27 |
| Mississippi Valley State | 5 | 9 | 12 | 17 |
| WEST | W | L | W | L |
| Grambling State | 16 | 5 | 24 | 18 |
| Southern | 12 | 6 | 24 | 14 |
| Texas Southern | 8 | 15 | 12 | 32 |
| Prairie View A&M | 5 | 15 | 8 | 41 |

**ALL-CONFERENCE TEAM: C**—Leroy McKinnis, Jr., Jackson State. **1B**—Ronald Smith, Sr., Southern. **2B**—Wesley Marshall, Jr., Grambling State. **3B**—Derrick Calvin, Sr., Southern. **SS**—Lamar Rushton, So., Grambling State. **OF**—Jason Ford, Sr., Grambling State; Rod Burnette, Jr., Alcorn State; Larry Allen, Jr., Grambling State. **DH**—Tommy Fuller, Sr., Southern. **P**—Rod Jackson, Sr., Jackson State; Courtney Mitchell, Jr., Grambling State; Hector Hernandez, Jr., Southern; Bryan Webb, So., Alcorn State.

**Player of the Year**—Courtney Mitchell, Grambling State.

## INDIVIDUAL BATTING LEADERS
### (Minimum 100 At-Bats)

| | AVG | AB | R | H | 2B | 3B | HR | RBI | SB |
|---|---|---|---|---|---|---|---|---|---|
| Calvin, Derrick, Southern | .420 | 131 | 40 | 55 | 13 | 2 | 7 | 38 | 11 |
| Goree, LaShaun, Jackson St. .. | .402 | 107 | 26 | 43 | 7 | 2 | 1 | 19 | 20 |
| Jeppesen, Elgin, Jackson St. .. | .397 | 131 | 43 | 52 | 10 | 5 | 2 | 28 | 35 |
| Rushton, Lamar, Grambling St. | .372 | 156 | 44 | 58 | 12 | 0 | 3 | 31 | 2 |
| Bady, Edward, Ala. St. | .357 | 140 | 43 | 50 | 9 | 4 | 2 | 23 | 44 |
| Harper, Charles, Alcorn State.. | .353 | 102 | 20 | 36 | 7 | 0 | 0 | 12 | 0 |
| Smith, Ronald, Southern | .349 | 109 | 37 | 38 | 4 | 0 | 12 | 39 | 5 |
| McKinnis, Leroy, Jackson St. .. | .346 | 127 | 33 | 44 | 6 | 2 | 3 | 40 | 3 |
| Ford, Jason, Grambling State.. | .346 | 136 | 38 | 47 | 12 | 1 | 8 | 48 | 1 |
| Gilkey, Corey, Southern | .345 | 116 | 29 | 40 | 8 | 2 | 1 | 21 | 12 |
| Boleware, Marlin, Ala. St. | .342 | 117 | 26 | 40 | 6 | 1 | 2 | 26 | 2 |
| Jordan, Fouston, Jackson St. .. | .340 | 106 | 19 | 36 | 4 | 1 | 0 | 16 | 6 |
| Marshall, Wesley, Grambling St. | .340 | 159 | 41 | 54 | 8 | 3 | 4 | 42 | 12 |
| Burnette, Rod, Alcorn State.... | .333 | 123 | 25 | 41 | 10 | 1 | 0 | 15 | 19 |
| Gilbert, Derrick, Jackson State | .331 | 142 | 37 | 47 | 5 | 1 | 0 | 19 | 16 |
| Jackson, Andree, Prairie View.. | .331 | 133 | 19 | 44 | 15 | 0 | 4 | 22 | 0 |
| James, Willie, Jackson State.... | .329 | 158 | 34 | 52 | 8 | 1 | 0 | 17 | 17 |

## INDIVIDUAL PITCHING LEADERS
### (Minimum 40 Innings)

| | W | L | ERA | G | Sv | IP | H | BB | SO |
|---|---|---|---|---|---|---|---|---|---|
| Jackson, Rod, Jackson State.... | 8 | 0 | 1.74 | 13 | 0 | 72 | 45 | 40 | 75 |
| Hernandez, Hector, Southern .. | 6 | 3 | 1.99 | 12 | 0 | 63 | 54 | 20 | 36 |
| Pinson, Bobby, MVSU | 4 | 5 | 2.94 | 10 | 0 | 49 | 33 | 36 | 35 |

| | W | L | ERA | G | Sv | IP | H | BB | SO |
|---|---|---|---|---|---|---|---|---|---|
| Driver, Terrence, Ala. St. | 3 | 4 | 2.95 | 12 | 0 | 55 | 46 | 38 | 30 |
| Lynch, Michael, Jackson St. | 6 | 1 | 3.00 | 13 | 1 | 57 | 51 | 26 | 42 |
| Webb, Bryan, Alcorn State | 6 | 4 | 3.00 | 10 | 0 | 63 | 55 | 23 | 52 |
| Broomer, Bradley, Ala. St. | 5 | 6 | 3.04 | 11 | 0 | 74 | 63 | 30 | 63 |
| Collins, Stephen, Jackson St. | 3 | 2 | 3.42 | 12 | 0 | 47 | 51 | 21 | 32 |
| Brown, Eric, Ala. St. | 3 | 7 | 4.00 | 13 | 0 | 57 | 64 | 25 | 38 |
| Wilson, Shannon, Jackson St. | 4 | 4 | 4.01 | 10 | 0 | 49 | 57 | 16 | 34 |
| Owens, Damon, Grambling St. | 5 | 3 | 4.66 | 14 | 0 | 66 | 70 | 31 | 34 |
| Mitchell, Courtney, Grambling St. | 7 | 4 | 4.72 | 18 | 3 | 80 | 70 | 78 | 80 |
| Shelton, Jeffrie, Texas South. | 3 | 3 | 4.91 | 10 | 0 | 48 | 52 | 34 | 18 |

## SUN BELT CONFERENCE

| | Conference | | Overall | |
|---|---|---|---|---|
| EAST | W | L | W | L |
| South Alabama | 11 | 6 | 37 | 21 |
| Arkansas State | 11 | 10 | 33 | 26 |
| Jacksonville | 11 | 10 | 33 | 26 |
| Western Kentucky | 11 | 10 | 30 | 22 |
| Arkansas-Little Rock | 5 | 13 | 24 | 29 |
| **WEST** | | | | |
| *Lamar | 13 | 5 | 44 | 18 |
| Louisiana Tech | 11 | 8 | 25 | 25 |
| Southwestern Louisiana | 10 | 9 | 25 | 29 |
| New Orleans | 9 | 10 | 25 | 28 |
| Texas-Pan American | 5 | 16 | 23 | 33 |

**ALL-CONFERENCE TEAM: C**—Chris Unrat, Sr., Arkansas State. **1B**—Bill Weyers, Sr., Western Kentucky. **2B**—Pat Murphy, Jr., South Alabama. **3B**—Joe Jumonville, Sr., Southwestern Louisiana. **SS**—Doug Angeli, Sr., New Orleans. **OF**—John Smykla, Jr., Arkansas-Little Rock; Bruce Aven, Jr., Lamar; Tyrone Dixon, Sr., South Alabama. **DH**—Shane Eaker, Sr., Arkansas State. **P**—Phil Brassington, Fr., Lamar; Sam Arguto, Jr., Jacksonville.

**Player of the Year**—Bill Weyers, Western Kentucky.

### INDIVIDUAL BATTING LEADERS
(Minimum 125 At-Bats)

| | AVG | AB | R | H | 2B | 3B | HR | RBI | SB |
|---|---|---|---|---|---|---|---|---|---|
| Weyers, Bill, WKU | .422 | 192 | 59 | 81 | 16 | 0 | 7 | 46 | 4 |
| Dixon, Tyrone, USA | .391 | 207 | 66 | 81 | 17 | 0 | 3 | 30 | 45 |
| Aven, Bruce, Lamar | .380 | 229 | 53 | 87 | 14 | 5 | 13 | 67 | 20 |
| Escala, Andy, Jacksonville | .379 | 227 | 54 | 86 | 18 | 2 | 5 | 40 | 15 |
| Murphy, Pat, USA | .366 | 246 | 48 | 90 | 13 | 5 | 2 | 51 | 30 |
| Hayes, Chris, Jacksonville | .361 | 144 | 26 | 52 | 13 | 1 | 4 | 37 | 6 |
| Angeli, Doug, UNO | .350 | 214 | 54 | 75 | 12 | 1 | 10 | 43 | 18 |
| Hawkins, Wes, La. Tech | .350 | 183 | 40 | 64 | 16 | 0 | 4 | 22 | 8 |
| Jones, Charlie, La. Tech | .349 | 166 | 39 | 58 | 12 | 0 | 18 | 53 | 3 |
| Hunt, Jeremy, USA | .347 | 170 | 42 | 59 | 9 | 2 | 3 | 34 | 6 |
| Bledsoe, Jim, USA | .344 | 163 | 36 | 56 | 13 | 2 | 3 | 29 | 4 |
| Mathews, Jonathan, UNO | .342 | 193 | 38 | 66 | 10 | 1 | 2 | 42 | 2 |
| Johnson, Dave, Jacksonville | .341 | 179 | 37 | 61 | 14 | 2 | 4 | 35 | 9 |
| Smykla, John, UALR | .333 | 177 | 37 | 59 | 12 | 1 | 14 | 55 | 8 |
| Culotta, Dean, UNO | .329 | 164 | 35 | 54 | 9 | 0 | 11 | 42 | 1 |
| Jumonville, Joe, SW Louisiana | .327 | 220 | 31 | 72 | 19 | 0 | 6 | 46 | 4 |
| Hatcher, Paul, UNO | .326 | 193 | 45 | 63 | 14 | 1 | 8 | 44 | 0 |
| Anderson, Marlon, USA | .326 | 138 | 24 | 45 | 5 | 5 | 3 | 31 | 7 |
| Bako, Paul, SW Louisiana | .326 | 175 | 39 | 57 | 9 | 5 | 7 | 43 | 3 |
| Millar, Kevin, Lamar | .324 | 216 | 53 | 70 | 18 | 1 | 5 | 54 | 12 |
| Nesbitt, Barry, WKU | .320 | 147 | 32 | 47 | 7 | 1 | 3 | 29 | 9 |
| Lacy, Marty, SW Louisiana | .316 | 174 | 39 | 55 | 4 | 1 | 1 | 22 | 8 |
| Unrat, Chris, Arkansas St. | .316 | 187 | 47 | 59 | 7 | 3 | 10 | 43 | 2 |
| Iapoce, Anthony, Lamar | .315 | 232 | 62 | 73 | 9 | 4 | 5 | 34 | 34 |
| Southard, Scott, USA | .315 | 213 | 49 | 67 | 7 | 2 | 8 | 43 | 11 |
| Diaz, David, USA | .314 | 137 | 34 | 43 | 2 | 0 | 1 | 21 | 12 |
| Thiedig, Gary, UALR | .310 | 174 | 41 | 54 | 13 | 0 | 10 | 39 | 1 |
| Scott, Bobby, Texas-Pan Am | .309 | 178 | 21 | 55 | 8 | 1 | 2 | 12 | 6 |
| Rivera, Triny, Lamar | .309 | 149 | 34 | 46 | 7 | 0 | 2 | 30 | 7 |
| Fowlkes, Troy, La. Tech | .309 | 175 | 46 | 54 | 14 | 1 | 8 | 34 | 11 |
| Hancock, Jay, La. Tech | .308 | 156 | 32 | 48 | 4 | 0 | 7 | 31 | 0 |

### INDIVIDUAL PITCHING LEADERS
(Minimum 50 Innings)

| | W | L | ERA | G | Sv | IP | H | BB | SO |
|---|---|---|---|---|---|---|---|---|---|
| Jenkins, Mike, Lamar | 5 | 3 | 2.25 | 30 | 2 | 64 | 48 | 21 | 55 |
| Lane, Kevin, Lamar | 8 | 1 | 2.76 | 15 | 1 | 65 | 50 | 22 | 51 |
| Green, Kyle, Lamar | 3 | 1 | 2.79 | 16 | 2 | 52 | 38 | 20 | 49 |
| Pasqualicchio, Mike, Lamar | 6 | 3 | 2.96 | 18 | 1 | 73 | 63 | 34 | 61 |
| Daly, Brendan, SW Louisiana | 3 | 4 | 2.99 | 17 | 0 | 75 | 71 | 26 | 40 |
| Patrick, Scott, USA | 5 | 3 | 3.00 | 28 | 4 | 75 | 72 | 28 | 59 |
| Lopez, Alan, La. Tech | 5 | 4 | 3.03 | 15 | 0 | 74 | 71 | 32 | 43 |
| Gunsalius, Paul, La. Tech | 5 | 5 | 3.09 | 15 | 0 | 93 | 85 | 31 | 74 |
| McLeod, Roy, SW Louisiana | 5 | 5 | 3.10 | 21 | 2 | 78 | 81 | 16 | 50 |

| | W | L | ERA | G | Sv | IP | H | BB | SO |
|---|---|---|---|---|---|---|---|---|---|
| Brassington, Phil, Lamar | 10 | 7 | 3.19 | 22 | 1 | 110 | 93 | 43 | 76 |
| Arguto, Sam, Jacksonville | 8 | 3 | 3.30 | 22 | 2 | 131 | 112 | 65 | '87 |
| Langlois, Darren, UNO | 3 | 2 | 3.54 | 19 | 0 | 56 | 49 | 25 | 28 |
| Terminie, Chad, UNO | 4 | 7 | 3.61 | 18 | 1 | 107 | 111 | 33 | 98 |
| Ybarra, Jamie, USA | 8 | 5 | 3.68 | 16 | 0 | 95 | 83 | 53 | 88 |
| Alepra, Andy, WKU | 2 | 4 | 3.72 | 18 | 3 | 58 | 57 | 24 | 51 |
| Monahan, Pat, Arkansas St. | 3 | 5 | 3.79 | 15 | 0 | 71 | 76 | 25 | 36 |
| Horn, Keith, Arkansas St. | 5 | 2 | 3.86 | 16 | 1 | 63 | 52 | 30 | 52 |
| Sweitzer, Chad, La. Tech | 2 | 3 | 3.91 | 16 | 1 | 51 | 44 | 15 | 19 |
| Lyons, Dan, Arkansas St. | 6 | 4 | 3.99 | 17 | 0 | 79 | 72 | 40 | 71 |
| Jumonville, Joe, SW Louisiana | 6 | 3 | 4.28 | 13 | 1 | 67 | 79 | 14 | 53 |
| Miller, Taylor, Texas-Pan Am | 3 | 7 | 4.46 | 15 | 1 | 75 | 88 | 25 | 44 |
| Ottmers, Marc, Texas-Pan Am | 3 | 7 | 4.50 | 16 | 2 | 72 | 47 | 55 | 94 |

## TRANSAMERICA CONFERENCE

| | Conference | | Overall | |
|---|---|---|---|---|
| EAST | W | L | W | L |
| Stetson | 11 | 7 | 38 | 17 |
| *Central Florida | 9 | 9 | 31 | 31 |
| Charleston | 9 | 9 | 18 | 24 |
| Florida International | 7 | 11 | 27 | 29 |
| **WEST** | | | | |
| Southeastern Louisiana | 19 | 5 | 38 | 17 |
| Centenary | 15 | 8 | 27 | 25 |
| Samford | 9 | 15 | 16 | 32 |
| Georgia State | 7 | 14 | 12 | 35 |
| Mercer | 6 | 14 | 15 | 34 |

**ALL-CONFERENCE TEAM: C**—Jason Moore, Jr., Florida International. **1B**—Brett McCabe, Jr., Centenary. **2B**—Mike Lowell, Fr., Florida International. **3B**—Brian Stier, Jr., Centenary. **SS**—Kiley Hughes, Sr., Southeastern Louisiana. **OF**—Aaron Iatarola, Sr., Stetson; Corey Boudreaux, Sr., Southeastern Louisiana; Brandon Allen, So., Charleston. **DH**—Kevin Millican, Jr., Southeastern Louisiana. **P**—Aaron Gallo, Jr., Stetson; Sean Gates, Jr., Southeastern Louisiana. **RP**—Jason Schlutt, Jr., Central Florida.

**Player of the Year**—Aaron Iatarola, Stetson.

### INDIVIDUAL BATTING LEADERS
(Minimum 125 At-Bats)

| | AVG | AB | R | H | 2B | 3B | HR | RBI | SB |
|---|---|---|---|---|---|---|---|---|---|
| Boudreaux, Corey, SE La. | .404 | 188 | 56 | 76 | 14 | 2 | 4 | 60 | 9 |
| Vindivich, John, SE Louisiana | .393 | 191 | 68 | 75 | 7 | 9 | 7 | 33 | 20 |
| Magee, Wendell, Samford | .376 | 141 | 22 | 53 | 8 | 0 | 6 | 32 | 7 |
| Iatarola, Aaron, Stetson | .372 | 199 | 56 | 74 | 6 | 12 | 51 | 17 |
| Lowell, Mike, FIU | .371 | 197 | 41 | 73 | 13 | 0 | 3 | 33 | 12 |
| Minacs, Derek, Samford | .352 | 165 | 30 | 58 | 11 | 2 | 9 | 34 | 2 |
| McCabe, Brett, Centenary | .343 | 169 | 31 | 58 | 10 | 0 | 4 | 30 | 7 |
| Millican, Kevin, SE Louisiana | .341 | 164 | 39 | 56 | 11 | 0 | 9 | 35 | 2 |
| Stier, Brian, Centenary | .335 | 167 | 41 | 56 | 18 | 0 | 12 | 51 | 2 |
| Phillips, Rick, Mercer | .331 | 166 | 32 | 55 | 12 | 0 | 12 | 47 | 4 |
| Hughes, Kiley, SE Louisiana | .327 | 202 | 47 | 66 | 11 | 1 | 14 | 44 | 2 |
| Glover, Jason, Ga. State | .324 | 173 | 36 | 56 | 8 | 1 | 15 | 41 | 7 |
| Marrillia, Tony, Cent. Fla. | .323 | 226 | 32 | 73 | 10 | 5 | 1 | 29 | 21 |
| Gann, Lee, Samford | .323 | 161 | 29 | 52 | 10 | 0 | 4 | 35 | 7 |
| Munoz, Juan, FIU | .322 | 174 | 30 | 56 | 6 | 4 | 2 | 20 | 10 |
| Angulo, Gabby, Cent. Fla. | .321 | 159 | 28 | 51 | 11 | 2 | 6 | 32 | 3 |
| Tribble, Scott, SE Louisiana | .305 | 200 | 39 | 61 | 13 | 1 | 10 | 42 | 7 |
| Isenhower, Gary, Mercer | .303 | 145 | 29 | 44 | 3 | 0 | 0 | 14 | 5 |
| Kroeker, Tim, Centenary | .296 | 186 | 44 | 55 | 12 | 3 | 8 | 38 | 8 |
| Parker, Jason, Centenary | .294 | 160 | 38 | 47 | 12 | 1 | 15 | 43 | 2 |
| Bolton, Doug, Stetson | .291 | 182 | 39 | 53 | 12 | 2 | 1 | 29 | 13 |
| Corbett, Craig, Stetson | .290 | 162 | 39 | 47 | 8 | 1 | 7 | 40 | 3 |

### INDIVIDUAL PITCHING LEADERS
(Minimum 50 Innings)

| | W | L | ERA | G | Sv | IP | H | BB | SO |
|---|---|---|---|---|---|---|---|---|---|
| Schlutt, Jason, Cent. Fla. | 9 | 2 | 2.62 | 34 | 8 | 76 | 72 | 29 | 75 |
| Gomez, Javier, Stetson | 7 | 3 | 2.72 | 15 | 0 | 76 | 64 | 39 | 68 |
| Keagle, Greg, FIU | 3 | 9 | 3.13 | 14 | 0 | 95 | 65 | 60 | 110 |
| Gallo, Aaron, Stetson | 8 | 3 | 3.14 | 15 | 0 | 77 | 68 | 34 | 52 |
| Kester, Tim, FIU | 6 | 4 | 3.26 | 14 | 0 | 97 | 76 | 41 | 82 |
| Schneider, Tom, Centenary | 6 | 6 | 3.47 | 18 | 1 | 106 | 105 | 42 | 87 |
| Halperin, Mike, Cent. Fla. | 6 | 8 | 3.47 | 17 | 0 | 91 | 109 | 32 | 71 |
| Hipp, Mike, SE Louisiana | 4 | 2 | 3.60 | 20 | 0 | 50 | 59 | 14 | 40 |
| Johnson, Chad, Charleston | 3 | 5 | 3.62 | 12 | 0 | 60 | 60 | 26 | 37 |
| Williams, Jeff, SE Louisiana | 7 | 2 | 3.90 | 16 | 0 | 81 | 64 | 53 | 69 |
| Foxhall, Scott, Charleston | 5 | 5 | 3.99 | 12 | 0 | 65 | 54 | 42 | 58 |
| Brown, Willard, Stetson | 4 | 1 | 4.02 | 15 | 1 | 81 | 66 | 42 | 109 |
| Wagner, Joe, Cent. Fla. | 4 | 6 | 4.19 | 19 | 0 | 97 | 96 | 42 | 75 |
| Gates, Sean, SE Louisiana | 10 | 2 | 4.34 | 14 | 0 | 85 | 90 | 42 | 67 |
| Beale, Chuck, Stetson | 9 | 5 | 4.64 | 20 | 0 | 64 | 72 | 37 | 36 |

# WEST COAST CONFERENCE

| | Conference | | Overall | |
|---|---|---|---|---|
| | W | L | W | L |
| **Pepperdine** | 24 | 6 | 41 | 17 |
| San Diego | 19 | 11 | 36 | 17 |
| Santa Clara | 16 | 14 | 27 | 29 |
| Loyola Marymount | 14 | 16 | 23 | 33 |
| St. Mary's | 12 | 18 | 19 | 34 |
| San Francisco | 5 | 25 | 8 | 44 |

**ALL-CONFERENCE TEAM: C**—Scott Vollmer, Sr., Pepperdine; Kevin Herde, Sr., San Diego. **1B**—Anthony Napolitano, Jr., Loyola Marymount. **2B**—Dave Pingree, Sr., San Diego. **3B**—Mark Wasikowski, Sr., Pepperdine. **SS**—Eric Ekdahl, Sr., Pepperdine; Nick Mirizzi, Sr., Santa Clara. **OF**—Mike Peters, So., Loyola Marymount; Keven Dell'Amico, Jr., Pepperdine; Ryan Radmanovich, Jr., Pepperdine; Larry Williams, So., San Diego. **DH**—Brian Oliver, Jr., St. Mary's. **Util**—Jesse Ibarra, So., Loyola Marymount. **P**—Steve Duda, Sr., Pepperdine; Mike Saipe, So., San Diego; Jason LeBlanc, Fr., Pepperdine.

**Player of the Year**—Kevin Herde, San Diego.

## INDIVIDUAL BATTING LEADERS
(Minimum 125 At-Bats)

| | AVG | AB | R | H | 2B | 3B | HR | RBI | SB |
|---|---|---|---|---|---|---|---|---|---|
| Stepner, Josh, San Diego | .386 | 145 | 33 | 56 | 8 | 4 | 4 | 30 | 3 |
| Herde, Kevin, San Diego | .372 | 196 | 43 | 73 | 18 | 1 | 10 | 46 | 2 |
| Peters, Mike, LMU | .365 | 208 | 34 | 76 | 14 | 1 | 7 | 36 | 12 |
| Bulanti, Billy, USF | .335 | 182 | 21 | 61 | 10 | 2 | 2 | 27 | 1 |
| Donati, Lou, Santa Clara | .328 | 201 | 49 | 66 | 8 | 0 | 1 | 23 | 7 |
| Pittman, Demerius, St. M. | .325 | 160 | 27 | 52 | 9 | 2 | 3 | 25 | 20 |
| Vrankovich, Russ, St. M. | .325 | 157 | 32 | 51 | 13 | 4 | 2 | 22 | 9 |
| Ekdahl, Eric, Pepperdine | .324 | 207 | 42 | 67 | 10 | 2 | 3 | 34 | 16 |
| Williams, Larry, San Diego | .321 | 209 | 41 | 67 | 5 | 3 | 13 | 45 | 9 |
| Thompson, Tommy, SCU | .317 | 205 | 39 | 65 | 16 | 1 | 3 | 33 | 9 |
| Napolitano, Anthony, LMU | .315 | 219 | 34 | 69 | 15 | 1 | 5 | 38 | 2 |
| Boyd, Chad, San Diego | .313 | 163 | 25 | 51 | 7 | 0 | 0 | 30 | 1 |
| Dell'Amico, Keven, Pepp. | .313 | 179 | 30 | 56 | 8 | 3 | 2 | 31 | 11 |
| Wasikowski, Mark, Pepp. | .313 | 224 | 37 | 70 | 12 | 0 | 6 | 38 | 4 |
| Mirizzi, Nick, Santa Clara | .308 | 201 | 25 | 62 | 11 | 0 | 5 | 49 | 3 |
| Oliver, Brian, St. Mary's | .306 | 147 | 18 | 45 | 12 | 0 | 3 | 17 | 1 |
| Radmanovich, Ryan, Pepp. | .305 | 167 | 41 | 51 | 5 | 3 | 13 | 41 | 17 |
| Pingree, Dave, San Diego | .304 | 194 | 49 | 59 | 17 | 1 | 3 | 26 | 23 |
| Lovell, David, Pepperdine | .301 | 193 | 30 | 58 | 14 | 2 | 1 | 26 | 12 |
| Seal, Mike, LMU | .299 | 194 | 30 | 58 | 10 | 3 | 6 | 34 | 5 |
| Ibarra, Jesse, LMU | .299 | 154 | 33 | 46 | 6 | 0 | 17 | 52 | 1 |

## INDIVIDUAL PITCHING LEADERS
(Minimum 50 Innings)

| | W | L | ERA | G | Sv | IP | H | BB | SO |
|---|---|---|---|---|---|---|---|---|---|
| Duda, Steve, Pepperdine | 12 | 3 | 1.64 | 18 | 0 | 137 | 108 | 20 | 114 |
| Gregory, Greg, Pepperdine | 7 | 3 | 2.65 | 15 | 0 | 76 | 71 | 25 | 47 |
| LeBlanc, Jason, Pepperdine | 7 | 4 | 2.83 | 15 | 0 | 86 | 77 | 20 | 55 |
| Mooney, Eric, St. Mary's | 5 | 6 | 3.54 | 15 | 0 | 84 | 80 | 19 | 74 |
| Saipe, Mike, San Diego | 7 | 3 | 3.69 | 15 | 0 | 110 | 93 | 39 | 79 |
| Pailthorpe, Bob, Santa Clara | 4 | 4 | 3.75 | 18 | 0 | 122 | 109 | 46 | 108 |
| Burgus, Travis, San Diego | 7 | 2 | 3.75 | 14 | 0 | 86 | 90 | 38 | 57 |
| Spaulding, Jon, Santa Clara | 5 | 0 | 3.88 | 30 | 1 | 51 | 50 | 15 | 31 |
| Collins, Chris, San Diego | 8 | 2 | 3.91 | 32 | 7 | 53 | 55 | 24 | 31 |
| Pogacar, Jay, St. Mary's | 5 | 8 | 4.30 | 19 | 0 | 103 | 112 | 39 | 45 |
| Bowers, Shane, LMU | 6 | 8 | 4.55 | 17 | 0 | 113 | 121 | 38 | 88 |

# WESTERN ATHLETIC CONFERENCE

| | Conference | | Overall | |
|---|---|---|---|---|
| **EAST** | W | L | W | L |
| Brigham Young | 16 | 6 | 39 | 18 |
| New Mexico | 15 | 9 | 35 | 21 |
| Utah | 14 | 9 | 31 | 19 |
| Wyoming | 6 | 16 | 19 | 31 |
| Air Force | 5 | 16 | 28 | 22 |
| **WEST** | | | | |
| *Fresno State | 14 | 8 | 41 | 22 |
| **Cal State Northridge** | 13 | 11 | 36 | 20 |
| Sacramento State | 13 | 11 | 36 | 22 |
| **Hawaii** | 11 | 13 | 34 | 25 |
| San Diego State | 7 | 15 | 22 | 36 |

**ALL-EASTERN DIVISION TEAM: C**—Adam Sessins, So., Utah. **1B**—Mark Gulseth, Jr., New Mexico. **2B**—Brent Turley, Jr., Brigham Young. **3B**—Antonio Fernandez, So., New Mexico; Dave Madsen, Jr., Brigham Young. **SS**—Manny Robinson, Jr., Air Force. **OF**—Brian Banks, So., Brigham Young; Luke Oglesby, Jr., New

Mexico; Brett Feauto, Sr., Wyoming. **DH**—Clint Kelson, Sr., Utah. **P**—Kurt Hildebrandt, Jr., New Mexico.

**Player of the Year**—Antonio Fernandez, New Mexico.

**ALL-WESTERN DIVISION TEAM: C**—Todd Johnson, Sr., Fresno State. **1B**—Will Fitzpatrick, Sr., Sacramento State. **2B**—Matt Martinez, Sr., Sacramento State; Pat Mummy, Sr., San Diego State. **3B**—Heath Hayes, Jr., San Diego State; Andy Small, Sr., Cal State Northridge. **SS**—Andy Hodgins, Sr., Cal State Northridge. **OF**—Kenny Harrison, Sr., Hawaii; Gary McNamara, Sr., Fresno State; Franz Yuen, Jr., Hawaii. **DH**—Ray Brown, Jr., Sacramento State. **P**—Roland DeLaMaza, Sr., Sacramento State; Mike Salazar, Sr., Fresno State; Rich Juarez, Sr., San Diego State.

**Player of the Year**—Kenny Harrison, Hawaii.

## INDIVIDUAL BATTING LEADERS
(Minimum 125 At-Bats)

| | AVG | AB | R | H | 2B | 3B | HR | RBI | SB |
|---|---|---|---|---|---|---|---|---|---|
| Fernandez, Antonio, NM | .430 | 221 | 56 | 95 | 16 | 4 | 6 | 71 | 4 |
| Madsen, Dave, BYU | .415 | 205 | 62 | 85 | 16 | 2 | 15 | 64 | 5 |
| Abbs, Steve, Wyoming | .404 | 171 | 48 | 69 | 13 | 2 | 5 | 33 | 11 |
| Clark, Geoffrey, BYU | .402 | 214 | 53 | 86 | 13 | 2 | 12 | 66 | 11 |
| Harrison, Kenny, Hawaii | .389 | 208 | 44 | 81 | 21 | 2 | 8 | 60 | 6 |
| Banks, Brian, BYU | .389 | 216 | 67 | 84 | 11 | 2 | 20 | 73 | 21 |
| Ray, Brown, Sac State | .384 | 164 | 45 | 63 | 7 | 1 | 7 | 35 | 6 |
| Larsen, Erik, BYU | .378 | 225 | 62 | 85 | 11 | 2 | 7 | 30 | 12 |
| Oglesby, Luke, New Mexico | .377 | 204 | 82 | 77 | 8 | 2 | 2 | 22 | 56 |
| Martinez, Matt, Sac State | .374 | 195 | 55 | 73 | 17 | 2 | 1 | 31 | 36 |
| Mullis, Vern, Air Force | .374 | 163 | 46 | 61 | 14 | 3 | 9 | 55 | 4 |
| Cooper, Chris, BYU | .372 | 223 | 68 | 83 | 19 | 1 | 15 | 56 | 0 |
| Feauto, Brett, Wyoming | .371 | 140 | 31 | 52 | 12 | 2 | 4 | 27 | 25 |
| Robinson, Manny, Air Force | .366 | 172 | 51 | 63 | 9 | 8 | 4 | 59 | 15 |
| Thrasher, Bill, Fresno St. | .364 | 206 | 52 | 75 | 21 | 2 | 3 | 35 | 8 |
| Mummy, Pat, SDSU | .364 | 217 | 24 | 79 | 10 | 3 | 2 | 36 | 14 |
| Johnson, Todd, Fresno St. | .357 | 258 | 47 | 92 | 10 | 4 | 3 | 46 | 8 |
| Santini, Aaron, New Mexico | .356 | 191 | 57 | 68 | 11 | 1 | 3 | 54 | 15 |
| Iveson, Mark, Wyoming | .356 | 163 | 27 | 58 | 11 | 2 | 6 | 38 | 11 |
| Quigley, Keith, New Mexico | .354 | 189 | 36 | 67 | 21 | 1 | 3 | 42 | 2 |
| Espiritu, Mike, BYU | .351 | 148 | 31 | 52 | 10 | 0 | 4 | 30 | 4 |
| Copeland, Kenny, New Mexico | .350 | 214 | 55 | 75 | 14 | 1 | 5 | 46 | 8 |
| Turley, Brent, BYU | .346 | 153 | 43 | 53 | 16 | 2 | 12 | 46 | 2 |
| Roe, Mike, Fresno St. | .345 | 194 | 49 | 67 | 16 | 2 | 6 | 39 | 1 |
| Arambula, Chris, Utah | .345 | 171 | 43 | 59 | 10 | 0 | 7 | 43 | 3 |
| Shepard, Greg, CSN | .345 | 229 | 60 | 79 | 18 | 2 | 11 | 64 | 4 |
| Jones, Shane, Utah | .342 | 202 | 46 | 69 | 13 | 0 | 11 | 45 | 5 |
| Dandridge, Brad, Fresno St. | .339 | 274 | 63 | 93 | 15 | 3 | 14 | 59 | 7 |
| Ishigo, Corey, Hawaii | .338 | 231 | 61 | 78 | 3 | 0 | 3 | 22 | 3 |
| McNamara, Gary, Fresno St. | .338 | 237 | 54 | 80 | 14 | 3 | 10 | 56 | 0 |
| Sims, Mike, CSN | .338 | 237 | 45 | 80 | 17 | 0 | 7 | 42 | 0 |
| Gulseth, Mark, New Mexico | .335 | 212 | 70 | 71 | 12 | 3 | 18 | 82 | 2 |

## INDIVIDUAL PITCHING LEADERS
(Minimum 50 Innings)

| | W | L | ERA | G | Sv | IP | H | BB | SO |
|---|---|---|---|---|---|---|---|---|---|
| Juarez, Rich, SDSU | 7 | 7 | 2.91 | 16 | 1 | 118 | 96 | 27 | 73 |
| McNally, Andrew, Hawaii | 9 | 5 | 3.15 | 18 | 0 | 137 | 137 | 26 | 103 |
| DeLeMaza, Roland, Sac State | 11 | 2 | 3.17 | 16 | 0 | 114 | 94 | 46 | 113 |
| Fernandez, Jared, Fresno St. | 7 | 3 | 3.54 | 19 | 0 | 81 | 94 | 14 | 57 |
| Apana, Matt, Hawaii | 11 | 6 | 3.57 | 19 | 0 | 126 | 115 | 61 | 102 |
| Salazar, Mike, Fresno St. | 13 | 3 | 3.60 | 20 | 0 | 147 | 159 | 43 | 131 |
| Wheeler, Dan, BYU | 6 | 3 | 3.67 | 30 | 7 | 56 | 55 | 18 | 69 |
| Soderstrom, Steve, Fresno St. | 6 | 5 | 3.80 | 19 | 0 | 107 | 100 | 49 | 114 |
| Cruise, Mark, Fresno St. | 7 | 6 | 3.82 | 16 | 0 | 106 | 115 | 24 | 70 |
| Contreras, Marco, CSN | 8 | 4 | 3.98 | 17 | 1 | 122 | 119 | 53 | 82 |
| Kempton, Keven, CSN | 10 | 4 | 3.99 | 15 | 0 | 120 | 134 | 32 | 70 |
| Eby, Mike, Sac State | 7 | 5 | 4.14 | 13 | 0 | 87 | 100 | 41 | 73 |
| Baum, Chris, New Mexico | 7 | 1 | 4.36 | 13 | 0 | 64 | 75 | 28 | 40 |
| Bushart, John, CSN | 10 | 4 | 4.38 | 14 | 0 | 96 | 108 | 36 | 61 |
| Cutler, Mike, Utah | 11 | 4 | 4.38 | 16 | 0 | 111 | 137 | 36 | 66 |
| Mills, Roger, Hawaii | 3 | 4 | 4.90 | 17 | 0 | 68 | 79 | 23 | 36 |
| Minor, Tommy, Fresno St. | 7 | 1 | 4.92 | 18 | 3 | 64 | 82 | 14 | 60 |
| Richardson, Mike, SDSU | 4 | 4 | 5.03 | 22 | 0 | 106 | 127 | 42 | 61 |
| Sagas, Mike, Utah | 6 | 1 | 5.09 | 14 | 0 | 69 | 83 | 37 | 29 |

# INDEPENDENTS

| | W | L |
|---|---|---|
| **Miami** | 36 | 22 |
| UNC Greensboro | 23 | 22 |
| Grand Canyon | 24 | 32 |
| Chapman | 22 | 32 |
| Wisconsin-Milwaukee | 10 | 19 |
| Northeastern Illinois | 25 | 25 |
| Chicago State | 8 | 36 |
| Southern Utah State | 6 | 46 |

# SMALL COLLEGES

## NCAA DIVISION II

### Tampa Defends Title

Junior outfielder David Dion slugged two home runs in the title game as Tampa beat Cal Poly San Luis Obispo 7-5 to win its second straight NCAA Division II College World Series championship.

The Spartans (43-21) hit 13 home runs in winning four straight games, includ-

**David Dion**

ing four homers in the deciding game. Dion tied the game at 2-2 in the second inning with a two-run shot off Broncos starter Dan Chergey, then broke a 3-3 tie with a solo homer in the third. Dion, a former walk-on, homered five times in the Series and was named MVP of the Montgomery, Ala., tournament.

"That first one was sweet, but this one was sweet too just to show everyone it wasn't a fluke last year," Tampa coach Lelo Prado said. "Not many people repeat as national champions."

Tampa went undefeated in winning both the 1992 and 1993 titles.

On the opening day of the 1993 Series, Troy State's (Ala.) Steve Charles threw the first no-hitter in the 26-year history of the tournament, beating Mansfield State (Pa.) 5-0. That must have seemed easy for Charles, at least compared to an accident he suffered in February 1990. He lost control of a chain saw which bounced back into his face, knocking out 11 teeth and leading to nine hours on an operating table and 216 stitches.

### FINAL POLL

| | |
|---|---|
| 1. Tampa | 43-21 |
| 2. Cal Poly San Luis Obispo | 39-19 |
| 3. Troy State (Ala.) | 39-17 |
| 4. Mansfield (Pa.) | 38-15 |
| 5. South Carolina-Aiken | 46-18 |
| 6. North Alabama | 39-18 |
| 7. California-Davis | 43-14 |
| 8. Missouri-St. Louis | 31-11 |
| 9. Adelphi | 32-17 |
| 10. Florida Atlantic | 41-17 |

■ Fort Hays State (Kan.) first baseman Derek Pomeroy hit in his last 27 games of 1992 and first seven in 1993 to break the Division II record of 33 set by Florida Southern's Bobby Green in 1985.

■ The Storm of the Century canceled games all over the East Coast in mid-March, but Shippensburg (Pa.) and Lewis (Ill.) played on in Boca Raton, Fla. With 40-mph winds blowing out to all fields and gusting up to 60 mph, Shippensburg won 37-17 in seven innings to set a slew of Division II records. The teams combined to establish marks for runs, total bases (91) and RBIs (47). Shippensburg third baseman Tut Bailey hit two three-run home runs in the Raiders' 11-run fourth inning to tie another record, and Flyers' reliever Brad Skritch gave up 15 earned runs in 1⅓ innings to set yet another mark.

**—JIM CALLIS**

---

# NCAA DIVISION II

## WORLD SERIES

**Site:** Montgomery, Ala.
**Participants** (final records): Adelphi, N.Y. (32-17); Cal Poly San Luis Obispo (39-19); Mansfield, Pa. (38-15); Missouri-St. Louis (31-11); North Dakota (29-14); South Carolina-Aiken (46-18); Tampa (43-21); Troy State, Ala. (38-17).
**Champion:** Tampa (4-0).
**Runner-Up:** Cal Poly San Luis Obispo (3-1).
**Outstanding Player:** David Dion, of, Tampa.

## ALL-AMERICA TEAM

| Pos. | Player, School | Yr. | AVG | HR | RBI |
|---|---|---|---|---|---|
| C | Kevin Brown, Southern Indiana | So. | .442 | 14 | 62 |
| 1B | Sean Starratt, Livingston (Ala.) | Sr. | .386 | 16 | 72 |
| 2B | Chris Hodge, Augusta (Ga.) | Sr. | .407 | 18 | 58 |
| 3B | Brian Zaletel, Tampa | Sr. | .333 | 15 | 62 |
| SS | Rodd Kelley, Tampa | Jr. | .319 | 7 | 43 |
| INF | John Stratton, Jacksonville St. (Ala.) | Sr. | .408 | 26 | 71 |
| OF | Dom Gatti, Adelphi (N.Y.) | Sr. | .466 | 9 | 50 |
| | Mike Myers, Mansfield (Pa.) | Jr. | .445 | 5 | 41 |
| | David Dion, Tampa | Jr. | .340 | 20 | 67 |
| | Bob Mutnansky, Missouri-St. Louis | Sr. | .363 | 11 | 47 |
| DH | Mari Munoz, Mesa State (Colo.) | Sr. | .398 | 15 | 67 |
| | | Yr. | W | L | ERA |
| P | Andy Runzi, Missouri-St. Louis | Sr. | 9 | 2 | 2.15 |
| | Dan Chergey, Cal Poly SLO | Sr. | 11 | 2 | 4.15 |
| | Bryan Shover, Valdosta State (Ga.) | So. | 12 | 3 | 1.67 |
| | Eddy Gaillard, Florida Southern | Sr. | 12 | 2 | 2.44 |
| | Steve Charles, Troy State (Ala.) | Sr. | 5 | 1 | 1.40 |

**Player of the Year—**Dom Gatti, of, Adelphi.

## NATIONAL LEADERS

### BATTING AVERAGE
(Minimum 125 At-Bats)

| | AB | H | AVG |
|---|---|---|---|
| Gatti, Dom, Adelphi (N.Y.) | 189 | 88 | .466 |
| Myers, Mike, Mansfield (Pa.) | 173 | 77 | .445 |
| Brown, Kevin, Southern Indiana | 154 | 68 | .442 |
| Newsome, John, West Georgia | 148 | 64 | .432 |
| Ricuparo, Dennis, Bentley (Mass.) | 151 | 65 | .430 |
| Keipert, Brian, Northern Kentucky | 156 | 66 | .423 |
| Santucci, Steve, Assumption (Mass.) | 149 | 63 | .423 |
| Keck, Brian, Fort Hays (Kan.) State | 162 | 68 | .420 |
| Ladjevich, Rick, Central Missouri State | 129 | 54 | .419 |
| Palmer, Randy, Delta State (Miss.) | 144 | 60 | .417 |
| Van Engelenhoven, Terry, South Dakota St. | 161 | 67 | .416 |
| Cox, Gaines, Carson-Newman (Tenn.) | 212 | 88 | .415 |

#### Department Leaders: Batting

| Dept. | Player, School | G | Total |
|---|---|---|---|
| R | Young, Steve, Armstrong State (Ga.) | 58 | 72 |
| H | Kelley, Rodd, Tampa | 64 | 89 |
| TB | Dion, David, Tampa | 64 | 158 |
| 2B | Wright, David, Carson-Newman (Tenn.) | 56 | 24 |
| 3B | DeFlorio, Chris, Adelphi (N.Y.) | 47 | 8 |
| | Waymire, Jeff, UC Riverside | 53 | 8 |
| HR | Stratton, John, Jacksonville (Ala.) State | 45 | 26 |
| RBI | Starratt, Sean, Livingston (Ala.) | 46 | 72 |
| SB | Green, Stacey, Shaw (N.C.) | 31 | 54 |

### EARNED RUN AVERAGE
(Minimum 60 Innings)

| | IP | ER | ERA |
|---|---|---|---|
| Ohme, Kevin, North Florida | 100 | 18 | 1.61 |
| Shover, Bryan, Valdosta (Ga.) State | 102 | 19 | 1.67 |
| Muglia, Ralph, Oakland (Mich.) | 63 | 12 | 1.71 |
| Shores, Steve, Saginaw Valley (Mich.) | 61 | 12 | 1.78 |
| Boyd, Daryll, Armstrong State (Ga.) | 80 | 16 | 1.79 |
| Harris, David, Florida Southern | 128 | 26 | 1.83 |
| Bigelli, Bob, Springfield (Mass.) | 81 | 17 | 1.88 |
| Byrd, Matt, Oakland (Mich.) | 66 | 14 | 1.91 |

#### Department Leaders: Pitching

| Dept. | Player, School | G | Total |
|---|---|---|---|
| W | Ohme, Kevin, North Florida | 17 | 13 |
| SV | Shepherd, Greg, Missouri-St. Louis | 17 | 11 |
| SO | Harris, David, Florida Southern | 18 | 143 |

**Ferrum Flash.** Lefthander Billy Wagner earned Small College Player of the Year award by striking out 133 in 75 innings.

# NCAA DIVISION III

## Jersey Comes Up Roses

Montclair State became the second straight New Jersey school to win the NCAA Division III World Series, defeating Wisconsin-Oshkosh 3-1 for the 1993 title in Battle Creek, Mich.

The Red Hawks (37-11) went through the eight-team tournament undefeated, allowing just five runs in five games. Lefthander Drew Yocum won the final game and was named the tournament's most valuable player.

Wisconsin-Oshkosh, which won the 1985 Division III title, has appeared in 12 of the last 14 national tournaments. The Titans (28-15) have lost in the title game three times since winning.

William Paterson (N.J.) won the 1992 title.

■ Ferrum (Va.) junior lefthander Billy Wagner continued to dominate Division III hitters en route to winning Baseball America's Small College Player of the Year award. A first-round pick of the Houston Astros, Wagner went 6-3, 1.56 with 133 strikeouts in 75 innings. He set an NCAA record in 1992 by averaging 19.1 strikeouts per nine innings.

### PREVIOUS WINNERS
**Small College Player of Year**
1989 —Steve DiBartolomeo, rhp, New Haven
1990 —Sam Militello, rhp, Tampa
1991 —Sid Roberson, lhp, No. Florida
1992—Michael Tucker, ss, Longwood

■ Don Schaly became the first Division III coach ever to reach 1,000 wins when Marietta (Ohio) beat West Liberty State (W.Va.) 9-8 April 16. Known for focusing on the task on hand, Schaly couldn't help but enjoy the monumental accomplishment.

"There's no place like Marietta," Schaly said as his voice cracked. "I never thought I'd live this long to see this day."

Schaly hasn't had a losing season in 30 years with the Pioneers, and won national championships in 1982, 1983 and 1986.

—JIM CALLIS

# NCAA DIVISION III

## WORLD SERIES

**Site:** Battle Creek, Mich.
**Participants** (final records): Anderson, Ind. (31-15); California Lutheran (32-9); Carthage, Wis. (30-14); Eastern Connecticut State (29-11); Ithaca, N.Y. (32-10); Montclair State, N.J. (37-11); North Carolina Wesleyan (29-11); Wisconsin-Oshkosh (28-15).
**Champion:** Montclair State (5-0).
**Runner-Up:** Wisconsin-Oshkosh (3-2).
**Outstanding Player:** Drew Yocum, lhp, Montclair State.

## ALL-AMERICA TEAM

| Pos. | Player, School | Yr. | AVG | HR | RBI |
|---|---|---|---|---|---|
| C | Brian Detwiler, Wm. Paterson (N.J.).... | Sr. | .346 | 6 | 54 |
| 1B | Scott Govoni, Ohio Wesleyan............. | Sr. | .407 | 10 | 73 |
| | Pete Misiaszek, Southern Maine......... | Jr. | .420 | 17 | 68 |
| 2B | Dan Bartolomeo, Wm. Paterson......... | Sr. | .354 | 1 | 29 |
| 3B | Paul Pedone, Ithaca (N.Y.)............... | Sr. | .378 | 7 | 48 |
| SS | Bob Eddy, Marietta (Ohio)............... | Jr. | .388 | 5 | 44 |
| OF | Rob Carpenter, Southern Maine ......... | Jr. | .436 | 14 | 48 |
| | Tom D'Aquila, N.C. Wesleyan ........... | So. | .458 | 16 | 57 |
| | John Graham, Mass.-Dartmouth ........ | Sr. | .459 | 9 | 50 |
| | Chris Hoeppner, Anderson (Ind.)........ | Sr. | .426 | 9 | 50 |
| DH | Eric Roepsch, Framingham (Mass.) .... | Fr. | .454 | 8 | 53 |
| UT | Harry Torgerson, Ill.-Benedictine........ | Sr. | .436 | 10 | 62 |

| | | Yr. | W | L | ERA |
|---|---|---|---|---|---|
| P | Jeff Berman, Cal Lutheran................. | Sr. | 9 | 2 | 1.58 |
| | Doug Drumm, Rensselaer (N.Y.)........ | Sr. | 10 | 2 | 2.51 |
| | Billy Wagner, Ferrum (Va.)................ | Jr. | 6 | 3 | 1.56 |
| | Harry Torgerson, Ill.-Benedictine........ | Sr. | 8 | 1 | 2.13 |

**Player of the Year**—Tom D'Aquila, of, N.C. Wesleyan

## NATIONAL LEADERS

### BATTING AVERAGE
(Minimum 100 At-Bats)

| | AB | H | AVG |
|---|---|---|---|
| Carey, Jamie, North Adams State (Mass.) ........ | 100 | 50 | .500 |
| Serafin, Doug, Emory (Ga.) ................................. | 137 | 67 | .489 |
| Faessler, Scott, Framingham (Mass.) ............... | 116 | 56 | .483 |
| Patzinger, Darrell, Marietta (Ohio) .................... | 127 | 59 | .465 |
| Jilek, Craig, Wis.-Eau Claire ............................... | 104 | 48 | .462 |
| Graham, John, Mass.-Dartmouth ...................... | 135 | 62 | .459 |
| D'Aquila, Tom, NC Wesleyan ............................. | 142 | 65 | .458 |
| Roepsch, Eric, Framingham (Mass.) .................. | 130 | 59 | .454 |
| Cook, Steve, Allegheny (Pa.)............................. | 144 | 65 | .451 |
| Wanner, Chris, St. John's (Minn.) ..................... | 105 | 47 | .448 |

**Department Leaders: Batting**

| Dept. | Player, School | G | Total |
|---|---|---|---|
| R | Misieszek, Pete, Southern Maine .................. | 39 | 61 |
| H | Hoeppner, Chris, Anderson (Ind.).................. | 46 | 72 |
| TB | Carpenter, Rob, Southern Maine ................... | 39 | 136 |
| | D'Aquila, Tom, NC Wesleyan ........................ | 40 | 136 |
| 2B | Govoni, Scott, Ohio Wesleyan ...................... | 45 | 24 |
| 3B | Grubb, Chris, Elizabethtown (Pa.) ................. | 32 | 8 |
| | Lauterhahn, Mike, Wm. Paterson (N.J.)........ | 42 | 8 |
| | Murray, Shawn, Trenton (N.J.) State ............. | 33 | 8 |
| HR | Misieszek, Pete, Southern Maine ................... | 39 | 17 |
| RBI | Govoni, Scott, Ohio Wesleyan ...................... | 45 | 73 |
| SB | Bridgers, Brandon, Methodist (N.C.) ............. | 37 | 54 |

### EARNED RUN AVERAGE
(Minimum 50 Innings)

| | IP | ER | ERA |
|---|---|---|---|
| Gomez, Dennys, William Penn .......................... | 70 | 9 | 1.15 |
| Fryzowicz, Travis, FDU-Madison ...................... | 58 | 8 | 1.24 |
| Atkinson, Joel, Mount Union (Ohio) ................... | 64 | 10 | 1.40 |
| Wagner, Billy, Ferrum (Va.) .............................. | 75 | 13 | 1.56 |
| Hanson, Kris, Wis.-Whitewater ......................... | 63 | 11 | 1.57 |
| Grubb, Chris, Elizabethtown (Pa.) .................... | 63 | 11 | 1.58 |

**Department Leaders: Pitching**

| Dept. | Player, School | G | Total |
|---|---|---|---|
| W | Thompson, Jim, Anderson (Ind.)..................... | 15 | 11 |
| SV | Peterson, Dean, Allegheny (Pa.) ................... | 23 | 12 |
| SO | Wagner, Billy, Ferrum (Va.) ........................... | 17 | 133 |

# NAIA
## Gillespie's Year To Remember

It was a year that Gordie Gillespie and St. Francis (Ill.) never will forget.

After starting the 1993 season 3-13, the Fighting Saints (46-16) won 38 of their last 39 games, making Gillespie the winningest coach in college baseball history and capturing the school's first NAIA World Series title.

Gillespie passed retired Southern California great Rod Dedeaux April 28 when he got win No. 1,333 of his 41-year coaching career, a 13-3 victory over McKendree (Ill.).

**Gordie Gillespie**

"There are two records that I see as never being broken: John Wooden's string of 10 championships in 12 years and Rod Dedeaux' five straight World Series," Gillespie says. "Those records will never be duplicated. Both John and Rod are one of a kind in their sports, and I am truly honored to be mentioned in the same breath as Rod."

St. Francis didn't stop winning after Gillespie reached his milestone, at least not until beating Southeastern Oklahoma 4-2 in the NAIA championship game at Des Moines. Paul Chovanec picked up the victory to improve his record to 14-0, while Ivan Lawler was named tournament MVP after winning two games to improve to 13-1, including a 13-inning, 1-0 decision over Cumberland (Tenn.) in the semifinal.

Chovanec, a senior righthander, won two games at the national tournament and was named the NAIA Player of the Year.

■ A decade of dominance for Lewis-Clark State (Idaho) came to an end at the NAIA Far West Regional. The Warriors, winners of six straight and eight of the previous nine NAIA championships, fell short of the NAIA World Series for the first time since 1981. They had played in the title game every year since.

Hawaii Pacific eliminated Lewis-Clark State with an 8-4 win in the losers' bracket.

"It's tough to see it end this way," senior third baseman Jake Taylor said. "But it was a great reign. I hope to hell these guys can come back next year and get it going again."

■ Southern California College made news when it signed Whittier (Calif.) Christian High lefthander Ila Borders to a partial 1993-94 scholarship. Borders will become the third woman known to have played college baseball.

Susan Perabo played one game at second base for Division III Webster (Mo.) in 1985, and Julie Croteau played first base for Division III St. Mary's (Md.) from 1989-91. Croteau hit .171 (13-for-76) in three seasons, and established several NCAA firsts for women, including getting the first hit, the first run and the first RBI.

**—JIM CALLIS**

# NAT. ASSOC. of INTERCOLLEGIATE ATHLETICS

## WORLD SERIES

**Site:** Des Moines, Iowa.
**Participants** (final records): Carson-Newman, Tenn. (41-15); Cumberland, Tenn. (23-11); Geneva, Pa. (30-11); Marian, Ind. (38-13); Point Loma Nazarene, Calif. (40-19); St. Francis, Ill. (46-16); St. Mary's, Texas (46-14); Southeastern Oklahoma (43-19).
**Champion:** St. Francis (5-0).
**Runner-Up:** Southeastern Oklahoma (3-2).
**Outstanding Player:** Ivan Lawler, rhp-of, St. Francis.

## ALL-AMERICA TEAM

| Pos. | Player, School | Yr. | AVG | HR | RBI |
|---|---|---|---|---|---|
| C | Adam Rodriguez, Oklahoma City | Sr. | .403 | 19 | 62 |
| | Beck Wells, Howard Payne (Texas) | Sr. | .446 | 13 | 68 |
| 1B | Mike Evans, Lubbock Christian | Jr. | .382 | 26 | 81 |
| 2B | Steve Gann, Dallas Baptist | Sr. | .392 | 15 | 58 |
| 3B | Kurt Huizenga, Aquinas (Mich.) | Jr. | .467 | 13 | 73 |
| SS | B. Bengoechea, Lewis-Clark St. (Idaho) | Jr. | .347 | 1 | 33 |
| INF | Derek Smith, St. Andrews (N.C.) | Sr. | .461 | 0 | 28 |
| OF | Ben Agbayani, Hawaii Pacific | Jr. | .385 | 10 | 35 |
| | Jeff Boatner, Brewton-Parker (Ga.) | Sr. | .430 | 21 | 105 |
| | Todd Dunn, North Florida | Jr. | .352 | 19 | 60 |
| | Mike Reyes, Wayland Baptist (Texas) | So. | .503 | 17 | 72 |
| DH | Neal Wozniak, Ohio Dominican | Jr. | .397 | 4 | 43 |

| | | Yr. | W | L | ERA |
|---|---|---|---|---|---|
| P | Paul Chovanec, St. Francis (Ill.) | Sr. | 14 | 0 | 1.80 |
| | Joe Daw, Arkansas-Monticello | Sr. | 15 | 5 | 4.35 |
| | Kevin Ohme, North Florida | Sr. | 13 | 1 | 1.62 |

**Player of the Year**—Paul Chovanec, rhp, St. Francis (Ill.)

## NATIONAL LEADERS
### BATTING AVERAGE
(Minimum 125 At-Bats)

| | AB | H | AVG |
|---|---|---|---|
| Reyes, Mike, Wayland Baptist (Texas) | 187 | 94 | .503 |
| Huizenga, Kurt, Aquinas (Mich.) | 197 | 92 | .467 |
| Smith, Derek, St. Andrews (N.C.) | 141 | 65 | .451 |
| Dietrich, Derrick, St. Mary's (Texas) | 164 | 74 | .451 |
| Tibbs, Cory, Lindenwood (Mo.) | 134 | 60 | .448 |
| Wells, Beck, Howard Payne (Texas) | 186 | 83 | .446 |
| Erwin, Monte, Arkansas-Monticello | 157 | 70 | .446 |
| Cardona, Ruben, Belhaven (Miss.) | 160 | 71 | .444 |
| Cheatum, Paul, Kansas Newman | 133 | 59 | .444 |
| Coffey, Josh, Dominican (N.Y.) | 132 | 58 | .439 |
| McLenagahn, Jason, Ozarks (Mo.) | 137 | 60 | .438 |
| Carroll, Sean, Geneva (Pa.) | 147 | 64 | .435 |

**Department Leaders: Batting**

| Dept. | Player, School | G | Total |
|---|---|---|---|
| R | Reyes, Mike, Wayland Baptist (Texas) | 54 | 70 |
| H | Koester, Jerry, Siena Heights (Mich.) | 69 | 95 |
| 2B | Huizenga, Kurt, Aquinas (Mich.) | 58 | 24 |
| 3B | Dietrich, Derrick, St. Mary's (Texas) | 50 | 13 |
| HR | Evans, Mike, Lubbock Christian (Texas) | 65 | 26 |
| RBI | Boatner, Jeff, Brewton-Parker (Ga,) | 69 | 105 |
| SB | Smith, Derek, St. Andrews (N.C.) | 48 | 50 |

### EARNED RUN AVERAGE
(Minimum 60 Innings)

| | IP | ER | ERA |
|---|---|---|---|
| Muhs, John, St. Andrews (N.C.) | 83 | 13 | 1.41 |
| Ochman, Steve, St. Francis (Ill.) | 71 | 12 | 1.52 |
| Flach, Jason, St. Ambrose (Iowa) | 62 | 11 | 1.60 |
| Ohme, Kevin, North Florida | 100 | 16 | 1.62 |
| Chovanec, Paul, St. Francis (Ill.) | 120 | 24 | 1.80 |
| Stein, Blake, Spring Hill (Ala.) | 119 | 24 | 1.82 |

**Department Leaders: Pitching**

| Dept. | Player, School | G | Total |
|---|---|---|---|
| W | Paul Chovanec, St. Francis (Ill.) | 20 | 14 |
| SO | Pete Magre, St. Mary's (Texas) | 21 | 131 |

# JUNIOR COLLEGE

## Sac City Falls Short Again

For the third straight year, Sacramento City College advanced to the championship game of the California community college tournament. For the third straight year and fifth time in the last seven, the Panthers finished second.

Rancho Santiago (41-9) beat the host Panthers twice in two days, including a 5-3 decision in the finale, to win its first state title. Dons reliever Steve Thobe struck out Brian Brewer with the tying run at second to earn his 11th save and preserve the win for Jason Dietrich (6-1).

**Don Denbow**

Thobe tied the school record for saves set in 1991 by his brother J.J., now a rising prospect in the Cleveland Indians system.

Dons outfielder Tony Truel went 8-for-11 with two home runs as Rancho Santiago went undefeated in three games.

■ Yavapai (Ariz.) capped a comeback from a dismal 20-25 season in 1992 by winning the 1993 National Junior College World Series. The Roughriders beat Triton (Ill.) 6-3 in the championship game at Grand Junction, Colo., for their first title since Oklahoma State's Gary Ward coached them in 1975 and 1977.

"This is what we've been waiting for all year," Roughriders all-tournament catcher Travis McClendon said. "Last year with a losing record and all, we didn't think we could do it. If a team deserves to win it, I think we do."

Yavapai starter Bobby Howry went the distance in the finale, beating Jason Ruskey, who had won three previous games and was selected the tournament's outstanding pitcher. Tournament MVP Kevin Pitts homered twice for the Roughriders.

■ Blinn (Texas) outfielder Don Denbow won Baseball America's Junior College Player of the Year award after batting .384 with 16 homers and 51 RBIs. He signed with the San Francisco Giants after being drafted in the third round. It marked the second year in a row that the recipient was San Francisco's third-round pick—Benji Simonton from California's Diablo Valley JC was the 1992 winner.

### PREVIOUS WINNERS
**Junior College Player of Year**
1989—David Evans, rhp, San Jacinto JC
1990—Kelly Stinnett, c, Seminole JC
1991—Frank Rodriguez, ss-rhp, Howard JC
1992—Benji Simonton, of, Diablo Valley JC

■ Massasoit (Mass.) got a homer and five RBIs from tournament MVP Michael Terceira to defeat Potomac State (W.Va.) 8-3 in the NJCAA Division II title game at Millington, Tenn.

■ Gloucester (N.J.) CC won the NJCAA Division III crown for the second year in a row with a 12-0 victory over Manchester (Conn.) CC at Jamestown, N.Y. Tournament MVP John Broome tossed a two-hitter in the final for the Roadrunners, who were 45-3 on the season.

# JUNIOR COLLEGE

## NJCAA DIVISION I
### WORLD SERIES

**Site:** Grand Junction, Colo.
**Participants:** Galveston (Texas), Hagerstown (Md.), Indian Hills (Iowa), Indian River (Fla.), Meridian (Miss.), Northeastern Oklahoma, Rockland (N.Y.), Southern Idaho, Triton (Ill.), Yavapai (Ariz.).
**Champion:** Yavapai (4-1)
**Runner-Up:** Triton (4-2)
**Outstanding Player:** Kevin Pitts, 1b, Triton.

### ALL-AMERICA TEAM

**C**—Rick Fisher, Montgomery (Md.) JC. **INF**—Louis Collier, Triton (Ill.) JC; Jose Padron, Hill (Texas) JC; Jason Jameson, Trinidad State (Colo.) JC; Tim Forkner, Seward (Kan.) CC. **OF**—Martin Dewett, Mesa (Ariz.) CC; Ledowick Johnson, Louisbury (N.C.) JC; Chris Pearce, North Florida JC. **DH**—Kevin Nichols, Wallace State (Ala.) JC. **P**—Ryan Franklin, Seminole (Okla.) JC; Bubba Dixon, Mississippi Gulf Coast JC; Mike Martin, Walters State (Tenn.) JC.

### NATIONAL LEADERS
#### BATTING AVERAGE
(Minimum 100 At-Bats)

| | AB | H | AVG |
|---|---|---|---|
| Zabatta, Dan, Nassau (N.Y.) | 100 | 50 | .500 |
| Flores, Jose, New Mexico | 145 | 71 | .490 |
| Slemmer, Dave, Crowder (Mo.) | 125 | 61 | .488 |
| Forkner, Tim, Seward County (Kan.) | 175 | 85 | .486 |
| Rodgers, Brian, Barton County (Kan.) | 114 | 55 | .482 |
| Johnson, Justin, Eastern Utah | 138 | 66 | .478 |
| Collier, Louis, Triton (Ill.) | 192 | 90 | .469 |

#### Department Leaders: Batting

| Dept. | Player, School | G | Total |
|---|---|---|---|
| HR | Dunavon, Chad, Howard (Texas) | 54 | 20 |
| RBI | Montano, Manuel, Trinidad State (Colo.) | 59 | 104 |

#### EARNED RUN AVERAGE
(Minimum 50 Innings)

| | IP | ER | ERA |
|---|---|---|---|
| Orr, Pat, Bossier Parish (La.) | 58 | 8 | 1.23 |
| Dixon, Bubba, Mississippi Gulf Coast | 103 | 15 | 1.31 |
| Mattson, Craig, Triton (Ill.) | 58 | 10 | 1.54 |
| Ruskey, Jason, Triton (Ill.) | 100 | 18 | 1.61 |
| Stierlen, Tom, Bethany Lutheran (Minn.) | 53 | 10 | 1.70 |

#### Department Leaders: Pitching

| Dept. | Player, School | Total |
|---|---|---|
| W | Ruskey, Jason, Triton (Ill.) | 15 |
| SV | Saylor, Jon, Allen County (Kan.) | 12 |
| SO | Ruskey, Jason, Triton (Ill.) | 129 |

## NJCAA DIVISION II
### WORLD SERIES

**Site:** Millington, Tenn.
**Participants:** Brookdale (N.J.), Carl Albert (Okla.), Grand Rapids (Mich.), Kirkwood (Iowa), Lincoln Land (Ill.), Longview (Mo.), Massasoit (Mass.), Potomac State (W. Va.).
**Champion:** Massasoit (4-0).
**Runner-Up:** Potomac State (3-2).

## NJCAA DIVISION III
### WORLD SERIES

**Site:** Jamestown, N.Y.
**Participants:** Allegheny (Pa.), Cedar Valley (Texas), DuPage (Ill.), Gloucester County (N.J.), Manchester (Conn.), Mohawk Valley (N.Y.), Rochester (Minn.), SUNY Farmingdale.
**Champion:** Gloucester County (4-0).
**Runner-Up:** Manchester (3-2).

## CALIFORNIA JUCOS
### STATE CHAMPIONSHIP

**Site:** Santa Ana, Calif.
**Participants:** Laney, Orange Coast, Rancho Santiago, Sacramento City.
**Champion:** Rancho Santiago (3-0).
**Runner-Up:** Sacramento City (2-2).

# HIGH SCHOOLS

# Arizona School Hits Top Of Prep Charts

**By ALLAN SIMPSON**

Greenway High of Phoenix, which won its first state title in 12 years and became the first Arizona high school ever to win 30 games in a season, finished 1993 atop the Baseball America/National High School Baseball Coaches Association poll.

The Demons (33-2), who hit .373 and averaged 12 runs per game, won their final 14 games of the season, beating Flowing Wells High of Tucson 20-0 in the championship game of the Arizona 4-A tournament. The school's only losses came at the hands of 5-A schools.

Greenway's top player was 5-foot-9, 150-pound pitcher-outfielder Jeff Strasser, who led the team in hitting (.447) and also went 12-0, 1.18. His twin brother John, a shortstop drafted in the 42nd round by the New York Yankees, hit .425.

Ted Blake, who started the Greenway program in 1973 and has been the school's only head coach, previously won a state title in 1981 when the Demons competed at the 5-A level. Because of declining enrollment, his team dropped to 4-A after the 1989

**Trot Nixon**

ROBERT GURGANUS

season.

Greenway, whose most famous baseball alumnus is 1993 American League rookie of the year Tim Salmon, fended off a late challenge by traditionally strong schools in California, Florida and Texas to capture the top spot in the BA/NHSBCA poll.

Bullard High (26-3) of Fresno was ranked No. 2 after winning its fifth California Interscholastic Federation Central Section title.

Another California school, Simi Valley High (27-4), was primed for a run at the mythical national title after winning the prestigious Upper Deck tournament, which annually attracts some of the nation's top high school teams. But the hard-hitting Pioneers lost 3-0 to Anaheim's Esperanza High in the CIF Southern Section championship game, and were relegated to fifth.

California schools do not compete in a state tournament.

Martin High (34-5) of Arlington, Texas, which eliminated powerful Duncanville High (28-1) in the first round of regional play and went on to win the Texas 5-A title, finished No. 3. Duncanville, which had four players selected in the draft and was generally regarded by scouts as the nation's best team, held the top spot in the poll before its only loss of the season. Duncanville, relegated to 10th, had defeated Martin earlier in the year.

Sarasota High (28-6) won the Florida 4-A title and featured the pitching duo of Yankees' first-round draft pick Matt Drews and projected '94 first-rounder Doug Million. But six early-season losses cost the Sailors a chance at a top 10 ranking. They finished at No. 14.

## Player Of Year: Nixon

Meanwhile, Baseball America's 1993 High School Player of the Year, pitcher-outfielder Trot Nixon, almost singlehandedly led his school, New Hanover High of Wilmington, N.C., to the national title. The Wildcats dropped their opening game of the year, then won their final 26 to capture the North Carolina state 4-A title. They finished No. 7 nationally.

Nixon hit .519 with 12 home runs and a state-record 56 RBIs. As a pitcher, he was a perfect 12-0 with a 0.40 ERA and 120 strikeouts in 71 innings.

"It was a dream come true," said Nixon,

## HIGH SCHOOL TOP 25

Baseball America's final 1993 Top 25, selected in conjunction with the National High School Baseball Coaches Association.

| SCHOOL, CITY | W-L | Achievement |
|---|---|---|
| 1. Greenway HS, Phoenix | 32-2 | State 4-A champion |
| 2. Bullard HS, Fresno, Calif. | 26-3 | CIF sectional champion |
| 3. Martin HS, Arlington, Texas | 32-5 | State 5-A champion |
| 4. First Colonial HS, Virginia Beach, Va. | 28-0 | State group 3-A champion |
| 5. Simi Valley (Calif.) HS | 27-4 | CIF sectional finalist |
| 6. Oak Park HS, Kansas City, Mo. | 22-0 | State 4-A champion |
| 7. New Hanover HS, Wilmington, N.C. | 26-1 | State 4-A champion |
| 8. Oak Grove HS, Hattiesburg, Miss. | 31-1 | State 4-A champion |
| 9. Arundel HS, Gambrills, Md. | 21-1 | State 4-A champion |
| 10. Duncanville (Texas) HS | 28-1 | |
| 11. Bishop Amat HS, La Puente, Calif. | 27-1 | CIF sectional finalist |
| 12. Moeller HS, Cincinnati | 27-4 | State Division I champion |
| 13. Elmhurst, Fort Wayne, Ind. | 33-2 | |
| 14. Sarasota (Fla.) HS | 23-6 | State 4-A champion |
| 15. Cheshire (Conn.) HS | 23-0 | State 2-L champion |
| 16. Eldorado HS, Albuquerque, N.M. | 23-2 | State 4-A champion |
| 17. Churchill HS, San Antonio | 25-1 | |
| 18. St. Thomas Aquinas HS, Ft. Lauderdale, Fla. | 30-2 | |
| 19. Santa Teresa HS, San Jose, Calif. | 22-2 | CIF sectional finalist |
| 20. Green Valley HS, Henderson, Nev. | 30-2 | State 3-A champion |
| 21. Monroe HS, New York | 34-3 | |
| 22. Marist HS, Atlanta | 30-3 | State 3-A champion |
| 23. Jefferson HS, Shenandoah Junction, W. Va. | 35-4 | State 3-A champion |
| 24. Seaford (Del.) HS | 21-1 | State Class B champion |
| 25. Westminster Christian HS, Miami | 28-5 | |

# BASEBALL AMERICA'S 1993 HIGH SCHOOL ALL-AMERICA TEAMS

## FIRST TEAM

| Pos. | Player | School, Hometown | Drafted | AVG | AB | H | HR | RBI | SB |
|------|--------|------------------|---------|-----|-----|-----|-----|-----|-----|
| C | John Roskos | Cibola HS, Rio Rancho, N.M. | Marlins (2) | .613 | 62 | 38 | 15 | 42 | 8 |
| IB | Derrek Lee | El Camino HS, Sacramento | Padres (1) | .459 | 98 | 45 | 10 | 47 | 33 |
| INF | Alex Rodriguez | Westminster Christian HS, Miami | Mariners (1) | .505 | 93 | 47 | 9 | 36 | 35 |
| | Kelly Dransfeldt | Morris (Ill.) HS | Twins (7) | .516 | 118 | 61 | 20 | 63 | 41 |
| | Scott Rolen | Jasper (Ind.) HS | Phillies (2) | .547 | 75 | 41 | 8 | 35 | 17 |
| OF | Trot Nixon | New Hanover HS, Wilmington, N.C. | Red Sox (1) | .519 | 79 | 41 | 12 | 56 | 20 |
| | Torii Hunter | Pine Bluff (Ark.) HS | Twins (1) | .436 | 55 | 24 | 6 | 30 | 12 |
| | Charles Peterson | Laurens (S.C.) HS | Pirates (1) | .449 | 49 | 22 | 6 | 26 | 21 |
| DH | Brad Fullmer | Montclair Prep, Van Nuys, Calif. | Expos (2) | .569 | 86 | 49 | 14 | 60 | 6 |

| Pos. | Player | School, Hometown | Drafted | W | L | ERA | IP | H | BB | SO |
|------|--------|------------------|---------|-----|-----|-----|-----|-----|-----|-----|
| P | Kirk Presley | Tupelo (Miss.) HS | Mets (1) | 15 | 0 | 0.58 | 97 | 37 | 15 | 161 |
| | Troy Carrasco | Jesuit HS, Tampa | Twins (3) | 15 | 0 | 0.32 | 87 | 31 | 26 | 176 |
| | Matt Drews | Sarasota (Fla.) HS | Yankees (1) | 10 | 2 | 1.27 | 88 | 47 | 30 | 125 |
| | Jeff Suppan | Crespi HS, Encino, Calif. | Red Sox (2) | 11 | 1 | 0.92 | 91 | 52 | 14 | 127 |
| | Nate Yeskie | Carson HS, Carson City, Nev. | Dodgers (6) | 12 | 0 | 0.65 | 85 | 41 | 22 | 157 |
| | R.A. Dickey | Montgomery Bell Academy, Nashville | Tigers (10) | 15 | 3 | 0.46 | 119 | 54 | 27 | 216 |

## SECOND TEAM

C—Steve Hagins, University HS, Irvine, Calif. (.507-3-29). **1B**—Nate Thomas, First Colonial HS, Virginia Beach (.575-7-26). **INF**—Mike Bell, Moeller HS, Cincinnati (.400-5-28); Anthony Medrano, Jordan HS, Long Beach (.351-2-20); Mike Torti, Newman Smith HS, Carrolton, Texas (.535-6-42). **OF**—Chris Schwab, Cretin-Derham Hall HS, Eagan, Minn. (.507-9-39); Tyrone Frazier, Woodlawn HS, Shreveport, La. (.482-2-19, 52 SB); Andre King, Stranahan HS, Fort Lauderdale (.492-5-13). **DH**—David Gibralter, Duncanville, Texas, HS (.484-11-54). **P**—Dan Perkins, Westminster Christian HS, Miami (10-1, 0.58, 73 IP, 72 SO); Jamey Wright, Westmoore HS, Oklahoma City (7-2, 0.57, 62 IP, 94 SO); Mark Watson, Marist HS, Atlanta (13-1, 0.80, 80 IP, 128 SO); John Phillips, Bullard HS, Fresno (14-0, 2.46, 97 IP, 120 SO); Matt LaChappa, El Capitan HS, Lakeside, Calif. (10-1, 1.57, 71 IP, 123 SO); Jason Middlebrook, Grass Lake, Mich. (12-1, 0.36, 77 IP, 192 SO).

---

also an All-American prep quarterback. "I'd been waiting for four years to win a state championship in football or baseball. In the last few years, we'd sputtered at the end.

"I worked my butt off to get recognition for New Hanover and our baseball team. I'm really proud of the guys. This wasn't a one-man team, or just me and Fletcher Bates (Mets, fifth round). They never gave up, even when I chewed them out as a coach on the field a couple of times. It was all 24 of us."

Nixon won a spirited three-way battle to earn Baseball America's 1993 High School Player of the Year award. He edged out shortstop Alex Rodriguez of Miami's Westminster Christian High and righthander Kirk Presley from Tupelo (Miss.) High.

Not coincidentally, the trio were the first three high school players selected in the June draft. Nixon went seventh overall to Boston and was signed to an $890,000 bonus contract that guarantees he'll be in a Red Sox uniform by September 1994. Rodriguez was drafted first by Seattle, while Presley went eighth to the Mets.

Nixon's father William, who is a leading kidney specialist, grew up with Hall of Famer Catfish Hunter in Hertford, N.C., and was Hunter's high school catcher.

"I've grown up in a baseball family," Nixon said. "Catfish is a real good friend."

Like the previous year's winner, infielder Preston Wilson of Bamberg, S.C., who was drafted in the first round and signed with the Mets, Nixon signed too late in the summer to begin his pro career in the same season he was drafted. Nixon signed in late August, after he had begun fall football practice at North Carolina State University.

Alex Rodriguez

LARRY KINKER

Rodriguez and Presley also came to terms with the Mariners and Mets, respectively, in 11th-hour deals.

## Heavy Interest In Rodriguez

Rodriguez, in particular, was under a microscope all of the 1993 season, with close to 100 scouts observing some of his games.

"It was the Alex Rodriguez Sweepstakes," said Westminster Christian coach Rich Hofman. "You can't imagine the pressure he has had to go through. We had big crowds everywhere just to see him play. And every pitcher pitched to him like it was the last out in the World Series.

"I've never seen a player command so much attention, yet he's handled it with a great deal of humility. There's been a crush of agents and scouts everywhere we've gone this year and it's been tough on him."

Rodriguez hit .505 and reached base 89 times in 125 plate appearances. Over his three-year career, Rodriguez hit .419 with 17 homers and stole 90 bases in 94 attempts.

Westminster Christian, the 1992 national champion and '93 preseason No. 1, lost in the semifinals of the Upper Deck tournament and failed to even qualify for the Florida 2-A playoffs when Rodriguez uncharacteristically committed a pair of costly last-inning errors in a qualifying game. In all, Westminster Christian lost five times in 1993, yet still produced Rodriguez and a second-round pick, righthander Dan Perkins.

Presley gained a great deal of notoriety because he is the third cousin of Rock 'n Roll legend Elvis Presley. Over the course of his high school career, Presley never lost a starting assignment, finishing at 37-1 overall. He was 15-0 in 1993 and also hit .422 with nine homers and 49 RBIs.

# AMATEUR
# BASEBALL

# Cuba Displays Its Usual Dominance

**By JIM CALLIS**

The New York Yankees of yore had nothing on Cuba when it comes to baseball dynasties. Again in 1993, Cuba's national team dominated the international stage.

Team USA's summer season, meanwhile, began with promise and ended in a riot in Nicaragua.

After beating Australia three times in four tries to kick off its 1993 schedule, the U.S. national team headed to Italy for the Intercontinental Cup, the highlight of the summer schedule. Defending Olympic champion Cuba beat the United States 9-4 in the finale to win the 14th straight major international tournament it has entered and run its unbeaten streak to 83 games in such events. But for the first time since the 1988 Olympics, Team USA reached the championship game of a tournament.

It was an especially significant accomplishment in a post-Olympic year when recruiting players is usually difficult. It also was the highlight of Team USA's summer.

The next major event for Team USA was the World University Games in Buffalo, where it didn't fare nearly as well. After winning its first three games, the United States lost its next three and had to settle for

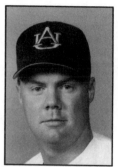

**Team USA Stalwarts.** Third baseman Todd Walker, left, and righthander John Powell led Team USA to a 30-16 record in 1993.

fifth place after beating Chinese Taipei 5-3. Team USA coach John Anderson (Minnesota) said his players took the college-age competition too lightly.

"I think our kids need to develop a little better passion about being the best in the world," said Anderson, who noted that Cuba has no other stage on which to achieve glory besides international tournaments, while U.S. players have college baseball. "Forget about your college, your league and worry about being the best in the world. They need to grasp that concept and realize these are once-in-a-lifetime opportunities."

Cuba, which didn't have a single player from its Olympic or Intercontinental Cup champions, beat Korea 7-1 for the gold medal. While the Cubans won another tournament, they lost two players.

Pitcher Edilberto Oropesa jumped the back fence at Sal Maglie Field in Niagara Falls, N.Y., where he fled in a car with a relative and headed to Miami to seek political asylum. Shortstop Reynaldo Ordonez defected from the athletes' village a few days later. They became the ninth and 10th players to leave the island nation since July 1991.

The Cubans continued to torment Team USA, which rebounded from the World University Games to beat Japan three games to two in an annual series. The United States lost four games to three in a hard-fought series with Cuba, which it has won only once since the teams began an annual series in 1986.

"They just made some unbelievable plays when we had some chances to win some games," said Anderson, an assistant on the 1990 edition of Team USA that beat Cuba two games to one. "We got through their pitching, but their defense takes it away from you. Because of their defense, we couldn't get that last hit.

"I think we gained some respect back, though. We got their attention, anyway."

## Violence Dampens Season

Team USA finished its summer season at a World Championship qualifying tournament in Managua, Nicaragua, a nation then on the brink of civil war. Dozens of hostages had been seized by armed rebels

## TEAM USA

### OVERALL STATISTICS

| BATTING | AVG | AB | R | H | 2B | 3B | HR | RBI | SB |
|---|---|---|---|---|---|---|---|---|---|
| Hinch, A.J., c | .372 | 86 | 15 | 32 | 4 | 0 | 2 | 12 | 4 |
| Helton, Todd, 1b | .352 | 122 | 28 | 43 | 10 | 2 | 2 | 24 | 2 |
| Wagner, Bret, p-of | .341 | 91 | 21 | 31 | 6 | 1 | 3 | 13 | 5 |
| Clougherty, Pat, of | .321 | 140 | 29 | 45 | 13 | 1 | 2 | 35 | 8 |
| Johnson, Russ, ss | .310 | 174 | 34 | 54 | 16 | 3 | 2 | 32 | 16 |
| Bellhorn, Mark, 2b | .294 | 34 | 9 | 10 | 2 | 0 | 0 | 5 | 2 |
| Walker, Todd, 3b-2b | .289 | 173 | 33 | 50 | 12 | 2 | 7 | 46 | 11 |
| Nelson, Charlie, of | .285 | 151 | 21 | 43 | 5 | 0 | 1 | 13 | 13 |
| Merila, Mark, 2b-3b | .280 | 143 | 42 | 40 | 10 | 0 | 1 | 16 | 7 |
| Martin, Mike, c-3b | .242 | 33 | 5 | 8 | 2 | 0 | 0 | 5 | 2 |
| Grass, Darren, c | .233 | 86 | 8 | 20 | 3 | 0 | 3 | 15 | 0 |
| Dunn, Todd, of | .226 | 62 | 13 | 14 | 3 | 0 | 1 | 9 | 4 |
| Barkett, Andy, 1b | .203 | 74 | 5 | 15 | 6 | 0 | 0 | 8 | 0 |
| Powell, Dante, of | .173 | 156 | 30 | 27 | 5 | 1 | 5 | 16 | 19 |
| Taylor, Richie, of | .083 | 12 | 1 | 1 | 0 | 0 | 0 | 0 | 0 |
| Hills, Rich, ss | .000 | 2 | 0 | 0 | 0 | 0 | 0 | 0 | 0 |
| Fernandez, A., 3b | .000 | 2 | 0 | 0 | 0 | 0 | 0 | 0 | 0 |
| Davis, Tommy, 3b | .000 | 2 | 0 | 0 | 0 | 0 | 0 | 0 | 0 |
| TOTALS | .281 | 1543 | 294 | 433 | 297 | 10 | 29 | 249 | 93 |

| PITCHING | W | L | ERA | G | SV | IP | H | BB | SO |
|---|---|---|---|---|---|---|---|---|---|
| Haynie, Jason | 0 | 0 | 0.00 | 1 | 0 | 2 | 1 | 2 | 1 |
| Powell, Brian | 0 | 0 | 0.00 | 1 | 0 | 2 | 2 | 0 | 1 |
| Hermanson, Dustin | 0 | 0 | 0.81 | 22 | 7 | 22 | 14 | 5 | 28 |
| Scafa, Bob | 3 | 1 | 1.91 | 10 | 0 | 28 | 21 | 12 | 19 |
| Graves, Danny | 2 | 0 | 2.29 | 21 | 2 | 39 | 29 | 18 | 35 |
| Reich, Steve | 2 | 1 | 2.48 | 17 | 0 | 36 | 34 | 3 | 38 |
| Kelly, John | 2 | 0 | 2.81 | 4 | 0 | 16 | 15 | 7 | 14 |
| Wilson, Paul | 5 | 4 | 3.06 | 10 | 0 | 62 | 61 | 15 | 61 |
| Loewer, Carlton | 3 | 3 | 3.21 | 9 | 0 | 42 | 33 | 20 | 36 |
| Wagner, Bret | 1 | 0 | 3.24 | 9 | 0 | 8 | 5 | 3 | 10 |
| Harvey, Terry | 4 | 2 | 3.43 | 7 | 0 | 42 | 47 | 7 | 24 |
| Powell, John | 8 | 3 | 3.58 | 12 | 0 | 75 | 66 | 25 | 69 |
| Codrington, John | 0 | 0 | 4.50 | 1 | 0 | 2 | 3 | 0 | 1 |
| Beaumont, Matt | 0 | 2 | 5.40 | 8 | 0 | 23 | 32 | 13 | 16 |
| Helton, Todd | 0 | 0 | 16.20 | 1 | 0 | 2 | 5 | 0 | 2 |
| TOTALS | 30 | 16 | 3.04 | 46 | 9 | 403 | 368 | 130 | 355 |

# SUMMER BASEBALL
## CHAMPIONS
### INTERNATIONAL

| Event | Age Group | Site | Champion | Runner-up |
|---|---|---|---|---|
| Intercontinental Cup | Unlimited | Italy | Cuba | United States |
| World University Games | College | Buffalo | Cuba | South Korea |
| World Championships Qualifying/Americas | Unlimited | Managua, Nicaragua | Nicaragua | Puerto Rico |
| Asian Championships | Unlimited | Perth, Australia | Japan | South Korea |
| European Championships | Unlimited | Stockholm, Sweden | Holland | Italy |
| World Junior Championships | 18 and under | Windsor, Ontario | Cuba | United States |

### NATIONAL

| Event | Age Group | Site | Champion | Runner-up |
|---|---|---|---|---|
| National Baseball Congress World Series | Unlimited | Wichita | Kenai, Alaska | Beatrice, Neb. |
| All-American Amateur Baseball Assoc. | 21 and under | Johnstown, Pa. | Baltimore | Columbus, Ohio |
| U.S. Olympic Festival | 18 and under | San Antonio | USA North | USA South |
| American Legion World Series | 19 and under | Roseburg, Ore. | Rapid City, S.D. | Las Vegas |
| Junior Olympic Super Series | 15-16 | Beaumont, Texas | Bayside, N.Y. | Meridian, Miss. |

### LITTLE LEAGUE

| Event | Age Group | Site | Champion | Runner-up |
|---|---|---|---|---|
| Big League World Series | 16-18 | Fort Lauderdale | Chinese Taipei | Broward County, Fla. |
| Senior League World Series | 13-15 | Kissimmee, Fla. | La Vega, Dom. Rep. | Chinese Taipei |
| Junior League World Series | 13 | Taylor, Mich. | Cayey, P.R. | Reynosa, Mexico |
| Little League World Series | 11-12 | Williamsport, Pa. | Long Beach | Panama |

### AMERICAN AMATEUR BASEBALL CONGRESS

| Event | Age Group | Site | Champion | Runner-up |
|---|---|---|---|---|
| Stan Musial World Series | Unlimited | Battle Creek, Mich. | San Juan, P.R. | Chicago |
| Connie Mack World Series | 17-18 | Farmington, N.M. | Cincinnati | Dallas |
| Mickey Mantle World Series | 15-16 | Scottsdale, Ariz. | Glendale, Calif. | Cincinnati |
| Sandy Koufax World Series | 13-14 | Spring, Texas | Pico Rivera, Calif. | Dallas |
| Pee Wee Reese World Series | 11-12 | Las Cruces, N.M. | Cardiff, Calif. | Kansas City, Kan. |
| Willie Mays World Series | 9-10 | Rex, Ga. | Spring, Texas | Levittown, P.R. |
| Roberto Clemente World Series | 8 and under | Jonesboro, Ga. | Villa Padres, P.R. | Tulsa |

### NATIONAL AMATEUR BASEBALL FEDERATION

| Event | Age Group | Site | Champion | Runner-up |
|---|---|---|---|---|
| Major World Series | Unlimited | Louisville | Long Island, N.Y. | Bridgeport, Conn. |
| College World Series | 22 and under | Cincinnati | Cincinnati | Macomb, Mich. |
| Senior World Series | 18 and under | Youngstown, Ohio | Marietta, Ga. | Bayside, N.Y. |
| High School World Series | HS students | Apopka, Fla. | Apopka, Fla. | Orlando |
| Junior World Series | 16 and under | Northville, Mich. | Bayside, N.Y. | Dearborn Hts., Mich. |
| Sophomore World Series | 14 and under | Northville, Mich. | Baltimore | W. Bloomfield, Mich. |
| Freshman World Series | 12 and under | Sylvania, Ohio | Joliet, Ill. | Dayton, Ohio |

### BABE RUTH LEAGUE

| Event | Age Group | Site | Champion | Runner-up |
|---|---|---|---|---|
| 16-18 World Series | 16-18 | Newark, Ohio | San Gabriel, Calif. | Lincoln Park, Mich. |
| 13-15 World Series | 13-15 | Ewing, N.J. | Carolina, P.R. | Sarasota, Fla. |
| 13 World Series | 13 | Springdale, Ark. | Taylorsville, Utah | Lexington, Ky. |
| Bambino World Series | 5-12 | Lebanon, Mo. | Connersville, Ind. | Willamette, Ore. |

### PONY LEAGUE

| Event | Age Group | Site | Champion | Runner-up |
|---|---|---|---|---|
| Palomino League World Series | 17-18 | Greensboro, N.C. | Houston | Honolulu |
| Colt League World Series | 15-16 | Lafayette, Ind. | Fountain Valley, Calif. | Maui, Hawaii |
| Pony League World Series | 13-14 | Washington, Pa. | Joliet, Ill. | Bayamon, P.R. |
| Bronco League World Series | 11-12 | Monterey, Calif. | Bayamon, P.R. | Joliet, Ill. |

### DIXIE BASEBALL ASSOCIATION

| Event | Age Group | Site | Champion | Runner-up |
|---|---|---|---|---|
| Dixie Majors World Series | 17-18 | Lufkin, Texas | Lufkin, Texas | Goodlettsville, Tenn. |
| Dixie Pre-Majors World Series | 15-16 | Lake Charles, La. | Meridian, Miss. | Columbus Cty., N.C. |
| Boys World Series | 13-14 | Covington, Ga. | Bossier City, La. | Lexington, S.C. |
| Youth World Series | 11-12 | West Monroe, La. | Columbus County, N.C. | Glencoe, Ala. |

### CONTINENTAL AMATEUR BASEBALL ASSOCIATION

| Event | Age Group | Site | Champion | Runner-up |
|---|---|---|---|---|
| | 18 and under | Russiaville, Ind. | Olympia, Wash. | Licking County, Ohio |
| High School | HS students | Euclid, Ohio | Bergen Beach, N.Y. | Miami |
| | 16 and under | Laredo, Texas | San Diego | Aguas Bunas, P.R. |
| | 15 and under | Crystal Lake, Ill. | Knoxville | Columbus, Ohio |
| | 14 and under | Dublin, Ohio | Stow, Ohio | Wichita |
| | 13 and under | McCook, Neb. | Marietta, Ga. | Dallas |
| | 12 and under | Omaha | San Juan, P.R. | Honolulu |
| | 11 and under | Tarkio, Mo. | Kansas City, Mo. | Southgate, Calif. |
| | 10 and under | Aurella, Iowa | Dallas | Honolulu |
| | 9 and under | Charles City, Iowa | Honolulu | Southgate, Calif. |

# TEAM USA '93
## INTERCONTINENTAL CUP
Italy
June 24-July 5, 1993

### STANDINGS

| ROUND-ROBIN | W | L | RF | RA |
|---|---|---|---|---|
| Cuba | 9 | 0 | 82 | 10 |
| Japan | 8 | 1 | 81 | 21 |
| United States | 6 | 3 | 61 | 31 |
| Nicaragua | 5 | 4 | 42 | 24 |
| South Korea | 5 | 4 | 56 | 32 |
| Australia | 5 | 4 | 41 | 46 |
| Mexico | 3 | 6 | 36 | 60 |
| Italy | 2 | 7 | 41 | 57 |
| Spain | 2 | 7 | 23 | 90 |
| France | 0 | 9 | 25 | 117 |

**SEMIFINALS:** Cuba 10, Nicaragua 1; United States 6, Japan 3.

**GOLD MEDAL:** Cuba 9, United States 4. **BRONZE MEDAL:** Japan 9, Nicaragua 0.

**ALL-TOURNAMENT TEAM: C—**Hideaki Okubo, Japan. **1B—** Orestes Kindelan, Cuba. **2B—**Toshihisa Nishi, Japan. **3B—**Omar Linares, Cuba. **SS—**German Mesa, Cuba. **OF—**Ermidelio Urrutia, Cuba; Marco Ubani, Italy; Aaron Harvey, Australia. **DH—**Lourdes Gourriel, Cuba. **P—**Hidekazu Watanabe, Japan; Omar Ajete, Cuba.

### ROUND-ROBIN LEADERS
#### INDIVIDUAL BATTING
(Minimum 20 At-Bats)

| | AVG | AB | R | H | 2B | 3B | HR | RBI | SB |
|---|---|---|---|---|---|---|---|---|---|
| Linares, Omar, Cuba | .576 | 33 | 16 | 19 | 2 | 1 | 6 | 13 | 1 |
| Okubo, Hideaki, Japan | .458 | 24 | 8 | 11 | 2 | 0 | 1 | 5 | 0 |
| Helton, Todd, USA | .448 | 29 | 11 | 13 | 4 | 0 | 0 | 5 | 0 |
| Mesa, German, Cuba | .444 | 27 | 6 | 12 | 0 | 1 | 0 | 4 | 0 |
| Scott, Andrew, Australia | .429 | 35 | 7 | 15 | 4 | 0 | 3 | 7 | 1 |
| Pacheco, Antonio, Cuba | .429 | 35 | 14 | 15 | 2 | 1 | 2 | 9 | 0 |
| Matsumoto, Naoki, Japan | .429 | 21 | 5 | 9 | 2 | 2 | 1 | 4 | 2 |
| Garcia, Luis, Mexico | .424 | 33 | 8 | 14 | 4 | 0 | 1 | 6 | 0 |
| Gourriel, Lourdes, Cuba | .424 | 33 | 6 | 14 | 3 | 0 | 3 | 13 | 0 |
| Trinci, Guglielmo, Italy | .407 | 27 | 6 | 11 | 4 | 0 | 1 | 6 | 0 |
| Urrutia, Ermidelio, Cuba | .400 | 35 | 9 | 14 | 5 | 0 | 3 | 4 | 1 |
| Fau, Arnaud, France | .400 | 30 | 3 | 12 | 0 | 3 | 0 | 5 | 0 |
| Taniguchi, Hidenori, Japan | .394 | 33 | 11 | 13 | 1 | 0 | 4 | 16 | 0 |
| Roa, Jenrry, Nicaragua | .389 | 36 | 4 | 14 | 4 | 1 | 1 | 12 | 0 |
| Mesa, Victor, Cuba | .382 | 34 | 3 | 13 | 2 | 2 | 1 | 6 | 1 |
| Johnson, Russ, USA | .375 | 32 | 4 | 12 | 3 | 1 | 0 | 5 | 3 |
| Kindelan, Orestes, Cuba | .371 | 35 | 10 | 13 | 3 | 0 | 5 | 16 | 1 |
| Walker, Todd, USA | .371 | 35 | 9 | 13 | 5 | 0 | 1 | 14 | 1 |
| DeFranceschi, Roberto, Italy | .364 | 22 | 7 | 8 | 3 | 1 | 1 | 3 | 0 |
| Kanaya, Yasunari, Japan | .346 | 26 | 8 | 9 | 1 | 0 | 1 | 6 | 2 |
| Takabayashi, Takayuki, Japan | .345 | 29 | 9 | 10 | 3 | 0 | 2 | 7 | 4 |
| Porras, Nemesio, Nicaragua | .345 | 29 | 6 | 10 | 2 | 0 | 1 | 7 | 0 |
| Harvey, Aaron, Australia | .344 | 32 | 4 | 11 | 2 | 1 | 0 | 5 | 1 |
| Estrada, Jose, Cuba | .343 | 35 | 8 | 12 | 1 | 0 | 0 | 5 | 3 |
| Ubani, Marco, Italy | .342 | 38 | 6 | 13 | 2 | 0 | 1 | 9 | 0 |

#### INDIVIDUAL PITCHING
(Minimum 10 Innings)

| | W | L | ERA | G | SV | IP | H | BB | SO |
|---|---|---|---|---|---|---|---|---|---|
| Watanabe, Hidekazu, Japan | 2 | 0 | 0.00 | 3 | 0 | 17 | 5 | 4 | 16 |
| Ajete, Omar, Cuba | 1 | 0 | 0.00 | 3 | 0 | 12 | 2 | 2 | 19 |
| Graves, Danny, USA | 1 | 0 | 0.00 | 4 | 0 | 10 | 5 | 6 | 7 |
| Takiguchi, Kasatsugu, Japan | 2 | 0 | 0.00 | 4 | 0 | 10 | 7 | 2 | 13 |
| Ceccaroli, Paolo, Italy | 0 | 1 | 0.79 | 3 | 0 | 11 | 14 | 1 | 4 |
| Arrojo, Rolando, Cuba | 2 | 0 | 0.82 | 2 | 0 | 11 | 7 | 2 | 17 |
| Saito, Mitsuhiro, Japan | 1 | 0 | 0.84 | 3 | 0 | 11 | 7 | 2 | 7 |
| Quiroz, Jose, Nicaragua | 1 | 0 | 1.08 | 3 | 1 | 17 | 7 | 5 | 9 |
| Pulido, Jose, Spain | 1 | 0 | 1.23 | 2 | 0 | 15 | 9 | 8 | 6 |
| Choi, Young-Pil, Korea | 1 | 1 | 1.79 | 5 | 0 | 20 | 13 | 2 | 30 |
| Perez, Epifanio, Nicaragua | 1 | 1 | 1.84 | 3 | 0 | 15 | 13 | 6 | 15 |
| Valle, Lazaro, Cuba | 1 | 0 | 2.03 | 2 | 0 | 13 | 8 | 8 | 18 |
| Hernandez, Orlando, Cuba | 1 | 0 | 2.08 | 2 | 0 | 13 | 6 | 2 | 17 |
| Powell, John, USA | 1 | 1 | 2.40 | 2 | 0 | 15 | 10 | 4 | 15 |

# WORLD CHAMPIONSHIP QUALIFYING TOURNAMENT
Americas
Managua, Nicaragua
Aug. 12-22, 1993

### STANDINGS

**FIRST ROUND**

| Group A | | | Group B | | |
|---|---|---|---|---|---|
| Team | W | L | Team | W | L |
| Puerto Rico | 5 | 0 | USA | 5 | 0 |
| Nicaragua | 4 | 1 | Panama | 3 | 1 |
| Canada | 3 | 2 | Mexico | 3 | 1 |
| Colombia | 2 | 3 | Dom. Republic | 2 | 3 |
| Costa Rica | 1 | 4 | Honduras | 1 | 4 |
| Guatemala | 0 | 5 | Argentina | 0 | 5 |

**SECOND ROUND**

| Group 1 | | | Group 2 | | |
|---|---|---|---|---|---|
| Team | W | L | Team | W | L |
| Puerto Rico | 3 | 0 | USA | 3 | 0 |
| Nicaragua | 2 | 1 | Panama | 2 | 1 |
| Canada | 1 | 2 | Dom. Republic | 1 | 2 |
| Colombia | 0 | 3 | Mexico | 0 | 3 |

**PLAYOFFS SERIES A (1st-2nd Place Finishers):** Puerto Rico 6, Panama 0; Nicaragua 6, United States 1. **Gold Medal—**Nicaragua 8, Puerto Rico 5. **Bronze Medal—**Panama by forfeit over United States. **SERIES B (3rd-4th Place Finishers):** Canada 7, Mexico 2; Dominican Republic 5, Colombia 4. **Fifth Place—**Canada 11, Dominican Republic 9.

**Qualified for 1994 World Championships:** Canada, Dominican Republic, Nicaragua (host team), Panama, Puerto Rico, United States.

**ALL-TOURNAMENT TEAM: C—**A.J. Hinch, United States (Stanford). **1B—**Miguel Figueroa, Puerto Rico. **2B—**Julio Medina, Nicaragua. **3B—**Todd Walker, United States (Louisiana State). **SS—**Russ Johnson, United States (Louisiana State). **OF—**Freddy Garcia, Nicaragua; Alberto Bracero, Puerto Rico; David Rivas, Panama. **RHP—**Carlton Loewer, United States (Mississippi State). **LHP—**Wilfredo Velez, Puerto Rico. **MVP—**Alberto Bracero, Puerto Rico.

---

from both sides of an eight-year war that had been in remission since 1990.

Violence also touched Team USA, which won all eight of its games in the tournament's first two rounds, then was upset 6-1 by Nicaragua in the semifinals Aug. 20. A mob of roughly 75 fans set upon Team USA's bus after the Nicaragua game, begging and grabbing for souvenirs.

As the bus pulled away from the stadium, a reportedly intoxicated man shattered a window with either his fist or a rock. Shards of glass stuck in righthander John Kelly's (Connecticut) eye and scratched other players.

"I saw the window shatter and I didn't know what was going to happen," said Kelly, who wasn't seriously injured but also sustained a black eye and bloody nose. "We didn't know if people were going to jump through the window."

"After a tough loss to Nicaragua and having fans yell obscenities at us all day, we would have gone at it," lefthander Steve Reich (Army) said. "Luckily, we were on the bus because we were kind of outnumbered."

The bus escaped without further incident. USA Baseball declined to play for the bronze medal the next day, forfeiting its game against Panama and returning to the United States Aug. 22.

Nicaragua beat Puerto Rico 8-5 in a tournament that Cuba didn't have to enter because it already had qualified for the 1994 World Championships by winning the Olympics. In addition to the medal-round participants, Canada and the Dominican Republic also qualified for the 1994 tournament, also scheduled for Nicaragua.

Despite the frightening ending to Team USA's season, the coaching staff still felt it was a positive summer. Taking a cue from the 1990 team on which players such as David McCarty and Aaron Sele emerged, Anderson wanted to emphasize player development.

Todd Walker (Louisiana State) led the team with seven home runs and 46 RBIs, continued to show why he's college baseball's best pure hitter and received valuable defensive experience after moving from second base to third. First baseman Todd Helton (Tennessee) had a team-high .352 average, but didn't accompany the team to Nicaragua because he had to report for football practice.

Righthanders Paul Wilson (Florida State) and John Powell (Auburn) picked up wins over Cuba and were the staff aces all summer. Another righthander, Dustin Hermanson (Kent State), was nearly untouchable as a closer, posting a 0.81 ERA and seven saves while striking out 28 in 22 innings.

"We were kind of prepared for this club not to be as good as some of the others, especially early, but we won 11 of our last 12 games and that was encouraging," Team USA assistant coach Ray Tanner (North Carolina State) said. "There was a lot of youth on the team, mostly freshmen and sophomores. It took some time for us to gel together."

## Deja Vu At World Junior

Cuba's junior (18-and-under) team is nearly as dominant as its Olympic champions. The Cubans won the World Junior Championships for the second straight year and seventh time in 10 tries by beating Team USA 5-1 in the championship game at Windsor, Ontario.

The result was strikingly similar to the 1992 finale, won by Cuba over the United States, 6-1. Righthander Livan Hernandez threw complete games in both outings.

There was one difference. In 1992, Hernandez allowed six hits and struck out seven. A year older and a year stronger, he yielded five hits and fanned 17.

Chinese Taipei finished third for the second straight year, defeating Canada 14-2 in the bronze-medal game. Taipei catcher Lin Hung-Yuan was named tournament MVP after batting .459 and leading all hitters with three home runs.

First baseman Danny Peoples (Round Rock, Texas) and outfielder Chad Green (Mentor, Ohio) were the only Team USA players to make the all-tournament team. Peoples, a University of Texas recruit, hit .412 with six extra-base hits and nine RBIs. Green, who enrolled at the University of Kentucky, hit .448 and led all players with 15 runs and seven stolen bases.

The U.S. team consisted of standouts from the U.S. Olympic Festival in San Antonio, where the North beat the South 13-7 in the championship game. Peoples, who played for the South, led all Festival hitters in batting (.615), home runs (two) and RBIs (eight).

## Long Summer For Rodriguez

No. 1 draft pick Alex Rodriguez sat out the entire

# WORLD JUNIOR CHAMPIONSHIP

Windsor, Ontario
Aug. 13-22, 1993

### STANDINGS

| ROUND ROBIN | W | L | RF | RA |
|---|---|---|---|---|
| United States | 7 | 0 | 65 | 22 |
| Cuba | 5 | 2 | 41 | 22 |
| Canada | 4 | 3 | 40 | 58 |
| Chinese Taipei | 4 | 3 | 44 | 43 |
| Australia | 3 | 4 | 46 | 47 |
| Netherlands | 2 | 5 | 34 | 46 |
| Brazil | 2 | 5 | 36 | 49 |
| Mexico | 1 | 6 | 24 | 43 |

SEMIFINALS: United States 3, Chinese Taipei 2; Cuba 9, Canada 0.
GOLD MEDAL: Cuba 5, United States 1. BRONZE MEDAL: Chinese Taipei 14, Canada 2.

ALL-TOURNAMENT TEAM: C—Lin Hung-Yuan, Chinese Taipei. 1B—Danny Peoples, United States. 2B—Yang Chao-Shin, Chinese Taipei. 3B—Luis Valle, Cuba. SS—Eric Boisjoly, Canada. OF—Chad Green, United States; Travis Loft, Australia; Miguel Luiz Batista, Brazil. P—Christiaan Ruggenberg, Netherlands; Livan Hernandez, Cuba.

## ROUND-ROBIN LEADERS
### INDIVIDUAL BATTING
(Minimum 20 At-Bats)

| | AVG | AB | R | H | 2B | 3B | HR | RBI | SB |
|---|---|---|---|---|---|---|---|---|---|
| Peoples, Danny, USA | .461 | 26 | 9 | 12 | 2 | 2 | 1 | 9 | 0 |
| Lin, Hung-Yuan, Chin. | .458 | 24 | 7 | 11 | 0 | 0 | 3 | 5 | 1 |
| Green, Chad, USA | .448 | 29 | 14 | 13 | 3 | 1 | 0 | 7 | 6 |
| Craig, Darryl, Canada | .417 | 24 | 5 | 10 | 1 | 0 | 0 | 2 | 1 |
| Higgins, Kym, Australia | .417 | 24 | 10 | 10 | 1 | 0 | 0 | 6 | 5 |
| Loft, Travis, Australia | .400 | 25 | 4 | 10 | 4 | 0 | 0 | 5 | 2 |
| Jimenez, Abdiel, Cuba | .381 | 21 | 3 | 8 | 3 | 1 | 0 | 5 | 3 |
| Yang, Hua-Lung, Chin | .381 | 21 | 3 | 8 | 1 | 0 | 0 | 2 | 2 |
| Spencer, Sean, USA | .375 | 32 | 7 | 12 | 3 | 0 | 0 | 6 | 1 |
| Chen, Chih-Yuen, Chin | .364 | 22 | 3 | 8 | 0 | 0 | 1 | 9 | 0 |
| Konerko, Paul, USA | .360 | 25 | 7 | 9 | 1 | 0 | 1 | 9 | 0 |

### INDIVIDUAL PITCHING
(Minimum 10 Innings)

| | W | L | ERA | G | SV | IP | H | BB | SO |
|---|---|---|---|---|---|---|---|---|---|
| Lopez, Jesus, Mexico | 0 | 2 | 0.87 | 2 | 0 | 10 | 6 | 5 | 6 |
| Nunez, Vladimir, Cuba | 1 | 0 | 1.32 | 2 | 0 | 14 | 13 | 3 | 11 |
| Mitchell, Scott, Australia | 0 | 0 | 1.38 | 6 | 0 | 13 | 8 | 3 | 6 |
| Hernandez, Livan, Cuba | 2 | 0 | 1.59 | 2 | 0 | 17 | 11 | 5 | 21 |
| Hsu, Ming-Chieh, Chin | 2 | 2 | 1.71 | 6 | 0 | 21 | 19 | 1 | 13 |
| Butler, Steve, USA | 1 | 0 | 2.13 | 2 | 0 | 13 | 7 | 8 | 13 |
| Zimmerman, Jordan, Canada | 0 | 1 | 3.97 | 2 | 0 | 11 | 11 | 8 | 6 |
| Nunez, Juan, Mexico | 0 | 2 | 4.15 | 3 | 0 | 17 | 21 | 5 | 10 |

## TEAM USA
### WORLD JUNIOR STATISTICS/OVERALL

| BATTING | AVG | AB | R | H | 2B | 3B | HR | RBI | SB |
|---|---|---|---|---|---|---|---|---|---|
| Haskell, Mike, c | .625 | 8 | 1 | 5 | 0 | 0 | 0 | 1 | 1 |
| Peoples, Danny, 1b | .412 | 34 | 9 | 14 | 2 | 3 | 1 | 9 | 0 |
| Konerko, Paul, 3b-c | .387 | 31 | 9 | 12 | 1 | 0 | 2 | 11 | 0 |
| Green, Chad, of | .378 | 37 | 15 | 14 | 4 | 1 | 0 | 7 | 7 |
| Shultz, Brian, of | .375 | 32 | 7 | 12 | 2 | 0 | 1 | 4 | 0 |
| Spencer, Sean, of | .342 | 38 | 7 | 13 | 3 | 0 | 0 | 7 | 1 |
| Johnson, Mark, c | .300 | 20 | 5 | 6 | 2 | 0 | 0 | 2 | 0 |
| Booty, Josh, 2b | .257 | 35 | 5 | 9 | 2 | 0 | 0 | 9 | 0 |
| Dransfeldt, Kelly, ss | .219 | 32 | 5 | 7 | 1 | 0 | 1 | 9 | 0 |
| Brannon, Tony, 3b | .200 | 5 | 2 | 1 | 0 | 1 | 0 | 3 | 0 |
| Elarton, Scott, p | .100 | 10 | 0 | 1 | 0 | 0 | 0 | 1 | 0 |

| PITCHING | W | L | ERA | G | SV | IP | H | BB | SO |
|---|---|---|---|---|---|---|---|---|---|
| Haskell, Mike | 0 | 0 | 0.00 | 1 | 1 | 4 | 1 | 1 | 6 |
| Eilers, Chris | 1 | 0 | 0.90 | 4 | 0 | 10 | 8 | 1 | 13 |
| Smolky, Chris | 1 | 0 | 1.29 | 2 | 0 | 7 | 7 | 7 | 5 |
| Elarton, Scott | 1 | 0 | 1.74 | 5 | 2 | 10 | 10 | 3 | 8 |
| Yarnell, Eddie | 2 | 0 | 2.79 | 3 | 0 | 10 | 13 | 3 | 14 |
| Butler, Steve | 1 | 0 | 3.00 | 3 | 0 | 15 | 12 | 9 | 18 |
| Spencer, Sean | 1 | 0 | 3.00 | 1 | 0 | 3 | 5 | 0 | 3 |
| Middlebrook, Jason | 1 | 1 | 4.05 | 3 | 0 | 13 | 11 | 7 | 12 |
| Kuklick, Brian | 0 | 0 | 4.05 | 2 | 0 | 7 | 4 | 4 | 5 |

summer while negotiating with the Seattle Mariners, who eventually gave him a $1.3 million package that included a $1 million signing bonus. Rodriguez wanted to spend his spare time playing for the U.S. national and junior national teams, but was derailed in each case.

The star shortstop from Westminster Christian High in Miami became the first high school player ever invited to try out for the U.S. national team. He played well enough to make the team, but was cut because he wouldn't sign a consent form allowing the Topps Company, Inc., to make a baseball card with his likeness.

**Alex Rodriguez**

Topps sponsors USA Baseball, which requires its players to sign an agreement allowing Topps to produce their cards. Because Rodriguez was a minor at the time, his mother had to sign the form. She refused, presumably on the advice of agent Scott Boras.

"It's unfortunate for Alex," said Team USA coach John Anderson (Minnesota), who was dazzled by Rodriguez' skills. "He's a 17-year-old who just wants to play. He probably doesn't understand all the long-term implications from this. His mother and family basically decided this. He's a wonderful young man, and I hope it doesn't come out that all he wanted was money."

The U.S. junior national team has no sponsorship agreement with Topps, and Rodriguez seemed a natural fit. He went 4-for-8 in two games with the South team at the U.S. Olympic Festival in San Antonio before an errant throw during the North team's infield practice struck him below the right eye while he was sitting in a dugout.

Rodriguez sustained a broken cheekbone and required cosmetic surgery, which sidelined him until he signed with Seattle.

## Another Holdout Thrives

Unlike Rodriguez, catcher Jason Varitek (Georgia Tech) made productive use of his free time. Varitek, a first-round pick of the Minnesota Twins and the only first-rounder not to sign, dominated the Cape Cod League for the Hyannis Mets.

Varitek won the batting championship with a .371 average, won league MVP honors and was named the Cape's top prospect in a Baseball America survey of managers.

"It's better that I'm here than home sitting on my rear," Varitek said. "I know my work ethic and what I have to do, and I think I'll get something out of this summer."

The only thing Varitek couldn't do was lead Hyannis to a championship. The Orleans Cardinals hadn't even qualified for the playoffs by the end of the regular season, but won an Eastern Division tiebreaker and went on to capture the title by sweeping the Wareham Gatemen in two games for the title. Orleans righthander Chris Ciaccio (Georgia) was named playoff MVP after pitching two complete-game victories, including a 5-1 triumph over Wareham in the finale.

Other stalwarts on the Cape included Yarmouth-Dennis Red Sox righthander Andy Taulbee (Clemson), who was named pitcher of the year after going 7-2 with a Cape-best 1.08 ERA and 84 strikeouts in 84 innings; and Wareham outfielder Roy Marsh (Ohio State), who set league records for stolen bases in a game (six) and season (48) and tied another with four hits in the all-star game.

## Kenai Wins NBC World Series

After a slow start, the Kenai Peninsula Oilers recovered with a vengeance. The Oilers won 17 of their last 20 games, including seven of eight at the National Baseball Congress World Series in Wichita to claim their first championship since 1977.

Kenai trounced the Beatrice (Neb.) Bruins 9-1 in the final, marking the 12th time in the last 25 tournaments that an Alaska team emerged victorious. The Oilers' lone NBC loss came at the hands of the Alaska Central League rival Anchorage Glacier Pilots, who beat Kenai in the 1991 championship game.

"You don't have a great season in Alaska unless you come here and win this tournament," said Kenai catcher Jeff Poor (Los Angeles Harbor JC), who was named tournament MVP after hitting .353 with 11 RBIs. "That's the truth."

The Glacier Pilots did win the Alaska Central League championship and shared the first-ever title of the Alaska Baseball Federation, which brought together the two Alaskan leagues' five Alaskan teams in what may be the first step toward a reconciliation. Anchorage and the Alaska Goldpanners of Fairbanks both went 16-8 in Federation games, though the Anchorage Bucs did edge the Goldpanners for their fifth straight Alaska League championship.

Bucs outfielder Geoff Jenkins (Southern California) batted .421 and led all Alaskan players in home runs (10) and RBIs (67) to win Baseball America's Summer Player of the Year Award. The top Alaskan pitcher was Mat-Su Miners righthander Phil Olson (Florida State), who went 8-2, 2.49 with 72 strikeouts in 90 innings and pitched for Kenai at the NBC World Series. He was named Alaska's top prospect in a BA survey of managers.

## Long Beach Defends Title

Long Beach, which won the 1992 Little League World Series title after a Phillipines team was stripped of the crown for using ineligible players, actually won the 1993 championship on the field.

A year after getting crushed 15-4 by Zamboanga City in the finals, Long Beach edged the David Chiriqui (Panama) Little League team 3-2 to become the first U.S. team to win consecutive titles in the 47-year history of the tournament.

Pinch-hitter Jeremy Hess delivered a two-out, bases-loaded single in the bottom of the sixth to give Long Beach the win. Sean Burroughs, son of Long Beach coach and former American League MVP Jeff Burroughs, was the undisputed star of the tournament. He pitched a pair of 16-strikeout no-hitters and batted .600.

Though Long Beach won the 1993 title on the field, scandal still tinged the Little League World Series as the Far East and Latin American regional champions were disqualified for using ineligible players.

# SUMMER PLAYER OF THE YEAR

## USC's Jenkins Earns Honor In Alaska

Outfielder Geoff Jenkins finished the college baseball season on a hot streak, and continued to sizzle during the summer. Jenkins tore up Alaskan pitching for the Anchorage Bucs, a perennial summer power, and won Baseball America's Summer Player of the Year Award.

Jenkins began his college career at Southern California last spring by going 10-for-47 (.213) in his first 18 games, then hit .358 afterward to finish at .323 and earn a spot on Baseball America's Freshman All-America second team.

For the Bucs, Jenkins hit .421 and led all Alaska players in home runs (10) and RBIs (67). He also had a 21-game hitting streak and set a Bucs record with a .723 slugging percentage.

Jenkins, whose brother Brett played three years of infield for Southern Cal and was a third-team All-American in 1991, joined a select group. Of the 13 previous winners of the summer

**Geoff Jenkins.** Southern Cal freshman outfielder enjoyed a big summer in Alaska.

award, 12 were first-round draft picks and the other was, like Jenkins, a smooth left-handed hitter: John Olerud.

The complete Summer All-America first team, with summer teams and leagues, colleges and statistics:

**C**—Jason Varitek, Hyannis/Cape Cod (Georgia Tech), .371-3-22. **1B**—Todd Helton, Team USA (Tennessee), .352-2-24. **2B**—Chris Allison, Nevada/Jayhawk (Bradley), .364-1-28, 27 SB. **3B**—Todd Walker, Team USA (Louisiana State), .289-7-46, 11 SB. **SS**—Nomar Garciaparra, Orleans/Cape Cod (Georgia Tech), .327-1-18, 17 SB. **OF**—Jeff Abbott, Cincinnati/ Great Lakes (Kentucky), .392-4-30, 13 SB; Geoff Jenkins, Anchorage Bucs/Alaska

(Southern California), .421-10-67; Travis Lee, Fairbanks/Alaska (Capital HS, Olympia, Wash.), .365-5-40, 12 SB. **DH**—Tristan Paul, Anchorage Glacier Pilots/Alaska Central (Los Angeles Harbor JC), .422-4-49.

**P**—Dustin Hermanson, Team USA (Kent State), 0-0, 0.81, 7 SV, 22 IP, 28 SO; Phil Olson, Mat-Su/Alaska Central (Florida State), 8-2, 2.49, 90 IP, 72 SO; John Powell, Team USA (Auburn), 8-3, 3.58, 75 IP, 69 SO; Andy Taulbee, Yarmouth-Dennis/Cape Cod (Clemson), 7-2, 1.08, 84 IP, 84 SO; Paul Wilson, Team USA (Florida State), 5-4, 3.06, 62 IP, 61 SO.

—JIM CALLIS

### PREVIOUS WINNERS

1984—**Will Clark**, 1b, Team USA
—**Rafael Palmeiro**, of, Hutchinson (Jayhawk)
1985—**Jeff King**, 3b, Team USA
—**Bob Zupcic**, of, Liberal (Jayhawk)
1986—**Jack Armstrong**, rhp, Wareham (Cape Cod)
—**Mike Harkey**, rhp, Fairbanks (Alaska)
1987—**Cris Carpenter**, rhp, Team USA
1988—**Ty Griffin**, 2b, Team USA
—**Robin Ventura**, 3b, Team USA
1989—**John Olerud**, 1b-lhp, Palouse (Alaska)
1990—**Calvin Murray**, of, Anchorage Bucs (Alaska)
1991—**Chris Roberts**, of, Team USA
1992—**Jeffrey Hammonds**, of, Team USA

# GOLDEN SPIKES AWARD

## Dreifort Claims Top Prize

Wichita State righthander Darren Dreifort became the fifth straight player to achieve a significant double: first college player drafted and winner of the Golden Spikes Award.

Dreifort, taken by the Los Angeles Dodgers as the

**Darren Dreifort**

second overall choice in the 1993 draft, followed in the footsteps of previous winners Ben McDonald (1989), Alex Fernandez (1990), Mike Kelly (1991) and Jeffrey Hammonds (1992). All but Kelly played in the major leagues in 1993.

Dreifort appears on a similar fast track after a stellar three-year career with the Shockers that included two first-team All-America berths and two summers with Team USA. In 1993, he went 11-1, 2.48 with 120 strikeouts in 102 innings, and added a .327 average with 22 homers as a DH.

### PREVIOUS WINNERS

1978—**Bob Horner**, 3b, Arizona State
1979—**Tim Wallach**, 3b, Cal State Fullerton
1980—**Terry Francona**, of, Arizona
1981—**Mike Fuentes**, of, Florida State
1982—**Augie Schmidt**, ss, New Orleans
1983—**Dave Magadan**, 1b, Alabama
1984—**Oddibe McDowell**, of, Arizona State
1985—**Will Clark**, 1b, Mississippi State
1986—**Mike Loynd**, rhp, Florida State
1987—**Jim Abbott**, lhp, Michigan
1988—**Robin Ventura**, 3b, Oklahoma State
1989—**Ben McDonald**, rhp, Louisiana State
1990—**Alex Fernandez**, rhp, Miami-Dade CC South
1991—**Mike Kelly**, of, Arizona State
1992—**Phil Nevin**, 3b, Cal State Fullerton

USA Baseball annually gives the award, college baseball's equivalent of the Heisman Trophy, to the nation's top amateur player. Selections are based on athletic ability, sportsmanship, character and overall contribution to the sport.

Other finalists were Wright State lefthander Brian Anderson, Texas A&M lefthander Jeff Granger, Texas DH-righthander Brooks Kieschnick, Arizona State catcher Paul LoDuca, Auburn righthander John Powell, Miami Westminster Christian High shortstop Alex Rodriguez, Georgia Tech catcher Jason Varitek and Louisiana State second baseman Todd Walker. Rodriguez was just the second high school player ever to become a finalist, following Ken Griffey Jr. in 1987.

# COLLEGE SUMMER LEAGUES

## CAPE COD LEAGUE

| EAST | W | L | T | PCT | Pts |
|---|---|---|---|---|---|
| Chatham | 25 | 19 | 0 | .568 | 50 |
| Orleans | 23 | 20 | 1 | .535 | 47 |
| Brewster | 23 | 20 | 1 | .535 | 47 |
| Yarmouth-Dennis | 22 | 20 | 2 | .524 | 46 |
| Harwich | 11 | 31 | 1 | .262 | 23 |

| WEST | W | L | T | PCT | Pts |
|---|---|---|---|---|---|
| Wareham | 25 | 17 | 2 | .595 | 52 |
| Hyannis | 25 | 19 | 0 | .568 | 50 |
| Cotuit | 24 | 20 | 0 | .545 | 48 |
| Falmouth | 22 | 21 | 0 | .512 | 44 |
| Bourne | 15 | 28 | 1 | .349 | 31 |

**PLAYOFFS:** Orleans defeated Chatham, 2-1, and Wareham defeated Hyannis, 2-0, in best-of-3 semifinals. Orleans defeated Wareham, 2-0, in best-of-3 league championship series.

**ALL-STAR TEAM: C**—Jason Varitek, Hyannis (Georgia Tech); Steve Puleo, Brewster (Maine). **1B**—Mike Mitchell, Chatham (UCLA); Brian Buchanan, Brewster (Virginia). **2B**—Lionel Hastings, Orleans (Southern California); Mike Metcalfe, Hyannis (Miami). **3B**—Tommy Davis, Wareham (Southern Mississippi). **SS**—Nomar Garciaparra, Orleans (Georgia Tech); Geoff Blum, Brewster (California). **OF**—Darin Erstad, Falmouth (Nebraska); Roy Marsh, Wareham (Ohio State); Bruce Thompson, Hyannis (Miami); Paul Ottavinia, Chatham (Seton Hall). **DH**—Ryan Beeney, Wareham (Kent State). **P**—Andy Taulbee, Yarmouth-Dennis (Clemson); Steve Stapleton, Wareham (Salem State, Mass.); Lyle Hartgrove, Hyannis (East Carolina); Ryan Frace, Orleans (Arizona); Ray Ricken, Cotuit (Michigan); Matt Morris, Hyannis (Seton Hall); Bill King, Brewster (Birmingham-Southern); Chris Clemons, Yarmouth-Dennis (Texas A&M).

### INDIVIDUAL BATTING LEADERS
(Minimum 75 At-Bats)

| | AVG | AB | R | H | 2B | 3B | HR | RBI | SB |
|---|---|---|---|---|---|---|---|---|---|
| Varitek, Jason, Hyannis | .371 | 105 | 20 | 39 | 8 | 1 | 3 | 22 | 4 |
| Beeney, Ryan, Wareham | .357 | 129 | 22 | 46 | 10 | 1 | 0 | 21 | 14 |
| Davis, Tommy, Wareham | .349 | 152 | 27 | 53 | 10 | 2 | 3 | 25 | 11 |
| Blum, Geoff, Brewster | .331 | 154 | 24 | 51 | 8 | 1 | 1 | 17 | 9 |
| Mitchell, Mike, Chatham | .331 | 124 | 23 | 41 | 10 | 0 | 4 | 29 | 1 |
| Metcalfe, Mike, Hyannis | .328 | 134 | 25 | 44 | 2 | 6 | 0 | 12 | 33 |
| Garciaparra, Nomar, Orleans | .327 | 153 | 23 | 50 | 10 | 2 | 1 | 18 | 15 |
| Monahan, Shane, Y-D | .309 | 162 | 18 | 50 | 7 | 1 | 4 | 17 | 8 |
| Puleo, Steve, Brewster | .305 | 131 | 16 | 40 | 7 | 1 | 0 | 15 | 6 |
| Ottavinia, Paul, Chatham | .304 | 191 | 32 | 58 | 8 | 3 | 0 | 24 | 8 |
| Erstad, Darin, Falmouth | .302 | 162 | 29 | 49 | 11 | 1 | 4 | 29 | 10 |
| DaSilva, Manny, Cotuit | .301 | 113 | 22 | 34 | 6 | 0 | 4 | 14 | 8 |
| Prodanov, Pete, Brewster | .299 | 127 | 13 | 38 | 8 | 0 | 2 | 15 | 11 |
| Hastings, Lionel, Orleans | .295 | 139 | 18 | 41 | 7 | 0 | 2 | 16 | 5 |
| Roberge, J.P., Chatham | .292 | 171 | 25 | 50 | 16 | 0 | 1 | 19 | 5 |
| Donato, Dan, Hyannis | .292 | 154 | 23 | 45 | 5 | 1 | 0 | 14 | 8 |
| Taylor, Brian, Orleans | .287 | 87 | 12 | 25 | 4 | 1 | 0 | 6 | 8 |
| Buchanan, Brian, Brewster | .285 | 172 | 21 | 49 | 7 | 0 | 5 | 27 | 9 |
| Knight, Bill, Hyannis | .282 | 131 | 20 | 37 | 12 | 3 | 4 | 19 | 2 |
| Kritscher, Ryan, Chatham | .279 | 122 | 26 | 34 | 8 | 0 | 1 | 10 | 7 |
| Thompson, Bruce, Hyannis | .278 | 162 | 33 | 45 | 8 | 8 | 2 | 31 | 23 |
| Martin, Mike, Falmouth | .275 | 167 | 33 | 46 | 8 | 3 | 0 | 21 | 18 |
| Farley, Rick, Bourne | .274 | 135 | 15 | 37 | 2 | 0 | 0 | 11 | 7 |
| Bellhorn, Mark, Cotuit | .270 | 126 | 12 | 34 | 2 | 2 | 2 | 14 | 10 |
| Stumberger, Darren, Cotuit | .269 | 78 | 13 | 21 | 4 | 0 | 2 | 8 | 2 |
| Boretti, Brett, Wareham | .268 | 149 | 40 | 54 | 6 | 1 | 2 | 25 | 6 |
| Boni, Chris, Wareham | .268 | 97 | 18 | 26 | 4 | 0 | 0 | 11 | 15 |
| Spears, Shane, Wareham | .266 | 79 | 6 | 21 | 3 | 0 | 0 | 14 | 5 |
| Pinoni, Scott, Chatham | .264 | 121 | 14 | 32 | 3 | 1 | 4 | 24 | 2 |
| Dunnett, Mike, Bourne | .264 | 144 | 22 | 38 | 4 | 1 | 1 | 13 | 4 |
| Marsh, Roy, Wareham | .263 | 167 | 39 | 44 | 3 | 1 | 0 | 12 | 48 |
| Newhan, David, Y-D | .261 | 142 | 27 | 37 | 6 | 3 | 4 | 28 | 13 |

### INDIVIDUAL PITCHING LEADERS
(Minimum 30 Innings)

| | W | L | ERA | G | SV | IP | H | BB | SO |
|---|---|---|---|---|---|---|---|---|---|
| Telgheder, Jim, Chatham | 2 | 0 | 0.29 | 15 | 3 | 31 | 19 | 7 | 26 |

**Phil Olson.** Florida State freshman righthander was selected Alaska's player of the year.

| | | | | | | | | | |
|---|---|---|---|---|---|---|---|---|---|
| Taulbee, Andy, Y-D | 7 | 2 | 1.08 | 11 | 0 | 84 | 50 | 23 | 84 |
| Hall, Yates, Y-D | 1 | 1 | 1.11 | 19 | 0 | 32 | 14 | 20 | 29 |
| Clemons, Chris, Y-D | 1 | 2 | 1.49 | 20 | 10 | 36 | 24 | 11 | 25 |
| Stapleton, Steve, Wareham | 7 | 1 | 1.59 | 12 | 0 | 62 | 51 | 24 | 42 |
| King, Bill, Brewster | 4 | 1 | 1.68 | 12 | 2 | 59 | 47 | 12 | 34 |
| Bigelli, Robert, Orleans | 2 | 2 | 1.93 | 14 | 3 | 42 | 35 | 14 | 40 |
| Drumright, Mike, Wareham | 2 | 2 | 2.02 | 10 | 1 | 71 | 45 | 35 | 56 |
| Saipe, Mike, Cotuit | 5 | 3 | 2.07 | 9 | 0 | 70 | 61 | 24 | 56 |
| Hartgrove, Lyle, Hyannis | 8 | 1 | 2.12 | 10 | 0 | 85 | 73 | 10 | 42 |
| Bell, Jason, Cotuit | 1 | 3 | 2.14 | 13 | 1 | 34 | 22 | 25 | 31 |
| Frace, Ryan, Orleans | 7 | 1 | 2.17 | 10 | 0 | 75 | 70 | 24 | 36 |
| Beardsley, Scott, Bourne | 3 | 6 | 2.20 | 15 | 0 | 70 | 52 | 34 | 63 |
| Morris, Matt, Hyannis | 7 | 2 | 2.24 | 10 | 0 | 72 | 61 | 11 | 53 |
| Ricken, Ray, Cotuit | 8 | 1 | 2.31 | 9 | 0 | 74 | 59 | 18 | 59 |
| Cummins, Brian, Falmouth | 4 | 2 | 2.38 | 8 | 0 | 57 | 54 | 11 | 35 |
| Maynard, Wally, Wareham | 4 | 4 | 2.38 | 19 | 6 | 34 | 22 | 15 | 39 |
| Ketterman, Mike, Hyannis | 0 | 3 | 2.41 | 11 | 0 | 37 | 24 | 12 | 32 |
| Gonzalez, Jess, Chatham | 5 | 2 | 2.43 | 9 | 0 | 70 | 50 | 27 | 54 |
| Halperin, Mike, Hyannis | 5 | 5 | 2.46 | 10 | 0 | 80 | 65 | 28 | 76 |

## ALASKA LEAGUES

| | League | | | | Overall | |
|---|---|---|---|---|---|---|
| **ALASKA** | W | L | PCT | GB | W | L |
| Anchorage Buccaneers | 13 | 7 | .650 | — | 37 | 23 |
| Alaska Goldpanners | 11 | 9 | .650 | 2 | 36 | 24 |
| Hawaii Island Movers | 6 | 14 | .300 | 7 | 23 | 26 |

| | League | | | | Overall | |
|---|---|---|---|---|---|---|
| **ALASKA CENTRAL** | W | L | PCT | GB | W | L |
| Anchorage Glacier Pilots | 26 | 14 | .650 | — | 42 | 21 |
| Kenai Peninsula Oilers | 24 | 19 | .558 | 3½ | 41 | 22 |
| Mat-Su Miners | 16 | 26 | .381 | 6 | 17 | 31 |

**ALL-ALASKA TEAM: C**—Jeff Poor, Kenai (Los Angeles Harbor JC). **1B**—Travis Lee, Alaska (Capital HS, Olympia, Wash.). **2B**—Robert Harris, Bucs (Texas A&M). **3B**—Tristan Paul, Glacier Pilots (Los Angeles Harbor JC). **SS**—Jed Hansen, Bucs (Stanford). **OF**—Geoff Jenkins, Bucs (Southern California); Shawn Rogers, Bucs (Hawaii). **DH**—Jesse Ibarra, Mat-Su (Loyola Marymount). **Util**—John McAninch, Bucs (Walla Walla, Wash., CC). **P**—Dan Boone, Alaska; Mike Brandley, Glacier Pilots (Wichita State); Chris Granata, Glacier Pilots (Ohio State); Phil Olson, Mat-Su (Florida State).

### INDIVIDUAL BATTING LEADERS
(Minimum 100 At-Bats)

| | AVG | AB | R | H | 2B | 3B | HR | RBI | SB |
|---|---|---|---|---|---|---|---|---|---|
| Paul, Tristan, Pilots | .422 | 206 | 43 | 87 | 13 | 2 | 4 | 49 | 4 |
| Jenkins, Geoff, Bucs | .421 | 202 | 49 | 85 | 19 | 6 | 10 | 67 | 7 |
| Rogers, Shawn, Bucs | .392 | 194 | 43 | 76 | 15 | 7 | 1 | 37 | 2 |
| Lee, Travis, Goldpanners | .365 | 159 | 37 | 58 | 11 | 4 | 5 | 40 | 12 |
| McAninch, John, Bucs | .347 | 193 | 36 | 67 | 14 | 7 | 6 | 38 | 2 |
| Napolitano, Anthony, Pilots | .344 | 183 | 30 | 63 | 11 | 3 | 3 | 30 | 3 |
| Poor, Jeff, Oilers | .334 | 206 | 33 | 70 | 16 | 3 | 8 | 55 | 1 |
| Hall, Carl, Pilots | .334 | 215 | 52 | 73 | 14 | 2 | 1 | 30 | 12 |
| Harris, Robert, Bucs | .330 | 197 | 47 | 65 | 15 | 1 | 4 | 26 | 6 |
| Ahu, Jamie, Island Movers | .329 | 161 | 27 | 53 | 10 | 2 | 0 | 22 | 13 |
| Monroe, Darryl, Oilers | .326 | 184 | 33 | 60 | 7 | 3 | 2 | 12 | 16 |
| Darcuiel, Faruq, Gpanners | .321 | 106 | 27 | 34 | 1 | 3 | 0 | 10 | 18 |
| Galvin, David, Gpanners | .317 | 101 | 18 | 32 | 5 | 0 | 1 | 17 | 4 |
| Gibbs, Kevin, Bucs | .315 | 130 | 28 | 41 | 7 | 1 | 0 | 6 | 16 |
| Thomas, Aric, Oilers | .315 | 143 | 36 | 45 | 4 | 1 | 1 | 13 | 15 |
| Dunckel, Bill, Goldpanners | .314 | 175 | 35 | 55 | 20 | 3 | 1 | 31 | 26 |
| Judge, Mike, Pilots | .312 | 141 | 21 | 44 | 7 | 1 | 2 | 15 | 2 |

Hunter, Randy, Gpanners.... .312 109 16 34 3 0 0 12 12
Cheff, Tyler, Bucs.... .307 189 18 58 10 2 2 39 1
Cady, Todd, Goldpanners.... .305 187 29 57 9 3 6 44 8

## INDIVIDUAL PITCHING LEADERS
(Minimum 40 Innings)

| | W | L | ERA | G | SV | IP | H | BB | SO |
|---|---|---|---|---|---|---|---|---|---|
| Brandley, Mike, Pilots.............. | 9 | 2 | 1.57 | 12 | 0 | 64 | 71 | 21 | 54 |
| Arffa, Steve, Pilots.................. | 5 | 0 | 1.62 | 20 | 5 | 39 | 26 | 14 | 34 |
| Foulke, Keith, Bucs ............... | 4 | 0 | 1.98 | 8 | 0 | 50 | 32 | 11 | 38 |
| Granata, Chris, Pilots............ | 7 | 0 | 2.05 | 11 | 0 | 66 | 49 | 32 | 42 |
| Walton, Tim, Oilers................ | 4 | 3 | 2.17 | 11 | 0 | 54 | 40 | 26 | 42 |
| Minor, Tommy, Bucs ............ | 6 | 2 | 2.23 | 11 | 0 | 65 | 54 | 10 | 57 |
| Boone, Dan, Goldpanners.... | 5 | 3 | 2.28 | 29 | 15 | 51 | 36 | 14 | 46 |
| Kawabata, Kyle, Isl. Movers.... | 5 | 2 | 2.45 | 10 | 0 | 66 | 50 | 20 | 72 |
| Olson, Phil, Miners/Oilers ........ | 9 | 2 | 2.51 | 13 | 0 | 93 | 76 | 29 | 76 |
| Estavil, Mauricio, Bucs ........ | 4 | 4 | 2.76 | 18 | 3 | 49 | 33 | 33 | 38 |
| Stein, Blake, Pilots ............... | 3 | 3 | 3.03 | 15 | 0 | 77 | 72 | 20 | 54 |
| Kishita, Kirt, Pilots................. | 5 | 0 | 3.05 | 12 | 2 | 44 | 40 | 19 | 34 |

## ARIZONA SUMMER COLLEGIATE

| | W | L | PCT | GB |
|---|---|---|---|---|
| Phoenix Braves | 26 | 9 | .743 | — |
| Scottsdale A's | 23 | 12 | .657 | 3 |
| Mesa Yankees | 19 | 16 | .543 | 7 |
| Chandler Giants | 14 | 21 | .333 | 12 |
| Glendale Angels | 13 | 22 | .317 | 13 |
| Sun City Royals | 10 | 25 | .286 | 16 |

## INDIVIDUAL BATTING LEADERS
(Minimum 85 At-Bats)

| | AVG | AB | R | H | 2B | 3B | HR | RBI | SB |
|---|---|---|---|---|---|---|---|---|---|
| Grazier, Ryan, Mesa ............ | .419 | 106 | 26 | 44 | 7 | 1 | 0 | 25 | 1 |
| Wilson, Vance, Phoenix ...... | .406 | 138 | 24 | 56 | 11 | 2 | 2 | 31 | 8 |
| Wickey, Menno, Scottsdale... | .383 | 120 | 33 | 46 | 11 | 10 | 1 | 30 | 17 |
| Cruz, Paul, Sun City............ | .375 | 104 | 20 | 39 | 6 | 3 | 0 | 20 | 4 |
| Kaitfors, Josh, Scottsdale.... | .365 | 104 | 21 | 38 | 6 | 4 | 1 | 13 | 6 |
| Homestead, Dax, Chandler .. | .358 | 98 | 20 | 35 | 3 | 2 | 0 | 5 | 12 |
| Sturges, Brian, Phoenix...... | .351 | 114 | 19 | 40 | 6 | 2 | 0 | 16 | 4 |
| McCormick, Andrew, Pho.... | .347. | 121 | 34 | 42 | 5 | 7 | 0 | 11 | 20 |
| Frederickson, Bob, Phoenix.. | .339 | 109 | 24 | 37 | 9 | 2 | 0 | 23 | 5 |
| Smaler, Josh, Mesa ............ | .336 | 119 | 23 | 40 | 12 | 4 | 0 | 21 | 7 |

## INDIVIDUAL PITCHING LEADERS
(Minimum 40 Innings)

| | W | L | ERA | G | SV | IP | H | BB | SO |
|---|---|---|---|---|---|---|---|---|---|
| Barrett, Darrel, Phoenix....... | 7 | 0 | 2.28 | 8 | 1 | 56 | 40 | 22 | 35 |
| Baum, Chris, Phoenix .......... | 9 | 0 | 2.61 | 12 | 2 | 35 | 46 | 36 | 47 |
| Freehill, Mike, Glendale ...... | 3 | 1 | 2.63 | 8 | 0 | 41 | 32 | 19 | 36 |
| Dixon, Keith, Sun City ......... | 1 | 2 | 2.99 | 18 | 3 | 39 | 37 | 19 | 37 |
| Wolger, Mike, Mesa ............ | 5 | 0 | 3.29 | 8 | 0 | 41 | 32 | 24 | 40 |

## ATLANTIC COLLEGIATE LEAGUE

| KAISER | W | L | PCT | GB |
|---|---|---|---|---|
| New York Generals | 23 | 17 | .575 | — |
| Long Island Sound | 21 | 19 | .525 | 2 |
| Nassau Collegians | 21 | 19 | .525 | 2 |
| Brooklyn Clippers | 15 | 25 | .375 | 8 |

| WOLFF | W | L | PCT | GB |
|---|---|---|---|---|
| Quakertown Blazers | 29 | 11 | .725 | — |
| Monmouth Royals | 21 | 19 | .525 | 8 |
| New Jersey A's | 15 | 25 | .375 | 14 |
| Jersey Pilots | 15 | 25 | .375 | 14 |

**PLAYOFFS:** Monmouth defeated New York and Quakertown defeated Long Island in one-game semifinals; Quakertown defeated Monmouth, 2-0, in best-of-3 final.

## INDIVIDUAL BATTING LEADERS
(Minimum 80 At-Bats)

| | AVG | AB | H | R | 2B | 3B | HR | RBI | SB |
|---|---|---|---|---|---|---|---|---|---|
| DeRosa, Jim, Long Island.... | .421 | 114 | 21 | 48 | 9 | 1 | 0 | 20 | 6 |
| McNally, Sean, New York ...... | .415 | 94 | 24 | 39 | 5 | 3 | 2 | 24 | 4 |
| Miller, Michael, Long Island .. | .376 | 93 | 22 | 35 | 8 | 1 | 5 | 25 | 2 |
| Taylor, Tim Jersey.............. | .364 | 121 | 32 | 44 | 7 | 1 | 0 | 14 | 10 |
| Barthol, Blake, Quakertown.. | .348 | 132 | 27 | 46 | 11 | 1 | 0 | 36 | 4 |
| Irey, Sean, Quakertown ........ | .331 | 127 | 33 | 42 | 4 | 4 | 3 | 27 | 22 |
| Rentschler, Kirk, Quakertown .328 | 119 | 31 | 39 | 3 | 3 | 1 | 14 | 10 |
| Manuelian, Jon, Brooklyn .... | .317 | 120 | 23 | 38 | 5 | 1 | 2 | 22 | 6 |
| Mitchell, Ed, Monmouth ...... | .315 | 111 | 22 | 35 | 9 | 3 | 0 | 15 | 9 |
| Howard, Richard, Nassau...... | .310 | 113 | 19 | 35 | 2 | 1 | 0 | 16 | 11 |

## INDIVIDUAL PITCHING LEADERS
(Minimum 35 Innings)

| | W | L | ERA | G | SV | IP | H | BB | SO |
|---|---|---|---|---|---|---|---|---|---|
| Forster, Scott, Quakertown ...... | 5 | 0 | 1.08 | 9 | 1 | 50 | 27 | 38 | 54 |
| Dudeck, David, Jersey ............ | 2 | 1 | 1.96 | 9 | 0 | 46 | 42 | 11 | 31 |
| Kibbey, Mike, Quakertown...... | 4 | 3 | 2.26 | 10 | 0 | 56 | 41 | 16 | 42 |
| Golden, Matt, New Jersey........ | 3 | 2 | 2.30 | 10 | 0 | 47 | 40 | 16 | 50 |
| Mackey, Joe, New York .......... | 3 | 0 | 2.33 | 8 | 0 | 39 | 39 | 20 | 27 |

## CENTRAL ILLINOIS LEAGUE

| FIRST | W | L | PCT | GB | SECOND | W | L | PCT | GB |
|---|---|---|---|---|---|---|---|---|---|
| Decatur | 14 | 4 | .777 | — | Champaign | 12 | 6 | .667 | — |
| Danville | 13 | 7 | .650 | 2 | Springfield | 11 | 7 | .611 | 1 |
| Fairview Hts. | 10 | 10 | .500 | 5 | Fairview Hts. | 9 | 7 | .563 | 2 |
| Springfield | 8 | 11 | .421 | 6½ | Decatur | 9 | 8 | .529 | 2½ |
| Champaign | 7 | 11 | .388 | 7 | Danville | 6 | 11 | .353 | 5½ |
| Twin City | 5 | 14 | .263 | 9½ | Twin City | 4 | 12 | .250 | 7 |

**PLAYOFFS:** Springfield (4-0) won six-team postseason tournament.

## INDIVIDUAL BATTING LEADERS
(Minimum 90 Plate Appearances)

| | AVG | AB | R | H | 2B | 3B | HR | RBI | SB |
|---|---|---|---|---|---|---|---|---|---|
| Asche, Mike, Springfield ...... | .372 | 156 | 36 | 58 | 11 | 4 | 2 | 26 | 16 |
| Wells, Forry, FH .................. | .371 | 124 | 33 | 46 | 8 | 10 | 4 | 19 | 5 |
| Manary, Alex, Twin City ...... | .349 | 86 | 15 | 30 | 2 | 2 | 0 | 2 | 4 |
| Sinak, Tom, FH .................... | .336 | 122 | 28 | 41 | 7 | 4 | 5 | 27 | 15 |
| Barner, Doug, FH ................ | .327 | 104 | 13 | 34 | 2 | 0 | 0 | 15 | 3 |
| Ladehoff, Dan, Springfield .. | .320 | 122 | 25 | 39 | 4 | 2 | 0 | 14 | 6 |
| Gadlage, Stephen, Decatur . | .317 | 126 | 23 | 40 | 8 | 1 | 2 | 12 | 15 |
| Jetel, Jason, Springfield ...... | .317 | 142 | 27 | 45 | 8 | 1 | 5 | 29 | 11 |
| Vallone, Gar, Champaign...... | .314 | 102 | 21 | 32 | 6 | 1 | 1 | 16 | 9 |

## INDIVIDUAL PITCHING LEADERS
(Minimum 38 Innings)

| | W | L | ERA | G | SV | IP | H | BB | SO |
|---|---|---|---|---|---|---|---|---|---|
| DeBrower, Ed, Danville............ | 5 | 2 | 1.07 | 10 | 1 | 67 | 56 | 13 | 46 |
| Ruch, Rob, Decatur ............... | 4 | 4 | 1.31 | 10 | 0 | 62 | 44 | 25 | 45 |
| Price, Tom, Champaign .......... | 5 | 1 | 1.39 | 13 | 1 | 71 | 54 | 13 | 45 |
| Sander, Matt, Champaign ...... | 4 | 2 | 1.65 | 12 | 1 | 49 | 40 | 19 | 28 |
| Noblitt, Andy, Decatur ............ | 3 | 1 | 1.74 | 9 | 0 | 57 | 40 | 18 | 48 |

## GREAT LAKES LEAGUE

### FIRST HALF

| NORTH | W | L | PCT | GB | SOUTH | W | L | PCT | GB |
|---|---|---|---|---|---|---|---|---|---|
| Motor City | 11 | 9 | .550 | — | Columbus | 14 | 6 | .700 | — |
| Lima | 11 | 9 | .550 | — | Cincinnati | 11 | 9 | .550 | 3 |
| Sandusky | 9 | 11 | .450 | 2 | Central Ohio | 9 | 11 | .450 | 5 |
| Toledo | 7 | 13 | .350 | 4 | Grand Lake | 8 | 12 | .400 | 6 |

### SECOND HALF

| NORTH | W | L | PCT | GB | SOUTH | W | L | PCT | GB |
|---|---|---|---|---|---|---|---|---|---|
| Lima | 13 | 7 | .650 | — | Central Ohio | 12 | 8 | .600 | — |
| Sandusky | 10 | 10 | .500 | 3 | Cincinnati | 10 | 10 | .500 | 2 |
| Toledo | 8 | 12 | .400 | 5 | Grand Lake | 10 | 10 | .500 | 2 |
| Motor City | 8 | 12 | .400 | 5 | Columbus | 9 | 11 | .450 | 3 |

**PLAYOFFS:** Lima defeated Central Ohio, 2-1, in best-of-3 final.

## INDIVIDUAL BATTING LEADERS
(Minimum 112 Plate Appearances)

| | AVG | AB | R | H | HR | RBI | SB |
|---|---|---|---|---|---|---|---|
| Abbott, Jeff, Cincinnati .............. | .392 | 143 | 27 | 56 | 4 | 30 | 13 |
| Freeman, Sean, Sandusky........ | .375 | 120 | 25 | 45 | 6 | 26 | 2 |
| Ayette, Joe, Motor City.............. | .369 | 130 | 33 | 48 | 1 | 25 | 11 |
| Koester, Jerry, Motor City ......... | .366 | 123 | 27 | 45 | 0 | 7 | 8 |
| Walker, Morgan, Sandusky...... | .357 | 98 | 20 | 35 | 4 | 17 | 1 |
| Stover, Greg, Columbus ............ | .355 | 138 | 23 | 49 | 0 | 16 | 16 |
| Dellucci, Dave, Cincinnati ........ | .350 | 137 | 36 | 48 | 5 | 23 | 17 |
| Engleka, Matt, Lima ................ | .348 | 89 | 18 | 31 | 1 | 10 | 12 |
| Lehrman, Dan, Lima ................ | .341 | 129 | 17 | 44 | 2 | 22 | 5 |
| Young, Kevin, Cincinnati .......... | .341 | 126 | 24 | 43 | 1 | 17 | 12 |

## INDIVIDUAL PITCHING LEADERS
(Minimum 32 Innings)

| | W | L | ERA | G | SV | IP | H | BB | SO |
|---|---|---|---|---|---|---|---|---|---|
| Reed, Brian, Cincinnati ............ | 5 | 1 | 1.53 | 12 | 1 | 59 | 50 | 11 | 55 |
| Hickman, Chad, Cent. Ohio .... | 7 | 1 | 1.69 | 9 | 1 | 48 | 49 | 16 | 31 |
| Decaminada, Scott, CO .......... | 4 | 1 | 1.72 | 10 | 2 | 37 | 34 | 17 | 23 |
| Payne, John, Columbus .......... | 4 | 2 | 2.11 | 8 | 0 | 55 | 56 | 12 | 37 |
| Golden, Steve, Central Ohio .... | 3 | 2 | 2.32 | 7 | 0 | 43 | 44 | 16 | 10 |

## JAYHAWK LEAGUE

| EAST | W | L | PCT | GB |
|---|---|---|---|---|
| Nevada Griffons | 37 | 15 | .712 | — |
| Clarinda A's | 24 | 26 | .480 | 12 |
| Topeka Capitols | 19 | 22 | .463 | 12½ |
| Red Oak Red Sox | 16 | 23 | .410 | 14½ |
| St. Joseph Cardinals | 12 | 29 | .293 | 24½ |

| WEST | W | L | PCT | GB |
|---|---|---|---|---|
| Liberal Bee Jays | 32 | 20 | .615 | — |
| Elkhart Dusters | 31 | 20 | .608 | ½ |
| Wichita Broncos | 24 | 17 | .585 | 2½ |
| Amarillo Texans | 23 | 17 | .575 | 3 |
| Hays Larks | 13 | 29 | .310 | 14 |

### INDIVIDUAL BATTING LEADERS
(Minimum 90 At-Bats)

| | AVG | AB | R | H | 2B | 3B | HR | RBI | SB |
|---|---|---|---|---|---|---|---|---|---|
| Allison, Chris, Nevada | .356 | 191 | 46 | 68 | 8 | 1 | 0 | 25 | 24 |
| Dean, Chris, Liberal | .342 | 111 | 25 | 38 | 7 | 4 | 2 | 10 | 8 |
| Hacker, Steve, Wichita | .333 | 135 | 29 | 45 | 3 | 0 | 5 | 26 | 1 |
| Wilcox, Luke, St. Joseph | .333 | 117 | 13 | 39 | 9 | 1 | 0 | 16 | 2 |
| Aven, Bruce, Liberal | .325 | 160 | 42 | 52 | 11 | 6 | 8 | 44 | 14 |
| Lewis, Ed, Liberal | .325 | 154 | 26 | 50 | 9 | 0 | 3 | 28 | 6 |
| Rivera, Triny, Amarillo | .323 | 133 | 18 | 43 | 7 | 4 | 2 | 23 | 20 |
| Gronowski, Craig, Amarillo | .319 | 91 | 26 | 29 | 8 | 4 | 1 | 12 | 12 |
| Priest, Adam, Liberal | .317 | 180 | 46 | 57 | 9 | 3 | 1 | 17 | 19 |
| Hughes, Bob, Nevada | .315 | 181 | 30 | 57 | 8 | 2 | 1 | 32 | 8 |
| Rich, Tony, Wichita | .314 | 159 | 34 | 50 | 11 | 1 | 0 | 18 | 10 |

### INDIVIDUAL PITCHING LEADERS
(Minimum 35 Innings)

| | W | L | ERA | G | SV | IP | H | BB | SO |
|---|---|---|---|---|---|---|---|---|---|
| Eddings, Jeff, Nevada | 6 | 1 | 1.48 | 13 | 2 | 73 | 47 | 10 | 45 |
| Driskill, Dan, Wichita | 6 | 1 | 1.84 | 9 | 0 | 68 | 47 | 22 | 68 |
| Corn, Chris, Hays | 3 | 1 | 1.95 | 7 | 1 | 37 | 27 | 12 | 45 |
| Jordan, Jason, Elkhart | 5 | 0 | 2.00 | 9 | 0 | 36 | 27 | 13 | 24 |
| Burgis, Travis, Clarinda | 2 | 2 | 2.23 | 7 | 0 | 40 | 30 | 17 | 20 |
| Frafjord, Bret, Nevada | 6 | 3 | 2.25 | 11 | 0 | 60 | 43 | 21 | 52 |
| Vermillion, Grant, Liberal | 4 | 3 | 2.25 | 10 | 0 | 56 | 47 | 14 | 58 |
| Kosek, Kory, Red Oak | 2 | 4 | 2.29 | 10 | 1 | 55 | 54 | 7 | 54 |

## NORTHEASTERN LEAGUE

| EAST | W | L | PCT | GB |
|---|---|---|---|---|
| Little Falls Diamonds | 30 | 13 | .698 | — |
| Schenectady Mohawks | 23 | 17 | .575 | 5½ |
| Utica-Rome Indians | 20 | 22 | .476 | 9½ |
| Schenectady Blue Jays | 16 | 24 | .400 | 12½ |
| Kanata Junior Selects | 8 | 34 | .190 | 21½ |

| WEST | W | L | PCT | GB |
|---|---|---|---|---|
| Cohocton Red Wings | 28 | 16 | .636 | — |
| Broome Rangers | 24 | 20 | .545 | 4 |
| Ithaca Lakers | 22 | 22 | .500 | 6 |
| Cortland Apples | 22 | 22 | .500 | 6 |
| Horseheads Generals | 22 | 22 | .500 | 6 |

**PLAYOFFS: Division**—Little Falls defeated Mohawks, 2-1, and Ithaca defeated Cohocton, 2-1, in best-of-3 series. **Finals**—Little Falls defeated Ithaca in one-game championship.

### INDIVIDUAL BATTING LEADERS
(Minimum 70 At-Bats)

| | AVG | AB | R | H | 2B | 3B | HR | RBI | SB |
|---|---|---|---|---|---|---|---|---|---|
| Mapes, Mark, Diamonds | .382 | 76 | 12 | 29 | 11 | 1 | 1 | 13 | 1 |
| Durkac, Bo, Mohawks | .366 | 71 | 10 | 26 | 4 | 1 | 0 | 11 | 1 |
| Carter, Byran, Rangers | .348 | 89 | 20 | 31 | 3 | 0 | 0 | 8 | 14 |
| Migita, Lance, Diamonds | .341 | 88 | 19 | 30 | 5 | 3 | 0 | 5 | 14 |
| Smith, Eric, Red Wings | .338 | 145 | 23 | 49 | 11 | 2 | 0 | 22 | 9 |
| McHugh, Ryan, Indians | .336 | 110 | 25 | 37 | 8 | 2 | 1 | 21 | 9 |
| Buckley, Matt, Red Wings | .336 | 110 | 16 | 37 | 7 | 2 | 0 | 19 | 9 |
| Schaefer, Rob, Diamonds | .333 | 78 | 16 | 26 | 4 | 2 | 0 | 8 | 10 |
| Mighton, Art, Lakers | .328 | 116 | 22 | 38 | 5 | 2 | 0 | 9 | 16 |
| Faircloth, Kevin, Red Wings | .323 | 93 | 22 | 30 | 3 | 1 | 0 | 14 | 10 |

### INDIVIDUAL PITCHING LEADERS
(Minimum 30 Innings)

| | W | L | ERA | G | SV | IP | H | BB | SO |
|---|---|---|---|---|---|---|---|---|---|
| Davidson, Scott, Mohawks | 7 | 1 | 0.00 | 19 | 3 | 35 | 18 | 5 | 39 |
| Dent, Hal, Selects | 3 | 3 | 0.90 | 6 | 0 | 30 | 25 | 10 | 23 |
| Hunt, John, Lakers | 3 | 1 | 1.12 | 7 | 0 | 32 | 20 | 10 | 26 |

---

| | | | | | | | | | |
|---|---|---|---|---|---|---|---|---|---|
| Heim, Joe, Red Wings | 6 | 0 | 1.17 | 8 | 0 | 38 | 29 | 12 | 24 |
| Kramer, Jeff, Generals | 3 | 3 | 1.19 | 6 | 0 | 38 | 28 | 9 | 51 |

## SAN DIEGO COLLEGIATE LEAGUE

### FIRST HALF

| AMERICAN | W | L | PCT | GB | NATIONAL | W | L | PCT | GB |
|---|---|---|---|---|---|---|---|---|---|
| Indians | 11 | 4 | .733 | — | Cubs | 12 | 3 | .800 | — |
| Royals | 7 | 7 | .500 | 3½ | Mets | 4 | 10 | .286 | 7½ |
| Angels | 7 | 8 | .467 | 4 | Padres | 3 | 12 | .200 | 9 |

### SECOND HALF

| AMERICAN | W | L | PCT | GB | NATIONAL | W | L | PCT | GB |
|---|---|---|---|---|---|---|---|---|---|
| Angels | 9 | 6 | .600 | — | Cubs | 14 | 1 | .933 | — |
| Indians | 8 | 6 | .571 | ½ | Mets | 4 | 10 | .286 | 9½ |
| Royals | 7 | 8 | .467 | 2 | Padres | 2 | 13 | .133 | 12 |

**PLAYOFFS: Semifinal**—Indians defeated Angels in one-game American Division playoff. **Finals**—Indians defeated Cubs, 2-1, in best-of-3 series.

### INDIVIDUAL BATTING LEADERS
(Minimum 72 Plate Appearances)

| | AVG | AB | R | H | 2B | 3B | HR | RBI | SB |
|---|---|---|---|---|---|---|---|---|---|
| Gunther, Scott, Cubs | .425 | 73 | 21 | 31 | 4 | 3 | 2 | 27 | 7 |
| Melero, Sam, Angels | .410 | 61 | 11 | 25 | 5 | 0 | 2 | 13 | 3 |
| Sanchez, David, Cubs | .389 | 72 | 17 | 28 | 1 | 4 | 2 | 15 | 6 |
| Thompson, Eddie, Royals | .372 | 78 | 15 | 29 | 3 | 1 | 0 | 16 | 7 |
| Morton, Eric, Cubs | .349 | 83 | 25 | 29 | 6 | 3 | 1 | 18 | 7 |
| Marsh, Brock, Padres | .348 | 66 | 11 | 23 | 5 | 3 | 0 | 8 | 2 |
| Chavez, Chris, Cubs | .341 | 88 | 24 | 30 | 3 | 3 | 0 | 13 | 7 |
| Barry, Chad, Angels | .324 | 71 | 8 | 23 | 1 | 0 | 0 | 2 | 4 |
| Mitchell, Spike, Indians | .323 | 62 | 15 | 20 | 3 | 1 | 0 | 5 | 2 |
| Simoneau, Bob, Cubs | .315 | 73 | 12 | 23 | 3 | 3 | 0 | 18 | 1 |

### INDIVIDUAL PITCHING LEADERS
(Minimum 30 Innings)

| | W | L | ERA | G | SV | IP | H | BB | SO |
|---|---|---|---|---|---|---|---|---|---|
| Buckles, Brandall, Indians | 4 | 1 | 0.18 | 8 | 0 | 39 | 24 | 9 | 39 |
| McWilliams, Joe, Indians | 6 | 1 | 0.86 | 10 | 0 | 41 | 19 | 19 | 34 |
| Barry, Chad, Angels | 4 | 1 | 0.90 | 6 | 0 | 31 | 12 | 12 | 20 |
| Nelson, Chris, Cubs | 5 | 0 | 1.17 | 10 | 2 | 42 | 34 | 3 | 38 |
| Rios, Mike, Angels | 3 | 1 | 1.33 | 7 | 0 | 42 | 33 | 24 | 43 |

## SHENANDOAH VALLEY LEAGUE

| | W | L | PCT | GB |
|---|---|---|---|---|
| Staunton Braves | 23 | 17 | .575 | — |
| Winchester Royals | 22 | 18 | .550 | 1 |
| Front Royal Cardinals | 21 | 19 | .525 | 2 |
| New Market Rebels | 19 | 21 | .475 | 4 |
| Harrisonburg Turks | 18 | 22 | .450 | 5 |
| Waynesboro Generals | 17 | 23 | .425 | 6 |

**PLAYOFFS: Semifinals**—Winchester defeated Front Royal, 3-0, and Staunton defeated New Market, 3-1, in best-of-5 series. **Finals**—Winchester defeated Staunton, 3-2, in best-of-5 championship series.

### INDIVIDUAL BATTING LEADERS
(Minimum 75 At-Bats)

| | AVG | AB | R | H | 2B | 3B | HR | RBI | SB |
|---|---|---|---|---|---|---|---|---|---|
| Munoz, Juan, Waynesboro | .374 | 171 | 23 | 64 | 16 | 5 | 1 | 23 | 11 |
| Wilson, Matt, Front Royal | .344 | 122 | 25 | 42 | 9 | 1 | 0 | 7 | 6 |
| Weaver, Scott, Staunton | .337 | 172 | 34 | 58 | 15 | 3 | 5 | 24 | 10 |
| Ficklin, Willando, FR | .336 | 119 | 30 | 40 | 5 | 1 | 6 | 20 | 12 |
| Copeland, Travis, New Mkt. | .335 | 155 | 24 | 52 | 6 | 3 | 0 | 13 | 7 |
| Raynor, Mark, New Market | .335 | 176 | 24 | 59 | 11 | 2 | 3 | 22 | 14 |
| Lopez, Luis, Winchester | .324 | 170 | 29 | 55 | 18 | 3 | 2 | 39 | 2 |
| Cooper, Chris, Harr. | .311 | 122 | 30 | 38 | 8 | 1 | 0 | 15 | 8 |
| Jordan, Jason, Harr. | .309 | 81 | 8 | 25 | 6 | 0 | 1 | 13 | 1 |
| Hernandez, Luis, Staunton | .296 | 169 | 45 | 50 | 7 | 1 | 2 | 12 | 28 |
| Adams, Brett, Waynesboro | .296 | 136 | 18 | 39 | 5 | 1 | 0 | 11 | 3 |

### INDIVIDUAL PITCHING LEADERS
(Minimum 30 Innings)

| | W | L | ERA | G | SV | IP | H | BB | SO |
|---|---|---|---|---|---|---|---|---|---|
| Loewe, Kevin, Winchester | 6 | 2 | 1.43 | 11 | 0 | 82 | 72 | 11 | 74 |
| Speer, Scott, New Market | 5 | 2 | 1.89 | 11 | 0 | 71 | 59 | 18 | 57 |
| Wallace, Jason, New Market | 4 | 5 | 2.09 | 10 | 0 | 65 | 55 | 29 | 48 |
| Parker, Eric, Harrisonburg | 0 | 2 | 2.54 | 8 | 2 | 39 | 33 | 19 | 37 |
| Paasch, Steve, Staunton | 4 | 2 | 2.68 | 10 | 0 | 54 | 47 | 15 | 52 |
| Casillas, German, Harr. | 6 | 2 | 2.78 | 10 | 0 | 74 | 76 | 23 | 36 |
| Eaddy, Brad, New Market | 2 | 2 | 2.91 | 7 | 0 | 43 | 33 | 21 | 50 |
| Cruz, Charlie, Waynesboro | 5 | 3 | 2.97 | 10 | 0 | 67 | 43 | 29 | 78 |

# AMATEUR DRAFT

# Seattle Plays It Straight, Takes Rodriguez

**By ALAN SCHWARZ**

The baseball world was expecting a curve in the 1993 draft, but instead got a fastball right down the middle.

No one really listened when Seattle Mariners scouting director Roger Jongewaard said a week before the draft: "If anything, I learned that you don't go the safe way. You don't worry about who will get there quicker."

The public still thought Seattle's selection would be influenced by manager Lou Piniella, who coveted a college pitcher capable of pitching for the Mariners in 1993. That meant taking Wichita State University righthander Darren Dreifort, the year's marquee quick fix. Miami high school shortstop Alex Rodriguez, considered the best long-range talent but at least two years away from the big leagues, would slip to the Los Angeles Dodgers at No. 2.

But it didn't happen that way. In the final days, Jongewaard managed to convince everyone in the organization that Rodriguez was their man. And with that, Seattle called Rodriguez' name with the first pick of baseball's 29th amateur draft June 3.

"There's nothing wrong with Dreifort," said Jongewaard, who with the Mets in 1980 and the Mariners in 1987 passed up proven college pitchers to take Darryl Strawberry and Ken Griffey Jr. with the draft's top selections. "Most years with the No. 1 pick you'd feel lucky he was out there for you. But a guy like Rodriguez doesn't come around very often."

At Westminster Christian High, the 6-foot-3, 190-pound Rodriguez hit .505 with nine home runs as a leadoff man and stole 35 bases in 35 attempts. His quickness in the field, strong and accurate arm and deft hands make him a potential all-star major league shortstop. Many scouts called him the best position player they had evaluated in 20 years.

Piniella was convinced of Rodriguez' skills before the draft and conceded to Jongewaard's judgment.

"Lou watched tapes of Alex and was very impressed with his bat," Mariners general manager Woody Woodward said. "His comment was he liked what he saw and will respect any decision the scouts make."

**Alex Rodriguez.** Miami high school product earned a $1 million bonus as Seattle's No. 1 draft pick.

a year near his Miami hometown. He called the Mariners and reinforced that stand the night before the draft. Seattle took him anyway, figuring it still could convince him to sign.

With a scholarship to the University of Miami and hard-line agent Scott Boras at his side, Rodriguez immediately insisted on a $2.5 million bonus with a major league contract. Never before had a player received more than $1.55 million, and baseball scoffed at such demands.

But Rodriguez' family, primarily his sister Susy Dunand, remained steadfast and asked that all negotiations go through her first.

The Mariners made their first offer to Rodriguez on the phone after midnight in late June: either a $1 million bonus or a $500,000 bonus and a three-year major league contract,

## Business Before Pleasure

Next, the Mariners had to sign Rodriguez. And that proved a far more sticky proposition than simply drafting him.

Rodriguez let it be known beforehand that he wanted to be drafted by the Dodgers at No. 2 because he could play several times

| TOP 12 SIGNING BONUSES | | |
|---|---|---|
| Drafted Players Only | | |
| Rank, Player, Pos. | Club, Year | Bonus |
| 1. Brien Taylor, lhp | Yankees, '91 (1) | $1,550,000 |
| 2. Darren Dreifort, rhp | Dodgers, '93 (1) | 1,300,000 |
| 3. Alex Rodriguez, ss | Mariners, '93 (1) | 1,000,000 |
| 4. Jeffrey Hammonds, of | Orioles, '92 (1) | 975,000 |
| 5. Kirk Presley, rhp | Mets, '93 (1) | 900,000 |
| 6. Trot Nixon, of | Red Sox, '93 (1) | 890,000 |
| 7. Calvin Murray, of | Giants, '92 (1) | 825,000 |
| 8. Matt Brunson, ss | Tigers, '93 (1) | 800,000 |
| 9. Steve Soderstrom, rhp | Giants '93 (1) | 750,000 |
| Wayne Gomes, rhp | Phillies, '93 (1) | 750,000 |
| 11. Phil Nevin, 3b | Astros '92 (1) | 700,000 |
| Derek Jeter, ss | Yankees '92 (1) | 700,000 |

with a guaranteed callup for September 1993, worth an additional $500,000.

Dunand, on Boras' advice, then insisted that the Mariners communicate with them only via fax.

"At this point, I don't trust them," Dunand said. "This is not a negotiation. I was up-front with them before the draft and after. They broke very simple ground rules. This is a negotiation and they'll go to the weakest person, the player."

Not surprisingly, there was little contact until days before Rodriguez would attend his first scheduled college class (Aug. 26) and become ineligible to sign. But by then, three things had occurred: one, Rodriguez broke his cheekbone during an infield-practice accident at the July Olympic Festival; two, Mariners president Chuck Armstrong became involved and faxed a late offer; and three, Rodriguez decided amidst all the arguing around him that he simply wanted to be a professional baseball player.

Hours before Rodriguez was to go to school, he decided to accept a decidedly smaller sum.

**Darren Dreifort.** Wichita State righthander was the second overall pick in the 1993 draft, going to Los Angeles.

Rodriguez received a $1 million bonus and a three-year major league contract beginning in 1994, roughly a $1.3 million package. The Mariners barely had to budge off their original proposal. In a rare treat for an industry complaining about the escalation of draft bonuses, Major League Baseball had to look at the signing as a victory.

Rodriguez sounded exhausted at a press conference the afternoon after the 3 a.m. Aug. 30 signing.

"I'm glad the negotiations are over," said Rodriguez, 18. "It's been a long process. I never wanted this to be a bad thing, a long summer thing. One day I'll get my market value, when I prove myself as an impact player. I just want to get started.

"Most of the summer, I thought I was headed for school. Education is very important to me. At the time, I didn't like what was offered or how the negotiations were handled."

Seattle has high hopes for Rodriguez reaching the major leagues in similar fashion to Griffey, who debuted for the Mariners less than two years later.

"I think that Alex already has proven to this point that college baseball would have been a step down for him," Woodward said. "He's about the most advanced infielder I've seen."

The intrigue didn't end after Rodriguez came to terms. Boras instigated a grievance Oct. 14 by the Major League Baseball Players Association that accused the Mariners of failing to respect Rodriguez' right to an agent when they signed him. The grievance, which had yet to be resolved in early November, asked that the contract be voided, making Rodriguez a free agent, or renegotiated.

## Trickle-Down Effect

The evidence of baseball's victory against escalating bonuses came one week later when Dreifort signed with the Dodgers for far less than his original demand.

Dreifort held out all summer for a bonus and three-year major league contract worth approximately $2 million. But when the Mariners signed Rodriguez, the Dodgers quickly got Dreifort to accept a $1.3 million bonus with no major league contract.

The bonus was the second-highest ever, behind the $1.55 million Brien Taylor received from the Yankees as the No. 1 pick in 1991.

John Dreifort, Darren's father who handled the negotiations, clearly was upset by the outcome.

"The negotiations weren't easy," he said. "I think this really could have been one of the highlights of Darren's life, and one of the highlights of our whole family. But I'm not sure if I feel that way . . . I think Darren, frankly, was just tired of the whole thing."

After sitting out a week of classes to keep himself eligible to sign, Dreifort accepted the Dodgers' offer after talking to Los Angeles GM Fred Claire. He previously had been involved only marginally in contract talks, and fliers had begun to appear on the Wichita State campus urging him to stop being greedy and sign.

Chances were good Dreifort could have reached the majors in 1993 had he signed quickly after the draft. Instead he began his professional career in the Dodgers' Arizona instructional league camp.

The Rodriguez and Dreifort "victories" for baseball came late in the summer, so bonuses still went up markedly. The first-round average for 1993 was $611,000, compared to $482,000 in 1992 and $355,000 in 1991.

## College Arms Dominate

Dreifort headlined a first round that was the most college-pitching dominated in history. Fourteen experienced arms went in the first 28 picks.

"If they don't have good arm action, and Dwight Gooden was an exception, high school pitching is too risky," one scouting director said. "A college pitcher will at least get to the big leagues faster, which will hold the job of the scouting director. They don't get rid of managers anymore. They fire the general manager

# High Stakes On International Stage

Two international players not subject to the draft made headlines in 1993 by signing lucrative contracts after bidding wars between several major league organizations.

The Atlanta Braves added to their already deep farm system with the signing of Australian shortstop Glenn Williams, considered by many the top international player available in 1993.

Williams, 16, received a signing bonus of $800,000, about what high first-round draft picks obtained in 1993. Toronto's involvement, in particular, drove up the ante. A year earlier, the Blue Jays outbid Atlanta for 16-year-old Jose Pett, signing the Brazilian righthander to a $700,000 signing bonus—then far and away the highest bonus paid to a foreign player.

Williams is 6-foot-2 and 175 pounds, but the Braves believe he'll continue to mature physically. He might even outgrow shortstop, though Chuck LaMar, Braves director of player development and scouting, said Atlanta will start him at that position.

"He's so young and talented at shortstop, we definitely see him staying there for the next few years," LaMar said. "He's a switch-hitter with power ability from both sides of the plate, and we think he has a chance to be an offensive shortstop."

While Atlanta and Toronto have pursued top foreign players most aggressively recently, the Seattle Mariners finally made an impact by signing Makato Suzuki, a Japanese-born righthander who was clocked at 97 mph playing for co-op San Bernardino in the Class A California League. Suzuki, 18, had offers from at least a dozen other clubs, including

**Glenn Williams**

two which bid higher than the Mariners.

Seattle had several advantages in their courting of Suzuki. The club is owned largely by Nintendo, a company based in Japan, and Seattle's largest minority population is Japanese. In addition, Suzuki is a native of Kobe, which is Seattle's sister city.

The Mariners shelled out $750,000 to sign him.

"We treated him like a high first-round draft pick because that's what he would have been if he'd been in the draft," said Roger Jongewaard, Seattle's director of scouting and player development.

Suzuki, 6-foot-3 and 195 pounds, came to the United States in 1992 to pitch one inning for Salinas, a California League club which had Japanese ownership, including his agent, Don Nomura. The franchise was sold and moved for the 1993 season to San Bernardino, where Suzuki went 4-4 with a 3.68 ERA and 12 saves.

In a rare international twist to the 1993 draft, the Oakland Athletics lost their 15th-round pick, Long Beach State All-America righthander Daniel Choi, to South Korea's professional league for an announced bonus of $200,000 but reportedly closer to $1 million.

Choi, a Korean-American who grew up in southern California, went 17-2 for the 49ers and led the nation's college pitchers in wins.

No treaty exists between the Korean league and Major League Baseball, although the Korean government has resticted the movement of its players in the past.

**—ALAN SCHWARZ**

---

and the scouting director."

Selected right after Dreifort were Wright State lefthander Brian Anderson (Angels), Old Dominion righthander Wayne Gomes (Phillies), Texas A&M lefthander Jeff Granger (Royals) and Fresno State righthander Steve Soderstrom (Giants).

Anderson and Granger signed contracts that guaranteed September callups for 1993, making them the first players to debut in the big leagues their first summer since the Cubs' Lance Dickson and the White Sox' Alex Fernandez in 1990. Soderstrom encountered arm problems at Fresno State and as a precaution didn't begin his pro career until the Arizona Fall League.

After that string of five college pitchers, the Red Sox and Mets scooped up the draft's consensus top high school hitter and hurler, both of whom also were all-America prep quarterbacks with commitments to major colleges. Boston selected outfielder Trot Nixon from New Hanover High in Wilmington, N.C., and New York took Tupelo (Miss.) High righthander Kirk Presley.

Nixon hit .519 and went 12-0 on the mound for the North Carolina Class 4-A state championship team to earn Baseball America's 1993 High School Player of

the Year award. He held out all summer and was attending football practice at North Carolina State when the Red Sox managed to sign him for $890,000.

"It was my goal to play professional baseball," said Nixon, whose contract included a gentleman's agreement for him to be called up to the majors in September 1994. "It's been my dream to do that. But I had every intention to play football at N.C. State. I was going to be a good football player. Not this year or next year, but down the road."

Presley, who surely will have difficulty in New York escaping the attention he gets for being Elvis Presley's third cousin, was considered the toughest first-rounder to sign. He easily might have slid out of the first round entirely because his signability was so in question, but the deep-pocket and deep-trouble Mets determined they could satisfy his bonus demands. He finally signed for $900,000 and passed up a scholarship to Mississippi State.

"Baseball is my career," said Presley, who went 15-0 for the Mississippi Class 5-A state champions and never lost a high school start. "There was no need for me to beat around the bush and play football. I'd just be wasting my time."

Presley had no clause in his contract for any specific major league callup.

"The callup would not be fair to the Mets or me," Presley said. "I want to go through the system, make sure I'm ready."

## Few College Hitters

As much as pitchers—19 of the first 28—were the story of the first round, the lack of position players—especially collegians—figured just as prominently.

The only lock to go in the first round was Georgia Tech catcher Jason Varitek, a player known as much for his defensive prowess and leadership qualities as for his switch-hitting skills. But his alignment with Boras may have scared teams off. Varitek lasted until No. 21, when Minnesota grabbed him. The Twins refused to budge from their $450,000 bonus offer and Varitek became the only first-round pick not to sign.

The Twins also had difficulty signing a number of their other early-round selections. They failed to come to terms with 12 picks in the first 19 rounds, though the previous winter's free-agent defections of Greg Gagne (Royals) and John Smiley (Reds) provided four extra picks in the first three rounds.

The Cubs, with the 10th pick, pulled the biggest surprise of the first round, taking Texas' Brooks Kieschnick, Baseball America's 1993 College Player of the Year. Kieschnick's lefthanded bat and gamesmanship are unquestioned, but defensive shortcomings and frequent pitching duties relegated him to Longhorn DH duties most of 1993.

Kieschnick and Varitek were the only college position players taken in the first round, the lowest total since 1976, years before college baseball's growth spurt in the early 1980s.

**Jason Varitek**

In fact, there were fewer college hitters taken in the opening round than relatives of former major league athletes. All were selected out of high school.

Englewood, Colo., shortstop Matt Brunson (No. 9, Tigers) is the son of Larry Brunson, a National Football League wide receiver and kick-return specialist from 1974-80.

Sarasota, Fla., righthander Matt Drews' (No. 13, Yankees) is the grandson of Karl Drews, who played eight years in the big leagues, three for the Yankees, from 1947-54.

Sacramento first baseman Derrek Lee (No. 14, Padres) is the son of Leon Lee and the nephew of former major leaguer Leron Lee, who were two of the most prolific imports in Japanese League history.

## Three Cubans Drafted

The 1993 draft included a historic twist, as a group of Cuban players were eligible for the first time. Through a special agreement with Major League Baseball, five Cuban defectors were made available for selection, but few clubs appeared moved by the novelty as eight rounds passed before the first was selected.

Lefthander Ivan Alvarez, 22, whose fastball hits 92 mph, was the first player picked, going to the Giants in the ninth round. Osmani Estrada, 23, a sure-handed infielder who batted .290 over five seasons in Cuba's elite Serie Selectiva, was taken by the Rangers in the 13th round. Alexis Cabreja, 23, a slugging outfielder with a six-year average of .330, also went to the Rangers two rounds later.

More than 120 Cubans have played in the major leagues, and 26 were on big league rosters when Fidel Castro took power in 1959. But Castro banned professional sports in the early days of the revolution and, by 1961, contact between Cuba and the U.S. professional

### NO. 1 DRAFT PICKS, 1965-93

| Year | Club, Player, Pos. | School | Hometown | Highest Level (G*) | '93 Status | Bonus |
|------|--------------------|--------|----------|--------------------|-----------|-------|
| 1965 | A's. Rick Monday, of | Arizona State U. | Santa Monica, Calif. | Majors (1,996) | Out of Baseball | $104,000 |
| 1966 | Mets. Steve Chilcott, c | Antelope Valley HS | Lancaster, Calif. | Triple-A (2) | Out of Baseball | 75,000 |
| 1967 | Yankees. Ron Blomberg, 1b | Druid Hills HS | Atlanta | Majors (461) | Out of Baseball | 75,000 |
| 1968 | Mets. Tim Foli, ss | Notre Dame HS | Sherman Oaks, Calif. | Majors (1,696) | Out of Baseball | 75,000 |
| 1969 | Senators. Jeff Burroughs, of | Wilson HS | Long Beach, Calif. | Majors (1,689) | Out of Baseball | 88,000 |
| 1970 | Padres. Mike Ivie, c | Walker HS | Decatur, Ga. | Majors (857) | Out of Baseball | 80,000 |
| 1971 | White Sox. Danny Goodwin, c | Central HS | Peoria, Ill. | Majors (252) | Out of Baseball | DNS |
| 1972 | Padres. Dave Roberts, 3b | U. of Oregon | Corvallis, Ore. | Majors (709) | Out of Baseball | 60,000 |
| 1973 | Rangers. David Clyde, lhp | Westchester HS | Houston | Majors (84) | Out of Baseball | 125,000 |
| 1974 | Padres. Bill Almon, ss | Brown U. | Warwick, R.I. | Majors (1,236) | Out of Baseball | 90,000 |
| 1975 | Angels. Danny Goodwin, c | Southern U. | Peoria, Ill. | Majors (252) | Out of Baseball | 125,000 |
| 1976 | Astros. Floyd Bannister, lhp | Arizona State U. | Seattle | Majors (431) | Out of Baseball | 100,000 |
| 1977 | White Sox. Harold Baines, of | St. Michael's HS | St. Michael's, Md. | Majors (1,962) | Orioles | 40,000 |
| 1978 | Braves. Bob Horner, 3b | Arizona State U. | Glendale, Ariz. | Majors (1,020) | Out of Baseball | 175,000 |
| 1979 | Mariners. Al Chambers, of | Harris HS | Harrisburg, Pa. | Majors (57) | Out of Baseball | 60,000 |
| 1980 | Mets. Darryl Strawberry, of | Crenshaw HS | Los Angeles | Majors (1,323) | Dodgers | 210,000 |
| 1981 | Mariners. Mike Moore, rhp | Oral Roberts U. | Eakly, Okla. | Majors (400) | Tigers | 100,000 |
| 1982 | Cubs. Shawon Dunston, ss | Jefferson HS | New York | Majors (923) | Cubs | 100,000 |
| 1983 | Twins. Tim Belcher, rhp | Mt. Vernon Naz. Coll. | Sparta, Ohio | Majors (207) | White Sox | DNS |
| 1984 | Mets. Shawn Abner, of | Mechanicsburg HS | Mechanicsburg, Pa. | Majors (392) | Royals (AAA) | 150,000 |
| 1985 | Brewers. B.J. Surhoff, c | U. of North Carolina | Rye, N.Y. | Majors (945) | Brewers | 150,000 |
| 1986 | Pirates. Jeff King, 3b | U. of Arkansas | Colorado Springs | Majors (523) | Pirates | 160,000 |
| 1987 | Mariners. Ken Griffey Jr., of | Moeller HS | Cincinnati | Majors (734) | Mariners | 169,000 |
| 1988 | Padres. Andy Benes, rhp | U. of Evansville | Evansville, Ind. | Majors (143) | Padres | 235,000 |
| 1989 | Orioles. Ben McDonald, rhp | Louisiana State U. | Denham Springs, La. | Majors (117) | Orioles | 350,000 |
| 1990 | Braves. Chipper Jones, ss | The Bolles School | Jacksonville | Majors (8) | Braves | 275,000 |
| 1991 | Yankees. Brien Taylor, lhp | East Carteret HS | Beaufort, N.C. | Double-A (27) | Double-A | 1,550,000 |
| 1992 | Astros. Phil Nevin, 3b | Cal State Fullerton | Placentia, Calif. | Triple-A (123) | Triple-A | 700,000 |
| 1993 | Mariners. Alex Rodriguez, ss | West'er Christian HS | Miami | | Did Not Play | 1,000,000 |

*No. of games at that level   DNS–Did not sign

# DRAFT '93

## FIRST-ROUND PICKS

**Brooks Kieschnick**
10th pick, Cubs

| Team. Player, Pos. | School | Hometown | Bonus | B'date | B-T | Ht. | Wt. | AVG | AB | H | HR | RBI | SB | '93 Assignment |
|---|---|---|---|---|---|---|---|---|---|---|---|---|---|---|
| 1. Mariners. Alex Rodriguez, ss | West'ster Christian HS | Miami | $1,000,000 | 7-27-75 | R-R | 6-3 | 190 | .505 | 93 | 47 | 9 | 36 | 35 | Signed late—DNP |
| 7. Red Sox. Trot Nixon, of | New Hanover HS | Wilmington, N.C. | 890,000 | 4-11-74 | L-L | 6-2 | 195 | .507 | 73 | 37 | 11 | 50 | 20 | Signed late—DNP |
| 9. Tigers. Matt Brunson, ss | Cherry Creek HS | Englewood, Colo. | 800,000 | 9-2-74 | B-R | 5-11 | 160 | .429 | 35 | 16 | 0 | 12 | 16 | Signed late—DNP |
| 10. Cubs. Brooks Kieschnick, 1b-of | U. of Texas | Corpus Christi, Texas | 650,000 | 6-6-72 | L-R | 6-4 | 228 | .376 | 245 | 92 | 19 | 80 | 3 | Daytona (A) |
| 14. Padres. Derrek Lee, 1b | El Camino HS | Sacramento | 600,000 | 9-6-75 | R-R | 6-5 | 195 | .459 | 98 | 45 | 10 | 47 | 33 | GCL Padres (R) |
| 20. Expos. Chris Schwab, of | Cretin-Derham HS | Eagan, Minn. | 425,000 | 7-25-74 | L-R | 6-3 | 215 | .500 | 62 | 31 | 8 | 32 | 5 | GCL Expos (R) |
| 20. Twins. Torii Hunter, of | Pine Bluff HS | Pine Bluff, Ark. | 450,000 | 7-11-75 | R-R | 6-1 | 190 | .436 | 55 | 24 | 6 | 30 | 12 | GCL Twins (R) |
| 21. Twins. Jason Varitek, c | Georgia Tech U. | Altamonte Springs, Fla. | DNS | 4-11-72 | B-R | 6-2 | 207 | .404 | 228 | 92 | 22 | 72 | 5 | Did not sign |
| 22. Pirates. Charles Peterson, of | Laurens HS | Laurens, S.C. | 420,000 | 5-8-74 | R-R | 6-4 | 200 | .449 | 49 | 22 | 6 | 26 | 21 | GCL Pirates (R) |

### SUPPLEMENTAL FIRST ROUND

| Team. Player, Pos. | School | Hometown | Bonus | B'date | B-T | Ht. | Wt. | AVG | AB | H | HR | RBI | SB | '93 Assignment |
|---|---|---|---|---|---|---|---|---|---|---|---|---|---|---|
| 29. Cubs. Kevin Orie, 3b | Indiana U. | Pittsburgh | 255,000 | 9-1-72 | R-R | 6-4 | 205 | .358 | 201 | 72 | 9 | 59 | 6 | Peoria (A) |
| 30. Rangers. Mike Bell, 3b | Moeller HS | Cincinnati | 310,000 | 12-7-74 | R-R | 6-2 | 185 | .407 | 81 | 33 | 4 | 22 | 23 | GCL Rangers (R) |
| 31. Expos. Josue Estrada, of | Madardo Carazo HS | Rio Piedras, P.R. | 165,000 | 12-1-75 | R-R | 6-0 | 185 | No high school team | | | | | | GCL Expos (R) |
| 32. Reds. Pat Watkins, of | East Carolina U. | Garner, N.C. | 235,000 | 9-2-72 | R-R | 6-1 | 180 | .445 | 220 | 98 | 19 | 57 | 29 | Billings (R) |
| 34. Pirates. Jermaine Allensworth, of | Purdue U. | Anderson, Ind. | 194,000 | 1-11-72 | R-R | 6-0 | 180 | .294 | 194 | 57 | 9 | 44 | 18 | Welland (A) |
| 35. Brewers. Todd Dunn, of | U. of North Florida | Jacksonville | 240,000 | 7-29-70 | R-R | 6-5 | 215 | .352 | 179 | 63 | 19 | 60 | 13 | Helena (R) |
| 37. Blue Jays. Matt Farner, of | East Pennsboro HS | Enola, Pa. | 300,000 | 1-15-74 | L-L | 6-4 | 175 | .417 | 60 | 17 | 3 | 19 | 9 | GCL Blue Jays (R) |
| 38. Twins. Kelcey Mucker, of | Lawrenceburg HS | Lawrenceburg, Ind. | 267,500 | 2-17-75 | L-R | 6-4 | 205 | .436 | 55 | 24 | 6 | 28 | 11 | GCL Twins (R) |
| 42. Pirates. Andy Rice, 1b | Parker HS | Birmingham | 160,000 | 8-31-75 | R-R | 6-1 | 225 | .519 | 52 | 27 | 6 | 25 | 6 | GCL Pirates (R) |

| Team. Player, Pos. | School | Hometown | Bonus | B'date | B-T | Ht. | Wt. | W | L | ERA | IP | H | BB | SO | '93 Assignment |
|---|---|---|---|---|---|---|---|---|---|---|---|---|---|---|---|
| 2. Dodgers. Darren Dreifort, rhp | Wichita State U. | Wichita | $1,300,000 | 5-3-72 | R-R | 6-2 | 205 | 10 | 1 | 2.23 | 93 | 58 | 30 | 110 | Signed late—DNP |
| 3. Angels. Brian Anderson, lhp | Wright State U. | Geneva, Ohio | 680,000 | 4-26-72 | B-L | 6-1 | 195 | 10 | 1 | 1.14 | 95 | 62 | 6 | 98 | Midland (AA) |
| 4. Phillies. Wayne Gomes, rhp | Old Dominion U. | Hampton, Va. | 750,000 | 1-15-73 | R-R | 6-2 | 215 | 2 | 2 | 2.03 | 27 | 7 | 22 | 55 | Batavia (A) |
| 5. Royals. Jeff Granger, lhp | Texas A&M U. | Orange, Texas | 695,000 | 12-16-71 | L-L | 6-4 | 193 | 14 | 3 | 2.72 | 119 | 82 | 51 | 143 | Eugene (A) |
| 6. Cardinals. Steve Soderstrom, rhp | Fresno State U. | Turlock, Calif. | 750,000 | 4-3-72 | R-R | 6-3 | 220 | 6 | 5 | 3.80 | 107 | 100 | 49 | 114 | Injured—DNP |
| 8. Mets. Kirk Presley, rhp | Tupelo HS | Tupelo, Miss. | 900,000 | 4-17-75 | R-R | 6-3 | 192 | 15 | 0 | 0.58 | 97 | 37 | 15 | 161 | Signed late—DNP |
| 11. Indians. Daron Kirkreit, rhp | UC Riverside | Norco, Calif. | 600,000 | 8-7-72 | R-R | 6-6 | 225 | 6 | 6 | 3.15 | 103 | 107 | 33 | 112 | Watertown (A) |
| 12. Astros. Billy Wagner, lhp | Ferrum (Va.) Coll. | Tazewell, Va. | 550,000 | 7-25-71 | L-L | 5-11 | 180 | 6 | 3 | 1.56 | 75 | 22 | 55 | 133 | Auburn (A) |
| 13. Yankees. Matt Drews, rhp | Sarasota HS | Sarasota, Fla. | 620,000 | 8-29-74 | R-R | 6-8 | 210 | 10 | 2 | 1.27 | 88 | 47 | 30 | 125 | Signed late—DNP |
| 15. Blue Jays. Chris Carpenter, rhp | Trinity HS | Manchester, N.H. | 580,000 | 4-27-75 | R-R | 6-5 | 220 | 8 | 1 | 1.20 | 60 | 16 | 27 | 90 | Signed late—DNP |
| 16. Cardinals. Alan Benes, rhp | Creighton U. | Lake Forest, Ill. | 500,000 | 1-21-72 | R-R | 6-4 | 205 | 7 | 5 | 2.73 | 105 | 88 | 45 | 122 | Glens Falls (A) |
| 17. White Sox. Scott Christman, lhp | Oregon State U. | Tualatin, Ore. | 450,000 | 12-3-71 | L-L | 6-3 | 190 | 14 | 1 | 2.20 | 111 | 84 | 38 | 119 | GCL White Sox (R) |
| 19. Orioles. Jay Powell, rhp | Mississippi State U. | Collinsville, Miss. | 492,000 | 1-9-72 | R-R | 6-4 | 221 | 3 | 8 | 3.56 | 73 | 58 | 36 | 73 | Albany (A) |
| 23. Brewers. Jeff D'Amico, rhp | Northeast HS | St. Petersburg, Fla. | 525,000 | 12-27-75 | R-R | 6-6 | 235 | 2 | 1 | 0.75 | 24 | 7 | 7 | 48 | Signed late—DNP |
| 24. Cubs. Jon Ratliff, rhp | LeMoyne Coll. | Clay, N.Y. | 355,000 | 12-22-71 | R-R | 6-5 | 195 | 10 | 1 | 2.04 | 84 | 67 | 17 | 64 | Geneva (A) |
| 25. Athletics. John Wasdin, rhp | Florida State U. | Tallahassee, Fla. | 365,000 | 8-5-72 | R-R | 6-2 | 190 | 10 | 1 | 3.15 | 114 | 104 | 34 | 138 | AZL A's (R) |
| 26. Brewers. Kelly Wunsch, lhp | Texas A&M U. | Houston | 400,000 | 7-12-72 | L-L | 6-5 | 192 | 7 | 1 | 4.46 | 81 | 59 | 52 | 106 | Beloit (A) |
| 27. Marlins. Marc Valdes, rhp | U. of Florida | Tampa | 410,000 | 12-20-71 | R-R | 6-0 | 165 | 8 | 6 | 3.67 | 123 | 113 | 59 | 119 | Elmira (A) |
| 28. Rockies. Jamey Wright, rhp | Westmoore HS | Oklahoma City | 395,000 | 12-24-74 | R-R | 6-6 | 205 | 7 | 2 | 0.57 | 62 | 40 | 34 | 94 | AZL Rockies (R) |

### SUPPLEMENTAL FIRST ROUND

| Team. Player, Pos. | School | Hometown | Bonus | B'date | B-T | Ht. | Wt. | W | L | ERA | IP | H | BB | SO | '93 Assignment |
|---|---|---|---|---|---|---|---|---|---|---|---|---|---|---|---|
| 33. Twins. Marc Barcelo, rhp | Arizona State U. | Tucson | 235,000 | 1-10-72 | R-R | 6-3 | 205 | 12 | 4 | 2.72 | 142 | 133 | 35 | 113 | Fort Myers (A) |
| 36. Athletics. Willie Adams, rhp | Stanford U. | LaMirada, Calif. | 240,000 | 10-8-72 | R-R | 6-5 | 200 | 8 | 5 | 4.23 | 121 | 132 | 26 | 114 | Madison (A) |
| 39. Brewers. Joe Wagner, rhp | U. of Central Florida | Friendship, Wis. | 210,000 | 12-8-71 | R-R | 6-1 | 190 | 4 | 6 | 4.19 | 97 | 96 | 42 | 75 | Helena (R) |
| 40. Blue Jays. Jeremy Lee, rhp | Galesburg HS | Galesburg, Ill. | 165,000 | 10-20-74 | R-R | 6-7 | 205 | 4 | 0 | 0.40 | 35 | 16 | 13 | 53 | GCL Blue Jays (R) |
| 41. Blue Jays. Mark Lukasiewicz, lhp | Brevard (Fla.) JC | Secaucus, N.J. | 250,000 | 3-8-73 | L-L | 6-5 | 230 | 10 | 3 | 1.94 | 88 | 71 | 38 | 62 | Signed late—DNP |

## SIGNING BONUSES

### SECOND-ROUND PICKS

| | |
|---|---|
| 43. Brewers. Brian Banks, c-of | $180,000 |
| 44. Cardinals. Nate Dishington, c-1b | 200,000 |
| 45. Angels. Ryan Hancock, rhp | 215,000 |
| 46. Phillies. Scott Rolen, 3b | 250,000 |
| 47. Blue Jays. Anthony Medrano, ss | 157,500 |
| 48. Giants. Chris Singleton, of | 207,500 |
| 49. Red Sox. Jeff Suppan, rhp | 190,000 |
| 50. Mets. Eric Ludwick, rhp | 210,000 |
| 51. Tigers. Tony Fuduric, rhp | 176,000 |
| 52. Rangers. Edwin Diaz, 3b | 130,000 |
| 53. Indians. Casey Whitten, lhp | 165,000 |
| 54. Pirates. Kevin Pickford, rhp | 165,000 |
| 55. Expos. Martin Mainville, rhp | 181,000 |
| 56. Padres. Matt LaChappa, lhp | 115,000 |
| 57. Blue Jays. Ryan Jones, 1b | 181,000 |
| 58. Cardinals. Jay Witasick, rhp | 150,000 |
| 59. White Sox. Greg Norton, 3b | 133,200 |
| 60. Expos. Brad Fullmer, 3b | 152,500 |
| 61. Orioles. David Lamb, ss | 417,500 |
| 62. Reds. Scott Sullivan, rhp | 200,000 |
| 63. Twins. Dan Perkins, rhp | 156,000 |
| 64. Pirates. Jose Delgado, ss | 195,000 |
| 65. Brewers. Danny Klassen, ss | 125,000 |
| 66. Braves. Andre King, of | 180,000 |
| 67. Athletics. Jeff D'Amico, ss | 325,000 |
| 68. Athletics. Mike Moschetti, ss | 165,000 |
| 69. Marlins. John Roskos, c | 175,000 |
| 70. Rockies. Bryan Rekar, rhp | 120,000 |

### SUPPLEMENTAL SECOND ROUND

| | |
|---|---|
| 71. Giants. Macey Brooks, of | DNS |
| 72. Giants. Brett King, ss | 125,000 |

Signing bonuses do not include college scholarships, incentive bonus plans or salaries from a major league contract.

leagues was cut off.

Alvarez, Estrada and Cabreja defected together in October 1992, risking 30-year prison terms by walking away from their team hotel during a regional tournament in Merida, Mexico.

"I decided not to return to Cuba because I'd like to play professional baseball," Alvarez said. That sentiment was echoed by Cabreja, who added, "I want to play with the best in the world. I want to play professionally."

## Players Union KOs Deadline

Though it generally was seen as just a goodwill gesture to college coaches, an Aug. 15 deadline MLB set for teams to sign draftees was thrown out after the Major League Baseball Players Association challenged the change.

Rights to high school and four-year college players still lasted until the player entered his first class, which varies widely from school to school. College coaches had asked for a set deadline so that they could know as soon as possible if a player was turning pro, so his scholarship could be used for someone else.

The Players Association, though, objected to the change based on a 1992 union victory in challenging sweeping draft-rule alterations. An arbitrator ruled that MLB can change virtually no aspect of the draft without union approval, because doing so could alter the value of picks used as compensation for major league free agents.

"They just didn't have their thinking caps on," union general counsel Gene Orza said.

A ruling that limited the number of rounds to 50 in 1992 and 45 in 1993 previously was overturned in arbitration. Clubs again were free to draft at will and the draft didn't stop until after the expansion Florida Marlins picked in the 91st round.

In all, a record 1,719 players were drafted in 1993, topping the previous record of 1,600 in 1991.

## All In The Family

The White Sox made draft history by selecting Carey Schueler, 18, the daughter of White Sox general manager Ron Schueler. She was picked in the 43rd round but never seriously considered signing.

"It's pretty cool to be drafted in baseball, but I'm definitely going to DePaul (University) to play basketball," said Schueler, who played on the boys' junior varsity baseball team as a 10th grader at Campolinda High in Moraga, Calif.

Two of college football's marquee talents—Florida State quarterback Charlie Ward (Brewers, 59th round) and San Diego State running back Marshall Faulk (Angels, 43rd round)—were drafted, though neither had played baseball in college.

Ward's selection raises his chances of becoming the first athlete drafted in three sports since Dave Winfield in 1973. Ward also is the starting point guard on the Florida State basketball team.

Washington quarterback Billy Joe Hobert, a former Rose Bowl MVP and central figure in a scandal that rocked the Huskies football program, also was drafted (White Sox, 16th round) without having played baseball in college. He signed with both the White Sox and National Football League's Los Angeles Raiders.

# DRAFT '93
## CLUB-BY-CLUB SELECTIONS

### ATLANTA BRAVES (24)

1. (Choice to Cubs as compensation for Type A free agent Greg Maddux).
2. Andre King, of, Stranahan HS, Fort Lauderdale, Fla.
3. Carl Schutz, lhp, Southeastern Louisiana University.
4. James Franklin, of, Larue County HS, Hodgenville, Ky.
5. Del Mathews, 1b-lhp, Fernandina Beach (Fla.) HS.
6. Danny Magee, ss, Denham Springs (La.) HS.
7. Travis Cain, rhp, T.L. Hanna HS, Anderson, S.C.
8. Micah Bowie, lhp, Kingwood (Texas) HS.
9. Jason Green, rhp, Contra Costa (Calif.) JC.
10. Robert Sasser, of, Oakland (Calif.) HS.
11. Kevin Millwood, rhp, Bessemer City (N.C.) HS.
12. Jerrod Miller, rhp, Ferris HS, Spokane, Wash.
13. Wes Culp, of, Anderson HS, Austin, Texas.
14. Doug Brewer, of, Snowflake (Ariz.) HS.
15. John Leroy, rhp, Sammamish HS, Bellevue, Wash.
16. John Reece, of, University of Nebraska.
17. Jermaine Dye, rhp, Cosumnes River (Calif.) CC.
18. John Rocker, lhp, First Presbyterian Day HS, Macon, Ga.
19. David Wells, rhp, Wabash Valley (Ill.) JC.
20. Roosevelt Brown, of, Roosevelt HS, Vicksburg (Miss.) HS.
21. David Knoerr, rhp, Mesquite (Texas) HS.
22. Andrew Tolbert, of, John Jay HS, San Antonio, Texas.
23. Darold Brown, lhp, Laney (Calif.) JC.
24. Jarod Erdody, c, Gladstone (Mich.) HS.
25. Darren Grass, c, University of Minnesota.
26. Rich Betti, lhp, Quinsigamond (Mass.) CC.
27. Casey Burrill, c, University of Southern California.
28. Ralph Denman, of, Dallas Baptist University.
29. Michael Warner, rhp, Bellaire HS, Houston.
30. Wayne Newman, of, American River (Calif.) JC.
31. Bennie Tillman, of, Jackson State University.
32. Eric Olszewski, rhp, Concordia Lutheran HS, Spring, Texas.
33. Jason Dailey, of, Lee (Texas) JC.
34. Chris Cox, 3b, University of North Carolina.
35. Gregory Feris, rhp, Plainview (Texas) HS.
36. William Faile, rhp, Greenwich (N.Y.) HS.
37. Gator McBride, 2b, Logan (Ill.) JC.
38. Charlie Gann, rhp, Jurupa Valley HS, Mira Loma, Calif.
39. Rickey Carter, 3b, North Marion HS, Sparr, Fla.
40. Adrian Lollie, rhp, Windsor HS, Kirkwood, N.Y.
41. Brian Cruz, c, Anderson (Ind.) College.
42. Brandon Wooten, lhp, Davidson Academy, Goodlettsville, Tenn.
43. David Catlett, 1b, Laney (Calif.) JC.
44. Justin Rigney, lhp, Tallahassee (Fla.) JC.
45. Marcus Tyner, rhp, Laney (Calif.) JC.
46. Cam Browder, of, University of North Carolina-Charlotte.
47. Jason Simmons, rhp, Bradley University.
48. Brent Moore, lhp, Midland Valley HS, Clearwater, S.C.
49. Kenneth Mullen, lhp, Beaufort (S.C.) HS.
50. Wonderful Mons, of, Tennessee State University.
51. (void) Pat Murphy, 2b, University of South Alabama.
52. Steven Lay, rhp, Roane County HS, Kingston, Tenn.
53. John Morris, 1b, Valley Christian HS, Lakewood, Calif.
54. Reginald Swilley, rhp, Santa Teresa HS, San Jose, Calif.
55. Ryan Martin, c, Highland HS, Pierron, Ill.
56. Brian Steinbach, rhp, Arrowhead HS, Pewaukee, Wis.
57. Andre Shaw, of, Lufkin (Texas) HS.

### BALTIMORE ORIOLES (19)

1. Jay Powell, rhp, Mississippi State University.
2. David Lamb, ss, Newbury Park (Calif.) HS.
3. Jimmy Walker, rhp, University of Kansas.
4. Jason Hackett, lhp, Caravel Academy, Bear, Del.
5. Mike Gargiulo, c, Bishop McDevitt HS, Harrisburg, Pa.
6. Brian Brewer, lhp, Sacramento (Calif.) CC.
7. John Lombardi, rhp-of, Central Arizona JC.
8. Harry Berrios, of, Louisiana State University.
9. Edwon Simmons, ss, Leo HS, Chicago.
10. Wes Hawkins, of, Louisiana Tech.
11. Tim Karns, rhp, Regis (Colo.) College.
12. Eric Mooney, lhp, St. Mary's (Calif.) College.
13. Brandon Bridgers, of, Methodist (N.C.) College.
14. Kimera Bartee, of, Creighton University.
15. Kevin Curtis, of, Long Beach State University.
16. Delshon Bowman, of, Brandon (Fla.) HS.
17. Lincoln Martin, 2b, Birmingham-Southern College.
18. Kenny Reed, 1b, Ball State University.

19. Rocky Coppinger, rhp, Coronado HS, El Paso, Texas.
20. Mike McKinlay, rhp, Marriott HS, White Rock, B.C.
21. **Alex Pena, rhp, New Mexico JC.**
22. **Jim Foster, c, Providence College.**
23. **Jeff Michael, ss, University of Kentucky.**
24. **Michael Lane, rhp, Belmont (Tenn.) College.**
25. John Batts, 2b, Penn Charter HS, Philadelphia.
26. **Jesse Garcia, 2b, Lee (Texas) JC.**
27. **Trovin Valdez, of, New Mexico JC.**
28. **Ron Shankle, ss, Essex (Md.) CC.**
29. Robert Conway, rhp, Tallahassee (Fla.) CC.
30. **Rocco Cafaro, rhp, Polk (Fla.) CC.**
31. **Michael Trimarco, rhp, Aurora (Ill.) University.**
32. **Bryan Link, of, Austin Peay State University.**
33. Paul Barry, rhp, Sacramento (Calif.) CC.
34. James Fritz, c, North Eugene (Ore.) HS.
35. Michael Sak, 1b, West Leyden HS, Melrose Park, Ill.
36. Jacques Landry, 3b, San Jacinto North (Texas) JC.
37. Dennis Gilich, rhp, Peninsula HS, Gig Harbor, Wash.
38. Jeff Westerman, rhp, Kennedy HS, La Palma, Calif.
39. Aaron France, rhp, Meridian (Miss.) JC.
40. Josh Itzoe, ss, Calvert Hall HS, Towson, Md.
41. Mike Bohny, 3b, Baylor University.
42. **Kendrick Singleton, rhp, Chamberlain HS, Tampa.**
43. Tim Giles, 1b, Arundel HS, Gambrills, Md.
44. James Esparza, lhp, Cedar Valley (Texas) CC.

## BOSTON RED SOX (7)

1. **Trot Nixon, of, New Hanover HS, Wilmington, N.C.**
2. **Jeff Suppan, rhp, Crespi HS, Encino, Calif.**
3. **Ryan McGuire, 1b, UCLA.**
4. **Shawn Senior, lhp, North Carolina State University**
5. **Kevin Clark, 3b, Cypress (Calif.) JC.**
6. Peter Munro, rhp, Cardoza HS, Bayside, N.Y.
7. **David Gibralter, 3b, Duncanville (Texas) HS.**
8. Sean DePaula, rhp, Cardinal Cushing Central HS, Derry, Mass.
9. **Dean Peterson, rhp, Allegheny (Pa.) JC.**
10. **Lou Merloni, ss, Providence College.**
11. **Kurt Bogott, lhp, College of St. Xavier (Ill.).**
12. **Pat Murphy, 2b, University of South Alabama.**
13. **Wilfredo Rivera, of, Vega Alta, P.R.**
14. **David Smith, ss, LeMoyne College.**
15. **Jacob Cook, rhp, Greenville (Ohio) HS.**
16. **Andy Abad, of, Middle Georgia JC.**
17. **Greg Patton, ss, George Washington University.**
18. Keith McDonald, c, Cypress (Calif.) JC.
19. **Courtney Arrollado, ss, Valhalla HS, El Cajon, Calif.**
20. Edward Westfall, rhp, Deltona (Fla.) HS.
21. **John Graham, of, University of Massachusetts.**
22. **Craig Phillip, rhp, Aurora (Ill.) University.**
23. Mark Ballard, rhp, University of Maine.
24. **Greg Kennedy, lhp, University of Southern Mississippi.**
25. **Shayne Bennett, rhp, JC of Du Page (Ill.).**
26. Christian McCarter, of, Northeast Louisiana University.
27. Scotty Hartfield, c, Hattiesburg (Miss.) HS.
28. **Steve Hayward, rhp, Seton Hall University.**
29. Jeff Belcher, of, Calhoun (Ala.) CC.
30. **Jim Larkin, 3b, Holy Cross College.**
31. **Aaron Fuller, 2b, University of California.**
32. **Nathan Tebbs, 2b, JC of Southern Idaho.**
33. Ricky Rodriguez, ss, Miami Springs (Fla.) HS.
34. **James Fernandes, rhp, Brandeis University.**
35. **John Walker, 2b, Grand Rapids (Mich.) JC.**
36. **Gavin Jackson, ss, Chipola (Fla.) JC.**
37. **Mark Dewalt, rhp, Upper Arlington (Ohio) HS.**
38. Wayne Slater, of, F.D. Roosevelt HS, Brooklyn, N.Y.
39. **Tony Brannon, 2b, Johnstown-Monroe HS, Ohio.**
40. Patrick McLendon, c, Lee HS, Baytown, Texas.
41. Daniel Ardoin, c, Texarkana (Texas) CC.
42. Chad Helmer, rhp, East Bay HS, Ruskin, Fla.
43. **Eric Ford, of, Jacksonville State University.**
44. Kenneth Davis, lhp, Chipola (Fla.) JC.
45. **Joseph Hayward, of, Boston College.**
46. Scott Brewer, rhp, Southern Union State (Ala.) JC.
47. Alphonso Johnson, ss, Hollandale Simmons HS, Miss.
48. Ricky Joe Redd, of, Mississippi State University.
49. Michael Davis, rhp, Northwest Whitfield HS, Rocky Face, Ga.
50. Chris Ciraulo, c, Cardinal Newman HS, Santa Rosa, Calif.

## CALIFORNIA ANGELS (3)

1. **Brian Anderson, lhp, Wright State University.**
2. **Ryan Hancock, rhp, Brigham Young University.**
3. **Matt Perisho, lhp, McClintock HS, Tempe, Ariz.**
4. **Andrew Lorraine, lhp, Stanford University.**
5. **Jose Cintron, rhp, Yabucoa, P.R.**

**Trot Nixon.** North Carolina high school outfielder was picked by Boston with the seventh pick of the 1993 draft.

KEN BABBITT

6. **Geoff Edsell, rhp, Old Dominion University.**
7. **George Arias, 3b, University of Arizona.**
8. **Tim Harkrider, ss, University of Texas.**
9. **Jamie Burke, 3b, Oregon State University.**
10. **Willard Brown, rhp, Stetson University.**
11. Greg Romo, rhp, Wasco Union HS, Wasco, Calif.
12. **Todd Greene, of, Georgia Southern University.**
13. **Kevin Ham, of, Eastwood HS, El Paso, Texas.**
14. John Pollard, of, Jersey Village HS, Houston.
15. Terrance Freeman, 2b, Bloomingdale HS, Brandon, Fla.
16. Sidney Newman, ss, Cordova HS, Rancho Cordova, Calif.
17. **Derrin Doty, of, University of Washington.**
18. **Bryan Harris, lhp, Florida State University.**
19. **Jeffrey Bawlson, lhp, Hillsborough (Fla.) CC.**
20. **Geoff Grenert, rhp, University of Nevada-Reno.**
21. **Aaron Iatarola, of, Stetson University.**
22. **Aaron Puffer, rhp, Creighton University.**
23. **Brooks Drysdale, rhp, Santa Clara University.**
24. **John Bushart, lhp, Cal State Northridge.**
25. Carl Caddell, lhp, Wyatt HS, Fort Worth, Texas.
26. **Shawn Slade, rhp, University of Tampa.**
27. Kevin Culmo, rhp, Sacramento (Calif.) CC.
28. Casey Snow, c, Crespi HS, Encino, Calif.
29. Timothy Moran, 1b, Chabot (Calif.) JC.
30. Steven Goodell, ss, Chabot (Calif.) JC.
31. Daniel Petroff, rhp, Gulf Coast (Fla.) CC.
32. Carlos Pagan, c, Vega Baja, P.R.
33. Keith Luuloa, ss, Modesto (Calif.) JC.
34. Brendon Cowsill, 3b, Crescenta Valley HS, La Crescenta, Calif.
35. Scott Rivette, rhp, Citrus (Calif.) JC.
36. Todd Stubblefield, rhp-1b, Cooper City (Fla.) HS.
37. Bryan Smithson, lhp, Santa Barbara (Calif.) HS.
38. Everard Griffiths, rhp, Miami-Dade CC North.
39. Adam Brick, c, Brandon (Fla.) HS.
40. David Johnson, rhp, Baxter Springs (Kan.) HS.
41. Gary Stevenson, rhp, Hart HS, Valencia, Calif.
42. Howard Pride, of, Butler HS, Huntsville, Ala.
43. Marshall Faulk, of, San Diego State University.
44. Richard Gonzalez, c, Indian River (Fla.) CC.
45. Richard Nadeau, of, Kennedy HS, Granada Hills, Calif.
46. Ryan Folmar, c, Chambersburg (Pa.) Area HS.
47. Brian Boeth, rhp, Pensacola (Fla.) JC.
48. Kyle Richardson, 3b, Casa Grande (Ariz.) HS.
49. Randi Mallard, c-of, Gainesville (Ga.) HS.
50. Alvin Casillas, rhp, Caguas, P.R.
51. William Perusek, rhp, Hillsborough (Fla.) CC.

52. David Robinson, of, Gulf Coast (Fla.) CC.
53. Rafael Gutierrez, of, Levittown, P.R.
54. Matt Schafer, c, Hillsborough (Fla.) CC.
55. Shawn Coolidge, of, Dunedin (Fla.) HS.
56. Daryl Porter, of, St. Thomas Aquinas HS, Fort Lauderdale, Fla.
57. David Supple, c, Notre Dame HS, Northridge, Calif.

## CHICAGO CUBS (10)

1. **Brooks Kieschnick, of-rhp, University of Texas.**
1. **Jon Ratliff, rhp, LeMoyne College** (Choice from Braves as compensation for Type A free agent Greg Maddux).
1. **Kevin Orie, ss, Indiana University** (Supplemental choice—29th—for loss of Maddux).
2. (Choice to Rangers as compensation for Type A free agent Jose Guzman).
3. **Vee Hightower, of, Vanderbilt University.**
4. **Miguel Montilla, ss, North Bergen (N.J.) HS.**
5. Matt Miller, lhp, Monterey HS, Lubbock, Texas.
6. **Pat Cline, c, Manatee HS, Bradenton, Fla.**
7. **Scott Kendrick, rhp, Monroe-Woodbury HS, Central Valley, N.Y.**
8. **Chris Bryant, lhp, Brandon (Fla.) HS.**
9. **Bob Morris, 3b, University of Iowa.**
10. Jamey Price, rhp, Texarkana (Texas) CC.
11. **Steven Rain, rhp, Walnut (Calif.) HS.**
12. **Gabe Whatley, of, Vanderbilt University.**
13. **Tony Locey, rhp, Columbus College.**
14. **Jose Molina, c, Vega Alta, P.R.**
15. **Brad Chambers, of-rhp, Midlothian (Va.) HS.**
16. **Wade Walker, rhp, Northeast Louisiana University.**
17. Robert Duncan, 3b, Central Florida CC.
18. Nathan Dunn, ss, Vestavia Hills HS, Birmingham, Ala.
19. **Alfredo Garcia, rhp, Buena Park (Calif.) HS.**
20. **Nate Thomas, lhp-1b, First Colonial HS, Virginia Beach, Va.**
21. **David Hutcheson, rhp, University of South Florida.**
22. Gary Burnham, of, South Windsor (Conn.) HS.
23. **Gilbert Avalos, ss, Alvin (Texas) CC.**
24. **John Rodgers, c, Rice University.**
25. James Hamilton, lhp, Turner Ashby HS, Weyers Cove, Va.
26. **Andrew Devries, lhp, Manatee (Fla.) JC.**
27. **Ronald Smith, 1b, Southern University.**
28. **John Sauer, of, Patterson HS, Baltimore.**
29. **Gregory Hillman, lhp, University of Texas.**
30. **David Weber, rhp, Marist HS, Jersey City, N.J.**
31. **Kenneth Jones, of, Middle Georgia JC.**
32. **Gabe Duross, 1b-of, University of Maine.**
33. **Doug Alongi, of, Rutgers University.**
34. **Sean Fric, of, Alvin (Texas) CC.**
35. **Jared Snyder, c, Nicholls State University.**
36. **Frank Cicero, c, La Mirada (Calif.) HS.**
37. Adam Robinson, 2b, West Morris Central HS, Long Valley, N.J.
38. **Daniel Gil, of, Mission Bay HS, San Diego.**
39. Kelvin Barnes, ss-of, Lake City (Fla.) CC.
40. **Bo Porter, of, University of Iowa.**
41. **Gary Beashore, rhp, Missouri Western State College.**
42. **Jose DeJesus, 3b, Patillas, P.R.**
43. **Jason Dunn, rhp, Raritan Valley (N.J.) CC.**
44. **Mark Lavenia, lhp, University of South Carolina-Aiken.**
45. **James Young, of, Valdosta State College.**
46. Jose Peraza, lhp, Norwalk (Calif.) HS.
47. **Shawn Hill, rhp, Nicholls State University.**
48. **William Vieilleux, ss, Hartford HS, White River Jct., Vt.**
49. **Gamalier Castro, lhp, Aguadilla, P.R.**
50. **Thomas Ball, lhp, Cal State Dominguez Hills.**
51. **Sean Hogan, lhp, Morehead State University.**
52. **Demetrius Dowler, 2b-of, Indiana State University.**
53. **Rodd Kurtz, lhp, University of Texas-Pan American.**
54. **Greg Twiggs, lhp, Brewton Parker College.**
55. **Stephen Kulpa, ss, Quinnipiac College.**
56. Javier Herrera, rhp, Miami (Fla.) HS.
57. **Michael Gibson, of-2b, Bowie State University.**
58. **Artis Johnson, of, Florida A&M University.**
59. **Ralph Eusebio, of, Brevard (Fla.) CC.**
60. **Joe Biernat, ss, University of South Carolina.**
61. **Brett McCabe, 1b, Centenary College.**
62. **Thomas King, of, Valdosta State College.**
63. **Tony Khoury, c-rhp, Ohio State University.**
64. **Sean Davisson, 2b-of, Long Beach State University.**
65. Dustin Wilkinson, 3b, Shaw HS, Columbus, Ga.
66. Rob Carpenter, of, University of Southern Maine.
67. Gregory Denly, rhp, Valdosta (Ga,) HS.
68. Scott Stephens, lhp, Eau Gallie HS, Melbourne, Fla.
69. Anthony Dellamano, rhp, Pierce (Calif.) JC.
70. Chris Price, rhp, Goddard HS, Roswell, N.M.
71. Cory Lima, 1b-of, Redan HS, Stone Mountain, Ga.

72. Danier Anderson, of, Tioga HS, Pineville, La.
73. Jose Castillo, lhp, Falfurrias (Texas) HS.
74. **Jason Maxwell, ss, Middle Tennessee State University.**
75. Shawn Knight, ss, College of William & Mary.
76. **James Farrow, rhp, Brewton Parker College.**
77. **Jamil Cunningham, ss, Bethune-Cookman College.**
78. Steve Everson, of, Valdosta (Ga.) HS.
79. Robert Baldwin, of, Duke University.
80. Clarence Williams, c-1b, Crescent City (Fla.) HS.
81. Anthony Rich, ss, Rollins College.
82. James Huntley, ss, West Mecklenburg HS, Charlotte, N.C.

## CHICAGO WHITE SOX (17)

1. **Scott Christman, lhp, Oregon State University.**
2. **Greg Norton, 3b, University of Oklahoma.**
3. **Joe Bales, rhp, Reed HS, Sparks, Nev.**
4. Dennis Twombley, c, Patrick Henry HS, San Diego.
5. **David Lundquist, rhp, Cochise County (Ariz.) CC.**
6. **Craig McClure, of, Columbine HS, Littleton, Colo.**
7. **Ben Boulware, 2b-of, Cal Poly San Luis Obispo.**
8. **Jason Goligoski, ss, Western Montana College.**
9. **Rich Pratt, lhp, University of South Carolina.**
10. **Zane Leiber, rhp, Central Arizona JC.**
11. **Tom Fordham, lhp, Grossmont (Calif.) JC.**
12. **Sandy McKinnon, of, Middle Georgia JC.**
13. **Steve Friedrich, of, Fullerton (Calif.) JC.**
14. **Bill Proctor, rhp, Western Oregon State College.**
15. **Mike Sirotka, lhp, Louisiana State University.**
16. **Billy Joe Hobert, of, University of Washington.**
17. **Scott Vollmer, c, Pepperdine University.**
18. Bill Mobilia, ss, University of Minnesota.
19. **Rich Carone, c, University of Mississippi.**
20. **Brian Woods, rhp, Fairleigh Dickinson University.**
21. **Andrew McCormack, lhp, University of South Florida.**
22. **Curtis Broome, rhp, University of Evansville.**
23. **John Quirk, lhp, Westchester (N.Y.) CC.**
24. **Jim Dixon, rhp, New Mexico State University.**
25. Joel Peters, ss, Lincoln HS, Vincennes, Ind.
26. **Harold Williams, of, Livingston University.**
27. Chris Olson, lhp, Alvin (Texas) HS.
28. Alex Prejean, rhp, Clear Lake HS, Houston.
29. Travis Rapp, c, Sebring (Fla.) HS.
30. Tim Fuhrman, rhp, Casa Roble HS, Orangevale, Calif.
31. Jory Diamond, rhp, Tallahassee (Fla.) CC.
32. Jeff Abbott, of, University of Kentucky.
33. **Jim Schlotter, rhp, Rider College.**
34. **David Moore, 3b, Dr. Phillips HS, Orlando, Fla.**
35. Ricky Garcia, rhp, Mesa (Ariz.) CC.
36. Brad Harker, 1b, Lawrence (Kan.) HS.
37. **William Baldwin, rhp, Florida Memorial College.**
38. Jim Gargiulo, c, Coconut Creek (Fla.) HS.
39. Ryan Roberts, ss, Utah Valley CC.
40. Joshua Whittenton, 3b, Auburndale (Fla.) HS.
41. Brandon Berger, c, Beechwood HS, Fort Mitchell, Ky.
42. Anthony Guerra, c, North Miami (Fla.) HS.
43. Carey Schueler, lhp-1b, Campolindo HS, Moraga, Calif.
44. **Todd Hall, ss, Cal State Sacramento.**
45. **Frank Menechino, 2b, University of Alabama.**
46. Marty Patterson, c, Croswell-Lexington HS, Croswell, Mich.
47. Gorky Estrella, 3b, George Washington HS, New York.
48. Mario Valdez, 1b, Miami (Fla.) HS.
49. Placido Polanco, 2b, Miami-Dade CC Wolfson.

## CINCINNATI REDS (20)

1. (Choice to Twins as compensation for Type A free agent John Smiley).
1. **Pat Watkins, of, East Carolina University** (Supplemental choice—32nd—for loss of Type A free agent Greg Swindell).
2. **Scott Sullivan, rhp, Auburn University**
3. **Steve Wilkerson, rhp, Grand Canyon University** (Choice from Astros as compensation for Swindell).
3. **Brad Tweedlie, rhp, Western Carolina University.**
4. **Samuel Osorio, of, Loiza, P.R.**
5. **Paul Bako, c, University of Southwestern Louisiana.**
6. David Caldwell, lhp, Northeast Texas CC.
7. **Darran Hall, of, Lincoln HS, San Diego.**
8. **Pete Harvell, lhp, University of Tennessee.**
9. John Ambrose, rhp, Memorial HS, Evansville, Ind.
10. **Chris Sexton, of-2b, Miami (Ohio) University.**
11. **Joel Franklin, rhp, Southwestern (Calif.) JC.**
12. **Doug Durrwachter, ss, University of Texas-Arlington.**
13. **James Lofton, ss, Los Angeles CC.**
14. J.J. Picollo, c, George Mason University.
15. Jason Ruskey, lhp, Triton (Ill.) JC.
16. **Jackie McCroskey, of, Male HS, Louisville, Ky.**

17. Matt Purkiss, 3b, Redwood HS, Visalia, Calif.
18. Jeff Niemeier, c, University of Kansas.
19. **Trey Rutledge, rhp, Louisiana State University.**
20. **Peter Magre, rhp, St. Mary's (Texas) University.**
21. James Emiliano, rhp, Odessa (Texas) JC.
22. **David McKenzie, rhp, Northwood (Texas) Institute.**
23. Anthony Johnson, of, Brookdale (N.J.) CC.
24. **Stephen Gann, 2b, Dallas Baptist University.**
25. **David Chandler, rhp, Morehead State University.**
26. **Donald Broach, of, Cincinnati.**
27. Alejandro Sanchez, rhp, Ontario (Calif.) HS.
28. **Jason Baker, of, Allegany (Md.) CC.**
29. **Jon Hebel, rhp, Auburn University.**
30. Scott Shores, of, Arizona State University.
31. **Michael Moses, lhp, University of Wyoming.**
32. **Cobi Cradle, of, Long Beach State University.**
33. **Steven Eddie, ss, University of Iowa.**
34. **Chad Akers, ss, West Virginia State College.**
35. Scott Wilson, 3b, San Dieguito HS, Carlsbad, Calif.
36. Brian Jergenson, of-1b, Lacrescent (Minn.) HS.
37. Michael Bauder, lhp, Western HS, Las Vegas.
38. Chad Allen, of, Duncanville (Texas) HS.
39. Rommel Motley, of, Riverside (Calif.) CC.
40. **Jonathon Dold, of, St. John's (Minn.) University.**
41. James Debruin, rhp, Calhoun HS, Seadrift, Texas.
42. Damon Miller, c, Washington HS, Cherokee, Iowa.
43. **Danny Hagan, lhp, Louisville, Ky.**

## CLEVELAND INDIANS (11)

1. **Daron Kirkreit, rhp, UC Riverside.**
2. **Casey Whitten, lhp, Indiana State University**
3. **J.J. Done, rhp, Pace HS, Miami.**
4. **Travis Driskill, rhp, Texas Tech.**
5. **Kris Hanson, rhp, University of Wisconsin-Whitewater.**
6. **Matt Hobble, of, Sarasota (Fla.) HS.**
7. Seth Greisinger, rhp, McLean HS, Falls Church, Va.
8. **Steve Kline, lhp, West Virginia University.**
9. **Greg Thomas, 1b, Vanderbilt University.**
10. Derrick Cook, rhp, Robert E. Lee HS, Staunton, Va.
11. **Jason Mackey, lhp, Lower Columbia (Wash.) JC.**
12. Jeffrey Haag, c, Florida Southern College.
13. **Steven Soliz, c, Cal State Los Angeles.**
14. Todd Betts, 3b, Northeastern Oklahoma A&M JC.
15. **Roland De la Maza, rhp, Cal State Sacramento.**
16. **Mike Neal, 3b-ss, Louisiana State University.**
17. **Robert Lewis, c, Texas A&M University.**
18. **Todd Johnson, c, Fresno State University.**
19. **Blair Hodson, 1b, Yale University.**
20. **Brett Palmer, lhp, Idaho Falls (Idaho) HS.**
21. **Eric Chapman, of, University of South Carolina-Aiken.**
22. **Chris Plumlee, rhp, Arkansas State University.**
23. Steve Hagins, c, University HS, Irvine, Calif.
24. **Rich Sexson, 1b, Prairie HS, Brush Prairie, Wash.**
25. **Robert Kulle, of, LeMoyne College.**
26. **Norman Williams, of, Chipola (Fla.) JC.**
27. **Ryan Lefebvre, of, University of Minnesota.**
28. **Richard Prieto, 2b-ss, Carmel, Calif.**
29. **Richard King, ss, Concordia (Texas) College.**
30. Greg Tippin, 1b, Cypress (Calif.) JC.
31. Jamie Coons, of, Edgewood (Md.) HS.
32. **Richard Lemons, of, University of Arizona.**
33. **Gerad Cawhorn, 3b, San Jose State University.**
34. Ken Westmoreland, rhp, Austin HS, Decatur, Ala.
35. Randy Woodall, rhp, Sheffield (Ala.) HS.
36. **Rodney Holland, of, Schriener (Texas) College.**
37. Ted Warrecker, c, Hancock (Calif.) JC.
38. Michael Rodriguez, c-of, Brandeis HS, New York.
39. David Townsend, rhp, Hinds (Miss.) CC.
40. Ara Petrosian, rhp, Fountain Valley (Calif.) HS.
41. **Jason Lyman, 2b, Cal State San Bernardino.**
42. Nisam Bean, ss, Kennedy HS, Richmond, Calif.
43. **Dalton Dempsey, lhp, Southwest Texas State University.**
44. Marvin Pierce, rhp, Lassen (Calif.) JC.
45. **Darnell Batiste, of, Sam Houston HS, Arlington, Texas.**
46. Jeff Bell, ss, Pinson Valley (Ala.) HS.
47. David Roberts, of, UCLA.
48. David Stevenson, of-1b, Los Angeles Valley JC.
48. Larry Dobson, of, Putnam City HS, Oklahoma City.
50. Poncho Ruiz, 2b, Esperanza HS, Placentia, Calif.
51. Samuel Mitchell, rhp, Navarro (Texas) JC.
52. Bret Soverel, rhp, Martin County HS, Palm City, Fla.
53. Aaron Gentry, ss, Claremore (Okla.) HS.
54. **Kevin Dinnen, rhp, Barry University.**
55. Robert Kinnee, rhp, Marshall HS, Portland, Ore.
56. Carlos Arellano, rhp, Granada HS, Livermore, Calif.

**Daron Kirkreit.** Cleveland selected the former UC Riverside righthander and U.S. Olympic team pitcher with the 12th pick.

57. Angelo Rodriguez, rhp, Isabella, P.R.
58. **Tony Runion, rhp, Duke University.**
59. Brian Basowski, of, Pierce (Calif.) JC.
60. Vincent Griffin, of, South Suburban (Ill.) JC.
61. Brian Norris, rhp, Stephen F. Austin HS, Port Arthur, Texas.
62. Ken Vining, lhp, Cardinal Newman HS, Columbia, S.C.
63. Jeffrey Kober, lhp, Jefferson (Wis.) HS.
64. Roger Walker, c, Florida CC.
65. Casey Swingley, rhp, Lower Columbia (Wash.) JC.
66. Jason Vorhauer, 1b, Fairfield HS, Suisun City, Calif.
67. **Bryan Garrett, of, Florida International University.**
68. Keith Cowley, 3b, Westminster (Calif.) HS.
69. Joseph Adams, rhp, Freeman HS, Richmond, Va.
70. Travis Peterson, of, Edmonds (Wash.) CC.
71. **Pedro Marte, 2b-of, Florida Memorial College.**
72. **Jason Marshall, c, Baylor University.**

## COLORADO ROCKIES (28)

1. **Jamey Wright, rhp, Westmoore HS, Oklahoma City, Okla.**
2. **Bryan Rekar, rhp, Bradley University.**
3. **Joel Moore, rhp, Bradley University.**
4. **Doug Walls, rhp, Muscatine (Iowa) CC.**
5. **Mike Zolecki, rhp, St. Mary's (Texas) University.**
6. **Chad Gambill, of, Clearwater (Fla.) HS.**
7. **John Thomson, rhp, Blinn (Texas) JC.**
8. **Kyle Houser, ss, Duncanville (Texas) HS.**
9. **John Myrow, of, UCLA.**
10. **Edgard Velazquez, of, Guaynabo, P.R.**
11. **Jacob Viano, rhp, Long Beach (Calif.) CC.**
12. **Keith Grunewald, ss, University of North Carolina.**
13. **Derrick Gibson, of, Haines City (Fla.) HS.**
14. **Bob Lasbury, rhp, Manhattanville (N.Y.) College.**
15. Casey Davis, of, Corsicana (Texas) HS.
16. **Nate Holdren, 1b, University of Michigan.**
17. **Kevin Wehn, rhp, Florida International University.**
18. **Morgan Burdick, rhp, Clovis HS, Dunlap, Calif.**
19. **Jason Johnson, rhp, Auburn University.**
20. **John Giudice, of, Eastern Connecticut State University.**
21. **Derrick Calvin, rhp, Southern University.**
22. **Mike Higgins, c, Rutgers University.**
23. **Martin Dewitt, lhp, Mesa (Ariz.) CC.**

STAN DENNY

24. Jason Smith, c, University of Texas-Arlington.
25. Jamie Anderson, ss, Hanover (Ind.) College.
26. Curt Conley, lhp, Ball State University.
27. Raymond Hoover, c, Cedar Cliff HS, Camp Hill, Pa.
28. Mario Munoz, 3b, Mesa State (Colo.) College.
29. Dan Barry, lhp, West Virginia University.
30. Mark Brownson, rhp, Wellington (Fla.) Community HS.
31. Patrick McClinton, lhp, Bellarmine College.
32. Dennis McAdams, rhp, Palomar (Calif.) JC.
33. Dominic Demark, of, Mesa (Ariz.) CC.
34. Ben Ortman, of, University of Portland.
35. Philip Davis, rhp, Yuma (Ariz.) HS.
36. Dan Butcher, rhp, Diablo Valley (Calif.) JC.
37. Enrigue Melendez, ss, Ensenada, P.R.
38. Darin Baugh, ss, Serra HS, San Mateo, Calif.
39. Brandon Nickens, rhp, Pierce (Calif.) JC.
40. Terry Jones, of, University of North Alabama.
41. Justin Liniak, of, San Dieguito HS, Encinitas, Calif.
42. Brian Culp, c, Kansas State University.
43. Larry Green, c, JC of Eastern Utah.
44. Johnathan Delya, rhp, Crescent-Iroquois HS, Crescent City, Ill.
45. Andrew Keehn, rhp, Central Arizona JC.
46. Joshua Jensen, rhp, Mountain Crest HS, Providence, Utah.
47. Marc D'Allessandro, lhp, St. John Vianney HS, Hazlet, N.J.
48. Bradley Molcak, ss, Cardston (Alberta) HS.
49. Philip Schneider, lhp, Rutgers University.
50. William Eden, lhp, Motlow State (Tenn.) CC.
51. Michael Dewitt, rhp, Pine Plains (N.Y.) HS.
52. Ryan Ware, ss, Jersey Village HS, Houston.
53. Marty Remmers, rhp, Riverbank HS, Modesto, Calif.
54. Brett Bibeau, rhp, Bishop Kelly HS, Boise, Idaho.
55. Brandon Knight, 2b, Buena HS, Oxnard, Calif.
56. Chris Cooper, 2b, Mesa (Ariz.) CC.
57. David Melendez, rhp, Blinn (Texas) JC.
58. Anders Stahl, c, Anderson (Calif.) HS.
59. Frank Chelbian, lhp, Middlesex (N.J.) CC.
60. David Mineer, rhp, Utah State University.

## DETROIT TIGERS (9)

1. Matt Brunson, ss, Cherry Creek HS, Englewood, Colo.
2. Tony Fuduric, rhp, Cardinal HS, Middlefield, Ohio.
3. Cameron Smith, rhp, Ithaca College.
4. Michael Wilson, rhp, Blinn (Texas) JC.
5. Jason Bass, of, O'Dea HS, Seattle.
6. Brian Moehler, rhp, UNC-Greensboro.
7. Greg Granger, rhp, Lake City (Fla.) CC.
8. Drew Christmon, of, University of Oklahoma.
9. Lonny Landry, of, Flagler (Fla.) College.
10. R.A. Dickey, rhp, Montgomery Bell Academy, Nashville.
11. Glen Barker, of, College of St. Rose (N.Y.).
12. Bryan Corey, ss, Pierce (Calif.) JC.
13. Eddie Gaillard, rhp, Florida Southern College.
14. Keith Foulke, rhp, Galveston (Texas) JC.
15. Bobby Jones, of, Riverside (Calif.) CC.
16. David Crafton, c, Lyons Township HS, LaGrange Park, Ill.
17. Mike Salazar, lhp, Fresno State University.

**Matt Brunson.** Detroit tabbed the slick-fielding Colorado high school shortstop with the ninth overall selection in the 1993 draft.

18. Sean Wooten, c, Mt. San Antonio (Calif.) JC.
19. Javier Cardona, c, Dorado, P.R.
20. Brandon Kent, rhp, Duncanville (Texas) HS.
21. Chris Wyrick, ss, University of Missouri.
22. Billy Thompson, c, University of Kentucky.
23. Corey Broome, c, University of North Carolina-Wilmington.
24. Matt Beech, lhp, University of Houston.
25. Shawn Brown, 2b, Rider College.
26. Matt Skrmetta, rhp, Jacksonville University.
27. Eric Danapilis, of, University of Notre Dame.
28. Steve Dietz, ss, San Diego State University.
29. Jason Hamilton, 1b, St Joseph's (Pa.) University.
30. Joshua Neese, rhp, Southwestern Oklahoma State Univ.
31. Will Hunt, lhp, Louisiana State University.
32. Roderick Jackson, rhp, Jackson State University.
33. Craig Tupper, c, Cal State Hayward.
34. Mike Wiseley, of, Eastern Michigan University.
35. George Abernathy, of, Pensacola (Fla.) JC.
36. Kirk Ordway, 2b, Portland State University.
37. Michael Goralczyk, lhp, Niles (Mich.) HS.
38. Gabe Sollecito, rhp, UCLA.
39. David Malenfant, rhp, Kearsley HS, Flint, Mich.
40. Samuel Arguto, rhp, Jacksonville University.
41. Adam Rodriguez, c, Oklahoma City University.
42. Scott Conant, ss, Western Michigan University.
43. Michael Richardson, rhp, San Diego State University.
44. Joel Hillebrand, rhp, Roosevelt HS, Wyandotte, Mich.
45. Brandon Reed, rhp, West HS, Lapeer, Mich.
46. Brian Rios, ss, Riverside (Calif.) CC.
47. Tyrone Dixon, of, University of South Alabama.
48. Justin Bettencourt, lhp, Cabrillo (Calif.) JC.
49. Anthony Jackson, of, Louisburg (N.C.) JC.
50. Brian Wilkes, c, Bishop Kenny HS, Jacksonville.
51. Michael Martino, rhp, Grand Blanc (Mich.) HS.
52. Rich Hartmann, rhp, Long Island University.
53. Gary Goldsmith, rhp, New Mexico State University.
54. Kiko Palacios, c, Southwestern (Calif.) JC.
55. Lloyd Wade, c, Escambia HS, Pensacola, Fla.
56. Bradley Lee, lhp, Delaware Tech & CC.
57. Jeffrey Barker, rhp, Riverside (Calif.) CC.
58. Anthony Williams, rhp, Fort Walton Beach (Fla.) HS.
59. Rob Welles, 1b, Pepperdine University.
60. Graham Koonce, of, Julian (Calif.) HS.
61. Carlton Washington, of, University of Texas-El Paso.
62. Nathan Smith, ss-of, Bonanza HS, Las Vegas.
63. Adam Finnieston, of, Gulf Coast (Fla.) CC.
64. Justin Duckwiler, c, Bonanza HS, Las Vegas.
65. Terry Tripp, ss, Harrisburg (Ill.) HS.

## FLORIDA MARLINS (27)

1. Marc Valdes, rhp, University of Florida.
2. John Roskos, c, Cibola HS, Rio Rancho, N.M.
3. Dan Ehler, rhp, South Hills HS, Covina, Calif.
4. Thomas Howard, lhp, Titusville (Fla.) HS.
5. Ernie Delgado, rhp, Sunnyside HS, Tucson.
6. Paul Thornton, rhp, Georgia Southern University.
7. Todd Dunwoody, of, Harrison HS, West Lafayette, Ind.
8. Billy McMillon, of, Clemson University.
9. Brady Babin, ss, St. Amant HS, Gonzales, La.
10. Ryan Filbeck, rhp, Rancho Santiago (Calif.) JC.
11. Damon Johnson, 3b, Crossett (Ark. ) HS.
12. Jason Fawcett, rhp, Robert E. Lee HS, Montgomery, Ala.
13. David Jefferson, of, Palo Alto (Calif.) HS.
14. Mike Sims, c, Cal State Northridge.
15. Erik Robinson, of, West Orange HS, Winter Park, Fla.
16. Scott Southard, ss, University of South Alabama.
17. Don Matthews, rhp, Lower Columbia (Wash.) JC.
18. Thomas Giles, lhp, Thomas Jefferson HS, Carter Lake, Iowa.
19. Richard Seminoff, lhp, Grand Canyon University.
20. Bryan Ward, lhp, University of South Carolina-Aiken.
21. Greg Mix, rhp, Stanford University.
22. Dan Chergey, rhp, Cal Poly San Luis Obispo.
23. Ivory Jones, of, Contra Costa (Calif.) JC.
24. Ronnie Brown, of, Mississippi State University.
25. Richard Dishman, rhp, Archbishop Molloy HS, Jamaica, N.Y.
26. Matt Martinez, 2b, Cal State Sacramento.
27. Andy Small, 3b, Cal State Northridge.
28. Tony Darden, ss, Northeast Texas CC.
29. Samuel Minyard, lhp, The Masters (Calif.) College.
30. Justin Long, ss, Riverside (Calif.) CC.
31. Justin Mark, rhp, Lassen (Calif.) JC.
32. Matthew Wells, rhp, Quincy (Calif.) HS.
33. Zachary Stark, lhp, David Lipscomb (Tenn.) College.
34. Jeffrey Lewis, of, Dundalk (Md.) CC.
35. Eric Genden, of, Taravella HS, Coral Springs, Fla.

JOHN LEYBA

36. Brett Ames, lhp, Pima (Ariz.) CC.
37. Brandon Villafuerte, rhp, Live Oak HS, Morgan Hill, Calif.
**38. Dave Berg, 2b, University of Miami (Fla.).**
39. James Merritt, rhp, South Georgia JC.
40. Derrick Johnson, of, Ewing HS, Trenton, N.J.
41. Eric Sees, ss, Santa Margarita HS, San Juan Capistrano, Calif.
42. Chad Phillips, lhp, Clemson University.
43. Ian Roberts, of, Mountain View HS, Vancouver, Wash.
**44. Greg Hubley, of, JC of San Mateo (Calif.).**
45. Bobby Howry, rhp, Yavapai (Ariz.) JC.
**46. Jon Van Zandt, rhp, UCLA.**
47. (void) Rafael Corrales, rhp, Niles West HS, Skokie, Ill.
48. Josh Deakman, of, Riverside (Calif.) CC.
49. Michael Reyes, of, Wayland Baptist University.
50. Mark Creelman, 1b, Ulster (N.Y.) JC.
51. Leslie Sean, lhp, Mendocino (Calif.) CC.
52. Ward White, 1b, Hug HS, Reno, Nev.
53. Jason Russell, rhp, Chattahoochee Valley (Ala.) CC.
54. Charles Bivens, of, Taft (Calif.) JC.
55. Diallo Banks, rhp, West Point (Miss.) HS.
56. David Harper, rhp, Mansfield (Texas) HS.
57. Michael Myers, c, Gaithersburg (Md.) HS.
58. Marc Lee, of, Calvert HS, Tiffin, Ohio.
59. Chad Ricketts, rhp, East Lake HS, Palm Harbor, Fla.
60. Daniel Sousa, of, Mendocino (Calif.) CC.
61. Michael Rios, rhp, University of the Pacific.
62. Casey Baker, of, McLane HS, Fresno, Calif.
63. Chris Sauritch, ss, Southern Illinois University.
64. Robert Cowan, rhp, Saugus (Calif.) HS.
65. James Gann, rhp, Norman (Okla.) HS.
66. Todd Teeter, c, West Orange HS, Winter Park, Fla.
67. Chris Hendrix, c, Oakland HS, Murfreesboro, Tenn.
68. Anthony Longueira, ss, Cooper City (Fla.) HS.
69. Larry Barnes, 1b, Bakersfield (Calif.) JC.
**70. Brian Deskins, lhp, University of Nebraska.**
71. Cameron Jones, ss, Millwood HS, Oklahoma City.
**72. Franklin Roberts, rhp, Seaford (Del.) HS.**
73. Brent Yarrow, of, Chemainus (B.C.) HS.
74. Brian Reid, 2b, Corona del Sol HS, Phoenix.
75. Eric Johnson, of, South Georgia JC.
76. David Bernhard, rhp, Monterey Peninsula (Calif.) JC.
77. Kenny Williams, of, Independence HS, San Jose, Calif.
78. Allen Stalvey, of, Columbia HS, Lake City, Fla.
79. Charles Roberson, rhp, Franklin HS, Seattle.
80. Dustin Spencer, ss, Santa Barbara (Calif.) HS.
81. Michael Logan, rhp, Dougherty HS, Albany, Ga.
82. Richard Bell, rhp, Crater HS, Central Point, Ore.
83. John Woodard, rhp, Cartersville (Ga.) HS.
84. Theron Truitt, of, LaGrange (Ga.) HS.
85. Jerry Whaley, c, McIntosh County Academy, Darien, Ga.
86. Stephen Haggard, rhp, Southern Arkansas University.
87. Jason Mann, rhp, First Colonial HS, Virginia Beach, Va.
88. Cabott Woods, rhp, Princeton (Ind.) Community HS.
89. Jason Dyer, of, Shawnee (Okla.) HS.
90. Tom Buckman, rhp, Broward (Fla.) CC.
91. Shawn Summers, of, University of Tennessee.

## HOUSTON ASTROS (12)

**1. Billy Wagner, lhp, Ferrum (Va.) College.**
2. (Choice to Pirates as compensation for Type A free agent Doug Drabek).
3. (Choice to Reds as compensation for Type A free agent Greg Swindell).
**4. Steve Verduzco, ss, San Jose, Calif.**
**5. Derek Root, 1b, St. Edward HS, Lakewood, Ohio.**
**6. Jamie Saylor, ss, North Garland HS, Garland, Texas.**
7. Jaime Bluma, rhp, Wichita State University.
**8. Mike Diorio, rhp, Seward County (Kan.) CC.**
**9. Brett Callan, c, San Diego Mesa JC.**
**10. Kary Bridges, 3b, University of Mississippi.**
**11. Edward Lewis, rhp, Central Missouri State University.**
**12. William Hartnett, rhp, Northeastern University.**
13. Rolando Avila, of, Los Angeles Harbor JC.
**14. Tim Forkner, 3b, Seward County (Kan.) CC.**
**15. Troy Schulte, rhp, Creighton University.**
**16. Grant Gosch, of, Serra HS, San Mateo, Calif.**
**17. Mark Dorencz, ss, Illinois State University.**
**18. Tim Kester, rhp, Florida International University.**
**19. Jon Phillips, lhp, St. Bonaventure University.**
**20. John Vindivich, of, Southeastern Louisiana University.**
**21. Jason Turley, rhp, Brighton HS, Sandy, Utah.**
22. Jay Vaught, rhp, University of Texas.
23. Landon Hessler, rhp, Brooksville-Hernando HS, Brooksville, Fla.
24. Jon Cannon, lhp, Gunn HS, Los Altos, Calif.
**25. Michael Walter, rhp, Palomar (Calif.) JC.**

26. **Tom Czanstkowski, rhp, University of Arkansas.**
27. **Trevor Froschauer, 1b-c, Lincoln Land (Ill.) CC.**
28. **Klint Klaas, 2b, Iowa Western CC.**
29. Steven Keen, rhp, Baldwin (Fla.) HS.
30. David Green, rhp, Port Hope (Ont.) & District HS.
31. **Brock Steinke, rhp, Washington HS, Cedar Rapids, Iowa.**
32. Duane Eason, rhp, Hackensack (N.J.) HS.
33. **Ted Wieczorek, 1b-3b, Southern California College.**
34. Joseph Painich, rhp, West Monroe (La.) HS.
35. Jerry Brandon, 2b, Airline HS, Bossier City, La.
36. Ryan Kelly, rhp, Amarillo (Texas) HS.
37. Rafael Corrales, rhp, Niles West HS, Skokie, Ill.
38. Joshua Halemanu, of, Mission (Calif.) JC.
39. **Daniel Dolney, c, New Trier HS, Wilmette, Ill.**
40. Todd Cook, rhp, Tavares (Fla.) HS.
41. Jonathan Lawrence, ss-2b, Columbus (Ga.) HS.
42. **Terry Beyna, 3b, Illinois State University.**
43. Anthony Mack, of, Los Angeles Harbor JC.
44. **Bryant Nelson, ss, Texarkana (Texas) JC.**
45. Ryan O'Toole, rhp, Irvine (Calif.) HS.
46. Mike Bustamonte, lhp, Eisenhower HS, Rialto, Calif.
47. Chris Bowker, rhp, Dillon (Mon.) HS.
48. Jeremy Miller, ss, Connelsville HS, Mill Run, Pa.
49. James Sapp, of, Geneva (N.Y.) HS.
50. **Ryan Campbell, rhp, Hoover HS, Fresno, Calif.**
51. Paul Powell, lhp, Denison (Texas) HS.
52. Nassim Hijazi, lhp, Downey HS, Bellflower, Calif.
53. **Scott Eidle, c, Yale University.**
54. Patrick Bell, rhp, Asheboro (N.C.) HS.
55. **Shawn Bartle, rhp, McLennan (Texas) CC.**
56. **Chad White, of, University of Maine.**
57. **Richard Humphrey, rhp, Liberty University.**
58. **Yamil Lopez, ss, Puerto Nuevo, P.R.**
59. **Chad Crossley, rhp, University of South Florida.**
60. Pat Maxwell, c, Cherry Creek HS, Englewood, Colo.
61. Dwayne Crawley, of-lhp, Prince George's (Md.) CC.
62. Eric Plooy, rhp, Hanford (Calif.) HS.
63. Michael Myro, rhp, West Torrance HS, Torrance, Calif.
64. Jeffrey Hook, rhp, Ventura (Calif.) JC.
65. Robert Poland, lhp, Southwood HS, Shreveport, La.
66. Carl Franzten, c, Fredericksburg (Texas) HS.
67. Leo Nunez, ss, Fresno (Calif.) CC.
68. Shaw Casey, ss-3b, Green Valley HS, Henderson, Nev.
69. Colland Felts, c, Brighton HS, Sandy, Utah.
70. Robert Slomkowski, rhp, Rutherford (N.J.) HS.
71. Jermaine Timberlake, 2b, Louisa County HS, Louisa, Va.
72. Anthony Sciola, c, Bullard HS, Fresno, Calif.
73. Aaron Martin, lhp, Angelina (Texas) JC.
74. Kiwane Garris, of, Westinghouse HS, Chicago.
75. Jack Jones, ss, Downey HS, Modesto, Calif.
76. Anthony Peters, c, Cardinal HS, Middlefield, Ohio.
77. Aaron Baker, rhp, Bellmont HS, Decatur, Ind.
78. Raphael Baro, lhp, LaSalle HS, Miami.
79. John Anderson, rhp, Chaffey (Calif.) JC.
80. Raul Plasencia, rhp, Jordan HS, Long Beach, Calif.
81. Chad Pittman, of, Haltom (Texas) HS.
82. Kelvin Parker, of, Montgomery (Md.) JC.
83. Jason Meier, of, Bluevale HS, Waterloo, Ont.

## KANSAS CITY ROYALS (5)

**1. Jeff Granger, lhp, Texas A&M University.**
2. (Choice to Blue Jays as compensation for Type A free agent David Cone).
3. (Choice to Twins as compensation for Type A free agent Greg Gagne).
**4. Phil Grundy, rhp, Western Carolina University.**
**5. Phil Brassington, rhp, Lamar University.**
**6. Tyrone Frazier, of-ss, Woodlawn HS, Shreveport, La.**
**7. Pat Flury, rhp, JC of Southern Idaho.**
**8. O.J. Rhone, of, Central Missouri State University.**
9. Chad Green, of, Mentor (Ohio) HS.
10. Tom Buchman, c, Shawnee Mission South HS, Lenexa, Kan.
**11. Larry Smith, of, Broomfield (Colo.) HS.**
**12. Kevin Rawitzer, lhp, Arizona State University.**
**13. Malcolm Cepeda, 1b, Solano (Calif.) CC.**
**14. Braxton Hickman, 1b, University of Texas.**
**15. Bill Dunn, 2b, Arizona State University.**
**16. Dustin Brixey, rhp, Northeastern Oklahoma A&M JC.**
**17. Glendon Rusch, rhp, Shorecrest HS, Seattle.**
**18. Kenneth Ray, rhp, Roswell (Ga.) HS.**
**19. Jimmie Byington, of, Seminole (Okla.) JC.**
**20. Eric Anderson, rhp, Blue Springs (Mo.) HS.**
**21. Kris Ralston, rhp, Central Missouri State University.**
**22. Michael Evans, c-of, Lubbock Christian College.**
**23. Jeremy Carr, 2b, Cal State Fullerton.**

24. Nevin Brewer, rhp, Southeastern (N.C.) CC.
25. Leonard Weathersby, of, Hamilton HS, Los Angeles.
26. Luke Oglesby, of-2b, University of New Mexico.
27. Jason Huffman, rhp, Southeastern (N.C.) CC.
28. Gadiel Medero, rhp, Trujillo Alto, P.R.
29. Justin McCoy, c, Bingham HS, South Jordan, Utah.
30. Lino Diaz, 3b, University of Nevada-Las Vegas.
31. Jacque Jones, of, San Diego (Calif.) HS.
32. Toby Smith, 1b-rhp, Wichita State University.
33. Brian Meyers, rhp, George Fox (Ore.) College.
34. Stephen Wojtkowski, 3b, Montgomery (Md.) JC.
35. Neil Atkinson, lhp, St. Mary's (Texas) University.
36. Jeff Ramos, c, Power-St. Joseph's HS, Toronto.
37. Sal Fasano, c, University of Evansville.
38. Daron Dondero, ss, Mt. San Jacinto (Calif.) JC.
39. Derek Dubois, lhp, Ft. William Collegiate HS, Murillo, Ont.
40. Ryan Stover, 1b, Winter Haven (Fla.) HS.
41. Matt Aminoff, rhp, George Washington University.
42. Cody Kosman, rhp, University of Nevada-Reno.
43. Frank Stewart, of, Julian (Calif.) HS.
44. Thornton Davis, 3b, Liberty County HS, Bristol, Fla.
45. Donovan Delaney, of, Bossier Parish (La.) CC.
46. Jeff Terrell, ss, Tri-City Christian HS, Blue Springs, Mo.
47. Ricardo Calderon, 1b, Carolina, P.R.
48. Howard Rosenberry, lhp, Hagerstown (Md.) JC.
49. Montrell Pride, 1b, Oak Ridge HS, Orlando, Fla.
50. Brian Paluk, rhp, Catholic Central HS, Plymouth, Mich.
51. Jess Utecht, of, Kamiakin HS, Richland, Wash.
52. William Roland, 3b, Galveston (Texas) JC.
53. Toussaint Waterman, of, Country Day HS, Pontiac, Mich.
54. Patrick Johnson, c, Taylorsville HS, Salt Lake City.
55. Jeffrey Peck, lhp, Ryan HS, Denton, Texas.
56. Jason Hueth, rhp, Norte Vista HS, Riverside, Calif.
57. David Trentine, rhp, Foothill HS, Santa Ana, Calif.
58. Christopher Jackson, of, Brownsboro HS, Chandler, Texas.
59. Sal McCullough, Muir HS, Pasadena, Calif.
60. Bubba Dixon, lhp, Seminole (Okla.) JC.
61. Mike Klostermeyer, 1b, Seminole (Okla.) JC.
62. Tremain Mack, of, Chapel Hill HS, Tyler, Texas.
63. Andrew Bernard, rhp, Highland HS, Bakersfield, Calif.
64. Anthony Barrett, rhp, Athens (Texas) HS.
65. Jeff Phipps, rhp, Palo Verde Valley HS, Blythe, Calif.
66. Scott Seal, of, Irvine (Calif.) HS.
67. Gordon Hegeman, 2b, Bakersfield (Calif.) JC.

## LOS ANGELES DODGERS (2)

1. Darren Dreifort, rhp, Wichita State University.
2. (Choice to Cardinals as compensation for Type B free agent Todd Worrell).
3. Dax Winslett, rhp, Arizona State University.
4. Nathan Bland, lhp, Mountain Brook (Ala.) HS.
5. Scott Hunter, c-of, Northeast HS, Philadelphia.
6. Nate Yeskie, rhp, Carson HS, Carson City, Nev.
7. Doug Newstrom, 1b, Arizona State University.
8. Jose Prado, rhp, University of Miami (Fla.).
9. Matt Schwenke, c, UCLA.
10. John Vukson, rhp-3b, Sanger HS, Fresno, Calif.
11. Josh Rash, of, Lamar HS, Arlington, Texas.
12. Craig Scheffler, lhp, University of Wisconsin-Milwaukee.
13. Brian Rolocut, rhp, Miami-Dade CC Wolfson.
14. Brett Binkley, lhp, Georgia Tech.
15. David Steed, c, Meridian (Miss.) CC.
16. Dan Hubbs, rhp, University of Southern California.
17. Mike Biltimier, 1b, Purdue University.
18. Joe LaGarde, rhp, East Forsyth HS, Winston-Salem, N.C.
19. Eric Maloney, rhp, Creighton University.
20. Michael Kinney, of, Texas Tech.
21. Mark Watson, lhp, Marist HS, Atlanta.
22. Charlie Nelson, of, University of Minnesota.
23. Eddie Davis, of, Long Beach State University.
24. Carl South, rhp, Marist HS, Atlanta.
25. Paul LoDuca, c, Arizona State University.
26. Corey Coggburn, of, Ada (Okla.) HS.
27. Bryan Coyle, rhp, Hudson's Bay HS, Vancouver, Wash.
28. Jeffrey Astgen, 2b, El Camino Real HS, Canoga Park, Calif.
29. Anthony Cellars, of, Texas HS, Texarkana, Texas.
30. Adrian Black, of, North Brunswick HS, Leland, N.C.
31. Douglas Davis, lhp, North Gate HS, Pleasant Hill, Calif.
32. Jordan Zimmerman, lhp, Brenham (Texas) HS.
33. Dwayne McCray, of, Sumter (S.C.) HS.
34. Raul Correa, rhp, Juana Diaz, P.R.
35. Tracy Johnson, of, Deer Valley HS, Phoenix.
36. Matthew Wagner, rhp, Iowa State University.
37. Richard Shaw, rhp, Sandwich HS, LaSalle, Ont.
38. Mark Manbeck, rhp, Round Rock (Texas) HS.

39. David Propst, of, West Charlotte HS, Charlotte.
40. Dion Rhodes, of, Hudson's Bay HS, Vancouver, Wash.
41. Eric Yanz, rhp, Arvada West HS, Golden, Colo.
42. Bruce Yard, ss, Indiana (Pa.) University.
43. Thomas Cody, c, Fort Vancouver HS, Vancouver, Wash.
44. Brian Piddington, rhp, Southwestern HS, Hazel Green, Wis.
45. Ben Padilla, ss, Carson (Calif.) HS.
46. Gustavo Rubio, 1b-c, Leuzinger HS, Lawndale, Calif.
47. Jason Smith, rhp, Meridian (Miss.) CC.
48. Jeff Falardeau, lhp, Notre Dame HS, Welland, Ont.
49. Julio Colon, rhp, Long Beach State University.
50. Richard Condon, 2b, Crossroads HS, Culver City, Calif.
51. Kendall Hill, rhp, Escambia HS, Pensacola, Fla.
52. Nathan Rasmussen, 1b, Lakeville (Minn.) HS.
53. Victor Sobieraj, rhp, Catholic Central HS, Windsor, Ont.
54. David Wease, 1b, Chesnee HS, Gaffney, S.C.
55. Jaymie Bane, lhp, Paradise Valley HS, Phoenix.
56. Steve Huls, ss, Rocori HS, Cold Spring, Minn.
57. Brian Carpenter, rhp, University of Texas.
58. Matthew Powell, rhp, Miami-Dade CC Wolfson.

## MILWAUKEE BREWERS (23)

1. Jeff D'Amico, rhp, Northeast HS, St. Petersburg, Fla.
1. Kelly Wunsch, lhp, Texas A&M University (Choice from Blue Jays as compensation for Type A free agent Paul Molitor).
1. Todd Dunn, of, University of North Florida (Supplemental choice—35th—for loss of Type A free agent Chris Bosio).
1. Joe Wagner, rhp, University of Central Florida (Supplemental choice—39th—for loss of Molitor).
2. Brian Banks, c-of, Brigham Young University (Choice from Mariners for loss of Bosio).
2. Danny Klassen, ss, John Carrol HS, Port St. Lucie, Fla.
3. George Preston, rhp, Brenham (Texas) HS.
4. Shane Sheldon, rhp, Gordon (Ga.) JC.
5. Steve Duda, rhp, Pepperdine University.
6. Josh Zwisler, c, St. Vincent-St. Mary HS, Akron, Ohio.
7. Mark Loretta, ss, Northwestern University.
8. Tano Tijerina, rhp, Navarro (Texas) JC.
9. Jon Hillis, rhp, Rice University.
10. Chris McInnes, ss, Ricks (Idaho) JC.
11. Chris Junghans, c, McDonough HS, Waldorf, Md.
12. Brian Blessie, rhp, Burke HS, Omaha.
13. Brian Luna, 1b, Craigmont HS, Memphis, Tenn.
14. Peter Benny, rhp, Wooster HS, Carson City, Nev.
15. Scott Perkins, rhp, University of Southwestern Louisiana.
16. James Wallace, rhp, Kellenberg Memorial HS, Wantagh, N.Y.
17. Chad Kopitzke, rhp, University of Wisconsin-Oshkosh.
18. Gabriel Mercado, rhp, Indian Hills (Iowa) CC.
19. Sean Maloney, rhp, Georgetown University.
20. Pedro Fuertes, 3b, Carolina, P.R.
21. Chris Schmitt, lhp, University of West Florida.
22. Rick Gutierrez, 2b, University of Oklahoma.
23. Ron Wallech, rhp, Hagerstown (Md.) JC.
24. Gregory Martinez, of, Barstow (Calif.) JC.
25. Jarod Fryman, 3b, Jefferson Davis (Ala.) JC.
26. Allen Mealing, of, Strom Thurmond HS, Edgefield, S.C.
27. James Cole, rhp, Mercer University.
28. Matt Murphy, lhp, University of Vermont.
29. Todd Cutchins, lhp, Westlake (La.) HS.
30. Chris Carter, c, Clemson University.
31. Todd Landry, 1b, University of Arizona.
32. James Reames, rhp, Seneca (S.C.) HS.
33. Jim Hodge, rhp, Mercer County (N.J.) CC.
34. Michael Kimbrell, lhp, Jefferson Davis (Ala.) CC.
35. Mark Wasikowski, 3b, Pepperdine University.
36. Clayton Hill, of, McLennan (Texas) JC.
37. Julio Ayala, lhp, Guaynabo, P.R.
38. Jamie Bass, 2b, Pine Bluff (Ark.) HS.
39. Brian Conley, ss, Glen Este HS, Cincinnati.
40. Ronald Fawley, c-of, Santaluces HS, Lantana, Fla.
41. Chris Ciaccio, rhp, University of Georgia.
42. Lorne Rosas, of, Hilo (Hawaii) HS.
43. Peter Jenkins, c, Redlands (Calif.) HS.
44. John Cromwell, rhp, Lake Howell HS, Winter Park, Fla.
45. Jose Calderon, rhp, San Juan, P.R.
46. Mandy Jacomino, c, Westminster Christian HS, Miami.
47. Joseph Walls, rhp, LaSierra HS, Hesperia, Calif.
48. Eduardo Acosta, ss-of, Muscatine (Iowa) CC.
49. Jason Greuel, rhp, South HS, Waukesha, Wis.
50. Kerry Mikulski, of, Pope John Paul HS, Boca Raton, Fla.
51. Miguel Villaran, ss, Loiza, P.R.
52. Francisco Garcia, c, Lewistown, P.R.
53. Daniel Jordan, ss, Thomasville (Ga.) HS.
54. Ken Wagner, rhp, Palm Beach (Fla.) JC.
55. Anthony Pavlovich, rhp, Thomasville HS, Pavo, Ga.

56. Bret Hemphill, c, Cal State Fullerton.
57. Marty Bourgon, c, Central Florida CC.
58. Michael Ribaudo, of, Sarasota (Fla.) HS.
59. Charlie Ward, ss-of, Florida State University.
60. Cameron Andrews, 1b, Milton (Fla.) HS.
61. Brian Scutero, rhp, Valencia (Fla.) CC.

## MINNESOTA TWINS (21)

1. **Torii Hunter, of, Pine Bluff (Ark.) HS** (Choice from Reds as compensation for Type A free agent John Smiley).
1. Jason Varitek, c, Georgia Tech.
1. **Marc Barcelo, rhp, Arizona State University** (Supplemental choice—33rd—for loss of Smiley).
1. **Kelcey Mucker, of, Lawrenceburg (Ind.) HS** (Supplemental choice—38th—for loss of Type A free agent Greg Gagne).
2. **Dan Perkins, rhp, Westminster Christian HS, Miami.**
3. **Troy Carrasco, lhp, Jesuit HS, Tampa** (Choice from Royals as compensation for Gagne).
3. **Jose Valentin, 3b, Manati, P.R.**
4. Toby Dollar, rhp, Graham (Texas) HS.
5. Jesse Ibarra, 1b, Loyola Marymount University.
6. **Benj Sampson, lhp, Ankeny (Iowa) HS.**
7. Kelly Dransfeldt, ss, Morris (Ill.) HS.
8. **Ryan Lane, ss, Bellefontaine (Ohio) HS.**
9. **Kevin Ohme, lhp, University of North Florida.**
10. Mark Merila, 2b, University of Minnesota.
11. **Troy Fortin, c, Lundar (Manitoba) HS.**
12. Alex Cora, ss, Caguas, P.R.
13. Pete Forster, lhp, Oak Park HS, Kansas City, Mo.
14. **Ryan Radmanovich, of, Pepperdine University.**
15. Mike Torti, ss, Newman Smith HS, Carrollton, Texas.
16. Wylie Campbell, ss, Southwest HS, Fort Worth, Texas.
17. Danny Kolb, rhp, Walnut (Ill.) HS.
18. L. J. Yankosky, rhp, West Springfield HS, Springfield, Va.
19. Chris Granata, rhp, Ohio State University.
20. **Aaron Santini, ss, University of New Mexico.**
21. **Shane Bowers, rhp, Loyola Marymount University.**
22. Robert Radlosky, rhp, Central Florida CC.
23. **Scott Stricklin, c, Kent State University.**
24. Ronrico Harris, of, Englewood HS, Jacksonville, Fla.
25. **Brian O'Brien, lhp, Creighton University.**
26. Mauricio Estavil, lhp, Pepperdine University.
27. **Russel Lehoisky, rhp, University of New Haven.**
28. **Mike Stadelhofer, rhp, Calistoga (Calif.) HS.**
29. Javier Encina, rhp, North Mesquite HS, Mesquite, Texas.
30. Doug Rheaume, rhp, Santana HS, Lakeside, Calif.
31. **Jacob Patterson, 1b, Neosho County (Kan.) CC.**
32. Jessie Thompson, of, Wingfield HS, Jackson, Miss.
33. Kenny Harrison, c, University of Hawaii.
34. **Deron Dowhower, rhp, University of Virginia.**
35. **James Motte, ss, University of Arizona.**
36. **Daniel Venezia, ss, Concordia (N.Y.) College.**
37. Emil Brown, of, Harlan HS, Chicago.
38. Jason Ford, lhp, North Idaho JC.
39. Stephen Watson, rhp, Westwood HS, Austin, Texas.
40. Douglas Beddinger, rhp, Manatee (Fla.) JC.
41. Lance Carter, rhp, Manatee HS, Bradenton, Fla.
42. Jason Adge, rhp, Sacramento (Calif.) CC.
43. Robert Landstad, of, Indian Hills (Iowa) CC.
44. **Chad Rupp, 1b, University of Miami (Fla.).**
45. Matt Freeman, c, Seminole (Fla.) HS.
46. **Justin Tomberlin, 3b, University of Maine.**
47. Spencer McIntyre, lhp, Texas A&M University.
48. **Eric Anderson, lhp, Parkland (Ill.) JC.**
49. Matthew Gondini, rhp, Green Valley HS, Henderson, Nev.
50. Aaron Sellner, rhp, Naugatuck (Conn.) HS.
51. Sandy Lopez, rhp, CC of Morris (N.J.).
52. **Chris Phillips, 2b, Western Kentucky University.**
53. J.T. Messick, ss, Seminole (Okla.) JC.
54. Anthony Lucca, lhp, South San Francisco (Calif.) HS.
55. William Stone, lhp, Delight (Ark.) HS.
56. Eddie Medlin, c, Billings (Mon.) HS.
57. Andrew Burt, rhp, University of Wisconsin.
58. Christopher Kilen, lhp, Janesville, Wis.
59. Danny Peoples, 1b, Round Rock (Texas) HS.
60. **Aaron Schooler, rhp, Columbia Basin (Wash.) CC.**

## MONTREAL EXPOS (18)

1. **Chris Schwab, of, Cretin-Derham HS, Eagan, Minn.**
1. **Josue Estrada, of, Rio Piedras, P.R.** (Supplemental choice—31st—for loss of Type A free agent Spike Owen).
2. **Martin Mainville, rhp, Marquette HS, Montreal** (Choice from Yankees for loss of Owen).
2. **Brad Fullmer, 3b, Montclair Prep HS, Chatsworth, Calif.**
3. **Jason Baker, rhp, Robert E. Lee HS, Midland, Texas.**

4. **Ronnie Hall, of, Tustin (Calif.) HS.**
5. **Nate Brown, lhp, University of California.**
6. **Jeff Foster, 3b, University of Tennessee.**
7. Donnie Fowler, rhp, Spring (Texas) HS.
8. **Neal Weber, lhp, Cuesta (Calif.) CC.**
9. **Jayson Durocher, rhp, Horizon HS, Scottsdale, Ariz.**
10. **Trace Coquillette, of, Sacramento (Calif.) CC.**
11. Richard Giannola, rhp, Boca Raton (Fla.) Community HS.
12. **Aaron Knieper, rhp, Central Michigan University.**
13. **Randy Culp, c, Ellison HS, Killeen, Texas.**
14. **Tom Schneider, lhp, Centenary College.**
15. Jason Bond, lhp, St. Mary's HS, Glendale, Ariz.
16. Troy Mattes, rhp, Riverview HS, Sarasota, Fla.͏
17. **Angelo Thompson, of-1b, Shaw (N.C.) University.**
18. Ricardo Spears, of, University of California.
19. Scott Needham, c, Bentonville (Ark.) HS.
20. Kevin Nykoluk, c, Simi Valley (Calif.) HS.
21. Darryl Monroe, of, University of Kansas.
22. Peter Bezeredi, 1b, Seminole (Fla.) CC.
23. Dirk Lewallen, 1b, Hesperia (Calif.) HS.
24. **Matt Harrell, c, Duke University.**
25. Donzell McDonald, of, Cherry Creek HS, Englewood, Colo.
26. Jason Romine, rhp, Omak (Wash.) HS.
27. Shane Gift, c, Gilbert (Ariz.) HS.
28. Stephan Neill, rhp, John Carroll HS, Port St. Lucie, Fla.
29. Ryan Fisher, lhp, Unity HS, Milltown, Wis.
30. David Moraga, lhp, Armijo HS, Suisun City, Calif.
31. **Chris Grubb, of, Elizabethtown (Pa.) College.**
32. Daniel Albrecht, lhp, Butler (Kan.) CC.
33. **Brian Detwiler, c, William Paterson College.**
34. **Scott Quade, ss, Austin Peay State University.**
35. George Elmore, rhp, Louisburg (N.C.) JC.
36. Robert Lentz, ss, Bloomingdale HS, Brandon, Fla.
37. Shawn Lopez, rhp, Lewis Clark State College.
38. Christopher Weidert, rhp, Butler (Kan.) CC.
39. Walter Owens, of, Odessa (Texas) JC.
40. Nole Elizer, c, Cape Coral (Fla.) HS.
41. Scott Kidd, ss, DeAnza (Calif.) JC.
42. Stephen Kokinda, ss, Cardinal Newman HS, Palm Beach, Fla.
43. Shawn Painter, of, Beaconsfield (Quebec) HS.
44. **Jeff Mitchell, rhp, Harvard University.**
45. Brett Rapozo, rhp, American River (Calif.) JC.
46. John Portugal, rhp, Oceanside (Calif.) HS.
47. Logan Miller, c, Marin (Calif.) CC.
48. Richard Matteson, rhp, Diablo Valley (Calif.) JC.
49. Orin Hirschkorn, rhp, Kerman (Calif.) HS.
50. Brian Cummings, rhp, Iona Prep HS, East Chester, N.Y.
51. Michael Lincoln, rhp, Casa Roble HS, Orangevale, Calif.
52. Ryan Gause, ss, Temecula (Calif.) HS.
53. Brian Downs, c, Don Lugo HS, Chino, Calif.
54. Nason Beckett, c, Port Angeles (Wash.) HS.
55. John O'Brien, of, Malvern HS, Chester, Pa.
56. Jeffrey Howard, rhp, Spartanburg Methodist (S.C.) JC.
57. Brett Lockwood, 3b, Mesa (Ariz.) CC.
58. **Jason Woodring, rhp, Trinidad State (Colo.) JC.**
59. **Michael Leon, lhp, Western New Mexico University.**
60. Greg Morris, 3b, University of California-Davis.
61. **Joseph Tosone, of, Dartmouth College.**
62. Adam Housley, rhp, Pepperdine University.

## NEW YORK METS (8)

1. **Kirk Presley, rhp, Tupelo (Miss.) HS.**
2. **Eric Ludwick, rhp, University of Nevada-Las Vegas.**
3. **Mike Welch, rhp, University of Southern Maine.**
4. Bill Koch, rhp, West Babylon (N.Y.) HS.
5. **Fletcher Bates, of, New Hanover HS, Wilmington, N.C.**
6. **Matt Terrell, of, Western Michigan University.**
7. Scott Adair, rhp, Norte Vista HS, Riverside, Calif.
8. **Paul Petrulis, ss, Mississippi State University.**
9. **Joe Atwater, lhp, South Alamance HS, Graham, N.C.**
10. **Derek Sutton, lhp, Indian Hills (Iowa) CC.**
11. Jared Camp, rhp, East HS, Huntington, W.Va.
12. **Ethan McEntire, lhp, Habersham Central HS, Cornelia, Ga.**
13. John Powell, rhp, Auburn University.
14. **Jeff Cosman, rhp, University of Mississippi.**
15. **Rodney Mazion, of, University of Nevada-Las Vegas.**
16. **Paul Bowman, rhp, Garrett (Md.) CC.**
17. **Sean Kenny, rhp, Eastern Michigan University.**
18. Jason Middlebrook, rhp, Grass Lake (Mich.) HS.
19. Ryan Rupe, rhp, Northbrook HS, Houston.
20. **Jarrod Patterson, 1b, Jefferson Davis (Ala.) JC.**
21. Billy Oliver, rhp-3b, Monta Vista HS, Cupertino, Calif.
22. **Kevin Lewis, c, Florida Atlantic University.**
23. **David Zuniga, ss, San Jose State University.**
24. **Brian Mast, rhp, David Lipscomb (Tenn.) College.**

**Kirk Presley.** Elvis' third cousin was drafted in the first round by the Mets—the eighth overall pick.

25. Brandon Welch, of-1b, Butler County (Kan.) CC.
26. **Thomas Wolff, rhp, Kellogg (Mich.) CC.**
27. **Robert Gontkosky, lhp, Rider College.**
28. **Tad Smith, 1b, Eastern Illinois University.**
29. **Scott Winterlee, c, University of Michigan.**
30. **Benny Agbayani, of, Hawaii Pacific University.**
31. **David Fellhauer, 1b, Gaither HS, Tampa.**
32. Burdette Greeny, rhp, Port Angeles (Wash.) HS.
33. **Jesus Morales, ss, East Los Angeles JC.**
34. **Ross Ferrier, of, University of Waterloo (Ont.).**
35. **Gary Collum, of, Pace University.**
36. Ken Harrell, c, Alamogordo (N.M.) HS.
37. Joseph Robinson, ss, Burlington (Iowa) HS.
38. Carlos Morrison, of, Cimarron HS, Las Vegas.
39. Keith Maxwell, of, Liberty County HS, Bristol, Fla.
40. Santiago Sanchez, ss, Lodi (Calif.) HS.
41. Barrett Short, rhp, Three Rivers (Mo.) CC.
42. Michael Ruhmann, lhp, St. Louis CC-Meramec.
43. **Brandon Newell, rhp, University of Washington.**
44. Vance Wilson, c, Mesa (Ariz.) CC.
45. **Michael Johnson, 2b, Union (N.Y.) College.**

## NEW YORK YANKEES (13)

1. **Matt Drews, rhp, Sarasota (Fla.) HS.**
2. (Choice to Expos as compensation for Type A free agent Spike Owen).
3. (Choice to Blue Jays as compensation for Type A free agent Jimmy Key).
4. **Sloan Smith, of, Northwestern University.**
5. **Mike Jerzembeck, rhp, University of North Carolina.**
6. **Kurt Bierek, 1b, University of Southern California.**
7. **Jim Musselwhite, rhp, University of Georgia.**
8. **Rob Trimble, c-rhp, Texas A&M University.**
9. **Clint Whitworth, rhp, Oklahoma City University.**
10. **Derek Shumpert, of, Aquinas-Mercy HS, St. Louis.**
11. **Jason Rathbun, rhp, Baylor University.**
12. **Anthony Shelby, lhp, Triton (Ill.) JC.**
13. **Jim Musselwhite, lhp, Mt. Vernon Nazarene (Ohio) College.**
14. **Jim Palmer, 3b, St. Thomas Aquinas HS, Fort Lauderdale.**
15. **Gregory Resz, rhp, Southwest Missouri State University.**
16. John Peters, lhp, Texarkana (Texas) JC.

17. **Frank Lankford, rhp, University of Virginia.**
18. **Joe Wharton, rhp, Baylor University.**
19. Terry Harvey, rhp, North Carolina State University.
20. **Casey Mittauer, rhp, Florida International University.**
21. Andrew Remala, ss, El Dorado HS, Placentia, Calif.
22. **Mike Schmitz, 1b-of, Florida State University.**
23. Jason Dietrich, rhp, Rancho Santiago (Calif.) JC.
24. **Scott Standish, rhp, Bellevue (Neb.) College.**
25. Chad Moeller, c, Upland (Calif.) HS.
26. **Kent Donnelly, rhp, University of Southern California.**
27. Jason Clark, 1b, Poly HS, Riverside, Calif.
28. Chris Druckrey, rhp, Kankakee HS, St. Anne, Ill.
29. Frisco Parotte, rhp, Toa Baja, P.R.
30. Jay Evans, lhp, Indian River (Fla.) CC.
31. Jason Smithberger, rhp, Watkins Mill HS, Gaithersburg, Md.
32.. Craig Dour, ss, Tarpon Springs HS, Palm Harbor, Fla.
33. Jarred McAlvain, 1b, Stigler (Okla.) HS.
34. Tom Bernhardt, of, Columbus HS, Miami.
35. James Kerr, ss, Coral Springs (Fla.) HS.
36. Craig Dingman, rhp, Hutchinson (Kan.) CC.
37. Matthew Aden, of, Northwest HS, Omaha.
38. **Jason Berry, rhp, Miami-Dade CC Wolfson.**
39. Cade Gaspar, rhp, Saddleback (Calif.) CC.
40. Joseph Victery, rhp, Ninnekah (Okla.) HS.
41. Eric Knutson, ss-2b, Benson HS, Omaha.
42. Brett Schlomann, rhp, Owasso HS, Collinsville, Okla.
43. Dietrich Johnson, cf, South Dorchester HS, Cambridge, Md.
44. Eddie Yarnall, lhp, Thomas Aquinas HS, Fort Lauderdale, Fla.
45. Dale Brandt, lhp, Indian River (Fla.) CC.
46. John Strasser, ss, Greenway HS, Glendale, Ariz.
47. Shawne Ware, of, Sacramento (Calif.) CC.
48. Phillip Haigler, rhp, Faulkner State (Ala.) JC.
49. Brandon Marsters, c, Sarasota (Fla.) HS.
50. Luis Flores, c, Columbus HS, Miami.
51. Roy Reis, c, Diman Vocational Tech HS, Fall River, Mass.
52. Oliver Harwas, rhp, Okeechobee (Fla.) HS.
53. Brent Southall, 1b-of, Manatee (Fla.) JC.
54. Isreal Barnes, rhp, King HS, Tampa.
55. Michael Massey, c, Indian River (Fla.) CC.
56. Greg Smitherman, of, Hartshorne (Okla.) HS.
57. Chris Wright, c, West Jones HS, Laurel, Miss.
58. Ken Shelly, ss, Ely HS, Pompano Beach, Fla.
59. Chris Dickerson, ss, Alvin (Texas) HS.
60. Wyley Steelmon, c, Enid (Okla.) HS.
61. Chris Halliday, c, Evans HS, Martinez, Ga.
62. Nolan Lofgren, c, East HS, Rockford, Ill.
63. Scott Carley, rhp, Crescent City HS, Milford, Ill.
64. Matt Dornfeld, of, Harding HS, St. Paul, Minn.

## OAKLAND ATHLETICS (25)

1. **John Wasdin, rhp, Florida State University.**
1. **Willie Adams, rhp, Stanford University** (Supplemental choice—36th—for loss of Type A free agent Dave Stewart).
2. **Jeff D'Amico, ss, Redmond (Wash.) HS.**
2. **Mike Moschetti, ss, La Mirada (Calif.) HS** (Choice from Blue Jays as compensation for Stewart).
3. Tucker Barr, c, Maclay HS, Tallahassee, Fla.
4. **Jason McDonald, ss, University of Houston.**
5. **Andy Smith, rhp, A.L. Brown HS, Kannapolis, N.C.**
6. **Scott Spiezio, 1b, University of Illinois.**
7. **Tim Kubinski, lhp, UCLA.**
8. **Leon Hamburg, of, Casa Roble HS, Orangevale, Calif.**
9. **Damon Newman, rhp, Fullerton (Calif.) JC.**
10. John Phillips, rhp, Bullard HS, Fresno, Calif.
11. **Jason Rajotte, lhp, University of Maine.**
12. **Chris Michalak, lhp, University of Notre Dame.**
13. **Scott Baldwin, lhp, Lewis Clark State College.**
14. **Willie Morales, c, University of Arizona.**
15. Daniel Choi, rhp, Long Beach State University.
16. **Mat Reese, of, Indiana State University.**
17. Stephen Fuller, rhp, St. Charles (Ill.) HS.
18. **Brian Whatley, c, Long Beach State University.**
19. **Pat Sanders, 1b, Cumberland (Tenn.) College.**
20. **Aaron Huber, rhp, Panola (Texas) JC.**
21. **Tony Banks, of, Cal State Fullerton.**
22. **Jeff Richardson, of, Long Beach State University.**
23. **Eric Harris, of, Columbia State (Tenn.) CC.**
24. Toby Larson, rhp, Lassen (Calif.) JC.
25. **Joe Montelongo, rhp, Truett-McConnell (Ga.) JC.**
26. **Derek Manning, lhp, University of North Carolina.**
27. **Ryan Whitaker, rhp, University of Arkansas.**
28. **Jason Lowe, rhp, University of Mississippi.**
29. Felix Martinez, ss, Rio Piedras, P.R.
30. Jeff Poor, c, Los Angeles Harbor JC.
31. **Brandy Bengoechea, ss, Lewis Clark State College.**

32. Michael McLeod, of, University of South Carolina.
33. Randy Ortega, c, Santa Clara University.
34. Jon Farmer, 1b-lhp, Porterville (Calif.) JC.
35. Peter Cervantes, of, Lincoln HS, Los Angeles.
36. Thomas Luft, rhp, Warner Southern (Fla.) College.
37. Robert Moore, rhp, Lassen (Calif.) JC.
38. Brandon Kolb, rhp, Chabot (Calif.) JC.
39. Matthew Weisbruch, rhp, Bradley University.
40. Bryan Warner, of, Monrovia (Calif.) HS.
41. Matt Walsh, rhp, Boston College.
42. Jeff Carr, c, Mission Viejo (Calif.) HS.
43. Chad Griffin, 2b, Garinger HS, Charlotte.
44. Santos Cortez, of, Millikan HS, Long Beach, Calif.
45. Tal Light, 3b, Seminole (Okla.) JC.
46. Eric Fuller, ss, West HS, Bakersfield, Calif.
47. Frank Harmer, c-rhp, Lake Brantley HS, Altamonte Springs, Fla.
48. Jay Wiebe, of, Foothill HS, Bakersfield, Calif.

## PHILADELPHIA PHILLIES (4)

1. Wayne Gomes, rhp, Old Dominion University.
2. Scott Rolen, 3b, Jasper (Ind.) HS.
3. Josh Watts, of, Ironwood HS, Glendale, Ariz.
4. Jeffrey Key, of, Newton County HS, Covington, Ga.
5. Thomas Franek, rhp, Mesa State (Colo.) College.
6. Blair Fowler, rhp, Everett (Wash.) HS.
7. Scott Sladovnik, of, Westside HS, Omaha.
8. Bo Hamilton, rhp, Cleveland (Texas) HS.
9. Nelson Metheney, rhp, Clinch Valley (Va.) College.
10. Silvio Censale, lhp, University of Miami (Fla.).
11. Jarrod Mays, rhp, El Dorado Springs (Mo.) HS.
12. Chris Mayfield, rhp, McNeese State University.
13. Brian Costello, of, Dr. Phillips HS, Orlando, Fla.
14. Richard Hunter, rhp, The Linfield School, Temecula, Calif.
15. Tom Danulevith, lhp, St. John's University.
16. Doug Angeli, ss, University of New Orleans.
17. Eric Ekdahl, ss, Pepperdine University.
18. Mark Gardener, lhp, Fountain Valley (Calif.) HS.
19. Jeff Gyselman, c, Portland State University.
20. Charles Tinsley, of, Cumberland HS, Lynch, Ky.
21. Nate Rodriquez, ss, Cal State Fullerton.
22. Andrew Szarko, rhp, University of Richmond.
23. Mark Foster, lhp, University of Richmond.
24. Tyrone Swan, rhp, University of LaVerne.
25. Matthew Brainard, c-3b, Wilmington (Del.) College.
26. Derek Stingley, of, Triton (Ill.) JC.
27. Dave Doster, 2b, Indiana State University.
28. Neal Murphy, c, Iona College.
29. Brian O'Connor, rhp, Creighton University.
30. Mike Muncy, ss, Ventura (Calif.) CC.
31. Danton Pierre-Louis, 1b, Dwight HS, New York.
32. Joseph Madden, of, Cal State Hayward.

**Wayne Gomes.** Old Dominion closer went to Philadelphia as fourth overall pick in 1993 draft.

DAVID GREENE

33. Kevin Sefcik, ss, St. Xavier (Ill.) College.
34. Shawn Fouch, rhp, Virginia HS, Bristol, Va.
35. Michael Boucher, rhp, Saddleback (Calif.) CC.
36. Larry Karpinski, rhp, Eisenhower HS, Rialto, Calif.
37. Darin Wood, c, Redwood HS, Visalia, Calif.
38. Jacob Esteves, rhp, Placer HS, Auburn, Calif.
39. Barry Fitzgerald, c, West Hills HS, Santee, Calif.
40. Karl Chatman, of, Nacogdoches (Texas) HS.
41. Michael Neal, rhp, Seymour (Tenn.) HS.
42. Daniel Held, c, Waukesha County HS, Neosho, Wis.

## PITTSBURGH PIRATES (22)

1. Charles Peterson, of, Laurens (S.C.) HS.
1. Jermaine Allensworth, of, Purdue University (Supplemental choice—34th—for loss of Type A free agent Doug Drabek).
1. Andy Rice, 1b, Parker HS, Birmingham (Supplemental choice—42nd—for loss of Type A free agent Barry Bonds).
2. Kevin Pickford, lhp, West HS, Clovis, Calif. (Choice from Astros as compensation for Drabek).
2. Jose Delgado, ss, Carolina, P.R.
3. Derek Swafford, of-2b, Ventura (Calif.) HS.
4. Kerry Ward, rhp, Edison (Fla.) CC.
5. Jason Temple, rhp, Woodhaven (Mich.) HS.
6. Shane McGill, rhp, Campbell HS, Smyrna, Ga.
7. Akili Smith, of, Lincoln HS, San Diego.
8. Sean Hagen, ss, Brighton HS, Sandy, Utah.
9. Rayon Reid, rhp, Miami-Dade CC North.
10. Tarrence Staton, 1b-lhp, West HS, Elyria, Ohio.
11. Matt Chamberlain, rhp, Louisiana State University.
12. Joseph Serna, rhp-c, Mt. San Antonio (Calif.) JC.
13. Kane Davis, rhp, Spencer HS, Reedy, W.Va.
14. Craig Mattson, rhp, Triton (Ill.) JC.
15. Kevin Keener, lhp, Arkansas HS, Texarkana, Ark.
16. Richard Luna, ss, Cosumnes River (Calif.) JC.
17. Jacob Eye, rhp, Windham (Ohio) HS.
18. Jeff Isom, lhp, Purdue University.
19. Francisco Lebron, 1b, Toa Baja, P.R.
20. Alan Purdy, ss, Vanderbilt University.
21. Heath Henderson, rhp, Huffman HS, Birmingham.
22. Jeff Pickich, rhp, Southern Mississippi University.
23. Anthony Sharer, rhp, Tyrone Area (Pa.) HS.
24. Matt Brown, rhp, Boone HS, Orlando.
25. Matt Ryan, rhp, University of Mississippi.
26. Matt Torres, c-3b, American River (Calif.) JC.
27. Ben Goldman, rhp, Sacramento (Calif.) CC.
28. Ryan Cunningham, 3b, Lancaster (S.C.) HS.
29. Trevor Leppard, rhp, Simi Valley (Calif.) HS.
30. John Yselonia, 1b, University of Georgia.
31. Jeffery Henry, rhp, George C. Wallace (Ala.) CC.
32. Trevor Skjerpen, rhp, University of North Dakota.
33. John Brammer, rhp, Logan HS, West Logan, W.Va.
34. Joel Williamson, c, University of Texas.
35. Ronald Ricks, rhp, Florida HS, Tallahassee, Fla.
36. Pete Pryor, 1b, Sacramento (Calif.) CC.
37. Chris Peters, lhp, Indiana University.
38. Michael Butts, ss-2b, Hillsborough HS, Tampa.
39. Johnny Mitchell, of, University of South Carolina-Aiken.
40. Nate Coleman, c, Northwest HS, Omaha.
41. Bruce Stanley, rhp, Shenandoah HS, Middletown, Ind.
42. Keith Finnerty, 2b, Rockland (N.Y.) CC.
43. Robert Matlack, c, Madill (Okla.) HS.
44. Jeff Lutt, rhp, Wayne State (Neb.) College.
45. Brian Harris, ss, Carmel (Ind.) HS.
46. Robert Dulli, rhp, Fairfield (Ohio) HS.
47. Tonka Maynor, of-1b, University of North Carolina-Greensboro.
48. Freddy Perez, c, Miami (Fla.) HS.
49. Brandon Griffith, rhp, Sibley HS, Heflin, La.
50. Derek Mitchell, ss, Waukegan HS, Gurnee, Ill.
51. Justin Ludington, rhp, Sacramento (Calif.) CC.
52. Patrick Gosselin, ss, Montmorency HS, Sherbrooke, Quebec.
53. Steve Hueston, rhp, Skyline (Calif.) JC.

## ST. LOUIS CARDINALS (16)

1. Alan Benes, rhp, Creighton University.
2. Nate Dishington, 1b, Hoover (Calif.) HS (Choice from Dodgers for loss of Type B free agent Todd Worrell).
2. Jay Witasick, rhp, University of Maryland-Baltimore County.
3. Elieser Marrero, c, Coral Gables (Fla.) HS.
4. Darrell Nicholas, of, University of New Orleans.
5. Marc Ottmers, rhp, University of Texas-Pan American.
6. David Carroll, lhp, Manatee (Fla.) JC.
7. Jeff Berblinger, 2b, University of Kansas.
8. Rantie Harper, of, Point Loma (Calif.) HS.
9. Mike Windham, rhp, University of North Florida.
10. Mike Martin, rhp, Walters (Tenn.) State CC.

**Alan Benes.** Younger brother of San Diego's Andy Benes was first pick by St. Louis in 1993 draft.

11. **Scott Marquardt, rhp, Galveston (Texas) JC.**
12. **Chris Christopher, of, Auburn University.**
13. **Anton French, of, Lafayette (La.) HS.**
14. **Dave Madsen, 3b, Brigham Young University.**
15. **Dee Dalton, ss, Virginia Tech.**
16. **Tom McMillan, of, Guaynabo, P.R.**
17. **Travis Welch, rhp, Sacramento (Calif.) CC.**
18. **Jeremy Current, of, Mt. Zion (Ill.) HS.**
19. **Steven Santucci, of, Assumption (Mass.) College.**
20. **Osmel Garcia, of, Miami-Dade CC Wolfson.**
21. **Armando Almanza, lhp, New Mexico JC.**
22. Kristren Detmers, lhp, Lincoln Land (Ill.) CC.
23. **Keith Conway, lhp, Gloucester County (N.J.) JC.**
24. **Greg Almond, c, North Carolina State University.**
25. Ronald Johnson, lhp, Rice University.
26. **Greg Deares, of, George Mason University.**
27. Jeremy Ross, rhp, Dixie (Utah) JC.
28. **Richard Lopez, of, Mt. San Antonio (Calif.) JC.**
29. **Joe Jumonville, 3b, University of Southwestern Louisiana.**
30. **Cory Corrigan, rhp, Ohio University.**
31. **Daniel Pontes, rhp, Long Island University.**
32. **Michael Matvey, ss, Berry (Ga.) College.**
33. **Freddie Parker, rhp, Northeast HS, Clarksville, Tenn.**
34. **Ron Scott, lhp, University of Florida.**
35. **Matt Arrandale, rhp, University of Illinois.**
36. **Mark Dean, ss-of, Georgia Southern University.**
37. **Anthony Magnelli, rhp, Dominican (N.Y.) College.**
38. **Kevin Herde, c, University of San Diego.**
39. **Robert Battles, rhp, Southern (Ga.) Tech.**
40. **Sheldon Cain, rhp, Berry (Ga.) College.**
41. **Eric Alexander, rhp, Florida International University.**
42. **Joseph Henson, 1b-of, David Lipscomb (Tenn.) College.**
43. **Kurt Grashaw, rhp, University of Hartford.**
44. **Troy Barrick, rhp, North Carolina Wesleyan College.**
45. **Mark Cruise, rhp, Fresno State University.**
46. **Curtis Williams, of, Connors State (Okla.) JC.**
47. **Tighe Curran, lhp, Ventura (Calif.) JC.**
48. Kortney Paul, c, University of Arkansas.
49. **Chris Stewart, rhp, Memphis State University.**
50. **Edward Kehrli, rhp, Pace University.**
51. Alfred Hughes, 1b, Vernon Regional (Texas) JC.
52. Brad Gore, rhp, Oklahoma State University.
53. Matthew Leach, rhp, Long Island University.
54. Joshua Bradford, rhp, Hutchinson (Kan.) CC.
55. Keith Bradley, ss, Connors State (Okla.) JC.
56. Matt Johnson, 2b, South Park HS, Library, Pa.
57. Tim Bradley, rhp, Dixie (Utah) JC.
58. Anthony Fisher, of, Cretin HS, Oakdale, Minn.
59. Mark Cridland, rhp, Ball HS, Galveston, Texas.
60. Phillip Bailey, of, Westark (Ark.) CC.
61. **Eric Iverson, of, Wilson HS, Fargo, N.D.**

1. **Derrek Lee, 1b, El Camino HS, Sacramento.**
2. **Matt LaChappa, lhp, El Capitan HS, Lakeside, Calif.**
3. **Matt Clement, rhp, Butler (Pa.) Area HS.**
4. Tim Miller, rhp, Williamsport (Pa.) HS.
5. **Hal Garrett, rhp, Brentwood (Tenn.) Academy.**
6. **Greg Keagle, rhp, Florida International University.**
7. **Jason Schlutt, lhp, University of Central Florida.**
8. **Derek Mix, rhp, San Bernardino Valley (Calif.) JC.**
9. **Jason Thompson, 1b, University of Arizona.**
10. Stacy Kleiner, c-3b, Taft HS, Tarzana, Calif.
11. **Faruq Darcuiel, of, Fresno (Calif.) CC.**
12. **Darrick Duke, of, University of Texas.**
13. Gary Matthews Jr., of, Mission (Calif.) CC.
14. **DeVohn Duncan, rhp, Marist HS, Jersey City, N.J.**
15. Jose Colon, of, Eau Gallie HS, Melbourne, Fla.
16. **Brad Kaufman, rhp, Iowa State University.**
17. **Daniel Harpe, rhp, Serra HS, San Mateo, Calif.**
18. **Bryan Wolff, rhp, Oral Roberts University.**
19. Chris Logan, c, University of Southern Mississippi.
20. Dan Cey, ss, El Camino Real HS, Woodland Hills, Calif.
21. Mark Hendrickson, lhp, Washington State University
22. **Daniel Zanolla, ss, Purdue University.**
23. Chris Humphries, rhp, Cochise County (Ariz.) CC.
24. **Chris Prieto, of, University of Nevada-Reno.**
25. **Santiago Rivera, ss, Arizona State University**
26. Mike Schiefelbein, rhp, University of Arizona.
27. Frankie Sanders, ss, Riverview HS, Sarasota, Fla.
28. **Alan Meyer, rhp, Edison HS, Huntington Beach, Calif.**
29. **Chris West, 3b, East Carolina University.**
30. Nathan Koepke, 1b, Millikan HS, Long Beach, Calif.
31. **Dickie Woodridge, 2b, LeMoyne College.**
32. **Leroy McKinnis, c, Jackson State University.**
33. **James Bostock, 2b, Eastern Michigan University.**
34. Corey Dillon, of, Franklin HS, Seattle.
35. Dietrich Evans, c, Arizona Western JC.
36. Travis Boyd, ss, UCLA.
37. Kelan Washington, of, Lanier HS, Austin.
38. Carlos Smith, ss, Anson County HS, Wadesboro, N.C.
39. Chris Havens, rhp, Central HS, Elkhart, Ind.
40. Ivan Loochkartt, of, Jordan HS, Long Beach, Calif.
41. **Daniel Drewien, rhp, San Diego State University.**
42. **Obed Martinez, of, Rio Piedras, P.R.**
43. Brian Baklik, ss, El Campo (Texas) HS.
44. Brent Bearden, rhp, Baylor University.
45. Brent Stentz, rhp, Hernando HS, Brooksville, Fla.
46. Etienne Hightower, of, Mt. Lebanon (Pa.) HS.
47. Brian Thompson, rhp, Northwest HS, Omaha.
48. Robbie Reid, lhp, Spanish Fork (Utah) HS.
49. William Bland, of, Dr. Phillips HS, Orlando.
50. Oscar Hirschkorn, rhp, Kerman (Calif.) HS.
51. Dexter Davis, ss, Jordan HS, Long Beach, Calif.
52. Ken Wilson, c, South Mecklenburg HS, Charlotte.
53. Brian Bejarano, ss, Alhambra HS, Laveen, Ariz.
54. Jason Kendler, c, Corona del Sol HS, Tempe, Ariz.
55. Greg Aiken, rhp, Temecula Valley (Calif.) HS.
56. Rodrick Meyer, c, Stanford University.
57. Justin McConico, ss, Burke HS, Omaha.
58. Gary Paul, 3b, Buena HS, Ventura, Calif.
59. Jonas Armenta, rhp, Bloomfield (N.M.) HS.
60. Jeff Van Every, lhp, Benson HS, Omaha.
61. Kyle Griffiths, c, Lake Michigan JC.
62. Ryan Vandeweg, rhp, Grand Rapids (Mich.) JC.
63. Kevin Coe, of, Simeon HS, Chicago.
64. Russ Chambliss, of, Tucker HS, Glen Allen, Va.
65. Terry Adams, 3b, Eastern Commerce HS, Toronto.
66. James Moore, ss, Sweetwater (Texas) HS.
67. Byron Tribe, rhp, St. Thomas HS, Katy, Texas.
68. Keith Dilgard, rhp, Raritan HS, Bridgewater, N.J.
69. Roger Main, 3b, Dundalk (Md.) CC.
70. Larry Smith, c, DeMatha HS, Lanham, Md.
71. Donald Whitney, of, Cahokia (Ill.) HS.
72. Scott Keithley, ss, Alvin (Texas) HS.
73. Isaac Byrd, of, Parkway Central HS, St. Louis.
74. Stan Conti, of, Seneca Valley HS, Mars, Pa.
75. Keith Whitner, of, Lincoln HS, Los Angeles.
76. David Yocum, lhp, Columbus HS, Miami.
77. Donn Cunnigan, of, University of Southern California.
78. Terrence Johnson, 1b-of, Guilford HS, Rockford, Ill.
79. **Byron Clark, lhp, Western New Mexico University.**
80. Chris Corn, rhp, University of Kansas.
81. Joshua Gibbons, rhp, Lincoln Way HS, New Lenox, Ill.
82. Rob Bonanno, rhp, University of Florida.
83. Larry Husted, 1b-of, Chaffey (Calif.) JC.

84. Theodore Persell, of, East Los Angeles JC.
85. Michael Brown, ss, Hazelwood West HS, Florissant, Mo.
86. Tim Farris, rhp, Newbury Park (Calif.) HS.
87. Keith Evans, rhp, Crespi HS, Encino, Calif.
88. Eric Skaife, rhp, South HS, Torrance, Calif.
89. Jesse Shanon, 1b, Dos Pueblos HS, Goleta, Calif.
90. Mark Harriger, rhp, St. John Bosco HS, Lakewood, Calif.
91. Trevor Preston, rhp, Temecula Valley HS, Temecula, Calif.

## SAN FRANCISCO GIANTS (6)

1. **Steve Soderstrom, rhp, Fresno State University.**
2. **Chris Singleton, of, University of Nevada-Reno.**
2. Macey Brooks, of, Kecoughtan HS, Hampton, Va. (Supplemental choice—71st—for loss of Type C free agent Mike Felder).
2. **Brett King, ss, University of South Florida** (Supplemental choice—72nd—for loss of Type C free agent Chris James).
3. **Don Denbow, of, Blinn (Texas) JC.**
4. **Jay Canizaro, ss, Blinn (Texas) JC.**
5. **Heath Altman, rhp, University of North Carolina-Wilmington.**
6. Pat Ryan, rhp, Apopka (Fla.) HS.
7. **Keith Williams, of, Clemson University.**
8. **Brent Smith, rhp, Arizona State University.**
9. **Ivan Alvarez, lhp, Canoga Park, Calif.**
10. **Jason Myers, lhp, Chaffey (Calif.) JC.**
11. **Brook Smith, lhp, Bradley University.**
12. **Kristin Franko, lhp, Ohio University.**
13. **Joel Galarza, c, Yabucoa, P.R.**
14. **Michael McMullen, rhp, Glendale (Calif.) JC.**
15. **Bill Mueller, ss, Southwest Missouri State University.**
16. Mickey Callaway, rhp, Germantown (Tenn.) HS.
17. **Chris Gump, 2b, University of Arizona.**
18. **Doug Drumm, rhp, Rensselaer (N.Y.) Polytechnical Institute.**
19. **Mark Gulseth, 1b, University of New Mexico.**
20. **Robert Rector, rhp, Southwestern (Calif.) JC.**
21. **Steve Bourgeois, rhp, Northeast Louisiana University.**
22. **Steven Day, lhp, Mesa State (Colo.) College.**
23. **Dan Barrett, c, Purdue University.**
24. Tim Conklin, rhp, Madison (Ore.) HS.
25. Chris Ratliff, rhp, Laney (Calif.) JC.
26. Tim Hicks, ss, Southwest HS, Macon, Ga.
27. **Rodney Bonds, rhp, Union City (Tenn.) HS.**
28. Jason Grote, rhp, Centennial HS, Gresham, Ore.
29. Notorris Bray, of, Central Alabama CC.
30. Rachaad Stewart, lhp, Triton (Ill.) JC.
31. **David Tessicini, ss, University of Vermont.**
32. **Brian Lootens, of, Arizona State University.**
33. **Matt Baumann, rhp, University of Maryland.**
34. **Clark Anderson, rhp, George Fox (Ore.) College.**
35. **Brian Zaletel, 3b, University of Tampa.**
36. Andrew Kalcounos, ss, DeMatha HS, Silver Spring, Md.
37. Daniel Fagley, c, Holy Cross HS, Riverton, N.J.
38. Jeff Tagliaferri, 1b, Kennedy HS, Granada Hills, Calif.
39. **Brian Benner, rhp, Capistrano Valley HS, Mission Viejo, Calif.**
40. Chad Dube, rhp, Cambridge, Ont.
41. Anthony Hilde, of, Pendleton (Ore.) HS.
42. Duane Stewart, of, Chino HS, Ontario, Calif.
43. Leonard McMillan, rhp, Crowder (Mo.) JC.
44. Ryan Miller, ss-2b, JC of the Sequoias (Calif.).
45. William Dicken, ss, Bloomington (Ill.) HS.
46. Tio Beall, rhp, South Salem (Ore.) HS.
47. Stephen Logan, 3b, Oak Grove HS, Hattiesburg, Miss.
48. David Russell, c, Bishop McGuinness HS, Lewisville, N.C.
49. **Jon Sbrocco, 2b, Wright State University.**
50. **Todd Petering, of, Kansas State University.**
51. Micah Terrell, ss, Mitchell (Ind.) HS.
52. **Chris Stasio, 1b, Barry (Fla.) University.**
53. **Michael Cecere, c, Rollins (Fla.) College.**
54. **Paul Reynolds, c, University of North Florida.**
55. **Andrew Mason, of, University of Washington.**

## SEATTLE MARINERS (1)

1. **Alex Rodriguez, ss, Westminster Christian HS, Miami.**
2. (Choice to Brewers as compensation for Type A free agent Chris Bosio).
3. **Ed Randolph, 3b-of, Roosevelt HS, Dallas.**
4. **Mike Collett, rhp, University of Southern California.**
5. **David Cooper, rhp, Hesperia (Calif.) HS.**
6. **Kenny Cloude, rhp, McDonough HS, Baltimore.**
7. **Tim Schweitzer, lhp, University of Arizona.**
8. Greg Hillengas, of, Seminole (Fla.) HS.
9. **Rob Krueger, lhp, Western Michigan University.**
10. **Dean Crow, rhp, Baylor University.**
11. **Casey Craig, rhp, Napoleon HS, Jackson, Mich.**
12. **Randy Jorgensen, 1b, University of Washington.**
13. **Rafael Carmona, rhp, Indian Hills (Iowa) CC.**

**Steve Soderstrom.** Fresno State righthander was selected sixth overall in the 1993 draft by the Giants.

14. **Brian Sosa, rhp, San Bernardino Valley (Calif.) JC.**
15. **Chris Green, rhp, Grossmont (Calif.) JC.**
16. **John Daniels, rhp, Mt. San Antonio (Calif.) JC.**
17. **Chad Dunavan, of, Howard (Texas) JC.**
18. **Tim Bruce, rhp, University of Detroit Mercy.**
19. Douglas Forde, lhp, Riverview HS, Sarasota, Fla.
20. Chris Dean, 2b, Seminole (Okla.) JC.
21. **Chris Dumas, of, Alabama Southern JC.**
22. **Matt Apana, rhp, University of Hawaii.**
23. **Mike Barger, of, Saint Louis University.**
24. **Joe Berube, c, Presbyterian (S.C.) College.**
25. **Daleon Isom, of, Benton Harbor (Mich.) HS.**
26. **Russell Jacobs, rhp, Winter Haven (Fla.) HS.**
27. **Joe Mathis, ss-of, Strom Thurmond HS, Johnston, S.C.**
28. **Jon Updike, rhp, Pensacola (Fla.) JC.**
29. **Andy Augustine, c, Triton (Ill.) JC.**
30. **Manny Patel, 2b, Yale University.**
31. Brandon Hoalton, rhp, Rancho Santiago (Calif.) JC.
32. **John Tejcek, of, University of Arizona.**
33. Chris Parker, rhp, Gonzalez Tate HS, Pensacola, Fla.
34. Grant Jondahl, rhp, Amador Valley HS, Pleasanton, Calif.
35. John White, c, University Christian HS, Jacksonville, Fla.
36. **Willie Wilkins, of, Atlantic HS, Boynton Beach, Fla.**
37. Brad Brasser, rhp, Grand Rapids (Mich.) Christian HS.
38. **Kelvin Mitchell, lhp, Choctaw County HS, Butler, Ala.**
39. Brandon Kleitch, of, Cibola HS, Rio Rancho, N.M.
40. Anibal Ramirez, ss, Miami-Dade CC Wolfson.
41. Chris Champanois, c, Columbia Central (Mich.) HS.
42. Heath Webster, rhp, Peninsula HS, Rancho Palo Verde, Calif.
43. Matt Wimmer, of, University of Washington.
44. Thomas Redd, of, El Camino (Calif.) JC.

45. Jeremy Morris, c, Monroe HS, Quincy, Fla.
**46. Johnny Cardenas, c, Texas Christian University.**
47. Marcus Jones, rhp, Esperanza HS, Yorba Linda, Calif.
48. Bryan Belflower, rhp, Oak Ridge HS, Orlando.
49. Jeremy Reeves, lhp, Lincoln Trail (Ill.) JC.
50. Jeff Harris, rhp, Contra Costa (Calif.) JC.
**51. Roy Miller, ss, Washington State University.**
52. Ryan Mullen, rhp, Boca Ciega HS, St. Petersburg, Fla.
53. Kevin McCoy, rhp, Triton (Ill.) JC.
54. Matt Wise, rhp, Bonita HS, LaVerne, Calif.
**55. Jason Cook, ss, University of Virginia.**
56. Chris Knowles, 1b, Blinn (Texas) JC.
57. John Romero, rhp, San Fernando HS, Sylmar, Calif.
58. Chris Kelly, lhp, Hamilton HS, Inglewood, Calif.
59. Ricky Tutson, of, Willow Run HS, Ypsilanti, Mich.
60. Barret Markey, rhp, St. Petersburg (Fla.) HS.
61. Robert Coddington, c, Grossmont HS, El Cajon, Calif.
62. Michael Rodgers, lhp, Olney (Ill.) HS.
63. Arnold Brathwarte, ss, St. Joseph's HS, Frediksted, Vt.
64. Justin Bice, rhp, Kentwood HS, Kent, Wash.
**65. Scott Smith, of, Texas A&M University.**
66. Aaron Keal, rhp, Labette County (Kan.) CC.
67. George Rayborn, rhp, Purvis (Miss.) HS.
68. Cirilo Cruz, 3b, Miami-Dade CC North.
**69. Rob Ippolito, rhp, University of Arizona.**
70. Jonathon Choate, of, Blinn (Texas) JC.

# TEXAS RANGERS (15)

1. (Choice to Blue Jays as compensation for Type A free agent Tom Henke).
**1. Mike Bell, 3b, Moeller HS, Cincinnati** (Supplemental choice—30th—for loss of Type A free agent Jose Guzman).
**2. Edwin Diaz, 2b, Vega Alta, P.R.** (Choice from Cubs for loss of Guzman).
2. (Choice to Blue Jays as compensation for Type B free agent Manny Lee).
**3. Andrew Vessel, of, Kennedy HS, Richmond, Calif.**
**4. Toure Knighton, rhp, Tucson (Ariz.) HS.**
**5. Rod Walker, ss, Hyde Park HS, Chicago.**
**6. Mark Ocasio, rhp, Carolina, P.R.**
**7. Dan Smith, rhp, Girard (Kan.) HS.**
**8. Jack Stanczak, 3b, Villanova University.**
**9. Pete Hartmann, lhp, Oklahoma City University.**
**10. Brian Thomas, of, Texas A&M University.**
**11. James Franklin, rhp, Carson Newman (Tenn.) College.**
**12. Osmani Estrada, ss, Canoga Park, Calif.**
**13. Marc Sagmoen, of, University of Nebraska.**
**14. Alexis Cabreja, of, Canoga Park, Calif.**
**15. Chris Unrat, c, Arkansas State University.**
**16. Tim Cossins, c, University of Oklahoma.**
**17. Brian Clark, of, University of Houston.**
**18. Ryan Falmier, rhp, Goreville HS, Tunnel Hill, Ill.**
**19. Wesley Sims, 2b, Austin Peay State University.**
20. Cesar Cerda, c, Southridge HS, Miami.
**21. Leland Macon, of, St Louis CC-Meramec.**
**22. Michael Jackson, rhp, Texas HS, Texarkana, Texas.**
23. Jason Dyess, rhp, McLaurin HS, Florence, Miss.
**24. Eric Moody, rhp, Erskine (S.C.) College.**
**25. Larry Ephan, c, Hawaii Pacific University.**
**26. Eric Dominow, 1b, Western Michigan University.**
**27. Lonnie Goldberg, 2b, George Mason University.**
**28. Jeffrey Davis, rhp, Massasoit (Mass.) CC.**
29. Michael Spence, rhp, South Gwinnett HS, Lithonia, Ga.
**30. Steve Ouimet, 1b, North Shore HS, Glenwood Landing, N.Y.**
**31. Michael Hill, of, Harvard University.**
**32. Scott Smith, rhp, University of Kentucky.**
33. Richard Collins, rhp-1b, Stockbridge (Ga.) HS.
34. Jamil Phillips, c, Redan HS, Stone Mountain, Ga.
**35. Gardner O'Flynn, lhp, University of New Hampshire.**
**36. Robert Kell, lhp, Temple University.**
**37. Gregory Lewis, of, University of New Hampshire.**
**38. Dom Gatti, of, Adelphi University.**
39. Ivan Zweig, rhp, Tulane University.
**40. Ray DeSimone, ss, Long Island University.**
**41. Mike Cather, rhp, University of California.**
**42. Greg Willming, rhp, University of Evansville.**
**43. Joe Morvay, rhp, Ohio University.**
44. Cajen Rhodes, 1b, Berkmar HS, Lilburn, Ga.
**45. Matt Huff, of, Northwestern University.**
46. Bryan Cunningham, rhp, Monte Vista HS, Spring Valley, Calif.
47. Rex Stevens, rhp, Wheeler HS, Marietta, Ga.
48. Michael Jackson, of, JC of Marin ( Calif.).
49. Nicholas Caiazzo, c, Deering HS, Portland, Me.
50. Brian Tickell, rhp, Grand Prairie (Texas) HS.

51. Juan Veras, ss, Palm Beach (Fla.) JC.
52. Stephen Cardona, rhp, San Joaquin Delta (Calif.) JC.
53. Daniel Schourek, rhp, Montgomery (Md.) CC.
54. William Pepper, 1b, Houston (Miss.) HS.
55. Kenneth Payne, 1b, St. Louis CC-Meramec.
56. Robert Tucker, 1b, Robert E. Lee HS, Huntsville, Ala.
57. Steve Frascatore, rhp, C.W. Post University.
58. Rayvon McGriff, of, Del Mar HS, San Jose, Calif.
59. Frank Chapman, rhp, MacArthur HS, San Antonio.

# TORONTO BLUE JAYS (26)

**1. Chris Carpenter, rhp, Trinity HS, Manchester, N.H.** (Choice from Rangers as compensation for Type A free agent Tom Henke).
1. (Choice to Brewers as compensation for Type A free agent Paul Molitor).
**1. Matt Farner, of, East Pennsboro HS, Enola, Pa.** (Supplemental choice—37th—for loss of Type A free agent David Cone).
**1. Jeremy Lee, rhp, Galesburg (Ill.) HS** (Supplemental choice—40th—for loss of Henke).
**1. Mark Lukasiewicz, lhp, Brevard (Fla.) CC** (Supplemental choice—41st—for loss of Type A free agent Jimmy Key).
**2. Anthony Medrano, ss, Jordan HS, Long Beach, Calif.** (Choice from Royals as compensation for Cone).
**2. Ryan Jones, 1b, Irvine (Calif.) HS** (Choice from Rangers as compensation for Type B free agent Manny Lee).
2. (Choice to Athletics as compensation for Type A free agent Dave Stewart).
**3. Mike Romano, rhp, Tulane University** (Choice from Yankees as compensation for Key).
**3. Joe Young, rhp, Ainlay HS, Fort McMurray, Alberta.**
4. Thad Busby, c-of, Pace (Fla.) HS.
**5. Charles Bourne, ss, Muir HS, Altadena, Calif.**
6. Rob DeBoer, c, University of South Carolina.
7. Donny Barker, rhp, Leander (Texas) HS.
**8. Matt Stone, lhp, Vista (Calif.) HS.**
**9. Oreste Volkert, rhp, La Habra (Calif.) HS.**
**10. Ruben Corral, rhp, Arroyo HS, El Monte, Calif.**
11. Larry Mohs, rhp, Nutley (N.J.) HS.
**12. Brent Coe, lhp, Franklin Central HS, Indianapolis.**
**13. Adam Melhuse, 3b, UCLA.**
14. Chris Freeman, rhp, University of Tennessee.
**15. Tyson Hartshorn, rhp, Lamar (Colo.) HS.**
16. Shane Dennis, lhp, Wichita State University.
**17. Michael Johnson, rhp, Salisbury Composite HS, Edmonton.**
**18. David Morgan, c, Harvard University.**
**19. David Sinnes, rhp, University of Notre.Dame.**
20. Aaron Gardin, of, Chaparral HS, Scottsdale, Ariz.
21. Daniel Crawford, rhp, Jersey Village HS, Houston.
22. Steve Johnson, of, Michigan State University
**23. Rob Steinert, rhp, North Carolina State University.**
**24. Brian Grant, lhp, Diablo Valley (Calif.) JC.**
**25. William Daunic, 1b, Vanderbilt University.**
**26. Victor Davila, ss, Westchester (N.Y.) CC.**
**27. Michael Toney, rhp, Cochise County (Ariz.) CC.**
28. John Nape, rhp, Lewis (Ill.) University.
**29. Rob Mummau, ss, James Madison University.**
**30. Richard Lutz, c, Elizabethtown (Pa.) College.**
31. Brad Feldewerth, rhp, Fort Zumwalt North HS, Wentzville, Mo.
32. James Bowman, rhp, Highline HS, Seattle.
33. Jon Phillips, rhp, South Cobb HS, Austell, Ga.
34. Eric Booth, of, Bassfield (Miss.) HS.
35. Michael Diebolt, lhp, Mayfield HS, Mayfield Village, Ohio.
36. Scott Henderson, rhp, Villa Park (Calif.) HS.
**37. Christian Roggendorf, 1b, Dowling (N.Y.) College.**
38. Ryan Brannan, rhp, Huntington Beach (Calif.) HS.
39. James Smith, of, Greensboro HS, Quincy, Fla.
40. Adrian Poindexter, ss, Caldwell HS, Columbus, Miss.
41. David Sumner, of, University of Pittsburgh.
42. Mane Gavric, of, Mather HS, Chicago.
**43. Ivan Nobles, of, Brandon (Fla.) HS.**
44. David Meyer, lhp, University of Kansas.
45. Brian Haebig, lhp, Sahuaro HS, Tucson.
46. Mark Macias, rhp, Ridgewood HS, Norridge, Ill.
47. Herman Gordan, of, El Camino HS, Oceanside, Calif.
48. Ronald Dempsey, of, Lufkin (Texas) HS.
49. Jason Monk, rhp, Mississippi Gulf Coast JC.
50 David Fogle, rhp, Torrance HS, Lomita, Calif.
51. Brian Thomas, rhp, Mt. Pleasant (Texas) HS.
52. Joseph Nelson, ss, Notre Dame HS, Alameda, Calif.
53. Jaime Roque, 2b, Vernon Regional (Texas) JC.
54. James Mann, rhp, Massasoit (Mass.) CC.
55. Michael Hannah, of, Bremen (Ga.) HS.
**56. Victor Rodriguez, rhp, Okaloosa-Walton (Fla.) CC.**

# INDEX

## GENERAL INFORMATION

# INDEX
## MAJOR, MINOR LEAGUE CLUBS

# Here's The Pitch

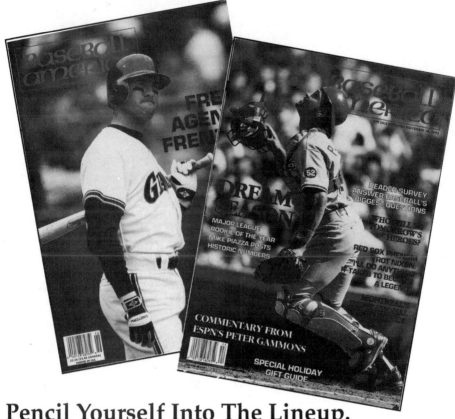

## Pencil Yourself Into The Lineup.
## Don't Get Caught Looking.

We take the mound 26 times a year. And as a 12-year veteran, we've developed quite a repertoire. We paint the corners with our special reports and insightful examinations of trends of the game.

Our colorful features, both major and minor league, will entice you like a lollipop curve. Our draft coverage and prospect lists are nothing but heat, right down the middle. And we may surprise you with an occasional knuckleball, just a tinge of humor and irreverence that helps weave the fabric of baseball.

We blaze the trail for you to follow your favorite prospects up the ladder to stardom, with complete minor league statistics and reports. And even before they sign their first professional contract, we've got our eye on them with college and amateur news.

From Lynchburg to Pittsburgh, Tokyo to Omaha, **Baseball America** keeps you in touch with the game.

## BaseBall america

### "BASEBALL NEWS YOU CAN'T GET ANYWHERE ELSE"

BASEBALL AMERICA
P.O. BOX 2089 • DURHAM, NC 27702
1-800-845-2726

---

**Baseball America**
**P.O. Box 2089 • Durham, NC 27702**

Please send me:

❑ 2-Year subscription at
**$67.95** (52 issues)

❑ 1-Year subscription at
**$38.95** (26 issues)

❑ My check or money order is enclosed ( in U.S. funds)

❑ Charge to my:  ❑ Visa  ❑ MC  ❑ AmEx

Exp. Date _____

Card No._____

Name _____

Address_____

City _____

State_____ Zip _____

Phone (_____)_____

For faster service on credit card orders, call
**1-800-845-2726**   ALM